W9-DJO-516

The New Collegeville Bible Commentary

THE NEW COLLEGEVILLE BIBLE COMMENTARY

SERIES EDITOR

Daniel Durken, O.S.B.

LITURGICAL PRESS

Collegeville, Minnesota

www.litpress.org

Nihil Obstat: Reverend Robert Harren, J.C.L., *Censor deputatus*.
Imprimatur: ✠ Most Reverend Donald J. Kettler, J.C.L., Bishop of St. Cloud, October 13, 2017.

Maps created by Robert Cronan of Lucidity Information Design, LLC.

1	2	3	4	5	6	7	8	9

Library of Congress Cataloging-in-Publication Data

Names: Durken, Daniel, series editor.
Title: The new Collegeville Bible commentary : in one volume / Daniel Durken, O.S.B.
Description: Collegeville, Minnesota : Liturgical Press, 2017.
Identifiers: LCCN 2016008113 (print) | LCCN 2016020010 (ebook) | ISBN 9780814646595 (hardcover) | ISBN 9780814646830 (ebook)
Subjects: LCSH: Bible—Commentaries.
Classification: LCC BS491.3 .D87 2017 (print) | LCC BS491.3 (ebook) | DDC 220.7—dc23
LC record available at https://lccn.loc.gov/2016008113

CONTENTS

Preface

A little more than fifty years after the close of the Second Vatican Council, with the publication of this one-volume edition of the *New Collegeville Bible Commentary*, Liturgical Press continues to respond to the call of the Dogmatic Constitution on Divine Revelation that "access to sacred Scripture ought to be open wide to the Christian faithful" (*Dei Verbum* 22).

The *New Collegeville Bible Commentary* draws richly on the expanding field of scholars who are opening up the sacred Scriptures to ever-new generations of Catholics. Following the time-tested criteria of the Collegeville Commentary these scholars offer accessible and up-to-date interpretation of the Scripture for preachers, teachers, Bible study participants, and all readers of the Bible who seek a deeper understanding of what *Dei Verbum* so beautifully describes as "the speech of God as it is put down in writing under the breath of the Holy Spirit" (9).

The *New Collegeville Bible Commentary* traces its form and purpose back to 1960 with the publication of the *Old and New Testament Reading Guides* by Liturgical Press. In the 1980s the original series was replaced with the *Collegeville Bible Commentary*, and for the first time the series was offered in both individual booklets and in collected Old and New Testament volumes. The first two editions have sold more than 2 million copies combined, amply demonstrating their effectiveness and appeal.

The third edition—the *New Collegeville Bible Commentary*—is now complete, and we are pleased to offer this one-volume edition. As the late Fr. Daniel Durken, O.S.B., editor of this third edition, said in concluding his preface to the New Testament volume in 2009: "May these commentaries, together with frequent reading of Scripture, inspire you and lead you to greater knowledge and love of Jesus Christ."

Peter Dwyer
Director
Liturgical Press

ABBREVIATIONS

Books of the Bible

Acts—Acts of the Apostles
Amos—Amos
Bar—Baruch
1 Chr—1 Chronicles
2 Chr—2 Chronicles
Col—Colossians
1 Cor—1 Corinthians
2 Cor—2 Corinthians
Dan—Daniel
Deut—Deuteronomy
Eccl (or Qoh)—Ecclesiastes
Eph—Ephesians
Esth—Esther
Exod—Exodus
Ezek—Ezekiel
Ezra—Ezra
Gal—Galatians
Gen—Genesis
Hab—Habakkuk
Hag—Haggai
Heb—Hebrews
Hos—Hosea
Isa—Isaiah
Jas—James
Jdt—Judith
Jer—Jeremiah
Job—Job
Joel—Joel
John—John
1 John—1 John
2 John—2 John
3 John—3 John
Jonah—Jonah
Josh—Joshua
Jude—Jude
Judg—Judges
1 Kgs—1 Kings

2 Kgs—2 Kings
Lam—Lamentations
Lev—Leviticus
Luke—Luke
1 Macc—1 Maccabees
2 Macc—2 Maccabees
Mal—Malachi
Mark—Mark
Matt—Matthew
Mic—Micah
Nah—Nahum
Neh—Nehemiah
Num—Numbers
Obad—Obadiah
1 Pet—1 Peter
2 Pet—2 Peter
Phil—Philippians
Phlm—Philemon
Prov—Proverbs
Ps(s)—Psalms
Rev—Revelation
Rom—Romans
Ruth—Ruth
1 Sam—1 Samuel
2 Sam—2 Samuel
Sir—Sirach
Song—Song of Songs
1 Thess—1 Thessalonians
2 Thess—2 Thessalonians
1 Tim—1 Timothy
2 Tim—2 Timothy
Titus—Titus
Tob—Tobit
Wis—Wisdom
Zech—Zechariah
Zeph—Zephaniah

Other Abbreviations

Ant.—*Antiquities of the Jews*
Apoc. Bar.—Syriac Greek Apocalypse
   of Baruch
H.E.—Eusebius, *Historia Ecclesiastica*

KJV—King James Version
LXX—Septuagint
NAB—New American Bible
T. Moses—*Testament of Moses*

INTRODUCTION TO THE BIBLE

Gregory W. Dawes

INTRODUCTION

The book we know as the Bible is not so much a single book as a library. It is a collection of books, written by different authors, at different times, and dealing with a wide range of concerns. We recognize this fact when we refer to the Bible as "the Scriptures," a term that implies we are not dealing with one book but with many. Even our English word "Bible" was originally not a singular noun but a plural one, for it comes from the Greek term *ta biblia*, which means simply "the books." Only very late in its history did the corresponding Latin word *biblia* come to be treated as a singular noun.

Imagine that you were to walk into your local public library and pick up a book entirely at random off the shelves. As you opened the book, there would be a number of questions that would immediately spring to mind. First of all, you might ask yourself, "What sort of book is this? Is it a 'how-to' book, such as a car repair manual, or a work on home decorating? Is it a work of fiction, such as a novel? Is it a history book, telling what purports to be a true story of a person or place? Or is it a textbook, setting out the fundamental ideas of some field of study?"

If you were not able to answer these questions, you would hardly know what to do with the book you were holding. What use would it be to you? How could you begin to understand it? As you continued turning the pages, other questions might occur to you. You might ask, for instance, "Who wrote this book? When was it written? For what purpose was it written? How is it set out? Does it, for example, tell a story with a beginning,

a middle, and an end?" These questions, too, would help you to understand the book better and to use it more intelligently.

Each volume in the New Collegeville Bible Commentary series will deal with one or more of the books that form the biblical library. In studying that book, it will ask precisely these questions. What sort of book is this? When was it written? By whom was it written and for what purpose? How does it organize its material and present its message? It is important to try to answer such questions if we are to read biblical books intelligently.

This volume, however, is intended as an introduction to the series as a whole. For this reason it is not devoted to any one of the biblical books; it is intended to be a guide to the library as a whole. What we will be looking at in the following pages is the history of this collection of writings and the ways in which it has been used. The questions we will be interested in are: Who founded this library? What books are found in it, and why were they selected? How has the collection developed over time? The following pages will also discuss how the library has been used over the long period of its history. What authority has been given to this particular collection of books and why? What instructions have been given for their interpretation during the long period that they have been regarded as Sacred Scripture?

In a word, this short work is intended to provide an initial orientation to the Bible for the general reader. It aims to help you read both the Bible itself and its commentaries with a sense of the

1

contexts out of which they have come. It will therefore discuss all the matters traditionally dealt with in an introduction to the Bible. To use some technical terms, which we will come across later, it will deal with issues of the biblical text, the biblical canon, biblical authority, and biblical criticism. But rather than discussing these matters in the abstract, it will do so in a broadly historical context. It will examine the origin of the biblical writings and the ongoing story of their interpretation by reference to wider changes in the Christian community and in the society to which it belongs.

The focus of this short book will be on the Christian churches and—in more recent times—the Catholic Church. But it is important to realize that the Christians are not the only people for whom the Bible is Sacred Scripture. The first part of the Bible, which Christians call the Old Testament, is also Jewish Scripture, read and studied in the synagogue in the same way as the Christian Bible is read and studied in the churches. The Jewish Bible, otherwise known as the Hebrew Bible, is often referred to simply as *Tanak*, a word made up of the initial letters of the Hebrew names of its three principal parts: the *Torah* (Law), the *Neviʾim* (the Prophets), and the *Ketuvim* (the Writings).

Insofar as it deals with the origins of the Old Testament books, the present volume will also be dealing with the origins of *Tanak*. To the extent that both Jews and Christians make reference to these writings, they share a common set of Scriptures. But when it comes to the interpretation of these writings, the two traditions part company. Jews and Christians read and understand these common Scriptures very differently. The present work will deal only with the history of Christian biblical interpretation; it will not try to deal with the Jewish. It would take another book to do justice to that topic, one written by an author with a more profound knowledge of Judaism. All I want to do here is to offer a warning. The attitudes towards the Bible described here are not the only attitudes that can be taken by people of faith. There is a parallel and very rich history of interpretation with which this introduction cannot deal.

In fact, there is a second history that this short work does not cover. This is the history of the use of the Bible outside the world of religious thought. It is the history of the Bible as a cultural artifact: its use by painters, musicians, poets, and playwrights and the role it has played in the develop-

ment of our thinking on a range of issues, from politics to psychology. This would be a fascinating field of study, for—whatever one thinks of the Bible's message—it would be hard to overestimate its cultural significance.

One could study, for instance, the changing ways in which painters and sculptors have depicted biblical scenes or the ways in which poets have used biblical themes to add resonance to their works. One could trace the influence of biblical patterns of thought on thinkers as apparently irreligious as Karl Marx (1818–1883) and Sigmund Freud (1856–1939). Sadly, however, I cannot deal with this topic either. In fact, no one person could hope to do it justice. A proper treatment of the Bible's cultural significance would require a whole team of authors with expertise in these different fields of study.

Finally, there is a third history of the Bible that the present study will not be able to discuss. This is the history of how the Bible has actually been used within the Christian community but at the grassroots level (as it were), outside the relatively rarified world occupied by bishops and theologians. A history of this sort would look at the use of the Bible by popular preachers, by teachers in classrooms, and by leaders of church discussion groups.

It would also examine the ways in which individuals have used the Bible, irrespective of what their teachers may have taught them. For instance, there exists a long-standing custom of solving personal dilemmas by opening the Bible at random and seeking an answer in whatever verse comes to hand. While widely condemned by church authorities and theologians, the practice continues to be used in our own time. In previous ages, biblical verses have also been used in charms and amulets, to ward off the power of evil in ways that many would regard as magical.

A history of such unofficial practices would be an extraordinarily interesting one, but it also falls outside the scope of the present work. What we are interested in here is what has been said about the Bible by its officially sanctioned interpreters and by those who have sought to influence them. It is a history of what we might call the institutional interpretation of the Bible within the Christian churches.

The present work falls naturally into two parts. The first will concentrate on the origins of the

Bible. It will offer a glimpse of the ways in which the people of Israel and then, in later centuries, the early Christians gathered this collection together and gave it the status of Sacred Scripture. This is the foundational section of the present study. After all, until there was an official collection of biblical writings, there was nothing for later Christians to interpret.

The second and larger part of our work will deal with the history of biblical interpretation. The survey found here will be divided into four periods. The first period is the longest, embracing both the age of those who are known as the church fathers and the Middle Ages. If we were to assign dates to this period, it would take us from about the year 200 to about the year 1500. Our second major period, that of the Protestant Reformation and Catholic Counter-Reformation, takes us from approximately the year 1500 to about 1650. This is a much shorter period, but it is one in which Western Christianity experienced revolutionary changes.

Our third period is the one I have described as the modern era. This may be said to begin with the scientific revolution of the mid-seventeenth century and continue through to our own time. However, we cannot stop there. Recent decades have witnessed a series of revolutions in scholarly attitudes to the Bible. These developments may conveniently be dealt with in a fourth and final section, under the heading of postmodern approaches to biblical interpretation.

While this represents a very broad overview of a very complex history, it may offer the general reader a helpful framework within which to begin to understand the Bible. In particular, it should enable you to appreciate the variety of ways in which the Christian Scriptures can be interpreted. It will also highlight the fact that these methods of biblical interpretation are not timeless. They did not fall from heaven as a user's guide to a divinely inspired collection of books. They represent attempts by devout but limited human beings to make sense of a set of writings they believed to be God's word for their time. However much the Bible may be thought to embody an eternal truth, its interpreters remain fallible human beings, bound by the limitations of their time and place.

The Origins of the Bible

The question with which this first section of our study deals seems simple enough: Where have these writings come from? But in dealing with this topic we are faced with almost insurmountable difficulties. Biblical scholars have spent more than two hundred years trying to trace the origins of the biblical writings, and yet this remains one of the most hotly debated topics in contemporary religious scholarship.

To make the present task more manageable, I will begin by making a distinction. I will distinguish between the material found in the Bible and the Bible in its present form as a collection of works from different times and places. Some of the material found in the Bible is probably very ancient, but the task of tracing its origin is best left to the authors of the individual commentaries in this series. All I can do here is try to trace the origin of the Bible in its present form. The question I will be trying to answer is: Where has this particular collection of books come from? I will begin by discussing the way in which Jews and Christians gradually assembled their sacred writings. I will describe how these Scriptures have been transmitted to us before glancing briefly at some major biblical translations.

THE BIBLICAL CANON

We may begin with what is generally described as the formation of the biblical canon. The word "canon" is derived from a Greek word meaning a rod or a rule, in the sense of a rod of fixed length that could be used for measurement. When used metaphorically, the same word indicated a fixed standard, a norm against which other things could be judged. The word could be used, for instance, of the models artists used to ensure correct proportions or of the models grammarians used to indicate correct speech. When such models were set out in the form of a table, the table as a whole could be described as a canon. At this point, the word had come to mean something like an authoritative series or list.

This is the sense in which Jews and Christians speak about the canon of the Bible. It is the list of biblical writings that is considered to carry authority within the synagogue and the churches. It is interesting to note that the word canon is today sometimes used in non-religious contexts. In literary studies, for instance, there have been some lively debates over the canon of English literature. The key question here has been: Which works should one include as worthy of study in a university course? More importantly, which works have traditionally been excluded, as unworthy of our attention, and why? Has the time come to incorporate previously marginalized voices—perhaps those of women or of African-American writers—into the canon?

Of course, similar questions can be asked of the Bible. There are, for instance, a number of early Christian gospels that the church came to regard as extra-canonical, that is, as not having authoritative status. (Such works are sometimes referred to as apocryphal works.) Often such works were excluded from the canon because they were thought to embody false teachings. Some of the non-canonical gospels, for instance, were connected with groups that are described today as Gnostic, a term that embraces a number of religious movements that flourished in the second century of the Christian era. These movements combined Christian beliefs with elaborate myths about the origin of the world in ways that made many of the church fathers deeply uneasy.

In recent decades, theologians have sometimes wanted to revisit these judgments. They have argued that such marginalized Christian groups may have something to tell us. In effect, this means questioning the limits of our present canon by suggesting that certain works should not have been excluded. But it is not only theologians who sometimes question the limits of the canon; the same is true of historians. If historians are in search of the history of biblical Judaism and early Christianity, they will make use of canonical and non-canonical works alike. For instance, some contemporary writers on the "historical Jesus" will refer to the non-canonical Gospel of Thomas, believing that this work embodies historically reliable information.

Whatever one may think of the limits of the canon, the existence of a canon of Scripture is a historical fact. For better or for worse, the canon of Scripture constitutes the Bible as we know it. It is the formation of the biblical canon that is of interest here. When did this particular collection of books come to be formed? Who was involved in its formation? What books were included? What criteria were used in the selection of these particular writings?

Before we begin looking at the details of this process, the reader may wish to note a particular feature of biblical scholarship. Because such scholarship is engaged in by Jews and Christians alike, one often finds the religiously more inclusive abbreviations B.C.E., "Before the Common Era," and C.E., "Common Era," which are used in place of the more common B.C., "Before Christ," and A.D., *Anno Domini*, "in the year of [our] Lord." While these two sets of terms have different meanings, they divide history in exactly the same way. As a matter of consistency, the New Collegeville Bible Commentary uses B.C. and A.D.

THE FORMATION OF THE OLD TESTAMENT CANON

First of all, we should examine the collection of writings that Christians customarily call the Old Testament. It is difficult to be certain about the events that led to the formation of the Old Testament canon. Some Old Testament books may contain material that is much older than the books in the present form, reaching back into the early centuries of the first millennium B.C. The traditions that constitute these books probably first circulated by word of mouth, since the Old Testament seems to have its origins in an oral culture.

Other traditions may have existed in written form before being incorporated into the books we now have. Biblical scholars have spilled much ink researching the formation of individual books and debating the date of the materials they contain. (For further information, the reader should consult the individual commentaries in this series.) But my concern here is not with the process by which individual books were formed; I am interested in the process by which these books were collected into an authoritative body of literature.

(a) The crisis of the Exile

A key event in this development seems to have been the Babylonian Exile, a series of tragedies that befell the Jewish people in Palestine in the sixth century B.C. On two occasions—first in the year 597 B.C. and then in the year 586 B.C.—the armies of the great empire of Babylon swept down from the north to destroy the Jewish kingdom in southern Palestine. This was not the first political catastrophe to be experienced by the Jewish inhabitants of the land. In the year 722 B.C. the armies of a previous Mesopotamian superpower, Assyria, had laid waste to the northern part of the Jewish-occupied land of Palestine. But according to the biblical history, the Jewish population of the North had long formed a separate kingdom, following a schism that had occurred in about the year 922 B.C.

At the time of the destruction of this Northern Kingdom the inhabitants of the Southern Kingdom, that of Judah, had escaped relatively unscathed. It seems from the account offered by the prophet Jeremiah (see, for instance, Jeremiah 7) that by the sixth century B.C. the inhabitants of Judah felt secure. They believed that the dynasty established by King David in Jerusalem enjoyed divine protection and that the Temple of God established in that city would never be destroyed.

The catastrophe of 586 B.C. put an end to this complacency. The Babylonians not only destroyed the city of Jerusalem and its temple and took a large part of the population of Judea into exile, but they also captured the ruling Jewish king and put his sons to death before his eyes prior to blinding him and taking him into exile as their prisoner. (One can read the biblical account of these events in 2 Kings 25.)

It would be difficult to overestimate the religious crisis brought on by these events. What had happened to God's promises to Israel? What had become of the promise of the land of Israel, the promise that the descendants of David would rule as kings in the city of Jerusalem? Israel's identity as a nation seemed to be in ruins. It fell to the prophets of that period, particularly the prophets Jeremiah and Ezekiel, to interpret the crisis and to give hope to the nation once again. The memory of their words helped to shape the Old Testament as we have it.

Of particular importance were the collected sayings of the prophet Jeremiah that seem to have been shaped by traditions now found in the book of Deuteronomy. According to the books of both Deuteronomy and Jeremiah, the promises of God were conditional. Their fulfillment was dependent on Israel's obedience to the Torah, the law given to Moses. On these grounds, the catastrophe of the Exile was explicable. It was not the case that God had abandoned Israel. On the contrary, Israel had abandoned God by failing to observe the law God had given. The defeat suffered at the hands of the Babylonians was a divine punishment. But it was not the last word. God may punish but would also restore, bringing Israel back to the land and rebuilding its temple. The book of Jeremiah could even speak of a "New Covenant," comparable to that originally made with Moses on Mt. Sinai (see Jeremiah 31).

The words of Jeremiah are important for many reasons. Not least among these is the fact that Christians would later claim to be the heirs of this New Covenant (or New Testament). The traditions found in Deuteronomy and Jeremiah are also of importance for the formation of the Old Testament canon, since it was this interpretation of the Exile that seems to have prompted one of the earliest attempts to compile and edit Israel's religious traditions. The traditions in question are those that make up our biblical books of Joshua, Judges, Samuel, and Kings. Many scholars believe that these books have been edited into a more or less unified story, often described as the "Deuteronomistic History," because of its similarity in spirit to the book of Deuteronomy.

The formation of this early collection of biblical materials remains a matter of scholarly conjecture. It is widely believed to have been completed toward the end of the years of exile, which lasted from 586 to about the year 538 B.C., when the Persian king Cyrus, the new ruler of the Mediterranean world, permitted the Jewish exiles to return to Palestine. We should probably not describe the compilation of the Deuteronomistic History as an attempt to produce "Sacred Scripture"; we know too little about the circumstances of its origin and about the attitude of its editors. But the compilation and editing of these traditions represent an early attempt to make sense of Israel's history in the light of a firm faith in Israel's God. If this is correct, the formation of the Deuteronomistic History is an important step toward the Bible as we know it.

(b) The growth of the canon

Much of the history I have presented to this point is conjectural. While it seems well supported by the biblical writings themselves, the interpretation I have offered is still open to dispute. If we want clearer evidence of the formation of an Old Testament canon, we must look to the time of the Jewish scribe Ezra in the mid-fifth century B.C. As we have seen, the Deuteronomistic History was probably assembled in the final years of the Exile. During those years, or in the period immediately following the Exile, other parts of what was to become the biblical canon were also being collected. In particular, the book of Deuteronomy was soon linked to the books of Genesis, Exodus, Leviticus, and Numbers to form what has come to be known as the "Pentateuch," the first five books of our present Bible. Within the Jewish world, these first five books are deemed particularly worthy of the title "Torah": the revealed law of God for Israel.

Ezra is remembered as a pious and learned Jewish leader who came from Babylon to the land of Palestine, perhaps about the year 458 B.C. Once in Palestine, he set about inaugurating a strict religious reform. As part of this reform (we are told in the book of Nehemiah) Ezra set up a wooden pulpit in the Water Gate Square in Jerusalem. From this pulpit he read aloud to the people from what seems to have been a set of Sacred Scriptures. These Scriptures are described as "the book of the law of Moses which the LORD prescribed for Israel" (Neh 8:1). As a result of Ezra's reading, the people repented of their sins and committed themselves afresh to keeping this law of God. What were these Sacred Scriptures that Ezra is reported to have read?

From the context it seems likely that what Ezra read were the first five books of our present Old Testament. There is much debate about the origin of these books—the books of Genesis, Exodus,

Leviticus, Numbers, and Deuteronomy—each of which seems to have been gradually assembled from oral and written sources sometime before this date. This discussion need not concern us here. All I am interested in is the process by which they became a single unit.

The story of Ezra suggests that by the mid-fifth century B.C., the first five books of the Bible were already regarded as forming a collection that is thought to have divine authority. This collection does not just represent the law of Israel; it represents the law of God. If we assume that the books that form the Deuteronomistic history reached their present form in the previous century, and if we assume that the oracles or pronouncements of some of the prophets had also been preserved, then it seems that by the mid-fifth century a fair portion of the present Old Testament is already in existence.

This is certainly the case by the mid-second century B.C. The author of the preface to the book of Sirach, for instance, writing shortly after 132 B.C., can speak of "the law and the prophets and the other books of our fathers." Given the later Jewish division of the Old Testament into three parts—the Law, the Prophets, and the Writings—it seems that by the mid-second century at least the first two of these parts were already assembled and were being studied as Sacred Scripture. The third category, described here as "the other books of our fathers," is unclear; we cannot know for certain which books it contained.

By the time of the New Testament, the situation seems little changed. In a story found at the end of Luke's Gospel, the risen Jesus appears to his disciples and explains to them the passages "in the law of Moses and in the prophets and psalms" that were about himself (Luke 24:44). Once again, the first two terms refer to what are now familiar parts of the Old Testament, but the precise composition of the third category seems unclear. It presumably includes a book of Psalms but probably embraces a wider range of writings.

It follows that by the time of the New Testament, the Old Testament canon as we know it was largely established, although its boundaries remained uncertain. (In Jewish circles it was not, of course, known as the Old Testament; this is a later, Christian title.) It is not entirely clear, for instance, which writings the New Testament authors would have considered to be Sacred Scripture. Their Bible may have included a larger number of writings than those that form our present Old Testament. On the other hand, one or two of the books in our present Old Testament may not have been regarded as Sacred Scripture by the New Testament writers. (The rabbinic literature records Jewish debates, apparently from the late first century A.D., about the canonical status of both Ecclesiastes and the Song of Songs.) At least one New Testament book (Jude 14–15) quotes from what would later be regarded as a non-canonical work (the book of Enoch) in the same manner as one would quote from Sacred Scripture. It seems that the process by which the canon was formed was not yet complete.

(c) Canonical and deuterocanonical books

These remarks highlight the difficulties that surround the question of what is called the closure of the Old Testament canon: the process by which these particular books, and these particular books alone, came to be regarded as having divine authority. With regard to the closure of the canon within Judaism, it used to be believed that the decision was made by an authoritative Council of Jewish teachers in the Palestinian town of Jamnia (or Yavneh) about the year 90 A.D. In more recent times scholars have questioned this tradition. However the decision was made, the end of the first century A.D. does seem to have marked a turning point within Judaism. After this date there seems to have been little significant disagreement about which books should be read as Sacred Scripture.

Among Christians, on the other hand, the limits of the Old Testament canon have remained a matter of debate. In particular, there exists a disagreement between the Eastern Orthodox and Roman Catholic churches and those churches that emerged from the sixteenth-century Protestant Reformation. What are rather misleadingly called "Protestant Bibles" contain thirty-nine Old Testament books, while what are sometimes called "Catholic Bibles" contain forty-six Old Testament books. (There are also small differences between the canon of the Orthodox churches and that of the Roman Catholic Church, but I will not deal with that matter here.)

The disputed books are often referred to by Protestants as the apocrypha, a term that originally meant "hidden" (or perhaps "obscure") books. Among Catholics these books are often referred to as deuterocanonical books, that is to say, books belonging to the second canon. Neither term is entirely satisfactory. The word "apocrypha" is often taken to imply that these books are somehow spurious, which is unfair. The term "deuterocanonical" is also inappropriate since—as we will see in a moment—there never was a second canon. Unfortunately, there is no alternative designation. In more recent Bibles, intended for use by Christians of different churches, the disputed books are sometimes included but are separated from the body of the text in an appendix or are placed between the Old and New Testaments.

How did this rather awkward situation come about? The decisive factor in this development was the existence within Judaism of a translation of the Old Testament into Greek. This translation is generally known as the Septuagint (the Latin term for "seventy," abbreviated LXX), because it is said to have been produced in the third century B.C. by seventy (or seventy-two) translators. (We will come back to this story when discussing ancient translations.) Understandably this translation was widely used by Greek-speaking Jews outside of Palestine, whose knowledge of Hebrew was often minimal. When the New Testament writers, for instance, cite Sacred Scripture, they generally refer to the Septuagint Greek translation rather than the original Hebrew text.

The problem is that the Septuagint does not merely include the books of the Hebrew Bible as this was later defined. This collection of Jewish religious texts also includes other works, whether originally written in Hebrew or in Greek. It is easy to see how this broader collection could have been compiled. After all, the Septuagint was being formed at a time when the limits of what we call the Old Testament canon were still unclear. So there was no one authoritative canon to which the translators could refer. The Septuagint's larger collection of books is sometimes known as the Alexandrian canon, after the city of its production (hence the term "deuterocanonical" meaning "belonging to the second canon"). But to speak of an Alexandrian canon is misleading, since it implies that the biblical canon was already fixed.

Within early Christianity the most common practice seems to have been to follow the larger collection found within the Septuagint. When

some local church councils in the fourth and fifth century, for instance, produced lists of Old Testament books, it was the larger collection that they cited. On the other hand, at least one early Christian writer disputed the value of the Septuagint. The writer in question was none other than the great biblical scholar St. Jerome (ca. 342–420). Jerome vigorously defended his translations from the Hebrew text against the suggestion of St. Augustine (354–430) that he rest content with the Septuagint.

As far as the canon was concerned, Jerome's preference seems to have been for the smaller, Hebrew collection. In any case, this collection was the unambiguous choice of the Protestant Reformers of the sixteenth century. Their decision may well have been motivated by theological concerns. The deuterocanonical books of Maccabees, for instance, encourage prayer for the dead, which could lend support to the Catholic doctrine of purgatory. It was also motivated by the same desire that motivated St. Jerome: a desire to return to the original languages of the Bible and to interpret the biblical text afresh. By way of reaction to the Reformers, the Catholic Church reiterated its traditional preference for the larger collection, defining this collection as canonical in 1546 during the Council of Trent.

THE FORMATION OF THE NEW TESTAMENT CANON

While the origins of the Old Testament canon are sometimes difficult to discern, we know more about the formation of the New Testament. As was the case with the formation of the Old Testament, this was a gradual process that took place over several hundred years. In a way that seems remarkable to us, it appears that the decision about the New Testament canon was not made by any one authority. Nor does there seem to have been any one moment at which one could speak of an agreement being reached. As we will see, various church fathers and various local councils did draw up lists of canonical New Testament books. In the end the matter seems to have been decided by a process of lively debate and gradually emerging consensus among the local Christian churches. In the following pages I will try to trace this process by looking at some of its significant moments.

Fig. 1: The Canon of the Old Testament

The books of the Old Testament are listed here in the order of the Hebrew (Jewish) canon, with the addition of the deuterocanonical works which are accepted as canonical by Catholics.

Pentateuch (*Torah*)
  Genesis
  Exodus
  Leviticus
  Numbers
  Deuteronomy

The Prophets (*Neviʾim*)
  Joshua ⎫
  Judges ⎬ also known as the "Former Prophets" or (in modern times) the
  1–2 Samuel ⎪ "Deuteronomistic History"
  1–2 Kings ⎭

  Isaiah
  Jeremiah
  Ezekiel

Hosea	Jonah	Zephaniah
Joel	Micah	Haggai
Amos	Nahum	Zechariah
Obadiah	Habakkuk	Malachi

  sometimes known as the twelve "Minor Prophets"

The Writings (*Ketuvim*)

Psalms	Lamentations	Daniel
Job	Esther	Ezra
Proverbs	Song of Songs	Nehemiah
Ruth	Qoheleth (Ecclesiastes)	1–2 Chronicles

The Deuterocanonical Works (also called the Apocrypha)

Judith	1–2 Maccabees
Tobit	Ecclesiasticus (Sirach)
Baruch	Wisdom of Solomon

(a) The Old Testament as Christian Scripture

As was the case with the Old Testament Scriptures, the writings of the New Testament seem to have emerged from a lively oral culture. The focus of early Christian faith was not a set of writings. It was a proclamation of the death and resurrection of Jesus and of its significance for human beings. In addition to this central proclamation, individual sayings of Jesus seem to have been preserved and handed on, particularly for use in moral exhortation. If the earliest Christians required biblical support for their message, then they found plenty of support in their Jewish Scriptures, for—even if the limits of the Old Testament canon were not yet fixed—Judaism already had its Sacred Scriptures. The Law and the Prophets along with a number of other writings were regarded as the word of God.

It was true that the followers of Jesus sometimes had to employ new styles of interpretation in order to uncover the Christian meaning of these Jewish Scriptures (see, for instance, Gal 4:21-31). The earliest Christians were in no doubt that their message about Christ could be found in what we call the Old Testament, even if it was sometimes

Fig. 2: The Canon of the New Testament

The Gospels
    Matthew
    Mark   }   The Synoptic Gospels
    Luke
    John

The Acts of the Apostles (a continuation of the Gospel of Luke)

The Letters of Paul

Romans	Colossians
1–2 Corinthians	1–2 Thessalonians
Galatians	1–2 Timothy
Ephesians	Titus
Philippians	Philemon

The Letter to the Hebrews

The Letters to all Christians (also known as the Catholic Epistles)
    James
    1–2 Peter
    1–3 John
    Jude

The Book of Revelation (also known as the Apocalypse)

ties with their text is also revealing: it suggests that these four gospels had not yet achieved a fixed status as Sacred Scripture.

The formation of a closed New Testament canon with authoritative status was encouraged by the work of Marcion, who also died about the year 160. Marcion was an early Christian thinker who believed there was a radical opposition between the God of the Old Testament and that of the New Testament. This belief led him to a thoroughgoing revision of the existing Christian Scriptures, which were purged of all elements that referred to the Old Testament. Needless to say, not much was left. From the existing gospels, for example, Marcion accepted only a highly edited version of the Gospel of Luke. The church as a whole rejected Marcion's position, but in doing so it was forced to name certain writings as authoritative.

A key figure here seems to have been Irenaeus of Lyons (ca. 130–200), who insisted that our four gospels, and only our four gospels, should be accepted as reliable and authoritative. Although there continued to be some debate regarding the Gospel of Luke, probably because of its use by Marcion, Irenaeus' position soon became widely accepted. It seems, therefore, that by the end of the second century there existed a fixed and authoritative collection of four gospels.

As far as the canonical status of the other books of the New Testament is concerned, there continued to be some debate through to the end of the fourth century. Between the end of the second century and the end of the fourth century we find two contrary tendencies. On the one hand, a few of the books that were eventually accepted into the canon continued to be regarded with suspicion. Particularly debated were the letter to the Hebrews and the book of Revelation. On the other hand, some early Christian writings that were eventually rejected from the canon were still competing for acceptance. For instance, the Christians of this period showed a particular fondness for an early second-century work known as the letter of Barnabas.

This state of uncertainty is reflected in the writer Origen, who in about the year 253 can speak of three categories of writings. The first

11

category is that of "undisputed" books, whose authority all Christians accepted. The second is that of "doubtful" books, whose status was undecided. The third is that of what he calls "false" books, whose claim was to be rejected. A similar threefold classification can be found in the work of the church historian Eusebius of Caesarea (ca. 260–340). A key figure in bringing these controversies to an end seems to have been the theologian and church father Athanasius of Alexandria. In a letter dating from Easter 397, Athanasius set out our current list of twenty-seven books and insisted that only these were to be accepted as authoritative. This position was soon accepted by all the churches.

TEXTS AND TRANSLATIONS

(a) The transmission of the biblical text

It is one thing to have established a collection of canonical writings; it is quite another to transmit those writings unchanged from one generation to another. Before the European invention of printing in the mid-fifteenth century, biblical manuscripts had to be painstakingly copied by hand, either onto papyrus (a material similar to paper but made from the reed-like papyrus plant) or onto vellum (specially prepared calfskin). While medieval scribes developed remarkably efficient methods of copying, the process was still liable to error and produced works that were expensive for a reader to purchase.

As far as writing materials are concerned, in the Old Testament period the typical form was the scroll, which continues to be used for liturgical purposes within Judaism today. However, a scroll is not a very convenient object for a reader to consult. It requires two hands—one to hold the scroll while the other hand unfurls it—and it must be rewound after use in preparation for the next reader. A scroll can also be very long, so that in this respect too it is an unwieldy artifact. For instance, the sixty-six chapters of Isaiah require a scroll more than twenty-one feet (about seven meters) in length. This meant that it was all but impossible for the entire Old Testament to be recorded on one scroll. Very often separate scrolls were used for individual books.

This process was revolutionized by the invention of the *codex*, probably late in the first century of the Christian era. The codex consists of individual pages bound together into something resembling our modern book. Indeed the development of the codex seems to have been pioneered by Christians out of their desire to preserve and consult their sacred writings.

If biblical texts were copied by hand and if this process was of necessity subject to error, then how can we be sure that our Bibles are accurate copies of the original documents? The short answer to this question is that we cannot. Despite some extraordinary discoveries in recent times, we do not have a Hebrew manuscript of the entire Old Testament that is older than the tenth century A.D. We do, however, have ancient manuscripts of the entire Greek New Testament, some of which take us back to the fourth century A.D. We also have ancient manuscripts of individual biblical books, both of the Old and New Testaments, as well as many papyrus and vellum fragments. These provide a rich resource for the student of the biblical text. The Bible is certainly no worse off in this respect than any other ancient work. Indeed we have a much richer supply of manuscript evidence for the Bible than we have for the classical authors of Greece and Rome.

Nonetheless, the task of piecing together a reliable text—a task known as textual criticism—remains a difficult one in which capable scholars can reasonably adopt different positions. It is also a highly specialized task, requiring detailed knowledge of the individual manuscripts, their relationship to one another, and the history of their transmission. Where uncertainties remain, our modern biblical translations will frequently contain footnotes that indicate that at this point different manuscripts have different texts. These footnotes typically have the form: "some witnesses read . . . ," or perhaps "other ancient authorities read . . . ," with the variant text following. A quick glance at such footnotes will show the reader how minor such variant "readings" (as they are known) generally are.

Of particular significance for textual critics has been the discovery, beginning in 1947, of a series of ancient manuscripts by the shore of the Dead Sea near an ancient settlement known today as Khirbet Qumran. This discovery has been an important one for a number of reasons. For instance, these "Dead Sea Scrolls" have shown us how diverse Judaism was around the beginning of the

Christian era. While making no direct reference to the Christian movement, the Scrolls have shed light on the world in which that movement developed.

What is worth noting here, however, is that the Qumran scrolls include much biblical material. In particular, they include both a complete copy of the book of Isaiah and fragments of all the other Old Testament books (i.e., the books of the Hebrew canon), except that of Esther. These texts and fragments are all much older than any previously extant manuscripts. While these discoveries have provided new evidence for textual critics to use, they have also demonstrated how reliable the traditional Hebrew text was. This traditional text, known as the Masoretic text (after the Masoretes, the Jewish scholars of the sixth to ninth centuries A.D. who edited it), remains the basis of our present-day editions and translations.

(b) Ancient translations

The books of our Christian Bible were originally written in three different languages. Most of the Old Testament was written in Hebrew, although small sections were written in a language that is a close relative of Hebrew, namely, Aramaic. While Jesus himself apparently spoke Aramaic, the whole of the New Testament was written in the common language of the Mediterranean world, namely, Greek. It follows that for most readers who have little or no knowledge of the biblical languages, access to the Bible will be through translations. (For serious study, of course, access to the original languages is indispensable.) For this reason the student will find it helpful to know something about some of the better known biblical translations.

The best known ancient translation of the Bible has already been mentioned. It is the Greek translation of the Old Testament that is known as the Septuagint (LXX). While the Septuagint was in all likelihood produced by a number of translators over several centuries, the traditional story of its origin highlights the authority it had within the Greek-speaking Jewish world. The story is found in a work known as the Letter of Aristeas, which probably dates from about the second century B.C. According to this source, a certain King Ptolemy (probably Ptolemy II Philadelphius [285–247 B.C.]) wished to have copies of all the books of the world. He therefore commissioned a translation of the Jewish Scriptures by sending a letter to the High Priest in Jerusalem. The High Priest sent the King seventy-two translators (six from each of the twelve tribes), who completed the work of translation in precisely seventy-two days.

Modern scholars consider the Letter of Aristeas to have all the marks of legend, and the real history of the Septuagint is much debated. While its oldest sections may well have been produced by the Jews of Alexandria in the third century B.C., as Jewish tradition suggest, it does seem to have undergone a series of later revisions. In any case, the Septuagint was an important work for Greek-speaking Jews for several hundred years. It fell out of favor among Jewish scholars only after the first century A.D., possibly because of its widespread adoption by Christians. But the Septuagint remained important within the Christian world, being the preferred biblical text not only of the New Testament writers but also of many of the church fathers. St. Augustine, for instance, believed that its translation was divinely inspired. To this day, the Septuagint continues to be a widely used translation of the Bible among Greek-speaking Orthodox Christians.

The second ancient translation worthy of mention is that known as the Vulgate, a name that suggests that this was an *editio vulgata*, or "common edition," of the biblical text. The Vulgate is a translation of the Bible into Latin, traditionally attributed to the early Christian scholar and ascetic, St. Jerome. Concerned by the lack of agreement among the existing Old Latin versions, Pope Damasus (ca. 304–384) commissioned Jerome, the leading biblical scholar of his age, to undertake a new Latin translation. While Jerome began his translation, as was customary at that time, from the Septuagint, he soon became aware of its deficiencies. This led him to undertake a more thorough translation, this time from the Hebrew text whose authority he vigorously defended. This new Latin version appeared between the years 390 and 405.

The Vulgate as we have it today, however, is not identical to the text produced by St. Jerome. Indeed our present Vulgate seems to be a composite work: some coming from Jerome, some representing surviving Old Latin translations, and some freshly revised after Jerome's time. Its importance lies in the fact that it remained the most influential version of the Bible throughout the

Middle Ages. After a decree of the Council of Trent in 1546, the Vulgate became the official Latin Bible of the Catholic Church, being published in an official edition in 1592. For this reason, most Catholic translations of the Bible in the modern period were made from the Vulgate. This remained the case right up until 1943 when translations from the original languages were officially sanctioned. A revised edition of the Vulgate was published by Pope John Paul II in 1979 under the title *Nova Vulgata* (New Vulgate).

(c) Modern translations

No attempt can be made here to cover the diversity of modern translations of the Bible that today cover more than 350 of the world's languages. But it may be worth mentioning the most famous early English translations, both Protestant and Catholic.

The first complete translation of the Bible into English was made from the Latin Vulgate by John Wycliffe and his supporters, between 1382 and 1384. Wycliffe's translation became the common English Bible of the fifteenth and early sixteenth centuries. The earliest printed biblical translations in English were those of William Tyndale, his New Testament first appearing in 1525. Tyndale later published some parts of the Old Testament, but he died as a Protestant martyr in 1536 before his translation could be completed. Tyndale's translation is noteworthy not only for its lively English, which left its imprint on later translations, but also because he worked from the original languages.

Because Tyndale's translation was never completed, the honor of being the first complete printed English Bible falls to the translation of Miles Coverdale, published in 1535. But the most famous English Bible ever produced is undoubtedly the Authorized Version, commonly known as the King James Version, of 1611. This edition became so popular that among many Protestant Christians it achieved almost canonical status in its own right. The King James tradition was continued in the Revised Version of 1881 and 1885, the Revised Standard Version of 1946 and 1952, and the New Revised Standard Version of 1989.

Some of these early editions of the Bible in English were regarded by Catholics with suspicion. Generally speaking, this was not so much because of their translations as because of the notes that

often accompanied them, notes that continued the Protestant Reformers' attacks on the Catholic Church. Catholics therefore undertook their own translations of the Bible into English. Up until the mid-twentieth century, these translations were generally based on the text of the Latin Vulgate. Noteworthy among these was the Douay-Rheims version, the New Testament of which was published in 1582 and the Old Testament in 1609. The language of this translation was somewhat improved by a revision undertaken between 1749 and 1763 by Bishop Richard Challoner of London.

More recent Catholic translations from the original languages include the New American Bible of 1952 and 1970 (the New Testament of which was extensively revised in 1987), a translation entitled the Jerusalem Bible (published in 1966 but originally produced in French), and the significantly revised New Jerusalem Bible (published in 1985). In more recent times the cooperation of Protestant and Catholic scholars in the work of biblical translation, as well as the inclusion of the deuterocanonical books in most scholarly editions, seems to be bringing an end to the age of separate, confessional biblical texts.

With regard to contemporary biblical translations, it may be useful to make some comment on the philosophies that underlie the different versions. An attentive reader of Bible translations will soon realize that they may be located on a spectrum. At the one end of the spectrum are those translations that attempt, as much as possible, to render one Greek or Hebrew word with a corresponding English word. Of course, a completely word-for-word rendering would produce a terribly stilted style of English. Indeed it would border on the unintelligible. But some translations do try to keep as close as possible to this ideal. Some of the early English translations seem to have followed this principle. The King James Version, for instance, even printed in italic type words added by its translators that do not correspond to words in the Greek or Hebrew text.

At the other end of the spectrum are those translations that attempt to discover the sense of a Greek or Hebrew phrase and then to reproduce this meaning freely in English. The correspondence aimed at here is not that of words, but that of meaning. If that meaning is thought to be best conveyed by an entirely idiomatic English phrase, then that phrase will be chosen even if it is far removed from the manner of speech adopted by the biblical writers. Both types of translation undoubtedly have their use, but the reader who wishes to undertake a close study of the biblical text will normally choose the former.

(d) Division into chapters and verses

It may also be helpful to comment on the division of our Bibles into chapters and verses. The Old Testament was already divided into sections in ancient times; such divisions may even be found among the manuscripts at Qumran. But these divisions of the text do not correspond to our modern chapters. Generally speaking, they marked off sections of text for weekly study, a practice that continued within Judaism. Similarly, the oldest Greek manuscripts of the New Testament are also provided with chapter divisions. But these, too, do not correspond to our modern chapters. It was only in the thirteenth century that the entire Bible came to be divided into chapters. This development occurred at the University of Paris in the course of developing a standard biblical text. The chapter divisions were then carried over into the Hebrew manuscripts in the fourteenth century.

As far as verse divisions are concerned, ancient Hebrew manuscripts did sometimes contain numbered verses. But the verses were not numbered by chapter as is our practice today. The present verse numbering of the Old Testament dates only from some printed editions of 1563 and 1571. The verse numbering of the New Testament is of a similar date. It is first found in the fourth edition of the Greek New Testament printed in 1551 by the Parisian publisher Robert Estienne (also known by his Latin name Stephanus). Indeed Stephanus is said to have divided the New Testament into verses while on a journey between Lyons and Paris.

These remarks indicate that the present chapter and verse divisions of our Bible were imposed upon the text at a relatively late date. While they are convenient, they have no particular authority and can sometimes be misleading. For this reason they should not be regarded as a guide to the interpretation of the text. The careful student of the Bible would be well advised simply to ignore them.

The Interpretation of the Bible

THE TASK OF INTERPRETATION

We are about to study the history of biblical interpretation. A devout reader may find this strange and may ask why it should be considered important. Why devote so much time to studying how the Bible has been understood? If the Bible is the word of God, then surely its message is the same in every age. There should be no need to speak about its "interpretation." If the Bible is the word of God, surely we should be able simply to pick it up and understand it. All this talk about interpretation—is it not merely complicating what is at heart a simple matter of faith?

Faced with the bewildering variety of biblical interpretations, one can understand this objection. However, it is fundamentally mistaken. For better or for worse, there is no such thing as a simple reading of the Bible. The Bible is always interpreted, even when it is read by an unsophisticated reader who would never think of being an interpreter. If we do pick up the Bible and understand it immediately, without any conscious reflection on its meaning, it is not because we are failing to interpret. It is because the act of interpretation is spontaneous: it happens so quickly that we fail to realize it has occurred. There is no reading of the Bible without interpretation, even if that interpretation is performed in an entirely unself-conscious manner.

While this idea may be surprising to many who think of themselves as "simple believers," it should not be a cause for alarm. Even if one believes that the Bible is God's word, it remains true that this divine word has been revealed in human words. The Second Vatican Council embraced this idea in its statement on divine revelation (*Dei Verbum*) where it insisted that "God speaks to men and women in sacred Scripture in human fashion."

Indeed the Council went further, writing that there is a certain parallel between the humanity of Sacred Scripture and the doctrine of the incarnation. Just as the eternal Word of God took upon himself the weakness of human nature, so in Scripture the words of God are expressed in human language. While the Bible may be God's word, it is also an artifact, a product of human culture.

Not only is the Bible a human artifact, as a written work it is also a collection of signs. For this reason it requires interpretation. A sign by definition is something that refers beyond itself. It has a double existence. First of all, it is a physical object (in this case, marks on a page) that can be seen, touched, tasted, heard, or smelled. But as a sign it points beyond the impression it makes on our senses: it acts as a bearer of meaning. When someone speaks to us, a sound is uttered that can be analyzed as a pattern of wave-like disturbances in the air. But that is not normally what we think of when we are addressed. What we think of are those realities to which the speaker's words refer. Similarly, when we look at a painting, it is not normally to admire the texture of the canvas on which it is painted. It is to appreciate the impression the painting is meant to convey. The sound of the speech and the paint on the canvas are physical realities that the physicist or chemist could describe. But they are much more than that. As products of human culture, they refer beyond themselves to other realities that they in some sense represent.

We may illustrate this fact by a famous example, first given by the English philosopher Gilbert Ryle. When we see someone rapidly close and open an eyelid, we must immediately decide whether this was a mere twitch—an involuntary act, perhaps in response to a floating grain of dust—or a deliberate act. If it was an involuntary act, then it can be described scientifically as a physiological reaction. In this case it remains simply a physical act, although it may have been triggered by a number of events. There is nothing more that needs to be said about it. But if it was a deliberate act, then it becomes a gesture, a wink, a small but significant artifact of human culture. As such it carries a meaning.

The problem is that it is not immediately clear what meaning it carries. This will depend very much on the situation in which it was performed. Was it a friendly gesture, directed to ourselves, intended to establish a rapport? Was it not only a friendly gesture but a sexually loaded gesture, an invitation to greater intimacy? Or was it an ironical gesture, a warning that there is something in the present situation that is not quite what it appears? On the other hand, perhaps the wink was not directed to us at all. Perhaps it was directed to someone else. If so, it may have been a signal, an indication that the other person should initiate some course of activity, one perhaps detrimental to us. Even so simple a gesture as a wink is deeply ambiguous. It requires interpretation.

Gilbert Ryle points out how complex this process can become. Suppose that the person winking is merely imitating another person. Suppose that the gesture is really a parody of someone who is prone to giving significant winks. It might be performed behind someone's back as a way of causing amusement to the onlookers. In this case, the wink takes on a new level of meaning that the interpreter will have to take into account. Suppose, once again, that the gesture is being performed by someone alone, in front of a mirror. He may, perhaps, be intending to practice his parody of someone's habit of winking so as to amuse his friends later on. In this case, there is a third level of meaning. Someone wanting to interpret the act of winking, to say what it means in this context, would have to take all three levels of meaning into account.

Unfortunately the task of interpretation is still more complex in the case of a written work. In the examples just given, the winker and the observer have at least one situation in common, namely, that in which the wink is being performed. In this situation the significance of the wink may appear obvious to the observer. It is understood immediately, without any apparent need for interpretation. (Once again, however, this does not mean that the gesture is not being interpreted. It means only that the act of interpretation is very rapid, perhaps automatic.) But when it comes to the interpretation of a written work, the situation may be very different. Such a work endures even after the death of its author and the loss of the context in which it was written.

The prophet Isaiah may be dead, but we have his words collected in the biblical book that bears his name. In this case the writer and the interpreter are far removed from one another in time. The prophet Isaiah's words may make reference to realities in the situation in which he was living. He will refer, for instance, to reigning Israelite monarchs and to the political situation in which his nation found itself. To understand what this text meant when it was written, the interpreter will have to reconstruct the context in which it was written, the situation in which it first served as an act of communication. As we will see shortly, it was a new awareness of the distance between the author and the interpreter of biblical texts that contributed to the rise of a self-consciously historical approach to biblical interpretation in the seventeenth century.

Discussions of these matters generally go under the heading of the term "hermeneutics," from the Greek verb meaning "to interpret." Hermeneutics, that is, the theory of interpretation, should be distinguished from exegesis, which refers to the very act of interpreting particular texts themselves. (The word "exegesis" comes from a Greek phrase meaning "to draw out," in the sense that one "draws meaning out" of a text.) Neither term is limited to discussions of biblical interpretation; they can be used with regard to the interpretation of any body of literature. Hermeneutical discussions can become very complex as we will see later when we consider what are sometimes called postmodern approaches to biblical interpretation.

For the moment I wish only to indicate that there is no reading of the Bible without some kind of interpretation. Indeed to read a translation of the Bible is to take for granted other peoples' interpretations, for at many points their translations will be based on interpretive decisions. For this reason alone it is important to appreciate the many and various ways in which the Bible has been interpreted throughout Christian history. It is to this task that we must now turn.

Patristic and Medieval Interpretation
(ca. 200–1500)

Having looked briefly at the origins of our Bible, it is time to begin our survey of the history of its interpretation. That survey begins with a very long stretch of history, one that embraces what is customarily described as the age of the church fathers (the patristic age: ca. 200–750 A.D.) and the medieval period (ca. 750–1500). In most fields of study it would be foolhardy to try to discuss so long a period, which embraces so many changes in European society and thought. In the late medieval period, for instance, the focus of European cultural life shifted from the countryside with its villages and monasteries, to the newly emerging cities with their commerce and their universities. This social change went hand-in-hand with an intellectual Renaissance that involved the rediscovery of many philosophical and scientific texts from the ancient world. This in turn prepared the way for the cultural Renaissance of the fourteenth and fifteenth centuries that contained the seeds of both the Protestant Reformation of the sixteenth century and the scientific revolution of the seventeenth.

PRINCIPLES OF PATRISTIC AND MEDIEVAL INTERPRETATION

All of these changes are important, and I will return to them shortly for they have their impact on biblical interpretation. When it comes to the understanding of the Bible, however, this long period of history has a certain unity, for virtually all Christian interpreters throughout these centuries accepted a basic set of assumptions. These are all the more important because they are assumptions that later centuries were to call into question. The first assumption was that of a harmony between the message of the Old Testament and that of the New Testament. The second was that of a harmony between the message of the Bible and

that of the church. The third assumption was that of a harmony between sacred and secular knowledge. The first two of these assumptions require little explanation and will be discussed only briefly. The third will require a slightly more extended treatment.

(a) Old and New Testaments

With regard to the harmony of the Old and the New Testaments, patristic and medieval thought was dominated by the idea of the divine inspiration of the Bible. The Bible may have had a diversity of human authors. These authors may have lived at different times and written for different audiences using a variety of literary genres. Its authors may have been Jewish rather than Christian. But insofar as patristic and medieval thinkers recognized these facts at all, they regarded them as insignificant when set alongside the divine inspiration of Scripture. The Bible may have a number of human authors, but it had one divine author whose voice could be heard throughout.

This meant that Scripture could contain messages about which its human authors were only dimly aware. For instance, the author of Isaiah 7:14 (". . . the virgin shall be with child, and bear a son, and shall name him Immanuel") may have lived in the eighth century B.C. In the normal course of affairs, one would not expect an author of that date to know about the birth of Jesus occurring some seven hundred years later. But this expectation has no force when it comes to a work inspired by God. Even if Isaiah did not know about the birth of Jesus, God surely did.

Those who believed in the divine authorship of Scripture could quite naturally take this verse as a reference to Jesus. It was not just isolated verses that were interpreted in this way: the patristic and medieval interpretation of the Old Testament was

18

thoroughly Christocentric ("Christ-centered"). If Jesus was indeed the eternal Word of God made flesh (John 1:14), then one would expect the entire Scripture to speak of him even if only in veiled and mysterious ways. As we will see, this assumption was to endure until the rise of historical criticism in the seventeenth century with its all-but-exclusive focus on the human authors of Scripture.

(b) Bible and church

With regard to the harmony between the message of the Bible and that of the church, patristic and medieval Christians did not just believe in the divine inspiration of Scripture; they also believed in the divine establishment of the church. The same God who was the author of the Bible had also founded an enduring institution on earth, an institution that spoke with divine authority. Nor was this institution some loose-knit and intangible community of believers; it was a very tangible and historically concrete body. It was nothing other than the Catholic Church founded on the apostles and governed by their successors the bishops, under the guidance of the successor of the Apostle Peter, the Bishop of Rome.

The same Spirit of God who had inspired the biblical writers guided the leaders of that church and kept them from error, particularly when they were called upon to define some central Christian doctrine. The teachings of the earliest church fathers, of church councils, and of individual popes provided the taken-for-granted interpretive lens through which patristic and medieval commentators viewed the biblical text. As we will see, this assumption was to endure until the Protestant Reformation of the sixteenth century, and it would be reaffirmed in the Catholic response to that Reformation.

(c) Sacred and secular knowledge

The third assumption, that of harmony between sacred and secular knowledge, is a more complex affair. We may begin by noting that for patristic and medieval Christians, the distinction between what we would call sacred and secular knowledge was not primarily a distinction between two fields of knowledge. We might be tempted to think that secular and religious knowledge—science and religion, to use our modern distinction—are distinct because they deal with two quite different objects. We might argue, for instance, that science deals with the structure and mechanism of the world, while religion deals with the relationship of that world to God. But for patristic and medieval thinkers, the distinction lay elsewhere.

Sacred and secular knowledge were distinguished not so much by their contents (which could overlap) as by their *source*. Sacred knowledge was knowledge derived from divine revelation. It included matters inaccessible to human reason, such as the mystery of the Trinitarian nature of God, but it also included matters that we would regard as the province of science, such as the origin of the world. Secular knowledge, on the other hand, was knowledge obtained not from revelation but by the exercise of human reason. It dealt primarily with this-worldly matters, but it was not restricted to some non-religious realm. Patristic and medieval thinkers believed that human reason could also attain to some knowledge of God by reflection on the world God created. It follows that for the church fathers and for medieval thinkers, sacred knowledge included knowledge of the structure of the world, while secular knowledge could include knowledge of God.

To many modern believers this view seems deeply problematic. Many Christians today argue that the objects of sacred and secular knowledge are distinct: sacred and secular knowledge are distinguished not so much by their source as by their *content*. This position betrays a very modern anxiety. It is driven by the fear that if science and religion did have the same object, if their content did overlap, the result would be conflict. This anxiety is a legacy of our modern debates about religion and science; it is foreign to the world of the patristic and medieval writers.

Even ancient Christian authors do not simply identify what we would call religion and science; they recognize that revelation and natural philosophy have different aims. But they also assume that their conclusions may overlap. For the church fathers this idea was relatively unproblematic. They take it for granted that there can be no irresolvable conflict between sacred and secular knowledge. Truth was ultimately one, whether that truth came directly from God or from the results of rational enquiry. If your interpretation of Scripture brought you into conflict with the assured results of rational enquiry, it could be assumed you were misunderstanding the meaning of Scripture. If, on the other hand, the results of rational enquiry were not assured and they seemed to contradict Scripture, it could be assumed that one's rational enquiry had gone astray.

PATRISTIC AND MEDIEVAL EXEGESIS

Under the guidance of these assumptions the church fathers and medieval theologians interpreted particular biblical passages. I say "medieval theologians" because up until about the thirteenth century, the interpretation of Scripture stood at the very heart of the theological enterprise. Our modern faculties of theology and divinity schools customarily make a distinction between biblical studies and systematic theology. This modern distinction would have been foreign to a patristic or early medieval theologian; it has its roots in developments that occurred only in the twelfth and thirteenth centuries with the growth of the universities. For the patristic or early medieval theologian, theology was the study of the *sacra pagina*, the sacred page.

When we examine the particular methods of exegesis adopted by patristic and medieval scholars, what is most striking is their flexibility. Where a modern interpreter might seek to discover the meaning of a biblical passage, patristic and medieval interpreters regularly offer several differing interpretations of the same passage without any sense that these are in conflict. There seem to be two factors at work here to produce what to us is a remarkable result.

The first is that patristic and medieval writers did not judge the correctness of an interpretation by reference to textual features alone. Rather, the most important mark of an acceptable interpretation was the conformity of its content to the *regula fidei*, the rule of faith. If two differing interpretations both conformed to the rule of faith, they were both (in principle) acceptable. There was no need to choose between them. The second factor is a strong sense that the biblical text, as an inspired text, could have several levels of meaning. This belief in the multileveled character of the Bible encouraged patristic and medieval interpreters to understand each biblical passage in

several different ways. Both these features of ancient and medieval biblical interpretation deserve closer scrutiny.

(a) The *regula fidei* (rule of faith)

The modern biblical interpreter is inclined to judge the correctness of an interpretation by the method through which it is achieved. In other words, the rules of interpretation are methodological: if one observes certain safeguards in dealing with the text, then one can be confident about one's result. The church fathers and medieval scholars, on the other hand, enjoyed a great freedom when it came to methods of interpretation. Even these were not entirely arbitrary—there were rules of interpretation that the fathers followed—but at the end of the day an interpretation was judged acceptable primarily on the basis of its content. St. Augustine, for instance, can accept the possibility of many legitimate interpretations, but only if they are all "in harmony with our faith." Similarly, he will dismiss an interpretation that he regards as unacceptable with the simple judgment: "This is against our Catholic faith."

This body of belief against which interpretations were measured was often described as the rule of faith (*regula fidei*), a phrase that first seems to have been used by Christian writers of the second century. St. Augustine suggests that the content of this rule of faith can be derived from the clearer passages of Scripture and from the teachings of the church. It follows that those writers who employ the rule of faith as a mark of correct biblical interpretation are merely reflecting the second assumption named above. They are affirming a unity between what is taught by the Bible and what is taught by the church.

(b) The spiritual sense of Scripture

A second feature of patristic and medieval exegesis is its readiness to offer spiritual interpretations of biblical texts. (These are often described as "allegorical interpretations," but the phrase "spiritual interpretation" better expresses the understanding of the fathers.) The church fathers believed that just as the human being is composed of body and soul, so the Scriptures have both a bodily and a spiritual meaning. Spiritual interpretation involved finding new levels of meaning in the biblical text, hidden (as it were) beneath its surface or literal sense. Even if they were perhaps not entirely clear to the human author of the text in question, these meanings were placed in the text by the divine author of Scripture.

This approach to the Bible may be illustrated by the story of Jesus' miraculous feeding of five thousand people (Mark 6:35-45). On a spiritual interpretation, such as that followed by St. Augustine in his sermons, the five loaves might be understood to represent the five books of the Pentateuch, the first five books of the Bible. Similarly, the boy who carried the loaves to Jesus could be seen to represent the Jewish people who carried the loaves without being able to break them open. Jesus' breaking of the loaves represented his explanation of the true sense of the Old Testament. This example also highlights a dark side of such spiritual interpretations: the fact that it often reinforced traditional Christian stereotypes about Jews.

Christians were by no means the first to use spiritual interpretation. This approach to texts had both Jewish and Greek roots. (The fact that it has Jewish roots is deeply ironic, given the way in which Christians often used the technique against Judaism.) Greek commentators on classical works had long employed allegory to offer morally uplifting interpretations of what were sometimes rather brutal stories. In the Jewish world, Philo of Alexandria (ca. 15 B.C.–A.D. 50) had used allegory to discover philosophical wisdom in the biblical narratives. But it was Christians who developed spiritual interpretation to a fine art in their attempts to bridge the gap between the Old and New Testaments, to avoid scandalous interpretations, and to find contemporary meanings in ancient texts.

(c) The four senses of Scripture

As early as the fifth century, the idea that biblical passages could possess a spiritual meaning had developed into the doctrine of the "four senses." In this doctrine, each biblical text could be read literally, according to its historical meaning. But it could also be read spiritually, and there existed three levels of spiritual interpretation. The allegorical sense spoke of the mysteries of faith. The moral sense spoke of how one was to live. The anagogical sense, as it was called, spoke of the hoped-for homeland of heaven. In the thirteenth century, this doctrine was encapsulated in a famous Latin verse:

Littera gesta docet,	The letter teaches what was done,
quid credas allegoria,	allegory what you are to believe,
moralis quid agas,	the moral sense what you are to do,
quo tendas anagogia.	the anagogical sense where you are to go.

If a psalm, for instance, spoke of a love for Jerusalem, then the literal meaning of this verse would refer to the Palestinian city of that name. Allegorically, Jerusalem could be understood to refer to the church. Morally, it could be understood as the human soul. Anagogically, it could be seen as a reference to the heavenly Jerusalem. While this doctrine of the four senses of Scripture was widely accepted in principle, it was rarely employed in practice. When patristic and medieval commentators came to study particular biblical passages, they tended to speak of just two senses: a literal and a spiritual. The latter could be an allegorical, a moral, or an anagogical meaning, depending on the passage being interpreted and the aim of the interpreter.

Biblical commentators of the late Middle Ages continued to speak of the spiritual sense of Scripture but laid increasing emphasis on the literal meaning. The great theologian St. Thomas Aquinas (ca. 1225–1274), for instance, insisted on the priority of the literal sense, that sense intended by the human author of the Bible. All other interpretations of Scripture, he insisted, were to be related to this literal or historical sense, and only the literal sense may be appealed to in theological debate. Nothing was lost by such restrictions, since every important Christian doctrine was somewhere contained in the literal meaning of the text.

In Thomas' view, the literal sense refers to certain historical realities. By controlling history, God has arranged that these historical realities can carry new levels of meaning. It is these new levels of meaning—in the events of history rather than in the text itself—that are the spiritual interpreter's task to discern. In effect, Thomas' teaching picks up and brings to a compromise solution some debates of the patristic period, when exponents of the spiritual sense (associated with the city of Alexandria) had competed with defenders of the literal sense (often associated with the city of Antioch).

However untenable it may seem to us, this patristic and medieval doctrine of the spiritual senses of Scripture has great religious power. Indeed it is hard to see how certain texts, such as some of the psalms, could be used in prayer in any other way. Not only does spiritual interpretation enable Christians to avoid otherwise insoluble difficulties in biblical interpretation (such as passages in which God appears to be acting in brutal ways), it also enables believers to read the Old Testament as Christian Scripture that speaks (in veiled terms) of the life, death, and resurrection of Jesus.

Finally, spiritual interpretation frees the interpreter from the tyranny of history. For spiritual interpretation not only links the Old and New Testaments, but the patterns of divine activity and human response found in the Bible can be projected forward (as types) into the reader's own time. In this way even the biblical history that on the face of it has little to do with our own time can offer a pattern by which our own lives can be understood.

The power of this method of interpretation is easily illustrated by reference to the Old Testament story of the Exodus. The biblical story speaks not only of the escape of the Hebrews from Egyptian slavery under Moses but also of the wandering in the wilderness of Sinai and the conquest of the land of Canaan. On the first level, that of a literal interpretation, the story can be read as a historical account of the origins of God's people: the events by which they became a nation, received the Law of Moses, and inherited the promised land.

Read spiritually, however, the same events could be projected forward to our own time to provide an explanation of contemporary events. (This was the way in which the Exodus story was read by nineteenth-century African-American slaves.) On a more personal level the events of the Exodus could represent the individual's journey of faith: from baptism (a release from the slavery of sin), through the desert wandering of this present life, across the Jordan River (that is, death), and into the promised land of eternal life. In all these different ways, spiritual interpretation provided a means of bridging the gap between past and present. It provided a way of incorporating later events, including the reader's own life, into the biblical framework. The collapse of this imaginative method of interpretation, at least among theologians and biblical scholars, would be one of the most significant developments of the modern period.

Reformation and Counter-Reformation (ca. 1500–1650)

The Protestant Reformation that begins with the work of Martin Luther (1483–1546) marked a new stage in Christian attitudes to the Bible. The degree of novelty, however, should not be overstated. For all their rebellion against the authority of the medieval Catholic Church, the Protestant Reformers maintained many of the attitudes of their medieval forebears. In the previous section of this study, for instance, I spoke of the three assumptions that were characteristic of patristic and medieval exegesis: namely, a unity between the Old and New Testaments, a conformity between the message of the Bible and that of the church, and a harmony between sacred and secular knowledge. It was only the second assumption—the unity of Bible and church—that the Protestant Reformers wished to call into question. Even here, what the Reformers were questioning was a particular conception of the relationship of Bible and church. They did not want to see the Bible removed entirely from the community of believers. There is, therefore, a real continuity between the Protestant Reformers and the medieval church.

Similarly, the Reformers had much in common with the period we know as the Renaissance, the "rebirth" of interest in the world of classical thought and literature that occurred in the fourteenth and fifteenth centuries. It was the humanist scholars of that period—people like Lorenzo Valla (1407–1457)—who pioneered the learning of classical languages (including New Testament Greek) and the art of textual criticism. This interest in classical antiquity led humanist scholars to a new sense of the distance between the world of the New Testament and that of the late medieval church. The first Protestants would draw on this sense of distance in order to call for a reform of the church by appeal to its New Testament model.

In this section of our study I will be concerned only to highlight what was new in the Reformers' attitudes to the Bible. To do this I have chosen three issues, all related to the relationship between the Bible and the church. The first two issues have to do with the question of religious authority. Does the Bible require some authority outside of itself to make its meaning clear? More seriously, does the Bible require some authority outside of itself to authenticate its teachings, to assure us they are true? The third issue has to do with the nature of the biblical message. Do biblical texts have only one meaning, or are there—as patristic and medieval commentators believed—levels of meaning that the interpreter can discover? On all three questions the answers given by the Protestant Reformers would be unequivocal and would have consequences far beyond those they themselves intended.

THE BIBLE AND THE CHURCH

As they embarked on the task of calling for a reform of the church—a task that had become increasingly urgent in the preceding centuries—the first Protestants were faced with a problem. Their model for church reform was the picture of early Christianity that we find in the pages of the New Testament. But the New Testament had been traditionally interpreted in the light of the teaching and traditions of the church. To embark on their program of reform, they had to weaken the link between Bible and church, to insist that, while the Bible was clearly the church's book, at the end of the day the church stood under its authority.

There were two principles in particular that allowed them to take this stand: the principle that the Bible interprets itself and the (closely related) principle that the Bible authenticates itself. But if the church's authoritative intervention was to be truly redundant, a third principle was needed, one that protected Scripture from potentially obscure, spiritual interpretations. These three principles allowed the Reformers to argue that the word of God was accessible to the individual believer without any need for the intervention of bishops or theologians.

(a) The Bible interprets itself

The first of these principles, that the Bible interprets itself, was perhaps most characteristic of the thought of Martin Luther. Luther takes his stand on the traditional principle (echoed in 1965 by the Second Vatican Council) that the Bible is to be interpreted "according to that Spirit by which it was written." He argues that this is a general interpretive principle: every book must be understood in the spirit of its author. But where can the Spirit of the Bible be found if not in those writings he himself wrote? Therefore it is to the Bible itself we must look if we are to understand it correctly. In a word, Scripture is "its own interpreter." This assertion in turn assumes that the meaning of Scripture is clear. It is only because its meaning is accessible to all that it requires no external interpreter to elucidate its secrets. This represents another important Reformation principle: namely, "the clarity of Scripture."

At first sight these claims might seem to be evidently false. The meaning of the Bible is apparently not clear, since the same text gives rise to many apparently divergent interpretations. Indeed many people seem unable to understand its message at all. But for Luther the clarity of Scripture, its ability to interpret itself, is not a matter that could be proven or disproved by studying what actually happens. It is a matter of faith. It is only on the basis of biblical authority that the Bible can be known to have a clear meaning.

If, for instance, Jesus and the apostles argued from Scripture, we must assume that its meaning was sufficiently clear to establish their case. Similarly, 2 Peter 1:19 speaks of Scripture as "a lamp shining in a dark place," which would not be true if its meaning were obscure. If many interpreters are unable to grasp this clear meaning, it is merely an indication of human sinfulness. Similarly if interpreters claim to find hidden meanings in the Bible, this merely suggests they are imposing their own meanings on the sacred text

rather than submitting themselves to its authority. In this sense, the external clarity of Scripture is only obvious to one who enjoys the inward illumination of the Holy Spirit. It is the Holy Spirit, by whom the Bible was inspired, who transforms this external clarity of Scripture into the inner clarity of perception.

(b) The Bible authenticates itself

Luther not only held that Scripture interprets itself; he also insisted that the Bible authenticates itself. It is, in itself, sufficient witness to its own authority. Once again this idea needs to be understood in relationship to the claims of the Catholic Church. Catholics could argue that the Reformers could not consistently reject the authority of the church, since it was the church that gave us the Bible. After all, it was the church that decided which books would form the New Testament canon. But for Luther the decision regarding the canon was merely an act of recognition. The church points out the authority of the Bible to us; she does not grant authority to the Bible. The Bible's authority comes from within. The Scripture bears witness to itself as God's word, and the church merely recognizes this fact. The church's decision regarding the canon does not mean that the church stands above the Bible any more than the fact that John the Baptist directs us to Christ means that John the Baptist stands above Christ.

This fundamental Reformation principle—that the Bible itself is sufficient evidence of its own authority—was developed by John Calvin (1509–1564) into the doctrine of "the internal testimony of the Holy Spirit." In effect, this doctrine spells out how it is that the Bible can be said to authenticate itself. It authenticates itself, Calvin argues, by way of the witness of the holy Spirit within the believer, a witness that is available only to one who grasps the biblical message in faith. This acceptance in faith yields a form of knowledge that is both direct and certain. To ask how one knows that the Bible is the word of God is like asking how we know light from darkness or how we distinguish sweet and bitter tastes. Just as sugar, for instance, is sufficient evidence of its own sweetness to one who tastes it, so the Bible is sufficient evidence of its own truth to one who is prepared to accept its message.

This evidence, we might note, is private rather than public. Each individual must make the act of faith and experience for oneself the internal testimony of the Bible's truth. (I don't know that sugar is sweet unless I have tasted it myself.) Calvin also believes that there exist what are sometimes called external evidences in support of biblical authority (such as accounts of miracles and of the fulfillment of prophecy), which are matters open to public scrutiny. But Calvin seeks certainty, the certainty on which the troubled believer can base one's assurance of salvation. No merely human authority, no merely human argument, can offer the certainty that divine revelation can provide. It must therefore be God who witnesses to the authority of the Bible by way of the voice of the Holy Spirit within the believer.

In all these discussions, we should note, the Reformers are not only trying to establish the authority of Scripture over against that of the Catholic Church. They are also trying to avoid the subjectivism (as we might call it) of the radical wing of the Reformation, the enthusiasts, who appealed to the voice of the Spirit within each believer as the final source of religious authority. For Luther and Calvin, the alleged voice of the holy Spirit within must be tested against the assured voice of the holy Spirit without, in Scripture. In this sense, the Reformers regarded the character of the Bible as a fixed, written document (its objectivity, as we might say) as a bulwark against individualist forms of interpretation. (One could, of course, argue from the subsequent history of Protestantism that this bulwark is not as strong as they supposed.)

(c) The Bible has a single meaning

There is one feature of the Reformers' attitude to the Bible that is often regarded as standing in clear contrast to the attitude of patristic and medieval thinkers. The Reformers appear at first sight to reject allegorical interpretations of the Bible. The Reformers' suspicion of allegorical interpretation is closely related to the first principle discussed above: that the Bible interprets itself and that its meaning is therefore clear. If the meaning of the Bible is clear, then one cannot speak of hidden meanings in the text, for this suggests the Scripture requires some external authority for its elucidation.

The Reformers insisted that the Bible has one simple meaning and that this meaning was accessible to any true believer. Luther, for instance,

speaks of "the one constant and simple sense of Scripture," while Calvin asserts that "the true meaning of Scripture is the natural and simple one." This one meaning of Scripture is nothing other than the message of Christ. While the New Testament proclamation of the gospel speaks explicitly of Christ, even the Old Testament Law is designed to lead us to him.

Yet if we are to find the message of Christ in the Old Testament, we cannot avoid reading certain passages in other than their immediate sense. In particular, we must argue that certain Old Testament events and individuals somehow foreshadow the events of the New Testament. The Reformers did not want to remove this possibility; on the contrary, they practiced such spiritual interpretations themselves. Luther, for instance, could see the Old Testament festival of Passover that commemorated the Exodus from Egypt as an image (or type) of the deliverance from sin that Christians celebrate at Easter.

In other words, what the Reformers objected to was not so much the discovery of a spiritual sense in Scripture as the neglect of the literal sense. A spiritual sense was acceptable provided it was clearly related to the literal sense. They were not the first people in Christian history to argue this way. As we have seen, the late Middle Ages saw a growing emphasis on the literal sense, a feature that we find, for instance, in the work of St. Thomas Aquinas. Here, too, the Reformers were not far removed from at least some of their medieval forebears.

There is a final qualification to be added that relates particularly to Martin Luther's attitude to Scripture. While Luther insists that the whole of the Bible witnesses to Christ, he also argues that not all parts of Scripture do so with equal clarity. The Old Testament Law, for instance, witnesses to Christ primarily in a negative way by making human beings aware of their sinfulness and of their need for God's grace. Even within the New Testament, the witness to Christ is not equally clear throughout. It is in the letters of St. Paul that we find the gospel message of justification by faith expressed most clearly. The letter of James, on the other hand, while well-intentioned, only obscures that message. Individual passages of the Bible and even individual books need to be judged against the message of God's grace, a message that stands at the heart of the Bible.

THE CATHOLIC RESPONSE

The Catholic response to these developments was to reaffirm and to clarify the link between Bible and church. A key document here is a decree passed in 1546 by the great Council of the Counter-Reformation, the Council of Trent. With regard to the text of the Bible, the decree first of all defined the canon of Scripture (over against the Reformers' rejection of the apocrypha or deuterocanonical books) and declared that the Vulgate Latin version of the Bible was to be taken as an authoritative translation.

With regard to the interpretation of the Bible, the decree made two points. First, it insisted that divine revelation was to be found not just in the written Scriptures but also in the unwritten traditions that the church has handed down from age to age. Second, it decreed that "no one . . . should dare to interpret Sacred Scripture in matters of faith and morals in a way that runs contrary to that meaning which the Holy Mother Church has held and holds . . . or even contrary to the unanimous consensus of the Fathers." In other words, the Council of Trent stated that it is the right of the church, and not of any individual, to decide on the true meaning of Scripture. It also insisted that a proposed interpretation of Scripture must be in conformity with church tradition as represented by "the consensus of the Fathers."

The intention of the Council is clear and—from a Catholic point of view—seems reasonable. In opposition to the apparent individualism of the Protestant Reformers, the Council wished to locate the interpretation of the Bible firmly within the life of the church. Unfortunately in this matter as in so many others, the Council did not simply re-establish the position held by the church before the Reformation. It hardened that position, stating it in very strict terms and surrounding it with penalties. For this reason the Council of Trent's decree on biblical interpretation made it difficult for Catholics to engage in the necessary task of biblical reinterpretation in succeeding centuries. It contributed, for instance, to the church's tragic condemnation of the astronomer Galileo Galilei (1564–1642), less than a hundred years after the Council at which this decree was promulgated. Galileo was himself a devout Catholic and defended his religious position with vigor. But even if Galileo's heliocentric view of the universe was not, strictly speaking, contrary to church teaching (since it had never been explicitly discussed), it could be said to be contrary to the unanimous consensus of the church fathers (who took the older view of the universe for granted). Another 350 years would pass before Catholic biblical scholars could begin to enjoy the freedom they so desperately required.

The Bible in the Modern Era
(ca. 1650–today)

THE DEVELOPMENT OF HISTORICAL CRITICISM

Between the age of the Protestant Reformers and our own time lies a great gulf, created by the emergence of what is often described as historical criticism of the Bible. (The word "criticism" here does not imply finding fault; it has its original sense of "analysis," in the same sense as one speaks about literary criticism. Older writers sometimes distinguish between lower criticism, the textual criticism discussed in the first part of this study, and higher criticism, the focus of the present discussion.) What is the historical criticism of the Bible? When and how did it emerge?

The simplest way of approaching this momentous shift in attitude is by way of the question of authorship. Christians had always recognized that the Bible had human authors. Its authors were believed to be Moses (in the case of the first five books) and the prophets of the Old Testament, as well as the evangelists and apostles of the New Testament. But if the Bible had human authors, this fact was not regarded as terribly significant; it was overshadowed by belief in the Bible's divine inspiration. As an inspired work, the Bible could be said to have God as its author.

This attitude began to change in the seventeenth century. In a process that began in the mid-1600s and accelerated in the eighteenth and nineteenth centuries, the divine authorship of the Bible came to be overshadowed by a new focus on its human authorship. Very often, the divine inspiration of Scripture was not denied. Many biblical interpreters remained devout Christians who continued, at least in principle, to hold to the doctrine of inspiration. But their focus was now on the Bible as a document of human history, a work comparable to any other, produced by human beings and able to be studied using the same methods as other documents of history.

What lay behind this shift? The religious thought of the seventeenth and eighteenth centuries was characterized by a crisis of biblical interpretation and (at a deeper level) a crisis of biblical authority. The wars of religion that followed the Protestant Reformation had contributed to this crisis, with both sides claiming biblical authority for their persecution of those who disagreed. The deepest reason for this crisis lay in the new knowledge of the age, both scientific and historical, and the challenge this posed to biblical interpretation.

There were, for instance, tensions between the biblical view of the universe and that emerging from the new Copernican astronomy espoused by such thinkers as Galileo Galilei. With the voyages of discovery that opened up the cultures of Asia and the Americas to European thought, there also emerged difficulties with the Bible's view of history. The approximately six thousand years of the biblical chronology seemed unable to accommodate either the diversity of human cultures or the existence of ancient nonbiblical civilizations such as that of China.

There were, of course, many thinkers for whom this new knowledge simply discredited biblical authority. To such thinkers, Christianity appeared to be merely one religion among others, no longer able to enjoy its taken-for-granted place in human life. Similarly, its Scriptures seemed to be merely one set of sacred writings among others, all too obviously the product of human beings whose knowledge was limited to that of their time and place. Even those who wished to maintain their traditional faith were forced to admit that the biblical writers had been very much men of their age. Divine inspiration had not lifted them above the limited knowledge of their own cultures. If the Bible was to have a message for today, that message needed to be understood as shaped by the particular historical context in which it was received.

It was these developments that lay behind the emergence of historical criticism. The earliest forms of such criticism focused on the Old Testament, particularly the first five books (the Pentateuch). Nineteenth-century scholars began to dismember these books, to see them as the product of a long period of transmission—both by word of mouth and in writing—and of editing. The most famous outcome was the division of the first five books of the Bible into four written sources: the Yahwist (J), the Elohist (E), the Deuteronomic (D), and the Priestly (P), a division that arose from the work of Julius Wellhausen (1844–1918).

This analysis allowed one, for instance, to distinguish between the first and the second chapters of Genesis. Genesis 1 came to be seen as a composition belonging to the so-called Priestly tradition, from relatively late in Israel's history, while Genesis 2 was a work from the Yahwist tradition, containing material from much earlier in Israel's history. These forms of analysis were soon applied to the New Testament where a key issue was that of the composition of the gospels. Here the most notable achievement was the two-source theory of the gospels, first formulated by Heinrich Julius Holtzmann (1832–1910). According to this theory, the Gospel of Mark was the earliest of our canonical gospels, while Matthew and Luke were composed using both Mark and a now-lost written collection of Jesus' sayings that has come to be known as Q (probably from the German *Quelle,* "source").

There is no need to dwell on these developments or on the fate of these theories in more recent times. (Those matters will be discussed in the later volumes in this series.) In this context we need only note some of the consequences of historical criticism. One of the most noteworthy was a gradual widening of the gap between the academic study of the Bible and its use in the churches. The historical criticism of the Bible seemed to require no particular religious commitment: it was a work of secular scholarship. Therefore the biblical scholars who pioneered these methods often thought of themselves as historians rather than as theologians.

From many points of view, this was a good thing. It allowed, for instance, Catholic, Protestant, and even Jewish scholars to work together in a common academic undertaking, setting aside for the moment their confessional commitments.

But when one took their results back into the life of the church (or synagogue), it was difficult to know what use could be made of them. To put it bluntly, once one had understood what the Bible meant to those for whom it was written, the question remained of what it means to the contemporary believer. Ancient Babylonian creation myths may well shed light upon the book of Genesis, but they are not the kind of thing that would inspire your average congregation.

This widening gap between biblical scholarship and church life was exacerbated by another feature of historical criticism: its complete neglect of the spiritual interpretation. Patristic and medieval writers, convinced of the divine authorship of the Bible, were prepared to find meanings in the biblical text that would have been inaccessible to their human authors. For instance, while the eighth-century B.C. author of Isaiah 7:14 (". . . the virgin shall be with child, and bear a son, and shall name him Immanuel") could hardly be expected to know about the yet-to-occur virginal conception of Jesus, the God who inspired him certainly did. This could therefore constitute a new level of meaning above and beyond that intended by the human author.

The Protestant Reformers condemned the more fanciful forms of allegorical interpretation, but they continued to believe that the Bible spoke of a divinely guided history in which the events of the Old Testament could be seen to foreshadow those of the New Testament, as well as shedding light on the events of their own time. Among historical critics such ways of reading the Bible seemed entirely discredited. Since historians, as historians, could not speak of divine inspiration or of a divinely guided history, all they could do was to describe the one meaning intended by the human author. Believers found themselves marooned in the past with no way of building a bridge to later times or to the present.

THE RECEPTION OF HISTORICAL CRITICISM

It is perhaps a tribute to the adaptive power of religious traditions that what began as a serious challenge to biblical authority was gradually absorbed into mainstream Christian practice. This positive reception, however, was far from universal. The nineteenth and early twentieth centuries witnessed a strong conservative reaction against historical criticism among both Protestant and Catholic Christians.

(a) The Protestant Churches

Given the uniquely important role the Bible plays within Protestant Christianity, one would expect a certain suspicion of historical criticism among conservative Protestants. Historical critics argued that the Bible needed to be understood as a human work, the product of particular historical contexts. In practice this suggested that the authority of the Bible was a limited authority: it was limited by the assumptions of its authors who were people of their time and place. Sometimes we must judge their ideas to have been simply mistaken.

To many conservative Christians, such claims seemed to overlook the divine inspiration of the Bible. If these authors were divinely inspired, God would at the very least have protected them from making false statements. God could also have raised their minds above the limitations of their own cultural context to transmit truths that were of divine and not merely human origin. The Bible, such Christians insisted, was not merely a record of human thought or of religious experience; it was a record of, or at least a witness to, divine revelation.

The great rallying point for conservative Protestants soon became the doctrine of biblical infallibility or inerrancy, the belief that the Bible was without error. This was the first doctrine defended in a famous series of booklets entitled *The Fundamentals*, published in the United States from 1909 onward and distributed to large numbers of Christian teachers and leaders. (Over three million copies were eventually circulated.)

A similar list of doctrines was adopted by the General Assembly of the North Presbyterian Church in 1910. On this occasion, too, the first of the "fundamentals of faith" to be defended was belief in the inspiration and infallibility of the Bible. Incidentally, the term "fundamentalist" dates from this period. It seems to have been coined following a similar defense of basic Christian beliefs at the Northern Baptist Convention in 1920. The word was initially used on both sides of the debate, being willingly embraced by those to whom it was applied. Only gradually has it become a term of opprobrium.

It is easy to ridicule the more extreme manifestations of this movement. It achieved notoriety, for example, in 1925 during the trial in Dayton, Tennessee, of John T. Scopes, a secondary school teacher who taught Darwin's theory of evolution in defiance of a religiously motivated state law. Although Scopes was convicted (the decision later being overturned on a technicality), there were many who saw the trial as a symbol of religious ignorance in the face of scientific knowledge. Such tendencies have not gone away. On the contrary, resistance to the theory of evolution seems to have increased, particularly in the United States. A 1991 survey suggested that 47 percent of Americans believe that "man was created pretty much in his present form at one time within the last 10,000 years," a statement that implies a remarkably literal interpretation of Genesis 1. To avoid the constitutional implications of introducing religious beliefs into public classrooms, defenders of a literal reading of Genesis 1 have recently begun describing their position as creation science (offering it as a scientific rather than a religious position) or simply as evidence against evolution. However, its roots lie in the same reaffirmation of biblical authority that prompted the Scopes trial of 1925.

Not all conservative Protestants, however, have adopted such extreme views. The great British evangelical J. I. Packer (b. 1926), a defender of conservative Christianity, insists that the inerrancy of the Bible does not necessarily imply a woodenly literal interpretation of what it teaches. For instance, there is nothing to prevent the devout Christian from reading the story of Adam and Eve as a symbolic expression of revealed truth. Packer also argues that one should not confuse the message of the Bible (what it actually teaches) with those beliefs about the world that the biblical writers simply took for granted. Belief in the inerrancy of the Bible need not extend to the latter any more than it implies that the biblical authors always wrote grammatically perfect Hebrew, for "they do not claim to teach either science or grammar."

Even in the early twentieth century there existed evangelical Christians who combined a reaffirmation of biblical authority with attempts to take seriously the claims of history and the sciences. A key figure here, particularly for American evangelicalism, was J. Gresham Machen (1881–1937), who had been trained in German New Testament scholarship and who could use at least some of its methods in defense of traditional Christian doctrines. Machen also realized that the crisis of biblical authority transcended the divisions established by the Reformation. On the matters that divide Protestants from Catholics he stood firmly with the Reformers, but he could see that on central matters of doctrine conservative Protestants and Catholics had much in common.

(b) The Catholic Church

While the leading biblical scholars of the nineteenth century were from the Protestant world, it was not long before Catholic scholars became interested in their work. They were hampered, however, by a conservative reaction on the part of the Catholic authorities, one that in many ways parallels that found among Protestants. The mood of the Roman authorities in the mid-nineteenth century was not conducive to freedom of thought. In 1864, for instance, Pope Pius IX issued a *Syllabus of Errors*, a list of eighty propositions that he regarded as worthy of condemnation. These propositions covered a very wide range of topics. Among the condemned propositions were those that asserted that Scripture was no more than a record of human experience and that the Bible's account of events is not always historically accurate. The same Pope summoned the First Vatican Council (1870), which strongly reaffirmed the Council of Trent's position on the canon, divine inspiration, and biblical interpretation.

In 1893 there was a change of mood. In that year Pius IX's successor, Pope Leo XIII, issued an encyclical on biblical interpretation entitled *Providentissimus Deus*. In many respects this encyclical was exceedingly cautious. It reaffirmed both the inspiration and inerrancy of Scripture, insisted on the traditional Catholic principles of interpretation, and condemned the pretensions of higher criticism, which it associated with the rationalist attack on the idea of revelation. The encyclical did, however, encourage serious biblical scholarship: the study of biblical texts in the original languages using the best methods of analysis available. It also addressed the apparent conflict between the biblical worldview and that of modernity. It suggested that, while it was not permissible to limit the authority of the Bible to matters of faith and morals, we should recognize that the sacred writers were not trying to teach scientific truths. Rather, they were concerned to teach those things that are "profitable to salvation" (a principle first enunciated by St. Augustine). In doing so, the sacred writers sometimes expressed their message in language that was "more or less figurative" or "in terms that were commonly used at the time."

A year before the publication of this encyclical, Leo XIII had commended the work of Marie-Joseph Lagrange (1855–1938), a Dominican priest who in 1890 had founded the École Biblique, a school of advanced biblical studies in Jerusalem. Lagrange is perhaps the greatest pioneer of historical criticism among Catholics. To open the door to historical criticism, Lagrange had been forced to rethink the doctrine of divine inspiration.

Whereas previous descriptions of inspiration had suggested that the sacred writers were merely passive recipients of the divine message, Lagrange insisted that they were truly authors. They were responsible for the entire process by which the Scriptures were composed: namely, gathering sources, both written and oral, selecting material, and shaping it into its present form. Throughout this process they were guided by God so that what they taught was indeed without error. What they taught, however, must be sharply distinguished from the forms in which the teaching is clothed. With regard to the latter we need to take into account the existence of different literary genres so that we may judge some stories to be edifying fiction rather than historical fact. (One thinks, for instance, of the story of Jonah and the large fish.) We also need to take into account the intention of the sacred writers. Sometimes, for instance, they simply repeat the account of Israel's history that they find in their sources without intending to endorse its accuracy.

While these seem bold statements for a Catholic to make at the beginning of the twentieth century, Lagrange could appeal to sections of *Providentissimus Deus* in support of his views. However, if the pontificate of Leo XIII represented a cautious opening of the door to historical criticism, that door soon closed. Alarmed by developments in a number of fields, his successor Pope Pius X issued a series of documents in 1907 condemning a number of propositions under the heading of modernism. Among the Pope's targets was the proposition that the biblical interpreter should approach Scripture as a "merely human document." While critics such as Lagrange were also devout believers who did not regard the Bible as a merely human document, the change of tone was clear.

One of the first victims of this crisis was the French biblical scholar and theologian Alfred Loisy (1857–1940). While Loisy's work included a defense of the Catholic view of religious authority, his critical attitude toward the historical value of the gospels resulted in his excommunication in 1908. In 1905 Père Lagrange himself was forbidden to publish on any controversial question and, after failing to obtain permission to publish works in Old Testament studies, switched his attention to the New Testament. In 1912–1913 he was also removed for a time from his post at L'École Biblique. Although he was later restored to his position, he no longer dared to tackle such a dangerous question as that of inspiration.

The effect of what has come to be known as the modernist crisis was to drive Catholic biblical scholarship underground. The moment at which it emerged was the publication in 1943 of an encyclical by Pope Pius XII entitled *Divino Afflante Spiritu*. The encyclical endorses the view of inspiration defended by Lagrange, according to which the sacred writer is a true author, using all his human powers in the composition of what he writes.

It follows that the interpreter must try to understand the character of these human authors, the context in which they were writing, the sources they used, and the forms of expression they employed. In other words, the primary task of the biblical scholar is to uncover the literal meaning of the biblical text, that is to say, the meaning intended by its human authors. To discover this meaning the interpreter ought to use the same methods of interpretation as would be used for any other human document. While repeating the traditional Catholic view that the final arbiter of the sense of Scripture must be the church, in accordance with her own tradition, the encyclical notes that relatively few passages of Scripture have had their meaning fixed in this way. There is still plenty of freedom for the biblical scholar. With these remarkable statements, the highest authority of the Catholic Church formally endorsed the program of historical criticism.

The publication of *Divino Afflante Spiritu* was a watershed in the Catholic Church's attitude to modern biblical scholarship. The Second Vatican Council with its Dogmatic Constitution on Divine Revelation (*Dei Verbum*, 1965) offers a further endorsement of historical criticism but adds little to the program set out in *Divino Afflante Spiritu*. Nor has this endorsement been withdrawn in more recent times.

Indeed a 1993 statement by the Pontifical Biblical Commission, while approving a wide range of new methods of interpretation, describes the historical-critical method as "the indispensable method for the scientific study of the meaning of ancient texts." In this respect the Commission is surely correct. Whatever criticisms it may meet at the hands of its detractors, it is difficult to see how one could dispense with the historical-critical approach to the Bible. As we will see shortly, even some "postmodern" critics have recently returned to the historical study of the Bible, although in a more nuanced and self-conscious way. It seems that the best insights of the historical critics are here to stay. If the next section of this work is entitled "Postmodern Biblical Interpretation," this is not intended to suggest that the historical criticism, so characteristic of the modern age, is now superseded. It suggests only that it must now be supplemented by more sophisticated approaches to the meaning of the biblical text.

Postmodern Biblical Interpretation

THE INDETERMINACY OF MEANING

At the beginning of this second part of our study, I made a few remarks about what it means to interpret a work. In particular, I insisted that one cannot escape the obligation of interpretation. To read a work and understand it *is* to interpret it. We must now return to these questions, for in our own time there has been an explosion of new approaches to biblical interpretation. What these new approaches have in common is a new sense of what is involved in interpreting a text.

In particular, many contemporary interpreters insist that the act of interpretation is a much more complex matter than was previously thought. They focus on those dimensions of the act of interpretation that destabilize textual meaning by suggesting that the biblical text cannot be given a single, definitive interpretation. (This is sometimes described as the "indeterminacy" of textual meaning.)

In this section of our study, I will look at those dimensions of interpretation highlighted by postmodern critics. If I deal with these matters in some detail, it is because such interpreters do not always make their intentions clear. Their work is all too often marred by confusing jargon and inflated rhetoric. I have therefore tried to set out as clearly as possible what they are attempting to do.

(a) Part and whole

The first dimension of the act of interpretation to be highlighted by postmodern thinkers is one that has long been familiar to students of the Bible. It is often described as the hermeneutical circle. (As we will see, this phrase has at least two meanings; we will look at its second meaning shortly.) The act of interpretation involves a circular movement in which the individual parts of a text are understood in light of the text as a

whole, and the text as a whole is understood in light of its individual parts. In principle, this process has no end.

To explore this insight we may start with a simple and familiar idea. It is the idea that one cannot properly understand any particular passage of a written work in isolation; it must be understood in context by reference to the larger work to which it belongs. To take a well-known example, it would seriously misrepresent the meaning of Psalm 53 to take the second part of its first verse, namely, "There is no God," in isolation from its setting where it is prefaced by the words, "Fools say in their hearts." But it is not just the other part of the verse that is important; you cannot properly understand Psalm 53:1 until you have read the psalm as a whole. For only at the end of the psalm does it become clear why the psalmist believes it is foolish to deny the existence or the power of God.

As a general rule, then, each part of a text must be read with reference to the text as a whole. Of course, the converse is also true. It may be stating the obvious but the point is worth making: the whole text can be understood only after reading each of its parts. These two facts together give rise to a circular movement. The parts of a text must be understood by reference to the whole, but the whole can be understood only by reference to its parts. In the case of simple texts, such as a single sentence, this process need not continue very long. A single reading may be enough to establish a satisfactory understanding of what we are reading. In the case of more complex texts (such as a Shakespearian play or a biblical book), each new reading may well alter our perception of the work as a whole. Having achieved this new perception, we can go back and find new significance in passages that we have already read.

A moment's reflection will suggest that this procedure has, in principle, no natural conclusion.

The interpreter can continue to travel this circle indefinitely. Having achieved our new understanding of the text as a whole, we go back and reread each of its parts. But in the case of a complex text, this process of rereading may lead us to alter our understanding of the whole work. This would lead us back into yet another reconsideration of individual passages, and so on.

Of course, there are lots of practical reasons for bringing this process to an end. Interpreters will soon tire of this task. They will decide they have achieved a sufficient understanding of the work before them. But that is not the point. The point is that, in principle, the hermeneutical circle could continue indefinitely. If this is the case, then no one interpretation of a complex text can claim to be final, once and for all. It represents nothing more than the point at which the interpreter has abandoned the work of interpretation.

The problem is particularly acute in the case of the Bible, since it is not clear to which whole any individual biblical text belongs. In the case of Psalm 53, for instance, it is clear that each verse should be read as part of the psalm as a whole. But what about the whole of the Psalter? If we insist, for example, that Isaiah 7:14 is to be read in the light of the book of Isaiah as a whole, then should we not read Psalm 53 in the light of the Psalter as a whole? But has the Psalter as a whole any real unity? Is it truly a "book"? Or is it merely a collection of writings related by nothing more than their literary genre? And while we may insist that the Bible as a whole is a collection of books, does that collection also have a certain unity? If it does, should Psalm 53 not be understood in the light of the Bible as a whole? (This has been the issue raised by those who espouse a canonical approach to biblical interpretation.) But if so, whose Bible should we choose? The Hebrew Bible (*Tanak*) or the Christian Bible? And why stop with the covers of our Bible? What is the largest possible literary whole in the light of which individual biblical texts should be read? One may wish to stop with the limits of the canon. But on historical or literary grounds, it is not clear why these limits should be so significant.

(b) The historical context

A second cause of uncertainty in interpretation arises from a matter that lies at the heart of a historically oriented approach to the Bible. It has to do with the question of the historical context in the light of which the text is to be understood. There are two problems here. First, the historical context of biblical texts is enormously rich. With regard to the New Testament in particular, we know almost too much about the world from which it emerged. This means that the interpreter must make a choice of certain features of this rich social and cultural environment in order to shed light on the text to be interpreted. To take a well-known example, John's Gospel begins by speaking about the "Word" of God, which became flesh in the figure of Jesus. How are we to understand this term "Word"? Should we understand it against the background of the Word (*logos*) doctrine of popular Greek philosophy? Should we understand it in the light of the Old Testament's descriptions of the Word of God? Or should both understandings of the term "Word" be taken into account? How are we to decide?

There is a second problem that seems even more intractable. While we may agree that a biblical text is to be understood in its historical context, there are no apparent limits to what this term can embrace. The problem is not just that the Bible emerged from a complex historical context. It is that the borders of that context can be continuously redrawn, like a series of concentric circles, with no obvious end in sight. Every artifact of human culture is created against the background of an indefinitely large set of assumptions. When you begin to trace these assumptions, you find that one rests on another, so that the process of explication has no natural end. Understanding one social institution involves understanding another, and this in turn involves understanding a third.

To take a simple example, when the New Testament authors refer to Jesus as the "Messiah" (in Greek, *Christos*), what does this term mean? To understand their use of this term, we may need to understand the Old Testament notion of kingship. But to understand kingship we may need to understand how ancient Near Eastern thinkers thought about society. To understand their view of society, we may need to understand their view of human nature. And so the process continues. Indeed the situation is even worse than might appear from this brief description. Each element in this series is itself susceptible to many different interpretations: it can be understood in many different ways, depending on the context in which it is placed.

Now once again these arguments may seem rather abstract, having little practical significance. In practice we are rarely deterred by such considerations. Whatever the student of interpretation may say, we do in fact arrive at decisions about textual meaning. We believe that we have understood enough of the biblical world to make such decisions. This is, of course, true. But it does not mean we can dismiss the arguments put forward by postmodernists.

Such interpreters are not arguing that we can never arrive at a decision regarding the meaning of a text. They are arguing that such decisions are always revisable. There is always another fact about the biblical world, another way of regarding it or a larger context in which it may be set that would reopen the question of what the biblical text means. Nor is this difficulty merely theoretical. We see its practical consequences every day in the world of biblical scholarship. That scholarship is characterized by the apparently endless production of books and articles on already heavily interpreted texts, such as—to take but one example—the letter to the Romans.

(c) The "intentional fallacy"

One way in which historical critics tried to control the process of interpretation was to focus on what is often called authorial intent. Many historical critics insist that our task is to try to understand what the human author of the Bible was attempting to say. So we can restrict our study of the biblical world to those features that would be known to the author in question. For instance, if we knew that the author of a particular New Testament book belonged to a predominantly Palestinian Jewish world, then we might choose to neglect currents of thought that were operative only in Hellenistic (Greek-speaking) Judaism. If one adopts this approach, there are clear limits to what evidence should be brought forward in favor of a particular interpretation.

In the 1940s and 1950s, however, a series of literary critics—often known as the New Critics—began to attack this assumption, not (admittedly) in biblical studies but in the study of literature. Such critics dismissed the attempt to discover the author's intended meaning as the intentional fallacy. First of all, they insisted, the author's intention is a psychological fact that is inaccessible to us (at least if we can no longer question the author in person). In the case of most works of literature, the author is dead. All that survives is the author's intention as embodied in the work.

If this is the case, then the focus of our attention ought to be the work, not its author. Even if the author were here to be questioned, these critics argued, why should his or her account of the meaning of the work be privileged? After all, whatever the authors' intention may have been, they may have failed to embody it in what they wrote. The final work, in other words, may fall short of their intended meaning. More commonly, however, skillful authors will create a work that goes beyond their intentions. By marshaling the resources of human language, with all the echoes and resonances that such language can convey, they will put more into their work than they are aware of. To restrict interpretation to what the authors intended is to miss out on the richness of human literature, its power to speak to new generations in new ways.

This line of argument has led to a plethora of what are sometimes called *literary* readings of the Bible that study the text with a view to discovering its possible meanings rather than its original meaning. Insofar as they focus on the text rather than its author, such readings also imply that the act of interpretation should be open-ended. One can never decide that this *is* the meaning of the text, since new readers, living in a new situation and having new sets of concerns, may find features in the text that we have overlooked. They should not be dissuaded from doing so by the fact that the new meanings they discover may not have been what the author intended. One could even argue that skillful authors will intend meanings of which they are unaware, insofar as they intend that their works be read in new ways by new generations of readers. If this is the case, one could argue that the interpreter would be faithful to the authors' intentions only by ignoring them!

(d) Text and reader

A later generation of interpreters would pick up and develop these reflections on the role of the reader. This would lead them to be critical of our customary ways of talking about textual meaning. In particular, they would question the idea that meaning somehow resides *in* a text. The meaning of a text, they argued, is not already there, fixed on the page, needing only to be drawn out (as the Greek origins of the word "exegesis" would suggest). Rather, meaning emerges from the interaction of text and reader. If the reader did not bring certain assumptions to the act of reading, the text would have no meaning at all.

It follows that what we call the text is merely a series of traces, out of which a meaning needs to be constructed on each occasion it is read. Rather than having a meaning, a text has a certain potential for meaning. It is the reader who decides (consciously or unconsciously) in what ways that potential is to be realized.

The written text, it is argued, resembles a musical score. A musical score is not itself music. To become music it must be performed. Similarly, a written text does not yet have a particular meaning. It acquires a particular meaning only when it is appropriated by a particular reader. It follows that there is a second sense in which we may talk about a hermeneutical circle. This is the circle of interpretation that takes us from text to reader and then back to the text. What we call the meaning of the text emerges only from this process. The reader's understanding of the text is at least partly shaped by the assumptions brought to the act of reading.

At its most extreme, this position would hold that the reader actually creates the text through what appears to be merely an act of interpretation. In this situation, one can say that there are as many texts as there are readers. A less extreme form of this view would hold that readers fall into interpretive communities, each holding more or less common sets of assumptions. We may then say that there are as many texts as there are interpretive communities.

A still weaker but perhaps more defensible form of this argument would avoid saying that readers create their text. Any text has features that are independent of its readers or (more precisely) features that can be recognized by different communities of readers. Even if readers do not create the text, they certainly complete it. The text has meaning only because of the interaction between its independently existing features and its readers' assumptions, which will be drawn from the interpretive community to which they belong.

Whatever form of this argument one accepts, it has some interesting implications. For instance, interpreters who hold such a view may spend as much time talking about themselves as they talk about the text. They would argue that it is their assumptions, or those of their interpretive community, that will determine the shape of their interpretation.

Indeed many postmodern interpreters will begin their work with a brief statement of who they are and of the communities to which they belong. Since the interpreters' backgrounds inevitably shape their interpretation, they would argue, these matters are best made explicit so that the reader may be warned in advance. Another expression of these ideas is the tendency toward autobiographical criticism, in which autobiographical facts are brought into interaction with the text to be interpreted. We have come a long way from the scientific objectivity with which the pioneers of historical criticism wished to escape the clutches of confessional religious commitments!

(e) A hermeneutics of suspicion

There is yet another dimension to postmodern approaches to interpretation. This is the realization that biblical readers may not be innocent. They may claim to be neutral and disinterested, objective interpreters of the text. While these professions of objectivity may be made in good faith, they should not be taken at face value. Postmodern interpreters insist that all our knowledge of the world is shaped by who we are and by our location in society. Of particular importance here is the idea of ideology, first developed by Marxist theorists.

The word "ideology" can sometimes be used in a neutral way to refer simply to a particular set of ideas. But since the time of Karl Marx (1818–1883) the term has had a more specialized use. It refers to the way in which the members of a dominant social group become so involved in the maintenance of their social position that their thinking becomes distorted. They are simply unable to see any facts that might undermine their dominant role in society. Ideology in this sense is a way of thinking that blinds us to what is really going on in a society that gives legitimacy to existing structures of domination and oppression.

The idea that interpretations of the Bible may be shaped by ideological factors is a major theme of postmodern biblical criticism. But postmodernists suggest that it is not only biblical interpretation that may be shaped by the interests of some dominant group. The message of the Bible itself may also have suffered various forms of ideological distortion. As we have seen, even if we regard the Bible as the word of God, we must recognize that the divine word is expressed in human words. Would divine inspiration have protected the biblical authors from the distortions of knowledge that we now know affect us all? If our answer to that question is "no," then the task of the interpreter should surely include ideological criticism—the process whereby these misleading and oppressive patterns of thought are unmasked for what they truly are.

Depending on which oppressed group is the focus of the interpreter's concern, this ideological criticism of the Bible can give rise to a number of different approaches. The first expression of this concern was found in the work of the liberation theologians who read the Bible in the light of the situation of the poor, particularly in the countries of the Third World. Among Catholic liberation theologians, the criticism of ideology has often been coupled with the idea of a preferential option for the poor, an idea that has been given cautious approval by a number of popes.

A similar concern is to be found in the feminist theology that emerged into public prominence in the 1970s (although feminist interpretations of the Bible date back to 1895, the year in which Elizabeth Cady Stanton published *The Woman's Bible*). A distinctively feminist hermeneutics does not merely criticize what it sees as patriarchal interpretations. It also seeks to recover the role of women in Jewish and early Christian history, women whose voices have been silenced by the dominant male ideology of the biblical writers.

Still more recently, a number of biblical critics have adopted a post-colonialist approach to the Bible. This starts from the modern experience of Western colonial power from which so many nations today are struggling to emancipate themselves. Once again, this approach not only criticizes those interpretations of the Bible that have lent support to colonial domination. It also seeks to destabilize the meaning of those passages within the Bible itself that seem to be shaped by a similar ideology. Such critics might reexamine, for instance, the much-celebrated conquest of the land of Palestine but from a new point of view,

namely, that of the Canaanites whose land was invaded.

What is striking about these developments is that they are leading interpreters back to a new interest in history, since one cannot understand the ideological slant of a text without understanding the social (and thus the historical) context occupied by its authors. This fact has given rise to what is called a new historicism—a revival of interest in the historical and cultural contexts in which texts were produced. Despite the warnings of the New Critics about authorial intent, postmodern interpreters have become interested once again in the role of the biblical authors, but now as social actors in the ancient Israelite or early Christian world. For instance, recent Old Testament criticism has focused on the way in which the writers and compilers of the Hebrew Bible occupied a particular place in Israelite society and were involved in the political struggle to define Israel's identity.

Incidentally, it was not only Marx who alerted us to the role of ideology in human thought. Postmodern interpreters will also appeal to two other thinkers whom French philosopher Paul Ricoeur famously described as "the masters of suspicion." These include the philosopher Friedrich Nietzsche (1844–1900) and the founder of psychoanalysis Sigmund Freud (1856–1939). These thinkers also warned us about the hidden forces shaping our knowledge, forces that may operate in ways of which we are unaware. Following Ricoeur, this general approach to biblical interpretation has become known as a hermeneutics of suspicion, which balances the hermeneutics of trust with which Christian interpreters have generally approached the Bible.

CONCLUSIONS

There is much more that could be said about the work of postmodern biblical interpreters, which continues to be controversial. For instance, their observations regarding the plurality of possible interpretations raise the question of how conflicting interpretations are to be judged. What are the marks of a better or a worse interpretation? Are some interpretations to be excluded? If so, on what grounds?

At the very least these new developments in biblical study have served to underline the fact with which we began our discussion, namely, the complexity of the act of interpretation. If we are to take the task of biblical interpretation seriously, we must try to understand this complexity and to think seriously about its consequences. Remarkably, postmodern critics also share some of the concerns of earlier Christian interpreters, particularly those of the patristic and medieval periods. Their work is often marked, for instance, by a strong pastoral concern. They want to uncover not just what the text meant at the time it was written but what it means to its readers today. They also insist that biblical texts have not just one meaning but a variety of possible meanings. Unlike the church fathers, however, postmodern interpreters rarely defend this claim by reference to divine inspiration!

It is too early to say what the Catholic Church's response will be to these trends, although in 1993 the Pontifical Biblical Commission very cautiously endorsed what it described as liberationist and feminist approaches to the Bible. The caution is understandable. At first sight, postmodern critics seem to stand in a deeply ambiguous relationship to the Christian tradition. Insofar as they adopt a hermeneutics of suspicion and call into question the authority of the biblical text, they might appear to be openly hostile to traditional forms of faith.

On the other hand, there are other aspects of postmodern criticism that have proven attractive to theologians. For instance, by highlighting the role of the reader and her or his interpretive community, postmodern approaches may allow us to interpret the Bible—as Catholics have traditionally wanted to do—in the context of the life of the church. It may be that there are at least some forms of postmodern criticism that the Catholic Church could welcome.

In more general terms, postmodern criticism could be seen as continuing the project embraced by *Divino Afflante Spiritu* and the Second Vatican Council: understanding the Bible as a work of human beings. However much the believer may insist that the Bible is the word of God, this word comes to us only in the form of deeply ambiguous human words. To understand those words requires all the skills of the interpreter and all the insights we can bring to bear. At a time when it might have seemed there was nothing more to say about this most interpreted of texts, postmodern writers have opened up new possibilities for understanding the Christian Scriptures. The history of biblical interpretation is clearly far from over.

THE
OLD TESTAMENT

THE BOOK OF
GENESIS

Joan E. Cook, S.C.

INTRODUCTION

Genesis is a story about beginnings: of the universe, of humans, of joys and sorrows, successes and failures. The book focuses on the relationships between God and people as well as those among different people. These themes are simple in principle, but often complex in our lives. While the themes of Genesis are universal they can be complex because they are expressed in the styles and settings of the ancient Near East. Before we look at the book itself, several introductory points will facilitate our reading of Genesis.

Themes

Genesis introduces several themes that permeate the entire Bible. The first of these is divine causality; that is, the ancient people believed that the deities caused everything that happened in life. The ancient Israelites came to believe in only one God, whose name they eventually learned was Lord or "I AM" (Exod 3:14). They believed that the one God who caused everything to happen took a special interest in them. This divine-human relationship was understood as essential, and it applied not only to the relationship between God and the people, but also among people.

An implication of the importance of relationships is the setting of boundaries between God and creatures, including human beings, and between different creatures. The boundaries involved right relationships among all creatures and also between humans and God. In addition,

boundaries factored into the topic of land and the possession of land. Finally, intimately connected to the theme of relationship is the theme of promise and blessing. The Creator promises to remember and care for all creation, and carries out that promise in spite of the many ways that creatures violate divinely set boundaries.

Ancient storytelling

Another important topic is the way in which ancient people expressed their beliefs and values and told their story: it is quite different from the way we today record our past. We strive to record information with great attention to the details of the event, such as when and where it took place, who was involved, what they did and said. Then we use these details in our efforts to interpret the event we record. But in the ancient world, the project of remembering the past took a different form. People were not as concerned with recording the precise details of an event as they were in probing its meaning. To that end they told stories.

This means of communication was ideally suited to nonliterate cultures, peoples who depended on oral communication because very few could read and write. The stories they told embodied the larger meanings they found in situations and events, and related them in ways their listeners would remember and pass down to their descendants. In fact, we will note throughout Genesis that some events were recounted more

41

than once, with different points of focus and emphasis. The variations were included because each one added to the meaning of the event, and to the overall picture of the people's relationship with one another and with their God.

Ancient Near Eastern parallels

Several Genesis stories have parallels in other ancient Near Eastern cultures. The best-known of these are the Mesopotamian creation myth called *Enuma Elish*, of which echoes can be seen in the Genesis creation stories, and a Mesopotamian myth about the quest for immortality called the Epic of Gilgamesh, of which traces are evident in the Genesis flood story. Other parts of Genesis include what appear to be allusions to ancient stories. The parallel stories provide plots and themes onto which the Genesis narratives superimposed the ancient Israelites' beliefs. We will comment on *Enuma Elish* and the Epic of Gilgamesh in our discussion of the biblical creation and flood stories.

Documentary hypothesis

As the ancient Near Eastern people continued to tell their stories throughout the generations, the stories took on characteristic themes and motifs typical of their particular geographical localities and political and socioeconomic situations. When the people eventually began to write down their stories, these particularities became part of the narrative. The process of recording the material was a complex one that extended over hundreds of years. In the past 150 years, scholars have studied this question and have developed a theory as to how the first five books of the Bible (also known as the Pentateuch, which includes the book of Genesis) developed into the form we have today. That theory is known as the Documentary Hypothesis. We will look at the contemporary understanding of this theory with regard to the book of Genesis, because an understanding of how the book probably came into its present form is helpful to an understanding of the book's content.

According to the theory, the process of setting the stories in writing took place over a period of several hundred years, from about 1000 B.C. to about 500 B.C. Before that the stories circulated by word of mouth in families and clans. Then around 1000 B.C. when David was King of Israel, he took

steps to unite the twelve tribes into one people. One of those steps was to commission his scribes to write down the people's stories, weaving them into one. This early strand of Genesis (in fact, of the entire Pentateuch) is called J to represent the German spelling of the word Yahweh (Jahweh), the name by which this strand of the Pentateuch refers to God.

After King Solomon's death about one hundred years later, the kingdom David had established broke into two: the northern and southern kingdoms. The southern kingdom, Judah, believed it was the one that remained loyal to God and to the divine promises. The northern kingdom, Israel, set about establishing a new identity, and one of its steps was to rewrite parts of the early J story, inserting new details and substituting different names according to their own regional usage. This strand was woven into the earlier story, and the new strand became known as E because it calls God Elohim.

About five hundred years later, the city of Jerusalem and the entire southern kingdom of Judah endured a traumatic defeat by the Babylonians. They destroyed the temple, which had become the central place of worship. They also imprisoned the king and took into exile many leading members of the Jerusalem community. This defeat represented not only a political act but also the violation of the divine promises that had sustained the people since the time of Abraham and Sarah, over one thousand years before. The upheaval caused the people to rethink the beliefs that had sustained them throughout those one thousand years. The result was two additional strands. The first is known as D and represents the efforts of the people to understand their exile in terms of the message of the book of Deuteronomy: reliance on the covenant, or the formal terms of the relationship between God and the people. The D writers understood the exile as punishment for their own violation of the terms God had set down for the people. They believed that the exile was not a failure of the deity to keep the divine promises, but rather the failure of the people to live up to them.

Finally, a group of priests, also working to understand the meaning of the exile, preserved a record of how they had practiced their religion when it was centered in the Jerusalem temple. They did this because they saw the temple worship as the norm for public practice of religion. They wanted to preserve this record in the hope that one day they would return to Jerusalem, rebuild the temple, and resume temple worship according to the record they left for future generations. And if the exile did not end, at least there would be a record of how religion was practiced in the "good old days" of temple-centered religion. This strand is called P for the priestly authors who are believed to have written it. These last two groups, D and P, were probably not simply writers but also editors, who worked their strands into the earlier ones and gave the entire Pentateuch the shape we know today.

This summary gives an idea of the stages in the writing of Genesis. We can also categorize the four strands in terms of their characteristic features. We have seen that the writers and editors used different names for the deity: the Yahwist, or J, used the term Yhwh, the name God gave to Moses at the burning bush in response to Moses' request in Exodus 3:13-14. The Elohist, on the other hand, used the name Elohim, a term that originally meant "gods" and that ancient Israel used in referring to their own God. A shortened form of the word is "El," another term we find in Genesis. The editors we call P also used the term Elohim to refer to the deity.

The four sources have other characteristics, too. The J strand is the storytelling piece, with details that enable us to see, hear, and feel the events described in that strand of the narrative. Its descriptions of the deity are vivid and concrete: they describe God in ways that we humans can identify with, as we will see in Genesis 2. On the other hand, the E strand tends to focus on the transcendence of God, describing the divine presence in dreams and other ways that highlight the mysterious quality of divine presence and action. The D strand tends to be solemn and formal, and to emphasize the cause-and-effect quality of human actions while at the same time recognizing divine inbreakings in unexpected and surprising ways. Finally, the P strand focuses on concerns relating to the public practice of religion: the details of rituals, the place of different people within society, the relationships among different people that are often expressed in genealogical lists. Genesis is composed primarily of the J and P strands; we will point them out in the places where it enhances our understanding of the story.

Ancient literary genres

Another element to consider in our reading of the book of Genesis is the ancient genres or types of writings that comprise the book. The people spoke and wrote according to the conventions of the day. There are three main types of writing that appear frequently in Genesis: myths, sagas, and genealogies. The first two are narrative forms. Myths, in the biblical sense, are not make-believe stories. Rather, they are stories that convey the beliefs and values of the people. We will get a better idea of what this means when we look at the myths in the book. The other narrative genre, the saga, is a story that tells about the past and relates it to the present. The Genesis sagas tell about the beginnings of the world and about events within families. Sagas are predominantly the work of J.

The genealogies appear throughout the book, enumerating the relationships among different generations. These lists are among the latest parts of the book, added during or toward the end of the exile in Babylon to produce a record of who belonged to the group of exiles from Judah. Such a record served several important purposes: it established the record of the family ties of different people, identifying how they belonged to the chosen people. In addition, it supported the claims to the land that became vitally important when the exiles returned to their land and needed to legitimate their claim to it, because others had settled there in their absence. The genealogical lists are the work of P, and they not only identify the relationships among the different people, they also provide an organizing principle for the book of Genesis. We will look at these lists and the information we can learn from them.

By taking note of the three genres—myths, saga, and genealogy—we can understand what the Second Vatican Council document on revelation, *Dei Verbum*, meant in referring to the Bible as the word of God in human language. We believe that the Bible is the word of God, that is, revelation from God. At the same time we believe that it is recorded by human beings who put down the information in the ways people communicated with one another at the time the words were put into writing, according to the genres of the day.

Keeping all these facets in mind—the overall themes of Genesis; the lengthy process of recording and editing that brought the book to the form in which we know it today; the characteristics of the four different strands J, E, D, and P; the literary forms in which the ancient writers and editors wrote their messages; and the ancient Near Eastern parallel literature—gives us useful tools for understanding the book of Genesis. Now let us look at the contents of the book.

Divisions of the book of Genesis

The Genesis story consists of three parts. The first is the Primeval Story, the story of the earliest beginnings of the universe and of human beings on earth. It is found in chapters 1–11 of Genesis. The second part is the Ancestral Story, the story of several generations who became the ancestors of God's people. They were Abraham and Sarah; Rebekah and Isaac; Jacob and his two wives Leah and Rachel, their maids Bilhah and Zilpah, and their twelve sons and one daughter. This part of the story is found in chapters 12–36. The final part of the Ancestral Story focuses on one of Jacob's sons, Joseph, and his adventures that resulted in the family of Jacob being given a privileged place in the land of Egypt. This part of the story is found in chapters 37–50. We will now begin our reading of the book, looking at each of these three sections and the stories in each in some detail.

As we read, we will keep in mind that we are looking simultaneously at two different historical periods: the time described and the time when the story was written down. The way in which each historical, or prehistoric, episode is recorded reflects not only the people's understanding of what happened but also the context in which they wrote: the political, economic, and religious concerns that were important at the time, and through which they found meaning in the ancient narrative.

COMMENTARY

THE PRIMEVAL STORY

Genesis 1:1–11:28

The Primeval Story in Genesis 1–11 is the story of the earliest beginnings of the universe and of the human race. It talks of prehistoric times, naming a few places that we can identify today such as the Tigris and Euphrates Rivers, but for the most part it recounts stories whose details we cannot identify with precision; often we can find parallel stories and themes in other ancient Near Eastern myths. The Primeval Story consists of two creation stories, followed by several examples of humans who missed the mark in their efforts to live up to the ideals of creation. The best known are the stories of Adam, Eve, and the serpent; the murder of Abel by his brother Cain; the Flood; and the tower of Babel. Each of these stories invites us to look at life's challenges and how we respond to them as individuals and communities.

The Primeval Story takes us back to that primordial time when God created the world. Today we struggle to weigh different theories of how the universe came into being: whether by divine fiat, by evolution, by intelligent design, or by some other means that we do not yet understand. Ancient peoples also struggled to understand how the world came into being. They expressed their questions and theories in stories, rather than in the scientific theories we propose today. This difference is an important one to note when we read the Old Testament. Ancient peoples used stories to express their beliefs and values. These stories were not primarily concerned with relating the facts of a given situation; rather, they expressed the contemporary meaning their tellers found in ancient events and circumstances.

The first two chapters of Genesis tell two stories of how the world came into being. The two stories have several common elements: one Creator made the universe by shaping and organizing everything within the confines of time and space to make sure that every creature belonged in it and nothing was destroyed. Among all the creatures, humans were given a special place.

Each of the two stories has distinctive features as well. These give each story its unique character.

1:1–2:4a First creation story

Genesis 1:1–2:4a describes a seven-day process during which the Creator's word, "Let there be . . ." brings the different elements of the universe into being. The first three days witness the creation of the environment, and the second three days parallel the first, with the creation of creatures to live in the different spaces in the environment. We can chart this parallel in the following way:

Days 1-3	Days 4-6
Light, Day and Night	Greater Light, Lesser Light, Stars
Water and Sky	Fish and Birds
Land and Sea, Plants	Earth Creatures, Animal and Human

Creation begins with a powerful wind sweeping over the waters. Then the activity of each day begins with the formula, "God said: Let there be . . ." Then the narrative reports the specific activity for the day. At the end of the first, third, fourth, and sixth days, God saw that it was "good." On the sixth day, after all the creatures had been created, God looked over all of creation and saw that it was "very good" (1:31). The description of each day's work ends with the notation, "Evening came, and morning followed . . .," then gives the number of the day. The account illustrates the power ancient people associated with the spoken word: to speak was to set an action in motion; thus speech had a sacramental quality insofar as it caused what it signified. The formulas suggest the unfolding of a ritual: creation occurs according to an organized plan by which God first creates the environment, then populates it with creatures suitable for that particular part of the universe.

In verse 6 the dome, or firmament, represents the ancient Near Eastern concept of a divider between the heavens and the earth. We can picture it as a large bowl inverted and set on a flat surface. Everything under the bowl is inside the firmament, and the rest is outside it.

One of the first acts of creation is to harness the waters by assigning them to specific places in the cosmos. This attention to water highlights its necessity for life, and the need to protect and preserve it in the arid ancient Near Eastern climate.

The separation of light from darkness in 1:14 makes it possible to count the passage of time, not only according to days but also to seasons and years. God blesses the creatures of the sea, air, and earth (v. 22), commanding them to be fertile and multiply, assuring the continuity of creation.

The Creator gives a special place to humanity in 1:26. Humans, male and female, are made in the image of God. This is a puzzling statement, for which several explanations have been suggested. For example, we were made with the ability to make decisions, just as God does; or we are the visible "image" of the invisible God in the world. As God's human counterpart, we have the ability to communicate with God and to ask "Why?" when we do not understand. We also have dominion over all the other creatures. This awesome responsibility involves nurturing and protecting all the other creatures in the universe. The biblical story contrasts with the Mesopotamian *Enuma Elish*, which is full of violence and oppression. In that version the gods compete for the opportunity to create the universe. The victor, Marduk, creates humans to serve the gods.

The seventh day is designated as holy because it is God's day of rest (2:3). In the ancient world "holy" meant "set aside for God." Legislation concerning sabbath observance relied on this model of divine rest. It gives us an example for how to spend the day of the week that is set aside for God. A summary statement marks the end of the first creation account.

This first creation account is the work of the P editor. At the time of its compilation the people of Jerusalem were in exile in Babylon as a result of the Babylonian takeover of the ancient Near East. They were searching for the meaning of their exile, and for evidence that God still cared for them and maintained the universe. The insertion of the account, one of the last to be composed, at the beginning of the entire Bible introduces the themes of one God, divine concern for creatures, the dignity of human beings, and the orderly division of creation into different habitats for different creatures, different times for different activities, and the importance of honoring God in difficult times as well as moments of celebration.

2:4b-25 Second creation story

Immediately after the first story of creation, a second one follows. Like the first, it highlights the special place of humans in creation, relating it in a storytelling mode. We can picture the divine creative actions: shaping things out of clay, planting a garden, instructing the human on how to act in the garden. The breath of God suggests the same kind of energy found in the first creation story: the blowing wind is an invisible force that causes things to happen. God's first act of creation in this account is to shape a human being from the dust of the earth. Again we notice the importance of water: a stream waters all the ground, making it possible to work the soil, and becomes four rivers. Two of these rivers, the Tigris and Euphrates, run through Turkey, Syria, and Iraq.

The prohibition in verse 17 not to eat from the tree of knowledge of good and evil carries with it the threat of death. Death is not explained here; its meaning is already known by the time the story is set in writing, probably around 1000 B.C. The mention of it foreshadows the snake's temptation of the humans in the next chapter, where punishment by death is best explained as an etiological detail, which is an explanation of one of life's realities.

This creation story highlights the importance of relationships: God makes all the other creatures in an effort to provide a suitable companion for the human (v. 18). Only another human can offer that companionship, which finds its ultimate expression in marriage. The solemn wording of verse 24, "That is why . . ." identifies this verse as another etiology, or explanation of the reality of marriage.

This second creation story is the work of J, the storyteller who first collated the ancient stories in an effort to establish a common memory for the tribes united under David. It depicts the work of creation by giving concrete details and describing God in immanent terms. In other words, it depicts God with descriptions that enable us to know God's nearness to us. We can contrast this description with that in the first creation story, which depicts God as transcendent, or far beyond our ability to comprehend. The juxtaposition of the two stories illustrates the belief that God is both transcendent and immanent: infinitely beyond our ability to grasp and at the same time here in our midst.

After the two creation stories, the Primeval Story describes incidents in which humans begin to violate the boundaries the Creator has estab-lished between God and creatures. Each of the stories describes the way the boundary is violated, gives a divine declaration of that violation and the tendency to evil, and reports divine actions to restore the balance in the relationship between God and humans. Interwoven with these are etiological tales about place names, customs, or human realities; for example, marriage, the wearing of clothes, the reality of shame, evil, and death. At different points throughout the stories, genealogies name those who belong to the different tribes and clans and specify the relationships among them. The names are often eponymous: names of individuals become the names of groups such as Israel, the name given to Jacob in 32:29.

3:1-24 Adam, Eve, and the serpent

The creation story in chapter 2 includes the divine prohibition against eating the fruit of a particular tree that God gave to the first human before the creation of the woman. Here a new creature enters the picture, described only as a snake. No physical description is given until the creature receives the divine punishment for leading the humans into sin (vv. 14-15). At that point the creature loses its legs and is condemned to crawl on the ground, eat dirt, and reach up only to the heels of humans. The creature is a tempter, but is not the devil in the modern sense of that term.

The snake approaches the woman while the man is with her (v. 6), misquoting the divine prohibition by applying it to all the fruit trees (v. 4). She in turn adds to the original prohibition the command not even to touch the forbidden fruit under pain of death (v. 3). The snake's words immediately characterize him as cunning, and the woman's words portray her as eager to observe the divine prohibition. The snake capitalizes on the reason for avoiding the fruit: death will follow. Even though death has not been explained, the story makes clear that the Creator, the snake, and the woman all see it as something to avoid. Here the story resembles other ancient Near Eastern myths that describe the futile efforts of creatures to become immortal. The snake then insinuates that the divine prohibition has a different motive: eating the fruit gives to humans divine knowledge of good and evil; eating the fruit will make the humans like gods.

This is a complex idea: God made the humans in the divine image; the temptation is to eat in order to become more like God by knowing as much as God, ironically, about good and evil. The fruit promises to have more benefits than the snake first mentions: it tastes good, is beautiful, and gives wisdom. The woman eats some, then gives some to the man who does the same. As soon as they have eaten, the snake's promise proves true: they have increased knowledge that shows itself in their awareness of their nakedness. Ironically, the couple now know about good and evil through experience: they have taken it into themselves.

The divine question in verse 9, "Where are you?" underscores the tragic rupture of the divine-human relationship caused by human efforts to usurp divine power. The sin is thus in crossing the boundary that God set for them. They attempt to go beyond the limits of humanity and usurp power that belongs only to God.

The Lord God punishes all three: snake, woman, and man. Of the three, the words to the woman are the fewest, and she is not accused of committing the first sin. That idea does not appear in the Bible until Sirach 25:24: "With a woman sin had a beginning, / and because of her we all die." The punishments are etiologies that explain such human questions as "Why are women and men attracted to each other?" "Why do some people try to dominate others?" "Why do we wear clothes?" "Why is childbirth painful?" "Why is work difficult?" "Why do snakes crawl on the ground?" "Why do we die?" Finally, the divine words recall the second creation story, in which God fashioned the human being from the ground, and reminds Adam that he will return to the earth from which he came. Immediately after hearing this, the man names his wife Eve. Naming her is an act of domination, and at the same time the name he gives her acknowledges the mutuality between man and woman, announcing the beginning of motherhood and Eve's role as the first mother, illustrating the complexity of human relationships.

God punishes the couple, but does not abandon them. Immediately after announcing the punishment, God arranges for their needs by providing clothes for them. In covering their nakedness, God removes their shame. This act of compassion establishes a precedent for what fol-lows repeatedly throughout the Old Testament: when humans violate the terms of the divine-human relationship God finds a way to restore the balance by providing for the needs of the people.

4:1-16 The first murder

The story of humanity continues with the births of Cain and Abel to Adam and Eve, as God promised after the first sin. The divine acceptance of Abel's sacrifice but not Cain's is troubling, as it appears to show that God plays favorites. We are not told how the brothers know whether their sacrifice is accepted, nor do we know why God rejects Cain's sacrifice. Perhaps the fact that Abel offers the first of his flock, while Cain offers the first of his crops, attests to the high regard for shepherds in the eleventh century, when the story was most likely put in writing. The main point of the story, though, is in Cain's reaction to the divine rejection of his offering. The Lord's speech to him suggests that rejecting Cain's offering does not in any way mean divine rejection of Cain himself. Cain's task is to do what is right, rather than give sin a chance to overtake him.

Cain's response is to kill his brother, violating the divine-human boundary by trying to exercise control over life and death. The divine question that follows in verse 9 reminds us of the question to Adam in 3:9, "Where are you?" Here the Lord asks Cain, "Where is your brother Abel?" high-lighting the alienation that results from sin (4:9). The divine question holds Cain responsible for his brother Abel's welfare. Cain's contemptuous response illustrates his nonconcern for his brother and his disregard for the deity. The Lord's punish-ment of Cain is an example of *lex talionis*, the law of retaliation that specifies that the punishment must fit the crime in both kind and degree: it must relate to the wrong that has been done, and must equal and not exceed the amount of wrong that was done. Cain will no longer be able to subsist as a farmer because he has violated the very soil that he works. As with Adam and Eve, God pun-ishes Cain, but does not abandon him, instead marking him for special protection.

4:17-24 Genealogical note

The genealogical note that follows in verses 17-24 shows that Cain has several generations of descendants who develop different professions important to civilization.

4:25–5:32 Adam's descendants

The narrative returns to Adam and Eve, reporting that they have additional children. The comment that people then begin to call on the Lord by name is puzzling because it seems to come too early: the Lord reveals the name YHWH to Moses at the burning bush (Exod 3:14), long after the time of the first humans. It might reflect the religious practices in the eleventh century, when the passage was most likely set down in written form. It also attests to the beginning of formal acts of worship, associating them with the descendants of Adam from earliest times.

A detailed genealogy records Adam's line to Noah's three sons: Shem, Ham, and Japheth. The narrative points out that the people are made with the same characteristics as the first humans: in God's image, male and female, and blessed. The list in chapter 5 includes many of the same names that we find in 4:17-24, but they are not identical. The lists represent different traditions, both of which were preserved when the stories were written down. The list in chapter 5 involves ten generations from Adam to Noah, a number that is parallel to the number of generations from Noah to Abraham in chapter 10. We cannot know the precise ages of these early people, partly because we do not know how they reckoned time and partly because the ages are unrealistic by modern calculations. Life expectancy today is the longest it has ever been, but does not approach the ages recorded here. The ages highlight the passage of a long time after the creation, during which humans thrived but also sinned. Verse 29 singles out Noah, identifying him as the one who will reverse the curse of the ground that began with Adam in 3:17-19 and continued with Cain in 4:10-12.

6:1–9:17 The Flood

A brief incident about the Nephilim seems to draw on an ancient story no longer known to us. It recounts further actions that blur the distinction between humans and God, with the result that God regrets having created human beings. Ancient people thought the heart was the locus of thinking and decision making. The statement that God's heart is grieved announces God's realization that something is out of place among human

beings, and the consequent decision to destroy all life, with the exception of Noah, who finds favor with God (see 5:29). This note introduces the story of the Flood and its aftermath, when creation is destroyed and then re-created.

The earth returns to its primeval chaos when the waters cover the earth, bursting forth from the boundaries to which they were assigned at the creation. And just as a divine wind swept over the waters in the beginning, so the same divine act returns the waters to their boundaries after the Flood. (In contrast, in the Epic of Gilgamesh the gods are terrified, once they see the destructive flood they have caused, and which they are powerless to control.) Once the people are back on dry land, Noah's sacrifice convinces God never to flood the earth again. God re-creates the people, providing for their needs in the same way as at the creation, with one exception: permission is granted to eat meat as long as the lifeblood has first been drained out. The reason for this stipulation is that blood is the symbol of life, and therefore belongs only to God. The rainbow sign of covenant flashes back to the seventh day after the six days of creation, the day set aside for honoring the Creator. Now God makes the rainbow the solemn sign of the promise never to destroy the earth in this way again. Thus the Flood story ends with the reestablishment of the relationship between God and all creatures.

The repetition of the names of Noah's sons in 6:9-10 (see 5:32) is the first indication that the narrative includes different versions. These two versions are not separate accounts, as we have in the two creation stories; rather, the two are woven together throughout the story, giving different sets of details that express the two different points of view while telling a single story.

Other signs of two versions are that humanity is corrupt, and that the Creator decides to destroy it according to J in 6:5-7, and according to P in verses 11-13. God instructs Noah to build an ark in preparation for a devastating flood in verses 14-22. The details suggest the P strand of the story: specific measurements and precise instructions. This ark, or box, will have no steering mechanism; God will be its pilot. The J strand does not include instructions for building, but gives instructions for entering it (7:1-3). The J instructions for entering the ark call for seven pairs of clean and one pair of unclean animals, all of which enter two by two (7:1-5, 8-9), while P reports that one pair of each enters the ark in 7:13-16a. The death of all other creatures appears in 7:21 (P version) and 7:22-23 in the J strand. The report of the end of the flood comes in 8:2b-3a (J) and 8:3b-5 (P). The J strand includes sending out birds to check the progress of the receding waters (8:6-12). Finally, the divine promise never again to destroy the earth by flood appears in 8:21b-22 (J) and 9:11-17 (P).

The P strand relates that God establishes a covenant, or solemn agreement, with Noah and all creatures, never again to destroy the earth by flood. The sign of the covenant will be the rainbow: whenever it appears, God will remember the solemn promise made to Noah. The narrative repeats the word "covenant" seven times, highlighting its solemn significance for God and all creation.

Several narrative elements in the Flood story parallel the first Creation story, illustrating God's creation and re-creation of the world. The chart below shows the similarities between the two stories according to P.

9:18-28 Noah and his sons

A brief genealogical note introduces the vague and puzzling incident between Noah and his son Ham. The story most likely alludes to an ancient Near Eastern story no longer available to us. From an etiological point of view it introduces viniculture and its positive and negative consequences, and also explains the negative attitude of ancient Israel toward the Canaanites: while it was Ham who violated his father, the narrative condemns his son Canaan for Ham's act.

10:1-32 Table of nations

A genealogy of Noah's sons and their descendants illustrates the widespread populating of the earth after the Flood. The genealogy is primarily the work of P, with narrative parts in verses 8-19 and 24-30 ascribed to J. The list, typical of Genesis, does not differentiate between people and nations, but names seventy descendants of Noah through his three sons. Japheth's descendants settle in the area north and west of the Fertile Crescent; Ham's around the Red Sea, northeastern Africa, and Canaan; and Shem's in the Fertile Crescent and Arabian Peninsula. This list of ten generations from Noah to Abraham parallels the ten generations from Adam to Noah in chapter 5. It does not prioritize any of the peoples, but names all of them as beneficiaries of the covenant God makes with Noah after the Flood.

11:1-9 The tower of Babel

The episode brings together three motifs: the development of technology, the dispersion of humanity throughout the world, and the confusion of languages. It specifies that all the people just named in the genealogy speak the same language, highlighting the unity of all humanity under God. In verses 1-4 we learn of a plan and its implementation by the humans, and in verses 5-8 we see the

Narrative elements	*Creation in 1:1–2:3*	*Re-creation in 7:11–9:17*
Wind over waters/earth	1:2	8:1
Watery chaos	1:1-2	7:11-12, 17-20
Separation of water and dry land	1:9-10	8:3b-5, 13a
Birds and animals brought forth	1:20-21	8:17-19
Blessing on animals: "Be fertile"	1:22	8:17
Humankind made "in the image of God"	1:26-27	9:6
Humans brought forth, blessed: "Be fertile"	1:27-28	9:1, 7
Humankind given dominion over animals	1:28	9:2
Provision of food for humankind	1:29-30	9:3
God saw . . . it was "very good/corrupt"	1:31	6:12
Covenant signs of Sabbath and rainbow	2:2-3	9:9-17

Lord's plan and its implementation. The people use their technical skills to try to construct a substantial, very tall building that will reach up into the sky, threatening to blur the boundary between the heavenly domain of God and the earthly dwelling of creatures. The Lord sees what the people are building, and realizes the potential threat to the divine-human boundary. Rather than risk a recurrence of chaos the Lord confuses their language and disperses the people all over the earth, thus populating the entire world and removing the danger that chaos will return. In an etiological note, the narrative specifies the name given to the place: Babel or Babylon. The words are similar to our modern term "babble," or incomprehensible talk, characterizing Babylon as a technologically advanced place where confusion thrives.

11:10-28 Shem's descendants

The narrative returns to the genealogy of Shem from 10:22-31, repeating the names of his descendants and adding information about the ages of the different people. The names are the same through Shem's great-grandson Eber, who has two sons: Peleg and Joktan. The list in chapter 10 focuses on Joktan's descendants, while chapter 11 lists those of Peleg. Five generations after Peleg, Abram and his two brothers Nahor and Haran are born. This point marks a transition in the narrative, away from the universal history of the human race to the particular saga of a single family: that of Abram. The genealogies illustrate Abram's ancestral link to the early generations of humankind, and establish a geographical tie to his ancient home in Ur, near the confluence of the Tigris and Euphrates Rivers (2:14). The stage is now set for the ancestral story.

THE ANCESTRAL STORY
PART I: ABRAHAM AND SARAH

Genesis 11:29–25:18

With the end of chapter 11 the narrative begins to focus on the family of Terah and four generations of his descendants: Abraham and Sarah, Isaac and Rebekah, Jacob and his two wives Leah and Rachel and their maids Bilhah and Zilpah, and finally Joseph. Chapters 12–36 recount the saga of the first three of these generations, and

chapters 37–50 focus on Jacob's son Joseph. The stories, like those in Genesis 1–11, were passed along by oral storytellers over hundreds of years. They were gradually collected and arranged into the narrative we have today. The different episodes in the saga reflect the concerns of the tellers and compilers, who used the stories to address the issues of their day. In this section we will focus on Abraham and Sarah (11:29–25:18). Then we will consider Isaac and Rebekah (25:19–28:9); next, Jacob and his wives (28:10–36:43); and finally Joseph in 37:1–50:26.

Chapters 12–36, like Genesis 1–11, are organized around genealogical summaries that mark the generations. In what is called the Abraham cycle, or stories about Abraham, a genealogical statement about Terah appears in 11:27 and of Ishmael in 25:12; in the Jacob cycle we find a genealogical summary about Isaac in 25:19; and in the Joseph cycle, a genealogical focus on Jacob appears in 37:2. Throughout these cycles the themes of divine promises of land, descendants, a nation, and blessing form the nucleus of the ancestral stories. Chapters 12–36 are a series of sagas, that is, prose narratives based on oral traditions, with episodic plots around stereotyped themes or topics. The episodes narrate deeds or events from the past as they relate to the world of the narrator. The sagas in these chapters are family sagas, or sagas about the family's past. They incorporate ancient Near Eastern literary conventions such as type scenes and specific family-centered motifs, which we will discuss as we meet them in the sagas.

11:29–12:9 The call of Abram

The transitional comments at the end of chapter 11 set the stage for the Abraham cycle by giving biographical information about Abram and Sarai. First, they link Abram with his ancestors. The narrative reports Sarai's childlessness twice, foreshadowing the importance of that detail in the narrative. The couple takes part in the family's migration from their ancient home in Ur to Canaan, but their travels are cut short when they settle in Haran, near the northernmost part of the Fertile Crescent. There Abram hears the divine commission to leave his family and go where the Lord shows him. In 12:2-3 the divine promise to Abraham includes a great nation and blessing; in fact, the word "bless" appears five times here.

The Lord will bless Abram, and in turn he will be a blessing to all the communities on earth.

For a great nation two things are necessary: children and land. The first is a problem because, as the narrative mentions twice, Sarai is childless. In ancient times childlessness was thought to be the woman's problem; that information helps us appreciate the stories from within their cultural point of view, even though modern medicine has given us a broader understanding of the causes of infertility. We will pick up this motif of childlessness several times in the ancestral story.

The second necessity for a nation, land, is also problematic because Abram and his family are nomads; they have no land of their own. This second problematic motif also appears frequently in the Genesis stories.

Verse 4 does not record any reaction to the divine command on Abram's part; it simply reports that Abram obeys the Lord's directive, taking his family and all his possessions to Canaan. Abram's nephew Lot, whose deceased father Haran was Abram's brother, travels with the family to Shechem. The account gives Abram's age: seventy-five; he is not a young man when they begin this journey.

Shechem was already an established worship center by the time Abram and his family arrived there; in verse 6 the narrative refers to a holy place near a certain tree. Abram responds to the divine promise of land by putting his own religious mark on the place: he builds an altar to the Lord. The promise of land is problematic because, as the narrative points out, the Canaanites were already living there. The dilemma of land use and ownership recurs throughout the book of Genesis and the rest of the Old Testament as well. Abram then built a second altar to the Lord near Bethel, south of Shechem, along their route southward toward the Negeb.

In the ancient Near East the building of altars marked sites as places of worship to honor a particular deity. The altars Abram builds identify the sites as places holy for the worship of Abram's God. The building of altars also marks the piece of land as sacred to the builders. Abram, in building an altar, makes an initial claim to the land. The book of Genesis takes for granted the existence of other gods worshiped by other peoples. In contrast, the book of Exodus describes in great detail the cosmic competition between the Lord and Pharaoh, whom the people believed was the personification of the sun god. That contest ends with the Lord's great victory over Pharaoh and the Egyptians, assuring the escaping Israelites that their newly identified Lord can care for them as he promised Moses.

12:10-20 Danger to Sarai

The family's survival depends on finding adequate sustenance in the face of famine, leading Abram and his family to travel southwest toward Egypt. This episode is told in the form of a type scene, that is, a story that includes several standard plot elements. A couple prepares to enter foreign territory, and the husband fears for his life because his wife is beautiful and the hosts might try to kill him in order to marry his wife. He arranges with his wife that she will pose as his sister, rather than his wife. She does so; the hosts see her, find her attractive, and take her to their leader. Difficulties arise in the leader's house because of the wife-sister; the leader discovers the truth about the woman; and the couple departs. The scene occurs three times in Genesis; twice with Abram and Sarai and once with Isaac and Rebekah.

The incident that begins in 12:10 includes the above elements. Abram's words to Sarai on the outskirts of Egypt lay out the background information: she will pose as his sister. Sarai makes no reply to his request; we are left wondering whether she agrees or merely acquiesces. No genealogical information is given about Sarai when the family is first introduced in 11:27-30. We assume that she and Abram were related in some way before their marriage because the narrative implies that they both came from the city of Ur. Furthermore, the terms "sister" and "brother" had a broader range of meanings in the ancient world than today; Abram might simply have intended to acknowledge that he and Sarai were relatives.

When they enter Egypt events unfold exactly as Abram predicted, and the Egyptian officials take Sarai to the house of Pharaoh and heap gifts on Abram in return. But the Lord intervenes and brings suffering to Pharaoh's house on account of Abram's deceit. The story does not tell us how Pharaoh learns the cause of his sufferings; it reports only that once Pharaoh realizes what has happened, he orders Abram to leave with his wife and possessions. The type scene includes several noteworthy details. First, Abram seems to be looking out only for himself. He fears for his own life because his wife is beautiful, but does not seem to consider the possible consequences for Sarai, who he anticipates will be the cause of his own danger. A further concern is that Abram jeopardizes the Lord's promise of family because the arrangement threatens to destroy Abram and Sarai's marriage, thus eliminating the possibility that they will have the children God promised them.

The narrative specifies that the punishment to Pharaoh comes from the Lord, assuring that the Lord protects the promise to Abram in the midst of Abram's actions that threaten to negate it. This episode is the first of many that address threats to the divine promises of land and descendants. The threat sometimes comes through human action, either of Abram or one of his family members, or by someone outside his family. At other times the threat comes from nature and the people's ability to find enough food to eat. In every instance someone does something that jeopardizes the divine promise, and then the Lord takes steps to avert the danger and assure that the promise is carried forward. In this episode Abram himself risks cutting off the possibility of having the children God promised by pretending that he and Sarai are not married. The Lord intervenes when events take their normal course, and assures that the promise will move forward in spite of human interference.

13:1-18 Separation of Abram and Lot

Leaving Egypt, Abram and his family retrace their path back toward Bethel and Ai, where he built an altar on his earlier journey through that region. By this time both Abram and Lot have accumulated great wealth in the form of livestock, precious metals, and tents. As the number of animals increases, the need for grazing land to feed them begins to strain the relationship between uncle and nephew. A further complication is that the Canaanites and Perizzites inhabit the land. Abram's solution to the problem is to offer Lot whatever part of the land he wishes, a very magnanimous offer by Abram who, as the older of the two, has the first right of selection. Lot chooses the more fertile area along the Jordan River banks. The narrative foreshadows troubles to come by noting that, even though the area is fertile, its inhabitants are wicked. Lot then moves his flocks to his selected area, and Abram stays in the central region of Canaan.

The episode illustrates Abram's willingness to provide for his nephew, even at significant cost to himself. In verses 14-15 God immediately rewards Abram's generosity by repeating the promise of land and descendants. This time the promises are more expansive than before: Abram is promised land as far as he can see, with descendants too numerous to count. The Lord invites Abram to move about in the land that will be given to him. Abram travels to Mamre, at Hebron, his first stop in the land of Canaan; he builds an altar to the Lord as is his custom.

14:1-24 Abram and the kings

Lot's choice of territory quickly becomes complicated when four kings attack Sodom and four other cities. The episode itself is complex in several ways. The historical and geographical details cannot be verified. Furthermore, Abram is portrayed here in a different light from the surrounding chapters; there he was a patriarch and shepherd; here he is the commander of an army. His troops set out in pursuit of Lot's captors, traveling as far as Damascus, far to the north. This incident in the Genesis narrative is probably a later addition, inserted to address a question that was pertinent to the writer, but beyond the scope of this commentary. We will focus on another incident, namely, Abram's meeting with the two kings, the king of Sodom and Melchizedek of Salem, on his return from Damascus. Melchizedek welcomes Abram and Lot by performing a priestly ritual.

Several of the geographical locations have been identified; for example, Salem is the ancient name of the city of Jerusalem. The climactic scene in the chapter is Melchizedek's priestly ritual to welcome Abram back from his rescue mission. This scene sets the stage for David's reign and the years that followed it: Melchizedek is both king and priest. The narrative identifies him as king of Salem, and then describes a ritual that involves bread and wine and a blessing of Abram by Melchizedek. Melchizedek blesses Abram in the name of "God Most High," the chief deity among the Canaanite gods. The serving of bread and wine might be a simple act of hospitality, or might also represent a religious ritual to celebrate

Abram's success. Its larger significance is thought to lie in its foreshadowing of three realities: the religious importance of Jerusalem, the combined royal and priestly offices of the king of the area, and the eventual loyalty of Abram's descendants to the Israelite king in Jerusalem. In a similar incident in 2 Samuel 6:13, David offers a sacrifice to the Lord during the ceremony of bringing the ark into Jerusalem (see also Ps 110:4). These foreshadowings of future situations suggest that the material is among the latest in the Genesis narrative. From the vantage point of the monarchy, the Priestly editor included details about the past that link the people's current reality with those long-ago days when Abram was new in the land, demonstrating that the Lord's protection of the people extended back into their earliest history. In a manner consistent with the early Christian custom of linking Christ to figures in the Old Testament, the author of Hebrews drew a resemblance between Melchizedek and Jesus Christ (Heb 7:1-4).

15:1-21 The promise to Abram

The narrative resumes with another divine promise that the Lord will protect Abram and give him a great reward. The first announcement, in verse 1, is vague compared to the earlier ones, but Abram's response articulates the profound problem foreshadowed above: the Lord promises offspring, but Abram's wife is barren. The conversation has a prophetic tone. The phrase "the word of the LORD came to . . ." appears frequently in the prophetic books, as does the context of a vision. The expression, "Do not fear" also occurs frequently in the prophetic books, when the Lord offers assurance to the prophet about a pressing problem, and the prophet in turn reassures the people. This prophetic language in the Lord's words to Abram speaks to the special relationship that Abram enjoys with the Lord. What is more, even though Abram still has no children, the divine speech foreshadows a change by which Abram will have many descendants.

The exchange resembles other biblical forms as well: verses 1-6 resemble a call narrative and verses 7-21 include elements of a covenant ritual. We will look at the narrative from these two points of view individually. First, a call consists of a theophany or appearance of God, a commission from God to perform a particular task, a question or objection on the part of the one receiv-

ing the call, and a reiteration of the call followed by a sign of confirmation. Here Abram has a vision (v. 1) in which the Lord makes a promise to him. Abram questions the promise on the grounds that he is childless (vv. 2-3). The Lord repeats the promise, expanding on it and adding the sign of the heavens: Abram's descendants will be as numerous as the stars in the sky (vv. 4-5). The text then asserts that Abram's faith in God is a righteous act; that is, Abram is in a right relationship with the Lord.

In verse 7 the commission seems to begin all over again in the form of a covenant ritual. The passage includes a historical introduction, an enumeration of the terms of the covenant, a sign confirming it, a list of the blessings and curses to follow obedience or disobedience, and an arrangement for promulgating the covenant. Verses 7-21 include most of these elements. The historical introduction announces that the same Lord who first brought Abram out of Ur is now giving him the land. In 12:1, when the Lord first instructed Abram to begin his journey, he was already in Haran. Here the text extends divine guidance all the way back to the family's departure from Ur (11:31), suggesting that it was the Lord who prompted Terah to move his family to Canaan. Then, as in call narratives, Abram responds with a question. (See, for instance, Exod 3:11; Jer 1:6).

The divine response is a call for a covenant ritual. This ancient Near Eastern ceremony involved cutting prescribed animals in two; then the two covenant parties walked between the pieces, binding themselves to the terms of the covenant under penalty of a fate similar to that of the slaughtered animals. The precise significance of the swooping birds of prey is not known; it can be understood as a way of expressing Abram's willingness to abide by the terms of the agreement even when danger threatens. Likewise, the liminal light of sunset highlights the unknown dimension of Abram's agreement with the Lord.

In verse 13 the text interrupts its description of the covenant ceremony to reiterate and elaborate on the Lord's promise of land. In addition, it alludes to a period of slavery that anticipates the exodus. Finally, a sign in the form of fire witnesses and confirms the sacred agreement the Lord has made with Abram. This particular ceremony does not include a list of blessings and curses or an arrangement to promulgate the treaty, as Abram still does not have a family among whom to publicize it. The covenant ritual solemnizes the divine promise to Abram, and also sets the stage for the next episode in the couple's efforts to have children.

Here the type scene of the barren mother appears. This kind of story involves a childless woman who gives birth to a son as a result of divine intervention. She takes specific steps to assure that her son will be successful, and often the son becomes a leader at a time of transition or crisis. The barren mother type scene has three models: promise, competition, and request. According to the promise model, a divine messenger appears and promises a son. That promise is confirmed, even though the recipient does not believe it. The son is born and receives a name that bears some significance to his life and work.

The Bible includes this kind of promise in the stories of Sarai here in Genesis, and also in the story of Hannah in 1 Samuel 1–2. The promises of sons to Zechariah and Mary in Luke's Gospel follow this model as well (Luke 1–2). Here the initial promise is not specific, only that the Lord will give Abram a great reward. Abram's question responds to the earlier promises in 12:2-3 and 12:7 that refer to descendants. In the formal covenant section that follows (v. 13), the divine response confirms the initial promise of biological descendants to Abram. Later in the narrative the remaining elements of the promise model appear.

16:1-16 The birth of Ishmael

The narrative returns to the dilemma of Abram and Sarai's childlessness in the story of the birth of Ishmael to Abram and Hagar, Sarai's maid. Sarai proposes, in keeping with ancient Near Eastern custom, that Abram father a child through Hagar. While we today find this a disconcerting arrangement, it illustrates the importance of children in the ancient world. Large families with many hands to do the work were a necessity for subsistence. In addition, it was a point of honor for a man to father a large family who would carry on his name.

This very human story depicts Sarai's frustration, embarrassment, and jealousy; Hagar's disdain for Sarai; and Abram's quiet lack of involvement in the controversy that ensues. In fact, Abram responds to Sarai just as he did to God: he heeds her request. When Sarai blames him for causing the problem, he responds to her accusation by returning Hagar to Sarai's care as the law provided for slaves who overstepped their boundaries. But Sarai's punishment exceeds Hagar's crime, and as a result of Sarai's mistreatment the maid runs away.

Hagar, like Abram and Sarai, receives divine promises when the Lord's messenger finds her, questions her, and sends her back to Sarai. She will have many descendants beginning with the son she carries in her womb. The messenger gives a name to the unborn child, and interprets the name for Hagar. The naming of a child had several layers of meaning in the ancient world. The significance of the one who gives the name foreshadows the importance of the child. In addition, the specific name foretells something about the character of the child, or about the life the child will live. Here the message promises divine care for Hagar and her son; it also hints that the tension between his mother and her mistress will continue in her son's generation between him and other peoples. Hagar in turn gives a name to the Lord, expressing her own incredulity that she survives the experience of seeing the Lord. The incident takes place by a spring, and the account ends with the etiological note that the spring, now referred to as a well, is named to acknowledge Hagar's religious experience in that place. We can assume that the place was known among the people who told the story throughout the generations.

The incident is significant in several ways. First, it demonstrates the Lord's continuing care for all the people, including Hagar. It also teases the reader, suggesting a possible solution to the problem of Abram and Sarai's childlessness. That possibility seems all the more realistic in light of Abram's advancing age.

This episode introduces another model of the barren mother type scene: the competition model. That model includes five elements: a wife is childless; her husband has another wife; the rival wife gives birth to a child, causing conflict; God intervenes to give a child to the childless wife; and finally, a significant name is given to the child. Here Sarai has no children; she gives her maid Hagar to Abram for the purpose of bearing him a child; Hagar bears a son, causing conflict between herself and Sarai; and the child receives the name Ishmael. At this point Sarai still does not bear a child; that element comes only after several more delays in the narrative.

17:1-27 The covenant with Abraham

The chapter relates an additional development that, on a narrative level, postpones yet again the fulfillment of the promise of children to Abram and Sarai. This episode is P's version of the incident told by J in chapter 15. Thirteen years have passed since Ishmael's birth when the Lord appears again to Abram and begins with a formal introduction, and then changes Abram's name to Abraham to reflect his role as father of nations. The terms of the agreement ask something of both parties. God repeats the promise of descendants and land, and promises to be their God. The people are enjoined to keep the covenant, that is, to adhere to the terms of the divine-human relationship, and all the males are expected to be circumcised. The origins of this requirement, given in some detail, are puzzling to us, but were undoubtedly understood by ancient peoples. What we do know is that the people living in exile in Babylon during the sixth century b.c. looked upon circumcision as the sign of their identity as exiles from Judah, in contrast to the Babylonians, who did not practice it. In keeping with the theory that the Priestly writers and editors lived and worked in Babylon during the exile, it is quite possible that this became an important sign of identity at that time.

Sarai also receives a new name, Sarah, from God, confirming that she will be the mother of the promised son. Abraham's incredulity, amazement, and joy on hearing the promise cause his marvelously human reaction, which is all the more touching because heretofore his response was simply to do what he was asked. His laughter foreshadows the name of his promised son: Isaac, or "laughter." But he remains incredulous, and gives God an alternative proposal, to make Ishmael the favored one. This suggestion gives God the opportunity to clarify that Ishmael will receive the divine blessing and promise of a great nation; but the son of the covenant will be Isaac, whom Sarah will bear within the year.

The divine announcement that the birth of the child will take place within a year moves the promise a step closer to fulfillment. Then the narrative reports that Abraham circumcises all the males in his family as the Lord commanded. This brief note illustrates yet again Abraham's unwavering obedience to God's commands. The vivid storytelling details characteristic of J are combined with P's solemn description of circumcision as the mark of the Lord's people.

The promise model of the barren mother type reappears in this episode. The Lord appears to Abraham (still Abram at the beginning of the episode), promising generations of descendants in verses 2-10. Then in verse 16 God explicitly announces that Sarah will be the child's mother. In response to Abraham's incredulous response God reiterates the promise and gives a name to the promised child. But several more events must intervene before the child is born.

18:1-16a The three visitors

Once again Abraham receives the divine promise of a child. The text juxtaposes the appearance of the Lord with the coming of three visitors in the heat of the day, creating several questions about the meaning of the text. Is the Lord one of the three visitors? Do all three guests represent the Lord? How is it that Abraham sees three people and bows down in respectful welcome; but when he speaks he seems to address only one person? As the text stands, it points out that God is revealed through humans, and through what is at first glance a visit from three travelers.

Many details suggest extremes: the heat of the desert afternoon, the three men who are related to the divine in some mysterious way, ninety-nine-year-old Abraham's energetic greeting, the feast he asks Sarah to prepare for the visitors. Then one of the guests asks a question that would seem impertinent in ancient Near Eastern society, "Where is your wife Sarah?" Women did not share the table with men, and the visitors were surely aware of that custom. The question seems inappropriately familiar until the visitor's next statement reveals the reason for his inquiry: when he returns in a year, Sarah will have a son. The Lord made the same promise in 17:21; this assertion by the visitor confirms both the promise and the date.

Now it is Sarah's turn to laugh. We learn that she has been listening to the conversation from her place out of sight, and she reacts as did Abraham: she laughs at the thought of bearing a child at her advanced age. Without realizing, she anticipates the name to be given to the boy. The follow-up question, "Why did Sarah laugh?" comes from the Lord, not from one of the three guests, and is directed to Abraham. But Sarah herself responds, denying that she laughed. Yet the visitor/the Lord hears the laugh: the narrative explains that it is a sign of her fear in response to the awesome announcement she has heard, and the amazing future it represents for her.

The entire incident bespeaks complexity—the human and divine realms are blurred, singular and plural forms intermingle, the normally reticent Abraham extends gracious hospitality, seemingly impossible promises are made, private responses become public—in keeping with the complicated reality the visitors announce: this elderly couple will soon be parents. As readers, we are tempted to join in the laughter with mixed emotions of relief, amazement, and puzzlement in the face of the seemingly insurmountable obstacle of the very advanced ages of husband and wife.

Here the promise model of the barren mother type scene highlights Sarah: it is she who cannot believe the messenger's word, and expresses her amazement in laughter. The messenger confirms the promise, not directly to Sarah but to Abraham: when he returns in a year, Sarah will have a child.

18:16b-33 Abraham intercedes for Sodom

The narrative returns to Sodom, where it left off in chapter 14. While Abraham accompanies his three guests on their journey, the Lord reflects on whether to let Abraham know about coming events. The incident is not simply about the destruction of Sodom; in larger terms it is about the developing relationship between the Lord and Abraham. The Lord has made him the father and teacher of many nations; therefore the Lord gives him information that will help him fulfill that responsibility. The Lord decides to investigate the rumors of sin in Sodom and Gomorrah.

Verse 22 takes us back to the puzzling identity of Abraham's three visitors. We learn that the men continue walking while the Lord stays behind with Abraham, who engages the Lord in conversation. He starts with the assumption that the Lord will completely destroy the sinful city and questions the Lord about destroying innocent people. He persuades the Lord to think again about this plan that is out of character for the

Deity. Abraham continues to press the question until the Lord agrees that ten innocent people are enough to warrant saving the city. Abraham has grown from silently obedient to passionately protective, an essential trait for the one destined to father many nations; he convinces the Lord to spare the city for the sake of the few righteous ones. This scene does not mention the possibility of repentance to forestall the destruction of the city, as we find in the prophetic books. (See, for instance, Jer 8:6; 9:4; Ezek 14:6; 18:30.)

19:1-29 Destruction of Sodom

Chapter 19 begins with the visit of the other two of Abraham's guests to Lot. The word "angels" is the English translation of the Hebrew word meaning "messengers," and designates anyone who delivers a word on behalf of another person. Here the two are called "angels," highlighting the ambiguous identity of the three visitors in chapter 18. Later in this chapter they announce on God's behalf, "We are about to destroy this place" (v. 13). Their visit begins with events that parallel the visit of the three men to Abraham: Lot receives the two visitors and bows to them in respectful welcome. He invites them to stay, and when they agree he prepares a meal for them.

At that point the similarities end: the meal Lot prepares is quite simple in contrast to the elaborate feast Abraham arranged for his guests. This detail does not begin to foreshadow the horror that is about to take place. Immediately the sinfulness of the Sodomites becomes apparent in their determination to violate the guests. While today we find Lot's offer to give his daughters to the men horrific, it speaks to the high priority given to hospitality among ancient Near Eastern nomads: a host protected his guests, regardless of the cost. This incident clarifies the sins of the city of Sodom alluded to in chapter 18: rampant lack of hospitality and sexual aberrations.

The quick action of the guests saves both Lot and his daughters from the horror that might have ensued. The NABRE translation of 19:11, "with such a blinding light that they were utterly unable to find the doorway" is a bit ambiguous; the Hebrew text reads, "And they struck with blindness the men who were at the door of the house, both small and great, so that they were unable to find the door." The incident confirms the Lord's assessment of the wickedness of the place, and the visitors urge Lot to remove his family at once, before the city is destroyed for its sins.

After all that transpires with the two guests during the night, we expect Lot to depart immediately. Instead, the angels must cajole and negotiate with him throughout the night. First, the fiancés of Lot's two daughters refuse to take the warning seriously. Then at dawn the angels press him to take the other members, but Lot hesitates. The visitors remove them from the house and insist that they depart immediately and not look back or stop. Lot still resists, and begs to be allowed to go to a small town nearby. The response comes from one angel, implying, as in the story of Abraham's guests, that the angel is actually the Lord, who agrees to accommodate Lot's request.

After all these steps Lot's wife violates the command not to look back, and she becomes a pillar of salt (see also Wis 10:7). This detail is a bit of etiological folklore: at the southern end of the Dead Sea, the salt deposits create bizarre shapes, some of which resemble human beings; tour guides point out which is their own favorite "Mrs. Lot." Here in the story the presence of a salt formation is explained as Lot's wife's punishment for her disobedience. In fact, the woman probably suffered the same end as all those who remained in Sodom: the sulphur and salt destroyed everything. (Salt is a symbol of death and destruction; see Judg 9:45.)

Verses 27-28 recount that Abraham witnesses the destructive scene. Again we learn nothing about the reaction of this very reticent man, but we do find out that it is for his sake that God spares Lot from the debacle.

19:30-38 Lot and his daughters

The action of Lot's daughters suggests they are living in very isolated circumstances after the destruction of Sodom. While the incident with their father would be offensive to modern sensitivity, it shows the daughters' desperation and ingenuity in assuring offspring for their family. The incident also serves another purpose; that is, the two sons become the ancestors of the Ammonite and Moabite peoples. Both of these groups were neighbors of Israel; this brief account establishes the reason for the animosity between them and the Israelites. In addition, the episode highlights the importance of having children in ancient Near

Eastern society. It also serves as a reminder that Sarah still has not given birth to the promised child, a concern that becomes acute when the following incident threatens yet again to thwart the divine promise of a son.

20:1-18 Sarah endangered again

The story returns to Abraham and Sarah, repeating the plot of the wife-sister story in chapter 12. This time the couple is in Gerar, and it is the local king Abimelech who takes Sarah into his house. This time Sarah explicitly supports Abraham's ruse by agreeing that she is his sister. God's warning to Abimelech saves him from punishment and saves Abraham and Sarah from further complications to their marriage. Abraham admits that fear has motivated him, and explains that Sarah is in fact the daughter of his father but not his mother; she is his half-sister. (We recall that the initial genealogy in Gen 11:27-29 does not include any mention of Sarah's lineage.) Once again we are reminded that Sarah still has no son, in contrast to the women of Gerar, whom God healed after their wombs had been closed in punishment for Abimelech's unwitting action. The event raises a question: Abraham puts the life of his wife in jeopardy because of his fear for his own life. How will he care for a newborn child, when he cares more for his own life than for his wife's?

It is problematic for us today to see the extent to which other people suffer the consequences of Abraham's efforts to protect himself. It is helpful to keep in mind that ancient people had a much stronger appreciation for the consequences of individual actions than we do today: they realized that every action affects all of creation. They understood that Abraham's actions to protect himself had ramifications for everyone: his family members, Abimelech, and all the people. In addition, we see an example of *lex talionis*, the law of retribution that insists that a punishment fit the crime. Here, the life of Sarah's promised child is endangered, and in consequence the future of Gerar is jeopardized.

But Abraham becomes the intercessor for the inhabitants of Gerar. Verse 17 reports that Abraham prays for Abimelech and his women, and as a result the Lord removes the punishment of sterility from them. Abraham's concern for a family other than his own represents a broadening awareness for the well-being of everyone. (We recall that Abraham urges God to spare the city of Sodom if a few righteous people can be found there; here Abraham convinces God to reverse the punishment he and Sarah caused by their ruse.)

21:1-21 Birth of Isaac and banishment of Hagar and Ishmael

At last the narrative reports that Sarah is pregnant and bears the promised son. He is circumcised and receives the promised name of Isaac. This time his name, "Laughter," relates to the joy his birth brings to his parents and all their acquaintances. The detail about Isaac's circumcision illustrates P's attention to details about religious practice: here we learn that Abraham carefully observes the covenant.

But in verse 9 the threats to the promise continue; Sarah works to ensure a future for her son in spite of her fear that Ishmael is a threat to him. Abraham's love for both his sons is evident in his distress over Sarah's demand (v. 11). The Lord reassures him that Ishmael, too, will receive divine protection and will himself become the ancestor of a great nation for Abraham's sake. This incident reminds us of Sarah's earlier insistence that Hagar leave, when the slave woman lorded it over Sarah because of Ishmael (ch. 16). This time it is Sarah's jealousy that prompts her to request that Hagar and Ishmael go away.

In verses 14-17 grief permeates the separation of Hagar and Ishmael from Abraham. The narrative describes in detail Abraham's preparations to send the two away, followed by Hagar and Ishmael's hopeless meandering and forlorn cries in the wilderness. The divine reassurance is more than words: God promises a future for Ishmael, then provides a well, insuring they will have as much water as they need. (We will meet Ishmael's Egyptian descendants in chapter 37, when they rescue Joseph from the cistern, another place associated with water, where his brothers leave him.) Here the narrative anticipates the agonizing scene in chapter 22, when God asks Abraham to give up his son Isaac: both describe God's instructions to Abraham to give up his son, both enumerate Abraham's preparations in measured detail, both tell us the boy cries out, and in the end both tell of divine intervention on behalf of the boy.

Sarah's action to ensure her son's future completes the type scene of the barren mother. She does what she considers necessary in order to guarantee that Isaac will be the son who receives his father's inheritance.

21:22-34 The pact between Abraham and Abimelech

In a flashback to chapter 20, we learn that Abimelech and Abraham negotiate a settlement to assure that their families can live in peace with one another, and that both groups will have access to water. Then Abraham plants a tree to stake his claim to the territory and mark it as a worship site, like the altars he built earlier.

22:1-19 God tests Abraham

Chapter 22 tells one of the most poignant stories in the Bible: God's test of Abraham. In Hebrew, Abraham's first response to God is *hinneni*, a word that has no exact English equivalent. It translates, "Here I am," and connotes attentiveness, readiness, willingness. The word appears again in verses 7 and 11. Abraham responds before he knows that God is about to make an unthinkable request. God describes Isaac in three phrases that intensify the dreadful irony of the divine instruction: "Take your son Isaac, your only one, whom you love."

After all the promises of a son, and all the times the promise was jeopardized before Isaac was finally born, now, before giving the command to Abraham, God highlights how precious Isaac is to Abraham by describing his uniqueness in three phrases of increasing intensity. Only then does God give the command to sacrifice Isaac in the land of Moriah, a place that cannot be located today. Second Chronicles 3:1 refers to Mount Moriah as the location of the Jerusalem temple, establishing a connection between the test of Abraham and the offering of sacrifices in the temple. Today the Muslim Dome of the Rock stands over the rock that tradition identifies as the place of Abraham's sacrifice.

The pace of the narrative resembles that of chapter 21: it gives measured details of Abraham's preparations, prolonging the suspense for both Abraham and Isaac, and also for the reader. We wonder how God can possibly ask this ultimate sacrifice of Abraham after all the years of promises that culminate in the gift of laughter that Isaac brings to his aged parents. The chapter continues the theme of jeopardy to the promise that permeates the entire Abraham narrative even after

Isaac's birth, as we saw in chapter 21. But this time it is the Lord, who made the promise of children to Abraham and repeated it over and over again throughout many threats to its fulfillment, who seems to jeopardize the promise. In the previous chapter, Abraham hesitates to banish his son Ishmael, but God insists; now Abraham has only Isaac, and God directs him to sacrifice that one whom he loves. This is to be a burnt offering, or holocaust. The expression appears six times in this chapter, highlighting its importance. In the time of Abraham it was the father who offered the sacrifice; after the temple was built and worship was institutionalized, the requirements stipulated that the offering was to be an animal without blemish, and that the priest would burn the entire offering at the temple (see Lev 1:3-17).

These details about the divine command suggest that the episode became part of the narrative late in the monarchy, when political and military events were testing the faith of the entire people. The scope of the divine command grows in horror with each added detail; here we realize that Isaac is a fitting offering because he is unblemished. Abraham's silence after his initial "Here I am!" is typical of his quiet acceptance of divine instructions throughout his life. Here it is all the more poignant in light of the dreadful act he is asked to perform: no words can adequately respond to this divine command. Just as God heard the cry of Ishmael in 21:17, Abraham hears Isaac's cry in 22:7; he responds "Here I am" a second time. Isaac's question about the sacrificial animal indicates that he, too, expects a holocaust, but does not at all envision himself as the actual sacrificial victim. In 21:17 God hastens to reassure Hagar; here in 22:8 Abraham reassures Isaac that God will provide.

The narrative continues at its infinitely slow pace, recounting the details of preparing the sacrifice with Isaac on top of the firewood. The matter is almost too much to bear. Not until Abraham holds the knife above his son does the angel stop his hand from performing the sacrifice and announce that Abraham has passed the test. The expression "fear of God" connotes awe, reverence, and obedience. After Abraham completes the sacrifice by offering a ram, the messenger repeats the divine promise of offspring, this time relating it to Abraham's obedience to God. After that the scene ends with the ambiguous note that they

return home; even the narrator is too exhausted to specify who: only the servants? Isaac?

There is no mention of Sarah in this story. We can only wonder about her reaction to the entire affair. In his tapestry that hangs in the foyer of the Knesset, or Parliament, building in Jerusalem, Marc Chagall depicted Sarah present at the sacrifice. Her presence in the tapestry expresses her agonized love for the son who brought laughter to her, and also intensifies the pain in the event: what mother could bear to watch her child become a sacrificial lamb?

The narrative explains that this is a test of Abraham's faithfulness, and that he passes it with flying colors. But the portrayal of Abraham the father is problematic. In previous episodes, he pleads with God on behalf of others. He begs God not to destroy the city of Sodom if a few righteous people can be found there (18:22-32). He objects when Sarah wants Hagar and Ishmael banished (21:11). But here, when God asks him to kill his only son Isaac, the son who has been promised repeatedly, the son whom he loves, Abraham's only response is "hinneni."

A brief genealogical note follows, informing Abraham and the reader that Abraham's brother Nahor has twelve sons including one named Bethuel, the father of Rebekah. This information foreshadows future generations of Abraham's family: Isaac will eventually marry Rebekah, and Isaac's son Jacob will marry Rebekah's nieces and will father twelve sons and one daughter.

23:1-20 Sarah's death and burial

Now that Abraham has passed his final test he spends his remaining days settling his affairs: purchasing a burial plot for his wife Sarah, securing a wife for his son Isaac, and distributing his assets before his own death. Verses 1-2 provide the background information in the style of P, the probable source for the episode. In verses 3-18 Abraham negotiates the purchase of land for a burial site. The negotiations proceed in stages: first, as a sojourner in the land, he petitions the local people for a burial place. They respond favorably and respectfully, inviting him to select the piece of land he prefers (vv. 3-6). In verses 4-15 the expression "bury one's dead" appears seven times, always with a possessive word that expresses relationship, love, and respect and highlights the purpose of Abraham's request. In verses

7-11 he designates the cave he would like, and asks the council to make his request to the owner of the plot, according to the custom. The owner offers to give the cave and its surrounding field to Abraham.

We learn in verses 12-18 that Abraham prefers to buy the land, and weighs out the stipulated price. His request to purchase the property raises two difficulties: first, he is an alien and is normally not entitled to buy land (Lev 25:23); and second, landowners are very reluctant to give up their land (1 Kgs 21:3). These negotiations take place in the presence of witnesses because it is an oral, rather than written, agreement.

The process of acquiring land for burial resonated with the people during the exile in Babylon, when they were without land to call their own. The P editors incorporated that concern into the ancestral story in such a way that the episode fits both the ancestral narrative and the exilic loss of land.

24:1-67 A wife for Isaac

One more task remains for Abraham in order to assure the continuation of the divine promise of progeny to him and Sarah: that is to find a wife for Isaac from among his own people. The text does not include Isaac in these arrangements; after the heart-stopping account of his near-death experience, there is no further record of interaction between father and son. The episode revolves around Abraham's servant, whom Abraham sends to his people in Haran. The importance of both family ties and land is highlighted in the servant's question as to whether to take Isaac back to that land if the chosen woman refuses to accompany the servant back to Canaan. Abraham's emphatic response assures the servant that the Lord will find him a wife. The servant's gesture in verse 9 (putting his hand under the thigh of his master) relates to an ancient custom of swearing by the genitals in acknowledgment of their sacred importance for passing life along to the next generation. (The thigh is a euphemism for genitals.) A further consideration is the need for Isaac to remain in Canaan because he embodies the divine promises of descendants and land. Later the Lord instructs him not to leave the land, even in time of famine (Gen 26:2).

Abraham's wealth and his eagerness to make a good impression on his relatives are evident in the sizeable gift the servant takes with him as a bride-price. The journey is surely lengthy, given the distance involved and the number of cattle in the servant's care; but the narrative skips over any mention of the trip, and focuses immediately on the scene at the well.

This story is an example of another kind of type scene: the betrothal. The type involves a man traveling to foreign territory to find a wife for himself or someone else. Once there he goes to a well and meets young women of the area. Someone provides water from the well for the visitor and for the animals gathered there. Then the girls return home to announce the visitor's presence. He receives an invitation to their home, and a betrothal follows. This scene appears here and also in Genesis 29, when Jacob is looking for a wife. The type scene appears again in abbreviated form in Exodus 2:15-22, when Moses takes a wife after fleeing from Egypt.

Here, in accordance with the type scene, the servant goes to the well at the time when the women come to get water for the evening meal. The servant prays to God, then sets up the scenario by which he will know whom to request as a wife for his master. It is a simple device: he will ask for a drink of water, and if a young woman agrees to give water not only to him but also to his camels, he will know she is the one he seeks. The narrator tells the reader that Rebekah is the granddaughter of Abraham's brother Nahor, and thus Abraham's grandniece, but the servant does not yet know this.

The particulars give the story its unique character. The text describes Rebekah in an unusual amount of detail. Specifically, we learn that she is a very beautiful virgin, an ideal choice for a wife for Isaac. The type scene continues when the servant poses his question and Rebekah responds, giving him water and then making several trips back and forth to water the ten camels as well. These details depict Rebekah as energetic, industrious, and generous, further augmenting her desirability as a wife for Isaac. The servant's two questions remind us that he still does not know who she is until she unwittingly identifies herself as a member of Abraham's family. The type scene continues as the girl rushes home to announce the servant's coming while the servant prays in thanksgiving to God for leading him there.

In keeping with nomadic hospitality, Rebekah's brother Laban rushes out to the servant and invites him to his home. The servant insists on telling his story, explaining why he has come and reminding the reader that the Lord is guiding the events that take place. The family members readily agree to the servant's request that Rebekah return with him to become Isaac's wife because they recognize that the request is from the Lord. Their statement, "Here is Rebekah, right in front of you; take her and go" in verse 51 is the formal ratification of the betrothal. The Hebrew formula includes the word *hinneh* that we met in chapter 22 and that connotes attentiveness, readiness, and willingness.

The next morning, in verse 54, her family suggests that the party stay awhile before leaving, in keeping with customs of hospitality. But the servant is eager to return to Abraham and report the successful outcome of his trip. The family members ask Rebekah's consent to the arrangement. This is a necessary step in ancient Near Eastern societies, because the betrothal involves two special circumstances: the marriage is arranged by her brother rather than her father, and it will take her away from her homeland. As soon as she gives her consent the family members send her and her nurse with the servant and all his retinue. The fact that her nurse accompanies her suggests that Rebekah is still quite young at the time of the betrothal. Her family members bless her with the hope of many descendants as well as victory over enemies. (See Ruth 4:11 for a similar blessing.)

In verse 62 Isaac reappears in the story for the first time since his near-sacrifice. We learn that he is living in the Negeb, and that one day in the late afternoon he sees the approaching caravan. The Hebrew text is not clear here, so we do not know whether he has been expecting them. The narrative switches immediately to Rebekah, who looks up at the same time and sees Isaac. The simple description of their meeting is anticlimactic after the lengthy account of the servant's journey to find Rebekah and bring her home with him. Rebekah veils herself for their meeting, signaling to Isaac that she has come to marry him.

The servant's response, "That is my master," is puzzling here, as his master is actually Abraham, but the person in front of them is Isaac. It is possible that Abraham has died by the time the party returns. That would explain the servant's comment in verse 36 that Abraham has given everything he owns to his son Isaac, and also the note that the servant reports on his journey to Isaac

(v. 66). Abraham's death is actually announced in chapter 25, immediately after the finding of a wife for Isaac, perhaps so as not to interrupt the flow of events in chapter 24. The touching note that Rebekah is a comfort to Isaac after his mother Sarah's death suggests that Isaac misses her keenly.

25:1-18 Abraham's death and burial

Chapter 25 begins with a genealogical summary of Abraham's descendants through his second wife Keturah. It specifies that Isaac receives his entire inheritance (see 24:36); but Abraham made settlements with his other sons, and sent them away to the east. This arrangement honors his relationship with all his sons, and at the same time protects the divine promises and the special status of his son Isaac who will carry the promise into the next generation.

Abraham dies, having left all his affairs in order. His sons Isaac and Ishmael bury him next to his wife Sarah. Another genealogical note lists the twelve sons of Ishmael, who become tribal chieftains. The narrative then records Ishmael's death, and gives the extent of the territory in which his descendants live in fulfillment of the promise in 21:13. This section brings to a conclusion the account of Abraham's and Ishmael's lives. It now picks up the thread of Isaac's life at the point of his marriage to Rebekah and the beginning of a new generation who will carry forward the divine promises of descendants and land.

THE ANCESTRAL STORY
PART 2: ISAAC AND REBEKAH
Genesis 25:19–28:9

25:19-28 The births of Esau and Jacob

The stories about Isaac are far fewer than those about Abraham. Many of them are incorporated into the narratives about his father Abraham and his sons Jacob and Esau. The Isaac account continues the theme of divine promise of descendants and land. In the narrative the betrothal and barren mother type scenes reappear, as does the wife-sister motif. In addition, we meet here another motif that occurs throughout Genesis: that of the younger before the older. We will discuss these as we come to them in the Isaac stories.

After a brief genealogical note we learn that Rebekah, like Sarah before her, is sterile—an immediate threat to the promise, just as in the Abraham and Sarah saga. This time the childlessness is quickly overcome when Isaac prays to God and Rebekah becomes pregnant. Her pregnancy, however, is not without difficulty. She carries twins who jostle each other in the womb, making her pregnancy very uncomfortable. Rebekah brings her concern to the Lord, and the divine response confirms that she will bear twins who will father opposing nations; indeed the tension between them has already begun in Rebekah's womb. The Lord informs Rebekah that the older will serve the younger, an unusual arrangement in ancient Near Eastern families.

The story follows the plot of the barren mother type scene: the childless Rebekah has a son (Jacob) and takes steps to insure his success. This account follows the request model, in which Isaac asks God for a son for his wife, and the Lord grants his request. The story alludes to the competition model as well, in the struggle between the two boys. Rebekah does not have a rival wife, but she carries the strife between her two sons even before they are born. The divine response to her prayer in the face of her difficult pregnancy explains the conflict, confirms that it is of divine origin, and announces the reversal of roles between the two brothers. This divine word forms the backdrop for all Rebekah's actions to ensure the success of her younger son Jacob.

In addition, the story alludes to the promise model in the divine explanation to Rebekah while her sons are still in her womb. The threefold promise announces that the tension between the two boys will continue throughout their lives: they will form two different nations; they will struggle for power; and their roles in the family will be reversed.

When the twins are born, Esau comes first, followed by his brother Jacob. Their names foreshadow the defining characteristics of each: Esau is hairy and reddish, and Jacob is the heel-gripper. With their contrasting personalities the two appeal to different parents: Esau the impetuous outdoorsman is his father's favorite while his mother prefers Jacob, the methodical and conniving tent-dweller.

25:29-34 Esau sells his birthright

The first illustration of the boys' contrasting personalities comes when Jacob is preparing a stew. Esau refers to it as "red stuff"; the narrative calls it lentil stew (v. 34). We recall that when Esau was born he was reddish, probably a reference to a ruddy complexion (v. 25). Here the color of the stew attracts his attention; perhaps he thinks it contains blood, which would appeal to his hunter's tastes. In fact, the color comes from the lentils, which would appeal to a vegetarian.

Jacob seizes the opportunity to strike a bargain with his brother, and agrees to give him a bowl of stew in exchange for Esau's birthright. This is a hard bargain, considering the inequality of the tradeoff. It highlights both Jacob's scheming personality and Esau's utter lack of concern for a matter with long-term implications. It also foreshadows Jacob's deception of his father Isaac when he arranges to receive the blessing intended for his brother Esau in chapter 27.

26:1-35 Rebekah endangered

The narrative returns to Isaac, who must care for his family in the midst of a famine. Just as his father did previously, Isaac prepares to migrate in search of food. Egypt is not an option for him because the Lord insists that he stay in the land of promise. At this point the Lord repeats to Isaac the promise of descendants, a nation, and land that was made so many times to Abraham. Instead of going to Egypt, Isaac travels to Gerar, as Abraham did during the second famine (ch. 20).

In verse 6 the wife-sister motif appears again, in the same location, Gerar, that was problematic for Abraham and Sarah in chapter 20. This time there is no prior arrangement between Isaac and Rebekah; the narrative simply tells us that Isaac identifies Rebekah as his sister when the men of Gerar approach him because of her. (Like Sarah, Rebekah is beautiful.) Isaac's first concern is for his own safety, as was Abraham's before him; he fears for his life at the hands of the inhabitants of Gerar.

This time there is no attempt on the part of Abimelech the king to take Rebekah; instead, he happens to see Isaac and Rebekah enjoying each other as husband and wife. The Hebrew word that describes their action comes from the same root as the word "Isaac," which means "laughter" and recalls the joy of Isaac's parents at his birth. But the moment creates the opposite of joy for Abimelech when he realizes that Rebekah and Isaac are husband and wife. The conversation that follows between Abimelech and Isaac shows that Isaac's fears are in vain. Abimelech has no intention of violating Isaac's wife, and he forbids his people to mistreat either of them. This mandate confirms Isaac's earlier fear: the people might indeed have violated Rebekah. It also highlights Isaac's duplicity: if the people had violated Rebekah, it would have been Isaac's fault.

The next episode describes a second incident when tensions arise between Isaac and Abimelech. This time the cause is Isaac's hugely successful farming in Gerar. In an effort to drive him away the Philistines stop up the wells that Abraham dug, and Abimelech directly asks him to leave. Isaac moves to the area where Abraham stayed (21:34), re-digs his father's wells, and discovers a spring in one of them. This valuable water source causes a new round of conflict, so Isaac moves again and digs other wells. These incidents highlight the scarcity of water in the region, and the desire of each family to protect its water sources, particularly during a famine.

Eventually (v. 23) Isaac returns to Beer-sheba, where he had lived with his father Abraham. Here the Lord appears to him and repeats the promise of descendants. Isaac builds an altar to mark the place where the Lord appeared, just as his father had done. After praying to the Lord, he sets about digging a well. Again he must reckon with Abimelech, who recognizes the power that Isaac has accrued by his economic success. In verse 26 Abimelech and his men ask for a nonaggression pact between the two peoples. Isaac agrees, and they make a formal agreement. A brief genealogical note follows in verse 34, listing Esau's marriages to a Hittite woman and a Hivite woman, a cause of bitterness to his parents. It foreshadows Rebekah's determination that Jacob, not Esau, will receive Isaac's blessing now that Esau has married outside the family.

27:1-45 Isaac blesses Jacob

The saga continues as Isaac arranges to bestow his blessing on his son before he dies, like Abraham before him. This episode, in which Rebekah helps Jacob to usurp the blessing intended for Esau, takes place in seven steps, permeated by the motif of younger-older.

The first step (vv. 1-4) involves Isaac and Esau. We learn that Isaac's eyesight is failing, and he instructs his son Esau to hunt game with which

to prepare him a meal, so Esau might receive his father's blessing. The formality of the request is evident in several details: first, Esau responds with "Here I am!" the formal acknowledgment of readiness and willingness. In addition, the meal his father requests has a ritual connotation; here it suggests a formal ceremony for bestowing the blessing.

The second step (vv. 5-17) involves the other two people, Rebekah and Jacob. Rebekah repeats what she heard Isaac say to Esau, adding the solemn words, "with the Lord's approval." She quickly formulates a plan and explains it to Jacob. She brushes aside his hesitation because she remembers the Lord's words, "the older will serve the younger," when the twins were still in her womb (25:23). They both make the necessary preparations, and Rebekah sends him in to his father.

The third step (vv. 18-29) takes place between Isaac and Jacob. Jacob lies to his father in order to receive the blessing intended for his brother. Because Isaac is losing his eyesight, he does not recognize Jacob, but questions the voice that sounds like Esau's. He blesses Jacob, assuring him of prosperity, political and military power, and divine protection.

The fourth step (vv. 30-41) brings together Isaac and Esau for the second time, when Esau returns after making the preparations his father directed. He and Isaac both realize what has happened, but it is too late to retract the blessing that has been given to Jacob. When Esau pleads for a blessing for himself, Isaac responds with the blessing of prosperity. He then announces that Esau will live a life of violence and subservience to his brother until he breaks free of him. Esau makes up his mind to kill his brother once their father is dead.

The fifth step (vv. 42-45) brings together Jacob and Rebekah for the second time. She urges him to leave at once and go to her brother Laban rather than risk being killed by Esau. She fears losing both of her sons at once: Jacob if Esau kills him, and Esau if he is condemned for killing his brother.

The sixth step (v. 46) takes place between Rebekah and Isaac. Rather than admit to her husband that she masterminded the deceitful events, she picks up the theme of 26:34-35: Esau's marriages outside the family have brought grief to his parents. Rebekah wants assurance that Jacob will marry within the family, to avoid further sorrow. Her request to send Jacob away has the added advantage of protecting the promise of children and land.

The seventh step (28:1-5) brings together Isaac and Jacob for the second time. Isaac formally sends Jacob to Rebekah's brother Laban to find a wife for himself. He repeats to Jacob the divine promise of land, children, and a nation in the name of his father Abraham, and Jacob sets out on the journey. This is the first time Jacob receives the promise; it comes from his father Isaac.

The episode brings out the deceptive aspect of Jacob's character even more strongly than the incident with the stew. Here Jacob deliberately lies to his father (at the encouragement of his mother) in order to get what he wants. It is true that the Lord intends for Jacob to win out over his brother. The means to this end are questionable, though, and Jacob's deception will come back to haunt him. The incident also highlights the extent of Esau's bitterness at his own situation. He arranges to marry one of Ishmael's daughters, to exacerbate his parents' displeasure with him. In addition, in this scene Isaac passes on the promise of descendants, land, and nation to his son Jacob. The event marks the successful completion of Isaac's primary role: he has carried the promise forward to the next generation and entrusted it to the son chosen by God.

Here the narrative leaves Isaac and focuses on Jacob until it announces Isaac's death in 35:27-29. We learn of Jacob's journey to his uncle Laban, his marriages and the births of his children, the tensions between him and Laban, and his meeting with his brother Esau before he returns home. Twice on his journey, once on the way to Haran and once on the way back home, he encounters God.

THE ANCESTRAL STORY
PART 3: JACOB AND HIS WIVES
Genesis 28:10–36:43

28:10-22 Jacob at Bethel

Just as in the report of the servant's journey to find a wife for Isaac, here we learn only the essentials of Jacob's trip, except for one event that takes place along the way. He stops for the night, apparently out in the open, at a place that has

something special about it. There he has a dream in which the Lord gives Jacob the promise of descendants and land. Jacob received that promise from his father before setting out on his journey. Now he receives it directly from God. The deity's name is "LORD," the God of his father and grandfather. This identification makes it clear that, even though Jacob is probably sleeping at a shrine to a local deity, the God who speaks to him there is not the local god but the God who has cared for his family for several generations.

The Lord reiterates the promises of land, descendants, a nation, and divine blessing. When Jacob realizes that he has met the Lord he takes the stone pillow, sets it up vertically, and pours oil on it to designate it as holy because his head rested on it during his revelatory dream. It is thus a witness to the event (see Josh 24:27). Jacob does not build an altar, as his grandfather Abraham did to mark the places where he met the Lord. Instead, he consecrates the stone, then formally accepts the terms of his encounter with God. He names the place Bethel, or House of God, the place near where Abraham once built an altar (12:8).

This story has an element of the E strand in which dreams are an important means of divine communication with humans. Dreaming is an act beyond human control, which takes place in a realm we cannot access by our own efforts. We often gain valuable insights while dreaming; ancient people understood these as revelations from God.

29:1-30 Jacob's marriages

The narrative resumes with Jacob's arrival in the general area of his uncle's home. The plot follows the elements of the betrothal type scene. By looking at those elements we can see the story unfold, and can also compare and contrast Jacob's experience with that of Abraham's servant when he went to Haran in search of a wife for Isaac. Jacob arrives at a well that is covered with a large stone, surrounded by several flocks of sheep. Shepherds are with them; when Jacob asks if they know Laban he learns that Laban's daughter Rachel is arriving at that moment with her father's flock.

These details set the stage for a very different experience from that of Abraham's servant who came with a large retinue of gifts for Laban and his family. Jacob comes on the one hand as one sent by God and on the other as a fugitive. He brings nothing with him. Instead, Jacob offers his services, the first of which is to remove the stone from the well. He manages the stone singlehandedly, even though it is huge, because he is thrilled at the sight of Rachel. It is not clear whether he is responding to the sight of a relative or to an attractive young woman; perhaps to both. Then Jacob, instead of asking for water and receiving it from the woman, offers to water Laban's sheep. He further expresses his delight by tearfully kissing Rachel, a gesture of delight and gratitude at meeting his relative (v. 11).

True to the type scene, Rachel hurries to tell her father of Jacob's arrival. He greets the visitor and invites him into his home. Then the narrative tells us only that Jacob told the story of his adventures; it does not repeat Jacob's words as Abraham's servant did.

The arrangements for the betrothal proceed much more slowly here than with Abraham's servant. A month passes before the subject comes up, and then Jacob mentions it in response to Laban's offer to pay Jacob for his services. Jacob offers to work for Laban for seven years in exchange for Rachel's hand (29:18). (Jacob must work for the privilege of marrying Laban's daughter because he does not bring gifts with him, as did Abraham's servant.) The narrative points out that Rachel is the younger of Laban's two daughters, bringing into play the younger-older motif. Jacob meets his match when Laban gives him his older daughter Leah in marriage instead of Rachel, then falls back on ancient tradition as his excuse for the deceitful arrangement. He assures Jacob that, after the customary seven days of celebration of the first marriage, Jacob may work seven more years for Rachel, and Jacob agrees.

Then the story picks up the barren mother type scene, and the competition model begins to unfold. Two women are married to the same husband; one has children and the other does not. The narrative highlights the divine action on behalf of Leah for her unfavored status. Leah bears four sons: Reuben, Simeon, Levi, and Judah. The names she gives the boys reflect her situation as the unloved wife. The note that she then stops bearing sons foreshadows further difficulties to come.

The request model of the barren mother type scene overlaps with the competition model when

Rachel pleads desperately with Jacob to give her children in 30:1. But Jacob does not accept responsibility for her childlessness, and reminds her that children are gifts from God. In her despair she offers her maid Bilhah to Jacob, just as Sarah offered Hagar to Abraham. Rachel arranges that Bilhah will bear surrogate children for her; she clarifies her own maternal status by arranging to hold Bilhah's children on her own knees. The act of holding a child on one's knees legitimates him as the son of that parent (see 48:12 and 50:23). Bilhah bears two sons, whom Rachel names Dan and Naphtali, referring to the competition between her and Leah.

Not to be outdone, Leah then gives her maid Zilpah to Jacob (v. 9). Zilpah bears two sons, giving them names that suggest Leah's own good fortune: Gad and Asher. Jacob now has eight sons, but none by his favored wife Rachel. Leah's son Reuben offers his mother some mandrakes, known for their aphrodisiac qualities. When Rachel asks for some of them she learns of Leah's bitterness at her own unloved status, so Rachel makes a deal: Rachel will have the mandrakes, but Leah will spend the night with Jacob. Leah bears two more sons, whom she names Issachar and Zebulun, reflecting her awkward relationship with Jacob. The narrative then reports that she also bears a daughter whom she names Dinah. No interpretation of her name or other details are given about Dinah.

Only after Jacob already has ten sons and a daughter does Rachel bear a son (v. 22). The narrative specifies that God remembers her; that is, God focuses attention on her. She bears Joseph, whose name suggests both removing her past shame and adding hope and joy to her future. By now eleven sons are born to Jacob and his four women: six to Leah, two to each of the two maids Bilhah and Zilpah, and one to Rachel. In addition he has one daughter by Leah. Throughout the narrative, all the women compete with one another for Jacob's love and for children. While the humans strive to control the situation, the narrative repeats frequently that it is God who gives children, assuring that the promise of descendants moves forward into the next generation.

30:25-43 Jacob tricks Laban

The story shifts back to the relationship between Jacob and his father-in-law Laban, and continues the motif of trickery that permeates the story of Jacob's marriage, his wives, and his children. After fourteen years of working for Laban in exchange for his two wives, he works for Laban six more years. By the end of the twenty years he has twelve children. In accordance with the divine promise to Jacob in his dream at Bethel to bring him back to his father's land (28:15), Jacob asks Laban's permission to return home. The history of trickery between the two men leads us to suspect that the leave-taking will not be a simple one. They bargain for a fair arrangement: Laban realizes he will lose the valuable services of his son-in-law, who has been a blessing to him; and Jacob wants compensation for all his labor.

Jacob requests some of the animals from Laban's flocks: he asks for the dark sheep and the spotted goats. These animals, a small proportion of Laban's flocks, do not have the usual coloring. The arrangement will, however, be a foolproof way to determine which animals belong to which of the men. Laban separates the flocks according to color as agreed, and puts his sons in charge of those flocks destined for Jacob. Jacob alludes to their history of trickery when he asserts his honesty to Laban in verse 33. Laban moves his flocks a three-day journey away, but Jacob takes advantage of the isolation of those flocks to breed animals selectively, thus increasing the size and quality of his own flocks and other holdings (v. 43). Eventually he justifies this practice by attributing the idea to a dream (31:10-13), thus intimating that it is God's plan.

Jacob's scheme is so successful that he arouses the suspicion and mistrust of Laban and his sons. The time to depart has arrived, and once again we expect complications.

31:1-54 Jacob takes leave of Laban

After the payment for Jacob's services is settled and Jacob's continued presence with his uncle has become very problematic, Jacob receives word from the Lord to return home with the assurance of divine protection. But several more complications arise before the men finally separate. The plot reflects the duplicity, not only of Jacob and Laban, but also of Rachel. The episode takes place in five stages.

In the first, verses 1-16, Jacob sends for his two wives and explains that the Lord has instructed him to leave Laban and return to his own land in fulfillment of the agreement made at Bethel. He gives a detailed description of the situation, putting his own actions in a good light and Laban's in a bad light. Both wives agree with Jacob that their father has been unfair in dealing, not only with Jacob, but also with them. It is unusual that the two are of one mind; their agreement expresses their bitterness at their father's treatment of them. They encourage Jacob to do as God instructs.

In the second, verses 17-21, the family flees. They depart while Laban is away, taking with them all Jacob acquired over the years. In addition, Rachel steals her father's household gods. The reason for the theft is not clear: perhaps she wants simply to deprive him of them, or perhaps to use them for her own benefit, either by claiming them as an inheritance or by using them for religious purposes. In 27:43 Rebekah insisted that Jacob flee from his father's house; now he flees from his father-in-law's house.

In the third, verses 22-35, Laban learns that the party has fled and sets out in pursuit. After seven days, as he nears the fugitives, he has a dream warning him not to interfere with Jacob. He confronts his son-in-law, accusing him of deceit and kidnapping. He bemoans his lost opportunity to give a proper farewell to his daughters and grandchildren, and then refers to the stolen household gods. Laban's complaint is filled with irony in light of his own treatment of Jacob from the time they first met. Jacob knows nothing of the stolen household gods, and assures Laban that he may have anything he finds that belongs to him.

Laban immediately begins to search the tents of each member of the party, saving Rachel's until last. She is ready for him: she had hidden the statues in a camel cushion, a combination saddle and storage box that is placed on a camel to provide seating and storage for the rider. She sits on the camel cushion, and protests that she cannot get up because she is menstruating. This adds to the irony of the situation: Rachel will not stand up to allow her father to search for the idols; in fact, he ought not to be in her presence under pain of defilement (Lev 15:19-23); but she defiles the idols by sitting on them in her claimed state of ritual uncleanness while at the same time protecting them from harm. Her action suggests that she herself does not believe the statues possess any power; otherwise she would treat them with respect. She accomplishes her purpose, however:

Laban gives up his search for the idols. She also demonstrates that she is as capable of trickery as her husband and her father.

In the fourth stage, verses 36-42, Jacob takes the offensive, rehearsing all the injustices he has suffered at Laban's hands since his arrival at his home twenty years ago.

In the fifth stage, verses 43-54, Laban proposes that the two of them make an agreement. This will assure him that his family will be safe in Jacob's care, and that the two families will not interfere with each other but will live in peaceful coexistence. They formalize the agreement by erecting a stone pillar and then sharing a meal. This meal probably includes only the two men, as Jacob then invites his men to share the meal in verse 54, after he offers a sacrifice. Both men give a name to the place, each in his own native language, further highlighting the separation that is taking place between the two families. Laban invokes the God of Abraham and the God of Nahor, the ancestral deities of both families. Jacob invokes his father's name, offers a sacrifice, and invites his men to the sacrificial meal to finalize the treaty.

32:1-3 The final leave-taking

Both parties spend the night in proximity to each other, and then Laban bids his family farewell and the two parties separate. This final scene is stark in its simplicity after the many duplicitous actions throughout Jacob's stay with Laban. As Jacob begins his journey homeward, angels appear, just as they did when he first left his parents' home at the beginning of his journey to Haran (28:12). While they do not take an active part in events, they mark the stages of Jacob's journey and the presence of God with Jacob in his travels.

32:4–33:20 The meeting of Jacob and Esau

When Jacob sets out, his first project is to make contact with his brother Esau. Jacob fled from his parents' home after he usurped the blessing intended for Esau, and Esau vowed to kill him (27:41). Now he returns home with a large family, and must protect both them and himself from harm. His honor as head of his family and also his promise to Laban demand that he take whatever steps are necessary toward this end.

Verses 4-22 describe four steps he takes in preparation for meeting his brother. First, he sends messengers with a conciliatory word to Esau, who sends word in return that he and his army will meet Jacob. Next, fearing for the safety of himself and his family, he divides his party into two groups. That way, if harm comes to one, the other will be spared. Then he prays to the God of his ancestors for help, recalling the promises God made to him when he started out from home (28:13-15) and when he began his journey home from Haran (31:3). Fearing what his brother might do to him and his family, he reminds God of the divine promise of descendants. His prayer calls on God's faithfulness rather than any claim of his own to divine care. Finally, he selects an extravagant number of livestock to give to his brother, and sends them ahead in droves, each in the care of one of his servants. After making all these preparations, he sends his family across the Jabbok, and he stays behind for the night. Crossing the Jabbok marks the family's entry into Jacob's homeland.

Verses 23-33 give a vague description of a curious incident: an unidentified man wrestles with Jacob until dawn. The narrative does not identify the person or give information about where he came from or how he happened to find Jacob until the end of the incident. When the stranger realizes he cannot defeat Jacob he injures his hip, leaving Jacob with a limp. Then the man asks to be released, suggesting that Jacob the heel-grabber has him in his grasp. Jacob agrees on condition that the man bless him. He gives Jacob the new name of Israel, but refuses to tell Jacob his own name, and then disappears as mysteriously as he came. The name Jacob gives to the place, Peniel, lets us know that his assailant is God. This mysterious episode describes a universal human experience of passing a restless night wrestling out a dilemma. By the time the sun rises Jacob has faced down the enemy and has come to a new awareness that God is with him. A brief etiological note follows, connecting Jacob's hip injury with the custom of not eating the sciatic nerve. Here for the first time the narrative uses the term "Israelites" in honor of Jacob's new name; it appears frequently throughout the Old Testament.

After all the preparations including Jacob's night of wrestling with the angel, the brothers meet in 33:1-20. The meeting is affectionate, respectful, yet guarded. When Jacob sees his brother coming with his four hundred men, he arranges his wives and their maids with their respective children, in order of importance and affection. Jacob's bow repeats Abraham's gesture when he received the three visitors in 18:2. It is also ironic in light of the divine words to Rebekah when the twins were still in the womb (25:23) and Isaac's blessing of Jacob in 27:29. Esau's tender, affectionate greeting reverses the kiss Isaac gave Jacob when Jacob stole Esau's blessing.

After their greeting the conversation becomes cautious when Esau inquires about all the gifts Jacob has brought. He demurs, perhaps according to custom, perhaps in an effort not to be beholden to his brother. Jacob remains respectful and deferential, and makes a connection between seeing Esau and encountering his assailant the previous night when he refers to the face of God. Esau accepts Jacob's gifts but does not offer any in return: Jacob's gifts are restitution for past wrongs rather than fraternal offerings.

The brothers arrange to continue their travels, negotiating whether to journey together or separately. The narrative suggests hesitancy on Jacob's part when he prefers to travel apart from Esau's men. In fact, Jacob does not follow Esau as he said he would, but goes in the opposite direction and establishes a temporary home for his family. The brothers leave each other on that somewhat wary note.

Jacob and his family stay temporarily at Succoth, then continue on to Shechem where the Lord appeared to Abraham when he first came into the land (12:6). There Jacob purchases land from the Shechemites and builds an altar to the God of Israel, his new name. This is the second purchase of land recorded in Genesis; the first is the burial place for Sarah. The narrative does not specify the purpose for which this purchase will be used; it seems to represent Jacob's belief that God will continue to care for him and his family in their new home. But the following chapters show that Jacob's hope of peaceful settlement in the land is mistaken.

34:1-31 Dinah among the Shechemites

The narrative then focuses on Dinah, who goes out to meet her new neighbors. By specifying that she is Leah's daughter the narrative casts her in a negative light. Her action has been interpreted in both positive and negative ways: either she is innocently exploring her new neighborhood or looking for companionship, or she acts inappropriately in going among Canaanites or leaving the family compound (see 24:3, 37). Perhaps the ambiguity of the statement leaves open all the above possibilities. She goes out to see the women, and is seen by the son of the chief, Hamor. She goes out as an active young woman and immediately becomes a passive victim. Things happen quickly, as the rapid succession of verbs indicates. The actions that follow are equally startling because of the abrupt shift they express.

In verse 5 the scene shifts to Dinah's father Jacob, who hears about the incident but decides against taking any action because his sons are working in the fields. This is an odd stance for Jacob, who usually takes matters in hand and finds ways to deal with complicated situations. Jacob apparently sends for his sons, who arrive to find Shechem's father Hamor making his request to their father. The brothers react with indignation to what Shechem has done: he did not simply violate Dinah and her entire family, but violated the moral climate of the community.

Several aspects of the narrative are complicated by layers of editing within the text. From a legal perspective Dinah's family is entitled to the bride-price for a virgin, but because Jacob is a resident alien, his claim to restitution is unclear. The relevant law in Exodus 22:15-16 reflects a time later than the ancestral period. In addition, the second half of verse 7 judges Shechem's sin in language typical of the monarchic period rather than the time of the ancestors.

In verse 8 Hamor ignores the moral question and focuses on the political and economic benefit to Jacob's family if Dinah is given to Shechem in marriage. Shechem then enters the conversation and offers to give whatever is appropriate, apparently acknowledging that his defilement of Dinah requires some sort of restitution.

Jacob's sons outwardly maintain their focus on the religious and ethical dimension of the situation; they object to their sister marrying an uncircumcised man. Only if all the Shechemite males agree to be circumcised can Dinah's brothers agree to the marriage. In fact, in making this assertion they show themselves as capable of deception as their father (v. 13). Their intent is not to observe the religious custom; it is rather to set a trap for the men of Shechem.

Hamor and Shechem agree immediately to the brothers' request. One wonders if they realize the implications of the request: do they see it as a religious act? a political bargain? a ruse? The narrative does not specify. We suspect they anticipate the economic gain because, when they urge the men of the city to comply, they add a detail that is unknown to Dinah's brothers: the people of Shechem will then possess the livestock that belong to Jacob's family. The men of the city readily agree to the procedure.

The loyalty among Dinah and her full brothers is evident in their next move. While the men are recuperating from the procedure, and are in great pain, two of her full brothers (that is, the sons of Leah), Simeon and Levi, kill all the males including Hamor and Shechem, then take Dinah from Shechem's house. Again the text leaves us wondering: is this a forceful removal or a rescue? Is Dinah eager to leave or reluctant? The text does not specify. Then Jacob's other sons completely sack the city and take the spoils for themselves.

Jacob finally takes a stand in verse 30, chastising Simeon and Levi for destroying Shechem. (Jacob's deathbed curse of these two sons in 49:5-7 reflects his outraged response to this destruction.) His response is startling: Jacob reprimands the two sons who come to Dinah's rescue, after he seems to have chosen not to make an issue of the terrible violation to her and to the entire family. Now that he has purchased a piece of land in the area, he hopes to live there in peace with the neighboring people who greatly outnumber them. He thinks of the number of his men, small in comparison to his neighbors. The brothers think of avenging the outrage to their sister and their entire family. Their final question summarizes the ambivalence and lack of resolution between father and sons and between competing values as the family settles in the land. Family concerns must be weighed in relation to relations with neighbors, and there are no easy answers.

35:1-29 Jacob settles in the land

Chapter 35 includes several episodes that seem at first glance to be isolated incidents in Jacob's life. In actuality each one relates to the whole cycle of stories about Jacob, showing that his life has come full circle during his absence from his father's house. The conniving, energetic youth who fled from his brother Esau has become a cautious father and protector of his land. This part of the narrative appears to be a compilation of stories from different sources; as a result we find incidents that appear to duplicate previous episodes. The chapter includes Jacob's visit to Bethel, the birth of his and Rachel's son Benjamin and the death of Rachel, Reuben's violation of Rachel's maid Bilhah, and the death and burial of Isaac.

After the massacre of the Shechemites, Jacob leaves that area at God's command and goes to Bethel. Jacob's threefold instruction depicts the preparations for departure as a liturgical act: he instructs them to dispose of their idols, purify themselves, and change clothes. Jacob follows the route taken by Abraham from Haran to Shechem and then to Bethel (12:4-8). The episode alludes to Jacob's night at Bethel when he fled from his brother Esau after stealing the blessing from their father (28:10-22). This time Jacob and his entire family are fleeing from the neighbors of the Shechemites. During his first stay at Bethel God promised to be with him in all his travels; now the family returns to the site to build an altar in thanks to God for fulfilling that promise. The people obey Jacob's three commands, and they set out on their journey of purification after the defilement of chapter 34. God continues to protect the travelers from the local people as they make their way to Bethel, where Jacob reiterates his earlier promise to honor God (28:19-22).

A very brief announcement of the death of Rebekah's nurse Deborah follows in verse 8, with the note that she is buried under a particular oak at Bethel. With her death Jacob's family relinquishes one of the few remaining ties with Laban and his land. Earlier they gave up another tie when Jacob buried their idols near Shechem (perhaps these were idols the family members brought with them from Haran, or perhaps they were part of the booty seized at Shechem).

In verse 9 the narrative relates another experience of Jacob at Bethel. God appears to him and gives him the name Israel; earlier the mysterious stranger gave him the name (32:29); here it comes directly from God. God also promises him descendants, a nation, and land in language similar to the promises to Abraham in 17:6-8, and to Jacob on his earlier visit (28:13-15). God specifies that these are the same promises given to his father and grandfather: now Jacob inherits them. Jacob sets up a stone pillar to mark the spot, blesses it, and names the place Bethel (see also 28:19). The similarities between this and earlier episodes suggest that they come from different sources; this version is associated with E.

Once again the family sets out and travels southward (v. 16). Rachel goes into very difficult labor and gives birth to a boy, thus bringing to fruition the name she gave Joseph when he was born: a prayer that the Lord would give her another son (30:24). Rachel's last act is to name her newborn son, characterizing him as the son of her distress. Jacob, however, gives him the name Benjamin ("Son of the Right Hand"). Rachel dies and is buried on the road to Bethlehem, where the narrator specifies that the monument Jacob set up still marks the spot. Today the site designated as Rachel's tomb remains a place of pilgrimage, especially for pregnant women.

That incident is followed by the very brief note that Reuben, Leah's first son, sleeps with Bilhah, Rachel's maid, and Jacob finds out about it. Other biblical stories point to taking the concubine of the conquered enemy as a symbol of taking the defeated kingdom (see 2 Sam 3:7-8; 12:7-8; and 1 Kgs 2:13-25). In this case there is no further comment about the incident until Jacob condemns the act in his final testament in 49:3-4. Reuben's act backfires; he loses the birthright to which he is entitled as Jacob's first son just as Jacob's older brother Esau had done. A brief genealogical note follows in verses 22b-26, listing Jacob's twelve sons according to their mothers. Dinah is not included in the list.

A second brief note observes that Jacob returns to his father Isaac at Mamre, the place where both Isaac and Abraham had lived. Then Isaac dies and his two sons bury him, just as Isaac and Ishmael buried their father Abraham. In both instances, despite all the tensions among the siblings, they honor their fathers in death. Isaac's role in life was to carry forward the divine promises; he lives to see them handed over to his son Jacob.

36:1-43 Esau's descendants

A detailed genealogy of Esau's descendants follows, interspersed with two other lists, the indigenous tribes of Seir and the Edomite kings. The lists are complicated because some of the information is given elsewhere, with a few variations. Verses 1-8 give the names of Esau's three wives and their children and grandchildren. Here the wives' names are Adah, a Hittite; Oholibamah, a Hivite; and Basemath, daughter of Ishmael; these

differ slightly from the names given in 26:34 and 28:9: Judith, Basemath, and Mahalath. Adah and Basemath (according to the list in chapter 36) both bear one son to Esau; Oholibamah bears three.

Verses 9-14 list the children born to each of Esau's wives in Seir, where they settle after Jacob returns home. Adah's son has six sons of whom one is born to a concubine, and Basemath's son has four sons. The list does not name the grandsons of Basemath. The names are repeated in verses 15-19 with the inclusion of one additional grandson to Adah's descendants. Amalek, the son of the concubine, is listed as a full son with his brothers.

Verses 20-30 list the descendants of Seir, who become seven clans. Then verses 31-39 name the eight kings of Edom who ruled before the establishment of the monarchy in Israel. Finally, verses 40-43 name the eleven Edomite clans. These lists, attributed to P, represent the fulfillment of Isaac's blessing to Esau in 27:39-40: Esau will live far away and will be a warrior rather than a farmer. They also fulfill the Lord's words to Rebekah when the twins were still in her womb (25:23) that the older would serve the younger: Esau's descendants eventually serve the descendants of Jacob.

The lists attest to the long history of the early inhabitants of the land, and illustrate the ongoing intermingling of the peoples throughout history. They also witness to the ongoing divine protection of the people throughout all their comings and goings in the region. After these genealogical notes the focus of the narrative shifts to Jacob's son Joseph, the first son of his beloved wife Rachel, who died giving birth to her second son Benjamin.

THE ANCESTRAL STORY
PART 4: THE JOSEPH STORY
Genesis 37:1–50:26

Both the focus and the genre of the narrative shift at this point. While the ancestral story in chapters 12–36 consists of a series of anecdotes arranged in episodic order (that is, separate episodes, loosely connected to one another but not moving toward a climax), the Joseph story has a unified plot that reaches toward a climax. The narrative is called a novella, or short novel. The term implies that the story is fictional; in fact, just as we do not know the precise historicity of the previous chapters, neither do we know the exact historical details of the Joseph narrative. What we do know is that the ancient narrative recounts God's continuing care for the people as promised from the time of Noah to the people in general, and promised in particular to Abraham and his family. The story of Joseph relates that ongoing care for the people as they move to Egypt, setting the stage for the exodus to come.

We have seen that the sons of Leah have a penchant for getting into trouble. Here we learn that the sons of Jacob's beloved, deceased Rachel, and especially Joseph her firstborn, are their father's favorites. This favoritism exacerbates the relationships among the twelve brothers, creating the conditions for several complications, expressed in familiar themes that continue to weave their way through the narrative; for example, competition among the brothers, similar to that between wives and brothers in previous generations; and younger versus older as was the case between Esau and Jacob, and between Ishmael and Isaac.

Articles of clothing figure prominently here. Likewise, dreams also play a prominent part in the story, as does the theme of divine promise in jeopardy, protected by God. The story also records reversals of various kinds: in geographic locations, weather conditions, relationships among the family members, the fortunes of different brothers, Jacob's hopes and fears, to name a few. A further characteristic of the story is the influence of the wisdom tradition, which emphasizes human wit. Divine intervention is indirect: there are no visions, but the narrative specifies at different points that God continues to direct the affairs of Joseph and his family.

37:1-36 The sale of Joseph into slavery

The story resumes where it left off at the end of chapter 35: Jacob and his family are settled in Hebron. The narrative now focuses on Joseph, a seventeen-year-old shepherd who works with his brothers. The narrative immediately introduces the tension among the brothers, reporting that Joseph tells his father tales on Bilhah's and Zilpah's sons, with whom he works as an assistant (he is younger than ten of his brothers and also his sister Dinah). We are not told whether his reports to his father are true or false, only that Joseph breaks ranks with his brothers by reporting on them.

Then the cause of the tension is revealed: Joseph is his father's favorite, and his father singles him out for preferential treatment.

Jacob gives Joseph a special garment. This item has been the subject of much discussion and illustration, including the title of the musical *Joseph and the Amazing Technicolor Dreamcoat*. The actual meaning of the Hebrew word is uncertain: translations include a long-sleeved garment, one with many colors or special ornamentation, and one that reaches to the floor. While the meaning is uncertain, the idea is clear: Joseph receives a special garment from his father who dotes on him, and this creates bitter envy and rivalry on the part of his brothers, to the point that they can barely speak to him.

Joseph has a talent for interpreting dreams, understood in the ancient world as a gift from God, since dreams were thought to be divine revelations. In the Joseph narrative the dreams are symbolic in contrast to the straightforward words from God in earlier chapters of Genesis. The dreams appear in pairs, with different symbols giving the same message. This duplication assures that the dreams are genuine, and that their message is clear.

Joseph's report of his dreams exacerbates the tension between his brothers and him for two reasons: first, because the fact of his having the dreams singles him out as the recipient of a special gift; and second, because of the subject of the dreams. Both the dream of the crops and that of the stars deliver the same message: his brothers will be subservient to him. Here the younger-older motif begins to factor into the story.

The second dream includes not only his brothers but also his parents among those who will be subservient to him. The mention of his mother is puzzling here since she has already died (35:19). Even Jacob questions Joseph about the second dream, but he "kept the matter in mind" (37:11). Throughout his own life Jacob received significant revelations in dreams; he can appreciate the importance of his son's dreams.

In Jacob's case it was his mother Rebekah who arranged that Jacob would receive his father's blessing, thus depriving Esau of what was rightfully his and feeding the tension between the two brothers. Now Jacob himself feeds the tension between Joseph and his brothers by showing favoritism to him. Joseph's awkwardly privileged position comes, then, partly from his father's actions and partly from the dreams.

In verse 13 Jacob sends Joseph to his brothers, who are tending the flocks at Shechem. Joseph's response, "hinneni," recalls other willing responses on the part of the ancestors when they are asked to do some significant task. Here Jacob directs Joseph to find his brothers and bring back a report on them. Perhaps he is concerned about their safety after their disastrous destruction of Shechem in chapter 34. The brothers have continued to move along with the grazing flocks, so by the time Joseph finds them they are at a considerable distance from home. The distance gives the brothers the opportunity to devise a plot against him without likelihood of detection: they plan to kill him and throw him into a cistern. Such an end would deprive Joseph of a proper burial, and thus dishonor him and them; the brothers are blinded to this possibility by their hatred and envy of him.

Reuben, the firstborn son, objects to killing his brother and offers an alternative: that they simply throw him into the cistern and not kill him. The narrative adds that Reuben hopes to rescue Joseph and return him to Jacob. As firstborn, he made an unsuccessful bid for power in violating Bilhah (35:22); here he unsuccessfully attempts to use his position in a positive way. Joseph reaches his brothers, wearing the infamous garment, which his brothers take from him; they throw him into the empty cistern, then sit down to enjoy a meal, indifferent to Joseph's plight and to their own evil.

In verse 25 the unexpected arrival of Ishmaelites offers an alternative opportunity, and the brothers arrange to sell their brother. (Egypt had a slave trade at the time.) Ironically, they explain their own hesitation to kill him because he is their brother, but that does not stop them from selling him or from deceiving their father about what they have done to him. A further irony rests in the family relationship among the descendants of Abraham: the brothers sell Joseph to their own relatives. (Recall that Ishmael was the son of Abraham by Hagar, the Egyptian maidservant of Sarah.) The mention of Midianites in verse 28 is puzzling. It might be a detail from the E strand in a passage that is primarily a J and P story, or it might relate that Joseph is sold several times before the Ishmaelites purchase him. Twenty shekels is the price of a slave between the ages of five and twenty, according to both the Code of Hammurabi

and Leviticus 27:5; the weight of the pieces of silver in this passage is not known, but is most likely comparable. The passage very likely predates Leviticus, with the detail about the price coming from a later P insertion.

Reuben is not with his brothers when they sell Joseph. Later, when Reuben returns to the cistern to retrieve him, he discovers that Joseph is gone. The text is ambiguous as to whether his brothers know about his plan to rescue Joseph. But his anguished question expresses his consternation when he realizes Joseph is gone.

In verse 31 the brothers determine a way to break the news of Joseph's disappearance to their father. They use the infamous garment and the blood of a kid, two items that Jacob used long ago when he deceived his own father into giving him the blessing intended for Esau. When Jacob receives the bloody garment, his three exclamations show his gradual realization of what it means: his beloved son Joseph is dead (37:33). Joseph's robe is the sign of his apparent death; Jacob's torn clothes are the sign of his grief. (Tearing one's garment was the customary sign of mourning.) Sheol, where Jacob expects to go after death, was the place deep under the earth where the spirits of all the deceased were believed to rest forever. It was not a place of reward or punishment.

Here the reader knows that Joseph is still alive. Jacob assumes his son is dead, and it is not clear what Joseph's brothers know about him. Meanwhile, the Midianites sell him into slavery to Potiphar, a courtier in the court of Pharaoh. This development jeopardizes the longstanding promise of descendants to Abraham, Isaac, and Jacob: Joseph is clearly his father's favorite and the one on whom we assume the promise rests; now he is a slave in Egypt.

38:1-30 Judah and Tamar

On the surface chapter 38 appears to be a digression from the Joseph narrative, but a closer look shows its connection. The narrative is vague about the chronology, stating simply, "About that time." Judah, who encouraged his brothers to sell Joseph rather than kill him, leaves his brothers and settles near Hirah the Adullamite. He marries a Canaanite woman and they have three sons. There is no stigma attached to marrying a Canaanite woman, unlike the situations for Isaac and Jacob (24:3; 28:6). Judah makes the customary arrangements for the marriage of his firstborn son Er to Tamar. Er sins (we are not told what his sin was) and the Lord takes his life in punishment. In keeping with the custom, Judah instructs his second son Onan to marry Tamar. Onan refuses to cooperate, interrupting intercourse and thus avoiding the conception of a child with Tamar. It is not clear whether he refuses to honor his deceased brother's name or whether he does not want to share his inheritance with a son. Whatever the reason, his negligence with regard to Tamar is a sin of disobedience for which the Lord takes Onan's life, leaving Judah with only one living son. At the time the levirate duty of a father-in-law to give his next son to the widow was obligatory; later law provided for the son to refuse this duty (Deut 25:5-9).

Judah does not wish to lose his only living son (v. 11), so he puts Tamar in an impossible position: he sends her back to her father's house, but does not release her from his family. Consequently she does not really belong to her father's family, but neither is she under the protection of Judah.

Years later Tamar takes an opportunity to force Judah's responsibility toward her (v. 12). She dresses like a prostitute (again clothing factors into the story) and places herself where he will see her as he travels to shear his sheep. The text is careful not to judge him harshly: he does not recognize her because of her veil, and he had not planned to engage a prostitute, as he has nothing with which to pay her. (The usual fee was a kid.) Instead, she requests three items that can positively identify him: his seal, cord, and staff. Cylinder seals with a hole through the middle, through which a cord was run to hang the seals around the neck of their owners, were a means of marking documents: the seal was rolled in soft clay. When the clay hardened the mark of the seal remained, identifying the sender of the document and assuring that it had not been tampered with. The staff or walking stick probably had some particular mark of identification on it.

Tamar conceives a child, and returns to her widow's life. Judah, true to his word, sends his friend Hirah to deliver the promised goat to Tamar (v. 20). Just as a kid played a role in notifying Jacob that Joseph was thought to be dead, likewise a kid plays a role here in maintaining Judah's anonymity. Hirah inquires about the whereabouts of a cult prostitute, but there is no cult prostitute in the town. (Tamar posed as a prostitute, not a cult prostitute. The Hebrew words mark this distinction.) Hirah reports to Judah that he is unable to locate the woman, and Judah prefers to let the matter go rather than risk embarrassment.

In verse 24 Judah learns that Tamar is pregnant, but has no idea that he is the child's father. Acting on his authority as head of the family, he orders that she be burned, an exceptionally harsh means of death. But Tamar produces the three items to identify the father of her child, and Judah realizes what he has done. Tamar's words to Judah resemble those of the messenger who delivers Joseph's garment to Jacob in 37:32. Judah acknowledges his sin: he did not give his third son to Tamar, as the ancient custom required. He uses his prerogative as her father-in-law to condemn her, but he neglected to use it earlier when he refused to give his third son to her. Again the text is careful not to condemn him harshly: it specifies that he does not have intercourse with her again. The narrative also exonerates Tamar: Judah says about her, "She is in the right rather than I" (38:26). In fact, Judah placed Tamar in an impossible position by not giving his third son Shelah to her but at the same time not relieving her of any obligation to him as her father-in-law. Tamar does what is necessary to provide a son for her deceased husband and still remain faithful to her obligations as Judah's daughter-in-law.

Tamar gives birth to twins in verse 27. The red thread tied around the first hand to come out of the womb recalls the birth of Rebekah's twins: Esau, whose name means "red," was born first but was not the favored son (25:25-26). Zerah is Tamar's firstborn, but Perez, the second, is the favored one; we learn in Ruth 4:18-22 that he is the ancestor of David.

The chapter began by depicting Leah's fourth son in trouble, like her first three. But it ends with indications that he assumes responsibility for his actions. The next time we meet Judah is in 43:3, when he and his brothers are back at home with their father.

39:1-23 Joseph in the household of Potiphar

The Joseph story resumes where it left off in 37:36, with Joseph in the household of Potiphar, his new owner. For the first time in the Joseph story we read that the Lord is with Joseph. Throughout the Joseph story the Lord guides and protects Joseph, but the narrative seldom mentions him. In this chapter, however, the word "Lord" appears six times. Its only other appearance in the Joseph story is in Jacob's testament in 49:18. The word "God" appears much more frequently in the Joseph story.

Here another of Jacob's sons faces a critical situation with a woman. (Jacob himself had his own difficulties over women: he was given Leah, after being promised Rachel for a wife in 29:14-30.) Joseph fares well under Potiphar, thanks to divine protection and guidance. Furthermore, he is handsome, an additional sign of divine favor. His master leaves all the household responsibilities to Joseph. The description of Potiphar being attentive only to the food he eats suggests that he neglects his wife. The juxtaposition of contrasting descriptions of Potiphar and Joseph foreshadows trouble in his household, and it is not long in coming.

Potiphar's wife's speaks as a slave owner to a slave in her efforts to seduce him (v. 7). Joseph attributes his refusal to his faithfulness both to Potiphar and to God. But she refuses to give up, and finds a way when the two are alone. Once again Joseph's garment is a source of trouble for him. She takes it to use against him by blackmailing him, just as his brothers did earlier when they took the garment his father gave him, and used it to insinuate that Joseph was dead. Tamar, on the other hand, took Judah's seal, cord, and staff for a different purpose. She held them in pledge until he would pay his debt to her, and eventually used them to identify him as the father of her children, saving her own life in the process.

Potiphar's wife is vengeful in her rejection and embarrassment, and she immediately accuses her husband of neglect in bringing a foreigner into the household. She claims to have screamed as evidence of her innocence; eventually the law required such an act if one was raped in a public place (Deut 22:23-27). Potiphar's lack of involvement continues, and he condemns Joseph, to whom he has entrusted his entire household, without even asking for his side of the story. Joseph is imprisoned in the royal prison, but the Lord is with him. The chief jailer puts Joseph in charge of the prison, just as Potiphar put him in charge of his household, and trusts him implicitly.

40:1-23 Joseph in prison

Eventually Pharaoh has two royal officials incarcerated in the same prison as Joseph. His gift for interpreting dreams serves him well when both officials have troubling dreams in the same night. Joseph offers to interpret the dreams, acknowledging that his ability comes from God. This statement dissociates his ability from that of the magicians in Pharaoh's court, whose duties include interpreting dreams. Both dreams involve the number three, a number that signifies completion. Here the number represents the number of days until the dreams come to pass. Numerology was often associated with wisdom in the ancient world. Joseph's ability to interpret numbers demonstrates that he has the divine gift of wisdom.

The cupbearer's dream, which he repeats in verses 9-11, relates to his duty in the court: as cupbearer he holds the cup from which the Pharaoh drinks. His character must be above reproach because it is his responsibility to be sure no one poisons the Pharaoh. Joseph interprets the dream, announcing to the cupbearer that he will soon be released from prison. Joseph asks in return that the cupbearer arrange for his release as soon as it is possible.

Then the baker repeats his own dream that, like the cupbearer's, relates to his office. This time Joseph's interpretation foreshadows an unfortunate outcome. In three days, the time designated in both dreams, both of Joseph's interpretations prove to be accurate: the cupbearer is restored to his office and the baker is impaled during a birthday banquet in Pharaoh's honor. The cupbearer does not remember Joseph, but completely forgets about him. His forgetting foreshadows the eventual experience of Jacob's descendants in Egypt when "a new king, who knew nothing of Joseph, rose to power" (Exod 1:8).

41:1-56 The exoneration of Joseph

Joseph's gift of interpreting dreams continues to serve him well. This time it is Pharaoh who has a troubling dream. It includes several ominous elements: the Nile, on which all the people depend for subsistence, and also cows that figure prominently in the economy of the people. It involves the number seven, a number that denotes completion. Furthermore, it shows the seven unhealthy cows eating the healthy ones. Then, as with Joseph's earlier dream, a second one follows, verifying the message of the first. This one also involves a subsistence item, corn, the number seven, and the unhealthy consuming the healthy. Pharaoh calls on his magicians to interpret the dream. When they fail to do so, the cupbearer finally remembers Joseph.

Verse 14 expresses the urgency of the situation in the rapid succession of preparatory actions. When Pharaoh explains his need to Joseph, Joseph is quick to point out that it is God, not himself, who interprets dreams. He repeats this three more times in his conversation with Pharaoh. Pharaoh reports the dreams to Joseph, adding details that highlight his anxiety. For instance, he says about the cows, "Never have I seen such bad specimens as these in all the land of Egypt!" (41:19).

Joseph immediately explains to Pharaoh that the dreams are a revelation from God about what the next fourteen years will bring: seven years of plenty, followed by seven years of severe famine. Joseph offers a plan to prepare for the coming famine by stockpiling the surplus during the seven years of plenty to tide the people over during the impending years of famine. Pharaoh is so impressed with Joseph's wise advice that he makes him second in command only to himself, hoping that God will care for Egypt through Joseph (vv. 37-41). There is an implicit statement of faith in God here: Pharaoh relies on the God of Israel rather than on the Egyptian deities to see them through the imminent crisis.

An installation ceremony follows, beginning in verse 42. Once again clothes factor into the story when Pharaoh clothes Joseph in the trappings of rank: signet ring, linen robes, and chain around his neck. The three items are a flashback to the Tamar story: seal, cord, and staff were Judah's identification; here seal, chain, and linen robe are Pharaoh's signs of office. Then he is given a public ride in a royal chariot, probably horse-drawn. This is the first mention of the vehicle in the Bible. The meaning of the salute, "Abrek!" is not known; it is similar to an Egyptian word that means "Attention!" Joseph's new name is Egyptian, and has been interpreted several ways that relate to his gift for interpreting dreams or his new position in Pharaoh's court. His marriage makes him a member of a noble family (41:45). Joseph implements his plan of storing food during the time of plenty so it will be available for the time of famine. The surplus is huge beyond measure.

During the time of prosperity Joseph fathers two sons, Manasseh and Ephraim (vv. 50-52), whose names relate to Joseph's past difficulties and present circumstances. Then the famine comes as predicted, and Pharaoh relies on Joseph to distribute the surplus grain so that everyone has plenty to eat. Eventually people come to Egypt from all over the world, seeking relief from the famine. This development sets the stage for Joseph's brothers to come to Egypt and be reunited with their brother.

42:1-38 The brothers' first journey to Egypt

Jacob and his family feel the effects of the famine, suffering from hunger and also from inability to find a solution for their desperate situation. It is Jacob who suggests a way out of their difficulty: he sends them to Egypt for rations. Ironically, he is sending them to their brother Joseph, just as he sent Joseph to his brothers long ago, precipitating his sale into slavery. He has resumed his place at the head of his family, after suffering the heartbreaking loss of his son Joseph. In fact, on account of losing Joseph he does not permit Benjamin to go with his brothers to Egypt because he does not want to risk losing the only living son of his beloved Rachel. The ten brothers travel together because there is safety in numbers, and perhaps because they hope to secure more rations for the family.

In verse 6 the ten brothers come to Joseph and pay the appropriate homage to him. They bow low just as his boyhood dream predicted. Joseph recognizes them immediately, but does not identify himself to them. On the contrary, he treats them harshly, remembering his dreams and their mocking reaction to them. His accusation that they are spies is plausible because the route into Egypt from Canaan was vulnerable to attack. In their effort to convince him that they are not spies they begin to give him information about the family. The more they tell him, the more he persists in his accusation: his memories of their abuse urge him to be harsh, while his eagerness for news of his father and brother presses him to learn as much as possible from his brothers.

His solution is to impose a series of tests; the first of these is for one brother to go home and bring the youngest while the others wait in prison for them to return. Three days later he changes his orders, sending all of them home with food for their families. In this way he assures himself that Jacob and Benjamin will not go hungry. The brothers, still in Joseph's presence, interpret his orders as punishment for their earlier abusive treatment of him, but they do not recognize him.

Reuben's chastisement of the others in verse 22 touches Joseph: he realizes that Reuben tried to save him from the brothers' plot. He leaves the room rather than weep in their presence and divulge his identity. Joseph takes the second-oldest, Simeon, hostage rather than Reuben, the oldest, in light of Reuben's earlier efforts to save him. He arranges for the others to have grain, money, and provisions for the return trip; then the brothers begin their journey home.

They are unaware that their money has been returned until one of them opens his bag and finds it (v. 28). Then the brothers realize that their situation is extremely precarious: they must eventually return to Egypt with their brother Benjamin in order to rescue Simeon and procure more grain, but they risk being accused of stealing the money once they arrive there. The brothers find themselves at the mercy of God in their predicament. Joseph's reason for ordering the money to be returned is not given: does he mean for the brothers to have the money because it is theirs? Or does he mean to give them grief? Or is he imposing another test on them?

Once back home, the brothers tell their father about their experiences in Egypt. Ironically they report that they called themselves honest men, still not realizing that they were speaking to the brother they tried to destroy. Then they discover that all their money has been returned, not just one person's. Their father is particularly stricken, fearing that he will lose his youngest son Benjamin to Egypt. Even though Reuben suggests that his own two sons could be ransom for Benjamin, Jacob will not agree to let Benjamin go. This is the last time the narrative depicts Reuben taking leadership in his position as firstborn. From now on it is Judah who assumes responsibility for his brothers. Judah is Jacob's fourth son; the first three (Reuben, Simeon, and Levi) have disgraced themselves: Simeon and Levi in the destruction of Shechem in chapter 34, and Reuben by sleeping with his father's concubine in 35:22.

43:1-34 The second journey to Egypt

The family gradually uses all the rations the brothers brought home from Egypt, and Jacob suggests a second trip to buy more food for them. Judah reminds him of the terms: Benjamin must go with them, or they will all be condemned as spies. Jacob now realizes how precarious their situation is: the brothers must take Benjamin with them if they return to Egypt. Jacob is distraught that his sons gave the Egyptian official so much information about their family, but they reply that he pressured them into it, and they complied, not knowing how the information would be used against them. Judah pleads with his father that this is their one hope of survival, because only in Egypt will they be able to find food for their families. Judah makes another offer to his father, commenting that they are wasting precious time by debating the inevitable. He pledges that, if the mission fails, he personally will assume the responsibility.

Jacob finally and reluctantly relents in verse 11. He tells his sons to take gifts with them; ironically they include the same items (balm, gum, and resin) the Ishmaelite traders had with them when they bought Joseph from his brothers in 37:25. He also advises them to take double the amount of money that was returned to them, on the chance that it was mistakenly placed in their bags. He sends Benjamin with them as well, calling on the ancient name of God to protect all of them, in the hope that both Benjamin and Simeon will be allowed to return to him. He expresses his own resignation to the possibility of not seeing either of his two sons again. The brothers make the necessary arrangements, taking along twice the amount of money they owed for the first provisions, and taking their brother Benjamin with them.

In verse 15 the brothers arrive in Joseph's house. When he sees Benjamin with them, he arranges a banquet. His steward makes the arrangements and brings the brothers into the house for the banquet, but they suspect a trap. The narrative describes the reason for their fright: they expect to be enslaved as punishment for stealing the money. In an effort to forestall what they fear is inevitable they immediately explain to the chief steward that they did not, in fact, steal the money on their first trip to Egypt, but it was put back into their bags without their knowing. The chief steward then assures them they have nothing to fear; their God is behind what happened. He then brings their brother Simeon to them and treats the brothers hospitably while they wait for the arrival of their host.

When Joseph comes in, they bow down to him as they did before, and as Joseph's dream predicted. He inquires about their father, using the Hebrew word "shalom" or "wholeness," the expression for health and well-being, in verses 27-28. Joseph then acknowledges Benjamin, but still does not identify himself to his brothers. Then his feelings wash over him, and he leaves the room rather than weep in his brothers' presence. When he returns he orders the meal served. He hosts a feast for his brothers; earlier they enjoyed a meal after throwing him into the cistern (37:25). They are served separately according to the Egyptian custom of not eating with foreigners. (They were considered unclean because they were shepherds.) The brothers are seated according to age, and are amazed at the gracious hospitality of their host. Benjamin receives portions five times larger than the other brothers, but the reason is not given: is Joseph heaping special treatment on his full brother because he is so happy to see him? Or is he watching for signs of envy from his other brothers, like their envy of him when they were young?

44:1-34 The final test

Joseph has still not identified himself to his brothers. He instructs his steward to pack the men's bags with provisions as they prepare to start on their journey home. In addition, the money is to be put back in their bags, and Joseph's own silver goblet is to be packed in Benjamin's bag. The silver goblet reminds us that the brothers originally sold Joseph for twenty pieces of silver; now he plants a silver vessel in the bag of Benjamin, who had nothing to do with the brothers' earlier abuse of Joseph. His orders are carried out, and early in the morning the party begins the journey home. Very soon after they depart, Joseph sends his steward after the men, to accuse them of stealing the goblet. The steward is not to refer explicitly to the goblet, but only to make an inexact accusation, to heighten the brothers' anxiety.

In verse 7 the brothers are aghast at the steward's accusation. Judah speaks for them all, protesting that they demonstrated their honesty by returning the money and questioning how he could accuse them of stealing something else. He offers to allow the guilty one to be killed, and all the rest of them will become slaves. This spontaneous protestation comes from his own conviction that his brothers are innocent, from the wariness they all experience after the previous incident with the money, and also from his eagerness to resolve the matter as quickly as possible. Judah's response is reminiscent of Jacob's assertion to Laban when he was accused of stealing the household gods in 31:30-35. But the steward insists that only the guilty one will be enslaved, and no one will be killed.

The brothers open their bags one after another, beginning with the oldest (v. 11). This procedure encourages the brothers, as one bag after another proves not to have the missing vessel. But for the reader, who knows the vessel is in the youngest brother's bag, the suspense mounts as his turn comes closer and closer. When the vessel is found in Benjamin's bag, the brothers are dumbstruck. They tear their clothes, reminiscent of their father's action when he received Joseph's blood-stained garment (37:34). For the third time they go to the city.

When they reach Joseph's house in verse 14, they prostrate themselves again, but this time the narrative uses the intensive form of the verb, expressing the brothers' sense of hopelessness that they will ever be exonerated. Joseph speaks harshly to them, accusing them and wondering how they could do such a thing: do they not realize he knows what happened because of his special powers? Judah, the spokesperson, speaks from the depth of his despair, wondering how the brothers can possibly break free of the misunderstandings and accusations they have suffered since they first arrived in Egypt. Again he asserts that all the brothers will stand together and accept the punishment of slavery. Joseph insists that only the guilty one will be punished, as his steward had specified.

Then Judah recounts the entire story of the brothers' first arrival in Egypt, the pain and grief their father suffered over the loss of Rachel and over the possible loss of Rachel's only remaining son, the brothers' concern that their father will die of grief if Benjamin does not return to him, and even his own pledge to Jacob that he will assume the guilt if anything happens to Benjamin. With these words Judah brings the story back to its beginning: the one who sold Joseph into slavery is now willing to accept slavery himself rather than devastate their father.

45:1-28 Joseph reveals himself to his brothers

Judah's words touch Joseph so deeply that he can no longer hide his identity from his brothers. He dismisses his attendants, then weeps for the third time. But this time he stays with his brothers, says simply, "I am Joseph," then inquires about his father (45:3). The image of his father's grief over the loss of his two sons by Rachel ultimately moves Joseph to identify himself to his brothers. The brothers are speechless. Joseph repeats his identity, adding that he is the one they sold into slavery. His words highlight both his identity and his former strained relationship with them. He then explains that, even though the brothers acted sinfully, everything has happened through God's care, to pave the way for them in Egypt. He sends them back to their father with instructions to bring him back to Egypt, where he will have enough fertile land for his family, livestock, and all his possessions, so they can survive the five years of famine that remain. They will live in Goshen, in the northeastern part of Egypt, where the land is ideal for cattle grazing. Joseph and Benjamin embrace (v. 14), then Joseph embraces each of his other brothers. Finally they are able to talk to him after his shocking revelation, and after all the years of strained relationships (37:15).

In verse 16 Pharaoh himself sends greetings to Joseph's brothers, and encourages Joseph to send for his father and the entire family. He repeats the offer in a formal order. Joseph gives his brothers provisions for their travel; to Benjamin he gives extra gifts, and sends gifts and provisions to his father as well. His final word is puzzling; the Hebrew text can mean, "Do not fear for your safety" or "Do not recriminate."

When Jacob hears that Joseph is not only alive, but a ruler of Egypt, it is his turn to be incredulous (v. 26). When he sees all the provisions Joseph has sent for their journey, he determines to go to Egypt to see Joseph.

46:1–47:12 Jacob's migration to Egypt

Jacob leaves his home, most likely in Hebron (37:14) and goes first to Beer-sheba where he lived

with his parents before traveling to Haran (28:10), and where his father Isaac received the Lord's blessing (26:23-25). The connection with Isaac seems to be his reason for going to that place, as the narrative specifies that he offers sacrifices to "the God of his father Isaac" (v. 1). There he has a vision in which God calls to him and he responds, "Here I am," expressing his readiness to do whatever God asks of him. God reassures him, repeats the promise of a great nation, and promises to bring him back after Joseph closes Jacob's eyes in death. The divine promises provide a clue as to why Jacob visits the shrine: he is leaving this land that has been promised to him, and the future is full of uncertainties. The divine reassurance convinces him that his decision to go to Egypt is a sound one.

It was the custom (and is still so in Jewish families) for the oldest son to close his father's eyes when he dies. Joseph is Jacob's first son by his beloved wife Rachel; here he receives a divine promise that Joseph will be with him at the moment of his death (see 49:33–50:1).

A genealogical list follows in verses 8-27, enumerating all those who travel with Jacob to Egypt. The list is arranged according to Jacob's twelve sons and one daughter by their respective mothers. The list includes Er and Onan, Judah's two deceased sons; it also includes Joseph along with his two sons who were born in Egypt. The total number given in verse 26 is sixty-six, not counting Er and Onan, who had already died, or Joseph's two sons who were born in Egypt, or Leah's daughter Dinah, even though she is listed in the genealogy. Then verse 27 gives the number seventy, after adding Joseph's two sons to the count.

Much effort has been made to reconcile these numbers, which have several problematic aspects in addition to the puzzling difference in the totals. For example, the list of Benjamin's sons differs here from corresponding lists in Numbers 26:38-40; 1 Chronicles 7:6; and 8:1-2; each of which is slightly different from the others. Quite possibly the significance of the number seventy, rather than the exact count, is the important aspect of it, as seventy is considered ten times the perfect number seven. (In Exod 1:5, the number of Jacob's family who migrate to Egypt is given as seventy.) The genealogy solemnly testifies that the entire family goes to Egypt, as Genesis 15:13 predicts. The list marks the end of the ancestral period in the land, and provides a transition to the next stage of the family story.

As the party approaches Goshen where they will live, Jacob sends Judah ahead to alert Joseph of their arrival. Thus Judah, who suggested selling Joseph and thus caused his separation from his father, now arranges their reunion. Joseph hurries out to meet his father as the caravan approaches. This time it is he who is overcome; his father expresses his sentiment that now that he has seen Joseph, his life is complete (v. 30). Joseph explains that he will formally notify Pharaoh of his family's arrival, and coaches his brothers that they are to identify themselves as owners of livestock like the Egyptians. This statement is puzzling in view of his final remark, "all shepherds are abhorrent to the Egyptians."

Joseph takes several of his brothers with him when he formally notifies Pharaoh of his family's arrival in 47:1. They state their occupation as shepherds and explain that they have come to stay on a temporary basis because of the famine. Pharaoh gives his formal approval to Joseph, authorizing them to stay in Goshen and serve as royal officers. This designation affords them legal status to which they would not otherwise be entitled as aliens. The approval implicitly makes Joseph responsible for the family.

The next audience is between Pharaoh and Jacob (v. 7). Pharaoh asks Jacob about his age, and his reply indicates that he has lived beyond the Egyptian ideal of 110 years. Jacob refers to himself as a wayfarer, perhaps in reference to his life as a journey, perhaps to emphasize his many travels, or perhaps to call attention to his alien status in Egypt. Joseph arranges for his family to have what they need for their stay in Egypt.

47:13-27 Joseph's land policy

The narrative picks up the story from 41:57 when the famine begins to affect everyone. The situation is dire, and Joseph takes drastic steps to keep the people from starving. First he collects all the money in the land as payment for grain, but keeps none of it for himself. Then he barters livestock for grain. When the people have no more livestock they give over their land and become slaves of the state. Thus the state comes to own all the money, livestock, land, and people except for the priests who have a special allotment from Pharaoh. Then Joseph gives the people seed to plant, with the stipulation that they give one-fifth of the crops to Pharaoh at harvest time. The people are profoundly grateful to Joseph, and readily accept the terms of the agreement. Meanwhile, Jacob's family thrives in their new home in Egypt (v. 27).

It is difficult to understand this arrangement in contemporary Western terms. In the ancient Near East, during the time of Hammurabi, a tax such as the one Joseph imposed could be as high as two-thirds. In Babylon the rate was between one-fifth and one-third. All these rates seem exorbitant to us; perhaps the narrator thought so, too, and avoided placing the responsibility for the policy on Joseph by having the people suggest enslavement. A brief note follows, that the practice became law, and was still in effect at the time the narrative was written.

By removing any moral stigma from Joseph, the narrative focuses on the wise policies Joseph introduces, portraying him as a concerned and creative administrator who takes bold action in a time of crisis, and thus saves Egypt from devastation.

47:28–48:33 Jacob's last days

When Jacob first arrives in Egypt he rejoices at the opportunity to see Joseph again before he dies; in fact, his sojourn in Egypt extends to seventeen years. This is the same as the amount of time before the two were separated (37:2), giving a sense of completion to Jacob's sojourn in Egypt. Jacob exacts a solemn oath from Joseph not to bury him in Egypt but to return his remains to the family burial place in the cave of Machpelah. Of all the ancestors, Jacob is the only one to die on alien soil. We can assume from the divine assurance to him at Beer-sheba before leaving for Egypt that Jacob was concerned about leaving the land. The divine promise highlights the importance of his being buried with his forebears in the land promised to him (46:4). Joseph swears to the agreement with the same gesture that Abraham's servant used when he agreed to go to Haran to find a wife for Isaac (24:2-9). Then Jacob bows his head in gratitude, perhaps to Joseph, perhaps to God, or perhaps to both.

Jacob's next act in preparation for death is to establish Joseph's sons as tribes. Joseph receives word in 48:1 that his father is not well. Joseph and his two sons visit his father, who is called Israel here because he is the father, not only of twelve sons, but of twelve tribes. He finds the strength to sit up in bed when his guests arrive. The next few verses are an E variation on the previous scene. Jacob recalls that at Bethel when he was starting out on his way to Haran (28:18-19), a dream established him as the keeper of the divine promise. Now he formally adopts his two grandsons as his own sons, thus passing the divine promises along to them.

Jacob follows a legal ritual: he formally states his intent to adopt the two boys, asks Joseph to name them, embraces them, and bows profoundly. Verse 6 suggests that Joseph has other sons as well, but Jacob adopts only the first two. Jacob's recollections of Rachel might suggest that she would have had more children if she had lived; but since she died so young Joseph's sons take the place of the children Rachel never had. He highlights his past grief and present joy, commenting that he once thought he would never see his son Joseph again, and now he sees Joseph's children.

Joseph places his sons close to Jacob to receive his blessing, with Manasseh the firstborn in a position to receive the blessing of the firstborn. At this point the text refers to Jacob by his name of Israel, focusing on his role as father of the twelve sons who become the twelve tribes of Israel. He puts his right hand on the head of his younger grandson Ephraim. Then, before blessing either grandson Israel blesses Joseph, the boys' father. When Joseph tries to reposition Israel's hands so the firstborn will receive the blessing, Israel insists that the younger will be the greater. Thus Israel establishes the younger over the older, just as he received his father Isaac's blessing before Isaac died. The blessing highlights Joseph's privileged place among his brothers, ten of whom are older than he is.

49:1-27 Jacob blesses his sons

Chapter 49 is a complex collection of poems, with sections devoted to each of Jacob's twelve sons. They are arranged in the form of a testament, that is, last words that leave a legacy for his family. Jacob alternates between speaking to the sons and speaking about them; this is awkward for modern readers but was frequent in ancient speech. Jacob first addresses Leah's six sons, then the four sons of the maids, beginning and ending

with one of Bilhah's children. Finally he speaks to Joseph and Benjamin, his two youngest sons and his children by his beloved Rachel. Even though he has just adopted Joseph's two sons as his own, they are not included in this testament. In some instances Jacob's words relate to different sons' previous actions; in others the words seem to relate to the lives of the tribes after they settled in the land.

Reuben (vv. 3-4): Jacob voices his condemnation of Reuben for sleeping with Bilhah in 35:22. Historically the tribe of Reuben actually disappeared very early.

Simeon and Levi (vv. 5-7): Jacob speaks of the two together, condemning their wanton destruction of the Shechemites in chapter 34, and predicting that they will not remain together. Historically, in time the tribe of Simeon became part of Judah, and the tribe of Levi was given priestly duties rather than land.

Judah (vv. 8-12): After condemning his first three sons for their previous sins, Jacob blesses Judah with the status of firstborn in verse 8b, and assures his authority, especially in verse 10. Historically, Judah remained after the Assyrians destroyed the northern kingdom in 722, bringing to an end the ten tribes who lived in that area.

Zebulun (v. 13): Jacob addresses Zebulun, Leah's sixth son, before her fifth son. Jacob foretells that Zebulun will live by the sea. In fact, his land was inland; perhaps its inhabitants worked along the coast.

Issachar (vv. 14-15): Jacob foresees that this son's tribe will work in servitude.

Dan (vv. 16-17): Dan, whose name is related to the Hebrew word "judge," will promote justice in his tribe and will fend off his enemies.

A brief prayer for deliverance comes next. In its position after the words about Dan it reinforces the divine source of Dan's ability to judge.

Gad (v. 19): Gad will successfully wage war against his enemies. Historically, his tribe, who lived east of the Jordan River, fought against the other peoples of that area.

Asher (v. 20): Asher inhabited the fertile land along the northwestern coast. It was a rich farming area.

Naphtali (v. 21): The reference to a female, fast-moving animal that bears young is obscure.

Joseph (vv. 22-26): Jacob's words about Joseph, like those about Judah, are lengthy. Parts are obscure; verses 25-26 promise him the blessings of children and land.

Benjamin (v. 27): Jacob predicts that this son will be a successful warrior. That depiction does not match the portrayal of the young Benjamin in Genesis. It does, however, address the strategic location of the tribe, dividing the northern tribes from Judah to the south.

49:28–50:14 Jacob's death and burial

After Jacob blesses his sons the story returns to the deathbed scene from 48:22. Jacob's final words repeat the instructions given privately to Joseph, to bury him with his family in the cave of Machpelah (47:29-31). This P version is more formal than the earlier J version. When Jacob dies, Joseph gives instructions for him to be embalmed. This was not the usual ancient Israelite custom, but it preserved Jacob's body so it could be transported back to Hebron as Jacob had requested. The people observe the period of mourning, then carry out Jacob's request, traveling in a large and solemn caravan. After they bury their father the sons all return to Egypt.

50:15-26 Final reconciliation

Now that their father is dead, the brothers fear that Joseph will exact revenge for their earlier mistreatment of him. They beg for his forgiveness, and Joseph is moved by their pleading. He answers them in words reminiscent of Jacob's when Rachel begged him for a child (30:2), reminding them that ultimately forgiveness comes from God. Then he sums up the message of the entire Joseph story, pointing out that God uses human actions, no matter how evil or inadequate, to achieve the divine purpose: in this case the survival of Jacob's family.

Then the story jumps ahead to the last days of Joseph, who assures his brothers that God will eventually take them back to the land that has been promised to them. He instructs his brothers to take his body with them when they leave Egypt (Exod 13:19). Joseph, like his father Jacob, is embalmed to preserve his body for its eventual return to the land of promise.

CONCLUSION

Our journey through Genesis began with God's creation of the universe and the first humans, whose early efforts to live in relationship with God and each other formed the basis of life within the human community. The story narrowed its focus from the universal to the family of one couple, Abraham and Sarah. Each time the people took missteps, God took action to reestablish the balance between the divine and human, and within the human community.

Throughout all these events God continued to provide for the peoples' needs. The ancestors were far from perfect or worthy. God guided them, with all their dignity and their frailty, in their comings and goings. Joseph summarized it for his brothers when he pointed out that God uses our actions to achieve the divine end (50:19-20). God continues to use our actions, redeeming what is evil and celebrating what is good. Genesis offers us the models; our lives continue the saga.

THE BOOK OF
EXODUS

Mark S. Smith

INTRODUCTION

The significance of the exodus

Exodus tells the story of Israel's divine deliverance and the freedom it gained in the covenant relationship with God on Mount Sinai. Many people think of the exodus as Israel's escape from slavery in Egypt, but freedom in the book of Exodus is not completely sealed until Israel completes the covenant with God at Mount Sinai. Freedom in Exodus is not only freedom from oppressive conditions or the evil of human power; human freedom becomes complete in the context of the covenantal relationship with the God of Israel. For the book of Exodus, to be free means not only freedom *from* evil but also freedom *through* responsible relationships *with* and *for* others, human as well as divine. Exodus expresses this twofold reality about human freedom through the geographical structure of the book: Egypt dominates the first major part (Exod 1–15), while Sinai is the focus of the second (Exod 16–40).

The book of Exodus is therefore not simply the record of physical journeys. It is also the journey of Israel and God. Following the end of Genesis, with its narrative about Jacob, his sons, and their families in Egypt, the beginning of Exodus shows how this family has become a people, the people of Israel. In the very first verse, they are collectively called "the sons of Israel." Exodus identifies Israel's origins as an oppressed people, one not at home in the foreign land of Egypt (Exod 1:8-14). It is a people heard by God (Exod 3:7) even before

the divine name is revealed to them (4:29-31); God relates to Israel even before Israel knows fully who their God is and well before they enter into the formal covenant relationship (Exod 19–40). Because Israel is God's people, "the God of Israel" is one key way for identifying the Lord. From the book of Exodus on, the Lord is "the God of Israel," and knowledge of the One God in the universe, whether for the Egyptians or for other peoples, comes through Israel (Exod 7:5; 8:6, etc.). Exodus not only tells the story of Israel's identity; it also explains who God is.

The exodus provided a model for expressing Israel's collective passage from persecution to freedom in a renewed relationship with God. In the sixth century B.C., the book of Isaiah could proclaim the impending return from exile in Babylon to Jerusalem precisely as a second exodus: "In the wilderness prepare the way of the LORD! / Make straight in the wasteland a highway for our God!" (Isa 40:3). Echoing Exodus, the first-century author of the book of Wisdom addresses the problem of reward for the just and punishment for the wicked: "For by the things through which their foes [the Egyptians] were punished / they [the Israelites] in their need were benefited" (Wis 11:5). The exodus was also celebrated in Israel's worship and used as an ongoing model for exploring its relationship with God. Psalm 105 focuses on the exodus for examples of God's "wondrous deeds" (v. 5), and Psalm 106 uses the same story to illustrate Israel's failures.

The early church likewise drew on the exodus for inspiration. As Jews, the early Christians adopted and adapted Passover and Pentecost in their experience of Jesus as the Paschal Lamb (Paschal referring to Passover) and the coming of the Spirit. The imagery of the Passover is explicit in the events of Easter, as the gospels locate the events of Jesus' death and resurrection at the time of the Passover (also called the feast of Unleavened Bread). The Last Supper was evidently understood by some of the gospel writers as a Passover meal. Luke explicitly uses the language of Exodus for Jesus' passage from persecution to the exaltation of the Father (Luke 9:31). Paul uses a traditional Jewish preaching strategy in referring symbolically to human corruption as food with yeast or leavening (removed from Jewish households during the feast of Passover/Unleavened Bread): "Clear out the old yeast, so that you may become a fresh batch of dough, inasmuch as you are unleavened. For our paschal lamb, Christ, has been sacrificed. Therefore let us celebrate the feast, not with the old yeast, the yeast of malice and wickedness, but with the unleavened bread of sincerity and truth" (1 Cor 5:7-8).

The Christian use of the imagery of Weeks may not be as obvious for the feast of Pentecost, but it is there in a very deep way. Following seven weeks after Passover, Weeks celebrates the giving of the Law through Moses in order to guide the Jewish people. So too in a parallel way, following fifty days after Easter, Pentecost celebrates the giving of the Spirit through the figure of Jesus in order to guide the Christian community. The coming of the Spirit in fire on Pentecost Sunday (Acts 2:2-3) echoes the fire of God blazing on Mount Sinai (Exod 19:18).

Passover, commanded as one of three annual pilgrimage feasts, becomes the occasion for retelling and reliving the exodus, and this celebration is complete in the pilgrimage feast of Weeks (Pentecost), which in late biblical tradition celebrates the giving of the covenant and law on Mount Sinai. Exodus tells its audience that Passover is a feast "which your future generations will celebrate with pilgrimage to the LORD . . . as a statute forever" (12:14). The book is designed not simply to convey information about the past; it also invites readers to participate in this event for themselves. Accordingly, Exodus was intended to be both informative and performative: it provides information about where Israel's ancestors came from and who they were; and it invites participation by their descendants to ritually perform this identity story for themselves.

The later Jewish celebration of the Passover beautifully captures the performative spirit of the book of Exodus: the identity story of the Israelite ancestors becomes the identity story of their Jewish descendants forever. The Jewish retelling of the Passover story says, "In each generation, every person should feel as though he or she had actually been redeemed from Egypt, as it is said [quoting Exod 13:8]: 'You should tell your children on that day, saying, "It is because of what the Lord did for me when I went free out of Egypt."' For the Holy One (Blessed be He) redeemed not only our ancestors; He redeemed us with them." The past is not simply celebrated in the present, nor is the past merely the model for the present. The present experience is the reality shaped and informed by the past event.

Thanks to the early church's Jewish foundations, Christians participate in their own way in this narrative of freedom and relationship with the God of Israel. In their eucharistic meal, Christians experience the ancient events surrounding the Last Supper as a living, present reality made possible through Jesus' mystical presence. Reading the book of Exodus, too, was meant to be a "sacramental" experience: not simply a reading of some past events, but a reading of present reality informed and shaped by the foundational events of the past.

Historical background of the exodus

Egyptian records are as silent as the Sphinx regarding the event of the exodus. Yet it is not surprising that Moses' dealings with Pharaoh do not get even a footnote in Egyptian history. Egyptian texts serve to exalt the glory of the Pharaohs and their deities. Moreover, from the Egyptians' perspective the Israelites were a relatively unimportant group, one that merited their attention only years after the event of the exodus. (There is only one reference to Israel in Egyptian records before the time of David and Solomon.)

The lack of Egyptian evidence is hardly proof that the exodus did not happen at least in some form. As the famous scholarly dictum expresses the point, "Absence of evidence is not evidence of absence." It is plausible that despite Egyptian silence about it, the exodus took place (even if the biblical memory elaborated the event). There are reasons to think that a historical event might lie behind the biblical account. It has been long noted that the names of Moses, Aaron, Hur, Merari, and Phinehas are Egyptian in origin and not Hebrew (Moses' name is related to the Egyptian element contained in the name of the Pharaoh Thut-mose, "the god Thut is born"). Some scholars would regard it as odd for these Egyptian names to be in the Israelite record if some major contact with Egyptian culture had not been a part of the Israelite historical experience. A further argument has also been marshaled in support of seeing an event behind the book of Exodus. If the exodus was originally a "made-up story," it seems odd to many that a people would have concocted a story of slavery for their origins (kingship in Mesopotamia, in contrast, was thought to have descended from heaven). Because of these considerations, a number of scholars see some historical kernel embedded in the exodus account.

The skepticism of some scholars about the exodus event helps all researchers to be as honest as possible in examining historical claims. Scholarship reminds us that the book of Exodus, as handed down to us, was written hundreds of years after the events that it narrates. As a result, the precise nature of the historical kernel is impossible to discern from the biblical record. Did the exodus involve as many people as the 600,000 Israelite males, "not counting the children" or the "crowd of mixed ancestry," as claimed in Exodus 12:37-38 (compare the 603,550 of Num 1:46 and the 601,730 of Num 26:51)? Did God really intervene miraculously at the Sea of Reeds by creating walls of waters through which the Israelites crossed (Exod 14:22), or did it involve a more naturalistic picture of an escape attributed to God's saving power (Exod 15)? Did the exodus really take place all at once, or could it have involved multiple departures, with different memories as to the routes taken (possibly with even different interpretations attached to them)? Was the God of the exodus really Yahweh, or was it El (cf. Num 24:8) before the two deities were identified (cf. Exod 6:2-3)?

Such questions lay beyond the grasp of historians to answer clearly. Instead, the biblical record

as it now stands expresses Israelite faith in a single exodus event made possible by the God of Israel. There are many layers of material in the text of Exodus, identified by many scholars according to the so-called Documentary Hypothesis. This theory holds that four sources of the Pentateuch (the first five books of the Old Testament) as well as their arrangement together by one or more later scribes were produced during the reigns of the Israelite kings and afterward. These multiple levels alert us to the fact that the book of Exodus itself contains not only the record of Israelites leaving Egypt but also several interpretations of the event. For example, the crossing of the sea in the poem of Exodus 15 looks natural, but the prose account of the same event in Exodus 14 contains elements that might be characterized as supernatural. Both natural and supernatural are expressions of faith in a God who has the power and will to redeem. Our biblical text combines event and interpretation.

The setting of the exodus

Although neither Egyptian records nor the biblical accounts provide any historical report in the modern sense of the term, there are some indications about the setting of the exodus in the Bible. Most scholars place the exodus in the thirteenth century B.C. According to these scholars, the Pharaoh who oppressed the Israelites was Rameses II (sometimes called Rameses the Great), the great builder who ruled around 1290 to 1224 B.C. One reason given for this view is the testimony in Exodus 1:11 that refers to the supply city of Raamses, which this Pharaoh is thought to have had built. It is known that Rameses II established his capital in the Nile Delta and that the term "city of Raamses" was not used after 1100 B.C.

Exodus 1–2 suggests a more complicated picture, if it is historically accurate. These chapters refer to three Egyptian kings: one who knew Joseph; a second who did not (1:8) and who oppressed the Israelites (1:8-14); and a third who continued the Israelites' slavery while Moses was in Midian (2:23). Rameses II is sometimes thought to be the Pharaoh of the exodus for whom the Israelites help build the store-cities mentioned in Exodus 1:11 and that it was his predecessor with whom Joseph and his family enjoyed such good relations. Other authorities would identify Rameses II as both the oppressor and the Pharaoh of the exodus as a single Pharaoh. Either way, the exodus would have occurred around 1250 B.C.

In contrast, other scholars wish to date these events to the fifteenth century B.C., in part based on 1 Kings 6:1, which dates the exodus to 480 years before Solomon's construction of the temple (ca. 970 B.C.). If this date were to be preferred, then it would be possible to situate the exodus against the backdrop of Egyptian records that complain about the activities of foreign Habiru; some scholars would like to identify them with the biblical word Hebrews, but many other scholars dispute this equation. Despite these uncertainties, most scholars still prefer a date in the thirteenth century. At the same time, one must openly admit that the precise dates are simply not known.

Literary forms, structure, and features

Modern readers often come to the Bible with the expectation that it provides accurate historical reporting of the events it depicts; it is often thought that the divine inspiration of the Bible guarantees its historical accuracy. Yet the book of Exodus is not history writing in the modern sense of the term. It includes a wide variety of genres or types of literature: genealogies (in chs. 1 and 6); stories of various sorts, including the call narrative of Moses (chs. 3–4), the plague stories (chs. 7–11), a poem (ch. 15), the travelogues and complaint narratives (chs. 15–17), and the story of Moses' intercession with God after the worship of the Golden Calf (chs. 32–34); commandments (chs. 20–23) and priestly instructions for worship (chs. 25–31 and 35–40). The variety of literary genres suggests that the exodus events were sources of reflection at various points in Israel's tradition. The core message proclaiming divine redemption of Israel from Egyptian oppression and the salvation of the eternal covenant on Sinai was celebrated throughout Israel's history. Scholarly analysis of Exodus has led commentators to see the book itself as the product of such reflection on the foundational events in Egypt and Sinai.

Within the book, scholars have discerned not only different genres but also different styles, vocabulary, and perspectives belonging to various writers or traditions. For decades, the dominant theory used to explain these differences was the Documentary Hypothesis, which holds that four sources of the Pentateuch as well as their arrangement together by one or more later scribal editors

were produced during the reigns of the Israelite kings and afterwards. Other theories emphasizing different concurrent traditions in dialogue with one another have been proposed as well.

Whatever approach proves true, it is evident that priestly concerns mark the prescriptions in chapters 25–31 and their execution in chapters 35–40. Moreover, priestly emphasis on the figure of Aaron (the prototype for the chief priest), for example, in Exodus 6:13–7:6 (over and above 4:10-17) likewise suggests a priestly hand. Accordingly, we may see the priestly concern for priestly personnel and space (often abbreviated as P) in these chapters and elsewhere (for example, in the priestly description of the tabernacle, etc., in chs. 25–31 and 35–40). This priestly tradition probably extended over a long period of time, from at least the eighth century down through the period following the return from exile in Babylon, when priestly rule governed the internal workings of Israel under the Persian Empire.

The other narrative material in Exodus, according to the Documentary Hypothesis (also called "source-criticism"), was divided into three other sources: the Yahwist (J), whose popular, suspenseful storytelling was produced in Judah anywhere from the tenth century to the sixth; the Elohist (E), a northern source with its emphasis on the fear (or better, reverence) of God, variously dated to the ninth through seventh century, and familiar with the prophetic milieu that produced the Elijah and Elisha stories of 1 Kings 17–2 Kings 13; and the Deuteronomist (dtr), a source identified largely based on similarities with the book of Deuteronomy (for example, in the Passover prescription in Exod 13). Material to be attributed to the Deuteronomist editor is relatively rare, and the E source is often tightly worked into the J material (in fact, one may represent the redaction of the other). Some scholars have further divided priestly material into priestly texts (P) and "Holiness School" (H) texts that have terms and expressions found in the Holiness Code of Leviticus 17–26 rather than other priestly material.

Without getting bogged down in the technical details of this source-criticism, for the purposes of this commentary it is sufficient to understand that the book of Exodus basically divides into priestly material (P and H) on the one hand and non-priestly material on the other (JE with some of the Deuteronomist material occasionally included) as well as regulations that may not derive from any of these sources. In the commentary these sources are mentioned, but issues about sources do not dominate the discussion.

There is an important theological value in noting the diversity of authors and their styles. It shows that ancient Israel cherished a variety of literary means to present its story: what is entertaining (the dramatic poem of Exod 15, or the suspenseful stories of the J source) as well as what is perhaps a bit shocking to modern sensibilities (for example, Moses as magician or his marriage to a non-Israelite) are preserved along with the morally uplifting tenor of E's theme of fear of God and with priestly narrative and ritual. Furthermore, these layers of material show that the biblical tradition reflected more and more deeply on the events that shaped the identity of ancient Israel. Finally, the tradition retained the variety of viewpoints expressed in the book. As a result, the canonized book preserves not only a record of past events but also the history of Israel's dialogue over their meaning.

Despite their variety, the genres (or categories) and sources (or traditions) did not result in a haphazard collection of material. Instead, the material now contained in Exodus passed through the hands of various scribal editors who shaped it in a way intended to provide a sense of literary balance and religious connection. The final editors seem to have belonged to the priestly tradition in ancient Israel. These priestly editors of Exodus placed a tremendous emphasis on Mount Sinai as the site of God's definitive revelation and covenant. As a result, priestly material dominates in the Sinai covenant not only in Exodus 25–31 and 35–40 but also the entire priestly book of Leviticus.

These priestly editors also seem to be responsible for the placement of the older poem into chapter 15. This piece of poetry marks the book's thematic midpoint between Egypt, the land of slavery, and Sinai, the mountain of freedom. As the book's fulcrum, the poem helps to create a literary balance that relates the Egypt story beforehand to the Sinai covenant afterwards. As a result, the journey of Moses to the mountain of God in chapter 2 seems to anticipate the journey of Moses and the people to the mountain of God in chapters 15–18. Both journeys are modeled on the audience's experience of making pilgrimage journeys to sanctuaries that were traditionally

regarded as the mountain of God (for example, Ps 15:1 referring to Jerusalem as God's "holy mountain"). Similarly, the two divine calls of Moses and his confrontations with Pharaoh in Exodus 3–15 seem to structurally echo the two sets of covenant tablets in Exodus 19–40. In the case of both, the initial effort fails, only to be followed by a second effort that is successful. Moses' initial call in chapters 3–4 is followed by an unsuccessful meeting with Pharaoh, a turn of events reversed following Moses' second call in chapters 6–7. Similarly, the Israelites' worship of the golden calf in chapter 32 represents an initial failure (signaled by Moses' smashing of the first set of tablets), evidently reversed with the second set of tablets. As a result of this priestly handling of various older texts, there emerges a picture of divine care for Israel which does not end on the first try. Instead, despite initial failure because of human resistance, God persistently works for Israel's deliverance.

Finally, it is important to note that the ancient authors and editors of Exodus often used language that deliberately echoes other passages in Scripture, especially the book of Genesis. The effect of such verbal resonances often indicates a pattern of divine purpose and redemption from the beginning of creation through the Sinai covenant (e.g., the Genesis creation story echoed in Exod 1 and 39–40). These writers enjoyed a high level of literary sophistication. Some of the techniques that they used and the religious message which they intended to convey through these techniques are noted in the commentary.

The sort of scholarly discussion involved with the Documentary Hypothesis and its four sources can be difficult to handle as readers try to read the Bible for spiritual benefit. It may be helpful to think of such scholarly notions as indicating that behind the Bible is a long tradition that discussed and wrestled with the hard issues: Does God care? What is the nature of God? How does Israel know God? How should Israel respond to God's actions in its midst and in the world? Out of this tradition emerged a number of voices: some prophetic (this seems to be the view of E); others priestly in concern and tone (so the P source or tradition). The prophetic and priestly voices had long been associated with God's own voices, while others, such as the material associated with J, show the hallmarks of a more popular voice, one that might not have been viewed as originally revelatory. Yet in time these voices were melded into a single literary progression that presented an original divine word as the last word.

The ongoing message of the exodus

The exodus story continues to inspire readers of the Bible. Throughout Jewish communities around the world and in Israel, the exodus is the single most celebrated holiday. The exodus story in the Passover meal returns Jewish families year in and year out to its fundamental message that God brought Israel out of oppression and into an eternal covenant. The story has provided inspiration and calls to action through various episodes of oppression against Jews.

The influence of the exodus story runs deep also in the church's struggle for justice in various parts of the world. In Central and South America, liberation theology has used the exodus story to understand and work against political oppression. Liberation theology applies the ancient story of Israel's bondage and subsequent deliverance to the circumstances of exploitation that have characterized a great deal of Latin American history, including the actions of the church itself. Closer to home in churches in the United States,

the exodus story has continued to move people to justice, again within and outside the church. Time and time again, Martin Luther King Jr. returned to the story of the exodus to exhort his audiences to work for freedom in their communities. On the night before he died, Reverend King at a church in Memphis delivered a speech that would become famous, "I've Been to the Mountaintop." Responding to a hypothetical question from God Almighty as to what age he would like to live in, Reverend King begins, "I would take my mental flight by Egypt, and I would watch God's children in their magnificent trek from the dark dungeons of Egypt through, or rather, across the Red Sea, through the wilderness, on toward the Promised Land. And in spite of its magnificence, I wouldn't stop there." In Reverend King's speech the struggle for freedom did not end with the exodus but is part of human history down to his own time with his struggle for civil rights. For Reverend King, the time of the exodus that ultimately mattered was his own time; and so too it is for us now. The exodus is not only an ancient story of a great, divine deliverance. It is also today's story, calling all people to work against oppression and to participate in a covenant relationship with one another and with God.

COMMENTARY

PART I: OUT OF EGYPT

Exodus (1:1–15:21)

The first part of Exodus relates the beginnings of Israel as a people, Moses' origins and his relationship to the people, and God's redemption of the people from slavery in Egypt. The various sources or traditions embedded in the book explore many questions: How did the Israelites become slaves in Egypt? How did Moses become their leader? What did it take for Moses to be leader? How did Moses deal with Pharaoh? What finally made Pharaoh agree to release the Israelites? What happened at the Reed Sea as they departed? What did God do for them at the Sea?

1:1-7 Israel in Egypt

This introduction begins by listing "the sons of Israel" (an expression for the Israelites). Verses 1-5 briefly retell the story of Jacob (Israel) traveling with his household down to Egypt, a story that refers back to Genesis 46. Verse 6 refers to the end of Genesis 50, with the death of Joseph. The mention of the earlier circumstances of Jacob and Joseph reminds readers of God's earlier deliverance of the family from the famine in Canaan, and it sets the stage for Exodus' story of danger and redemption. These verses provide further information about the Israelites in Egypt. They are "fruitful and prolific . . . the land was filled with them," which is an echo of the divine command in the Priestly (P) creation story of Genesis 1:28 ("Be fertile and multiply; fill the earth . . ."). The genealogy and the echo of the priestly passage of Genesis 1:28 suggest that the priestly tradition provided this introduction to the exodus story. The priestly prose of Exodus is thought to have been written any time during the end of the monarchy, the exile in Babylon, or after the return to the land under Persian authority. Apart from some brief exceptions, all these periods were ones of significant testing of Israelite faith. The introduction faces these difficulties and offers an expression of encouragement and a sign of hope that the divine promise made to Abraham (Gen 17) began to be fulfilled in Egypt and will continue to come to pass despite difficult circumstances.

1:8-14 The oppression of God's people

The passage introduces new circumstances between Egyptians and Israelites, mentioned at the beginning and end of the unit (vv. 7-8 and 13). Like a new boss or political leader who does not recognize earlier working relationships or ways of doing things, the new pharaoh introduces a note of tension into the scene. Both his lack of a prior relationship with Joseph and Israel's increased growth fuel fear in the new pharaoh. Despite the Israelites' positive relationship with his predecessor, the new pharaoh expresses his fear of a potential threat of an alliance with outsiders in wartime. It is unclear why Pharaoh thinks such things about the Israelites, but because he speaks his words "to his people" (instead of just saying them to himself), the pharaoh sets up a divide between himself and his people over and against the Israelites; perhaps he perceives them as outsiders. Fear of outsiders was a common theme of Egyptian texts of the New Kingdom, and it may serve as reason enough. Yet this is only implicit (v. 9); readers are left in the dark as to any further reasoning behind Pharaoh's thinking. By leaving unanswered the question as to why one in a position of superior power comes to fear the Israelites, the story opens with a heightened level of anxiety.

The Egyptians join Pharaoh in taking action against the Israelites (1:11-14). Enslavement provides a profitable mechanism of control, and it leads to an increased death rate. The story, however, gives no reason for the choice of slavery as the response to the perceived threat (and in any event, the readers of this story know that it will not work). The story introduces an Egyptian flavor into the story in referring to Egyptian store-cities by name. Raamses was a city built by Rameses II; it is generally identified with Qantir. Its full name in Egyptian was "Houses of Rameses, Beloved of the god Amun, great of victories." Pithom means "House [or domain, i.e., estate] of the god, Atum"; its location is debated. Yet even within the difficult circumstances, the divine promise was not thwarted, as the Israelites "multiplied and spread" (v. 12). At this point, Pharaoh's fear has become the dread of the Egyptians as a whole. In a sense, the Egyptians and the Israelites are mysteries to one another. The Israelites have no understanding of why they are enslaved, and the Egyptians do not understand why the Israelites continue to grow despite enslavement. The gaps in understanding generate an unresolved tension. With the new threat of danger introduced, the remainder of part 1 of the book continuously builds toward its resolution.

1:15-22 From enslavement to the threat of genocide

In verses 15-16 Pharaoh decides to act against the Israelite population increase by forcing the help of two Israelite midwives, Shiphrah ("Beauty") and Puah ("Girl"?). The episode reflects what many critics regard as a motif of the Elohist (E) source, the fear or reverence of God (see Gen 20:11; Exod 20:20). It is this emphasis on fear of God (v. 17) that leads to the midwives' civil disobedience. Before any male leadership appears in Exodus, the two women know how to act rightly without God's telling them, even in the most difficult of circumstances. Thanks to the midwives, the people of Israel continue to increase (v. 20), a reward that is highlighted for their households (v. 21). The narrative introduces God into the story for the first time, in this case not as a divine agent acting center stage but as standing behind the scene while the two women act courageously. Failing to enlist the aid of the two midwives, Pharaoh turns to his own people to have every male Israelite drowned (v. 22). While Pharaoh needs the help of others to carry out his will, God's will is enacted without any divine action taken.

The passage reads nicely in a straightforward manner, yet it also creates a structure which arranges phrases in an inverted series of parallels (called chiasms):

A Pharaoh's directive to the midwives to kill the male infants (vv. 15-16)

    B The midwives' fear of God and their refusal to obey Pharaoh (v. 17)

        C Pharaoh's reaction to the midwives' refusal and the midwives' response (vv. 18-19)

        C' God's reaction to their refusal and the effect on the people (v. 20)

    B' The midwives' fear of God and their reward (v. 21)

A' Pharaoh's command to his people to kill the male infants (v. 22)

One basic contrast reflected in this structure is the vast superiority of the Israelites to any power wielded by Pharaoh. Even humble Israelite midwives are presented as outsmarting the Pharaoh, who has aspirations to divinity. These women are the first model of spirituality presented in Exodus. They do not receive communication from God, yet they know what is right and they act on this knowledge. Here they differ not only from Moses and Aaron later in Exodus but also from the male models of Genesis: Abraham, who enjoys direct communication with God; Isaac, who shows no such initiative or brave act as do the midwives; and Jacob, who struggles with God. As the midwives do not enjoy communication with God yet know how to act rightly, they are emblematic not only of women but of Israelites in general. The Bible's human models of spirituality differ rather dramatically, yet God chooses to work through all of them.

2:1-10 The birth and salvation of Moses

This passage highlights the role of women in Israel's salvation, for the unnamed women help Moses survive. Being born to parents of the priestly tribe of Levi (v. 1), Moses stands within the ranks of priestly leadership. (This non-priestly passage does not seem to have a tradition of the parents' names, unlike Moses' priestly genealogy in Exod 6:20, which gives Amram and Jochebed

as their names.) Moses' mother sees that Moses is "fine," or, literally, "good" (apparently echoing priestly creation language in Gen 1:4, 10, 18, 21, 31), and she bravely hides her son (v. 2), an act that again reflects the female courage. Her hiding Moses in a "basket" also echoes the story of Noah. The Hebrew word chosen for "basket" in verse 3 is the same word for Noah's ark in Genesis 6–9; these are the only biblical passages that use this word. The word choice suggests that like Noah's ark, Moses passes through the threatening waters and survives. His passage through the waters also anticipates his passage with the Israelites through the sea in Exodus 14–15. With him at this point in his life (v. 4) is his sister; here she goes unnamed, but later she is Miriam, who will lead the singing with the women of Israel after the Israelites pass through the sea (Exod 15:20-21). In Exodus 2:4 Moses' sister shows a concern that captures and directs the audience's concern for Moses: what will happen to him?

In verse 5 yet another female acts on Moses' behalf. This time Pharaoh's daughter enters the picture. Opening the basket (v. 6), she sees the baby crying, perhaps anticipating the cries of Israelites later in this chapter (v. 23). Her compassion for the baby crosses ethnic boundaries, and she reverses the will of her father in saving Moses; she recognizes that the baby is a "Hebrew" (a term sometimes used by non-Israelites for Israelites). In verse 7 Moses' sister returns to the story at just the right moment to offer to find a nurse, and the passage comes full circle in reintroducing Moses' mother in verse 8. Moses' mother returns to her maternal role in verse 9. Together all of these women act heroically in saving the human hero from destruction.

The name given to Moses in verse 10 offers a summary of the action in this section. His name makes a wordplay on the Hebrew word "to draw" (*mšh). The name is actually Egyptian (as in the name Thut-mose). The "cultural amnesia" about the origins of Moses' name suggests that his Egyptian background or experience may bear some kernel of historical authenticity. The Hebrew interpretation given to Moses' name aims to proclaim the message of divine salvation from life-threatening peril represented by the waters (cf. 2 Sam 22:17 and Ps 18:17 where the same word is used in David's describing his divine rescue from the waters of the underworld).

As in the preceding passage, this one uses a structure that highlights the role of the women in the action:

A Moses' parents and his birth
    B His mother hides him in a basket
        C The sister positions herself
            D The princess finds him
        C' The sister makes an offer
    B' The mother becomes his nurse
A' Moses is adopted and named

The structure highlights Moses' salvation through the Egyptian princess (D), flanked by the help of his sister (C and C') and his mother (B and B'). The story of Moses' miraculous delivery enjoys important parallels in ancient Middle Eastern literature. The birth legend of Sargon, which was current during the later part of Israel's monarchy, may even have inspired this account of Moses. According to the legend of Sargon, his mother (a priestess, perhaps not permitted to have children) places him in a basket of rushes that she seals with bitumen. After he is found and drawn out (by Aqqi, drawer of water), he was adopted and later becomes king. The similarities between the baby stories of Sargon and Moses are quite striking. The biblical story further stresses the role of the various women in advancing the divine plan.

2:11-22 From manslaughter to Midian

These passages link Moses' life to the destiny of his people. Faced with the conflict between an Egyptian taskmaster and a Hebrew slave, the adult Moses is moved to intervene (vv. 11-12). The text presents the act neutrally, neither praising nor condemning it, and the author evidently presupposed that an Israelite audience would assume that Moses is siding with his "kindred" (as he calls them in 4:18) and against his adopted people. Moses' effort to conceal his crime is unsuccessful. When he intervenes a second time, this time between "two Hebrews," they question his authority (a motif that will be picked up again in Exod 16–17 when the people quarrel with him in the wilderness). Now he knows that his crime is known (v. 14). Knowledge of the deed reaches Pharaoh, who seeks justice of "a life for a life." Facing the possibility of a death sentence, Moses flees to the land of Midian (v. 15).

Other figures of ancient Middle Eastern literature leave their homeland for refuge in the wilds of Syria-Palestine, for example, Sinuhe of Egypt and Idrimi of Alalakh; in both cases, such journeys eventuate in their elevation back at home. Sinuhe in particular flees Egypt, lives with a tent-dwelling Bedouin and marries his daughter, and later returns to Egypt. The same is true of Moses. His deed stands in some contrast to the midwives' of the preceding chapter: where they fear God (1:17), he fears for his life (2:14). Where their deed of saving Israelite life is regarded as a righteous act rewarded by God, Moses' deed of killing an Egyptian is relatively ambiguous in its moral quality, and it leads to self-imposed exile. Despite mixed signals, the divine plan proceeds toward Midian.

The land of Midian was a desert area located in the northwest corner of modern-day Saudi Arabia (reflected in St. Paul's mention of "Sinai, a mountain in Arabia," in Gal 4:25). In early biblical tradition the area, which is designated by a number of names (Seir, Teman, Paran, and Edom), is associated with God's southern mountain of Sinai (cf. Judg 5:4-5; Deut 33:2; Ps 68:9; Hab 3:3, 7). Moses is said to dwell there for some amount of time before he comes and sits at a well, a traditional site of meetings between men and women, where he meets Reuel's seven daughters (cf. Rebecca in Gen 24:15 and Rachel in 29:10). Their father is called Jethro in Exodus 3:1; 4:18; and 18:1; in Judges 4:11 he is named Hobab, but Numbers 10:29 regards Hobab as the son of Reuel. In the case of Judges 4:11 and Numbers 10:29 there seems to be some conflicting recollection about Hobab's identity; in contrast, both Reuel and Jethro are names only for Moses' father-in-law. Attempts have been made to see one of these two names as a mistake, either in the tradition or because of a scribal error. Another possibility is to regard Reuel as a tribal name and Jethro as the man's specific name. It is also possible that multiple traditions for the name existed.

After Moses helps the sisters fend off intruders, he is invited to their father's household (vv. 17-21). This sort of story was evidently quite popular. The Egyptian tale of Sinuhe narrates the hospitality that the hero receives from a local leader in Syria-Palestine, followed by marriage to one of his daughters. In Moses' case, hospitality leads to his marriage to Zipporah and the birth of their son, Gershom, whose name emblemizes Moses' situation as a "stranger residing in a foreign land." Moses' marriage echoes an ancient tradition linking the Midianites with the Israelites. Early, the Midianites were probably traders allied and intermarried with Israelites; later this positive relationship turned hostile (see Judg 6–7).

2:23–3:22 The burning bush and the call of Moses

The scene goes back to Egypt with information that the king of Egypt died (v. 23). The slavery of the Israelites continues despite the change of pharaohs, and as a result, the Israelites groan and cry out to God, who hears and recalls the covenant with the patriarchs (vv. 23-24). This presentation recalls the communal liturgy of lamentation in the psalms that ask God to hear their prayer and remember the covenant (e.g., Ps 74, in particular v. 20). The prayer is thought to go up to God in heaven (v. 23), who then hears the prayer and is reminded of the covenant (v. 24). The model for such prayer is human petition made to a superior in the treaty or covenant relationship, who then is reminded of the urgent matter. As the superior party, God pays attention to the prayer of the Israelites; God is said to see them and know (v. 25). The phrasing is a bit awkward in English (note the inconclusive dots at the end of v. 25), but the verb "to know" is a hallmark of covenantal language, indicating that God, the overlord of Israel, is now prepared to act on behalf of the treaty-vassal, the Israelites. In setting the stage for the call of Moses, these verses hint that he will carry out God's response to the Israelite crisis in Egypt.

The narrative returns to Midian, where Moses works for his father-in-law. The brief mention of Jethro as a priest (3:1) may be intended to suggest an appropriate marriage for Moses since he comes from a priestly family. Tending the family sheep, Moses journeys to the mountain of God, here called Horeb. This name appears in the E and D traditions, their alternative to the better-known name of Sinai (found in the J and P traditions). Moses has arrived unknowingly at a site of divine presence represented by a bush that burns but is not burned up ("consumed," v. 2). Moses does not initially see anything more than a natural wonder, inspiring his curiosity (v. 3).

An "angel of the Lord" then appears in the burning bush, reflecting a traditional idea about

angels appearing with fire—the angel and the fire in the call story of Gideon in Judges 6:21-22, or the appearance of the angel and the fire to Manoah and his wife in Judges 13:20. Whereas in these cases this association is made to confirm a revelation at the end of the story, for Moses such a revelation is signaled as a hallmark at the outset of the story. Moreover, this particular story adds the specific word for the bush, *seneh*, which was apparently chosen (by J) to connect to the name of Mount Sinai and the fiery appearance of God on the mountain (see 19:18). Moses' journey to the mountain anticipates both his journey with the people to the same mountain of God in chapters 15–18 and the experience of the divine that follows.

Moses' experience of the burning bush is the first element in a pattern of call stories of leaders such as Gideon (Judg 6) and the prophets, Samuel (1 Sam 3), Isaiah (ch. 6), Ezekiel (chs. 1–3) and Jeremiah (ch. 1). These narratives often begin with some experience or contact with the divine. In Moses' case this is the burning bush (in Isaiah's it is the vision of the enthroned God and the burning seraphim). This initial experience is followed in varying order by a divine address informing the figure about the job description (or commission); the would-be leader's objection to being called (often citing some personal inadequacy as an excuse, for Isaiah his feeling of unholiness, for Jeremiah his not knowing how to speak because of his young age); and the divine response of assurance and a sign meant to aid the leader.

For an ancient Israelite audience, the application of this format to Moses would serve to emphasize that he is chosen by God like other leaders, especially prophets. Additional details in Exodus 3–4 will suggest further that Moses was not only prophetic but also greater than all the prophets who would come after him (Deut 34:10). Moreover, the elaborate extension of the prophetic objection and of the divine reassurance in Exodus 3–4 serves a variety of purposes, including showing Moses' humility (cf. Num 12:3: "very humble, more than anyone else on earth") and revealing the character of God.

The discussion between the divine and Moses that ensues from verse 4 can be somewhat confusing, as it switches so much between "Lord" and "God" (not to mention the angel who drops out of the scene). The Documentary Hypothesis considers this alternation one of the hallmarks of different sources ("the Lord" in J, and "God" in both E and P). Whatever the precise literary development lying behind this passage, it may be simpler to regard it as a combination of JE. In context, it would seem that "Yahweh" (the translation "the Lord" is actually a traditional substitute used out of reverence for the actual name of God) is the name of the deity who serves as "the god," specifically in the role called "the God of your father" (3:6), or the family god who accompanies and protects the clan. In the ancient Middle East, the family god was often identified with a high god; for ancient Israel, the Lord often served in both capacities.

The deity twice calls the name of Moses (v. 4), just as with the call of Samuel (1 Sam 3:10); Moses responds "Here I am," just as Isaiah responds (Isa 6:8; cf. 1 Sam 3:4, 6, 8). Warning Moses, God then informs him about the location as a sacred site and commands him to remove his footwear (v. 5), now a traditional practice for Muslims when entering mosques. God provides identification through the chain of time back to Abraham, Isaac, and Jacob. Shielding his face in fear, Moses understands the fiery bush to be the chosen medium of the divine presence. Moses' concern is echoed by Isaiah, who laments: "Woe is me, I am doomed! . . . my eyes have seen the King, the Lord of hosts!" (Isa 6:5). This fear is familiar from other experiences of "seeing God" (Gen 32:31 and Judg 6:22-23; 13:20-22). To see the divine, it was believed, was to run the risk of death, and to be able to do so was viewed as a mark of divine approval. This belief was rooted in popular conceptions of divine purity that regarded holiness not only as absence of impurity and unholiness but also as a dangerous power intolerant of unholiness. Yet unlike the stories of other leaders, Moses' call shows no concern about holiness or about the danger of seeing God. The absence of such concerns marks Moses as a man unlike others. The response additionally anticipates Moses' later experience of seeing God on the mountain (Exod 24:11; 33:20).

God continues with the description of the past divine relationship to Israel and leads up to Moses' new job description (vv. 7-10). The cry of the Israelites first mentioned in 2:23-24 is now acknowledged by God; it serves as a framing motif in verses 7 and 9 around God's stated purpose in verse 8: to rescue them and lead them to the land of the ancestors. This divine speech concludes with Moses' designation as the divinely sent instrument of this plan (v. 10). Prophets are said to be sent in order to speak on God's behalf (Jer 1:7; 26:12, 15), and Moses' speeches directed against Pharaoh and the Egyptians are similar to prophetic oracles against foreign nations. Yet Moses' job description involves more than speaking. He is sent to the Israelites, like angels sent to help or accompany God's human servants (Gen 48:16; Exod 23:20-22, 23; Tob 5–6). The cumulative effect of the presentation of Moses is to elevate him to a status as close to God as is humanly possible without calling him "divine" or a "god."

Yet such an exaltation does not inspire pride or confidence in Moses. Instead, his dialogue with God in verses 11-14 opens with a question of modesty, "Who am I that . . . ?" A similar formulation conveying humility appears in Psalm 8:5 ("What are humans that . . . ?"), where God's universe overawes the speaker, who feels his modest place within this wondrous creation. The initial divine response is one of the assurances of the divine presence. It is backed up further by an unusual sign. Most biblical "signs" are ones perceptible and operative in the present (see 4:1-17), but the "proof" given in verse 12 involves the future. Here the anticipation of the return to the mountain in Exodus 19 is made explicit, and it says something further about Moses' mission: it is not only to lead out of Egypt but also to bring the people to God at the mountain. With verse 13 Moses presents a new objection concerned with the response he will get from the Israelites.

The divine response in verse 14 picks up from the assurance God provided in verse 12: both start with the same form "I will be/I am." Yet the response in verse 14 gives the full divine identity: "I am who I am" is the one who has sent Moses (connecting with the end of v. 13). The presentation presupposes that the name derives from the verb "to be"; Yahweh ("the Lord" in translation) is the third-person form, while the form given in verse 14 is first person. Accordingly, the first-person formulation given here is perhaps not the literal name of the Lord (which is the third-person form, meaning either "He is/will be" or "He causes/will cause to be," possibly a way of expressing the divine role of creation). In context, it is a first-person explanation of the name, conveying the point that the being of God means *being with*, conveying divine involvement and participation with those human parties in relationship to this God.

The Lord confirms this name for eternity as the one and only divine name, unlike any other name or title. As a result, "The LORD" now heads up the references to the "God of your ancestors" (vv. 15, 16; 4:5). The name is expressive of God having "observed" (v. 16) the Israelites, and it helps to explain the divine effort to rescue Israel from Egypt and to lead the people to the land of the Canaanites, etc. (returning full circle to vv. 7-8). God predicts the acceptance of Moses' message to the elders, and together with them Moses is told how to carry out his commission, namely, to go before Pharaoh with the elders to plead for permission to journey in the wilderness to worship God (vv. 18-19). The three-day time period matches the three encampments between Egypt and Sinai in 15:27; 16:1; 17:1; and 19:2. God concludes this speech with a second prediction, that Pharaoh will not let the Israelites go until God exercises divine power. Like a victorious army that takes spoils from an enemy, the Israelites will go with goods taken from the Egyptians, goods that will serve for proper offerings (vv. 21-22). The phrase, "you will not go empty-handed" (v. 21), echoes the command for Israelite pilgrims to bring goods as proper offerings for the three major annual feasts (23:15).

4:1-17 Further objections and divine assurances

After two rounds of question and answer, Moses persists with his reservations. In this third round, Moses backs up to the rejection he fears from the people (vv. 1-9). In order to allay his concerns about being regarded as a fraud ("The LORD did not appear to you"), the Lord offers Moses three powerful signs. Though considered beyond the capability of most people, they are common for magicians and not supernatural. Magical acts were not uncommon for older Israelite prophets such as Elijah and Elisha, whose powers Moses later manifests (see 15:22-27).

In the fourth round of dialogue (vv. 10-17) Moses raises another objection: that he is unable to speak. Jeremiah (1:6) offers a similar excuse. In Jeremiah's case he is too young to know how to speak well, but Moses claims to be "slow of speech and tongue," perhaps a speech impediment. Moses does not deny his relationship to the Lord in referring to himself as "your servant" (v. 10), but he acknowledges his inadequacy in speech. The Lord responds that such bodily capacities are divinely given (v. 11) and that the Lord will assist Moses in speaking (v. 12; similarly in Jer 1:7-9).

Continuing his objection, Moses angers the Lord, who offers an alternative strategy of employing his brother Aaron to serve as his spokesperson, while Moses stands in the role of "God" toward him (v. 16), namely, in telling him what to say. The two brothers will serve as a team whom the Lord will aid (vv. 15-16). Here divine anger does not issue in punishment or rebuke from the Lord; instead, it moves the Lord to undertake a new strategy that works with human limitations. Biblical heroes are often deeply flawed individuals rather than ideal heroes; the divine choice of leaders often involves selecting ordinary individuals called to do extraordinary things on behalf of the people.

The extended call narrative of 3:1–4:17 presents the identity and character of both God and Moses. The divine identity is communicated in the name, itself an expression of divine care and concern for Israel. Moses' responses show humility as his heroic quality, and in turn the Lord's response to his self-perceived limitations shows divine compassion willing to bend to human weakness.

4:18-23 From Midian back to Egypt

Moses respectfully asks permission from his father-in-law to return to his people in Egypt (cf. Jacob's request to Laban in Gen 30:25). Moses does not mention his experience of God, but his words reflect a concern for the life-threatening effects of Egyptian slavery on his people. Speaking again to Moses, the Lord declares that it is safe to return to Egypt since "those who sought your life are dead" (v. 19); this opposition was principally identified in 2:15 as Pharaoh. Perhaps another pharaoh was thought to have assumed the throne in the interim, but the text does not clarify this matter. Moses sets out with his household, using a donkey for transportation (like "Asiatics" depicted in Egyptian art). With the reference to the staff (v. 20), the Lord's speech (vv. 21-23) to Moses about his mission begins with the wonders to be worked. These will not move Pharaoh, whose heart, we are told for the first time in verse 21, God "will harden."

In biblical thought the heart was regarded as the seat of intellectual, moral, and spiritual faculties, and so "hardening" suggests a lack of proper functioning, in Pharaoh's case a lack of compassion or reason. The idea that God would harden Pharaoh's heart (in 7:3; 9:12; 10:1, 20, 27; 11:10) and then punish him with plagues seems unfair, yet the motif is complicated. Over the course of the first five plagues, it is Pharaoh who is said to be obstinate (7:13, 14, 22; 8:11, 15, 28; 9:7, 34-35), not God who makes him so. When Pharaoh hardens his heart, the story (often J) stresses his responsibility. God's hardening or stiffening his heart over the course of the last five plagues (in E and P) indicates Pharaoh's habitual, irreversible attitude as well as divine control over the chain of events. Divine involvement also evokes an atmosphere of warfare (cf. Josh 11:20: "For it was the LORD's doing to make their hearts obstinate to meet Israel in battle," but literally, "It was from the Lord to stiffen their heart . . ."). First Samuel 6:6 cites the hardening of Pharaoh's heart as an object lesson to Israel's enemies, the Philistines. The divine speech anticipates a struggle to the death (Exod 12), with the death of the firstborn son as retribution for enslaving God's metaphorical "firstborn," a term that expresses Israel's special relationship to God. The notion of this conflict as a war continues in Exodus 14–15, with Pharaoh and his army pursuing the enemy Israel saved by its warrior-god. The plagues as "holy war" is also suggested by Israel being designated by army terms: "company by company" (6:26; 12:51), "armies, my people the Israelites" (7:4; cf. 12:41), "your armies" (12:17).

4:24-31 Meeting in the desert

The circumstances and motivations for the circumcision in verses 24-26 are hard to understand. The circumcision may use older ideas associated with adult circumcision (that accompanies marriage—hence "spouse of blood"— perhaps to avert demonic threats thought to menace the occasion) in order to express the idea that as Moses returns to the scene of his crime of manslaughter (2:12), he still bears bloodguilt considered punishable by divine retribution. In any case, the scene brands Moses in his identity before exercising his divinely appointed role (cf. Jacob's wrestling with the unnamed divine figure in Gen 32:24-32).

The setting of this conflict may confuse modern readers, since Moses has left the mountain here, only to be described back on "the mountain of God" in verse 27. Contrary to expectations, biblical narrative does not always follow linear order; instead, it sometimes is ordered thematically. In the case of verses 24-26 the theme of circumcision is associated with the notion of the firstborn son mentioned in verses 22-23 (cf. circumcision in 12:43-49 followed by the theme of the firstborn in 13:1-2, 11-15). The meeting of Moses and Aaron in verses 27-31 sets up the structure of authority between the brothers. The passage then moves without comment to Egypt. In this context Aaron operates as spokesperson; it would also seem that he, and not Moses, performs the signs. As a result, the people believe, and they bow down after learning not simply about divine power but of divine compassion for their suffering.

5:1–6:1 Pharaoh versus Moses

Six short scenes set into motion the events that increase the severity of the Israelites' situation. The *first* (vv. 1-5) involves Moses' message and Pharaoh's response. As with the prophetic style of his call in 3:1–4:17, Moses is presented like biblical prophets. His message begins by stressing the commission's divine origin and authority ("Thus says the LORD, the God of Israel") and is followed by the message proper ("Let my people go . . ."). Compared with the ultimate outcome of the plague stories, Moses' request for permission for proper worship (and not complete freedom from Egypt) appears modest. Yet Pharaoh's response is not simply to question the significance of Moses' God and deny the request.

The *second* scene (vv. 6-9) shows an increased work quota for the Israelite slaves. They are to continue to make bricks with straw that they themselves must now gather. Straw is a necessary element that served as a binder; it is thought that the acid released by the decay of the straw further enhanced the cohesion of the bricks. (Egyptian villagers today make bricks by piling mud bricks in large square stacks that can be burned from fire made in the hollow area left inside.) The increased labor is to put thoughts of departure out of the slaves' minds.

The *third* scene (vv. 10-13) depicts the taskmasters' aggression in implementing the royal order. It results in the people's failure to comply, which leads to the *fourth* scene of Israelite foremen getting flogged and complaining (vv. 14-18). The passage seems to blame Pharaoh ("you" in v. 16), but the Hebrew wording aims the point indirectly at "your people," namely, the Egyptian taskmasters enforcing his command. The royal response is to repeat the original directive.

The *fifth* scene (vv. 19-21) returns the story back to Moses, now faced with failure. The foremen's wish that God judge between them and Moses (v. 21) does not challenge God or God's power; they question Moses' commission from God, which should have been successful; instead, it has only made the Israelites' situation worse. The *sixth* scene (5:22–6:1) brings Moses back to God, who redirects the lament of the Israelites. This speech before God exhibits a further characteristic of Israelite prophets (such as Jeremiah) who not only deliver divine messages to human parties but also plead human concerns before the Almighty. Here Moses pleads the case of the Israelites and his own case as well. The divine response in 6:1 is not to deny Moses' concerns but to demonstrate divine power. This final section provides a transition between the failure of this section and the renewed commission of Moses in 6:2–7:7.

6:2–7:7 The recommissioning of Moses

Up to this point the story consists mainly of JE passages. They are largely *descriptive*: they evoke an earlier era of Israelite origins and life. They offer a good suspenseful story with entertaining details (such as Moses' magical staff) or exotic elements (including the mysterious circumcision). At this point in the story, priestly compositions are added to the mix. Priestly narratives bear a *prescriptive* force: they often relate what is supposed to be taught and then followed, according to the priestly view. Matters such as the high status of Aaron and the miraculous character of divine power come to the fore in these compositions. In the narrative context of 6:2-13, Moses receives a recommissioning that enhances his capabilities following the failures related in chapter 5. From the perspective of the sources, this priestly version repeats many of the themes found in the earlier JE commission in 3:1–4:17 and adds some priestly thematic emphases. (In a sense, the priestly commission offers a sort of inner-biblical commentary on the JE commission.)

Verses 2-10 lay out Moses' commission again in prophetic style. As expected of the priestly narrative, the divine name switches back to God (cf. "LORD" in preceding J material), since it is only at this point that the divine name is being revealed, according to the view of the priestly tradition. The divine self-identification acknowledges both the equation of this deity with "the God of the fathers" and the fact that the proper name of the deity had not been revealed before. For the priestly tradition the revelation of the divine name marks a new era of revelation, one that will culminate in the second half of Exodus with the giving of the covenant on Mount Sinai. Compared with the JE history of the divine relationship with the patriarchs in 3:4-10, which verses 3-5 closely parallel, the priestly source here adds the distinctive theme of the covenant. For priestly theology this is the most important event of world history (see 31:18); after Sinai, Israel and the world are changed forever. Verses 6-8 state the central meaning of the covenant: it binds God and people together, with divine destiny cast with Israel forever, and so the Lord is about to act miraculously on its behalf. With the commission, the people believed and then Moses was rebuffed by Pharaoh; this time, the people now rebuff Moses (v. 9).

Verses 10 and 28, together with verses 13 and 26, form a frame around the genealogy that follows, with verse 28 through 7:7 continuing the story of the commission. This technique of repetition (vv. 10 and 28; 13 and 26) is sometimes used by scribes to insert material, in this case the genealogy of Moses and Aaron. Genealogies do not normally belong with a commission; the priestly genealogy inserted at this point traces the line of Moses and Aaron in order to connect their origins with the lines of the priesthood as known to ancient Israelites. For the priestly tradition, Aaron was thought of as the model chief priest, and his high priestly line was traced through Phinehas and Eleazar (v. 25), as opposed to the Korahites (v. 24), considered a lesser priestly family and known from the books of Psalms and Chronicles as temple singers. This priestly view of Aaron's priesthood became the established norm in the Jerusalem temple in the postexilic period.

Exodus 6:28–7:7 echoes the conversation in 4:10-17. It repeats the divine commission and Moses' objection about his speech, but this time the priestly account introduces two themes: the

Lord promises divine power in a manner never seen before, and it will show not just Israel but also Egypt who the Lord is. The One God is to be known not just by Israel but also by foreigners, with power wielded only by this One God. In this way the priestly version of Moses' commission adds a monotheistic perspective to the earlier JE rendering of Moses' commission. The section ends by mentioning the advanced years of Moses and Aaron. The two begin their important life's work at ages when most have long completed theirs. Is this intended to highlight the heroic nature of the two men, or does it signal the strength and support that God gives them? According to Deuteronomy 34:7, Moses' strength lasted right up to his death at 120 years of age.

7:8-13 Last chance before the plagues

The renewed conflict is a competition between Moses and Aaron, on one side, and the Egyptian magicians, on the other. It involves not supernatural signs but the sort of magic that the Egyptians are capable of performing. It is interesting that magic here is no religious issue, as the two Israelite leaders are presented as superior magicians. This section introduces the so-called ten plagues, which are rendered in various ways in the Bible. In matching poetic parallel lines, Psalm 78 has only six or seven plagues, and Psalm 105 enumerates seven plagues in a slightly different order. Exodus 10:2 implies that these traditions were transmitted orally, and some variation is to be expected from processes of transmission that involved a combination of written and oral modes that possibly influenced one another. Scripture's truth lies not in its specific historical detail as much as its moral truth (2 Tim 3:16: "for teaching, for refutation, for correction, and for training in righteousness").

7:14-25 First plague

The first plague involves turning the Nile into blood, a traditional sign of trouble in ancient Egyptian literature. Chaotic conditions in Egypt are characterized by one Egyptian wisdom text (the Admonitions of Ipuwer): "the river is blood" and "as one drinks from it, one . . . thirsts for water." Natural explanations for the first plague have been long sought in the Nile's reddish appearance in the summer months due to reddish particles of soil and/or flagellates flowing to

Egypt from the Sudan. If correct, it would suggest that the ten plagues take place roughly over a single year, as they apparently end with Passover in the following spring.

This plague shows Egyptian magicians performing the same feats as Moses and Aaron (see also 7:11). The initial plagues were not understood as "supernatural" in the sense of coming from outside the natural order; instead, they were within the power of superior magicians (v. 22). Egyptian texts record wondrous tricks of legendary magicians. A late Egyptian text (Setne Khamwas II and Si-Osire) describes a competition between Egyptian and Nubian magicians; if the Nubians prove successful, then water would take on the color of blood (turning water into blood is a common ancient Middle Eastern theme). Verse 22 also pokes fun at the Egyptian magicians: in their zeal to show off their power, they add to the Nile's destruction.

In the story of the first plague God fights the Egyptians on their own terms in order to show the Israelites the ultimate source of the magic of Moses and Aaron (v. 17). The two appear every bit as much as prophets commanded to deliver a divine accusation against Egypt; in Ezekiel 29 the prophet is ordered to face Pharaoh and Egypt and announce a divine punishment that kills the Nile's fish (cf. Isa 19). The scene of Moses and Aaron versus the Egyptian magicians highlights the question as to whether God or Pharaoh is more powerful, and perhaps by implication, which one is really divine.

It has been thought that various plagues imply a polemic against different Egyptian deities and therefore against Egyptian polytheism in general, since in Egyptian culture different deities were associated with the Nile and its inundation, with frogs, etc. For Exodus 8:22-23 and Numbers 33:4 (cf. Exod 12:12), the plagues represent the Lord's judgment against not just the Egyptians but also their gods. It is unclear whether Israelite authors had this level of knowledge about such Egyptian religious matters, but the possibility cannot be ruled out.

7:26–8:11 Second plague

This plague may have been inspired by frogs known to invade the land during the Nile's inundation in September and October. In the context of the story, the first plague sets off a chain reaction: as a result of the fouling of the Nile, frogs invade the land in massive proportions. The frogs that "come up" (v. 29; cf. the river "will teem" with frogs in v. 28) may resonate as a just punishment against the Egyptians who tried to kill Israelites, who were "fruitful" and "filling" the land (1:7). Once again the Egyptian magicians add to the destruction, and again Moses is shown to be superior, this time in being able to end it. Unlike the first plague, the second induces Pharaoh to relent, if only temporarily.

8:12-15 Third plague

The plague of gnats may have been suggested by mosquitoes reproducing quickly in pools of water left by the Nile following its inundation, but the story presents this plague in terms of dust turning into gnats. The picture evokes the image of a dust storm transforming into gnats. In this brief plague story the Egyptian competition finally recognizes the divine power behind Moses' superior ability: "This is the finger of God" (v. 15). Once again Pharaoh does not respond (as with the first plague, but not the second).

8:16-28 Fourth plague

The plague of flies is similar to the preceding, and Psalm 78:45 does not distinguish them, speaking only of "insects," placed in matching poetic lines with the frogs (before them and not after). Psalm 105:31 speaks of "flies" and "gnats" in matching poetic terms, suggesting that for this psalm the two together represented a single plague. The authors of the exodus story evidently understood the poetic parallelism of "gnats" and "flies" as separate plagues. (This reading might also help to explain the relative brevity of the third plague.) This plague marks a new level of drama in the story. Verse 18 introduces a new element: the Lord will protect the Israelites from the effects of this plague. (Readers may perhaps assume that the same was true of the previous plagues, but the story does not address the issue.) This new element is aimed at helping to persuade Pharaoh, who enters into negotiations with Moses and Aaron for the first time. Verse 21 shows Pharaoh offering limited concessions. As a result, Moses ends the plague only to have Pharaoh stubbornly refuse once again.

9:1-7 Fifth plague

Pestilence here applies specifically to livestock plague. In Habakkuk 3:5 pestilence personified appears as one of the Lord's destructive agents. Here pestilence is regarded as the smiting by God's "hand" (in the ancient world, diseases are described as the "hand" of destructive deities). Underlying the presentation of the destruction of land and animals is the idea that their well-being depends on the righteousness of its human inhabitants (Lev 26; Deut 28). The distinction made between Egypt and Israel continues, and no negotiations defuse the tension that only continues to rise.

9:8-12 Sixth plague

The plague of boils is the first to afflict humans as well as livestock. Boils afflict the knees and legs, according to Deuteronomy 28:35. Boils may refer to skin inflammations (the Hebrew literally means "to be hot"), and their "festering" suggests malignant pustules that characterize anthrax. In Deuteronomy 28:27 boils are associated specifically with Egypt. It is to be noted that Aaron's role in this plague is minimal when compared with the other plagues where Moses and he function as a team. The story of the boils brings the Egyptian magicians back into the picture, but this time they do not copy Moses and Aaron in creating the plague; instead, for the first time they are said to be afflicted with the plague. Their mention here perhaps caps the middle set of plagues four through six, just as the magicians' special role in acknowledging God in the third plague provides a fitting climax to the first three plagues. After plague six, the magicians drop out of the narrative.

9:13-35 Seventh plague

The plague of hail makes the conflict seem less like a human drama. Instead, the next three plagues shift the story's focus away from the competition between Moses and Aaron and the Egyptian magicians. It moves the drama from the water and land to the heavens. As a result, the third set of three plagues offers an almost apocalyptic conflict between God and Pharaoh. This shift heightens the divine agenda, moving from a simple request for proper worship to the divine cosmic plan to "unleash all my blows upon" all the Egyptians in order that Pharaoh will learn there is no one like the God of Israel (v. 14). Up to this point

God has spared them only in order to demonstrate the cosmic power of this deity (v. 16). The warning is unlike anything that came before, as all the Egyptians are given a chance to respond in bringing in their livestock from the fields. Here Pharaoh more than concedes; he admits fault (v. 27). Yet the tension only builds, as Pharaoh once again refuses (v. 35).

The plague involves a massive rainstorm (v. 33). In Psalm 78:47 the plague of hail is combined with frost, and in Psalm 105:32 hail comes with lightning. Hail is common to Israel and its immediate neighbors, less so in Egypt. In some contexts it is combined with burning sulfur (Gen 19:24), there evoking the east wind storm (called the *khamsin* in Arabic) blowing off the desert from the east during the dry season. Verses 31-32 give one of the few clues as to the time of year imagined by the authors, after the flax and barley ripened but before the wheat crop comes in. In Egypt, flax comes in late January and barley in February. This description implies a rain after the normal rainy season (roughly October to March) and moving into the dry weather season (approximately April to September). For ancient Israelites the lateness of the rain would be considered extraordinary, possibly a sign of divine intervention (1 Sam 6:10). Here it serves as one of the Lord's weapons (Josh 10:11; Isa 30:30; Ps 18:13-14).

10:1-20 Eighth plague

No longer aimed simply at persuading the Israelites or the Egyptians, the plague of locusts is to teach the descendants of the Israelites (v. 2). This theme anticipates the celebration of Passover in Exodus 12–13. Here, for the first time, Pharaoh's own servants plead for the Israelites' release (v. 7); Pharaoh is presented as the only Egyptian who still needs convincing. He again negotiates with Moses and Aaron, but to no avail; also for the first time, the story depicts Pharaoh's suspicions about some hidden agenda on the part of Moses and Aaron (vv. 8-11).

A massive east windstorm (v. 13) brings the locusts, which were a major problem all around the ancient Middle East. The poetic traditions of the plagues are no less graphic: in Psalm 78:46 locusts are paired in poetic parallelism with "the caterpillar," and in Psalm 105:34-35 with "grasshoppers." Psalm 78:46 mentions the locusts in the

context of a harvest, and Psalm 105:35 mentions the destruction of crops; the authors seem to have in mind the destruction of the spring or summer harvests. The book of Joel likewise describes a locust plague in the context of an east windstorm. Verse 19 uses the western wind (literally "sea-wind") to drive off the destructive locusts into the Reed Sea, anticipating the hurling of the Egyptians into this body of water in Exodus 14. The presentation of the east wind likewise heralds the dry wind mentioned in the account of the crossing of the sea (14:21).Israel's experience of westerly rainstorms and dry east windstorms helped to inform its story of Egypt's destruction.

10:21-29 Ninth plague

The plague of darkness is not mentioned in Psalms 78 and 105. The preceding plague (10:15) mentions the covering of the entire land, while this one blankets the entire sky (10:21-22). A late Egyptian text (Setne Khamwas II and Si-Osire) similarly presents a magician casting darkness over Pharaoh's court. Like the preceding plague, this one presupposes the picture of a massive *khamsin*, the destructive east wind darkening the sky (Joel 2:2, 10; 3:4; 4:15). Perhaps because of the massive severity of this plague, Pharaoh again attempts to negotiate with Moses (v. 24). He refuses the request to release the Israelites' animals, ironic given that they are needed for the sacrifice (vv. 25-26). Ultimately Pharaoh refuses, increasing the tension by refusing future audiences with Moses (vv. 27-29). This plague ends with a stalemate that requires a different sort of persuasion.

11:1-10 Tenth plague

The command from God declares not that the Pharaoh will simply let the Israelites go but that he will drive them away (v. 1). They are to depart with goods from the Egyptians (v. 2) due to their positive attitude toward them (v. 3); the picture might suggest spoils of war. This plague is different from all the others because the death of the firstborn is the only plague presented as the result of direct divine intervention and not an act of nature (v. 4).

The various plagues were evidently understood as three sets of three, or triads, capped by the tenth and final plague. The first triad is marked by the Egyptian magicians' admission of "the finger of God" (8:15), the second by the same magicians suffering from the plague (9:11), and the third by Pharaoh's isolation in his deadlock with Moses and Aaron (10:28). Each triad moves the conflict to a higher level of dramatic tension. The first triad operates mostly on a basic human level of which Egyptian magicians are nearly as capable as Moses and Aaron. The second triad adds the idea of divine protection of the Israelites from the plagues. The last set of three plagues moves the drama from the human level between the Egyptian magicians and Moses and Aaron to a cosmic plane of conflict between Pharaoh and God. In the tenth plague God's force and intervention reach a climax.

In verses 4-10 the divine message about the tenth plague is delivered to Pharaoh without description of his response. The message shows the ultimate effects of Pharaoh's refusal: all Egyptian firstborn will die because of him. The firstborn extends to male offspring of people and animals, as well as crops, which serve as offerings to God (see 4:23; 13:12; cf. 22:28-29, 34:19-20). In the case of Israelite human firstborns, a further ritual provides for their redemption (Exod 34:19-20; see also Num 3:40-51). Such ritual borrows from the literal notion of redemption as financial compensation paid to get a family member out of slavery entered into because of debt (cf. Exod 22:2). The presentation is metaphorically dense: Israel's salvation (which literally refers to military help) is here understood as God's exercising the divine right to Egyptian firstborns without their recourse to financial redemption. In Numbers 3:12-13 and 8:17-18 the Lord's slaying of the Egyptian firstborn appears as an explanation for when the Israelite practice of firstborn redemption started. These passages give the impression that the Israelite tradition of the tenth plague was celebrated in the ritual of redeeming the firstborn. The exodus story connects the narrative of the Egyptian's destruction of their firstborn to Passover.

In the context of the story, because of Pharaoh's refusal to release Israel, the Lord's firstborn son (4:22; cf. Hos 11:1), the Egyptians will experience the destruction of their own firstborn with no possibility of redemption (see Num 3:12-13). Sacrificial imagery appears in other descriptions of Israelite warfare (Isa 34, especially v. 6). Under oppressive conditions, war can show that a deity is both willing and able to act on behalf of Israelites, who call to this deity for help and call this

deity "the God of Israel." This ultimate sacrifice will reverse the situation between the Israelites and the Egyptians. Before it was the Israelites who cried from their suffering (Exod 3:7, 9); now it is to be the Egyptians' turn (11:6). There will be no sign of hostility against the Israelites: "not even a dog will growl" at them (v. 7). As a result, the Egyptians will act like the "servants" to Israel (just as the Israelites had been Egypt's servants), and they will beg them to leave (v. 8). Moses departs from Pharaoh's presence not with fear or disappointment but with "hot anger," evidently mirroring God's own attitude against Pharaoh (v. 8). Although the quoted words of verses 4-8 begins as God's speech that Moses is to deliver to Pharaoh, in verse 8 Moses is the one referred to as "me," the one to whom the Egyptians will come and beg, implying overlap in the identity of God and Moses (cf. 7:1, where the Lord predicts that Moses will be "a god to Pharaoh"). A brief divine report (11:9) and a narrative notice (v. 10) indicate that Pharaoh refuses. A description of Pharaoh's response is delayed until 12:29-36, after the description of the Passover ritual (12:1-28).

12:1-20 The Passover ritual (initial description)

This chapter contains a complex set of materials centered on Passover. The core description of the holiday in verses 1-10 is followed by a series of elaborations, verses 11-13, 14-20, 21-27. Verses 11-13 and 21-27 are somewhat redundant, suggesting two versions of the ritual instructions for this festival. Like a magnet, this chapter attracted various texts originating from different traditions (vv. 1-20 = P, possibly the specific priestly tradition of the Holiness Code [H] of Lev 17–26; vv. 21-28, 29-39 = J[E]; vv. 43-49 = P, possibly H, similar to Num 9:11-12; cf. 13:3-13 = dtr).

The initial part of the Passover ritual is marked by time: Passover occurs in the first month of the year, specifically on the tenth day (vv. 2-3). With Passover the story enters into the holy time of the spring pilgrimage feast, suggesting that this is the time when God acts on Israel's behalf. This sacred time lasts through the book of Exodus, as the covenant on Mount Sinai (Exod 19:1) corresponds to the time of the feast of Weeks (Pentecost). The next pieces of ritual information concern the sacrificial animal and the setting of this ritual in homes (v. 3). According to verse 5, the animal may be the young of a sheep or of a goat (in colloquial English a "kid"). The blood of the animal is a significant element of the ritual (v. 7). The meat of the animal is to be eaten with unleavened bread and bitter herbs (v. 8). The description reflects the domestic setting of Passover, designed to overcome the limits of any family's poverty ("too small," v. 4). The ritual prescription also reflects the understanding of Passover as a national holiday ("the whole community of Israel assembled," v. 6), elsewhere listed as one of the three great pilgrimage feasts to the temple (Exod 23:14-17; Lev 23:4-14; Num 28:16-25).

Verses 11-13 elaborate on the unleavened bread and the blood. Verses 11-12 link those celebrating the ritual of Passover with the Israelite ancestors who experienced the first Passover. The departure from Egypt serves as an explanation for the Passover celebration. Verses 12-13 describe the Lord as the direct executor of the plague. (An alternative interpretation appears in the J version of vv. 21-23.) Verses 14-20 contain provisions designed specifically for the feast of Unleavened Bread, without reference to Passover. (The well-known interpretation of the unleavened bread as a remembrance of the haste with which the Israelites had to leave Egypt does not appear here, but in the narrative of 12:24 and 39.) The two feasts are thought to have been originally separate but were linked at an early point in Israel's history.

12:21-28 Passover instructions revisited

The instructions here vary from verses 1-20. Verse 21 does not specify the animals (cf. 12:5), with the Hebrew for "lambs" being generic for small animals of the flock. Verse 22 adds hyssop as the instrument for applying the blood. Because of its thin branches, hyssop was suitable for use in ritual cleansing (Lev 14:4; Num 19:6; cf. Ps 51:9). The detailed location given for the blood (v. 22) and the "destroyer" (v. 23) may point to an old belief that paschal blood averts the springtime demonic power that kills its victims, except where the ritual commanded by God prevents execution. Although an older tradition might have held that the demon thinks that, because of the blood, the inhabitants of those houses are already dead, in the context of the exodus story the blood was regarded as purifying the houses, which become zones of holiness repellent to demonic force and attractive to the Lord.

The Hebrew word *pasach* seems to mean "to shield" in Isaiah 31:5, and the idea of the Lord's protection is explicit in Exodus 12:13, 23. In Psalm 78:49 the plagues, generally regarded as the unleashing of divine "fiery breath, / roar, fury, and distress," are personified as divine "storming messengers of death." The idea of the divine "destroyer" also underlies the two divine figures with the Lord who "destroy" Sodom and Gomorrah (Gen 19:13; cf. 1 Chr 21:15; according to Isa 54:16 God created this "destroyer"). These passages show considerable imagery of the destructive east wind (Ps 35:5), and this spring-summer wind perhaps inspired the destructive dimension of this divine figure, whose force was modeled on the military units called "raiders" ("strike forces" in colloquial English) in 1 Samuel 13:17; 14:15. The destroyer embodies the power of death passing by under God's authority (cf. Isa 28:18-19). Exodus 12:13 and 23 present the divine destruction in different ways, but both differ from the later idea of devils or Satan. Verses 24-27 add a ritual instruction addressed to Israel's descendants; they are to ask questions and provide answers about the meaning of the ritual, which infuses events with meaning. The people's compliance in verses 27-28 echoes their compliance in 4:31.

12:29-36 The story resumes

With the prescriptions for Passover laid out, the narrative picks up again. This section fulfills the divine words of 11:5-8: destruction of the Egyptian firstborn results in lamentation; in turn, Pharaoh demands the Israelites' departure. Verses 33-36 add the Egyptian people to the picture. Missing from the ritual prescriptions is the detail that the Israelites should take their dough before it was leavened (12:34). Verses 35-36 echo the divine words of 11:1-3 regarding the Egyptians providing the Israelites with goods. Given the resonances between 11:1-8 and 12:29-36 (as well as the crossing pattern or "chiasm" achieved by their reversal of sections), the two passages form a literary frame around 12:1-28, highlighting its importance.

12:37-42 The beginning of the departure

As recalled in Numbers 33:5, the first stage in the journey from Egypt to Sinai involves the trip from Raamses to Succoth (v. 37). The number of six hundred thousand Israelite males, "not counting the children" or the "crowd of mixed ancestry" in verses 37-38 (cf. Num 1 and 26), has been doubted by scholars; some prefer to view the word "thousand" instead as a homonym (words spelled and pronounced alike but different in meaning) for "clan" or "unit." The narrative refers in v. 39 to the unleavened dough mentioned in verse 34; the duplication may suggest that the two units were not written down by the same author. In verses 40-41 the chronological notice of 430 years spent in Egypt contrasts with the 400 years offered for the same period in Genesis 15:13 (cf. the 480 years that 1 Kgs 6:1 counts from the time of the exodus until the building of the temple); it would seem that these numbers represent a reckoning of generations (generally twenty years in biblical terms). With these sorts of numbers, ancient scribes were perhaps trying to make sense of the vagaries in the historical record that they inherited.

Verse 42 closes the unit by underscoring the relationship between the ancient event of the Passover and its ritual celebration in the time of its author.

12:43-51 Passover: Further regulations

Verse 19 had mentioned the possibility of the problem with a "resident alien," but had not fully clarified his status in the actual celebration; verses 43-49 address the matter of the "foreigner." This style of inserting or adding paragraphs of material to the core of the ritual (itself embedded within the larger narrative) suggests a growing priestly corpus of texts, which further clarify issues as needed. Verse 46 adds a note about the manner of eating the meal; it must take place in the house, and eating may not go as far as breaking the animal's bones (to get at the marrow for further nourishment?), a directive quoted as prophetic of Jesus' crucifixion in John's Gospel (19:36).

The team of Moses and Aaron suggests a priestly hand for this section, which adds specifications about the participants in the Passover celebration. Ancient Israelite households could include non-Israelites (specifically servants), and the priestly tradition here clarifies who is eligible to participate in the Passover. Verse 51 virtually repeats verse 41, picking up the story line of verses 37-41. This technique of repetition is used

by scribes to insert material, in this case the regulations of verses 43-50.

13:1-16 Unleavened bread

Using language closer to the book of Deuteronomy than to priestly tradition, this presentation focuses on the redemption of the firstborn (vv. 1-2, 11-16) and the feast of Unleavened Bread (3-10). In this version Passover is not mentioned at all. Redemption of the firstborn represents a ritual strategy (see 11:4-10) to avoid the practice of child sacrifice known among Israel's neighbors and evidently in early Israel as well (Isa 30:33; Mic 6:7; cf. Ezek 20:25-26). The sacrifice of the firstborn son endured as a powerful image, one that would heavily inform the Christian presentation of Jesus as the Son of the Father.

For several decades scholars have viewed Passover and Unleavened Bread as unrelated festivals: Passover has been thought to have originated as a spring rite to ensure the protection of the group and its flocks against death as they move to summer pasture, while Unleavened Bread has been interpreted as ritual for a settled agrarian community celebrating the first spring grain harvest. Israelites, however, took care of both flocks and crops, and participated in the festivals of spring associated with their care (just as they celebrated a group of holidays in the early fall, at the end of the dry season and just as the rainy season is to commence). The shift from the rainy season to the dry season in the spring brought potential threats to both flocks and crops, and the rituals of this period may have been designed to ward off dangers associated with the east wind (including pestilence, locusts, darkness, and death), captured in the personification of the destroyer (12:23). The Passover story perhaps moves from plagues associated most directly with Egypt (in particular, the first three or four plagues) closer to the Israelite experience at home.

Throughout its history Passover–Unleavened Bread remained largely a family affair, even as it served as one of the three pilgrimage festivals. After the Roman destruction of the Jerusalem temple in A.D. 70, Passover–Unleavened Bread remained preeminently a family celebration. The Samaritan community, which traces its origins to the northern kingdom of Israel, today adheres to the ancient tradition of family sacrifice spelled out in Exodus 12. Although sacrifices stopped in

Jewish tradition following the temple's destruction, Passover celebrations ritually remember this sacrifice by including an animal bone on the Passover plate. The Last Supper was understood as a Passover meal by three of the gospel writers (Matt 26:17; Mark 14:1; Luke 22:1, 7, 11, 15; cf. John 13:1).

Christianity further reinterpreted various aspects of Passover ritual. The unleavened bread and wine are the elements transformed by the Eucharist into the body and blood of Christ. Jesus himself becomes the sacrificial "paschal" Lamb of God who takes away the sin of the world (John 1:29, 36; 1 Pet 1:19; Rev 5:6-14; 17:14). The English word "paschal" derives from Jewish Aramaic *pascha*, itself derived from the biblical Hebrew word for Passover, *pesach*. Jesus as the sacrificial lamb (Acts 8:32) was modeled on Isaiah 53:7's application of this notion to a prophetic figure. Paul makes a classic rabbinic move in using unleavened bread as a symbol of personal renewal, thanks to Jesus the paschal lamb (1 Cor 5:7-8). The bitter herbs endure in the Jewish Passover as a powerful reminder of the Israelites' bitter life in Egypt.

As these examples show, the Jewish use of these symbols, as well as their Christian reuses, gains meaning when considered in the larger context of the ancient Israelite-Jewish sacrificial system prior to the temple's destruction. In more recent decades, Christians have been invited into Jewish homes to celebrate the Passover meal, helping Christians to appreciate Judaism in itself as well as the Jewish background of Jesus and the Christianity inspired by his life, death, and resurrection.

The Passover instructions in 13:1-16 capture the personal side of the exodus, as it is commanded that the child shall be instructed that this is "what the LORD did *for me*" and "so that the teaching of the LORD will be on *your lips*" (vv. 8-9; emphasis added). For Jews of each generation, to remember (v. 3) is to reexperience the exodus for themselves (v. 8). This is to be recalled with the help of memory aid devices put on the hand and head (vv. 9, 16), comparable to amulets in the ancient world, but without magical incantations (cf. Deut 11:18). This Passover memory from one generation to the next is expressed in the title of the Jewish Haggadah, the book used for the Passover ritual meal, which derived from the biblical expression in verse 8, "you will explain" (*wehiggadta*).

13:17–14:9 Succoth to the sea

The route taken by the Israelites does not follow the direct route "by way of the Philistines' land" (v. 17); instead, God directs them toward the sea. Following the early Greek translators, the NABRE translation renders this sea as the "Red Sea" (v. 18), but the Hebrew word involved better suits either "Reed Sea" or "Sea of the Edge." "Reed Sea" would point to the marshes at the north of the Nile Delta or perhaps even the Gulf of Aqaba (cf. 23:31), while "Sea of the Edge" evokes a watery peripheral area. The march is couched in military language as Israel goes "arrayed for battle" (v. 18).

The passage mentions "Joseph's bones" (v. 19), in fulfillment of the oath in Genesis 50:24-25 and anticipating their interment at Shechem. For an Israelite audience these bones would have evoked the connection of the Shechem sanctuary with the patriarchs Joseph and Jacob. For that was the holy place where Jacob earlier "set up an altar there and invoked 'El, the God of Israel'" (Gen 33:20) and where the bones will be ultimately buried (Josh 24:32). Verse 20 then includes a geographical reference of the type found in 12:37 and paralleled in Numbers 33:6. The list in Numbers 33 may have provided the names for the stops made by the Israelites in the books of Exodus and Numbers. The columns of fire and cloud (v. 21), dramatic signs of divine presence and protection (Isa 4:5), anticipate one version of the battle at the sea in 14:11-31. Finally, 14:1-10 presents the Egyptians mobilized as a military force, this time obstinate beyond belief and ultimately for the sake of God's glory (v. 4).

Much speculation has gone into the route taken by the Israelites. A journey across the north of the Sinai Peninsula has been thought to underlie the place names (13:20, also 14:1-2), since the only known place name is Baal-zephon, believed to be located about twenty-seven miles south-southwest of modern Port Said (on the Mediterranean Sea). The mention of the "wilderness road" in 13:18 had been thought to suggest a way farther south. Some scholars speculate further as to whether different Israelite groups or tribes went by different routes, but such reconstructions lie beyond any known evidence. During the period of these texts' writing, accurate information about the route may have been unknown.

14:10-31 A double version of the crossing

The frightened, lamenting Israelites caught between the Egyptians and the sea set the stage for the Lord's military action (vv. 10-14). The better-known version of the victory presents it as a miraculous splitting of the sea. This version (usually considered priestly) begins in verses 15-18 with the divine command to Moses to part the waters. The Egyptians will be obstinate and learn the lesson of who the true God is. This version continues in verses 21-23 with the execution of the command and its supernatural effect. With the Egyptians following the Israelites (v. 23), the Lord instructs Moses again to stretch out his hand for the waters to return (vv. 26-27a) to engulf the Egyptians (v. 28). This version, summarized in verse 29, stresses the miraculous divine help (cf. Ps 78:13: "He split the sea and led them across, / piling up the waters rigid as walls"; see also Neh 9:11a; Isa 63:11-14). This presentation closely resembles the Israelites crossing the Jordan (Josh 3–4, esp. 4:23; the two may have influenced one another). This version, dramatically rendered in the Hollywood movie *The Ten Commandments*, is not the complete story in Exodus 14, however.

Another version, often attributed to JE (vv. 19-20, 21b, 24-25, 27b, 30-31), involves the help of an angel and the column of cloud (see 13:21-22; Josh 24:7). Together they protect the Israelites by separating the two camps. The Lord uses the east wind (v. 21a) to allow the Israelites to move forward at the sea. With the Egyptians in hot pursuit, the Lord throws them into a panic. Their wheels get clogged in the mud and they try to retreat (vv. 24-25), but the Lord hurls them into the sea. This natural account evidently takes place at the edge of the sea (not in the middle of it), resulting in the Egyptians "lying dead on the seashore" (v. 30). This version seems to inform the mention in Numbers 20:16. Partially similar to this version is Psalm 106, which stresses the drying of the sea through a divine roar (v. 9; cf. Ps 105, with no crossing of the sea).

15:1-21 The song at the sea

The poetic song celebrates the victory (v. 1). With its numerous ancient Hebrew grammatical features, the poem offers the oldest surviving witness to the victory at the sea, and the later JE and P authors used it to craft their own prose accounts. The poem has three parts: verses 1b-8 offer an initial picture of divine victory, verses 9-12 recapitulate verses 4-8, and verses 13-18 shift the focus away from the battle to events after the victory. The initial section presents God as the divine warrior who saves Israel (vv. 1-2). In its literal sense, to save is a military image. The Lord is also the personal deity of the family, "the God of my father" (vv. 2-3). It is this God who throws Pharaoh and his military force into the sea, with the water piling up on them (vv. 4-8). The picture focuses not on the Israelites' progression through the sea but on the drowning Egyptians. How this exactly took place is not spelled out (which is not expected of a poem). To reconcile the versions requires one to reinterpret the piling up of the water as happening during the Israelites' movement (as they are in 14:22), even though the Israelites are not mentioned in this part of the poem.

The enemy is presented as an individual warrior who wrongly believes the victory to be already his, but just then the divine power in the wind defeats him (vv. 9-10). Verse 10, like verse 8, suggests a picture of drowning Egyptians. The poem asks a hymnic question that suggests no god compares with the Lord (v. 11). Other gods are known to Israel, yet only the Lord acts for Israel, and no other god can rival this one. This account concludes with the enemy ending up in the "earth" (v. 12), which can mean either "world" or "underworld." Context suggests the underworld, though not the fiery hell of later tradition but a shadowy sort of postmortem existence.

Verses 13-18 shift the focus to post-victory events. The victory is complete with the people at the Lord's "mountain" (v. 17). This is also a victory insofar as it panics the other peoples in Canaan and its environs (v. 15). Accordingly, this section of verses 13-18 balances the victory over the Egyptians in verses 1-12; both show the Lord as the warrior-king. Verses 19-21 present a sequel of song. Verse 19 reiterates the priestly summary of the events at the sea (cf. 14:22), followed by Miriam and the women breaking into song, apparently the same one (vv. 20-21). The quote of the first line of the poem (v. 1b compared with v. 21) may suggest that the women answer in song not just with one line but with the contents of the whole poem. Moses' sister, who went unidentified in 2:4, 7-9, is named here as Miriam and as Aaron's sister. She is provided with the important title of prophet. The use of the title in this context perhaps suggests that hymnic celebration by the people is a prophetic witness to God (like the psalms in later tradition).

The poem stands in its present position as a sequel to the battle. Poems in narrative contexts offer a sort of punctuation point to events; the shift to poetry marks their great importance. Finally, the poem functions as a pivotal point: verses 1-12 look back to events surrounding the departure from Egypt while verses 13-18 anticipate coming events, namely, the journey to God's mountain. Exodus 15 originally celebrated the exodus tradition at a shrine in the land (which would account for the peoples in and around the land in v. 15); the language in verses 13, 16-18 is used for sanctuaries (cf. Ps 78:54-55, with v. 60 suggesting Shiloh). Placed in its new context in Exodus by priestly tradition, the poem anticipates the journey to Mount Sinai (Exod 19:1) and not a shrine in the land. The poem's placement constitutes a priestly reinterpretation of its meaning.

The prose and poetic versions all treat the scene as a battle conflict. Unlike chapter 14, the poem does not mention Moses or his holding his hand over the sea. Nor is there any reference to an angel, the divine cloud, or the nighttime setting of the conflict. Yet the prose versions are literarily dependent on the poetic version. The east wind in 14:21a reflects the poetic rendering of the same wind in 15:8 and 10, and the image of the waters standing like a mound in 15:8 evidently inspired the priestly reading of the walls of water to the Israelites' left and the right in 14:22.

The tradition of composition reflected by these connections presupposed that authenticity was based not on eyewitness testimony to the event but on the capacity of the witness to proclaim God's victorious nature on Israel's behalf. One more supernatural, the two others more natural, all three versions attest to God's glory. The result was a collection of different viewpoints from different times, set in a literary progression that could speak to Israelites across time. This may contradict modern ideas about truth in the Bible, that only one original version can be true, or that to be true it must be a historically original eyewitness account. Yet these are not biblical ideas about truth (note that texts like Ps 18 and 2 Sam 22 contain both cosmic and naturalistic presentations of an event). The versions in Exodus 14–15 witness to the truth that against powerful evils in this world, the Lord has the capacity and desire to act on Israel's behalf.

PART II: FROM EGYPT TO SINAI
15:22–40:38

This part begins with the movement to God's mountain by Moses and the Israelites (15:22 through ch. 18). After arriving at the mountain, they enter into the covenant with God (chs. 19–31). This covenant fails on the first try as the Israelites fall into idolatry with the golden calf (ch. 32). A second set of tablets is made, and the threat of the failed covenant is averted (chs. 33–34). This covenant includes both the Ten Commandments (ch. 20) and the Covenant Code (chs. 21–23). The collections of commandments in Exodus widely differ in form and function: the Ten Commandments of chapter 20 are general in formulation; the Covenant Code in Exodus 21–23 deals mostly with civil and religious matters often in the form of case law; and Exodus 25–31, 35–40 consist of priestly instructions for the sanctuary, sacrifices, priestly vestments, and other cultic provisions.

These collections are set in a single literary progression designed to suggest that all of them belong to a single covenant on Mount Sinai. This literary presentation of the collections stresses their eternal source, yet it is evident that the different collections came from different times and backgrounds. To illustrate this apparent contradiction, three different calendars of holidays show ongoing additions and modifications (Exod 23:14-17; 34:18-26; Lev 23; cf. Deut 16), yet appear as part of the same Sinai covenant. This is a paradox: commandments both early and later in the order of human time now belong to a single ancient divine order. The covenant is eternal and timeless yet also added to over time.

15:22-27 Conflict at Marah and Elim

Exodus 15:22–18:27 contains a series of episodes that take place at three places listed in the travel itinerary in Numbers 33. These episodes, including 15:22-27, often begin with an Israelite complaint about the situation (this motif begins back in 14:10-14). In Exodus the needs voiced by Israelite complaints are not regarded as unwarranted. Instead, they show the Lord's benevolent care for a people who do not fully grasp the divine plan or capacity to save Israel. These episodes are regarded as a series of tests for the Israelites (Exod 15:25; 16:4; cf. 20:20). The book of Numbers resumes and sharpens these stories of the Israelites' complaints after they leave Sinai (Num 11–21); there the emphasis falls on the Israelites as sinners. Exodus is the book of promise moving toward the Sinai covenant, while Numbers is the book of disappointment in the old generation that fails the tests.

Exodus 15:22–18:27 stresses divine concern during the Israelite journey toward Mount Sinai, echoing the same journey made by Moses alone at the outset of Exodus. The place name of Marah ("bitter") inspired the story of "bitter" water (v. 23); this verse provides a folk explanation for the name of the place. The miracle (v. 25) recalls the prophetic figure of Elisha, who "heals" bad water (2 Kgs 2:19-22); the association with healing appears in verse 26 (cf. Ezek 47:12 for water and healing). As the channel of divine healing, Moses is the preeminent prophet (see Exod 3–4, 6–7). Underlying the complaint stories is the Lord's providing food and drink for his prophet Moses in the wilderness; Elijah in the wilderness similarly receives divine provisions (1 Kgs 17:1-6). As these comparisons suggest, E sees Moses as a prophet like Elijah, only greater (see Exod 33–34). In the context of the complaint stories in Exodus, the Israelites benefit from the Lord's regard for the prophet.

16:1-36 The manna and the quail

The stop in the wilderness of Sin (v. 1) is the setting for this complaint story (primarily P). The preceding episode is a classic story of providing water; this one addresses the problem of not having food in the wilderness. Like the recurring complaint over water in the wilderness, the manna-quail theme appears elsewhere (for quail as a replacement for the manna, see Num 11:5-6, 31-33). Manna was the secretion of insects living on the tamarisk tree and is said to be prized by Bedouin for its sweetness (see Exod 16:14, 31). Quail migrate to Europe in the spring and return in the fall when they can be captured. Verses 1-15 show the solicitous care of the Lord, who appears to the Israelites. "[T]he glory of the LORD . . . in the cloud" (v. 10) reflects a priestly picture of the divine presence in the temple (cf. Exod 19, esp. v. 9; the divine glory in Isa 6). A folk explanation for

the word manna is provided in verse 15; the Israelites ask "What is this?" (Hebrew, *man hu'*). In this largely priestly passage, the manna becomes the occasion for a spiritual test over working on the sabbath (vv. 16-30; cf. Deut 8:2-3; Ezek 20:10-13).

A final commandment in verses 32-33, perhaps authored by an additional priestly hand, shows the manna as a memorial to the Lord's care for the forty years of Israelite journey in the wilderness (in contrast, the quail was not provided over the course of the forty years; see Deut 8:3, 16 and Neh 9). With verse 36 a later writer or editor added a sentence to correlate the ephah, perhaps a unit of measure better known to the audience of his time, with the measurement of the omer mentioned in verse 32.

17:1-46 Water from the rock and the Amalekites

In the next stop at Rephidim, two episodes take place. First is another episode regarding water (see 15:22-27), largely an E narrative (possibly with J material) fronted by the P itinerary notice in verse 1a. The story line of water needed by the Israelites is paralleled quite closely in an episode about Samson (Judg 15:18-19). The wilderness stories of this sort add the idea of God's testing the Israelites found in 15:25 and 16:4 (cf. Ps 81:8), which is turned on its head with the Israelites testing God (vv. 2, 7; cf. Num 14:22, "put me to the test ten times"). Both sorts of testing were a teaching theme at sanctuaries, especially northern shrines (Pss 78:18, 41, 56; 81:8; 95:9; 106:14; cf. the preaching theme about wilderness as a "honeymoon period" among prophets of the northern tradition, Hos 2:17, Jer 2:2).

These complaint stories also stress Moses as a prophetic mediator between the Lord and the people. Moses pleads before the Lord, who answers with the command to strike the rock (vv. 5-6). Verse 6 suggests that the episode takes place at Horeb (= Sinai in J and P). The episode (v. 7) then locates this episode at Massah (literally, "test") and Meribah ("contention"). In the rain-starved Middle East, water was a source of strife (see Exod 2:17; Judg 7:24), and the names of some springs reflect competition (Gen 14:7; 26:18-33). Deuteronomy 33:8 as well as Psalms 81:8 and 95:7-11 associate Massah and Meribah with the complaint tradition. The section ends on the assumption that the people are satisfied and Moses acts correctly;

in contrast, Numbers 20:11-13, the replay of this episode, dramatizes Moses' disobedience, which prevents him from entering the Promised Land. The different handling of this story idea in Exodus versus Numbers reflects the contrasting purposes of the two books: graciousness in Exodus, disappointment in Numbers.

Reconciling the place names in this section is a problem. The priestly editor of Exodus 17:1-7 locates Massah and Meribah at the stop at Rephidim (v. 1a), evidently because of the framework of place names he is apparently using; Numbers 33 locates the complaint about water there (v. 14). This list, however, does not mention Massah and Meribah or Horeb. Massah and Meribah are known in the northern tradition (Ps 81), and it is not surprising to find them in E material.

The reference to the Massah-Meribah incident "in Horeb" (v. 6) is confusing, since this is the mountain of God (Sinai in J and P). The theory that "in Horeb" is a later addition makes little sense, given the later tradition's presentation of the Israelites arriving at Sinai in 19:1. Instead, Massah and Meribah in the tradition known to E were apparently located at or near Horeb (cf. Meribath-kadesh in context with Sinai in Deut 33:1-2). Exodus 17:1b-7 was perhaps relocated to the pre-Sinai wilderness because the association of Massah and Meribah with Horeb-Sinai was unknown to the priestly writer of verse 1a, for whom the complaint episodes traditionally occurred in the wilderness (see also Num 27:14). For the biblical writers (especially the priestly tradition), themes influenced the representation of geography: Egypt was the land of slavery and death, the desert was a place of divine care for human anxiety and neediness, and Sinai was the Mount Everest of divine revelation.

The placement of the battle with the Amalekites (vv. 8-16, E) was perhaps suggested by their living in the territory generally south of Israel. As camel nomads and traders, they interacted with the Israelites. Before the monarchy the two enjoyed good relations at some times (Judg 5:14a, literally "Ephraim whose root is in Amalek"). With the royal exercise of territorial control (1 Sam 15:6-7; 27:8-9; 30:1-2; 2 Sam 8:12), conflict with the Amalekites ensued, perhaps over economic turf, which influenced monarchic period renderings of the Amalekites as Israel's enemies (see also Judg 6:3, 33; 7:12). This view of military conflict with the Amalekites informs Exodus 17:8-16. The first part of the story (vv. 8-13) focuses on the battle proper, anticipating Joshua's later leadership in the biblical book bearing his name. Unlike the prophetic (E) or priestly treatments of Moses elsewhere, in this E piece Moses channels divine power, apparently reflecting what prophets accompanying armies into battle were thought to contribute in military conflicts. The second part (vv. 14-16) serves as a commemoration of the victory yet paradoxically contains a divine command to blot out the memory of Amalek (also Deut 25:17-19).

18:1-27 Moses and Jethro

Tacked onto the stories situated at Rephidim in chapter 17, chapter 18 (E) describes a meeting between Moses and his father-in-law, here called Jethro (but Reuel in 2:18). His Midian background reflects an older, friendly relationship between the Midianites and Israelites, despite later enmity (cf. Num 25:16-18; 31:1-12; Judg 6–8). The description of Moses' family (vv. 1-6) echoes Exodus 2. The explanation of Gershom's name in 2:22 ("I am a resident alien in a foreign land") is repeated in 18:3, which adds the meaning of the name of Moses' second son, Eliezer ("The God of my father is my help"). The appearance of the second son reflects the passage of time since Exodus 1–2.

These connections also highlight the parallel between Moses' journey to Midian in chapters 1–2 and his journey with the Israelites in chapters 15–18. As with 17:6, verse 5 locates the episode "at the mountain of God," evidently a sign of an older E tradition that located this story at the mountain in the wilderness (P distinguishes the wilderness episodes from the events at the mountain). The initial meeting continues with Moses' witness to divine care and power, and Jethro's joy at the news and belief in the Lord, followed by a covenant meal (vv. 7-12); these features are suggestive of the E source of the northern kingdom (cf. 2 Kgs 5:15). Verse 12 shows Jethro acting in his priestly role (v. 1) in preparing the covenant meal for Moses, Aaron, and the elders. Given Jethro's Midianite background and the later tradition's relative silence about him, the tradition about him in E material bears signs of authenticity, even if it was elaborated.

Verses 13-27 seem to presuppose a large, sedentary population. The judicial appointments to be made are "God-fearing" (v. 21), reflecting E's theme of reverence for God (1:17, 21). It has been suggested that this passage reflects judicial appointments made during the reign of King Jehoshaphat (2 Chr 19:4-11). The judicial system balances the military mobilization of chapter 17. For the E material represented in chapters 17–18, the tradition of Horeb involved the establishment of a Levitical priesthood, an army with Joshua (17:8-13), a judiciary (ch. 18), writings (possibly including holy battles) to be read and remembered (17:14), a covenant meal at the mountain (18:5, 7-12)—in short, many of the basic ingredients of a covenant with God. These mountain episodes fulfill the promise made in 3:12 (also E). This earlier E tradition of covenant making at the divine mountain was obscured in part by the priestly tradition, which positioned these episodes after its own wilderness traditions (in chs. 15 and 16) and incorporated other E episodes at Horeb into the priestly organization of material set at Sinai in chapters 19 and following. For the priestly tradition, the Israelites arrive at Sinai in the next section.

19:1-2 Arrival at Sinai

With this section dawns a new day in the history of the Israelite people; in fact, it is the central moment of world history for the priestly tradition in particular and for Judaism in general. Sinai looms as the Mount Everest of the covenant and torah (teaching, often rendered "law"), overshadowing and shaping later Jewish traditions. Already in pre-rabbinic Judaism, covenant giving was celebrated at the feast of Weeks (though the exact day was debated at this time, e. g., Jubilees 6:17). Christian tradition echoes this association in celebrating the Spirit's coming at the same time on Pentecost (Acts 2). The coming of the Spirit in "tongues as of fire" (Acts 2:3) echoes the fiery divine appearance (theophany) in Exodus 19:18.

Chapter 19 is introduced by a double itinerary notice (vv. 1-2a), which locates the Israelites' arrival at the time of Weeks (Pentecost). Unlike the association of Passover with the departure from Egypt in Exodus 12–13, Weeks is not mentioned here. The priestly itinerary notices are deliberate, and sacred times are very much in evidence with Passover in Exodus 12–13 and in Numbers 10; it seems odd for priestly tradition to omit reference to Weeks in Exodus 19 (unless it was reticent to

fuel the debate over the feast's precise date). In any case, the Jewish association of the covenant with Weeks predates rabbinic Judaism or Christianity (e. g., Jubilees 6:17).

The exact location of Sinai is unknown. Later tradition locates it at Jebel Musa in the southern Sinai Peninsula, but Paul and other Jewish writers located it "in Arabia" (Gal 4:25), which accords with older poetic references to Sinai used sometimes in conjunction with Seir, Edom, and Teman (Deut 33:1-2; Judg 5:4-5; cf. Ps 68:8; Hab 3:3, 7), all thought to be located to the southeast of ancient Judah and not in the Sinai Peninsula. Later disagreements suggest that Sinai's location was forgotten or disputed, perhaps even within the biblical period.

19:2-25 Meeting the Lord

Because of its initial position at Sinai, chapter 19 constitutes an important presentation of the relationship of God and Israel. The divine speech of verses 3b-8 has been thought to derive from an older poetic piece. Given its resonances with Deuteronomy, this passage is attributed by other scholars to the Deuteronomist editor, but the later priestly tradition may have incorporated older elements, whatever their origin. Verses 4-6 contain a series of memorable expressions for the covenant relationship. The journey from Egypt to Sinai is couched in terms of the Lord bearing the Israelites "on eagles' wings" (v. 4). The image, known also from Deuteronomy 32:11, at once conveys majestic power and care.

The covenant relationship is to make Israel into God's "treasured possession" (v. 5), an economic expression referring to one's personal financial accumulation (1 Chr 29:3; Eccl 2:8). In this metaphorical usage, Israel has special value for the Lord. The covenant relationship will result in Israel's transformation into "a kingdom of priests, a holy nation" (v. 6). This metaphorical application of the priestly status to the wider community is not a challenge to the traditional priesthood but a recognition of the people's special character to partake of divine holiness (cf. Isa 61:6). The people accept the terms of the divine mandate for them, which is reported to the Lord (vv. 7-8).

In verses 9-15 (JE), Moses, the covenant mediator, is to prepare the Israelites for their meeting with God. The ritual preparations and the precise details regarding observing distance from the mountain to which the divine glory is to come suggest a priestly model of liturgy. It also ties into the earlier description of Israel as "a kingdom of priests, a holy nation." The third day signals the arrival of the Lord in the thunderstorm (vv. 16-19, JE). The result is the divine mountain blanketed in smoke, which at once signals yet hides the divine presence. Corresponding to the natural effects of the thunder is the human trumpet blasts: both announce the coming of the Lord to the mountain. Precisely because of the common experience of the rainstorm in ancient Israel as well as its paradoxical quality, the storm served as a wonderful expression for the Lord's appearance.

Verses 20-25 (J) report the second encounter between Moses and the Lord. Whereas before the encounter was verbal (v. 3), this one envisions a divine fire (v. 18), which "came down . . . to the top of the mountain" (v. 20). A common way of making divine appearances (theophany) in the ancient Middle East, divine fire appears in the poetic description of the divine appearance at Sinai in Deuteronomy 33:2. As in Exodus 19–20, divine fire precedes the giving of teaching (Deut 33:4). The desire of the people "to see" the Lord (v. 21), also expressed in liturgical contexts (Ps 42:3), was thought to be reserved for the upright (Ps 11:7). As the restrictions imposed in Exodus 19:20-25 suggest, the divine presence was regarded as potentially deadly to the unworthy who see God (Gen 16:13; 32:31; Judg 13:22; cf. Judg 6:22). The sacred space is delimited according to priestly norms: Moses and Aaron enter into the divine presence, while the lesser priests and people are commanded: "Set limits around the mountain" (v. 23). Holiness is not simply the absence of fault or sin; it is also a positive power proportioned within the community according to priestly rank. The description of the divine presence, the restrictions placed on the Israelites, and their desire to "see God" are heavily liturgical in sensibility. The book of Exodus is religious literature inspired on several levels by religious experience.

20:1-26 The Ten Commandments

Framed by theophany on either side (19:16-19; 20:18-21), the Ten Commandments (more accurately, the Ten Sayings or Words) are unlike either the civil and religious regulations of Exodus 21–23 or the priestly instructional literature in Exodus

25–31. They provide general statements applicable to a variety of circumstances. Some are provided with motivations (e.g., v. 11, with a priestly justification; cf. the Deuteronomistic motivation provided in Deut 5:15). The variations between the two versions of the Ten Commandments in Exodus 20 and Deuteronomy 5 point to a tradition later modified separately by priestly and Deuteronomistic hands. These may not postdate the Ten Commandments by much, but they may represent distillation and elaboration of earlier material, reflecting the traditional ethos of Israelite society based on family units and their inherited land.

Despite consensus about their number, the Ten Commandments are divided differently. Jewish and Protestant traditions view verses 3-4 as two different commandments (Judaism takes v. 2 as the beginning of the first commandment) and follow Exodus 20:17 in taking the rule of coveting as a single commandment. Catholic tradition regards verses 1-6 as the first commandment and follows Deuteronomy 5:21 in treating coveting as two commandments.

Verse 2 details the background of God's relationship to Israel. Many scholars compare this introduction and the obligations that follow it to ancient Middle Eastern treaties between kings and their vassals. This treaty style (which is more heavily marked in Deut) presupposes a royal model of relationship that binds the Divine Lord and Israel as overlord and servant. Verse 3 has been understood as a monotheistic declaration of belief in only one God (NABRE "beside me"), but the Hebrew expression (literally, "before me") suggests a prohibition against any worship of another god; the issue concerns cultic practice, which is to lead to proper regard of only the Lord. Within the context of treaty imagery, Israel is to serve only one divine Lord.

Verse 4 forbids images of any sort, but verse 5 restricts the prohibition to religious images. As "a jealous God" (v. 5), the Lord has a singular claim on Israel, which demonstrates its loyalty through the body language of worship (cf. the corresponding command made in terms of verbal prayer, 23:13). The biblical period witnessed a debate over whether a form of the Lord was perceptible, for example, Numbers 12:8 versus Deuteronomy 4:15-18. The latter connects its denial of a form to God to the prohibition against images.

The motivation clause in verses 5b-6 appears in longer form in 34:6-7, reflecting an older liturgical context.

Prohibition against the improper invocation of the divine name (v. 7) may include a number of abuses, such as cursing and swearing by the divine name in blasphemy (Lev 24:10-11; cf. Middle Assyrian Palace Decree 10). The divine name was regarded as sacred, reflected by the substitution of the word "Lord" in the early Greek translation of the Bible and in many later Bible translations, including the NABRE. In the Dead Sea Scrolls, sometimes the divine name was written in archaic Hebrew letters, at other times only with four dots. This substitution illustrates why calling Jesus "Lord" was scandalous by Jewish standards of the time.

The sabbath law in its form here (vv. 8-11) is the first of two "positive" commandments (i.e., what to do versus what not to do). The elaboration reflects priestly influence (Exod 16:25-30; 31:12-17), with its connection to the priestly creation story known from Genesis 1. The term refers to cessation from work, and the sabbath provision perhaps originated not to rest after a week's time but to mark cessation from labor after six days of harvesting. For this reason the sabbath rule in Exodus 23:12 follows regulations pertaining to harvesting, and in Exodus 34:20-25 it stands between the regulation for bringing offerings at the pilgrimage feasts and their listing (cf. the Mesad Yeshavyahu inscription).

The sabbath cessation fits with the lunar reckoning of the year, in particular for the months of the spring and fall major harvests, which is reflected by the phrase "new moon and sabbath" (Isa 1:13; Amos 8:5; cf. 2 Kgs 4:23). The seven-day celebration of Passover and Booths (Lev 23:6, 34; Num 28:17; 29:12) corresponds to the week-long effort involved in the harvests. This may explain why the sabbath, although it was distinguished from holidays in priestly reckoning, begins priestly calendars (Lev 23; Num 28–29). In the sixth-century book of Ezekiel, the new moon would be separated from the sabbath (46:1), which would be sanctified on a weekly basis (cf. Ezek 20:20; 44:24). The seventh year of land rest (Exod 23:11) and the jubilee year (Lev 25) of rest for the land may have developed as an extension of the harvest sabbath and not the weekly sabbath. Later development of the sabbath's significance is here enshrined at the original moment of the Sinai covenant.

The second "positive" commandment is to honor one's parents (v. 12). Extending into adulthood, this responsibility included not hitting parents (21:15; cf. Code of Hammurabi 195) or cursing them (21:17). Honoring parents included honoring their memory, perhaps including offerings to them in their afterlife. Traditionally verses 2-12 have been counted as five commandments in the Lord's honor, with honoring parents considered an extension of divine respect.

The last five commandments govern human relations. Verse 13 outlaws murder (not warfare or capital punishment). Verse 14 forbids adultery, namely, sexual relations involving a married woman and any man (cf. Code of Hammurabi 129). Married men were permitted sexual relations with prostitutes (Gen 38; Hos 4:14 rejects this double standard); regulations governing sexual relations with single women do not specify married versus single men (e.g., Exod 22:15; Deut 22:22). The commandment not to steal (v. 15) covers theft of goods (including slaves). "False witness" (v. 16), a legal problem in Israel (1 Kgs 21), perhaps was expanded to include lying (Hos 4:2) and slander (Lev 19:16). The last commandment (v. 17) may cover a covetous disposition (cf. Code of Hammurabi 25) as well as actions taken in efforts to seize another's property (cf. Mic 2:1-2). In this listing, women hold a status just above slaves and animals.

The storm of the divine glory resumes in verses 18-19. According to the story, the storm as occurs during the giving of the Ten Commandments. The presentation adds dramatic effect by describing the people's reaction. They are frightened by the thunder and lightning, and their speech shows fear at hearing the divine speech (v. 19); the divine words are presented as being heard as thunder (cf. "voice" is thunder in Ps 29:3-8). This is to test and inspire reverence in Israel (v. 20); only Moses can withstand the full brunt of the divine presence (v. 21). Verses 22-26 add miscellaneous instructions about proper worship. Some scholars view this section as the beginning of the Covenant Code of Exodus 21–23, though verses 22-26 hardly look like an opening, in contrast to 21:1. Nonetheless, the section (esp. v. 22) functions to connect the Covenant Code to the Sinai theophany of chapter 20.

21:1-11 Regulations about slaves

Verse 1 uses a standard opening formula (as in 35:1; Deut 1:1; 4:45; cf. Exod 19:6; 36:21). It signals the start of a collection called the Covenant Code (based on the expression "book of the covenant" in 24:7). At its core are regulations governing property loss and damage (21:33–22:14), framed by rules concerning the social realm (21:12-32 and 22:15–23:9), with 23:10-33 perhaps added as a closing exhortation. Like the great law codes of ancient Middle Eastern societies, the code reflects a patriarchal society engaged in agriculture; social identity was based not on the individual but on the multigenerational family and its inherited land. The regulations strongly correspond in form, content, and principle to ancient Middle Eastern law codes, such as the Code of Hammurabi (also spelled Hammurapi). The Covenant Code mostly follows ancient Middle Eastern legal tradition, reflected in the citations below to law codes from Mesopotamia. Contrary to common perception, the laws in the Covenant Code do not show a generally higher moral standard in Israel as opposed to its neighbors; in some cases, the more humanitarian ruling occurs in the extra-biblical material. Provisions for the poor and noncitizens (22:20-24) are poignant, but they compare with the concern shown the "commoner" in Mesopotamian law codes, which, unlike the Covenant Code, provide some concrete rulings on their behalf. Women and descendants of slaves will find little noble and uplifting in the Covenant Code. Like its monotheistic ideal, Israel's moral sensibilities developed over time.

Exodus 21:1-11 reflect standard rulings for the ancient world (cf. Code of Hammurabi 117–19); only later would the tradition outlaw Israelite slaves (Deut 15:12-15; Jer 34:8-10). In verses 1-6, a male slave may go free in the seventh year (like an indentured servant), but various conditions are placed on family members. If a slave chooses not to go free, he is brought "to God" at the door and marked as a "slave forever" (v. 6). The word "God" may be also translated "divine ones," perhaps household gods (or deceased ancestors?) who participate in marking the slave as a permanent member of the household (see 22:27). In an attempt to stem potential abuses, regulations (21:7-11) nonetheless show women's terrible vulnerability in the patriarchal structure: they could be sold by their fathers, they do not go free like male slaves (v. 7), and they may suffer the difficulties of polygamy (v. 10). An alternative for some women in dire economic trouble was prostitution (see 38:8).

21:12-32 Personal injury law

This section addresses damages and conditions involving the death penalty (cf. Code of Hammurabi 195–214). It does not provide procedures for ascertaining guilt, but largely assumes it. Verses 13-14 distinguish conditions between accidents ("God caused death to happen," v. 13) and premeditated murder (v. 14). Other cases result in the death penalty (vv. 15-19), including kidnapping (Code of Hammurabi 14). The means used ("stone or . . . fist," v. 18, as opposed to a lethal weapon, such as a sword or knife) are considered an indicator of intent. Since some Mesopotamian law codes at times permit payment instead of the death penalty in cases involving persons of higher social status than their victims, Israel's silence at such a "solution" has been taken as a higher moral standard; it may instead reflect a less stratified society in Israel. Additional provisions hold damage to slaves to a lower standard than injury to free persons (vv. 20-21). Miscarriage due to injury merits a fine (v. 22; Sumerian Laws 1–2, Code of Hammurabi 209–13). Damage is viewed from a patriarchal perspective: the loss is incurred by the male head of the household and damages are paid to him.

Otherwise, the standard for justice is premised on the logic of equivalence summarized in what is called the *lex talionis* ("life for life, eye for eye . . . ," vv. 23-25; cf. Gen 9:6; Lev 24:17-22; Judg 15:11): the severity of punishment is to be proportionate to the magnitude of the crime's damage. This principle runs from the Code of Hammurabi to modern Western norms of justice. It has been wrongly thought to reflect Old Testament legalism because of the contrast drawn in Matthew 5:38-39 between the Old Testament *lex talionis* and the supposedly "higher" New Testament norm. Matthew's gospel, however, is not addressing civil case law but personal interactions, and no "Christian" society relies on the Christian standard for adjudicating legal cases.

The formulation of correspondence in verses 23-25 is almost poetic; here it is not applied literally in cases of mutilations, which issue instead in compensation, as reflected in verses 26-27 (cf.

Lev 24:19-20; Code of Hammurabi 196–208). Without forbidding physical abuse by slave owners, the two provisions penalize it. Verses 28-32 address the problem of an ox that gores others (Laws of Eshnunna 53; Code of Hammurabi 250–51; cf. Sumerian Laws 10). The responsibility for the ox's behavior belongs ultimately to the owner (v. 29). This section presupposes a patriarchal hierarchy, with free men at the top, women in the middle, and slaves and animals ("living property") at the bottom.

21:33–22:14 Property loss

Shifting from damage by oxen (vv. 28-32) to damage to oxen (vv. 33-36), this section continues the idea of payment of like for damage of like ("an ox for an ox," v. 36); verse 37, however, requires a higher compensation, possibly as a deterrent. Exodus 22:1-14 addresses loss due to theft, accident, and negligence. Verses 1-2 defend the right of the homeowner against a thief caught at night, but not during daytime when it would be easier to detain him (Job 24:15b-16). A thief may enter servitude to cover the debt incurred by legal penalty (v. 2; cf. the death penalty in Code of Hammurabi 21). The compensation required in verse 3 perhaps acts as a deterrent in cutting down on the thief's margin of profitability.

Though liable to unintended damage, burning fires to destroy stubble and thorns in fields and vineyards (vv. 4-5) was common agricultural practice and a well-known metaphor for divine destruction (e.g., Isa 5:24; 9:18; 10:17; 27:2-4; 33:11-12). Without banks or safety deposit boxes, ancients used neighbors to safeguard "money" (silver, not currency or coinage, which began in the Middle East in the sixth century) or property (vv. 6-12; cf. Code of Hammurabi 122–25). The procedures include an appeal to God in the form of an oath taken in God's name, perhaps at a shrine (cf. 20:7). Verses 13-14 add rules about borrowing and hiring the use of an animal.

22:15–23:9 Social regulations

This passage shifts from property loss to social matters, which also include damages potentially incurred by the household patriarch. Premarital sexual intercourse between a man—married or single—and an unengaged single woman potentially is not forbidden but it may damage the household's welfare. This situation (vv. 15-16) is somewhat similar to Genesis 34. Both reflect the perception that a "virgin" (v. 15), literally an unmarried or married woman who has not yet born children (Joel 1:8), needs protection from men (cf. Ruth 2:9, 22; Songs 8:8-9), sometimes even to the point of rape (Sumerian Laws 7–8). Marriage is a financial arrangement involving a "bride price" (v. 15) paid to the woman's father (1 Sam 18), whether or not he allows her to marry (cf. Code of Hammurabi 159–64).

Sorcery, bestiality, and sacrifice to multiple deities were known in ancient Middle Eastern cultures, including Israel (vv. 17-19). Sorcery, legislated in neighboring cultures (e.g., Code of Hammurabi 2), refers primarily to spells to harm others, and not to divination (cf. Num 23:23). The formulation in Hebrew refers to a female practitioner; magical acts performed by a female are also singled out in neo-Babylonian laws (7). Hittite laws (187–88, 199–200) and Middle Assyrian laws (199, 200) forbid bestiality with cows, sheep, pigs, or dogs. The lines of what was considered idolatry in Israel shifted over time, and strictures against worshiping other deities reflect the attitudes of those who made the rules, and not necessarily the view of the entire culture.

Rules show concern for weaker groups in the society, namely, the noncitizen who lives in Israel as well as the widow and the orphan (vv. 20-23; see Prov 23:10-11). The Bible reflects the ancient Middle Eastern norm. The three categories lack a patriarch who provides for and protects them. The poignant cases in verses 24-26 (cf. Prov 22:22-23) show a concern for the poor comparable to the "commoner" defended in Mesopotamian law codes. Cloaks taken as pledges must be returned by nightfall so that the poor can keep themselves warm (Job 22:6; Prov 20:16; 27:13; Amos 2:8; a seventh-century Israelite inscription from Mesad Yeshavyahu). When the family unit fails to provide, the system is designed to compensate. Moreover, justice is more than just compensation for individual loss; it advocates care for the weaker in society who, if necessary, have recourse to God, who will hear their cry. In the Covenant Code, these high ideals lack concrete punishment or motivation to help the poor.

The ordinances of verses 27-30 overlap between the religious and social spheres, but ancient Israelites did not conceptually separate the two. Second Samuel 16:1-12 illustrates the reviling

(v. 27) that even "a leader" could experience. In 22:27 the word "God" may be an honorific title for "judges" (or perhaps the household "gods"). Verses 28-29 offer no distinction in the treatment of human or animal firstborns. Child sacrifice was a known Israelite practice (Isa 30:33; Mic 6:7), though later it was not followed (Ezek 20:25-26). Human firstborns could be redeemed with an animal (Exod 34:19-20). Verse 30 includes an old dietary restriction against eating the meat of an animal carcass. Divine self-reference ("to me") in verses 28-30 is unusual in the Covenant Code; it perhaps adds the authority of the divine persona to the prohibition's force.

Exodus 23:1-9 addresses behavior in lawsuits. Verses 1-3 cover individual testimony as well as conspiracy with others. They also extend to wrongful favoritism of the poor (see also Lev 19:15; Deut 1:17). Verses 4-5 require neighborly help, even for someone "who hates you." This is not simply an emotional designation but refers to someone outside the kin group or someone otherwise lacking a social bond to the addressee. The legal context may seem odd for this regulation, but it offers safeguards against accusations of theft. In the Hittite laws (later version of 45) the return of a lost animal is treated under livestock theft rules. Someone "who hates you" may be more prone to suspect theft, and so it is strongly advisable to be neighborly under such circumstances. Verses 6-9 apparently address judges (cf. 18:13-27). The famous command, "Justice, justice alone shall you pursue" (Deut 16:20), belongs to a legal section concerning judges. Bribes could be a problem.

23:10-33 Religious law

Land use and animal labor are tied to the sabbatical year and the sabbath (vv. 10-12; see Exod 20:8-11). Israelites are expected to keep the sabbath on the same day, but it is unclear whether all are to observe the sabbatical year in the same year or whether all the fields of a single Israelite must lie fallow in the same year. The regulations are not simply ecological in providing for a term of fallow land; the provisions are also "conservationist" with respect to people and animals in aiding both the poor and noncitizens ("the resident alien") as well as one's "living property," animals and servants. These provisions have no explicit religious association, but elsewhere they are treated in more religious terms, which may explain the rationale for their inclusion here.

A provision to invoke only the name of the Lord and not those of other gods (cf. body language of homage forbidden in the Ten Commandments, 20:5) heads up the calendar of holidays (vv. 14-17). These are the three pilgrimage feasts when males are to bring their produce as offerings to the Lord (v. 17; also not "empty-handed," v. 15). Males are required; women could be excused for cause (Hannah stays home to nurse her baby Samuel, in 1 Sam 1). This calendar lacks provisions for Passover with the feast of Unleavened Bread (see Exod 12–13). Passover was perhaps still a separate home celebration at the time of the Covenant Code (cf. 2 Kgs 23:21-23). The grain harvest here (v. 16) does not have a religious connection with the giving of the Covenant at Sinai; this was probably a postexilic association. The same applies to the feast of Ingathering (v. 17), which later is connected with the wandering in the wilderness. Further provisions (for example, the Day of Atonement) are added in other versions of the annual calendar commanded on Mount Sinai (Exod 34:18-26; Lev 23; Deut 16), yet other additions are made to the cultic calendar commanded in the wilderness (Num 28–29). Historical progression of the Jewish calendar did not end with the Pentateuch; Purim was added in the Persian period (Esth 9), and Hannukah was included in the Maccabean era (1 Macc 4:36-60).

The provisions in verses 18-19 are connected to Unleavened Bread and the produce for the three pilgrimage festivals in verses 14-17. Blood in sacrifices is addressed in the priestly Holiness Code, which provides a rationale: "the life of the flesh is in the blood" (Lev 17:11; cf. 19:26). When animal consumption shifts from shrines to family communities, the associated provision for avoiding blood carries over (Deut 15:19-23).

The provision not to boil a kid in its mother's milk (v. 19) was once interpreted as an Israelite reaction against Canaanite practice, but this idea was based on a Ugaritic text now understood differently. The placement of this provision with the annual calendar may suggest that the dietary rules generally were to maintain temple holiness (cf. Exod 34:26); such provisions were perhaps followed in homes, though probably not at the same level (cf. Deut 14:21). The rule of verse 19 (and related passages), perhaps inspired by economic strategy (to maintain either the mother or her kid as a source of benefit) or humanitarian concerns (cf. 22:29), became the basis for separating milk (dairy) and meat products in Jewish dietary practice.

23:20-33 Promise of divine protection

This passage concerns divine protection on the journey to the land. In this E speech, the Horeb covenant is nearing conclusion, and travel to the Promised Land lies on the horizon. In context, it links the Covenant Code to the following narrative. For E, the angel would serve the expected role of divine accompaniment, fueled with the firepower of the divine name ("my authority," literally "my name," v. 21; cf. Ps 29:2). The angel reinforced with the name represents the Lord in battle (vv. 22, 23, 27; cf. Isa 30:27). Proclamations of divine victory over the peoples of the Promised Land (vv. 23, 27-31) preface commands to avoid them and their gods (vv. 24-26, 32-33).

24:1-11 Covenant meal

Verses 1-2 specify the company Moses is to bring, but only he is to come near the Lord. The others are to bow down to the Lord from afar, language used in royal letters to denote the submission of a vassal to his overlord. Because verses 9-11 again name those who are to accompany Moses, commentators suggest that these verses originally followed verses 1-2. This theory assumes verses 3-8 as a second version of covenant renewal, with reading the law, its acknowledgment by the people, and blood manipulation ritual. In context, verses 1-11 (JE) are designed to be read as a single version that functions to show the acceptance of the Ten Commandments and the Covenant Code: in verse 3, "words" refer to the Ten Commandments (20:1) and "ordinances" to the Covenant Code (21:1). In verse 8 blood binds the people and God (symbolized by the altar, v. 6). Verses 9-11 in context serve to seal the covenant of verses 3-8.

The company mentioned in verse 1 may advance to enjoy the vision of God in verses 9-10 (cf. 19:20-25), a biblical example of mystical experience and forerunner to what Catholic tradition calls the "beatific vision" in heaven. They look up through the floor of the heavenly palace and see God's feet (presumably resting on a divine footstool before the heavenly throne on which God

sits enthroned; cf. Isa 6:1; 66:1). The "sapphire tilework" (v. 10) refers to the stonework of the heavenly palace (cf. the sapphire in the heavenly throne in Ezek 1:26). Sapphire evokes the color of the heavens (the word also means skies), as suggested by the simile at the end of verse 10. Verse 11 reflects the common belief that only the righteous may see God and live (see 19:20-25). The picture closes with a covenant meal, a eucharistic communion, on the mountain (Exod 18:12).

Verses 12-15a (E) follow unevenly from verses 1-11. In verse 12 Moses is ordered up the mountain, but according to verses 9-11 he is there already, and the word for regulations in verse 12 differs from the terms used in verse 3. In general, ancient and modern readers can read such shifts without noticing; they show a high capacity to read ambiguity out of a text presented as a single work. In context, this section narrates how Moses receives the written form of the commandments. He already has a "book" (more exactly, "a document"), but a permanent copy in the form of "stone tablets" is to be given to Moses (v. 12).

Clay tablets were the norm; standing stones (such as the Code of Hammurabi) served for public display of writing. The tablets, however, are of conventional scale, given so that Moses carries them down the mountain (Exod 32:15). A seventh-century rectangular stone tablet about eleven inches square has Aramaic writing on one side; the two tablets inscribed on both sides (32:15) could have contained the contents of the Ten Commandments. The ark is also the correct size for tablets (see 25:10, 15). The idea of the tablets was apparently created with the scale of the Ten Commandments in mind.

Verses 15b-18 (P) shift into priestly imagery of divine glory and the formula of seven days. Presupposing the covenant context of verses 1-15a, the description of the glory in verses 15b-18 anticipates the tabernacle's construction in Exodus 25–31, a mechanism for maintaining holy, divine presence in the midst of a people that sometimes sins. The divine glory and the tabernacle are linked in the book's finale in chapter 40 (Exod 24:15-17 parallels 40:34-35; cf. Lev 1:1; 9:6, 23-24). Verses 15b-18 also anticipate the story of the golden calf in Exodus 32. Instructions to Aaron and Hur to adjudicate disputes (v. 14) foreshadow Aaron's role in the calf story (32:1-3), and Moses is up on the mountain for forty days (v. 18) at the time of the beginning of chapter 32 (v. 1). These connections provide "narrative room" for including Exodus 25–31 in the Sinai covenant, and the two tablets mentioned at either end (24:12; 31:18) frame the chapters and connect them to the larger story line.

25:1-9 The collection of materials

The first phase in the standard format for the construction of sanctuaries involves instructions for gathering building materials, the actual building and furnishing of the tabernacle or temple; these appear in the priestly chapters 25–31 (to be carried out in chs. 35–40). This section shows priestly adaptations to the older biblical and ancient Middle Eastern pattern that appears in Solomon's temple in Jerusalem (1 Kgs 5–8) as well as the palace of the storm god Baal (the Ugaritic Baal Cycle). A command is given to take up a collection from the Israelites for the various materials needed (vv. 1-7). The metal and wood are for furnishings and tent frames, the cloth materials for the tent curtains, the stones for the priestly vestments.

A first-person divine speech explains the sanctuary's purpose: it is for the Lord to dwell in its midst (v. 8). A transition from named materials to instructions for construction refers to the "pattern of the tabernacle" (v. 9), the model to be followed in the construction (25:40; 26:30). Like Moses' vision, King Gudea of Lagash has a vision showing the pattern of the temple commanded by his patron-god. Though following a traditional motif of building stories, these passages show that, for Israel, Moses was a leader who possessed prophetic capabilities.

25:10-22 The ark

The wooden box of the ark, gold plated inside and out, measures about 3.75 feet in length, and 2.5 feet in width and height (v. 10). The attached rings and poles (vv. 12-15) equip the ark for being carried. Gold plate expresses the ideal that the furnishings of the gods consist of gold. The ark is to provide storage for the tablets (vv. 16, 21), a purpose mentioned also for them in the Jerusalem temple (1 Kgs 8:9). The ark was imagined as God's footstool (1 Chr 28:2), but this may be an old idea. In an Egyptian-Hittite treaty, the copy of the treaty is deposited "beneath the feet" of the patron gods of the contracting parties. In contrast to this idea

in the Jerusalem tradition, the Shiloh tradition recalls "the ark of the Lord of hosts, who is enthroned upon the cherubim" (1 Sam 4:4).

The ark's measurements are the same for the "propitiatory" (the gold cover known as the "mercy seat" where the presence of God was believed to dwell) placed on top of it, flanked by cherubim with outstretched wings (vv. 17-21). According to 1 Kings 6:19-28, the cherubim throne without the ark or propitiatory appears in the holy of holies in the Jerusalem temple. Biblical cherubim are not the winged babies depicted in Western art but large creatures of the mixed form of a human's head, an eagle's wings, and a lion's body (cf. Ezek 1:6-11; 10:14-22) who protect the abode of their divine masters. Cherubim guard the garden of Eden (Gen 3:24), and they mark the walls of the Jerusalem temple (1 Kgs 6:29-32; cf. Ezek 41:18-19). In 2 Samuel 22:11 (Ps 18:11) the Lord rides his cherub on the wind. Two cherubs make up two sides of a royal throne on a piece of ivory from Megiddo; the comparison suggests that the ark had a propitiatory function as a throne, with the Lord as divine king. Adding the sizes of the ark and the propitiatory heights, the seat of the throne stands five feet in height and conjures a picture of a superhuman-size divine king.

"Propitiatory" is the same word as *kippur* ("atonement," a metaphor from the word "to clean, purge"), as in the name of the holiday, Yom Kippur ("Day of Atonement"). It implies a place where the deity cleanses the priests' sins. The context explains the propitiatory's function as the site where the Lord addresses the priests to "tell you all that I command you regarding the Israelites" (v. 22; cf. 40:20). A broader revelatory function appears in Psalm 80:2, which asks the Lord to "From your throne upon the cherubim reveal yourself." Unmentioned outside of priestly contexts (except 1 Chr 28:11), the propitiatory may reflect a priestly understanding of the cover placed on the ark.

25:23-40 The table and menorah

The table is to be constructed with gold and equipment for being carried as well as an accompanying set of dishes (vv. 23-29). The table is designed for the placement of the "showbread" always set before the Lord (v. 30). Replenished every sabbath, these loaves of unleavened bread are twelve in number for the twelve tribes of Israel

(Lev 24:5-9; cf. 1 Sam 21:2-7). The gold stand (vv. 31-40) holds seven lamps (cf. the ten lampstands in Solomon's temple, 1 Kgs 7:49; and the lamp taken in the sacking of the temple depicted on the Arch of Titus in Rome). These are equipped with items used to remove burned wicks (v. 38).

The temple's menorah is commemorated in Jewish tradition by the seven-branched "menorah" lit for the holiday of Hanukkah. The menorah has branches, blossoms, and petals, all of which suggest the image of a tree, possibly evoking or replacing the sacred tree. In Israel one sacred tree symbolized a goddess by the same name (*asherah*), and later the tree symbolizes the personified female wisdom (Prov 3:18). Cherubs flank trees in the temple walls (1 Kgs 6:29-32). The menorah also served as an "eternal light" (Exod 27:20; Lev 24:2-3), and its seven branches may have evoked the seven heavenly bodies, perhaps understood as the hosts of the Lord, the divine assembly of angelic powers.

The showbread and other items reflect the idea that offerings are food consumed by people and their God in a communion mediated by priests, a norm in ancient Middle Eastern religion and evident in biblical characterizations of sacrifices as the Lord's food (e.g., Lev 3:11; 21:6, 8, 17, 21; for God consuming offerings in fire, see Lev 9:22-24). This human representation of God was not transcended in biblical religion, as shown by criticism of the idea (see Pss 40:7; 50:8-15, 23; 51:18; Isa 1:10-17; Jer 7:21-22; Hos 6:6; Amos 5:21-25; Mic 6:6-8). This criticism does not call for abolishing sacrifice but for a deeper understanding of the meaning of the sacrificial system. Along with prayers and body language (gestures and postures), sacrifice represents part of a communication system expressing the covenant relationship between human vassals and their divine king; the terms for sacrifices include "tribute" and other payment owed the divine overlord. Critiques call for understanding sacrifice as an offering of the self to the Lord.

26:1-37 The sanctuary

The items in chapter 25 are to be housed in the structure mandated in this chapter. Behind the temple traditions at Jerusalem and Shiloh and the Exodus tabernacle stands a long line of tent-tabernacle shrines going back to the pre-Israelite tradition (the Baal Cycle), which portrays the god

El issuing decrees from his tent-home. From the second millennium site of Mari to modern Bedouin culture, large tents have been used, sometimes for sacred purposes. In the priestly conception here, the sanctuary is a portable tent half the size of Solomon's temple (1 Kgs 6:2, 16-17). It is implicitly identified with and thereby supersedes the tent of meeting in the E tradition (see Exod 33:7-11 and 40:34-38). Sheets of cloth are sewn together to make two large sheets joined together by means of clasps and loops (vv. 1-6) and woven with the image of the cherubim (compare the cherubim on the temple walls, 1 Kgs 6:29-32). Sheets woven of goat hair overlay the cloth sheets of verses 1-6 and hang down on both sides (vv. 7-13). Dyed ram skins cover the whole structure of wooden frames, which form a rectangular structure, about forty-five feet long, fifteen feet wide, and open to the east (vv. 15-29). In addition, one veil (vv. 31-37) is over the entrance and another inside splits the interior space between an outer area ("the holy place") and an area in the back ("the holy of holies"). The outer area is for the divine table setting and menorah (v. 35), while "the holy of holies" (a way of expressing superlative degree in Hebrew, so "the holiest place") is the space reserved for the propitiatory and the ark (v. 34). The model for this structure is the interior space of temples and shrines, regarded as palaces of the divine king with back spaces of the "holy of holies," the divine throne-room served by the king's servants, the priests. The colors of the clothes used (v. 1) recall the colors of the high priest's garments (Exod 28:5).

27:1-21 The altar and the courtyard

Today, altars are located inside churches, but in ancient Israel the altar was located outside the temple building in a courtyard area accessible to the people. The altar (vv. 1-8), about 7.5 feet in length and width and about 4.5 feet high, is a hollow wood box with bronze plating (cf. Exod 20:24). The altar's horns (v. 2) are marked with blood in sacrifices (29:12), and an offering for God could be brought to the altar and bound to its horns (Ps 118:27). The horns were also grasped by persons seeking asylum at the sanctuary (see Exod 21:13-14; 1 Kgs 1:50; 2:28; cf. Num 35). In these instances, the horns are a contact point with the divine. Horns generally denote power and belong to the symbolism of several gods, which is perhaps reflected in the altar's horns (cf. ox imagery for God, Num 24:8).

The enclosure (vv. 9-19) functions as an uncovered outside courtyard for the altar. A note (vv. 20-21) is added about oil, which was extracted by pounding the olives in a mortar rather than grinding and then passed through a strainer (and thereby free of dregs, hence "clear"). How the priesthood conceived the sacrificial process is spelled out in Leviticus 9:22-24: following his blessing of the people and various sacrifices, Aaron along with Moses would enter and exit the tabernacle, blessing the people. Then the divine glory would be revealed to the people through the divine presence producing fire that consumes the offering; at the sight of the fire the people would respond in worship (Exod 25:23-40; 29:43-46; cf. Sir 50).

28:1-43 Priestly vestments

Aaron and his sons in 27:21 connect to their mention in 28:1. For the priestly writer, Aaron's family was the preeminent priestly line (in contrast to the Korahites and other lesser Levitical priests, regarded by P as worthy not of high sacrificial service but of temple duties considered of lesser importance; see 6:10-27). The items to be made are listed (v. 4) before the materials to be used (v. 5). The priestly garments correspond in color to the tabernacle's cloth, suggesting a color-coded identification of the priests with the service in the sanctuary (27:16). Many of the garments and their colors echo royal dress (39:30 calls the plate a "diadem").

The ephod (vv. 6-12) was an ancient robe of priests (1 Sam 21:10; cf. 1 Sam 2:18; 22:18; 2 Sam 6:14). Fastened to the ephod was a robe to be worn over the priest's chest (vv. 13-35). Because the priest is the representative of the twelve tribes, his clothing bears two stones inscribed with those names "as a reminder before the LORD" (v. 12). The priest serves as mediator, bearing a reminder and offerings of the Israelites before the Lord and in turn the Lord's commands to the people.

Priests also convey to the people the Lord's oracles via the Urim and Thummim (v. 30), mentioned several times in the Bible (Lev 8:8; Num 27:21; Deut 33:8; 1 Sam 28:6; Ezra 2:63; Neh 7:65; cf. Septuagint of 1 Sam 14:31). Worn over the priest's heart in "the breastpiece of decision," these stones are used in a divinatory practice to indicate answers to questions posed to them. A Mesopotamian text describes a "shining" divinatory stone like the Urim ("Light"). A Mesopotamian myth tells of divinatory stone called "true word stone," similar to the Thummim ("Truth").

Worn on the priest's head was a gold plate secured to his miter and inscribed (vv. 36-38) with the formula, "Sacred to the LORD," found also in Zechariah 14:20 (cf. Ezek 48:14). Pertinent in view of the pomegranates of verse 33 is an excavated pomegranate written with these very words. The priests are so marked as living vessels of holiness.

The new clothing along with an ordination ritual (v. 41) prepares the priests for service in the sanctuary. Anointing was a common ritual marker to denote the new, elevated status of new priests or royalty. "Ordain" is here literally "filling the hands" (perhaps referring to priestly instruments placed in a new inductee's hand at the time of his ordination), an old idiomatic expression designating priestly consecration (Lev 21:10; Num 3:3; Judg 17:5, 12; 1 Kgs 13:33; 2 Chr 13:9). The chapter closes with a description of additional garments (vv. 39-43). "The clothes that make the man" in this case communicate priestly identity (see Num 20:22-29). The high priest, exiting the tent in his magnificent robes and making offerings with his brother priests, would be remembered as glorious, comparable to the shining sun and the moon (Sir 50:6).

29:1-46 Priestly consecration

Aaron's induction mentioned in 28:41 involves three ritual steps: purification offerings and washing (vv. 1-4), clothing (vv. 5-6), and anointing (v. 7). The other priests are to follow Aaron's lead (vv. 8-9; see also Lev 8:1-38). Purification is a prerequisite for entering into the holy area of the tabernacle. The offerings, laid out in verses 10-28 (cf. Lev 1–7), distinguish between their purpose, manner, and material. The "purification offering" (v. 14), reflecting its purpose to purify of sin, uses blood toward that end; the interior organs and fat go as offerings to the Lord, and the rest is burned outside the camp. The "burnt offering" (v. 18) refers to the manner of the offering as completely made to the Lord, with the blood on the altar and the entire animal burned on the altar, but the name for this offering in Hebrew denotes its purpose as literally "one that ascends" to heaven in order to gain the Lord's attention. Washing (v. 17) offerings of meat is ancient (see 1 Sam 2:13-17; cf. Ezek 46:19-23's vision of the priestly kitchens in the temple for cooking offerings). The "ram for installation" (v. 22) provides blood of purification for the priests (on their right ears, vv. 19-20; cf. Lev 14:14), for the altar (v. 20), and then in a mixture with oil for all the priests as well as their vestments (v. 21).

The rest of this meat, combined with cereal offerings, shows how priestly income derived from offerings: the Lord receives the generally less (humanly) edible inner organs and the priests receive the meat of the brisket (vv. 22-27; cf. Lev 7:28-34). The division of sacrificial income is mandated also for "elevated offerings" and "communion offerings" (vv. 27-28); the first term refers to an act of elevation signifying the transfer of items to priestly use, while the second means greetings or good, peaceful relations between the Lord and the offerer (see Lev 3). In addition to the priests, their vestments are anointed and ordained for the seven-day ritual, which focuses on the altar's purification through offerings (vv. 29-30, 35-42). Verse 37 reflects the understanding that holiness can be conveyed by contact. These rituals relate the human mechanics involved, but the first-person divine speech (vv. 43-46) explains their religious significance: the ritual site and its priestly officiants are consecrated by the Lord's presence experienced in the ritual. As a result, the Lord will meet Israel at the altar and dwell in its midst. Through this experience, the Israelites will come to the knowledge of God begun by the exodus (cf. 6:7; 7:4-5).

30:1-38 Final ritual ordinances

The incense altar (vv. 1-10) follows the regulations for sacrifices in chapter 29. It is to provide a sweet smell of aromatic smoke specially reserved for the deity (Lev 4:7). Unlike the bronze altar (Exod 27:1-8), this one is gold, corresponding to the gold altar in Solomon's temple (1 Kgs 6:22) used for burning incense (2 Chr 26:16). Sites from the period of Israel's kings have yielded forty-five limestone altars, thirty-three horned and twelve unhorned; they were apparently used for burning incense. The incense altar is reserved for the atonement rite of Yom Kippur (v. 10; cf. Lev 16:18). A census tax (vv. 11-16) is mandated for all in the community.

"Ransom" (v. 12) is an economic application of the word used for "atoning" in verse 10 (also related to the word for "propitiatory"), here for buying a person's life out of debt, conceptualized as a payment owed to God, which if unmet may result in divine plague. The words "atoning" in verse 10 and "ransom" in verse 12 help to explain the placement of the census tax in this context of ritual purification. The "service of the tent of meeting" (v. 16) could refer to priestly service in general or to the work of construction (as in 39:32); the former seems preferable, given the future use imagined for the other items here.

The bronze basin (vv. 17-21; cf. 1 Sam 2:14) is used for priestly washing (cf. 40:30-32), like the laver belonging to Solomon's temple (2 Chr 4:6). Yet according to 1 Kings 7:23-26, the laver in front of Solomon's temple was the bronze "sea," which was far too large for washing, probably a symbol of the divine victory over the cosmic sea celebrated at the temple (cf. Ps 29); this old religious theme is not transmitted by the Exodus tradition of the laver, which prefers a purpose and scale suitable for priestly use.

The anointing oil (vv. 22-33) is to be applied to the tent and its various items, symbolizing their consecration like the anointing of priests and their vestments (28:41; 29:29). Forbidden to laypersons, it is not for "any ordinary anointing" (v. 32), as it is composed of imported aromatic substances from southern Arabia, Somalia, and various places in Asia. As valuable trade items (cf. Gen 37:25), they were stored in the royal treasury (2 Kgs 20:13). Their mixing required professional expertise (v. 25). The incense (vv. 34-38) too is made up of imported spices. Frankincense (v. 34) and myrrh (v. 23) are gum resins deriving from trees growing in the southern Arabian Peninsula and Somalia. The subject of the incense connects the end of the chapter to its opening topic of the incense altar in verses 1-10.

31:1-11 Choice of artisans

The selection of craftsmen is a standard element in ancient building stories, especially in the Bible and texts from nearer neighboring areas (e.g., the Ugaritic Baal Cycle). Sometimes the divine spirit is regarded as supernatural, but in verse 3 it is the divine spirit of knowledge and skill that goes into craftsmanship, including embroidery, metalwork, working in precious stones, and wood carving (v. 4-5). The names of the craftsmen, Bezalel (v. 2) and his assistant Oholiab (v. 6), relate to the task at hand. Bezalel means "in the shadow [or protection] of God," which suggests the tabernacle's function in providing divine aid. Oholiab means "the tent of the father" or "the father is my tent," suggesting the paternal divine care embodied by the tent of meeting (v. 7). Verses 7-11 offer a recapitulation of chapters 25–31 in listing all the items commanded in them.

31:12-18 The sabbath and the tablets

The building instructions end with the sabbath observance. Like the week of six days of work followed by the sabbath, so too the labor commanded in the preceding sections culminates in a final command to keep the sabbath. The creation account known from Genesis 2:2-3 is given as the sabbath's rationale (for discussion, see Exod 16 and 20:8-11). Ceasing from work provides "ease" (v. 17) or, more precisely, a person's refreshment. Unlike other discussions of the sabbath, this one regards the sabbath as a sign of "an everlasting covenant" (v. 16) and "an everlasting sign" (v. 17). The sabbath thus represents the climax of the eternal covenants made with Noah (Gen 9:8-17) and Abraham (Gen 17:9-14).

The sign of the rainbow for Noah's covenant is perceptible by humanity, which is included under this covenant. The sign of the covenant with Abraham is circumcision, which marks him along with his male descendants. The sign of the Sinai covenant for the priestly tradition is specified to Israelite observance of the sabbath. Just as the sabbath represents the week's culmination, it completes and crowns the Sinai covenant for the priestly tradition. The mention of the divinely written tablets (v. 18; see 32:16; 34:1, 28) offers a narrative endpoint for Exodus 25–31, and it picks up the context of the story back in 24:12-18.

32:1-35 The golden calf

The narrative of Exodus 32–34 differs from the priestly instructions of Exodus 25–31, yet both may be viewed in terms of the ancient Middle Eastern pattern of building stories, which interrupt the construction project with an insurrection that must be subdued. The story is largely E or JE with a handful of priestly additions apparent. Despite the difficulty posed for analysis, the complexity of this section with its varied traditions is

witness to the importance attached to this point in Israel's covenant with God. With the priestly placement of the story between chapters 25–31 and 35–40, and with further priestly additions, the priestly tradition molds older material to illustrate the priestly understanding of the covenant.

In its present priestly form, the story demonstrates the need for the tabernacle; it serves as a means for God to dwell in the midst of Israel despite the vast gulf between divine holiness and human sinning illustrated by chapters 32–34. The tabernacle preserves boundaries between God and the Israelites even as God is in their midst. The various sacrificial rituals provide a means for purifying sin as it arises. As an example of covenant-threatening sin and the divine desire to rectify it, the golden calf story powerfully dramatizes the relationships of the Lord and Moses on one side and Moses and the people on the other.

Behind chapters 32–34 stands a long complex tradition. The idolatry of the golden calf is not straightforward, especially if the calf is to be regarded not as an attempt to represent a god but as a support for the divine throne (like the cherubim in 25:10-22). Prophets such as Hosea (13:2), however, criticize the young bull as a symbol of idolatry, perhaps suggesting then that the people did not always distinguish between the deity and the symbol of the calf.

Hosea's criticism is directed at the calf symbol that was set up by Jeroboam I (ca. 931–910). As the first king of the northern kingdom after Solomon, he erected a young bull image at his two royal shrines at Dan and Bethel (1 Kgs 12:26-32) so that northerners would make their pilgrimages to northern shrines instead of the traditionally important site of the Jerusalem temple, which was favored by the southern kingdom. Jeroboam did not think of himself as setting up idols to other gods, but he used a form of imagery in order to distinguish his royal sanctuaries from the Jerusalem temple, which used the symbol of the cherubim.

The golden calf story is related to Jeroboam's calves. Following the contribution of the people, Aaron—in Moses' absence on the mountain—accepts their offering and makes "a molten calf" (vv. 1-4). The people respond (v. 4) with an identification of the calf as "your gods, Israel, who brought you up from the land of Egypt," the very same line used in Jeroboam's shrines (see v. 8;

1 Kgs 12:28). The word "gods" here is ambiguous; it may also mean "God." Aaron proclaims a feast of holocausts and peace offerings in honor of the Lord (vv. 5-6; Lev 1, 3), indicating that the calf is not dedicated to another god. Instead, the idolatry may lie in a confusion of symbol and deity, in other words, an idolatrous symbol used for the right God. The divine response (vv. 7-10) suggests that it is Moses who brought the Israelites out of Egypt (v. 7) and not the calf (v. 8). The sin may not be so much apostasy against God as against his choice of a leader in Moses, who then responds in the classic role of covenant mediator, imploring God in prayer (vv. 11-13). The prayer (v. 12) draws on traditional lament asking why the foreign nation such as the Egyptians should impugn God's relationship with Israel (Pss 79:10; 115:2). Moses also appeals to the divine promise to the patriarchs (v. 13). As a result, the Lord relents (v. 14), but this does not solve the problem at hand.

In the next section, Moses seems ignorant of the idolatry. Carrying the tablets down the mountain (vv. 15-16), Moses is unaware of the activity in the camp below, and in this version, Joshua accompanies Moses (cf. 24:12). The noise sounds like "a battle in the camp," in other words, "noise of victory" (vv. 17-18; cf. the victory celebration in Isa 9:2). Moses then sees the calf and the dancing (v. 19). His wrath here mirrors the divine wrath displayed in verses 7-14. Verses 1-14 and verses 15-20 were alternative versions sewn together, achieving a larger thematic whole regarding divine and human anger as responses to sin. Moses breaks the tablets, symbolizing the breaking of the covenant relationship, and he instructs the Israelites in a ritual for completely destroying the calf (vv. 19-20; cf. Num 5:12-31; the Ugaritic Baal Cycle's description of the goddess Anat destroying the god, Mot).

Moses interrogates Aaron for his side of the story (vv. 21-24). Aaron excuses himself as responding to the people and offers the further explanation that the calf "came out" from the fire as if on its own power (v. 24); yet the verb may be—or may be a pun on—"come out" as a technical term of metallurgy (Prov 25:4; cf. English expression of how "a cake turns out"). Moses summons the Levites to purge the camp of sinners (vv. 25-29).

The story then describes the process of Israel's atonement for Israel, another prayer by Moses offering to be the mediator in place of the people

(vv. 30-32). He would prefer to see himself rather than the people stricken from the heavenly book that keeps a record of good and bad human deeds (Ps 69:29; cf. Dan 7:10). A divine promise to destroy only those who have sinned is at odds with the earlier verses presenting the people as a whole participating in the revelry. Such a distinction recalls a liturgical setting of prayer that God postpone divine judgment; Israel averts the evil decree, for now.

The divine answer also states that an angel will lead the people. At this point, such a divine statement seems a favorable omen, a positive promise. In context here it also sets up the question of the nature of divine presence that chapters 33–34 address. Overall these chapters show a polemic directed against the priestly line of Aaron in favor of the Levitical priests, perhaps by priests of Shiloh who disapproved of Jeroboam's shrines (cf. the story praising a comparable action taken by the descendant of Aaron in Num 25:6-13). Yet chapters 32–34 are also concerned more broadly with important questions of divine presence and sin. How can a holy God move forward with Israel as it sins?

33:1-11 Moses in the middle

Chapter 32 illustrates the need for human mediation between God and the people: how now shall God accompany Israel to the Promised Land? Chapters 33–34 answer this question with a masterpiece structured with thematically inverted sections (chiasm) to dramatize Moses' crucial role in convincing God to help Israel and in representing the divine presence to Israel:

A: 33:1-11 An angel to accompany the Israelites (vv. 1-6); Moses' mediation (vv. 7-11)

   B: 33:12-17 Moses' intercession

      C: 33:18-23 Moses asks to see God

      C': 34:1-8 Moses sees God

   B': 34:8-9 Moses' intercession

A': 34:10-35 The Lord to accompany the Israelites (vv. 10-28); Moses' new mediation (vv. 29-35)

Exodus 33:1-11 (marked A in the chiasm above) continues the theme of angelic accompaniment from 32:33-34, but here it is an insufficient sign of presence contrasted with the actual divine presence. The scene (vv. 1-6), which draws on Deuteronomistic language used elsewhere for the Promised Land and for the foreign peoples there, ends with the Israelites in mourning ("no one wore any ornaments," v. 4, see v. 6). Verses 7-11 stop the story momentarily to describe how God and Moses used to interact at the tent of meeting. After noting that anyone could go to the tent in order "to consult the LORD" (v. 7), Moses, along with Joshua, is said to enter it (vv. 8-11). As a mark of Moses' special favor, the divine column of cloud descends over the tent (this E tradition of the tent will be superseded by the priestly tradition's "tabernacle, with its tent," 35:11; see 40:34-38). The Lord is said to speak face-to-face with Moses, establishing a proximity with the divine unachieved by any other mortal. This passage falls just short of stating that Moses sees God. According to an older tradition, Moses does see God (cf. 24:11; cf. Moses and God directly speaking with direct vision in Num 12:8). This chapter modifies and explores this notion and its significance for Israel's relationship with God.

33:12-17 (B) Moses' intercession

The dialogue alternates between Moses and God in a manner not seen in Scripture since Abraham. Moses, as the Lord's "intimate friend" who has found divine favor, frames this section (vv. 12, 17); it is this special relationship, and not the Israelites themselves, that motivates the Lord's willingness to accompany them. Moses appeals to his special relationship with God and complains that God has not told him whom God will send with him (vv. 12-13). God has mentioned the angel (v. 2); perhaps Moses' returning to the issue represents an indirect way of suggesting that an angel is not good enough. The divine response (v. 14), agreeing to God's very self instead, seems to answer the implicit request for divine rather than angelic accompaniment. In his statement (v. 15), does Moses detect divine reluctance? Moses pursues the implication: divine absence implies divine disfavor (v. 16). God restates his agreement to Moses' request and reiterates Moses' favor with God (v. 17).

33:18-23 (C) Moses' request to see God

Moses pursues his special relationship with the Lord in asking to see the divine glory (v. 18).

The Lord responds with an offer of divine beauty accompanied by a pronouncement of the divine name (v. 19), yet Moses is denied direct vision of the divine face (v. 20). Instead, God offers a partial vision, the sight of the divine back as the divine glory passes by (v. 23; cf. Jer 18:17).

This scene recalls the prophet Elijah, who travels forty days to Mount Horeb following his conflict with idolaters (1 Kgs 18–19). Moses in similar fashion has been on the mountain for forty days during the Israelite idolatry (Exod 32; cf. 24:18; 34:18). Moses' experience (vv. 22-23) echoes other features of Elijah's experience of God on Mount Horeb. Just as Elijah goes to the entrance of the cave to experience God (1 Kgs 19:13), so Moses will station himself on the rock (v. 22). Just as the Lord passes by Elijah (1 Kgs 19:11), so too Moses is to experience the Lord passing by (vv. 19, 22). Whereas Elijah covers his eyes (1 Kgs 19:13), God covers Moses' sight with the divine hand (vv. 22-23). Revelation to both figures expresses the ineffable quality of the divine. For as close as Elijah gets, the Lord is—contrary to older biblical revelations of God—not in the wind, nor in the earthquake nor in the fire but in "a light silent sound" (1 Kgs 19:11-12), a medium mysterious yet appropriate for a prophet who speaks as God's agent.

For the northern E tradition of this passage, Moses was the prophet of the original covenant, Elijah its fiery enforcer. Malachi 3:22-24 mentions Moses, the prophet of the ancient covenant on Horeb, with Elijah, a figure of the prophet who heralds the coming day of the Lord. The ancient and future covenant prophets in the Old Testament inform the New Testament understanding of John the Baptist as an Elijah figure who heralds the coming of Jesus the Lord (e.g., Matt 11:10, combining Mal 3:1 with Exod 23:20); in this way, the end of the Old Testament connects to the start of the New Testament. Given the parallels between Elijah and Moses, the tradition of 1 Kings 18–19 informed Exodus 33's prophetic picture of Moses, greater than even the great Elijah. Yet the chapter is more complex. Moses can witness divine glory, beauty, and name, but not God's face. By drawing on Israelite liturgy (Pss 27:4; 13; 29:2; 42:3), these terms connect the audience's experience with Moses' desire for communion with God. Moses' greatness is more than being greater than Elijah; he also nearly attains the ideal of

Israelite pilgrimage feasts—divine presence and vision of God.

34:1-8 (C') Moses and God

This section does not describe the divine manifestation first but returns to the tablets (v. 1). The placement of the tablets before the theophany points to an additional sign of Moses' greatness. His divine communion advances Israel's covenant with the Lord; Moses and the covenant literally go together in this section (vv. 2-4). The narrative (vv. 5-9) then offers a unique moment of liturgical transcendence. In the cloud denoting the paradox of presence hidden from view, "the LORD . . . stood with him" and proclaimed the divine name to him (v. 5). The presentation has a liturgical atmosphere like the Day of Atonement, when the high priest is said to pronounce the divine name (cf. Sir 50:20, Mishnah, Yoma 6.2, and Sotah 7.6). The proclamation of divine attributes (vv. 6-7) is likewise the stuff of prayer (Neh 9:17; Pss 86:15; 99:8; cf. Num 14:17-18), showing hope for divine compassion even as divine justice is acknowledged.

34:8-9 (B') Moses' response

Continuing the liturgical picture, Moses bows down in worship (v. 8). Moses again asks for the Lord to accompany the people (v. 9). Despite its brevity, this section echoes the dialogue over divine accompaniment in chapter 33 (cf. 34:9 with 33:3, 5). This interlude also provides an introduction to the refashioning of the commandments. Divine presence is premised on the commandments.

34:10-35 (A') The terms of the covenant

The commandments to be written on the second set of tablets include variants of three of the Ten Commandments (20:2-17): prohibitions against worship of other deities (v. 14) and against making "molten gods" (v. 17) as well as the sabbath requirement (v. 21). The commandments are otherwise a cultic calendar (vv. 18-25) that compares with 23:12-19. The passage gives the impression of being a second Ten Commandments (v. 28), but it combines some of the Ten Commandments with material from the calendar of pilgrimage festivals in Exodus 23. This new form of the Ten Commandments (v. 28) presents an implicit claim that the regulations of the Covenant Code

in Exodus 21–23 hold the same divine authority as the original Ten Commandments in Exodus 20.

Moses writes down the commandments, echoing his earlier forty-day stay on the mountain (vv. 27-28; cf. 24:12, 18). He returns, burnished with the frightening radiance of the divine presence (vv. 29-31). Moses summons the people and presents the commandments: the mediator and the commandments go together (v. 32). As a new way to mediate (vv. 33-35), the veil is removed whenever Moses meets with God and he speaks to the Israelites; otherwise, his face is veiled. The divine radiance is imprinted on Moses, and the divine word is heard by him; in turn, he conveys the divine presence and word to the people. Overall, Exodus 32–34 places Moses at the center of God's relationship with Israel. It partially identifies Moses with God, whom Moses can partially glimpse, and it separates him from the people in his special service as the bearer of the divine presence. No golden calf or any other lifeless image can symbolize the divine. Moses becomes the living icon of the God alive in Israel's life. While these chapters mark a highpoint in the story, one final moment of divine glory awaits at the end of Exodus.

35:1–36:7 Sabbath, contribution, and craftsmen

Shifting from the JE story back to the priestly dwelling construction, the next major stage in the building pattern is the execution of the divine instructions. The command to observe the sabbath (vv. 1-3) is a priestly modification of this standard pattern. Two standard preparations for building commands follow: the command to secure materials (vv. 4-9) and the execution (vv. 20-29), and the summoning of craftsmen reiterated (vv. 10-19) and the execution (35:30–36:7). These topics connect to the beginning and end of chapters 25–31: sabbath (vv. 1-3) and craftsmen (vv. 10-19) connect the end of the commands (ch. 31) with the beginning of their execution, while the discussion of materials (vv. 4-9) connects to the beginning of the commands (25:3-7). The mention of the sabbath here adds a limitation on the use of fire (v. 3).

36:8–39:43 Execution of the instructions

The next major component of building stories is the construction of the items commanded (chs. 25–31). The tabernacle's construction (ch. 36) precedes the making of the ark, table, and the menorah (chs. 37–38) that go inside it, in contrast to the commands for them (chs. 25–26). The progression is from the outside inward. This section largely follows chapters 25–31 with the emphasis that the final product corresponds to the instructions. For the tent cloth, coverings, wood frames, and veils (36:8-38), see 26:1-29, 31-37. For the ark with the propitiatory, table, and menorah (37:1-24), see 25:10-39. For the altar of incense (37:25-28), the anointing oil, and fragrant incense (37:29), see 30:1-6, 23-25, 34-36. For the priestly vestments (39:1-31), see 28:1-43. For the census tax (30:11-16), see 38:21-31, which adds a balance sheet for the amount of metals used for the various items of the tabernacle.

Exodus 38:8 adds that the bronze basin (30:18-21) is made from the mirrors of the women who serve at the entrance of the tent. The service is unspecified, but the parallel in 1 Samuel 2:22 suggests it is sexual in nature. In the latter verse, Eli's sons "were behaving promiscuously" with women (literally, "lying with the women") at the Shiloh sanctuary. The sexual offense was evidently neither rape nor failure to pay for sex, but sexual relations considered improper for priests (Lev 21, esp. v. 7). In Genesis 38:15-24, Tamar, disguised as a "sacred" woman, is also called a prostitute. Sexual relations evidently transpired around sanctuaries (cf. Hos 4:13-15; Amos 7:17) and were perhaps sponsored by them in order to generate revenue (cf. Lev. 19:29; 21:9). Women of families in deep economic trouble had limited options; prostitution was one alternative, slavery another (Exod 21:7).

The items made are now brought to Moses (39:32-43). Their listing (vv. 33-41) is framed by the statement that the Israelites did the work just as it had been commanded (vv. 32, 42). The paragraph ends with a deliberate echo of the Genesis creation story: Moses' seeing the work and blessing it (v. 43) echoes God's looking at all that God had made (Gen 1:31) and blessing the work of creation (Gen 2:3). This resonance sets up an implicit comparison between cosmic creation and the divine dwelling.

40:1-38 Conclusion

The last major element in building stories involves the structure's dedication, culminating in the deity's entry into the newly built abode. The divine speech (vv. 2-15) opens with an important date (v. 2): the first day of the first month is New Year (Rosh Hashanah), later symbolizing creation and renovation of the world. In context here, the completion of the tabernacle marks a moment of new creation. The items are to be brought into the erected tabernacle (vv. 2-8). The order of items begins with the ark, the item belonging in the most sacred area of the tabernacle, and then proceeds from inside to outside. All the items are to be anointed (vv. 9-11) in order to mark their elevated, holy status. The priestly personnel to serve the tabernacle are also to be anointed (vv. 12-15). Reflecting its hereditary nature, the priesthood is a family household consisting of a priestly "father" and his "sons" (Sir 50:12-13). It is also "a perpetual priesthood," serving as maintainer and sign of the "eternal covenant" with Israel.

The final instructions (vv. 2-15) are matched by their implementation (vv. 16-33), stressing that Moses followed the directions exactly. Overall Moses' work is recounted in more elaborate terms than the divine instructions. To follow the instructions exactly does not mean a word-by-word copying of the commands, but following them to the utmost, both explicitly and implicitly. The description does not mention the anointing of the priests commanded in the instructions (vv. 12-15); instead, it substitutes a discussion of the washing of the priests in the water in the basin (vv. 31-32).

The description ends (v. 33b) with an echo of the Genesis creation story: "Moses finished all the work" resonates with the statement that "God completed the work" (Gen 2:2). This echo, like those at the end of chapter 39, may seem slight to readers today, but in the verbally sensitive circles of the priestly tradition that produced both the Genesis 1:1–2:3a creation story and the priestly sections of Exodus 25–31 and 35–40, these verbal links were strongly heard as casting the dwelling in terms of cosmic creation, as found in other creation and tabernacle/temple-building accounts ("He built his shrine like the heavens, / like the earth which he founded forever," Ps 78:69). These resonances indicate that the completion of the tabernacle is to be understood as an event of cosmic importance.

The final act of Exodus now takes place (vv. 34-38). With the work completed, the divine cloud covers the meeting tent, and the divine glory fills the tabernacle. The wording corresponds to the description of the divine glory on Mount Sinai (24:15-17; see also Lev 1:1; 9:6, 23-24; cf. 1 Kgs 8:10-11; Isa 6:3). The new tabernacle replaces the divine mountain by providing a mobile mechanism for divine presence and communication. The cloud replaces the older pillar of cloud and pillar of fire (see 13:21-22; 14:19-20; 33:7-11), which will indicate when and how long the Israelites will encamp (Num 9:15-23; 10:11-28). Just as Moses was promised (Exod 32–34), they will be accompanied by God as they travel in stages to the Promised Land. Absorbing the insights of older traditions, the priestly tradition's new theological creation brilliantly addressed Israel's situation whether at home or in exile. At home it provided a standard for worship in Jerusalem, and it also offered hope of divine presence despite exile and utter loss.

THE BOOK OF
LEVITICUS

J. Edward Owens, O.SS.T.

INTRODUCTION

Leviticus often seems a strange and antiquated book to the modern reader. Its prescriptions regarding cleanliness, diet, and liturgy hardly resonate with modern science, culture, and religion. However, it is noteworthy that the first chapters of Leviticus were traditionally a primer for Jewish children at the synagogue. The rationale for this choice deserves comment. Let the children who are pure learn about sacrifices that are pure. Let the pure begin their educational journey with what is holy, wholesome, and whole.

Although the modern reader may question such reasoning, I suggest that it bespeaks timeless pedagogical values on at least two levels. First, Leviticus teaches us to appreciate rules of right conduct based on clear and measurable standards. Small children have yet to understand abstract thinking and complex moral issues, so how "age appropriate" it is to introduce them to material of some catechetical nature, i.e., moral lessons about the fundamentals of one's religion. Second, education promotes ongoing cultural and religious values. What are the abiding canons of right conduct, liturgical integrity, accountability to the community, and building a better future for the next generation?

This is the stuff of Leviticus that speaks to the Old Testament theology of "teaching to remember" that begins with the exodus story of the first Passover: "When your children ask you, 'What does this rite of yours mean?' you will reply, 'It is the Passover sacrifice for the Lord, who passed over the houses of the Israelites in Egypt; when he struck down the Egyptians, he delivered our houses'" (Exod 12:26-27). The saga must ever be retold lest it be forgotten.

With the emergence of Judaism in the postexilic periods (the Persian [539–333 B.C.] and subsequent Greco-Roman period), preservation of Israel's heritage took on great importance. The Torah (the first five books of the Bible, also called the Pentateuch) became canonical. The Israelite monarchy had ended with the Babylonian exile and new groups assumed leadership roles in Judaism, among them the Sadducees, Pharisees, priests, scribes, and elders. The second temple cult held sway in Jerusalem, but the Diaspora Jews had the synagogues in communities outside of Palestine.

With such cultural and religious diversity, the saga of Israel as a people and nation had to be preserved. This agenda led to the designation of canonical books, i.e., the scriptural heritage that was inspired and authoritative as God's timeless word. The book of Leviticus played a role in this task via its preservation of liturgical, social, and other prescriptions that acknowledge God's holiness and seek to inculcate such holiness in the people.

Stylistically, Leviticus is dominated by laws and regulations pertaining to priest and laity. The Israelites are by definition a priestly people: "You will be to me a kingdom of priests, a holy nation. That is what you must tell the Israelites" (Exod 19:6). The narrative flows from the book of Exodus and leads into the book of Numbers. Moses is the chief spokesperson who receives revelations from the Lord at the tent of meeting (1:1). Moses calls all the people to holiness and to atone for ritual and personal sin. Holiness pervades all of life and is not limited to the realm of the sacred. Holiness flows through creation: from the tabernacle to the home, from the sacrificial offering to the fields where the grain and animals are raised.

These initial observations serve to orient the reader to this commentary. The book of Leviticus at first glance may seem dated, but it offers lessons for today. The ancients had different canons of purity, social contact, and religious observance. However, upon a closer reading of the text, their needs, motivations, and practices resonate with our own. Their God of the ancestors (Abraham, Isaac, and Jacob) is our God as well. Their intentionality to stand before God in sincerity and truth was as strong as ours. In sum, the book of Leviticus has much to teach us today once we grapple with its essential messages and apply them to our religious life.

The historical background of Leviticus

The books of the Hebrew Scriptures are designated by initial words in the text. Genesis is called *běrē˒shit*, "*In the beginning* [when God created the heavens and the earth]." Exodus is designated as *shěmôt*, "[These are the] *names*." Leviticus is titled *wayyiqrā˒*, "[The Lord] *called* [Moses]." The opening word "called" in Leviticus introduces a long speech wherein Moses speaks to the people of Israel regarding various laws and observances. The English title Leviticus comes from the Greek word *Levitikon*, i.e., what is levitical and priestly in nature. However, the Levites are mentioned but once in the book regarding the redemption of their houses at the jubilee year (25:32-34). Leviticus relates more to practices of the Israelites as a people than to duties of the Levites and priests.

Leviticus is dominated by the Priestly source/tradition (called P) that runs from Genesis into parts of Deuteronomy. This tradition highly influenced the final redaction of the Pentateuch. The literary and theological characteristics of the P tradition include attention to genealogies, laws, God's abiding presence in the midst of Israel, and the power of blessing. Sabbath rest, the Sinai covenant, and proper cultic observance are related themes. Further, the P tradition offers a lasting diatribe against pagan religion.

Pagan religion in the Scriptures is typically depicted as capricious, malevolent, and coercive of creation in general and humankind in particular. The gods demand to be fed, and sacrifices offered by humans serve to satisfy the gods' hunger and sometimes calm their rage. Demons are all around and affect many aspects of life. In pagan religions the celestial bodies were typically divine and maintained creation in its seasonal cycles.

The parade example of a P diatribe against such paganism is the description of the celestial bodies in Genesis 1, the six-day creation account after which God rests from work. Therein, the narrative describes a greater and lesser light in the heavens: "God made the two great lights, the greater one to govern the day, and the lesser one to govern the night; and the stars" (Gen 1:16). Neither object is named sun or moon; neither lamp does more than provide the light God had designated to it. The stars are mentioned almost in passing.

The P tradition demands monotheism and being holy as God is holy. Religious life must mirror the order and cyclic pattern seen in creation. Such order is not about dry legalism and forensic justice. To live well and stand sincerely before God bespeak peace (Hebrew *shālôm*). Peace means health, happiness, abundance, and a good name in the community: "May the Lord bless you from Zion, / may you see Jerusalem's prosperity / all the days of your life, / and live to see your children's children. / Peace upon Israel!" (Ps 128:5-6).

The P tradition evidences that all cultures hope to elicit the help of supernatural powers in controlling nature and society. Each religion has its unique ritual observances to that end. Humans seek to court or appease spiritual beings with sacrifices thought to be pleasing and appropriate. The ancient Israelites and their neighbors used animal and grain sacrifices for the most part. Some engaged in child sacrifice. Other cultures, such as Native American, offered tobacco and food to their spiritual entities. In many cultures the priest, shaman, or other figure often led the rituals in the hope of some good: a bountiful harvest, victory in warfare, or relief from a plague. Ancient Israel was much caught up in purity, atonement, and thanksgiving to their Lord. Festivals were also times of covenant renewal.

The P tradition reminds the contemporary reader that our religious world shares common ground with the ancients. We, too, are solicitous of liturgy that is valid, licit, and observed in its proper season. We embrace annual observances that characterize our religious heritage and bring the past alive in the present. Such practices as the Advent wreath, ashes on Ash Wednesday, fast and abstinence during Lent, fronds on Palm Sunday, and water at Easter come to mind. Certain phrases in Leviticus speak to every age and religion. These include "You shall love your neighbor as yourself" (19:18; see Luke 10:27) and "For I, the Lord, am your God. You shall make and keep yourselves holy, because I am holy" (11:44; see Matt 5:48).

In sum, I invite the reader of this commentary to look for timeless values and theological connections that transcend primitive science and time conditioned practices. Let us look to themes and motifs that make Leviticus a book still worth reading and a source of biblical-spiritual reflection in every age. To this end, I suggest that the reader begin by perusing the review aids and discussion topics at the end of the commentary.

The literary artistry of Leviticus

Recent biblical studies have given attention to fresh "lenses" through which to read and understand the Scriptures. One is socio-cultural criticism, a method that investigates the real cultural world in which the biblical texts emerged and grew. What seem to be their values? Why was something a social given or a taboo? Another is narrative criticism, a method that utilizes such techniques as repetition, symmetry, *inclusio* (key words or phrases that begin and end a section), irony, conflict, resolution, and character development. These devices help the reader appreciate the literary artistry of biblical texts. One intention of such criticism is to help the reader understand the text in its own terms (a task of exegesis) and then find meaningful applications for the present (a task of hermeneutics). This commentary will utilize these methods among others.

Great themes and motifs in Leviticus

The literary artistry of Leviticus raises themes and motifs deserving mention as an orientation to this commentary. First, holiness is the primary theme in the book. The intrinsic characteristic of God is being holy (Hebrew *qādôsh*). Holiness in the Scriptures denotes being somehow set apart by nature or by vocation. Thus a priest is set apart by vocation to serve liturgically in holiness and consecration: "You are consecrated to the Lord, and the vessels are also consecrated" (Ezra 8:28). God is holy and sinful humanity seeks holiness.

This perspective leads to a second theme in Leviticus, i.e., the divine presence among the people. How can the all holy God be present to a sinful people? God does not compromise intrinsic holiness in order to engage with creation, and creation is good from the beginning (Gen 1). Humans must grow in holiness to meet the God they love and worship. Leviticus addresses this theological issue throughout. Although the book has a complex history of development toward its final canonical form, the message is clear. Humans strive to grow in holiness but are hindered in that progress by falling into error and sin, both unintentional and intentional. Unintentional errors call for purification; intentional sin demands atonement.

The book also delimits boundaries of cleanness and uncleanness. The issue is not about compliance or non-compliance to dry, constricting laws but about growing in holiness, wholeness, and sincerity before God. Further, Leviticus is not simply about attaining holiness before God in a totally personal relationship. Holiness also bespeaks a holy and wholesome relationship with family and neighbor.

Leviticus 19 introduces in the Scriptures what we call the Golden Rule: love your neighbor as yourself (v. 18). This chapter also mandates care for the poor by leaving a portion of one's crops behind at harvest time (vv. 9-10), and honesty in keeping with the Ten Commandments (vv. 11-12). Rules of sexual conduct serve to maintain integrity in the family and social harmony in the community. Blood and its shedding are closely regulated because life is in the blood (17:11). All the sacrifices, holy days, dietary laws, rules of sexual relations and other bodily contacts, and charity to the poor serve to draw one closer to God. All these instructions are rooted in God's covenant as human obligation: "These are the commandments which the Lord gave Moses on Mount Sinai for the Israelites" (27:34). This intentionality colors all that we read in Leviticus.

Finally, a former Old Testament professor of mine once quipped that in a commentary we read what struck the author's fancy as he/she moved along. That remark came to my mind as I began to research and write this commentary. I hope to highlight what strikes my fancy without becoming fanciful. My goal is that this commentary will offer the popular audience a reading that helps make sense of the book of Leviticus in itself and offer associations for contemporary faith. In sum, the Scriptures are the *Living Word*, and Leviticus still speaks to that lived tradition, both oral and written.

COMMENTARY

SACRIFICES AND OFFERINGS

Leviticus 1–7

Leviticus 1–7 covers a variety of sacrifices and offerings. The chapters also introduce holiness/ sacredness (Hebrew *qādôsh,* literally, to be set apart; 6:9, 19, 22; 7:6), an important theme that runs through the book. The narrative may be subdivided into two basic sections. Chapters 1–5 relate to sacrifices of the Israelites in general, while chapters 6–7 relate first to sacrifices of the priests and then flows back to the Israelites in general. This sequence creates an "a: b: a" pattern (people: priests: people) in the narrative, centering on the activity of the priests. This narrative technique highlights the central role of the priest as presider and cultic mediator for the priestly nation of Israel.

Chapters 1–5 repeat the phrase "If/when . . ." and then moves to the specific sacrifice involved (1:3, 10, 14; 2:1, 4, 14; 3:1, 6, 12 and so on). The four sacrifices are as follows: burnt offerings, grain offerings, communion sacrifices, and purification offerings. Chapters 6–7 are punctuated by the phrase "This is the ritual . . ." for the priests (6:2, 7, 18; 7:1, 11 and so on) and "Tell the Israelites . . ." (7:22, 29) for the people in general. Such narrative techniques give some order and symmetry to the book.

Moses is the central figure and mediator *par excellence*, harking back to his characterization in Exodus 3–5 and anticipating his role in Numbers and Deuteronomy. That Moses is called and then commanded to speak to the people (Lev 1:1) reflects his biblical characterization as prophet and spokesperson for God in word and deed. Moses is called at the burning bush and sent to speak the Lord's message to Pharaoh: "Let my people go . . ." (Exod 5:1). At first Moses is a reluctant leader: "Who am I that I should go to Pharaoh and bring the Israelites out of Egypt?" (Exod 3:11; cf. 3:13; 4:1, 10, 13). Later he comes into his own and assures the frightened Israelites as they head toward the Red Sea (Exod 14:10-14). In the book of Leviticus Moses addresses the people in a lengthy discourse wherein he shows his character as a decisive leader with privileged access to the Lord. He is the valid and authoritative lawgiver.

1:3-17 Burnt offerings

The sacrifice of a domesticated herd animal (cattle, sheep, or goat) was the primary food offering to gods in the ancient world. The sweet-smelling oblation (vv. 9, 13, 17; cf. Gen 4:1-5; 8:20-22) was voluntary for the most part, motivated by such occasions as a vow, an annual festival, or purification rite. Immolation of the entire animal, apart from the hide, gave full recognition and glory to the Lord. The laying on of a hand (Lev 1:4) was not so much about transferring the sins of the offerer to the animal (cf. 16:20-28, the scapegoat) but affirming the identity of the owner and that person's benefit from the sacrifice. The offerer received a benefit or atonement for making the sacrifice.

The categories of suitable animals are cited in their descending value. The first category is the male bovine (Hebrew *bāqār*: variously the ox, bull, or calf). In the ancient world only the wealthy could own large herds of bovines. The animal must be without blemish, i.e., not blind, crippled, or maimed; not with running sores, mange, or ringworm (22:22-24). The priest is also prohibited from physical defect (21:17-21).

The second category is the male ovine (sheep, goat), the most common domesticated animal in the ancient world. Their hair, milk (and milk products), skin, meat, bones, and horns were useful to humans. Goats can produce milk even in arid climates, making them useful to nomadic peoples. Like the bovine offering, the ovine must be without blemish.

The third category is the bird (Hebrew ʿôph), specified as a turtledove or pigeon. This offering is basically a substitution offering available to the poor (see 5:7; cf. Luke 2:24 [presentation of Jesus]). The text makes no mention of the bird being without blemish. This detail may stem from the fact that a feathered animal would not exhibit blemishes as easily as on a bull, sheep, or goat. The seasonal molting of feathers may have been another case.

The role of blood in the burnt offering deserves comment. Blood is an essential element of sacrifice; it is either sprinkled or squeezed on the altar. Blood joins the human and the divine in a sacred moment. People share in God's holiness through sprinkling of blood. The Day of Atonement highlights the ritual use of blood (16:14-19) and is related theologically to the Israelite covenant at Sinai sealed by blood (cf. Exod 24:3-8). On that occasion Moses sprinkled the holy blood on the people, saying, "This is the blood of the covenant which the LORD has made with you according to all these words" (v. 8).

Chapter 1 sets the tone for the book of Leviticus. First, a relationship with God demands sacred moments of encounter. Liturgy provides such occasions. Second, sacred moments demand a precise order of worship. The ancients valued ritual integrity as much as moderns do: Who presides? What vestments are worn? What are the proper gifts? What benefit comes from this practice? Third, the gifts brought to worship flow from God's fruits of creation as animal or grain (Gen 1:1–2:4 [P creation account]; 4:1-16 [Cain and Abel]). Fourth, gifts offered to God include some human benefit in return. The subsequent chapters may seem repetitive at times, but the repetition drives home the important lessons of Leviticus. Repetition aids stories rooted in oral tradition, such as much of biblical literature.

2:1-16 Grain offerings

Like the bird offering, the grain offerings are available to the poor. Several recipes were acceptable, and any offerings mixed with frankincense were burned and not eaten.

Frankincense is a large succulent with aromatic sap. Many ancient civilizations imported its expensive gum for ritual use. Its reputed medicinal value was acclaimed in the ancient world. A portion of a cooked offering without frankincense went to the priests as a gift (v. 10). The reasons for the prohibition of leaven or honey remain obscure. Leavened bread was an acceptable thanksgiving offering but never a burnt offering. It may be that these ingredients put off a displeasing smoke and odor unbefitting of a sweet-smelling oblation.

Salt, however, is required of all cereal offerings. Salt was considered a necessity of life and used as a condiment, preservative, and healing agent. It was also a symbol of covenant alliance and friendship as attested here and elsewhere in the Old Testament (Num 18:19 ["covenant of salt"]; 2 Chr 13:5; cf. Mark 9:49-50; Col 4:6).

3:1-17 Communion sacrifices

The essence of peace (Hebrew šālôm) is well-being in every aspect of life. The communion sacrifice (also called a peace offering) affirms the harmony and right relation with God and others in the community. Like the burnt offering this offering demands an unblemished bovine or ovine. Selected portions were offered to God, the priest, and the offerer. In practice this offering provided blessed meat for special occasions, since meat was not a daily staple in the ancient world. As with the burnt offerings, blood is splashed on the altar. The occasion for the sacrifice could be thanksgiving for a divine favor, one's completion of a vow, or simply out of generosity. The joyful nature of this offering sets it apart (see 7:11-21).

One can see that chapters 1–3 present a variety of sacrifices that include sensitivity to the poor in the community. The various rubrics bespeak not mechanical actions that coerce things from God, but a relationship involving right order, often including the laying on of the hand and each person assuming a specific role in the ceremony. The gifts are not random but appropriate to the occasion and offered with care.

The opening chapters of Leviticus show the importance of offerings occasioned out of free will and not just need. The reader may too readily associate Old Testament sacrifice with placating God or atoning for sin. Although atonement informs many sacrifices, the foundation of worship is the covenant. Covenant includes God's commitment to the good creation (Gen 9:1-17 [Noah]; Gen 15 and 17 [Abraham]; 2 Sam 7 [David]) and the human obligation to live as God's people (Exod 24 [Moses]; Josh 24:16-28). Covenant is a two-sided coin in the Scriptures. It offers God's free commitment and, in turn, the human obligation to live by God's laws.

4:1-12 Purification offerings for priests

The occasional designation "sin" offering is misleading. More recent studies distinguish between unintentional ritual impurity and intentional wrongdoing, both of which may demand a sacrifice. This distinction highlights that not all these offerings relate to sin. Some relate to normal bodily functions (menstruation, childbirth), personal ignorance of the law, or acting out of necessity (burial of the dead). Certain actions may make a person *ritually* impure but not all of them are sinful.

The first purification offering belongs to the priests serving in the sanctuary and thus bound to exemplary holiness. This offering involves the threefold sprinkling or pouring of blood. "Horns" of the altar are mentioned for the first time in Leviticus (v. 7). These ornaments projected from the four corners of the altar and probably represented the strength and abiding presence of God, drawing on the mythical qualities of the bull. Cutting off the horns of the altar was an act of desecration (Amos 3:14). The horns are also cited as a place of refuge for transgressors (e.g., 1 Kgs 1:50; 2:28).

Particular attention is given to the fatty parts of the animal, which along with blood were the best gifts. Fat offered in sacrifice must not be consumed by humans (see 3:17; 7:23-25) and blood can never be consumed. Non-sacrificial fat may be eaten. The entire animal is burned outside the camp and its ashes deposited there. The ashes symbolize the reality and efficacy of the purification (cf. Num 19 [ashes of the red heifer]; Heb 9:13).

4:13-21 Purification for the community

The whole community includes the priests and the people. This sacrifice closely mirrors the purification offering of the priest discussed above. However, on this occasion the community, not the priest, brings the bull forward (v. 14). The exact nature of this assembly remains obscure. Has the entire community sinned, or the community leaders who corporately represent them all? Whichever the case, this sacrifice acknowledges the reality of communal need for atonement. Offering a bull purifies the sanctuary and brings the community back into a right relationship with God. The greatest time of purification is the Day of Atonement discussed later in Leviticus.

4:22-26 Purification for the tribal leaders

The tribal leader (Hebrew *nāśîʾ*, literally, "one raised up") comprises a variety of officials in ancient Israel. For example, the term can designate the head of a small group or a tribe. Since he is a leader of the community, the sin of a tribal leader has broader impact. He is called to a higher level of accountability, but his subordination to the priests is reflected in the fact that a goat suffices as an offering. One can see that the value of a sacrificial animal sometimes reflects the status of the offerer and not just one's wealth.

4:27-35 For the general populace

The so-called private person (of the general populace) is literally an individual from among "the people of the land" (Hebrew *ʾam hāʾāres*). The designation "people of the land" has several meanings in the Scriptures, depending on the historical period or context involved. It can mean citizens in good standing (excluding foreigners and slaves), the powerful elite, or even lower classes. In this account such persons are citizens enfranchised with rights and responsibilities representative of their status in society. They may bring a goat or lamb of sacrifice. The option of a bird or grain purification offering by the poor is discussed in chapter 5.

5:1-13 For special cases

Attention to special cases shows that Leviticus wants to be as thorough as possible about purification and atonement. Several representative examples are cited: failure to give legal testimony (v. 1), touching an unclean animal or person (vv. 2-3), and making a rash oath (v. 4). These laws take economic hardship into consideration, a theme that began in chapter 1 and is highlighted in this chapter by the twofold repetition of the phrase "If, however, the person cannot afford . . ." (vv. 7, 11). The appropriate sacrifice in such instances is a female ovine, a bird, or a cereal offering.

It is noteworthy that special cases are not all about economic hardship. Poverty is no excuse for not making eventual atonement. Responsibility demands performing the required ritual even if realized well after the fact.

5:14-26 Reparation offerings

This offering, sometimes called a guilt offering, includes occasions of intentional and unintentional impurity. The first case is the unintended act of cheating in sacrificial dues (v. 17). An unblemished ram of a certain monetary value suffices for atonement. The exact worth of a sanctuary shekel remains uncertain because coinage was valued by weight and not by face value. The second case relates to the first, citing instances of an unintentional breaking of a commandment. The third case relates to intentional dishonesty and is discussed in greater detail (seven verses, the length of the previous two cases combined).

The various offerings in chapters 4 and 5 distinguish between inadvertent and intentional wrongdoing. Both occasions demand reparation and restitution. It would be "cheap grace" for a person to atone via a simple offering and not compensate the person wronged. The prophets railed against sacrifices driven by formalities but without the proper interior disposition. Legal justice demands moral justice as well.

6:1-6 The daily burnt offering

Chapters 6–7 discuss instructions for the priests regarding the various offerings. The narrative is punctuated by the phrase "This is the ritual . . ." (Hebrew *tôrâ* or *tôrat*, literally, "instruction," 6:2, 7, 18; 7:1, 11, 37). The commands are enjoined on Aaron and his sons, a designation for a class of priests more than succession by bloodline. Aaron and his sons are the only priests who preside at rituals in Leviticus. The ordination of the Aaronide class is discussed in chapters 8–9.

The whole burnt offering comes from the verb meaning "to go up" (Hebrew *ʿōlâ*). The offering ascends to the Lord as a fragrant offering with spatial and visual symbolism. Attention is given to the priest's vestments for this sacrifice. The linen robe and drawers represent fine fabric befitting the priest (Exod 28:4-5). Linen, usually bleached to shades of white, was cool to wear in hot and humid weather. Removal of ashes occurs in two stages: to the side of the altar and then outside the camp. The altar is sacred as the place of divine presence and a traditional place of covenant-making. The priest dresses appropriately and makes a change of clothes during the removal. This re-vesting respects the distinction between the holy sanctuary and all space outside of it.

The continuous fire on the altar also highlights the holiness of the sanctuary. Maintaining the fire is an obvious convenience, but it also offers a point of continuity between sacrifices and a vigilant respect for God's abiding presence even when people are absent. A modern parallel would be the perpetual sanctuary lamp in some Christian churches.

6:7-16 Daily grain offering

This offering of the priest actually comprises two separate laws (vv. 7-11 and 12-16) and takes up the discussion of the grain offering in chapter 2. The first law highlights the priest eating the offering in a sacred place, i.e., the court of the meeting tent. The second law demands that the grain be a whole burnt offering to God. These daily sacrifices are cited in Hebrews 7:27 to explain how the perfect sacrifice of Jesus the high priest is once and for all.

6:17-23 Purification offerings

This offering, first mentioned in chapter 4, highlights which offerings the priest may consume, as well as his sacred duties in the slaughter of burnt offerings. The details here exceed those of previous chapters and reiterate the importance of holiness (v. 20). Holy blood is a powerful element in sacrifice and must be handled with care. Sacred vessels are treated with utmost care because they come into contact with the holy. Both clay and bronze vessels are cited. Earthenware must be broken and metal scoured. Earthenware was probably disposable because of its absorbency and fragility.

Shattering pottery is a vivid symbol of divine punishment in the Old Testament: "Thus will I smash this people and this city, as one smashes a clay pot so that it cannot be repaired" (Jer 19:11; cf. Ps 2:9). Metal vessels are more durable and must be purified before further ritual use. Such details in the narrative bespeak reverence of the sacred and the proper care of liturgical objects. In the New Testament Jesus uses cups, jugs, and kettles to condemn token ritual washing without the proper inner disposition (Mark 7:1-8).

7:1-10 Reparation offerings

This offering, first mentioned in 5:14-26, gives particular attention to the fatty portions offered on the altar. The smoke that fat produces would enhance the visual effect and aroma. One may also present a grain offering. The distinction between the grain eaten by one priest or to be shared by all the priests remains obscure. Whatever the reason, laypersons do not partake of this offering.

7:11-21 Communion sacrifices

First mentioned in chapter 3, this ritual has the distinction of being eaten by priests and laity alike. Thanksgiving for release from affliction or prayers answered may occasion such a ritual meal. Particular attention is given to the meal being consumed that day and kept from anyone and anything unclean.

This section introduces the notion of being "cut off" (Hebrew *kārat*, 7:20, 21, 25, 27) from the people, a state that bespeaks excommunication and even death. The emphasis is on divine judgment, for the Lord sees through human cover-up or oversight. Even if the guilty person is acquitted in a human court, God's eventual judgment is certain. The theme of being cut off recurs in chapters 17–20.

7:22-27 Prohibition against blood and fat

This section highlights the sacredness of *sacrificial* fat and blood of *any* kind, neither of which is to be consumed (3:16-17). These portions are set apart to the Lord as holy. In pagan religions fat was food for the gods, but ancient Israel never embraced the idea that their God was dependent on food (Ps 50:12-14). Fat bespeaks offering the best of what one has, a metaphor that calls to mind the phrase "the fat of the land" (Gen 45:18).

7:28-38 The portions for priests

Certain delicacies from the sacrificial animal go to the priest as a gift. The elevated offering, sometimes called a wave offering, includes upward gestures representing the object being dedicated to God and certain parts blessed for the priest's meal. Such elevation rites are also cited of gold for the tabernacle (Exod 35:22) and new grain at the harvest (Lev 23:15-17).

Verses 37-38 close Leviticus 1–7 and introduce the ordination offering. The term for ordination (Hebrew *mālē*, literally, "to be full") suggests the portions of a sacrifice placed in the hands of the priest, as well as his being set apart by divine choice and his hand "filled" with a special duty. This imagery of filled hands bespeaks the privilege and responsibility of the priest.

In sum, Leviticus 1–7 discuss a variety of laws and sacrifices unified by the call to holiness, the value of communal ritual, and the benefits that come from embracing and maintaining right relationship with God. The priests and attendants of the sanctuary must have the proper interior disposition and perform their duties according to proper form. These values flow into the theme of ordination in chapters 8–10. The priest has prestige and responsibilities, but his vocation is fraught with danger as the death of Nadab and Abihu will show.

CEREMONY OF ORDINATION
Leviticus 8–10

Moses presides at the ordination of Aaron and his sons and instructs that priestly line about rules of right conduct (cf. Exod 29). Several points are noteworthy. First, Moses literally bathes and then dresses Aaron in his vestments (8:6-9), an intimate gesture that recalls the Lord dressing Adam and Eve before their banishment from Eden (Gen 3:21) and personally shutting Noah and his remnant in the ark at the great flood (Gen 7:16). Second, the repetition of the phrase "as the Lord had commanded" (8:4, 9, 13, 17, 21, 29; 9:7, 10; 10:15) and similar statements emphasize the valid and licit nature of the rite and create a bold contrast to the disobedience of Nadab and Abihu (10:1). Third, the themes of summoning, assembling, and bringing forth inform the narrative (8:1-6, 14, 18, 22; 9:1, 5, 8, 15). The liturgical style of these chapters is striking.

The narrative also highlights the mediatory character of Moses as he facilitates the Lord's will for valid ordinations. Moses enjoys such a status because he is a friend of God, a relationship beautifully described in Exodus 33:7-23. Verse 11 is a key statement in that passage: "The Lord used to speak to Moses face to face, as a person speaks to a friend."

The modern reader can better appreciate this section by associating it with lived experience. Life stages bring so-called "rites of passage" to which all can relate in some way: birthdays, receiving sacraments, graduations, becoming parents or grandparents. Ordinations and other calls to ministry characterize modern faith as much as they did for the readers of Leviticus 8–10. Being called, consecrated, instructed in proper service, and embracing moral living remain perpetual values.

8:1-13 Ordination of Aaron and his sons

The items mentioned in verse 2 equip Moses for leading the ceremony. The vestments denote distinctive attire associated with the temple and sacrifice (see Exod 28 and 39 for details about the vestments). The anointing oil is used to consecrate the sacred furnishings and the priests, setting both apart from others (Levites and laypersons). The rams and unleavened bread are gifts for sacrifice. More will be stated below about oil and the sacrificial animals.

8:14-36 Ordination sacrifices

This ritual mirrors the account in Exodus 29:10-14. Moses' purifying the altar (v. 15) prepares it for consecrating the many offerings to be laid upon it. The two rams cited in verse 2 are then sacrificed. The first ram, like the bull, is a burnt offering. The second is called the ordination ram (see 7:37). It atones for any sins of Aaron and his sons and dedicates them to the Lord.

The details in verses 22-24 highlight the central moment of ordination itself. Blood is daubed on parts of the right side of the body, from upper to lower extremities: ear, thumb, and toe. In ancient societies (and some Middle Eastern countries today), the right hand was "clean" and used to touch another person. Sitting at someone's right hand was the position of honor at banquets and ceremonies (Ps 110:1, 5). The ear, thumb, and toe symbolize, respectively, listening to God's words, having hands pure for leading sacrifices, and walking with God (see Deut 30:16). In every aspect of his life the priest is consecrated by the blood. His whole being belongs to divine service. His dedication calls to mind Psalm 19:15, "Let the words of my mouth be acceptable / the thoughts of my heart before you, / Lord, my rock and my redeemer."

The elevation offering of unleavened food, placed in their hands by Moses, is a gift from Aaron and his sons to the Lord. Reciprocally, their sprinkling with oil and blood from the altar further consecrates the priests and their vestments. After a ritual meal, the newly ordained must stay at the entrance of the meeting tent for seven days, seven being the biblical number of completion, perfection, and wholeness (cf. Gen 2:1-3).

Verse 36 closes the chapter. The newly ordained, Aaron and his sons, now do all the things commanded by the Lord through Moses. Proper authority and protocol have been observed as the many details in the chapter confirm. Chapters 9–10 move from hearing about the proper conduct of the priest to their acting it out in their daily duties.

9:1-24 Octave of the ordination

On the eighth or octave day of ordination, Aaron and his sons officiate at their first sacrifices. The list comprises the variety of offerings enjoined so far: burnt offering, purification, communion, grain, etc. The presence of the Lord confirms the efficacy of their ordination (vv. 4, 6). Divine presence at these ritual moments affirms the great events at Sinai as abiding and now present in the meeting tent. The awesome divine powers of Sinai are demonstrated anew in fire coming forth from the Lord's presence and consuming the burnt offering and remnants of fat on the altar (v. 24). This awesome event anticipated the death of Nadab and Abihu that follows. It also calls to mind Elijah's encounter with the prophets of Baal where fire from heaven consumed his burnt offering: "The Lord's fire came down and devoured the burnt offering, wood, stones, and dust, and lapped up the water in the trench" (1 Kgs 18:38).

Verses 22-24 create a fitting climax to the chapter. With preparations ready and sacrifices offered, Aaron raises his hands in blessing. Though his words of blessing are not quoted, the blessing of Aaron in Numbers 6:24-26 would be a fitting selection: "The Lord bless you and keep you! / The Lord let his face shine upon you, and be gracious to you! / The Lord look upon you kindly and give you peace!"

Now for the first time Moses and Aaron enter the tent of meeting. The elaborate preparations lead to this climactic moment. It is noteworthy that the phrase "all the people" is stated twice at the end (vv. 23-24). This sacred moment is not just about Moses, priests, and attendants in their realm of the sacred. The presence and response of the Israelites is also essential. God's glory is revealed to all present. Finally, the theme of obedience punctuates this chapter. Such repetitions as "then he/they brought . . ." (vv. 5, 12-13, 16, 18) show the order and careful execution of every step. The priests must not forget what they have been taught lest they receive the fate of Nadab and Abihu.

10:1-5 Nadab and Abihu

This tragic episode is triggered by the offering of an unauthorized fire (Hebrew *ʾēsh zārâ*, literally, "alien fire"). The exact nature of the offense remains unclear. In some manner the fire was not pleasing to the Lord. Perhaps they substituted embers from another source, thus cutting corners and violating the integrity of the altar fire. Other suggestions include acting at the wrong time, not being properly vested, or even being intoxicated while on duty (see v. 9). Whatever the case, the penalty of death reminds the people that God sees into the heart and makes strict demands of priestly service. Further, the poetic statement in verse 3 is telling. It juxtaposes holiness and glory as divine attributes. Holiness is the intrinsic characteristic of God; glory is God's extrinsic expression in creation: "Holy, holy, holy is the Lord of hosts! / All the earth is filled with his glory!" (Isa 6:3).

10:6-11 Conduct of the priests

Moses tells Aaron and his sons not to engage in mourning, leaving that duty to the people. Because contact with a corpse defiles a person, priests are to stay away except in the case of a next of kin (21:1-4; cf. Luke 10:31-32 [The Good Samaritan]). Notably, this is one time in Leviticus where Aaron speaks face to face with the Lord and not through Moses. The prohibition of alcohol probably relates to its impairing effects (Prov 20:1; 23:31-32; Hos 4:9-11). The most pointed condemnation of such abuse by those in leadership roles occurs in Isaiah: "Priest and prophet stagger from strong drink, / overpowered by wine; / They are confused by strong drink, / they stagger in their visions, / they totter when giving judgment" (28:7). This point flows into the following verses

about the priest distinguishing the clean from the unclean and instructing the laws of the Lord to the Israelites. Impairment affects right judgment, so stay sober and alert.

In sum, this section speaks to a theology of priesthood. Privilege must not erode into being "intoxicated" by power and prestige. The priest is called from among the people, is accountable to the community, and is answerable before God. The priest is commissioned with *tôrâ* (instruction of the law), meaning that the people turn to him for understanding the Lord's will. This responsibility must be taken seriously because it impacts on the entire community; it does not remain insulated in a hidden sacred realm. Kingly duties are much the same. The king must exact justice impartially and is condemned for injustices (see 2 Sam 12:1-12 [Nathan judges King David]).

10:12-20 The eating of the priestly portions

This section focuses on the incident of the uneaten goat. Recalling the fate of Nadab and Abihu, the reader might expect divine wrath to fall upon these priests as well. However, Moses accepts the explanation of Aaron and his sons that fear of the Lord motivated their offering up the goat and not partaking of it (v. 19). Memory of the fate of Nadab and Abihu may account for the actions of these priests.

Once again Moses acts as judge in a tense situation. One can justify Moses' anger at their insubordination because eating the priestly portion is required and not optional. The priest eating his portion serves to "swallow up" the unholy and is essential to the efficacy of the ritual. Although the precise interpretation of this section remains obscure, one may suggest that the integrity of the purification offering, entirely offered up to God, supersedes any questions about portions to the priest. Moses' satisfaction with Aaron's explanation is stated but not explained.

The incident juxtaposes clear laws and noncompliance to those laws, a tension that highlights the fragile and sometimes dangerous nature of human encounter with the divine. Further, this episode bespeaks divine and human freedom. God can have a change of heart, e.g., Adam and Eve never die for eating the forbidden fruit (Gen 2:17; 3:3-4). Humans can change their mind as Moses does here.

The tense and somewhat unhappy ending to chapter 10 seems awkward, but it certainly sets the stage for chapters 11–16 that deal with issues of purity. The priests must clearly understand their role and duties if they expect to judge rightly between the clean and unclean. Issues surrounding clear categories, proper boundaries, and distinct identities come into play with legal purity. The situations are different but the principles are much the same.

LAWS REGARDING RITUAL PURITY

Leviticus 11–16

This section discusses topics of which Leviticus is most popularly associated, i.e., ancient customs and matters of daily life. To the modern reader such detailed attention to unclean food, defilement at childbirth, leprosy, personal hygiene, and scapegoats seems primitive and superstitious. However, as with the ceremony of ordination, the *values* underlying these laws are timeless. The reader must remember that purity and holiness underlie these regulations.

The origins of clean and unclean things are rooted in a variety of needs and experiences, no one of which can be deemed definitive. Anthropologically, some foods become forbidden because they easily spoil and cause illness. Others do not fit into distinct categories and thus seem abnormal, such as reptiles that dwell both in water and on land, and birds that cannot fly. Animals that eat carrion consume what is dead and thus unclean. Boundaries are also involved. Skin lesions cross the boundaries of inner and outer parts of the body. Something is out of order. Theologically, order shows itself in fidelity to the categories and boundaries of creation (Gen 1, the Priestly account). God made birds of the air, fishes of the sea, and the land animals. Phenomena that blur this order are abnormal and unclean. They bespeak primordial chaos.

In sum, purity and holiness comprise more than personal and social hygiene. These values are at once physical, ritual, and moral, all demonstrating obedience to God. Holiness demands wholeness. This obedience harks back to the intentionality of creation in Genesis 1–2. Human dominion over other creatures includes a sense of limits and commitment to stewardship (Gen 1:28-31; 9:1-7).

11:1-23 Clean and unclean meats

This section echoes the classes of animals in Genesis 1: water, land, and flying creatures (cf. Deut 14:4-21). Edible land animals must be cloven-footed and chew the cud. These standards thus exclude the pig and the camel. The ancient world did not have the sophisticated biology of fauna we have today, so some of the biblical understanding of animals is imprecise. For example, the hare reputedly chews the cud (v. 6). This error is based on the sideways chewing habits of the animal and not actual cud behavior. The bat is listed among the birds, though it is a mammal (v. 19). Clean water creatures have both fins and scales. Hence, scale-less water scavengers and shellfish are forbidden. The list of forbidden birds embodies three taboos. They are either flightless, predatory raptors, or eat carrion. Winged insects that hop on hind legs are edible (v. 22). All others that swarm or crawl on all fours are forbidden.

In sum, one must avoid the abnormal in creation. Land animals walk on all fours; fish swim with fins and have gills; and birds fly with wings and walk on hind legs. The primary concern is properly distinguishing what God deems clean or unclean in the created order (v. 47).

Not to be lost in the details of this chapter is the fact that God's covenant extends through all creation. It is significant that Genesis 1 depicts the created order as essentially vegetarian: "See, I give you every seed-bearing plant . . ." (1:29-30). Not until the great flood and covenant with Noah does violence among the creatures emerge: "Any living creature that moves about shall be yours to eat; I give them all to you as I did the green plants" (Gen 9:3).

This theological perspective helps the reader understand the laws enjoined here. The wanton and unregulated consumption of meat is forbidden from "the beginning" (Gen 1:1) and violates the call for humankind to be stewards of creation (Gen 1:26). The message of the prophets includes a dream of the initial harmony in creation: "Then the wolf shall be a guest of the lamb . . ." (Isa 11:6-9). That harmony would be characterized by peace and justice in the world. Indeed, a theology of ecology emerges from Leviticus 11.

11:24-47 Pollution by animals

This section moves from what may be consumed to what may be touched. The main point is the taboo of any dead creature, regardless of its cleanness in life. Those contaminated by the dead must bathe and remain unclean until the evening (v. 24). Contaminated earthenware vessels must be shattered (cf. 6:21). An exception is given to springs and cisterns (v. 36). These natural bodies provide water from the ground or from rain. Their connection with the waters of God's ordered creation makes them distinct and ever pure, unless contaminated by humans.

The repeated rationale for all these laws is the divine holiness in which only the pure may share. Everything holy remains "apart" in some way: apart from the pagan nations, apart from uncleanness as God commands, and set apart in communal morality and personal vocation. The words in 10:10 state it all succinctly: "You must be able to distinguish between what is sacred and what is profane, and between what is clean and what is unclean."

12:1-8 Uncleanness of childbirth

Behind the laws enjoined here is the value of life from cradle to grave. Life is in the blood (17:11; Deut 12:23), a belief that pervades the Scriptures. To understand this law the modern reader should call to mind the common human reaction to the sight of blood. Bleeding is typically abnormal and a sign of something dangerous at work in the body or violence done to it from the outside. The ancients shared such emotional reaction and gave blood a rich variety of meanings. It was at once the source of life and a symbol of death. It is bright red and stains what it touches. It also has the ability to ward off evil (see Exod 12:21-23 [Passover blood]). Hence, one must not dismiss as superstitious what are innate and pervasive ideas in the human psyche. Some people even faint at the sight of blood.

The blood of menstruation and childbirth ultimately bespeaks holiness, not displeasure or rejection. The emphasis is not on defilement but purification and restoration. Blood "defilement" here is a condition that must be set aright to bring healing and harmony to the family and community. During childbirth blood unites life and death in a mysterious tension. Miscarriage and infant mortality were high in the ancient world, so the survival of mother or child was fragile, fraught with mystery and bittersweet experience. These realities and emotions inform the meaning of this passage. The events that follow childbirth (circumcision of a son and the purification of the mother) guarantee purity, social harmony, and the hope of a happy life for all involved. May all enjoy peace (*shālôm*).

13:1-59 Scaly infection

This lengthy chapter addresses a variety of skin diseases, none of which can be associated directly with leprosy (Hansen's disease). Skin ailments render persons unclean, with consequences that ostracize them from the community for shorter or longer periods (vv. 4 and 45-46). The chapter is divided into several sets of criteria: diseases of the skin, scars, burns, hair problems, and even articles of clothing. Houses can be "leprous" as well (14:33-57).

It is noteworthy that the accusation of sin is absent in this chapter. Although skin disease may be the result of sin, it is not necessarily so. One can surmise that eruptions of the skin were so common in the ancient world that one could hardly presume a connection with sin. On the one hand, no one wanted to contract the disease by proximity or touching. On the other hand, drawing the afflicted person back into the community was a value. Probably victims of skin disease were more pitied than judged.

The tragedy of such conditions shows itself in other biblical passages. So-called lepers wander in bands (2 Kgs 7:1-13) and are shunned no matter their status in life (2 Kgs 5:1-27; 2 Chr 26:16-21). In the New Testament Jesus shows compassion to lepers and enjoins his disciples to care for them (Mark 1:41; Matt 10:8).

In sum, the pervasiveness of skin disease in life and its variety of manifestations commends such diseases to the interests of Leviticus. To be holy means to be whole and without *dis*-ease. What modern society would refer to physicians, they referred to priests. Their perspective is surely primitive, but every age grapples with diseases it does not understand and that can evoke panic among the people and ostracism of the victims. One thinks of HIV, SARS, avian bird flu, and other diseases today. Social lepers in every age are often the victims of misinformation and false labeling.

14:1-57 Purification after scaly infection

This section builds on chapter 13 and addresses how to deal with cured scaly infections and the victim's ritual purification. It is important to note that culpability is not a central issue. Rather, those ostracized are drawn back inside the camp from which they were excluded. Such persons are no longer "outside the camp" (v. 3).

The length of the purification ritual and its stages are noteworthy. The process begins outside the camp and moves toward the camp. The list of items for the ritual is specific: two birds, cedar wood, scarlet yarn, and hyssop. One bird is sacrificed; the other is set free as a sign of the person's restoration (cf. 16:20-28, the scapegoat). The malady is symbolically carried off. The wood, yarn, and hyssop are used to fashion a sprinkler to splash the blood mixed with spring water. The sevenfold sprinkling bespeaks perfection and wholeness. The person is now restored to the community. In sum, purification and atonement are the heart of the ritual as reiterated in verses 8, 9, and 20.

Purification follows with a sacrifice on the eighth day. Animals, grain, and oil are involved. Since sensitivity to the poor is a value in Leviticus, doves or pigeons may be substituted for lambs (vv. 21-32). The sacrifice is one of thanksgiving but also one of precaution. The affliction may have been coincidental or may have been occasioned by some offense unknown to the victim. Cover all the bases.

By extension scaly infection can infect dwellings and their contents (vv. 33-57). Probably mold, mildew, and rust are involved. The fact that these conditions are often bright in color, spread across surfaces, and are hard to scrub off lends to the perception that they are "leprous" like skin infections. Pagan cultures attributed such nuisances to demonic powers. Ancient Israel believed that God created all things and can use all things to teach and punish (v. 34).

Further, the house or home (Hebrew *bēth*) in biblical theology is more than a structure. It bespeaks the family and its members. The home is the dwelling where sabbaths and annual Passovers are observed. Home is the locus of hospitality. Care for the purity of the house symbolized the integrity of the family. It is noteworthy that synagogues are often named as "House of . . .," e.g., Beth El (House of God), Beth Shalom (House of Peace), and Beth Israel (House of Israel).

The summary in verses 54-57 wraps up the scaly infection laws in chapters 13–14. The impor-

tance of cleanness is reiterated as a criterion of holiness. Skin disease and mold on surfaces bespeak disorder and "*dis*-ease," i.e., loss of health, stress, and even intimations of death. The priest must be familiar with these phenomena and diagnose them rightly.

15:1-33 Sexual uncleanness

These laws resume the topic of childbirth (ch. 12) but relate more directly to male and female emissions and matters of intercourse. The process of purification for men and of women parallel one another in the narrative (cf. vv. 1-18, 19-30).

The modern reader must not assume a universal and timeless understanding of sexual morality. Sexuality in every culture enjoys a unique understanding and canons of appropriate and inappropriate behavior. Again, the priestly tradition that underlies much of Leviticus is informed by Genesis 1 and the divinely blessed human stewardship of all creation stated therein (Gen 1:26-28). Sexual union that brings life is godly by its very nature; no view of sexuality as dirty or a tolerated sin for the sake of procreation can be found here. Ancient reproductive science was primitive by our standards. The male fertilized the woman, and she as the "nest" produced the child. Hence, one never reads of barren men in the Bible, only barren women. Yet an appreciation of the mystery and the holiness of life remains a timeless value.

Chapter 15 teaches that the mysteries of physical sexuality expressed in genders, male and female, are gifts that bind God and humankind together. An essential aspect of blessing is fertility: "God blessed them and God said to them: Be fertile and multiply; fill the earth and subdue it" (Gen 1:28). Blessing shines forth in children, abundant flocks and fields, a good name in the community, and ultimately peace: "May the Lord bless you from Zion, / may you see Jerusalem's prosperity / all the days of your life, / and live to see your children's children. / Peace upon Israel!" (Ps 128:5-6).

Personal uncleanness of men comes from an ongoing genital discharge, probably referring to symptoms of gonorrhea and related sexually transmitted diseases. The striking distinction of this impurity is that the victim can remain in the community and at home, not banished outside the camp as with leprosy. Genital area contact with objects such as a bed, chair, or saddle makes those items unclean. Human to human physical contact and spitting also bring uncleanness. In sum, direct contact (or perceived direct contact) of the genital discharge with another person or object generates impurity.

The meaning of verse 18 deserves comment because, if read superficially, it may appear to suggest that sexual union is immoral. The emissions associated with sexual intercourse, not the act itself, are the major issue as the surrounding material affirms. When a man gives his life-giving seed to the woman, there is no certainty that an offspring will be born. The potency of seminal discharge and the fragility of conception and birth create a delicate balance of life and death. In Leviticus it is appropriate that the partners bathe in water as an act of purification. Water is essential for life, cleanses what it touches, and offers refreshment and replenishment of energy. These associations underlie this law.

The counterpart to male seminal emission is the woman's menstruation. Both men and women are impure for seven days, and curiously the woman transmits her impurity to the man (vv. 13, 24). The reason for these designations is unclear. It may relate to the ambiguity of blood as both a symbol and instrument of life *and* death. Also the loss of powerful and life-giving fluids (semen and blood) may be in mind. The cure of uncontrolled menstruation is one of Jesus' miracles in the New Testament (Matt 9:20-22; Mark 5:25-34; Luke 8:43-48) and creates a foil to this law in Leviticus. Jesus is not made impure by the woman's contact but rather he purifies her. Jesus demonstrates the power to work a wonder that transcends the sacred law.

Verses 31-33 conclude this section. Emphasis is given to the fact that these laws prevent the defilement of sacred spaces, particularly the Lord's dwelling, also called the tabernacle or holy of holies. This summary leads nicely into the next section about the Day of Atonement. This festival was the grand occasion on which the high priest would sprinkle blood of the bull and goat on the mercy seat in the holy of holies.

16:1-19 The Day of Atonement

The modern reader often associates Judaism with its annual observances, including the New Year (*rōsh hashānâ*) and the climactic Day of Atonement (*yôm kippûr*). This chapter speaks to these sacred calendared events of the fall harvest so deeply rooted in Israel's history and self-understanding. Some ideas borrowed from ancient Israel's surrounding neighbors may be behind these observances, e.g., the need to quell blood vengeance among clans and the exorcism of demons from a temple. However, the content and meaning of these observances sets Judaism apart and highlights the complexities of cultural borrowings and religious self-identification in any age.

A day of atonement for priests and the people recognizes that the rituals cited in Leviticus have their effect, but the community must not overlook other acts of ritual impurity and personal sins that accumulate during the year. These, too, require purification or atonement. Further, the altar used for the offering of animals and cereals merits reconsecration over time.

Only on the Day of Atonement may the priest enter the inner sanctuary (Holy of Holies) to purify the sacred space. He cannot enter whenever he pleases (v. 2), a warning that harks back to the fate of Nadab and Abihu (10:1-2). Further, the priest must properly dress for the occasion and offer a bull for purification and atonement, followed by a sacrificial goat. The censer smoke and the sprinkling of blood on the ark and the people add to the solemnity.

The purification of the sanctuary begins in verse 11. Sprinkling of the animal blood is essential to the ritual. The priest brings the bull (v. 6); the people bring the goat (v. 15). The collective blood atones for the whole community, priests and laity alike. The abundant incense fills the holy of holies (vv. 12-13). The volume of smoke befits the utter holiness of the inner sanctum. It may also serve to shield the priest from gazing clearly about this sacred space lest he be struck dead (v. 13). The sprinkling of the animal bloods in the holy of holies is described in some detail (vv. 14-15). From there the priest moves to the altar and performs much the same ritual (vv. 18-19). He then purifies the people, the point where the scapegoat comes into play.

16:20-28 The scapegoat

The scapegoat (Hebrew "goat for *ʿăzāʾzēl*," vv. 8, 10 [twice], 26) deserves some comment. A number of explanations of its meaning have been proposed. The animal may symbolically carry away the guilt of the people, or may represent a geographical location or formation. Probably Azazel is rooted in a legendary male demon of the desert evidenced in Mesopotamian literature. In the Scriptures this figure is merely symbolic and represents the removal of sin for all the people. The goat for Azazel is distinct from the sacrificial goat and selected by casting lots (v. 8). Casting lots leaves the choice of each goat's fate to the Lord's will. The laying on of both hands by the priest and sending of the goat into the wilderness "carries off" the burden of sins and restores spiritual and communal harmony. The desert has several meanings in the Scriptures, one of which is its being the place of sinners and evil spirits. This meaning applies here (cf. Isa 34:13-14; Matt 12:43).

In sum, blood purifies and re-consecrates the sacred space. The scapegoat takes away the sins of the people. This observance also involves fasting (literally, "afflicting the soul/spirit"), an ancient custom that was an act of piety as well as an expression of mourning or one's preparation to receive some divine revelation. In many Christian churches today the season of Lent is an annual time of fasting and penance, often associated with almsgiving and sharing the fruits of self-denial.

CODE OF LEGAL HOLINESS
Leviticus 17–26

The Holiness Code comprises a large block of laws enjoined on all the people, priests and laity alike. The reader should note that many of these laws take up matters that began in Leviticus 1–6 but now with more universal application. Unlike the laws regarding crime and civic duty found in Exodus and Deuteronomy, the Holiness Code focuses on religion and cult. As already noted, these liturgical laws find their theological foundation in the repeated call to holiness: "Be holy, for I, the LORD your God, am holy" (19:2; also 20:7, 26; 21:6, 8). In fact, reading chapter 19 first is a helpful way to become oriented to Leviticus 17–26 and the overall theological perspective of the Holiness Code.

17:1-16 Sacredness of blood

The chapter may be divided into two sections: verses 1-9 and 10-16. The first section relates to the slaughter of animals, and the second to the special treatment of blood. Both issues are intimately connected in the realm of the sacred. The narrative proceeds with a description of various circumstances (inside or outside the camp, Israelites or aliens in their midst, offerings destined for total sacrifice or eventually for table food). All animal sacrifice is regulated with an eye to communal and personal holiness. There is no provision for any "non-sacrificial" or secular slaughter of animals. The draining and burying of the blood, even of hunted animals for sport or food, speak most directly to this point (v. 13).

The discussion of blood in Leviticus 17 remains essential for our understanding of blood in the Scriptures. Blood is life and all animate creatures (animals and humans) have an inner component apart from the body but intimately related to it. A close reading of verse 11 helps our understanding of Old Testament anthropology: "the *life* of the *flesh* is in the *blood* . . ." (emphasis added). The life (Hebrew *nephesh*) refers to the spirit or spark of animation in a creature. It resides throughout life in the blood. The flesh (Hebrew *bāśār*) means a living being that grows, becomes old, dies, and returns to the dust of the earth. It is essentially the meat on the skeleton. The blood (Hebrew *dām*) is the seat of life in animate creatures. Its shedding depletes life and brings on death.

These three components helped the ancients understand corporal life and death. This understanding is primitive by modern standards but bespeaks the perennial fascination with life, death, and the fragile mysteries of mortality. The modern reader must not confuse *nephesh* (spark of life, spirit, soul) with the Christian understanding of an immortal soul separate from the body. Those categories arose in later Greek philosophy (body vs. soul) and went on to inform Christian theology. The biblical meaning of the body is more holistic.

The end of chapter 17 addresses the eating of carrion or animals killed by other beasts. Animals that eat decaying flesh are already forbidden as food (ch. 11). By extension human consumption of animals found dead is forbidden. The ritual washing harks back to 11:25 and reiterates the uncleanness that can come from contact with the dead. Again, the issue is not sinfulness (burial requires human contact). Rather, ritual purification informs the meaning of such laws.

18:1-30 The sanctity of sexuality

Major issues surround the sanctity of sex: life and death, property and boundaries, rights and obligations, penalties for misconduct, and most importantly the tragedy of innocence lost and the violation of right relationships. Thus the Scriptures emphasize that all creation is sacred and answerable to God for the abuse of the gifts of life. Recent socio-cultural biblical criticism has informed our understanding of the ancient biblical world, including the rationale for many of the customs that were important in those times.

To the modern reader some of these laws seem antiquated or are illegal in modern jurisprudence. Others seem universally correct and simply common sense. One must strive to distinguish between any particular practice and the morality behind it. For example, in ancient societies a girl of thirteen or so was of marriageable age, and degrees of separation (the marriage of cousins) were more proximate than many modern laws allow. Ancient marriages were normally arranged by families rather than by falling in love and announcing marriage to the family.

These perspectives inform the reader's thoughtful reading of Leviticus 18. One must not be immediately presumptive or judgmental, but rather ask what moral values ground a particular law. One must avoid the tendency to pick and choose based on one's own canons of morality. Such subjectivity is not helpful to understanding biblical texts. While condemning certain practices (e.g., brother-sister marriage, cultic prostitution, and child sacrifice), nowhere do the laws in Leviticus forbid intermarriage with other nations. That prohibition is extant, however, in other biblical laws (Exod 34:11-17; Deut 7:3-4). In sum, such differences demand a contextual reading of all biblical laws.

In verses 1-18 the Egyptians and Canaanites serve as examples of practices abhorrent to Israel. The command not to serve other gods is repeated throughout this section (vv. 3 [twice], 24, 26, 27, 29, 30). Israelites must not conform to pagan customs, but no ban on intermarriage is stated. The laws begin with the closest degrees of kinship. Intercourse with blood relatives or those in the family by marriage is strictly forbidden. The repetition of "disgrace" (vv. 7-19; literally, "uncover the nakedness of") deserves comment. Intercourse with one's closest kin brings shame on the family, whether the act becomes known or not. Social justice is also involved. Widows must not become prey to sexual aggression or male opportunism at the death of a spouse.

Verses 19-23 begin with the prohibition of intercourse with a woman during menstruation or with another man's wife. Adultery is forbidden in the Ten Commandments (Exod 20:14; Deut 22:22), and Leviticus 20:10 imposes the death penalty for this offense. It is noteworthy that the laws of adultery were less strict for a male. A man committed adultery *against another man's marriage*; a woman committed adultery *with any man*. Hence, a married man's liaison with an unmarried woman, such as a prostitute, was not forbidden.

Child sacrifice to Molech (v. 21) refers to a Canaanite practice that was an abomination for ancient Israel. The name Molech occurs here and in 20:2-5. Sacrificing children is evidenced throughout Old Testament as a pagan ritual and, at times, crept into Israelite worship (cf. 2 Kgs 16:3 [Ahaz]). The primary motivation in verse 23 is the integrity of Israelite worship. The Lord is their God, whose name is profaned by calling on other gods.

As seen in previous sections, chapter 18 ends with a closing exhortation (vv. 24-30). This exhortation is more decisive than others so far, and the Lord speaks most personally and directly to all the people ("your" is plural): "I, the Lord, am *your* God" (v. 30; emphasis added). No ritual of purification is available to right a sexual abomination. The very land must be purged of sexual violence because life and blessing underlie the scriptural understanding of sexuality.

19:1-37 Various rules of conduct

The reader will notice that chapter 19 calls to mind the Ten Commandments and the two essential foci of all scriptural law: to God and to one's neighbor. Holiness is the primary theme here: be holy as the Lord is holy (19:2). The intrinsic nature of God (holiness) must inform human morality. Moral behavior is more than what seems right or serves good social order. The very actions of God observed in creation inform all human law, whether simple or complex. As the heavenly bodies and the seasons obey God's laws in creation, so must humankind (Gen 1; Job 38).

19:3 Revere parents and keep the sabbath

Respect for parents and elders was a primary value in ancient society, and certain laws impose a harsh penalty for insubordination (Deut 21:18-21 [stoning to death]). The wisdom literature offers the widest discussion of family values and raising children (Prov 3:11-12; 13:1; 31:28; Sir 3:1-16; 30:1-13). Many modern societies have an understanding of child development very different from the ancient world. While we may give consideration to age-appropriate behavior, the ancients saw children as untamed and gradually tamed by discipline.

Further, we must realize that respecting parents in the Old Testament speaks more directly to adult children. Revering father and mother in the Ten Commandments means not to abandon them in their old age. In nomadic society, the cultural root of many ancient laws, seniors may not be able to keep up with the caravan. Their children must not abandon them or neglect their needs. This basic understanding informs parental respect in later settled societies. As the book of Sirach notes, "My son, be steadfast in honoring your father; / do not grieve him as long as he lives" (3:12).

Sabbath rest harks back to Genesis 2:1-3 where God rests on the seventh day. The history of sabbath observance is complicated. The essence of this law is freeing people from endless work, making time for the rest and worship, and behaving as God behaves. Rest even for the land is an extension of the sabbath ideal (see 25:1-7).

19:4 Prohibition of idols

Some Christian groups cite this and related passages as evidence for the prohibition of any divine iconography. However, the prohibition of idols is more nuanced than that. The Israelites must not understand God as confined to a molten image and believe that whatever happens to the object happens to God. Statues have no magical power. Divine freedom knows no compromise, and the true image of God is the human person (Gen 1:26-27).

The reader need but look at Genesis 31:25-35 (Rachel's theft of her father's gods) to see that Israel's early history included some use of images, especially statues. Early Christianity evidences frescoes and statues, e.g., the iconography in catacombs and ancient Christian churches. Modern Christians who use sacred images and statues should explain that these objects do not confine God or saints. They represent artistically some image or attribute that fosters piety and prayer, much like a photograph evokes the memory of a person.

19:5-8 The acceptable communion sacrifice

This section continues the communion sacrifice discussed in chapters 3 and 7. Food offered to God and then left to spoil is a desecration, so the offering must be consumed before the third day. The number three has the symbolic value of completeness and wholeness. There are three sections of the sanctuary, three times for daily prayer, and Jonah is in the belly of the fish for three days. Hence, three symbolically represents the completion of the offering in a timely manner.

19:9-10 Sharing the harvest

This law bespeaks care for the poor in ancient Israel (see 23:22; Deut 24:19-22). The compassion of Boaz for the widow Ruth returning from famine speaks eloquently to the spirit of these verses (Ruth 2). It is noteworthy that widow-orphan-alien was the sacred triad of the poor and disenfranchised in the Old Testament. The book of Deuteronomy speaks most directly to these persons as a sacred triad (10:18; 24:17; 27:19). Hence, care for the poor enjoys a foundational place in ancient Israelite law and social justice.

19:11-18 Duties to one's neighbor

Right conduct with one's neighbor demands social justice in every area of life. Injustice shows itself in theft, deception, false witness, and most powerfully in hatred and revenge. Hence, this section begins with representative behaviors and builds up to the basic attitudes that motivate such behavior. The ultimate motivation for social justice is love of neighbor as oneself, the great Golden Rule.

Verses 11-12 juxtapose four interrelated verbs that condemn "robbing" one's neighbor of something. To steal (Hebrew *gānab*) bespeaks more than property theft. It includes kidnapping as well, a crime that robs a person of rightful freedom. To deceive (Hebrew *kāhash*) connotes the withholding of relevant information that robs another of justice. To speak falsely (Hebrew *shāqar*) means to engage in deception and fraud, a designation given to false prophets in Israel (Jer 14:14; 23:25-27). To swear falsely (Hebrew *shābaᶜ*) usurps the uncompromised testimony an oath demands, i.e., to tell the truth, the whole truth, and nothing but the truth. Swearing falsely offends God who stands as the ultimate judge and sentence-giver. To promote the wrongful sentencing of a person in the name of God (perjury) is a great blasphemy.

In sum, stealth in all its forms sins against God and the community. The moral decay caused by "robbing" another person of some right affects the community and is not lost from God's judgment, even when done in secret. This value was powerful in the ancient world. The modern reader must acknowledge that physical evidence and sworn testimony have guided forensic justice for most of human history. Tales of perjury and payoffs abounded (see Dan 13 [Susanna's virtue]). There were no lie detector machines, DNA testing, and video surveillance. The sworn word held sway.

Verses 13-14 continue the theme of social justice. One must not withhold rightful payments to another. That, too, is a form of oppression. The person intended in verse 13 may well be the day laborer who lives off wages hand to mouth. Such persons need the constant trickle of minimal income to feed the family (cf. Deut 24:14-15). Such constant need flows well into care for the disabled person. Their situation is likewise chronic. In ancient Israel disabilities were often considered the consequence of sin (Deut 28:29). The blind and other disabled persons were banned from priestly service (Lev 21:18) and at times barred from the temple (2 Sam 5:8), but charity toward them was still enjoined on all of Israel. Verse 14 probably reflects the ban of cruel practical jokes at the expense of a disabled person. Amid uninformed social perceptions and biased laws, care for the disabled is a holy responsibility. Jesus' healing ministry in the gospels bespeaks this value. He reaches out to those often shunned by society.

Verses 15-16 juxtapose the unfair legal decision and slander against a neighbor. It is noteworthy that in verse 15 the poor are paired not with the rich but with the mighty. Abuse of power, not wealth in itself, is the issue. Leniency out of pity has its place but should not be a key factor in legal decisions. Likewise, deference to those with power and influence compromises the equality of all persons that true justice demands. Verse 16 makes two points related to commission and omission. First, spreading gossip never serves the good. Such information is usually biased, and the victim is not there to make a defense. Second, standing idly before a person in danger is a sin of omission. This law probably embraces a variety of circumstances, everything from personal injury to capital punishment. In sum, social justice demands vigilance against sins of commission and omission, doing and failing to do.

Verses 17-18 contrast hatred and love. These feelings come from the "heart" (Hebrew *lēb, lēbāb*), which in Israelite thought was not merely the seat of emotion and sentiment but rather intellect, will, and understanding. Hence, intention and memory are involved. This is the first of three occurrences in Leviticus of the term "heart" (also 26:36, 41), a grand motif in the Old Testament, occurring some eight hundred times. The Great Commandment ("Hear, O Israel!") in Deuteronomy 6:4-9 includes loving the Lord with all one's heart. The psalms proclaim the heart as the place where the Lord sees one's inner self (Ps 44:22) and tests one's intentions (Ps 7:3).

More deeply, the call to love and not hate rests on the fact that vengeance ultimately belongs to God: "You know, LORD: / Remember me and take care of me, / avenge me on my persecutors" (Jer 15:15; cf. Ps 94:1). God must delegate vengeance to humans. This belief, rooted in Israelite law, finds an early expression in Moses' killing of the Egyptian taskmaster (Exod 2:11-14). Moses acts alone and apart from God's revealed laws. Though filled with righteous indignation, he emerges not as the hero but a fugitive from justice. Moses flees to Midian and there encounters the Lord at the burning bush. Only later, after the exodus and the events at Sinai, do divine laws emerge that govern the human taking of life. Vigilante justice in any age never bespeaks divine justice.

These verses culminate in what we call the Golden Rule: love your neighbor as yourself. Recalling that the motif of the heart bespeaks more than emotions, this command includes intentionality. One's attitudes, behaviors, and choices must bespeak love. We love God by observing the revealed commandments. We love our neighbor by acts of social justice in line with God's commandments.

19:19-37 Miscellaneous laws

The laws discussed in this section are random and unsystematic. Basically, the matters concern secondary human relationships and material possessions.

Verse 19 is curious and has occasioned a variety of explanations. Literally, taking care to breed animals within their species bespeaks harmony in creation. God made the beasts and humankind in their intended order and relationship with one another. Indiscriminate interbreeding bespeaks primordial chaos. This law may also be a metaphor for illicit human relationships. One must not intermarry indiscriminately and engage in unlawful unions.

The laws regarding farming and clothing are extensions of the basic principle here, i.e., one must not mix foreign things and blur proper distinctions or boundaries. It may be that the farming and clothing laws are rooted in practical wisdom. Farming two crops in the same plot sometimes results in a poor harvest as each competes for nutrients from the soil or one overtakes the other. Different threads in sewing can shrink and cause clothing to pucker when washed. Such folk wisdom shows metaphorically that some "mixtures" in life do not do well. Water and oil do not mix.

Verses 20-22 address the case of a female slave betrothed to one man and seduced by another. Because the woman is property, her seducer atones with a simple offering. In terms of social justice, this violation bespeaks an abuse of the powerless. Such a violation is clearly against the Ten Commandments (Exod 20:17; Deut 5:21). This law seems out of place. Some suggest that it belongs after 20:12. For more on slave laws see Exodus 21:7-11.

Verses 23-25 discuss laws regarding fruit-bearing trees. The details indicate an appreciable knowledge of horticulture in the ancient world. Young fruit trees are left to bear unpicked fruit until the fourth year and such early fruit is metaphorically "uncircumcised." The fourth year crop is like a firstborn gift to the Lord and offered in the sanctuary. People can begin eating the fruit of the tree in the fifth year. This practice bespeaks the value of waiting and anticipation. Gifts of the earth take time, patience, and skilled handling. The time it takes to enjoy eventually the grain, wine, and oil in their proper seasons relates to practical folk wisdom. As Ecclesiastes notes, "There is an appointed time for everything, / and a time for every affair under the heavens / . . . a time to plant, and a time to uproot the plant" (3:1-2).

Verses 26-28 address random pagan practices foreign to genuine Israelite worship. The practices in and of themselves are not the focus here. Rather, it is the presumed magical power or benefit therein that is condemned. In some ancient societies the hair represented the unique life force of an individual. Its color and shape bespoke one's personal uniqueness and, like bones and teeth, remained more or less intact after other body parts deteriorated. Hairstyles could represent a special office, which is much behind the grooming of the priest cited later in 21:5-6. He must not clip the crown of the head or spoil the edges of his beard. The same goes for lacerating himself. The pagans would lacerate themselves to get the gods' attention (1 Kgs 18:25-29 [the prophets of Baal]). Incised markings, piercing, and branding were methods of marking slaves (Exod 21:6; Deut 15:17).

Verse 29 speaks of prostitution, a practice not in itself prohibited in ancient Israelite law. Adultery is a separate matter because it violates a man's marriage. To degrade one's daughter in such a manner for profit is an abomination. It affects the very fabric of the family and social order.

Verse 30 reminds the reader that the sabbath is holy and its observance a way to holiness. A time of rest gives the people an opportunity to worship and is rooted in God's plan of creation (Gen 2:2-3).

Verse 31 resumes verses 26-28 and the rejection of certain pagan practices. To consult the dead via fortune-tellers and other mediums was a way of seeing into the future and perhaps manipulating one's fate. Such superstition, though evidenced in ancient Israel (Isa 8:19-20), is censured here and elsewhere (20:6, 20; Deut 18:10-12).

Verse 32 resumes the spirit of respect for the disabled enjoined in verse 14. Reverence of parents and elders stems from the Ten Commandments and finds its fullest expression in the Old Testament wisdom literature. Proverbs and Sirach discuss this theme in various places (Prov 10:1; 23:22-25; Sir 3:1-16).

Verses 33-34 remind the Israelites to care for the alien in their midst out of the remembrance that they were once themselves slaves in Egypt. This law echoes the spirit of Exodus 22:20 where care of the disenfranchised triad of widow-orphan-alien is motivated by the memory of the slavery of the Hebrews (also Exod 23:9; Deut 10:17-19; 24:17-18).

Verses 35-37 speak of justice in the marketplace, with verse 37 summing up the chapter. The term used to express dishonesty (Hebrew *ʿāwel*) bespeaks an unjust and sinful deed, not merely shady business practices to be winked at. Cheating in weights and balances was typical in the ancient world, so customers regularly bargained with vendors. The ephah was approximately six gallons and the hin one gallon, so the law concerns bulk sales.

The prophets (Hos 12:8; Amos 8:5; Mic 6:10-11) and the wisdom literature (Prov 11:1; 16:11; 20:10) railed against such dishonesty. The sin was most heinous when done against the poor and those with limited income (Amos 8:4).

20:1-27 The death penalty for the integrity of the land

This chapter contains various laws divided into two sections: the penalty of death (vv. 1-21, 27) and the integrity of the land (vv. 22-26). "Shall be put to death" is repeated through these laws and forms an *inclusio* for the chapter (vv. 2, 27). Certain sins are so heinous that the sinner must be blotted out from the community, and the community members exact the execution. The term "people of the land" (Hebrew *ʿam hāʾāreṣ*) means "fellow citizens" here. These are probably the adult males who represent the community in the act of stoning, along with any formal witnesses against the person. Their act bespeaks a communal punishment that typically takes place outside the city (24:14).

Such violence seems harsh to the modern reader, but to the ancients the integrity of the land and the community superseded the individual. To their mind much was at stake with some sins, and the community good must take precedence. The stoning of Stephen in the New Testament indicates the gravity of the charges laid against him by his accusers. In their eyes he blasphemed the Mosaic law, the temple, and the stature of Moses (Acts 6:8-15).

20:1-21, 27 The death penalty

Similar laws are evidenced elsewhere in the Old Testament. Murder (Gen 9:6; Exod 21:12),

adultery (Deut 22:20-21), kidnapping (Exod 21:16), and even striking parents (Exod 21:15) called for capital punishment. Stoning and burning were the most typical forms of execution.

Verses 2-5 discuss an abomination that combines murder and idolatry. The Lord will notice and punish attempts to abet or cover up child sacrifice. The fourfold repetition of Molech, a pagan god associated with human sacrifice, contextualizes the ban. The details of this prohibition are telling. Sacrificing one's offspring is rooted in the idea that returning "first fruits" to the gods would assure fertility in the future. While acknowledging that the first male offspring belonged to God (Exod 22:29-30), Israelite law called for a substitute animal offering (Exod 13:12-13; Num 18:15). Further, such an abominable sacrifice defiles the sanctuary. The Lord is intrinsically holy, so such a practice is impure and desecrating by its very nature. At times ancient Israel dappled in such pagan practices, but authentic worship demanded allegiance to the Lord.

Verse 6 condemns the consultation of mediums and fortune-tellers. Such persons engage in necromancy, i.e., the consultation of ghosts to learn secrets of the future. The secrets allow someone to know the future in advance or try to alter the intended future. The manipulative nature of such superstitions is foreign to divine freedom and human openness to the will of God.

Verses 7-8 again exhort holiness, the quality that sets authentic worship apart from pagan superstitions and practices. Obedience is a way to holiness, and God shows holiness in mighty deeds that evoke awe and reverence.

Verses 9-21 list numerous acts that bring disgrace on the family. Any one of these acts breaks the fabric of familial and communal integrity. Parental disrespect heads the list. The modern reader may find the death penalty harsh, but the foundational importance of father and mother underlies this teaching. All other family relations stand on honor of parents as one's human creators and first teachers.

Sexual misconduct violates another man's property (spouse, children, slaves, animals), but more profoundly tears at the fabric of the household and the extended family (cf. 18:1-18). The abuse of power is also involved. Sexuality is a strong symbol of human power used to humiliate, subjugate, and steal from others, both physically and emotionally. Leviticus demands the harshest of penalties.

Verse 27 picks up on verse 6 and further condemns those who act as mediums and fortune-tellers. Its position is awkward in the flow of the narrative, but it does add an element of personal responsibility for engaging in superstitions. The verse sums up all the laws in the chapter: "their bloodguilt is upon them."

20:22-26 The integrity of the land

These five verses form a smoother end to the chapter if verse 27 is read immediately after verse 6. The fourfold repetition of "land" or "ground" (Hebrew ʾeres or ʾădāmâ [each twice]) punctuates this section, as well as the twofold repetition of holiness (Hebrew qādôsh). The land and its people must be holy as God is holy. The land is a gift the Lord is bringing them to, not a land they earn for themselves (vv. 22, 24). Therein, the Israelites must distinguish and separate the clean from the unclean, a command that harks back to 10:10 and 11:47. The Israelites themselves are a people set apart.

Leviticus 18–20 forms a splendid unit in its own right. Though many of its laws are time conditioned, the content demonstrates that ancient Israel and many neighboring cultures valued social harmony and ethical human relationships. The Golden Rule in 19:18 succinctly teaches that charity and justice bespeak fidelity to God. This rule also affirms that ritual sacrifice without the proper inner disposition is empty. The same spirit governs the New Testament. In Jesus' warning against anger he admonishes the crowd to leave their gifts at the altar if there is need of reconciliation (Matt 5:21-26). The letter of James affirms that faith and good works go hand in hand (2:14-26).

21:1-15 Sanctity of the priesthood

Though priesthood and priestly duties are discussed earlier in Leviticus, the subject gets its most focused attention here. The priest, set apart to mediate and officiate for the people, must embody distinct qualities and a particular lifestyle. First, he must not touch the dead except for the burial preparation of nearest relatives. This taboo extends from his duty to distinguish between the clean and unclean (10:10) and to act as guardian of the sanctuary.

Second, he must keep laws regarding shaving the head or beard, which are related to ancient mourning practices. The same applies to self-laceration (cf. 19:27-28). His ministry centers in the sanctuary and its environs, so he must not become ritually defiled or appear bodily unkempt. The modern reader must remember that the dead were not brought into the temple for a memorial service but buried with dispatch. Different customs of mourning and burial apply to biblical texts.

The sanctity of the priests demands that they marry only women of pure lineage. The bride could not be a prostitute or any non-virgin, even if the previous victim of rape. The daughter of a priest incurs the harshest of penalties for shaming her lineage. The death penalty indicates that any sexual misconduct of the priest's children, even a consensual act, was more heinous than with commoners.

Verses 10-12 relate to the high priest, literally, "the priest who is exalted above his fellows." He is anointed on the head, while the other priests' clothing is anointed (see 8:30). The application of oil and special vestments bespeaks his consecration and mandate to fulfill his duties as high priest.

Verses 13-15 complement verses 7-8, adding to the list of unqualified brides for the priest. Virginity is the issue, not the character of the woman. One should recall that a widow could face economic hardship if her deceased husband's family disowned her and she was unable to reunite with her family.

21:16-24 Priestly blemishes

Defects were prohibited on all beings associated with sacrifices, human and beast alike (cf. 22:19-25). However, a priest with a bodily defect could serve in areas not associated with the altar, the place "to offer the food of his God" (v. 17). In the ancient world deformities were often considered signs of divine punishment for personal sin or that of one's ancestors. The book of Job uses being without defect as a metaphor for moral living (11:15; 31:7; see also Prov 9:7), and the New Testament draws on such imagery to describe Jesus as the unblemished Lamb of God (Heb 9:14; 1 Pet 1:19).

22:1-16 Priestly purity

The impurities in verses 4-9 hark back to sections in chapters 13–15. Intentionality distinguishes the cases cited here. Intentional sin merits being cut off from the Lord and the community (v. 3). Unintentional impurity renders a person unclean for a period of time (v. 4).

Lay persons become the focus in verses 10-16. Those in some relationship with the priest (his slaves and their children, his hired laborers, or a daughter returned to his house) may partake of the sacrificial food. Those with no such status are excluded.

22:17-30 Unacceptable victims

As the priest must be unblemished, so must the sacrificial animal. Certain blemishes are easily recognizable and make for immediate rejection; other defects are minor and acceptable for a free-will offering but not a votive offering (22:23). Minor defects include the stunted growth of an otherwise healthy animal. Waiting until the eighth day to take a sacrificial animal from its mother bespeaks the spirit of the seven days: a symbolic value associated with rest, completion, and a parallel with the seven-day creation schema in Genesis 1. This waiting period also calls to mind the octave of ordination discussed in chapter 9. Timing is often significant in these laws.

22:31-33 A closing exhortation

These verses are punctuated with the call to holiness. The profane is incompatible with the sacred, and the true Israelite must make a choice. God's intrinsic holiness remains the standard of all human choices. When one brings a sacrifice to the altar, the holy name of God is invoked. This gesture joins the grain or animal sacrifice to God. The memory of slavery in Egypt remains a timeless reason for observing the commandments and is repeated throughout the Old Testament.

23:1-44 Holy days

Communal celebrations through the liturgical year give identity and order to the religious community. Hence, the emphasis on second-person *plural* pronouns and verbs in this section highlights the communal nature of the laws enjoined. Spring and fall festivals, three in each season, characterize the worship calendar of ancient Israel. In the spring season Passover and Unleavened Bread (vv. 4-8), First Fruits (vv. 9-14), and Pentecost (vv. 15-22, also called Weeks) occur. In

the fall the New Year (vv. 23-25), the Day of Atonement (vv. 26-32), and Booths (vv. 33-44, also called Succoth) take place. Woven through these annual feasts is the weekly sabbath observance (v. 3).

It is noteworthy that the sabbath observance is enjoined on the Israelites as a people (v. 2), not the priests as its presider. The laity has the primary responsibility for regular sabbath observance through the weeks of the year. This observance is rooted in creation where God enjoins humankind to be vigilant of the days and years (Gen 1:14) and to rest as God rests (Gen 2:3). Sabbath recurs weekly in the calendar; the other celebrations are moveable feasts in their proper season.

23:1-3 The sabbath

This observance sets a weekly day of rest and mirrors God's rest after creation: "On the seventh day God completed the work he had been doing; he rested on the seventh day from all the work he had undertaken. God blessed the seventh day and made it holy . . ." (Gen 2:2-3). God is intrinsically holy, so what better way to emulate that holiness than to act as God does. Sabbath imitates the cycle and rhythm of creation, that order that God brought out of chaos. Sabbath is for everyone: free persons, slaves, and even the animals.

23:4-14 Passover and Unleavened Bread

These feasts are discussed more fully in Exodus 12:1-20 and Numbers 28:17-25. They were originally separate festivals celebrating the first fruits of the harvest: the Passover of the shepherd and his flocks, the Unleavened Bread of the farmer and his crops. Once combined, they celebrate the memory of freedom from slavery in Egypt and the exodus journey (Exod 1–15, especially chs. 12–13).

First sheaves or fruits (vv. 9-14) celebrate the barley harvest. Barley is planted in the fall/winter season and reaped in the spring. This grain is generally heartier than wheat and can grow in less than ideal soil. This quality lends to the grain's inclusion in the list of produce that symbolizes blessings for Israel in the Promised Land (Deut 8:8). The elevation of the sheaf expresses thanks in the present and prayers for continued abundance in the future.

The theology of remembering and retelling informs the meaning of this festival: "When your children ask you, 'What does this rite of yours mean?' you will reply, 'It is the Passover sacrifice for the LORD, who passed over the houses of the Israelites in Egypt; when he struck down the Egyptians, he delivered our houses'" (Exod 12:26-27). To remember these saving events is not simply a recollection of the past. By sharing in this family meal the participants become exodus people in the present.

The history of Passover is rich and complex. A family celebration in its origins, it later becomes a pilgrimage festival to Jerusalem (Deut 16:1-8). Today the Jewish Passover Haggadah (Sedar Meal) continues this annual festival. Appreciation of Passover theology also informs our understanding of the Eucharist in the church. The gospels place Jesus' death at the time of Passover and Unleavened Bread (e.g., Mark 14:12-15), and Paul uses these feasts in exhorting Christians to moral living (1 Cor 5:6-8).

23:15-22 Pentecost

Also called Weeks, this feast celebrates the first wheat harvest and occurs seven weeks after Passover and Unleavened Bread (hence Pentecost or "fiftieth"). Bread from the wheat harvest, several sacrificial animals, and libations are included (vv. 18-19). The libation is typically wine poured on the altar. The association of wine with festivities offers a vivid metaphor for ritual abuses and dappling in paganism: "Indeed, you poured out a drink offering to them, / and brought up grain offerings. / With these things, should I be appeased?" (Isa 57:6).

As with Passover and Unleavened Bread, Pentecost later became a pilgrimage feast (Deut 16:9-12). Its origins are in the farmer bringing first fruits of the harvest to a local shrine. In the postexilic period (Second Temple Judaism) the association with agriculture waned and the feast became associated with the making of the Sinai covenant, based on its timing in the spring (see Exod 19:1; 2 Chr 15:8-15).

Verse 22 echoes the spirit of the second harvest (19:9-10). Amid all its ritual laws, Leviticus repeatedly enjoins the care of the poor. The repetition of this law reminds the hearer that charity is an ongoing obligation throughout the year and not a seasonal time of almsgiving. Such charity is grounded in that fact that the Lord demands it: "I, the LORD, am your God."

23:23-25 The New Year

Leviticus now moves to the autumn feasts on the calendar. New Year was the time of celebration and renewal. Ancient societies record a myriad of New Year rites, including parading statues of the gods and holding lavish banquets. The trumpet blasts were festive accents rooted in calling on the gods' attention to ongoing fertility, including abundant rainfall and productive flocks and crops. People made wishes for the coming year, believing at the same time that the gods were setting their destinies. New Year also invites attention to remembering what God has wrought for the people. This point harks back to the theology of remembering in Passover and Unleavened Bread (vv. 4-14).

23:26-32 The Day of Atonement

The Day of Atonement caps off the fall festivals that begin with New Year (see ch. 16). This is a time of introspection, penance, and prayer. It has a certain sabbath character to it: a ritual retreat from the routine of daily life. Most important, the day provides an occasion for necessary atonements that are overlooked by the various sin and purification offerings. There would always be residual sins, both communal and individual, for which the community must render accounts. This day filled the gap. The gravity of this observance comes across in the penalty of being cut off from the community, with God actively removing that person from their midst (23:30). The meaning and message of this day informs our New Testament understanding of Christ's redemptive atonement for the sins of humanity (Heb 8–9).

23:33-44 The feast of Booths

This third fall festival and last of the pilgrimage feasts is sometimes called Tabernacles and lasts for seven days. It celebrates the harvest of grapes and olives, acknowledging the end of the annual agricultural seasons. As a vintage feast it has some parallels with the Greco-Roman feasts of Dionysius/Bacchus. The designation "booths" reflects the shelters built to house the many pilgrims that came to Jerusalem for its observance.

The festiveness of this occasion can hardly be exaggerated. Celebration included candle processions, dancing through the night, and the generous consumption of wine by revelers. Though rooted in celebration of the harvest and an appeal to God for another fruitful season, the festival evolved into a time of anticipating the coming of the Messiah and the independence of Israel (see 2 Macc 1:9-36). This change in focus shows that festivals are very much living traditions, often rooted in one reality and later given other meanings.

The colorful information in verses 39-43 deserves comment. The Hebrews camped in temporary shelters on their exodus journey to the Promised Land. They were a people "on the move." Now enjoying the abundance of the land, the people reenact that simple living with memory and gratitude. On their minds would be words like those from Psalm 136:10-12: "Who struck down the firstborn of Egypt, / for his mercy endures forever; / And led Israel from their midst, / for his mercy endures forever; / With mighty hand and an outstretched arm, / for his mercy endures forever."

Most people live by a daily calendar, caught up in routines and deadlines, places to go and people to see. Reading about holy days in Leviticus offers hermeneutical insights for the modern reader. First, men and women in ministerial leadership will probably better relate to these observances. Their lives are caught up in church duties and presiding at ceremonies. Second, Leviticus invites the laity to reflect on their personal calendar. Are weekly observances in a faith tradition—sabbath, Sunday, etc.—more than interruptions? Are these days simply obligations to fulfill or are they moments of rest and grace? Third, Old Testament rituals remind us that liturgy means celebration of the gifts of creation. Beneath the many details of observance in ancient Israel lie values that speak to holy worship in any faith tradition.

24:1-4 The sanctuary light

Care of the sanctuary lamp follows nicely from the previous section because olive oil, a gift of the autumn harvest, is involved. The first extraction of oil was the purest and most valuable. Modern terminology uses "extra virgin" to describe this squeezing. The purest and clearest of oil was typically used for cooking and medicinal purposes. Later presses of oil were for lighting lamps and other secondary functions. The stipulation of clear oil indicates that only the best was fit for the sanctuary, setting the holy place apart from household use of oil for lighting, medicinal needs, and other purposes.

24:5-9 The showbread

Bread offerings to gods are evidenced throughout ancient Near Eastern cultures. However, the showbread or bread of the presence in the Israelite temple was not to feed God but to represent the offering of a staple of life (see Exod 25:23-30). The twelve loaves or cakes represent the twelve tribes in covenant with God. The placement of the bread so near the holy of holies affirms its holiness and being set apart to God. The story in 1 Samuel 21:2-8 where David and his soldiers eat the showbread comes to mind. Such a bold action would be an abomination except for the fact that they were in a state of holiness, having refrained from sexual activity during time of war (cf. Mark 2:23-28).

24:10-23 Punishment of blasphemy, and the *lex talionis*

Blasphemy is essentially cursing God. Although a curse may be a personal act, there is a communal element to such a transgression that calls for a communal response. The power of invoking a divine name and the efficacy of blessings and curses were powerful in the mind of the ancients. Hence, to curse another person in God's name bespeaks assuming a prerogative not given to humans. Who can dare to assume for oneself what God can or will do? Who can coerce God to fulfill a curse? To curse God directly is thus a capital offense.

The damning nature of blasphemy relates well to the so-called *lex talionis*: an eye for an eye, a tooth for a tooth. Punishments for violent acts must be proportional to the damage and not in excess. In sum, curses are often emotional and disproportionate, so excess must be avoided in acts of retribution as the *lex talionis* demands (cf. Matt 5:38-42).

The principle of equality also informs our understanding of the *lex talionis*. In an unfair world the wealthy can buy themselves out of a crime, while the poor must serve their time. This law provides no monetary or other material compensation for damages against another person. All must make equal restitution for the same crime. Further, this law demonstrates that violations against the sanctuary do not stand over and above violations of daily life. God's holiness pervades every aspect of life. Violence against one's neighbor is violence against the God in whose nature that person is made. To strike and injure another person for no justifiable reason evokes divine judgment. One must act under the law and not out of unbridled anger or vigilante justice.

25:1-22 The sabbatical and jubilee years

These observances represent a time of rest and release. God's rest after creation and the memory of slavery in Egypt are the theological foundations of sabbath and jubilee (cf. Exod 20:8-11; 31:12-17; Deut 5:12-15). The laws cited here emphasize rest for the land and care of the poor. Such a reprieve may have been more an ideal than a practice, given the delicate balance of feast and famine in ancient Palestine. Most people eked out a daily living and had little time for a day of rest. Crops had to be managed and animals tended to.

Whatever the socio-cultural realities, the value of a time of rest enjoys an enduring theological meaning. This meaning includes the call to be compassionate as God is so. Such virtue includes stewardship of creation and relief for the poor. Further, sabbath and jubilee embody the spirit of *shālôm* (peace). Peace in Israelite thought was more than the absence of war; it bespoke harmony and welfare in every facet of life. Leviticus 25 envisions a world in which labor is embraced as a gift, people can rest as needed, and no family lacks hearth and home.

The jubilee year is a grand ideal. At that time land held in debt was returned to its heirs, and those enslaved to pay off debts were freed. The theological meaning of this year is noteworthy. The land ultimately belongs to God, and the people must remember the heritage of having been slaves in Egypt (v. 23).

The modern reader may see the very idea of jubilee as poor fiscal policy, but the spirit of jubilee remains timeless. No one has a right to hold permanently what belongs rightfully to another. No one must lock other persons in a cycle of debt from which they cannot break. Our understanding of jubilee in the Old Testament informs the New Testament parable about writing off debts and showing compassion toward those who owe us (see Matt 18:21-35). Show compassion, and judge not lest you be judged (Jas 2:12-13).

25:23-55 Redemption of property

This section elaborates on specific circumstances that concretize the ideals of sabbath and jubilee. The land belongs to the Lord (v. 23); family land must revert to its intended heirs (v. 28); the Levites traditionally hold a special position among the tribes because no parcel of land in Canaan was given to them (Num 18:21-24; Deut 18:1-4). The Levites supported themselves by ritual services and have a perpetual right to their property (v. 32). Further, Israelite countrymen may be pressed into service but not remain slaves in perpetuity (v. 39-43). Non-Israelite slaves bought from neighboring nations may be held in perpetuity (v. 44-46). Israelite slaves must eventually be redeemed by the next of kin (vv. 46-49).

The reason for these laws stems from the memory of Egypt: ". . . whom I brought out of the land of Egypt, I, the LORD, your God" (v. 55). The Lord is the creator and redeemer who led the Israelites out of Egypt and later out of Babylon. No permanent captivity can be found in the divine plan for Israel, and neither must it endure in Israelite society. No land and no people are perpetually lost. Sabbath and jubilees celebrate this vision of harmony and social justice.

26:1-13 The reward of obedience

Leviticus draws to a close with an exhortation to obedience as the path to blessing. Obedience is intimately related to hearing in Israelite thought. To hear means to follow through, to obey (Deut 6:4). The God who frees the Israelites from oppression demands obedience in turn.

The path to blessing through obedience is multifaceted. This section offers a variety of ways in a condensed and unsystematic order. The people should reject idols (v. 1) and keep the sabbath (v. 2) so that rain (v. 4) and peace (v. 6) will abide in the land. Freed from placating idols, the people enjoy the patronage of the one God. Freed from endless toil, the people can embrace the rhythmic time of sabbath. Rain provides gifts of the earth, while peace ensures domestic and social order. Divine presence binds these gifts together: one God and one people (v. 12). The Israelites were freed from slavery in Egypt but are now the Lord's servants. Their vassal state is transferred from Pharaoh to the Lord.

26:14-39 The punishment of disobedience

The curses for disobedience are more specific than the blessings for obedience. Further, the repetition of sevenfold penalties punctuates this section (vv. 18, 21, 24, 28), emphasizing the severity of the curses enjoined. The curses begin with the individual and dovetail to the larger community. That God, in turn, will give the people what they deserve reflects the *lex talionis* (24:20): eye for an eye, tooth for tooth.

The mounting gravity of the curses stems from the persistent defiance among the people (vv. 18, 21, 23, 27). God is forced to escalate the curses to such horrors as cannibalism (v. 29) and the destruction of the holy places (v. 31). But eventually the stiff-necked people will give in, even if they be just a remnant of what was before. The survivors will carry their own guilt and sometimes that of their ancestors (v. 39). The notion of sins of the fathers visited on the sons recurs at several points in the Old Testament (Exod 34:6-7; Num 14:18; Jer 5:7; Lam 5:7). Most famous is the proverb in Jeremiah: "The parents ate unripe grapes, / and the children's teeth are set on edge" (31:29; cf. Ezek 18:2).

26:40-46 Repentance and return

Restoration of a right relationship with God depends on human contrition and the Lord's remembering of the covenant with the ancestors. The theme of remembering (Hebrew *zākar*) is reiterated in this section (vv. 42, 45) and has a rich tradition through the Old Testament. Remembering harks back to God's saving Noah and his family at the great flood (Gen 8:1) and preserving his line as a remnant of humanity. God also remembers childless women and hears their prayers (Gen 30:22-24 [Rachel]; 1 Sam 1:9-19 [Hannah]). Covenant requires that the Lord remembers the promises made long ago: "Remember! Do not break your covenant with us" (Jer 14:21). Further, Deuteronomic theology demands that the people remember the wonders God has wrought for them through the generations (Deut 5:15; 7:18; 8:1-5).

The land is also important in repentance and return; it must be purified of human sin (v. 43). The land motif also speaks to a theology of exile. The deportation of the people to Babylon gives the Promised Land time to rest and grow back to its fertile self. A later remnant will repopulate the land and live according to God's laws. Remembrance of the Sinai covenant remains foundational to this event (vv. 45-46).

REDEMPTION OF OFFERINGS

Leviticus 27

Most commentators consider this chapter an appendix to Leviticus. Numerous vows and related gifts to the Lord are discussed. These gifts can be persons or property and involve a serious commitment that can only be annulled in special cases. Several Old Testament passages warn against making impulsive or frivolous vows: "When you make a vow to the LORD, your God, you shall not delay in fulfilling it; for the LORD, your God, will surely require it of you and you will be held guilty" (Deut 23:22; cf. Eccl 5:3-6; Sir 18:22-23). The payment scale in shekels, estimated by age and gender, is so high that it would deter the average person from making rash and imprudent vows. The amounts cited in each case bespeak that person's ability to redeem a votive offering, i.e., small children and seniors over sixty years old produce less service. It is also noteworthy that the distinctions in payments do not figure in wealth and social status. All persons are suitable gifts to the Lord who sees into the heart and is not swayed by worldly power and status.

The dedication of house or land (vv. 14-24) sets that property apart for sacred purposes. The offering need not be permanent. The owner can redeem the property for a certain fee. The most colorful example of this principle occurs in Ruth 4:1-12. Boaz redeems the property of his deceased kinsman, Elimelech, in a protracted episode set at the city gate before assembled elders. Boaz must also take Ruth (daughter-in-law of Elimelech and widow of his son Mahlon) as his wife and so continue that family line. His action shows his love for Ruth and respect for due process.

Mention of the jubilee year shows that inheritances must not be permanently taken from a family, even for cultic purposes. This provision bespeaks the spirit of the prophets who railed against kings and creditors permanently seizing the rightful inheritance of others, especially the poor (e.g., Isa 5:8-10; Mic 2:1-3). Ancient empires were known to seize tracts of land to build temples and related structures. Though sometimes engaging in such practices, Israel is warned not to do so. Such is an egregious injustice.

The property of a person given in vow to the Lord cannot be sold or ransomed (vv. 28-29). The Hebrew term used here (*hērem*, a ban) has various meanings in the Old Testament, including things banned from use by God or peoples doomed to destruction. For example, Deuteronomy bans or dooms the indigenous peoples of Canaan as the Israelites engage in conquest (20:15-18). Here the ban (things "doomed" to the Lord) must remain in perpetuity for the gift is consecrated and set apart to God.

Tithes (vv. 30-33) in the Old Testament took on various expressions and served a variety of sacred purposes. Some offerings went to support the Jerusalem temple and sanctuaries. The offering of grain, wine, oil, and firstling animals was typical. Those unable to transport their produce or animals could send a monetary equivalent.

Levites were supported from this income as well (Deut 14:22-29). Tithing included an element of social justice. The material goods and monies accrued provided care for the widow, orphan, and alien. The prophets warned that such giving must include the proper inner disposition; lip service while oppressing the poor brings divine judgment (Amos 4:1-5).

Verse 34 concludes Leviticus. As noted above, chapter 27 appears to be an appendix added by a later redactor. The intention behind this addition remains unclear, but Leviticus 27 certainly offers a conclusion that softens the curses in chapter 26. The repetition of "Sinai" serves an *inclusio* with 26:46 and binds these chapters together as narrative.

I would invite the reader to read Psalm 119, the longest in the Psalter, in its entirety as a closing prayer to this commentary on Leviticus: "I long for your salvation, Lord; / and your law is my delight" (v. 174).

THE BOOK OF
NUMBERS

Irene Nowell, O.S.B.

INTRODUCTION

Title

The English title of this book is Numbers, a fitting name for a book that contains not only two censuses of the people (chs. 1 and 26) and a separate census of the Levites (ch. 3), but also many lists: the offerings of the tribes to the tabernacle (ch. 7); the measurements of grain, wine, and oil to accompany sacrifices (ch. 15); the designated sacrifices for all occasions (chs. 28–29); the stages of the wilderness journey (ch. 33); and the boundaries of the land (ch. 34). The Hebrew title of the book is *Bemidbar*, "in the wilderness," a word found in the first verse of the book, which aptly describes its contents.

Chronology and geography

Most of the stories in Numbers seem to be clustered around the first two years and the fortieth year after the exodus event. The book opens on the first day of the second month of the second year after the exodus from Egypt. The people have been encamped at Sinai almost a year, since the first day of the third month of the first year after the exodus (Exod 19:1). There is a flashback of a month in Numbers 7–9: The tribal leaders make their offerings when Moses completes the construction of the tabernacle, the first day of the *first* month of year two (Num 7:1; see Exod 40:2, 17). The Passover is celebrated in the same month, on the fourteenth day of the first month of year two (Num 9:1-5). The flashback ends and the chro-

nology resumes with the people's departure from Sinai on the twentieth day of the second month of year two (Num 10:11).

Thus the events of Numbers 1:1–10:10 occur in the first twenty days of the second month of the second year after the exodus. Then there is a gap in the chronology. No dates are indicated until chapter 20 and the date that appears in that chapter is incomplete: The Israelites arrive at Kadesh in the wilderness of Zin in the first month; neither the day nor the year is mentioned (Num 20:1). A clue to the year may be found in the announcement of Aaron's death in 20:22-29. Elsewhere his death is reported to be on the first day of the fifth month of the fortieth year after the departure from Egypt (Num 33:38). No further dates appear in the book.

For the first several chapters the people are encamped at Mount Sinai (1:1–10:10). From there they travel to two otherwise unknown wilderness locations whose names recall the people's murmuring against the Lord: Taberah and Kibroth-hattaavah (11:3, 34-35). From there they travel to Hazeroth where Miriam and Aaron complain against Moses (11:35). These places seem to be in the southern part of the Sinai Peninsula.

Then the people turn north and come to the wilderness of Paran in the northeastern part of the Sinai Peninsula. From here Moses sends spies to scout out the land (13:3). A problem arises when the place is also named Kadesh (13:26).

Figure 1: Chronology

First census (1:1)	Day 1	Month 2	Year 2
Tribal offerings (7:1; see Exod 40:2, 17)	*Day 1*	*Month 1*	*Year 2*
Passover (9:1-5)	*Day 14*	*Month 1*	*Year 2*
Departure from Sinai (10:11)	Day 20	Month 2	Year 2
Arrival at Kadesh (20:1)	---	Month 1	---
Aaron's death (20:22-29; 33:38)	Day 1	Month 5	Year 40

Apparently in one version of the wilderness story Israel arrived at Kadesh fairly soon after the departure from Egypt, since they are told in the wilderness of Paran that they will wander for forty years before entering the Promised Land (14:29-34). Another version of the story puts their arrival at Kadesh in what seems to be the fortieth year of their sojourn in the wilderness (20:1). Both traditions were preserved. Kadesh is located in the northern part of the wilderness of Paran, close to the wilderness of Zin. See map on page 1524.

From Kadesh the people begin their approach to the Promised Land. They arrive at Mount Hor on the border of Edom where Aaron dies (20:22-27). They take the Red Sea road according to God's instructions (14:25), possibly going as far south as the Gulf of Aqaba (called the Red Sea in 21:4). They then go north to bypass Edom on the west, camping at two otherwise unknown sites, Oboth and Iye-abarim. From there they travel around Moab to the west, camping first at the Wadi Zered between Edom and Moab and arriving at the Wadi Arnon, which forms the northern border of Moab (21:11-13). The remaining sites are all in the plains of Moab. Mount Pisgah is, according to Deuteronomy, the site of Moses' death (Deut 34:1-6).

Structure

The basic structure of the book is set by the censuses of two generations and the primary stages of the itinerary: (1) preparation for the departure from Sinai (1:1–10:10); (2) forty-year wandering of the exodus generation from Sinai to the plains of Moab (10:11–25:18); (3) a new generation on the plains of Moab (26:1–36:13).

Another important characteristic of the structure of the book is the interweaving of narrative

and law. After chapters 1–10, which consist mostly of legislative and organizational material, stories set the stage for laws. Stories of murmuring and rebellion (chs. 11–14) lead to the legislation concerning sacrifices and sin offerings (ch. 15). Korah's challenge that all the people of God are holy and should be allowed to handle holy things (ch. 16) is followed by the legislation concerning priests and Levites (chs. 17–18) and preparation of purification water (ch. 19).

Even as the murmuring continues, the report of the deaths of Miriam and Aaron (ch. 20) introduces the last leg of the journey toward the Promised Land (ch. 21). The oracles of Balaam show Israel as blessed by God (chs. 22–24), but the incident at Baal-Peor reveals their weakness (ch. 25). In chapter 26 a new generation is introduced and counted. The rest of the book is filled with legislation for this new generation in the Promised Land: inheritance and allotment of the land (chs. 27, 32, 34, 36), observance of festivals (ch. 29), validity of vows (ch. 30), and cities of asylum (ch. 35). Even this collection of laws, however, is interrupted by narrative, the battle against the Midianites (ch. 31); this story provides the model for waging Holy War. Chapter 33 is a summary of the stages on the journey.

Sources

For almost two centuries the Documentary Hypothesis was considered the best way to analyze the sources in the pentateuchal (first five books of the Old Testament) narrative. According to this theory there were four major sources that threaded their way through the narrative from creation to the entrance into the land: Yahwist (tenth-century Judah); Elohist (ninth-century Israel); Deuteronomist (seventh-century Jerusalem);

Figure 2: Itinerary (compare Numbers 33)

Mount Sinai	1:1–10:10
Wilderness: Taberah, Kibroth-hattaavah, Hazeroth	10:11–12:15
Wilderness of Paran (at Kadesh?)	12:16; 13:3 13:26
Wilderness of Zin (Kadesh/Meribah)	20:1, 13, 14, 16, 22
Mount Hor on the border of Edom	20:22-27
The Red Sea road	21:4; see 14:25
Oboth and Iye-abarim across from Moab	21:11
Wadi Zered	21:12
Wadi Arnon north of Moab	21:13
To the plains of Moab: Beer, Mattanah, Nahaliel, Bamoth, Pisgah Shittim/Peor in the plains of Moab	21:17-20 25:1, 3

Priestly (sixth-century Babylon). According to the theory, these sources, each a written version based on oral tradition and the situation of the intended audience, were finally compiled in the sixth-century Babylonian exile to form the final edition of the Pentateuch. It has become increasingly clear, however, how difficult it is to follow any one of these sources throughout the Pentateuch. So different models are being proposed to assist the reader in understanding the contradictions, duplicate stories, and different styles that appear in these books, sometimes in close proximity to each other.

The assumption in this commentary is that various traditions are represented in the book of Numbers. One tradition is interested in matters of worship and law, and is probably also responsible for the various censuses and lists. This tradition will be called "Priestly." Other traditions supply some of the murmuring stories and a variant report of the itinerary of the wilderness wandering. These traditions will be called collectively "pre-Priestly." No attempt is made to date any of these traditional sources.

Content

The Hebrew title of the book indicates one of its major themes: the wilderness. The wilderness (or desert) is both a positive and a negative sym-

bol in the Old Testament. It is a place of constant murmuring and rebellion (e.g., Exod 15:22–17:7; Num 11–14), but it is also the place of Israel's "honeymoon" with God, the place where they were totally dependent on God who provided for them abundantly (e.g., Jer 2:1-3; Hos 2:16-17). Both connotations often appear together (see Num 20:2-13; Deut 8:1-5). It is in the wilderness where those who were slaves in Egypt make covenant with God and become God's people (Exod 19:1-8). The book of Numbers describes their testing in the wilderness and the implications of being God's covenant people.

A significant implication of being God's people is that God chooses to live in their midst, literally to pitch a tent with them. The "tent of meeting" is mentioned almost sixty times in the book of Numbers. In this book the tent is ordinarily understood to be in the center of the camp (2:17; 3:38). The tribes encamp on all four sides of it with the Levites, as guardians of the tent, encamped between the other tribes and the tent itself (chs. 2–3; see Figure 4, p. 157). Careful instructions are given for the dismantling of the tent and its transport in the midst of the line of march (4:1-33).

The ark of the covenant is inside the tent (3:31; 4:5) and sacrificial worship is offered at the tent (6:18). God speaks to Moses at the tent, makes decisions and gives instructions (see 7:89; 17:7-8,

19). The sacred place in the midst of the camp is also called the tabernacle (Hebrew *mishkan*; e.g., 1:50, 51, 53) and the sanctuary (Hebrew *miqdash* or *qodesh*; e.g., 3:28, 31, 38). God's presence in the tent is the reason for the purity laws in chapters 1–10. The holy God lives in their midst. Thus they must be a holy people.

An alternate tradition (pre-Priestly) places the tent outside the camp (11:24-27; 12:4-5). According to this tradition God speaks to anyone who comes to this tent (Exod 33:7), but sacrifice is not offered here and the ark is separate from the tent (10:33-35; 14:44).

The Levites are set apart throughout the book of Numbers. They are given the responsibility to care for the tent: to guard it (1:47-53), transport it (3:21-38; 4:1-33), and to assist the priests who minister before it (3:6-10). They camp between the tent and the rest of the people in order both to protect the sanctuary and to protect the people from straying too close to the holy place. They are also designated as substitutes for the firstborn sons who are God's own possession (3:5-13, 40-51).

The goal of Israel's journey through the wilderness is the Promised Land. In traveling toward this land and taking possession of it, they will need to do battle against the native populations. God instructs them to do battle in a certain way, which has been paradoxically called "Holy War." First of all, they must always recognize that it is God who gives the victory; they do not win by their own power. At the beginning of their journey the song of the ark indicates God's leadership: "Arise, O Lord, may your enemies be scattered" (10:35). They forget this principle in an unsuccessful attack against the Amalekites and Canaanites (14:39-45). When other peoples attack them, however, they remember God's power and are successful (21:1-3, 21-35).

Second, they must not go to war for gain; they must dedicate all the spoils to God. This dedication is sometimes called the "ban" and the spoils as "doomed" (Hebrew *herem*). Carrying out the *herem* happens in two ways: If the defeated people are not inhabitants of the Promised Land, all or some of the spoils may be given to the sanctuary both through sacrifice and for the support of the priests and Levites (18:14; 31:9-12, 25-47; see Deut 20:10-15). If the defeated people are one of the five Canaanite groups, everything may be destroyed and all the people killed (21:1-3). The reason for the distinction is that the native Canaanites may lead the Israelites into worship of other gods (see Deut 20:16-18).

Reading the book of Numbers

The book of Numbers rarely makes the top ten list of favorite biblical books. But there are several insights regarding how to live as God's people that can be gained from a thoughtful reading of this book. First, it is true for us also that the holy God lives in our midst. How then should we act? What kind of people should we be? Second, we too are a people on the way. We too journey through the wilderness; we too grumble when we do not get what we want. It is vital to remember that the living God supplies all our needs with care and generosity. Third, God chooses people to lead us on our journey. How can we learn to trust those leaders and to trust God who chooses them?

Fourth, we too have enemies who would prevent us from entering into the land God has promised us, most notably our own sinfulness. We must realize that we do not conquer evil by our own strength but only through God's power. We are called to sing God's praise, dedicating everything that has been given us back to our generous God. Finally, although the message is serious, several of the stories in Numbers are humorous. It is a gift to recognize God's gentle humor in our own lives.

COMMENTARY

CENSUS AND PREPARATION FOR THE DEPARTURE FROM SINAI

Numbers 1:1–10:10

1:1-3 The census

The book of Numbers begins with a numbering, a census of all the men able to fight. The opening sentence is typical of the Priestly source of the Pentateuch (see introduction): identifying everything that happens as a direct command of the Lord to Moses and setting the stage by giving the date and the place of what follows.

God orders the census taking on the first day of the second month in the second year after the departure from Egypt. The exodus is the central event for Israel just as the life, death, and resurrection of Jesus Christ is the central event for Christians. Just as Christians set the beginning of their calendar by Christ, marking all the years as *Anno Domini* (Year of the Lord), so here Israel dates these happenings as if time began with the exodus. The community has been at Sinai since the third month of the first year after the exodus (Exod 19:1). In less than a month they will depart on the twentieth day of this second month of year two (Num 10:11). It is time to make final preparations.

Mount Sinai is the place of covenant making. God has been revealed to them in a great theophany (manifestation), given them the law, and sealed the covenant, promising to make them a chosen people, a priestly kingdom, and a holy nation (Exod 19–24). God has given them instructions for building the tabernacle as a divine dwelling place (Exod 25–31; 35–40). They have already broken the covenant and God has renewed it (Exod 32–34). Now they must get ready to go on through the wilderness toward the Promised Land.

The Lord orders Moses to take a census of the whole community. The specific terms used to identify these people indicate two important realities: They are a worshiping community (the *edah*) and they are bound together by familial ties (the "house of the father" or "ancestral house," and the "clan" or extended family). The persons to be numbered, however, are only the men over twenty years old who are thus eligible for military service. Moses and Aaron are to take a head count

(literally, "by the skull") and register each eligible male by name. They will not only be numbered, but they will be assigned to military divisions or "companies."

1:4-19 Moses' assistants

Moses and Aaron do not have to take this census alone. They are to enlist the assistance of a leader from each of the twelve tribes. The assistants are named, tribe by tribe. First, the tribes from Leah's own sons are named in birth order: Reuben, Simeon, Judah, Issachar, Zebulun. Then the tribes named for Rachel's two sons are listed: Joseph (represented by his sons, Ephraim and Manasseh) and Benjamin. Finally, the tribes representing the four sons of the maids, Bilhah and Zilpah, are named in no apparent order: Dan, Asher, Gad, and Naphtali (see Gen 29:31–30:24). Since the tribe of Levi is omitted (see 1:47-54), the tribe of Joseph is divided between Ephraim and Manasseh (Joseph's two sons) in order to fill out the number twelve.

With the exception of Nahshon, son of Amminadab of the tribe of Judah (Exod 6:23), the individual representatives of each tribe appear only here and in chapters 2, 7, and 10. Many of their names, however, are based on the divine names El and Shaddai: for example, Elizur, "my God is rock"; Shedeur, "the Almighty gives light"; Shelumiel, "God is my peace"; Zurishaddai, "the Almighty is my rock." None, however, are based on the sacred name, Yahweh. After the assistants are named, Moses and Aaron carry out God's instructions exactly.

1:20-46 Count of the twelve tribes

The results of the census are reported tribe by tribe. The same formula is repeated for each tribe. Only the first two tribes have some different phrases. Reuben is identified as the firstborn (1:20). Those registered for Reuben and Simeon are identified as males who are counted "individually" (literally, "by head" or "polled"). The order of the tribes is similar to the order in the list of assistants. The only exception is the tribe of Gad, which is inserted between Simeon and Judah.

The total number of men eligible for military service registered from the twelve tribes is

Figure 3: Listing of Tribes

| Genesis 29–30 | Genesis 46 | Genesis 49 | Numbers 1 | Numbers 2, 7, 10 |
Birth Order	*To Egypt*	*Blessing*	*1st Census*	*Order of March*
Reuben	Reuben	Reuben	Reuben	Judah
Simeon	Simeon	Simeon	Simeon	Issachar
Levi	Levi	Levi	Gad	Zebulun
Judah	Judah	Judah	Judah	Reuben
Dan	Issachar	Zebulun	Issachar	Simeon
Naphtali	Zebulun	Issachar	Zebulun	Gad
Gad	Gad	Dan	Ephraim	Ephraim
Asher	Asher	Gad	Manasseh	Manasseh
Issachar	Joseph	Asher	Benjamin	Benjamin
Zebulun	Benjamin	Naphtali	Dan	Dan
Joseph	Dan	Joseph	Asher	Asher
Benjamin	Naphtali	Benjamin	Naphtali	Naphtali

603,550. The number is unrealistic. If there were 600,000 able men among the Israelites at Sinai, the whole people, including women and children, would have numbered around two million. The Sinai desert could not have supported a group that size. Thus the number must have another meaning. First of all, the large number indicates that Israel need not fear anyone who resists its entrance into the Promised Land. Second, the same number of men were assessed the half-shekel sanctuary tax. That tax payment covered the exact cost of the pedestals for the sanctuary along with the veil and the hooks and silver-plating for the columns (Exod 38:26-28).

Third, the number may have symbolic value. In ancient Israel the same symbols were used for letters and numbers (analogous to the use of letters for numbers in Roman numerals). Thus the symbol for the first letter of the alphabet was also used for the number one; the symbol for the second letter served also as the number two, and so on. If the letters for *bene-yisraʾel* ("sons of Israel" = Israelites) are added up, they equal 603. So 603,000 would be the Israelites times a thousand. Finally, since Babylonian mathematics worked from a base of sixty and the Priestly source for this section of Numbers was probably completed during the Babylonian exile, it is not surprising to find a number close to 600,000.

1:47-54 Levites omitted in the census

The Levites are not included in the census because they have other duties. They are not expected to take up arms. Rather they are responsible for the tabernacle and everything that belongs to it. They put it up, take it down, and carry it whenever it is moved. They are responsible to guard it and to perform the liturgical services. Any other person who approaches this sacred tabernacle is subject to the death penalty. A census of the Levites will be taken in Numbers 3.

The chapter closes with the notice that God's command to Moses (v. 1) had been fulfilled exactly.

2:1-34 Arrangement of the tribes

The Lord issues a new command to Moses (see 1:1 ["said"], 1:19 and 54 ["commanded"], 1:48 ["told"]). This command has to do with the arrangement of the tribes in their encampment and the placement of the tent of meeting (see introduction: tent of meeting). The twelve tribes, minus Levi who is replaced by the division of Joseph into the tribes of Ephraim and Manasseh, are set up in groups of three tribes each on the four sides of the tent of meeting. The tribal leaders identified in 1:5-15 are named again and the census count from 1:20-42 is repeated. A major tribe leads each of the four tribal divisions: Judah on the east,

Figure 4: Arrangement of Tribes around the Tent of Meeting

	Asher	DAN	Naphtali	
Benjamin		*Merari*		Issachar
EPHRAIM	*Gershonites*	TENT OF MEETING	*Moses with Aaron & his sons*	JUDAH
Manasseh		*Kohathites*		Zebulun
	Gad	REUBEN	Simeon	

Reuben on the south, Ephraim on the west, and Dan on the north.

The listing of the tribes is not in the same order as chapter 1 (see Figure 3, p. 156). Nor is it related to the geographical locations of the tribal settlements in Israel. It seems rather to be by later importance. Judah, the tribe favored in Jacob's farewell address (Gen 49) and the ancestor of David, holds the prime location: the east at the entrance to the tent of meeting. Reuben, the firstborn, follows at the south. Ephraim, the primary tribe of the northern kingdom, Israel, is next at the west. Dan, a tribe that did in fact move to the north and fell to the Assyrians in Tiglath-Pileser's invasion during the eighth century, is last.

This order represents not only their encampment but also their order of march. The census was taken for military purposes and the arrangement of the tribes sets the order of military divisions. In this order the tribes will leave Sinai in chapter 10 and march toward the Promised Land. After chapter 10 the order of march is never again mentioned.

The Levites are again singled out. Their position in the midst of the camp and the midst of the line of march is stated at the exact center of the chapter, verse 17. More detail regarding their arrangement will be found in 3:21-39.

The chapter ends with two statements indicating the fulfillment of God's commands. The Levites were treated specially "just as the LORD had commanded Moses" and the tribal divisions, both in the camp and on the march, were arranged "just as the LORD had commanded Moses" (2:33-34).

3:1-4 The sons of Aaron

Now that the other tribes have been counted and put in order, chapters 3–4 turn to focus on the Levites: their genealogy, their special status as substitutes for the firstborn, their census, their

order of service and march, and their duties. The genealogy of Aaron, ancestor of the priests, sets the stage. (Moses' sons are not mentioned.)

Nadab and Abihu died after they offered "unauthorized fire" (Lev 10:1-7; 16:1-2) perhaps an unapproved kind of incense (see Exod 30:9). So the priestly descent continues only through Aaron's sons Eleazar and Ithamar. A description of their anointing as priests is found in Exodus 40:12-16.

3:5-13 Levites in place of the firstborn

The special status of the Levites is now explained: they are substitutes for the firstborn. After the tenth plague, when the Egyptian firstborn were killed but the Israelite firstborn were spared by the blood of the lamb, the Lord claimed for himself every firstborn male (Exod 13:2, 11-16). Every firstborn son must be given to the Lord, even those born in the wilderness. Since human sacrifice is not allowed among the Israelites, these firstborn must be redeemed in another way. The Levites stand in as substitutes, consecrated to the Lord. Their service redeems the firstborn. They are not priests, but are subordinate to them, assigned to serve them and to care for the tent of meeting and the tabernacle.

3:14-39 Census of the Levites and duties of the Levitical clans

The census of the other tribes was taken for military purposes; the census of the Levites is taken in order to determine how many firstborn are redeemed by their service. In the previous census only men over twenty years old were counted; this census includes all male Levites one month old or more. Even the infants can be substitutes for the firstborn. Infants younger than one month are not included since only after a month was an infant considered likely to survive. Just as the others were counted by tribes, each with a tribal leader, and were assigned places to camp and an order for the march, so also the Levites are counted by ancestral houses, each with a leader, and were given a specific place in the inner circle of the camp around the tent of meeting (see Figure 4, p. 157).

In addition, each ancestral house is given a specific responsibility in service of the tent of meeting. The Gershonites care for the hanging materials: the tent and its two-layer covering, the curtains and other hangings, and the necessary ropes for these materials (see introduction, "tent of meeting," pp. 153–54). The Kohathites were responsible for what was inside the sanctuary: the ark, table, menorah, altars, and utensils. Since Aaron is descended from this ancestral house, his son, the priest Eleazar, is named here. He has authority over the other three Levitical leaders and over all those who minister in the sanctuary. The third ancestral house, the Merarites, was given responsibility to care for and transport all the supports of the structure: the boards, bars, columns, pedestals, fittings, pegs, and ropes. Finally, Moses with Aaron and his sons encamped in the favored spot to the east in front of the entrance of the tent of meeting. Presumably they are numbered with the Kohathites.

3:40-51 Census and ransom of firstborn

The purpose of the census is stated again: the Levites are substitutes for all the firstborn. But the number is short. There are 22,273 firstborn males among the Israelites and only 22,000 Levites. So a new principle for redemption is established. The remaining 273 firstborn may be redeemed with money collected from the Israelites and paid to the priests (see Num 18:16). In this passage the cattle of the Levites also are designated as substitutes for the cattle of the rest of the Israelites here; however, the usual practice with regard to domestic animals of the other tribes is that the firstborn males must be sacrificed (see Num 18:17-18).

4:1-33 Duties further defined

A second census of the Levites is taken for a different purpose. In chapter 3 all the male Levites one month and older were taken for the purpose of setting them aside as substitutes for the firstborn males of the rest of Israel. In chapter 4 the male Levites between thirty and fifty years old are to be counted in order to assign them duties

regarding the tent of meeting, its contents, and furnishings. The responsibilities of the three clans, which were briefly mentioned in 3:25-26, 31, 36-37, are now specified in greater detail.

The Kohathites, who have the most honorable responsibility, are discussed first. They are to carry the sacred objects that are housed in the tent of meeting along with their utensils (4:4, 15). No Levite may touch these sacred objects, however, not even the Kohathites. Thus the priests, Aaron and his sons, must first prepare these objects for transport (4:5-14). These priests take down the curtain that screens the ark of the covenant from view and use it to cover the ark. Then they are to wrap the ark in two additional coverings and insert the poles by which the Kohathites may carry the ark without touching it.

The first covering is a yellow-orange skin (*tahash*), probably either dolphin skins or leather; the second covering is an "all-violet," or perfectly violet cloth. Violet or purple cloth is valuable because the dye is difficult to obtain. Thus the ark is covered richly. The table of the Presence on which the bread offering is laid along with the bread and the other utensils is to be covered in similar fashion, with violet and crimson cloths and the yellow-orange skin. The table too is provided with poles for carrying.

The menorah, along with its lamps, tongs for holding the wicks, oil containers, and trays for pouring the oil are wrapped in two coverings and placed on a litter. The incense altar is doubly covered and its carrying poles inserted; the other utensils are also doubly wrapped and placed on a litter. Finally, the bronze altar of sacrifice is cleansed of the ashes from burnt offerings and covered with a purple cloth. Then all its utensils—forks for turning and removing the meat of the sacrifice, basins for blood and other juices, fire pans and shovels for the coals—are covered with a yellow-orange skin and placed on top of the altar. The altar is also provided with poles for carrying.

All of this careful wrapping and covering is done by the priests to protect the Kohathites, because any non-priest, even a Kohathite, who touches these sacred objects will die (4:15, 18-19). No one but the priests may even look upon these holy things, even for an instant (4:20). The Hebrew word used to describe this "instant" means "a swallowing" (*bala*ᶜ); the English equivalent would be the blink of an eye. So the sacred objects are prepared by the priests for the Kohathites to carry. The objects that are too sacred even for the Kohathites to carry—the oils, incense, and grain offering—are to be carried by the priest Eleazar, who is in charge of everything regarding the transport of the altar.

The tasks of the Gershonites (4:22-28) and the Merarites (4:29-33) are described more simply because the objects they carry are not so sacred and thus not so dangerous. The Gershonites carry all the fabric of the tent of meeting, the hangings and draperies. The Merarites carry the boards and braces, all the solid objects that form the structure of the tent of meeting. These two clans are under the supervision of the priest Ithamar.

4:34-49 Number of adult Levites

The males between thirty and fifty years old belonging to these three clans must be counted in order to enroll them for this service regarding the tent of meeting (see 4:2-3). The Kohathites number 2,750, the Gershonites 2,630, and the Merarites 3,200. The total number of Levites available for service at the tent of meeting is 8,580. The minimum age for service noted here is thirty (see also 1 Chr 23:3). In chapter 8 the minimum age for Levitical service is given as twenty-five (Num 8:24), and in Chronicles it is twenty (1 Chr 23:24, 27; 2 Chr 31:17; cf. Ezra 3:8). This discrepancy may reflect different sources or different practices at different times. It also suggests that there may have been a lengthy period of training before a young Levite was allowed to perform the duties regarding the tent of meeting.

The narrator is careful to note that this count was made at the Lord's direction through Moses (4:37, 41, 45). Everything they did was in obedience to the Lord's command to Moses (4:49). Censuses taken without the Lord's command do not turn out well (cf. Exod 30:12; 2 Sam 24).

5:1-4 The unclean expelled

The holy God, symbolized by the tent of meeting, is present in the midst of the Israelite encampment. Thus the people must be holy and whatever threatens that holiness must be expelled or healed. The chapter begins with the "unwholeness" of disease and death. God's holiness is the source of life; disease and death must be removed from the camp.

Three groups are to be expelled: those with a scaly skin infection, those suffering from abnormal genital discharges, and those who have touched a corpse. The detailed legislation regarding scaly skin infections is outlined in Leviticus 13–14. This condition is not to be equated with Hansen's disease, commonly called leprosy. Rather it is any condition that renders the skin scaly and hard. According to this legislation in Numbers the person so affected must be expelled from the camp, not because of fear of infection but because the scaly skin is a sign of death. These persons are allowed to return to the camp only after the priest has declared them clean and the proper sacrifices have been offered (see Lev 13–14).

Men or women afflicted with abnormal genital discharges, pus or bleeding, form the second group. (This legislation does not apply to normal menstruation or seminal emission.) The abnormal genital discharge is a sign of contradiction: at the place where life is engendered, there is an indication of disease and death. According to Leviticus, these persons are allowed to return to the camp seven days after the affliction ceases; they too must offer a designated sacrifice (see Lev 15:1-15, 25-30).

The third group has become unclean by contact with a corpse, the ultimate sign of death. (See Num 19:11-22 for the full legislation.) This group includes those who perform the needed care of washing, dressing, and burying the body. These persons may re-enter the camp after they have performed the necessary purification rites on the third and seventh days after contact with a corpse (see Num 19:11-22).

5:5-10 Unjust possession

If external afflictions render a person impure, broken relationships do so even more. The next situation is clearly universal. The offender may be a *man or woman* (5:6). This inclusive phrase is unusual in biblical law (see Exod 21:28-29; Lev 13:29, 38; 20:27; Num 6:2; Deut 17:2, 5); usually "man" is the only one named. Also, the one offended is identified as any *ʾadam*, any human being.

The wrong has to do with misappropriation of property, cheating, or stealing. The offender must confess the wrong, offer a sacrifice of atonement, and make restitution with twenty percent interest (5:7-8). But a problem arises if the one wronged is dead. In that case the restitution must be paid to the next of kin, the redeemer (Hebrew *goʾel*).

This redeemer is responsible to ransom a person who has been sold into slavery or to buy back the ancestral land that had been lost through debt (Lev 25:25-26, 48-49). The redeemer is also called to avenge a person's death (Num 35:18-21, 26-28; Deut 19:5-6, 11-13). Possible redeemers include father, mother, daughter, son, brother, uncle, or first cousin.

What happens if the wronged person is not only dead but has no redeemer? Then the restitution belongs to God (5:8). The priest accepts it in God's name. Whatever priest accepts the offering has the right to keep the offering (5:9-10).

5:11-31 Ordeal for suspected adultery

If the broken relationship is marriage, the situation is even more critical and must be healed if the encampment of God's people is to remain holy. The husband has the right to take action and divorce his wife if he has evidence of adultery or serious sexual misconduct (see Deut 24:1). If, however, he only suspects his wife but does not have evidence, he may subject her to an ordeal. If she fails the test, she is dishonored and physically impaired and he may divorce her. If she passes the test, she is exonerated and he may not divorce her.

The ritual for the ordeal combines several elements: an oath, a magical water test, and a grain offering. The grain offering is necessary because one may never appear before God empty-handed (Exod 23:15; Deut 16:16). This offering differs from the ordinary grain offering in that it is made of barley meal instead of coarse flour (semolina), no oil is smeared on it, and no frankincense accompanies it. The offering is starker because it is an "offering of jealousy" and a memorial of wrongdoing. It is offered for the woman (5:15) after she has taken the oath and before she drinks the bitter water (5:25-26).

The oath is administered after the woman has been made to stand before the altar with her head uncovered and the grain offering in her hands. The action shames the woman, whose hair is uncovered and probably disheveled by a man not her husband. The husband is also shamed by this public display. The oath has two parts. The first is an oath of innocence. If she has not been unfaithful, the bitter water will not hurt her. The second part is a self-curse if she is guilty. The priest concludes with a curse that assumes the

woman's guilt (5:21-22) and she swears her agreement to the two-part oath, "Amen, amen!"

The base for the water of bitterness is "holy water" (5:17; the only appearance of this phrase in the Old Testament). It may be water from the basin that is set between the tent of meeting and the altar (Exod 30:18; 40:30). Dust from the floor of the tabernacle is put into this water and the ink of the oath's words written by the priest is washed into it. The water thus symbolizes purification (the water from the basin) as well as death (dust). The dust and ink, no doubt, make the water taste bitter and suggest danger or poison. When the woman drinks the water, she is taking into herself the oath with its curse (ink) as well as physical elements from the sacred place (water and dust).

The effect of the water depends on the woman's guilt or innocence. If she is guilty, her uterus will fall and her belly swell. If she is innocent, the water will have no effect and, literally, "she will be sown with seed" (5:28). There are two possible meanings here. If the woman is pregnant and that is the reason that her husband suspected her, she will either miscarry if guilty or bear a healthy child if innocent. If the woman is not pregnant, she will either suffer a prolapsed uterus if guilty or remain fertile if innocent. In any case, the husband remains free of guilt even if he suspected his wife falsely.

The Code of Hammurabi (eighteenth century B.C.) also has a water ordeal for suspected adultery. "If the 'finger is pointed' at a man's wife about another man, but she is not caught sleeping with the other man, she shall jump into the river for her husband" (no. 132, translated by L.W. King; see also nos. 131, 133, 143). If she drowns, she was guilty; if she survives, she is innocent.

6:1-21 Laws concerning Nazirites

Another relationship is so important that its disruption also causes defilement of the sanctuary: the relationship between the Nazirite and God. Nazirites willingly take a vow to dedicate their lives to God for a certain time (6:1-8). (The stories of Samson [Judg 13:4-5] and Samuel [1 Sam 1:11, 22] indicate that a Nazirite vow could also be taken for life, but the legislation in this chapter is primarily directed to those who make the vow only for a time.) It is specifically stated that either men or women are permitted to make this vow. (The phrase "men or women" is rare in biblical law, appearing only here in 6:2 and in Exod 21:28-29; Lev 13:29, 38; 20:27; Num 5:6; Deut 17:2, 5; 29:17.)

The language in this section is particularly dense, with significant words repeated several times. The root *nzr*, from which "nazirite" is derived, means "to separate or set apart"; it occurs twenty-four times in 6:1-21. Related roots, which have similar meanings, are interwoven with *nzr*. The root *ndr*, usually translated "vow" or "dedicate," occurs six times; the common root *qdsh*, usually translated "holy" but which connotes setting apart, occurs four times. This rich interweaving of words describing the dedication of the Nazirite to God indicates the solemnity of this action.

Three restrictions characterize the Nazirite: abstention from wine and any other grape product including raisins, refraining from cutting the hair, and avoidance of any dead body including that of any immediate family member. Drinking wine, especially to the point of intoxication, was associated with the Canaanites, particularly their agricultural way of life. Critiques of the agricultural economy appear in the story of Noah's drunkenness (Gen 9:20-27) and in the seventh-century protest of the Rechabites, who insisted on maintaining their nomadic way of life, neither building houses nor planting crops nor drinking wine (see Jer 35).

Hair was considered an extension of a person's vitality. Not cutting the hair was a way of preserving strength (see Samson, especially Judg 16:17-20). Offering one's hair to God symbolized the total dedication of one's life.

The strict legislation concerning avoidance of a corpse is a protection against a cult of the dead like that practiced in the rest of the ancient Near East. The dead were not transformed into immortal gods and were not to be worshiped. In this society where there was no belief in resurrection, the dead were not considered even to remain as part of the human community. Holiness has to do with life, not death, and the consecrated Nazirite must thus avoid any contact with the dead.

The Nazirite who transgressed these three prohibitions, even accidentally, had to go through a seven-day ritual of purification and begin the whole period of Nazirite consecration again (6:9-12). The hair must be shaved off because the consecration has been lost. No doubt this shaved hair

is to be burned with the sacrifice just as it is at the normal end of the period of consecration (6:18). Sacrifices must be offered to God: first an offering to purify the sanctuary, which has been defiled, and then a burnt offering to restore the relationship with God. Finally a lamb is offered as reparation for the broken vow. Only then can the person begin again to be a Nazirite for whatever period of time had been initially set.

A complicated ritual signifies the end of the designated period of time for the Nazirite vow. One does not lightly move from a consecrated state to ordinary life. In addition to the purification offering and the burnt offering, the person brings a ram for a communion offering along with grain and drink offerings. These last offerings symbolize an ongoing sharing of life with God, the gift of *shalom*, peace and well-being. After these are offered, the consecrated hair is shaved off and burned in the fire of the sacrifice. Only then may the former Nazirite return to an ordinary way of life.

The detailed instructions for Nazirites and the solemnity of the ritual at the end of the period of dedication indicate the degree of holiness attached to this vow. The restriction regarding contact with the dead, for example, is more stringent even than that placed on the priests (Lev 21:1-4); it is as strict as the demands on the high priest (Lev 21:11). Nazirites were a living symbol of holiness in the midst of God's holy people.

6:22-27 The priestly blessing

The blessing assigned to the priests, descendants of Aaron, is very old and is still in common use. Similar blessings have been found on a jar from the eighth century B.C. at Kuntillet ʿAjrud in the upper Sinai Peninsula and on small silver pieces, possibly amulets, in seventh-century graves in the Hinnom Valley outside Jerusalem. The second-century sage, Ben Sira, describes the high priest's daily blessing: "Then coming down he would raise his hands / over all the congregation of Israel; / The blessing of the LORD would be upon his lips, / the name of the LORD would be his glory. / The people would again fall down / to receive the blessing of the Most High" (Sir 50:20-21). The blessing found here in Numbers is currently used at the end of Evening Praise in the Liturgy of the Hours and sometimes as the concluding blessing of the Eucharist. In the Roman

Lectionary it is the first reading for New Year's Day.

God's blessing signifies a sharing in God's life and power. To be blessed by God is not only to be endowed with spiritual grace; it is also to receive material abundance. In Genesis human beings are blessed with fertility and the gift of land (see Gen 1:28; 27:27-29; 35:9-12). God's blessing also brings prosperity and peace. To be blessed by God is to be strengthened to live as true human beings, images of God.

7:1-88 Offerings of the tribal leaders

This chapter is a flashback to the day of dedication of the tabernacle: the first day of the first month of the second year from the departure from Egypt, according to Exodus 40:2-17. Thus this chapter describes events a month earlier than the first chapter of Numbers (see 1:1). All the legal traditions in Leviticus and Numbers 1–5 are, in a sense, outside of time. Here we resume the temporal sequence.

The tabernacle and all its equipment, including the altar, have been anointed. Anointing with sacred oil was a common practice in the ancient Near East to set something apart for special use or to indicate the special status of a person such as a king or priest. This dedication (Hebrew *hanukkah*) prepares the sacred space for its intended use as a meeting place between God and the covenant people.

The first set of offerings brought by the tribal leaders (see commentary on 1:4-19) consists of the means of transportation for the tabernacle and all its equipment. The wagons and oxen are assigned to the ancestral houses of the Levites according to their responsibilities (see commentary on 3:14-40; 4:1-33). The Kohathites do not need wagons and oxen since they carry on their shoulders the sacred objects from inside the tabernacle.

The next section (7:10-88) seems to be the verbal presentation of a table of offerings. Each of the twelve tribal leaders is named and his offerings listed (see Figure 3, p. 156, for the order of tribes). From the third tribal leader on, there are no verbs. The use of numbers is out of the ordinary: instead of "two bulls, five rams, five he-goats," for example, the Hebrew says: "bulls–two, rams–five, he-goats–five." The donations are listed, not according to the ordinary order of sacrifice with items for the purification offering first, but accord-ing to value with the gold and silver items first and then the animals large and small. It is easiest to imagine someone reading this list aloud from a table. At the end (7:84-88), the "bottom line" is read, the total of all the offerings.

Each tribe brings the same offering, regardless of the size of the tribe. Each tribe shares equally in the worship of God at the tabernacle. The tribes appear, not in birth order as in chapter 1, but in the same sequence as chapter 2 with Judah appearing first (see Figure 3, p. 156, and commentary on ch. 2). It seems that these sacrifices are not being made at the dedication; rather their offerings provide the resources for future offerings of all the major sacrifices in the priestly tradition (see Lev 6–7) except the guilt offering.

7:89 The voice

The final verse of this chapter is a transition from the twelve days of offerings outside the tabernacle to the arrangement of the inside. The sacred place is identified as the tent of meeting. In contrast to the Priestly description earlier (e.g., 2:17; 3:38) where the tent is in the center of the camp, here the tent is outside the camp (also at 11:24-27; 12:4-5; see introduction: tent of meeting/ tabernacle). God comes to the tent to speak with Moses (see Exod 33:7-11). God is revealed only by word, only by voice. The voice comes from between the cherubim, guardians of the ark. God's instructions continue in the next chapter with the phrase so frequent in Numbers 1–10: "The LORD said to Moses."

8:1-4 The menorah

The final detail in preparing the tabernacle is the instruction on the function of the menorah, the seven-branched lampstand. The making of the menorah was described in Exodus (25:31-40; 37:17-24). Regarding its use, the Israelites are all commanded to supply the oil (Lev 24:2), but only the priest Aaron (and his sons) may care for this sacred object (Exod 30:7-8). It must be so situated that the light shines toward the altar, the sign of God's presence. This is how God instructs Aaron (8:1-2), and this is what Aaron does (8:3).

8:5-22 Purification of the Levites

The Levites must now be prepared for their ministry. The ritual begins with three outward signs of purification. They are sprinkled with water, shave their whole bodies, and wash their clothes (see Exod 19:10). Then a sacrifice of purification is offered. The congregation, through designated representatives, lays hands on the Levites, designating them as special ministers and offering them to God. The Levites in turn lay hands on the two bulls, one for the purification sacrifice and the other for the burnt offering. Thus the Levites are identified with the animals for sacrifice. Aaron the priest offers the Levites to God in the name of the people and sacrifices the two bulls according to the appropriate sacrifices. The first is a sacrifice to purify the Levites; the second is a whole burnt offering, asking God to accept their service.

The Levites are cleansed but not "consecrated" or "ordained" as are the Aaronide priests (see introduction, Levites, p. 154). They are not sprinkled nor touched with sacrificial blood or anointed with oil. They do not have the power or status of the priests. They may neither touch the sacred objects nor offer sacrifice or enter the tabernacle. This designation of the Levites' duties reflects the period from Josiah onward (seventh century B.C.) after all sacrificial worship was limited to the temple (see also Ezek 44).

The Levites are set aside, however, as God's own possession. They substitute for the firstborn of all the Israelites (see commentary on 3:5-13). They, who have been purified by sacrifice, form a bridge between the Israelites and the holiness of God and serve as a protection for the Israelites who may not come too near the tabernacle. They also serve as assistants to the priests.

This is what God commands (8:5-19); this is what is done (8:20-22).

8:23-26 Age limits for Levitical service

Levites are to begin their service at age twenty-five and retire to minor duties at age fifty. This instruction differs from the age limits in the census (4:2-3), where the Levites undertake their tasks at age thirty. Perhaps there was a period of training before full responsibility was given to a young Levite.

9:1-14 Second Passover

This chapter concludes the flashback that began in 7:1. This section is set on the day that the tabernacle was finished, the first day of the *first* month of the second year after the people left

Egypt (cf. Exod 40:17), whereas Numbers begins in the *second* month of the second year after the departure from Egypt.

Passover, the memorial of the deliverance from Egypt, is the most significant liturgical celebration for God's covenant people. Passover celebrations are described only a few times in the Old Testament, but all of these are at critical junctures in the people's history. The first Passover is an anticipatory celebration of deliverance (Exod 12; cf. Num 33:3). The second Passover is described here as the people prepare to leave Sinai and continue their trek through the wilderness. The third mention of a Passover celebration occurs just after Joshua and the people cross the Jordan River to enter the Promised Land (Josh 5).

There are only three other stories describing the observance of this important liturgy: Hezekiah's attempt during his reform to reunite with the remaining people of the northern kingdom after the Assyrian invasion (2 Chr 30), at the conclusion of Josiah's reform (2 Kgs 23//2 Chr 35), and after the Babylonian exile when the second temple was finished (Ezra 6:19-22). Instructions for how to observe the festival are found in Exodus 34, Leviticus 23, Numbers 28, and Deuteronomy 16 (cf. Ezek 45).

The familiar pattern of the Lord's command (9:2-4) and the people's obedience (9:5) appears again. The regulations, which are outlined in detail in Exodus 12, are stated here only briefly. A problem arises, however: what to do with those who are ritually unclean? Moses waits for a command from the Lord.

The Lord's instruction extends not only to those who cannot celebrate because of ritual uncleanness, but to everyone who finds it impossible to keep the Passover feast for whatever reason. This is the only feast that all Israel is required to keep. No one is to be excused from this memorial of Israel's creation as a people. Anyone who is prevented from celebrating at the appropriate time during the first month of the year must keep the feast at the prescribed time during the second month. Anyone who neglects to keep this feast is to be cut off from the people. To be "cut off" is equivalent to death. By failing to keep the Passover the offender has symbolically already separated from the community's life and identity.

The reasons listed that persons may be unable to keep the Passover at the appropriate time are:

ritual uncleanness, travel, or non-Israelite status. Those who are ritually unclean are put outside the camp for a prescribed number of days and are not allowed to participate in any worship (see 5:2-3). The other two reasons, however, suggest that these laws belong to a time after Israel is well settled in the land. Travel is a difficulty only if the celebration of Passover is limited to a certain place. In the time of Josiah (seventh century) all formal worship was centralized in the Jerusalem temple. As for the third reason, resident aliens were part of Israel only after they had their own land. During the wilderness period they themselves were "resident aliens." Throughout the Pentateuch we find similar evidence that later laws were inserted into earlier material. Almost the whole legal tradition in particular gravitated toward the story of Israel's stay at Sinai (Exod 19–Num 10).

9:15-23 The fiery cloud

In the middle of the chapter is another reminder that this is the first day of the *first* month of the second year after the departure from Egypt, the day on which the tabernacle was completed. The time at Sinai is coming to an end. The previous description of Passover bound together the section from Exodus 12 to Numbers 9; now the story of God's taking possession of the tabernacle, symbolized by the cloud, is repeated (see Exod 40:34-38).

The cloud is a common biblical symbol for God's presence. The radiant cloud both reveals and conceals God's presence. When the Israelites were encamped by the sea, God protected them by day in a pillar of cloud and by night in a pillar of fire (Exod 13:21-22; 14:19-20, 24; cf. Deut 1:33; Ps 78:14). Apparently the fire burns constantly in the middle of the cloud but is invisible in daylight. The glory of the Lord appeared as a shining cloud when Aaron announced that God would give the people bread (manna; Exod 16:10). When Moses received the Ten Commandments, the cloud covered Mount Sinai (Exod 24:15-18). When Moses went to the tent of meeting to speak with God, the cloud signaled God's arrival (Exod 33:9-10). When the priests dedicated the temple that Solomon had built in the tenth century, the cloud filled the temple so completely that the priests could not continue their ministry (1 Kgs 8:10-11). The

cloud as a symbol for God's glorious presence is also common in the rest of the ancient Near East as well as in Christian iconography. The halo around a holy person's head is a stylized image of the cloud.

God, present in the cloud, is the leader of the people on their journey from Sinai to the Promised Land. When the cloud moves, the people follow; when the cloud stops, the people rest. They go nowhere except where the cloud leads. They are completely obedient to the Lord's direction.

10:1-10 The silver trumpets

The final preparation for Israel's departure from Sinai is the making of the two silver trumpets. Josephus, a first-century Jewish historian, describes these silver trumpets as somewhat less than eighteen inches long (less than a cubit), straight, and bell-shaped at the end (*Antiq.* III, xii, 6). Their sound must have been piercing. These straight trumpets (Hebrew *hatsotserah*) are different from the ram's horn (*shofar*) and the *yobel* (also a ram's horn, from which "jubilee" gets its name). Trumpets are used to announce feasts and heighten the celebration (Ps 98:6; Ezra 3:10; Neh 12:35, 41; and throughout Chr) as well as to summon warriors to battle (Num 31:6; Hos 5:8).

The Aaronide priests are assigned to blow the trumpets. Different signals are sounded on them. The difference between the signal for an assembly (10:3-4, 7), the signal for breaking camp and departing (10:5-6), and the signal for battle (10:9) is not described. Possibly the signal for an assembly is only a long sound and signals for the other two events are a series of tones in a certain rhythm.

The trumpets are not only signals for the people, however. When the trumpet is sounded for war, God remembers the people and saves them (10:9). The trumpet sound during liturgical celebrations serves as a memorial for the people before God (10:10). Throughout the Old Testament God's remembering means well-being for the people. When God remembers Noah, the floodwaters begin to abate (Gen 8:1). When God remembers the covenant, he calls Moses to deliver the people from Egyptian oppression (Exod 2:24). When God remembers Hannah, she conceives Samuel (1 Sam 1:19-20). The trumpets become a signal for God to continue remembering just as the bow in the clouds does (Gen 9:16).

DEPARTURE, REBELLION, AND WANDERING IN THE WILDERNESS FOR FORTY YEARS

Numbers 10:11–25:18

10:11-28 Departure from Sinai

The Israelites, having arrived at Sinai on the first day of the third month after their departure from Egypt (Exod 19:1), now set out to continue their journey through the wilderness. They have been camped at Sinai almost a year. There they have made covenant with the Lord, broken the covenant by forging a golden calf (Exod 32:1-4), and been granted a new covenant (Exod 34:1-28). They have received the gift of the law, beginning with the Ten Commandments (Exod 20:1-17). Since all Israelite law is covenant law, the later law codes have also been inserted into the Sinai story; these laws form the bulk of material from Exodus 21, through Leviticus, to Numbers 10. Now instructions for the rest of the journey have been given and the cloud has risen from the tabernacle of the covenant (so called because the ark is traditionally believed to have contained the tablets of the commandments; see Exod 25:16, 21; 40:20; Deut 10:2, 5; 1 Kgs 8:9; 2 Chr 6:11). It is time to move on.

The tribes set out in the order given in Numbers 2 (see Figure 3, p. 156). The Levitical clans join the march according to their respective duties. The Gershonites and Merarites, who carry the structural elements of the tabernacle (Num 4:21-33), set out after the first division led by the Judahites. They are to have the structure set up before the arrival of the Kohathites, who are carrying the sacred objects (Num 4:4-15) and who set out after the second division led by the Reubenites.

The journey will take the people from the wilderness of Sinai to the wilderness of Paran (10:12; 12:16). On the way they will camp at Taberah (11:3), Kibroth-hattaavah (perhaps the same place, 11:34); and Hazeroth (11:35). The exact location of these places is difficult to determine. It is generally accepted that Mount Sinai is Jebel Musa in the southern tip of the Sinai Peninsula. The wilderness of Paran is a more or less large area in the north-central part of the peninsula. Kadesh-barnea, in the wilderness of Zin, seems to be at the northern edge of the wilderness of Paran (20:1; cf. 13:26). See map on page 1524.

10:29-32 Hobab as guide

The section from 1:1–10:28 represents priestly interests and is considered to be from the Priestly tradition. A pre-Priestly source, which seems actually to be a combination of several different traditions, begins with 10:29. Thus there are several contradictions evident in this section: Moses' father-in-law, who is named Jethro throughout most of Exodus (3:1; 4:18; 18:1-12) but Reuel in Exodus 2:18, is here called Hobab, who is the son of Reuel (cf. Judg 4:11). Moses asks him to be their guide, although God, signified by the cloud (9:15-23; 10:11-12) or the ark (10:33-34), is supposed to show them the way. The cloud itself forms a pillar (Exod 13:21-22; Num 12:5) or covers the tabernacle and/or the tent (Exod 40:34-38; Num 9:15-16), but appears rarely with the ark as it does here (Lev 16:2; cf. 16:13).

Perhaps this last item is not a contradiction, since the ark is to be set within the tabernacle (Exod 40:5, 21) and the cloud hovers over the people when the ark leads them (Num 10:34). But where is the ark found in the order of march? According to the detailed instructions from the Priestly tradition the ark is to be carried by the Kohathites (Num 4:4-5, 15) and they march behind the Reubenite division, close to the center of the line. In 10:33-36, however, the ark goes before the people.

These contradictions must be noted but need not be disturbing. They reveal the great respect of the ancient biblical editors for the traditions they have inherited. These editors seem to have operated according to the principle, "Don't throw anything away because it may contain some truth." When Christians gathered the books of the New Testament they had the same respect for sources. The four gospels contradict each other in many details, but the church has kept them all.

10:33-36 Into the wilderness

The ark of the covenant has many functions. It is a sign of God's abiding presence with the people. It is a throne for God (1 Sam 4:4; 2 Sam 6:2; 2 Kgs 19:15/Isa 37:16; Pss 80:2; 99:1; 1 Chr 13:6); God's footstool (1 Chr 28:2; Pss 99:5; 132:7); the Lord rides upon the cherubim (Pss 18:11; Ezek 10:18-20; 11:22). It is used as a palladium to be carried into battle (see 1 Sam 4–7). It is a container, holding the tablets of the commandments (Deut 10:2-5; 1 Kgs 8:9). In Christian tradition it is also thought to contain a jar of manna and Aaron's rod that blossomed (Heb 9:4). In Numbers 10 it is a symbol of God's guidance of the people through the wilderness.

The song of the ark is a battle song. The Lord advances into battle, scattering the enemies, and returns to camp with the army. The placement of the song here indicates that the journey from Sinai to the Promised Land will not be entirely peaceful.

11:1-15 Discontent of the people

The murmuring of the people that characterized the journey from Egypt to Mount Sinai returns and intensifies. In the period before their arrival at the covenant mountain they grumbled about genuine needs. They cried out and God, in response to Moses' prayer, gave them what they needed (see Exod 16–17). Now they complain where there is no need and their grumbling rouses God's anger. They have made covenant with the Lord and have experienced generous care for more than two years, but still they do not trust God to continue sustaining them. This is a critical moment in Israel's history. Will their lack of trust destroy the covenant? Moses, caught in the middle between a rebellious people and an angry God, must continually intercede for them.

The first murmuring story is told in general terms and functions as a pattern for the rest. The people complain, apparently for no good reason. God overhears their grumbling and with blazing anger burns the outer edges of the encampment. After the people cry out, Moses prays and God quenches the fire. The event gives the place its name: The Burning (Taberah).

Thus the pattern is set: (1) the people complain for no good reason; (2) God punishes them in anger; (3) they cry out; (4) Moses prays for them and God removes the punishment; (5) finally they name the place for the event.

The second murmuring story in this chapter is more complex. Two issues are interwoven: the people's weariness with the manna and Moses' weariness with leadership. Food has been a cause for grumbling since they left Egypt (see Exod 16); now leadership becomes a primary source of conflict. The story begins with the food issue. The grumbling begins with the mixed crowd that left Egypt with the Israelites (see Exod 12:38).

The people complain that they are tired of manna; God's gift is not sufficient for their taste.

According to Psalm 78 they cry out, "Can God spread a table in the desert?" (Ps 78:19). They remember fondly the meals in Egypt. Ironically they list the foods they got *without cost*, but forget that they paid with their slave labor. The second issue arises immediately. Moses hears their grumbling and voices his own complaint to God: "Why are you so displeased with me that you burden me with all this people?" Moses points out that he is not their mother; God is! God conceived them and gave them birth, so why does Moses have to nurse them? The people may be tired of manna, but Moses is tired of the people. He begs God to just let him die.

Imaging God as mother rather than father may seem surprising. Masculine images for God do outnumber feminine images in the Bible. This passage, however, is not the only biblical example of imaging God as mother (e.g., Ps 131; Isa 49:15; 66:13; Sir 4:10).

11:16-23 The seventy elders

The Lord outlines a plan to resolve both issues. Moses is to gather seventy elders at the tent of meeting where God will bestow on them a share of the spirit that is on Moses (see Exod 24:1-11). Second, Moses is to prepare the people for the gift of meat.

Seventy is a common biblical number for completion or for inclusion of the Gentiles (see Gen 10). Here it seems to be an indication that Moses will have plenty of help. In Exodus 18, Moses' father-in-law advised him to appoint minor judges to help him in settling disputes. In this passage God promises to give a share of Moses' charismatic gift to reputable elders so that they may share his leadership tasks. Apparently Moses' grumbling came out of a real need as did the people's grumbling before they arrived at Sinai. Thus God will supply what he needs.

The tone of God's reply regarding the people's desire for variety in their diet signals that the response to this complaint will not end so happily. God sounds like a disgusted mother: "You want meat? You will get meat! You will eat it until it comes out your noses!" Why is God so angry? The people want to undo the exodus, God's gracious rescue of them. They want to undo the covenant: they would rather be people of Egypt than people of God. Moses attempts to intercede by reasoning with God: "Do you know how many people we have? Can you really give them that much meat?" God replies, "Wait and see!"

The number of people Moses claims to lead agrees with the number given when Israel set out from Egypt: 600,000 men, not counting women, children, and the "crowd of mixed ancestry" that went with them (Exod 12:37-38). The number is no doubt inflated. If the others were included, the count would reach approximately two million, an impossible number for this trek across the desert.

11:24-30 The spirit on the elders

Now the final resolution of the two issues begins. The leadership question is treated first. Moses gathers the seventy elders at the tent of meeting where the Lord appears in the cloud (see Exod 33:9-10). The location of the tent outside the camp and the appearance of the Lord in the cloud indicate the source of the passage to be the pre-Priestly tradition. (In the Priestly tradition the tent is in the center of the camp; see Num 2:2). Moses has been filled with the spirit of prophecy throughout his ministry. The description of his call in Exodus 3 is a model for the call of later prophets (see Isa 6; Jer 1; Ezek 1–3). Now the Lord will take some of that spirit and bestow it on the elders who are to be his assistants. The effect is immediate: they fall into a prophetic trance. Saul will have a similar experience when the spirit of God comes upon him (1 Sam 10:10-13; 19:20-23). This ecstatic experience is not lasting, but their commission as assistants to Moses continues.

The spirit of God, however, cannot be constricted by human limitations. Two of the elders were on the list but for some reason did not go out to the tent of meeting. The spirit found them anyway and they too fell into a prophetic state. Joshua wanted Moses to stop them. But Moses has no desire to control God's spirit, nor is he protective of his own prophetic gift. He wishes that all God's people might be prophets. In the next chapter God will reconfirm Moses' own special status.

11:31-35 The quail

The leadership question has been settled; now it remains to satisfy the appetite of the people. So God again sent a wind. A wind sent by God had also split the Red Sea and turned it into dry land so that the people could cross (Exod 14:21-22). A mighty wind hovered over the waters when God began to create (Gen 1:2). This time the wind sent by God drives in an abundance of quail. Underlying this story is the fact that many birds migrate across the Sinai Peninsula. Often they are exhausted from the trip across the Mediterranean. So many quail are driven in by the wind that they pile up on the ground a yard deep! (A cubit is about eighteen inches.) An alternate view is that they can fly only about a yard above the ground. In either case, the weakened birds surround the camp for the distance of a day's journey.

For two days the greedy people gather as many quail as they can. Everyone got at least forty to fifty bushels of them. God, however, is still angry. Before they have even swallowed their feast, they are struck with a great plague. They wanted the tasty foods of Egypt; instead they suffer a plague just as Egypt did. The place, according to the pattern, is named for the event: The Graves of Greed, Kibroth-hattaavah. The survivors then continue their journey, stopping at Hazeroth. (See Ps 78:26-31 for another version of this story.)

12:1-9 Jealousy of Aaron and Miriam

In chapter 11, Moses expressed a wish that all God's people might be prophets. Now the two other desert leaders, Miriam and Aaron, challenge Moses' singular authority as a prophet: "Is it through Moses alone that the Lord has spoken?" (12:2). A prophet is first and foremost God's messenger, one who speaks in God's name. Moses has certainly done that. But are there not others in the wilderness community who also speak God's word? Moses, truly humble, seems to pray for that (11:29).

The challenge is introduced with what seems to be an unrelated issue, Moses' marriage to a Cushite woman. Cush is somewhere south of Egypt and is usually identified with Ethiopia. This woman is almost certainly not Zipporah, who is identified as a Midianite. It is not likely that the problem is Moses' taking a second wife. Abraham had three wives (Sara, Hagar, and Keturah); Jacob had two wives and two concubines (Rachel, Leah, Bilhah, and Zilpah). David and Solomon will have multiple wives.

The problem is also not one of race, even though a Cushite may be black. Racial discrimination against blacks is not known in biblical times. The difficulty may center on the fact that the great lawgiver has married a foreign woman.

Especially after the Babylonian exile there is a fear of marrying foreign women (see Ezra 9–10; Neh 13).

The danger of foreign women also appears in reports of other events: Rebekah's fear that Jacob will marry a Hittite or Canaanite (Gen 27:46; 28:1), Moabite and Midianite women leading Israel astray (Num 25:1, 6-18), Solomon seduced into idolatry by foreign wives (1 Kgs 11:1-2). All these stories were probably written during or after the Babylonian exile. If the fact that the wife is foreign is the problem, however, why is Zipporah the Midianite not a problem also? Among the patriarchs, Judah married a Canaanite (Gen 38:2) and Joseph an Egyptian (Gen 41:45). The book of Ruth (perhaps also postexilic) identifies a Moabite woman as David's ancestor. The difficulty with Moses' Cushite wife remains a mystery.

The Lord responds to the other difficulty: prophetic status in the wilderness community. The three leaders are summoned to the tent of meeting where the Lord appears in the column of cloud (see Exod 33:9-10; Num 11:24-25). He addresses Aaron and Miriam directly and declares in no uncertain terms the priority of Moses. Other prophets receive the Lord's message in visions or dreams, but the Lord speaks to Moses face to face (literally "mouth to mouth"). Moses sees the form or the likeness of the Lord. By contrast, Israel at Sinai saw no form but only heard God's voice (Deut 4:12). The Lord declares that Moses is truly unique. Aaron and Miriam may have some prophetic gifts, and indeed each is named "prophet" (Exod 7:1; 15:20); however, they will never equal Moses.

12:10-16 Miriam's punishment

The complaint of Miriam and Aaron is another murmuring story in this series. They have complained where there was no need, and thus the anger of God is roused against them. Miriam is struck with a scaly infection and thus must be expelled from the camp (see Lev 13:1-46; Num 5:1-4). Aaron pleads with Moses who begs God to heal her (thus following the pattern set in Num 11:1-3). As is the case in the other murmuring stories in Numbers, God heeds Moses' plea, but not before some of the punishment has been carried out. Miriam will suffer excommunication for seven days.

Why is Miriam punished and Aaron not? There is a hint that the story may originally have

been only about Miriam and Moses. It is odd to find Miriam's name before Aaron's. More convincingly, however, the Hebrew verb in 12:1 is feminine singular even though the subject is the compound "Miriam and Aaron" saying literally, "Miriam and Aaron, she spoke against Moses." "Aaron" seems to have been added to the sentence. All the remaining verbs are plural and Aaron is mentioned first in verses 4 and 5.

Is there a deeper meaning here also? It surely is not that a woman cannot hope to be a prophet. Both Deborah (Judg 4:4) and Huldah (2 Kgs 22:14) will later be called prophets. Or is Miriam punished because she is also challenging Aaron's priestly authority? Aaron has been set aside as priest and the ancestor of the priestly clan (Exod 28–29; 40:12-15; Num 17:16–18:7). Is Aaron spared the uncleanness because of his priestly status? This text too remains a mystery.

13:1-24 The twelve scouts

The story of the twelve scouts as it appears here represents a combination of sources and viewpoints. An early version appears in verses 17b-20, 22-24, and 27-31. Another version, possibly Priestly, is represented in verses 1-17a, 25-26, 32-33. In the early tradition the people are at Kadesh (see 13:26) and the object of the expedition is to discover whether an invasion of Canaan from the south is possible. In the Priestly tradition the community is encamped in the wilderness of Paran (see 13:3, 26) and arrives in Kadesh only in 20:1. The scouts are to explore the whole land that God has promised. Both traditions are attempting to explain why the Israelites did not enter the Promised Land from the south shortly after the exodus and Sinai experiences.

The story begins with the Priestly tradition. God gives the order to spy out the land and Moses and the people obey. There is another list of tribal leaders similar in form to the list in Numbers 1:4-19, but the names are different. Hoshea, representative of the tribe of Ephraim, is renamed Joshua by Moses. The two names are similar: Hoshea means "he saves"; Joshua means "The Lord saves." Although Joshua appeared in chapter 11, it sounds here as if he is just being introduced.

A pre-Priestly tradition begins in the middle of verse 17. The scouts are instructed to determine the possible success of an attack: the fortifications of the towns and the strength of the inhabitants.

They are also to evaluate the fertility of the land. From Kadesh they travel through the Negeb as far as Hebron, thus exploring only the southern part of the Promised Land. (The P tradition inserts v. 21, extending the scouts' journey to the northern limits of the land; see 34:8.) They discover that the land is indeed rich; to prove this they cut down a cluster of grapes so large it has to be carried on a pole by two men. They name the place "Grape Cluster" (Hebrew: *eshcol*).

13:25-33 Their return

In the early version of the scouts' return (13:27-31), they report the results of their search into the two questions of fertile land and possible conquest. First they show the immense cluster of grapes and declare that this is indeed a land of milk and honey (see Exod 3:8, 17; 13:5; 33:3). Then they acknowledge that the cities are indeed fortified and the inhabitants strong. Some are descendants of the legendary Anakim, widely believed to be giants. Others are the traditional enemies mentioned throughout the settlement period: Amalekites, Hittites, Jebusites, and Amorites (see Exod 17:8-16; 33:2; Josh 3:10). If the Israelites invade they will be surrounded by powerful foes! Apparently the people respond in fear, but Caleb, the Judahite scout, reassures them that, if they attack, they will prevail. The other scouts, however, counter his encouragement with a prediction of certain failure.

The Priestly tradition shifts the emphasis of the scouts' report (13:32-33). Instead of describing the goodness of the land, they announce that this land consumes its inhabitants (a direct contradiction of verse 27). This land is like Sheol that swallows up the unwary (see Prov 1:12; Isa 5:14). They heighten the terrifying appearance of the inhabitants: They are Nephilim ("fallen ones," translated "giants" in the Septuagint), descendants of gods and human women (see Gen 6:1-4); they are so huge that the scouts felt like grasshoppers. The scouts' discouraging report is called *dibba* in Hebrew. This word *dibba* usually connotes slander. God has promised this land and the scouts are disparaging it. Their report is a rejection of God's gift.

14:1-9 Threats of revolt

The story continues with the Priestly editing of the earlier story (14:1-7a). The Israelite community wails in despair at the grim report of the scouts. Once more the murmuring begins. Now, however, the complaint is not about conditions in the wilderness, but about the difficulties of entering the Promised Land. In the earlier stories the people remembered how wonderful Egypt seemed; now they would prefer even to die in the wilderness. Moses prayed to die in chapter 11; now the people pray to die. Anything is better than attempting to take possession of the land that God has promised them. The only solution they can think of in their distress is to replace Moses as leader and return to Egypt. They not only want to forfeit God's gift of the land; they also want to undo God's liberation of them in the exodus event. They are undoing the covenant relationship with God from Abraham to Moses.

Moses and Aaron fall on their faces at the news. Prostration is an expression of reverence. Usually one prostrates before God in worship (see Gen 17:3; Lev 9:24) or before another person out of respect (see Gen 44:14). In Numbers Moses (sometimes with Aaron) is often seen prostrating before God in intercession for the people (see 16:22; 17:10; 20:6). In this passage they fall on their faces before the community (see also 16:4). Is this also intercession for the people or is it an expression of horrified anger? Joshua and Caleb rip their clothes in a traditional sign of grief.

Inserted into this Priestly rendition of the event is a speech of the scouts from the earlier tradition. This speech is put into the mouths of Joshua and Caleb. They plead with the people, repeating their earlier praise of the land (see 13:27). They will be able to take possession of the land not by their own strength but because the Lord is with them. The fierce inhabitants will be helpless because their "protection" has left them. The gods in whom the current inhabitants of Canaan place their trust have deserted them. The Lord will serve the Canaanites up to Israel as a banquet.

14:10-38 The Lord's sentence

The whole community responds in anger, threatening to stone the leaders: Joshua and Caleb and perhaps also Moses and Aaron. They are stopped, however, by the appearance of the Lord's glory at the tent of meeting. The story of the Lord's response to the people's murmuring is told twice, first from an early tradition (14:11-25) and then from the Priestly tradition (14:26-38). In each version the Lord complains "How long!"

(14:11, 27) and takes an oath to punish the grumblers, swearing "by my life" (14:21, 28).

In the earlier tradition the Lord decides to wipe out the people and begin again with Moses. (The whole section is remarkably similar to Exod 32–34.) Moses, however, acts as a true prophet. Having pleaded with the people for the sake of God, now he pleads with God for the sake of the people. His argument is simple: "If you destroy this people, Lord, it will ruin your reputation!" He points out that God has been associated publicly with this people ever since the exodus and is still visibly present with them (in Hebrew, revealed "eye to eye") by means of the pillars of cloud and fire. If the Lord wipes them out, the whole world will think that God did not have the power to bring this people into the land promised to them.

Moses' second and final argument trumps the first. God has revealed the divine name and nature to this people (see Exod 34:5-7). The Lord is not a God of anger and revenge but of love and forgiveness (Num 14:18). The punishment is limited but God's mercy lasts forever. This statement is Israel's most frequent definition of who God is; it defines the "God of the Old Testament" (see Joel 2:13; Jonah 4:2; Pss 86:15; 103:8; 145:8; Neh 9:17). Moses ends with a plea that God live up to this divine nature and continue to forgive the people.

The Lord submits to Moses' arguments and agrees to pardon the people. This is still a murmuring story, however, and there will be a limited punishment (see chs. 11–12). God swears that all who still refuse to trust in spite of *seeing* the wonderful signs from the exodus onward will never *see* the Promised Land. So Moses is instructed not to travel north toward the Promised Land but to turn south toward the Red Sea in order to circle around Edom and Moab and enter the land from the east. (The Red Sea here probably represents the Gulf of Aqaba/Eilat.) See map on page 1524.

Even Moses is not excused from this judgment. Only the faithful Caleb will be brought into the land. This continual separation of Caleb from the rest of the scouts may be an indication that a small group did succeed in invading from the south (see Num 21:1-3). In the later division of land by Joshua, Caleb is given Hebron (the area he explored) and is reported to have driven out from there the three Anakim mentioned in Numbers 13:22: Sheshai, Ahiman, and Talmai (Josh 15:13-14).

In the Priestly version of the story (vv. 26-38), the Lord complains to both Moses and Aaron. The Lord's oath is a tit-for-tat response to the grumbling of the community: They wished to die in the wilderness (14:2), so everyone registered in the census (see Num 1) will die in the wilderness. Only the children that they feared would be taken captive (14:3) will survive to take possession of the Promised Land. The children, however, will suffer for the sins of their parents. They will be forced to roam the wilderness for forty years—one year for each day of the scouting expedition—until the whole exodus generation has died. This announcement of punishment is sealed by another solemn oath: The Lord has spoken and will do it.

The first to die are the scouts who spoke evil words about the Promised Land. Only Joshua and Caleb are spared. In the earlier tradition Caleb is the one who speaks favorably about the land (13:30) and is the sole survivor of the scouts (14:24); in the Priestly tradition Caleb is joined by Joshua (14:6, 30, 38).

14:39-45 Unsuccessful invasion

The earlier tradition picks up the story again to report a further rebellion by the people. They have been told to turn back and make a long journey to enter the land (14:25), but now they regret their murmuring and decide to attempt an invasion of Canaan anyway. Moses warns them that this is not a "Holy War." God, symbolized by the ark of the covenant, is not going with them and neither is Moses. In their stubbornness the people attempt an attack anyway and are soundly defeated. See map on page 1524.

15:1-21 Secondary offerings

The purpose of most of this chapter (vv. 1-31) is to supplement the ritual laws given in Leviticus 1–7, adding the ingredients and measurements for the grain and wine offerings that accompany the animal sacrifices. This legislation will apply both to the native-born Israelite and to the resident alien (15:14-16, 26, 29-30). The chapter also provides the story of the scouts with a more hopeful ending. Twice the legislation begins, "When you enter the land" (15:2, 18). God's promise of the land has not been taken away altogether; it has only been delayed.

The first set of sacrifices are burnt offerings, whether whole burnt offerings (see Lev 1:1-17) or

Figure 5:
Measurements of Offerings to Accompany Animal Sacrifice

ANIMAL	FLOUR	OIL	WINE
Sheep or goat	1/10 ephah 2.35 lb.	1/4 hin 1 qt.	1/4 hin 1 qt.
Ram	2/10 ephah 4.7 lb.	1/3 hin 1.35 qts.	1/3 hin 1.35 qts.
Ox	3/10 ephah 7.05. lb.	1/2 hin 2 qts.	1/2 hin 2 qts.

the portion burnt for a communion sacrifice, a sacrifice in fulfillment of a vow, or a voluntary offering (see Lev 3:1-17; 7:16). The ingredients and measurements vary with regard to the animal offered (see Fig. 5). An ephah of flour is about 23.5 pounds (2 quarts dry); a hin is just a little more than a gallon. The oil was apparently mixed with the flour or poured over it and the wine poured out as a libation.

In addition, a portion of the first batch of dough is to be offered to God. Paul mentions this practice in the Letter to the Romans: "If the first-fruits are holy, so is the whole batch of dough" (Rom 11:16). This remains a Jewish custom to this day. A small pinch of every batch of dough, about the size of an olive, is burnt in the fire as an offering to God.

15:22-31 Purification offerings

The purpose of this section is similar to that of the previous: the stipulations regarding supplementary offerings to accompany animal sacrifices (15:24). The sacrifices are offered to atone for inadvertent offenses, transgressions committed in ignorance. For example, an individual might eat forbidden food without knowing it was forbidden until later. Even these transgressions must be made right. Anyone, however, who sins willfully and with premeditation (Hebrew: "high-handedly") will not be forgiven. Such a person is to be expelled from the community.

The animals to be sacrificed in this section are different from those required for similar offenses in Leviticus (Lev 4:3-21): here a bull is to be sacrificed as a burnt offering and a goat as a purification offering; in Leviticus the bull is the purification offering. Perhaps this section in Numbers is a further development of the legislation in Leviticus.

15:32-36 The sabbath-breaker

The legislation applying to life in the Promised Land is interrupted by a story of a man gathering wood on the sabbath day. The act of gathering wood may be considered work, which is forbidden on the sabbath (Exod 20:8-11), or the offense may be the intention of making a cooking fire on the sabbath, which is also forbidden (Exod 35:3). The offender is held in custody until the appropriate action can be determined. Since the sabbath law is already clear, the uncertainty must be regarding the type of punishment. Moses is told by the Lord that he should be stoned. The community executes the offender outside the camp according to the Lord's command. Breaking the sabbath is an offense directly against God and is thus a capital crime.

15:37-41 Tassels on the cloak

The final directive in the chapter is the requirement to put blue-violet tassels on the corners of one's garments. This blue-violet is an expensive dye made of a certain kind of snail. It is thus considered precious and associated with royalty and worship. The command is given to "the Israelites" but seems to apply only to men. The purpose of the tassels is to remind the covenant people of their obligation to keep all God's commandments. Whenever one is tempted to stray, the tassel will remind him to be faithful. God promised in the covenant making that the people would be holy

(Exod 19:6); the tassels are a simple means to that end. The directive closes with the opening statement of the commandments: "I, the LORD, am your God who brought you out of the land of Egypt" (15:41; cf. Exod 20:1-2).

16:1-11 Rebellion of Korah

Like chapters 13–14, chapter 16 is two stories woven together: the challenge of Dathan and Abiram concerning Moses' civil leadership from the early tradition (16:1, 12-15, 23-34) and the challenge of Korah and his faction concerning Moses' priestly leadership from the Priestly tradition (16:1-11, 16-22, 35 + ch. 17). The method of weaving the stories together was to insert the name of Korah in the Dathan and Abiram story (16:24, 27, 32) and the names of Dathan and Abiram in the Korah story (16:1).

The story of Korah begins the chapter. Korah is a Kohathite and thus belongs to the most highly respected clan of the Levites. The Kohathites were assigned to care for and carry the sacred objects of the sanctuary: the ark, the veil, the table, the menorah, the altars, and all the other utensils within the tabernacle (Num 3:27-32; 4:1-14). But they have been expressly warned not to touch or even look at these sacred objects until they are wrapped by the priests (4:15-20). Only those who are specifically designated may approach so near to the Holy One and the sacred objects used in worship.

This limitation is the basis of the challenge against Moses and Aaron. (Moses has functioned primarily as a prophet up to this point, but this challenge has to do with priestly authority.) Korah and his faction declare that the whole community is holy, so why do Moses and Aaron think they have special authority over this ministry? Their argument is soundly based: God did promise to make the people holy if they kept the covenant (Exod 19:6) and the Israelites have just been told to put tassels on their garments so that they will remember to be holy (Num 15:40). But does this holiness mean that they are all called to be priests?

The situation is complicated by the fact that Moses and Aaron are also Kohathites! They are sons of Kohath's son Amram (see Exod 6:18, 20), whereas Korah is a son of Kohath's son Izhar. (According to this genealogy, Korah is the first cousin of Moses and Aaron.) The priesthood, however, has been limited to descendants of Amram, specifically Aaron and his descendants. Is Korah asking, "Who do you think you are?" He says to them, "You go too far!"

Moses responds to this challenge by falling on his face. Is he responding in anger? Or is he prostrating before God asking for help in this tricky situation? In any case, he turns the situation over to God. Korah and his faction are to appear at the tabernacle with censers and incense and the Lord will choose who will draw near to him.

Moses also warns Korah and company: "It is you who go too far!" God has chosen the rest of the Kohathites for a most honorable ministry. Is this not enough? Do they want to be priests too?

16:12-15 Rebellion of Dathan and Abiram

Korah and Aaron both disappear from the scene as a second challenge arises. Moses sends for Dathan and Abiram and they respond, "We will not go." Their challenge has to do with Moses' civil leadership. They followed him out of Egypt because he told them God had promised them a land flowing with milk and honey. Now they have been told they will die in the wilderness (14:22-23). Looking back, Egypt seems wonderful in their eyes. Egypt is the land of milk and honey, not the Promised Land. As for Moses, he has not only seduced them with false claims, he is also lording it over them.

The argument of Dathan and Abiram fails on two counts. They seem to have forgotten that the reason they will die in the wilderness is their refusal to believe Caleb and go up to enter the Promised Land (13:30–14:4). Second, they are wrong that Moses is flaunting his authority. Moses has been interceding with God for this people from the very moment that they left Egypt (Exod 15:25). When his authority has been challenged, he has prayed for the challengers (Num 12:13). He has begged to be relieved of this burden and has accepted help (Num 11:11-15, 24-29). So Moses is furious with the two because of these false charges and prays that God will not accept their offerings.

16:16-24 Korah

The scene shifts again to Korah and his faction. All of them plus Aaron are to appear at the tent of meeting to offer incense. Each one shall take his censer, gather burning coals from the altar fire, and burn incense. Moses had told Korah and company that the Lord would choose those who would draw near to him. So as they offered the incense, the glory of the Lord appeared to the whole community. Then the Lord makes a choice, telling Moses and Aaron to stand back because the whole community will be consumed by fire. This is the third time God has threatened to destroy the Israelites (see Exod 32:10; Num 14:12). Twice Moses has persuaded God not to do it.

Again Moses and Aaron fall prostrate and beg the Lord not to destroy the whole community. The Priestly interpretation of their plea reflects themes from the period of the Babylonian exile and later. God is appealed to, not as covenant partner with and redeemer of Israel, but as creator of every living thing (see Isa 40:28; 43:15; 45:18). The argument turns on individual responsibility (see Ezek 18): Will God destroy everyone for the sin of one person? Can that be just? This third time the plea of Moses is again effective. God does not destroy the whole people.

16:25-34 Punishment of Dathan and Abiram

This section begins at 16:23. Just as God warned Moses and Aaron to stand back from Korah and company, now God instructs Moses to warn the people to stand back from the tents of Dathan and Abiram. (Note: Aaron has again disappeared and Korah has been inserted into this sentence.) Moses carries out God's command, telling the people not even to touch anything that belongs to these two insurgents. Moses informs Dathan and Abiram that God will decide between them and Moses. If they die an ordinary death at an expected time, then they were right and Moses had usurped authority over them. If the earth opens up and swallows them, however, then God has indeed chosen Moses and Dathan and Abiram are in the wrong. Moses has barely finished his speech when the earth opens and swallows them, their families, and everything they owned. All the people are terrified and flee from this horror.

The refusal of Dathan and Abiram to go up when Moses calls may reflect the conflict with the Reubenites (and other Transjordanian tribes) to help the other tribes to take possession of Canaan (see Num 32:1-15). God has promised to "lead them up" out of Egypt into the Promised Land (Exod 3:8, 17; 33:3). At the report of the scouts the people refused to "go up" to the land (Num 13:30-31) and then, too late, went up in rebellion (Num 14:44). In Numbers 32 the Reubenites eventually agree to cross over with the rest of the tribes until they have won the land; then they will return to their good grazing land across the Jordan (Num 32:16-33).

16:35–17:15 Punishment of Korah

Korah (who undoubtedly belongs here in verse 35 rather than in 16:32) and his faction were last seen offering incense at the tent of meeting. Moses and Aaron stepped back when God threatened to consume the whole community. Their prayer saved the community, but not those who were guilty. Fire blazed out from the Lord and consumed Korah and his 250 companions.

The censers and the incense that they used, however, are holy, because they have been offered to God. So Eleazar, who is in charge of all things inside the tabernacle (3:32; 4:16), is summoned to take care of them. He is carefully identified as a son of Aaron, a priest, and so authorized to approach holy things. Eleazar scatters the coals with the incense at some distance away where there is less danger of profanation. Then, in accord with the Lord's instructions, he has the censers hammered into plates to cover the altar. There they will function as a sign (17:3; Hebrew *'oth*) and a reminder (17:5; Hebrew *zikkaron*) that no unauthorized person may attempt to exercise a liturgical role.

The language is significant here. In the Priestly tradition covenants are marked by "signs": the covenant with Noah by a rainbow (Gen 9:12-13); the covenant with Abraham by circumcision (Gen 17:11); the Sinai covenant by the sabbath (Exod 31:13, 17). Throughout the Old Testament the wonders that God worked in delivering Israel from Egypt are known as "signs" (e.g., Exod 4:8-9; 10:1-2; Num 14:11, 22; Deut 4:34; 7:19; Pss 78:43; 105:27; 135:9; Neh 9:10). The Passover is called a *zikkaron* (Exod 12:14); liturgical objects such as the ephod worn by Aaron (Exod 28:12) and the trumpets blown to announce festivals also function as a remembrance before the Lord (Num 10:10).

The warning that no unauthorized person (literally "strange man") may approach the altar parallels the story of Nadab and Abihu (Lev 10:1-7). These two sons of Aaron were authorized persons, but they presented unauthorized incense (literally "strange fire"). The Hebrew phrase for "strange man," *ʾish zar*, echoes that for "strange fire," *ʾesh zara*. In liturgical matters anything that is unauthorized is potentially fatal. This is the negative answer to Korah's challenge. Moses has said that God will make known who is chosen to approach the sacred (16:5); the hammered cover on the altar warns that God has not chosen everyone. The positive answer will follow in 17:16-26.

Another murmuring story separates the two responses to Korah's challenge. The pattern is familiar: The whole community grumbles without cause; God is angry and punishes; Moses (through Aaron) intercedes with God; God relents and the punishment ceases. The complaint against Moses and Aaron has to do with the deaths in the previous chapter. The two leaders are seen as murderers. (Ironically, Moses was justly accused of murder in Egypt [Exod 2:11-15], but here he is innocent.) As the community joins together against them, the glory of the Lord appears once more (see 14:10; 16:19). Once more God warns Moses to stand back (16:21; see 16:24, 26). Moses and Aaron, however, prostrate themselves once more before God in intercession (16:22; see 14:5; 16:4).

Moses instructs Aaron to perform his priestly duty to make atonement for the people. Usually atonement rituals require blood, but here Aaron is to do exactly what Korah and his faction did and offer incense (16:6-7); Aaron, however, is authorized to do this and Korah was not. What the Levites were authorized to do was to form a buffer zone between the people and the tabernacle so that a plague would not strike them (Num 8:19). In reaching for priestly status, however, they have failed in their assigned duty. The plague has already begun and some people have died, so Aaron does not hesitate. He *runs* from the tent of meeting into the midst of the people, identifying with them as he makes atonement for them. Through his action the plague is stopped, but not before almost fifteen thousand people have died.

17:16-26 Aaron's staff

The positive response to Korah's challenge follows the murmuring story. Moses has said that God will choose the holy one who may draw near (16:5, 7); now that choice will be made. There is a play on the Hebrew word *matteh*, which can mean either "tribe" or "staff"; the leaders of each ances-

tral house (i.e., "tribe") will present a "staff." In addition to these twelve staffs, Aaron shall also submit a staff for the house of Levi (17:18, 21). (Levi has not been included in the list of the twelve tribes throughout the book of Numbers; the count has remained twelve because of the division of the tribe of Joseph into Ephraim and Manasseh; see 1:47-54; 2:33.) Whichever staff sprouts will signal God's choice. The choice is first of all between tribes, but there is a suggestion that God will also choose a specific person (17:20).

The thirteen staffs are placed in front of the ark of the covenant, which contains the tablets of the commandments. The very next day Aaron's staff has not only sprouted, but even blossomed and produced almonds! There is now no doubt about the person God has chosen. Aaron's staff lives and the others are dead; just so Aaron may approach the sanctuary, but if unauthorized people do they will die. Moses is to put Aaron's staff in front of the ark as a sign (Hebrew *ʾoth*) to warn the people so that their grumbling will cease. Later tradition will include Aaron's rod as one of the objects kept within the ark of the covenant (Heb 9:4).

Korah's clan does not disappear altogether. In later tradition the Korahites are recognized as singers (2 Chr 20:19; Pss 42, 44–49; 84–85) and as gatekeepers for the temple (1 Chr 9:19; 26:1).

17:27–18:7 Charge of the sacred things

The people have finally gotten the point, but their response shows a typical exaggeration. Now they are terrified that they will all die because they have seen Aaron's staff, which is now holy. The section that began with Korah's challenge that, since all the people are holy, they should all be allowed to touch holy things and exercise sacred ministry, ends with the people's terror in the presence of the holy.

In order to alleviate the people's fear the Lord gives Aaron instructions regarding the boundaries of the sanctuary. The Lord usually speaks to Moses but, outside of this chapter (18:1, 8, 20), speaks to Aaron only one other time (Lev 10:8). All of these passages treat the prerogatives of the priesthood and the danger of improperly approaching God.

Aaron is told that from now on he and the whole house of Levi will be responsible for the sin of anyone who crosses the sacred boundaries; they must guard the sanctuary or they will bear the punishment. Aaron and his sons, the priests, are responsible for all ministry within the sanctuary as well as the purity of the priesthood. The other Levites will maintain and guard the tent of meeting and serve the priests who minister there. Each group has its own duties and its own boundaries. No one, including Levites, may usurp the prerogatives of the priests; none of the other Israelites may usurp the prerogatives of the Levites.

18:8-20 The priests' share of the sacrifices

The priests are given no inheritance in the land; God is their heritage. But they must have some compensation for their ministry in order to survive. Thus they are given a share in all the sacrifices and offerings at the sanctuary except holocausts, which are totally consumed by fire. A distinction must be made, however, between the "most holy" oblations and other offerings. The "most holy" offerings include the grain offerings, purification offerings, and reparation offerings (see Lev 6:7–7:10). Only a portion of each of these offerings is burned. The rest may be eaten only by ritually clean priests and only within the precincts of the sanctuary. The various kinds of communion sacrifices—the thanksgiving sacrifice, the free-will offering, the sacrifice in fulfillment of a vow—however, are divided differently. The portion that is given to the Lord may be eaten not only by the priests, but by anyone in their families who is ritually clean; the rest of the sacrifice is eaten by the offerer and those to whom he gives it (see Lev 7:11-21). The same is to be done for elevated offerings (see Lev 7:28-36). In addition the priests and their families may have the best (literally "fat") of grain and wine and oil as well as first fruits, which the Israelites donate to the sanctuary (see Deut 18:4; 26:2).

Two other occasions provide contributions for the priests and their families. First, whatever is put under the ban (Hebrew *herem*) is to be given to them (18:14). *Herem* means that everything is set aside for God: spoils of war (including prisoners), property of those condemned to death, or any other condemned or dedicated property. In this chapter the ban applies primarily to hereditary land or any goods that someone has vowed to dedicate to the Lord (see Lev 27:21, 28; Num 30:2-17) or the property of those condemned to death (see Exod 22:19; Lev 27:29). (See commentary on Num 31 regarding the ban applied to spoils of war.)

Second, the firstborn that belong to the Lord are to be given to the priests. Firstborn sons and animals unfit for sacrifice are redeemed with money; firstborn of clean animals must be sacrificed. Both the money and the meat belong to the priests.

These stipulations for the upkeep of the priests are sealed in a covenant of salt. This designation presumably refers to the stipulation of offering salt with sacrifice (Lev 2:13; Ezek 43:24) and the custom of eating salt together as a symbol of permanent bonding (Ezra 4:14; 2 Chr 13:5; Mark 9:50).

18:21-24 Tithes due the Levites

The Levites, like the priests, inherit no land and need compensation for their services at the tent of meeting. The Israelites are reminded that the Levites protect them from the dangerous holiness of God in the sanctuary. Thus they have been assigned all the tithes that the Israelites must give to the Lord. Tithing is not voluntary in Israel; it is a kind of tax due to the Lord. The people are to give a tenth of all the produce of their land: the fields, vineyards, and orchards. (Legislation regarding tithes is not consistent; compare Deut 12:17-19; 14:22-29). Anyone who wishes to pay a tithe in money instead of produce must give an additional twenty percent (see Lev 27:30-31).

18:25-32 Tithes paid by the Levites

The Levites in their turn must also pay a tithe to the priests. Since they have no land and thus cannot give the regular tithe to the priesthood, they are required to give one-tenth to the priests from all the tithes that they receive. This tithe frees them to do what they wish with the other nine-tenths. The produce and money that the Israelites have given them were dedicated to the Lord, but once the Levites pay their own tithe from this offering, the rest is no longer sacred. They may consume it with their families just as the rest of the Israelites consume the rest of the produce from their land.

19:1-10 Ashes of the red heifer

The legislation regarding purification from contamination by a corpse is intense and unique. Every other legislation regarding purification involves at least some ritual action at the sanctuary;

the ritual preparation of this purification water, however, takes place not only outside the sanctuary but even outside the camp. All those who are involved in the preparation of this water of purification are defiled by the ritual; nowhere else is a priest said to be defiled as a result of ritual action. Contamination by a corpse threatens to defile not only the person involved, but even the tabernacle itself.

The preparation of the water begins with the acquisition of the proper animal: a red cow who has no defects and who has never been used for ordinary work. Even though virtually every translation identifies this animal as a "heifer" (i.e., a young cow who has never borne a calf), the Hebrew word is the ordinary word for "cow" (*parah*). The cow must be red, probably to symbolize blood. Blood is a powerful agent for purification. The cow must never have been used as a draft animal. An animal offered to God should not have been previously used for human purposes. The same stipulation is required of the two cows (who have borne calves) that in Samuel's time bring the ark home from the Philistines (1 Sam 6:7).

Eleazar the priest supervises the ritual. Eleazar is rising to prominence at this point in the story. Aaron's eldest sons, Nadab and Abihu, died after offering unauthorized incense (Lev 10:1-2). Eleazar is next in line and will succeed Aaron. He has already been put in charge of everything within the sanctuary (Num 3:32; 4:16). It is he who scattered the coals and incense after the incident with Korah and who had the censers hammered into a covering for the altar (17:1-3).

Eleazar's role in this ritual is central but limited. He takes the blood of the slaughtered cow and sprinkles it seven times toward the tent of meeting. The tent, which here is understood to be in the center of the camp, is at some distance from the action that takes place outside the camp. Nevertheless, since it is threatened with defilement, it must be included symbolically in the purification. Sprinkling blood seven times is part of the ritual in the standard purification offerings (Lev 4:6, 17), on the Day of Atonement (Lev 16:14, 19), and for the cleansing of those suffering from skin disease (Lev 14:7, 27; cf. 14:51). The whole cow is burned, including its blood. The burned blood in the ashes of the cow will still have power to purify.

While the cow is being burned, Eleazar throws cedar, hyssop, and scarlet yarn in the fire. The cedar is used no doubt because of its aromatic properties. Hyssop, also highly aromatic, is used twice in the ritual: it is burned with the cow and its branches are used to sprinkle the water. The scarlet yarn may also symbolize blood. The same three elements are used with blood in the ritual to purify someone who has been healed of skin disease (Lev 14:4, 6; cf. 14:49-52). "Cleanse me with hyssop, that I may be pure" (Ps 51:9) is a reminder of these purification rituals.

Several men assist Eleazar. Someone brings the red cow and slaughters it in Eleazar's presence. Someone burns the red cow; someone who is ritually clean gathers up the ashes of the cow and puts them in a place outside the camp where they will not be defiled. The priest and the one who burned the cow are unclean and must bathe and wash their clothes. The one who gathers the ashes is also unclean, but apparently less so. He is only required to wash his clothes. They all remain unclean until evening.

19:11-22 Use of the ashes

These ashes of the red cow, which have been so carefully prepared, must be mixed with living water, that is, water flowing from a spring or other source. The resulting "purification water" is to be used to purify someone who is unclean because of having touched the dead body of a human being. A human corpse is regarded as having the potential for powerful contamination. If someone dies in an enclosed space, a tent or building, everything within the tent and everyone who is in the tent or enters it is unclean for seven days. The only things that are protected are things in closed pots. The contamination is somewhat less severe out in the open. Only the person who touches the dead body is unclean for seven days. In either case, however, everything and everyone that the unclean person touches also becomes unclean. Even the person who sprinkles the purification water is also rendered unclean until evening.

The person made unclean by contact with a dead body must be cleansed by the purification water. On the third and seventh day this water is to be sprinkled on him or her by someone ritually clean (not a priest). The same water must be sprinkled on whatever object has become unclean. After the seventh day the unclean person must bathe and wash clothes and will then be declared clean. This process is absolutely necessary. Twice it is stated that anyone who fails to submit to this ritual of purification remains unclean forever and will be cut off from the community. Otherwise the person's very presence in the camp would defile the Lord's sanctuary.

The purpose of this ritual is not simply hygienic. According to this legislation even the bone of a person long dead or a grave renders someone unclean. The purpose therefore must be sought somewhere else. There is a strong resistance in ancient Israel to anything suggesting worship of the dead. Ancestors are remembered, but they are not to be consulted about future actions (Lev 19:31; 20:6, 27; Deut 18:11; 2 Kgs 21:6; 23:24; Isa 8:19). Saul forbade the summoning of the dead by necromancers; when he was in desperate straits and asked the medium in Endor to call up Samuel, Samuel's response is to scold him (1 Sam 28:7-20; see 1 Chr 10:13). Manasseh, regarded as Judah's most wicked king, consulted the dead (2 Kgs 21:6; 2 Chr 33:6); his grandson Josiah "purged the consultation of ghosts and spirits, with the household gods, idols, and all the other horrors to be seen in the land of Judah and in Jerusalem" (2 Kgs 23:24).

Most of the peoples in the ancient Near East from Egypt to Mesopotamia had a cult of the dead. God's covenant people are not allowed to succumb to this practice. Declaring a dead body to be a powerful source of uncleanness is a deterrent against turning to the dead person for advice and assistance. It is a short step from consulting the dead and asking them for help to worshiping them. Israel is to look to God who leads them into the future rather than depending on the dead who are buried in the past.

20:1 Death of Miriam

Chapter 20 signals the end of the wilderness period. Miriam dies in the first verse; Moses and Aaron are informed in verse 12 that they will die before the entrance into the land. Aaron dies in verse 28. The exodus generation has been told they will all die in the wilderness; this warning indicates these three major leaders of the community will die with the rest of their generation. Miriam's death is reported simply with no comment about mourning.

Because of the interweaving of traditions there is some confusion in the geography. The Priestly tradition seems to indicate that the people have

just arrived at Kadesh, whereas the earlier tradition located them at Kadesh already when the scouts went up to spy out the land (13:26). The same inconsistency is probably the reason no year is mentioned in this verse. Later Aaron's death is dated to the fortieth year after the departure from Egypt (33:38).

20:2-6a Need for water at Kadesh

Again the people complain. This story, however, is not like the other murmuring stories in Numbers. This story follows the pattern seen in Exodus: the people have a genuine need; they murmur; Moses prays; God provides. This is the first murmuring story in Numbers where there is a genuine need; it is the Priestly parallel to the earlier water story in Exodus 17. The people's complaint looks like mutiny; they hold an assembly against Moses and Aaron. They bemoan the fact that they did *not* perish in their previous episodes of murmuring: in their desire for meat (Num 11:33), in their refusal to believe Caleb's report (Num 14:11-20), in their rebellion against the leadership of Moses and Aaron (Num 17:6-15; see 17:27-28). They repeat the now-familiar refrain: "Why have you brought us out of Egypt?" The wilderness is no land of promise! The inclusion of Aaron as a leader along with Moses identifies the source of this story as the Priestly tradition. Both of them hear the complaint and fall prostrate in petition at the tent of meeting. The final element in the pattern, God's response to the people's need, follows in the next section.

20:6b-13 Sin of Moses and Aaron

Once more the glory of the Lord appears at a critical moment (see 14:10; 16:19; 17:7). The Lord gives Moses instructions to provide the people with the needed water. He is to take the staff—his or Aaron's that is in the tent of meeting—and command the rock to give water. An abundance of water will pour forth at his word alone. The Lord is not angry as in the other murmuring stories in Numbers because now the people have expressed a genuine need. Moses, however, *is* angry. First, he scolds the people, calling them rebels and suggesting that they are unworthy of having water come from the rock for them. Then, instead of commanding the rock to yield water, he strikes it not once but twice.

God keeps his part of the bargain; the water gushes out in abundance and the people are satisfied. But Moses and Aaron do not get off so easily. (Aaron is complicit in the failure simply by his presence; he does not escape here as he did in the incident with Miriam in ch. 12.) These two leaders neither followed God's command nor imitated God's generosity to the people. They did not trust God's goodness. Thus they have not demonstrated God's holiness to the people. Therefore they too will die in the wilderness with the rest of their generation.

Other attempts are made to explain the reason that Moses and Aaron are prevented from entering the Promised Land. In Psalm 106 the people are blamed (Ps 106:32-33; see Deut 1:37; 3:26; 4:21-22). Some interpreters say they are punished because Moses struck the rock twice instead of once; however, Moses was not told to strike the rock at all. He was told just to speak to the rock. Other commentators point out that from the exodus generation only Caleb and Joshua are permitted to enter the land (14:21-24, 29-30). Whatever the reason, it is clear from this chapter that a new generation will pioneer in the land God promised to their ancestors.

The passage ends, as most of the murmuring stories do, with an explanation of the place names: "Meribah" is derived from the Hebrew word *rib*, which means "to contend against." The name "Kadesh" is suggested by the comment that there God displayed divine holiness (Hebrew *yiqqadesh*).

20:14-21 Edom's refusal

In the earlier tradition, after the Israelites refused to go up to the land at Caleb's urging, God told them two things: first, the whole adult generation would die in the wilderness; and second, they would not enter Canaan from the south but would go back to the Red Sea (probably here the Gulf of Aqaba) and come around to enter from the east (14:25). Thus Moses sends messengers to the king of Edom to gain permission to travel through his land toward the eastern side of the Dead Sea. His appeal to Edom as a brother is not without merit. Edom is another name for Esau, just as Israel is another name for Jacob (Gen 25:30; 32:29; 35:10). The twin sons of Isaac and Rebekah are believed to be the ancestors of the Edomites and the Israelites.

Moses reports to the Edomite king the whole story from Jacob's going down into Egypt to their arrival back at the borders of Edom. He tells how God sent an angel to deliver them from Egyptian persecution and slavery (see Exod 14:19; 23:20-23; 32:34). Now Moses has sent a messenger to the king of Edom. (In Hebrew the same word is translated both "messenger" and "angel.") Then Moses makes his request: "Please let us pass through your land" (20:17). He promises they will take absolutely nothing. The King's Highway is an ancient caravan route, stretching from the Red Sea (modern Gulf of Aqaba) to Damascus. It passes through Edom and runs up the eastern side of the Dead Sea and the Jordan valley. Traces of it, rebuilt by the Romans, can still be seen today. See map on page 1525.

The king of Edom refuses, threatening violence against the Israelites if they cross their borders. Even when the Israelites insist, Edom rejects their request. So the Israelites turn back to go all the way around Edom's southern and eastern borders. Deuteronomy tells the story somewhat differently. The Israelites pass through Edom and Moab, but the Amorite king, Sihon, refuses to let them pass (see Num 21:21-35). Israel's attack against him is the first battle of the entry into the land (Deut 2; see Num 21).

20:22-29 Death of Aaron

Miriam died at the beginning of this chapter; Aaron dies at the end. Much more attention is given to his death, however. The Israelites have traveled some distance along the Edomite border to Mount Hor, an unidentified location; the name "Hor" means "the mountain." Aaron and his son Eleazar are to be brought up this (small?) mountain and to perform the ritual transfer of authority in the sight of all the people. The priestly vestments are taken off Aaron and put on Eleazar, who thus assumes the office of high priest (see Lev 8:7-9). When this is accomplished Aaron dies; only Moses and Eleazar descend from the mountain. The community mourns for thirty days, much longer than the traditional seven-day period (see 1 Sam 31:13; Jdt 16:24; Sir 22:11). Deuteronomy reports that the mourning period for Moses was also thirty days (Deut 34:8). The Egyptians mourned Jacob for seventy days, but Joseph later observed the traditional seven days of mourning (Gen 50:3, 10).

21:1-3 Victory over Arad

This puzzling little passage seems the direct opposite of the Israelites' earlier experience at Hormah (14:39-45). At that time they had refused to go up and take possession of the land in spite of Caleb's advice. After God declared that they would indeed die in the wilderness as they had asked, they attempted to attack even though Moses warned that God would not go with them. In that event they were soundly defeated. Now, only a short time later, they are attacked by the king of Arad (in the southern Negeb near Hormah) and some Israelites are taken captive. They plan to attack but they also promise God that they will abide by the customs of holy war: (1) they will recognize that the victory is won by God's power, not their own; (2) they will not enrich themselves with plunder but will dedicate it all to God. As a result, they are victorious.

The first principle of holy war is based on the exodus experience. Pharaoh pursues the fleeing Israelites, who are unarmed, with all his chariots and horses. The victory clearly belongs to God (Exod 14:13-14). Throughout the Old Testament there is a consistent warning not to trust in armaments (horses and chariots) or in the size of the army, but to trust in God (see Judg 7:1-7; Ps 20:8-9; Isa 31:1; Mic 5:9-12).

This second principle is called *herem* in Hebrew and is translated either as "the ban" or "doom." War must not be waged for profit. God wins the victory; the spoils belong to God. Either all the plunder is destroyed—all living beings killed and all property burned (Deut 2:34; Josh 6:18, 21)—or some of it is offered to God at the sanctuary (Lev 27:21; Num 18:14).

This story of victory in Canaan seems out of place here; a more likely victory at Hormah is reported in Judges 1:17. The next passage about the bronze serpent (21:4-9) seems to follow directly from chapter 20 with the departure from Mount Hor; the story of Hormah looks like an insertion. There are two possible reasons for this anticipation of the entrance into the Promised Land. First of all, Caleb was exempted from God's decision that the exodus generation would all die in the wilderness (14:24). This story may explain the report in Joshua that Caleb holds the territory in the southern Negeb (Josh 14:13-14; Judg 1:12-15; 1 Sam 30:14). Second, this story, taken with the earlier failed attempt to enter Canaan from the south, may illustrate the way by which Israel should take possession of the Promised Land. This second experience in the southern Negeb, in contrast to the first attempt, results in victory. In the first attempt the people act on their own in disobedience to God and they fail. In this second attempt they trust God to give them the victory and they subsequently give both the credit and the spoils to God. The place is named (again) "Hormah," a word that suggests the practice of *herem* (see 14:45).

21:4-9 The bronze serpent

Following God's instructions (14:25), the Israelites set out by way of the Red Sea road to go around Edom. But before they leave the wilderness there must be one more murmuring story. This story is like all the murmuring stories in Numbers (except the grumbling about water in chapter 20): the people's complaint again seems unfounded. They claim there is no food or water, yet they are disgusted with the food they have. As usual, when there is grumbling without cause, God grows angry and punishes the people. Moses then prays and God relents.

The punishment is in the form of "seraph serpents." *Saraph* in Hebrew means "burning." Perhaps this name refers to the poisonous (thus burning) bite of the serpents. In Isaiah 14:29 and 30:6 *seraphim* (plural of *saraph*) are clearly serpents, associated with vipers and adders, and they also fly. *Seraphim* appear once more in Isaiah during his call vision (6:2, 6). The six-winged *seraphim* hover aloft and cry out, "Holy, holy, holy is the LORD of hosts." One of them brings a *burning* coal to cleanse the prophet's lips. Seraphim in Isaiah's vision seem to be guardians of God's throne. They may be modeled on the hooded cobra, a sacred animal in Egypt imaged even on the pharaoh's headdress.

God instructs Moses to provide for the people's healing with a kind of sympathetic magic. He is to mount a bronze *saraph* on a pole, and anyone who looks at it will live. The *saraph* serpent thus becomes associated with healing as well as with death. This ambiguous meaning of the serpent as a symbol is found throughout the ancient world and still today. Moses' own staff was turned into a serpent (Exod 4:3; 7:15). In the eighth century Hezekiah removes a bronze serpent from the temple because apparently it had become a temptation to idolatry (2 Kgs 18:4). The serpent in Genesis 3 becomes in later tradition a symbol for the devil (see Wis 2:24). In the Gospel of John the evangelist sees the raised serpent as a type of Christ on the cross (John 3:14-15). Today the symbol of medicine, the caduceus, consists of serpents entwined around a winged staff.

21:10-20 Journey around Moab

The story of the bronze serpent marks the transition from the wilderness wandering to the purposeful movement toward the Promised Land. The Israelites have journeyed around Edom and rapidly move around Moab. Most of this section is a simple listing of places. The first two camping sites mentioned in this brief itinerary are unknown: the name "Oboth" means "mediums" or "necromancers"; "Iye-abarim" means "ruins of the crossing" or "ruins on the other side."

The Israelites move on from these two places with ominous names to the Wadi Zered and from there to the Arnon, which forms the northern boundary of Moab. They arrive at Beer, which means "well," and there the Lord gives them water. Further stations on the journey bring them to the headland of Pisgah that overlooks Jeshimon ("wasteland"). Pisgah is the traditional site for the death of Moses (see Deut 34:1-5). This itinerary is a summary of Israel's whole journey from Mount Hor to the edge of the Promised Land. The entry into the land, however, is a long way off and there are several stories that illustrate the details of the journey summarized here.

Two songs interrupt the itinerary. The first is a song about the river Arnon, the northern border of Moab. Its source is said to be the "Book of the Wars of the LORD." The book is unknown, but the title is an introduction to the stories that will follow. The Lord is about to go to battle in order to give the land to the Israelites just as he swore to their ancestors Abraham, Isaac, and Jacob. The second song is a celebration of the well. The well itself is a sign that the wilderness period is over; the gift of water will be available in the land they are approaching.

21:21-32 Victory over Sihon

The Israelites, having crossed the Arnon, now reach the territory of the Amorites. They make the same request of Sihon that they made to the king of Edom omitting the recital of previous history

and reminder of family relationship (see 20:14-16). Edom had refused the request and threatened violence; Sihon not only refuses but engages Israel in battle. The Israelites are victorious and seize the territory of the Amorites. Then they sing a song just as they did after the crossing of the sea. This song, however, does not celebrate Israel's victory. Rather it commemorates Sihon's earlier victory over Moab when the Amorites pushed the Moabites back south of the Arnon. Is the recollection of this song a taunt against Sihon who has now lost this same territory? Or is it just a familiar song, remembered because they are now in Heshbon, Sihon's former capital?

21:33–22:1 Victory over Og

As the Israelites press farther north, another king, Og of Bashan, engages them in battle. Israel, however, cannot lose as long as they are faithful to the Lord and acknowledge that they win only by God's power. So Israel takes possession of the whole area on the east side of the Jordan River. The capture of the territory legitimates Israel's later settlement in the area east of the Dead Sea and the Jordan. The tribes of Reuben and Gad will settle in the area of Sihon to the south and half the tribe of Manasseh will settle to the north in Og's former kingdom (see Num 32; Deut 3:12-20; Josh 1:12-16; 12:6).

Sihon, king of the Amorites, and Og, king of Bashan, are well known throughout biblical literature. Deuteronomy repeats the story of their defeat (Deut 2:24–3:11) and adds the detail that Og was one of the giants that the people feared so much (see Num 13:32-33); his bed was almost fourteen feet long (Deut 3:11). Rahab of Jericho and the Gibeonites know the story when Israel enters the land (Josh 2:10; 9:10). After the Babylonian exile Nehemiah praises God for this victory as part of his recital of God's gifts to the people (Neh 9:22). Everyone who prays the Psalms acknowledges this event as a sign of God's great love for the people (Pss 135:11; 136:19-20).

After the victory over Sihon and Og, Israel encamps by the Jordan River across from Jericho. There they will stay until Joshua leads them across to take possession of the land of promise.

22:2-14 Balaam summoned

A cycle of stories about the seer Balaam is inserted into the narrative about Israel's advance toward the Promised Land. Balak, king of Moab, is fearful of the power of the Israelites. He has seen how they defeated Sihon and Og; he is aware that this great multitude of people is using up the resources of the surrounding area. So he summons Balaam, son of Beor, to place a curse on Israel. Balak's hope may be that the curse will weaken Israel to the point that he can defeat them and drive them away. When Balak's messengers arrive, however, Balaam tells them he does not act on his own; he must ask God. God forbids him to go because the people he is to curse are already blessed, so Balaam sends a refusal to Balak.

It is unclear from the biblical stories where Balaam's home is. It is sometimes assumed that he is from Syria. In his first oracle (Num 23:7) Balaam says that he has come from Aram (= Syria), from the mountains of Qedem (or the eastern mountains), a mountain range in Syria. Numbers 22:5 states he is from "Pethor on the river"; the "river" is usually a reference to the Euphrates. This same text, however, also says that Pethor is "in the land of the Amaw," which may mean simply "his people." NABRE emends to "Ammonites." Not only is it more likely that Balak would look for a seer close to his own neighborhood, but evidence outside the Bible also supports the conjecture that Balaam is from the Amorite territory east of the Jordan. A seer named Balaam, son of Beor, is known through texts found at Deir ʿAlla, a site in the Valley of Sukkoth not too far north of where Israel is said to be encamped in Numbers 22:1.

22:15-21 Second appeal to Balaam

Balak is not so easily deterred; he sends a more impressive delegation to pressure Balaam into coming and promises a handsome reward. Balaam insists he can act only with God's authorization, so again he awaits a night vision. This second time God permits him to go, but warns that he must act totally according to God's design. Throughout this section God is identified through the generic term *ʾelohim* (God; 22:9, 10, 12, 18, 20) and by the proper name of Israel's God *Yahweh* (English, LORD; 22:8, 13, 18, 19). The Israelite author assumes that the only god who could be inspiring Balaam is the Lord. This non-Israelite prophet does God's work just as Israel's prophets do. A prophet is a messenger and must deliver the message exactly as the sender intends. Israel's

prophets speak the Lord's word; Balaam too will speak only the message God gives him.

22:22-40 The talking donkey

This section is a fable inserted to illustrate the dependence of the prophet on God. The insertion is marked by two repetitions: First, in 22:21, Balaam goes off with the princes of Moab and in 22:35 it is again noted that the princes go with him. In between he seems to be accompanied only by two servants and his donkey. Second, in 22:20 God tells Balaam to go with the men but to say only what God tells him; a similar phrase is repeated in 22:35. In between God seems to be angry that Balaam has set off on this journey.

The story makes fun of Balaam. Three times the angel of the Lord stands in his way to stop him; three times the donkey sees the angel but the seer does not. When Balaam beats the donkey a third time, she asks why he is being so cruel. Then the Lord, who opened the donkey's mouth, also opens Balaam's eyes and he sees the angel. The angel (who is really the Lord himself) tells him that he is against this journey. Had Balaam not stopped, the angel would have killed him but spared the donkey. Balaam pleads ignorance and turns to go back home. Here the fable is woven back into the first story: the Lord allows him to go, but only on condition that he delivers God's message.

In the Pentateuch the "angel of the LORD" is often a disguise for the Lord himself as is the case here. Often the angel disappears and the Lord is revealed as the one who is speaking (see Gen 16:7-13; 22:15-16; Exod 3:2-4). The angel also reveals that he is acting as an adversary, who has come to hinder Balaam (22:22, 32). The Hebrew word is *satan*. Throughout the Old Testament period anyone, even God, can be a *satan*; it is only in the New Testament that the developed figure of Satan appears as the personification of evil.

Balak is angry because Balaam has been slow in arriving, but Balaam informs Balak of the truth that has been emphasized throughout this chapter: He can act only when God sends him and speak only when God gives him the words. Balak then offers a sacrifice for the purpose of having meat for a feast to celebrate Balaam's arrival.

22:41–23:12 The first oracle

Early the next morning Balak and Balaam prepare for Balaam's task. Tension rises from the different motives of the two men: Balak is intending that Balaam will curse Israel and thus weaken it (22:6, 11, 17); Balaam has been insisting that he can speak only what God puts in his mouth (22:38, see 22:13, 18-19). Balak chooses the spot for the event, a place where Balaam can see "some of the people" whom he is to curse. Balaam gives instructions for inviting God to be present: Balak is to build seven altars and offer a bull and a ram on each. This is a significant sacrifice. Bulls and rams were valuable animals; the number seven signifies completeness. Surely God will respond.

Balaam goes out to meet the Lord. This non-Israelite seer cannot assume that Israel's God will speak to him even though he knows God's proper name, Yahweh (22:8, 13, 18, 19; 23:3), and claims him as his own God (22:18). Thus he walks around seeking an omen indicating what he should do. God, however, has a relationship with this man and not only comes to meet him but puts a word in his mouth just as he does with the other prophets (see Jer 1:9).

Balaam returns to Balak and recites his *mashal*. The *mashal* is a wisdom saying, either short (a proverb) or long (a parable). Usually the *mashal* has a "sting in its tail," a message that the hearer may not want but really needs. The use of the word *mashal* suggests that Balaam is a wise man, a sage, since the *mashal* is usually not associated with prophets. (Ezekiel, however, does tell several parables and contradicts several proverbs [Ezek 12:22-23; 17:2; 18:2-3; 24:3] and is even called a "spinner of parables" [Ezek 21:5].) Philo, a first-century Jewish writer, calls Balaam a *magus*, that is, "wise man" (compare the *magi* in Matt 2).

Balak's first *mashal* begins with his impossible task: he was summoned to curse Israel, but where can he find power to curse one whom God has not cursed? Thus, instead of cursing (or blessing), he expresses his awe at the greatness of this people spread out below him. This people lives independently without need of allies among the nations. Their multitude, which frightened Balak just as it worried Pharaoh (Exod 1:9), is beyond counting. God's promise to Abraham that his descendants would be like the sand on the seashore (Gen 22:17) has been fulfilled: they are like the dust that their travels have stirred up in the desert. Balaam is so overcome at the sight of this people that he prays to be like them.

Balak is enraged and claims that Balaam has even blessed the people although he has not. Balaam's defense is simple: He can say only what the Lord puts in his mouth. He is a faithful prophet.

23:13-26 The second oracle

Balak decides to try another place; perhaps at the previous site Balaam could see too many of these people. The same sacrifices are offered; Balaam again goes out to seek the Lord, who meets him and puts a new word in his mouth. When Balaam returns to Balak, the king asks, "What did the Lord say?" Balak has at least learned the source of Balaam's oracles even if he does not like them.

Balaam's second *mashal* is addressed to Balak. It is a lesson regarding who the Lord is. This is not a weak human being who can be manipulated; rather, this is the faithful God who has power to bring his word to fulfillment. Balaam was summoned to bless and he must bless. What is more, this people whom Balak fears is stronger than he imagined. The Lord, who brought them out of Egypt, remains with them and gives them terrible strength. Balak has miscalculated: these people are not an ox eating up the grass of the field (22:4); they are a lion ready to attack and devour their prey. Balak cannot defeat them.

Balak now tries to minimize the damage. He orders Balaam neither to curse nor to bless these people. Balaam, however, cannot even agree to this: Whatever the Lord says, he must announce.

23:27–24:13 The third oracle

Balak stations Balaam at yet a third place. This time he is not concerned about what Balaam can see (23:13) but about whether God will approve a curse from here. Gradually Balak is learning who is in charge. The same sacrifices are again offered.

Balaam, however, has changed his method. He recognizes that God will be pleased not with a curse but with a blessing for Israel. He does not need to walk around to seek omens; he is filled with the spirit of God. This puts him in good company: The spirit of God (or the Lord) inspires leaders (Othniel, Judg 3:10; Gideon, Judg 6:34; Jephthah, Judg 11:29; Samson, Judg 13:25; 14:6, 19; 15:14; Saul, 1 Sam 10:6, 10; 11:6; 19:23; David, 1 Sam 16:13; 2 Sam 23:2; the ideal king, Isa 11:2), wise persons (Joseph, Gen 41:38; Bezalel, Exod 31:3; 35:31), and prophets (Elijah, 1 Kgs 18:12; Ezekiel, Ezek 11:5, 24; 37:1; Micah, Mic 3:8).

Thus inspired, Balaam recites his *mashal*. He begins with a solemn introduction: This poem and the next one are identified by the technical term "oracle" (Hebrew *neʾum*; 24:3-4, 15-16). This term is commonly used by prophets (356 times) to identify a message from the Lord (e.g., Isa 41:14; Jer 1:8; Ezek 37:14; Hos 11:11; Joel 2:12; Amos 2:11; Mic 4:6; Nah 2:14; Zeph 1:2-3; Hag 1:13; Zech 1:3-4; Mal 1:3). Not only Balaam's vocabulary, but also his claim to authority puts him squarely in the prophetic tradition. He describes himself as one who sees as God sees, hears what God says, and knows what God knows. The message he delivers will be the message of God; he has received it in a prophetic trance but with his eyes open.

He identifies God with three names that were originally the names of Canaanite gods but that have become descriptions of Yahweh, the God of Israel: El, the head of the Canaanite pantheon; Shaddai (translated "Almighty"; see Gen 17:1; 28:3; 35:11; Exod 6:3), god of the mountains; and Elyon ("Most High"), the god whom Melchizedek serves (Gen 14:18-22).

This oracle is addressed to the people, Israel ("you/your" in 24:5, 9). It is a hymn of praise, echoed in the psalms: "How lovely your dwelling, / O LORD of hosts" (Ps 84:2); "How good it is, how pleasant, / where the people dwell as one!" (Ps 133:1). Israel itself is a testimony to God's fidelity: God's promise of fertility has been fulfilled (see Gen 17:5-6); the prophet sees this people like well-watered trees. The promise of land (see Gen 12:7) is also about to be fulfilled, but it will require struggle. The people will crush all their enemies as a lion devours prey. The refrain from the second oracle recurs (see 23:22), along with a reference to a later victory. As an example of Israel's power, the final editor anticipates King Saul's tenth-century defeat of the Amalekites under their king, Agag (1 Sam 15:1-8). Balaam ends his oracle with a beatitude and a curse, repeating the promise to Abraham: "I will bless those who bless you and curse those who curse you" (Gen 12:3).

Balaam's blessings and curses are not according to Balak's wishes, however. In his fury the king dismisses Balaam and refuses to pay him. But Balaam had never agreed to the payment (22:18); instead he has consistently told Balak that

he can proclaim only what the Lord gives him. He can bless and curse only those whom God blesses and curses.

24:14-25 The fourth oracle

Balak may be finished with Balaam, but the prophet is not finished with the king. He has a warning for Balak regarding Israel. This last oracle begins with the same claim to authority as the previous one. Balaam warns Balak, king of Moab, that a future ruler of Israel will crush Moab along with the rest of Transjordan. The future ruler is imaged as a star and a scepter. In the tenth century David did defeat Moab and made it a vassal state; Moab remained under Israelite control until the revolt of the Moabite king Mesha (see 2 Kgs 3:4-5). In the ensuing centuries as further difficulties arose, the people began to look for a new David, an anointed king (=messiah) who would shepherd them with his scepter/staff as David did (see Mic 5:1-4; 7:14).

Early Christian writers understood Balaam's words in terms of Christ and connected his vision of a star to the story of the magi in Matthew 2. Jewish interpreters also regarded this passage as an expression of messianic hope. The messianic aspirations that circled around Simon ben Kosiba who led a revolt against Rome (132–135 A.D.) are indicated by his nickname, Bar Kokhba, "son of the star."

Balaam continues his oracle by describing the fate of the Sethites, Edomites, Amalekites, Kenites, and Ishmaelites. Edom is just south of Moab, south of the Dead Sea. Although their name (another name for Esau) indicates a family tie with Israel (=Jacob), they are traditional enemies. David conquered Edom but they regained independence during the reign of Solomon. They were among those who plundered what was left of Judah after Nebuchadnezzar's invasion in 587 B.C. The Amalekites are described as "first of the nations," either because they were the first to engage Israel in battle (Exod 17:8-16) or because they were an ancient Canaanite people. Although they were "first," their "end" is to perish before Israel. They were finally subdued by David (1 Sam 30:1-18). The Kenites are usually regarded as friendly to Israel (see 1 Sam 15:6; 27:10). Perhaps the oracle against them reflects the traditional belief that they were descended from Cain and a distrust of their profession as metalworkers (Gen 4:22).

The other two groups are more difficult to identify. Sethites, descendants of Seth, Adam's son, may be a generic term for human beings (see Gen 4:25) or they may be a people otherwise called the Shutu, who are mentioned in the Amarna letters of the fourteenth century B.C. The final group named in the oracle (Hebrew *sumo ʾel*) is unknown. The Septuagint interprets this word to connote Og (see Num 21:33-35). The NABRE translators have interpreted it to mean the Ishmaelites, descendants of Abraham's son, who live in the southern desert. Whoever these people are, Balaam announces that they will be attacked by the Kittim, people of Cyprus, after they have conquered Assyria and the otherwise unknown Eber. The point of the oracle is that Israel's enemies, including Moab, will not survive.

After these chapters in which Balaam claims the Lord as his God and faithfully proclaims his word, his reputation suffers. Only the prophet Micah recalls his steadfastness in resisting Balak's plans (Mic 6:5). He is blamed for Israel's infidelity at Baal Peor (Num 31:15-16; see Josh 13:22) and, in contrast to the story here, is portrayed as actually proclaiming a curse against Israel, which God turned into a blessing (Deut 23:6; Josh 24:9-10; Neh 13:2). He fares even worse in the New Testament where he is not only made responsible for the Baal Peor incident (Rev 2:14) but is also described, in direct contradiction of this story, as greedy for gain (2 Pet 2:15; Jude 11).

25:1-5 Worship of Baal of Peor

Careful reading is necessary to understand this chapter. Two stories have been woven together, producing several ambiguities. The first story involves Moabite women; the second centers on a Midianite woman. The first story concludes with the execution of the guilty parties as does the second, but at some indeterminate point a plague also breaks out. In later literature both stories have been interpreted in sexual terms, but nowhere in the chapter is there an explicit description of sexual activity.

The first story represents the earlier, pre-Priestly tradition. It is introduced with the announcement: "[T]he people profaned themselves by prostituting themselves with the Moabite women." Two verbs describe their action: "profaned" and "prostituting themselves." The verb

translated "profaned" (Hebrew *hillel*) is used in many contexts, most having to do with breaking God's law. For example, one profanes oneself by working on the sabbath (Exod 31:14), by sacrificing children to Molech (Lev 18:21), by swearing falsely (Lev 19:12), or by not keeping a vow (Num 30:3). The verb translated "prostituting themselves" seems to suggest a sexual context. However, it is a common idiom also for worshiping other gods. The covenant relationship with God is compared to a marriage relationship, most notably by Hosea (chs. 1–3; cf. Jer 3:1). So worshiping another god is imaged as adultery against the people's "husband," Yahweh (e.g., Lev 20:5-6; Deut 31:16; Judg 2:17; 1 Chr 5:25). This is the context for the story in Numbers 25:1-5.

The Moabite women invite the people—presumably both men and women—to share in the sacrifices to their god, the Baal of Peor. In one sense, this is as simple as inviting them to dinner. In most of the ancient Near East during this period, meat was not eaten unless the animal had first been offered to a god in sacrifice. (The same problem, whether to eat the meat set before one in someone else's house, faced Christians in Paul's time; see 1 Cor 8.) The Israelites attended the sacrifice, ate the meal, and thus honored the god.

The meal itself is the central element of the sacrifice and the greatest problem. To eat together, to share the same food, is to share the same life. For this reason, a meal is one way of sealing a covenant (see Gen 31:45-54; Exod 24:11). This principle is evident also in Israel's sacrificial tradition: in sacrifices other than the whole burnt offering, part of the sacrifice is offered to God (by burning) and part is consumed by the worshipers (e.g., Lev 7:11-21). Thus by eating the sacrifice "with" the Baal of Peor, the Israelites have attached themselves to another god and been unfaithful to the Lord. The people's sin is idolatry.

In anger the Lord commands Moses to execute all the leaders of the people by impaling them in the sun (i.e., "publicly"). The leaders are apparently considered responsible for the wrongdoing of the people. The punishment is unusual in the Old Testament, occurring only one other time (2 Sam 21:5-9). Not only is the execution public, but burial is probably denied the victims (see Deut 21:23). Moses modifies the Lord's command, however, by instructing the judges to kill only those who are guilty.

25:6-15 Zeal of Phinehas

The second story is from the Priestly tradition. As it begins the community is weeping at the entrance to the tent of meeting, presumably in mourning for those who have been killed. An Israelite man brings a Midianite woman in before the whole community. Immediately Phinehas assassinates both of them. Then the plague is stopped.

There are more questions than answers in this story. No reason is given for the woman's presence and no description is given of what the man and woman do. No reason is given for the action of Phinehas, but the consequence is the cooling of God's anger and the cessation of the plague. The plague also comes as a surprise. When did it begin and why? The only information provided is that twenty-four thousand people have been killed.

Interpreters have assumed that the Israelite man, later identified as Zimri, married the Midianite woman. There is a great fear that marriage to non-Israelite women will lead men into worshiping other gods (Exod 34:15-16). Even Solomon is said to have been led astray by his foreign wives (1 Kgs 11:1-8). Interpreters also assume that Zimri and Cozbi were having sexual intercourse when Phinehas killed them. Neither assumption is explicitly supported by the text, however. Phinehas follows them to "the tent" (Hebrew *qubbah*). This Hebrew word occurs only here in the Old Testament and signifies something like a canopy or alcove. It is not clear whether this is part of the tent of meeting or a separate enclosure. Perhaps it is related to the tent shrines of nomadic Arabs called *qubbah* in Arabic. In that case, Zimri may have brought Cozbi in to perform a cultic ministry, pleading with God to end the plague just as Balak brought Balaam in to curse Israel. Whether it is intermarriage with a foreigner or a cultic ritual performed by a foreigner, however, the action is understood by Phinehas as an affront to the Lord. The wrongdoing in this story is the same as that in the first story: the movement toward worship of other gods.

Phinehas is praised for his rapid response to the threatening situation: "Then Phinehas rose to intervene, / and the plague was brought to a halt. / This was counted for him as a righteous deed / for all generations to come" (Ps 106:30-31). He is promised a covenant of peace and a covenant of everlasting priesthood. The covenant of peace suggests that, first of all, he will be protected from vengeance by the family of Zimri. It also indicates that he will remain in God's favor and friendship. In the book of Malachi God states that the covenant with Levi is just such a covenant: "My covenant with him was the life and peace which I gave him, / and the fear he had for me, / standing in awe of my name" (Mal 2:5). Through this action Phinehas is also established as the one through whom the priestly line continues. He is the only son of Aaron's son Eleazar according to the genealogy in Exodus (Exod 6:25; see Num 20:26-28). After the people are settled in the Promised Land he ministers to the ark of the covenant in the shrine at Bethel (Judg 20:28).

Phinehas is said to have been as jealous among the Israelites as the Lord is. The words "jealousy" and "to be jealous" occur twice each in 25:11-13. The Lord is often said to be jealous for the chosen people (e.g., Isa 9:6; 26:11; 42:13; 59:17; Joel 2:18) or for Jerusalem (e.g., Zech 1:14; 8:2). God is even named "the Jealous One": "You shall not bow down to any other god, for the LORD—'Jealous' his name—is a jealous God" (Exod 34:14; cf. Deut 4:24; 5:9; Josh 24:19). English speakers must remember that the words "jealous" and "zealous" have the same root even though their current meanings have separated into negative and positive connotations. To speak of God's "jealousy" or "zeal" is to say that God is passionate about these people and cares deeply. Phinehas has mirrored that passionate zeal.

25:16-18 Vengeance on the Midianites

The incident with the Midianite woman leads to a command to crush the whole people. The Midianites were somehow involved with Balak in arranging with Balaam to curse Israel (see Num 22:4, 7). Cozbi, the catalyst for the previous event, was the daughter of a Midianite prince. The battle against the Midianites will be described in Numbers 31.

Women from the two groups of people who are held responsible in this chapter for Israel's apostasy, the Moabites and the Midianites, have also been a great blessing to Israel. Zipporah, daughter of the priest of Midian, saved the life of Moses, her husband (Exod 4:24-26). Ruth, the Moabite, is an ancestor of David, the king (Ruth 4:13-17).

SECOND CENSUS OF A NEW GENERATION, PREPARATION TO ENTER THE PROMISED LAND

Numbers 26:1–36:13

25:19–26:51 The second census

The primary tradition represented from this point to the end of Numbers is the Priestly tradition. A major interest in this tradition is genealogies, so it is no surprise that another census begins this last section. This is a new generation, however. Apparently the last of the generation that came out of Egypt has died in the plague at Shittim, as God said they would (14:21-23, 28-33). (The pre-Priestly tradition suggests that the old generation has died at the end of Num 20.) Only Caleb, Joshua, and Moses remain from that generation (see 26:64-65). The "little ones" who were under twenty when the spies scouted out the land are now to be counted. The first purpose of the census is to assess military strength (v. 2). Are there enough fighting men to prevail in the struggle for the Promised Land? A second purpose has to do with the allotment of the land (see 26:52-56). How much land can each tribe settle and does each tribe need?

This second census parallels the first (see Num 1). The Lord's command to Moses is similar and the order of the tribes is the same with one exception: Manasseh is placed before Ephraim (see Figure 3, p. 156). There are other differences: There is no indication of the date except the notice that the plague has ended (25:19). Eleazar has replaced Aaron who has died. No tribal leaders are designated to assist them. Several generations of each tribe are listed and stories are attached to several individuals.

The significant material in this census is found in the stories, all of which have to do with inheritance. From the tribe of Reuben, Dathan and Abiram from the third generation of descendants are singled out (26:9). They were killed for rebelling against Moses and so their line is removed from the tribal inheritance (see ch. 16). Korah, from the tribe of Levi, is also mentioned here, since the story of his rebellion is told in chapter 16. The narrator is careful to note that, even though Korah died, some of his descendants survived (26:10-11). Several psalms are later attributed to the "sons of Korah" (Pss 42; 44–49; 84–85; 87–88).

The story of Judah's three sons by his first wife is the next to appear (26:19; see Gen 38). Judah arranged for Er to marry Tamar and, when he died, to marry Onan according to the levirate custom. Onan refused to father a son with Tamar, however, and he also died. Judah did not want to lose his third son, so he made Tamar wait. After a long period of time she tricked Judah into having intercourse with her. Tamar's twin sons, Perez and Zerah, appear in this genealogy, replacing the two lost sons of Judah. The line of Perez is taken to the next generation, presumably because he is the ancestor of David. The inheritance will continue through him.

Manasseh is listed before Ephraim, thus holding the significant seventh place in the genealogy (compare Figure 3, p. 156). One reason for this distinction is the story of the daughters of Zelophehad, who occupy the seventh place in the genealogy of Joseph (Joseph, Manasseh, Machir, Gilead, Hepher, Zelophehad, his five daughters). They will initiate a change in the law of inheritance, which previously had applied only to sons. Their full story is told in the next chapter and in chapter 36. The tribe of Manasseh has also increased more since the first census than any other tribe: from 32,200 to 52,700. They will be one of the dominant tribes throughout Israel's history.

In the tribe of Asher a daughter, Serah, is named (26:46). Besides the daughters of Zelophehad, she is the only woman named in this genealogy. There are no stories about her, but she is also listed in other genealogies (Gen 46:17; 1 Chr 7:30). The situation of the daughters of Zelophehad does not apply to her since she has brothers and the inheritance continues through them.

26:52-56 Allotment of the land

The second purpose of the census, the allotment of the land, appears next. Two apparently contradictory methods of distribution are described. The first (vv. 53-54) relates directly to the census: tribes with more people get more land. The second (v. 55) calls for distribution of land by casting lots. This lottery method seems to ignore the relative size of each tribe. Verse 56 is an attempt to combine the two methods, which seems to be what Joshua did for each tribe, with the exception of the tribes that remained in Transjordan: Reuben, Gad, and the half-tribe of Manasseh (see Josh 13–20).

Figure 6:
Comparison of the Population in the First and Second Censuses

Tribe	Numbers 1	Numbers 26	Tribe	Numbers 1	Numbers 26
Reuben	46,500	43,730	Manasseh	32,200	52,700
Simeon	59,300	22,200	Ephraim	40,500	32,500
Gad	45,650	40,500	Benjamin	35,400	45,600
Judah	74,600	76,500	Dan	62,700	64,400
Issachar	54,400	64,300	Asher	41,500	53,400
Zebulun	57,400	60,500	Naphtali	53,400	45,400

26:57-65 Census of the Levites

The Levites are again omitted from the regular census (see 1:47-53). They are not to inherit the land along with the other tribes (Num 18:20-24; 26:62; Deut 10:8-9; compare Josh 21). The genealogy of Levi begins as usual with Gershon, Kohath, and Merari (see Gen 46:11; Exod 6:16; Num 3:17). The next verse (26:58), however, interrupts the list with clans that, in other genealogies, belong to the next generations: Libni, son of Gershon (Exod 6:17; Num 3:18, 21); Hebron, son of Kohath (Exod 6:18; Num 3:19, 27); Mahli and Mushi, sons of Merari (Exod 6:19; Num 3:20, 33); Korah, son of Izhar and grandson of Kohath (Exod 6:21).

The genealogy resumes with the line of Amram, son of Kohath. Amram married Jochebed, his father's sister (see Exod 6:20). Their children are the wilderness leaders: Aaron, Moses, and Miriam. The story of Aaron's sons, Nadab and Abihu, ends the genealogy. These two offered "unauthorized fire" (incense) before the Lord and they died (see Lev 10:1-2; Exod 30:9). They too are removed from the line of inheritance.

The chapter concludes with a summary: Moses and Eleazar took a census of the Israelites; no one remained of the previous generation except Caleb and Joshua (and, of course, Moses himself).

27:1-4 Zelophehad's daughters

Zelophehad had no sons, as was already noted in the previous chapter. Thus, according to the prevailing custom, he had no heirs; his claim to the land was lost. His five daughters, however, did not want their father's name to disappear. In the presence of the whole community at the tent of meeting, they make a direct appeal to those in authority, Moses, Eleazar, and the tribal leaders. Their appeal is simple and straightforward; they state the situation and make their request. Zelophehad has died, not because he participated in Korah's rebellion but because he was part of the generation that refused to enter the Promised Land at Caleb's urging (Num 14:1-35).

Their protest suggests that, if Zelophehad had been a member of Korah's faction, his land would have been forfeit under the law of *herem*. The land (along with all the other possessions) of those condemned to capital punishment was turned over to the priests (see Commentary on 18:8-20) or to the king (see 1 Kgs 21:13-16). Zelophehad's death as a member of his generation is not the main problem, however; the problem is that he has no sons. His daughters object that his name will be "cut off" from his clan, just as the names of those who were guilty of rebellion or sacrilege: Dathan, Abiram, Korah, Nadab, and Abihu. Their proposed solution is simple: Allow daughters to inherit if there are no sons.

Several elements in this story are noteworthy. First of all, the daughters are allowed to speak in the presence of the assembly gathered at the cultic site, the tent of meeting. They are not required to transmit their request through a man. Second, the request they make is for a woman's right to inherit. The request is limited to an extraordinary situation and will be further limited in chapter 36; nonetheless, it demonstrates that women could be considered as legal persons in the community. Third, however, their proposed solution will affect only one generation. The land the daughters inherit will subsequently be inherited by their sons, who will be counted not in the clan of their mother but in the clan of their father. This situation will be addressed in chapter 36.

The daughters of Zelophehad are all named, a fact to be noted since only six to eight percent of the persons given names in the whole Bible are women. Some of their names also appear as the names of cities or territories in the central highlands, the area of the northern kingdom. In the Samaria Ostraca, an eighth-century record from Samaria reporting the arrival of wine and oil from several territories, Hoglah and Noah are named as two of the territories. Hoglah is near Geba and Noah is near Socoh. (The Samaria Ostraca also names some of the men mentioned as Manassite in the previous chapter: Iezer, Asriel, Shechem, and Shemida; see Num 26:29-32.) Tirzah is an important city in the territory of Manasseh; it is the capital of the northern kingdom from the time of Jeroboam until Omri built Samaria (ca. 922–870 B.C.; see 1 Kgs 14:17; 15:21, 33; 16:6, 8, 9, 15, 17, 23). The beauty of the beloved in the Song of Songs is compared to Jerusalem and Tirzah (Song 6:4). This echo of their names shows another consequence of their request: the establishment of part of the tribe of Manasseh in the territory west of the Jordan. The Manassite clans of Machir and Gilead settled east of the Jordan in the area of Gilead and Bashan, the territory they claimed before the people crossed the Jordan (see Num 32:29-42; 34:13-15; Deut 3:12-17). But Manasseh was also given ten shares west of the Jordan because the daughters of Zelophehad each received a portion along with Manasseh's sons (Josh 17:1-6).

27:5-11 Laws concerning heiresses

The request of the daughters of Zelophehad leads to a change in the law of inheritance. Just as he had done in other cases for which there were no legal provisions (e.g., making arrangements for those unable to celebrate Passover at the prescribed time, 9:6-14; determining the punishment for breaking the sabbath, 15:32-36), Moses takes the daughters' request to the Lord.

The Lord validates the request and instructs Moses to add these specifications to the law: In the case of a man who dies without sons, a daughter has first right of inheritance, followed by male relatives in order of relationship: brothers, uncles, and then the next relative in line. The basic principle that men inherit still holds, but, at least in one situation, women also have property rights.

27:12-23 Joshua to succeed Moses

None of the exodus generation will enter the Promised Land except Caleb and Joshua. The transfer of priestly leadership has already taken place: Eleazar has succeeded Aaron (20:25-29). The transfer of civil leadership from Moses to his successor must still be arranged. (The third wilderness leader, Miriam, has no successor.) Moses has already been told that he will die with the rest of his generation because of his own infidelity at the waters of Meribah (Num 20:7-13). So he prays that the Lord will appoint a new leader for the people who will be both mighty in battle and wise in leadership. He calls upon the Lord as "the God of the spirits of all humanity." Moses and Aaron addressed God by this same title when they appealed for mercy during Korah's rebellion (16:22). Now Moses is appealing to God's compassion that the people not be left as sheep without a shepherd.

God responds with instructions for a ritual to appoint Joshua as Moses' successor. Joshua is an ideal candidate. He is "a man of spirit," a charismatic leader like Joseph (see Gen 41:38). He was victorious in the first battle of the wilderness journey (Exod 17:8-16). He stayed on Mount Sinai with Moses for forty days and nights (Exod 24:12-18). He is devoted to God, remaining in the tent of meeting when Moses leaves (Exod 33:11). In his objection to the prophesying of Eldad and Medad he is perhaps overprotective of Moses' rights or of following proper procedure, but he accepts Moses' rebuke (Num 11:28-29). According to the Priestly tradition he is one of the two scouts to give a positive report and encourage the people to go up and take the Promised Land (Num 13:16; 14:6-10). Thus he is one of the two from the exodus generation who will enter the land (14:29-30, 38).

In the presence of the priest Eleazar and the whole community, Moses is to lay hands upon Joshua. Thus he will convey some of his own power and dignity (Hebrew *hod*) on Joshua just as some of his spirit was given to the seventy elders (Num 11:25). This is the only occurrence of *hod* in the Pentateuch; the word appears most often in the Psalms (8x) and is usually applied to God (Pss 8:2; 96:6; 104:1; 111:3; 145:5; 148:13). The Lord confers this majesty on the king (Ps 21:6; see Ps 45:4). Thus Joshua is greatly honored.

Joshua will not be the sole leader of the people, however. He is dependent on the priest Eleazar to inform him of the Lord's decisions, especially regarding when to go into battle. Eleazar will seek these divine decisions by means of the Urim (the Thummim is undoubtedly also meant even though it is not mentioned here). These objects are mentioned only seven times in the Old Testament (Exod 28:30; Lev 8:8; Num 27:21; Deut 33:8; 1 Sam 28:6; Ezra 2:63; and Neh 7:65) and are never described. They seem to be two small objects, probably stones, which could either be cast on the ground or drawn out of a vessel. The two stones can be distinguished from each other and one side of each stone indicates "yes" and one side indicates "no." When cast, if the two show the same side, the Lord's answer is a definite "yes" or "no." If one shows "yes" and the other "no," the answer is inconclusive. When drawn out, the Urim indicates "yes" and the Thummim "no" (see 1 Sam 14:41).

At the end of his life Saul complains that he gets no answer from the Lord by the use of Urim and Thummim (1 Sam 28:6). It is likely that the Urim and Thummim were cast as a way of determining the guilty party when a battle was lost (Josh 7:14; 1 Sam 14:36-44), of deciding who will lead an attack (Judg 1:1-3; 20:17-18; see 2 Sam 5:23-24), in selecting Saul as king (1 Sam 10:20-22), and for any other decision requiring a "yes" or "no" answer (see 1 Sam 23:7-13; 2 Sam 2:1-2). They are carried in a pocket of the ephod, a priestly vestment (Exod 28:30; Lev 8:8).

The conclusion is typical of the Priestly tradition: Moses did exactly as God had commanded him.

28:1-2 General sacrifices

Chapters 28–29 outline procedures for offering the appropriate sacrifices throughout the year, beginning with the daily offering and ending with the yearly festivals. The primary audience is thus the priests who will be offering the sacrifices. The first seven chapters of Numbers were concerned with the place where sacrifice should be offered. These chapters prescribe the time and the material for the offering. These offerings are to be burned so that their aroma may rise to the Lord.

28:3-8 Each morning and evening

The first sacrifice to be described is the regular daily offering (Hebrew *tamid*). The same offering is to be made both morning and evening: one

male yearling lamb with the amount of grain and oil established in 15:4. A libation of strong drink is to be poured out with each lamb also according to the amount named in 15:5. The reason for the legislation is said to begin at Sinai although there is no mention of such a daily sacrifice there. Even after the temple is built, the daily sacrifice of a lamb seems to have occurred only in the morning with a grain offering in the evening (see 2 Kgs 16:15; Ezek 46:13-15). Only postexilic texts—the Priestly tradition in the Pentateuch and the Chronicler—describe animal sacrifice in the evening as well as in the morning (Exod 29:38-39; 1 Chr 16:40; 2 Chr 31:3).

The tradition of morning and evening prayer, however, is ancient. Offerings are made to God in the morning in thanksgiving for a new day and in petition for blessings on the work of the day; offerings are made in the evening in thanksgiving for the blessings of the day and repentance for faults committed as well as for protection from evil throughout the night.

28:9-10 On the sabbath

Other sacrifices are to be offered on special days, but these special sacrifices do not replace the daily offering. The daily sacrifice of a lamb morning and evening must continue unabated. On the sabbath day two additional lambs are offered with the same accompanying grain, oil, and strong drink. In no other sabbath legislation in the Pentateuch is a sacrifice mentioned. The emphasis is always on refraining from work (see Exod 16:29-30; 20:8-11; 31:13-16; 35:2-3; Lev 23:3; Num 15:32-36; Deut 5:12-15). Besides this passage in Numbers only Ezekiel and 2 Chronicles mention sacrifice on the sabbath (Ezek 46:4; 2 Chr 31:3).

28:11-15 At the new moon feast

Months in Israel's calendar began at the new moon. The sacrifice to be offered at the beginning of each month (in addition to the regular daily sacrifice) consists of two bulls, one ram, and seven yearling lambs, each with the amount of grain, oil, and wine established in 15:1-12. A further offering of a male goat is required for a purification offering. This purification sacrifice was probably offered first as a way of atoning for any inadvertent failings of the people during the last month. Then the sacrifice for the new month was offered.

28:16-25 At the Passover

The focus in this passage is not on the Passover celebration itself, which is a family celebration (see Exod 12:1-11), but on the sacrifices to be offered during the Festival of Unleavened Bread during the seven days after Passover. These two feasts originated separately: Unleavened Bread is a harvest festival, celebrating the new grain that is as yet unleavened. Passover is related to nomadic rituals for protecting the flock during the move from winter to summer pasture. Legislation such as this is a reminder that the two feasts are separate even though they are celebrated at the same time.

The first day of the Festival of Unleavened Bread is a pilgrimage feast (Hebrew *hag*; see Exod 13:6; 23:15; 34:18; Lev 23:6). Before the seventh century B.C. the people could congregate at any sacred site to celebrate the feast. Josiah, however, decreed that the only legitimate place for sacrifice was the temple, so if they wished to participate, pilgrims were required to travel to Jerusalem. In addition to the sacred assembly, no heavy work is to be done. The sacrifice to be offered each day for seven days includes two bulls, one ram, and seven yearling lambs with the appropriate offerings of grain, oil, and the libation of wine or other strong drink. On the first day a goat is also to be sacrificed as a purification offering. The seventh day is a holy day on which heavy work is prohibited.

28:26-31 At Pentecost

The feast of Weeks, also called first fruits, celebrates the wheat harvest. Its time is determined by counting seven weeks (or seven sabbaths) after the barley harvest, celebrated at Passover (see Exod 34:22; Lev 23:15; Deut 16:9-10). The feast of Weeks was called Pentecost in Greek because of the fifty days (Greek *pentekonta*) between Passover and Weeks. The sacrifice for this feast (in addition to the regular daily offering) is the same as that for the seven days of Unleavened Bread. It includes two bulls, one ram, and seven yearling lambs with their offerings of grain and oil and the libation of strong drink. A goat is to be offered also as a purification offering.

29:1-6 On New Year's Day

Three celebrations are held during the seventh month: the New Year on the first day, the Day of Atonement on the tenth day, and Booths on the fifteenth day. New Year's Day is announced with trumpet blasts; it is a holy day on which no heavy work may be done (see Lev 23:24). The sacrifices to be offered are: one bull, one ram, and seven yearling lambs with their grain and oil and presumably with the libation of wine also. The purification sacrifice of a male goat is also to be offered.

It may seem odd to name the first day of the seventh month "New Year's Day." Two calendars were in effect during the biblical period. In one calendar the year began in the spring. Nisan, the month of Passover, was the first month (see Exod 12:2). In the other calendar followed by the Babylonians but also represented by the tenth-century Gezer calendar, the year began in the fall. The Jewish New Year, Rosh Hashanah, is still celebrated on this autumn day even though Nisan continues to be called the first month. Compare this to the Christian practice of designating the First Sunday of Advent as the beginning of the liturgical year even though it falls during the eleventh or twelfth month of the civil calendar.

29:7-11 On the Day of Atonement

Just as the first day of the seventh month is not specifically named "New Year's" in the previous verses, so the tenth day is not specifically named "Day of Atonement" here (Hebrew *yom kippur*). It is so named elsewhere, however (Lev 23:27-28; 25:9), and is clearly signified by the additional instruction to "humble oneself," which frequently indicates fasting (see Isa 58:3, 5; Ps 35:13). The celebratory sacrifice consists of one bull, one ram, and seven yearling lambs with their grain and oil (and, no doubt, the libation of wine). In addition to the customary goat sacrificed as a purification offering, a bull is also offered as a purification offering for the tent of meeting (see Lev 16:11-12). The full legislation for the Day of Atonement is found in Leviticus 16.

29:12–30:1 On the Feast of Booths

The Feast of Booths (Sukkoth) is the third harvest festival (along with Passover and Weeks) in the calendar. It is sometimes called "Ingathering" (Hebrew *ʾasiph*; Exod 23:16; 34:22) because of the harvest of fruits (mostly grapes and figs) and nuts in the fall of the year. It is a pilgrimage feast and a holy day on which no heavy work may be done. It is sometimes called *the* festival, indicating its importance (1 Kgs 8:2, 65; 12:32; Ezek 45:25; 2 Chr 5:3; 7:8-9; see Ps 81:4). The number of animals sacrificed during the seven days of celebration also demonstrates the significance of this feast. Every day for seven days two rams and fourteen yearling lambs are sacrificed along with a goat for a purification offering.

On the first day thirteen bulls are also sacrificed, on the second day twelve bulls, on the third day eleven bulls, and so on. On the seventh day seven bulls are sacrificed along with the two rams and fourteen lambs, making a grand total of seventy bulls as well as fourteen rams, ninety-eight lambs, and seven goats for purification offerings. The number seven signifies completion, so the seven bulls sacrificed on the seventh day to make a total of seventy bulls emphasize the fullness of the offering. It is not quite enough, however. On the eighth day (one past the perfect number) at a public assembly, one final sacrifice is offered: one bull, one ram, seven yearling lambs with their grain and oil and libations, along with one male goat for a purification offering. Throughout these eight days the regular sacrifice of one lamb in the morning and one lamb in the evening has also been offered daily. As usual, the Priestly tradition assures us that Moses followed the Lord's instructions exactly.

30:2-17 Validity and annulment of vows

Two types of voluntary obligations are treated in this chapter: a vow (Hebrew *neder*), which is a promise to offer something to God if God first grants a request; a pledge (Hebrew *ʾissar*, literally "a binding"), which is a promise either to do something or refrain from doing something (e.g., to fast). Sometimes the pledge is confirmed by an oath (Hebrew *shebuʿah*). The chapter begins with the flat statement that men are obligated to pay their vows or fulfill their pledges.

But the point of the chapter is the placement of restrictions on women who make such vows or pledges. Women had the freedom to make these promises voluntarily. Since these promises most frequently involved the gift of real property, however, the means to fulfill them usually depended on the willingness of whichever male figure had legal control of the woman: her father or her husband. (See Lev 27 for legislation regarding the payment of vows.) The only women who had free control of their property were widows, divorced women, or prostitutes.

If an unmarried woman still in her father's house makes a vow or pledge, her father has two choices (vv. 4-6). He may either approve her action by remaining silent or immediately refuse to allow her to make such a promise, in which case her vow or pledge is invalid. If her father remains silent, he is liable for payment, possibly an animal for sacrifice. If he opposes her promise, then neither the father nor the young woman is obligated. She is released from her vow or pledge because she has no power to fulfill it.

A husband has the same options and obligations if his wife makes a vow or a pledge (vv. 11-13). Other conditions also apply (vv. 7-9). If a woman is already obligated to fulfill a vow or a pledge when she marries, her husband has the power to annul it immediately even though her father presumably approved it. But in either case—whether the woman had made the promise before or after marriage—if the husband delays and remains silent, then he takes on the obligation to supply the means for fulfilling the promise. He cannot annul her commitments at a later time; he is responsible for either making the payment or bearing the guilt of an unfulfilled vow or pledge.

A woman who is not under the legal control of a man, such as a widow or divorced woman, bears the obligation for her own vows and pledges just as a man does (v. 10). Perhaps her husband approved her vow before he divorced her or died. Now she bears the responsibility alone. This situation may place a serious burden on the woman, since she has few economic resources. The third circumstance in which a woman is independent is that of a prostitute. That situation is not mentioned here, but Deuteronomy specifically forbids the payment of a vow with resources gained through prostitution (Deut 23:19; see Prov 7:14).

There are not many examples of women making vows or binding themselves to a pledge. Hannah makes a vow to God: If God gives her a son, she will give him back to God as a Nazirite serving in the sanctuary (1 Sam 1:11). The Nazirite vow itself is open to both men and women (Num 6:2). Lemuel's mother calls him the "son of my vows," suggesting that she too promised to offer something to God if God gave her a son (Prov 31:2). Jeremiah complains that both men and women are fulfilling their vows to offer something to the "queen of heaven," probably the goddess Astarte. For either a man or a woman the fulfillment of a vow is a serious matter. Qoheleth advises, "It is better not to make a vow than make it and not fulfill it" (Eccl 5:4; see Prov 20:25).

31:1-12 Campaign against the Midianites

Chapter 31 begins where chapter 25 left off, with the Lord's command to crush the Midianites because of the incident at Baal Peor (25:16-17). Moses is warned that this is virtually his last task. The people are almost ready to enter the Promised Land and he will not go with them.

The purposes of the Priestly writers in telling the story of this battle are two: to explain why the previously friendly Midianites become enemies after the Israelites enter the Promised Land, and to outline the customs for holy war. First of all, what happened with the Midianites? They are identified as the descendants of Abraham through his third wife, Keturah (Gen 25:1-2, 4). Moses lived with the Midianite priest Reuel (also known as Jethro) when he fled from Pharaoh; Reuel's daughter Zipporah became his wife and saved his life (Exod 2:15-22; 4:24-26). Moses even invited his brother-in-law Hobab to accompany Israel on its march through the wilderness (Num 10:29-31).

The situation turned when Midian joined with Balak in attempting to curse Israel (Num 22:4, 7) and when Zimri brought a Midianite woman into the camp in the midst of the Baal Peor incident (Num 25:6-15). Perhaps the Priestly authors have inserted Midian into these events in order to explain how they became a mortal enemy when Israel was settling the land. They remained a problem in the time of the judges when God raised up Gideon to free Israel from their power (Judg 6:1–8:28; see Ps 83:10; Isa 9:3).

Second, the Priestly writers use this battle as a model for the conquest of the land and an example of how to fight a holy war. When Moses musters the troops, a thousand men from each tribe, to attack Midian, there is no mention of a general, not even Joshua. The troops are accompanied by the priest Phinehas who has the sacred vessels and the trumpets with him. The "sacred vessel" is probably the ark of the covenant, symbolizing God's presence with Israel in the battle (see Num 10:35-36; 1 Sam 4:1-3). The trumpets are used to sound the alarm (see Num 10:1-10).

Israel goes to war under God's command. The amazingly successful result is what Israel can expect if they are faithful to God and do only what they are commanded to do. According to the narrator, all the Midianite men are killed including their five kings and Balaam, son of Beor. All the Midianite towns and encampments are burned. Everything the Midianites owned, including their women and children, are taken as spoil. All the spoil is brought to Moses and Eleazar the priest. Its disposition will also illustrate the customs of holy war.

31:13-18 Treatment of the captives

The rules for dealing with spoils are usually called *herem*, the ban or doom. The word is not used here, but the principles reflect the instruction in Deuteronomy 20–21. If the conquered enemy is within the Promised Land, everything is to be destroyed—all the people and all the property (Deut 20:16-18). Everything must be put under the ban lest Israel be led into worshiping other gods. If the conquered enemy is at a considerable distance, however, then only the men (perhaps also boys) must be killed; it is permissible to keep everything else—women, children, livestock, and anything else that is valuable (Deut 20:13-15). Captive women may be taken as wives after a period of mourning for their parents (Deut 21:10-14). The Midianites are not regarded as a people of the Promised Land, so the Israelites kill only the adult men.

Moses interprets the law more strictly, however. When he discovers that all the women have been spared, he is furious. He blames the Midianite women for the infidelity of Israel at Baal Peor and commands that only women who are virgins (including female children) be spared. All other captives—married women and boys—are to be killed. The virgins may be taken as wives. Apparently they are not seen as a threat to lead the people into idolatry.

31:19-24 Purification after combat

All those involved in the war—soldiers and captives—must go through a ritual of purification before they are allowed into the camp. Even if this is a holy war, killing and contact with the dead corrupt the participants. They must follow the ritual described in Numbers 19, using the purifying water prepared with the ashes of the red heifer. In addition, all material objects must be purified. Anything made of metal that can endure burning must be purified both by fire and with the water of purification. Other objects need only be cleansed with the water of purification.

31:25-31 Division of the spoils

Eleazar is again a major participant in the action as he was with the purification ritual. He and the ancestral leaders are commanded to inventory all the spoils and then divide them in half. Half will go to the soldiers and the other half will be divided among the rest of the community. This principle is explained later by David: "the share of the one who goes down to battle shall be the same as that of the one who remains with the baggage—they share alike" (1 Sam 30:24). The tax for the two groups is different, however. The soldiers are taxed at a rate of .2 percent; the people are taxed at a rate of 2 percent. The soldiers' tax is paid to Eleazar the priest and the sanctuary; the people's tax is paid to the Levites. This is consistent with another principle of *herem* that what is "doomed" is given to the sanctuary (Lev 27:21; Num 18:14).

31:32-47 Amount of the plunder

The staggering amount of plunder is also a clue that this story has been idealized. The pattern of the list is similar to that of Numbers 7. It seems to be an oral report from a table: oxen, 72,000; donkeys, 61,000, etc.

31:48-54 Gifts of the officers

The officers take a census of the soldiers and discover that not one soldier has fallen in the battle (one more clue that this story is idealized). From their plunder they bring articles of gold as a donation to the sanctuary. This offering is intended either as atonement or a ransom for their lives. Perhaps they need to make atonement because they have attacked and killed other human beings. Perhaps they need to pay a ransom because their lives now belong to God who has saved them all from death. The gold is put in the tent of meeting as a memorial, a reminder before God.

32:1-5 Request of Gad and Reuben

Three issues dominate chapter 32: the question of inheritance, specifically inheritance on the east side of the Jordan; the question of just how far the Promised Land extends; and the demands of holy war. The request of two tribes, Gad and Reuben, will have an impact on all three issues.

Representatives of these two tribes address the full leadership of Israel: Moses, the priest Eleazar, and the community leaders. The economy of these two tribes is based on shepherding and their desire is to remain in the good pastureland in Gilead on the east side of the Jordan, the land that was taken from the Amorite king Sihon (see Num 21:21-32). This land with its towns lies between the Arnon (the northern border of Moab) and the Jabbok. But their plea not to be forced to cross the Jordan implies that they do not want to participate in the battles necessary to wrest the land west of the Jordan from the Canaanites.

32:6-15 Moses' rebuke

Moses does not look favorably on their request. His first objection indicates that the land requested by Gad and Reuben is not the land the Lord has given the Israelites, and thus is not part of the Promised Land. He compares their intention to the action of the scouts whose unfavorable report prevented Israel from entering Canaan from the south (Num 13–14). Just as Israel begged to stay in the wilderness rather than face the "giants" of the scout's report, so now these two tribes plead to stay here rather than fight the Canaanites on the other side of the Jordan. Moses comes close to laying the primary blame for God's anger against the exodus generation on the Gadites and Reubenites, the "sinful stock" from which these tribes come. If their offspring persist in their refusal to cross the Jordan it will bring about the ruination of the whole people.

32:16-19 Counter proposal

The Gadites and Reubenites not only promise to cross the Jordan and fight, they volunteer to lead the charge. The question regarding holy war is thus answered: all the tribes must participate in the conquest of the Promised Land. Inheritance is a different matter, however. As security for their families and property, they propose to construct sheepfolds for their flocks and rebuild and fortify the towns east of the Jordan. They will not claim any heritage in the land west of the Jordan. They repeat their request to claim as their heritage the land east of the Jordan. Does this mean that they will live outside the Promised Land or is Transjordan also part of the Promised Land?

32:20-32 Agreement reached

Moses agrees to the proposal of the Gadites and Reubenites. If they march at the head of the troops and persevere until the land west of the Jordan is subdued, then they may return and claim the land east of the Jordan. If they fail to keep their promise, however, not only will that be a sin against the Lord but their sin will pursue them and they will never escape its consequences. The Gadites and Reubenites repeat their intention to keep their promise and fight for the land across the Jordan.

The question regarding the status of these two tribes and the land east of the Jordan is left ambiguous. They promised to march "before the Israelites" (v. 17) and they are told to march "before the LORD" (v. 21). Does this mean that the Lord is with Israel and, by implication, not with them? Or is the meaning simply that they will march in front of the ark of the covenant as they go into battle? In either case, they are separated from the rest of Israel. They are further told that if they keep their promise, they have no more obligation to the Lord or to Israel. Does this apply only to the taking of the land or is it a more permanent separation? In spite of the questions, the land in Transjordan is identified as their "possession before the LORD," which seems to indicate that they are still full members of Israel and that their land is part of what God had promised their ancestors.

Moses solemnizes the decision by commanding the two leaders who will lead the Jordan crossing, Eleazar the priest and Joshua the leader of the troops, to allow Gad and Reuben to inherit Gilead as long as they cross the Jordan with the rest of Israel to fight for the land. If, on the other hand, the two tribes fail in this commitment, they will be deprived of any holding east of the Jordan and will be forced to accept land with the rest of the tribes on the west side of the Jordan.

A third time the Gadites and Reubenites pledge to keep their promise (32:31-32; see 32:17-18, 25-27). Moses then officially designates the land taken from Sihon and Og as their heritage. A surprise in verse 33 is the assignment of part of this land to half the tribe of Manasseh. The heritage of Manasseh west of the Jordan has already been secured with the right of the daughters of Zelophehad to inherit their father's land (27:1-11). Other clans of Manasseh settled in northern Gilead and Bashan, territory taken from Og (21:33-35). The presence of all three tribes in Transjordan is legitimated by Moses' proclamation.

32:39-42 Other conquests

The story of the Manassite clans is expanded in these verses. The assignment of Transjordanian land to the clans of Machir and Jair is reported in Deuteronomy in greater detail (Deut 3:13-15).

Israelite communities in Transjordan lasted from the settlement period until the Assyrian deportations began under Tiglath-Pileser III in 734 B.C. Their legitimacy as full participants in Israel continued to be questioned. Their building of an altar east of the Jordan leads to the threat of war (Josh 22:10-34). The confrontation is settled only by their assurance that no sacrifices will be offered on this altar. (The controversy may reflect the seventh-century designation of the Jerusalem temple as the only site where sacrifice may be offered; see Deut 12.) When the kingdoms divided in 922 B.C., the territory of Reuben, Gad, and Manasseh became part of the northern kingdom, Israel. Elijah the prophet was a Gileadite, from east of the Jordan. The Transjordan settlements flourished under Omri (876–869 B.C.) but came to an end with the final deportation when Samaria was conquered in 722 B.C.

33:1-4 Stages of the journey

These final chapters of Numbers set the stage for the crossing of the Jordan and the conquest of the Promised Land. Israel has been encamped on the plains of Moab since the victories over Sihon and Og (22:1). Matters of inheritance and regulations for worship in the land have predominated in chapters 26–32. Chapter 33 is a recapitulation of the journey from the exodus to the plains of Moab; the chapter concludes with orders for the taking over of Canaan. Israel is described as an army on the march, company by company. Only forty camping sites between Rameses, the point of origin, and the plains of Moab, the arrival point, are listed for the forty years. The journey can be divided into three sections: Egypt to Sinai, Sinai to Kadesh, Kadesh to the Plains of Moab. The itinerary is written down by Moses. Besides writing down the law (Exod 24:4; 34:27; Deut 31:9, 24) the only writing Moses is said to have done is the curse against Amalek (Exod 17:14), his final song (Deut 31:22), and this itinerary.

The exodus is presented as a great victory of the Lord over the Egyptians and their gods (Exod 12:12). Israel leaves, not secretly as in the pre-Priestly tradition (Exod 12:37-39), but in full view of all Egypt (Exod 13:18).

33:5-15 From Egypt to Sinai

This section of the itinerary corresponds substantially to the itinerary in Exodus 12–19: Rameses to Succoth (Exod 12:37) to Etham (Exod 13:20). Next they encamp at Pi-hahiroth, opposite Baal-zephon, opposite Migdol. As the story is told in the book of Exodus, this is the site of the deliverance at the sea (see Exod 14:2, 9), identified in song and tradition as the Red Sea (Exod 15:4; Deut 11:4; Josh 2:10; 4:23; Ps 136:15). In Numbers 33, however, this sea is unnamed and there is no report of an encounter with Pharaoh's chariots, only that the people crossed over through the sea into the wilderness. The unidentified sea here is probably one of the marshy lakes in the area of today's Suez Canal, around Lake Timsah or the Bitter Lakes. Then between Elim (see Exod 15:27) and the wilderness of Sin (Exod 16:1), the people camp beside the Red Sea. What is probably meant here is the northern tip of the Gulf of Suez. The next two sites are otherwise unknown: Dophkah and Alush. From Alush they move to Rephidim where the people complain about lack of water and where they are attacked by the Amalekites (Exod 17). From Rephidim they go to Sinai.

33:16-36 From Sinai to Kadesh

The first two sites of this section correspond to the narrative in Numbers. At Kibroth-hattaavah the people cried for meat (Num 11:4-15, 18-24, 31-35). At Hazeroth Miriam and Aaron complained against Moses (Num 12:1-16). The next seventeen sites are unknown. Ezion-geber, at the head of the Gulf of Aqaba, became a shipping port for Solomon in the tenth century (1 Kgs 9:26). From there the people went to Kadesh in the wilderness of Zin (Num 20:1). The Priestly tradition represented here portrays the people spending most of the forty-year sojourn in the Sinai peninsula and arriving at Kadesh only in the fortieth year (see Num 20:1, 22-29). It was there that the first of the wilderness leaders, Miriam, died. The

other tradition represented in these stories has the people arrive at Kadesh much earlier, perhaps little more than a year after the exodus event. From there Moses sends the scouts to reconnoiter the land and there God condemns the exodus generation to wander in the wilderness for forty years until all of them have died except Caleb and Joshua (Num 13–14).

33:37-49 From Kadesh to the Plains of Moab

This section of the itinerary begins with the story of Aaron's death on Mount Hor. New details are added: the year of Aaron's death (the first day of the fifth month in the fortieth year after the exodus) and Aaron's age (123 years). This corresponds to the notice in Exodus 7:7 where Aaron was said to be 83 years old at the time of the exodus. The notice that the king of Arad heard of Israel's approach is probably an allusion to the victory over Arad in 21:1-3.

Of the stages between Mount Hor and the plains of Moab, Oboth and Iye-abarim are mentioned elsewhere as camping sites after the incident with the fiery serpents (Num 21:10-12). God sends Moses up the Abarim Mountains to glimpse the Promised Land, which he is not allowed to enter (Num 27:12). From there the people arrive at the plains of Moab where they will encamp until they cross the Jordan under Joshua's leadership (Josh 3).

33:50-56 Conquest and division of Canaan

At this point in the chapter the focus turns to the future. Moses is told to give instructions to the Israelites regarding their entrance into Canaan. They are to be careful to do four things: (1) to drive out all the inhabitants; (2) to destroy all the signs of worship of other gods—carved and molten images as well as high places; (3) to divide the land both by size of clan and by lot (see ch. 26); and (4) to take possession of the land. The current inhabitants will remain a problem if they fail to drive them out and the Lord will begin to treat the Israelites like Canaanites. In other texts the danger of allowing the current inhabitants to remain is the likelihood that Israel will be drawn to worship their gods (Exod 23:24, 33; Deut 7:16). This apostasy will lead to Israel's punishment.

34:1-15 The boundaries

The preparation for entering the Promised Land continues. The land of Canaan is Israel's heritage, in other words, the land promised to Abraham by God. The land east of the Jordan is not included, so only nine and a half tribes will live in what is here considered the Promised Land. The Transjordanian tribes live outside the Promised Land proper.

The boundaries of the land are outlined, beginning in the south. Judah, the major tribe of the south, leads the list of tribal leaders (v. 19), so the southern boundary is the first to be declared. The southern boundary begins at the Dead Sea, bends south as far as Kadesh-Barnea (60–80 miles), and then runs northwest to the Mediterranean Sea south of Gaza. The western boundary is easy to chart: the Mediterranean coastline. The northern boundary begins close to Mount Hor (50–60 miles north of Sidon; not the Mount Hor where Aaron died) and extends about 90 miles east to Hazar-Enan. The eastern boundary runs straight south from there about 125 miles and then runs west to just south of the Sea of Galilee (Chinnereth). From there it extends along the east side of the Jordan River to the Dead Sea. The territory east of the Jordan—the territory given to Reuben, Gad, and half of Manasseh—is not included in Canaan, however, nor is Moab or Edom.

On today's map, the territory would include most of modern Israel and Palestine except the southern tip that extends to Eilat and the Gulf of Aqaba. It also includes a portion of northern Sinai just west of the Gaza strip. On the north it includes most of Lebanon and the western part of Syria.

These boundaries are obviously idealized. The greatest surprise is the extent of territory to the north and east. The territory enclosed by these boundaries was never totally under Israelite control. The boundaries compare most closely to the Egyptian province of Canaan from the fifteenth to thirteenth centuries B.C. Ezekiel describes the ideal Israel with similar boundaries (47:13–48:29). See map on page 1525.

34:16-29 Supervisors of the allotment

The leaders who shall oversee the division of this land among the nine and a half tribes are Eleazar the priest as religious leader and Joshua as civil and military leader. Only ten tribal leaders

are named to assist. Reuben and Gad already have their territory and so need no one to represent them in a later division of land. Manasseh, however, is included in order to represent the half of that tribe that will settle west of the Jordan. None of the names correspond to the tribal leaders who assisted Moses in the census of chapter 1. None of the scouts chosen in chapter 13 appear either except Caleb, whose survival is a reward for his fidelity. Otherwise this list represents a new generation.

35:1-8 Cities for the Levites

The Levites have been treated separately from the rest of the Israelites throughout this book. They were omitted from the original census (1:47-54; 2:33) and counted as substitutes for the first-born (3:5-16, 40-50). They were numbered again (4:34-49) and purified for service to the sanctuary (8:5-26; see 18:2-6). They are granted special tithes and obligated to pay tithes in turn (18:21-32; see 31:30, 47). When the second census was taken for the purpose of apportioning the land, the Levites were again omitted and then numbered separately (26:57-62) because the Levites have no share in the inheritance of the land (18:23-24; see Deut 10:8-9; 14:27-29; 18:1-2).

Therefore another arrangement has to be made for the Levites, since they will not share in the division of land. They are to be given cities with pastureland by each of the other tribes, more from the larger tribes and fewer from the smaller tribes. (The number of cities assigned for each tribe to donate is set and the cities named in Josh 21.) The measurements of these grants are unclear, but apparently the cities are to be 2,000 cubits square and the pasturelands extend outward from the city walls for another 1,000 cubits. Thus the whole plot would be 4,000 cubits square. The total number of cities is to be forty-eight, six of which are to be cities of asylum.

35:9-15 Cities of asylum

The cities of asylum are places of refuge where a killer may flee until it is determined whether he is guilty of murder or manslaughter. (The cities are further described and named in Josh 20; see also Deut 19:1-13.) This place of refuge is necessary because, without it, the next-of-kin might avenge the killing before a reasoned judgment can take place. The next-of-kin (Hebrew *goʾel*, often translated "redeemer" or "restorer" but here as "avenger"; 35:12, 19, 21, 24, 25, 27; see Josh 20:3, 5, 9) has the responsibility to ransom a relative who is enslaved (Lev 25:48-49), to redeem land that has been lost due to debt (Lev 25:25; see Num 5:8), and to avenge the relative's murder. These cities of asylum must be spaced so that it is possible for a fugitive to reach one before the next-of-kin catches up.

Traditionally sacred places have been considered places of safety for fugitives (see 1 Kgs 1:50-51). Some of the cities named as cities of asylum may have a reputation as sacred sites: Shechem was the site of a temple to Baal Berith; the name of Kedesh is based on the word for "holy" (*qadosh*). Perhaps their reputation as sacred places is the reason for their designation. This association with sacredness may also be the reason that the term of an offender's confinement in the city of asylum is linked to the life of the current high priest.

35:16-30 Murder and manslaughter

Several examples are given for distinguishing between premeditated murder and manslaughter. If someone kills another deliberately with a weapon or if the one who kills another hates the victim and has planned the killing, that person is a murderer and must be put to death. The *goʾel* is designated as the executioner. If the death is accidental, however, and there is no history of conflict between the two, then there is no cause for the death penalty. The one who caused the death is to be taken back from the place of judgment to the city of asylum and must remain there until the death of the high priest. After the death of the high priest, the one who killed accidentally may return to home in safety. If the killer leaves the city of asylum before the death of the high priest, however, the *goʾel* may execute that person without penalty.

35:30 Judgment

The testimony of at least two witnesses is necessary to convict someone of a capital crime and to execute that person (see Deut 17:6). Deuteronomy expands this law: No one may be convicted of any crime without the testimony of two or three witnesses (Deut 19:15).

35:31-34 No indemnity

A person who is subject to the death penalty cannot be rescued by either a ransom or a bribe. Nor can one who is confined to a city of asylum buy freedom before the death of the high priest. These legal decisions are final and must be carried out in full.

This legislation is based on the principle that life is sacred and bloodshed pollutes the land. In the story of the first murder, God says to Cain, "Your brother's blood cries out to me from the ground!" (Gen 4:10). The pollution must be removed, because of God's presence in the land. The understanding in these laws is that the only thing that can cleanse the land from this pollution is the blood of the perpetrator. Blood is the sign of life; blood cleanses blood.

36:1-11 Inheritance of daughters

The daughters of Zelophehad have been given the right to take possession of their father's share of the Promised Land since he died with no sons (see 27:1-11). The men from the same clan as Zelophehad now raise a concern. They speak to the same group that the daughters addressed: Moses, Eleazar the priest, and the tribal leaders. They recognize that the right given to the daughters of Zelophehad was commanded by the Lord. But they point out that this may lead to a diminishment of the land allotted to the tribe of Manasseh.

According to custom, the land owned by these women will be inherited by their sons. But sons are counted as members not of their mother's but of their father's tribe. If the daughters of Zelophehad marry men from another tribe than Manasseh, the land will transfer to that tribe. Not even the jubilee will solve this difficulty. At the jubilee land that has been sold or lost because of debt is returned to the original tribe (Lev 25:13-17, 23-28), but the jubilee does not apply to land that transfers because of inheritance. Thus, although the daughters of Zelophehad have ensured that their father's heritage will not be lost in their generation, it may be lost in the next generation.

Moses resolves the difficulty by issuing a new command, restricting the rights of daughters who inherit the family property. Because the land of any tribe should not be lost, these women must marry within their ancestral tribe. The daughters of Zelophehad, therefore, must marry someone from the tribe of Manasseh. Tribal rights to the land supersede women's rights. The daughters of Zelophehad obey the command by marrying their first cousins. Because of them two laws have been initiated: the right of daughters to inherit if they have no brothers and the obligation of the same daughters to marry within their own tribe.

36:13 Conclusion

The book of Numbers concludes with the statement that the prescriptions in this book were commanded by the Lord and announced to the Israelites through Moses. The statement that what is being promulgated is what the Lord has commanded Moses appears several times (33x) throughout Numbers (1:19, 54; 2:33, 34; 3:16, 42, 51; 4:49; 8:3, 20, 22; 9:5; 15:22-23, 36; 17:26; 20:9, 27; 26:4; 27:11, 22, 23; 30:1, 2, 17; 31:7, 21, 31, 41, 47; 34:13; 36:5, 10). The same declaration is made at the end of Exodus (40:16, 19, 21, 23, 25, 27, 29, 32), Leviticus (27:34), and Deuteronomy (34:9-12). In Exodus and Leviticus Israel is still at Sinai. In Numbers and Deuteronomy Israel is on the plains of Moab, poised to cross the Jordan into the Promised Land.

THE BOOK OF
DEUTERONOMY

J. Edward Owens, O.SS.T.

INTRODUCTION

The book of Deuteronomy has a profound influence on both Testaments. It forms the basis of what scholars call the Deuteronomistic History, which extends from Joshua to 2 Kings; in the prophetic literature Hosea and Jeremiah show its influence as well. Some influence is also seen in the Chronicler and Tobit. The New Testament cites or alludes to Deuteronomy over one hundred times, including words from the lips of Jesus (Matt 4:4, 7, 10; John 8:35). With great breadth the Deuteronomic tradition informs our understanding of the Scriptures and offers an abiding theological message to believers in every age. In sum, Deuteronomy is panoramic, offering a bird's-eye view of the saga of Israel and informing later Jewish and Christian traditions.

Deuteronomy is essentially a book of torah, i.e., instruction in life and faith for curse or blessing (29:20; 30:10; 31:26). Homiletically, it is a proclamation to be read aloud. Moses is presented as writing the instructions at the end, and his message is to endure as a proclamation in the assembly (31:9-13). This attitude reflects ancient literacy in which communication and understanding came more through the ear than the eye, even though the eye was a metaphorical window to knowledge (4:9).

The historical background of Deuteronomy

It is beyond the scope of this introduction to discuss at length the complex history and redaction (changes and additions by later authors) of Deuteronomy. Numerous books and articles are available on the subject. However, a few observations will demonstrate the issues and ongoing scholarly debate involved.

First, the general dating of the book is disputed. Many scholars date Deuteronomy to the seventh century B.C. when the Assyrian Empire held sway and the Judean kings Hezekiah and Manasseh reacted, each in his own way, to the crises at hand. Other opinions range from the thirteenth to the fifth century B.C. Second, did Deuteronomy originate in the northern kingdom (perhaps as an internal reform or the reaction of a disenfranchised group) or are its origins in the southern kingdom? Third, as with many biblical books, authorship is another question. Were the authors priests, Levites, prophets, sages, scribes, elders, or a combination of circles with a common agenda? Fourth, there remain issues surrounding redaction toward the canonical text we now have. Many scholars speak roughly of Deuteronomy 5–26, 28 as the core of the book, with the opening and closing chapters as later additions in light of the exile. Others suggest alternative delimitations. Further, there is the account of the high priest Hilkiah finding a scroll of the law in the temple during Josiah's reign (2 Kgs 22–23; cf. 2 Chr 34–35). Whether that account is fact or fiction, there are affinities between Deuteronomy and the Josianic reform, which share numerous parallels. One should also note the connection between the basic Deuteronomic Code (Deut 12–26) and the Book of the Covenant (Exod 20–23). Even a casual reading of these two legal documents finds striking parallels. Law is not univocal in the Scriptures but informed by intertextual analysis. Finally, a comparison of the Ten Commandments in Deuteronomy 5:6-21 and Exodus 20:1-17 offers insights into the development of legal traditions.

Despite differences of opinion regarding these and other issues in the history of tradition, one cannot dismiss the impact of the Babylonian exile on Deuteronomistic history and theology. The Lord God was not responsible for the fall of Israel and then Judah. The people were unfaithful to the vision of the great themes of promise, election, covenant, and law. They were in the grip of a great crisis to which the nations' ancient traditions still offered a message of hope and a challenge to return to the Lord. An example is the story of the monarchy in 1–2 Kings. These books represent a review of a sacred Israelite institution in light of Deuteronomic concerns, particularly the legacy of corrupt kings and emphasis on the centrality of the Jerusalem cult.

In sum, Deuteronomy is about reform and restoration, looking to the past with an eye to the future. Its tone is urgent and appeals to the individual as well as the community. Everyone is called to respond to the Lord's statutes and commandments *today* (4:40).

The literary artistry of Deuteronomy

Deuteronomy picks up where Numbers leaves off. However, these two books have different emphases. Numbers is essentially indirect discourse while Deuteronomy is mostly direct speech. Further, Deuteronomy tends to present a more refined and humane legal spirit. A good example is the distinction of wives from other property in the ninth commandment (5:21). Deuteronomy is not a recounting of past events that no longer impact on life and faith, but a program for the future.

Building on the contributions of the modern historical-critical method, more recent studies have moved to the literary analysis of biblical texts. Such analysis pays close attention to techniques such as repetition, comparison, contrast, irony, wordplay, chiasm, inclusion (also called *inclusio*), and numerical symmetry. The book of Deuteronomy lends itself to such methodologies (rhetorical, narrative, canonical, structural, reader-response, etc.).

Perhaps more than any other Old Testament book Deuteronomy is characterized by repetitive themes and motifs, many of which should be familiar to those who have read the book in its entirety or heard its liturgical proclamation through the years. One thinks of the motif of the land, or the theologies of love, remembering/forgetting, time, and retribution, the Divine Name and the Lord as warrior, the Ten Commandments, the great Shema (Deut 6:4ff), and the enjoining of humane interaction among persons of every class. The Ten Commandments and the great Shema are central to Deuteronomy. Both are relational in nature. The commandments spell out the essentials of a proper relationship between God and others. The Shema complements the Ten Commandments with a counterpoint, i.e., what are the characteristics of this proper relationship? They are love, fidelity, and obedience. Such themes and motifs will be highlighted in the course of this commentary to inform the reader's understanding of the theological message therein. Where notable, attention will also be given to more recent methodologies, including feminist and sociocultural approaches, which have enriched the understanding and appreciation of Deuteronomy. Attention to intertextuality, i.e., interconnections with other biblical texts, will also be noted in course.

In Deuteronomy the reader encounters a grand sermon by Moses on the plains of Moab as the Israelites prepare to cross the Jordan from the east and enter Canaan. This sermon is usually divided into four addresses delimited by editorial superscriptions: "These are the words" (1:1), "This is the law" (4:44), "Moses summoned all Israel" (29:1), and "This is the blessing" (33:1). Each speech has its own emphases while at the same time harking back to what precedes and anticipating what follows. Indeed, "These are the words" is an appropriate beginning and title for Deuteronomy. More than in any other book in the Pentateuch or subsequent historical books words are important in Deuteronomy, words repeated over and over to instruct the people and drill torah into them and future generations (6:7).

It is noteworthy that Deuteronomy characterizes Moses with all the complexity of human nature, including its shadow sides. Moses presents not so much a code of laws (though laws are enjoined) as an impassioned exhortation to live in covenant with the Lord, the one God of Israel. Moses, that reluctant but ever-growing leader in the book of Exodus, has been condemned not to enter the land (32:48-52; cf. Num 20:7-12); he neither becomes bitter nor turns from God but remains an example of unwavering loyalty and service. He obeys the Lord's command to impose hands upon Joshua and commission him as the new leader of journeying Israel. Such steadfastness contrasts with Moses' characterization in the book of Exodus where he doubts his ability (Exod 3:11; 4:1) and argues with the Lord (Exod 5:22-23). Despite his fate Moses is remembered at the end

of Deuteronomy as a prophet without equal and an incomparable worker of signs and wonders (34:10-12). Moses' trust in the Lord is praised in later wisdom literature. His memory is held in benediction and God's honor conveyed to him (Sir 45:1-5).

The reader is encouraged to use the commentary with an eye to the Review Aids and Discussion Topics provided at the end. It is also helpful to utilize other biblical resources in studying the rich, complex, and timeless message of Deuteronomy. These resources include other commentaries, concordances, dictionaries, and, of course, the Bible itself.

Outline of the Book of Deuteronomy

Deut 1:1–4:43	Moses' First Address
Deut 4:44–28:69	Moses' Second Address
Deut 29:1–32:52	Moses' Third Address
Deut 33:1–34:12	Moses' Fourth Address

COMMENTARY

MOSES' FIRST ADDRESS

Deuteronomy 1:1–4:43

1:1-5 The introduction to Deuteronomy

The Hebrew title for Deuteronomy comes from its opening words, *'ēlleh haddĕbārîm*, "These are the words . . ." It is from the Greek translation, called the Septuagint, that we get the name Deuteronomy or "second law." As with many biblical books, the opening verses set the stage for what follows. Moses, Israel, and the Lord stand in opposition to the kings and kingdoms of Canaan. The striking geographical details in these few verses call to mind Exodus 14:1-9 where Israel takes its stand against Pharaoh and his army at carefully designated points by the Red Sea. In both scenes the Lord is the guarantor of Israel's security. Further, *all* of Israel is gathered to hear *all* the commands of the Lord through Moses (vv. 1, 3). This is a communal event of grand propor-

tions and with lasting implications. As at the Red Sea, Israel must take its stand as it prepares to cross the Jordan, and takes a stand against Sihon and Og. Israel's victory over them is reiterated later in Deuteronomy and remembered in tradition (Neh 9:22; Pss 135:10-11; 136:17-22). With this introductory information, Moses commences his extended discourse on torah.

1:6-18 Departure and appointment of elders

The motif of the land is introduced in the context of promise and fulfillment (vv. 7, 8 [2x]). Promise recalls divine commitment in the covenant relationship with the ancestors (Gen 12:1-3; 15:18-21), and fulfillment now demands abiding trust in the Lord. The land bestowed is the Lord's gift to Israel and ideally encompasses a variety of terrain and climates from the Euphrates River in the north to the Negeb (reclaimed desert) in the south. The land motif is important in Deuteronomy because it recalls that the landless people journeyed in trust of the promise of a fertile land, a memory that stirs (in readers and hearers of the book) thoughts both of the exodus and the return from Babylonian exile in Israelite later history and theology. Further, the land is intimately connected to observance of the law (5:31; 12:1). The land could be lost, as Israel found out in the course of time. In sum, going forth under divine promise, trust on the journey, and observance of divine commands in the land are intrinsically related.

The selection of elders in 1:9-18 may seem to interrupt the flow of the narrative. However, this episode anticipates the important theme of leadership in Deuteronomy (e.g., judges, priests, and prophets in 17:8–18:22) and culminates in Joshua's marching before the people under the protection of the Lord (31:1-6). Shared leadership by elders and other persons is a response to increase in numbers among the Israelites (an aspect of blessing) and the people's occasional murmuring (an important and widespread motif in the Old Testament). Increase harks back to the book of Exodus where Pharaoh reacts with oppression to counter the prolific growth of his Hebrew slaves (Exod 1:7-10; cf. Gen 1:28).

The star motif (v. 10; 10:22) highlights fertility, a reference back to the promise of descendants to Abraham (Gen 15:5; 22:17; 26:4), and anticipates in Deuteronomy the warning against the worship of celestial bodies (4:19; cf. Gen 1:16). Further, this motif underscores that for Israel God's throne is set above the stars and celestial bodies. These objects are under divine control (Job 22:12; Ps 147:4; Sir 43:9-10).

The motif of the resident alien (Hebrew *gēr*) emerges in verse 16. Together with the widow and orphan, this triad of vulnerable and often exploited persons enjoys special protection in Deuteronomic theology. In sum, this opening section affirms the perennial value of collaborative leadership and equal justice under the law. Israel must be careful to keep all the laws cited in the course of Moses' grand speech, because judgment belongs to God (v. 17).

1:19-46 The debacle at Kadesh-barnea

The land is a promised gift, but at the same time it must be taken by force. Will the Israelites trust that the Lord is present with them as they

march forth? This tension recalls the Israelites' fear at the Red Sea, which is later juxtaposed with their breaking into joyful song (Exod 14:10-14; 15:1-3). The psalms extol the Lord as warrior (Pss 68:1-4; 114:1-8; 124:1-8) despite numerous military defeats recounted in Israel's history. The book of Deuteronomy concludes with an affirmation of security under the Lord (32:10-14).

At this juncture the tension between security and fear is dramatized via engagement between the Israelites and the indigenous peoples. Israelite scouts reconnoiter the land and bring back an encouraging report, including some token fruit from the land. This good news is met with murmuring and fear. The Israelites must face the great and tall indigenous peoples, including the Amorites and the Anakim. The Anakim (9:1-2; cf. Num 13:30-33) are eventually conquered by Joshua and take refuge in Philistine cities (Josh 11:21-22). Such references to the enemy are probably more symbolic than references to real geography and history. They represent the arousal of fear and certainty of defeat against the enemy, calling to mind the David and Goliath story (1 Sam 17) and other such narratives.

In addition to fear, seeing is another theme. The Israelites already saw a fearful desert but safely crossed it (v. 19). Will they remember what they saw and see it happening now as the Lord carries them along (vv. 30-31)? Will they let the sight of threatening opponents compromise their trust in the Lord?

Fear and disobedience overwhelm trust and confidence at this juncture. Longing for the past overshadows their envisioning of a bright and promising future in the land (v. 25). It is noteworthy that their failure to trust (v. 32) is expressed by the Hebrew active participle. This verbal subtlety highlights the ongoing and pervasive nature of their distrust and unbelief. The tentative and unsuccessful first scouting of the land leaves the Israelites sojourned for a long time at Kadesh-barnea.

2:1–3:11 From Edom to Bashan

Edom, Moab, and Ammon permit easy transit for the wandering Israelites in Transjordan, while the Amorites and Bashan resist and engage in battle. The Deuteronomic tradition differs to some degree from similar accounts in Numbers 20–21 and 33:37-49. For example, in Numbers the

Israelites must circumvent a hostile Edom, and the land is specifically referred to as Edom rather than the descendants of Esau (Num 21:4; cf. Gen 25:21-26).

The narrative moves from a description of peaceful passage to warfare, with the Lord in control of Israel's movement at every turn. During their crossing through Edom, Moab, and Ammon, the Israelites are ordered not to fight because the Lord has given these lands to other peoples from among the wider family of Abraham (2:5, 9, 19). In warfare against the Amorites and Bashan, the Israelites are assured victory through divine intervention, including the Lord's hardening of Sihon's heart (2:30; cf. Exod 4:21; 8:15 on Pharaoh). Ironically, the Israelites who so recently were fearful of the indigenous people are now feared themselves (2:4, 25).

It is noteworthy that the lands not given over to the Israelites are identified with their own kin, Esau and Lot. Esau's hairiness (Gen 25:25) is related by folk etymology to the name of the region of Seir where he eventually settles. Ancient Seir (meaning "hairy") was situated along a rugged, thickly forested mountain range, the appearance of which gave rise to the association with hairiness. Lot is the great ancestor of the Ammonites and Moabites (Gen 19:30-38). The lands given over to the Israelites are bestowed on the tribes of Reuben and Gad, as well as two clans of Manasseh. Whether by entitlement or bestowal, the new land is linked to kinship among the tribes. Deuteronomic theology highlights the fact that the Lord's gift of land is more than violent conquest and that blood ties have an abiding value. Relationships engage people with God and with one another despite conflict and mutual claims to the same territory. The Lord is not solely the God of Israel but also of the nations. Gratitude for divine favor must not be exclusive but celebrated with and for others.

The ecological destruction and human genocide against the Amorites and Bashan may strike the modern reader as extreme and morally distasteful (2:34; 3:6-7). Only spoils of livestock and loot, not human persons, are of value to the conqueror. However, war is inherently a violent enterprise and says more about human nature and desire than divine will. Decimation of the enemy is more about military strategy and taking spoils than moral values (20:10-20). Nations tend to presume that God goes forth with *their* armies. So-called Holy War (perhaps better "Wars of Yhwh" or "Wars of the Lord") and the theology of warfare are more reflective of perceived ideals than of historical fact. Any claims, territorial or otherwise, are not solely the result of human prowess but the will of God at work in the created order. Theologically, the narrative highlights the tension between divine freedom and the vagaries of human freedom.

3:12-29 Allotment of the land and plight of Moses

The first apportionment of land to certain tribes of Israel is more than simply a geographical division. Taking possession of the land is the result of a struggle that includes conflict and loss of life on the battlefield. However, the land is ultimately a gift and the fulfillment of divine promises. This gift stems from divine love of Israel (7:6) and judgment on the wicked indigenous nations (9:5).

This first gift of land leads to the first prayer of Moses in Deuteronomy (vv. 24-25). He begs to touch the land beyond the Jordan, only to be rebuffed by God. The priestly tradition (P) offers an explanation, i.e., Moses' breaking faith at the waters of Meribah (32:51-52; cf. Num 20:12), but in Deuteronomy the explanation is mitigated in line with Deuteronomic theology. Here Moses takes on a punitive judgment for the sake of the people, a hint of the scriptural theme of vicarious suffering of one for the many (Isa 53:4-6). Moses is barred from the land on their account, a detail repeated in the narrative to emphasize the point (1:37; 3:26; 4:21), but Moses is not passive; he makes an appeal (vv. 23-25; cf. Gen 18:22-33 on Abraham).

One more time Moses climbs a mountain. Pisgah is a mountain in northwestern Moab and close to Mount Nebo, the mountain on which, according to tradition, Moses died and was buried. Pisgah is also the site where Balak built seven altars and Balaam spoke oracles over Israel (Num 23:14-26).

4:1-40 The call to fidelity

The first discourse of Moses concludes with a reminder of what God has done for the Israelites and what they in turn must observe. Observance is concretized and lived out by means of statutes, ordinances, decrees, and commands. This exhortation is highlighted by an inclusion, i.e., repetition of a word or phrase at the beginning and end of a unit (vv. 1, 40), where the theme of statutes given by the Lord for long life is repeated. "Life" is a word that echoes throughout Deuteronomy (4:1; 5:29, 33; 6:24; 30:19-20; 32:43).

Various themes and motifs run through the speech. First, the people are directed toward observance. The Hebrew verb for "observance" denotes having charge over, tending, and keeping watch like a sentinel. Such vigilance characterizes observance of the commandments. Second, teaching children is emphasized throughout. Instruction must be passed down to subsequent generations (6:7). This mandate both harks back to the Passover ritual question: "What does this rite of yours mean?" (Exod 10:2; 12:24-27) and anticipates the pedagogy of wisdom literature (Prov 1:8; Sir 2:1-6). Third, the sevenfold repetition of "fire" punctuates the recounting of the theophany at Horeb (vv. 11, 12, 15, 24, 33, 36 [2x]). Fire both illumines and consumes, a fitting metaphor for the divine presence and activity in the created order. The reference to consuming fire in verse 24 (the very center of the fire motif here) links fire to divine jealousy. The Hebrew word for jealousy means fiery red, a fitting image. Fire remains today a liturgical appointment in many Christian liturgical settings, including the Easter candle, altar candles, and the sanctuary lamp.

The dangers of idolatry are also noted. The phrase "You heard the sound of the words, but saw no form . . ." (vv. 12, 15) emphasizes divine transcendence and the futility of incantations and the use of similar practices to manipulate God. Such conduct is not in compliance with the Ten Commandments (5:7-8). Idols, objects of false worship, can either be the powerful, observable forces of nature that impact life and the cycle of seasons (sun, moon, and stars) or works of human hands that tell more about human need than divine attributes.

Finally, the speech introduces another important theme in Deuteronomy, i.e., the grand theology of remembering/forgetting (v. 23; see 5:15; 7:18; 8:2, 18-19, etc.). The faithful must remember the covenant with the Lord, a value closely connected to teaching children. Not to remember and not to teach suppress the great saga of the people,

a lesson reprised in the wisdom literature (Sir 28:6-7).

4:41-43 Cities of refuge

Mosaic law provides places of asylum to those who kill without malice. This institution is unique to Israel in the Scriptures. The topic is added on here and discussed in more detail later (19:1-13; cf. Num 35:9-15 where six cities are provided to harbor the refugee from blood vengeance). Joshua 20 calls for a trial and actually names the six cities. The book of Numbers focuses on harboring the culprit in a limited area until he makes an appearance before the community. Since clan vengeance would pollute the land, Deuteronomy emphasizes the protection of the innocent blood of accidental death from such clan vengeance. The caring spirit of Deuteronomy comes through on this issue. The Lord is the source of justice, and human life is sacred. Vigilante justice must never be allowed to gain the upper hand.

MOSES' SECOND ADDRESS

Deuteronomy 4:44–28:69

4:44-49 Introduction

These verses are similar to the introduction to the first address (1:1-5) in that they cite precise geographical locations. From this point in the narrative, references to statutes, ordinances, decrees, and similar terms become more common. The address dovetails into the Ten Commandments and the great Shema, followed by various laws sanctioned by curses and blessings.

5:1–6:3 The Ten Commandments

All Israel is summoned to hear the statutes and decrees that stem from covenant with the Lord. The call to "hear" (v. 1) implicitly includes response and obedience, as well as anticipates the great Shema (6:4). The Mosaic covenant is characterized by human obligations, in contrast to the Abrahamic covenant that emphasizes what the Lord will do for Israel (Gen 12:1-4; 15:1-6). Both aspects of covenant complement one another, i.e., the gift of the land fulfills God's promises to the ancestors and in turn demands obedience from the people. The land is not an outright gift with guaranteed security. Further, 5:1-5 shows that

Moses speaks to the present and to future generations, and is not simply reciting a nostalgic recollection of past events that have no further impact.

This background sets the stage for the revelation of the Ten Commandments (cf. Exod 20:1-17; the sequence here follows the Catholic and Lutheran division. Other traditions divide the material differently). In both Exodus and Deuteronomy the commandments are offered in the context of a covenant relationship. Further, the Ten Commandments are a monumental revelation mediated and communicated by Moses (5:5). His mediation characterizes other climactic moments in the saga of Israel, such as in Pharaoh's court (Exod 5:1), at the Sea of Reeds (Exod 14:10-16), and the revolt at Kadesh (Num 14:1-25). Despite starting out as a reluctant leader, Moses is remembered as the Lord's preeminent envoy.

The Ten Commandments are not burdensome decrees but an invitation to a relationship characterized by mutual freedom. The God of Israel is free of coercion by magic; the Israelites are free of the burdens of polytheism. The prologue offers an ageless reason for fidelity to these commandments, namely, the Lord freed the people from slavery in Egypt (v. 6).

The first commandment (vv. 7-10) is essentially a demand that Israel have no other gods besides the Lord, a mandate that would often be compromised in the course of Israelite history. This commandment relates both to human and divine freedom. Having no other gods frees the Israelites from the burden of placating a pantheon of gods. The prohibition of carved images preserves the Lord from the superstitious controls of magic and idol worship. The meaning and practice of authentic religion are in mind here; salvation history spans the promises to the ancestors, the exodus and wilderness experience, the covenant and other key events. Freedom in the land demands total fidelity to the Lord.

The second commandment (v. 11) relates to the first. It preserves the Lord from superstitious control through the use of the divine name. In the ancient world to bestow a name, know a name, or change another's name implied certain authority over the individual. Hence, Adam names the animals and gains stewardship over creation (Gen 2:19-22; cf. 1:28); the Lord designates Abram/ Abraham as father of the nations (Gen 17:3-8); and the Lord reveals the divine name Yhwh to Moses because an unnamed god is an unknown god in Semitic thought (Exod 3:13-15).

The third commandment (vv. 12-15) regarding the sabbath associates holiness with relaxation from work. To be holy means to be set apart, so the sabbath is set apart as a special day. Sabbath preserves the Israelites from constant labor by providing a day of rest. The spirit of this commandment is reiterated in Deuteronomy 15 where release from debt is discussed. The sabbath is essentially a gift of rest from habitual toil. The ancient world lived under the demand of daily toil in order to eke out a living and the possibility of rest was more an ideal than a reality, given the daily demands of ancient pastoral and agricultural life. The sabbath ideal is found in the prophets as well (Isa 66:22-23) and anticipates the vision of apocalyptic hope of a world with no toil, pain, or death (Rev 21:1-4).

The fourth commandment (v. 16) is a hinge amid the commandments as they move from divine/human relationship to relationships between people. Its original wording may have paralleled the other apodictic commandments here and may have appeared as something like "You shall *not* curse your father and your mother." This commandment preserves the dignity of family life, especially that of the aged when they lose productivity and become burdensome. Old Testament wisdom literature echoes this value (Prov 19:26; 30:17; Sir 3:16; cf. Eph 6:1-3). Hence, this law relates more to the adult children of the sick or elderly than to youths. It is noteworthy that this commandment has a promise attached, i.e., long life in the land. Promises fulfilled permeate Deuteronomy and are associated with reciprocal obedience (4:40; 5:33; 6:2).

The fifth commandment (v. 17) prohibits killing as an individual prerogative apart from divine law and judicial process. The commandment is more related to preserving Israelite life than a universal regard for life in general (Lev 19:17-18; cf. Matt 5:21-22; Luke 10:29-37).

The sixth commandment (v. 18) against adultery preserves the sanctity of marriage and family. The patriarchal society of the ancient world had different standards for men and women. A man committed adultery with a married woman (i.e., against another man's marriage); a woman committed adultery with any man. By most modern standards this seems biased, but the commandment is intended to protect the paternity of offspring and the innate sanctity and exclusivity of marriage.

The seventh commandment against stealing (v. 19) deals more with human persons than property, but the issue of property theft is included in Israelite law as well (Exod 22:1-3, 11). Stealing in this sense includes extended servitude of any kind that exploits another's indebtedness and compromises human freedom. The spirit of the commandment is more forcefully stated in 24:7 and deemed a capital offense. On a higher level, this mandate speaks to the opportunistic abuse of one's neighbor, especially the powerful over the powerless (1 Sam 12:1-12; 1 Kgs 21:1-16).

The eighth commandment (v. 20) forbids false witness in order to preserve an Israelite's reputation and legal rights in the community. Harmony in human relations requires telling the truth, especially before the court. Hence, Israelite law prescribes the sworn testimony of two or three witnesses against a defendant (19:15; cf. Dan 13:52-59; Matt 18:16). The psalms cry out for a just hearing (Pss 4:2; 10:3-10).

The ninth and tenth commandments (v. 21) speak, respectively, to coveting a neighbor's wife and material possessions. These laws preserve the Israelite's spouse and property from loss through theft or scheming. The most powerful example of coveting another's wife in the Old Testament is David's adultery with Bathsheba (2 Sam 11:1-5). One should note that Deuteronomy distinguishes the wife from material property and uses a distinct verb for her; compare verse 21 with Exodus 20:17.

The promulgation of the Ten Commandments concludes with an exhortation to obedience. Why should one obey? The reasons are clear. As 5:22 states, Moses brings down tablets of chiseled stone from the Lord, tablets given to him apart from the people. These tablets contain the statutes and decrees to be lived in the Promised Land flowing with milk and honey. Observance is the key to long life in the land. Such is the motivation for the human obligation to observe the decrees with which the covenant is expressed.

6:4-25 The great commandment

The Shema (the word *shĕmac* is a Hebrew imperative, which means "Hear!") reiterates the Lord's claim on Israel. However one chooses to translate the exclusivity or oneness of God in verse 4, Israel's covenant relationship is highlighted in this exhortation. Further, love of God in verse 5 is intimately tied to the heart, the seat of intellect and will in Semitic thought. The Deuteronomic theology of love expressed here pervades the entire book. It is out of the Lord's first love of Israel that the nation finds its self-understanding (4:37-40; 7:6-8; 10:15). Such affection is rooted in the Lord as God of the ancestors and is echoed in the gospels (Matt 22:37-39; Mark 12:29-31). Further, the soul is not conceived as an isolated entity that survives after death but a principle of life in all its forms. The soul (the same Hebrew word is sometimes translated as "spirit" or "being") bespeaks a needy humanity full of appetites, desires, and mortality (Job 6:7; Isa 29:8). Strength reflects a single-minded zeal to fulfill the Lord's will.

The call to teach future generations is also part of the commandment. To "keep repeating them" (v. 7; the word literally means to "sharpen" or "whet") to your children expresses getting to the heart of the matter with no ambiguity. Indeed, teaching children is a repeated mandate in Deuteronomy because Moses' speeches communicate rights and obligations that span generations (6:2; 20-25; 32:46-47). The details in verses 8-9 are metaphorical but become in early Judaism the phylacteries (leather bands with attached boxes worn on the left arm and forehead during prayer) and the *mezuzah* (a receptacle placed on the right-hand outer doorjamb which contains words from Deuteronomy).

The rewards of fidelity (vv. 10-19) are more than a reprise of previous statements in Deuteronomy. They serve as a bridge between the great Shema and the instructions to children because what the Lord commands must be lived out and passed on. In this light, what would arrival in the land mean in terms of gift and responsibility? As a gift, the land means reaping benefits at no great labor or cost. As responsibility, the narrative harks back to the Deuteronomic theology of remembering/forgetting. The mention of cisterns, vineyards, and olives is quaintly artful in the narrative. These three motifs refer to abundance in the land. Cisterns denote security through the availability of channeled and potable water (2 Kgs 18:31-32; Isa 36:16-17). The vineyard is a sign of divine blessing and a refuge to the widow, orphan, and resident alien in need (24:21-22; see Lev 19:10). Sharing the fruits of the vineyard is informed by the remembrance of having once been slaves in Egypt. Elsewhere in the Old Testament the vineyard is a metaphor for Israel itself (Isa 5:1-7). The olive tree is hardy, growing well even in rocky soil and, like the vineyard, a source of sustenance for those in need (24:20). The olive and its multipurpose oil represent all the traditional staples of the Promised Land: grain, wine, and oil (7:13; cf. 30:9).

7:1-26 Victory over the enemy

The text offers readers a striking example of the vagaries of war and conquest. Taking no prisoners is a military option that reaches its lowest level in genocide. But here the emphasis is more theological than historical. For example, the doom of the enemy protects the Israelites from possible intermarriage with them (v. 3). The social institution of marriage is a perennial litmus test of the current social climate, whether dealing with political opportunism (see 1 Kgs 11:1-8), cultural bias, or lovers who break from tradition. In sum, whatever else it is about, this text deals with the issue of whether my child can or should marry a person of another race, nationality, or religion.

7:1-11 The identity of Israel

The identity and cultic integrity of Israel are highlighted here (cf. Exod 34:11-16). The prohibition against making covenants or showing mercy to other peoples relates to Israel's holiness (v. 6), a status which implies that they must be somehow set apart in a special way. Holiness is an intrinsic characteristic of God (Exod 3:5; Isa 6:3) and requires harsh judgment on priests who abuse their cultic responsibilities via apostasy (Hos 4:4-19).

Israel's self-understanding is intimately associated with its covenant relationship with God. Israel is not worthy on its own merits but chosen out of love. They are in a strict sense the Lord's property (v. 6) and observing the commandments is a constant duty (v. 11). This self-understanding underpins all Old Testament theology and informs Christian identity as well (Rom 8:28-39).

7:12-15 The blessings of obedience

The motif of blessing punctuates these verses. Blessing is intrinsically related to fertility and by extension is related to all prosperity in the created order (Gen 1:28; 12:1-3; Num 6:22-27; Ps 127:3-5).

Ideally, no family is childless, no livestock barren. Blessing is also relational, i.e., one can bless or be blessed in anticipation of some benefit that fosters goodness and well-being. Absence of disease is also connected to blessing. Infidelity brings on maladies of all sorts (28:58-62). Health is peace (Hebrew: *shālôm*) and associated with covenant loyalty.

7:16-26 The Lord as victor

Israel is encouraged not to fear in the face of its enemies. The imagery in these verses recalls the exodus from Egypt, especially details in the Song of the Sea (Exod 15:14-16). The enemy will panic in the face of the Lord's incomparable power and suffer defeat amid Israel's victory. The command not to covet idols of silver or gold is intrinsic to Israelite law and theology. Idol worship is an abomination as seen in the incident of the golden calf (9:7-21; cf. Exod 32), because idols represent the religions of the surrounding nations, something that compromises holiness as being "set apart."

8:1-20 The temptations of prosperity

This chapter reiterates the Deuteronomic theology of remembering/forgetting and the temptations of the land. Observance demands ongoing recollection of God's mighty deeds on behalf of Israel, specifically the wandering in the desert with its tests of faith and divine sustenance by miraculous food and drink.

The temptations of prosperity relate to a universal aspect of human nature. Guaranteed security leads to laxity as time goes on because of the false presumption that it has always been so and will always be so. Smug self-assurance becomes more pervasive as successive generations enjoy unthreatened comfort (v. 14), so remembering a time of want is essential to true religion. Each generation must embrace the stories which are told over and over: "My father was a refugee Aramean . . ." (26:5; cf. Exod 12:26-27). Such humble beginnings, fraught with danger, contrast with the dream of the Promised Land and its securities.

The terrain is depicted as well-watered, with grain and fruits, olive trees, and honey. Such bounty can be wrongly accredited to human ingenuity and accomplishment, not cooperation in covenant with God. Israel must remember and retell each generation that the Lord is the master of the arable land, providing the rainfall to replenish the soil (11:10-12; cf. Gen 8:22).

9:1-29 Israel's stubbornness

The chapter is punctuated by repeated themes and motifs: possession of the land in place of the enemy, divine commitment to ancestral promises, rebellion occasioning divine anger, fire, forty days and forty nights, etc.

9:1-6 The Lord's fidelity

The opening verses hark back to themes already addressed, e.g., the fear of the Anakim (1:28), and highlight that Israel cannot boast of its own merits, for the people are habitually stiffnecked (vv. 6, 13, 27) and rebellious (vv. 7, 23, 24). The Lord will drive out the enemy because of their pagan wickedness and the promises made to Israel's ancestors. The Lord and Israel work together in reaching victory, a detail noted in verse 3.

9:7-29 The intercession of Moses

This section presents a touching portrait of Moses, a multifaceted character in Israelite theology. He appeals on behalf of the people and wants to set things right. The Israelites are reminded of the golden calf debacle and Moses' intercession at that juncture (Exod 32). The pattern of pronouns is striking in the narrative. The discourse begins with "you," i.e., Israel, leaving Egypt and subsequent moments of rebellion in the wilderness, then moves to "I," i.e., Moses' intercessory fasting, prayer, and reception of the Ten Commandments. The section concludes with these two pronouns juxtaposed to highlight the sin of the people and the intervention of Moses (vv. 18-19). Even Aaron, who so much embodies Israelite priesthood, is indicted. Moses stands alone as righteous amid their rebellion; he is ever Israel's intercessor in the face of divine anger (cf. Exod 32:11-14; Sir 45:1-5).

The motif of forty days and nights deserves comment, given its fourfold repetition (vv. 9, 11, 18, 25). Numbers in the Bible relate only secondarily to counting. Forty represents a complete cycle or major event, such as the flood (Gen 7:12), the wandering in the wilderness (Exod 16:35; Num 14:20-23), and Jesus' temptation in the desert (Luke 4:1-13). Here the number forty marks the sequence of events that culminate in Moses'

prayerful intercession in the wake of divine anger (vv. 25-29). Moses is on the mountain and then descends after forty days; he lies prostrate for forty days in intercession for the sinful people.

Further, anthropomorphic images of God inform the narrative. The finger of God etches the stone tablets (v. 10; cf. Exod 8:15; 31:18), and God's outstretched arm frees Israel from bondage (v. 29; cf. Exod 6:6). Such images reveal divine presence and intervention, while also limiting any depiction of God in iconography.

Moses' prayer concludes this section. The tone may seem manipulative to modern canons of piety, i.e., the plea "remember . . . lest" (vv. 27-28). The Lord's honor is at stake before other gods and nations. Such intercession is not foreign to Old Testament prayer (Exod 32:11-14; Num 14:15-16; Ps 22:3-6). The prayer also illustrates the theology of divine freedom in that the Lord can have a change of heart. In the Scriptures cause and effect, mercy and justice, are all mysteries that defy a systematic theology. Such is the case with Abel's offering being accepted over that of Cain (Gen 4:3-4) and David's selection from among his brothers as the Lord's anointed (1 Sam 16:11-13).

10:1-11 The ark of the covenant

New stone tablets of the Ten Commandments are commissioned, to be deposited in the ark of the covenant. This chest of acacia wood represented the divine presence on journeys and in the cult (Num 10:35-36; 1 Sam 5), but by the time of Solomon references to the ark all but vanish. Symbolically, the ark represents God's going forth with the people, especially in battle. Besides the Ten Commandments, the ark reportedly contained Aaron's staff and a vessel of manna from the wilderness. It had rings on its sides through which poles were inserted for easy transport (Exod 25:10-16).

10:12–11:9 The great equation

This section presents the gist of Deuteronomic theology. What does the Lord ask? The answer is fourfold: that one love the Lord, fear the Lord, keep the commandments, and walk in the Lord's ways (10:12-13).

The circumcision of the heart is a metaphor for repentance and a new way of living. As stated above (see 6:5-6), the heart is the seat of the will and intellect, so its "circumcision" describes an irreversible change of heart that draws one closer to God. This inward transformation supersedes the outward mark of physical circumcision that serves as a visible symbol of religious identity. Humans judge by appearance; God sees into the heart.

The orphan, widow, and alien cited together in a triad (10:18) stand for the disenfranchised in society who depend on the kindness of others (14:28-29; cf. Exod 22:20-23; 26:12; Ps 10:14-18).

11:10-17 The gift of rain

The Nile River of Egypt (some 4,000 miles in length from its source to its estuary) creates a climate that contrasts strongly with the seasonal rainfall in Palestine. Egypt receives little rain and depends on the flow of water along the Nile and irrigation for sustenance. The river's annual flooding deposits silt along its banks to promote agriculture. Before modern dam construction, desert lay beyond the banks of the Nile. The imagery here extols the gift of the seasonal cycle "that drinks in rain from the heavens" (v. 11). However, as with the flow of the Nile, unpredictable weather patterns create cycles of feast and famine. The theological point of the rain motif is its connection with loyalty to the covenant. The temptation of apostasy to pagan gods (e.g., the Canaanite Baal was god of the thunderstorm) brings disaster on the Israelites; the Lord will withhold rain and thus blessing (vv. 16-17).

11:18-32 The need for fidelity

This statute harks back to the great Shema. The Lord alone is God of Israel; all other gods are as naught, so decision for the Lord is at the heart of this exhortation and will result in either blessing or curse. Blessing reinforces the rain motif discussed previously, i.e., the blessing of creation by means of rain and other positive forces of nature represents order brought out of chaos, seasonal harmony, and fruitfulness in the land. Obedience brings blessing, but disobedience brings a perennial curse.

12:1–26:19 Deuteronomic law

This lengthy section elaborates on a wide variety of legislation, creating what many refer to as the Deuteronomic Code. These laws build on the Ten Commandments and the great Shema;

these two guiding principles are used to inform more specific circumstances. The legislation is not systematic and is rooted in traditional values handed down over generations. The integrity of this unit is indicated by the inclusion (12:1 and 26:16-19) that enjoins Israel to observe these statutes and decrees as a people of divine promise and set apart in holiness to serve the Lord.

12:1-19 Conquest and centralization

The narrative is divided into three parts (vv. 1-7; 8-12; 13-19) and punctuated by the threefold repetition of "rejoice" (vv. 7, 12, 18). Merriment is a celebration of the divine blessing for the individual and the community. At the center of this section the theme of rest is highlighted (vv. 9-10). Successful conquest and prosperity in the land are celebrated in the Psalter as well (Pss 21; 110).

Conquest and centralization of the cult evoke a variety of associations. Conquest realizes the Lord's promise of the land to Abraham and his descendants and the curse of Canaan (Gen 9:25-27; 13:15). Thus it also reflects the extermination or banishment of indigenous peoples, a theme that is troublesome to the modern reader, given the Holocaust, ethnic cleansing, and other events, but theologically the issue is the integrity of true religion and covenant fidelity. Pure worship cannot tolerate the deification of natural phenomena, the carving of images that compromise divine freedom, and the manipulation of God by incantations, fertility rites, child sacrifice, etc. Centralization, a key theme in Deuteronomy and related Deuteronomic literature, bespeaks purity and integrity of worship. A plethora of holy sites imitates the multiplicity of Canaanite local shrines and increases the possibility of dabbling in pagan practices. In Israelite theology no place is inherently sacred; a site is holy because of the divine presence and communication which take place there. At the burning bush the ground was holy because the Lord was present, and Moses took off his sandals in reverential awe (Exod 3:5; cf. Isa 6:1-4).

12:1-7 Destruction of Canaanite sanctuaries

This mandate is riddled with verbs of utter destruction: destroy, tear down, smash, burn up, shatter. Ultimately, the goal is to suppress any memory of pagan practice (v. 3), an irony in light of Israel's own Deuteronomic theology of remembering for itself.

The place of the Lord's dwelling (v. 5) refers in a veiled way to the centralized cult in Jerusalem, an anachronism here, given that David's reign is still in the future (2 Sam 5:6-12). Likewise, the list of sacrificial offerings reflects a more defined cult.

12:8-12 Centralization

After crossing the Jordan, Israel will move toward more centralization of the cult. In principle, no longer can someone simply do what seems right (v. 8; literally, "what is right in one's own eyes." Compare that phrase with "What is right in the sight of the LORD," 13:19; 21:9). That such centralization took place is not a mere fiction. Efforts to consolidate the cult are reflected in the programs of Hezekiah and Josiah (2 Kgs 18:4; 23:19-20). Most probably, historical events such as war, loss of territory, and economic crisis were the driving forces behind centralization of the cult, but centralization had a deeper theological meaning. For instance, it allowed for precise seasonal celebrations on an annual basis by all the people, including covenant renewal under a defined priestly heritage (18:1-8).

12:13-19 The nature of right sacrifice

A distinction is made between the ordinary and the ritual slaughter of animals, a detail inserted at this point because of the centralization of the cult in place of multiple shrines. In a sense all slaughter of meat in the ancient world was "sacred" in that it provided nourishment. Universally, the act of saying grace before meals gives thanks for bounty from God. Although the narrative describes abundance of meat as a blessing (v. 15), the daily diet of the ancient world was more dependent on grains. Meat was by and large reserved for special banquets (Exod 16:12; Amos 6:4; Dan 10:3). Partaking of the blood of slaughtered animals was taboo because blood was essential to life and a vicarious means of atonement (v. 23; cf. Lev 17:11). Further, the references to grain-wine-oil, the firstborn, and vowed or voluntary offerings add to the breadth of what constituted a sacred meal. As noted above, the grain, wine, and oil formed a triad of staples in the ancient Near East; the firstborn held a privileged position; and the disenfranchised (widow, orphan, and resident alien), along with the Levites, deserved

charity and hospitality (12:12; 26:11-12). All these blessings are cause to make merry and rejoice.

12:20-28 Further comments

These verses expand on the preceding section and elaborate further on the sacred nature of blood. Blood is not to be consumed with its flesh, a point reiterated four times (vv. 23-25). Such abstention assures prosperity in the land and is rooted in the primeval history, the instruction to Noah in the covenant (Gen 9:4; cf. Acts 15:20, 29). However, blood which has been set apart is an acceptable component in certain circumstances. A blood ritual seals the covenant with the Lord (Exod 24:3-8). Atonement involves blood (Lev 16:15) and is also found in the ordination sacrifice and priestly consecration (Exod 29:20). Verse 28 is a fitting conclusion to this section as it reiterates the benefits of observance for later generations. Such conduct is right in the sight (literally, "in the eyes") of the Lord. The eyes of God see all; idols have eyes but cannot see (Pss 115:4-5; 135:15-16).

12:29-31 The lure of idols

These verses hark back to 12:1-7 and emphasize that Israel's victory is essentially the work of God. As already warned, a temptation in the Promised Land will be attraction to pagan idols (11:16). The Bible paints a thoroughly negative picture of Canaanite religion, and the prophets berate Israelite kings for adopting foreign images and rituals. Paganism is an abomination (v. 31) because it includes such sins as eating unclean animals, unchaste behavior, idol worship, and human sacrifice. All are contrary to true religion.

13:1-19 Leading astray

The chapter is punctuated by the threefold repetition of "straying" (literally, "to thrust out, or banish"; vv. 6, 11, 14). This verb is rooted in shepherding where the flocks serve as a vivid metaphor for straying (Jer 23:2; 50:17). By extension the verb suggests seduction of the faithful away from the right path. Each usage here highlights a particular circumstance, i.e., false prophesy, enticement to idolatry by a family member, and being led astray by the broader community.

Given this background, the prophet and the dreamer come under scrutiny because their vocation includes admonishing the sinner and calling the errant people back to covenant fidelity. Deuteronomic law offers a fine and often overlooked nuance to the characteristics of true prophecy. What comes to pass in prophecy is not as important as the message's conformity to true religion as outlined in Deuteronomy. False prophecy may come true, but the event is a test from the Lord. Finally, family members can have a negative impact by enticing a relative to paganism (vv. 7-10; cf. Matt 10:34-38).

Perhaps the most powerful warning relates to communal apostasy (vv. 13-19). The abominations of false prophecy and familial misguidance crescendo into social sin on a grand scale. The narrative depicts citywide apostasy (v. 14) that results in vast retribution (v. 16). This calls to mind the Tower of Babel where the escalation of sin in the primeval history came to affect all human life (Gen 11; cf. Jonah 3 on the conversion of Nineveh). Yet this section ends on a positive note. Heeding the Lord's voice brings mercy and renewed blessing (vv. 18-19), a reward for keeping the commandments.

In sum, Deuteronomy offers timeless laws that warn against being led astray by human voices that may not reflect divine will. Deuteronomic law, written down and proclaimed to the assembly, fosters remembrance and long life in the land (32:45-47).

14:1-29 Children of the Lord

To be children of the Lord (v. 1) involves a right relationship. Specifically, it demands obedience, a challenge emphasized throughout the Scriptures (21:18-21; cf. Sir 3:1-16; Matt 21:28-31). When properly observed, rituals, dietary laws, tithing, and other demands demonstrate fidelity to the covenant and stewardship of the created order.

14:1-2 Ritual custom

In the ancient Near East canons of mourning often involved an emotional display with wailing, the chanting of dirges, rending of garments, wearing of sackcloth, sitting in ashes, and self-mutilation. Shaving the head and gashing the body are expressly prohibited because they mirror Canaanite rituals (1 Kgs 18:28; Jer 47:5; Ezek 9:14-15).

14:3-21 Dietary laws

The exact names of these forbidden foods are obscure in Hebrew and their English equivalents are not certain. Whatever the rules of clean/unclean, dietary laws distinguish one's religious identity apart from other faiths. In conjunction with the blood laws cited above, certain kinds of animals are not to be consumed at all. Fish with fins and scales, as well as quadrupeds with cloven hooves and chewing cud, are acceptable (Lev 11:3-12). Clean animals reflect order in creation (birds, fish, land animals; Gen 1:26), unlike hybrid creatures that represent lack of distinction and embody the primordial chaos before creation. Some commentators suggest that food hygiene is at the root of some forbidden items, given the lack of refrigeration and preservatives. Whatever the exact origin of these dietary laws, their observance shows that Israel belongs to the Lord and is set apart in holiness.

14:22-29 Tithes

The practice of tithing (offering a tenth of one's income) is an enduring institution used to support political and sacral activities. In the ancient world when distance prohibited bringing an offering of grain-wine-oil and firstlings to the sanctuary, a cash donation was acceptable (Lev 27:30-33). Care of the poor by tithing adds a charitable dimension to the practice. Such a duty is to be carried out with joy and happiness, returning in kind what God has given in creation (Sir 35:7-14). Support of the Levites (v. 29) reflects consideration of those with no inheritance who serve in the sacral realm (Num 18:21-32; Neh 10:37-38).

Such right conduct brings divine blessing. Once again Deuteronomy reiterates that blessing is intimately related to fertility, expansion, and well-being in life. It also acknowledges that bounty is a gift in a Promised Land that ultimately belongs to the Lord.

15:1-23 Ownership and relaxation of debt

The chapter discusses laws regarding a variety of issues: the waiving of debts, emancipation of Hebrew slaves, and the offering of animal firstlings. These regulations are intimately linked to sabbath ideals, particularly the value of a regular day of rest and relief from indentured service.

15:1-11 No one in need

Ideally, no Israelite should be in need, although in reality there would always be needy people in the land (Matt 26:11). Tensions between ideals and realities in life mandate the periodic relaxation of debts on a communal level. The seven-year period enjoined here is rooted in the principle of protecting the poor from economic exploitation and endless service in paying off debts (Exod 22:24-26; Lev 25:35-38). This sabbatical year does not benefit foreigners, and its exact nature remains a point of debate. Is the debt canceled, or is it merely suspended for a grace period? Whatever the case, the effort to ease debts reflects the great Deuteronomic call to love one's neighbor.

15:12-18 Slavery

The seven-year period of relaxation continues in regard to Hebrew slaves. This commandment is rooted in the abiding recollection of Israel having been ransomed from slavery in Egypt. Such indentured servitude is always one way of paying off a debt, but the practice is ripe for abuse. An Israelite's integrity and identity with the whole body of the Israelite nation transcend monetary debt, so freed slaves deserve assistance in making the transition from involuntary service back to freedom. Not being sent away "empty-handed" (vv. 13-14) recalls the flight of the Israelites from Egypt when the Hebrews went on their way laden with gifts (Exod 3:22; 12:36).

15:19-23 Firstlings

Offering the firstlings of the flocks or the first fruits of the harvest is an ancient institution. The firstlings belong to God and are offered back in anticipation of ongoing fertility. For Israel the first Passover in Egypt initiated this practice in that the firstborn males of Israel were saved during the tenth plague by the blood of a lamb sprinkled on the lintel and doorjamb of the house (Exod 12:22-23). Except under special circumstances, a firstborn ranks first in inheritance. Blemished firstborn animals are handled differently (vv. 21-22; cf. 17:1).

16:1-17 The great feasts

Religions typically observe annual celebrations that embody their collective experience of God and give cause to assemble ritually. For Israel the calendar includes Passover (Unleavened Bread), Weeks, and Booths. These feasts are cited elsewhere in the Pentateuch (Exod 23:14-17; 34:18-23;

Lev 23; Num 28–29) and in Deuteronomy are connected to the central sanctuary.

Passover is the celebration of the wandering shepherds' firstlings and is rooted in an annual nomadic feast where the blood of the slaughtered animal was used to assure safe passage during migration. Unleavened Bread recognizes the barley harvest and the leaven used by the settled farmer. Despite their distinct origin, both are integrated into the exodus from Egypt (Exod 12:1-28).

The feast of Weeks (also called Pentecost; Acts 2:10) is another agricultural feast, a spring agricultural feast rooted in the farmer's offering of the first fruits of the barley harvest. Deuteronomy gives precision to this observance by placing it seven weeks after the sickle is put to the standing grain, broadening what was probably an individual offering of the harvest into a national pilgrimage.

The feast of Booths (also called Tabernacles, Succoth, or Ingathering) is an autumn celebration, especially of such fruits as grapes, olives, and dates at the end of the annual harvest season. Traditionally, Booths related to Israel's wandering in the wilderness and living in tents. This memory occasions a time of celebration that lasts for a week, from sabbath to sabbath (cf. Lev 23:39-43; Neh 8:13-18). Temporary shelters are erected in the orchards while the harvesters make merry over the agricultural bounty. Speaking of a much later time, Josephus says that its observance included menorah lamps, music, dancing, and generous libations of water and wine. The feast became associated with messianic hope and restoration of the fortunes of Israel via Hanukkah, also called the feast of Dedication (1 Macc 4:54-59).

16:18–18:22 Leadership in Israel

This section describes leadership roles over the course of Israelite history, beginning with the Judges. The material in 16:21–17:7 may appear to interrupt the flow of the narrative, but it does establish canons of right judgment through dutiful leadership. Further, we learn that pagan practices and blemished sacrifices are unacceptable in the cult. The worship of celestial bodies patently contradicts the Israelite theology of creation (Gen 1:14-19; Ps 19:1). False witness is also dismissed as contrary to the Ten Commandments and related laws (5:20; 19:15; cf. Exod 20:16). Fidelity and right judgment foster peace, social order, and long life in the land.

16:18-20; 17:8-13 Judges

The role of the judge in the Scriptures is not univocal. In the historical books (Josh–2 Kgs) this was the institution that provided the Israelites with leadership before the monarchy. This is clearest in the beginning of the book of Judges where these leaders are not simply justices in legal matters. They are military leaders who rescue errant Israel from the enemy and oversee a time of peace. Deuteronomic theology colors this portrait: Israel sins, is punished, cries out for help, and the Lord sends a judge to the rescue. A time of peace then follows.

In the book of Deuteronomy the tasks of judges are more strictly legal in nature, and they are presented as vigilant protectors of the law whose verdicts must be accepted. Levitical priests are included as a balance to the judges. In sum, Israelite tradition enjoins judges not to take bribes (16:19) and to defend the triad of needy persons: the widow, orphan, and resident alien.

17:14-20 Kings

The origins of the monarchy in Israel are complicated. Old Testament tradition preserves both pro- and anti-monarchy traditions (1 Sam 8–18), and the rise of kingship is associated with the Philistine threat and the need for a more consolidated government, over and above the tribal federation. The people want a king like all the surrounding nations (1 Sam 8:19-20) and eventually get one. Unique to Israelite monarchy is the monarch's subordination to the Lord as a vassal king. He is subject to the law and expected to embody covenant ideals and mete out justice impartially (v. 20). Israel's kings are never made into gods.

The extent to which the portrayal of the Israelite monarchy found in the Bible reflects objective history is debated. Some scholars think there is less history here than theology, but the ancients did not understand "history" in the modern sense of the word, i.e., objective recorded events in chronological order.

Curiously, the narrative highlights certain royal prerogatives that remain in check, i.e., horses and wives (vv. 16-17). These items have a metaphorical value that should not be overlooked. As is the case even today, horses are much associated with the upper class, because the wealthy can afford their care and maintenance. The Philistine threat cited above comes into play because of the recollection of their chariots and horsemen against King Saul (1 Sam 13:5; cf. 2 Sam 15:1-6 on Absalom). Further, horses represent the hidden dangers of military prowess and royal privilege, i.e., human pride. Deuteronomy insists that reliance on the Lord supersedes "horse and chariot," a tenet sung in Israel's worship and prophecy (Pss 20:8; 33:16-19; 76:7-8; 147:10; Isa 43:16-17; Ezek 26:7).

Many wives represent polygamy and the luxury of a harem. Such is the issue behind Absalom's invasion of his father's harem in the sight of the people (2 Sam 16:20-22). This action is tantamount to pretensions to the throne of David his father.

18:1-8 Levites and priests

The history of the Israelite priesthood is complex. Religions define themselves by concepts of sacred space, times and seasons, and chosen representatives who serve as intermediaries between the human and divine. Here the Levites are portrayed as dependent on the beneficence of others, devoid of property and assets (vv. 6-8). Whatever the actual historical background, the Deuteronomic concern about priestly rights stems from the suppression of local shrines and the centralization of the cult in Jerusalem. In Deuteronomy the levitical priests gain prominence (v. 8; 27:9-10; 31:9-13).

Levites also embody a perennial value, that being sponsored and subsidized by others is not a burden on the religious community but a gift that frees a person to serve the wider community without extraneous burdens. Fiscal self-sufficiency is not the litmus test of dignified ministry in any age. By definition benefactors support persons and groups that depend on their largesse. At the heart of such service is the acknowledgement of one's ultimate dependence on God (cf. Luke 12:22-34). By the time of Chronicles, Levites would be given a more defined history, claiming a clear genealogy from the ancient tribe of Levi (1 Chr 6).

18:9-22 Prophets

Genuine prophecy is regulated in the Deuteronomic Code and viewed with a certain guardedness. Here the discussion picks up from 13:1-6 and its warning against false prophets. The narrative can be divided into two parts: vv. 9-14 and vv. 15-22, the latter building on the former prohibitions.

It is noteworthy how Moses is idealized as prophet par excellence (vv. 15, 18). Moses the prophet is one biblical portrait of Israel's exodus leader, but he was also thought of as liberator, priest, judge, model of humility, and privileged intimate of God. He speaks the word of the Lord and commands obedience. The task of Old Testament prophecy is characterized as one that ensures covenant fidelity and proclaims the word of God. Indeed, emphasis on the "word" from Moses punctuates verses 18-22. Obedience brings peace and prosperity; disobedience brings disaster, often via invasion by foreign adversaries. Such elements of the Deuteronomic theology of prophecy color other books as well (2 Kgs 17:13-18).

19:1-13 More on cities of refuge

Refer to 4:41-43 for a discussion of this provision in Deuteronomic law. The city of refuge protects a fugitive from indiscriminate vigilante justice and emotionally driven blood vengeance, especially from the traditional redeemer of blood (2 Sam 14:7).

The city of refuge is a sparsely attested but powerful theme in the Old Testament. Later rabbinic tradition elaborates on its provisions. The city should be near a water supply and street markets so that the refugee lacks nothing, in a populous district so that a cry for help can be heard, without any trafficking of arms or traps lest the avenger purchase his goods there. Elsewhere, refuge is depicted in the metaphors of the tent, rocky fastness, secure dwelling, or shelter (33:27-28; cf. Isa 33:16; Ps 142:5-6). Ultimately, God is our refuge (Ps 14:6; 71:7).

19:14 Boundaries and landmarks

This small piece of legislation bespeaks the Deuteronomic theology of the land. No one can violate the inheritance of another by moving boundary markers. Ahab's seizure of Naboth's vineyard with the complicity of the notorious Jezebel is a good example of such abuse (1 Kgs 21). Deuteronomic theology emphasizes that landmarks and boundaries are a sacred value and related to the protection of inheritance (v. 14; 27:17). The Lord apportions the nations their inheritance (32:8). As the prophets proclaim, human greed cannot rationalize such injustice and avoid divine retribution (cf. Mic 2:2).

19:15-21 False witness

Prior to the benefit of modern forensic tools like fingerprinting and DNA analysis, the sworn testimony of witnesses has been a given in human history. In the Scriptures two or more firsthand witnesses were needed for conviction (17:6; cf. Num 35:30). Obviously, such a system is open to abuse. Perjury is difficult to prove when false witnesses conspire, and especially when they are considered pillars of the community. Such is the suspense of the Susanna tale (Dan 13). Hence, this statute takes a defensive stance and imposes harsh penalties for such obstruction of justice (vv. 16-19). False witness deserves the *lex talionis*: "eye for eye, tooth for tooth," i.e., retribution not excessive but equal to the injury. It remains debated whether this law is to be interpreted literally or is simply a guiding dictum in deciding cases.

20:1-20 The rules of war

This legislation builds on 7:1-26 and anticipates further items (chs. 21–25). The opening section (vv. 1-4) once again recalls the Song of the Sea (Exod 15:1-18). The Israelites should not fear military prowess, for the Lord brought forth the Israelites from Egypt and continues to go forth with them into battle. Further, the call to hear (v. 3) reiterates the great Shema, i.e., if the Lord is God alone, live righteously and fear not the vagaries of war.

The following three sections build on this spirited introduction: exemption from military service (vv. 5-9), negotiating with the enemy (vv. 10-18), and the ecological impact of war (vv. 19-20). The narrative assumes a compassionate tone. Soldiers with a new home, vineyard, or wife are exempt from immediate military duty. A human value is celebrated here. Each person should enjoy property, marriage, and family before being put in harm's way. Even modern military law allows for compassionate leave, deferment from service because of siblings killed in battle, and other exemptions. One's name and inheritance should not cease to exist in the land, a violation often at the hands of those most empowered (2 Sam 12:9; 1 Kgs 21:3).

The destruction of trees while laying siege (vv. 19-20) raises hermeneutical questions. At first glance, the preservation of fruit trees seems an agricultural nicety, speaking to the theology of ecology. However, one may ask a deeper question: Why and under what circumstances do trees supersede the value of human life? This point is all the more troubling in light of the mandate to kill the men, while holding women, children, and livestock as valuable booty (v. 13-14). Deuteronomy reflects the time in which it was written, but the book also speaks perennially to the violence of war, as well as the abuse of people who have suffered devastation and are zealous for retribution.

21:1–25:19 Various laws

This section contains a variety of laws, many of which apply general principles to specific problems. Such laws are couched in an "If . . . then" pattern. Compliance secures inheritance, long life, and prosperity in the land (21:9, 23; 22:7; 23:21; 25:15; 26:8-11).

21:1-9 The guilt of innocent blood

This law demands communal responsibility for a rural murder and links the crime to the nearest city. The slaughter of a heifer and the ritual hand washing by the elders atone for the offense. Special to this law is the prayer therein (vv. 7-8). The elders pray for absolution, noting that neither hand nor eye was involved, i.e., neither committing nor aiding and abetting the crime. In ancient anthropology the hand symbolizes responsibility. Hand washing is thus a declaration of innocence (Matt 27:24). Further, the eye is not understood in terms of light entering the body but a transmission outward from the person. Hence, vision intrinsically stems from the living being. God sees all (11:12), idols have eyes but cannot see (Pss 115:5; 135:16), and humans see God incompletely (Num 24:4; Jer 5:21). Deuteronomic laws regarding homicide remind the reader that the loss of human life is not an isolated event but a tragedy that impacts the entire community.

21:10-14 War brides

Although monogamy was the usual social practice for economic reasons in the ancient world, polygamy remained an option. In practice only monarchs and the wealthy could afford multiple wives, technically called polygyny. To the

point, this rule of war is baldly sexist by modern standards. Women are among the spoils of war and objects of forced marriage. The one-month grace period is deemed a kindness (v. 13), but the fact that consummation of the marriage is imminent and the husband can easily dismiss her makes the grace period more a formality than anything gracious.

The high female mortality rate in the ancient world due to death in childbirth is often cited as a pretext for polygyny. The stipulation that the war bride assumes the status of an Israelite woman assures her technical freedom (v. 14). The best the modern reader can see here is a primitive effort to establish some military justice. However, protocols of warfare (e.g., the 1864 Geneva Convention) are never acted out judiciously when humans get caught up in the violence and mass carnage that are often involved.

21:15-17 The firstborn

Ancient laws tended to defer to the firstborn son. Canons of seniority and inheritance were involved, as well as maintaining family order. In Deuteronomic thought, parental favoritism and sibling rivalry must not supersede birthrights and due process.

The firstborn is a grand motif in the Scriptures, extending even to animals. Such new life belongs to God as first fruits and is the focus of the tenth plague against Egypt (Exod 12:29-30; 13:2, 12-16). Israel itself is described as the Lord's firstborn (Exod 4:22; cf. Matt 1:25; Heb 12:23).

21:18-21 Family discord

This law seems excessive by modern standards, but the intent is maintaining good social order. Rebellious children reach beyond the family and impact on the entire community (cf. 21:1-9). The communal aspect brings town elders into the picture as mediators, and justice is meted out at the city gate (v. 19; cf. Josh 2:4; Ruth 4:1). In the best circumstances mediation settles the domestic dispute and avoids bloodshed. The death penalty is a communal event (v. 21). Stoning is a corporate act to purge an offense against the people and is often executed outside the town or city (Lev 17:5-7; 24:14). The gist of this legislation is that grievous and habitual sinning against family and community demands a communal response.

21:22-23 Hanging on a tree

The statute does not reflect hanging as a form of capital punishment but public exposure after execution. Such an act serves as a warning to others. The corpse is not to remain exposed overnight. Timely burial is dictated in Israelite law. Nonburial of the dead, even in time of war, or later desecration of a grave is an abomination (Tob 1:17-18; 4:3-4). The violent end of Jezebel, wife of Ahab, serves as an example of the desecration of a corpse (2 Kgs 9:30-37). She is humiliated and her memory erased in the land.

22:1-4 Respect for livestock

Return of lost property is a universal value, especially when of high monetary or sentimental value (cf. Exod 23:4-5). The famous parable of the ewe lamb illustrates attachment to animals (2 Sam 12:1-6). Harmonious community life depends on respect for what belongs to others and rendering aid when necessary.

22:5 Rules of dress

Appropriate and fashionable dress is culturally conditioned and much associated with gender. In an oblique way, such order speaks to harmony in creation and is spoofed in burlesque when men and women wear one another's clothing or dress outlandishly. This law relates to other prohibitions that define accepted boundaries, e.g., kosher foods, clothing made of one thread, etc. Although the Scriptures offer no detailed record about men's and women's clothing, certain passages identify dress according to status and role (Gen 38:14; Isa 3:18-24).

22:6-7 Nestlings

This short precept speaks again to the theology of ecology and harks back to 20:19-20. Apart from modern sensitivities about the ethical treatment of animals, the spirit of the law is to ensure survival of the species. Taking only eggs or nestlings allows the mother to reproduce. In addition, the ancient world lacked our refined ornithological nomenclature and broke birds into three basic categories: kosher food, votive offerings, and forbidden food. Many names for birds cited in Bible translations are tentative.

22:8 Sound construction

Although not motivated by malice, involuntary manslaughter by negligence or random chance has ramifications (cf. 19:4). In the ancient world accidental death on one's property could trigger the retaliation of blood vengeance.

The parapet is a short wall on the edge of a roof to prevent people from falling. Ancient roofs were mostly flat and used as guest quarters, working space, and even a site for sacrifices and ritual mourning (Josh 2:6; 1 Sam 9:25-26; Jer 19:13; Zeph 1:5). The use of roof space for such purposes is still evidenced in Eastern countries and requires sturdy construction to handle the weight and foot traffic involved.

22:9-12 Combined objects

On one level these directives regarding agriculture and clothing represent an abiding respect for order in creation. The first creation account in Genesis 1 depicts order out of chaos and the human stewardship of creation as seminal values. These principles lie behind legal concerns about whatever causes or symbolically represents chaos. Hence, elements in nature that do not naturally commingle are anomalous and taboo (Lev 19:19).

A diatribe against magic may also be involved. Magic and incantations in the ancient Near East involved supernatural powers channeled and controlled by ritual activity. The concoction of unrelated ingredients in precise measurements (herbal folk medicine, potions, etc.) and verbal incantations were perceived as powerful forces. Hence, the mixing of otherwise distinct agricultural categories is suspect in Deuteronomic theology. Rabbinic Judaism picked up on these laws, elaborating and systematizing them in the Mishnah. The mention of tassels or twisted cords (v. 12) is an item that gained prominence in rabbinic Judaism. Attitudes, behaviors, and appearances speak to covenant loyalty and serve to distinguish the community member from others around them.

22:13-29 Rules of betrothal and marriage

Marriage law in the ancient world was highly patriarchal and sensitive to human sexuality as a powerful force in nature. Pagan religions took this energy into the realm of the cult to curry favor from the gods and promote fertility in the land.

The laws here address a number of issues, that is, attraction, virginity, and alleged adultery. A husband may no longer find his bride attractive and bring the accusation of nonvirginity as a pretext for divorce. The woman's family may intervene to challenge such alleged shame upon their name. The penalty for the husband's false accusation is harsh. He must pay a fine and have no further recourse to divorce her. Should he prove to be right, she is to be stoned (v. 21; cf. 21:21). The penalty for consensual violation of another man's marriage is death for both parties. This precept illustrates the penalties for adultery as in the sixth commandment. The point about sexual assault in the city or in the open field (vv. 23-27) refers to the victim's ability to cry for help and be heard. Such mitigating circumstances are a means of protecting the powerless from falsely accused complicity. Rape of an unbetrothed virgin incurs a fine upon the man and disallows recourse to divorce (vv. 28-29; cf. 18-19). But for all practical purposes, the woman is treated like damaged goods.

Like other passages in Deuteronomy, this section is punctuated by the threefold repetition of purging evil from the midst of the people (vv. 21, 22, 24; cf. 19:18-19; 24:7). False witness, adultery, rape, kidnapping, and other heinous crimes impact the family and larger community. Purging sin is a communal responsibility in the land.

23:1 Incest

Although the Scriptures have no precise term for "incest," illicit familial sexual union is a taboo. Degrees of licit and illicit sexual union are not as refined as in most modern law codes, but certainly such cases as the one described here (marrying one's stepmother) are widely forbidden and are cited as so in the New Testament as well (1 Cor 5:1-5).

23:2-9 The assembly of the Lord

The phrase "assembly of the Lord" punctuates this section (vv. 2, 3, 9). This particular Hebrew term for community (*qāhāl*) represents a variety of situations, including national identity and admission to worship. The term does not specifically include legislative or judicial contexts. Despite Deuteronomic sensitivity to the resident alien (1:16; 10:18-19), the law emphasizes what is distinctive in Israel's social and cultic life. Hence, genital mutilation is taboo. The exact reason for this exclusion is not stated but does relate to rejection of pagan fertility rites and the loss of procreation in the individual. The rejection of children born of an incestuous union relates to boundaries of blood and marriage. It also implies the rejection of children conceived in the context of fertility rites.

With the average life span in the ancient world being forty years or so, the tenth generation bespeaks a lengthy period of time. The list of nations is also informative. Ammonites and Moabites are excluded, while Edomites and Egyptians enjoy some status. Ammon and Moab are linked to alliances against Israel (Judg 3:12-14) and tied to fertility rites between gods and consorts. Moab is a traditional enemy of ancient Israel (1 Sam 14:47). In contrast, Edom is related to Esau, the brother of Jacob. Egypt, while the land of exodus, is also remembered as a place of refuge in famine or flight. Abraham and Jacob migrate to Egypt (Gen 12:10-20; 46:1-7); Judahites flee there in the wake of Babylonian encroachment (Jer 41:11-18). Israel is admonished not to abhor Egypt because its people were aliens in that land.

23:10-15 Purity during war

This law reflects rules of personal and ritual hygiene while on military duty. The depiction is not absolute, since the Lord's Tent of Meeting itself is described elsewhere as pitched outside the camp (Exod 33:7). "Outside the camp" in Deuteronomy is the place for impurity (vv. 11, 13, 14). In mind is the demand that soldiers observe a fastidious purity as they go forth in battle. The Lord goes forth with Israel's army, so its ranks must maintain holiness in the presence of the Holy. For example, Uriah the Hittite stays encamped with his troops rather than spend the night with his wife Bathsheba while back in Jerusalem (2 Sam 11:6-11). Even human bodily fluids represent impurity (Lev 15; Num 5:1-4).

23:16–25:19 Various communal precepts

These laws address aspects of personal integrity and social harmony. They are not organized systematically. The spirit herein emphasizes care of the poor and marginalized who are members of the community or enter its midst and must be welcomed. The memory of past kindness must not be forgotten, a point that echoes the Deuteronomic theology of remembering/forgetting.

23:16-17 Slaves in flight

This precept deals with asylum for runaway slaves from foreign masters. Such refugees must be granted sanctuary at whatever place they choose. Two key issues are at work here. First, Israel must maintain its covenant loyalty to the Lord, remembering that its ancestors were once slaves in Egypt. Second, although the biblical evidence and historical data of the time provide no systematic and overarching provisions for extradition, ancient Near Eastern codes evidence harsh penalties for runaway slaves and those who help them. Slavery as spoils of war and as debt-bondage is the predominant scenario (15:1-18). Deuteronomy is quite unique in its protection of runaway slaves and other persons at risk. In the New Testament an example of the negotiation of slave ownership and manumission is the Letter to Philemon.

23:18-19 Cultic prostitution

This prohibition is another bald diatribe in Deuteronomy against the pagan practice of associating sexual relations with attaining divine access and favor. The power involved is tied to the energy of fertility and procreation. Further, the mention of any kind of votive offerings indicates rejection of tainted money. This detail deserves comment because it represents in every age monetary or bartered exchange for goods and services, as well as selling a person at a paltry price. The "dog's pay" (v. 19) is especially pejorative. In the Old Testament dogs are dirty scavengers that roam about and interbreed indiscriminately. To call someone a dog is deemed a vile insult (1 Sam 17:43; Ps 22:17).

23:20-21 Interest on loans

As already evident in Deuteronomy, modern standards of social order and justice do not always apply. Such is the case with making loans for profit. In the Scriptures usury among family and community members is frowned upon, while more acceptable and widespread with outsiders. This prohibition guards against the economic exploitation of the Israelite. Further, in any age uneven monetary structures involve conversion rates that can be manipulated for unfair profit (Matt 21:12). Profiting on loans smacks of exploitation, a concern in several aspects of Old Testament literature (Prov 19:17; 28:8; cf. Exod 22:24;

Pss 15:5; 37:26; Ezek 18:7-8). Ideally, a loan is not opportunistic but saves another person from economic disaster.

23:22-24 Keeping vows

In general a vow is a promise to perform or refrain from something that fosters personal happiness and spiritual life. Vows can be private or public. In the Old Testament vows take a variety of forms. For example, Nazirites vow to live a distinct lifestyle that sets them apart and leads them to holiness (Num 6:1-21). Individuals take vows in hope of divine favor or rescue from distress (1 Sam 1:9-11; Ps 66:14). Once made, vows must be fulfilled and are not to be trivialized. To compromise a vow brings on disaster, because such conduct breaks a promise to the Lord (v. 24; cf. Prov 20:25; Eccl 5:4).

23:25-26 Gleaning

This law speaks once more to the theology of ecology. The gifts of the earth come from the Lord and belong to all creatures. A careful balance is offered, i.e., the resident poor and the traveler are fed while the integrity of the owner's property is basically respected. The donee must not cart off what cannot be eaten along the way. A notable example of this tenet is Ruth's gleaning of the field of Boaz (Ruth 2). Such openness represents hospitality, a value in Israel and the broader Greco-Roman world as represented in tales of gods or angels disguised as travelers seeking hospitality (Gen 18:2-8; Tob 5:4; Heb 13:1). This section anticipates Deuteronomy 26 and thanksgiving for the harvest.

24:1-5 Marriage legislation

In Deuteronomy someone cannot remarry his divorced wife who subsequently marries another man. The exact nature of this law is unclear but may represent a desire to preserve the traditional and legal boundaries of marriage, divorce, and adultery. A document of divorce allows a woman to remarry without the penalty of adultery. However, remarriage to a former spouse blurs laws regarding adultery and somehow violates another man's marriage. Jeremiah metaphorically picks up on this theme in relation to prophetic judgment on wayward Israel (Jer 3:1-5).

Exemption from military duty for the newly-wed husband harks back to 20:5-8 where this point is discussed in greater detail, as well as the purity-in-the-camp laws in 23:11-12. Normal bodily functions and willful sexual activities can create ritual impurities in various ways. Further, in the ancient world tales of the perils of newly-weds and even wedding night death are note-worthy (Tob 3:7-9; 8:1-21). But on a positive note, Deuteronomy shows loving concern for those just married. To enjoy a one-year exemption from military service allows a couple to grow closer and perhaps bear a child. Military life includes the possibility of war and death, an eventuality that includes the possibility of widowhood and orphaned children.

24:6 Objects taken in pledge

Goods held in pledge should not impact on the debtor's essential needs. Given the fact that in the ancient world bread was prepared daily from the mill, such seizure disrupts family life. Hence, the millstone is unjust collateral. Meta-phorically, the silence of the grinding mill repre-sents desolation (Jer 25:10; Rev 18:21-22).

24:7 Kidnapping

The matter of holding someone for ransom is probably secondary here. More to the point, sell-ing another Israelite into slavery is an outrage and capital offense (cf. Exod 21:16). Kinship in cove-nant with God precludes such misconduct and is a clear violation of the Ten Commandments.

24:8-9 Skin diseases

In the ancient world this malady was not lim-ited to the modern medical definition of Hansen's disease discovered in the nineteenth century. Any scaly infection was included and referred to the Levitical priests or other authorities for diagnosis and treatment. Laws regarding scaly infection are more fully discussed in Leviticus 13–14. Symp-toms such as flakes and boils were included. Even clothing and dwellings could be condemned as infected (Lev 13:47-59; 14:34-57). Social order and canons of purity/impurity were the driving forces behind such laws, not medical expertise. Moses and Miriam are both remembered as victims of scaly infection and show, respectively, divine power and divine judgment (Exod 4:6-7; Num 12:9-15). The New Testament largely departs from the traditional shunning of persons with a scaly infection, which is a splendid metaphor for Jesus' association with sinners and other outcasts (Matt 10:8; Mark 1:41).

24:10-13 Further on pledges

Collecting debts should not be intrusive or vio-late the canons of honor and shame. By not enter-ing the house, the creditor allows the debtor to have charge of whatever pledge is brought out-side. The home is not violated. Whether actually an observed law or more an expression of charity, to return garments taken in pledge shows sensi-tivity to the poor (v. 17). Clothing is personal, and the poor lack the wardrobe of the wealthy. Cloth-ing also symbolizes one's social status and must not impact the integrity of the community and its worship (Jas 2:2-3).

24:14-15 Just wages

Once again Deuteronomy shows care for the poor, whether native or resident alien. Many people live hand-to-mouth and cannot afford to lose a day's pay due to an unscrupulous employer (Lev 19:13). The prophets railed against defraud-ing the poor (Jer 22:13; Mal 3:5).

In ancient times employment depended on seasonal agricultural conditions, weather, and related factors. Wages were traditionally negoti-ated rather than regulated. Services included such tasks as midwifery, construction, farming, shep-herding, and fishing.

24:16 Individual responsibility

Although seemingly contrary to the spirit of Deuteronomy 5:9, this stipulation is valid. Even though the ancient world had a larger sense of corporate personality than many moderns do, the individual held a level of personal responsibility. Read together, these verses recall the deepest trag-edy of crime, i.e., the individual is responsible, but there are always ramifications for the larger community. Personal guilt and communal guilt are not mutually exclusive.

The Scriptures do not take a single position on sin and punishment. Such is the point of the prov-erb about eating "sour grapes" (Jer 31:29; Ezek 18:2-3). Sirach 15 complements this issue with its sage reflection on free will and the individual conscience.

24:17-22 The memory of Egypt

This section is delimited by the inclusion, "You were slaves in Egypt" (vv. 18, 22). This grand memory is so much a part of Israel's self-understanding. Ransom from Egypt does not involve an exchange of money (7:8; 13:6; cf. Mic 6:4). In the book of Exodus the Lord never speaks to Pharaoh, never negotiates a diplomatic compromise, and basically sets the people free at no cost. In fact, they leave Egypt with impressive spoils (Exod 3:22; 12:36). In the Israelite cult the ransom motif expresses itself in redemption of the firstborn by a sacrificial animal or monetary donation.

This theological perspective provides a motive for the prosperous in Israel to share their wealth. During the harvest allow no second harvest; let the poor glean from the leftover produce. Such virtue shows compassion to the needy and reminds the wealthy of the humble lesson that the land belongs to the Lord.

25:1-3 Human dignity and punishment

The gist of this regulation is the preservation of human dignity when punishing a convicted criminal. A maximum number of stripes sets boundaries that guard against unbridled retribution. Corporal punishment in the ancient world (and much of human history for that matter) was largely a public event intended to warn others and bring shame on the culprit's family. Corporal punishment, especially of children, is more and more questioned today but has wide biblical attestation, particularly in the wisdom literature (Prov 19:29; 26:3; Sir 30:1-13). However, one must not use the Bible to condone gross physical abuse. Such harsh laws must be read in their temporal and cultural context, not cited to rationalize abuses today. For example, the modern sentence of community service is an alternative to corporal punishment or incarceration.

25:4 Animal care

This pithy law harks back to 22:4, 6-7 and reflects the humane treatment of animals. Oxen were valuable animals in the ancient world and a status symbol. Given their size and strength, they were useful for plowing, treading grain, and other agricultural tasks. The New Testament draws on this verse to encourage the communal support of itinerant missionaries and local ministers (1 Cor 9:9; 1 Tim 5:18).

25:5-10 Levirate marriage

The word "Levirate" comes from the Latin word *levir*, "brother-in-law." This practice concerns providing an heir for a man who dies childless. The intent is to preserve the deceased person's name and inheritance via his nearest kinsman. The discussion is divided into two parts (vv. 5-6 and 7-10). The first part relates details of this arrangement and emphasizes maintaining what we call today the nuclear and extended family. Other issues include keeping the widow's dowry in the family and, on a more charitable level, providing her with financial and material security. The second part concerns the kinsman's shirking of Levirate duty. In that case the widow brings her suit to the elders and, if the kinsman remains obstinate, she shames him openly. Her actions serve as a public display of her innocence and his guilt in the matter. Removing his sandal is an invasive gesture by a woman upon a man (cf. vv. 11-12). Spitting is a sign of contempt (Job 30:10; Mark 15:19). Genesis 38:8-18 recounts the death of Onan for not performing the duty of Levirate marriage.

25:11-12 Intervention

This law may seem extreme to the modern reader but is rooted in the violation of gender boundaries, a sociocultural demand in many cultures even today. The severity of the penalty emphasizes the gravity of the offense. The punitive loss of a hand, especially the right one, made the person a social outcast and left visible evidence of a serious criminal act.

25:13-16 Weights and measures

Lacking modern weights and standards, dishonesty in the marketplace was rampant in ancient times and protested by the prophets (Amos 8:5). Retail bargaining was a common if not expected practice. In Deuteronomy fair trade reflects social justice and fosters communal harmony.

25:17-19 The memory of Amalek

This diatribe against Amalek and the Amalekites (a notorious Bedouin tribe) is anachronistic. The group no longer exists by the time of Deuteronomy, so this is not a statute of current relevance. The text speaks more to the Deuteronomic theology of remembering/forgetting. Forget not your enemies and all they did against you during the exodus. The modern reader may take a dim view of this stance. Forgiveness and healing cannot be attained when past abuses and hurts are held onto and handed down to later generations.

26:1-15 Remembrance and thanksgiving

"When . . ." serves to divide this section into two parts (vv. 1, 12). The first part relates to entering the land and offering some of the first fruits as an annual tithe. The second part concerns offering the fruits of the land in a triennial tithe. As stated earlier (14:22-29), tithes are portions set aside for sacred rites and services. Verses 1-11 highlight remembrance of past oppression, the exodus, and entrance into the Promised Land. The first fruits of the land are gifts from the Lord and thus holy. Without a symbolic ritual offering as return to the Lord, blessing on the rest of the crops is at risk. The prosperous must invite the disenfranchised and needy to their celebrations of the harvest.

Verses 12-15 relate a local triennial celebration that emphasizes sharing stored foods with those most at risk. It is noteworthy that again in Deuteronomy the traditional classes of needy persons are cited (v. 12). The prayer (vv. 13-15) summarizes the spirit of this cultic law. The prayer includes three denials that distance the Israelite from what represents foreign practice, i.e., eating the tithes of a mourner, personal uncleanness in the cult, and making death offerings. The person has obeyed the voice of the Lord (v. 14, literally "listened to"), a common biblical phrase that emphasizes obedience. The prayer ends with a plea for continued blessing in the Promised Land.

26:16-19 Covenant as time of decision

This point in Moses' second address is punctuated by the threefold repetition of "this day" or "today" (vv. 16, 17, 18). Now is the opportune time to rededicate oneself to the commandments and life in covenant. The narrative is also highlighted by motifs from earlier in Deuteronomy: today is the time of decision (5:1) for Israel is the Lord's own people (7:6; 14:2). Such repetitions serve to emphasize key teachings in Deuteronomy. Finally, true religion is rewarded by divine favor and the esteem of surrounding nations (v. 19).

27:1–28:69 At the border of the land

With the people about to cross the Jordan River, the narrative reemphasizes curses and

blessings. The assertions are oriented toward the future, from the day the people cross the Jordan (v. 2). Subsequent generations must learn and heed what the ancestors swore to embrace as they entered the Promised Land.

This section recalls the grand story of passing through the Sea of Reeds (Exod 13:17–15:27). Both sea and river share symbolic value in the saga of Israel. Wandering eastward, the people leave Egypt on their journey from slavery to freedom. The Promised Land is ever the destination during the symbolic forty years of wandering and murmuring. Now they turn back and journey westward across the Jordan and enter the land. Crossing water is a key geographical and intertextual link between the exodus and entrance into Canaan.

27:1-13 Crossing the Jordan

The Jordan is mentioned three times (vv. 2, 4, 11). The first citation of the river relates to the writing of the Deuteronomic laws on plastered stones, an event that is to take place immediately after the people cross over. The second citation calls for a stone altar of sacrifice on Mount Ebal (by Shechem and Mount Gerizim). The third citation juxtaposes the two mountains, Ebal and Gerizim, as staging points for the ritual announcement of curses and blessings by members of the twelve tribes. In the Bible the Jordan is a geographical locus and memorial marker for a variety of important events (Gen 50:10-11; Josh 12:1-24; Matt 3:13-17; Mark 10:1).

27:14–28:69 Curses and blessings in the land

Interspersed with other material, a litany of curses and blessings informs this section. The pronouncements are in random order and touch on a variety of topics.

27:14-26 Twelve curses

A number of Hebrew words denote a curse. The verb here (Hebrew *'arar*) has the semantic range of casting spells, banning persons or things, and the withdrawal of some strength or benefit. It is noteworthy that the element of secrecy is included in the curses (vv. 15, 24). Even when not explicitly defined as secret, a number of the curses imply stealth (e.g., vv. 17, 18, 20, 25).

In Israelite thought the power of a curse (or blessing) is rooted not in the human person but in the holiness of God and divine will. The "Amen" response to each one proclaims these laws as steadfast truths.

28:1-14 A pattern of blessings

Blessing brings prosperity and is connected to hearing the Lord's voice (vv. 1, 2; cf. v. 15 on curse). These blessings are artfully presented in a merism, a figure of speech that cites extremes but presumes everything between them (e.g., high and low, young and old). Blessing is caught up in fertility of the soil and the womb, bringing forth plant and animal life in all its forms. However, in ancient thought plants were deemed not to be alive because they did not move about. Verses 7-14 elaborate on some specific benefits of blessing: victory over the enemy and international renown. These favors are contingent on keeping the Deuteronomic laws (v. 9). Ideally, divine blessing is associated with peace among the nations, despite the pervasive presence of war in the Old Testament.

Picking up from 11:10-17, rain nourishes the land in due season (v. 12). In the Scriptures the Lord is the one who causes rain and the one who makes possible life and happiness in the Promised Land (Deut 11:10-17; cf. Job 28:26; Jer 14:22).

28:15-69 Curses for disobedience

This lengthy section begins with another series of curses (vv. 16-19) that contrast with the blessings cited above. Moses' second address ends on a negative note but also serves as a firm exhortation to obedience. Although not outright apocalyptic, the language borders on this genre as depicted in the book of Revelation.

Among the overarching themes and motifs depicted here, several are notable. First, the repetition of the voice of the Lord (vv. 15, 45) and rain (v. 24) stitch the narrative to the motif of blessing discussed above. Second, the horrific physical afflictions and other disasters recall the plagues in Exodus 7–11 and the more historically proximate sieges of Jerusalem (597–587 B.C.) surrounding the Babylonian exile. Third, oppression connotes speaking falsely of or doing wrong to another, especially by extortion (Lev 19:11; Ps 146:7). Fourth, exile and indentured service are symbolized by the yoke (v. 48), a fitting motif for oppression as a consequence of sin. However, in the Scriptures the yoke also has a positive meaning

when one hears the voice of the Lord and lives rightly (Sir 6:24-26; Matt 11:28-30).

MOSES' THIRD ADDRESS

Deuteronomy 29:1–32:52

This address is informed by the theme of time, i.e., past favors from the Lord, the current exhortation to fidelity, and what lies in the future. In sum, the speech is sweeping and comprehensive in scope. The gist of the address is a call to decision: "See, I have today set before you life and good, death and evil . . . Choose life . . ." (30:15-19).

29:1-8 Remembering the past

This brief section repeats elements of Israel's saga noted already, namely, Egyptian exile and exodus, wandering in the wilderness, and conquest of the Promised Land. Divine care is remembered as a constant on the journey. The mention of clothing in verses 4-5 reminds the reader of the Lord's tender care in spite of sin. Adam and Eve exit Eden not dressed in fig leaves but dressed by the Lord in durable leather garments (Gen 3:21); Cain is marked against random human retribution (Gen 4:15). Later, in the long wilderness experience, Israel's needs are met through divine power (Exod 16–17).

All these blessings inform the people's knowledge of God who manifests divine will in promise, election, covenant, and law. Deuteronomy echoes that Israel comes to know the Lord in the course of remembering and retelling (Exod 7:17; 11:7).

29:9-14 Assembling in the present

Deuteronomy again emphasizes Israel's covenant relationship. Here the people stand before the Lord and renew their obligations. To stand (v. 9; literally, "take one's stand") bespeaks a certain purposefulness, being appointed to fulfill a duty. The people must take courage, for the Lord goes forth with them and is ever present to them, even when the Lord is seemingly hidden or absent.

29:15–30:20 Fidelity in the future

As the book of Deuteronomy draws to a close, future generations are emphasized (29:21). In Hebrew a generation (*dôr*; literally, "circle") spans about forty years. Covenant abides through the cycle of life, beginning with the ancestor Abraham

(Gen 17:7) and later figures. Hence, the covenant people must shun idolatry and other forms of syncretism. The explicit command against idols of wood and stone (29:16; cf. 7:5, 25) sets Israel apart from its neighbors. The theological diatribe behind this law is more than simply the fashioning of religious objects. In the ancient world gods were deemed somehow present within the figure and experienced that object's fate. Hence, statues, divination figurines, etc., could be kidnapped (Gen 31:19-35) and people actually harmed in the object's destruction (1 Sam 5:1-5). Even though early Israelite tradition acknowledged the existence of other gods, later tradition took a firmer stance that satirized pagan iconography (Ps 115:4-8).

Coming generations must not become complacent in the land. Divine wrath is powerful and effective (29:22, 27). Most references to anger in the Old Testament have God as the subject and God's responding to Israel's sinning. Yet, divine wrath is balanced by divine love (Exod 34:6-7; Ps 103:8-10).

The allusions to dispersion, scattering, and return refer to exile (30:1-7). Rhetorically, Israel is asked, "What have you learned? What will you do now in light of experience?" God's great act of love in renewal is circumcising their hearts (30:6). The physical act of circumcision distinguishes Israel from its neighbors, but inner disposition is equally important. As noted earlier, a positive change of heart is behind this metaphor and echoed elsewhere in the Scriptures (10:16; Jer 4:4; 9:25; cf. Rom 2:29).

Now Deuteronomy reaches its climax in a moment of decision. Israel must choose life (30:19). In doing so the people must keep the commandments for blessings in the land. Decision is highlighted by extremes, i.e., life and prosperity or death and doom. Moses' call to heaven and earth as witnesses (30:19; cf. 21:1) reflects an element in ancient Near Eastern treaties. Powerful and potentially violent forces in creation will mete out retributive justice on the noncompliant party.

The exhortation emphasizes that choice is a demand for every generation, not simply a perfunctory covenant renewal ceremony recounting the past and answered by lip service. In this regard, it is noteworthy that the people do not audibly respond to Moses' speech here. "Choice" remains a perennial question and awaited re-

sponse. This pattern contrasts with the collective response of "Amen" to curses and blessings (e.g., 27:14-26).

31:1–32:52 The legacy of Moses

Now the death of Moses begins to unfold. There is a sense of peace and security amid the impending turn of events. Whatever happens, the Lord marches with the Israelites and will never forsake them (20:3-4; 31:6). Joshua is commissioned to lead the conquest and tribal allotment of Canaan. He is greatly revered in later Old Testament literature (Sir 46:1-7).

Between Joshua's call and commission, a reading of the law is mandated before the full assembly (31:9-13). This is a grand and broadly inclusive liturgical event. A key admonition is, once again, to teach the law to their children lest its memory and observance be lost.

As Moses prepares the people for an orchestrated transfer of leadership to Joshua, the narrative is highlighted by references to "that time" (literally, "that day," 31:17 [2x], 18; cf. v. 21). Verses 17-18 say that divine wrath is an appropriate response to the people's disobedience, which has already occurred and is to be expected in the future. At the same time, all is right at this sacred moment. The Lord remains present to the people (Exod 3:12).

32:1-43 The Song of Moses

This song has a juridical color, akin to the ancient *rîb* or covenant lawsuit leveled by the Lord against Israel. The *rîb* is a basic form of prophetic speech (Mic 6:1-8). Heaven and earth are called as witnesses, and the disobedience of the people is contrasted to the fidelity of the Lord. Israel is accused, "Yet his degenerate children have treated him basely . . ." (v. 5), and called to remembrance, "Remember the days of old . . ." (v. 7). Divine loyalty is expressed in rich poetic imagery that echoes other biblical passages. God protects Israel on the wilderness journey, metaphorically spreads wings like an eagle (Exod 19:4), and blesses them with gifts from the earth.

The song is artfully informed by the eightfold repetition of "rock" (vv. 4, 13, 15, 18, 30, 31[2x], 37). This motif is often a title of God and here emphasizes the Lord's faultless deeds, divine sustenance in the wilderness, and incomparability before the gods. Rock, a hard element sometimes an instrument of violence, is balanced by its association with a softer motherly imagery, "the Rock that begot you" (32:18; cf. Ps 18). The reference to God as "father" is rare in the Old Testament (v. 6; cf. Ps 103:13; Prov 3:12).

Moses gets to view the Promised Land from across the Jordan before his death (32:48-52; cf. Num 27:12-14). This moment is full of pathos. After his great legacy— the call and commission at the burning bush, confrontation with Pharaoh, leading a murmuring people through the Red Sea and during the wilderness experience—Moses never enters Canaan. Divine freedom remains a mystery amid justice and mercy.

Moses' death outside the land is punishment for disobedience in the priestly (P) tradition; in the Deuteronomic (D) tradition Moses dies by taking on the sins of the people (1:37-38; 3:23-29). His burial is recorded as on Mount Nebo. The name Nebo is often associated with a Semitic root for height and geographically located at a site some 2,700 feet above sea level. Such a vantage point offers a spectacular and panoramic view of the Promised Land.

MOSES' FOURTH ADDRESS

Deuteronomy 33:1–34:12

33:1-29 Blessing upon the tribes

The poem is a final eulogy to the ancient tribes. It is delimited by praise of the Lord (vv. 2-5, 26-29) and particularly the repetition of "Jeshurun," an obscure Hebrew name meaning "upright" (vv. 5, 26; see 32:15; Isa 44:2). This name is considered by some commentators to be a poetic term of endearment for Israel because of the similarity in sound between the names Jacob, Israel, and Jerusalem in Hebrew. Curiously, Simeon is not included among the twelve tribes, and the number is balanced by Joseph praised as Ephraim and Manasseh.

Bodily imagery pervades the blessing; the Lord is present with hand and foot (vv. 3, 7), favor falls on the head and brow of Joseph (v. 16), and Gad seizes the arm and head of prey like a lion.

34:1-8 Death and burial of Moses

This section harks back to 3:23-29 and the denial of Moses' entry to the Promised Land. The book of Deuteronomy now comes full circle. The

carefully cited geographical details speak to the cherished memory of Moses (1:1-5). Moses' burial site is unknown today. He is memorialized as a robust man who never succumbed to the vagaries of premature death and physical aging. He was blessed with divine favor in life and fondly remembered in death. Such a life is extolled in the psalms (Pss 39:5-8; 62:10; 128:5-6).

34:9-12 Praise of Joshua and Moses

Joshua is characterized as filled with the spirit of wisdom, a fitting gift from his mentor Moses. Wisdom is the gift of knowing how to live well in the world and attain the fullness of life. Sages are to teach their students well, as does Moses in the book of Deuteronomy.

Apart from the other models of Moses in the Scriptures (liberator, model of humility, judge, priest, and king), here his role as prophet is again accented. He is incomparable in his prophetic vocation. Like the classic Old Testament prophets, he serves the Lord in word and deed; he also suffers in his mission (Jer 37:15). His characterization in the Scriptures remains an abiding paradigm of service to the Lord, even amid the twists and turns of human frailty and sin.

These final verses in the book of Deuteronomy succinctly describe Moses. He performs signs and wonders before the Egyptian Pharaoh and manages to gain the trust of reluctant Hebrew slaves. At first a reluctant leader himself, he eventually comes into his own. In Deuteronomy his confidence shines.

The end of Deuteronomy is punctuated by the sixfold repetition of "all" (the Hebrew *kōl* is omitted in some translations). Moses is incomparable in *all* signs and wonders against Pharaoh and *all* his servants in *all* his land, as well as *all* the great might and *all* awesome power displayed before *all* Israel (vv. 11-12). The legacy of Moses is timeless.

To conclude, the book of Deuteronomy is both about the law and Moses the lawgiver. The book exhibits a complexity akin to human nature, i.e., nothing is simply two-dimensional; there are always contradictions and shadow sides. Hence, Deuteronomy exhorts care of the widow, orphan, resident alien, and Levite, while also presenting a plan of conquest that wipes out indigenous peoples. In the Ten Commandments wives are a separate category from other goods, but women are still in some sense a man's property. These and other realities offer material for reflection in the review aids and discussion topics below.

By New Testament times the role of Moses as the great lawgiver becomes paradigmatic. The canonical status of the torah in early Judaism makes Moses a key figure, and the New Testament gospels make clear parallels between Jesus and Moses. For example, Jesus' Sermon on the Mount mirrors Moses as lawgiver on Mount Sinai/Horeb. The Transfiguration places Jesus amidst Moses and Elijah, who were, respectively, the great lawgiver and the most esteemed prophet in Israel (Matt 17:1-8; Mark 9:2-8; Luke 9:28-36).

THE BOOK OF
JOSHUA

Roland J. Faley, T.O.R.

INTRODUCTION

The book takes its name from its central character, Joshua, son of Nun, the faithful aide of Moses. He is the designated leader of the Hebrew people as they take possession of Canaan, the Promised Land. In him the leadership of Moses finds its continuation, even to the point of echoing moments of the Mosaic exodus, the crossing of the Jordan (Red Sea) (chs. 3–4) and the renewal of the covenant at Shechem (Sinai) (ch. 24).

In the figure of Joshua, the author(s) of the book continues the early history of Israel, recounting the fulfillment of the promise of land possession, a promise which stands at the heart of the Deuteronomistic history.

The Deuteronomistic History

Although complete in itself, the book of Joshua is actually part of a much longer historical record which proceeds from a particular school of religious thought. As is commonly held today, the book of Deuteronomy served as the inspiration for the historical books which follow it, viz., Joshua, Judges, 1–2 Samuel, and 1–2 Kings. It is the theological perspective of that fifth book of Torah which colors the entire history of Israel from the occupation to the time of the Babylonian exile. That viewpoint can be summarized in the oft-repeated admonition: Fidelity to the Lord's commands brings success, while infidelity brings only failure and rejection (Deut 5:32; 6:24f; 7:4). It is against this background that the dominantly successful career of Joshua is judged.

The record of this history was long in the making, extending over six centuries and comprised of various documents and sources (not all of them in total agreement). If any moment was central in this process, it would have to be the reign of King Josiah (620–609 B.C.) who inaugurated a reform strongly influenced by the thinking of Deuteronomy. In fact, the discovery of a lost book of laws at the time of Josiah's temple renovations (2 Kings 22) is often identified by scholars as an early copy of Deuteronomy. Whatever the evolution of this historical corpus may have been, the final result is clear enough. The accounts of the Israelite monarchy and its precedents, extending back to the twelfth century B.C., provided the Deuteronomists with a framework in which to explain the country's successes and failures from a distinctly theological point of view. If the Assyrians were to destroy the Northern Kingdom of Israel in the eighth century B.C. and Babylon were to do the same in the sixth, the reason was not military or political inferiority but the failure of the Israelites to live as a sacred, covenanted people.

The final editing of the Deuteronomistic History, which included Joshua, comes from a period shortly after the destruction of Jerusalem in 587–586 B.C.

The theology of Joshua

It is the religious perspective on Israel's successes and failures that permeates the book of Joshua. If the occupation of Canaan was marked by success in the invaders' military undertakings, this was simply due to their obedience to the Lord's directives.

The book of Joshua brings to fulfillment the promise initially made to Abraham. That promise was twofold: many descendants and the making of a great nation (Gen 12:2ff). It is with the last part of that promise that this book primarily deals, i.e., the occupation of Canaan, the land of promise.

Covenant fidelity, so important to the Deuteronomist, is centered principally in this book on the first precept of the Decalogue, i.e., the exclusion of false deities. Canaan was a land wherein foreign cult abounded, especially the worship of fertility gods. It is clear throughout that the Hebrews are to see any form of religious compromise as categorically excluded. To underscore the exclusivity of YHWH's sovereignty the book ends with a ceremony of covenant renewal.

The book's division

There are two main sections of Joshua, the first dealing with the occupation of the land of Canaan (chs. 1–12), and the second with the distribution of the land to the twelve tribes (chs. 13–21). The final chapters deal with a dispute regarding a Transjordanian altar (ch. 22), the renewal of the covenant, and the death of Joshua (chs. 23–24). The account of the occupation does not extend to the entire territory which later made up the country but is more limited and centered around the land of the tribe of Benjamin. The documentation underlying this narrative of seizure is considered very ancient, probably dating from the twelfth century, whereas the text dealing with land distribution dates from the time of the established monarchy.

Joshua and history

When it comes to a historical appraisal of the Joshua narrative, the reader must proceed with a measure of caution. The book forms part of the "historical" literature primarily because it is a broad record of the country's origins and early development. That is not to make of it a totally objective picture of what actually transpired, refraining for the moment from the question of whether historical accounts are ever objective. The book, for example, presents the occupation of Canaan in lightning fashion, with little or no strong military opposition. That the actual occupation was a much slower process of elimination and incorporation is evident from both biblical (see Judg 1–3) and extra-biblical sources. The destruction of Jericho and Ai is evidently more idealistic than real, with archeological evidence pointing to no significant occupation of those cities during the period of the Israelite incursion. As we shall see, there are other instances of difficulty in squaring the biblical data with other historical sources. What is intractable, however, is the appearance of the Hebrews in Palestine in the twelfth century B.C.

All of this is but to say that a theological perspective is dominant in this and the other historical books of the Old Testament. The land was a gift of the covenant God to the Israelite population and, regardless of the actual circumstances that made this a reality, the basic belief is never compromised. This accounts for the marked idealization which is present in the story of the occupation.

The figure of Joshua

While Joshua was certainly a towering figure at the time of the conquest, historical accuracy does not permit us to see him as responsible for all the remarkable strides taken in the book that bears his name. He is presented as the idealized hero of the conquest and the one who presided over the subsequent distribution of the land. But the fact is that much of the activity presented in the first twelve chapters is localized, largely related to the single tribe of Benjamin and its sanctuary at Gilgal. The land of Canaan was brought under control only after a century of Israelite expansion, and the account of the allotment of the land largely reflects the period of the monarchy.

Yet in all of this Joshua stands as a larger than life figure. Not unlike Moses, he has been drawn to some events recorded in this book more in spirit than in fact. It is under the mantle of his leadership that the events of the occupation of the land find their appropriate setting.

COMMENTARY

POSSESSION OF THE LAND

Joshua 1–12

1:1-18 Preparatory injunctions

The chapter is clearly Deuteronomistic in character and style: YHWH's assurance of success in return for law observance (1:1-9); Joshua's injunction to prepare for the conquest (1:10-11); and the admonition to the three Transjordanian tribes to participate in the military action (1:12-18).

In the promise of divine protection and the injunction to fidelity (1:3-7. cf. Deut 30:15-20), there are elements of both the real (v. 3) and the ideal (v. 4), with the latter granting borders extending from the Mediterranean in the west to the Euphrates in the east. The law to be strictly observed (1:7-8) is that enunciated by Moses after the battle of Sihon and Og (Deut 1:3-5) and later in its written form to be read in assembly every seven years (Deut 31:9-11). It is the book of Deuteronomy which is intended.

Joshua allows three days of preparation prior to the Jordan crossing from the east, the locale of Moses' death at Nebo at the conclusion of Deuteronomy (1:10-11). The injunction to the three tribes—Reuben, Gad, and one half of Manasseh—is based on an important historical antecedent (1:12-18). These tribes settled in Transjordan and never occupied "the land of Canaan" properly so called (Deut 3:12-20). However, their legitimate status as part of Israel is repeatedly brought to the fore in underscoring the part they played in the occupation. They were not excused from military duty in bringing the Canaanites into subjection. In their submissive response to Joshua's exhortation (1:16-18), they echo the customary response of the covenanted people.

2:1-24 Rahab and the spies

The heroic action of the harlot Rahab wins her recognition in both Testaments (cf. Heb 11:31; Jas 2:25) and finds her a place in the genealogy of Jesus (Matt 1:5).

The account, which has experienced a process of editorial redaction, revolves entirely around the person of Rahab, the only person identified by name. Its present location argues for its independent origin, now located somewhat artificially between the preparations for occupation (ch. 1)

and its beginning (ch. 3). Joshua's spies are sent to reconnoiter the enemy terrain. In the course of the actual battle, all enemy forces, military or civilian, were to be destroyed. The present narrative explains why one family, "the house of Rahab," was ultimately saved. This may well be the original reason for its preservation.

In addition, it represents the conflict between two forces: the pagan king of Jericho and the faith-filled Hebrews under Joshua. These two forces converge dramatically around the person of Rahab, who handles both with consummate cunning. She deceives the king's emissaries in the matter of the spies' whereabouts and sends them on a vain pursuit (2:3-5). She protects the Israelite spies by hiding them in the flax stalks drying on her roof prior to their being made into linen (2:6). She wrests from them assurance of future protection for herself and her family (2:13-14). Her plan succeeds and the spies are saved. The conflict between the two forces of the chapter clearly points to success for the invaders and destruction for the inhabitants.

Finally, the story is cast in a faith-filled mold, reflecting the final stage of its composition. Rahab recognizes the God of the Hebrews (2:9) and recalls his saving action in the exodus (2:10). It is in recognition of YHWH's power and might that she asks for her own deliverance (2:11-12). The departing spies agree to her request but, in Deuteronomistic form, with certain conditions. The scarlet cord is to be exposed and none of her relatives are to leave the house (2:18-19). The experience shores up the confidence of the spies, who in returning to Joshua assure him of success (2:22-24).

3:1–4:24 The crossing of the Jordan

The crossing begins at Shittim (3:1) or Abel-shittim (Num 33:49), east of the Jordan, and concludes at Gilgal, later an important cultic site, east of Jericho. What is presented is primarily a liturgical procession, situating the historical event in what later became a cultic celebration of the crossing. The underlying sources of the narrative are complex and intertwined although the story line itself remains clear enough. In various ways it is a theological duplicate of the Exodus-Sinai experience.

3:1-17 Preparation and crossing

The pre-crossing injunctions are Deuterono-mistic in character. The order for the people to "sanctify" themselves involved ritual washing and even abstinence from sexual intercourse (3:2-5; Exod 19:10-14). The ark of the covenant, the throne or footstool of the invisible Yhwh also contained the tablets of the law. A reverent distance separated the ark from the people, excluding any physical contact (Exod 19:12; 2 Sam 6:6-7). The role of Levitical priests as ark-bearers at this early stage may be later editorializing, in substitution for the twelve men who were originally designated (3:12). The combination of different sources makes it difficult to distinguish between the role of the priests and the twelve laymen.

The occupation is to bring to Joshua the type of recognition reserved for Moses, the original deliverer of God's people (3:6-7; 4:14). The presence of the ark highlights the intervention of Yhwh. As the priests reach the river's edge, the waters recede and dry land appears (3:13). An interesting sidelight is the mention of various peoples that occupied Canaan at the time, pointing to the fact that it was not only native Canaanites who were dispossessed (3:10). In fact, the term Canaanite was frequently used for the various ethnic groups occupying the country. In this listing the Hittites were a non-Semitic people known in the south from the time of Abraham (Gen 23:10). The Amorites were well known from pre-Israelite times. The Jebusites occupied Jerusalem. The Hivites are sometimes identified with the known Hurrians, and the Perizzites and Girgasites, generally unidentified.

The crossing takes place at the time of the spring harvest (3:15), coinciding with the time of Passover (5:10). It was a season when the Jordan was swollen from spring rains and the melting snow of Mt. Hermon. The passage of the people is facilitated as the priests and the ark remain motionless in the bed of the river (3:10-13). The account is evocative of Israel's earlier passing through the Red Sea (Exod 14).

4:1-24 The remembrance

Etiology—a way of explaining the causes or origins of something that occurs later—is central to any understanding of much of Old Testament narrative. This is a linkage between memorials or important sites and historical events in the life of the people. The site then served to evoke the memory. The collection of stones from the Jordan, linked with the Gilgal sanctuary, so important to the Benjaminite tradition, became a concrete reminder of the Jordan crossing. It is also a refrain from the Exodus-Sinai experience when twelve pillars were erected to commemorate the covenant with the twelve tribes (Exod 24:4). It would also seem that two traditions are combined in this chapter, the one centering on the memorial stones at Gilgal, the other on the stones set up in the Jordan itself (4:9). The full complement of the people, including the military forces, then complete the crossing (4:10-13), with the Deuteronomist not failing to mention the cooperation of the three Transjordanian tribes (4:12).

Speculation centers on the historical character of the event and the possibility of an unforeseen landslide blocking the flow of water, thus making the passage possible. Such a fortuitous occurrence at the right moment would retain its "miraculous" character. But beyond all of that is the recognition that this is primarily a theological statement, not historical replay. The ark is a clear sign of Yhwh's ongoing protection of his people. The earlier crossing of the Red Sea and the Jordan passage form parallel brackets incorporating this central idea (4:23-24).

5:1-15 Arrival in Canaan

Three unrelated events are woven together with the exodus theme as the thread. These are the circumcision ritual (5:2-9), the Passover celebration (5:10-12), and the vision of the warrior God (5:13-15).

The battle lines are clearly drawn at the chapter's beginning (and the favorable outcome foreshadowed; 5:1). According to Jewish law only the circumcised could eat the Passover (Exod 12:43-49). In a stylized, even too tidy, presentation of the data, there were no circumcised Hebrews at this point since those who had departed Egypt were now deceased and the rite had never been performed on their sons (5:2-8). This called for a performance of the rite. Two theories are at work here to explain the site of this ritual, both centering around Gilgal. The first gives a popular explanation for a site known as Gibeath-haaraioth, "hill of the foreskins" (5:2-4). This is, however, only loosely connected with Gilgal, even phonetically, but it may have been a more primitive name of the site. Another possible origin is more closely related to the sanctuary after the circumcision is completed and the pagan state of uncircumcision removed (5:8-9); "I have removed" or "rolled away" employs the Hebrew verb *gallothi* in a very free allusion to Gilgal. The actual meaning of Gilgal is probably related to a "circle of stones."

The ritual of a later time appears in the account of the Passover (5:10-12). *Pesah* or Passover was originally a nomadic or pastoral feast, centering on the killing and eating of the spring lamb; Unleavened Bread was an agricultural feast joined to Passover only after the period of occupation, with bread eaten in its pure unfermented state. Here by retrojection the combined ritual is remanded to the time of the crossing, just as had been done in relating the exodus experience itself (Exod 12). In addition, now that the land of plenty has been reached there is no need for the miraculous manna formerly provided.

The heavenly warrior who appears to Joshua (5:13-15) is clearly YHWH himself, visible to humankind only in some form of apparition (Gen 18). This is a replay of Moses' experience at the burning bush; the command to remove the sandals is practically identical (Exod 3:4-10). Gideon will have a similar experience (Judg 6). Again Joshua's status is elevated and the stage is set for the subsequent battle in which the "warrior God," the leader of the heavenly forces, is the protagonist.

Standing now on covenant soil and with the sacred events of the past recaptured, the Hebrews are poised for the conquest.

6:1-27 The siege of Jericho

There is probably no other biblical battle that has attained the notoriety of Jericho. And yet it is a narrative beset with historical and literary problems. The first thing to note is that there was no battle. The city was besieged and the walls collapsed. In addition, few biblical sites have received as much archeological attention, even as late as the 1950s. Although much has been recovered, the evidence points to Jericho having been destroyed centuries before the Hebrew incursion. It seems clear that the Jericho which Joshua found was already in ruins.

There are a number of sources underlying the narrative, with overlapping inconsistencies. The ark for example, so important for the victory, receives no mention after verse 13. Was there one set of trumpeters or two (6:8-9, 13)? Was there a constant din in the horn blasts (6:13) or silence until the single blast gave the signal to shout (6:16, 20)? There are doublets as well, e.g., the shout of the people (6:16, 20) and the injunction to save Rahab (6:17, 22).

The account is primarily theological. That Canaan eventually became the land of the Hebrews is incontestable. That this was accomplished by the power and protection of YHWH is central to Israel's belief. This is all reflected in the conquest of Jericho. A city already in ruins could very well have become a symbol of the entire conquest. The account is more liturgical than military: the role of the ark (6:6), the priests with the trumpets (6:8), the procession around the city walls (6:7), the significant biblical number seven (6:13), and the shout of the people (6:20). The siege takes place with no military intervention. The Hebrews see the walls fall; they storm the city; and victory is theirs. This was accomplished because of their obedience to YHWH in every detail. No life was lost; no damage experienced.

The notion of *herem* or "the ban" is alien to modern thought (6:18-19). Evil was the antithesis of YHWH himself. Its force had to be eliminated or kept at a distance lest it affect God's people. Evil was seen as infectious and had to be rooted out (Deut 7:1-4); this meant people, livestock, and property (Deut 13:13-19). In the case of Jericho, only the precious metals were to be saved and placed in the sacred treasury, an anachronistic reference to the later constructed temple (6:19).

There are a number of etiologies in the narrative. The deliverance of Rahab and her family explained the later custom of allowing non-Israelite peoples to live in the community (6:22-24); the prohibition to rebuild Jericho alludes to the precept violated during the reign of Ahab (6:26; 1 Kgs 16:34); the central etiology probably explained the ruins of Jericho itself. If Jericho was already in ruins at the time of the occupation, it could well have taken on the symbolism of a fallen country. For this reason it was never to be rebuilt.

In their initial foray the Hebrews met an unqualified success, always by the power of YHWH, the "warrior God."

7:1-24 Defeat at Ai

The sin of Achan is related to the defeat and subsequent victory at Ai (ch. 8) but was probably originally an independent tradition. It tells the story of a single person's disobedience in taking goods that were under the ban (7:1; cf. 6:15-19), and the first defeat of the Hebrews as a result (7:2-9). The guilty man pays for the crime with his life and only then is the reproach lifted (7:16-24). The event may well have been originally associated with another time and place and later attached to the Ai campaign. It serves well the Deuteronomist's theme of inevitable punishment following upon evil.

Joshua's scouts are sent to reconnoiter sites in the interior and central part of the country, in the region of Bethel (7:2). This leads them to the city of Ai and leads us to another historical quandary. Excavated in the last century, Ai, as its name signifies, was a long standing "ruin" by the time of the Hebrew invasion. Once again the name "Ruins" theologically suggests an important battle took place there. But the forces of Ai rout the Hebrews, killing thirty-six warriors and causing the first Israelite defeat (7:4-5).

This was a defeat viewed in ethical terms. Joshua is unable to explain the defeat (7:6-9), but YHWH explains it is due to moral default (7:10-15). In the theft of goods under the ban, the contagion of evil reached the people as a whole. Success will only come when the sin is excised at its core. The people must first go through purification rites (7:13; cf. 3:5), then through a process of elimination to determine the guilty party.

By narrowing possibilities by tribe, clan, and family, in casting sacred lots (1 Sam 14:38-42), Achan emerges as the sinner (7:16-23). After the restoration of the sacred booty, he, along with his family and possessions, is taken away and stoned in a classic example of sin spreading its contagious net. The death not only of the culprit but his entire retinue is an example of solidarity in guilt.

A twofold significance is attached to the site of the death of Achan. His name is connected with the place, Achor (Hebrew for "misery"; cf. 7:25), and a heap of stones at the site recalling his death (7:26). This location later separated the territories of Benjamin and Judah, the latter being Achan's tribe of origin (7:1).

8:1-35 The conquest of Ai

At Jericho there had been no military action; at Ai, there is, with the capture centering on an ambush of the city. With moral guilt now removed, victory is in the hands of the Israelites. At the Lord's injunction, the Hebrews are to destroy the city and its inhabitants. However, unlike Jericho, the ban is not total; booty is permitted from livestock and possessions (8:1-3). As happens frequently, the number of soldiers is evidently inflated (8:3; some texts read three thousand). Joshua gives orders for an ambush. Some troops are to remain concealed, while Joshua and his party draw the enemy forces out of the city. Once the city's forces have been sufficiently diminished, the concealed troops are to besiege and burn the stronghold (8:3-9).

The tactic is executed exactly as planned (8:10-15). That victory belongs to the Lord is reflected in Joshua's extended javelin, a parallel to Moses' earlier posture during battle (8:18, 26; Exod 17:8-13). With the city destroyed and the booty taken, the dead king is exposed but only till sunset (Deut 21:22-23). His burial place remains a permanent reminder (8:29), just as the ruins of Ai speak permanently of the sacred conquest.

The historical problem present in the capture of Jericho appears again at Ai. If the settlement is to be identified with the present day el-Tell, a site slightly southeast of Bethel, as many scholars maintain, there is no support for its existence at the time of the conquest. The archeological findings indicate that it was destroyed in about 2000 B.C. and had a limited resettlement for about two centuries after 1200 B.C. The occupation at that later time may well have been Israelite, or more specifically Benjaminite.

The Joshua narrative, then, would be largely based on the end result of the conquest. It would have been composed as a composite of historical memories dealing with various battles and etiologies connected with important sites. It is also suggested that a later Israelite presence there would have found its justification in the limitations placed on the destruction of property in the story (8:1-2). Joshua then became the over-arching victor with his javelin extended in Moses-like fashion.

The ceremonial conclusion (8:30-35) carries out the injunction of Moses (Deut 27) and is clearly Deuteronomistic in character. If historically accurate it would posit a major jump into Canaanite territory some twenty miles to the north. It may actually date from a later time; it takes place in the region of Shechem, the place of covenant renewal in chapter 24. Shechem, standing between Mt. Ebal and Mt. Gerizim, is where this ceremony seems to have taken place (see v. 33) rather than on Mt. Ebal (8:30). There is an altar constructed from uncut stone (Exod 20:25), a sacrifice, and the reading of the law (8:30-35).

The reading of the law is strongly Deuteronomistic in fulfilling the directive of Deuteronomy 27. At this religious high point, Joshua and all the people assemble in the presence of the ark to offer sacrifice and listen to the law of the Lord. There are the blessings and curses (8:34; Deut 28); more than simple utterances, they are truly effective instruments of prosperity or destruction.

9:1-27 The alliance with Gibeon

The dealings at Gibeon bring the Israelites into the central hill country. It lay only ten miles north of Jerusalem. It appears repeatedly in the Old Testament as one of the cities of Benjamin (18:25); it was a Levitical city (21:17) and the scene of warfare in the time of Samuel (2 Sam 2:12-16; 20:4-13). It became an important cultic site by the time of Solomon (1 Kgs 3:4).

This chapter contains the Gibeonite ruse to deceive Joshua (9:1-15) and the subordination treaty made with them. A number of etiologies come into play. It explains how this part of the central hill country came into Israelite control. Like the story of Rahab, it explains the peaceful coexistence between Israel and certain foreign peoples, despite the order of extermination (Deut 7:1-2). Joshua is the central figure (9:6, 8, 15), with another tradition highlighting the community leaders (9:7, 14, 16). Although Gibeon is central, other cities are mentioned as well. Even though certain features of the deception strain its credibility, the story is well told. The reference to the Gibeonites as Hivites relates them to a larger ethnic body; at another point they are also termed Amorites (2 Sam 21:2). They are presented as being conversant with past Hebrew victories in the Transjordan. Disguised as poor exhausted foreigners, the Gibeonites succeed handily in deception (9:12-15), but not without the ironic surmise of the Israelites: "You may be living in land that is ours" (9:7).

A treaty once made is irrevocable. Thus, there is nothing to be done now except to spare the Gibeonites. Fortunately for Israel the treaty offered minimum benefits, only life itself. Nothing precluded the Gibeonites from being relegated to an inferior social class, as choppers of wood and bearers of water for the community and the sanctuary (9:27). From their designated state there would be no escape (9:23), even though they were to live peaceably in the Hebrew community. In fact, violent action against the Gibeonites in monarchical times was seen as a serious covenant violation (2 Sam 21:1-6).

10:1-43 The Southern campaign

The chapter contains three originally unconnected accounts: the siege of Gibeon (9:1-15), the death of the five kings (9:15-27), and the invasion of southern Palestine (9:28-43). Their original separation with resultant overlapping does not detract from the author's intent of placing the land as far south as the Negeb in Israelite hands.

10:1-11 War at Gibeon

When the treaty with the Gibeonites reached royal ears, the king of Jerusalem enlisted the help of four other kings to attack Gibeon (10:1-4). The Amorite cities of Jarmuth, Hebron, Lachish, and Eglon were situated to the south of Jerusalem, all seen as closely related to Judah in later times. Faced with this grave danger, the Gibeonites logically looked to their covenant partner, Israel, for help. With the Deuteronomistic assurance of success, Joshua sets forth with his troops (10:7-8). They have an unparalleled victory and relentlessly pursue their enemy. Divine assistance provides a storm of hail which causes more damage than the human battle (10:11).

The quotation from the book of Jashar, a record of Israel's mighty deeds (10:12-13; 2 Sam 1:18), originally commanded an "astonished" sun and moon to stand still before God's might. The quotation is often interpreted as a plea for the prolongation of daylight. However it is better seen as a plea for the darkness to continue, with the sun obscured by the hailstorm. The darkness worked to the advantage of Israel in overcoming the enemy.

10:16-27 The murder of the kings

The murder of the kings at Makkedah is etiological, with the presence of the memorial stones commemorating their death. The kings were left concealed in caves until the battle was finished

(10:16-19). They are killed only after suffering the humiliation of having their necks stamped upon (10:24; Ps 110:1). With their death and public exposure until sunset (10:26; Deut 21:22-23), Israel's victory is definitively assured.

10:28-42 The conquest of the South

This is primarily a list of the sites taken by Israel in settling in southern Palestine, many of which attained notoriety in later history. Those conquered are Libnah, Lachish, Gezer, Eglon, and Debir, all belonging to the tribe of Judah (15:39-44). This is a summary list with no indication of the time it took to assimilate the entire region from the central hill country to the southern Negeb desert. Not all of the cities included in the original hostile coalition are mentioned, e.g., Jerusalem and Jarmuth. Jerusalem was not taken until David's time (2 Sam 5:6-9). *Herem* (the ban) is dutifully executed on the whole region. At this point Joshua is clearly seen as an agent of the Lord, bringing the country into subjection in what is presented as a "blitzkrieg" attack.

11:1-25 The Northern campaign

This chapter is thematic in character, painting in broad strokes a conquest of the north of Canaan which even other biblical sources indicate took a much longer time. This is theological history which has to be understood on its own terms. The chapter existed as an independent and separate source, now utilized by the Deuteronomist to match his overall purpose. Except for the reference to Jabin's hearing of the southern campaign (11:1), there is no other reference to preceding events. The two time references (11:10, 21) are vague and are not necessarily sequential. The chapter is made up of three main sections: the formation of a confederacy (11:1-9), similar to that of the south (9:1-2); the battle (11:10-15); and a survey of the conquest (11:16-23). All of these have their parallel in the southern campaign.

11:1-9 The Northern confederacy

The fear of the Israelites moves the northern kings to form a confederacy. Hazor is north of the Sea of Galilee (Genesareth), a prominent city in the Middle Bronze era, and impressive ruins in later times. It was rebuilt in the time of Solomon (1 Kgs 9:15). Madon is identified with a site also close to the Sea of Galilee, while the cities of Shimron and Achshaph cannot be identified with certainty (11:1-2). The list of tribal peoples inhabiting the north corresponds to what is known from other sources; only the presence of the southern (Jerusalem-inhabiting) Jebusites is rather surprising (11:3). The actual location of Merom, the place of battle, remains enigmatic, other than its general location in the upper Galilee region (11:5). Following the Lord's directives exactly, the Israelites cripple their enemies' defense, pursue them to the far north, and then kill them all (11:6-9).

11:10-15 Conquest of Northern Canaan

After the defeat of the armed forces, the Israelites turn on the cities themselves. The entire population is eradicated; the city of Hazor is put to the torch; the spoils and livestock are taken as booty. This is *herem* at its strongest, enjoined on Moses by the Lord himself (Deut 7:2). It can only be understood against the background of the pernicious and contagious properties of evil, calling for a type of total eradication foreign to the modern ear. It also underscores the invincibility of YHWH in the face of any pagan threat.

11:16-23 Survey of the conquest

Joshua's conquest is idealized here and is more reflective of events that only came about gradually, as verse 18 indicates. The boundaries extend from the Negeb in the far south to the northernmost point of Mt. Hermon. The conquest goes much farther than anything seen so far, with some territories, still unconquered, appearing later in the book itself (13:1-6; 15:63; 16:10). There are forays against foreign inhabitants still flourishing in the time of the Judges. The total elimination of the Anakim (v. 22) is at odds with their later presence in the territory of Caleb (14:6-15; 15:13-19).

Divine causality is overarching in biblical thought. It was YHWH who hardened pharaoh's heart (Exod 7:13) so that the liberating plagues might take place. Here too the Lord encourages the enemy to wage war so that they may be justifiably defeated and not killed as innocent landowners (11:20). With nothing happening without his authorization, the Lord manages "to write straight with crooked lines."

12:1-24 Summary of the conquest

This chapter links the two major sections of the book, the conquest and the distribution of the land. It has two parts, one dealing with the taking of the land east of the Jordan under Moses (12:1-6), the other, with the victories of Joshua (12:7-24). The first is more broadly geographical; the second, centering on the royal fiefdoms overcome.

The account of the Hebrew victory over Sihon, king of the Amorites, and Og, king of Bashan, is found in Numbers 21:21-35. From south to north in the land east of the Jordan, the territory extended from the Arnon River at the Dead Sea to Mt. Hermon in the far north (12:1). The territory of the two kings was divided by the Jabbok river, Sihon being the king to the south with his capital at Heshbon (12:2-3), and Og ruling in the north (12:4-6). Legend had the people of Bashan as being tall of stature, hence the Rephaim (12:4; i.e., "giants").

The significance of recounting the capture of Bashan and Og lies in the fact that the Israelite tribes of Reuben, Gad, and one half of Manasseh were allotted that territory at the time of distribution (ch. 13).

The territories west of the Jordan are succinctly enumerated, with a simple mention of the kings and their land. Some of these locations are already known to us from Joshua itself or from other sources; others are not. The evidence points to an early independent source used and adapted by the Deuteronomist, whose imprint is present in the sequence and ordering of the names. In addition to Jericho and Ai, there are the five cities listed in 10:3 (12:10-12) and the four of 11:1 (12:19-20).

While it is not possible to identify each of the cities with certainty, those which are known extend to the farthest points of Canaan in the south and north. The chapter is a tribute to the leadership of Moses and Joshua. It points to the end of petty fiefdoms and the emergence of a theocratic and unified country with a clear religious, if not yet national, identity. It will have its finest hour under David in a lifespan that was destined to be all too short.

DIVISION OF THE LAND

Joshua 13–21

Following upon the rather idealized picture of Joshua's conquest of Canaan, the second major part of the book deals with the allotment of the land, bringing to a conclusion the objective enun-

ciated by Moses (11:23). This begins with the land east of the Jordan, promised to two and one-half tribes (13:8-32; Num 32:32-33), with the territory in Canaan itself given to the remaining eight and one-half tribes (chs. 14–20). In addition, there is added clarification of the special status of the tribe of Levi (ch. 21). Due to the limitations of space, and possibly reader interest as well, geographical detail is absent here, for which the reader is directed to lengthier and more critical commentaries. These chapters have special interest for the Deuteronomist in reminding his readers, at a much later date and in a time of dispersion and disappointment, of the truly felicitous conclusion to the exodus, a realization of promise, which was initially theirs.

13:1-7 Land to be conquered

This is a touch of realism brought to an idealized presentation of the land's possession. There were still pockets of resistance, some of which were to continue into monarchical times. The territory mentioned here includes the coastal land of the Philistines with its five major cities (13:2-3), which remained hostile and inimical well into the time of David (2 Sam 5:17-24), and the Geshurites (2 Sam 27:8), a people distinct from the Transjordanian group of the same name (12:3). Mention is also made of northern Canaanites, near Amorite country (13:4), and a territory further north in the Lebanon region (13:5). These are presented as part of Israel's heritage, although still unconquered in the time of Joshua (13:6).

13:8-29 The Eastern tribes

Once again the tribes to which Moses had assigned territory in Transjordan—Reuben, Gad, and one-half of Manasseh—are highlighted (12:6; Num 32:32). The allotment moves from south to north: Reuben's is the land between the Arnon river and the region of Heshbon, slightly north of the Dead Sea (13:15-23). This was the land of the Amorites with its former king Sihon, recalled here for its association with Moses (Num 21:21-31).

Gad is allotted the region beyond Heshbon which was part of Ammon and Gilead in northern Transjordan (13:24-25). Its northern boundary is not clear from the text since most of the cities mentioned cannot be identified with certainty. Manasseh receives Bashan, the land of Og (Num 21:33-35), including a part of Gilead (13:29-31). In summary, the Transjordanian tribes occupied a territory extending roughly from the Dead Sea in the south to the Lake of Chinnereth in the north, although the full conquest was not realized until the period of the monarchy and David's military successes in the region. The text notes that no land was allotted to Levi, the priestly tribe. Since the Lord was their "heritage," they received no geographical territory (13:14). In fact, because of their unique vocation, the Levites would be found throughout the country as a whole.

14:1-15 Special considerations

Land distribution is carried out by the leaders designated by Moses: Joshua, the priest Eleazar, Aaron's son (Exod 6:25), and the tribal family heads (14:1-2; Num 32:28). This was done by lots, a customary way of determining God's will (Num 26:55-56). However, prior to distribution, two other issues are considered, both connected with distinct traditions. One explains the number twelve even though one tribe, Levi, has been excluded. The tribe of Joseph was traditionally divided in two: Ephraim and Manasseh, named for Joseph's two sons and accorded patriarchal status at the time of Jacob's death (Gen 48:5).

14:6-15 Caleb

The second etiology of the chapter centers on the Calebite clan and their unique status within the tribe of Judah. Caleb's claim to settle in the city of Hebron sprang from the scouting expedition he had made with Joshua to reconnoiter the land of Canaan at Moses' behest. He and Joshua were the only two to encourage Moses to undertake the occupation. For that reason Caleb was accorded a position of status in Israel's tradition (Num 13–14). Interestingly, he is presented as both a Judahite and a Kenizzite (14:6, 14), the latter evidently an indigenous tribe which was incorporated into Israel. This foreign origin would have been added reason to attempt to legitimate the Calebite claim to one of Judah's most important sites, the first capital of David's kingdom (2 Sam 2:1-4).

These inserted etiologies, springing from independent sources, interrupt the flow of the narrative between chapters 13 and 15; this only underscores, however, the importance in which they were held. Caleb swears to remove the enemy Anakim from his territory (14:12), even though

another tradition had them eliminated earlier by Joshua (11:21).

15:1-12 Boundaries of Judah

The preeminence of Judah gives it first place in presenting the geographical configuration of the tribes. Its location in the south places it near the Dead Sea touching the border of Edom and part of the Negeb desert (15:1). In the north (15:6-11) it went beyond the Dead Sea to the region north of Jerusalem. The western boundary is said to be the Mediterranean (15:12), although in Joshua's time this territory was occupied by the Philistines and would remain so into the time of the monarchy.

15:13-19 Caleb and Othniel

Once again it is etiology which accounts for the narrative. It is again stated that Hebron was allotted to the Kenizzite Caleb, who took it by conquest (15:13-14; 14:6-15). The presence of evidently important pools in the area is explained as the gift of Othniel, Caleb's nephew, to his wife Achsah after their marriage (15:17-19; cf. Judg 3:7-11).

15:20-61 List of cities

This is evidently an administrative list of the different jurisdictions within Judah from the time of the southern kingdom. The four major regions are the south land (15:21-32), the foothills (Shephelah) (15:33-47), the hill country (15:48-60), and the desert (15:61-62). These major regions are then divided into smaller sectors, each section punctuated in the text by citing the number of cities. An interesting footnote is the continued presence of the Jebusites, from whom Jerusalem was taken by David (2 Sam 5), still maintaining a presence in the city at a much later date (15:63). The major Philistine cities, to be taken only at a later date, are also listed (15:45-47).

16:1-10 The Joseph tribes

The geographical sequence is again interrupted, with Benjamin and Dan to the north of Judah bypassed, to treat the important Joseph tribes, named for Ephraim and Manasseh, the patriarch's sons. Ephraim bordered Benjamin and Dan in the south and met Manasseh in the north at Taanah-shiloh on the east and the gorge of Kanah in the west. Its eastern boundary reached the Jordan (16:7) and on the west the Mediterranean at some point (16:8). Again reference is made to a non-Israelite population present in the region (16:10).

17:1-18 More on Joseph

The chapter deals with added issues concerning Manasseh and Ephraim, including Manasseh's allocation west of the Jordan (17:1-10), the continued presence of Canaanites within the territory (17:11-13), and the tribes' request for more territory (17:14-18).

17:1-10

The western territory of Manasseh lay between Issachar on the north and Ephraim on the south. Its western boundary was the Mediterranean coast, and, despite verse 7, it touched on Asher at one coastal point only. Its location in central Palestine later became the hub of Samaria. The tribal land was divided among twelve clans: two in Transjordan and ten west of the Jordan, with five of the latter identified with women, the daughters of one Zelophehad (17:1-6).

17:11-13

The cities which remained unconquered and occupied by Canaanites correspond to those cited elsewhere (Judg 1:27). While located in the territory of Manasseh, they were evidently identified as well with Asher and Issachar as border cities in the Jezreel valley. The author attempts to reconcile the two viewpoints with an oblique reference to the two tribes (17:11).

17:14-18

Two traditions are reflected in Joseph's request for more land. In the first Joshua responds to the request by urging them to clear the forest and settle in the land already designated (17:14-15). The second deals with the threat of the Canaanites in the region with their formidable military prowess in the Josephite territory (17:16), with Joshua again urging continued expansion (17:17-18). The reference to iron chariots (17:16) recalls the earlier introduction of the chariot in Near Eastern warfare by the Hyksos (17:16).

18:1–19:51 Land distribution to the seven remaining tribes

There is a time lapse here to allow for the subduing of hostile forces and surveying the territory

(18:1-10). From another point of view, it provides sufficient separation from the allotment given to the major tribes, Judah and Joseph, before turning to the less important tribes: Benjamin (18:11-28), Simeon (19:1-9), Zebulun (19:10-16), Issachar (19:17-23), Asher (19:24-31), Naphtali (19:32-39), and Dan (19:40-48).

18:1-10

The action is now situated in Shiloh, an important sanctuary in later times, identified with the prophet Samuel. The mention of the meeting tent is unusual in the Deuteronomistic tradition. It was a vital part of the religious experience during the desert sojourn and is prominent in the priestly (P) tradition. It may show the influence of priestly sources in the final text.

Land assignment is judiciously and cautiously executed. Scouts from each tribe are to survey the land; the cities are listed in seven sections. With fair distribution among the seven, Joshua then cast lots to determine the Lord's will for each tribe (18:4-7). Excluded from consideration were Judah, Reuben, Gad, and Manasseh, already determined, and Levi, the priestly tribe (18:5-7).

18:11-28

The relatively small but politically important territory allotted to Benjamin lay between Ephraim in the north and Judah in the south. It was bound by the Jordan (east), the region of Jericho and Bethel (north), by Kireath-jearim (west). On the south its boundaries with Judah correspond to those already cited (15:6-11).

The list of cities (18:21-28) was evidently one of the administrative subdivisions mentioned earlier in connection with Judah (15:20-63), pointing to a period in which the boundaries between the two tribes were more fluid. Here the list includes important cities such as Jericho and Bethel. There is reference to the "Jebusite city (that is, Jerusalem)" (18:28). The city was probably unidentified originally, since Jerusalem would hardly be listed as Benjaminite or Judahite on an administrative list. Moreover, the importance of its being conquered by David would hardly permit a reference to it as a Jebusite city. That Jebusites remained in the region, however, is entirely likely.

In chapter 19, portions are allotted to the remaining tribes. For clarity the reader is referred to a map indicating the location of the tribes throughout the land. Here we shall paint with a broad brush, limiting our comments to the more salient features.

Simeon

(19:1-10) seems to have lost its original identity, if indeed it ever had one, in being entirely absorbed in the larger tribe of Judah. It is a relationship alluded to in the present text (19:1, 9). No geographical boundaries are noted; most of the cities cited are already found on the Judah list (15:20-63). This section may well be a Deuteronomistic construct of a tribe which no longer enjoyed an independent existence.

Zebulun

(19:10-16) occupied the Plain of Esdraelon in the lower hills of Galilee. Moving clockwise, it was bounded by Naphtali, Issachar, Manasseh, and Asher. A small northern tribe, it claimed twelve cities and their villages.

Issachar

(19:17-23), another northern tribe, was also located on the Plain of Esdraelon. Bounded on the east by the Jordan and the southern end of the Lake of Galilee, it reached Naphtali in the north, Manasseh in the south, and Zebulun and Manasseh in the west.

Asher

(19:24-31), one of the northernmost tribes, went as far as the boundary of Phoenicia. A large territory, it extended as far as the Carmel mountains in the south. It was contiguous with Zebulun and Manasseh.

Naphtali

(19:32-39) parallels Asher in the northeast. Geographically it extended from the Jordan valley in the south to Lake Huleh, above the Sea of Galilee, in the north. On its west and south it touched on Asher, Zebulun, and Issachar.

And finally the tribe of Dan

(19:40-48) was originally assigned a small portion of land in the region of Judah and Ephraim. Oppressed by the Amorites, they could not appropriate their land (Judg 1:34-35). Their further oppression is recounted in the Samson story (Judg

13–16). The tribe finally moved north. Their conquest of Leshem (Laish; 19:47) is recounted in Judges (ch. 18). This was the northernmost tribe, reaching the Valley of Lebanon and Mt. Hermon.

As his personal inheritance, Joshua received the city of Timnah-serah in Ephraim which he restored as his personal home. It may be identified with the later Khirbet Tibneh in the central region of Shechem (19:49-50).

20:1-9 Cities of refuge

The recompense for serious sin moved toward the guilty person with an almost physical sense of inexorability. This was the "boomerang" quality of sin as the ancients envisioned it. In the case of homicide, the avenging agent was the next of kin with the act to be executed as soon as possible (Gen 9:6). Far from being sinful, such revenge was a moral imperative. Hence, provision had to be made in the case of accidental killing. Mosaic legislation (Num 35:9-28), spoken of here (20:1-2) provided for cities to which the offender could flee and be safe from harm until his case could be adjudicated (20:6). If he was proved innocent he could remain safe within the city. Judgment was passed by the elders (20:4). An awkward attempt to include other legislation accounts for the mention of community judgment as well (20:6). The death of the main priest in the community left the person free to leave.

Needless to say, these cities had to be readily accessible. Distance could mean death at the hands of the avenger. Conveniently, three were located east and three west of the Jordan (20:7-9).

21:1-45 The Levitical cities

The often repeated injunction that no land allotment was to be given to the tribe of Levi left the question of their future provision unresolved. Thus this final chapter on land distribution treats exclusively of the Levites. They were to be given a number of cities throughout the country with surrounding pastureland to serve as a home for them and locations where priestly service could be offered to the people. This was done in accord with the Mosaic directive (Num 35:1-8). This did not mean that Levites alone occupied these cities; they were situated among the tribes whose citizens lived there as well, as would be seen clearly in the case of places like Hebron, Shechem, and Ramath-gilead.

Some authors argue that the list is artificial, with its neat division of four cities for each tribe in a territory which in early times would have been very vast. All of this points to the fact, it is said, that the list lacks historical accuracy. On the other hand, some see considerable historical possibility, especially in light of the expansion that took place during David's reign, which could see the cities as placed within a royal administrative territory. In addition, the rather clumsy clustering of the cities is hardly consonant with a neat idealized list. In view of the administrative as well as cultic role of the priests, the Levitical cities make considerable administrative sense, especially in the far flung regions of the country.

The descendants of Levi, in an admittedly artificial setting, are listed under three headings: Kohathites (12:3-5), Gershonites (21:6), and the Merarites (21:7). Highlighted as a group are the descendants of Aaron (Kohathites), who receive thirteen cities in Judah, Simeon, and Benjamin (21:4), with ten given to the remaining Kohathites (21:5); thirteen to the Gershonites (21:6); and twelve to the Merarites (21:7). The total number of Levitical cities was forty-eight. Four cities were allotted to each tribe, with the exception of Judah/Simeon (nine) and Naphtali (three). The list includes all of the cities of refuge (ch. 20) where the priestly presence was particularly important.

APPENDIX

Joshua 22–24

22:1-34 Problems in Transjordan

The story is clear enough in its broad outline. The two and one-half tribes given land east of the Jordan were sent back to their homeland by Joshua. Once there they constructed an altar which was seen as a secessionist gesture and cultically objectionable as opposed to the single sanctuary within Canaan proper. Before military action was taken, a delegation was sent to investigate the matter, only to be reassured that the altar was not for sacrifice but rather a symbol of unity. The delegation returned and reported their favorable findings to Joshua and the Israelites.

Two underlying motifs important to the Deuteronomist are significant in the narrative. The first lies in the preeminence accorded Canaan itself, "the land the LORD possesses" (22:19). The repeated efforts to legitimate the Transjordanian tribes in the biblical narrative is a clear indication of their secondary, even controversial status. In fact there were moments when they were opponents of Israel proper (Judg 12:1-6). The second motif underscores the later centralization of all cult in Israel under king Josiah in the seventh century. Jerusalem alone was the place of worship, and all other places of cult were destroyed (2 Kgs 22–23). This was a reform particularly close to the Deuteronomist, who gives this centralization repeated emphasis.

22:1-9 The commission of the tribes

The legitimacy of the claim of the Transjordanian tribes as being true Israelites is highlighted in Joshua's statement, as they are exhorted to continued fidelity in strongly Deuteronomistic language (22:1-6). They return home with a more than sufficient share of the booty from the conquest (22:7-9).

22:10-20 The construction of the altar

From the initial mention it is not clear on which side of the Jordan the altar was built (22:10), but it is quickly clarified as being in Transjordan (v.11). The act was seen as immediately provocative in compromising the singular character of the sanctuary at Shiloh, and a call to arms was issued (22:10-11; cf. 18:1). The diplomatic embassy consisted of the priest Phinehas and one prince from each tribe west of the Jordan (22:13-14). The accusation was of serious cultic violation and possible secessionist intent. The action of the Transjordanians was compared to the idolatry of the Baal of Peor in the desert where illicit cultic sex and other pagan rites had prevailed (Num 25). The present action was seen as having collective consequences as in the case of Achan (7:20). The people were advised that if they saw their land as unclean, they always had the right to cross the Jordan and worship there.

22:21-31 The response

The episode ends on a positive note, with the presence of the altar taking on etiological importance (22:34). It was intended as a symbol of unity, not a place of sacrifice (22:21-29). It was not to compete with Shiloh where the Tent of the Lord's Dwelling was located. Rather it was to be a "witness" to the exclusive worship of Yʜᴡʜ in the duly designated sanctuary, as well as to the unity of all the tribes. The name "witness" was given to the altar (22:34), and peace was restored within all of Israel.

23:1-24 Final exhortation

The chapter is Deuteronomistic in content and style. Its strong parallelism with chapter 24 may point to the incorporation of two distinct documents. It is certain that the present chapter has been reworked and edited by the Deuteronomist. The next chapter is located in Shechem; the present one is presumably in Shiloh. The parallels between Joshua and Moses have been mentioned earlier in the commentary. Here again it appears between Moses' farewell address (Deut 32–33) and the present discourse. The passage also bears similarity with the final words of David to his son Solomon (1 Kgs 2:1-10).

The literary form, common to many ancient treaties and documents, contains a recall of past benefits and assurance for the future (23:3-5), an exhortation to fidelity (23:6-13), and a conclusion (23:14-16). In reviewing past benefits, Joshua speaks of the invasion and occupation of the land and the tribal allotments. But there is clear indication that some foreign elements still remain to be dislodged (23:4-5). The land of Canaan from the Jordan to the Mediterranean is the unmerited, wholly gratuitous heritage of Israel. It is the Lord who has led the way, fought the battles, and vanquished the foe. This recounting is intended to elicit sentiments of gratitude in the people's hearts.

For their part, the Israelites must adhere to the laws and statutes which Yʜᴡʜ has given. Apostasy is the great sin and it appears repeatedly in the final exhortation. Categorically excluded is any form of homage to foreign deities, as well as any form of inclusive contact or intermarriage (23:7-8, 12).

As in Deuteronomy 27, there are threats as well as blessings. If the love of God and the observance of his laws are abandoned, the pagan countries that remain will be a continuous source of enmity and hostility (23:13). If necessary, this will lead to Israel being overcome and dislodged from the land of its inheritance.

In reading this final exhortation, there is the mounting realization that, regardless of the liter-

ary setting, the historical moment is that of the Babylonian exile of the sixth century. It was Israel's continued infidelity that led to the destruction and deportation of 586. What appears as a future warning in the text recalls the sad reality of Israel's history at the time the text was written.

24:1-33 Conclusion

This celebrated chapter recounts the renewal of the covenant (24:1-28) and the burial of the patriarchal figures (24:29-30). An earlier document has been edited by the Deuteronomist to bring the book to a close on a very positive note. Differences from the body of the book, pointing to original independence, can be readily noted, e.g., a military conflict at Jericho (24:11), and the repeated emphasis on the Amorites as the nearly exclusive enemy (24:6, 15).

24:1-28 Covenant renewal

A covenant (in Hebrew *berith*) was the most common form of agreement between nations, groups, or individuals. In the Bible this is extended to God and his people. The earliest biblical precedent for the Joshua covenant was that made with Noah after the flood (Gen 9). This was a unilateral covenant requiring nothing of the contracting party. It was Yʜᴡʜ who pledged himself never to destroy the earth by flood again. The visible sign of this covenant was the rainbow. The covenant with Abraham (Gen 15) can be considered bilateral if the circumcision imposed upon the patriarch is considered part of the agreement (Gen 17:9-14). However the major initiatives come from Yʜᴡʜ, who pledges himself to grant Abraham a large and numerous progeny (Gen 14:2-7) and a bountiful country (Gen 15:18-20).

The major covenant is, of course, that of Sinai, which is the prototype of all others (Exod 19–24). Therein, following a customary covenant or treaty form, Yʜᴡʜ presents himself and recounts his benefits (Exod 20:2). He then lists the terms of the agreement (Exod 20:3-17; chs. 21–23). If the terms are agreed upon, Yʜᴡʜ will be the protector and deliverer of his people (Exod 19:5-6). The people agree and in a solemn ritual the covenant is concluded (Exod 24:3-8).

The Joshua covenant renewal takes place in Shechem, one of Israel's central sanctuaries. Following the customary form, there is a recounting of Yʜᴡʜ's saving action, beginning with Abraham and the early settlement of the patriarchs (24:2-4), to Moses and the exodus (24:5-10), and the eventual settlement in Canaan (24:11-13). The recital of this creed placed emphasis on foreign gods and soothsayers, underscoring their ineffectiveness (24:2, 9-11). No mention is made of the pivotal Sinai covenant, as is the case also in other liturgical expressions (e.g., Exod 15). The most likely reason for this is that it would have been redundant and anticlimactic in a ceremony which was itself a covenant ratification. The mention of the hornets leading Israel alludes to Exodus 23:28.

After the litany of the Lord's favorable action, as on Sinai, the people are asked to express their gratitude. Once again the emphasis falls on a strictly monotheistic worship, excluding completely any foreign gods (24:15). Acceptance of the absolute sovereignty of Yhwh is initiated by Joshua (24:15) and reaffirmed by the people four times (24:18, 21, 22, 24), a distinct echo of the Sinai agreement (Exod 24:7). The book of the law again comes to the fore (24:25-26; cf. 1:8; 8:30-35), as well as the memorial stone, both related to Sinai (24:26-27; Exod 24:4). With the creedal formula, acceptance by the people, the written terms, and the memorial stone, covenant renewal is complete. The memorial stone is etiological, a perpetual reminder of the covenant bond. It should be noted that a tradition such as this probably reflects also the incorporation of other people encountered in the conquest into the covenant relationship.

Further development of the covenant theme is seen in the later prediction by Jeremiah of a new covenant not written on stone but one which will find a deeply personal response within the human heart (Jer 31:1-34). All of this is brought to a stirring conclusion at the Last Supper when Jesus initiates a new covenant in his blood (Luke 22:20).

24:29-33

Joshua's death at an advanced age brought the patriarchal period to a close. Patriarchs and priest were laid to rest: Joshua in the land allotted to him in Ephraim (24:30; 19:50), Joseph, whose remains had been brought from Egypt (Gen 50:25), was appropriately buried in Josephite territory (24:32), and Eleazar, son of Aaron, in the mountains of Ephraim (24:33). The chapter as a whole, as well as the burial of Joseph, underscore the importance of Shechem in Israelite history.

THE BOOK OF
JUDGES

Roland J. Faley, T.O.R.

INTRODUCTION

Were it not for the book of Judges, we would be ignorant of Israelite life from the time of the settlement under Joshua (ca. 1200 B.C.) to the rise of the monarchy (ca. 1050 B.C.). During this span of 150 years considerable importance is attached to the religious and political development of the tribal life of the Israelites. Although not intended as a strict historical presentation, Judges fills in many gaps in its extensive and colorful presentation of the six "major judges" and its summary account of the six "minor judges." This is well before the time of national unity, during a time when the people were bound together solely by their faith in YHWH. This was the period in which the twelve tribes, now settled in various parts of the country, were in the ascendancy and played a singular role in the history of God's people.

The book is divided into three parts: a presentation of tribal coexistence with pagan peoples (1:1–3:6), the accounts of the judges (3:7–16:31), and an appendix with events related to the tribes of Benjamin and Dan (17:1–21:25).

The judges

The Hebrew name of the book, *shopetim*, the participial or substantive form of the verb *shapat*, means to execute justice or to do justice. The notion of judicial magistrates comes to mind at once, but the fact is that none of the judges, with the possible exception of Deborah (4:4), were involved in legal proceedings. Several of them, such as Ibzan, Elon, and Abdon, are said to have "judged Israel," but we are given no explanation of what that means. The major judges are not called such in the text itself, and all of them were involved in acts of liberation. That one of these, Jephthah, is also said to "[have] judged Israel" (12:7) may point to a meaning of "hero" or "savior." The overall relation to justice seems to lie in the fact that they were instruments of God's justice in liberating the people from their enemies, and therefore they may best be seen as liberators or saviors.

Formation and theme

Various documents have been assembled in Judges in something of a patchwork fashion. These existed independently and were brought together from various sources. They include records of Israelite-Canaanite coexistence (ch. 1) and the tales of the charismatic judges from various tribal sources (chs. 3–16). While the judges are regularly spoken of as leading all of Israel, this inflation of personal stature is more editorial than historical. These personalities were all originally identified with particular tribes. There is, furthermore, a list of judges about whom very little is said (e.g., 12:8-13).

The editing of the various strands was the work of the Deuteronomistic school, which has assembled the documents, linked them, and edited the material to point up the major themes of its theological approach. The major idea is the same as that in Joshua, taken from Deuteronomy: infidelity assures defeat, while fidelity is crowned with success. The major motif that sounds throughout Judges has four major moments: sin, punishment, repentance, and deliverance. The Deuteronomist has woven this intricately into his text.

Historical character

Much of Judges reflects early pre-monarchical times, and credence can be accorded to much that it presents regarding the religious, social, and geographical scene. In fact, it surpasses Joshua in more accurately portraying the mix of the Israelite and non-Israelite population long after the occupation. Tribal life dominated Israel's history during this period, as is clearly portrayed in this book.

By the same token, it must be admitted there is a considerable embellishment of the facts in creating the book's *Heldensleben* (i.e., a focus on the life of national heroes) theme. This is clearly seen in the deeds of Judge's principal protagonists. Moreover, major editing has been done to highlight the ideals and values of a later time. In short, the history which is present is always at the service of Deuteronomistic theology.

Theology of Judges

To look to many of the personalities of Judges for ethical inspiration is to look in vain. Ehud is a ruthless murderer who fortunately is on the right side. Jephthah runs a great risk in making his vow and pays the unfortunate price. In a class all by himself, Samson champions the cause of God only in the final moments of his life when he brings catastrophe upon the Philistines. In the main, these are not people on a par with Abraham, Joseph, or Samuel; yet with all their inadequacies, they still play their part in salvation history. They lived before there was national unity, at a time when both the social and religious practices of the Israelites were disorganized and disparate. Their faith was still young; their centers of cult, few; their laws and rituals were still in a formative stage.

The judges play a formidable role. Their stories are an important part of the Bible, and not solely because they link two significant moments in history. In a rudimentary and even crass way, the stories of the judges show the God of Israel still guiding the life of his people. The judges are fully aware of the sacredness of their spiritual allegiance, part of a history which was quite singular. While moral failure met them along the way, they never stood in opposition to Yhwh. Repeatedly the Israelites recognized their own wrongdoing and knew that repentance could make things right. And so it did. In the book of Judges the Deuteronomistic thesis is more than vindicated: a people of faith, even if they wander, cannot fail.

COMMENTARY

COEXISTENCE

Judges 1:1–3:6

1:1–2:5 A mixed population

The picture of Israel's conquest of the land differs considerably from that depicted in Joshua. By the time of Joshua's death, and much later, there were many pockets of resistance to Israel's presence in the land from indigenous elements that still held sway. This chapter, part of an earlier document, was appended to this section of the Judges narrative at a later date and is, in the main, a credible listing of parts of the country which remained in foreign hands. It is brought into relationship with the preceding volume by the mention of Joshua's death (1:1) in introducing the Judahite campaign. The desecration of the "mixed population" with its attendant problems moves from south (Judah/Simeon) to north (Dan). The subordination of Simeon to Judah points to its eventual assimilation. The Perizzites (1:4) were not ethnically distinguished from the Canaanites, the name being more descriptive ("unwalled cities") than ethnic. The dismemberment of Adonibezek rendered him incapable of bearing arms at any future date. He shared the fate of many to whom he had meted out the same punishment (1:6-7). The mention of Jerusalem is an erroneous gloss (1:8), contradicting verse 21. David captured Jerusalem at a much later date.

The preeminence of Judah continues in the account of its forays in the south (1:9-13). The wedding gift from Caleb to his daughter in the form of two pools explains the claim of Othniel's descendants in Debir (1:13-15) and parallels the same account in Joshua 15:13-19. Etiology is also dominant in the reference to the Kenites, Moses' in-laws (Num 10:29-32). The efforts of Judah farther north meet with only limited success. They took the hill country (1:17-20) but had no success on the coastal plain and gained no access to Philistine territory.

Indigenous populations were not dislodged in the territories of Benjamin (1:21), Ephraim and Manasseh (1:22-29), Zebulun (1:30), Asher (1:31-32), Naphtali (1:33), and Dan (1:34-36). Mention is made, however, that some of the native population were pressed into slave labor by the Israelites (1:35).

The reason for this ambivalent picture of the occupation is explained at the beginning of chapter 2 (vv. 1-5), and it is clearly Deuteronomistic. In view of their disobedience to the Lord's wishes and their entrance into forbidden pacts with the resident population, the Israelites were unsuccessful in making the land their own. This message was relayed by a divine messenger at Bochim, an unidentified locale but perhaps related to the important sanctuary at Bethel. The name, however, is significant; it is related to the Hebrew verb "to weep." Bochim then is "weeper's land," a lasting reminder of Israel's infidelity.

2:6-36 The apostasy of Israel

The chapter is the Deuteronomist's introduction to the book as a whole. It picks up where Joshua ended, with the death and burial of Joshua (2:8-9 cf. Josh 24:29-32) and the retirement of the tribes to their designated territories (2:6; Josh 13–19). This supports the thesis that the first chapter of Judges was a late addition, perhaps placed here for historical reasons.

The continued presence of pagan elements is explained solely in terms of Israel's wanton disregard of Yhwh's commands. The population is cited as the generation that followed Joshua, a generation which departed from the fidelity of their predecessors (2:7, 10). Not adhering to the faith of their forebears, this generation turned to idolatry in the worship of Canaanite gods, as well as the gods of neighboring countries (2:10-13). Baal (a word which means "lord") was the chief god of the Canaanite pantheon and Astarte, his consort, was the goddess of love and fertility. The plural references here look to the various forms and images of the two which were used in popular worship, rather than a plurality of deities (2:11, 13).

The judges were raised up to deliver the oppressed people. In a departure from the common motif of sin-punishment-conversion-deliverance, there is no explicit mention here of conversion ("crying to the Lord"); repentance is at best implicit. The deliverance is simply an act of Yhwh's pity (2:18). Variations in the narrative also point to different sources. In one instance, the people failed to pay any heed to the judges but simply abandoned themselves to their pagan practices (2:17); in another, there is recidivism or backsliding after deliverance when the judge dies (2:18-19). In any case, the foreign nations remained in place as a continued test of the people's fidelity (2:20-23). Testing was necessary since the present generation had not participated in the battles under Joshua (3:2).

Israel's hostile neighbors included the Philistines on the central coastal plain, Canaanites throughout the country, and the citizens of Lebanon in the north (3:2-3). The stereotypical list of non-Israelites affords little knowledge of the actual identity of some of them (3:5; cf. Josh 3:10; 24:11). At the time there was both cultic abuse and inter-marriage as well (3:6). In all of this, the Deuteronomist's point is clear. The people in exile for whom he writes, one half of a millennium later, should see their unfortunate lot as a part of a continuous history of infidelity. The continued presence of pagan elements was due not to YHWH's original design but to human sinfulness.

THE JUDGES
Judges 3:7–16:31

3:7-11 Othniel

Little is said about the first of the judges. Othniel is a paradigm of much that is to follow: the people sin, YHWH punishes, the people turn to the Lord, YHWH sends a deliverer. This introductory piece is probably Judahite in origin, with Othniel's origin found in the Calebite clan of Judah. Neither the king nor the location of his kingdom can be identified with certainty. Central to the account is the spirit of the Lord which takes possession of the judge (3:10), a divine force which enters into the Lord's emissary enabling him or her to perform feats beyond any human expectations.

3:12-30 Ehud

The story of Ehud's triumph over Eglon, king of Moab, seemingly existed originally as an account of bravado on the part of a rustic Israelite in effectively countering the king of a hostile Transjordanian realm. This is contained in the murder narrative (3:15-25), quite complete in itself, which was then adapted to fit the basic Judges framework.

The threat from an expanding Israel aroused its Transjordanian neighbors and led to its sub-jugation for eighteen years, but the defeat is attributed to Israel's moral waywardness (3:12-14). Then Ehud of Benjamin is designated by the Lord, without any mention, however, of his receiving the spirit. His left-handedness would have been considered a human defect or imperfection, which in this case proved an asset in enabling him to conceal his dagger on his right thigh (3:16) The account is somewhat gross in its bloody description of the fat king's death (3:22); and its humor coarse in the servants' imagining that the king was relieving himself (3:24). However, it would have been seen as a striking example of YHWH's power over an evil opponent, even to the point of ridicule. There is drama in the narrative, seen in the ruse Ehud uses to see the king alone, the impending death described as a message, the departure of Ehud with doors locked behind him, and the king inaccessible until he is certainly dead.

The account ends on a note of military prowess. Ehud drew on Ephraimite forces and subdued the forces of Moab, resulting in an eighty-year period of peace (3:26-30).

A single verse is given to the judge Shamgar, who followed Ehud and was engaged in military exploits against the Philistines (3:31).

Chapters 4–5 Deborah

The account of Israel's woman judge comes to us in two forms, one prose (ch. 4) and the other, a poetic canticle (ch. 5). The latter, although at times unclear due to errors in literary transmission, is one of the oldest extant pieces of poetry, thought to be written very close to the time of the events depicted. The two accounts converge around essentials but are at variance in secondary features. In the narrative, the principal characters on the positive side are Deborah, Barak, and Jael. As judges, the roles of Deborah and Barak coalesce. Although the victory is his, the direction is hers. Although the action of Jael is applauded, she is not considered a judge. Her story seems to have arisen out of a context of tales of popular heroism. The two antagonists are Jabin and Sisera.

4:1-23 The prose account

Contained within a Deuteronomistic introduction (4:1-3) and conclusion (4:23), the chapter is made up of battle preparations (4:1-9), the battle itself (4:10-16), and the death of Sisera (4:17-21). The provenance is in the north from Bethel in Ephraim (4:4) to Hazor, north of the sea of Galilee (4:2). To speak of Jabin as the "Canaanite king" (4:2) is as much an overstatement as it is to call the tribal battles of the book the responses of "Israel." He is more accurately seen as the Canaanite king of Hazor. A Jabin of Hazor has been met before and overcome by Joshua (Josh 11); his name may have anachronistically attached itself to the present tradition. Attention passes quickly to Jabin's military leader, Sisera, whose non-Canaanite name may well be of Philistine origin (4:2).

Deborah was a prophetess and a judge, exercising a threefold office in the account. As a prophetess, she was a diviner of the divine will (4:4); she also handed down judicial sentences (4:5); and she was a charismatic leader (judge) as well. Barak is summoned by Deborah to assume a "judging" role by YHWH's design, i.e., the liberation of his people from Canaanite oppression (4:6-7; cf. Heb. 11:32). Barak's plea for Deborah's presence is an effort to place Sisera's defeat clearly in YHWH's camp, with his falling into "a woman's power" (4:8-9). In the battle itself Deborah plays only a directive role; the actual victory is Barak's. The battle takes place at the Kishon river on the Plain of Esdraelon in the region of Mt. Tabor, placing the event clearly in relationship to the north (4:12-13).

The parenthetical mention of the Kenites, Moses' in-laws (Num 10:29), serves to introduce Jael at a later point (4:17). The Kenites originally settled in southern Judah (1:16), with a segment separating and settling in the north (4:11).

With the defeat of Jabin's forces, attention passes to the fate of his general Sisera. Like the story of Ehud in the previous chapter, this has all the characteristics of an epic tale which originally constituted a separate and isolated account. It is here attached to Deborah and Barak possibly for historical reasons, but more importantly for theological emphasis. It is a woman ally of the Hebrews who, even though she violates the important law of hospitality, overcomes pagan military prowess with a tent peg (4:17-22)! Barak's pursuit proves unnecessary. Not a warrior's might but the hand of a woman had dispatched the enemy. It was another victory for YHWH. Later, in the face of disgrace and defeat, Jabin himself succumbed (4:23).

5:1-31 The poetic account: Deborah's canticle

This is basically an ancient victory song (5:12-30), given a cultic setting as a hymn of thanks (5:1-11, 31). An ancient piece of Hebrew poetry, it focuses on the victory attained in chapter 4.

This is the song of Deborah and Barak, the charismatic leaders of the preceding chapter (5:1). Formerly Barak had been engaged in the battle; here he is largely an onlooker in a battle which is fought by YHWH, the warrior God. The Lord makes his entry from the south, from Sinai through Edom, accompanied by the cataclysms of nature which are regularly the trappings of mythological poetry (5:4-5). He comes to liberate a people reduced to slavery, excluded from human commerce and contact (5:6-7); yet, in true Deuteronomistic fashion, the cause of disaster is Israel's own apostasy. It has left the people bereft of any form of self-defense (5:8). It is the ingenuity of Deborah which now galvanizes Israel's forces (5:9-11).

The location of the battle is Taanach on the Kishon, the same region identified in chapter 4 (5:19-21). In the prose account, however, the forces were drawn from Zebulun and Naphtali; here it is extended to Ephraim, Benjamin, Manasseh (Machir), and Issachar (5:14-15a). Reproved are the tribes that failed to respond: the Transjordanians, as well as Dan, Asher, and the unidentified locale of Meroz (5:15b-17, 23). It is clear that the battle has taken on national proportions in the hymn, yet no mention is made of Judah, which may have already begun its independent stance.

It is the forces of nature that combine to spell defeat for the Canaanites, with the role of the military left undefined (5:19-20). This is clearly YHWH's victory.

The account of Jael is Hebrew poetry at its most vivid, with its striking contrast between the generous offering of refreshment and the cunning of the plan to kill (5:25-26). More than touching is the description of Sisera's mother awaiting his return from battle, with its feminine conjectures on the reason for the delay—that the victors are dividing the spoils—an imagining far from reality.

The dichotomous final plea prays for misfortune to plague the evildoer and blessings to surround the observant, an oft-repeated Hebrew invocation.

Chapters 6–9 Gideon and Abimelech

The complexity of the Gideon narrative is rooted in various distinct and even disparate sources which are here interwoven. It appears evident that the Gideon (chs. 6–8) and Abimelech (ch. 9) stories were originally separate and unrelated narratives, with many authors seeing the link based on family ties as being artificial (8:31). Gideon clearly fits the profile of a judge; Abimelech is simply an example of a failed attempt at kingship. Other sources will be indicated at a later point; they blur but do not extinguish the basic idea: the blessings of virtue and the tragedy of evil.

6:1-40 Gideon's call and mission

The threat at this point comes from the Midianites, a people related to Moses by marriage (Exod 18:1), who proved to be more than a thorn in his side during the exodus experience (Num 25:6-18; ch. 31). They were a nomadic people largely identified with the Sinai peninsula who, with other tribes, were making incursions into Israel.

Oppressed by the Midianites, Israel cried out to the Lord, and this leads to the call of Gideon. The Lord's messenger (6:11) is actually Yhwh himself (6:14,16). Like Jacob before him (Gen 32:31), Gideon is granted this visible contact without incurring death (6:22-23). Before accepting his call, Gideon asks for a sign, a literary device which allows for the introduction of two distinct sources. The two are etiologies, one explaining the name of the altar at Ophrah (6:19-24; "the Lord is peace"), the other explaining Gideon's name change (6:25-32; Jerubbaal means "Let Baal take action"). The first authenticates the call of Gideon through the fiery consumption of the offering; the second, the successful destruction of the pagan altar and sacred poles, connected with the cult of Astarte, the female fertility goddess (6:25; cf. Exod 34:13), and the construction of a new altar. The failure of Baal to act in his own defense explains Gideon's name change (6:32).

The Lord's spirit takes possession of Gideon as he goes forth to battle (6:34). Even with the help of four tribes (6:35), the skeptical judge still seeks assurance of victory, which is granted in the signs of the wet and dry fleece (6:36-40).

7:1-23 War with the Midianites

The Israelites are now battle ready. However, a significant reduction in forces takes place first.

If Yhwh was to be recognized as the victor, human forces had to be reduced (7:2). The fearful were sent home, leaving a force of ten thousand (7:3). Further reduction was obtained by distinguishing between those who drank water with cupped hands and heads erect and those who bent down to drink. The more cautious and alert "heads up" group remained, whereas the others were dismissed. This reduced Gideon's forces to three hundred men (7:6-8).

A spying foray into enemy territory led to Gideon's hearing the dream recounted; it clearly pointed to an Israelite victory, with the barley loaf standing for the agricultural Israel (7:9-15). The battle took place with no military engagement at all. The noise level created confusion and self-destruction (7:16-22). The scene is reminiscent of Jericho, a prior victory without military engagement (Josh 6). In pursuit of the fleeing enemy, Israel now had the upper hand. With their water supply cut off, the Midianites were vanquished and their two princes beheaded. The recall of Israel's tribal force is historically unlikely (7:23-24); it was a way of again adjusting the numbers after the victory of the three hundred in order to present the victory as accomplished by a united Israel. This was clearly a triumph for Gideon, but more so for the Lord.

8:1-22 The Midianite kings and idolatry

Varied and disconnected narratives are here linked together in bringing the Midianite threat to an end. The similarities between the two kings of this chapter and the two princes formerly mentioned (7:25) may point to parallel traditions regarding the same persons. Here a number of accounts are connected: discussion with the Ephraimites (8:1-3), the reproof and reprisal against Succoth and Penuel (8:4-17), and the sentencing of the Midianite kings (8:18-20).

The discussion with Ephraim underscores that tribe's importance and the need for consultation when any action was taken in that region. There were, however, advantages for Ephraim to be obtained out of the conflict, as indicated in the adage (8:2). War had been waged by the Abiezerites, but the Ephraimites gleaned the fruits of victory; it was the latter who had captured the enemy princes (7:24-27).

The dealings with Succoth and Penuel in Transjordan find these settlements hostile and arrogant (8:4-12). Food was to be given only with the removal of the threat (8:6). When Gideon captured the fleeing kings at Karkor, an unidentified location east of the Jordan and a Midianite attack point, he returned to Succoth and Penuel and inflicted severe penalties on the city leaders and the male population, notwithstanding the fact that they were part of the Israelite population (8:13-17). The point of this and the Ephraim account underscores the importance of Israel's acting in concert in the face of a threat, brooking no opposition.

The death of the two kings is said to be in reprisal for the death of Gideon's brothers, about which we have been told nothing (8:18-21). Such a vendetta would have been customary, however, in keeping with the law of retribution (Deut 19:21; Lev 24:17). The only concession made was that the execution was carried out by Gideon and not his inexperienced son.

8:22-29 The death of Gideon

This is the earliest mention of kingship and its tone is clearly anti-monarchical (8:22-23). This train of thought will emerge strongly in the time of Samuel (1 Sam 8). An earthly kingship inevitably compromised the singular sovereignty which belonged to YHWH.

Unfortunately Gideon turns to idolatry, bringing his story to a disappointing end (8:24-27). Midianites and Ishmaelites were interchangeable, both finding their origins in nomadic tribes (8:24; cf. Gen 37:25-28). Out of the gold collected, Gideon made a cult object. The ephod (8:27) was part of the priestly attire (1 Sam 2:18) but was also an instrument for discerning the divine will (1 Sam 14:3, 18-19). In Judges, it is connected with idols (17:5; 18:14), which is its obvious meaning here. It leads to the ruin of Gideon and his family. This unfortunate event notwithstanding, the Deuteronomist's cycle ends with a forty-year peace (8:28).

The chapter's ending attempts to bring the Gideon and Jerubbaal traditions together (8:29-32). It is Jerubbaal's son who will come to the fore in the next chapter. Noted again is the Israelite's reversion to former idolatrous practices in honor of Baal-berith (the lord of the covenant) after the death of Gideon.

9:1-56 The reign of Abimelech

The chapter views Israel's first experience of kingship in a very negative light. It contains Abimelech's bid for the throne (9:1-6), the prophetic opposition of his brother Jotham (9:7-21), the battle at Shechem (9:22-45) and Migdal-shechem (9:46-49), and the death of Abimelech (9:50-56).

Abimelech, son of Jerubbaal, made an ambitious appeal for the throne in Israel before his maternal relatives at Shechem, claiming preference over the other sixty-nine sons of Jerubbaal. With his end in sight, he eliminated any possible opposition by killing his brothers, with the exception of one, the young Jotham. He attained his goal and was proclaimed king at Shechem (9:1-6).

Jotham's presentation of the choice in figurative and poetic language cannot conceal the obvious conclusion. The selection would be based not on quality but political greed and inferior ambition. In choosing Abimelech, a man guilty of fratricide, they would have a king amounting to little more than the common buckthorn plant (9:7-12). In Jotham's warning, there is a clear indication of Shechem's destruction by the king (9:20).

The people's eventual disenchantment with their king found them receptive to the revolutionary overture of Gaal (9:22-29). However, the king retained an ally in the city in the person of Zebul (9:30-33). The revolt proved unsuccessful and Gaal's forces were defeated in a pitched battle (9:34-41); Abimelech then took the city of Shechem by ambushing the local population (9:42-45). "[S]owing it with salt" (9:45) remains unclear, except for the fact that a salted earth was a symbol of devastation (Jer 17:6)

Another source speaks of the tragedy of the Tower of Shechem (*Migdal-Shechem*; 9:46-49). Ironically the people were killed during idolatrous worship of the pagan god of the covenant (9:46; 8:33). Abimelech had completed his task, and the prophecy of Jotham was fulfilled. The Shechemites were put to the torch by the buckthorn (9:13, 20).

There is incredible irony in the death of Abimelech at Thebez, an unknown location, identified by some with modern Tubas. He was killed by a falling stone thrown by a woman (9:50-55). In ordering his armor bearer to dispatch him, he was assured that his death will be given a more honored place in history. With this tragedy, the beginnings of kingship were brought to a bitter end. For the Deuteronomist it was due retribution for a fratricidal king and an unfaithful population (9:56).

10:1-5 Minor judges

Passing reference is made to two judges, Tola of Issachar and Jair of Gilead, who "judged" Israel for twenty-three and twenty-two years respectively. Jair was a man of means (who possessed saddle asses, cf. Judg 5:10). The mention of the two of them in a climate of peace and harmony contrasts with the turmoil of Abimelech's reign. The absence of any mention of military undertakings points to the broader understanding of "judgeship" in the sense of leadership.

10:6-17 Ammonite oppression

The Deuteronomistic framework reappears forcefully in this prelude to the story of Jephthah, and, more broadly, to the second part of the book. There is the reference to idolatry (10:6), punishment (10:7-9), and repentance (10:10). There is specific reference to the Ammonite incursion east and west of the Jordan, an appropriate introduction to the role of Jephthah (10:8-9). Moreover, the repentance of the Israelites is here more detailed, with a twofold plea to the Lord (10:10, 15) and concrete steps to eliminate idolatry (10:16). With hostilities running high, the opposing forces prepare for battle (10:17-18). The chapter ends with a prophetic allusion to the forthcoming role of Jephthah.

11:1-40 Jephthah

The tribes of Gad and Manasseh occupied the region of Gilead in Transjordan. Jephthah, whose birth was illegitimate, was a native of the region, the son of a man bearing the region's name. His father's other sons disowned their half brother because of his illegitimate origins; distanced from his home, Jephthah joined ranks with a band of brigands (11:1-3).

At this point, the family of the man named Gilead merges with the Gileadite tribes. Thus, it is the elders of Gilead whom Jephthah accuses of driving him from his father's house. Jephthah is seen as a credible warrior. He assumed leadership to wage war against Ammon, with his future position secure (11:9-10).

The new judge's first ploy was diplomatic, sending a delegation to the king of Ammon. After first obtaining the Lord's assurance (11:11), he learned of Ammonite intentions in the Transjordan to "repossess" the land lying between the Arnon and Jabbok rivers (11:11-13). Jephthah rejected the demand through a second delegation, illustrating the legitimacy of Israel's claim. The account of Israel's dealings in the past with Moab, Edom, and the Amorites is in basic agreement with the Pentateuchal narrative found in Numbers 20–24. The disputed territory, now occupied by the Israelites in the Transjordan, had been taken in the war against the Amorites; Israel's claim is legitimate. Since Ammon's designs on westward expansion had been thwarted, war was seen as the only solution. In holding that each country's god establishes boundaries, Jephthah is speaking in diplomatic, not theological, terms (11:24). Either the author or a later copyist has confused the god of the Moabites, Chemosh, with the god of the Ammonites, Molech (cf. Num 21:29; 1 Kgs 11:7). But Jephthah's voice fell on deaf ears. War was now inevitable (11:28).

That the spirit of the Lord has empowered Jephthah does not suffice. He further makes a vow to the Lord in what may have originally been a separate and isolated incident. In exchange for victory, he will sacrifice the first person to emerge from his house upon his return (11:29-31). Human sacrifice was not uncommon among Israel's pagan neighbors but was not practiced in Israel (Lev 18:21; 20:2-5; Deut 12:31; Mic 6:7). The possibility of its limited toleration in early premonarchical times cannot be categorically ruled out. Here the author passes no judgment on Jephthah's decision; it was secondary to the vow itself, which had to be upheld at all cost.

The Ammonites were defeated. The vow was fulfilled even though it meant the sacrifice of Jephthah's only child. That she was a virgin and therefore childless was cause for mourning in itself. This was an unwanted fate for any Israelite woman and called for a period of mourning. For this the daughter was granted a two-month reprieve (11:32-39). The final verse indicates that this may have been written to explain a local annual mourning ritual (11:40).

12:1-7 Internal conflict

The civil conflict between Gilead and Ephraim may have been originally unrelated to Jephthah.

It is inserted here to complement his position as a major judge. A contentious Ephraim has appeared before (12:1, cf. 8:1). The confrontation with Jephthah took place at Zaphon in Gileadite territory. The account reflects the uneasiness of tribal isolation in the absence of any national unity, clearly seen in the case of the insurgent Abimelech in chapter 9. There would seem to be an indication here of Ephraim's intent to move beyond the Jordan, insinuating a claim to territory there (12:4). The charismatic Jephthah and his forces thwarted them. Differences in pronunciation between Ephraimites and Gileadites afforded the opportunity to unmask the fleeing Ephraimites and put them to death (12:6). After a relatively short judgeship, Jephthah died and was buried in his native city (12:7).

12:8-13 More minor judges

Elon and Abdon were from Zebulun and Ephraim respectively. Abdon was from Pirathon on the Ephraim–Manasseh border. Ibzan is identified with Bethlehem, which many authors see as the northern town in Zebulon not the more familiar Bethlehem of Judah. Once again, the judges here seem to have had administrative functions. They ruled after the death of Jephthah in a twenty-five year period marked by peace and harmony.

13:1–16:31 Samson

Referred to by one biblical scholar as a "wenching lout," Samson is one of the most enigmatic persons in the Bible. The accounts of his life have the aura of legend and folklore. Rather than a person raised up as a judge to liberate his people, his exploits seem to be more personal in character, underscoring his personal prowess or vindicating his own position. In this he differs from the other judges. His personal life leaves much to be desired—rash responses, lust for women, disregard of his vowed status. Yet it is in his weakness that the power of YHWH appears most strongly. In Samson the Lord often triumphs not because of him but in spite of him. The narrative comes from a variety of independent sources and is divided: birth (13:1-24), marriage to a Philistine (14:1-9), Philistine defeat (15:1-20), prostitute encounter (16:1-3), Delilah (16:4-22), and finally death (16:23-31).

13:1-24 Birth

The Philistines occupied the coastal region of central Canaan in the twelfth century B.C., close to the time of the Israelite occupation of the land. Formerly in Judges, the enemy threat came principally from the east; here it lies to the west. In Samson's time the Philistines dominated the central part of the country (13:1). Samson's father, Manoah, was a Danite from Zorah in the south, a town which had been allotted to Dan (Josh 19:4); this was before the migration of the tribe north, leaving Zorah as part of Judah (Josh 15:33).

There are several accounts of the announcement of important births in the Old Testament, e.g., Isaac (Gen 15:1-6) and Samuel (1 Sam 1). Here the angel of the Lord is a visible manifestation of YHWH himself (13:21-22). The exceptional character of the forthcoming birth is clear: the barren wife conceives by divine design (13:3), and Nazirite features are connected with his birth (13:4-5; see Num 6:2-8). The law of abstinence is imposed on the child's mother and his hair is not to be cut. These are external features of his consecration to the Lord (13:5b).

Solemnity is added through the double announcement, first to the mother (13:3-7) and then the father (13:13-14). The son's mission will be the liberation of his people, in a departure from the usual formula of this promise following upon a plea for deliverance (13:5). Underscoring the divine character of the vision, the angel vanishes in flame, the holocaust is offered, and there is the refusal of identification (13:17-20). Knowledge of the name gave authority or dominion over the one named and is thus excluded (Gen 2:20; 32:30). Soon after his birth Samson was spirit-empowered and his destiny was fixed (13:25).

14:1-20 Marriage

In the twofold prediction about Samson, he was to be consecrated to the Lord and would initiate deliverance from the Philistines (13:5). The first is highlighted in the circumstances of his birth (13:24-25); the second, in the account of his marriage.

Timnah was in Philistine territory but a short distance from Zorah. Samson's impulsive attraction to an unnamed Philistine woman manifested more lust than discernment (14:1-2). His parents' objection to the marriage on religious grounds is overridden by the editorial comment in verse 4:

this was God's way of inserting Samson into Philistine life.

The role of the parents in obtaining the girl's hand is confusing. They are said to accompany their son (14:5) and yet are distant from the events described; in fact, there is an allusion to his second trip to marry the girl, wherein the mother and father are mentioned (14:6-9) and subsequently the father alone (14:10). There is evidently here an uneven blending of sources. The slaughter of the lion exemplifies the hero's exceptional strength (14:6), and the later presence of bees in the carcass is prelude to the riddle in the subsequent episode (14:8).

Samson's character as a rogue comes to light in the marriage account. Being the sole outsider puts him at a disadvantage in his in-laws' eyes. He is thus presented with thirty male companions, not only as part of the wedding party but also as future companions in a foreign culture (14:11). The riddle proposed by Samson could never have been solved without knowledge of his prior encounter with the lion: sweet food (honey) comes from the predatory beast. Here it serves as a literary device to enhance Samson's superiority. The use of the wife to obtain the solution subtly foreshadows the following Delilah story (14:13-17). Samson alludes to his wife's role in obtaining the solution to his riddle in his retort, which contains its own ribald nuance (14:18).

Samson has lost his bet but resorts to slaughter to make good on his promise. Acting impulsively he then annuls his marriage. His attack on the Philistines is cruel and boorish. It serves, however, to highlight his superiority and ability to humiliate his foes, all accomplished in "the spirit of the Lord" (14:19).

15:1-20 Philistine defeat

The chapter contains a number of Samson stories which may well have existed independently. There is no essential inter-relatedness in the loss of his wife (15:1-3), the burning of the fields (15:4-5), the defeat of the Philistines (15:6-7), and the annihilation at Lehi (15:9-19). There are, in fact, a number of incongruities in the editorial attempt to unify these stories, e.g., Samson's return to a repudiated wife, a massive response against the Philistines because of his in-laws' limited action against him, then a later strong reaction against the Philistines on behalf of the same despised rela-

tives. However, in the editing of the final text, these are a series of inter-locking episodes highlighting Samson's prowess and charismatic spirit.

The loss of his wife should have come as no surprise to Samson after he had abandoned her (15:1-2; 14:19-20). In Hebrew law, at least at a later date, he could not have taken her back after remarriage (Deut 24:1-4). Rejecting her younger sister, he plans retaliation not against the families but against the Philistine population (15:3). The use of the foxes for incendiary purposes, with its sudden and unforeseen character, was a guerilla tactic (15:4-6). Violence escalates with the killing of his wife and relatives by the Philistines (15:6), which then leads Samson to single-handed revenge against a great number of his opponents (15:7-8).

The following episode takes place in Judahite territory, a tribe not thus far involved in the Samson narrative. But Judah was also under Philistine domination (15:11); thus they capitulated readily to the occupiers' demand for Samson's extradition. Judah took no chances against their powerful countryman in sending three thousand men to arrest him (15:11). Taking no action against his own people, Samson surrendered without incident. But before being handed over to his enemy, again empowered by the Lord's spirit and with the jawbone of an ass as a weapon, he dispatched one thousand Philistines (15:12-15). The rhyme in 15:16 causes one to wonder to what extent the jingle has influenced the formation of the narrative.

Two etiologies complete the chapter, both of them connected with local sites. Ramath-lehi ("the heights of the jawbone") and En-hakkore ("the spring of the caller") are connected with the battle and the later slaking of the hero's thirst (15:17-19). The conclusion points to an earlier ending of the Samson story at this point (15:20).

16:1-22 A further adventure and Delilah

What this chapter lacks in moral refinement it supplies in vivid drama. The fateful romance between Samson and Delilah is preceded by a bit of folklore surrounding the protagonist (16:1-3). Samson's amorous visit to Gaza in the heart of enemy territory was ruled more by passion than good sense. But once again moral weakness is overshadowed by physical prowess as he carries the city gate from Gaza in coastal Philistia to

Hebron in eastern Judah! The account is clearly didactic in character: a morally weak but empowered Samson renders his pagan foe inept and ridiculous by carrying off the gates of the city.

Still on Philistine soil, Samson became enamored of Delilah (i.e., "flirtatious"). The theme of the story is enunciated by the enemy: to determine the source of this Hebrew's strength (16:5). The threefold attempt by Delilah to obtain the answer strains the reader's willingness to accept the unlikely as much as it carries the drama forward. In a match of wits employed by Samson, Delilah is left without the answer (16:6-14). Persistence crowns her efforts as she finally attains her end; his strength is in his hair (16:15-17). This follows logically from his Nazirite vow which forbade the cutting of hair (13:5). With the secret known and the locks shorn, Samson is rendered powerless. The Nazirite vow at this point has become completely unraveled, since he has presumably already broken the other two prohibitions through contact with corpses and the presumed drinking of wine (cf. 14:10). The wounded hero is blinded and subjected to forced labor. Only the mentioned regrowth of the hair sounds an ominous note (16:22).

16:21-31 The death of Samson

As colorful, and even unsavory, as much of the Samson story is, it serves the Deuteronomist's purpose. Regardless of how dire the situation, a return to the Lord brings deliverance. This is clear in the climax of the narrative. In the pagan temple to the god Dagon, the blind Samson is brought to a scene of cultic revelry and taunted by his captors (16:23-25). This has now become a contest between deities: Dagon and YHWH. As weakened as he may have been, Samson stations himself in a strategic position to effect the collapse of the temple. Nothing transpires before his prayerful invocation of the Lord (16:28). But unlike former judges, he pleads not for deliverance of the people but for personal vindication. The prayer is heard and a massive destruction of the pagan enemy follows (16:29-30).

After a twenty-year judgeship, Samson was laid to rest (16:31), following a life which, if it was not always marked by virtue, was certainly expressive of faith and an abiding trust in the God of Israel.

APPENDIX

Judges 17–21

The final chapters of Judges come from the Deuteronomistic editors and are different thematically from the rest of the book. There are no judges, no vindication of Israel over pagan oppressors, no impressive leaders. In the main, they are a sad commentary on tribal life in Israel before unification. Their pro-monarchical bent emerges from a negative assessment of social life without a king and cultic life without central control. These are tales of moral turpitude, civil war, and priestly patronage. The section is easily divided into two: the migration of Dan to the north (chs. 17–18) and the civil war against Benjamin (chs. 19–21).

17:1-13 Micah and the Levite

Micah, whose name ironically means "Who is like YHWH?" was an Ephraimite placed under a curse for stealing from his mother (17:2). Even restored, the stolen goods remained tainted, with part of the silver used to fashion an idol (17:4). His religious interests also led to his making a priestly garment (ephod) and consecrating his son a priest (17:5). His actions were reprehensible. Images, especially of YHWH, were prohibited by law (Exod 20:2-5) and priesthood, while perhaps less regulated at this early stage, was limited to Levites by the time of Judges' composition.

The locale eventually became a sanctuary for which Micah obtained the services of a Levite from Judah (17:9-10). That an Ephraimite consecrated a Levite a priest may reflect early custom when norms were less fixed (17:12; cf. Lev 8–9). Micah became the priest's patron to whom the latter was beholden (17:13).

18:1-31 Dan

The tribe of Dan had been allocated territory in the southwest, contiguous with Judah and Benjamin. However, they never succeeded in gaining a foothold and so eventually migrated to the north (Josh 19:40-48; Judg 1:34). At the time of the divided kingdom, there were two major sanctuaries in the north, one at Bethel, the other at Dan (1 Kgs 12:28-30). Both were involved in illicit worship from their beginnings. The present account of the sanctuary in Dan clearly points to its unseemly origins.

Five scouts are sent from the south to reconnoiter the land, and they meet Micah and his priest (18:3-6). It may have been a different accent that makes the Levite recognizable (18:3). His credentials are tested by asking him to divine God's will, which leads to a favorable response (18:5-6).

The scouts proceed to the farthest point north, Laish, at the base of Mt. Hermon, which is the source of the Jordan river (18:7-8). They make a positive report upon returning home (18:7-10). With military force, they proceed north to make the conquest, making a stop in Judah in the region of Kiriath-jearim, gifting a part of the region with a second name, Mahaneh-dan ("the camp of Dan").

Iniquity is compounded as the Danites steal sacred objects in Micah's sanctuary and prevail upon the priest to accompany them. Certain that they will be pursued by Micah and his compatriots, the Danites invert the line of march, with families and livestock going first and the military as a rear guard (18:13-21). Micah pursues but is intimidated by the superior forces (18:22-26). Reaching the peaceful and unprotected citizens of Laish, the Danites unleash a deadly force in a fiendish and brutal fashion. It is an unwarranted slaughter (18:27-31).

Dan loses no time in constructing their sanctuary and installing their priest, who is now identified as Jonathan of the line of Moses; it is his descendants who will continue in priestly ministry (18:30). Like Bethel, the Dan sanctuary lasted until the Assyrian invasion in 734 B.C. (18:30). Its life was co-extensive with that of the authentic sanctuary of YHWH at Shiloh (18:31), and it appears here in a very negative light. Its origins were related to stolen gods; it had enthroned idols, a subordinated priesthood, and was established in the wake of a ruthless invasion.

19:1–21:25 Civil War

There is little of redeeming value regarding tribal life in this final segment of the book; rather, the picture is one of increasing moral disintegration. It is quite possible that we are dealing with originally distinct and detached events in the story of the Levite and his concubine (19:1-14), the incident at Gibeah (19:15-29), the assembly and war against Benjamin (20:1-48), and the parallel accounts of providing women for Benjamin (21:1-14; 21:15-25). These accounts have been skill-fully edited to form one continuous narrative. The pro-monarchical slant, seen especially in the events surrounding the survival of Benjamin, is much to the fore.

19:1-30 The Levite from Ephraim

Like Micah, the unnamed Levite is from Ephraimite territory (19:1; 17:1). An alternate reading for verse 2 in some manuscripts has the concubine leaving the Levite because she was angry rather than unfaithful. At any rate, the move was unusual because the woman could not initiate divorce proceedings according to Hebrew law. The Levite's attempt at reconciliation found him and his father-in-law in remarkable accord, enjoying five days of feasting (19:4-10). The sentiments of the concubine, however, are never mentioned. On the return journey home, they bypass pagan Jebusite Jerusalem to lodge among their own in Benjaminite territory (19:10-14).

The hospitality of the man in Gibeah, who is also from Ephraim, contrasts sharply with the conduct of the townspeople (19:15-21). In fact, the repulsive gesture at Gibeah earned for it a name of poor repute. The efforts of the men to abuse the guest sexually mirrors very closely the scene at Sodom (19:22-24; cf. Gen 19:4-8), and the retaliation against Gibeah resembles that of Saul at Jabesh-gilead (1 Sam 11:7-8). In demanding the overnight guest, the men of Gibeah violated the sacred law of hospitality, but the alternative solution was equally abhorrent. By modern standards, the treatment of the concubine was unconscionable. Both her husband and the Gibeahites share the guilt in her death, although it is the latter who appear reprehensible in the narrative. There is no criticism of her dismemberment, an action which was geared to create a strong reaction (19:25-30). From an editorial vantage point, the death of the concubine was seen as so serious that it resulted in an Israelite assembly.

20:1-48 War with Benjamin

As formerly noted, the war with Benjamin over the death of a single person may be more literary than historical. The picture is one of Israelites in battle array, with numbers that are undoubtedly inflated (20:2). The Levite's account of the event at Gibeah attempts to color the facts (20:4-5). He mentions an attempt on his life not heretofore indicated, and does not state that he gave his concubine to the men who abused her. The first overture made by the indignant Israelites was to ask for the extradition of the men of Gibeah guilty of the crime (20:11-13); this failing, a full-scale battle ensued (20:20-48). In the first two encounters, the Benjaminites were victorious (20:20-29), in the third, they were defeated through a clever ruse (20:30-35). The two defeats of the Israelite forces gave the impression of an inadequate military force (20:20-25). With the third attack the Benjaminites felt more secure and moved their troops out of the city in pursuit of the enemy (20:30-32). In abandoning Gibeah, they left their rear flank unprotected. The concealed Israelites then staged an ambush, entered and destroyed the city, putting it to the torch (20:36-42). Caught in this "pincer" strategy from the front and behind, the Benjaminite troops were in disarray and quickly defeated (20:43-47). Thus, the Gibeahites, their city, and the forces of Benjamin were decimated. This proved to be a serious insurrection and brought great damage and loss to one of Israel's tribes.

21:1-25 The future of Benjamin

Following the defeat of Benjamin, Israel was faced with a dilemma. In the heat of the assembly, the other tribes had sworn not to have their daughters marry Benjaminites. This now meant that one of the twelve tribes was faced with extinction (21:17). In determining who had not been present at Mizpah for the vow, the name of Jabesh-gilead in Transjordan emerged (21:8). Once again the decision involved an act of terror. The city was destroyed with all its inhabitants, except for the unmarried women, four hundred in number. These were then given to the Benjaminite male population (21:1-14).

In what may well be a parallel source, now made complementary to the preceding, the number of women was not sufficient. An annual feast at Shiloh offered the opportunity for abduction, and this the Benjaminites were counseled to do (21:15-22). The proposed response to be given the girls' families was disingenuous. In accepting the fact of their abduction and generously letting things stand, the families would not be guilty of violating the vow, since the women had not been offered (21:22). Benjamin was thus assured a future, the tribe was reinstated, and peace returned (21:23-24).

The Deuteronomist gives his assessment of such unwarranted and unruly conduct. Without a king, people made their own choices (21:25). From his perspective, the argument has been well made, and the reader is now prepared for the rise of the monarchy.

THE BOOK OF
RUTH

Irene Nowell, O.S.B.

INTRODUCTION

THE FESTIVAL SCROLLS

Five Old Testament books are identified in the Hebrew Bible as the Festival Scrolls, or *Megilloth* (Hebrew: "scrolls"): Song of Songs, Ruth, Lamentations, Ecclesiastes (also known as Qoheleth), and Esther. These short books are read at important Jewish festivals during the year: The Song of Songs is read in the spring on Passover as a testimony of God's love for the chosen people. The book of Ruth is read on Pentecost (Weeks) because the date of this festival is set by counting the seven weeks between the beginning of the barley harvest and the beginning of the wheat harvest; the story of Ruth is set in that time frame. Lamentations is read in some Jewish communities on the ninth of Ab, the commemoration in late July or early August of the destruction of the temple in 587 B.C. and A.D. 70. Ecclesiastes is read on the feast of Booths, the last harvest festival of the year (September–October). The book of Esther provides the foundation for the celebration of Purim in the winter month of Adar (February–March).

These five books have a tangled history in Jewish and Christian Bibles. Jews debated into the first century A.D. whether Song of Songs, Ecclesiastes, and Esther belonged in the Scriptures at all. Esther is the only book of the Hebrew Scriptures that was not found among the Dead Sea Scrolls. The Hebrew version of Esther (see Introduction to Esther) and the Song of Songs are the only two

biblical books that never mention God, which may be why they were questioned. All five books have been put in different places in different versions of Scripture. The Septuagint (the Greek translation of Jewish Scripture) placed Ruth where the story fits chronologically, between Judges and 1 Samuel, which is where it is found in Christian Bibles. In the Septuagint (followed again by Christian Bibles) Lamentations is found after Jeremiah, who was traditionally considered its author. All five books have always been included in the third section of the Hebrew Scriptures, called the Writings, where they are found in Jewish Bibles today. Even in the Writings, however, their arrangement has varied in different manuscripts. The Hebrew text used by scholars has an arrangement from the eleventh-century Leningrad manuscript: Ruth, Song of Songs, Ecclesiastes, Lamentations, Esther. Hebrew Bibles used by most Jews today arrange the books in liturgical order as they are in this commentary. In Christian Bibles Esther is found with the historical books—after Tobit and Judith in the Roman Catholic canon and after Nehemiah in the Protestant canon. Ecclesiastes and Song of Songs are found after Proverbs among the wisdom books.

Despite their "wandering ways," each of these little books has a poetic beauty and a powerful message. Having them gathered in one small volume gives the reader a wealth of God's word to ponder.

Literary quality

The book of Ruth is a masterpiece of storytelling. The narrative is fictional, but the memory of David's ancestry may be historically accurate. The author's literary artistry is evident especially in the rhythmic prose and pace of the story. Care is taken with the dialogue: the older characters, Boaz and Naomi, speak in more formal and archaic language than the younger characters. Word play hints at hidden meaning, such as the echo between the words for "redeem" (*ga'al*) and "uncover" (*galah*) in the scene at the threshing floor and the double entendre of "knowing" in this emotionally charged scene (ch. 3). Other key words weave through the story: return/go back, kindness/loyalty (*hesed*), cling, empty, worthy/powerful (*hayil*), wings.

The characters are complex and well drawn. The reader is left to wonder whether Naomi did not want companions or why Boaz did not help the women sooner, why Ruth turned her attention to the older Boaz or what either woman thought would happen at the threshing floor. The plot is carefully structured. The two central chapters have similar patterns, with conversation between Ruth and Naomi surrounding the encounters between Ruth and Boaz. The first and last chapters mirror each other with discussions of kinship and the appearance of the women of Bethlehem. The story, however, does not go in a circle but moves resolutely from emptiness to fullness, desolation to redemption.

Context

The setting of the story is the time of the judges (1250–1050 B.C.) when the tribes were semi-autonomous. There was no ruler over all the twelve tribes, no capital city or central shrine. Stories in the book of Judges show it to be a rough period, a time of conflict between tribes and with neighboring peoples. A particularly horrific story is set in Bethlehem (Judg 19). Moab is the "off-stage" scene. Moab, east of Judah, on the other side of the Dead Sea, is often regarded negatively in the Bible. Its origin is traced to the incest between Lot and his elder daughter (Gen 19:37). The Moabites are remembered for their refusal to give supplies to the Israelites when they came out of the desert on their way to the Promised Land (see Judg 11:17-18). Balak, king of Moab, summoned the prophet Balaam to curse Israel (Num 22:4-6). Because of these things, there is a prohibition against admitting Moabites into the community up to the tenth generation (Deut 23:4-7; see Neh 13:1-2). In the desert Moabite women lured the people into idolatry (Num 25:1-5). In the time of the judges the Moabite king, Eglon, oppressed Israel for eighteen years (Judg 3:12-14). Later, however, David took his parents to stay in Moab for protection while he was fleeing from Saul (1 Sam 22:3-4) suggesting that he may indeed have had Moabite ancestors.

Date

The book of Ruth is virtually impossible to date. The story probably circulated orally before it was written down. The style and content suggest the time of the monarchy, perhaps the ninth–eighth century.

Theology

The most important theological question for the reader of Ruth is "where is God?" God acts only once, causing Ruth to conceive (4:13). It is reported that God has given the people food (1:6). All other mention of God is in blessings, prayers, or laments (e.g., 1:8-9, 13, 20-21). Throughout the book, however, the characters expect God to act. Most striking is the fact that the characters themselves fulfill these expectations (compare 2:12 with 3:9; 1:21 with 3:17). Is the storyteller saying that God works through the courageous actions of faithful people?

COMMENTARY

NAOMI IN MOAB

Ruth 1:1-18

The story is situated between the time of the judges and the beginning of the monarchy. The refrain at the end of the book of Judges—"there was no king in Israel; everyone did what was right in their own sight"—suggests a longing for a more stable situation (Judg 17:6; 21:25; see 18:1; 19:1). The book of Ruth ends with the name of Israel's best beloved king: David.

The need to relocate because of famine is mentioned more often with the patriarchs than in the period of judges (see Gen 12:10; 26:1; 42:5). It is ironic that a man from Bethlehem, which in Hebrew means "house of bread," should have to leave home with his family and go to Moab (see Introduction) because there is no bread (1:1). The occasion sets up a theme in the book of "empty" and "full" (see 1:21; 3:17). At the beginning of the story the family leaves empty of bread but full of sons.

The questions "when" and "where" are answered. Now "who" is involved in this story? In the first five verses six characters are introduced and three—all the men—die. The action of the story begins with their three widows: a Judahite woman and her two Moabite daughters-in-law.

Immediately the three women set out on the road back to Judah (1:6). The repetition of two Hebrew words for "go" (ten times) and "return" (twelve times) sets the tone of this chapter. Naomi returns because her family is dead and she has heard that the famine is over. Why do the two younger women set out? Do they plan to accompany her a short distance on the road, or is their original plan to go the whole way? Three conversations turn on this question.

In the first conversation (1:8-10) Naomi indicates to her daughters-in-law that they have come far enough and prepares to say goodbye. She blesses them for their kindness (Hebrew *hesed*), the faithful love that characterizes the covenant bond, and she prays that God will grant them security. Two "houses" frame her words. She sends them back to their "mother's house." This phrase is much less frequent than "father's house." It occurs only in the betrothal scene of Rebekah (Gen 24:28) and the Song of Songs (3:4;

8:2). The phrase is probably equivalent to the "father's house." It may be used here because the conversation is between women; the mother-in-law urges them to return to their mother's house. It seems also to be used in the context of marriage. Naomi prays that each will soon be in her "husband's house."

Naomi becomes more insistent in the second conversation (1:11-14). The young women have no hope with her; she cannot give them husbands. She herself is without hope. There is a suggestion here of the practice of levirate marriage, where a man's brother marries his widow in order to raise up children for him (see Deut 25:5-10). Naomi says this is impossible; Mahlon and Chilion left no surviving brothers. Then she turns to the question of security again. The only security for women she can imagine—and the reality of the cultural situation is on her side—is in marriage. Orpah obeys her mother-in-law and sensibly turns back. But Ruth "clung," a word suggestive both of marriage and of covenant. In Genesis 2 a man leaves father and mother and clings to his wife (Gen 2:24); Ruth will not leave her mother-in-law but clings to her. In Deuteronomy the covenant people are urged to cling to God (Deut 4:4; 10:20; 11:22; 13:5).

Covenant language appears in the third conversation (1:15-18). Naomi now insists that Ruth identify with her sister-in-law and thus with the Moabite people and their god. Ruth insists on bonding with her mother-in-law and, in the best-known passage of the book, makes a lifetime commitment to Naomi, her people, and her God (see Exod 6:7; Lev 26:12). She seals the commitment with an oath in the name of YHWH, Israel's God. Naomi says no more.

THE RETURN TO BETHLEHEM

Ruth 1:19-22

Did Ruth and Naomi travel in silence the rest of the way to Bethlehem? What does Naomi's silence mean? When the two arrive, her bitterness overflows. The women of the town (who will reappear in ch. 4) seem both excited and shocked to see this woman who left more than ten years ago with a husband and two sons (1:19). Now she reappears with only a woman companion. She responds to their question by changing her name from Sweet to Bitter (1:20). There is no attempt to introduce Ruth, who will be forever known as "the Moabite woman."

Naomi blames God for her troubles (1:21). She accuses God of trying her in court and condemning her to a harsh sentence. She claims that God has made her life bitter, bringing her back to Bethlehem empty. She cries out in the tradition of the lament psalms (see especially Ps 88) and the book of Job. The lament psalms almost always turn to hope in the end. Naomi's bitter cry is the first move toward that hope.

God appears several times in this first chapter and with several names. As "LORD" (Hebrew *yhwh*) God is the one who relieved the famished people's need (1:6). Naomi prays that the Lord will take care of her daughters-in-law (1:8-9). But it is also the Lord who caused Naomi's distress (1:13) and brought her back empty (1:21). In her final outburst (1:20-21) Naomi names God "Almighty" (Hebrew *shaddai*), an ancient name going back to the time of Abraham (see Gen 17:1).

The chapter closes with a note of hope: Bethlehem, house of bread, is about to begin the barley harvest. Thus it is Passover time.

THE MEETING

Ruth 2:1-23

2:1-2 Ruth at home with Naomi

This chapter can be divided into three scenes: Ruth at home with Naomi (2:1-2); Ruth in the field of Boaz (2:3-17); Ruth at home with Naomi (2:18-23). The first scene is very brief but provides two hints that better times are ahead. The narrator introduces a rich and powerful relative of Naomi's husband. Will he come forward to help the two women? Why has he not done so already? Ruth ventures out to seek food for herself and Naomi. She has a triple right to glean, according to the law (Deut 24:19): she is a widow, "fatherless" (having left her parents), and a stranger. But will she, "the Moabite," be allowed to do so? Will this action cheer up her mother-in-law?

Ruth's intention to glean reveals an important theme in this book: the presence of the needy poor. Naomi and her family went to Moab "empty" because of famine; now she and Ruth

are hungry, even though God has provided food for the people in this "house of bread" (2:6). The vulnerable remain dependent on the generosity of others.

2:3-17 Ruth in the field of Boaz

The narrator cannot wait to announce more good news: The field Ruth chooses belongs to Boaz and soon the man himself appears (2:3-4). Boaz speaks first to the laborers hired to harvest his crop, greeting them with a common blessing. Then he asks the overseer about Ruth (2:5). Apparently he has spotted her among the gleaners, those following the harvesters. He asks not her name but her identity: Whose is she? Whose daughter or wife? The overseer recites the essentials—still omitting her name: She is not the daughter of anyone you know but is a foreigner, a Moabite; she does not have a husband but came with Naomi (2:6). This information, along with the observation mentioned twice that she is young, reveals Ruth to be very vulnerable. She has no protector, and Moabites are associated with illicit sexuality (see Introduction). The overseer also mentions her request to glean and her perseverance.

Next Boaz speaks to Ruth with a series of staccato commands: "Listen," "Do not go," "Stay," "Watch," and "drink" (2:8-9). He is the owner and in charge of gleaners as well as harvesters. His speech (like Naomi's) is formal and somewhat archaic, possibly indicating that he belongs to the older generation in contrast to all the young people around him: Ruth, whom he calls "daughter" (2:8; see 2:5, 6), the overseer (2:5, 6), and the young men (2:9, 15, 21) and young women (2:8, 22, 23) harvesters. His instructions indicate three things: his desire to have Ruth remain in his field, his awareness of her vulnerability, and his attentive care of her (permission to drink from the harvesters' water supply). In the conversation that follows she acknowledges her vulnerability and his attentive care. She had set out to glean in the field of someone in whose eyes she might find favor; now she is amazed that she has found favor (2:2, 10, 13).

Boaz, it turns out, knows who Ruth is, having heard the Bethlehem gossip (2:11-12). He prays that the Lord will reward her. The idea of taking shelter under God's wings, found in the Psalms (Pss 36:8; 61:5; 91:4), suggests the image of a mother bird protecting her young (see Exod 19:4;

Deut 32:11) and also the wings of the cherubim on either side of the ark in the temple (see 1 Kgs 8:6; Isa 6:2). Ruth takes what Boaz says and turns it back toward him: *He* is the "lord" in whose eyes she hopes to find favor (2:13). In the next chapter she will ask *him* to spread his wing over her (3:9).

Boaz continues his kindness, inviting her to eat with the harvesters and making sure she has more than enough food. He also makes sure she has more than enough to glean (2:14-16). At the end of the day she has about an ephah of barley, somewhere around thirty pounds (2:17)! It has been a very good day!

2:18-23 Ruth at home with Naomi

When Ruth produces the abundance of grain plus the leftovers from lunch, Naomi is amazed. After two "where" questions, she pronounces a blessing on the man who has helped her. Naomi does not yet know who this is, but she is sure some man must have made all this possible. The reader has been waiting since verse 1 for this revelation, but Ruth keeps Naomi in suspense until the end of the sentence (2:19). As soon as Naomi hears the name Boaz, she tells Ruth that he is someone on whom they can count for help. He is a *go'el*, a "redeemer" (2:20). The *go'el* had responsibilities to help a debtor regain land (Lev 25:25) or be released from slavery (Lev 25:48); he also had responsibility to avenge one's murder (Num 35:19, 21). The responsibility of a man to marry his deceased brother's widow is nowhere included among the responsibilities of a *go'el*, and Naomi herself seems to think that this duty of levirate marriage applies only to a brother (1:11), not to a larger kinship. So what does she expect of Boaz, a member of Elimilech's clan? Naomi's words are also ambiguous: who is it "who never fails to show kindness to the living and to the dead"? The Hebrew allows for either subject: the Lord or Boaz ("he").

Naomi has been transformed by this good news. She is now speaking to Ruth in full sentences. She is blessing the Lord whom she earlier accused. She now thinks of Ruth as part of the family: "near relative of *ours*, one of *our* redeemers" (emphasis added).

In the final interchange between the two women there is an amusing confusion of words (2:21-22). Ruth reports (incorrectly) that Boaz has told her to stay with his "young men"; Naomi, well aware of her daughter-in-law's vulnerability,

points out that it would be better to work with his "young women." The word translated "stay" is the same verb translated as "cling" in 1:14, emphasizing the inadvisability of "clinging" to the young men. Ruth obeys Naomi, staying with the young women throughout the grain harvest. The time between the beginning of the barley harvest and the end of the wheat harvest is usually calculated as seven weeks, the time between Passover and Pentecost (see Deut 16:9-10).

RUTH AGAIN PRESENTS HERSELF
Ruth 3:1-18

3:1-6 Ruth at home with Naomi

Chapter 3 can also be divided into three scenes: Ruth at home with Naomi (3:1-6); Ruth at the threshing floor with Boaz (3:7-15); Ruth at home with Naomi (3:16-18). In chapter 2 Boaz addressed Ruth with a series of commands (2:8-9); in the first scene of chapter 3 a revived Naomi gives the commands. Naomi had prayed that her two daughters-in-law would find rest in the home of a husband (1:9). Now she sets out to find that "rest" for Ruth (3:1). Ruth is to beautify herself and find Boaz at the threshing floor (3:3). This instruction already seems scandalous; should a young woman go alone at night to a place where men have been working all day and drinking through the evening? Naomi's second instruction is even more shocking: uncover the sleeping Boaz and lie down next to him (3:4)! Ruth is to uncover his "feet." But this is not the common word for "feet"; it may also connote "legs." In addition, "feet" is the common euphemism for genitals. So it is unclear how much of Boaz Ruth is supposed to uncover, but Naomi's words are certainly suggestive. Ruth's response is simple assent (3:5). Her words echo Israel's response to God in the covenant making at Sinai: "Everything the LORD has said, we will do" (Exod 19:8).

A question arises concerning why Boaz is winnowing barley at the end of the wheat harvest. Were the sheaves stored and all the grain winnowed at once?

3:7-15 Ruth at the threshing floor with Boaz

This section is characterized by the absence of proper names; each character is only named once

(3:7, 9). It is night at the threshing floor and whatever happens is shrouded in secrecy. Ruth has indeed followed Naomi's instructions. Boaz is startled awake in the middle of the night—because he is cold? Or aware of another presence? The narrator takes the viewpoint of Boaz: He groped around and look! a woman at his feet (3:8)! He demands: Who are you! Her response recalls their conversation in the field, but there are significant differences. Earlier she said she was not his servant (2:13); now she identifies herself as "servant" (3:9). But she has changed the term for "servant" from *shiphhah* to *amah*; the *amah* was eligible for marriage with her master whereas the *shiphhah* was not. Boaz had described her taking shelter under the Lord's wing; she asks Boaz to spread the wing of his cloak over her. In this context the request suggests sexual relations and is tantamount to a proposal of marriage (see Deut 23:1; Ezek 16:8). She continues: You are a redeemer, a *go'el*. What does Ruth expect? Nowhere else does the responsibility of the *go'el* include marriage to a relative's widow. Does Ruth, a Moabite, not know that? Is she only picking up the word from Naomi, understanding it (correctly) to be someone who is responsible to help family members in need? Is Ruth being creative? Is this part of the law that we simply do not know? (Notice also that it is Ruth who is telling Boaz what to do, not the reverse as Naomi suggested.)

Boaz describes Ruth's second act of loyalty (*hesed*) as greater than the first (3:10). Is the first act her commitment to Naomi, which Boaz mentioned earlier (see 1:8; 2:11)? Is her offer of marriage to Boaz a further commitment to Naomi? Ruth was not bound by the laws of levirate marriage. She has no brothers-in-law and she is a foreigner. She could have married any of the young men. But such a marriage might have separated her from Naomi, whereas marriage to a relative will not.

Now Boaz echoes Ruth's words: whatever you say (3:11). He identifies her as "a worthy woman" (Hebrew, *eshet hayil*). He was introduced with the same adjective, "powerful, worthy" (2:1, *ish gibbor hayil*). He has erased the social distinction between them; she is no longer to be identified as "servant." In some versions of the Jewish Bible the book of Ruth comes immediately after the book of Proverbs. The final poem in that book begins with the question: "Who can find a woman of worth?" (*eshet hayil*; Prov 31:10). Boaz says, "I have."

Boaz accepts Ruth's identification of him as a "redeemer" and uses the root word "redeem" six times in verses 12-13. But there is a further twist in the plot, a closer relative. So secrecy must be maintained. Ruth leaves at the first light of dawn (3:14-15).

3:16-18 Ruth at home with Naomi

This is the last conversation between the two women; neither will speak again. Ruth reports on the night's happenings and gives her mother-in-law the gift of grain. Boaz admires Ruth's care for Naomi; he too cares for her. He has again acted in the Lord's name, not sending Ruth back to Naomi "empty" (3:17; see Naomi's complaint against the Lord in 1:21). Naomi assures Ruth (and the reader) that the complication will be solved "today" (3:18).

BOAZ MARRIES RUTH

Ruth 4:1-22

In this chapter the scene returns to the public view: Boaz and the "other redeemer" at the town gate (4:1-12); the women's celebration over the birth of a son (4:14-17); a closing genealogy (4:18-22). Only in verse 13, which reports in short order the marriage of Boaz and Ruth and the birth of their son, is there the suggestion of a private space.

4:1-12 At the town gate

The town gate is the setting for the exercise of law, business, and political judgment. Every man could be expected to pass through the gate to the fields and back every day. Boaz summons the "other redeemer" and ten elders who will function as witnesses to settle the matter (the reader thinks) of his marriage to Ruth (4:1-2). He calls the "other redeemer" *peloni almoni*, a Hebrew way of saying "Mr. So-and-So." Why does he do this? Surely he knows the man's name! There is no need to protect him since there is no negative judgment against him. The narrative effect of his "non-name" is to diminish this character even more than Orpah in chapter 1; he is simply not worth naming!

The reader is surprised that Boaz begins not with the issue of marriage but with the sale of a piece of land (4:3-4). Why did we not know Naomi had land? Why does she seem so destitute? What has happened to the land since Elimelech and his family left Bethlehem? How does Boaz have authority to dispose of the land? The narrator does not answer these questions. The issue of land, however, is appropriate to the responsibility of the *go'el*. (The root word "redeem" occurs four times in verse 4.) A reasonable scenario is this: When Elimelech left Bethlehem, someone else began to farm the abandoned land. Naomi's return coincided with the harvest, and no claim to the land could be made until the harvest was complete. In reclaiming the land Naomi seems to have two choices: find someone to cultivate it or sell it. If she puts it up for sale, the *go'el* has the responsibility to acquire it (Lev 25:25) so that the land will remain within the clan (see Lev 25:10; Num 36:8). Even if she sells it, the land is to be returned at the next jubilee year (see Lev 25:28). Thus Boaz seems to be acting out of courtesy to the man who has the first right of refusal. The man no doubt recognizes that he will have to return the land and that he is also taking responsibility for Naomi's welfare by purchasing it. He agrees to act as *go'el*.

Then Boaz reveals the surprise: Ruth is part of the package (4:5)! This is not only to be an act of "redemption" but also a levirate marriage. The Hebrew is confusing here. What is written is *"I will acquire Ruth,"* but the transmitters of the text in early medieval period revocalized it to say, *"you must acquire Ruth."* (The NABRE translation clarifies that "responsibility for Ruth" is the object of acquisition.) Although the two options change the plot considerably, the consequence is similar: economic loss. If Boaz marries Ruth, there will probably be an heir to whom the land will revert in the name of Ruth's first husband. If the "other redeemer" marries her, he will have to support her, plus any children she may have. In the situation of levirate marriage no attention is given to the *levir's* current marital situation. "Mr. So-and-So" probably already has a wife and children. In addition, Ruth is a Moabite, which may cause the man to hesitate. It is too much. He relinquishes his right and responsibility (4:6). The ritual of relinquishing is otherwise unknown. The "other redeemer" takes off his sandal and gives it to Boaz as a sign that Boaz now has the right and responsibility to act (4:7-8). There are echoes of the ritual

when a widow is rejected by her brother-in-law: she is to take off his sandal and spit in his face (Deut 25:8-10). In that ritual the potential husband is shamed; here there is no shaming.

Boaz calls on the witnesses to confirm the transaction: he acquires the land and Ruth; he acts as *go'el* and *levir* (4:9-10). All the people at the gate—the ten elders and the crowd that has gathered—bless Boaz and his marriage (4:11-12). (Note: they ignore the land.) They pray for the prosperity of Boaz and that the marriage be blessed with children—thus he will be able to "Bestow a name." They pray that Ruth may be like the matriarchs of Israel: Rachel, the beloved wife; Leah, mother of six of the twelve tribes (plus two from her maidservant, Zilpah); and Tamar, ancestor of Boaz. Each of these women endured unusual marriage circumstances. Leah was substituted for Rachel on Jacob's wedding night and Rachel wedded only later (Gen 29:21-30). Like Ruth, Tamar was a foreign woman caught in a troublesome situation of levirate marriage (see Gen 38). After the death of two husbands, she disguised herself and tricked her father-in-law Judah into fathering her twin sons. Judah judged her "more righteous" than himself. Each of these women was *eshet hayil*, a woman of worth.

The Lord has been mentioned in blessings throughout the book, but only twice does the Lord act: giving food to end the famine (1:6) and now giving Ruth and Boaz a son (4:13). Although the plot demands it, this conception is not at all certain. Ruth was married to her first husband for ten years without bearing a child; Boaz is no longer young. The child is a gift of God.

4:14-17 The women's celebration

The women of Bethlehem, who listened to Naomi's challenge to God in 1:21, now bless God for providing for her. She has been given a redeemer, a *go'el*. This is the new heir who will care for her old age, not Boaz, although he too is now her *go'el*. The catalyst for God's action is Ruth, mother of the child, wife of Boaz. The word "love" appears only here in this book; redemption has come through Ruth's love of Naomi. Ruth, to whom Naomi hardly spoke in her bitterness, is worth more than this new baby, worth more than even seven sons! Seven is the number for fullness. The new baby boy helps heal Naomi's heart from the loss of her two boys in Moab. The neighbor women name the baby, a unique occurrence in the Old Testament (4:17). Usually either the mother or father gives the name. In the New Testament, however, the neighbors attempt to name Elizabeth's baby Zechariah for his father (see Luke 1:58-59).

4:18-22 A genealogy

The book closes with a genealogy, possibly a later addition. The genealogy begins with Perez, son of Tamar, and ends with David, Israel's best-loved king. At the significant seventh and tenth positions in the list are found Boaz and David. The story has moved the reader from the time of the judges to the time of the monarchy; the genealogy reaches farther back to the time of the patriarchs. It is ironic that no women are mentioned in the genealogy that closes this story of two valiant women. The only genealogy in which Ruth will appear is the genealogy of Jesus (Matt 1:5).

THE BOOKS OF

FIRST AND SECOND SAMUEL

Feidhlimidh T. Magennis

INTRODUCTION

Composition

The books of Samuel are part of a larger continuous history of the Israelites, from their entrance to Canaan under Joshua to the deportation to Babylon in 587 B.C. This extensive narrative is called the Deuteronomistic History because its editors based their theology on the teachings of the book of Deuteronomy. The Deuteronomists were a reformist movement in seventh century Judah who promoted fidelity to the Mosaic covenant: God had chosen and liberated Israel from slavery and granted them the land where they would live out their relationship with God. Through Moses, God offers the people a choice: if they are faithful to the covenant laws, they will prosper; if they are disobedient, they can expect punishment through disaster, invasion, or exile. The Deuteronomistic History is the story of the people's response. The history was first composed in the time of King Josiah (640–609 B.C.) and underwent expansion and revisions during the Babylonian exile. The History was divided into "books" for ease of handling. In the later Greek translation, known as the Septuagint, such division created 1 and 2 Samuel as we know them.

Sources

The composers of 1–2 Samuel made use of older materials, both oral and written. Two sources probably date back to the time of David and Solomon. Scholars call one of the narratives "The History of David's Rise" (1 Sam 16–2 Sam 5). Although the other has been called "The Succession Narrative" (2 Sam 9–20), the narrative seems to focus more on relations within David's family than on the actual succession. The composers of 1–2 Samuel also incorporated shorter narrative cycles and other traditions to create a complex, yet sustained account of a significant period of Israelite history. These Deuteronomist editors tell a story that illustrates their theological views, but they do not completely suppress the views of older material. Thus a multiplicity of "voices" enriches the presentation of the transition taking place.

Narrative art

The subject matter deals with political, personal, and theological issues. To allow these different aspects to be heard and to interact, the writers make use of artistic storytelling; they create a skillful narrative which presents the events, the personalities, and the issues. A key component of this art is the use of speech. Both in the longer set speeches and in the interplay of dialogue, characters interact to influence and persuade, to express motivation and desire, and to shape the reader's understanding of issues. The conscientious reader will pay attention to what the narrator shows, while keeping the larger picture in sight. In doing so, some key ideas emerge.

A period of transition

A transition is occurring in Israelite society, from a scattered, tribal confederacy to a unified, centralized state. The certainties of the old ways have been giving way to an uncertain future. The old ways were not ideal: change is needed to save the people from injustice and oppression. Yet there are aspects of the old ways that must not be left behind: the fundamental nature of the covenant society must be retrieved and represented in the new order. From Hannah's opening prayer, these agendas of change and conservation compete within the books.

Key to the covenant relationship is the question of leadership. Israel has only one true King, the Lord. God's leadership is manifested through human intermediaries. In the period of the Judges, leaders were chosen individually by God for specific tasks. Under the monarchy, leadership is permanent and dynastic. New circumstances require new leaders, yet God's freedom to choose and de-select leaders must be protected. The resolution of this tension is a key issue of the books of Samuel.

Displacement

The long succession of leaders in 1–2 Samuel—Eli, Samuel, Saul, Jonathan, David, Absalom—serves to illustrate the tension between divine choice and human planning. The narrative tells of several attempts to pass power from father to son that are thwarted by the Lord (Eli, Samuel). As a result, accession to power is by displacement. Even when the old guard seeks to exercise paternal control over the new (cf. Samuel over Saul in chaps. 10–15), the Lord guards his prerogative to cast down the old and raise up new leaders (cf. 1 Sam 2:6). The dynastic principle seems to rule out the Lord's freedom to choose. But displace-ment creates instability and uncertainty. While various human actors attempt to smooth the dynamics of displacement by transfer of allegiance (Jonathan, Michal, Abner), it is the Lord alone who can change the dynamics of displacement to allow for dynastic succession (cf. 2 Sam 7). But even here, the Lord retains the freedom to choose which son will succeed.

Power and prophecy

The ability to choose a successor is a clear demonstration of power over the future. The books of Samuel are deeply interested in the possession, use, and abuse of power. All power and authority devolves from the Lord, and in a covenant society the use of power must comply with the norms of the covenant. In simple terms, humans must obey the Lord in their dealings with one another. Leaders must also be faithful to the Lord's commands or forfeit their position. A critical issue emerges: how is one to know God's will on specific occasions? As well as the emergence of monarchy, the narrative tells of the development of new forms of divine guidance, whether priestly or prophetic. Kings cannot use power for personal benefit without reference to the divine plan. The prophetic vision supplies reminders of God-given norms. Mistakes will be made, as Saul and David amply demonstrate, but divine guidance is on hand to correct and rectify sin.

By the end of 2 Samuel, the key institutions of a monarchical form of covenant society are in place. The transition has been negotiated and a new future opens for Israel. These books enable the modern reader to grow in hope that the God of the covenant will remain faithful to his people as they struggle to find contemporary forms of community in a changing world.

Outline of the Books of Samuel

1 Sam 1–3	Hannah's Gift
1 Sam 4–6	The Ark Narratives
1 Sam 7–15	The Transition to Monarchy
1 Sam 16–2 Sam 5	The Rise of David
2 Sam 5–8	The Reign of David
2 Sam 9–20	The Family of David
2 Sam 21–24	Appendices

COMMENTARY

HANNAH'S GIFT

1 Samuel 1–3

The opening chapters of 1 Samuel are dominated by Hannah and her prayer. In a situation where "everyone did what was right in their own sight" (Judg 21:25), she does what she thinks best for herself and for Israel: the provision of a new leader attuned to the Lord's will who shall replace uninformed priestly corruption. To understand her predicament, and Israel's, the reader should review Judges 17–21.

1:1-28 Hannah's prayer

As in Judges 17:1 and 19:1, this story begins with a man from the hill country of Ephraim (1:1). The anarchy of the closing chapters of Judges is not far away. That chaos is attributed by the narrator to the absence of a king (Judg 17:6; 18:1; 19:1; 21:25). While Elkinah's background is foreboding, the echoes of Judges 13:2 are hopeful: there, a barren wife became the mother of a savior. Will the same happen to Hannah, despite the fraught familial relationships? The family travels regularly to worship in Shiloh, a place most recently associated with the abuse of women (Judg 21:19-21). While Elkinah favors Hannah with a double portion, his action seems self-centered: "Am I not better for you than ten sons?" (1:8). This triggers Peninah's vindictive treatment of her co-wife. Hannah's situation is distressing, but the narrator suggests a deeper conflict. The Lord has made Hannah barren (1:5). Hannah's problems with Elkinah and Peninah are due to the Lord (1:6). It is with the Lord that she must take issue. In verses 1-8, the narrator has sketched out a family crisis which is both theological in nature and national in scope. Hannah's problems reflect Israel's crisis of relationship with the Lord. What will Hannah do?

1:9-19 Hannah's case

Hannah takes up her case with the Lord. Her prayer leads to a resolution of sorts. Hannah passes from fasting and weeping (1:8) to eating and being no longer downhearted (1:18). But appearances are misleading. When Eli learns that she is not drunk but pouring out her troubles to the Lord, he assures her that the request will be granted without knowing its content. As a solution to her affliction she had asked for a male child and then vowed to dedicate the child to the Lord (1:11). The terms of the dedication echo the angel's description of Samson (Judg 13:4-5). Hannah's concern may appear personal, but her vow has national implications. She wants a judge! The child who will save her from torment will also save Israel. As the official representative of the Lord, Eli accepts and blesses a plan at odds with the Lord's usual manner of appointing a judge. His reply in verse 17 plays on the consonants of the Hebrew verb "to ask" which also spell out the name, Saul. Is there a gap between what Hannah asks for and what the Lord plans?

1:20-23 Samuel's birth

The action moves quickly to the birth of the child. But while this is the child "asked for" (Saul), Hannah calls him Samuel. The confusion over the name may indicate a tension between divine and human intentions. Furthermore, when Elkinah asserts his role as dominant parent, Hannah refuses to release the child (1:21-22). This is a strange assertion of female rights, not only against the husband but against the Lord. Hannah will fulfill the vow on her terms. Elkinah's acquiescence introduces another note of foreboding: "Do what you think best" (1:23; cf. Judg 21:2).

1:24-28 Samuel's dedication

At last Hannah brings the child to Shiloh and hands him over to Eli (1:24-25). Her comments acknowledge that the child is the answer to her prayer, as Eli promised (1:17). Hannah will now fulfill her vow to the Lord. The verbs of verse 28 ("give," "dedicate") are various forms of the verb "to ask." Samuel is the child asked for; he is now given to the Lord. Samuel is dedicated to the Lord by his mother to save her from affliction (and Israel from anarchy). Hannah's intentions complicate the birth of a savior. The child is given by the Lord, but is also given to the Lord. There is a double origin and claim on the child which could lead to confusion. This very personal problem foreshadows some confusing national solutions to Israel's crisis.

2:1-10 Hannah's song

Hannah closes her conflict with the Lord, the cause of her barrenness, by praising the God who grants her a child. Her song expands beyond her personal situation to include the Lord's dealings with his people. That double focus is suitable for a story which has personal and national dimensions.

The opening six lines (2:1-2) express praise and exaltation in the God who grants victory. The descriptions of God are similar to Psalm 113: this is a God who saves those who call on him. The song then addresses the audience and establishes its theme; a contrast is outlined between boasting and silence (2:3). The haughty will be deposed in favor of the humble by the God who knows and judges all actions.

The core section (2:4-8b) outlines a series of reversals in which the proud are humbled and the lowly raised up. In verses 4-6a there is a downward movement as the established are deposed. At the lowest point, death, an upward movement towards life begins (2:6).

The reason for reversal is outlined, beginning with "For" in verse 8c. The celebration of reversal and exaltation is a celebration of the power of God who establishes life and death. Such power is rooted in God's creative activity (2:8c-9a). The Lord creates and establishes order. God sets all things in place and supervises their unfolding. The song ends with a prayer that God will include the king in this manifestation of his saving care (2:10c). The saving help experienced by the poet ("my horn," 2:1) is to be experienced by all in the action of the king ("horn of his anointed," 2:10). This is the first explicit mention of a king. It does not seem to flow from the story. But, following on from Judges 17–21, Hannah's problem occurs in the absence of a king. Hannah took the initiative and forced the hand of the Lord to produce a savior. The song put in her mouth gives a positive understanding of God's salvation as liberation from the mighty. Still, such salvation requires an agent. Hannah looks for a judge, while the book's compilers look for a king. There is a divergence between the expectations of the traditional materials and of the book's editors. At best, God's anointed will be one who implements God's defeat of the haughty and exaltation of the humble. But will Samuel, Hannah's child, achieve that ideal?

The song resembles the Magnificat of Luke's gospel (Luke 1:46-55) at various points: a song of a virgin mother who is gifted with a child, a celebration of reversals, praise of the saving God who grants a king. Yet that child-king is different. He is God's gift and initiative and so can fully implement God's will for his people.

2:11-36 The haughty fall; the humble rise

The remainder of chapter 2 contrasts the rise of Samuel with the fall of the house of Eli. Thus the reversal proclaimed in Hannah's song begins to take place. The unit is punctuated by references to Samuel in the service of the Lord (2:11, 18; 3:1), a role in which he grows in stature and estimation (2:21, 26; 3:19). Between these framing references are two passages about Eli's sons and a further report about Hannah, contrasting the fortunes of the two families. This sets the scene for the announcement of doom for Eli's family in 2:27-36.

2:12-17 The sons of Eli

The sons of Eli were introduced in 1:3 as ministers at the Shiloh sanctuary. This passage tells how they abuse their position. Contrary to customary practice (outlined in vv. 11-14), their servant would take sacrificial portions that still have fat on them (2:15-16). As this practice is not described in the Pentateuch, the details are uncertain, but it would seem that the fat of the sacrificial animal was reserved to the Lord and so burnt in sacrifice: boiling the meat removes the fat to prepare it for human consumption. The sons of Eli claim the fatty portions and display a lack of reverence for the Lord (2:17). They are the haughty whom Hannah seeks to overthrow.

2:18-21 Eli blesses Elkinah and Hannah

In contrast, Samuel's parents visit regularly to offer sacrifice and to bring Samuel garments appropriate for a servant of the Lord. Eli blesses Elkinah and his wife with words that recall Samuel's status as "dedicated to the LORD" (1:28; 2:20), implicitly contrasting Samuel with his own sons. Hannah is clearly blessed as she bears five more children, almost reaching the total listed in her song (2:5b).

2:22-26 Reversing positions

The narrative returns to the crisis of Eli's sons. Verse 22b makes the crime explicit and contrasts it with the zeal of another Phinehas (Num 25:6-15) who saved the people by killing the sinners. Eli's sons are doomed to die for their sins. The words of Eli (2:24-25) spell out the warning while the narrator supports Eli's concern by noting that the Lord has already decided on their death. They have grown great in sin while Samuel continues to grow in the presence of the Lord (2:26). The reversal of positions is almost completed.

2:27-36 A prophetic oracle

A mysterious man of God delivers an oracle of doom to Eli concerning the displacement of his family, descendants of Moses, from the priesthood, and its replacement by descendents of Aaron in the person of Zadok. In common with other prophetic oracles, the passage recalls past gracious action and present sins and pronounces judgment. The description of past graces (2:27b-28) climaxes in permission to offer fire offerings; the actions of 2:12-17 are transgressions of this privilege. The accusation goes beyond 2:22-26 to implicate Eli in the sin: "fattening yourselves with the choicest part" (2:29).

It is a key characteristic of the prophetic strands of these books to show that God's word is fulfilled. This oracle looks forward to the deaths of Phinehas and Hophni (2:34) in chapter 4; the slaughter of Eli's house (2:33) in 22:18-19; and the survival of one priest, Abiathar (2:33) in 22:20-23 and 1 Kings 2:27. This pattern of prophecy and fulfillment demonstrates that history unfolds under God's direction. The prophecy ends by looking forward to the establishment of a "faithful" priest and a "lasting" house (2:35); both adjectives translate the same Hebrew term. Such language will also be used in Nathan's oracle (2 Sam 7:16) to describe David's house. The narrator is providing hints of the outcome of national change, the establishment of a royal Davidic dynasty and a priestly dynasty of Zadok. At the same time, the oracle contains ominous warnings that promises made "forever" can be annulled if the recipients do not give full obedience to the Lord (2:30). Through his prophetic word, God can both promise and punish. The theme of reversal celebrated in Hannah's song is not far away.

3:1–21 Samuel encounters the Lord

The well-known story of Samuel's first encounter with the Lord is the fulfillment of Hannah's plan to provide a replacement for Israel's failed leadership. Replacement implies reversal. Samuel begins "under Eli" (3:1), dependent on the old man for guidance, but ends by revealing God's word to the dependent Eli (3:18). Replacement is needed because divine guidance is missing; verse 1 notes the rarity of divine word and vision. Eli's condition symbolizes the problem for Israel which Samuel shares (3:7): blindness parallels a lack of knowledge of the Lord. In the end, Samuel will be acknowledged by Israel as a prophet; revelation is once more available.

To reach this outcome the Lord initiates the action by calling Samuel (3:4). Ironically, Samuel needs the guidance of Eli to answer this call (3:4-10). The one to be displaced prepares the way for the Lord. This story takes a nasty turn as the Lord announces his decision (3:11-14). The harsh judgment summarizes what the reader learned in 2:27-36, but without qualifications or exemptions. It is a darker and more complete condemnation. Even Eli's complicity is deepened by the accusation that he did not "reprove" his sons (a better translation of verse 13 would be "he did not restrain them"). Just like the man of God, Samuel conveys the Lord's word to Eli, but reluctantly! It requires a threatening oath (3:17) to overcome his fear. Eli's reaction is reminiscent of his willingness to accept God's will in answer to Hannah's prayers (3:18). Samuel's reluctance is reminiscent of his mother's delay in giving him up (cf. 1:22-23).

The final paragraph completes the reversal of roles (3:19-21). Samuel is now the accredited prophet of the Lord (note the same Hebrew word lies behind "trustworthy" and, in 2:35-36, "faithful" and "lasting"). The passage also contains a subtle theology of revelation. It distinguishes between Samuel's words and God's word. They are not identical but the latter inspires and makes firm the former. God's revelations to Samuel authorize him to speak for God. Thus the words of Samuel must be heeded (3:19) as the concrete, historical expression of the divine will, yet they are not that divine will itself. The Bible itself struggles to prevent a fundamentalist identification between the divine will and its temporal expression, and requires the reader to do the same.

THE ARK NARRATIVES

1 Samuel 4:1–7:1

The stories about the ark form a coherent narrative which may seem primitive in its theology yet is highly developed in its narrative skill. The narrator allows the story to unfold, using the speeches to offer insights. The chief "character" is the ark of the Lord, the gold-plated wooden box made to contain the tablets of the covenant (Exod 19–20). It is the symbol of God's presence and power. The main theme of the narrative is the freedom of the God of the exodus: free to take the initiative, to depart or return, but always to act for his own sake. References to exodus and exile abound. A secondary theme is the destruction of the Elides, the old priestly leadership in Israel, clearing the way for the judgeship of Samuel in chapter 7.

4:1-11 The defeat of Israel

The Philistines were more advanced than the Israelites in culture and technology. They dwelt on the coastal plain and were a continuing menace to Israel's survival. Battle is engaged and lost (4:1-2). No reason is given for the attack or defeat, but the elders ask why the Lord allowed it to happen. At one level this reflects their admirable faith in the reality of God's power. But their call for the ark is, at another level, suspect. Can God be brought to heel, his mere presence assuring victory? (4:3-4). The narrator notes the presence of Phinehas and Hophni with the ark. After chapters 2 and 3, this is not a good sign.

Faced with the ark, the Philistines' comment expresses surprising knowledge of the Lord (4:7-9). They, not the Israelites, recognize the God of the exodus and the free, sovereign power manifested in those events (4:8). Even more surprisingly, that knowledge emboldens them to a major victory over Israel. Almost in passing, the narrator notes the death of Phinehas and Hophni (4:11b). Such narrative structuring suggests that the key to these battles lies in the different perceptions of God: one manipulative and the other recognizing gracious freedom.

4:12-22 Reactions to defeat

The remainder of the chapter deals with the reactions to the rout. The narrator uses a common device of the report from the battlefront (4:12-18; cf. 2 Sam 1:3-4) to build dramatic suspense. The messenger breaks the news to Eli in stages, culminating with the capture of the ark (4:12). The shock of this disaster, not the personal loss of his sons, brings about his collapse and death. Only

now does the narrator comment that Eli was a judge (4:18). Perhaps the absence of any prior comment emphasizes his ineffectual judgeship, suggesting Eli is more an anti-judge, the last of a failing system of leadership.

Phinehas' wife goes into labor on hearing the news (4:19). In naming her child, she interprets the reversal of fortunes taking place: "The glory has gone into exile from Israel" (translating vv. 21-22 literally). God has seized the initiative from presumptuous Israel and taken the ark out of the sinful hands of the Elide leadership. As a result, Israel is bereft of God's presence.

5:1-12 The ark among the Philistines

Having broken free from Israelite control, the ark is apparently spoils of war for the Philistines, who lodge this trophy in the temple of Dagon (5:1-2). Thus begins an entertaining account of the humiliation of the Philistines. They will learn also that the Lord cannot be manipulated. A key word in this chapter is "hand," meaning power to act. Dagon loses his hands (5:4), but the Lord's hand proves to be heavy upon the Philistine cities (5:6, 7, 9, 11). The plagues, reminiscent of the Lord's actions in Egypt, demonstrate who has the power of life and death. In acknowledging that the Lord's hand is heavy, the Philistines confess God's glory (the same Hebrew root lies behind "heavy" and "glory"). They witness the glory in exile by its exodus-like manifestations. In a sense, they testify to the liberation of God to act freely for God's own sake. Those who sought to tame God by manipulating the ark find themselves crying out in dismay (the people of Shiloh in 4:13-14, and the Philistines in 5:12).

6:1-12 The ark's exodus

Having decided to get rid of the ark (5:11), the Philistines consider what tribute must be sent with it (6:3-6). Just as the Hebrew slaves did not leave Egypt empty-handed, so the ark must be accompanied by gifts of value (gold), indicative of the giver (five cities), and of the circumstances (models of the plagues). Once again, the Philistines' comments in verses 5-6 make the exodus analogy explicit. They know Israel's faith-story and they recognize Israel's God. They have learned proper humility and avoid the hardened heart of a Pharaoh. Still, they set up tests for the ark (6:7-9). The new cart, the milk cows separated from their calves, and the lack of a driver are all obstacles to be overcome by a god who takes the initiative. This is the key lesson in these narratives. The Lord is not led but takes the lead. And the Lord brings the ark directly to Israelite territory (6:10-12).

6:13–7:1 The ark's homecoming

The Lord's homecoming from exile is met with an appropriate response by his people. There is rejoicing (6:13), sacrifices and worship (6:14-16), and a memorial stone is erected (6:18). The correct attitude towards the ark is to rejoice in God's presence, rather than attempting to use or abuse that presence. However, some lack that reverence (6:19). Such behavior caused the ark's exile in the first place. The death of these men is a sharp reminder of the need to root out such attitudes. Chastened by this reminder, the people of Beth Shemesh transfer the ark to Kiriath-jearim (6:20–7:1) where it is tended by Eleazer. At this point the ark disappears from the book, its narrative role complete. Its movements have demonstrated the freedom of God to initiate change in Israel. The Elides have been removed from office. Now God can use the one gifted to the Lord without obligation to the giver's plans. Samuel can step forward as God's agent for leadership in Israel.

THE TRANSITION TO MONARCHY

1 Samuel 7–15

The transition from judgeship to kingship is fraught with uncertainty and conflict, particularly at the level of ideology and theology. This narrative was composed using materials from various sources with different viewpoints on monarchy and is often described as a patchwork of pro- and anti-monarchical accounts. The editors have created a sustained narrative reflecting on the complex changes that took place in Israel, which required an accommodation between covenantal theology and a new political ideology of monarchy. Monarchy had advantages—sustained leadership in times of constant military threat— but it also had disadvantages in the social and economic spheres. Israel, however, was created from those who escaped slavery under a king, Pharaoh, to be a new type of society with God as king. How will the organization of a theocratic society accommodate a human king? Fundamentally, the narrative is attempting to answer the key question: can divine freedom of action and the human demand for stable leadership be reconciled? The narrative tells how Saul came to be king, using Samuel to voice the concerns of the old order. By chapter 12, an accommodation is brokered, but will it work? Chapters 13–15 suggest it will not, at least not for Saul.

7:2-17 Samuel the Judge

This passage can be read in several contexts. At one level, it is a reversal of the Israelites' defeat in chapter 4. The location is once again called Ebenezer, but now the Israelites fear the enemy and express faith in God, and the Philistines are routed. The crisis of the recent chapters is over as Samuel mediates the Lord's presence to Israel. However, on a wider horizon, this short passage raises many thoughts about the nature of Israelite society.

There seem to be two paradigms at work. One is the paradigm of judgeship. As sketched in Judges 2:16-19, the people turn from God and experience difficulties; in response to their cries, God sends a judge; the judge saves the people; and the judge leads the people for a period of security. Following the death of the judge and a new apostasy, the cycle begins again. This passage fits that pattern. The Philistine threat prompts the people to cry out (7:7-8). Samuel intercedes and God delivers the people (7:9-11). Then Samuel is established as judge for a period of peace (7:15-17). Using this pattern, the narrator presents Samuel as a successful and effective judge, in the line of the great judges of Israel.

But another paradigm is visible in the earlier part of the text. Samuel's call for an undivided heart in verse 3 is reminiscent of Moses in Deuteronomy 6:4-5. There are also echoes of Moses' summons to Israel at Sinai (Exod 19:5-6) and Joshua's at Shechem (Josh 24:14-15). A covenant renewal is taking place in verses 3-6. The people "put away" other gods, and they return to the Lord alone. They constitute themselves as the covenant people in faithful obedience to the Lord, with Samuel as the Moses of their day.

These two paradigms overlap: the Israelites put away Baals and Astartes, gods frequently mentioned in the judgeship cycles (cf. Judg 2); when threatened by the Philistines, their mediated cry is an expression of covenantal faith to which God responds as the faithful Lord. Even more boldly, the narrator links covenant and judgeship in verse 6b; the ceremony at Mizpah is when Samuel begins to judge Israel. Using the two paradigms, the narrator presents a dense, theological declaration about the nature of Israelite society and its governance. Israel is, in essence, a covenantal society obedient to one God who is its Lord and king. This society lives covenantal faith boldly in the face of danger, sure of God's power to save. This power is mediated through human intermediaries. This happens most successfully when the roles of priest, prophet, and judge are aligned in a Moses-like figure who calls the people to covenant, intercedes with God, and judges them regularly.

Hannah's personal request has answered Israel's national crisis. During Samuel's lifetime, Israel need not worry about leadership, supplied fully and extensively by him. But Samuel began to judge in 7:6b, and verse 15 reads like the summation of his career. Will Israel have to undergo another exile experience (cf. chapters 4–6) after Samuel's day? The question hangs in the air.

8:1-22 "Give us a king to rule us."

Like Eli, Samuel appoints his sons as successors, but with similar results. The sons pervert "justice" (v.3) just as Eli's sons disregarded the priests' "duties" (2:13 uses the same term, *mishphat*). Hereditary succession does not work. So, just like Hannah, the elders take the initiative. They sum up the situation correctly and then, in the language of Deuteronomy 17:14 which foresees such an eventuality, demand a king (8:5).

Samuel is displeased (8:6). He finds himself in Eli's place (cf. chapter 1) but reacts very differently. Note that three times he will be told to "listen to them" (8:7, 9, 22). Is this a hint that Samuel is not a reliable intermediary because of his vested interests? God accedes to the people's request but describes it as apostasy (8:8). Such behavior could trigger a new judge cycle (cf. 7:3) but times have changed! Note the shift from "judges" (8:1) who pervert "justice" (8:2), to a request for a king "to judge" (8:5-6 where the Hebrew verb "to judge" has been translated "to rule us") and a description of the justice of the king (8:9, translated "rights of the king"). The solution to apostasy will now lie with kingship and not judgeship.

8:10-22 King and covenant God

Samuel's description of the "rights of the king" focuses on the socio-economic demands made by the monarchy on the people. Just how negative this report is can be seen by comparing it to Deuteronomy 17:16-20. Samuel seems strongly opposed to having a king, even if there are provisions within the covenantal relationship for such a post. His onslaught climaxes in a warning that the people will become slaves (reversing the benefits of the exodus experience) without recourse to God's help (8:15). Despite this critique, the people repeat their demand, balancing the internal effects ("a king to rule us") with the external advantages (8:20; "lead us in warfare"). Samuel listens and passes on their words. The Lord tells him to grant the request, but he does not. Samuel sends them home (8:22). An impasse has been reached when God's representative does not carry out God's word.

The arguments about a king's behavior have been made, but the real issue is the relationship of king and covenant God. The echoes of Deuteronomy 17:14-20 suggest that kingship could be accommodated in covenantal relations. The Lord is willing to accept the people's initiative (though describing it as apostasy) and to work with it, just as God accepted Hannah's prayer, but Samuel stands in the way. If this is personal pique, he is told to forget it (8:7). Samuel's description of the rights of the king suggests that Deuteronomy 17:14-20 is too idealistic. The reality for Israel will be much worse, as later history shows. Perhaps Samuel's report represents the voice of the exilic editors who can look back in regret on the failure of Israelite monarchy to implement the covenant ideals.

9:1–10:16 Saul searches for donkeys and finds a kingdom

A prosperous Benjaminite, Kish, loses some donkeys and sends his son to find them. But the son's quest takes a strange turn when he meets Samuel. He is anointed and transformed in preparation to become king. The son's name is Saul.

9:1-10 A fruitless search

The narrator keeps the reader's attention on the search for the donkeys in the first section of the story. Saul's search is long and fruitless. Obstacles have to be overcome so help is needed.

Saul is assisted by his servant, who suggests that they consult an unnamed man of God (9:6). Saul agrees and the quest moves to the next stage (9:10). The narrator uses various terms for this personage—"man of God" (9:6-8, 10), "seer," and "prophet" (9:9)—so that the attentive reader wonders if this is Samuel whose word is always effective (compare 9:6 with 3:19).

9:11-26 Saul's new role

The two travelers are guided to the seer who is indeed Samuel (9:11-13). Now this becomes a quest for leadership in Israel. Revelation becomes the help, rather than human guides. The narrator reports a prior revelation given to Samuel (9:15-16). The Lord is sending his choice to Samuel to be anointed as "ruler" (an archaic term, *nagid*, meaning "designated one" is used here and in 10:1). He is to "save my people," a very covenantal concept (9:16). The Lord is doing this in response to the people's misery and cry for help. It is not obvious that this refers to the request for a king in 8:5. Instead, the Lord seems to be taking the initiative to supply a covenant savior of his choosing. This chosen one will "govern" (9:17) and "save" (9:16) as God intends.

When Saul appears before Samuel, the Lord confirms his selection. Samuel prepares Saul for the amazing change in his quest: the donkeys have been found but something else is missing (9:20). The cryptic comments about Israel's desire in verse 20 suggest that Samuel perceives Saul as the answer to the people's request in chapter 8. But Saul is the Lord's chosen, not Israel's. This will create tension later. Samuel now invites Saul to the sacrifice as guest of honor (9:22-24). Saul's new role has a deeply religious character. He belongs more to God than to Israel.

9:27–10:16 Shifting relationships

Before letting them continue their journey, Samuel takes Saul aside to reveal God's intentions (9:27). This is the signal for the anointing of Saul as *nagid*, the one to govern and save (10:1). Saul now knows the contents of God's revelation (9:15-16), but Samuel goes further. He outlines a series of three signs that will authenticate the message (10:1b-6). Following the signs, Saul will be a new man, able to do whatever comes to hand because God is with him (10:7). But will he be his own

man? Verse 8 immediately ties down Saul's freedom under Samuel's direction: he is to remain idle at Gilgal until Samuel arrives and conducts a sacrifice; then, he will be given instructions. None of this was mentioned in the Lord's instructions. Is Samuel giving concrete expression to the divine word (cf. 3:19-22), or is he voicing his own desire to subordinate the new leader to the old? There is no clear answer here, but the problem will dominate later chapters.

The narrative moves quickly. Already Saul's transformation has commenced (verse 9 refers to a new heart), so the narrator jumps to the last sign where the transformation is completed. The spirit of God takes hold of Saul and he enters a prophetic state (10:10). The public reaction raises the central question: what has become of Saul? (10:11). The Lord designated him as leader, and Samuel anointed him for that role, but now he acts prophetically. There is confusion. Someone adds the astute question, "who is their father?" (10:12). Is Samuel, the leading prophet in Israel, the superior over Saul? His instructions in verse 8 suggest Samuel wants this to be the case. Saul's natural father disappears from the story: when Saul returns home, he meets his "uncle" (10:14-15). Has Kish been demoted to "uncle" now that Saul is among the prophets under Samuel's jurisdiction? The narrator may be signaling that events place Saul in a very awkward set of relationships. At home, Saul is silent about what has happened. His anointing does not become public knowledge. A similar situation develops after the anointing of David (16:1-13) and of Jehu (2 Kgs 9–10). Divine designation is always distinct from public affirmation.

10:17-27 Saul chosen by lot

This passage is ambiguous in content and in relation to the surrounding texts. It does not follow on from 10:16. Rather, it flows more smoothly from the dismissal at 8:22. In that context, Samuel is gathering the people to continue the previous assembly, this time at Mizpah. Read in this way, one expects Samuel to complete the Lord's instructions and appoint a king. However, he does not. Verses 18-19 take the form of an oracle of judgment. Speaking for the Lord, Samuel reformulates 8:7-9 to describe God's deliverance in the past and to denounce Israel's sin: it has rejected

God by asking for a king. Comparing these two texts raises the possibility that Samuel is concretizing the Lord's word in terms of his own evaluation of the request; where the Lord puts stress on granting the request, Samuel stresses the rejection of the Lord. But he cannot ignore God's intention completely and so, in place of the usual declaration of punishment, "Now, therefore . . ." starts a process of lots (10:19b).

What does Samuel intend? The process of "taking one's stand before the Lord" and "choosing" is used elsewhere to identify a guilty party (see Josh 7:11-26; 1 Sam 14:36-43). Used in the context of an oracle of judgment, the candidates take their stand for judgment (10:20-22). When Saul is discovered and brought forward, he takes his stand among the people. This should be for judgment but the Lord has intervened to present Saul (10:22). The people are struck by his appearance (10:23). Samuel focuses their attention on the one "whom the LORD has chosen" (10:24). But, together with his description of the people's sin (10:19 recalling Deut 17:14) and his comments in verse 24 (recalling Deut 17:15), Samuel unwittingly has shifted the focus from judgment to the search for a king. The people react positively to Saul's appearance and acclaim him king.

Whatever his motives for selection by lot, Samuel proceeds to explain the "law of royalty" (10:24; the *misphat* of the kingdom). It is unlikely that this is a repeat of 8:11-18. Since it is written in a book (10:25), this teaching may be in line with Deuteronomy 17:16-20. Samuel, willingly or not, is complying with the divine instruction to grant the people's request. All can go home again.

Saul has been chosen by lot, a public ritual which, in addition to the private anointing, authenticates his position as the Lord's choice. He has support from some warriors (literally, worthy men) who have been influenced by the Lord as Saul was (compare v. 26 with v. 9). But there are others, worthless men, who are not convinced. Just as Saul's possession by the spirit did not impress, so choice by lot leaves some unmoved. Saul's position is not secure.

11:1-15 Can Saul save?

The key task of God's chosen one is to save the people. And Saul has not yet done so. Hence the last episode ended with the question, "How can this fellow save us?" (10:27). Salvation is the key issue of this episode. The narrative is in three parts: describing a need for salvation, discovering the means, and bringing about salvation.

While Saul is chosen to save Israel from the Philistines, an urgent need develops when Nabash threatens to humiliate the people of Jabesh-gilead. The Ammonites were quarrelsome neighbors on the north-eastern shores of the Dead Sea and a regular threat to Israelite settlements such as Jabesh. The inhabitants play for time as they seek someone to rescue them (11:3).

At first the search is fruitless (11:4). Saul's actions depict him as one of the great saviors of old: called away from farming (11:5; cf. Gideon in Judg 6:11-12), seized by the spirit of the Lord (11:6; cf. Samson in Judg 14:19), and summoning the people (11:7; cf. Judg 19:29-30). The mobilization of the people brings joy to Jabesh-gilead (11:9).

The resolution of the crisis happens swiftly (11:10-11). Saul emerges as the triumphant hero. This prompts a resolution of the doubts expressed about Saul. The narrator brings Samuel on scene as the people seek to punish the doubters of 10:27 (11:12). Saul intervenes for clemency with a classic declaration of faith in the covenant God, "today the LORD has rescued Israel" (11:13). Such a declaration marks him out not just as a military hero, but also as a faithful servant of the Lord. Can Saul save? Yes, and such a man is suitable to lead Israel. Samuel seizes the opportunity to renew the kingship after the last faltering attempt (11:14). The episode culminates at Gilgal when the people make Saul king (11:15).

This narrative incorporates allusions to previous judges, so is Saul more a judge than a king? Like judges he saves, so one more episode is needed to outline how a king in Israel might act. Furthermore, Saul is marked out as belonging to the Lord—the anointing, the seizures by the spirit, his declaration of faith in the savior God—but it is the people who make him king as the answer to their request. Will there be a struggle for ownership of this king? Finally, Samuel appears suddenly and moves the assembly to Gilgal where he sacrifices peace offerings. Is this the Gilgal event that Samuel announced in 10:8, when Samuel took control of the king? There are several questions of role and loyalty yet to be resolved, and the answers will pull Saul in different directions. His kingship is far from secure.

12:1-25 Samuel sets kingship within the covenant

Chapter 12 completes the transition to monarchy. After several digressions and tentative starts, Samuel has acceded to the people's request for a king, as he notes in verse 1. However, the process has not been straightforward. The Lord chose the candidate, Saul, who had to be authenticated by various means. That process resolved opposition to Saul. Samuel voiced his opposition to kingship (8:11-18; 10:18-19), and once more he moves to subordinate the realities of the new leadership to the old covenantal faith structures. This is a key moment in the emergence of monarchy, and consequently in this history of Israel. The compilers of the history place major speeches at key moments (cf. Josh 24 and 1 Kgs 8) to provide theological reflection on what has happened and what lies ahead. Samuel's speech not only addresses the Israelites at Gilgal, but also conveys the biblical writers' understanding to the reader. For these writers, monarchy was a serious risk from the very beginning.

12:1-5 Facing the people

Samuel seeks to vindicate his leadership as a new leadership emerges (12:2). This is a bipartite process. Samuel faces the people: will they accuse him or vindicate his leadership? The Lord and his anointed (Saul) act as witnesses (12:3, 5), nothing more. Interestingly, Samuel's list of possible crimes parallels the "rights of the king" (8:11-18) with its frequent use of "take." Implicitly he is claiming that the old leadership was good; the new is bad. The people vindicate Samuel (12:5) so a new process can commence in which Samuel acts as arbitrator between the Lord and Israel (a tripartite process). This shift in procedure is important: Samuel is carving out a role for the future.

12:6-15 Conditions of the covenant

In the new process, the people take their stand as the accusations are made. The many "acts of mercy" of the Lord are contrasted with his continual rejection by Israel. Yet when they cried out, the Lord delivered them, from Jacob to Joshua (12:8) and throughout the period of the judges (12:9-11). The Lord is faithful, the people fickle, but the Lord always provided a savior, so why change the system? If one listens carefully, this summary applies not only to the judges (some

ancient texts read "Samson" instead of "Samuel" in verse 11) but also to the career of Samuel (cf. 1 Sam 7). Even in the present crisis the Lord provided a judge-like savior (verse 12 looks to chapter 11), but the people insist on a king. They now have their king (12:13) but he has been given by the Lord and his role is circumscribed within the Lord's covenant. Verses 14-15 are the heart of the speech. In a two-part conditional statement, reminiscent of the book of Deuteronomy, Samuel offers blessing and curse. The conditions are typical of the covenant relationship: fear of the Lord, exclusive service, obedience. This is a reaffirmation of the covenant. The new element comes in those addressed: the "you" of the people becomes "you and your king." The king is part and parcel of the people under covenant Torah, subject to the same demands for obedience and sharing the same blessing or curse.

12:16-25 Covenantal kingship

Having made this adjudication, Samuel calls the people forward to witness a sign (12:16-18). The sign not only demonstrates the Lord's displeasure (12:17) but also Samuel's position within the new dispensation: *he* calls, the Lord sends. As a result, Samuel is placed with the Lord (12:18) while the king is placed among the people. The people beg for intercession for their sins (12:19) and Samuel responds with an oracle of salvation ("Do not fear . . ."; 12:20-22). The old pattern of crying out for deliverance still functions in the hands of the old leadership! The Lord recognizes their evil but promises not to "abandon his people" (12:22) who must not "turn from the Lord" (12:20).

Samuel concludes by emphasizing his role in the new dispensation as intercessor and teacher (12:23). But he ends with another two-part condition offering blessing or curse (12: 24-25). While the former would end the discourse on a positive, hopeful note, the latter sounds an alarming note of doom for the future.

The effect of this speech is to locate kingship within covenantal relationships. A new leadership has been inaugurated but heavily circumscribed by the dynamics of the old. The guardian of the old ways, Samuel, has a key role to play in arbitrating, teaching, and interceding for the people (and their king). Israel may now live under a monarchy, but that monarchy is under the Torah and its representatives. The initiative taken by Israel in asking for a king has been granted, but in a form which allows God the freedom to act for blessing or curse. The people are given Saul ("the one asked for"), but will he be what they wanted? Or will he perish under the tensions of conflicting demands of ownership?

13:1-22 Saul rejected by Samuel

Chapter 13 begins the account of Saul's reign with a regnal formula (13:1), used throughout the history to mark the start of a reign (cf. 2 Sam 5:4), but Saul's age and length of reign are missing. This verse was perhaps introduced at a late stage in the composition of the book, but its faults are consonant with what follows. Saul's reign lacks something. His exploits in the opening verses (13:2-7) suffer setback after setback. The narrator gives special prominence to the perceptions of the people. The people make the king: now they see what Saul makes of the role.

At Gilgal, Saul waits seven days for Samuel (13:8) as he was told to do (cf. 10:8). When Samuel does not appear, Saul begins the sacrifices. Then Samuel appears and rebukes Saul (13:9-14). Both men agree that an appointment was made and not kept, but what then? Saul's excuse (13:11-12) summarizes his predicament. He has too many masters and is the victim of competing demands: the people's desertion, Samuel's orders, and the need to sacrifice to the Lord. He is not free to trust totally in the Lord. Samuel says that Saul has failed to obey the Lord and so the curse of 12:15 comes into play (13:13-14). But more accurately, Saul has failed to obey the command of Samuel, who planned to maintain control over the new king. In a fit of rage, Samuel abandons his protégé. While Saul had been given a new heart (10:9), it is not pliable enough for Samuel's liking. The Lord will look for a man after his own heart (13:14).

Abandoned by Samuel, Saul and the remnant of his forces take up position (13:15-18) while the Philistines move freely in and out of their base camp. Nothing is done to prevent their advance (13:23). The narrator darkens the prospects with a digression (13:19-22) on the technological gap between the Philistines and the Israelites. In such a situation, victory can only be gained by the Lord. Poor Saul was chosen to be the savior, but everything is going wrong for him.

14:1-23 Jonathan's exploit

In contrast, his son Jonathan moves forward (14:1-6). Jonathan does not inform his father (14:1) nor the troops (14:3). Is he distancing himself from Saul? Jonathan expresses faith in the Lord's power to save, no matter the circumstance (14:6), and his armor-bearer commends him to do all that is in his heart (14:7). Is Jonathan the man after the Lord's heart for whom Samuel yearned? Jonathan's choices and actions are constantly announced in faith-filled terms, and the Lord does help Jonathan to a significant victory (14:8-15). The ensuing earthquake is a clear sign of divine victory over the Philistine garrison (14:15). Meanwhile Saul's posture and entourage send the wrong signals: he sits, and he is accompanied by one of the disgraced Elide priesthood (14:2-3). When action is needed, he turns to ritual once again (14:16-19) and nearly misses the opportunity. Saul seems unable to read the signs of the Lord's victory which are plainly visible to his troops (14:16). Other Israelites are less obtuse: Jonathan's victory triggers a wholesale uprising (14:21-22). Thus the Lord saves Israel (14:23) despite the overwhelming power of the Philistines and the underwhelming caution of Saul.

14:24-46 Jonathan caught in Saul's oath

With the Lord's victory assured, the narrative can focus on Saul's handling of the situation. At once, he complicates the action with an oath (14:24) cursing anyone who eats that day while battle continues. At one level, such fasting is part of a holy war, a means of devoting oneself to the Lord's cause. But victory *has been* granted so such preparations are redundant. The oath hinders progress by weakening the soldiers who hear and keep it (14:25-26) while creating a snare for Jonathan who does not (14:27). A soldier witnesses Jonathan eating honey and reports the negative effects of the oath. This leads Jonathan to voice the pragmatic interpretation: had the people eaten, the victory would be greater (14:30). Further, he describes Saul as one who "brings trouble to the land" (14:29), a serious accusation calling to mind the crimes of Achan (cf. Josh 7).

The oath creates another transgression (14:31-35). In their hunger, the army fails to prepare meat in the ritually correct manner (cf. Lev 3:17). Saul responds in an efficient manner: he can deal with ritual if not with its spirit.

Saul takes the initiative at last to continue the plunder (14:36). The army's response is non-committal and the priest has little difficulty in deflecting Saul into another ritual. But engagement in a ritual does not guarantee communication with the Lord (14:37). Saul assumes a sin has been committed and begins an investigation using the Urim and Thummim, or sacred lots. With another oath he vows that the guilty will die (14:39). The people's silence suggests they are not happy with this turn of events. The process is carried through until Jonathan is taken and admits that he ate the honey. Saul is consistent in demanding his son's death (14:44). However, the army intervenes to stop this becoming a tragedy (14:45). They declare their evaluation of the day's events: Jonathan is the one who brought victory (not Saul) and shall not die (despite Saul's oaths). Thus, the people end Saul's initiative and close the sorry episode.

Chapters 13 and 14 contrast Jonathan, trusting in the Lord and willing to be the means of victory, with a hesitant, ritual-bound Saul for whom events go very wrong. Bereft of Samuel's guidance, he struggles to uncover the Lord's will without success. He therefore stumbles from one mistake to another in an attempt to appease the Lord. This becomes too much for the people, who block his ritual-driven destruction of the victory. The narrator has shaped the story to share the people's perceptions with the reader: it was the people (and Samuel) who made Saul king, and in these chapters the people come to regret their choice. Saul's kingship cannot be maintained if these key players no longer back him.

14:47-52 Summary of Saul's reign

Despite the negative picture of the last narrative, the reign of Saul did last many years and he achieved some notable successes which the narrator lists in this summary. Also listed are the names of his family. But the summary ends by noting that Saul never brought the Philistine threat to an end.

15:1-35 Saul rejected as king

This chapter opens with a concise statement of the settlement reached in chapter 12: Samuel stands as the voice of the covenant God and the king must listen to that voice (15:1). This narrative sets up a specific case study of the theological settlement: Saul will be judged on his ability to obey. The Lord's will is the extermination of the Amalekites (15:2-3; cf. Deut 25:17-19). Extermination is abhorrent to modern ears, but the ban is actually a consecration of Amalek to the Lord. That nation is set aside for the Lord's use and destruction ensures that it is beyond human interference.

15:4-9 Disobedience

Saul initially obeys the Lord's command and is successful. The narrator then reports what "He and his troops" do. Saul and the people are acting together, as expected when Samuel outlined the conditions of the new settlement (12:14-15). Contrary to instructions (15:9) they spare the best of the booty when the Lord said, "Do not spare . . ." (15:3).

15:10-23 Punishment

Verses 10-11 are the heart of the narrative. The Lord reveals his decision: "I regret having made Saul king." The reason is expressed in terms of apostasy and disobedience, two sides of the one coin. After initial opposition to the Lord's willingness to appoint a king (ch. 8), Samuel had invested his hopes in a pliable Saul (ch. 10), but was disappointed by Saul's independence (13:13-14). Saul was Samuel's foothold in the new dispensation. If the Lord rejects Saul, Samuel has nothing either. Perhaps this explains Samuel's anger in verse 11.

Samuel's confrontation with Saul is clinical and penetrating (15:12-23). Saul states his obedience to the Lord's command (15:13), but the evidence contradicts him and Samuel cuts through his subtle distinctions (15:14). Two excuses form Saul's defense: he distinguishes between his actions and those of the people, and he claims that the spared booty was for sacrifice. There is no evidence for the latter excuse. The former is contradicted by the reported facts (15:9) and the theological frame within which monarchy is to function: it is not a valid excuse. Samuel cuts through the excuses to the main accusation: disobedience of the Lord's command (15:19). Samuel's prophetic word of judgment (15:22-23) poetically balances "obedience" against "sin," "rebellion," "arrogance," and "idolatry," in summation, rejection of the Lord's command. The punishment for disobedience is measured: rejection for rejection.

15:24-35 Setting the stage for a new beginning

Saul acknowledges his sin in two stages (15:24-25 and 30) in the hope of reconnecting with Samuel and thus with the Lord. His first request for forgiveness (15:25) is rebuffed by a repetition of judgment. Looking forward to 2 Samuel 12, David will find himself in a similar position and be forgiven. Why Saul is not forgiven is a mystery unresolved in this text. In desperation, Saul grasps at Samuel's cloak, and the torn fragment only becomes a prophetic sign to underline the rejection of Saul (15:27-28). Samuel's concluding remark creates more difficulties for the reader (15:29). He claims that the Lord does not repent, yet the Lord said in verse 11 that he does, and in verse 35 the narrator will confirm this repentance. In the story of Saul's rejection, the reader comes face to face with the mystery of the Lord's ability to change.

Once more Saul acknowledges his sin and asks Samuel to maintain the appearance of support (15:30). Without comment, Samuel agrees, and completes the extermination commanded in verses 2-3 (15:31-33).

The narrator offers some parting observations about Samuel. He goes home (15:34), and he never sees Saul again (15:35). Samuel's grief arises from the failure of the arrangements he had established in chapter 12. Saul's disobedience places him under the curse of 12:15 and Samuel's hopes to create a prophet-led monarchy collapse. But the double failure of Saul and Samuel is based in the deeper dynamics of the Lord's plan. Samuel declared, "The Glory of Israel neither deceives nor repents" (15:29). Saul's monarchy was of the people's making, not the Lord's. The Lord's plan for Israel continues to unfold even when complicated or thwarted by human initiatives. Saul was one such initiative: he will always be the king "asked for." Now that his failure is clear, and his rejection declared, the Lord can create a new beginning for a monarchy of his own choosing.

THE RISE OF DAVID

1 Samuel 16:1–2 Samuel 5:12

In chapter 16, David is introduced and begins his long rise to become king of Israel and Judah (2 Sam 5). It is generally accepted that the Deuteronomists incorporated a very old document, possibly put together in the court of David or Solomon, which has been called "The History of David's Rise" (1 Sam 16:14–2 Sam 5:12). The document explains why Saul's monarchy disappears and legitimates David's accession. It affirms that the Lord was with David (16:18; 17:37; 18:12, 14, 28) and had departed from Saul (16:14).

16:1-13 Samuel anoints David

With 16:1, a new initiative begins. This time, the Lord is in charge of the action, prompting and directing each step. The Lord's beginning reverses the ending of Saul's kingship. Verse 1a echoes the content of 15:35b to effect this transition from rejection to selection of a new anointed.

There are close similarities between the anointing of David and of Saul (9:1–10:16). Both are carried out by Samuel under a cloak of secrecy; this time it involves a visit to a city to conduct a sacrifice to which certain people are invited. After each anointing, the spirit of the Lord rushes upon the anointed. Yet there are striking differences. The Lord is much more prominent in directing Samuel and explicit in naming his choice in 16:4-13. And there is an interesting exploration of the importance of appearances (16:7). These similarities and differences further support the notion of a new beginning which corrects the previous attempt to choose a king.

Saul's appearance distinguished him and his stature marked him out as a suitable candidate (cf. 9:2 and 10:23-24). Samuel continues to be influenced by appearances (16:6) but the Lord stops him: "God does not see as a mortal" (16:7). Samuel has not fully grasped the essence of divine discernment; he rejected Saul (13:14) for not having a heart attuned to the Lord, but he has not yet abandoned judgments based on appearances. The mystery for humans is to understand the criteria of the Lord and to live accordingly. It is ironic that David will be described as "ruddy, a youth with beautiful eyes, and good looking" (16:12), since all of this is supposedly irrelevant.

Anointing David is Samuel's last prophetic act. He retires to Ramah. The initiative started by Hannah's request is now complete and the Lord's own response to her situation can commence.

16:14-23 Saul appoints David

The spirit links these two accounts of David's selection: where the spirit of the Lord seizes David

(16:13), it abandons Saul and is replaced by an evil spirit (16:14). The replacement of spirits in Saul also signals the start of his replacement by David.

David is summoned to court to deal with Saul's torment (16:15-18). Again, appearance provides part of the reason for David's advancement. More notable is the servant's comment that the Lord is with David, in contrast to Saul from whom the Lord has departed (16:18). This story is setting up conflicts to come. A further complication enters the story in verse 21: Saul loved David greatly (translating literally). In these stories, "love" refers to allegiance and fidelity. In effect, Saul adopts David and becomes his surrogate father (16:22), thus binding their fates very closely indeed (cf. 10:11-12). Will Saul's efforts to repeat Samuel's attempt at paternal control be equally disastrous? Or will David be able to escape and become "son" to the Lord?

17:1–18:30 David in the court of Saul

The text of chapters 17 and 18 has a complex compositional and transmission history. Major portions are missing from the oldest Greek translation, preserved in Codex Vaticanus (17:12-32, 41, 48b, 55-58 and 18:1-5, 10-11, 12b, 17-19, 26b, 29b-30), but are contained in the Hebrew manuscripts. Scholars believe that the Old Greek translation is witness to the original version of these chapters. In the fourth century B.C., the text was expanded to incorporate a second storyline. The older storyline develops from David's arrival at court and appointment as armor-bearer (16:14-23), and tells of his willingness to volunteer as champion against the Philistine. This story assumes that Saul knows David throughout. The added storyline grows out of 16:1-13 (David as shepherd, at home with his family), and tells how he arrives at the battle scene, meets Saul for the first time, and volunteers as champion. The editors skillfully merge the two traditions to create one of the most memorable narratives of the Old Testament.

17:1-11 The challenge of Goliath

Saul was anointed to end the Philistine threat but he failed to do so (cf. 14:52). This story opens with a major confrontation between the two peoples (17:1-3). The balance of power is tilted heavily in the Philistines' favor. They have a champion (17:4) who strikes fear into the Israelites (17:11). Three things about Goliath are described.

Goliath is very tall, but appearances should not count for people of faith (cf. Eliab in 16:6-7). Secondly, he is well-armored, but this did not deter Jonathan in chapter 13. Finally, he is boastful (17:8-10), but God's people should believe the affirmations of Hannah's song (2:3). Yet Saul and the troops do not express covenant faith, nor do they mention the divine name.

17:12-31 David's faith

Into this reign of terror comes David, exuding curiosity and enthusiasm. Using the second storyline, the narrator recaps David's origins and describes how he is transferred from minding sheep to bringing provisions to his older brothers (17:12-19). David arrives in time to hear Goliath's morning challenge to the cowering troops (17:20-24). As in all good adventure stories, there is talk of a reward—wealth and the hand of the king's daughter—for the man who kills Goliath. David is not motivated by reward but by faith. He boldly declares his faith in God's power to save (17:26). David's use of the term "the living God" contrasts the God of Israel with idols such as Dagon, whom God has already knocked down in chapter 5. While not a common term, it is the first declaration of faith in this story.

17:32-40 The Lord's deliverance

David's declaration brings him to Saul's attention and David promptly volunteers to be Israel's champion (17:32). Saul demurs because David is only a "youth." The Hebrew term, *na'ar*, has a range of usages (infant, youth, attendant, soldier, royal official) arising from a root meaning of dependence, either within the family or in service. This flexibility of meaning allows the editor to weave together the two storylines. David responds with another speech expressing faith in God as savior (17:34-37). He describes his own experience as shepherd when he would rescue the prey from wild animals (17:35). He was able to do so then because the Lord "delivered" him, and the Lord will deliver him again. At the center of the speech, David restates his anger at the insult to the living God (17:36) and names the Lord as the one who delivers his people. This faith alone makes the difference in battle. Yet Saul, cautious and not so bold in faith, tries to arm David (17:38-39). This would give him a comparable appearance to Goliath, but is not how God wins victories! Appearances or weapons are immaterial to one with faith; David takes the basic armaments of a shepherd or foot soldier (17:40).

17:41-54 Victory in battle

The two champions square off (17:40b-41), and each hurls insults and threats (17:43-47). But David's speech is framed with declarations of faith. He names his God in contrast to the anonymous Philistine gods of Goliath's curse: "the LORD of hosts, the God of the armies of Israel" (17:45). The battle shows that "the LORD shall deliver you into my hand" (17:46). David is proclaiming the same good news of salvation for all to hear, as did Jonathan (compare 14:47 with 13:6).

Following the declaration, the account of the battle is swift and decisive (17:48-51). The real issues have been dealt with. Appropriately, the Lord's victory causes panic among his enemies and a rout ensues (17:51-53). Verse 54 is anachronistic; Jerusalem is not yet an Israelite city.

17:55-58 A failure of recognition

It is strange that Saul and Abner do not know who David is. This is understandable as part of the second, added storyline, but creates a certain tension in the final text. Is Saul's failure to recognize David a sign of his failure to recognize the Lord's support of this savior of the people?

18:1-30 Relations at Saul's court

This chapter describes the complex relationships between David, Saul and his family, and the public. David's successes win him the "love" of almost all, while Saul grows embittered towards the rising star. "Love" carries tones of personal affection, but the political dimensions of loyalty and allegiance are never far away. The narrative shifts between the reactions of Saul's children and the public. Much of the narrative reports events from Saul's perspective; his thoughts and intentions are revealed by the narrator. This enables the reader to appreciate Saul's ironic intimation of David's goal (18:8) while failing to see the reason until the end: the Lord is with David (cf. 18:12, 14, 28). David's thoughts are hidden. This reticence means he is a blank page for both reader and Saul.

Verses 1-4 emphasize Jonathan's love for David. Jonathan identifies with David and gives him his regalia, treating him as an equal. But the Hebrew verb underlying "to be bound to" (18:1) can also mean "to be in conspiracy with." Where Saul attempted to hold on to Samuel's garment (symbol of the kingdom) in 15:27, Jonathan hands over his cloak. Jonathan's actions may be read as generosity or treachery. The covenant made by Jonathan in verse 3 will prove critical. Saul and David will react differently to his "love."

The song of the women, a public acclamation of both Saul and David, prompts the first indication of Saul's resentment (18:6-9). He interprets the song with faulty literalism, but if his suspicions are poorly based, his intuition is accurate: David is the one who will receive the kingship (cf. 13:14). But Saul fails to see the Lord's hand at work. Tension mounts as David's task of soothing Saul only provokes more rage (18:10-11). Appointing David to the field provides temporary respite but advances David's popularity (18:13-16). Nothing is going right for Saul. No wonder, the narrator comments, since the Lord is with David and has departed from Saul (18:12).

The next two incidents deal with Saul's daughters. Saul uses the ploy of marriage to entice David into dangerous exploits in the hope that he will be killed. The first attempt (18:17-19) involving Merob fizzles out as David declines the king's offer. By contrast, Michal loves David (18:20). David's claim to be unworthy allows Saul to set the trap. For once, the narrator reports David's reaction: he "was pleased" to become the king's son-in-law (18:26). Perhaps this is a hint that Michal's love is reciprocated. At the least, Michal's love for David suggests she is willing to transfer her loyalty to make him a royal figure. David is more than successful in passing the test (18:27) and Saul realizes that the Lord is with David, as are his children and his people. But still, it is not clear that Saul yet realizes that David is the Lord's chosen one to replace him. Saul continues to oppose David and his unstoppable rise to the throne.

19:1–21:1 Jonathan and David

Jonathan is the key character in chapters 19–20. As Saul moves beyond placing David in harm's way to openly plotting to kill him (19:1), David withdraws from court. Throughout that process, Jonathan acts as intermediary between king and servant in an attempt to resolve their conflict. In terms of the overall narrative, this mediation serves a more profound purpose. As Saul's son,

Jonathan stands to inherit the throne. But he aligns himself with David and transfers allegiance ("love" and "kindness") to him. Jonathan thus "abdicates" and allows David to replace him. He becomes the human legitimation of David's accession. These chapters play a pivotal role in the justification of David's rise to power.

19:1-7 Jonathan defends David

The narrator emphasizes Jonathan's place at court: he is called "son" twice in verse 1 and he speaks of Saul as "father" (19:2) and "king" (19:4). Jonathan is located firmly on Saul's side of the conflict, yet he is "very fond" of David (19:1). Friendship prompts him to defend David and argue his case before the king (19:4-6) to good effect. Jonathan is an effective mediator (19:7) and restores harmony for a time.

19:8-17 The flight from Saul

But renewed evidence that the Lord is with David reopens the divisions, or, put theologically, the evil spirit comes on Saul again. Verses 9-10 repeat 18:10-11 but with greater intensity. Saul strikes with the spear this time. Saul then sets up an assassination attempt, but Michal saves David (19:11-17). David is passive throughout these incidents. David is gifted by the Lord with protectors and deliverance. In the tradition of strong biblical women (e.g., Rahab in Josh 2), Michal is successful in her subterfuge and enables David to escape (19:12, 18). His flight from Saul begins.

19:18-24 David meets Samuel

David's first destination is with Samuel. The narrative does not report Samuel's reaction to what has happened, but he sides with David by accompanying him to Naioth. Divine protection is also displayed by the prophetic frenzy which overtakes the sets of messengers. When Saul arrives, he too comes under prophetic influence. Prophetic ecstasy marked Saul's appointment as leader (10:10-12) and now it is the public manifestation that he is stripped of appointment (19:23-24). His fall from grace is complete, though his removal from office will take many more chapters.

20:1-24 Testing covenant loyalty

Next on his flight, David visits Jonathan and speaks for the first time since 18:24 to protest his innocence (20:1). Jonathan is again characterized in relation to his father (20:1-3) so that, as one on Saul's side, he can declare David innocent. David then mentions Jonathan's friendship (20:3), which he uses to cast doubt on Jonathan's knowledge of Saul's intentions, but he is also subtly moving Jonathan onto his side of the conflict. Jonathan is willing to make the move (20:4) and so David outlines a plan to test Saul's true intentions (20:5-7). David commits Jonathan to his plan by recalling the covenant between them (20:8; cf. 18:3). This is not a bond between equals. David calls himself Jonathan's "servant," and it was Jonathan who made the pact. They may view the relationship differently. For Jonathan it seems more emotional, but David appeals to covenant loyalty ("kindness," *hesed*).

Jonathan's response comes in two parts. The first (20:11-17) may have been a secondary development during the composition of the book: it does not focus on the immediate context but looks beyond David's rise to his reign, and specifically to 2 Samuel 9. Jonathan replies to the invocation of covenant kindness (cf. vv. 14-15 with v. 8). After piling up oaths to do as David requests (20:12-13), Jonathan prays, "May the LORD be with you even as he was with my father." The heir whom the Lord helped mightily (ch. 14) hands over divine blessing to the future king. In doing so, he can now strike a bargain with that king. Jonathan recognizes that David's accession will involve the destruction of the house of Saul (20:15b), so he binds David to covenant loyalty either to himself (20:14) or to his family (20:15a, 16). The pact of friendship is reformulated to reflect future political realities. (Verse 17 is better translated, "Jonathan made David swear.") Jonathan's "love" for David may be more personal, but he is making political use of it.

The second part of Jonathan's speech (20:18-24) sets up a method for communicating the outcome of David's plan.

20:25-34 The stratagem unfolds

All the key players are at the feast except David. Saul notes his absence: one day is excusable but not two. Perhaps it was Jonathan's assumption of authority to dismiss David, or his favoritism to the son of Jesse, but Jonathan's explanation triggers a violent response (20:30-31). Saul is abusive of his son and wife, because

Jonathan is not acting as *his* son. The breach of father and son is complete when Saul tries to skewer Jonathan, just as he attempted to kill David (cf. v. 33 with 19:10 and 18:11). Jonathan is now fully transferred to David's side and identified with him.

20:35–21:1 A farewell between friends

Jonathan informs David by use of the signal with the arrow. It is a nice elongation of the suspense but irrelevant, since the two actually meet for a final farewell. David's prostration before Jonathan is a reminder of the unequal nature of the friendship. But Jonathan summarizes the oaths made as a divinely protected relationship between two equals, and between their posterities (20:42). Jonathan has demonstrated his faithfulness to David, almost at the cost of his life. David must reciprocate. This final insistence again hints that the relationship was unequally perceived: more a friendship for Jonathan, more a political alliance for David. And if that is so, David's loyalty has yet to be tested. Will he show *hesed* to those who have committed themselves to him: Jonathan, Michal, the Lord?

21:2–22:5 David's flight continues

Since Michal spirited him away (19:12), David has been on the run while others act for him. Now he starts to act on his own, and a new, unflattering portrait emerges, David as deceitful and evasive. Three more stages of his escape are narrated before his flight ends.

His third stop is in Nob to visit Ahimelech the priest (21:2). His solitary arrival frightens Ahimelech and David lies. He needs food and weapons for his escape. His story of a top-secret mission is contrived. Under questioning, the lie is elaborated almost to breaking point. Where are the consecrated men he speaks of (21:3), and can he honestly expect that men would apply holy war strictures (21:6; see Deut 23:10-15) to ordinary forays? Ahimelech accepts the story at face value, even when the so-called secret agent admits he is weaponless (21:9-10). Either he is very trusting or works on a need-to-know basis. It would not matter, but the presence of one of Saul's henchmen will create devastating consequences for David's deceit (21:8).

Next, David flees to a Philistine city, an indication of his desperation to escape Saul's grasp (21:11). David will go so far, even to joining the enemy! The Philistines are well-versed in Israelite affairs and recognize David's potential as king (21:12). This is a very dangerous moment and David shrewdly creates another deceit (21:13-14). Madness cancelled Saul's hold on monarchy (16:14; 18:10; 19:9) and put David in mortal danger. Now David feigns madness to get out of danger by cancelling his royal identity.

Finally, David escapes to the land of Judah (22:1). The empty-handed and deceitful fugitive is home. He has lost everything but now begins to build his own power base. His followers are either fellow Judahites or members of the disaffected. This power base seems to have two aspects. It is a Judean counterbalance to a northern, Benjaminite coalition around Saul. This north-south division will plague Israel throughout the period of monarchy. Secondly, it reflects a division between the haves and the have-nots. This has populist appeal and also taps into covenant consciousness of Israel as slaves granted freedom. David's provision for his parents indicates careful planning for a long rise to power, and this rise is blessed from the start by the unrequested prophetic guidance of Gad.

22:6-23 Slaughter of the priests

Saul begins his pursuit. His spear signals his murderous intent (22:6). He begins to encourage his officers, reminding them of their advantages under his leadership (22:7), but paranoia sets in. Where one may have opposed him, Saul sees all of them as conspirators (22:8). Saul's fellow Benjaminites are silent, suggesting that relations are strained.

Doeg the Edomite, a non-Israelite, reports what he saw at Nob (22:9-10). Now the consequences of his presence unfold (21:8). Two points must be made. Ahimelech is now called the son of Ahitub: so he is the brother of Ahijah who served Saul in chapter 14, and great-grandson of Eli (cf. 14:3). Secondly, Doeg gives pride of place in his report to Ahimelech consulting the Lord for David, something not mentioned previously. Whether Ahimelech did so or not, this act triggers Saul's anger more than any other; it will be the culminating charge in verse 13. Saul was unsuccessful in consulting the Lord in chapter 14; now this family of priests assists David in doing just that. Hence, all the family are summoned (22:11) and condemned (22:17). Ahimelech's defense is an accurate description of affairs from his perspective, but reminding Saul of David's loyalty and position (22:14-15) does not endear him to the paranoid king.

Doeg's treachery does not end there. The Benjaminite servants refuse to execute the king's command. They will not strike fellow Israelites, especially the Lord's priests (22:17). Doeg steps in to do his master's bidding with ruthless efficiency (22:18-19). (The inclusion of Saul's name in verse 19 is incorrect.) The prophecy of 2:31-33 is being fulfilled. The family of Eli is wiped out, but one escapes and flees to that other fugitive from Saul (22:20). When told what happened, David admits partial responsibility (22:21-22), but David does not admit that his deception put Ahimelech in danger to start with! Still, David has started to repay others' loyalty to him. With words that sound like an oracle of salvation ("Stay with me. Fear nothing . . .") he offers his protection to Abiathar (22:23).

23:1-28 Saul pursues David

Saul's pursuit of David, begun at 22:6, continues. Both protagonists must abandon their conflict to deal with the continuing Philistine threat. Their responses bracket various incidents of the pursuit. All the time, the key player ensures that the pursuit is futile; the Lord will not give David up to Saul (23:14). Whatever happens in the wilderness, David is the Lord's choice for king.

23:1-13 David saves Keilah

The Philistines attack the Judean town of Keilah (cf. Josh 15:44), which is deep in Philistine territory and of dubious loyalty (cf. 23:11a, 12a). David's rescue is a risky venture, but he reacts in response to divine guidance, asking the Lord twice if he is to save the town (23:2, 4). Saul knows David's location and David can be trapped there (23:7). Once more, David consults the Lord using the ephod. The process involves prayers (23:10-11a) followed by specific questions requiring a yes/no answer (23:11b-12). Like Saul in chapters 13–14, David makes use of a range of consultation methods. Unlike Saul, the Lord answers him clearly. Saul is without prophet or priest, while David has both. More importantly, the Lord is with him.

23:14-18 Jonathan's return

Still, David is apprehensive. The narrator reintroduces Jonathan to serve as another means of divine assurance (23:16). His words are an oracle of salvation ("Have no fear"; 23:17). Jonathan renounces his claim to the throne, making explicit what was implied in 20:12-17. However, surprisingly, he claims that Saul knows David will be king. This looks forward to David's encounter with Saul in the next chapter (24:21). Jonathan has been the human mediator of kingship from Saul to David. His task is done now. For the first time, David makes covenant with Jonathan as a partnership between equals (cf. 18:3; 20:8, 14-17).

23:19-28 David's escape

Treachery once more assists Saul to close in. Some Ziphites betray David's location (23:19-20). Saul is grateful but suspicious of any support (23:21-23). Pursuit quickens through the Judean wilderness and David is in grave danger of being encircled. (The NABRE translation uses "gorge" in verse 25 for a Hebrew word meaning "crag, rock" [cf. 14:4-5], which completely changes the topography of the chase! In the Hebrew, David is on one flank of a hill with Saul circling around from the far side.) But just as David is about to be trapped, rescue comes in the unlikeliest of forms. A report of a Philistine attack draws Saul away (23:27-28). The Israelite leader's duty to save the people supersedes a personal vendetta. Is this a fortuitous escape or a divine intervention?

24:1-23 David spares Saul

This chapter is parallel to chapter 26. They are possibly alternative traditions of the same event. This version follows from Jonathan's assertion in 23:17 in a dramatic fashion. Saul the pursuer falls into David's hands; David spares him and makes use of the incident to protest he is innocent of harming Saul. The passage plays two apologetic functions: it absolves David of guilt for Saul's death, and it has Saul acknowledge David as his successor.

24:1-9 Loyalty over opportunity

The action is brief: it sets up the two speeches that form a bipartite judicial process or *rib* (24:10-23). Verses 1-3 pick up the action after the Philistine interruption (23:28). Saul goes to relieve himself in the cave where David is hiding (24:4).

David's men urge him to kill Saul but he does not (24:5), nor will he allow the men to do so (24:8). What is God's will? The men cite a divine word, but such freedom does not allow David to strike the Lord's anointed. Loyalty triumphs over opportunism. David does, however, cut off the corner of Saul's mantle (24:5-6). While he regrets the action, he will make use of it later: it is deeply symbolic of snatching the kingdom (cf. 15:27-28 and 1 Kgs 11:26-40).

24:10-23 Saul's response

When Saul leaves, David calls after him and begins the *rib*, a process in which the accuser seeks to have the accused recognize and confess to a crime. David makes his accusation and outlines the evidence proving his innocence (24:10-12). Saul believed David meant to harm him; this day David could have harmed Saul but did not. David invokes God as witness in verses 13 and 16. In between, he again states the issue. This is a powerful declaration of innocence on David's part.

Saul's response is simple: he has no defense, only an expression of guilt, namely his weeping (24:17). In this context, "voice" probably denotes "speech," the content rather than the tone of what is said. He resolves the case by declaring David to be "in the right" and his actions to be "gracious" (24:18-20). As David invokes God as witness, Saul prays that the Lord will reward David who was wrongly accused. His reply reaches a climax in verses 21-22. Forced to admit he was in the wrong, Saul must now face the realization that David will be king. The corner of the mantle is proof here, recalling Saul's own attempt to snatch Samuel's cloak (15:27-28) and Samuel's words in 13:13-14, which Saul now echoes. Like Jonathan before him, Saul now asks that his family will not be exterminated (cf. 20:14-15). As in the previous episode, when David's kingship has been acknowledged, he gives his oath to Saul.

This is an important moment in the history of David's rise. This *rib* absolves David of the charge of regicide. The Lord will ensure that David gains the throne after Saul dies, but it will be the Lord's doing, not David's grasping.

25:1 Death of Samuel

This report interrupts the story but it may be necessary for the narrator to remove Samuel, who

sought control over the king, before David begins entry into that kingship.

25:2-44 The story of Abigail

The story of David, Nabal, and Abigail interrupts the wider drama but casts light on the options facing David. Given the inconsistent behavior of Saul, David has two options: do battle with a paranoid Saul, or make peace with a repentant Saul who recognizes David's future. This story illustrates the options: Nabal (meaning "fool") obstructs; Abigail assists. One path involves bloodshed, the other wealth and a wife! Which will David choose? But the story is more than an illustration of options because Abigail is no mere cipher. She is "intelligent and attractive" (25:3). Her husband is defined by possessions (25:2), but she seeks to create relationships. Like Hannah and Michal, this is a powerful woman whose actions shape the ensuing history. This is her story, so what does she want?

25:2-13 A negative portrayal

David is portrayed negatively here. He is a criminal godfather demanding protection money from Nabal. Nabal refuses to pay this leader of malcontents (cf. 22:2), and David vows vengeance (cf. 25:21-22). David is rapacious, ready to kill to grasp his goals.

25:14-23 Nabal's household

Nabal has household problems. His servant (25:14-17) and his wife (25:18-19) do not support his action. Contempt drips from every word. If no servant can talk to Nabal, Abigail does not even try. She acts quickly, decisively, and freely with her husband's possessions to save the household from David's anger. Or so it would seem. She demands full attention from David, but to what end?

25:24-35 Abigail's judgment

She addresses David as "my lord" and calls herself "your maidservant," appropriate terms of address to a social superior, or of a wife to a husband. But Abigail never acknowledges Nabal as her husband, only referring to him as "that scoundrel" (25:25). This attractive woman is making a play for David! Her main task is to divert David from bloodshed, though demurely she attributes this action to the Lord. The shedding of blood could tarnish David's standing within the covenant community. It is a key concern of the narrative to absolve David from the charge that he was a usurper. David cannot be seen to seize the throne; it is, and must be seen to be, the gift of the Lord. He cannot be seen to "gain victory by your own hand" (the literal translation of "rescuing yourself personally" in verses 26 and 31). Astutely, Abigail presents herself as the Lord's instrument to keep David safe in this venture, but her foresight is greater still. She looks forward to David's victory and predicts a "lasting house" (25:28), something not even the Lord has mentioned! She recognizes David is going to be "ruler over Israel" (25:30). This is the sort of language Samuel would use. Is she making a play to be kingmaker? It takes a woman to build a dynasty: "remember your maidservant" (25:31)!

David blesses her good judgment (25:33). She has averted the danger to her household, but more importantly she has protected David from bloodguilt and vengeance. He is happy to take her wealth (25:35a), but does he acknowledge her request to be remembered? His final comment is very obscure (25:35b).

25:36-44 Nabal's death

Abigail leaves the future king and returns to her drunken "king." She says nothing until Nabal is at his most fragile, and then delivers her news. In a society based on honor/shame, her report is devastating. Nabal suffers a stroke (25:37; "his heart died within him"). She has all but killed him, but the Lord intervenes to protect her from bloodguilt (25:38). With Nabal out of the way, David is free to take his wife. Abigail's response sounds bashful (25:41), but she wastes no time and travels to David with a full retinue to signal her status (25:42). She is no coy trophy wife but David's equal in cunning. However David has one final trick. He marries Ahinoam at the same time (25:43), so Abigail does not get her way in full. She has a new rival, even as Saul gives David's first wife, Michal, to another man.

In the emergent, monarchical Israel, sexual relations and power politics intertwine. Royal polygyny is a mark of status and a means to form alliances. By removing Michal, Saul is cutting David off from his house. David builds his own harem in opposition, but perhaps he is preventing Abigail gaining too much influence in that household. In this chapter a pattern begins to emerge, by which David's sexual relationships will constantly affect his monarchy for good and ill.

26:1-25 David spares Saul again

Chapter 26 parallels chapter 24. While this important encounter deserves to be reported from several angles, the second account must move the overall narrative forward. Chapter 24 looked back to Jonathan's claim (23:17) and brought that narrative thread to fulfillment. Chapter 26 looks forward; it speaks more clearly of Saul's death (26:9-11), and it prepares for David's exile from the land (26:19-20).

This episode recalls the treachery of the Ziphites (23:19-24) and reactivates Saul's pursuit (26:1-4). This time David is ready for Saul's arrival and takes the initiative to enter the enemy camp (26:5-7). Saul and David have their seconds with them, Abner and Abishai, making the incident more public and preparing for events after Saul's death (2 Sam 3). Once again, David gives a strongly theological argument for not harming Saul (26:9-11), but goes further to state his belief that the Lord will handle Saul's death. It will not be David's doing. David takes Saul's spear, the weapon used in attempts on David's life. The narrator's comment in verse 12 confirms that the Lord is backing David on this occasion.

The dialogue is more complex than in chapter 24. Firstly, David speaks with Abner (26:15-16). It is a clever speech which both praises and condemns him for dereliction of duty. It acknowledges Saul as king, thus underlining David's loyalty. David then addresses Saul. He complains that Saul's action is driving him from the land (26:19). In exile, he would be cut off from the Lord. Saul admits this is wrong and invites David back (26:21). But David is not willing, and he brandishes the spear to remind Saul of his murderous attempts. David has just spared Saul, so he prays that the Lord will spare his life (26:24) as reward for David's righteousness and faithfulness (26:23). David wants a blessing for protection during exile. Saul confirms this request so David can now go on his way (26:25).

This second encounter attempts to re-establish justice and loyalty between the two protagonists, but the divine plan makes this impossible. David must be king and Saul must go, but they cannot live together. The resolution removes both combatants from the scene of conflict, Israel. David is to leave the land of the covenant under the protection of the Lord. Saul returns home but will also cross boundaries of covenant law. The narrative incorporates strange new twists to the history.

27:1–28:2 David among the Philistines

The author of the "History of David's Rise" had a major problem. Tradition remembers that David once served the Philistines. Was he a traitor, then? Is he still a vassal of Israel's enemies? The narrative must incorporate this period into David's story and defend him against such charges. On the theological level, chapter 26 has cleared David of the suspicion of "serv[ing] other gods" (26:19)—the Philistine sojourn was blessed by the Lord (26:25). Now the narrator deals with the historical memory. David's move into Philistine territory successfully ends Saul's pursuit (27:1-3). David's exile serves the greater goal of avoiding civil war.

David returns to Achish who dismissed this madman earlier (cf. 20:11-16). Somehow, David is given Ziklag, a Philistine town, which becomes a personal fiefdom of the Davidic family (27:6). There are narrative gaps here which gloss over elements which may reflect badly on David. Why did Achish welcome David? Why did he give David a stronghold?

Instead, the narrator moves swiftly to make use of David's darker characteristic, deception, to celebrate success in the Philistine venture (27:8-12). David raids non-Israelite peoples in the Negev, and while he takes no prisoners, he does take lots of booty. He reports back to Achish and lies (27:10-11). He is pretending to raid Israelite settlements, so he leaves no one alive who may betray this trick. Achish trusts David and the situation lasts for some time.

However, a Philistine campaign against Israel begins (28:1) and David must choose. Will he continue as a Philistine vassal and attack Israel, or will he side with his own people? His reply to Achish is a masterful piece of noncommittal ambiguity (28:2). But Achish trusts David and appoints him to his elite troop. The narrator stops the story at this critical moment of decision!

28:3-35 The medium of Endor

The resolution of chapter 26 permitted David to leave the land and enter the domain of other gods. Saul makes a similar journey. Having banished mediums from the land (28:3), he departs to consult one (28:8). She dwells in Endor, behind Philistine lines, so Saul also enters Philistine territory where other gods hold sway! Exile helps the narrator surmount the standoff of chapters 24 and 26. Saul will reenter the land as one marked for death in battle (ch. 31). David reenters the land to become king (2 Sam 1-2).

The central character of chapter 28 is a powerful woman who reintroduces the dead Samuel into the story to mediate its final resolution. The medium of Endor plays a complementary role to Hannah: both bring Samuel into the world, both are intent on unblocking the flow of Israelite history, and one stands at either end of the canonical book. To call this woman a witch introduces a negative evaluation which the text does not support. Certainly, Deuteronomy 18:9-22 prohibits occult practices and the woman has been banished, but not even the Deuteronomic editors condemn her. The one evaluation, spoken by Saul, acquits her of blame (28:10).

The Philistines are advancing and Saul is in great fear (28:4-5). He is isolated from the Lord who appointed him for this task (cf. 9:16) but will not answer him (28:6). Saul steps outside his own law to consult the medium at Endor (28:8). He disguises himself as another man (cf. 10:6) in an attempt to get back to the start and reconnect with the Lord through Samuel.

The medium deals with Saul in a mixture of efficiency and caution. Does she recognize Saul despite the disguise? Is she protecting herself from incrimination by having the lawmaker exempt her from blame (28:10)? Her moment of recognition is confusing, suggesting she knows more than she admits (28:11-12).

The ghost is recognizable to Saul by its mantle, last seen in 15:27. Samuel is as cantankerous as ever and not in the least impressed by Saul's great distress (28:15). Saul's description of affairs ends with his hope, "I have called upon you to tell me what I should do," a direct echo of 10:8. Samuel failed to fulfill this instruction then, but will he do so now? No, Saul is doomed to be the one who asks—a play on his name—but is never answered (28:16). Instead of recalling chapter 10, Samuel cites 15:28 and specifies who will receive the kingdom: David. Then he announces a terrible doom which subverts the normal saving activity of the

Lord to bring death to Saul and his sons (28:19), just as God used the Philistines to destroy Eli and his sons in chapter 4.

The apparition disappears and Saul collapses from a combination of terror and hunger (28:21). He is marked for death. The woman's remarks are measured and reassuring. She cannot deflect his spiritual trauma, but she revives Saul with a kingly meal. As a result, he is able to leave to face his doom. Saul's journey beyond the boundaries brought him into contact with the dead. He returns, but he does not stand among the living. There can be no respite for him. He has begun his journey to the grave.

29:1-11 David rejected

To prolong the tension of the choice facing David (28:1-2), the narrator jumped forward to the eve of battle (28:4). Now, the narrator returns to the Philistine muster (29:1-2) and picks up the story. Ironically, it is the Philistine lords who extricate David from his dilemma by refusing to allow him to march into battle on their side (29:3-5). They are deeply suspicious of his duplicity, and once more the chant of the Israelite women is quoted as evidence of the solidarity between David and Saul (cf. 18:7; 21:11). Achish protests David's innocence (29:3); either he is a fool, or the narrator is trying to suggest loyalty is David's main character trait.

Achish dismisses David with regret and fulsome praise for his loyalty (29:6-7). David protests his innocence (29:8), too much perhaps. He professes loyalty to his king, but which king does he mean, Achish or Saul? Were the Philistine lords correct in guessing that David would switch sides in battle to emerge as the savior of Israel? Do David's protestations arise out of frustration as this plan collapses? The wider narrative would suggest that David is duplicitous but in good cause. However, this text leaves as many gaps as it supplies answers. The narrator struggles to respect the traditional memories of David's absence in Israel's hour of need, while attempting to nudge the reader towards a positive evaluation of his role in the downfall of Saulide Israel.

30:1-31 Ziklag in ruins

Having removed David from the battlefield, the narrator explains what he was doing in Israel's hour of need. He was engaged with another enemy whom Saul failed to destroy, the Amalekites of chapter 15. David "bring[s] about a rescue" (30:8) through the guidance of the Lord. Where Saul fails to exterminate the Amalekites, a failure which underlies his continued rejection (cf. 28:18), David does destroy the enemy (v. 17). The episode continues the contrast with Saul. Both men find themselves in "great distress" (28:15 and 30:6 use the same verbal construction) because of enemy assault, but David's reaction is one of "courage in the LORD his God" which leads to victory (30:6), and the means to build support among the elders of Judah (30:26-31).

The narrative has various folkloric elements—the captured wives, the obstacles of hunger and exhaustion, the chance find of a slave who acts as guide—and makes a good tale, an encouraging war story before the account of Saul's final defeat. However, some aspects have wider importance. Verse 6 is a rare moment of popular unrest against David. It could be a narrator's flourish to tighten the straits David finds himself in. Or it could prepare for the later dissent over the spoils (30:21-25). The division of forces into an advance party and a rearguard was a regular strategy of David's (cf. 25:13), but there was no previous hint of tension between the two groups. David moves to establish new rules of conduct for dividing the spoils. The rules are egalitarian, but they are rules for a king to make. David is acting as a king, victorious in battle and supported by his God, able to establish "a law and a custom" (*misphat*) in Israel (30:25). David is establishing that his *misphat* will not be that described by Samuel (8:10-18); this king will give rather than take.

31:1-13 The death of Saul

The narrator returns to the main battle (cf. 28:4) and the outcome of Saul's doom-laden encounter with Samuel (28:15-19). Samuel's declaration of Philistine victory unfolds with unstoppable momentum. They press the attack and the Israelites flee (31:1, 7). They close in on the royal party and slay Saul's sons (31:2). Saul is now alone and mortally wounded (31:3). In the midst of battle, the narrator gives space to Saul's last actions (31:4-5). The narrator marks these deaths in verse 6 with a dignified notice. The whole account of the battle is free from evaluation or editorial touches. It is as if Saul's death is to be accorded the dignity of a faithful record, affording him one last opportunity for an almost heroic end. Samuel has already passed judgment on Saul (28:16-19), yet Saul was the Lord's anointed, the king of Israel. Even in failure that must be honored.

The victory is so complete (31:7) that the Philistines declare it "good news" (31:9). Saul's failure means that the Lord has not saved Israel; it is also a failure of the Israelite god before the Philistine idols. As before (cf. 5:1-2), the Philistines place the visible emblems of the Lord's supposed saving power (Saul's armor) in one of their temples. They use his body as a warning to a conquered people (31:10), an act of desecration meant to instill fear in Israel.

Saul has failed to save Israel from the Philistines; but he did save the people of Jabesh-gilead (ch. 11), and they respond in loyalty by rescuing his body and those of his sons (31:11-13). Cremation was not usual Israelite practice. Some suggest that the narrator is mimicking the honor given to heroes in the Greek world, but cremation may have been demanded by the unusual circumstances of Saul's death.

The narrator has brought the history of Saul to a close with a masterful symmetry—one last encounter with Samuel in an attempt to recapture the promise of chapter 10; David tying up the loose ends of the material cause of Saul's rejection in chapter 15; and, finally, burial by those Saul first delivered in chapter 11. The burial of Saul brings 1 Samuel to a close, but this is merely a formal division of the ancient history. Many aspects of the narrative lack resolution: the outcome of the Philistine invasion, the position of David, and, most importantly, the provision of salvation by the Lord for his people.

THE RISE OF DAVID (continued)

2 Samuel 1:1–5:12

1:1-16 Report of Saul's death

With the death of Saul, a new and dangerous phase of David's rise begins. The way is clear to the throne, but David's claim must be seen to be legitimate and acceptable to the people. He still must avoid the two dangers Abigail named (cf. 1 Sam 25:30-31): implication in the destruction of the Saulide monarchy, and seizure of the throne. While his presence in Ziklag (1:1) clears him of

involvement in Saul's death, the arrival of the messenger focuses attention on David's use of this disaster.

At first, this is a typical report from the battlefront (cf. 1 Sam 4:12, 16-17). There is nothing untoward in the man's appearance, identity, or message. It is only when pushed for details about Saul and Jonathan that a story very different from 1 Samuel 31:1-7 emerges. This man is no mere messenger but an eyewitness and participant in Saul's last moments (1:6-10). He is an Amalekite who killed the king! And he presents the royal insignia as evidence (1:10). Whatever his motivation, he creates a major temptation for David to grasp the royal regalia.

David's response is not what the Amalekite expects. David and his troops grieve deeply for the slain (1:11-12), and then David executes the Amalekite (1:15). David is consistent, as he has frequently argued against harming the Lord's anointed (1 Sam 24:7; 26:9). For one last time, David recalls the argument and demonstrates loyalty. The king's death is not a time for grasping but for mourning (1:17).

1:17-27 Elegy for Saul and Jonathan

David's lament is a powerful expression of public grief. Saul may have been rejected by the Lord, but he was still the leader of Israel. His death is a moment of defeat for the people. The warriors have fallen, Israel has been unmanned, and the women are summoned to mourn their fallen heroes. The incomprehension caused by death and defeat act as a refrain, "How can the warriors have fallen!" (1:19, 25, 27). This is a crisis of faith in a god who promises life and salvation. The crisis deepens because the Philistine women rejoice at the "good news" (1:20; cf. 1 Sam 31:9). What should have been a place of blessing has become a place of curse (1:21a). The battle was glorious (1:22) even if it was disastrous (1:21b). Grief is the only response to this crisis, a grief that voices the contradictions and thus opposes them. Only from such remembering can the grief-stricken reclaim the joy of past blessings (1:23-24) as an assurance for future comfort.

This grief is public and personal. All Israel mourns with David for the lost leaders, as he mourns for one he loved. Verse 26b is more precisely translated: "More precious have I held your love for me than love of women." Even here, the unequal nature of the relationship cannot be avoided. Jonathan's commitment to David has been consistently noted (1 Sam 18:1, 3; 19:1; 20:3, 17), but there was no such expression of David's feeling for Jonathan. Jonathan's affections motivated him to assist David, protecting him, saving him, and encouraging him. Others have acted similarly, particularly the women of 1 Samuel (Michal and Abigail), but none did as much (nor were given as much narrative space) as Jonathan. David is deeply in Jonathan's debt both on a personal and a political level. Only now, when Jonathan is dead, does David acknowledge this (as it was only when Jonathan abdicated his succession rights that David entered a mutual covenant with him in 1 Sam 23:18). David's grief is personal, but one wonders if the political, public dimension still dominates his reckoning.

2:1-11 Rival kings

This unit contains two accounts of king-making following Saul's death. The narrator draws them together using a Deuteronomistic regnal formula. Such formulae provide a chronological framework for the monarchies of Israel and Judah. In this case, elements of the formula are divided between Ishbaal and David (2:10-11). As in its previous usage (1 Sam 13:1), there is something incomplete and unstable about the formula and the monarchy at this moment.

David's accession results from an inquiry of the Lord (2:1). The Lord clearly moves David into position at Hebron where the men of Judah anoint him king. This public anointing is minimally described (2:4a); there is no religious dimension as in 1 Samuel 16:1-13. It is a sign of public acceptance of the Lord's choice. This acceptance will be a key element in David's efforts to woo the northern tribes. He contacts Jabesh-gilead (2:5-7), a key center of Saulide support, and praises their "kindness" (*hesed*, loyalty) to Saul. Such loyalty calls forth and manifests divine blessing, but how will that blessing be maintained? David presents himself as the partner of Jabesh-gilead in actions which continue loyalty (2:6). This is a bold move to win their support and establish himself as a legitimate successor to Saul.

But David has a rival. Abner takes the Lord's role in moving Saul's surviving son, Ishbaal, into position and establishing him as king (2:8-9). Abner is Saul's general and the power behind the

northern throne. There are now two claimants for loyalty, and two powers moving the kings. Hence the regnal formula fragments. A Saulide monarchy continues in the north while David is installed in Hebron. Civil war looms.

2:12-32 Skirmishes and combat

Civil war places the focus of attention on the generals. Abner and Joab lead out forces which are described in equivalent terms (2:12-13). This balance leads to a standoff. Abner proposes a gladiatorial contest in an attempt to break the deadlock with minimal casualties (2:14), but even here, the sides are evenly matched (2:15-16). Fighting escalates into battle. The three sons of Zeruiah are David's key warriors and constantly enmeshed in violence. On this occasion, the speedy Asahel chases the fleeing Abner (2:19-23). The drama intensifies as Abner tries to avoid killing Asahel for fear of vengeance. His attempts fail; he kills Asahel; bloodshed triggers vengeance (2:24).

The scene is set for a bloody showdown (2:25) when Abner succeeds in parleying a truce (2:26-28). Joab accepts the need to halt the fratricidal bloodshed, but almost too quickly. He is willing to stop the people killing fellow Israelites, but he makes no commitment that his personal vendetta is over. Both sides withdraw to count and bury their dead.

The seeds of this conflict were sown in 1 Samuel 26 when the conflict between Saul and David was widened to include their generals. While the principals refrained from bloodshed, their seconds show little restraint. Violence begets vengeance and threatens to destroy the very thing the kings are quarrelling over, as Abigail warned in chapter 25. Abner emerges in this episode as an honorable man who seeks to limit the bloodshed, but will Joab cooperate? Or will he drag his leader into guilt by association?

3:1-5 Civil war

The civil war is long but unequal. David's "house" is winning and its position becomes more secure: political strength and sexual prowess mirror each other in this culture. This is an appropriate point to list David's sons by his many women. This successful harem will contrast with the competition over Saul's concubine (3:7).

3:6-39 Abner, kingmaker betrayed

The quarrel over Rizpah, Saul's concubine, initiates a move by Abner to transfer the allegiance of the north to David. In effect, Abner, who, apart from David, is the only character to cite the Lord, becomes the agent of David's rise to the throne of all Israel, until Joab complicates the plot. The result is an intriguing narrative which illustrates the danger of bloodlust.

3:6-11 Ishbaal's accusation

Women play a crucial, if normally passive, role in Israelite politics. Ishbaal is accusing Abner of usurping the kingdom by taking Saul's concubine (3:6-7). Abner's anger derives from this slight to his loyalty to Saul's house (3:8). Like the people of Jabesh-gilead, his loyalty to the Lord is expressed in concrete terms by loyalty to Saul's family. Ishbaal's accusation pushes Abner to express that loyalty to the Lord in a new political form. He will bring about the Lord's promise to David (3:9-10).

3:12-21 Abner's gift

David is shrewd enough to facilitate Abner. His condition is the return of Michal (3:13). Once he has Saul's daughter (3:14-16), David becomes Saul's son-in-law and legitimate claimant to the loyalty owed to Saul's house, so easing Abner's transfer of allegiance. Abner persuades the elders to make the same transfer by highlighting David's claim to divine approval (3:17-19). In all their dealings Abner acts honorably and David reciprocates (3:20-21). David is the recipient of Abner's gift, but happily plots with him to achieve it. Together they arrange a peaceful transfer of power. David has learned well from Abigail that persuasion and patience outweigh violence as the path to power.

After these negotiations, the narrator begins to refer to David as "the king" (vv. 24, 33, 36, 37, 38) and gives him the title "King David" in verse 31. Abner's negotiations have effectively made David king of all Israel, even if the coronation lies some chapters away.

3:22-39 Joab's crime

However, Joab's actions threaten David's claim to the kingdom. Joab's desire for vengeance colors his reactions to events in his absence (3:22-25). He may be David's chief officer, but he is not under David's control. He acts for his own goals. The narrator stresses the independence (3:26) that results in Abner's murder (3:27). David is shocked and swears his innocence (3:28). He quickly and profusely pins responsibility and punishment on Joab (3:29), while he orders a burial with full honors for Abner. This is a very public show of grief (3:31-35). It is probably heartfelt, but it also serves as a public demonstration of innocence. This crime threatens to wreck the unification of Israel and to besmirch David's kingship. The danger is so great that even the narrator declares David innocent (3:37), as do the people (3:36). Clearly the compilers of the history felt a great need to exonerate David of involvement in the death of an honorable general.

Comparing David's last speech with verse 11 shows that both he and Ishbaal are unable to control their generals. Both are effectively hostage to these men and can be destroyed by their actions. Abner ends Ishbaal's reign by withdrawing support. David's reign is almost destroyed by Joab's crime. The monarchical system threatens to unleash forces which even kings cannot control. The Lord has raised David to the throne, but this will not save the institution from human failings.

4:1-12 Death of Ishbaal

With Abner dead, the northern kingdom collapses (4:1). Ishbaal is powerless and is assassinated by two officers. Their identity is given in detail (4:2) to state clearly the assassins' family backgrounds and to dissociate them from David's entourage. The murder is swift and brutal, using three verbs: "[they] struck and killed him, and cut off his head" (4:7).

The assassins bring their trophy to David expecting a reward. Their presentation is logical and assured (4:8), but fails to take account of David's loyalty to the family of Saul. His reaction and words recall a similar incident after Saul's death (1:1-16). David has the assassins punished, again using three verbs: "the young men killed them and cut off their hands and feet, hanging them up near the pool in Hebron" (4:12). The punishment fits the crime. As with Abner, David ensures that Ishbaal's remains are buried with dignity. Once again, the narrator demonstrates David's loyalty to the house of Saul and his innocence in planning or benefiting from their deaths. The kingship will come to David, but not by vengeance (contrary to claims in v. 8b).

The narrator inserts one ray of hope for Saul's family. An aside informs the reader of the survival of Jonathan's son, Meribbaal (4:4). The child is crippled and so cannot attain political power, but his existence will provide David with an opportunity to fulfill his oaths to Jonathan (1 Sam 20:14-17) and Saul (1 Sam 24:22-23).

5:1-5 David, king of all Israel

The story of David's rise reaches its conclusion. David is crowned king over Israel and establishes his capital. The coronation of David happens in two movements. First, the tribes of Israel meet David and resolve their alarm (5:1-2; cf. 4:1). The tribes stress their solidarity with David as fellow Israelites (5:1), and affirm David's leadership (5:2). They quote a word of the Lord (previously unmentioned) to demonstrate their recognition of his divine appointment to rule ("shepherd") the people. The term, "ruler" (*nagid*), has several echoes: it emphasizes David's role as military leader (cf. Saul's appointment in 1 Sam 9:16), it picks up several predictions of David's rise (1 Sam 13:14; 25:30), and it prepares for anointing (cf. 1 Sam 10:1). It catches the covenantal understanding of the king as leader of God's people, filled with God's spirit and subject to God's word.

Secondly, the scheme of Abner is ratified by the elders (5:3; cf. 3:17-18). David enters a covenant ("agreement") with the elders (cf. Abner's agreement with David in 3:12). Such an action is missing from David's enthronement over Judah: his rule of Israel must recognize and respect the covenant traditions of the whole people. The passage ends with a Deuteronomistic regnal formula. David has begun his reign over all Israel (5:5).

5:6-12 Jerusalem's capture

The formula's reference to Jerusalem is quickly sorted out by the account of Jerusalem's capture. Jerusalem lies between the tribal areas of Judah and Benjamin. It was not an Israelite city. David captured it with his own men so that it is truly his city, an autonomous place from which he can rule both Judah and Israel with impartiality. An account of the capture is also given in 1 Chronicles 11:4-9 with less attention to the blind and lame. The comments about the blind and lame stress

the city's apparent impregnability, which David overcomes. It is conjectured that his troops broke into the city by climbing up a well shaft linking the city to a spring in the valley below. With David established in Jerusalem, the narrator concludes the story of his rise with two statements of God's support (5:10, 12). The last statement is a fitting summary for this phase in Israel's history.

THE REIGN OF DAVID

2 Samuel 5:13–8:18

Between the major narratives of David's rise (1 Sam 16–2 Sam 5) and of his family (2 Sam 9–20), the compilers of the Deuteronomistic History inserted a collection of stories about David's monarchy. Framed by lists of his family (5:13-16) and his officers (8:15-18), these accounts tell how his monarchy developed. There are stories of his battles and of his dealings with the Lord. Militarily, David moves from defense to expansion. Religiously, attention shifts from the ark to the dynasty of David as the sign of God's continuing presence.

5:13-25 The defeat of the Philistines

David's family is already extensive. Now he adds concubines to his harem. While the later narratives will deal with his children born in Hebron, one son born in Jerusalem should be noted in passing, Solomon.

As David's reign begins, there is unfinished business with the Philistines. It is possible that the Philistines assembled their troops to punish their renegade vassal, so David goes into hiding (5:17). The situation is critical for the new kingdom. The valley of Rephaim gives access from the coast to Jerusalem; controlling it, the Philistines can split the kingdom and dominate its capital. As before, David consults the Lord (5:19; cf. 1 Sam 23:4; 30:7-8; 2 Sam 2:1) and is given clearance to proceed. The first encounter drives the enemy back. The place name means "Lord of the breaking through," signifying the breaking of the Philistine line (5:20). But the Philistines return to the fray and this time the Lord gives quite specific directions (5:23-24). This second battle becomes the occasion of a theophany; the sound of the wind rustling the treetops suggests the footsteps of

Israel's divine warrior charging into battle. The rout is complete. The Philistines are driven out of the hill country and confined to the coastal plain. The Lord has marked the beginning of David's reign with a decisive defeat of Israel's greatest enemy as promised (cf. 3:18). The people know for certain that David is the Lord's chosen king.

6:1-23 The ark is brought to Jerusalem

The defeat of the Philistines by the warrior Lord recalls the traditions of holy war. This is a suitable moment to reconnect with the ancient symbol of the Lord of hosts, the ark, which was deposited in Kiriath-jearim (1 Sam 6:21–7:1). By retrieving the ark, David connects his new regime to covenant tradition and thereby gives it further legitimation.

The ark is transported on a new cart and with significant rejoicing (cf. 1 Sam 6), and as before, the narrator highlights the dangers of taking God's presence lightly. Like the descendants of Jeconiah (1 Sam 6:19-20), Uzzah is struck down (6:6-7). David, belatedly, asks "How can the ark of the LORD come to me?" (6:9). Curiously, this is one venture which David initiates without consulting the Lord. His attempt to co-opt the old traditions is checked temporarily by a reminder of the freedom of the Lord of hosts, a key theme of the earlier ark narratives.

The journey resumes with even more religious festivities. Sacrifices (6:13) and communion feasts (6:17-19) are added to the song and dance (6:5, 14-15). David is at the center of worship, dressed in a priest's linen tunic (6:14). He dances with abandon. Is there an echo of Saul's possession by the Spirit (1 Sam 10:5-6) with its combination of music and ecstasy? Is David caught up in the charismatic exuberance which overpowered Saul? Does Michal despise him for this behavior, reminiscent of her father's darker moments (6:16)?

Following the joyous celebrations, the private encounter picks up this jarring comment. Michal vents her anger about three things: honor, slave girls, and common behavior (6:20). David is reduced in her esteem from king to commoner! David's response ends with her three points in reverse order: lowliness, slave girls, and honor in verse 22. It was for the Lord that he danced (6:21). What right has she to complain? The Lord chose David over Saul. What Michal sees as shame (David exposing himself), David claims as a sign

of honor. The theme of reversal of Hannah's song (1 Sam 2) is operating, and it rebounds on Michal, the king's daughter who remains childless and so dishonored in comparison with the slave girls.

7:1-29 The Lord's promise to David

While 5:17–6:23 show David engaging with the old traditions of Israel to secure his kingdom, chapter 7 marks a new beginning in Israel's relationship with the Lord. David wants to incorporate the ark and its symbolism into the new settlement to ensure the stability of the monarchy. The symbol of the Lord's freedom to move with nomadic tribes and to act independently of the people is to be housed in one location, the royal capital. The Lord resists this imposition but responds with a startling promise which makes the kings the living testimony to God's presence. The oracle of 2 Samuel 7:4-16 is one of the central texts of the Old Testament.

The keyword "house" gives unity to the chapter. Reflecting the tension between freedom and presence, mobility and stability, it has several connotations: dwelling, palace, temple, dynasty. After the introduction (7:1-3) outlining David's plan comes the Lord's oracle through Nathan (7:4-16). A short narrative interlude (7:17-18a) introduces David's prayer as the response to the oracle (7:18b-29).

7:4-16 Nathan's oracle

Scholars suggest that the oracle has been elaborated several times, a sign of constant reflection within the tradition prior to the composition of the book. An original account, possibly dating from David's time, focused on the Lord's rebuttal of David's plan to build a house (temple). Instead the Lord would build David a house (dynasty) and kingdom which would last forever (7:11b, 16). This promise underwent elaboration in prophetic circles to stress David's role as *nagid* (7:8-10) and to focus on Solomon as the particular successor (7:14-15). Nathan's role was also enhanced (7:3, 17). The notion of a temple as God's permanent residence generates mixed reactions throughout the Bible, different views which also affect this text. Verses 5-7 were revised to show that such a building compromised God's freedom. Those who saw Solomon's temple as the pinnacle of Israel's relationship with the Lord added verse 13.

Such a textual history is complex, but the struggle to understand God's promise today continues a process of interpreting God's will which goes back to its first revelation.

David wishes to build God a house (7:1-2). At best, this gives glory to God (so Nathan interprets David's motive); at worst, it is a domestication of the Lord of Israel. The Lord's intervention rejects such domestication, which runs counter to the fundamental religious experience of Israel, the exodus (7:6-7). In the new dispensation, that experience of the liberating God must be maintained. God's saving presence will not be limited to a place or object, but will be manifest in a people established in security (7:10). To achieve this, the Lord has chosen to raise up an individual as leader (7:8). Just as monarchy is established by divine choice rather than a human one, its stability will be provided by a divine "building" rather than a human "building." The Lord will establish a dynasty for David (7:11b). The present text focuses first on David's immediate successor (7:12-15) before expanding to consider a permanent dynasty (7:16).

The presentation of David's heir is particularly noteworthy. Normally, God's promises are conditional on ethical requirements. While the oracle does warn of ethical/religious requirements for the members of the dynasty (7:14b), the conditional "if" is not present in the Hebrew text. Instead, the promise is unconditional: "but I will not withdraw my favor from him" (7:15). This is a new departure in Israel's experience of God. In these individuals, the house of David, is invested the hope of Israel. It is the human incarnation of God's promise that is truly messianic: a human being now bears the symbolism of God's presence and power in the world. For Jews and Christians reflecting on this oracle, this human being is the instrument for establishing the reign of justice and peace, covenant fraternity, and integrity.

7:18-29 David's prayer

David's prayer is a fitting response to the oracle. He moves from prostration before the Lord's grace (7:18-21), to praise (7:22-24), and on to petition (7:25-29). The oracle outlined what the Lord will do for David; now David acknowledges the graciousness of God's attention to one who has nothing to recommend him (7:18-21). David locates what the Lord has done for him in the

context of God's saving actions for his people (the exodus, 7:22-24). This new revelation is a continuation of that fundamental revelation. This display of humility and praise only emboldens David to petition the Lord to keep his promise! This is a bold faith. Like Jacob (Gen 32:27), David will not let God go until the Lord blesses him and confirms the promise (7:25-29).

8:1-14 David's wars

Chapter 8 offers a summary of David's campaigns. Some material looks back to round off stories already told (e.g., v. 1 parallels 5:17-25); other material anticipates and provides context for later stories (e.g., the campaign against Hadadezer in 8:3-6 supports 10:15-19). This unit shows David moving from defense to offense, saving Israel by conquering its neighbors. It is a celebration of his military prowess. It also raises questions about excessive use of power. Moab, an ally during David's rise (1 Sam 22:3-4), is now conquered and most of its fighting men executed (8:2).

War against the Arameans accounts for a significant part of David's campaigns. The campaign against Hadadezer (8:3-6) leads into the gathering of booty and tribute (8:7-12). The focus is on David's accumulation of wealth. Only in verse 11 does the narrator add that the materials were "consecrated to the LORD." The passage as a whole celebrates David's abilities and fame (8:13), but the narrator reminds the reader twice (8:6b and 14b) that the true source of success is the Lord.

8:15-18 David's government

This section of the book (5:13–8:18) concludes by outlining the key officials in David's government. The government covers all areas of public life: justice, the military, administration, and religion. The list suggests a more complex administration than the family-based government of Saul (cf. 1 Sam 14:49-51). David's administration incorporates the need to establish justice, a key covenantal theme. The success of the king will be measured by his ability to provide justice (cf. Ps 72:1-4; Jer 22:15-16). It is also noteworthy that David's administration includes the Elide priesthood (Abiathar), as well as the Zadokite priesthood which will eventually replace the former (cf. 1 Sam 2:27-36).

THE FAMILY OF DAVID

2 Samuel 9–20

Many scholars identify 2 Samuel 9–20 and 2 Kings 1–2 as a continuous narrative which deals with the question: who will succeed David? It has been called the Succession Narrative. It is suggested that this narrative was composed in court circles soon after the succession was achieved. However, debate still continues about the details of this hypothesis.

2 Samuel 9–20 is a sustained literary masterpiece which skillfully explores the ambiguity of human personality, success and failure, and the tensions that arose in David's household. There is little direct involvement of God, his prophets, or priests. This more secular drama is played out in a strongly religious context. The overall direction of events is set by God's promise to establish this family as a dynasty, but the foibles and faith of human beings complicate yet enrich the unfolding of that plan. It is this aspect that the narrator is particularly keen to explore.

9:1-13 David and Meribbaal

This episode looks back to David's oaths to Jonathan (1 Sam 20:14-17) and Saul (1 Sam 24:21-23). Jonathan made David swear to protect Jonathan's descendants. David now recalls that loyalty ("kindness," *hesed* in vv. 1, 3, 7) and seeks to carry it out. Loyalty is David's key characteristic in chapters 9 and 10. As the narrative opens, David is unaware of any survivor of Saul's house (9:1): the Hebrew text suggests he grows more doubtful (literally in v. 3: "Is there no one still belonging to Saul's house?"). Ziba, however, gives a positive answer (9:3).

The survivor is introduced by description only. The reader can deduce his identity since the description fits 4:4. But the survivor is anonymous and located in a nameless place ("Lodebar" actually means "no word"): clearly he is a nonentity! Yet this insignificant person exists in tension with his status as Jonathan's son. Both narrator and David name him (9:6), because he is significant in their eyes.

For David, he is the means to fulfilling oaths. Loyalty is shown by the double gift of restitution and a place of honor at court (9:7). But Meribbaal clings to his nonentity status ("a dead dog"; 9:8). Perhaps he is aware how much safer he is being left alone. David's act of loyalty must be made concrete, and Ziba reenters the drama as the means to carry out David's wishes (9:9-11). A place of honor at the king's table is both a concrete sign of loyalty and a means of watchful control over a potential rallying point for opposition. David is both magnanimous and cautious.

Meribbaal is important in the narrator's eyes. He is named formally as the successor of Saul (9:6), and he has a son (9:12), but he is crippled (9:3, 13). The narrator is teasing the reader to pay attention to Meribbaal, an incapacitated source of danger to David, a test whether David will keep his word, a potential focus for opposition, and an added complication in a crowded royal household.

10:1-19 War with the Ammonites

David not only displays loyalty to individuals, but also in his dealings with surrounding nations. In chapter 10 he intends to maintain "kindness" (*hesed*) with the Ammonites. Saul had defeated Nabash (1 Sam 11), so presumably some form of nonaggression pact had been established. By sending ambassadors to Nabash's son, Hanun, David seeks to continue the pact (10:2). However, Hanun is encouraged to reject David's offer in a particularly shaming fashion (10:3) by unmanning the messengers (10:4) and sending them packing. David's concern for his servants illustrates why he inspires tenacious loyalty (10:5). The Ammonite action, however, is a declaration of war.

The Ammonites hire mercenaries from the Aramean kingdoms in Syria-Lebanon (10:7) so that Joab and the standing army (10:8) must fight on two fronts. Joab emerges as a skilled general (10:9-10) who can also invoke the rhetoric of holy war (10:11). His strategy is successful, but for no reason he withdraws, leaving the Ammonite city intact.

The Arameans rally their forces, and Hadadezer is named as leader (10:16). The outcome is therefore already known (cf. 8:3-6). David takes the field with an all-Israel force. The details of the battle are brief (10:17-18), sufficient to record a major victory which leads to the submission of the Arameans and the isolation of the Ammonites (10:19). The narrator uses this second account of the campaign to provide background for the story to come in chapters 11–12. David's loyalty to his treaty obligations, to his honor, and to his troops also provides an appropriate background to his treatment of Uriah. This man of *hesed* is about to sin spectacularly.

11:1-27 David's sin

The narrative of chapter 11 is cleverly composed. While seeming to present all the facts, it refrains from showing the feelings or motives of the characters. The reader sees and hears "from outside," while the inner lives are hidden. The reader unconsciously fills in these gaps with hypotheses to assist evaluation of the action. To fully appreciate the narrative as art, the reader should restrain from guessing, pay attention to what is actually said, and accept that there is room for conflicting interpretations. The full richness of the ambiguity of human action should be allowed to emerge.

11:1-5 Sending for Bathsheba

A good example of the need for restraint occurs in verse 1. The contrast between "when kings go to war" and "David himself remained in Jerusalem" is often read as criticism of David. Perhaps this criticism is warranted, but such arrangements were usual on David's campaigns (cf. 10:7). It is better to pay attention to the verb "to send." This verb occurs masterfully in the narrative to express the sender's control over others. It is a verb of power, even manipulation. David is in control from verse 1. He is the subject of a long series of verbs in verses 2-4a, from rising after a siesta to lying down with the woman. He does what he wants. The flow of David's activity ends with a parenthetical reference to Bathsheba's menstrual cycle. This is beyond David's control, and she now becomes the subject of the verbs (11:4b-5). She is no passive object, but had power over David. She sends him a message that changes everything, "I am pregnant" (11:5).

11:6-14 Sending Uriah

The next scene opens with more sending (11:6). Uriah is the pawn of others' schemes. Usually speech links actions with motives, but here speech does not match action. The suspicion of deception adds new layers of ambiguity. The narrator reports that David asks after the wellbeing of Joab, the troops, and the war (11:7), all in line with previous displays of his loyalty (cf. 10:5). But his speech (11:8) contains two commands, "Go down

to your house and bathe your feet" (a euphemism for sexual intercourse). His sole interest is to conceal his paternity of the child. However, Uriah disobeys the king! Throughout verses 9-10, the verb "did not go" keeps repeating. Why did Uriah disobey? Should his speech in verse 11 be read as the words of a pious soldier, or is it an implied criticism of David arising from Uriah's suspicions of the king's motives? The narrator hides the answers. How far can David push Uriah without revealing his hand? How much does Uriah know? The lack of clarity frustrates both David and the reader! Eventually David gives up and sends Uriah with a letter to Joab (11:14), and there is that verb again!

11:15-27 Evaluating David

The narrator allows the reader a clear view of David's plans in the letter (11:15), but texts are no sure guide to events. Joab does not follow David's plan (11:16-17). Joab instructs the messenger on how to report the death of Uriah (11:18-21) but the messenger does not follow Joab's plan, either (11:22-24). Such complications of the plot to kill Uriah implicate more people: Joab, the messenger, and the unfortunate soldiers killed with Uriah. Joab betrays a realization of what is going on in his speculative description of David's outburst (11:20-21) by alluding to the death of Abimelech (Judg 9:50-55), a king whose reign was destroyed by a woman!

In the end, David responds mildly, "Do not let this be a great evil in your sight" (11:25) and is content that the sword devours here and there. Uriah's wife—note the description—grieves for her husband (11:26). But when mourning is over, both she and David carry out two verbs of action (11:27). Is she really a victim of a grasping king? Adultery is concealed. All's well, then? The narrator reports one evaluation completely the opposite of David's (11:25). "But in the sight of the LORD what David had done was evil" (11:27).

12:1-31 The Lord's response

Just as David achieves control, a new sending occurs (12:1). The Lord is in control and delivers judgment. Nathan's parable (12:1a-4) is "the thing wherein I'll catch the conscience of the king" (*Hamlet*, Act 3 Scene 1). The parable contrasts the unfeeling rich man with the doting poor man. The rich man is characterized by the verb "to take," the verb of kings (cf. 1 Sam 8:11-18). David is able to read the parable, but he fails to apply it. Nathan does that for him: "You are the man" (12:7a).

12:7-14 The verdict

Nathan cuts through the ambiguity of chapter 11 and delivers the Lord's verdict. The opening verses sum up the Lord's graciousness towards David (12:7-8) in a way that both echoes the Lord's promise in 7:8-9 and sets the context for David's infidelity. The accusation and condemnation come in two parts. In both, David is accused of spurning or despising the Lord (12:9, 10b). In the first case, infidelity is specified as Uriah's murder; since he died by the sword (which David so casually accepted in 11:25), the sword will hang over David's house (12:9-10a). In the second, the crime is adultery; for taking Uriah's wife, David's wives will be taken from him (12:10b-12). The punishment fits the crimes. The future story of David's family is plotted.

After all the ambiguity of David's actions, his response is a flash of clarity: "I have sinned against the LORD" (12:13). This simple, unelaborated declaration cuts through the web of self-deception and allows God the freedom to create a new future. The Lord responds by "transferring" the consequences of David's sin (the significance of "has removed your sin" in v. 13). The relationship with the Lord remains intact but the implications of the sin must be worked out, starting with the death of the child (12:14).

12:15-25 Repentance

David's actions are reported from the "outside" (12:15-20). Again, this creates confusion about his motives. His explanation ends the opaqueness of the narrative (12:22-23). He has left behind his attempts to manipulate events and people, and now his actions unfold from faith in the Lord as controller of human affairs. David does not send for Bathsheba but goes to her (12:24). This new series of verbal actions ends with the birth of Solomon. Now it is the Lord who sends (12:25), and the special name denotes the child as a sign of hope in the midst of sin and punishment.

12:26-31 The war and its aftermath

The war has provided the backdrop to these events. Now the narrator can wind it up. As before (10:15-19), David goes forth for the decisive battle when prompted by Joab. David takes the crown of the Ammonite idol (12:30) and much other booty. He also enslaves the population.

David's adultery with Bathsheba triggers the drama of the remainder of 2 Samuel. Nathan's oracle links the turmoil of David's family to that moment of passion, one spring afternoon, as if it were the original sin of the dynasty (cf. Gen 2:8). Clearly, adultery and murder are serious crimes. The narrator refrains from providing motive or extenuating factors, elements which the modern reader seeks in order to make a moral evaluation. Is the narrator suggesting that these are not relevant, or that they offer no diminution of the act? Perhaps. The struggle to interpret and explain the actions of David is an important struggle, but it does not excuse him of his sin. After the ambiguity of human affairs in chapter 11 comes the all-seeing clarity of judgment in chapter 12. In the former, we strive for clarity of motive; in the latter, faithful receptivity provides guidance.

13:1-22 Amnon rapes Tamar

Chapters 13–14 describe a new family crisis. Absalom's sister is raped by her half-brother and Absalom takes revenge. The sins of David are repeated in the next generation. The narrator provides much more access to the inner lives of the characters, exploring particularly the interplay of action and emotion. In the opening episode (13:1-22), familial ties pepper the narrative. The reader is not allowed to forget such relationships, which set limits on proper behavior and create hierarchies of power and responsibility. Uncontrolled desire confuses proper relations; the language of "brother/sister" can also express passionate love (cf. Song 4:9-10).

Amnon is in love with his half-sister Tamar (13:1, 4), but this is a consuming emotion that renders him irrational (13:2). His wily cousin, Jonadab, concocts a scheme to give Amnon private access to Tamar (13:5). Everyone plays along without a hint of suspicion (13:6-10). Does no one else notice Amnon's dejection, or ask why?

In contrast to Amnon's irrationality, Tamar speaks with cool argument. She names the crime immediately. "Do not force me" (13:12; cf. 13:14, 22, 32) denotes the humiliation of a woman by sexual violence. The action is both wrong and unwise, she argues. Committing this "terrible crime," Amnon will be classed as a "fool." Both words translate the Hebrew root, *nabal* (cf. 1 Sam 25). However, Amnon does not listen to her voice (13:14, 16b), because he is driven by lust, nothing more. Once that is satisfied, his "love" is spent. Verse 15 succinctly records this psychological change.

Now Amnon wants rid of her (13:15b-17) but she refuses to be hidden (13:18-19). This crime will not be suppressed; others must respond to it. Absalom's response is twofold. He takes her into his home. His words may seem to dismiss her grief (13:20), but a better translation is, "Do not set your heart on saying anything." He will act for her. Secondly, to Amnon he says nothing, but he bears his sister's shame with a hatred that drives the story on. The other respondent is David. All references to him in the story hint at his love for Amnon: he would do whatever his firstborn asked (13:13). Now he is very angry but does nothing (13:21). Is this extreme indulgence, or is it paralysis as his own failings are mirrored in his son? His inaction only causes the hatred to ferment.

13:23-39 Absalom's revenge

Absalom bides his time (13:23). A shearing festival (cf. 1 Sam 25) provides the opportunity to act. Verses 24-27a allow the narrator to explore the relationship between David and Absalom. On the surface, all is pleasant consideration (13:24-25), but when Absalom mentions Amnon, David panics (13:26). David is suspicious and needs persuading. Is he conscious of Absalom's unexpressed hatred?

The murder is swift and efficient (13:28a-29). The narrator reports Absalom's instructions to highlight the motive of personal revenge. Then attention focuses on the reaction to this murder. The other brothers panic and flee. The first rumors of a massacre prompt extreme grief. It is ironic that now all tear their garments but no one did so for Tamar (cf. 13:19). Up pops Jonadab to stem the panic by reminding David of Amnon's rape of Tamar (13:32-33). "Now let my lord the king not take so to heart that report" echoes Absalom's words to Tamar in verse 20. David is being encouraged to react to Amnon's death as he reacted to the rape, by doing nothing. The arrival of the fleeing princes confirms Jonadab's words (13:34-35), but the grief is not much diminished. David fails to respond appropriately once again.

Meanwhile, Absalom flees (13:34, 37) and is in exile for three years. Revenge took time (13:23), but so also does reconciliation (13:39), all because of David's failure to respond correctly to the crimes of his sons. He has lost his firstborn. Will he now lose the second-born for whom he longs?

14:1-33 Absalom's return

Joab acts to break the stalemate and enable David and Absalom to be reconciled. He prepares a gifted woman from Tekoa (14:2-3) to create a fictional case which, like Nathan's parable, will enable David to see his situation in a new light.

14:4-20 Absalom's case

The fictional story is simple: her two sons quarrel, one is killed, and the other is under sentence of death. Can David save her surviving son (14:4-7)? David is moved to help her, but the woman extracts an oath that her surviving son will not be harmed (14:8-11). Once David binds himself by oath (cf. 12:5-6), the woman can use the fictional scenario to change David's real situation. Her argumentation is subtle, shifting between real and imaginary cases (14:12-17). The king has responded to a parent's plea. Will he now act as a parent himself? The king keeps his son in exile because he interprets the law to require Absalom's execution (14:13), but such a punitive view ignores how God acts. People die, but God does not banish (14:14). If God can resolve this predicament, so can his people and their king. In her fictional case, the woman considered David wise enough to save her son (14:15-17). Now let him do the same for his own son!

In struggling to come to terms with her rhetoric, David guesses that Joab is involved (14:18-19). The woman admits this is so, but stresses the need for a decision (14:20). The fictional tale has enabled David to view his predicament in a new light, and he moves to bring back Absalom.

14:21-33 The verdict

Joab responds gratefully and quickly (14:21-23), but the restoration does not result in reconciliation. Absalom may return to Jerusalem, but David will not meet him (14:24).

The narrator pauses to describe Absalom's beauty. The praise is glowing (14:25-26) but disconcerting. Bathsheba and Tamar were beautiful, but it only caused them trouble. Saul was handsome (1 Sam 9:2) but a failure. The Lord warned against judgment by appearances (1 Sam 16:7). Like his father, Absalom is attractive; he looks as a king should look. Such praise warns of trouble to come. The reference to luxuriant hair (abundant by royal standards!) will be picked up later.

Two years pass and the situation becomes unbearable for Absalom. He seeks Joab's help, but Joab refuses to see him (14:29). He gains Joab's attention with a wanton act of destruction reminiscent of Samson (Judg 15:4-8), another ominous note. Even his speech is rushed and confused (14:32). A meeting is quickly arranged. Absalom's prostration acknowledges the king's authority, but does it express contrition? The king's kiss is according to protocol, but is it reconciliation? Appearances can deceive. Has the long estrangement done irreparable damage to relations?

15:1-12 Absalom's rebellion

A new phase of the narrative begins as Absalom usurps the trappings of a king (15:1). He also seeks to preempt the royal prerogative to administer justice (15:2-6). With promises of favorable judgments, he wins over individuals from the northern tribes. The narrator's concluding remark sums up the irony (15:6b): good judgment from a thief, affection for the disaffected.

After cultivating support for four years, Absalom initiates rebellion. The pretext of a vow allows him to go to Hebron, where David was crowned king (2:1-4; 5:1-3). He is as devious as his father, and David is taken in (15:9). Once in Hebron, Absalom sounds the signal for the uprising. The description of the uprising is mixed. It has widespread support in Israel (15:10), yet those from Jerusalem are not involved (15:11). However, at least one counselor, Ahithophel, joins Absalom (15:12). The narrator sums up the ambiguity: this is conspiracy. It may be gathering strength, but this negative evaluation suggests an action lacking in real loyalty.

15:13–16:14 David's flight

A report of the transfer of Israelite affection to Absalom precipitates David's flight from Jerusalem (15:13). This retreat forms the narrative thread linking dialogues between David and those he meets. The real drama lies in these revealing speeches that explore the motivations of the characters.

15:14-16 David and his household

The first dialogue is between David and his household. David's motive for flight is to avoid slaughter. The sword of the Lord's punishment (12:10) looms large in his thinking. His officers' response is immediate and unswerving. In Hebrew, the verbs "to flee" and "to choose" have the same consonants, and the word play brings out the closeness between master and servants. David leaves ten concubines behind. While he seeks to spare others his punishment, his actions nonetheless prepare for the fulfillment of the oracle (12:11-12).

15:19-22 David and Ittai

As the troops pass in review (15:17-18), the second dialogue occurs with Ittai. Following the general affirmation of devotion, Ittai's is a particular case. He is a non-Israelite, an exile already, and David seeks to spare him further disruption. Ittai's response is a heartfelt oath of devotion (cf. Ruth 1:16). There is a pragmatic dimension to David's solicitude. He invites Ittai to stay behind "with the king" (15:19). This is a test of loyalty and Ittai passes. David may be in flight, but he is consolidating his forces for further action. Even so, such foresight does not minimize the grief of the flight (15:23).

15:24-29 David, Zadok, and Abiathar

David encounters Zadok and Abiathar bringing the ark from Jerusalem. David instructs them to take the ark back. His first statement expresses a trusting faith in God (15:25-26). He subjects himself completely to the Lord's will, yet this attitude is combined with political cunning. In his next breath, David sets up a spy ring involving the priestly families (15:27-29). Acceptance of God's will does not rule out human planning, because it is through human action that God carries out his will.

15:32-36 David, Ahithophel, and Hushai

The mourning continues as David's entourage ascends the Mount of Olives (15:30). David learns of Ahithophel's betrayal and prays that his counsel will be thwarted (15:31). Again, petitioning the Lord is paired with human scheming. The next encounter provides the means to thwart Ahithophel: Hushai. A consistent plan is being hatched. David goes into the wilderness with the military, while the rest of his administration is deployed in Jerusalem to safeguard his possessions and to undermine the conspiracy. Hushai's task is the most difficult. He has to pass himself off as a turncoat to enter Absalom's confidence and confuse his counsel (15:34). With Hushai in place, David's deployment is completed before Absalom enters the city (15:37).

16:1-4 David and Ziba

The next encounter is more ambiguous. Ziba arrives with provisions, taken presumably from Meribbaal's estate (cf. 9:9-13). David's interrogation suggests suspicion of this gesture (16:2-3). Ziba claims that Meribbaal has sided with the rebels in the hope of restoring Saul's kingdom (16:3). David accepts this strange claim without question and transfers the family property to Ziba, a revocation of his loyalty to Jonathan in response to an alleged act of disloyalty.

16:5-13 David and Shimei

There follows a hostile encounter with a supporter of Saul. Shimei curses and stones David in the midst of his troops. His curses link the rebellion to David's murderous dealings with Saul's house (16:8). Just as David displaced Saul, so the Lord is displacing David. Guided by the narrator, the reader knows the linkage is inaccurate. The narrator has been at pains to exonerate David of bloodguilt for the house of Saul, yet the perception remains, both for characters in the story and within the historical memory. When the bloodthirsty Abishai wants to kill Shimei, David invokes the Lord's will to stop him (cf.1 Sam 26:8-9). David detects something prophetic in Shimei's words (16:10b). Once again he accepts whatever the Lord plans for him, yet with a prayer that acceptance may lead to mitigation. These final comments (16:11-12) speak to a wider audience in the language of faith using the style of psalms of lament: may the Lord see his affliction and come to his rescue. David's journey of affliction has reached its lowest point, the Jordan River, and comes to a halt (16:14).

16:15–17:14 Absalom's counselors

Attention now shifts to Absalom's triumphant entry to Jerusalem (16:15), to tell of the struggle between Absalom's counselors. This struggle will decide the fate of Absalom. The narrative revolves around Ahithophel's advice, which is as respected as a divine oracle (16:23). His counsel is divided in two: the first part is followed successfully to fulfill the oracle of 12:7-12, but the second part is thwarted by Hushai in fulfillment of David's prayer (15:31). Hushai plays a key role, but the attentive reader will be guided by the narrator's concluding comment about the Lord's involvement (17:14b).

Hushai ingratiates himself into Absalom's service (16:16-17). With flattery he overcomes Absalom's suspicions and offers to serve the son as he served the father, or so it seems. It is all doublespeak, but nonetheless effective. Nevertheless, Absalom turns to Ahithophel for advice.

His advice neatly fulfills the Lord's judgment. Absalom has intercourse with David's concubines in full view of the people (16:22; cf. 12:11-12). As in 3:7-8, sexual relations serve as a symbol for political power. Seizure of the concubines is equivalent to seizing the throne. Ahithophel advises a speedy operation to kill David (17:1-3). His wisdom is clear: David is weary, with few supporters, and quick action will reduce bloodshed and animosity later. Yet, amazingly, Absalom seeks another opinion from Hushai (17:5-6).

Hushai begins by playing on their fear of David and his warriors (17:7-10). With extravagant rhetoric, he uses half-truths and lies to undermine Ahithophel's plan. He claims it is too late to catch David without risking a demoralizing defeat. Having magnified the danger, he proposes to maximize the size of the Israelite army, and use overwhelming force in open battle or a siege (17:11-13). Of course, such force takes time to assemble and gives David breathing space to organize. Secondly, Absalom should lead the troops, placing his life at risk. Thus Hushai counters the two main elements of Ahithophel's plan, speed and security.

Rousing rhetoric is effective. All the Israelites support Hushai, whereas older, wiser heads (the elders) back Ahithophel (compare v. 14a with v. 4). However, the deeper reason Absalom heeds Hushai is that the Lord is involved (17:14b). This is one of three places in the Succession Narrative that the narrator clearly reports the Lord's involvement (cf. 11:27 and 12:24). These deft touches remind the reader that human affairs, driven and confused by human motivations, are ultimately under divine guidance. That influence is rarely apparent but nevertheless effective. This narrative style challenges modern readers to develop a similar ability to tell their stories in the light of faith.

17:15–18:5 Preparations for war

David's scheme was to confuse Absalom's counsel and to gather intelligence. Having done the first, Hushai uses the spy ring to forewarn David of Ahithophel's advice (17:15-16), just in case it is followed. The narrator complicates the plot to increase the excitement of the story (17:17-21). Helped by a quick-witted woman (cf. Josh 2:4-7), the messengers reach David, and the company crosses the Jordan (17:22).

Ahithophel took a risk in defecting to Absalom, and his counsel has been rejected. He knows the rebellion is doomed. His suicide preempts the coming destruction (17:23). Amasa takes command of the army (17:24). This is a family affair: father against son, cousin against cousin. Amasa, Joab, and Abishai are all nephews of David, sons of his two sisters, Abigail and Zeruiah (cf. 1 Chr 2:13-17).

David receives ample support from three non-Judahites of importance: the Ammonite prince, Shobi; Machir who had sheltered Meribbaal (cf. 9:4-5); and Barzillai (17:27-29). He is also able to place his forces under three able generals: Joab, Abishai, and Ittai (18:1-2). Even in this moment of difficulty, devotion to David is high and provides him with ample backing. David planned to fight with the troops, but they resist the idea (18:2b). They place a high value on the king's life (18:3), a nice contrast to the risk Absalom has been persuaded to take (cf. 17:11). However, David then complicates issues: "Be gentle with young Absalom for my sake" (18:5). This will be a critical battle for the throne, but now David hampers his generals by commanding gentleness towards the usurper. The narrator notes who heard the command. Everyone knows that David is torn between royal necessity and fatherly love.

18:6–19:1 The death of Absalom

The account of the battle is brief (18:6-8). Given David's command, attention is on Absalom. The odd statement in verse 8b about the consuming thickets may be to lessen internecine guilt (more died by misadventure than were killed by fellow Israelites). It also prepares for Absalom's misadventure. His luxuriant hair (cf. 14:26) catches in branches; his royal mount abandons him; and he hangs "between heaven and earth," in a limbo while others debate his future (18:9). The soldier did not and will not touch him. Joab is furious and does the job himself (18:10-14). The dialogue recalls David's command, which the soldier stubbornly obeys, and thus highlights Joab's disobedience. Joab does not waste time over David's sensibilities, either political (when he killed Abner, cf. 3:24-27) or emotional (in this case). Joab does David's dirty work and secures the throne. With Absalom dispatched, the battle can end (18:16). Absalom is buried unceremoniously, as a criminal (cf. Josh 7:26; 8:29; 10:27). (The pillar Absalom erected is problematic. The claim that he had no son contradicts 14:27. It is probably a late addition.)

The king must be told the news. The standard pattern of such messages from the front (cf. 1 Sam 4:12-18) is elaborated to increase suspense. Joab refuses to permit the eager Ahimaaz to go because he is aware of the risk (18:19-20). David has killed previous messengers of bad news (cf. 1:15-16). Instead he sends an anonymous Cushite (18:21). However, Joab finally gives way to Ahimaaz's pleading (18:22-23). The narrator is setting up expectations that the son of Zadok may be killed as he races ahead of the Cushite. The narrator shifts to the viewpoint of David, responding overoptimistically to each fragment of the lookout's reports (18:24-27). Suspense mounts as Ahimaaz arrives and his eloquent proclamation slithers into confusion (18:28-29), because he cannot tell the king of Absalom's death. He is safe, but how will the king learn? The Cushite's report is equally verbose (18:31), again prompting David to ask about the "young Absalom." The Cushite delivers the news in glorious terms (18:32), but the king's reaction breaks all expectations. David breaks down in tears (19:1). His grief is more heartrending than for Saul and Jonathan (1:17-27), or for his other sons (12:16-17; 13:31, 36). Five times in the inchoate sobbing he calls Absalom "son." Never before has he done so, preferring "young Absalom." If only David had treated Absalom as a son, perhaps he would not be weeping over his death now.

19:2-9a Joab reproves David

David's grief has serious repercussions. The troops valued David's life above their own (18:3), but now he values the traitor more than himself. The death of Absalom turns victory into defeat (19:4). Throughout this unit, "today" is mentioned frequently. This is a critical moment: rebellion is defeated, but will David throw victory away? Joab's actions are the cause of grief, because he killed the son to save the father. Now he must suppress the father's grief for the son (19:6-8). Against this rebel (son), the troops have saved father, sons, daughters, wives. This is the cold truth of political survival. David must choose between the dead Absalom and his living supporters, and he must do so quickly! David obeys Joab and greets the troops (19:9). The correct protocol saves the day, but at what personal cost?

The narrative exonerates David of guilt for Absalom's death and highlights his love for his son. But David's response to his sons' deaths is increasingly unbalanced. He is a paragon of faith in chapter 12; he mourns bitterly when Amnon dies (ch. 13); but now he is unhinged by Absalom's death (ch. 18). The punishment announced in 12:7-14 is bearing a heavy toll on David's character and on his ability to pass the crown to the next generation.

19:9b-44 David returns

The narrative of Absalom's rebellion has an artful symmetry. The contest between counselors (16:15–17:14) is balanced by the contest between the warriors (17:15–19:9a). The flight from Jerusalem (15:13–16:14) is now balanced by a return to the city (19:9b–20:3). During the flight David encountered three groups: the loyal (Ittai, the priests, and Hushai), the doubtful (Ziba), and the opponents (Shimei). On his return he meets these three groups in reverse order. The rebellion has been presented as a family affair, yet there are hints of wider political divisions. Absalom played on the tension between the northern tribes and the southern monarchy, threatening to turn rebellion into civil war. Nevertheless, he began the rebellion in Hebron, heartland of Judah, and there has been silence on Judah's stance. The king must negotiate these tensions to rebuild support and reunite his kingdom.

19:9b-16 Dealing with division

The northern tribes are divided (19:9b-11), but opinion is swinging towards David. However, it is Judah that worries David more. Using the priests, he prods the Judahite elders to remember clan loyalty (19:12-13), and he makes a bold offer to replace Joab with Amasa, Absalom's general (19:14). This would indicate that support for Absalom was strong in Judah. It also suggests a breach between David and Joab, caused by the death of Absalom. The king's move wins support, but what is Joab's response?

9:17-41 Further dialogues

As David approaches the Jordan, he has three encounters. First, Shimei, who cursed him (16:5-14), comes to beg pardon (19:16-24). Again Abishai wants to kill Shimei (19:22), but with an identical retort (in the Hebrew) David stops him (19:23a; cf. 16:10a). Before, David offered a theological explanation, but now his argument is royal. Joab has succeeded in suppressing the personal under the political, at least where the sons of Zeruiah are involved.

The second encounter involves Meribbaal (19:25-31). His appearance suggests a total lack of self-attention while David was absent (19:25). This is not easy to fabricate. David's question flows from Ziba's allegation (cf. 16:7), and Meribbaal bluntly accuses Ziba of betrayal (19:27). Who is to be believed? Meribbaal throws himself on David's mercy (19:29-30). David cuts him short and makes a quick decision to divide the property (19:31). David's judgment indicates that he cannot decide who is telling the truth. Meribbaal's reply is a dramatic gesture of loyalty, but brings about the final dispossession of the house of Saul.

The encounter with Barzillai is warmer. This wealthy elder, who supported David in exile, is offered a place in Jerusalem (19:32-34). Barzillai politely refuses (19:35-38b): perhaps he wishes to maintain a certain independence from the Jerusalem establishment. Instead, he sends Chimham (his son, according to some ancient versions) to bind the alliance. This final encounter completes the crossing of the Jordan to Gilgal (19:16-41), and the narrator returns to the simmering tension between north and south.

The Judahites have been present throughout (19:16), but now some Israelites are mentioned (19:41b). Which group will show greater loyalty by escorting David home? Each side stakes its claim. Judah focuses on kinship, while Israel focuses on the office of king (19:42-44). These differences were implicit in David's coronations (2:1-4; 5:1-3), but now they are in the open. In later generations, they will divide the kingdom. Absalom's rebellion failed, but it exposed an inherent weakness in the Davidic monarchy.

20:1-22 Sheba's revolt

The quarrel endangers David's return. Sheba's cry of rebellion (20:1b) will be repeated when the kingdom divides after Solomon's death (1 Kgs 12:16). David reaches Jerusalem with only the people of Judah loyal to "their king" (20:2). Sheba's rebellion is presented as the conclusion to Absalom's revolt, but it is potentially more dangerous (20:6).

Clearly, Amasa is a lynchpin in David's relations with Judah (20:4), but his delay places him under suspicion (20:5). Curiously, David turns to Abishai. Has Joab fallen out of favor? Suddenly, Joab appears again (20:7), and he acts with his usual murderous efficiency to regain his position (20:8-10b), with a hidden weapon, a disarming gesture of friendship, and a swift blow. The troops are taken aback, but such doubts are quickly quashed (20:11-13), and Joab is in control again. His campaign takes the usual course of pursuit followed by siege (cf. 10:6-14; 11:1). His brutality is checked by another wise woman (20:16-21). Joab used the wise woman of Tekoa to change the king's mind about Absalom (14:1-20), and this woman now tells Joab what to do about Sheba. In each case, the women strive to avoid bloodguilt and alienation. They appeal to covenant categories to change royal decisions. The woman of Tekoa rescued one man, while this woman saves a city by setting aside one man. The rebellion of Absalom prompted by the first decision is finally laid to rest by the second.

20:23-26 Listing government officials

Joab is back in charge of the army as Absalom's rebellion ends (20:23). Just as 2 Samuel 9–20 was prefaced by a list of David's officials (8:15-18), so it is rounded off by a similar list. There is some rearrangement, but little overall change in government. A new post is added, that of Adoram in charge of forced labor (20:24). Such an addition suggests that David's government is moving towards the ominous pattern of 1 Samuel 8:11-18.

APPENDICES

2 Samuel 21–24

The chapters that follow the long narrative of 2 Samuel 9–20 interrupt the consideration of David's family and the succession. When the continuous Deuteronomistic History was divided into scrolls of relatively equal length, these chapters became the concluding "appendices" of 2 Samuel. This miscellany of independent traditions is arranged in a concentric fashion. In the center are two poems attributed to David (22:1-51; 23:1-7). They are bracketed by two lists of heroes and their exploits (21:15-22; 23:8-39). The miscellany opens and closes with two narratives about public disaster resolved by ritual intercession (21:1-14; 24:1-25).

21:1-14 Gibeonites and a famine

This is a relatively independent tradition with little connection to other stories about David. While placed at the end of the book, some think that these events happened prior to David's meeting with Meribbaal (ch. 9). This story reflects a theology which links public disaster to God's anger, which then needs appeasement. Faced with famine, David consults the Lord and learns of the bloodguilt of Saul's house (21:1). He approaches the surviving Gibeonites to arrange expiation of the treaty breach (21:2-3). The Israelites' oath to the Gibeonites alludes to Joshua 9:3-27, but there is no reference to Saul's campaign against them. Their response is cautious. They will not name a price until the king gives his word to carry it out, thus absolving them from any future retaliation. They demand the execution of seven descendants of Saul. Such an execution is both punishment for breach of the treaty and an offering to the Lord to remove the sin of bloodguilt. David agrees, but spares Meribbaal, son of Jonathan, in consideration of his own obligations to Jonathan (21:7).

Rizpah's act of loyalty to the dead spurs David to demonstrate similar loyalty (21:10). Curiously, he focuses on the remains of Saul and Jonathan, disinterring their bones for reburial in the family grave (21:11-12, 14). Almost in passing, the bones of the seven are gathered up (and presumably buried also).

This episode could be read as a positive portrait of David, who is here attentive to the Lord, seeking to remove bloodguilt, showing loyalty to oaths, and honoring Saul's house. Furthermore, the Lord answers his efforts (21:14b). In contrast, Saul is portrayed in violation of ancient obligations (cf. his breach of the Amalekite ban in 1 Sam 15). However, there is another negative reading. David benefits politically as seven close relatives of Saul are eliminated. Such action would explain Shimei's curse (16:7-8). With so little to go on, both evaluations are valid interpretations of the story.

21:15-27 David's warriors

This collection of exploits by David's warriors dates from the early Philistine wars (5:17-25). The warriors defeat members of the Rephaim, probably an elite military band dedicated to a Philistine god, Rapha. In contrast to the prowess of his servants, David is portrayed as weak and vulnerable (21:15-16). The soldiers then decide that he should not risk himself in battle, a strategy which was reflected in 11:1 and 18:3-4. Their reference to the "lamp of Israel" (21:17) becomes apparent in 22:29. David's relationship with the Lord is a sign of hope and confidence for his followers. First Chronicles 20:5 corrects verse 19 to say that Elhanan killed Goliath's brother, leaving David as Goliath's slayer (1 Sam 17:48-51).

22:1-51 Psalm of thanksgiving

The song of chapter 22 is a duplicate of Psalm 18. The poem is part hymn, part thanksgiving. It celebrates the Lord as savior of Israel and of the individual believer, in this case, David. Within the hymnic opening and closing frames (22:2-4 and 22:47-51), there are two panels which celebrate God's deliverance in mythic and historic terms (22:5-20 and 22:33-46 respectively). At the center is a more reflective passage on the poet's relationship to God (22:21-32).

The opening frame establishes the key relationship of psalmist to God. An accumulation of substantives dealing with rescue describes this God (22:2-4). Moving into the first panel, the need for rescue is made clear using the mythic language of chaos (22:5-6). The psalmist is overwhelmed by death and despair, and does the only thing possible for a person of faith: "I called out: LORD!" (22:7). In response, God "heard my voice." This is the fundamental relationship of Israel's faith experience. The remainder of the panel describes the theophany of deliverance in powerful, majestic language (22:8-20). God's coming overpowers

the nothingness of chaos: "he drew me out of the deep waters" (22:17). The imagery is allusive to both creation and exodus. It is elemental yet personal. All this "because he loves me" (22:20).

The gracious condescension of God in verses 8-20 is put to one side in the central reflection (22:21-32). Now God rescues because I deserve it, the psalmist declares (22:21-25). Given David's moral behavior, such a claim is both ironic and inaccurate in a strict theory of distributive justice. But David stands in a vassal-master relationship with God. In 1 Samuel 26:23, he challenged Saul for a failure of *hesed* (loyalty). Loyalty works both ways within a covenantal relationship. David lives in a covenantal relationship with God and has kept that covenant, so he can rely on God to keep loyalty to him (22:26-32). Verse 29 sums up the effect of the relationship: darkness becomes like day for David. The relationship is a "lamp" for David, and through him for the people (cf. 21:17).

Renewed by reflection, the psalmist returns to celebrate deliverance in more historical terms (22:33-46). Taking his cue from verse 29, the confidence of deliverance strengthens the psalmist in the face of his foes (22:30). There is success on the battlefield, but constantly this personal success is attributed to the Lord. The celebration of "I" gives way to thanks to "You." Thus, the poem moves into the final hymnic frame (22:47-51). Once more, God is described with a series of substantives of rescue. The rescue is focused on the "king . . . anointed . . . David and his posterity" (22:51). The key word is *hesed* ("kindness"). David's success—his very life—is determined by his relationship with the Lord. The Lord is sovereign and when David (or his posterity) forgets that, he fails. The sentiments of the hymn echo Hannah's song (1 Sam 2:1-10). Both celebrate the sovereignty of the Lord and his power to save and protect, and both focus attention on the Lord's anointed as the concrete expression of the Lord's continuing help. Ideologically, kingship is incorporated into the faith of Israel, even if the practical experience of monarchy falls short of the ideal.

23:1-7 Last words of David

The second poem is written in a sapiential style: the opening (23:1a) is similar to the oracle of Balaam (Num 24:3,15) or the sayings of Agar (Prov 30:1). Like 22:51 and 1 Samuel 2:10, verse 1 speaks of God's determination to choose an anointed one as his instrument for wellbeing in Israel. Thus, the monarchy is intimately related to God (23:1-3a) as the concrete manifestation of God's will to establish justice in the world (23:3b-4). Justice is central to social life and is God's gift. God has established the monarchy to mediate that gift into the life of Israel, not just in David's day but forever (23:5). The promise of 2 Samuel 7 is now called an "eternal covenant." In that chapter the key words were "firm" and "forever" (cf. 7:16), but covenant was not used. The language of "eternal covenant" is more often used of creation (cf. Gen 9:16; Isa 54:9-10) and refers to a promise without time limits, part of the very fabric of reality. God's promise to David has come to be part of God's created order (cf. Jer 33:17, 20-22). The historical reality of the Davidic dynasty stands in considerable tension with these theological affirmations.

23:8-39 David's warriors

A second catalogue describes two groups. The Three (23:8-12) are champions who fought single-handed against the Philistines and were instrumental in the Lord's victory. The Thirty may be a company of David's bodyguards (23:18-39). The thirty-seven names listed suggest that "The Thirty" is the name of the company whose membership changed over time (note Uriah's inclusion in the list). Some members of the Thirty are singled out for individual exploits (23:18-24), which nevertheless do not elevate them to the level of champions (the Three). Note Joab's absence from both groups. His position is singular among David's men.

An interesting vignette (23:13-17) from David's time in the wilderness (1 Sam 22) separates the two lists. It illustrates the devotion of his bodyguards, ready to risk their lives to fulfill a whim of David. David reciprocates by pouring the water on the ground as a libation (23:16-17). The water becomes symbolic of lifeblood, the loyalty between David and his men, and so is holy to the Lord.

24:1-25 Census of the people

This narrative concludes the miscellany of 2 Samuel 21–24 with a second story of ritual appeasement warding off disaster. At one time, the pair of stories may have been linked (note the

"again" in v. 1). The opening phrase serves as a title, "The LORD's anger against Israel flared again," rather than a prior cause of the census.

David orders a census to count those fit for military service (24:9). By doing so, he places the people on standby for war and perhaps subjects them to the purity laws associated with warfare (cf. Deut 23:10-15). Breach of such rules contaminates the land; in the ancient mind, disaster would ensue. Having completed the census, David belatedly recognizes the ritual predicament in which he has placed the people and confesses the sin as his own (24:10). The Hebrew behind "Take away your servant's guilt" means "transfer the guilt" from the people to David (cf. 2 Sam 12:13).

As in 2 Samuel 12, a prophet brings God's answer (24:11-12). Gad was last mentioned in 1 Samuel 22:5. The Lord offers David three choices of disaster for the people (24:12-13), in effect ignoring David's prayer. David ignores the command to pick one (contrary to the narrator's comment in v. 15), opting instead to throw himself on the Lord's mercy (24:14). This is an expression of trust in God similar to 2 Samuel 15:25-26 and 16:12.

The punishment takes the form of pestilence (24:15) carried out by a destroying angel (cf. the "destroyer" of Exodus 12:23). The angel draws near to strike Jerusalem. The narrator offers two simultaneous accounts from different angles: firstly, the Lord relents (cf. 1 Sam 15:11) his action and stops the angel (24:16); secondly, David sees the angel and repents his sin (24:17). The two simultaneous acts of repentance enable each other. Both together create the possibility of a new future.

This new future will build on the relationship between David and the Lord. Its concrete form will be an altar (24:18). The threshing floor belongs to Araunah, one of the original Jebusite inhabitants of Jerusalem. David proceeds to purchase the site in a deal reminiscent of Abraham's purchase of a burial site in Hebron (24:19-24; cf. Gen 23:3-16). Purchase of the land makes it an inalienable possession of the people. First Chronicles 21:26-30 makes the explicit link between this altar and the altar of holocausts in Solomon's temple.

There are some interesting parallels between this narrative and 2 Samuel 11–12. In both cases, David sins. A prophet announces the Lord's condemnation and punishment. David throws himself on the Lord's mercy and begs that the sin be transferred. Following punishment, a new future opens up. In chapter 12, it is the birth of Solomon, and in chapter 24 it is the construction of the altar.

From David's sins and repentance emerge the two mainstays of dynasty and temple which are central to the continuing history of Israel in the land.

THE BOOKS OF

FIRST AND SECOND KINGS

Alice L. Laffey, S.S.D.

INTRODUCTION

More than twenty years ago I wrote a commentary for the two books of Kings in the first Collegeville Bible Commentary. Since the biblical texts changed little in the New American Bible Revised Edition, why would I set out to write another commentary of approximately the same length on these same texts for the same or a similar audience? The answer is simple. I have been teaching these texts every year for the past twenty years and because of that I have come to know them far better than I did when I wrote the original commentary. Moreover, I have the benefit of an additional twenty years of biblical scholarship by myself and my colleagues that hopefully will improve the quality of this commentary. Finally, I love the texts and would like another opportunity to distill their treasures so that others might also deepen their appreciation of them.

Kings in the context of the Deuteronomistic History

Christians have traditionally considered the books of Kings to be historical and thus identified them as part of the "historical books" of the Old Testament. Even today they are listed under that heading in the front of many Bibles, along with the books of Joshua, Judges, 1–2 Samuel, 1–2 Chronicles, Ezra, Nehemiah, Tobit, Judith, Esther, and 1–2 Maccabees. These historical books are contrasted with the Pentateuch, the prophetic books, and the wisdom books. In 1926, however, a German biblical scholar, L. Rost, proposed that the books of Joshua through 2 Kings comprise a literary unit that narrates the history of the rise of King David and the narrative of his succession. This hypothesis was later refined by Martin Noth, who further established that the biblical literature we now refer to as 1–2 Kings is part of a larger literary piece, the Deuteronomistic History. Though this history is comprised of sources once independent of each other that were edited and reedited, still, as it now stands it is a carefully constructed literary unit governed by the editors' theology. God is Israel's God, and Israel is God's people. God has given his people the land, and they are to give their total allegiance to God. As Deuteronomy 28 makes clear, adherence to God's teachings brings blessing, while neglect of God's teachings brings curses.

The literature that comprises the Deuteronomistic History has been analyzed to determine its structure. There are farewell speeches on the lips of Israel's early leaders, e.g., Moses in Deuteronomy 31; Joshua in Joshua 23; Samuel in 1 Samuel 12.

These speeches provide perspective on the past and, building on that past, advice and admonition for the future. In addition, the editors of the History evaluate the performance of Israel's later leaders, both the judges and the kings. Most of the judges emerge to lead the people out of oppression, the source of which is their unfaithfulness to the Lord. The judges help the people secure a victory over their oppressors and a return to covenant faithfulness. Each king's behavior is evaluated, and the success of his reign is described in proportion to his faithfulness to the Lord.

Although 2 Kings ends with the fall of Jerusalem to Babylon, the last four verses of the book, and of the entire History, provide a literary hint of the reemergence of Israel. The new Babylonian king releases Jehoiachin, the imprisoned king of Judah; he speaks kindly to him and gives him a privileged seat among the other exiled kings. Jehoiachin, every day for the rest of his life, dines in the king's presence and receives an allowance. The unfaithful nation has been punished, but all hope is not lost. There is a root, a seed, an ill-defined but real future embodied in the person of the exiled king whose life is not snuffed out, but who is, on the contrary, freed and, at least limitedly, honored.

Prophets in the books of Kings

Jews, in contrast to Christians, speak of their Bible as the TaNaK, that is, the Torah, the Prophets, and the Writings. Jews do not identify any books as historical; rather, they consider books such as Judges and 1–2 Kings in the same category as the books of Isaiah and Jeremiah, all books of prophets. That is because of the importance of the role of the prophets in each of the books. Nathan, David's loyal prophet, participates in anointing David's son Solomon as king (1 Kgs 1:8-45); Ahijah predicts the division of Solomon's kingdom (1 Kgs 11:29-30); Elijah predicts the death of Israel's evil king, Ahab, and of his wife Jezebel (1 Kgs 21:20-24). Michaiah predicts Ahab's death in the battle against Ramoth-gilead (1 Kgs 22:15-18); Elisha predicts the end of the siege of Samaria (2 Kgs 7:1-2); Isaiah predicts the victory of Babylon over Judah (2 Kgs 20:16-18); and Huldah predicts the demise of Judah for its unfaithfulness to the Lord, a defeat that will take place only after Josiah's death (2 Kgs 22:14-20). The books of Kings record that each of the prophetic predictions that

in some way or other involved one of Israel's or Judah's kings was fulfilled. Prophets speak and act with the power of God and can be seen, therefore, as being even more important characters in the Jews' sacred story than their kings.

Women in the books of Kings

Though men seem to dominate the books of Kings, a close reading of the texts uncovers numerous women—some more important than others to be sure. Bathsheba and Abishag play prominent roles in the opening chapters. Jehosheba and an unnamed nurse appear in 2 Kings 11; both act with courage to preserve Joash and by doing so preserve David's dynasty. Other women are named because of their status; they are the wives of reigning kings who become the mothers of future kings: Zeruah (1 Kgs 11:26); Naamah, (1 Kgs 14:21, 31); Maacah (1 Kgs 15:2, 10); Azubah (1 Kgs 22:42); Athaliah (2 Kgs 8:26); Zibiah (2 Kgs 12:1); Jehoaddin (2 Kgs 14:2); Jecoliah (2 Kgs 15:2); Jerusha (2 Kgs 15:33); Abi (2 Kgs 18:2); Hephzibah (2 Kgs 21:1); Meshullemeth (2 Kgs 21:19); Jedidah (2 Kgs 22:1); Hamutal (2 Kgs 23:31; 24:18); Zebidah (2 Kgs 23:36), and Nehushta (2 Kgs 24:8).

In contrast, at least nine unnamed women appear in the texts: the daughter of pharaoh who became Solomon's wife (1 Kgs 3); the widow who was Hiram's mother (1 Kgs 7); Tahpenes' sister, who became Hadad's wife and Genubath's mother (1 Kgs 11); Jeroboam's wife who was his messenger to Ahijah (1 Kgs 14); the widow at Zarephath who fed, obeyed, and trusted Elijah (1 Kgs 17); a widow who trusted and obeyed Elisha and who prospered (2 Kgs 4); the wealthy Shunammite woman who fed Elisha, and who is rewarded with a son and whose son Elisha resuscitated (2 Kgs 4 and 8); the little Israelite maid who, along with Naaman's wife, set the wheels in motion that led to Naaman's cure from leprosy (2 Kgs 5); the nurse who cared for Joash (2 Kgs 11), and the woman who bore Zedekiah's two sons (2 Kgs 25).

Animals in the books of Kings

It is helpful to look also at the relationship of the people of the Ancient Near East, as depicted in the biblical texts, to animals. When in 1 Kings 22, for example, the prophet Micaiah informs Ahab that he will die in battle, he proclaims: "I see all

Israel / scattered on the mountains, / like sheep without a shepherd" (v. 17). Such a proclamation traces its roots back to the relationship of tribal leaders to the people of Israel (2 Sam 7:7) and ultimately to David. Comparing humans to animals would not be heard, in that culture, as at all degrading. Sheep, in fact, were valued as a significant source of prosperity. Close reading of the biblical texts reveals significant roles for the lion (e.g., 1 Kgs 7, 10, 13, 20; 2 Kgs 17), the donkey (1 Kgs 13), and the lamb (2 Kgs 3).

The books of Kings' contemporaries

Solomon began his reign in approximately 960 B.C. The kingdom of Judah fell to Babylon in approximately 586 B.C. An account of the intervening approximately four hundred years is contained in the two books of Kings. But 1–2 Kings are not the only biblical source for that period. The books of Amos and Hosea, for example, are addressed to the northern kingdom of Israel during the eighth century B.C. reign of Jeroboam II. The books of Isaiah (chs. 1–39) and Micah are addressed to the southern kingdom of Judah, also during the eighth century B.C. Zephaniah, Habakkuk, and Nahum are addressed to Judah in the late seventh century B.C., while the content of both Jeremiah and Ezekiel extends through the fall of Judah to Babylon. What this means for us as readers of 1–2 Kings is that if we read these other books together with Kings, we will have a fuller

version of the story and an opportunity to gain a deeper appreciation of what the inspired authors wanted us to understand.

A final word

In 1993 the Pontifical Biblical Commission produced a document entitled "The Interpretation of the Bible in the Church." The document encourages us to use every means at our disposal to better understand the biblical text. It encourages us to strive to understand, as best we can, the world that produced the text so very many centuries ago, but it also encourages us to bring the text into the present. The books of Kings, though in real ways foreign to the twenty-first century world in which we live, do contain content that resonates with our experiences. In the concrete nitty-gritty of our day-to-day lives, in the power struggles, in the relationships between and among individuals and between and among nations, what constitutes loyalty? What behaviors execute justice? What are the demands of being in a covenant relationship with God? What does it mean to be faithful to that relationship? What risks are we willing to take? How do we pray? Where do we look for the power of God?

The commentary below seeks to integrate insights from Israel's history that serve to elucidate the text in its original context as well as insights from contemporary perspectives and the believing community. Let us begin. . . .

CHRONOLOGY OF THE KINGS OF ISRAEL

United Kingdom

King	Approximate Years of Reign	Books of Kings
Saul	1020–1000	
David	1000–961	1 Kings 1:1–2:12
Solomon	961–922	1 Kings 1:11–11:43

Divided Kingdom

South			North		
King	**Approximate Years of Reign**	**Biblical Text**	**King**	**Approximate Years of Reign**	**Biblical Text**
Rehoboam	922–915	1 Kgs 14:21-31	Jeroboam	922–901	1 Kgs 12:26–14:20
Abijam	915–913	1 Kgs 14:31–15:8			
Asa	913–873	1 Kgs 15:8-24	Nadab	901–900	1 Kgs 15:25-31
			Baasha	900–877	1 Kgs 15:33-34
			Elah	877–876	1 Kgs 16:8-14
			Zimri	876	1 Kgs 16:15-20
			Omri	876–869	1 Kgs 16:23-28
Jehoshaphat	873–849	1 Kgs 22:41-51	Ahab	869–850	1 Kgs 16:28–22:40
			Ahaziah	850–849	1 Kgs 22:52–2 Kgs 1:18
Joram (Jehoram)	849–843	2 Kgs 8:16-24	Jehoram (Joram)	849–842	2 Kgs 3:1–9:28
Ahaziah	843–842	2 Kgs 8:25–9:29			
Athaliah	842–837	2 Kgs 11:1-16	Jehu	842–815	2 Kgs 9:3–10:36
Joash (Jehoash)	837–800	2 Kgs 11:19–12:21	Jehoahaz	815–801	2 Kgs 13:1-9
Amaziah	800–783	2 Kgs 14:1-20	Joash (Jehoash)	801–786	2 Kgs 13:10-13
Uzziah (Azariah)	783–742	2 Kgs 14:21; 15:1-7	Jeroboam II	786–746	2 Kgs 14:23-29
			Zechariah	746–745	2 Kgs 15:8-11
			Shallum	745	2 Kgs 15:13-15
Jotham	742–735	2 Kgs 15:32-38	Menahem	745–738	2 Kgs 15:14-22
			Pekahiah	738–737	2 Kgs 15:22-26
Ahaz	735–715	2 Kgs 16:1-20	Pekah	737–732	2 Kgs 15:25-31
			Hoshea	732–724	2 Kgs 17:1-6
			The Destruction of Israel		
Hezekiah	715–687	2 Kgs 18:1–20:21			
Manasseh	687–642	2 Kgs 21:1-18			
Amon	642–640	2 Kgs 21:19-26			
Josiah	640–609	2 Kgs 21:26–23:30			
Jehoahaz	609	2 Kgs 23:30-33			
Jehoiakim (Eliakim)	609–598	2 Kgs 23:34–24:6			
Jehoiachin	598–597	2 Kgs 24:8-16; 25:27-30			
Zedekiah (Mattaniah)	597–587	2 Kgs 24:17–25:21			
The Exile of Judah					

COMMENTARY: *1 KINGS*

THE REIGN OF SOLOMON

1 Kings 1–11

The transfer of monarchic power from David to Solomon was not without struggle. Nevertheless Solomon, Bathsheba's son, became king and ruled a peaceful and prosperous land. He built the Lord's temple and all went well until his greed and the oppression of his own subjects led to political discontent and the people's revolt.

1:1-4 Abishag the Shumamite

The narrator connects David's sin with Bathsheba to the circumstances surrounding his death. Just as Saul's sin in letting the Amalekite king live (1 Sam 15:20) resulted in Saul's death at the hand of an Amalekite (2 Sam 1:7-10), David, who lusted after and violated Bathsheba (2 Sam 11) is now no longer interested in and/or capable of sexual relations, even with a beautiful young woman whom his culture places at his disposal. Since blankets did not enable David to keep warm, a woman would surely enable him to get warm; Abishag is brought in to nurse the king and she does just that; twice the word "warm" appears; twice reference is made to nursing; twice Abishag's beauty is noted. Yet despite her beauty and her nursing, the warmth which sexual relations should provide, eludes David. For Israel's beloved King David, it seems that his sin with Bathsheba continues to have consequences.

1:5-10 Adonijah's bid for David's throne

While David lies dying, his son Adonijah seeks to take his place as king. According to 2 Samuel 3:2-5, David's first-born is Amnon, his second Chileab, his third Absalom whose mother was Maacah, and his fourth son Adonijah whose mother was Haggith. By now Amnon was dead (cf. 2 Sam 13:28-29), as was Absalom (cf. 2 Sam 18:15); nothing is known of Chileab; his name appears only in 2 Samuel 3:3. To identify Adonijah here as next in age to Absalom is consistent with 2 Samuel 3:3-4. Comparing (cf. 2 Sam 14:25; 15:1-10) and contrasting (cf. 2 Sam 13:37; 14:28) Adonijah with Absalom may be intended to recall Absalom who was so loved by David (cf. 2 Sam 13:39; 14:33; 19:5-7).

Adonijah, who declares himself king, is not without powerful supporters, including the army general Joab and one of Israel's very influential priests, Abiathar. However, certain other leaders of the kingdom including Zadok, another influential priest, the prophet Nathan, the head of David's bodyguards, and military officials do not support Adonijah. Clearly the text suggests significant political division among David's inner circle. Adonijah excludes from the celebration of his kingship those who do not support him. He excludes also his brother Solomon, although he has invited "all his brothers" (1:9). The narrator seems to suggest that Adonijah considers Solomon more a contender for the throne than a brother.

1:11-31 David appoints his heir

The prophet Nathan realizes what Adonijah's kingship will mean for Bathsheba (cf. 2 Sam 11:26b) and Solomon (cf. 2 Sam 12:24-25) and probably also for himself (1:8). They will be considered criminals (1:21) and put to death (1:12). Nathan, therefore, convinces Bathsheba to help him execute a plan that is intended to put David's support behind Solomon as his heir. The text is reminiscent of the aged Isaac's deception by Rebakah and Jacob (cf. Gen 27). Here, Bathsheba and Nathan convince David that previously he promised the throne to Bathsheba for her son Solomon and that what Adonijah is doing in having himself declared king lacks David's support. Their plan succeeds.

1:32-40 The anointing of Solomon

David then summons Zadok the priest, the prophet Nathan, and the head of his bodyguards, and gives directions for the anointing of Solomon as king (cf. 1:8). Solomon is to sit on David's own mule. Both prophet and priest are to participate in the anointing, after which the horn is to be sounded and the attendants are to cry, "Long live King Solomon!" They execute these instructions. David designates Solomon to sit on his throne and reign as king.

1:41-53 Adonijah gets the bad news

Jonathan, the son of the priest Abiathar, Adonijah's supporter, brings Adonijah the news that David has made Solomon king. He describes who is involved and what has taken place, as well as David's satisfaction. Adonijah then realizes the implications of Solomon's anointing. He will likely be killed just as Nathan and Bathsheba expected Solomon would be killed (1:12, 21) if Adonijah had become king. Adonijah seeks protection by the altar, by law a place of sanctuary. Solomon agrees not to have Adonijah killed unless he is found guilty of a crime (cf. 1:21).

The narrative repeats with variation a theme that began in Genesis 4 with rivalry between the siblings Cain and Abel. Sarah saw the brothers Ishmael and Isaac as potential rivals (Gen 21:9); Rebecca saw her sons Esau and Jacob as rivals for their father's blessing (Gen 27); the sisters Leah and Rachel were rivals for Jacob's affection (Gen 30:1, 15), and Joseph's brothers clearly envied him (Gen 37:11). The stakes here are high: leading the Davidic line.

2:1-11 David's advice and directives to Solomon

Precedent for a last will and testament occurs elsewhere in the Deuteronomistic History. See, for example, the farewell speeches of Moses (Deut, especially ch. 33), Joshua (Josh 23), and Samuel (1 Sam 12). Here David imparts his last advice to his chosen heir. He exhorts Solomon to conform to the behavior Samuel described as that of a good king when addressing the first king of Israel, Saul (1 Sam 12:14), and alludes to the specific promise God has made through Nathan to David (2 Sam 7:11-16). David then directs Solomon to see that Joab, who killed Absalom (2 Sam 18:9-18), and Shimei, who cursed David (2 Sam 16:5-8), are punished and to make sure that the sons of Barzillai (2 Sam 19:31-37), who faithfully supported David, are rewarded. The narrator depicts David as wanting to even old scores before his death and wanting the demise of those who could undermine Solomon's rule. Since Solomon becomes the first expression of dynasty in Israel's history, one can assume that his ascension to the throne did not occur without challenge. This fact underscores the importance of David's support of Solomon. Finally, then, David's reign is complete (2:10-11), and he dies. Both the number forty (e.g., Gen 7:4, 12, 17; Exod 24:18; Num 14:33; Deut 8:2; Judg 5:31; 8:28; 1 Sam 4:18; 2 Sam 2:10) and seven (e.g., Gen

7:2, 4, 10; 8:10; Exod 12:15; Lev 4:6, 17; Num 19:11; Deut 16:3; Josh 6:4; Judg 16:19; 1 Sam 2:5; 2 Sam 21:6) symbolize completion.

2:12-25 Adonijah seeks Abishag

Adonijah is here identified, not as having the same mother as Absalom (cf. 1:6) but having Haggith for a mother (cf. 2 Sam 3:4). He approaches Solomon's mother Bathsheba with a request. Prefacing his request with assertions intended to win Bathsheba's sympathy, and make her disposed to honor his request, Adonijah reminds Bathsheba that he, not Solomon, is David's eldest living son. Therefore the kingdom rightfully belongs to him—except for the fact that the Lord has given it to Solomon (cf. Gen 25:23b). Adonijah appears to accept the Lord's decision. He asks only that Abishag (cf. 1:3-4) be given to him for a wife. The narrative teases out the dramatic tension by having Adonijah first ask Bathsheba to ask Solomon about Abishag, and then it narrates Bathsheba's asking Solomon.

Seeking to possess a woman already possessed by another man is tantamount to seeking to take over the power and prestige of that other man. Abner had been accused of taking Saul's concubine (2 Sam 3:7-8), Absalom had gone in to the concubines of David (2 Sam 16:20-22); both acts were considered treason. Now Adonijah wants David's Abishag. This request is rightly judged by Solomon to be what it is, a criminal act (cf. 1:52), for which reason Solomon appears justified in having Adonijah put to death. By requesting Abishag, Adonijah continues to stake a claim to David's throne.

Verse 25 functions also as the final fulfillment of Nathan's prophecy to David that the sword will never depart from his house (2 Sam 12:10), if "house" is understood as David's nuclear family. (However, the prophecy continues through 2 Kgs 25 if "house" is understood as David's dynasty.) David's family has suffered several losses: the death of his first son with Bathsheba (2 Sam 12:19); Amnon's rape of Tamar (2 Sam 13:11-14); Amnon's violent death (2 Sam 13:29); the contestation of David's throne by his son Absalom (2 Sam 15:10-12); Absalom's violent death (2 Sam 18:14-15); the contestation of David's throne by his son Adonijah (1 Kgs 1:5-6); and finally, Adonijah's violent death (1 Kgs 2:24-25).

2:26-46 Solomon secures the kingdom

Because Abiathar and Joab remain supporters of Adonijah, Solomon uses Adonijah's "treason" as an opportunity to have Joab, the head of the army, put to death (2:5-6; cf. 2 Sam 3:28-30; 20:10). Shimei, who cursed Solomon's father David, he puts to death also (2:8-9; cf. 2 Sam 16:5-8). With these deaths Solomon eliminates potential opposition and settles David's score.

2:28-35a Joab punished

Just as Adonijah had done, Joab seeks protection from Solomon by fleeing to the tent where he clings to the horns of the altar (cf. 1:50). Ordinarily this proto-temple would not be an appropriate place to kill anyone. The priest Jehoiada, for example, explicitly directed that Athaliah be taken outside the temple to be killed (cf. 2 Kgs 11:15). Still, because Joab refuses to leave the tent, Benaiah kills him there. After Joab's death, Solomon promotes Benaiah to Joab's position as general of the army.

2:35b Abiathar punished

Although, like Joab, the priest Abiathar supported Adonijah, Solomon does not have Abiathar put to death. He shared David's hardships, including Absalom's conspiracy attempt. He, along with Zadok, carried the ark of the covenant back to Jerusalem. Consequently, Abiathar is merely demoted and sent away from Jerusalem to his home at Anathoth. Solomon then promotes the priest Zadok who had not supported Adonijah to be Abiathar's replacement.

2:36-46 Shimei punished

Shimei was of Saul's house and supported Absalom's conspiracy against David. Still, when David proved victorious, Shimei sought David's forgiveness, for which reason, contrary to Abishai's advice, David allowed Shimei to live. Yet before David's death he asked Solomon to even his score with Shimei. At first Solomon punishes Shimei by requiring him to live in Jerusalem and to remain there. For three years Shimei complies with the restraining order, but then he risks its violation, leaving Jerusalem in order to retrieve two escaped servants from Gath. Solomon uses that occasion as the pretext to have Shimei put to death. The narrative thus justifies Solomon's removal of other potential opposition, further securing his place on the throne.

3:1-3 The first days of Solomon's reign

Having eliminated internal threats to the throne, Solomon next turns his attention to establishing external ties. He forms a political alliance with Egypt by marrying the daughter of Pharaoh. He also begins his famous building projects—his palace, the Lord's temple, and the walls of Jerusalem. These undertakings require negotiations with two Lebanese cities, Tyre and Sidon. That the people "were sacrificing on the high places" and that even Solomon was offering sacrifices and burning incense on the high places can be explained by the absence of a temple (3:2). However, after Solomon builds the temple—one place to worship for the people who are now united under one Lord, one king, and one capital—the phrase "offering sacrifices and burning incense on the high places" comes to infer that neither the king nor his subjects are fully faithful to the Lord. The placement of the phrase here may be a literary foreshadowing of behaviors to come, but for now, the text comments, "Solomon loved the LORD" and obeyed the statutes of his father David.

3:4-15 Solomon seeks and receives wisdom

Deuteronomistic theology posits that obedience brings blessings. Usually blessings consist of a long life, many children, health, and prosperity. Solomon, at a sacred site (cf. Josh 10:12), in a dream (cf. Gen 20:6; 31:11), is depicted as a king faithful to God who requests a blessing. He does not request the long life, progeny, and prosperity that are usually the content of blessings, but an understanding heart with which to distinguish between right and wrong and then to be able to judge between the Lord's people. God grants his request and goes on to add incomparable riches and glory. Finally, God makes a conditional promise: *if* Solomon follows David's path of obedience to the Lord's commandments and statutes, then he will have a long life. The very conditioning of the promise suggests the possibility of—if it does not prefigure—unfaithfulness and punishment (cf. Deut 28:15).

3:16-28 Solomon exercises wisdom

Solomon has indeed received the ability to judge the Lord's people and to distinguish between right and wrong. At a time when a woman's status was closely linked to the children she bore, when a mother would grieve over the death of any offspring, never mind an accidental death that she herself had caused, acknowledging that she had smothered her own child—even to herself—would have been difficult. The natural temptation would be to deny what had happened and claim another woman's child as her own. Without blood tests, when there was no "evidence," except one woman's word against the other, how could the true mother be determined? The narrator obscures the differences between the two women by the way he tells the story, just as the characters of the two women are difficult to distinguish in the story itself; neither is named. Yet a wise king Solomon devises a way to distinguish between the liar and the true mother. The woman who prefers that the child be put to death—for surely that would be the effect of cutting the child in two—cannot be the child's true mother. Solomon reunites the true mother with her child. Solomon has devised a brilliant solution to a predicament that would have stymied most. Truly he possesses the wisdom of God: the child reunited with its actual mother is evidence.

4:1-19 The organizational structure of Solomon's monarchy

Naming Solomon's officials, although some of the names appear only here in the Old Testament, serves to concretize and thus authenticate Solomon's bureaucracy. The list serves to formalize roles and differentiate between tasks. High officials include at least three priests, two scribes, a chancellor, a commander of the army, a head of the officials of the commissaries, a companion to the king, a major-domo of the palace, and a superintendent of forced labor. An official is over each of the twelve commissaries that provide food for the king's household—one for each of the twelve months of the year. Twelve, like forty, seven, and ten, is a symbolic number for completion or totality (e.g., Gen 35:22; Exod 15:27; 24:4; Num 1:44; Josh 4:2).

Reading between the lines we see that royal officials were given the task of providing food for the king's household. While we do not know the size of the household nor have a detailed accounting for how this food was obtained, a careful reader might recall Samuel's warning in 1 Samuel 8:11-12. The text reads: "The governance of the king who will rule you will be as follows . . . . He will appoint from among them his commanders of thousands and of hundreds. He will make them do his plowing and harvesting."

5:1-8 The prosperity of Solomon's reign

Contemporary translators have rearranged the verses in an attempt to put the actions described into a more logical sequential order. The verses depict an extensive empire, with Solomon ruling over kingdoms from the Euphrates River in the east to the land of the Philistines in the west down to the border of Egypt at the south, all of which territories paid tribute to him and were his vassals. The extent of his empire (cf. 5:4) recalls the promise made to Abraham (cf. Gen 15:18). Solomon's empire was greater in expanse than David's and greater than that of any Israelite king who succeeded him. Because of his strength, the borders of his empire knew peace; Judah and Israel were secure.

The population of Solomon's kingdom was as extensive as the "sands by the sea" (cf. Gen 22:17; 32:13). Moreover, the food provided for Solomon's table was abundant: thirty, that is, three times ten (both three and ten signify completion and assert the fullness of what is provided) kors of fine flour; sixty, that is, three times two times ten kors of meal; ten fattened oxen; twenty pasture-fed oxen; a hundred sheep, as well as harts, gazelles, roebucks, and fatted fowl. The number and variety of the animals indicate the grandeur of Solomon's kitchen! Hidden in the text, however, is a subtle connection to the potentially oppressive power of a monarch over his subjects (cf. 1 Sam 8:11-18).

Contemporary First World readers often fail to notice that a major component of Solomon's wealth was the capability to produce food: flour, meal, and animals. The enumeration of these valued possessions expresses the authors' consciousness of the people's dependence on the earth for survival.

5:9-14 Solomon's gifts

Not only were the inhabitants of Judah and Israel as numerous as the "sand on the seashore" (cf. 4:20) but, the narrator tells us, Solomon's wisdom and exceptional understanding and knowledge were also as vast as the "sand on the seashore." His wisdom was greater than that of all the peoples of the East, including the Egyptians, and individuals known for their wisdom.

The Old Testament book of Wisdom has been traditionally attributed to Solomon because in it he speaks of his experience with wisdom (Wis 7:7-12). While the book of Wisdom is considerably later than Solomon, or even the book of Kings in which Solomon's wisdom is first recorded, it nevertheless witnesses to the association of Solomon with wisdom throughout the tradition.

The text then documents the accomplishments that Solomon's talents made possible: the utterance of 3,000 proverbs and the composition of 1,005 songs. Similar to the book of Wisdom, the biblical book of Proverbs identifies Solomon as the author of some of its material (Prov 1:1; 10:1; 25:1), as does the book known as the Song of Songs. Like Wisdom, Proverbs and the Song of Songs are later biblical books, though some of the content of Proverbs may derive from a considerably older tradition.

Other of Solomon's accomplishments included his knowledge of plants and animals. Such knowledge was of incalculable value in the world of the ancient Near East. It was the key to survival and even prosperity. These talents and accomplishments made Solomon famous even beyond the borders of his empire.

5:15-26 Solomon's treaty with the king of Tyre

The political alliance that existed between David and Hiram, king of Tyre (2 Sam 5:11), is strengthened when Solomon enlists Hiram's aid—in the form of men and cedar, for which Solomon promises to pay Hiram—to help his own men build a temple for Solomon's God, the Lord. Because there is now peace in Solomon's kingdom, he can begin to fulfill the promise God made to David—that his son would build the Lord a temple (2 Sam 7:13).

Hiram agrees to Solomon's terms. He will provide the cedar and the manpower to deliver the cedar by sea to a destination of Solomon's choosing. Solomon will, in exchange, give Hiram whatever household provisions he requests. Hiram provides the cedar and fir trees; Solomon pays Hiram annually twenty thousand kors of wheat and twenty kors of pure oil. The alliance seems, at least on the surface, to work well and benefit both kingdoms.

5:27-32 The cost of Solomon's building project

In addition to the payment of wheat and oil, however, Solomon also provides Hiram with Israelite workmen. He conscripts thirty thousand men, whom he sends in relays of ten thousand each month to Lebanon. The numbers are symbolic of large totalities. Each of the groups spends one month working in Lebanon and two months at home, that is, four months of every year working for Solomon. But in addition to them, Solomon puts to work eighty thousand stonecutters, seventy thousand carriers of stone, and thirty-three hundred overseers. His workers are organized hierarchically to accomplish his ends. Less subtle than in 1 Kings 5:1-8 is the connection with 1 Samuel 8:11-18, the oppressive methods and greedy manner of a monarch over his people.

6:1-10 Building Solomon's temple

Dating the beginning of the construction of the temple to a precise month and year establishes the building's credibility as a concrete historical fact (6:1). Verses 2-10 then describe the details of the building project, which give a sense of the building's grandeur. The measurements of the temple itself, in addition to its porch and its three-story annex, project a massive building complex. The building materials—dressed stone and cedar—suggest its splendor.

6:11-13 The Lord makes Solomon a promise

The narrator interjects into the middle of his description of Solomon's building project a word from the Lord to Solomon. The Lord's promise to David—that his son would build the temple (cf. 2 Sam 7:13)—is being fulfilled. Taking the material promise one step forward, the Lord affirms the relationship that the temple implies: He will be in Israel's midst and not abandon the people. However, the further promise contains a conditional element; it is contingent on the king's faithfulness to God. This is the second time that a promise from the Lord to Solomon is expressed conditionally (cf. 1 Kgs 3:14). The reader might begin to suspect that Solomon will not remain faithful.

6:14-36 The temple's interior

The narrator continues to describe the grandeur of the Lord's dwelling: cedar paneling for the walls, fir planking on the floors, a well-proportioned inner sanctuary to house the ark of the covenant, an altar and nave made of intricately carved cedar, and generous overlays of gold throughout. The builders place two cherubim (6:22-28) in the holy of holies. They make doors either of olive wood or fir wood for both the entrance to the sanctuary and the entrance to the nave (6:31-35); everything is elaborately carved and overlaid with gold. Contemporary American English would describe the temple (or at least the authors' description of the temple) as being enormously elaborate, "over the top."

6:37-38 The temple's completion

Just as 1 Kings 6:1 dates the beginning of the construction of the temple, verses 37-38 date the completion of its foundation and then, seven years later, the completion of the temple itself. Seven is frequently used in biblical texts to symbolize completion. The narrator notes that the temple is completed "in all particulars, exactly according to plan" to emphasize the perfection associated with the undertaking.

7:1 Solomon's palace: its construction

Whereas the final verse of chapter 6 functions as both a climax and a statement of completion, the narrator introduces chapter 7 with a seemingly deliberate literary contrast. Whereas it took seven years to build the house of the Lord, it takes thirteen years to build the house of the king. Although thirteen is not a number used frequently in the biblical texts, it too may be used symbolically to indicate completion (ten and three). The unusual character of the number may be a literary device that the authors use to subtly imply some inappropriateness related to the king's palace. The fact that it takes almost twice as long to build the king's house as it does to build the Lord's house can imply that the king's house was not worked on by as many builders, or with as much zeal as was the Lord's house. Or, it could imply that the grandeur of the Lord's house paled beside the grandeur of the king's. If the latter is true, the text is hinting at future difficulties.

7:2-8 Solomon's palace: its size

Verse 2 answers the question implied by verse 1. Solomon's palace is even larger than the Lord's temple. Whereas the temple's measurements are sixty cubits by twenty cubits by twenty-five cubits, one cedar hall of the palace measures one hundred cubits by fifty cubits by thirty cubits. In addition, Solomon's palace also includes a throne room and living quarters. Both the temple and the palace have a porch, but the palace's porch is more than seven times the size of the temple's porch. Seven here implies a porch of completely greater size, suggesting the magnitude of the palace's porch. And it seems that Solomon built another palace, the second one being for his wife.

7:9-12 Solomon's palace: its grandeur

Constructed with at least some of the same materials as the Lord's temple—fine hewn large stones and cedar wood—Solomon's "house" is very grand. The Hebrew word *bayit* may be translated "house," meaning "temple," if the term refers to the Lord's house (cf. 6:1) or, as here, "palace," if it refers to the king's house.

7:13-51 The temple's furnishings

Just as the editors seem to have inserted into the narration the Lord's conditional promise to Solomon regarding temple building (1 Kgs 6:12-13), the editors seem also to have inserted the description of Solomon's palace (1 Kgs 7:1-12) into their detailed account of the temple construction. Are the insertions deliberate—to interrupt the narrative flow, to disturb the reader, and thus to prepare the reader for the larger disruption (Solomon's unfaithfulness and its consequences) that will follow? Once completed, the temple has to be furnished. Solomon arranges for Hiram, an outstanding metal worker of mixed blood (mother from an Israelite tribe, father from Lebanon) to fashion most of the temple furnishings from bronze. Is this Hiram the king of Tyre who was David's friend, and who helped with the building of the temple by providing manpower and materials? That he is married to a woman from the Israelite tribe of Naphtali would only reflect the political alliances common at that time and help to explain the cooperation between Hiram and Solomon. After all, Solomon is himself married to an Egyptian (1 Kgs 3:1). On the other hand, it is likely that more than one citizen of Tyre had the name Hiram. That the Hiram referred to here is not the king is supported by his work in metal.

In any case, the text describes in detail certain temple furnishings: the two hollow bronze columns that are located on each side of the temple porch; the sea, that is, a large basin that could hold two thousand measures of water and that the priests used for purification purposes; ten very ornate stands, and ten other basins. The narrator's style both describes what is being made (7:15-39) and summarizes what has been made (7:40-45). Hiram makes everything of burnished bronze, the weight of which is undetermined.

To these bronze furnishings Solomon adds certain gold articles (7:48-50). In addition, Solomon places in the temple's treasury all of the precious objects that David had dedicated to God (7:51). This survey of the temple's contents functions to confirm the temple's opulence.

8:1-21 Preparing the temple's dedication

After the temple is built and furnished, it has to be dedicated. It is not any building; it is God's dwelling place, and has to be formally set aside as such. The narrator describes the circumstances surrounding the temple's dedication. The dedication is set during the seventh month in spite of the fact that 1 Kings 6:38 says that the temple was not completed until the eighth month. The discrepancy was apparently unimportant to the author, suggesting that the seven was here used symbolically, to signify completion.

Those high in the pecking order—elders, princes, and priests—come to Jerusalem, as well as "the whole people of Israel." The priests and the ancestral family of the priests, that is, the Levites, bring up from Zion the provisional tent-sanctuary built by David, the ark of the covenant, and the meeting tent that contains the sacred vessels. They sacrifice many sheep and oxen before the ark and then carry the ark that contains the two tablets of the law, representative of the Lord's covenantal relationship with the people of Israel, to its place in the new temple. When the Lord's glory (i.e., God's presence) fills the temple in the form of a cloud, Solomon declares the temple a place where the Lord can abide "forever." He reminds the people of the Lord's promise to his father David and its fulfillment in himself and the temple (2 Sam 7:8-16).

8:22-26 Dedicating the temple

Solomon's prayer begins with a declaration of the Lord's uniqueness and of his faithfulness to his promises. He then asks God to confirm God's promise to David that David's line will continue on the throne of Israel. In 2 Samuel 7:15 God promises David that if his heir does wrong, he will correct him, but he will not withdraw his favor from him. Here the text becomes conditional. Solomon reiterates God's promise to David that David will always have someone from his line on Isarael's throne, *but* Solomon repeats the promise specifying the condition that David's descendents are faithful and "live in God's presence" as he, David, had done. Those who come after David will be measured against David; David's line will continue *if and only if*, their behaviors conform to his, because David's conformed to faithfulness to God.

This is the third time that the fulfillment of God's promise to Solomon is conditioned by Solomon's faithfulness (cf. 1 Kgs 3:14 and 6:12).

8:27-29 The dwelling for God's name

Solomon then articulates to God the paradox of the temple as a place that contains the presence of God at the same time that the presence of God cannot be contained in any one place. Often this paradox has been explained as "name theology," (8:29), that somehow God's "name" dwells in the temple as a way of talking about God's being there in a special way but not in an exclusive way that prevents God from being somewhere else also. This same use of God's "name" can be found in Exodus 20:7 and Deuteronomy 5:11. Whereas a superficial reading of those texts suggests a prohibition against swearing, the command is considerably broader. God, and all that pertains to God, is not to be taken lightly.

8:30-50 Sin and forgiveness

Solomon's prayer repeatedly acknowledges his and the people's sin (8:31, 32, 33, 35, 46) and asks the Lord to listen to their prayer (8:30, 32, 34, 36, 39, 43, 49, 52) and to forgive them (8:30, 32, 34, 36, 39, 50). The date of the passage is uncertain. Clearly its content is Deuteronomistic and may suggest a late seventh-century authorship: the people sinned and were punished, they cried out to God in their distress, God heard their prayer, and God restored them. On the other hand, verse 34 requests that the Lord return them to their land, verses 41-43 support an inclusive attitude toward the foreigner, and verses 46-50 describe the people's being deported and asking God to grant them mercy from their captors. These passages indicate that either the entire prayer, or at least this section of it, was composed later, during the exile.

8:51-53 Recalling the exodus

The foundation of the people of Israel as God's people is the exodus. They were the people the Lord brought out from Egypt (cf. 8:21). The liberating initiative of God on behalf of a motley group of enslaved people has become the basis for Israel's covenant identity. Who they have become, God's people, is the basis on which Solomon makes his requests.

8:54-66 Blessing the people

Concluding his prayer to God, Solomon then addresses the people, praising and thanking God for having fulfilled the promises. Solomon then commits the people to covenant faithfulness, to being "wholly devoted" to God, that is, to being monotheistic and obedient (8:54-61). The festival that began with the offering of many sacrifices "before the ark" (8:5) concludes with the offering of many more sacrifices in "the middle of the court facing the house of the LORD" (8:62-64). The festival, which lasts seven days, includes "all the Israelites," what has become a numerous people, a large kingdom (8:65-66).

We as readers need to be aware of the role of animal sacrifices. Offering God their valuable possessions expressed their recognition of God as the provider of all.

9:1-24 Reiterating God's conditional promise

The Lord appears again to Solomon and reminds him of both the promise and the conditions that limit it: *if* Solomon lives "in the Lord's presence" and is obedient, God will fulfill for Solomon what he had promised to David. However, *if* Solomon and his descendants fail to live up to covenant faithfulness and worship strange gods, the Israelites will lose their land and the temple will be destroyed (9:1-9). The people of Israel have been tempted to idolatry since their arrival in the land but now its consequences are being spelled out. They will lose the land (cf. Josh 23:15-16).

After the temple's completion, payment to Hiram, king of Tyre, for all the materials and manpower he provided for Solomon's building projects is just. Hiram adds one hundred talents of gold and receives from Solomon in return twenty cities in Galilee, that is, he enlarges his territory. When Hiram sees the cities, however, he is dissatisfied with them, which leaves the reader to wonder whether the text's authors are insinuating that Solomon cheated Hiram. Solomon has enslaved non-Israelites for his building projects and organized his own people for the smooth operation of his kingdom (9:10-23); would cheating Hiram be so out of character? Solomon's additional building projects include the queen's palace and a fortification (9:24).

9:25-28 Worship and wealth

Solomon practices covenant faithfulness insofar as he offers sacrifices to the Lord and maintains the Lord's temple. But the text adds another building project—a fleet through which Solomon gains considerable wealth. One gets the impression that Hiram, though also a king, is not by this time Solomon's equal. Hiram's seamen work with Solomon's servants to Solomon's advantage (cf. 10:11-12). The text enhances Solomon's profile by diminishing Hiram's.

10:1-13 International confirmation of Solomon's success

First Kings 5:11 attests to the fact that Solomon's "fame spread throughout the neighboring peoples" and 5:14 confirms that "People came from all nations to hear Solomon's wisdom, sent by all the kings of the earth who had heard of his wisdom." The Queen of Sheba confirms Solomon's fame and wisdom, and marvels at the abundance of his wealth. She has heard of Solomon, but she now sees his situation firsthand. Her praise is extensive and she presents Solomon with extravagant gifts. Hiram delivers to Solomon gold, "almug wood and precious stones" from abroad. What more can be said about the power and prestige of the king?

10:14-29 Solomon's wealth

More is said about the wealth and prestige of the king: more gold, large and smaller shields of gold, an ornate ivory throne, drinking vessels of gold, and imported silver, apes, and peacocks. Verse 23 summarizes by saying that Solomon surpasses all other kings in wealth and wisdom. Yet verses 24-25, while connecting Solomon's wisdom to his receipt of lavish gifts, also hint that much of Solomon's wealth is acquired at other people's expense, by their payment of an annual tribute.

Another source of Solomon's wealth is trade. He imports chariots and horses and exports them to other kings. We can expect that this undertaking is not without profit.

11:1-13 Solomon's downfall

Whereas 3:3 asserted that "Solomon loved the LORD," 11:1 asserts that "Solomon loved many foreign women" and then continues that these foreign women turned Solomon's heart to their gods. To express the magnitude of his sin, the narrator says that he had seven hundred wives: seven, a symbolic number for completion, times ten, another symbolic number for completion, times ten again! And as if they were not enough, he had three hundred concubines! The text now contrasts Solomon with David and details his egregious behavior—in spite of the fact that the Lord had appeared to him twice (cf. 1 Kgs 3:5; 9:2).

As a consequence of this infidelity, the Lord punishes Solomon by declaring that he will give Solomon's kingdom to his servant. Saul's kingdom went to Saul's servant David, after Saul's sin (cf. 1 Sam 24:21). Yet, Solomon will not lose the kingdom during his lifetime but during his son's reign. Nor will the loss be total: for the sake of David and Jerusalem, Solomon's son will rule over one tribe. The text manages to condemn Solomon's wrongdoing—theologically understood as idolatry—and to award Solomon fitting punishment according to the condition set out in 1 Kings 9:5, but the text also manages to maintain God's promise to David that his dynasty will stand (2 Sam 7:13).

11:14-22 Solomon's adversary Hadad of Edom

To support the theological judgment of the Deuteronomistic editors that Solomon and his kingdom will be punished for his polytheism and idolatry, the text describes some of Solomon's political opponents, including Hadad of Edom. The narrator explains one reason for Hadad's opposition to Solomon: When David conquered Edom, David's general, Joab, put to death all the men of Edom over a six-month period. Hadad was only a boy at the time. As a member of Edom's royal family, he had been able to escape to Egypt and

was there given refuge. Still, despite his faring very well in Egypt, when he learned of David and Joab's deaths, he chose to return to Edom as its king. While in Egypt he contracted a political marriage with Pharaoh's sister-in-law. The narrative serves to legitimate Hadad and to justify Edom's hostility toward Solomon.

11:23-25 Solomon's adversary Rezon of Aram

This is the first and only mention of Rezon in the Bible. He is identified as having fled from his own king, and having gathered a band of men around him. This may be intended to indicate that he is less reputable than a royal heir. In any case, he eventually becomes king of Damascus. The reference to him here functions to reinforce that Solomon received punishment as a consequence of his sins. Rezon was Israel's enemy during the entirety of Solomon's reign.

11:26-28 Solomon's adversary Jeroboam of Ephraim

Solomon had appointed Jeroboam, an Ephraimite, a "very able man," over the labor force that was working to build the Millo in order to close up "the breach of the City of David, his father." The reference to the Millo in 9:24 appears as a positive statement of another of Solomon's building projects. Perhaps, however, the reference is intended to foreshadow the implication here, that Solomon is taking advantage of Jeroboam and his wealth (in addition to the labor force?) to further his building projects (cf. 1 Sam 8:10-18). Jeroboam's response is to rebel.

11:29-39 God's choice of Jeroboam

Ahijah (11:29) prophesies to Jeroboam that he will be king over ten of the tribes of Israel. This will not occur during Solomon's lifetime. Moreover, one tribe will be left for Solomon's son (cf. 11:12). Ahijah explains to Jeroboam the reason Solomon is losing the kingdom. He reiterates the polytheism and idolatry cited above (11:5): Solomon worshiped other nations' gods including Astarte, Chemosh, and Milcom, thus displeasing the Lord. Yet the prophet proclaims that the kingdom will not be lost during Solomon's lifetime (cf. 11:12) for the sake of David and Jerusalem, whom the Lord chose and who had proven faithful. A third time the prophet reiterates that one tribe will be given to Solomon's son (11:12, 32), so that David might always have a lamp before the Lord in Jerusalem. David's sins against God pale (2 Sam 11; 24) in comparison to Solomon's idolatry. Ahijah declares that Jeroboam will be made king of Israel and then conditionally promises Jeroboam that he will have a lasting dynasty *if* he is like David, that is, *if* he obeys the Lord's statutes and commandments (11:26-38).

Jeroboam, though not a Davidic heir, is given the same promise Solomon was given, a lasting dynasty dependent on his fidelity. Jeroboam's relationship to Solomon is, at least literarily, similar to what David's relationship to Saul had been. When Saul had proven unfaithful and an unfit king, David, who was not related to Saul but who had once been in good standing with him, emerged as Saul's successor. When Solomon proves unfaithful and an unfit king, Jeroboam, who was not related to Solomon but who had once been in good standing with him, emerges as Solomon's at least partial successor. Just as Saul tried unsuccessfully to have David killed (1 Sam 19:1), Solomon attempts, also unsuccessfully, to have Jeroboam killed. Both David and Jeroboam flee the land to escape (cf. 1 Sam 21:11). Whereas David fled to Ramah, a Benjaminite city, Jeroboam flees to Egypt where Shishak, a later opponent of the southern kingdom of Judah, was king.

Ahijah's final word to Jeroboam, that the Lord will not punish David's line "forever" (11:39), reinforces God's faithfulness to David.

A word should be said about the role of prophets in the books of Kings. Nathan, who supported Solomon over Adonijah (1 Kgs 1:8), had served as David's wise counselor. Now Ahijah emerges to predict Jeroboam's rule in Israel. First and Second Kings contain stories of other prophets (e.g., Elijah, Elisha, Micaiah, and Hulda). The prophet speaks and acts with the power of God; to them even kings must listen.

11:40-43 Solomon's final days

The "chronicles of Solomon" apparently refer to court records that are no longer in existence and which would have provided a fuller account of Solomon's reign. Presumably they contained an account of Solomon's accomplishments as king; to the extent that they contained royal propaganda we can suspect that they were filled with praise for the king's judgments and deeds. One

can presume that they lacked the theological judgment of the Deuteronomistic editors. The length of Solomon's reign, like that of his father David (2:11) was forty years.

Deuteronomistic editing provides the official declaration of the king's death, the length of his reign, the site of his burial, and his successor. Almost all of David's successors rested with their fathers in Jerusalem. Solomon's son Rehoboam succeeded his father as king.

JUDAH AND ISRAEL TO THE TIME OF KING AHAB
1 Kings 12–16

With Solomon's death came the division of a once-united kingdom into two parts, Judah and Israel. During the years between the reigns of Jeroboam (922–901 B.C.) and Ahab (869–850 B.C.) in the North, several Davidic kings reigned in Judah.

12:1-25 The North rejects Rehoboam

The opening verses acknowledge the heavy burden Solomon imposed on the people, a burden that had only been implied in the previous chapters. When the people request that the new king lighten their burden, Rehoboam postpones giving the people a reply to their request for three days. He consults with the elders who advise him to listen to the people and honor their request. He then consults with his contemporaries who advise him to assure the people that he will place an even heavier burden on them than his father did. Rehoboam has to choose which advice to follow. In the world of ancient Israel, the advice of the elders was clearly to be preferred. They had been blessed by God and had lived long lives, and they possessed the wisdom that comes from experience. Nevertheless, Rehoboam prefers his contemporaries' advice and informs the people accordingly. The narrator interjects that he did this to fulfill the prophecy the Lord uttered to Jeroboam (cf. 1 Kgs 11:31). The response of the northern tribes is to rebel; Jeroboam returns from Egypt and becomes king over them (1 Kgs 11:35). Rehoboam flees to Judah. Though Rehoboam attempts to muster troops from the tribes of Judah and Benjamin against Israel, Shimaiah, a man of God, assures Rehoboam that his efforts are futile, that the Lord has brought this about.

The text functions to confirm the division of the kingdom as an expression of Deuteronomistic theology. Solomon sinned, which is why ten tribes will be given to Jeroboam. Now Rehoboam has behaved at least stupidly—if not also sinfully (e.g., Deut 27:1). The punishment that follows their sin, the division of the kingdom, is, according to the text, clearly God's will.

The two cities that Jeroboam chooses for his residence, Shechem and Penuel, both have long histories. While the Hebrews' difficulties with the Shechemites can be traced back to the rape of Dinah (i.e., Gen 34) and then to Abimelech's slaughter of his brothers (Judg 9), Penuel, a town on the northern bank of the Jabbok River, was associated with Jacob's encounter with God (i.e., Gen 32:23-31). Together the sites symbolize Jeroboam's separation from Judah as well as his divine mandate.

12:26-33 Jeroboam's religious restructuring

In order to avoid his subjects' return to Jerusalem to worship the Lord at the temple, which Jeroboam concludes would result in the people's return to Judah and loyalty to Rehoboam, Jeroboam makes two golden calves and sets them up at two worship sites, Bethel and Dan. Just as Shechem and Penuel each had a long history, so Bethel (e.g., Gen 12:8; 35:14-15) had a sacred history of worship and sacrifice. Dan's history was associated with the establishment of the city of Dan as a cult center by the Danites (Judg 18:27-31).

The text describes Jeroboam as doing all the wrong things: making golden calves (cf. Exod 32; Deut 9:16); using priests who were not Levites (cf. Num 3:5-10); establishing a pilgrimage feast in Bethel, not Jerusalem; setting it at a seemingly arbitrary time—the eighth month on the fifteenth day—not the fifteenth day of the seventh month that was traditionally stipulated for sacrificial offerings (cf. Lev 23:39 and Num 29:12). Jeroboam himself was even going to offer the sacrifice, a text that recalls Saul's inappropriate sacrifice (1 Sam 13:9).

13:1-10 Jeroboam's condemnation

No sooner has Jeroboam done evil than a prophet from Judah comes to the Bethel shrine to denounce Jeroboam and the altar he set up there. The prophet announces that King Josiah of Judah

will slaughter the priests who sacrifice on the altar and who burn human bones on it. As a sign that his prophecy will be fulfilled, that Josiah will slaughter Jeroboam's priests—the prophet says that the Bethel altar will be broken up and its ashes strewn about. Jeroboam tries to silence the prophet, that is, he orders the prophet to be captured. But the prophet is a man of God with the power of God. Jeroboam's hand withers and the altar, as the prophet predicted, breaks into pieces. The withered hand and the destroyed altar convince Jeroboam of the prophet's power and authority. He asks the prophet to intercede with God for him, that his hand might be restored. According to Deuteronomistic theology (sin, punishment, crying out to God for deliverance, the Lord hearing the plea, and restoration), the prophet does intercede with God for Jeroboam and Jeroboam's hand is restored.

The prophet is God's intermediary; he does not accept Jeroboam's invitation to go to the king's home, to place himself under the king's authority. Rather, the prophet obeys the Lord: he does not have bread or water in Bethel nor does he return by his original route.

13:11-22 Prophetic obedience

The narrator records an encounter of the prophet from Judah with a prophet of Bethel. The prophet of Bethel lies to the prophet from Judah. He tricks the Judean prophet into believing that he has received the word of the Lord through an angel, and that, contrary to what the Judean prophet himself heard from the Lord, it is all right for the Judean prophet to eat bread and drink water in Bethel. The Judean prophet listens to the prophet of Bethel, disregarding the word of the Lord. Because the prophet from Judah does not hold fast to the Lord's word, the prophet of Bethel predicts he will not be buried with his ancestors. Ironically, the prophet of Bethel who lies to the Judean prophet now prophesies regarding the Judean prophet's fate. The narrative teaches that a prophet must obey the word of God that he has received. A prophet's refusal to obey the word of the Lord in favor of the word of another prophet can only result in punishment.

13:23-32 The Judean prophet's death

When the prophet of Judah is en route back to Judah the prediction of the prophet of Bethel regarding the death of the prophet from Judah is fulfilled. A lion kills the prophet. He who did not obey the Lord is punished. However, the lion does not eat the prophet, nor does the lion harm the donkey. The lion stands by the prophet's body. The description is hardly the behavior one would expect from a lion. But this is not any lion; this is a lion who is the instrument of the Lord, helping to fulfill the word of the Lord that came through the prophet of Bethel about the fate of the prophet from Judah. According to the text, the Lord is clearly in control.

The Judean prophet had been faithful; he had condemned Jeroboam and predicted the demise of the Bethel altar; his prophecy was fulfilled. But he was also unfaithful; contrary to the word he had received from the Lord, he ate and drank in Bethel. So he was punished, and he was not buried with his ancestors (e.g., 14:31; 2 Kgs 9:28). But his punishment could have been worse; not to have been buried at all would have been far worse punishment (cf. 1 Sam 31; 1 Kgs 14:11; 16:4; 21:23-24; 2 Kgs 9:36).

Similarly, the prophet of Bethel was faithful and unfaithful, or more accurately, unfaithful and then faithful. First he lied to the Judean prophet, but afterward, he claimed his body, buried it in his own grave, and confirmed that the Judean prophet's word against the altar in Bethel and against all the high places in the cities of Samaria would be fulfilled. He instructed his sons that he should be buried in the same grave as the prophet from Judah. Though the prophet from Bethel had deceived the prophet from Judah, he was truly a prophet who spoke the word of the Lord; the word of the Lord would come to pass.

13:33-34 Jeroboam's continued evildoing

In spite of God's warning to Jeroboam—his withered hand, the smashed altar (and the death of the prophet from Judah)—Jeroboam continued to disobey the Lord: he made priests for the high places not from among the Levites but from among the common people (cf. Num 3:10). Deuteronomistic theology provokes the reader to await God's punishment of Jeroboam for his sins.

14:1-16 Ahijah's prophecy against Jeroboam

When Jeroboam's son becomes sick, he seeks out Ahijah, the prophet who made him king over Israel (cf. 11:31)—despite Jeroboam's unfaithfulness to the Lord. The reader may be waiting for Jeroboam's punishment, but Jeroboam appears to have no such expectation. Because Ahijah's prediction regarding the kingship was fulfilled, he seeks Ahijah's word regarding his son's fate. But Ahijah is in Jerusalem. Jeroboam built the shrines at Bethel and Dan so that his people would not return to Jerusalem. How could Jeroboam go to Jerusalem to consult a prophet of Judah?

Lest he be seen and captured, or lest it become known among the people that he is seeking out the Lord's prophet in Jerusalem, Jeroboam sends his wife, disguised, to Ahijah. Ahijah's failing eyesight and her disguise would have prevented the prophet from recognizing Jeroboam's wife except that the Lord identifies her to him and gives Ahijah a message for her to deliver to Jeroboam. In spite of God's gift to Jeroboam of ten tribes, he did not behave like David; he did not obey the Lord's statutes and commands (cf. 11:38); he behaved worse than his predecessors (Saul? Solomon?); he made idols and forsook the worship of the Lord. Because of these sins, the Lord promises to cut off the line of Jeroboam completely. In effect, the Lord revokes the conditional promise made to Jeroboam through Ahijah; he failed to meet the condition.

But the prophecy against Jeroboam continues: the son about whom his wife had consulted Ahijah would die; Jeroboam's house would be replaced; Israel itself would be destroyed; Israel's people would be scattered outside the land, and the flesh of Jeroboam's dead descendants would be devoured by dogs and birds and not honored by burial. The prophet uses an image taken from the natural environment, a reed tossed about in the water, to depict the helplessness of Israel. The text condemns Jeroboam's egregious sins of polytheism and idolatry and declares a harsh punishment that will extend to future generations. Deuteronomistic theology holds: unfaithfulness to God has consequences.

14:17-18 Jeroboam's son's death

Jeroboam trusts the word of the prophet or he would not have sent his wife to seek out Ahijah. Now, lest he or his wife doubt that the prophet's word will be fulfilled, his sick son dies when his wife returns home. And, according to the word of the prophet, this son does receive a proper burial.

14:19-20 Jeroboam's death

Jeroboam has a twenty-two year reign, considerably shorter than the reigns of David and Solomon, after which he is buried with his ancestors. His son Nadab succeeds him. We have been warned to expect that Nadab will suffer a violent death.

14:21-31 Rehoboam of Judah's reign

While Jeroboam was ruling in Israel, Rehoboam was reigning in Judah. He lived a lifetime (forty years) by the time he became king, and he reigned for seventeen years. The narrator records the name of his mother—Naamah—to differentiate which among Solomon's wives was his mother. That she is identified as an Ammonite (14:31) may help, from the editors' perspective, to explain the evil behavior of her son. (Ammonite women were associated with idolatry; cf. 1 Kgs 11:4-5.) The Deuteronomistic judgment of Rehoboam's reign is not a good one. Rehoboam allows high places, pillars, sacred poles, and cult prostitutes; these latter perform the abominable practices of the polytheists who preceded them. Not surprisingly then, Judah is punished. The kingdom is attacked by Egypt and suffers material loss; its wealth is diminished. Also, Judah and Israel are in constant conflict. Consistent with Deuteronomistic theology, sin has consequences.

Nevertheless, when David's descendent Rehoboam dies, he is buried with his ancestors; his son Abijam succeeds him as king. The chronicles of the kings of Judah, like the chronicles of Solomon (cf. 1 Kgs 11:41) and the chronicles of the kings of Israel (cf. 1 Kgs 14:19) are, to our knowledge, no longer extant. No archaeological dig has so far unearthed them.

15:1-8 Abijam of Judah's reign

Dating was done in relationship to other major events, and so Rehoboam's son Abijam is said to have become king of Judah in the eighteenth year of the reign of King Jeroboam. The text assumes the same year for the beginning of the reigns of both Jeroboam and Rehoboam. Abijam's reign lasts for three years. Maacah, among what are presumed to be the many wives of Rehoboam, was Abijam's mother. Even if polygamy was diminishing at this time, which it may have been, those in positions of power and wealth who could afford to support many wives and children most likely possessed them.

Abijam, like his father, does evil. War between Judah and Israel continues during his reign. All—both the king's behavior and the political climate—is not well. Still, for the sake of David, God allows the dynasty to continue. The Deuteronomistic editors, while pronouncing against the unfaithful behavior of Abijam and many of Judah's kings, nevertheless defend the continuation of the dynasty because of David. Since David, too, sinned, we may conclude that it was his humble acknowledgment of his sin and his request for forgiveness that were credited to him as faithfulness. Abijam's son Asa succeeds him.

15:9-22 Asa of Judah's reign

Asa reigns forty-one years and in contrast to his father and grandfather, resembles David in his faithfulness toward God. He banishes the cult prostitutes, removes the idols, and deposes his grandmother as queen mother because of her idolatry.

Still, he allows the high places to remain and war continues between Israel and Judah (15:16-22), though it would appear from the description of the war that Judah is gaining the upper hand. Baasha, king of Israel, attacks Judah and fortifies Ramah, a city near the southern border of the northern kingdom, in order to prevent the Israelites from going south to Jerusalem to worship. Asa's response is to appeal to Ben-hadad of Aram, with whom Judah has a treaty. Asa sent Ben-hadad tribute—silver and gold from the treasuries of the Lord's temple—as an incentive for Aram to break its treaty with Israel; Aram then attacks several Israelite cities. Baasha retreats. Asa is then able to dismantle the fortifications that Baasha had been setting up at Ramah and use the materials for his own building projects.

Verses 16-22 seem to be out of logical/historical order. First Kings 14:20 asserts that Jeroboam's son Nadab succeeded him as king (cf. 15:25). Baasha reigned in Israel after Nadab (see 15:33–16:8 below). The war that is here described between Asa and Baasha (15:16-22) might be better placed between 16:4 and 16:5.

15:23-24 Asa's death

The Deuteronomistic editors judge Asa as faithful and consequently determine his reign a success: faithfulness to God is rewarded. They also indicate that a record of his accomplishments can be found in the chronicles of the kings of Judah. By referring to this second witness to Asa's kingship, they confirm the veracity of their judgment. Asa's son Jehoshaphat succeeds him as king; David's line continues.

15:25-32 Nadab of Israel's reign

Jeroboam's son, Nadab, succeeds him as king (cf. 1 Kgs 14:20); he reigns for only two years. The Deuteronomistic editors compare his reign to that of his father: Nadab did evil. Baasha, a non-relative, uses the opportunity of Nadab's battle with the Philistines to kill him; he thus fulfills the word of the prophet Ahijah (cf. 1 Kgs 14:5-11), that Jeroboam's line would be totally eliminated. Baasha then succeeds Nadab as king. War continues between the kings of Judah and Israel, Asa and Baasha respectively, as long as they live (cf. 15:16-22).

15:33–16:7 Baasha of Israel's reign

Baasha reigns over Israel for twenty-four years. He too sins against God just like Jeroboam sinned. And just as the prophet Ahijah condemned Jeroboam's sins and his line (cf.14:10-11), the prophet Jehu here condemns Baasha and his line. Baasha's house, like Jeroboam's, will not last. The same imagery that was applied to Jeroboam's house is here applied to Baasha's: dogs and birds will devour Baasha's offspring. Yet just as Jeroboam's son Nadab succeeded him, Baasha's son succeeds him. Elah becomes king of Israel.

16:8-14 Elah of Israel's reign

Elah, like Jeroboam's son Nadab, reigned for only two years (cf. 1 Kgs 15:25). Zimri, not a relative of Elah, assassinated him and reigned in his stead. Zimri fulfilled the word of the Lord to Jehu, totally eliminating Baasha's line (cf. 16:1-4). Elah, like his father Baasha and like Jeroboam, sinned against God and caused Israel to sin. The text conforms to Deuteronomistic theology: sin has consequences.

16:15-22 Zimri of Israel's reign

Zimri's reign lasts seven days; though its duration is brief, seven is a symbolic number for completion, nevertheless. He too is judged as "walking in the way of Jeroboam and the sin he had caused Israel to commit." He too is punished; he is unable to secure his place on the throne. Zimri seems to have preferred suicide to assassination (cf. the suicide of King Saul in 1 Sam 31:4), but still, he meets an untimely death.

Omri, the general of Israel's army, is intent, with the support of the army, to take over the throne. In spite of an even split among the people over who should be Israel's next king, with half of them supporting Tibni and half supporting Omri, Omri prevails. He, after all, has the support of the army. The succinct comment that "Tibni died and Omri became king" suggests that an untimely death eliminated Tibni as a contender for the throne. Recall Adonijah's untimely elimination by Solomon (2:24-25) and other conspiracies leading to the deaths of the reigning kings of Israel (e.g., 15:27-28; 16:10; 2 Kgs 15:25).

16:23-28 Omri of Israel's reign

Omri reigned for twelve years. Whereas the previous kings of Israel ruled from Tirzah (cf. 1 Kgs 14:17; 15:33; 16:8, 15), Omri moves the capital, building Samaria and establishing it as Israel's new capital. From a theological perspective, he is denounced as being even more evil than his predecessors, and is compared to Jeroboam. One should note at this point that Jeroboam, Nadab, Baasha, Elah, Zimri, and Omri all reigned in Israel during the forty-one year reign of Asa in Judah. Despite Israel's size and prosperity, it lacked Judah's political stability. From the Deuteronomistic editors' theological perspective, the source of its difficulties is its lack of faithfulness to God. When Omri dies his son Ahab succeeds him.

16:29-34 Ahab of Israel's reign

Like the reign of his father Omri, Ahab's twenty-two year reign was characterized as being evil; it is described as being more evil than any that preceded it. This is explained by the fact that, in addition to being guilty of all of the sins Jeroboam committed, Ahab married Jezebel, a daughter of the king of the Sidonians, and worshiped Baal. Jezebel became the symbol of female power and female evil in the northern kingdom. Performing a similar function in Israel as Athaliah, also a powerful and evil queen, came to perform in Judah (2 Kgs 11) Jezebel usurped a power not willingly provided by society, and she was condemned for it.

The narrator informs us that Ahab even erected an altar to Baal in the temple that he built to Baal in Samaria and that he also made a sacred pole. Moreover, during his reign Jericho was rebuilt; God through Joshua had explicitly forbidden the rebuilding of Jericho (cf. Josh 6:26).

STORIES OF THE PROPHETS

1 Kings 17–22

When the evil king Ahab was confronted by the power of God expressed in the words and deeds of the Lord's prophets, he realized that he was no match for God. Yet the unfaithful northern kingdom continued in its idolatrous ways.

17:1-6 Elijah predicts a drought

The Lord warns Ahab through his prophet Elijah of an impending drought. Whereas drought is life threatening, the Lord provides for his prophet. Evil is punished and good is blessed. Elijah is given sufficient food and water to survive. Ravens care for him; they bring him bread and meat. In contrast, birds devour the sons of evil kings who die in the field (cf. 14:11; 16:4). The Wadi Cherith provides Elijah with water, at least until the stream dries up. Water nourishes life but its absence leads inevitably to death. The Israelites experience keenly their dependence on water for survival.

17:7-16 Elijah satisfies the widow's hunger

When the Wadi Cherith dries up, Elijah, obeying the Lord, moves to Zarephath of Sidon. There, at the city's entrance, he asks a widow for bread and water. She replies that she has little, and that she is gathering sticks to prepare a last meal for herself and her son. She doesn't actually refuse the prophet's request, but she admits to her dire situation. Elijah tells her not to be afraid (cf. Deut 7:18; Josh 8:1; 10:25; Judg 4:18), and assures her that God will provide flour and oil for her and her son. She and her son will be able to sustain themselves for an entire year—until it rains. The widow obeys Elijah and through him the Lord's word regarding food for her and her son is fulfilled. When the drought led to famine and was starving those around them, the widow's handful of flour and small amount of oil continued to sustain them. The prophet speaks and acts with the power of God; his word is effective.

17:17-24 Elijah raises the widow's son

When, however, the widow's son gets sick and dies, the woman asks Elijah why he allowed this to happen; she blames Elijah for the child's death, presuming that his death was punishment for her sin. Elijah does not understand why God has done this, and asks God why he would so punish Elijah's hostess. Elijah then proceeds three times to breathe the breath of life back into the child, and the child revives. The widow's faith in the man of God, established by the enduring flour and oil, is strengthened by the resuscitation of her son. Again, the prophet of God acts with the power of God.

18:1-20 Elijah confronts Ahab

After three years (cf. 11:3; 17:21) of drought, the Lord directs Elijah to present himself again before Ahab; his intention is to end the drought. Three years of drought had destroyed pastureland. Ahab therefore divided up his land between himself and his vizier, Obadiah, and the two went out in search of water. Ahab was hoping to find enough grass to be able to provide a little food for his animals so that they would not have to be slaughtered. While on this mission, Obadiah, a zealous follower of the Lord, encounters Elijah.

Obadiah's first instinct on seeing Elijah is to honor him; Obadiah, when Jezebel was murdering the Lord's prophets, had hidden a hundred of them in two caves, and had provided them with food and water. Presumably by doing so he had saved their lives.

Jezebel comes to be judged so harshly, feminist scholars believe, not only because she kills the Lord's prophets but because she demonstrates blatant disregard for her subordinate status and authority at large. She exercises an autonomy and power that her society denies her.

When Elijah directs Obadiah to tell Ahab his whereabouts, Obadiah pleads for mercy. He is afraid to obey the word of the prophet. He fears that Ahab will come after Elijah, Elijah won't still be there, and Ahab, frustrated and angry, will kill Obadiah. Elijah assures Obadiah that he will be there, that he intends to meet with Ahab.

With this reassurance, Obadiah obeys the prophet. He reports to Ahab Elijah's whereabouts, and Ahab then comes to meet him. Each of the men accuses the other of being bad for Israel. Ahab brought idolatry; Elijah brought drought. Elijah instructs Ahab to bring all Israel including the prophets of Baal and the prophets of Asherah to Mount Carmel. The king obeys the prophet.

18:21-40 Elijah triumphs over the prophets of Baal

Elijah confronts the people whose loyalty has been divided between God and Baal. He asks the people to choose either the Lord or Baal (cf. Josh 24:14-15). When the people refrain from choosing, Elijah proposes a test. The people are to provide two bulls, and the Baal prophets are to choose between the bulls and then prepare a sacrifice. Elijah will take the other bull and likewise prepare it for sacrifice. Neither Elijah nor the Baal prophets will use fire. Rather, they are to pray to their respective gods; whichever god produces the fire is God. The biblical text describes in great detail how the Baal prophets proceed. Despite their prayers, however, they have no success. Elijah mocks their efforts. Then he prepares a sacrifice. Again the text is very detailed. Elijah builds in impediments to his success. He has water poured over the altar that collected in the trench that he built around the altar. Still, when he calls on God, the Lord sends fire to consume the sacrifice. The people witness the power of God and the impotence of Baal. They claim the Lord as their god. Elijah orders the prophets of Baal killed.

The text contains some of the same drama and suspense found in 1 Kings 3:16-28, where Solomon identified the real mother of the surviving baby. The people wait to see what will happen, how the test will be resolved. In this case, it is not the king but the prophet, not God's gift of wisdom but God's intervening power that resolves the conflict.

18:41-46 The drought ends

God has shown the people that the Lord and not Baal is God. In case King Ahab is not yet convinced that the Lord is God and that Elijah is his prophet, Elijah predicts to him the end of the drought. He even warns Ahab to go down from the mountain before the rain becomes an impediment to his getting down. When Elijah goes to the top of Mount Carmel and prays, he sends his servant to look toward the sea seven times. Finally, the servant sees a small cloud that signals imminent rain. The scene ends with both king and prophet departing toward Jezreel, the prophet running ahead of the king.

19:1-8 Elijah flees Jezebel

Jezebel did not witness the fire Elijah's God had sent to consume the bull, nor was she there when Elijah predicted to Ahab the rain that ended the drought. What she focuses on is that Elijah has slain the Baal prophets. She therefore determines to kill him. These verses seem transitional. Elijah is afraid and flees to Beersheba, beyond Jezebel's grasp. Yet once there, seemingly in solidarity with the other prophets Jezebel killed, Elijah asks God to take his life. His request is not granted. Rather, he remains in Judah, gathering his strength, sleeping and being fed by the Lord's messenger (*malʾak* is also translated "angel"), and then he sets out for Horeb (cf. Exod 3:1; Deut 5:2). The duration of his journey is forty days and forty nights, the "complete" time from the start of his journey to its end.

19:9-18 Elijah's encounter with God

At Horeb God speaks with Elijah, just as God spoke with Moses at Horeb (Sinai; cf. Exod 3:1-15). Elijah identifies himself: he is a faithful prophet at a time when Israel has forsaken the covenant and killed the other prophets; at present they are seeking to kill him. God tells Elijah to go out from the cave to which he has retreated, that God will pass by. What happens next are powerful displays of nature: a strong wind, an earthquake, and then fire. But Elijah does not recognize God in those forces. They, however, are followed by a "light silent sound," in which Elijah does recognize the Lord. The encounter is framed with a literary inclusion, that is, a phrase repeated at the beginning and end of a structural unit. Just as Elijah originally identified himself to God as a zealous prophet whose life was being sought by Israelites who had forsaken the covenant (v. 10), he now responds to the question of why he is there with the same answer (v. 14).

At this point Elijah is commissioned for historical tasks he is to accomplish. Just as Moses was sent to Pharaoh with the ultimate goal of delivering the Israelites from Egypt, the Lord directs Elijah to take a specific road back to the desert near Damascus. He is then to anoint Hazael as king of Aram, Jehu as king of Israel, and Elisha as his prophetic successor.

He then tells Elijah that because of the actions of Hazael, Jehu, and Elisha, almost all of the Israelites will be destroyed; only seven thousand who did not practice idolatry will be spared. While seven thousand as a percentage of all Israelites may have been a relatively small number, the number does represent a totality according to the symbolism of numbers used throughout the book.

19:19-21 Elisha is commissioned as God's prophet

The narrative dramatizes the call of Elisha, Elijah's successor. Elisha was plowing with twelve yoke of oxen when Elijah "threw his cloak over him" (cf. 1 Kgs 11:29-30). Elisha apparently understands the symbolic gesture and responds with a willingness to follow the prophet. The text does not say that Elisha kissed his father and mother, but the reader can presume that he did. He sacrificed the pair of oxen closest at hand, gave their boiled flesh to the people, and then joined Elijah.

The intent of Elisha's sacrifice is unclear. Just as David went from following the sheep to being prince over the Lord's people (2 Sam 7:8), Elisha, when called, seems to totally leave behind his role as a farmer in order to become the Lord's prophet.

20:1-12 Aram provokes Israel

Ben-hadad, king of Aram, with a well fortified army, attacks Samaria, the capital of Israel. He sends messengers to Ahab who demand from him his gold, his silver, his wives, and his sons. Ahab, under siege, capitulates to these demands. But then Ben-hadad ups the ante, promising that his servants will infiltrate the king's house and take from it everything they want or deem of value.

When the king consults the city's elders regarding how to respond to Ben-hadad's increased aggression, they advise him not to capitulate. Ahab takes their advice and reports that he will comply with Ben-hadad's first demands, but that he cannot agree to the latter. Ahab's response escalates into "a war of words;" Ben-hadad promises to pulverize Samaria and Ahab counters that bragging should follow victory, not precede it. Ahab's response to Ben-hadad makes war inevitable.

20:13-21 A prophet's prediction fulfilled: Israel defeats Aram

A prophet predicts Ahab's victory over Ben-hadad's army; Ahab should learn by this victory—if he hasn't already learned (cf. 1 Kgs 18:39, 45)—that God is the Lord. Ahab asks the prophet two questions: through whom will Ben-hadad's army be delivered up and who will attack first? The prophet answers that Ben-hadad's army will be delivered up through the retainers of the governors of the provinces and that Ahab should attack first. Ahab does as the prophet directs; he puts the retainers of the governors of the provinces at the head of his army and launches a surprise attack. Just as the prophet predicted, Ben-hadad's army is defeated. Ben-hadad himself flees. The episode presents another opportunity for Ahab to take seriously the word of a prophet.

20:22-30 Prophetic counsel continues: another Israelite victory

The prophet warns Ahab to maintain his army because the Aramean army will attack again in the spring. Meanwhile, the Aramean king's advisors support another attack. They advise Ben-hadad to muster another army as large as the one that had been defeated. They persuade the king that the Israelites' god is a god of the mountains, and like other nation's gods, is geographically limited. If they fight Israel on level ground, they will doubtless be victorious.

The Aramean army far outnumbers the Israelites; the narrator provides an image of "two small flocks of goats" doing battle with an army that "covered the countryside." Nevertheless, a man of God predicts to Ahab that the Israelites will defeat the Syrians. He explains that this will happen for the same reason that Israel was victorious against the Arameans the previous year, that is, so that Israel will know that the Lord is God (cf. 20:13). Israel's God is not just god of the mountains, but God. After seven days of encampment opposite each other, they join in battle. The Israelites kill one hundred thousand foot soldiers in one day and are decisively victorious. Again, Ben-hadad flees (cf. 20:20), this time seeking refuge in the city of Aphek.

20:31-34 The wages of war

Ben-hadad, having been defeated, is persuaded by his servants (the same servants who convinced him that he would be victorious if he attacked the Israelites on level ground?; cf. 20:23) to plead for his life. They don sackcloth and approach the king of Israel. Ahab consents. An agreement is worked out between Ben-hadad and the king of Israel by which Ahab spares Ben-hadad's life in exchange for Ben-hadad's restoration of Israelite cities that his father had captured and allowing the Israelites to set up bazaars in Damascus. Aramean aggression has failed; Aram is worse off than before they attacked Israel.

20:35-43 Israel's king deserves death

Ahab allows Ben-hadad to live. According to the rules of holy war, when the Lord fights for Israel and is victorious, to the Lord belong the spoils of war. They should be destroyed. Saul lost the kingship partly because he failed to kill King Agag (1 Sam 15:9). The narrator justifies Ahab's condemnation to death on the grounds that he allowed Ben-hadad to live. He tells two condemning parables (cf. 2 Sam 12:1-7). The first has to do with disobedience. When a man, even a prophet, disobeys the word of a prophet, he is condemned to death; a lion kills him. Another man, in contrast, obeys the word of the prophet and lives. The prophet then disguises himself and appears before Israel's king. He tells a second parable, a story about particular behavior in battle; he implies that he wants the king's judgment about the incident. Should a man who fails to do what he was charged to do on pain of death be put to death? The king renders the judgment in the affirmative, that the man who failed to guard another on threat of death should indeed die. The prophet then makes himself known to the king and assures him that he has condemned himself. The Lord will punish him and the Israelites with death because of their failure to do what they should have done, that is, put Ben-hadad to death. For their perceived benefit, but against the rules of holy war, they allowed Ben-hadad to live. As we have seen throughout 1 Kings, obedience is essential, whether that obedience is to the word of the prophet or, as in this case, to the rules of holy war.

21:1-16 The theft of Naboth's vineyard

The power imbalance between king and subject allows Ahab to expect that Naboth will hand over to him his vineyard, either in exchange for another vineyard or for monetary recompense. But Naboth understands his land as "ancestral heritage" (cf. Num 36:2-7). He therefore understands himself as incapable of acceding to the king's request even if he wants to. He therefore refuses the king's offer, which makes the king angry and depressed. How dare Naboth refuse the king? The power struggle is not just between king and subject but between God, whose law Naboth was obeying, and king. Jezebel, Ahab's wife whose god is Baal (e.g., 1 Kgs 16:31; 18:13), ridicules the king for accepting Naboth's refusal. She assures Ahab that she will get the vineyard for him. Using Ahab's authority—his name and his seal—Jezebel brings about Naboth's death, which secures his vineyard for Ahab (21:8-16). The reader is admitted to the details of Jezebel's conniving in such a way that her injustice is clearly evident.

What Abraham and Isaac had feared according to the accounts in Genesis 12, 20, and 26 (that is, that they would be killed so that a king could take their "property," in that case their wives), and what indeed had taken place with respect to Bathsheba (Uriah's death so that King David could take possession of Uriah's wife; cf. 2 Sam 11:26-27) is recounted here as having taken place with respect to Naboth. Naboth is put to death so that Ahab can take his property. In spite of the opportunities for Ahab to know the Lord (e.g., 20:13, 28), Ahab takes possession of property that could not rightfully be his. Like David's indirectly causing Uriah's death to take possession of Bathsheba, Ahab's taking possession of what is not rightfully his will have dire consequences. Whereas David, the Lord's chosen, escaped death but paid the price of his son's death (2 Sam 12:14) and the sword not departing from his house (2 Sam 12:10), Ahab will die.

Feminist scholars challenge the description of Jezebel's behavior and believe that her behavior was condemned because it defied her status as a woman, that is, her subordinate status in a patriarchal society, and also as a Sidonian in Israel. They contend that these factors were responsible for her bad reputation. After all, David eliminated Uriah when Uriah stood in the way of David's gaining the possession he craved (2 Sam 11). Feminist scholars hypothesize that a male in Jezebel's position performing the same deed might have been regarded as shrewd rather than evil.

21:17-26 Elijah denounces theft and murder

Just as Nathan condemned David (2 Sam 12:5-6), the word of the Lord comes to Elijah who confronts Ahab with the Lord's condemnation. In Jezreel where Naboth's blood was shed, Ahab's blood will also be shed. But the imagery is even more devastating: dogs licked up Naboth's blood; dogs will lick up Ahab's blood. Moreover, Elijah tells Ahab that because of his evildoing, what happened to Jeroboam (cf. 14:11) and to Baasha (cf. 16:4) will also happen to him: his line will be utterly cut off. Dogs and birds will devour them. Further, Elijah declares that dogs will devour Jezebel, also in the district of Jezreel. The reason for this condemnation is, cumulatively, Ahab and Jezebel's idolatry, which was worse than their predecessors', comparable to that of the Amorites (cf. Josh 24:15) who had preceded the Israelites in the land.

21:27-29 The punishment postponed

Ahab's response to the prophetic condemnation is to mourn—to tear his garments, to don sackcloth, and to bear a posture of remorse (cf. 2 Sam 12:16-17). Because of this attitude, the Lord postpones the execution of the full extent of Ahab's punishment until after his death. Because of David, Solomon's kingdom was not divided until his son's reign (cf. 11:34); because of Josiah's faithfulness, despite Manasseh's sins, Judah will not be destroyed during Josiah's lifetime (cf. 2 Kgs 22:19-20). Here, the full extent of Ahab's punishment that will affect his line is postponed until after his death.

22:1-5 Military tensions resurface

There was peace between Aram and Israel for three years (cf. 1 Kgs 20:30). The reader might assume that the cities Ben-hadad promised to return to Israel had been returned (22:34). Apparently, however, one city, Ramoth-gilead, had not been returned. The king of Israel asks Jehoshaphat, king of Judah, to help reclaim Ramoth-gilead. The king of Judah, represented here as faithful to God (cf. 22:43), asks the king of Israel to seek the word of the Lord.

22:6-14 Israel attacks Aram

The king of Israel consults four hundred prophets (the number that had been associated with the prophets of Asherah, cf. 18:19), all of whom support his attack. When Jehoshaphat asks if there are any other prophets to consult, the king of Israel admits that there is one other, Micaiah. However, Ahab acknowledges that Micaiah never prophesies to Ahab anything good. Nevertheless, we can presume that, because of pressure from Jehoshaphat, though the text does not say so explicitly, the king of Israel sends for Micaiah. He is informed how the other prophets have spoken and advised to proclaim a similar message. Micaiah assures the messenger that he will only proclaim the word of the Lord (cf. Num 23:26).

22:15-23 Micaiah's message

Micaiah first proclaims what the king of Israel wants to hear: victory against Ramoth-gilead. When, however, the king of Israel insists that Micaiah declare the truth, he predicts the king's death in battle. Ahab repeats to Jehoshaphat that Micaiah never proclaims any good for Ahab (cf. 22:8). Micaiah then explains how the Lord has actually willed that Ahab go into battle at Ramoth-gilead and fall there, and that, to accomplish this, one of the spirits of the Lord volunteered to put a lying spirit into the mouth of all of Ahab's prophets. That way he would heed their word and go into battle.

22:24-28 Prophetic differences

The prophet Zedekiah confronts the prophet Micaiah because Micaiah's word contradicts his own. Micaiah, confident, responds to Zedekiah that the time will come when he will see whose prophecy is true. Ahab then orders Micaiah to be imprisoned and given only small rations until Ahab returns safely from battle. Micaiah, however, has the last word, which Ahab can only have received ominously. He assures Ahab that if he returns, then the Lord has not spoken through him (cf. Deut 18:22). The interchange dramatizes, and Micaiah's prophecy reinforces, Elijah's prophecy against Ahab (1 Kgs 21:19).

22:29-38 Ahab's death

Ahab goes into the battle in disguise. To further dramatize the situation, the king of Aram has ordered his soldiers not to fight against anyone except the king of Israel. Yet, despite the precaution taken by Ahab and the limitation imposed by the king of Aram, the word of the Lord through Micaiah will be fulfilled: a stray arrow hits Ahab between the joints of his breastplate. Neither a disguise nor armor, nor even being surrounded by other soldiers can prevent the word of the Lord through Micaiah from being fulfilled. Ironically, a soldier struck him, not even knowing that he was the king. Ahab bled to death in his chariot. Ahab was brought back to Samaria to be buried, where they washed his chariot—the bottom of which was filled with the king's blood—at the pool of Samaria; dogs licked Ahab's blood. The action fulfilled the prophecy made to Ahab by Elijah (cf. 21:19). Further, though the original prophecy did not mention this detail, the chariot-washing took place at that same pool where harlots bathed. Ahab had played the harlot insofar as he had supported the worship of Baal (cf. Hos 4:10, 15).

22:39-40 Ahab's successor

The narrator informs the reader that Ahab's other achievements, including the ivory palace and the cities that he built, are documented in the chronicles of the kings of Israel. He then reports that Ahaziah, Ahab's son and Omri's grandson, succeeded Ahab as king of Israel.

22:41-51 Jehoshaphat of Judah's reign

A logical historical order would have placed the Deuteronomistic addition that introduces Jehoshaphat's reign (22:41-44) before his meeting, as already king of Judah, with Ahab. The editors' purpose for displacing the introduction may have been to emphasize the close connection between Elijah's prediction of Ahab's death (1 Kgs 21:19), and then its reinforcement by Micaiah (22:17), and its fulfillment (22:34-35).

In any event, Jehoshaphat succeeds his father Asa (cf. 15:24) as king of Judah in the fourth year of Ahab's reign in Israel. Azubah, one of Asa's wives, bore Jehoshaphat. He reigns in Jerusalem for twenty-five years, and like Asa, Jehoshaphat does "right in the Lord's sight," except that he allows the high places to remain, at which the people continue to sacrifice and burn incense. He removes the remainder of the cult prostitutes. His international efforts include making peace with the king of Israel (the prelude to the incident described above, 22:4-33), and appointing a regent in Edom. When his attempt to bring gold from Ophir is aborted because the ships he built for that purpose are wrecked, he turns down Ahaziah's offer to collaborate. The text gives no explanation for why Jehoshaphat turned down Ahaziah's offer; the reader may speculate that, because of Ahab's behavior and its punishment, Jehoshaphat does not wish to become indebted to Israel. After Jehoshaphat's death and burial, his son Jehoram succeeds him as king.

22:52-54 Ahaziah of Israel's reign

Jehoshaphat has already been reigning in Judah for seventeen years when Ahab dies and is succeeded by his son, Ahaziah (cf. 22:40). Like Jeroboam's son (cf. 15:25) and Baasha's son (cf. 16:8), Ahab's son reigns for only two years. Like Jeroboam and like Baasha (16:13) and like his own father and mother, Ahaziah worships Baal and provokes the Lord.

CONCLUSION

First Kings documents the history of Israel from the death of the first king of its united monarchy, David, through the division of the kingdom into Israel (the northern kingdom) and Judah (the southern kingdom). Only the South preserved the dynasty of David. The North was ruled by a series of unrelated kings who came to power by conspiracy and assassination, and by short-lived dynasties. Because the geographical area of Israel was considerably larger than Judah's and the economic prosperity of Israel was greater than Judah's, Israel was frequently threatened with assaults from its neighbors.

The biblical perspective from which this history is viewed clearly understands that the fate of the nation is dependent on the faithfulness of its king and implicitly, of its people, to the Lord. Idolatry and greed were the reasons for Israel's political instability, whereas David's fidelity, and the relative fidelity of his descendants, explains the political stability of Judah. Despite the prophetic activity of Elijah and Micaiah, Israel did not change its evil ways.

Nothing could be clearer than the lens through which this history is viewed; it is theological. Actions have consequences and these consequences are determined by the faithfulness or unfaithfulness of the actors to the God of Israel and the covenant. While a critical historical approach to the text can challenge the neatness of the editors' framework, and suspect more complicated political causes and effects, the editors' message to their audience is crystal clear: the monarchy stands or falls on its faithfulness to its God.

COMMENTARY: *2 KINGS*

THE KINGDOMS OF ISRAEL AND JUDAH

2 Kings 1–17

Whereas the reign of King Solomon over a united kingdom and the reign of King Ahab over Israel dominate much of the text of 1 Kings, the Second Book of Kings records the reigns of many kings of Israel and of Judah. Their accomplishments, the political struggles they endured, and the wars they waged are condensed in the biblical record. Clearly, and consistent with 1 Kings, the text's editors were intent on convincing their audience that behavior faithful to the Lord yielded good, but the toleration and/or implementation of polytheism, not surprisingly, led to disaster.

1:1-8 Ahaziah's idolatry

The period immediately following the removal or death of any ruler is often volatile. During the time of transition, before a new ruler is firmly in place, insurrections can occur. It is not surprising then that shortly after Ahab's death, the people of Moab rebel against Israel. To add to Ahaziah's vulnerability, he is hurt as the result of a fall and becomes bedridden. In response to his dilemma, Ahaziah seeks the word of Baalzebub, the god of Ekron, one of the Philistine cities; he wishes to learn if he will recover from the fall. Elijah, however, intercepts the messengers that Ahaziah sent to Baalzebub. He then sends the messengers back to Ahaziah with a message whose content Ahaziah feared but from a source that Ahaziah did not anticipate. The answer to the question of whether he will leave his bed is no; but the answer does not come from Baalzebub, the god of Ekron. The answer comes from the prophet of Israel's God, Elijah. And it comes in the form that it does because Ahaziah sought the god of Ekron as if there were no god in Israel. The first of Ahaziah's

actions that the history records assumes idolatry; its consequence is death.

1:9-18 Elijah's prophecy fulfilled

The narrative continues to dramatize Ahaziah's relationship with Elijah. Because Elijah is the prophet of God who speaks and acts with the power of God, two separate times Elijah effects the deaths of a captain and his fifty men. Each time Elijah eludes Ahaziah's efforts to capture him. Knowing from the Lord that he will be safe, Elijah heeds the plea of a third captain and agrees to accompany him and his company to meet Ahaziah. There, in Ahaziah's very presence, Elijah reiterates the prophecy he made earlier (1:6). Ahaziah will not leave his bed but will die. Ahaziah does die, leaving no heir, and so his brother Joram succeeds him.

2:1-8 Elisha follows Elijah

Elijah is about to be taken up in a whirlwind; Elisha knows it and does not want to leave Elijah's side. They travel together to Bethel. When they arrive guild prophets confirm Elijah's imminent departure. Elisha again insists on accompanying Elijah, this time to Jericho; again guild prophets confirm Elijah's imminent departure to Elisha. A third time Elisha insists on accompanying Elijah, this time to the Jordan; this time they are accompanied by fifty guild prophets. When they arrive at the Jordan Elijah uses his mantle (cf. 1 Sam 18:4) to strike the river so that the water divides and both prophets cross the river on dry ground (cf. Exod 14:16). The prophets have traversed the country, from Bethel, a symbolic site in the North (e.g., Gen 28:19) to Jericho, a symbolic site in the South (e.g., Josh 2:1), and arrive at the river the Lord had miraculously separated so that the Israelites could cross over (cf. Josh 3:13-17) into "the land the Lord had promised to give them" (e.g., Exod 12:25; 32:13).

2:9-12 Elisha receives Elijah's prophetic spirit

Elijah, knowing that he is about to be taken from Elisha, asks Elisha if there is anything he can do for him. Elisha requests a double portion of Elijah's spirit. Elijah is not certain that Elisha's wish will be granted. However, *if* Elisha witnesses Elijah's departure it will be. As the two of them walk on, a flaming chariot with flaming horses comes between the two men and sweeps up Elijah. Elisha witnesses Elijah's departure. Elisha tears his own garment in two, perhaps as a symbol of the double spirit. Torn clothing has symbolic significance (e.g., 1 Kgs 11:29-32).

2:13-15 Elisha receives Elijah's mantle

Elisha retrieves Elijah's mantle, which fell off of him when he was swept away, and walks back to the bank of the Jordan. He strikes the water with Elijah's mantle (cf. 2:8), the water parts, and he crosses the river. The prophets from Jericho confirm that Elisha has indeed received Elijah's spirit.

2:16-18 Elijah's departure confirmed

Elisha reluctantly consents to have fifty men search for Elijah for three days; as Elisha predicts, they are unable to find him. Elisha is not surprised at their lack of success. After all, he saw Elijah's departure, and he himself has now done marvelous things. To the prophet of God marvelous things are possible.

2:19-22 Elisha's prophetic power purifies water

Elisha responds to the complaint of the inhabitants of the city that their water is bitter and their land unfruitful by purifying the spring, and declaring that in the future it will not be a source of death or miscarriage. The narrator confirms that the water has remained pure according to Elisha's word. What the narrator is really confirming is Elisha's ability to act with the power of God, that is, to purify the water. Implied also is an affirmation of the prophet's ability to speak a word that

is effective, to promise a future in which the water is pure. Because of the prophet's act, the prophet's word can be trusted: the prophet acts and speaks with the power of God.

2:23-25 Elisha's prophetic curse

Elisha, en route to Bethel, is made fun of by some small boys because of his bald head (cf. Lev 13:40-41). He curses the boys. As a result two she-bears come out of the woods and tear to pieces forty-two of the children. The prophet of God possesses the power of God; he is not to be treated with contempt! Again, Deuteronomistic theology is expressed. Misbehavior has consequences. The prophet who proclaims the words and deeds of God is, like God (cf. Exod 20:7), to be taken seriously. Not surprisingly, failure to do so results in death.

A passage that resonates with 2 Kings 2:23-25 occurs in Mark 11:12-14. In the Markan passage, Jesus is hungry. When he sees leaves on a distant fig tree he approaches it in hopes of finding something to eat. Unfortunately, there are only leaves on the tree, no figs. The text makes a point of saying that it was not the season for the tree to bear fruit. Nevertheless, Jesus curses the tree, that it might never again produce fruit. While Jesus' action seems totally out of character, it points to the severity of not taking seriously God's prophet—even if your behavior is not deliberate.

From Bethel Elisha traveled to Mount Carmel and then to Samaria.

3:1-8 Joram of Israel's reign

Ahab's son Joram, Ahaziah's brother, reigns in Israel for twelve years. He is evil but not as evil as his parents; he removes the pillar of Baal, yet he does evil as Jeroboam did. During Ahab's reign, Mesha, king of Moab, pays Ahab what is here depicted as an exorbitant amount in tribute: a hundred thousand (that is, ten times ten times ten times ten times ten) sheep and the wool of a hundred thousand rams. Keeping peace with Ahab proves costly. After Ahab's death, therefore, Moab takes the opportunity to rebel (cf. 1:1), refusing to pay the tribute Ahab had extracted. Jehoshaphat, king of Judah, unites with Joram to fight Moab (cf. 1 Kgs 22:4). This text contrasts with 1 Kings 22:5 because here there is no initial effort to consult a prophet to determine the battle's outcome, and with 1 Kings 22:49 where Jehoshaphat is unwilling to collaborate with Joram's brother.

3:9-19 Elisha prophesies Moab's destruction

The king of Israel, allied with the kings of Judah and Edom, sets out toward Moab. Seven days into their journey, they have exhausted the water supply; neither the army nor their animals have water. The king of Israel laments that the three kings will be delivered into the hands of the king of Moab. The king of Judah suggests that they seek a prophet from whom to inquire the word of the Lord (cf. 1 Kgs 22:5, 7). Elisha is found. When the kings approach Elisha, he clearly distinguishes between the king of Israel and the king of Judah. Associating the king of Israel with the Baal prophets and the idolatry of Ahab and Jezebel, he wishes to reject Joram. Joram, however, affirms his belief that it was the Lord of Israel who brought the three kings together to deliver them to the king of Moab. Implied is Joram's belief that only Israel's Lord can address their need. Elisha, disgusted with Joram, assures him that if it were not for the king of Judah, he would ignore them and their request. However, he tells them to get him a minstrel.

The minstrel's music induces the power of the Lord to come upon Elisha, who then declares the word of the Lord. The men are to provide catch basins. Though the men will see no wind or rain, the wadi will become filled with water sufficient for themselves, their livestock, and their pack animals. In addition, Elisha prophesies, the Lord will deliver Moab over to them. Their destruction of Moab will be total; they will conquer all their fortified cities, fell their fruit trees (source of food), stop up all their springs (source of water), and ruin every fertile field with stones (agriculture). The influence of the faithful King Jehoshaphat is greater than the influence of the unfaithful King Joram and secures the blessing of the Lord, the victory over Moab.

3:20-27 Elisha's prophesy fulfilled

Just as Elisha predicted, water comes. That very water tricks the Moabites. When the sun shines on it, the water looks from a distance like blood (cf. Exod 7:17). The Moabites conclude that the three kings fought with each other and shed each other's blood. So they proceed to the Israel-ites' camp to collect spoils. However, when they arrive the Israelites attack them. They flee, only to be pursued by the Israelites. The Israelites proceed to destroy their cities, throw stones on their fertile fields, clog up their springs, and fell their trees. In short, the Israelites behave as Elisha foretold with the consequences for Moab that Elisha foretold. When only one city remains to the Moabites, the king of Moab attempts to get military aid from the king of Edom, but is unsuccessful. Desperate, he offers his own son as a holocaust. The Israelites give up their siege of Moab—victory is established—and return home. The prophet's word is fulfilled.

4:1-7 Elisha empowers a widow

The poverty of a guild prophet's widow is about to cause her to lose her children into slavery. Elisha responds to her request for help by seeing to it that her one resource, a jug of oil, produces enough oil to pay the woman's creditor and to provide for the maintenance of herself and her children. The incident reinforces what the people should know: the prophet possesses the power of God and can act on their behalf. In this case, the prophet acts on behalf of the powerless, that is, the poor widow.

4:8-37 Elisha twice gives a son to his mother

Elisha acts not only on behalf of the powerless, but also on behalf of the relatively powerless, in this case, a woman. Though married and wealthy, she is nevertheless dependent on her husband in the society's social structure. Elisha rewards this woman who provided lavishly for him and for his servant by promising her that she will bear a son. At a time when there was no belief in life after death, children very explicitly represented a person's future. In addition, they represented a woman's major contribution to the society. Elisha promised and his word came to pass.

But the narrative is complicated first by a threat to the child's life and then by his death. When her son is old enough to go out to his father among the reapers, he becomes sick and dies soon after. His mother sets out to find Elisha, who knows nothing of the young boy's death. She begs him to return with her, which he does. Elisha brings the boy back to life. Here again, the power of the Lord's prophet—the one who speaks and acts on behalf of the Lord—is confirmed. The two events also parallel Elijah's experience with the widow of Zarephath (1 Kgs 17). Elisha is clearly Elijah's successor. Elisha sent his servant to lay his staff on the boy; Gehazi had gone ahead and tried to bring the boy back to life but had failed. Obviously Gehazi is not Elisha!

4:38-44 Elisha neutralizes poison and multiplies bread

Elisha made bitter water pure (2:19-22) and increased the amount of oil in a jug (4:1-7); now, during a famine when food of any kind is scarce, he changes stew that has been poisoned with wild gourds into edible stew. When offered twenty barley loaves and fresh grain, he orders it to be given to the people; contrary to logic and expectation, it not only feeds a hundred men (symbolic of a totality), but there is even some left over. Acting with the power of God, God's prophet provides food during famine, thus alleviating the people's suffering.

5:1-8 A slave girl seeks Elisha's help

Naaman, the commander of the Aramean army, was a leper. The Israelite servant girl of Naaman's wife, no doubt part of the booty of war, assures her mistress that if only Naaman will seek out "the prophet in Samaria," he will be cured. Naaman, with a letter from the king of Aram, goes to the king of Israel, asking him to cure Naaman of leprosy. Note the hierarchical transference: from servant girl to mistress to master to king to king. The prophet, the one whom the servant girl recommended, is passed over. The king of Israel tears his garments (cf. 1 Kgs 21:27) when he reads the letter, knowing that he lacks power over life and death. He rightly attributes such power to a god. Elisha, however, hears of the incident and asks for the man to come to him.

5:9-14 Elisha cures an Aramean's leprosy

Elisha instructs Naaman to wash in the Jordan seven times. Naaman was expecting hands-on treatment and goes away angry. Again, the assumption is hierarchical; he assumed his importance. Only when he is successfully persuaded by his servant (note the reversal of hierarchy) does Naaman finally relent and wash in the Jordan; he

is cleansed. He expected the extraordinary; the ordinary was sufficient to his need. What he needed was to believe the word of the prophet!

5:15-27 Naaman's conversion to the Lord

Naaman professes faith in the God of Israel and offers Elisha a gift that Elisha refuses. Naaman is so convinced of the God of Israel that he asks for two mule-loads of earth so that he can henceforth offer holocausts to the Lord. He asks that the Lord will forgive him when he goes with his master to worship at the temple of Rimmon. Elisha sends him off in peace. Elisha seems unconcerned that Naaman is an Aramean. He seems uninterested in any payment, and he even seems unconcerned that Naaman will accompany his master to a foreign god's temple. Rather, what seems to be important to Elisha is the fact that Naaman has been converted to Israel's God.

Gehazi, Elisha's servant, wants some of the "gift" Elisha refused. (The episode recalls Aachan in Josh 7 who wants some of the Lord's booty.) Gehazi therefore goes after Naaman, unbeknownst to Elisha; he lies to him, saying something about Elisha wanting silver and festal garments for two visitors; he is thereby able to retrieve some of the gift from Naaman. On his return Gehazi lies again, this time to Elisha, about where he has been. Elisha knows what happened and condemns Gehazi and his descendants to the leprosy from which Naaman was cured (cf. the comment on 2 Kgs 4:31-37). The episode reinforces the power of God's prophet who knows the truth despite Gehazi's lie. Elisha is able not only to cure, as with Naaman's leprosy, but to curse, as with Gehazi and his descendants' leprosy.

6:1-7 Elisha recovers an ax

The guild prophets come to the conclusion that there is not enough room for all of them and Elisha to live together (cf. Gen 13:9). They therefore determine to go to the Jordan where they can build their own house. Elisha agrees to accompany them there.

While felling trees to build the guild prophets' house, a borrowed iron ax head falls into the water. The prophet who lost it asks for Elisha's help. Despite impossible odds, Elisha locates the ax blade in the water and retrieves it for the prophet. Lest anyone have doubt, Elisha is the prophets' prophet.

6:8-12 Elisha warns the king of Israel of Aram's attack

The prophet Elisha thwarts the efforts of the king of Aram to launch successful attacks against Israel. Every time the king of Aram determines a specific location from which to launch an attack, Elisha warns the king of Israel of the place of the attack. Elisha not only predicts a future event, he knows of events before they occur (cf. 5:26). The king uses Elisha's knowledge to avoid the place, and to alert his men of the planned ambushes by the Arameans so that they can take the necessary precautions.

The king of Aram logically concludes that there must be an informer among his men. When confronted, his men respond that it is the prophet Elisha who is responsible for the king of Israel's learning about their planned attacks; they know that he knows what is spoken in secret. The king of Aram then seeks to capture Elisha, thereby acknowledging the power of Israel's prophet.

6:13-23 Elisha opens and closes eyes

Strong Aramean forces with chariots and horses come to Dothan to capture Elisha. Elisha's servant is afraid when he sees that the Arameans have surrounded the city, and asks the prophet what they should do. Elisha comforts the servant, telling him not to be afraid and asking the Lord to open his servant's eyes. The Lord grants Elisha's request so that his servant sees the mountainside filled with horses and fiery chariots around Elisha. He too has an army.

When the Arameans arrived to capture Elisha, he prays again to the Lord. This time he requests closed eyes, that the Arameans be struck blind. The Lord grants Elisha's request. Ironically, Elisha then offers to take them to the man they seek to capture. They permit him to lead them, and he brings them to Samaria. Once they are inside the capital of Samaria, Elisha asks God to open their eyes. Again God grants Elisha's request. About the time they realize where they are the king of Israel asks Elisha if he should kill them. Elisha does not wish them killed, but rather he wants them fed and then returned to their own country. Elisha's intent is accomplished. He used the power of God to quell the fear of his servant and, by putting the Arameans in harm's way and then delivering them (cf. 1 Sam 24:6; 26:21-23), he teaches the Arameans the power of Israel's God. The king of Aram will know better than to ever again try to capture or otherwise best the Lord's prophet. The narrator's comment is almost superfluous; there were no more Aramean raids on Israel.

6:24–7:2 Aram's siege of Samaria

The text gives no indication of how much time has passed before, despite the content of the preceding verses, Ben-hadad of Aram and his whole army lay siege to Samaria and provoke a famine in the city. The famine is so severe that mothers eat their children. Although the king wants to kill Elisha, he recognizes that the Lord has brought about the suffering that he and the people are experiencing because of the famine. When he asks Elisha why he should continue to trust in the Lord, the Lord assures him through Elisha that by the very next day plenty of food will be available to them. Because the king's adjutant is skeptical of Elisha's prediction, not trusting in the Lord, Elisha tells him that though he will see the food, he himself will not eat it. Obviously the prophet of God has the power of God to effect what he promises. However, those to whom he speaks must trust his word if they are to benefit. Faithfulness to God and to the word of God through the prophet are essential and will result in blessing—in this case, food. Lack of trust will result in being cursed.

7:3-16 Lepers aid the military

The narrative records an episode in which those lowest on the power scale, rejected because of their leprosy, become Israel's saviors. Four lepers are faced with a dilemma. Currently situated at the city gate, if they remain there, suffering as they are from the famine, they will die. But what are their alternatives? If they go into the city, because of the famine, they will die there. They therefore decide to desert to the Aramean camp, where they might be allowed to live. That alternative is no worse than the others, and may, in fact, be a better one.

When they reach the Aramean camp, they are surprised to find it deserted. The text reports that the Lord caused the Arameans to hear the sound of chariots and horses as if a large army was approaching. Because they concluded that the Israelites were attacking with help from mercenaries, the Arameans fled. The deserted camp enables the lepers to enter the tents of the Arameans and pillage. The lepers then go back to inform the Israelite palace of their good fortune. At first the king distrusts that the Arameans have abandoned their camp; he believes that they have deserted the camp as a trick. One of the king's servants suggests that they have nothing to lose if they go to investigate. Scouts are dispatched and when they return the people go to the Aramean camp and plunder it, taking for themselves the food that is within it.

The narrator presents here another story of role reversal. The lowest people in Israel's social structure, the lepers, are the ones who save the people from starvation. Their logic and their courage save the day. But even the king's servants are presented as being wiser than the king. When he hesitates, despite the obvious crisis, they suggest a plan. Their recommendation minimizes risk and has the potential to produce good effect. Because of the judgment and courage of those not in authority, the otherwise deadly famine is ameliorated.

7:17-20 Elisha's word fulfilled

Indeed then, plenty of food becomes available to the Israelites just as Elisha promised (7:1). However, the king's adjutant, who had been skeptical of Elisha's prediction, who had not trusted the word of the Lord, is not able to eat the food. He is trampled to death. The prediction of the prophet that he would see the food but not eat it was thus fulfilled (7:2). The prophet possesses the power of God to effect the word of God. Failure to believe in the word of God spoken through the prophet—no matter how fantastic that word may seem—can have no good outcome.

8:1-6 Elisha warns of famine

Elisha predicts to "the woman whose son he had restored to life" (notice that she is not named but is identified as the recipient of Elisha's marvelous deed on her behalf) that there will be a seven-year famine in the land, and that she and her household should depart to escape it. She

obeys Elisha and moves to the land of the Philistines. After seven years she returns to Israel and seeks to reclaim her house and property. When the king learns that Elisha had raised the woman's son from the dead, he restores her house, her field, and all that her field produced during her seven-year absence. King Joram saw fulfilled the victory of Israel over Moab that Elisha had prophesied (3:18). Apparently he learned to recognize Elisha as a prophet of God who spoke and acted with the power of God. Because of the woman's previous history with Elisha, the king accedes to her request.

8:7-15 Elisha predicts Ben-hadad's death

When Ben-hadad, king of Aram (cf. 6:24) becomes ill, he sends his servant Hazael to inquire of Elisha whether or not he will recover. Elisha instructs Hazael to tell Ben-hadad that he will recover, but Elisha tells Hazael that that is not true, that Ben-hadad will die. After that prediction, Elisha goes on to tell Hazael that Hazael will wreak terrible devastation on the Israelite people. At first Hazael doesn't understand how this can be so; he is only a servant. Elisha, however, explains to Hazael that he will become king of Aram (cf. 1 Kgs 19:15 where this task of anointing Hazael king of Aram is given to Elijah, suggesting that the roles of the two prophets have been conflated). When Hazael returns home, he does as Elisha has instructed him. He tells Ben-hadad that he will recover; however, the very next day Hazael kills Ben-hadad and usurps the throne. Whereas in 1 Kings 22, Micaiah at first predicted a false prophecy to Ahab and then a true prophecy, here Elisha predicts a false prophecy regarding Ben-hadad and then predicts a true prophecy regarding Hazael.

8:16-24 Joram of Judah's reign

Jehoshaphat's son Joram succeeds him as king of Judah. He lives for forty years, eight of which are spent as king. The Deuteronomistic editors determine that he was an evil king, comparing him to the kings of Israel and explaining that his wife was the daughter of Israel's evil king Ahab. Not surprisingly, punishment follows. Both the Edomites and the people of Libnah revolt against Judah. Nevertheless, "for the sake of David," God does not destroy Judah.

8:25-29 Ahaziah of Judah's reign

Joram's son Ahaziah succeeds him as king, but reigns for only one year. His mother is Athaliah, the granddaughter of Omri, the former king of Israel. The text suggests that Ahaziah's parents had been joined in a political alliance (cf. 1 Kgs 3:1). The South (i.e., Joram) had been married to the North (i.e., Athaliah).

Ahaziah too, like the kings of Israel and like his father, does evil. Ahaziah and the king of Israel, Joram, become allies against Aram. When Joram is wounded at Ramoth-gilead, he retreats to Jezreel. Ahaziah also goes to Jezreel, which was a place of refuge for Ahab also (1 Kgs 18:45).

9:1-10 Jehu's anointing

While the Israelite forces are still at Ramoth-gilead, Elisha sends one of the guild prophets there to single out Jehu and to anoint him as the future king of Israel. The prophet obeys Elisha, goes to Ramoth-gilead, singles out Jehu from among the commanders of the army, and, separating him from his companions, pours oil on his head, thus anointing him king over the Lord's people, Israel. (In 1 Kgs 19:16 the task of anointing Jehu is given to Elijah, suggesting that the roles of the two prophets have become conflated.) The prophet declares to Jehu that through him the Lord will destroy Joram and his entire line, thereby avenging the blood of the prophets and God's other servants that Jezebel shed. Just as the Lord did to Jeroboam's house (cf. 1 Kgs 14:11) and Baasha's house (cf. 1 Kgs 16:4), so will he do to Ahab's house. The prophet predicts that dogs will devour Jezebel in the confines of Jezreel, to the extent that no one will be able to bury her. In 1 Kings 21:23 the Lord through Elijah uttered a similar prophecy regarding Jezebel, another indication that the sources of some prophetic predictions have become blurred.

9:11-13 Jehu's circumspection and conspiracy

The narrator heightens dramatic tension. When Jehu returns to his companions, at first he declines to answer their questions about the content of the prophet's message. Then, since their urging persists, he informs them first of what the prophet said; then he tells them that the prophet anointed him. They respond by spreading their

garments (cf. Matt 21:8; Mark 11:8; Luke 19:36) before him and declaring him king.

Jehu mounts a conspiracy against Joram; Joram has been fighting Hazael, king of Aram, but has retreated to Jezreel in order to recover from wounds the Arameans inflicted on him. The narrator reports that Ahaziah, the king of Judah, is with him (cf. 8:25-29).

9:14-20 Jehu's conspiracy

The verses heighten the suspense by slowing down the action. Jehu is to confront Joram but their encounter is delayed by narrative detail. For Jehu to be able to successfully wrest the kingship from Joram, it is imperative that no one leak the news of his intent, so Jehu first secures the loyalty of his men. He then proceeds to Jezreel. When Jehu approaches the city, the watchmen see at a distance both him and the chariots that accompany him, and they report what they see to Joram. Joram, unsuspecting, sends a driver to meet Jehu and to inquire if everything is all right. When the driver meets Jehu, Jehu obliquely informs him of his conspiratorial intent and the driver joins with Jehu. The watchman reports to Joram that the driver reached Jehu but that he is not returning. The same behavior is repeated a second time. A second driver is sent out from Jezreel but does not return. Finally, with the watchman reporting that the man approaching is probably Jehu, Joram, still suspecting nothing, decides to go himself to meet him.

9:21-26 Joram's assassination

Joram goes in his chariot. The narrator informs us, almost parenthetically, that King Ahaziah of Judah went out also in his own chariot. They meet up with Jehu near Naboth's vineyard. Joram, apparently still unsuspecting, asks for a third time, this time to Jehu himself, what the other drivers asked, whether everything is all right. Jehu's response is an explicit condemnation of Joram. How could things be all right when Joram has allowed the evils of Jezebel to continue? Joram frantically warns Ahaziah of Jehu's treason, but is himself unsuccessful in his attempt to flee. Jehu puts an arrow through Joram's heart. Afterward, Jehu bids his adjutant to throw Joram's body onto Naboth's vineyard in order that the word of the prophet might be fulfilled, that is, in order that Naboth's blood might be avenged on the very field where it was shed (cf. 1 Kgs 21:19). Evil behavior can only result in evil consequences.

9:27-29 Ahaziah's death

Finally, Jehu sees to it that Ahaziah, who was allied with Joram (cf. 9:16, 21) and who fled, is also killed. They wound him as he flees, so that he is able to get only as far as Meggido before he dies. Ahaziah, a descendant of David, is then brought to Jerusalem and buried with his ancestors in the City of David.

9:30-37 Jezebel's death

When Jehu arrives finally in Jezreel, after both Joram and Ahaziah are dead, Jezebel tries to curry his favor, or at least to make an impression. She does what she can to make herself beautiful and then greets Jehu with a salutation that is intentionally assertive and seductive, addressing him as Zimri, the Israelite servant who also assassinated a king (cf. 1 Kgs 16:10). However, Jehu is not impressed; in fact, he makes short shrift of her. In response to his request, two or three eunuchs throw Jezebel out her window so that as she falls to the ground, her blood spurts "against the wall and against the horses," providing a rather gruesome sight.

Jehu then proceeds to get something to eat and drink. Only after he has done so does he turn his attention back to Jezebel. He suggests that, because she was a king's daughter—no mention is made of her being Ahab's wife!—she should be buried. However, when they go out to retrieve her body for burial, there isn't much left of it. Jehu's response to this news is to remark that the word of the Lord through Elijah the prophet concerning Jezebel's death has been fulfilled (cf. 1 Kgs 21:23). Again, according to Deuteronomistic theology, one could only expect that Jezebel's evil behavior would result in evil consequences.

10:1-11 Jehu destroys Ahab's house

The narrator details the defeat of the house of Ahab. He had seventy (seven times ten) descendants, in Samaria. Jehu sends two letters to the guardians of Ahab's descendants and the city's elders and leaders. The first letter suggests that these prominent men should choose the one among the seventy of Ahab's descendants that they consider the best and fittest to be king, and that they should "fight for" their master's house.

The men, intimidated by Jehu and his military victories, respond to Jehu by pledging to him their obedience and loyalty. Jehu then writes back a second letter based on their response to his first, telling the men that they should count the heads of Ahab's descendants and meet him in Jezreel with them the following day. Thereupon they slay the seventy, and send their heads the following morning to Jehu in Jezreel (cf. 1 Kgs 21:21). Then Jehu, in a gesture reminiscent of David's slaughter of the Amalekite who had slain Saul (cf. 2 Sam 1:1-16), uses this opportunity to denounce to the people those who killed Ahab's descendants and to justify their slaughter. Jehu thus indirectly sees to the removal of Ahab's descendants from Israel in fulfillment of Elijah's prophecy, and creates circumstances that legitimate the elimination of all those who had supported Ahab's descendants. The end of Ahab's dynasty has almost arrived, just as Elijah predicted (l Kgs 21:20-24).

10:12-14 Jehu eliminates Ahaziah's kinsmen

On the way to Samaria, Jehu encounters "kinsmen" of Ahaziah, king of Judah (cf. 2 Kgs 9:27-29). They are traveling to visit the queen mother, that is, Athaliah, who is a daughter of Omri and a worshiper of idols. Jehu apparently understands this declaration by Ahaziah's kinsmen as a clear admission of their own unfaithfulness to the Lord, and uses the opportunity to eliminate them. Jehu systematically destroys any potential royal opposition to his reign, potential conspirators, and even any potential southern opposition.

10:15-17 Jehu destroys the remainder of Ahab's family in Samaria

Also en route to Samaria, but in contrast to his meeting with the kinsmen of Ahaziah, Jehu meets Jehonadab, son of Rechab. Jehonadab pledges loyalty to Jehu and accompanies him to Samaria. There, Jehu finishes the slaughter of those who remain of Ahab's line, thus fulfilling Elijah's prophecy (1 Kgs 21:21-22). The narrator clearly supports Jehu's deeds, asserting them to be acts that fulfilled the will of God as proclaimed through the prophet Elijah (1 Kgs 19:17).

10:18-27 Jehu destroys Baal's temple

The narrative dramatizes how Jehu tricked all the followers of Baal in order to lead them to their deaths. He gathers all of Baal's followers in Baal's temple for a sacrifice. He directs all of Baal's followers, without exception, to be there. They consent. When they are all present inside the temple it is filled to capacity. Jehu then continues the deceit. He brings out festal garments for the worshipers and tells them to make sure that none of the followers of the Lord is with them inside the temple. They proceed with the offering of sacrifices and holocausts to Baal. Meantime Jehu stations men outside and warns them not to let anyone leave the temple for fear of their own lives.

After Jehu himself offers the holocaust, he orders the guards and officers to go into the temple and slay those inside. The guards and officers obey, and then they go into the inner shrine of Baal's temple, remove the stele (an upright slab with inscriptions that would have been the central memorial of the shrine), and burn the shrine. They smash the stele, destroy the building, and convert it into a latrine. While Jehu's deception of the people is distantly reminiscent of Jacob's deception of Isaac (cf. Gen 27), it enables him to fulfill the word of the Lord, just as Jacob's had (1 Kgs 19:17; cf. Gen 25:23b).

10:28-33 Jehu's limitations

Because Jehu eliminated Baal worship in Israel, he is rewarded with a dynasty of four generations' duration; faithfulness leads to blessing. However, Jehu, like other kings of Israel, does not receive the judgment of the Deuteronomistic editors of being "good in the eyes of the Lord." In fact, like all the other kings of Israel, he is compared to Jeroboam; specifically, he allows the golden calves at Bethel and Dan (cf. 1 Kgs 12:28) to remain. Because he is "not careful to walk in the law of the Lord," he is punished. Hazael of Aram (cf. 1 Kgs 19:25) defeats territories of the northern kingdom east of the Jordan River.

10:34-36 Jehu's death

Jehu's death notice includes that he reigned over Israel for twenty-eight years, that he was buried with his ancestors in Samaria, and that more information about him and his reign can be found in the chronicles of the kings of Israel. Though these chronicles are no longer extant, the reader can presume by this allusion to them that a fuller historical record of the kings' accomplish-ments had been produced. It is likely that the chronicles of the kings celebrated their achievements in glowing terms. To what extent these accounts were merely royal propaganda or to what extent they represented a reasonably accurate record of the kings' activities we will never know. What we do know is that the editors did not feel compelled to share more, perhaps because of the Deuteronomistic judgment of Jehu's unfaithfulness. In any case, Jehu's son Jehoahaz succeeds him as king.

11:1-3 Athaliah's reign in Judah

Athaliah is the wife of Joram, former king of Judah, and the mother of Ahaziah, former king of Judah; she is also the granddaughter of Omri, king of Israel (cf. 2 Kgs 8:25-26). All three kings have been judged as being unfaithful to the Lord (2 Kgs 8:18, 27; 1 Kgs 16:25). Athaliah uses Ahaziah's death as an opportunity to seize the throne of Judah. She tries to kill off the entire royal family and would have succeeded except that Jehosheba, a sister of Ahaziah—perhaps Jehosheba and Ahaziah had different mothers—took Joash, Ahaziah's son, and fled. During the six years that Athaliah rules Judah, the royal line in the person of Joash is kept alive, hidden in the temple.

While Athaliah is considered the most evil queen of Judah, a usurper of the throne who tried to destroy the Davidic dynasty so that she could reign, feminist scholars believe that her condemnation as evil is really about her rejection of both her subordinate status in a patriarchal society and her inferior status as a foreigner in Judah (2 Kgs 8:26). Assassination of contenders to the throne was not uncommon in the ancient Near East. Solomon had even killed his brother Adonijah (1 Kgs 2:24-25). Yet that a woman should dare to seek the throne was unthinkable and had to be forcefully condemned. She had to be demonized. The denunciation that Jezebel suffered in Israel (e.g., 2 Kgs 9:10) finds its counterpart in the judgment against Athaliah.

11:4-8 Joash revealed

In the seventh year, Jehoiada, the high priest, summons the Carians and the guards into the temple, makes them swear loyalty, and then shows them Ahaziah's son, the Davidic heir. Seven years represents the passage of a sufficient period of time for Joash to have grown from infancy when he needed a nurse (11:2) to childhood. Jehoiada has devised a plan that he orders the Carians and guards to carry out; one third of the men, those who would ordinarily come on duty on the Sabbath, he directs to guard the palace. The other two-thirds of the men he directs to surround the temple. In other words, the entire contingent of mercenaries and guards is to be on duty and focused on the king's protection. They are instructed to kill anyone who tries to approach.

11:9-16 Joash anointed king

The narrative detail contributes to a heightened tension. Who will try to approach? Will Athaliah's supporters, presuming that she has some? Will Athaliah herself? Will not the people rejoice that the Davidic line has been preserved? What will happen?

All the captains do as Jehoiada directs. He equips them with David's weapons that were in the temple. Then, with the armed guard surrounding the area, Jehoiada brings out Joash and places the crown on his head and the other royal insignia on him. The men proclaim Joash king and anoint him.

When Athaliah hears the commotion, she comes to the temple and sees Joash. Only when she has fully taken in the scene—the king standing by the pillar, surrounded by captains and trumpeters, all the people rejoicing and blowing trumpets—does she tear her garments (cf. 5:7; 6:30) and cry treason (cf. 9:23). Despite her protest, she and any who would support her rule are brought out of the temple (cf. 1 Kgs 1:49-51) and slain.

11:17-20 Jehoiada's covenant renewal

The priest then makes two covenants, one between the Lord and the king and people, recommitting the people to faithfulness to the Lord as their God; the other, between the king and the people, recommitting the people to faithfulness to David's heir. The destruction of Baal's temple and the slaughter of Baal's priest follow soon after the people's recommitment to the Lord.

The final scene depicts the crowned King Joash being led triumphantly from the temple to the king's palace where he takes his seat on the throne of the kings amid his people's rejoicing. The city can then return to quiet. The verdict is still out on the faithfulness of Joash but certainly, within the theology of the Deuteronomistic historians, the

evil Queen Athaliah has suffered the consequences of her wrongdoing.

12:1-9 Joash of Judah's reign

Joash was seven years old when he became king, beginning his reign in the seventh year of the reign of Jehu, king of Israel. He reigns for forty years (all symbolic numbers we've seen many times in the text). Ahaziah's wife, Zibiah, was his mother. Joash's behavior is pleasing to the Lord throughout his lifetime; the priest who anointed him king guides him. The only shortcoming of his reign noted by the Deuteronomistic editors is that he, like Asa (cf. 1 Kgs 15:11) and Jehoshaphat (cf. 1 Kgs 22:43-44) before him, allows the high places to remain.

Zibiah is mentioned only here and in the parallel account in 2 Chronicles 24:1. No doubt she would not have been referred to by name except that she is the mother of a king. The hierarchical structures of ancient Israel were not only patriarchal but also social and political.

12:10-17 Temple repairs

The narrator details how Joash sought to provide for the priests and for the upkeep of the temple. Originally he allowed all the money of the temple offerings to be given to the priests on the condition that they would be responsible for repairing the temple whenever it needed repair. However, after the passage of twenty-three years without any repairs being made to the temple, the king revised his provision. The priests were to be allotted the funds from guilt-offerings and sin-offerings; all the other money was to be set aside for temple repair. The reader might conclude from this detail that the priests had put their own financial gain or material well-being over the well-being of the Lord's house, but the Deuteronomistic editors do not explicitly condemn their behavior.

The text may be similar to 1 Kings 5:13, where the manner in which Solomon made provisions for the building of the temple is not condemned but later on it becomes clear that it at least indirectly contributed to the division of the kingdom (cf. 1 Kgs 12:4).

12:18-22 Joash buys off Aram

The aggression of Hazael of Aram is reported in his successful takeover of the Philistine city,

Gath. When Hazael of Aram advances to attack Jerusalem, however, he is deterred by King Joash who repels the attack by paying him a very generous and costly tribute.

It would seem here, as elsewhere in 2 Kings (i.e., 18:3, 13; 21:1, 16), that Deuteronomistic editing does not conform proportionally to Deuteronomistic theology. While Joash is judged to be better than some kings of Judah (e.g., Manasseh), he does not die a natural death. Rather, more in keeping with the final outcomes of many of the kings of Israel, Joash is assassinated. His own servants kill him. One might stretch to say that from the Deuteronomistic editors' perspective, Joash's diminished fidelity to the Lord results in diminished blessing, but the curse of an unnatural death was usually reserved for greater infidelity than his. Still, Joash is buried with his ancestors and his son, Amaziah, succeeds him as king.

13:1-9 Jehoahaz of Israel's reign

Jehu's son Jehoahaz succeeds him as king (cf. 10:35) and reigns for seventeen years. Like Jeroboam, he does evil in the Lord's sight. Not surprisingly therefore, the Deuteronomistic editors highlight the fact that during his reign Israel is severely and for a long time oppressed by Aram. Only when they entreat the Lord does God send a savior to deliver them (cf. Judg 3:15; 6:7; 10:10). Yet they persist in their unfaithfulness to the Lord. The Deuteronomistic editors emphasize that the military force of Israel has been greatly reduced, clearly a punishment for their infidelity. Jehoahaz is succeeded by his son Joash.

13:10-25 Joash of Israel's reign

The Deuteronomistic editors pass judgment on the reign of Joash. The king does evil in the sight of the Lord, and persists in the sins of Jeroboam. Verses 12 and 13 are probably misplaced. There is a very brief reference to Joash's valiant fight against Amaziah, king of Judah (cf. 14:1), and the editorial comment that more about his reign can be found in the book of the chronicles of the kings of Israel. With no details regarding anything that transpired during his reign, the text then records his death and his burial in Samaria with the other kings of Israel.

After the comment regarding his death and burial, an incident is described in which Joash has an opportunity to finally defeat Aram. Joash, however, comes up short. Shortly before Elisha's death Joash visited him. He received from the prophet an opportunity finally to defeat Aram, but Joash falls short of the prophet's directive. He shoots arrows to the ground three times when he might better have shot more arrows. Elisha gave the good news that he would be victorious against Aram three times, but like the arrows that were insufficient in number, Joash's efforts would fall short of the effort needed to totally defeat Aram. Deuteronomistic editing presents Joash's evildoing and his ultimately unsuccessful campaign against Aram. Still, Hazael does not totally defeat Israel, but rather, in fulfillment of the prophet Elisha's word, after Hazael's death when his son Ben-hadad has succeeded him, Joash is able to defeat Aram three times and recover some Israelite towns.

The text asserts that Israel is protected from destruction because of the Lord's covenant with Abraham, Isaac, and Jacob. Stepping out of the expected Deuteronomistic theology, Israel is spared not because of what it does but because of who it is. It is not faithfulness in the form of specific concrete action by the people that leads to blessing but rather the original and primary covenant relationship of God with his people.

During Joash's reign, the prophet Elisha dies. In contrast to the faithful kings of Judah who died and were then buried with their ancestors, or to Elijah who was taken up to heaven in a whirlwind, the circumstances related to Elisha's death and burial start out to be ordinary and then become extraordinary. Elisha is buried but then through unusual circumstances, a dead man's bones come into contact with his bones. The dead man comes back to life. Lest anyone have doubts, this shows Elisha was no ordinary prophet. King Joash is succeeded by Jeroboam II.

14:1-7 Amaziah of Judah's reign

Joash's son Amaziah succeeds him as king (cf. 12:22) and reigns in Jerusalem for twenty-nine years; Joash's wife Jehoaddin was his mother. Amaziah is compared to his father (cf. 12:3). Although he is pleasing to the Lord, he is unlike David insofar as he allows the high places to remain where the people continue to offer sacrifices and burn incense. He is credited with slaying his father's assassins. He also obeys the law of Moses insofar as he permits the sons of his father's assassins to live (cf. Deut 24:16). The narrator records his military success against the Edomites. Faithfulness leads to blessing.

14:8-14 Amaziah challenges Israel

Amaziah, buoyed up by his conquest of Edom, seeks to confront Israel's King Joash in battle. Joash's reply to Amaziah's challenge takes the form of a parable: a thistle sought for its son the hand of the daughter of a cedar, but meanwhile an animal walked by and trampled the thistle. Joash tries to dissuade Amaziah from seeking a confrontation, claiming that Judah is no match for Israel and will lose. Note the use of the thistle and the cedar here. The ancient authors took advantage of their natural surroundings to create their analogies.

Despite Joash's advice, Amaziah persists. The two armies meet in battle and Judah's army is defeated. Amaziah is captured. Moreover, Israel's army pursues the fleeing Judahite army and, upon arriving at Jerusalem, proceeds to tear down part of the wall of the city. Joash strips the temple and the palace of their precious metals and takes hostages with him back to Samaria.

14:15-16 Jehoash's death

More was recorded regarding the accomplishments of Joash, just as more was recorded about the accomplishments of most of the kings of the northern kingdom—in the chronicles of the kings of Israel. When Joash dies, his son Jeroboam succeeds him as king.

14:17-22 Amaziah's death

Despite his loss to Joash, Amaziah himself was not killed in battle but, in fact, survived Joash by fifteen years. However, when a conspiracy forms against Amaziah, although he tries to escape by fleeing to Lachish, he is unsuccessful. He is killed there and then brought back to Jerusalem to be buried. His sixteen-year old son Azariah succeeds him as king. Deuteronomistic editing judges Amaziah as doing right in the sight of the Lord, but not entirely. His reign corresponds to that judgment. He overcame the Edomites but not the Israelites. He reigned for a long time, twenty-nine years, but he was killed by a conspiracy. Still, he was buried and his son became his successor.

14:23-29 Jeroboam II of Israel's reign

Despite the fact that Jeroboam II is cited as guilty of the same wrongdoing as Jeroboam I, he nevertheless reigns for forty-one years, and is geographically and militarily successful. He restores Israel's boundaries in fulfillment of a prophecy that was made by Jonah, son of Amittai, from Gaththepher. (There is no record in the text of the prophecy.) While Jeroboam's success would seem not to conform to Deuteronomistic theology since the king's evil seems not to have been cursed, the text explains that Israel's obliteration is not the Lord's intent (cf. 2 Kgs 13:23). Jeroboam's son Zechariah, the fourth of the descendants of Jehu, succeeds Jeroboam II as king.

15:1-7 Azariah of Judah's reign

Amaziah's son, Azariah, becomes king in Judah (cf. 14:21-22). Amaziah's wife Jecholiah is his mother. The Deuteronomistic editors compare Azariah to his father (cf. 2 Kgs 14:3) and to his grandfather (cf. 2 Kgs 12:3), pleasing the Lord but allowing the high places to remain. Sometime during his fifty-two year reign, he becomes a leper so that his son Jotham functions as the vizier and regent for the kingdom of Judah during his lifetime; at Azariah's death his son Jotham succeeds him as king. The Deuteronomistic theology allows Azariah, who was pleasing to the Lord, to be blessed with a fifty-two year reign. On the other hand, his leaving the high places may help to account for his leprosy.

15:8-12 Zechariah of Israel's reign

Zechariah, son of Jeroboam II (cf. 14:29), succeeds his father as king and reigns over Israel for six months, that is, until he is assassinated. His assassin, Shallum, succeeds him. The Deuteronomistic editors confirm that the descendants of Jehu to the fourth generation sat upon Israel's throne (cf. 10:30), but the dynasty ended when Shallum took the throne. That Zechariah lasted on the throne only six months attests to the political instability of the northern monarchy.

15:13-16 Shallum of Israel's reign

Shallum reigns for only one month before he is assassinated by Menahem who then reigns as king. The Deuteronomistic editors omit any judgment on the brevity of Shallum's reign, but one might conclude that its brevity is connected with the king's unfaithfulness. In contrast to Shallum, the editors do give an insight into the character of his successor, Menahem. They comment that he punished the people of Tappuah and the whole surrounding area (geographically extensive punishment), even to ripping open all the pregnant women (exceedingly cruel punishment). The text explains that he did this because they did not let him into their territory when he was on his way to assassinate his predecessor Shallum.

15:17-22 Menahem of Israel's reign

Menahem reigns for ten years. Like his predecessors, including Jeroboam, he is judged by the Deuteronomistic editors as doing evil in the eyes of the Lord. According to Deuteronomistic logic, because of Menahem's evildoing, he should be cursed. As it turns out, during Menahem's reign Assyria invades Israel. Menahem is able to successfully buy Assyria off, but only by giving the Assyrian King Pul money that he extorted from the wealthy people in his kingdom. His evildoing is indeed punished. At the end of his reign, Menahem's son Pekahiah succeeds him as king.

15:23-26 Pekahiah of Israel's reign

Pekahiah does evil in the Lord's sight and is also compared to Jeroboam I. He reigns for two years in Samaria before his adjutant Pekah, with fifty men, assassinates him (cf. 2 Kgs 1:9-14). Pekah then succeeds Pekahiah as king of Israel.

15:27-31 Pekah of Israel's reign

Pekah reigns for twenty years in Israel. He commits the same sins as Jeroboam. During his reign the Assyrian army captures several key cities of the northern kingdom and exiles their inhabitants. Deuteronomistic theology is here highlighted: evil behavior results in evil consequences; the perpetrators of evil, in this case the follower of the behaviors of Jeroboam, will be punished. This northern king is also assassinated. His assassin, Hoshea, takes over the kingdom and reigns in Pekah's place.

15:32-38 Jotham of Judah's reign

Jotham succeeds Uzziah (Azariah, cf. 15:7, 13, 30) as king of Judah and reigns, with his father and independently, for a total of sixteen years.

Uzziah's wife, Jerusha, was Jotham's mother. Like his predecessors, Jotham pleases the Lord but he also leaves the high places. Among his accomplishments, he builds the Upper Gate. During his reign Aram and Israel form an alliance against Judah and eventually attack Judah (i.e., 15:37; cf. Isa 7:1-2). In Deuteronomistic terms, good but not totally good yields blessing but not total blessing. In this case, Jotham's pleasing the Lord can only result in good; but his having left the high places can result in evildoing, the attack against Judah. When Jotham dies, his son Ahaz becomes the next king.

16:1-9 Ahaz of Judah's reign

In contrast to his predecessor who pleased the Lord, Ahaz does not please the Lord. He is not like David; he is like the kings of Israel. He practices child sacrifice, offering up his own son (cf. Abraham and Isaac in Gen 22:1-19; Saul and Jonathan in 1 Sam 14:24-30; but Jephthah and his daughter in Judg 11:29-40). When Aram and Israel attack him, he seeks protection from Assyria, and pays the Assyrians handsome tribute. The Assyrians take the tribute, attack Aram, and exile the inhabitants of its capital (cf. Isa 7:1-17).

16:10-20 Ahaz's idolatry

While it might seem that Ahaz is successful in protecting Judah, Ahaz's reign, according to the narrator, is hardly independent and prosperous. He meets with the king of Assyria in Aram. He then orders the Lord's temple in Jerusalem to be adorned with foreign objects of worship. The Jerusalem priest Uriah complies with his request to have an altar built in Jerusalem comparable to one that Ahaz saw in Damascus. This new altar replaces the Lord's old altar in the temple for sacrifice; the old altar will now be used only for the king's "consultation." Also, in deference to the king of Assyria, Ahaz removes from the Lord's temple accoutrements that are associated with Judah's king. Such behavior, from the Deuteronomistic editors' perspective, clearly signifies that Ahaz accords greater respect to the king of Assyria than to the Lord. That Judah suffers because of its king's sins is quite consistent with Deuteronomistic theology. Yet Ahaz dies a natural death. When Ahaz dies, after his sixteen year reign, his son Hezekiah succeeds him as king.

17:1-6 Hoshea of Israel's reign

Hoshea succeeds Pekah as king of Israel (cf. 15:30). He is credited with being better than the other kings of Israel although he is still not a good king. During his reign Assyria successfully attacks Israel. First Hoshea, like Ahaz of Judah, is able to buy off the Assyrians by paying them tribute. However, the feelers he puts out toward Egypt and his failure to pay the tribute lead to his arrest and imprisonment, to a three-year attack on Samaria by Assyria, and finally to the fall of the capital and the exile of the Israelites from their land. Deuteronomistic theology functions here insofar as Hoshea's doing evil in the sight of the Lord results in the fall of Samaria. On the other hand, since Hoshea is described as being better than his predecessors, the punishment seems disproportionate to his offense. Clearly the exile is the consequence of the evil behavior of Israel's kings understood cumulatively. From a historical perspective, the increasing military power of Assyria was far superior to Israel's, so Israel's defeat at the hands of Assyria was inevitable.

17:7-18 Israel deserved destruction

The Deuteronomistic editors could only understand the fall of the northern kingdom to Assyria as a result of the kings' continued and severe unfaithfulness to the Lord. They venerated other gods, built high places, and set up pillars and sacred poles. They burned incense and served idols. In spite of the Lord's repeated warnings through the prophets, they rejected their covenant with the God who had delivered them from Egypt. They were stiff-necked; they rejected the Lord's statutes. They pursued vanity and imitated the surrounding nations. They worshiped all the host of heaven and served Baal. They sacrificed their children and practiced fortune-telling and divination. God's punishment for their unfaithfulness comes in the form of removing "them from his presence," that is, allowing them to be exiled to Assyria.

17:19-23 A warning for Judah

Inserted almost parenthetically, but functioning as a foreshadowing of things to come, is the assertion that Judah did not keep the Lord's commandments but followed the rites practiced by Israel. The narrator continues with a concise summary of Israel's history: Israel's separation from the house of David, Jeroboam's kingship, Jeroboam's evildoing, the Israelites' imitation of Jeroboam, and Israel's exile. Unfaithfulness will be punished.

17:24-33 Relocation of peoples

The land of Israel is repopulated, under Assyria's direction, with people from other places—from Babylon, Cuthah, Avva, etc. These were not the Lord's people but people from round about who worshiped other gods and not the Lord. Not worshiping the Lord clearly worked to the people's detriment (e.g., lions killed the people), so the king of Assyria directed that an Israelite priest should return to Israel to teach the immigrants how to worship the god of the land, the Lord. Nevertheless, even if they also worship the Lord, most of the peoples eventually return to worshiping their own gods. The Babylonians, for example, worship Marduk and his consort; the men of Cuth worship Nergal; and the men of Hamath worship Ashima. Some people do worship the Lord, but like the Israelites before them, they also sacrifice on the high places and in their case, to their native gods.

The Assyrians' strategy for securing their conquests was to displace the educated and influential of a conquered nation's people and replace them with people from other conquered lands. This diminished the likelihood of an insurrection. The practice was cruel insofar as it separated families. It consequently earned the hatred of those affected. Later, when Judah's exiles were able to return to their land (after 539 B.C.), they rejected the people of the North because of their post-exilic history of intermarriage and worshiping multiple gods (e.g., Hag 2:14).

17:34-41 Observe the Lord's statutes

The text reiterates what the people should have known: the importance of keeping in mind the covenant and what constitutes covenant faithfulness. There should be no worship of other gods; rather, there should be worship of the Lord alone, and there should be obedience to all of the Lord's statutes and ordinances. However, the people who had been the nation of Israel, now intermixed with peoples of other lands, worship the Lord but they also worship the gods of the peoples from whom they came. This behavior continues into subsequent generations. This compromised behavior is unacceptable to the Deuteronomistic editors. One can only expect that Israel as a nation will have no future.

THE KINGDOM OF JUDAH AFTER 721 B.C.

2 Kings 18–25

After the conquest of Israel by Assyria in 722 B.C., Judah survives as a more or less independent nation for almost another 150 years. Survival demands both political prudence and political alliances. The Deuteronomistic editors understood Judah's survival as the result of the faithfulness of two of Judah's kings, Hezekiah, and especially, Josiah. Manasseh, however, reigned between these two just kings, and Manasseh was, from the Deuteronomistic editors' viewpoint, very evil. He worshiped the whole host of heaven in the Lord's temple and even sacrificed his son.

In fact, Assyria was defeated. Meanwhile, Babylon emerged as an ever-expanding and encroaching empire. The conquest of Judah by Babylon became ever more likely. This could only be explained theologically by the fact that the Lord, despite Josiah's reforms, was going to punish Judah's unfaithfulness, for which Manasseh became the symbol. In 586 B.C. Judah falls to Babylon, Jerusalem is captured, the temple is burned, and the king is taken into exile. Despite this doom, the book of 2 Kings ends on a hopeful, if guarded, note.

18:1-12 Hezekiah of Judah's reign

Ahaz's son Hezekiah succeeds him as king of Judah; Ahaz's wife, Abi, was Hezekiah's mother. Hezekiah, in contrast to most other Judean kings is described as not only pleasing the Lord but as removing the high places and destroying all the associated instruments of idol worship. Further, he puts his trust in the Lord; there is no Judean king who compares to him. The Lord is with him, and he is always fully faithful to the Lord. Blessings accompany his fidelity; he successfully rebels against the king of Assyria to whom his father paid high tribute (i.e., 2 Kgs 16:10-20) and he extends Judah's boundary by subjugating Philistine territory.

If the description of Hezekiah's reign ended here, one would conclude that Deuteronomistic theology is fully implemented: Hezekiah was extraordinarily faithful and as a consequence, he was extraordinarily blessed. It was during Hezekiah's reign that Assyria destroyed Israel (cf. 17:4-6), explicitly interpreted here by the Deuteronomistic editors as the consequence of Israel's unfaithfulness to the Lord.

18:13-26 Sennacherib's invasion of Judah

Eight years after Assyria destroyed Israel, it captures the fortified cities of Judah. Hezekiah responds to this assault by consenting to the payment of a generous tribute to Assyria, three hundred talents of silver and thirty talents of gold. To provide such a (symbolically) complete tribute, Hezekiah had to take not only all the gold and silver from the temple and palace treasuries, but also he had to give over the gold that overlaid the door panels and uprights of the temple. These events of his reign hardly seem appropriate for such a faithful king.

Worse, the king of Assyria bullies Judah. He sends his army to Jerusalem and when they arrive, they send for Hezekiah. Hezekiah does not respond to their call but rather sends messengers out to them—the master of the palace, a scribe, and a herald. Assyria's delegation sends a message back to Hezekiah through these messengers, asking him on what basis he dares to confront the king of Assyria? Surely he doesn't do it based on his military might or on the strength of an alliance with Egypt or even on the basis of his faith in the Lord in Jerusalem?

The messengers of Sennacherib ridicule Hezekiah and his faith in the Lord by assuring him that it is the Lord's will that the Assyrians come up to Jerusalem to destroy it. At this point Hezekiah's messengers request that the messengers of Sennacherib speak in Aramaic, a language with which the common people would not be familiar. They do not wish the people of Judah to understand the Assyrian taunts.

The text does not (cannot?) conform to Deuteronomistic theology because a faithful king, Hezekiah, is suffering military domination and personal humiliation. Clearly the political and military strength of Assyria could not be denied.

18:27-37 Sennacherib's messengers continue the verbal assault

The Assyrians respond to Hezekiah's messengers' request with the assertion that their words are intended for all the people, since all the people will bear Hezekiah's fate. All the people of Judah will suffer from famine, the gravity of which is here graphically described as eating their own excrement and drinking their own urine. One of Sennacherib's chief court messengers then appeals directly to the people of Judah, encouraging them to surrender and promising them that if they do they will have food in the land to which the Assyrians will deliver them like they used to have in their own land. Again the imagery is graphic: they will have wine and water to drink; they will have figs, grain, and bread to eat; and they will have olive oil and honey. To a starving people, what greater temptation could possibly be offered—if only they cease their support for Hezekiah and their trust in the Lord, Hezekiah's God. Using a strategy of rhetorical questions to intimidate, he asks them if any other nation's gods have been able to deliver their people from Assyria. Citing many kingdoms the Assyrians conquered as examples, including Israel, he asks if any of these people's gods were able to deliver them. The people of Judah remain silent before this Assyrian messenger, obeying Hezekiah's directive to them. After this encounter, Hezekiah's messengers, garments torn (cf. 5:7; 6:30; 11:14), return to the king to report what the commander has said. Hezekiah's messengers remain obedient and loyal to their king.

19:1-19 Isaiah's warning to Hezekiah

When Hezekiah hears how Sennacherib's representative has taunted the people of Judah, he sends his own representatives to the prophet Isaiah, asking Isaiah to pray and hoping that the Lord will rebuke Assyria. The word of the Lord that comes through the prophet Isaiah declares that Sennacherib will return to Assyria and be killed there. Before this happens, however, Sennacherib sends his envoys again to Hezekiah, assuring him that Judah's God will not be any more successful in saving Hezekiah's people than the gods of the other nations whom Assyria has defeated were in saving their people. Hezekiah responds to this message with prayer to the Lord, asking that the Lord deliver them from Assyria, and that the others whose gods were no gods would come to know that Judah's God was indeed God, the only God. Hezekiah remains faithful and trusting in the midst of great distress.

19:20-37 Sennacherib's punishment

The Lord speaks through the prophet Isaiah in answer to Hezekiah's prayer, proclaiming the downfall of Sennacherib and Assyria's defeat as well as Judah's restoration. Jerusalem will be spared.

An angel of the Lord slays so many of Sennacherib's forces that he returns to his capital, Nineveh. Then, in the temple of Nisroch, when Sennacherib is worshiping his god—obviously he had not learned to trust the Lord—his sons slay him (cf. 19:7).

Finally, Deuteronomistic theology is expressed in a manner that highlights Hezekiah's faithfulness to the Lord. Jerusalem was spared Assyria's assault and the enemy army retreated. Moreover, it was Hezekiah's prayer that prompted God's marvelous intervention to save the people of Judah. Not military forces but the Lord's messenger effected the victory. Obviously this was a holy war, just as the Lord had fought for Israel so that Joshua and his men could take Jericho (Josh 6:16) or just as the Lord had fought for Israel so that Saul could take the land of the Amalekites (1 Sam 15:7). The text is not meant to convey historical detail but rather to assert how the power of God accomplished the word of God on behalf of the one faithful to God.

20:1-11 Hezekiah's illness

When Hezekiah is deathly sick, the prophet Isaiah proclaims his imminent death. Hezekiah, however, prays to the Lord who hears his plea. The prophet Isaiah then reports to Hezekiah that God has heard his prayer and that because of Hezekiah's prayer, God will allow him to live another fifteen years. In an exchange reminiscent of the dialogue between Nathan and David (2 Sam 7:3-7), the prophet Isaiah makes a statement that is then contradicted by word of the Lord. The word of the Lord changes the prophet's original judgment.

Knowing that Hezekiah is going to live, Isaiah proceeds to order a remedy to facilitate the king's recovery. Hezekiah then asks for some indication that the Lord will heal him. Hezekiah and Isaiah agree that the sign will consist of a shadow moving backward ten steps. The shadow moves accordingly.

Hezekiah is unusual among the kings in that the text twice records his praying (2 Kgs 19:15 and

20:2). He is also unusual in that he asks for a sign. Gideon asked for a sign, also a reversal of nature's laws (Judg 6:36-40). The evil King Ahaz refused to ask for a sign (Isa 7:10-14).

20:12-21 Hezekiah's Babylonian visitors

When visitors from the king of Babylon arrive in Jerusalem bearing gifts—since they had heard of Hezekiah's illness—he welcomes them. Moreover, he shows off to them the treasures of his storehouses. The prophet Isaiah's reaction to the foreign visitors is to inform Hezekiah that the Babylonians will indeed take from Judah all the treasures that Hezekiah has shown them; they will even take some of Hezekiah's own descendants to become their servants, a foreshadowing of Judah's exile to Babylon. Hezekiah receives this as favorable news since it isn't going to occur during his reign.

According to Deuteronomistic theology, because of Hezekiah's faithfulness, the disaster of exile would not occur during his reign. In a similar manner because of Josiah's faithfulness, the disaster of exile will not occur during his reign (cf. 2 Kgs 22:20).

Hezekiah is credited with constructing the pool and conduit through which water was brought into Jerusalem. The significance of such an undertaking cannot be overestimated. Access to water in Jerusalem meant survival, the possibility of prosperity, potentially greater independence from attacking enemies, etc. Whether or not this attribution is historically accurate, the text as it reads is an assertion of the importance of Hezekiah. When he dies, his son Manasseh succeeds him.

21:1-18 Manasseh of Judah's reign

Hezekiah's wife Hephzibah was Manasseh's mother. As elsewhere throughout the descriptions of the reigns of Judah's kings, the mother of the future king is named. This has to do with the polygamy of the kings, to distinguish which of the king's wives was the mother of the next king, and because of the power and prosperity of the monarchy. Consistent with the patriarchal culture that produced these texts, the names of women associated with lesser men ordinarily are not specified.

Manasseh does evil in the Lord's sight. Note that the narrator not only compares Manasseh's evildoing to Ahab's (cf. 2 Kgs 8:18), but he also

compares it to the evil of those nations that the Lord originally expelled when the covenant people first came into the land that the Lord had promised to give them (e.g., Judg 1:4, 17). In other words, the evil that Manasseh perpetrates recalls not only the wrongdoing of the northern kingdom, but also the idolatrous behavior that the Israelites confronted even before there was a Davidic monarchy.

Manasseh reverses the reforms of his father. Whereas Hezekiah destroyed the high places, Manasseh rebuilds them. He erects altars to Baal and to other gods in the Lord's own temple and he himself practices idolatry. He reintroduces the practice of consulting ghosts and mediums (cf. 1 Sam 28:3). Like Ahaz before him (cf. 2 Kgs 16:3), he sacrifices his son.

The Lord's response to Manasseh's behavior is to declare through the prophets that the Lord will destroy Judah and Jerusalem, delivering them to their enemies. The reader has already seen such a prediction (i.e., 2 Kgs 20:16-18), but now the prediction is repeated and this time it is linked to the evils of Judah's king.

Still, the prophets' prediction is not effected in Manasseh's lifetime. On the contrary, Manasseh reigns for fifty-five years. Ordinarily one would associate such a long life and reign with the Lord's blessing for faithfulness. This detail, because it does not conform to Deuteronomistic theology, is especially likely to have some historical accuracy. When Manasseh dies, his son Amon succeeds him.

21:19-26 Amon of Judah's reign

Manasseh's wife Meshullemeth was Amon's mother. Her naming, similar to the naming of the mothers of all the kings of Judah, points not to any personal accomplishment but to her connection to men of political and economic stature.

Amon does all the very evil things that his father Manasseh did. In contrast to his father, Amon reigns only two years and does not die a natural death. He is slain as a result of a conspiracy instigated by his own subjects. But the people also kill those who have slain him. They make sure that Amon's son Josiah succeeds his father as king and that the Davidic line is preserved. The details of Amon's reign that are presented in the text are consistent with Deuteronomistic theology: Amon's unfaithfulness results in his being cursed, that is, in a short reign and an unnatural death.

22:1-7 Josiah of Judah's reign

Amon's wife Jedidah was Josiah's mother. Josiah pleases the Lord and is compared favorably to David. Josiah orchestrates the repairs of the temple with the money collected at the temple from the people. A careful reading of this passage in conjunction with the final verses of chapter 21 suggests that the people had become disgusted with their rulers' religious corruption. Perhaps there were some people, not the establishment certainly, who would provide even a somewhat receptive audience for the preaching of prophets like Jeremiah.

22:8-20 The restoration discovery

In the process of doing repairs on the temple, the high priest recovers the book of the law. This he takes to the scribe who then reads it to the king. Josiah reacts to the contents of the book with grave concern because the book lays out the behaviors that are associated with faithfulness to the Lord, behaviors with which Judah has not complied. Josiah orders the high priest, the scribe, and others to consult the Lord through the prophet Huldah regarding the implications of the content of the book.

The Lord condemns Judah for its unfaithfulness and confirms that the punishments stipulated in the book will be executed against them (cf. 2 Kgs 20:17-18; 21:12-15). Josiah, however, because of his faithfulness to the Lord, and his grieving in response to Judah's unfaithfulness and the book's threats, will not have to witness the nation's destruction. He will die before the judgment against Judah is carried out (cf. 2 Kgs 20:19).

23:1-20 Covenant renewal

Josiah has all the contents of the book of the law read to the people. He then sets about making a covenant with the Lord binding the people to follow God and obey his laws, and reviving the terms of the covenant that were set out in the book of the law. Josiah then promulgates religious reforms to make possible the Israelites' observance of the covenant that they just renewed. These reforms include the removal from the temple and the destruction of all objects associated with other gods—Baal, Asherah, the whole host of heaven (cf. 2 Kgs 21:2-4, 7); the removal/slaughter of the pseudo-priests who burned incense either at the high places or to Baal or to one or more of the heavenly bodies; the removal of the high places dedicated to Astarte, Chemosh, and Milcom, (cf. 2 Kgs 21:3); the destruction of the housing of the cult prostitutes; the termination of the practice of offering sons and daughters by fire to Molech, and the removal of the shrines at or near Bethel and Samaria. The statement included by the Deuteronomistic editors regarding Josiah's turning to the Lord (23:25) is consistent with the king's reforms.

23:21-25 Passover observance

In addition to terminating practices inconsistent with faithfulness to Judah's God, Josiah institutes or reinstitutes the celebration of the Israelites passing over from Egypt to freedom. The formalizing of this commemoration is usually credited to Josiah. Not surprisingly, the Deuteronomistic editors evaluate Josiah's behavior as dissimilar from the kings that precede or follow him. He is associated with Judah's last attempt, its most serious attempt in a divided kingdom, to fulfill the responsibilities of covenant faithfulness.

23:26-27 Judah's condemnation

Yet, according to a Deuteronomistic reading of the history, in spite of the righteous leadership of Josiah, the Lord does not forgive Judah for the many and egregious sins they committed during the reign of his predecessor Manasseh. For this reason, the downfall of Judah, even Jerusalem, though delayed (cf. 22:18-20), is inevitable.

A contemporary historian might argue that Judah was destroyed not because of idol worship, not even idol worship in the Lord's temple, or human sacrifice, or even, for that matter, any of the behaviors that disregarded the Lord's covenant; rather, Judah was destroyed simply because of the superior military might of Babylon. This would explain why the fall of Judah did not occur after Manasseh's reign but only later. But the Deuteronomistic editors were not historians in our time. They were historical theologians or theological historians in their own time. They tried to understand their people's experience in relation to their people's God; the only way they could understand what was happening to them was related to the action of God in their midst.

23:28-30 Josiah's death

Egypt and Assyria become allies against Babylon. Josiah unsuccessfully attempts to thwart

Egypt's advance toward Assyria and is killed in battle at Meggido. Jehoahaz, Josiah's son, succeeds him as king.

23:31-35 Jehoahaz of Judah's reign

Josiah's wife Hamutal was Jehoahaz's mother. Again, the prestige of her male family members, and the impetus to distinguish her among Josiah's wives, may explain why her name was included in the record. Apparently Egypt asserted itself as a dominant power, at least superior to Judah. It was responsible for the death of Josiah (2 Kgs 23:29) and had taken control of Judah. It exacted tribute from Judah and after Jehoahaz's three-month reign, took the king into exile. The same strategy (remove a king less amenable to your agenda and replace him with a supporter) had been a strategy of the Syro-Ephraimite Alliance (cf. the historical background to Isa 7:1). Jehoahaz's brief reign and exile were, no doubt, thought by the Deuteronomistic editors to be fitting punishment for a king of Judah who "did evil in the LORD's sight, just as his ancestors had done."

Pharaoh Neco, now temporarily in control of Judah, places another of Josiah's sons, Jehoahaz's half-brother Eliakim, whom he renames Jehoiakim, on the throne of Judah. The change of name is significant because it represents a different identity. Judah's king Eliakim now reports to an Egyptian.

Jehoahaz and Jehoiakim had different mothers, accentuating the importance of naming the women. Pharaoh Neco forced Judah to pay him tribute, and Jehoiakim did so with silver and gold that he extracted from the people.

Though Judah was not conquered by Egypt, that is, its capital was not destroyed, for all purposes it had become politically and economically dependent, characteristics of its situation after the exile.

23:36–24:7 Jehoiakim of Judah's reign

Josiah's wife Zebidah was Jehoiakim's mother. Jehoiakim reigns for eleven years and also does evil. Sometime during his reign the power shifts so that he turns his allegiance from Egypt to Babylon. Babylon's King Nebuchadnezzar makes Jehoiakim his vassal for three years. When Jehoiakim finally rebels, he meets with opposition not only from the Chaldeans (Babylonians), but also from the Arameans (Syrians), the Moabites, and the Ammonites. In other words, Judah is attacked with force from the north and the east (the south had already been subdued). Babylon, for all practical purposes, annexed Egypt. Egypt's king would remain a captive in his own land. Judah was also destined to be destroyed. The theological explanation for Judah's defeat is, broadly speaking, Judah's sinfulness, but especially the sins of Manasseh and the shedding of innocent blood. Still, by the time Jehoiakim dies, the kingdom has not yet been totally obliterated. Jehoiakim's son Jehoiachin succeeds him.

24:8-16 Jehoiachin of Judah's reign and exile

Jehoiakim's wife Nahushta was the mother of Jehoiachin. Again, as with the other mothers of Judah's kings, it is her marital and maternal relationships that are responsible for her name being recorded.

Like his father and grandfather before him, Jehoiachin does evil in the Lord's sight. He reigns for only three months. It is during Jehoiachin's reign that Jerusalem is attacked. Nebuchadnezzar takes the king and the royal family captive, confiscates the temple treasures, and exiles from Jerusalem all of the city's citizens, except the poor. He takes into exile ten thousand officers and men of the army, as well as a thousand craftsmen and smiths.

Note the class distinctions recorded here. The elite of the citizenry are exiled: the king, the king's mother and wives, the king's functionaries, the military officers and many men of the army, as well as educated smiths and craftsmen. The poor remain in the land. One can hypothesize that the military are exiled lest they mount a rebellion, the king and his court because of their symbolic power, and the smiths and craftsmen because of their potential contribution to the well-being of Babylon. Although the number of those exiled may represent only a small percentage of Judah's entire population, the exile represented the final stage in Babylon's conquest of Judah.

24:17-20 Who was Zedekiah?

According to 2 Kings 24:17, Jehoiachin is not succeeded on the throne in Jerusalem by his son but by his uncle, Mattaniah, who is a brother of Jehoahaz. He and Jehoahaz had the same mother,

Hamutal (cf. 23:31). The king of Babylon changes Mattaniah's name to Zedekiah. Here again, as in 2 Kings 23:34, the titular king of Judah, now for all practical purposes devoid of power and under the control of outside forces, this time of Babylon, has his name changed, this time to Zedekiah. Judah is in dire circumstances. Its defeat is inevitable, since the king is mere putty in Babylon's hands. Like his predecessors, Zedekiah does evil in the Lord's sight. Deuteronomistic theology reminds the reader that sin has consequences.

25:1-7 Babylon destroys Jerusalem

Jerusalem's final defeat begins on the tenth day of the tenth month. The city is surrounded and driven to famine. When the city walls are breached, the king tries to escape with his army but is unsuccessful. When Zedekiah is captured and brought to the king of Babylon at Riblah, his punishment is to see his two sons slain and then to have his eyes gouged out. He is then taken to Babylon. The gouging out of Zedekiah's eyes recalls the gouging out of Samson's eyes (i.e., Judg 16:21); in Zedekiah's case, he is treated so cruelly perhaps because he tried to escape. Nothing really is said about his faithfulness or unfaithfulness to the Lord, perhaps because he is not in control of his own behavior.

25:8-12 The Lord's temple burned

Seven months later on the seventh day of the month, the captain of the bodyguard, Nebuzaradan, goes to Jerusalem. He burns the temple, the king's palace, all the houses, and every large building in Jerusalem. The Babylonian forces then tear down the city's walls. Finally, all those who have not yet been deported—except some of the poor who are left behind as farmers and vine dressers—are led out of Judah to Babylon.

The final blow to Judah's identity is the destruction of the temple, willed by David (2 Sam 7:2-3) and built by Solomon (1 Kgs 7:51). The centralization that had occurred politically (the monarchy), geographically (Jerusalem), and religiously (the temple) is now totally destroyed.

25:13-21 The spoils of war

The Babylonian soldiers break into pieces valuable bronze artifacts from the temple and take booty; the captain of the guard also takes silver and gold accoutrements. In addition, the captain also takes two chief priests, three gate keepers, a scribe, a courtier, and various and sundry others, all of whom he brings to the Babylonian king at Riblah in Hamath. Nebuchadnezzar has them executed there. Not only is the Lord's house burned, its personnel are killed. The religious center of Israel's identity has been eliminated.

25:22-26 Gedeliah appointed governor

Although Gedaliah tries to convince the army commanders who had come to him at Mizpah (cf. 1 Sam 7:6) that they should serve the Babylonian king, and that if they do, all will go well with them, not everyone is convinced. One of the commanders, a certain Ishmael, assassinates Gedaliah in the seventh month. Was he hoping to mount an insurrection? If so, he fails. The other commanders flee to Egypt for fear of Babylonian reprisal. This brief account suggests that at least some of the people of Judah were not yet totally subdued.

25:27-30 Jehoiachin's release

In the twelfth month of the thirty-seventh year of Jehoiachin's exile, in the first year of Evil-merodach's reign as king of Babylon, he releases Jehoiachin from prison. He allows him to eat with him and gives him a daily allowance. It was common and considered a wise political strategy for new kings, on their ascension to the throne, to give amnesty to their predecessor's enemies. The final word of the Deuteronomistic History is a form of amnesty for Judah's king (cf. Jer 52:31-34). Both the kingdom and the temple may have been destroyed, but the dynasty has not ended (cf. 2 Kgs 11:3).

CONCLUSION

During the long reign of Ahab, the evil king of Israel, the prophet Elisha repeatedly confronted him with the superior power of the Lord. God did through his prophets what Ahab could not do—cause a famine, end a famine, raise a dead child to life, multiply food, neutralize poison, etc. Ahab angrily admitted this when he responded to the king of Aram's request that he cure Naaman's leprosy: "Am I a god with power over life and death, that this man should send someone to me to be cured of leprosy?" (2 Kgs 5:7). While the prophet of God could act with the power of God, the evil king could do nothing. Nevertheless, after Ahab's death, Israel continued with a succession of evil kings. According to the judgment of the Deuteronomistic editors, because of Israel's idolatry and injustice, finally, Israel was destroyed.

As for Judah, all of its kings were descendants of David; several behaved in a manner pleasing to God, like David, except for allowing the high places to continue. Hezekiah and Josiah were singled out as being more faithful than the others, but Ahaz was particularly evil, even to the point of sacrificing his son. Yet the Deuteronomistic editors lay at Manasseh's feet the final responsi-

bility for Judah's fall to Babylon. The kings' cumulative unfaithfulness exceeded the limits of God's tolerance. And yet . . .

The final three verses of 2 Kings parallel the final three verses of the book of the prophet Jeremiah. Exiled in Babylon, the king nevertheless was let out of prison, given a daily allowance, and permitted to eat each day at the king's table. It would seem as if, despite the demise of the kingdom, which the Deuteronomistic editors clearly saw as deserved, there was tangible hope for some sort of restoration of the Davidic line in the release of King Jehoiachin. Sin has consequences, but God forgives.

THE BOOKS OF

FIRST AND SECOND CHRONICLES

John C. Endres, S.J.

INTRODUCTION

During the era of Persian rule (539–332 B.C.), when the land of Israel was known as the province of Yehud, a Jewish writer with close connections to the Jerusalem temple authored a new version of Israel's sacred story. Crafted for the Jewish people of his time, Chronicles spans the time from the creation of the world through the end of the Babylonian exile and Cyrus' permission for Jews to return home in 538 B.C. These books tell the story from a special perspective. They emphasize the relationship with God centered at the temple and focus on Israel's monarchs as leaders in political and religious matters, cooperating with Levites, priests, and prophets. For example, in Chronicles there is little concern for the split between the northern and southern kingdoms after Solomon. Jerusalem is God's chosen city, the temple is God's special place of presence, and public worship and song are critical aspects of Israel's public life. God appears as mighty power, transcendent divinity, creator and sustainer of the world. There are no other gods as rivals.

These views come from the same storyline as that in the books of Deuteronomy through 2 Kings, often referred to as the Deuteronomistic History. The Chronicler, however, paints this picture with different shades and accents. Often, such differences can be easily traced when the Chronicler follows the story in the Deuteronomistic History rather closely. In fact, one can read 1–2 Chronicles synoptically, comparing it with Samuel and Kings, much as one reads Matthew, Mark, and Luke in synoptic fashion. In this commentary we will attend to the Chronicler's alterations of the older text as he rewrites Israel's history. As we observe his changes to the story, some very obvious, many very subtle, we will notice how his theological perspective differs greatly from the earlier history. One difference is striking: the Deuteronomistic History views the era of the monarchy as a downward spiral leading to the Babylonian exile, and blames the regression on sinful actions of the kings. The Chronicler, on the other hand, presents a far more positive view of kings, especially those of Judah. He implies that their ways of conduct, especially their faith and their attention to God through worship, can lead to bountiful blessings for Israel. For the Chronicler, "Israel" is the Jewish people in Judah in the postexilic era, so the message to his audience is that they can enjoy more blessings if they wholeheartedly dedicate themselves to their God.

Israel's early history is recounted in these books quite differently than in the Pentateuch. 1 Chronicles 1–9 consist of a series of genealogies, which cover time from the creation of the world up to the reign of Saul. While many connections exist between people in the genealogies and persons known from stories elsewhere, Chronicles does not entirely depend on narratives. Rather the story is carried through the genealogical connections. King David's reign constitutes the second part of this book (1 Chr 10–29). Here, the Chronicler repeats much of the material in the books of Samuel and describes David's plans for the temple and its personnel in much greater detail (1 Chr 22–29). Solomon's reign (2 Chr 1–9) was a wonderful time for later Israel to remember and to emulate; it includes his building and dedication of the temple and lacks the negative evaluation of him found in 1 Kings 11:10–22. 2 Chronicles 10–36 narrates the history of the kingdom of Judah, with special focus on the exemplary rule of kings Jehoshaphat, Hezekiah, and Josiah. Chronicles generally omits criticism of kings in the northern kingdom of Israel, so the Chronicler may be seen to favor a reunion of the northern and southern kingdoms. In short, we can say that the Chronicler rewrites the Pentateuch by way of genealogies, and the books of Joshua through 2 Kings by a new version of the history emphasizing David's line.

It is very helpful to keep a copy of the books of Samuel and Kings handy while reading this text, since Chronicles clearly uses these sources. The differences between them will catch our attention and suggest to us important emphases for the Chronicler. In particular, the Chronicler rewrites Kings with subtle and substantial differences (e.g., the story of Solomon, 2 Chr 1–9) and completely omits stories well known from Kings (e.g., the narratives about the prophets Elijah and Elisha, 1 Kgs 17–2 Kgs 9). The Chronicler almost ignores the kings of the North, whereas the author of Kings had evaluated them as consistently evil and guilty of idolatry. Along these lines, the Chronicler omits 2 Kings 17 and 18:9-12, a detailed examination of Israel's various offenses against God and how they fulfill God's word through the prophets.

This commentary will focus on some special themes and expressions in Chronicles that differ from the Deuteronomistic History. The Chronicler's idiosyncrasies show a great interest in how Israel (i.e., Judah in postexilic times) should pray and worship, and ultimately what religious practices can help the divided sectors of Israel come together in unity.

COMMENTARY: *1 CHRONICLES*

GENEALOGIES

1 Chronicles 1–9

Genealogies offer people a sense of their identity by linking them to their past, giving them a type of connection to those who gave birth to them and to their ancestors. Frequently we think of building links backwards in a line of ancestry; these we may call linear genealogies. Other genealogies spread out and display all the relations (e.g., siblings) in a certain generation, offering a sense of the breadth of connections; some people call these segmented genealogies. Occasionally, the two mix, with a genealogical line described for one or more members of a broad list of siblings. The manner and order of presentation gives a good idea of what values are most important to the writer. For example, a genealogy might trace a "line" by naming the parental relationships of one to another, going through several generations. If several members of one generation are mentioned, then you may observe which members of the line are carried through, and in what order they are described. Often they save the most important for the last.

For the people of the Chronicler's age, hard questions persisted: how did their identity connect with the twelve tribes of Israel? What happened to the ten lost tribes? How did Israel fit into the whole of the human race? What would be their future: a small group or all Israel (represented by all twelve tribes)? Which tribes and families of Israel were most important to their self-understanding? The genealogies offer subtle answers to these questions. Much of this information can be found in the Pentateuch, interspersed with narratives well known to all Israelites. The genealogical lists in chapters 1–9 call to mind many stories and narratives recounted elsewhere.

1:1–2:2 Descendants of Adam to Israel

This chapter demonstrates that Israel's origins go back to the origins of all peoples—i.e., Abraham's ancestry in Adam and Noah; it places Israel in this wider scope of human history envisaged by the Bible. Verses 1-4 list thirteen names of the ancestors of all human beings, distributed in ten generations. These names differ somewhat from the stories in Genesis 2–5, but they match closely a genealogical list in Genesis 5:1-32. Only in the case of Noah are all the sons listed: Shem, Ham, and Japheth (1:4).

1:5-23 lists the descendants of the sons of Noah, drawing from a genealogy in Genesis 10:1-32. Japheth's fourteen descendants (1:5-7) seemingly relate to Noah's sons' settling in Europe and Asia. Ham's thirty descendants (1:8-16) point to specific peoples and lands in Africa and Syria-Palestine; they include Canaan and other peoples later connected to lands to be dispossessed: Jebusites, Amorites, etc. Then come twenty-six descendants of Shem, the Semites localized in Arabia and Mesopotamia, with some familiar names: Asshur (Assyria) and Aram (Arameans, near Damascus) (1:17-23). Verses 24-27 contain another list of Shem's descendants, in generations from Noah to Abraham, which parallels the genealogy in Genesis 11:10-26. In verse 27, the Chronicler says "Abram, that is, Abraham," the name first given him in Genesis 17:1. Thus the Chronicler jumps from Genesis 11 to Genesis 17 with a new focus on Abraham, father of Israel. The rest of this chapter lists Abraham's descendants: Ishmael (1:29-31; cf. Gen 25:13-16), Keturah his concubine (1:32-33; cf. Gen 25:1-4 where she is called a "wife"), Isaac his son (1:34), with a long genealogy for Esau (1:35-54; cf. Gen 36:10-42).

Notice how the less-favored descendants (e.g., Ishmael, Keturah, Esau) appear first, followed by the most important line. Chapter 2 begins the line of the twelve sons of Jacob, though the Chronicler never uses the name Jacob, but rather Israel. These are the heads of the twelve tribes of Israel. There are parallel lists in Genesis (35:16-18; 35:22-26; 29:31; 30:24) and Exodus (1:1-4). Although Dan and Zebulun are found in this list (2:1-2), the Chronicler does not give them a genealogy, and Dinah, Jacob's daughter (Gen 34), goes unmentioned in the genealogies.

2:3–4:23 Descendants of Judah

This is the major tribe of the southern kingdom. Judah's family has the largest genealogy of all, about one hundred verses. It includes several complex genealogies and brings the house of David into immediate prominence.

The genealogies of Judah provide evidence about the occurrence of intermarriage in Israel; this is quite interesting because exogamy, i.e., marrying outside family/tribal lines, is condemned elsewhere (especially in the book of Nehemiah). There are at least six cases of intermarriage in this genealogy: 2:3 ("these three, Bathshua, a Canaanite woman, bore to him"); 2:17 (Abigail, David's sister, bears Amasa, whose father was Jether the Ishmaelite); 2:34-35 (Sheshan has his daughter marry his Egyptian slave Jarha); 3:2 (David's wife Maacah is daughter of King Talmai of Geshur); 4:18 ("sons of Bithiah, the daughter of Pharaoh"); 4:21-22 (Saraph, who marries into Moab). The Chronicler does not critique any of these intermarriages. This may be the way that the Chronicler incorporates marginal figures or clans into the central group. Clearly it is one of the ways for Judah to expand its population.

2:3-55 Judah

This list ultimately focuses on David. For the reader already familiar with other biblical histories, this genealogy recalls several well-known biblical stories, such as Judah and Tamar in Genesis 38 (2:3-4), Samuel's anointing of Jesse's youngest son (cf. 1 Sam 16:1-13), and Ruth (2:5, 9-15; cf. the genealogy in Ruth 4:18-22).

3:1-9 David

The genealogy lists names of various mothers of his children and differentiates children born in Hebron from those born in Jerusalem, paralleling 2 Samuel 3:2-5. Another list of his children is in 1 Chronicles 14:3-7.

3:10-24 Solomon

Here is a list of kings of Judah to the Babylonian exile (3:10-16) and their descendants after the exile (3:17-24). This list corresponds to information from the books of Kings up to Josiah (died ca. 609 B.C.), where there is divergence. A post-exilic list of about eight generations shows that for the Chronicler the lineage of David remains important after the return from exile.

4:1-23 Judah

This list of his descendants derives from various lists. In 4:9-10 we hear the story of a man named Jabez, whose name is derived from the verb for pain (in childbirth), and who is honored above his brothers. Jabez asks for a sizeable blessing from God, who grants his request. Though consistent with the Chronicler's theology of prayer, this request is more self-referential than most prayers in 1–2 Chronicles.

4:24-43 Descendants of Simeon

Simeon traditionally occupies territory close to Judah, in the south of the land. The list of names in 4:24-27 draws on two sources: Genesis 46:10 and Exodus 6:15. Verse 27 recounts Shimei's offspring, surprisingly mentioning six daughters (plus sixteen sons) and that he has more offspring than his brothers, suggesting a problem with underpopulation in the time of the Chronicler. A list of cities and towns follows, drawing on a list in Joshua 19:1-9 (land allotments after the conquest) but implying that Israelites have been here from time immemorial. Verses 39-43 narrate two events in which Simeon increases its territory, pushing out earlier inhabitants (Meunites and Amalekites) when they needed more space for their flocks. The warlike nature of this group corresponds to their characterization in Genesis 34, 49:5-7 and Judges 9:2.

5:1-10 Descendants of Reuben

Reuben occupies territory east of the Jordan River. His four descendants are known also from Genesis 46:8-9, Exodus 6:14, and Numbers 26:5-6. In verses 1-2 Reuben, though firstborn, loses his birthright to the sons of Joseph, since he defiled his father's bed by having sexual relations with Bilhah, his father's concubine (Gen 35:22). Moreover, the real power of the firstborn is exercised by Judah.

5:11-17 Descendants of Gad

The names of members of this tribe, situated in northern Transjordan, do not resemble his brief genealogies in Genesis 46:16 and Numbers 26:15.

5:18-26 Descendants of the two-and-a-half tribes

This unusual section describes the situation of the tribes of Reuben, Gad, and the half-tribe of Manasseh, all situated east of the Jordan River. The Chronicler mentions their initial conquests, their sin of idolatry (5:25) which led to their demise, and their (later) exile by the Assyrians ca. 722 B.C.

5:27-41 Descendants of Levi

This is another complex genealogy, which includes various kinds of information about Levites and priests (Aaronites and Zadokites). The passage begins with Levi, mentions three of his sons (Gershon, Kohath, and Merari), and traces the line through his second son, Kohath: Amram, who fathers Aaron, Moses, and Miriam (5:27-41). The Chronicler traces a line through Aaron, Eleazar, Phinehas . . . all the way to Zadok (6:34), a priest in the time of David and Solomon. The line of priests then continues into the post-exilic era (including, incidentally, another Zadok). Zadok seems to be the center of the family—i.e., twelve generations (of forty years) precede him and twelve follow him. So the Chronicler has provided an Aaronite ancestry for Zadok, a fact not mentioned during his more prominent appearances in the books of Samuel (cf. 2 Sam 15–19). The Levi family's antiquity points to the importance of this family to the entire constitution of Israel. This is part of the Chronicler's view.

6:1-15 Another listing of Levi's sons

This list includes Gershon, Kohath, and Merari, with a number of offspring for each of these family groups. Important figures include: Mushi (Moses), son of Merari in verse 4, and Samuel in verse 12 (from Kohath).

6:16-32 Levites trusted with song

Levites are entrusted with the "service of song in the Lord's house" (6:16), after the ark is installed there. From the house of Kohath are: Heman (6:18), a descendant of Korah (6:22), a name found in several psalm titles. From Gershon, standing at Heman's right, is Asaph (6:24), another name well known from titles of various psalms. Standing on Heman's left are the sons of Merari (6:29). Since Levitical temple singers in the First Temple are mentioned only in Chronicles, their presence here may be a bold move to give Levites in the Second Temple era (516 C.E. ff.) an ancient heritage and function. This link with antiquity, i.e., David and Moses, increases their religious significance for Chronicles. From Merari, again, comes Mushi (Moses in 6:32).

6:33-34 Priestly institutions

These lists portray a traditional view of priestly institutions, i.e., Levite singers (6:16), Levites in charge of "all the other services of the tabernacle of the house of God" (6:33), and priests descended from Aaron, who are responsible for burnt offerings, incense offerings, and all the work of the "holy of holies" (6:34). Service corresponds to our notion of liturgy, so Levites have responsibility for everything but the three tasks assigned to the priests.

6:35-38 Aaronite priests

These verses list Aaronite priests in charge of burnt offerings and incense offerings to make atonement for Israel, according to Moses' commands. This list concludes in the time of David, with Zadok and his son Ahimaaz.

6:39-66 Levite cities

This listing of the cities of the Levites, given to them by all the tribes of Israel, probably derives from Joshua 21:1-42. In order to more closely follow the account in Joshua, the original NAB translators transposed verses 46–50 and the NABRE revisers followed suit. Members of the tribe of Levi receive no allotment of land because they are dedicated to God (Josh 14:4), so the Chronicler clearly indicates the names of their cities.

7:1-5 Descendants of Issachar

Issachar is a northern tribe, located southwest of the Sea of Galilee. Many of this family are warriors, numbered in a census in David's time. The only biblical parallels for this list are Genesis 46:13 and Numbers 26:23-25, so the Chronicler may have had other sources of information. Here the Chronicler only details three of the five Galilean tribes: Issachar, Naphtali, and Asher. Zebulun is missing and so is Dan (except for a possible reference noted in verse 12). Altogether, these tribes merit only sixteen verses. Clearly, the Chronicler was much more interested in southern tribes, especially Judah, and in Levi. But his information

on the Galilean tribes suggests his ongoing interest in the return of the lost northern tribes.

7:6-12 Descendants of Benjamin

Benjamin is a small territory, lying north of Judah and south of Ephraim. Parallels include Genesis 46:21 and Numbers 26:38-41. There is a longer genealogy of this family in 1 Chronicles 8:1-28, with many different names. In 7:12, "The sons of Dan: Hushim," Dan is not actually mentioned in the Hebrew text, but many commentators interpret the Hebrew word as another, unnamed brother and think of it as a reference to Dan, who is not mentioned elsewhere in these genealogies.

7:13 Descendants of Naphtali

A single verse, this genealogy draws on parallels in Genesis 46:24 and Numbers 26:48-50. Since it is so brief, scholars think the actual genealogy was lost. Naphtali's territory was north of Issachar, in the region known to us as Galilee.

7:14-19 Descendants of Manasseh

This territory lies north of Ephraim and south of Issachar, from the Jordan River west to the Mediterranean Sea. Biblical parallels include Numbers 26:29-34 and Joshua 17:1-6. This brief notice mentions more women family members than most others (7:15), including the concubine of Manasseh, wives for his sons, and the name of his sister, Maacah. It also mentions Zelophehad, who had only daughters. Zelophehad's five daughters play an important role in Numbers 27:1-11 and 36:1-12, where they challenge traditional laws of heredity (restricted to sons) and invite Moses to reinterpret law to meet changing circumstances. Here the Chronicler provides a clear reference to their family.

7:20-29 Descendants of Ephraim

This tribe inhabits the central hill country north of Benjamin. The genealogy is somewhat convoluted, but we do learn that Ephraim's sons were killed by the people of Gath and that he and his wife subsequently had a third son, Beriah (7:23). His daughter Sheerah, however, is more prominent. She builds three towns, two of which guard the routes from the coastland up into the hill country (7:24). Joshua appears in this genealogy (7:27), which concludes with a list of famous places inhabited by Ephraimites and Manassites: Bethel, Gezer, Shechem, Beth-shean, Taanach, Megiddo, and Dor.

7:30-40 Descendants of Asher

This group's territory is far north, along the coast south of present-day Lebanon. Like the genealogies of Issachar and Benjamin, it focuses on names and references to military leaders (7:4-5, 9, 11, 40). Here are also listed two women: Serah, a daughter of Asher (7:30), and Shua, daughter of Heber, son of Asher (7:32). Biblical parallels are found in Genesis 46:17 and Numbers 26:44-47.

8:1-28 Descendants of Benjamin

Here is a second Benjaminite genealogy (cf. 7:6-12, above). This tribe, just to the north of Jerusalem and Judah, is important because Saul came from it, and after the loss of the ten northern tribes it continued in association with Judah. The five sons of Benjamin found in 8:1-2 differ from three sons in 1 Chronicles 7:6 and larger numbers in Genesis 46:21 and Numbers 26:38-39. The Chronicler lists the sons of Bela in 8:3-7, and in 8:8-14 lists the sons of Shaharaim.

Again, women are featured in the story: Shaharaim's wives Hushim and Baara, whom he "put away" (i.e., divorced) (8:8); his wife Hodesh, by whom he had sons (8:9-10); and a later note that he also had children by Hushim (8:11). Some familiar towns, Lod and Ono, were built by Hushim's descendants, a sign of blessing through a divorcee. Two more families are introduced in verses 13-14: Beriah and Shemah. In 8:15-28, the Chronicler lists a number of families, some members already mentioned, which were said to live in Jerusalem (8:28), which was located on the border of Benjamin and Judah.

8:29-40 Genealogy of Saul

A nearly identical genealogy appears in 1 Chronicles 9:35-44. Saul provides the transition from the period of the judges to the monarchy, described in the books of Judges and 1 Samuel but presented in Chronicles only through genealogies. This genealogy carries Saul's family through approximately ten generations after his death (1 Chr 10), into the eighth century B.C. So Saul's line remains important even after being displaced by David's family. Three names in this list refer to the Canaanite god Baal: Baal (8:30),

Eshbaal (8:33), and Meribbaal (8:34). Elsewhere the "baal" in these names is modified, eradicating any reference to Baal, but the Chronicler seems not to be worried about the dangers of such worship in his own day.

9:1-44 Inhabitants of Jerusalem

This chapter begins by summarizing the descendants of Israel of chapters 2–8 (9:1-2). Then the Chronicler lists the ancestral houses of Jerusalem (9:3-34), repeating the genealogy of Saul (9:35-44; cf. 8:29-40). The section, 9:3-34, divides itself according to postexilic views of how Israel was constituted: Israel (laity, non-clerics) in verses 3-9 (naming four tribes: Judah, Benjamin, Ephraim, Manasseh); and the clergy—i.e., the priests (9:10-13) and the Levites (9:14-34). An unusual section lists the gatekeepers and describes their functions (9:17-32), and there is similar attention to gatekeepers in 1 Chronicles 26:1-19. Singers are mentioned in verse 33. Verse 34 concludes the entire list of Levites, reiterating their habitation in Jerusalem. This chapter shows the social dimensions of Judah's population and concludes with the first ruling family, that of Saul (9:35-44).

THE REIGN OF DAVID BEGINS

1 Chronicles 10–14

10:1-14 [cf. 1 Sam 31:1-13] The death of Saul and his sons

Up to this point, the Chronicler has recounted history through detailed genealogies, so this chapter begins the narrative part of the book. Saul's genealogies are in 1 Chronicles 8:29-40 and 9:35-44. This chapter of Chronicles begins abruptly with the death of Saul, who is killed in a battle with the Philistines. The narrator does not call him a king in this narrative, even though he notes that God had "turned his kingdom over to David" (10:14). The Chronicler emphasizes the death of Saul's household because his theological perspective is that David's reign came immediately and completely (10:12). The Chronicler omits some details from the book of Samuel, e.g., the all-night walk of the Jabeshites and the description of hanging corpses on the city walls of Beth-shan. Verses 13-14 are additions by the Chronicler which place the kingdom squarely in David's hands. They show that the Chronicler knows stories about Saul which he opts not to narrate, like Saul's consultation with the witch at Endor (1 Sam 28). He mentions Saul's unfaithfulness which leads to his death and the transfer of his kingship to David, all the results of Saul's sin. Neither the book of Samuel nor Chronicles comments on Saul's taking his own life. Saul's sin consisted in consulting a medium rather than consulting God. The kingdom is at God's disposal, and he turns it over to David.

11:1-3 [cf. 2 Sam 5:1-5] David is made king in Israel

In verse 1 "all Israel" suggests an inclusive view of Israel which the Chronicler offers rather than "the tribes of Israel" in 2 Samuel 5:1. The Chronicler does not distinguish between Judah and the northern tribes of Israel. Verse 2 is the one place in Chronicles where Saul is referred to as king. In verse 3 the phrase "in accordance with the word of the Lord given through Samuel" is an addition by the Chronicler. It might refer to 2 Samuel 7:7-8 (cf. 1 Chr 17:6-7), but it might also hearken back to 1 Samuel 15:28 and 16:1-13. It underlines God's choice of David to be king, an important part of the Chronicler's theology.

11:4-9 [cf. 2 Sam 5:6-10] David captures Zion

As in Samuel, David's capture of this Canaanite city as capital of his kingdom is an important part of David's military strategy. The Chronicler narrates David's capture of Zion more briefly and less dramatically than Samuel. For the Chronicler, the event has a much more theological tone, showing God's final plan for David and Jerusalem. In verse 4, David "and all Israel" (instead of "the king and his men" of Samuel) furthers the Chronicler's notion of inclusivity, especially regarding the northern tribes. The Chronicler omits the difficult saying about the blind and the lame (2 Sam 5:6, 8). Verse 6 has a play on words: the one who "first" strikes down Jebusites will be chief (i.e., "first"), so Joab becomes the chief ("first"), even though he is not included in the lists of David's supporters (1 Chr 11:10–12:40).

11:10-47 [cf. 2 Sam 23:8-39] David's mighty men

As David's story begins, the Chronicler includes lists of the mighty men who gave him solid support from the very start. Moreover, the Chronicler omits all the stories of David's rise to power in 1 Samuel. Therefore, a different portrait of David emerges: a divinely chosen leader with resounding support from various groups in Israel, both north and south.

Verse 10 shows the Chronicler's theology: David was made king according to the word of the Lord concerning Israel. Here and at 12:23, the Chronicler asserts that David's kingship was God's doing, and not David's own accomplishment. Verses 11-47 are drawn mostly from 2 Samuel 23:8-39, except for the last six verses. In 2 Samuel this list of mighty men comes after all the David stories, almost like an appendix. Here the list resembles a list of characters in the great capture of Zion that was just narrated. The "Three" and the "Thirty" are groups of David's elite warriors and officers. One story lies within these lists of warriors: the Three who brought water from the cistern at Bethlehem (11:15-19) demonstrate their great loyalty to David, while he shows his own humility in face of their courage. Verses 41b-47 are drawn from sources other than Samuel. These names, including Uriah the Hittite, refer to locations east of the Jordan River.

12:1-23 David's helpers at Ziklag

This section, with no parallel in Samuel, is a composition by the Chronicler. It refers to David's time with the Philistines at Ziklag (cf. 1 Sam 27:6), depicts the widespread support for David, and recalls the time before he was acclaimed king. He has the support of Benjaminites, Saul's own tribe (12:2b-8, 17), of the Gadites (12:9-16; not well known in Deuteronomistic History) and Manassites in the north (12:20-21, a story which summarizes some incidents in 1 Sam 28–30). In verse 19, Amasai, chief of the Thirty, speaks with prophetic inspiration of David's beneficial relationship (peace is mentioned three times) with his supporters. This language of closeness points to the unity that exists when David takes the throne. This feeling of intimate relationship will be sundered in the time of Rehoboam, when the kingdom is divided (2 Chr 10:16).

12:24-41 David's army at Hebron

Composed by the Chronicler, this section offers a more inclusive listing of Israel's troops which come to David at Hebron, not just the heads or the commanders. It includes soldiers from all the tribes of Israel (including divisions of Levi, into Zadokites and Aaronites) and the two sons of Joseph (Ephraim and Manasseh as two separate half-tribes) so that the total could be considered fourteen. Verses 39-41 contain language typical of the Chronicler: David's kingdom as "all Israel" drawn up in battle array with "resolute intention," with all the rest of Israel "of one mind," i.e., in agreement. Verses 40-41 mention three days of festive celebration, with much eating and drinking of various delicacies which were brought by donkeys, camels, mules, and oxen by three northern tribes: Issachar, Zebulun, and Naphtali. No wonder there was rejoicing in Israel! This word "rejoicing" (12:41) also appears in 2 Chronicles 30:23, 26 (Hezekiah's Passover festival) and in other post-exilic worship festivals (Neh 8:12, 17, and 12:43). Rejoicing describes a characteristic mood of festive celebration. Joyful eating and drinking characterize most public worship events in Chronicles.

13:1-4 David proposes to bring the ark to Jerusalem

David's transfer of the ark to Jerusalem continues for four chapters: 1 Chronicles 13:1–16:43. The Chronicler rearranges the story found in 2 Samuel 5–6. David's concern for the ark of God comes first, before he negotiates with Hiram of Tyre and defeats the Philistines, and before the record of his posterity (in 2 Samuel, these events precede his decision to move the ark). For the Chronicler, David's concern for the ark, for Israel's worship of God, is his primary role as chosen king.

In this section, composed by the Chronicler, David consults his commanders, and then the assembly of Israel, about the ark. They all participate in the decision to lead the ark to Jerusalem, since it had been neglected in the days of Saul. All the people demonstrate the correct attitude toward the ark (modeling a proper attitude toward symbols of the Lord in the Chronicler's own day). Special mention of priests and Levites in verse 2 indicates his religious concerns.

13:5-14 [cf. 2 Sam 6:1-11] David goes to bring the ark

The Chronicler follows the source in 2 Samuel, with a few differences. In verse 5 "from Shihor of Egypt to Lebo-hamath," i.e., from Egypt to Lebanon, denotes the widest boundaries ever claimed by Israel and suggests David's total inclusion of all peoples ever considered part of Israel. Next the Chronicler follows the story in 2 Samuel: David and all Israel go to bring the ark, which they transport on a cart drawn by oxen to the house of Abinadab, while singing and dancing in great liturgical procession. When the oxen stumble and Uzzah tries to save the ark from falling, God's anger flares forth because of the command not to touch the ark. In anger, David discontinues the journey, leaving the ark at the house of Obed-edom, which is abundantly blessed by its presence.

14:1-2 [cf. 2 Sam 5:11-12] Hiram's recognition of David

The Chronicler follows the Samuel text closely. Hiram of Tyre's international recognition of David occurs after David demonstrates his concern for the ark. Thus, David's concern for worship brings benefits in the political realm.

14:3-7 [cf. 2 Sam 5:13-16; cf. 1 Chr 3:5-9] David's children born at Jerusalem

The Chronicler follows Samuel, though he does not mention David's concubines (2 Sam 5:13). In a comparable genealogical section (1 Chr 3:5-9), the Chronicler does mention David's concubines, as well as Tamar his daughter, whose narrative in 2 Samuel 13 is not reproduced in Chronicles. Theologically, a large household, as here attributed to David, is a blessing from God. This blessing of progeny also follows the king's initiative concerning the ark and worship of God.

14:8-17 [cf. 2 Sam 5:17-25] David defeats the Philistines

The Chronicler follows 2 Samuel, adding the comment that David's fame spread to all the nations (14:17). This victory again follows David's concern for the ark, suggesting that his military strength depended on his concern for worship.

LITURGY FOR INSTALLING THE ARK

1 Chronicles 15–16

These chapters constitute a very important text for the Chronicler, who transforms a brief notice in 2 Samuel 6:12-19a (about David's transfer of the ark to Jerusalem) into a major liturgical festival of transfer and dedication of the ark. It also includes a lengthy psalm of thanksgiving, which portrays the spiritual climate of the celebration.

15:1–16:6 [cf. 2 Sam 6:12-19a] David brings the ark to Jerusalem

In 15:1-24 David prepares for the transfer of the ark, i.e., the arrangement of a grand liturgical action. The Levites should carry the ark in procession and they must prepare (i.e., "sanctify") themselves for the ceremony. The Levites Obed-edom and Jeiel should be the doorkeepers at the sanctuary after this liturgy. This liturgy seems an example of the kind of worship the Chronicler recommends for people of his day. This unit is an original composition of the Chronicler and it highlights his interest in worship, its texts, its music and song, and its officials.

Levites have prominent roles at the temple and in worship. They carry the ark (15:2). In fact, the first attempt to bring the ark to Jerusalem (13:9-11) had failed because Levites did not carry it (15:13). They carry the ark on their shoulders, as Moses had commanded (15:14-15). They are responsible for song and music—a song of joy. So they appoint their kindred to play musical instruments (e.g., cymbals, harps, lyres) and to sing (15:16-22). Finally, some Levites serve as doorkeepers for the ark (15:23, 24). Priests are appointed to blow trumpets before the ark (15:24). Processions with the ark, music, and song are important parts of this type of worship.

First Chronicles 15:25–16:6 is the second part of this narrative. The Chronicler rewrites 2 Samuel 6:12-19, following the sources fairly closely, but with the following changes. First, when David goes to the house of Obed-edom to bring the ark, he is accompanied by the elders of Israel and the officers of the thousands (15:25). Then, in the next verse, the Chronicler says "God helped the Levites to carry the ark of the covenant" (15:26). The Levites enjoy divine favor in Chronicles.

David's clothing and that of the Levites in 15:27 is also distinctly priestly: fine linen robes, and also the ephod in both Samuel and Chronicles. As in Samuel, Michal (Saul's daughter and David's wife) looks on David's dancing with disgust (15:29). Here her reaction is hard to understand, for she has observed a liturgical procession, not the bawdy, raucous parade of 2 Samuel. She

and David's family appear just to be petty. At this point, the Chronicler omits the ugly scene between David and Michal in 2 Samuel 6:20-23.

In 16:1-3 the Chronicler returns to issues of worship. After this procession reaches the tent, the ritual continues as they make burnt offerings and thanksgiving offerings, and David blesses the people and distributes food delicacies to all. As usual in Chronicles, this type of ceremony is conducted with rejoicing. Then, in 16:4-6, the Chronicler further describes duties of Levites. They serve before the ark, appointed to "celebrate, thank, and praise the Lord" (we prefer "invoke" rather than "celebrate" of the NAB). The Chronicler may indicate three types of psalm-prayers found in the book of Psalms: lament-petitions to God, thanksgiving psalms, and hymns of praise. Asaph the Levite and his family receive important musical tasks (interestingly, there are twelve psalms attributed to Asaph: Psalms 50 and 73–83). Two priests are appointed to make music on trumpets.

16:7-36 [cf. Pss 105:1-15; 96:1-13; 106:1, 47-48] David's psalm of thanksgiving

The Chronicler adds this long psalm adapted for the occasion by Asaph and his brothers. It includes verses from several canonical psalms. Psalm 105 praises and thanks God for good deeds done for Israel, especially the covenant. Psalm 96 is a hymn of praise, which claims that the Lord is king and calls the people to worship. Psalm 106 is a thanksgiving psalm, but the Chronicler incorporates only its beginning and ending verses (1 Chr 16:34-36; cf. Ps 106:1, 47-48). Verse 34 repeats a favorite refrain of postexilic Judah: "Give thanks to the Lord, who is good, whose love endures forever." Verse 35 changes tone, petitioning God their savior to gather and deliver them from the nations. The Chronicler might be reflecting postexilic Judah's desire to be freed of Persian interference and domination. The Chronicler implies that two different kinds of song go together at this point, praise and invocation of God.

16:37-42 Priests and Levites lead worship at Gibeon and Jerusalem

The Chronicler concludes the ceremony by assigning different tasks to priests and Levites at two different sites: Gibeon and Jerusalem. The altar of burnt offering remains at Gibeon, where Zadok and the other priests continue regular sacrificial offerings, and some Levites (Heman and Jeduthun) lead the music and song (16:39-42). At Jerusalem, where the ark is installed in the tent, Asaphite Levites lead the worship (without sacrifices). This sung worship seems to be an innovation of the Chronicler and probably mirrors worship patterns of his day. For the Chronicler, the time of Solomon saw both kinds of worship merge in the first temple, an example for his later era.

GOD'S COVENANT WITH DAVID AND HIS RESULTING SUCCESS

1 Chronicles 17–21

17:1-15 [cf. 2 Sam 7:1-16] God's covenant with David

David's concern for worship results in God's promise to establish his house, i.e., Solomon his son, and a lasting temple to be built by him. David's petition (16:35) has a response from God: the "favor" promised to David (17:13). This pattern of petition and response suggests that those who call upon God will find salvation.

The Chronicler's source is 2 Samuel 7, God's promise through Nathan the prophet to establish a lasting dynasty. The Chronicler states some conditions for the behavior of his successors and also changes the story in subtle ways. He omits the warning against sin by David's son (2 Sam 7:14b). Rather he focuses on the promise to confirm Solomon, who will build the temple. The Chronicler shifts the focus from David's dynasty to Solomon's temple. This alteration corresponds with the Chronicler's views on the importance of worship. David's proposal to build a house is transformed into a divine promise: a temple (i.e., house) built by his son, Solomon. Another subtle change of the Chronicler concerns "rest." David as a "man of rest" (2 Sam 7:1, 11) is omitted by the Chronicler in favor of Solomon who will be the "man of rest" (1 Chr 22:9). "Rest" in Chronicles seems to be a quality Israel experiences in association with the temple (2 Chr 6:41). Perhaps the Chronicler adjusts the promise to reflect the reality of his day, i.e., a temple without a king. Thus, his community can find a new person of "rest" and a place of "rest" in the temple of their day.

17:16-27 [cf. 2 Sam 7:18-29] David's prayer

David utters a prayer of praise and thanksgiving to God for his "house" (i.e., family, dynasty), for Israel, and for God's promise of a temple. It begins with David's humble question, "Who am I" that I should be here? (17:16), which is also a confession of God's graciousness to him. One of the Chronicler's changes stands out: David claims that God has already blessed his household (17:27), whereas in Samuel God's blessing would be a future event (2 Sam 7:29). The Chronicler's David appears more secure and confident because God has already fulfilled his promises. The fate of David (recipient of God's gracious promise) intertwines with Israel's well-being, and the themes and the mood of David's prayer inspire his descendants, especially those of the Chronicler's era.

God's graciousness and David's receptivity work their way out in the next several chapters (1 Chr 18:1–20:8), where David enjoys overwhelming military success against various foes in surrounding countries: Edom, Moab, Ammon, and Philistia. We readers may wonder whether his victories in battle result from his desire to build God a house to dwell in (ch. 17) or from God's pleasure in the great worship ceremony (ch. 15–16). We may view this success as God's promise playing itself out in David's actions. To put it more theologically, David's success in battle demonstrates God's blessings for him.

18:1-13 [cf. 2 Sam 8:1-14; Ps 60:2] David's victories

David defeats Philistines (north and west, especially along the coast), Moabites (east, across the Jordan valley), Hadadezer of Zobah (north and east of Aram), and the Arameans (north and east). These victories demonstrate how God makes David victorious everywhere (18:6b, 13b). The Chronicler mentions that booty from battle and the bronze taken from battle with Hadadezer are later used by Solomon to construct the bronze sea and other temple vessels. Here in Chronicles David's nephew Abishai, rather than David himself, defeats the Edomites (1 Chr 18:12; cf. 2 Sam 8:13).

18:14-17 [cf. 2 Sam 8:15-18] List of David's officers

The Chronicler's only change is to redefine David's sons as officials rather than priests (2 Sam

8:18). Since they are not of the line of Aaron, the Chronicler presents a more cautious view (18:17).

19:1-19 [cf. 2 Sam 10:1-19] David defeats the Ammonites and Arameans

The Chronicler omits the story of David's graciousness to Meribbaal (2 Sam 9), the crippled son of his friend Jonathan. This story would contradict the Chronicler's assertion that all of Saul's household died with him at Mount Gilboa (1 Chr 10:6). The Chronicler, unlike Samuel, omits the ongoing power struggle between David and the house of Saul. For the Chronicler, the old order has passed away and a new one begun. In verses 6, 7, and 18, the Chronicler changes some details to magnify David's role, since enemies make peace with David rather than with Israel (2 Sam 10:19).

20:1-3 [cf. 2 Sam 11:1-12:31] Joab besieges and defeats Rabbah

The Chronicler mentions that Joab besieges and defeats Rabbah (present-day Amman), while David remains behind in Jerusalem. In 2 Samuel 11, David arranges from Jerusalem for the death of Uriah the Hittite, husband of Bathsheba. The stories of David and Bathsheba and Nathan's reproof of David (2 Sam 11–12) are not told in Chronicles.

20:4–21:27 Chronicles Omits the "Court History" of 2 Samuel 11–20

The Chronicler reproduces only eleven verses from ten chapters of 2 Samuel. The stories the Chronicler omitted include many incidents in which David's loyalty and character seem compromised, where he appears weakened by sin that affects him and most of his household negatively. Omitted are: David, Bathsheba, and Uriah; the rape of Tamar (daughter of David) by Amnon; the anger and rebellion of Absalom, son of David; the flight of David from Jerusalem; the death of Absalom; the revolt of Sheba; and the final quelling of the rebellious groups. The Chronicler omits much of the negative portrayal of David ("whitewash"), perhaps to make him appear more religious and saintly. The Chronicler pictures David as the initiator and leader of Israel's worship life at the Jerusalem temple. The Chronicler also includes stories (e.g., battle victories) that demonstrate the blessed outcomes of a life of dedicated worship.

20:4-8 [cf. 2 Sam 21:18-22] Giants slain by David and his men

Like David's victory over the Ammonites (20:1-3), his defeat of Philistines shows how God fulfills his blessings for David. For some reason, the Chronicler omits the beautiful psalm of David's thanksgiving (2 Sam 22:1-51, which is a nearly exact version of Ps 18). Likewise, the Chronicler skips David's "last words" in 2 Samuel 23:1-7. Though both poems present magnificent religious and spiritual motifs, they differ from the public liturgical songs of praise and thanksgiving which the Chronicler seems to prefer.

21:1-27 [cf. 2 Sam 24:1-25] David's census of Israel and Judah

This is a pivotal chapter, since the Chronicler presents David's first personal encounter with sin. This story provides an opportunity to select a site for the temple. Theologically, God seems to respond to those who are seeking him, with the temple as symbol of God's readiness to grant mercy. So the Chronicler emphasizes this event, which was merely one of the "miscellaneous" stories in 2 Samuel 21–24.

The Chronicler alters the story significantly. In 2 Samuel 24:1, God's wrath has flared against Israel, so he incites David to sin by ordering the census. The Chronicler says a satan or "an adversary"—and not God—stands against Israel and incites David (21:1). This Satan is like the Satan in Job 1–2, a troublemaker opposed to Job in the heavenly court. The Chronicler thus removes from God any responsibility for tempting David to this sinful action. Next, where 2 Samuel speaks of the threshing floor, the Chronicler changes it to "the place" (21:22, 25), signifying that it would be a site of something special. Some Jewish writings use "the place" as a synonym for the temple, and even refer it to God.

This section comprises four parts. First comes a census, i.e., a military draft (21:1-7); the story implies that all these soldiers belong to David, rather than to God. Second, the prophecy of Gad occurs when David becomes aware of his sin and asks for forgiveness (21:8-13). Through Gad God presents David with three options: famine, enemy attack, or pestilence. David chooses the third, presuming it comes directly from God (whom he offended) and leaves open possibility of divine compassion (21:13). Third, the plague results in the death of seventy thousand (21:14-17). After-wards, God sends a divine messenger to destroy Jerusalem, but at the last moment the Lord sees and repents, telling the messenger to stop the slaughter. This messenger is standing at the threshing floor of Ornan the Jebusite (Araunah, in 2 Sam), between earth and heaven with his drawn sword in his hand (21:16). This terrible sight symbolizes only a lull in the killing, for the sword is still drawn. So David and the elders make a gesture of penitence, and David confesses his sin—his alone—and begs mercy for his people, "these sheep" (21:17). Fourth, David purchases the threshing floor and the plague ends (21:18-27). Afterwards, David offers sacrifices (21:23, 27) together with his prayer of petition. When fire descends from heaven on the offerings, it demon-strates God's favor, just as at other key moments in biblical tradition (Lev 9:24, the beginning of Aaron's priesthood; 1 Kgs 18:38, Elijah on Mt. Carmel. Later in 2 Chr 7:1 fire will descend on offerings in Solomon's temple, showing divine acceptance of sacrifices and divine hostility com-ing to an end).

21:28–22:1 The site for the temple

The Chronicler points to this "place" for a con-tinuing encounter with God in the temple, for David sacrifices at the threshing floor of Ornan the Jebusite. The key point is in 22:1: "This is the house of the Lord God, and this is the altar for burnt offerings for Israel." This verse points to the ultimate religious symbol in this place, the temple to be built by Solomon, with its altar of burnt offering. But for the present (and until Solomon), the tabernacle and altar for offerings are still at the high place at Gibeon. Even though David will not build the temple, he prepares the site for con-struction. For the Chronicler, worship of God in the temple was the final goal of David's reign.

PREPARING FOR THE TEMPLE

1 Chronicles 22–29

These chapters have no parallel source else-where in the Bible, so they highlight the Chroni-cler's concern with the temple, its construction, and all its personnel. All these events occur dur-ing David's reign instead of Solomon's, while some verses in Kings about Solomon constructing

the temple are omitted. Thus, the Chronicler's goal seems clear: to show that David really planned the temple and its worship. Chapters 22, 28, and 29 contain narratives about David's ac-tions, while chapters 23–27 contain lists of person-nel for the temple. These chapters give detailed lists of priests and Levites (chs. 23–24), musicians (ch. 25), gatekeepers and overseers (ch. 26), and officials of the kingdom (ch. 27). The Chronicler portrays David positively, showing him as a good king, worthy to be remembered by Israel and by God.

22:2–23:1 David's preparations for the temple

In verses 2-4, David gathers stones, iron, bronze, and cedar for temple building because Solomon is still "young and inexperienced" (22:5). Then he addresses Solomon privately, telling him to build the temple (22:6-16). David cannot do so because he has shed so much blood (22:8). It seems that waging war disqualifies David from enacting his religious program. But Solomon is a "peaceful man," so he will bring Israel peace and quiet all his days (22:9). Some of the language in this speech reflects Nathan's message to David in 1 Chronicles 17:1-15. In 1 Chronicles 22:17-19 David instructs Israel's leaders to help Solomon in this task. Next, in 1 Chronicles 23:1, David makes Solomon king. In Samuel–Kings, there are many struggles in David's family over the succes-sion to the throne, including an attempt to usurp it by his elder son Adonijah while David is lying on his deathbed. Here, in Chronicles, political intrigue and infighting evaporate, just as the struggles between David and Saul have vanished.

23:2-32 Division and duties of Levites

David assigns 38,000 Levites to four different tasks: 24,000 for service of the temple; 6,000 as officers and judges; 4,000 as gatekeepers; and 4,000 for choral music and song (23:3-5). The divi-sions of Levites correspond to the sons of Levi: Gershon (23:7-11); Kohath (23:12-20); and Merari (23:21-23). David then outlines Levitical duties (23:26-32). They do not carry the tabernacle or its instruments (23:26), but they do assist the priests for the service in the temple (23:28-29). They sing thanks and praise at morning and evening worship and whenever the priests offer burnt offerings, especially at sabbaths, new moons, and festivals

(23:30-31). Levites also oversee the tent of meeting and the sanctuary (23:32). The responsibilities and rights of Levites all depend on decisions made by King David.

24:1-31 Divisions and duties of priests and of additional Levites

The postexilic priests are divided up into twenty-four courses or groups, which take turns officiating at the Jerusalem temple, alternating week after week. These are listed as deriving from Aaron's surviving sons, Eleazar and Ithamar, since Nadab and Abihu died in the desert (cf. Lev 10:1-3; Num 3:4). The Chronicler depicts priests of the line of Eleazar as superior, with Zadok listed among them (24:3-4). Shemaiah the Levite writes down this list in the presence of King David and some prominent priests (24:6). There follows another list of Levites (24:20-30), who cast lots for their positions, just like priests (24:31).

25:1–26:32 Additional Levitical officers: musicians, gatekeepers, and overseers

David and his army officers set up the families of Asaph, Heman, and Jeduthun as musicians for the temple (25:1, 6) and divide them by lot into twenty-four divisions of Levites, paralleling the priests in chapter 24. These Levites prophesy on lyres, harps, and cymbals (25:1). So the music ministry of Levites has a prophetic character, which indicates high regard for their work. David, then, is also responsible for the twenty-four courses of Levite singers with prophetic powers. Moreover, in 2 Chronicles 20 an important Levite will prophesy to King Jehoshaphat in time of grave danger from enemy armies. Chapter 26 lists those Levites serving as gatekeepers and overseers of finances and other civil matters.

27:1-34 Officers of the kingdom

David now lists other officials, not Levites, associated with the king: military leaders (27:1-15), tribal leaders (27:16-24), stewards of the king's property (27:25-31), and members of the royal cabinet (27:32-34). He lists 24,000 workers for each month (27:1-15), and then mentions some well-known advisors of the king: Ahitophel, Hushai, Jehoiada son of Benaiah, Abiathar, and Joab. Many names in this list mirror names in 1 Chronicles 11–12 (i.e., David's supporters from the time

of the monarchy), but they mix with new names that may come from the Persian era, the time of the Chronicler.

28:1–29:9 David entrusts temple building to Solomon

In verses 2-10, David addresses an assembly of all royal and civil officials of Israel in a speech that pulls together all the motifs and themes of chapters 22–27. This speech reflects many issues from David's private address to Solomon in 22:6-16, including God's promise to David through Nathan the prophet (1 Chr 17). Solomon would build the temple (28:6-10) and be blessed with a dynasty if he would remain faithful to God's commands (28:7). David exhorts the leaders to study all God's commands and ordinances; then they will receive the divine blessing (28:8). David turns next to say to Solomon: "know the God of your father and serve him with a whole heart" because God "searches all hearts and understands all the mind's thoughts" (28:9). God's knowledge of human hearts echoes language used before the Flood (Gen 6:5). There God knows human hearts, especially their evil inclinations, and this grieves God. But here the Chronicler takes an optimistic turn: the phrase "perfect heart" shows up several times in Chronicles to describe total devotion to God (e.g., 1 Chr 12:38; 28:9; 29:9, 19; 2 Chr 15:17; 16:9; 19:9; 25:2). It probably comes from Deuteronomy 6:5 ("You shall love the Lord, your God, with all your heart"). This spiritual stance leads to a hopeful saying in verse 9: "If you search for him, he will be found." David concludes: since God has chosen you, Solomon, to build the temple, you must act on it.

In verses 11-19 David transfers to Solomon the temple plans (of the building, of the priests and Levites, of the vessels and decorations), which he had received in writing from God (28:19). He then exhorts Solomon to be courageous and not fearful, for God is with him and will support him, even with all the human assistants he may need (28:20-21).

In 29:1-9 David delivers a third farewell speech (cf. 22:6-16 and 28:2-10) to the assembly, admonishing them to cooperate with Solomon. David lists his generous gifts (29:2-5) and those of others in his administration (29:6-8). All these gifts lead to great rejoicing (29:9), for "[the offerings] had been contributed to the Lord wholeheartedly."

Recounting all those donations is probably intended to challenge the hearers to respond generously themselves. Verse 9 begins and ends with the notion of joy (joyful celebration), while the notion of a whole heart stands in the center of this verse. For the Chronicler total devotion to God leads to joyful celebration.

29:10-22a David's farewell liturgy

Here the Chronicler articulates the lofty theology of his postexilic age. He begins with praise and thanksgiving for the God of Israel, expressed in expansive and abstract terms like greatness, power, and glory; and he acknowledges that the kingdom belongs to the Lord (29:11). This language, by the way, resembles the final doxology in the Lord's Prayer: "For the kingdom, the power, and the glory are yours, now and forever." God has the power to make everything strong and lasting. Therefore, David and everyone with him join in praising and thanking God (29:12-13). All is gift from God, so David and his people are grateful recipients of divine grace, as he says, aliens and guests before God (29:14-15). David changes from praising God (29:10-13) to confessing utter dependence on God (29:14-17). His prayer concludes with two petitions: keep your people strong in this spirituality (29:18) and give Solomon a "wholehearted desire" so that he can obey your commands and build the temple (29:19).

These same three elements characterize David's prayer in 1 Chronicles 16:8-36: confession of our sad state as landless patriarchs (16:8-22); praise of God as king (16:23-33); and a petition (16:35). These two prayers (in chs. 16 and 29) pull together key elements of David's ministry for Israel: installing the ark of God at its place in Jerusalem and passing on the reign and temple-building to his son Solomon. The Chronicler's audience should always be able to discern the influence of King David in his views of the temple and its worship.

Afterwards, David invites the others to participate in vocal prayer (praising God, 29:20a) and in gesture (prostration, 29:20b), and in the offering of sacrifices (29:21). This ceremony concludes with "great rejoicing," i.e., with the entire congregation eating and drinking joyfully. Joyful worship, not political intrigue and infighting, are King David's final legacy, as the Chronicler retells this story for his Jewish community.

29:22b-30 [1 Kgs 2:10-12] Solomon becomes king after David's death

In 23:1 David had declared Solomon king, but here the Chronicler repeats it, mentioning the appointment of Zadok as priest (29:22). We learn in advance that Solomon will receive the allegiance of all David's sons, as well as countless riches and blessings. Then follow the basic statistics of David's reign (forty years: seven years in Hebron and thirty-three years in Jerusalem) and the simple statement that David has died (29:27-28). This chapter concludes with a typical note about the sources of the Chronicler's information: Chronicles of Samuel the seer, of Nathan the prophet, and of Gad the seer (29:29).

COMMENTARY: 2 CHRONICLES

SOLOMON

2 Chronicles 1–9

Acclaimed as king by all Israel (1 Chr 29:20-25), Solomon was not the candidate of any particular group. Like David, his father, he proved to be an avid patron of divine worship at the temple, which he constructed and dedicated, following David's instructions. Solomon's role in worship overshadows his wise actions, so strong in 1 Kings and in other biblical traditions. The Chronicler makes a very significant change in his portrayal of Solomon. Here he is not a man of sin, as in 1 Kings 11, where his many wives and concubines lead him astray. The Chronicler simply omitted all the offending sections of 1 Kings, just as he skipped over most of David's sins and problems in 2 Samuel 11–20. Here is an idyllic picture of national solidarity and prosperity.

1:1-13 [cf. 1 Kgs 2:12b; 2:46b; 3:1-15; 4:1a] Solomon prays for wisdom at Gibeon

In this version Solomon took hold of royal power unhindered, since the Lord supported him (1:1; cf. 1 Kgs 2:12b, 46b). The Chronicler omits information in Kings about the king's political marriage with the daughter of Pharaoh (1 Kgs 3:1). He journeys to Gibeon (1:2-6), the great high place where the tent of meeting (with the ark) and the bronze altar were located (1:3-5). Solomon and all the people go in procession to Gibeon (2 Chr 3:3).

The ark of God was the central religious symbol in the books of Joshua and Samuel, while the tent was the major religious symbol of priestly traditions in the Pentateuch; here the Chronicler joins them all together. Since 1 Kings waged a verbal campaign against worship at the high places, the writer needed to justify Solomon's trip there—i.e., the temple had not yet been built. The Chronicler has a more complex view of Israel's worship during the time of Solomon. The tabernacle built by Moses in the wilderness, with its altar for sacrifices, was still at Gibeon, where they conducted full worship ceremonies: sacrifices and song. After David moved to Jerusalem, the ark and the tent were symbols of another religious movement: music and song.

The Chronicler solves two problems of Israel's worship. First, he shows why Solomon could go to Gibeon to pray; second, he provides a smooth transition between the older pattern of worship, established by Moses and practiced by the priests in the desert, and the newer worship which also includes choral music and song by the Levites, representing David's liturgical innovations. This story in Chronicles helped people of the Chronicler's day appreciate worship with both sacrifice and song at their temple.

Solomon goes to Gibeon, offers sacrifices, and then makes his famous prayer (1:8-12; cf. 1 Kgs 3:6-15). The Chronicler reduces the content in 1 Kings by about half, especially by omitting some of the typical Deuteronomistic language (e.g., 1 Kgs 3:6-8, 10). Here Solomon asks for gifts more closely resembling those God gives him, "wisdom and knowledge"; in 1 Kings 3:9 he had requested an "understanding heart to judge your people." In Chronicles, Solomon wants these gifts so that he can lead this people and govern appropriately. As in Kings, Solomon receives more gifts than he asks for: wisdom, knowledge, riches, treasures, and glory (1:11-12). But the Chronicler omits verses in Kings which demonstrate Solomon's wisdom: the story of Solomon's judgment between the two harlots and the one living child (1 Kgs 3:16-28), and the lists of Solomon's administrators and officials, which demonstrated his wisdom at governance (1 Kgs 4:1-19).

1:14-17 [cf. 1 Kgs 4:20–5:14; 2 Chr 9:25-28; 1 Kgs 10:26-29] The wealth of Solomon

The Chronicler describes Solomon's wealth: chariots, horsemen, horses, silver and gold, and cedar for (temple) construction. Mentioning them right after Solomon's prayer shows how God's gift of wisdom also resulted in wealth. Information about Solomon's wealth, wisdom, and horses is repeated in 2 Chronicles 9:25-28. By repeating this information, the Chronicler shows that Solomon's wisdom and wealth do not fail him (unlike 1 Kgs 11, where his reign ends disgracefully, in sin).

1:18–2:17 [cf. 1 Kgs 5:15-32] Solomon's treaty with King Huram

This story shows that Gentile kings now recognize Solomon. The decision to build a temple is Solomon's first action after receiving the gift of wisdom (1:18). Here, unlike Kings, Solomon initiated correspondence with Huram of Tyre (Hiram in Kings), which gives him a bit more stature. Since the Chronicler has more interest in worship than the book of Kings, he describes temple vessels, furnishings, and rituals not mentioned in Kings: incense and bread offerings for daily morning and evening sacrifice, and for Sabbaths, new moons, and appointed festivals. Each of these practices is known from the Pentateuch, but the Chronicler implies that all should take place in the temple of his day. Later kings will be judged by their fidelity to these criteria (e.g., 2 Chr 13; 28; 29–31).

All these negotiations with Huram of Tyre focus on building and equipping the temple, as Huram's response emphasizes in his letter to Solomon (2:10-15). He realizes that the Lord loves Solomon and ought to be blessed for appointing Solomon to such a task, so he will send to him a skilled helper, Huram-abi. In 2 Chronicles 2:16-17 Solomon counts as workers all the aliens, probably the Hittites, Amorites, Perizzites, Hivites, and the Jebusites not from Israel (2 Chr 8:7). By speaking of aliens [resident aliens], he implies that they are no longer foreigners but are still not incorporated into Israel. Here is another occasion where the Chronicler includes all the various groups in the land in Israel.

3:1-14 [cf. 1 Kgs 6:1-31] Solomon builds a house for the Lord

Now Solomon accomplishes his plan; this description is about half as long as its counterpart in Kings. The Chronicler omits completely 1 Kings 6:4-18; 29-38; and 7:1-12. Curiously, the Chronicler abbreviates descriptions of the temple, its construction and furnishings, even though he puts more emphasis on worship and the temple. Apparently the Chronicler has more interest in what went on in the temple than in its furnishings. Also, many details mentioned in Kings may not have existed in the second, rebuilt temple of the Chronicler's era.

Solomon chooses to locate the temple at the site of David's sacrifice (1 Chr 22:1). The Chronicler also names the site Moriah, the place of Abraham's offering of Isaac (Gen 22:2, 14), so this may be the first witness to an ancient tradition that the temple stands on Mount Moriah, site of Abraham's sacrifice. Thus the Chronicler connects traditions about Abraham and Isaac with those about David's sacrifice and plan for the temple.

3:15–5:1 [cf. 1 Kgs 7:15-51; 2 Kgs 25:17; Jer 52:21-23] The work in the temple

Many details about the physical construction and appearance of the temple derive from Kings, but much of that is not reproduced here, esp. 1 Kings 7:27-37. The Chronicler describes the two columns, Jachin and Boaz (3:15-17), which are also known from 2 Kings 25:17 and Jeremiah 52:21-22. He then describes the bronze altar (4:1), the molten sea (4:2-5), ten basins (4:6), ten menorahs of gold (4:7), the ten tables (4:8), the courtyards for priests and the great court (4:9), pots, shovels, and bowls (4:11) and then describes the placement of all these sacred objects (4:11-16). Then he describes Solomon's work with all these sacred objects (4:17-22) and says that Solomon put them all in the temple treasuries (5:1). The only object here that is not found in Kings is the bronze altar (4:1), though it does appear elsewhere in the source (1 Kgs 8:64; 2 Kgs 16:14).

5:2-14 [cf. 1 Kgs 8:1-11] Solomon brings the ark into the temple

In the seventh month Solomon summons all Israel to bring the ark into the temple (5:2-3). The elders enter along with the Levites, who carry the ark to the tent, while priests help to carry the sacred vessels and solemnize the ritual with animal sacrifices (5:4-6). In a solemn assembly of all Israel, they carry the ark to its place, "the inner sanctuary of the house, the holy of holies, beneath the wings of the cherubin" (5:7).

Three times during this worship service the Chronicler mentions sacred song: in 5:11-14 (esp. 5:13); in 7:1-3; and in 7:4-6. Song does not appear in the parallel passages in Kings. The Chronicler emphasizes that David established sacred song and he fashioned the musical instruments. It was sung by Levites and priests, and presumably all the people. The Chronicler also notes how huge public sacrifices were accompanied by song with joy, contrary to some scholars who think that Israel's sacrifice was always a silent affair.

A different kind of liturgy occurs in 5:11-14: the priests exit from the shrine and are joined east of the altar by large numbers of Levites singing along with the one hundred and twenty priests making music on trumpets. Then a cloud fills the temple as a sign of divine presence (5:14); smoking incense may have carried this meaning in the Chronicler's community. The Chronicler creates this liturgy of choral song (5:11-14), just like his other two descriptions of sung worship within the temple dedication service. Levites sing "praise to the Lord, who is so good, whose love endures forever" (5:13).

This antiphon is very characteristic of postexilic texts. It already appeared in the psalm of thanksgiving at the worship ceremony in David's era (1 Chr 16:34). In general it praises the Lord's ongoing goodness and steadfastness in language that reminds us of the covenant with Moses. We may imagine a cantor and a choir singing this antiphonally, like Psalm 118, reminding us of the covenant and praising God wholeheartedly in grateful acceptance. The Chronicler redefines the style of worship for this moment by introducing Levites and their choirs as a central element. Finally, the cloud that fills the temple reminds Israel of God's presence (5:14), a symbol drawn from old priestly traditions: Exodus 24:17; 40:34; and Numbers 17:7.

6:1–7:10 [cf. 1 Kgs 8:12-66; Ps 132:1, 8-10; Ps 136:1] Temple dedication

This long, complicated ceremony owes much to the Chronicler's source in Kings, but there are significant changes. Israel's heritage in Egypt is downplayed. When speaking of the ark "of the covenant," the Chronicler fails to mention their ancestors coming out of Egypt as God's covenant partners (as in 1 Kgs 8:21). At the end of this prayer, the Chronicler omits the verse in Kings describing Israel as a people brought out of Egypt and set apart by God, as Moses the prophet had proclaimed (1 Kgs 8:53).

Solomon's prayer (6:12-42) is the centerpiece of the service in both Kings and Chronicles, but the Chronicler introduces changes. In 1 Kings the king was simply standing before the altar at prayer (1 Kgs 8:22), but here he was standing on a bronze platform (6:13), possibly the liturgical practice of the Chronicler's era.

Solomon's long prayer (6:13-42) highlights the temple as a house of prayer (as in 1 Kgs 8:22-54), a place for petition to God for God's people Israel, especially when they suffer distress. This prayer petitions God, as do psalms of lament, and it seems to fulfill a task that the Chronicler assigns to Levites, to "invoke" God in petitions. Here Levites also fulfill their role in choral song, and later they give thanks. The prayer refers to seven occasions for the people Israel to approach God, so it is often called a Prayer of the People. The crises that call for such prayer are: improper oaths (6:22-23); defeat in war (6:24-25); drought (6:26-27); famine and pestilence (6:28-31); a foreigner praying to God in the temple (6:32-33); God's people going out to battle (6:34-35); and God's people sinning against God (6:36-39).

In the postexilic context one petition stands out: foreigners (e.g., Gentiles) coming to pray in the temple characterizes the Chronicler but contradicts views of Gentiles in other postexilic books (e.g., Ezra and Nehemiah). The second and sixth occasions for prayer concern Israel at war or battle, praying here in the temple for divine help. After the time of Solomon, the Chronicler will show the effectiveness of such prayer in seven different situations. Each time God saves Israel (Judah) against their enemies: Egypt (12:1-8); the northern kingdom of Israel (13:13-16); Zerah of Cush (14:11-12); the Arameans (18:31-32); Moab and Ammon (20:5-17); Edom (25:7-11); and Assyria (32:20-22). This lesson of history shows proper recourse to God in times of crisis.

The Chronicler continues Solomon's prayer with words drawn from Psalm 132, an ancient psalm for processions with the ark. This psalm glorifies David as he brings the ark to Jerusalem, and it celebrates God's choice of David, of the temple, and of the ark. It suggests that Israel—after the exile, in the Chronicler's era—should return to their ancient style of worship, bringing the ark to the temple and singing Psalm 132. In verse 41 the words "Arise, Lord God" come from an ancient song Israel sang when they carried the ark into battle (Num 10:35). This song's theology envisions God's presence moving into the temple. This is a more priestly theology than that in Kings, which describes the temple as the place where God's name dwells.

The Chronicler changes other words of Psalm 132. Priests should clothe themselves with salvation (i.e., saving, delivering properties) rather than with clothing of righteousness (1 Kgs). This small change suggests a desire for God's decisive military aid in the Chronicler's era. The Chronicler says that God's priests should rejoice in goodness (they sing out in Kings). "Rejoice" is a technical word for festive worship, which the Chronicler recommends. The Chronicler's use of Psalm 132 gives the sense of solemn procession and worship.

In 2 Chronicles 7:1-11, like his source in Kings, the Chronicler describes the consecration of the middle court (7:7), the seven-day festival and consecration of the altar (probably the Feast of Booths/Tabernacles, the harvest festival in autumn), and an additional seven days (7:8-9). They rejoiced because of all the good the Lord did for them. This liturgical celebration leads to great benefit and blessing from God, so the Chronicler shows the proper response of the people: sacrifice and also song, always expressed with great joy.

7:11-22 [cf. 1 Kgs 9:1-9] God responds to Solomon's temple dedication

God appears to Solomon during the night after he dedicates the temple (7:12), concluding the dedication liturgy. God has heard the prayer of the temple and confirms the power of Solomon's prayers of petition (6:13-39). God promises Solomon an enduring kingly line if he will walk faithfully according to God's commands, as David his father did (7:17-18). Then God challenges Israel: if you turn aside from me and my commands then I will pluck you up, and the fate of your temple will shock everyone who sees it (7:19-22). Although the Chronicler follows the words of 1 Kings closely, the tone is different after the exile. The Chronicler focuses more on God's promise of blessing than on warnings.

8:1-18 [cf. 1 Kgs 9:10-28] Solomon's further activities

The Chronicler surveys Solomon's accomplishments on a more political front, i.e., the cities which he captured, controlled, built, and fortified. One telltale change by the Chronicler is the following: in 1 Kings 9:11 Solomon seems to hand over to Hiram (Huram in Chronicles) twenty cities in Galilee, but the Chronicler does not mention Solomon's subservience to Huram, so he suggests that Huram actually gave these twenty cities to Solomon (8:2). Solomon needs "forced labor" for his extravagant building projects, but the Chronicler points out that he enlisted descendants of the land's original inhabitants—Hittites, Amorites, Perizzites, Hivites and Jebusites—for this work, but not native Israelites (8:7-9).

Solomon marries Pharaoh's daughter, but the Chronicler abandons Kings' interpretation of this marriage (as evidence of Solomon's wisdom and wealth). For the Chronicler her presence in the city where the temple now stands presents a problem; his wife cannot reside in the palace because of its sacred precincts (8:11). Some think that these verses suggest Jerusalem is to be a sex-free zone, as the temple scroll from Qumran indicates, but others propose a more likely view: she must reside outside the zone of holiness if she keeps worshiping her ancestral gods.

The Chronicler gives more details about Israel's worship practices at the temple (8:12-16). Kings mentions three annual festivals with burnt offerings, peace offerings, and incense offerings (1 Kgs 9:25). Here Solomon arranges the proper sacrificial system (8:12) with its worship calendar: daily offerings, Sabbaths, new moons, and three annual festivals, as Moses commanded (8:13). He also arranges the divisions and work of the priests, Levites, and gatekeepers. Here Solomon finalizes the worship arrangements given by his father David.

9:1-12 [cf. 1 Kgs 10:1-13] Visit of the queen of Sheba

In this popular story she travels a long way to visit Solomon and her goal is to test him with riddles, to see if his wisdom matches his reputation (9:1). His correct answers demonstrate his wisdom, just as the wealth and beneficence of his house and temple give signs of wisdom (9:2-4). She praises his wisdom and acclaims him as king appointed to administer "right and justice" (9:8), further signs of wisdom. She brings magnificent gifts to Solomon, who uses them to furnish both his palace and the temple. Solomon even uses some of the precious cabinet wood he receives to make lyres and harps for temple singers (9:9-11). In the view that wisdom begets the good life—especially opulence—his wisdom is being recognized. Since wisdom crosses boundaries, it seems fitting that Solomon's wisdom is tested and pro-claimed by someone from another country. That this person is a woman and a queen adds to the perennial appeal of the story.

The Chronicler shows how Solomon's greatness was recognized by Gentiles both at the start (ch. 2) and end (ch. 9) of his story. The final sentence (9:12) claims that Solomon gave her all that she desired, more than she brought to him. His largesse is appropriate for a great and wise king.

9:13-28 [cf. I Kgs 10:14-29] Wisdom and happiness of Solomon

The opulence of this golden era of Israel's life is a measure of Solomon's wisdom, how he was gifted by God (9:22-23). Solomon's horses and stables and his trade in horses with rulers in Egypt, Aram, and the Hittites (9:25-28) again remind us of his wisdom. Often the horse with chariot is the equivalent of a modern war machine. The Chronicler ends the story of Solomon just as he began it, with his great wealth and riches (1:1-17). The comment here about his horses recalls 1:14-17; this is a literary repetition and it binds the entire Solomon section together and alerts readers to see what the Chronicler considers to be most important in Solomon's story.

The Chronicler omits from the older story of Solomon (1 Kgs 11:1-40) a description of the sin and errors of Solomon's life, especially all his wives and concubines. In Kings this chapter sets the theological stage for the division of the kingdom after his death; it also contains much historical information about opposition faced by Solomon, both external and internal. All that is absent in Chronicles. Solomon's faults and sins have vanished, and he emerges as the most faultless of the kings of Israel (even more so than David).

9:29-31 [cf. I Kgs 11:41-43] The death of Solomon

The Chronicler narrates Solomon's death and Rehoboam's succession to the throne with only minor changes to the account in Kings. In verse 29, the Chronicler omits Solomon's wisdom (1 Kgs 11:41) as a topic of discussion. For the Chronicler there were three additional prophetic sources of information to consult for further information: the acts of Nathan the prophet, the prophecy of Ahijah, and the visions of Iddo the seer. Only

Nathan and Ahijah are mentioned elsewhere. For the Chronicler, telling history becomes another of the tasks of the prophets.

THE DIVIDED MONARCHY

2 Chronicles 10–28

10:1–11:4 [cf. I Kgs 12:1-24] Israel's revolt

After Solomon's death Rehoboam goes north to Shechem to be made king, so Jeroboam returns home from Egypt to confront Rehoboam. Since the Chronicler skipped 1 Kings 11 with its justifications for rebelliousness against Solomon, he can blame this rebellion on Jeroboam and his followers. Jeroboam and his northern companions ask Rehoboam for lighter treatment than they received from Solomon.

Rehoboam consults first with his elders. They understand that a kingdom united North and South as under David and Solomon depends on the good will of all parties, but especially on Rehoboam's style of rule. They recommend a kindly approach in negotiations to render the Israelites generous (10:7). But Rehoboam also consults his impetuous younger advisors, who counsel forceful and harsh actions to make the northerners submit (10:10-11), and they insult their northern brothers. Unfortunately, Rehoboam prefers their advice, so he reacts harshly to the northerners and alienates them. Israel's rebellion against the house of David begins here (10:19).

Later, the Chronicler has King Abijah summarize this view of Jeroboam as a rebel (1 Chr 13:6-7). But Rehoboam, indecisive son of Solomon, could not stand up against his young counselors, so the Chronicler also hints that the rebellion was due to Rehoboam's ineptitude. But the Chronicler still follows Kings in explaining Rehoboam's rejection of advice as somehow intended by God (10:15; cf. 1 Kgs 12:15). Thus, the Chronicler remains ambivalent: the rebellion and division were brought about by God, but the willfulness of Jeroboam was responsible for its continuation.

The Chronicler changes the picture in Kings because he cannot admit a hint that Jeroboam's reign was legitimate. The Chronicler omits Kings' statement that all Israel went out to meet Jeroboam when he returned in order to make "him king over all Israel" (1 Kgs 12:20). In Chronicles, "all Israel" is the entire people, though it refers only to the North in Kings. In 11:4 Rehoboam and "all Israel" obey the words of the Lord by deciding not to go against Jeroboam. Now Rehoboam demonstrates a sensitivity to God's word (as in 11:17 and 12:5-6), a change from before.

11:5-23 The prosperity of Rehoboam

The Chronicler here paints a positive portrait of King Rehoboam. His building projects symbolize divine blessing on his reign (11:5-12). These projects demonstrate his prosperity and suggest a sound strategy: cities for defense, fortified with ample supplies of food, oil, wine, and weapons. Religious matters and reforms come up when the Chronicler speaks of Levites who had lived and worked in the northern kingdom of Israel but were prevented by Jeroboam from being priests to the Lord. Many decide to move south after being deprived of office by Jeroboam, who reforms northern religion by appointing his own priests. This detail, not found in Kings, proves quite interesting, since many scholars think that northern Levites moved south to Judah, bringing with them the Moses traditions which comprise the core of the book of Deuteronomy. The Chronicler describes the spirituality of those who joined Israel in the South. They had "set their hearts to seek the Lord, the God of Israel" (11:16), so they came to Jerusalem to make sacrifices there to God.

Altogether Rehoboam had eighteen wives, sixty concubines, twenty-eight sons, and sixty daughters (11:21). These statistics show God's blessings for Rehoboam. Rehoboam also appoints Ahijah as crown prince (11:22) and then distributes his sons to every region of the country, a very strategic move. This information is unique to Chronicles. Comparing this section with the book of Kings is instructive. The Chronicler omits the long account of Jeroboam in 1 Kings 12:25–14:20, so his account of Rehoboam is unique and seems designed to present a story parallel to Jeroboam in Kings. This king will set a pattern for viewing later kings in Judah.

12:1-16 [cf. 1 Kgs 14:21-31] Rehoboam's demise as Shishak invades Judah

Then Rehoboam and all Israel forsake God's law (12:1), so the Egyptian King Shishak attacks Jerusalem in his fifth year. Shemaiah the prophet delivers a warning to Israel (12:5-6): since they have abandoned the Lord, so the Lord will abandon them. This kind of speech can be used either to evaluate the past or prepare for the future. Here the prophet warns people to change their future behavior. They humble themselves so that God determines not to destroy them but rather to provide a means of escape, even though they must serve Shishak (12:6-7). Servitude to Shishak is intended to teach Israel the difference between serving others and serving God (12:8). Rehoboam humbles himself by agreeing to hand over significant wealth and taxes to the Egyptians, so God's wrath turns away from total destruction of Judah. But the Chronicler's final assessment of Rehoboam is fairly negative; it concludes with an ominous remark about continuing wars between Rehoboam and Jeroboam.

13:1-23 [cf. 1 Kgs 15:1-8] The reign of Abijah (Abijam)

The Chronicler expands the eight verses in Kings to twenty-three verses for this three-year reign, but also omits the negative conclusion in 1 Kings 15:3-5. The Chronicler's fairly positive account focuses on a battle with Jeroboam not included in Kings. Although greatly outnumbered, Abijah stands on a mountain slope in southern Israel (Ephraim) and delivers a long theological speech to his opponents, Jeroboam and Israel (13:4-12). His speech develops these points. God established a covenant with King David, but Jeroboam opposed him, and worthless young men surrounded Rehoboam, who was too young and inexperienced to stand up to them. He challenges the northerners: you cannot oppose David, God's choice. You banished the priests of the House of Aaron and the Levites and set up your own priesthood. Remember that we are faithful, that our priests and Levites continue to perform their duties—burnt offerings morning and evening, spicy incense, the rows of bread, and the lamp they light each evening (13:10-11). God is with us Judeans, so you Israelites should not fight us, or the Lord. You will not succeed!

This speech does not persuade Jeroboam, so he sets out for battle and surrounds the southerners. But the Judahites cry out to God while the priests blow their horns (13:14). As is normal for those who cry out to God, the Lord responds: Jeroboam and his men are routed, the northerners flee and many thousands are killed. Theologically speaking, the Israelites are humbled, while the Judahites prevail because they rely on the God of their ancestors (13:18). Abijah's fortunes include fourteen wives, twenty-two sons, and sixteen daughters, signals of a blessed life. The witness to his success is evident.

14:1–17:1 [cf. I Kgs 15:9-24] The reign of Asa

Asa begins well, calling Judah to seek the Lord, so they prosper. When King Zerah and the Cushites (Ethiopians) attack Judah, Asa cries to the Lord. He professes reliance on God, so they defeat the Ethiopians and other peoples around Gerar. Still Azariah son of Oded receives "the spirit of God" (15:1) and he urges Asa in a type of sermon to seek God (15:2-7). The message is: God is found by those who seek him. Therefore, do not weaken, do not give up, but seek God and persevere. Asa responds by reforming worship in Jerusalem and gathering the people of Judah, Benjamin, and sojourners from the North to celebrate Weeks/Shabuot (15:8-15). Three times the Chronicler says the people sought God (15:12, 13, 15). Here is the key to his auspicious beginning: no war (with Israel) for his first thirty-five years (15:19).

In his latter years, Asa responds poorly to the menacing of Baasha, King of Israel (16:1-10). Asa seeks an alliance with the king of Aram instead of renewing the covenant with God; this leads to initial success (16:2-6). Then Hanani the seer excoriates Asa for relying on Ben-hadad rather than on God, reminding him that he overcame the Ethiopians by relying on God (16:7-9). Asa is angered and imprisons the seer and oppresses many others. When he contracts a serious foot disease, he seeks the help of physicians rather than God (16:12). Asa had sought and trusted God in his earlier years, but he changes in his later years. This turn of events challenges the audience to persevere in seeking God.

The Chronicler moves on to the reign of King Jehoshaphat, passing over without mention several kings of Israel (Nadab, Baasha, Elah, Zimri, Omri, Ahab), plus Elijah and Elisha the prophets (1 Kgs 15:25–21:29). The Chronicler normally omits the history of northern kings, all of whom were evaluated very negatively in the book of Kings.

17:2–21:1 [cf. I Kgs 22:1-51] The reign of Jehoshaphat

The Chronicler expands Jehoshaphat's story from one chapter in Kings to four chapters in Chronicles. Chapter 17 has no parallel in Kings. Jehoshaphat begins positively: he does not seek the Baals but the God of his fathers, and he avoids the practices of Israel. The result is predictable: Jehoshaphat's reign is firmly established and he receives tribute and wealth (17:5). As proof of his piety (17:6), he sends officials and Levites throughout Judah to teach the Torah, so the people can live according to God's law (17:7-9). The Chronicler lists this king's projects, his success in international relations, and the numerical strength of his warrior allies (17:10-19). This data sets the stage for his alliance with Ahab in chapter 18 and it raises an intriguing question: why does a king so devoted to the Lord align himself with Ahab through a marriage alliance (18:1)?

In chapter 18 Jehoshaphat and Ahab of Israel conspire to battle against Aram. Seeking God's word (18:4) will be tricky, especially since Ahab hates his own prophet by whom he has sought God's word; Micaiah ben Imlah has spoken words that displease Ahab (18:7). Asked about Ahab's proposal to go to battle at Ramoth-gilead, Micaiah describes a terrifying image: Israel will be scattered on the mountains, with no shepherd to guide or guard them, so that all the sheep return home alone (18:16). In the ancient near East the shepherds symbolize kings, so Micaiah effectively says that Israel will be without its king, i.e., that Ahab will die in battle. Ahab disregards this unpleasant word, goes to battle, and dies of combat wounds. But Jehoshaphat cries out, so God helps him by luring away his attackers. Once again, crying out to God brings success. The Chronicler's message is: trust more in God than in human means, including political alliances.

Chapters 19–20 contain more events not included in Kings. A prophet named Jehu, son of Hanani, rebukes Jehoshaphat for aligning with Ahab, one who hates God (19:1-2). Still, Jehoshaphat dedicates his heart to seek God (19:3), with happy results. He reforms Israel's judicial system by appointing judges dedicated to ancient notions of justice (parallels from Deut 1:16-17; 10:17; and 16:18-20). The most important guide for justice, however, is the divine model: "with the Lord, our God, there is no injustice, no partiality, no bribe-taking" (19:7).

The Chronicler now relates in chapter 20 a victory in battle over the Ammonites and Moabites, a story not known from Kings. When enemies advance from the East, Jehoshaphat's fear leads him to "consult the Lord" (20:3), the proper religious approach for the Chronicler. This going to God forms part of a larger service of worship, a communal fast and lament service (20:5-12), which leads to God's clear protection of the people. This story shows how postexilic Israel could address God in time of crisis with prayer in the form of communal laments (which address God, complain of their sufferings, petition God to intervene). A similar event is found in a communal fast alluded to in Joel 1–2, when they are facing a natural disaster (probably a plague of locusts).

Then a prophetic figure stands up—the Levite Jahaziel (20:14)—and proclaims God's response to the king's outcry; they should not fear, for God will be with them (20:17). Responding to this promise of victory, the king and people of Jerusalem bow down and worship the Lord (20:17-18). Then Levites arise to praise God with a very loud voice, which they are appointed to do, but here it seems premature, for the victory is still in the future. Jehoshaphat then rises and delivers a speech that sounds like a sermon. Believe God and you will be set firm (20:20); here the Chronicler adapts an old prophetic saying: "Unless your faith is firm / you shall not be firm!" (Isa 7:9). The Chronicler gives a theological commentary on this event: Jehoshaphat faces a test of faith, just as Ahaz faced a test of faith when Isaiah uttered the word to him.

Again the Chronicler views Levites as prophetic speakers. God's spirit came on Jahaziel the Levite in the assembly (20:14) and he publicly utters a salvation oracle in response to the king's lament prayer (20:14-17). This Levite's concern seems more spiritual than tactical; Judah and its leader are to conduct themselves in utter humility and confidence in God, whose deliverance can be expected. The Chronicler seems to address the spiritual yearnings and laments of his own day (Persian-era Judeans). They can realize that God is about to work a new saving action in their day, in the tradition of God's earlier saving acts for Israel.

Jehoshaphat did not always seek God, but he followed the ways of his father Asa, who ended

badly (20:35-37). This shift toward unfaithfulness stands as a powerful reminder to the Chronicler's audience: persevere in seeking God. Chapters 21–28 are filled with Judean kings who fail because of disobedience, who do not seek God.

21:2–22:1 [cf. 2 Kgs 8:16-24] The reign of Jehoram of Judah

The Chronicler's additions tend to highlight the evils of this reign. The Chronicler lists Jehoram's brothers, who received many gifts from their father Jehoshaphat (21:2-3); Jehoram kills them all as soon as he takes power (21:4). After marrying Athaliah, the daughter of Ahab of Israel, he follows the evil ways of the kings of Israel (21:6; cf. 2 Kgs 8:18). God's anger is provoked, so this king might have been put away except for God's covenant promise not to destroy the royal line of Judah (21:7). His punishment comes in the form of a revolt by Edom and Libnah against Judah (21:10). The Chronicler adds a theological reason for these revolts: Jehoram built high places and led Jerusalem and Judah astray in false worship, thus forsaking God (21:11).

The Chronicler adds a letter from the prophet Elijah to Jehoram (21:12-15). His prophecy of doom explains how his evil conduct (especially killing his brothers and infidelity to God) will lead to a plague on his people and a horrible death by sickness of the bowels for himself. Elijah's appearance here is intriguing. First, all the stories about Elijah in 1 Kings are omitted by the Chronicler, so this appearance is unique. Nevertheless, Elijah opposes the house of Ahab in Chronicles as in Kings. Just as he proclaims disaster, so it happens for Judah and for Jehoram. The king dies of some terrible disease of the bowels (21:19), and though he was buried in Jerusalem, it was not in the tombs of the kings. After his death, Jerusalem's inhabitants make his surviving son Ahaziah (Jehoahaz) king in his place (22:1).

22:2-9 [cf. 2 Kgs 8:25-29] The reign of Ahaziah of Judah

The Chronicler adds very little new material and seems to blame his evil on the counsel he followed, much of it from Athaliah and the house of Ahab (22:3-5). So Ahaziah appears as a kind of victim in this text. His ruin came from God because he had sided with Joram, and he was killed in the executions of the house of Ahab conducted by Jehu (22:8-9). In deference to his grandfather Jehoshaphat who sought the Lord, they gave him a burial, though the Chronicler does not mention where. So another unfaithful king of Judah has now passed, and the house of David stands at a precarious point, with no obvious successor to the rule (22:9).

22:10–23:21 [cf. 2 Kgs 11:1-20] Athaliah usurps the throne

When Athaliah realizes that her house and that of David are facing extinction and she is the only adult who could claim the throne, she prepares to put to death all of Ahaziah's sons. But Jehosheba, daughter of King Jehoram and sister of Ahaziah, steals away Joash, the only son of Ahaziah still living. She acts to save him from the murderous intentions of Athaliah and to preserve the line of the house of David. The Chronicler emphasizes that Jehoshabeath was married to the priest Jehoiada. This detail fits well with the fact that she and her husband hid the child in the temple for six years, while Athaliah reigned (22:12). The Chronicler says that the child was with "them" in the temple, i.e., husband and wife, rather than with "her" (as in 2 Kgs 11:3). Saving this child involved more than a single person, including cooperation between priests (Jehoiada) and royal family to preserve the Davidic line.

In 23:1-15 the Chronicler retells the story of the coronation of Joash as king of Judah. The leaders go out to the towns of Judah to enlist support of the Levites and leading families. The Chronicler thus demonstrates widespread support and participation to save the royal line because an unbroken succession in the line of David was so important for all. Levites generally replace the military conspirators of 2 Kings (23:2, 4, 6, 7, 8) and priests are added in two places (23:4, 6). The Chronicler implies that danger to the king is also danger to the temple. In Chronicles these events involve all the people, not just a group of military conspirators. The people of the land sound their trumpets along with singers with their musical instruments and praise songs (23:13). Worship is the overall horizon. Then follows the assassination of Athaliah (23:14-15).

Jehoiada the priest acts as a kind of regent for the young king Jehoash after Athaliah's death. He begins with a covenant ceremony between himself, the people, and the king, so they will be a

people of the Lord (23:16). Thus they destroy all signs of Baal worship (23:17) and Jehoiada the priest appoints people to rule the temple. The Chronicler specifies that all these officials were responsible to the Levitical priests who had been organized and appointed by David to offer sacrifices with rejoicing and song. The Chronicler mentions gatekeepers for the temple to protect it from entry by people who were unclean; this was clearly a Levitical concern (23:19). Ultimately the Chronicler is more interested in the cultic purity of the temple than in the political plotting. The Chronicler concludes that the whole city was quiet after Athaliah was executed, so the people of the land rejoiced: God has indeed preserved the line of David and his promise to that line (1 Chr 17).

24:1-27 [cf. 2 Kgs 12:1-22] The reign of Jehoash

Jehoash, the young survivor of Athaliah's massacre, becomes king at age seven and reigns for forty years (24:1). The Chronicler describes a good and blessed reign, as long as his patron Jehoiada is living, and the king restores the temple. The Chronicler has special emphases. First, Jehoash is rewarded for upright behavior; Jehoiada provides him with two wives and he fathers numerous sons and daughters (24:3). Second, the collection to restore the temple features Levites (in addition to priests) following regulations given by Moses (24:9). Third, the officials and people participate enthusiastically in the collection (24:10). The Chronicler thus portrays the project as a joint venture of priest and king; it probably reflects his vision for cooperation in his own day. In contrast to Kings, where money was not spent for temple vessels, they spend leftover money on temple worship vessels and they actively continue the schedule of burnt offerings in the temple (24:14). Thus far Jehoash seems a model king.

After Jehoiada's death, however, things change dramatically in the Chronicler's version—with no parallel in Kings. Judean officials approach Jehoash, who heeds their advice and shifts worship back to the old idols (24:18). Divine anger follows (24:18), but God sends prophets to bring them back. They do not heed the prophets (24:19), so God endows Zechariah, son of the priest Jehoiada, with a prophetic spirit and he issues a stern oracle of judgment. Angered, the king orders his officials to stone the priest/prophet in the temple court, a horrifying sacrilege (24:21). The Chronicler accuses Joash of ingratitude, not remembering Jehoiada's kindness to him, i.e., of breaking the covenant they had made (24:22). The result is a punishment from God in the form of an Aramean invasion (24:23-24). Joash is killed by a conspiracy of his own servants because he spilled the blood of the sons of Jehoiada the priest (24:25). Because of the murder and sacrilege recounted here, the Chronicler claims that he was not buried with the kings of Judah, although his grave was in Jerusalem (24:25). This murder of Zechariah seems to be mentioned in a woe-saying of Jesus against unfaithful people of his own time who shed the blood of prophets (Luke 11:49-51).

25:1-28 [cf. 2 Kgs 14:1-20] The reign of Amaziah

Amaziah reigns for twenty-nine years in Jerusalem. The Chronicler includes most of the material in Kings and concludes that he acted correctly in God's eyes, except "not wholeheartedly" (25:2). His adherence to God's ways is partial. His first move, political and tactical, is to kill those servants who had killed his father, but he does not kill their children, reasoning from Deuteronomy 24:16 that children should not be put to death because of the sins of their fathers (25:4). The Chronicler adds a story that Amaziah organized his military and hired one hundred thousand northern Israelites. This action invites a prophetic rebuke to rely not on Israel and Ephraim but on God alone (25:7-8). There follow details of acrimonious relations with the North, a successful battle against peoples of Edom and Mt. Seir, and disturbing reports that he then worships the gods of Seir (25:9-14). Another prophet comes to express the Lord's anger that he would trust other gods to deliver him (25:15). Many other disastrous interchanges follow. He is carried back to Jerusalem on horses and is buried there with his ancestors (25:28). The initial evaluation is correct; he acted uprightly, but only partially. Like Jehoash before him, he begins well but does not persevere.

26:1-23 [cf. 2 Kgs 14:21–15:7] The reign of Uzziah (Azariah)

This king also begins well but ends badly. He becomes king at age sixteen, when his father was killed, and he reigns fifty-two years. The Chroni-

cler gives a much longer account than Kings. At first he seeks God, as instructed by his advisor Zechariah, so God made him prosperous. The Chronicler describes victory on the battlefield, his construction of cisterns and towers, and his development of farms and vineyards because of his love for the earth. Under him the kingdom is prosperous and secure, and much the same situation prevails in the North. This era, the early eighth century B.C., is a time when superpowers were weakened and Israel and Judah could grow strong. Later he grows proud and personally enters the sanctuary to offer incense (26:16). Usurping the authority of the priests brings the punishment of leprosy for the rest of his days (26:19-20). He lives in seclusion, excluded from the temple, while his son Jotham takes over his judicial duties (26:21). After his death, Uzziah is buried adjacent to a royal burial ground. One of the Chronicler's sources for this story was written by the prophet Isaiah, son of Amoz (26:22). Like his father, Uzziah's richly prosperous reign turns sour at its end as pride guides his actions.

27:1-9 [cf. 2 Kgs 15:32-38] The reign of Jotham

This report is quite positive, a welcome interlude among many negative accounts. He follows the best paths of his father Uzziah, especially in his construction projects in Jerusalem (Ophel hill) and the hill country of Judah, as he established his ways before God (27:6). In one important detail he does not imitate his father: he does not presume to enter the temple (27:2). Ammonites pay him tribute (27:5), and after his death he rests with his ancestors in the city of David (27:9).

28:1-27 [cf. 2 Kgs 16:1-20] The reign of Ahaz

This king reverses the positive pattern of his father, Jotham, so the Chronicler narrates nothing positive about his reign. He is responsible for much idolatry. He personally produces metal images of the Baals (28:2), makes incense offerings in the Ben-hinnom valley, and engages in child sacrifices (28:3). Because he has forsaken his ancestral God (28:6), who is thereby enraged (28:9), Ahaz suffers defeats at the hands of the Arameans (28:5), Israelites (28:6-15), Edomites (28:17), and Philistines (28:18), and is oppressed by Assyria (28:16, 20-21).

The Chronicler tells a much more detailed story of battle with northern Israelites. The prophet Oded exhorts the northerners to curb their rage and return Judean captives, arguing that both Judah and Israel have sinned equally (28:9-11). This unusual speech succeeds and many captives are returned. With regard to Damascus and the Arameans, the Chronicler has Ahaz sacrificing to their gods. He collects temple vessels and uses the metal to pay tribute, closes the temple doors (i.e., causes normal worship to cease), and builds altars everywhere. This thoroughly disobedient king was buried in Jerusalem, but not in the royal cemeteries. The Chronicler will move directly to Ahaz's son, Hezekiah, the next king of Judah.

At this point, the Chronicler omits crucial texts: 2 Kings 17 and 18:9-12. The Kings account begins with the reign of King Hoshea of Israel and includes the attack by Shalmaneser, King of Assyria, and his siege of Samaria. Eventually the Assyrians capture the Israelite capital and send its people into exile. The Chronicler does not comment on these events, since he does not specifically narrate the history of the northern kingdom. Some scholars suggest that the condemnations of Israel are not included by the Chronicler so that northerners, the lost tribes of Israel, could be more clearly invited back to union and worship with the southern kingdom of Judah.

HEZEKIAH

2 Chronicles 29–32

Hezekiah ranks as one of Judah's three most important kings, after David and Solomon. The Chronicler devotes four chapters to him, most of them without parallels in Kings. The unique material recounts issues of worship at the temple, whereas Kings focuses more on military and political events, especially the invasion of Assyrian King Sennacherib. The Chronicler links Hezekiah's concern for worship with the accomplishments of David and Solomon. The Chronicler transforms the Hezekiah story into a renewal program for the entire people, including northerners who were presumably cut off after 722 B.C. In chapters 29–30 Hezekiah cleanses the temple from the impurity introduced by Ahaz and re-

establishes the proper rituals and the joyful celebration of Passover and Unleavened Bread. He delineates duties and roles of Levites and priests, focusing on status and responsibility for the Levites. Thus the Chronicler underscores the importance of worship for Israel's common life. His attention to Sennacherib's invasion and defeat is quite abbreviated when compared with its parallels in 2 Kings 18–19 and Isaiah 36–37. This commentary will emphasize the Chronicler's favorite issues: temple worship, personnel, and the great Passover festival.

29:1-36 [cf. 2 Kgs 18:1-12] Hezekiah restores temple service

Hezekiah reigns for twenty-nine years and does what God considered right and honest, like David. He restores the temple for worship and for the Passover, after the reign of Ahaz left it with a polytheistic atmosphere. First, he cleanses the temple and rededicates it (29:3-30). Then he assembles the priests and Levites and exhorts them to participate in the cleansing and consecration of the temple (29:5-11). The Levites are prominent in their enthusiastic response. In verses 12-14 the Chronicler lists fourteen Levitical families that participated. The first eight come from the four great Levite families: Kohath, Merari, Gershon, and Elizaphan (29:12-13a), and the next six names derive from three families of singers: Asaph, Heman, and Jeduthun (29:13b-14).

To purify the temple, the priests bring out unclean things, while the Levites receive and dispose of them in Wadi Kidron. The ceremonies take eight days for the outer court and another eight days for the inner house of the Lord; so this entire process takes them to the sixteenth of the first month. Since Passover begins on the fourteenth of the first month, they cannot begin on time since the temple is not yet consecrated. Their only alternative is celebrate Passover in the second month.

The consecration ceremony (29:20-30) begins with various sacrifices (sin offerings and sprinkling blood against the altar) to make atonement for all Israel. During the public sacrifices Levites are stationed in the temple and begin their music and song, while the priests sound their trumpets. At the same time the assembly bows down in prostration. Hezekiah arranges for burnt offerings accompanied by the Lord's song and the playing of trumpets and other musical instruments of David. Having music, song, and burnt offerings together seems to be a liturgical innovation of Hezekiah. The Levites praise God using the ancient words of David and Asaph.

When the assembly brings thank offerings and burnt offerings (29:31-33), Levites assist the priests to prepare the offerings, until enough priests had consecrated themselves. The Chronicler notes that the Levites "were more careful than the priests to sanctify themselves" (29:34). This was a time of great rejoicing over the revival of worship and the Chronicler offers a message for his own era. Postexilic Israelites should adhere to the great worship traditions, especially Passover and Unleavened Bread, which recall Israel's covenant with their God. Worship should include public sacrifices, music, and song, along with physical prostration; it concludes with personal sacrificial offerings, many of them shared in a liturgical meal with great rejoicing.

30:1-27 The celebration of Passover

This chapter has preparations for the Passover (30:1-12) and the ceremony itself (30:13-27). Invitations to come to Jerusalem for Passover go out also to the northern tribes Ephraim and Manasseh (30:1-2). It seems that the Chronicler aims at some kind of reconciliation with the lost northern tribes. He also invites them for a festival in the second month, as explained in 29:17. The invitation to "return to the Lord" in penitence intends that God might bring back all the exiles to their homeland (30:6). This spirituality of repentance deepens; when you turn to the Lord you will find mercy before your captors, for your God is merciful and compassionate (30:9).

His invitation to Passover finds two distinct responses. Many northerners ridicule the messengers who bring the invitation, while others humble themselves and go to Jerusalem. For some northerners, answering Hezekiah's invitation carries political ramifications that they could not overcome. Southerners from Judea accept the invitation unanimously (30:12). They celebrate with a huge assembly in Jerusalem for the Unleavened Bread. The Passover sacrifices on the fourteenth of the month (30:14-20) follow prescriptions of the Torah of Moses. There were so many people who needed assistance but had not consecrated themselves that many Levites assisted them in their sacrifices (30:17). The Chronicler mentions large numbers of northerners who had not purified themselves but still ate the Passover meal against regulations. This act poses a challenge for the king. He prays to God for them, especially those who set their heart to seek the Lord (30:18). This shows the importance of a right heart, a spiritual intention in celebrating the festival sacrifice. The Chronicler focuses on inner spirituality in a balance with ritual actions. God listens to the king's prayer and heals the people (30:20). The feast of Unleavened Bread follows for another seven days, and it combines thanksgiving sacrifices and feasting with thanksgiving songs and music; it is another occasion of great joy.

The entire assembly decides on an additional festival of seven days, a festival not required by Torah and not characterized by burnt offerings or Levitical song and music. However, the notion of joy or rejoicing appears three times in the space of four verses (30:23-26), so typical for the Chronicler. This was an inclusive celebration—with Judeans (community, priests, and Levites), northerners from Israel, and resident aliens (from Judah and Israel). Joy and inclusiveness were sufficient reasons for the Chronicler's enthusiasm: he exclaims that Hezekiah's Passover was like none since the days of David and Solomon (30:26). This celebration shows five important aspects of Israel's public worship. First, it should be an inclusive celebration. Second, it recognizes God's past generosity to Israel, especially the exodus from Egypt. Third, speaking of the Lord as merciful and compassionate highlights the notion of God's everlasting compassion, often related to the exodus tradition. Fourth, a whole heart was crucial for good worship. Fifth, there should be great joy and rejoicing. The Chronicler uses the word for joy six times in these chapters (29:30, 36; 30:21, 23, 25, and 26), suggesting that the rituals of worship, exercised with a full heart, actually lead to great rejoicing and to the experience of unity with each other and their entire tradition (30:26).

31:1-21 Hezekiah provides for priests and Levites

This chapter adds more information about religious matters during Hezekiah's reign. They continue to remove vestiges of idolatry after the Passover feast. Hezekiah also establishes the work rotations of priests and Levites, similar to the specifications of David in 1 Chronicles 23–27 (31:2). The monarch is responsible for providing animals for sacrifice; royal funding of sacrifices was likely the historical practice in postexilic times. Financial remuneration for priests and Levites is assigned to voluntary offerings of the people, who respond generously (31:4-13). Moreover, one document specifies the organization of Levites and priests for the distribution of tithes to them (31:14-19). The chapter ends with a positive summary of Hezekiah's actions; he has acted with a whole heart, so he prospers. The only other king who prospered, according to the Chronicler, was Solomon (1 Chr 29:23), which means that they both follow God's Torah.

32:1-33 [cf. 2 Kgs 18:13–20:21; Isa 36:1–39:8] Invasion of Sennacherib and other events during Hezekiah's reign

The challenges brought on by the Assyrian invasion of Judah take up only one chapter here, but two chapters in Kings (2 Kgs 18:13–20:19) and Isaiah (chs. 36–37). The Chronicler's interest in Hezekiah's political and military affairs focuses more on their religious and theological significance, though his reign was apparently a time of great construction projects in Jerusalem (32:27-30). The discussions and negotiations between Judeans and Assyrians in Kings are shortened by the Chronicler, who then mentions that Hezekiah and the prophet Isaiah pray to God (32:20), who delivers them just as he had delivered Israel during the reigns of Abijah (13:3-20), Asa (14:9-15), and Jehoshaphat (20:1-30). Finally, a very brief version of Hezekiah's illness is mentioned (32:24), distilled from 2 Kings 20:1-11 and Isaiah 38:1-22 (with the famous prayer of Hezekiah).

Still, there are danger signs. Hezekiah is affected by pride (32:25), though he later humbles himself, thus delaying God's anger until after his time (32:26). Sin is followed by repentance, but it seems possible that the exile was occasioned by his pride. Hezekiah's repentance repairs the breach, for he is greatly successful again. Great construction projects date to this era, including diversion of the spring Gihon (32:30), corroborated by Hezekiah's tunnel (visible to this day), with an inscription describing its construction. Also, envoys came to him from Babylon to make inquiries. Finally comes his death notice (32:32-33), with the positive note that he was buried in royal tombs in Jerusalem.

THE FALL OF JUDAH

2 Chronicles 33–36

33:1-20 [cf. 2 Kgs 21:1-18] The reign of Manasseh

The Chronicler transforms a very negative view of Manasseh in the book of Kings into a vision of hope. Here is a great idolater who becomes a king who is humbled and repents of his sin. His reign of fifty-five years must be seen as a blessing. At first he does evil (as in Kings), rebuilding high places that Hezekiah had torn down, and conducting child sacrifice in the valley of Ben-hin-nom (i.e., Gehenna, as in the New Testament: Matt 5:22; Mark 9:43; Jas 3:6). The Chronicler's new version in verses 10-17 is surprising. God warns Manasseh and the people to repent (33:10), and then Assyrians capture him and take him to Babylon (33:11). There he prays to his God and humbles himself (33:12; cf. 2 Chr 7:14); his petition is heard and God returns him to Jerusalem, so Manasseh knows that the Lord is God (33:13). Then he pursues ambitious construction projects in the city of David, removing idols and altars, and installing an altar for the Lord. Although his life is changed, the people keep sacrificing on high places, though to the Lord (33:17). In conclusion the Chronicler mentions particularly Manasseh's prayer to God after he had been humbled and that he was buried in his house (33:18-20). These verses replace the condemnation in 2 Kings 21:10-16. The Chronicler omits mentioning that his sin and the evil of Manasseh were the reason for the downfall of Judah in the South.

Unlike other Judean kings, Manasseh's life pattern went from bad to good. The Chronicler seldom invents stories, so this account may be considered historical in some way. Still, his repentance, return, and actions are not portrayed as historical but as acts of God. The Chronicler uses his life as an excellent example of the possibility of repentance, forgiveness, and grace, especially for postexilic Israel. In this tradition is the beautiful Prayer of Manasseh, a prayer of penitence found in the Apocrypha but not in the biblical canon.

33:21-25 [cf. 2 Kgs 21:19-26] The reign of Amon

Manasseh's son, Amon, follows the evil in his father's life rather than humbling himself, as Manasseh had done. Rather, he increases his own guilt (33:23). As in Kings, he was assassinated by conspiratorial servants, who were in turn struck down by the people of the land (33:25). Unlike the Kings account, there is no burial notice or regnal notice for this king.

34:1-7 [cf. 2 Kgs 22:1-2] The reign of Josiah: early reform movements

After Amon's murder the people of the land make the eight-year-old Josiah their king. Surely other officials administer the kingdom until he reaches his majority at age twenty, the twelfth year of his reign (34:3). Josiah is a notable religious reformer, but the Chronicler's description differs greatly from 2 Kings; there Josiah initiates the reform after his officials find the book of Torah in the temple. For the Chronicler, Josiah's religious concerns come first. At age sixteen he begins to seek the God of David his forebear, removing high places from Judah and Jerusalem. At age twenty, when he begins to rule himself, his religious reforms begin. He removes and destroys idol altars and images in Jerusalem and Judah; then they pulverize all these objects and spread their dust on the graves of their worshipers (34:4). Since corpse pollution is considered a terrible degradation in Israel, these actions would be especially harsh. As elsewhere, the Chronicler extends the reform to northern Israel (34:6). Josiah's religious devotion and concerns come first in his career, which is the Chronicler's preferred order of events (also evidenced in the lives of David and Solomon). The Chronicler also emphasizes that worship and liturgy typify Israel as God's people, more than politics, economics, or warfare.

34:8-18 [cf. 2 Kgs 22:3–11] The Torah book discovered

Josiah's religious concern continues. At age twenty-six he orders his officials to repair the Jerusalem temple, using funds collected by the Levites from Israel, Judah, and Jerusalem. They give the money to the appointed workers, honest workers supervised by various Levites. In the midst of these operations Hilkiah the priest finds the book of the Torah given through Moses (34:14). He hands it over to Shaphan, an official, who takes it to Josiah to read aloud before the king (34:18). When Josiah hears the words of the Torah he weeps and tears his garments and is moved to repentance by what he has heard. Many scholars today think that this scroll discovered in the temple was a version of the book of Deuteronomy. For the Chronicler, this discovery results from his reforms, whereas in Kings this discovery motivates Josiah to reform.

34:19-33 [cf. 2 Kgs 22:12–23:3] Confirmation by the prophetess Huldah

Eager to learn the status of this document, Josiah sends Hilkiah, Shaphan, and other officials to inquire of the prophetess Huldah. She responds in an oracle which describes the evil about to overcome Jerusalem and Judah because of their sins (34:23-28). She answers their question only indirectly. She says that God is about to enact all the curses written in the book (presumably those listed in Deut 28:15-68), which implies that Israel deserves the fulfillment of God's word in Deuteronomy. So she implies that this book of Torah is authentic, i.e., it is God's word for Israel. But she also prophesies that Josiah will die in peace rather than in battle, because he repented (34:27-28). She is the prophet who authenticates the Torah document and exhorts the king and people to adhere to it and the covenant with God. She is the one woman prophet of the era of Israel's monarchy.

35:1-19 [cf. 2 Kgs 23:21-23] Josiah keeps the Passover

Josiah's religious reform also includes a great Passover celebration at the Jerusalem temple, just as Hezekiah has done. Here again the festival is not family-oriented as in contemporary practice but is an act of public worship. It includes slaughtering Passover lambs, burnt offerings, arrangements for the priests and Levites, singers, and gatekeepers. It is followed by the Feast of Unleavened Bread for seven days. This celebration proceeds according to plan.

One unique aspect of this celebration is the description of roles for the Levites. The Chronicler identifies them as teachers of Israel and changes their responsibilities; no longer do they carry the ark, but they assist in temple liturgy and they help in the flaying of the Passover lambs (35:11). The

Chronicler emphasizes that the Levites follow God's word found in the Scriptures: verses 6 and 12 connect their roles with the book of Moses. The Chronicler was very impressed with this festival, noting that nothing comparable had occurred since the days of Samuel the prophet. The Chronicler uses this pattern of an authentic Passover celebration to encourage his community's practice.

35:20–36:1 [cf. 2 Kgs 23:28-30] The death of Josiah

Despite his religious reforms and despite Huldah's prophecy about Josiah dying peacefully, this king gets caught in the war between Egypt and Assyria. He moves into the path of Pharaoh Neco on his northward battle march through Israel. Chronicles reflects the basic narrative in Kings, but the Chronicler seems troubled by Josiah's untimely, unmerited death. Neco, the Egyptian ruler, proclaims to Josiah that he intends to attack the house of Judah but not him, so he should cease his opposition. Josiah does not obey Neco, but the Chronicler explains it in a startling way: "he would not listen to the words of Neco that came from the mouth of God" (35:22). Even an enemy king can mediate God's word to Israel! Perhaps his downfall relates to disbelief in God's word through the Pharaoh, for Josiah is soon shot by archers, mortally wounded, and dies after his servants carry him back to Jerusalem. Judah and Jerusalem all mourn for Josiah (35:24), and Jeremiah utters a lamentation for him, while male and female singers mention him in their lamentations (35:25). These lamentations remind us of the book of Lamentations, usually connected with Jeremiah the prophet. Josiah has a glorious burial, for he has been loyal and faithful to God's Torah (35:26). This death notice is extremely positive for Judah's last independent king.

36:2-4 [cf. 2 Kgs 23:31-35] The reign and dethronement of Jehoahaz

Made king by the people of the land, Jehoahaz reigns only three months before being deposed by the king of Egypt. Neco imposes tribute on the land, replaces Jehoahaz with his brother Eliakim (his name is changed to Jehoiakim), and exiles him to Egypt. The Chronicler's account is so brief—an indignity in itself—that it even omits negative comments about his evils.

36:5-8 [cf. 2 Kgs 23:36–24:7] The reign of Jehoiakim

The Chronicler greatly abridges Jehoiakim's story in Kings. He removes much of the information in 2 Kings, including hints of the great historical shifts of this time, when Egypt was defeated by Babylon and Judea shifted loyalties from Pharaoh Neco to Nebuchadnezzar of Babylon. He also omits the king's revolt against his Babylonian overlord. For the Chronicler it seems sufficient to mention his reign of eleven years, the evil and abominations of his reign, and his capture and exile to Babylon by Nebuchadnezzar. As usual, the Chronicler's interest focuses on his king's religious posture, so he adds the information that Nebuchadnezzar took vessels from the Jerusalem temple to his temple in Babylon. This deed is noted also in Daniel 1:1-2. The Chronicler's brief account demonstrates his negative evaluation of Jehoiakim based on his religious posture.

36:9-10 [cf. 2 Kgs 24:8-17] The reign of Jehoiachin

This brief reign (three months and ten days) lasts long enough for him to do evil in God's sight, so Nebuchadnezzar takes him to Babylon along with the best vessels from the temple, and in his place installs Zedekiah his brother as king. Overlooking the details of Jehoiachin's surrender to his enemy and the detailed account of exiles to Babylon (2 Kgs 24:14-16), the Chronicler pinpoints religious attitudes and objects as his main interest in this king.

36:11-17 [cf. 2 Kgs 24:18-20; Jer 52:1-3] The reign of Zedekiah

Appointed by Nebuchadnezzar, this king also does evil in God's sight. The Chronicler summarizes the problem: Zedekiah should have repented and humbled himself before the word of God uttered through Jeremiah (36:12). The prophet Jeremiah contains eight chapters of oracles during Zedekiah's reign, so we cannot identify a specific act of disobedience but rather a general failure to heed God's prophetic word. The Chronicler composes his own version of Judah's end (36:13-17). Zedekiah rebels against Nebuchadnezzar, even though he had sworn by God to serve him: so he offends God and also errs politically (36:13a). More seriously, he hardens his heart against returning to God (36:13b); in biblical language, he refuses to repent, so he is cut off from God. Leaders of the priests and people also act unfaithfully, like the Gentile nations; thus they help to pollute the temple. The Chronicler speaks of the sin and evil in more general terms, but mocking God's prophetic messengers is serious enough to bring divine anger.

Still, the Chronicler claims that God has compassion on his people and temple and keeps sending messengers to call them back (36:15). Even as the Chronicler spells out Israel's sins he carefully juxtaposes God's compassion on the people and temple. God's ultimate action, bringing the enemy to victory over Jerusalem, seems almost an act of divine desperation (36:17). The Chronicler states tersely that God brings against them the Chaldeans, who destroy the temple and its vessels and slaughter the people.

36:18-21 [cf. 2 Kgs 25:8-21; Jer 52:12-30] The fall and captivity of Judah

Nebuchadnezzar exiles to Babylon all those who survive the sword in Jerusalem, until the rise of Cyrus the Persian. For the Chronicler, this exile fulfills Jeremiah's prophetic saying about seventy years of exile (Jer 25:11-12; 29:10). In this connection, Leviticus 26:34 mentions times of exile for the people as a time for the land to make up its lost sabbaths with sabbatical years. For the Chronicler this is an opportunity for transformation and change in relationship with God.

The Chronicler follows the story pattern of 2 Kings, but not its details or theology. Missing here is the international political scene, especially struggles between Babylon and Egypt and their impact on Judah. Missing also is the notion that exile to Babylon mostly involved higher echelons

of Judeans, with the poorer farmers and peasants left around the destroyed city. Lacking also is the tendency in 2 Kings to blame the Babylonian invasions on the sin of Manasseh (e.g., 2 Kgs 24:3; not repeated in 2 Chr). Manasseh has repented in Chronicles. More significant, the Chronicler tends not to blame present evils on past generations; rather he finds the evil in the kings and Judean social groups of the generations after Josiah's untimely death.

36:22-23 [cf. Ezra 1:1-4] Cyrus' proclamation about a return to Jerusalem

The Chronicler concludes this history quite differently than Kings, which ends with the image of Jehoiachin, the last king of Judah, under house arrest in Babylon. Here the reader is moved to the next historical period, the Persian Era when Jews return to Jerusalem and Judah. Cyrus the Persian has come to power after defeating the Babylonians, and with him has come a new policy of allowing subject peoples to return to their homelands, under watchful conditions. His proclamation begins the book of Ezra (Ezra 1:1-4) but also concludes 2 Chronicles. It includes a startling image of Cyrus in the service of the Lord God of heaven, i.e., as an instrument of Israel's God. The Chronicler also transforms the doom of exile into a moment of blessing for those who belong to God: May God be with them as they return. Here is a final word of hope, consistent with a theology which envisions the conversion and transformation even of Judea's worst king, Manasseh. In the last sentences the Chronicler looks forward, to a time of renewed hope and blessing, when Israel strengthens its covenant bond with God through committed worship and faithful service.

THE BOOKS OF
EZRA AND NEHEMIAH

Thomas M. Bolin

INTRODUCTION

The Historical and Theological Importance of Ezra-Nehemiah

The books of Ezra and Nehemiah (originally a single literary work, hence Ezra-Nehemiah) deal with one of the more fascinating and, until recently, little known eras in ancient Israelite history. Because it was long thought that most of the Old Testament had been written before or during the Babylonian exile (586–539 B.C.), many biblical scholars paid little attention to the period immediately following the exile known as the Persian period (539–330 B.C.). It was understood simply as that era when the final editorial touches were placed on the larger biblical books and when some of the smaller texts (e.g., the books of Jonah, Esther, and Ecclesiastes) were written.

However, there has been a great change in attitude concerning the historical importance of the Persian period, as it appears more and more to be the formative era for the Old Testament texts. This current interest in the Persian period underscores the importance of Ezra-Nehemiah, since it is the main literary source of historical data for Jerusalem during that era. Just how much reliable information it provides is a matter of some debate.

Additionally, Ezra-Nehemiah has played an important role in biblical theology. Since the nineteenth century, Christian biblical scholars saw the Persian period as the beginning of Judaism, a religion they maintained to be distinct from the Israelite religion that existed prior to the exile.

Christian scholars characterized postexilic Judaism as a nationalistic faith that believed that God had reserved blessing for Jews alone. Ezra-Nehemiah, with its condemnation of intermarriage with non-Jews, was held up as evidence for this unflattering portrayal of postexilic Judaism. The alleged contrast served to divorce Judaism from its own historical and religious roots. This allowed some Christian biblical scholars to use the Old Testament to support a theological claim that Christianity had replaced or superseded Judaism. Advances in historical and theological study, along with the great strides made recently in Jewish-Christian relations, have revealed this kind of biblical interpretation to be flawed. Instead, when one engages in a careful, informed reading of Ezra-Nehemiah, a compelling story emerges which tells of a people's attempt to reassemble the fragments of their lost heritage in order to face the future.

BRIEF OVERVIEW OF THE PERSIAN EMPIRE

No careful reading of the Bible can take place without knowledge of the relevant historical and cultural contexts at work behind the text. This is particularly necessary when reading Ezra-Nehemiah. Both Ezra and Nehemiah are functionaries of the Persian crown, and the biblical text makes clear that none of the work of resettlement and restoration would have taken place were it not for imperial support. Several of the ancient Achaemenid kings (what the Persian kings called themselves because they traced their descent from a royal ancestor, Achaemenes) are mentioned in the text, and the imperial government plays a major role throughout the story. The Persian Empire began with Cyrus the Great (559–530) and came to an end in 330 with the defeat of Darius III by Alexander the Great. Please note that *all* dates discussed in this book are B.C. unless otherwise noted.

Sources for the study of the Persian Empire

Knowledge of the ancient Persians for most people comes from study of classical Greek sources.

Sadly, despite the power and magnitude of Persian imperial power, very few Persian texts have survived to offer first-hand information about the empire. Apart from one royal inscription—the famous text of King Darius I (522–486) carved on an inaccessible cliff face at Behistun—there are no existing Persian historical records of significant length. Knowledge about ancient Persia must come from other areas, most notably the writings of peoples who were either Persian subjects or enemies (or, at times, both). These writings include the biblical books of Esther, Daniel, Ezra-Nehemiah, and ancient Greek writings (i.e., the histories of Herodotus, Thucydides, and Xenophon). However, one must use caution when consulting these writings. They are written from noticeably biased viewpoints (either pro- or anti-Persian) and often emphasize things that the Persians themselves would have found less important, such as the role of Judah and Jerusalem in the political designs of the empire, or the significance of the Persian defeats in Greece.

Many other written sources survive in addition to these literary texts. First are the numerous archives from various parts of the empire that contain records of mundane but necessary day-to-day activities. Special mention must be made here of the archive of Aramaic letters from the Jewish military garrison at Elephantine on the Nile River in Upper (Southern) Egypt. These texts date from the fifth century, i.e., almost contemporaneous with Nehemiah's work in Jerusalem, and offer a precious glimpse of life in the service of the Persian king and the practice of Judaism outside of Palestine. When this latter information is set alongside the texts in Ezra-Nehemiah concerning the building of the Jerusalem temple and establishment of Jewish religious practice, the contrasts are illuminating.

Equally important evidence comes from seals and coins which, by their reference to local political leaders and use of religious iconography, can furnish much knowledge about political and cultural developments. Seals and coins mentioning several Persian governors of Judah from the period after Nehemiah who were otherwise unknown have shed invaluable light on a little-known historical period in ancient Israel. Finally, but not least important, are nonwritten archaeological data, ranging from the ruins of the stunning Persian palaces in Persepolis and Susa to the evidence concerning population and settlement in Jerusalem and its environs. Such data serve both to complement and correct the picture provided by written sources.

The extent and organization of the Persian Empire

Greatness is a term often bandied about, but it is a well-deserved title for the founder of the Persian Empire, Cyrus, whose military exploits became legendary. By 539, he had gained mastery over almost all the major political forces in the ancient Near East, culminating with the defeat of Nabonidus, king of the Neo-Babylonian Empire. It is as the conqueror of Babylon that Cyrus figures prominently in the Old Testament, and this will be discussed more below. It was left to Cyrus's successors to solidify Persian power. At its greatest extent in the fifth century, Persian control encompassed three continents, extending south from the Black Sea to the Persian Gulf and west from India all the way to Ethiopia (see maps section). Kings built opulent royal residences at Susa, Persepolis, and Ecbatana (all in modern-day Iran), and made elaborate rock-cut tombs for themselves set in the side of a mountain. Persian relief sculptures and inscriptions repeatedly stress the multinational nature of their empire and the vast array of different peoples who live under Persian dominion.

After this rapid period of expansion, Persian imperial policy focused mainly on the consolidation and maintenance of power. To this end an elaborate governmental system was devised. At the top was the king, who ruled as an absolute monarch. He spent the bulk of his time moving seasonally between the magnificent palaces of his imperial cities. A large retinue accompanied the king wherever he went. In addition to nobles and grandees from around the empire, an elite corps of bodyguards protected the king. Priests and other religious personnel attended to the gods on the king's behalf. A harem comprised of a small number of wives along with a large contingent of concubines was always available to the king.

All of the conquered lands were understood as the king's private property and all subject peoples his servants. The administrative system reflected this, since it served to centralize all authority and resources in the person of the king. The imperial holdings were arranged into organizational units known as satrapies, a term derived from an Old Persian word meaning "protecting the kingdom" and known in the New American Bible Revised Edition as "provinces." The administrator was known as a satrap (in the New American Bible Revised Edition called "governor"). The governor was not exactly a ruler, but functioned as a representative of the king. He served to remind Persian subjects that the power of the king was ever present, even though the king himself might be far away, and this paradoxical combination of absolute power with remoteness surrounded the king with a sense of mystery. Indeed, in most of the major Greek writings of this period, including Plato and Aristotle, the Persian king is simply referred to as "the Great King."

Satrapies themselves were further divided into subunits also called "provinces" in the Bible. These were usually based upon preexisting political boundaries. Judah with its capital in Jerusalem was its own province that in turn was part of the satrapy called "Beyond the River" (translated "West-of-Euphrates" in the New American Bible Revised Edition). This satrapy comprised roughly the modern states of Syria, Lebanon, Jordan, and Israel and took its name from the fact that it was located across the River Euphrates from the vantage point of Persia. Samaria also at this time was a provincial capital in the same satrapy. Residents of Judah were called in Hebrew *yehudim*, which can be translated as either "Judeans" or "Jews." In Ezra-Nehemiah both of

these meanings are used, as the author attempts to show that only people who belong to the community of Israel are the rightful occupants of the land of Judah.

Beneath the satraps were various regional overseers (also known in the Bible as governors) responsible for smaller administrative units within an individual satrapy. Often these offices were given to local elites, which offered the Persians a degree of political stability. People whose status and well-being were dependent upon the king may be less likely to engage in seditious behavior. The Israelite functionaries Sheshbazzar, Zerubbabel, and Nehemiah played this role in Judah.

Kings in the ancient Near East extended their dominance to neighboring people for two main reasons. The first was to provide a buffer to protect the homeland from rival powers. The second was to exploit the conquered territories for their resources. This was accomplished in the form of tribute, which took many forms: agricultural produce, manufactured products, precious metals, and people. When Alexander the Great destroyed the Persian capital at Persepolis in 330, he was said to have confiscated an astronomical amount of wealth from the treasury there.

The regional governors and satraps were responsible for the collection of tribute and its payment to the king. In many cases, temples were used as administrative clearinghouses for the collection of tribute, and this helps to explain Persian interest in restoration of the Jerusalem temple. The primary role of satraps and regional governors was to ensure the orderly collection of tribute and its payment to the royal court. They were also required to maintain peace in their territories.

Satraps and governors could become very powerful in several ways. First, they too were supported by tribute and so, prior to sending payment to court, the local official was first given his due. Second, through loyalty to the king they could be granted large land holdings and estates throughout the empire. Because of this, a satrap could amass revenue and military power in an attempt to free himself from the rule of the king. In the middle of the fourth century a number of satraps in Asia Minor undertook just such a revolt which eventually failed. Some scholars believe that certain messianic expectations in Jerusalem concerning Zerubbabel led to his being eliminated by the Persians, given the fact that he disappears abruptly from the narrative. Caught in the midst of this system were the conquered populations and, whether they provided economic support for satrap and king or were pawns in an armed struggle between Persia and her enemies, the burdens on them were very great.

One may well ask how the Persians were able to maintain absolute control over such a large geographic area for two centuries. In addition to their military strength and administrative mechanisms, the Persians, like all conquerors, used art and writing as propaganda with great effect. Persian kings never failed to stress the continuity between their rule and older, well-established monarchies. By the sixth century, Egypt and Babylon already possessed heritages that were over two thousand years old, and in both regions the Persian kings placed inscriptions in which they claimed to be the legitimate successors to the pharaohs of the Nile and the kings of Babylon. The Persians often described themselves as worshipers of the gods of conquered peoples, which portrayed divine support for Persian rule. The success of this strategy is apparent in the Bible, where the Israelite author of Isaiah portrays Cyrus the Persian as the chosen instrument of God.

LITERARY AND HISTORICAL QUESTIONS

Attempting to use any biblical book as a historical source presents many obstacles. We do not know exactly when most of the biblical books were written, and hence how close they are to the events they describe. Moreover, whatever sources biblical authors used to write their texts are now lost and must be reconstructed through painstaking, speculative work. Finally, the biblical books have been subjected to extensive editing by ancient copyists who sought to "correct" the text wherever they saw any historical, literary, or even theological deficiencies. Ezra-Nehemiah has posed some of the most difficult problems to those who hope to learn about its history and composition. Discussion below will reflect these problems by focusing on the several viable alternatives proposed by scholars.

The use of sources in Ezra-Nehemiah

It is not known exactly what sources the author of Ezra-Nehemiah used, but the text shows evidence that it draws upon earlier writings of various kinds. Ezra-Nehemiah contains numerous lists of names. These lists denote different groups of Israelites, such as those who returned from exile (Ezra 2:1-70; 8:1-14; Neh 7:5-68); men who had married non-Israelite women (Ezra 10:18-43) and those who signed the covenant agreeing to put away their foreign wives (Neh 10:3-27); those who worked to rebuild the walls of Jerusalem and dedicate them (Neh 3:1-32; 12:31-42); those who took up residence there (Neh 11:3-36); and the list of high priests and Levites in the rebuilt temple (Neh 12:1-26). These lists may come from archival sources, or they may be remnants of an oral tradition, which also makes extensive use of lists. What is clear in Ezra-Nehemiah is that these lists do not always fit the context in which they are placed and in some instances date from a later period.

There are also several decrees from Persian kings in the text (Ezra 1:1-4 [Cyrus]; 4:17-22 [Artaxerxes]; 6:3-5 [Cyrus]; 6:6-12 [Darius]; 7:12-26 [Artaxerxes]). These texts, as well as the letters written to the Persian king (Ezra 4–5) may draw upon or reproduce actual Persian administrative documents. This is especially so for those texts written in Aramaic rather than Hebrew (Ezra 4:17-22; 6:3-5, 6-12; 7:12-26), since Aramaic was the official diplomatic language of the Persian Empire. However, neither the presence of official correspondence nor the use of Aramaic is any guarantee that historical sources lie behind the text. Works of creative literary fiction in the Old Testament such as Esther and Daniel also make use of royal decrees and Aramaic.

Parts of Ezra-Nehemiah are written in the first person and give the appearance of direct speech to the reader from Ezra and Nehemiah. Scholars have maintained that the first-person sections of Nehemiah (1:1–7:73; 11:1-2; 12:31-43; 13:4-31) draw upon a memoir written by Nehemiah that was deposited in the temple archives. These first-person passages in Nehemiah resemble other texts from the ancient Near East in which the author addresses his god and gives an account of his actions. Naturally the rhetoric of these texts is one of self-justification, but that does not make them devoid of authentic historical information.

With the first-person sections of Ezra there is less scholarly consensus. Some think that a text written by Ezra has been incorporated into Ezra-Nehemiah, while others maintain that the first-person sections in Ezra have been written in imitation of the genuine Nehemiah memoir.

Ezra-Nehemiah and 1–2 Chronicles

Ezra-Nehemiah and 1–2 Chronicles have long been associated with each other. The last verses of 2 Chronicles are repeated in the opening of Ezra. Both texts seem to focus on the importance of the temple in Jerusalem and proper worship there, especially the function of the Levites. Both are written from a postexilic perspective. If one were to begin reading at 1 Chronicles and read through 2 Chronicles and on to Ezra-Nehemiah, the entire history of Israel is presented from the creation of the world to the restoration of the temple after the exile.

Because of these features, many biblical scholars maintain that 1–2 Chronicles and Ezra-Nehemiah have the same author, called the Chronicler for lack of a better name. However, attempts to determine the authorship of ancient works are notoriously difficult and many scholars now doubt the existence of the Chronicler as author of 1–2 Chronicles and Ezra-Nehemiah. Ultimately, what is important to remember is that Ezra-Nehemiah may be profitably read as part of a larger narrative work that includes 1–2 Chronicles, regardless of whether or not the books originate from a single author or group of scribes.

Ezra and Nehemiah in the canon and in later Jewish and Christian traditions

Ezra-Nehemiah was originally a single literary work before Jerome divided it into two separate books when he made the Vulgate translation. For centuries the two books were known as 1 and 2 Esdras in Catholic Bibles. In Judaism the work was not divided until the Middle Ages, although in modern printed Hebrew Bibles the two books are still united. Throughout the ancient Jewish and Christian world, many traditions grew up around the figure of Ezra. In Jewish tradition he is the second great lawgiver, esteemed as highly as Moses, and is also credited with the collection and publication of the Jewish scriptures.

One tradition in the Talmud states that if God had not called Moses, then he would have given the law to Ezra. The Jewish philosopher Baruch Spinoza expanded on this tradition and claimed that Ezra was the author of the Pentateuch. There are many apocryphal stories written by both Jews and Christians about encounters between Ezra and divine figures. These stories often have an apocalyptic tone, much like the book of Revelation, which shows that early Jews and Christians saw Ezra as a mediator between God and humankind. With Nehemiah things are simpler. Apart from his presence in Ezra-Nehemiah, Nehemiah is mentioned only in Sirach 49:13, a long poem praising the great Israelites of the past, and in 2 Maccabees 2:13, which recounts his efforts at collecting the lost sacred books after the exile.

Historical background to Ezra-Nehemiah

A very curious feature about all of these later traditions surrounding Ezra and Nehemiah is that the two figures never occur together in any of them. The only place where they are connected is in Ezra-Nehemiah, yet even here there are problems. First, the two men appear to have no knowledge of each other at all, an odd situation given the prominent role both are given in the rebuilding of Jerusalem. They are only mentioned together in Nehemiah 8:9; 12:26, 36, but because neither man speaks or acknowledges the other in any of these instances, most biblical scholars see these texts as editorial glosses inserted to create a relationship between the two men.

Additionally, the chronology of Ezra-Nehemiah as it now stands poses problems. According to Ezra 7:7, Ezra left for Jerusalem in "the seventh year of King Artaxerxes," while in Nehemiah 2:1 we are told that Nehemiah goes to Jerusalem in "the twentieth year of King Artaxerxes." But if Ezra in fact arrived before Nehemiah, there are logical inconsistencies in the story recounting their deeds. When Ezra arrives, he finds a populated, walled (depending on how one reads Ezra 9:9) city, which makes it difficult to explain why Nehemiah, arriving after Ezra, should have to rebuild the wall of Jerusalem and arrange for the city to be inhabited. Also, Ezra 10:6 mentions that Johanan was high priest during Ezra's stay in Jerusalem. We know from other records that a Johanan was high priest ca. 410 and was the grandson of Eliashib, who is the high priest in Nehemiah 3:1; 13:10. If Ezra came first, then how could Johanan have been high priest before his grandfather?

The obvious solution to these problems is to reverse the order of Ezra and Nehemiah's journeys to Jerusalem. Some biblical scholars have done this, based upon different historical and literary proposals. One such solution argues that the King Artaxerxes who sent Ezra back is a different Artaxerxes from the one who commissioned Nehemiah's trip to Jerusalem. Since it is almost certain that the Artaxerxes with whom Nehemiah dealt is Artaxerxes I, some maintain that Artaxerxes II (405–359) is the king who commissions Ezra. This makes the "seventh year of King Artaxerxes" in Ezra 7:7 the year 398 rather than 458. According to this reconstruction, Nehemiah arrives in Jerusalem in 445 and Ezra follows in 398:

Nehemiah: "twentieth year of Artaxerxes"
  (Neh 2:1) = Artaxerxes I (445)
Ezra: "seventh year of King Artaxerxes"
  (Ezra 7:7) = Artaxerxes II (398)

Another solution claims that Artaxerxes I is the king who deals with *both* Ezra and Nehemiah, but that the text of Ezra 7:7 should read "the thirty-seventh year" rather than "the seventh year." In Hebrew, the word "thirty" (*sheloshim*) is spelled similarly to the words for "year" (*shenah*) and "seven" (*sheva*). It would be easy for a copyist to accidentally omit the word "thirty." There is a similar instance of a number having dropped out of the Hebrew text of the Bible in 1 Samuel 13:1 which reads: "Saul was a year old when he began to reign, and he ruled two years over Israel." Given the implausible nature of the statement as it stands, it is certain that the actual age of Saul upon his accession has been lost, most likely due to a copyist's error. With this proposed change to Ezra 7:7, Nehemiah came to Jerusalem in 445 and Ezra followed in 428.

Nehemiah: "twentieth year of Artaxerxes"
  (Neh 2:1) = Artaxerxes I (445)
Ezra: "[thirty]-seventh year of King
  Artaxerxes" (Ezra 7:7) = Artaxerxes I (428)

Neither of these solutions is without problems, and other scholars argue that the biblical order of Ezra followed by Nehemiah is also historically plausible, although their arguments too are fraught with gaps and inconsistencies. One factor worth mentioning is that most of the chronological problems occur in the book of Ezra. The first half of the book telescopes almost a century of history into a time span that gives the impression of being much shorter. There is evidence of multiple returns from Babylon behind the portrayal of a single great return in Ezra 1–3. The depiction of Ezra is also highly irregular. He is nowhere mentioned as the governor of Judah, as is Nehemiah, nor is he a high priest. It is clear that the author of Ezra-Nehemiah wants to place the work of Ezra at the same time as that of Nehemiah and, further, that the author had literary and theological reasons for doing so. Exploring these reasons is a fruitful enterprise, despite the fact that the historical background to Ezra-Nehemiah remains a puzzle.

Literary considerations and ancient history writing

The author may have had other priorities than historical accuracy. Often the questions that modern readers bring to biblical texts are conditioned by assumptions and sensibilities foreign to the biblical authors. That history is only about the retelling of events in the order that they happened is a modern idea that often is at odds with how ancient authors wrote about the past. For the biblical writers, history writing must always have a moral or didactic purpose. It did not exist simply to tell readers about the past, but instead it drew upon traditions about the past to teach readers a lesson.

Many examples of this kind of historical writing are in the Bible. The author of Judges arranged traditional material about early Israelite heroes into a repeated pattern of apostasy, oppression, repentance, and salvation to stress the importance of fidelity to Yahweh for peace and prosperity. Similarly, 1–2 Kings arranges its material through the lenses of "good" and "bad" kings, i.e., those who were either faithful or disobedient to the covenant. Even in the New Testament, one finds that in each gospel, stories about Jesus handed on in the tradition are arranged and shaped according to theological rather than historical aims. Witness in John the fact that the cleansing of the temple is placed at the beginning of the gospel, rather than at the beginning of the Passion as in the Synoptic Gospels of Matthew, Mark, and Luke.

In addition to the fact that the biblical writers had a different understanding of history than we do, it is also the case that in many instances they did not intend to write about the past simply as past. Once one understands this, many of the so-called "contradictions" in the Bible disappear because they are revealed to be texts driven by theological or literary concerns rather than historical ones. This is most apparent in the case of the many doublets in the Old Testament, i.e., two (or more) versions of the same story. Examples of these abound, from the two creation stories in Genesis 1–3, to the stories of Abraham and Isaac passing off their wives as their sisters in Genesis 12, 20, and 26, to the two traditions of the slayer of Goliath in 1 Samuel 17 and 2 Samuel 21, to the two different versions of the Ten Commandments in Exodus 20 and Deuteronomy 5.

Turning to Ezra-Nehemiah, one gets the impression reading the text that the book is telling parallel stories simultaneously, rather than recounting a single story in a strict, linear fashion. In response to this, some biblical scholars maintain that the present text of Ezra-Nehemiah is jumbled and needs rearrangement. The following changes are often proposed: Ezra's reading of the law in Nehemiah 7:72–8:18 is placed right after Ezra's arrival in Jerusalem in Ezra 8:36. Ezra's prayer in Nehemiah 9:6-37 is combined with his prayer in Ezra 9:6-15. The people's lament in Nehemiah 9:1-5 about having taken foreign wives is placed in the assembly of the people in Ezra 10. The covenant made by the people in Nehemiah 10:1-40 is placed after Nehemiah 13:31, so as to be the final chapter of the book. The list detailing the inhabitants of Jerusalem in Nehemiah 11:1-19 is placed after Nehemiah 7:72, the end of the list of returned exiles.

Such wholesale emendation of the text is necessary, however, only if the assumption is that the author of Ezra-Nehemiah placed the highest priority on linear coherence. But perhaps the author was more concerned with trying to show how the distinct missions of Ezra and Nehemiah paralleled and complemented each other. Of course some chronological integrity was then sacrificed for the sake of this larger purpose. This would explain why, in the text's present form, the missions of both men contain the same elements:

return, reconstruction, assembly, covenant renewal, and reform.

These elements, it should be added, form a larger narrative pattern known from the Greek world involving stories of colonization. During the classical Greek period, roughly contemporaneous with the events depicted in Ezra-Nehemiah, several Greek cities sent groups of citizens to found colonies. Many of these Greek colonies were founded in southern Italy and Sicily, which is why those regions now have some of the most impressive Greek ruins. The leader of the expedition was required to seek divine sanction for the new colony from the gods, to oversee the colony's foundation and governance, and to ensure the proper transfer and institution of the mother-city's religious practices.

Ezra-Nehemiah contains all of the essential elements needed to describe the colonization of a new settlement in antiquity. Here, the two main characters share the duties of the founder. To Ezra is given the task of ritual purification, which involves offering prayers on behalf of the people and giving instruction in the law of Yahweh. To Nehemiah fall the activities of building fortifications, populating the city with worthy inhabitants, and establishing commercial, cultic, and social regulations.

In addition to shaping the stories of Ezra and Nehemiah along the lines of the Greek colonization process, the author also arranged his material according to a handful of stylized type-scenes that are repeated for both Ezra and Nehemiah. Type-scenes are standardized vignettes that ancient authors and storytellers used to arrange their source material. The type-scene signals the reader to make connections between a particular story and others like it. Here, the purpose of the type-scenes is to draw the reader's attention to the similarities between the figures of Ezra and Nehemiah and the significance of their respective missions.

Among the type-scenes in Ezra-Nehemiah is the return from exile, the first led by Sheshbazzar, Zerubbabel, and Jeshua (Ezra 1:5; 2:1), and a second led by Ezra (Ezra 7:7; 8:15-36). Another type-scene involves the attempt by enemies to halt the reconstruction of Jerusalem and the temple (Ezra 4:1-6; 5:3; Neh 2:10; 3:33–4:2; 6:1-14). The enemies are variously understood as the "people of the land," or other regional governors, such as Sanballat or Tobiah. Both Ezra and Nehemiah say lengthy prayers (Ezra 9:6-15; Neh 1:5-11; 9:6-37) that function much like the long speeches placed into the mouths of main characters in ancient history writing, for example, Peter and Paul in Acts. Ancient authors used such monologues to interpret events in the narrative or to give them historical context. Finally, there is the type-scene which involves the assembly of the entire people (Ezra 3:1; 10:1; 10:9; Neh 8:1; 9:1). This type-scene can coincide with either a rededication to the law of Moses (Neh 10:29-40) or the observance of a religious festival (Ezra 3:4; Neh 8:13-17). This type-scene is also found in other Old Testament texts (e.g., 2 Kings 22; 2 Maccabees 2) and plays a significant role in ancient Israelite self-understanding.

Theology in Ezra-Nehemiah

If the author was subordinating historical concerns to his theological agenda, then the text of Ezra-Nehemiah can be understood without recourse to changing the order or the contents of the text, although it is helpful to know exactly how the author has rearranged his source material in order to understand the author's literary and theological concerns. From the author's perspective, he was telling a tale of the distant past when the people of Israel were brought home to Jerusalem by God in fulfillment of the divine promise. This tale was one of hardship and conflict. Fidelity to the covenant and perseverance in its observance were the only remedies for the people's troubles.

The theology of Ezra-Nehemiah consequently stresses the connection between God's people and God's law, the latter being the defining characteristic of the former. The role of the law is paramount. Ezra comes back to Jerusalem for the sole purpose of bringing the law of Moses to the newly reconstituted community. Nehemiah rebuilds the wall of Jerusalem before he repopulates the city with Israelites and enforces observance of the law. Both of these missions, Ezra's to bring the law and Nehemiah's to build the wall, serve to create a people set apart in both the literal and metaphorical senses. The law and the wall mark the boundary and maintain the distinction between insiders and outsiders. Indeed, in his great prayer, Ezra brings the metaphorical and the literal understanding of walls together when, in reference to

the law, he proclaims that God has given his people "a protective wall in Judah and Jerusalem" (Ezra 9:9). The connection is clear: both the law of God and the walls of Jerusalem serve to preserve God's people.

This connection is strengthened later in the history of Judaism. There is a famous Greek text called the Letter of Aristeas, which tells the story of how the law of Moses was translated from Hebrew into Greek. Written sometime in the second century, the text is also a defense of the Jewish law. One of the images the author uses for the law is a wall, claiming that through Moses God has surrounded his people with "iron walls" to separate them from other people and their false beliefs.

This concern for adhering to the law through maintenance of community boundaries has been misunderstood by non-Jews for over 2,000 years. This misunderstanding has sadly led many Christians to characterize Judaism as legalistic, rigid, nationalistic, or even xenophobic. Doing so overlooks the larger historical context that led postexilic Judaism to stress fidelity to the law in the manner that it did. Those who came to Jerusalem under the auspices of the Persian authorities saw themselves as returning exiles, descendants of a people who had been brutally deported by the Babylonians in 587. Deportation was a common military strategy in the ancient Near East. Thousands of conquered people were moved great distances and forcibly resettled. Deportation was an effective means of controlling conquered people for the very reason that it destroyed their identity as a people. After three or four generations, people were assimilated to their new habitat, one provided for them by conquerors who were now seen as the guarantors, rather than the destroyers, of a people's identity.

Thus, those who came to Jerusalem saw themselves as the fortunate recipients of another chance to be the people God had intended them to be. Consequently they were determined not to let this opportunity pass them by. Out of this arose a critical reflection, begun already during the exile, in which Israelite intellectuals explored the question: "Why did God allow us to be taken into exile?" Finding an answer to this question would help ensure that such a calamity never happen again.

For the author of Ezra-Nehemiah, part of the answer could be found in Deuteronomistic History, the scholarly designation for that great body of work comprising the books of Deuteronomy–2 Kings that chronicles Israelite history from their arrival in the Promised Land through the division into two kingdoms that culminates in the exile. There, God repeatedly makes explicit that any violation of the covenant will result in the Israelites' expulsion from the land (see, for example, Deuteronomy 28). Then when both the northern and southern kingdoms are destroyed, the author adds the editorial comment that these disasters were deserved divine punishments for the faithlessness of the people (2 Kings 17, 24).

Ezra-Nehemiah stands in this tradition when it affirms that the exile was the deserved punishment of a just God on a disobedient people. Yet that is only half the picture for Ezra-Nehemiah, since it also chronicles the return from exile. Here, the text takes a cue from the prophetic literature in the Old Testament, which often uses a stylized pattern of sin, punishment, and forgiveness to describe the relationship between God and the Israelites (Amos and Hosea are good examples of this pattern). So too in Ezra-Nehemiah, the return to Jerusalem is seen as a gracious act of mercy on the part of God, a second chance that, because it is undeserved, is not to be squandered.

The Deuteronomistic vision of a just God who punishes wrongdoing and the prophetic proclamation of a merciful God who ultimately forgives come together in Ezra-Nehemiah, most notably in Ezra's great prayer on behalf of the people: "Yet in your great mercy you did not completely destroy them and you did not forsake them, for you are a gracious and merciful God. . . . In all that has come upon us you have been just, for you kept faith while we have done evil" (Neh 9:31, 33). This affirmation of God's just punishment and gracious mercy is at the heart of the Old Testament's theology. It is expressed most forcefully perhaps in the doxological poem that God proclaims about himself during the theophany to Moses on Mt. Sinai:

> The LORD, the LORD, a God gracious and merciful, slow to anger and abounding in love and fidelity, continuing his love for a thousand generations, and forgiving wickedness, rebellion, and sin; yet not declaring the guilty guiltless, but bringing punishment for their parents' wickedness on children and children's children to the third and fourth generation! (Exod 34:6-7)

Studying Ezra-Nehemiah at once opens the reader to a time in the history of ancient Israel in which many of the foundational texts and ideas at work in the Old Testament came together and were crystallized in what was seen as a providential opportunity, a graced moment not to be missed. The intensity with which Ezra and Nehemiah exhorted their compatriots to "seize the day" should not be lost on us. Living with one's eyes open to the sweep of history and aware also of the presence of God and the responsibilities of following God are perennial necessities for the life of faith.

COMMENTARY: *EZRA*

THE RETURN FROM EXILE

Ezra 1–6

Scholars have divided Ezra into two parts. Ezra 1–6 deals with events spanning the first return of exiles in 539 until the sixth year of Darius I (516). Ezra 4 seems to leapfrog into the reign of Artaxerxes I (beginning in 465). Ezra 7–10 presupposes a completed temple and begins with the arrival of Ezra in Jerusalem during the seventh year of the reign of Artaxerxes I (458). Text divisions and subheadings below are taken from the New American Bible Revised Edition. A Greek paraphrase of parts of 2 Chronicles and Ezra-Nehemiah exists. It is part of the Catholic apocrypha known as 3 Esdras (but in Greek it is called 1 Esdras; biblical studies can be confusing). In certain instances, this Greek version contains interesting variants from the Hebrew text of Ezra-Nehemiah. Where appropriate, these variants will be noted below.

1:1-11 The decree of Cyrus

Cyrus of Persia (d. 530) was the founder of the first true empire in the ancient Near East. In the space of twenty years, he completed a series of stunning military conquests, defeating the Medians, Lydians, Babylonians, and Egyptians (the final conquest of the Egyptians completed by his son Cambyses). In the *Histories* of Herodotus, Cyrus is portrayed as an ambitious and brilliant general, destined for greatness from before his birth.

In October 539 Cyrus entered the city of Babylon after having defeated the armies of the Babylonian king, Nabonidus. The decree in Ezra 1:2-4 is dated immediately after Cyrus' conquest of Babylon ("the first year," 1:1) and implies that one of his first acts was to send the exiles home. This decree is also found in 2 Chronicles 36:22-23, and functions as the bridge between 1–2 Chronicles, which tells the story of the Israelites from creation to the return from exile, to Ezra-Nehemiah, which continues that story until roughly the year 400.

The decree in Ezra 1 is prefaced by the author's belief that Cyrus was moved to send the exiles back to Jerusalem at the urging of God. The anonymous author of Isaiah 44 expands on this belief

and not only has God call Cyrus but also declare him to be his "anointed":

> I say of Cyrus, My shepherd! / He carries out my every wish, / Saying of Jerusalem, "Let it be rebuilt," / and of the temple, "Lay its foundations." / Thus says the LORD to his anointed, Cyrus, / whose right hand I grasp, / Subduing nations before him, / stripping kings of their strength, / Opening doors before him, / leaving the gates unbarred: / I will go before you / and level the mountains; / Bronze doors I will shatter, / iron bars I will snap. / I will give you treasures of darkness, / riches hidden away, / That you may know I am the LORD, / the God of Israel, who calls you by name. / For the sake of Jacob, my servant, / of Israel my chosen one, / I have called you by name, / giving you a title, though you do not know me. / I am the LORD, there is no other, / there is no God besides me. / It is I who arm you, though you do not know me (Isa 44:28–45:5).

Worth noticing in the biblical portrayal of Cyrus is not only the fact that he is understood as the instrument of God, but also that God is understood as the god of the entire world. Belief in the universal dominion of God appears to have originated in ancient Israel during and after the exile. The fact that the entire known world was under the rule of a single king doubtless played a role in this theological speculation.

The Cyrus decree preserved in the Old Testament is not the only evidence of his astute political policy. The British Museum in London houses a clay barrel on which is a cuneiform inscription that Cyrus had placed in Babylon. This inscription, known as the Cyrus Cylinder, sheds valuable light on Cyrus' return of the exiles to Jerusalem in that it is Cyrus' justification for his takeover of Babylon.

In the ancient Near East royal legitimacy was based on continuity. The king was rightfully so because he continued the line, beliefs, prayers, and activities of the ancient kings. By 539, when Cyrus conquered Babylon, the city's culture and traditions were already 2,500 years old. In the inscription, Cyrus demonstrates his rightful place as king both by claiming that the Babylonian king, Nabonidus, had abandoned the correct traditions and that he, Cyrus, had been chosen by the Babylonian god Marduk to restore right worship:

> Nabonidus turned the worship of Marduk into an abomination. . . . Marduk searched all the lands for a righteous ruler. He chose Cyrus and anointed him as the ruler of all the earth. Because Marduk . . . was pleased with Cyrus . . . he ordered him to march against Babylon. They walked together like friends. . . . Marduk allowed Cyrus to enter Babylon without a battle. . . . I [Cyrus] entered Babylon as a friend of Marduk. . . . Every day I offered sacrifices to Marduk who made the people love and obey me (Victor Matthews and Don C. Benjamin, eds., *Old Testament Parallels: Laws and Stories from the Ancient Near East*, 2nd edition [New York: Paulist Press, 1997], 193–94).

Then the text turns to the reestablishment of order under Cyrus after the chaos of life during the rule of Nabonidus. The hallmark of good kingship in the ancient Near East was the creation and maintenance of a divinely ordained order. The king thus functioned as an agent of the gods, and proper worship is a necessary component of right rule. Thus Cyrus proclaims in the Cylinder:

> I returned the statues of the divine patrons of every land . . . to their own sanctuaries. When I found their sanctuaries in ruins, I rebuilt them. I also repatriated the people of these lands and rebuilt their houses. Finally, with Marduk's permission, I allowed statues of the divine patrons of Sumer and Akkad [traditional name of Babylon] to be returned to their own sanctuaries, which I rebuilt (ibid., 195).

In both the biblical and cuneiform decrees, Cyrus the Persian is portrayed as the chosen instrument of the vanquished peoples' god, be it the Hebrew god Yahweh or the Babylonian god Marduk. Cyrus has been sent to restore order, understood specifically as the return of exiled peoples and the reestablishment of temples.

It is a matter of debate whether or not Cyrus actually promulgated decrees specific to each of the many peoples he conquered and repatriated. Scholars disagree over the authenticity of the decree in Ezra 1. The title "King of Persia" is not the customary title Cyrus and his successors used. Many think it highly unlikely that a Persian decree would mention the name of Yahweh, as in Ezra 1:2, although the Cyrus Cylinder freely uses the name of the Babylonian god Marduk. It also seems implausible that Cyrus would have authorized offerings for the reconstruction of the temple in Jerusalem.

The phrase "let them go up" in verse 3 is problematic in that, although it is a standard biblical phrase for going to Jerusalem, this is due to the fact that the city sits on a relatively high elevation in comparison to other areas in Palestine. That is to say, the expression "to go up to Jerusalem" would only make sense to someone who lived in Palestine. It is extremely unlikely that Cyrus would use a phrase that draws upon the geographic features of Palestine.

In Ezra 6:3-5 is an Aramaic version of the decree that seems to have more in common with surviving Persian correspondence, yet it too is not without difficulty. However, the Cyrus Cylinder and the praise of Cyrus in Isaiah, when placed alongside the decrees in Ezra and 2 Chronicles speak strongly in favor of an authentic tradition of Cyrus authorizing people in Babylon to return to Jerusalem, regardless of whether the decrees quoted in the Old Testament come from any archival sources now lost.

One may well ask why a Persian king would have had any interest in the destroyed temple of a small people on the southern borders of his empire. As mentioned in the introduction, temples, because they were places that collected offerings, were natural choices for administrative centers and hence facilitated the collecting of tribute. The Persians viewed their empire as a source of revenue and were very efficient at exploiting their holdings in order to amass vast wealth. It made good sense to rebuild temples. It won the goodwill of the conquered peoples, or at least of the local elites whose support would be necessary. It showed the ruler to be the favored one of the conquered people's god, thus emphasizing his right to rule. Finally, it allowed the ruler to collect tribute with a minimum of effort.

Sheshbazzar is a mysterious figure, mentioned only here and in Ezra 5:14-17. Although he is called a prince of Judah in the text, it is unlikely that he was of Davidic descent. Instead, as the first governor of Judah, Sheshbazzar is an elite member of the Jewish community whom the Persians designated to establish an administrative structure. The name Sheshbazzar is Babylonian, a not unusual feature for Jews who lived in exile. Such is also the case with the name Zerubbabel. Remember too that Daniel and his companions are given Babylonian names in Daniel 1.

The account of the return in Ezra is most concerned with the rebuilding of the temple and the reestablishment of worship. Thus, there is the list of all the precious vessels returned to Jerusalem by Cyrus. The total amount of goods in verse 11 does not match the specific amounts listed in verses 9-10. All of the gifts are of an extraordinary amount, no doubt a literary exaggeration. It is doubtful that Cyrus would have given gold to the returnees, although the name of his treasurer in verse 8, Mithredath, is Persian. The picture of Jews departing a place of foreign captivity laden with riches is a motif that draws upon Exodus 12:35-36, in which the departing Israelites are given gold and other precious metals by the Egyptians. The author here is trying to draw the comparison between the exodus and the return from the exile. Both are a release from bondage due to an act of divine grace that allows God's people to return to their land.

Historical records show that not all the Jews who lived in Babylon returned to Jerusalem. Indeed, Babylon went on to become one of the major centers of Jewish intellectual life in the following centuries. In verse 5 the author mentions that the only people who returned to Jerusalem were those who had been inspired by God. Implicit in this remark is that not everyone who could go back to Jerusalem did indeed go. There would be many reasons why some exiled Jews chose not to return. After a period of fifty years, people would have become acclimated to their "new" surroundings. Children born in exile would have already been fully grown with children of their own. Babylon would have been the land that they knew, and Jerusalem would have been new and different.

Underlying the decision of whether to stay in Babylon or return to Jerusalem is a profound theological question. Can one properly worship God outside of the Promised Land and the Holy City? For many Jews in Babylon the answer to this question was "yes," and they developed a way to be faithful to the covenant without the temple in Jerusalem. Centuries later, when the temple was destroyed by the Romans, the way of life developed by the expatriate Jewish community in

Babylon would become part of the norm for all Jews, even to this day.

2:1-70 A census of the returned exiles

Strictly speaking, this is a list of returnees from Babylon, led by Zerubbabel rather than Sheshbazzar. Sheshbazzar curiously drops out of the narrative until chapter 5, and some scholars maintain that the author of Ezra-Nehemiah has combined two separate returns in chapters 1–2, or that Sheshbazzar and Zerubbabel were the same person. The list in this chapter itself is clearly composite and much of it dates from later periods. The Nehemiah mentioned in verse 2 is not the same Nehemiah who builds the wall of Jerusalem. Of particular interest is the name Bigvai in verse 2, since it is a Persian name. It is highly unlikely that a returning Jewish exile would have a Persian name in the first year of Cyrus's reign.

The list is comprised of several subcategories. First is the "people of Israel," noting people by their family names, i.e., "descendants of X," in verses 3-21 and then shifting to designation by place (of settlement or origin?) in verses 22-28, before reverting to family designations in verses 29-35. Curiously, many of the family names are clearly place names, e.g., "descendants of Bethlehem" in verse 21, or "descendants of Jericho" in verse 34. Perhaps the author has combined two lists that used different formulae for designating family/town groups. Next, temple functionaries are listed in descending order of importance: priests (2:36-39), Levites (2:40), singers (2:41), gatekeepers (2:42), and slaves (2:43-54). After the temple personnel are "descendants of Solomon's servants," a curious designation. Finally, and significantly in the last position, are those returnees who could not prove their Israelite ancestry. Of these latter groups, those who claimed to be of priestly families had their ancestry checked against "family records." While designating Jews from non-Jews will be a main priority for the returned exiles, it is more acute for the priesthood, since anyone with even a remote chance of impurity or unworthiness must be kept away from the sacred meals in the temple.

The governor (Zerubbabel rather than Sheshbazzar) temporarily bars these men from the sacrifice until a priest can determine their ancestry for certain. The Urim and Thummim (v. 63) are mysterious devices, mentioned only a handful of

times in the Old Testament, mainly in the Pentateuch. They appear to have been some sort of
means of divination, i.e., determining the divine
will through manipulation of an object. Numerous means of divination existed in the ancient
world, from reading the entrails and livers of sacrificed animals to casting lots. The ancient Israelites were no exception in the practice of divination,
since it was of vital importance to know that one
was not going against the will of God. While some
divinatory practices are condemned in the Bible,
others are sanctioned (the Eleven cast lots in Acts
1 to find the successor of Judas). The Urim and
Thummim are divinely approved means of divination, and so Zerubbabel calls for their use here.
Interestingly, the Greek version of Ezra does not
mention the Urim and Thummim at all but says
rather that these men were barred from food in
the temple until there arose "a high priest clothed
in clarity and truth" (1 Esdr 5:40).

The total number of the returned community
given in verse 64, excluding slaves and singers, is
42,360, a number evenly divisible by twelve (12 x
3,530), perhaps significant, given that the returnees are the reconstituted twelve tribes of Israel.
The total in verse 64 does not correspond with the
numbers given in the census, which when added
together give the figure 29,818. No explanation
has yet been found for the discrepancy. It is also
clear, given the most recent archaeological data,
that the population of Judah throughout the
Persian period was many times smaller than the
numbers of returning exiles in Ezra-Nehemiah
(not to mention the people who were already living in Judah).

The freewill offerings of the people in verses
68-69 form a frame with the offerings of 1:6-11
given to the departing Israelites in Babylon. The
sums here are exaggerated. The mention of the
drachma in verse 69 occurs only here and in the
other occurrence of this census in Nehemiah 7.
The drachma is a Greek coin introduced in the
fifth century that could not have been in the possession of Jewish returnees of the preceding century. Some have translated the Hebrew word
darkemon as "daric," an imperial Persian coin.
However, this coin was not introduced until the
reign of Darius I. In either case, the reference is
clearly an anachronism. The chapter ends with a
brief notice that the returnees settled in their
ancestral homes and in Jerusalem.

3:1-5 Restoration of worship

This continues the narrative of Zerubbabel and
Jeshua, who can be dated on the basis of Ezra 4:24
and Haggai 1:1 to the second year of the reign of
Darius I (521) but are here placed in the narrative
of the first returnees from Babylon in 538 under
Sheshbazzar. The seventh month referred to in
verse 1 is ambiguous but helps to explain the celebration of the feast of Booths in verse 4. A major
reason that temples were important was the fact
that in antiquity the relationship between humanity and the gods was understood as reciprocal. Offerings were concrete, usually of animals
or produce, and were made in order to express
gratitude for past benefit or to request future
blessing. To shirk one's duty in offering was to
court disaster. It is thus natural that Zerubbabel
and Jeshua ensure that the altar and offerings are
established first before seeing to the actual building that will house the place of offering.

The notice in verse 4 that the feast of Booths
was kept parallels Nehemiah 7–8, which begins
with the same census of Ezra 2 and then also notes
that the people kept the feast of Booths. The two
passages in Ezra-Nehemiah themselves are an
echo of the dedication of the first temple under
Solomon in 1 Kings 8 (paralleled in 2 Chronicles
7), which also coincides with the celebration of
the feast of Booths. The author of Ezra-Nehemiah
is at pains to show connections between the return
of the exiles and the exodus as well as the dedication of the rebuilt temple with the building of
Solomon's original. Continuity is of prime importance, for in its resemblance to its Solomonic
prototype the new temple derives its validity.

3:8-13 Laying the foundations of the temple

Ezra continues to stress the similarities with
the building of Solomon's temple, as Phoenician
craftsmen from the port cities of Tyre and Sidon
are enlisted here to help with the building of the
new temple. "[T]he year after their coming" is
ostensibly after the decree of Cyrus in 539 but,
on the basis of other evidence, actually 520 (3:8).
"[T]he second month" was also when building on
the first temple commenced (1 Kgs 6:1).

Stories of the founding of temples were very
popular in the ancient world. Kings were fond of
restoring or improving temples (in essence re-

founding them) both to please the gods and exalt their own glory. This stressed the continuity and, hence, the legitimacy of the king's rule. This is apparent in the stories of the founding of the first temple in the Old Testament, especially those in 1–2 Chronicles, which serve to show the obedience and piety of David and Solomon. Here in Ezra there is no king present to extol and Zerubbabel, as the designated Persian functionary, does not take center stage. Still, continuity with the temple of Solomon is stressed. Of interest is the role of the Levites in the rebuilding. The work is in and of itself a liturgical act, also part of the standard practices surrounding temple building in antiquity. The antiphonal singing of Psalm 100 strikes yet another note of continuity, binding this event with David (3:11).

One interesting anomaly from this emphasis on continuity is the observation in verse 12 of the tears of those who remembered the first temple as the foundations of the second were laid. Again, the author wants us to picture this event occurring immediately after the first return of exiles in 539. However, by the time Zerubbabel laid the foundation of 520, it is unlikely that anyone old enough to remember the temple destroyed almost seventy years earlier would have been alive.

The Hebrew text of this verse reads: "Many of the priests, Levites, family heads and elders who had seen the first temple on its foundation—this was the temple in their eyes—they wept with a loud cry, but many others shouted on high with joy." The phrase "this was the temple in their eyes" has been omitted in the New American Bible Revised Edition, since it is determined to be a copyist's editorial insertion. The phrase is ambiguous. Did those who had seen the first temple not view this new structure as a valid place of worship? In the centuries after the exile there is evidence of numerous disputes within Judaism concerning proper worship of God. The Samaritans had their own temple (see more below). Two rival temples were built in Egypt, one at Elephantine and the other in Leontopolis. Part of the theology of the Qumran community involved what they perceived as illegitimate worship in the Jerusalem temple. Or were these returnees simply anguished at the modest structure before them when compared to the splendid building erected by Solomon? This is the explanation of Haggai 2:3 and the Jewish historian Josephus.

4:1-5 Outside interference

Here local groups from the former northern kingdom of Israel request permission to help with the temple and are rebuffed. The reason given is that Cyrus specifically charged those returning from Babylon to rebuild the temple, and that to allow local assistance would somehow be a disobedience of an imperial command. What lies behind this, however, is also imperial status. As mentioned above, temples functioned as powerful administrative tools and ideological symbols for ruling powers. Those local elites who functioned as the proxies of imperial power stood to gain greatly in their role as brokers between the ruler and his subjects. Add to this the returning exiles' desire for holiness and purity in the wake of their understanding of the cause of the exile, and their refusal of the offer of help makes more sense.

It is widely assumed that Ezra 4 is one of the earliest references to the Samaritans in the Old Testament, although this is based more on the paraphrase of this incident found in the Jewish historian Josephus, since the Samaritans are not mentioned by name in Ezra. Today, the Samaritans are a small Jewish group in Israel numbering less than five hundred people. Their sacred scriptures consist of a version of the Pentateuch that differs from the version used by other Jewish denominations. They do not acknowledge Jerusalem as a holy site but rather worship on Mount Gerizim just outside the ancient city of Samaria, the capital of the ancient northern kingdom. Their origins are shrouded in mystery and conjecture but appear to be in the destruction of the northern kingdom by the Assyrians in 721. According to their own traditions, Samaritans are descended from the remnant of Israelites not deported by the Assyrians. According to the Old Testament and other later rabbinic traditions, they are descended from the non-Israelites repopulated in Israel by the Assyrians after they destroyed Samaria. Firm historical evidence of the Samaritans is not available until the Hellenistic period in the late fourth century, and perhaps in Ezra the author is placing contemporaneous historical tensions back at the origins of the Second Temple.

Samaritans and other Jews have been bitter enemies for centuries, as is often the case involving disputing groups of co-religionists. Much of the animosity has centered on worship, since Samaritans deny the sanctity of Jerusalem and continue to worship at a temple on Mount Gerizim. This dispute lies at the heart of important New Testament texts, such as the Parable of the Good Samaritan, in which knowing that Jews and Samaritans are bitter enemies helps one to understand the parable. It also clarifies Jesus' remark to the Samaritan woman in John's gospel that "the hour is coming when you will worship the Father neither on this mountain nor in Jerusalem" (John 4:21).

In Ezra the local inhabitants claim to have been settled in the land by Esharhaddon, Assyrian king from 680–669. Historically, the northern kingdom was destroyed some forty years earlier by Sargon II. Verse 4 uses the phrase "people of the land" (translated in the NABRE as "local inhabitants"), which in rabbinic texts is a clearly derogatory term and certainly bears negative connotations in Ezra-Nehemiah. In verse 5 the author has a summary statement noting the continuation of such opposition for the twenty-year period between the decree of Cyrus in 539 to the beginning of the reign of Darius I in 522.

4:6-24 Later hostility

This incident of local tensions in the rebuilding of the temple allows the author to develop this theme in the remainder of the chapter, which covers a period of approximately 100 years, spanning the reigns of Persian kings from Cyrus to Artaxerxes I. The summary statement of verse 5 is continued in verse 6 and notes opposition to rebuilding during the reign of Xerxes I ("Ahasuerus"). This theme is furthered in verse 7 for the reign of Artaxerxes I, but the author now takes time to relate a particular incident. Here a Persian, or someone with the Persian name Mithredath, along with Tabeel and other Persian local functionaries, complain to Artaxerxes I about the rebuilding of the temple.

The text appears to be quoting official correspondence, especially because in verse 8, where the letter begins, the text switches from Hebrew to Aramaic, which a Hebrew scribe noted by inserting the remark "in Aramaic" at the end of verse 7. It bears mentioning here that Hebrew and Aramaic share significant features as well as an alphabet. This Aramaic portion runs from 4:8–6:19 where it reverts to Hebrew. There is probably an Aramaic source being used by our author here. Besides the change in language there are some divergences in historical facts between the Aramaic and Hebrew portions of Ezra 1–6. These are noted below.

There appear to be two separate complaints sent to Artaxerxes, one from Mithredath and Tabeel, which is not quoted, and another from Rehum and Shimshai. Rehum is called literally "the master of decrees." He and Shimshai the scribe are Persian officials. In verse 10 the local population claims to have been settled by the Assyrian king Assurbanipal (668–ca. 631), contrary to their claim in 4:2 that Esharhaddon had settled them.

Scholars have long debated the authenticity of the Aramaic portions of Ezra-Nehemiah in general and of the correspondence and royal decrees in particular. They do exhibit certain grammatical features from correspondence of the time and Aramaic was the diplomatic language of the Persian Empire. The letter here purports to come from a large representative body of the Persian satrapy "West-of-Euphrates," of which the province Judah was a part. The letter does not exactly fit the context here, since it refers to a return of Jews to Jerusalem during the time of Artaxerxes I (4:12) over half a century after the decree of Cyrus. That, and the fact that the letter makes more sense if Jerusalem is being fortified, rather than if the temple is being rebuilt, lends credence to the opinion that this letter is better associated with Nehemiah than Zerubbabel.

The idea of an archival search, as the letter writers advise the king in verse 15, reappears in the following chapter within a similar letter to Darius I. It is also a significant plot device in the book of Esther (Esth 6:1-2), which takes place in the Persian court. In an interesting variation of the theology in Ezra-Nehemiah, the letter points out that Jerusalem was destroyed because its inhabitants were disobedient subjects to their overlords, while for the author it was disobedience to God and the covenant that led to the city's downfall. Verses 17-23 purport to relate the imperial reply to the letter and order the cessation of work in Jerusalem. Verse 23 notes that this cessation lasted until the second year of Darius I (520). This poses a major chronological problem, since Darius I reigned before Artaxerxes I. Josephus and I Esdras correct this by omission, and scholars have proposed many different historical reconstructions. Looking at the text as it stands, it appears that the troubles of Ezra 4 are more consistent with the work of Nehemiah, which occurred during the reign of Artaxerxes I and involved the refortification of Jerusalem, rather than the building of the temple. Perhaps the author wanted to group here all the formal appeals to the Persian kings challenging the work in Jerusalem and underscore the futility of those challenges by having the narrative's climax be the completion of the temple in Ezra 6. The fact that the temple was completed in the reign of Darius I, while further challenges to the refortification of Jerusalem occurred half a century later in the reign of Artaxerxes I, would not have bothered our author.

5:1-17 The work resumed under Darius; further problems

As it stands, Ezra 5–6 relates a nearly identical situation as Ezra 4, i.e., a letter to the king from Persian officials hostile to the reconstruction in Jerusalem, requesting that the king both make an archival search and halt the work in Jerusalem (compare 4:8-11 with 5:6; 4:14-15 with 5:17). Doubtless the author has shaped both stories according to a similar literary pattern. The difference between the two anecdotes lies in the fact that Darius' search in the archives allows work in Jerusalem to continue, while the search of Artaxerxes results in his ordering the cessation of work. Again, it bears repeating that the lack of chronological integrity is due to the fact that the author's tradition stated that the temple was completed under Darius I, and he wanted to end the story of opposition to the work of the returned exiles with their triumph over the opposition.

The prophecies of Haggai and Zechariah mentioned in verse 1 are preserved in the two biblical books of the same names. The book of Haggai is a collection of four oracles that are all dated to the second year of Darius I (520). They urge the community in Jerusalem to rally around Zerubbabel and Jeshua and to complete the rebuilding of the temple. Speaking through Haggai, God makes clear that the delay in building the temple is the cause for want among the community of returned exiles. Zechariah, a much longer and more complicated book with messianic and apocalyptic themes, contains an oracle in 4:4-10 praising Zerubbabel for constructing the temple.

The second challenge to the rebuilding comes from Tattenai, the governor, or satrap of the satrapy West-of-Euphrates; he is also mentioned in Babylonian sources. Sheshbazzar, Zerubbabel, and Nehemiah also are called governors but they were provincial governors of the province of Judah, a part of the satrapy West-of-Euphrates, and hence under the jurisdiction of the satrap. The intervention of Tattenai here might be his attempt to assert his newly granted authority over his provincial governors. The satrapal system was conducive to corruption and treachery, and Persian kings had always to be wary of powerful satraps who themselves acted like kings. For example, records of a certain Arsames, satrap of Egypt in the latter half of the fifth century, show that he controlled lands in Babylon, Syria, and Egypt, and that he even made gifts of some of these lands to other Persian nobles.

Tattenai and his secretary, Shethar-bozenai, write to Darius requesting an inquiry into the archives to see whether Persian permission has been granted to rebuild the temple in Jerusalem. While this letter does not have the polemical edge of the letter of Rehum and Shimshai in 4:11-16, it serves the same function as that letter in this incident in that it is a challenge to the rebuilding in Jerusalem. The letter is long and includes a sizable amount of secondary quotation of the Jewish leaders' explanation of their actions. Interestingly, 5:16 states that Sheshbazzar laid the foundation of the temple, contrary to 3:8, which attributes this act to Zerubbabel. Additionally, 5:16 also claims that work on rebuilding the temple has been ongoing since the return under Cyrus, while 4:24 states that work was halted after the complaint of Rehum and Shimshai. This latter verse, however, is at the crux of the chronological mix-up in Ezra 4 and should be read more as a literary device rather than an accurate historical datum. Tattenai requests a search of the archives in Babylon for the Cyrus decree, a logical choice given that those exiles who returned home had been deported to Babylon.

6:1-12 The decree of Darius

The reply of Darius I is an imperial order which reiterates the original decree of Cyrus, also quoted in full. Historically, Darius was a usurper of the Persian throne, having murdered the legitimate king in 522. Herodotus preserves a vivid account of this. After assuming the throne, Darius worked hard to prove his legitimacy and to consolidate his power. If the decree in Ezra 6 is authentic, coming early in the reign of Darius, then it would be consistent with these aims, since in it Darius reiterates the decree of Cyrus and thus places himself in continuity with the founder of the empire.

The citation of the Cyrus decree gives the impression of an authentic archival document, especially the presence of the scribal note "Memorandum" in verse 2. The decree was written in Aramaic on a parchment scroll and deposited at Ecbatana, the former capital of the Medes (in modern-day Iran) that was the summer residence of the Persian king.

After quoting the Cyrus decree, which is not verbatim with the Hebrew version in Ezra 1:4-11, but quite similar in content, Darius goes on to order measures intended to enforce the Cyrus decree. Thus, not only are Persian officials in the satrapy forbidden to interfere with the building of the temple, but they are also to supply resources for the construction and the offering of sacrifices (verses 8-10).

This action clearly places the temple and its function under the imperial aegis, a relationship that benefits both the temple and the king. Verse 10 shows that this relationship requires that offerings be made for the well-being of the king and his family. This is a standard expectation of those who endow religious sites that has continued to the present.

6:13-18 The task finally completed

The decree of Darius, citing and enacting the prior order of Cyrus, rounds out Ezra 1–6, which began with Cyrus' order to rebuild the temple in Jerusalem and now ends with Darius enacting that order and the returned exiles completing the temple. Tattenai works quickly to enact the king's instructions. "[T]he sixth year of the reign of King Darius" (6:15) is 516/15.

An interesting historical parallel to the letters exchanged between Tattenai, Shethar-bozenai, and Darius I involves the fortunes of the Jewish community at Elephantine about a century after the incident in Ezra 5–6. Elephantine is an island in the Nile River situated in Southern Egypt immediately downstream (i.e., north) of the First Cataract of the Nile. During the fifth century a Persian military garrison was placed there to secure the southern border of Egypt and ensure

the peaceful flow of goods from Nubia and the rest of Africa. Among the troops at the garrison were Jewish soldiers and their families. Archives of letters, contracts, and administrative records written in Aramaic on papyrus have been discovered that have shed light on the life of this Jewish community during the Persian period.

These valuable historical witnesses reveal that the Jewish community at Elephantine had a temple to Yahweh on the island, and that in 411 this temple was destroyed by Egyptians living there also. In 407, the leaders of the Jewish community then wrote to Bigvai, the Persian governor of Judah, Johanan the high priest in Jerusalem (mentioned also in Ezra 10:6, see below), and to Delaiah and Shemaiah, the sons of Sanballat, the Persian governor of Samaria, requesting permission to rebuild their temple. Some of these men are also mentioned in Ezra-Nehemiah. The letter of the Elephantine Jews resembles the explanation of the Jewish leaders to Tattenai in 5:11-16 for why the temple in Jerusalem is being rebuilt. Specifically, both groups speak of the antiquity of their temples and refer to Yahweh as "the god of heaven," a term used by Jews in the Persian period to speak of Yahweh to non-Jews (see, for example, Jonah 1:9). The response from Bigvai is also preserved, and just as in the case of the Darius decree in Ezra 6, it is called a "memorandum" and authorizes rebuilding of a temple for "the god of heaven."

6:19-22 The Passover

Here the text reverts from Aramaic to Hebrew. The dedication of the completed temple followed by the observance of the Passover parallels the rite of laying the foundation and keeping the feast of Booths recounted in chapter 3. The community kept itself pure for the festival, both the priests making the offerings and the people who kept themselves separate from outsiders. In verse 21 are mentioned non-exiles who, because they adopted the religious practices of the exilic community, were allowed to share in the festival. The phrase "king of Assyria" in verse 22 is curious, but probably not unintentional, although why the author chose this rather than "king of Persia" is open to speculation.

The joyous observance of Passover closes a major section of Ezra-Nehemiah, spanning the time from the edict of Cyrus allowing the exiles to return to Jerusalem and rebuild the temple to the completion of the temple by the community. The author has used his sources, sometimes with a great deal of freedom, to tell a compelling story of the return of the exiles, the obstacles they encountered in refounding the temple, and how their fidelity to God and his covenant resulted in their ultimate triumph. In many respects, the plot comes to resolution here and the story to an end. The author now will jump ahead in time over half a century to deal with the work of Ezra as a new plotline opens and a new crisis faces the descendants of those who rebuilt the temple.

THE DEEDS OF EZRA

Ezra 7–10

The remainder of the Book of Ezra deals with the work of Ezra who, with permission of the Persian king, came to Jerusalem to promulgate a social and religious law. Curiously, the main figure of Ezra 1–6, Zerubbabel, simply disappears from the story. The narrative slows down considerably, with the remainder of Ezra and all of Nehemiah spanning a period of less than fifty years. About Ezra himself there is considerable historical speculation. Did he come during the reign of Artaxerxes I or Artaxerxes II? Was he a governor of Judah or did he occupy some other Persian office? Was he sent to introduce and enforce a new law, or to ensure that existing law was being observed? Was the law that Ezra enforced a formal, written law code? If so, then was it the final form of the Pentateuch? Some have argued that the figure of Ezra himself is a literary creation meant to act as a significant religious figure alongside the political ruler, Nehemiah, in much the same way that Zerubbabel the governor and Jeshua the priest work in tandem in Ezra 1–6. These questions will be explored below.

7:1-10 Ezra, priest and scribe

This section functions as an introduction to Ezra, and the author is clear about Ezra's exalted status. His genealogy makes him a direct descendant of Aaron, founder of the priesthood (7:1-5). Genealogies are often used to make theological claims about the person whose genealogy it is (think here of the radically different genealogies for Jesus in Matthew and Luke and the evange-

lists' respective theological reasons for tracing Jesus' lineage back to Abraham, as does Matthew, or Adam, as does Luke). Ezra's genealogy is problematic. His father Seraiah is the last high priest killed by the Babylonians in 586 (2 Kgs 25:18), a biological impossibility given that Ezra is working over a century later but rhetorically important to the author in emphasizing the priestly legitimacy of Ezra.

In tandem with Ezra's priestly pedigree is his role as a scribe versed in the law, whose pleasure lies in studying the law and teaching it to his fellow Israelites. The language used here is similar to that found in Deuteronomy, which speaks of the law given by God to Moses consisting of ordinances and statutes to be taught to the people. While the term "scribe" is used elsewhere in Ezra-Nehemiah to speak of Persian functionaries, e.g., Shimshai in Ezra 4:8, here the term has religious connotations. The scribe is the person dedicated to study of God's law.

This special understanding of the scribe in ancient Judaism grew out of the wisdom traditions of ancient Israel and its neighbors. Scribes in the ancient Near East (Israel included) understood themselves as devoted to the pursuit of wisdom and, in later Judaism, when wisdom became equated with the written law of Moses, the scribe's object of devotion was both concrete and inexhaustible. The great hymn to the scribe as a scholar of the law in Sirach would make an apt description of Ezra:

How different the person who devotes himself / to the study of the law of the Most High! / He explores the wisdom of all the ancients / and is occupied with the prophecies; / He preserves the discourses of the famous, / and goes to the heart of involved sayings; / He seeks out the hidden meaning of proverbs, / and is busied with the enigmas found in parables. He is in attendance on the great, / and appears before rulers.

He travels among the peoples of foreign lands / to test what is good and evil among people. / His care is to rise early / to seek the Lord his Maker, / to petition the Most High, / To open his mouth in prayer, / to ask pardon for his sins.

If it pleases the Lord Almighty, / he will be filled with the spirit of understanding; / He will pour forth his words of wisdom / and in prayer give praise to the Lord. / He will direct his knowledge and his counsel, / as he meditates upon God's mysteries. / He will show the wisdom of what he has learned / and glory in the Law of the Lord's covenant.

Many will praise his understanding; / his name can never be blotted out; / Unfading will be his memory, / through all generations his name will live; / Peoples will speak of his wisdom, / and the assembly will declare his praise. / While he lives he is one out of a thousand, / and when he dies he leaves a good name. (Sir 39:1-11)

In Ezra 7 then, two distinct offices in ancient Judaism—namely, that of priest with knowledge of cultic regulations and the mechanics of sacrifice, and that of scribe with knowledge of the written Torah—are combined in Ezra, who is called by the hybrid term "priest-scribe" in verse 11.

References to "the seventh year of King Artaxerxes" in verses 7-8 have posed many chronological problems for scholars (see discussion in the Introduction). Whenever the historical Ezra may have been active, in the context of Ezra-Nehemiah he is placed in the time of Nehemiah, who worked during the time of Artaxerxes I. Thus, apart from any historical issues, which are highly speculative at this point, but instead on purely literary grounds, the Artaxerxes of Ezra 7 will be understood below to be Artaxerxes I.

7:11-26 The decree of Artaxerxes

This is the fourth royal decree in Ezra (Cyrus in 1:1-4, Artaxerxes I in 4:17-22, Darius I in 6:1-12, and Artaxerxes I here in 7:12-26). The Artaxerxes in this decree is the same as the Artaxerxes who halted construction on the temple in 4:17-22, but the author has neglected to mention his change of heart. As was mentioned above, however, the author is more interested in pursuing his literary and theological themes than in recounting a chronologically coherent story. The fact that the decree is given in Aramaic lends an air of authenticity to it, as does the presence of Persian words in the phrase "copy of the rescript" in verse 11.

While the decree may draw upon some archival document, the author of Ezra-Nehemiah has shaped the text to fit into his theological vision. The decree is deliberately evocative of the Cyrus decree in Ezra 1. Both texts authorize the return of Jewish exiles to Jerusalem and make provision for government funding of the temple's construction and ongoing maintenance. Thus Ezra 7–8

forms a parallel with Ezra 1–2, which recounts a royal decree that results in a mass journey of Jews to Jerusalem.

Scholars have long thought that Ezra held an official position in the service of the Persian king. Some have argued that Ezra was governor of the province, although he is never called by that title and in the narrative he is contemporaneous with Nehemiah, who is the governor of Judah. The decree simply says that Ezra has been sent by the king to lead Jewish subjects back to Jerusalem and to supervise the province of Judah in the observance of the "law of your God" (7:13-14). But the decree then goes on in verses 25-26 to give Ezra much broader powers: to appoint judges and to enforce "the law of your God and the law of the king" in the entire satrapy of West-of-Euphrates, of which Judah was but a single province. Ezra's broader powers in verses 25-26 seem to be at odds with his charge in verses 13-14. These expanded powers come at the very end of the decree and give the impression of being an appendix to it. Moreover, they appear very similar to legendary or fictional accounts of Jews who are given broad powers by foreign kings (e.g., Joseph in Gen 37–50, Daniel in Dan 1–7, Esther and Mordecai in Esth 6–10). Cumulatively, these observations support the conclusion that verses 25-26 are an editorial insertion made to exalt the status of Ezra.

Yet the question still remains concerning the nature of Ezra's mission. Scholars have noted the presence of inscriptions from the reign of Darius I that show the Persian imperial authority engaged in codifying and enforcing local religious law throughout the empire. Another example of Persian interest in local religious law comes from a letter written in 419 found in Elephantine (mentioned above). This letter appears to relate an order from Darius II authorizing observance of the Passover among the Jewish soldiers in service to the Persian king. There is nothing particularly distinctive about this policy on the part of the Persians. With some exceptions, rulers in the ancient Near East were content to allow conquered peoples to continue their ancestral worship.

The main concern of the Persians was in the efficient exploitation of resources from their imperial holdings. To the extent that local religious practices aided, or did not hinder, in this exploitation, these practices were tolerated. Rarely were they instituted or financially supported by the

Persians. In Ezra-Nehemiah the statements about the lavish monetary gifts given by the king to the Jerusalem temple are in all likelihood due to the rhetorical aims of the author. Moreover, the author is at pains to stress that the reforms of Ezra are consonant both with the will of God and of the king, thus giving them ironclad legitimacy.

What exactly was "the law of God" that Ezra was supposed to apply in Judah? The classic, or standard, opinion in biblical scholarship has been that Ezra brought the completed Pentateuch to Jerusalem and was instrumental in having the books of Moses assume sacred status among the Jewish community. Others have argued that the law of Ezra was his own particular interpretation and application of the legal traditions that are found in the Torah. The text of Ezra is ambiguous in this respect. While verse 14 refers to the law of God as a specific written text, literally "the law of your God which is in your hand," the exact nature and relationship of the laws referenced in Ezra-Nehemiah and the final form of the Pentateuch are still a matter of debate.

7:27-28 Ezra prepares for the journey

Here begins a portion of the text written in the first person that continues through chapter 9. Some scholars believe these first-person passages come from memoirs written by Ezra himself, although there is considerable debate about this (see Introduction).

Ezra 8:1-14 Ezra's caravan

Ezra 8:2-14 is a list of those who went to Jerusalem with Ezra. The list is organized according to family/clan name, most likely the name of a patriarch who may be from the distant past. The list is highly stylized, giving first priestly clans ("the descendants of Phinehas" and "the descendants of Ithamar," 8:2) and a royal clan ("the descendants of David," 8:2), and then giving the names of twelve different clans who sent people to Jerusalem. This grouping is meant to evoke the exodus, in which Moses and Aaron led the twelve tribes into the Promised Land. Closer to home, it also calls to mind the return from exile in Ezra 2, led by a priestly and royal figure, Jeshua and Zerubbabel, respectively. Indeed, each of the twelve clan names in 8:3-14 are included in the list of Ezra 2:1-70. The exact relationship between the two lists is unclear.

8:15-30 Final preparations for the journey

Ezra realizes that he has no Levites or temple servants in his party and makes provisions for adding some. The journey of Ezra, although it presupposes a reconstructed temple in Jerusalem, appears not to be aware of the list of returnees in Ezra 2 which included Levites and temple servants, all of whose descendants would be in Judah at this time.

The journey to Jerusalem is here depicted more like a religious procession, similar to the way the wandering in the wilderness is portrayed in the Pentateuch as an orderly liturgical procession around the ark. Here the journey begins with fasting and prayer (8:21-23), and offerings to God, symbolized in the weighing out of precious metals to the priests, who will then convey the valuables to the temple. A talent is approximately seventy-five pounds, and so the amount of gold and silver mentioned here totals to more than twenty-eight tons, a patent exaggeration.

8:31-36 Arrival in Jerusalem

Again recalling the wandering traditions of the Pentateuch, the text here notes that the only protection the party needed on the long journey from Babylon to Jerusalem was "[t]he hand of our God" (8:31). No imperial troops accompanied the party. The journey from Babylon to Jerusalem would have taken approximately a month, with a large caravan only covering 15–20 miles a day. However, based upon the statement in 7:8 that Ezra came to Jerusalem in the fifth month, combined with the remark here in verse 31 that he left Babylon in the first month, a journey of one hundred days is implied. Upon arrival the party rests for three days (8:32), mirroring the three-day encampment at the outset of the journey in verse 15.

Significantly, the people in Ezra's party are called "those who had returned from captivity, the exiles" (8:35), even though none of these would have been alive when the exile occurred in 586. Here, the idea of exile transcends generations. People can have a homeland even if they have never seen it. The place where one is born, raised, and has lived can be understood as exile. How can this be? In his novel *The Plague*, Albert Camus brilliantly describes the pain of exile, summed up in the fact that to be an exile is to carry the burden of a memory that serves no purpose. What made the Jews who had been born and raised in Babylon view it as exile, and Jerusalem, a city they had never seen, as home was memory.

The traditions and, probably in some instances, texts that went into exile in 586 apparently played a vital role in the identity of those who chose to make the journey "home" to Jerusalem. Unable to bear these memories in an environment in which they were out of context (so the famous line of Psalm 137:4: "But how could we sing a song of the LORD in a foreign land?") the people who came to Jerusalem from Babylon for the first time understood themselves as captive exiles free to come back home.

The offerings made at the temple in verse 35 parallel those made at the temple's dedication in 6:16-17. Verse 36 notes the fulfillment of the Artaxerxes decree given to Ezra in chapter 8. As mentioned in the Introduction, many scholars believe that Nehemiah 7:72–8:18 is the continuation of the narrative in Ezra 8. However, the author has arranged his source material to connect the figures of Ezra and Nehemiah and point out the parallel nature of their missions. Consequently, the reforms of both Ezra and Nehemiah are intertwined.

9:1-2 The crisis of mixed marriages

Ezra is here informed, presumably in his capacity as the king's legal authority, of members of the returned exiles marrying with local women. The passage is clearly a cursory summary and is unclear concerning the difference between the "leaders" who report the infractions to Ezra in verse 1 and the "leaders" who are responsible for illicit marriages in verse 2. The list of peoples in verse 1 is a deliberate archaism, meant to group the indige-nous population with the enemies of Israel from the stories of the conquest of Canaan after the exodus. The contrast between the "peoples of the land" and the "holy seed" in verse 2 is stark. The passage draws upon Deuteronomy 7:1-6:

> When the LORD, your God, brings you into the land which you are about to enter to possess, and removes many nations before you—the Hittites, Girgashites, Amorites, Canaanites, Perizzites, Hivites, and Jebusites, seven nations more numerous and powerful than you—and when the LORD, your God, gives them over to you and you defeat them, you shall put them under the ban. Make no covenant with them and do not be gracious to them. You shall not intermarry with them, neither giving your daughters to their sons nor taking their daughters for your sons. For they would turn your sons from following me to serving other gods, and then the anger of the LORD would flare up against you and he would quickly destroy you.
>
> But this is how you must deal with them: Tear down their altars, smash their sacred pillars, chop down their asherahs, and destroy their idols by fire. For you are a people holy to the LORD, your God; the LORD, your God, has chosen you from all the peoples on the face of the earth to be a people specially his own. (See also Exod 34:16.)

In the vast majority of Old Testament texts, the greatest sin is apostasy from the sole worship of Yahweh. One of the favorite images used to describe this sin is sexual immorality. In some instances, God is the aggrieved husband and Israel the faithless wife, as in Hosea 1–2 and, graphically, in Ezekiel 16. Oftentimes, however, apostasy is not symbolized as marital infidelity but rather is attributed to invalid marriages with foreign women who lead their Israelite husbands to abandon the sole worship of Yahweh. The most famous instance of this in the Bible is Solomon. 1 Kings 11 recounts how Solomon built shrines to other gods because he had married foreign women who worshiped these gods. Another example is Ahab, whose Phoenician wife, Jezebel, led him to abandon the worship of Yahweh in favor of Baal (1 Kgs 16:31). Indeed, the foreign woman is a powerful biblical image, evoking temptation and danger; remember what Delilah did to Samson!

There are two sociological factors at work in this fear of foreign women. First is the fact that ancient Near Eastern cultures were almost exclusively patriarchal. Thus, literature was written by males for other males. Most gender-based or sexual imagery, therefore, is written from a male perspective and hence is focused on the female. Thus in Proverbs 9, the two paths of wisdom and folly are portrayed as two different types of women (although a notable exception to this is the vivid language of the woman describing her beloved in the Song of Songs).

Second is the practice of endogamy (marriage only within one's ethnic group) which is common particularly among groups made up of people who are immigrants or otherwise minorities in a larger social structure. Endogamy is a way to preserve a group's identity, customs, religion, and tradition, by way of perpetuating the group without recourse to the outside, dominant society. Endogamy is a concern of many biblical texts, most notably Abraham's efforts to secure a wife for Isaac from his own kin in Haran (Gen 24) or the rumblings against Moses for having married outside of the Israelite community (Num 12:1), or the biblical condemnation of Solomon mentioned above.

However, the biblical stance on intermarriage between Israelites and outsiders is not univocal. First, it is only Canaanite women who are placed off-limits to the Israelites. Second, other texts see no problem with the practice. For example, despite the fact that Moses is criticized in the narrative for marrying outside of Israel, the text is clear that those criticizing Moses are in the wrong. Perhaps the most striking example of an alternative opinion is the book of Ruth. The heroine Ruth is a foreign woman who not only marries an Israelite (actually two of them, since her first husband who died was also an Israelite, as is Boaz, her second husband) but becomes one of the forebears of David. Even more dramatically, Ruth is a Moabite, a people with whom God explicitly forbids the Israelites any contact (Deut 23:4).

9:3-5 Ezra's reaction

The depth of Ezra's reaction is a vivid demonstration of his zeal in this matter. Tearing of garments and pulling of hair are traditional symbols of mourning. Sitting motionless in mourning recalls the attitude of Job and his companions in Job 2:13. Those who mourned with Ezra are described literally as "all who trembled at the words of the God of Israel" (9:4; compare with the NABRE translation above). This phrase occurs also in 10:3, and in 10:8 the assembly trembles in fear at God's wrath against them for violating the principle of endogamy. Scholars have noted that this reference to those who follow the law as "tremblers" (Hebrew: *haredim*) occurs only here and in Isaiah 66 and seems to denote a particular way of interpreting and following the law which involves intense devotion and piety. Ultra-Orthodox Jews today

refer to themselves as *haredim*. Indeed, this language is also present in Christianity, where both the Shakers and the Quakers take their name from reference to their attitude before God.

Use of this special term for Ezra and those who followed him in his interpretation of the law lends credence to the fact that Ezra was not enforcing any new law on the Israelites but rather was demanding adherence to a particular interpretation of the law they already knew. That is to say, Ezra and those around him represent a particular way of living out God's law which was not seen as normative by all who revered the law. Catholics are no strangers to disagreements among people of the same religious community concerning how religious laws ought to be interpreted and implemented. Sadly, history has shown time and again that people often reserve the greatest anger for their disagreeing coreligionists. It was no different for the author of Ezra, who was obviously sympathetic to Ezra's interpretation of the law.

9:6-15 A penitential prayer

Ezra's prayer in verses 6-15 reads like many of the penitential psalms of lament, such as Psalm 51. The prayer is essentially an admission of guilt framed by a lengthy historical review of God's relationship with Israel. This historical component to prayer is even more pronounced in Nehemiah 9:6-37. Worth noticing in the prayer is the ambiguous portrayal of the Persians, for although God "has turned the good will of the kings of Persia toward us" (9:9), servitude to the Persians is still viewed as divine punishment. The prayer also alludes to the prohibition on intermarriage in Deuteronomy 7:3 (9:12) and makes reference to a protecting wall given to Israel by God (9:9). Many scholars have interpreted this to mean that the city of Jerusalem was walled when Ezra arrived and use this as a reason to move the activity of Ezra after that of Nehemiah, who built the wall. However, the Hebrew word for "fence" in this verse (*gader*) is not the same as the word used to describe the walls of Jerusalem (*homah*). The meaning in Ezra's prayer is metaphorical but related with the work of Nehemiah (see Introduction).

10:1-17 Response to the crisis

The text here shifts back to the third person. Ezra's fervent prayer convokes a spontaneous assembly of people who are moved to tears by his words. Equally spontaneous is the decision that the community swear an oath to dissolve any marriages with foreign women and to send them and their children away. There are apparently six different men named Shecaniah in Ezra-Nehemiah (Ezra 8:3, 5; 10:2; Neh 3:29; 6:18; 12:3). The particular Shecaniah mentioned in verse 2 is from a nonpriestly family.

Mention of Johanan son of Eliashib in verse 6 has perplexed scholars. According to Nehemiah 3:1, Eliashib was the high priest during the rebuilding of the walls of Jerusalem. Moreover, the list of high priests in Nehemiah 12:10 makes Johanan the grandson of Eliashib, and not his son. Additionally, Johanan is mentioned in the letter of the Elephantine Jews to the Persian governor of Judah written in 407 that is discussed above. If Ezra came before Nehemiah, Johanan could not have been old enough to have his own quarters in the temple or even to have been born.

A second assembly is then convened in verses 9-15. The author adds the poignant touch that a cold winter rain, consistent with "the ninth month" (10:9), fell on the crowd, chilling them to the bone. Given that the assembled exiles were deciding to send away their wives and children, the dreary weather fit the somberness of the occasion.

It is important not to pass over the magnitude of what is being asked of the community: to send away their wives and children if they are not of Israelite stock because it is the will of God. It is not surprising then to find the protest of some mentioned in verse 15. The human toll in emotional suffering would be incalculable, as those who had married local women were faced with the harrowing choice between their love for their families and their love for God. It is fitting here to remember a more famous version of that awful choice—namely, Abraham's decision in Genesis 22 to follow the divine command and to offer Isaac as a sacrifice. Sadly, here in rainy Jerusalem there would be no last-minute divine intervention on behalf of the women and children. The process of determining the origins of every married woman in the community takes three months (10:16-17).

10:18-44 The list of transgressors

The names of those who had to send away their wives and children are grouped, like the other long lists in Ezra, according to family name, with priests and Levites listed first. Scholars have noted that the number of people who actually sent away their families is very small when compared to the number of people said to have returned from exile in Ezra 2 and 8. Perhaps the list only names those from distinguished families who carried out the decision, or maybe Ezra's reform was ignored by the majority of the community. Verse 44 is grammatically unclear in the Hebrew and its abrupt nature gives the ending of Ezra a sense of incompleteness. Many think that Ezra 10 should be read in conjunction with Nehemiah 9, but having this incident occur at the end of Ezra links the work of Ezra and Nehemiah together, since Nehemiah will have to continue with the work of reform. This was probably deliberately done so by the author for that purpose (see Introduction).

COMMENTARY: *NEHEMIAH*

THE DEEDS OF NEHEMIAH

Nehemiah 1–7

Unlike Ezra, the book of Nehemiah is a relatively straightforward narrative. Nehemiah, a Jew and a member of the Persian royal court, was appointed the governor of Judah in the twentieth year of Artaxerxes I (445, see Neh 2:1). During his tenure, Nehemiah rebuilt the decrepit city wall, enacted economic reform to aid the poor, and populated the city with people descended from each of the tribes of Israel. Nehemiah held the post of governor for twelve years and then returned to the royal court (13:6). At an unknown later date, Nehemiah came back to Jerusalem and stayed for an unknown length of time (13:6). A good deal of the book is written in the first person, and scholars believe these sections draw upon a memoir written by Nehemiah (see Introduction). The book can be divided into two equal sections. Chapters 1–7 deal with Nehemiah's arrival in Jerusalem and his building of the wall. The remainder of the book, chapters 8–13, focuses on implementation of the law in the newly refortified Jerusalem.

1:1-11 Nehemiah hears bad news

The story begins in Susa, the former capital of the Elamites (in modern-day Iran) and the site of the Persian kings' winter residence. Excavations of the Persian royal palace have revealed a vast complex with an audience chamber over 10,000 square feet in area with a roof supported by thirty-six columns over sixty feet tall. Verse 1 notes that it was during the ninth month (Chislev) of the twentieth year of Artaxerxes I. In the Elephantine letter of 407 requesting Persian permission to rebuild the temple to Yahweh discussed above, reference is made to one of the Jerusalem nobles named Hanani. The Hanani mentioned in verse 2 may be related. The description Hanani provides of Jerusalem is dire and fails to mention the work of rebuilding done by Zerubbabel recounted in Ezra 3–6. Indeed, the picture of the city is of a ruin left to decay after the Babylonian destruction of 586. The implausibility of this has led some scholars to speculate that Jerusalem had taken part in a rebellion against Persian rule sometime in the generation before Nehemiah. It is known from other records that during the first half of the fifth century Egypt twice succeeded in temporarily throwing off Persian control.

Nehemiah offers a prayer to Yahweh in verses 5-11 that is reminiscent of Ezra's lament in Ezra 9, which emphasizes the sinfulness of the people, the justice of the exile as divine punishment, and God's mercy in allowing the exiles to return to Jerusalem. As is the case with Ezra's prayer, the theology here is heavily indebted to Deuteronomy (see in particular 1:7-10). The reference to the "God of heaven" found in verse 5 is typical of Persian era biblical texts.

2:1-10 Appointment by the king

Nehemiah's role as royal cupbearer offers him privileged access to Artaxerxes in the royal palace. Nisan is the first month of the year, which would seem to be at odds with the notice in 1:1 that Hanani came to Nehemiah in the ninth month of the same year. However, the year referred to in the text is not a calendrical unit, as we count years, but rather the twentieth regnal year of Artaxerxes, which obviously could span portions of two different twelve-month cycles.

The scene with the king is similar to those in Esther and Daniel, other texts that show faithful Jews enjoying the favor of Persian royalty. Although not explicit, Nehemiah's request involves being granted authority in Judah. He requests letters of introduction to the other governors of the satrapy (2:7), as well as access to the royal timber supply for his official residence. The word "woods" in verse 8 is actually a Persian loanword from which we get our word "paradise." Greek writers often referred to the royal gardens and forests of the Persian kings. As befits a provincial governor, Nehemiah is sent to Jerusalem with his own detachment of troops (2:9).

Similar to the local interference that halted construction of the temple under Zerubbabel (Ezra 4), here too Nehemiah encounters resistance, but from other regional governors in the satrapy. These opponents appear throughout the first half of the book of Nehemiah. Sanballat was the governor of the province of Samaria. He is mentioned in the Elephantine letter of 407 as the father of two grown sons. Tobiah is the governor of the province of Ammon. Nehemiah's use of the term "slave" ("official" in the NABRE) could simply mean that Tobiah, like all governors, was the servant of the king, but here it may also have a derogatory sense. In Nehemiah 13:4 Tobiah is linked with the high priest Eliashib. Extrabiblical records show that the family of Tobiah was politically prominent in the region of Ammon during the third and second centuries. Nehemiah portrays the opposition of his fellow governors as motivated by hatred for God and his people. Rivalries between royal functionaries are ancient and legion. An archive of letters dating from the fourteenth century B.C., a thousand years before the time of Nehemiah, was found in the Egyptian royal city of Amarna. These letters preserve the dispatches of mayors of cities in Palestine to the pharaoh. The majority of these letters contain the mayors' accusations of their fellow mayors for treasonous behavior and the denial of the same accusations that have been levied against the letter writers by the other mayors. Although Nehemiah came a long time after the authors of the Amarna correspondence and was working for the Persians instead of the Egyptians, the dynamic of constant mutual blame among imperial middle management had changed little.

2:11-16 Circuit of the city

As is the case with the journey of Ezra to Jerusalem (Ezra 8:32), Nehemiah rests for three days upon his arrival. Nehemiah's secrecy concerning his plan to rebuild the walls is curious. As duly appointed governor with a royal mandate he could have simply announced his intentions upon his arrival. Instead, he takes a small party of loyal attendants under cover of darkness and makes a partial circuit of the ruined walls. The implication is that the religious and political authorities in Jerusalem would oppose the rebuilding efforts. The symbolism of Nehemiah's walking tour of Jerusalem should not be overlooked, for it signifies his taking possession of the city as governor. A similar incident occurs in Genesis 13:17 where God commands Abraham to "[g]et up and walk through the land, across its length and breadth, for I give it to you."

The layout of Jerusalem's walls and gates that is described here and in chapter 3 has long puzzled scholars. The walls and gates of the present-day Old City of Jerusalem were built by Suleiman the Magnificent in the sixteenth century A.D. Even though one of the gates in Suleiman's wall, the Dung Gate, has the same name as a gate mentioned in Nehemiah, Suleiman's gate does not occupy the same place as its biblical namesake. Biblical Jerusalem was situated on a narrow ridge running on a north-south axis between two steep valleys (or wadis). To the west ran the Tyropoeon Valley, while the Kidron Valley lay on the east. At the southern end of the ridge was the Hinnom Valley. The oldest settled part of Jerusalem is the southernmost part of this ridge, called in the Bible the Ophel (see Neh 3:27). David expanded the city north from the Ophel and this new area was called the City of David. Solomon continued this expansion northward when he built his temple-palace complex (the site of the present-day Temple Mount and Al Aqsa Mosque). Excavations on the southern ridge of the Ophel near the modern village of Silwan have uncovered artifacts dating from nearly every period in the city's history, including the Persian period. Additionally, in the Muslim Quarter of the Old City one can see the remains of a wall built by the Israelite king Hezekiah in the eighth century. Only a small portion of Nehemiah's wall has been excavated on the eastern end of the ridge. The full extent of the city walls during the Persian period remains a mystery.

2:17-20 Decision to rebuild the city wall

Nehemiah now addresses the leaders in Jerusalem ("them" in 2:17 refers to those listed in the preceding verse). The leaders embrace Nehemiah's plan to rebuild the walls without hesitation, which seems to render his secrecy in inspecting the walls unnecessary. Sanballat, Tobiah, and another regional governor, Geshem (whose name has been found on inscriptions dating from this time), offer resistance. Their challenge, "Are you rebelling against the king?" (2:19), may mean that they were intending to accuse Nehemiah of treason before Artaxerxes as Rehum and Shimshai did to Ezra in Ezra 4. The reader already knows, however, that Nehemiah is working with the blessing of the king. Interestingly, however, Nehemiah does not mention this in his retort to Sanballat, Tobiah, and Geshem. Rather he points out that the work is done under the protection of God. Nehemiah's threat to the other governors that for them there is to be "neither share nor claim nor memorial in Jerusalem" (2:20) is significant in that he makes clear to them that the city will not acknowledge their authority nor will it be a part of their legacy. This is particularly harsh. In the ancient Near East walls were a way for a ruler to ensure his legacy and, after a fashion, to enjoy some kind of enduring life after death. In Mesopotamia, rulers often had their names stamped on the bricks used to build walls or placed inscriptions in the foundations of walls they had built or restored. The oldest surviving written story, *The Epic of Gilgamesh*, makes use of this practice. Gilgamesh, the king of Uruk (a ruin in present-day Iraq), boasts to a companion about the walls of his city, his enduring legacy that will survive him after he has gone to his death. Why the other governors would have been interested in having a legacy in Jerusalem is unclear. Scholars have speculated that because Sanballat had given his sons names that contain a shortened form of the name "Yahweh" in them (Delaiah and Shelemiah), as does the name Tobiah, that these governors worshiped the God of Israel, and hence would want to be involved in any work in Jerusalem. The context, however, seems to speak against this.

3:1-32 List of workers

Most scholars agree that this list draws upon some archival sources, but its exact relationship with the narrative in Nehemiah is puzzling. The list implies that Jerusalem is populated, since it mentions people who worked on sections of the wall nearest to their homes (3:10, 23-24, 28-30) alongside people who hailed from the surrounding cities, such as Tekoa (3:5) or Mizpah (3:15). This is curious in light of the fact that Nehemiah takes measures to populate the city in chapter 11 and that the city is described as a ruin in chapter 1. The work is described in a counterclockwise motion around the city, beginning and ending at the Sheep Gate (3:1, 32). Meshullam, son of Berechiah, is mentioned both at the beginning and the end of the list (3:4, 30). Not all members of the community chose to take part in the rebuilding (3:5). Among the workers were women (3:12). Of particular interest is the reference to workers who were "district administrators," which casts valuable evidence on the organization of Judah under the Persians. Based on the list, Judah was divided into districts centered on the cities of Beth-haccherem, Mizpah, Jerusalem, Beth-Zur, and Keilah. Some

of these districts were further divided, witnessed by the fact that some individuals are referred to as the leaders of half a particular district (3:9, 12, 16-18). Archaeological evidence bears this out. Seals and stamped jar handles attest to the importance of some of these cities as administrative centers during the Persian period.

3:33–4:17 Opposition from Judah's enemies

Sanballat and Tobiah appear again to offer mockery of the work on the wall, specifically pointing out the impossibility of restoring the destroyed wall and the inadequacy of the finished product. "Jews" in verse 33 might be better read as "Judeans," i.e., residents of the province. The Hebrew is ambiguous (see Introduction). Reference to the troops of Samaria in verse 34 adds a note of danger to the narrative, since taunting was common before battle. Nehemiah responds to the taunt with a prayer for divine punishment of his enemies reminiscent of many psalms of lament. The determination of the people is vividly expressed in verse 38, which may be literally translated as "the people had a heart to work."

A second episode now commences, introduced by the formulaic "When Sanballat . . . heard" (cf. 2:10, 19; 3:33). With every new appearance of Sanballat the number of his confederates grows. First, Tobiah the Ammonite appears with him in 2:10. Geshem the Arab is added in 2:19. Now in 4:1, in addition to Samaria, Ammon, and the Arabs, the city of Ashdod is against Jerusalem. Ashdod is a Philistine city on the Mediterranean coast and, in the books of Judges and Samuel, one of the enemies of Israel. Plotting these places on a map reveals that Jerusalem is now completely surrounded by hostile neighbors, making the situation especially dire. To add to this sense of urgency, the threat of attack implicit in verse 34 is realized as the enemies of the rebuilding now plan a military intervention to stop the work in Jerusalem. In verse 4 the demoralized Judahites quote a poetic couplet expressing their fatigue and hopelessness at finishing the task in the face of such opposition. Nehemiah responds in verse 8 with encouragement that echoes through the history of humankind, urging the workers to remember their God and to fight for their families and homes. Nehemiah's "work force" in verse 10 (literally "young men") probably denotes his own personal detachment of troops, customary for a governor, who have access to the finest weaponry. Readying his own troops and arming the workers seems to have been enough for Nehemiah to turn back the proposed assault. It is curious that the author did not take this opportunity to emphasize the cowardice of the attackers. However, in light of the continuing danger, Nehemiah now has to remove half of his workforce from the restoration and set them to guard duty. Furthermore, even those who are still working are now armed. Verses 15-16 emphasize the hardship of the labor: the people worked from dawn to dusk and did not return to their homes to sleep.

5:1-13 Social and economic problems

The narrative thread of Nehemiah's construction of the wall and the strident opposition to it is interrupted here in chapter 5 only to be taken up again and concluded in chapter 6. Now Nehemiah must face an internal problem concerning the economic hardship of the small landowners. The situation described here is, unfortunately, perennial, involving the predatory actions of some people who, for their own gain, take advantage of their brothers and sisters during difficult times. Life for the average person in ancient Palestine was always difficult and precarious. Food supplies were at the mercy of powers beyond the farmer's control, be they natural or political forces. Throughout the biblical period, wealth, mainly in the form of land, was often concentrated in the hands of a few elites who were most likely part of a royal court or a temple complex.

Small farmers were put under crushing tax or tribute burdens by these elites. When they defaulted on these debts, they were forced to offer something else of value to their creditors, usually their land or its equivalent in human labor. Often a peasant would enter into a sort of temporary bondage or indentured servitude to pay the debt, or he would offer one of his children to be put at the disposal of the creditor. During Nehemiah's time, there was also royal tribute to be paid, and the Persians created a complex bureaucratic system to help them exploit their conquered peoples to the greatest extent possible (see Introduction). Regional governors and satraps, acting in the name of the crown, collected this tribute, usually in the form of goods rather than coin. However, many of these imperial bureaucrats abused their authority and lined their own pockets with tribute. Records indicate that some satraps owned vast estates throughout the empire, which they disposed of at their pleasure.

The complaint of the people in verses 2-5 speaks of hard times. A famine has put a strain on farmers as they struggle both to pay their tribute and to feed their families. Added to this, the people as inhabitants of the province of Judah were also faced with imperial taxes. Some took loans against their fields in order to get through the famine and pay their tribute. Defaulting on these loans forced some to give up their land or, in extreme cases, to offer their children as indentured servants to forgive the debt. This is similar to the situation in Genesis 47 where Joseph enslaves the Egyptians by cornering the food supply during a seven-year famine. In Nehemiah's situation, however, the creditors are also Jews, most likely those belonging to the local elites (see the condemnation of the nobles and magistrates in verse 7). Thus there exists the unhappy situation of members of the same community taking part in a system that exploits the weak to the benefit of the rapacious.

Biblical law is explicit in its condemnation of unjust economic practices. In Exodus 21, debt slaves are to be freed every seventh year. In Leviticus 25, God mandates that every fiftieth year be declared a jubilee in which debts are forgiven, slaves are freed, and land returned to its original owners. God's reasoning for this is clearly tied to divine sovereignty. No land can be sold in perpetuity, "for the land is mine, and you are but resident aliens and under my authority" (Lev 25:23). Moreover, and especially relevant in Nehemiah's case, no Israelite may own another as a slave. "Since they are my servants, whom I brought out of the land of Egypt, they shall not sell themselves as slaves are sold" (Lev 25:42). The logic behind the biblical laws is the preservation of the community as the people of God, as well as the continued relationship of a particular family to its particular plot of land, itself understood as a gift of God.

Drawing on the concern for economic justice found in the Bible, the social teaching of the church has affirmed that gospel charity ought to characterize economic relationships. And so, while the church affirms the right to own private property, that right is not understood as absolute. One's right to private property does not trump the obligation to help a fellow human being in need:

> In using them, therefore, people should regard the external things that they legitimately possess not only as their own but also as common in the sense that they should be able to benefit not only themselves but also others. On the other hand, the right of having a share of earthly goods sufficient for oneself and one's family belongs to everyone. The Fathers and Doctors of the Church held this opinion, teaching that human beings are obliged to come to the relief of the poor and to do so not merely out of their superfluous goods. Those who are in extreme necessity have the right to procure for themselves what they need out of the riches of others. (Second Vatican Council, Pastoral Constitution on the Church in the Modern World [*Gaudium et Spes*] 69)

Nehemiah is in a delicate position, for as governor of the province he is part of the system helping to create the unjust situation, yet as governor he alone has the authority to alleviate the matter. He acts quickly and with passion, summoning those magistrates and nobles who have increased their wealth while increasing the misery of their fellow Jews. He orders them to stop lending at interest (something prohibited in Deut 23:20). Nehemiah points out in verses 7-10 that he has been paying off the debt of those Jews who have become servants to their Gentile debtors. He is also quick to mention that neither he nor his retinue has loaned anything at interest (although the words "without charge" in 5:10 do not occur in the Hebrew text, the sense is that Nehemiah has been a responsible creditor). Interestingly, after securing the nobles' agreement to cease from unjust economic practices, Nehemiah also subjects them to a binding oath in the presence of priests (5:12). This is not the only mention of Nehemiah's suspicion of the Jerusalem elites. In 2:16 Nehemiah notes that his nocturnal inspection of the city walls was done without their knowledge. The image of shaking a garment in verse 13 is also used in Job 38:13 to speak of the rejection of the wicked. Nehemiah uses the action in conjunction with an oath, again perhaps demonstrating his mistrust of the Jerusalem elites' sincerity in this regard.

5:14-19 Nehemiah's record

The episode of intra-community economic oppression ends with Nehemiah's *apologia*. In it we are given a precious piece of historical information concerning exactly when and for how long Nehemiah was the governor of Judah. In order to understand Nehemiah's protestations, one must call to mind the power of regional governors and how often that power was abused. Nehemiah is fervent in stating that not only has he not abused his position (5:15), but also that he has not even availed himself of the ordinary allowance entitled to him by his province (5:14). In addition, not only has Nehemiah forgone the labor of his subjects for his own support, but to the contrary he has drawn upon his own private wealth to support certain members of the community with regular meals.

There is a careful rhetoric at work here that requires an understanding of ancient social attitudes. In Mediterranean societies of the ancient world, honor was a prized commodity. One did things to increase and maintain honor. Conversely, shame was to be avoided at all costs. One of the ways one's honor was enhanced was through hospitality, literally playing the host. Doing so demonstrated one's power and dominance over guests, albeit in a noncoercive way. People who wished to enhance their honor in their own cities did so by temporarily hosting their fellow citizens to a feast. Usually a religious sacrifice would be performed and the offering distributed to the populace as a meal. The entire affair would be underwritten by a prestigious citizen who would, by doing so, enhance his honor. Similarly, rulers would demonstrate their largesse and increase their honor by supporting many people at court with food. 1 Kings 4 lists the astounding amounts of food gone through by Solomon's court in a day. Shrewdly, it also reinforces the king's superiority while making any potential rivals to his power dependent upon him. Usually those people who shared the king's board were themselves elites, and the food was taken as tribute from the peasantry. In Nehemiah's case, however, while the guests at his table are from the elite class, the food is provided from his own stores. Nehemiah ends his *apologia* with a prayer that God will remember his goodness. This is a standard formula found in numerous ancient inscriptions that seek to extol a person's good deeds as a ruler. All the other prayers of Nehemiah asking for God's remembrance are in chapter 13. Some believe that this prayer was once a part of those others, but that it has been moved here, along with the story of Nehemiah's reforms.

6:1-14 Plots against Nehemiah

The story of the building of the wall in the face of opposition interrupted by chapter 5 now resumes and comes to a climax. Verse 1 demonstrates that work on the wall has been progressing. It is now complete with the exception of gates (compare the summary statement about the construction in 3:38–4:1). Sanballat, Tobiah, and Geshem now undertake their most aggressive tactic, an attempt on Nehemiah's life, which they couch under the guise of a diplomatic meeting. Nehemiah politely but firmly denies their request that he meet them on "neutral" ground, adding that he is too busy working on the wall to take time out for superfluous meetings! Finally, Nehemiah receives an "unsealed" letter from Sanballat, so that the charges against him will be made common knowledge, accusing him of treason to Persia. Before the charges reach the king, Sanballat writes, let us meet together. Treachery on the part of satraps and governors was a commonplace in the Persian Empire. Any such charges would have been taken seriously by the king. Mention of unnamed prophets giving legitimacy to Nehemiah as king in Jerusalem calls to mind the activity of Haggai and Zechariah in Ezra 5. Nehemiah denies the allegations. The thoughts of Sanballat and his associates quoted in verse 9 call to mind the taunt of the Judeans in 4:4.

Nehemiah now goes to the house of Shemaiah, the son of Delaiah. Two men of the same names were the sons of Sanballat, as is known from the Elephantine letter discussed above, but this Shemaiah is clearly another person who is a temple prophet. Commentators are uncertain as to the exact meaning of the remark that he was unable to leave his house. Was he in a state of ritual impurity? Was he in an ecstatic trance? Shemaiah's message to Nehemiah in verse 10 is a prophetic oracle, appropriately in poetic form, which counsels that Nehemiah take refuge from his enemies in the temple. Nehemiah quickly ascertains that Shemaiah is in league with Tobiah and Sanballat and that to enter the temple would cause Nehemiah to lose the support of the people. His rhetorical questions in verse 11 are ambiguous. The phrase "A man like me" could mean that Nehemiah is not a priest and so cannot enter the temple, or it could mean that Nehemiah is a man who has placed his trust in God and consequently will not shrink from his duty. As in 3:36, Nehemiah calls for divine judgment on his enemies in verse 14. Noadiah the prophetess is mentioned nowhere else inside or outside of the Bible, but female ecstatics were not unknown in the ancient Near East. What is clear from this episode is that Nehemiah had opponents who were temple functionaries. This also squares with further conflicts Nehemiah will have with temple officials in chapter 13.

6:15–7:3 Conclusion of the work

The summary statement in verse 15 functions as a climax of the first part of the book of Nehemiah. In the face of all opposition, both within and without, and despite the enormity of the task, the wall of Jerusalem was completed in the record time of fifty-two days. Indeed, the Jewish historian Josephus probably found this short time frame too much to swallow and in his account of the story states that the rebuilding took over two years. The completion of the walls is seen as a victory over Nehemiah's enemies and is cast in the language of honor and shame. Sanballat and his associates had tried to shame Nehemiah by getting him to take refuge in the temple. Instead, Nehemiah had persevered in completing the wall and so brought shame onto Sanballat and his associates. The first half of the book of Nehemiah thus parallels the first half of Ezra; in both instances the community overcomes local opposition in its quest to rebuild the temple and walls of Jerusalem. These parallel plot lines are part of how the author arranged his source material.

This is not the end of the intrigue for Nehemiah, unfortunately. Some of the Jerusalem elites, who have already had conflict with Nehemiah over the issue of debt slavery, are sympathetic to Tobiah. Tobiah's father-in-law, Shecaniah, is not the same as the man who takes the lead in the marriage reforms of Ezra 10. Tobiah is also linked by marriage to Meshullam son of Berechiah, who figures prominently in the rebuilding of the wall in chapter 3. Tobiah's sworn associates in Jerusalem posed a continual threat to Nehemiah. Accordingly, as security measures, Nehemiah appoints Levites as guards over the walls and gates and orders the gates to be open only in complete daylight.

7:4-72 Census of the province

Now that the city wall is built and guarded, Nehemiah must deal with populating Jerusalem. Again, there is the conundrum of Nehemiah's description of a ruined Jerusalem (see his remark in verse 4 that "none of the houses had been rebuilt") and the fact that in the book of Ezra, Jerusalem appears to be inhabited. This problem is further compounded by the fact that material dealing with Ezra begins here in Nehemiah 7:6 and runs through chapter 10.

The author now skillfully recycles the genealogy of Ezra 2 in the form of an archival search (a motif occurring already in Ezra 4 and 6). Using the list again allows the author to further connect the originally separate traditions of Ezra and Nehemiah. It also portrays Nehemiah's restoration of the wall, dated roughly to 445, as the continuation of the return from exile and restoration of the temple done by Zerubbabel almost a century before. The list in Nehemiah is not identical to that in Ezra 2, but the differences are minor, and many may be attributed to copyists' errors. The list also functions as a conclusion to the first half of Nehemiah. The wall has been built; the listing of the peoples who constitute the people of Israel has been recalled. The remainder of the book of Nehemiah focuses on bringing the people and their city together through observance of God's law, so that a holy people will dwell in a holy city.

PROMULGATION OF THE LAW

Nehemiah 8–13

The remainder of the book of Nehemiah is devoted to the reading and implementation of the law of Moses. Almost half of these six chapters describe a liturgical service led by Ezra, who makes a curious appearance for the first time in the book of Nehemiah. These remaining chapters appear to have been arranged from a variety of source materials and are more than a little puzzling when looked at from a strict linear perspective.

8:1-12 Ezra reads the law

This liturgical ceremony is parallel to that of Ezra 3, when Zerubbabel and the exiles return to Jerusalem. Both begin with the same phrase, "Now when the seventh month came, the whole people gathered as one" (Neh 8:1; see Ezra 3:1). Both mention observance of the feast of Booths (Ezra 3:4, Neh 8:17). Both speak of the sadness and weeping of the people (Ezra 3:12-13, Neh 8:9). Mention of Nehemiah in verse 9 is most likely a gloss inserted by the author or a copyist in order to make it fit more smoothly in the Nehemiah story. Additionally, the entire passage has been stylized so as to make it conform to a synagogue service. Ezra stands on a platform to read the law (8:4). He holds the scroll up before the people, who respond by paying it respect (8:5-6). Ezra offers a blessing and then begins to read (8:6). The law is then interpreted for the people by the Levites (8:7). Although the exact date of the origins of synagogue worship in Judaism is unclear, and indisputable evidence for synagogues dates only from the century immediately prior to Christ, many scholars would agree that it was during the exile that Jews learned to worship God apart from the temple and without sacrifice. If that is the case, then the liturgical features of Nehemiah 8 make sense.

There is some confusion in verses 7-8, due mainly to editorial glosses. As the text stands now, it makes little sense to have the Levites interpret the law in verse 7, when verse 8 says that it was already being ably interpreted by Ezra, "so that all could understand." Although the remark that Ezra "read clearly" could refer to clear pronunciation and inflection of the Hebrew text of the law, thus leaving explanation of the law's content to the Levites, it is still likely that a copyist wanted to give the Levites an important role in this liturgical event. The sadness of the people at hearing the law not only echoes the tears of those at the dedication of the temple in Ezra 3 but also calls to mind the story of Josiah in 2 Kings 22, who upon being read the forgotten book of the law, weeps and tears his garments. In response to the people's sadness, the Levites prescribe rejoicing, "for today is holy" (8:10-11). Acknowledging the power of God and remembering the great acts of divine mercy should be a cause for joy. As the psalmist says, "In your statutes I take delight. . . . I study your statutes, which I love" (Ps 119:16, 48). Importantly, in verse 12 the author notes that the reason the people were joyful was because they had understood the law. In modern Judaism, the last day of the feast of Booths is known as *Simchat Torah*, or "joy of the law." On that day the final liturgical portion of the Pentateuch from Deuteronomy 34 is read for the year and the cycle started over again at Genesis 1. As in Nehemiah 8, the people spend all morning listening to the reading of the law and then go home to enjoy a sumptuous feast. In both the service in Nehemiah 8 and in modern Jewish practice there is an important religious lesson here: God's will should not be a burden or source of sorrow. On the contrary, walking in the path of God should bear the fruits of joy and happiness. This is the sentiment behind the remark of Jesus that "my yoke is easy, and my burden light" (Matt 11:30).

8:13-18 The feast of Booths

After the general assembly, at which even women and children were present (verse 2), on the next day family heads gather to more closely study the law in order to fully enact it. Here they discover the divine mandate for the feast of Booths (see Exod 23:14, Lev 23:33-36). The festival is then observed by means of a decree and the author notes that this celebration was unlike any other since the days of Joshua ("Jeshua" is an alternative spelling in Hebrew). The entire episode here gives the curious impression that the people have never heard of the festival or are indeed not even aware of the law of Moses. The passage thus seems to ignore the celebration of Booths in Ezra 3 by the returning exiles and the frequent reference to the law of Moses throughout the Book of Ezra (for example, Ezra 3:2, 6:18). Perhaps the author wishes to note that this particular celebration of the festival was the most fervent and observant in a long time. The reference to Joshua helps to portray Ezra as a new leader of the people of Israel who have come into the Promised Land to live under the law of God. As with the liturgical assembly in verses 1-12, here there is an interesting connection with the story of Josiah and the finding of the law in 2 Kings 22–23. There, after reading the law of Moses which apparently had been forgotten in a temple storeroom, Josiah commands that the Passover be celebrated. The narrator remarks that "[n]o Passover such as this had been observed during the period when the Judges ruled Israel, or during the entire period of the kings of Israel and the kings of Judah" (2 Kgs 23:22).

9:1-37 Public confession of sin

Another solemn assembly is convoked, this one of a decidedly penitential nature, in contrast to the command for joyousness in 8:9-12. Given that the purpose of the assembly is for the people to atone for marrying outside the community, many scholars argue that verses 1-5 constitute the "missing" ending to the book of Ezra and opt to place them immediately after Ezra 10:44. The mention of "the twenty-fourth day of this month" in verse 1 could easily be a reference back to "the first month" noted in Ezra 10:17. Again, the assembly follows a formal liturgical format with a Torah reading, public confession, and antiphonal singing led by the Levites. The blessing and response in verse 5 are very similar to the doxologies that occur at the end of certain psalms (for example, Pss 41; 106).

The remainder of the chapter is a lengthy address to God, most likely originally attributed to Ezra (compare his other long prayer in Ezra 9:6-15). Many think that verses 6-37 should be placed right after Ezra 9:15, and indeed the Greek text of verse 6 contains the phrase "Then Ezra said," showing perhaps that this is part of a longer prayer which had already made reference to Ezra as the speaker.

The prayer is a summary of Israelite history contained in the books of Genesis–2 Kings. It borrows heavily on language from the book of Deuteronomy and is also reminiscent of Solomon's long prayer during the dedication of the temple in 1 Kings 8. After a brief treatment of creation and the call of Abraham in verses 6-8, there is a lengthy description of the exodus and the wandering in the wilderness in verses 9-19. The settlement in the land of Canaan and the period of the judges comprise verses 20-28, ending finally with the destruction of Jerusalem and the exile in verses 29-31. The prayer emphasizes three main themes: first is the fidelity of God in contrast to the faithlessness of his ungrateful people (9:7, 16); next is the justice of God in punishing the Israelites for abandoning his covenant (9:26-28); finally alongside God's justice, however, is his mercy in not allowing the people to be utterly destroyed (9:17-19, 27-28, 31). These themes all come together in the summary contained in verses 32-35, which begins with the word "Now." Of them all, it is the mercy of God which is emphasized the most.

Rhetorically, the prayer strikes a fine line between the expression of guilt and the request for divine assistance once more. There is a subtle shift in verse 36 where Ezra points out that, while the people presently live in the land promised their ancestors, the land no longer belongs to them. Rather, they are subjects (literally "slaves") of the Persian king. In effect, the status of being subject to the Persian king has created a situation in which God's promise of the land to his people cannot be fulfilled. Instead, the land's "rich produce goes to the kings you set over us because of our sins, who rule over our bodies and our cattle as they please" (9:37). Thus, Ezra is able to ask for God's assistance for the people, but not because the people deserve it. Indeed, Ezra makes it clear that their servitude to Persia is fully deserved. Instead, Ezra wants God to intervene once more *in order that God may continue to be faithful to his own promise.* The prayer is striking in its clearly negative portrayal of the Persians (contrast the view of Cyrus and God's chosen in Ezra 1; see also Ezra 9:7). The accuracy of the complaint in verse 37 about Persian exploitation of their subjects fits known historical data about Persian imperial policy (see Introduction).

10:1-28 Signatories of the pact

Chapter 10 appears to reproduce the text of a written document signed by the Jerusalem elites (priests, Levites, and lay leaders) swearing fidelity to the law of Moses. The word "covenant" is not used, but instead "a firm pact" (*amanah*). The term comes from a root meaning "to be firm," which also lies behind the Hebrew term "Amen." The use of the first person plural "we" in this chapter is also noteworthy. The list of names in verses 3-28 draws extensively from the list of returnees in chapter 7 and of high priests in chapter 12. However, in most ancient contracts the signatories are listed at the end rather than at the beginning as they are here. The list is headed by Nehemiah, here referred to by the Persian honorary title translated as "governor" (see also 8:9 and Ezra 2:63 in reference to Zerubbabel). Noticeably absent from the list of signatories is Ezra, yet another piece of evidence that he and Nehemiah have been artificially linked in the story (although it has been argued that the name Azariah in 10:3 is a variation on the name of Ezra, analogous per-

haps to the way that the name Megan is a variant form of Margaret).

10:29-40 Provisions of the pact

The actual terms of the covenant are arranged thematically. First, marriage outside the community is prohibited (10:31). Although no stipulation is made that those who have already married non-Jews must send their spouses away, the fact that forbidden marriage partners are now called "local inhabitants" (literally, "peoples of the land") rather than named specifically as they are in Ezra 10 could signify a more rigorous enforcement of the ban. Next, sabbath observance is mandated, specifically in that no commerce will be transacted with outsiders, the assumption being that inside the Jewish community all commerce already ceased on the sabbath (10:32). As an extension of the notion of the holiness of the seventh day, the sabbath year is also affirmed (10:32). This, of course, would help to prevent the kind of economic abuses that Nehemiah dealt with in chapter 5. The longest set of provisions deals with the maintenance of the temple. Most of these laws are drawn from the Pentateuch, especially concerning the first fruits and tithing. Thus, the people commit themselves to maintaining the temple through payment of an annual tax (10:33-34), providing firewood for the sacrifices (10:35), offering of first fruits of both animals and produce (10:36-38), and tithing their produce (10:38). The laws here progress in an outward direction in an attempt to sanctify the people on every level of their lives, beginning with their families, progressing to their economic relationships, and then encompassing all that they produce: children, livestock, crops. A similar progression of sanctification can be seen in the holiness code contained in Leviticus 17–26. A portion of the offerings made by the people to the temple would doubtless have been passed on to the Persian crown as provincial tribute, which was why the Persians usually supported the building of local temples among their subject peoples. This may also explain the rather strict supervisory roles of the Levites and the Aaronite priests in collecting the tithes that are described in verses 38-39.

11:1-24 Resettlement of Jerusalem

Continuing the extension of holiness outward found in the provisions of their pact, the people now make a tithe of themselves. Naturally, the elites will live in Jerusalem, but one-tenth of the community will also move inside the walls. Lots were often used in the ancient world to determine the divine will (see the discussion of Ezra 2:63). Again, the picture of Jerusalem in the book of Nehemiah is of a ruined and deserted city, in contrast to that found at the end of the book of Ezra. Scholars continue to be puzzled by this. Verse 2 contains an interesting aside and may imply that taking up residence in Jerusalem was not a desirable thing. Perhaps those on whom the lot fell were reluctant to leave their extended families and lands behind.

Verse 3 begins a collection of disparate lists grouped by the author or an editor. As in the case of the liturgical services and the covenant in Nehemiah, this list describes in great detail the Levites and their various roles in the temple. First are the names of those elite families ("the heads of the province," 11:3), both lay and priestly, who took up residence in Jerusalem. The number of elites totals 3,044. Adding in one-tenth of the remainder of the population, said to be over 42,000 people a century before under Cyrus, would put the population of the city somewhere around 7,200 souls. While little is known of Jerusalem during this period, the most recent population estimates claim that the city was no larger than 1,500 people at this time.

The list is very revealing about certain offices and provincial organization at some unknown point in the later Persian period. Reference to "people of substance" and "warriors" in verses 6, 8, and 14 implies some sort of standing army or professional soldiery. The Seraiah called "the ruler of the house of God" in verse 11 may be the same person as the Seraiah mentioned in 10:29, but the Hebrew text of 11:11 has been subject to copyists' errors. The name of Nehemiah does not appear in the list, further indication perhaps that the list dates from a later period.

11:25-36 Other settlements

This is an independent list appended to the list of settlers in Jerusalem that speaks of settlements outside the city according to the ancient distinction between the tribes of Judah and Benjamin. It has been noted that the list of cities here most closely resembles the settlement lists in the book of Joshua, yet another connection the author

makes between the return from exile and the exodus regarding settlement in the Promised Land.

12:1-9 Priests and Levites at the time of Zerubbabel

Yet another independent list is inserted here; this one continues the focus on temple personnel. There are several chronological and logical inconsistencies in this list and those that follow in verses 10-25, all of which point to the fact that they come from a much later period. The list of priests "who returned with Zerubbabel" (12:1) has nothing in common with the list of priests in 7:39-42 that is part of the larger census of those who came back with Zerubbabel. Interestingly, Ezra is mentioned in verse 1 of the list in chapter 12, although according to the book of Ezra he came to Jerusalem seventy years after Zerubbabel. Some have argued, therefore, that this Ezra is another person. Comparing the Levites listed in verses 8-9 with the names in 7:43, Jeshua, Binnui, and Kadmiel are the only names occurring in both lists.

12:10-11 High priests

Here is another independent list of high priests beginning with Jeshua and ending with Jaddua in a father-to-son succession. Chronologically there are problems with this list. Jeshua may be dated with some certainty to the time of Zerubbabel (ca. 520). Johanan, the next-to-last name on the list, can be dated to the end of the fifth century (ca. 410) on the basis of the Elephantine letter discussed above. However, his "son" Jaddua is said by the historian Josephus to have met Alexander the Great when the latter came to Jerusalem sometime around 335. This would make the time span between Johanan and his son Jaddua too long. Obviously, some names have dropped out of this list. Several ingenious proposals have attempted to restore the lost names, but none has met with widespread acceptance.

12:12-26 Priests and Levites under Joiakim

This list continues the list of verses 1-9 into the second generation after the return under Zerubbabel. The names of the priests in the list of verses 1-9 have now become family names in this list.

With the exception of Harim in verse 15, all the names of this list are found in verses 1-9, although some have undergone minor changes due to copyists' errors, e.g., Shebaniah instead of Shecaniah, or Miamin for Mijamin. The names of the priestly members of the clan of Miamin in verse 17 have dropped out in the history of transmission. This is represented in the New American Bible Revised Edition by an ellipsis.

For the names of the priests and Levites during the reigns of the other high priests treated here, the author refers the reader to "the Book of Chronicles" ("the book of the deeds of [past] days"). This is a generic title denoting any kind of archival document and is not to be understood as a reference to the two biblical books of the same name. For some reason, this archival source omitted the names of the priests for the time of Joiakim, and so the author chose to include them here. Darius the Persian in verse 22 could either be Darius II or Darius III. Johanan the high priest functioned during the reign of the former, while his "son" Jaddua apparently was alive during the reign of the latter. Given the chronological irregularities in these lists, however, it is unlikely that our author knew the difference. Verse 23 states that Johanan was the son of Eliashib (as does Ezra 10:6), contrary to the independent list of verses 10-11, where Johanan was Eliashib's grandson. With the list of Levites in verses 24-25, again the only common names with the previous Levitical lists are Jeshua, Binnui, and Kadmiel. In keeping with the stress on the liturgical importance of the Levites, reference to their duties in temple worship and administration is made again here.

The summary statement of verse 26 contains another chronological error in that neither Ezra nor Nehemiah appear to have been in Jerusalem during the time of Joiakim the high priest (see Ezra 10:6 and Neh 3:1). This is yet another sign of later editorial activity meant to relate a plethora of source material to the work of the heroes Ezra and Nehemiah.

12:27–13:3 Dedication of the wall

Here the original narrative thread of the book of Nehemiah, the rebuilding of the walls of Jerusalem, is taken up again after the intervening material concerning Ezra and the various lists. The rededication of the walls constitutes the third great liturgical service of the book, after the initial reading of the law in chapter 8 and the communal confession in chapter 9. Nehemiah divides the elites ("administrators of Judah," 12:32) into two "choirs." The Hebrew word *todah* also denotes a sacrifice made to God or the songs of praise that accompany it. The sense here is one of jubilant praise. Each group contains seven priests and eight musicians. The first group, beginning at the Valley Gate on the western end of the city, proceeds southward ("to the right," 12:31; note that the text assumes that the choirs are facing inward from the wall) around the southern end of the city and part of the way up the eastern wall (compare the similar route taken by Nehemiah in his initial inspection of the walls in 2:11-16). The second proceeds northward along the western wall ("to the left," 12:38) and continues along the entire length of the northern wall, stopping just past the Sheep Gate at the northeast corner. Making a ceremonial procession around a city's walls in order to ensure their role as protectors of the city was a common practice in the ancient world. Herodotus recounts the story of a king of the city of Sardis (now in Turkey) who carried a lion cub around the walls because he had been told that to do so would render the city impregnable to attack. Coincidentally, Sardis was besieged and captured by Cyrus the Great of Persia in 546.

There is yet more editorial evidence in this chapter attempting to link the independent figures of Ezra and Nehemiah. In verse 33, Ezra is listed as among the priests of the first choir. It is perhaps significant that his name occurs right after that of Azariah, which is a variant form of the name Ezra. Then, in verse 36 is an aside noting that "Ezra the scribe" was at the head of the first choir, a clear reference to the Ezra who brought the law to Jerusalem (see Neh 8:1). What has possibly occurred here is that the name Ezra was inserted after Azariah in verse 33 to clarify that Ezra was present at this great ceremony. Then another explanatory note was added in verse 36 to ensure that readers knew that it was *the* Ezra who took part in the ceremony as opposed to someone else with the same name.

The two groups are next gathered in the temple and the narrative is clear about the extent of the exuberance of the celebration, recalling the command to the people to rejoice in 8:9-12. The remark in verse 43 that the sound of rejoicing could be heard from far off is reminiscent of Ezra 3:13, except here the joyful sounds are not tinged with mourning, as was the dedication of the temple under Zerubbabel. With the completion of the walls and their dedication, the main narrative thread of the book of Nehemiah comes to rest on a triumphant note.

Continuing with the focus on the Levites in the second half of the book of Nehemiah, verses 44-47 are rather loosely appended to the story of the dedication of the walls, that affirm not only that the people followed the prescriptions of David and Solomon concerning the administrative role of the priests and Levites but that they did so joyfully (12:44), perhaps an instance of protesting too much (see below the discussion of 13:4-14). The role of the Levites in overseeing temple revenues in verse 44 echoes the provisions of the covenant in 10:38-40. The reference to David, Solomon, and Asaph gives Levitical authority, the added weight of tradition, and connection with the glorious Israelite past. Verse 47 shows this passage deals with the time of Zerubbabel. The reference to Nehemiah is most likely an editorial edition from a later time (use of the phrase "in the days of . . ." implies reference to the distant past) to help connect the passage with the surrounding material. Nehemiah's name is not in the Greek text.

The final chapter of the book of Nehemiah consists of four independent stories appended here and linked by the loose chronological connective "In those days" or "At that time." Such vague introductory phrases are often used in the Bible to connect independent stories, as is seen in, for example, the gospels or Genesis 22:1. The first episode (13:1-3) appears to be a variant of the reforms of Ezra in Ezra 9–10 and follows the pattern of Nehemiah 8, in which a directive is found during a reading of the law and is immediately put into place. The quotation here is a summarizing paraphrase of Deuteronomy 23:3-6. Verse 3 is emphatic: "When they had heard the law, they separated all those of mixed descent from Israel." This seems much harsher than the biblical injunction that forbids interaction specifically with Ammonites and Moabites, and also with the reforms of Ezra, in which only the foreign women who had married into the community were to be sent away. In all likelihood, this paragraph is an editorial summary inserted here to connect the reforms of Ezra with those of Nehemiah.

13:4-14 Reform in the temple

Beginning here, the remainder of the book is drawn from the Nehemiah memoir and consists of three separate episodes, each of which ends with Nehemiah's request that God remember his good deeds. Each episode shows the people in direct violation of a stipulation of the covenant they agreed to in chapter 10 and Nehemiah's decisive reaction to these infractions. The placement of these episodes at the end of the book emphasizes a theme prevalent throughout the Old Testament that stresses the continual need for repentance due to the persistence of sin. This situation is not distinct to the children of Israel but, as Paul makes clear, is part and parcel of the human condition (see Romans 5–7).

The introductory phrase "Before this" in verse 4 is vague in the present context, and we do not know exactly to what it refers. Here, Nehemiah recounts that after he had served for twelve years as the Persian governor of Judah he was recalled to Artaxerxes I, here called the "king of Babylon," perhaps because the Persians had conquered Babylon, which allowed the exiles to come to Jerusalem. At one time Babylon was part of the satrapy "West-of-Euphrates," but during the reign of Xerxes I some 50 years before Nehemiah, it had been separated and made into its own satrapy. During the time Nehemiah was away from Jerusalem, the high priest Eliashib allowed Tobiah, one of Nehemiah's enemies in the rebuilding of the wall, to have chambers in the temple. Nehemiah does not specify exactly when Artaxerxes I sent him back to Jerusalem, how long he stayed there, and if he was appointed governor again or was a special envoy of the king. His reaction to Tobiah's residence in the temple in verses 8-9 is swift and decisive, denoting the same degree of authority that he exercised during his twelve years as governor. Tobiah's belongings were thrown out and the chamber purified. The shame that would have accrued to Tobiah should not be lost on the modern reader. The need to "purify" a place of someone's presence still carries with it today the highly derogatory connotations at work here.

The other matter needing Nehemiah's attention involves a lapse in the people's support of the Levites. There is a precious historical kernel underlying the book's exaltation of the Levites worth looking at. First, contrary to the claims in 10:38-40 and 12:44 that the people gladly gave of their own resources to support the Levites, the episode here shows that perhaps they were reluctant to support the daily upkeep of a large temple personnel. Once the governor who instituted these taxes left, they naturally stopped paying them. It makes sense for Nehemiah in verse 11 to ask the local elites why the offerings have stopped, since it is they who would have been responsible for ensuring that they continue in his absence. Here we see the temple's role in the Persian imperial policy of regular, continual reliance on subject peoples for revenue. Not surprisingly, when their upkeep was withheld, those Levites who had come to Jerusalem simply went home to earn their livelihood (13:10). Nehemiah now appoints a council consisting of a priest, a Levite, and a scribe to ensure the proper collection and distribution of the offerings for the Levites.

13:15-22 Sabbath observance

An independent episode is introduced by the phrase "In those days. . . ." Here there is a twofold violation of the sabbath, in direct contradiction of the agreement sworn to by the people in 10:32. First, those in the Jewish community are engaged in work on the sabbath (13:15). Additionally, they also conduct commercial transactions on the sabbath with non-Jews. Tyrians denote residents from Tyre on the Phoenician coast. Tyre once had good relations with Israel in the time of Solomon (1 Kgs 5) but by the time of the exile it was one of the enemies of Israel (see the oracle against Tyre in Ezek 26–28). Again, Nehemiah must upbraid the Jerusalem elites. Interestingly, in a book that repeatedly stresses the necessity of the Jewish community to separate itself from outsiders, the text here does not condemn the Tyrians for selling on the sabbath. The reason is clear when one realizes that the law of the sabbath was given by God to Israel, and they alone are responsible for its observance. There is to be no passing of the buck for the people of God.

In 7:3 Nehemiah ordered the city gates shut for security measures. Here in 13:19 he has them shut for the duration of each sabbath. Ancient gates were more than simply openings in city walls. They could also contain a complex of buildings suitable for commercial, judicial, or religious functions. In Ruth 4 the gate is where the elders of the city meet to conduct legal business. Excavations in the city of Hazor in Galilee have revealed

a shrine housed in the city gate dating to the Israelite monarchy. The gates are closed as the shadows grow long on the sabbath eve. In both ancient and present-day Judaism, the new day begins at sundown (see the repeated phrase in Genesis 1: "Evening came, and morning followed—the first day," etc.) Those merchants who would come to Jerusalem to sell their wares on the sabbath apparently thought that these measures would not last long. "Once or twice" they spent the night outside the city (13:20) until Nehemiah warned them off.

13:23-30 Mixed marriages

Despite the people's agreement in 10:31 and 13:3 not to marry outside the community, Nehemiah finds foreign wives among the Jews. Ammonites and Moabites are expressly forbidden to the children of Israel in the text of Deuteronomy 23 paraphrased in Nehemiah 13:1-2. Ashdod is mentioned in 4:1 as an ally of Sanballat in opposing Nehemiah.

Nehemiah's concern about the languages spoken by the children in the community reflects a perennial interest among groups who feel their culture and identity are threatened by larger cultural forces. One of the most tangible signs of cultural assimilation is when the children of a particular group do not grow up as native speakers of that group's language. In the U.S., where English is the de facto official language, this usually happens by the third generation after immigration. Exceptions are when a particular group chooses to live in close-knit communities where there are enough native speakers for everyone to conduct necessary daily activities in the native language. Losing the language of one's origins entails the loss of more than just the ability to communicate. Every language is a "world" unto itself, denoting a particular cultural vision and way of understanding reality. To lose a language is really, then, to lose that world. "Ashdodite" in verse 24 is not a known ancient language, but since the West Semitic family of languages encompassed many local dialects in Palestine, of which Hebrew was one, it probably denotes a Phoenician dialect now lost. "The language of Judah" in verse 24 denotes the Hebrew language. By this time Aramaic had become the international *lingua franca*, as is made clear by the citation of Aramaic documents in Ezra and the documents from

Elephantine. It was to remain so until the conquests of Alexander the Great replaced Aramaic with Greek (although as the gospels show, residents of Palestine in the time of Jesus still used Aramaic for their everyday language). That Nehemiah stressed the use of Hebrew here is significant in demonstrating his concern that the community not lose its cultural identity. Archaeological evidence bears out the impact of Nehemiah's concern. Many of the seals and coins that date from the Persian period after the time of Nehemiah bear their inscriptions in Hebrew rather than Aramaic. Nehemiah reminds the community of their pact by quoting their very words back to them (compare 13:25 with 10:31). He also reminds them of the negative example of Solomon, who is condemned in 1 Kings 11 for marrying foreign women who led him astray from the worship of God (see above the discussion of Ezra 9:1-2).

Nehemiah now deals with a particular and dramatic example of inappropriate intermarriage involving the families of the high priest Eliashib and Nehemiah's old nemesis Sanballat. This episode forms a parallel with that of 12:4-9 where another of Nehemiah's enemies, Tobiah, has made an inroad into the Jerusalem temple. The phrase "One of the sons of Joiada, son of Eliashib the high priest," in verse 28 may denote the time before Eliashib's death and the assumption of the office of high priest by his son Joiada. However, the fact that Joiada himself has a grown son of marriageable age would mean that Eliashib lived to a ripe old age. This particular son of Joiada is probably not the Johanan who became the high priest himself (see 12:10-11).

Verses 30-31 are probably an ending added by an editor to round out the book. The editor writes in the first person and borrows the language of the Nehemiah memoir in asking God to remember his (Nehemiah's) good deeds. To this he adds a summary of the episodes collected in chapter 13 and appended to the book of Nehemiah: the separation of the people from foreign elements and the establishment of the Levites and their offerings. The ending of Nehemiah forms a fitting counterpart to the opening of Ezra. There, God remembered his prophecy to Jeremiah and so roused Cyrus to send the exiles back to Jerusalem. Here, Nehemiah asks God to remember his good deeds. The fidelity of God stressed in the beginning of the book of Ezra is a powerful witness that Nehemiah's hope is not in vain.

CONCLUSION

Reading Ezra-Nehemiah can be a daunting task. There is a good deal of history one needs to know in order to make sense of the text. Then there are all those difficult names to keep track of, not to mention the minute discussion of worship regulations that can seem to a modern reader to be nothing more than museum pieces of a lost and forgotten past. This commentary has tried to show that the difficult parts of a biblical book cannot be soft-pedaled or ignored. Responsible readers of the Bible are obligated to work through those rough spots that seemingly have no relevance for one's spiritual development. Indeed, doing so reveals many timely and important lessons that may be profitably applied to the lives of modern readers. Among those from Ezra-Nehemiah are the following.

First is that while God is just, he is also merciful. Moreover, his mercy thankfully trumps his justice. The people knew that the exile had been a deserved punishment. Yet they also knew with just as much certainty that this punishment was not the last word in their relationship with God. Mercy had come in the person of Cyrus and in the form of the opportunity to return to Jerusalem and to start over. They had been given another chance, and they were determined to make the most of it.

Part of making the most of God's gracious offer to start over is the realization that being part of God's people may demand a radical reorientation of one's life and relationships. No arena of human life, be it personal relationships, business affairs, or one's livelihood, is immune or quarantined from one's "religious" obligations. Indeed, relating the law to the category of religious duties is more a reflection of the thoroughly modern idea of separating religion from the scope of one's "everyday" life. Such a distinction would have been meaningless to an ancient Israelite. The members of Nehemiah's community were asked to scrutinize their lives in the light of the law and to make changes where necessary, even though some of these changes required drastic measures.

A life lived following God's law is not one of drudgery, nor is it devoid of joy. Many people think this, however, due in part to the connotations that surround modern perceptions of law. For us, law is often seen as prohibitive and restricting and, given the emphasis on personal freedom, rights, and autonomy in our culture, anything that imposes limits on a person may naturally be viewed negatively. The Hebrew word *torah*, usually translated as "the law," has a much wider range of meaning, including the ideas of instruction, custom, and even philosophy, understood as a way of life. In the Old Testament, the law is not a prison that binds the individual but rather a blueprint or guide given by a loving God to help his children live joyous and fulfilled lives in a fully realized community with each other and in genuine relationship with God. The rejoicing of the people as they realized not only that God's will was made plain to them, but also that they had it in their power to carry it out, should not be overlooked. The genuine happiness at following the divine will has been a trademark of Judaism even to this day and one from which Christians could learn much.

In addition to a heightened sense of personal autonomy that chafes at the idea of laws as limitation, Christians are also influenced by the theology of the early church in such a way as to view the Old Testament law in a negative light. One of the first great theological debates among early Christians involved whether or not following Jesus should be understood as an alternative way of being Jewish or as a completely new thing. The major player in this debate was Paul who, although he was Jewish, was firmly committed to the idea of Christianity as a radically new way of being in relationship with God. For Paul, this meant that the requirements of the Old Testament law were no longer in effect. However, many people, especially since the Reformation, have misinterpreted Paul's attitude and read him as

saying there was something deficient in the law itself. For Paul the problem lay not in the law, but in a flawed human nature damaged by sin (see Rom 1–3, 5–7).

This particular misunderstanding of Paul has had a direct bearing on how Ezra-Nehemiah has been read by Christians. Many Christians understand Judaism to be a rigid, legalistic religion based on outmoded and deficient laws. Consequently, they see in Ezra-Nehemiah a picture of an almost sectarian or fundamentalist faction rigidly imposing laws on its members and openly hostile to any outsiders. Of course, as the analysis here has shown, this particular reading of Ezra-Nehemiah overlooks much crucial contrary evidence in the text and also from modern knowledge of the strategies that subcultures use to help preserve their identity. Christians in the U.S. have no firsthand experience of being in a religious minority (although that was certainly not the case for Catholics two or three generations ago), and that makes it difficult to understand the logic at work behind the reforms of Ezra and Nehemiah. However, reading literature generated by Christians when they were a minority group, such as the letters of Paul or the book of Revelation, reveals some of the same concerns as those expressed in Ezra-Nehemiah. For example, there is Paul's stricture in 1 Corinthians 6 that Christians not use the civil authorities to settle their legal disputes so that they will not be judged by unrighteous nonbelievers, or his rather harsh judgment concerning an inappropriate marriage in 1 Corinthians 5 that the offending party be excluded from the Christian community, a striking parallel with Ezra-Nehemiah.

"All scripture is inspired by God and is useful for teaching, for refutation, for correction, and for training in righteousness" (2 Tim 3:16). Often overlooked by modern readers, Ezra-Nehemiah is a good example of this affirmation of the worth of the Scriptures. Written about an eventful period in the history of Israel and full of drama and emotion, the books show vividly the responsibilities facing all who claim to walk the path of the God of Israel, and how walking in that path can lead to hope and joy.

THE BOOK OF
TOBIT

Irene Nowell, O.S.B.

INTRODUCTION

Who is Tobit?

Tobit is a good and holy man. He makes every effort to observe God's law and to teach his son Tobiah to do the same. His goodness is attested by Raphael, who praises his prayer and his attention to burying the dead (12:12-13), and by Raguel, who describes him as "righteous and charitable" (7:7). But Tobit has his flaws. In the early part of the story he seems preoccupied by money. He will send his only son on a dangerous journey to regain the money he deposited with Gabael (4:2; 4:20–5:3). It is Tobit's wife Anna who declares that the son's life is more important than the money (5:18-20). But money is still uppermost in Tobit's mind. Weeks later when Tobiah is delayed he worries that there was no one to give him the money (10:2). He also, however, gives alms to the poor and encourages Tobiah to do the same (4:7-11). At the end of the story he is willing to give the guide Azariah (Raphael) half the money they have brought back (12:4-5). Tobit is also greatly distressed by his need to be supported by his wife's work. He shares the sentiment of his contemporary, Ben Sira, who says, "Harsh is the slavery and great the shame / when a wife supports her husband" (Sir 25:22; cf. Tob 2:11-14).

At the end of the story it is evident that Tobit also is a person of hope. His prayer begins with a strong encouragement to trust in God even in the midst of suffering (13:1-8). Then he proclaims the glory of a future Jerusalem, rebuilt with a glorious temple as its center (13:9-18). In his final exhorta-

tion to Tobiah and his family Tobit assures them that, after the exile, Jerusalem will be rebuilt and faithful people will be gathered to it again (14:4b-7).

Theology: prayer and almsgiving

The theological stance of the book of Tobit is based on the book of Deuteronomy. Fidelity to the law and the conviction that Jerusalem is the place one must offer sacrificial worship are strong Deuteronomic themes. There is also a belief that God rewards fidelity and punishes wrongdoing. This story, however, challenges that belief somewhat. Tobit, a faithful man, is eventually rewarded, but he initially endures heartrending suffering.

Two primary virtues are emphasized in this book: prayer and almsgiving. The characters turn to prayer frequently and in all situations. There are several formal prayers. When it seems their lives are all but lost, both Tobit and Sarah pray to God (3:2-6, 11-15). "At that very time" God heard the prayer of both and sent Raphael to heal their distress (3:16), although the two characters will have to wait some time to know their prayer has been answered. Tobiah and Sarah pray for blessing and safety on their wedding night, as Raphael has instructed them to do (8:4-8). Raguel with Edna blesses God that the disaster he feared has not happened and asks for blessings for the newlyweds (8:15-17). Tobit blesses God for the gift of renewed sight (11:14-15). Finally Tobit sings a long song of thanksgiving and hopeful praise for the new Jerusalem (ch. 13).

It is not only formal prayers, however, but the spirit of prayer that permeates the book. All the characters are drawn to prayer frequently. At the very beginning Tobit testifies to his fidelity in worshiping in Jerusalem (1:6). When Tobiah and Raphael leave on their journey, Tobit blesses Raphael and, ironically, prays that God will send an angel to protect Tobiah (5:17). Both Raguel and Edna pray for safety for Tobiah and Sarah as they marry (7:12, 17). Gabael, who holds Tobit's money, also blesses Tobiah and Sarah (9:6). As Tobiah and Sarah set out to return to Nineveh, both Raguel and Edna bless the two and Tobiah blesses them in turn (10:11-13). When Sarah arrives in Nineveh, Tobit blesses her and her parents and Tobiah (11:17). Raphael instructs Tobit and Tobiah to thank God for all the blessings they have received, and informs them that he was sent in answer to their prayers (12:6, 12-14). He encourages them to "bless God every day" (12:18, 20). In the last verse of the book we read that Tobiah "blessed the Lord God forever and ever" (14:15).

The other major virtue that is stressed throughout the book is almsgiving. In the early second century b.c. this became a prominent theme in both Tobit and Sirach (see Sir 3:30; 7:10; 29:8, 12; 35:4). In Tobit's instruction to Tobiah he emphasizes the necessity of giving to the poor. This generosity is tempered by wisdom: "Give in proportion to what you own" (4:8). He returns to the theme a few verses later: "Whatever you have left over, give away as alms" (4:16). But his strongest statement is in the center of his speech: "almsgiving delivers from death" and "is a worthy offering in the sight of the Most High" (4:10, 11). Almsgiving is praised above every other virtue. It is better than wealth; it is even better than "[p]rayer with fasting." It removes sin and is the way to "a full life" (12:8-9). Tobit gave alms throughout his life, and at the end exhorted Tobiah and his children "to do what is right and to give alms" (14:9). He also used the story of Ahiqar as an example. Ahiqar escaped the plot his nephew set for him because he gave alms (14:10-11). Tobit's final exhortation is to give alms.

The book also contributes much to the developing theology of angels. Raphael identifies himself as one of the seven angels who stand in the presence of God. He is sent as a messenger, the essential meaning of the word "angel." He hides his identity in order to allow the human charac-

ters to be free throughout the story. But at the end he reveals himself and, after encouraging them to praise God, ascends to heaven.

Intertextuality

A major characteristic of this book is the allusion to earlier biblical texts. In his prayer, Tobit is so discouraged he prays to die. Here he is following the example of noble predecessors: Moses (Num 11:15) and Elijah (1 Kgs 19:4; see also Jonah 4:3). At the end of the story Tobit, like Moses, dies outside the Promised Land but looks forward to its future (see Deut 31:7-8; 32:44-52). The meeting between Tobiah and the family of Raguel (7:1-6) is patterned on the meeting between Jacob and the family of Laban in Genesis (Gen 29:4-14). In Tobiah's prayer he suggests that he and Sarah are modeled on Adam and Eve (Tob 8:6). Raphael's character echoes that of earlier biblical angels: the angel who appeared to Manoah and his wife who asks, "Why do you ask my name?" and who also ascends to heaven (Judg 13:18, 20; Tob 5:12; 12:20).

Genre and date

The book of Tobit is a biblical novella, that is, a short, fictional tale told to make a point and to encourage its readers to greater fidelity. Its purpose is not to recount history but rather both to entertain and to edify. This story is rich with irony, the situation where the reader knows more than the characters. For example, the reader knows that Raphael is an angel, but Tobit and Tobiah do not. The irony is often amusing, but this story is not a comedy. It is a serious meditation on the mystery of human suffering and God's justice.

There is a consensus that it was written in the early second century b.c. at which time the novella became a popular form (see also Judith and Esther). There is no evidence in the book of a belief in meaningful life after death, a belief that began to emerge in the mid-second century around the time of the Maccabees. It shares its theology and worldview with the book of Sirach, which was written around the same time.

Original language, place of composition, and canonical status

The original language was most likely Aramaic, although this is still a subject of debate. Fragments of the work in both Aramaic and

Hebrew were found among the Dead Sea scrolls. There are two major Greek translations, one represented by Codex Vaticanus and Codex Alexandrinus and the other by Codex Sinaiticus, plus other fragmentary manuscripts. It is also included in the Vulgate even though Jerome did not want to translate it. He was only persuaded to do it by some friends who were bishops and he claims he made the translation in one day. He also made several additions, which are not found in the Semitic fragments or the Greek translation.

The question of provenance is also debated. Was this book written in Palestine or in the Diaspora? The situation of the main characters in the story, especially Tobit himself, suggests that it was written in the Diaspora. Emphasis on family and kinship, rather than city and temple, as a way of preserving identity as God's people is also a hint that the writer was not "at home." The book ends with Tobit's vision that eventually all God's people will be gathered in the new Jerusalem.

The book of Tobit was not included in the Hebrew canon, which was closed around the end of the first century A.D. One reason may be its late composition; another may be its fictional character.

COMMENTARY

TOBIT'S VIRTUE AND COURAGE

Tobit 1

Tobit is introduced with a seven-member genealogy, tracing him back to the tribe of Naphtali. The names of his ancestors all end in "el," meaning "God." Tobit's own name seems to be a nickname. In the Aramaic version of the story, probably the original, he is called "Tobi," perhaps short for "Tobi-el" or "Tobi-yahu," meaning "God/YHWH is my good." Tobit lived in the area settled by his tribe, that is, the northern kingdom known as Israel. The ten tribes making up this northern kingdom had separated from the southern tribe of Judah in the tenth century. Tobit's story is set toward the turn of the eighth–seventh century B.C., the time of the collapse of the northern kingdom.

The Assyrian kings had been harassing Israel for some time, demanding tribute and taking over territory. When King Jeroboam II, whose reign was one of the longest in Israel's history (786–746), died, his son Zechariah, who was pro-Assyrian, was killed within six months by the anti-Assyrian, Shallum. Shallum's reign, however, only lasted a month and he was assassinated by Menahem. Menahem paid tribute to the Assyrian leader Tiglath-Pileser III, and managed to hold the throne from 745 to 738. He was succeeded by his son, Pekahiah, who was pro-Assyrian. But before the year was out, Pekahiah was murdered by one of his officers, Pekah, who was anti-Assyrian. Pekah attempted to organize a coalition against Assyria (see Isa 7) and was killed by Tiglath-Pileser III. The Assyrians put Hoshea on the throne, but he rebelled against Assyria when Tiglath-Pileser died. Shalmaneser V, his successor, then attacked in 724 and Israel fell to his successor Sargon II in 722.

There is a problem with the listing of kings in the book of Tobit. Shalmaneser V (727–722 B.C.) was succeeded by Sargon II (722–705), not Sennacherib (705–681), as Tobit says (1:15). Sennacherib was the son of Sargon II, but Sargon was not a son of Shalmaneser V. Sennacherib, however, was indeed murdered by his sons and was succeeded by his son Esarhaddon (681–669 B.C.; Tob 1:21).

It is possible that Tobit himself was taken captive to Nineveh during the reign of Pekah in an earlier Assyrian raid led by Tiglath-Pileser III on the northern territory of Naphtali (see 2 Kgs 15:29; Tob 1:2), although he names Shalmaneser as the king. In the midst of this turbulent time, Tobit remained completely faithful to his tradition. He reminds the reader of the separation of the twelve tribes into two political entities at the death of Solomon in 922 B.C. (Tob 1:4-5). Judah (with tiny Benjamin) pledged allegiance to Solomon's son Rehoboam, but the ten northern tribes followed another king, Jeroboam, who had been in charge of forced labor under Solomon (see 1 Kgs 12). Jeroboam, not wanting his subjects to go to Jerusalem, the capital of Judah, to worship, established two shrines: one at Bethel and the other at Dan. Tobit, however, insists he continued to go to the temple in Jerusalem to worship God (Tob 1:6-8). He is there for the three established feasts: Unleavened Bread (Passover), Weeks, and Booths, and also makes the offering of first fruits (Deut 16:16; 18:4).

Tobit is particularly careful about the required tithes, perhaps even scrupulous. Besides the first fruits and firstlings for the priests (cf. Deut 12:4-7; 18:1-5), he offers the "first tithe," which is the tenth of the harvest of grains and fruits (Deut 14:22-23). He also offers a "second tithe" of money, which seems to be a misreading of the Deuteronomic regulation that allows for the offerer to bring an equivalent sum of money if it is too difficult to bring the first fruits, firstlings, and the harvested material itself (Deut 14:24-25). In addition to all these, Tobit offers a "third tithe" for the relief of orphans and widows who live in Nineveh where he resides (Deut 14:28-29; 26:12). The original meaning of these three tithes, however, is this: The required tithe was to be brought to Jerusalem either in kind (Tobit's "first tithe") or in money (Tobit's "second tithe") in years 1, 2, 4, and 5. Then in years 3 and 6 the tithe (Tobit's "third tithe") was to be kept in the offerer's home area for the relief of the poor (Deut 14:22-29; 26:12). Tobit interprets these offerings as separate and is contributing them all. This understanding of tithing reflects the practice in the second century, the time the book was written.

Tobit was also careful to marry someone of his ancestral family (endogamous marriage), a practice that is described as common among the early tribes (1:9; see 4:12-13). Perhaps the most significant quality of his righteousness, however, is his care for the weak and vulnerable, especially his practice of burying the dead. All these qualities of wise and holy living he learned from his grandmother, Deborah, who appears in only one sentence (1:8), but whose influence permeates the whole book. From her he learned to obey the law. He must also have learned from her the Deuteronomic principle that obedience brings success and disobedience brings punishment (see Deut 28). His confidence in this principle, however, is about to be tested.

In the early years of his time in Nineveh, Tobit's life was peaceful and profitable. He worked for Shalmaneser and traveled east to Media as his purchasing agent. On one of his trips he deposited a sum of money with a relative, Gabael, who lived in Rages. Retrieving that sum of money will become a major factor in the plot of this story. But before that becomes necessary, Tobit's situation changes for the worse. A new king, Sennacherib, returns from Judea angry because of a humiliating defeat (see 2 Kgs 19:35-36). He takes out his revenge on the Israelites who are captive in Assyria. Tobit, faithful to the Deuteronomic code of charity to the vulnerable, steals the bodies of Sennacherib's victims and buries them. When he is found out, he is forced to flee and everything he owns is confiscated. In addition, the roads to Media are no longer safe, so he cannot obtain the money he left with Gabael. All he has now is his family.

His distress is short-lived, however. Sennacherib is assassinated and succeeded by his son Esarhaddon (681–669 B.C.). The new king appoints a man named Ahiqar as his chief administrative assistant. Ahiqar intercedes for Tobit, and Tobit returns to Nineveh. Who is this Ahiqar? He was known as a wise man in Assyria, and several of his sayings were preserved in Syriac. Then in the early twentieth century, a papyrus document was discovered in Egypt that contained in Aramaic a short biography of a certain Ahiqar and several of his proverbs. The biography sets his work in the time of Sennacherib and Esarhaddon. The writer of the book of Tobit makes him Tobit's relative and helper. So the stage is set for the main action of the story.

TOBIT'S BLINDNESS

Tobit 2

The scene moves to Tobit's home, which has now been restored to him. The family is preparing to celebrate Pentecost. This feast is sometimes called "Weeks," because it is seven weeks after

Passover. "Pentecost" is the Greek term that signifies the fifty days of those seven weeks (Lev 23:15-16). Passover celebrates the barley harvest and Pentecost celebrates the wheat harvest. Deuteronomy prescribes that the offering should be "in proportion to the blessing the LORD, your God, has given you" (Deut 16:10). The instructions continue with the exhortation to celebrate with one's family, one's servants, the Levites, "as well as the resident alien, the orphan, and the widow among you" (Deut 16:11). Tobit will follow these commands as closely as he can in his exile. He cannot go to the temple, and there may be no Levites in his neighborhood. But he can certainly invite those less fortunate than he is. So he sends his son Tobiah to find a poor person among the exiled Jews and bring him to this festal meal (2:2).

But the situation soon turns for the worse. Instead of bringing a poor person to the dinner, Tobiah returns with the news that there is a dead body in the marketplace. Tobit, true to form, immediately goes out and collects the body to bring home until sunset when he can bury him without being detected. Because he has touched a dead body, Tobit is now unclean and so performs the necessary purification ritual (see Num 19:11-13). That night, after the burial, he again purifies himself and sleeps outside in order to avoid bringing the uncleanness into the house.

Tobit's neighbors mock him, reminding him that he was already in danger of death once before for burying the victims of violence. But another affliction awaits this good man. The droppings of sparrows fall into his eyes from the roof and blind him. Doctors cannot heal him, but he is not totally without resources. His kinsman Ahiqar cares for him for two years and his wife Anna goes to work to support the family. Anna thus becomes our first example of a working mother. She must have been good at her work, because her employers also give her a bonus, a young goat, probably for the celebration of the Purim festival (see Esther). Tobit, however, is so depressed by his blindness and his dependence upon others that he strikes out at his wife, accusing her of bringing home stolen goods. Anna does not take this abuse quietly. She repeats the truth that this goat was a bonus and then she aims sharp words at the heart of Tobit's confidence: his faithfulness to the law. How can he continue to believe the Deuteronomic principle that those who are faithful will be blessed and those who disobey the law will suffer? Tobit is clearly suffering. Thus he must be unfaithful to the law.

TOBIT AND SARAH PRAY FOR DEATH; GOD'S ANSWER
Tobit 3

Anna, it seems, has done her husband a favor. Her sharp words drive Tobit to prayer. In this chapter two suffering people will pray for death. The prayers of both will be answered, but not quite as they expected. The first petitioner is Tobit. He begins his prayer with praise of God. Tobit's own righteousness has been challenged, but he acknowledges that, even though he is afflicted, God is completely righteous. Whatever God does, however mysterious it may seem, is characterized by faithful love.

Now that he acknowledged God's righteousness, Tobit prays for God's mercy. He asks God to remember him. He knows the tradition. When God "remembers," something happens. In the story of the great flood, when God remembers Noah, the rains stop and the water begins to recede (Gen 8:1). When the descendants of Jacob are enslaved in Egypt, they cry out to God and God remembers the covenant. That sets in motion the great exodus event (Exod 2:23-25). Now Tobit hopes for the same mercy. He acknowledges that he and his ancestors have sinned. He declares that God's judgment against them is fair and that they have deserved the misery of exile, but still he hopes that God will hear him. What Tobit asks, however, shows the depth of his despair. He begs God to just let him die. He has lost his will to live and cannot face another day of such suffering.

At this point a new central character is introduced, Sarah, daughter of Raguel. She too is in terrible anguish. Her father, like Tobit, is committed to the principle of endogamous marriage (marriage within the clan). But although Sarah has been married to seven appropriate husbands, all seven have died on the wedding night. As if that were not enough tragedy, she is now attacked verbally by her maid, who accuses her of killing her husbands herself. The maid, angry because apparently Sarah has abused her, wants Sarah to follow her husbands into death and prays she never has children. So Sarah too longs for death and plans to hang herself. But then she recognizes the shame this would bring upon her father, and decides rather to ask God to take her life.

Now Sarah, like Tobit, turns to God in prayer. She has been well trained; she knows how to pray. She stretches out her hands presumably toward Jerusalem and begins by blessing and praising God and makes her petition for death. Then she describes her situation. Her purity is undefiled; her love for her father is clear. But she does not know the way out of this anguish. Then, surprisingly, she surrenders to God's will. If God does not wish to take her life, she will accept it. But she still begs God to take away her suffering if she must continue to live.

These two people of different ages in different places both turn to God in prayer when they are in trouble. They set the stage for the many prayers that characterize this book. At virtually every turn, one or more of the characters pray to God. They pray in sorrow and they pray in joy. But prayer is never far from their hearts. Their trust is not misplaced. A clue that God is at work in these lives has already been suggested by the phrase, "On that very day" (3:7). Tobit and Sarah pray to God at the same time, and "[a]t that very time" the prayer of both is heard and answered (3:16). They do not know this, however. They will have to wait to see how God will respond. But God has already set in motion the events that will bring them more joy than they could have imagined.

God answers their prayer by sending the angel Raphael to heal both Sarah and Tobit. The reader does not yet know that Raphael is an angel. That news will not be revealed until chapter 5. Tobit and Tobiah will not discover Raphael's true identity until the end of the story. But the angel's name, given only to the reader and not to the characters in the story, gives away his identity and mission. Raphael means "God heals." The word "angel" means "messenger," and Raphael is God's messenger sent to heal these suffering people. The other non-human character in this story is the demon Asmodeus, who is afflicting Sarah by killing her bridegrooms. The name Asmodeus means "demon of wrath." The conflict in this story has now moved to the superhuman realm. Raphael is assigned the task of subduing the demon.

TOBIT'S INSTRUCTION TO TOBIAH

Tobit 4

"That same day," the day that Tobit and Sarah prayed and God sent Raphael to them, Tobit remembers that he has money deposited with Gabael in Rages. He must take care of this matter immediately, since he has asked God for death. But God will answer the prayer of the two petitioners differently than Tobit imagines. The trip is part of God's plan, but not because of the money. Tobiah's journey to Rages will be guided by Raphael, who will arrange a detour to Ecbatana, which will join the two petitioners and heal both of them. The deposited money becomes almost an afterthought.

The main characters in the story, however, do not know the details of this plan. Tobit is focused on the money, and decides to send his son to recover it. But before Tobiah makes this potentially dangerous journey, Tobit wants to be sure he has absorbed his teaching on how to live a holy life. Tobit was instructed by his grandmother Deborah; now he instructs his son. His instruction follows closely the pattern of farewell discourses found throughout biblical literature (see Gen 47:29–49:33; Josh 22–24; 1 Chr 28–29). Particular characteristics of this form that are emphasized in Tobit's speech are the mention of the speaker's death, the exhortation to keep the commandments, and the promise that God will be with Tobiah. The content of Tobit's instruction closely resembles biblical wisdom literature, especially the Wisdom of Ben Sira, a contemporary of the author of Tobit (see the introduction regarding almsgiving and Sir 3:1-16; 7:27-28 regarding the instruction of one's children).

Tobit begins with family duties, specifically care for Anna, Tobiah's mother. Even though Tobit and Anna have their disagreements, they clearly love one another. Tobit is also concerned about proper burial and wishes to be buried in the same grave with his wife. He also instructs Tobiah concerning his own marriage. He should follow the custom of endogamy, and marry a woman of his own tribe. To support this instruction, he lists the example of the patriarchs and the bonds of kinship.

In the midst of this instruction Tobit exhorts Tobiah to be generous in giving alms. Tobiah should not impoverish himself, but he should share in proportion to whatever he has. Later in his speech Tobit gives specific examples of how this should be done: giving food to the hungry, clothing the naked, and paying workers promptly. The benefits of almsgiving are great, equal to the offering of sacrifice to God. Almsgiving saves one from death and the darkness of Sheol. This theme of almsgiving is a major contribution of the book of Tobit and forms a foundation for the gospel message.

Tobit wants his son to be wise, so he advises him to seek out other wise persons and listen to what they teach him. Tobiah should be wise regarding himself, cultivating discipline. He should be wise regarding other people, following the golden rule: "Do to no one what you yourself hate" (4:15). He should be wise in relationship to God, blessing God and asking God to guide his way. The commandments should be written on his heart.

One of Tobit's instructions seems odd to modern readers: "Pour out your wine and your bread on the grave of the righteous" (4:17). This may reflect a practice of sharing food at the grave of family members, or it may be another example of almsgiving, bringing food to the bereaved family.

After all these instructions about how to live a holy life, Tobit tells Tobiah about the money deposited with Gabael. But he also reminds him of the Deuteronomic principle that God rewards those who are faithful. Tobit has a very clear idea of how this Deuteronomic principle is supposed to work. He promises Tobiah that, if he obeys God's law, he will be very wealthy. Today's readers have a more nuanced understanding of the Deuteronomic principle, especially because of the belief in life after death, a belief that Tobit was not fortunate enough to share.

THE ANGEL RAPHAEL

Tobit 5

Tobiah is a good son. He will obey his father. But he does not know how to do what his father asks. He needs a guide and he needs identification so that Gabael will believe him. The identification is simple; Tobit will give him half a bond (the document on which the terms of the deposit were written), which will match the other half that Gabael holds. The guide, however, will be more than either father or son expects.

When Tobiah goes out to search for his guide, he immediately encounters the angel Raphael. Here the irony begins. The human characters do not know that Raphael is an angel. They do not even know his name, because he identifies himself as Azariah, a relative of Tobit. But young Tobiah should be surprised at his opening words. Tobiah has asked only if he knows the way to Media. This Azariah claims not only to have that knowledge, but even to know Gabael who lives in Rages. He also adds a comment about Ecbatana, the home of Sarah. But neither Tobiah nor Tobit have any interest in going there. This man seems to be an amazingly perceptive guide. He also seems to be very speedy, since he claims that the journey from Ecbatana to Rages takes two days, when it took Alexander's army eleven days of forced march to cover the 180 miles. The reader knows what is happening but Tobit and Tobiah have no idea.

Tobiah is happy with this guide, so he goes in to inform his father. When Raphael enters, Tobit begins with a heartrending complaint about his blindness. Raphael, whose name means "God heals," encourages him with the words, "God's healing is near." He exhorts him to "take courage," a phrase that will appear frequently in the book (5:10). Tobit then begins his inquiry. Does this man know the way to Media? Indeed. But to what family does he belong? Tobit will not entrust his son to a stranger. After a little teasing about why Tobit wants not only a guide but a tribe, Raphael gives his name as Azariah, which means "Yhwh is my help," son of Hananiah ("Yhwh is merciful"), and claims to be from Tobit's own family. That is enough for Tobit, who states the terms of Raphael's employment, the standard laborer's wage, and promises a bonus. Raphael in turn promises that the two of them will go in good health and return in good health.

Tobiah collects what he needs for the journey and prepares to set out. His father blesses him and prays that a good angel will accompany him. But his mother, Anna, is terrified that now she will lose her son. She scolds Tobit for wanting more money and begs him to consider the deposited funds as Tobiah's ransom. But Tobit reassures her by repeating the words with which he blessed his son: "a good angel will go with him" (5:22). Little do Tobiah's parents know how true those words are. The good angel is already in their midst.

THE JOURNEY AND RAPHAEL'S INSTRUCTIONS

Tobit 6

Raphael may know all the roads to Media, but he starts out in the wrong direction. The Tigris River is west of Nineveh and Rages is to the east. Nonetheless, what Raphael does know well is in accordance with his name, "God heals." Tobiah is threatened by a very large fish who threatens to swallow him, just as his family's distress threatens to engulf him. But Raphael instructs him to seize the threat itself and gut it. He is to keep the gall, heart, and liver, but throw away the rest of the entrails. Then Tobiah cooks and eats part of the fish. Symbolically he has defeated the "sea monster" and now it becomes a source of life and healing for the characters in the story.

Finally, days later, Tobiah can no longer stand the suspense and he asks Raphael why he is keeping the inner organs of the fish. He has already surmised they are medicine, but does not know how or when to use them. Raphael informs him that the fish gall is used to heal blindness, a purpose Tobiah readily understands. The practice of using fish gall to restore the sight was well known in ancient Assyria and elsewhere. Raphael goes on to tell the boy that the heart and liver are to be used to drive demons out of an afflicted person. Tobiah must wonder why he needs that medicine.

When the travelers approach Ecbatana, Raphael tells Tobiah two things: first, they will spend the night in the house of a relative, Raguel; second, Tobiah should marry Raguel's beautiful daughter Sarah, because he is her closest relative. Raphael will arrange the details with Raguel to set up the marriage for that very evening. Tobiah is not only startled, he is terrified. Apparently news of this young relative's affliction has spread as far as Nineveh. She is possessed by a demon who kills her bridegrooms on the wedding night. One of the Qumran manuscripts (4QTob\u1d43) says that this demon is in love with her. Tobiah does not want to die, and he is sure his parents do not want that either.

Raphael reassures the young man and reminds him of the remedy he has in his possession, the fish organs that will repel the demon. He also exhorts Tobiah to pray with Sarah that God will protect them and bless them. Raphael knows that Sarah and Tobiah have been destined to be together since the beginning of creation. But he does not know everything. Just as Tobiah does not know Raphael's true identity, Raphael does not know if Tobiah and Sarah will have children. Only the reader knows the work that God is doing here. Twice Raphael tells Tobiah not to worry (6:16, 18), and the young man heeds the angel's advice. He immediately sets his heart on Sarah.

RAGUEL'S HOUSE: ARRIVAL AND MARRIAGE

Tobit 7

Tobiah has made up his mind that he is destined to marry Sarah and so he wishes to go straight to Raguel's house. Before he can express his intention, however, there are greetings and introductions to be made. Raguel, whose name means "friend of God," is as hospitable to strangers as Tobit is. But he is struck by the resemblance of the young man to his relative Tobit. Tobiah then reveals that he is Tobit's son. At this news, the whole family bemoans Tobit's affliction; they have clearly heard of his blindness. Hospitality then moves to the forefront as Raguel prepares a great feast. This welcome and feast are reminiscent of the welcome of three strangers by Abraham, another friend of God (Gen 18:1-8). The strangers who arrive at Abraham's tent also include angels as well as the Lord.

Tobiah, however, will not eat until he has accomplished the mission revealed to him by Raphael. He asks Raphael to ask Raguel to give Sarah to him as his wife, but Raguel overhears the young man. From this point on, Tobiah takes responsibility for his own destiny. Raguel informs him of Sarah's affliction (which he already knows) and warns him of the danger. But Tobiah will not be put off until the wedding takes place. So the arrangements are made and Sarah is given to Tobiah as his wife. The wedding ceremony is typical of the period. A fifth-century Egyptian text, the decree of Mibtahiah's third marriage, describes the wedding formula: "She is my wife and I am her husband from this day forever." Raguel states it similarly: "from now on you are her brother, and she is your sister" (7:11). The terms "brother" and "sister" are frequent references to husband and wife at this time (see Tob 5:21; 7:15; 8:4, 21; 10:6, 12; Esth 15:9[D:9]; Song

4:9-10, 12; 5:1-2). Then the marriage contract is drawn up and sealed. Only after this wedding ceremony will they begin the meal.

Raguel then asks his wife to prepare a bedroom for the newlyweds and to take Sarah there. The young woman must be terrified, knowing that seven bridegrooms have already been killed by the demon Asmodeus. Her mother too dreads this night, fearing another tragedy. But Edna is a strong mother. She weeps, but she also attempts to strengthen her daughter. She prays a blessing on her, and twice she reminds her to "take courage" (Greek *tharsei*). This word is closely connected to the healings that God has set in motion (3:16-17). Tobiah himself will encourage his father Tobit with this same word (11:11). Prayer is also never far from the hearts of each of the characters in this story.

RESOLUTION:
DEMON EXPELLED, WEDDING FEAST, MONEY RECOVERED

Tobit 8–9

The critical moment has arrived. Each of Sarah's bridegrooms has been killed by the demon Asmodeus on the wedding night. But Tobiah and Sarah have, unbeknownst to them, one of God's angels to advise them and defend them against the demon. Raphael has already instructed Tobiah to put the fish entrails on the coals left there for the incense. The aroma from the fish's liver and heart certainly is not as pleasant as incense, but it is effective. The demon is repulsed by the odor and flees all the way to Egypt, where he is pursued and bound by Raphael. The young newlyweds are safe from the demon's anger and lust.

But they have also been advised by Raphael to pray, not surprising in this book so full of prayer. Tobiah quotes Raphael exactly as he asks Sarah to get up and pray with him: "let us pray and beg our Lord to grant us mercy and protection" (8:4; see 6:18). Tobiah composes a prayer and Sarah confirms it with her Amen. The prayer is a beautiful request for a happy and holy marriage. After blessing God, Tobiah refers to the original couple, Adam and Eve. This is one of the few places in Scripture after Genesis where the two are named and it is the only place outside of the genealogies (1 Chr 1:1; Sir 49:16; Luke 3:38; Jude 14) where

there is no reference to sin (see Rom 5:14; 1 Cor 15:22, 45; 2 Cor 11:3; 1 Tim 2:13). This prayer is all about blessing, and especially the gift of a healthy and holy marriage. Tobiah ends with a prayer for God's mercy, enabling them to "grow old together." The Old Latin version adds the request to be blessed with children. In the Latin Vulgate Tobiah adds an exhortation to Sarah before the prayer that they not have intercourse for three nights (8:4, Vulg.). But this restriction does not appear in any other ancient version of the text.

Meanwhile Sarah's father Raguel has gone out to dig a grave for Tobiah. He is sure that the demon will have killed Tobiah and wants to bury him secretly so the neighbors do not mock the family. Will the neighbors not have noticed that two men came to Raguel's house and only one is left? Raguel is too distressed over his daughter's affliction to consider that complication. After he has dug the grave, Raguel asks Edna to send a maid to see if Tobiah is still alive. When the maid returns with the news that the newlyweds are sleeping peacefully, Raguel and Edna immediately begin to pray. Their prayer is a joyful song of thanksgiving to God and a petition that God will protect these two only children through long lives of happiness. Then Raguel sends the servants out to fill the unnecessary grave.

Sarah's parents do not get much sleep this night. Raguel is now ready to prepare a grand celebration. He asks Edna to do the baking and goes out himself to choose the animals to be slaughtered for the fourteen-day feast, twice as long as a normal wedding celebration. In the morning he informs Tobiah that they will spend the next two weeks rejoicing in this surprising and delightful turn of events. He claims Tobiah as his own son and Edna's and promises him half the inheritance immediately and the other half when he and Edna die. Twice he uses the phrase, "take courage," the same phrase that Edna used twice in preparing Sarah for the wedding (7:17) and that Raphael said to Tobit at their first meeting (5:10).

In the midst of all this festivity, however, there is still the matter of the money that Tobit had deposited with Gabael, the reason Tobiah thought he made the journey in the first place. Now the young man is concerned that his parents will worry about his delay. So Tobiah, who has now assumed responsibility, commissions Raphael to go to Gabael's house in Rages and collect the money. He also invites Gabael to the wedding celebration. The angel follows Tobiah's instructions and makes amazing speed in traveling to Rages, which is at least a two-day journey. Raphael tells Gabael the news and, after packing the moneybags, the two of them make haste to Ecbatana. Tobiah, ever kind and polite, leaps up to greet Gabael when he arrives and Gabael prays a blessing on the whole family (9:1-6).

PARENTS' ANXIETY; DEPARTURE FROM ECBATANA

Tobit 10

This chapter tells of the overwhelming joy of one family and the overwhelming sorrow of another. Tobiah's parents are worried sick about their son. He is late and they imagine the worst. Tobit imagines various difficulties Tobiah might have encountered, but Anna is convinced her son has died. Tobit attempts to encourage her by reminding her of the trustworthy guide that accompanies their son. The reader knows that he is quite right, but Anna will hear none of it. Their conversation echoes the sharp tone of chapter 2. He tells her to be still; she replies, "You be still!" Paradoxically, however, as she continues to declare that Tobiah is dead, she goes out every day to watch for his return. She is eating nothing and crying all night. Tobit too must be getting little food and sleep.

The situation at Raguel's house stands in direct contrast to the grief at Tobit's house. The wedding celebration has ended, but Raguel wants Tobiah and Sarah to stay in Ecbatana with him and Edna. He promises to send messengers to inform Tobiah's parents of the wedding and the whereabouts of their son. But Tobiah is a wise son; he knows his parents and knows how worried they must be. So preparations are made for the departure. The farewells are tender. Both Raguel and Edna pray blessings upon the newlyweds. They remind Sarah that Tobit and Anna are now also her parents, just as Tobiah is now their son. Raguel encourages Sarah to be good and Edna instructs Tobiah never to bring grief upon his wife. Tobiah in turn blesses his father-in-law and mother-in-law. After lengthy good-byes, he thanks God for all these gifts and sets off "full of happiness."

HOMEWARD JOURNEY AND HEALING

Tobit 11

The return journey to Nineveh is told with dispatch. What is most important now is the second healing promised by God. Sarah is free of Asmodeus and married to Tobiah; now Raphael and Tobiah are focused on the removal of Tobit's blindness. Even the dog, whose last appearance was in chapter 6 as the travelers set out, now is hurrying to get home (6:2; 11:4).

Anna, who has been watching the road every day, finally spots Tobiah in the distance. She, who has been calling Tobiah "*my* son" since he left, now says to Tobit, "Look, *your* son is coming" (11:6). She runs up to him, hugs him, and declares that now she can die! Everything she had hoped for is fulfilled. Anna never fails to express her strong emotions. Meanwhile, Tobit, having heard Anna's declaration, stumbles out of the gate. The stage is set for the second healing. A painting by the nineteenth-century artist Jean-François Millet titled *Waiting* portrays this scene poignantly. An old woman has started down the road and a blind old man stands hesitantly in the doorway.

Raphael has already instructed Tobiah about the use of the gall and the method he is to use to heal his father. But it is Tobiah who performs the action that restores Tobit's sight. Tobit is also overcome with joy and is delighted that his first vision is that of his dearly beloved son. Immediately Tobit expresses his gratitude to God, blessing God and all God's angels. He does not yet know that God has sent an angel to bring about his healing and that this angel is standing right in front of him.

Tobiah tells his father the whole story of all that has happened in Ecbatana. Tobit rushes out to meet his new daughter-in-law. His brisk stride amazes his neighbors and a crowd gathers to rejoice with him. Tobit greets Sarah with many blessings and claims her as his daughter. Then all the Jews of Nineveh join in the celebration of God's goodness in healing Tobit and Sarah. Another seven-day wedding feast follows; the newlyweds have now celebrated for twenty-one days! Ahiqar, Tobit's relative who helped him before his blindness, is among the guests along with his nephew, Nadin. A treacherous story about Nadin will soon be revealed.

RAPHAEL'S IDENTITY

Tobit 12

Tobit is now ready to wrap up the details of the journey. He has been healed of his blindness. His wife is happy again. His son has come home with a new wife. All that remains is to pay their debt to the guide who not only led Tobiah safely on the journey, but who brought him to his new wife and taught him how to heal her and his father. The money, the original purpose of the journey, has also been recovered from Gabael. How can they possibly reward this extraordinary guide? In the original agreement (Tob 5:15-16) they promised him a drachma per day, the normal daily wage, and a possible bonus. Now they decide to offer him half the ten talents that have been brought back (see 1:14). So Raphael's payment would be raised from about $1.20 per week, so presumably no more than $10 total, to almost $7,000 for the journey.

But Raphael has a surprise of his own. When they offer him this generous sum, he changes the subject. First, he gives them an instruction, which echoes Tobit's instruction to Tobiah before the journey. They are to continue to give thanks to God with all their energy and devotion. They are to proclaim their thanks before all the living. In the biblical tradition thanksgiving requires a crowd or at least another person. The Hebrew word for "thank" (*todah*) also means "praise." Thanksgiving is proclaiming to someone else how good God is. This move to gratitude is something they have been doing throughout the book and they are not to forget it now that their troubles are diminished. But even this public prayer and thanksgiving are not enough. They are also to continue to give alms to the poor and needy. This emphasis on almsgiving is characteristic not only of this book, but of second-century Jewish piety. Ben Sira emphasizes the same action, and also says that almsgiving is more valuable than gold and will "save [them] from every evil" (Sir 29:8-13; see Tob 4:7-11, 16-17; 14:2, 9-11).

The second part of Raphael's speech reveals a big surprise. He is not Azariah, one of Tobit's kinsmen (see Tob 5:13); he is Raphael, one of the seven angels who stand before God. His true name corresponds to his task; Raphael means "God heals." He was sent by God right after Tobit and Sarah prayed for relief from their anguish (3:16-17). He

is, in fact, the one who presented their prayer to God as well as Tobit's charitable deeds. But he was sent to them, not only to heal, but also to put them to the test to determine their perseverance and to strengthen their faith.

Raphael claims to be one of the seven angels standing before God. Traditionally these angels are called "archangels." Three of them are named in Scripture: Michael, who is the protector of the people (Dan 12:1; Rev 12:7-9); Gabriel, who announces the births of John the Baptist and Jesus (Luke 1:19, 26; cf. Dan 8:16; 9:21); and Raphael, who appears only here. Tradition has given us the names of four more: Uriel (or Phanuel), Raguel, Sariel, and Remuel. In the book of Revelation there are seven angels who stand before God and blow the seven trumpets (Rev 8:2-6).

Tobit and Tobiah are terrified, but Raphael encourages them with a typical angelic phrase, "Do not fear." He exhorts them again to give praise and thanks to God. Then he ascends to heaven and they can no longer see him. The scene foreshadows Jesus' ascension into heaven (Acts 1:9).

TOBIT'S SONG OF PRAISE

Tobit 13

Tobit's thanksgiving becomes an extended song of praise. The first eight verses are praise of God who both "afflicts and shows mercy" (13:2). Tobit has come to a new understanding of the Deuteronomic principle regarding prosperity and suffering. After stating this renewed principle, Tobit encourages his people, the Israelites, to thank God who, because of their sins, has afflicted them through exile but who will also have mercy on them when they turn back to God (13:3-6ab). Then he uses himself as an example, giving thanks even in captivity and rejoicing in God, "King of the ages" and "King of heaven" (13:6c-8a).

Verses 9-18 are an exultant praise addressed to Jerusalem, the holy city that has also been afflicted but will again enjoy God's mercy. Tobit hopes the temple will be rebuilt and that peoples from the ends of the earth will again come to worship God (13:9-11). He proclaims a curse against all who hate and attack the holy city (13:12). Then, he balances the curses with a series of beatitudes, proclaiming the happiness of those who love

Jerusalem and rejoice over her (13:13-14). Tobit himself blesses God and anticipates his own happiness if his descendants see the rebuilding of the temple and the renewed glory of the city (13:15-16a). Finally he sings the praises of the new Jerusalem he envisions, and closes as he began, by blessing God (13:16b-18).

EPILOGUE

Tobit 14

Tobit's long life is coming to an end, so he has one more set of instructions for his son, and now he includes his seven grandsons, a perfect number. He begins by predicting the destruction of Nineveh in 612 B.C. and the final defeat of the Assyrians by the Babylonians in 609 B.C. Tobit himself had been taken captive to Nineveh; now he foresees the end of Assyrian power and the rise of the Babylonians who will eventually destroy Jerusalem with its temple and kill many of its inhabitants (587–539 B.C.). He relies on prophetic announcements for this knowledge. Manuscripts differ regarding which prophet he is reading, however. One tradition names the prophet Nahum, who not only foretells the destruction of Nineveh but delights in the rout of this terrible enemy. The other tradition names Jonah, who announces the fall of Nineveh, but who then must endure God's forgiveness and rescue of this hated people. Nahum is the more likely candidate as the original reading, because he is clear about the fall of Nineveh.

Tobit also predicts the return from exile, which begins in 538 B.C., and the rebuilding of the Jerusalem temple, which is dedicated in 516 B.C. Echoing the Deuteronomic theory that the good will be blessed and the wicked punished, he hopes not only for this restoration, however, but envisions that "[a]ll the nations of the world" will worship God in truth and bless God in righteousness (14:6-7). The just will rejoice but the wicked will be wiped out from the land.

Tobit's advice to Tobiah, in the face of the impending disaster, is to return to Media, specifically to Ecbatana, Sarah's home. There he will be sheltered from the upheaval to the west. Tobit also reemphasizes the instructions he gave his son before the first journey to Media. He should remember to give alms, because those who are diligent in this virtue will be saved from death. He tells the story of Ahiqar and his nephew as an example. The nephew, Nadin, tries to kill Ahiqar, who is saved because he gave alms.

As is appropriate for the righteous according to Deuteronomy, Tobit lives a long life and dies at the age of 112. He lives long enough to see his predictions fulfilled and blesses God for removing the threat of the Assyrians. Just as the story began with Tobit's care for burying the dead, now Tobit is concerned that Tobiah will bury him and Anna appropriately. The faithful son carries out these instructions and then moves with his family to live with his in-laws. He cares for them in their old age and he buries them with honor as well. Finally he inherits the estates of his father and father-in-law and lives a good life to the age of 117, blessing God "forever and ever."

THE BOOK OF

JUDITH

Irene Nowell, O.S.B.

INTRODUCTION

Who is Judith? Who is the maid?

Judith is a complex character. Her name means "Jewish/Judean woman," and she acts to deliver the town of Bethulia, which means "virginity." Or is her name taken from the hero, Judas Maccabeus, who delivers the people from the threat of Antiochus Epiphanes (see 1–2 Macc)? Is she modeled on Jael, who hammered a tent peg through the head of the enemy General Sisera (Judg 4:17-22)? Or is she modeled on the earlier deliverer, David, who killed Goliath with a stone and then cut off his head (1 Sam 17:48-51)? Perhaps all of these stories form the portrayal of Judith, who saves her people from destruction at the hands of a terrible enemy.

Judith is a paradoxical character. She takes charge of the situation, assuming a man's role, but she uses feminine wiles to accomplish her task. She is described as a faithful and pious woman, yet she seems aloof from her people, unaware of their distress until it is desperate. She has a maid, who remains nameless and somewhat invisible throughout the story. Is this maid a slave, an indentured servant? Is she a Jew or a Gentile? Is it accurate that Judith "frees" her maid only at the end of her long life? If the maid is Jewish, the law demands that she be freed in the seventh year of her servitude. In any case, the maid is faithful and trustworthy. Judith could not have carried out her daring deed without the essential assistance of the maid.

Judith is not a hero, even though the Jerusalem leaders identify her as such (15:9-10). She consistently names God as the hero who saved the people; she is simply God's servant, who carries out God's plan (13:11-14; 16:5).

Judith also has a rich afterlife. Saint Jerome holds her up as an example for Paula's daughter Eustochium (Ep 22.21.8). Other patristic writers praise her highly, including Clement, Origen, Ambrose, Fulgentius, and Augustine. She becomes a type of Mary and selections from her story appeared in Catholic liturgy before Vatican II for the feasts of the Immaculate Conception and the Assumption. In the current Lectionary a selection from her introduction (8:2-8) is suggested for votive Masses for widows. Artists also delight in painting the scene of Judith's victory over Holofernes. The subjects range from the gory scene of the beheading by Artemisia Gentileschi (1611–12) to the calm and subdued scene of Botticelli's *Return of Judith to Bethulia* (ca. 1472).

Genre and date

The story of Judith is a novella, somewhat longer than a short story and shorter than a novel. The writer has made great efforts to show that this work is fictional. Historical figures are placed in the wrong time and place; historical events are deliberately combined and rearranged. The purpose of the story is not to outline historical facts but to highlight the faithfulness of God who can always be counted on to rescue the people in both ordinary and extraordinary ways.

The book is difficult to date. It was written sometime between the beginning of the Maccabean revolt against the persecution of Antiochus IV Epiphanes (167 B.C.) and the Roman capture of Jerusalem (63 B.C.).

Original language and canonical status

The book of Judith was probably written in Hebrew, although there are no surviving manuscripts in this language. It is one of the few biblical books not found among the Dead Sea Scrolls. Also it was not included in the Hebrew canon, possibly because it was written so late. Thus it is not found in English Bibles from the King James and Revised Standard traditions. It is, however, included in the Septuagint and thus is in the Catholic canon, both Roman and Greek Orthodox. It is also found in the Latin Vulgate thanks to some friends of St. Jerome. He did not intend to include the books not found in the Hebrew canon, but his bishop friends persuaded him to translate Judith and Tobit for them.

Power of prayer

The book of Judith is punctuated by prayer. As soon as the army of Holofernes threatens Bethulia, the people cry out to God and begin to fast (4:9-15). God immediately hears their prayer (4:13), but the people will not know this for many days. In the meantime Achior, expelled by Holofernes, arrives in Bethulia and describes the army's intentions. Immediately the people again turn to prayer (6:18-21). Nonetheless Holofernes besieges the city and the Israelites again cry out to God and blame their leaders (7:19, 29-30). When Judith appears, she exhorts the leaders once more to pray (8:17-26). Then she herself turns to God with a lengthy prayer (9:1-14). As she departs for the Assyrian camp, the leaders bless her and she bows to God (10:8-9). Even Holofernes praises God, mistakenly thinking God is on his side (11:22-23). Throughout her stay in the camp Judith goes out to the spring to pray with her maid every morning (12:6-8). As she prepares to behead Holofernes, Judith begs God for strength (13:4-7). Then arriving back in Bethulia she encourages the people to praise God for their deliverance (13:11-14, 17-20). The Jerusalem leaders pray a blessing over her (15:9-10). Finally Judith sings a long song of praise (16:1-17). Prayer strengthens all the Israelites. The people are losing hope, but still cling to prayer. Judith never doubts God's presence with her, but prays for courage and the ability to save her people. God hears all their prayers but answers in ways they do not expect.

The prayers are expanded in the Latin Vulgate. The elders not only encourage the people to pray, but add the example of Moses defeating the Amalekites "by holy prayers" (4:12-14, Vulg.). The prayer of the people who have heard Achior's report is also extended (6:14-18, Vulg.). When the people blame the leaders for their distress, they add a prayer of repentance for their sins and beg for mercy (7:19-22, Vulg.).

Who is God?

The central question in this book is "Who is God?" In the early chapters Nebuchadnezzar portrays himself as God, destroying all the gods of the lands he conquers and demanding that all peoples "invoke him as a god" (3:8). Later, in response to Achior's testimony about the God of the Israelites, Holofernes challenges him, "Who is God beside Nebuchadnezzar?" (6:2). For him Nebuchadnezzar is "lord of all the earth," whose words will be effective (6:4). Judith, in her prayer to the Lord, counters Nebuchadnezzar's boasting: "Make every nation and every tribe know clearly that you are God, the God of all power and might" (9:14). Holofernes ironically tells Judith that, if she does what she claims, "your God will be my God" (11:23). Little does he know that he will not have a chance to fulfill that promise. When Judith returns to Bethulia, carrying Holofernes's head, Achior "believed firmly in God," the God of Israel (14:10). In her song, Judith proclaims, "O Lord, great are you and glorious, / marvelous in power and unsurpassable" (16:13). The God of Israel is the one and only God.

COMMENTARY

NEBUCHADNEZZAR'S VICTORY AGAINST ARPHAXAD

Judith 1

This first chapter of Judith suggests that the story is about Nebuchadnezzar rather than the woman for whom the book is named. Nebuchadnezzar seems to have godly power. He summons all the inhabitants of the lands from Persia (modern-day Iran) to the Mediterranean and from the Black Sea to Egypt. When these peoples scorn him, he sets out to destroy them all. The first enemy he confronts and defeats is Arphaxad, ruler of the Medes.

The story seems to be a straightforward tale of kings and battles and greed for power, and it is about all these things. But there are hints already in this first chapter that not everything is what it seems. First of all, there are historical problems. Nebuchadnezzar ruled over Babylon, not Assyria, and his reign was from 605 B.C. to 562 B.C. By the time of his reign Nineveh, the capital of Assyria, was already gone, having been destroyed in 612 B.C. Arphaxad, named here as king of the Medes (1:1), is otherwise unknown, but it is worth noting that Assyria was conquered by the Medes and Babylonians, not the other way around.

Exaggeration also characterizes this introductory chapter. The walls Arphaxad builds to defend Ecbatana are, by our measurements, about 105 feet high and 75 feet wide. (A cubit is about 18 inches long.) The stones in the walls are 9 feet long and 4½ feet wide. The towers are 150 feet high and 90 feet wide. Remains of such massive structures would certainly be evident around the area of Ecbatana, but none have been found. The list of peoples summoned by Nebuchadnezzar is also exaggerated. It includes every group living in the Middle East, "the whole land" or "all the land" (a phrase occurring ten times in chs. 1–2). His ambitions include everything from "sea to sea," perhaps the Persian Gulf to the Mediterranean. Finally, in an echo of Artaxerxes's banquet in the book of Esther, Nebuchadnezzar holds a victory banquet lasting a third of a year (see Esth 1:4-5).

The exaggerations and the historical anomalies lead the reader to seek a different purpose for this introduction. What is the author trying to say here? First of all, it is clear that this work is not intended as a historical account, but rather a fictional tale. The confusion of dates and persons must point to another reality. So the second task of the reader is to probe the meaning of these dates and persons. The story opens with the twelfth year of Nebuchadnezzar, 593 B.C. At that time Judah is in trouble. King Jehoiakin and the leading citizens have already been exiled to Babylon. In 593 King Zedekiah, who had been put on the throne by the Babylonians, is invited to join a coalition against them but refuses. In only a few years, however, Zedekiah changes his position and Nebuchadnezzar besieges and conquers Jerusalem and takes many more people into exile.

The confusion of rulers and their territories also calls up significant events in the people's history. The Assyrians conquered the ten northern tribes, known as Israel, in 722 B.C., deported many of the people, and repopulated the territory with other conquered peoples. The Babylonians under Nebuchadnezzar took the remaining southern tribe, Judah, into exile in 587 B.C. By making Nebuchadnezzar, who was actually the ruler of the Babylonians, the ruler of the Assyrians, the author is suggesting both deportations, the worst tragedies in the people's history. The irony of Nebuchadnezzar's attempt to rule from "sea to sea" is that in the Psalms that phrase describes the rule of the ideal king (Ps 72:8).

REVENGE AGAINST THE WEST AND HOLOFERNES'S CAMPAIGNS

Judith 2

In the eighteenth year of his reign, Nebuchadnezzar constructs his plan to destroy all the peoples who had scorned him. The year is 587 B.C., the year that, in historical fact, Nebuchadnezzar destroyed Jerusalem with its holy temple and took its people into exile. It is the worst year in biblical history for God's people. The date is a warning for the reader to be prepared for disaster—but disaster for whom?

Exaggeration again characterizes the description of Nebuchadnezzar's plan. He will cover the whole land with his soldiers and fill all their watercourses with the dead. He appoints Holofernes as his army commander and commissions him to slaughter and plunder the whole land to the west.

So Holofernes sets out with a large force to destroy "all the lands of the western region" (2:19). His army is incredibly swift, marching three hundred miles in a mere three days (2:21), and amazingly successful, ravaging every people he encounters.

Throughout this chapter Nebuchadnezzar continues to be described in language usually reserved for God. He calls himself "the great king, the lord of all the earth" (2:5). Psalm 47 describes God with similar phrases: "For the LORD, the Most High, is to be feared, / the great king over all the earth" (Ps 47:3). Psalm 95 declares, "the LORD is the great God, / the great king over all gods" (Ps 95:3), and Jerusalem is called "the city of the great king" (Ps 48:3). In Psalm 97:5 "[t]he mountains melt like wax before the LORD, / before the Lord of all the earth" (see also Ps 97:9). "Fear and dread" of Holofernes, Nebuchadnezzar's army general, fall upon all the peoples of the coastland. In Deuteronomy God promises that "fear and dread" of the Israelites will fall on "the peoples everywhere under heaven" as they march into the Promised Land (Deut 2:25; see Deut 11:25; Josh 2:9).

Nebuchadnezzar declares, "as I live, and by the strength of my kingdom, what I have spoken I will accomplish by my own hand" (Jdt 2:12). But in the prophetic literature, especially at the time of the Babylonian exile, it is God who continually asserts "as I live" (Isa 49:18; Jer 22:24; 46:18; Ezek 5:11; 14:16, 18, 20; 16:48; 17:16, 19; 18:3; 20:3, 31, 33; 33:11, 27; 34:8; 35:6, 11; Zeph 2:9). Deuteronomy also exhorts the people to "observe carefully" all God's commandments (Deut 4:6; 6:25; 7:11; 15:5; 17:10, 19; 19:9; 24:8; 28:1, 13, 15; 29:8; 31:12; 32:46; see Josh 1:8; Neh 10:30; Ezek 43:11). Nebuchadnezzar commands Holofernes, "Do not disobey a single one of the orders of your lord; fulfill them exactly as I have commanded you" (Jdt 2:13).

It seems clear that Nebuchadnezzar is portrayed as a god, using divine language to declare his authority and issue his commands. In Israel's history the exodus from Egypt has been described as a battle between gods. Pharaoh has declared himself a god and YHWH is his opponent. God's people reading the story of Judith will recognize the echoes of that struggle and remember the outcome. Already there are suggestions that this "false god," Nebuchadnezzar, and his general, Holofernes, will never be able to resist the power of the God of Israel.

SUBMISSION OF VASSAL NATIONS AND ISRAEL'S PREPARATION FOR WAR

Judith 3–4

The people of the coastlands, having seen what Holofernes has done to their neighbors, now plead for peace. They offer him everything they have and twice they tell him to do what he pleases (3:2, 4). When Holofernes arrives in their territory with his armies, they welcome him with honor. Will this save them? No! Holofernes destroys their whole territory including their sacred shrines. Nebuchadnezzar must be honored as the only god; all rivals must be deposed (3:8).

Holofernes has now arrived at the edge of Judean territory and is poised to attack, but he delays for a month to restore his troops and supplies. At last we begin to recognize what this story has to do with God's people even though we have not yet met the title character. Once more we have a confusing suggestion of dates (4:2-3). The narrator reports that the people had recently returned from exile, presumably the Babylonian exile. The return from that exile was around 538 B.C., but, as has been already noted, Nebuchadnezzar ruled from 605–562 B.C. and has set out on this campaign to destroy all the nations in 587 B.C., the year the Israelites went into exile. So what the author of this story has done is to combine into one year the people's worst disaster—the deportation in 587 B.C.—and their greatest rescue by God—the return from exile in 538 B.C. So even though a terrible threat looms over them as Holofernes approaches, the reader already knows that they will be saved by God.

So the people begin to prepare for war. They notify the whole region, gather up their resources, and secure the mountain passes. Then they begin the most significant preparation: they fast and pray. They not only put on sackcloth, a sign of penitence, but they even drape the altar in sackcloth. It is as if God is a penitent too! They also remind God that their defeat would result in the profanation of God's own sacred sanctuary. God hears their prayer (4:13). Just as in the book of Tobit (Tob 3:16-17), however, the people do not yet know that God has heard them and is coming to their rescue. It will be some time before they realize that they are saved.

Their cry to God is based on age-old tradition. During their enslavement in Egypt they finally cry out to God and "God heard their moaning and God was mindful of his covenant" (Exod 2:24). Their cry sets in motion the great rescue of the exodus. In the book of Judges over and over the people sin against God and God strengthens their enemies. But when they cry out, God sends a judge to rescue them (see Judg 3:9, 15; 4:3; 6:6-7). Again and again the Psalms assert that when the people cry out, God hears: "On the day I cried out, you answered; / you strengthened my spirit" (Ps 138:3; see Ps 18:7; 22:6, 25; 30:3, 9; 34:7).

We know that God has rescued them before. We know the hope the author has given us through the confusing dates. We know that God has already heard their cry. Yet we must wait to see how God will work the wonder of saving them from this awesome military power at their gates.

ACHIOR IN THE ASSYRIAN WAR COUNCIL

Judith 5

Holofernes is astounded at the audacity of the Israelites, who are preparing to do battle with him. He summons the leaders of the peoples whom he had just recently devastated (Moab, Ammon, and the coastlands) and asks, "what sort of people is this?" His questions are revealing. It is not surprising that he asks, "How large is their force?" But the other questions suggest that Holofernes may unwittingly recognize that he is in more trouble than he realizes. "In what does their power and strength consist?" The story will reveal that their power and strength is in their faith in God. "Who [is] their king?" (5:3). It is the all-powerful God who is their king. If Holofernes heard the true answers to those questions, he would know why these people alone have refused to come out to meet him. He has finally met a power greater than his own.

The person who attempts to reveal this threat to Holofernes is the Ammonite Achior. Achior's name suggests that he is modeled on the wise teacher, Ahiqar, who appears in the book of Tobit (see commentary on Tob 1:21-22; 2:10; 11:18; 14:10), where he is clearly an Israelite. Here he is identified as the leader of the Ammonites, a people said to have descended from Lot's younger daughter (Gen 19:38) and who were enemies of Israel in the pioneer period (see Ps 83:2-8; Deut

23:4-5). Whatever his ancestry, however, Achior clearly understands both the history and the power of the Israelites. He is the ideal person to answer Holofernes's questions.

Although he names no names, Achior's recital of the history begins with Abraham, who, according to Genesis, came from Mesopotamia (Gen 11:27-31). He continues with the story of Joseph and the migration of the whole family of Jacob to Egypt (Gen 37–50). He knows the exodus-wilderness stories and the entrance of the people into the Promised Land. He even moves on to the story of the destruction of Jerusalem in the sixth century and the deportation of the people to Babylon. He ends with the news that the people have returned from exile and restored Jerusalem, possibly the temple as well. In other words, he has summarized in two paragraphs the story of God's people from around the nineteenth century B.C. to the sixth century B.C. (Note again the discrepancies with the regnal years of Nebuchadnezzar.)

But Achior knows more than the history. He also understands the theology of this people, particularly Deuteronomic theology. A major principle in the book of Deuteronomy is that if the people are obedient they will be blessed, whereas if they are disobedient they will be punished (see especially Deut 28–29). This principle is the basis of Achior's advice to Holofernes. If these people are sinning, conquering them will not be a problem. But if they are faithful to God, "their Lord and God will shield them" (Jdt 5:20-21; cf. 5:17-18). The soldiers of Holofernes and all those who heard Achior misjudge the Israelites and encourage Holofernes to attack. They expect an easy victory, but they will be greatly disappointed.

RESPONSE TO ACHIOR AND HIS ARRIVAL IN BETHULIA

Judith 6

Holofernes continues the blasphemy of exalting Nebuchadnezzar as God. He begins by challenging Achior: "Who are you" to speak against Nebuchadnezzar (6:2)? Judith will echo that challenge later in her words to the town elders: "Who are you to put God to the test . . . ?" (8:12), but she is not referring to Nebuchadnezzar but to YHWH. Holofernes clarifies his meaning by adding, "Who is God beside Nebuchadnezzar?" He calls Nebuchadnezzar the "lord of all the earth" and declares that "his words will not be in vain" (6:4). These phrases all suggest divinity. Psalm 97 asserts, "The mountains melt like wax before the LORD, / before the Lord of all the earth" (Ps 97:5; see Zech 6:5). In Isaiah 55 God declares, "So shall my word be / that goes forth from my mouth; / it shall not return to me empty, / but shall do what pleases me, / achieving the end for which I sent it" (Isa 55:11). The question, "Who is God?" continues to move the plot of this story.

Achior is to be tested by the truth of his words. He has said that the Israelites cannot be defeated if they are faithful to God. So Holofernes sends him to Bethulia to experience whatever its citizens experience. Holofernes taunts him that he should not be downcast, but ironically Holofernes is correct. Achior is much better off with the people of Bethulia than with the army of Holofernes. He is left bound at the foot of the hill in front of Bethulia where the Israelites find him. They convene the city council and question him about what is happening in Holofernes's camp. Thus he becomes an asset to Bethulia, although its people do not know that yet.

The people's first response is to turn to God in prayer. They know where their power lies, as indeed Achior has stated. They contrast their humility with the arrogance of Holofernes and his army and beg for God's mercy. Then Uzziah holds a banquet for the elders with Achior as the honored guest. The banquet is in marked contrast to the situation that will soon face the Israelites as they suffer the effects of Holofernes's siege. But on this night they have confidence in God's rescue even as they continue to pray until morning.

THE SIEGE OF BETHULIA

Judith 7

Holofernes now musters his whole army to move against the little town of Bethulia, the only place that has refused to surrender to him. His army, made up of his own forces plus those of the peoples who have joined him, consists of 182,000 soldiers, not counting the support troops. This force is only slightly larger than the number of Allied troops who landed at Normandy on D-Day, June 6, 1944. That force numbered 160,000. The extent of the encampment of Holofernes's army

is impossible to determine, since Bethulia itself appears nowhere outside the book of Judith. The locations of Balbaim and Cyamon are also unknown. The geographic data may well be an invention of the author whose intent is clearly to demonstrate that the threat against this little town is immense.

The Israelites' immediate neighbors to the south, Edomites and Moabites, as well as the generals of the coastal region suggest a plan to Holofernes by which he can conquer Bethulia without losing a single soldier. Israel's troubled history with the Edomites and Moabites goes back to the pioneer period when the people were entering the land under the direction of Joshua. The Edomites refused to allow the Israelites to go through their territory (Num 20:14-21), and the Moabite king hired the prophet Balaam to curse the Israelites, which he was unable to do (Num 22–25). Now the Edomites and Moabites advise Holofernes to weaken the people of Bethulia by cutting off their access to water. All the besieging army needs to do is wait. Holofernes agrees to the plan and the siege begins. The local armies of Edomites and Ammonites guard the springs and the hills surrounding Bethulia.

At this point in the story (7:19) the focus moves from Holofernes's camp to the town of Bethulia. As Achior warned Holofernes, the Israelites immediately turn to God. They knew, as Esther knew, that they have no help but God (Esth 14:3[C14]; 14:14[C:25]). But after thirty-four days, when they have no water and people are collapsing from thirst, they go to the elders of the city and beg them to make peace with the Assyrians. They consider themselves to be in the same situation as their ancestors in the settlement period who, when they sinned, were "sold" by God to their enemies (Judg 2:14; 3:8; 4:2; 10:7; cf. Esth 7:4). As Esther argued before Ahasuerus, it would be better to be slaves than for all the people to die (Esth 7:4). They blame Uzziah, the leader, just as their ancestors blamed Moses: "You have made us offensive to Pharaoh and his servants, putting a sword into their hands to kill us" (Exod 5:21). Uzziah pledges to do as they say, but only after waiting five more days. God now has a time limit to deliver the people.

Thirty-four days seems a strange number for the end of the people's patience. Is there more significance to this number? It is one shy of a multiple of seven, a perfect number. Does this suggest that it is not quite God's time yet? The thirty-four days also match the time of God's rescue: Judith will spend four days in the Assyrian camp and after Holofernes's death the Israelites will spend thirty days plundering that camp.

ARRIVAL OF JUDITH AND HER RESPONSE TO THE CRISIS

Judith 8

Finally, after seven chapters setting the stage, we meet the title character of this book. Her introduction is impressive. She is given a sixteen-member genealogy, tracing her ancestry all the way back to Jacob/Israel. Rarely are genealogies given for women in the Old Testament and this one is certainly the most impressive. A second bit of information concerning her identity is that her marriage was endogamous, that is, her husband was from her own clan. This practice was common in the late Old Testament period (see Tob 1:9; 4:12-13). Thirdly, she has been a widow for forty months. But she is also a rarity in this category. Widows did not generally inherit their husband's property; it went to other male members of the clan. Widows are among the most vulnerable persons in society along with Levites, resident aliens, and orphans; faithful people are exhorted to support them (see Exod 22:21-22; Deut 14:29; 24:17-21; 26:12-13; 27:19). But Judith has inherited her husband's property, and she is very wealthy. A characteristic that will become important as the story continues is that she is also very beautiful.

More important than her external characteristics, however, is her internal character. Judith is a very pious and God-fearing woman. She is faithful to the liturgical calendar of feasts and holidays, but on all other days she fasts and wears sackcloth, a penitential garment. She is highly respected in Bethulia. But she is not a shy, retiring hermit. She feels free to summon the leaders of the city and to scold them for their lack of faith. In a surprising reversal she teaches them the ways of God and warns them not to pretend to limit God's power or freedom. She reiterates the Deuteronomic theory of retribution, but asserts that she knows they have been faithful to God, so God will certainly rescue them. She warns that they themselves will be blamed if Bethulia falls and all Judea after it. Finally she gives the leaders advice:

wait for God's salvation, call on God for help, set an example for the common people, and even thank God for putting them to the test. To support her argument she recites their history, beginning with Abraham. She is a fearless woman.

Uzziah acknowledges her wisdom and her piety, but has no imagination that God will save them in any other way than by sending rain. He dismisses Judith's strength and, in effect, pats her on the head and says, "We know you are a good woman. Go home and pray for rain." But Judith has other plans that neither Uzziah nor the reader suspect. Uzziah has not realized that she has included herself with the leaders by saying, "let *us* set an example" (8:24, emphasis added). She announces that she has a plan that will astonish everyone and again gives instructions to Uzziah and the leaders to do what she says. Uzziah's time limit for God will be upheld and he will not be embarrassed. But their rescue will come in a way he cannot imagine. Judith is not a woman to be dismissed easily.

But there are also problems in this scenario. Why, when this mortal threat to the city has been going on for days, does she seem to have just heard of it? Does she not know about the lack of water? Where is she getting water? She exhorts the leaders to call upon God, but they have been doing that for days already. Is she so isolated on her rooftop that she is unaware of the terrible distress of her fellow townspeople? Has her maid not brought her any news until this day? The reader is challenged to accept these contradictions and submit to the flow of the story.

THE PRAYER OF JUDITH

Judith 9

Judith follows the accepted ritual for prayer in the postexilic period. Like Esther's uncle Mordecai, she wears sackcloth and ashes (Esth 4:1; see Esth 4:3; 1 Macc 3:47; Dan 9:3). Like Daniel and Ezra, she prays at the time of the evening offering (Ezra 9:5; Dan 9:21; 2 Chr 13:11; 1 Macc 4:50; 2 Macc 10:3; see Exod 30:8). But her prayer indicates the violence she intends to do. She begins by telling the story of her ancestor Simeon, one of Jacob's sons. When Jacob's daughter Dinah went out to visit the neighboring women, she had sexual relations with Shechem, the son of the region's leader (Gen

34). Hamor, Shechem's father, went to discuss the matter with Jacob, hoping to make peace by proposing that Shechem marry Dinah. But Dinah's full brothers, Simeon and Levi, have a more sinister plan. They demand that all the men of Hamor's clan be circumcised. Then, when the men are weakened and in pain, Simeon and Levi massacre all of them and take all their possessions including their wives and daughters. Judith speaks admiringly of their action and declares that it was God who inspired it. She will also give God credit for what she plans to do.

She describes the pride of the Assyrians and their ignorance of God's power. She echoes the song of Miriam and Moses in Exodus 15, declaring that the Assyrians think their horses and chariots will save them when, in fact, the Lord is the one "who crushes wars" (Jdt 9:7; Exod 15:1-3, 21; Ps 46:9-10; 76:4-5). She is equating this rescue of God's people with their most central event, the exodus. She gives God reasons to destroy these enemies. God must protect the holiness of the sanctuary, the place where God's name resides. God is also the protector of the lowly and weak. She names all the titles for God that she knows (9:12). She declares that no one can save her people but the Lord. She has persuaded the elders of Bethulia; now she is using everything she can in order to persuade God.

She asks for two things for herself: a strong hand and deceitful lips. She will indeed deceive Holofernes, often by telling the truth, but telling it in such a way that he misunderstands her. Her strong hand will not only kill Holofernes, but it will shame him and all the Assyrians. To be defeated by the hand of a female is the height of disgrace. To emphasize this point, she does not use the word for "woman" (*gyne*) in verse 10, but the generic word for "female" (*theleia*).

JUDITH AND HER MAID
GO OUT TO WAR

Judith 10

Now that she has completed her prayer, the most important part of her plan, Judith goes on to make other preparations for battle. Her weapons are beauty and wit (cf. Esth 15:5[D:5]); she intends to entice Holofernes and all his soldiers. Her ritual is careful and thorough, from inside to outside.

(Again it is puzzling where she got the water to bathe.) The narrator cannot stop repeating the success of her efforts. The elders are amazed at her beauty (10:7). The Assyrian guards are so impressed that they send a hundred men to escort her to Holofernes (10:14-15). All the men in the Assyrian camp are astounded at her beauty. Paradoxically they exclaim that all the men of her people should be killed since they have the power to outwit the whole world (10:19). Even Holofernes and his attendants are awestruck by her appearance (10:23). They will all soon discover to their dismay that even one Israelite woman has the power to outwit all their might!

Beauty is not Judith's only weapon. She plans carefully. She takes food that she can eat in accordance with kosher laws. She will use another religious ritual, daily purification with water, to ensure her escape route (12:7). More importantly, she takes her faithful maid, who will assist her in her plot. The maid is successful at remaining invisible. When the two women leave Bethulia and cross the valley, the men keep only Judith ("her," 10:10) in view. When the two women meet the Assyrian patrol, they take "her" into custody (10:12). The hundred men escort both women to Holofernes's tent, but the news in the camp is of "her" arrival (10:17-18). Holofernes is informed about "her" and the attendants usher "her" into the tent (10:18-20). Presumably at this point the maid remains outside the tent, but she is still unnoticed. This invisibility makes it possible for the maid to be not only a companion for Judith, but a sentinel outside Holofernes's tent.

Judith begins her strategy of deceit as soon as she meets the Assyrian patrol (10:12-13). She is not fleeing from her people. (She calls them "Hebrews," a term sometimes used by foreigners for the Israelites; see Gen 40:15; 43:32; Exod 2:6, 13.) They are not "about to be delivered up." It is the Assyrians who will be delivered up. She is not going to give Holofernes a "trustworthy report." He will not "take possession of the whole hill country," and his men will be killed and the survivors will flee for their lives. The only true sentence she utters is, "I have come to see Holofernes" (10:13).

Before Judith set out, she prostrated before God and prayed. When she is brought into the presence of Holofernes, she again falls prostrate and pays homage. Her motive, however, is far different this second time. She will do everything she can to encourage Holofernes in the misperception that he has absolute power and is the total focus of her attention.

JUDITH AND HOLOFERNES

Judith 11

When Judith comes into Holofernes's presence, he says at the beginning and end of his speech, "Take courage" (Greek *tharseo*, 11:1, 3). It is the same word that Uzziah used in encouraging the people to hold out for five more days (7:30). This word is common in the postexilic novellas. In the book of Tobit Raphael twice tells the blind Tobit to "take courage" (Tob 5:10). Sarah's mother encourages her daughter twice before her wedding with Tobiah (7:17). Sarah's father, Raguel, echoes his wife in encouraging the young people as they return to Tobiah's family (8:21). Finally Tobiah says, "Courage, father" to Tobit as he applies the fish gall that will remove his blindness (11:11). In the Greek additions to Esther, Ahasuerus revives Esther from her faint by saying, "Take courage" (Esth 15:9 [D:9]). By contrast, the word appears only four times in the rest of the Old Testament (Gen 35:17; Exod 14:13; 20:20; 1 Kgs 17:13). Courage is clearly a necessary virtue for the Jews in the late postexilic period.

Judith's conversation with Holofernes is a study in the advice a nineteenth-century poet gave: "Tell all the truth but tell it slant" (Emily Dickinson). She declares that she will "say nothing false to [her] lord." She also asserts that her lord "will not fail to achieve his designs" (11:5-6). Holofernes assumes that he is "her lord," but the reader suspects it is the Lord God. When she states that she swears by Nebuchadnezzar's life and by the power of the one who has sent Holofernes to guide all living things, the reader is certain that she has her fingers crossed behind her back. Everything she says in this first speech can be applied to the Lord God, and it is virtually certain that this is the power Judith has in mind. Judith is deceiving Holofernes, but she is doing it with a mixture of truth and falsehood and flattery. In his pride Holofernes misses the irony and this failure will bring his demise.

Judith then turns to Achior's speech and declares truly that Achior is correct about the Deu-

teronomic theory that the good are blessed and the wicked punished. But then she states falsely that the people have sinned or are planning to sin by eating forbidden food. She has no evidence that this is true and she herself is very careful to observe these same dietary laws. It is false also that she has fled from her people, but it is true that God has sent her to perform amazing deeds (11:16). It is no wonder that Holofernes is confused! Unwittingly he even begins to mix truth and falsity. He is correct that God has done well in sending Judith and that destruction will come to those who have despised the true Lord, but he is fatally wrong that the victory will come to him (11:21-22). It is true that Judith will be renowned, but false that she will live in Nebuchadnezzar's palace (11:23).

Judith is not only focused on deceiving Holofernes in this encounter. She also sets up her escape route. Having convinced the general that she is on his side, she describes her piety to him. She says truly that she is a God-fearing woman; she serves "the God of heaven night and day." So she plans to go out of the camp into the valley every night to pray (11:17). When the critical moment comes, the two women will be able to leave the Assyrian camp with no challenge. Judith is indeed wise, as Holofernes says (11:20). He is so impressed by her holiness that he promises to abandon his god and worship Judith's God if he is successful in destroying Bethulia! It becomes ever clearer that he does not know what he is saying. He will destroy the Israelites and their sanctuary and then will worship their God? Poor Holofernes is totally befuddled!

JUDITH IN THE ASSYRIAN CAMP AND AT HOLOFERNES'S TENT

Judith 12

Judith sets up a pattern for her life in the Assyrian camp that will ensure her security when she carries out her plot. She has been given a certain amount of freedom. She has her own tent and keeps her own schedule. She continues to observe the dietary laws, refusing the delicacies that Holofernes orders for her. She also goes out every night with her maid to the valley of Bethulia to purify herself and pray for wisdom to succeed in her venture. She keeps to this rhythm for four days and waits. Holofernes is also waiting. He is concerned that she will run out of the food she can eat and he has no idea how he can get more for her. She reassures him that she will have enough to last until "the Lord accomplishes by [her] hand what he has determined" (12:4). Holofernes is completely blind to what her plan is.

Judith's insistence on eating the proper food described in Leviticus (see Lev 11) is not just part of her plot. It is a common practice in the postexilic period. During the Babylonian exile, the best way the Jews had to preserve their identity was through the ritual laws. They had no temple; they had no land. But they could still keep the laws of circumcision and proper diet. Tobit insists that during the Assyrian captivity he, unlike his fellow captives, never ate the Gentile food (Tob 1:10). Esther asserts that she has not eaten at the banquets of either the king or Haman (Esth 14:17 [C:28]). During the persecution by the Syrian Antiochus IV Epiphanes, the Jews were willing even to suffer torture and martyrdom rather than eat forbidden food (1 Macc 1:62; 2 Macc 6:18-31; 7:1-2). Daniel convinces King Nebuchadnezzar of Babylon to give him and his companions only proper food (Dan 1:8-16).

By the fourth day Holofernes cannot stand it any longer. He sends his personal attendant, Bagoas, to persuade Judith to come and enjoy a meal with him. The irony continues. Holofernes calls Judith "the Hebrew woman." Does he not even know her name? He certainly does not know her intentions. He intends to seduce her, but she has already seduced him. Bagoas persuades her, the Hebrew woman, to come to Holofernes's tent and act like the Assyrian women. Her reply seems to indicate agreement, but the ambiguity again turns on the meaning of "her lord." She will never refuse her Lord and throughout her life will do "[w]hatever is pleasing to him" (12:14). She is delighted at the opportunity. She will declare to Holofernes that "today is the greatest day of [her] whole life" (12:18). Indeed it is. Her actions on this night will define her and bring her fame.

Again Judith beautifies herself and dresses up in "all her finery." One wonders how much luggage the women carried across the valley! Her maid goes ahead of her to Holofernes's tent to spread out fleece for her to recline to eat. The maid is going to have a much more significant role as the evening progresses, but Holofernes certainly does not even notice her. He is besotted by Judith's beauty and drinks far too much. His overindulgence will prove to be his undoing.

JUDITH BEHEADS HOLOFERNES AND RETURNS TO BETHULIA

Judith 13

The stage is set for the execution of Judith's plan. Holofernes is unconscious. His servants are also all asleep. Judith's maid is on the watch. The guards assume that both women will go out for prayer. Even Bagoas expects their regular predawn departure. Judith makes her final preparation by turning to God in prayer. She calls on the Lord as the "God of all might" (13:4). It is God's strength on which she depends. But she also mentions again her own hands, the hands of a woman. She reminds God that Jerusalem and this people belong to God in a special way as the divine heritage. Everything is now in readiness.

With one hand Judith takes hold of Holofernes's hair. After another prayer for strength, she takes hold of Holofernes's sword with the other hand and decapitates him. She may have been strengthened by God, but it is still a woman's hand that does the deed. It takes her two blows to cut off his head. But she is not a weak woman; she does not faint at the sight and smell of blood. With cool determination she rolls the body off the bed, takes the canopy as part of her proof, and goes out of the tent with Holofernes's head. The maid is not excitable either. Judith hands the head to the maid, who puts it in the food bag, and the two women go out toward the valley as usual for prayer. The whole action is completed calmly and quietly in a mere seven verses.

This portrayal of Judith reflects earlier biblical stories. When Deborah was judge over Israel, she predicted that Sisera, the general attacking them, would fall "into a woman's power" (Judg 4:9). And so it happened. Sisera fled to the tent of Jael, who lured him in with kind words, covered him with a rug, and then gave him milk to drink. Then this tent-dwelling woman hammered a tent peg through his head. When Barak, the general of the Israelite tribes, arrived, Jael presented him with the corpse (Judg 4:17-22). Later, when the people are threatened by their archenemy, the Philistines, David slays their champion, Goliath, with a slingshot and cuts off his head with Goliath's own sword (1 Sam 17:40-51). The figure of Judith is modeled on these earlier heroes.

Judith and her maid do not go into the valley, however. Rather they go around it and up the mountain to Bethulia. When they reach the gates, Judith cries out to the guards to open the gate and immediately gives credit to God for her success in defeating their enemy (13:10b-11). All the people gather around her and Judith strongly urges them again to give praise to God who has shattered the enemy. Judith will not claim the role of hero; she is simply God's helper in their rescue. She demonstrates her success by showing Holofernes's head and declares again that God has defeated him by the "hand of a female" (13:15). She also insists that she has not been dishonored by Holofernes, but has seduced him only by the beauty of her face.

The people follow her direction and begin to praise God. But Uzziah, who could only imagine their rescue in terms of rain, now praises Judith and declares her "blessed among women." Two other biblical women receive a similar praise, Jael in the Old Testament and Mary in the New Testament (Judg 5:24; Luke 1:42). All three women have been used by God to defeat the enemy who threatened their people. Jael defeated Sisera; Judith defeated Holofernes. Mary, through her Son, has defeated Satan. All three women have performed a "deed of hope" that "will never be forgotten" (13:19). All the people who hear Uzziah's praise of Judith respond, "Amen! Amen!"

THE PEOPLE'S VICTORY OVER THE ENEMY

Judith 14

Judith's plan is not finished, even though the people of Bethulia are already celebrating. Holofernes is dead, but the Assyrian army is still encamped outside their walls. It is not yet daybreak and the Bethulians must act quickly. Judith has one more plan of deceit. She instructs the people to hang Holofernes's head on the parapet of the wall and then to rush out of the city armed for attack. But they are not to engage the Assyrians. They are simply to wait and let the enemy see them. When the Assyrians muster for battle, they will discover that they are without a leader and will flee demoralized.

One more task remains, however, before this plan can be carried out. Achior, who has met Holofernes, must be summoned to verify that the severed head is indeed that of the Assyrian leader. In contrast to Judith and her maid, who were cool and collected at the crucial moment, Achior faints at the sight of Holofernes's head. When he is revived, he too praises Judith and calls her blessed. He also wisely realizes that every enemy of Israel will be terrified to hear her name. Then he asks Judith to retell the story, which gives the people another chance to cheer for joy. Achior is so moved by her courage and the power of God that he asks for circumcision and embraces the faith of Judith's people.

The people obey Judith's instructions, and, as planned, the Assyrians prepare for battle. They assume that they will slaughter the Israelites because of their superior numbers and weapons. But they have not yet realized the effects of Judith's trickery. Bagoas presumes she is still in Holofernes's tent, but he is shocked to find his master dead on the floor. He is even more dismayed to realize that Holofernes's head is missing, a fact that is repeated twice. The startling news does indeed demoralize the Assyrian troops and they flee in terror.

CELEBRATION OF VICTORY; PRAISE OF JUDITH

Judith 15

As the Assyrian troops flee, the Israelite soldiers attack them. But now they are not alone. All the Israelites from Galilee in the north to Jerusalem in the south and Gilead to the east come to join the battle. They drive the Assyrians even as far north as Damascus. All this military force has apparently been waiting to see the fate of Bethulia before they took action.

The report of plundering the Assyrians is equally exaggerated. The people of Bethulia first plunder the camp, then all the soldiers who returned from the slaughter. Towns and villages all around take their share. They spend thirty days gathering up the plunder. It seems the whole country is enriched with the goods in the Assyrian camp. Judith too gets her share of the goods, everything of value that was in Holofernes's tent. Ever resourceful, she hitches up her mule cart and takes the bounty home. She is now even more wealthy than before. The description is amazing. Why was all this wealth in the camp of a besieging army? Did they leave nothing behind for Nebuchadnezzar? The point seems to be that the Assyrians are totally defeated and the Israelites now totally secure.

The celebration is not only about riches, however. The officials from Jerusalem come to see what has happened and to congratulate Judith. They sing another blessing over her and all the people respond with their Amen. These leaders also note that the victory was won by the hand of Judith. Their blessing is now sung for feasts of the Blessed Virgin Mary, another woman who contributed to the salvation of her people.

Finally, in the tradition of holy war, the women perform the victory dance. The tradition begins with Miriam, who leads all the women in celebrating God's deliverance of the people at the Reed Sea (Exod 15). A more tragic example is that of Jephthah's daughter, who, not knowing that her father had promised to give thanks by sacrificing the first living thing that came out of his house, rushes out with song and dance to celebrate his victory over the Ammonites (Judg 11:34). There is no thought of tragedy in Judith's victory dance, however. All the women crown themselves with olive leaves, while even the men join in the singing. The words of Judith's song follow in the next chapter.

JUDITH'S THANKSGIVING SONG

Judith 16:1-17

Judith's song is modeled on the songs of thanksgiving in the book of Psalms. This form is more fluid than the lament or the hymn, but there are some standard elements that appear frequently. Often the grateful person turns first to God with thanksgiving and then gathers a crowd and tells the story of rescue. Gathering a crowd is described at the end of chapter 15. Judith's song then begins like a hymn, with a call to everyone to sing praise (16:1; cf. Ps 33:3; 96:1; 98:1; 147:7; 149:1; 150:5) and an announcement of the reasons for praise (16:2; cf. Ps 46:9-10). The reasons for praise, which lead into the formal thanksgiving, echo David's song of thanksgiving when he had been rescued from Saul (2 Sam 22:4; Ps 18:4).

The story of rescue begins in verse 3. In order to show how great God's deliverance was, the distress is described in exaggerated terms, balancing the description of Holofernes's force in the opening chapters (16:3-4; cf. 2:4-18; 7:1-3). The rescue is equally dramatic (16:5-12). First of all, Judith describes herself and how God worked through her. The enemy is destroyed "by the hand of a female," a great humiliation. The point is driven home by naming possible foes of great strength, Titans and giants. However, it was not power that overcame Holofernes, but the beauty of a woman. Judith has prepared for battle by beautifying herself, and God has worked through that beauty. After the lavish description of her loveliness, the brutality of the final line is a shock: "the sword cut through his neck!" (16:9).

The Persians and Medes are a surprise (16:10). Nebuchadnezzar has been introduced as the king of the Assyrians, and Holofernes is the general of the Assyrian army (1:1, 7, 11; 2:1, 4; 4:1). It is the Assyrian army that has besieged Bethulia (7:17; 8:9; 9:7) and that has now fled before the people of Bethulia (14:3, 19; 15:1-6). Historically, Nebuchadnezzar was king of the Babylonians, who destroyed Jerusalem in 587 B.C. and took its people into exile. The Babylonian empire was later defeated by a coalition of Persians and Medes under Cyrus, king of Persia. It is Cyrus who in 538 B.C. allowed the Jews to return home from the Babylonian exile. The author of this story of Judith is again gathering every possible threat against Judah and Israel to show how great God's rescue was. As the wisdom literature continually asserts, God works through the lowly and the humble to defeat the strong (16:11-12; cf. Sir 10:14-15).

Judith now returns to a song of praise, speaking again to God, who is great and glorious and powerful (16:13-15; cf. Ps 21:6; 66:2; 118:14). God is the one who created everything by the word, filling creatures with the divine spirit (see Gen 1:3, 6, 9, 11, 14, 20, 24, 26; Gen 2:7; Ps 33:9; 104:30; 148:5). God's word is so powerful that even the "mountains melt like wax" (Ps 97:5; cf. Mic 1:3-4). Those who fear the Lord, however, will be exalted and treated with mercy (cf. Ps 31:20; 33:18; 34:8, 10; 40:4; 103:13; 115:11). Fear of the Lord is awe at God's greatness and God's compassion. It is a spirit of wonder at all God's goodness and a dread of ever offending God. Fear of the Lord is the way to everything good (Sir 1:11-30). The song of thanksgiving often concludes with a pilgrimage to the sanctuary to offer sacrifice to God. In Judith's hymn the fear of the Lord is described as even better than sacrifice (16:16). But the ritual offering will be performed as soon as the song is over (16:18).

Judith's song ends with a woe (16:17). In this final verse there is a suggestion of belief in life after death. There will be punishment for the enemies of God's people on the "day of judgment." The punishment will include "fire and worms," a description of hell. Their suffering will last "forever." This signals a transition from the idea that all human beings, good and bad, went to Sheol when they died, to a belief that the good went to heaven and the bad to hell. Sheol was not a place of punishment; rather it was more like our earlier concept of limbo. But once the belief in everlasting life developed, Sheol was transformed into hell. This transition is illustrated in the book of Sirach. The Hebrew version, from the original author, says, "More and more, humble your pride; / what awaits mortals is worms" (Sir 7:17). The grandson's translation into Greek, however, says, "Humble yourself to the utmost, / for the punishment of the ungodly is fire and worms" (Sir 7:17, NRSV). The grandfather thought everyone went to Sheol; the grandson believed that only the "ungodly" went there, and that it was now a place of suffering and fire. The author of Judith's song agrees with the grandson.

HAPPILY EVER AFTER

Judith 16:18-25

After the song, the people go to Jerusalem to worship God. Those who had touched the dead body of Holofernes must spend seven days being purified according to the Torah legislation (Num 19:11-13). Then they offer three types of sacrifice: burnt offerings, which are wholly offered to God (Lev 1; 6:1-6); voluntary offerings, which must be eaten within two days (Lev 7:16); and various donations. Deuteronomy remarks that, in the context of the feast of Weeks, voluntary offerings should be "in proportion to the blessing" the Lord has granted (Deut 16:10). The people of Bethulia must be making very generous offerings, since their blessing is nothing short of rescue from certain death. Their joy is evident in the length of time of the celebration: three months!

Judith also donates all Holofernes's things and puts his canopy under the ban. This "ban" is part of the restrictions of holy war in Israel's early history. The people are not to profit from making war; whatever spoils they take are "doomed" (Hebrew *herem*) or put under the ban. In the pioneer period, if the defeated people were not residents of the Promised Land, a share of the spoils was donated to the sanctuary for sacrifice or for the support of the priests and Levites, and the rest could be shared among the people (see Num 18:14; 31:9-12, 25-47; but compare Deut 20:10-15).

When the celebration is over, Judith returns to her estate and lives in relative seclusion. Before she died she made arrangements to distribute her wealth to her own family and to her in-laws. She also set her maid free, but it is not clear when this happens. Is it immediately? Is it an instruction to be followed at the end of her life? Perhaps the maid continued to live with her until she died at the ripe old age of 105. Throughout her life she, like the judges before her, was a protection for the Israelites (cf. Judg 3:11, 30; 5:31; 8:28). At her death the people mourned her for the customary period of seven days (cf. Sir 22:12a).

THE BOOK OF
ESTHER

Irene Nowell, O.S.B.

INTRODUCTION

See "The Festival Scrolls" on page 254.

The book of Esther tells the story of a Jewish woman and her uncle who, by their courage and wit, deliver the Jews from threatened genocide. The drama and humor of the story, which is characterized by exaggeration and irony, is appreciated best when the book is read aloud. Esther, one of the Megilloth ("scrolls"; see introduction to the Festival Scrolls on pages 425–26), is known in Jewish tradition as the Megillah, *the* Scroll.

Versions and canonicity

The book of Esther has come to us in Hebrew and Greek versions. The Greek version is a free translation of the Hebrew but with some significant differences. The major difference is found in the six additions, lettered A–F in the NABRE. In the Hebrew version, probably closest to the original, God is never mentioned, nor is the covenant or the observance of the law or customs regarding diet and marriage. The primary festivals—Passover, Pentecost, and Booths—are missing; the only festival that appears is Purim. The silence about faith is remedied in the Greek version: God is mentioned by name or title over fifty times (in the additions but also in the main text); addition C presents the prayers of Mordecai and Esther, and Esther bemoans her marriage to a Gentile. Addition D heightens the drama as Esther risks

her life for her people. Additions B and E are supposed copies of official decrees. Additions A and F set an apocalyptic tone with the description of a dream and its interpretation. The reader will discover that the story has a different emphasis in the two versions. In the Hebrew version Esther and Mordecai are the heroes; in the Greek version God is the hero. In the Hebrew version the focus is on the deliverance of the Jews and the establishment of Purim; in the Greek version the focus is on God's work through Esther.

The Hebrew version is accepted as canonical in the Jewish and Protestant traditions; the Greek version is canonical in the Roman Catholic and Orthodox traditions. The NABRE translation represents the Hebrew version with the Greek additions.

History or fiction

The background of the story is the reign of the Persian king Xerxes the Great (485–465 B.C.). The representation of fifth-century Persia and the court seems to be accurate, judging by the descriptions of the contemporary Greek historian Herodotus. Details such as court customs, the efficient postal system, the winter court at Susa, as well as several Persian loan words in the text, give a sense of historicity to the book. Other elements, however, indicate the fictional character of the story: Persian kings could choose queens from only seven noble families and Xerxes' queen was

441

named Amestris. The official language of Persia was Aramaic, and it is unlikely that decrees would be sent out in "all languages." Exaggerations such as the six-month feast and the over-reaction to Vashti's refusal also show the work of a master storyteller, as do ironic details such as Haman's execution on the very scaffold he prepared for Mordecai.

Structure

The book is carefully structured. The dream (add. A) is balanced by its interpretation (add. F). The banquets of the king and queen in chapter 1 are balanced by Esther's two banquets in chapters 5 and 7. The decree authorizing the annihilation of the Jews (ch. 3 and add. B) is balanced by the decree authorizing the Jews to kill their enemies (ch. 8 and add. E). The prayers of Mordecai and Esther and Esther's approach to the king are at the center of the book (adds. C–D).

Purim

The establishment of the festival of Purim as the celebration of deliverance is described in 9:20-32. The name is derived from the Babylonian word for "lot," *puru*. Its observance is characterized by feasting and gift giving. The story of Esther is told (and dramatized) with much cheering and jeering. The Talmud suggests drinking to the point that one can no longer distinguish between "Blessed be Mordecai" and "Cursed be Haman." The secular nature of the celebration may indicate its non-Jewish origins, possibly a festival marking the Persian New Year.

COMMENTARY

PROLOGUE

Esther A:1-17

A:1-11 Dream of Mordecai

The story of Esther begins with a prelude, the first of the Greek additions. (Much of the material here, with some differences, is also found in 2:5-6, 19-23 of the Hebrew version.) In the NABRE the name of the king (see Introduction) has been rendered throughout as "Ahasuerus," although in the Greek additions he is called "Artaxerxes." The first paragraph sets the stage. The time is the second regnal year of Ahasuerus, thus a year before the events of the first chapter of the Hebrew story (see 1:3). The date is the first of Nisan, the first month of the Jewish year, two weeks before Passover (see Exod 12:6). Mordecai, one of the two main characters, is introduced with a four-member genealogy that associates him with Saul, son of Kish (1 Sam 9:1). This relationship will prove significant. Mordecai is an exile, supposedly part of the first deportation under Nebuchadnezzar (see 2 Kgs 24:10-12). The place is Susa in Persia.

Mordecai has a dream full of apocalyptic imagery: dragons, darkness, total war (A:4-11). The message of the dream is also typical of apocalyptic worldview: "the nation of the just" is threatened with mortal danger but God saves them. The beginning of their salvation is symbolized by a mighty river that rises from a tiny spring. Mordecai cannot understand the dream; neither can we. It will be explained at the end of the story in addition F.

A:12-17 Mordecai thwarts an assassination

Mordecai's service to the king extends to saving his life. The consequence of his action is twofold: the king gives him a court appointment and Haman becomes his mortal enemy. Was Haman in on the plot? In any case, he is already portrayed as a villain. Both the king and Mordecai write down an account. These events lead to the major action of the story.

ESTHER BECOMES QUEEN

Esther 1:1–2:23

1:1-9 The banquet of Ahasuerus

The Hebrew version of the story also opens with significant information concerning the situation and themes of the book. The king is again identified by name and a description of his power is given. While it is true that the empire of Xerxes stretched from India to Ethiopia, the number of governmental divisions (satrapies) is usually given as about 30, not 120. The court is in Susa, the winter capital. The Greek historian Xenophon describes the unbearable heat of Susa in the summer. Other royal cities were Babylon, Ecbatana, and Persepolis. The time is the third year of the king's reign, thus a year after the events of addition A. The setting is a lavish royal banquet. The exaggeration that characterizes the whole book is evident here. All the important people of the whole realm are present for half a year (180 days). The king displays the extraordinary wealth of his palace and kingdom. The furnishings and the table service are lush! The Greek historian Herodotus reports on the extravagance of Persian drinking bouts, and this festivity is no exception. By the king's order everyone is to be given as much to drink as he desires.

Actually three banquets are described in this chapter: the 180-day banquet for all the prominent people of the kingdom (1:3-4); the seven-day banquet for the citizens of the royal district of Susa (1:5); and the banquet for the women given by the queen (1:9). The first banquet raises the question: "Who is minding the kingdom while all these officials are partying?" The third banquet makes it clear that the participants in the king's banquet are all men. It is also worth noting that the Hebrew word for banquet, *mishteh*, is derived from the word meaning "drink."

1:10-22 Refusal of Vashti

The first crisis emerges at the end of the king's second banquet. He already showed off all his glorious wealth; now, happily drunk, he wants to show off the beauty of his queen. Vashti is to come in all her finery, wearing the royal crown. He sends seven eunuchs to bring her from her banquet to his. The eunuchs are literally the middlemen who pass freely from the men's area of the court to the women's. But Vashti will not come! Does she refuse simply because she will not demean herself (and him) by appearing before a roomful of drunken men? Is she too busy with her own party? The narrator does not reveal the reason.

The consequence, however, is clear. The king is furious. The rest of the scene reveals the character of the king and of his advisors (1:13-22). The king does not know what to do, so he confers with his lawyers and advisors. Several times throughout the story this king will not know what to do. One of his major advisors escalates the problem to the whole kingdom: Since Vashti has disobeyed the king, all the women of the province will disobey their husbands (1:17)! Vashti is banished from the king's presence (perhaps to her delight?) and one "better than she" will be chosen. (This raises the question of how Esther will be "better": more compliant, more beautiful?) The king is persuaded to issue an irrevocable decree that all wives will honor their husbands! A place is now opened for Esther to become queen. The decree is sent by the efficient postal service of the Persians (1:22). Throughout the book local problems will escalate to a national level. More irrevocable decrees will appear with sweeping demands on the population, and this amazing postal service will be used again.

In Memucan's suggestion concerning the deposing of Vashti, he says that the royal dignity will be taken from her and given to a neighbor who is better than she (1:19). The phrase echoes what Samuel says to Saul in the controversy over Agag (1 Sam 15:28; see commentary on 3:1-4).

Several elements indicate the comic and farcical nature of this story: the exaggeration, the impossible decree, the playing with numbers. On the seventh day of the banquet seven eunuchs are sent to bring the queen; when she refuses, the king consults seven advisors. Seven is the number for completion. The king's response to his wife's disobedience—sending a decree that all wives shall obey—is ironic to say the least. The pervasive exaggeration makes the Persian court an object of ridicule.

2:1-15 The search for a new queen

The king has a dilemma; he remembers Vashti and what happened but, because of the irrevocable decree, he has no solution (2:1). This king needs advice for all his decisions! His servants suggest a roundup (what else could it be called?) of *all* the beautiful young virgins of the kingdom to find a woman "better than" Vashti (2:2-4). Many stories of such gatherings of women to please a potentate exist; perhaps the most familiar is found in the *Arabian Nights*. The fictional nature of this story is again indicated since by law Persian kings had to choose their queens from specific noble families.

The flow of the story is interrupted by the introduction of "Mordecai the Jew" (2:5-7; see A:1-3) The wording is virtually identical to the introduction of Saul in 1 Samuel 9:1; the ancestry of Mordecai also links him to Saul. The impossibility of his deportation in 597 B.C. is one of many indications that this is not a historical narrative. Xerxes began to reign in 485 B.C., so Mordecai would now be over one hundred and Esther would be in her sixties. The mention of the deportation in 597 rather than the one in 587, however, indicates that Mordecai belonged to a noble family (compare 2 Kgs 24:14-16 with 25:11-12). Esther is also introduced here (2:7). The only details are that she is orphaned and beautiful. The names Mordecai and Esther may be from the Mesopotamian gods Marduk and Ishtar. Each of them probably also has a Jewish name (see Dan 1:7) although only Esther's is given: Hadassah, meaning "myrtle."

The process of preparing the gathered virgins for the king's enjoyment is thorough and complex (2:8-15): a year of massages with aromatic oils and instructions regarding cosmetics and perfumes. Already Esther stands out: she gains the favor of Hegai (2:9) and of everyone else (2:15), presumably even the other young women! In one respect she is certainly "better" than Vashti: she is almost too compliant! She obeys Mordecai and does not reveal her Jewishness; she relies solely on Hegai's advice regarding what she should take with her for her night with the king.

2:16-18 Ahasuerus chooses Esther

Esther is taken to the king in the seventh year of his reign (another seven!), thus four years after Vashti's banishment. She not only pleases him and gains his favor, she wins his love. The word "love" to describe the relationship between a man and a woman appears only here (2:17). Ahasuerus crowns her as Vashti's replacement (with the crown Vashti was supposed to wear? see 1:11) and holds yet another great banquet.

2:19-23 Mordecai thwarts an assassination

But all is not well in the kingdom. Mordecai, who may be at the gate because he holds an official position (see commentary on Ruth 4:1), discovers a plot to assassinate the king (see A:12-15). He sends word to the king through Esther and the plotters are executed in a manner common in

Persia. Questions arise: Why must Esther not reveal her Jewish origins? Is there a fear of anti-Jewish sentiment? Why does Esther's association with Mordecai not give away the secret? Why is Mordecai not rewarded? The plot demands that these not be answered here. Esther must not be known as a Jew; otherwise Haman's villainy would not be possible. Mordecai's reward must wait until it exposes Haman's ambition.

HAMAN'S PLOT AGAINST THE JEWS
Esther 3:1-15; B:1-7

3:1-4 Mordecai refuses to honor Haman

After Mordecai saves the king, the reader expects him to be raised to a high position. Instead another man, Haman, is promoted. This promotion precipitates the crisis: Mordecai will not bow down to Haman. Why? The text does not reveal the reason, but several possibilities have been proposed: (1) Mordecai is arrogant; (2) he will bow to no one except God; (3) Mordecai will not bow to Haman because he is an Agagite; or (4) he refuses because Haman was part of the plot to assassinate Ahasuerus. The first two suggestions are not likely. Nowhere else in the story is Mordecai portrayed as arrogant; even when he saves the king's life he is self-effacing. Mordecai must already be in the habit of bowing to the king; otherwise he would have been noticed before this. However, compare C:7! The other two suggestions are more plausible. The Amalekites have been under a curse since they refused to let the Israelites pass through on their way to the Promised Land (Deut 25:17-19; see Exod 17:14). Saul, son of Kish, lost his throne because he failed to wipe out the Amalekites and kill Agag, their king (1 Sam 15:20-26). Mordecai is identified as a Benjaminite like Saul and a descendant of Kish. So it is no surprise that there would be mortal hatred between Haman and Mordecai. If the Greek additions are taken into consideration, there is enmity between them because Mordecai foiled the assassination plot (see A:17).

3:5-7 Haman's reprisal

Haman apparently does not notice Mordecai's refusal to bow until the other officials bring it to his attention (3:4). Then, just as Ahasuerus was enraged at Vashti's refusal, Haman is filled with anger. Ahasuerus responds to Vashti by issuing a decree regarding *all* women. Haman now plans a decree regarding *all* Jews (3:6). But whereas the response of Ahasuerus seemed ridiculous, Haman's plan is murderous.

Haman has lots cast, presumably to determine the most propitious date for the annihilation of the Jews. Verse 7, possibly a later insertion in the text, provides two critical bits of information. The "lot" is called *pur* from the Babylonian word *puru*. This provides an explanation of the name for the feast that the Jews will establish to celebrate their deliverance: Purim. The day on which the lot fell, the thirteenth of Adar, establishes the date for the proposed annihilation but will actually determine the date for the celebration (see 9:24-28).

3:8-15 Decree against the Jews

Just as Memucan proposed a solution to Ahasuerus regarding Vashti, Haman proposes a solution to the king regarding the slight to his own honor. The solution, however, is cleverly disguised so it seems that it is the king whose honor is being injured. He describes an unnamed people who are (1) dispersed throughout the kingdom but (2) distinct because of their own laws and customs. Then he accuses them of (3) refusing to obey the king's laws (3:8). The accusation is equivalent to treason. Haman begins with the truth, but his subtle move to untruth plants unwarranted suspicion in the king's mind. Haman concludes that the king must not tolerate these people but should have them destroyed (3:9). But before the king can respond, Haman offers ten thousand silver talents! This amount represents about two-thirds of the gross national product of Persia! It would seem that Haman is working for his own interests, not those of the king! It may also be true that the money convinces the king better than the argument does. The king authorizes Haman to do what he wishes with the people and hands over the signet ring to seal the decree in the king's name (3:10; see Joseph in Gen 41:42). Ahasuerus seems to refuse the money, but this may simply be Middle Eastern bargaining—saying "no" while accepting payment (3:11).

The letters, dictated to scribes by Haman and sealed with the signet ring, are sent throughout the kingdom by the efficient Persian postal service (3:12-15). The summary is brutal: "to destroy, kill, and annihilate *all* the Jews, young and old, includ-

ing women and children" (emphasis added). There is to be no mercy. *All* the people of the realm are to be prepared for that set day (3:14). The final sentence reveals the heartlessness of the king and Haman, who sit down to drink while the city of Susa is thrown into confusion (3:15). Greek historians say that the Persians either made or reconsidered decrees while they were drunk. The city of Susa refers to the city outside the royal precinct proper. Does the confusion indicate that the citizens are shocked at this command to slaughter their neighbors?

B:1-7 A copy of the letter

In the Septuagint a supposed copy of the letter interrupts the chapter between verses 13 and 14. (Compare the letters in Ezra 4:11-22; 7:11-26.) This addition, in contrast to addition A, was almost certainly written in Greek, not translated from an earlier Hebrew text. Ahasuerus is called the "great King," a title of Xerxes (see Introduction). The king is presented as acting in the best interests of the people. He is dependent particularly upon Haman, who "excels . . . in discretion" and is "outstanding for constant good will and steadfast loyalty" (B:3). This fulsome praise, which contradicts what is known of Haman from the rest of the story, reminds the reader that Haman himself dictated the letter! The description of the Jews (B:4-5) is even more damning than Haman's words to the king (3:8). The date set for their annihilation (without mercy) is the fourteenth of Adar, a day later than the date set in the Hebrew text. The author may have been confused by the fact that the celebration of Purim is a day later than the proposed slaughter.

ESTHER AND MORDECAI PLEAD FOR HELP

Esther 4:1–5a; C:1–D:16

4:1-17 Mordecai exhorts Esther

This chapter presents a dialogue between Mordecai and Esther through the intermediaries of her servants, especially the eunuch Hathach. Mordecai opens the conversation by not only exhibiting the traditional signs of mourning—torn garments, wearing of sackcloth and ashes—but by doing this at the very threshold of the royal gate. He is inches away from disobeying a royal law (4:2). His actions are reported to Esther, who is horrified. Is she afraid he will violate the law? Is she embarrassed by his behavior? In any case, she, secluded in the harem, does not know of the decree against the Jews (4:5).

Esther first sends clothes, but Mordecai refuses (4:4). Then she sends Hathach to discover the reason for his risky actions. Hathach returns with detailed information: a copy of the decree and a report of the exact amount Haman promised to pay Ahasuerus (4:7-9). Mordecai also sends instructions to Esther to plead with the king for the Jews.

Hathach carries Esther's reply. The use of "know" is ironic. Mordecai learned ("came to know") all that was happening (4:1), but Esther did not know! She sent Hathach to find out (4:5). Now Esther tells Mordecai what everyone knows (4:11): to go to the king unbidden means certain death! Mordecai wins this interchange, however: "Who knows—perhaps it was for a time like this that you became queen?" (4:14)! It must be observed that through all this the servants (at least Hathach) know everything!

The Persian law that anyone who approaches the king without being summoned is subject to death is confirmed by the Greek historian Herodotus. But Herodotus also reports that it was possible to request an audience with the king. Somehow Esther had managed to get word to the king earlier concerning the assassination plot (2:22). The story is enhanced, however, by the queen risking her life.

Mordecai points out two significant things: Esther will not escape death by keeping silent; if she does not respond, help will come from another source (4:13-14). She will not escape death because either Haman will find her out or the Jews who are saved will take vengeance on her as one of the perpetrators of the violence. This is a no-win situation. The other "source" from which help will come has often been interpreted as God (clearly so in the Septuagint, the Greek version of the Old Testament). God's help, however, may be indirect, perhaps through another palace coup. In any case, Mordecai has faith that the Jews will be delivered.

The crisis leads Esther to a transformation. She is faced with several life-threatening choices. She can choose to identify with the Persians and escape recognition as a Jew. She can choose to identify with the Jews and risk her life by going to the

king to plead for them. She cannot, as Mordecai has pointed out, refuse to choose at all. At this point the woman who has obeyed every command given to her begins to issue commands. She commands Hathach (4:5) and Mordecai through Hathach (4:10). Now she sends Mordecai both her acceptance of his challenge and her instructions to him (4:16). She will risk her life, but everyone else must fast for three days on her behalf. (It is difficult not to see a request for prayer here!) Mordecai now obeys Esther, doing exactly what she has commanded (4:17). In later Jewish tradition there is observance of the Fast of Esther on the day before Purim.

C:1-11 Prayer of Mordecai

This addition from the Septuagint makes explicit what is never found in the Hebrew text of Esther: the main characters pray. Their prayer also reveals the theology and preoccupations of the Jewish people in the late second–early first century B.C.

Mordecai not only calls the Jews to fast but also pleads with God to save them. The structure of his prayer is simple and traditional: praise of God (C:2-4), description/defense of his own situation (C:5-7), plea for God's help (C:8-10). Mordecai consistently uses the title "Lord" for God (eight times, plus two in the introduction), reflecting the privileged personal name of God revealed to Moses, Yhwh. He praises God's power in creation and in history and God's knowledge of all things. No one can resist God; no one knows all that God knows. In the middle section Mordecai defends his actions and gives a clear reason for his refusal to bow down to Haman: he will only bow down to God. (This contradicts the reality of the Hebrew story where Esther bows to the king in 8:3 and Mordecai surely does also.) In his plea to God Mordecai points out that it is in God's own interests to help the people: *your* people, *your* inheritance, *your* portion, redeemed for *yourself*, praise to *your* name. This line of persuasion is typical of biblical prayer (see Exod 32:11; Ps 74:1-2; 79:12-13).

C:12-30 Prayer of Esther

Esther too prays (compare Jdt 9). She identifies with her people (not the Persians) who are wearing sackcloth and ashes (see 4:3). She too cries to God as "Lord" (eight times, plus one in the introduction). She prays for her people and speaks a communal confession: we have sinned; we worshiped their gods (C:17-18). She also prays for herself. Twice she declares that she is alone and only God can help her (C:14, 25). She begs for courage (C:23, 30). Her description/defense of her own situation (C:26-29) illustrates the concerns of second-century Judaism: prohibition of marriage with non-Jews (see Neh 13:23-27) and dietary laws (see Dan 1:8-16). (Neither of these customs seems to be a problem in the Hebrew form of the story.) Esther's persuasion of God takes the form of remembering God's former acts of love and salvation (C:16) with the implication: "You saved us once; do it again!" (see Ps 77:11-13). She too declares that saving the people is in God's best interests: these enemies want to turn God's own people to praise of other gods and to lead them to honor a mortal king rather than the Lord who alone is their king (C:20). The enemy now seems to be all Gentiles and their false worship; there is only a suggestion of the threat of genocide. Her final sentence reveals the depth of her anguish.

D:1-16; 5:1-5a Esther goes to Ahasuerus

The Hebrew text gives a straightforward account of Esther's approach to the king (5:1-2). She is literally clothed in royalty, the same royalty that Mordecai suggested was given her for just this purpose. With dignity she stands in the courtyard; she does not bow. She waits—for death or the king's invitation. He spies her and grants permission to approach by extending the royal scepter. The Greek addition D dramatizes the story, emphasizing Esther's courage in the face of mortal danger and God's rescue of her. God's presence is evident throughout the chapter. Esther has finished her long prayer but perhaps makes another short one (D:2). God changes the heart of the king from anger to gentleness when she approaches (D:8). Esther is both radiant and terrified (D:5). She goes all the way into the throne room, passing through "all the portals." Thus she has apparently defied the law, although the king later says that she is exempt. In her terror, she faints—twice (D:7, 15)! (But remember, she has been fasting for three days.) As for the king, his rage has been seen several times, but this is the first time that he appears truly regal. Interestingly, when he is majestic he is compassionate. Esther describes him as others described David: like an angel of God (D:13; see 2 Sam 14:17, 20). He describes himself simply as

Esther's brother, a typical term for husband (D:9; see Song 4:9-12; Tob 7:11).

The reader expects Esther to plead for the lives of her people. The king has offered half his kingdom (5:3). Instead she invites the king and Haman to a banquet! Banquets have been critical occasions in this story. What will happen now? The delay contributes to the narrative tension. Ironically the king instructs Haman to make haste to fulfill whatever Esther wishes. Neither the king nor Haman knows what Esther really wants!

HAMAN'S DOWNFALL

Esther 5:5b–8:2

5:5b-8 First banquet of Esther

The question of Esther's request appears again at the banquet. Its importance is signaled by the threefold repetition of the double phrase: "ask/petition" and "request" (5:6, 7, 8; see 7:2-3). Again the king promises half the kingdom. Esther seems about to make her petition and request, but then she stops and instead invites the two guests to a second banquet. At the second banquet, she promises, she will reveal her petition and request. Why the second delay? It seems risky! Haman may discover her relationship to Mordecai; the king may change his mind about granting her request. Perhaps she wishes to increase the king's curiosity; perhaps his repeated offer of half the kingdom will shame him into granting her request whether he wants to or not. Perhaps she is securing the trap against Haman, lulling him into a proud security and suggesting to the king, ever so subtly, that she regards Haman as his equal. In any case, the reader's suspense is heightened.

5:9-14 Haman's plot against Mordecai

This section is framed by the image of Haman happy and in good spirits (5:9, 14). By contrast, Haman's mood is dark throughout the rest of the verses. Mordecai has great power over Haman rather than the reverse. Mordecai, now threatened with death, refuses to cower in Haman's presence. Not only does he not bow, he will not even stand (5:9)! Haman is enraged by this man who still sits at the gate! Like the king, however, Haman needs advice on how to deal with his rage. He calls his friends and his wife and begins by describing, not his troubles with Mordecai, but his own greatness

(5:10-12). His wounded pride really needs comfort! When he finally admits that Mordecai is ruining his life, his wife and friends make an outlandish suggestion: Set up a stake seventy-five feet high (5:14). The stake will be higher than the palace. Haman will look as foolish as Ahasuerus did in chapter 1. The stake will be ready, so that Mordecai can be impaled on it as soon as Ahasuerus gives permission. Thus the king cannot change his mind! The end of the chapter is reminiscent of the end of chapter 3. After arranging for the execution, Haman can go to the party in good spirits.

6:1-13 Mordecai's reward from the king

In this chapter the comic nature of the story is stunningly evident. The irony (where the audience knows more than the characters) is rich and reversals of fortune are everywhere. The king cannot sleep. Why? Has he eaten or drunk too much at Esther's banquet? Is he plagued by curiosity regarding Esther's request? Is he nervous that Esther keeps honoring Haman? Perhaps there is no reason except narrative necessity—or the providence of God hidden in the events. Also, apparently by chance, the particular passage from the chronicles that is read to him is the story of Mordecai's saving his life (6:1-2). The king's desire to honor Mordecai (belatedly) sets up the rest of the chapter.

This king will do nothing without advice, so he asks for anyone who might be present in the court (6:4). It seems that Haman has not slept much either, for it must be very early in the morning. Both Haman and the king have something to ask. The king asks first. Just as Haman did not reveal the name of the people who were to be annihilated, so the king does not reveal the name of his intended honoree. This creates the opportunity for Haman to arrange his own undoing.

The key phrase, "the man whom the king wishes to honor," occurs four times. The king introduces it (6:6). Haman assumes it refers to himself (6:6). He uses it three times in his answer (6:7, 9 [twice]). Adele Berlin says that Haman is a "glutton for honor." His plan for honoring this favored person is excessive. It is similar to the pharaoh's honoring of Joseph (Gen 41:42-43), but here the honoree is wearing the king's own clothes and riding the king's own horse. It is unclear whether the horse is wearing the crown (what the Hebrew says) or whether this is the horse the king rode

when he was crowned. Or perhaps Haman is so excited that his words are confused and he means that he should wear the crown! Clearly Haman wants to be king! The Hebrew root *mlk*, meaning "to be king/royal," is repeated seven times in verses 8-9.

One can only imagine Haman's humiliation when he finds out the true honoree and then has to carry out what he himself has "proposed" (as the king reminds him twice; 6:10). The king identifies Mordecai as "the Jew." But it is unclear whether the king knows that the murderous decree is against the Jews, or whether he even remembers the decree.

Both Mordecai and Haman return to their places, but now Haman has all the signs of mourning as Mordecai did earlier (6:12). Again Haman repeats the events of the day to his wife and friends. This time, however, their advice is ominous: If (as is certainly true) Mordecai is a Jew, you will surely fall before him (6:13). How do they know this? Or are they speaking in the voice of the all-knowing narrator? They seem to be modeled on other non-Jews who announce such success (see Balaam in Num 23–24; Rahab in Josh 2:9-11; Achior in Jdt 5:5-21).

6:14–7:8 Esther's second banquet

Much has happened in the hours between Esther's first and second banquets. At this banquet Haman's fate will be sealed. Esther finally answers the king's question, using the two words he has consistently repeated. Literally she says, "Let my life be given to me according to my *petition* and my people according to my *request*." She has prefaced this with stock phrases: "finding favor" and "pleasing your majesty." She has indeed found favor with everyone throughout the book (see 2:15, 17). She has subtly changed the phrase, "if I have found favor with the king" (see 5:8), to "if I have found favor with *you*, O king." She is gradually aligning herself with the king against Haman.

She explains her plea for her life and her people by quoting the decree authorizing the annihilation of the Jews: "destroyed, killed, and annihilated" (7:4; see 3:13). (Mordecai had sent her a copy of the decree; 4:8.) She contrasts two possible "sales" of herself and her people—to slavery or to death—and says that she would not have troubled the king if it were slavery. Here she appeals to his love of money. Presumably the king would have profited from their sale into slavery, but what can he gain from their deaths? She also indicates that the villain has usurped the king's power. No one can seize and sell people or property in a kingdom except the king. So Esther too has uncovered a plot against the king.

The action speeds up (7:5-8). Ahasuerus barks out the question: Who and where? Esther identifies Haman. The king leaves the room. Haman falls on Esther's couch (Persians reclined at meals) to beg for his life. The king returns and accuses him of attempted rape of the queen in his presence. Haman is a dead man.

Two questions arise concerning the king: Why did he leave? Why did he accuse Haman of rape when that must have been the last thing on Haman's mind? The king has a terrible dilemma. He has been confronted with a choice between his prime minister and his queen. Complicating the matter is the fact that the king has approved the slaughter of the Jews, even though he may not have known or remembered which people were involved. Almost certainly he and Haman did not know that Esther was endangered by the decree. The appearance (however slight) of attempted rape gives the king a different reason to condemn Haman and thus gets him off the hook.

7:9–8:2 Punishment of Haman

Now the king needs advice on what to do. As always, someone else provides not only a suggestion but also another reason to condemn Haman. Haman has conspired against a benefactor of the king (Mordecai). The stake is already prepared for the execution of the king's enemy (now recognized to be Haman). The reversal of fate is finalized with the gift of Haman's house to Esther and his position, along with the signet ring, to Mordecai (8:1-2). It seems that the next line should be, "and everyone lived happily ever after." But the irrevocable decree against the Jews still stands.

JEWISH VICTORY AND THE FEAST OF PURIM

Esther 8:3–9:23; E:1-24

8:3-17 The second royal decree

The king may think he is finished, but Esther knows better. Just as Haman fell before her, pleading for his life, she falls pleading before the king.

The same verb indicates that she is obeying Mordecai's injunction to plead for the people (4:8). Haman is again identified as the Agagite, the age-old enemy of the Jews. The king indicates his willingness to listen by holding out the scepter.

Standing before him Esther begins with a four-part introduction (8:5). (Two or three clauses have previously been sufficient; see 5:4, 8; 7:3.) Two parts appeal to his love for her ("found favor" and "pleasing in his eyes"); two parts appeal to his good judgment in administering the kingdom ("good to the king" and "right"). Then she requests that the decree concerning the Jews be revoked. (By naming only Haman, she removes the king's responsibility for the decree.) The request is impossible, since royal decrees are irrevocable (1:19). The king responds by listing all the things he has already done—given her Haman's house and impaled him on a stake (8:7). Then, distancing himself even more from this unpleasant situation, he proposes an alternate solution: he gives to her and Mordecai authority to write whatever they wish in the king's name and to seal it with the royal seal. The decree is written at Mordecai's command, sealed, and sent by royal pony express (8:9-10; compare 3:12-13).

Authority shifts throughout this scene. Initially all authority belongs to the king (8:3-4). Esther pleads with him; he responds to Esther and Mordecai (8:7). The decree is then dictated by Mordecai alone (8:9). The first decree regarding the Jews was dictated by the prime minister Haman (3:12); the second, dictated by the man who takes Haman's place, parallels the first.

The wording of this decree also echoes the former one: "to destroy, kill, and annihilate . . . along with their wives and children, and to seize their goods as spoil" (8:11; see 3:13). But the command is ambiguous. The Jews are authorized "to gather and defend their lives." Does this allow them a preemptive strike or only defensive action? The note about women and children is chilling. It comes from the "ban" (Hebrew *herem*) exercised in the Holy War tradition, where the Canaanite peoples were supposed to be completely exterminated (see Deut 7:1-2). The final event in Saul's collapse was his failure to kill Agag and all the Amalekites as required by the *herem* (1 Sam 15:3, 9-29).

The date of writing is puzzling: the twenty-third day of the third month (8:9). Haman's decree was issued on the thirteenth day of the first month (3:12). Mordecai's appeal to Esther, the fasting of the people, and the two banquets seem to follow in very close order, perhaps even in the space of a week. Why the delay before the second decree is issued? Is the date perhaps symbolic? There are seventy days between decrees. Is this intended to suggest the seventy-year exile? Another dating issue is also troubling. The three-day fast seems to be between the thirteenth and fifteenth of the first month, Nisan. Esther's first banquet (on the third day; 5:1) would then be the night after Passover (see Exod 12:2, 6). Symbolically this is highly significant as the day of deliverance. But why is there no mention anywhere of anyone celebrating Passover? Are all the Jews really fasting during Passover?

E:1-24 A copy of the letter

Another Greek addition is inserted here, a supposed copy of Mordecai's letter. This addition was almost certainly written in Greek (perhaps by the author of addition B) and at least a century after the Hebrew version of the story. In the letter Ahasuerus is portrayed as wise, generous, and concerned for the welfare of his people—and totally innocent of the previous decree authorizing the annihilation of the Jews. The king also seems to know Jewish belief: God is identified as "the Most High, the living God of majesty," and "the ruler of all" (E:16, 21). God is also given credit for the deliverance of the Jews in contrast to the Hebrew story in which God is not mentioned.

Haman is portrayed as thoroughly wicked. Most damning is his identification as a Macedonian (E:10). The Macedonians under Alexander the Great defeated the Persians under Darius II in 333 B.C. So Haman, who throughout the Hebrew version is identified as an Agagite and thus an enemy of Saul's descendants and all Jews, is here identified by another ethnic tag as the enemy of the Persians.

The people are instructed to "ignore" Haman's letter and to help the Jews (E:17-20). Is the king saying here that his letter really was not a royal decree, in spite of the royal seal? Does this second letter actually revoke the decree issued by Haman?

Two bits of information are anticipated: the death of Haman's sons (E:18), which in the Hebrew version happens in 9:7-10, and the establish-ment of Purim (E:21-22), which will be described in 9:17-23.

8:13-17 Public response

The mood changes with the return to the Hebrew story. The Jews are to be prepared to avenge themselves (8:13). Vengeance is a strange term here. No one has yet done them any harm! In contrast to the actions of Haman after the first decree, Mordecai appears in public (8:15). He is regally clothed: Purple and crimson are expensive dyes and signs of royalty; the crown is also a sign of status, but it is called by a different Hebrew word to distinguish it from the king's crown. The response of the Jews everywhere to the new decree is great rejoicing. Especially in Susa, where there had been great confusion, there is now great joy.

Many people identified themselves as Jews (8:17). This can only mean that they sided with the Jews in preparing for the upcoming conflict. There has been a singular absence of overt religious practice throughout the book; thus it is unlikely that this sentence indicates religious conversion. The "fear of the Jews" should not be interpreted as a hidden reference to fear of the Lord. The Hebrew word (*pahad*) is not the ordinary word used in that phrase, and there is no reason to deny that the Persians are simply afraid of the Jews who have this newfound power!

9:1-17 The massacre reversed

The remaining chapters of the book of Esther represent several endings. This first ending brings to a head the theme of reversal, which is pervasive throughout the story. The thirteenth of Adar has arrived, the day on which the royal decree is to be carried out. But which decree—Haman's or Mordecai's? Apparently both! Those who expected to carry out the first are defeated by those empowered by the second (9:1). But there is no description of battles; it seems that the Jews meet little or no resistance. Somehow, however, they are enabled to make distinctions between "those who hated them" and those who supported them. Fear fills all the non-Jews, their enemies and their supporters: fear of the Jews as a people (because their fortunes have been so wonderfully reversed?) and fear of Mordecai, who grows ever more powerful (9:2-4). No Jewish casualties are reported. The other casualties are enormous, part of the exaggeration of the book: five hundred in the royal precinct of Susa, three hundred in the lower city of Susa, seventy-five thousand in the provinces (9:6, 15-16). The ten sons of Haman are also killed, those of whom he was so proud (9:7-10). Jewish tradition calls for reading the ten names in one breath, a reminder that even here the story is a comedy!

In the midst of recounting the slaughter, a little conversation between Esther and Ahasuerus appears (9:11-13). This vignette inspires laughter too. The king has only two things to say. First, he gleefully repeats the number killed in the royal precinct of Susa and wonders what has been achieved in the provinces. He has become the Jews' cheerleader! Second, he offers again to give Esther whatever she asks and whatever she requests (see 5:6; 7:2). Does he know no other question? Esther's request is surprising in its boldness: impale the corpses of Haman's ten sons and allow the people of the lower city of Susa to continue killing tomorrow (9:13). Haman's sons are thus publicly shamed as he was, and a reason is given for the custom of celebrating Purim on two different days.

Three times it is reported that the Jews did not engage in plunder (9:10, 15, 16), even though the decree permitted them to do so (see 8:11). This is the final echo of the story of Saul and Agag in 1 Samuel 15. Saul's undoing was the taking of plunder, thus disobeying the rule of Holy War. The Jews will not repeat his mistake.

9:17b-23 The feast of Purim

The remaining verses of the chapter record the establishment of the feast of Purim. There are several explanations given for the feast. It must be well grounded since this feast is not found in the torah. Also, it seems that some festival was already celebrated and needed a foundation story (see 9:23). Finally, this festival was by custom celebrated on two different days, on the fourteenth in the rural areas and on the fifteenth in the walled cities. So a reason had to be given for the discrepancy. In Susa they fought an extra day (see 9:15-19).

What is being celebrated, according to the story, is not the battle but the "rest" from enemies (9:22). Thus the celebrations are set on the day *after* the battles (whether the fourteenth or the fifteenth). The way the festival is celebrated fits the story attached to it. This has been a story of banquets. So the celebration is characterized by

much feasting, by giving presents—usually of food—to one another and also to the poor. The custom of including the poor in festivals is found throughout biblical tradition (see Deut 16:11; Neh 8:10-12; Tob 2:1-2).

EPILOGUE: THE RISE OF MORDECAI
9:24–10:3; F:1-11

9:24-28 Summary of the story

The date, the reasons, and the way of celebrating have been determined. Now it remains to explain the name: Purim. The Babylonian term *pur* (the "lot" that Haman cast; see 3:7), which sounds like "Purim," is made the basis of the festival name (9:26).

9:29-32 Esther and Mordecai act in concert

All that remains is to establish the authority for the feast. Esther and Mordecai have worked in partnership to deliver the people from their enemies, so the introduction of the feast of Purim must be attributed to both. The letter attributed to Esther in verse 32 is credited to both Esther and Mordecai in verse 29. Mordecai's first letter (9:20-22) is attributed to both Mordecai and Esther in verse 31. Thus Purim is now firmly established.

10:1-3 The rise of Mordecai completed

The end of the story returns to the beginning (see 1:1). Ahasuerus is again in complete control of the whole world (the land and the distant islands). But one important difference suggests that his kingdom is in better shape now, both for himself and for the Jews: Ahasuerus has Mordecai as his right-hand man! All these things are written down. In this story everything must be written down to be valid (see 1:22; 2:23; 3:12, 14; 4:8; 6:1-2; 8:8-13; 9:20, 23, 27, 29, 32). The book of Esther, after all, is known as *the* Scroll (see Introduction).

F:1-10 Mordecai's Dream Fulfilled

This Greek addition, an interpretation of the dream in addition A, also returns to the beginning. Throughout the Greek additions everything that has happened is attributed to God. The interpretation of the dream does not quite fit the story, however. It is not true that "not a single detail has been left unfulfilled," or at least unexplained (F:2).

451

Esther is the river; is she also the tiny spring? Haman and Mordecai are the two dragons, but how is Mordecai like Haman, a dragon whose great cry inspires the nations to fight against the just (A:5-6)? What about the light and the sun (F:3)? Is this the splendid light that shone for the Jews when they heard Mordecai's decree (8:16)? The Greek interpreter does not tell us. A further discrepancy has to do with the question of "lots." God arranged two lots, one for God's people and one for others (F:7). The purpose of these lots is not the same as the single lot cast by Haman, although the mention of "the hour, the time, and the day" echoes that event (see 3:7). The plural "lots" may be an attempt to justify the apparent plural "Purim." (The "-im" ending signifies the plural in Hebrew.) In spite of all these differences, addition F wraps up the story one more time. God has saved his people (F:9)!

F:11 Colophon

A colophon is a later addition to a book, indicating critical information such as the author, the date, and the work's authenticity. This colophon does not clear up all the mysteries. Someone who claimed to be a priest and Levite identified this "letter of Purim" and its translator. Apparently the "letter of Purim" is the book of Esther in one of its versions, probably the Greek. Since there were several rulers named Ptolemy who had wives named Cleopatra, the date remains unclear—sometime between 116 and 48 B.C.

THE FIRST BOOK OF
MACCABEES

Daniel J. Harrington, S.J.

INTRODUCTION

First and Second Maccabees, along with Tobit, Judith, Wisdom, Sirach, and Baruch, belong to the canon of biblical books recognized by the Catholic and Orthodox Church traditions as Holy Scripture. They appear in early manuscripts of the Greek Bible (Septuagint). These books, however, are not recognized as canonical by Jews and Protestants (who follow the Hebrew canon in the Old Testament). The seven books are often referred to as the "Apocrypha" or "Deuterocanonicals." All agree, however, that they provide important historical information and illustrate some major theological concerns of Jews around the time of Jesus. For a full discussion of this collection, see my *Invitation to the Apocrypha* (Grand Rapids, MI: Eerdmans, 1999).

The Maccabean revolt

The expression "Maccabean revolt" refers to a series of events in the mid-second century B.C. by which one Jewish family, known as the Maccabees, gained political, military, and religious power in Judea. The adjective "Maccabean" derives from the nickname (usually interpreted as "the hammerer") given to Judas in 1 Maccabees 2:4. For the historical context and course of events of the Maccabean revolt, see the chronological tables on page 497.

The primary sources for the Maccabean revolt are the two books known as 1 Maccabees and 2 Maccabees. First Maccabees covers the period

from roughly 175 to 134 B.C., and it reports the exploits and achievements of three generations of the Maccabee family: the priest Mattathias; his sons Judas, Jonathan, and Simon; and Simon's son John Hyrcanus. Second Maccabees provides important background information about the intrigues surrounding the Jewish high priesthood before the revolt started in earnest and takes the story of the revolt up to 161 B.C., shortly before the death of Judas. The focus of its interest is God's concern for and defense of the Jerusalem temple through the agency of Judas Maccabeus.

The book of Daniel seems to have been composed in 165 B.C., around the time of the events described in the early chapters of 1 and 2 Maccabees. Thus it is a precious resource for understanding the circumstances leading up to the Maccabean revolt. Whereas the book of Daniel looks for imminent divine intervention to put Israel's enemies to fight and establish God's kingdom, 1 Maccabees presents the Maccabee dynasty as bringing about Israel's salvation. Whereas 2 Maccabees focuses on Judas in his role as savior of the Jerusalem temple, 1 Maccabees considers three generations of the Maccabee family and attends to their military exploits as well as their ability to deal in the political arena.

The historical consequences of the Maccabean revolt have been great. From being a small and insignificant client people in the Seleucid Empire, the Jews of Judea moved toward political independence with their own native rulers and with Rome as a powerful ally. From being on the edge of cultural and religious extinction, the Jews of Judea moved toward a form of religious life that was both traditional to their heritage and adaptable to the realities of the Greco-Roman world. In the crisis period under the high priests Jason and Menelaus (175 to 162 B.C.) the fate of Judaism (and with it Christianity and Islam) was uncertain. The result of the Maccabean revolt was a renewed Judaism that had both clarity and flexibility. The revolt established the Torah and the Jerusalem temple as the central features in Second Temple Judaism.

First Maccabees

The basic outline of the book reveals its purpose. After describing the crisis initiated by King Antiochus IV Epiphanes and the resistance begun by the Jewish priest Mattathias (1:1–2:70), it recounts the military, political, and religious exploits of Judas Maccabeus (3:1–9:22), his brothers Jonathan (9:23–12:53) and Simon (13:1–15:41), and Simon's son John Hyrcanus (16:1-24). The author wants to show how God used Judas and his family to remove the yoke of Seleucid (Syrian) oppression, and how the Jewish high priesthood came to reside in this family. Judas and his brothers constitute God's dynasty, the family "through whom Israel's deliverance was given" (5:62).

First Maccabees ends with the accession of John Hyrcanus, who served as Judea's leader from 134 to 104 B.C. The work may have been composed near the end of his reign or shortly afterward (in the early first century B.C.). The canonical text of 1 Maccabees is in Greek, part of the Septuagint manuscript tradition. Most modern scholars assume that 1 Maccabees was originally composed in Hebrew and then translated into Greek, though it is conceivable that it was written in a "semitizing" Greek. In either case, the present text is in "biblical" Greek, much like the versions of the early historical books in the Greek Bible.

The Greek text incorporates some "official" documents (for example, 8:23-32; 10:18-20, 25-45; 11:30-37, 57-59; 12:5-23; 13:36-40). The authenticity of these documents is disputed, though current scholarship tends to support them in the main. Of course, if 1 Maccabees was composed in Hebrew, then we may be dealing with Greek or Latin documents translated into Hebrew and back again into Greek. Some scholars argue that 1 Maccabees and 2 Maccabees used a common source in their accounts about Judas Maccabeus (1 Maccabees 1–7 and 2 Maccabees 3–15). However, even if that is so, it does not seem possible to recover the exact wording of that source, given the complicated transmission of both books. The poems, speeches, and prayers are best viewed as free compositions by the author.

In its literary style the book seems anxious to link the Maccabee family with the great heroes of Israel's past. An important element in this program is the device of biblical re-creations or echoes, that is, deliberate attempts at showing how the actions of the Maccabean dynasty stand in line with the words and deeds of the early heroes of the Bible. The not-so-subtle message, of course, is that the Maccabee family carries on the heritage of Israel's past.

The reading of 1 Maccabees presented here gives particular attention to the book's distinctive angle in viewing events in the second century B.C. In this commentary I have drawn on, adapted, and developed some material from my earlier publications, especially *The Maccabean Revolt: Anatomy of a Biblical Revolution* (Collegeville, MN: Michael Glazier, 1988); my notes on 1 Maccabees in the *Harper Collins Study Bible* (2006) and the *New American Bible, Revised Edition* (2011).

COMMENTARY

CRISIS AND RESPONSE

1 Maccabees 1:1–2:70

1:1-9 The historical setting

First Maccabees begins by sketching the historical context from which Antiochus IV arose and set in motion the events that led to the Maccabean revolt. The starting point is the amazingly fast and complete conquest of the Persian Empire and beyond by Alexander the Great (356–323 B.C.). Alexander is said to have come from the land of the "Kittim," a term derived from "Kiti," the ancient capital of Cyprus (see Gen 10:4; 1 Chr 1:7), and extended to include not only Cypriots but also Greeks in general (and eventually the Romans). When his father, Philip II of Macedon, was assassinated in 336 B.C., Alexander assumed command of his army and defeated the Persian emperor Darius III between 334 and 331 B.C.

Alexander succeeded in extending Greek rule well into Egypt and as far east as Afghanistan. His swift rise to power and fierce exploits are described allusively at several points in the book of Daniel (see 2:33, 40; 7:23; 8:5-8, 21; and 11:3). With his military conquests also came Greek influences in military strategy, politics, economics, language, and culture. At the same time, the Greek invaders were influenced to varying degrees by the indigenous peoples and their cultures.

The description of Alexander as "proud and arrogant" (1:3) foreshadows how Antiochus IV will be portrayed in 1 Maccabees, Daniel, and 2 Maccabees. The ideal scene of Alexander on his deathbed dividing his empire among his faithful lieutenants obscures the historical complexity of events after his death. The division was only really completed around 305 B.C. However, it was in the interests of his successors to depict the division as smooth and peaceful, with everything proceeding according to Alexander's last will and testament. In that way they could point to themselves as legitimate successors of the great king and bask in his glory. Alexander died in Babylon, at the age of thirty-two or thirty-three, in 323 B.C., some twelve years after taking over from Philip.

The two kingdoms within Alexander's empire that most affected the Jews in the land of Israel were based in Egypt (the Ptolemies) and in Antioch of Syria (the Seleucids). The Ptolemies exercised a relatively loose administrative and political control over Judea from about 300 to 198 B.C. Then the Seleucids under Antiochus III annexed Judea to their kingdom. The author of 1 Maccabees gives a very negative assessment of the whole period from Alexander the Great to Antiochus IV (336 to 175 B.C.). He accuses Alexander and his successors of "multiplying evils on the earth" (1:9).

1:10-15 The major figures in the crisis

According to 1 Maccabees, the chief external villain was the Seleucid king, Antiochus IV Epiphanes, who reigned from 175 to 164 B.C. He was a son of Antiochus III and had been taken as a hostage to Rome as a penalty against his father under the stipulations of the treaty of Apamea in 188 B.C. His brother, Seleucus IV, reigned between 187 and 175 B.C. The name "Epiphanes" means "[God] manifest" and suggests some pretensions to divinity on his part. Antiochus IV was famous for his erratic behavior, such as dressing up as a commoner and mixing among his subjects. His critics gave him the nickname "Epimanes," meaning "madman." The story about the mad king in Daniel 4 may allude to this negative evaluation of him.

The accession of Antiochus the "sinful offshoot" (1:10) of Alexander and his successors in the 137th year of "the kingdom of the Greeks" (175 B.C.) is computed from the beginning of the Seleucid era in 312 B.C. The dates in 1 Maccabees are complicated by the presence of two systems of calendar reckoning. The Seleucids themselves marked the beginning of their era in October of 312 B.C., while the Jews, following Babylonian practice, regarded April 311 B.C. as the beginning of the Seleucid era. The author of 1 Maccabees seems to have dated political events according to the Seleucid calendar (with a fall new year) and religious events according to the Jerusalem temple calendar then in force (with a spring new year).

In 1:11-13a the author hints at some influential Judean collaboration behind Antiochus IV's intervention in Jewish affairs. He describes these Jews as "transgressors of the law" and suggests that they wanted all Judeans to become more fully integrated culturally and religiously, as well as economically and politically, into the Seleucid kingdom. They reasoned that things would go better for Judeans if they were more fully assimilated and less separate within the Seleucid realm. Indeed, 1 Maccabees indicates that these Judeans took the initiative in approaching the king and managed to seduce many other Judeans to join them. For a more detailed account, see 2 Maccabees 4:7-50. According to 2 Maccabees 4:7-17, the chief instigator was Jason, the brother of the legitimate high priest Onias III, and himself the high priest from 175 to 172 B.C. But the author of 1 Maccabees provides no names or details about the conspirators. Their omission may be deliberate as a way of not giving enemies within Israel too much prominence or notoriety (the technique is known as *damnatio memoriae*, damning by silence). This author was more interested in the exploits of his Maccabean heroes than in the renegades and their threat.

According to 1:13b-15, Antiochus IV authorized the Judeans to "introduce the ordinances of the Gentiles." Whereas Antiochus III had allowed the Judeans to follow their ancestral law (the Torah, or law of Moses), now the king at the urging of some Judean leaders was proposing a program that would make Judeans indistinguishable from their neighbors. The program involved observing a non-Jewish legal system, building a "gymnasium" in Jerusalem, removing the marks of circumcision, and abandoning the traditional Jewish religion ("the holy covenant").

In Greek society the gymnasium was more than a facility for physical exercise. It also involved philosophical and cultural education, as well as military training. Thus it was an important vehicle for Hellenistic culture that would help initiate the sons of elite Judeans into the Greek world and into the Seleucid vision of a united empire.

The surgical removal of the marks of circumcision is called "epispasm." For Jews it may have reflected a desire to conform to the Greek practice of nudity in physical exercise and athletics. Whether many Jewish men actually underwent this operation is debated. In either case, the author's point is that these Jewish men under the influence of certain renegades were abandoning one of the distinctive features of Jewish life in the second century B.C.

1:16-40 The despoiling of Jerusalem

According to 1:16-19, Antiochus IV in 169 B.C. invaded Egypt in the hope of conquering the Ptolemaic kingdom and making it part of his empire (see Dan 11:25-27). The Egyptian ruler then was Ptolemy VI Philometor, a nephew of Antiochus IV. The Seleucid and Ptolemaic royal families often intermarried as a way of giving unity to the two kingdoms. The practice is sometimes described as "marrying one's enemies." Antiochus' use of elephants in battle as the ancient equivalent of tanks was a Seleucid military practice going back to Seleucus I around 300 B.C.; see 1 Maccabees 6:34-37 for a vivid description of their role in a battle against the Maccabees. Although Antiochus had success in his invasion, he failed to capture Alexandria, and Ptolemy VI Philometor survived to rule in Egypt until 145 B.C. His second invasion of Egypt in 168 B.C., while noted in Daniel 11:29 and 2 Maccabees 5:1, 11, is not mentioned here.

According to 1:20-24, Antiochus returned in 169 from his victory in Egypt by way of Jerusalem and plundered the temple there. Like other temples in the ancient world, the Jerusalem temple not only possessed valuable sacred vessels but also served as a bank where wealthy persons could store their money and other possessions (see 2 Macc 3:10-11). Following the examples of his father Antiochus III (who died while robbing a temple) and his brother Seleucus IV, Antiochus took the opportunity to rob the Jerusalem temple. At the very least, the spoils would have enabled him to pay his soldiers. The furnishings and sacred vessels of the temple are described in Exodus 39:32–40:11 and 1 Kings 6:23-36. Daniel 11:28 and 1 Maccabees place Antiochus' temple robbery after his first Egyptian campaign (in 169), while 2 Maccabees 5:11-21 dates it after his second Egyptian campaign (in 168). The author continues his negative characterization of Antiochus IV by charging him with "great arrogance" in speech and accusing him of shedding "much blood." The poetic lament in 1:25-28 is reminiscent of the book of Lamentations and emphasizes the social disruption at all levels in Judean society that was caused by the despoiling of the Jerusalem temple. For other such poetic laments, see 1:36-40; 2:7-13; and 3:45.

According to 1:29-35, Antiochus sent "the Mysian commander" against Jerusalem in 167 B.C.

The Mysians were mercenary soldiers from northwest Asia Minor. The Greek translator of 1 Maccabees seems to have misread the Hebrew expression *sar hamûssîm* ("chief of the Mysians") as *sar hamîssîm* ("chief collector of tribute"). Whereas Antiochus focused his plundering on the temple, the Mysian commander despoiled the city as a whole and took as captives women and children, probably to sell them as slaves.

The most lasting result of this campaign was the establishment of a Seleucid fortress or garrison near the temple area. The precise location of this citadel (also known as the Akra) has been a topic of longstanding debate among scholars. However, according to the lament in 1:36-40, it was clearly somewhere very near the temple complex, probably to its northwest. The garrison was manned by foreign troops and some renegade Judeans, altogether forming "a sinful race" (1:34). Despite the Jewish recapture of Jerusalem and the rededication of the temple, the citadel remained under enemy control for over twenty-five years. It finally fell to Simon in 141 B.C. (see 13:49-50). The poetic lament (1:36-40) attached to this episode stresses the threat posed by the citadel to the temple complex and the shame that its presence brought to the people of Jerusalem.

1:41-63 A new program and religious persecution

Having plundered the Jerusalem temple and established a citadel nearby, Antiochus IV is said to have issued a decree that would have erased the distinctive features of Judaism and have brought the Judeans into the mainstream of his empire. According to 1:41-42, it was his intention that all should be "one people" and give up their "particular customs." There is no non-Jewish evidence that supports the claim that Antiochus imposed such a program on "his whole kingdom." In fact, it seems to have been confined to Judea. Moreover, such a program of compulsory cultural and religious universalism does not fit the ancient world in general or Antiochus in particular. Note that 1 Maccabees does not mention going over to the "Greek" way of life, as in 2 Maccabees. Antiochus' "religion" (1:43) was the cult of the "Lord of heaven" (*Ba'al Shamen*). He and his Jewish supporters most likely understood the "Lord of heaven" as the generic equivalent of Yahweh the "Most High God" of Israel. However, the pious

in Israel viewed this program as idolatry and a sharp break with Israel's sacred religious traditions such as sabbath observance. See 1:54 for another expression of their negative attitude toward the new form of worship.

The prohibitions directed to Jerusalem and the cities of Judea in 1:44-50 would have effectively abolished many of the distinctive features of Judaism in the Second Temple period: temple worship and its system of sacrifices, observance of the sabbath and the Jewish holy days, circumcision of male children, and the laws of ritual purity. Moreover, the animals to be sacrificed were pigs and other ritually unacceptable animals. According to 1:50 the penalty for not observing these decrees was death.

Having promulgated these decrees, Antiochus appointed inspectors to ensure that they would be carried out (1:51-53). He also ordered that each city in Judea should offer sacrifices according to the new order of worship. The author observes that many Jews (whom he regarded as apostates) participated in the new regimen. However, he reserves the name "Israel" only for those who resisted and even went into hiding (see 2:29-38; 2 Macc 6:11).

The results of Antiochus' program and the prohibitions are presented in a catalogue of horrors in 1:54-63. The most dramatic step was the erection of "the desolating abomination upon the altar of burnt offerings" (1:54) in the Jerusalem temple in mid-December of 167 B.C. The "desolating abomination" derives from the Hebrew expression *shiqqus meshomem* ("the abomination that makes desolate") in Daniel 11:31. It is a play or pun on *Ba'al Shamen* ("Lord of heaven," 1:43) in which *shiqqus* ("abomination") is substituted for *Ba'al* ("Lord") and *Shamen* is interpreted not as "heaven" but rather as "makes desolate." For New Testament uses of this expression, see Matthew 24:15 and Mark 13:14. The precise nature of the "abomination" is uncertain, with learned suggestions ranging from a statue of the Greek god Zeus or an altar dedicated to him, to stones that had fallen from meteors to the earth.

Other steps included erecting pagan altars throughout Judea, burning incense in the streets, destroying scrolls containing the traditional Jewish law and executing those found possessing them, and forbidding mothers to have their sons circumcised. There was also to be a special sacrifice on the 25th day of every month, in honor of the king's birthday (see 2 Macc 6:7). As in 1:53, the author reports on opposition among the faithful in Israel who were willing to face death rather than give up the "holy covenant." He describes the situation as "very great wrath" (1:64) upon Israel. But his interests lay more with the need for bold leadership than with additional martyrs.

2:1-28 The revolt begins

In 2:1-5 the author traces the beginning of organized Jewish resistance to 166 B.C. (see 2:70) under the leadership of Mattathias from the priestly family of Joarib (1 Chr 9:10; 24:7). The first act of resistance takes place at Modein, about seventeen miles northwest of Jerusalem. Mattathias is said to have moved there from Jerusalem.

His five sons, who constitute the focus of attention in 1 Maccabees, are listed in 2:2-5: John (9:35-42), Simon (13–15), Judas (3:1–9:22), Eleazar (6:40-47), and Jonathan (9:23–12:53). Their surnames or nicknames remain mysterious, though "Maccabeus" is generally interpreted as "hammerer" and is the source of the name commonly given to the dynasty. They are also called "Hasmoneans," perhaps derived from the name of Mattathias' grandfather, Simeon.

According to 2:6, the reason for their resistance was the sacrileges being committed in the Jerusalem temple and in cities in Judea under the new order. The language of Mattathias' lament in 2:7-13 echoes Lamentations and various Psalms (44, 74, 79). The focus is the shame that has come upon the people with the defiling of the temple and the city by the Gentiles (and their Jewish collaborators). By tearing their garments and putting on sackcloth (2:14), the Maccabee family engages in traditional mourning rituals (Gen 37:29, 34).

The occasion for their resistance in 2:15-28 was the arrival at Modein of royal officers who were sent to organize and enforce the pagan sacrifices. They promise Mattathias and his sons great rewards, even the rank of nobility in the Seleucid Empire as "the King's Friends" (see 10:65; 11:27), if they will participate (2:17-18). But in response (2:19-22) Mattathias stands firm in his dedication to his ancestral religion and its commandments: "We will not obey the words of the king by departing from our religion in the slightest degree." He would not participate in what he perceived to be pagan worship.

His words are followed by an act of resistance in 2:23-26. When a Jew comes forward to offer sacrifice on the pagan altar, Mattathias kills him and the king's officer and tears down the altar. This act of "zeal" evokes the memory of Phinehas, the grandson of Aaron, who killed an Israelite man and a Midianite woman engaging in the cult of Baal at Peor (Num 25:6-15; see also Ps 106:28-31; Sir 45:23-24). This dramatic incident that sparked off the Maccabean revolt according to 1 Maccabees is not mentioned in 2 Maccabees. What motivated the rebels, according to 2:27, was zeal for the Jewish law and fidelity to the covenant. The "mountains" where they found refuge (2:28) were most likely in the district of Gophna, northeast of Modein and bordering on Samaria (cf. 2 Macc 5:27).

2:29-48 Two other Jewish groups

The active military resistance shown by Mattathias contrasts with the passive response of the pious Jewish group described in 2:29-41. Seeking to live according to "righteousness and religious custom," they fled to the Judean Desert (see 1 Sam 23:14) in the hope of escaping the new religious order and remaining faithful to the Torah (2:29-30). When the king's officers and soldiers heard of their attempts at evading the new order, they went out to the Judean Desert and found their hiding places. When their pursuers attacked on the sabbath, the members of the group offered no resistance, lest they profane the sabbath. Their rationale is stated in 2:34: "We will not come out, nor will we obey the king's command to profane the sabbath." They preferred death to breaking the sabbath commandment. The result was the death of a thousand persons. For an account of the same or a similar incident, see 2 Maccabees 6:11 and *Assumption of Moses* 9. Their sad fate led Mattathias and his supporters to decide in 2:39-42 that they would fight defensive wars on the sabbath if they were attacked. Otherwise, their enemies could destroy Israel entirely by waiting to attack on sabbath days.

In contrast to the group described in 2:29-38, the Hasideans ("the pious ones") join forces with the Maccabees. They were "mighty warriors of Israel" and zealous for the law (2:42). According to 2 Maccabees 14:6, Judas was the leader of the Hasideans. However, in 1 Maccabees 7:12-13, there is a report of rift between Judas and the

Hasideans. Their alliance with the Maccabees attracted still other Jewish rebels and gave substance and definition to the revolt (2:43). The newly organized army struck down sinners and lawless men (Jewish apostates), tore down pagan altars, circumcised boys, and hunted down the arrogant (2:44-47). Their program is summarized in 2:48: "They saved the law from the hands of the Gentiles and of the kings and did not let the sinner triumph." Their aim was to do away with the program described in 1:41-50 and to reestablish traditional Judaism.

2:49-70 The farewell discourse of Mattathias

The first stage of the Maccabean revolt reaches its climax with the death of Mattathias in 166 B.C. (2:70). As he faces death, he gives a farewell speech, or testament, after the pattern of Jacob (Gen 49), Moses (Deut 33), and Samuel (1 Sam 12). After urging his sons to show zeal for the law and to give their lives for the covenant (2:49-50), he appeals in 2:51-60 to biblical characters who underwent testing and were rewarded by God: Abraham (Gen 22), Joseph (Gen 39–45), Phinehas (Num 25), David (2 Sam 7), Elijah (1 Kgs 18; 2 Kgs 2), and Daniel and his three companions (Dan 1–6). Their rewards—priesthood, rule, deliverance from danger, and the land—foreshadow the rewards that Judas, Jonathan, and Simon will gain. This catalogue of heroes of faith (see Heb 11) shows that the author knew the book of Daniel or at least the stories told in Daniel 3 and 6.

In conclusion (2:61-68), Mattathias foretells the fall of Antiochus IV ("his glory ends in corruption and worms" [2:62; see 2 Macc 9:5-10, 28]); appoints Simeon (Simon) as chief counselor and Judas as commander of the army (2:65-66); and urges his sons to "[P]ay back the Gentiles what they deserve, and observe the precepts of the law" (2:68). His death takes place in 166 B.C., and he is buried in his ancestral tomb in Modein (2:69-70).

JUDAS

1 Maccabees 3:1–9:22

3:1-26 Judas' early victories

The leadership exercised by Judas Maccabeus is described in 3:1–9:22. He is primarily a daring

military leader, and his career is covered until his death in 160 B.C. He is introduced as his father's replacement in 3:1-2, where he is said to have had the support of his brothers and all who had joined their cause (see 2:42-48). The poem celebrating his military exploits in 3:3-9 portrays him as an enemy of the apostates among his people and of Gentile kings. The many kings he defeated included the Seleucids Antiochus IV, Antiochus V, and Demetrius I. He is celebrated as a redeemer or savior of his people, and his renown certainly reached as far as Rome (3:9).

Judas' first battles resulted in dramatic victories over Apollonius (3:10-12) and Seron (3:13-26). Apollonius, the military commander and governor of Samaria, may have also been the commander of the Mysian mercenaries mentioned in 1 Maccabees 1:29 (see 2 Macc 5:24). Whether his army included Samaritan Jews is not clear. By taking the sword of Apollonius and using it in subsequent battles, Judas followed the example of David who seized the sword of Goliath after killing him (1 Sam 17:54; 21:9-10).

In the hope of taking revenge on Judas and winning a great reputation for himself, Seron gathered a large army (3:13-15). The description of Seron as "commander of the Syrian army" probably exaggerates his rank and importance (which is something that the author wanted to do). The mention of a "large company of renegades" in his army (3:15) suggests that it included some apostate Jews opposed to the Maccabees and their movement.

The battle against Seron (3:16-26) took place at the Ascent of Beth-horon, a site on the main road running from the west to Jerusalem in the east. About twelve miles northwest of Jerusalem there was a narrow pass between Lower and Upper Beth-horon. Since Seron and his army had to go through that pass, it would have been relatively easy for Judas to ambush them. Joshua had won an important battle there (Josh 10:10-11), and in A.D. 66 a Roman army led by Cestius was ambushed there.

In trying to calm his soldiers in the face of Seron's numerical superiority (3:17), Judas echoes the speech given by Jonathan in 1 Samuel 14:6, "in the sight of Heaven there is no difference between deliverance by many or by few" (3:18). Rather than using the titles "Lord" and "God" too frequently, the author of 1 Maccabees often used

"Heaven" (see Matthew's preference for "the kingdom of heaven") or personal pronouns to refer to God. The estimate of eight hundred enemy casualties (3:24) seems realistic and is less of an exaggeration than most of the other battle totals in 1 Maccabees. The country of the Philistines (3:24) refers to the Hellenized cities in the south coastal plain of Palestine. A common etymology of "Palestine" derives the name from the Philistines. Instead of Seron making a name for himself (3:14), his rashness in pursuing Judas only contributed to the growing fame of Judas as a mighty warrior (3:25-26).

3:27-37 Lysias as regent

According to 3:27-31 Antiochus IV wished to pursue the campaign against Judas but found himself in need of money. So he went off to Persia to raise funds. Again, the author seems to be exaggerating the significance of the uprising in Judea to give the impression that it was the focus of all of Antiochus' attention. In fact, he had other rebellions to deal with in the eastern part of his empire. The author traces Antiochus' financial problems to his excessive generosity to his soldiers in response to the seriousness of the Judean threat. The historian Polybius and other ancient writers confirm that Antiochus IV was lavish in giving gifts. His solution to his troubles, according to 3:31, was to go to Persia and raise a large sum of money there. Polybius (*Histories* 31.9) and Appian (*Roman History* 11.66) claim that Antiochus IV died while robbing a temple in Elam (see 1 Macc 6:1-16). According to 3:32-37, Antiochus IV left Lysias in charge of his political and military affairs in the western half of his empire and made him the guardian of his son Antiochus V, who was then seven or eight years old. Lysias held the title of Kinsman of the King and was later to be prominent in the battles at Beth-zur (4:26-35) and Beth-Zechariah (6:28-63). Antiochus IV gave to Lysias half of his army and the elephants and ordered him to destroy the people of Judea and Jerusalem and to resettle the land with foreigners. Antiochus IV set out in the spring of 166 B.C. (3:37) from Antioch in Syria to the eastern part of his empire, beyond the Euphrates River. Antioch on the Orontes River had been founded in 300 B.C. by Seleucus I and served as the western capital of the Seleucid Empire. Lysias was left in charge there, with Antiochus V under his supervision.

3:38-60 Preparations for another battle

In carrying out Antiochus IV's order to destroy Judea and Jerusalem (3:38-41), Lysias chose three of the King's Friends as leaders and prepared a large army of forty thousand men. "Friends" were officials who belonged to the lowest rank of Seleucid nobility. According to 2 Maccabees 8:8-9, Gorgias was Nicanor's superior, and Ptolemy ordered Nicanor and Gorgias into battle. Also, according to 2 Maccabees 8:9, there were only twenty thousand soldiers in Lysias' army. The Seleucid army camped at Emmaus, about twenty miles west of Jerusalem (this is probably not the Emmaus of Luke 24:13). Since an easy Seleucid victory was expected, this army attracted slave merchants eager to buy and sell the anticipated Jewish captives as well as military support from Israel's traditional enemies, the Idumeans and Philistines.

Meanwhile, according to 3:44-60, Judas took the current state of the Jerusalem sanctuary as a rallying point, carefully observed the biblical regulations for warfare, and followed various biblical precedents in his actions. At the first assembly (3:44-45) there was lamentation over the sad state of the temple now occupied by Gentiles. The city was "uninhabited, like a wilderness" in the sense that no true Israelite (now identified as Judas and his followers) was there.

The second assembly (3:46-54) took place at Mizpah, eight miles north of Jerusalem, a traditional place for assemblies and prayers before battles (see Judg 20:1; 1 Sam 7:5-9; 10:17). The meeting there is full of religious symbols: fasting, mourning rituals, unrolling Torah scrolls, and so on. Instead of using pagan divination techniques as omens, the Jews discerned the future from the Torah (3:48). Since the temple was now in pagan hands, the presence of the priestly vestments and the sacrificial offerings and tithes were reminders that Jews no longer controlled the temple and its rituals (3:49). Nazirites, according to Numbers 6, took temporary vows of consecration to God. Since the temple was in pagan hands, the rituals marking the end of their consecration could not be observed. The prayer at the Mizpah assembly (3:51-53) emphasizes that the Jerusalem temple is being desecrated and the Gentile armies were poised to destroy God's people led by Judas.

In marshaling his army (3:55-59), Judas carefully follows biblical precedents and rules. He divides the army into numerical groups, exempts those legitimately released from military service (Deut 20:5-8), and gives a short speech (after the pattern of Deut 20:3-4) to the effect that it is better to die in battle than to witness the destruction of the Jewish people and its sanctuary. Having duly prepared his troops, Judas and his army leave Mizpah and camp to the south of Emmaus.

4:1-25 Victory at Emmaus

By his wise military strategy Judas managed to divide Gorgias' army and to defeat both the main contingent camped at Emmaus and the expeditionary force led by Gorgias. At every point Judas conducts himself as the exemplary biblical warrior.

According to 4:1-5, Gorgias took a force of five thousand soldiers and one thousand cavalry to pursue Judas by night. Again, the numbers are very likely exaggerated. The guides from the citadel in Jerusalem (4:2) may have been Jews who were familiar with the terrain. Meanwhile, Judas was preparing to attack the main camp since a large part of the army had left Emmaus with Gorgias (4:3-4). Since it apparently did not occur to Gorgias that Judas might attack the main camp, he brought his troops to the mountains where he thought Judas would be hiding (4:5).

When Judas and his army arrived at the main camp (4:6-11), they found themselves outnumbered (they were only three thousand men) and lacking the fine weapons that the Seleucid soldiers had. As in 3:18-19, Judas has to remind them that large numbers and good equipment do not necessarily win battles (see Deut 20:3-4). With God's help the judge Gideon won a great battle with only three hundred men (Judg 7), and Moses triumphed over Pharaoh's army at the Red Sea (Exod 14–15). The Jews' victory in battle will prove to the Gentiles that "there is One who redeems and delivers Israel" (4:11).

Taken by surprise, the main army is defeated (4:12-15), suffering as many casualties (three thousand) as there were soldiers in Judas' army (4:6). Moreover, many of the Seleucid soldiers fled to Gezer, Ashdod, and Jamnia—cities presumably that were not supporting Judas. Thus Judas' surprise attack on the main camp turned into a rout. Recognizing that Gorgias and his force would soon return, Judas in 4:16-18 ordered his men to hold off from taking plunder. When in 4:19-22 Gorgias' soldiers saw what had happened to their

main camp and that their gear and other possessions were being burned, they fled to Philistine territory (see 3:24). The gold, silver, cloth, and other treasures noted in 4:23 probably belonged in part to the slave traders (see 3:41) who had come in expectation of doing much business. Finally, Judas and his soldiers celebrate their victory by singing Psalm 136:1 in praise of the One "who is good, whose mercy endures forever." The author's comment about Judas' victory being a great deliverance for Israel (4:25) echoes Judges 15:18 (Samson) and 1 Samuel 14:45 (Jonathan).

4:26-35 Victory over Lysias

In the absence of Antiochus IV, Lysias was in charge of the western part of the Seleucid Empire and was serving as guardian for Antiochus V (see 3:32-33). He had been ordered by Antiochus IV to destroy Jerusalem and to resettle it with foreigners (3:35-36). Therefore in light of the defeat of Gorgias' army in 165 B.C., he organized in the year 164 an even larger army, consisting of sixty thousand soldiers and five thousand cavalry (4:28). His strategy was to approach Judea from the south, so he camped at Beth-zur on the southern border of Judea and Idumea. Sometimes called the "fishhook" strategy, his plan was to take advantage of the less mountainous terrain there and the longstanding hostility toward Israel from its neighbors to the south and east.

As the exemplary biblical warrior, Judas prays in 4:30-33 to God as the "Savior of Israel" and recalls the great victories won by David (1 Samuel 17) and Jonathan (1 Samuel 14) against all odds. Then he asks that God strike fear into Lysias' warriors and strike them down by the swords of Judas' soldiers. At the battle of Beth-zur (4:34-35), Lysias lost about five thousand men. He came to recognize that Judas and his followers would be difficult to defeat. As the Seleucid armies got larger, their casualties grew greater, and so did Judas' army and his fame as a warrior. Therefore Lysias returned to Antioch in the hope of fighting another day. For a second battle at Beth-zur, see 6:28-31.

4:36-61 The rededication of the temple (Hanukkah)

The first phase of Judas' leadership reaches its climax with the rededication of the Jerusalem temple to the God of Israel. After defeating the Seleucid armies in spectacular fashion, Judas restores the temple furnishings and restarts the proper rituals there. The initial goal of the Maccabean revolt was reached when the temple altar was rededicated to Yahweh. The festival of Hanukkah, which commemorates the rededication of the temple under Judas, takes its name from the Hebrew verb *hanak* ("dedicate"). For another account of the first Hanukkah, see 2 Maccabees 10:1-8.

When Judas and his brothers arrive at Mount Zion (the temple area), they find it in total disrepair (4:36-38) and so perform the appropriate gestures of mourning (4:39-40). Why the site was in such bad condition presents a mystery. Had the new order based on worship of Baal Shamen been a failure that gained no popular support? Or did Judas purposely delay rededicating the temple to highlight his role in bringing about this event? Or was the author so overcome with dislike for the former pagan worship and so enamored with the renewal of proper Jewish worship that he exaggerated how bad things had become?

In order to proceed with purifying and rededicating the sanctuary, Judas first had to defuse the possibility of attacks from the citadel overlooking the temple area (1:33). The troops stationed there remained a threat to the temple and the Maccabees for over twenty more years. The "blameless priests" of 4:42-43 were those who had refused to participate in the worship of Baal Shamen (the "Abomination") and were found to be ritually pure in accord with Leviticus 21:17-23. The defiled "stones" (perhaps from meteors?) were those used in the altar connected with the Baal Shamen cult. Since the altar of holocausts had been defiled (4:44-46), the decision was made to store them away and await enlightenment from "a prophet" in the future (see Deut 18:15; Mal 3:23; 1 Macc 14:41). For building the new altar with "uncut stones" (4:47), see Exodus 20:25 and Deuteronomy 27:5-6. The temple furnishings (4:48-51) that had been pillaged by Antiochus IV (1:21-24) were restored according to the directives in Exodus 25–27.

The rededication of the Jerusalem temple (4:52-55) took place on December 14 of 164 B.C., three years to the day from when it had been defiled to make way for the new cult of Baal Shamen. The celebration of the first Hanukkah (4:56-59) lasted eight days, as did earlier consecrations of the Jerusalem temple under Solomon (1 Kgs 8:65-66) and Hezekiah (2 Chr 29). There was great rejoicing because "the disgrace brought by the Gentiles"

(4:58) had finally been removed. Therefore Judas and his supporters decreed (4:59) that Hanukkah should be an annual observance to last for eight days, from the 25th of Chislev (roughly our December). (See 2 Macc 1:1-9 for a plea that Jews in Egypt should also observe Hanukkah.) They also fortified Mount Zion to protect against further attacks from the citadel, and Beth-zur to prevent more invasions of Judea from the south (see 4:29).

5:1-68 Jewish victories in all directions

The end of the first phase in Judas' leadership found him in control of the Jerusalem temple and environs, as well as the fortress at Beth-zur about twenty miles south of Jerusalem. In the next phase (163 B.C.), Judas and his companions attack in all directions: Idumea to the south (5:3-5, 65), Ammon and Gilead east of the Jordan River (5:6-13, 24-51), Galilee to the north (5:14-23), and the coastal plain (5:66-68). Their attacks are portrayed as revenge for the harm visited on Jews in those territories or to ward off the threat of their destruction there. They echo the example of David in 2 Samuel 8 and 10. Those who act apart from the leadership of the Maccabees (5:55-62, 67) suffer defeat, while Judas and his brothers are honored in all Israel and among the Gentiles (5:63). The author's comment on those defeats summarizes the major themes of the entire book: "But they were not of the family through whom Israel's deliverance was given" (5:62).

Judas' success in capturing the Jerusalem temple and environs and in rededicating it led his Gentile enemies to take revenge on Jews living in areas not controlled by Judas (5:1-2). In response (5:3-5) Judas attacks first the Idumeans ("sons of Esau") at Akrabattene (southwest of the Dead Sea), and then the "sons of Baean" (nomads who attacked caravans, see 2 Macc 10:14). When they took refuge in towers, Judas burned the towers and killed those who were inside.

The account of Judas' attacks against the Ammonites in 5:6-8 may be out of place here. Some scholars suggest that these attacks were in retaliation for the massacre of the Tobiads mentioned in 5:13 and might fit better between 5:36 and 5:37. Timothy may have been the local ruler of the Ammonites in Transjordan or the Seleucid commander mentioned in 2 Maccabees 8:30-33. Jazer was near Heshbon in Transjordan (see Num 21:32).

When Gentiles in Gilead (east of the Jordan, see Josh 22:9) threatened to attack the Jews settled in their territory, the Jews there fled to Dathema (location unknown, see 5:29) and wrote an urgent letter to Judas and his brothers, asking for help. In their letter (5:10-13) they note that the Tobiads had been killed and their wives, children, and possessions taken away. The Tobiads were Jews who lived at et-Taiyibeh, twelve miles east and slightly north of Ramoth-gilead. Meanwhile, a similar message (5:14-16) arrived from the Jews in Galilee that the Gentiles in the seacoast towns as well as "the whole of Gentile Galilee" (see Isa 9:1; Matt 4:15) were joining forces to attack them.

In response the three most prominent Maccabean brothers devised a plan in 5:17-20 according to which Simon would go to Galilee with three thousand soldiers, and Judas and Jonathan would go to Gilead with eight thousand soldiers. They left Joseph and Azariah (not their brothers) in charge of Judea, with the warning not to engage the Gentiles in battle until the brothers should return.

According to 5:21-23, Simon had great success in Galilee. He pursued the Gentiles to Ptolemais (named after Ptolemy II of Egypt, and also known as Acco and Acre) and brought the Jews who were in Galilee and "Arbatta" (Narbatta?) back to Judea.

On the basis of information from some Nabatean travelers, Judas and Jonathan rescued the Jews besieged in Gilead and defeated Timothy near Raphon (5:24-44). The Nabateans (5:25) were based in southern Transjordan and traveled the caravan routes as traders. They seem friendly toward Judas and Jonathan here and in 9:35 and may have shared the Jews' hopes for independence from the Seleucids. Bozrah (5:26) was seventy miles south of Damascus and appears at the head of the list of cities east and north of the Yarmuk River. The Gentiles in these cities probably sided with the Seleucids, and felt threatened by their Jewish neighbors in the light of Judas' recent victories. The Nabateans informed them that the Gentiles were prepared to massacre the Jews on the next day (5:27).

In response Judas attacked and destroyed Bozrah (5:28), and went to the Jewish stronghold at Dathema (5:29; see 5:9). As the Gentiles began to besiege Dathema at dawn, Judas and his army came up from behind them and routed them, with more than eight thousand casualties and Timothy's army put to flight. Then Judas moved against the other cities in Gilead (5:35-36) mentioned by the Nabateans. See 5:6-8 for an earlier (and perhaps misplaced) reference to Timothy.

According to 5:37-44, Timothy amassed an even larger army and camped opposite Judas' army, with a stream or river between the two armies. The Seleucids often used Arabs as mercenaries (2 Macc 12:10). Timothy reasoned that if Judas crossed over the river to engage his army, then Judas had confidence that his army was large and strong enough to defeat Timothy's army. If Judas had to retreat, he and his troops would be hampered by the river behind him. In fact, Judas did cross over (5:43) and won the battle decisively. The name "Carnaim" (5:43-44) means "horns," and suggests that the goddess Astarte, depicted as having cow's horns, was worshiped there. The Gentiles may have fled there in the hope of gaining asylum, but Judas did not respect the pagan shrine at Carnaim as a legitimate sanctuary.

According to 5:45-54, Judas brought the Israelites from Gilead to Jerusalem and its temple by way of Ephron and Beth-shan. Ephron was nine miles east of the Jordan River, opposite Beth-shan. In offering peace terms to Ephron and then (when they were refused) destroying it totally, Judas in 5:46-51 acted as the perfect biblical warrior in accord with the rules laid down in Deuteronomy 20:10-20. Beth-shan (5:52), also known as Scythopolis and Nysa, was on the western side of the Jordan River. The caravan of Jews from Gilead and elsewhere arrived in Jerusalem without losing anyone, and they celebrated their arrival with sacrifices at the Jerusalem temple. According to 2 Maccabees 12:31-32, they arrived just in time to observe the feast of Weeks (Pentecost).

While Simon was off in Galilee and Judas and Jonathan were in Gilead, the two men left in charge in Judea, Joseph and Azariah, disobeyed Judas' command not to engage the Gentiles in battle (5:18-19) and attacked Jamnia in the hope of making a name for themselves (5:55-62). The result was a rout at the hands of Gorgias and the loss of two thousand men. Their fault lay in not listening to Judas and his brothers. Jamnia, also known as Yavneh, was the capital of the province of Azotus (Ashdod) and a center of hostility to the Jews (2 Macc 12:8-9). Their folly and defeat served to highlight the pivotal role of the Maccabees in bringing about Israel's "deliverance" (5:63-64).

The long narrative of Jewish victories in all directions ends in 5:65-68 with battles against Idumea (to the south) and Philistia (to the west). The use of the archaic biblical expressions "the sons of Esau" and "the land of the Philistines" contributes to the presentation of Judas as the ideal biblical warrior. The priests who fell in battle (5:67) may also (see 5:56-62) have failed to follow Judas' command in their search for personal glory. Azotus may refer to the province rather than the city of the same name.

6:1-17 The death of Antiochus IV

According to 1 Maccabees, Antiochus IV died after the rededication of the Jerusalem temple in December 164 B.C. (see 4:36-61). While the occasion is his inability to rob a temple in Elymais, the real reason, according to this author, was his arrogance in plundering the Jerusalem temple and desecrating it with the cult of Baal Shamen. For other (conflicting) accounts of his death, see Daniel 11:40-45 and 2 Maccabees 1:13-17; 9:1-29.

Elymais, or Elam, was a district to the west of Persia; the city that Antiochus tried to rob may have been Persepolis (6:1-4). His plan to rob the temple there was thwarted when the local population learned about his intentions. So he returned to Babylon, the eastern capital of the Seleucid Empire.

While in Babylon (6:5-7), Antiochus received a report not only about the defeat of Lysias but also about the success of Judas' army, his rededication of the temple, and his fortification of Beth-zur. In fact, Antiochus was probably dead by the time of the temple's rededication. The shift in chronology was part of the author's effort at making Antiochus' outrages against the Jerusalem temple into the real reason for his death.

According to 6:8-13, Antiochus in his misery and frustration came to the realization that the cause of his death was "the evils I did in Jerusalem" (6:12). The "Friends" who were keeping watch at his deathbed (6:10) were advisers to the king. Antiochus' description of himself as "kindly and beloved in my rule" (6:11) is confirmed by the name "Eupator" (meaning "of a good father") given to his son in 6:17. The Jewish sources, however, are unanimous in making him into a horrible villain because of what they perceived he had done to their temple and their people.

By appointing Philip (6:14-15) as regent and guardian of his son, and placing him in the same

office as Lysias (3:32-33), the dying king set up a rivalry between the two men. Antiochus IV died (6:16) in October or November of 164 B.C., shortly before the rededication of the Jerusalem temple. But news of his death may not have reached Judas and his supporters before the rededication. The author of 1 Maccabees, by placing his death after 4:36-61 (in December 164) and Judas' spectacular military successes in 5:1-68 (in 163) has him die with full knowledge of these setbacks. On learning of Antiochus IV's death, Lysias established Antiochus V Eupator as king (6:17) at Antioch, though he was still a boy.

6:18-31 The siege of the citadel

Taking advantage of the confusion surrounding Antiochus IV's death, Judas decided to launch an attack against the citadel overlooking the temple complex (6:18-21). For other references to the citadel, see 1:33-34; 4:41; 9:52; 10:6-9; 11:41; and 14:36. The citadel was finally captured and dismantled under Simon in 141 B.C.

Some of the Seleucid soldiers who escaped from the citadel were joined by "some renegade impious Israelites" (with the high priest Menelaus at their head, see 2 Macc 13:3) and formed a united delegation that lodged a complaint with the new king (6:22-27). Their complaint was that despite their loyal support for and cooperation with the program set forth by Antiochus IV (1:40-45), they were being abandoned by the king and harassed by Judas and his supporters. They contended that it was in the king's best interests to do everything to stop Judas now.

Although the boy-king may have been involved in the response (6:28-31), it was surely Lysias who was directing the planning and execution. The huge army (6:30) that he assembled, even allowing for exaggeration, was an indication of how seriously the threat from Judas was being taken. Lysias repeated his "fishhook" strategy (see 4:29) by approaching Judea from the south, through Idumea. The battle was joined at Beth-zur (6:31), the site of an earlier battle with Lysias (4:29-35), which Judas had fortified as an outpost against attacks from the south.

6:32-47 The battle at Beth-zechariah

The author seems to obscure the fact that the battle at Beth-zur (6:31) ended in defeat for the Jewish forces (see 6:49-50). Beth-zechariah, south of Jerusalem, was six miles north of Beth-zur. The site was chosen in the hope of stopping the advance of the Seleucid army. According to 6:33, King Antiochus V Eupator was leading the charge. This is highly unlikely, since he was still a young boy. Lysias or a subordinate must have been directing the military operations.

The description of the battle in 6:38-46 is quite vivid, perhaps based on eyewitness testimony. That Judas was defeated is glossed over, and the focus is on the courage displayed by his brother Eleazar (2:5) and the superior numbers and equipment of the Seleucids. Despite the overwhelming strength of the Seleucid army, Judas' forces managed to kill six hundred soldiers at the start of the battle. In the midst of the battle, Eleazar thought that he could get at the king by killing the elephant on which Eleazar thought the king was riding. In carrying out his plan, however, the elephant that he stabbed fell on Eleazar and crushed him to death (6:43-46). Meanwhile, the king was elsewhere. The Jewish defeat is marked by a brief notice (6:47) of the army's retreat.

6:48-54 The siege of Jerusalem

With the defeat at Beth-zechariah, the surrender of Beth-zur, and the siege of Jerusalem, the Maccabean movement was close to complete defeat. Matters were made worse by the observance of the sabbatical year (6:49) in which sowing and reaping were prohibited (see Exod 23:10-11; Lev 25:2-7). However, it should be noted that food shortages would be even more severe in the following year (6:53), since little food would have been stored away.

The Seleucids (6:48) recognized the symbolic significance of Mount Zion (see 4:36-61) for the Jews, which also explains the intense Jewish resistance there. The surrender of Beth-zur (6:49-50) confirms the impression that the battle there (6:31) had been a defeat for the Jews. The combination of relentless attacks from the Seleucids and near famine induced by food shortages (6:51-54) made the prospect of total death almost inevitable for the Jews.

6:55-63 Peace treaty

The Jews were rescued by developments in the Seleucid court. Lysias, who had been named regent and guardian of the new king (3:32-33), learned that Philip, who had been given the same

offices by Antiochus IV on his deathbed (6:14-15), was returning to Antioch in Syria with a large army (6:55-56). Since Lysias had to get to Antioch to prevent Philip from taking control there, he decided to make a quick settlement with the Jews.

The speech attributed to Lysias in 6:57-59 provides a list of reasons why a peace treaty then was appropriate and promises to allow the Jews "freedom to live according to their own laws as formerly" (6:59). Their laws were those found in the Torah, and this concession effectively canceled the program that Antiochus IV had decreed according to 1:41-50. The concession suggests that Lysias and Antiochus V had no interest in forcing the Jews to become part of the "one people" in the Seleucid Empire and to give up their particular customs (1:41-42).

In 6:60-61 we are told that Lysias' offer of a peace treaty was acceptable to both sides, and that the king swore an oath and left Jerusalem. But the Seleucids did not leave (6:62) without first destroying the wall around the temple complex that Judas had recently built (4:60). And the citadel remained in Seleucid hands. So the year 162 B.C. ended with the Maccabean revolt in deep trouble. There had been military defeats at Beth-zur and Beth-zechariah. Eleazar was dead. The Jewish defenses in Jerusalem had been weakened. And the peace treaty with the Seleucids, while timely, was also shaky.

7:1-25 Trouble from Bacchides and Alcimus

According to 7:1-4, in the spring of 161 B.C., Demetrius I Soter ("savior"), the son of Seleucus IV (whom Antiochus IV, his brother, deposed in 175), returned to Syria from Rome where he had been held as a hostage. When he was nine years old, Demetrius was brought to Rome to take the place of his uncle, Antiochus IV. Now at the age of twenty-five he escaped from Rome and landed at Tripolis by the sea, some 170 miles south of Antioch. From there he moved to Antioch and deposed Antiochus V and Lysias, and seized the Seleucid kingship from them. When the soldiers seized Antiochus V and Lysias, Demetrius refused to meet with them and allowed the soldiers to execute both of them. Thus he came to rule as Demetrius I.

Having removed Antiochus V and Lysias from power, Demetrius I, according to 7:5-7, sought to stabilize affairs in Judea by sending a large army under the command of Bacchides and by appointing Alcimus as high priest and political leader. Alcimus (Yakim in Hebrew) apparently came from a priestly family (7:14; see 1 Chr 24:12) and may have already been appointed as high priest under Antiochus V. He represented a faction in Judea that was favorable to the Seleucids and opposed to Judas and the Maccabees. The author of 1 Maccabees describes him, probably unfairly, in very negative terms. He portrays him as a magnet for "all the lawless men and renegades of Israel" (7:5). Those men petitioned the new king to send a high official to inspect all the damage done by Judas and to punish him and his supporters.

Demetrius I chose Bacchides, the governor of "Beyond the River" province, that is, the territory west of the Euphrates River, as his emissary to Judea (7:8-11). Meanwhile, the new king was occupied with putting down the revolt of Timarchus in the east. Bacchides and Alcimus arrived in Judea with a "great army" and sent messengers to Judas with offers of peace. But in the view of the author, Judas saw through their deceitful words and paid no attention to them.

However, according to 7:12-18, Bacchides and Alcimus did get a positive hearing first from a group of scribes (7:12) and then from the Hasideans ("the pious ones"). The latter group had previously allied themselves with Judas (2:42). Now they were impressed with the priestly credentials of Alcimus and assumed that he would do them no harm (7:13-16a). But for no apparent reason, Alcimus had sixty of the Hasideans killed in one day (7:16b-18). Perhaps their past allegiance to Judas was behind their execution, which was said to fulfill the words of Psalm 79:2-3. This act of treachery dissuaded many of the people from accepting Bacchides and Alcimus as champions of peace for Judea.

According to 7:19-20, Bacchides had his army camp at Beth-zaith, about twelve miles south of Jerusalem and three miles north of Beth-zur. The "pit" into which many who had come over to his side were thrown was probably a large cistern no longer used for storing water (see Jer 41:7). It appears that Bacchides intended to install Alcimus as a political ruler in Judea, as earlier high priests had been. From 7:21-25 it seems that while Alcimus had some success, Judas was still strong enough to carry out guerilla actions and prevent Alcimus

from really controlling Judea. Therefore, Alcimus went back to Demetrius I and accused Judas of more terrible crimes, in the hope of getting the king to send a still more powerful army against Judas.

7:26-50 Trouble from Nicanor

In 7:26-28 the author describes Nicanor as "a bitter enemy of Israel" and a deceiver. There is a more favorable portrait of Nicanor in 2 Maccabees 14:18-25, where he cultivates a genuine friendship with Judas and seeks to mediate between various Jewish factions. Their friendship is then destroyed by meddling from Alcimus (14:26-30). Nicanor's mission was to prop up Alcimus and his party and to defuse the threat from Judas. His first action in Judea was to request a peaceable meeting with Judas (7:28).

The peaceable meeting was only a ruse to ensnare Judas, who then refused to meet with Nicanor again (7:29-32). Having failed with personal diplomacy, Nicanor then provoked a battle with Judas at Caphar-salama, north of Jerusalem. But when Nicanor lost five hundred soldiers, he returned to the citadel in the "City of David" (Jerusalem).

Nicanor's threat to destroy the Jerusalem temple unless Judas was handed over to him reflects his frustration with his personal, political, and military failures (7:33-38). At this point the temple was in the hands of priests who were loyal to Alcimus and so to the Seleucids. These priests pointed out to Nicanor that they were regularly offering sacrifices to God on the king's behalf. However, Nicanor responded by spitting on them, thus not only insulting them but also rendering them ritually unclean for their temple service. The prayer offered by the priests in 7:37-38 echoes that of Solomon in 1 Kings 8 by identifying the Jerusalem temple as God's dwelling place on earth and in asking God to punish the enemies of Israel.

According to 7:39-50, Nicanor's threat against the temple resulted in his defeat by Judas and the dismembering of his corpse (see 2 Macc 15:1-36). According to 7:39-40, Nicanor gathered his army at Beth-horon (see 3:13-26), while Judas camped at Adasa (somewhere between Jerusalem and Beth-horon) with only three thousand men. In his prayer before battle (7:41-42), Judas recalls the expedition of Sennacherib against Jerusalem in 701 B.C. when the Judean forces were vastly outnumbered but were miraculously rescued by the "angel of the Lord" (2 Kgs 19:35; Isa 37:36).

The battle (7:43-46) took place in March of 160 B.C. Judas' strategy was to kill the commander Nicanor first in the hope of panicking his troops. It worked, with the result that Nicanor's soldiers tried to flee to Gazara (ancient Gezer), where there was a Seleucid fort. Emboldened by Judas' success, the local people joined forces with Judas and wiped out Nicanor's army.

In the aftermath of the battle (7:47-50), the Jews cut off Nicanor's head and right arm. Originally a Persian punishment, this was interpreted by the Jews as just punishment for his threat against their temple (7:47). In the first century "Nicanor's Day" was celebrated as a Jewish holiday, but it eventually dropped from the calendar. In 7:50 the author echoes a formula familiar from the book of Judges (3:30; 5:31; etc.), but modifies it with the phrase "for a few days" in light of the continuing threat from the Seleucids. In fact, the peace lasted only about a month (see 1 Macc 9:1-18).

8:1-16 Praise for the Romans

In the effort to protect himself and his people, Judas sought to establish an alliance with the Romans. The terms of the alliance are preceded in 8:1-16 with an idealized and somewhat inaccurate description of Roman military successes and the help that they gave to their "friends" in the past. Judas probably initiated the process before Nicanor's death, and foresaw that having an aggressive and powerful ally outside the Near East would allow Israel to survive as a people.

The Gauls, subdued by the Romans (8:2), were most likely those on the southern side of the Alps, in northern Italy and southern France, who were defeated in 222 and again in 191 B.C. Spain (8:3) came under Roman control in the late third century B.C. The kings (8:4) defeated by the Romans included Philip V of Macedon in 197 B.C. and his son Perseus in 168 B.C. (8:5), as well as Antiochus III who was defeated by the Romans at Magnesia in 189 B.C. and forced by the Treaty of Apamea to give some of his territory to Eumenes II of Pergamum (8:6-8). Among the "hostages" (8:7) was the future king Antiochus IV. Neither India nor Media (8:8) was ever ceded to Eumenes, although they made their way into manuscripts, probably through scribal error. The textual revision "Ionia [or, Lycia], Mysia," in 8:8 is more accurate.

The report of the Roman defeat of the Greeks (8:9-10) refers to the revolt of the Achaean League in 146 B.C. that was crushed by Lucius Mummius, who then destroyed Corinth. This victory took place fifteen years after the Jewish embassy went to Rome. The summary in 8:11 highlights the Romans' military success, thus providing one good reason why Judas sought an alliance with them.

Another reason is supplied in 8:12-13: Rome's alleged faithfulness in protecting and empowering its allies. Prior to the emergence of the Roman Empire under Julius Caesar and Augustus (63 B.C. to A.D. 14), Rome was a republic ruled by two consuls and the senate. The senate (8:15) had three hundred members (not three hundred twenty) and did not meet every day. Moreover, two consuls, not one, were elected every year. The statement that "there is no envy or jealousy among them" (8:16) does not fit well with what Roman historians reported.

8:17-32 An alliance with Rome

The Jews needed a defender against the Seleucids, and the Romans were displeased by the actions of Demetrius I and eager to extend their influence in the east. However, according to 1 Maccabees, nothing much came of the alliance until Simon came to power (see 14:16-24). Eupolemus (8:17), from the priestly clan of Hakkoz (1 Chr 24:10), was the son of the man who had won concessions from Antiochus III (see 2 Macc 4:11). His journey with Jason to Rome probably lasted over a month (8:19) and may have taken place in 161 B.C., even before Demetrius I arrived in Syria and Nicanor was defeated. According to 8:18-21, they made their proposal for an alliance in the senate chamber, and it was accepted unanimously. The original Latin text on the bronze tablet (8:22) would have been kept in Rome, while a copy in letter form (in Hebrew or Aramaic, or perhaps even Greek) would have been sent to Jerusalem.

Most scholars today regard the text of the treaty in 8:23-30 as basically authentic. After an opening statement of mutual good will (8:23), there are parallel statements in 8:24-26 and 8:27-28, stipulating that each side would come to the other's aid if war broke out. However, the clause "as the occasion shall demand" (8:25) provides a good measure of flexibility. Alterations could be made only with the consent of both parties (8:29-30). The threatening message about King Demetrius in 8:31-32 may not have been part of the original treaty text. It is written in biblical idiom ("Why have you made your yoke heavy . . . ?"), and was never acted upon by the Romans.

There is evidence that the Romans were not very scrupulous about fulfilling their obligations in this kind of treaty. They usually acted when it best suited their interests. However, a small constituency like the Maccabees had little to lose from such a treaty. Its existence might scare off the Seleucids, who would not know whether this might be one of those occasions that might bring about Roman intervention. It also gave the Maccabees and their supporters the status of speaking on behalf of Israel and so constituting a kind of government.

9:1-10 The return of Bacchides

To avenge the defeat of Nicanor, Demetrius I sent Bacchides back to Judea (see 7:8-9). In 9:2 the Greek text reads "Gilgal" and "Mesaloth in Arbela." But the geography and the context demand the changes to "Galilee" and "the ascent at Arbela." There, Bacchides won a victory and killed many, and at the beginning of 160 b.c. he and Alcimus camped against Jerusalem (9:3).

Then in verse 4 Bacchides went to Berea (ten miles north of Jerusalem) with a huge army, while Judas camped opposite him at Elasa with a much smaller force of three thousand men. Moreover, wide-scale desertions depleted Judas' army down to eight hundred (9:6), and this fact helps to explain his defeat.

Faced with an apparently hopeless situation, Judas proposed seizing the initiative from Bacchides ("Let us go forward to meet our enemies" [9:8]) as a way of taking his numerically superior opponents by surprise. But even his remaining troops balked at the suggestion. Nevertheless, Judas urged them forward as a mark of courage and in the hope of personal glory.

9:11-22 The death of Judas

The description of Bacchides' army in 9:11-13 is remarkably vivid and contributes to the mood of the impending doom that Judas faces. The "phalanx" in verse 12 refers to an infantry unit made up of soldiers carrying spears and shields.

According to 9:14-18, Judas' plan was to make a run at Bacchides himself and the right wing of his army. The change to "mountain slopes" (9:15) replaces the Greek text's obvious error of "Mount Azotus." Apparently the Greek translator mistook the Hebrew word for "slopes" (*ashdot*) for Ashdod/Azotus. While Judas had initial success against the right wing, he soon found himself trapped when the left wing doubled back around him in a pincer movement. The result was death for Judas, and the defeat and scattering of his remaining soldiers (9:17-18).

Jonathan and Simon attended to the burial of Judas in the family tomb at Modein (9:19; see 2:70; 13:27-30). The people's lament in 9:21 echoes 2 Samuel 1:25, 27, and Judges 3:9. And the formula concluding the exploits of Judas in verse 22 is reminiscent of the language used regarding the various kings of Israel and Judah in 1 and 2 Kings. Thus Judas dies as a biblical hero. But once more the Maccabean movement is in serious trouble. It needs a new leader and a new way of dealing with its enemies. It will find both in Jonathan, the brother of Judas.

JONATHAN

1 Maccabees 9:23–12:53

9:23-31 Jonathan succeeds Judas

While Judas was a daring and brilliant military leader, his brother Jonathan became a skillful politician. His greatest successes came from playing off one claimant to the Seleucid throne against another, and so gaining more territory and security for his people. With the death of Judas it looked like the Maccabean revolt was over. What gave it new life was Jonathan's political skill.

In 9:23-27 the author describes the terrible state of affairs after Judas' death. The "lawless" in Israel and "all kinds of evildoers" emerged. There was famine in the land. And Bacchides put "renegades" in charge, who punished the remaining followers of Judas. In a time of famine the rulers had charge of the food supplies and thus could win over the common people to their side. The "prophets" mentioned in 9:27 were the postexilic prophets such as Haggai, Zechariah, and Malachi. For hope for the appearance of a new prophet, see 4:46 and 14:41.

The choice of Jonathan to succeed Judas (9:28-31) echoes the dynamics of how the "judges," the charismatic leaders in ancient Israel before the monarchy, came to power. This impression is confirmed in 9:73. Why the friends of Judas passed over the older Simon to be the leader is not explained.

9:32-49 Vengeance for John's death

Recognizing that Bacchides wished to kill them, Jonathan and Simon fled to the "wilderness of Tekoa," fifteen miles southeast of Jerusalem. Tekoa had been a place of refuge for Saul's son Jonathan (see 2 Sam 14:1-17; 2 Chr 20:20) and was the home of the prophet Amos. The pool of Ashpar (9:33) may have been a cistern. The report of Bacchides' movements in 9:34 is out of place and belongs more properly in 9:43 where it is repeated.

The brother whom Jonathan sent (9:35) was John, also known as Gaddi (2:2). For the Nabateans as friends of the Maccabees, see 5:25. Whether the family of Jambri from Medeba (northeast of the Dead Sea) were Nabateans is not clear. However, they seized John and stole all that he had. That they killed John becomes clear in 9:38, 42.

According to 9:37-42, Jonathan and Simon took their vengeance on the family of Jambri for having killed John by ambushing their wedding party. As the family of Jambri were leading a bride from a Canaanite family to the household of one of their own, the Maccabees attacked the procession, killed the people, and seized all their goods. What in this context "Canaan" meant and where Nadabath was (9:37) remain mysteries. The massacre is interpreted as legitimate vengeance for the murder of John (9:42).

From 9:43-49 it is difficult to discern the movements of the armies. The events take place in the swampy area north of the Dead Sea, by the Jordan River (9:43). This is the first report of the Maccabees fighting on the sabbath since the decision announced in 2:40-41. In his speech to the troops (9:44-46), Jonathan acknowledges the problem posed by the terrain and prays for divine deliverance. We are told in 9:47-48 that Jonathan almost killed Bacchides but then had to flee by swimming across the Jordan. While 9:49 gives the impression that the battle was a victory for Jonathan, it was more likely a defeat, as what follows in 9:50-57 indicates.

9:50-57 Bacchides and Alcimus secure their power

When he returned to Jerusalem (9:50), Bacchides had forts constructed in Judea and southern Samaria (Timnath, Pharathon, and Tephon), as well as in Beth-zur and Gazara/Gezer (9:52). He also strengthened the citadel in Jerusalem and put under guard as hostages there the sons of the leading men of Judea as a way of securing their cooperation (9:53).

In 159 B.C. the high priest Alcimus embarked on a project to remodel the temple complex (9:54-55). He ordered torn down "the wall of the inner court of the sanctuary," that is, the wall separating the Holy of Holies (reserved for Israelite priests) from the rest of the temple area. The "prophets" mentioned in 9:54 are Haggai and Zechariah who encouraged and oversaw the rebuilding of the Jerusalem temple in the late sixth century B.C. The author suggests that the stroke suffered by Alcimus and his subsequent death (9:55-56) were fitting punishments for daring to change the design of the temple. The notice of rest for two years (9:57) again evokes the book of Judges. Who succeeded Alcimus as high priest between 159 and 152 B.C. is not clear.

9:58-73 More battles and another peace treaty

In 157 B.C. Jonathan's opponents, described as "the lawless," pleaded with Bacchides to return to Judea and destroy Jonathan and his supporters once and for all (9:58-59). However, according to verses 60-61, Jonathan found out about the plot and killed fifty of the local ringleaders.

To escape from Bacchides, Jonathan and Simon withdrew to Bethbasi, near Bethlehem and north of Tekoa, and settled in there (9:62-64). On learning of their move, Bacchides brought his army there and laid siege to Bethbasi. However, Jonathan took a small force and struck down some local allies of Bacchides, here identified as Odemera and the sons of Phaseron. Then Simon engaged Bacchides' forces directly and defeated them (9:67-68). Out of frustration at having been called upon repeatedly to resolve disputes in Judea, Bacchides directed his anger at "the lawless men" there, killed many of them, and returned to his own country (9:69).

In response Jonathan proposed to Bacchides another peace treaty and a release of prisoners (9:70-72). Since Jonathan was apparently the only significant military and political leader left in Judea, his offer was acceptable to Bacchides who in turn agreed to leave Jonathan alone in the future.

According to 9:73, there was peace in Judea and Jonathan "began to judge," an expression that again links him to the "judges" of old. However, all the forts established by Bacchides (9:50-53) and Jerusalem itself were still in the hands of the Seleucids and their local supporters. Michmash, nine miles north of Jerusalem, had been the center of an earlier Israelite kingdom under Saul (1 Sam 13:2) and of the earlier Jonathan's victory over the Philistines (1 Sam 14:5-31). It served as headquarters for Jonathan Maccabeus from 157 to 152 B.C.

10:1-14 The appearance of Alexander Balas

In 152 B.C. Alexander Balas appeared on the scene (10:1) as a claimant to the Seleucid throne occupied by Demetrius I. Claiming to be the son of Antiochus IV, he took the title "Epiphanes" ("[God] manifest") and secured a base at Ptolemais (also known as Acco and Acre). The name "Balas" most likely derives from the Semitic title "Baal," meaning "lord" or "master." He was accepted not only by the local populace but also by the Romans who were angry with Demetrius I for becoming king without their permission. Eager to stop Alexander's revolt as quickly as possible, Demetrius I wrote to Jonathan "in peaceful terms" (10:3), in the hope of getting to Jonathan before Alexander did. He recognized that Jonathan was the only leader in Judea worth cultivating.

According to 10:6-14, Jonathan took full advantage of his newfound recognition by Demetrius I. Not only did Demetrius I allow Jonathan to raise an army and equip it with arms, but he also gave him the honor of overseeing the release of the hostages from the citadel (see 9:53), let him take up residence once more in Jerusalem, and oversee the repairs made in the temple area ("Mount Zion"). Jonathan's quick rise to prominence frightened both the non-Jews installed in the forts built by Bacchides and the Jews who had opposed Jonathan. The latter found refuge at Beth-zur (10:14) and are dismissed by the author as "those who had abandoned the law and the commandments."

10:15-21 Jonathan becomes the high priest

Alexander Balas recognized that it would be better to have Jonathan as his "friend and ally" than as his enemy (10:16). And so he entered into a bidding war with Demetrius I for Jonathan's services (10:15-16). In his letter to Jonathan (10:18-20), Alexander promised to make him "high priest of your nation" as well as the "King's Friend" (part of the Seleucid nobility) and to allow him to wear the purple robe and golden crown befitting those offices. Although Jonathan was from a Jewish priestly family (see 2:1), he was not one of the descendants of Zadok, which was the legitimate high priestly family. The high priesthood seems to have been vacant since the death of Alcimus in 159. This is called the *intersacerdotium*, the period of time between priestly administrations, lasting until 152. Seleucid kings had routinely appointed Jewish high priests in the past (see 2 Macc 4:7, 23-24).

According to 10:21, Jonathan saw his opportunity and took it. In late October of 152 B.C., Jonathan put on the high priestly regalia at the feast of Booths (Tabernacles) and gathered an army. Thus he usurped leadership in Judea on three levels: religious, military, and political. Jewish opposition to his moves may have occasioned the beginning of the Qumran sect and the building of the temple by Onias IV at Leontopolis in Egypt (see 2 Macc 1:1-9).

10:22-50 Demetrius I's offer and his death

Anxious to top Alexander in the bidding for Jonathan's support, Demetrius I wrote a letter with so many extravagant promises that it defied credibility. In his prologue (10:25-28) Demetrius addresses his letter to "the Jewish nation" and promises to bestow upon it various tax exemptions and other gifts and privileges. The body of the letter offers exemptions from all kinds of taxes, recognition of Jerusalem as a holy city, freedom for Jewish prisoners, provisions for Jewish soldiers in his army, annexation of some neighboring territories, subsidies for Jerusalem and its temple, the right of asylum in Jerusalem, and funds to rebuild Jerusalem (10:29-45).

By addressing "the Jewish nation" and mentioning "the high priest" (10:32, 38) without referring to Jonathan by name, Demetrius may have hoped to lure the people away from Jonathan and his supporters. That may help to explain why Jonathan and his supporters so quickly and completely rejected Demetrius I's offers (10:46), besides the obvious fact that these promises were too good to be true. Therefore they allied themselves firmly with Alexander Balas. Despite what is said in 10:47, Demetrius had been the first to seek peace (see 10:3-6, 15). In this case, Jonathan backed the successful Seleucid claimant, since in 150 B.C. Alexander defeated Demetrius I in battle, and "Demetrius fell that day" (10:50).

10:51-66 The marriage alliance

Having gained control of the Seleucid kingdom, Alexander saw the need to make peace with the Ptolemaic kingdom based in Egypt by proposing a marriage alliance. The "king of Egypt" in 150 B.C. (10:51) would have been Ptolemy VI Philometor (see 1:18), and his daughter would have been Cleopatra Thea (see 10:57-58). She later married Demetrius II and still later his brother Antiochus VII. The marriage alliances between the Seleucids and the Ptolemies were not always successful (see Dan 2:43; 11:17). Alexander's proposal was that Ptolemy give Cleopatra to him as his wife, and Alexander give in return many appropriate gifts (10:54). While not rejecting the proposal, Ptolemy suggested (10:55-56) a personal meeting at a neutral site, Ptolemais. The meeting apparently went well, and Alexander and Cleopatra were married "with great splendor" (10:58).

According to 10:59-66, Jonathan once more seized or even created an opportunity for his greater advancement. Invited by his new ally Alexander to Ptolemais, Jonathan met with both kings and won their favor. Despite the protestations of his Jewish opponents, Jonathan was clothed in royal purple, seated beside the king, and granted immunity from any charges made against him. Moreover, Alexander promoted him to the rank of "Chief Friend" and named him military commander and governor of Judea (10:65). Jonathan's Jewish accusers were clearly beaten and so they fled, while Jonathan returned to Jerusalem "in peace and happiness" (10:66).

10:67-89 Jonathan's victory over Apollonius

In 147 B.C. Demetrius II Nicator, the son of Demetrius I and then about fourteen years old, appeared on the scene (10:67-68) to challenge Alexander Balas (and his loyal supporter Jonathan). The name "Coelesyria" (10:69) originally referred to the area between the Lebanon and anti-Lebanon mountains but later came to include

Palestine. As governor of Coelesyria, Apollonius would have been Jonathan's superior. Having gathered a large army on the Mediterranean coast at Jamnia (Yavneh), Apollonius sent a message to Jonathan (10:70-73) decrying his lack of cooperation and challenging him to a battle on the plain rather than attacks in the mountains. The two earlier Jewish defeats alluded to in 10:72 refer to the battles at Beth-zechariah (6:47) and Elasa (9:18).

According to 10:74-76, Apollonius' taunting of Jonathan achieved the desired effect of drawing him out of Jerusalem and into battle. Joppa was on the coast, north of Jamnia and about forty miles northwest of Jerusalem. Jonathan's capture of Joppa not only gave the Maccabees a seaport for the first time but also cut off Apollonius from Demetrius II.

By heading south to Azotus (ancient Ashdod), Apollonius hoped to lure Jonathan out into the plain (10:77-78) where his advantage in the size of his army could be better exploited. By leaving behind a thousand cavalry, Apollonius set an ambush for Jonathan and had him trapped. However, according to 10:81-83, Jonathan managed to hold out against Apollonius' forces and Simon defeated his phalanx.

Following the example set by Judas (5:44, 68), Jonathan showed no mercy to those of Apollonius' army who sought refuge in the temple of Dagon (an ancient Semitic deity) at Azotus (10:84-85). From there he went to Askalon (a port south of Azotus) where he received a hero's welcome, and returned to Jerusalem with much plunder. As a reward for his loyalty, Alexander Balas promoted him to the rank of the "King's Kinsman" (10:89) and gave him Ekron and its surroundings. In ancient times Azotus, Askalon, and Ekron had been Philistine strongholds.

11:1-19 Ptolemy's attempted coup

According to 11:1-2, Ptolemy VI Philometor sought to add Alexander's Seleucid kingdom to his own, despite the fact that he was Alexander's father-in-law (see 10:58). Indeed, his close relationship with Alexander allowed him to enter freely (and deceitfully) the cities that belonged to Alexander, and once there to station his own troops (11:3). He took note of the damage done by Jonathan at Azotus (11:4; see 10:83-85) and listened to accusations against him (11:5). He met up with Jonathan (11:6-7) at Joppa (see 10:76), who accompanied him as far as the River Eleutherus, two hundred miles north of Joppa and the southern border of the Syrian territory of the Seleucids.

Ptolemy began (11:8) to put his plan against Alexander into action by seizing "Seleucia-by-the-Sea," the port city of Antioch that was loyal to Demetrius II. Then he proposed a marriage alliance with Demetrius II that would involve giving his daughter (then Alexander's wife; see 10:51-58) to be his wife. There had been an attempt to kill Ptolemy, and the assassin (a friend of Alexander) claimed that Alexander had been the instigator. However, according to 11:11-13, Ptolemy's real reason for making the marriage alliance was to force a sharp break with Alexander and to make the Seleucid kingdom part of his own kingdom. Thus in 145 B.C. Ptolemy II Philometor came to wear the crowns of both the Ptolemaic and Seleucid kingdoms.

But Ptolemy's success was short-lived. When Alexander who was putting down a revolt in Cilicia to the west learned of Ptolemy's coup, he rushed back to engage Ptolemy in battle at the River Oenoparus near Antioch. According to 11:15-17, Ptolemy won the battle, and Alexander fled to "Arabia" (the northern desert east of Damascus) where he was beheaded by Zabdiel. However, Ptolemy himself (11:18) died from wounds incurred in the battle, and the men in his garrisons were also killed off. That let Demetrius II become king by default in 145 B.C. (11:19).

11:20-37 Jonathan's agreement with Demetrius II

The political confusion surrounding the Seleucids and Ptolemies afforded Jonathan another opportunity to try to gain control over the citadel in Jerusalem (11:20-22). Acting on information from other Jews (who are dismissed by the author as "some transgressors of the law"), Demetrius II summoned Jonathan to a meeting to be held at Ptolemais (Acco), on the Mediterranean coast.

While ignoring the king's order to stop besieging the citadel, Jonathan went with his retinue and many gifts to Ptolemais (11:23-28). There he "found favor with the king" and got himself confirmed in his office as the Jewish high priest and in his rank as one of the king's Chief Friends. This gave him the boldness to request that Judea and the three districts of Samaria (see 10:30, 38) be exempted from taxes in return for a payment of three hundred talents.

The king's acceptance of Jonathan's request takes the form of a letter contained in 11:30-37. Addressed to Jonathan and the Jewish nation, it purports to be a copy of the king's letter to Lasthenes, who is described as the "kinsman" and "father" to Demetrius II. Lasthenes was the leader of Demetrius' mercenary soldiers from Crete and served as his chief minister. He was undoubtedly the real power behind the throne of the young king. The body of the letter (11:33-36) confirms the addition of three districts to Jonathan's territory of Judea and exempts them all from paying taxes to Demetrius II. Those revenues were to go instead to the Jerusalem temple (where Jonathan was the high priest). The agreement was to be made public (11:37; see 8:22) by displaying the text at the Temple Mount (the "holy mountain").

11:38-40 The intrigues of Demetrius II and Trypho

Since both Alexander Balas and Ptolemy were dead, Demetrius had no real opposition. Emboldened by the peace, he dismissed his native or local soldiers and handed his military affairs over to his Cretan mercenaries ("from the islands of the nations," 11:38). This strategy undoubtedly was the work of Lasthenes, and the plan was to absolve Demetrius from paying the local soldiers and to give him tighter control over what was in effect his private army. However, the native soldiers resented the new policy, since it left them without jobs and salaries. The plan eventually backfired and led to the king's loss of power (see 11:55).

Meanwhile, according to 11:39-40, Diodotus Trypho ("the luxurious one") persuaded Imalkue the Arab, who had been serving as the guardian for Alexander Balas' son, to allow the boy to become known as King Antiochus VI. See 13:31-32, where Trypho kills Antiochus VI and sets himself up as king. While Trypho was with the boy, he painted a dark picture of Demetrius II and suggested that the native soldiers' hatred of Demetrius II could be used to their advantage.

11:41-53 Jonathan helps Demetrius II

Only at 11:41-43 does it become apparent that Jonathan's siege of the citadel in Jerusalem had failed. But when Jonathan requested that Demetrius II should withdraw his troops from the citadel and other garrisons (see 9:50-51), Demetrius readily acceded (at least verbally) and asked for help in putting down a revolt by the disgruntled native soldiers.

The account of the battle at Antioch (11:44-51) features inflated numbers of troops and very likely exaggerates the role of Jonathan's army in winning the battle. The bulk of the work was probably done by the Cretan mercenaries. Nevertheless, the presence of the Jewish soldiers may well have saved the king's life (11:48). The result was that the Jewish force won glory in battle and took home "much plunder" (11:51). However, once the crisis was over (11:52-53), Demetrius II reneged on all his promises and became hostile to Jonathan. Losing Jonathan as an ally probably contributed to the king's downfall.

11:54-59 Jonathan's alliance with Trypho and Antiochus VI

When Trypho brought the boy to Antioch and set him up as King Antiochus VI, the native soldiers rallied to their cause and drove Demetrius II out of the city. By capturing the elephants (the ancient equivalent of tanks), Trypho gained the military advantage and took over Antioch. Ever the shrewd politician, Jonathan went over to the new regime. In turn, Antiochus VI confirmed Jonathan as the Jewish high priest and ruler and appointed him as one of the King's Friends. The permission for Jonathan to wear the "gold buckle" (see 10:89) also made Jonathan one of the King's Kinsmen. Moreover, the appointment of Simon (11:59) as governor of the coastal area from the southern border of Lebanon (the "Ladder of Tyre") to the northern frontier of Egypt expanded Maccabean control of the land of Israel westward.

11:60-74 The campaigns of Jonathan and Simon

According to 11:60-62, Jonathan traveled around Palestine and Coelesyria, apparently in order to recruit soldiers to fight against Demetrius II. Although he was welcomed in Askalon, he met opposition in Gaza. So he did great damage to Gaza and sent the sons of the leading men to Jerusalem as hostages.

Since Jonathan was now openly supporting Antiochus VI, the generals of Demetrius II wanted to stop him from recruiting troops and to remove him from his offices. As recent archaeological investigations have revealed, Kadesh in Galilee (11:63) was used as an administrative center by the Seleucids. Meanwhile, in 144 B.C. Simon recaptured Beth-zur (see 9:51; 10:14), thus providing the Maccabees with a southern stronghold.

From his camp near the Sea of Galilee ("the waters of Gennesaret"), Jonathan went to the plain of Hazor (see Josh 11:10-11), ten miles north of the sea. The description of his Seleucid opponents as "the army of the foreigners" in 11:68 suggests that they were Cretan mercenaries. At first the battle went badly for Jonathan, and many of his troops deserted him. Nevertheless, following the example of Joshua (see Josh 7:6-9), Jonathan prayed for God's help and returned to the battle from which he emerged as the victor. The deserters returned, and his army camped at Kadesh, supposedly having killed three thousand of the "foreign troops" (Cretan mercenaries). His return to Jerusalem (11:74) served as the occasion to renew contact with the Romans and find a new ally in the Spartans.

12:1-23 Alliances with Rome and Sparta

Up to this point in his career as a leader, Jonathan had skillfully and successfully played off one claimant to the Seleucid throne against another, and gained religious and political authority for himself and additional territories for the Judeans. However, he recognized how precarious his political situation was and decided in 144 B.C. to renew his alliance with the Romans and to explore the possibility of a new alliance with the Spartans.

The earlier embassy to Rome was described in 8:17-32. The emissaries sent by Jonathan on this occasion (12:1) are identified in 12:16 as Numenius, the son of Antiochus, and Antipater, the son of Jason. Note the non-Jewish names, though surely they were Jews. Their request for renewing the "friendship and alliance" (12:3) led the Romans to give them letters that attested to the reality of the Jewish alliance with Rome and ensured their safe conduct in territories friendly to the Romans. The Roman response also gave Jonathan a powerful protector that was eager to expand its influence in the ancient Near East.

In 146 B.C. the Romans had defeated the Greeks who belonged to the Achaean League (see 8:9-10) and gained a foothold in Greece. However, the Spartans had not been part of the Achaean

League, and their nonparticipation helped them to become important once again. The Jewish ambassadors to Rome (12:1, 16) were supposed to return home by way of Sparta after delivering a letter to the Spartans from Jonathan. In that letter (12:6-18), Jonathan presents himself as the Jewish high priest and spokesman for the "senate" (the Jewish council of elders), the high priests, and the Jewish nation (12:6). He bases his request for an alliance on a letter sent from Arius (the king of Sparta from 309 to 265 B.C.) to Onias I (the Jewish high priest around 300 B.C.). The "sacred books" mentioned in 12:9 are most likely "the law, the prophets, and other books" noted in the prologue to the book of Sirach, that is, the basic components of what came to be the Hebrew Bible. The body of Jonathan's letter gives the impression that Onias I failed to answer Arius' letter. Glossing over that embarrassing fact, Jonathan notes that the Jews have been mindful of the Spartans in their "sacrifices and prayers," and have rejoiced over their fame (12:11-12). Then in 12:13-15 he uses two familiar excuses for not replying to Arius' letter: We were too busy with our own problems, and we did not want to be a bother to you.

Appended to Jonathan's letter is a copy (12:20-23) of Arius' letter to Onias I, sent about 150 years before. In that letter Arius claimed a common descent of the Spartans and the Jews from Abraham. That claim was surely fictional. But it was meant to give a genealogical basis for a friendship between the two peoples. However, Arius' letter did not go so far as to propose a formal alliance. Why it was ignored by the Jews around 300 B.C. is not clear.

12:24-38 The further exploits of Jonathan and Simon

When the "generals of Demetrius" (see 11:63) returned with an even greater force (12:24-30), Jonathan seized the initiative by going out to meet them at Hamath, in the Orontes Valley, between the Lebanon and Anti-Lebanon mountains. But the opponents learned of Jonathan's plan to attack them, and they withdrew under the cover of night, to beyond the River Eleutherus. Perhaps out of frustration, Jonathan overwhelmed and plundered the Zabadeans, who lived about thirty miles northwest of Damascus (12:31). From there Jonathan went to Damascus and traveled about the region (12:32). Meanwhile, according to 12:33-34, Simon, who was now governor of the coastal region (see 11:59), put down a planned rebellion among supporters of Demetrius II at Joppa and left a garrison there.

When Jonathan arrived at Jerusalem (12:35-37), he worked out a plan for a series of strongholds in Judea (see 9:50; 10:12) under his control. Moreover, since his efforts at taking control of the citadel in Jerusalem had failed, he devised a scheme to wall it off and isolate it from the city. The part of Jerusalem called "Chaphenatha" is usually identified as the Mishneh (or, Second) Quarter, northwest of the temple (see 2 Kgs 22:14). The fortress built up by Simon (12:38) at Adida (near Lydda) would have served as a Maccabean stronghold between the hill country of Judea and the coastal plain.

12:39-53 The capture of Jonathan

According to 12:39-42, Trypho's plan was to make himself the king of "Asia" (another name for the Seleucid kingdom) and do away with Antiochus VI when the time was right. (This is what he finally did according to 13:31-32.) Only fear of Jonathan prevented him from doing so then. Part of his plan was to seize and kill Jonathan at a meeting in Beth-shan, also known as Scythopolis, at a strategic point in the Jordan Valley. When Jonathan arrived with a very large army (though forty thousand is surely an exaggeration), Trypho was taken aback and pretended that he had been misunderstood by Jonathan. He claimed that he only wanted to honor Jonathan and give him even more territories and authority. As a sign of his alleged friendship, he invited Jonathan to accompany him to Ptolemais (Acco) on the coast.

Since Jonathan trusted Trypho's words (12:46-48), he sent most of his army back to Judea and kept only three thousand troops with him. And of that group, he sent two thousand off to Galilee and left himself with only a thousand as he went off to Ptolemais. What he found at Ptolemais was a trap for him and his men. Once the gates were closed behind them, there was a massacre, though Jonathan was not yet killed (see 13:23). Then Trypho tried to finish off Jonathan's army in Galilee and "the Great Plain" (Esdraelon), the western section of the valleys and plains separating Galilee from Samaria (12:49-52). However, Jonathan's army fought back and managed to escape to Judea. All Israel recognized that Jonathan was as good as dead, and expected that their enemies would soon attack them since the Jews now had "no leader or helper" (12:53).

SIMON AND JOHN HYRCANUS

1 Maccabees 13:1–16:24

13:1-11 Simon as Israel's new leader

Of the five brothers (2:1-5) only Simon remained alive. In the face of the attack planned by Trypho, Simon went up to Jerusalem and exhorted the people there. In his short speech (13:3-6), he recalled that his family had fought for "the laws and the sanctuary," and that "for the sake of Israel" his four brothers had died: Eleazar (see 6:46), Judas (9:18), John (9:36-42), and Jonathan (13:23). Simon then promised to carry on their work and bring vengeance on Israel's enemies. The crowd responded in 13:8-9 by acclaiming Simon as their new leader and promising to obey him. After raising an army, Simon (13:10-11) completed the fortification of Jerusalem (see 12:36-37) and sent Jonathan, the son of Absalom, to Joppa to secure it (see 12:33-34).

13:12-24 The defeat of Trypho

When Trypho made his move from Ptolemais against Judea, he found himself blocked by Simon at Adida, which Simon had only recently fortified (see 12:38). So he decided to use trickery against Simon by claiming that Jonathan owed the royal treasury a large sum of money (perhaps the crown tax, see 13:39) and by promising to free Jonathan if Simon would send to him a hundred talents of silver and two of Jonathan's sons as hostages (13:15-16). His offer put Simon on the defensive. If Simon refused, he might be criticized for failing to do everything possible on Jonathan's behalf or even suspected of wanting to take over Jonathan's offices and possessions. But when Trypho received the money and the boys from Simon, he did not release Jonathan.

Having outwitted Simon, Trypho turned to military action in the hope of capturing Jerusalem by force (13:20-24). Following the example of Lysias (see 4:29; 6:31), Trypho first tried to approach Jerusalem from the south by way of the road leading to Adora, five miles southwest of Hebron. But Simon's army again blocked Trypho at every point. Then the men in the citadel sug-

gested that he approach "by way of the wilderness" (13:21), that is, from the Judean Desert and so from the south and southeast. However, this plan was ruined because of a surprise snowstorm that made the attack impossible. On the way to Gilead (or perhaps Galilee), Trypho had Jonathan killed and buried near Baskama (whose location is uncertain). He probably had Jonathan's two sons (being held as hostages, see 13:16, 19) killed at the same time, in the winter of 143–142 B.C.

13:25-30 Jonathan's tomb

After retrieving Jonathan's body from Baskama, Simon buried it in the family tomb at Modein (see 2:70; 9:19) and turned the funeral into a period of national mourning. Moreover, he erected an elaborate monument over the tomb and set up seven pyramids (possibly as symbols of hope for life after death), one each for his parents, his four brothers, and himself. The representations of suits of armor commemorated the Maccabees' achievements as warriors, while those of the ships may refer to their success in capturing Joppa and other coastal cities. That the latter carvings could be seen from the sea is unlikely, since Modein was twelve miles from the coast.

Thus ended the life of Jonathan. He was a brilliant strategist and a shrewd politician. His skillful dealings with the various claimants to the Seleucid throne rescued the Maccabean revolt from apparent defeat at the death of Judas and did much to make the people of Judea and beyond into an independent nation once again.

13:31-42 An agreement between Simon and Demetrius II

In 142 B.C. Trypho deposed Antiochus VI and made himself the king of "Asia" (a name for the Seleucid Empire). He eventually had Antiochus VI killed in 139 B.C. Thus Trypho finally achieved what he seems to have sought ever since he discovered Antiochus VI (see 11:38-40; 12:39-40). His murder of Jonathan had made him an enemy of the Maccabees. And so Simon prepared for war, strengthened his fortifications in Jerusalem and Judea, and sought new allies.

Acting on the principle that "the enemy of my enemy is my friend," Simon in 13:34 opened up negotiations with Demetrius II. In particular, he requested that Judeans be exempted from the land tax. The letter (13:36-40) containing Demetrius II's response indicates that Simon had sent him a gold crown and a palm branch as peace offerings. For his part, in a rather formulaic manner, Demetrius II welcomed Simon's offer of peace and agreed to forgive past offenses (see 11:63-74; 12:24-32) and to exempt the Judeans from the crown tax, which was the annual tribute from Jerusalem paid to the Seleucid king. He closed by inviting Jews to enlist in his royal army (see 11:47-48).

Since Demetrius II did not have any real power at this time, these concessions were not objectively significant. Nevertheless, Simon seized upon them and took the removal of "the yoke of the Gentiles" (perhaps the crown tax) as symbolic of Judean independence and as the beginning of a new era in Jewish history. The sense of liberation and new beginnings was made concrete by the practice of dating events and documents from the first year of Simon's reign (142 B.C.).

13:43-53 The capture of Gazara and the citadel

With Trypho and Demetrius II occupied in their own struggle for power, Simon took the opportunity to besiege Gazara (Gezer). The reading "Gaza" in the Greek manuscripts must be incorrect; for references to the Maccabees' capture of Gazara, see 13:53; 14:7, 34; 15:28, 35; 16:1, 19, 21. The siege machine mentioned in 13:43 was a large movable tower, containing battering rams and catapults, and capable of accommodating many soldiers. When Gazara's inhabitants begged for peace, Simon relented and made them vacate the city. Then he turned Gazara into a Jewish city by purifying it of idols and settling observant Jews in it. Thus he ensured the loyalty of Gazara to him and rewarded his soldiers and other supporters with property there. Moreover, he built a residence for himself (13:48) and appointed his son, John Hyrcanus, as leader there.

Jonathan's plan to wall off the citadel and isolate its soldiers from the city (see 12:36) seems to have been successful (13:49). In June of 141 B.C. its occupants surrendered to Simon, and he let them leave in peace (13:50). The capture of the citadel by Simon and his supporters became the occasion for a celebration (13:51). It marked the final success in the revolt that had begun some twenty-five years before. As long as the citadel remained in enemy hands, the Maccabees had not yet achieved their goal of freedom from foreign

and pagan rule. As a symbol of victory, Simon decreed that the day of the citadel's Jewish occupation should be observed as an annual holiday, and he and his companions took up residence in the citadel. The chapter ends in 13:53 with a note introducing John Hyrcanus, the son of Simon, who was being groomed to succeed his father.

14:1-3 The capture of Demetrius II

In 140 B.C. Demetrius II entered Media, where he was taken captive by King Arsaces, the dynastic name of Mithradates I, the Parthian king from 171 to 138 B.C. The author claims that Demetrius II went there to gain more military support for his struggle against Trypho. However, another reason was that the Parthians had seized the eastern part of his Seleucid Empire, including Babylon, and the Greeks and Macedonians left there needed his help. Arsaces treated Demetrius II well and even gave his daughter to him in marriage.

14:4-15 In praise of Simon

The first part of the poem in praise of Simon characterizes his reign as time of peace and contentment for the people and lists his achievements, with particular attention to his military successes at Joppa, Gazara, Beth-zur, and the Jerusalem citadel (14:4-7). It stresses the popular support that he was attracting: "His rule delighted his people" (14:4).

The second part celebrates Simon's exploits in terms taken largely from various biblical passages: Leviticus 26:3-4 (14:8), Zechariah 8:4 (14:9), and Micah 4:4 (14:12). Thus it continues the motif of biblical re-creations or echoes with regard to the Maccabees. The "lawless" and "wicked" (14:14) probably were those Jews who had encouraged and supported the program instituted by Antiochus IV back in 167 B.C. (see 1:11-15).

14:16-24 The renewal of foreign alliances

When there was a change in leadership, it was customary to renew the alliances made in the past. The renewals of the alliances with Rome and Sparta probably took place shortly after Simon's accession in 142 B.C. According to 14:16-19, the Romans sent a copy of their treaty inscribed on bronze tablets to Jerusalem where it was read in public. They were undoubtedly pleased with Simon's early successes and the chaos that had overtaken the Seleucid Empire. According to

14:20-23, the Spartans sent a letter confirming the agreement produced by the recent visit of Numenius and Antipater (see 12:16) and provided a copy of their friendship alliance. The notice in 14:24 gives the impression that Simon sent Numenius back to Rome with his gift of a large golden shield.

14:25-49 Simon is honored as a benefactor of the Jewish people

Simon's benefactions on behalf of the Jewish people were recognized in an official decree inscribed on bronze tablets and posted at Mount Zion for all to read. The decree is dated September 13, 140 B.C. The word "Asaramel" may have been Hebrew for "the court of the people of God."

The first part of the decree provides as a kind of historical preamble a summary of the major events narrated thus far in 1 Maccabees (14:29-40). It portrays Simon as a great benefactor to his people not only in his military successes but also in spending his own money (see 13:15-19; 14:24) in order to equip his army and foster the welfare of his people. It also highlights his success in filling the offices of high priest and leader of the people, and his skill in renewing the alliance with the Romans.

The second and most important part of the decree (14:41-43) confirms Simon in what had become his three official positions: military leader, high priest, and governor of the Jews (or ethnarch). Thus Simon was granted by the people (or, more likely, had already taken to himself) all military, religious, and political authority. There is, however, a provision that this arrangement should last only "until a trustworthy prophet arises" (14:41). This condition may have been a way of stifling opposition to what amounted to dictatorship by Simon. Or it may also have been meant cynically, on the assumption that such a prophet was not likely to arise at any time soon. For earlier references to a future prophet, see 4:46 and 9:27. For the dating of contracts in Simon's name, see 13:42. And for purple and gold as insignia of the high priesthood and being the King's Friend, see 10:20, 89.

The third part is a warning to the people not to change any of these decisions or disobey any of Simon's orders (14:44-45). According to verses 46-49, all the people agreed to these decisions, Simon accepted the three offices, and the decree

was inscribed on bronze tablets and made public (with a copy deposited in the temple treasury).

It is often difficult to pinpoint the end of a revolution. A successful revolution results in a stable government and a restoration of civil life. The transition to the new order is sometimes vague, because one phase leads to another. One clear marker for the end of the Maccabean revolt was the capture of the citadel in Jerusalem by Simon in 141 B.C. This military installation lasted a long time (twenty-five years) and caused the Maccabees and their supporters a good deal of trouble. Another marker was the concentration of military, religious, and political authority in one man, Simon Maccabeus, in 140 B.C. His rise to power gave Judea at least the semblance of a stable government and the restoration of civil life. It also turned Judea into an independent political entity.

Yet the concentration of all power in the Maccabee family would eventually prove to be a seed of the revolution's undoing. The family soon fell victim to the dynastic struggles that had long plagued the Seleucids and the Ptolemies. And a new era began when in 63 B.C. the Roman general Pompey intervened at Jerusalem to settle a family dispute among descendants of the Maccabees about who was to be the successor of Queen Salome Alexandra.

15:1-14 Antiochus VII appears on the scene

Antiochus VII was the son of Demetrius I and the brother of Demetrius II. Because he grew up in Side in Pamphylia, he was known as Sidetes. In his letter to Simon in 15:2-9, he complains about "certain villains" (15:3) who had gained control of his kingdom. By this he surely meant Trypho, and perhaps also Alexander Balas and Antiochus VI. He wrote to secure Simon's support when he landed in Seleucid territory in his effort to wrest control of the kingdom from Trypho. He promised to exempt Simon and the Judeans from various taxes, to allow Simon to keep and expand his military resources, and to cancel various debts owed to the royal treasury. The one new promise was the permission for Simon to issue his own coinage, which would have been still another symbol of Judean independence. See 15:27 where he breaks all these agreements.

In 138 B.C. Antiochus VII, at the age of twenty, launched his invasion from the island of Rhodes.

When Trypho learned of this move and of Antiochus VII's designs on his kingdom, he fled to Dor, a port city nine miles north of Caesarea Maritima and south of Mount Carmel. There Trypho found himself trapped, facing a large army by land and a blockade off the seacoast.

15:15-24 Renewal of the Roman alliance

Having brought the gold shield to Rome (see 14:24), Numenius (see 12:16; 14:22) took away with him letters reaffirming the friendship alliance between Rome and the Jews. The sample letter preserved in 15:16-21 is from Lucius, consul of the Romans. This may be Lucius Catullus Metullus who was consul in 142 B.C., or Lucius Calpurnius Piso who was consul in 140–139 B.C. It is addressed to King Ptolemy, who was Ptolemy VIII Euergetes II (Physcon), who reigned from 145 to 116 B.C. It mentions the renewal of the friendship alliance in the reign of Simon and his welcome gift and warns the king not to harm Simon's emissaries and not to harbor the opponents of Simon. According to 15:22-24, similar letters were sent to Demetrius II of Syria, Attalus II of Pergamum, Ariarathes V of Cappadocia, and Arsaces of Parthia. The "countries" listed in 15:23 were independent states in Greece, the Greek islands, and Asia Minor. A copy was also sent to Simon.

As we have seen, revolutions often sow the seeds of their own destruction. Besides the concentration of all power in one family, another seed of the destruction of the Maccabean revolt was excessive reliance on Rome for protection. Although the Romans were eager to make treaties but slow to follow through on them unless it suited their interests, the fact is that treaties existed between the Romans and the Jews because Judas, Jonathan, and Simon sought out a relationship with the Romans. In the short run the official link suited both parties. The Jews gained a powerful defender against the Seleucids and the Ptolemies, and the Romans had a client state in Judea and a foothold in the Near East. However, in the first centuries B.C. and A.D. the Romans began to take much more direct control of Judea and the whole of Palestine until the independence that the Maccabees had gained was lost again.

15:25-36 Hostility from Antiochus VII

The narrative begun in 15:10-14 is resumed in 15:25, and the reader is reminded that Antiochus VII had Trypho trapped by land and sea at Dor. When his new ally Simon sent troops along with gold and silver (15:26), Antiochus VII refused to accept his help and rescinded all the concessions made in his letter in 15:2-9. Antiochus VII probably felt that victory over Trypho was in his grasp, and that there was no need to share the spoils with Simon. Indeed, he began to regard Simon and his people as enemies and as resources to be exploited.

Antiochus VII sent one of his Friends, Athenobius, with a message to Simon (15:28-31) that accused him of occupying cities (Joppa and Gazara) and seizing property (the Jerusalem citadel) that belonged to Antiochus VII's empire. He gave Simon this ultimatum: Either give those territories back to him as the Seleucid king or pay to the king a thousand talents. Otherwise, the king threatened that he would come and make war against Simon. According to 15:32, Athenobius was amazed at Simon's great wealth, and came away impressed with Jerusalem. Its splendor probably confirmed the perception that Simon and his people were resources to be exploited.

In his reply, however, Simon claimed that these cities and territories were part of the Jews' ancestral heritage and were in enemy hands only for a time (15:33-35). Simon was undoubtedly basing his claim on the biblical promises about the land of Israel as well as on international Greek law. He went on to explain that he had taken Joppa and Gazara only because they were harming his people. Nevertheless, he agreed to give the king a hundred talents for them. Simon's response angered both Athenobius and Antiochus VII, and they moved to carry out their threat of making war against Simon.

15:37–16:10 Victory over Cendebeus

Trypho managed to escape from Dor and to travel to Orthosia, a port between Tripolis and the Eleutherus River. Antiochus caught up with Trypho and had him killed at Apamea. Meanwhile, Antiochus VII appointed Cendebeus as the governor of the coastal region of Palestine and ordered him to move against Judea and Simon. Cendebeus made his base at Kedron (four miles southeast of Jamnia) and from there made incursions into Judea with great success.

The Maccabean outpost that was closest to the area of Cendebeus' activity was Gazara, where Simon's son, John Hyrcanus, was in charge (see

13:53). When John and his brother Judas consulted with their father Simon about what they should do, Simon, according to 16:2-3, gave them a "pep talk," in which he reminded them of all that he and their uncles had done for Israel and urged them to "go out and fight for our nation." In the description of the battle that follows in 16:5-10, there are many allusions to Simon and his brothers and to their exploits.

The description of John's army in 16:4 contains the first mention of Jewish horsemen. John's first stop on the way to battle was Modein, the ancestral home of the Maccabees and the site of the monumental tomb erected by Simon. In taking the initiative crossing the stream (16:6), John follows the pattern set by his uncle Judas in 5:40-43. By setting his cavalry between the two wings of his infantry (16:7), John probably threw his opponents into confusion and thus won the battle. His brother Judas was wounded, though he would recover only to be murdered shortly afterward (see 16:14). Meanwhile John pursued Cendebeus back to Kedron and killed two thousand of his troops who sought refuge in the towers on the plain of Azotus. His uncle Jonathan had already burned Azotus according to 10:84. From there John returned to Jerusalem in peace.

16:11-17 The death of Simon and two of his sons

Simon had appointed his son-in-law, Ptolemy the son of Abubus, to be the governor of the area around Jericho (16:11-12). However, Ptolemy planned to kill Simon and his sons, and get all their territories and possessions for himself. And so in the winter of 134 B.C. he arranged a banquet for Simon and two of his sons, Judas and Mattathias, at a fortress called Doq, three miles northwest of Jericho. When Simon and his sons were drunk, Ptolemy sprang his plot and had them killed. The narrator's comment is tersely eloquent: "By this vicious act of treachery he repaid good with evil" (16:17).

16:18-24 The escape and accession of John Hyrcanus

Ptolemy's report to the king suggests that they expected Antiochus VII to come to his aid with military help to fend off the remaining supporters of Simon and to appoint him to be Simon's replacement as ruler over Judea. His plan to kill John Hyrcanus (16:19-22) was foiled when John learned about what had happened to Simon and his brother at Doq. When his would-be murderers arrived at Gazara, John was ready for them and had them put to death.

First Maccabees ends in 16:23-24 with a summary of John's accomplishments cast in a formula familiar from 1 and 2 Kings (see 9:22, where it was applied to Judas). It is also noted that John took over the Jewish high priesthood from his father, Simon. John served as the high priest as well as the military and political leader in Judea from 134 to 104 B.C. The closing of the book in this way suggests that it was completed near the end of John's reign or shortly after his death.

THE SECOND BOOK OF

MACCABEES

Daniel J. Harrington, S.J.

INTRODUCTION

The work known as 2 Maccabees provides important information about the events leading up to the revolt led by Judas Maccabeus and describes his exploits up to 161 B.C. when he defeated Nicanor. It explores the political intrigues surrounding the Jewish high priesthood before the revolt and portrays Judas as the ideal Jewish warrior who prays before and after his battles, and observes the sabbath and other Jewish rituals.

The body of the book (3:1–15:39) concerns three attacks on the Jerusalem temple by Israel's enemies and their defeats by divine help and by Judas and his companions. In the first attack (3:1-40) under Seleucus IV, Heliodorus seeks to plunder the temple treasury. The second attack (4:1–10:9) occurs under Antiochus IV and ends with Judas' capture of the temple and its purification. The third attack (10:10–15:37) takes place under Antiochus V Eupator and Demetrius I, and concludes with the defeat of his general Nicanor in his attempt at killing Judas. These three attacks provide a broad outline for the book and serve as the framework for conveying much other information. They are preceded by two letters from Jews in Jerusalem to Jews in Egypt that are designed to persuade the latter to observe Hanukkah (1:1-10a; 1:10b–2:18), and a preface by the author in which he describes the content of his work and explains why and how he wrote it (2:19-32).

In the preface, the author notes that his work is the condensation of a five-volume composition by Jason of Cyrene. Relying on Jason for his data, he observes that his goal is to tell the story of Judas and the attacks on the temple in a way that will be pleasurable, memorable, and profitable to his readers. Jason's work is no longer extant, and there is no way to know how closely the author followed its wording or content. Jason may well have written shortly after the events described in the work. At least, the narrative breaks off before the death of Judas in 160 B.C. The condensed version that we know as 2 Maccabees may have been completed by 124 B.C., the date of the first cover letter. Both Jason and his condenser most likely wrote in Greek, probably in Palestine.

As a historical source 2 Maccabees is especially valuable for its information about the disputes surrounding the Jewish high priesthood involving Onias III, Jason, and Menelaus, as well as the religious-cultural program of Hellenization carried out under Antiochus IV and his supporters. Its accounts of battles and other events tend to be less detailed, reliable, and vivid than the parallel material in 1 Maccabees. It is possible that the writers of 1 and 2 Maccabees had access to a common source. But there is no way to reconstruct that source in any detail. There is no evidence that one writer used the other's work.

The major theme of 2 Maccabees is the holiness and inviolability of the Jerusalem temple under the protection of the God of Israel, who works through both angelic and human agents (especially Judas Maccabeus). The work has been described as "pathetic history" in the sense that it often plays on the reader's human emotions (*pathe* in Greek). However, it is probably most famous and influential for its accounts of the martyrdoms of Eleazar (6:18-31), the mother and her seven sons (7:1-42), and Razis (14:37-46). These stories have served as models for Jewish and Christian martyrs throughout the centuries. The dialogues between the wicked king and the mother and her seven sons in 7:1-42 provide especially important evidence concerning Jewish beliefs about life after death, rewards and punishments, and bodily resurrection. The author's interpretation of Judas'

sin offering on behalf of his dead soldiers (12:39-46) has sometimes served as the theological basis for praying on behalf of the dead and even the existence of purgatory.

The reading of 2 Maccabees presented here gives particular attention to the book's distinctive angle in viewing events in the second century B.C. In this commentary I have drawn on, adapted, and developed some material from my earlier publications, especially *The Maccabean Revolt: Anatomy of a Biblical Revolution* (Collegeville, MN: Michael Glazier, 1988); my notes in the *Harper Collins Study Bible* (2006) and *The New American Bible Revised Edition* (2011).

COMMENTARY

TWO LETTERS AND A PREFACE

2 Maccabees 1:1–2:32

1:1-10a A letter to the Jews in Egypt

The first letter was written in 124 B.C. (1:10a) from the Jews in Jerusalem and Judea to the Jews in Egypt. It urges them to celebrate the festival of Hanukkah. After the salutation with its customary greetings (1:1), there are four wishes or prayers on behalf of the Egyptian Jews (1:2-5) and an assurance of prayers for them from the Judean Jews (1:6). The prayers may be alluding to a persecution of Jews in Egypt ("in time of adversity," 1:5). The prayers may also be indirectly criticizing the Jewish temple at Leontopolis in Egypt that was founded around 160 B.C. by the Jewish priest Onias IV.

The body of the first letter (1:7-9) refers to a previous letter written in 143 B.C. that recounted the troubles brought about earlier by the Jewish high priest Jason (see 4:7-22; 5:5-10). However, with God's help in response to the prayers and sacrifices of the people, that crisis had passed. Through the courage and military skill of the Maccabees, the temple worship had been restored to its rightful ritual patterns. The point of the letter becomes clear only in 1:9. It requests that the Egyptian Jews celebrate Hanukkah, the commemoration of the rededication of the Jerusalem temple, on the 25th of Chislev (November–December). The festival of Booths or Tabernacles

(see Lev 23:33-43) is celebrated on the 15th of Tishri (September–October). For similarities between Booths and Hanukkah, see also 1:18 and 10:6. The letter in 1:1-10a may have been composed to introduce and accompany a copy of 2 Maccabees (or its original version by Jason of Cyrene) being sent to the Egyptian Jews so that they might understand better why they should celebrate Hanukkah.

1:10b–2:18 A letter to Aristobulus and other Egyptian Jews

The second (undated) letter also tries to convince the Egyptian Jews to celebrate Hanukkah. Part of their resistance may have stemmed from the fact that the first Hanukkah celebration took place in 164 B.C. in Jerusalem. The Jews in Egypt may have felt that this festival was too recent in its origin and had no foundation in the Hebrew Scriptures. Moreover, they may have regarded it as too closely tied to the Maccabee family and Jerusalem, and therefore too parochial and narrow in significance.

The second letter comes from the Jews of Jerusalem and Judea, as well as the senate (the council of Jewish elders) and "Judas." If this is Judas Maccabeus, the letter would have to have been written between 164 and 160 B.C. The addressees are Aristobulus, an Egyptian Jew from a priestly family who had been a teacher of Ptolemy VIII, and the Jews in Egypt.

The strategy of this letter seems to be to connect Hanukkah with great figures in Israel's past and earlier events in Israel's history. But it first describes the event that Hanukkah celebrates and the figure (Antiochus IV Epiphanes) who brought about the crisis and how he met his death.

In 1:11-12 the letter gives thanks to God as the one who was really responsible for rescuing the holy city from its enemies. Then in 1:13-17 it recounts how Antiochus IV died in Persia while trying to rob a temple dedicated to the goddess Nanea, a deity of Sumerian origin, who was a goddess of love and fertility comparable to the Greek goddess Artemis. The priests of Nanea lured Antiochus inside the temple, sprung their trap on him and his companions, threw stones down upon them, and dismembered their corpses. For the Jews of Jerusalem, this manner of death was appropriate for the one whom they blamed for defiling their temple in Jerusalem. There are other, quite different, and conflicting accounts of the death of Antiochus IV in 2 Maccabees 9, as well as 1 Maccabees 6 and Daniel 11:40-45.

The first figure in the letter's attempt at connecting Hanukkah to Israel's past is Nehemiah. The point of contact is the festival of Booths (see 1:9; 10:6) and the legend of the miraculous fire. There are a few historical imprecisions in 1:18-19. Nehemiah rebuilt the walls of Jerusalem, not its temple. That was done earlier by Zerubbabel. Also, the Jews were exiled to Babylon, not Persia, though Babylon then became part of the Persian Empire. At any rate, in this letter the legend of the miraculous fire is loosely connected with the Jerusalem temple and its rededication through Nehemiah.

According to the legend, devout priests going into exile had hidden some fire from the altar. When Nehemiah came much later as governor, he found a thick liquid, a kind of petroleum, which went up in flames when smeared on wood and exposed to the sun. In 1:36 the liquid is identified as naphtha (a highly flammable petroleum substance). The fire was regarded as miraculous, and its occurrence prompted a prayer led by Jonathan (perhaps the Mattaniah of Neh 11:17; both names mean "gift of God" in Hebrew).

Many people associate Hanukkah with the story of oil that miraculously lasted eight days in an altar lamp during the rededication of the temple. The story goes that only one vial of specially prepared oil could be found to light the altar lamp after Judas and his men took back the temple. However, that oil miraculously lasted eight days. That story is not in 1 or 2 Maccabees. It appears in rabbinic sources. However, the account of the dedication in 2 Maccabees with its mention of miraculous fire offers a reason for calling Hanukkah "the festival of lights."

The prayer (1:24-29) stresses the power of the God of Israel, his justice and mercy, and his election of Israel as his people. These themes were as appropriate to Israel's situation in the second century B.C. as they were in Nehemiah's day, as was the plea for God to rescue his people and punish their enemies.

After the prayer and sacrifice, Nehemiah had the rest of the liquid poured out on large stones (1:30-36). However, the brilliance of their fire was eclipsed by the brilliance of the fire emanating from the altar in the temple. Fire was sacred to the Persians, and they sometimes built their temples around it. The miracle of the fire demonstrated the sacredness of the altar in the Jerusalem temple. For Hanukkah as a "purification" (1:36), see also 2:18; 10:3; and 14:36.

In 2:1-8 the figure of Jeremiah is also (loosely) associated with Hanukkah through the legend of the fire. It is said that Jeremiah ordered the exiles to take some of the fire with them as he warned them against the allures of idolatry (see Jer 10:2-15; 29; and the *Letter of Jeremiah*). The prophet Jeremiah is also said to have hidden the tent, the ark, and the altar of incense in a cave at Mount Nebo, where Moses looked over into the Promised Land before his death (see Deut 32:49). These sacred vessels are to remain hidden until the gathering of God's people and the return of God's presence to the Jerusalem temple ("the Place"). For references to the glory of the Lord and the cloud, see Exodus 40:34-35 (Moses and the tent of meeting) and 1 Kings 8:10-11 (Solomon and the temple).

The motifs of miraculous fire and the rededication of the temple are continued in 2:9-12 with reference to Solomon and Moses. When Solomon dedicated the first temple, it was said that fire came down from heaven (see Lev 9:23-24; 1 Chr 7:9). For the words of Moses cited in 2:11, see Leviticus 10:16-19. For the eight-day observance of the dedication of the first temple (2:12), see 1 Kings 8:65-66 and 2 Chronicles 7:9. The point of all these biblical allusions is to suggest that the celebration of Hanukkah, the rededication of the second temple, has old and deep biblical roots.

The "memoirs" of Nehemiah contained in Nehemiah 1–7 and 11–13 say nothing about his building the temple or the miraculous fire. Perhaps the reference is to some apocryphal work now lost. The mention of the "books about the kings and the prophets, the books of David" (2:13) provides important evidence for the early development of the canon of the Hebrew Bible. The "royal letters about votive offerings" may refer to something like what is now in Ezra 6:3-12 and 7:12-26. The Jewish books "scattered because of the war" (2:14) may refer to the Torah scrolls destroyed in the persecution under Antiochus IV (see 1 Macc 1:56-57). The "Judas" noted here is presumably Judas Maccabeus, who may also have been a coauthor of this letter (see 1:10b).

The final plea (2:16-18) to the Egyptian Jews to celebrate Hanukkah (see 1:18, 36) as the purification of the temple is expressed in biblical language taken from Exodus 19:6 and Deuteronomy 30:3-5. As in 2:7 the temple is referred to as God's holy "place." The letter's appeals to famous characters from Israel's past and its abundant use of biblical language constitute a concerted effort to suggest that the celebration of Hanukkah was not a complete innovation.

2:19-32 The author's preface

The materials presented so far in 2 Maccabees are really cover letters sent to Jews in Egypt to encourage them to celebrate Hanukkah along with Jews in Judea. The hope is that when they read the full story of the first Hanukkah and related events that begins in 3:1, they will understand better why they should do so. Before that, however, the "author" of the main story needs to introduce himself and explain his undertaking in the preface contained in 2:19-32.

The first part of the author's preface provides a synopsis of the book's content and a statement about its source (2:19-23). The narrative that follows will describe the exploits of Judas Maccabeus and his brothers during the reigns of Antiochus IV Epiphanes (2 Macc 4:7–10:9) and Antiochus V Eupator (10:10–13:26). No mention is made here of the reigns of Seleucus IV (3:1–4:6) and Demetrius I (14:1–15:37). There is a reference to the "heavenly manifestations" or epiphanies that appear throughout the book (see 3:24-26;

10:29-30; 11:8; 12:22; 15:27), as well as the first extant use of the term "Judaism" (2:21; see also 8:1; 14:38). While the NABRE translates the word as "the Jewish people," the Greek has *Ioudaismos*.

The most important information contained in the first part of the preface, however, concerns the origin and nature of what we call 2 Maccabees (2:23). It is based on the much longer work in five volumes that was written by Jason of Cyrene. Jason was undoubtedly a Jew from North Africa (modern Libya) who in all likelihood wrote in Greek. The present work is a digest or condensation of Jason's original composition.

This frank admission leads the author to explain his purpose and method more fully in 2:24-32. Rather than including all the details contained in Jason's work, he wants to produce a narrative that will be pleasant, memorable, and useful (2:24-25). He defends what he has done as hard work and compares his efforts to those of someone who is responsible for preparing a festive banquet (2:26-27). In both cases, the work is harder than it may appear to be on the surface. While relying on Jason's data for the accuracy of his details, the author proposes to offer an outline of the events (2:28) in a way that will involve and entertain the reader (see 15:38-39).

In 2:29 the author goes on to compare Jason to the architect of a building and himself to the interior decorator. He admits in 2:30 that he is not a professional historian, and that he has not carried out independent research on the topics treated in this book. Instead, his contribution will be to tell the story concisely (2:31) and in a pleasing way. And so in the interests of brevity he cuts off his preface in 2:32 and begins his narrative with the story of Heliodorus' attack upon the temple.

HELIODORUS

2 Maccabees 3:1-40

3:1-14a Simon's treachery and Heliodorus' mission

Heliodorus' attempt at despoiling the temple treasury is really an overture to, or preview of, the other two attacks on the Jerusalem temple. The main character in this episode is Heliodorus, who was sent by King Seleucus IV Philopator (187–175 B.C.) to confiscate the wealth stored at the temple treasury. Seleucus probably needed the money to pay the reparations to the Romans agreed to by his father Antiochus III in the Treaty of Apamea in 188 B.C. The lesson that Heliodorus will learn is that there is "some divine power about the place" (3:38).

Onias III was the Jewish high priest from 196 to 175 B.C. He was the son of Simon, the great high priest celebrated in Sirach 50. The author in 3:1-3 describes Onias as an exemplary leader, so successful that foreign rulers admired and supported the Jerusalem temple ("the place"), and Seleucus IV even defrayed the cost of sacrifices there.

But a certain Simon had a disagreement with Onias about "the administration of the city market" (3:4), which very likely involved money. Simon was from the priestly clan of Bilgah (see Neh 12:5, 18; 1 Chr 24:14), and his brothers were Menelaus (4:23) and Lysimachus (4:29). Failing to get his way against Onias, Simon went to Apollonius, the governor of Coelesyria (which included Judea), with the report that the temple treasury in Jerusalem contained enormous sums of money, and that Seleucus IV could gain control of it (3:5-6). In antiquity it was common practice for private individuals to deposit money and other precious items in the temple treasury at Jerusalem and elsewhere. This practice made temples attractive sites for robbers, especially kings in need of quick money (see 1:13-17).

Apollonius conveyed Simon's report to the king, who in turn sent Heliodorus to check out the situation (3:7). Heliodorus had been raised with Seleucus IV and was later involved in the plot to kill him in 175 B.C. When he arrived in Jerusalem, Heliodorus inquired from Onias about the extent of the temple treasury (3:8-9). His mission very likely had a historical basis, though in 2 Maccabees 3 the story is told in a dramatic and legendary style.

According to 3:10-12, Onias explained that some of the money belonged to a fund for the charitable support of widows and orphans, and that another part belonged to Hyrcanus, from the powerful Jewish Tobiad family that had settled in Transjordan and were known to be sympathetic to the Ptolemies. Onias further contended that Simon's estimate of the treasury's wealth was much too high, and that the real figure was four hundred talents of silver and two hundred talents of gold. Finally he declared that for Heliodorus to confiscate this money would be an offense

against all those who put their trust in the temple and against the holiness and inviolability of the temple itself. However, Onias could not dissuade Heliodorus from carrying out his mission from the king, and he insisted on making his own inventory of the temple treasury (3:13-14a).

3:14b-28 The people's anguish and the divine intervention

The prospect of Heliodorus profaning the temple sent the people into a panic (3:14b-21). The author describes how the various groups—priests, people, and women—reacted with fear and sadness. The passage is an example of playing on the reader's emotions ("pathetic history") to heighten the intensity of the threat. According to 3:15, the priests prayed that the God who made the laws about the security of deposits (see Exod 22:7-13) would see that they were enforced in the case of Heliodorus. The high priest was visibly shaken, the people offered prayers in the streets, and the women observed rituals of mourning by putting on sackcloth (see Esth 4:1). The author's comment about their "pitiful" state (3:21) makes explicit what the reader is expected to feel.

Just as Heliodorus and his companions arrived at the temple treasury, they were driven off by a fearsome rider and "two other young men" who defend the sanctity of the temple and thrash Heliodorus to the point of death (3:22-30). Other miraculous appearances of a horse and rider occur in 5:2-3; 10:29; and 11:8. The young men were angelic figures, and the whole event is miraculous and supernatural. The result of their intervention is that even members of Heliodorus' bodyguard recognized "the sovereign power of God" (3:28). The Jewish people praised God for defending "his own place," and rejoiced that "the almighty Lord had manifested himself" (3:30). As in many biblical texts, there is no sharp distinction between the actions of God and those of his messengers or angels.

3:31-40 Heliodorus' healing and confession

Having witnessed the power of the Most High, the companions of Heliodorus beg Onias to pray for his healing. And Onias, fearing that the Jews might be blamed for killing Heliodorus, offers a sacrifice of atonement on his behalf (3:31-32). In praying and offering sacrifice for a Gentile sinner, Onias follows the example of Moses (see Exod

8:26-27) and Job (see Job 42:7-9). The "same young men" reappear and tell Heliodorus to proclaim to all people the power of the God of Israel (3:33-34). Without necessarily becoming a Jew, Heliodorus offers sacrifice and acknowledges Israel's God as supreme (3:35; see Dan 2:47; 4:1-3; 4:34; 6:26-27).

When Heliodorus left Jerusalem and returned to the king at Antioch, he obeyed the command of the two young men and bore witness to the power of the Most High (3:36-37). When asked by the king whom he should send next to Jerusalem, Heliodorus suggests that the king should send his worst enemy (3:38). What Heliodorus came to see was that "the one whose dwelling is in heaven watches over that place and protects it" (3:39). This is the major theme of 2 Maccabees.

In several respects the Heliodorus episode is a preview of what follows and so alerts us to what we should expect in the next two episodes. There are tensions within the Jewish community in Jerusalem, in this case between Onias III and Simon. When Simon tries to resolve the tensions by appealing to the Seleucids, they involve themselves in Jewish affairs. The result of the Seleucid intervention is the threat that the Jerusalem temple will be profaned. The attempt at profaning the temple fails only because God intervenes to protect the temple and his people.

The chief difference between the Heliodorus episode and those that follow concerns the manner of God's intervention. The divine intervention in the Heliodorus episode is miraculous or supernatural. The rider and the two young men appear out of nowhere, do their job, and disappear. They seem angelic rather than human. In the two remaining threats to the temple, God works through human beings, notably Judas Maccabeus and his companions.

ANTIOCHUS IV

2 Maccabees 4:1–10:9

4:1-9 Simon's treachery and Jason's priesthood

Even after the Heliodrous incident, the intrigues surrounding the high priesthood in Jerusalem continued. Simon (whom we met in 3:4-6) claimed that Heliodorus had been incited by Onias III to seize the funds in the temple treasury. We are to presume that Heliodorus and Onias III were now friends, and that this slander was Simon's way of getting revenge and keeping his own interests alive. Simon also had the governor, Apollonius, as an ally (see 3:7) and even resorted to murder (4:3). Onias sought to warn Seleucus IV about his true enemies and their plots (4:5-6), but he was prevented by the death of Seleucus IV (at the hands of Heliodorus) and the eventual succession of his younger brother, Antiochus IV Epiphanes, who reigned from 175 to 164 B.C.

The accession of Antiochus IV gave Onias' brother Jason the opportunity to take over the Jewish high priesthood by outbidding Onias for it (4:7-8). Jason promised Antiochus IV 360 talents of silver and 80 talents more from another source. It was not unusual that the Seleucid ruler should have final approval over the office of the Jewish high priesthood. Nor was it unusual that Antiochus IV should need quick money and so be willing to accommodate the desires of Jason. Nor would all Jews be outraged at this transition, since Jason (whose Hebrew name was Joshua) belonged to the same legitimate high priestly family as his brother Onias did.

What was unusual was Jason's proposal to pay 150 more talents if he could institute the program outlined in 4:9. Jason wanted to establish in Jerusalem a gymnasium (an institution for physical exercises and for imparting Greek education and culture), as well as an ephebate (the body of youth enrolled in the gymnasium), and to "enroll Jerusalemites as citizens of Antioch." Whether he hoped to have men in Jerusalem made into honorary citizens of Antioch in Syria, or (more likely) to turn Jerusalem itself into a Greek city (*polis*) called "Antioch," is a matter of debate.

4:10-17 The Greek way of life

The author presents Jason's program as a wholesale shift over to Hellenism, or "the Greek way of life" (4:10). How radical this shift appeared to Jerusalem Jews around 175 B.C. who were already accustomed to Greek ways in many areas (language, economics, military strategy, etc.) is also a matter of debate. But the author was clearly disturbed by what he regarded as a radical move on Jason's part away from Judaism and toward Hellenism.

The references to Jason's setting aside the existing royal concessions and destroying the lawful ways of living to introduce new customs contrary to the Jewish law (4:11) describe his efforts to replace the Torah as the official law in Israel with Seleucid law. John, the father of Eupolemus (see 1 Macc 8:17), had negotiated with Antiochus III the right for Jews to be ruled according to the Torah rather than Seleucid law. The placement of the gymnasium right under the citadel near the temple and inducing young men to wear the wide-brimmed Greek or "Hermes" (the god of athletic skill) hat (4:12) are put forward as further examples of the craze for Hellenism and the "outrageous wickedness of Jason, the renegade and would-be high priest" (4:13). While Jason was from the right high priestly family, he was not a genuine high priest in the writer's eyes because he had obtained the office by bribery and carried out a program hostile to Judaism. So great was the impact of his program of Hellenization that priests serving at the temple were more interested in attending wrestling matches than in caring for the sanctuary and carrying out the sacrifices (4:14-15). According to 4:16-17, the evils that were to befall the Jewish people and the temple were the result of following the Greek way of life (see 6:12-17; see Dan 9:4-19).

4:18-22 Further outrages

The tensions involved in joining Judaism and Hellenism became apparent with an incident at the athletic games held in Tyre in honor of the god Melqart/Heracles/Hercules (4:18-20). Jason sent as his envoys some "Antiochians of Jerusalem" (see 4:9) with three hundred silver drachmas for a sacrifice to be offered to the pagan god Hercules. However, the envoys seem to have developed scruples and put the money toward the construction of "triremes," that is, Greek ships with three rows of oars on each side.

Through Apollonius (see 3:7; 4:4), Antiochus IV learned that his nephew Ptolemy VI Philopator had designs on his kingdom (4:21-22). On his way down the coast to Egypt, Antiochus went east to Jerusalem where he was warmly received by Jason and the people of Jerusalem in 172 B.C.

4:23-29 Menelaus becomes high priest

Jason served as high priest from 175 to 172 B.C. If the author was outraged with the high priesthood of Jason, how much more was he angered at the accession to that office by Menelaus, the brother of the wicked Simon (3:4; 4:3-4)! In 172 B.C.

Menelaus obtained the high priesthood from Antiochus IV when he outbid Jason by three hundred talents—just as Jason had done in outbidding Onias III (4:7-8). The author viewed this twist of fate as an appropriate punishment to Jason for his arrogance. But Menelaus was even worse in character than Jason and had no qualifications for the office of the Jewish high priest. At least Jason was from the legitimate high priestly family. Menelaus, however, was merely from the priestly clan of Bilgah (see 3:4). Nevertheless, he retained the office from 172 to 162 B.C. Jason is said to have sought refuge among the Ammonites in Transjordan, perhaps with Hyrcanus (3:11) or the Nabateans (5:8).

However, according to 4:27-29, Menelaus failed to make the payments that he had promised to Antiochus IV for the high priesthood, despite the demands of Sostratus, the non-Jewish commander of the citadel in Jerusalem (see 4:12). When both were summoned to Antioch, Menelaus left his brother Lysimachus as high priest and Sostratus left Crates (the commander of the Cypriot mercenaries) as his substitute.

4:30-38 The death of Onias III

The evil character of Menelaus is further revealed by his mistreatment of the temple vessels and his role in the murder of Onias III. While Antiochus IV went off to put down a revolt in two cities in Cilicia (across the Syrian border, to the northwest), he put Andronicus in charge, who had been the murderer of the young son of Seleucus IV in 175 B.C. According to 4:32, Menelaus took the opportunity to steal vessels from the Jerusalem temple and present them to Andronicus, presumably in payment of his debts. After Onias III made a public protest against both Menelaus and Andronicus, he sought asylum at an "inviolable sanctuary" in Daphne, five miles from Antioch (4:33). Acting on a suggestion from Menelaus, Andronicus lured Onias out of the sanctuary by false promises of safe conduct and immediately put him to death (4:34).

The revulsion of both Jews and Gentiles at these acts of treachery led to public outcry (4:35) and an audience with Antiochus IV on his return (4:36). There was a growing Jewish community in Antioch, as the presence of Onias III indicates. According to 4:37-38, Antiochus too became enraged at the murder of Onias, and so he had

Andronicus stripped of his purple robe (emblematic of his status as the King's Friend), paraded through the streets, and executed at the very place where Onias had been killed. While the author interprets Antiochus' action as just punishment for the scoundrel Andronicus, the king may have also recognized Andronicus as a threat to his own rule.

4:39-50 Public outrage against Lysimachus and Menelaus

The practice of robbing temple vessels being carried out by Menelaus and his brother Lysimachus provoked opposition at Jerusalem (4:39). As a result, Lysimachus was killed in a riot in Jerusalem, and Menelaus escaped from a court at Tyre only by bribery. When Lysimachus tried to put down a riot with excessive force, he became in turn the victim of the riot at the very place he was robbing (the temple treasury). The author dismisses him as a "temple robber" (4:42).

At Tyre (4:43-50) a delegation of three men from the Jewish senate (council of elders) was allowed to plead their case against Menelaus before Antiochus IV. Knowing that he was going to be convicted, Menelaus bribed Ptolemy, the son of Dorymenes (who was later governor of Coelesyria and Phoenicia, 8:8; see 1 Macc 3:38), to win the king over to his side. The result was that Menelaus was acquitted and his Jewish accusers were put to death (4:47). The author observes that the three men would have been declared innocent even by Scythians, a people from north of the Black Sea who were famous for their cruelty. And he notes that even the Tyrians recognized the enormity of this travesty of justice and describes Menelaus as "scheming greatly against his fellow citizens" (4:49-50).

5:1-10 Jason's attempt to regain power

Antiochus' second campaign against Egypt took place in 168 B.C. (see 1 Macc 1:29-35; Dan 11:29-30). According to 1 Macc 1:16-28, there had been an earlier invasion of Egypt and sack of Jerusalem in 169. When forced by the Romans to retreat, he vented his anger and frustration on Jerusalem. The apparition of the horsemen arrayed for battle (5:2-4) turned out to be a bad omen, unless it looked forward to Judas (see 5:27).

According to 5:5-6, Jason took the reports of Antiochus' defeat as including his death. And so

Jason tried to seize back the high priesthood and political power in Jerusalem from his rival Menelaus (who was hiding in the citadel). Although Jason did great damage to Jerusalem, he failed in his attack and fled back to the Ammonites (see 4:26). The author takes delight in 5:7-10 in describing Jason's miserable end. Driven from Transjordan by the Nabatean king Aretas I, he traveled to Egypt and then to Sparta (see 1 Macc 12:5-23) where he died in exile.

5:11-27 Antiochus IV's sack of Jerusalem

Smarting from his defeat by the Romans in Egypt and assuming that all Judea was in revolt, Antiochus took Jerusalem by storm and massacred a huge number of people and sold many others into slavery—all in three days (5:11-14). Moreover, he dared to enter the temple precincts, laid his impure hands on the sacred vessels, and appropriated them for himself (5:15-16). What irritates the author most is that the high priest Menelaus served as his guide.

In 5:17-20, the author offers his theological interpretation of these events. They were punishments for the people's sins, especially those of their leaders. The temple ("the place") was profaned in solidarity with the people. However, reconciliation and restoration will come in time for both the people and the temple. Then Antiochus will be punished for his arrogance.

In the aftermath of Antiochus' theft of eighteen thousand talents from the temple, there was even greater pressure on the Judeans (5:21-26). Menelaus was still the high priest, barbarous governors were appointed in Jerusalem (Philip the Phyrgian) and Samaria (Andronicus), and Apollonius the Mysian was sent to attack Jerusalem on the sabbath.

The only note of hope comes in 5:27 with the first mention of Judas Maccabeus and his companions. They were in the hill country, faithfully observing the Jewish food laws. There is no mention of Judas' father or brothers (see 1 Macc 2:1-5). Judas reappears in chapter 8.

6:1-11 The abolition of the law and the desecration of the temple

The forced assimilation to Greek culture and religion is interpreted in 2 Maccabees as an attack on Judaism. In 167 B.C. an "Athenian senator" (or, "Geron the Athenian") was sent to abrogate the

Torah as the law in Judea and to transform the Jerusalem temple into a shrine honoring "Olympian Zeus" (6:1-2). The deity to be worshiped there was to be the "Lord of heaven" or its Semitic equivalent, "Baal Shamen." Pious Jews rejected and resented identifying this deity with the God of Israel (see Daniel). The practice of cultic prostitution was more at home in Semitic religions than in Greek religions (where it does not seem to have been at all common). For prophetic suggestions that it took place even in ancient Israel, see Amos 2:7-8, Ezekiel 23:36-49, and Isaiah 57:7-8. While there is a reference to "abominable offerings" in 6:5, there is no mention of the "abomination of desolation." Instead of observing the sabbath or the traditional festivals, Jews were expected to celebrate the king's birthday on the 25th of every month as well as the festival of Dionysus (also known as Bacchus), the god of the grape harvest and wine.

According to 6:8-11, the penalties for noncompliance were severe. The people of Ptolemais (Acco) suggested that those who refused to participate in the pagan sacrifices or to adopt Greek customs should be put to death. The author gives two examples in which Jewish resisters were killed: the two women who circumcised their sons (see 1 Macc 1:60-61) and those who died in caves rather than profane the sabbath (see 1 Macc 2:31-38).

6:12-17 A theological reflection

The author interrupts his catalogue of martyrdoms to offer a theological interpretation of the sufferings being endured by Jews. He regards them as a divine discipline for the people and insists that God never abandons his people. Rather, they are God's way of correcting his people promptly, so that they will not persist in their sins and fall more deeply into even greater sins. While God allows other nations to reach the full measure of sinfulness and will punish them severely then, it is a sign of God's care and mercy to punish his people right away, thus saving them from greater sins. In this way it is possible to find God's loving kindness and mercy even in the midst of the terrible sufferings of the people of God.

6:18-31 The martyrdom of Eleazar

Resuming the narrative, the author tells the story of the martyrdom of Eleazar the scribe, an elderly man (ninety years old) who was being forced to eat pork in public. Pork was a food forbidden to Jews according to the Torah (see Lev 11:7-8). The Jewish food laws, along with circumcision and sabbath observance, made Jews a distinctive people in the Greco-Roman world.

Even when his torturers offer Eleazar the opportunity only to pretend to eat the forbidden food, he refuses lest he provide a bad example to the young people in Israel. His references to "Hades" (the abode of the dead, 6:23) and the possibility of punishments from God (6:26) suggest that Eleazar acts in part out of his belief in life after death and divine judgment. His torturers reject such talk as madness (see Wis 3:1-4; 5:4) and proceed with his execution. For his part, Eleazar goes to his death with joy and out of devotion to the God of Israel. The author portrays him as a model of courage and virtue not only for the young but also for all other people in Israel (6:31).

7:1-42 The martyrdom of the seven brothers and their mother

This chapter is the most famous and theologically influential part of 2 Maccabees. The wicked king, later identified as Antiochus IV (7:24), tries to force the seven brothers to eat pork, which the Torah forbids Jews to consume (Lev 11:7-8). Each brother is subjected to gruesome tortures before death, including scalping, dismemberment, and roasting. Each explains why he is willing to go to his death rather than disobey the divine commandment against eating pork. At two points their mother intervenes and encourages her sons to remain firm in their faith (7:20-23 and 7:26-29). She dies last of all, after seeing her sons die (7:41). This narrative has provided an archetype for Jewish and Christian martyrs throughout the centuries. Each son bears witness to his devotion to the God of Israel and his identity as a Jew and chooses death rather than compromise those ideals.

The most prominent motive for the martyrs to undergo these terrible sufferings leading to their death is their belief in the bodily resurrection of the dead and in postmortem rewards and punishments. The second son affirms that "the King of the universe will raise us up to live again forever" (7:9). The third son hopes that he will receive again from God his tongue and hands that are to be cut off (7:11). The fourth son dies "with the hope that God will restore me to life" (7:14). The mother assures the sixth son that God "will give you back both breath and life" (7:23). At the same time there are several warnings that the wicked king will not share in the resurrection of the righteous but rather will experience great suffering and even annihilation (7:14, 19, 23, 31). This passage is among the earliest witnesses to Jewish belief in resurrection and, in particular, resurrection of the body (or whole person). See also 12:43-45.

Another important theological theme is the idea of suffering as divine discipline. The author has already given his reflections on this motif in 6:12-17. It appears here in the sixth brother's admission that "we" (meaning the people as a whole) are suffering because "we have sinned against our God" (7:18, see Dan 9:4-19). The seventh brother's similar admission in 7:32 is balanced by his conviction that although God may treat "us" harshly for a while in order to correct "us," God will again be "reconciled with his servants" (7:33). By dying for "our ancestral laws" (7:37), the seventh brother hopes to hasten the fulfillment of the discipline imposed on Israel and the just punishments owed to the wicked king.

The mother is praised as a model of "manly emotion" (7:21), who willingly gives back her sons to God who gave them to her in the first place. Her appeal to the seventh son to look at the heavens and the earth is meant to encourage him to recognize that "God did not make them out of existing things" (7:28; see also 7:11, 22-23). Her statement has often been interpreted as a biblical basis for the philosophical concept of *creatio ex nihilo* ("creation out of nothing"), though it is doubtful that the writer intended it as a philosophical statement.

8:1-7 Judas Maccabeus

The narrative about Judas Maccabeus ("the Hammerer") begun in 5:27 is resumed. Most of the material in 1 Maccabees 2:1–3:26 is absent. In 8:1 Judas emerges as Israel's hero against the Seleucids (see 1 Macc 3:41) and manages to assemble an army of six thousand men consisting of relatives and other Jews "who remained faithful to Judaism." Their prayer in 8:2-4 summarizes what has happened so far in the book regarding the people, the temple, the city of Jerusalem, and the martyrs. The formation of this army is presented as a sign that "the Lord's wrath had now changed to mercy," thus echoing the author's theological reflection in 6:12-17. The strategy that Judas adopts is classic guerilla warfare (8:6-7), featuring sudden attacks and ambushes under cover of night. Being familiar with the terrain, the Judean soldiers had the advantage over the foreign (Seleucid) forces.

8:8-36 Judas' early victories

The early military successes of Judas and his army alerted the Seleucid officials that he might be a serious threat to their rule over Judea. And so Philip, the governor of Jerusalem (see 5:22), informed his superior Ptolemy, the governor of Coelesyria and Phoenicia (see 4:45-46), who in turn chose Nicanor (one the king's Chief Friends) and Gorgias (an experienced military strategist) to put down the Jewish uprising. Another motive driving the Seleucid concern becomes clear in 8:10-11. They needed quick money to pay off their debts to the Romans (see 8:36) that were part of the Treaty of Apamea in 188 B.C. under Antiochus III. Their plan was to capture the Jewish soldiers and sell them into slavery, and so obtain the money to pay the Romans. The projected price of one talent for ninety slaves was very low and indicates their contempt for the Jews.

The description of Judas' preparation for battle in 8:12-20 portrays him as the ideal biblical warrior. With the news of Nicanor's approach some of Judas' troops deserted (8:12-13), since they were now facing a formidable army of twenty thousand troops and no longer engaging in guerilla warfare. However, according to 8:14-15, Judas also attracted other soldiers who dedicated themselves to the cause "for the sake of the covenants made with their ancestors" and the "holy and glorious name" of God. Having assembled his army of six thousand, Judas exhorted them not to give in to fear but rather to recall the outrages perpetrated against the temple, the city of Jerusalem, and their ancestral way of life (8:16-17). While urging them to trust in God, he invokes two examples in 8:18-20 where Jews succeeded with God's help against numerically superior forces: against the army of Sennacherib in 701 B.C. (see 2 Kgs 19:35-36; Isa 37:36), and against the Galatians in Babylonia who were defeated by a force of Jewish mercenaries and Seleucids (Macedonians). Nothing else is known about the latter battle.

In defeating Nicanor and Gorgias (8:21-29; see 1 Macc 4:1-25), Judas acts again as the exemplary biblical warrior. He first divides his troops into four sections, placing himself, Simon, Joseph, and Jonathan each over fifteen hundred men (8:21-23). "Joseph" may be Judas' brother John, or he may be the Joseph mentioned with Azariah in 1 Maccabees 5:18, 55-62. The watchword "The help of God" may be connected with the meaning of the Hebrew name Eleazar (as well as Azariah). The battle results in a victory for Judas (8:24), and he even seizes the money intended for the purchase of the Jews as slaves (8:25). Then Judas and his companions are careful to observe the sabbath rest (8:26-27), divide the spoils according to biblical principles (8:28; see Num 31:25-47; 1 Sam 30:21-25), show care for widows and orphans (see Deut 26:12-13), and join in prayer (8:29).

The summary of Judas' victories in 8:30-36 notes how he conducted himself against Timothy and Bacchides (see 1 Macc 5:6-7; 7:8-25), the chief of Timothy's Arab mercenaries (see 1 Macc 5:37-44), and Nicanor (see 8:24). It was only fitting that Nicanor, who planned to enslave Judas and his men, had to escape "like a runaway slave" (8:35). Nicanor and the others learned that "the Jews had a champion" (8:36) in their God, and that they were invulnerable as long as they followed his laws.

9:1-10 The punishment of Antiochus IV

While Judas was winning battles in Judea, Antiochus IV was in Persia in his ongoing efforts to raise money to pay his soldiers and to make good on his debts to the Romans. According to 9:1-2, he was foiled in his attempts at robbing a temple in Persepolis (the ancient capital of the Persian Empire, founded by Darius I) and at capturing the city. When he arrived at Ecbatana (northwest of Persepolis), he learned about Judas' victories over Nicanor and Timothy, and decided that he would go to Jerusalem and make it "the common graveyard of Jews" (9:4). According to the author, his arrogance merited "the condemnation of Heaven."

In his rush to take vengeance on the Jews, Antiochus suffered one gruesome punishment after another: excruciating pains in his bowels (9:5-6), a fall from his chariot (9:7), worms in his body, and a terrible smell emanating from it (9:9-10). These maladies are interpreted by the author as fitting punishments for his arrogance (9:8; see 5:21) and manifestations of the power of the God

of Israel. For worms as punishments on evildoers, see Isaiah 14:11; 66:24; and Acts 12:23. There is little correlation between these maladies and Antiochus' own description of his medical condition in 9:21: "I fell victim to a troublesome illness." This is probably a case of our author exaggerating the seriousness of his sickness, and of Antiochus not wanting to reveal it to his subjects.

9:11-29 Antiochus IV's letter and his death

According to 9:11-12, the "scourge of God" in the form of these maladies brought Antiochus IV to his senses and to the recognition that "[i]t is right to be subject to God" (9:12). His acknowledgment parallels those of various kings in the book of Daniel (see Dan 2:46-49; 4:1-3; 4:34-37; 6:26-27). This makes sense, since the kings in Daniel are meant to be ciphers or symbols for Antiochus IV.

Not only does Antiochus IV acknowledge the sovereignty of the God of Israel, but in 9:13-17 he makes extravagant promises about setting Jerusalem free (from taxes, most likely), allowing all Jews to live in freedom (like Athenians), redecorating the temple and paying for the sacrifices there, and even becoming a Jew. No other ancient source confirms that Antiochus ever made such promises, and they are historically most unlikely. In any case, the author observes that God did not accept them, since he "would never again show him mercy" (9:13).

Recognizing that his death was imminent, Antiochus IV wrote to the Jews a letter in the form of a "supplication." But the letter in 9:19-27 is hardly a supplication. Rather, it is the notification that Antiochus IV was appointing as his successor his son, Antiochus V. Because the content of the letter does not fit at all well in its present context in 2 Maccabees 9, it is very likely to have been genuine in another context.

The letter is addressed by Antiochus IV to "the worthy Jewish citizens" (9:19), but it has the feel of a form letter being sent to various peoples who made up the Seleucid Empire. After the greeting and customary words of thanksgiving in 9:19-20, Antiochus IV comments on his own health ("a troublesome illness") but expects that he will soon recover (9:21-22). However, as a precaution Antiochus IV has decided to name a successor, just as his father Antiochus III did when he named Seleucus IV (the older brother of Antiochus IV) as his successor in 187 B.C. His successor will be his son, Antiochus V Eupator ("of a good father"). He was still a boy and would need a regent (see 1 Macc 3:33; 6:14-15). The letter closes with Antiochus IV's hope that his subjects will treat his son well and that he will treat them well (9:26-27).

The authors of Daniel, 1 Maccabees, and 2 Maccabees would not agree that Antiochus IV's policy had been one of "equity and kindness" (9:27). The author of 2 Maccabees calls him a "murderer and blasphemer" (9:28) and interprets his miserable end as just punishment for the sufferings that he inflicted on others. For different accounts of the death of Antiochus IV, see Daniel 11:40-45; 1 Maccabees 6:1-17; and 2 Maccabees 1:13-17.

While 1 Maccabees says that Antiochus IV died after the rededication of the Jerusalem temple, 2 Maccabees places his death before the temple's purification. In fact, Antiochus seems to have died shortly before the restoration of the temple worship in late 164 B.C., though word may not have reached Jerusalem in time for the festival. According to 1 Maccabees 6:55-56, 63, Philip (9:29) fled from Antioch because his coup against Lysias (and Antiochus V) had failed.

10:1-9 The purification of the temple

Whereas 1 Maccabees 4:36-59 presents the restoration of the traditional temple worship in late 164 B.C. under Judas Maccabeus as a "dedication," 2 Maccabees 10:1-8 emphasizes its character as a "purification." There is no mention in 1 Maccabees about the destruction of the Gentile altars and sacred enclosures (10:1-2). For the connection of fire (10:3) with Hanukkah, see 1:19–2:1. According to 1 Maccabees 1:54 and 4:52, the sacrifices had been interrupted for three years rather than two years. According to 10:4, Judas and his companions accepted the author's interpretation of the desecration of the temple as a punishment for Israel's sins and a divine discipline (see 6:12-17). The purification of the temple was celebrated on the 25th of Chislev (November–December), on the anniversary of its desecration, and lasted for eight days like the feast of Booths (Tabernacles) (see 1:9). For Judas and his companions living in the mountains, see 5:27. The use of "rods entwined with leaves" (10:7) sounds like the ivy-wreathed wands (*thyrsoi*) carried in processions honoring Dionysus (see 6:7), but they were prob-

ably not viewed as distinctively pagan. For efforts to convince Jews in Egypt to celebrate Hanukkah, see the two letters in 1:1–2:18.

NICANOR

2 Maccabees 10:10–15:39

10:10-13 The death of Ptolemy

With the passing of Antiochus IV in late 164 B.C., his son Antiochus V Eupator succeeded him as the Seleucid king (10:10). He would be overthrown in 162 B.C. by Demetrius I. Since he was only about nine years old, his regent Lysias was responsible for making policy. Lysias took over as governor of Coelesyria and Phoenicia (10:11), replacing Ptolemy the son of Dorymenes who had held that office (8:8). Surnamed "Macron" ("Large Headed"), Ptolemy had formerly been hostile to the Jews but seems to have had a change of heart and was now treating them fairly (10:12). Moreover, when Cyprus was invaded in 168 B.C., Ptolemy had gone over from supporting Ptolemy VI Philometor to the side of Antiochus IV. Thus Ptolemy was suspect to Lysias on two counts: being "soft" on the Jews, and being a "turncoat" and therefore not trustworthy. When Ptolemy found that he could no longer win the respect that went with high office, he committed suicide by taking poison (10:13).

10:14-23 Victory over the Idumeans

Idumea was the region to the southeast of Judea, and Gorgias who had become its governor was an aggressive opponent of the Judeans. Moreover, the soldiers at the strongholds held by the Idumeans were harassing the Jews (10:14-15). After offering public prayers for God's help, Judas and his companions quickly gained control of the strongholds. The various numerical figures in this section (10:17, 18, 23) are obvious exaggerations.

According to 10:18-23, Judas' army would have had quicker success in besieging the two towers if some of Simon's men had not accepted bribes and allowed some of the enemy to escape. When Judas learned of their treachery, he had the Jewish malefactors executed and then took the towers without delay. The point is that Judas succeeded in almost every military endeavor. And where he lacked complete success, that was due to the treachery of his soldiers.

491

10:24-38 Victory over Timothy

For an earlier victory over Timothy, see 8:30-33. The account of this battle (see 1 Macc 5:30-34) emphasizes once more Judas as the model biblical warrior who prays before his battles and gives thanks to God after them. In the face of the huge force assembled by Timothy, Judas and his men perform rituals of supplication (10:25-26) and win the battle not only by their valor but especially because of their reliance on God. In the midst of the battle a vision of five men on golden-bridled horses (10:29-30; see 3:25-26; 5:2-3; 11:8) throws the enemy into confusion.

Meanwhile, Timothy fled to Gazara (or perhaps Jazer), where his brother Chaereas was in command. After a five-day siege, Judas and his men stormed the fortress and tracked down and killed Timothy who was found hiding in a cistern. After their victory they blessed God "with hymns of grateful praise" (10:38).

11:1-12 The defeat of Lysias at Beth-zur

According to 1 Maccabees 4:28-35, the siege of Beth-zur by Lysias took place before the death of Antiochus IV. Here, Lysias is identified as the guardian of Antiochus V and "kinsman" of the king (a member of his inner circle of advisers). Displeased at the several defeats that his Seleucid forces had suffered at the hands of Judas, Lysias was determined to turn Jerusalem into a Greek city and to increase royal revenues by taxing the temple and putting the high priesthood up for bid every year.

With thousands of soldiers and eighty elephants, Lysias set out to approach Jerusalem from the south and to attack the Jewish fortress at Beth-zur, some twenty miles south of Jerusalem (11:4-5). Before rushing out to defend Beth-zur, Judas and his men prayed that God would "send a good angel to save Israel" (11:6). Their prayers were answered with the appearance of a horseman clothed in white garments and equipped with gold weapons (11:8; see 3:25-26; 5:2-3; 10:29-30). They regarded him as their "heavenly ally" (11:10), and so they won the battle against their numerically superior opponents. According to verse 11, eleven thousand foot soldiers and sixteen hundred horsemen were slain. First Maccabees, which also tends to exaggerate the numbers of the enemy killed in battles, places the count of those slain at Beth-zur at five thousand (see

1 Macc 4:34). Lysias escaped death only by a "shameful flight."

11:13-38 A peace treaty

In light of his defeat at Beth-zur, Lysias decided that it would be in everyone's interests to work out a peace treaty with Judas. According to 11:13, he realized that the "Hebrews" (here used as a religious term; see 7:31; 15:37) had as their ally a divine protector (see 3:39; 8:36). The terms of the peace treaty are presented by means of four letters, which may be substantially authentic. While these four letters may not be in their correct chronological order, they will be treated here as they appear in 2 Maccabees.

The first letter (11:16-21), which is dated 164 B.C., is from Lysias to the Jewish people. It accepts the requests that Judas made in writing to Lysias (see 11:15), though it leaves some room for flexibility in responding to them, and calls for further talks about matters of detail by representatives of both sides. It also insists that Judas maintain loyalty to the Seleucid government (11:19).

The second letter (11:22-29), undated, is from Antiochus V to Lysias. Since the king was a boy and Lysias was his regent, Lysias was effectively writing to himself. This letter gives the Jews permission to live again according to their own laws and customs and effectively ends the program of forced Hellenization promulgated under Antiochus IV. The Torah once more could be the law of Judea. Moreover, it grants that the temple be restored to the Jews, and that the traditional rituals be carried out there. Of course, according to 10:1-8, that had already happened.

The third letter (11:27-33), which is dated March 164 B.C., is from King Antiochus to the senate and other Jews. It grants an amnesty to Jews who stop fighting before the end of the month and allows Jews to observe again their food laws and other customs (the Torah). If the date is correct, the author would have to have been Antiochus IV (who died in late 164). It is possible that the high priest Menelaus went to Persia and convinced Antiochus IV to rescind his decrees against the Jews. However, it is suspicious that the date for both the third and the fourth letters is the same. If the correct date was 163, then the author would have been Antiochus V.

The fourth letter (11:34-38), which is also dated March 164, is sent from two Roman consuls to the

Jewish people. It consents to the arrangements being made between Judas and Lysias and requests that further details be made available to the Roman consuls as they make their way to Antioch.

12:1-9 The peace breaks down

The peace treaty seems to have had a short lifespan. When Lysias returned to Antioch and the Jews tried to resume their normal lives, local Seleucid governors refused to let the Jews live in peace (12:1-2). The names of Timothy, Apollonius, and Nicanor may not refer to the figures who already have been (or will be) mentioned in the narrative, since they were common Hellenistic names.

An incident at Joppa, a port thirty-two miles from Jerusalem, prompted Judas to return to his role as defender of all Israel (12:5-7). Some people in Joppa lured two hundred Jews into boats and caused them to drown. In response to this outrage, Judas sprang into action and took revenge on the perpetrators and the city of Joppa. He did so only after "calling upon God, the just judge" (12:6).

Since Judas heard that the people of Jamnia (twelve miles south of Joppa) were planning to do to the Jews there what the people of Joppa had done, Judas made a preemptive strike against Jamnia and caused a huge fire that supposedly could be seen even in Jerusalem (12:8-9). Thus, from these two episodes Judas emerged as the champion of all Jews, even those outside Jerusalem and Judea.

12:10-37 Judas' campaigns in Gilead and elsewhere

The incidents described in this section are treated in greater detail in 1 Maccabees 5. The notice "from there" in 12:10 cannot refer to Joppa or Jamnia, since most of what follows occurred in Gilead, east of the Jordan River. In the first incident Judas wins a battle with Arab mercenaries "with God's help," and even makes peace with them to the point that they become allies and live in peace (12:10-12). See 1 Maccabees 5:25 where the Nabateans become Judas' friends.

In the second incident Judas attacks "Caspin" ("Chaspho" in 1 Macc 5:26, 36) and manages to overcome the arrogance of its inhabitants and their strong fortifications by invoking "the aid of

the great Sovereign of the world" (12:13-16). Here Judas' victory is compared to Joshua's conquest of Jericho (see Josh 6:1-21).

In the third incident (12:17-25; see 1 Macc 5:37-43), Judas meets up with the "Toubians," the remnants of a military unit commanded by the Jewish Tobiad family, at Charax. There, Dositheus and Sosipater, two of Judas' captains, win a great victory. Meanwhile, Judas sets off in pursuit of Timothy and catches up with him at Karnion ("Carnaim" in 1 Macc 5:43-44). There, the enemy melts away in fear "at the manifestation of the All-seeing" (12:22). Timothy escapes only after convincing Dositheus and Sosipater that, if he were allowed to leave alive, he could intercede for the lives of other Jews, most likely those associated with the Tobiads.

Judas' further successes (12:26-31; see 1 Macc 5:46-54) occur at Karnion and its shrine to Atargatis (a Syrian goddess identified with Astarte and Artemis in the Hellenistic times) and at Ephron (opposite Beth-shan/Scythopolis) where the Jews invoke "the Sovereign who powerfully shatters the might of enemies" (12:28). On the word of local Jews who testified that they were well treated there, Judas spared Scythopolis and moved on to Jerusalem to celebrate the feast of Weeks/Pentecost (in the late spring). Judas recognized that he owed his success as a warrior to the God of Israel.

In the final campaign (12:32-37; see 1 Macc 5:55-68) Judas confronted the army of Gorgias, the governor of Idumea, who narrowly escaped with his life to Marisa. Meanwhile, in the midst of a long battle, Judas "called upon the Lord to show himself their ally and leader in the battle" (12:36). And so he and his men prevailed over another numerically superior enemy.

12:38-46 Judas cares for his dead soldiers

In the account of Judas' battle against Gorgias' army, it was noted that "a few of the Jews were slain" (12:34). After his victory Judas assembled his army at Adullam (eight miles northeast of Marisa) where they purified themselves (by ritual bathing) from contact with dead bodies and observed the sabbath rest. After the sabbath they decided to care for the bodies of their fallen comrades. In doing so they made the startling discovery that those Jews who had been killed in the battle had been wearing "amulets sacred to the idols of Jamnia" (12:40). For the author, this fall into idolatry explains why those Jewish soldiers died.

The reaction of Judas and the author's interpretation of it have had important consequences in theology and religious practice. Judas and his men regarded their shocking discovery as proof of the justice of God, "the just judge who brings to light the things that are hidden" (12:41). Then "they prayed that the sinful deed might be fully blotted out" (12:42) and took up a collection to provide for an "expiatory sacrifice" at the Jerusalem temple (12:43). In the Old Testament context one would assume that Judas and his men were concerned with the collective guilt that might adhere to the living soldiers, and that their prayers and sacrifices were intended to render the surviving soldiers spiritually ready for battle again.

The author of 2 Maccabees, however, gives these actions a different interpretation. In 12:43b-46, he takes as his starting point his firm belief in the resurrection of the dead (see 1 Macc 7) and explains the prayers and sacrifices as having atoning or expiatory value for the dead sinners so that they too might fully participate in the resurrection of the dead. The Catholic practice of prayers for the dead finds some of its Old Testament roots in this author's interpretation of Judas' actions on behalf of his dead soldiers.

13:1-23a A Seleucid invasion and the death of Menelaus

Judas learned that the new king, Antiochus V Eupator, and his adviser Lysias were planning an invasion of Judea with a huge army in 163–162 B.C. Their "Greek army" (13:2) was likely composed mainly of mercenaries. The scythes on their chariots were intended to ward off the opposition's infantry.

The account of the invasion is interrupted in 13:3-8 by the story of the death of Menelaus, the Jewish high priest from 172 to 162 B.C. Menelaus at first supported the new invasion in the hope that he could return to Jerusalem and take over from the Maccabees. However, "the King of kings" (God) turned the Seleucid king against Menelaus, and he was blamed for the continuing troubles in Judea. At Beroea (the name given to Aleppo in Syria by Seleucus I), Menelaus was put to death by a Persian method of execution in which the person died either by burning (if the

ashes were hot) or by asphyxiation (if they were cold). The author's judgment on Menelaus is harsh ("transgressor of the law," 13:7), and he regards Menelaus' way of dying and lack of decent burial to be fitting for such a scoundrel.

The account of the invasion is resumed in 13:9-17, with the description of Judas' preemptive strike against the Seleucid army near Modein (the home base for the Maccabees). Before the battle (13:9-14) Judas is careful to prepare his troops spiritually. He urges them to call upon God in prayer and to remember what is at stake for them: "their law, their country, and their holy temple" (13:10). He encourages them in this strike against the superior Seleucid army out of reliance on God's help. And "[l]eaving the outcome to the Creator of the world" (13:14), he and his troops make a nighttime attack on the Seleucid camp. They are said to have killed two thousand soldiers and to have slain the lead elephant and its rider (13:15; see 1 Macc 6:43-46). Again the victory is attributed to "the help and protection of the Lord" (13:17).

According to 13:18-23a, the king and Lysias made another attempt at approaching Jerusalem from the south by way of the Jewish fortress at Beth-zur (see 1 Macc 6:31, 49-50). While the author presents the episode as a victory for Judas and his forces, he admits that one of the Jewish soldiers, Rhodocus by name, betrayed his people and gave out military secrets (probably about the lack of provisions inside the fortress) to the enemy.

13:23b-26 Another peace treaty

The new peace treaty between Antiochus V and the Jews was due in large part to developments back in Antioch. Philip (see 9:29) seems to have also been appointed by Antiochus IV as the guardian of Antiochus V while both were in the eastern part of the Seleucid empire (see 1 Macc 6:14-15). After the death of Antiochus IV, Philip returned to Antioch and took control of the city (see 1 Macc 6:63). Therefore, it was necessary for Lysias to get back to Antioch as soon as possible and to reestablish his authority there.

On hearing that Philip had control of Antioch, Lysias and the king proposed another peace treaty with the Jews and even made Judas the governor of the coastal area from north (Ptolemais-Acco) to south (Gerar), despite the objections of the people of Ptolemais (13:25; see 6:8).

14:1-11 Alcimus as high priest

To add to the confusion surrounding Seleucid affairs, in 161 B.C. Demetrius I, the son of Seleucus IV, arrived in Tripolis and managed to do away with Lysias and Antiochus V (see 1 Macc 7:1-4), and to seize power for himself.

The change in rule gave Alcimus (Hebrew "Yakim") the opportunity to get himself appointed as the Jewish high priest in place of Menelaus. The author of 2 Maccabees dismisses Alcimus as "a former high priest" and suggests that he had collaborated with the new order of worship at the temple and so "willfully incurred defilement" (14:3). However, it is likely that Alcimus had a legitimate claim upon the Jewish high priesthood and regarded Judas as responsible for the continuing troubles in Judea. In 14:6 Alcimus describes Judas as the leader of the Hasideans and lumps them all under the epithet of "warmongers" (see 1 Macc 2:42 and 7:12-17 for a different picture of the relationship between Judas and the Hasideans). Moreover, in 14:10 he advises the new king's council that "[a]s long as Judas is around, it is impossible for the government [that is, the Seleucid kingdom] to enjoy peace."

14:12-25 Nicanor's mission

According to 14:12-13, Demetrius I sent Nicanor (see 8:9-36) to be governor of Judea. His task was to kill Judas and his followers and to establish Alcimus as the high priest. His appointment pleased the local Gentile population but terrified the Jews who immediately took to prayer (14:14-15). After glossing over Nicanor's defeat of Simon at Adasa as a "slight setback" (14:17), the author explains that Nicanor had a change of heart and decided that the most effective strategy was to arrange a peace treaty with Judas (14:18-22).

Even more remarkable is the claim that, according to 14:23-25, Nicanor developed a personal friendship with Judas. Compare 1 Maccabees 7:27, which suggests that Nicanor behaved treacherously from start to finish. However, according to 2 Maccabees, Nicanor not only befriended Judas but even served as his mentor or guide and urged him to marry, have children, and settle down in peace.

14:26-36 The friendship ends

According to 14:26-27, it was Alcimus' intervention that destroyed the friendship between Nicanor and Judas, and the peace in Judea. Alcimus took the latest peace treaty as evidence that Nicanor was failing to carry out the king's orders (see 14:13). Although Nicanor was reluctant to break his agreement with Judas, he recognized that "there was no way of opposing the king" (14:29). The increasing coldness with which Nicanor treated Judas led Judas to suspect a problem and so he went into hiding.

Nicanor's attack on the temple (14:31-36) comes in the form of a threat; unless the Jews handed over Judas to him as a prisoner, he would "level this shrine to God to the ground . . . tear down the altar, and erect here a splendid temple to Dionysus" (14:33). In response, the priests prayed to God as "the unfailing defender of our nation" (14:34) to protect the temple that had so recently been purified (10:1-8). For the fulfillment of their prayer, see 15:34.

14:37-46 The death of Razis

For earlier accounts of martyrdoms, see chapters 6 and 7. Perhaps even a convert to Judaism (see 15:38), Razis was an elder of Jerusalem and a supporter of Judas ("a patriot" from the author's perspective). To make an example of him, Nicanor sent a huge force to arrest Razis on account of his fidelity to the Jewish cause.

Rather than be arrested and executed, Razis preferred to "die nobly" (14:42) by turning his sword against himself. For a biblical precedent, see the case of Saul (1 Sam 31:4). However, his first attempt at suicide was not entirely successful. And so he then threw himself down from the tower where he had been hiding. But his second attempt was also unsuccessful. Finally as he was making his last stand, he tore out his innards and threw them on the crowds. The author insists in 14:46 that Razis undertook "suicide" out of his conviction that in the resurrection he would get back his bodily parts (see 7:11, 22-23).

15:1-5 Nicanor's arrogance

Learning that Judas and his men controlled the northern approaches to Jerusalem ("Samaria"), Nicanor decided to attack them on the sabbath (15:1). Nothing is said about the Maccabees' decision to defend themselves on the sabbath (see 1 Macc 2:41). The Jews who had been forced to serve Nicanor pleaded with him to respect the sabbath rest on the grounds that it was a divine command (15:2). The ensuing conversation between Nicanor and his Jewish collaborators (15:3-5) concerns sovereignty in heaven and on earth. When the Jews protest that there really is a ruler in heaven, Nicanor replies that he is the ruler on earth, and that therefore his order to attack Judas on the sabbath is to be carried out. At the same time he seems to be arrogantly putting himself above the one who is sovereign in heaven, or at least denying his sovereignty on earth.

15:6-19 Preparation for battle

In contrast to the arrogant Nicanor who was already planning a public monument commemorating his victory over Judas (15:6), Judas provides spiritual encouragement for his men. He first reminds them of God's help in their past victories and reads to them from "the law and the prophets" (15:7-10). Then in 15:11-16 he recounts to them a dream or vision featuring the former high priest Onias III and the prophet Jeremiah. He portrays these two revered figures as praying on their behalf and interceding for them with God. And finally, Jeremiah presents Judas with a golden sword as a gift from God to be used in crushing the enemy. Encouraged by Judas' words, his soldiers go into battle eagerly, with their primary concern the defense of "the consecrated sanctuary," that is, the Jerusalem temple (15:17-18). Thus the theme that has run through 2 Maccabees comes to a climax.

15:20-36 The defeat and death of Nicanor

According to 1 Maccabees 7:40-50, the battle took place at Adasa. In the face of Nicanor's huge and well-arrayed army (15:20), Judas turns to prayer out of a recognition that victory is won only through "the Lord's decision" (15:21). In his prayer he recalls again (see 8:19; also 1 Macc 7:41-42) the miraculous defeat of Sennacherib's army in 701 B.C. (see 2 Kgs 18:13–19:35 and Isa 36–37) and asks God to send "a good angel" to frighten away the enemy.

Whereas Nicanor's army goes into battle with trumpet blasts and battle songs, Judas' army engages in supplications and prayers (15:25-26). They come out of the battle with a complete victory, which they celebrate with shouts in Hebrew in praise of God (15:27-29). Among the thirty-five thousand slain, they find the body of Nicanor in all his armor (15:28).

In response, Judas orders that Nicanor's head and right arm be cut off and brought back to Jerusalem (15:30). There he puts them on display, giving a special message to the Seleucid soldiers and their supporters who were manning the citadel. Judas' actions are presented as just punishments visited upon the one who threatened the temple with his mouth and raised his arm against it (see 14:33). With God's help, the prayer of the priests in 14:35-36 has come to pass. The concluding prayer—"Blessed be the one who has preserved undefiled his own place" (15:34)—summarizes the book's central theme. And by public vote the day of Nicanor's defeat and death is to be celebrated as "Nicanor's Day" annually (15:36).

15:37-39 Epilogue

The author/summarizer breaks off his narrative at this point and brings the reader back to his preface in 2:19-32. He claims that he has done his best both to inform and to entertain and hopes that readers will have found his work "well written and to the point" (15:38). He defends his artistic contributions by the analogy of mixing water and wine. In antiquity the wine was often so strong that it had to be diluted with water to make it enjoyable.

CHRONOLOGICAL TABLES

Seleucid Rulers

223–187:   Antiochus III

187–175:   Seleucus IV Philopator

175–164:   Antiochus IV Epiphanes

164–162:   Antiochus V Eupator (and Lysias)

162–150:   Demetrius I Soter

150–145:   Alexander I Balas

145–139:   Demetrius II Nicator

145–142:   Antiochus VI (and Trypho)

138–129:   Antiochus VII Sidetes

Key Dates in the Maccabean Revolt

175:   Antiochus IV Epiphanes as Seleucid ruler; Jason as Jewish high priest

172:   Menelaus as Jewish high priest

169:   Antiochus IV's first Egyptian campaign; plunder of the Jerusalem temple

168:   Antiochus IV's second Egyptian campaign; founding of the Jerusalem citadel

167:   Desecration of the temple; persecution of Judeans

165:   Judas leads the revolt

164:   Rededication of the temple; death of Antiochus IV

162:   Alcimus as Jewish high priest

161:   Judas' victory over Nicanor; alliance with Rome

160:   Death of Judas; accession of Jonathan

159:   Death of Alcimus

152:   Jonathan as Jewish high priest

142:   Death of Jonathan; accession of Simon

141:   Conquest of the citadel

134:   Death of Simon; accession of John Hyrcanus

THE BOOK OF
JOB

Kathleen M. O'Connor

INTRODUCTION

The book of Job is vivid testimony to pain, a plea for justice, and a wrenching theological debate about suffering and its causes. Central to this debate are questions about the roles God and humans play in causing human suffering and whether divine-human relationship can proceed in the midst of overwhelming anguish. Like a riddle, the text grasps readers' minds and emotions, inviting them to participate in Job's story and to work toward their own solution to the dilemmas of both Job and his friends.

Literary features

The book's literary components do not fit easily together. It sets conflicting characters and discordant speeches side by side without providing interpretive clues. But rather than producing a mish-mash of ideas, the resulting tensions summon readers to engage in Job's struggle, to stay with him on the ash heap and stand with him before God in search of healing. Because the book refuses to leave our present understandings intact, reading means undertaking mental and emotional labor. Job and his friends argue with each other in dense, beautiful poetic speeches, and they complain at length to wear the reader down. In the process, the poems bring us into Job's despair and his friends' frustration and growing rigidity.

But the effort required to read and study the book is worth it because the book's unsettled nature puts us either in Job's place or in sympathy with his friends or, perhaps, both. Precisely be-

cause it refuses to settle for easy answers about any of its subjects, the book of Job is a classic of world literature.

Most interpreters believe the book as we now have it is a composite, built upon an ancient tale about an innocent sufferer. The outlines of Job's story were well known across cultures in antiquity. Peoples of the ancient Near East produced several texts with affinities to the biblical book where an innocent person undergoes suffering, argues with the gods, and is inexplicably restored to well-being. Job also appears by name in a biblical list of heroes (Ezek 14:14, 20), adding to the sense that his basic story was widely known.

It is likely that a writer in ancient Israel took this folktale, adapted it, cut it open, and then set the poetic speeches in the midst of it. The prose narrative appears in the prologue (1:1–2:13) and epilogue (42:7-17). By using both forms of literature, folktale and poetry, the book presents a totality of suffering, an overwhelming portrait told from outside by a third person narrator in the prose and from the inside in the poetic testimony of Job and his friends. The prose describes Job's external losses, while the poetry portrays Job's more internal sufferings.

Poetry is particularly suited to the task of spiritual struggle because its dense imagery, compactness of speech, and allusiveness create an artistic world something like music. It appeals to the full humanity of readers, summoning forth our own ghosts, unsettled sorrows, and hidden angers. It can transport us into realms of spirit and lead to new discoveries. But the poetry of Job makes best sense when read in the context of the prose narrative that lays out the book's initial problem. Job is an innocent person yet enormous catastrophes befall him because of a deal made in heaven. This predicament gives rise to the poetry.

The prose and the poetry belong together, but there are great differences between them. In the prologue, for example, Job is patient and trusting while his friends are silent. By contrast, in the poetry Job is furious and impatient and his friends flood him with words. This is one of the many gaps that raise questions about characters and their motivations, thereby engaging us in Job's plight.

Job's poetry uses a great deal of legal imagery as a way for Job to imagine that God might acknowledge his innocence. Job appeals to a third party to assist him in his search for justice because his informal appeals to God seem to produce nothing but more sorrow. He declares legal oaths of innocence by which he offers his self-defense at the end of his speeches. But legal language is only one way Job voices his complaints. Language of creation and observations from the world of plants and animals help him build his protests.

Much of Job's speech takes the form of lamentation. Over one third of the book of Psalms and the entire book of Lamentations are laments. These are prayers in the form of complaint. The one who prays cries out to God in pain, describes various forms of affliction, and seeks redress. Laments are a form of truth-telling to God. They open up rather than deny suffering, and they present to God the affliction of the one who prays and demands action. In Old Testament laments, anger at God and fury close to blasphemy are instruments of fidelity because they keep the relationship with God alive in the midst of suffering. They are acts of faith that God cares for the afflicted and can bear to hear the truth. By using laments, Job grows strong and courageous as he clings to God under the worst conditions.

Wisdom literature

The book of Job belongs in a grouping of biblical books called the wisdom literature that includes Proverbs, Ecclesiastes, Sirach, and the Wisdom of Solomon. These books differ from other biblical literature in their attention to daily struggles of ordinary human life. By contrast, the prophetic books speak of God's word to the people, and the historical books tell of God's actions on behalf of Israel. Wisdom starts neither with God nor with large political and national events, but from human efforts to live wisely from day to day. Life's challenges give rise to theological reflection, not the other way around. Job is merely going on with his daily life when disasters overtake him, and those events propel his theological questions. In wisdom thinking, at least in the book of Proverbs, faithful living should yield material blessing. When Job loses everything, his fidelity to God is suspect.

Job's cultural world

Job lived in a different cultural world from that of contemporary Western readers, though people in tribal communities on various continents may find many affinities with aspects of the book. Job lived in a community-oriented culture. The family and clan were of high value, and one sought to become wise and learn proverbs in order to create harmony for in the community, not for self-advancement as in individual-oriented cultures.

Israel's culture as reflected in Wisdom literature was deeply concerned about the authenticity of speech, about proper use of the tongue, and about wise sayings or proverbs as a key to right behavior. Proverbs are short sayings that were instruments of wise living and the storehouse of tradition. Because the culture was an oral one, the right use of words was critical for communal well-being. Wisdom drawn from animal and plant life instructed humans in how to maneuver in daily life and how to contribute to the community. Both Job and his friends apply proverbs to his situation, but their proverbs usually conflict with one another.

Other features of Israel's culture important for understanding the book include the values of honor and shame. Shame was a communal judgment, often implicit, that one's behavior or attitude brought dishonor to the community. To be shamed means one has been disrespectful of persons or basic values in the community. Job begins the story as a most honorable person, but his disasters cause him shame and isolation from his friends. He loses his good name and his community no longer recognizes his honor, isolating him and causing him great anguish. Many Asian and African cultures structure themselves with similar values.

Outline of the book

The book divides into the following literary units:

The Prologue (1:1–2:13)

Three Rounds of Speeches among Job and His Friends (3:1–14:22; 15:1–21:34; 22:1–31:37)

Hymn to Wisdom (28:1-28)

Job's Self-Defense (29:1–31:37)

Elihu's Speech (32:1–37:24)

The Encounter with God in the Storm (38:1–42:6)

The Epilogue (42:7-17)

COMMENTARY

PROLOGUE

Job 1:1–2:3

The prose prologue begins with a depiction of a contented Job, residing in security, wealth, and domestic tranquility. A narrator describes events that move through the slow but complete unraveling of these good things and end in grief on the ash heap. Events alternate in the five scenes between earth and heaven; events in heaven determine what happens on earth. The narrative unfolds in highly stylized fashion with sparse detail and repeated patterns typical of a folktale. The effects of this narrative style are to present a hammering sequence of events that shatters Job's world and leaves many unanswered questions about divine and human characters and their motivations.

1:1-5 Job's goodness

The opening scene takes place on earth where every detail contributes to a portrait of Job as innocent man, beloved of God. The narrator calls him "blameless and upright," one who "feared God," and "avoided evil" (1:1). To "fear God" is a common term of the wisdom literature that has less to do with fright before God and more to do with right relationship with God. "Fear of God" is not easy to translate into English but conveys qualities of obedience, reverence, and awe before God. One commentator calls it a synonym for true religion. Job's fear of God marks him as a wise

and righteous man. His large family and vast wealth in animal holdings confirm his blamelessness and special relationship with God. In antiquity, material wealth signified that its bearer was a worthy recipient of divine favor.

Job's uprightness receives further confirmation from the size of his family and the peaceful generosity of his children. His seven sons invite his three daughters to their feasts, showing their hospitality to exceed the bounds of their culture where women had little status. And perhaps most indicative of Job's righteousness is a detail in which he exceeds all obvious requirements of care for his family by offering sacrifice on behalf of his children in case they have sinned "in their hearts" (1:5). In its spare telling, the story leaves readers to ponder Job's behavior. Is he an overly scrupulous parent? Does he act to protect the children? Or is this one more instance of his absolute devotion to God? The folktale genre of the prologue, however, may preclude suspicions about Job's character, for folktales typically tell actions as straightforward events to be taken at face value. The next scenes support the view that fidelity alone motivates Job.

1:6-12 Deal in heaven

The action starts when messengers, called "sons of God," come before "the LORD" in the heavenly court. Heavenly courts with semi-divine beings of the spirit world appear elsewhere in the Old Testament (1 Kgs 22:19-23; Dan 7). Among the heavenly messengers is "the Satan," whose name means "the adversary," an official court title, not a proper name. He is not yet the demonic figure of later Jewish and Christian thinking, but one of the Lord's faithful servants, though it is easy to see from his role here how he might later come to personify evil.

The Lord starts the action by asking the Satan if, when traveling to and fro on the earth, he had noticed "my servant Job" (1:7). Should readers still question Job's innocence, God's authoritative boasting repeats the narrator's assessment of Job's innocence. Job is "blameless and upright, fearing God and avoiding evil" (1:8). The Satan, however, suspects Job is faithful only because God has given him good things. He accuses God of purchasing Job's fidelity, for if God were to remove them, "surely [Job] will curse you to your face" (1:11). The Hebrew word translated "curse" means literally "to bless," but here "bless" is a euphemism, that is, a polite way to say the opposite.

Without hesitation and without debate, the Lord gives the Satan control of Job's life with one caveat—he is not to touch Job. Why God acquiesces to this deal is not clear. It may be that refusing the Satan's challenge would cause God shame in this ancient Israelite culture where honor is of high value. Or it may be that God is so confident of Job's loyalty that a positive outcome of the deal seems assured. Whatever God's reasons for abdicating power, Satan goes forth to loose tragedy upon Job.

1:13-22 Job's first test

Back on earth, catastrophes roll over Job in quick succession. In simple, unadorned prose, the story unfolds in parallel episodes so each disaster appears like the one before in a persistent drumbeat of loss. Events concerning Job's children form a literary frame around his other losses (1:13, 18-19). By setting the other disasters during one of their feasts, the text creates a foreboding sense of doom and foreshadows the fourth and most horrible of Job's devastations. A messenger comes to announce each tragedy and says, "I alone have escaped to tell you" (1:15, 16, 17, 18). And "He was still speaking when" the next messenger appears with a similar report. Finally, in the horrible climax, the narrator gives extra description to the children's destruction. A great wind destroys the

house where they are feasting and kills all of them. Within a few verses, Job loses everything in a whirlwind of calamity, a blitz of overwhelmingly bad news.

To this point in the telling, Job has made no response to any of the reports, but then in customary rituals for expressing grief, he tears his clothes, cuts his hair, and falls upon the ground. At last he speaks in carefully balanced sentences typical of Hebrew poetry. "Naked I came forth . . . naked shall I go back . . . The LORD gave . . . the LORD has taken away" (1:21). Then he blesses God's name. Job does not curse God and the narrator confirms that Job does not "sin, nor did he charge God with wrong" (1:22).

2:1-6 Another bad deal in heaven

The story might have ended in the previous chapter where, even in the aftermath of the unrelenting assault upon him, Job proved himself blameless and upright, a God-fearer, and a refuser of evil. Instead, when the heavenly messengers come before the Lord again, the tension escalates. The narrative follows the first heavenly scene of the previous chapter, but with some important changes. Again God asks the Satan where he has been and if he has seen his "servant Job" who remains "blameless and upright, fearing God and avoiding evil" (2:3). In still a further affirmation of Job, God accuses the Satan of manipulation in order to harm Job "without cause."

The Satan replies "skin for skin," a short saying that probably means, if you harm someone's skin, they will harm yours in turn. His principle of human behavior is that people may remain faithful when you take their things or their loved ones, but if you attack their bodies and threaten their lives, they will do anything. The Satan applies his principle to Job, insisting that Job will "curse you to your face" (2:5). Again without explanation, God relinquishes Job into the Satan's power. The only constraint on Satan is that he preserve Job's life.

2:7-10 Job's second test

Satan goes forth again and afflicts Job with severe boils that cover his body. To convey the horror of Job's physical condition, the narrator mentions the simple detail of a potsherd, a piece of broken pottery Job uses for wound-scraping as he sits on the ash heap (2:8). Job's nameless wife appears only in this scene, but her question intones a theme of both the prologue and the book. "Are you still holding to your innocence?," she asks. The Hebrew word translated "innocence" also means "integrity" or "wholeness" in the sense of deeply held honesty and blamelessness. Job's wife's motivations have provoked debate among interpreters. When she advises him to curse God and die, is she betraying him? In the ancient world, people believed cursing God brought certain death. Does his wife want him to die because she cannot bear to see him suffer? Or is her question a literary device to provoke Job's response? Everything comes from God, he proclaims, so should we not accept both good and evil? Job has passed the second test in patient fidelity.

2:11-13 The friends

Job's three friends hear of his tragedy and travel to see him, but they do not recognize him, so altered is he by his suffering. So stunned are they, they can find no words adequate to comfort him. They lament, tear their clothes, and put dust on their heads according to ancient mourning rituals. For a week they sit with him, mercifully silent, and perhaps numbed themselves, companions who see "how great was his suffering" (2:13). Their silent companionship may be their deepest act of friendship.

FIRST ROUND OF SPEECHES
Job 3:1–14:22

To cross from the prose prologue into the poetry in the book is to move into an altered world. Job is no longer the "patient man" of popular opinion but an enraged, impatient, and broken human. His friends, provoked by his outburst in chapter 3, also break their silence and offer advice to comfort and guide him into their version of the "truth"of his situation. Job's suffering expands in the poetic speeches for they add to his suffering internal anguish that compounds his pain. His friends fail to understand him and cannot relinquish their belief that he must be guilty of sin and so he must have caused his own suffering. Job himself has no other explanation for his overwhelming misery than that God has betrayed him. Together the speeches of Job and his friends offer conflicting interpretations of Job's suffering without indicating which one might be correct.

This mode of theological debate encourages readers to weigh each view and to come to terms with the drama of Job's life themselves and perhaps also with the suffering within and around them.

3:1-10 Job curses his birth

Job curses both the day of his birth (3:1-6) and the night of his conception (3:7-10), two continuous moments in the creation of his life. His curse is actually a series of wishes, impossible appeals, not only to undo his life but also to unmake, to cancel out God's creation of his birthday. As a way to develop dramatic tension, the poem withholds the reason for his curse until verse ten. Prior to that, Job presents his suffering as part of the larger cosmic battle between light and darkness, order and chaos, life and death. Upon the day of his birth, he heaps a series of synonyms for darkness. He wishes to obliterate his day of birth from the calendar, as if it were possible to reach back in time and blot out his life from human history. Job wants to turn the day of his birth, normally a time of joy, into empty gloom. Daylight should turn to darkness, no light should shine, darkness should claim his day, and the dark night itself should frighten the day from even existing.

When Job steps back further in time to the night of his conception, he wishes to destroy the joyful night of his parents' love-making and the beginning of his life in the womb (3:7-10). Underlying his curse of the night are ancient Canaanite myths in which chaos struggles with order and life with death. Chaos was represented as the sea and sometimes as a mythic sea monster, here called "Leviathan" (3:8). Job desperately seeks a mysterious group of people who are able to raise up Leviathan to help him curse his conception. The poem poetically turns the night into a person who cannot find the morning light or gaze at the "eyes of the dawn" (3:9). The climax of the poem comes when Job finally proclaims the reason for his curses—the night did not shut the door to his mother's womb (3:10). Had he never been born or conceived, he would not have to face his present troubles.

3:11-19 Job's despair

Job elaborates on his desire never to have been born with a series of questions about his birth (3:11-12). Since his conception was unavoidable, he would rather have been a stillborn or an abandoned infant with no one to nurse him. Then death would have come quickly, and he would be at rest rather than living in turmoil and pain. Death attracts him because it is a state of rest, free of pain. He imagines the world of the dead as a place occupied by many elite people who, in a democracy of the underworld, rest together with captives and slaves. In death everyone is free from oppression and from distinctions of class. Small and great are the same. To be there is better than to be alive in misery.

3:20-26 Why does anyone suffer?

Job's suffering expands his imagination and compassion. He moves in his mind from the world of the dead to the plight of other suffering people. His afflictions lead him to wonder why anyone suffers, why anyone would know so much anguish to make them long for death and to desire the grave. Job's sudden and colossal misery enables the once rich, powerful man to see beyond his own world to the larger torments of others. In Job's view, the reason people suffer is because God "hems" them in (3:23). Job sighs and groans and has discovered that he has little control over anything. Death is preferable because in death there is rest.

4:1–5:26 Eliphaz's first speech

Eliphaz from Teman is the most gentle of Job's three friends, all of whom are deeply rooted in the theology that people bring suffering upon themselves. Often called the "theology of retribution," the thinking is that if you do good things, you receive good things in return, and vice versa. Across the book, Job's friends will defend this view and interpret Job's life through it. But no matter their theology, the three friends care deeply for Job and wish to see him released from his suffering.

Respectfully, Eliphaz asks Job if he is willing to hear, if he is open to wise counsel. Implying that Job was once a vocal proponent of the theology of his friends, Eliphaz reminds him of his past support of people who faltered along life's journey (4:3-4). Now Job must preach to himself. With a rhetorical question, Eliphaz goes to the heart of the theology Job once shared with these friends (4:7). In his view, the innocent and the upright do not perish. Instead, they are safe and therefore Job can face the future in confidence.

Using a style of argument typical of wisdom literature, Eliphaz contrasts the fate of the innocent with the fate of trouble-makers (4:8-11). "Those who plow mischief" will get what they deserve, because God's angry breath will destroy them. The moral dynamic is clear; humans determine their own fate and Job must choose which group, the innocent or the wicked, he wishes to be among. And again using a common speech form of wisdom, Eliphaz speaks in proverb-like sayings that draw wisdom from the animal and plant world. His reference to lions is not connected grammatically to the fate of the wicked, but it probably means that even these powerful beasts have to put up with travail and loss, so Job should expect no less.

Eliphaz claims that theological authority for his advice comes from his experience of "visions of the night," a dream-like revelation experienced by him alone (4:12-21). A spirit visits, frightens, and questions him, and then answers the questions. All creatures are sinful before God, even heavenly beings. Humans, made only of clay and dust, are even more sinful than corrupt denizens of the spirit world. Humans die and may never learn wisdom, presumably the wisdom of their true sinful condition. Depicting the fragility of human life, the visiting spirit speaks of human bodies as houses and tents, temporary dwellings that crush, shatter, or pluck up easily (4:19-21). That life is fragile and humans sinful should be a warning to Job.

Eliphaz's advice grows less gentle when he points to Job's isolation in his suffering (5:1-2). There are no holy ones to whom Job might appeal for help. Whereas some interpreters believe Eliphaz's claim about holy ones is a putdown of ancient beliefs in lesser gods who intervene with the high god, others think Eliphaz is merely underscoring the vast gap between humans and the spirit world. Job cannot expect assistance; all rests with him alone. Although Eliphaz does not say Job is an impatient fool directly, in typical wisdom style, he implies as much. The fool's fate includes loss of his household and the endangerment of children (5:4). In his most callous and insensitive statement, Eliphaz interprets the tragic death of Job's children as both something avoidable and the result of Job's own malfeasance (5:7).

Pain and loss are clear and understandable for Eliphaz. He says this in a number of striking ways

(5:2-7). The fool's impatience slays him; the fool spreads his roots but around him his family collapses; the hungry will eat what they reap, and mischief does not emerge from the ground. In other words, suffering is not built into the created order of the world; instead, humans manufacture it. Accordingly, Job has brought his anguish upon himself. Eliphaz's belief that humans are responsible for what happens in life, his "theology of retribution," also contains hope for Job. If he caused his pain, he can also act to remove it.

Eliphaz truly wants his friend to escape his suffering and live a renewed life (5:8-16). His advice rests on his assumptions about Job's situation. If I were you, "I would appeal to God, and to God I would state my plea" (5:8). Job did not do so in his cursing laments in chapter three. Parallel statements about God's treatment of the earth and its inhabitants emphasize the urgency of Eliphaz's hopes for his friend (5:10-13). To motivate Job to appeal to God, Eliphaz points to saving characteristics of the divine. God is creator and rain giver, rescuer of the lowly and mournful, and frustrator of the schemes and craftiness of the so-called "wise." It is the poor whom God saves, so "the needy have hope" (5:16). Eliphaz reminds Job of a theological tradition of which Job has long been a part; God is on the side of the broken and the humble.

Eliphaz then moves from the subject of how God behaves to a theological interpretation of Job's predicament (5:16-27). Using the "happy is the one" saying common among wisdom sayings (e.g., Ps 1:1 and Prov 29:18), Eliphaz thinks God's reprimand is a blessing that should not be rejected. He assumes that Job's suffering is a punishment to benefit him. Job will escape his suffering because of God's character. God both wounds and binds up, smites and heals (5:18). Eliphaz applies his thinking directly to Job's life by changing from third person plural speech (they) about the unfortunate in general to the second person singular "you" of direct address. God will deliver "you" from evils, threats, swords, wars, scandals, fear, want, and beasts of the earth (5:18-23).

Extremely appealing blessings cap Eliphaz's advice to Job (5:23-27). He continues to address Job directly to assure him he will be in covenant with the earth and its inhabitants (5:23). Job will be at peace with stones and beasts alike. He will live in security in a household lacking nothing;

he will see his offspring and live to old age, like grain in its season (5:26). Eliphaz concludes with a clinching warrant for the advice he has offered Job. "We," presumably, he and his wise friends, have "searched" it out (5:27). From the sages' long study of human experience, they have known that Eliphaz speaks the truth, or so he claims.

6:1–7:21 Job's reply to Eliphaz

Set next to Eliphaz's tranquil vision of Job's future, Job's response appears all the more bitter. His experience no longer complies with Eliphaz's optimistic picture of the life of the faithful. Whereas Eliphaz believes Job must be responsible for his suffering, so he can also anticipate a beautiful future once he appeals to God, Job believes God has viciously turned against him. Nor does Job believe Eliphaz has heard or understood him. His suffering is so enormous that it cannot be measured, for it is heavier than "the sands of the sea" (6:2-3).

Job's complaint about the enormity of his misery indicates the depth of the chaos in which he now lives (6:2-7). His immeasurable pain leads him to speak freely. Without restraint, he interprets his suffering as the consequence of God's attack on him. Like a vicious hunter, God shoots poison-tipped arrows into him (6:4). God is a terrorist who both attacks and poisons him. Like his friends, Job also uses proverb-like sayings from the animal world to give authority to his speech. Neither the wild donkey nor the ox make noise without reason, and so Job, too, has reasons for his emotional lament.

Verses six and seven are obscure even in the Hebrew, but they focus on food as a metaphor for life. Job's food is tasteless and loathsome to him.

After his sharp outburst in the previous verses, it is as if he were so alienated from God, he cannot even pray (6:8-10). Job does not address God but speaks indirectly in a wishful manner about the deity. He wants God to respond to a startling request—that God would crush him and cut him off. His death would be a comfort because he is innocent. He insists he has been obedient to divine commands and, therefore, did not create his own suffering, as Eliphaz maintains. The rhetorical questions of the next three verses reinforce Job's despair and desire to endure no longer (6:11-14). He ponders his own strength, his limits, and his support group, and all fall short.

Particularly unsatisfactory is the support of his friends (6:14-17). Job's remarks about his friends increase readers' sense of his isolation. Rather than speaking directly to his friends, he speaks about them in the third person as though they are not present. The ideal friend owes kindness to one "in despair," even if he has abandoned the "fear of the Almighty" (6:14). "Fear of God" in the Old Testament means a spirit of true religion, of obedience and awe before God. Hence, friends owe loyalty to the wounded. Even if he has broken loyalty with God, they should not. In Job's culture, loyalty among friends is of very high value. Job's friends fail him like a dried up stream in the desert or a raging, icy torrent in winter (6:15-16). Jeremiah makes similar accusations against God who, like a treacherous stream, disappears in times of need (Jer 15:17).

Though the next verses appear to change the imagery from water courses to caravans, they are probably continuing the same search for reliable sources of water (6:18-21). Merchant caravans may leave their routes to find water in desert streams only to be frustrated, as Job is with his friends who offer him no nourishment. That only one friend has spoken so far in the book may not be important for Job's conclusion, if he understands Eliphaz to be speaking for all of them. But Job's language of the deceptive waters and the frustrated caravans are not offered indirectly as in Eliphaz's style of speech. Job uses second person address to apply the deception to his friends. "It is thus you have now become for me" (6:21). Then Job interprets the cause of their betrayal. They see and "are afraid." They see Job's terrible suffering that might become their fate, too, if their theology proves wrong. Fear blinds them to his true circumstances.

The subject of their friendship continues to occupy Job's thoughts for the rest of the chapter (6:22-30). He wants to know how he has failed them, or if he has asked too much from them. Humbly he begs them to teach him where he has gone wrong. Once he knows, he will stop speaking. But he does not believe he is wrong for he accuses them of dishonest speech. He mocks their words as lacking proof and having the windy quality of the desperate. He attacks their moral character as callous enough to "cast lots" for an orphan and to sell away a friend. Then he pleads with them for a full and attentive hearing and

tries to convince them of his honesty and his innocence (6:30).

Job now reflects on human misery in general and his experience of it in particular (7:1-10). Rhetorical questions embrace the lot of humanity. Is human life not drudgery, the life of a "hireling," a laborer with little or nothing in the way of rights or pay or dignity? Like a slave without protection, Job too lives in misery. The verb translated, "I have been assigned" indicates Job's self-understanding as a victim of some design (7:3). He laments his nights when he talks to himself, is restless, and his skin crawls (cf. 2:7-8). His days, in contrast to his nights, are brief and hopeless (7:10). Despair prevails in his imagination, for he cannot conceive of any future different from the present except for death, an event he expounds with images of life's fleetingness. Eyes will no longer see him, clouds will dissolve like those who go to the underworld, and the dead will not return home.

But it is Job's very despair that empowers him to speak and to express his resistance to God's designs upon him. He has nothing to lose, so he will not even try to be quiet (7:11). He hurls a bold challenge to God. Does God think he is a sea monster or the sea itself, those mythic images of unbridled force and chaos that Job mentioned in 3:8? Job accuses God of watching him and attacking him as if he were one of the sea creatures, and he demands to know why God makes him a target. In Job's view, God assaults him without reason and misunderstands his own being. He cannot escape this treachery in the comfort and oblivion of sleep because God continues to attack him even in his dreams. He would prefer to die and, unlike most religious people, asks only for God to leave him alone (7:16).

To express his plight, Job alludes to Psalm 8 and inverts its meaning. The question of the psalm, "What are human beings that you make so much of them, mortals that you care for them?" (Ps 8:5, NRSV) becomes in Job's mouth not thanksgiving for God's care but a promise of judgment, threat, and menacing presence. Job's despair continues to drive him. Depending on how one translates verse 20—Job either acknowledges he is a sinner, "If I sin" (NABRE) or in other translations, "Though I sinned"—the consequences are the same. God does not pardon guilt of anyone. But even if Job has sinned, he has done nothing to deserve the calamities that have befallen him. He calls God a "watcher" of humans (7:20), not to speak of divine protection but to accuse God of vigilance in search of human sin. Like a petulant child, he reminds God of his mortality. Time is running out and the two of them are split asunder.

8:1-22 Bildad's first speech

When Job's second friend speaks, it is to jump to God's defense and to call Job a chattering windbag. God's justice cannot be challenged, argues Bildad. After he applauds God's reliable governance of the world, he strikes a piercing blow against his friend. Indirectly but unmistakably, he interprets the death of Job's children as the result of their sin (8:4). Bildad cannot think for a minute that the innocent would perish. Like Eliphaz, Bildad believes there is still hope for Job (8:5-7). If he appeals to God and is "blameless and upright," God will act on his behalf. Readers, of course, know from the prologue that Job is "blameless and upright" (1:1). But for Bildad, Job's moral state has become a matter of doubt. Even so, if Job appeals to God in righteousness, then God will restore him as if nothing ever happened.

Besides turning back to God, Bildad advises Job to appeal to the ancestors and the wise traditions of the past that have sustained many (8:8-19). What they will teach Job is the dismal fate of the wicked, once again implying that Job is among them and must take action to escape their company. Bildad offers a proverb drawn from the natural world to make his point (8:11-13). Papyrus and reeds grow only in water; even so humans live only in God. God-forgetters will perish like the "gossamer" threads of a spider's web (8:14). The godless appear to be filled with life energy, but they cannot grow among the rocks, and they have no safe place.

In these allusions, Bildad places Job among the godless but, confident that God overcomes the suffering of the righteous, he also promises Job a glowing future. Job will again know overflowing laughter and his lips will rejoice even as his enemies meet their demise (8:21-22).

9:1–10:22 Job's reply to Bildad

In anguish, Job affirms what Bildad had just said, "I know well that it is so" (9:1). Certain that no human can stand before God in complete innocence, he knows the human condition is sinful and broken. Once he had been a proponent of his friend's theology, but now his experience challenges his old theology. Yet no new understanding of suffering and God's relationship has emerged to ease his way. He is in a liminal position outside of solid explanations.

By contrast to human creatureliness, God's awesomeness intimidates Job (9:3-13). The Hebrew word translated "to contend with" has legal implications (9:3). If Job wanted to take God to court, he would be unable to speak because God's power and distance from humans contribute to Job's feelings of helplessness. Job extols God's strength in a hymn containing a series of parallel verbs about divine deeds (9:4-11). But unlike other creation hymns that sing of the harmonious beauty of God's creative work (Gen 1; Ps 104), in Job's hymn, God's deeds are terrifying. God removes and overturns mountains, shakes the earth out of its place, seals off sun and stars.

This God is dangerous, beyond comprehension, and invisible even when present (9:11-21). Divine presence is not a blessing for Job. God might seize him and who would be strong enough to resist? Even the helpers of the powerful, mythic sea monster, here called "Rahab" (9:13; cf. 3:8) cannot resist the relentless power of God. If God overpowers them, all the more, God's presence silences Job (9:14). Even if Job were to get God to come to court, Job's fear would force him to say the opposite of what he intended. God would not hear him out and would surely overcome him with a storm (some translations read "tempest"), a great whirlwind (see 38:1). Even if Job is in the right, he has no hope in a courtroom. He declares he is innocent, but he cannot experience the legal results of innocence, so he despairs (9:21).

Job's suffering leads him to reflect more broadly on the inadequacies of divine justice in the world (9:22-24). God treats the good and the bad equally, destroying both at whim. God gives the earth into the power of the wicked and even blinds judges to the plight of the innocent. If the powerful God is not the one who overturns justice in the world, then who is it? Job asks. He turns again to the fragility of his life, speaking in the first person to describe his pains and loss, but he knows God will not recognize his innocence (9:25-31). There is nothing he can do to establish it. Using second person speech, he accuses God of altering the facts, for God has plunged him into the ditch (9:31). Physical cleaning would symbolize his innocence. In Job's imagination that cannot be accomplished.

A court of law is one place wherein he might declare his innocence, but God is not human, and the gap between them is so enormous, only an arbiter or mediator could help Job. He imagines someone who could control God and protect him from God's might. Such a mediator could make a meeting between them possible and Job might then speak without fear. But this hope is contrary to fact, for no one can tell God what to do. Job sinks back into despair and hates his life (10:1a).

Rather than being cowed by his fearful despair, Job speaks for another chapter and grows more courageous. He announces his determination to speak the truth before God, imagining what he will say and demanding justice (10:1b-2). Boldly, he demands an accounting of God's treatment of him (10:3-7). His questions challenge God's very identity as a divine being. He accuses God of acting no differently than a human oppressor who delights in the pain of others. He reminds God of their deep relationship, for Job is the work of God's hands (10:3). God knows Job is innocent yet searches for sin and guilt in him regardless of the true state of Job's heart.

Job switches rhetorical tactics from blaming interrogation to gracious appeal, returning to the intimate relationship God has had with him from the time of his conception (10:8-13). Unlike his curse of his conception and birth in chapter 3, this appeal emphasizes God's tender care in fashioning his being, knitting him together in his mother's womb (see Ps 139:13). God has forgotten this past relationship between them (10:13). The rest of the speech resumes Job's bitter attack on God (10:14-22). There is no hope for a just hearing for God watches, will not forgive, attacks, and hunts Job like a lion no matter whether he is guilty or innocent. Now Job resumes thinking about his birth as a tragedy God should have averted by not letting him be born. Now Job wants God to leave him alone as he faces death.

11:1-20 Zophar's first speech

Job's third friend is immensely impatient with him. He thinks Job is full of hot air, babbling words, and arrogant self-righteousness (11:2-3). Job, he contends, has claimed doctrinal and ethical purity for himself. But Zophar is confident

that if God were to speak, Job would learn wisdom and pay for his guilt. Zophar bases his authority on traditional theological doctrine, expressed in a hymn praising divine power and knowledge (11:8-12). Humans cannot know the designs of God for they are impenetrable to humans. But then Zophar contradicts himself. He himself knows the mind of God regarding "worthless" people, a point he emphasizes with a proverb-like saying that indirectly attacks Job as an empty, untamable wild jackass (11:12).

Despite his scathing denunciation of Job, Zophar joins Eliphaz and Bildad to advise Job about how to escape from his suffering (11:13-19). The conditions he sets assume Job's guilt. Job must set his heart aright, abandon iniquity, and cast out injustice. Then he will have a future without fear or shame, and his misery will fade from memory like receding waters. The picture is utopian, for Job's life will be brighter than the noonday; he will live in safety and be at rest.

12:1–14:22 Job's reply to Zophar

Job counters Zophar's speech with denunciations of his own. Sarcastically, he ridicules his friends' advice as the product of wisdom they alone seem to possess. But immediately Job asserts his equal intelligence and skill in expressing wisdom (12:2-3). From the perspective of relationships of honor and shame typical of ancient Israelite culture, he describes his suffering from yet another angle (12:4-6). His neighbors' mockery disgraces him and amplifies his suffering, for he has lost his place in society. He names robbers and God-provokers among the prosperous in order to contradict his friends' theology. When he claims that humans can learn from living creatures, he turns his friends' wisdom tactics back on them because he draws opposite conclusions (12:7-10). Instead of claiming that other creatures teach God's providential care of the work, the beasts, birds, reptiles, and fish know God controls all that lives and human suffering.

In another hymn, Job reflects on God's strength (12:13-25). He portrays divine actions in the world, beginning mildly enough (12:13), but the examples of divine power he draws upon are violently fearsome. God breaks down, imprisons, creates drought, releases prisoners, imprisons kings, and disperses rather than gathers water. God overturns expectations concerning leaders, nations, and the patterns of just political relationships in the world. Though Job affirms traditional notions of divine power, he believes God's power is both unconstrained and destructive of human life.

From experience and observation as a sage, Job claims equality with his friends in discerning God's ways (13:1-2). Yet despite his belief that God is unpredictable and dangerous, he declares his desire to argue his case with God. His friends lie and he begs them to show their wisdom by being silent; God will rebuke them when judgment comes (13:4-13). His passion for speaking grows and he refuses to be silenced; he says he will go so far as to "carry my flesh between my teeth" (13:14). Although this expression does not occur elsewhere in the Old Testament, the next verse clarifies its meaning. Job will speak at the risk of his life. He will defend himself before God, even if God kills him. To speak before God would vindicate him, for no "impious" person can come before God (13:16). Job has prepared his case and reasserts his innocence but would be silent if anyone can build a case against him. Job's confidence rests in his belief that he has not committed any actions against God or humans that warrant his present suffering.

Job shifts from addressing his friends to speaking directly to God, a shift marked by a move from plural to singular verbs (13:20-27). Legal dealings inform Job's imagination about his relationship with God and provide a way for him to describe himself as one unjustly accused, imprisoned, and monitored. But the courtroom can also become a place in Job's hopes that will reveal his innocence. He demands protection from God in the court. God must stop hurting him by withdrawing the "hand," a term meaning to have "control over," and God must prevent Job from being too terrified. If God does these things, then Job will speak and listen. His questions set out his sense of his own victimhood (13:23-25). He insists on being told where he went wrong and why God, who had been his friend, is now his enemy. He accuses God of placing false legal charges against him, imprisoning him in the stocks for offenses of long ago, and stalking his footsteps.

The fragility of human life and the hopelessness of the human condition continue to occupy Job's attention (14:1-22). Job's speeches are the words of a distraught and broken individual. Their principal logic is the expression of pain in its multiple aspects, the results of which are circular and repetitive while Job retells his sorrows again and again. Humans have but a short life, full of trouble, as ephemeral as a flower or a shadow (14:2). Still addressing God, he wonders why God bothers with such insignificant creatures as humans. And though Job has just asserted his innocence, he wonders if any human lives free of some guilt. All Job wants is for God to leave feeble humanity alone as each one lives out its life of hard labor.

A tree, although it withers and dies, has the possibility of revival, but when a human dies, nothing is left (14:7-12). Ancient Israel did not believe in the afterlife of the individual, except in the memory of one's children and in the goodness of one's name, so Job wants his present life to be rich and full, or at least free of his misery. He wishes God would hide him in the underworld until divine anger has passed. He imagines a new beginning when God would call him, esteem him, and stop watching for his misdeeds (14:13-17). But not only are these aspirations merely wishes, they are impossible because God actively prevents a better life with the inevitability of falling rocks or flooding waters (14:17-20). Job may be referring to his sacrifices on behalf of his children (1:5), when he mentions honor or shame of children eluding the parent. All that Job has now is bodily pain and a grieving spirit.

SECOND ROUND OF SPEECHES
Job 15:1–21:34

This cycle of speeches pursues the theme of the fate of the wicked. The friends concentrate on the dire punishment of evildoers, while Job ponders the ways evildoers escape all punishment even as the innocent suffer torment.

15:1-35 Eliphaz's second speech

Although Eliphaz was kind and somewhat gentle in his first speech, he begins his second speech angrily blasting Job for his windy words, airy opinions, and arrogant arguments (15:1-6). Job's speech is dangerous; it does away with "fear of God," here translated "piety" (15:4). Job's own words serve as testimony against him.

In his second speech, Eliphaz challenges Job's wisdom and responds with "wisdom" of his own.

Unlike all previous speeches by the friends, this one does not propose a means of escape. After dismissing Job's words, Eliphaz continues to attack Job's wisdom with a series of questions that undermine Job's authority as a sage (15:7-13). If he was not there at creation, "brought forth before the hills," and if he has not stood in the divine council, how can Job know anything his friends do not know? (15:7-9). The divine council is the heavenly court where God presides over heavenly servants and messengers (Job 1–2). Eliphaz thinks God's consolation should be adequate for Job, perhaps found in Eliphaz's first speech, but Job is not experiencing any such comfort at present. Job is being carried away by false ideas and foolishly voicing anger.

Then, sounding like Job (14:4), Eliphaz exclaims that no one born of a woman's body, that is, humans, can be blameless or righteous. The problem for Eliphaz is probably not women's bodies but the human condition itself. If the holy ones and the heavens are unacceptable to God, all the more lowly is someone who drinks "iniquity," meaning Job himself (15:16).

Eliphaz draws from the established and conventional wisdom of the ancestors about the fate of the wicked in his appeal to get Job to listen (15:17-35). The speech is a harsh warning to Job, and though Eliphaz has abandoned his more gentle approach from the first speech, and though his own anger at Job seems to be mounting, he surely presents his warning to alter his friend's behavior. The wicked one is in torment and terror for his whole life. And referring directly to Job's situation, Eliphaz declares that destruction comes when "all is prosperous" (15:21). About the wicked, Eliphaz piles up statements of disdain (15:21). They despair, wander, face destruction, become food for vultures, and dread overtakes them. They bring suffering upon themselves by stretching out their hand against the Almighty (15:25). Their fate is to live among ruinous poverty only to die young. Eliphaz confirms the wisdom of his warnings by using proverbial sayings. To clinch his argument, he indirectly compares Job to plants in an environment that yields only barrenness (15:30-35).

16:1–17:16 Job's second reply to Eliphaz

Job angrily names the conventional, boring, and useless nature of Eliphaz's advice. But he also admits that were their situations reversed, Job might have spoken in the same "windy" way as his false comforters and presented the same interpretation of suffering as they have (16:1-6). This acknowledgement underscores Job's pain. His former explanations of misery once shared with his friends no longer fit his life. His pain will not end no matter what words he uses.

Whereas Job's friends blame him for his suffering, Job interprets the cause of his disaster to be God's attacks on him. The betrayal of his friends amplifies his anguish. Verses 7-8 contain grammatical difficulties in the Hebrew, but their general movement is clear. Job laments his devastation and speaks of a witness who betrays him like a wild beast (16:9-10). By verse 11, however, God emerges as Job's betrayer. Job heaps up charges against God with a series of violent verbs, accusing God of handing him over to the wicked, dislodging him from his peace, dashing him to bits, and setting him up as a target. God does these things like a warrior without mercy (16:11-14).

Grief for his own broken life accompanies his anger as he laments his suffering and expresses grief in traditional forms of weeping and wearing sackcloth (16:15-17). The poetry's continual return to Job's grief and vulnerability keeps readers' empathy for him alive by making him a complicated character whose anger at God cannot be easily dismissed as the words of a madman. The interlacing of Job's grief and anger make him human, but his insistence on his innocence, of which readers are aware, makes him a figure of compassion. He suffers at God's hands even though he is innocent (16:17).

Job looks for an ally in the earth itself, personified here as a witness to his suffering (16:18). By commanding the earth not to cover his blood, he appeals to the story of Cain and Abel. There God says to Cain, "your brother's blood cries out to me from the ground" (Gen 4:10; cf. Ezek 24:8). In this poetic way of thinking, blood itself calls for justice as Job begs the ground to keep his cry alive. But the implicit witness of the earth is not enough. Job proclaims he also has a witness in heaven who will speak on his behalf against his friends (16:19). Who this witness might be is not certain. Because Job has just been accusing God of causing his pain, it seems unlikely to be God, although in these verses he admits weeping before God and hoping for a just decision in his dispute with his friends. Job's desired witness might be a member of the heavenly council who could argue on his behalf, just as the Satan argued against God in the prologue (chs. 1–2). Or the witness may be the imagined arbiter he wished would stand between him and God in the courtroom (9:33). But Job's hope for justice grows dim because death comes quickly toward him (16:22).

His approaching death continues to haunt him and words about it frame the next chapter (17:1 and 13-16). The imminence of death accentuates his despair, because everything will be over before his world is set right; consequently, justice will elude him. The Hebrew of verses 3-6 is not clear. Job appears to be complaining to God about the wrongful critique his friends are making about him and he appeals for help, for someone to offer "surety" on his behalf. He has no one who will guarantee his innocence, but he appeals to God for such a one anyway (17:3). But then Job claims God is the one who darkens his friends' minds.

To be mocked and turned into a "byword" or popular symbol of brokenness in Job's culture means to be cut off from the community (17:5-6). Job's anguish expands and among his friends he finds only fools who name reality by its opposite (17:11-12). They lie about the world and claim darkness is really approaching light (17:12). As Job resumes his reflections on death, he finds companionship only with corruption and worms that attack the body. These join him with the intimacy of family members on his journey to the nether world. Job's morbid reflections bespeak his hopelessness and isolation in his suffering.

18:1-21 Bildad's second speech

From Bildad's perspective, Job's words appear thoughtless, endless, and harmful. They are self-lacerating and powerless to change either the reality of the earth or the solidity of a rock. Bildad thinks Job has made himself the center of creation, for Bildad does not understand how profound pain can shrink one's world and alter one's perceptions.

The body of Bildad's speech, however, concerns the fate of the wicked (18:5-21). Like Eliphaz (15:20-25), he presents a frightening picture of the life and death of a person who does not know God (18:21). Perhaps he hopes to terrify Job into altering his speech and changing his attitude, but his didactic approach is harsh and further deepens the alienation between Job and his friends. Like Eliphaz, Bildad fails to mention the bright future toward which his previous speech tried to lead his friend.

Imagery of light and darkness creates an envelope around Bildad's depiction of the wicked person (18:5-6 and 18). Bildad asserts that light and harmonious life elude the wicked in their tents. Darkness, here depicted as an encroaching, deathlike force, awaits the evil ones (18:18). The life of the wicked is one of claustrophobic captivity. They are hemmed in and cast down, entrapped and ensnared by nets and a noose. Once captured, the wicked experience more terrifying tortures (18:11-15). Disaster, death's child, and perhaps a reference to disease, stands ready to consume them. Fire destroys the household of the wicked who are like a dried up tree that disappears from memory (see Ps 1:1-3). Because ancient Israelites believed the afterlife of the individual occurred only in the memory of one's children and in the goodness of one's name, the absence of offspring ensures the utter obliteration of the wicked.

All these terrors evoke Job's own condition. He is covered in sores (2:7-8) and his children are dead (17:18-19). No one will remember him and his spirit is dried up. Bildad's vivid accounting of the destiny of the wicked speaks of Job indirectly, but no less transparently, as the wicked one whose fate will appall later generations.

19:1-29 Job's second reply to Bildad

Job begins with the now-expected criticism of the previous speaker (19:2-4). Using a phrase common in lament psalms, he asks no one in particular, "How long?" How long will his friends continue to assault him and endlessly revile him "without shame." In the central section of Job's reply, however, he speaks of his suffering life in terms that parallel and expand Bildad's depiction of the fate of the wicked (19:5-22). The two friends see the reality of Job's suffering but draw radically different interpretations from it. In Job's view, he suffers not because he is wicked, but because God is unfair (19:3). He does not address God in this speech as he has in every speech before. Instead, he speaks to his friends (19:1-6, 21-22, 28-29) and complains to them about God's treatment of him in their triangulated relationship (19:6-12).

Job's complaint shows him to be an angry, grieving person who cannot find enough ways to describe his experiences of claustrophobia and hopelessness. If his friends continue to reproach him, they should know it is God who "has dealt unfairly" with him and trapped him with a net (19:6). In Job's interpretation of his suffering, God is the active agent who initiates all his mistreatment and, like his friends, gives no hearing to Job's cries of "violence" (some translations read "injustice"). In a depiction of his life that echoes Bildad's speech, Job piles up accusations against God who bars his way, puts darkness across his path, strips him of glory, treats him like an enemy, and sends disciplined, unified troops against him (19:7-12). To Job, God resembles a military commander who sends unnamed forces to attack him.

Job then shifts the focus of his lament from God to companions who have betrayed and abandoned him (19:13-22). He lists friends, servants, wife, and other members of his extended household—all his "intimate friends hold [him] in horror" (19:19). He feels the heartbreaking pain of abandonment and isolation, made all the more torturous because it is his closest friends and intimate members of his household who have betrayed him. In a verse difficult to translate, he complains that his own body turns against him as he wastes away and has escaped only "by the skin of my teeth," as some translations put it (19:20; NRSV). Whatever the Hebrew means, it is part of the evidence of God's attack on him and one reason he begs his arrogant friends to pity him (19:21-22).

Though death may be near, Job is not dead yet. Laments in the prayer of ancient Israel often turn from complaint to an act of hope, to wishing for someone who would vindicate the speaker so that the present situation would not be the last word (19:23-29). Job wants his own lament to be chiseled in stone as a permanent record of his innocence, a kind of witness on his behalf. But he also wants a redeemer, translated here as "vindicator," one who will legally establish his innocence. He wants to be declared blameless in his "flesh," that is, in his own body with his "own eyes" before his death. In these dramatic verses Job affirms that his "vindicator lives" (19:25).

The Hebrew title translated "vindicator" is a legal one and refers to the "redeemer" who buys back kinfolk from slavery, pays their debts, and

buys back land taken by creditors (cf. Lev 25:23-24, 47-55; Deut 25:5-10). Some interpreters think Job's vindicator personifies his own cry, witnessing on his behalf. Others propose that Job seeks someone who can act as a mediator between himself and God (cf. 9:33; 16:19). Still others think Job expresses faith that the redeemer is God who will judge him to be innocent. However one understands Job's redeemer, the desire to "see God" consumes Job with longing, for only God can declare him in the right (19:26). Though later Christian tradition finds hope for personal resurrection in this verse, ancient Israel did not believe in the afterlife of the individual until the very end of the Old Testament period (see 14:10-22).

Job ends his speech by quoting his friends who find the problem to be him, and he warns them of judgment to come (19:28-29).

20:1-29 Zophar's second speech

Rebuking speech introduces the words of a new speaker. The purpose of these reproaches is to counter the authority of the previous speaker, in this case, of Job (20:2-3). Zophar claims Job has provoked him and thereby enabled him to understand Job's plight. After these words, readers might expect Zophar's counsel to take a new direction, since this is the only remark by one of Job's friends to indicate someone is actually listening to him. But like Eliphaz and Bildad before him, Zophar devotes his second speech to a dramatic depiction of the fate of the wicked. His words reveal his growing frustration with Job and his deepening belief in Job's guilt. Unlike his previous speech, he offers no advice to his friend on how to escape his predicament (11:14-19). His words merely warn Job that his present course leads to greater calamity.

The torments awaiting the guilty occupy Zophar's imagination. Four times he names God as the one who enacts the torture due to the wicked (20:15, 23, 28, 29). On this point, he seems to agree with Job's view of God, but Zophar thinks God is justified in tormenting people. Job claims he is innocent and God tortures him anyway (19:3-12). By contrast to the brutal power of God, the wicked are ephemeral beings, according to Zophar. They perish like the "dung he uses for fuel" and fade like "a vision of the night," finally to disappear from the human community (20:6-8).

Outward appearances of the wicked are deceptive (20:11-19). They seem to be healthy and vigorous, hiding wickedness under their tongues, that is, under wise and appropriate speech, and they may be rich as well. But wickedness resides inside them like a poison gaining dominion over their bodies. God will intervene to force the disgorgement of riches like food from a poisoned stomach. And even if the wicked enjoy some benefits in life, they experience no joy.

Zophar's accusations identify specific evil deeds among actions of the wicked; they oppress the poor (20:19). The Hebrew, however, specifies that oppression more strongly as the crushing and abandoning of the poor and as the violent taking possession of a house that the wicked did not build. These acts of treachery result from greed; therefore, the wealth of the wicked will provide no respite (20:21-22). Nor can the wealth of the sinner be interpreted as a sign of divine blessing, as many in the ancient world believed. Instead, for Zophar, wealth is as the sign of devious and evil dealings so it will neither endure nor save (20:20-22).

Beyond lack of enjoyment of the good life, the wicked will experience horrific torments whose originating source is the fury of God (20:23-29). The NABRE and other translations supply the word "God" as the subject of verse 23, but the text uses the pronoun "he" and reveals who "he" is only in the last word (20:29). The effect of withholding the identity of the attacker until the poem's end is shock, since the assault upon the wicked is vicious. Though the Hebrew of verse 23 is unclear, it is clear that the attacker will rain down fury upon the guilty, bring weapons of war against them, set them in darkness, and consume them in fire. The cosmos will conspire against the wicked and reveal their guilt. Floods of anger will sweep them away. The last line of Zophar's speech names these disasters as the "portion" and "heritage" of the wicked, reversing traditional understandings of these terms as divine blessings. Zophar presents a bleak future for Job, whom he assumes to be among those he has been describing.

21:1-34 Job's second reply to Zophar

Job closes this cycle of speeches by responding to his friends' accounts of the fate of the wicked, often alluding to their speeches. He speaks directly to them in this chapter and neither calls

upon God nor engages in a long monologue. Job interprets the destinies of the innocent and the wicked quite differently from his friends. He thinks it is shocking that the wicked get away with their crimes, live abundantly, and go to the grave after a life of contentment. He wants to know why.

Job begins by demanding what he needs from his friends (21:1-6). He needs them to "listen." His friends should be able to "bear with" him as he describes his life. Were they able to hear him, he could find comfort. If they listened, they would be able to see his deep pain from his point of view, even if they did not agree with him. If they listened, they would accord him personal dignity and honor, and, like him, they too would be horrified.

Job shows in this speech that he has been listening to them. He responds to their understanding of the wicked and the just punishment the friends believe they receive. Job asks a question to show his perspective: "Why do the wicked keep on living, grow old, become mighty in power?" (21:7). Job does not answer his own question, but instead sets up the opposite case in rhythmic parallel sentences (21:8-16). Their offspring are secure, their homes peaceful, and God's punishment is absent from their lives. Even their cattle thrive, and their children are healthy, safe, and happy. The wicked and their families sing, dance, and make merry; then they die in peace. No harm seems to come to these people. Yet despite the evident harmony of their lives, they have turned from God and deserve none of these blessings. The text quotes them to reveal the depth of their sin. They are adamantly alienated from God, deny the Almighty's power, and refuse to serve (21:14-15).

Job's observations contradict the reigning beliefs of his friends who hold that sin affects one's entire family, especially offspring. Job now asks how often the wicked pay for their sins? (21:17). In his view, they escape suffering and avoid just punishment. He utters curses against them, hoping for God to do justice by punishing the sinner and not deferring it to the children (21:18-21). Like Ecclesiastes, Job maintains that there is no justice because death treats the good and the bad alike (Eccl 3:16-20).

This cycle of speeches concludes with Job's challenge to his friends (21:27-34). He knows they think he is wicked, but the real evildoers go un-challenged. Because his friends are completely wrong about God's distribution of suffering among the wicked and the innocent, they can offer Job no comfort. And, Job adds, they are un-reliable because of the duplicity of their speech (21:34).

THIRD ROUND OF SPEECHES

Job 22:1–31:40

The final round of speeches among the friends differs from the previous two in a number of ways and disrupts patterns established there. The speeches of Eliphaz and Bildad are much shorter than their previous discourses, while Zophar has no speech at all. By contrast, Job's last speech in reply to Bildad is the longest in the book (chs. 26–31). Surprisingly, in these chapters Job often appears to take up the positions of his three friends. Interpreters explain these features in a variety of ways. Some interpreters believe the text was disrupted when it was copied, omitting Zophar's speech and parts of the others. Some think editors added material to Job's speech, namely chapter 28.

In the book's present form, however, altera-tions in the previous arrangement of speeches probably imply a great deal more than editorial error or addition. If the present arrangement is deliberate rather than chance confusion and dis-order, then the shortening of the friends' words and the increase in Job's words provokes reflec-tion on the debate. On the one hand, the friends' words have lost their power. Lacking further crea-tive insight, their speech fades away as if their point of view has come to an impasse. Job's words, on the other hand, grow in length and authority, revealing increasing strength. His character has changed across the book from the one who wanted to die (ch. 3) and for whom words were futile and inadequate (9:20-12), and who knew only terror before God (9:3-15) to become, in his final speech, a forceful, potent spokesperson on his own behalf.

When Job espouses aspects of his friends' arguments, he is probably employing a device known in Babylonian literature where an oppo-nent takes up the opposite position so no point

of view completely triumphs over the other. In this way, the book of Job invites readers to take competing interpretations of Job's suffering with equal seriousness and to struggle with his dilemma.

22:1-30 Eliphaz's third speech

Clearly, Eliphaz was not moved by Job's previ-ous appeals to his friends to listen to him. Eliphaz begins with a series of rhetorical questions about human relationship with God (22:2-5). The ques-tions start innocently with humanity in general, but then move to accuse Job of "great" wicked-ness (22:2-5).

In Eliphaz's understanding, God is unmoved by human self-worth or by their efforts to be just and pious. Self-sufficient and detached from hu-mans, God's judgments are fair and impartial. The questions addressed to Job in second person sin-gular ask him if it is not his own doing that God has brought judgment upon him (22:3b-5).

From these unforgiving but general questions, Eliphaz turns to attack Job directly (22:6-18). First, he accuses Job of injustice (22:6-9). Job, he claims, has wrongly garnered the goods of poor kinfolk, stripped them of clothing, withheld water and nourishment from the hungry, and failed to aid widows and orphans. These sins involve attacks on the poor and those without protection in the society. Such actions grievously violate torah and covenant relations in Israel. Job's sins against the poor have led to his misery (22:10-11). But Eliphaz fabricates these charges against Job, for readers know that Job is "blameless and upright"; he "feared God and avoided evil" (1:1). Eliphaz must be motivated to this extreme misreading of Job's life because, if Job is innocent, then Eliphaz's own worldview, his understanding of God, and his sense of his place in the world would collapse upon him.

Instead of listening to Job, Eliphaz hurries to defend God. He asks Job if God is not higher than the heavens, to which Job would surely reply "yes." Then, having set Job up, he accuses him of turning from God. He quotes words Job has not spoken, claiming that clouds and darkness blind God's just judgment. But Job accused God of see-ing well his innocence and deliberately distorting justice (9:20; 10:7). In Eliphaz's view, Job acts wickedly just like Noah's generation (22:16; cf. Gen 6).

Eliphaz makes one more appeal to his friend to repent and turn back to the Almighty (22:21-30). Assuming Job's guilt, Eliphaz promises goodness and restored relationship between Job and God will follow Job's repentance. The choice is in his hands. If he turns to God and rejects iniquity, then life will be good again, "light shall shine" (22:28). Eliphaz sums up his theology that God delivers the innocent with more proverbial instruction (22:30). Through spiritual practices, Job can save himself.

23:1–24:25 Job's third reply to Eliphaz

Despite Eliphaz's efforts to change his friend, Job grows stronger in his own interpretation of his predicament. He wants to meet the Almighty in a courtroom (23:3-6). Legal metaphors reappear in his speech (9:13-21; 13:14-27) as he pictures himself at trial. He imagines God hearing and receiving his arguments. God and he would have a reasonable exchange, and though the Hebrew of verse seven is unclear, Job clearly anticipates an outcome of justice, of gaining his rights (23:7).

But his present experience of God's absence dampens confidence in a just legal outcome (23:8). God is nowhere to be found, although Job searches in every direction. He uses the compass points to lament divine absence, hidden from him no matter how hard he searches. In the next verses (23:10-12), he reasserts his belief that God knows he is innocent (cf. 10:7) and reiterates his claim that he has lived in constant fidelity, treasuring God's word in his inmost being (cf. 13:15). The problem in their relationship lies with God (23:13-17). No matter the injustice of divine decisions, God cannot be challenged (23:13-14). When he thinks of God, Job lives in conflict between hope and despair, but despair seems stronger (23:17).

Job reflects on the fate of the wicked, the subject that has dominated speeches in this cycle, but here Job also considers the fate of their victims. He yearns for God to set times, presumably for justice, and for God to make them visible. Instead, the wicked steal property by moving landmarks and steal people's livelihoods. They feed on the orphans, widows, and the poor. The poor, in turn, are forced into the wilderness to lead onerous, dangerous lives, exposed to the elements and enslaved to the wicked. And, observes Job, God does not act on their behalf, even though they are dying in the dust (23:12).

Imagery of light and darkness dramatizes Job's perceptions of the good and the wicked (24:13-20). The wicked rebel against the light, against wisdom and right relationship with God and humans. They commit all kinds of evil in the dark, treating time as the domain of wickedness. They hide from light and roam about in darkness. The powerful seem to have God on their side, but ultimately they disappear. Of course, that may be a long time in the future, but Job thinks his words are irrefutable.

25:1-6 Bildad's third speech

Bildad concludes with a hymnic appreciation of divine power (25:1-3) contrasted with the lowly state of humanity (25:4-6). His words present major opinions of the friends and act as a succinct summary of their theological positions on Job's messy life. He views God as the creator who brings about harm and peace in a mythic battle against chaos. He affirms his friends' sense of the world as a static place, evident in the order of the heavens and sure to be enacted on earth. Before such a powerful God, what human can be judged to be righteous? No human, born of woman, can be pure if even the moon and stars are not clear before God (25:4).

Bildad's reference to women and childbirth is probably not a negative comment on womanhood so much as it insists that humans are mere mortals who participate in the cycle of birth and death over and against divine awesomeness. But Bildad's view of humanity is dismal, indeed, for humans are no better than maggots and worms (25:6). His friends share this point of view (4:17-21; 11:11; 15:14-16; 22:2-3). Humans are hopelessly trapped in their situation and cannot expect justice before God. This perspective conflicts with another view consistent among them that Job is at fault for his own transgressions, hidden and not so hidden. He has power to escape his suffering, if he would only turn to God (5:8; 8:5-7; 11:13-14; 22:21-30).

26:1–31:40 Job's final reply

Job's last speech to his friends comprises six chapters, though many interpreters subdivide it because it contains a variety of literary forms and themes. Job begins typically enough, complaining to his friends and questioning God's abusive power (26:1–27:21), but in chapter 28, he changes both his subject and the genre of his discourse. Called a hymn to Wisdom, chapter 28 appears to interrupt Job's tone, because it is tranquil and hopeful. Many interpreters think it was simply inserted here by a later writer and not an original part of Job's speech. In the next three chapters, Job laments his lost past (ch. 29), complains about the bitter present (ch. 30), and utters oaths asserting his innocence. Together these chapters mount Job's self-defense as if he is in a divorce court where one partner is betrayed by the unfaithfulness of the other. He insists that God name the charges against him (ch. 31). The text unifies disparate poetic pieces into one bumpy whole that expresses Job's anger and doubt along with his last grasp at hope. Perhaps Job's defense functions in the book to draw God forth from hiding.

26:1–27:21 Job's reply to his friends

Job begins sarcastically, demanding an explanation of his friends' words to help the "powerless," namely himself. Their counsel is insulting, verbose, and without wisdom. Since wisdom in Israel attends to human experience, they have failed in their role as wise elders and friends because they have disdained his words about his experience.

Some interpreters think the next verses (26:5-14) actually belong to Bildad since they pick up creation language Bildad uses (25:5). When Job has spoken of creation before (9:5-13; 10:8-3; 12:13-25), he has portrayed it as chaotic and evidence of God's lack of justice and wisdom. Job seems to offer a more orderly view of "the outlines of [God's] ways" than is characteristic of him (26:14). But if that is so, Job may be using a tactic of ancient argument that presents the opponents' views in order to keep any one perspective from complete domination in the debate. Yet Job echoes themes and language in this chapter that he used in the hymn in chapter nine (9:4-13).

To whomever the verses should be ascribed, they contain beautiful imagery arising from ancient Near Eastern creation myths. The underworld, known both as Sheol and Abaddon, lies open and exposed before the powerful deity. The earth and the North, mythic realms of the gods, hang in space. The Creator controls the rain and the clouds and marks out light and dark in a circle. The created world and the pillars upon which the world is set tremble as God rebukes them.

Job's account of creation exalts divine power against the sea monster Rahab and the dragon, the mythic figures of chaos (26:12). Angry storms heed God's design. The Creator is powerful and magnificent. Job's words laud that power of combat against sea monsters, hidden from humans, and cause of fear. This stirring hymn is not completely alien to Job's way of speaking.

The introduction to chapter 27, "Job took up his theme again," smoothes out the interrupting boundary between this chapter and the previous chapter. After chiding his friends and promising to teach them God's ways, Job uses the oath, "as God lives," to declare his innocence with solemnity and to stake his innocence in the highest authority (27:1-6). He cannot agree with his friends and promises to maintain his innocence with a clear conscience until death.

The fate of the wicked reappears, and Job turns the criticism against his friends who, with their "empty words," are his implied enemy (27:7-21). This is where he begins to sound like his friends because he agrees that God will punish the wicked while the just will prevail in the long run (26:17). Some interpreters believe these words are the missing final speech of Zophar, yet the text assigns them to Job. These words may again follow the practice of some ancient Near Eastern texts of assigning the opponent's viewpoint to the final speaker. Borrowing imagery from Bildad (8:14), Job claims the houses of the wicked are no more sturdy than "cobwebs" (27:18). Storms will sweep the wicked away. These last lines anticipate the storm in which Job meets God, though different vocabulary appears there and no one is swept away (38:1).

Job 28:1-28 Hymn to wisdom

The problems of this chapter become immediately apparent to any careful reader. Job changes the subject from his suffering and the fate of the wicked in the previous speeches to the search for wisdom. The tone of the passage changes, too, from discontent to tranquility. It ends with a renewal of traditional wisdom embraced by the book's prologue where "the fear of the Lord is wisdom" (28:28; cf. 1:1, 8; 2:3). For these and other reasons a great number of scholars think this passage is a late addition to the book, added by a subsequent reader to make the debate between Job and his friends more orthodox. That may be so, but in its present place in the book, the chapter serves as a theological comment on the book itself, voiced by its principal character Job. It is as if he has temporarily stepped aside from the debate to comment on it.

In places the Hebrew is obscure. Though some literary sense can be made of the chapter in its original state, this interpretation will follow the NABRE arrangement. The Old Testament personifies Wisdom as a woman (Prov 1:20-33; 3:13-18; 4:5-9; 8:1–9:6), and because the noun "wisdom" is a feminine form in Hebrew, references to Wisdom herself may be present here. She is a controversial figure present at creation and witness to God's creative works (Prov 8:22-36). God acquires her, delights in her, and she, in turn, becomes the bridge between God, creation, and human beings. Some think Wisdom is another way to speak of God, but minimally, at least, she is closely connected to God.

Job begins with an impersonal set of observations about the human endeavor of mining for precious minerals (28:1-6). He observes that humans are able to draw silver and gold, iron and copper, even sapphires from the earth. The earth itself is a vast mystery, for though it produces bread, great fires burn within (28:5). Amazing as is the human capacity to extract things from the ground, the deeper puzzle resides elsewhere and is the theme of the poem. As for wisdom—where can she be found? Where is the place of understanding?" (28:12, and rephrased slightly, 28:20).

Yearning for wisdom centers the poem, as if Job imagines that it is located in a physical spot. He knows that for humans nothing is as precious as wisdom; neither gold nor silver can match its importance (28:13-18). As the sages traditionally hold (Prov 3:14-15; 8:10-11, 19; 16:16), even the most treasured jewels pale compared to the value of wisdom. This observation leads back to the question of verses 12 and 20. Wisdom cannot be found. It is hidden from beasts, birds, and even birds of prey, who sail above the earth and excel at finding food. Nature cannot find it. Both the unfathomable abyss and the sea, here given voices, acknowledge they do not have wisdom. Death and Abbadon, the mythic place of the dead, have only heard rumors about it. The cosmos itself is ignorant of the way to wisdom.

The climax of this hymn is that only God knows the way to her and knows her place (28:23-28). This conclusion surprises because Job has been accusing God of misrule, injustice, and disdain for Job himself, and thus, lack of wisdom. Now in a surprising turn, he identifies the Creator as one who sees the earth, maintains it, splits rocks, fixes boundaries of the waters, and, then, seeing wisdom, becomes one with her. Even more surprising, Job quotes God instructing humans in behavior Job already does: he fears God and avoids evil (28:28; cf. 1:1, 8; 2:3).

Job's hymn comments on the speeches thus far in the book. The debate has not yielded wisdom, though readers know that Job lives a wise life because of his righteous behavior. The chapter also anticipates the speeches in the storm where God appears again as Creator whose wisdom transcends human capacities to grasp. Finally, the poem serves as a tranquil interlude, a space for reconsideration, and an invitation to readers to ask where wisdom resides in this book and in the world.

29:1–31:37 Job's final defense

These three chapters form another subunit within Job's long speech (chs. 27–31). They begin with a new introduction (29:1) and proceed as if the hymn to wisdom had never been spoken. Chapter 29 presents the good old days of Job's relationship with God. As if in a divorce court, he sets out the beauty of their former friendship. In the next chapter, he laments the humiliation and loss that characterizes his present life (ch. 30). In chapter 31, he utters a series of solemn oaths to declare his incontestable innocence in very specific terms. His self-defense concludes his words with poignant wishes that someone would hear his case and the Almighty would answer him.

29:1-25 Nostalgia for the past

Job's description of the past is filled with lyric beauty. Nostalgically, he wishes he were back in the times when God watched over him and shed light upon him even as he walked through darkness. In those days God watched over his tent and Job flourished. Interpreting life in a way that echoes the Satan's view (1:9-10), Job claims his familial and material blessings as signs that "the Almighty was still with me" (29:5). He speaks of his "footsteps," that is, all his endeavors, in language of wellbeing and fertility, "bathed in cream" and sustained by "streams of oil" (29:6).

During that idyllic past, God's blessings extended to Job's social relationships. In a culture of honor and shame, he was a most honored man. When he recalls the way young people and elders, chiefs and princes showed him respect, he is not bragging in an arrogant fashion (29:7-25). Instead, he is remembering evidence of divine blessing upon his life. In contrast to the behavior of his three friends, his community was deferential, gave him proper space, listened to his every word, and waited for him as if they were anticipating the needed rains in spring. Not only was Job personally blessed and honored, he blessed others by his compassionate concern for them. He reassured, comforted, and led them.

Eliphaz had accused him of injustice, of failing to live according to torah, and of refusing to maintain solidarity with the poor (29:11-17). Job argues to the contrary. He rescued the poor, the widow, and the orphan. He lived honestly and justly and helped the disabled like a father to the needy. He fought evil rather than performed it. Because he lived a righteous life and had so many blessings, he expected his good life to continue into his old age. The beauty and power of Job's past was strong and his inner life was rich, for his glory was "fresh within" him and his bow was renewed in his hand (29:20).

30:1-31 The miserable present

Grief and mourning quickly replace the beauty and joy of Job's past in this lamenting speech. His depiction of the present stands in sharp contrast to the golden past of the previous chapter. Instead of honor, his community now holds him in derision (30:1-15). In this hierarchical society, people who themselves are dishonorable treat Job as lower than they. Young men whose fathers would rank with dogs, who suffer want and hunger and scavenge for food, irresponsible men without names of honor are among his deriders (30:1-8). They mock him and scorn him and lord it over him recklessly (30:11). As they approach him like an army advancing through the breach, terror overtakes him and all seems lost (30:12-15).

Job replaces the plural of the enemies with the singular "he pierces my bones . . . he has cast me into the mire" (30:17-19). God has become his "tormentor" (30:21). The object of Job's complaint switches from his human enemies to the divine enemy who has cast him off. It is the failure of

Job's relationship that has destroyed his life and propelled him into his present. The "mire" is a metaphoric description of his suffering that also alludes to Job's place on the ash heap (2:8) and anticipates his response to God in the storm (42:6).

Job then speaks directly to God, continuing the divorce proceedings (30:20-25). Their relationship is utterly broken. When Job cries to God there is only silence and mute staring back. He charges God with abuse as God's strong hand strikes him and casts him off into the tempest (30:21-22). God is sending him to death, "the house destined for everyone alive" (30:23). Yet Job appeals again. Should he not receive a helping hand in this calamity, particularly since he had shown compassion and care for the hardships of others?

From his indirect appeal to God, he returns in grief to his own relentless experiences of gloom and hopelessness, as if he knows help will not come (30:26-31). His suffering is constant and its effects are physical (30:17, 30), spiritual (30:16), and psychological (30:26, 28). His only companions are jackals and ostriches, creatures with whom he shares experiences of human hatred. He mourns the fate of his body and imagines his whole being as a musical instrument of weeping (30:31).

31:1-40 Job's solemn oaths

Perhaps because he has mourned, complained, and expressed his fidelity and innocence, perhaps because he has spoken back to both God and his friends, Job has grown strong and courageous in his sorrows. His expressive words have expanded even as his friends' words have disappeared. Again, Job calls on God to give him a hearing and court and for God to answer his charges (see 13:13-19 and 23:2-7). In this final chapter of his speech, he sets out the case for his innocence in legal terms. He speaks in solemn oaths.

An oath follows the form, "If I have done X, then let Y happen to me" (see Ps 7:4-6). In an oral culture like ancient Israel, words alone guaranteed the reliability of business transactions and legal dealings; hence, their validity was essential to communal life. By uttering oaths, people gave solemnity to their statements, calling curses upon themselves if they were lying. Job uses oaths to force God to declare him guilty or innocent. If Job is guilty, God will execute the curses, but if God keeps silent, then Job will be publicly vindicated. The catalogue of sins Job offers to vindicate himself presents a highly moral picture, for Job declares all his relationships to be honorable and just. To modern readers, Job may appear as a privileged male presiding over women and servants as their superior, but Job is righteous in the terms of his own culture.

With sixteen oaths, Job catalogues sins of which he declares himself innocent. The chapter begins with general claims about God's legacy to humans, a legacy that appears to contradict Job's own experience (31:2-6). He asks if calamity befalls the unrighteous. His next question directly charges God with failure to see. He knows if God weighs him in the scales of justice, he will be shown to be innocent.

Job begins his oath with a central virtue of communal life, honesty (31:5-7). He has not lied, deceived, or stained his hands with bribery or thievery, or any kind of offense. If he has, then he will plant like a laborer, but his neighbor will reap the rewards.

The next cluster of oaths concerns Job's life of social justice (31:13-23). He has treated fairly all claims of his servants against him, and he acknowledges the common humanity they share (31:15). He has never denied the poor, the widow, or the orphan, the naked or the hungry, nor has he harmed the innocent in league with other important men at the city gates. If he has, then his own arm will be severed from his body and God will overpower him (31:22).

If he has abused the land (31:38-40), then the land will retaliate by producing weeds instead of food (31:1, 9-12). If he has even been tempted by a woman or stalked her, then may his wife become a sexual slave to others. Because women were second-class citizens in much of the ancient world, assaults on one's wife were a dishonor to their husbands who could not protect them.

The theological side of injustice is idolatry (31:24-28). Job neither worshiped gold nor gloated over his wealth, nor did he deny God by worshiping the sun and moon as did some in ancient Israel (2 Kgs 21:3ff; Deut 4:19; Jer 8:2; Ezek 8:16). He treated his enemies well and extended hospitality toward the stranger, as required not only by custom in the ancient world but also by Hebrew law. Nor was Job self-righteous and hypocritical, never hiding his sins to save his reputation (31:33-34).

Job's oaths make clear that he believes himself innocent of moral transgression in all phases of his life. If he has committed sins to deserve his suffering, he is unaware of it. As readers have known from the beginning, he is a blameless and upright man who fears God and avoids evil (1:1), but no one else among his community knows this. He does not deserve his suffering as his friends maintain, and God has abandoned him.

Job concludes his words with a final wish for someone to hear his case (31:35-37). Perhaps, like his earlier desire to have a mediator bring him and God together in a courtroom (9:33), he wants his adversary to write out an indictment. This would make the charges public and, above all, evident to him. Or perhaps the document would be a writ of exoneration, since Job has declared his innocence. Either way, Job would be so liberated and empowered by this document that he would wear it before the public and present himself like a prince. He concludes with a challenge for the Almighty to answer him (31:37).

Job began his speeches in chapter 3 with a desire for death to come and for his life and its beginnings to be obliterated from creation. He ends his words, having lamented his many sorrows, raged at God, despaired of his friends, and protested with full force the theology of which he had been a former proponent. No longer does that theology stand. The wicked are not punished and the innocent are not protected from the horrors of this world. One does not always and inevitably reap what one has sown.

Job protests this theology and in the process begins to undergo transformation. His rage at God emerges not as blasphemy but as an expression of his fidelity. Throughout his long, dark night he has clung to God, even if in biting critique of God's management of the world. He shouts at God, disparages God, but he never abandons God, even though he believes God has abandoned him.

Readers now expect God to step forward and reply to Job, but, instead, a fourth friend named Elihu comes onto the stage.

ELIHU SPEAKS

Job 32:1–37:24

Elihu appears suddenly in the book of Job. He has not been mentioned before, nor counted among the three friends who comfort Job on the ash heap, and he completely disappears after his speeches. For a number of reasons, including his abrupt appearance, many interpreters think Elihu's speeches are a later addition to the book, perhaps by a writer who wanted to make the book more orthodox. Elihu both repeats some of the claims of the friends and anticipates some of God's speech in the whirlwind, making his words seem unnecessary. But from a literary point of view, Elihu's speech creates a dramatic delay and builds tension before God appears in the storm. Moreover, Elihu asserts that humans cannot discover God, so God's appearance becomes more striking and unexpected.

By introducing Elihu (32:1-5) and repeatedly announcing across the chapters that he is continuing to speak (34:1; 35:1; 36:1), a narrator divides Elihu's speeches into four parts (32:6–33:33; 34:1-37; 35:1-16; 36:1–37:24). These announcements of continuation may indicate the work of an editor who incorporated pre-existing material into the book or, more likely, they may highlight one of Elihu's character flaws. He is long-winded.

32:1-5 Introduction

Though debated among interpreters, the introduction offers clues to what follows. This is the first significant intrusion of a narrator since the prose prologue (chs. 1–2). The narrator introduces Elihu as an angry man (32:2). Next he presents Elihu's family tree, an honor provided for no other character in the book. It is possible that the Hebrew names of Elihu's ancestry mock him by referring to a contemptuous one who is high and mighty. The narrator expands Elihu's motivation for speaking. He is angry because the friends failed either to answer or to condemn Job. He waited to speak only because he was showing respect to his elders. Then for the fourth time, we learn about his wrath; it was "inflamed" (32:5). Elihu's words are passionate, but they are not necessarily judicious.

32:6–33:33 Elihu's first speech

Elihu introduces himself as a youth, and then chides his elders for not speaking words of wisdom. He spends the entire first chapter introducing himself and telling why he must speak. In the process, he confirms the narrator's suggestions about his character. The three friends are not inspired by the Almighty because the spirit, not experience, gives understanding. He commands everyone to listen to him, implying that he alone has received the spirit. He accuses the friends of failing to refute Job (32:12-14). He even admits he is full of words given by the spirit and is ready to burst (32:18-19). That he does not know how to flatter is evident already to readers (32:22).

In the next chapter (33:1-33), Elihu appeals directly to Job and demands that he listen. Offering some comic relief in this otherwise somber book, he continues to announce that he is going to speak, that the spirit of God inspired him to speak, and that Job should prepare to rebut him without fear of him (33:2-7). Finally, he gets to his point in a direct manner. He claims to quote Job in order to argue against him. His quotes, however, convey the sense of Job's words but not his direct speech (33:9-11). Elihu tells Job he is unjust to God. Because God is greater than humans, Job has no place in demanding an account. When God does speak, one may not even know it. When God warns with terrors of the night or sends illness and suffering, it is to save the person from death (33:14-22).

Like Job, Elihu also hopes for a mediator between God and humans, not to control God as Job had hoped (9:32-35), or to witness on Job's behalf (16:19), but to bring Job around and save him. Elihu and Job have opposite opinions as to the role of the heavenly mediator. The effects of the mediator's guidance will be to restore Job to singing and rejoicing as God restores his soul from the realm of death (33:25-30). In an arrogant manner, Elihu urges Job to listen silently, unless he has something to say. As a younger man speaking to an elder in a culture that honors the elder, he is quite overbearing. Perhaps he thinks he is Job's mediator.

34:1-37 Elihu's second speech

Elihu treats Job's three friends with the same disrespect he shows Job, addressing them as wise men while he mocks their wisdom. He invites them to discern the truth with him, though he has already decided what it is. Again he quotes Job to discredit his speech, interpreting his words and his person as evil. With even more arrogance, he instructs the friends about God's justice in traditional terms (34:10-15). God does not respect humans for wealth or power but focuses on their ways and dispenses justice with inescapable speed. He condemns Job further by assuming that the wise will agree with him in dismissing Job's claim to wisdom. He deserves punishment because his rebellious words compound his sins.

35:1-6 Elihu's third speech

Elihu continues interrogating Job. Why does Job think it proper to claim he is just and God is not? (35:1-3). He wants Job to recognize and submit to the transcendence of God beyond all things human (35:4-12). No human behavior can affect God, even that of the oppressed who cry out. God does not respond to human cries. The Hebrew of the next verses is not entirely clear, but Elihu maintains that Job's words are meaningless (35:16).

36:1–37:24 Elihu's fourth speech

Elihu keeps his windbag character by telling us again that he is going to speak to illuminate Job's situation (36:2-4). When he finally gets to the knowledge he brings "from afar" (36:3), it amounts to reiteration of arguments already given by the friends that God rewards the good and punishes the wicked (36:4-21). Though God is not affected by any human behavior according to the previous chapter, God does respond to human behavior by punishing the wicked. God reveals sins to correct the disobedient and causes the disobedient to perish. Suffering and distress are educational for some and God sends affliction to save them (36:15). Verses 16-21 are nearly unreadable in the Hebrew.

Much of the remainder of Elihu's speech anticipates the words of God in the storm (36:22–37:22). His theme is the power and wonder of creation. He advises Job to consider that God is transcendent, beyond human connection, as revealed in God's providential control of the cosmos (36:22-25). In the ancient world, the workings of sun and rain, of stars and seasons, were profound mysteries. Elihu finds a nearly sacramental sense in the world, an expression of divine life when God uses the rains to nourish nations and provide food (36:26-32). Offering personal testimony, he speaks of storms as God's angry and controlling voice (36:33–37:9). Even hail and frost serve God's purposes (37:10-13).

Elihu commands Job to listen and contemplate God's works. He demands to know if Job understands how God creates light behind clouds, and if Job participates in creating the firmament with God (37:15-18). After six long chapters, he concludes that humans cannot discover the Almighty

because God is beyond all accounting. None can see him (37:22-24).

Surely Elihu is an intruder on the scene, but his speech acts as a thematic bridge between the debates of Job and his friends and the speeches of God still to come. In comic, bombastic terms that violate the customs of the day and disrespect the previous speakers, Elihu builds anticipation and makes Job's three older friends look good by comparison.

THE SPEECHES IN THE STORM
Job 38:1–42:6

Elihu's insistence that "we cannot find" God (37:23) makes God's appearance in the storm all the more dramatic and surprising. Job alone hoped for such a meeting, but the friends insisted God was inaccessible and did not need to speak because divine justice was already clearly revealed in human life and in the world of animals and plants. In these speeches, as in the prologue, God's name again becomes Yahweh, ("the LORD"), the personal name revealed in Exodus 3. Throughout the long debates between Job and his friends, God was often called by the ancient title, El Shaddai, translated by the NABRE with the traditional "the Almighty." The name Yahweh reveals the God of the storm to be the God of Israel's story, even though the book's characters are foreigners and the book makes no clear reference to historical events.

Although the primary speaker in the storm is the Lord, Job also speaks to create a form of dialogue between them (40:3-5 and 42:1-6). These speeches appear in the book as one more set of arguments in the debate, yet their climactic position and the divine authority of the main speaker grant them significance beyond the others. Carefully structured thematically, they progress through the creation of the cosmos to the wonders of the animal world, and then concentrate on particular animals called Behemoth and Leviathan.

38:1–40:2	Creation of the cosmos and its nonhuman inhabitants
40:3-5	Job's silence
40:6–41:26	Creation of Behemoth and Leviathan
42:1-6	Job's Enigmatic Response

These speeches are as puzzling as they are beautiful. A major interpretive question of the book is how the speeches relate to what precedes and follows them. To this point, the major question of the debate has been why Job suffers, and thus far, no consensus has emerged among the speakers. Readers might, therefore, expect God to settle matters between Job and his friends. Instead, God changes the subject, interrogating Job about his knowledge of creation. Equally puzzling are Job's responses to God's words. In his first response, he silences himself; in the second, he ignores his promise not to speak again, and the words he speaks are ambiguous.

Another interpretive issue regarding events in the storm is how to understand God's questioning of Job. Do God's questions disrespect or belittle Job and his suffering? Is God introducing new themes to set Job's suffering in a different perspective? Some scholars think the speeches portray God as a bully who uses superior knowledge and power to silence, shame, and overpower Job. In this view, God appears as the stronger one who out-talks Job the talker, and God disrespects and intimidates Job. But by attending to the poetic imagery of creation, the subject about which Job is ignorant, other interpretations are possible. Rather than doing battle with Job by means of the creation, God celebrates it in its beauty, wildness, and freedom. The speeches portray the breath-stopping creativity of God, the generative beauty of the cosmos and its inhabitants, and the wild freedom of God's creatures. This experience transforms Job.

To grasp the power of these chapters, it is best not to think of God's words as didactic answers to Job's questioning, angry laments. Rather than prosaic instruction, these speeches are lyric poetry, hymn-like speeches, celebrating creation, the amazing web of life in its awesomeness and beauty. They describe what ecologists might call "the household of life," overflowing with energy and freedom. But, of course, readers wonder how these divine speeches relate to Job's suffering?

Together God's speeches form a thematic symmetry between Job's first outburst and events in the storm. Job himself introduced the subject of creation in the curse of his birth (3:1-26). There he tries to "uncreate" the cosmos, to turn day into night, light into darkness, and life into death. God replies to Job's rhetorical destruction of creation with rhetorical reconstruction and recreation. These questions reestablish the world from the bottom up, from the waters, to the stars, to the animal inhabitants.

The setting of the encounter is a tempest, a whirlwind or fierce storm (38:1). In the Old Testament storms are sometimes the setting for theophanies, that is, appearances of God to humans (Exod 19:16-20; 1 Kgs 19:11-13; Ps 18:7-17; Hab 3:14). Besides being a conventional place of divine-human encounter, the storm conveys divine power and mystery. But the storm also evokes Job's stormy life of suffering, as well as the deaths of his children who lost their lives in a "great wind" (1:19). Job meets God face to face in the stormy chaos of his destroyed world, not in a safe haven protected from harm and tragedy. Finally, if the storm is not only the venue for God's appearance but also an aspect of revelation itself, then the storm implies a deity who is wild, beautiful, free, and deeply unsettling. The speeches do not explain suffering, but they do present Job's anguished sorrows as the place of divine encounter.

38:1–40:2 Yahweh's first speech

The many ambiguities of the divine speech begin in the introductory verses (38:1-3). God interrogates Job like an impatient judge speaking before a courtroom. Annoyance with Job appears to drive the first question. What does God mean by asking "Who is this who darkens counsel with words of ignorance?" God surely knows who Job is, since God previously called him "my servant Job" (1:8; 2:3). Is this question a literary device by which God draws attention to Job's words? Could it be Elihu to whom these words refer? Is this a statement of divine impatience, or is it a testing of the character, as if to ask, "What are you made of Job? Can you stand toe to toe with the Creator of the cosmos?" God then commands Job to prepare for battle by girding his loins. He calls Job by a Hebrew word, translated "man" in the NABRE, that means specifically a "man who is charged as military protector of women and children," that is, one ready for battle. Then God turns the tables to announce that it is now Job's place to be interrogated.

The subject of the interrogation is Job's knowledge of creation. Asking if Job knows who, where, and when, God picks up the creation theme Job introduced in his curse of his birth where he wanted to unmake God's creation of him (ch. 3). God depicts the cosmos as if it were a habitat, a large building for living creatures. Where was Job when God founded the earth? Does Job know its size, how it rests upon pedestals, or who placed its cornerstone? Was Job a witness when the morning stars sang like a choir? Of course, Job knows nothing about creation, nor can he reach back in memory to the beginnings of the world and the joyous chorus of stars that sang at creation. The ancients believed that the earth itself rested on pedestals and a great dome held the planets and the stars and separated the waters above from the waters below (Gen 1:6).

In a reimagining of the creation story (Gen 1:1–2:4), God asks about Job's knowledge of the sea (38:8-11), conceived as a newborn babe emerging from God's womb, dressed by mother God in swaddling clothes of clouds and darkness, and kept within its limits like a baby in its playpen. From there God speaks of light (38:12-15), asking Job if he has commanded the day to begin and understands how the morning light changes the earth's appearance. Echoing the hymn to Wisdom (ch. 28), verses 16 and 17 attend to the sources of the sea, depths of the abyss, and gates of death.

These verses express ancient understandings of creation, its beginnings, the existence of the underworld, and sources of light, snow, hail, the winds, and the rain (38:22-38). With exquisite beauty, they set forth cosmic imagery of birth and nourishment. The heavenly constellations, in their mysterious appearances in each season (38:31-33), challenge Job's understanding of the rules governing heavenly bodies and his command of thunder and lightning. But Job is out of his depth. Only Wisdom was there with God at creation's beginning (Prov 8:22-36). God proudly points to each facet of the cosmos, showing it off to Job like a new homeowner delighting and bragging about her new home.

After God describes the wonders of the cosmic habitat, God interrogates Job about the inscrutable ways of its animal inhabitants (39:1-30). Equally beautiful and filled with the wild life-energy, diverse and unique, these creatures also confound Job. It is possible these animals come from royal lists of hunted animals and the icons that symbolized kings and their power. Some interpreters propose that these animals are negative in their

association with wilderness and chaos, but if so, here they come firmly within divine control. Yet God's control of the earth and its animal inhabitants is not a subject of these speeches. Rather God appears to be bragging about the animals who occupy this magnificent habitat in their mysterious ways and stunning freedom. Regardless of the origins of this mixed list of creatures, each of them is beautiful, as well as joyously alive. With God's approval and expressive pride, each acts independently according to its own rhythms.

God's focus with the first three animals concerns the care and sustenance of their young (38:39–39:4). Lions, ravens, and mountain goats feed and give birth to their progeny. Does Job understand the various ways of birth in the animal world, each creature following its own times of gestation? The wild ass, the ox, and ostrich also live in freedom, resist human control, and act each according to their own kind (39:5-18). God has given the wild ass its freedom and gave it the wilderness for a home. Similarly, the wild ox cannot be bound with rope or domesticated to suit Job. Only the ostrich is subject to divine control, for the Creator has withheld wisdom from her. Yet even this ungainly animal is alive, "swift of foot," and "makes sport" of horse and rider; the ostrich is free and wondrous (39:18). The horse, too, is powerful and fearless, racing on the plains and into battle, while the eagle and the hawk elude human discernment and control (39:19-30).

God's depiction of the animals is one of pure delight in their variety, strength, and prowess. Job is a know-nothing in this arena. He cannot fathom the ways of his fellow creatures, in their assortment and inscrutability, and their freedom to grow and flourish in their dwelling places. In this first speech, God has expanded horizons of the debate from Job's suffering to the glories of the created world, a world characterized by beauty and energy of life.

Has God been bullying Job? Surely divine interrogation is terrifying and overwhelming. At the same time, God brings Job into a new frame of reference within which to view his own plight and to consider the way God relates to the world. Chapter 40 continues God's speech for two verses and ends with an intimidating question and a challenge that seems to say that God will brook no criticism from a "faultfinder" like Job.

40:3-5 Job's first response

Uncharacteristically, Job responds to God's speech by silencing himself. He announces that he is "of little account," a lightweight who has no answer to these many questions. Has he been cowed by an intimidating, interrogating God, or does his silence signify something further. Has he finally come to a place of wonder where he can step back and contemplate the beauty that has passed before him? Does his silence mean that he has become contemplative and now has room to come to grips with what he has lost and has been lamenting for many chapters? Perhaps his silence opens him, at last, to hear a response and to reframe his own experience. But the book, in its ambiguities and gaps, leaves interpretation to the readers, providing few clues to settle our many questions. No stage direction accompanies these speeches.

40:6–41:26 Yahweh's second speech

God's second speech repeats the opening challenge of the first (38:3) and amplifies it by asking Job if he would condemn God in order to justify himself (40:8). Although this challenge is indeed daunting, it does reveal that God has been listening to Job's accusations. God treats Job as a serious challenger, proposing that if Job can bring justice upon the earth by the power of his arm and the terror of his glance, then God would acknowledge that Job could save himself (40:9-13). Job, however, has not sought equality with God or the acquisition of power. He has been driven, instead, by a desire to understand his predicament.

After hurling this contest at Job as if he were a serious claimant to divine power, God turns to two specific and extremely frightening animals to further interrogate him. The first creature, Behemoth, is a land monster (40:13-24), and the second, Leviathan, is a sea monster (40:25–41:26). Some interpreters think Behemoth and Leviathan represent the hippopotamus and the crocodile, but it is more likely that they are mythic creatures who symbolize primordial chaos that God overcame at the creation of the world. They may be examples of the wicked ones that God challenges Job to "tear down the wicked in their place" (40:12). But God's relationship with these creatures is not adversarial; it is full of boastful pride.

The first statement about Behemoth addresses Job directly and asserts Behemoth's creaturely equality with Job. "Look at Behemoth, whom I

made along with you" (40:15). An animal of marshy waters, Behemoth is far stronger than Job, but both are creatures of God. Stiff-tailed and iron-boned, Behemoth is wild, ferocious, and makes sport of other wild animals (40:20). He is not disturbed by turbulence, and no one can capture him in his idyllic domain that provides for all his needs. Job and he are equals in God's creation.

The Leviathan (40:26–41:26) is an even more fearsome creature. Job has already mentioned this monster twice: once, in his opening speech, when he wishes "those skilled at disturbing Leviathan" to curse the night of his conception (3:8), and again, when Job asks if he must be watched like the sea monster for being chaotic and uncontrollable (7:12). Now God brings that beast before Job for his reflection, perhaps as a kind of mirror. Again God brags about the power, strength, and awesome beauty of this creature. Again interpreters see here evidence of ancient Ugaritic creation myths where God does battle with chaos monsters. But although those traditions are probably present, they are greatly tamed in this speech, since a battle does not occur.

God asks Job if he can curb, tame, domesticate, or do battle with this creature (40:25-32). Job must answer God's question with a resounding "No!" He cannot control this creature, but neither does God claim to do so. Instead, God shifts from questioning Job to a stance of ebullient delight in the wondrous Leviathan (41:2-26). In the style of a hymn of praise, God praises Leviathan's fierceness, his strong limbs, terrible teeth, scales on his back, fire from his nostrils, and his general imperviousness to attack. Even the "mighty" are afraid when this creature rises up from the sea (41:17). "Upon the earth there is none like him" and "he is king over all proud beasts" (41:26). Although Leviathan is a fierce, proud creature suited for combat, this poetry is not about warfare between God and the wild creature. It is about divine joy in this most intrepid and fearsome animal. God does not repress Leviathan and Behemoth nor act in hostility toward them. Instead, the Creator leaves them in their natural state, uncontrolled and free to be themselves, wild and beautiful.

Rather than waging war with the creatures or even with Job, God opens up before Job the panorama of creation in its energy, variety, and wild beauty. Surely Job would be in fear and awe before this display, yet something more than intimidation is at work here. In the midst of the storm, God draws Job's attention away from himself to the awesomeness of the cosmos and its residents, kin to him, fellow creatures, untamed, and following their own paths. Some scholars note the absence of human creatures from God's speeches, yet humans are present in Job who is the one whom God addresses. God shows Job a world of immense marvels and beauty. Job participates in this glorious world and is one with it. This changes everything.

42:1-6 Job's second response

Job's final response reveals that his experience in the storm satisfies him and transforms his life, even if his words leave interpreters in doubt. Although Job promised previously to remain silent, he speaks again, acknowledging God's sovereignty and unstoppable will (42:2). Humbly he declares his know-nothing status before the glories of God's unfathomable creation. And he testifies that his encounter with God has altered him, as if he has become happily content with the experience of mystery and made alive again.

Job used to know about God through the words of other people, "by hearsay," but now in a marvelous declaration, he claims, "my eye has seen you" (42:5). Such seeing may refer to a vision, a common means of revelation in the Old Testament, but surely it signifies more. Job evokes Jeremiah's famous passage where the new covenant will mean that people will no longer teach one another because "Everyone, from least to greatest, shall know me" (Jer 31:34). Job is no longer reliant upon the word of others to have connection with God. Now he knows God directly from his own experience. With his own eye, in his own body, he has met God face to face.

The last line of his response, however, complicates interpretation of Job's words. Traditionally translated, "Therefore I despise myself and repent in dust and ashes" (42:6), the verse actually allows for several translations. In the NABRE translation, Job disowns his words and repents even though he is a righteous man. Both translations create problems. The former leaves Job in self-hatred, a defeated man beaten down by God. The latter shows Job renouncing the truthful laments he has set before God, who, in turn, praises Job's speech in the epilogue (42:7). But the Hebrew word often

translated "repent" can also mean "be comforted," or "regret." Other translations create different nuances. In one, Job retracts his words and "is comforted by dust and ashes." In another, Job "rejects" the "dust and ashes," meaning that Job has stopped grieving and gotten on with his life.

The ambiguities of this line resist oversimplification. In light of the book's puzzling structure and unresolved debate, it is likely that the ambiguity is deliberate, a means to invite readers to enter Job's experience and come to terms with it for themselves. Whereas many interpreters find the speeches in the storm to be marked by chaos that Job learns to accept, this commentary concentrates the beauty of both the language and events in the storm. The breath-taking attraction of God's creation draws Job in and transforms him. The beauty of God and God's world allures, takes him outward from his suffering, and enables him to relinquish his imaginary position at the center of the world. Experience of beauty sharpens attentiveness, creates a contemplative spirit, provokes gratitude, and opens one to care for the world.

Job's long, angry laments have helped to heal him and opened him to the life-affirming greeting from God. However we deal with the many lingering puzzles of the book, its beauty points to the beauty of the Creator and summons readers to the possibility of encounter with God in any of life's circumstances.

EPILOGUE
Job 42:7-17

The book surprises readers again by returning in a short epilogue of ten verses to prose narrative. These verses not only resume the folktale genre of the prologue to form a narrative frame around the book, they also return to the worldview of the book's beginning. There coherent themes of cause and effect rule in contrast to the poetry where ambiguity, complexity, and contradiction dominate the debates. The epilogue adds further complications to the book, even as it provides a satisfying happy ending. It brings readers back to a life where the good are rewarded and the wicked punished, as if the anguishing debates about God and human suffering only lead back to the beginning, having achieved little. The epilogue divides into two scenes: Job and friends (42:7-9) and Job's new life (42:10-17).

42:7-9 Job and friends

The narrator connects the epilogue with the speeches in the storm by setting events immediately "after the Lord had spoken these words to Job" (42:7). In these verses, God finally grants what Job desired all along, vindication of his righteousness or, at least, of the righteousness of his speech. But this honoring of Job's words is indirect, for it occurs in speech addressed to Eliphaz and comes only after God rebukes the friends, for "You have not spoken rightly concerning me, as has my servant Job" (42:7). It is strange that God does not affirm Job's words in the storm nor affirm him directly here. It may be that when Job sees God with his eye his needs are met and there are no other requirements of healing gestures between them.

The epilogue does not re-impose the theology of the prologue completely. Although the epilogue rewards Job, the innocent one, God does not punish the friends, so the chain of cause and effect is broken. God sets in place dynamics for rebuilding the friendship that fell upon the rocks of their disputes about Job's suffering. God tells Eliphaz and his two friends to offer sacrifice and Job will pray for them. God will not punish them because of Job's prayer. Job's experience of God in the storm enables him to intercede on his friends' behalf, altering his relationship with them and effecting a renewal of community. Job, the victim, extends a gesture of reconciliation to his persecuting friends.

42:10-17 Job's new life

God does more than approve of Job's words. In the second scene, God rewards him with good things, returning once again to the theology of the prologue. Job never asked God for restoration of anything he had lost except for their relationship. Now that Job has seen God himself, God gives him double what he had before (42:10-12). Among the doublings, Job's community comes first. Friends and family gather around him, feast with him, present gifts, and offer genuine comfort, "for all the evil the Lord had brought upon him" (42:11). Then he receives doubled numbers of animals and material wealth to make him twice as rich as before.

It is probably mistaken to ask where this community has been all along, since folktales tell their stories for the sake of the narrated events rather than to raise unanswered questions. Similarly, the replication of his family of ten children in the same gender balance as before does not address what all parents know, that lost children can never be replaced by new ones. The new children signify, instead, that Job has a full life, replete with a large family. But even this blessing is in some ways altered from the prologue because Job's daughters are not only named, they are given an inheritance with their brothers. By naming the daughters, and even more strikingly, listing them among inheritors, Job acts in ways his culture would find suspect (but see Num 27:1-11). Here the daughter's inheritance underscores Job's vast wealth as sufficient to include them, and for modern readers, it suggests that Job is not bound by the usual constraints of his society.

Job, the blessed servant of Yahweh, has come full circle. Restored to health, wealth, and community, he lives to see his children's children and dies old and full of years. And his latter days were more blessed than the former (42:12). Is this as a reward for his innocence, or is it a case of God pouring forth grace upon the beloved?

CONCLUSION

The book of Job is too rich in meaning and metaphoric power and complex in literary structure and theological debate to be reduced to one interpretation. Here are some ways to reflect upon the book as a whole.

A dramatic process

From a literary perspective, the book of Job evokes experiences it is trying to express. The prologue positions readers as privileged interpreters, sympathizers with Job, because we know he is the innocent victim of a deal made in heaven. The seemingly endless debates between Job and his friends immerse us in Job's despair, the friends' frustration, and Job's rage at them and God. The book's spiraling, contradictory interchanges wear us down, as if it were designed to force us into the depth of the struggle, to wrestle with it, examine it from many sides, only to be surprised and unbalanced again by events in the whirlwind and epilogue.

Against Elihu's confident denial, God appears in the storm. With a literary beauty that replicates the beautiful wildness of creation itself, God draws Job and readers into a world beyond ourselves. There, no intellectual answers resolve the conflicting voices, but God and Job meet, and Job changes. Finally, we rest with Job in the epilogue, a rest foreshadowed by the hymn to wisdom (ch. 28). Although Job lives happily ever after in peace, many questions remain because Job, the righteous one, receives rewards.

Rather than restating orthodoxy or hammering home one interpretive viewpoint, the book implies that the hymn to wisdom is a key to interpretation. Humans can do many things, but wisdom is hidden to everyone but God, a point the book illustrates. By leaving unanswered questions, the book provokes active participation in the drama of Job's life from its collapse to its restoration. Such participation is potentially transformative for readers.

Innocent suffering

Rather than explain why the innocent suffer, the book spreads a feast of understandings and theological positions about the matter. In telling of Job's life it presents injustice, life-stopping losses, grief, and the collapse of the worlds. This narrative is capable of embracing the sufferings of individuals and of whole peoples. Rich Job loses all to join the poor and outcast, symbolized by his place on the ash heap or garbage dump of his village. This broken figure reappears in the homeless, frightened refugees, displaced persons, and the hungry millions of our rich world. Job's suffering is undeserved, and his friends further isolate him in their inability to see him as he really is. The book calls readers to face our responses to the suffering around us, near and far, and to note the suffering, like Job, are God's favored.

By undermining easy interpretations of Job's plight, the text reminds readers of the limited grasp on truth of our theological positions. Repeatedly, through structural juxtapositions of conflicting parts and voices, the book displaces each voice, interpretation, and point of view regarding Job's suffering. Such unsettling argument summons us to openness to other understandings, to humility in holding our own truth, and to recognition that theologies and spiritualities change with new human circumstances. In times of uncertainty and meaninglessness, Job also calls us to stubborn fidelity to the God who transcends all reduction to rigid and narrow doctrine.

The prologue presents Job's disaster as a calculated design made in a heavenly bargain. Job suffers physically, mentally, and spiritually. His friends believe Job sinned and God merely responded by punishing him. Job thinks God betrayed him and, by extension, treats the world unjustly. When God speaks, it is to change the subject from Job's suffering to the beauty and wild freedom of creation. The book does not explain Job's suffering, nor does any text of the Bible settle the matter. Rather than explaining suffering, the New Testament presents another One who suffers innocently and whose suffering and death on the cross culminates in the gift of new life.

God humbles Job

Another way to view the same literary evidence is to understand the book as a divine putdown of Job. Some interpreters believe that when God changes the subject from Job's suffering to the creation, God disrespects and abuses Job who complains for legitimate reasons. In this view, divine interrogation in the storm emphasizes God's power and humiliates Job. The book, therefore, conceives of divine-human relationship as continuing combat. Job curses and God overpowers, bullies, and silences Job. Job's second response, in the traditional, although disputed, translation, "I despise myself and repent in dust and ashes" (NRSV, 42:6), expresses Job's diminishment. God's attempt to restore Job's life shows Job's charges against God are correct. In this interpretive approach, the book reinstates divine power and keeps humans humbled in the chaos of life.

Divine-human relationship

The book's primary concern, however, may not be the suffering of the innocent but the larger question of human relationship to God in the midst of suffering. Job's catastrophe provides the flesh and blood mess within which to debate the character of divine-human relationship. The Satan thinks divine-human relationship is a mercenary one. God buys human loyalty by giving gifts and putting a hedge of protection around Job. Job's words and actions in the prologue refute that point of view, for he remains utterly faithful. The Satan disappears from the book because his role in the story is finished. He lost his bet.

Job's friends reverse the Satan's perspective but are equally mechanistic. They insist that humans buy God's blessings or curses with their behavior. This theology of retribution gives humans controlling power over the actions of God. For both the friends and the Satan, divine-human relationships are one-sided arrangements. The Satan thinks God controls humans by giving or withholding good things. The friends think humans control God by loyalty or disloyalty. God has no choice but to bless or punish accordingly. Either way, divine-human relationship is compulsive and rule-driven.

Job breaks through these rigid patterns. In his experience, humans cannot control God, whom he finds to be both free and unreliable. He thinks God transcends human understanding, abides by no rules, and is inaccessible to humans. He thinks the sovereign God is beyond human capacity to understand and is also capricious and unjust. For him, God's being is deep mystery laced with cruelty.

When God appears, God not only affirms divine freedom, wildness, and beauty, but also the freedom and wild beauty of creation including Job. By implication, divine-human relationship is a mutual one where neither party controls the other, but both are free. In the epilogue, God approves Job's words. Is even Job's anger and despair about God's absence from the world evidence that Job has "spoken rightly" about God? (42:7). Are all Job's charges and accusations correct?

When God rejects the friends' words and declares Job to be right, the book appears to dismiss the friends' theology in the most authoritative way. But with great irony, the epilogue reinstates retribution. God blesses Job, the righteous one, and doubles all good things in his life. We are back where we started, but things are not the same.

Movement to mature faith

From another interpretative standpoint, Job's experiences resemble human struggles toward adult faith. As the story begins, Job is rich, secure, powerful, and surrounded by family and servants. Even when the Satan removes his blessings, he remains righteous. His piety is pre-critical and unquestioning, and his life has clarity of purpose, driven by acceptance and trust.

But in the poetry, Job's trust evaporates as rage, doubt, and despair displace it. The collapse of his life brings with it loss of the traditions that had supported him. Formerly, he was a comforter of others and a leader among them. After the breaking of his world, his theology no longer holds. It cannot explain, support, or illuminate his life. Instead, his life challenges his theology. Adding to his pain, no new way of understanding emerges except his assumption that God has betrayed him. He faces what later contemplatives might call the "dark night of the soul," when all support for faith unravels and one plunges into divine absence.

Yet in the process, Job remains faithful. He grows in power and rhetorical expansiveness. He laments what he has lost, voicing his anger and grief to his friends and to God. His truthful, angry speech becomes a vehicle of his loyalty. Job holds fast to his integrity despite efforts of his friends to talk him out of his experience of the world. It enables him to dare to challenge God and to demand that God step forward and explain matters to him.

Job's life propels him from a faith of few challenges into a chaotic spiral of doubt where faith no longer has any buttress or external support. Yet in the midst of bitter strife, he never lets go of God. Instead, he cries and yells angrily at God, telling his truth and keeping their relationship alive. When Job and God meet in the storm, Job knows a "reorientation," a new way of being that exceeds doctrinal or philosophical answers. His encounter with the beauty of divine revelation, of the cosmos, and by implication, the beauty of God, provide him with direct spiritual experience and a sense of oneness with all life. He shares life with the Behemoth, the Leviathan—proud and joyous expressions of divine life. In the storm, Job glimpses a world energized by the creative power of God.

That glimpse of the absolute wondrousness of the Creator and of creation reorders his relationships. His communal life becomes more open, inclusive, and peaceful. He repairs friendships, interceding on behalf of his friends and extending extraordinary care to his daughters. In the storm, Job receives a life-affirming greeting from another world, and however we deal with the book's many lingering questions, its beauty calls us to glimpse God's amazing creativity divinely loosed in the cosmos. It summons us to care for creation and all its inhabitants, especially those who know Job's suffering and abysmal pain. It urges us toward lives of worshipful gratitude.

THE BOOK OF
PSALMS

Dianne Bergant, C.S.A.

INTRODUCTION

About the book

The book of Psalms, also known as the Psalter, is really a collection of books, each of which ends with a short doxology or hymn of praise: book 1, Psalms 1–41; book 2, Psalms 42–72; book 3, Psalms 73–89; book 4, Psalms 90–106; and book 5, Psalms 107–50. The book of Psalms itself is composed of even earlier collections. Several psalms, found principally in the first book, are attributed to David. (This may account for the popular but probably not historically accurate tradition that David himself wrote most of the psalms.) Several psalms in the second and third books are ascribed to Korah or Asaph, the two great guilds of temple singers of the Second Temple period (cf. 1 Chr 6:33ff; 25:1-2). The fifth book consists of a number of songs of ascent and psalms of praise known as Hallel or the Hallelujah collection. There are also variations in the preferred name for God. *Yahweh* (rendered Lord), generally used in the first, fourth, and fifth collections, suggests an earlier "Yahwist Psalter," while *Elohim* (God) is preferred in the second and third books, suggesting an earlier "Elohist Psalter."

Some psalms include a superscription or an informative statement that precedes the psalm itself. This information might include identification of the earlier collection to which the psalm belonged (e.g., "A psalm of David" [Ps 3] or "A psalm of Asaph" [Ps 82]), liturgical directions (e.g., "For the leader" [Ps 68] or "On stringed instruments" [Ps 55]), lyrical classification (e.g., "A

maskil" [Ps 54] or "A *miktam*" [Ps 59]), and a purported historical setting (e.g., "for the dedication of the temple" [Ps 30]). This information, which may have little meaning for contemporary readers, was probably included when the psalms were being collected. Since superscriptions are found in the Hebrew text, some English versions begin the numeration of the verses of the psalm with the superscription. The New American Bible Revised Edition follows this custom. Other versions begin the numeration with the first verse of the psalm itself. This explains why there is not always agreement among various translations or versions as to the number of verses in certain psalms.

LITERARY CHARACTERISTICS

The psalms are first and foremost lyrical creations, poems that are rich in metaphor and fashioned according to the patterns and techniques of ancient Israelite poetry. One of the most distinctive characteristics of this type of poetry is its parallelism. In this feature, the second half of a poetic line somehow echoes the sense of the first. Thus we read in Psalm 61:

hear	my cry, O God
listen to	my prayer

This poetic technique serves to intensify the point being made.

Another very important feature found in several psalms is the acrostic structure. In this structure the first letter of the first word of successive poetic lines follows the order of the alphabet. The structure is meant to suggest comprehensiveness, similar to the English expression "from A to Z." Unfortunately, this alphabetic pattern is usually lost when the psalm is translated. However, identification of the acrostic or alphabetic pattern has been retained in Psalms 37, 111, 112, and 119.

A third important feature of the psalms is meter. This is a form of poetic rhythm that is determined by the number of accents in the words that comprise the line of poetry. Since this is a feature of Hebrew poetry, it is also lost in translation.

Finally, a single word, *selah*, is found in several psalms. It is probably an indication of some kind of pause, but it does not always follow the sense of the poem. Many scholars believe that it might have originally functioned as a liturgical or musical directive. However, this is not clear. Nonetheless, it has been retained in the Hebrew and so it does appear in many versions of the Psalter.

Types of psalms

The major classifications of psalms are lament, hymn, prayers of confidence, and prayers of thanksgiving. There are also royal psalms, wisdom poems, historical recitals, ritual or liturgical, and some psalms that might fit more than one classification.

Laments

Nearly a third of all psalms are laments. Some of them are complaints of an individual; others are communal complaints. Laments usually consist of an actual complaint, a plea for deliverance from hardship, an expression of praise of God or confidence that God will intervene and deliver the one(s) suffering, and a promise to perform an act of devotion in gratitude for God's intervention. Some laments include an acknowledgment of guilt or a claim of innocence. Finally, there is frequently a curse hurled at the one(s) believed to be responsible for the intolerable situation that called forth the lament in the first place. Many people believe that originally the lament included several distinct religious sentiments. The first was the lament or complaint. This was followed by

expressions of confidence that God would hear the complaint and remedy the situation. The lament would then end with expressions of gratitude for the divine graciousness of which the psalmist was confident. While traces of all three sentiments can still be found in some laments, the confidence and thanksgiving often comprise individual psalms.

Hymns

The hymn consists of a call to praise God and an account of the wondrous acts of God that elicited the praise. These marvelous divine acts might include glories of creation or the marvelous feats performed in history on behalf of Israel. Hymns praising the Lord's kingship are a distinct group of psalms. Their focus is God's cosmic sovereignty and exclusive reign over all the heavenly bodies. Songs of Zion extol God's holy mountain, the place of God's dwelling on earth, and Jerusalem, the city built on that mountain from which God chose to rule.

Prayers of confidence

Although confidence or trust is often found in laments, the Psalter also contains prayers that focus primarily on such sentiments. The motives for confidence in God's protection and care include divine justice that the people believe will be shown on their behalf, God's faithful commitment to the covenant that God chose to initiate with Israel, and the promises made to Israel's ancestors and renewed from generation to generation. As is the case with laments, there are both individual prayers of confidence and those that are communal in character.

Thanksgiving

Scholars do not agree as to which psalms belong to this category because expressions of confidence and gratitude are often found in laments. Consequently, this type of psalm is usually classified according to its content rather than its form. Thanksgiving psalms are similar to hymns, in that they extol the marvelous works of God. However, hymns call forth praise because of these wonders, while thanksgiving psalms include expressions of gratitude for God's graciousness.

Royal psalms

Some psalms seem to have sprung from various occasions in the life of the king. They are often referred to as "messianic psalms," since messiah means "anointed one" and kings were anointed. On occasion, they might celebrate the king's success in battle. However, they usually extol the special covenant relationship that God established with the king and the divine protection bestowed on the Israelite rulers because of it. Royal psalms take on new meaning when they are included in the Christian tradition and are applied to Jesus who is king par excellence and the one uniquely anointed by God. In such instances, it is not that the original psalmist had Christ in mind when composing the poem. Rather, the early Christian community began to view Christ from the perspective of the Davidic ruler and to interpret the psalm from a Christian point of view.

Wisdom poems

Wisdom poems clearly differ from other psalms in both content and style. They call people to listen and to learn, not to pray. Although they do not follow a uniform style, they do possess some distinctive literary characteristics. One such characteristic is the acrostic arrangement in which the alphabet determines the initial letter of the first word of each successive line. This is recognizable only in the original Hebrew. A second characteristic is the recourse made to order in the world of nature. This order is employed as an incentive for establishing social order. One of the most prominent topics of the instruction found in these poems is the theory of retribution: the wise or good will be rewarded with happiness and prosperity while the foolish or wicked will suffer misfortune. Descriptions of situations that illustrate this teaching are intended to exhort people to live life in a way that will lead to happiness.

Various other psalms

The songs of ascent, one of the early collections mentioned above, were probably sung during pilgrimages to or processions around Jerusalem and the temple. A few other psalms appear to have been composed in the style of prophetic speech. Finally, a small number of psalms defy classification. They are either historical recountings of the feats of the Lord, composites of other psalm forms, celebrations of the kingship of the Lord, or liturgical songs.

THE THEOLOGY IN THE PSALMS

The God of Israel

The portrait of God sketched in the psalms draws together all the characterizations of God found in the rest of the Israelite tradition. God is depicted as the creator of the universe and the source of all life, victoriously enthroned in heaven, yet dwelling in the city of Jerusalem. Initially believed to be exclusively Israel's liberator, God's reign was ultimately perceived as universal, and all people were invited to worship this God in Jerusalem. The God depicted in the psalms inspires both fear and confidence because of God's breathtaking divine power and majesty as well as the care and protection that God provided for Israel's ancestors in the past. This God demands compliance to the law and yet forgives infraction of it, regardless of the seriousness of the violation. Perhaps the key characterization of the Lord is that of "covenant partner." Fundamental to this understanding of God is the firm conviction that God initiated the covenant, not because Israel in any way deserved it, but because God is "gracious and merciful, slow to anger and abounding in love" (Pss 145:8; 103:8).

Humankind

The psalms come from a society in which men are the norm and so the language and imagery reflect this gender bias. Honored as the culmination of creation, humankind is made responsible for all other living creatures. Still, humans live a fleeting life, perishing after a short life span like field flowers. The absence of a clear notion of life after death underscores the starkness of life's impermanence. Though all humans are dependent on God's providence, God seems to be the special guardian of the poor and afflicted, the defenseless widows and orphans.

Natural creation

The psalms reveal a special regard for creation as the handiwork of God's power and ingenuity. Furthermore, Israel reinterpreted many ancient Near Eastern concepts of divinity, arguing that its own God is the one revealed through the elements of nature, in the exquisite design of the natural world, in the power of the thunderstorm, and in the gentleness of refreshing rain. In many psalms creation itself is called on to join in the praise of this wondrous creator-God.

The future

Israel's view of the future, known as eschatology, stems from its faith in the goodness of God toward all creation. Despite the struggles that it faced throughout its history, Israel believed that the final victory would be God's. The psalms say very little about possible life beyond the grave, but they frequently mention the shadowy existence known as Sheol. This netherworld was not a place of reward or punishment, but of darkness, dust, and inactivity. Israel may not have had a clear idea of life after death, but it did not seem to believe that the dead ceased to exist. The people awaited a final divine victory that would unfold in history, but in a history that included the cosmic realm of the heavens as well.

THE PSALMS TODAY

Contemporary devotion

The psalms continue to play a significant role in the official and private prayer of both the Jewish and Christian communities today. In this way they shape the minds and hearts of modern believers. One result of the various liturgical reforms of the twentieth century is that verses from a particular psalm serve as a response to the first reading. When there is a thematic connection between that first reading and the gospel passage, the responsorial psalm often acts as a prayerful summation of the readings.

Reflective reading of the psalms enables us to immerse ourselves in the religious dispositions of the psalmist. Though the sentiments with which we come to the psalms may not be identical to those expressed in those prayers, we can still recognize the world that they project. At the moment, we may not be living in a world similar to what is depicted there, and our sentiments may not correspond to the sentiments expressed by the psalmist. Most likely, however, there are people somewhere for whom those sentiments accurately express their present situation. Standing in solidarity with those people, we can make our prayer

their prayer. In this way our religious consciousness can be profoundly shaped by the psalms.

Troublesome images

The psalms come from worlds that are very different from those of contemporary society. They frequently reflect cultural customs and values that are foreign to us or might even offend our sensitivities. Examples of the first would be ancient patriarchal marriage practices or family customs; an example of the second would be the role that honor and shame play in determining one's social status. In such situations it is important to discover the meaning behind the uncommon expression or figure of speech in order to appreciate its theological message. This can usually be accomplished through an examination of the historical circumstances from which the psalm originated.

There are other aspects of the psalms that many people today find offensive. Examples of these would include the male bias that is apparent in the gender-specific language used, the ethnocentrism that reveals itself in a measure of disdain for nations other than Israel, and the prejudice in presuming that physical disabilities are punishment for sin. These offensive features are not easily overlooked, but careful historical analysis can help us realize that they are historically and culturally conditioned perspectives that need not be carried into a contemporary point of view.

What is perhaps most troublesome today in many circles is the violence that seems to enjoy divine sanction in so many of the psalms. The psalmists perceive God as a warrior who can be called on to wreak vengeance on the heads of Israel's opponents. God is called on to "crush the heads of his enemies" and then directs the people to "wash your feet in your enemy's blood" (Ps 68:22, 24). Who can comfortably pray: "Blessed the one who seizes your children / and smashes them against the rock" (Ps 137:9)? This kind of characterization of God and these kinds of directives must be carefully interpreted if we are to continue to maintain that they have revelatory value for us today.

Without in any way minimizing what is offensive, we should realize that the psalmists understand the violence that they attributed to God as a form of divine retribution. God was being called on to punish the wicked. When these wicked people were the national enemies of

Israel, God was envisioned as a defending warrior, fighting on Israel's side. Since the image of a conquering god was already present in the ancient myths of creation, it is not difficult to see how such an understanding of God might be employed to describe how God acted in Israel's military history.

As is the case with all characterizations of God, the image of the divine warrior is a metaphor, a figure of speech that applies traits of one object to a second and very different object. A metaphor is never a definition, nor does it exactly parallel the two objects being compared. It simply states how these two objects have certain attributes in common. If we are to understand the metaphor of God the warrior, we will have to discover what traits traditionally attributed to the warrior are being applied to God.

COMMENTARY

BOOK ONE: PSALMS 1–41

Psalm 1 (wisdom psalm)

1-6 The two ways

The Psalter begins with a wisdom psalm. This suggests that the final editors of the book intended that the Psalter itself be used for instruction, not merely for prayer. The prosperity of the righteous is contrasted with the fate of the wicked. In typical wisdom style, the psalm lays out two divergent ways of life: one leads to happiness, the other to misfortune. The choice is up to the individual. The psalm opens with a macarism, or beatitude ("Happy" or "Blessed"). The righteous flourish because they reject the influence of the wicked and follow the way of the Lord. A metaphor derived from nature characterizes prosperity. Just as a tree thrives on the life-giving properties of nearby water, so those rooted in the law of the Lord bring forth fruit in abundance. The righteous are rooted in the Lord; the wicked are rootless, like worthless chaff. Deprived of life-giving water, they wither and blow away. The way of the righteous is under God's protection; the way of the wicked ends in ruin.

Psalm 2 (royal psalm)

The psalm describes the enthronement of a human king by the divine king who sits enthroned in heaven. Psalm 2, which ends with a macarism, is frequently linked with Psalm 1, which opens with that same literary form. This pattern creates a kind of *inclusio* (bookend frame).

Together they provide a twofold lens through which the entire Psalter is read. The lens is one of wisdom and messianic expectation (from the Hebrew word *māshîah*, or anointed one).

1-3 Kings of the nations rise up

The relationship between God and the king is clearly drawn. Any kind of rebellion against God or against God's anointed one is doomed to failure, because the power of God sustains both God's own dominion and the dominion of God's chosen king.

4-9 Divine oracle

A divine oracle bestows God's legitimation on the monarchy and it identifies Jerusalem, also referred to as Zion after the mountain on which it was built, as the divinely chosen shrine. The divine decree that establishes the king's legitimacy reflects the royal covenant that God made with the house of David (cf. 2 Sam 7:14). The notion of the royal covenant is derived from the ancient Near Eastern belief that the king was in some way the son of the god. Hence the father-son relationship. "Today" implies that the king was not always the son of God, but became so, probably at the time of enthronement. (Christians have applied this verse to Jesus and have incorporated it into their Christmas liturgy.) The divine decree also endorses the king's rule over all other nations. The shepherd metaphor was quite common in the ancient Near East. Kings were often characterized as shepherds with responsibility for the well-being of the people.

10-11 Warning from God

Finally, in the style of a wisdom admonition, the rebelling nations are exhorted to listen and to learn, to serve the Lord lest they perish on their rebellious way. The psalm closes with a macarism ("Blessed are all").

Psalm 3
(prayer of confidence of an individual)

2-4 Cries of complaint

The psalm opens with one of the standard cries of complaint to God: "How many?" The suffering persists; enemies taunt the psalmist and claim that God is not concerned with the misfortune into which the psalmist has fallen. Despite experiencing derision, the one suffering is confident that God will eventually hear these cries for help and will respond. A military image of a shield characterizes God's protection that, when it is granted, will enable the psalmist to stand proudly with head held high.

5-7 Confidence in God

God's "holy mountain" can be a reference either to a sacred mountain on which God dwells or to the temple where God is found in the midst of the Israelites. Because God has answered prayers in the past, the psalmist is confident that God will answer again. With God as protector, the psalmist claims to have nothing to fear from human attacks.

8-9 Cry for help

A final cry for help arises out of extreme distress. Violent means may be necessary to defend the psalmist. The parallel construction demonstrates the character of the reprisals the psalmist suggests that God may have to take:

| shatter the jaws | of all my foes |
| break the teeth | of the wicked |

This construction also shows how the psalmist's foes are likened to the wicked. When deliverance finally does come, it will not be as the result of military might, but as a gift graciously given by the Lord.

Psalm 4
(prayer of confidence of an individual)

2 Cries for help

The psalm opens with a threefold petition: "Answer me . . . take pity . . . hear. . . ." The multiple nature of this petition underscores the urgency of the psalmist's need. Despite this, the psalmist is confident that God will eventually respond favorably to the prayer that is offered. This confidence is based on remembrance of the blessings of God that were granted in the past ("you cleared a way").

3-6 Warning to the wicked

In the throes of suffering, a threefold accusation is hurled at enemies: "you be hard of heart, / love what is worthless, chase after lies." The threefold accusation balances the earlier threefold prayer for help. It underscores the psalmist's deep resentment of those who act as enemies. Their treachery is futile in the face of God's defense of the faithful. It is interesting to note that after pleading for their punishment, the psalmist seeks their repentance and reform, exhorting them to change their lives, offer sacrifice in reparation, and trust that God will look kindly on them.

7-9 Trust in God

Though the idea of complaining to God may be disconcerting, this psalm ends, as do most laments, on a note of confidence. According to the psalmist, the joy of having been heard by God far exceeds the delight experienced over a bountiful harvest of grain or the pleasures of rich wine. Peace (*shalom*) really means prosperity and contentment because one possesses everything that is needed to live a full and meaningful life. It is the Lord alone who grants the psalmist the sense of security that comes with having been blessed.

Psalm 5 (lament of an individual)

2-9 Prayers to God

The psalm itself resembles a temple liturgy. (This may explain the liturgical directives found in the superscription.) It opens with a triple petition: "Give ear . . . Attend . . . hear." Prayer at dawn suggests an all-night vigil in the temple, a common devotional practice, particularly when an important favor is being asked of God. The psalmist seems confident that by the end of the vigil the prayer will be heard. To stand in God's presence is to enjoy some degree of intimacy, a privilege that the wicked are denied. A second privilege is access to the temple. It is granted because of God's love, not as a reward for the psalmist's devotion. The Hebrew word used is a technical term for God's covenant love. It describes a love that is steadfast and enduring. The psalmist's reverential devotion is a response to this love; it is not its cause. Wisdom language ("Guide" and "way") reflects the psalmist's desire for divine direction in life. The psalmist seeks to follow the way of righteousness.

10-11 Attacks of the wicked

In many laments, the sinfulness of enemies is asserted. In some psalms the evil that they perpetrate is the affliction that the psalmist must endure. In other psalms its offensiveness is meant to provoke God's wrath. Here the offenses appear to be sins of the tongue rather than violent physical oppression, and God is called on to execute the justice that this sinfulness warrants. To persecute the righteous was considered rebellion against God. Therefore, those who attacked them deserved to be chastised.

12-13 Confident of God's justice

The psalm ends on a note of confidence, not vengeance. Despite the distress that initially prompted the lament, the righteous seek refuge in God and trust that God will hear their cries for help and will come to their aid. Just as the earlier indictment was based on one dimension of the theory of retribution (the wicked will be punished), so the confidence expressed here is grounded in the other dimension of that theory (the righteous will be rewarded).

Psalm 6
(lament of an individual; penitential)

In Christian devotion, this psalm is considered one of the seven penitential psalms (cf. Pss 32, 38, 51, 102, 130, 143).

2-8 Complaint to God

Terror in the face of divine wrath is all consuming, even causing physical weakness and trembling. The psalmist begs for pity and healing. The complaint ends with the stereotypical cry of lament: "How long?" The reason for God's anger is not given. However, since Israel did not consider God capricious, inflicting pain and suffering for no apparent reason, and since there is no explicit declaration of innocence, the one suffering is probably considered guilty of some offense. Since suffering was thought to result from God turning away in anger, God's turning back to the one suffering was seen as a sign of divine forgiveness or blessing. The word translated "mercy" is the covenant term often translated "steadfast love." In an attempt to secure deliverance from suffering, the psalmist appeals to God's covenant commitment. Since Israel did not yet have a clear teaching about reward or punishment after death, Sheol was considered a place of neutral existence with neither suffering nor contentment. However, it was still undesirable. Rescue from this place of murky existence would allow the psalmist to praise God, something that God would surely prefer.

9-11 Confidence in God

Just as God is asked to turn toward the psalmist with love and mercy, so the evildoers are charged to turn away and allow this afflicted individual some respite. Confident that God has heard these ardent pleas for help and will respond favorably to them, the psalmist is certain that these enemies will face the just wrath of God.

Psalm 7 (lament of an individual)

2-6 Prayer for help

The psalmist cries out to the Lord for refuge from brutal enemies, whose savagery is compared to that of lions mauling their prey. This psalmist claims to be innocent, never even having retaliated against those who might have deserved some form of retaliation. Verbs depicting forcefulness and the resulting terror describe the punishment that the psalmist is willing to bear if found guilty of any serious transgression. Dust is a symbol of mortality (cf. Gen 3:19). Used here, it suggests fundamental human insignificance and vulnerability (lacking value and subject to death).

7-14 Divine justice

What appears to be the psalmist's vindictiveness is really a plea that God will execute justice in the face of the enemy's unjustified oppression.

Several images point to the exalted prominence in which God is held by the psalmist. Enthronement on high is a reference to divine kingship established after the battle against cosmic chaos had been won. The military shield signifies protection from danger of any kind; the sword, the bow and arrows, and the deadly shafts are armaments of war that God will use against the wicked if necessary. The concept of God the warrior, an image that many currently find troubling, captures important theological themes that are relevant even today. These include God's commitment to justice and right order both in heaven and on earth, undisputed divine power, and God's willingness to defend the chosen people in the face of mortal danger. The dire circumstances of Israel's history prompted the people to depict God in this military fashion.

15-18 Punishment of the wicked

The psalm does not really suggest that God delights in savagery. Rather, it demonstrates that by their sinfulness the wicked provoke their own punishment. They bring on themselves the evil that their hearts conceive; they fall into the holes that their wickedness digs for others; they are crowned by their own violence. In the mind of the psalmist, any form of retribution is simply the consequence brought on by the wicked's own actions. The psalm concludes with praise of God's divine justice, not divine vengeance.

Psalm 8 (hymn)

2-3 Invitation to praise God

The simple structure of this psalm perfectly exemplifies the pattern of a hymn. It contains an initial acclamation of praise of God. This is followed by a list of reasons for this praise and a concluding invocation of praise. Names were important in ancient Israel, as they continue to be in many traditional societies today. They were thought to capture part of one's essence. For this reason in many instances they were held secret, revealed only to those with whom one shared an intimate relationship. This explains the reverence shown the personal name of God. In this psalm we see that to praise God's name is really to give glory to God. This glory shines forth both on the earth and in the heavens. The contrast between the most vulnerable ("babes and infants") and the

powerful ("enemy and avenger") suggests that the praise of the former is able to silence the opposition of the latter.

4-5 Splendor of creation

The reason for praising God is the wondrous creation that God has brought forth. Attention is drawn first to the principal heavenly bodies, whose splendor and greatness prompted many cultures to consider them deities. This resplendence is compared with the relative insignificance of human beings. Two Hebrew words characterize the lowly nature of humankind: *enosh*, weak human being; and *ben-adam*, mortal or, literally, son of the one formed from the ground. Just as earlier in the psalm the most vulnerable were contrasted with the powerful (v. 3), so here, limited humankind is compared with the glorious heavenly bodies.

6-9 Extraordinary human dignity

Though inferior to heavenly wonders, human beings are still exalted creatures. Royal imagery describing their lofty status ("crowned him with glory and honor") is complemented by a sketch of the rule over the rest of the created world to which they are appointed (cf. Gen 1:26-28). Thus, when beholding the resplendence of the heavenly bodies, the psalmist is in awe of the exalted position to which God has raised limited human beings.

10 Invitation to praise God

The psalm ends as it began, with an acclamation of praise of God.

Psalms 9–10

There are several reasons why Psalms 9 and 10 are analyzed together. First, many early Greek and Latin versions of the Bible consider them one psalm; together they form an acrostic pattern. Second, they share several linguistic and thematic features. Finally, Psalm 10 is one of the few psalms in the first book (Pss 1–41) that lacks a superscription, suggesting that it may be a continuation of what precedes it. Despite these similarities, there are significant differences between the psalms as well. Most of them can be seen in that Psalm 10 seems to contradict, almost point by point, the praise found in Psalm 9.

A (prayer of thanksgiving of an individual)

2-7 Defeat of enemies

The repetition of exclamations suggests that the psalmist cannot adequately express gratitude toward God for having been delivered from the hands of enemies: "I will praise . . . / I will declare . . . / I will delight and rejoice . . . / I will sing." Dynamic verbs describe the enemies' defeat by God: "turn back . . . stumble and perish . . . rebuked . . . blotted out . . . ruined . . . destroyed." The psalmist claims to be innocent, and so God's intervention, violent and destructive as it may be, is performed in the name of divine justice (see the explanation of God as warrior, Ps 7). The title "Most High," which may have originated in the cult in Jerusalem before the city's capture by David (cf. Gen 14:18-20), is here a designation of superiority. God is high above everything else.

8-11 The power of God

Enthroned as a king above all, God executes judgment over all the world. This divine judgment acts as a fortified stronghold of refuge and protection. Without it the vulnerable would continue to be oppressed, but with it they are safe from dangers of any kind.

12-15 In praise of the one who delivers from danger

The psalm moves from sentiments of thanksgiving to those of praise. The place of God's enthronement is Zion, the mountain on which the city of Jerusalem is built. From there God passes judgment on Israel's enemies. To call God the "avenger of bloodshed" might upset contemporary believers, but it means that God will execute justice and it was probably a reassuring concept for the ancient Israelites (cf. Deut 32:43). Though the psalmist cries out to God in the form of complaint, there is still confidence that God will hear this cry and will respond favorably. When this happens, the psalmist will praise God in a way that all will hear. The psalmist's deliverance by God corresponds with the enemies' demise, which is brought on by their own wickedness.

16-21 The fate of the enemies

The psalmist may have been rescued from the gates of death or Sheol, but the enemies are not. They face a bleak future, for the justice of God will not allow injustice to go unpunished. This does not mean that the righteous will never die. Rather, it means that they are saved from tragedies that shorten their lives or that are truly unbearable.

B (lament of an individual)

1-11 Complaint

The sentiments of this psalm take a decided turn toward complaint. The lament itself is quite pointed. Having witnessed the unexplained suffering of others, the psalmist accuses God of indifference. What appears to be divine disinterest allows the wicked to get the upper hand and the poor to become victims of their treachery. The wicked are not only free to plan and execute their selfish pursuits, they are also successful in doing so, and they gloat over their success. The psalmist is not alone in accusing God of disinterest. The wicked make this same claim, as do the helpless themselves. Everyone can see that God allows the arrogant to overpower the vulnerable and seems to do nothing about it. The section ends with an accusation against God.

12-15 God is not deaf

The psalmist cries again to God: "Rise up . . . Do not forget!" This second plea is followed by an expression of confidence. The psalmist insists that God does indeed care for the unfortunate. The orphans represent all those who, in a patriarchal society, lack a male defender. Once again God is called on to act as a warrior in defense of the vulnerable.

16-18 The divine king

Having begun in complaint and moved to confidence, the psalm ends with praise of the divine king who has delivered the people from their enemies. The psalmist praises God for having come to the aid of the needy, for having executed justice in their favor, and for having made them secure in the land.

Psalm 11
(prayer of confidence of an individual)

1b-3 Confidence in God

The psalmist, who is in an unidentified threatening situation, confesses total trust in God and challenges the plan of escape suggested by another. The psalmist employs dynamic imagery to depict the enemies as hunters who, with bow and arrow, lie in wait for some defenseless innocent victim. The idea of the hunt underscores both the vulnerability of the one threatened and the malice of those who do the threatening. The psalmist rejects the advice to flee from danger to safety in the high mountains and chooses refuge in God instead.

4-7 God rules from the heavens

The final statement of the one who offers an alternate plan for relief strikes a note of hopelessness: "what can the just one do?" (v. 3b). In response, the psalmist once again declares utter confidence in God who is portrayed as enthroned in heaven, attentive to everything that unfolds on earth. Divine justice is meted out to both the righteous and the wicked. Fiery coals, brimstone, and scorching wind here characterize the punishment of sinners, and may have contributed to the much later depiction of the "fires of hell." On the other hand, the righteous will behold the face of God, a concept that here suggests the return of a sense of security and good fortune, and in its own way may have contributed to the later characterization of reward in heaven as an intimate union with God. The psalmist's confidence is grounded in attachment to the divine sovereign who renders justice to all.

Psalm 12 (communal lament)

2-5 Cry for God's help

The opening plea in this psalm is direct and piercing: "Help!" The psalmist is the victim of lying speech and finds neither support nor comfort from others. Feeling forsaken at this time of great need, the psalmist concludes that there are no righteous people left to whom he or she can turn. God alone can be trusted, and so the psalmist prays for divine justice, not vengeance.

6 God speaks

In the words of this divine oracle, God promises to act promptly to remedy the exploitation of the weak and the needy. This promise is both comforting to those who turn to God for refuge and threatening to the wicked who might have to face God's just wrath.

7-9 Trust in God

Though the psalm began in lamentation, it ends in confidence. The psalmist believes that God's promises are trustworthy and priceless, since they have been tested and purified by fire. Still, this confidence is not foolhardy. Since the righteous will always be threatened by the wicked, the psalmist prays for God's continued protection.

Psalm 13 (lament of an individual)

2-5 Agonizing complaint

Four times this tormented individual cries out to God: "How long?" Though not specifically described, the psalmist assures us that the suffering is truly a heavy burden to bear. Probably the greatest trial is alienation from God, which is referred to in forceful poetic style:

Will you	utterly forget me?
Will you	hide your face from me?

The profound inner suffering is expressed in similar forceful poetic fashion:

sorrow	in my soul
grief	in my heart

The psalmist's suffering is soul-searing and heart-rending. Enemies have triumphed and God has not come to the rescue. The psalmist is bereft of comfort and aid from God or from anyone else. Plea upon plea compounds this lamentation: "Look upon me, answer me . . . / Give light to my eyes." Once again the psalmist speaks with poetic force:

Lest	my enemy	say, "I have prevailed"
Lest	my foes	rejoice at my downfall

To fail to come to the assistance of the psalmist is to give validity to the enemies' contention.

6 Confidence in God

As is the case with so many laments, this psalm ends on a note of trust in God. Despite the agony that is so clearly depicted, the psalmist is confident of God's faithfulness (the covenant word that characterizes God's steadfast love). Here again, confidence is grounded in the covenant relationship.

Psalm 14 (wisdom psalm)

1b Foolishness of the wicked

The genre of this psalm cannot be easily determined. It is rich in wisdom themes, and for this reason many commentators identify it as a wisdom psalm. Others see its confident longing as prominent and classify it as a psalm of trust. However it is ranked, its content is almost identical to that found in Psalm 53. The psalmist laments the despicable condition of the human race. Its total depravity is stated twice: "No one does what is good, / not even one." The foolish claim, "There is no God," is less a denial of God's existence than it is an assertion of God's apparent disinterest. They draw this conclusion because perversion rules on earth, and God seems to do nothing to rectify the situation.

2-6 God's response to foolishness

In response to the arrogant allegation of God's disinterest, the psalmist insists that God is indeed concerned. Though God dwells in heaven, what transpires on earth is not ignored. God looks among the foolish in search of the wise; God is aligned with the just and acts as a refuge for the poor. The wicked are not only arrogant in their apparent strength but also foolish to question God's commitment to the needy. Appearances are often deceiving, and even when they are not, fortunes can be reversed in the blink of an eye.

7 Deliverance from God

The psalm ends on a note of confidence. Divine assistance will come to Jerusalem, God's chosen city that is built on Mount Zion. Furthermore, this restoration will elicit universal rejoicing.

Psalm 15 (liturgical hymn)

1-5 An entrance ceremony

The psalm appears to be a ritual for use during the entrance into the sanctuary. In liturgical style, there is a question-answer exchange. God is questioned about the prerequisites needed for access to the place of worship. The poetic parallelism is obvious:

who	may abide	in your tent?
who	may dwell	on your holy mountain?

Both tent (which is reminiscent of the sacred tent of the desert) and holy mountain (presumably Zion on which the temple was built) are references to a place of worship. Remarkably, the responses to these questions are not found in Israel's extensive Holiness Code, the set of laws that clearly stipulate the ordinances that govern all liturgical matters (cf. Lev 17–26). Instead, the psalm claims that personal moral integrity is the condition for admission. All the behavior that comprises this moral integrity is conventional social conduct. This includes honesty in speech, living in harmony with others, judicial use of money, careful choice of companions. The character of one's life in community is the criterion for one's liturgical participation.

Psalm 16
(prayer of confidence of an individual)

1b-4 The loyalty of the psalmist

The psalm focuses on the psalmist's loyalty to God. The attributes of the Lord are contrasted with characteristics of "all the false gods of the land." The Lord, to whom alone the psalmist is faithful, is a secure refuge, while the other deities bring frustration and sorrow to their devotees. Using the name of a god in prayer or in making vows and offering blood libations are liturgical practices of tribute. The psalmist will never pay such homage to false gods.

5-6 The Lord is my portion

The Levites, who were responsible for religious ritual, were not assigned land when Joshua allotted territory to the tribes of Israel (cf. Josh 13:7). They were told that the Lord would be their heritage (cf. Deut 10:9), and that they would have to trust in God for their sustenance rather than the work of their hands. Because of the reference to allotted land, some commentators maintain that the psalmist was a Levite. However, the message of the psalm could be calling all Israelites, not just Levites, to trust in God for what they need to survive, and not in the fruits of their labor or in the produce of the land. The psalmist's adherence to God is not intermittent but is intense when there is a need. It is enduring, both in times of prosperity as well as in times of want.

7-11 Trust in God

To bless the Lord is to give praise to God. This should be done even at night, the time of vigil. Having God at one's right hand, the place of honor and importance, is an assurance of protection and blessing. Faithful to God, the psalmist is confident of being preserved from Sheol and of enjoying the blessings that life has to offer.

Psalm 17 (lament of an individual)

1b-8 A prayer for justice

This psalm has several features that characterize the lament. There are the cries for help, a description of the suffering endured, declarations of the psalmist's innocence, a list of the sins of the enemies, and a call for punishment of the wicked. Though the suffering is clearly meted out through the agency of human enemies, the psalmist considers misfortune a test from God, a trial by fire meant to discover the depth of the psalmist's commitment to God. God's covenant love gives the psalmist confidence that God will eventually come to the rescue. Metaphors highlight aspects of the psalmist's confidence. God is characterized as a military deliverer who rescues with a strong right arm, and as a protective bird whose wings guarantee safety and comfort. Perhaps the most tender image suggests God's special devotion to the psalmist: "Keep me as the apple of your eye."

9-14 Attacks of enemies

The psalmist is numbered among the friends of God who have been victimized by heartless enemies. These enemies are like voracious predators, animals that lie ready to devour their prey. Like lions, they are swift and vicious. Though they are certainly a danger to the psalmist, they are no match for God who can easily put an end to the threat that they pose. The psalmist is convinced that God is powerful enough to do this, and is indeed committed to the deliverance of those who are suffering. This conviction is clear in the psalmist's prayer.

15 Claim of innocence

The prayer ends with a declaration of innocence: "I am just." Therefore, "let me see your face." Such intimacy with God is the greatest reward for fidelity.

Psalm 18 (royal psalm)

With only minor variations, this prayer is also found in the mouth of David after he was rescued from the hand of his enemies and from the grasp of Saul (cf. 2 Sam 22). This explains the detailed historical note included in the superscription.

2b-4 Attachment to God

The psalm opens with a description of God's might made up of several literary images: "my strength . . . / my rock, my fortress, my deliverer . . . / my rock of refuge, / my shield, my saving horn, my stronghold." People who prefer the idea of a God of love and peace will be troubled by the military nature of these metaphors. However, when people are overwhelmed by the circumstances of life and they fear that they will not be able to survive, the thought of a powerful God who will overcome such obstacles can comfort and encourage them.

5-7 The threat of death

Death itself and Sheol seek to ensnare the psalmist, who cries out to the Lord enthroned in the heavens. Death is characterized as unruly water, the principal enemy of order in many Near Eastern myths of creation. As is the case in those ancient myths, God hears this cry for help, cancels the threat, and restores order. Since the very life of the psalmist is at risk, God descends from the heavenly throne established when the cosmic battle with chaos had been won, shaking the earth at its very foundations in the descent.

8-20 Cosmic victory over chaos

The destructive force of uncontrolled water so endangered the ancient Israelites that it became a symbol of threatening chaos. That chaos could be personal struggle, social disorder, or cosmic upheaval. This concept was so much a part of the ancient Near Eastern worldview that primeval creation itself was considered the act of reordering after a cosmic battle between the forces of order and those of chaos. Israel appropriated this mythological concept, envisioning its own God in the guise of the triumphant conqueror of chaos. It was their God and no other who rode on the clouds, whose voice was heard in the thunder, and whose arrows were the lightning bolts. It was their God who walked through the waters of the deep, held back the unruly sea, and sent gentle rain to quench the thirst of the earth and all that lived on it. This fearsome God reached into the depths of chaos, thwarted the designs of the enemies, and drew out the imperiled psalmist.

21-46 Reward of the righteous

God acted as deliverer out of commitment to the poor and needy, and because of the righteousness of the psalmist. Clean hands suggest moral integrity, not ritual purity. Turning directly to God, the psalmist acknowledges the justice with which God executes retribution, rewarding the faithful and punishing the wicked, upholding the lowly but humbling the proud. In so many ways God has reversed the fortunes of the righteous and the transgressors. God's superiority above all others is extolled. Praise is given for the way God has made the psalmist sure-footed like a deer, has girded and armed the psalmist like a warrior able to defeat a previously overpowering enemy. In this psalm, it is the psalmist who routs the enemies, punishing them with the sword, granting them no mercy. As is so often the case in laments, retribution is severe and justice is cloaked in the guise of vengeance.

47-51 Praise of God who rescues

The psalm ends as it began, praising God for deliverance, for though it may have been the psalmist who brought justice to those who had attacked without cause, the victory was really God's, for the psalmist would never have been able to succeed or endure without divine assistance.

Psalm 19 (wisdom psalm)

2-7 Praise of creation

The psalm opens with a hymn in praise of some of the heavenly bodies. The poetic construction is extraordinary:

the heavens	declare	the glory of God
the firmament	proclaims	the work of his hands

Creation itself stands in awe of the sun, the chief celestial body without which nothing would exist or have life. Its radiance is compared to a bridegroom who glows with the ecstasy of union with his beloved and an athlete who glistens with mus-

cular exuberance. As it rises in the east and traverses the expanse of the sky, the sun's heat is felt by all. Israel demythologized the ancient Near Eastern belief in the sun as the major god in the pantheon, seeing it simply as a brilliant creature, appointed to its rule of the heavens by the God of the universe.

8-15 Praise of the law

The second part of the psalm praises the law. Tight poetic construction describes this law and highlights several of its extraordinary features:

law	perfect	refreshing the soul
decree	trustworthy	giving wisdom to the simple
precepts	right	rejoicing the heart
command	clear	enlightening the eye
fear	pure	enduring forever
statutes	true	all of them just

It is clear that the psalmist considers the law a treasure rather than a restriction, as many people erroneously perceive it today. It is more precious than gold and sweeter than honey. In true wisdom fashion, the psalmist affirms the importance of learning from the law and following its direction in order to be rewarded in the end. Acknowledging human weakness, the psalmist prays to be preserved from serious sin. Only with God's help will this be possible; the Lord is the sure rock on which the psalmist depends.

The relationship between the two distinct parts of this psalm should be noted. The psalmist parallels the grandeur of the sun and the prominence of the law. Each is appointed by God to ensure order and well-being. Just as human beings would be fools to attempt to undermine the order within the universe, so they would be foolish to challenge the order established by the law. In other words, the very structure of the psalm gives cosmic legitimation to the law, and those who pray the psalm will perceive this and will stand in awe of both the sun and the law.

Psalm 20 (royal psalm)

1-6 A royal liturgy

The psalm contains both liturgical and royal references. The first category includes the temple:

Zion (the city of the king and the location of the temple), offering, holocaust, and prayer. The second category includes the anointed of the Lord and the king. Taken together, these two categories suggest that the psalm was used during some kind of royal liturgy. The king is addressed in the first part of the psalm. In the second part, the psalmist speaks to an unnamed assembly. Only the very last verse of the psalm is an actual prayer. Initially the king is under siege, and God is called on to come to the rescue. The king has fulfilled his duty in offering the appropriate prayers and sacrifice. He has only to wait for God's response.

7-10 Victory comes from God
The second part of the psalm indicates that God did indeed respond to the king's prayer, and granted victory to him. It is important to note that this victory is given to the king as a gift from God; he did not win it himself. Israel's royal theology clearly insists on the king's dependence on God. While other nations rely on the armaments of war and, as a consequence, are defeated, Israel relies on the name of the Lord and is ultimately triumphant. Finally, it is not only the king who prays to God. All of the people pray to God in the king's name.

Psalm 21 (royal psalm)

2-8 God's relationship with the king
This psalm continues the sentiments of Psalm 20. Addressing God, the psalmist declares that the victory in which the king rejoices was really given to him by God. The king prayed to God, and his prayer was heard. Not only is victory credited to God, but kingship itself is seen as a divine gift. God is the one who raised the king to the throne, placed a crown on his head, and conferred the royal attributes of majesty and splendor upon him. The king owes everything to God. The divine favor shown him flows from covenant love.

9-13 The king's victory
The psalmist next addresses the king. Although the victory is God's, the king does not stand by idly as God conquers the enemies. Rather, the king is the agent through whom God acts and vanquishes. In the description of the battle, the psalmist does not minimize the brutality of war. The comprehensiveness of slaughter, particularly

of the enemy's offspring, may offend contemporary readers. However, the psalm implies that this was a war of defense, not of aggression. Furthermore, without exonerating butchery, we must remember that ancient warfare usually included total destruction. This was a safeguard against any possible regrouping by the enemy, which would have posed a threat for the future.

14 A prayer to God
The psalm ends with a prayer that God might rise up again in all of the power and might of a military defender. When this happens, all the people will respond in praise.

Psalm 22 (lament of an individual)
2-6 The haunting cry of agony
The anguish expressed in this psalm is heartrending, bursting forth from a sense of abandonment: "My God, my God, why . . . / Why?" Day and night the psalmist cries out, and there is no relief. God is depicted in ways that should inspire hope, but they do not. The first picture is of the supreme deity who, enthroned as the Holy One, rules over both heaven and earth. Since this is the picture of the conqueror of cosmic chaos, such a God has the power to rescue the psalmist from this distress. But God does not. The second depiction envisions the glory of Israel, the God who heard the cries of the enslaved ancestors and drew them out of Egyptian bondage. God led them through the wilderness and fed them there, and then brought them successfully and safely into the land of promise. Certainly this God will save the psalmist. But God does not. The psalmist trusts in God's special affection for the chosen people, just as the ancestors did. Their prayer was heard, but the psalmist's prayer is not.

7-12 Human frailty
Affliction has stripped the psalmist of human dignity and has left the sufferer writhing in the dirt like a worm. It is probably the sight of this degradation that elicits scorn from onlookers. The description of their faces distorted in mockery is striking. Their cruel words cut the psalmist to the core. It is not only the suffering that they ridicule, but the psalmist's reliance on God during that suffering. Why should they offer relief to this pathetic individual when not even God seems

willing to do so? Hoping to evoke even a shred of divine compassion, the psalmist recalls the care that God showed in the past. Birth imagery represents the psalmist's vulnerability and total dependence on God as well as the intimate character of the bond that unites them, even though God seems to have disregarded this relationship. The psalmist pleads again for divine protection in the face of utter desolation.

13-22 The vicious attack

Attention turns to the psalmist's suffering. Animal imagery captures the ferocious nature of the enemies. The psalmist is no match for their savagery. Bashan, a powerful and populous nation east of the Jordan River, was defeated by the Israelites as they advanced toward the land of promise (cf. Deut 3:1-11). The psalmist's attackers are compared to bulls from that barbarous nation. Dynamic verbs describe the psalmist's physical deterioration: "drains away . . . are disjointed . . . melts away. . . ." Witnessing this diminishment, the enemies are in no way moved to pity. Where is God while all this happens? God is either very far away or totally unconcerned. Undeterred by this torment, the psalmist turns again to God and pleads for deliverance from almost certain death, which is characterized variously as the sword, the teeth of the dog, the lion's mouth, and the horns of the wild bull.

23-27 Confidence in God

As is frequently the case in laments, the sentiments of the prayer take a dramatic turn. Gone is the lament itself and in its place are expressions of confidence and thanksgiving. This may seem incongruous, unless we can appreciate the extent of the psalmist's confidence. So sure of deliverance, the psalmist thanks God in advance. The section opens with a promise to praise God for this deliverance. Such tribute will take place within the community so that God's saving goodness will be known to all. The psalmist's restoration will be evidence that God does indeed hear and answer the prayers of the poor.

28-32 Praise of God who rescues

Praise of God extends beyond the assembly of believers to the entire world. All will worship the God of Israel, because this God is the ruler of all. God's rule extends over both the living and the dead. God's sovereignty over the dead is a relatively new concept for the Israelites who believed that there was no worship of God in Sheol (cf. Ps 6:6). (This new concept has led some to view this as a late psalm, perhaps postexilic.) The psalmist makes a further promise, to serve the Lord and to ensure that generation after generation will do the same. It is clear why the early Christians would have employed images from this psalm to describe the passion of Jesus (cf. Matt 27:35-46).

Psalm 23
(prayer of confidence of an individual)

1b-4 The Lord is my shepherd

The psalmist's confidence rests in the experience of God's loving concern. In light of this concern, God is characterized by two moving metaphors, namely, the shepherd and the host. As a shepherd, God finds pasturage for grazing and water to quench the thirst of the flock. God is concerned with the sheep that stray or are lost and guards the flock from predators and dangers of any kind. This shepherd attends to both the physical needs of the sheep and to the soul. God's guidance is more than provident; it is also moral. God leads along the paths of righteousness. Darkness, whether a reference to the darkest part of the terrain, to personal gloom, or to death itself, does not instill fear in the psalmist, for the presence of the Lord is reassuring.

5-6 The Lord is my host

The second image is of a host who prepares a lavish banquet for guests. The strict Near Eastern code of hospitality obliged hosts to provide the very best provisions for guests, even those who might be enemies. The Lord spreads out such a banquet here. The feast affords not only nourishment but also a public witness to God's high regard for the psalmist. The psalmist has been under the loving guidance of the Lord and will remain there forever.

Psalm 24 (liturgical hymn)

1b-2 God is creator

The psalm opens with a statement claiming divine dominion over all creation. This clearly contradicts any idea of autonomous human jurisdiction stemming from an erroneous interpretation of the Genesis creation account (cf. Gen 1:26-28). The earth and everything that is in it belong to the Lord, and not to humankind. This is because the Lord made everything. The description of creation reflects the ancient Near Eastern concept of victory over chaotic waters (cf. Ps 18).

3-6 Criteria for access to the temple

The second part of the psalm is remarkably similar to Psalm 15. It opens with a question concerning the requirement for access to the place of worship.

who	may go up	to the mountain of the Lord?
who	can stand	in his holy place?

Here too Israel's stringent purity code (cf. Lev 17–26) is set aside in favor of personal moral integrity. Proper social behavior and exclusive devotion to the God of Israel summarize the requirements for admission to the place of worship. This behavior and devotion also summarize the requirements for obedience to the law.

7-10 Entrance ritual

The entrance ritual consists of a liturgical dialogue. A request for entrance is made by pilgrims who, led by the king of glory, approach the gates of the holy city. The attendants guarding the city inquire as to the identity of this king. The people respond that the king is the divine warrior, the cosmic champion who created the world. A second time they request entrance; a second time identity is demanded; a second time identity is given.

Psalm 25 (wisdom poem)

Though is it not evident in translation, this psalm follows the acrostic pattern. Adherence to this pattern often produces a poem that lacks thematic consistency or development and, consequently, is difficult to categorize. Some commentators consider this psalm a prayer of confidence, others list it as a lament. It is considered a wisdom psalm here because of its instructional character and its acrostic pattern. The pattern itself suggests that the psalm contains everything one needs to know about the matter at hand.

1b-7 Trust in God

The psalm opens with sentiments of trust. The psalmist fears being shamed before others. Honor and shame played very significant roles in ancient Israel, as they do in many community-based cultures today. These qualities, more than economic station or political status, determined one's position in society. A life without honor was not worth living. For the psalmist, honor is born of a life lived in fidelity to God. The wisdom tradition teaches that one must choose between two ways of life, the way of wisdom and the way of folly. The psalmist first prays to be shown the way of wisdom, the way of the Lord, and then appeals to God's covenant love and compassion. Compassion comes from the Hebrew word for "womb" and designates the love a mother has for her child. Here it signifies the intimacy of the covenant bond that unites God and the people.

8-15 The guidance of God

Perhaps the most significant wisdom concept is fear of the Lord. It is an attitude of awe and reverence that one should have toward God. While it does indeed include a measure of trepidation, it is more a stance of respect than one of terror. Wisdom teaching can be identified through some of its specific vocabulary. Standard wisdom words or phrases include: good and upright, guides rightly, the way, teaches, paths, and counsel. Here the teaching includes covenant themes as well, such as faithful love and covenant demands. The point of the teaching is clear: the way of wisdom is the way of covenant fidelity. The theory of retribution, which states that good is rewarded and evil is punished, is also part of wisdom teaching. Those who follow the path of wisdom will "abide in prosperity."

16-22 Prayers for deliverance

The psalm concludes with multiple pleas for deliverance. Though the psalmist suffers at the hands of enemies, there is an admission of guilt here. These circumstances suggest that the psalmist probably considers the enemies as agents of God's retribution. Despite the cry of lament, the psalmist still trusts that God will eventually intervene. The final verse fits neither the specific character of the psalm itself nor its acrostic pattern. Though the focus of the psalm has been on the rescue of an individual, this verse is a prayer for the deliverance of the entire nation.

Psalm 26 (lament of an individual)

1b-5 A cry for justice

The psalmist claims to have lived a blameless life, to have trusted in God, and to have remained faithful to God's covenant love. The psalmist is certain of being found innocent and so invites scrutiny: "Test me . . . / search my heart and mind." There is neither culpability for personal transgression nor guilt by association, for this person has diligently avoided associating with anyone involved in questionable behavior.

6-8 Liturgical practices

Washing hands was a common ceremonial act symbolizing purity. However, since worship frequently included animal sacrifice or the offering of grains and incense, hand washing was also necessary for hygienic reasons. Besides the washing of hands, walking around the altar and lifting one's hands in prayer were also liturgical practices. In addition to this, singing praise to God is a part of the worship of most peoples. Finally, the psalmist is attached to the temple itself, for it was considered God's dwelling place on earth.

9-11 A prayer to be spared

Following these assertions of innocence and fidelity, the psalmist cries out to God to be spared the fate of sinners. The assertions may have been meant to remind God of the psalmist's righteousness, a righteousness that God could not overlook, but would reward with deliverance. The enemies are guilty and deserve the retribution of God; the psalmist is guiltless and deserves God's good favor. The lament ends with a final declaration of innocence and a promise to praise God in the assembly of the people. To stand on level ground means to be firm in one's position, to avoid falling.

Psalm 27
(prayer of confidence of an individual)

1b-3 Confidence in God

The psalmist's confidence is seen in the images employed in describing God. God is the light that casts out fearsome darkness; God is true salvation and protection from all harm; and God is the only refuge for safety. It is obvious why there is no need to be afraid. The enemies are ruthlessly brutal: they seem to eat the psalmist alive; they surround the psalmist like an enemy force ready to do battle. However, they are unable to strike fear in the psalmist's heart, because God is there as the ultimate protection.

4-6 Access to the house of God

Besides the plea for deliverance from enemies and the harm that they might inflict, the psalmist prays for continued access to the house of the Lord, the place where God can be encountered. It is in the temple that prayer and sacrifice are offered and refuge from harm is provided. Secure in the protection of God that the temple affords, the psalmist promises continued devotion.

7-14 Cries for divine protection

The psalm moves from sentiments of confidence in the power and graciousness of God to cries for help in a time of distress. The trust expressed earlier now comes into play. Even if parents close their ears to the cries of their offspring, God will still hear and will answer. The way of the Lord, along which the psalmist seeks to be led, is both the way of wisdom and the way of righteousness. Adhering to that way will keep the psalmist away from the snares of enemies and directed toward the land of the living, the place where the faithful enjoy the blessings of God.

Psalm 28 (lament of an individual)

1b-3 Prayer for deliverance

The psalmist cries out for deliverance from the attacks of enemies. If God does not hear, the psalmist faces a bleak fate. The pit, which is usually a metaphor for death or whatever might lead to death, probably refers here to any serious misfortune. If God does not step in as deliverer, the psalmist faces the possibility of being dragged off to some form of punishment with those who have done wrong. The punishment of the wicked might very well be death or a form of social exclusion, which for community-centered people was a kind of death. If God turns a deaf ear to cries for help, the psalmist might as well be dead.

4-5 Divine punishment of enemies

The evil ones with whom the psalmist does not want to be associated have sinned in both word and deed. They deceived people with words of peace, only to take advantage of them when they were unaware. They have also perpetrated wicked schemes. It is only right that they should be punished for their wickedness, while the innocent psalmist be spared his or her fate.

6-7 Praise of God

Expressions of praise and thanksgiving are included within this prayer of complaint and petition for rescue. Some commentators maintain that the tenor of the prayers suggests that they have already been answered. More likely, confidence that God will hear these pleas leads the psalmist to praise God in anticipation of deliverance. The psalmist's confidence is evident in the characterizations of God. Strength and shield are military metaphors suggesting might and certain protection.

8-9 A prayer for the entire people

At the end of the psalm, the focus turns from the complaints of the individual psalmist to the needs of the community. The king is singled out for special mention because he represents the entire people.

Psalm 29 (hymn)

1b-2 A call to praise God

This hymn is rich in mythological imagery. It begins with a call to praise God. The summons is directed to the sons of God. Israel demythologized such minor deities, demoting them to mere heavenly creatures or angels (cf. Ps 8:6). In their subordinate rank, they are now summoned to praise and bow down in homage to the Lord.

3-9 God is victorious over chaos

The description of God found here reflects ancient Canaanite mythological imagery. Chaos was often characterized as stormy waters, and the deity who was able to control these waters was hailed as the major god. This phenomenal feat is here accomplished by the mere voice of the Lord, not by victory in a cosmic battle. God's thunderous voice is mighty and splendid. It exercises power over the cosmic forces of chaos as well as over the political nations that surround Israel. God's power is depicted in striking imagery. The northern country of Lebanon was known for its

spectacular cedar trees. Sirion was another name for the northern mountain Hermon. These two imposing natural phenomena are characterized as young bulls, the metaphor used to symbolize the strength and prowess of the Canaanite storm god. Here these two wonders cease to inspire awe and are under the control of Israel's god. Most commentators maintain that the Kadesh mentioned in this psalm is the Hittite capital located about eighty miles north of Damascus (cf. 2 Sam 24:6), not the city of the same name located in the southern Negeb Desert. Here too the voice of the Lord demonstrates astounding power. In the face of this divine strength and authority, the heavenly beings all exclaim: "Glory!"

10-11 God rules from on high

The final scene in the psalm is of the majestic divine ruler enthroned above the now subservient waters. From there the Lord reigns over all forever. The psalmist prays that from that awe-inspiring position the Lord will grant peace to the people of Israel.

Psalm 30
(prayer of thanksgiving of an individual)

2-4 A prayer of thanksgiving

The psalm itself contains no mention of the event identified in the superscription. Instead, it is a prayer of thanksgiving to God for deliverance from enemies. Having been cast down by some misfortune, referred to as Sheol, the psalmist is lifted out of it by God.

5-6 An invitation to praise God

In the face of this rescue, the psalmist invites others to praise God. The reversal of fortune is depicted in two major ways: temporary divine anger is replaced by everlasting divine favor; weeping at night, a time of darkness and fear, gives way to rejoicing at dawn, a time of new hope and promise.

7-13 God's blessings in the past

The psalmist reflects on past experience with God. In previous times of good fortune, the psalmist foolishly presumed that nothing would disturb that peace. Everything changed, however, with the sensation that God no longer looked with favor on the psalmist. Complacency was turned to terror, and the psalmist once again cried out to God for help. Lifeblood, grave, and dust reveal Israel's concept of the impossibility of an enduring relationship with God after death. At this point in its history, Israel viewed God as the God of the living, but not of the dead. Therefore, there was no way for the dead to continue to praise God. The psalmist uses this understanding as grounds for encouraging God to look kindly on the psalmist's request. This devoted person would be able to offer praise to God only if alive. The end of the psalm includes sentiments of thanksgiving. This gratitude is for the reversal of fortunes: the grief of mourning is replaced by the joy of dancing; the penitential garb of sackcloth is exchanged for attire that expresses gladness.

Psalm 31 (lament of an individual)

2-5 Cries for help

The psalmist cries out to God with a fourfold plea. "[I]ncline your ear" implores God to be attentive in any situation; "deliver" and "rescue" suggest that the psalmist is already afflicted with some kind of misfortune; "let me never be put to shame" asks for protection against dishonor in the future as well as the present. This last plea addresses the psalmist's social status. To be shamed is to lose one's acceptability in the group, a bitter sentence for members of a community-based society. "[R]ock . . . stronghold . . . fortress" characterize God as a sure source of refuge. One's name contains part of the very essence of the person. To call on God's name is to call on God's strength. The psalmist argues that God's protection and guidance will give witness to God's goodness and will enhance the reputation of God's name in the world. Enemies have laid a net, demonstrating the vulnerability of the psalmist and emphasizing the need for God's intervention.

6-9 Trust in God

In the midst of distress, the psalmist exclaims in utter confidence: "Into your hands I commend my spirit" (cf. Luke 23:46). Spirit can also be translated "breath." What is being handed over to God is the psalmist's very life. "Faithful" and "love" are words associated with the covenant. The psalmist's confidence in God's deliverance is rooted in the strength of that intimate bond estab-

lished by God. Others may serve false gods, but the psalmist has chosen the Lord and has remained loyal to that commitment.

10-14 A second cry to God

Another prayer for help is followed by a description of the distress that gave birth to the cry. The misfortune has cut to the very core of the psalmist's being. The grieving has wasted away all of the psalmist's strength. Whether the affliction has been physical or emotional, other people are repelled by it, and they actually avoid the despairing and pitiful individual. The psalmist is forgotten, forsaken, and broken. The whispering could be evidence of genuine conspiracy or a sign of paranoia. Whichever the case, the psalmist feels victimized and turns to God for comfort.

15-19 Expressions of trust

This second complaint is followed by sentiments of confidence, which contain a profession of faith and commitment: "You are my God." Psalms of lament often include not only a plea for one's own rescue but also a prayer for the punishment of those who constitute a threat or are actually guilty of assault. What the psalmist asks for is justice, not hateful revenge. Because of the covenant bond, whoever threatens the safety or good fortune of the psalmist will have to answer to God, who is the partner in this mutual relationship. Since there is no admission of guilt here, one can safely presume that any attack from the outside is unjustified. The enemies are in fact identified as being "wicked" (v. 18b). Their attacks are verbal and false, filled with contempt and scorn.

20-25 Words of praise

The psalmist extols divine goodness manifested in the way God protects those who have been loyal. In a lament, such praise demonstrates the afflicted one's recognition of God's power and goodness as already shown in other circumstances, and it indirectly indicates the way the psalmist hopes God will act in this particular situation. God has indeed acted out of covenant love and has rescued the one who has suffered so much. These sentiments suggest that God's rescue has actually taken place. However, they might simply flow from the psalmist's profound conviction that they will certainly take place in the near future. Overwhelmed by these sentiments, the psalmist encourages others to place their trust in the Lord who will hear their pleas and will come to their aid as well.

Psalm 32 (wisdom psalm; penitential)

1b-2 Happy those who choose the right path

The psalm opens with a double beatitude. It describes how God comes to the aid of those who trust in God. The first person described is a repentant sinner; the second is someone free from guilt. Since the blessedness of both individuals is held up as desirable, the paths that they choose, namely, repentance and righteousness, are advanced as paths to be followed.

3-7 The rewards of following God

The psalmist appears to be a repentant sinner, initially slow in acknowledging guilt. The consequences of sin are graphically depicted: wasting away, groaning, and withering day and night. There is no relief until guilt is admitted and reconciliation with God is sought. The admission of guilt and repentance prompted the church to set this psalm aside as one of seven penitential psalms (cf. Pss 6, 38, 51, 102, 130, 143). The psalmist offers this personal vignette for the instruction of others. Flood waters are a metaphor for chaos or danger. If the faithful turn to God in their need, they will not be overcome by them. God is the true refuge in the face of any threat.

8-11 The instruction

Though the instructional character of the psalm is obvious, it is not clear whether the instructor is God or the psalmist. This instruction includes an exhortation to be a docile student rather than one who is ornery or senseless like dumb and belligerent animals that have to be controlled in a forceful manner. The opposing ways of the wicked and of the righteous are compared. The path of the wicked leads to sorrow, while those on the second path enjoy the blessings of covenant love. The psalm ends with a threefold summons to the righteous: "Be glad . . . rejoice . . . exult." Such uplifting encouragement further suggests that the prayer will be answered.

Psalm 33 (hymn)

1-5 A call to praise God

This psalm is directed toward an assembly of people rather than toward God. The designations "righteous" and "upright" may be stereotypical ways of referring to believers, and not specific judgments of their moral character. Several references to musical instruments and singing suggest a liturgical context.

6-7 The creative power of God's word

The creative word of God is acclaimed. The spoken word has power and the more powerful the speaker, the more powerfully creative the words. God's word exercises cosmic power. The hosts of heaven are mythological heavenly armies, minor deities that fight the cosmic battles of warring gods. The psalm demythologizes these heavenly bodies and claims that they are simply creatures of God, brought into being by God's powerful word. In many ancient Near Eastern myths, the waters of the sea were depicted as chaotic monsters of the deep. Here, they too are merely creatures that are controlled by the mighty word of God.

8-12 God governs human affairs

Attention turns from natural creation to human society. A call to praise God is issued to all the nations. Fear of the Lord is an attitude of reverence shown to God, rather than terror experienced in God's presence. A poetic parallel construction demonstrates this:

all the earth	fear the LORD
all who dwell in the world	show him reverence

The performative power of God's word elicits reverence. The word that called forth the order and splendor of the universe is the same word that influences the course of human history. To say that the God of Israel governs the fate of other nations is to make a bold claim. It means either that God has usurped the power of other gods, or that there really are no other gods and so God has jurisdiction over all.

13-19 God rules from the heavens

In many ancient Near Eastern creation myths, a palace for the god who won the conflict against cosmic chaos is established in the heavens. From there, the victor rules over all creation. This mythic scene is the background for the reference of the Lord ruling from a heavenly throne and looking down on all who live on earth. The psalmist insists that no form of military strategy or weaponry can guarantee the success that trust in God is able to achieve. Only God can save one from the threats of death, and so attachment to God is the only sure defense.

20-22 Trust in God

The final verses of the psalm move from the earlier personal testimony to a direct prayer to God. After describing God's power in such moving terms, the psalmist praises and declares loyalty to God. Trust in God is rooted in God's own kindness or covenant love.

Psalm 34 (wisdom psalm)

Although the entire psalm is in an acrostic form, only the final section contains clear wisdom instruction.

2-4 A declaration of praise of God

The psalmist is overwhelmed with praise of God and promises to "bless . . . praise . . . glory in . . . Magnify" the Lord. Furthermore, such exuberance will be ongoing, "at all times . . . always." Besides giving homage to God, this devotion will give encouragement to others who are needy. The first part of the psalm ends with an invitation to these others to join the psalmist in praising God.

5-8 God is the deliverer

The psalmist has been delivered from distress. There does not seem to be any external cause of this trouble; no enemies are mentioned. Perhaps the suffering was something personal, some great inner turmoil. Whatever it may have been, the psalmist cried to God, and God heard the prayer and answered it. This fortunate consequence of turning to God for help can now encourage others suffering misfortune to act in like manner. "[A]ngel of the LORD" is an expression that signifies the presence of God. Appearing quite often in early texts (cf. Gen 31:11-13), it was a way of referring to God's undeniable presence in a manner that was somewhat concrete yet still other-worldly. There is not some other being active here; it is really God who delivers those who stand in awe and with reverence.

9-23 Instruction

Explicit instruction is found in the last part of the psalm: "Taste and see that the LORD is good" (v. 9). Fear of the Lord is *the* classic wisdom exhortation. The psalmist's experience serves as evidence that God does indeed hear the cry of the righteous, while the powerful (the Hebrew has "fierce young lions") are stripped of what strength they might possess. This theory of retribution is another characteristic of wisdom teaching: the good or wise enjoy happiness, while misfortune is the lot of the wicked or foolish.

The psalmist assumes the role of the teacher: "listen to me." (Though some translations have "children," the Hebrew has "sons," evidence of the gender bias in many patriarchal societies, such as was Israel.) Those who genuinely fear the Lord and live with integrity will enjoy the blessings of a long and prosperous life. God will hear their cries and will rescue them from danger. The psalm shows God as particularly committed to the needy, to those who are brokenhearted and crushed in spirit. Here they appear to be synonymous with the persecuted just ones. God's care might be an example of the requisite reward for righteousness, or it might reflect God's predilection for the needy. Whichever the case, God's provident care is unflinching. The psalm ends with assurances that the perpetrators of evil will be punished for their sin, while those who cling faithfully to God will be generously rewarded. The experience of the psalmist recounted at the beginning of the psalm is evidence of this. The experience here acts as an incentive to others to commit themselves to the Lord.

Psalm 35 (lament of an individual)

1b-3 A cry for redress

The psalmist is suffering opposition from enemies, is in need of protection from their assaults, and is being pursued by them in order to be shamed. Rather than launch a counterattack against these aggressors, the psalmist turns to God for assistance and refuge. God's protection is described in military terms, God's defense is depicted as fierce weapons of war: shield and buckler, lance and battle-ax. This characterization, distasteful to contemporary people who envision a God of peace, is probably reassuring to people of any period of time or religious persuasion who are under siege and who, in desperation, turn to God for help. God is asked to act not only as military defender but also as the protector of the psalmist's social status. Shame would accompany defeat, and the loss of honor is sometimes more devastating than the defeat itself. The psalmist asks for redress in the face of such opposition, not for hateful revenge.

4-6 Thwart the evil plans

The psalmist prays that the plans of the enemies be frustrated and that the enemies themselves be as ineffective as worthless chaff that poses no threat but is blown away by the wind. "[A]ngel of the LORD" is probably a reference to God (cf. Ps 34:8). Consistent with the military tone of the psalm, this angel probably belongs to the hosts of heaven, the heavenly army of God that is called on to war against the forces of evil.

7-21 Sins of the wicked

The devious plans of the enemies are laid bare, and the psalmist prays that they themselves become the victims of the ruin they planned for others. What makes their schemes so treacherous is that they sought to inflict them on the psalmist without cause. In fact, the psalmist is being attacked for having been righteous, for having performed acts of devotion on their behalf. The affliction described here is neither tribal nor national conflict. It consists of personal attacks by people who were close companions of the psalmist, and they are personal attacks without cause. God does not seem to hear the cries of the psalmist or respond with deliverance, but the psalmist continues to hope. When God eventually does come to the rescue, the psalmist promises to proclaim publicly the news of God's favor.

22-26 The cry of the innocent

The psalmist complains again to God about the heartless behavior of the enemies. They register false accusations. They repay evil for good. They rejoice over the psalmist's misadventure. The psalmist is clearly oppressed by them, and for no expressed reason. This is an innocent victim, and to seek redress is really a search for jus-

tice, not revenge. Turn the tables on them; reverse their fortunes. Put them to shame instead of allowing them to shame the psalmist. Their assaults against an innocent individual make them guilty of sin. Punish them!

27-28 A prayer for the righteous

The psalm ends with a prayer for those who have been supportive of the psalmist. Since they stood in solidarity with the innocence of this beleaguered individual, they deserve to rejoice in the deliverance that God saw fit to grant. As reward, they are invited to join in the psalmist's praise of God.

Psalm 36 (lament of an individual)

2-5 Behavior of the wicked

This psalm is difficult to categorize. Although it describes the behavior of the wicked, there is no soul-wrenching cry from out of the depths of suffering. However, the psalmist does pray for protection from the evil schemes of the wicked and for the just punishment that they deserve because of their schemes. There is a strong wisdom tone to both the criticism of the wicked and the praise of the goodness of God, prompting some commentators to place the psalm in the category of wisdom.

The people of ancient Israel believed that each individual was subject to two fundamental propensities, the inclination toward good and the inclination toward evil. The psalmist claims that the inclination toward evil has invaded the very heart of the sinner, spawning delusion, deception, and mischief of every kind. The wicked choose the path of evil rather than the path of righteousness, and everything along that path is tainted by sin.

6-8 Covenant love

The psalmist contrasts the motivating principle of the wicked with that of the righteous. While the former is governed by sin, the latter entertains a certain fear of God. The divine characteristics that the psalmist acclaims are associated with the covenant: love, which is thought to be steadfast love; fidelity, which is unwavering truth; justice, which is the standard of integrity; judgment, which is a just ordinance. These divine attributes govern the entire world: the heavens, the home of God; the clouds, formerly considered the garments of the storm god; the high mountains, the place where gods dwelt on earth; and the deep waters, thought to be a chaotic threat to the order of creation. The God who established a covenant with Israel is the very God who conquered all the forces of evil. Surely the evil that is perpetrated by wicked individuals is no match for the power of this God, and those who have chosen to be in covenant relationship with God can rest assured in divine protective care. The sheltering wings of God call to mind the image of a bird protecting its young.

9-13 God protects and nourishes

God nourishes the righteous, feeding them and providing them with life-giving waters to drink. In fact, God is the very source of life and of light. The psalmist prays to remain within the embrace of God's covenant love and to be safeguarded from the evil stratagems of the wicked, who will ultimately be brought to the tribunal of divine justice, there to answer for their sinful ways.

Psalm 37 (wisdom psalm)

1-40 Contrast between the fate of the wicked and that of the just

This psalm is an acrostic, though the alphabetic pattern is not rigorously followed. The psalm is actually a collection of discrete proverbs, each one able to stand alone on its own merits. On occasion the idea in one verse seems to be developed in the next, but this is not usually the case. It is very difficult to hold rigorously to the development of a particular theme or themes when one is constrained by this kind of alphabetic structure. Some of the proverbs found here are in the imperative form, giving explicit counsel. Others are written as declarative descriptions, succinctly capturing the consequences of acting in either a wise or a foolish manner.

The righteous are told not to envy the good fortune of the wicked. This good fortune may be conspicuous now, but eventually it will disappear. Wisdom teachers frequently employ illustrations from the natural world to exemplify the points they are making. A popular metaphor capitalizes on the short duration of life. Grass may be vibrant and lush for a time, but it quickly fades and withers. Such is the fate of the wicked. They may enjoy a certain degree of prosperity and contentment, but ultimately the consequences of their mischief will catch up with them.

The righteous are instructed to trust in the Lord and to find their delight there instead. In time, they will indeed be vindicated. The need for vindication (being cleared of the suspicion of wrongdoing) implies that the circumstances of their lives are not commensurate with the decency with which they live them. Rather, using only the theory of retribution (the good are rewarded, and the wicked are punished) as a guide, one might conclude that they were being punished for some transgression. This theory might serve well as a principle for encouraging social order, but it does not always describe the actual circumstances of life. Righteous people are often oppressed and suffer want, and at times it appears that crime does indeed pay. The wisdom tradition insists, however, that in the end, the justice of God will prevail.

In addition to describing the lives and fates of the righteous as diametrically opposed to those of the wicked, this psalm asserts that the righteous are frequently assaulted by the wicked. It further insists that even when this happens, the oppression will be of short duration. Since the righteous have committed themselves to God, God will be their refuge in such times of distress. The righteous may not be perfect, but they are not destined to the same kind of punishment that awaits the hardened sinner. Their goodness assures them of eventual blessing. Sinners are enjoined to turn from their evil ways. If they do repent and reform their lives, they too will be counted among the faithful and will deserve to enjoy the blessings of the Lord.

The importance of the land and the prosperity that it promised was never far from the mind of the ancient Israelite. Land, particularly the land that they believed was promised to their ancestors, gave the people meaning, security, and the resources needed for survival. Considered a gift from God in fulfillment of a divine promise, its possession was dependent on the people's fidelity to the will of God. The psalmist points to the land as *the* fundamental blessing bestowed as reward for living a righteous life.

The pedagogical technique of the wisdom teacher is frequently indirect. Following this method, a circumstance of life is described in such a way as to make it either desirable or repugnant.

The character of the circumstance encourages the student to either choose or reject the particular path that led to such consequences. The righteous, who speak words of wisdom and who in their hearts hold to the teaching of God, do not falter. As a consequence, if such stability is attractive, the path of wisdom will be chosen. Thus, what is described becomes an exhortation to action.

Psalm 38
(lament of an individual; penitential)

2-10 The suffering endured

The psalm opens with the standard cry to God for help, a prayer that suffering will be brought to an end. The psalm demonstrates ancient Israel's belief that sickness is the consequence of sin. This is the theory of retribution read backward (if evil is punished with suffering, then suffering is the consequence of sin). The description of the psalmist's suffering is graphic: afflicted flesh, aching frame, festering sores, stooped and bowed, fever. All of these afflictions are seen as the consequences of personal iniquity. Whether this is a description of actual physical ailment or a metaphorical characterization of some other kind of affliction, suffering itself is associated with guilt, and the affliction is perceived as chastisement from God for some transgression. Physical suffering is not the only affliction endured by the pathetic individual. The anger of God has cut the psalmist to the heart, and there is deep inner anguish as well.

12-15 Deserted by friends

As if bitter suffering was not enough, the afflicted one is abandoned by others just when the support of friends and family is needed the most. This might be the result of the repulsion that many people experience at the sight of human suffering, or it could stem from the belief that suffering was brought on by the individual's own sinfulness, and in such circumstances offering comfort would be inappropriate. Add to this the treachery devised by enemies, and it appears that the entire world has conspired against the psalmist. In the face of such compounded misfortune, the psalmist is bereft of resources needed to cope, stripped even of the powers of sense. This poor person is battered by others, broken by life, and forsaken by all.

16 Only in God is there help

Helpless, the psalmist turns to the Lord. It is this religious attitude of dependence on God in the face of affliction, not merely the frightful afflictions themselves, that prompted the church to rank this psalm with the other penitential psalms (cf. Pss 6, 32, 51, 102, 130, 143). Here, the expression of trust that is often found in laments is clearly stated: "it is for you that I wait." The psalmist is confident of being heard, but also willing to wait patiently for God's response.

17-23 Repentance

As is so often the case, there are unscrupulous people ready at hand to take advantage of others when they are down. They gloat over another's misfortune. Sometimes they even lay traps for the unwary. The psalmist had to face this hurdle as well. There was nowhere to turn, no one to offer refuge or solace—except God. Acknowledging guilt and grieving over sin, in the end the psalmist prays that God will intervene and will provide the saving help that comes only from God.

Psalm 39 (lament of an individual)

2-4 The need to speak

This lament contains some interesting parallels with the message found in other biblical books. It opens with the psalmist pledging to refrain from speech, yet ultimately being unable to contain the inner sorrow that demands expression. This recalls a similar experience of the prophet Jeremiah, who resolved never again to speak in God's name. However, the burning in his heart erupted into words (cf. Jer 20:9). The psalmist's concern is not prophetic proclamation, as was the case with Jeremiah, but complaint in the face of overwhelming affliction.

5-9 Life is so short

The transience of life has caused significant regret for people of every age and culture. Human impermanence has been compared to a fleeting breath, a vapor. One's life span (the Hebrew is really "handbreadth") is short, and life itself often seems pointless. (Though the Hebrew in v. 6 here is uncertain, it does include the word that is translated elsewhere as "vanity" or "pointless"; cf. Eccl 1:2). This view of the short duration of life is reminiscent of the perspective found in the book of

Job. He too was saddened by life's fleeting nature (cf. Job 7:6-7; 8:9; 14:1-2). In Job, the ephemeral nature of life is simply another aspect of the burden that human beings seem forced to bear. In this psalm, the realization of life's brevity opens the psalmist's eyes to the insignificance of everything in life except loyal attachment to the Lord.

10-14 Complaint

The actual complaint is found in the final section of the psalm. Here the psalmist explains the earlier attempt to be silent. Since the psalmist was in fact guilty of some transgression, complaining to God or to others about God seemed out of place. Without claiming innocence, the psalmist asks for a reprieve from the suffering. The argument used to persuade God to grant this request is striking. The fleeting nature of life is here compared to a journey, and the psalmist assumes the identity of a resident alien, similar to the situation of the ancestors of old (cf. Gen 23:4). In the earlier tradition, the ancestors were actual sojourners on their way to the land that God had promised them. In the psalm, life itself is characterized as a journey, and the psalmist is a sojourner with God. The psalmist prays that relief be given before life's short journey is over.

Psalm 40
(prayer of thanksgiving of an individual)

2-6 A prayer of thanksgiving

In the first section, the psalmist rejoices in the blessing that came from trusting in the Lord. That blessing is deliverance from some form of tribulation. Whatever the hardship might have been, it is compared to falling into a pit where there is no footing, into a swamp that sucks one deeper and deeper into its slime. Rescue from such adversity is like being lifted out of the quagmire and set securely on firm rock. This rescue prompted the song of thanksgiving and praise. The psalmist hopes that it will also encourage others to trust in the providential care of God. In typical wisdom fashion, the psalmist declares that those who trust in the Lord will be happy. Furthermore, if they trust in God, they will not turn for support to those who choose another and unacceptable path in life. God is praised for all the blessings human beings have been granted, blessings without num-

ber and beyond compare. The psalmist's deliverance is but one example of this divine goodness.

7-11 Commitment to God

Besides prayer, appropriate sacrifice was the standard way of showing gratitude to God for blessings received. By mentioning all four kinds of ritual sacrifice, the psalmist intends to show that no form of sacrifice is required. The return for blessings received is obedience, an obedience that is not merely external observance of social convention or religious practice, but a deep commitment of the heart. Because of the restrictive juridical connotation that law has today, the Hebrew word *Torah* might be better translated as "instruction." The psalmist stands open before God and is intent on conforming to God's will. This personal commitment is coupled with the resolve to announce God's goodness to the assembled congregation. The Hebrew word *qahal* suggests some form of religious gathering. Earlier references to sacrifice support this understanding. Covenant language (enduring kindness) throws light on the character of the relationship between God and the psalmist.

12-18 A cry for rescue

(Verses 14-18 are almost identical to Ps 70.) The tone of the psalm changes from gratitude to a prayer for continued deliverance. Covenant love is followed by a second covenant characteristic: compassion. In Hebrew, this word derives from the same root as does "womb," implying that compassion is related to the attachment that one has toward the child of one's womb or between individuals born of the same womb. Therefore, compassion might be called "womb-love." While appealing to this covenant attachment, the psalmist acknowledges personal guilt. These verses seem to serve as a link between the prayer of thanksgiving and commitment to God and the cry for help.

There is no admission of guilt in the lament itself. The afflicted one appears to be innocent, yet besieged by enemies. Besides pleading for personal rescue and protection, the psalmist prays that, as a penalty for their aggressiveness, these enemies themselves might be put to shame. In contrast to the fate of the wicked, the prayer pleads that those who seek God might be blessed with happiness.

The final verse is made up of a testimony to the care that God has shown the psalmist and a final plea for deliverance. The two parts of this verse seem to contradict each other. The first part implies that deliverance has already been granted; the second part suggests that it has not. Such inconsistency in temporal sequence is not uncommon in biblical poetry. In this case, the final request is consistent with the character of the lament.

Psalm 41
(prayer of thanksgiving of an individual)

This psalm appears to be a composite of various psalm forms. It opens with a beatitude, a form associated with the wisdom tradition. The main body of the psalm contains characteristics of the lament, ending with a cry for mercy and restoration. This is followed by a testimony that suggests the psalmist has indeed been delivered from adversity by God. The psalm ends on a note of praise.

2-4 Blessed of the Lord
The macarism is unusual. It claims that the happy or blessed ones are those who are concerned with the poor and lowly; they are not the poor and lowly themselves. The psalmist proclaims that the Lord will meet the needs of those who are attentive to the needs of others. These needs include prosperity in the land, security from enemies, and healing when afflicted by disease. Such graciousness is an example of how God cares for those who are concerned with the well-being of others.

5-10 Unmerited suffering
The psalmist's prayer to God shows an understanding that physical malady is somehow the consequence of infidelity. The taunting by enemies and the malicious slander that they devise casts a pall over the spirit of the psalmist. The prayer for healing with which this section opens shows that the psalmist is indeed suffering physical distress. The enemies claim that this is proof that the psalmist is guilty of grievous transgression. If this condition is the result of serious sin, the psalmist does not deserve the consolation and support that one might look for in friends. Disloyalty is added to treachery. Stripped of

human solace, the psalmist turns to God for mercy, deliverance, and redress.

11-13 Prayer for mercy
The psalmist speaks directly to God as if having been delivered from the affliction described. The cessation of the enemies' derision shows that God has indeed looked favorably on the psalmist. Admission of sin and expressions of repentance are evidence of the psalmist's fundamental integrity that has called forth God's consideration.

14 Doxology
The final verse is less a part of the psalm itself than it is the conclusion of the entire first collection of psalms (Pss 1–41). It is a doxology praising the God of Israel. It contains none of the specific concerns found in the psalm, and it redirects attention away from the immediacy of God's involvement in human affairs to an undefined openness to the future. This doxology is a fitting prayer to bring to closure this first collection of psalms. Like Psalm 1, it opens with a macarism, thus creating a kind of inclusion.

BOOK TWO: PSALMS 42–72
Psalms 42–43

Psalms 42 and 43 were probably originally one psalm. As was the case with Psalms 9 and 10, there are clues that point to this. The most obvious feature is a repetition of a refrain appearing throughout the verses of both psalms. Furthermore, Psalm 43 is one of the few psalms in this second book that lacks a superscription, suggesting that it is a continuation of the previous psalm. Finally, the two psalms contain many of the same themes.

Psalm 42 (lament of an individual)

Most of the psalms that comprise the first book (Pss 1–41) come from the Davidic collection. Many of the psalms in this second book are from the Korahite collection. Although one of the descendants of Esau was named Korah (cf. Gen 36:5), the reference here is probably to a Levitical priestly family (cf. Num 16:1) that, after the exile, came into prominence in the role of temple choir (cf. 2 Chr 20:19). This could explain why a collection of psalms would be credited to them.

2-5 Longing for God

The psalm is replete with expressions of longing that are characterized as thirst for the Lord. God, the source of life, appears to be absent. This absence is a searing experience, compounded by the mocking challenge of others: "Where is your God?" The psalmist has not always suffered the absence of God. Quite the contrary. In former times the psalmist was part of the throng that went in procession to the temple, probably as part of a pilgrimage festival celebration.

6 The downcast soul

The refrain is a kind of lament directed to the psalmist's own "soul" (vv. 6, 12). There is really no word in Hebrew for "soul." The word used here means "life force." The refrain implies that this life force is stifled by the sense of divine absence. The psalmist self-reflectively counsels trust in God who will eventually act as savior in the psalmist's life.

7-11 Melancholy

Burdened by a state of despondency, the psalmist turns to God, and uses geographic markers to continue the theme of living waters introduced in the first part of the poem. The Jordan River always plays a significant role in the history as well as the theological landscape of Israel. It supplies the land with life-giving water, and thus it became a theological symbol of the source of spiritual life. Hermon is a mountain in southwest Syria, considered the source of the headwaters of the Jordan River. Mount Mizar is a peak in the Hermon range. The waters on which Israel depended for life have become destructive waters for the psalmist (the deep represents waters of chaos; cf. Gen 1:2). The metaphor of chaotic waters is linked with the metaphor of darkness. The psalmist prays that chaotic darkness will give way to the light of covenant love, so that the darkness itself may be transformed.

This second and last section of the psalm is a prayer of lament. Once again the psalmist bemoans the sense of God's absence, especially at a time when enemies seem to have the upper hand and are able freely to torment the psalmist. For a second time they throw the taunt in the face of this tormented individual: "Where is your God?"

12 The refrain

The section ends with the refrain, which here again counsels trust in God.

Psalm 43 (lament of an individual)

1-4 Cries for justice and deliverance

The attacks against the psalmist are unwarranted, since those who pose a threat are judged to be unfaithful and deceitful. Like Psalm 42, this prayer addresses the sense of God's absence. This absence is particularly distressing because in the past God acted as a stronghold, a place of refuge for the psalmist, and now the psalmist feels rejected by God, and the prey of enemies. In the midst of this darkness, the psalmist prays for God's light and truth ("fidelity" is a covenant characteristic). They will act as guides, leading the psalmist to the place where God dwells. Although high mountains were often considered the dwelling places of deities, explicit mention of the altar of God is a clear reference to the temple. This is confirmed by mention of an instrument (the harp), which is often used during ritual celebration.

5 The refrain

The lament concludes with the refrain, which exhorts trust in God just as it did in the previous psalm (cf. 42:6, 12).

Psalm 44 (communal lament)

2-9 God's past favors

The psalmist appeals to the favors that God granted the ancestors of old, specifically at the time of the occupation of the land. It is clear from the story, which has been handed down from generation to generation, that the land was not captured through the military prowess of the people. Rather, it was the hand of God that rooted out the original occupants and planted the Israelites there. This was done in the way a gardener weeds the land and sets plants in place so that they might ripen and thrive. It was the strong right arm of God, the symbol of military force, that defeated those nations and seized their land.

Many people today find such images of God distasteful. The concept of a divine gardener who plants is probably not offensive, but the thought that God uproots one people for the sake of another might be. Certainly the image of a divine warrior is troublesome, especially at a time like ours when wars are accorded religious justification. Both images, however, give confidence to dispossessed and vulnerable people. They assure them that God is committed to their well-being, even if gaining and preserving that well-being might call for extreme measures. People in situations of war could easily become disheartened if they did not believe that God supported their efforts. Such images of God were meant to assure the people that God certainly did support them.

10-17 Present suffering

God may have been attentive to the needs of the ancestors of old, but the people at the time of the psalmist appear to have been bereft of divine protection. They have been defeated in battle and disgraced as a result of it. They feel that God has led them to their death. It is as if they have lost value in the sight of God, who now sells them to the lowest bidder. It is not enough that they must endure these misfortunes, but they must bear the shame of them as well, and in a society where honor and shame significantly influence one's social status, the loss of honor can be more grievous than the loss of life itself.

18-23 Suffering of the innocent

The psalmist insists that the people do not deserve such affliction. They have not forgotten God, and yet God seems to have forgotten them. They have upheld their part of the covenant; they have faithfully walked the path of righteousness. Despite this, God seems to have deserted them and left them in a place of desolation. They have been loyal to God, upheld God's name and have not turned to other gods, yet God has turned away from them. God, who should act as their shepherd, has handed them over to be slaughtered. The complaint is pointed and thrown directly in the face of God.

24-27 A prayer for help

The psalm does not end on a note of complaint, but with prayers of petition. Though the psalmist has just accused God of being the people's tormentor, here God is addressed as the one who can and does aspire to save. The psalmist offers an excuse for God's apparent disinterest. If God has allowed the people to suffer, God has not acted out of malice, but has been asleep, unaware of the plight of these unfortunate ones. Surely God will eventually awake from slumber and come to their aid, for, after all, these are God's chosen people. These are the people toward whom God looks with covenant love. It is to this love that the psalmist appeals for help.

Psalm 45 (royal psalm)

2-6 An extraordinary king

This psalm is like no other. It is directed toward the king and it offers praise to him, rather than to God. The psalmist intends that this oral praise should be as permanent as the written word ("pen of a nimble scribe"). The king is first acclaimed for his attractive appearance and pleasant manner of speech. This is not merely superficial flattery. The people believed that God would only choose for royal rule one who possessed the most appealing human qualities. Beauty and graciousness are two such attributes. Since one of the chief responsibilities of leaders is the protection of those under their jurisdiction, other attributes that one would look for in a king include military prowess in the cause of truth, meekness, and justice.

7-8 Royal dignity

It appears that the king is referred to as God, a feature that has prompted significant discussion as well as occasional emendation of the text. The psalmist is certainly not ascribing divinity to the Israelite king, as many ancient Near Eastern societies did. This reference is most likely an example of exaggerated court language, a way of expressing royal pomp and majesty. (Solomon is said to have been seated on the throne of the Lord [1 Chr 29:23], and the child born to the royal family is called the "God-Hero" [Isa 9:5]). The king's scepter is a symbol of royal rule. This king's rule is one of justice rather than might. Because of his commitment to justice, God has raised him up above all other kings. It is important to note that these extraordinary features are bestowed on the king from God; they are not earned by the king through his own power.

9-10 Royal attire

Although royalty lived lives of conspicuous opulence, the description of the king's garments suggests more than extravagant attire. Myrrh, aloes, and cassia were all aromatic substances that individually created a strong sensual response. One can only image the effect of the mixture of the three scents. The scene that is depicted here is one of extraordinary solemnity. The king is heavily perfumed; stringed instruments entertain; members of the royal harem are in attendance; and a woman adorned in gold stands at the king's right side. Some biblical versions identify her as the queen, but the Hebrew word used here is not the standard word for "queen." Other versions have "princess," but that designation is usually the translation of the Hebrew expression "daughter of the king." The Hebrew word found here is best translated as "consort," a word that carries a strong suggestion of sexual partnership. This translation fits well into the picture of a royal wedding.

11-16 Royal partner

The psalmist turns to the young woman. Kinship ties in patriarchal families are quite strong. They give identity to the individual and they guarantee legal protection and physical security. To sever these ties without serious cause is to place in jeopardy one's very survival. This is precisely the directive given the young woman. She is told to leave her father's house, but she is further told to embrace the house of the king. She is directed to shift her allegiance from one patriarchal household to another. The implication here is a marriage within which her partner will be her "lord" because he is her husband, not because he is the king.

17-18 Royal dynasty

In the final verses of the psalm, the king is assured of the continuation of the dynasty. As he inherited the throne from his ancestors, so his descendants will inherit it from him. The promise of a great name is reminiscent of that same promise made to Abram: "I will make your name great" (Gen 12:2). There is, however, a significant difference. The earlier promise was made to the entire nation; this promise is made exclusively to the royal family.

Psalm 46 (song of Zion)

2-3 The God of the great city

The psalm proclaims the greatness of the city of God. The name Zion refers to two distinct yet intimately related realities. First and foremost, Zion is the mountain on which the city of Jeru-

salem was built (cf. Isa 8:18). The name also refers to Jerusalem itself, the city within which the temple of the Lord was located (cf.1 Kgs 8:1). The plural form of the vocabulary indicates that the psalmist is speaking in the name of a community. God is depicted as the refuge to which these people can turn in times of distress. The upheaval in creation calls to mind the cosmic battle in which God was victorious over the forces of chaos. These mythological allusions lay bare God's unrivaled control and assure the people that they can indeed find safety in this God.

4 The refrain

The refrain is an acclamation of the strength and reliability of God. It continues the military and cosmic themes found in the preceding verses. The Lord, the patronal God of Jacob (a reference to the patriarch himself as well as the people who descended from him), is portrayed as commander of hosts of armies. This is the warrior who defeated cosmic chaos.

5-7 The glorious city

Having praised the triumphant deity, the psalmist next considers Jerusalem. This is not an accurate depiction of the city. Rather, it is one that captures something of the city's deep spiritual essence. Jerusalem is situated on a mountain, not next to a river. The use of the river in this psalm is significant, however, because streams of water are life-giving, both literally and metaphorically. Therefore, describing the city in this way points to its life-giving character. There is biblical evidence that the god who was worshiped in this city before David conquered it was named "Most High" (cf. Gen 14:18-20). Here we see that Jerusalem continued to be the home of "God Most High." What changed was not the divine name of the city's God, but the identity of the God who was worshiped there.

Mythological imagery is employed in describing the defeat of threatening national enemies. The thundering voice of God encompasses those enemies, just as it rolled through the heavens during the primeval cosmic battle.

8 The refrain

Refrains always suggest some kind of liturgical interaction. The content of this refrain is praise of the trustworthy divine warrior.

9-11 Invitation to behold the city

In the final section of the psalm all are invited to observe how God destroys the weapons of war. This armament is worthless before the great God who has conquered cosmic chaos and so there is no need to keep it. The divine oracle calls for an acknowledgment of the exclusive sovereignty of God.

12 The refrain

Once again the refrain acclaims the divine warrior who is the refuge of those who cry for help. The refrain brings the entire psalm to a close.

Psalm 47 (kingship of God)

2-5 In praise of the kingship of God

This psalm extols God's sovereign majesty. "Most High," which originally was the name of the god of the city of Jerusalem (cf. Gen 14:18-20), is here a descriptive title of the God of Israel. God is also identified as king over all the nations of the earth. It was in this capacity that God made Israel victorious on earth and gave it a land to call its own.

6-10 King of heaven and earth

God's rule is described in striking fashion. In ancient myths of creation, after the cosmic battle is won and order is reestablished, a palace is built for the victor. In a ceremony marked by great pomp and splendor, this triumphant warrior ascends the heavenly throne, there to reign absolutely and exclusively over all. This is the scene depicted in the psalm. The Lord is the conquering hero who now rules over all peoples, both the people of Israel and the people of the other nations. The singing, the shouts of joy, and the blasts of the horn (the ceremonial *shofar*) denote a cultic celebration. Not only is God enthroned on high, but all the peoples of the earth rejoice in this fact.

Psalm 48 (song of Zion)

2-3 Acclaim for the city of God

Any praise that is conferred on the city is really praise of God. This city is acclaimed, not because of its beauty, but because it is the dwelling place of God. Religious significance was attributed to various nature locations. Rivers contain life-giving waters; mountains rise above their surroundings. Mount Zion, on which Jerusalem was built, was considered a holy mountain. Because of the excellence of the God who dwelt there, Mount Zion was even considered the highest of all mountains, despite its modest elevation. Zaphon, the sacred mountain of the Canaanite god Baal, was located north of Ugarit in modern-day Syria. The psalmist transfers to Zion all of the glory previously ascribed to Zaphon.

4-8 The city's military strength

A citadel is a fortified dwelling, usually part of a royal complex. It is a bulwark of safety, assuring security to all within it. In this remarkable city, God is that bulwark, more secure than mere stone, striking fear in the hearts of invading armies. Two analogies characterize the terror that such armies might experience. The first is the pain of a woman in labor. This image usually refers to the agony that precedes the birth of someone or something extraordinary. Here, however, the focus is on the terror experienced by the woman as she is suspended between the possibility of death, which is always present during childbirth, and the expectation of new life. The second analogy employs the panic into which one is thrown at the time of shipwreck. Here too one is the victim of forces beyond one's control and is forced to face the possibility of death. If Tarshish was a southern port in ancient Spain, as most commentators maintain, then the treacherous storms referred to arose over the vast Mediterranean Sea. These storms traumatized people who experienced them while at sea.

9 The sight of the city

The reputation of this magnificent city has now been confirmed by firsthand experience: what was heard of is now seen. Though the actual city was certainly fortified, here the cause of its invulnerability was the unqualified power of the God who had chosen to dwell in it. Its real military prowess was the Lord of hosts (armies). The presence of this mighty God acted as a deterrence, striking fear in any invading army and holding it at bay. Should enemies presume to approach this city, they would be confronted by an indomitable force.

10-12 Within the temple

The psalmist speaks directly to God. An assembly within the temple implies a cultic celebration.

God's steadfast love refers to the covenant bond. The ancients believed that a dimension of one's essence was captured in one's name. To say that God's name reaches the ends of the earth is to assert God's omnipresence, and such absolute rule evokes boundless praise. The right hand was considered the powerful hand, the hand with which one held weapons. Mount Zion, here meaning the city of Jerusalem, and all of the other cities in the southern nation of Judah praise the divine majesty pictured in this psalm.

13-15 An invitation to visit the city

Finally, the psalmist invites the people to take inventory of the fortifications of this military stronghold in order to go out and proclaim its magnificence to the next generation. The psalmist is confident that praise of the city of God will lead people to praise the God of the city.

Psalm 49 (wisdom psalm)

2-5 The teacher calls for attention

The psalmist assumes the role of the wisdom teacher and calls all to hear the instruction about to be offered. This lesson is not meant merely for the privileged few. The teachings of wisdom are meant for all people.

Hear this	all you peoples
Give ear	all who inhabit the world

The pedagogical techniques of the wisdom teacher include simple maxims, clever riddles, the manipulation of numbers, various forms of problems for solving, even poems and songs that need to be interpreted.

6-13 It is foolish to envy the wealthy

The wisdom teacher counsels against envy of the wealthy. Their present lives may appear to be blessed, but they will die like everyone else, and besides, "you can't take wealth with you." Though not exactly a refrain, the final verse is very similar to an earlier one. In matters of life and death, human beings are subject to the same natural laws as are the undomesticated beasts (cf. Eccl 3:18-22). What sets them apart is insight into the meaning of life.

14-15 All die

The fate of the wicked is contrasted with that of the righteous. Some of Israel's images of death are quite different from today's. While death certainly meant the ultimate expiration of life, it also included the process of diminishment that frequently unfolded as one approached that final moment. Related to this, just as Sheol was considered the place or state of being of those who were definitively dead, so also it figuratively represented various steps along the path to that final end. The psalmist is probably speaking of death and Sheol in this second and broader sense, a stage of diminishment that could end in ultimate dissolution.

Death is characterized as a shepherd who leads to Sheol those who have chosen a path of foolishness that ends in punishment. On the other hand, the psalmist wisely chose the path that leads to blessing and, consequently, is confident of being preserved from both death and Sheol. In no way does this challenge the fact that ultimately death will overtake us all. Instead, it is a figurative way of portraying the contrasting fates of those who travel the two paths.

16-21 Wealth will not last

The theme of the lesson the sage is teaching is the fleeting nature of material wealth and the folly of placing one's trust in this unreliable resource. Lines of distinction are drawn between the psalmist, who appears to possess limited financial assets, and the psalmist's opponents, who enjoy significant prosperity. At issue is not the wealth itself, but the arrogant and oppressive attitude that frequently accompanies it. The psalmist is intimidated by these prosperous people and does not have the means to ward off this threat. Relying on the principles of the theory of retribution, that goodness will ultimately be rewarded and evil punished, the psalmist calls for continued trust in God rather than in wealth. One cannot use money to bargain with life. Besides, wise and foolish alike leave their wealth behind at death. Judging the value of the pursuits of life from the perspective of death is a common wisdom technique. Since death and the grave are the final destination of all people, it is foolish to waste life amassing treasures.

Psalm 50 (divine oracle)

With this psalm we come upon evidence of a third collection of psalms. Although Asaph is identified as a court official at the time of David, he became significant as the forebear of a group of postexilic temple singers (cf. 1 Chr 16:5-7). This association with cultic celebration could explain why a collection of psalms bears his name. Many commentators classify this psalm as a prophetic exhortation. Although both the prophetic exhortation and the divine oracle contain the words of God, in the first, God's words are delivered through a prophet, while in the second, God communicates directly to the people. This psalm consists of three distinct parts: an introduction to God's speech, a divine oracle of salvation, and a divine oracle of condemnation.

1b-6 The God who speaks

The psalm opens with a threefold identification of the one delivering the oracle: God (singular form), God (plural form), and the ineffable name Yhwh (Lord). God's words are a summons that can be heard from one end of the horizon to the other. As is so often the case in a theophany, God is revealed in the midst of fierce fire (cf. Exod 19:16-19). Heaven and earth alike are called on to witness the justice that God will pass on the people with whom God is in covenant.

7-15 Praise rather than sacrifice

The first oracle opens with an imperative: "Listen!" A similar word, "hear," is the first word of Israel's central call to covenant union: "Hear, O Israel! The Lord is our God, the Lord alone" (Deut 6:4). The word implies not merely listening but also opening oneself to the implications of the words heard on one's life. It is usually a call to some form of transformation. The oracle itself contains a strong rebuke. Despite the good intentions of the worshipers, God finds fault with any attempt to win divine favor through the means of sacrifice. Though Israel did not believe that animal sacrifice appeased divine hunger, as may have been the thinking in other cultures, it still believed that animal sacrifice pleased God. Here God declares: I don't really reject your sacrifices; I just don't need them. God does not seek external observance; what God desires is interior commitment. The oracle concludes with a promise of

blessing if the people follow God's will in this matter.

16-23 Divine rebuke

The oracle of condemnation is also a rebuke. The circumstances here are very different from those already considered. The people who are reproved in this psalm are guilty of explicit transgressions. They claim to be in covenant with God, but their commitment is insincere. They align themselves with sinners and they violate the commandments of God. They are not led to new insight, as was the earlier group. These people are called to judgment. Still, God does not utterly reject them. In the end, they are given an opportunity to change their lives. If they seize this opportunity, they too will enjoy the blessings of salvation.

Psalm 51
(lament of an individual; penitential)

This psalm is classified as one of the penitential psalms (cf. Pss 6, 32, 38, 102, 130, 143).

3-6 A cry for mercy

The opening words are a plaintive cry for mercy. The deliverance sought by the psalmist is from the onus of sin, not from the aggression of vicious enemies. The psalmist appeals to God's goodness and compassion, both characteristics of divine covenant care. There is no attempt to deny fault or escape from personal responsibility. The afflicted one is not ignorant of the evil perpetrated, is not innocently caught in a net set by others. The psalm contains a confession of guilt, and in confessing this guilt, the psalmist makes use of the rich vocabulary of sin: offense, guilt, sin, evil. The punishment is justified. What the psalmist seeks is mercy.

7-10 Personal guilt

The penitent sinner draws on hyperbole to emphasize the heinousness of personal transgression. Sin is a constant companion of this individual; iniquity is almost second nature. The psalmist lives in sin, having been conceived in it and born into it. (This exaggerated language should not be construed as a condemnation of sexual intercourse or a statement of belief in original sin, as some have claimed.) Still, the psalmist does not despair of personal repentance or divine forgiveness. Even lifelong sinners can learn wisdom. However, growth in wisdom will only occur because of the graciousness of God. Acknowledging this, the psalmist pleads: "Cleanse me . . . wash me." Such inner renewal will restore the psalmist to a life at peace with God, a life of joy and gladness.

11-19 Repentance

The psalm is replete with soul-wrenching petition: "Turn away . . . create for me . . . Do not drive me from . . . Restore . . . uphold . . . Rescue." The multiplicity of requests reveals the depth of the desire for restoration, a restoration that will be an example to others of the magnanimous mercy of God. Elements of Israel's sacrificial system are juxtaposed to an interior disposition of repentance. As important as worship may be, God prefers inner compunction. A heart that is contrite and broken is more inclined to be open to the mercy of God than one that is confident of its own righteousness.

20-21 Rebuild the city

The final verses of the psalm introduce a totally new and unrelated theme. Even the psalm form is different from what has preceded it. This is a prayer of petition, not one of lamentation. The fact that it entreats God to rebuild the city of Jerusalem has led many commentators to conclude that it is a postexilic addition to an earlier lament. With this addition, the pleading might be seen as flowing from the anguished guilt of one who endured the destruction of the city and understood that destruction as punishment for the sins of its inhabitants. With Jerusalem's restoration, cultic practices can be resumed, and once again honor and glory can be given to God.

Psalm 52 (prophetic exhortation)

3-6 Condemnation

It is difficult to classify this psalm. However, it resembles the prophetic oracle of doom in its denunciation of sin and its declaration of subsequent punishment. The Hebrew translated "deceitful tongue" suggests an arrogant attitude of self-sufficiency. The wickedness that has provoked the condemnation is deceitful speech (hence the

translation "deceitful tongue"). Though such sinfulness may not directly cause physical harm, it can undermine the social fabric of a community and result in irreparable damage.

7-9 Judgment

Judgment is rendered and the sentence is passed. In consequence of such behavior, the guilty person will experience a reversal of fortune. The one once considered mighty will be brought down, destroyed, snatched from the place of security, and cast out of the land of the living. Ruin will be complete. The righteous will be awestruck at the miserable condition of this once-powerful individual. Their jeers will compound the burden laid upon the guilty one. The mockery is not petty. It is grounded in the condemned person's decision to trust in wealth rather than to take refuge in God. The folly of this decision is now apparent to all.

10-11 Words of confidence

Attention turns from the wicked one and the jeering bystanders to the psalmist. Olive trees thrive in Near Eastern countries. They provide many staples for the people's diet and comforting shade from the fierce sun. Comparing oneself to such a tree implies sturdiness, dependability, and fruitfulness. The psalmist is the opposite of the sinner who has just been judged and sentenced. While the sinner spurns God's protection, the psalmist relies on God's covenant love. Addressing God, the psalmist vows to proclaim to others the certainty of divine judgment as well as the assurance of divine graciousness.

Psalm 53 (wisdom psalm)

This psalm is almost identical to Psalm 14. The superscriptions vary somewhat, and one or two verses use slightly different words to express basically the same idea. The striking difference is in the name used to refer to God. This psalm employs the generic word "God" (*elohim*); Psalm 14 uses the ineffable personal name (YHWH; LORD). The preference found in various psalms for a specific name for God has led scholars to conclude that many of the psalms that now make up the Psalter belonged to earlier collections before they found their way into this larger collection.

2 Foolishness of the wicked

The genre of this psalm cannot be easily determined. It is rich in wisdom themes, and for this reason many commentators identify it as a wisdom psalm. Others see its confident longing as prominent and classify it as a psalm of trust. The psalmist laments the despicable condition of the human race. Its total depravity is stated twice: "not one does what is right, not even one" (v. 4). The foolish claim, "There is no God," is less a denial of God's existence than it is an assertion of God's apparent disinterest. They draw this conclusion because perversion rules on earth, and God seems to do nothing to rectify the situation.

3-6 God's response to foolishness

In response to the arrogant allegation of God's disinterest, the psalmist insists that God is indeed concerned. Though God dwells in heaven, what transpires on earth is not ignored. God looks among the foolish in search of the wise; God is aligned with the just and acts as a refuge for the poor. The wicked are not only arrogant in their apparent strength but also foolish to question God's commitment to the needy. Appearances are often deceiving; fortunes can be reversed in the blink of an eye.

7 Deliverance from God

The psalm ends on a note of confidence. Divine assistance will come to Jerusalem, God's chosen city built on Mount Zion. Furthermore, this restoration will elicit universal rejoicing.

Psalm 54 (lament of an individual)

3-5 An appeal for rescue

In the thinking of the people, God's name possessed some of the very essence of God and, therefore, an appeal to the divine name was an appeal to divine power. The psalmist is assailed by cruel-hearted enemies who are intent on the psalmist's downfall. Unlike the psalmist who has taken refuge in God, these ruthless individuals have turned away from God.

6-9 Trust in God

Besides complaints, laments also frequently contain expressions of confidence. Such sentiments are clearly present in this psalm. The psalmist perceives God as a helper and a support.

The covenant term "faithfulness" suggests that this confidence is rooted in an intimate relationship with God enjoyed by the psalmist. Many laments also include a promise to accomplish some act of devotion once the prayer is heard. Here the psalmist promises to offer sacrifice and to continue to praise God's name.

Psalm 55 (lament of an individual)

2-9 Petitions for a hearing

This prayer demonstrates the dynamic meaning of "Listen," which includes acting on what has been heard. This is the point of the psalmist's plea: "Listen . . . do not hide . . . hear and give answer." The grieving person is assaulted by enemies. Their incessant attacks provoke intense inner agony such as a pounding heart, terror, fear, trembling, and shudders. The picture painted is turbulent, bleak, somber; the tormented individual dreams of escape. The vivid imagery sketches the simplicity and peacefulness of a dove and the uplifting nature of its wings. The place of refuge described is the wilderness where the fleeing bird would be safe from the turbulent winds and the storms of enemy attack. The series of complaints, which began with cries for help, ends with an appeal for an aggressive counterattack. The psalmist asks God to face the assailants and foil their assault.

10-13 Trials of the city

Attention is directed toward the city. Sentinels usually patrolled on the ramparts of a walled city. From there they exercised a dual role. They prevented danger from breeching the walls and invading the city, and they kept peace within the city itself. In this psalm, lawlessness and turmoil have taken the place of the sentinels. They make their rounds on the walls, ensuring access to those who would wreak havoc and allowing chaos free rein within the city itself. The sins of this city are many. They include violence, strife, mischief, evil, treachery, oppression, and fraud.

14-15 Treachery of a friend

As if attacks from an enemy were not difficult enough to bear, the psalmist is made to endure the betrayal of a close companion. This unfaithful friend is not explicitly identified. However, the description indicates that these two shared an intimate bond that was both personal ("my other self") and religious (being together "in the house of God").

16-24 Divine retribution

The psalmist's lament includes imprecations as well as pleas for deliverance. The condemnations are born of the desire for justice; the cries for help rise out of a profound sense of need. In both instances there is the assurance that God, who is enthroned as sovereign over all, will hear and will respond favorably. Prayer is directed to God three times a day: in the evening when the day begins, at dawn when light appears, and at noon when the sun is at its height. In this way, all of the day is dedicated to God. The imagery used to describe the treachery of the enemies is striking:

Softer than butter	is his speech	but war is in his heart
Smoother than oil	are his words	but they are unsheathed swords

The psalmist's complaint is a familiar exhortation to trust in God along with an assurance that God will always care for those who have been loyal. The psalm ends on a note of righteous vindication. The wicked will reap the consequences of the path they have chosen. The faithful psalmist will trust in God.

Psalm 56 (lament of an individual)

2-4 Complaint to God

The psalm opens with the classic plea for mercy. The oppression of enemies is unrelenting ("all the day"). The attacks only serve to turn the psalmist to God, confident that these assaults can accomplish nothing if the psalmist clings to God.

5 Prayer of praise

Following the complaint is a short prayer of praise. It states that the reason for the psalmist's trust is the promise of protection that God has made. After all, the enemies are only weak human beings, while God is omnipotent.

6-10 Enemy plots

The enemies not only disrupt the plans of the psalmist but resort to devious intrigues and outright attacks of their own. They "foil . . . ambush

. . . watch . . . lie in wait." They cannot be trusted. In the face of all of this, the psalmist turns to God for personal support and for divine retaliation against the evil ones. The simple prayer for help is enough to turn the enemies back, because they realize that God is on the side of the psalmist and this leaves them powerless.

11-12 Prayer of praise

The prayer of praise is repeated. This repetition serves to reinforce the psalmist's confidence.

13-14 The psalmist's piety

The psalmist's devotion to God is highlighted. Laments often contain promises to perform acts of piety in response to God's graciousness. This was frequently some kind of thank offering or sacrifice, as is the case here. God saved the psalmist from stumbling so that the psalmist was able to "walk before God / in the light of the living."

Psalm 57 (lament of an individual)

2-4 Cries for help

The cry for help is testimony to the psalmist's faith. God is enthroned in heaven as the Most High God. The psalmist directs cries for deliverance from enemies to that throne and, in return, God sends help from there. God is also characterized as a comforting bird with wings expanded. The shadow of those wings is a haven of refuge. This could mean that they offer some kind of respite from the fury of attack, or that they actually hide the one besieged by enemies. God's commitment springs from God's covenant attachment ("fidelity and mercy").

5-7 Enemy attacks

The enemies' attack seems to be verbal, their words like weapons of an invading army: spears, arrows, swords. Their speech wounds and threatens to kill. Oppressed in this way, the psalmist pleads that God will frighten these oppressors with a show of divine power, and that this power will be manifested over the entire world and across the span of the heavens. It is not clear what kind of traps the wicked have set. They could be actual traps for physical capture, or any kind of ensnarement. The rich metaphorical expressions in the rest of the psalm suggest that the latter is the case. Here God is asked to turn the tables on those who are afflicting the psalmist and to visit them with the very misfortune they had devised for others.

8-12 The psalmist's devotion

The remainder of the psalm is a testimony to the psalmist's piety. Praise of God springs from a faithful heart. It rises at dawn, most likely following a night of prayer. It is not offered privately, but publicly so that it can be witnessed by all. It is rooted in God's own covenant devotion, in the divine love and faithfulness that surpass anything earthly.

Psalm 58 (communal lament)

2-6 Complaints

The psalmist seems to be complaining to other gods, who themselves have judged unfairly and have perpetrated evil on the earth. It is probably through the agency of the wicked that this evil is spread. The psalmist maintains that they are intrinsically corrupt, evil from their very birth. Envisioning them as poisonous snakes underscores three threatening characteristics that they share with these hated reptiles. Their behavior is devious; they seem to slither about. They prefer to be unmanageable, refusing to listen to the one who might be able to charm or tame them. They are a mortal threat to everything around them.

7-12 Call for reprisals

In a series of metaphors, the psalmist implores God to punish these wicked people, to make them as ineffective as lions without teeth, or water that has no force, or grass that has been trampled, or the empty shell of a snail, and finally, as a stillborn with no promise of life. May they be tangled in a thicket of thorns, captured there and in pain. Without justifying the vengeance found in this prayer, it is important to realize that the righteous are really calling for just retribution, and they do not take matters into their own hands but look to God, the Righteous One, to render it.

Psalm 59 (lament of an individual)

2-6a Enemy attacks

The lament opens with multiple cries for help: "Rescue me . . . / lift me out of reach . . . / Deliver me . . . / Come near and see." The psalmist is an innocent victim of the attacks of others. The enemies are evil, bloodthirsty, and conspiratorial.

The psalmist is unable to withstand them alone and so turns to God for assistance. The psalmist appeals for deliverance to God as Lord of hosts, the special God of Israel.

6b-8 The ferocity of the enemies

The enemies are vicious, like growling dogs that frighten and run free through the city, seeking to scavenge wherever they can. They give no thought about the damaging effect of their harsh words, because they do not believe that they are accountable to anyone for their speech.

9-16 God's response to these attacks

Since God had not initially protected the psalmist from the attacks of these enemies, surely God will now step in as a deliverer. Confident that God will hear these prayers, the psalmist seeks retribution: "laugh at them . . . deride . . . Slay them . . . Shake them . . . destroy them." As is usually the case in such psalms, this is a cry for justice, not merely revenge. God laughs at the meager offensive of these adversaries. They are no match for God, but they are indeed a threat to the psalmist, who realizes that their lying words might easily deceive the unsuspecting. God's victory over these deceitful people will be a testimony to the sovereignty of the God of Jacob.

17-18 A promise to praise

The psalm ends with the psalmist praising God who is indeed a refuge and a fortress. More than this, God is the loving God of the covenant.

Psalm 60 (communal lament)

3-7 God allows hardship

Three times the psalmist recounts how the power of God has caused havoc in the lives of the people. God rejected them, broke them, and was angry with them. It is now time for God to revive them. The psalmist uses three metaphors to reinforce an understanding of the suffering of the people. The first metaphor employs a military image; the people's defense was breached because God allowed it to happen. The psalmist then describes God's fury, expressed through the destructive forces of nature. Finally, suffering so overpowered the people that they staggered as if intoxicated. After each report of distress, the psalmist pleads that this suffering be assuaged.

Appeal to divine military prowess is made: "Raise up a banner." The banner is a rallying point for the troops. It is meant to inspire courage and loyalty. The right hand is preferred because it wields the weapon.

8-10 God speaks

A divine oracle, issued from the sanctuary, calls to mind the promise that Israel will occupy the land. The military success needed to realize this promise functions here as grounds for hope of deliverance from present peril. Shechem was situated in northern Israel between Mounts Ebal and Gerizim. The Valley of Succoth was just east of the Jordan River. Gilead and Manasseh were regions in Transjordan, while Ephraim, a common name for the northern tribes, and Judah, the name given to the southern tribes, were regions west of the river. All these territories were part of the united kingdom of David. On the other hand, Moab and Edom were independent nations just south of Gilead on the eastern side of the Jordan, and Philistia was a nation west of Judah on the eastern coast of the Mediterranean Sea. The oracle promises that these nations will all be under the control of Israel's God. Their combined borders will constitute the boundaries of the kingdom of Israel.

11-14 Does God hear?

God may be the hero who conquers these territories, but the assaults that Israel suffers indicate that at this point God does not march with Israel's armies. God seems to have abandoned the people, or at least refused to listen to their pleading. The psalmist, however, is not deterred, but continues to cry to God for relief, for only divine assistance can ensure triumph.

Psalm 61 (lament of an individual)

2-6 Petitions for a hearing

The psalmist begs God to be heard. The phrase "ends of the earth" could refer to Sheol or to a place far from the temple, the sanctuary to which the psalmist yearns to be brought. Faint of heart, the psalmist hopes to receive assistance from God who is characterized as a secure rock, a tower of strength, and a place of refuge. Here the temple is seen more as a place of refuge than a place for sacrifice. The protective wings could be a reference to the winged cherubim that guarded the

temple, or the psalmist might be characterizing God as a bird under whose wings one could take refuge (cf. Ps 57:2). The vows mentioned by the psalmist are probably promises to perform acts of devotion when divine assistance is eventually granted.

7-9 Prayers for the king

Attention turns to the king. The long life for which the psalmist prays implies royal stability and prosperity. The covenant language of love and fidelity belongs to the fundamental Mosaic covenant (cf. Exod 34:6). However, the Davidic covenant (cf. 2 Sam 7:12-16) did not negate the privileges or responsibilities of this fundamental bond. The protection and blessing accorded the monarchy would have accrued for the nation as well. When this petition is granted, the psalmist will fulfill the vow mentioned earlier.

Psalm 62 (prayer of confidence of an individual)

2-5 Confidence in God

The psalmist's life force rests in God, who is as secure as a rock and who assures the psalmist of deliverance. Though the psalm opens with a very touching expression of trust in God, it moves back and forth between sentiments of trust and descriptions of attack. Accusations of oppression are hurled at the enemies, not at God. They plot against the vulnerable, who seem to crumble under their attack. They delight in treachery and lies. They appear to bless, but they are really cursing. There is nothing about them that can be trusted.

6-9 God alone is reliable

The psalm's opening words of confidence are repeated with slight variations. Images used to describe God include rock, salvation, fortress, and deliverance. They are all standard metaphors that characterize God as the only source of true stability and security. The psalmist summons other people to place their trust in this same God, who then will be a refuge for them as well.

10-13 There is no security in human beings

There is no comparison between the security that one can find in God alone and the ephemeral nature of human beings. The psalmist draws out the contrasts with undeniable precision. God is solid and secure, like a rock; humans are ephemeral, like a passing breath. Even what appears to be human power is a fleeting illusion that cannot be trusted. In the long run, neither physical force nor wealth can ensure protection. Real power and genuine faithfulness belong to God, and God will allot appropriately what is due to each one.

Psalm 63 (lament of an individual)

2-4 Longing for God

The psalmist's longing for God is captured in the poignant metaphor of parched land. The soul thirsts; the body yearns. The longing for God has taken over the entire person. Power and glory are divine manifestations that frequently occur at times of worship in the sanctuary. A desire to enjoy such a manifestation prompts the psalmist to turn toward the sanctuary. The psalmist considers being in covenant with God and experiencing covenant love, which is considered a greater value than life itself.

5-9 Piety of the psalmist

Various elements of devotion are mentioned. The lifting up of one's hands is a common posture of prayer. Calling on God's name and honoring God with joyful lips are references to prayer itself. The rich banquet of praise is probably an allusion to a sacred meal. Keeping night vigil in prayer was a common devotional practice. The shadow of God's wings could either refer to God's protective care or to the cherubim that flanked God's heavenly throne. In either case, the solace that these divine wings represent causes the psalmist to rejoice.

10-12 Punishment for the wicked

As with so many prayers of lament, this psalm includes a plea that enemies be severely punished for their treachery. The psalmist prays that they be banished to Sheol ("the depths of the netherworld"), that they suffer at the point of a sword, and that they be the prey of the wild jackal. Though not stated explicitly, what the psalmist desires is probably retribution rather than revenge. The very last sentiments confirm this. After a brief prayer for the king, the respective fates of the righteous and the wicked are stated: joyous

exaltation for the former, restrictive silence for the latter.

Psalm 64 (lament of an individual)

2-7 Plots of the wicked

The lament opens with an appeal to be heard. The mob of enemies is vicious and spiteful. They attack the psalmist with speech that is destructive. Their tongues are swords; their cruel words are like poisonous arrows. Furthermore, they launch their attacks from hiding, set nets, and ambush the innocent. In such situations, there is no opportunity for the unwary to defend themselves. In a society in which honor and shame play prominent roles in determining one's reputation, gossip, scorn, libel, or any form of verbal assault can seriously jeopardize one's social status. Frequently, the harm suffered in this way is more difficult to bear than physical injury; it is sometimes even feared more than death itself.

8-11 God intervenes

Convinced that the guilty will eventually be punished for their sin, the psalmist declares that these wicked enemies will be snared in the very traps they laid for others. God's arrows will pierce them; their wicked speech will be their own downfall; and they will be the ones who suffer shame in the sight of others. The psalmist's hope for retribution rests in God. When God does indeed act, the righteous who are vindicated will exult in God's power and justice.

Psalm 65
(communal prayer of thanksgiving)

2-6 Gratitude to God

The psalmist speaks in the name of the entire community and proclaims its gratitude to God. This gratitude is expressed liturgically through prayers and vows. These acts of devotion take place on Zion, the mountain on which the temple was built. It is there that the sins of the people are brought in order that they may be forgiven. A beatitude functions here as part of this expression of gratitude. It is a response to the marvels that God has accomplished for this chosen people. Chief among these blessings are the magnificent order and splendor of the universe, social harmony, and the fertility of the land.

7-9 Divine creator and savior

God acts as both creator and savior. As portrayed in this psalm, these two roles are not distinct from one another. It was as creator that God established the order in the universe, setting up the mountains and triumphing over chaotic cosmic waters. The cosmic order that God established is also manifested in the social harmony initiated on earth. Just as God stilled the roaring of unruly waters, so God quelled the tumult of warring peoples. Thus it is the creator God who has acted as savior. These marvels are acclaimed from east to west, from horizon to horizon, in other words, throughout the entire world.

10-14 Divine sustainer of life

God is not only the creator of the world but also the one who brings forth life and sustains it. God accomplishes this as well through divine regulation of water. The water that was originally destructive is now manageable, even life-giving. This is the water that makes the land abundantly fertile. Vivid metaphors are used to represent this fertility. The land is blanketed with life. This includes both the crops of the land meant for human consumption and the pasturage intended for the animals. All of creation cries out to God in praise.

Psalm 66 (composite psalm)

1b-9 A call to praise God

The psalm opens with a communal summons to praise God and it closes with an individual prayer of gratitude. All the people of the earth are called to praise God for the wonderful deeds that God has accomplished, deeds that cause God's enemies to tremble. These deeds were the miracles that attended God's deliverance of Israel from the Egyptian bondage and its safe passage into the land of promise. Changing the sea to dry land is a clear reference to the people's miraculous escape from Egypt (cf. Exod 14:22). Their passing through the river on foot is an allusion to the equally miraculous crossing of the Jordan as they entered the land (cf. Josh 3:16-17). Although there is no explicit cosmic imagery here, God's power over water always carries allusions to the primeval battle with chaos. Only the victorious creator God would be able to exercise such control over water. These feats should be a lesson to the nations of the earth: the God of Israel is the mighty one, and this God will tolerate no manner of defiance. Instead of rebellion, these nations are invited to bless Israel's God.

10-15 God tests the people

The psalmist next speaks directly to God. The testing to which the people were subjected is probably a reference to the hardships they underwent during their escape from Egypt and while they were in the desert. (Some translations of the Bible imply that these hardships refer to the oppression the Israelites suffered during the Babylonian exile [vv.11-12]). After having been delivered from misfortune, the psalmist fulfills the promises made earlier to offer various sacrifices in the temple.

16-20 Learn from my experience

A second summons is issued. It is a call to wisdom, not to praise. The fear of God, a central wisdom theme, is the awe that is to be shown to God because of divine power and splendor. It is the foundation of the life of the wise. Those who fear God in this way are called to listen to the psalmist's report and to marvel at the divine graciousness that is manifested in the deliverance of the people. Ultimately, God heard the pleading of the psalmist and showed the loving kindness that is expected in covenant commitment.

Psalm 67
(communal prayer of thanksgiving)

2 Thanksgiving at harvest time

The psalmist addresses two audiences, sometimes speaking to the community, sometimes praying to God. The opening words, directed toward the community, express a threefold wish for God's blessing.

3-6 May God be praised

The middle section of the psalm is directed toward God. It contains two reflections on God's beneficent rule, each followed by the same call for praise (vv. 4, 6). God's saving power has been such a blessing for the community that God's graciousness should be proclaimed to all the neighboring nations as well. More than being told of God's graciousness, the other nations will also experience God's saving rule.

7-8 Fertility of the earth

There is a brief yet clear reference to harvest, which is viewed as a blessing from God. The nations of the world will see all the ways that God has blessed this people, and they will join in praising God for such graciousness.

Psalm 68
(communal prayer of thanksgiving)

2-4 The promise of future victory

Although the word for "battle" is not found in the Hebrew, the description of God's actions clearly implies that divine power will rout the enemies. Their strength is illusory. Dynamic metaphors are used to describe their retreat. They will be dissipated like vanishing smoke and melted away like wax before the fire of divine fury. On the other hand, the righteous will rejoice and praise God. This is a good example of the reliability of the theory of retribution: the good are rewarded and the evil are punished.

5-7 Praise of God

There is a call to offer praise to God who is portrayed as the triumphant one who rides on the clouds. This is the picture of the great storm god, the one who mounts the heavenly chariot and surveys the expanse of the heavens. This great creator is none other than the Lord, the God of Israel. Though mighty in the heavens and on the earth, God is attentive to the needs of society's most vulnerable, namely, the fatherless and the widowed, the homeless and the imprisoned. In the tradition of Israel, care for these needy ones was a gauge of the righteousness of an individual or of the community. Israel itself had suffered indignities such as these, and God had delivered the people from them. It is now the peoples' turn to act toward the needy in society as God had acted toward them.

8-15 The marvels God performed in the past

Attention is now directed toward God. The psalmist recounts some of the divine blessings the people experienced from the time of their deliverance from bondage in Egypt to the time of their settlement in the land of promise. It was God who led the people through the desert. It was God who caused the earth to tremble at the time of divine manifestation on Mount Sinai. Finally, it was this same God who claimed the land of promise and made it fertile by supplying it with life-giving waters. At the time of the judges, it was God who gave the people military victory over any nation that tried to thwart God's plans to settle the tribes of Israel. The armies of those nations fled, leaving the spoils of war for the women to gather up, a custom that was practiced extensively throughout the ancient world.

16-19 The glories of the temple

The majesty of God's temple is exulted. Employing the poetic technique of personification, the psalmist chastises the towering peaks of Bashan, a fertile plateau east of the Jordan River in what is today the Golan Heights. These magnificent heights envy the modestly elevated Mount Zion, whose resplendence stems from its being the dwelling place of God on earth. What is described here as the journey from Sinai to Zion is probably really a formal liturgical procession, not a strenuous geographic trek. Military imagery can be seen in the description of a cortege that includes captives of war. The enemy has been vanquished, and those who have not been killed in battle are held as slaves. The sheer number of them gives testimony to the victorious might of God.

20-32 Procession with the spoils of war

The people of God are spared disaster, and they appear to take morbid delight in wading through enemy blood and in allowing ravenous dogs to lap up the gore. Though this gruesome image of revenge will trouble many today, it is probably meant to be an example of the justice of God directed against the wicked. The enemy is portrayed both as historical adversary (people from Bashan) and as mythological foe (found in the depths of the sea). Furthermore, the image itself is probably an exaggeration intended to emphasize God's anger in the face of wickedness.

The procession to the sanctuary includes musicians and singers as well as dignitaries of various tribes. We see Benjamin and Judah from the south and Zebulun and Naphtali from the north. The calls for divine retribution show this extravagant liturgical procession to be a celebration of military victory as well. The psalmist prays for a demonstration of divine power from the temple. Ferocious beasts represent foreign threats. These nations, along with the kingdom of Egypt, bring tribute to the temple and sing praise to the God of Israel.

33-36 Praise to the majestic God of heaven

God is called on for a display of the same divine power that was demonstrated throughout the days of Israel's history. The God that Israel claims as its own is really the creator God who rides the clouds of heaven and whose voice thunders over the earth. This is the God who dwells in the temple in Jerusalem. The psalmist exclaims: "Blessed be God!"

Psalm 69 (lament of an individual)

2-5 Cries for help

The psalmist feels overwhelmed by affliction, as if swallowed up by perilous waters. There is no foothold, no support. This tormented individual has cried for help, but to no avail; has looked to God, but found no comfort. Enemies beyond number afflict the psalmist without cause. The cry is soul-wrenching: "Save me!"

6-13 Afflictions endured

It is possible that the psalmist's affliction will affect others. The psalmist prays for those for whom this is in fact the case. The parallel construction emphasizes this:

Let those who wait in hope for you	LORD of hosts	not be shamed because of me
Let those who seek you	God of Israel	not be disgraced because of me

The psalmist has been shamed and ostracized by kinfolk. Shame is a severe trial in an honor-based society. In a community-based society, ostracism could be a death sentence. Though not totally guiltless, the psalmist is nonetheless filled with religious zeal and has practiced acts of devotion such as fasting and public penance. However, this piety has brought down the scorn of others. This unfortunate individual has even been reviled by those who themselves are upbraided by society.

14-22 Cries for help

The psalmist turns to God, hoping that God will respond at some favorable time. Appeals are made to God's kindness or generous love and to God's mercy, qualities associated with the covenant bond. Surely God will turn again to this loyal servant. From the depths of profound agony, the psalmist cries for help: "Rescue me . . . Answer me . . . Come and redeem my life." This miserable person is overwhelmed by reproach, shame, and disgrace, yet no one shows pity or compassion. Instead, people add to the torment by offering poison for food and vinegar to drink (cf. Matt 27:34).

23-29 Divine retribution

The psalmist begs God to act justly against those responsible for this misery. May the traps that they have set snare them instead. May God dim their sight and deprive them of strength, empty their military camps and leave them desolate. The psalmist prays that God will turn the fury of divine wrath against them, for they took advantage of the suffering of the one that God had already afflicted. And finally, the psalmist asks that God might strike their names from the book of life, disregard them when the just are granted the enjoyment of divine blessings. Though believers today are not accustomed to formulating hateful prayers such as these, vituperations are very common in the psalms of lament. However, they are usually appeals to divine justice.

30-32 Cries for help

The psalmist prays for divine assistance and protection, not merely for the sake of release from suffering, but in order to eventually testify to God's goodness through songs of praise and thanksgiving. This kind of grateful prayer from the heart is more pleasing to God than mere external signs of devotion such as sacrifice, regardless of how dramatic they might be.

33-37 Confidence in God

True to the character of a lament, this psalm ends with words of confidence in God. The lowly ones who seek God will not be disappointed. Then the entire universe, not only the world in which we live, but the world above as well as the world below, will praise God. The rescue of Zion and the rebuilding of Judah suggest an exilic promise. In the end, peace will return.

Psalm 70 (lament of an individual)

With only minor variations, this psalm is identical to Psalm 40:14-18.

2-6 A prayer for help

In this psalm, the afflicted one appears to be innocent, yet besieged by enemies. Besides pleading for personal rescue and protection, the psalmist prays that, as a penalty for their aggressiveness, these enemies themselves might be put to shame. In contrast to the fate of the wicked, the prayer pleads that those who seek God might be blessed with happiness. The final verse is a final plea for deliverance.

Psalm 71 (lament of an individual)

1-4 Prayers for rescue

With only minor variations, the first three verses of this psalm are the same as Psalm 31:1-3a. In asking for deliverance, the psalmist appeals to divine justice, not to God's compassion. This suggests the psalmist's innocence. Here God is perceived as a refuge, a rock, and a fortress. These are all images of strength and security, images that inspire confidence.

5-8 Trust in God

The trust that the psalmist has placed in God is not a disposition recently developed, one that functions only when the psalmist is in difficult straits. Rather, it has been the psalmist's attitude since birth. Current difficulties did not generate hope, nor do they diminish it. The psalmist's hope is a permanent disposition. This suggests genuine devotion to God. A portent or sign can represent either something positive or something negative. In this case, the psalmist might be an example either of how God punishes the guilty, or of how the confidence of the righteous does not waver even in the face of misfortune. The fact that the psalmist promises to praise God suggests that the latter meaning is intended.

9-13 The cruelty of enemies

The psalmist prays not to be abandoned when old age begins to sap former youthful energy. If this should happen, the enemies would take advantage of the situation and devise plots that, they presume, would not be foiled by God. From the perspective of retribution, the psalmist's misfortune has been sent by God as punishment. Added to this, God has made no effort to remedy the situation. God does not seem to be concerned, and no one else has intervened on the psalmist's behalf. What would prevent these enemies from taking advantage of the situation? Who would care?

14-16 Undeterred commitment

Despite all of this misfortune, the psalmist still trusts in God, still proclaims the news of God's acts of deliverance, and is still confident that divine justice will win the day.

17-24 Prayer in old age

The constancy of the psalmist's faithfulness is underscored. Having trusted God since youth, the psalmist trusts even into old age. The psalmist is convinced that just as God acted as deliverer in previous times, so God will intervene again. The psalmist promises to continue to proclaim to others God's power and might, God's justice and tender concern. The psalmist is confident that in the future refuge will be given and honor will be restored. Then the one rescued will praise God unceasingly.

Psalm 72 (royal hymn)

1-4 Royal rule

Prayer is offered for the king that, with God's help, he might execute his royal responsibilities. Chief among these obligations is fair judgment, especially toward those under his rule who have the least amount of political power. Since these are the ones most likely to be taken advantage of by those who are unscrupulous, it is the king's duty to act on their behalf. The rewards of such rule will be blessings in abundance. (The Hebrew has *shalom* [peace], which really means prosperity.) Protection against political or military oppression is another royal responsibility. Prayers for the success of the king are also prayers for a good life for the people.

5-7 Royal blessings

In exaggerated fashion, the psalmist prays for a long life span for the king. The ancient Israelite king enjoyed a special relationship with God (cf.

2 Sam 7:14), which made him the channel through which God blessed the nation. It was only right to pray for the long life of God's appointed king. The importance of the king is compared with that of both the sun and the moon. The significance of the sun is obvious. There would be no growth without it. The moon with its phases plays an important role both in the agricultural life of the people and in the calculation of the ritual celebrations. Similar blessings come to the people through the king. The psalm also contains prayer for the success of the king's reign, which is compared to fertility of the land.

8-14 Revered among the nations

The psalmist prays that the dominion of the king might span from the Mediterranean to the Red Sea and as far west as the Euphrates River. When this is accomplished, the enemies will be forced to pay homage and foreign nations will pay tribute. They will come with this tribute from Tarshish in southern Spain, from nations on the Arabian peninsula, and from Seba in northern Africa. It is not merely for military ingenuity and prowess that the king is revered, but for humanitarian rule at home as well. He is the protector of the poor and needy, the advocate of all the oppressed. This king rules in righteousness and compassion.

15-17 Blessings for righteous rule

The blessings for the king include a long and happy life, wealth, prosperity, and vast grain harvests that rival the glories of the forests of northern Lebanon. In addition to this, his name will be revered among the nations and he will be a source of blessing for all (cf. Gen 12:2). These are the royal blessings for which the psalmist prays, blessings that will overflow into the lives of the people of the realm.

18-20 Doxology

The last verses of this psalm are probably a doxology that closes the second book of psalms. It turns the focus away from prayers for the king to praise of God for all the marvelous feats that God has accomplished. The very last verse announces the end of the collection of psalms ascribed to David.

BOOK THREE: PSALMS 73–89

This third book of psalms contains the major collection of psalms from the collection associated with Asaph.

Psalm 73 (wisdom psalm)

The psalm is difficult to classify. However, since its chief focus is the theme of retribution, many commentators consider it a wisdom psalm.

1b God rewards the righteous

The psalm opens stating the first half of the theory of retribution: the good will be rewarded. It is a curious opening statement for a psalm that really describes the dilemma suffered by the psalmist at the sight of the prosperity of the wicked.

2-5 The wicked enjoy life

The psalmist is troubled by the prosperity (the Hebrew is *shalom*) of the wicked. These wicked people should be suffering the consequences of their sinful way of living. Instead, they seem to be thriving. It is not their ungodly behavior that is coveted by the psalmist, but the apparent ease of their lives. They are healthy and free of life's cares. They do not carry the burdens that many of the innocent do. Not only do the wicked seem to prosper, but it appears that those who should be enjoying life's blessings are not. In other words, the entire theory of retribution is reversed: those who should not be happy enjoy life; those who should be happy suffer. It is this incongruity that so troubles the psalmist.

6-12 The arrogance of the wicked

The wicked themselves realize that the circumstances of their lives do not fit the pattern established by the theory of retribution. However, unlike the psalmist, they are not bothered by this. Rather, they delight in it. They wrap themselves in their sinfulness as they would clothe themselves in garments. Their good fortune makes them haughty. They scorn whatever in heaven or on earth might challenge them. They even defy God, maintaining that God really does not know what is happening in the world. Such blasphemy challenges one of God's fundamental attributes, namely, divine omniscience. To say that God does not know implies that God will be unable to rectify the situation. This is an indirect challenge to divine omnipotence. The circumstances of the wicked are succinctly summarized: they are free of cares, and they amass wealth.

13-17 The heart of the psalmist

In the face of the prosperity of the wicked, the psalmist questions the value of loyal commitment to God. If the force of retribution has been turned upside down, why struggle to be faithful? A clean or pure heart and hands washed in innocence not only refer to personal moral integrity, but also are the criteria for access to the temple and the presence of God (cf. Ps 24:3-6). The psalmist has lived with this kind of integrity, yet has endured constant affliction. Despite this, any decision to join the ranks of the wicked is firmly rejected, because it would be a sign of betrayal of God's people. Still, like Job, the psalmist struggles to understand the incongruity of these circumstances.

Verse 17 announces a turning point in the psalmist's struggle. From a literary point of view, it also acts as a kind of hinge, connecting this struggle with insight into the ultimate end of the wicked, which is described in the verses that follow. This shift in understanding took place in the sanctuary. Hence the psalmist claims to possess the kind of integrity required for entrance into God's holy place.

18-20 The fate of the wicked

The ultimate fate of the wicked is described in graphic terms. God caused them to slip and fall from prominence into ruin. This fall was not gradual. It was total, unforeseen, and compounded by all of the surprise and terror that accompanies sudden disaster. The period of the wicked's prosperity is characterized as a time when God was asleep, unaware of the inequity of the situation. But now that the Lord is awake and the ungodly have been dealt the just desserts of their sinfulness, they are like a bad dream. They have no lasting force.

21-28 Confidence is restored

Personal affliction that is incomprehensible along with the apparent good fortune of the wicked left the psalmist deeply wounded and embittered and acting like a senseless brute animal. The psalmist should have known that God would eventually intervene and correct the

situation. Once confidence in divine fairness is restored, the psalmist professes enduring attachment to God alone and commitment to God's guidance. God is the rock on which the psalmist finds security, the portion to which the psalmist can lay claim. Though the wicked will perish, the psalmist will remain near to God and will announce God's goodness to all who will hear.

Psalm 74 (communal lament)

1-3 The lament and the prayer

The people feel that they have been cast off and forgotten by God. In their name, the psalmist cries in lament: "Why?" What have they done to deserve this? They are God's flock, God's own people, the tribe that God brought back. Mount Zion with its sacred temple is the place where God chose to dwell. Why has God turned against them? The plea is twofold: remember this people; return to the ravaged sanctuary. "Remember" means "turn back and remedy the situation." The psalmist is certain that walking through the ruins of the temple will cause God to relent.

4-9 The destruction of the sanctuary

The enemies of God ravaged the holy place, slashing away at the wood of the shrine as if it were an overgrown grove of trees, destroying what they could, and finally setting it on fire. As a result, the devout praise of God has given way to the enemies' mocking shouts of victory; the sacred furnishings have been replaced by their victorious standards of war. God's holy place has been both desecrated and destroyed. The evil foes have even issued the command to lay waste all the other shrines in the land. This detailed description has led many commentators to date the psalm at the time of the exile or shortly after it.

In the past, the people looked for signs that might have helped them discover God's will. Prophets also had arisen through whom God would speak to the people. Now they have neither signs nor prophets, so they have no way of knowing how long this devastation might last.

10-11 A second lament

Again the psalmist cries out: "How long?" This time the concern is with the way the enemy blasphemes God. How long will God allow this to last? Why does God not retaliate? The right hand represents the hand with which one fights, the hand that holds the weapon. It seems that God's right hand is idle.

12-17 The creative power of God

It is not that God is powerless. On the contrary, this God has not only been victorious throughout the earth, but in the beginning actually conquered the forces of creation as well. In the myths of creation, the sea was the god of chaos. Another fearsome threat was the dragon or mighty creature of the deep called Leviathan (cf. Isa 27:1; Job 3:8; 40:25). The psalmist declares that God exercised power over all these mythological beings as well. Creation, often characterized as victory over chaos, is here described as the simple ordering of nature. God's control of water embraces the management of springs and torrents on earth as well. Through governance of the heavenly bodies, God regulates days and nights and the seasons of the year.

18-23 A plea for divine justice

Once again the psalmist prays that God might remember. This time it is a prayer to remember justice, specifically punishment of the wicked who taunted God. Since part of one's very person was somehow contained in one's name, to profane God's name was to blaspheme God. This is what the enemy has done. On the other hand, just as the psalmist would have God recall the sinner, so would the psalmist have God be attentive to the needs of the righteous. "[W]ild animals" could be read literally or it might be a figurative way of referring to the enemies. The psalmist prays: Don't surrender your people to the beasts; don't forget their lives; look to the covenant and the promise of protection that it contains. The psalmist would have God look kindly on God's own people but punish severely those who stand against them and against God.

Psalm 75 (prophetic exhortation)

2 Praise of God

The psalm opens with words of praise and thanksgiving. (The phrase "call upon your name" might be better translated "your name is near," suggesting that God is already close to the psalmist.) Though the works of creation are often called

wondrous deeds, here the reference is probably to divine judgment.

3-6 God speaks

God claims to exercise universal and exclusive control: "I will choose . . . / I will judge . . . / I make steady." The time of judgment is probably a reference to divine intervention in the future, a time that only God knows. Though the judgment will be demanding, it will be fair. Though earth and everything on it will quake, God will not allow it to collapse. God warns the boastful and the wicked that they will be powerless when this comes to pass. The horn is a symbol of strength. When God comes to judge the earth, human strength will be useless.

7-9 God's judgment

The psalmist expands God's words about divine judgment. At different times in its history, Israel experienced attacks from enemy nations in the east and from some in the west. This included marauders from the wilderness. This does not constitute the judgment of which God or the psalmist speaks. The judgment referred to here comes from God, who lifts some up and puts others down. The cup mentioned is the cup of divine wrath (cf. Isa 51:17; Jer 25:15; Ezek 23:33). The guilty will be forced to drink of it.

10-11 Final praise of God

The psalm ends as it began, with praise of God. The title "God of Jacob" identifies God as the special divine patron of Israel. This suggests that the wicked are not merely sinners, but are the enemies of Israel. The reference gives a national character to this psalm.

Psalm 76 (song of Zion)

2-4 Praise of Zion

Judah is the name of the southern kingdom within which Jerusalem and the temple were located. It was God's choice of this place that gave the region its importance. Since God's name is an aspect of God's very being, the divine name itself is renowned. Salem may have been the original name of the city (cf. Gen 14:18). It is there, in the temple in that city on that mountain, that God decided to dwell. Though the city was won through war (cf. 2 Sam 5:6-12), God's presence makes the city secure and weapons of war are now unnecessary.

5-11 God's defense

God is described as a mighty and fearsome warrior, one before whom all else tremble. The ancient mountains could be a reference to the foundations of the universe. Since God established them, God's strength would certainly exceed theirs. Chariots and steeds call to mind God's triumph over the Egyptians at the time of the Exodus (cf. Exod 14:26-31). Divine anger is not capricious. It is righteous anger in the face of willful transgression. The punishment that God metes out is equitable judgment. God's roar could be the judgment that God pronounces from heaven.

Edom was one of the nations east of the Jordan River. It had a long and varied history with Israel. It was somehow linked with Israel through Jacob's twin brother Esau (cf. Gen 25:22-26), yet it was also considered an enemy because it refused passageway when Israel moved into Canaan (cf. Num 20:18). Hamath was part of the land in the north occupied by Israel (cf. Num 34:7-9). In this psalm, however, both nations pay homage to the God of Israel.

12-13 The people's response

The psalmist calls on the people to fulfill their religious obligations. They are to bring offerings to the temple. For the third time God is called awesome (vv. 5, 8, 12). In the previous instances the focus was on God's military prowess. Here it describes the status that God enjoys among the rulers of the earth.

Psalm 77 (lament of an individual)

2-4 Lament

The cry of lament is searing and prolonged. It rings out to God day and night, and the psalmist refuses to be consoled by anything or anyone other than God. However, it is actually the thought of God that causes the psalmist to lament. (Throughout the psalm, the perspective moves from the individual to the community.)

5-11 The psalmist's suffering

The psalmist suffers great mental anguish. This includes inner turmoil, sleeplessness, and the inability to communicate. Usually remembrance of "the days of old," a reference to the former time of deliverance, brings confidence in God. Such is not the case here. Instead, memory of past deliverance only exaggerates the present tribulation. God may have intervened in the past, but there is no indication that God will do so in the present. This only causes more anxiety. In fact, the psalmist wonders if perhaps God has terminated the covenantal relationship. Where are the covenant love, mercy, and compassion? Have God's promises been negated? The right hand of God is the hand that protects. It should have been raised in Israel's defense. The psalmist's suffering raises the question: has God's protection been withdrawn?

12-16 Past deliverance

These afflictions notwithstanding, the psalmist is intent on not only remembering the past gracious deeds of the Lord but also proclaiming them to others. The reference here is probably to the deliverance of the people of Israel. God could wield saving power in the land of another people, within the jurisdiction of another god. God did this at the time of the deliverance out of Egypt. Why not now? God was able to do this because there is no god greater than the God of Israel. Though the psalm speaks of Jacob and Joseph, names often given to the northern tribes, the psalmist probably has the entire nation in mind.

17-21 God's cosmic power

The warrior God who saved Israel is also the creator God who in the beginning brought order to the entire cosmos. Just as God conquered Israel's national enemies, so God subdued the cosmic forces. The waters of chaos were no match for the mighty God. They are now tamed and, by the power of God, have become mere natural phenomena. God is characterized as the storm deity who races across the heavens. It is this God who controls the rains, whose arrows are seen in the lightning, and whose chariot wheels can be heard in the thunder.

The image of a divine warrior traveling in a chariot remains the same, but the setting changes. The psalm moves from a cosmic setting in the heavens to a historical setting on earth. The waters, once a cosmic threat, are now the sea through which God's people pass. There is little difference between control of the waters of chaos and those of the Reed Sea, for the cosmic creator and the God who saved Israel through the leadership of Moses and Aaron are one and the same God.

Psalm 78 (historical recital)

1-11 Introduction

This historical recital is an unusual kind of psalm. While it recounts the marvelous deeds of God, it does so for the purpose of teaching others rather than praising God. Furthermore, the purpose of the teaching is clearly stated. Lessons are to be drawn from the past. Those who hear the report are to put their trust in God and not, like the ancestors who actually experienced the wondrous deed, rebel against God (cf. Deut 9:7, 24). In other words, the purpose of the retelling is obedience to the law (*torah*, v. 5).

The psalm opens like a wisdom psalm: "Attend . . . listen." The psalmist is about to explain a story. The Hebrew *mashal* might be better translated as the generic word "proverb," a lesson from life. The traditional accounts are well known: our ancestors knew them; we know them; and our children—even those yet to be born—will know them. The stories may be known, but the lessons to be drawn from them are more difficult to discern. An example was given from the dismal history of the northern kingdom. (Ephraim, the name of one tribe, also referred to all of the tribes of the north.) It is the psalmist's way of saying: let this be a lesson to you.

12-16 Egypt and the wilderness

The mighty power of God was seen in the marvels performed in the land of Egypt, where God split the sea just as the primordial waters of chaos had been defeated at the time of creation. The wondrous deeds did not end there. Just as God led the people through the waters, so God led them through the wilderness by day and by night and supplied them with water from the rock. God was not only their savior but also their provider.

17-20 The people sinned

The rebellion of the people is inexplicable. Deliverance did not seem to have been enough for them, nor was the miracle of water from the rock. They demanded food. This was not the first time that they had rebelled. The psalm says that they "went on sinning." In fact, they put God to the test, a sign that they lacked trust in God's power or in God's willingness to care for them.

21-32 God's response

God's initial response to their lack of trust was rage. What follows is curious. Rather than strike them down, God gave them what they demanded. The heavens opened and manna rained down; God stirred up the east wind and it brought winged fowl. The people ate and were more than satisfied. However, God's anger had not been abated. While they were still eating, it flared up and consumed the strongest among them, the promise of their future. As unbelievable as it may seem, the people continued in their rebellion and lack of faith.

33-39 The covenant relationship

When Israel recounts its history, it always underscores God's continued care despite the people's fickleness. God may be wrathful, but divine anger was always precipitated by infidelity. For a time the people might have remembered God's constancy toward them, but then they fell back into their old ways of sin. They were not faithful to the covenant, but God continued to be merciful toward them. The frailty of human nature is given as a reason for God's forgiveness.

40-55 Deliverance and entrance into the land

The remainder of the psalm repeats and enlarges many of the themes recounted in the preceding verses, almost as if these were two psalms joined together. The psalmist recalls the rebellion of Israel (cf. vv. 12-16) and adds an account of the plagues that struck Egypt but spared God's people (cf. Exod 7–11). All these marvels originated from the hand of God, and yet the people rebelled and tested God. Finally, God brought them to a holy land and allotted the territory to the various tribes. These were the events that established Israel as a nation chosen by God from among all other nations. Surely their gratitude would be shown in their obedience.

56-58 A second rebellious generation

The first part of this report of the sinfulness of the people resembles an earlier summary (cf. vv. 17-20). However, just as the previous verses added mention of the occupation of the land, so these verses tell of the idolatry of the people at that time in their history. That generation succumbed to the worship of Canaanite gods, worship that was performed at various high places in the area. These people were no better than their ancestors.

59-64 God's response

Once again, God's anger blazed against the sinfulness of the people. As before (cf. vv. 21-32), this anger was a response to their disregard for the covenant responsibilities to which they had agreed. As punishment for their transgressions in the land, God withheld divine protection and allowed victory to their enemies. The ark of the covenant, the symbol of God's presence in their midst, was captured and taken from the tribal shrine at Shiloh. Their warriors were killed and the rest of the nation suffered severely.

65-72 The choice of David

God's anger does not last forever. The earlier verses told of God's covenantal faithfulness and mercy (cf. vv. 33-39). This final section tells of another special relationship, the one God made with David. Here God's preference for the southern kingdom is obvious. God is said to have rejected the northern tribes of Joseph and Ephraim in favor of choosing a king from the southern tribe of Judah. Furthermore, Mount Zion, on which was built Jerusalem, the city of David, was the place God chose to dwell. David, the former shepherd, was appointed the shepherd of God's own people, the people who, generation after generation, sinned against God. Despite their weaknesses, this king was both a skillful ruler and a righteous man.

The psalm ends on this positive note. The extent of the people's sinfulness could never compare with the depth of God's love. As stated at the beginning, those hearing the story are encouraged to refrain from following the example of their ancestors, but rather to be faithful to the covenant made with God (vv. 6-8).

Psalm 79 (communal lament)

1-4 The cruelty of the enemies

The psalm has traditionally been linked with the destruction of Jerusalem and the desecration of the temple. The description of the horrors that befell the people is startling. Death and devastation are all around; blood runs deep throughout the city. Bodies are not even afforded the dignity of burial. Instead, they have been left on the streets, there to become carrion devoured by wild beasts and winged fowl. The people who prided themselves on being the chosen of God have become the butt of the mockery of neighboring nations. Comfort can be found nowhere.

5-7 The lament

The actual cry of lamentation opens in the traditional way: "How long, LORD?" Though the people suffer at the hands of others, they know that it is really God's wrath that they experience, a wrath that burns them like an unforgiving fire. This agonizing people pray that divine wrath might be turned away from them and toward their enemies. Despite the fact that these enemies have been instruments of God for the chastisement of Israel, they have wreaked havoc on the people of God and they have laid waste the land that was God's own heritage.

8-13 A prayer for release

The people acknowledge that they have been guilty of transgression. However, they pray that God's compassion might far exceed their culpability. Besides, they believe that the sufferings they have endured are punishment enough. Having called on the covenant characteristic of compassion, they now appeal to God's honor or reputation in the sight of the other nations. What would these nations think if God allowed this special people to be completely destroyed? Punishment for transgressions might be appropriate, but total destruction? Furthermore, these adversaries should not be able to gloat over the Israelite blood they have spilled. Such behavior might suggest that the God of Israel is powerless to act on behalf of the people.

Modern sensibilities could be offended by the prayer for the affliction of enemies. Without condoning revenge, we must remember that such a petition is simply the reverse side of a prayer for victory in battle. This psalm clearly shows Israel's belief that its own enemies were also enemies of God. They would probably consider this a prayer for just punishment for their iniquities.

Psalm 80 (communal lament)

2-4 A cry to God

God is called on as shepherd and as warrior, two metaphors that capture the notion of divine protection. The throne among the cherubim could be a reference to God's heavenly throne, which was believed to be surrounded by angels, or to a shrine, before which representations of cherubim were commonly set up. Joseph, Ephraim, Benjamin, and Manasseh were northern tribes, suggesting a northern origin for the psalm. This section ends with a prayer (v. 4) that serves as a refrain throughout the psalm (cf. vv. 8, 20). In it the people ask for restoration and salvation.

5-8 The lament

The military title, "LORD of hosts," is followed by the traditional cry of lament: "how long?" God, who previously fought on behalf of the people now seems to be fighting against them, for their affliction has come from the hand of God. They are forced to feed on sorrow as if it were food. Furthermore, now God has allowed warring neighbors to fight over the spoils of their defeat. This section ends, as did the first, with the same prayer for restoration and salvation.

9-20 Remember the blessings of the past

Prayers for deliverance are often rooted in remembrance of former blessings. Here God is reminded of the graciousness shown at the time of Israel's deliverance from Egypt and entrance into the land. Israel is characterized as a vine that was taken out of Egypt and transplanted in the land of promise. This vine grew larger and covered more territory than even mighty cedar trees—a reference to neighboring nations, specifically Lebanon. The sea (probably the Mediterranean) and the river (perhaps the Tigris or Euphrates) set the desired boundaries of Israel's land. Despite all of this care and magnificence, God allowed the nation to fall and the land to be overrun by wild animals.

Once again God is called on as the mighty "God of hosts" (v. 15) who has the power to save the people. The metaphor shifts back to that of a vine dresser: "Visit this vine." If God sees fit to restore this people, they will show their gratitude through praise and reverence. The man at God's right hand, the place of honor, is the king who is God's representative among the people. This third section ends with the refrain.

Psalm 81 (prophetic exhortation)

2-6b A call to praise

The liturgical elements of this call to praise are clear. The plural imperative form of the verbs suggests a joyful, even triumphant, community gathering: "Sing joyfully . . . / raise loud shouts." Singing to musical instruments is also directed. The sound of the trumpet (*shofar*) announced important liturgical commemorations such as the celebration of new moon, full moon, and solemn festivals. These celebrations were mandated by law (cf. Lev 23). The divine title "God of Jacob" and mention of the tribe of Joseph are usually associated with the northern tribes, suggesting a northern origin for the psalm.

6c-17 The oracle

The oracle from God consists of two reports: one of God's deliverance of the people from Egyptian bondage (vv. 7-11), the other of the people's rebellion in spite of God's graciousness (vv. 12-17).

Temple prophets frequently delivered an oracle from God as part of solemn temple liturgies. This is probably what is described here. The images used in the description of the people's release from servitude capture the essence of their hard labor. They called and God responded. God not only rescued them but also cared for them in the wilderness when they had no other means of support. The mention of Meribah is a reminder of their infidelity in the wilderness (cf. Exod 17:1-7; Num 29:6-13). In the face of God's protective concern, the people's transgressions are baffling. The sin of the wilderness was murmuring against God, not idolatry. Therefore, the admonition against false worship was probably added at a later time. Some form of the phrase "I am the LORD your God," is a divine title that appears more than a hundred times in early traditions.

For their part, the people refused to follow God's directions and so God abandoned them, allowing them to remain in their hardness of heart and to fall victim to the designs of dangerous enemies. Despite their sinfulness, however, God does not seem to be able to forsake forever this chosen people. If they return to God, God will once again defend them against their enemies. The oracle ends with the possibility of peace and prosperity. It is up to Israel to choose.

Psalm 82 (divine oracle)

1 The divine council

The setting is the familiar ancient Near Eastern council of gods (cf. Job 1:6; 2:1). In Israelite tradition, Israel's own God is the mighty sovereign who reigns there. The presumed gods of the other nations are simply celestial bodies or the forces of nature created by God.

2-5 Divine directives

God chastises the members of the council for their failure to judge justly. The favoritism they show to the wicked may simply be the psalmist's way of describing the common understanding of the bias that patron gods show to their devotees. Instead of condemning the people for such worship, here God denounces the gods. They should have been attentive to the needy and those who are oppressed by the wicked. In other words, God is calling the members of the divine council to shift their own loyalties and to favor those whom the God of Israel favors. God moves from directly addressing the others gods to speaking about them (v. 5). Their lack of understanding does not merely affect them; it also threatens the very foundations of the earth.

6-8 Condemnation

There is some question about the identity of the speaker here. Some commentators claim that it could not be God, since the existence of other gods is not questioned. They maintain that it is the psalmist who, like other Israelites of the day, believed that other nations worshiped minor deities. Whoever the speaker might be, the insignificance of these other gods is underscored. Like human beings, they are transient and have no enduring future.

The final verse is a prayer to God, and it clearly comes from the psalmist. To ask God to judge the earth is to acknowledge God's universal sovereignty, even over those gods to whom other nations look for protection and justice.

Psalm 83 (communal lament)

2-9 Lament

The people pray that God will step in and end the persecution that they are suffering at the hands of those who are identified as God's own enemies. These foes are so identified because they are enemies of God's people. They have conspired to destroy this people so completely that not even their memory will endure. For people who did not have a well-defined belief in life after this life, to be blotted out of memory was considered the ultimate threat. It would be as if one had never even existed. Conspiracy against God's people was conspiracy against God. The nations named were those neighbors who at some time in their history warred against Israel. Ishmael, born of the Egyptian Hagar, and the rival brother of Isaac, was associated with the Transjordanian country of Edom (cf. Gen 25:22-26), the nation that much later forbade the Israelite people from passing through it on their way to the land of promise (cf. Num 20:18). The Hagrites, probably linked with Hagar, also lived east of the Jordan. Gebal was near Petra in the east; Ammon and Amalek were also eastern nations. Only Philistia (cf. Josh 13:3) and Tyre (cf. Ezek 26:3) were to the west of Israel. The most threatening nation was Assyria, the superpower to the northeast (cf. 2 Kgs 17:6).

10-19 Prayers for redress

Those who oppressed the chosen people of God have also sinned against God and should be punished. They should be punished just as earlier nations that had similarly transgressed were smitten by the righteous wrath of God. The Midianites were a desert people who constituted a serious threat during the time that Israel was settling in the land. Zebah and Zalmunna were kings of that nation (cf. Judg 8:6), and Oreb and Zeeb were princes (cf. Judg 7:25). Under Gideon's leadership they were conquered. The Canaanite king Jabin and his general Sisera were defeated at the time of the judges (cf. Judg 4), as was the territory of Endor (cf. Josh 17:11).

The people pray that afflictions will devastate their adversaries. The enemies sought to erase from memory the name of Israel. Now Israel asks that those same enemies be withered up and blown away, or burned to ashes. In either case, nothing would remain of them and so they would be forgotten. They pray for terror and shame, for battles could be won because of terror, and shame is sometimes even worse than death. What the people are really asking is that the sovereign power of God be made manifest in the defeat of their and God's enemies.

Psalm 84 (song of Zion)

2-5 Happiness in the temple

In this psalm, devotion toward God extends to an overwhelming attachment to the house of God, the place on earth where God dwells in the midst of the people in a very special way. The yearning of the psalmist indicates distance from the temple at this time. This yearning is all-encompassing, affecting both body and inner being. Though the desired sense of security, which is compared with that experienced by nesting birds, introduces the idea of protection from harm, the overriding sentiments here are those of intimacy and serenity. The military designation "Lord of hosts" is softened somewhat by the reference "living God." The section ends with a beatitude "Blessed!" Those who dwell in God's presence are certainly happy or blessed.

6-8 Divine protection

This second section opens with a macarism. Here the focus shifts from the tranquility associated with God's presence to the divine protection that it guarantees. The picture sketched is that of a pilgrimage. Commentators have been unable to locate the Baca valley. The derivation of the word ("to weep," thus yielding "valley of tears"), along with the mention of God's gift of water, has led some to conclude that this is a reference to an arid stretch of land through which the people passed on their way to Jerusalem. It could also be a figurative way of describing the interior movement from thirsting for God's presence to enjoying the refreshment that experiencing that presence ultimately brings.

9-10 A prayer for the king

The military tone of these verses is seen in the divine epithet "Lord of hosts" and in the characterization of the king as the shield of the people. The focus here is on protection, not aggression.

11-13 Delight in the presence of God

The psalmist includes two examples of "better than" proverbs in this praise of the temple. The comparisons may seem exaggerated, but they clearly convey the high regard in which are held the temple itself and time spent within the temple. God protects ("shield") the righteous and provides everything ("sun") that is necessary for prosperous life. The psalm ends with a macarism that exhorts trust in God. The frequent use of "Lord of hosts" (four times) testifies to the divine power that inspires such trust.

Psalm 85 (communal lament)

2-4 Remember the past

Speaking in the name of the people, the psalmist reminds God of some of the favors they enjoyed in the past. This is done in order to encourage God to grant similar favors in the present. The verb "restore" became a technical term referring to the restoration of the nation after the Babylonian exile. This seems to be the sense of the psalm here. Since the exile was perceived as punishment for the sins of the people, their restoration would have been viewed as evidence of divine forgiveness, pardon, withdrawal of wrath, and turning back of anger.

5-8 Prayer for deliverance

The prayer is now explicit. Though specifics are not given regarding the situation within which the people now find themselves, they are definitely suffering. The psalmist would not speak of divine wrath if this were not the case, for Israel believed that misfortune was God's angry response to their infidelity. The prayer is fourfold: "Restore us . . . / restore our life . . . / Show us, Lord, your mercy; / grant us your salvation." The people bring these prayers to God, who is the savior from whom alone salvation will come.

9-14 Trust in God's graciousness

After past favors have been recalled and petitions for deliverance have been offered, the graciousness of God is praised. For the only time in this psalm, the psalmist speaks as an individual, as one who is confident that God will respond favorably to the people's prayer. In this trust, the psalmist waits for God's word of assurance. The role that the psalmist plays in the prayer of the people prompts some commentators to conclude that the setting is liturgical, the people having brought their needs to worship, with the psalmist acting as mediator between them and God. God's forgiving response depends on their repentance and promise of future faithfulness. Reconciliation with God results in the restoration of characteristics of the covenant bond that had been fractured by the people's sin: love, truth, justice, peace (*shalom*). God's good favor will be seen in the eventual prosperity that will surround the forgiven people.

Psalm 86 (lament of an individual)

1b-7 A call for help

The psalm opens with a series of petitions: "Incline your ear . . . answer . . . / Preserve . . . / save . . . be gracious . . . / Gladden . . . / hear . . . / listen." The psalmist claims to be a faithful covenant partner, and so this suffering is not punishment for sin. Rather, it is oppression caused by enemies, and God is called on to intervene. Although this section of the psalm is replete with petition, the tone of the prayers and the way God is portrayed subtly show that the psalmist perceives God as faithful and concerned about the welfare of the righteous. This is confirmed by the unflinching trust expressed in the psalm (v. 7).

8-10 Praise of God

The people of Israel worshiped only one God, but they did not always reject the possibility that other nations had their own gods. Even when they entertained this idea, they insisted that their God was superior to all other deities, being the maker of all that was created. Furthermore, they maintained that eventually other nations would recognize their God's superiority, would switch their allegiance, and would join them in paying homage to the Lord who was really the only true God.

11-17 Petitions repeated

A second set of petitions is directed toward God. Some of them repeat preceding sentiments, others do not. The first prayer arises from the wisdom tradition, which exhorts the student to choose one way of life over another. The psalmist prays for instruction in God's way, the way of

truth and commitment to righteousness. With this kind of training, the psalmist would be able to praise God's name appropriately. There is no explicit expression of thanksgiving; however, the acknowledgment of divine covenant love that prompted God to rescue the psalmist from some dimension of death (Sheol) certainly lays the ground for sentiments of gratitude. Those who rise up against the psalmist are identified as enemies of God. Therefore, any defense of the psalmist would be a defense of God's honor. What the psalmist seeks is the downfall of these enemies. Their defeat will be seen as a victory for God and a sign of God's partiality toward the psalmist. Once again, covenant language is used to represent God: merciful and gracious, loving and true. God is characterized in this same way in the Exodus tradition after the people had sinned with the golden calf (cf. Exod 34:6). This phrase became one of the standard ways of describing God.

Psalm 87 (song of Zion)

1-3 Jerusalem, the favored city

It is not uncommon that Israelites insist that Zion far exceeds in grandeur the cities of other nations. Here it is said to be more loved by God than any other Israelite city. In fact, it is God's own city, built on a high mountain so that all can see it and marvel at its splendor. The superiority of this city, also known as the city of David, could be a way of asserting God's preference for that southern king and all his descendants.

4-7 Jerusalem, the mother of the people

Cities were frequently personified as mothers of the inhabitants within them. Such a familial relationship with Jerusalem is here extended to others as well. The boundaries of this influence are remarkable. Babylon and Egypt (the Hebrew has Rahab, the mythological monster associated with Egypt [cf. Isa 30:7]) were the ancient and somewhat distant superpowers that set the general geographic boundaries of the ancient Near East. Philistia, Ethiopia, and Tyre were smaller nations immediately adjacent to Israel. Some commentators maintain that the psalmist is speaking about Jews living in Diaspora in these nations. They would certainly have claimed citizenship. Others think that the reference is to natives of these nations who had chosen the Lord as their God. Their membership would have been religious. Whoever these people might have been, the sense of the psalm is quite clear—there are people outside the geographic boundaries of Israel who claim Zion as their city and pay homage to its God.

Psalm 88 (lament of an individual)

2-3 The lament

Day and night cries for help rise to God. Loud cries suggest unrelenting anguish. The fact that pleas are made at all suggests a degree of trust in God. However, there is still a sense of foreboding here, as if God might not listen after all.

4-10 The psalmist's affliction

Sheol, the pit, and the abyss are references to the place of the dead. Israel did not believe in utter annihilation after death, but neither did it have a well-developed idea of life after this life. Therefore, Sheol was not considered a place of punishment. Israel dreaded it, not because of what happened to the dead when they were there, but because of the death that brought them there in the first place. Affliction of any kind was considered a foretaste of ultimate death. Therefore, the one who was in any way suffering was thought to be struggling with death itself.

Suffering was also ascribed to divine wrath, God's anger in the face of transgression. It crashed upon the tormented one like a series of waves cascading upon the shore. Unfortunately, people often tend to avoid those who are suffering, perhaps because suffering is so hard to witness, or because those who would like to help frequently feel so powerless before it. If it is punishment from God, then the one suffering will also have to endure the shame that accompanies culpability. All of this explains the sense of revulsion many experience in the face of suffering. Unfortunately, the one suffering is unable to escape.

11-13 God is questioned

The psalmist addresses a series of rhetorical questions to God. Besides underscoring the futility of suffering, Israel's understanding of the netherworld is revealed. At this point in its history, Israel did not believe that God's jurisdiction extended into the world of the dead. God's power was not

felt there, nor did those who dwelt there praise God. In other words, the God of Israel was revered as the God of the living, not of the dead.

14-19 Lament repeated

The cries of lament are repeated. The silence from God is interpreted as rejection. Affliction includes many of the signs of death, and the psalmist has endured this for a prolonged period of time. Furthermore, those who should support the tortured individual have turned their backs. Abandoned by all, the only companion is darkness. The psalm ends with not even a hint of hope.

Psalm 89 (royal psalm)

2-5 A royal covenant

The psalm opens with a hymn in praise of God who promised to make a covenant with the royal house of David and who has been faithful to that promise. The promise was prompted by God's love and faithfulness. Just as that faithfulness is enduring, so will this covenant last throughout the ages.

6-19 Praise of the creator

The scene reflects the ancient Near Eastern council of the gods. What other nations revered as minor deities, Israel considered created celestial beings. These creatures offer their homage to the Lord God of hosts, the one who rules over all other gods. The description is of the primeval cosmic battle in which God was triumphant over the forces of chaotic waters. Rahab is the name given to the monster of the deep (cf. Job 26:12; Isa 51:9). The orderly universe was established after the battle had been won.

The scene moves from the heavens to earth, from myth to the ancient world. Zaphon was the sacred mountain on which the Canaanite god Baal was believed to dwell; Amanus is a mountain in southern Turkey; Tabor and Hermon are found in Israel itself. These mountains, majestic peaks that inspired wonder and religious devotion in the people, now praise the God who fashioned them. God's own royal rule is extolled, a rule founded in righteousness and justice. Those who recognize and acclaim this rule are called "Blessed." By deftly drawing a line from primeval victory through the marvels of creation to the rule over the people, the psalmist has shown that the cosmic conqueror and creator of all is none other than the God of Israel.

20-38 The divine oracle

God speaks and briefly recounts the choice of David as commander of Israel's armies and king over all the people (cf. 1 Sam 16:1-3; 2 Sam 7:11-16). The faithfulness and love that were lauded earlier (v. 3) were bestowed in a special way on David (v. 25). He will be given rule over the unruly sea and rivers, making him the mightiest ruler of the earth, actually wielding some of the power that belonged to the divine warrior. Many ancient people believed that their king was a direct descendant of their god. Israel retained elements of that royal ideology, but reinterpreted them. The king did have a kind of father-son relationship with God, but it was one of responsibility, not descent. Though the Davidic dynasty was afforded divine legitimation, its human character is also clearly stated in the psalm. All Israelites, even the kings, were bound by the regulations of the law. All violators would have been punished, including the kings. The promise of the dynasty's enduring rule is firmly rooted in the establishment of cosmic order. It will last forever, like the sun and the moon.

39-52 Lament over the ruin of the king

Included in the royal covenant was the king's responsibility to uphold the law. What follows is an account of the afflictions that befell him when he was not faithful to that responsibility. Just as throughout this psalm "David" represents the dynasty generally and not merely the specific man, so these verses might contain a description of the failure of any of the kings. The report of ruined strongholds and the collapse of royal rule (vv. 41-45) lead some to believe that the reference is to the exile. God originally warned the kings that they would pay for their sinfulness by defeat at the hands of their enemies (cf. 2 Sam 7:14-15). That warning was not heeded and so calamity struck.

The psalmist cries out in typical lament fashion: "How long?" How long will God remain hidden? How long will divine anger rule the day? Human frailty is used as an incentive for divine forbearance. God made human beings weak: how can God expect more from them? The psalmist next appeals to the promises made to David. Even

though the kings have been unfaithful, surely God will remain constant. The psalm ends on that note.

53 Doxology

The last verse is less a resolution of the sentiments of this psalm than it is the conclusion of the entire third book. Though shorter, it resembles similar conclusions of the previous books (cf. Pss 41:14; 72:18-20).

BOOK FOUR: PSALMS 90–106

Psalm 90 (communal lament)

1b-6 The fleeting nature of human life

(This is the only psalm attributed to Moses.) The psalm opens with words of praise. God, who existed before all of creation, is acclaimed the everlasting God. What human beings would consider incalculable periods of time are as nothing to the God of all eternity. The fleeting nature of human life is compared to the short four-hour duration of a night watch. Human mortality, which is associated with the dust of death (cf. Gen 3:19), is compared to the daylong lifespan of grass. The themes of this first part of the prayer are reminiscent of wisdom teaching on the transitory nature of human life and its perishability (cf. Job 14:2).

7-11 Divine punishment

God's anger is fierce, like a consuming fire. It is also unrelenting, a fury that the people have brought on by their own sins. In the first verses of the psalm, the psalmist lamented the fleeting nature of life. A different perspective is expressed here. A longer life is also troublesome because it is usually filled with trouble and wearisome toil (cf. Job 7:1). In other words, life itself is a burden, regardless of its duration.

12-17 Prayers of petition

The psalm ends with a collection of prayers. The first plea is for wisdom. Several theological concepts are brought together in the second prayer. It asks God to "Relent," the traditional word for "change one's heart." This is followed by the familiar cry of lament: "How long?" Appeal is then made to the covenant features of mercy and steadfast love. The psalmist asks that the people be granted as many days of happiness as they have been forced to endure in affliction. In these prayers for restoration, the people are called God's servant, God's children—references to the covenant relationship. The final prayer is a general request for divine favor.

Psalm 91
(prayer of confidence of an individual)

1-2 God, a sure refuge

Two well-known names for God illustrate the role that God plays in this psalm. "Most High" is the title attributed to the original deity worshiped in Jerusalem and then appropriated to the God of Israel once David captured that city (cf. Gen 14:18). This high God provides a shelter in which one can find safety. "Almighty," the divine epithet of the patron God of Abram (cf. Gen 17:1), emphasizes God's superiority. In this psalm, this title too is associated with security. Both names signify that under the protection of the supreme God, one has nothing to fear. God is further described as refuge and fortress, two more references to security. By attributing to God these four titles, the psalmist means to generate trust in God.

3-13 Divine protection

The psalmist encourages an unnamed listener to trust in God. The troubles of which the psalmist speaks are depicted in various ways: a snare, the plague, darkness, deadly weapons. In each case, God will intervene and either ward off the attacks or release the afflicted one from distress. Covenant faithfulness (v. 4) is lifted up as a trustworthy defense. Others may fall victim to these assaults, but whoever trusts in God the Most High will be spared. God's protection is administered through angels who ward off all forms of danger (vv. 11-12). (This passage may have influenced our understanding of guardian angels.) Asp, viper, lion, and dragon denote dangerous animals, or they could be metaphors for threatening enemies.

14-16 God speaks

God promises to stand by all who are faithful and who honor the divine name. Since the name represents part of one's essence, to honor God's name is to honor God. Those who do so will enjoy divine protection. God will be their deliverer and will act as savior on their behalf.

Psalm 92
(prayer of thanksgiving of an individual)

2-4 Give thanks to God

The psalm opens with what appears to be a call to others to give thanks to God. It then moves immediately to a proclamation of praise directed to God. Such praise is appropriate all day long, both morning and evening. Reference to musical instruments suggests liturgical performance.

5-12 Reasons for gratitude

The "deeds" and "works of your hands," for which the psalmist is grateful, could be a reference to the wonders of creation or blessings that Israel experienced within its own history. If one interprets them from the context of the rest of the psalm, one could say that they refer to the justice that God will exact on Israel's enemies and the subsequent punishment meted out to them.

"Works" is in a parallel construction with "designs" (also translated "thought" or "device"). This suggests the wisdom tradition rather than history. God's purposes are not comprehended by fools and, therefore, the foolish will suffer the consequences of their foolishness. In the wisdom tradition, there is a very thin line between folly and sin. The psalmist crosses that line here. Sinners may think that they will escape punishment, but their good fortune will not last (short-lived like grass); retribution will ultimately overtake them.

The psalmist, on the other hand, is certain of God's favor. The Hebrew word translated "strength" is really "horn," a symbol of power; anointing with rich oil suggests extravagant blessing. The psalmist takes great delight in personal blessing as well as the downfall of the wicked.

13-16 The reward of the righteous

Nature metaphors are used to describe the blessings that the just will enjoy. Palm trees produce dates that are a staple in the diet of the Near East. The cedars of Lebanon were famous for their majesty. Wood from these trees was used to construct the temple. The righteous are said to be like these trees, established in the courts of God and bearing fruit for many years.

The psalm ends with a joyful shout of praise of God who is just and reliable.

Psalm 93 (kingship of God)

1-5 The majesty of the divine king

The psalm opens with what might be considered a shout of acclamation. "The Lord is king"—and no one else is! Both the shout and the scene described originated in a mythological account of the primordial chaos battle (cf. Ps 89:10-12). After this battle was won, a palace was constructed in the heavens for the conqueror, and a throne was set up. From there, the victorious king rules over all. The unruly waters were tamed during the battle and are no longer a threat to the order of the cosmos. God's rule extends to the earth as well. The one who ordered the heavens also established laws to be followed on earth. Furthermore, God's heavenly dwelling is mirrored in God's holy temple on earth.

Psalm 94 (communal lament)

1-2 A cry for retribution

The psalm opens with words that are quite jarring for those who think of God as being primarily gentle and merciful. However, God is also just, and the psalmist is calling on that justice to right the wrongs that have been committed against God's people and, therefore, against God. It is important to note that the psalmist acknowledges that justice and vengeance will be meted out by God (cf. Deut 32:35) and not by vindictive human beings.

3-7 The deeds of the wicked

The lament itself begins with the standard cry of complaint: "How long?" The sinners take pride in their sins; they even boast about them. How long will God allow this situation to last? In a patriarchal society, the widow, the orphan, and the resident alien have no male guardian and, consequently, lack a legal sponsor or protector. In the Bible, these three groups represent the most vulnerable in society. Here, oppression of them symbolizes the excessive cruelty of the enemies. Their boast is close to blasphemy; they claim that God does not even care about the fate of God's own people.

8-11 The wicked are chided

The psalmist turns on the wicked. "Brutish" might be a better translation of the Hebrew word than "stupid," for these wicked have acted like beasts toward the helpless as well as like fools before God. How could they think that the creator would bestow gifts on creatures and then not use the divine exemplars of those gifts to benefit these very creatures? Compared with God's wisdom, human plans are vapid.

12-15 Praise of God

Using themes from the wisdom tradition, the psalmist praises God's justice. Those who accept divine guidance and instruction will be blessed, while the wicked who refuse to heed God's directives will suffer misfortune. Contrary to what the foolish and wicked think, God will not abandon God's very own people. Justice will again rule in society.

16-23 Trust is in the Lord

Rhetorical questions set the stage for a confession of trust in God. Who will stand in defense of the psalmist? The Lord will. In fact, if God had not done so in the past, the psalmist would have been relegated to a life of silence. Though not in the Hebrew version, "in the grave" is added in some translations because of the association of silence with death (cf. Ps 115:17). God is addressed directly in this acknowledgment of divine protection (vv. 18-19). The care that God shows is the covenantal steadfast love. Once again the psalmist employs rhetorical questions. Here they prepare for a declaration of commitment. Will allegiance be entrusted to the unjust? No. Security can only be found in the Lord and, being just, the Lord will destroy the wicked. Therefore, commitment will be made to the Lord alone.

Psalm 95 (liturgical hymn)

1-7a A summons to praise God

A cry goes out to praise the Lord. The psalm is replete with liturgical allusions. Besides mention of praise and song, there is an invitation to enter, presumably, a place of worship, where the devout might bow, kneel, and worship God. The reason for such praise is the greatness of God as witnessed in the marvels of creation. The entire natural world belongs to God, the sea and the dry land, from the depths of the earth to the heights of the mountains. This great God is the special God of the very people called to give praise. They are cared for by God as a shepherd tends a well-loved flock.

7b-11 A warning

The psalm takes on an entirely different character. The people are admonished to listen to God and not follow the path taken by their ancestors who, despite God's solicitous care of them, revolted in the wilderness and turned away. God tells of their sin and describes their punishment. In consequence of their disloyalty, they were prevented from entering the land of promise. Instead, they were forced to sojourn in the wilderness for an entire generation (forty years). All but a few died there (cf. Deut 1:35-39). The psalm ends on this negative note.

Psalm 96 (kingship of God)

1-3 An invitation to praise

Three times the psalmist calls out: "Sing to the LORD." This is followed by two exhortations to proclaim God's wondrous deeds of salvation. These imperatives are addressed to all the earth, all nations, and all peoples.

4-6 Reasons for praise

The reason for the praise is the superiority of this God over the gods of the other nations. They are powerless to accomplish any good thing. The Lord, on the other hand, created the heavens. The holy place to which the psalmist refers here might be God's heavenly dwelling place. However, it could also connote the temple, since Israel believed that it was an earthly representation of that heavenly dwelling.

7-10 A second call to praise

Once again the nations are invited to give glory to God. Here the temple is clearly the focus of attention. It is to this holy place that gifts will be brought as offerings of devotion. It is here that homage will be paid and worship performed. The cry of divine enthronement goes out from this temple: "The LORD is king." God's rule assures that the earth is steadfast and justice reigns among the people.

11-13 Praise from creation

All of creation is called on to praise God. This includes the heavens and the earth. The sea, which in myths of creation is often the chaotic enemy, is here simply a creation of God. It is the habitat of the water creatures that are also called to praise. The God enthroned in the heavens governs the earth with justice and with the covenant characteristic "faithfulness."

Psalm 97 (kingship of God)

1-6 The majesty of the divine king

This enthronement psalm opens with the cry of acclamation: "The LORD is king." The scene is one of great power and majesty. All of creation responds to the approach of the mighty ruler. The description, reminiscent of the theophany at Mount Sinai (cf. Exod 19:16-19), signals the appearance of the great storm deity, who comes with clouds and darkness, fire and lightning. This fury causes the earth to tremble; the scorching heat melts the mountains. The God who is so powerful in the heavens is also the one who executes justice on earth.

7-9 Effects of the divine king's coming

Two different yet related consequences follow the coming of the divine king. The first is an acknowledgment of the worthlessness of idols and the shame that accrues for those who worship them. A second effect can be seen in the judgments of God that cause Zion (Jerusalem) and all the surrounding cities to rejoice. The connection between the two is found in the last verse of this section (v. 9). The Lord's superiority over all other deities is captured in the title "Most High." This divine epitaph is the name of the god worshiped in Salem (Jerusalem) before David conquered the city (cf. Gen 14:18).

10-11 The rewards of righteousness

The psalmist lists some of the rewards enjoyed by those who have chosen the path of righteousness. They are loved by God, protected and rescued from harm. They live in light rather than darkness, and they enjoy the happiness that comes from this choice.

12 A final exhortation

The psalm ends on a positive note. The righteous are invited to take delight in God and to continue in their praise.

Psalm 98 (kingship of God)

1-3 Praise to the victorious God

The particular divine victory that calls forth songs of praise is difficult to identify with certitude. "[R]ight hand" and "holy arm" are metaphors for military might. The victory took place on earth, not in heaven, for it was witnessed by the other nations. This witness functions as evidence of God's superiority over all other forces. Allusions to the covenant are present in the mention of God's faithful love and in reference to Israel as the recipient of that special love.

4-6 Liturgical celebration of divine kingship

The extensive description of the musical involvement suggests a liturgical celebration. It was probably at such an event that the kingship of God was celebrated.

7-9 Natural creation joins in the celebration

Forces of nature, which in other cultures were considered minor deities, join in the celebration. These include the sea and rivers, thought by some to be chaotic deities. Here they join with the mountains and the inhabitants of the earth in rejoicing in anticipation of the arrival of the divine king, who will come in justice.

Psalm 99 (kingship of God)

1-3 Praise of the divine king

The psalm opens with the standard cry of praise: "The LORD is king." Though God's primary place of enthronement is the heavens, details in the psalm indicate that the site of divine rule is the temple. It is people who tremble, not celestial beings; the cherubim are probably the guardians of the ark of the covenant (cf. Exod 25:18-22); Zion is a reference to Jerusalem, where the temple was built and where God's name was revered in a special way (cf. 1 Kgs 8:16-29). This praise ends with a declaration of God's holiness.

4-5 The God of justice

The praise of God is interrupted by a declaration addressed directly to God. In it God is acclaimed for being just and exercising this justice in Israel, referred to as "Jacob." God's footstool is a further reference to the ark. This acclamation also ends with a declaration of God's holiness.

6-9 Ancestors praise God

Moses, Aaron, and Samuel, significant figures in Israel's history, were rewarded for their devotion to God. The pillar of cloud led the people through the wilderness (cf. Exod 13:21). Once again God is addressed directly (v. 8), acknowledging both God's forgiveness and God's justice. The psalm ends with a final call to praise God who is acclaimed as holy.

Psalm 100 (hymn)

1b-2 An invitation to praise

Though the superscription classifies this as a psalm of thanksgiving, it has the features of a hymn: a call to praise followed by the reason to give praise. All the earth is invited to worship the Lord. The site where this will take place is the temple.

3-5 Reasons for praise

The Lord's identity as God and Israel's privilege as God's chosen people are cause for praise. This God is both the creator of the people and the one who cares for them. Love and faithfulness underscore the covenant bond, a bond that will endure from generation to generation.

Psalm 101 (royal psalm)

1b-3 The upright king

The king begins with praise of God's covenant love and justice, and then moves immediately into a promise to act righteously. (The Hebrew verb forms are future tense.) These promises probably apply more to the king's manner of ruling than simply to his personal life. Integrity of heart (v. 2) is a distinctive characteristic of the king (cf. 1 Kgs 3:6).

4-8 Righteous citizenry

The king not only pledges himself to principled living, but also promises to require the same righteousness of the people in his realm. This will be particularly true of those who serve in court. Since they execute the directives of the king, they must be trusted to do so with the same integrity with which those directives were initially enacted. The king further pledges to enforce this justice daily and with great severity. Most likely, the city of the Lord is Jerusalem.

Psalm 102
(lament of an individual; penitential)

2-3 A cry for help

The lament (considered one of the penitential psalms; cf. Pss 6, 32, 38, 51, 130, 143) opens with the standard cry for help: Hear me! Don't turn away. Don't allow me to linger in distress, but come to my aid quickly. The tenor of the prayers implies that God can indeed alleviate the suffering under which the psalmist labors.

4-12 The distress

The psalmist does not identify the exact nature of the affliction. Instead, metaphors are used to characterize it. Smoke signifies the emptiness and worthlessness of days as they pass; fire describes the burning nature of the physical pain; lifeless and useless grass characterizes the body that has withered away and is now skin and bones; finally, the afflicted one experiences isolation, like a solitary bird in the wilderness or alone on a roof. Added to these tribulations is the mockery hurled at the psalmist by enemies. Ashes, along with dust, symbolize human mortality (cf. Gen 18:27; Job 30:19; 42:6). Therefore, to eat ashes means to eat death. The psalmist acknowledges that all of this suffering comes from God. In fact, God is described as being somewhat capricious, for this tortured one was lifted up, only to be cast down again.

13-23 Divine mercy

Mention of divine enthronement implies God's conquest over chaos and consequent dominion over all creation. By appealing to this divine supremacy, the psalmist is acknowledging God's power, most likely hoping that this power will be employed to assuage the psalmist's own suffering.

Attention is directed to the misfortune suffered by Zion, the city of Jerusalem. Mention of its rebuilding indicates that the city has been destroyed, a factor that helps to classify the psalm as exilic or postexilic. The reconstruction of the city, a demonstration of divine compassion and

power, will garner praise for the Lord from the other nations. It also instills hope for those who, like the psalmist, are in agony and who turn to God for escape. Just as God will show mercy to Zion (v. 14), so God will hear the cries of the lowly (v. 18) and those who are imprisoned (v. 21). The psalmist appeals to such divine compassion, hoping to be the beneficiary of it as well.

Another approach is used to win divine assistance. The psalmist suggests that if a report of God's deliverance is preserved for the instruction of the generations to come, they will know that the God enthroned above has compassion on those on earth who are struck down by affliction. Such a report will redound to God's glory, and praise of God's goodness will resound in the restored city of Jerusalem. More than this, other nations and peoples will gather to worship this merciful God.

24-29 A plea for deliverance

The psalmist extols God's graciousness, perhaps hoping that this acclamation will soften God toward the psalmist's own suffering. Now the psalmist returns to lament. In order that God be persuaded to lift the burden of suffering, appeal is made to two other divine characteristics—God's everlasting nature and unwavering stability. God endures through generation upon generation; the psalmist simply asks to be granted a full complement of years and not be cut off in midlife. In addition to being steadfast, God has established the earth on a firm foundation. But even if the heavens and the earth crumble, God remains; the psalmist asks for some kind of endurance to live on through the future generations. The prayer that began with lament, moved to praise and back to lament, now closes with a request for continuity.

Psalm 103 (hymn)

1-5 An invitation to praise

The same invitation to bless or praise the Lord both opens and closes this psalm, thus acting as a kind of frame enveloping the sentiments expressed. The Hebrew word translated "soul" is actually the "life force" that sustains the entire individual. Thus the call to bless is issued to the most vibrant aspect of the person. Several reasons to praise God are given. Of the gifts bestowed on the psalmist, the most significant are divine love and compassion. Characteristics of God's covenantal commitment, these gifts are probably the reason and source of all other blessings. The eagle was a symbol of rejuvenation and strength (cf. Isa 40:31).

6-18 God's graciousness

The goodness of God is extolled, particularly God's mercy toward Israel, despite its continued disloyalty. First, God's care of the oppressed is acclaimed. This was most evident in the events surrounding the exodus from Egyptian bondage. The psalmist then expounds on God's merciful nature. "Merciful and gracious is the LORD, / slow to anger, abounding in mercy" (v. 8), the divine characterization proclaimed by God after the people had forged a golden calf for themselves in the wilderness (cf. Exod 34:6), became a standard way of describing God's mercy toward sinners (cf. Num 14:18; Neh 9:17; Ps 86:15). The extent of God's steadfast love is compared to the boundless expanse between the heavens and earth; God's willingness to forgive is compared to the vast distance between east and west, as well as the compassion of a human father for his children. Each example highlights a feature that cannot be calculated. In like manner, God's graciousness to those who have been disloyal is immeasurable.

The reason for God's compassion is humanity's fundamental frailty. Human beings are made of worthless dust; they live a very short time, and then they disappear like insubstantial vegetation. Once again a comparison is made. Though human beings are short-lived, God's steadfast love lasts forever. The blessings of the covenant continue through the ages from one generation to the next, to those who are faithful to their own covenant commitment.

19-22 Praise of the divine king

Celestial beings are invited to praise God who is enthroned in the heavens. The angels are divine messengers, and the hosts are the heavenly armies. They all serve God faithfully and are here called on to praise or bless the Lord. Finally, everything that God created is called to join the chorus of praise. The psalm ends as it began: "Bless the LORD, my soul!"

Psalm 104 (hymn)

1-4 The God of heaven

Commentators have long recognized the similarities between this hymn and various other ancient Near Eastern songs of praise, particularly the Egyptian "Hymn to Aton." While literary comparison can certainly be made, the major difference is theological. The Egyptian poem celebrates the divinized sun disk, while Israel praises its God as the sole creator.

Like Psalm 103, this psalm opens and closes with the same summons to bless or praise the Lord, but then it moves immediately to acclamations directed to God. In them, God is characterized as the triumphant cosmic warrior who now rules in the heavens as the mighty storm deity. God is clothed in the majesty and glory of the heavens, is housed in a palace that is erected over the defeated waters of chaos, and, like the sun, God travels across the heavens with the clouds and wind as celestial attendants. The flaming fire that accompanies God is probably the lightning.

5-13 Waters of the earth

The once chaotic waters have been tamed and are now an ordered part of the world. The earth was established on them, and boundaries were set so that these waters would not endanger it. God's authority over the waters is evident. They heed God's word, assume the place that God assigns them, and remain within the limits that God set. Once secured, they serve to water the land and quench the thirst of earth's wild animals. The waters that once threatened life now support it. All of this is accomplished by the mighty God who rules from the divine throne established in the heavens. God's distance does not suggest disinterest. Rather, it is evidence of God's supremacy over all.

14-23 God's care of the earth

The description of the earth depicts a peaceful and flourishing paradise. There is food for the animals and bread and wine for human beings. Oil for anointing suggests a level of economic prosperity. Bread, wine, and oil are not only fruits of the earth and staples of life, but also products of a society engaged in agriculture and viticulture. Cattle and beasts of burden are domesticated animals implying some form of animal husbandry.

The scene depicted is one of order, fulfillment, and stability.

There is also order and satiety outside the realm of human habitation. Trees thrive, as do the animals dependent on them. Topography that is inhospitable toward humans is ideal for certain animals. There they find not only safety but enough food and water to survive and flourish. The orderly movements of the heavens also serve the needs of earth's creatures. The sun and the moon, celestial bodies that were considered divine in other cultures, were demythologized by ancient Israel and now simply mark the seasons and the times of day. Even the regularity of night and day serves the needs of earth's animals. Many of them seek food under the cover of darkness, while human beings thrive in the light of day. Each follows the nature determined by the creator who oversees their activities and provides for their needs.

24-30 Divine providence

The psalmist marvels at the great variety of life-forms found in creation. Not only is this assortment vast and varied, but it also exhibits a kind of interdependence. All the different aspects of creation fit together and work together. This order in the midst of complexity testifies to the divine wisdom that brought it into being in the first place. The sea, once the unruly waters of chaos, is now the home of living creatures. These waters are reliable enough for ships to sail across them. Leviathan, once the monster that characterized chaotic waters (cf. Ps 74:14; Isa 27:1; Job 3:8; 40:25), is now one water animal among many that frolic in the sea. All the creatures of the land and of the sea are dependent on God for sustenance. Their very lives are in God's hands, and they live at the pleasure of the creator. Mention of dust recalls the early account of creation (cf. Gen 2:7, 19) and points to their vulnerability.

31-35 Prayer wishes

The psalm ends with several prayer wishes. The first is for the perpetual endurance of God's glory. This glory is seen in the power that God exercises over creation. The psalmist prays that these very prayers be pleasing to God and, finally, that sinners be punished. To the repetition of the opening summons to bless God is added a second acclamation: "Hallelujah!" Praise (*hallel*) the Lord (*jah*).

Psalm 105 (historical recital)

1-6 A call to give thanks

This historical recital opens with a series of imperatives: "Give thanks . . . / Sing praise . . . play music; / proclaim . . . / Glory . . . / rejoice . . . Seek out . . . / seek." Each in its own way is a summons to extol the greatness of God. While praise can be lifted to God at any time and in any circumstance, mention of playing music suggests a cultic situation. The last imperative, "Recall," explains why such a determined summons is issued. The psalm is addressed to the people of Israel, the descendants of Abraham. They are told to call to mind the wondrous deeds that God accomplished on their behalf.

7-15 The ancestors

Israel begins its story with an account of the promises made to the ancestors concerning numerous descendants and a land of their own (cf. Gen 15:2-18). Though ruler of all the earth, the Lord chose this particular people with whom to enter into covenant. Made first through Abraham, then renewed through Isaac and later through Jacob, this pact was meant to last forever (cf. Gen 17:7). Israel's subsequent history was an unfolding of the fulfillment of these covenant promises. Though in the beginning they were a wandering people (one of their earliest creedal statements identifies Abraham as "a refugee Aramean" [cf. Deut 26:5]), they were always under God's protection. The hand of a much later editor, one who was well acquainted with the monarchy, can be seen in the mention of the prophets and an "anointed." Prophets did not appear until several centuries later, and "anointed" refers to the king, the head of a form of government Israel would adopt centuries after the time of the ancestors.

16-22 Israel in Egypt

The story of Israel's ordeal in Egypt begins with the Joseph narrative (cf. Gen 37–47). This account contains several important aspects of Israelite faith. Besides explaining the arrival in Egypt of the ancestors of Israel, it underscores God's special care of them in a foreign land. The rise of one Israelite (Joseph) within the ranks of the Egyptian government demonstrates the superior nature of the entire people. Joseph surpassed the Egyptian sages and magicians with his wisdom, proving that the tradition of Israel outstripped that of Egypt. The exploits of Joseph gave the nation a reason to be proud of its heritage.

23-38 Bondage and deliverance

According to both the psalm and the account of Israel's oppression in Egypt (cf. Exod 1:7), Israel's swell in population contributed toward Egypt's resentment and the consequent hardships forced upon Israel. Ham was one of the sons of Noah. The land that bore his name included Egypt (cf. Gen 10:6). The land of Ham became a synonym for that country. The effects of the signs and wonders wrought by Moses and Aaron were both positive and negative. They were miracles for the Israelites, but plagues for the Egyptians (cf. Exod 7–11). Regardless of their degree of historical accuracy, these signs and wonders proclaim two major interrelated theological truths: a) The God of Israel has the power to perform marvelous works even in Egypt; b) The God of Israel is actually more powerful than the gods of Egypt.

39-45 Guidance to the land

Escape from Egypt was not enough. The people would have been perpetual wanderers had God not led them into the land promised to their ancestors. The trek from Sinai to Canaan was marked by miracle after miracle. This historical recital recounts only the graciousness of God, not the infidelity of the people, because it is a hymn of praise. (Ps 106 provides another view of the events of history). The psalm closes with the joyful acclamation "Hallelujah!" Praise (*hallel*) the Lord (*jah*).

Psalm 106 (historical recital)

1-3 A call to give thanks

Psalms 105 and 106 could be considered a pair. Both begin with a summons to give thanks to the Lord, both end with the joyful cry "Hallelujah," and both recount events from Israel's history. However, the psalms provide two very different views of this history. All the events recorded in the first psalm describe the marvelous deeds that God accomplished on Israel's behalf, while those

in the second recount the infidelity of the people even in the face of God's goodness. This psalm begins and ends with the joyful acclamation "Hallelujah!" This is followed by the summons to thank God for all of the goodness that God has shown, particularly for God's steadfast covenant love. Righteous living is affirmed by means of a beatitude.

4-5 A fervent prayer

The psalmist prays to be among those who are blessed by God. The reference is to the chosen people who have been delivered by God and granted a share in the land of promise ("your heritage").

6-12 Deliverance from Egypt

This section opens with an admission of guilt. Though the psalm recounts the sins of the ancestors, the psalmist includes the present generation in the company of those who have done wrong: "We have sinned . . . / we have done wrong." The events of escape from Egypt (cf. Exod 14) are condensed into a description of divine victory over waters, reminiscent of the ancient Near Eastern story of creation. Just as God had cut through the waters of primordial chaos and ordered the cosmic world, so God separated the waters that represent political oppression for the people and transformed them into a new nation. The primary purpose of this particular historical recital might be seen in verses 7 and 8; the people were oblivious of the magnanimous goodness of God, and yet God saved them out of even greater goodness. On the other side of freedom, they sang songs of praise. However, the remainder of the psalm will show that this piety was short lived.

13-18 Infidelity in the wilderness

The alternation between blessing and transgression continues in the wilderness (cf. Num 16). Each demonstration of divine providence is met with an act of rebellion. Despite this, when the people grumbled and made demands on God, God responded by granting their request. Eventually, however, their infidelity was requited; they were punished for their sinfulness. When they were disgruntled, they turned against their leaders and were punished for this as well. They did not learn from their misfortune, but continued their rebellious behavior.

19-23 The sin of idolatry

Perhaps their most ignominious betrayal occurred at the foot of the very mountain from which God delivered the law (cf. Exod 32:1-14). There they fashioned an idol for themselves, choosing to worship lifeless metal rather than the living God who had delivered them from bondage, provided for their needs in the wilderness, and protected them from harm. Moses, the very man they had turned against, intervened on their behalf and staved off the destructive hand of God. In each case recalled, despite their treacherous behavior, God's wrath is assuaged and the people are given another chance.

24-27 The people's distrust

The people left Egypt in order to settle in a land they could call their own. Their initial reluctance to enter that land, because of the fearsome reports about it that were brought by scouts (cf. Num 14:1-25), illustrated their lack of trust in God. The only explanation for their mistrust of the very God who showed such power in Egypt and such kindness and patience during their sojourn in the wilderness is their hardness of heart. Since they doubted the desirability of the land that God had chosen for them, God ordained that they would not live to enter it. Since the descendants of this generation did indeed enter the land, mention of the dispersal of descendants is probably a reference to a later generation that experienced the exile.

28-31 A second sin of idolatry

Peor, the site where the people of God sinned by worshiping the Canaanite storm god Baal, was located in Moab on the eastern shore of the Jordan River. This betrayal was associated with sexual impropriety with some foreign women. The punishment of the people was shortened by the retributive zeal of the priest Phineas (cf. Num 25:1-13). Once again the people sinned and were punished, but then God relented.

32-33 The sin of Moses

It was because of the incident at Meribah that Moses was prevented from entering the land of promise (cf. Num 20:2-13). The people's demand for water so angered him that he deviated from the trust in God that should have motivated him and he spoke rash words to them.

34-39 Infidelity in the land of promise

The people continued their sinful ways even after having been brought miraculously into the land of promise. The violence they were directed to execute on the original inhabitants of Canaan often offends the sensitivities of contemporary readers, because it appears that God directed it. Without defending the slaughter, it is important to understand why the people would think that this is what God would want. Though Israel was the nation moving into the territory of another people, as a nation it was still vulnerable. Realizing how susceptible they were to the religious practices of others, the Israelites believed that the best way to prevent such betrayal was to eliminate the other people. They did in fact succumb to idolatrous worship, even practicing child sacrifice and engaging in sex as part of the fertility cults.

40-46 God's response to sin

God's response to Israel's sinfulness in the land was the same as it had been when the people were in the wilderness. God's anger flared, the people endured chastisement for their transgressions, and eventually God relented. Once they were settled in the land, the punishment took the form of defeat at the hands of their enemies. The ultimate punishment was the defeat by the Babylonians and exile in the land of their conquerors. This was probably the captivity referred to here (v. 46). Even in that situation, God's steadfast covenant love for the people prevailed. The hearts of the captors were softened and they were kindly disposed toward God's people. The stage was set for their release.

47 A prayer for deliverance

The prayer to be gathered from among the nations suggests the dispersal of the people at the time of the exile. Their release, reunion, and return to their land will prompt them to thank and praise God continually.

48 Final doxology

The final prayer of praise is the conclusion of the entire fourth book of the Psalter. It contains many of the same sentiments found in the conclusions of the other books (cf. Pss 41:14; 72:18-20; 89:53). Unlike the others, this book ends as the psalm began, with the traditional acclamation of praise: "Hallelujah!" Praise (*hallel*) the Lord (*jah*).

BOOK FIVE: PSALMS 107–150

Psalm 107
(prayer of confidence of an individual)

1-3 A call to give thanks
The psalmist calls the people to give thanks to God. Mention of God's love suggests a covenant relationship. Identifying the people as those who have been redeemed and gathered from all directions suggests the period after the exile. The people's redemption and return to the land of promise would be ample reason for giving thanks.

4-9 Hardships en route
The hardships described in this section could refer either to the trials endured as the people traveled from their place of exile in Babylon back to their home in Israel, or to an earlier time when their ancestors moved from bondage in Egypt to the land promised by God. Most likely, this tradition of hardship was originally associated with the earlier period and then employed poetically in describing the latter one. Whichever period is the focus of this description, the point made is the same, namely, the people cried to God in their need, and God responded.

This is the first of four descriptions of suffering endured by some of the population. In each case the suffering is identified. This first description is followed by a report that serves almost as a refrain: "In their distress they cried to the LORD, / who rescued them in their peril" (vv. 6, 13, 19, 28). Finally, the people are called to give thanks: "Let them thank the LORD for his mercy [the word for covenant love], / such wondrous deeds for the children of Adam" (vv. 8, 15, 21, 31). Here, the people remember that they were wandering with no direction, and God guided them to safety.

10-16 Hardships of prison
The descriptions in these sections do not appear to follow any chronological order. The previous verses described the hardships with which the people were afflicted while they were on their return from exile. These verses revert to a time of imprisonment. The hardship may have been severe, but the psalmist maintains that it was justi-

fiable punishment. The people had violated their covenant agreement, rejected divine counsel, and rebelled against God. Initially, they were bereft of help, but eventually God relented and came to their rescue, releasing them from their bondage. Here too they cried out, were heard, and were subsequently summoned to give thanks to God.

17-22 Stricken with illness
A third type of suffering is described. Some of the company were stricken with illness, which was yet another consequence of their sins. Unable to eat, they almost died. However, after they cried for help, God snatched them from the jaws of death. Besides being called to give thanks, here the people are exhorted to offer sacrifice as well.

23-32 Deliverance of seafarers
The last descriptive section reports trials at sea. Such experiences would have been markedly unusual for most of the land-bound early Israelites, though quite common for those who lived near cities like Tyre and who made their living through maritime trade (cf. Ezek 27–28). The language used is highly mythological, which adds a sinister dimension to this description. The sea, the turbulent waters, and the storm winds were all manifestations of the Canaanite storm god. While these forces threatened the lives of sailors, they were no match for the God of Israel whose mere word first provoked their fury and then quelled it. The frightened mariners cried to God; they were heard and finally brought to safe harbor. Once again the people are called on to give thanks to the Lord, to praise God both in the religious assembly of the people and in the council of the ruling elders.

33-43 The providence of God
The preceding sections have been reports of past favors. The present form of verbs used here indicates that this is the way that God acts even now. The once-fertile land of the wicked is turned into a salty, barren wasteland, while the hungry are settled in a land that was once a desert but now yields an abundant harvest. Both the people and their flocks thrive and increase there. This description is reminiscent of the tradition of Israel's occupation of the land of promise where God dislodged one people in order to settle another. The reason given for such a reversal of fortune is the sinfulness of one people and the

neediness of the other. Such circumstances serve as a lesson for the future.

Psalm 108 (communal lament)

The psalm is a composite, consisting of sections from two earlier psalms: verses 2-6 repeat Psalm 57:8-12; verses 7-14 repeat Psalm 60:8-14.

2-6 The psalmist's devotion

The first part of the psalm is a testimony to the psalmist's piety. Praise of God springs from one who rises at dawn, most likely following a night of prayer. Mention of musical instruments suggests some form of liturgical celebration. The prayer is offered, not privately, but publicly so that it can be witnessed by all. It is rooted in God's own covenant devotion, in divine love and faithfulness that surpass anything earthly. The psalmist requests a manifestation of God originating in the heavens and visible over the entire world.

7 A plea for help

Speaking in the name of the entire community, the psalmist pleads for divine assistance. The right hand is traditionally considered the stronger hand, the one that wields the weapon of defense.

8-10 God speaks

A divine oracle, issued from the sanctuary, calls to mind the promise that Israel will occupy the land. The military success needed to realize this promise functions as grounds for hope of deliverance from present peril. Shechem was situated in northern Israel between Mounts Ebal and Gerizim. The valley of Succoth was just east of the Jordan River. Gilead and Manasseh were regions in Transjordan, while Ephraim, a common name for the northern tribes, and Judah, the name given to the southern tribes, were regions west of the river. All these territories were part of the united kingdom of David. On the other hand, Moab and Edom were independent nations just south of Gilead on the eastern side of the Jordan, and Philistia was a nation west of Judah on the eastern coast of the Mediterranean Sea. The oracle promises that these nations will all come under the control of Israel's God. Their combined borders will constitute the boundaries of the kingdom of Israel.

11-14 Does God hear?

God may be the hero who conquers these territories, but the assaults that Israel suffers indicate that at this point God does not march with Israel's armies. Instead, God seems to have abandoned the people, or at least refused to listen to their pleading. Still, the psalmist is not deterred, but continues to cry to God for relief, convinced that only divine assistance can ensure ultimate triumph.

Psalm 109 (lament of an individual)

1-5 The lament

The psalmist, who is described as the victim of lying enemies, turns to God for help. There is no reason for such ill treatment by others; the psalmist has shown love to and even prayed for the very people who are now acting in such a despicable manner. In this case, kindness is repaid with malice; love is met with hatred.

6-19 The treachery of the enemies

What follows is a very controversial section. The speaker is cursing enemies, calling calamities down on their heads. Many commentators are reluctant to ascribe such sentiments to the psalmist, and so some translations insert words at the beginning of this section (v. 5c) that suggest that it is really the enemies who hurl the imprecations at the psalmist rather than the psalmist speaking with such hatred. While such revision might exonerate the psalmist, it tends to minimize the depths of anger that the psalmist and righteous people sometimes feel in the face of oppression.

Curses are pronounced over various aspects of life. Since justice is necessary in all societies, lying in court is a serious offense and a serious threat to social order. The testimony of the accuser (the Hebrew has *satan*), will result in the innocent defendant suffering the consequences of guilt. The widow and orphaned children of one who meets an untimely death will be left with no male protector. If the family goods are confiscated, these poor people will be forced into deplorable destitution. Early Israel did not have a clear understanding of reward or punishment after death. They believed that restitution was frequently exacted in the next generation, children carrying the burden of guilt of their predecessors and suffering the punishment due such sins. The speaker calls this fate down on the stricken individual. The final and perhaps greatest misfortune would be the total eradication of one's name. With no one to do the remembering, it would be as if the person had never even existed. This would be a fate worse than death. The speaker next calls for punishment that fits the crime: the wicked one is accused of loving to curse, so let the curse fall back on the one cursing; since he did not engage in blessing, may he never know blessing. The final curse calls down a curse itself. May it surround this one like a garment; may it enter the deepest regions of his being.

20 Reversal or ratification?

If it was the enemies who were calling down the curses on the psalmist, in this section the psalmist prays that the curses hurled by these enemies fall on them instead. If it was the psalmist pronouncing these imprecations, here he prays that they be ratified by God and enacted against the enemies.

21-31 A plea for divine assistance

Turning to God in supplication, the psalmist appeals to God's faithful commitment to the covenant relationship (vv. 21, 26). The psalmist's miserable condition resembles the end of life as it ebbs away. The suffering is both interior (heart) and physical (tottering knees, wasted flesh). This sufferer's condition prompts mockery from enemies. The psalmist offers a second prayer for help and begs for some sign from God that will let the persecutors know that God is indeed on the psalmist's side. The psalmist asks for reversals: though enemies desire the psalmist's downfall, may God bestow blessing instead. The psalm ends on a note of confidence. God is the protector of the poor, and will stand in their defense.

Psalm 110 (royal psalm)

1-3 Royal enthronement

The first Lord is really YHWH, the personal name of Israel's God; the second lord (*adonai*) probably refers to the king. The enthronement scene is quite striking. It is God who enthrones the king in the ultimate place of honor, at God's right hand. Under the king's feet are his enemies, placed there by God. From Zion, the mountain on which Jerusalem stands, the king rules over all the nations. Traces of ancient Near Eastern royal

ideology can be seen in the reference to the father-son relationship between the deity and the human king. The metaphor of the daystar is rich with implications. It may refer to the divine origin of the king's rule, the freshness of its potential, or the enlightenment brought by this king. The fact that this is a divine oracle gives religious legitimation to the king and his rule.

4 Priestly dignity

A second oracle bestows priestly dignity on the king. The name Melchizedek comes from the Hebrew *melek* (king) and *zedek* (righteous). How the king will function as priest is probably not as important as the connections made between the ruler in Jerusalem and earlier religious traditions (cf. Gen 14:18; Isa 11:1-5).

5-7 Royal success

The scene has changed; it is no longer the place of enthronement, but the battlefield of the world. God, who is here referred to as "Lord," is now at the right hand of the king, acting with force and ensuring victory. It should be noted that the goal of this victory is justice ("judges nations"), not vengeance, and the end of such struggle is honor ("holds high his head").

Psalm 111 (hymn)

The psalm is acrostic, but this characteristic is lost in translation. Though an acrostic structure is a trait of a wisdom psalm, here the content suggests a different classification.

1 Praise of God

The psalm opens with a declaration of praise: *hallel* (praise) *jah* (the Lord). This is followed by a second summons to praise God publicly.

2-9 Reasons for praise

While other psalms describe the wonders of creation as "majesty and splendor" (cf. Ps 104:1), the reference here seems to be to the marvelous deeds that God performed in redeeming the people of Israel and granting them a land of their own. Besides the explicit mention of covenant (vv. 5, 9), there are other references to elements of the covenant: "gracious and merciful" (v. 4; cf. Exod 34:6), identification of the people as God's people (v. 5). Providing food for the people could be a reference to God's care of them during their sojourn in the wilderness (v. 5; cf. Exod 16:4-36; Num 11:31-34). There is explicit mention of God's gift of the land (v. 6). Decree (v. 7) is a traditional word for law. Finally, mention of deliverance recalls the people's escape from Egypt (v. 9; cf. Exod 14:10-22). All these wondrous deeds prompt the psalmist to call for praise.

10 True wisdom

The psalm ends with *the* classic wisdom adage. Fear of the Lord is really awe in the presence of the almighty God. Anyone with this attitude is on the right path to wisdom. The list of blessings found in this psalm should call forth the kind of awe or "fear of the LORD" that will lead to this wisdom. The psalm ends as it began, with praise of God.

Psalm 112 (wisdom psalm)

This psalm is a companion to Psalm 111. It begins with the same declaration of praise, and it follows the same acrostic structure.

1 Praise and fear of the Lord

The psalm opens with two very distinct literary forms. The first is a declaration of praise: *hallel* (praise) *jah* (the Lord). The second is a beatitude, a typical wisdom form that states the blessedness of those who choose a particular way of life. Here the blessed ones are those who fear the Lord. Using parallel construction, the psalmist defines fear of the Lord as "delight[] in [God's] commands."

2-9 Blessings that follow fear of the Lord

Various blessings follow this fundamental attitude of mind and heart. These blessings are not limited to one generation, but will flow over into the lives of descendants. In accord with the theory of retribution, those who fear the Lord will be granted wealth; their righteousness will be seen by all and will be remembered. Even if hardship befalls them, they will continue to trust in God. Finally, they do not hoard their good fortune to themselves, but they share it with those less fortunate. The horn is a symbol of strength; the strength of the righteous will be honored. Those who fear the Lord are people of integrity and unselfishness.

10 The envy of the wicked

The good fortune of the righteous will be the envy of the wicked. The wicked will not only be saddened by this but also be forced to endure the failure of their own aspirations.

Psalm 113 (hymn)

1-3 A call to praise

The psalm opens and closes with "Hallelujah!" The call to praise is issued twice in the first verse. Also identified three times in this section is the object of the praise, namely, the name of the Lord. God's servants are called to praise continually, from dawn to dusk.

4-6 God's universal reign

The Lord is said to rule over heaven and all the nations of the earth as well. The reference to God's enthronement on high suggests the honor bestowed on the divine conqueror of primordial chaos. It is from that singular vantage point that the creator rules over all. There, in the highest regions of the heavens, the glory of God is manifested.

7-9 God's care of the needy

God is not only glorious, but gracious toward the needy as well. Some commentators hold that the elevation of the destitute to the company of royalty is really a reference to the rise of David from humble means to the throne of Israel. Childless women suffered discrimination because they failed to make the contribution to society that was expected of them. This psalm praises God for the reversal of the fortunes of the unfortunate.

Psalm 114 (historical recital)

1-2 God's special people

The psalm describes Israel's release from Egypt. Though the name of the ancestor Jacob was changed to Israel (cf. Gen 35:10), both names are used in poetry to refer to the nation. The "sanctuary" in Judah is Jerusalem. The entire nation is the special place of divine rule.

3-6 Nature responds to God's deliverance of the people

Victory over the sea, the symbol of primordial chaotic waters, is the ultimate sign of divine sovereign power. Israel's release began with the people going forth from Egypt through the Reed Sea and ended with them crossing the Jordan River into the land of promise. The skipping of the mountains and hills is probably a reference to the trembling of Mount Sinai at the time of the manifestation of God. What must have originally terrified the people is, in the sight of God, mere playfulness.

7-8 A call to revere God
Just as the mountains and hills quaked before God, so the earth or land is called to tremble in God's presence. Divine power had already shown itself on the earth by means of the miracles performed for the people while they sojourned in the wilderness, where water came from the rocks (cf. Num 20:1-11). It was only right to revere the God who performed such wonders.

Psalm 115
(communal prayer of confidence)

Though some ancient manuscripts join Psalms 114 and 115, commentators today recognize the differences between them.

1-2 Glory belongs to the Lord
There appears to be a contradiction in the first two verses of this psalm. In the first verse, the people decline any praise for themselves and direct all praise to God. What is unusual is the absence of a reason for the people to have been praised in the first place. The second verse suggests an entirely different situation. The fact that other nations would ask, "Where is their God?" implies that the lot of the people was anything but praiseworthy or satisfying.

3-8 The worthlessness of foreign gods
A contrast is made between the sovereign majesty of Israel's God and the worthlessness of the gods of the other nations. On the one hand, the God of Israel is the only deity who rules from heaven and whose will is accomplished. On the other hand, the gods of the nations are merely ineffective idols. They may have been made of precious materials, but they are the products of human industry; they have no power in themselves. Furthermore, those people who worship these idols and who expect that they will act

mightily, will be as powerless as are these human artifacts.

9-11 Trust in the Lord
A kind of antiphonal litany in which three classes of Israelites are said to trust in the Lord: the house of Israel, the house of Aaron, and those who fear the Lord. (The verb forms are really present imperative rather than past, as many contemporary versions translate them.) The house of Israel probably includes the entire nation; the house of Aaron is the priests. Since fear of the Lord is the fundamental religious disposition of awe and reverence before God, those who possess this disposition would be the genuinely religious ones among the people. In each case, the Lord is their help and their source of safety.

12-15 Blessings from God
The psalmist declares that God will be mindful of the same categories of people and will bless them. It is significant that both small and great are mentioned; there is no class preference here. The psalmist next prays for blessings on the people, specifically in terms of increase in population. This blessing extends across generations, from descendants to descendants. This invocation is made to the mighty God who is the creator of heaven and earth.

16-18 The living bless the Lord
The psalmist acknowledges that earth is the stage on which human beings enact the drama of life. Though they believed that God rules over both the heavens and the earth, they did not have a clear idea of God's control over the realm of the dead, and so they could not envision the dead praising God. Therefore, praise would come from the heavens and from the earth. It is the latter praise that was the responsibility of human beings. The psalm ends with just such praise: "Hallelujah!"

Psalm 116
(prayer of thanksgiving of an individual)
1-4 God heard my cry
The psalmist responds with love to God who has heard the psalmist's cries for help. The ancient Israelites considered any form of serious distress as some dimension of destruction or death. Therefore, to say that one was seized by death or by

Sheol meant that one was afflicted with some form of grievous suffering, one that might eventually result in death, though not necessarily. It was from such a desperate predicament that the psalmist cried to God for help and was ultimately saved by God.

5-9 The graciousness of God

The graciousness and compassion of God's covenant commitment are coupled with fundamental divine justice. These dispositions have been turned toward those who are needy. The declaration itself is not impartial; the psalmist speaks from personal experience, having been the beneficiary of God's gracious care. There is no word in Hebrew for "soul." The word used might be better rendered "life force," a concept that is less abstract and thus makes this mysterious force more accessible to human understanding. It is the psalmist's entire vital being that has been freed and is now called to turn to God in thanksgiving.

10-11 Suffering alone

The psalmist claims to have been faithful to and trusting of God, even during past times of great distress. At such times, no one but God offered help; no one but God served as refuge. Now, having been rescued from harm, the psalmist promises to continue to live a life of faithfulness.

12-19 A life of fidelity

Out of gratitude for having been saved from distress, the psalmist chooses a life of total commitment to the Lord. This promise will be partially accomplished through public acts of worship. It was a common devotional practice to promise some kind of offering if prayers were heard. The psalmist's public thanksgiving sacrifice would be the fulfillment of such a vow. The cup of salvation is probably part of a thanksgiving offering (cf. Num 28:7). God had saved the life of the psalmist, and now, in the midst of other worshipers, the psalmist acknowledges God's graciousness. The psalm ends on a note of praise: Praise (*hallel*) the Lord (*jah*)!

Psalm 117 (hymn)

1-2 Praise of God's love

This is the shortest psalm in the entire Psalter. Despite this brevity, it contains the basic structure

of a hymn, opening with a call to praise God. This is a universal call, issued not only to Israel but to all nations, all peoples. True to the hymnic structure, the reason for praise is given. God has acted out of covenant love and faithfulness. Finally, the psalm ends as it began: Praise (*hallel*) the Lord (*jah*)!

Psalm 118
(prayer of thanksgiving of an individual)

1-4 Give thanks

This summons to give thanks to God is in the form of antiphonal prayer ("his mercy endures forever"). The same categories of people are called on as are found in Psalm 115. The house of Israel represents the entire nation; the house of Aaron includes the priests; those who fear the Lord are the most devout. All of these people have acknowledged and responded to God's covenant love, a love that is unfailing and will last forever. They are now called on to demonstrate their gratitude for God's goodness.

5-9 The psalmist's testimony

The psalmist recalls past troublesome times when God was the only sure source of refuge. God's deliverance enabled the psalmist to realize that no human being could be trusted, not even the royalty whose responsibility it was to safeguard the populace. Only God was dependable; only God was a firm defense against threatening enemies; only God could be trusted.

10-18 Victory over enemies

Once again the psalmist employs an antiphonal prayer ("in the LORD's name I cut them off"). Though the psalmist fought the enemies, it was the power of God working through the psalmist that triumphed. The victory is really God's. The enemies are compared to a swarm of bees, surrounding and attacking the poor victim from every side. But the Lord delivered the psalmist from the sting of their fire. Besides describing God as a strong and mighty savior, the psalmist uses powerful military images to characterize God's defense. The tents are probably the military encampment; God's raised right hand is the hand that wields the weapon with which God will frighten or even slay the psalmist's enemies.

Without divine assistance the psalmist would have succumbed to the enemies' advances. God intervened, however, and for this the psalmist is grateful.

19-29 Thanksgiving liturgy

What follows is the description of a liturgical celebration of thanksgiving. The liturgy begins at the gates of the sanctuary, where thanks for deliverance is given. The psalmist acknowledges having been rejected by enemies, but saved by God and raised up in importance. This day of celebration is a day of divine victory, which gives it its significance. Though the celebration is for the rescue of the psalmist, all people are invited to rejoice in the salvation wrought by God. Throughout this liturgy, communal petitions for deliverance and blessing are directed to God. What follows is a form of liturgical dialogue. The one who comes in the name of the Lord is probably the priest who gives the blessing (v. 26). The people respond with a shout of praise and an invitation to proceed to the altar. The psalm concludes with the psalmist's words of thanksgiving and the repetition of the summons to give thanks that was issued at the beginning of the psalm.

Psalm 119 (wisdom psalm)

This psalm is extraordinary not merely because of its length but also for its elaborate structure and the singular focus of its content. Like other acrostic psalms, it follows the alphabet sequence. However, where other such poems consist of twenty-two lines or verses, each beginning with a successive letter of the alphabet, this psalm is made up of sections of eight lines, each of which begins with the same letter. The psalm itself has one basic theme, the celebration of the law. There is no mistaking this praise, for each of the one hundred seventy-six verses acclaims the law and contains either the word *torah* (law) itself or a synonym of it. This group of synonyms includes words such as: way, teaching, decree, command, precepts, edict, word. Exaltation of the law is not an example of legalism. Actually, the word *torah* might be better translated "instruction." This rendering helps us to understand better the law as the fundamental teaching about life. It helps us to set our sights in the direction that will lead to

success and happiness. Such an approach is certainly not legalistic.

Each section of the psalm contains basically the same focus. In order to avoid excessive repetition this reflection will address the salient theological themes found throughout the verses as well as some of its important literary characteristics. It will not present a section-by-section commentary.

Wisdom psalms are usually instruction rather than prayer. Still, this wisdom psalm contains elements of other genres as well. There are prayers of petition through the entire psalm (vv. 5, 66), as well as rhetorical questions used as a pedagogical device (v. 9), words of praise (v. 120), and cries of lament (v. 28, 84).

The acrostic structure is a familiar characteristic of the wisdom poetry. It is a mnemonic device, providing a recognizable pattern for data retention. Since it consists of the entire alphabet, the structure itself suggests a universal sweep that encompasses the entire range of a particular issue, everything from *alef* to *taw*, or from A to Z. In other words, Psalm 119 tells us what we need to know about observing the law of the Lord.

The psalm opens with a double beatitude (vv. 1-2), which sets the tone of the entire poem. This introductory acclamation indicates that observance of the law of the Lord is not a heavy burden. Rather, it is the source of true happiness. As is the case with much of the wisdom teaching, this perspective is based on an understanding of a form of cause and effect or the theory of retribution: wise or righteous living will result in happiness or reward; unhappiness or punishment will follow a foolish or wicked way of life. Wisdom teaching generally, and this treatise on observance of the law of the Lord in particular, provides a way of living that is both pleasing to God and will lead to happiness and success.

Emphasis on law should be placed within the context of covenant. The psalmist is consistently identified as the servant of God (vv. 17, 23, 38, 49, 65, 76, 84, 124, 125, 135, 140, 176). This servant prays for and is enriched by the covenant attributes: mercy ("steadfast love" or "kindness" in other translations; vv. 41, 64, 76, 88, 124, 149), compassion (v. 77, 156), and truth (vv. 43, 142).

This wisdom psalm exhibits a definite attitude of docility, a desire to be taught and to be led along the way of fidelity. Though wisdom grows out of reflection on life experience, this psalm clearly underscores the need to be led by God (vv. 12, 29, 33, 66, 171). The law is not only a list of precepts to be obeyed but, more important, it is a way of life to be studied (vv. 97-100). The psalmist prays not only for obedience but also for insight (vv. 27, 34, 104) and direction (vv. 18, 35). Furthermore, a life lived in accordance with the law is often ridiculed by others (vv. 39, 51, 141). In the eyes of the psalmist, these others would be considered foolish. Nonetheless, their derision is difficult to endure, so the psalmist also prays for the fortitude needed to remain faithful in the face of such a trial. The psalmist is dependent on God for deliverance from hardship as well as direction for living. Enemies had oppressed the psalmist who had nowhere to turn but to the Lord (vv. 81-88, 121, 153-155, 161).

Although the psalm opens with a clearly defined poetic device (beatitude), it closes rather abruptly. The acrostic pattern has been faithfully followed and so there is nothing left to say.

SONGS OF ASCENT (120–34)

Although the next fifteen psalms are classified according to various standard genres, they comprise a discrete collection known as the Songs of Ascent. Most likely they were used during the pilgrimage to Jerusalem on the occasion of the major festivals. Some commentators suggest when and how these psalms might have been part of religious pilgrimages to the holy city. However, many of the psalms lack explicit references to such processions. In this commentary, whatever connections there might be to historical events will be made only when features within the psalm itself warrant them.

Psalm 120 (composite psalm)

1-2 Deliverance from enemies

Commentators debate the relationship between these two verses. Some say that the second verse is dependent on the first—that it is the prayer that was offered by the psalmist and heard by God. This would mean that the psalmist has been delivered and endures as a freed person. Others maintain that the verses are independent of each other. This reading would imply that the

psalmist was delivered in the past, but that this prayer springs from yet another situation of distress. Whichever version is the case, the fundamental meaning is the same: The psalmist was besieged by liars and God stepped in as deliverer.

3-4 The fate of the liars

The psalmist turns to the liars themselves and challenges them. What have they gained from their deceit? In punishment for their sins, they will become the victims of the sharp weapons of their own enemies.

5-7 A lament

The psalm ends with a lament. The psalmist cries out in the traditional form of woe: "Alas!" The psalmist, who cherishes peace, is forced to live as an alien among people committed to war. Meshech was land in the distant northeast, between the Black and the Caspian Seas; Kedar was an Arabian tribe that lived in tents in the southeast.

Psalm 121
(prayer of confidence of an individual)

1-2 God is a sure refuge

The initial scene envisioned is that of the psalmist either on flat land or in a valley, somewhat defenseless, looking toward the mountains for help. The identification of God as the maker of heaven and earth suggests that these are cosmic mountains on which God dwells and from which God comes to save.

3-8 The divine guardian

An unknown voice addresses the psalmist, designating God as a watchful and constant guardian. To underscore this characterization of God, the author uses some form of the word "guard" no less than six times in this short psalm (vv. 3, 4, 5, 7 [2x], 8). There are dangers in the psalmist's "coming and going." With God as guardian, however, the psalmist is guaranteed sure footing. Besides being a dependable guardian, God is described as ever-watchful, protective in the face of heat, and a source of strength ("right hand"). Reference to the sun and moon, revered by ancient Near Eastern people as celestial deities, could have cosmic significance. However, this may also be a poetic way of claiming that neither dangers of the day nor those of the night will have any power over the one who is guarded by God.

Psalm 122 (song of Zion)

1-5 Pilgrimage to the temple

The theme of pilgrimage is explicit in this psalm. Having been invited to join a procession to the temple in Jerusalem, the psalmist stands within that city, overwhelmed by his good fortune to have come to this place of both religious and political significance, and by the glory of the city itself. Like most important ancient settlements, Jerusalem was a walled city with carefully protected gates. It was the renowned seat of Davidic rule, the place where justice was meted out to all. The political grandeur of this city notwithstanding, the psalmist's visit was religiously motivated. All Israelites were required to make religious pilgrimage to Jerusalem to offer thanks to God there. It was for this reason that the psalmist made the journey.

6-9 A prayer for peace

There are three distinct prayers for the peace of Jerusalem, the city whose very name in Hebrew contains the root letters for the word "peace" (*shalom*). The first prayer is for peace for those who are favorably disposed toward the city. The second is that peace might reign within the city itself. The third prayer for peace is for family and friends. This may refer to those unable to make the pilgrimage. These prayers are for peace in the broadest sense, not merely for the absence of conflict. Such peace is really a state of wholeness and contentment, of fulfillment and prosperity. Jerusalem, chosen and blessed by God, was a symbol of this all-encompassing peace and a sign of promise for all those who traveled to it on religious pilgrimage.

Psalm 123 (communal lament)

1 Individual cry

The psalmist speaks in the singular. To raise one's eyes is to look for help. The psalmist looks for help from God who reigns as sovereign from heaven.

2-4 Communal cry

The psalmist develops further the theme of eyes, now speaking for the entire community. The comparisons employed are drawn from the social practice of servitude. As male and female servants look for blessings from the hands of their master and mistress respectively, so the people look to God. The cry for blessing is repeated twice. One must wait until the end of the psalm to discover the reason why the people turn to God for help. They have been the victims of the contempt of others. Now they turn to God for release.

Psalm 124 (communal prayer of thanksgiving)

1-5 Rescued by God

The psalmist describes how the people were rescued by God from the assaults of others. The serious jeopardy in which they found themselves is captured in the metaphors used to describe the fate that would have been theirs had they been vanquished. They would have been swallowed alive, engulfed by waters, swept away, and finally drowned. The choice of water imagery is significant, for water was the symbol of primordial chaos. Used here, it emphasizes both the ferocity of the enemies' attack and the character of the marvelous victory wrought by God.

6-8 Praise of God

The psalmist praises God for having rescued the people from their enemies. The imagery employed to describe this rescue has been borrowed from hunting practices. No longer are the people threatened by water. Here they face the possibility of being the prey of fierce animals or human hunters; however, God, who is the maker of heaven and earth, saved them from being ripped apart. God broke the snare that had entangled them and set them free.

Psalm 125 (communal prayer of confidence)

1-2 Trust in God

According to this psalm, those who trust God are guaranteed a security that is as grounded as the mountains. Israel claimed that Mount Zion, the very hill on which Jerusalem was built, was firmly established by God from the very beginning. By means of a different but related image of mountains, the psalmist then compares God's encircling protection to the mountains that surround Mount Zion and Jerusalem. Twice the psalmist states that such divine security will last forever.

3 Secure from the wicked

Security in the land, free from the rule of the wicked, is granted the just in order that they not fall under the influence of the wicked and turn to wickedness themselves.

4-5 Divine retribution

The psalmist prays for divine retribution, that the righteous be blessed by God and those who choose wickedness be made to endure the punishment meant for the wicked. The psalm closes with a wish that does not really flow from the sentiments expressed in earlier verses, but that is always relevant: Peace upon Israel!

Psalm 126 (communal lament)

1-3 Past deliverance

The people recall how, in the past, God restored the city that had been devastated. If this is a reference to the return to Jerusalem from Babylonian exile, the psalm might be dated in the postexilic period. This restoration was astounding. It amazed the delivered people themselves, and it became known throughout the world. Other nations marveled at the wonders God had worked for this people.

4-6 Present need

Relying on those past favors granted by God, the people pray again for the reversal of fortune. Some commentators maintain that the reference is to the same favor as mentioned above. However, here the people are not asking for deliverance, but for restoration in their homeland. The nature imagery is striking. The Negeb Desert is known for the sudden flooding of its riverbeds during the winter rains. It is for such remarkable reversals that the people pray. The agricultural image is not as easy to understand. It may have originated in the earlier Canaanite fertility cult. During that ritual, the people weep at the time of sowing when the land appears to be lifeless, but rejoice at harvest when clearly that life has returned. Here this ancient rite suggests the death that the exile represented and the new life experi-

enced at the people's return. The psalm seems to end abruptly.

Psalm 127 (wisdom psalm)

1-2 Limitations of human endeavor

The basis of wisdom is the insight into life that one gains through studious reflection on experience. Here the psalmist insists that the most important lesson that one could learn is the futility of every human endeavor pursued without direction from or the assistance of God. Building houses and guarding cities are simply representative of fundamental and necessary human ventures. Even the most basic activity of rising early to cultivate the land for food is considered useless, for it is really God who provides.

3-5 Children as a blessing

This society cherished its children, not simply out of emotional sentiment, but because they realized that children are the future of the nation. As with all other realities, they saw children as gifts from God. Children are also the defense (arrows) against whatever may be threatening. This could range from actual enemies to the diminishment that comes with aging. The psalm closes with a beatitude. It states that the one who has many children, who can ensure a prosperous future and care in old age, will be truly blessed.

Psalm 128 (wisdom psalm)

1-4 Fear of the Lord

This psalm opens with *the* beatitude: "Happy are all who fear the LORD." According to the wisdom tradition, this fear or awe before God is the fundamental religious attitude. Those who possess it follow the path set out for them by God. As a consequence, they will enjoy the rewards that come from such fidelity. While peace and prosperity are treasured blessings, the most meaningful blessing is children.

5-6 Words of blessing

The psalm ends with words of blessing. Zion or Jerusalem was the dwelling place of God on earth. It was from this hallowed place that God's blessings flowed. This final prayer consists of three petitions: that blessings will be granted throughout life; that those for whom the prayer is offered will share in the peace of Jerusalem; that they will enjoy a long life and see generations of descendants. The psalm ends with a prayer for peace for Jerusalem.

Psalm 129
(communal prayer of confidence)

1-4 Past deliverance
Although the psalmist speaks in the first person, the focus here is the deliverance experienced by the entire people. This is a nation that has been on the offensive from the very first days of its existence. Though assaulted, however, it has not been vanquished. With a vivid agricultural image, the psalmist depicts its former servile condition and the pain that it endured because of it. However, God intervened on the nation's behalf and released it from its bondage.

5-8 Fate of the wicked
In the manner of a curse, the psalmist wishes ill fortune on those who hate God's holy city. The first misfortune that the psalmist would have fall on them is the burden of shame. In many societies, even today, shame is sometimes considered a suffering worse than death. In addition to this adversity, the psalmist would have these people dry up and shrivel like the grass in thatched roofs. When the dry and scorching winds sweep over the houses, the burned grass is made worthless. The psalmist would have this happen to the enemies. Finally, may they never hear words of blessing addressed to them. Those who have scorned what God loves do not deserve God's blessing. The psalm ends on this note of imprecation.

Psalm 130
(lament of an individual; penitential)

1-2 The lament
In this penitential psalm (cf. Pss 6, 32, 38, 51, 102, 143), the situation of the psalmist appears to be dire; "depths" refers to deepest suffering. It is from there that the psalmist cries out to God for mercy. This is not the mercy associated with the covenant. It is the kind of pity that one shows toward another who is in great distress. The psalmist begs that God will hear the cry and will respond with some kind of relief.

3-4 A prayer for forgiveness
The psalmist does not ask for justice, but for forgiveness. Such a prayer suggests that this is not an innocent sufferer, but one who is guilty of some offense. In this prayer it is the mercy of God that is extolled, not divine justice.

5-6 A prayer of confidence
As is the case with so many psalms of lament, this prayer ends on a note of confidence. The psalmist has already acknowledged some degree of guilt and has appealed to God's mercy. There is nothing more to do but wait patiently and hopefully for God to respond. The vital life force waits for the Lord. The reference to dawn suggests that the long nightwatch is over. It also assures the sentinel that the terrors that fill the night will have no power in the light of day. The psalmist waits for God's mercy with the same degree of expectation.

7-8 Prayer for the community
The individual character of the psalm changes to one that is communal. Now it is the entire people who are urged to wait longingly for the Lord. The concept of covenant love is introduced, as is the notion of paying a ransom for another. It is God who will pay this ransom on Israel's behalf.

Psalm 131
(prayer of confidence of an individual)

1-3 Resting in the Lord
There is deep serenity in the words of the psalmist. A proud heart and haughty eyes are signs of great ambition, a trait that is absent in this humble individual. A weaned child is one whose hunger has been satisfied and who now rests contently at its mother's breast. This passage contains not only a moving description of the psalmist but also a tender characterization of God—a mother who has given of her very self for the life of her child. Such an understanding of God surely generated trust in the hearts of the people. The psalm ends with a summons to such trust.

Psalm 132 (royal psalm)

1-5 David's oath
The first part of this psalm recalls David's plan to build a sanctuary for the Lord (cf. 2 Sam 7:1-2).

Although the psalm suggests that this plan sprang from religious devotion, such a building project was expected of any successful ancient Near Eastern ruler. Therefore, political obligation was involved as well. The divine title "Mighty One of Jacob" is an ancient name for God. It is first found in the ancestral narrative (cf. Gen 49:24) and then, along with the designation "redeemer," in postexilic writings (cf. Isa 49:26; 60:16). Its inclusion in this psalm links the royal temple tradition with both the ancestral or tribal tradition and that of the postexilic prophet Deutero-Isaiah. This connection gives the temple tradition, which some within the community might have seen as a Canaanite innovation, both legitimation and continuity with more established religious traditions.

6-10 Liturgical procession

It is clear that temple worship has been established and the ark of the covenant, the religious symbol of God's presence in the midst of the people, has found a place within the sanctuary. The people are invited to join in procession to the temple to celebrate either its dedication or the anniversary of that event. The psalmist calls on a well-established Davidic tradition and asks God to be mindful of the present king for the sake of the founder of the dynasty. The psalm includes other Davidic connections. Ephrathah is associated with Bethlehem, the city of David (cf. Mic 5:1). The fields of Jaar is a district west of Jerusalem near Bethlehem. It was there that the ark of the covenant was kept (cf. 1 Sam 7:1) before David brought it to Jerusalem (cf. 2 Sam 6:12).

11-18 The divine oath

The psalm recalls the oath that God made to David to establish the family of David as a royal dynasty (cf. 2 Sam 7:12-16). The covenant made at this time was considered eternal, from generation to generation. However, the reign of each individual ruler was dependent on his fidelity to the Mosaic law that bound every Israelite. Not only was the Davidic family specially chosen, but Jerusalem, the city of David, was also set apart as the place where God dwelt on earth. The oath contains a promise to grant the city choice blessings. The horn is a sign of the strength of the dynasty. The lamp may be a reference to the flask of oil that remained burning in the temple. It is clear that the strength and endurance of the dynasty

and the splendor of the temple are grounded in this promise of God.

Psalm 133 (wisdom psalm)

1-3 A harmonious community

The wisdom saying that comprises this psalm extols the blessings that accrue for a community that lives together in harmony. The saying includes two vivid images that describe this harmony, both of which rely on the belief that these blessings really come down to the people from God. The first image originates in the cultic ceremony of priestly anointing. The precious ointment that was poured over the head of the priest ran down his head and over his beard, its luxurious aroma filling the air. In like manner, the pleasurable scent of harmonious community living brings joy to all. The second image is drawn from Mount Hermon, which stands majestic in the northern part of Israel. The dew from its peaks flows down to the valleys below and there waters the land, making it fertile and productive. Similarly, harmonious community living is the source of many other blessings.

Psalm 134 (liturgical hymn)

1-3 A call to worship

The collection of songs of ascent (Pss 120–34) appropriately closes with a liturgical hymn. This prayer contains several ritual elements. It opens with a call to praise God. It takes place in the temple, after the long hours of a night vigil. Included is a directive to raise one's hands in prayer, a traditional stance of petition. It closes with a prayer for blessing from God, who is the creator of heaven and earth but who dwells in the temple in Jerusalem.

Psalm 135 (hymn)

1-4 A summons to praise God

This hymn of praise opens with the traditional cry: "Hallelujah!" The call to praise either the Lord or the name of the Lord is repeated three times in this section. Many people believe that the name contains a dimension of the very essence of the person. Therefore, to praise God's name is to praise God. The house of the Lord is the sanctuary; the servants who stand in service in the sanctuary are probably the priests and Levites. They are called on to sing praise to God. Typical of the structure of the hymn, reason for praise is given: God has chosen Israel as a special people.

5-7 The superiority of the God of Israel

The psalmist continues to cite reasons for praising God. Israel's God is greater than all other gods, exercising dominion over the heavens and the earth alike. Seas and deeps are references to primordial chaotic waters. Many people of the ancient world believed that the great storm gods rode across the heavens in chariots of clouds, with bolts of lightning like arrows in their quivers. Here, such celestial phenomena are recognized as simple meteorological manifestations under God's supreme control.

8-14 God's salvific wonders

Israel's God is not only the creator but also a deliverer. A short account of God's salvific marvels is recited, beginning with a report of their deliverance from bondage in Egypt, the event that will forever mark Israel as God's chosen possession (cf. v. 4). This is followed by an allusion to the victories God granted the people as they moved through the wilderness and attempted to enter Canaan, the land of promise. The people would not have been able to accomplish such feats by their own power. They knew that it was God who, out of great concern ("mercy") for them, delivered and guided them. For that reason, God will be praised from generation to generation.

15-18 Worthlessness of other gods

Having extolled the marvels accomplished by the God of Israel, the psalmist proceeds to ridicule the gods of other nations. Though fashioned out of precious metals, they are simply the products of human making. They are not only devoid of divine powers, they cannot even do what human beings are able to perform. Finally, not only are they worthless, those who trust in them will be worthless like them.

19-21 A final call to praise

All are called on to bless or praise God. The house of Israel includes all the people. Explicit mention is made of those who serve in the sanctuary (cf. v. 2): the house of Aaron refers to the priests; the house of Levi refers to the Levites.

Since fear of the Lord is the fundamental religious disposition of awe and reverence before God, those who possess this disposition would be the genuinely religious ones among the people. All Israel has been called on to praise the Lord who dwells in Jerusalem. The psalms ends as it began, with "Hallelujah!"

Psalm 136 (liturgical hymn)

1-3 A call to praise God

The liturgical character of this psalm is quite clear. Each verse ends with the refrain: "for his mercy endures forever." While each invocation was probably spoken by a liturgical leader, the refrain is meant for the entire congregation. This refrain is a statement of assurance that God's covenant love is eternal. Each of the first three verses is a summons to praise God. Three divine titles are employed. The LORD (YHWH) is the personal name of the God of Israel. This verse also provides a reason for the praise, namely, that God is good. The other two titles indicate that this God is superior to all other gods and to all other ruling lords.

4-9 Praise of the creator

God's exclusive divine power can be seen in the rule that God exercises over all the wonders of the heavens. It is this God who created the heavens and assigned the celestial bodies their stations, there to give off their light at the appropriate time; it is this God who harnessed the waters of the deep and spread out the earth on them. Such a God certainly deserves the praise of all.

10-16 God's exploits during the exodus

This mighty God is not only the creator of and ruler in the heavens and on the earth but also the one who delivered the Israelites from their cruel bondage in Egypt, a deliverance that was accomplished through miraculous signs and wonders. "[M]ighty hand and outstretched arm" symbolize the wondrous feats that God performed on Israel's behalf. Chief among these is the conquest of the sea. Though the reference here is to the geographic Reed Sea, behind the reference are allusions to the primordial chaotic waters over which God was triumphant at creation. Many ancient myths of origin recount how those waters were split and order was eventually established.

In Israel's history, it was the evil of the pharaoh that was conquered, while the people of God were led to safety. The desert was a place of both testing and community consolidation. It was there that the motley group of survivors became a nation.

17-22 The land is occupied

In only a few short verses, Israel's struggle for the occupation of the land is recounted. It is important to note that Israel claims it was God, not simply the people's military prowess, that fended off those who would have prevented the occupation. In like manner, it was God who chose this land for the people in the first place. Israel would always regard this land as their heritage or inheritance, first promised and ultimately bestowed on them by a loving God.

23-26 God's continued providence

The goodness of God is not limited to past favors. The wonders of creation and the deliverance from servitude may have transpired in the past, but God continues to shower blessings on this favored people. Therefore, it is fitting to continue to praise God.

Psalm 137 (communal lament)

1-4 The captives mourn

The psalm begins with a description of the sorrowful situation of the captives. The suffering of the people is not the result of physical assault at the hands of their enemies or of social oppression because of unjust laws and customs. Rather, it is soul-wrenching sorrow over the loss of their beloved city Jerusalem. In contrast, the triumphant city of Babylon has rivers that provide water to thriving poplar trees. Those who have captured the people ask them to sing a song of Zion. If the reference is to Israelite folk music, the request is for entertainment, which, under the circumstances, would be considered quite demeaning. If it is to religious music, the request would be blasphemous, for the Israelites could not envision praising God on foreign soil. In either case, such a request would have been seen as a form of mockery.

5-6 Self-curse

The psalmist calls down a self-curse to take effect if Jerusalem is ever forgotten. The conse-

quences for infidelity are dire. A withered right hand would make one incapable of work and, therefore, would relegate one to the margins of society. A paralyzed tongue would prevent one from speaking and would prevent one from participating fully in community life. According to Israel's strict laws of purity, one with any such disability would be considered a sinner who was so afflicted as punishment for some sin.

7-9 A curse on enemies

The last verses of this beautiful psalm are considered quite troublesome by many people today. Israel is actually calling down curses on those nations that have in any way acted against it. Edom, one of its neighbors to the east, not only refused Israel access through its territory when the people were originally entering the land of promise, but also participated in the looting of Jerusalem and the murder of its inhabitants at the time of its destruction by the Babylonians (cf. Obad 11-14). The most violent and disturbing image is of the children of Babylon being smashed against the rock. Without exonerating the violence, it is important to understand that, since children are the future of a people, Israel prayed for safety from any future conflict with Babylon. This scene also reveals the far-reaching horrors of any war.

Psalm 138 (prayer of confidence of an individual)

1-3 The prayer of thanksgiving

The psalmist is filled with gratitude because God responded to a desperate call for help. Homage is given to God and thanksgiving is offered in the temple. The gods or heavenly beings were probably minor deities in the Canaanite pantheon, which, in Israel's religious scheme, remained a subservient part of God's council in heaven (cf. Ps 8:6; Job 1:6). Divine fidelity and steadfast love are characteristics of the covenant.

4-6 The exalted nature of God

Earlier, the psalmist sang of the greatness of the Lord. Now the rulers of other nations praise God. They too will exalt the goodness of God. The situation of the psalmist, once in need and then strengthened by God (cf. v. 3), is an example of how God cares for those who seek divine aid. Though God rules from the heavens, God is well aware of what transpires on earth and is attentive to the needs of the lowly.

7-8 Confidence in God

The psalmist knows from personal experience that God is ever-ready to help those in dire straits. God's right hand is the hand that wields salvific power. The psalmist declares that God's covenant love will last forever. This is the ground of all genuine confidence.

Psalm 139 (wisdom psalm)

1-6 God is all-knowing

This psalm is more a testimony to divine majesty than it is a prayer, though it does extol various divine characteristics. The psalmist maintains that God knows everything that happens and has insight into the innermost depths of an individual. In fact, God has such a grasp of one's thoughts that even the future is within the scope of divine comprehension. There is no place that is not under the all-knowing eye of God. Actually, God's comprehension is so thorough that it encircles the psalmist. This can be both reassuring and frightening. It all depends on the individual's disposition.

7-12 God is all-present

Besides being all-knowing, God is also omnipresent. The psalmist attempts to sketch the extent of the domain within which God reigns, a domain that reaches to the farthest limits of the heights and depths, as well as the expanse, of the earth. Early Israelite tradition did not include a well-defined notion of life after this life. While Israel did believe in a place inhabited by the dead, it was not clear that God exercised jurisdiction over it. The reference here seems to contradict that belief. The psalmist claims that God is indeed in Sheol. God rules over the highest heavens as well as the depths of Sheol. God is also present from the borders of the east, where dawn begins its flight across the horizon, to those of the west, the land on the other side of the sea. In other words, God is ever-present, guiding and caring for the psalmist. Finally, one might hope to look to darkness for concealment. Not so. Only creatures are hampered by the dark; light and darkness are the same to God. It is not that the psalmist is really

trying to escape God. Rather, this is a poetic way of describing God's all-pervasive presence.

13-18 God creates with care

The inmost being is literally the kidneys, the seat of emotion and conscience. God possesses intimate knowledge of the psalmist, because God is the creator. The psalmist is in awe of the delicate care with which God fashions the human body within the mother's womb, like a weaver blending skeins of material into an artistic creation (cf. Job 10:11). Although this marvelous fashioning takes place within the womb, hidden from sight like the mysteries of the earth's formation within the bowels of the earth, God is aware of every detail of human gestation. God's omniscience even includes divine foreknowledge. This detailed description demonstrates the psalmist's appreciation of God's comprehensive knowledge, the scope of which the psalmist cannot even begin to fathom.

19-24 A plea for retribution

The psalm concludes on a somewhat negative note with the psalmist appealing to the theory of retribution: may the wicked be punished for their sinfulness. It is important to note that the psalmist does not assume the role of arbiter of right and wrong. That is God's right, and it is for God to execute justice. These wicked have not only oppressed the psalmist, but have also blasphemed God's holy name. They are thus enemies of both, and so they are certainly deserving of punishment. Presumably, the psalmist has been faithful. Since God sees into the inmost recesses of the human heart, God would know this.

Psalm 140 (lament of an individual)

2-6 The cry of lament

The psalmist turns to God with two distinct yet very similar cries of lament. This double plea is for deliverance from the wicked, that is, those who set out to ruin the vulnerable psalmist with venomous lies and other traps. The violence from which the psalmist prays to be delivered is not physical assault. Rather, the Hebrew word employed means extreme wickedness. The psalmist is assailed by evil and seeks refuge from it in God.

7-8 A confession of faith

The titles with which the psalmist addresses God mark the manner in which the psalmist hopes God will act. The psalmist first declares, "You are my God." This statement claims that there is a relationship because of which the psalmist can presume divine assistance. The military title characterizes God as the bulwark of defense in time of battle. This is precisely the kind of help the psalmist needs at this time of crisis.

9-12 Punishment of the wicked

It is quite common for laments to include prayers that the wicked be punished for their sinfulness. The psalmist prays that the plans of the enemies be thwarted and the wickedness that they plotted against the psalmist be turned against them instead. Some commentators maintain that the punishment for which the psalmist prays is more vengeance than it is justice. This is particularly true with regard to the fiery end that is envisioned. However, one cannot underestimate the threat posed to the delicate fabric of society by the kind of deceit and exploitation described here. If the society is to survive, such threats must be addressed.

13-14 Expressions of confidence

The lament ends on a note of confidence. The psalmist is certain that the evil will fall on those who perpetrated it. The just will be rescued and will give appropriate thanks to God.

Psalm 141 (lament of an individual)

1-2 A cry for help

The cry for help with which the psalm opens is short and to the point: "hasten." However, its brevity does not make it curt. On the contrary, the psalmist sees it as sweet-smelling as incense rising to God, and the traditional prayer stance of upraised arms is likened to an evening sacrifice offered in the temple.

3-4 The need for divine assistance

The possibility of being tempted to sin is always present. Therefore, the psalmist asks to be strengthened so as not to fail. While sins of speech are explicitly mentioned, there is an acknowledgment that evil really originates in the heart.

5-7 The right choice of company

The Hebrew of these verses is obscure. However, while the thoughts do not always seem to follow logically, it is clear that the psalmist is contrasting the company of the just with that of the wicked. The psalmist is also willing to be disciplined by the just. Just chastisement is compared to the steadfast love ("mercy") associated with the covenant. It might be considered a blessing, since it is meant to strengthen the psalmist's resolve to be faithful. Those cast over the cliff are probably the wicked. When this happens, the prayers of the righteous psalmist will be recognized by all as having been pleasing to God. An agricultural metaphor is employed to describe the fate of the wicked. They will be plowed, broken, and scattered at the entrance of Sheol.

8-10 A prayer for help

The psalm ends as it began, with a prayer to God for assistance when in need and protection from the schemes of evil perpetrators. The final words are for reversals of fortune: May they be caught in their own traps while I escape.

Psalm 142 (lament of an individual)

2-3 A cry of complaint

The cry of the psalmist is not muted. Rather, it is full voiced and determined. The psalmist is intent on making God aware of the distress that has become such a terrible burden.

4-5 The path of suffering

The psalmist is vulnerable to the hidden traps set by attackers. There is no one along the way to help. God, who is aware of the course of events, is the psalmist's only hope, and so the afflicted one cries out to God for help.

6-8 The prayer for help

God is described as the psalmist's refuge, the only source of security. The land of the living signifies promise and full life. With God as surety, the psalmist is guaranteed life there and the peace and prosperity that come with divine blessing. Without God's help there is no hope, for the enemies are too strong for this sufferer. However, if God would step in and rescue the psalmist, this act of divine graciousness would be known to all, and all righteous people would marvel at God's goodness.

Psalm 143
(lament of an individual; penitential)

1-2 A cry for help

Appeal is made to divine faithfulness and righteousness, two characteristics of God's covenant relationship with the psalmist. This relationship is underscored by the psalmist's own self-identification as servant of God. This servant is well aware of the impossibility of a person being just before God. Therefore, the prayer is also one of humble acknowledgment of human limitation.

3-4 The enemy attack

In this last of the penitential psalms (cf. Pss 6, 32, 38, 51, 102, 130) the psalmist's suffering is described. Enemies have had the upper hand. They have hounded the psalmist and smashed this defeated one to the ground. More than that, they have relegated the psalmist to a state of darkness that is as grim as death. All of this distress has taken its toll on the distraught one's inner being as well. The psalmist's state is pitiful. Surely God will respond.

5-6 Remembering past favors

Recalling past blessings can serve two related pressing religious concerns. As a reminder of God's beneficence in the past, it can instill hope in those who suffer, assured that God will act in a similarly gracious manner in the present. It can also spur the sufferer on to turn to God with this confidence and plead for relief. The image of a parched desert strikingly describes the psalmist's condition of longing for God.

7-12 Prayers for assistance

The lament ends as it began, with prayers for God's help. The psalmist cries to be heard. The pit is a reference to Sheol, the fate of the psalmist if God chooses not to respond. The possibility of experiencing divine mercy (covenant love) at dawn suggests a night vigil of prayer. The psalmist asks for both rescue from distress and direction for living. Though the latter implies a recommitment to a way of life in concert with covenant fidelity, there is no indication that the affliction that burdens the psalmist is punishment for some

transgression. Rather, the psalmist has been faithful. It is the enemies who are guilty of transgression in their assault against this servant of God. The psalmist relies on God's kindness (covenant love) to set things right.

Psalm 144 (royal psalm)

1-2 Victory for the king

It is not until verse 10, with the mention of God's rescue of David, that the royal character of this psalm becomes apparent. The praise of God for having delivered the psalmist, with which this psalm opens, could have come from the mouth of any loyal Israelite. However, in this Davidic context, everything within the psalm takes on a decidedly royal character. Using military imagery, the psalmist ascribes all the king's military success to the power of God. God has been rock, fortress, stronghold, deliverer, shield, and defender. The king has simply been the beneficiary of divine goodness.

3-4 Human frailty

The psalmist marvels at God's concern for human beings (cf. Ps 8:5). Human strength, which is nothing compared with divine power, is as fragile as a breath of air, as fleeting as a momentary shadow. Despite such obvious frailty, God cares for humankind.

5-8 A prayer for help

This is a request for a manifestation of divine power. God was frequently revealed amid extraordinary occurrences in nature. Mountains quaked; the heavens thundered; lightning split the sky (cf. Exod 19:16). Here God is asked to rescue the psalmist in just such an awe-inspiring manner. This kind of phenomenal appearance of divine power would silence the psalmist's enemies and leave them quaking in the presence of such majesty.

9-11 A promise to praise God

The victory that God has already bestowed on various kings and on David in particular is employed as incentive for the deliverance of the psalmist from the lying speech of the enemies. This latter favor is then the occasion of singing a new song of praise to God.

12-15 A benediction

The section ends with a beatitude, a typical wisdom form that demonstrates the happiness that one finds by following the way mapped out by God. The entire section, however, contains several statements that are similar to beatitudes: May your sons be filled with life's potency so that the family bloodline will endure; may your daughters be beautifully fashioned so that they will honor the family; may your flocks increase and your fields produce abundantly; may your cities resist any attack from the outside. The actual beatitude (v. 15) gathers all of these people together and identifies them as blessed. They are particularly blessed because they are the Lord's own people.

Psalm 145 (hymn)

1-3 Praise of God

In traditional hymnic fashion, the psalm opens with an acclamation of praise. God is exalted as the divine king whose greatness cannot be fathomed. Words cannot even begin to describe God's wondrous nature, and so the psalmist resorts to repetitious exclamation and superlatives. In the midst of this exuberant praise, the psalmist promises to sing God's glories everywhere and forever.

4-9 Continuous praise

The psalmist is not alone in praising God. Generation after generation recalls the wondrous deeds performed by God, and each generation joins the next in singing God's praises. God's "mighty works" is usually a reference to the wonders God accomplished in delivering Israel from the bondage of Egypt. In this regard, God's justice was seen in the release of this chosen people from oppression. This interpretation of the reference is reinforced by the description of God: "The Lord is gracious and merciful, / slow to anger and abounding in mercy." The phrase first appears in the account of the renewal of the covenant in the wilderness after the people had sinned by worshiping the golden calf (cf. Exod 34:6). The phrase not only contains covenant vocabulary (mercy and love), but is a reminder that this promise was made with people who had only recently violated their covenant commitment. Divine mercy and love take on a distinctive character in such circumstances. It is precisely this mercy toward sin-

ners, and not merely divine splendor generally, that is being praised in this psalm.

10-14 Divine rule

The universal rule of God is extolled. This rule is characterized by its glory, its power, and its eternal duration. God has no rival; all creatures, generation after generation, are under this divine dominion, and all creatures praise God for the glorious nature of this rule. God seems particularly attentive to the needs of the weak and afflicted, lifting them up when they fall. Such kindness is in keeping with a nature that is merciful and compassionate.

15-21 God cares for the needy

God's prodigal generosity to the needy is proclaimed. God cares for them with open hands, refusing nothing. Covenant love ("merciful," v. 17) is extolled, as is another covenant characteristic, faithfulness ("truth," v. 18). Fear of God is the disposition of awe and reverence. Those who possess this disposition turn to God and rely on divine assistance. They will not be disappointed. God will hear their cry and come to their aid. This is reason for praising God.

HALLELUJAH PSALMS (146–50)

The last five psalms of this book and of the entire Psalter are known as the "Hallelujah Psalms," because they begin and end with that traditional acclamation. None of these psalms has a superscription, and all of them are hymns.

Psalm 146 (hymn)

1-2 Praise of God

The psalm opens with the standard call to praise God: "Hallelujah!" This is followed by a second call to praise and a promise that the psalmist will do so throughout all of life.

3-4 Human rule is not to be trusted

The psalmist warns against putting trust in human rule which is dependent on the person in power. Human beings are mortal and human rule collapses with the death of the ruler. Any security that may have existed in society is then lost, and the people are often thrown into confusion with no direction. It is foolish to trust in something so fragile and transitory.

5-9 The trustworthiness of God

In contrast to the futility of trust in human beings, the psalmist testifies to the wisdom of trusting in God. This wisdom is stated by means of a beatitude. Those who turn to God for help will find that God is more than trustworthy. God has the power and authority to accomplish whatever one requests, for God is the creator of heaven and earth. God is the one who formed the sea, once thought to be the primordial monster of chaos. God also exercises power and authority on earth. What follows may be reminiscent of some of the favors Israel experienced from the hand of God when the people were in dire straits. One item in the list also reflects an aspect of the social obligations on which Israelite society was based. This was care for the stranger, the orphan, and the widow, three classes of people who lacked male legal protection within the patriarchal society. Their mention here shows that the God of Israel is attentive to the needs of the most vulnerable in the community.

10 Praise of God

The final verse contains an acclamation of divine sovereignty. It is precisely the God of Israel who will reign forever. It is this God in whom all should place their trust. The psalm ends as it began, with an exclamation of praise: "Hallelujah!"

Psalm 147 (hymn)

1-6 The graciousness of God

The first section of the psalm opens with a declaration to celebrate God's saving power in song. This is followed by a listing of some of the wondrous deeds that God performed for the people of Israel. These are the reasons for giving praise. Mention of the restoration of Jerusalem and of the return of the scattered people dates the psalm in the postexilic period. God's goodness to the poor and needy is acclaimed.

7-11 The power of God

The second section opens with a summons to thank God in song. The reasons for praise are the glories of creation. In ancient Canaanite mythology, the clouds were the chariot of the great storm deity. Here they are simply the covering for the heavens, both of which are creatures of God. This same God is the source of water and fertility, the

one who provides food for all living beings. Despite all the marvels of the created world, God takes greatest delight in devout hearts.

12-20 The providence of God

For a third time, the people are called to praise God. Here the address is directed to the city of Jerusalem. There is no chronological order in the listing of favors granted by God. The city itself has been fortified, and peace reigns within it. Praise is given to the God who controls the powers of nature as well as the forces of history. All of this is done for the sake of the people of Israel. Mention of divine law is a reference to the covenant pact made with this chosen people. The psalm ends as it began, with the exclamation of praise: "Hallelujah!"

Psalm 148 (hymn)

1-6 Praise from the heavens

Besides the initial summons: "Hallelujah," the call to praise appears seven times in this section. All the celestial beings are invited to praise the Lord. The sun, moon, and stars, considered deities in other ancient cultures, are creatures of God called on to sing praise to the creator. The heights of the heavens is the place of greatest honor; the hosts are military units of angelic defenders; the waters above the heavens are part of the original chaotic flood that was quelled by God and then assigned its place above the firmament (cf. Gen 1:7). Every aspect of the heavenly realm was created by God and continues under God's control. They are all called on to sing praise to the Lord.

7-13 Praise from the earth

All the creatures of the earth are summoned to praise God. The sea monsters and the ocean depths have mythological connotations. Originally they were chaotic forces (cf. Isa 27:1; Gen 1:2). Storm elements were also considered minor deities, agents of the mighty storm god. Here, they are called on to praise the creator along with the wonders of the earth, the animals that live on it, and the fruits that it produces. Formerly the rulers of other nations paid homage to their respective gods. Now they too are invited to praise the God of Israel. Despite the class distinctions normally present in strict patriarchal societies, there is neither gender nor age exclusion. All are invited to praise the name of the Lord.

14 Israel is favored

The horn is a symbol of strength. This God who is to be praised by everything in the heavens and on the earth has singled Israel out for special honor. The psalm ends as it began: "Hallelujah!"

Psalm 149 (hymn)

1-5 A communal celebration

The psalm opens with the standard summons to praise: "Hallelujah!" The setting is a liturgical assembly with music, festive dancing, and banqueting. The occasion is the celebration of the kingship of God. The psalmist calls for a new song, perhaps because of some victory that God granted the people in return for their fidelity.

6-9 A victory celebration

It is clear that this is a celebration of victory over enemies. The two-edged sword, which cuts both ways, executes both justice and the punishment due those who have acted as enemies of God's people and, therefore, as enemies of God. The psalm ends as it began: "Hallelujah!"

Psalm 150 (hymn)

1-6 A liturgical celebration

The entire psalm is a paean of praise. With the exception of the last verse, every line begins with a call to praise. The long list of musical instruments indicates that the occasion is a liturgical celebration. There is some question about the setting of this celebration. The sanctuary is certainly the temple in Jerusalem, but the dome of heaven suggests God's celestial tabernacle. Every element in the psalm indicates that the celebration is on earth. It may be that the heavenly dome is mentioned for poetic reasons and because the earthly temple was considered a reflection of the heavenly sanctuary. The psalm ends as it began: "Hallelujah!" It is fitting that the entire Psalter ends in this way.

THE BOOK OF
PROVERBS

Katherine M. Hayes

INTRODUCTION

The Purpose and Ethos of Proverbs

In some ways the English word "proverb" is misleading as a title for this book because it gives the impression of folksy, simplistic advice that is familiar to the point of boredom. In fact the Hebrew word behind "proverb" is better translated as "memorable saying." This book resembles a collection of the wit and wisdom of Shakespeare or an anthology of Japanese haiku. The observations of Proverbs are carefully crafted: poetic, subtle, multifaceted, playful or ironic, and profound. Their wit prompts the reader to think more clearly about the various dimensions of human existence.

The intent of Proverbs, as stated in the prologue (1:1-7), is that this sort of thinking will lead to insight and understanding about the world that can inform the way one lives. Delightful as they are to read and ponder, the sayings of this book are devised to teach, furthering the growth in character we call wisdom and thus enhancing the quality of one's life.

The wisdom in which Proverbs aims to instruct its readers is comprehensive. It ranges from the practical to the psychological to the ethical. It includes management of one's own life, relations with others, and, in places, the governance of a nation. It is pervaded with reminders about the activity and presence of God in human life, and it is founded in awareness, or fear, of the Lord (1:7; 9:10; 21:30).

In its central contrast between the ways of the just and the wicked, the wisdom of Proverbs reflects a communal ethos evident also in the biblical law codes and the prophetic literature. This is clear in sayings that point to practices like the bearing of false witness, adultery, mistreatment of parents, accepting bribes, falsification of weights and measures, exploitation or indifference to the poor, and ritual observance that is unaccompanied by human decency. Proverbs explores the implications of these practices from various angles. The sayings extend beyond these areas, however, to encompass many others: neighborly relations, marital relations, child rearing, speech and conversation, friendship, work, and human emotions and individuality. They touch on the whole quality of a person's life.

In their range the sayings reflect an understanding of the integral relationship between the life of the individual and the life of the social body. What each individual does or doesn't do affects the quality and character of the community. The community as a whole attains stability and thrives when its members prosper and know how to live peaceably with each other. At the same time, the way an individual's life develops is influenced by the community's response to that person's decisions and actions. If these habitually cause conflict and trouble, if they are abusive or simply misguided and inept, the person will eventually face opposition or social stigma (shame). Hence the significance of honor and a good name, which bring the trust and good will that are vital if an individual is to flourish and that can be passed on to children. A good name is of more value than riches (Prov 22:1).

Overall, Proverbs can be seen as guiding members of the community, especially the young, in how to get on and how to get along in life. In some instances the observations and counsels of this book are culturally limited, but for the most part they are formulated in language that speaks universally of the human condition.

The Structure of the Book of Proverbs

The title "The Proverbs of Solomon" (Prov 1:1) applies to the entire book, yet the book encompasses collections of sayings clearly attributed to other figures. Proverbs is in fact a composite of various writings. Nine sections are usually distinguished.

1:1-7	Prologue
1:8–9:18	Introduction
10:1–22:16	The Proverbs of Solomon
22:17–24:22	The Sayings of the Wise
24:23-34	Other Sayings of the Wise
25:1–29:27	Other Proverbs of Solomon
30:1-33	The Words of Agur
31:1-9	The Words of Lemuel
31:10-31	The Worthy Woman

The overall structure of the book consists of a central core of sayings and instructions (Prov 10–29) that is prefaced by a long introduction (Prov 1–9), and ends with concluding reflections and a poem (Prov 30–31). The introduction creates a broad framework of wisdom for the sayings, the concluding reflections echo this framework, and the final poem transforms all that has been said about wisdom into a human portrait.

The Authorship and Origins of Proverbs

The titles of the discrete collections within Proverbs suggest diverse origins. The notation in Proverbs 25:1 that other proverbs of Solomon were transmitted by the "servants of Hezekiah, king of Judah," who lived several centuries after Solomon, points to stages of compilation and editing over time. The claim of Solomonic authorship for the book in 1:1 places the entire work

within the tradition associated with a wise and just king who "uttered three thousand proverbs" (1 Kgs 5:12). This claim is meaningful but does not tell the whole story.

Because the sayings of Proverbs elucidate fundamental human situations, they offer few clues to the particular contexts of their composition. The roles of both father and mother in teaching children are mentioned in the book, however, and some scholars propose that the sayings and instructions in their earliest forms were associated with the formation of character of the young in the home (23:22, 25; 29:15; 30:17; 31:1; cf. 1:8; 4:3; 6:20). That various proverbs speak of the role of the king or ruler suggests, further, a historical context under the monarchy (14:28; 16:10, 12-15; 20:8, 26, 28; 21:1; 29:4, 14), as does the reference to King Hezekiah in 25:1.

The literary quality of Proverbs makes it likely that colloquial sayings were not simply collected but also selected, refashioned, and composed by royal scribes: men trained in reading, writing, and composition and familiar with the language and literature of other cultures. Scribes were probably associated with the royal court before the exile (e.g., the "servants of Hezekiah"). To them may be attributed sayings that pertain to working closely with kings and rulers or holding positions of power (14:35; 22:11, 29; 23:1-8, 10-11; 24:21; 25:1-7, 15). The task of collecting and writing wise sayings, however, cannot be definitively traced or limited to the reign of Solomon in the 10th century B.C.

After the exile scribal activity may have been associated with both the temple and independent scribal schools. The introduction and conclusion to Proverbs (chs. 1–9 and 30–31) were probably added at a later stage of redaction, well into the postexilic period.

Some scholars propose that early written collections of sayings and instructions were read and copied in Israel, along with other forms of literature, in schools training young men as scribes (and possibly as potential leaders and officials as well). That scribal schools existed in Egypt and Mesopotamia is clear in texts preserved from these cultures. In a school setting the copying and reciting of proverbial material would have contributed to the moral and psychological development of students as well as to their literary skills. Schools in Israel may have ensured the preservation of the proverbs as part of a communal treasury of wisdom handed down within families over many generations.

Literary Forms in Proverbs

Wisdom is praised and taught in Proverbs in three major literary forms: (1) instructions, (2) wisdom poems, and (3) sayings. Following are examples of each type, (2) being an *excerpt* of a wisdom poem.

> (1) Hear, my son, and be wise,
>> and guide your heart in the right way.
> Do not join with wine bibbers,
>> nor with those who glut themselves on meat;
> For drunkards and gluttons come to poverty,
>> and lazing about clothes one in rags.
>> (Prov 23:19-21)

> (2) Long life is in her right hand,
>> in her left are riches and honor;
> Her ways are pleasant ways,
>> and all her paths are peace;
> She is a tree of life to those who grasp her,
>> and those who hold her fast are happy.
>> (Prov 3:16-18)

> (3) The naive believe everything,
>> but the shrewd watch their steps.
>> (Prov 14:15)

Instructions deliver advice in imperative form, either positive (a command) or negative (an admonition). As in example 1 above, many begin with a direct address ("my son") and an appeal to listen ("hear," "guide your heart"). The directive itself ("do not join") is often followed by an explanation ("for drunkards and gluttons come to poverty"). The parental speeches in chapters 1–9 are a form of instruction, as are many of the "Sayings of the Wise" in 22:17–24:22 and "The Words of Lemuel" in 31:1-9. Instructions are to the point and press the reader to take a specified course of action. They rely on the personal tone and conviction of the speaker (often the parent) to persuade.

Wisdom poems praising or speaking of wisdom as a distinct quality, as in example 2 above, are found in chapters 1–9, interwoven with the parental speeches. In these poems wisdom is often personified as a woman ("Long life is in her right hand"), and this is matched by the embodiment of wisdom in the worthy woman who is the sub-

ject of the book's concluding poem (31:10-31). The lyric tone, archetypal imagery, and cosmic language of these poems awaken in the reader an attraction to wisdom as a way of life.

Sayings in Proverbs typically take the form of a one line, two-part, aphorism, as in example 3, but include some multi-verse units, such as the lists of phenomena known as "numerical sayings" in Proverbs 30. "Saying" is a translation of the Hebrew word *mashal*, which is used in the Old Testament to refer to a range of types of speech (see, e.g., 1 Sam 24:14; Ezek 17:1-10; Jer 24:9; Num 23:7-10). As noted above, the word is probably best understood as a "memorable utterance."

Sayings, in contrast to instructions, are for the most part not explicit directives. Rather, they provide miniature sketches of human behavior and attitude. Often they contrast different types of behavior, as in example 3 above, where the unthinking acceptance of the naive person is contrasted with the careful reckoning of the shrewd. Often the consequences of specified behaviors or attitudes are contrasted as well. In these ways the sayings provide "food for thought" for the reader.

All of Proverbs is poetic in form. The kind of figurative language that is characteristic of poetry—image, metaphor, word play, personification, irony—is densely clustered in these writings. In terms of poetic structure, all exhibit the characteristic feature of Hebrew poetry called *parallelism*. This means that they are composed in poetic lines that divide syntactically into two-part (occasionally three-part) lines, which complement and interact with each other. *Synonymous parallelism* occurs when half-lines echo each other in some way, as in example 1 above. *Antithetic parallelism* means that the half-lines contrast with each other, as in example 3. Finally, *synthetic parallelism* refers to instances in which the half-lines simply complete each other, as in the last line of example 2. The natural but often inexact pairing of the half-lines allows for many possible points of connection and contrast.

The Artistic and Didactic Mode of the Saying

Because the two-part saying dominates in Proverbs, it is helpful to consider briefly its mode of expression and teaching. First, these sayings represent a particularly compressed form of poetry. There is no room in them for elaboration or explanation, and thus the resonant quality of the poetic language is intensified. The images they raise are concrete, yet evoke multiple associations (see, e.g., the image of the shrewd person watching his or her steps in example 3 above). In this respect the proverbial sayings are not unlike the seventeen-syllable poetic form of the Japanese haiku.

Second, many of the sayings effect a comparison or contrast, which is heightened by the parallelism of the compound poetic line. Antithetic parallelism sharpens a contrast, as in example 3, but the sayings include many other types of comparison and contrast. The "better than" sayings compare two situations by declaring the one named in the first half-line to be better than the one named in the second (15:17, 16:8, 32; 17:1; 19:1; 27:5; 28:6). The "happy are" sayings compare by implication those pronounced happy with those who are not (14:21; 16:20; 20:7; 28:14; 29:18). The "abomination" sayings, which declare certain types of behavior as an abomination to God or to others, can be seen similarly (11:1; 15:8; 21:27; 28:9).

"Like" sayings spread a simile over two half-lines (10:26; 11:22; 25:11-14, 18-20; 26:1, 8-10; 27:19; 28:15). Other sayings accomplish this sort of comparison without using the word "like" (26:7, 14; 27:17-18, 20), and many others employ similes or metaphors in one half-line or the other (16:31; 17:8; 18:8; 20:1, 27; 21:1; 22:4; 25:4). In all these instances the sayings instruct by inviting the reader to ponder just how the things compared are related or different, better or worse. As thoughts reverberate in the mind, one's understanding is expanded.

Each saying, then, opens up associations, and each is intended to be read as a small poem. For the most part, there is no discernible principle of order in the sequence of sayings in Proverbs. This need not be problematic if each is contemplated on its own terms.

At the same time, the sayings have been gathered together into different collections and into one overarching collection, and it is natural to read them in relation to each other. Apparent contradictions in perspective should not surprise the reader (e.g., 10:10 and 11:12; 10:15 and 11:4, 28; 11:15 and 11:24-25; 26:4-5; 28:1 and 28:15). Most sayings reflect a particular insight that sheds light on an aspect of human experience. None intends to encompass all the complexities of a situation or to preclude other angles of vision.

Rather, it is left to the reader to weigh the different perspectives and to consider their appropriateness in different contexts. When, for example, is it helpful to confront or reprove (10:10) and when to keep silent (11:12)? When is wealth (or equity) to be valued for the stability it brings to life (10:15) and when is it overvalued (11:28)? The gathering of distinct sayings into a collection makes possible a second level of comparison in Proverbs. The comparison *between* sayings also furthers the reader's growth in wisdom.

This is as true for the resemblances between sayings as for the differences. There are a few instances where sayings are repeated word for word, or practically so (18:8 and 26:22; 19:5 and 19:9; 20:16 and 27:13; 21:9 and 25:24; 22:13 and 26:13). Many more express similar perspectives with distinctive language and imagery. The recurrent patterns help the reader build up in his or her mind an impression of the contours of wisdom as an approach to life.

The Nature and Limits of Wisdom in Proverbs

The wisdom of Proverbs is optimistic. Its basic premise is that life is made up of choices, and its basic tenet that the ability to make good choices can be learned. By attending to the inherited ethos represented by parental instruction and reflecting on the connections displayed in the sayings (especially the connections between behavior and outcome), the reader sees life's realities and choices more clearly. He or she learns to discern what is appropriate and of lasting value and gains competence in responding thoughtfully in all the moments that compose a life. The result is well-being beyond price. In the words of Proverbs 19:8, those who acquire the sensibility of wisdom (literally, "gain heart") love themselves, and those who actively maintain understanding find what is good in life. It is a good that tastes sweet to the soul and that instills hope:

> If you eat honey, my son, because it is good
> if pure honey is sweet to your taste;
> Such, you must know, is wisdom to your soul.
> If you find it, you will have a future,
> and your hope will not be cut off. (Prov 24:13-14)

The speeches and poems of chapters 1–9 further assert that if one trusts in the promise of wisdom (and in the parental figures who teach it) and opens oneself to learn, wisdom will inhabit the heart, directing one's actions and saving one from serious missteps and wrongdoing as if by intuition (2:1-22; 3:21-26). Wisdom is ultimately a habit of being that is greater than the sum of its parts. It is, in fact, a transcendent quality that comes from God (2:6; 8:22-31). Personifying wisdom as a woman, chapters 8 and 9 show her delight in human beings and her desire to become the intimate companion of all (8:17, 31; 9:1-6; cf. 7:4).

Fools are those who have not pursued or who reject this possibility of companionship and well-being. They range from the naïve or unthinking, to the obtuse who are set in their own ways, to the arrogant and perverse who dismiss any thought of change or improvement. Fools are headed for trouble because they have not accepted wisdom's promise of protection and presence.

The focus of Proverbs, then, is on what can be learned from the contemplation of traditional teachings and of wisdom itself as a transcendent power. The book is not primarily concerned with life situations that are unexpected, inexplicable, or seemingly unconnected to human choice. There are sayings in Proverbs that depict these sorts of situations. Some speak of the ultimate role of God, rather than of human wisdom, in the unfolding of human experience. For example:

> The human heart plans the way,
> but the LORD directs the steps (16:9).

Or:

> Our steps are from the LORD;
> how, then, can mortals understand their way?
> (20:24).

Other sayings present certain existential or social realities as givens, such as anxiety and sadness (13:12; 14:10, 13), the shunning or oppression of the poor (13:23; 14:20; 18:23; 19:7; 28:3), the injustice of rulers (28:15-16; 29:4), and the allure of wrongdoing (17:8, 18:8) or foolishness (26:11). Such observations seem to foster a sense of realistic acceptance more than of proactive choice. Yet in light of the overall teaching mode of Proverbs, sayings like these can be seen as challenging the reader to work out their implications for living wisely. This challenge is taken up in depth in the books of Job and Ecclesiastes.

Gender in Proverbs

When the vantage point of gender is either specified or implied in Proverbs, it is almost entirely male. The speaker in the ten parental speeches in chapters 1–9, which serve as a literary frame for the book, is a father who addresses his son. It is true that the father links his teaching with that of the mother in 1:8 and 6:20, and we might presume that he serves as the spokesperson for a tradition of wisdom that is passed down from the older generation—mother and father alike—to the younger. But the mother's wisdom is generally articulated by her husband. It is the son, moreover, who is singled out as the novice in wisdom. He is repeatedly, and at length, warned against committing adultery with another man's wife (2:16-19; 5:1-23; 6:20-35; 7:1-27). The perspective given on this particular form of foolishness is clearly male.

The sayings in chapters 10–29 refer to the role of both father and mother in the formation of the young (10:1; 15:20; 23:22; 29:15; 30:17). "The Words of Lemuel" in 31:1-9, further, are identified as the teaching of Lemuel's mother (31:1), thus balancing at the end of the book the parental speeches delivered by the father at the beginning. Yet on the whole, when gender features in a saying or instruction in the body of the book, the focus is, again, on the male (11:16; 15:25; 23:25b; 29:15; and 30:23 could be considered exceptions). This is clear in sayings that speak of finding a spouse (11:22; 12:4; 18:22; 19:14), the experience of marriage (21:9, 19; 25:24; 27:15-16), and the dangers of adultery (22:14; 23:27-28; 30:20). The naming of King Lemuel as the recipient of his mother's teaching provides another example.

This imbalance in perspective may be related to the literary adaptation of traditional wisdom by scribal circles and to the use of such adaptations in scribal schools. The profession of scribe was limited to men, and the schools trained only boys and young men. As noted above, however, many scholars believe that the basic formation in character that underlies the sayings was centered in the home and naturally included children of both sexes.

The majority of the sayings and instructions in Proverbs make no explicit reference to gender and can be read from the viewpoint of both men and women. The personification of wisdom as a woman and potential companion in the introduction of the book (chs. 1–9) and the manifestation of wisdom in the worthy woman in the conclusion to the book (31:10-31) may have been intended to stir the imaginations of men. At the same time they cannot help but do the same for the women who, as seekers of wisdom, read Proverbs today.

Proverbs Today and Tomorrow

Proverbs represents the ongoing search for a way of being in the world that is life-giving and fruitful. It illuminates the varied realities and circumstances of human experience, while mindful of the presence and activity of God. John Henry Cardinal Newman's affirmation of the pursuit of knowledge in his *The Idea of a University* reflects this kind of conscious integration:

We attain to heaven by using this world well, though it is to pass away; we perfect our nature, not by undoing it, but by adding to it what is more than nature and directing it towards aims higher than its own.

In Proverbs, wisdom is a search that each person must undertake for him or herself. Wisdom is above all an endeavor. The sayings, instructions, and poems of Proverbs invite us to become students or disciples of wisdom, striving continually to comprehend what it means to be wise in our own time and place and as our circumstances change. In opening up this possibility for sincere seekers, wisdom's value is unchanging: "she is a tree of life to those who grasp her" (Prov 3:18).

COMMENTARY

PART I: PROLOGUE

Proverbs 1:1-7

These verses set out the purpose of the book: it is to be used in learning the full dimensions of wisdom. It will give resourcefulness, knowledge, and discretion to the "simple," those who are young and unformed (1:4), and assist those already committed to the pursuit of wisdom to expand their learning, gain in guidance, and grow in their understanding of wise writings (1:5-6). The sayings and instructions of Proverbs, then, hold out the promise of unfolding the ways of wisdom to novices and the experienced alike.

The qualities of wisdom in which readers will be instructed are varied (1:2-4). The Hebrew word translated "wisdom" in verse 2 is *hokmah*. It means, in a concrete sense, skill developed through experience (see, e.g., 1 Kings 7:14). In Proverbs *hokmah* conveys competence in building a fruitful and happy life. It is linked with discipline in verse 2 and in the concluding line of the prologue (1:7). The word "discipline" implies the active engagement of the student in learning. It draws out the element of skill and expertise in wisdom. Wisdom has an active component and entails ongoing growth in competence. The parallelism of verse 2 pairs this kind of active learning with the understanding of intelligent sayings, implying that both practice and contemplation are needed to grow in wisdom. The ethical dimensions of wisdom—righteousness, justice, and fairness—are brought out in verse 3, and the more practical virtues of resourcefulness, knowledge, and discretion are named in verse 4.

Verse 7 concludes the prologue by acknowledging that not all are open to wisdom and discipline. There are fools who despise both because fools lack the quality that makes knowledge of wisdom possible: "the fear of the Lord." This phrase conveys an elementary sense of the presence and power of God in human life, and it is frequent in Proverbs. Here it suggests that acknowledgment of divine presence and power is essential to the acquisition of wisdom (cf. 1:29; 2:5; 9:10).

PART II: INTRODUCTION

Proverbs 1:8–9:18

Proverbs 1:8–9:18 forms a sustained introduction to the book of Proverbs. It extols the value of wisdom as a quality of being that transcends particular wise behaviors. The longer literary compositions of the introduction are distinct from the short sayings and instructions that predominate in the body of the work. These longer forms offer a vehicle for persuasive, dramatic, and hymn-like language intended to move the reader to engage in the study of the proverbs that follow.

The introduction consists of a series of ten parental speeches interwoven with four poetic reflections on the nature of wisdom. A cluster of specific words of advice in 6:1-19 illustrates the range of wisdom.

The parental speeches share a similar form and familial tone, and they build on one another in laying out for the son a fundamental choice between the ways of wisdom and foolishness. The father impresses on his child the rewards of wisdom as well as its demands. The poetic reflections create a sense of wisdom as a quality so real and present that it takes on human shape and voice. In the imagination wisdom becomes a woman who invites all to enjoy her friendship and protection. Chapters 1–9 as a whole, then, can be seen as a duet of intertwining voices, each lyric in its praise of wisdom: the voice of the father (who represents the older generation) and the voice of wisdom herself.

1:8-19 First parental speech: the way of the violent

This is the first of ten parental speeches invested with the loving concern of the parents for their offspring's safe passage into responsible adulthood. The speeches represent a form of instruction or direct advice, and they have a consistent structure in chapters 1–9. Each begins with an initial address to the son and a plea to listen to the parents' teaching (e.g., 1:8-9), a set of commands and warnings (e.g., 1:10-18), and a concluding summation (e.g., 1:19).

The opening line of this first speech refers both to the instruction of the father and the teaching of the mother (1:8). The father is the speaker, but he stresses the value of the wisdom of both parents. Such parental guidance sets a child apart as especially favored, just as a diadem or pendant are signs of acclaim and adornment (4:9; cf. Song 4:9).

The content of the instruction (1:10-18) has to do with the son's choices in the social or public domain. How will he form a network of friends and associates and construct his livelihood? The

parents know the appeal of "sinners" who grasp at wealth by preying on others, and the father is able to produce a life-like imitation of their thoughts and words (1:11-14). He counters their enticements of riches and friendship ("we shall all have one purse!") with the metaphor of the way, a central image in Proverbs. The actions of the violent and unscrupulous track a way of life that leads beyond the immediate gains of wealth that preoccupy them. It is a path on which their feet "run to evil" as they "hasten to shed blood" (1:16), and it inevitably brings them to ambush and harm (1:18). Verse 19 offers a final pronouncement on this way of life: it is self-destructive.

1:20-33 First poem: Wisdom's lament

Wisdom's own voice now takes over from the father's. Wisdom is conceived as a whole quality of being and appears in the figure of a woman. In this poem she stands in the public domain: in streets and squares and at the city gates, the hub of the city's economic and civic transactions. The city gates are, further, traditionally associated with the hearing of disputes and dispensing of justice by the city's elders (Amos 5:15). Wisdom's appeal to the "naive," or unthinking, thus stands as an alternative to the appeal of the sinners in the previous speech.

Like the father's speech, wisdom's words are full of warning, but they depict the choices facing the young person in broader terms. Here the option lies between responding to wisdom's invitation or turning away from her (cf. 1:7b). The choice is an active one that involves transformation from a state of contentment with careless naiveté (1:22).

The question "how long" in verse 22 is characteristic of psalm laments (Pss 6:4, 74:10; 82:2). It occurs also in prophetic speeches where either the prophet or God laments over the intractability of the people of Israel (Hos 8:5, Isa 6:11, Jer 4:14, 21; 13:27). Wisdom's speech here has prophetic resonance as she reproves the simple for refusing her outstretched hand and ignoring her counsel and correction (1:23-25). This scenario of resistance is comparable to the deaf ears and closed eyes that the prophet Isaiah is told he must confront in Isaiah 6:10 (see also Jer 1:19; Ezek 2:3-7). Prophetic, too, is wisdom's foretelling of calamity for those who ignore her (1:26-31). The prospect of seeking wisdom too late (1:28) is reminiscent of the desperate but futile search for the word of the Lord in Amos 8:12.

Wisdom links the rejection of knowledge by the naive to their failure to choose the fear of the Lord (1:29). They have no sense of what is larger than their own experience, and their hatred of knowledge expresses itself in the spurning of all advice and correction (1:30). But they will be compelled to eat the fruit of the way they have chosen (1:31). The final summation in 1:32 is incisive: the turning away from wisdom by the naive "kills them." Verse 33 sounds a final note of hopeful contrast: those who listen to wisdom will live safely and without fear of harm.

2:1-22 Second parental speech: the safe way

The father's voice now picks up the theme of the choice *for* wisdom, and his assurances about the safety of the way of wisdom echo the promise of wisdom herself in 1:33.

Verses 1-11 describe the unfolding of wisdom in those who are receptive to it. The path to wisdom begins with openness to the father's words and commands. These are parental commands, not the stipulations of the law per se, although in Proverbs the one often evokes the other (see, e.g., the father's warning against adultery in 2:16-19).

Understanding the significance of the father's teaching entails an active response, as the sequence of verbs in verses 2-4 suggests: turn, incline, call for, raise the voice, seek, and search out. The student of wisdom must go after it, for it is not a given but a precious quality that is not easily acquired, like silver or "hidden treasures" (2:4). Only through persistent effort will the young come to understand what fear of the Lord means through gaining knowledge of God and God's ways in the world (2:5). Although the fear of the Lord is the *beginning* of wisdom, growth in wisdom involves movement toward understanding who God is (1:7).

In response to this movement, the Lord himself grants wisdom (2:8). It is a divine gift to those who are sincere, honest, just, and faithful, and it enables them to *understand* what is right, just, and honest and every path that is good in life (2:6-9). Wisdom enters deeply into the heart and soul of the seeker, transforming him or her (2:10). In Hebrew, the heart is the center of a person's thought, or discernment, and understanding. It includes

the concepts of "mind" and "sense" and is sometimes translated with these words. The Hebrew word represented here by "soul" means the whole being of a person, the life force that moves him or her.

In providing counsel for the upright, God shields them from harm (2:7-8). Just so, once wisdom has become rooted in the inner being, discretion and understanding watch over and guard the seeker (2:11). Wisdom in her various aspects is a beneficent force in the life of those who receive her.

Verses 12-19 provide two illustrations of the kind of protection wisdom offers. First, discretion and understanding will save a person, not necessarily from all harm, but from the way of the wicked: from those who "walk in ways of darkness" and whose ways are crooked and devious (2:13-15). The further identification of the wicked as those who "delight in doing evil" (2:14) recalls the sinners in 1:10, whose paths are rife with dangers.

Second, wisdom will save a young man from danger of a more personal nature: the woman married to someone else who is ready to forget her marriage vows. Literally, the Hebrew refers to the "stranger" or "foreign woman," one who is bound to another man. With her "smooth words" she attracts the susceptible but leads them on a path that turns downward. The imagery of death in verses 18-19 evokes, if not death itself, a banished and bereft form of existence that is irreversible. These verses sound a serious warning about the consequences of adultery.

The twin dangers of dishonest wrongdoing and adultery presented in verses 12-19 are representative of the seductive paths beckoning the unwitting. Wisdom guards those who listen to her by delineating those paths.

The speech concludes by recapitulating the metaphor of wisdom as a way: the way of the good and the just (2:20). At the same time verses 21-22 introduce a new metaphor based on the central biblical promise of land. Here the choice is between possession of the land and banishment, the finality of which is a lot like death (2:19). A similar theme runs through Psalm 37 (37:3, 9, 11, 29, 34). This choice also recalls prophetic language about exile from the land as well as restoration of the land (on exile, see Amos 7:17; Isa 5:13; Jer 9:15; on restoration, see Amos 9:13-15; Ezek

34:11-16; Jer 31:1-6; Isa 60:21; 65:9-10). The promise of tenure in the land echoes wisdom's promise of untroubled security in 1:33.

3:1-12 Third parental speech: what wisdom demands

This speech expands on the theme of divine grace in the conferring of wisdom. The opening address begins by urging the son to keep mindful of his father's teaching and commands because they will safeguard his life, bringing him both longevity and peace (3:1-2). Verses 3-10 then enunciate what taking the father's wisdom to heart demands and what it will ensure. In verse 3 it means wrapping oneself in the parental teachings as if around one's neck (6:21; 7:3; cf. Deut 6:8). The command to "write them on the tablets of the heart" further suggests the inner appropriation that is part of growth in wisdom (2:10; 7:3; cf. Jer 17:1 and 31:33). This will elicit favor and regard on the part of both God and others (3:4).

True wisdom, moreover, demands trusting in God for guidance and being mindful of the Lord "in all your ways," rather than relying on one's own insight (3:5-6). In essence the fear of the Lord means turning away from what is wrong, which preempts any other brand of human wisdom (3:7). This kind of lived out trust in God will bring about healing and vitality, penetrating deep into the flesh and bones, or self (3:8; cf. Gen 2:23).

The command to "honor the Lord with your wealth" in verse 9 refers to agricultural contributions to the temple. Ritual offerings, too, are part of a wisdom founded in fear of the Lord, and they result in productivity (3:10). This instruction overlaps with the prescriptions for worship in the law codes (Num 18:12; Lev 2:14; cf. Neh 12:44).

Finally, those seeking wisdom must accept discipline from the Lord (3:11), which is part of growth in knowledge (12:4). The phrase "the discipline of the LORD" represents a way of understanding unforeseen obstacles and hardships as a sign of the Lord's teaching and care. In this respect the Lord acts like parents who correct and challenge the child they love (3:12).

3:13-20 Second poem: wisdom's worth

This poem exalts the full scope of wisdom's value. Wisdom is better than the most treasured tangible objects: silver, gold, and corals (3:14-15).

She is, rather, like a living woman who holds out in one hand long life and in the other both "riches and honor." Her ways in the world are imbued with pleasantness and peace (3:16-17). Even more, she can be compared to a tree of life (3:18), an archetypal symbol of earth's fruitfulness in the ancient Near East (Gen 2:9). Those who find wisdom and stay close to her can be called "happy" (3:13, 18). The use of the world "happy" both at the beginning of the poem and at its end reinforces the concept of wisdom as a fortunate mode of being.

The last two lines of the poem (3:19-20) expand the implications of the tree of life as a symbol of creative power, linking wisdom with God's creation of the cosmos. It was by wisdom, understanding, and knowledge that God made the heavens, the earth, and the waters which make life possible (8:22-31; Ps 104:24; Jer 10:12-13). They are engrained in reality as we know it. Wisdom, understanding, and knowledge are the same qualities human beings are encouraged to seek at the beginning of the poem (3:13; see also 2:1-2), and they enable all to comprehend and live fruitfully within the created world.

3:21-35 Fourth parental speech: the particulars of wisdom

This speech begins by drawing attention to two important aspects of wisdom: deliberation and planning (3:21). Exercising these qualities will bring life, grace, and safety to the son (3:22-24). The young need not, then, be anxious about the kind of sudden or unexpected disaster that comes upon the wicked, for the Lord will be their confidence (cf. Job 4:6), keeping their feet from being caught in various snares (3:25-26). This, again, is not a promise that one's life path will necessarily be easy or painless, but that careful thought, along with trust in the Lord's protection, will see one through.

Verses 27-35 comprise specific points of advice that demonstrate the exercise of deliberation in social relationships. The neighbor in these instructions is any member of the community, and the father warns against behavior that irritates or erodes communal relations (3:27-30). Verses 31-32 pose the choice for or against the way of the violent and perverse in this context (cf. 1:10-19; 2:12-15). The behavior of such individuals is disruptive in the most damaging way, and those who adopt it are an abomination, or wholly unacceptable to God (cf. 1:10-19; 2:12-15). The upright, it is implied, contribute to communal harmony and are close to God (3:32).

The concluding verses of the speech fill out the concept of alternatives with a further set of parallel oppositions between the wicked and the just, the arrogant and the humble, and the wise and the foolish. Similar clusters of oppositions recur in chapters 10–29.

4:1-9 Fifth parental speech: get wisdom

In this speech the father shares his experience growing up under the care and guidance of his own father and mother, thereby heightening the personal tone that contributes to the persuasiveness of the parental speeches. The father insists that what he is teaching his children is good (4:2). It is not his own invention, nor does it represent the experience of his generation alone, but it comes from a tradition of wisdom that he received as a young man from his own father (4:3-4). The echoing of the father's appeal for attention in verse 1 with the grandfather's words in verse 4 illustrates this claim.

The repetition of the injunction "get wisdom, get understanding" in verses 5 and 7 suggests that the speech reduces to this essential point. The verb translated as "get" means to acquire and take possession. It implies active claiming as one's own and may include an element of acquiring through producing or creating (Gen 4:1). The son is urged in the clearest possible language to set his sights on getting wisdom in this full sense. For the young person beginning an independent life and concerned about acquiring many things, from material wealth to community standing to a spouse, wisdom must come first. All that is symbolized by the garland and crown (signs of special favor and recognition) comes with wisdom, once it is won (4:8-9). St. Paul's image of the Christian disciple as a runner straining to gain an imperishable crown recalls the father's advice here (1 Cor 9:24-27; cf. Matt 6:33).

4:10-19 Sixth parental speech: the two ways

In this speech and the next the father develops at length the metaphor of the way, juxtaposing the paths of the wicked and the just as alternative options (4:14, 18). As in previous speeches, the son is instructed with a direct imperative to steer clear of the way of wrongdoers (4:14; cf. 1:15; 3:31). When it comes to the way of the just, however, the father lets his description of it attract the son (4:18). Images of light show that, like the dawn, the promise of this way grows stronger and brighter as one proceeds (Ps 97:11). Not only the end of the way of the just but the way itself partakes in clarity and hope. The path of the wicked, in contrast, is dark, confused, and impassable (4:19). The prophet Third Isaiah uses similar images of light and darkness to characterize the courses of the just and the unjust (Isa 58:9-10 and 59:9-10).

4:20-27 Seventh parental speech: the straight path

The father now asks the son to fix his whole being on keeping to a straight path and away from evil. The child is implored again to listen to the father's words and hold them within the heart (4:20-21; cf. Deut 6:6). But more is required: one must guard one's heart carefully, for it is the source of inner sensibility, and from it a life takes shape (4:23; cf. Luke 6:45). Guarding the heart means rejecting what is devious and manipulative in one's speech, keeping one's eyes on the way of life the parent's words trace out (4:25; cf. 4:21), and steadying one's steps in that way (4:26-27).

This speech describes a deep appropriation of parental wisdom that affects how one engages with life (cf. 2:10). In this it is reminiscent of the "new heart" passages in Ezekiel 11:19-20 and 36:26 and the image of laws written on the heart in Jeremiah 31:33.

The opposition between what is upright or straight and what is dishonest or crooked is recurrent in Proverbs (2:13-15; 3:32; 4:11; 6:12; 11:3, 21:8; 28:6, 18). The book of Deuteronomy, further, uses the language of turning aside to the right or left in reference to obedience to the law (Deut 17:11, 20; 28:14).

5:1-23 Eighth parental instruction: the deception of adultery

This is the first of three parental speeches that focus on the dangers of adultery (see also 2:16-19). Adultery would have been a common threat to a young man for obvious reasons but also, perhaps, because of the practice of arranged marriages at a young age. Adultery serves as a premier example of the raison d'etre of wisdom because of the strong pull of sexual attraction, which has positive aspects in the right contexts and destructive impact in the wrong ones. Discernment, discipline, justice, and good sense are all called into play in confronting the possibility of violating the marriage of a neighbor. The extended focus on adultery in Proverbs 1–9 enables the readers to view different approaches to critiquing this paradigmatic form of foolishness.

In the opening address of the speech, the father calls the son to listen to his wisdom so that the young man may learn to act with discernment, which is needed because the appeal of adultery (and of the adulteress, or "stranger"; cf. 2:16) is misleading. The parallelism of verses 3-4 is both synonymous, within each verse, and antithetic, between verses. The adulteress's lips are honeyed (5:3), but her aftertaste is bitter (5:4); her mouth is smooth as oil (5:3), but, in the end, sharp and dangerous as a two-edged sword (5:4). In sum, the steps, or actions, of her way move toward death and the realm of the dead (2:18-19), and the tortuous wanderings of her paths prevent one from even seeing the way of life (5:6).

This is why the father pleads with his sons in no uncertain terms to stay away from her (5:7-8). Dalliance with another man's wife will take all the promise out of life (5:9-11). What the father describes is not simply the social stigma of adultery but the actual damages suffered by one who encroaches on the marriage of another. These include social shame, monetary reparations, and economic deprivation and physical exhaustion (cf. 6:32-35). The father envisions how the son will recognize after the fact that he has ruined his future through willful ignorance (5:11-14). Such visualizations of the end of a pattern of behavior (or of the whole pattern, from beginning to end) are the essence of the wisdom of Proverbs.

The alternative for the son is to delight in his own wife (5:18-19). She is referred to obliquely with images of water (cistern, well, streams, and fountain) in 5:15-17 (cf. Song 4:15). Water is a source of life. If one has such a source, why look elsewhere (5:20)? Why put that source at risk, allowing its waters to be scattered in the streets (5:16)? Although many interpreters have taken the last image as referring to the husband's aber-

rant sexuality, it is just as likely that this verse refers to the effect of the husband's adultery on the wife and on the integrity of his marriage. A betrayed wife may, in time, turn to others, and her springs and streams, once contained in the well of her home for her husband, will be dispersed outside and shared with outsiders (5:17; cf. 11:29).

The end of this speech places adultery within the broader framework of human ways in general: all lie open to the eyes of the Lord (5:21). From that vantage point it is possible to see that the wrongs done by the wicked inevitably entrap them (5:22). The wicked suffer this fate because they learn nothing through discipline, or instruction, and thus fail to grow in wisdom. Rather, by persisting in doing what will bring them serious harm—that is, in great folly—they are lost (5:23).

6:1-19 Interlude: A sampling of wisdom

The four sayings and instructions interjected here serve as snapshots of the path of wisdom and its terrain. The two instructions in verses 1-5 and 6-11 invoke qualities of good sense and enterprise and call the young person to take responsibility for managing his or her own life. The sayings in verses 12-15 and 20-35 address forms of troublemaking and wrongdoing in the community. The interrelation of individual and communal perspectives here anticipates a similar mix in the sayings of Proverbs 10–29.

Although the first instruction begins in verse 1 with the familiar address, "my son," it lacks the overall structure of the parental speeches. It resembles, rather, the shorter and more loosely structured instructions found in Proverbs 22:17–24:22.

Verses 1-5 warn against guaranteeing the debts of a neighbor, or fellow community member. This is a recurrent theme in Proverbs (11:15; 17:18; 20:16; 22:26-27; 27:13). The advice may seem to run counter to other exhortations to share generously with the poor (14:21, 31; 19:17; 31:8-9). It is consistent, however, with the ethos of careful management of one's own resources, which can be seen as a communal value. In effect the warning promotes a healthy realism about taking on someone else's debt. Verse 5 ends the instruction by comparing the person trapped by his or her unwise promises to animals trapped by hunters (6:2).

Verses 6-11 take up an even more frequent theme: laziness (24:30-34 and numerous sayings in chs. 10–29). Here the attention of the lazy person is directed not to a human pattern of behavior but to the ant. An example from the natural world sometimes provides a paradigm against which human life can be seen more clearly (see, e.g., the lists of human and natural phenomena in 30:18-19, 24-28, 29-31). The didactic mode of wisdom remains the same: "study her ways and learn wisdom" (6:6). In this case the ant demonstrates the foresight and hard work that result in a good harvest (6:7-8).

The depiction of the lazy person, in contrast, shows that lack of a work ethic makes one vulnerable to poverty and want (6:9-11). These verses illustrate the adeptness of Proverbs in making general concepts visual through image and metaphor. The reader is shown the lazy person sleeping with folded hands, as defenseless against the intrusion of poverty and want as against robbers or armed men.

Verses 12-15 draw a portrait of the person who is up to no good, showing how one's self as well as one's fate is shaped by a way of life. Here physical features express character and presage destiny. Everything about this person is twisted or crooked, from speech to glance to gait to gesture to thought (6:12-14; cf. 2:12-15). The impact of such a person is to destabilize: to plan harm or evil and to instigate strife (6:14). It is not unnatural, then, that he or she will in time suffer a sudden ruinous twist of fate (6:15).

Verses 16-19 place the preceding description in a theological light: the actions of people set on what is harmful are hateful to God. These verses constitute what is called a numerical saying because they enumerate a list of phenomena that share some feature or features. Such sayings typically begin with a formula that states the number of things listed in a two-part sequence, as in 6:16: "There are six things the Lord hates / seven are an abomination to him." This saying elaborates on the statement in 3:32: "To the Lord the devious are an abomination." Again, a composite picture approximates the whole person: eyes, tongue, hands, heart, feet (6:17-18). So, too, the propensities described—haughtiness, deception, bloodshed, wicked schemes, false witness, and the sowing of discord—coalesce in the person who is at odds with the Lord.

6:20-35 Ninth parental speech: the foolishness of adultery

The son is urged to impress the father's command and mother's teaching on his mind or heart in the same way that a necklace is tied around the neck (6:21; cf. 3:3). They will then serve as guides and guardians through life (6:22-24; cf. 4:4-6). The imagery here draws on the concept of the amulet, an ornament inscribed with words intended to protect its wearer from evil spirits.

The threat to the son takes the form, again, of the neighbor's wife, with her flattering overtures (6:24). This speech focuses on the disastrous consequences of adultery, adding detail to what was suggested in 5:7-14. The teaching of father and mother here emphasizes the inherent foolishness of cultivating desire for a married woman and letting oneself be caught by the signs of her interest (6:25). The relationship between these two steps—desire for what is not yours and susceptibility to desire returned—is perhaps reflected in the saying about committing adultery in the heart in Matthew 5:27-28.

The price paid for adultery is life itself, a cost far beyond what one might pay for a prostitute (6:26). The parents are not recommending that their son seek out a prostitute but explaining the far greater danger of violating a marriage.

The inevitable consequence of adultery is shown by comparison with a natural phenomenon: fire burns (6:27-29). But just as the warning "don't touch" to a child who reaches out toward a hot object is often insufficient, so the father adds another comparison, which shows up adultery as utterly senseless. Thieves may steal out of need because they are hungry and the community still retain some sympathy for their act (6:30). Yet if caught, thieves are held to the communal standard of justice and must repay sevenfold (in biblical idiom, many times over) for what they have taken, even to the point of emptying out their own houses (6:31). The adulterer's act is gratuitous, however, and brings down on him much worse: physical injury, contempt, and a permanent stigma (6:33). These consequences are unavoidable because the jealous anger of the offended husband will seek reprisal without pity and cannot be appeased (6:34-35).

The one who commits adultery lacks sense in that he needlessly destroys himself (6:32). Working against such blind self-destruction, the father's command, the mother's teaching, and the reproofs of parental discipline light a way to life (6:23; cf. Ps 119:105).

7:1-27 Tenth parental speech: the tragedy of adultery

Since all the parents' words may not be enough to dissuade the young man from the lure of adultery, the father summons up a lifelike drama before his son's eyes. This scenario of seduction is designed to resonate with the young man's fantasies but also to show their tragic end. In real life the outcome of mutual attraction is not necessarily evident in its initial stages, at least not to the naive. A dramatic narrative makes it possible for the inexperienced to witness the dynamics of adultery at a remove and look at them with a critical eye.

The father's introductory words in verses 1-3 encourage the son, again, to take parental instruction so seriously that it becomes part of his senses (eyes), his actions (fingers), and his understanding (heart). By fully appropriating the father's teaching, the son will in effect claim wisdom as an intimate friend and relation (7:4). The word "sister" is used of the beloved, or bride, in the Song of Songs, as well as in Egyptian love poetry, and it carries associations of deep bonding. The dual bonding of the son with wisdom and with the father's words (7:3) will keep him from being taken in by the "smooth words" of the adulteress (7:5). This advice goes beyond that given in Proverbs 5:18-20, where the son is urged to embrace his own wife. It is through embracing the wisdom inherent in parental guidance that the son will find true and lasting pleasure.

In verses 6-20 a vivid scene unfolds. The eyewitness narrative of the father brings the son (and the reader) to a window, looking out at the naive. Among these the father singles out one without sense (literally, "without heart," 7:7; cf. 6:32). This is a young man who is not only inexperienced but lacking an interior life of reflection. He is easy prey for the powerful attraction of adultery. This attraction is personified here, in dramatic fashion, as an adulteress ("stranger" or "foreign woman"; cf. 2:16) in the persona of a prostitute, brazenly soliciting a sexual partner (7:8-13).

She issues her invitation to the young man in verse 14. She has just sacrificed an animal in connection with a vow she has made (Lev 22:21;

1 Sam 1:9-11, 20-21, 24-25). Such a sacrifice, known as a peace offering, was consumed by the donor once the fat parts of the animal were burned on the altar (Lev 3:1-17; 7:11-15). The opening gambit of the adulteress, then, is to woo the young man with the promise of a festive meal.

She rapidly moves on to insinuate much more (7:16-18), assuring him that her husband is out of town and not due home until the end of the month (7:19-20). These inducements are what the smooth words of the adulteress sound like. They are the stuff of fantasy, blocking out any thought of unpleasant repercussions.

But the young man without sense is easily led (7:21). He follows his seductress without hesitation, like an unwitting animal, unaware that what he is dallying with is his own life (7:22-23). The image of the ox led to slaughter in verse 22 ironically recalls the woman's invitation to a sacrificial feast.

From this drama turned tragedy the father draws a conclusion in verses 24-27, connecting what has been vicariously witnessed with the "words of my mouth" (7:24). Unlike the hapless and helpless young man without sense, the son should exert direction over his heart (7:25). Those who fail to question or think twice and who succumb to adultery are many (7:26). But once they enter its realm (the house of the adulteress) they find that it is anything but festive and fun. Rather, it is the way to the dwelling place of the dead (Sheol), whose rooms are death chambers (7:27; cf. 2:18-19; 5:5).

8:1-36 Third wisdom poem: the scope of wisdom

The introduction to Proverbs reaches a literary summit in this incantatory revelation of wisdom's reach and roots, most of it uttered in the first person in her own voice. Much of what has been said about wisdom by the father and in the wisdom poem in 3:13-20 is declared here by the persona of wisdom herself, who commands attention as a living reality.

She stands in the center of human interaction and activity: at the city heights overlooking the road, at the crossroads, at the city gates (8:1-3). But instead of lamenting over and admonishing those who fail to respond to her, as in 1:20-33, she appeals to all to learn resourcefulness and sense and to trust her as a teacher (8:5-9).

She claims to speak honestly (8:6-7), in contrast to the smooth words of the seductress. Her words ring true to those with the intelligence and knowledge to understand them (8:8-9). Her teaching is as trustworthy as sterling or gold, but more valuable (8:10-11; cf. 3:14-15).

In verses 12-14 wisdom tells us herself who she is. She claims the qualities of prudence, useful knowledge, counsel and advice as well as strength (8:12, 14). We can infer that wisdom is able to see and assess the realities of life on the ground, however discomforting, and to respond to them capably. In all these respects wisdom embodies understanding of human life: "I am understanding" (8:14).

These are the attributes that enable kings and rulers to make justice a reality for those they govern (8:15-16). But wisdom is not reserved solely for rulers: she loves all those who love her and shows herself to all who look for her (8:17; cf. Wis 7:27-28). To all she holds out her rewards: riches, honor, and wealth (8:18). Yet these standard concepts of well-being are inadequate to express the fruits of a relationship with her (8:19). She moves in the ways of righteousness and justice, and the wealth she bestows on those who love her must be understood in these terms (8:20-21).

Wisdom now reveals her origins in a poem within a poem (8:22-31). The beauty of the cosmic imagination in these verses creates a moment of epiphany. Wisdom's origins are with God (8:22). She was formed by God and brought forth at the very beginning of creation, before the earth was fashioned (8:23-26). She was present when God marked out and set in place the heavens, the seas, and the earth's foundations (8:27-29). According to many interpreters (as well as to the translators of the NABRE), wisdom stood beside God as an artisan (Wis 7:22; 8:6). She is associated with the design and construction of creation, as in 3:19, where wisdom, understanding, and knowledge are used by God to found and sustain the heavens and the earth.

Thus God delights in wisdom, who is described in this poem as "playing," before God and over the whole of God's earth (8:30-31). The Hebrew verb "to play" also means "to laugh" and includes the meaning of dancing, singing, the playing of instruments, and rejoicing generally (1 Sam 18:7; 2 Sam 6:5; Jer 31:4). The image of wisdom playing suggests the personification of a quality that celebrates and rejoices in God's handiwork in creation, delighting in human beings, as God delights in her (8:31). Overall, the poem reveals that wisdom is founded in creation as God made it, that she articulates and rejoices in creation, and that she has a special affinity for human beings. She thus provides a link between human beings and the Lord, their creator.

Some scholars find similarities between wisdom's portrait here and goddesses of wisdom in other ancient cultures. Parallels have been drawn with the Egyptian goddess Isis in Hellenistic cults, for example, or to the Egyptian goddess of truth and justice, Ma'at. Yet in Proverbs 8:22-31 wisdom is presented as the first of God's creative works rather than as a separate deity (8:22-23, 27, 30). In the Christian tradition the concept of Christ as the preexistent logos in John 1:1 has been associated with this passage, and it is part of the lectionary readings for Trinity Sunday.

Proverbs 8 ends with wisdom turning to the human children in whom she delights and appealing to them directly, just as the father has done to his son (8:24). She summons them to listen to her, hear her instruction, and become wise. In this harmonizing of wisdom's voice with the father's, the parents' instructions take on universal overtones, and wisdom's, the loving intimacy of the parent. As in 8:4-21, wisdom now affirms from her own mouth what 3:13-20 declares: those who listen to her and are persistent disciples are "happy" (8:33b-34). The choice for wisdom is again as simple as that between life and death (8:35-36).

9:1-18 Fourth wisdom poem: the two invitations

The cosmic self-revelation of wisdom in chapter 8 shifts into more domestic images in the poem that concludes the introduction to Proverbs. The opposition between finding and missing wisdom stated in the last two verses of chapter 8 is developed here in the form of competing offers of hospitality. One comes from wisdom, again personified as a woman (9:1-6), and the other from "Woman Folly," a personification of foolishness (9:13-18).

The imagery of verses 1-6 builds on that found in 8:34, where the disciple of wisdom sits at her gates and doorposts. At the same time, it contrasts with the house of the adulteress, to which the unwitting are lured in 7:27. In chapter 9 wisdom extends a welcome to all the uninstructed, and she is amply prepared to provide for them as guests. Her house is solidly founded on seven pillars and spacious: the number seven conveys completion and perfection (9:1). As hostess, wisdom has spread her table with meat and wine and sent out her many assistants with invitations (9:2-3). In accepting her hospitality and eating and drinking with her, the naive will begin to leave behind their foolishness and grow in understanding (9:6).

Many of the features of this banquet are standard elements of the meal prepared for a guest in ancient traditions of hospitality (e.g., Gen 18:1-15). The meal itself is a sign of shared abundance and friendship, or good will, but also an occasion for listening, hearing, and the exchange of conversation (see Gen 18:9-15; Isa 55:1-3). In this poem the simple are invited to spend time with wisdom, to partake of her food, and to enjoy conversation with her.

Verses 7-12, inserted between the description of the two invitations, remind the reader that not all will be willing to enter wisdom's house or be glad of her company. Although her invitation includes all (9:4-6), paradoxically, a degree of inherent wisdom is needed to accept her corrections and teachings (9:8-9; cf. 8:9, 17). The nature of this prerequisite wisdom is stated in verse 10: fear of the Lord, or a sense of the reality of God, and knowledge of the Holy One, a sense of the nature of God (cf. 1:7; 2:5).

The possibility of rejecting wisdom's invitation has now been raised. Verses 13-18 pose an alternative invitation, from "Woman Folly." The description of this figure creates an antithesis to personified wisdom in 9:1-6. Woman Folly does not symbolize the foolishness of women, but the quality of foolishness in general, just as woman wisdom represents the quality of wisdom in the abstract. The depiction of Woman Folly soliciting passersby to enter her house in verses 15-17 resembles the solicitations of the adulteress in 7:10-20, but adultery is only one form of foolishness (5:20-23).

Folly is loud and restless (9:13; cf. 7:11). Steeped in foolishness, she knows nothing at all (9:13). Like wisdom, she invites the simple to enter her house (9:14-17). The contrast between the two invitations is obvious and laughable, however.

Folly has no assistants to send out but sits at her door and yells like a street vendor. She has prepared no genuine meal of meat and wine but offers bread and water stolen from someone else. Although she insists that there is special pleasure in consuming what is illicit and enjoyed on the sly, one would need to be very simple and foolish to take this bait. Verse 18, the last line, suggests that tragically there are those whose naiveté approaches the willful ignorance of Woman Folly. They do not know that her banquet is no treat, that her guests are ghosts, and that her house is a facade leading to the underworld (7:27).

On this note the introduction to Proverbs ends, leaving the reader with a solemn warning to weigh life's choices carefully and critically. Implicitly, the seeker of wisdom is encouraged to study and reflect on the proverbs that follow as an aid to doing just that. They will guide him or her step by step in considering the intricacies of living wisely. They are the meat and wine that wisdom invites all to share.

THE PROVERBS OF SOLOMON
Proverbs 10:1–22:16

Chapter 10 begins the first of a series of collections of sayings and instructions that provide a diverse texture for the basic choice between wisdom and foolishness set out in chapters 1–9. This initial collection bears the superscription, "The Proverbs of Solomon," and it consists entirely of short poetic sayings. It extends through 22:16 and consists of two sections that differ somewhat in both form and content: 10:1–15:33 and 16:1–22:16.

Despite common elements, each saying strikes its own chord. There are 375 separate sayings in this first collection, and it is not possible to comment on each one. Yet to speak of them only in broad thematic or formal groupings is to miss the wit, artistry, and profundity of the individual saying. This commentary will discuss overall thematic patterns where appropriate, but focus on selected sayings that are representative of the diversity and depth of the whole.

Section One (Proverbs 10:1–15:33)

The proverbs in this first section almost unvaryingly use antithetic parallelism to contrast a characteristic behavior or attribute described in the first half-line with one named in the second. The parallelism creates a set of recurrent oppositions, the most frequent being that between the just and the wicked. The basic choice between wisdom and foolishness is thus posed within a matrix of other choices, including uprightness and perversity, honesty and deviousness, hard work and laziness, restraint and lack of control, generosity and indifference. Often the contrast between ways of life is yoked to a second contrast between the consequences of each way, so that an overall pattern of act leading to consequence is evident.

10:1-32

Verse 1 situates wisdom, as in the instructions of chapters 1–9, within the domain of the family, where character is formed. The antithetic parallelism of this saying is clear: "wise son" in the first half-line is opposed to "foolish son" in the second, while "glad" contrasts with "grief." The opposition between wise and foolish in this first verse provides a rubric for the various contrasts delineated in succeeding verses, and in particular for the predominant opposition between the just and the wicked, which is introduced in verse 2 and repeated in verse 3.

The first half-line of verse 2 denies the profitability of ill-gotten wealth. It corresponds in aphoristic form to the first parental instruction in 1:8-19. The second half-line asserts that justice delivers what is lasting. Verse 3 brings the Lord into the picture. God does not allow the life of the just to waste away through hunger but actively opposes the greed of the wicked. This verse, moreover, begins with the just in the first half-line and ends with the wicked in the second, thus inverting the order of the contrast in verse 2. This literary structure is known as a *chiasm* (an x-shaped configuration), and it locks the thought in place. Acknowledgment of the divine role in the fates of the just and the wicked further reinforces the significance of this opposition within chapter 10 (where it occurs in eighteen out of thirty-two verses) and in chapters 10–15 as a whole.

Verses 4-5 introduce and reiterate the contrast between laziness and hard work. In verse 4 the slack hand that creates nothing but poverty is opposed to the busy hand that enriches. Verse 5 returns to a familial setting and offers a concrete illustration: the son who gathers grain during the summer wheat harvest is contrasted with the son who is asleep under the haystack. The first son is a success; the second, a disgrace, or object of public disfavor. As in verses 2-3, the repetition of the contrast in two guises at the beginning of the chapter marks its importance (see also 10:16; cf. 6:6-8).

In verse 8 the contrast between the wise and the foolish is presented in terms of one who listens to commands as opposed to the fool who is busily speaking his or her own mind. Here "commands" has the broad meaning of instructions, like those offered to the son in chapters 1–9 (2:1-2; 3:1; 4:4). The parallelism of this verse is not exact. The first half-line describes the receptive posture of the wise person toward instruction. The second contrasts the foolish talker who will be brought down to ruin, introducing a notion of consequence that is lacking in the first. The second half-line says something a little different and something more. Yet the association of ruin with the fool naturally raises implications for the wise listener: surely he or she will proceed from strength to strength. Further, the notion of instruction, explicit in the first half-line, is present as a backdrop in the second half-line, influencing how the "fool" or careless talker is understood. Such subtle asymmetry, which evokes unvoiced associations, is a powerful feature of biblical parallelism.

The phenomenon of speech is taken up again and again, under various aspects, in the sayings that follow. Such sayings attest to the power of words in human relationships. Unrestrained speech, deceptive speech, negative and trivial speech, or mistimed speech are arrayed before the reader in 10:10-11, 13-14, 18-21, 31-32. The positive effects of speech are stressed as well as the negative. In verse 11 the mouth of the just is a "fountain of life," in contrast to the concealed violence of the wicked, which destroys. In verse 21 the just one's lips nourish (literally, "shepherd") many.

In some of these sayings about speech the polarities of wise and foolish and just and wicked occur as well, bringing all three sets of categories into alignment with each other. In verse 31, for example, "The mouth of the just yields wisdom" (cf. 10:21).

Lack of restraint in speech is often linked with lack of emotional self-control, another frequent topic in the sayings. Verse 12 distinguishes between love in action and hatred in action. Whereas hatred stirs up conflict and rancor, love "covers over" or buries the memory of all offenses (17:9). This saying is quoted in 1 Peter 4:8 and alluded to in James 5:20.

Verse 26 is a "like" proverb that captures the essence of a situation in a memorable comparison. The images convey effectively just how irritating the lazy are to those who rely on them for various tasks. The comparisons sharpen one's recognition of this phenomenon, but the implications of the knowledge gained are left to each reader to consider.

By the end of this introductory chapter of the first collection of sayings, certain patterns are established. The wise are repeatedly associated with the just, and logically so, since the just enjoy blessing, joy, and long life. They withstand all challenges, while the hopes of the wicked come to nothing (10:28). Through the juxtaposition of various antitheses, wisdom and justice are associated with other qualities as well: willingness to work, to listen and learn, to speak thoughtfully and honestly. These initial impressions are filled out in the chapters that follow.

11:1-31

Verse 1 represents a type of proverb in which a practice or attribute is declared to be an abomination, thus weighting the typically more subtle contrasting of options (see also 15:8; 21:27; 24:9; 26:25). The term "abomination" is especially common in ritual language, where it marks what is unacceptable in terms of sacrifices and other ritual observances. It is used here in a moral sense of what is unacceptable to God in terms of community practices. The strong language reflects the central role of scales in the doing of business in Israel. Agricultural commodities like grain were measured by weight before being bought and sold. Skewing the scales could mean extra profit for one party but hunger for another. Sanctions against this practice must have formed part of the common ethos of the society, as the altering of weights and measures is condemned in the prophetic writings (Amos 8:5; Hos 12:8; Mic 6:10-11) as well as in the law code of Deuteronomy (Deut 25:13-16). Proverbs 20:10 reiterates this particular "abomination."

Many of the sayings in chapter 11 portray the outcome of dishonest practices wholly within the

framework of the contrast between the lives of the just and the wicked (11:3-11, 16-19, 21, 27-28, 30-31; but cf. 11:20). These proverbs do not mention God's favor or disfavor, but draw attention to the inherent malfunction of what is "crooked." The metaphor of the path or way comes into play explicitly or implicitly in several verses. A chosen path or mode of life can be straightforward or devious. One would expect the straight path to reach its destination but the twisted path to wander into undesirable byways and possibly never arrive (10:9). This imagery is latent in verse 3: the honesty of the upright or incorruptible "guides them," but the duplicity of the faithless or treacherous misleads and ruins them. In verse 5 the imagery is explicit: the virtue of the honest makes their ways straight, whereas the wicked stumble and lose their footing through their wickedness. In verse 6 the impression of self-destruction is even stronger: in contrast to the upright, whose virtue delivers them, the intrigue (literally, the "craving") of the wicked entraps them (cf. 11:8).

Verses 9-11 consider the impact of the just and the wicked on others in the community. Verse 9 refers to the destructive effect of uncontrolled talk against one's neighbor or fellow community member. Verses 10-11 extend the scope to the public arena. Verse 10 states that a city has cause to be happy when the just do well and the wicked fail. Verse 11 supplements this assertion: the blessing of the upright has power to raise or build up a city, whereas the mouth of the wicked can break down not just a neighbor, but the whole social body. Here again, the reference is to both the positive and negative powers of speech, which can generate life but also do violence (10:11; 18:21). The ancient concepts of blessing and curse represent forms of speech that wield life-giving and death-dealing power (Gen 27:1-39; Num 6:22-27; Num 22:1–24:25; Deut 27:1–28:69).

In addition to sayings that weigh the ways of the just and the wicked are some that speak directly of wisdom (11:2, 12, 14, 29). Verse 12 connects the wisdom attribute of intelligence (see 1:2) with speech toward a neighbor. The openness of this saying allows one to imagine scenarios of both the irritating and the blameless neighbor. The rule of thumb for many sorts of social interactions, it implies, is silence (10:19).

Verse 22 is another "like" proverb. The comparison here is striking, even bizarre. The image of the gold ring in the pig's snout, though taken in part from the world of animals, is anything but natural. So, it is implied, is a beautiful woman who lacks judgment. Like a gold ornament, good looks gleam and fascinate, but divert attention from the inner sensibility that ultimately defines a person.

Verses 24-25 add the dimension of generosity to the portrait of wisdom. Generosity has a paradoxical dynamic: it enriches the giver. Luke 6:38 and Acts 20:35 express similar thoughts. In a related vein, verse 26 refers to the commercial practice of withholding supplies of grain from the market so as to keep prices high. The public curses those who do this, but blesses those who forgo extra profit and sell their grain to supply those who need it.

Verse 30 is a classic expression of the association of wisdom with life (see 4:22-23; 10:11). The fruit of justice becomes a tree that bears its own fruit, thus engendering more life (cf. the comparison of wisdom to a tree of life in 3:18; 15:4). The New Testament parable of the mustard seed uses a similar image (Matt 13:31-32, Mark 4:30-32, Luke 13:18-19). The "sage" or wise person thus can be said to exert power over lives.

Verse 31 reaffirms the expectation of diverging outcomes for the just and the wicked. If the just are compensated for their acts in this life, those who are committed to wickedness face unthinkable reparations. This saying is quoted in 1 Peter 4:18.

12:1-28

Verse 1 presents a complex nesting of facets of wisdom. The first half-line asserts that those who love (and welcome) correction are the ones who love (and seek) knowledge. Correction is part of the process of active learning. The first half-line yokes correction with knowledge; the second contrasts the hater of criticism. Such a person is stupid, or unable to learn. See also verse 15, which speaks of the self-assurance of the fool, and 13:1, in which the wise person who loves correction is contrasted with the senseless (literally, "arrogant") person, who dismisses all correction (cf. 9:7-8).

Verse 4 conveys the vital importance of marriage in life, from the perspective of a man. A worthy wife is, literally, a "strong" or "outstanding," woman, one who pulls her weight in the

relationship and is a true life partner. Such a wife is the crown or garland of her spouse, setting him apart as specially graced (see also 18:22; 19:14; 31:10-31). The image of the crown probably reflects the wedding ceremony as well as signaling honor and favor (Song 3:11). Here the choice of a worthy spouse can be seen as an aspect of wisdom. To choose badly is to become yoked to one who brings disgrace or disappointment that eats into the very bones, or self. The Hebrew word for disgrace or shame means a kind of publicly acknowledged failure that is felt as utter defeat (Jer 14:3-4). The phrase "like rot in his bones" recalls the saying uttered by Adam when he first sees Eve in Genesis 2:23: "This one at last, is bone of my bones / and flesh of my flesh." The image implies the deep rooting of the human person in marriage, and the saying can be read in present contexts from the viewpoint of either spouse.

Verse 10 shows, with telling contrast, that justice is a deep and pervasive quality. The just are sensitive even to the needs of their animals, on whose labor they depend. In comparison, even the *compassion* of the wicked is cruel. The depth of the righteous person is also expressed in the image of the root in verse 12.

Verse 14 breaks with the predominant pattern of contrast and sews together two positive qualities to create a two-dimensional picture. Human speech is productive. It creates "fruit" that satisfies and fills a person with good things, just as the work of one's hands is productive and yields results.

Verse 16 suggests the linking of speech, as well as nonverbal responses, with emotion. Fools immediately reveal their anger, but the shrewd conceal contempt (10:12). The saying stresses the intelligence of such a strategy.

Verse 20 draws out the psychological benefit of promoting peace and well-being (the Hebrew word *shalom* means both). Contrasted with the machinations that fill the hearts of those who plot harm is the joy experienced by those who build positive relationships within the community.

13:1-25

Verses 7 and 8 address the topic of wealth and poverty, a recurrent theme in Proverbs. Some sayings link wealth to hard work and poverty to laziness (10:4; 12:11, 27), but others simply note the discrepancy between rich and poor (13:23; 10:15;

14:20). Verse 7 describes a type of pretense or delusion driven by the polarities of wealth and poverty. One can act as if rich and yet lack everything, or as if poor and yet enjoy great wealth (cf. 12:9). The saying sets the external appearance of wealth and poverty against the possibility of deeper, fuller meanings.

Verse 11 has a practical slant. A steady habit of economy builds up wealth penny by penny. It stands in contrast to the sudden acquisition of riches, which, without such a habit, are easily squandered (cf. 20:21). Despite the concrete tenor of this saying, it can be read on figurative levels as well.

Verse 12 is a classic example of a saying that addresses the psychological dimension of human life (cf. 12:25; 14:10, 13; 15:13). Like others of its kind, it offers a glimpse of the human condition without moving the reader toward a particular course of action. Nothing is suggested in the saying, for example, about avoiding the emotional hardship that comes from the repeated frustration of hope. In the interplay between the two half-lines, however, something is implied. That hope deferred makes one heartsick is a reality, the other side of which is the new life that springs up when a long-awaited desire comes to pass. In the twin assertions of the verse, neither reality cedes to or subjugates the other. Those who ignore one or the other court the dangers, emotional and otherwise, of ignorance.

Verse 19 draws an implication from the delight of realized desires. As often, the inexactness of the contrast between half-lines speaks indirectly, and the reader is impelled to fill in the gaps. That fools cannot break away from doing harm prevents the fulfillment of their desires. Evil is a subversive quality that hinders fulfillment.

Verse 23 makes an observation about poverty. It states baldly the injustice suffered by the poor without hinting at its redress. In this it differs from prophetic pronouncements, yet it shares with them awareness of injustice. The saying conveys knowledge about a pattern of human life that can inform the reader in any number of different ways.

Verse 24 is one of the most well known of biblical proverbs because of its currency in home and school settings throughout the centuries. It takes up the recurrent theme of child rearing (23:13-14; 29:15, 17). Changing cultural mores aside, to insist

on a narrow interpretation of this verse is to misread the mode of the sayings in Proverbs. The sayings use figurative language to make their points vivid, and they communicate within a network of comparisons and juxtapositions, not equivalents. In this saying the rod serves as a metonym for the whole concept of discipline, which encompasses correction and instruction generally (13:18; cf. 1:2, 7, 8; 4:1, 13; 12:1). To "spare the rod" in the first half-line is antithetically parallel to "discipline," in the second. But discipline is never simply equated with corporal punishment in Proverbs. See the similar metonymic use of "rod" in the phrase "the rod of discipline" in 22:15.

14:1-35

Verse 1 attributes to wisdom the accomplishment of building a house (9:1). A house, as here and elsewhere in the Old Testament, refers not simply to a building but to a household of children, extended family, servants, and guests (11:29; 31:15 and Gen 35:2) and often to an intergenerational family line, as in the "house of Israel" (Ruth 4:11) or the "house of David" (2 Sam 7:27). The house represents the locus of a way of life, and the whole bent of wisdom is to create a locus that is stable and generative. In contrast folly pulls down her house with her hands, or activities, illustrating the self-destructive potential of those who will not learn wisdom (9:18; 11:26).

Verse 4 seems anomalous in its practical agricultural focus, yet it is comparable to Hesiod's *Works and Days*, which combines wisdom instruction relating to familial, social, and religious life with specific advice on farming. This saying should be read in relation to others in Proverbs that encourage intelligent assessment of life's demands and realities (see, e.g., 13:11, 16). One might compare this saying with the New Testament parables of the tower builder and the warrior king in Luke 14:28-32.

Verse 8 can be interpreted as a general affirmation of knowledgeable choices. The wisdom of the shrewd keeps them conscious of the paths they make through life and where they lead. In contrast, foolishness is deceptive. The implication is that foolishness does not foster clear-eyed assessment but misleads fools about what they are doing and the decisions they are making (14:15; 15:14). Verse 12 qualifies these claims about human self-knowledge by reminding the reader that all are vulnerable to self-deception.

Verses 10 and 13 reflect on psychological realities. Verse 10 acknowledges the unique configuration of each human sensibility, which is never fully understood by or replicated in another. This assertion nuances the tendency of Proverbs to point to common patterns comprehensible by all. The idiosyncratic is also a component of human life. Verse 13 recognizes the element of sadness in life, even in moments of laughter. The second half-line links this reality to another: the grieving that comes with the end of joy. In acknowledging the sorrowful and transient in human experience, this saying is reminiscent of the wisdom of Ecclesiastes (Eccl 3:1-8; 7:2-4; 9:11-12).

Similarly resigned in tone is the observation in verse 20. Word choice makes an effective contrast here: the poor are "despised" or avoided even by their neighbors or fellow community members, whereas the friends or hangers-on of the rich are many.

Verse 21 evaluates this situation from two different angles. The first half-line flatly states that those who despise the hungry are deficient (or sinners). Those who share what they have and are kind, on the other hand, are "happy." The word for "happy" is used elsewhere in the Old Testament in contexts of divine blessing and good fortune (see, e.g., Pss 1:1-3; 34:9; 41:2-4). The saying draws out the implications of one's relationship to the poor for both the generous and the contemptuous. The connection between this relationship and the relationship with God ("their Maker") is compactly stated in verse 31 (cf. 17:5; 19:17).

Verse 25 makes the case for truthful testimony in court (12:17; 14:5; 19:5, 9, 28). This particular standard of honesty is deeply seated in the biblical tradition, as is evident in the programmatic prohibitions against false witness in the Decalogue (Exod 20:16; Deut 5:20), the insistence on at least two or three witnesses in legal disputes in Deuteronomy 19:15, and the narrative of false accusation in 1 Kings 21:8-14.

Verses 29-30 spotlight the value of restraining strong emotion and the danger of allowing it to predominate. The Hebrew phrase for "long-suffering" in verse 29 is literally "slow to anger" (16:32). It occurs in Exodus 34:6, where it is used of the Lord's divine forbearance and mercy. In verse 30, serenity is contrasted with jealousy, which "rots the bones," an expression for deep discomfort (12:4; Hab 3:16).

Verse 28 subjects the institution of kingship to an indirect critique by pointing out the dependence of a king's destiny on the proliferation (and hence well-being) of his people. Verse 35 looks at the relationship of servant to king. Wisdom and ineptitude have particular significance within the royal domain. The king is the dispenser of favor (for astute success) or wrath (for shameful failure). This saying would be particularly meaningful for those working within or for the court.

15:1-33

Verse 3 carries the genre of pure observation into the realm of theology. Nothing is hidden from the eyes of the Lord, the first half-line asserts (5:21). The second specifies divine watchfulness over both the wicked and the good. The verb "to watch" used here refers elsewhere to watchmen, whose job is to keep an eye out for danger of all sorts (1 Sam 14:16; Ezek 33:2-3). The "wicked" and "good" represent then not simply types of people but their destructive or constructive activities. Such activities do not go unnoticed but are monitored by God. The similar saying in verse 11 claims that even the realm of the underworld and dwelling place of the dead are open to the gaze of the Lord. These sayings, like others scattered throughout chapters 10–15, cast a theological light on the observations of the sayings as a whole. Theological sayings are clustered at the beginning of the section, in chapters 10 and 11 (10:3, 22, 27, 29; 11:1, 20) and at the end, in chapters 14 and 15 (14:2, 26, 27, 31 and 15:3, 8, 9, 11, 16, 25, 26, 29, 33).

Verse 8 has a prophetic ring, with its evaluation of ritual sacrifice in terms of ethical distinctions (the wicked and the upright). The term "abomination," which carries ritual associations, is used to condemn sacrifice that is perfunctory (6:16-19; cf. Amos 5:21-24; Isa 1:10-17). The parallelism of this saying with the next one in verse 9 suggests that the sacrifice of the wicked is an abomination to the Lord because the "way" of the wicked is abhorrent.

Verse 14 captures an irony of wisdom. The discerning heart (mind) continues to seek knowledge about life and the world. In contrast, the mouth of the fool feeds (literally, grazes) on what is foolish. The opposition of mind and mouth, the active seeking of knowledge and the sheep-like consuming of what lies in front of one sharpen this saying.

Verses 15-17 qualify the interpretation of poverty as the result of bad choices. Verse 15 observes that a given material situation is not determinative of one's whole state of being. The saying plays with the multiple meanings of the Hebrew words *ra*, which means both evil in the moral sense and what is harmful or onerous, and *tob*, which means both what is morally good and what is pleasant and beneficial. One's days may be difficult (evil), but gladness (goodness) of heart feeds one in abundance.

Verses 16 and 17 are examples of "better than" sayings in which two things are compared by measuring one against the other. These verses qualify the good of material prosperity. If surplus wealth is accompanied either by anxiety or by ill will, it is no longer better than modest means. Verse 17 makes the general evaluation of verse 16 concrete by situating it in the context of the daily meals that are a focus of family life. Good will and affection at mealtimes are of more worth than the richness of the food.

Verse 19 combines a "like" phrase in the first half-line with a contrasting parallel in the second. The way of the lazy seems to them like a thorny hedge through which progress is not possible, whereas the path of the diligent is a highway on which they move quickly forward. The image of the highway or level road reflects the concept of the straight way pursued by the upright (11:5; 16:17). The contrast of the lazy with the diligent in these terms illustrates the multidimensional aspect of wisdom and foolishness.

Verse 22 stresses the communal aspect of wisdom. Plans break down when they are made without consulting others, but succeed when many heads are involved (20:18). This is a particular facet of the emphasis on heeding correction and advice in Proverbs (see 15:31 and 32; 12:15).

Verse 23 extols the delight of well-considered conversation. A person's speech (literally, "the answer of the mouth") can be a joy. The second half-line specifies what kind of speech: a word suited to the occasion ("season"). The art of choosing words well is a wonder over which the proverb exclaims, "how good it is!" (cf. Gen 1:13). The constructive power of words is illustrated in verse 1, in which the mild answer turns back anger, as opposed to the aggravating word. In verse 4 a

soothing (literally, "healing") tongue is a "tree of life" in contrast to the perverse or disruptive tongue that breaks down the spirit (12:18). In verse 28 speech is related to careful deliberation. The heart of the just person weighs how he or she will respond, whereas the mouth of the wicked pours forth what is harmful (see 15:2, 7).

Verse 25 conveys in miniature the pattern of divine reversal of human fortunes found, for example, in the song of Hannah in 1 Samuel 2:1-10 and in prophetic texts like Isaiah 65:13-16. Widows were among the most vulnerable members of Israelite society, along with orphans and resident aliens (Exod 22:21-24). Without an adult male protector widows could fall prey to schemes that left them without land and property (Prov 23:10-11; Mic 2:9). The landmark refers to the boundary stone designating an allotment of land. According to the book of Deuteronomy such allotments were inherited within families and were not to be altered (Deut 19:14; 27:17). This saying asserts that the Lord preserves widows' rights against the encroachment of those who seek to enrich themselves. The saying has a less obvious basis in personal experience than many (although the story of Ruth might serve as a literary example), and its prophetic overtones are unmistakable (cf. Isa 5:8-10; Mic 2:1-2). It sets a pattern of divine protection of the vulnerable (and dislocation of the powerful) for the reader to ponder.

Chapter 15 concludes the first section of "The Proverbs of Solomon." It ends with reminders about the need for openness to correction (verses 31-33). Verse 33, the last verse, brings back the theme of the fear of the Lord with which Proverbs as a whole begins. As in 1:7 the fear of the Lord is linked to discipline or instruction in the pursuit of wisdom. Humility precedes honor (16:19), and to know what you do not know is fundamental to wisdom.

Section Two (Proverbs 16:1–22:16)

These chapters constitute a second section of "The Proverbs of Solomon." Sayings that use antithetic parallelism to contrast opposite types of behavior now give way to instances of synthetic or synonymous parallelism that probe the complexities of a single phenomenon. Comparisons are often made through "better than" or "how much more" sayings, and proverbs are sometimes grouped in short sequences that treat a common theme from different angles. There are some short instructions that use imperative forms in these chapters.

16:1-33

The section begins with a cluster of sayings that acknowledge the ultimate role of the Lord in overseeing and directing human life (16:1-7, 9, 25, 33; cf. 14:12; 15:3, 11). These proverbs speak of the outer limits of human wisdom, sounding a philosophical tone that calls to mind the books of Job and Ecclesiastes. Verses 1 and 2 use antithetic parallelism to contrast the provinces of the human and the divine. Each saying offers a different configuration of human senses (speech represented by the tongue, and sight represented by the eye) and internal disposition (the heart and the spirit). In verse 1 human beings make plans in their hearts, but the way they actually respond in situations or answer with their tongues stems from God (cf. 16:9). In verse 2 a person's ways may be pure in his or her eyes, but the Lord is the one who takes measure of the spirit or internal intent, trumping human insight as well as human execution. Verse 3 then sets out a logical conclusion: Give over what you do to the Lord, and he will bring your plans to realization.

Verse 4 offers an assurance with which to consider the existence and persistence of the wicked. The saying asserts that "the LORD has made everything for a purpose" (literally, "for its answer"). The wicked can be seen as "made" or destined for a day of disaster, which will be the divine answer to their lives. God's purposes affect the course of the wicked as they do everything else (cf. Ps 73).

Sayings relating to kingship are more prevalent in the second section of "The Proverbs of Solomon" than in the first. Verse 10 reflects the ideal of kingship in Israel and in the ancient Near East in general. The king was regarded as a "son of God" (Ps 2:7; 2 Sam 7:12-15), divinely anointed to maintain justice and order on earth (Pss 45, 72, 101). He was endowed with wisdom in order to bear this responsibility, as the story of Solomon in 1 Kings 3:3-28 illustrates. This ideal portrait of the king lies behind the saying in verse 10: the king's lips are an oracle that imparts inspired insights, and literally his mouth does not betray justice (see also 16:12-13).

Verses 14-15 concern the actual rule of the king. Like 14:35, they seem to be directed toward those who work directly for him. The special position of the king as God's agent and dispenser of justice on earth shows through in the language of these sayings. The king's wrath is like "messengers of death," his approval (literally, "the light of his face") is life, and his favor is like a cloud bringing welcome rain. Those who work closely with the king would do well to remember these realities and draw reasonable conclusions. The wise person, for example, will pacify the king's wrath (16:14).

The dynamic of human pride is underscored in verses 18-19. The verses are linked by the juxtaposition of "haughty spirit" in 16:18b with, "humble" (literally, "lowly spirit") in 16:19a. Verse 18 may be the most well known of Old Testament proverbs in its adaptation, "Pride goes before a fall." The biblical saying does not insist that pride causes disaster, however (as in 11:2). It leaves that possibility open, but it also suggests that pride does not survive disaster. Breakdowns and stumbling in life put an end to haughtiness (18:12). The saying is enhanced by the emphasis in chapter 16 on the role of the Lord in shaping human outcomes (16:1-3, 9, 25, 33). A major setback in life could be the medium through which a person recognizes this divine role.

Verse 19 asserts the superiority of humility, declaring that sharing a lowly spirit with the poor is better than dividing plunder with the proud (11:2; 15:33). The word "plunder" carries associations not just of treasure but of violent seizure by the powerful (1:13), and it recalls the kind of self-engineered disaster sketched in 1:10-19.

Verse 29 extends the warning given to the son in 1:8-19 to a more general audience. It is not only the young who are subject to peer pressure. The violent and lawless are apt to allure their neighbors into a way that is "not good." Again, the multiple meanings of "good" (morally upright, pleasant, beneficial) add depth to this saying. Verses 27-28, which directly precede, provide specific images of the negative effects of the scoundrel, the intriguer, and the talebearer: scorching fire and divisions between friends.

In verse 31 the praise of gray hair as a "crown of glory" makes a link between righteous living and the grace of longevity (3:16).

In verse 32 the twofold "better than" stresses the heroism demanded in restraining anger and ruling over one's temper (literally, "spirit"). The kingly associations of the verb "rule" are brought out in the image of capturing a city, as kings led their armies into battle. Those who can rule over their own spirits are then greater heroes than warriors and kings.

Verse 33 concludes the chapter by reminding readers of its opening theme: the involvement of the Lord in all that transpires in human life. Throughout the Old Testament, lots are cast to seek divine guidance in making decisions (18:18; Josh 18:6; 1 Sam 10:20-21; Jonah 1:7). Here the lot may be a metaphor for one's portion of life, as in 1:14. Whatever that portion may be, it is the Lord who determines how it will develop.

17:1-28

Verse 3 makes an implicit comparison between the refining of precious metals and the divine testing of the human heart. This metaphor is used of God's testing of Job (Job 23:10) and of the testing of the just in Wisdom 3:5-6 as well as in prophetic oracles of judgment against the people as a whole (Isa 1:25; Jer 6:27-30; Zech 13:7-9).

One of the key tests of the community's relationship with God in much of the prophetic literature is the treatment of the poor. Although several sayings refer to the active exploitation of the poor (14:31; 15:25), verse 5 speaks in terms of attitude. To look at the poor with disdain is to insult one's Maker, and to rejoice in (and benefit by) someone else's distress is to invite punishment.

Verse 6 expresses the primacy of familial relations. For the old, their grandchildren are their "crown," or emblem of blessing. For children, their parents are their glory: their mark of stature and favor (1:8-9).

Verse 8 spotlights the attraction of bribes as a strategy for making one's way in the world. A bribe seems to work like a magic charm, opening doors at every turn (17:23; 18:16; 19:6; 21:14). Injunctions against bribery are part of the basic standard of behavior in the Old Testament (6:35; Exod 23:8; Deut 16:19; Isa 1:23; Mic 3:11). This saying is framed from the perspective of those who offer bribes. It subtly suggests both the enthrallment of bribery as a path to success and the credulousness of those who practice it.

Verse 9 comments on an aspect of friendship. The language is similar to that in 10:12 but more specific. The one who overlooks, or literally "covers over" an offense genuinely seeks love or friendship (17:17). Whoever reveals the offense to others, however, estranges the friend.

Verse 14 offers a warning about the dynamics of conflict. The first half-line captures attention with an apt comparison between the beginning of an argument and the release of water, which cannot easily be recovered. The second half-line follows up with a logical corollary: avert a quarrel before it breaks out and something vital is lost (20:3).

Verse 19, similarly, supplies an image to rivet a point. The first half-line links offense to conflict: the one who loves to offend loves to contend. The second half-line supplies an analogy: one who raises a gate too high is asking for its collapse.

Several of the sayings in this chapter characterize the fool. The Hebrew word for fool used here (*kesil*) conveys obtuseness and inertia, qualities that are vividly illustrated in verse 10. A single correction is felt more deeply by a discerning person than a fool registers a hundred blows. A fool is not interested in new knowledge. Not even a barrage of warnings and suggestions has an impact, because the fool's aptitude for receiving them is closed (27:22). The dangerous aspect of this kind of fool is brought out by the dramatic comparison in verse 12: a bear bereft of her cubs is less threatening than a fool immersed in foolishness.

In verse 16, even if the fool has the means to buy or acquire wisdom, he or she lacks the heart or sense to learn it. The second half-line exposes the foolishness of thinking of wisdom as a commodity. Wisdom cannot be bought with money in the hand but is acquired by engaging the heart or mind (2:10; 4:20-27).

The contrast in verse 24 is telling as well. Whereas the face of the discerning person is turned toward wisdom, the eyes of the fool are on the ends of the earth: that is, everywhere else. Of the deeper search to understand what is seen and determine what is of lasting good, the fool is unaware. The implication is that the fool must keep looking but never finding. In this saying there is a hint of the personification of wisdom found in chapters 1–9. The intelligent person's face looks toward wisdom, as if toward a guide and companion.

18:1-24

Verse 2 targets the social isolation and self-absorption of the fool. He or she has no interest in understanding but only in laying bare his or her own mind and heart. Fools, it would seem, are very poor conversationalists, if not social misfits (18:13).

Verse 4, on the other hand, turns attention to the "deep waters" that one's words *can* represent, for the spring of wisdom is a brook that flows forth into words (4:23).

The temptation to listen to rumors is described in verse 8. The Hebrew verb behind "talebearer" means "to whisper" or "murmur," and it carries associations of disruptive activity (16:28, 26:20; Ps 106:25). Yet rumor is hard to resist. Like a delicious treat, it is swallowed and penetrates into one's inner recesses. How such a diet alters the listener is left to the imagination of the reader. This saying is repeated in 26:22.

Similarly frank is the comparison in verse 9. Those who are casual about their work are akin to those who destroy. Many levels of destruction can be envisaged here, including damage to the lives and well-being of all those affected by poor workmanship.

Verses 10-11 use related metaphors to express different perspectives, creating an interactive juxtaposition. Verse 10 represents the perspective of the just. For them, the name of the Lord is a strong tower that stands out in the landscape, and they run for refuge to it and are kept safe. Verse 11 conveys the point of view of the rich: their wealth is their strong city, in their imagination protecting them as does the city's wall against adversary and adversity. The contrast between verses 10-11 invites the reader to compare the impregnability of the two sources of safety.

Verse 12 adds an additional note to this interlinear dialogue. Before a breakdown or disaster one's heart may be inflated with self-confidence, but before true acclaim is won, humility must be realized (16:18; 15:33). The word for humility in Hebrew is related to words meaning "poor" and "afflicted" as well as "humble." Since riches are subject to dissolution (11:28; 13:11), the rich person's confidence in them (18:11) may be shaken, and he or she may experience the humility that precedes real honor (Sir 11:1-6).

Verses 17-19 offer wry observations on a more concrete topic: the settling of disputes between neighbors (community members). Verse 17 accentuates a common dilemma for those hearing the arguments in such conflicts. The argument of the first disputant sounds reasonable until the other starts to probe it. The saying prompts readers to think about not judging too quickly the truth of a matter.

Verse 18 implies that some disputes need a radical or "Gordian knot" solution. The casting of lots can effectively bring disputes to an end, even between the powerful. Verse 19 singles out the intensity of family disputes.

Verse 24 turns to one of the relationships that form the nexus of a person's life. An associate may do one harm, but a true friend (literally, "one who loves") is closer than a blood relative.

19:1-29

Verse 2 reaffirms the value of deliberation, or knowing and thinking before acting. Desire without knowledge is not a helpful motivator to action, and the one who pushes forward in a hurry is apt to lose his or her footing and miss out.

Verse 3 reveals an irony of flawed decision making. It is foolishness that subverts one's way and upsets one's hopes. But the same foolishness may cloud one's assessment of the blame for failure, as one's heart fumes against God. This saying does not refer to all cases of personal disaster but only to those that have clearly been brought about by thoughtless choices.

Both verses 2 and 3 move easily within the circuit of the saying in verse 8, which captures the essence of wisdom. Those who possess sense love themselves, and those who cultivate understanding will find good things (15:32). The similar saying in verse 16 employs the language of commands with the broader meaning of guidance and instruction (10:8). The opposition between life and death in this verse echoes that in chapters 1–9 between adhering to parental teaching and to wisdom, which means life (3:2; 4:22-23; 7:2), and following the way of the violent and wicked, which leads to death (1:32-33; 2:18-19; 5:22-23). It also recalls the choice between life and death in relation to the commandments of the Lord in Deuteronomy (30:15-20).

Verse 18 brings equal gravity to the subject of child rearing. The strong wording of the second half-line suggests the inherent difficulty of raising children. The command to the parent to discipline or instruct the child refers here to the formation of character in wisdom. The balancing of hope in the first half-line against death in the second insists on the possibilities latent within any child and any parent-child relationship during the formative period. From the child's side, verse 26 calls shame in the strongest terms upon those who mistreat or refuse to care for their parents (20:20).

The saying in verse 24 offers a devastating (if hyperbolic) sketch of the lazy person, who cannot even be bothered to bring the hand he or she digs into a plate of food back into the mouth. The picture serves as its own warning.

20:1-30

Verse 1 specifies alcohol as an ingredient in foolishness through the literary device of personification. Wine is arrogant, drink a troublemaker. These are strong characters who stand for no opposition and thus, like those intoxicated by alcohol, inherently unwise (23:29-35). Drunkenness as a symbol of communal oblivion and degeneration is also a prophetic motif (Amos 2:8, 12; 6:4-6; Hos 4:11; Isa 5:11-12; 28:7-8; 56:9-12).

Verse 5 is one of a number of enigmatic and philosophic sayings in this chapter. The image of deep waters found in 18:4 recurs here in relation to the intentions or plans of the human heart, which are both profound and hidden. Yet the person of intelligence and sense can draw them up like water from a well. The saying suggests that discernment is needed to access the depths of the heart's wisdom and to make it serviceable in particular situations.

Verse 7, one of the "happy are" sayings, suggests the imitative nature of wisdom. The just walk through life in integrity, and their children who follow after them are happy. In having such parents to imitate, they are fortunate (17:6).

Verse 8 offers an icon of the king in his primary role as executor of justice. He sits on an elevated throne, surveying his land, sorting out what is evil with his eyes, and scattering it as if in one motion (cf. 20:26).

Verse 9 points to the complexity of determining the purity of one's own heart. Like a number of others, this saying recognizes that the knowledge of what is good and evil sought through wisdom has limits (14:12; 16:2, 25; 21:2). Human judgment only goes so far.

In light of the preceding observations about the realities and limits of judgment, the assertion in verse 12 assumes greater complexity. From one perspective the saying affirms the role of the listening ear and the seeing eye in gaining knowledge and wisdom. Proverbs exalts the value of listening to instruction, and the sayings, with their sharp-edged depictions of human reality, rouse us to look knowingly at the world around us. God has made both ear and eye, and their activity is part of the divine intent.

From another perspective verse 12 can read as a qualification of the human pursuit of wisdom. It reminds the reader that however active the human eye and ear are in gaining knowledge, the knowledge of God, who has made the instruments of human perception, is immeasurably greater (16:1-2, 9; 19:21).

Verse 24 offers a paradox in the same vein. If the steps one takes or decisions one makes ultimately issue from God, what kind of understanding can one hope to achieve about one's way of life? This saying acknowledges the great unknown that surrounds our circumstances and choices: one can live deliberately only up to a point (16:9). The book of Job shows a man who is mystified about the way his life has unfolded, and the book of Ecclesiastes explores more generally the incomprehensibility of the divine order (3:11; 9:11-12) and the limits of human wisdom (1:12-18).

Perhaps the most enigmatic saying in this chapter is verse 27. The link of human beings to God through the breath is expressed in the creation tradition reflected in Genesis 2:4b-7, in which God breathes into the nostrils of the human creature made from the dust and brings it to life. The saying suggests that the breath of life, which comes from God, has the capacity to search out the inner being of a person as a lamp would do. The saying hints at a kind of synergy with God that is inherent in every person (cf. the first reading of 20:12). Yet this possibility must be balanced against verses 9 and 24 and the second reading of verse 12.

Verse 30 is strongly, even disturbingly stated. Again, the metaphorical mode of Proverbs must be kept in mind. The bloody beating of the first half-line is paired with the "inner scourging" of the second. The saying can be read in light of others that refer to physical punishment as part of the discipline of learning wisdom (13:24; 22:15) but can also be linked to the kind of correction that is felt more deeply than blows (17:10). Perhaps, too, this saying shares the perspective of 18:12, which observes that the human heart tends toward self-aggrandizement before experiencing disaster and the kind of real humility that precedes honor (cf. 15:33).

21:1-31

Verse 1 evokes, again, the ideal of kingship. The Hebrew word for "hand" also means "power," "force"; hence the unusual image of the heart of the king like a stream of water in the hand of the Lord. Only the Lord could hold a stream in the hand, turning it this way and that.

The insistence of the saying in verse 3 on the primacy of doing what is right and just over the offering of ritual sacrifices is a familiar prophetic theme (Amos 5:22-24; Hos 6:6; Mic 6:6-8; Isa 1:11-17; see also 1 Sam 15:22 and Matt 9:13; 12:7). The Hebrew word translated "acceptable" derives from the verb "to choose" found elsewhere in Proverbs in relation to wisdom (8:10, 19; 10:20; 16:16; 22:1). This saying is related to others that condemn the sacrifice of the wicked as an abomination (see 21:27 and 15:8).

The dramatic rendering of choices in the "better than" saying in verse 9 (and the similar saying in 21:19) leaves no ambiguity about the value of peace and good will in the family. Better to remove oneself to a corner of the roof (or, in 21:19, to the desert), away from any human interaction, than to be caught up in continual quarrels. Both alternatives are untenable: in one case squeezed into a corner exposed to the elements, in the other struggling to eke out existence in a lifeless terrain. These images convey the inescapable misery of a contentious marriage, though framed from the perspective of the husband. The observational mode of the saying allows various implications. The choice of an appropriate mate is certainly one, but the taking of steps within a marriage to avert chronic conflict is not precluded.

Verse 10 gives insight into how the character of the wicked is formed by their choices. The soul or life force of the wicked longs for what is wrong and harmful, and the correlative is that they do not look on their neighbors (fellow community members) with pity or good will. The parallelism in this saying is synthetic, in that the second half-line completes a thought begun in the first. The

parallel structure yokes the two features of the wicked together as if each were an aspect of the other.

The consequences of closing an ear to a poor neighbor are spelled out in verse 13. Those who do not hear the poor will not be heard when they cry out. The saying does not specify who, in this event, will turn a deaf ear to the indifferent: one's neighbors, or God, or both. The language echoes that of Exodus 22:22, 25-26 (cf. Deut 24:15), in which care for the poor—including the widow, orphan, stranger, and debtor—is rooted in the genesis of Israel as the people of God.

The poetic justice in this saying is also apparent in the synonymous parallelism of verse 17. The lover of pleasure and celebration will suffer deprivation, just as the lover of wine and perfume, fruits of the earth's richness, will never become rich. In our modern idiom, you cannot have your cake and eat it, too.

The military scenario sketched in verse 22 is hyperbolic but testifies to the superior power of wisdom over physical strength (24:5). Verse 30, however, reminds the reader that there is no wisdom, good sense, or counsel that can prevail over the Lord. And the military imagery of verse 31 qualifies all human endeavor (16:9; 19:21). The parallel structure of this saying links the horse that is made ready for battle to the larger movement of the Lord's victory. The second half-line does not discount the element of preparation but looks beyond it.

22:1-16

Verse 1 extols the value of a "good name." Simply put, a good name is a good reputation. It means that others trust you, welcome you, listen to you, and remember you (10:7). A name is the reputation of a person that is built up through one's actions and responses over time. Like riches, it has to be earned, but it is to be chosen above them because it is more fundamental and enduring. The language of choice is explicit in the first half-line (literally, "a name is to be chosen above great riches"), and the second adds specificity: it is better than silver and gold.

Among many sayings that point to the inevitable social gap between rich and poor (22:7; 14:20; 19:4), verse 2 lays down a more basic assumption. Rich and poor meet in their common origins: God has made them both (14:31, 17:5).

Verse 3 illustrates graphically the perspective of wisdom. The astute person sees evil or harm coming and gets out of the way. This is not necessarily a depiction of moral heroism but of good sense. The naive person keeps on walking, oblivious to what is coming, and pays the price.

Verse 9 raises up the virtue of generosity. Those who are generous are literally "good of eye," looking benevolently on others, and they themselves will be blessed. What generosity means is spelled out in the second half-line: giving from one's own sustenance to the poor. Other sayings warn against taking advantage of the poor and afflicted (14:31; 17:5; 21:13). This one promotes the positive act of caring for the less fortunate by asserting the paradox of 11:24-25: those who give away what they have will receive blessing (14:21; cf. Mark 12:41-44; Luke 21:1-4).

The "foreign woman," or adulteress, of chapters 1–9 appears in verse 14. As in the father's instructions, it is her mouth, or seductive words, that entrap (2:16; 5:3; 6:24; 7:5). In the poetic compression of this saying, her mouth not only leads downwards to the pit that is death, it *is* a pit (23:27; cf. 2:18; 5:5; 7:27).

"The Proverbs of Solomon" closes in verse 16 with a consideration of the inequity of rich and poor that looks at the obverse of verse 9. Enriching oneself by extorting from the poor is as unwise as giving money (possibly bribes) to the rich: both add up to loss and want. This is a suitable ending note for a collection assigned to a king who was legendary for taking seriously his royal commission to ensure justice (1 Kgs 3:9).

SAYINGS OF THE WISE

Proverbs 22:17–24:22

A new collection begins here under the heading "Sayings of the Wise." Scholars have found significant parallels between these sayings and the Egyptian wisdom composition known as *The Instruction of Amenemope*, which dates to the twelfth century B.C. or before. Parallels are especially evident in 22:17–23:11, where all but three verses correspond at least roughly to passages in the Egyptian work. Particularly striking is the reference in 22:20 to "thirty sayings." *Amenemope* comprises thirty chapters, and various scholars have divided the material in 22:17–24:22 into thirty discrete units.

The narrator of *Amenemope* presents himself as a royal official and scribe who wishes to instruct his son in the skills of a courtier as well as to guide him "in the ways of life," assuring his prosperity and steering him away from evil. The conclusion to the work suggests additional audiences: the inexperienced generally and scribes who aspire to higher positions within the court.

"Sayings of the Wise," in contrast, is not specifically designated for the training of royal officials. These verses, however, contain advice that could be useful to those working with the king or holding positions of power (22:22–23:11). The reference to learning how to give a "dependable report" in verse 21 occurs in the preface to *Amenemope* in connection with courtly skills. Further, the concluding verse of "Sayings of the Wise" yokes fear of the king with fear of the Lord (24:21).

There are also similarities in literary form between these two works. Like *Amenemope* (and in distinction to "The Proverbs of Solomon"), "Sayings of the Wise" largely consists of specific directives or instructions. These frequently occur, as in *Amenemope*, in a two-verse sequence in which the second verse provides a rationale for the instruction in the first. Clusters of related directives and extended instructions, both of which are characteristic of *Amenemope*, are also evident.

The authors and editors of 22:17–24:22 have by no means replicated the Egyptian work, however. They have adopted the concept of a handbook suitable for instructing the young (including future leaders), expressed some common concerns, and contributed their own reflections, especially in 23:12–24:22.

22:17-22

Verses 17-21 serve as a prologue to the "Words of the Wise," corresponding closely to chapter 1 of *Amenemope*. In verse 17 the invitation to incline the ear, listen, and attend to what is taught resembles the calls to attention that introduce many of the instructions in chapters 1–9 (see, e.g., 1:8; 2:1-2; 4:1, 10; 5:1-2, 7).

The instructions begin in verses 22-23 with a two-verse admonition against robbing the poor that corresponds to the beginning of chapter 2 in *Amenemope*. After this point the order of topics taken up in the two works diverges.

Verses 24-25 and 26-27 are also examples of two-verse admonitions, each of which begins with an imperative in the first half-line followed by an explanation or motivation in the second. Verse 27, for example, expresses in a single image why one should heed the directive in verse 26 against guaranteeing another's loan. You might lose your bed, becoming a debtor like the one you were trying to help—or like the one described in Exodus 22:25-26, who has only a cloak to lie on. Entanglement in the debts of others is a frequent topic in Proverbs (6:1-5; 11:15; 17:18; 20:16; 27:13; cf. Sir 29:14-20).

In verse 28, the "ancient landmark" set up by one's ancestors refers to the boundaries marking land owned by a family and passed on within it (Deut 19:14; 27:17). Stripping people of their legacy of land left them without resources and often drove them into slavery. The prophetic denunciations of such practices in, for example, Micah 2:1-2 and Isaiah 5:8-10 suggest that they were a common occurrence in the preexilic period (see also the narrative of 1 Kgs 21:1-29). Nehemiah 5:3-13 testifies to similar trends in postexilic Judah. Proverbs 23:10-11 echoes this admonition and indicates a particular type of land seizure: the fields of defenseless orphans (cf. 15:25). The dislocation of landmarks is also addressed in chapter 6 of *Amenemope*.

Verse 29 promises promotion to those who develop skill in their work. Promotion will mean serving directly under the king rather than under lesser figures. This saying points ahead to the opening verses of chapter 23, which elaborate on the fine points of working closely with a ruler.

23:1-35

Verses 1-3 address the situation of those who move within the close circle of a ruler or political leader. They take up the subject of proper protocol at official meals, such as state banquets. The advice is politic: (1) keep in mind where you are, or "who is before you," as well as what food is set before you; (2) guard your manners and consume in moderation; and (3) don't forget who *you* are by developing a taste for regal fare. Such food is deceptive: merely emulating the lifestyle of a ruler does not make one more powerful.

This last warning leads easily into verses 4-5, which caution against wearing oneself out in the pursuit of wealth. Chapter 7 in *Amenemope* uses a similar image of riches taking wings like a bird flying toward heaven. In verses 6-8 the discussion returns to the sharing of meals, this time with unwilling hosts (literally, the "evil of eye" as opposed to the "good of eye," or generous, in 22:9). Reading these verses in the context of verses 4-5, the reluctant hosts might be envisioned as those whose eyes have flown toward riches. In any case, their hospitality is poor.

Verse 9 urges discretion in conversation with fools (cf. the warning against throwing pearls before swine in Matt 7:6), and verses 10-11 return to the issue of appropriating land, a temptation to those holding power.

Taken as a whole, the sayings in 22:17–23:11 can be seen as a guide for those seeking or assuming leadership roles in the community. They warn against abusing or squandering advantage and advise on how to deal prudently with problematic characters (fools) and to interface with the powerful.

The admonitions and instructions in 23:12–24:22 have no exact parallels in *Amenemope*. This section of "Sayings of the Wise" resembles the parental instructions of chapters 1–9. The frequent use of the address "my son" and the references to the father and mother of the listener (23:22-25) create an intimate tone. Although different points are taken up, the entire unit flows like one long sequence. It begins in verse 12 with the characteristic appeal to apply the heart to discipline and the ears to words of knowledge. It ends in 24:21-22 with a summative counsel.

Proverbs 23:13-18 consists of three two-verse sayings: two admonitions and a personal appeal. Verses 13-14 address the listener as a parent and speak of the discipline required to raise children intentionally. Verses 15-16 address the listener as a son, who through his wisdom and integrity can bring deep joy to his father. These two sayings culminate in the instruction of verses 17-18. Verse 17 directs the son to guard against emulation of sinners and keep his focus on the fear of the Lord. It suggests an experience of hardship in which it is tempting to follow the model of the successful. Hence verse 18 encourages the son to think about the long term: "for you will surely have a future." In this future the Lord will not disappoint. The envy of wrongdoers is a topic that is resumed in 24:1-2, 19-20 and dwelt on at length in Job 24:1-25, Wisdom 1–5, and Psalms 37 and 73.

A new instruction begins in verse 19 with the call to "Hear, my son, and be wise." Verses 20-21 warn against over-consumption of food and drink, which represent youthful excess generally. The daze created by overindulgence clouds one's potential and in the end leaves one clothed only in rags. The theme of drunkenness is taken further in verses 29-35, and the instructions that lie between these two sections are drawn into relation with the warnings against excessive consumption. This kind of literary bracketing is known as an *inclusio*.

The instruction in verses 22-25, introduced by the plea to listen to both one's father and mother, lifts up a positive principle: what the child should invest in or "buy" is the full range of wisdom qualities: truth, wisdom, discipline, and understanding. These should not be sold or exchanged for anything else (3:13-18). The instruction ends with an appeal to the affection of the son for his parents, especially for his mother: "Let her who bore you exult" (23:25).

An invitation to give one's heart and attention to the ways, or example, of the parent begins the next instruction in verses 26-28. The concern here is sexual indulgence, which is represented by the images of the harlot and the adulteress (the "foreign woman"). As in 22:14, such women are a disaster: a "deep pit" and a "narrow well." As in 7:12, they lie in ambush to entrap young men and so add to the number of the faithless or treacherous.

Verses 29-35 return to the subject of alcohol, characterizing the serious drinker as both volatile and vulnerable (23:29-30) and giving a realistic impression of the physical state of drunkenness (23:31-34). The one who suffers all these pains and still asks for another drink is exposed as a sad case (23:35). Although verse 31 explicitly directs the reader to avoid wine, the description of the drinker that follows is eloquent warning in itself.

24:1-22

Verses 1-20 are framed by the matching warnings in verses 1-2 and 19-20 against the envy of wrongdoers (cf. 23:17-18). What lies between these two endpoints can be seen in relation to them (another example of *inclusio*).

Following the initial directive not to emulate or seek out wrongdoers, since they cause havoc and harm, verses 3-4 assert that a house or habitat is constructed, made firm, and enriched by wisdom, understanding, and knowledge (9:1-6). Similarly, in verses 5-6 battles are won by planning and much consultation (20:18; 21:22).

Foolishness, on the other hand, hinders one's effectiveness in the community, as verses 7-9 make clear. In verse 7 the assembly refers to the gathering of elders at the city gate to conduct civic business (Ruth 4:1-12). Fools are hampered in this arena by their lack of wisdom, which keeps them silent. Verse 8 observes that one who consistently schemes to bring about what is wrong and harmful becomes labeled as such, and is presumably avoided by others. Verse 9 concludes that above all other manifestations of harmful foolishness, the arrogant person who shows no respect for the thoughts and interests of others is regarded as an abomination by the community.

Verses 10-12 imply that the arrogant in fact shrink back in a time of adversity rather than intervening and rescuing those who are being taken off to death. The dramatic situation evoked here is not specified, but the virtue of standing up to abusive violence is clear and given divine backing. Those who plead ignorance will not deceive the Lord (24:12).

Verses 13-14 reassert the enduring goodness of wisdom, which, in an appealing metaphor, is like honey to the soul (Ps 19:11). The assurance about the future in verse 14 repeats almost word for word that in 23:18, where it is associated with the temptation to envy sinners.

Verses 15-16 warn against becoming one of the wicked by stalking those who are just. The verb "lie in wait" is the same used of the adulteress in 23:28 (see also 1:18). The just will repeatedly rise again, but the wicked will stumble and fall once and for all (cf. Job 5:17-22).

Yet in verses 17-18 the wise person does not gloat over an enemy's fall (cf. Exod 23:4-5; Lev 19:17-18; Matt 5:22). This kind of exulting is displeasing to the Lord and will cause him to withdraw from enacting justice. In Proverbs 20:22 vengeful intentions presume against the work of divine justice (cf. Rom 12:19).With consciousness of these facets of wisdom in relation to evildoers, the instruction repeats in verses 19-20 the admonition with which it began: do not envy the wicked. Whereas with wisdom one has a future, the wicked have neither (24:14).

What not envying the wicked means, as verse 1 states, is refraining from joining with them or imitating them. The verses between verses 1-2 and 19-20 show how the wise take a different route, one that includes relying on wisdom in all undertakings, avoiding violence, advocating for the abused, and leaving vengeance to God.

"Sayings of the Wise" concludes in verses 21-22 by offering the learner a final summation: "My son, fear the LORD and the king." Reverence of the Lord stands first: obedience to the king, God's guardian of justice and order on earth (21:1) follows. Both Lord and king have the power to bring disasters and calamity on those who set themselves against them and the justice they protect.

OTHER SAYINGS OF THE WISE

Proverbs 24:23-34

This small group of sayings is marked as a separate collection by the opening phrase: "These also are Words of the Wise." In its present placement it appears as an appendix to "Sayings of the Wise" (22:17–24:22). It combines short sayings and instructions with slightly longer sequences.

Verse 26 can be seen as part of the discussion of partiality in judgment that precedes it (24:23-25), but it also stands on its own as an example of proverbial wit. The one who returns a straight answer from his or her lips gives a kiss on the lips. Such an answer, in other words, is as delightful as a kiss, and the one who gives it is a true friend.

Verse 27 illustrates the essence of wisdom in a practical context. One's life must be planned out with thought and a long view of the desired outcome. In this case the *means* of living—the field and the work of cultivating it—must be attended to before one builds a house to live in and fills it (the Hebrew word for "house" also means "household"). This instruction serves as an excellent example of the need for deliberation in planning any endeavor, including life itself.

Verse 29 can be read in direct relation to the saying in verse 28 about giving false testimony against a neighbor. It can also be taken more broadly as a warning against retaliation and vengeance, as in 24:17-18.

Verses 30-34 offer a first-person narrative that illustrates the joining of wisdom to perception of life. The speaker passes the untended field of one

who is lazy and without sense, observes that it is overgrown with weeds, and reflects on what he has seen (24:30-32). The result is a lesson given not so much in the form of a dictum as of a visual impression of lazy behavior ("a little sleep, a little slumber, a folding of the arms to rest") and its outcome. Poverty will break into this comfortable oblivion as rudely as a burglar (24:33-34). This micro-narrative, which stresses the integral relation between wisdom and a way of seeing the world, forms a suitable conclusion for the collection of sayings of "the wise" in 22:17–24:34.

OTHER PROVERBS OF SOLOMON

Proverbs 25:1–29:27

These chapters are designated as a distinct collection in 25:1: "These also are proverbs of Solomon. The servants of Hezekiah, king of Judah, transmitted them." This verse, the only reference in Proverbs to the process of composition of the book, is taken by some scholars as a historical colophon, although this cannot be definitively established. Hezekiah, who ruled Judah in the late eighth century B.C., is lauded as a God-fearing and just king in 2 Kings 18–19 and Isaiah 36–37, and the hymn praising an unnamed future king as a "wonderful counselor" in Isaiah 9:1-7 may refer to Hezekiah. His royal legend, then, is similar to Solomon's.

Chapters 25–26 include some thematic sequences of proverbs, and the sayings of chapter 27 conclude with a multi-verse instruction. Chapters 28–29 resume the pattern of antithetically parallel sayings that opens the first collection of Solomon's proverbs. These features suggest some intentional literary shaping.

25:1-28

The series of sayings about the king in verses 2-7 follows naturally the attribution of this collection of proverbs to the servants (probably scribes) of King Hezekiah. In verse 2 the king works in tandem with God, but in a contrasting role. God knows everything, but does not reveal all. It falls to the king to search out and examine what is concealed from ordinary sight. King Solomon does just this in judging the case of the two women who claim the same child (1 Kgs 3:16-28). In verse 3, then, the heart of the king, like that of

God, is itself so wide and deep as to be unsearchable (Isa 40:28; Ps 145:3; Job 5:9; 9:10). Clearly the ideal face of kingship is shown here.

The realities of kingship are suggested in the metaphor of verses 4-5. Just as only after dross has been removed from silver is it purified and ready to be shaped into a useful object, so only when wicked hangers-on are purged from the court can the king's throne be firmly founded in justice.

Verses 6-7 speak of the proper attitude toward the king: respect and deference, as opposed to self-promotion and presumption. The "better than" contrast in verse 7 is echoed in the parable in Luke 14:7-11.

Many of the sayings in verses 8-28 heighten sensitivity to the dynamics of personal and social relations: with neighbors (25:8-10, 17, 18), with a ruler (25:15), with enemies (25:21-22), with a spouse (25:24), and with others generally. These verses coach the reader to think about which sorts of actions cause discord with others and which create good will. Among the former are lawsuits (25:8-10), empty promises (25:14), outstaying a welcome (25:7), testifying falsely against a neighbor (25:18), betraying trust (25:19), insensitive levity (25:20), gossip (25:23), argumentativeness (25:24–21:9), and lack of self-control (25:28). Actions and occurrences that build social harmony and well-being include suitable words (25:11), wise correction (25:12), trustworthy messengers (25:13), patience (literally, "slowness to anger") and a gentle tongue (25:15), and good news from those who are distant (25:25).

Among these sayings are a number of "like" proverbs that make an overt comparison, often between natural and human phenomena. Such comparisons help define what seem to be puzzling human experiences. In verse 14, for example, the appearance of clouds and wind that never produce rain is compared to one who boasts about a gift that never materializes. Verse 23 also draws on meteorological imagery: the north wind brings rain, and mean gossip, angry faces. On the positive side, a word spoken at just the right time is like something extraordinary: golden apples in silver settings (25:11; cf. 15:23). One who gives wise correction is, similarly, like a golden adornment to a listening ear (25:12; cf. 24:26).

The prescription in verses 21-22 to be generous to one's enemies is consistent with the admonitions against vengeance in 20:22 and 24:17-18 (cf. Matt 5:38-42). The metaphor that compares generosity to heaping coals on an adversary's head is taken up by St. Paul in Romans 12:20.

The potential magnitude of the impact of an uncontrolled temper (literally, "spirit") is considered in verse 28. The person without restraint is like a city whose walls have been breached by a hostile invasion. The consequences of military conquest in the ancient world were grim: slavery, looting, exile, and death. The language and imagery of this saying make it a mirror opposite of 16:32, in which one who rules over his or her spirit is declared to be better than one who *captures* a city.

26:1-28

Most of the sayings in this chapter concern what it means to be a fool. Some overlap with the sayings of the preceding chapter, since troubling or alienating others is characteristic of fools (11:29; 18:6; 20:3; 22:10). Again, many of these sayings are "like" proverbs that show up the futility of foolish behavior or ridicule the fool.

Verse 1 uses a natural image to highlight the inherent incompatibility of honor, or communal acclaim, with the fool. Like snow in summer or rain in harvest, honor for fools is out of the natural order of things. Verse 8 makes the same point but chooses a different analogy, having to do with the misuse of a slingshot.

Verses 4-5 provide a classic example of how even explicit instructions in Proverbs can appear contradictory. On the surface these verses appear to cancel each other out: should one answer fools according to their foolishness, or not? These verses could also be seen as balancing or moderating each other. Determining when it is sensible to answer or not to answer, and to what extent, is part of the discipline of discernment.

The point of verse 4 is to avoid descending to the level of fools in interactions with them: to remain careful and deliberate in one's "answers" or responses. The point of verse 5 is, on the other hand, to assess whom it is you are dealing with and to catch fools up or "answer" them when needed, i.e., "according to their folly." Both the negative ("Answer not") and positive ("Answer") instructions make sense. But both must be undertaken advisedly, with an awareness of the alternative strategy.

Discernment is what the foolish do not undertake, according to the image of verse 7. Even if fools can learn a proverb, it hangs limp or useless in their mouths because they don't know what to do with it (17:16). Verse 9 offers a different and more threatening image: a fool wields a proverb the way a drunkard handles a thorn stuck in his hand. The wit of this saying raises the possibility that the thorn represents a barb against fools and foolishness. In verse 10 the harm a fool can do is given further expression in the simile of the employer of a drunken fool, who is compared to an archer recklessly shooting off arrows.

The disinterest of fools in learning is the source of the insult in verse 11, a saying that is well known through its citation in 2 Peter 2:22. The comparison of a fool to a dog is in itself degrading (see, e.g., 1 Sam 17:43; 2 Sam 3:8, 16:9), even more the elaboration of the dog's behavior. The coupling of a natural canine habit with the reversion of a fool to foolishness implies that the latter is both habitual and instinctive.

Verse 12 measures the fool against what is even worse: one who is wise in his or her own eyes. At the same time the parallelism of the two half-lines encourages us to link the fool with this kind of self-delusion (26:5). Verse 16 asserts that the same defect is endemic to the lazy (26:16), who are vividly ridiculed in verses 13-16 (26:13 repeats 22:13). The comparison in verse 14 is particularly neat. As a door turns on its hinges but goes nowhere, so the lazy person moves in his or her sleep and dreams but does nothing. Within the overall perspective of Proverbs, the lazy embody a particular form of foolishness.

Similarly vivid and recognizable are the portraits of troublemakers in verses 17-19, both the one who interferes in someone else's quarrel and the one who misleads or cheats a neighbor and then tries to laugh it off. Verses 20-26 and 28 speak specifically of the role of negative and deceitful talk in strife and hostility. The sayings in chapter 26 as a whole, then, connect foolishness (26:1-16) with social disturbance (26:17-28), which is a predominant theme in chapter 25.

Verse 27 is often cited as a clear illustration of the wisdom principle of act leading to consequence. The metaphors chosen convey a kind of natural inevitability. The images of a person falling into a pit and a stone rolling back on the one who sets it in motion evoke the law of gravity. In its present placement at the end of chapter 26, this paradigmatic saying can be understood in terms of the negative reaction of the community to fools who disrupt the social order.

27:1-27

The sayings in chapter 27 are not grouped thematically, but many of them relate to the theme of social and personal relationships established in chapters 25 and 26. Verse 3 lights on the vexing effect of the fool, which is more burdensome than the weight of stones or sand. Verse 4 differentiates between negative emotions, singling out jealousy as the most difficult to resist (6:34). Verse 5 weighs open rebuke against hidden love. If love keeps thoughts secret, the saying insinuates, it may not be manifesting itself as love in action (24:26). Thus in verse 6 the blows of a friend are accepted as trustworthy.

Verse 10 affirms the value of cultivating supportive relations with friends (literally, "neighbors") and warns against writing them off in times of trouble in favor of distant relatives. Verse 14 offers a very ordinary example of behavior that irritates: a loud greeting to a neighbor early in the morning, no matter what its intention, will be taken as a curse.

Another facet of human interaction is addressed in verse 17. Just as iron striking against iron sharpens it, so one person draws out and sharpens the personhood of another. Verse 19, on the other hand, speaks of the inevitable distance between persons: just as physical appearances (faces) differ, so do internal sensibilities (hearts). Taken together these sayings exhibit the balance between the individual and the interpersonal that is fundamental in Proverbs.

Verse 20 compares the insatiability of the underworld for the dead, which is never exhausted, to that of human eyes, which are never satisfied either. The comparison evokes the concept of futility (in 17:24 it is the fool whose eyes are on the ends of the earth). This saying calls to mind the musings of Ecclesiastes on the vanity of human attempts to comprehend the ebb and flow of existence: "The eye is not satisfied by seeing" (Eccl 1:8; 4:8).

Verses 23-27 conclude the chapter with an instruction that speaks of knowledge in relation to the occupation of herding. A literal translation of verse 23 exhorts the listener to "take good care of your flocks" and "give careful attention to your herds." This sort of particular knowledge is placed within the framework of broader knowledge of the cycles and seasons of human and natural life. Wealth, or treasure, does not last forever (27:24). Grass, on the other hand, renews itself and can be gathered and stored to feed one's flocks (27:25). Flocks supply food, clothing, and even the equivalent of "the price of a field" to support an extended family (27:26-27). The wise farmer will be mindful of these realities and take animal husbandry seriously. This six-verse instruction is reminiscent of the advice on farming and herding that follows the counsels on religious, social, and family life in Hesiod's *Works and Days*. As a culmination of the shorter sayings and instructions in chapters 25–27, it marks the end of a literary section.

28:1-27

Antithetically parallel sayings, many of which display the fundamental divergence between the just and the wicked, predominate in Poverbs 28–29. Since the initial collection of proverbs begins with a similar section of sayings (Prov 10–15), chapters 28–29 form a literary *inclusio* bracketing "The Proverbs of Solomon" (Prov 10:1–22:16) with the "Other Proverbs of Solomon" (Prov 25–29).

Proverbs 28:1 is a prototypical saying that contrasts the fundamental instability of the wicked with the confident security of the just. This contrast is both heightened and made ironic by the comparison of the just person to a lion, a hunting animal. The unscrupulous wicked person, on the other hand, bolts even when no one is in pursuit. The parallelism encourages the reader to envision the wicked as prey.

Verses 4-5 illustrate the inherent clash of perspectives between the just and the wicked. In verse 4 the point of view is defined by instruction, which refers to the traditional teaching of the community (cf. 28:7). Those who abandon this teaching praise the wicked; those who hold onto it clash with wrongdoers (29:10, 27). The image of pitched conflict and the plural forms ("those who . . .") create an impression of social division.

Verse 5 presents a similar opposition. The wicked cannot understand what justice is. Those who seek the Lord, on the other hand, understand it fully. The Lord is the source of justice (Pss 50, 94, 96–97, 99), so those who seek to know God

come to understand it. The sights of the wicked are fixed elsewhere, and justice does not enter their view (21:15; 29:7, 10). Wisdom 2–5 features a similar disjunction between the perception of the wicked and that of the just.

Verse 13 steps beyond the stark contrast between just and wicked to speak of the reality of human transgression. Those who hope to get ahead by concealing their misdeeds won't, but those who openly admit and abandon their wrongdoing can expect mercy.

Verse 28 considers the wider social dynamics of the just and the wicked. The dominance of the wicked in a community establishes a climate of fear, sending people into hiding (28:15; Amos 5:13). Conversely, when the wicked vanish the just can multiply and thrive (cf. 28:12; 29:2, 16). In 29:16, crime increases when the wicked are many.

29:1-27

A number of sayings in this chapter continue the theme of the societal and political impact of the just and the wicked, the foolish and the wise. Several reflect on the character of the king or ruler. In verse 4 the king who brings stability to a land through justice is contrasted with the one who by overtaxing destroys its prosperity. Taxes, tithes, and voluntary contributions are not by definition unjust in the Old Testament (see, e.g., Deut 12:6, where they support the temple), but Deuteronomy 17:14-20 warns against excessive royal expenditures. Further, the account of Solomon in 1 Kings 4–12 links his taxation and forced labor policies with the eventual breakup of his kingdom. Verse 12 observes that if a ruler pays attention to false talk (including perhaps flattery), all who work for him will be wicked.

Verse 8 sets a contrast between the arrogant and the wise in terms of their impact on the social body. The arrogant inflame a city, presumably because they take counsel with no one and hold others in contempt. The wise in contrast are able to negotiate and to turn back the course of anger.

Verse 13 points out a mystery of the social body, in which poor and oppressor coexist in the same community. The saying observes only that the Lord gives light to the eyes of both (cf. 22:2). Read from one perspective, it points to divine tolerance of both oppressed and oppressor, and seems to counter the assertion in 13:9 that "the light of the just gives joy, but the lamp of the wicked goes out" (cf. 24:20). In this it echoes reflections on God's justice in wisdom writings like Job (Job 21:17; 24:21-23; but see 38:15), Ecclesiastes (Eccl 4:1-3; 7:15-18), and Sirach (Sir 33:10-15). Read from another perspective, it asserts that the poor are no less important to God than the powerful (Job 31:13-15; Sir 11:1-6).

The role of vision in the social body is the subject of verse 18. Vision in the Old Testament refers to divine communication, almost always in the context of prophecy. Without such communications from God, a people is unrestrained because they lack divine guidance (Amos 8:11-12). The second half-line of the verse contrasts with the first but makes a slightly different claim: the one who follows instruction is happy. Again, the full saying opens up many avenues of meaning. The antithetic parallelism implies: (1) that an unrestrained people is not happy, (2) that the imparting of divine vision enables the observance of traditional teaching (see the connection of *torah*, or priestly instruction, and prophetic vision in Lam 2:9), and (3) that even though the people as a whole abandon restraint, some members of the community may still respect the tradition by their actions. Altogether this proverb provides a glimpse of the interface of prophecy and the teaching of the wise (cf. Ezek 7:26).

Verse 26 reminds readers of the ultimate justice of the Lord, to which even the greatest holders of human power are subject. Those who seek a favorable hearing from a ruler might do best first to seek favor with God. Moreover, those who are eager to win favor from a ruler will not escape God's dispensation of justice.

The fundamental incompatibility of the upright and the unjust is pitched in strong language and with exact antithetic parallelism in verse 27. The two modes of being are mutually incomprehensible (29:27). The word "abomination" is used here to convey the mutually exclusive limits that define the perspectives and practices of the wicked and the just. This verse provides a suitable closing for chapters 28–29, which begin in 28:1 with a similar opposition. In the context of the proverbs of Solomon as a whole, it can be read as delineating with final clarity the choice between ways of life that is a constant theme in the sayings. This closing verse implies that the choice is both necessary because the ways do not coincide, and profound because each entails a world view.

THE WORDS OF AGUR
Proverbs 30:1-33

This chapter represents a further collection of sayings, attributed in verse 1 to Agur, son of Jakeh the Massaite. The collection is uniquely designated as a pronouncement or oracle and its tone and form are distinct from the collections of sayings that precede it. It begins with Agur's meditation on the limitations of human knowledge in light of the limitlessness and reliability of divine wisdom (30:1-6). This is followed by his prayer for an appropriate posture toward the Lord (30:7-9), a list of arrogant behaviors and attitudes (30:11-14), and a series of numerical sayings (cf. 6:6-19) that reveal the patterns of creation (30:15-31; cf. 6:16-19). Short instructions or sayings punctuate the chapter in verses 10, 17, 24, and 32-33. The words of Agur then break with the standard variation between short sayings and instructions, introducing new literary forms. In this respect the chapter resembles wisdom writings like Job, Ecclesiastes, and Sirach.

The identification of Agur as a Massaite in verse 1 makes him a member of one of the northern Arabian tribes. The tradition of legendary wisdom among the peoples to the east of Israel appears also in the book of Job, where Job and at least some of his friends are Edomites (Job 1:1; 2:11), and in the book of Obadiah, which refers to the wisdom of Edom (see Obad 8). The inclusion of a voice from outside Israel indicates the universal reach of wisdom.

The term *oracle* is used most often of divine revelation in prophetic contexts (e.g., Num 23:7, 18; 24:1-4, 15-16). Agur speaks for himself in the first person, yet his oracle draws attention to the "word of God" (30:5). Somewhat surprisingly, at the end of Proverbs this teacher of wisdom delivers an oracle that denies any claim to human wisdom.

Agur begins in verses 1-6 with a lament over the finitude of his own wisdom: "Neither have I learned wisdom, / nor have I the knowledge of the Holy One" (30:3). The series of rhetorical questions in verse 4 evoke a sense of the immeasurable knowledge of God and resemble those posed by God to Job in Job 38–39 (cf. Isa 40:12-17). The lament ends in verses 5-6 with an affirmation that God's words prove true against all challenges and that they should form the foundation and end of human knowledge ("Add nothing to his words"). By the word of God Agur means the law and prophetic revelation (cf. Deut 4:2). Agur's wisdom can only recognize the incomparability of divine wisdom and take refuge in it (30:5). All else is deceptive, and those who know this find true protection from life's ills.

The prayer of Agur in verses 7-9 reflects his orientation toward divine wisdom. As a teacher of wisdom, Agur asks God to keep him away from what is false (30:6). This request is coupled with his plea to be given neither poverty nor wealth, for either state might distance him from God. Agur asks, in effect, that he always be conscious of his dependence on the providence of the Lord. These verses are the only instance of a prayer in Proverbs.

Verses 11-14 list four categories of people, each of which can be seen as rejecting divine wisdom. The first group, who curse their parents (30:1), and the last group, who exploit the poor and weak (30:14), exhibit behavior that strikes at the heart of the ethical tradition of Israel (see Exod 20:12; 22:24-26). They frame two groups who are faulted for their attitudes: self-delusion (30:12) and pride (30:13).

Verses 15-33 contain a series of five longer sayings interspersed with shorter proverbs. The former are known as "numerical proverbs" because they take the form of a listing of diverse objects and phenomena. A characteristic numbering formula gives the number of things listed in a two-part sequence: for example, in verse 18: "Three things are . . yes, four. . . " (cf. 6:16-19). The common thread running through each list is stated in the opening lines. Yet the sayings retain a riddle-like quality in that the reader is left to ponder exactly how the phenomena named manifest the common feature and relate to each other. By joining unlikely phenomena these sayings of Agur convey a sense of the enigmatic patterning of creation that echoes his affirmation of the transcendence of divine wisdom.

Of the five numerical sayings, three join human and natural phenomena (30:15-17, 18-20, and 29-31), one names only human figures (30:21-23), and one only animals (30:24-28). The overall mix evokes the totality of creation in its various aspects.

The numerical sayings thus continue the theme of reverence for divine wisdom raised in verses 3-6. At the same time they encourage the student of wisdom to contemplate the face of creation. The interspersing of more typical proverbs among the numerical sayings in verses 17, 20, and 32-33 suggests that these riddles of the natural and human worlds are to be seen as an integral element in the acquisition of wisdom (6:6-8; cf. 1 Kgs 5:12-14).

The first saying (30:15-16) does not begin with the characteristic numerical formula but with an arresting image (the leech and his daughters) that signals the theme of the saying, which is insatiability. Four things are never satisfied: the underworld, or realm of the dead (27:20); a womb that cannot conceive; the dry earth; and fire. The first and last in this list concern death and destruction, which exert a continuous pull on life, and the middle two, the drive toward regeneration of life, which pushes forward simultaneously.

The saying in verses 18-19 is probably the best known, and its theme is wonder. The mystery of traversing the realms of sky, earth, and sea form a cosmic background for the climactic journey: the way of a man with a young woman. That this is the most wondrous phenomenon of all is implicit in its final position and in its contrast to what precedes. The flight of an eagle, the passage of a snake, and the course of a ship leave no trace, but the life of a man and woman together has the potential of generating new life.

In verses 21-23 what seems to hold the four situations named together is the anticipation of excessive behavior. This saying points to the granting of power (to the slave and the maidservant), position (to the hated woman), and satisfaction (to the fool) to persons who will probably not handle these states well (19:10; 26:1). The pattern of overcompensation for past deprivation is evoked in the cases of the slave, the maidservant, and the woman, and the fool is drawn into this pattern as well. Foolish behavior typically results in failure and shame, but the fool whose needs are satisfied may gain new confidence in his or her approach to life and act all the more foolishly.

Verses 24-28 trace a pattern in the animal world. As in 6:6-8, where the lazy son is urged to observe the ways of the ant, the reader is given examples in the form of various small creatures, including the ant. The point is that wisdom is more important than power and strength (24:5). With wisdom, ants think ahead to gather in summer their food for the winter, badgers are able to construct their houses in rocky cliffs, locusts move together in synchrony, and lizards small enough to be held in the hand reside in king's palaces. The lack of a human example in the list calls recalls Agur's question about what human wisdom amounts to (30:2-3). This numerical saying bears out the common assertion that biblical wisdom has to do with the contemplation of creation in all its aspects, though always with reference to enlightening human ways (cf., e.g., Job 38–39).

The mix of animals and a human king in verses 29-31 has, in one sense, a leveling effect. The common thread in this saying is the emergence of leaders in diverse species: the lion, the rooster, and the he-goat all have distinctive gaits that place them in front of those they lead, and so does a king. On the one hand, placing human kingship within the natural order of things demystifies royalty. The king's responsibility appears here in a different light than it does in the psalms that praise him as divinely anointed and a son of God (Ps 2, 45). At the same time, kingship is shown to be an inherent part of the creative design.

THE WORDS OF LEMUEL
Proverbs 31:1-31

The final chapter of Proverbs is presented as the words of a mother to her royal son, thus balancing the speeches of the father to his son in the introduction to the book (Prov 1–9). King Lemuel, like Agur, is a Massaite (31:1). He is also a king, a sign of the royal as well as the universal aspect of wisdom. As in 8:15-17, royal attributes of judgment and comportment are extended by implication to all (Wis 1:1; 6). Verses 1-9 are in the form of an instruction, a series of positive and negative guidelines. Verses 10-31 form a separate section as a poem or ode extolling the woman who embodies the virtues of wisdom.

31:1-9

This closing instruction echoes the claim of personified wisdom in 8:15: "By me kings reign." The voice of wisdom is heard in the words of the king's mother. A personal and serious tone is set by the repetition of phrases at the beginning and end of the instruction (31:2, 4, and 8-9), especially in verse 2: "What are you doing, my son! / what

are you doing, son of my womb; / what are you doing, son of my vows!" The phrase "Son of my womb" conveys the tenderness of the mother's pleading; the phrase "son of my vows" expresses gravity. The "vow" probably refers to a vow made by the mother to God in hopes of receiving a son, like Hannah's vow in 1 Sam 1:11. Such a vow might involve, as in the story of Hannah, a pledge to raise the child in a special relationship to God (see also the nazirite vow in the account of Samson's birth in Judg 13:3-7, 12-14). The vow of Lemuel's mother would have been answered by the birth of a future king, who would grow up to bear unique responsibilities. These are what the mother reminds her son of in what follows, as the twofold repetition of the phrase "it is not for kings, Lemuel" in verse 4 underscores.

The king's mother steers him away from excesses that could erode his royal role. Verse 3 concerns sexual relations and the diversion of the king's energies to them. The account of Solomon's relations with his many foreign wives in 1 Kings 11:1-13 illustrates this possibility (cf. Deut 17:17). In verses 4-7 the mother warns against the overuse of wine, a symbol of festivity that is carried too far (Amos 6:4-8; Isa 5:11-13; 28:1). Such overconsumption can lead a ruler both to forget his responsibility for upholding the laws of the land and to violate the rights of the powerless (31:5). Drink as a medium of escape is appropriate for those who live in misery and despair (31:6-7), but the king's mandate is different. It is spelled out in verses 8-9 with the repetition of the positive imperative, "Open your mouth." The king must speak out for the voiceless and destitute and by doing so, rule justly (29:4, 14).

Placed at the end of an anthology of diverse wisdom writings, this royal instruction is clearly intended for a wider audience. It can be read with broad implications for self-control, sobriety, and a fundamental commitment to upholding justice and advocating for the weak. The royal framework lends climactic significance to this final instruction, reminding the reader of the social as well as personal ramifications of wisdom.

31:10-31 The Woman of Worth

These verses form an acrostic poem, one in which each line or section begins with a successive letter of the Hebrew alphabet (see, e.g., Pss 119, 145). This poetic device is used here for a concluding poem that presents a summation of wisdom from, as it were, *a* to *z*.

The poem to the woman of worth parallels the poems praising wisdom in chapters 1–9, especially those in which wisdom is personified as a woman. In 31:10-31, however, wisdom takes the shape of a real woman in her daily activities. This is the companion to whom a young man should pledge himself, and this the life he can hope to share with her. She is essentially worthy (literally, strong) in her character and her actions. The larger than life depiction of her conveys this strength: she is outstanding in all she says, does, and feels (31:29).

The poem begins with three verses that express the value of the worthy woman in language that parallels the praise of wisdom in chapters 1–9. The question, "Who can find a woman of worth?" recalls the language of seeking and finding wisdom in the wisdom poems (3:13; 8:17, 35). Such a woman is to be valued beyond jewels (3:15; 8:11). She has, above all, judgment (literally, heart, the faculty of discernment) and will bring her husband abundance and good things as long as she lives (3:16-18; 8:5, 18-21). That a wife could do otherwise is implied in the qualification "good, and not evil" in verse 12.

Verses 13-24 are a portrait in motion of this woman. Her wisdom is manifest in what she does. As a doer she works with willing hands the wool and flax she gathers (31:13). The ambit of her efforts, like that of merchant ships, reaches far away (31:14), yet she does not neglect her household, rising early each day to make sure all within it are fed (31:15). The motif of active hands continues in verses 16-17, 19-20 and in verse 31, where "the work of her hands" is acclaimed.

Verses 21-22 and 24 highlight examples of her handiwork. Spinning and weaving were considered feminine arts throughout the ancient world. In the *Odyssey*, for example, Penelope, the wise counterpart to her shrewd husband Odysseus, spends her days weaving. One can compare the reference to the women skilled (literally, "wise") at spinning in Exodus 35:25-26.

The activities of the worthy woman are not limited to cloth-making, however. She is productive in many ways, for whatever she does yields positive results. She deliberates over a field, decides to buy it, and investing what she has already earned from her handiwork, plants a vineyard

(31:16). She shows her generosity by reaching her hands to the poor (31:20). Her helpful influence on her spouse is evident by the recognition and respect shown him at the city gate (31:23; cf. 24:7). What this woman does is known not just by her household but in the community at large.

All these activities build up a character that is described in verses 25-29. In an apt word play, the worthy woman is "clothed" with strength and dignity (31:25a). This clothing, too, she has made with her hands: with what she has done and the way she has lived. These qualities protect and enhance her like clothing, enabling her to face the future with hope: "[she] laughs at the days to come" (31:25b), just as wisdom herself plays or laughs before the Lord and over the entire earth (8:30-31).

The strength of character she possesses strengthens others as well. The woman of worth shares her wisdom, imparting kind advice: literally "the teaching (*torah*) of kindness is on her tongue" (31:26). As does the teaching of the mother in the parental instructions (1:8 and 6:20), her words form others in the essential values of wisdom. She protectively watches over the activities of those in her care and does so tirelessly (31:27; cf. 15:3).

For these reasons, those who know her best acclaim her worth. Her children call her blessed or happy, and her husband prizes her above all others (31:28-29; cf. 12:4).

Verses 30-31 offer a final summation, bringing praise of this woman's many strengths into alignment with the reverence toward God that is the beginning of wisdom (1:7). Charm can be deceptive and beauty fleeting, but what endures as praiseworthy over the long term is a woman who fears the Lord (31:30). Such a woman will experience herself the fruit of what her hands have nurtured, and all she has done will sing her praises well beyond her immediate circle in the public arena of the city gates (31:31).

The pairing of father's and mother's instruction and the invitation of woman wisdom to companionship in the introduction to Proverbs is thus matched at the end of the book by the marriage of the discerning man with the woman of strength. In this final poem, the promises of personified wisdom with which the book begins are realized in the union with a human woman who creates a life in accord with her reverence of the Lord.

THE BOOK OF
ECCLESIASTES

Irene Nowell, O.S.B.

INTRODUCTION

See "The Festival Scrolls" on page 254.

Name and attribution

The book of Ecclesiastes begins with a typical introduction of the speaker: "The words of So-and-So, son of So-and-So" (see Jer 1:1; Amos 1:1; Prov 30:1; Neh 1:1). The speaker's name is "Qoheleth," a word that appears only in this book in the Hebrew Bible (1:2, 12; 7:27; 12:8-10). The term is a feminine participle of the verb *qahal*, which means "to assemble or gather." (The feminine form is often used for an official status.) The related noun is the term for the gathered assembly of Israel. So Qoheleth is a gatherer or collector, whether of people or of wise sayings. In Greek the assembly is *ekklesia*, and the gatherer or member of the assembly is *ekklesiastes* (in Latin *ecclesiastes*). Thus the book is often named "Ecclesiastes." Because of the connection to the liturgical assembly, Luther interpreted the name to mean "The Preacher."

Qoheleth is identified as "David's son . . . king in Jerusalem." In 1:12, he claims to have been "king over Israel." So the speaker takes on the persona of Solomon, the only one of David's sons who ruled over all twelve tribes and could thus be called "king of Israel." Solomon (a collector of women, wealth, and wisdom) is the patron of biblical wisdom. When God offered to give him whatever he asked, he asked for wisdom, "a listening heart" (1 Kgs 3:9). Solomon was said to have greater wisdom than all the sages of the East (1 Kgs 5:10-14). Even the Queen of Sheba came to test his wisdom (1 Kgs 10:1-10). The book of Proverbs is put under his patronage (Prov 1:1). Song of Songs and the Wisdom of Solomon are written under his name. This book too, which challenges traditional wisdom, is given legitimacy by the claim of Solomonic authorship.

Date and authorship

Two clues help in the dating of Ecclesiastes: the form of Hebrew used (characteristic of the fifth century B.C. or later) and the presence of fragments of two manuscripts of the book among the Dead Sea Scrolls (which puts it earlier than the second century B.C.). The date confirms the fact that Solomon, who lived in the tenth century, is not the author. The author is a sage, probably also a teacher (see 12:9), living and writing in the environs of Jerusalem.

Structure

The book begins with a title (1:1) and ends with an epilogue (12:9-14), both written by a later editor. The turning point, exactly halfway through the book with 111 verses before and after it, is between 6:8 and 6:9. Beyond these observations, there is no agreement on the structure. The first half is characterized by the refrain "a chase after wind." The second half repeats the ideas of knowing/not knowing and finding/not finding.

Key concepts

The best-known word in Ecclesiastes is "vanity" (*hebel*), which occurs thirty-eight times in the book. The word means "vapor" or "puff of wind" and connotes futility, absurdity, unreliability. The repetition of the word in 1:2 and 12:8 sets the tone for this work. Another key concept is "profit" or "gain." Qoheleth, in the voice of an accountant, keeps asking of every human action, "What do we gain?" The reason that nothing is profitable is a third theme: death. At the time when this book was written there was no belief in meaningful life after death. So whatever humans do, death wipes out in the end. The view that this life is all there is leads to another preoccupation of Qoheleth, the unfairness of life. The just suffer and the wicked prosper; all is vanity!

Qoheleth's view of life is not unrelieved darkness, however. In his meditation on time he concludes that human beings cannot understand the proper time for things, but they can take hold of the present moment. Seven times he repeats the advice to enjoy the present moment because it is a gift of God (2:24-26; 3:12-13, 22; 5:17-19; 8:15; 9:7-10; 11:9-10). This advice (echoed almost exactly in 9:7-9) is found already in the third-millennium story of the Mesopotamian hero Gilgamesh, who goes off in search of immortality.

Qoheleth describes God as the one in control of all that happens and active in every event. Human beings can neither understand nor change God, so Qoheleth advises that fearing God is the best course of action. The term used to name God is Elohim, the generic word for "god"; the personal name of God, Yhwh, is never used.

How to read

On the one hand, the statements in this book seem straightforward and obvious. Certainly we work hard and then everything goes to someone else (2:18-23)! On the other hand, the book is full of contradictions. Wisdom is better than folly, but "in much wisdom is much sorrow" (1:18; 2:13). "[T]here is nothing better than to be glad and to do well during life," but "[t]he heart of the wise is in the house of mourning" (3:12; 7:4). The reader is encouraged to notice the contradictions and to relish them. Is human life not contradictory?

COMMENTARY

SETTING THE THEME

Ecclesiastes 1:1-11

After the title (1:1), verse 2 presents the theme of the book: "All things are vanity!" "Vanity" (*hebel*) is repeated six times in this verse (see Introduction). The phrase "X of X" is the Hebrew way of expressing a superlative, the "highest vanity." Over and over Qoheleth will demonstrate that human experience and knowledge, even human life itself, are fleeting and insubstantial. Human beings cannot cling to any moment, nor can they fully understand even themselves. "Every man is but a breath" (Ps 39:6, 12; see Pss 62:10; 144:4). Verse 2 is repeated at the end of the book (12:8), forming an inclusion (the same phrases or words repeated at beginning and end) and is echoed throughout the book.

1:3-11 Vanity of human toil

The futility of human toil is presented first in a poem (1:3-8) and then in a prose commentary (1:9-11). There is no profit in all this human striving. The word "profit" (or "advantage") occurs ten times in the book; it means the surplus created by human effort. "Under the sun," a phrase that occurs twenty-nine times in Qoheleth and nowhere else in the Hebrew Bible, means "during this earthly life." In Qoheleth's time it was believed that at death persons left the sunlight and entered into the silent darkness of a place called Sheol. Meanwhile, in human experience before death everything keeps running in its same course. Generation replaces generation. Every night the sun has to race (literally "pant") to get back to the place it began the previous morning. The winds have their regular cycle, and, for all their flowing, the rivers never produce more water. There is no profit! The same holds true for human desire: everything makes us tired, yet we are never satisfied. The prose commentary explains: Nothing new will ever happen; even what is past—people or events—is soon forgotten.

QOHELETH'S INVESTIGATION OF LIFE

Ecclesiastes 1:12–6:9

1:12-18 Twofold introduction

After his self-introduction, Qoheleth describes his experience, supporting his conclusions with proverbs. Even wisdom does not profit! God appears here for the first time in the book: Qoheleth concludes that God has set humans to a worthless task (1:13). The refrain that characterizes the first half of the book also appears for the first time: "all is vanity and a chase after wind" (1:14; see 2:11, 17, 26; 4:4, 16; 6:9). The word translated "chase" is related to "shepherd"; in vain does one "shepherd the wind." Chasing the wind is characteristic of a fool (see Sir 34:1-2). A proverb states the reason that even through wisdom one cannot acquire full knowledge. The implied actor is God: What God has made crooked, human beings cannot make straight (1:15; see 7:13). The first line of the proverb suggests ancient Near Eastern ideas concerning the purpose of education: to make stubborn students (the crooked) straight. Qoheleth says that not only does this not work in education, it is impossible in any other toil. The second metaphor is economic: What is lacking, one cannot count. The term, "lacking" (NABRE: "what is not there"), suggests the phrase from Psalm 23: "there is nothing I lack." Qoheleth says human beings do indeed lack, and what is lacking is understanding of what exists.

Qoheleth begins again by stating his qualifications for this search for understanding (1:16). His statement recalls the description of Solomon (1 Kgs 5:9-11). He expands his search to include wisdom's opposite, striving to understand by circling to the other side: madness and folly (1:17). This too is shepherding the wind. It is common knowledge that to acquire wisdom one may have to suffer (no pain; no gain), but Qoheleth's proverb declares that wisdom itself is a cause of pain and grief (1:18). In this introductory section Qoheleth turns traditional wisdom on its head: wisdom itself is futile!

2:1-17 Study of pleasure-seeking

Chapter 2 is divided into three sections by the refrain, "All is vanity and a chase after wind" (2:11, 17, 26). The word "vanity" appears eight times in this chapter (2:1, 11, 15, 17, 19, 21, 23, 26). Qoheleth is setting out "to know wisdom and knowledge, madness and folly" (1:17), but his move to specific experiences in chapter 2 shows that his quest is indeed vain!

The first area of Qoheleth's quest is pleasure (2:1-11). After testing merriment and intoxication (2:2-3), he moves to the pleasure of great accomplishments (2:4-6). Two of these verses begin with "I made/constructed" (2:5, 6; see also 2:8b). Qoheleth's list of great works recalls other descriptions of Solomon's accomplishments: palaces and vineyards (1 Kgs 3:1; 10:4; see Song 8:11), gardens and parks (Neh 2:8; 3:15), reservoirs and forests (Neh 2:14). The remains of three reservoirs south of Jerusalem are still known as Solomon's pools; the name comes from a first-century historian, Josephus (*Antiquities of the Jews* 8.186). Qoheleth also acquires everything his heart desires: slaves, livestock, wealth, and entertainers (2:7-9). This too recalls Solomon, who was known as the richest king in Israel and who had seven hundred wives and three hundred concubines (1 Kgs 10:23; 11:3). Despite the abundance, the only possible gain of this quest is delight in the toil itself (2:10). But even that is vanity; there is no profit (2:11).

Verse 12 is not clear in Hebrew. The NABRE has reversed the two halves of the verse and added the phrase "He can do only." The second half of the verse (first in NABRE) introduces the subject of the king's successor (see also 2:16, 18-19). He too can do nothing new. The first half of the verse (second in NABRE) reiterates the general subject of Qoheleth's quest—wisdom, madness, and folly (see 1:17).

2:13-17 Study of wisdom and folly

In the next section, Qoheleth turns to wisdom itself and its opposite, folly. "Wisdom/wise" and "folly/fool" appear in every verse in this section except the last. Qoheleth's first conclusion is that here, finally, there is "profit." There is more gain in wisdom than in folly (2:13). This gain is overwhelming—as much as light over darkness. Light and darkness are often symbols of life and death. The difference between wisdom and folly is as great as the difference between life and death.

Since the goal of wisdom is always the good life, this statement seems obvious. Qoheleth even supports it with a proverb (2:14). But this happy assertion collapses with the observation that both the wise and fools die. Death wipes out all "profit"—even the profit of wisdom (2:15).

When this book was written there was no belief in any meaningful life after death. All the dead were thought to go to a place called Sheol where there was no joy, no feeling, no communication, no memory. It was even debated whether God could be present in Sheol (compare Ps 88:11-13 with Ps 139:8). The only hope for immortality was through one's children and through being remembered. Even this, says Qoheleth, is vanity. Even the hope for immortality through being remembered is futile. Everyone is forgotten in death (2:16). The result of Qoheleth's quest is hatred for life (2:17).

2:18-26 Study of the fruits of toil

In verse 10 Qoheleth rejoiced in the fruit of his toil; in this third section he seeks the "profit" in toil. This quest too leads to despair, because whatever one has gained has to be left to one's heirs at death. The heir, who has not earned this gain, may be a fool. So not only is there no hope for immortality through one's children, there is not even the hope that what little one has gained through wisdom will be used wisely. No wonder Qoheleth despairs! Why should people work so hard? There is no profit; there is only grief (2:22-23).

The chapter closes with a slight glimmer of hope. The future holds no promise, but there is still the present. Verses 24-25 introduce an idea that will thread throughout the book: the present moment, with its joys and sorrows, is a gift from God. It is all that mortals have, and so there is nothing better than to enjoy it.

3:1-15 No one can determine the right time to act

The opening poem (3:1-8) is perhaps the best-known passage in Qoheleth, but without its prose commentary (3:9-15) it is easily misunderstood. The poem is a beautiful meditation on the proper time for everything in human life from birth to death. Each line sets out opposite experiences and each verse (with the possible exception of 3:5) has an inner parallelism. For example, seeking is opposed to losing, but seeking is related to keeping

and losing to casting away (3:6). Verse 2 opposes *giving* birth (not "being born") to dying; thus it parallels planting and uprooting. Various interpretations are given for verse 5a. Does scattering and gathering stones refer to counting, buying, and selling (see Deut 25:13, where the "weights" are literally "stones")? Does it relate to building fences and setting boundaries (see Gen 31:46-52)? Is it a sexual reference (see Exod 1:16, where the midwives are supposed to look at the "stones" to determine the gender of the baby)? This last interpretation would parallel the second half of the verse. The final verse of the poem (3:9) reverses the parallelism—love (A), hate (B), war (B'), peace (A')—thus ending the poem on a positive note. The mirroring pattern (ABBA), called chiasm, is a common technique in Hebrew poetry.

The prose commentary (3:9-15) returns to the problems of chapter 1: what profit (3:9; see 1:3), a bad business (3:10; see 1:13). Chapter 3 began with the statement that "there is an appointed time for everything." God has set this "appointed time," but human beings cannot find it. God has put "the timeless" into human hearts, but they cannot understand what God has done (3:11). The "timeless" (Hebrew, *'olam*), connotes a long time, or the distant past, or forever. The hunger for more than the present (the timeless) is planted in human hearts, but human experience is caught in this rhythm of events one after the other (within time). A characteristic of the wise, according to the rest of wisdom literature, is that they know the proper time (see, e.g., Prov 25:11; Sir 20:5-6; 51:30). In the midst of this ambiguity between time and the timeless, Qoheleth knows only two things, one about God's work and the other about human response. How human beings should respond has been stated before: enjoy the present moment; it is God's gift (3:12-13; see 2:24-26). Regarding God's work, it lasts forever; human understanding cannot grasp its immensity. What humans cannot hold onto, God retrieves. (Literally, "God seeks what was pursued"—the chase after wind?) The awareness that God is beyond human understanding leads to awe and fear of the Lord, the beginning of wisdom (3:14-15).

3:16-22 Problem of retribution

Qoheleth observes that life is not fair (3:16). Only God can judge with justice, because only God knows the appropriate time (3:17). Human beings are humbled because they cannot see as God sees (3:18). They are mortal like the animals. Both die; both return to the dust from which they were made (3:19-20; see Job 34:14-15; Ps 104:29). Qoheleth puzzles over where the "life-breath" goes. Does the breath of humans return to God (3:21)? It must be remembered that Qoheleth does not have a belief in meaningful life after death. Neither God's judgment of people nor the question about life-breath implies human immortality. Qoheleth knows simply that God is the only one who has power to judge and to give and take life. He concludes again that the only hope for mortals is in the present moment (3:22).

4:1-6 Vanity of toil

After declaring that there is "nothing better" for mortals than to rejoice now in their work (3:22), Qoheleth continues with two "better" sayings. Such sayings—this is better than that—are common in wisdom literature (e.g., Prov 15:16-17; 17:1; Sir 20:31). Having observed that life is unfair (3:16), he turns his attention to those who suffer violence (4:1). Twice he declares that "there is none to comfort them" (see Lam 1). So the dead who no longer suffer are more fortunate than the living, and the unborn better off than either (4:2-3). When he considers work, Qoheleth sees that all human accomplishments come out of competition (4:4). The observation is followed by two proverbial sayings, seemingly opposed to one another. Fools, who "fold their arms" and thus do no work, will starve to death ("consume their own flesh"). On the other hand, it is better to have little without worry than to work oneself to death, chasing the wind (4:5-6)! This last saying echoes the repeated advice to enjoy the present moment.

4:7-16 Companions and successors

Verses 7-8, at the center of chapter 4, link the preceding advice concerning overwork with the following "better" saying (4:9). Not only is it a "bad business" to spend all one's energy on work and never be satisfied, it is even worse if there is no one with whom one can or does share the results. (See Sirach's words against the miser: If ever he is generous, "it is by mistake"; 14:7.)

Several reasons are given that "two are better than one" (4:9-12). Living is more economical for two; one can help the other in trouble. They warm each other in sleep and defend each other in dan-

ger. The metaphor of the three-ply cord for strength in numbers is as old as the story of Gilgamesh (see Introduction).

The fourth "better" saying in chapter 4 opens a meditation on the fate of rulers (4:13-16). Wisdom is better than power; power does not make one person better than another. Verse 14 may reflect the stories of both people mentioned in verse 13. The poor but wise youth may come out of debtor's prison to reign. The foolish king may again become poor. In any case, the king will be succeeded by another (4:15), and later generations will neither remember nor rejoice in him (4:16).

4:17–5:6 Vanity of many words

Qoheleth turns to advice regarding one's relationship to God. With this section a common wisdom form begins to appear: admonitions ("do this," "don't do this"). The repetition of "dreams" and "a multitude of/multiply words" in 5:2 and 5:6 divides the section into two parts (4:17–5:2; 5:3-6).

The sage warns that people should watch their step in the temple (God's house). The purpose of worship is to listen to God's voice and obey, not to make a show of piety. Only the fool offers many sacrifices and then turns to evil. The verse is reminiscent of Samuel's warning to Saul: "Obedience is better than sacrifice" (1 Sam 15:22). The end of 4:17 can be interpreted sarcastically: "for they know not [or recognize not] how to keep from doing evil." The fool is too blind to recognize evil even in the doing of it. The fool also multiplies words (5:2). Jesus too warns against "babbling" in prayer (Matt 6:7-8). Thus to be wise is to be cautious and slow to speak in God's presence (5:1), aware of God's heavenly majesty. God is transcendent, totally beyond human imagination.

The warning about hasty speech becomes more specific in verses 3-5. The "vow" is a promise to take some action, for example, to offer a sacrifice; it does not refer to lifetime vows but to a temporary obligation. Qoheleth echoes Deuteronomy that it is better not to make a vow at all than to make it and not fulfill it (see Deut 23:22-24). One will be held guilty for failing to fulfill a vow. There is no excuse, no plea to God's representative that "it was a mistake." The "representative" (literally "messenger") is surely the priest or some other minister in the sanctuary who is expecting the sacrificial offering. The word for "mistake" is used in the legal tradition for inadvertent failings (see Lev 4:2; 5:15; Num 15:22-31), but the making of a vow is not inadvertent. God will have no pleasure in an unfulfilled promise, even if the promise was made lightly; rather God's anger will be aroused. (It is also possible that the "utterance" in verse 5 is an oath taken lightly or another sin in speech; the consequence is the same.)

Verses 2 and 6 remind us of Qoheleth's observation that everything is fleeting. Dreams evaporate with the morning; many words are useless. The word translated "futilities" in verse 6 is the plural of *hebel*, the word translated "vanity" throughout the book. Only one thing is sure: fear God! The fear of the Lord is the awareness that God is God and I am not (5:1; see Ps 115:16). For human beings fear of the Lord is the only way to wisdom (see Job 28:28).

5:7-19 Gain and loss of goods

The next two sections (5:7-19; 6:1-9) parallel one another. The primary concern is possessions: problems with them and the enjoyment of them. Two verses (5:7-8), which are difficult to understand, introduce the sections. The idea is clear: Do not worry about what you cannot control; you cannot uproot all injustice. The reason is less clear. Either the bureaucracy is such that at every level there are officials "watching out" for each other, even if they practice injustice. Or people who are "high," the arrogant and ambitious, keep climbing (and trampling the "lowly"), even though there always seems to be another level above them. Verse 8 is more ambiguous. Does it mean that a king who cares about the state of agriculture is good for the land? Does such a king balance the upwardly mobile people in the previous verse? Is this a cryptic criticism of those who amass land without caring for its ongoing fertility? It is difficult to know.

The next two paragraphs (5:9-11, 12-16) portray problems with possessions: they never satisfy and they cannot be relied on. No matter what one has, it is not enough. Wealth also draws others who will "devour" it (5:10). These may be "hangers-on" who want to enjoy the wealth earned by others, for example, the newfound friends of the lottery winner! They may be the laborers upon whom the wealthy person depends for the increase of riches. In addition, worry about protect-

ing wealth deprives the rich of sleep (5:11; see Sir 31:1-2). What good is wealth except to look at? All one needs is enough to eat and the sweetness of sleep.

A worse situation results from the sudden loss of riches when the hoarder has depended upon them (5:12-16). As Job says, "Naked I came forth from my mother's womb, / and naked shall I go back there" (Job 1:21). All human effort counts for nothing; there is not even anything to hand on to descendants. Why work so hard and deprive oneself of joy?

Qoheleth has only one solution: enjoy the gifts of God in the present moment (5:17-18). The final verse of the chapter may hold the most hope. There are two possible meanings. Either God gives joy so that human beings may be "preoccupied" with it and thus be distracted from the miseries and shortness of life. Or God "answers" human frailty with joy. In either case, joy is God's gift and happiness is found in the present moment.

6:1-9 Limited worth of enjoyment

At the beginning of chapter 6 the subjects of the previous section are repeated and reversed. Qoheleth advised the one to whom God gave "the power to partake" of riches to enjoy them (5:18). Now he acknowledges that sometimes this does not work. There may be someone to whom God grants riches but not "the power to partake" of them (6:2). The wealth is not even passed down to descendants (see 2:18-21) but goes to a "stranger," someone outside the family. This is in contrast to the one who has lost wealth and has nothing to hand down to descendants (5:13).

The next four verses (6:3-6) are bound off by exaggerated numbers: a hundred children, a lifetime of two thousand years. Just as great riches do not satisfy (5:9-10), neither do many children and many years of life (6:3). The common blessings of wisdom were understood to be wealth, old age, and descendants (see Job 42:16; Prov 8:18; Ps 112:2-3). These things provided a kind of pseudo-immortality, but Psalm 49 points out that everyone must die. Two thousand years (6:6) is twice the age of Methuselah (Gen 5:27)! But even that is not enough. If one does not enjoy one's goods, that is, if one does not enjoy the present moment, then all is worthless. The child born dead, the most hopeless example of mortality, is more fortunate, because the child does not know what it has missed (6:4-5). In the end, Qoheleth believes, everyone dies and goes to Sheol (6:6; see Introduction).

The goal of all human desire is life, beginning with food, but no one is ever fully satisfied (6:7). So the wise, whether rich or poor, have no advantage (6:8). Qoheleth quotes a proverb meaning that it is better to focus on the reality that is seen than what is only wished for. But even the proverb is vanity (6:9)! This is the last appearance of the phrase: "vanity and a chase after wind."

QOHELETH'S CONCLUSIONS
Ecclesiastes 6:10–11:6

The second half of the book is introduced in 6:10-12. The ideas have appeared before. What exists was created, that is, "called by name," long ago (see 1:9-10; 3:15). Human nature—the Hebrew word is *adam*—is known to be earthly (from the *adamah*, the earth) and mortal. Humans cannot contend with God (the one who is stronger), although there are several examples of those who have tried (see Job 9:3; 23:6; Jer 12:1). Human words are empty; in verse 11 the words themselves sound like babbling: *yesh-debarim harebbeh marbim habel*. Verse 12 introduces a key idea of the second half: "who knows?" Who knows what is good for mortals? Who knows what the future will bring? Human life vanishes like a shadow.

7:1-14 Critique of sages on the day of adversity

This is the first of three collections of proverbs in the book (see 9:17–10:4; 10:8–11:4). The key to interpreting this section lies in the characteristic ambiguity of the proverb in general and the juxtaposition of proverbs here. Proverbs are by nature ambiguous. The meaning of any proverb is shaped by the context. It takes wisdom to interpret and use a proverb, as is shown by the juxtaposition of two seemingly contradictory proverbs in the book of Proverbs (26:4-5). To take a modern example: Is it better to consider all the alternatives before acting ("Look before you leap") or to act immediately ("He who hesitates is lost")? Qoheleth capitalizes on this paradoxical character of proverbs. He seems to be responding to his own question: "who knows what is good?" (6:12). The

word "good/better" (*tob*) occurs eleven times in these fourteen verses.

The topic in verses 1-4 might well be St. Benedict's advice: "Keep death daily before your eyes" (RB 4.47). Verse 1 begins with a common idea: reputation is better than wealth and pleasure. The proverb is enhanced by its sound: *tob shem mis-shemen tob* (see commentary on Song 1:3). But the second half of the verse seems to subvert the first half. Why is the day of death better? Because a good name, a good reputation, is only certain at death. Before death it is possible to lose one's reputation. The opening proverb is simply carried to its logical conclusion. Therefore it is better to go to a funeral than a wedding in order to remember that death comes to everyone. Sorrow, acknowledging the whole reality of human life, is better than shallow merrymaking. Literally, by a bad/sad face the heart is made good (or glad or wise). Honesty in facing death distinguishes the wise and the foolish.

The contrast between the wise and the foolish is continued in verses 5-7. Heeding a wise rebuke leads to wisdom (Prov 13:1; 17:10). The fool's song may be empty praise. The Hebrew word for "song" (*shir*) leads to the image in verse 6: the crackling of thorns (*sirim*) under a pot (*sir*). Thorns used for fuel produce more sound than heat; the fool's noisy laughter and song do not produce wisdom. Qoheleth says, however, that even here is vanity. Why? Even the wise can be made foolish by too much stress, whether the distress of extortion or the potential pleasure of a bribe (7:7).

Verses 8-10 return to the question of the "better" time that was introduced in verse 1. The end is better than the beginning just as the day of death is better than the day of birth. Thus it is better to have the ability to wait, to have a "long spirit" (NABRE: "patient spirit") than to have a "high spirit" (NABRE: "lofty" spirit) arrogantly assuming at the beginning that something will come to a successful conclusion (7:8). Even this truth, however, is not absolute. Although one must not be too hastily upset by anger, neither must one be a fool and nurse anger patiently in one's heart (see Sir 27:30). Nor can one say that the past was a "better" time. One of Qoheleth's primary messages is that the best time to live is the present (see 3:11-13; 9:7).

In verses 11-14 Qoheleth concludes that wisdom is profitable, but he does not repeat the common tradition that wisdom is "better" than gold and silver (see Prov 3:14; 8:19). It is only *as good as* an inheritance. Verse 12 is ambiguous, as the Hebrew reads literally: "in the shadow of wisdom, in the shadow of money." Is wisdom a shelter, a protection, just as money can shelter one from some of the difficulties of life? Or is wisdom, like money, as fleeting as a shadow? The NABRE has opted for the former. In any case, the sage considers wisdom profitable because it enables one to live.

The bottom line in this collection of proverbs is that human beings cannot really know what is good because they can neither understand nor change the works of God (7:13-14). Qoheleth sees God as the source for both good and evil (see 1 Sam 2:6-7; Job 2:10), but in no way can human beings contend with God (see 6:10).

7:15-25 Critique of sages on justice and wickedness

Qoheleth now grounds his advice in experience. He has seen both good and bad, all manner of things. Worst of all he has realized that righteousness does not guarantee long life, nor do the wicked always die young. This contradicts traditional wisdom (see Prov 11:4-7) and prompts the advice to avoid extremes of righteousness and wisdom (7:16). The sage is not against striving to be righteous; he is against the presumption that one can be perfectly and completely righteous by one's own effort. He is also against the presumption that the possession of wisdom in its fullness is available to human beings. Such presumption and perfectionism will inevitably lead to psychological and physical disaster. On the other hand, one must not simply give up and go to the extremes of wickedness and folly (7:17). That too leads to death. Rather one must strive for good while recognizing one's own weakness. The fear of God, that is, the recognition of God's infinite power and one's own finite frailty, is the way to live well (7:18). There is true wisdom.

Verses 19-25 demonstrate the limitations of righteousness and wisdom. The inevitability of sin shows one's flaws (7:20). Awareness of others' weaknesses in speech reveals one's own similar faults (7:21-22). Try as he might, Qoheleth cannot attain the perfection of wisdom (7:23). Another characteristic question of this second half of the book appears here: Who can find out?

7:26-29 Critique of advice on women

These verses are the most difficult to interpret in the book and they have been the cause of much persecution of women. Qoheleth has declared his intention to seek wisdom and its design (7:25). In this section he continues his search (7:27-28). He begins, however, with a warning against "the woman" who is a trap (7:26). The warning may simply be an echo of the proverbial advice against adultery (Prov 2:16-19; 5:1-14; 6:20–7:27). In the context of the search for wisdom, however, this woman may be the personification of Folly, mentioned in verse 25, whose guests end up in Sheol (Prov 9:13-18). Wisdom, on the other hand, is the valiant woman: Who can find her (Prov 31:10; see Eccl 7:24)? The word "find" occurs seven times in this passage, the word "seek" three times.

Qoheleth has recognized the web of wickedness, folly, and madness (7:25). He still seeks the design, the answer. He has *not* found the proverb true that there is one [good] man in a thousand but no woman (7:28). ("I still seek and have yet to find.") He has found only this, that God made all humankind (*adam*) honest, but they have pursued many (devious?) designs (7:29).

This interpretation, adopted by the NABRE, softens but does not remove Qoheleth's misogynism. Other scholars consider verse 28b to be a later insertion in the chapter. The passage remains mysterious, open to many interpretations. All interpreters seek and have yet to find!

8:1-9 Critique of advice to heed authority

The previous chapter ended with Qoheleth still seeking wisdom and its design. Now he exclaims: Who knows! That statement about the search for wisdom in general leads to practical advice on how to behave in the presence of the king. Such advice is common in Proverbs (e.g., Prov 16:12-15). First of all, it is wise to look pleasant in the presence of authority (8:1). Usually it is God who illumines the face (Num 6:25; Pss 67:2; 80:4); here it is wisdom, and perhaps the practical wisdom of necessity. Respect for the authority of the king is demanded (8:2). Two phrases that describe his authority are otherwise used of God (8:3-4): "he does whatever he pleases" (see Ps 135:6) and "who can say to him, 'What are you doing?'" (see Job 9:12; Isa 45:9). The wise person considers when to stay with the king and when to yield

(8:3). Verse 5 seems to summarize the wisdom of the previous verses: obedience and knowledge of times.

But Qoheleth has said previously that humans do not know the appropriate times (see 3:11). They do not know the future (8:6-7). They cannot even control the extent of their lives (8:8). Even if it is possible to be exempt from war (see Deut 20:5-8) or to pay someone to substitute in the military draft as was done in the Persian period, no one can escape the final battle of death. Humans, who do not have power over breath or death, however, do have power to tyrannize one another (8:9). The sage continues to observe and ponder.

8:10-17 The problem of retribution

The violent injustice which ends verse 9 leads to a reflection on another injustice: the wicked are honored in burial and remembered for frequent visits to the temple while the just are forgotten (8:10). The wicked, who by rights should suffer for their wrongdoing, seem to prosper, and this inequity leads others into wrongdoing (8:11-12). It is the problem of Psalm 73: "I was envious of the arrogant / when I saw the prosperity of the wicked. / For they suffer no pain; / their bodies are healthy and sleek" (Ps 73:3-4). Qoheleth comes to the same conclusion as the psalmist. This injustice will not last (8:12-13). God sets the wicked "on a slippery road" and "suddenly they are devastated" (Ps 73:18-19). But good will come to the just. The distinguishing mark is again fear of the Lord.

After his declaration of faith that God will eventually make things right, Qoheleth returns to the problem that the wicked prosper and the just suffer. His solution is familiar: cultivate joy in the present moment (8:14-15).

The sage continues to search for wisdom, aware that no one can understand the work of God. The refrain, "find out," is repeated three times in verse 17.

9:1-10 Live in the present

Qoheleth redefines his problem: the commonness of common human experience! "Everything is the same for everybody." Mortals cannot understand the actions of God, whether apparently favorable (love) or unfavorable (hate). Yet no one can escape the hand of God. No matter how people distinguish themselves from one another,

everyone dies. Still the sage affirms the goodness of life (9:4-6). Even a dog, a despised animal, is better off when alive than the great lion that is dead. Qoheleth's understanding of the place of the dead, Sheol, is clear: the dead know nothing; they forget and are forgotten; they no longer have any relationship with anyone; they no longer have any purposeful activity. So Qoheleth returns to his advice to enjoy life now (9:7-9). The present moment is all anyone has. Take full advantage of whatever the moment brings.

9:11-12 The time of misfortune is not known

The question of the appropriate time returns (see 3:1-15). It is impossible to predict by human wisdom who will succeed and who will fail. It is as impossible for human beings to know what will happen in the future as it is for any animal.

9:13–10:14 The uncertain future and the sages

This section consists of an example story (9:13-18) and several loosely connected sayings. First Qoheleth turns to a story to illustrate a point: the wisdom of a poor man is more powerful than the siege works of a mighty king. However, the people saved by the poor man forget him, presumably because of his lower social status. It is a story of little and great: a great example ("magnificent," 9:13); a "small city" (9:14); a "mighty king" who "threw up great siegeworks" (9:14). It is also a story of misplaced priorities: the inhabitants of the city value wealth above wisdom. Two proverbial sayings lay bare the contradiction (9:17-18). What is "better" can be destroyed by just one "bungler."

The theme that it takes very little to destroy great good is continued in chapter 10. Just one or two dead flies may cause the perfumer's oil to ferment and possibly change the odor. Just a little folly can pervert wisdom (10:1). This observation leads to a meditation on folly. In biblical times the heart was understood to be the seat of intelligence and will. One thought and acted from the heart. The hearts of the wise and foolish go in opposite directions. The "right" is the direction of goodness and favor; the "left" is the direction of ignorance and disaster. (Compare "sinister" or "gauche" in English, both of which mean "left.") Fools, turning to the left, lack "heart" (i.e., understanding).

Thus they either call everyone else a fool or announce (by their actions?) that they themselves are fools (10:3).

The subject of conduct in the presence of a powerful person returns (10:4; see 8:2-4). This ruler is not a king but probably some high official. In contrast to 8:3, the advice here is to remain steadfast even in the face of anger. The attitude, however, seems to be similar: remain calm. The saying echoes a proverb: "By patience is a ruler persuaded, / and a soft tongue can break a bone" (Prov 25:15).

The anger of the previous ruler suggests the folly of another powerful person, a tyrant (10:5). His "mistake" (the word suggests an inadvertent error) turns the world upside down (10:6-7). Fools have replaced official advisors; commoners have replaced the elite. The horses upon which slaves are riding are a sign of wealth and power. Horses are not native to Israel; few could afford them. They are ordinarily used for military purposes or as regal transport. Ordinary people rode donkeys or walked. The stability of the social order is a value in the wisdom tradition.

Life is risky for everyone; the laborer faces danger also (10:8-9). The hunter digs a pit for an animal to fall into and camouflages it. But if he is careless and his camouflage works too well, he falls into it himself. The walls between fields and of houses were built of stones with smaller stones used as mortar, a perfect place for snakes to hide. The worker who takes down a wall risks a poisonous bite. Anyone who uses sharp tools is also in danger, both from the tools and from the material worked by them.

Practical wisdom teaches ways to diminish the risk (10:10). Sharpen the tools; charm the snake. The charmer is called the "master of the tongue," the master of languages even of snakes. There is advantage in wisdom, but sometimes even wisdom does not help (10:11). Sometimes danger comes unexpectedly or is more powerful than human prevention.

This last collection of sayings (10:12-15) is held together by the words "fool" and "fool" (compare 9:17–10:3). The subject is a favorite wisdom topic: speech. There is only one comment about the wise: the words of the wise win favor (but see 9:11). The sage's attention is on the babbling of fools. From beginning to end their words are folly, yet they cannot stop. They more than anyone do not know what is going to happen, yet they keep talking. They do not even know the way to town, a sign of absolute incompetence! The section ends with this repetition of "do not know."

10:16–11:2 No one knows what evil will come

Several sayings are gathered in this unit, bound off by the repetition in 11:2 of "not know." Verses 16-17 proclaim a woe and a beatitude concerning the character of leaders in a land. The word translated "youth" can also mean "servant." (This compares to the derogatory use of "boy" in English.) So the ruler in verse 16 may be immature or may belong to a lower class (see 10:6-7). His princes dissipate their strength by feasting and carousing in the morning, thus by implication all day. The contrast is a mature and well-born king whose princes know the proper time (see 8:5) and have good judgment. They too feast, but as strong men who have self-control.

The simple meaning of the proverbs in verses 18-19 is obvious: laziness brings disaster; feasting brings joy; money answers for everything! These are all themes that recur in traditional wisdom, although there are often warnings about money (Prov 11:4; 13:11). The joy in feasting is particularly important to Qoheleth (see 8:15; 9:7). It is also possible, however, to read these proverbs in the context of the previous verses. If the leaders of a land are dissolute and lazy (see 10:16), the "house," that is, the kingdom or the dynasty, may collapse. Perhaps such leaders, whose wealth makes them callous to the needs of others, focus only on feasting.

Verse 20 returns to the subject of rulers; the topic, however, is caution in criticism. The image of birds carrying one's voice is common in the ancient Near Eastern wisdom tradition and in the modern English proverb: "A little bird told me." In this context the proverb may be a warning to those who live in the land described in 10:16!

There is serious disagreement concerning the interpretation of 11:1-2. The traditional interpretation, both in Jewish and Christian tradition, is that one is advised to be generous. A good gift today may be rewarded in the future; give generously to many people, even if the future looks bleak. It is also possible to interpret the verses as economic advice: Send out your goods, you may get a return on your investment (hopefully also a profit).

Diversify your investments as a protection against disaster. Finally, Qoheleth may typically be commenting on the phrase, "you don't know." Do something that seems foolish. It may turn out well; it may not! In any case, these verses illustrate the rich ambiguity of proverbs!

11:3-6 No one knows what good will come

The final verses in this section emphasize human ignorance. Especially among farmers there are certain folk sayings about the weather that are frequently recited, but the most common wisdom is that no one can control the weather. Anyone who waits for the perfect conditions will never act. What human beings think they know is never certain. The comments on the weather lead to a meditation on a greater mystery: the coming of new life in the womb (11:5; see Ps 139:14-16). The repetition of words links the two subjects: "wind/breath" (Hebrew *ruah*) in verses 4-5; "full" and "the full one" (i.e., the pregnant one) in verses 3 and 5. "Wind/breath" has appeared several times. The wind constantly shifts (1:6). Human effort is "a chase after wind" (1:14, 17; etc.). Is the life-breath of humans and beasts the same (3:19, 21)? No one can master the breath of life (8:8). The mystery of breath and wind leads to Qoheleth's main point in this section: Mortals do not know the work of God (see 3:11; 7:13; 8:17). What is to be done? Act wisely; work regularly. Qoheleth implies but never says this: Trust God. The threefold repetition of "you do not know" closes this section (11:5-6).

POEM ON YOUTH AND OLD AGE

Ecclesiastes 11:7–12:8

The book opened with the cycles of nature that seemed endless; it closes with everything coming to an end. The final poem can be considered in two parts (11:7-10; 12:1-7). The first part is Qoheleth's final advice to enjoy life. It is addressed to a youth, a young man in full vigor. Two imperatives characterize the section: remember and rejoice. Remember that the "days of darkness," that is, old age and death, are coming; rejoice in the days of your youth (11:7-8). The rejoicing requires positive and negative actions (11:10): Remove pain from your heart and body; follow your heart

and eyes. The comment concerning God's judgment seems out of place (11:9). Throughout the book, however, Qoheleth has advised the reader to fear God and to remember God's judgment (see 3:17; 5:6; 6:10; 8:12). Enjoyment of the present moment is God's gift (see 3:13; 5:18; 8:15). God judges whether one has taken full advantage of what has been given.

The second part of the poem (12:1-8) opens with the key word "remember." The spelling of the next word in Hebrew leads to two interpretations: "Remember your Creator" can also be read "remember your grave." Qoheleth keeps the focus on the beginning and the end. The remaining verses have several layers of meaning. It is generally agreed that they have to do with old age and death. They may be read, at least in part, as an allegory of old age. In this reading the women who grind are the teeth; those who look through the window are the eyes; the guardians of the house are the limbs, and so on. Parts of the poem seem to be simple descriptions of aging: fear of heights, gray hair (the white almond blossoms), the failure of stimulants to rouse the appetite (caper berry). Second, the poem may be read as a description not only of the old age and death of one person but as the eschatological end of the world. The light of sun and moon and stars is darkened (see Matt 24:29). Even strong men tremble and bow down. "Two women will be grinding at the mill; one will be taken, and one will be left" (Matt 24:41). The human being (*adam*) goes to his lasting home. Third, there are suggestions of the funeral rite and death. Mourners are in the street. Pottery is shattered; broken pottery is often found in graves in the ancient Near East, a symbol that the human being, an earthen vessel, has been destroyed. The flesh returns to dust and the breath returns to God. Verse 7 does not reflect the Greek notion of body and soul; rather it indicates that at death there is no longer a living human person: the parts (dust and breath) have each returned to their source. The destruction of the lamp (the silver cord and golden bowl) and of vessels for water is also symbolic of death (12:6). There is no need to impose a single grid of interpretation. The poem is powerful precisely because all these layers of meaning are suggested.

Qoheleth's work concludes with a repetition of the opening statement: all things are vanity (12:8; see 1:2).

EPILOGUE

Ecclesiastes 12:9-14

An editor added these comments about Qoheleth and his book. Qoheleth is praised for his work and his wisdom, but there is a warning against an excess of searching for more wisdom or more books. The summary of Qoheleth's message is simple: Fear God and keep the commandments. Keeping the commandments is not clearly mentioned by Qoheleth in the body of the book, but it is a natural corollary to the fear of God (see Deut 5:29; 8:6). This comment too is followed by a warning about God's judgment (12:14).

THE SONG OF SONGS

Irene Nowell, O.S.B.

INTRODUCTION

See "The Festival Scrolls" on page 254.

Title

"Song of Songs" is the Hebrew way of conveying the superlative: the best song (compare "king of kings" or "holy of holies"). The Song is attributed to Solomon. This attribution is more like a dedication than a declaration of authorship. The work is put under the patronage of Solomon, who is mentioned in it seven times (1:1, 5; 3:7, 9, 11; 8:11, 12). This dedication links the Song to the wisdom literature. The wisdom books Proverbs and Ecclesiastes are also dedicated to Solomon, who is said to have "uttered three thousand proverbs, and his songs numbered a thousand and five" (1 Kgs 5:12). Wisdom is based on common human experience and its goal is the good life. God is found in ordinary life. When the Song of Songs is read through a wisdom lens, it reveals the goodness of God in the experience of human love.

Genre and structure

The Song is a collection of love poetry, celebrating the joys and longings of human love. The songs are so skillfully woven together that there is no agreement on how many songs are collected or where each song begins and ends. Repeated phrases act as refrains, however, giving some indication of structure. Different voices, evident in the Hebrew verb forms, are marked in many translations: M = the man; W = the woman; D = Daughters of Jerusalem.

Poetic artistry

The Song is rich in poetic beauty, especially metaphorical expressions. The comparisons are from both nature and human achievement such as architecture. Themes common to love poetry, such as searching and finding, weave throughout. Repeated words and phrases bind the whole work together.

Date

The Song of Songs is difficult to date. Parts of the work undoubtedly circulated orally before the book was written. Analysis of the language suggests that the writing occurred sometime after the Babylonian exile, perhaps around the fourth century B.C.

Interpretation

Early in Jewish tradition the Song of Songs was interpreted as an allegory of the love between God and the covenant people. In Christian tradition too the Song was understood to describe the love between God and the church or the individual soul. This tradition of interpretation flourished in the Middle Ages, especially among the Cistercians. In recent times interpreters have returned to the original sense of the Song as a celebration of human love.

COMMENTARY

A DECLARATION OF LOVE

Song of Songs 1:1-6

1:2-4 The woman speaks of her lover

After the title (1:1, see Introduction), the Song begins with the woman's passionate outcry of love. She speaks to her lover and about him in the same breath. He is eminently desirable and his love is intoxicating. The sound of his name fills her with sweetness. (In Hebrew "name" is *shem* and "perfume" is *shemen*.) She is certain that every woman loves him!

1:5-6 Love's boast

The woman's description of herself inserts a note of tension. She speaks to the "Daughters of Jerusalem," a group that functions as a chorus throughout the Song (2:7; 3:5, 10; 5:8, 16; 8:4). She is black and beautiful. The woman's color is compared to the desert tents made of black goat hair and to curtains either of Solomon's own tent or of Solomon's temple. The wealthy tribe of Qedar (a word which means "dark") lived in the Arabian Peninsula and is associated with Ishmael (see Gen 25:13; Isa 60:7), so "black" here suggests beauty and luxury. But the woman's blackness came at a price. She has been forced by her brothers to work outdoors and the sun has burned her. What does the "vineyard" mean? Her sun-blackened skin indicates work in a literal vineyard. Throughout the Song, however, the vineyard also symbolizes the woman herself, her beauty and fertility (see 8:12) and the love between the man and the woman (see 2:15; 7:13).

A CONVERSATION BETWEEN THE LOVERS

Song of Songs 1:7–2:7

1:7-8 Love's inquiry

Now the woman begins a conversation with her lover. She will seek him at the time of the midday rest. She names him "you whom my soul loves," a phrase that becomes a refrain in 3:1-4 where the theme of seeking is intensified. The agricultural metaphors continue. She cared for the vineyards; they both are shepherds.

1:9-11 Love's vision

A dialogue of mutual admiration ensues. In this first speech the man compares the woman to a mare among pharaoh's chariotry. Comparison to a beautiful horse is a great compliment in the worldview of the Song. She is adorned with precious jewelry like the trappings of a horse. In addition, a mare turned loose among the chariot horses—all stallions—would cause chaos. Her beauty, her strength, and her desirability are all praised in this metaphor.

1:12–2:7 Love's union

The woman returns to the subject of sweet smells (1:12-14; see 1:3). In her longing for him she gives off the sweet scent of spikenard, an aromatic herb from India used in making ointments. This is probably the ointment used in the various anointings of Jesus (see Mark 14:3; John 12:3). The man is a cluster of fragrant spices lying between her breasts. Myrrh is a sweet-smelling gum resin from various trees of Arabia and India. Henna is a shrub of the loosestrife family that has fragrant white or reddish flowers. Spices were valuable in the ancient world for fragrance, flavoring, and as an embalming agent. Stores of spices were a sign of wealth (see 2 Kgs 20:13).

The two lovers exchange compliments: "How beautiful you are" (1:15-16). He calls her "my friend." The feminine form of this word occurs nine times in the Song and only one other time in the Hebrew Bible (Judg 11:37). She calls him "my lover," a term she uses twenty-six times. He again uses a visual metaphor: her eyes are like doves. Soft, gentle, gray-brown? She responds with a metaphor of fragrance: their house is made of sweet-smelling wood. Inside a building or in a grove of trees?

The conversation between the man and the woman continues (2:1-3), building on the plant metaphors of chapter one. She compares herself to the first flowers of spring: the crocus or narcissus growing on the fertile coastal Plain of Sharon and the lotus flower (a lily) growing in the valleys. He emphasizes her uniqueness, "a lily among thorns." She responds with her own metaphor of his uniqueness. He is a fruit-bearing tree among the other trees of the wood. This tree is not our common apple tree, which is not native to Israel, but an undomesticated fruit tree. She proclaims her lover the bearer of sweet fruit and the giver of pleasant shade. These images lead to metaphors of eating and finally a direct statement of love. He brings her to the place of eating, the place of love. She is weak with passion and longing. He takes her in his embrace.

The final verse in this section (2:7) is a refrain that occurs several times in the Song. The woman puts the Daughters under oath not to arouse love until it is ready. Is this a plea not to disturb the two lovers? Or is it advice that genuine love has its own time and we must wait for it? The oath—"by the gazelles and the does of the field"—is a euphemism for names of God. The Hebrew words for "gazelles" and "does" (*tsebaoth, ayeloth*) sound like the words for "hosts" in the term "Lord of hosts" (*tsebaoth*) and for "God" (*eyl* or *eloah*). This is similar to our use of "gosh" for "God" or "jeepers creepers" for "Jesus Christ."

HER LOVER'S VISIT REMEMBERED

Song of Songs 2:8-17

This section is a passionate description of the delight of lovers in springtime. The song is beautifully structured. It is linked to the previous song by the images of gazelle and deer (2:7, 9). The end of the song echoes its beginning, forming what is known as an "inclusion." In verse 8 the lover arrives and in verse 17 he departs. He moves with the grace and speed of a gazelle or young stag (2:9, 17). An inner inclusion surrounds the description of the approaching spring; the phrase "Arise, my friend" is found in verses 10 and 13. The whole section is characterized by abundant images of sound, smell, sight, and anticipated taste. The verbs of springing and leaping, as well as the description of spring's rapid arrival, convey a sense of urgency.

The woman hears her lover's voice and sees him eagerly rushing toward her, but she stays hidden and forces him to search for her (2:8-9). He calls out to her with his favorite terms of endearment, "friend" and "beautiful one." He insists that she come out to enjoy the wonders of springtime (2:10). Spring is announced by the end of the rainy season, March or April in Israel, and the arrival of the first migrating birds. Vine-

dressers know that the grape vines must be pruned promptly, before the sap begins to rise. The description of spring appeals to all our senses. We feel the end of the winter rains; we see the flowers and the birds. We hear the doves cooing and anticipate the taste of grapes and figs (2:11-13).

The man continues his invitation to the woman, pleading with her to come out of hiding (2:14). He has compared her previously to a mare; now he compares her to a dove, a symbol of gentleness and love. The poetry of this verse is carefully worked, with the last four lines in a mirroring pattern: face, voice, voice, face. The woman answers with what may be a line of a song (2:15). The little foxes symbolize the other young men who would like to court her (the vineyard). She is warning her lover to pay attention to her. She continues with a declaration of her commitment (2:16) and an invitation to him to spend time with her, either the whole day or the whole night (2:17). It is difficult to tell whether the time she indicates is the evening, with its cool breezes, or the morning, when the shadows flee.

LOSS AND DISCOVERY

Song of Songs 3:1-5

The scene shifts to the woman's bedroom. She is alone and longing for her lover. The interweaving of repeated words and phrases carries the meaning of this scene: "seek/sought" (twice each in 3:1-2); "whom my soul loves" (3:1, 2, 3, 4); "not find/found" (3:1, 2, 3, 4); "go about/make rounds of the city" (3:2, 3). These repetitions make up over half the Hebrew words in verses 1-4 (26 of 50).

The woman's searching begins on her bed (3:1). Is this a dream? Or is her longing so intense that she gets up and goes out alone at night (3:2), an action uncharacteristic of women in that society? She seeks him but does not find him. Ironically, however, the watchmen find her! She is making her rounds of the city and so are they (3:2-3). She seeks "him whom [her] soul loves." This phrase identified her lover already in 1:7. Her love is so intense that she repeats this name for him four times. When she talks to the watchmen, she puts this phrase first: "Him whom my soul loves—have you seen him?"

Finally, when she finds him, new phrases appear (3:4-5). She clings to him and brings him to her mother's house (see also 8:2). The designation, "mother's house," is rare, occurring only twice more in the Old Testament, both times in stories of women and in the context of marriage (Gen 24:28, concerning Rebekah, and Ruth 1:8). She brings him to the room of her mother (literally, "the one who conceived her"). The passage begins and ends with the suggestion of a bed. The section ends with a repetition of the refrain of 2:7.

SOLOMON'S WEDDING PROCESSION

Song of Songs 3:6-11

Not only does this poem begin with a question, there are questions about it. Who or what is this coming from the desert? It seems to be Solomon, coming to his wedding, although another opinion is that the one arriving is the bride. A further dispute concerns the number of pieces of furniture: is the litter in verses 7-8 the same as the one in verses 9-10? The NABRE translation suggests it is the same single piece of furniture.

The procession from the desert suggests the arrival of a caravan of merchants with all their exotic wares (3:6). The columns of smoke in the desert suggest also the exodus journey (see Exod 13:21-22). Both images reveal the elegance of this procession. The identification of the traveler as Solomon also enhances the vision (see Introduction). Throughout the Song the lovers are compared to a royal couple (see 1:4; 8:11-12). The number of warriors is double the usual guard (see Judg 14:11; 2 Sam 23:18-23). They are prepared to defend the lovers against any danger (3:7-8).

Solomon's litter is made of precious materials: cedar of Lebanon, gold and silver (3:9-10). Purple cloth was a sign of royalty because purple (or blue) dye, obtained from the murex shellfish, was very difficult to process. The framework or interior of the carriage is "lovingly fitted" (literally: "inlaid with love"), another indication of the impending union of the lovers. The witnesses to the wedding will be the Daughters of Jerusalem, so often summoned by the woman (see 1:5). The groom will be crowned by his mother with the wedding wreath (3:11). This is the only mention of marriage in the Song of Songs.

THE BEAUTY OF THE WOMAN

Song of Songs 4:1-11

The next section begins with a poem in praise of the beloved's physical beauty. The style is that of the Arabic *wasf*, a love song that compares parts of the beloved's body (top to bottom or the reverse) to images in nature or human art. Here the song is set off by an inclusion—"beautiful you are, my friend"—in verses 1 and 7. The man declares that everything about the woman is beautiful, even though he will only describe her from head to breasts.

A second inclusion, "behind your veil," sets off the description of her head (4:1-3). She is tantalizingly hidden, but this is a hiddenness that enhances rather than conceals her beauty. Her hair is like a flock of goats streaming down the mountain. The movement of the black goats, leaping downward, suggests long, wavy black hair. In contrast, her teeth are white as newly washed sheep and no teeth are missing. Her cheek is like a plump, red pomegranate. The man's gaze moves down to her neck adorned with many necklaces and pendants, which he compares to a strong, straight tower hung with the small round shields of victorious warriors (v. 4). Finally, her breasts are as soft and beautiful as young gazelles (4:5). Both the pomegranate with its many seeds and the gazelle, drinking from the stream that waters the tree of life, are ancient Near Eastern symbols of fertility. The man concludes his description by accepting the woman's invitation to come to the fragrant mountains (her breasts?) as the day grows cool and the shadows lengthen (4:6; see 2:17).

The lover's longing is evident in his insistent call to her to come to him (4:8). She seems as inaccessible as the mountain range of Lebanon with its peaks of Hermon (called Senir by the Amorites, see Deut 3:9) and Amana (probably near Damascus, see 2 Kgs 5:12). She is as impossible to reach as if she were hidden in a wild animal's lair. The man now describes the effect of her beauty on him (4:9-11). He calls her "my sister," a frequent term of endearment for a wife (see Tob 5:21; 7:15; 8:4; 10:6), and "bride," a term that appears in the Song only in 4:9–5:1. He returns her praise of his love and fragrance (see 1:2-3). Her kisses are as sweet as honey and as nourishing as milk, images that recall the wonders of the Promised Land (see

Exod 3:8, 17). Two kinds of "honey" are mentioned here: the first is domesticated honey, dripping or strained from the comb; the second is wild honey or the syrup from grapes or dates. Her fragrance is like Lebanon, either the famous cedars or frankincense (Hebrew, *lebonah*, see 4:6).

THE LOVER'S GARDEN

Song of Songs 4:12–5:1

The man continues his praise by describing the woman as an enclosed garden, a sealed fountain, reserved for him alone. The garden suggests Eden, and the term for "grove" in verse 13 is a Persian loanword, *pardes*, from which we get the word "paradise." She is truly an extraordinary garden in which all sorts of wonderful fruits and spices grow, precious items that in ordinary life must be imported from far and wide (4:13-14). Not only is she a watered garden, she is living water, flowing from the mountains of Lebanon (4:15). The man calls all the winds to spread the intoxicating fragrance of his garden; the woman interrupts with an invitation to him to come enjoy his garden (4:16). He replies that he has indeed come. The narrator encourages the lovers to enjoy their lovemaking (5:1).

A FRUITLESS SEARCH

Song of Songs 5:2-8

This section seems to be a replay of 3:1-5. Many of the images and phrases are the same, but the differences are significant. In 3:1 the woman was on her bed; in 5:2 she is not only on her bed, but sleeping. Yet, she says, her heart—the seat of both thought and emotion—is awake. Is she dreaming? Is she simply dozing? In any case, the vigorous knocking of her beloved interrupts her. He calls to her with four terms of endearment. Three have appeared before; the fourth, meaning "perfect" or "whole," suggests his description of her as altogether beautiful (4:1, 7). In chapter 3 she could not find him, but here he is! Both sides of their conversation seem self-centered. He is wet and she is ready for bed (5:2-3). The rendezvous will not happen.

The description of their encounter is filled with sexual innuendo. He asks her to open to him; she replies that she is naked and has bathed her feet (a common Hebrew euphemism for genitals). He puts his hand through the opening (the keyhole?) and her "innermost being" (literally: "innards") are in turmoil (5:4). But the desire of the lovers is not to be satisfied. By the time she rises to open for him, he is gone. The door, however, is dripping with myrrh (5:5). Has he left the perfume as a gift? Is this further innuendo?

At his departure her heart sinks and she goes in search of him. The phrases of 3:1-3 are repeated but each with an addition. Now she not only seeks him, she calls out after him (5:6, see 3:1-2). The watchmen not only find her, but they also beat her and strip her of her mantle (5:7, see: 3:3). She adjures the Daughters of Jerusalem, but her request is now that they tell her beloved that she is lovesick (5:8, see 2:5; 3:5). In every instance the description of her longing is intensified.

THE LOVER LOST AND FOUND

Song of Songs 5:9–6:3

Two questions from the Daughters of Jerusalem and the woman's answers structure this section. The Daughters ask how her lover is better than others (5:9) and where he has gone (6:1). Both times they address her with a title given her by the man: "most beautiful among women" (see 1:8). The woman's answer to the first question is a *wasf* about her lover's physical beauty. In her answer to the second she returns to the image of the garden (see 4:12-16).

5:9-16 The lost lover described

The woman describes her lover much as he described her. She moves from head to foot and concludes with praise of his mouth (see 4:11). She begins and ends by emphasizing his complete desirability (5:10, 16; see 4:1, 7). The images differ, however. He used two terms for honey in describing her mouth; she uses two terms for gold in describing his head. (A third term describes his golden feet!) His hair is thick and luxuriant, like branches of the date palm or clusters of fruit (5:11). His eyes too are like doves (see 1:15; 4:1) bathed in milk (i.e., not bloodshot). His cheeks and lips are fragrant and intoxicating (5:13).

As she moves to a description of his torso, the imagery shifts, suggesting the statue of a god.

He is made of precious metals set with gemstones (5:14-15). He is as impressive as the cedars of Lebanon. He can be compared to the statue of Nebuchadnezzar (Dan 2:31-34), but unlike Nebuchadnezzar, he does not have clay feet. He is utterly desirable (5:16).

6:1-3 The lost lover found

The Daughters' second question suggests that the woman ought to know where this marvelous man has gone. Perhaps the Daughters would like to find him too (6:1). The woman's response makes it clear that he belongs to her alone. He has come to her, his enclosed garden (6:2; see 4:12-15). The section ends with the statement of mutual possession (6:3; see 2:16).

THE BEAUTY OF THE WOMAN

Song of Songs 6:4-10

The lover has returned and repeats much of a previous *wasf* in praise of the woman (compare 4:1-3 to 6:5-7) with some differences. The woman's eyes, like doves, which ravished his heart (4:9), have become even more exciting (6:5). His beautiful, perfect one (4:7) is better than any other woman; even queens sing her praises (6:9).

Just as the *wasf* in 4:1-7 was surrounded by an inclusion, declaring the perfect beauty of the beloved, so this *wasf* is enclosed ("beautiful" and "fearsome" in 6:4, 10). In 4:4 the man compared the woman's bejeweled neck to David's tower. Now he compares his beloved to two capital cities: Tirzah, capital city of the northern kingdom (Israel) from 910–870 B.C., and Jerusalem, capital city of the southern kingdom (Judah). Although Samaria is the best known of Israel's three capital cities, Tirzah may have been chosen because its root word means "to be pleased with." The repetition of the inclusion (6:10) does not compare the woman to cities but to cosmic realities. She is as beautiful as the moon, literally "the white," referring to the full moon; as pure as the sun, literally "the heat." These comparisons reach toward the divine, since sun and moon were sometimes considered gods in the ancient Near East.

The last phrase of the inclusion is difficult to translate. The woman is as fearsome as what? The last word, which occurs only here in the Old Testament, comes from a root meaning "banners," "signals," or "divisions." It has often been interpreted in a military context as "bannered troops." But in this context, with the sun and the moon, it may mean the stars, the armies (hosts) of heaven, thus "celestial visions."

LOVE'S MEETING

Song of Songs 6:11-12

It is not clear who is speaking in these verses. Previously the man came down to the garden (5:1; 6:2), which symbolized the woman (4:12-16). Here, however, the woman seems to be speaking. She goes down to enjoy the new growth of springtime. On the eastern end of the Mediterranean as soon as the rains stop there is an explosion of blossoms, flowering trees, and wildflowers. The vision overwhelms the woman.

THE BEAUTY OF THE BELOVED

Song of Songs 7:1-6

A third *wasf* about the woman (see 4:1-7; 6:4-10) is introduced by a mysterious verse addressed (apparently by the Daughters) to the "Shulammite" (i.e., the woman). The name "Shulammite" is unknown. It may be another spelling for "Shunammite," a woman from Shunem, a city in Galilee. Abishag, the last concubine of David, was a Shunammite (1 Kgs 1–2), as was the friend and benefactor of Elisha (2 Kgs 4). It may be a feminized form of Solomon (*shelomo* in Hebrew), indicating that the woman has royal status (see 7:2), or it may simply be derived from *shalom*, peace.

The woman is commanded to "turn" so that she may be seen, presumably because of her beauty (7:1). Her response indicates that they are watching her dance. The dance, otherwise unknown, is called "the dance of the two camps."

This third *wasf* sung by the man is the most explicitly erotic. The direction of his gaze from foot to head is the reversal of the other two. He begins with her feet, enticingly shod in sandals (see Jdt 10:4; 16:9). The word used here for "feet" refers to the beat of her steps (in the dance?). He moves upward to her thighs, her navel, her belly, describing her full roundness with symbols of richness and fertility (6:2-3). He again compares her breasts to the twins of a gazelle and her neck to a tower, but now the tower is precious ivory (6:4-5; see 4:4-5). Her nose is a tower too. We may not think that is a compliment, but Lebanon suggests the white moon (Hebrew *lebanah*, see 6:10) or white, sweet-smelling frankincense (*lebonah*). Damascus is the prosperous and powerful capital city of Aram (Syria); Heshbon, in Moab, was the capital city of Sihon, king of the Amorites. The two cities lie on the northern and southern ends of the Kings' Highway. This woman's face—eyes and nose—are as strong and compelling as cities on the caravan route. (Bath-rabbim is unknown, perhaps Rabbah, just north of Heshbon.) Finally, the woman's head is as commanding as Mt. Carmel, rising over the Mediterranean; her blue-black hair, precious as royal purple, captivates her king (7:6). His praise recognizes the strength of this woman.

LOVE'S DESIRES

Song of Songs 7:7–8:4

The man again exclaims over the woman's beauty (see 1:15-16; 4:1, 7) and desires to enjoy it. Her stature is that of a palm tree with its clusters of dates high and out of reach, but her inaccessibility will not be a barrier to him. Once more he begins to compare her to delicious fruits—dates, apples, grapes and their wine—but she interrupts him, offering herself (7:8-10). She reverses the statement in Genesis, where the woman is told, "*your* urge shall be for your husband" (Gen 3:16; emphasis added). This woman declares that her *lover's* yearning is for her (7:11). With images reminiscent of her visit to the nut garden (6:11), she invites him to come with her into the fields for lovemaking (7:12-13). The mandrake, an herb called *duda'im* in Hebrew (compare *dodi*, "beloved"), was considered an aphrodisiac because of its human-like shape (7:14). Rachel, longing for a child, bargained with Leah for mandrakes (Gen 30:14-16). This woman has treasured up all her fruitfulness for her lover.

The woman wishes the man were her brother so that she could show her affection without scandalizing others (8:1). This is different from the affectionate term, "sister," used by the man (see 4:9-10, 12; 5:1, 2); this is a wish for sibling relationship. Again she wants to bring him to her mother's house (see 3:4). The drinks she will give him

suggest the intoxication of love. Also the Hebrew word for "drink" in verse 2 (*shaqah*) echoes the word for "kiss" (*nashaq*) in verse 1. An almost verbatim repetition of earlier verses closes the unit (2:6-7; see 3:5).

REPRISE

Song of Songs 8:5-14

8:5 The return from the desert

The last ten verses of the Song of Songs are like a reprise of all the melodies heard throughout the work. The echo of "Who is this coming" appears here (see 3:6; 6:10). In chapter 3 we saw the litter of Solomon coming in a cloud of perfume; here it is the woman leaning on her lover. At the end of the same passage, his mother crowned him with the wedding wreath (3:11). This scene is set under the tree where his mother conceived him. The woman has compared her lover to an apple tree and delighted to rest in his shadow (2:3); she has asked the Daughters of Jerusalem not to arouse love before its time (2:7; 3:5; 8:4). Now she declares that she has aroused her lover under the apple tree.

8:6-7 True love

The most powerful statement of love in the Song is at the center of chapter 8. The seal is a sign of identity. It may be a cylinder seal worn around the neck or a scarab ring worn on the finger. Whoever sees the seal or its imprint recognizes the owner, just as a signature is used as identification today. She declares that she is as bound to him as his own identity. Love is as impossible to stop as death; passion is as devouring as Sheol, the home of the dead. Even chaos cannot sweep it away, nor is there anything that can buy it.

The nouns here suggest the names of Canaanite gods: Mot (Death), Resheph (translated "flames," the name of the god of pestilence, often portrayed with arrows), and Yamm (sea, or the waters of chaos). The name of Israel's god is suggested at the end of verse 6, which ends with Yah, a short form of Yнwн. The phrase may mean "flames of Yнwн" or "flames as powerful as a god."

8:8-10 An answer to the brothers

The woman's brothers, who were angry with the woman in 1:6, are heard again. They think their sister is too young to be courted by a man (8:8). They will protect her virginity with barricades made of precious metal and wood (8:9). She responds to their words with the announcement that she is indeed mature and strong. Her neck and her nose have been compared to towers (4:4; 7:5); now she says that her breasts, thought to be undeveloped by her brothers, are towers. She is a source of peace (*shalom*) to the man (compared to Solomon, *shelomo*) who courts her (8:10).

Guarding a sister's virginity, and thus her value, and arranging her marriage were tasks that often fell to brothers. See, for example, Laban's interest in Rebekah (Gen 24:29-31, 50-59) and the revenge taken by Simeon and Levi for the loss of Dinah's virginity (Gen 34:25-31).

8:11-12 A boast

Vineyards have been a place where the lovers went for lovemaking (7:13); the vineyard has been a symbol for the woman (1:6; 2:15). The man has been compared to Solomon (see Introduction and 3:6-11). Now Solomon's vineyard is described as extremely valuable (7:11), but the man boasts that he has his own vineyard and, unlike Solomon, needs no caretakers. He implies that his vineyard is more valuable to him than Solomon's (7:12).

Solomon's vineyard is at Baal-hamon, which means "the master of the multitude." Is Solomon the master of the multitude? Is his vineyard the harem? Solomon had seven hundred wives and three hundred concubines (1 Kgs 11:3). If so, the man is boasting that the woman is worth more to him than Solomon's entire harem.

8:13-14 The lovers' yearnings

The man has compared the woman to a garden (4:12–5:1) and she has agreed with the image (4:16; 6:2). Now he refers to the woman as one who dwells in gardens. Again he asks to hear her voice (see 2:14). She responds as she did previously, comparing him to a gazelle or young stag (see 2:9, 17) and calling him to hasten to her breasts, the mountains of spices (see 2:17; 4:6).

THE BOOK OF
WISDOM

Richard J. Clifford, S.J.

INTRODUCTION

Name, author, and audience

The book is known in the Septuagint (the early Greek version of the Old Testament) as Wisdom of Solomon and in the Latin tradition as The Book of Wisdom. Though neither Solomon (nor any individual for that matter) is ever named in the book, the author assumes the persona of the tenth-century Israelite king renowned for his wisdom. The book presupposes that its readers are familiar with the biblical portrait of Solomon, the wise king in 1 Kings 2–11, especially chapters 3; 5:9-14; 10:1-10. The author of another book categorized as wisdom literature, Ecclesiastes (fourth century B.C.), also assumes the persona of Solomon in Ecclesiastes 1–2 without naming him.

The author is not named, as in many biblical and apocryphal books. The practice enhances a book's authority by linking it to a tradition; the author's task is making that tradition relevant to a contemporary audience. Solomon represented the wisdom tradition. Though the author is unknown, a few biographical details can nonetheless be inferred from the book. The author is obviously a Jew with a fierce pride in Judaism, in God's call of the Jews, and in the relevance of the biblical story. The place of composition is generally assumed to be Alexandria, the Egyptian seaport on the Mediterranean Sea, on the Western Delta at the mouth of a branch of the Nile River, about 130 miles north of Cairo. The city, planned by Alexander the Great (356–323 B.C.) and built a few

years after his death, had a large Jewish community whose upper class would have nurtured and understood the complex ideas and language of the book. Though it seems that Jews of the time were not ordinarily admitted into the *gymnasium* to receive a Hellenistic education, the author must have been one of those allowed to study Greek literature, rhetoric, and philosophy. The author delights in virtuoso display, coining words, inventing arguments, and playing on biblical traditions. The author's project is similar to that of the prolific Jewish philosopher Philo of Alexandria (ca. 20 B.C.–A.D. 50). Philo likewise stood within the Jewish tradition of biblical study, was familiar with pagan learning, and interested in the spiritual dimension of individual life. Like Philo, the author of Wisdom of Solomon is confident in humans' capacity to know God and act virtuously, and confident too in the special vocation of Israel, whom God protects and endows with wisdom.

What audience does the author have in mind? Until recently, most scholars would have answered a Gentile audience, for they assumed that Judaism vigorously promoted itself in the Hellenistic world and that Jewish works written in Greek were part of that missionary effort. There are, to be sure, indications that many non-Jews found Judaism very attractive. Acts 13:16, for example, speaks of "those who fear God," "God-fearers" who were attracted to Judaism but stopped short of full conversion. And according to Wisdom 18:4, "the imperishable light of the law was to be given to the world." Recent scholarship, however, is divided on the issue, some feeling that the primary goal of Jewish literature written in Greek was to help Jews maintain and strengthen their identity and their faith in a pluralistic world, though they would not necessarily rule out apologetic and missionary goals as well.

It is likely that the primary audience envisioned by the book was Jewish, for only such an audience would have understood the esoteric commentary on the Bible and accepted the uncompromising monotheism and election of Israel as God's "son." The latter two teachings were contrary to the broad "philanthropic" outlook of educated pagans. Instruction of Jews was a necessity in the Hellenistic marketplace of ideas, for one could not assume young Jews would adopt the religion of their ancestors (see below). The biblical "base text" in Wisdom of Solomon is the wisdom books, especially the book of Proverbs. Like Ben Sira a century before within the Palestinian culture of Jerusalem, the author integrates those wisdom traditions with the historical books of the Bible, especially Exodus. The wisdom tradition, enriched with material from the historical books of the Bible, enabled both authors to deal with existential and national issues at one and the same time.

Date and place of composition

The book contains no specific historical references by which one can date it. The best evidence is literary; the affinities in phraseology and ideas with the writings of Philo of Alexandria suggest the authors were contemporaries in Alexandria (30 B.C.–A.D. 40). Specialized meanings of some words in Wisdom of Solomon match other writings of the period; tensions at the time between Jews and their urban neighbors would account for the book's concern with justice and its harsh criticism of Egyptian customs; Wisdom of Solomon presupposes its readership is literate and thoroughly Hellenized, which would have been true of the large Jewish community at Alexandria. Alexandria was the capital of Egypt and a brilliant center of Hellenistic philosophy and art, which was symbolized by its famous museum and library. The Greek translation of the Hebrew Bible (the Septuagint) was, according to Jewish tradition, initiated by Ptolemy Philadelphus (285–246

B.C.) for the library. It is tempting to imagine that Wisdom of Solomon was written for such a vibrant community, where Jews would see the grandeur of their traditions depicted by an author skilled in Hellenistic rhetoric and philosophy as well as biblical lore.

Hellenistic Judaism

The Judaism reflected in Wisdom of Solomon is largely a product of Hellenistic culture rather than the Palestinian culture reflected in the Hebrew Bible. One should not, however, regard the two cultures as totally distinct, for each was multifaceted and there was considerable overlap. "Hellenistic" is an adjective for Greek culture ("Hellenism") in its interaction with the native cultures of the East, an interaction initiated by Alexander the Great in the fourth century B.C. The age was the first great marketplace of ideas in the East. The old cultures and societies of the ancient East, ruled by tradition and custom, were confronted by new ideas, customs, and people. Two areas are especially relevant to this introduction—religion and philosophy. Enthusiastic advocates of the new religions traveled about expounding their views and looking for followers. The religions and philosophies were regarded as ways of life as well as doctrines; they were intellectual-ethical systems.

Of the many emphases of Hellenistic religion, three are especially important for Wisdom of Solomon. The first was miracles. Performing miracles was the mark of a god, and lists called aretalogies were kept of a god's miracles. The religions were also interested in immortality as a gift from god. Pre-Hellenistic Judaism did not use the concepts of immortality or eternal life to express the blessed future. Rather, it looked for divine restoration of the nation as a whole. But in the Hellenistic marketplace, a good religion had to promise immortality. Even in Egypt, where life after death had always been offered, it was now offered to more people than before. A third feature of Hellenistic religions was the claim of great antiquity. A religion had to be old to have credibility, for new ideas required validation by the tried and the true. Several ancient events were cited as standards of antiquity: the reign of Semiramis, the legendary founder of Assyria; the Trojan War, the oldest datable event in Greek history; and the Flood.

The above emphases appear in Wisdom of Solomon. Wisdom 11–19 portrays the central biblical event of the exodus as a series of miracles in which natural elements change their properties. Immortality is the dominant category of hope, which is a striking difference from earlier biblical books. As examples of antiquity, Wisdom of Solomon presents Adam as the first person guided by wisdom (10:1); among its heroes is Noah "when . . . the earth was flooded" (10:4-5). The author knows what attracts followers. What is most important, however, is that the author of Wisdom has entered the marketplace of ideas with the aim of persuading fellow Jews of the relevance of their Jewish faith.

Philosophical influences

Wisdom of Solomon engaged the same questions as the philosophies of the day, incorporating without apology whatever elements might make the biblical tradition more meaningful and credible to a Jewish audience. Ben Sira, the author of the book of Sirach, another piece of wisdom literature in the Old Testament, in an earlier century borrowed some concepts from Stoicism (e.g., Sir 41:14–42:8; 43:27; 36:1-4), but to a much lesser degree than this author. The principal Hellenistic philosophical movements were Stoicism, Epicureanism, and Skepticism. All were rooted in the great philosophical schools of the fourth century B.C., Plato's Academy and Aristotle's Lyceum. A widely-used division of the period shows that philosophy was conceived more broadly and integrally than in the modern West: logic (the study of reasoning and discourse), physics (the study of external nature), and ethics (the study of human nature and how life ought to be lived). All the schools agreed that philosophy was a serious affair and had the purpose of gaining life-enhancing wisdom.

Of these three schools, Stoicism was influential on Wisdom of Solomon. In physics, it was materialist, rejecting external entities such as Plato's forms and Aristotle's unmoved mover (God) as explanations of sensible reality and of motion. In ethics, it was strongly rationalist; happiness is attained by the right use of reason, and moral failures are failures in the functioning of reason. The most important philosophical influence on Wisdom of Solomon, however, was Middle Platonism (ca. 80 B.C.–A.D. 250), which is the scholarly

designation of the Platonic tradition from the first century to the third century A.D. Shapers of the tradition included several Alexandrians—Philo and the church fathers Clement (ca. A.D. 150–215) and Origen (A.D. 185–254). Elements of Stoicism and Aristotelianism had by this time become part of the Platonic tradition. Middle Platonism became increasingly a metaphysical or theological system, characterized, among other things, by ideas as thoughts in the mind of God, assimilation to God as an ideal of human life, and the hierarchy of being.

Aspects of Stoicism and Middle Platonism are found in popularized form in Wisdom of Solomon, especially in Wisdom 13–15. Examples of general Greek influence are the four virtues in Wisdom 8:7 (the Christian "cardinal" virtues), temperance, prudence, justice, and fortitude, and the viewing of fire, wind, stars, or water as animating forces in the world (13:2). Stoic influence is seen in the use of the concept of a world soul (7:24), materialist physics (8:1; 19:18), the proof from design (13:1), and the mode of argument called the *sorites* (chain argument) in 8:17-21. Borrowings from Middle Platonism include the pre-existence of souls (8:19), the sharp distinction between body and soul (8:20; 9:15), and the diminished reality of the material world compared to the spiritual world of heaven (9:15-16).

The author draws on one or another philosophical tenet without necessarily fully subscribing to the system of which they are a part. An example is the immortality of the soul (Wis 3:1-4), which in the book is a prelude to the establishment of the kingdom of God (see below).

The genre and the structure of the book

The genre of the book has been much debated. Indeed some scholars have even denied the book is a unity. In recent decades, a number of scholars have proposed that the book belongs to a type of literature mentioned in classical rhetorical treatises though no complete example has survived—the elaborate commendation of a way of life (which is sometimes called a protreptic). The author faced a situation unparalleled in Judaism—an educated community that required persuasion to *choose* afresh their ancestral traditions amid the clamor of competing and prestigious opportunities.

In recent decades, a consensus has formed about the broad structure of the book. The book has three parts: Part 1: 1:1–6:21, the depiction by means of typical figures and events of the authentic (though hidden) world and the justice that characterizes its governance; Part 2: 6:22–10:21, the gift of wisdom that enables one to understand this world and live happily in it; and Part 3: 11:1–19:22, the exodus as the great illustration of how the world operates. Ancient manuscripts were not provided with the visual guides of modern printed books. It was the responsibility of the author rather than copyists to indicate the structure. Authors used repetitions of key words to frame sections by using them at the beginning and end of a passage. This is called *inclusio*. The outline below, reflecting the consensus of biblical scholars, is a convenient guide to a complex and dense book. Some of the units below are marked by *inclusio* and the structure is chiastic. In a chiasm the elements are repeated in reverse, resulting in the pattern ABBA. It is common in ancient literature.

Part I (1:1–6:21) The Two Worlds

A. Exhortation to pagan kings: Rule according to divine justice and seek wisdom! (1:1-11)

  B. A drama in which the true nature of the world is revealed (1:12–2:24)

    C. Contrasting portraits: death of the just and impious (3–4)

  B'. Divine judgment against the wicked and for the righteous person (5:1-23)

A'. Repetition of the exhortation to pagan kings: Rule according to divine justice and seek wisdom! (6:1-21).

Part 2 (6:22–10:21) Wisdom and the Way to It

Wisdom 6:22-25 introduces the themes. Wisdom 6:22–8:21 is composed of seven passages.

A. The origin of the wise king is like any other human (7:1-6)

  B. I, Solomon, prayed for wisdom (7:7-12)

    C. Giving of wisdom of God to Solomon (7:13-22a; vv. 13b and 21a have an *inclusio* around "hide" and "hidden")

      D. Praise of wisdom—its nature, origin, and attributes (7:22b–8:1)

    C'. Solomon will marry wisdom who lives with God (8:2-9)

  B'. Thoughts of the young king (8:10-16)

A'. Young Solomon will ask for wisdom (8:17-21; vv. 17b and 21d, *inclusio*: "heart")

Chapters 7 and 8 prepare for the prayer at their beginning (7:7) and end (8:21). The Prayer of Solomon in chapter 9 has three parts: vv. 1-6 about human beings, vv. 7-12 about Solomon, and vv. 13-18 about human beings. The prayer is the center of book because the beginning of the prayer is concerned with creation (theme of Part I) and the end is concerned with salvation (theme of Part II).

Chapter 10 presents the eight "wisdom heroes" of Genesis, each of whom is involved in a contrast. Abel is opposed to his brother Cain. All except Cain were helped by wisdom who came to their rescue. The reference to prayer in 10:20 is an *inclusio* of 19:9, the final verse of the book.

Part 3 (11:1–19:22) The Exodus: God Provides for His Child Israel

The exodus is viewed as seven "comparisons" (Greek: *synkrisis*, 11:1-14 and 16:1–19:22). The plagues against the Egyptians (given in italics below) are contrasted with the blessings given to the Israelites during the exodus (given in roman type below). The comparisons are interrupted by two digressions in verses 11:15–15:19.

Comparison 1. 11:6-14 *flowing water*—water from the rock

  Digression 1: the moderation of God in punishing the wicked, Egypt, and Canaan (11:15–12:27)

  Digression 2: a critique of idol worshipers (13:1–15:19)

Comparison 2. 16:1-4 *frogs*—quails

Comparison 3. 16:5-14 *flies and locusts*—bronze serpent

Comparison 4. 16:15-29 *storm and hail*—manna

Comparison 5. 17:1–18:4 *darkness*—light

Comparison 6. 18:5-25 *death of first-born*—Israel spared

Comparison 7. 19:1-9 *drowning in the Red Sea*—passage through the Red Sea

Final statement and broadening of the perspective (19:10-22).

The meaning of the book of Wisdom

By making Solomon the speaker and by building on the wisdom tradition, the author is employing the most universal and least nationalist part of the Bible. The appeal is to the nations (in the person of their kings), especially in 1:1-15 and 6:1-21. Though the envisioned audience is primarily Jewish, the book addresses Gentile rulers in these passages; the same dynamic is found in Psalm 2 and Isaiah 40–55. They are called to recognize the just God's governance of the world and the coming judgment that was part of that governance. In part 2 (6:22–10:21) Solomon appears as the model king and seeker after wisdom. Thereafter Israel is the protected and wise "son/child" of God (part 3, 10:22–19:22). The universalist outreach of the wisdom literature has been enriched and qualified by the special role of Israel. Israel is a witness to the world of God's justice and protection.

Wisdom of Solomon seeks to demonstrate the reality of the "kingdom of God," or, in other terms, the sovereignty of Israel's Lord. To many Jews, that sovereignty was hidden in the sense that it was not yet fully realized and visible. Non-Jews denied the rule of Israel's God, like the gang in Wisdom 2 who say " by mere chance were we born" (2:2). They kill the righteous person, God's child (2:20); only at the judgment do they see the resurrection of the child and the reality of the "kingdom" or sovereignty of God (Wis 5). In Wisdom of Solomon, knowledge of "the kingdom" does not consist merely in an intellectual appreciation of the Lord's universal dominion. Rather, the book expresses the concrete hopes of Jews in the period at the turn of the era. Like many in Judaism, the author seems to regard Israel to be still in exile, awaiting the fullness of redemption. Jewish literature both in the Diaspora and Palestine attests to the deep and widespread conviction that the national story has not yet come to its proper conclusion. Psalm 106:47 expresses a widespread feeling: "Save us, LORD, our God; / gather us from among the nations." Another biblical book awaiting the restoration of Israel is Daniel, written during the Maccabean crisis in the mid-second century B.C. Daniel 12:2-3 also viewed restoration as resurrection: "Many of those who sleep / in the dust of the earth shall awake; / Some to everlasting life, / others to reproach and everlasting disgrace. / But those with insight shall shine brightly / like the splendor of the firmament, / and those who lead the many to justice / shall be like the stars forever." Wisdom of Solomon has the same spirit (e.g., Wis 3:6-8; 4:16–5:2). Wisdom 3:7-8 seems to allude to the Daniel text and says of the just who have been slain that "they shall judge nations and rule over peoples, / and the LORD shall be their king forever." The resurrection of the dead in Wisdom 5 seems to refer to the same intermediate state as Daniel, where the righteous who have died await the restoration of Israel and the full realization of the reign of God.

The teaching on immortality (Greek: *athanasia*, 3:4; 4:1; 8:13, 17; 15:3) and incorruptibility (6:18, 19) must be understood in the same context of the judgment preceding restoration. Though the book borrows the Platonic language of the immortality of the soul, the context is completely different. For one thing, the author is primarily concerned with the Lord's governing rather than with an individual soul's reward. For another, the governing has a historical context—the restoration of Israel who, the author believes, is still in exile.

Three affirmations of the book have a special resonance for modern Christians. The first is its distinctive understanding of the kingdom (sovereignty) of God, which is perhaps the most persistent theme of the Bible. God's justice actually rules the world even though human kings are under the impression they have the final say. Divine wisdom is required to see divine justice at work. Such wisdom is (paradoxically) granted only to those who earnestly seek it. Though operative now, divine justice is not yet visible to the world. It becomes visible when God's "son" (2:18; 12:21; 16:10, 26; 18:4; also rendered "child" in 2:13; 16:21; 19:6 and "servant" in 12:7) is faithful to his "father" (2:16; 11:10). Fidelity means allowing the justice of God to work. Israel is God's child and thus witnesses to the true King of the universe. From its very founding in the exodus, Israel was protected, its enemies punished, and God was revealed as Lord of the universe.

God's lordship is not timeless, however. Israel does not live outside of history. For the author, the Lord had not finished regathering Israel from its exile. The critical time of refounding the community is approaching. Divine rule has been hidden in that it has not yet appeared in its fullness. There are now, therefore, "two worlds," corresponding in a sense to the two ways in ancient wisdom literature. One world is all too familiar, for its law is that might makes right and that those faithful to God are at risk from violent and selfish people. It is ruled over by the kings of this world. Though the other world has not appeared fully, it is destined to last; it is eternal, for it is ruled by God. Each world has its adherents, its citizens. The citizens of this world are doomed, however, as their world is passing away. The citizens of the true world already possess eternal life, for their world will endure.

The real world is marked by life and the other is marked by death. Paradoxically, it is when the righteous are faithful and rescued that the real world appears. In part 1, the death of the (typical) righteous person who trusts in God shows forth the true world when God raises up that person in the sight of those who killed him. In part 3, the justice of God is shown forth in the rescue of the "child" of God, Israel. As they are rescued in the sight of the Egyptians, the latter come to acknowledge the true God. The true world is revealed in the trusting and obedient conduct of the chosen ones.

A second contemporary issue is that God is Lord of the universe, which consists of nature and history. Many believers instinctively make God the Lord of heaven but retreat from affirming the lordship of earth, nature, and history. They have difficulty seeing God at work in the world, in human history, and are disposed to think separately of God acting in history and in nature. Wisdom of Solomon affirms the central reality of God the creator and of God's choice of Israel. God acts in history (in the book's perspective) primarily by dealing with Israel, reshaping at will human activity and natural elements. "For the elements, in ever-changing harmony, / like strings of the harp, produce new melody, / while the flow of music steadily persists" (19:18). To recognize this rule takes divine wisdom. It must be sought earnestly in prayer, preferred to all else, and yet, paradoxically, is conferred as a gift. Its possession enables one to see the true nature of reality and to remain faithful to it.

A third point relevant to Christian readers is the outreach of God that is called wisdom. Despite the author's learning in Greek philosophy, God is not portrayed as "the prime mover" or transcendent ideal. God is engaged in human history and dwells with the human race. At times, divine wisdom is the energy that runs through the universe; at other times, it is the inspiration that enters into human beings, directing them to act justly and trust in God's fatherly protection. Christian readers will see in this wisdom aspects of their triune God, which will be made more explicit in the pages of the New Testament and in subsequent Christian reflection.

COMMENTARY

THE TWO WORLDS

1:1–6:21

Part 1 of the book of Wisdom develops and combines two biblical traditions. The first is the view of world history found, among other places, in Psalms 2, 48, 89, 96; Isaiah 10:5-19; 44:24–45:7; 55; and Jeremiah 27, 29: the Lord, Most High over heavenly beings and earthly kings, directs the course of history, and the Lord's servant Israel is, in principle at least, similarly "most high" over the nations. Rulers of the earth are thus agents of the Lord and will be judged according to whether they ruled justly and wisely (Wis 1:1-15 and 6:1-21). Israel is privileged and protected, though explicitly identified as "your [the LORD's] children" only in part 3 (19:6). In part 1, the "child of the LORD" (2:13) is left unspecified. The second biblical tradition used in part 1 is the doctrine of "the two ways" (found especially in Proverbs and Psalms), which portrays the moral life in dramatic terms as walking on either of two opposed paths—the way of the righteous and the way of the wicked, each path having its proper destiny. Wisdom 1–6 shows the wicked (usually referring to a group) plotting against the righteous individual (Wis 2) and the respective destinies of each way (Wis 5). One of the "Two Worlds" in part 1 is the world of everyday experience. Ruled over by earthly kings, it is characterized by rampant wickedness and is short-lived. The other "world" is not always visible. Ruled over by the Lord, it is inhabited by the righteous who trust in God their Father (2:16). The true world becomes visible when the righteous act faithfully in the face of opposition, for God intervenes to rescue them. Divine intervention functions as a judgment that the righteous will live forever and the wicked will perish (Wis 5).

Part 1 is framed by exhortations to the rulers of the world in Wisdom 1:1-15 and 6:1-21. Couched in the language of personal relationship, the first exhortation warns the rulers (and their subjects) against inviting death through wickedness; the second exhortation urges them to court wisdom. At chapter 6, the second exhortation is used to close this section and transition to the next.

1:1-15 Seek righteousness and wisdom to avoid death!

The instructions of Proverbs 1–9 urge the son or disciple to seek wisdom above all. Though wisdom must be earnestly sought, it is ultimately a pure gift of God. Wisdom brings life, which is defined as health, reputation, wealth, a suitable spouse, and children. Its opposite, death arrives prematurely as punishment. Wisdom 1 develops these ideas from wisdom literature, especially Proverbs 8:15, "By me kings reign," and Proverbs 8:35-36, "[Whoever] finds me finds life / . . . all who hate me love death." Wisdom retains Proverbs' language of love and courtship as a metaphor of the search for wisdom (see Wis 1:1, 12, 16).

The warning to "you who judge the earth" (Wis 1:1), as in Pss 2:10 and 96:9-10, presumes all kings are under the dominion of the Lord; rulers represent all lands and peoples, for wisdom's invitation is universal. The language of affection is used of the quest for wisdom in Wisdom of Solomon, to love, to seek (v. 1), to find (v. 2), to dwell (v. 4), to court (v. 12). Just as the son or disciple in Proverbs must submit to discipline (*paideia*), so also must kings/peoples of the earth in Wisdom 1:5, where *paideia* is translated "discipline." To oppose the process of discipline is to "test [God]" (1:2), which is the attitude of the wicked in 2:19. Wisdom literature usually gives reasons for the conduct it teaches; one finds "because" and "for" throughout the book (e.g., seven occurrences in

1:1-15 alone). The terms "justice," "goodness," "wisdom," "spirit of the Lord," "holy spirit," and "power," are chosen for their cumulative effect and in vv. 1-15 are virtually synonymous. Seeking wisdom is not a matter of the mind alone; one must be open to discipline, must act justly, and revere God. The spirit as "all-embracing" (1:7, literally: "holding all things together") was a Stoic expression for fiery air that was thought to hold each thing together. The book applies that function to God's spirit in 8:1.

Older wisdom literature promised that those earnestly seeking wisdom would gain life, which was understood in this-world terms as health, longevity, children, a suitable spouse, wealth, and reputation. Premature death was the lot of the wicked; it symbolized failure to gain blessings. Wisdom 1:13-15 asserts something new: God did not make death the final dissolution of human beings, for the universe has a positive goal. The overarching principle is stated in verse 14, "the creatures of the world are wholesome," i.e., all that is created preserves its being. The same verse conceives of "the nether world" as a place of lethal power; that power does not extend to earth. Human beings die because of their mortality, but the power of death to end life permanently is ended.

1:16–2:24 The wicked and their plans

The righteous-wicked contrast (the "two worlds") is dramatized as an encounter between two groups about their beliefs and plans (2:1-9). How will the gang deal with a righteous individual who believes in the very things they reject (1:10-16)? They decide to test which way of life is valid, theirs or that of the righteous individual who boasts God is his father who will deliver his "son" from foes (1:17-18). They decide to kill him to see if God will do anything (v. 20). The answer will come in Wisdom 5. Wisdom 2 is framed by two verses (1:16 and 2:24) that highlight the words "death" and "possession" (Greek *meris*).

Each of the two ways has its adherents (i.e., those "in possession of" it). The wicked reveal their beliefs and behavior as well as those of the righteous individual (2:12-20). Their irreverence, pleasure seeking, and violence are an allusion to the opening scene in Proverbs 1:8-19. The wicked are said to consider death a friend and to make a covenant with it (Wis 1:16). "Covenant with death" borrows from Isaiah 28:15, where "death" is a metaphor for Egypt with whom some in Israel allied themselves instead of trusting in the Lord.

The father-son language in Wisdom 2 is borrowed from wisdom literature, in particular from Proverbs. Proverbs 3:12 teaches that, "whom the LORD loves he reproves, and he chastises the son he favors." Wisdom of Solomon regards the sufferings of the just "child of God" as divine reproof through which the son learns about divine governance. From Proverbs the author borrows the concept of "discipline" (Hebrew *mûsār*, Greek *paideia*) by which the teacher helps the disciple to become wise and mature; it can involve suffering. Also from Proverbs is the idea that the conduct of children honors or dishonors their parents (see Prov 10:1; 15:20; 17:21, 25; 19:13, 26; 23:22-26). Such is the sense of the accusation that the wicked have sinned against their "training" (*paideia*, 2:12). It is also possible, as some scholars have suggested, that the example of the loyal servant who is humiliated and then rescued by God (e.g., Joseph in Genesis 37–50 and the servant in Isaiah 53) has influenced Wisdom 2 and 5.

If "the devil" is indeed a reference to the devil, as most scholars hold, blaming the devil for death here is a striking innovation of the book. "Devil," however, is most probably not a good translation of Greek *diabolus*, which reflects Hebrew *satan*. "The satan" (with the article) referring to a particular figure occurs in two post-exilic texts (Job 1–2 and Zech 3:1-2) with a different meaning: "the satan" is an official of the heavenly court who scrutinizes human conduct and accuses them before God. In these passages, the Hebrew term *hassatan* means literally "the Adversary" or "Accuser." *Satan* (without the article) in 1 Chronicles 21:1 is disputed, but can mean "adversary" according to recent commentators. Such uncertainty makes attractive the view of St. Clement (*Epistle to the Corinthians* 3–4, A.D. 96), followed by some modern scholars, that Greek *diabolos* simply means "adversary" in Wisdom 2:24 and refers not to the snake who tempted the man and the woman in Genesis 3, but to Cain who murdered his brother Abel out of jealousy. In Wisdom 10:1-2, the author does not consider the sin of Adam as particularly grievous, but in 10:3-4 blames Cain for three instances of death: the death of Abel, Cain's own spiritual death of exile, and the death of almost the entire human race by flood. It is

likely therefore that death entered the world through Cain's murder of Abel.

3:1–4:20 The hidden meaning of the suffering of the just, the barrenness of the virtuous woman, and premature death

Instead of the proper conclusion to the story of the wicked versus the righteous individual begun in Wisdom 2, the author treats three classical problems of divine justice: the just who suffer (3:1-12), the virtuous woman who cannot bear children (3:13–4:6), and the premature death of a righteous person (4:7-20). The proper conclusion to the story will be told in Wisdom 5, deferring it until it then heightens interest in the problem of justice. Wisdom 3–4 can be considered an excursus, like those on the moderation of God toward sinners (11:15–12:27) and false worship (13:1–15:19).

3:1-12 The meaning of the suffering of the just

The torment of the just person depicted in Wisdom 2 raised the perennial question, why should "a child of the LORD" (2:13), a just person, suffer? This is the question of Job, and it is an abiding dilemma in biblical religion. This question is answered in the very first verse (3:1), they are in the hand of God, not in the "hand of [their] foes" (2:18). The following verses give supporting arguments: the righteous only *seemed* to be punished, but they are at peace (3:2-4); they were being tested (3:5-6; see Prov 3:11-12). Found worthy, they shall shine like the stars and rule like the angels with God (3:7-9; see Dan 12:1-3). That the righteous will rule Israel after their death is a corollary of their being with the angels in heaven, who were seen as servants of God. In contrast, the wicked are truly punished, have no hope, and their wives and children are accursed (3:10-12).

3:13–4:6 The virtuous woman who cannot bear children

As in the preceding section, this opens with a portrait of a type of person generally considered to be an argument *against* divine justice, a virtuous woman who was childless. Children were the means of living beyond death; the barren wives of Genesis (Sarah, Rebekah, Rachel) experienced a kind of resurrection when they had children. Not only such women, but virtuous eunuchs will also have their reward (3:14). The children of adulterers, on the other hand, will have no issue or die prematurely or in dishonor (3:16-19). They are a tree with shallow roots, vulnerable to strong winds, leaving behind no lasting fruit (4:3-6; see Psalm 1). The virtuous barren woman and eunuch, on the other hand, leave behind an immortal memory (4:1-2).

4:7-20 The premature death of a righteous person

A third obstacle to believing in a just God is the death of a "son" of this God at a young age. If the fruit of righteousness is long life, how is God just in this case? The author reinterprets old age as mature ripeness rather than longevity as such (4:7-9) in view of immortality.

The example of Enoch (4:10-14) illustrates the teaching, though he is not named, following the convention of wisdom literature. Enoch was the seventh of the ten pre-Flood heroes in Genesis 5. Instead of dying, literally, "[he] walked with God after the birth of Methuselah three hundred years, and had other sons and daughters. Thus all the days of Enoch were three hundred sixty-five years. Enoch walked with God; then he was no more, because God took him" (Gen 5:22, 24, literal translation). He lived far fewer years than the other pre-Flood heroes, and the text does not explicitly say he died. Rather, he was "transported" (4:10), "snatched away" (4:11), because "he became perfect in a short while" (4:13); the latter phrase is an interpretation of Genesis 5:24, "Enoch walked with God."

The meaning of the death of the just person, however, is lost on the wicked (4:14c-19). Only at the final judgment will they understand. The nature of the judgment will be described in the next section.

5:1-23 The last judgment, confession of the wicked, and arming of the cosmos

The narrative of the gang's attack on the righteous individual, begun in Wisdom 2, is brought to its conclusion in Wisdom 5. The wicked presented their philosophy of life in their first speech (2:1-20) and retract it in their second speech (5:3-13). Both speeches are provoked by the righteous person, whom the wicked have failed to understand.

What is the scene? No details are given except that the wicked see the righteous person raised up from the dead. As noted in the Introduction, it is best interpreted as the judgment that precedes the new age when the righteous become rulers. Such judgment scenes are attested in classical biblical literature (e.g., Ps 82; Isa 41; 45:20-21; etc.). The scene that most closely resembles this one is Daniel 12:1-3; it too has those who have been killed in God's cause raised up, whereas their enemies are "in everlasting horror and disgrace." The view taken here is that this judgment precedes the final restoration; it is left vague because the author did not know the timetable, but only that those loyal to the Lord would rule in the new age.

Thematically and rhetorically, Wisdom 5 develops 4:7-20, for the series of initial verbs in 4:17–5:1 reach their climax in 5:1: "they [the wicked] see," "see," "shall afterward become," "shall be," "shall be," "shall they come," "the just one" will "confront." As in Wisdom 2, the just person is silent, the mere sight of the risen one provokes self-condemnation on the part of the attackers. Their confession in 5:5, "See how he is accounted among the heavenly beings" (literally "sons of God") evokes Matthew 27:54 and Mark 15:39, where the wonders accompanying the death of Jesus lead the centurion to cry out, "Truly this man was the Son of God!" The wicked, citizens of this world only, did not *know* until they saw the just one raised from the dead; now they understand "justice is undying" (Wis 1:15). They are shamed, in the biblical sense, i.e., what they relied on is shown to be illusory. The real world, normally hidden, becomes visible when the just person trusts in God and is raised from the dead.

The confession of the wicked in 5:6-13 is a vivid and even poignant description of the life they believe ends definitively with death. The point is made largely through variations on one image, "way": we strayed from the way (5:6-8); our own fleeting way is like a shadow, a word (5:9), the fleeting wake of a ship (5:10), the air unaffected by a bird's flight (5:11), the course of an arrow (5:12). Their conclusion is in 5:13: our wickedness is the cause of our demise. The comparisons are inspired perhaps by the poem on the "way" in Proverbs 30:18-20. The author confirms the self-judgment of the wicked, nicely picking up the images of air and water (Wis 5:14).

What is the divine protection that means life for the just? The final part of Wisdom 5 (vv. 16-23) describes the arming of the Storm God and the employment of the storm weapons against that which rebels against the justice implanted in the world. The Scriptures often portray the Lord as a Storm God (e.g., Exod 15:1-18; Judg 5; Ps 29). The imagery is even older than the biblical portraits; the Storm God used thunder, lightning, wind, and rain against his enemies to gain kingship over the universe. Wisdom 5:17 draws on Isaiah 59:17, "He put on justice as his breastplate, / victory as a helmet on his head; / He clothed himself with garments of vengeance, / wrapped himself in a mantle of zeal." The author gives a new emphasis, "[the Lord] shall arm creation to requite the enemy," i.e., creation itself will fight against injustice. The arming of creation will be particularly clear in part 3 in which the natural phenomena of the seven plagues of the exodus are used to punish the wicked (the Egyptians) and benefit the children of God (Israel).

6:1-21 Seek wisdom and avoid judgment

The author returns to the authoritative warnings and exhortations to kings that began part 1 (Wis 1:1-15), bringing the structure of this part to its conclusion. Wisdom 1:1-15 warned the kings they are being judged by God whose spirit fills the world and scrutinizes their performance; 6:1-21 again reminds them they rule only as servants of God who will judge them impartially (vv. 1-8). Wisdom 6:9-11 marks the transition from warning against lawless behavior to positive seeking of wisdom. Borrowing Proverbs' personification of wisdom and exhortation to seek her (Prov 1–9), the author retains Proverbs' paradox that one must earnestly *seek* wisdom so that God can *bestow* it as a gift. The relationship of the individual ideal king to wisdom is portrayed in Wisdom 6:12-16 with the language of love. The relationship culminates in wisdom's bestowing true sovereignty upon her faithful and loving friend ("the desire for Wisdom leads to a kingdom"). The section that concludes part 1 also introduces part 2 by its introduction of wisdom as lover who is to be courted.

In biblical categories, the kings represent the nations; in addressing kings, the author addresses all nations and every person, asserting that each is under the one Lord. In Wisdom 6:4, "the law" is not the Mosaic law as such but natural principles of justice, knowledge of which could be expected from every ruler and every person. The section is brought to its conclusion in Wisdom 6:17-20 by a rhetorical figure called a chain syllogism or *sorites* in which each proposition leads to another and the whole series ends with a surprise declaration ("desire for discipline," leads to "love," love means "keeping of her laws," which in turn is the "basis for incorruptibility," bringing one "close to God," in other words to the "kingdom"). To paraphrase: if you want to retain your ability to rule, pursue wisdom and you will attain the fullness of rule.

Part 1 has emphasized again and again that the world is ruled by the spirit and wisdom of God, not by the kings that one sees in daily life. There is thus operative in the world a *hidden* authority; unknown to most people, it becomes visible especially when a "child [or servant] of God" trusts completely in God. Can we know more about this mysterious power in the universe, and can we encounter it to enrich our lives? That question will be answered in the next section of the book.

WISDOM AND THE WAY TO IT
6:22–10:21

Part 1 warned kings to recognize that they owe obeisance to the Lord who rules the world through power, spirit, and wisdom (1:1-15 and 6:1-21). In 6:1-21, wisdom becomes the preferred term for divine rule (6:9, 12, 20, 21). In part 2 the wise king (Solomon, not named according to the typifying convention of wisdom literature), speaking in the first person, instructs the kings of the world. The wise king emphasizes the common humanity shared with all people and gives his secret: his ardent and unremitting quest of wisdom since childhood. The quest is something *all* can embark on and is not limited to one nation. Wisdom has guided the whole course of human history by raising up wise individuals in every generation (Wis 10). Wisdom 10 is the link between parts 2 and 3 (God's guidance of Israel in Egypt), for the eighth in the line of wisdom heroes is Moses, the leader of the exodus that will be the center of attention in part 3 (10:16).

This section has two parts. Seven passages (6:22–8:21) in chiastic order describe Solomon's quest; this is followed by his great prayer for wisdom (Wis 9) and eight episodes about wisdom heroes (Wis 10).

6:22-25 Introduction

The verses serve as a transition from part 1 and a preview of part 2. Up to this point in the book, kings (representing the Gentile nations) have been warned to seek wisdom or incur divine wrath in the coming judgment (Wis 1:1-15; 6:1-21). Now one king addresses the whole world ("I" in 6:22) with an authority gained from seeking and finding wisdom. This king will describe his own quest and gift of wisdom (7:1–8:2a; 8:2–9:18), what wisdom is (7:22b–8:1), and how she rules the world (ch. 10). In the Egyptian culture of the day, mystery cults had secret lore known only to the initiates. Following the example of Woman Wisdom in Proverbs (see Prov 1:20-21 and 8:1-3), the king speaks *openly* to all (6:22b). The Jewish philosopher Philo also attacked secretive pagan mysteries, citing Plato that "jealousy" (6:23) is incompatible with wisdom's freehanded pouring forth knowledge (Philo, *Quod omnis probus liber sit* 13–14). Moreover, "jealousy" provoked the adversary to bring death into the world (Wis 2:24). Going beyond the view of wisdom as enriching only individuals, 6:24 says that wise people benefit the world and a wise king benefits his people (cf. Prov 29:4); Wisdom 10 will illustrate this assertion.

The King's Quest for Wisdom and Celebration of Her Virtues (7:1–8:21)

For a detailed outline of this lengthy speech, see the Introduction. Wisdom is not a doctrine one human being can impart to another. Rather, it is a gift given by God to those who earnestly seek it. The king's "teaching" is therefore the story of his own strivings after it and of God's granting it, as well as a description of wisdom in herself (7:22b–8:1).

7:1-6 The origin of the king is like any other human

The beginning and end of the section are marked by the words "the same" / "one same

way" in verses 1 and 6. The king is wise not because of his kingship but because of his lifelong quest for wisdom. The Gentile kings were told to seek wisdom (1:1-15 and 6:1-21) and this king has done just that. Kingship, which in the ancient East and especially in Egypt was more than a human state, is here demystified. "Ten month period" is a Greek way of reckoning pregnancy; Hebrew tradition reckoned it as nine months (2 Macc 7:27).

7:7-12 So I prayed for wisdom

Given that wisdom is a gift, it is not surprising that the king now tells us of his constant prayer for it and *preference* of it over gold and silver. The text alludes to the famous dream in 1 Kings 3 where God, pleased that Solomon preferred wisdom to long life or riches, or for the life of his enemies, gave him "a heart so wise and discerning that there has never been anyone like you until now, nor after you will there be anyone to equal you" (1 Kgs 3:11-13). Preferring wisdom over gold and silver is a theme from Proverbs, e.g., Proverbs 8:10-11: "Take my instruction instead of silver, and knowledge rather than choice gold. / [For wisdom is better than corals, and no treasure can compare with her.]" "Wisdom is their leader , though I had not known that she is their mother." (7:12). Proverbs portrayed wisdom as a bride and lover, but not as a mother. Like a mother, wisdom brings to birth human possibilities for happiness.

7:13-22a Gift of knowledge of God to Solomon

The section is marked off by "hide away" in verse 13b and "hidden" in verse 21a. The king is about to expound what wisdom is (7:22b–8:1) and prepares for that auspicious moment by a prayer, "God grant I speak suitably" (v. 15). The king said, "I shall conceal no secrets from you" in the introduction (6:22), for no one can hide what is gratuitously given by the generous God (7:13). The author is careful not to make wisdom an entity separate from God. Rather, it is a divine gift enabling people to have a relationship with God (7:14-15). Verses 15-16 emphasize the close relationship of wisdom to God: "[God] is the guide of Wisdom and the director of the wise." Part 3 will no longer refer to wisdom as a subject who acts, replacing it with God who acts for Israel.

In both Hellenistic philosophy and traditional Near Eastern religions, wisdom included the knowledge of what moderns call science. The philosopher Aristotle (384–322 B.C.) wrote both philosophical and scientific treatises; Stoicism was a cosmology as well as a philosophy; and Solomon "spoke of plants, from the cedar on Lebanon to the hyssop growing out of the wall, and he spoke about beasts, birds, reptiles, and fishes" (1 Kgs 5:13, other versions 4:33). Wisdom makes people careful and discerning observers of the universe God made.

7:22b–8:1 Praise of wisdom, its nature, origin, action, and attributes

This section is the center and core of the king's speech, for it describes what the introduction promised, "what Wisdom is, and how she came to be" (6:22). The first section (7:22b-23) is a list of attributes of wisdom, using the sacred numbers three times seven to yield twenty-one attributes. The terminology and the genre are Greek. Hellenistic religions employed such lists, sometimes called aretalogies (literally, accounts of virtue), to gain adherents. Aretalogies were especially associated with Isis, originally an Egyptian goddess, who became popular in Greek and Roman religions as a model sister, wife, and great mother. The terms for wisdom are influenced by the Stoic world-spirit thought to be immanent in the universe. It permeates and pervades (the same words as Wis 6:24) all things, and communicates virtue to intelligent creatures.

The twenty-one attributes make their impression cumulatively rather than singly. The first cluster of seven underscores the intelligence, transcendence, and mobility of wisdom, the second cluster underscores her purity, benefits to humans, and reliability, and the third her subtlety and ability to enter within all things. These attributes go considerably beyond the portraits of wisdom in Proverbs 8 and Sirach 24, for they transpose wisdom into spirit and make her able to *animate* natural phenomena as well as human beings.

Wisdom 7:25-26 is a memorable five-fold metaphor for wisdom, each part of which relates wisdom to an aspect of God: "aura" (better: exhalation, breath) of the power of God, "effusion" or outflowing of the divine glory, "refulgence" or reflection of eternal light, a "spotless mirror" of the divine energy, "the image" of divine goodness. The language is daring especially for an author writing in the biblical tradition. Even Philo does not use such terms as "effusion" or "reflection" for the origin of the Divine Logos. Wisdom 7:27-28 speaks of wisdom's governance of the world. Wisdom herself remains unaffected as she affects others, which is a sure sign of transcendence and superiority.

Beyond assuring the cohesion and order of the universe, wisdom enters into humans, becoming the principle of their moral and religious life. She enters into certain people in every generation. Wisdom 7:27cd views the divine call as wisdom entering a person, "passing into holy souls from age to age, she produces friends of God and prophets." Luke 7:35, "wisdom is vindicated by all her children," seems to draw on this concept of vocation to portray Jesus as an emissary of wisdom. Wisdom 10 describes wisdom-inspired heroes in the book of Genesis. Wisdom has her own people in every age. Sirach 44–50 similarly viewed history as a series of spirit-inspired individuals.

Again, like Ben Sira (Sir 16:26-28; 42:15–43:33), the author credits wisdom with the operation of the universe (Wis 7:29-30). "Reaches from end to end" (8:1) draws on Stoic cosmology, in which the movement of the world was caused by a continuous outward-inward movement of air from the center to the outermost pole.

8:2-9 Solomon will marry wisdom who lives with God

The section balances 7:13-22a by repeating its themes of wealth, knowledge, wisdom's relationship to God (8:3), and virtues including "science" (8:8 = 7:17-22a). It speaks of them from a different perspective, however—that of the ardent suitor of Woman Wisdom. Her gifts are personal and given directly to her lover, the king. The beginning and end of this section is marked by the inclusion of "to take her" in both verse 2 and verse 9. The portrayal of Woman Wisdom as a beautiful woman seeking suitors (8:2) is traditional (e.g., Prov 1:20-33; 7:4; ch. 8; 9:1-6, 11; Sir 14:23-25; 15:2-6; 51:13-22).

Paradoxically, seeking *one* thing (wisdom) means that *all* things will be given (cf. Matt 6:33 and parallels.). Her closeness to God makes her lead into (Wis 8:4, Greek: *mustis*) divine knowledge. The Greek term was used in the mystery religions for the highest level of knowledge. Encompassing all knowledge, Wisdom can give all else, for knowledge is the central virtue in Wisdom of Solomon. Among wisdom's gifts are "moderation and prudence, justice and fortitude" (8:7c), which is the first mention in Scripture of the four cardinal virtues. The cardinal virtues (from Latin *cardo*, "hinge") occur in Greek philosophical debate from the time of Plato and Aristotle as a means of unifying the virtuous life. The author is integrating the Greek ideal with the biblical tradition. The cardinal virtues became a staple of Christian tradition, being later discussed by St. Ambrose, St. Augustine, and St. Thomas Aquinas.

8:10-16 Thoughts of the young Solomon

The section balances section 7:7-12 in that both sections allude to 1 Kings 3 and Proverbs 8, which tell of Solomon being granted wisdom, his preference for wisdom over gold and silver, and the necessity of wisdom for governing. Common to the two sections in Wisdom of Solomon is the mention of by-products of the quest for wisdom, riches (7:7-12), and fame (8:10-16). Fame in the latter passage has two aspects: prestige in this life (8:10-12, 14-15) and immortality in the next (8:13). Both aspects are characteristics of Solomon in 1 Kings 3–11. In 1 Kings 3:6-9, the young Solomon asked for wisdom to govern like his father David. Solomon also won "immortality" in the sense of enduring fame by his judgment on the true mother of the child (1 Kgs 3:28) and by his vast knowledge (1 Kgs 4:34; 10:6-10).

8:17-21 Young Solomon will ask for wisdom

The section, marked off by "heart" in verses 17b and 21d, balances 7:1-6. Both sections underscore the humanity the king shares with all people and that one needs wisdom to bring one's humanity to perfection. In both sections, the realization leads to prayer, in 7:7 and in Wisdom 9.

Wisdom 8:19-20, literally, "I was a well-favored child, / having a noble soul fall to my lot, / or rather, being noble, I entered an undefiled body," show an awareness of the Greek philosophical idea of the preexistence of souls. The view is classically stated in the myth of Er in Book 10 of Plato's *Republic*, "Now is the beginning of another cycle of mortal generation. . . . Let him to whom

falls the first lot first select a life to which he shall leave of necessity." The pre-existence of souls did not play a major role in Wisdom of Solomon. Wisdom 9:15 similarly has Greek vocabulary, "For the corruptible body burdens the soul."

The Prayer of the King for Wisdom (9:1-18)

The king's prayer is the center of the section and indeed of the entire book. In chapters 7–8, the king explained that his entire life has been dedicated to seeking wisdom, and now recalls how he acquired wisdom through prayer. Chapters 7–8 pointed to the prayer at their beginning (7:7) and end (8:21). Part 1 (Wis 1–6) demonstrated the hidden energy of the world (wisdom), warning kings they risk punishment if they overlook it. Part 3 (Wis 11–19) will show how that wisdom-energy benefited Israel and punished their enemy. Wisdom 9 shows the ideal king uttering a model prayer for wisdom. The prayer thus bridges parts 1 and 3. By its reference to creation ("you who have *made* all things . . . have *established* [humankind]," 9:1-2), it refers to part 1, and by its reference to salvation ("and people learned what pleases you, and were *saved* by Wisdom," 9:18), it alludes to part 3. The prayer itself is divided into three parts by its topics: verses 1-6 focus upon human beings, verses 7-12 the king, verses 13-18 human beings.

9:1-6 As a limited human being I stand in need of your wisdom

The first part builds on venerable texts about Solomon the wise king and wisdom as an attendant at God's throne. At the very beginning of his reign, Solomon confessed his inadequacy, "I am a mere youth, not knowing at all how to act" (1 Kgs 3:7; cf. Wis 9:5-6), and asked for "a listening heart to judge [govern] your people" (1 Kgs 3:9; cf. Wis 9:4). The royal prayer in Wisdom 9, however, is broader than its prototype in 1 Kings 3. It harks back to Genesis and Exodus by the use of the divine name, "God of my ancestors" (Wis 9:1; "the God of Abraham, Isaac, and Jacob," see Gen 28:13 and Exod 3:6) and to Genesis 1 by "you who have made all things by your word" (Wis 9:1) and the assignment to humans of governing the world (Wis 9:2-3; cf. Gen 1:26-28). "Wisdom, the consort at your throne" (Wis 9:4) echoes Prov 8:30, "then was I beside him as artisan."

The first section of Solomon's prayer (9:1-6) is concerned with Solomon as a human being rather than as king. It nonetheless presupposes that all humans, not kings alone, have a vocation to govern the world. For this reason, the warnings to kings in Wisdom 1:1-15 and 6:1-21 include *all* human beings, not kings only. Despite its occasional denunciations, Wisdom of Solomon has an extremely high evaluation of humans. Its high assessment of humans and their vocation in fact accounts for the severity of the criticism.

The book considers the gift of wisdom a *complement* to native human excellence, not a replacement for it. Though the book employs the fashionable body-soul language of Middle Platonism (e.g., 8:19-20; 9:15), its underlying view of the human person is biblical, i.e., an animated body. The body is regarded as good.

9:7-12 Send me wisdom to build you a house and help me govern

The second part of the prayer is concerned with Solomon *as king*. The account of Solomon's reign in 1 Kings 1–11 tells of the "wisdom" of Solomon in governing well—deciding, organizing, and building. Almost forty percent of the account in 1 Kings is devoted to his planning, building, and dedicating the temple. It is not, therefore, surprising that Wisdom 9:7-10 is devoted to constructing the temple. The temple is the symbol of a transcendent heavenly reality given from heaven. In biblical thought, realities existing in heaven could be copied on earth so that their virtues affected human beings. In Exodus 25:9, God tells Moses to make the tabernacle and all its furniture, exactly "according to all that I show you regarding the pattern" and rabbinic tradition included the torah among those things descended from heaven. The Platonic tradition also assumed a correspondence between heavenly reality and earthly copy. In Solomon's prayer, the temple is a symbol of the wisdom from heaven that enables humans on earth to do what is pleasing to God (9:10).

9:13-18 Humans require wisdom to be saved

The last section returns to the theme of humans as such. It stresses the limits of human knowing. For humans to know and do the divine will, God must take the first step and send wisdom. Reve-

lation is absolutely necessary for humans to be pleasing to God (9:18). The Platonic echo in 9:15, "the corruptible body burdens the soul," is less a statement about the constitution of humans than a psychological statement about ill-informed desire. Wisdom 4:12 is similar: "For the witchery of paltry things obscures what is right, and the whirl of desire transforms the innocent mind." The human race, in short, requires divine intervention if it is to do what is pleasing to God. This conviction provokes the last assertion of the king, people "were *saved* by Wisdom" (9:18; emphasis added). As the prayer began by addressing God as creator, it ends by addressing God as savior. The mention of salvation introduces the next chapter, on the seven plus one wisdom heroes who saved the world in their generations.

In Every Age Wisdom Forms Friends of God and Prophets (10:1-21)

Wisdom 10 is the story of the human race to the formation of Israel ("the holy people," 10:15) told as a series of personalities of the torah who were guided by wisdom. The eight contrasts are sketched with great variety: Adam/his fall (vv. 1-2a), Abel/Cain (vv. 2b-3), Noah/the flooded earth (v. 4), Abraham/the wicked nations (v. 5), Lot/the wicked (vv. 6-9), Jacob/Esau and Laban (vv. 10-12), Joseph/Potiphar's wife (vv. 13-14), and Moses/Pharaoh and enemies (vv. 15-21). Moses, the eighth, stands outside the series, for with him there begins something new, the story of Israel as the child of God. The feminine pronoun for "wisdom" (Greek *hautē*) begins verses 1, 5, 6, 10, 13, 15. The technique can be called midrashic, for scriptural data are elaborated through story to bring out their meaning for a contemporary audience. Sirach 44–50 also regards history as a succession of wisdom-inspired individuals.

Wisdom 10 looks backward and forward in the book. With its seven just individuals delivered by wisdom (vv. 6, 9, 13, 15), it illustrates the deliverance of the prototypical just individual in Wisdom 2 (see esp. 2:18). Wisdom 2 is schematic and abstract and Wisdom 10 is concrete and historical. Wisdom 10 also illustrates Wisdom 7:27, for Wisdom passes "into holy souls from age to age, she produces friends of God and prophets." Finally, Wisdom 10 looks forward in that the eighth wisdom hero, Moses, points to part 3 where Israel, child of God, is protected in the exodus.

10:1-4 Adam, Cain, and Noah

These three individuals are from Genesis 1–11, the time before Abraham. Adam is the first human being and the first sinner. Hence, wisdom "preserved" him and "raised him up" from his transgression (10:1, NAB "fall") and enabled him to exercise the ruling function assigned to human beings in Genesis 1:26-28. Because he murdered his brother Abel (Gen 4:1-16), wisdom destroys Cain, prefiguring the divine destruction of the Canaanites and Egyptians in part 3. Wisdom sees to it that the just Noah saved the earth flooded in punishment for Cain's offense.

10:5-9 Abraham and Lot

Abraham is remembered for his faith, most memorably expressed in his sacrifice of his son Isaac (Gen 22). By this time in Judaism, Abraham's paternal feelings had become a subject of much reflection; wisdom is credited with ensuring that such feelings did not prevent him from carrying out the divine will. Contrary to the less-than-admirable picture of Lot in Genesis 13–19, Lot here is described as a righteous man in contrast to his neighbors and his disbelieving wife. Their strange fates, smoking desert and salt pillar, are a memorial of their folly. "Pentapolis" refers to the five cities of the plain (Gen 14:1-12).

10:10-12 Jacob

The story of Jacob is concise but complete. "[K]ingdom of God," the only Old Testament instance of the phrase familiar from the New Testament, refers to Jacob's dream of the stairway to the heavens, with angels going up and down on it, and the Lord standing beside him and promising him land and descendants (Gen 28:12-15). Jacob's devotion gave him the prize in his struggle with the night visitor (Gen 32:23-33).

10:13-14 Joseph

The story ends when Joseph attains power in Egypt. The midrashic style is highly selective. Nothing is said, for example, about the bitter relationship of the brothers to Joseph or its resolution. Joseph's "scepter of royalty" prefigures the authority the entire people will later have over Egypt.

10:15-21 Moses

The emphasis changes from person to people, for verse 15 is concerned with "the holy people and that blameless race." Moses appears briefly in verse 16, and thereafter the people are the subject or objects of all subsequent verbs. The Red Sea is mentioned explicitly, another place the text makes a specific reference instead of relying on type. The emphasis falls on the same elements of the exodus as will later be singled out in chapters 11 and 15–19, the journey through the sea and through the wilderness. The allusion to the singing of God's praises is to Exodus 15, the Song of the Sea.

THE EXODUS: GOD PROVIDES FOR HIS CHILD ISRAEL

11:1–19:22

Part 1 described in schematic fashion how wisdom, the hidden energy of the world, protects the child of God, and how it becomes visible, especially when the child is threatened by the wicked. Part 2 showed what wisdom is, how to attain it, and its embodiment in a succession of righteous historical personages. Part 3 shifts the perspective by speaking of God rather than of wisdom. God is named as the one who guides and protects the righteous child, Israel. Wisdom is mentioned only twice in part 3, both times in connection with the origin of idolatry (14:2, 5). The shift from wisdom to God is less radical than it might seem, however, for wisdom represents the outreach of God to human beings. Another shift is that the child of God, who was left unidentified in part 1 (2:13, 16; 5:1), is now identified with Israel (18:13; 19:6).

Part 3 also contains two digressions on questions relevant to the theme of God's governance: (1) how could a "philanthropic" (= "people-loving") God destroy the Canaanite inhabitants of Palestine and give their land to Israel? and (2) how ought one evaluate other religions?

Part 3 is the most specifically Israelite part of the book. Up to this point, the author has dealt with "the nations," i.e., the human race generally. Part 1 is about the typical righteous and wicked person, and is addressed to "kings" (= Gentile kings and their subjects). Part 2 is about wisdom and how anyone can attain it, though an Israelite is the model king. Ancient Near Eastern wisdom literature had in view humankind as such; national consciousness did not generally play a large role. In Proverbs, Job, and Ecclesiastes, Israelite heroes and institutions are not mentioned. Only with Sirach (first quarter of the second century B.C.) do specifically Israelite themes appear. Like Sirach, Wisdom of Solomon similarly combines universal and national themes.

The author portrays Israel in its defining moment, the exodus. In ancient Near Eastern cultures, the moment of origin was deemed particularly important, for it was then that the imprint of the creating gods was clearest. In antiquity, people thought of the world as "given" at the beginning, having already the institutions (kingship, temples, marriage, etc.) and systems of the present. To understand a reality, therefore, one had to understand its founding moment. Hence, the founding moment of Israel, the exodus, took on a special importance.

The Israelite exodus is explained in a seemingly strange way—as seven plagues. In the book of Exodus, the exodus is a two-part process involving liberation and formation—the people cease serving Pharaoh in Egypt and begin serving Yahweh in Canaan. The ten plagues in Exodus 7–11 are viewed as a series of battles between Yahweh and Pharaoh in which the tenth, the death of the Egyptian firstborn, is the climax that signals victory for Yahweh. Why did Wisdom of Solomon take a relatively minor part of the story and make it *the* story? One reason is that the book can presume its readers are sufficiently familiar with the story so it can concentrate on one aspect. The major reason, however, seems to be that the plagues show the working of divine justice (rewarding the just and punishing the wicked) as divine control of nature. The judgment scene in 5:16-23 told how God "shall arm creation to requite the enemy" (5:17) and "the universe will war with him against the ungodly" (5:20). The plagues (to which Wisdom adds some wilderness miracles) illustrate God using creation to protect his child (Israel) against the wicked (Egypt).

Wisdom 11:6-14 and chapters 16–19 compare the effects of the seven plagues on Israel and Egypt. In addition, there is another system alongside the seven comparisons—five sketches showing how Egypt's faulty reasoning led them into an act that turned out to have bad consequences for them. Each sketch is introduced by the Greek preposition *anti*, "instead of, in return for" (11:6, 15; 16:2, 20; 18:3). At times, a sketch blends with a comparison.

11:1-5 Protection in the wilderness; the principle of divine activity

The first verse makes the transition from Moses the wisdom hero to Moses the leader of the exodus, which will be the topic henceforth. Before dealing with the exodus plagues, the author mentions the journey through the wilderness, which took place *after* the plagues. In the Bible, the wilderness is the environment most inhospitable to human beings. Miracles are required for humans to live there—bread from heaven (Exod 16:4; Neh 9:15), water from the rock (Num 20:8; Deut 8:15), valleys raised and mountains lowered (Isa 40:4). Great acts of God were required for Israel to survive (Wis 11:2-4). In that extraordinary period, the divine acts that benefited Israel were the same acts that punished their enemies (11:5). Verse 5 is important because it states succinctly the principle that will operate in the seven comparisons: by the act that benefits Israel, God punishes their foes. Actually, the principle has been operative so far in the book up to this point, e.g., in chapters 2 and 5, the death of the just person was at once his entry into eternal life and his killer's condemnation.

Comparisons of Egyptians and Israelites during the Exodus (11:6-14)

11:6-14 Comparison one: flowing water

The first of the seven comparisons (Greek *synkrasis*) between Egypt and Israel is the Nile turned into blood (the first plague, Exod 7:14-25) and the water given to Israel in the wilderness (Exod 17:1-7; Num 20:2-13). In the structure of the book, two digressions (11:15–12:27; chapters 13–15) will subsequently intervene before the second comparison in 16:1-4. Each of the seven comparisons illustrates the principle of divine justice enunciated in 11:5 and operative throughout the book.

The main difference is that the Nile ("the perennial river," 11:6), the sole source of water in Egypt, became undrinkable whereas there was abundant water in the desert. The Nile becoming bloody was punishment for Pharaoh's decree that every Hebrew boy was to be thrown into the Nile (Exod 1:22). The figure of Moses opens and closes the section. Moses is implicitly in Wisdom 11:7a, for he was one of the boys thrown into the Nile (Exod 2:1-4), and explicitly in Wisdom 11:14, for he is the one cast out and abandoned long ago.

The author addresses a problem for anyone making the case that God is just, i.e., punishes the wicked and rewards the good. The problem is that the good often suffer; in this case Israel suffered from thirst in the wilderness. The author's answer (11:9) is that such suffering is only temporary and it has an educational purpose: to teach the people how the wicked were being chastised, i.e., the Egyptians were suffering a deadly drought.

In verse 7, the author begins to address God in the second person singular; previously God was addressed as "you" only in the great prayer in chapter 9. From now on, however, God will frequently be addressed as "you" as the narrator turns the events of the exodus into praise. In 11:10a, God is a "father" to the Israelites and a "stern king" to the Egyptians. Both metaphors relate to the purpose of suffering. "Father," derived from Proverbs 3:12 ("For whom the Lord loves he reproves, and he chastises [like a father] the son he favors"), shows that Israel's sufferings are educational, teaching them about God's rule. "Stern king" shows that Egypt's sufferings are punishment for their wickedness.

The author's interest in psychology is particularly clear in 11:12-14, which explains the emotional discontent that increased the Egyptians' pain—the drinking water they were deprived of by the bloodying of the Nile was freely available to their enemies in the wilderness, the leader they had tried to remove turned out to be successful. The recognition leads to "shame" in that one loses face because what one hoped in has turned out to be false.

The First Digression:
The Moderation and Mercy of God
(11:15–12:27)

The mention of the animals worshiped by the Egyptians in 11:15 provokes the thought that God could, in poetic justice, have employed the most vicious animals ("bears," "fierce lions," 11:17) instantaneously to tear the worshipers apart. Instead, God acted mercifully, allowing time for the repentance that wins mercy and forgiveness (11:21–12:2). The digression then turns to another traditional enemy of Israel, the Canaanites (12:3-11). "The ancient inhabitants of your holy land," though sinners to their core (12:3-11), were not wiped out at one blow, but were "sent wasps as forerunners of your army" (Wis 12:8; cf. Exod

23:28; Deut 7:20; Josh 24:12) to warn them so they would repent. There follows a reflection on divine sovereignty and mercy in Wisdom 12:12-18. The section up to this point is developed with perfect symmetry: the Egyptians (11:15-20) and God's response of mercy rather than immediate punishment (11:21–12:2); the Canaanites (12:3-11) and God's response of mercy rather than immediate punishment (12:12-18). The conclusion of the section is the double lesson Israel should take from these events (12:19-27).

11:15–12:2 Opportunity for repentance of Egypt

The opening preposition, "in return for" (Greek: *anti*), introduces another instance of poetic justice (one is punished by the very thing through which one sins, 11:16). In this sketch, the Egyptians' animal worship (11:15) provokes God to send animals to punish them. The punishment has a point, however—"that they might recognize [God's hand]" (11:16a). God could have sent the most vicious animals, bears or lions, to kill at one stroke (11:17-20), but sent instead the smaller animals of the plagues, frogs (16:1-4; see Exod 8:1-15) and the flies and locusts (16:5-14; see Exod 8:16-32) that hurt but do not kill, allowing the Egyptians time for repentance. One reason for moderation is God's careful, almost mathematically exact, governance (11:20-22). The same notion occurs in other Jewish literature (1 Enoch 72-82; 2 Esdr 4:36-37) and in Hellenistic writings such as Plato's *Laws* 575B and Philo's *On Dreams* 2.193. The second reason is more specifically biblical, and especially dear to the author of Wisdom (1:13-15; 2:22-24)—God's loving commitment to creation, and willingness to give human beings the opportunity to repent and be renewed (11:23–12:2). Not all religious thinkers of the time were so positive regarding God's abiding commitment and the possibility of human renewal. Some Qumran sectarians, for example, viewed outsiders with harshness and suspicion and emphasized divine vengeance.

12:3-18 Opportunity for repentance of Canaan

The author is unusually negative in assessing the conduct of the Canaanites. The reason perhaps is that the Israelite conquest was used in anti-

Jewish polemic of the time as a sign of Jewish injustice and cruelty. The author, understandably, stresses the Canaanite practice of infant sacrifice, attested in Phoenicia, pre-exilic Israel, and the Phoenician colonies in North Africa. Polluted by such conduct, Canaan would be ennobled by "a worthy colony of God's children" (Greek = "children/servants of God" 12:7). Countering pagan criticism, the author emphasizes Israel's God is absolute and above human criticism (12:12-18). Yet the Canaanites, wicked as they were, had the opportunity to repent (12:8-11). It is always interesting to see how a later biblical author interprets an early reference. "Wasps," mentioned in Exodus 23:28 as a messenger of destruction preceding the Israelite armies, is reinterpreted in Wisdom 11:15-16 as a small animal punishing the Canaanites for their animal worship.

12:19-27 The double lesson for Israel

"Your people" (12:19) is contrasted with the people of Egypt and Canaan. "These deeds" are the divine acts that first warned and only afterward inflicted punishment, and giving an opportunity for repentance. The reason for the two-step process is given in verse 19b, literally, "because the just one must be philanthropic [= loving humanity]." God is preeminently just (12:15) and God's actions are "philanthropic" in providing an opportunity for repentance (Greek *metanoia*, 12:19c). God is a teacher, however, whose actions instruct Israel while punishing their enemies (12:21). Israel learns about God by watching God act in history. Like other wisdom books, Wisdom of Solomon puts a premium on learning through the "discipline" of the teacher.

Wisdom 12:23-27 returns to the principles stated at the beginning of the digression (11:15-16)—people are punished through the choices they make (cf. 12:23, 27), and worship of animals brings punishment by means of animals (see 12:24). In keeping with the Platonic philosophical tradition, the author sees virtue as right thinking and vice as faulty knowing. The unjust are foolish (12:24), they go astray on the paths of error and are deceived (12:24). Only at the end do they see and recognize "the true God whom formerly they had refused to know" (v. 27). Inability to see and know the nature of reality is also the fault of the wicked in chapter 2; only when they see the exaltation of the just person whom they persecuted

(Wis 5) do they recognize the true God whose actions they had failed to perceive.

The Second Digression:
False Worship (Wisdom 13–15)

Since the goal of Wisdom of Solomon is to persuade people, especially the Jewish community, of the nobility and truth of Judaism, the author has to point out the defects of other religions. In that market place of ideas, proponents of one religion had to make a case for its superiority over others. The author concentrates on a single theme—the object of worship, evidently presuming that the god one worships is the key to any religion. The author's division of the forms of cultic worship was common in Hellenistic commentary of the time. Philo makes a similar distinction between the worship of natural elements and of idols or animals in *On the Decalogue* 52 and *On the Special Laws* 1:13.

There are three critiques: (1) unreflective nature worship (13:1-9); (2) the worship of images (13:1–15:13); (3) the worship of images and animals (15:14-19). The first and the last are of approximately the same length, whereas the middle section is long and complex. The criticism becomes increasingly severe as the objects of worship become more reprehensible. Those in the first group are "foolish" (13:1), those in the second are "wretched" (13:10), and those in the third are "most stupid of all and worse than senseless" (15:14).

13:1-9 The critique of the philosophers

The critique is concerned with right and wrong knowing, as one might expect in a book in the Platonic tradition. The philosophers' basic fault is that "studying the works [they] did not discern the artisan" (13:1). Though their incorrect knowledge is here judged leniently, it is essentially the same fault as the violent gang in chapter 2 who did not know the just person was the child of God. The great difference between chapters 2 and 13 is that the unknowing philosophers "seek God and wish to find him" (13:6), whereas the unknowing gang does not, and plots to kill the child of God (2:12-20). The faulty knowledge of the philosophers is underscored: they are "in ignorance of God," "did not succeed in knowing," "did not discern" (v. 1), "considered" the elements gods (v. 2), etc. They did not know rightly, however, for they never went beyond sense impressions to reflect that the creator is seen in his works (vv. 1, 3-5). Verse 7 is the core. Having conceded in verse 6 that the philosophers sincerely seek God, the author is precise about their failure, literally translated as, "for, engaged with his works, they search / and are misled by the seeing because what they see is beautiful." To paraphrase, they are misled by over-reliance on sense impressions and by failure to reflect. Wisdom of Solomon repeatedly states an unseen world coexists with the world of daily experience. The philosophers stop at the world of daily experience, seduced by its beauty.

Does the author refer to a specific group who are "in ignorance of God"? The philosopher Philo's similar critique (*On the Decalogue* 52–54) clearly refers to Stoicism. They regarded the world as an enclosed system, and explained it without recourse to Platonic other-worldliness. Stoics were pantheists; god, who guides the world toward good, is present in everything as "spirit," conceived however in corporeal terms, for only the corporeal exists. The Stoics took nature as their guide, and it is easy to see why "natural law" originated with them. Wisdom of Solomon faults them for the philosophical materialism that makes them reject the hidden world advocated by the book. It also faults them for failing to see the universe as *created* by a being outside and greater than it, "the one who is," "the artisan" (13:1). "The one who is" is the same phrase found in Exodus 3:14, "I AM who am."

The kind of critique in this passage is used by Paul in Romans 1:18-23 to indict the Gentiles for failing to worship God: "Ever since the creation of the world, his invisible attributes of eternal power and divinity have been able to be understood and perceived in what he has made. As a result they have no excuse" (Rom 1:20). The body of knowledge that may be obtained by human reason alone is sometimes contrasted with "revealed theology." The distinction was worked out in the Middle Ages and is reflected in a definition of Vatican I in 1869. Reformation theology tends to reject the possibility of natural theology because of what it regards as the incapacity of fallen human nature to grasp such truths.

13:10–15:13 Worshipers of images

Unlike the short and simple first and third sections of the digression, the middle section is long and complex, shaped by a chiastic structure (a pattern where the second half of the argument is a parallel but inverted form of the one that comes before): A. 13:10-19, wooden images; B. 14:1-10, invocation of God, reference to history; C. 14:11-31, chastisement; B'. 15:1-6, invocation of God, reference to history; A'. 15:7-13, clay images.

13:10-19 Wooden images and their makers

The Greek word for this kind of false worshiper literally means "suffering hardship; toiling; wretched." "Wretched" is more severe than "foolish" (13:1), but less severe than the final judgment, "most stupid of all and worse than senseless in mind" (15:14). The first commandment of the Decalogue forbids images: "You shall not have other gods beside me. You shall not make for yourself an idol or a likeness of anything in the heavens above or on the earth below or in the waters beneath the earth; you shall not bow down before them or serve them" (Exod 20:3-5; Deut 5:7-9). The absolute prohibition inspired a vehement polemic against images, e.g., Psalm 115:4-8; Jeremiah 10:1-16; Isaiah 40:18-20; 41:6-7; 44:9-20. This passage draws on that tradition, especially Isaiah 44:9-20.

More blameworthy than the philosophers who worshiped natural phenomena (13:1-9), image-worshipers adore what their hands have made, fashioning inanimate material, gold, silver, stone (13:10), and wood. The last-mentioned, wood, is the author's chief concern in verses 11-19. It is the least permanent material, scrap wood useless for anything else. It is unsuitable as an image of god, for the wood must be laboriously carved simply to make it resemble a human being. When it has attained a human shape, it is utterly passive. Though immovable, people pray to the statue for help; though inanimate, people turn to it for vitality. In brief, image worship is irrational and utterly contrary to the true wisdom espoused by the book.

14:1-10 God, not images, is friend and benefactor to human beings

The topic of the previous section is continued. According to the author, to embark on a sea voyage is a daring act, for one entrusts oneself to a small wooden boat floating on the wild and unpredictable deep. To allay their fears and obtain protection for the voyage, people pray to a wooden image. The text may refer to images of Castor and Pollux, twin heroes in classical mythology, the Dioscuri. Castor was the son of Leda and Tyndareus, and Pollux was the son of Leda and Zeus; the half-brothers were famous for their exploits and devotion to each other. Saint Cyril of Alexandria (d. 444) says that Alexandrians put pictures of the twins to the right and left of prows of ships. How, asks the author (14:1), can one entrust oneself to a wooden image more fragile than the ship that carries it? What actually guides a ship over the threatening sea is not a paltry wooden image, but "your providence, O Father!" (14:3).

The author selects a particularly hazardous enterprise, commercial sailing in the Mediterranean, to show the foolishness of human behavior. Instead of recognizing the one power that can protect and guide them, sailors rather pin their hopes on wooden images that are far more frail than any boat. The author in no way denigrates the trades of shipbuilding or sailing, for wisdom inspires people to practice them (14:2, 5). The world is good (1:14) and intended to be developed. God gives wisdom to humans precisely that they might act wisely even in the most challenging and difficult enterprises. An example of someone successfully entrusting himself to a piece of wood is Noah (14:5-7; see Gen 6–9) who made an ark to escape the flood sent to wipe out the inhabitants of the world. But the wooden image and its maker will not be saved (14:8-10).

Two stylistic points are noteworthy, the address to God in the second person and the designation "Father" for God. The section, like its parallel section in the chiasm (15:1-6), refers to God as "you" (14:3, 5). The section is otherwise in third-person narrative style; the abrupt shift lends intimacy to the passages. Addressing God directly as "Father" develops the metaphor of God as the father who educates his son or disciple by discipline (Prov 3:12). By addressing God as father here, the author assumes the mantle of the just person mentioned in chapter 2 and of Israel that will be explicitly identified as God's child in Wisdom 18:13.

Though 14:7, "blest is the wood through which justice comes about," actually refers to the ark of Noah, some patristic authors took it as a reference to the wood of the cross by which the world was

saved. The Greek word used here, *xulon*, is used for the cross in New Testament passages such as Acts 5:30 and Galatians 3:13.

14:11-31 The origin and effects of image worship

The beginning (14:11-12) and the end (14:30-31) of the passage predict divine judgment on idolaters, for the Scriptures condemn false worship. Between the two sets of verses, the author describes the origin of image worship and the malice it provokes in those who practice it.

To show that images are wrong and pervert created objects to unnatural uses, the author gives a historical sketch of the rise of image worship. Image worship did not exist from the beginning, i.e., it is not "natural." Its origin can be assigned to two sources. It should be noted that in antiquity, writers often sought ultimate explanations in accounts of how a reality appeared for the first time, for the first appearance of something provided a privileged glimpse of its purpose. One origin of image worship was an incident in which a beloved son died prematurely, and the grieving father made an image by which to remember him The image eventually became worshiped as a god (14:15-16). Another source of image-worship was also a specific situation: in a country far from the dwelling of the king, his loyal subjects decided to honor his portrait in lieu of his person. Eager artisans encouraged the trade in images and, lo and behold, the king became a god (14:17-20). The origin of the worship of images is therefore shameful, arising from grief or greed (14:21, see also 14:13-14).

Wisdom 14:22 begins to describe the great evils that come upon idolaters, even though they themselves may not be aware they are suffering. Verse 22 expresses a sentiment remarkably close to a famous comment of the Roman historian Tacitus (56–ca. A.D. 120) on the Roman Empire: "To plunder, butcher, steal, these things they misname empire; they make a desolation and they call it peace" (*Agricola* 30). The following verses show the effects of such an unrecognized "war" upon the "combatants": they fall into corrupt practices such as child-sacrifice and orgies (14:23), adultery and murder (14:34), and a riot of passions and crimes in verses 25-26. The list of vices show that the worship of images is the cause of every evil (14:27). Retribution will come not from the lifeless images, but from the living God who is offended by the people swearing by them (14:29-31).

15:1-6 God, not images, is friend and benefactor to human beings

The section balances 14:1-10, which is also concerned with showing that it is God and not images who benefits the human race. After the grim description of image-worshipers and their depravities, the affectionate second-person address to the living God in 15:1-2 comes as a relief, "But you, our God, are good and true" and "we are yours." The author identifies himself with the people of God, "you, *our* God" (emphasis added). The passage is after all about the one God who is also the God of Israel, and the speaker is a member of this people. As was true in the previous section, the worshiper is transformed by the object of worship, "to know you well is complete justice" (15:3). Worshipers are no longer deceived by the forms and colors that stir up false hopes (15:4-5), which was the case with those venerating images. In sum, 15:1-6 is a warm and enthusiastic restatement of the biblical injunction to worship God alone, without using images. They are also thoroughly compatible with the Platonic philosophic tradition that distinguished earthly form and heavenly reality.

The four divine attributes that the section singles out in verse 1, "good and true, slow to anger, and governing all with mercy," are inspired by a famous passage in Exodus 34:6-7, "So the Lord passed before him and proclaimed, 'The Lord, the Lord, a God gracious and merciful, slow to anger and abounding in love and fidelity, continuing his love for a thousand generations . . .'" The context of the exodus confession was people's apostasy—worshiping the golden calf (an image) and God's decision to destroy them for the violation. When Moses intercedes, God relents and acts with mercy. The scene has influenced the Wisdom passage. Wisdom 14:11-31 described worship of images and the depravity that results (cf. Exod 32:6). Yet the Lord is merciful and loyal, restoring the broken relationship in Exodus 34:6, and here as well.

15:7-13 Clay images and their makers

In the chiastic structure of 13:10–15:13, the denunciation of makers of clay images matches that of makers of wooden images in 13:10-19. Though both sections mention makers of gold and silver images (13:10cd and 15:9cd), their chief concern is wood and clay images, and these materials provide the occasion for the rich ironies of the passages. The potter is implicitly contrasted with the Divine Potter who molds human beings and gives them life (e.g., Gen 2:7; Isa 43:1; 45:7, 9; 49:5; Jer 18:1-11; Sir 33:13). The human potter in contrast makes only lifeless objects. The potter "creates" from the very clay he or she was taken from only a short time before, and will return there soon (15:8). Bedazzled by greed, the potter competes with those who work in gold and silver, forgetting how miserable clay is compared to those precious and enduring metals (15:9). Not surprisingly, ignorance is the root cause of the folly. The potter is satisfied with the inert clay only because "he knew not the one who . . . breathed into him a quickening soul" (15:11). Some vessels are for ignoble purposes, whereas others are for noble uses; the final arbiter of value is the very human being who is also made from clay (15:7)! The ultimate driving force for the whole industry of image making is greed born of the conviction that life has no meaning (15:12). Money determines all. The underlying desperation recalls the attitude of the malicious gang in Wisdom 2:1-9 and 5:8-14. How can such clay figures ever represent the God who created and sustains the entire universe!

15:14-19 The Egyptians, enemies of God's people, venerators of images and animals

The third group, the Egyptians, also failed to know God. They are the worst of all, for they not only adopted other nations' images, but worshiped animals and were "enemies of your people who enslaved them" (15:14b). The epithet applied to them, *aphronestatoi*, "most stupid of all" (v. 14a), is the most biting of all. Like the "foolish" philosophers (13:1-9) and the wretched image venerators (15:10-13), the "most stupid of all" Egyptians are another instance of the ignorant gang that attacked the child of God in chapter 2. None of these three groups truly *knows* God; they think God is materially within creation, or in inert images, or in living animals. The last group does not know God is with the chosen people. The so-called digression is thus thematically related to Part 1 of the book.

The author makes no attempt to understand Egyptian religion sympathetically (nor the other religions in the book, for that matter). Wisdom of Solomon is a tract in the Hellenistic marketplace of ideas: criticize other religions, uphold your own. A defender of image worship might say that the image presents an aspect of the deity without containing it; its aim is to facilitate an encounter between deity and worshiper. The author, however, concentrates only on the dangers of such worship, and attributes the depravity of worshipers to their images.

The mention of image worship returns the reader to 11:15-16, which provoked the digression in the first place, where it is said that the Egyptians were punished for worshiping unknowing serpents and worthless insects. God sent them swarms of unknowing animals in punishment.

Comparisons of Egyptians and Israelites during the Exodus (11:1-14; 16:1–19:22)

The digressions on divine retribution (11:15–12:27) and on false worship (Wis 13–15) have come to an end. The mention of animals in 15:18-19 brings the reader back to the animals (gnats and frogs) of the exodus plagues. The author returns to the exodus, which is presented in the form of seven comparisons. The principle of divine activity that operates in the comparisons has already been stated in 11:5: the act that benefits Israel punishes their foes. Actually, the principle has been operative in the book from its very beginning, for the death of the just person meant entry into eternal life and death for the killers (chs. 2 and 5).

16:1-4 Comparison two: frogs and quails

The critique of animal worship in 15:18-19 provides a transition to the animal passage in 16:1-4. Wisdom 16:1-4 repeats words from the first comparison in 11:1-4, alerting the reader that the comparisons are starting up again, e.g., "punished" in 16:1 and 11:8, 16; "tormented" in 16:1 and 11:9; "swarms" in 16:1 and 11:15, 17; "benefit" in 16:2 and 11:5, 13.

The feeding of the people with quails is told in Exodus 16:13 (in a story otherwise concerned only with manna) and in Numbers 11 where the quail is given to the people dissatisfied with manna. In the Pentateuch and in Psalm 78:26-31

(though not in Ps 105:40), the quails are a curse rather than a blessing, for they bring a plague. Wisdom of Solomon regards it as a pure blessing. The author combines the exodus plagues of small animals, frogs (plague two, Exod 8:1-15), gnats (plague three, Exod 8:16-19), flies (plague four, Exod 8:20-32), and locusts (plague eight, Exod 10:1-20).

The themes of the first comparison are continued. The same thing brings punishment to the ungodly and benefit to God's people. The animals of the Egyptians are too loathsome to eat, whereas the animals of the Israelites, the quails, satisfy their hunger. The brief hunger that Israel felt (Wis 10:3d) is only to remind them of the gnawing want their enemies must endure. God is shown to be utter master of creation, playing it like an instrument (see 5:17-23) to ensure that the divine will is done (see 19:18-22).

16:5-14 Comparison three: flies/locusts and the bronze serpent

The third comparison is developed with considerable freedom. It emphasizes the bronze serpent, which Israelites who had been bitten by poisonous serpents had only to look on to be healed (Wis 16:5-8, 10-11). In contrast, flies (plague four, Exod 8:20-32) and locusts (plague eight, Exod 10:1-20) slew the Egyptians and no remedy was found to save their lives (Wis 16:9). The author is careful to state that those looking upon the bronze serpent were saved not by what they saw, "but by you, the savior of all" (16:7 and see vv. 12-13, 15).

The basis of this treatment is Numbers 21:4-9, the last of the complaint stories in the wilderness journey to the promised land. The people accused the Lord as well as Moses of bringing them into the wilderness to kill them by depriving them of food and water. The Lord sends poisonous serpents to punish them, the people cry out, Moses intercedes successfully, and the Lord provides a solution—a bronze image of a poisonous serpent. Those bitten had only to look at it to be healed. Serpents were associated with healing in antiquity; even today the caduceus, a representation of a staff with two entwined serpents and wings at the top, is a symbol of a physician. Wisdom of Solomon omits any mention of the rebellion that made the bronze serpent a necessary remedy, concentrating exclusively on its healing (Wis 16:10a).

The author interprets the whole episode as a teaching moment, an instance of "discipline" in the terminology of wisdom literature. The Israelites were terrorized "for a short time" (16:6) purely for an educational purpose—to make them aware of divine salvation (16:6 and 11). The bronze serpent is a perfect foil to the locusts and flies whose bites killed the Egyptians. Once again, God uses creation with utter freedom to bring about justice. By one and the same means—animals— the wicked are punished and the righteous are rewarded.

16:15-29 Comparison four: storm/hail and manna

Thunder and hail constitute the seventh plague in Exodus 8:13-35. As the previous comparison began with the benefit to Israel (the bronze serpent), this one begins with the punishment of Egypt, the thunderstorm (Wis 16:16-19, 22). The story concentrates on only one element of the storm, lightning (Exod 9:23, 24), which it calls "fire." The Hebrew word can mean both fire and lightning. Why concentrate on "fire"? Because fire provides the author with an opportunity to show how God changes the nature of things for the sake of justice. Despite the water of the thunderstorm, the fire was intensified (Wis 16:17), but was prevented from destroying the beasts already sent to punish. Wisdom 16:18, which presumes the animals were sent simultaneously rather than successively, is contrary to the Exodus account. The fire was again intensified to destroy Egyptian crops (16:19), but lessened so as not to harm the food of Israel (16:22). The alteration of the nature of fire shows that it is "your word that preserves those who believe in you" (16:26). The author is, as ever, careful to show that God uses created elements but is not identified with them.

The passage begins with the storm that none could escape and that devastated the produce of the land (16:15-19). According to Exodus 9:26, only the land of Goshen, where the Hebrews lived, was spared. That detail seems to have suggested to the author the contrast between the destroyed food ("the produce," Wis 16:19b) of Egypt and the protected food ("food of angels," 16:20) of Israel. Fire destroys the one (v. 19), but not the other (v. 22). The author expands the biblical depiction of manna, asserting that it was capable of taking on any taste (vv. 20-21). "Snow and ice" in verse 22 refers to the manna; it uses the figure of hendiadys (literally, one meaning through two words), "icy snow." Manna is also called snow in Wisdom 16:27 and 19:21. The metaphor comes from Exodus 16:14 where manna is "fine flakes like hoarfrost." In the somewhat strained connection, the author wants readers to marvel at the fire that destroyed the produce of Egypt's land, but left unharmed the ice-like manna, the food of "your children" (16:21a). Writers of the time compared manna to snow, (e.g., Josephus, *Antiquities* 3.1.6). The preservation of the manna from harm also had an instructional purpose, for it reminded Israel that their enemies' food was destroyed (16:22). Verse 24 seeks to explain philosophically the miracle of the fire that burned in water and of the ice-like manna that did not melt in fire. The language about creation being tense and relaxed derives ultimately from Plato, *Republic* 442A and *Phaedo* 86C, 94C and was current among the Stoics. According to the doctrine, the elements of fire and water were transformed by the heightening or lowering of their inherent "tension" (Greek *tonos*); the result was that their usual properties did not appear. Wisdom 16:26 adapts Deuteronomy 8:3 (see Matt 4:4): "[God] therefore let you be afflicted with hunger, and then fed you with manna . . . in order to show you that not by bread alone does man live, but by every word that comes forth from the mouth of the LORD." In another elaboration of the biblical data, Wisdom 16:27 declares that the manna not collected on one day did not remain for the next day because it melted by a single sunbeam.

17:1–18:4 Comparison five: darkness and light

In Exodus 10:21-29 the ninth plague is darkness over all the land of Egypt for three days, though the Israelites had light where they lived. Exodus 10:21 says there was "such intense darkness that one can feel it" and Exodus 10:23 adds that people "could not see one another, nor could they move from where they were."

Wisdom of Solomon expands these details in an elaborate antithesis between the Egyptians and the Israelites. It imagines Israel's captors themselves imprisoned in their dark chambers and terrified by strange noises (18:2-4). They are unable to light a fire to ward off the darkness (17:5). The only lights were momentary bursts which, when they subsided, left people more terrified than before (17:6). The description moves subtly to the psychological effects of darkness—loss of confidence by people who previously had great faith in their spiritual powers (17:7-8) and fear in every aspect of their lives (17:9-10). The author asks why fear spread so quickly and completely through the Egyptian community and answers that their wickedness made them vulnerable (17:11-12). Thick night took away their senses and made them subject to self-imagined terrors, locking them in a prison without bars (17:13-16). People of every class of society (even those who had fled to the desert from debts and hardships, 17:17b) were afflicted so that the pleasant sounds of wind and of birds or the brutal sounds of beasts inspired terror equally (17:17-19). Only the Egyptians had to endure darkness and its psychological devastation; the rest of the world went happily about its business, bathed in light (17:20-21).

After a lengthy description of the punishment inflicted on Egypt, the author turns to Israel (18:1-4) who enjoyed the natural light of day, the flaming fire by night ("the flaming pillar" in v. 3; see Exod 13:21), and, in climactic third place, "the imperishable light of the law" (18:4c). Israel, "your holy ones," enjoyed brilliant light so that even the Egyptians recognized they were favored and called them blest (18:1-2). Verse 4 sums up the comparison—the captors become captives, the captives escape, all this happening through divine mastery over the element of light. There is a deeper divine purpose, that the imperishable light of the law should be given to the world through the agency of Israel (v. 4c).

The promise that the light of the law would be made available to the nations is found in the Bible as early as Isaiah 2:3-4 (= Mic 4:2-3), "Come, let us go up to the LORD's mountain, / to the house of the God of Jacob, / That he may instruct us in his ways, /and we may walk in his paths. / For from Zion shall go forth instruction, / and the word of the LORD from Jerusalem." In the ancient Near East, the sun was hailed as the god of justice. Psalm 19 implicitly compares the torah to the sun, and Sirach 24:32 says that wisdom is found in the torah and shines forth like the dawn. Jewish-Hellenistic and rabbinic literature speak of Israel's obligation to bring the torah to the nations, e.g., Testament of Levi 14:4; 2 Baruch 48:40; 59:2. Inspired by a universalistic conception of the human

race rooted in Hellenistic and biblical ideals, Philo believed Israel to be a model for other nations and its law to be "a law for the world" (*Questions and Answers on Exodus* 2.42).

Wisdom of Solomon develops the biblical story with great rhetorical skill and originality. The story of the plague of darkness is enriched by psychological observation and broadened by symbols of light and darkness.

18:5-25 Comparison six: death of the Egyptian first born and the sparing of Israel

The first-born child plays a large role in the book of Exodus. After the call of Moses in Exodus 3–4, the Lord tells Moses to perform wonders before Pharaoh and say, "Let my son go, that he may serve me. Since you refused to let him go, I will kill your son, your first-born" (Exod 4:23). The high god was thought to have a claim on one's firstborn. One either sacrificed one's child directly or, as in biblical narratives (Gen 22:1-19) and legislation (e.g., Exod 13:1-16; 34:19-20), offered an animal in its place. Exodus 11–12 interpret the killing of the Egyptian first-born as both poetic justice for Pharaoh's refusal to "let my son go" and as an act of obeisance to the Lord.

Wisdom of Solomon interprets the tenth and climactic plague much differently. It sets it within the comparisons: (1) as the Egyptians tried to put to death the infants of the Israelites, God in punishment killed their children (Wis 18:5); (2) the Israelites interpreted it as "the salvation of the righteous and the destruction of their foes" (18:7); (3) God's all-powerful word killed the Egyptian first-born (18:15-19), whereas the plague that briefly touched Israel in the wilderness was stopped by the righteous Aaron (18:20-25).

Moses is the "boy" (Greek *teknon*, Wis 18:5) who is cast off and rescued yet saves his people like the wisdom-endowed individuals in chapter 10. The same Greek word is used for the Israelites in 16:21 (*tekna*, "children"). The "sworn covenants with their ancestors" (18:22) are the promises made to the patriarchs in Genesis, especially those in which God promises to be their God (e.g., Gen 17:8) and be *with* them (e.g., Gen 26:3; 31:3; cf. Ps 105:42-43). "In secret" in Wisdom 18:9 has occasioned much comment. Most probably, it suggests that Israel was already carrying out the rituals of Passover; "the ancestral hymn of praise " refers to the Egyptian Hallel (Psalms 113–118) sung before and after the Passover meal (cf. Matt 26:30 and Mark 14:26). The Egyptians' acknowledgment in Wisdom 18:13 "that this people was God's son" refers back to Wisdom 2 and 5 where the just person afflicted by the wicked is rescued by God and elicits the admission, "See how he is accounted among the heavenly beings!" (5:5). The impressive description of the descent of the all-powerful word from heaven's throne in 18:14-16 may owe something to classical descriptions of Athena leaping from the brow of Zeus. It also resembles the description of the powerful word of God in Hebrews 4:12.

"The blameless man" in 18:21 is Aaron, whose offering of incense among the people saved the people from the plague that was just beginning (Num 17:6-15): "standing there between the living and the dead. And so the scourge was checked" (Num 17:13). The reference to Aaron's robe on which was emblazoned the whole world, and the glories of the fathers carved in four rows upon the stones (Wis 18:24) elaborate Exodus 28, which is concerned with the vestments of the chief priest (Aaron). Exodus 28:9-10 prescribes that the ephod (a long vest) have two onyx stones inscribed with the names of the sons of Israel in the order of their birth, and Exodus 28:15-21 prescribes that the "breastpiece of decision" (a purse holding sacred lots) have four rows of stones inscribed with the names of the sons of Israel, i.e., the twelve tribes. The "crown" in Wisdom 18:24c, described in Exodus 28:36-38, is a golden rosette attached to the front of the high priest's turban. The priest represents the people and carries them into the presence of the Lord. The inscribed names of the tribes are sufficiently powerful to make the instigator of the desert plague flee; to disturb further the holy children would incur divine wrath (Wis 18:25). The phrase "on his full-length robe was [depicted] the whole world" (18:24) represents a Stoic-Cynic idea that the universe is a temple. Philo also has the idea in *On the Life of Moses* 2:117-135; Josephus mentions it in *Antiquities* 3:7.7; 3.7.5: the priestly robe is a likeness and copy of the universe, and the twelve stones reflect the zodiac symbolizing the four seasons, so that the high priest carries an image of the All.

The emphasis is on death of the Egyptian firstborn as retaliation for the attempt to kill the infant Moses. The holy priest Aaron stopped the incipient plague in the wilderness, but no one could stop the horrible plague in Egypt. Thus does God control the universe to punish the wicked and reward the just.

19:1-9 Comparison seven: drowning of the Egyptian in the Red Sea and the passage of Israel through the Red Sea

Exodus 14–15 tells of Israel's flight through the Red Sea and the drowning of the Egyptian pursuers. The Egyptians, at first numb from the death of their children, begged the Israelites to leave. Changing their minds, they pursued them, only to be struck down by the massive waters obedient to the Lord's command. In Wisdom 19:1-9, the antithesis of Egypt and Israel is not sharply drawn; the reader is left to infer the drowning of the Egyptians from verses 3-5. There are two emphases. One is the marvelous crossing and subsequent journey of "your children" (19:6), and the other is "a compulsion" (19:4; Greek *anagkē*, lit. "necessity") that drove the Egyptians to self-destruction. The author needs only to remind the reader that the principle of poetic justice is part and parcel of the holy people's history, and that creation preserves "your children unharmed" (19:6) as promised in 5:16-23 and 19:18-22. The people "ranged about like horses, and bounded about like lambs" (19:9), a reference to Psalm 114:3-4, which celebrates the crossing of the Red Sea, "the Jordan turned back. / The mountains skipped like rams; / the hills, like lambs."

In the seventh and final comparison, the Egyptians are finished as a threat to the holy people, for their young are destroyed (18:5-25) and their army wiped out (19:1-5). The Israelites are on their way to the promised land (19:7-9). There remains only a summary and an explicit statement that the experience of the exodus generation will be the experience of Israel for all future time.

19:10-22 Summary of the history, final critique of the wicked (Egyptians), and the statement that God glorifies his people at all times and places

The people now remember ("were still mindful," v. 10) the reversal of expectations in Egypt and the wilderness. Instead of the young of animals, the land produced gnats; instead of fishes, the river produced frogs; and the wilderness produced a new kind of bird, the quail from the sea. The comments generalize the specific reversals, implying that they are only a harbinger of the alterations of nature that will be made for the holy people. The author uses a favorite word "instead of" (*anti*) twice in verse 10 (cf. 7:10: 11:6, 15; 16:2, 20; 18:3).

Non-Jewish Hellenistic writers such as Diodorus and Hecataeus of Abdera accused the Jews of hatred of humankind on the grounds that they kept themselves apart by dietary laws and other customs. The Jewish philosopher Philo responded with spirit to these charges and, like Wisdom of Solomon, threw the charge back to the Egyptians (*On the Life of Moses* 1:36). Wisdom 19:13-17 does the same, comparing the Egyptians with the men of Sodom who attempted to rape the two angelic strangers despite their being under the protection of Lot. In punishment the men were struck with blindness and their city was destroyed (Gen 19). The men of Sodom come off much better than the Egyptians, for the latter at least were dealing with strangers, people they did not know (Wis 19:13-15). The Egyptians, in contrast, knew the Israelites full well, had profited from their work (Gen 41:37-57; 47:13-26), and had earlier welcomed them (Gen 47:1-12). They were without excuse, therefore, and rightly suffered the blindness inflicted also on the men of Sodom (Wis 19:17; cf. Gen 19:11; Exod 14:20). In keeping with the typifying tendency in the book, the acts are not named.

The last section of the book (vv. 18-21) expresses the wondrous guidance of God's people in the language of Stoic cosmology, as Stoicism and Epicureanism were also ways of life, and had explanations of the physical world (cosmologies) from which ethical principles were derived. Wisdom 19:18 apparently uses an analogy from music (varying the key while holding to the melody) to illustrate how elements within the universe can be altered without interrupting the orderly functioning of the universe. According to the Stoic cosmology (already referred to in 16:24), the tension (*tonos*) of the elements was heightened or lowered affecting their make-up, just as the tension of a musical mode is varied by the notes within it. Philo of Alexandria uses similar argumentation in describing the miracle of manna, claiming that the heavenly food, like the created world, was begun by God on the first of six days. As God called up his most perfect work, the world, out of non-being into being, so he called up abundance in the desert, changing the elements (see Wis 19:18a) to meet the pressing need of the occasion (*On the Life of Moses* 2:266-267).

Verses 19-21 illustrate the transposition of elements: "land creatures were changed into water creatures" refers to the Israelites crossing through the Red Sea (Exod 14–15 and Wis 19:1-9); "those that swam" were the frogs (Exod 8:1-15 and Wis 16:1-4); "fire" is the author's term for lightning that burned the Egyptians even in water (Exod 9:23-24; Wis 16:17); "flames" that spared and were gentle refers to Wisdom 16:18, 22.

The final verse is a doxology (a formula giving praise to God), common in Jewish religious literature and at the end of wisdom books. Each of the five books of the Psalter ends with a doxology (Pss 41:14; 72:18-19; 89:53; 106:48; 150). The verse is also a fine summary of the book.

THE BOOK OF

SIRACH

Jeremy Corley

INTRODUCTION

Title and author

The author's Hebrew name is Yeshua Ben (son of) Sira, which in the Greek translation became Jesus son of Sirach (50:27). Hence in Hebrew the book is known as the Wisdom of Ben Sira, and in Greek as Sirach. In Latin the work is called Liber Ecclesiasticus (the church book), because in the early Christian centuries it was widely used for instructing converts. This commentary employs the name Ben Sira for the author, and Sirach for the book.

Ben Sira composed his Hebrew work in Jerusalem, which plays a central role in his writing. He describes wisdom coming to dwell in Jerusalem (24:10-11) and pleads for divine mercy on the holy city (36:18-19). Furthermore, his depiction of the temple liturgy under the high priest Simeon II (50:5-21) appears to be the work of an eyewitness.

Ben Sira probably ran some kind of educational establishment in the city (51:23), though scholars dispute exactly when schools arose in ancient Israel. It is possible that Ben Sira was one of the "scribes of the temple" mentioned by Josephus (*Antiquities* 12.3.3 #142). The description of the scribe in 39:1-11 provides a kind of self-portrait of the author.

Date and place of composition

Scholars agree that Ben Sira's book dates from 195–175 B.C. Because the poem praising the high priest Simeon II speaks of him in the past tense (50:1-4), it must have been completed after his death around 196 B.C. Moreover, the Greek prologue speaks of the arrival of Ben Sira's grandson in Egypt in 132 B.C., which suggests that the author was active about half a century earlier. Additionally, there is no indication of the religious turmoil that followed the accession of the Seleucid king Antiochus IV Epiphanes, who reigned from 175 to 164 B.C. (1 Macc 1:10-64). Thus we may estimate Ben Sira to have been born soon after 250 B.C. and to have died around 175 B.C.

Throughout the sage's lifetime, the Holy Land was under the control of Greek-speaking rulers, first the Ptolemies of Egypt until the Battle of Panium (200 B.C.), and then the Seleucids of Syria. For most of that time the people of Jerusalem were heavily taxed, though a decree of the Seleucid king Antiochus III (around 198 B.C.) reduced the city's tax burden for a while (Josephus, *Antiquities* 12.3.3-4 ##138-146). Since Greek language and culture were dominant in civic life, some Jews wishing for social advancement were tempted to abandon their ancestral faith and instead seek favor from the pagan authorities.

Canonical status

The grandson's Greek translation of the book was included in the Septuagint, which became the Bible of the early Greek-speaking church. From there it was translated into Latin. Its canonicity for Roman Catholics was defined at the Council of Trent (1546), whereas many Protestant reformers followed St. Jerome and the rabbinic tradition in rejecting it as uncanonical. The fact that the Greek version of the work became popular in the Christian Church may have contributed to its dropping out of usage in rabbinic Judaism. According to the Jerusalem Talmud (tractate *Sanhedrin* 28a), its use was excluded by Rabbi Akiba (d. ca. A.D. 132).

Because some rabbis spoke against the book, the Hebrew text almost vanished, except for a few proverbs quoted in rabbinic writings. Nevertheless, ancient Jewish respect for the book is evident from the Hebrew copies that have survived. The Dead Sea sites of Qumran and Masada have yielded some Hebrew fragments from before A.D. 70. Other Hebrew manuscripts from the tenth to the twelfth centuries A.D., copied by a group of non-rabbinic Jews called Karaites, were preserved in the storeroom (Genizah) of a Cairo synagogue. In all, the surviving Hebrew fragments cover two-thirds of the book.

Greek and Latin additions

Over time, scribes copying the Greek and Latin versions added supplementary lines, which often came to be added to the verse numbering. For example, some Greek manuscripts of the opening poem (1:1-10) include additions, which many modern translations place in footnotes or omit. The New American Bible has left out all these additions from the main text.

Because the Second Vatican Council urged Catholics to return to the original scriptural texts (*Dei Verbum* 22), the New American Bible has omitted material that seems like later Christian (or Jewish) scribal additions or changes, made to "improve" or "update" Ben Sira's teaching. One example concerns the afterlife. Like other Hebrew biblical authors before him (Isa 38:18; Pss 6:6; 115:17), Ben Sira had no clear expectation of the afterlife (10:11; 17:27-28). Thus, the Hebrew text of 7:17 says: "More and more, humble your pride; / what awaits mortals is worms." To bring in a reference here to punishment after death, the Greek translation reads: "The punishment of the impious is fire and worms."

Place in the wisdom tradition

The ancient Near East had a long tradition of scribal education, especially in Egypt. Wisdom literature is the term used to denote texts probing philosophical questions or offering advice on how to behave. Hebrew wisdom literature includes the behavioral admonitions of the book of Proverbs and the search into life's mysteries provided in the book of Job. Closer in time to Ben Sira, the skeptical author of Ecclesiastes sought a purpose in life, while after Ben Sira's time the writer of the book of Wisdom adapted traditional Israelite insights for a Greek-speaking audience. Like the book of Proverbs, Sirach consists entirely of poetry, except for the grandson's prologue.

Sources

Ben Sira's ideas and language suggest familiarity with earlier biblical writings. For instance, the Praise of the Ancestors (44:1–50:24) makes numerous allusions to the Hebrew Scriptures, while many of the ethical sayings develop thoughts found in the book of Proverbs. Because Ben Sira builds on the teaching of previous biblical authors, the commentary provides many cross-references to other scriptural texts. References not naming the book are to Sirach.

It is likely that Ben Sira also had some direct or indirect knowledge of some non-Jewish ancient writings. For instance, 38:24-34 adapts an ancient Egyptian wisdom theme, the *Satire of the Trades*, while other passages echo the thought of a sixth-century B.C. Greek poet named Theognis.

Structure

Whereas most of the book of Proverbs consists of diverse aphorisms, the outer sections (Prov 1:1–9:18 and 30:1–31:31) are comprised of longer poems. Ben Sira's book is generally made up of longer passages on a particular theme. Significant for the structure of his book are eight poems focusing on finding wisdom (1:1-10; 4:11-19; 6:18-37; 14:20–15:10; 24:1-33; 32:14–33:18; 38:24–39:11; 42:15–43:33). Many scholars regard these poems as introducing the eight major sections of 1:1–50:24.

Influence on the New Testament

Ben Sira had a widespread, though often indirect, influence on the New Testament. Thus, Matthew's sermon on the church calls for humility, offers advice on fraternal correction, and appeals for forgiveness (Matt 18:4, 15-17, 21-35), echoing three themes of Ben Sira (3:17-18; 19:13-17; 27:30–28:7). Luke's parables of the rich fool and the unjust judge (Luke 12:16-21; 18:1-8) develop ideas found in Ben Sira (11:18-19; 35:17-21). Finally, the letter of James treats topics like divine testing and control of the tongue (Jas 1:12-15; 3:1-12) that already occur in Ben Sira (2:1-6; 5:9-14).

Problems for modern readers

Over and above Christian reservations about Ben Sira's lack of belief in the afterlife, modern readers may well question some of the sage's attitudes, which were often based on social views from his time. Most regrettably, he exhibits prejudice against women (25:13-26). His misogyny builds on warnings in ancient wisdom literature addressed to young men about the allures of women (Prov 5:1-14; 7:6-27). His attitude may be explained (but not excused) by his professional setting in the shadow of the male-dominated Jerusalem temple, while an additional factor influencing him was the exclusion of women from many aspects of Greek civic life.

COMMENTARY

GRANDSON'S PROLOGUE

Ben Sira's grandson supplied a prologue to his Greek translation of his grandfather's Hebrew work, just as Luke provided a prologue to the third gospel (Luke 1:1-4).

In the first paragraph, the grandson adopts a division of the Hebrew Bible into three parts, matching the subsequent rabbinic classification of law, prophets, and writings (compare Luke 24:44).

Because those who love learning have the duty to teach what they have learned (39:8), Yeshua Ben Sira (in Greek: Jesus son of Sirach) composed his book for the benefit of others (33:18). His purpose was that his audience would not feel pressured to seek wisdom in pagan Greek culture, but would remain steadfast in following the law of Moses (2:15-16; 42:1-2).

In the prologue's second paragraph, the grandson frankly admits the difficulty of translating from Hebrew to Greek, and there are many cases in Sirach where the Greek translation differs from the Hebrew (see notes on 4:10; 7:17; 48:11; 50:24). He is aware of the early Greek versions of several books of the Hebrew Bible. These translations, known as the Septuagint, were made in Alexandria in the third and second centuries B.C.

The prologue's third paragraph recounts the grandson's work of translation. The thirty-eighth year of the Egyptian king Ptolemy VII, known as Physcon Euergetes II, was 132 B.C. After his arrival in Egypt (presumably Alexandria) the translator found a copy of some valuable teaching, perhaps biblical books in Greek or other wisdom writings. Thereupon he felt obliged to translate his grandfather's work into Greek, not least because Alexandria had many thousands of Greek-speaking Jews.

The grandson's "many sleepless hours" may have covered more than fifteen years, since the Greek of the final paragraph suggests that King Euergetes (d. 117 B.C.) was already dead when the prologue was written. "Those living abroad" refers to the Jews dispersed outside Palestine, including those in Egypt.

UNDERSTANDING WISDOM

Sirach 1:1–4:10

1:1-10 Where to find wisdom

Ben Sira begins his book with a clear assertion: wisdom is not primarily an achievement of human endeavor, but rather a gift from God (1 Kgs 3:9; Wis 9:1-4).

In Ben Sira's time, the cosmological questions of 1:2-3 were important, because of a double threat to Israel's traditional faith in the one Creator. The twin worldviews threatening traditional Judaism were the apocalyptic speculations of esoteric Jewish circles and the intellectual currents of Greek philosophy. In this context, Ben Sira's intention was that investigation of the world should be undertaken with a humble attitude toward God, based on an acceptance of divine revelation in the Torah (39:6-8).

Ben Sira views wisdom as preceding all creation (1:4), while other texts equate the divine wisdom with God's creative word (Ps 33:6; Prov 3:19). Having been formed by the Creator (Prov 8:22), wisdom is not a goddess or source of creation in place of the one God. The main text does not have 1:5 or 1:7, because these verses are later scribal additions, not found in the earliest manuscripts.

The question about where to locate wisdom (1:6) finds an answer in 1:8-10. Ben Sira directs his students' attention to the Lord, who is both wise and to be feared (Prov 1:7; 2:6). Since God measured out wisdom originally in the Creation (Job 28:27), the best way to find wisdom is to be attentive to God the Creator.

Though wisdom is in principle accessible to all humanity, God gives it especially to "those who love him" (1:10). While this phrase could apply to anyone, it alludes especially to Moses' great commandment to Israel in the *Shema*: "You shall love the Lord, your God" (Deut 6:5). Here, therefore, it may refer particularly to Israel, which had been commanded to love God.

Besides intellectual knowledge, wisdom also involves the practical action of keeping the Torah (Deut 4:6). Thus, the poem that began with a universal scope (heaven, earth, the abyss) ends with a special focus on Israel's calling to observe the law of Moses. Only by following revealed truth can a person find God's wisdom.

1:11-30 What the fear of God offers

Having moved from intellectual wisdom (1:2-3) to practical wisdom as enshrined in the Torah (1:10), Ben Sira develops a picture of wise conduct, expressed as fear of God. This is not a craven submission, but a respectful reverence toward God (Prov 2:1-5). It also includes the idea of following one's conscience. On the basis of Deuteronomy 10:12 Ben Sira equates fearing God with loving him (2:15).

The poem begins with the assertion that the fear of the Lord means "glory and exultation" (1:11). All cultures have their own sense of honor, but this sense was acute in many parts of the Hellenistic world, including the Palestine of Ben Sira's day. Elsewhere the sage insists that one gains honor not by military exploits but by obeying God's law (4:20-21; 42:2).

Ben Sira treats fear of God at the start of his book because the fear of the Lord is the beginning of wisdom (Ps 111:10; Prov 1:7; 9:10). While other good things in life may bring more immediate pleasures, the fear of the Lord gives lasting joy (40:26). The sage follows earlier biblical teaching (Prov 3:2; Deut 30:20) in promising a "long life" on earth to the God-fearer (1:12).

According to 1:14-21, the fear of the Lord is not only the beginning of wisdom but also wisdom's fullness and crown and root. Because wisdom is formed with the faithful in the womb, it belongs innately to the Israelites as their heritage (24:8), and hence Ben Sira's students do not need to seek Greek philosophy to gain true understanding. Rather, wisdom is the inheritance of the devout, such as those listed in the Praise of the Ancestors (44:1–50:24). Through fear of the Lord the believer will receive wisdom's rich harvest and the gift of health (6:19; 34:17-20), as the book of Proverbs already promises (Prov 3:7-8; 8:19). According to 1:20, wisdom's root grows up to produce branches (14:26; 24:16), equivalent to long life on this earth (Prov 3:2).

The statement that "the fear of the Lord turns back all anger" (1:21) completes 1:14-20 and provides a link to the mention of anger in 1:22. Because human wrath does not accomplish God's righteousness (Prov 15:18; Jas 1:20), Ben Sira urges his students to control their anger. The self-controlled person will receive public praise for being patient (Prov 14:29).

Sirach 1:25-27 links wisdom, the commandments, and fear of God (Prov 2:5-6; Deut 4:5-6; 10:12-13). The fear of the Lord entails "faithfulness and humility," such as were shown by Moses (45:4). In 1:28-30 the sage recommends a sincere and reverent attitude toward God, because duplicity will lead to embarrassment. Ben Sira cautions his students against the double path of trying to remain faithful to Israel's God while accepting all the values of the pagan Hellenistic culture. Seeking to gain status in this way will lead to a disgraceful downfall (Prov 5:12-14; 16:18).

2:1-18 Be prepared for testing

After introducing the themes of wisdom and fear of God, the sage immediately warns that the way of God's wisdom can involve testing. This motif occurs elsewhere in the Bible (Gen 22:1;

Deut 8:2). In Ben Sira's view, wisdom is acquired at the cost of trials, but in the end produces blessings (4:17-18; 6:24-31).

The poem begins bluntly (2:1): the student is to be ready for trials (Acts 14:22). Already in the Jerusalem of Ben Sira's day, it was hard for the worshiper of Israel's God to resist the pressure to follow pagan Greek practices. This pressure increased after 175 B.C., following the accession of King Antiochus Epiphanes, who banned many practices of the Jewish religion (1 Macc 1:41-64). Christian readers might also recall Jesus' words about taking up the cross and following him (Mark 8:34). An illustration of 2:3-6 would be the story of Job's endurance of suffering (Job 1:1–2:10; Jas 5:11). The testing of human beings by trials can have a refining effect, as with gold in the furnace (Prov 17:3; Wis 3:6). Trust in God will be the prelude to divine help (Ps 37:3-6; Prov 3:5-6).

In 2:7-9 Ben Sira thrice urges his students to have faith and hope in God (1 Pet 1:21), so that like the redeemed Israelites they may have lasting joy (Isa 51:11). Sirach 2:10 uses three rhetorical questions to appeal to the past experience of the people of Israel (Deut 32:7). Ben Sira's confidence in divine help builds on the experience of the psalmist (Ps 34:8; 37:25). Even the sufferer who feels abandoned by God (Ps 22:2; Mark 15:34) will eventually be rescued (Ps 22:24-25; Acts 2:31-32). To be sure, Ben Sira's words of encouragement do not fully explain the mystery of suffering, as experienced by victims of genocide or famine, for instance. The sage boldly repeats the biblical proclamation that God is merciful, as first made to Moses (Exod 34:6) and often recalled since (Ps 111:4; Jas 5:11).

Ben Sira then launches into a threefold woe, addressed to the faithless (2:12-14). The fainthearted tread a double path by claiming to be members of the Israelite community yet also following pagan ways. Unlike the truly God-fearing (34:19), such faithless people will have nowhere to hide on the day of God's visitation (Wis 5:14-16). The devout person lovingly reverences God by humbly keeping the divine law and enduring trials (Deut 8:2; 10:12-13).

As a model for accepting suffering (2:18), Ben Sira alludes to David's choice to fall directly into God's hands by accepting a plague sent to punish Israel (2 Sam 24:14). Though God is great (18:5), God's mercy is just as great (Wis 11:21-23).

3:1-16 Honor toward parents

Because wisdom involves obeying the divine law (1:26), Ben Sira urges his students to obey the precept to honor father and mother (Exod 20:12; Deut 5:16). The commandment covers not only young children's obedience to their adult parents, but also the respectful care shown by adults toward their aged parents (Mark 7:10-12). Ben Sira lived in a traditional society where respect was due to parents and older persons (7:27-28; 25:3-6).

Sirach 3:2-6 recalls the biblical promise that obedience to parents will lead to a long life (Exod 20:12; Deut 5:16). Like almsgiving, caring for one's father is a good work that brings atonement for one's sins (3:3, 30), just as care of one's mother is a sort of financial investment (Tob 4:8-9) for the future. Moreover, those who honor their father will receive the blessing of their own children (Ps 128:1-3), and God will hear their prayer because they have fulfilled their duty (Prov 15:29). God-fearing children will serve their parents like slaves (3:7), an exaggerated way of expressing the devotedness of the care (7:27-28).

According to 3:8, those honoring their parents will be blessed for obeying the divine law (Deut 28:1-2). A blessing from parents can cause a family to take root and flourish (Prov 12:3). One is not to take pleasure in the disgraceful condition of a parent (3:10-11), because the glory of children is their parents (Prov 17:6). Indeed, cursing one's parents is self-destructive (Prov 20:20). Hence 3:12-16 urges proper filial care of senile parents, who deserve respect even in their infirmity (Prov 23:22; Tob 4:3). Kindness to aged parents counterbalances one's earlier sins, whereas despising parents is an offense against God (Prov 19:26; 30:17).

3:17-29 A humble attitude

While Moses was praised for his meekness (Num 12:3) and Proverbs inculcates a modest attitude (Prov 11:2; 15:33), Ben Sira makes humility one of his special hallmarks (1:27; 7:17), thereby anticipating Jesus' way of humility (Matt 18:1-4).

Sirach 3:17 urges the student to walk humbly (Mic 6:8), since paradoxically humility will lead to honor (Luke 14:11). The greater the humility that is shown, the more the favor that will be received from God. Ben Sira reminds readers that God's power is great, far beyond the power of any human being (18:5). God is glorified by the humble, because they know their own weakness (2 Cor 12:9). Some late manuscripts add a comment in 3:19.

Ben Sira's counsel (3:21-24) to avoid setting one's sights too high draws on Psalm 131:1. In the original context, the marvels beyond human knowledge may refer both to apocalyptic revelations and to the wonders of Greek science. Rather than attending to matters too great, students are invited to pay attention to what has been shown to them, namely, God's law (Deut 29:28).

Just as the eye needs to be open to receive light (3:25), so the mind must be open to receive wisdom (Luke 11:34-36). The person who stubbornly risks danger will come to a bad end (Prov 28:14). As in Wisdom 12:10, Ben Sira regards the arrogant person as the offshoot of an evil plant (40:15-16).

3:30–4:10 Principles of social justice

The opening point that almsgiving can atone for sin occurs elsewhere in the Bible (Dan 4:24; Tob 12:9). According to Ben Sira (7:1; 27:26-27), kindness produces its own reward, but evil recoils on the head of its practitioners (Tob 14:10-11; Prov 26:27). In fact, the sage holds the traditional Israelite view that good deeds are rewarded and evil deeds punished (Deut 28:1-68; Prov 11:8).

In 4:3 Ben Sira urges his students not to delay their giving to the needy (Prov 3:28), because those who attend to the plea of the poor will be like God (Ps 22:25; Tob 4:7). The one who ignores the needs of the destitute will become the victim of their curse (Exod 22:21-23; Prov 28:27), whereas the helper of the poor will receive their blessing (Job 31:20). Since one Maker created rich and poor (Prov 22:2; Job 31:15), all persons deserve respect (Prov 14:31).

According to 4:9, those who achieve positions of responsibility are to use their power to rescue the oppressed (Ps 82:2-4; Prov 31:8-9). If the Most High is "father of the fatherless, defender of widows" (Ps 68:6), one becomes like God by assisting these persons in their need (Job 29:16). Thereby a person becomes a true child of God (Ps 82:6; Luke 6:35). Whereas the Hebrew text speaks of God delivering a generous person from death (Tob 14:10-11), the Greek version of 4:10d employs maternal imagery for God: "He will love you more than your mother does" (cf. Isa 49:15; 66:13).

USING WISDOM PERSONALLY

Sirach 4:11–6:17

4:11-19 Learning wisdom

The poem opening the second section of Ben Sira's book presents the rewards of wisdom while also acknowledging the hardships involved in acquiring it. Ben Sira calls the recipients of personified wisdom "her children" (Luke 7:35).

Wisdom's basic reward is "life" (4:12), as in Proverbs 8:35. Ben Sira echoes the choice between life and death that Moses placed before the Israelites (Deut 30:15). The point of 4:12 is not only that the wise person will avoid dangerous situations (3:26; 9:13), but also that wisdom itself is a source of life (Prov 3:18). In 4:14 the sage seems to liken wisdom's servants to those serving God's sanctuary in the Jerusalem temple (24:10). According to 4:15, one who understands wisdom will judge nations (Wis 3:8; 1 Cor 6:2).

Ben Sira develops the female personification of wisdom in 4:17-19. The hardships of wisdom begin with the difficult task of going around with her while she seems a stranger. Then she will probe the student with trials, making the learner choose between wise and foolish actions. But eventually, when the learner's heart is filled with wisdom, she will reveal her secrets.

4:20-31 Honesty

By keeping from evildoing, a person will avoid shame, the disgrace dreaded by people in the Hellenistic world (5:13–6:1; 41:16–42:8). Sirach 4:21 distinguishes a wrongful shame (dependent on the opinions of others and leading to sin) from a modest shame (a careful avoidance of sin which in fact leads to honor). In 4:23 Ben Sira insists that a false sense of shame should not hold people back from uttering their wisdom at the right moment (20:30-31).

Because truth is like an unstoppable stream (4:25-26), it is pointless to cover up one's sinfulness. There is no disgrace in acknowledging guilt, though ignorant folly is a cause for real shame. The sage's admonition to fight for what is right, even to the point of death (4:28), was heeded a few years later by the Maccabean martyrs (2 Macc 6:18-20; 7:1-2). Sirach 4:31 commends giving rather than receiving (Acts 20:35).

5:1–6:4 Against presumption and insincerity

Sirach 5:1-3 warns against arrogant self-sufficiency. Dependence on wealth is insecure (Luke 12:15; 1 Tim 6:17), while human desires can lead a person astray. In 5:3 the sage urges a humble recognition that God is more powerful than we are (1 Cor 10:22).

It is wrong to boast if no punishment has followed one's sin (5:4), because God can show wrath as well as mercy toward humanity (16:11). Indeed, sinners are regarded as deserving divine anger (Rom 1:18). Hence the sage solemnly warns against postponing repentance, lest one suddenly become a victim of God's displeasure (5:7). Moreover, wealth gained by unjust means will be useless if God decides to bring punishment (Prov 10:2).

Using images from agriculture and travel, 5:9 advocates sincere and consistent speech. Common sense entails being quick to hear and slow to respond (5:11), an insight that the letter of James borrows from Ben Sira (Jas 1:19). Sirach 5:12 employs graphic imagery to inculcate silence when one has nothing sensible to say. Speech may bring honor or dishonor, and the tongue can be a person's downfall (Prov 18:21). Like thieves, the double-tongued deserve disgrace (Prov 18:7).

The final passage (6:2-4) warns of the danger of lustful desire which, if not controlled, can overwhelm someone. Sirach 6:3 compares such a person with a tree (Jer 17:5-6) destroyed by fire. Unrestrained desire can make people the laughing stock of their enemies.

6:5-17 The value of true friendship

Ben Sira has much to say on friendship (9:10-16; 22:19-26; 27:16-21; 37:1-6). While the book of Proverbs includes scattered sayings on the topic (Prov 17:17; 19:4-7; 27:10), Ben Sira collects his thoughts into longer passages.

Polite speech is a prerequisite of friendship (6:5), since a rude response will spoil any chance of making friends (Prov 16:21; 22:11). Yet though everyone deserves a polite greeting, few deserve to be trusted. Rather than trusting a person instantly, one should test the genuineness of the friendship (Matt 7:16), particularly by evaluating the friend's behavior in one's adversity.

The need for testing a potential friend is elaborated in 6:8-13. The sage's caution is based on the unreliability of fair-weather friends, who are happy to be table partners, but who run away at a time of need and even disclose confidences. Apparently Ben Sira had been betrayed by his former friends, and had been saved only with God's help (51:2-3). Hence, besides keeping away from enemies (as expected), one should also (unexpectedly) be on guard in dealings with friends.

After the negative tone of 6:8-13, the sage describes the loyal friend (6:14-17). The image of "sturdy shelter" suggests a good friend's protective quality. Such a person is a priceless treasure; in 26:15 the sage uses similar language for the chaste wife. Sirach 6:16 states that the God-fearing person will find such loyal friends, because like is attracted to like (13:15-16).

APPLYING WISDOM SOCIALLY

Sirach 6:18–14:19

6:18-37 Wisdom's blessings

The book's third part opens with a poem on the hardships and benefits of gaining wisdom. Students need to acquire wisdom in their youth through a disciplined approach to life (25:3; 31:22). Sirach 6:19 uses the imagery of sowing and reaping (2 Cor 9:6; Gal 6:7-9). A rich harvest results from the effort given to acquiring wisdom, though the fool regards discipline as a heavy burden to be cast aside. As the sage notes elsewhere (2:4-5; 4:17), the hardship of discipline is self-evident (Prov 12:1; Heb 12:11).

Sirach 6:24-25 compares this wise discipline to a yoke and fetters. Later rabbis spoke of the yoke of the law of Moses (*Mishnah Aboth* 3.5), while Jesus invites his followers to take his yoke upon themselves (Matt 11:29). The quest for wisdom is to be undertaken with one's whole soul and strength, like loving God (Deut 6:5). To find wisdom, a person must first seek it (Matt 7:7). Once found, wisdom should be held firmly (Prov 4:13), because it will eventually provide contentment (15:6).

Though discipline seems like fetters and bonds for a fool (6:29-30), it represents a glorious garment for the sensible person (21:19, 21). According to Numbers 15:38-40, the Israelites were to use a purple cord to tie tassels to the corner of their garments, as a visual reminder of all God's commands; Ben Sira sees wisdom as having a similar function. Indeed wisdom will provide the student with a glorious robe such as the high priest wore (50:11), as well as a splendid crown (Prov 4:9).

In 6:32-33 the sage invites the student to choose to become wise (15:15-17). Wisdom can be acquired by associating with sensible persons (8:8-9; 9:14-16). This biblical teaching (Prov 13:20) is matched by an Egyptian wisdom saying: "The friend of a fool is a fool; the friend of a wise person is a wise person" (*Ankhsheshonq* 13.6). The sensible student will also gain wisdom by reflecting on God's commands revealed in the Scriptures (1:26; 19:20).

7:1-17 Conduct in public life

The next poem outlines the practical implications of the wisdom commended in 6:18-37, in terms of upright and humble behavior in one's social life. The first verse (often quoted by the rabbis) reminds us that much of the evil we suffer comes to us from our own evildoing (Num 32:23). For instance, 2 Samuel traces David's family problems back to his adultery with Bathsheba (2 Sam 12:9-12). Using an agricultural metaphor, the sage warns against sowing injustice, since the harvest will be seven times worse (Job 4:8; Gal 6:8).

Since Ben Sira's students were young men from the upper classes, in 7:4-7 he warns them against ambition (Prov 25:6-7; Luke 14:8). It is unwise to claim to be upright before God, because everybody sins (Ps 143:2; Rom 3:9-10). Likewise, it is foolish to flaunt one's wisdom before the king, whose intentions may be unfathomable (Prov 25:3). A judge has the weighty responsibility to root out crime by withstanding the forces of evil (Lev 19:15), but disgrace results from yielding to unjust pressure from the powerful. For the sage, public shaming is a strong sanction against sin (1:30). Sirach 7:8-10 warns that proud sin is inevitably punished, and a multitude of offerings to God cannot be a substitute for upright behavior (Amos 5:21-24; Isa 1:11-15).

In 7:11-17 the sage again counsels upright and humble conduct. Mocking the unfortunate is stupid, since the God who raised you up and brought the other person down can reverse the balance (11:4-6). According to 7:13, lies produce evil results (Hos 10:13). Thoughtless words are inappropriate whether in a political meeting or in prayer. Moreover, physical work was allotted to humanity by God (Gen 2:15; 3:19) and thus has

its own dignity (38:24-34). The rabbis taught that Torah study should be combined with manual labor (*Mishnah Aboth* 2.2).

An incentive to humility is the realization that what awaits humanity after death is bodily decay (Job 25:6). In line with earlier biblical texts (Isa 38:18; Job 14:7-12), Ben Sira has no belief in an afterlife. However, whereas the Hebrew text asserts that "what awaits mortals is worms," the grandson's Greek version of 7:17b introduces the idea of penalties after death: "The punishment of the impious is fire and worms," using imagery as in other biblical books (Isa 66:24; Jdt 16:17; Mark 9:47-48). By the time the grandson made the Greek translation, the idea of rewards and punishments after death had become more widely accepted among the Jews (Dan 12:2-3; 2 Macc 7:14).

7:18-36 Duties toward others

Ben Sira next spells out duties toward members of society: family, friends, the priests, and the needy. Since friends are "beyond price" (6:15), one should not barter them for money. Ophir (perhaps in Arabia) was proverbial as a source of fine gold (1 Kgs 9:28; Job 28:16). Ben Sira praises a sensible and gracious wife, who is more precious than pearls (Prov 31:10).

Sirach 7:20-21 counsels fair treatment of a faithful household servant (33:31-33) and of a laborer (Deut 24:14). A wise servant is to be loved as oneself (Lev 19:18), and should be offered freedom in the seventh year as the Torah commands (Exod 21:2; Deut 15:12). As in many African countries today, cattle can be a source of wealth for people in the Near East (Gen 13:2), and so these valuable animals deserve to be looked after (Prov 27:23-27).

Rearing of sons involves disciplining them (Prov 13:24) and submitting their neck to the yoke of obedience (30:12-13). However, 7:23b in the Hebrew says: "Choose wives for them in their youth," referring to the Jewish tradition that a father should provide a wife for his son before he is too old (tractate *Qiddushin* 30b in the Babylonian Talmud). In a traditional patriarchal society, rearing of daughters involved guarding their chastity (42:9-10). Marrying off a daughter meant getting rid of a source of worry for a father, provided she married a wise husband. In 7:26 Ben Sira urges faithful love of one's wife in normal circumstances, but distrust of her if she is hated, perhaps meaning divorced. The law of Moses made provision for divorce (Deut 24:1-4), though Jesus forbade it (Mark 10:9).

Sirach 7:27-31 alludes to the *Shema* (Deut 6:5), with its command to love God with all one's heart and soul and strength. For Ben Sira, this precept includes love of parents and respect for the temple priesthood. While the command to honor and care for father and mother is included in the Ten Commandments (Exod 20:12; Deut 5:16), the sage emphasizes the motive of gratitude (Tob 4:3-4). Respect for God also involves revering the Aaronic priests as holy (Lev 21:8), and love of the Creator includes attending to the needs of God's ministers (Deut 12:19). Ben Sira urges his students to contribute the prescribed offerings to support the priests (Prov 3:9-10; Num 18:9-20).

Kindness to the poor (7:32) will be rewarded with the divine blessing (Deut 14:28-29; Tob 4:7). Indeed, it is good to be generous to everyone, and even contribute to burying the dead (Tob 1:17). Moreover, Ben Sira urges his students to share the grief of mourners and visit the sick (Rom 12:15; Matt 25:39-40). Finally, awareness of personal mortality will keep one humble (7:17; 28:6), with a healthy reverence for God and respect for one's neighbor.

8:1-19 Prudence in dealing with others

Sirach 8:1 warns against quarreling with influential persons, who might become hostile. Upsetting the rich could lead them to bribe the ruling powers against one (Prov 17:23). Arguing with a loud-mouthed person (Prov 26:20-21) only adds fuel to the fire (28:8-11).

Sirach 8:5-7 advocates a sympathetic understanding toward human weakness. All human beings need to repent (17:24-25), because everyone sins (1 Kgs 8:46; Eccl 7:20). A society that despises the elderly despises its own future. To express the idea of death, Sirach 8:7b echoes the biblical expression "to be gathered" to one's ancestors (Gen 25:8; Judg 2:10).

In 8:8-9 Ben Sira urges openness to learning from older and wiser persons (Lev 19:32). Ancient Hebrew society respected the wisdom of the elders, who were regarded as possessing insight gained from their life experience and their knowledge of tradition (25:4-6). A willingness to learn from the wise (9:14-15; 39:1-4) will enable the sensible student to advance in society (Prov 22:29). The valuable ability to give an appropriate

answer will come from listening to the spoken tradition of the elders (Prov 22:21).

Sirach 8:10-19 describes persons to be approached with caution. According to Ben Sira (28:10-11), a sinner's anger is easily kindled, with disastrous results (Prov 26:21). Lending to someone more powerful can mean saying goodbye to one's money (29:4-7), just as guaranteeing the loan of an influential person (29:16-19) can necessitate repaying it oneself (Prov 22:26-27). In the nature of things, it is impossible to win a case against a judge. Moreover, traveling with someone ruthless or angry will lead to harm. Sirach 8:17-18 warns against revealing a secret to a fool (who may pass it on to others) or to a stranger (who may misuse it). Indeed, any confiding in others may spoil one's happiness or prosperity.

9:1-9 Caution in relating to women

This is the first of several passages in which Ben Sira advises his students on relations with women (25:13–26:18; 42:9-14). The general attitude is cautious and even suspicious. As a teacher in a patriarchal society governed by rules of honor and shame, he warns his young male pupils of the moral danger of associating with loose women.

The sage begins by emphasizing respect for marriage. The young man is to avoid jealousy toward his wife, else she may be provoked to evil. In 9:2 Ben Sira displays his cautious outlook (33:20): giving power to a woman could enable her to disgrace her husband by trampling on his dignity (Prov 31:3). Moreover, the male student should avoid intimacy with a strange (or foreign) woman, who might catch him in her snares (Prov 7:23).

Sirach 9:5 advises against lustful thoughts toward a virgin (Job 31:1; Matt 5:28). Moreover, the student associating too closely with a married woman will go down in blood to the grave (Prov 2:18; 7:27), probably a reference to the death penalty stipulated for adulterers (Lev 20:10) or to the husband's revenge (Prov 6:34).

9:10-16 Caution in relating to men

An old mature friendship cannot easily be replaced by a new one (Luke 5:39); fidelity in friendship is important (6:14-16). The sage urges his students to distance themselves from sinners and the proud, who will receive retribution in this life

(11:24-28). Moreover, Ben Sira's pupils will do well to keep away from the ruling power if they want to avoid the danger of death.

Instead, the students are encouraged to associate with truly wise persons (9:14-16), namely, those who are righteous and God-fearing (Prov 13:20). The Greek writer Xenophon (d. ca. 354 B.C.) makes a comparable assertion: "The society of honest persons is a training in virtue, but the society of the bad is virtue's undoing" (*Memorabilia* 1.2.20). In 9:16 Ben Sira appeals to his students to dine only with upright people. According to one of the Dead Sea Scrolls, it is the virtuous who know the divine wisdom: "Her voice is heard in the gates of the just; their meditation is on the law of the Most High" (11Q5 18.12-14).

9:17–10:18 True greatness

The next section treats genuine greatness in two parts: on rulers (9:17–10:5) and on the sin of pride (10:6-18). Ben Sira first contrasts the skilled manual worker with the learned sage (38:24–39:11). Sirach 10:2 draws a parallel between ruler and ruled; either the people imitate their leader, or they get the government they deserve! According to 10:4-5, God is sovereign over all earthly rulers, and can grant them success or failure (10:14; 11:5-6).

In 10:6 the sage urges a humble response to a neighbor's evil action; here he anticipates the Sermon on the Mount (Matt 5:39). Since God hates arrogance, proud nations end by receiving divine retribution. Sirach 10:9-10 mocks human pride with a vivid proverb: "A king today—tomorrow he is dead." Then the human corpse becomes food for worms (7:17). According to 10:12-13, pride and sin are linked, leading to ruin (Gen 6:5-8). Hence, God dethrones the proud and raises the lowly (1 Sam 2:7-8; Luke 1:52). In the imagery of 10:15, God's destruction of the proud is like uprooting (Ps 52:7; Prov 2:22).

10:19–11:6 True glory

This finely crafted poem comments on the rise and fall of human beings. The powerful receive honor but may fall through foolish pride, whereas the powerless are often despised yet may rise through humble wisdom. According to 10:19, true honor comes not from status or wealth but from fear of God (Jer 9:22-23). Hence, honor is due to a wise pauper rather than a lawless person (Jas

2:1-4). Though civil rulers deserve appropriate respect, the greatest honor belongs to a God-fearing person. Indeed, a prudent slave may rise to have power over free persons (Prov 17:2). A well-fed laborer is better than a hungry boaster (Prov 12:9), because there is no shame in honest work (7:15).

Next, Ben Sira advises his students to have a realistic and positive appreciation of their own value (10:28-29), because no one will honor those who discredit themselves. Honor is available to the impoverished for their prudence, whereas the rich easily gain prestige through their wealth. A pauper's wisdom can lead to a position of honor among princes.

In 11:2-6 Ben Sira observes that appearances can be deceptive (1 Sam 16:7; Isa 11:3), since even a tiny bee can produce the sweetest honey. Sirach 11:4-6 is a reminder that God can bring about unexpected reversals in human situations (10:14). People can go from prison to become national leaders (Eccl 4:14). A biblical case is the patriarch Joseph (Gen 41:14-44), while a late twentieth-century example is Nelson Mandela of South Africa. By contrast, powerful dictators can be overthrown.

11:7-28 Moderation

Wishing to encourage thoughtfulness in his students, Ben Sira urges them to beware of criticizing others on the basis of preconceived judgments. Instead, they are to get the facts first and listen without interrupting (Prov 18:13). In 11:9 the sage urges them to stick humbly to their own business (3:21-23), without getting caught up in conflicts among the powerful (Prov 26:17). Sirach 11:10 asserts that those desperate to get rich cannot help sinning (Prov 28:20; 1 Tim 6:10), because their thirst for wealth is insatiable (Eccl 5:9).

Ben Sira then makes a contrast (11:11-13): one person may toil hard yet not attain success (Eccl 9:11), while a weak person may rise in the world because of God's blessing. Sirach 11:14 draws the conclusion: both success and failure are in God's hands. Thomas à Kempis (1380–1471) develops this biblical teaching (Prov 16:9; 19:21): "Humanity proposes, but God disposes" (*Imitation of Christ* 1.19). In view of the inevitability of death, it is stupid to be miserly (14:3-12). Comparable teaching appears in Ecclesiastes 5:12–6:2, and in Jesus' parable of the rich fool (Luke 12:16-21).

In 11:20 Ben Sira advocates concentrating on one's own task instead of being fascinated by the apparent success of sinners (9:11). In due course God can reward anyone who patiently trusts in God (Ps 37:1-3).

Sirach 11:23-24 refutes the claims of those seeking to live self-sufficiently, independent of God. As good times can make one forget the lessons of adversity, so hard times can blot out the happiness of earlier prosperity. The Hebrew text of Sirach has no place for retribution in the afterlife. Instead, the sage warns that God can repay the evildoer with a miserable death (11:26-27). Hence 11:28 echoes the saying of the sixth-century B.C. Greek poet Solon: "Until he is dead, do not yet call a person happy, but only lucky" (Herodotus, *Histories* 1.32).

11:29–12:18 Warnings about strangers, beggars, and enemies

Sirach 11:29-34, doubtless based on observation and bitter experience, warns against strangers taking advantage of hospitality. Talebearers will turn good to evil, and their words will start a whole fire leading to disastrous results (Jas 3:5-6). A wicked person will bring forth only evil (Luke 6:45), and a stranger can alienate people from their community.

In 12:1-6 Ben Sira advises a narrow realism in almsgiving. Whereas the good will benefit from generosity, kindness to bad persons will have only harmful effects. In a comparable way, a Greek poet asserts: "Doing a good turn to the inferior is an utterly useless act of kindness" (Theognis 105). While God will reward almsgiving to a good person, Ben Sira sees no merit in giving to an evildoer.

The sage justifies his teaching by asserting God's hatred of wicked persons (12:6). The Qumran community also saw as its task "to detest all the children of darkness, each one in accordance with his blame in God's vindication" (1QS 1.10-11). However, Wisdom 11:24 asserts God's love for all creation. As a whole, Sirach 12:1-6 offers a contrast with the Sermon on the Mount, where Jesus affirms God's loving care of the wicked as well as the good, and the consequent duty of his disciples to love evildoers as well as good persons (Matt 5:44-45).

Ben Sira observes that we recognize our true friends only in adversity (12:8-9), when fair-weather friends disappear (Prov 19:4). A Greek poet makes a similar observation: "No one wants to be a friend whenever hard times befall a person" (Theognis 299). In 12:10-12 Ben Sira warns his students to be cautious, or else someone hostile may usurp their place.

Sirach 12:13-14 plays on the Hebrew word *hober*, which can mean "snake charmer" or "companion." Just as no one pities a snake charmer who is bitten (Eccl 10:11), so an associate of someone proud will also suffer painful treatment. In 12:16 Ben Sira contrasts an enemy's pleasant words with the scheming in his heart (Prov 6:12-14; 26:24). In adversity the false friend will cause one's downfall, even while pretending to help. Sirach 12:18 mentions the traditional gestures of mockery with which the enemy will make fun of one's humiliation (Ps 22:8; Lam 2:15).

13:1-23 Caution toward the rich and powerful

The next poem urges caution in choosing associates. The opening proverb takes a lesson from the natural world: just as people cannot touch pitch without getting their hands covered in the sticky substance, so a scoffer's companion will learn his way of behaving. Likewise, a Greek poet warns against mixing with persons regarded as inferior: "If you mingle with the base, you will lose even the sense you have" (Theognis 35-36).

Associating with a richer person is like trying to carry something too heavy (13:2). Whereas the rich can get away with their crimes, the poor always have to ask for forgiveness (Prov 18:23). The wealthy can exploit the poor and then abandon them. Therefore, 13:8 warns against the senseless presumption of mixing with richer people (Prov 25:6-7; Luke 14:8-11).

A moderate humility is the best response to an invitation from the influential (13:9-13). Someone inordinately keen to approach them can risk outright rejection, while someone excessively reticent risks being left behind altogether. After using words to test one (13:11), the influential person will readily inflict mockery or punishment. Hence the sage advises his students to avoid keeping company with the powerful ruling class.

In the next part (13:15-20) Ben Sira utilizes comparisons from the animal world to inculcate caution. Like the Greek fables of Aesop, the Hebrew Bible sometimes employs animal imagery for people (Ezek 22:25-27; Ps 22:21-22). According to 13:15-16, it is natural for a human being to like someone similar. Aristotle (d. 322 B.C.) also observes: "We love those who are like ourselves" (*Nicomachean Ethics* 8.1.6). Hence Ben Sira recommends associating with one's own kind.

Sirach 13:17-19 contrasts the innocent parties (lamb, dog, wild donkey) with the predators (wolf, hyena, lion). Ben Sira first uses the proverbial comparison between wolf and lamb (Isa 11:6; Matt 10:16) to show the impossibility of allying sinners with innocent persons (2 Cor 6:14-15). Although Near Eastern street dogs could be wild, they were not as fierce as hyenas seeking food. Hence Ben Sira makes this second comparison to contrast the poor and the rich in their struggle to survive, marked by an economic "survival of the fittest." In 13:19 Ben Sira draws a third contrast between the wild donkeys of the desert and the predatory lion (Job 24:4-5). The parallelism suggests that he links the rich with evildoing and sees the poor as tending to be innocent victims (34:21-24).

Sirach 13:21-23 extends the contrast between rich and poor by describing general reactions to them. People rush to help a rich person who stumbles, but in a similar situation they push down someone poor (Prov 14:20; 19:4). Likewise, people acclaim the unsavory words of the wealthy, but shove aside the poor even if they speak sensibly (Eccl 9:15-16).

13:24–14:19 The use of wealth

Ben Sira's discussion of the proper use of material goods begins with the statement that wealth can be good for the sinless person (31:8-11). Sirach 13:25-26 suggests that people's generosity (or otherwise) can be seen on their faces (Prov 15:13; Eccl 8:1). According to 14:1-2, depression from having said or done harmful things can spoil a person's happiness (22:22; 28:26).

In 14:3-10 Ben Sira describes the sad situation of misers, who actually gain no benefit from their wealth (Prov 28:22). Indeed, the money they save will be spent by other people (Eccl 6:2-3)! Sirach 14:5 observes that those unable to be kind to themselves find it hard to be generous to others (10:28-29; 11:18-19). By their miserliness they punish only themselves (Eccl 5:9-12). Misers cannot even enjoy the food that they eagerly acquire, since they are not contented with what they have (Prov 30:8-9; 1 Tim 6:8).

Since death is inevitable (14:11-12), it is good to enjoy life while it lasts (Eccl 8:15). Using God's good gifts is not mere self-indulgence if it involves sharing with friends. Instead of leaving wealth to others, Ben Sira urges present enjoyment of it (Eccl 2:18-24). His lack of expectation of an afterlife (matching Eccl 9:9-10) contrasts with the hope of immortality expressed in the book of Wisdom (Wis 3:1-9).

Sirach 14:17-19 (like 41:3-4) speaks further about nature's law of death (Gen 2:17; 3:19). The image of the garment wearing out is biblical (Isa 51:6; Ps 102:27). The comparison of human generations with leaves on a tree (Job 14:7-10) occurs also in Homer's *Iliad* (6.146-149).

WISDOM IN SPEECH AND THOUGHT
Sirach 14:20–23:27

14:20–15:10 The blessings of searching for wisdom

The opening beatitude speaks of the happiness of one who meditates on wisdom (Ps 1:1-2). A Qumran poem makes a similar statement: "Happy is the person who attains Wisdom, and walks in the law of the Most High, and dedicates his heart to her ways" (4Q525 2.2.3-4). In 14:21-27 wisdom is personified as a woman. The sage urges his students to seek wisdom as assiduously as a young man courting his girlfriend, waiting patiently beside her house (Prov 8:34) and even looking through the window to see her (Song 2:9). Indeed, there is a progression from observing where wisdom dwells (14:22-23) to encamping near her house (14:24-25), and then setting up home with her as his bride (14:26; 15:2). In 14:26-27 wisdom is portrayed as a tree (Prov 3:18), providing refuge from the burning heat (Isa 4:6).

According to 15:1, wisdom is available to the God-fearing person who keeps the Torah (1:26; 19:20). Ben Sira declares that wisdom will be as caring as a mother (Isa 49:15; 66:13) and as loving as a young bride for the male student (Prov 5:18). Sirach 15:3 states that she will feed him with understanding (Isa 30:20; Prov 9:1-6). In old age he will be able to lean on her when he finds walking difficult. Wisdom will also grant eloquence to those who love her (Wis 8:10-11). This wisdom is as much moral as intellectual, not available to the impious or the arrogant (15:7-8) who reject God's words (Ps 50:16-17). The wise person is characterized by a readiness to praise God (Ps 33:1).

15:11-20 Human free will

A perennial theological puzzle lies in the balance between human free will and divine predestination. Whereas Genesis 3 narrates the sin of Adam and Eve after the serpent's temptation, some Jewish apocalyptic circles traced back the origin of sin to the fallen angels (1 Enoch 6:1–9:9), while various Greek writers blamed human shortcomings on fate. In 15:11-20 Ben Sira wishes to emphasize human responsibility in contrast to those who denied liability for their actions. Sirach 15:11 teaches that human sin cannot derive from God (Jas 1:13), who does not cause human beings to do things that God dislikes (Wis 11:24).

After creating human beings (15:14), God gave them into the power of their free choice, an inclination either to good or to evil (Gen 2:16-17). Human beings are capable of fulfilling the divine commands (Deut 30:11-14), because God does not demand what is impossible. Sirach 15:16-17 spells out the choice offered to human beings: either life or death (Deut 30:15; Jer 21:8), symbolized by life-giving water or destructive fire (3:30). God's commands are not narrow or stifling, because divine wisdom is immense, but God's eyes see every human deed (Prov 15:3; Heb 4:13). In conclusion, God never commands sin or authorizes deceit.

16:1-23 God's punishment of sinners

Sirach 16:1-4 considers what kinds of children are desirable. Ancient Israelite society viewed children as a sign of divine blessing (Deut 28:4; Ps 128:1-4) and childlessness as a curse (Deut 28:18; 1 Sam 1:6). Sinners with many children could therefore claim that they had God's blessing. What impresses Ben Sira, however, is not the quantity of children but the quality of their lives. Having numerous children is no cause for joy unless they are God-fearing (Wis 3:10-12; 4:3-6). Better a virtuous person who is childless than the parent of godless children (Prov 17:21; Wis 4:1).

Sirach 16:5-10 discusses examples of divine punishment (2 Pet 2:4-9; 3 Macc 2:4-7), as a warning to sinners not to presume on God's forgiveness. Thus, fire burned up Korah's rebellious group (Num 16:35), the ancient giants did not receive the divine pardon (Gen 6:4; Bar 3:26-28), and God did not spare Lot's proud neighbors

from punishment (Gen 19:24-25). Moreover, Joshua placed the doomed Canaanites under the ban (Deut 7:1-2; Josh 11:16-20). In 16:9 the sage assumes the sinfulness of the Holy Land's early inhabitants (Gen 15:16; 1 Kgs 21:26), though modern readers might regret the placing of nationalistic limits on God's universal mercy. Like the Canaanites, the Israelites could not presume on divine compassion. Sirach 16:10 refers to the six hundred thousand Israelite males (46:8) who died in the wilderness as a punishment for their unfaithfulness (Num 11:21; 14:26-30). Hence, if whole nations have been punished for rebelliousness, how much more should an individual avoid being irreligious!

According to 16:11, the wise recognize that God can be angry as well as merciful (5:6). God is capable of punishing sinners and rectifying injustice (16:12-13). The righteous person can be confident of eventually receiving a reward (51:30), even if present experience offers no sign of it. Two supplementary verses (16:15-16), found in some manuscripts, specify the unbelieving Pharaoh (Exod 7:3-4) as an example of a sinner.

Sirach 16:17-23 teaches that sinners cannot escape the eye of God, who punishes iniquity. Here Ben Sira refutes an opponent's view that human beings are too insignificant for God to take an interest in their faults (Ps 8:4-6; Jer 23:24). "If God's dominion extends through the vast universe," asks the skeptic, "will the Almighty bother to pay attention to my ways?" This opponent believes that God notices neither sins nor good deeds (Ps 10:11; Isa 29:15), but Ben Sira knows that God sees everything (23:18-19).

16:24–17:24 Divine wisdom seen in creation

According to 16:26-30, divine providence is evident from the creation (Ps 104:24; Rom 1:20). God's ordering of the universe provides for the needs of each created thing (39:33-34), and the world is governed by the divine word (Ps 147:18; 148:8). The sage's emphasis on the purposefulness of creation reflects biblical tradition (Ps 148:6; Jer 31:35-36), and also agrees with Stoic philosophy. While animals cover the earth in fulfillment of God's blessing (Gen 1:22), nevertheless they are mortal (14:17-18) and will return to the earth (Ps 104:29).

Sirach 17:1-14 deals with God's making of human beings. Their creation from the earth echoes Genesis 2:7, while their return to it in death recalls Genesis 3:19. While Genesis 3 sees death as a divine punishment for human sin, Ben Sira regards death as God's decree (41:3-4) and the providential completion of an allotted number of days (37:25; 41:13). God's gift to humanity of authority over creation recalls Genesis 1:28 and Psalm 8:6, while the making of them in God's image draws on Genesis 1:27. Animals' fear of humans is reminiscent of Genesis 9:2.

Sirach 17:6 varies the Greek notion of the five senses (Aristotle, *On the Soul* 2.5-12). While seeing and hearing are shared with animals, human beings have tongues not only for tasting but also for speaking. This power of speech, a capacity unique to humanity, appears in Genesis 2:20, where Adam names the animals. Instead of smell and touch, Ben Sira mentions discernment and a mind for thinking. The ability to distinguish between good and evil is an attribute of wisdom (Isa 7:15; 1 Kgs 3:9), which Adam and Eve lacked, despite the serpent's claim (Gen 3:5). Yet God enables human beings to see the divine glory reflected in the created world, and thus to praise the Creator (39:33-35; 42:15-17).

In 17:11-14 we move from the creation to the giving of the law of Moses (45:5), with its promise of life in exchange for obedience (Deut 30:15; Ezek 20:11). According to Deuteronomy 5:22-26, the Israelites saw and heard the divine glory. Sirach 17:14 may refer particularly to the Ten Commandments. The command to avoid all evil may refer to the prohibitions against idolatry and sabbath work (Deut 5:6-15), while precepts about how to treat one's neighbor occur in the second part of the Decalogue (Deut 5:16-21).

Sirach 17:15-24 speaks of Israel's national life after Sinai, with a particular focus on the people's sins. At Sinai God proposed the paths for Israel to take (Deut 10:12; 30:16). Yet human ways, even when sinful, are not hidden from God (Ps 90:8; 139:3), despite the sinner's claim in 16:17-22. The ruler assigned by God to each people may be either the civil leader (Dan 2:21; Wis 6:3), or a nation's angelic guardian (Dan 10:20). However, God rules Israel directly (Deut 32:8-9), as they are God's own possession (Exod 19:5; Deut 7:6). Therefore they cannot escape divine scrutiny, because God knows their sins (23:19) and will punish transgressors (16:11).

The care for Israel as the apple of God's eye (Deut 32:10) is the basis of Ben Sira's response to the skeptic's earlier question in 16:22. Sirach 17:22 uses language that recalls the divine concern for the leader of the postexilic Jerusalem community, Zerubbabel (49:11), who is compared to God's signet ring (Hag 2:23). In 17:24 the sage concludes this section with the assertion (4:26; 5:7) that the repentant are offered a way back to God (Ezek 33:11).

17:25–18:14 Call to leave sin behind

This poem appeals to human beings to repent, because God is both powerful and merciful. Sirach 17:25-26 echoes the prophetic calls to repentance (Jer 3:12-14; Joel 2:12-13). By hating wickedness, humans become like God (15:13). Sirach 17:27-28 expresses the view of Hebrew writers before the Maccabean revolt that nobody can praise God after death (Ps 88:11-13; Isa 38:18). Hence, living persons need to receive the abundant divine mercy (Ps 31:20; 86:5). By contrast, mortality sets limits to human mercy (Ps 103:13-18). If God can find fault with the angels, how much more with mortals (Job 15:15-16; 25:5-6), who are merely "dust and ashes" (10:9)!

Sirach 18:1-2 notes that unlike humankind, God is just (Ps 51:6-7; 145:17). Ben Sira next echoes biblical statements (Ps 145:3; Job 9:10) that no human being can fully declare the divine greatness (42:17; 43:31). No one can add to God's majesty (Eccl 3:14), or subtract from it (42:21). Unlike God, human beings are limited (Ps 8:5; 144:3). While a person's allotted lifespan may be seventy or eighty years (Ps 90:10), one hundred years is even now exceptional, yet God is everlasting (Ps 90:2).

Sirach 18:11 presumes that God's very majesty makes God compassionate (Wis 11:21-23; Ps 36:6-7). Human mortality evokes divine mercy (Ps 103:13-14). While a person will naturally be compassionate to a neighbor (13:15), God's mercy reaches out to all humanity, like a shepherd's care for a flock (Isa 40:11; Ps 23:1).

18:15–19:17 Prudential warnings

After a long section of theological teaching on the origin of sin (15:11–18:14), Ben Sira begins a lengthy section of ethical instruction (18:15–23:27). The present poem falls into three parts: on wise conduct (18:15-29); on control of the passions (18:30–19:4); and on the correct use of the tongue (19:5-17).

According to 18:15-18, a generous attitude when giving is as important as the gift itself; thereby we imitate our gracious God (2 Cor 9:7; Jas 1:5). A time of giving is the wrong occasion for reproving (20:1). Sirach 18:19-21 emphasizes the value of being prepared: it is better to have the cure before falling ill. Likewise, it is sensible to acknowledge one's fault repentantly, before others pass judgment (Matt 7:1; 1 Cor 11:31) and before death comes (5:7-8; 17:25). Sirach 18:22-24 urges the prompt payment of vows before death may strike (Deut 23:21-23; Eccl 5:3-4). For Ben Sira the thought of death is a motive for right conduct (28:6-7). The wise are aware that their situation in life can alter suddenly, just as the weather can quickly change.

Sirach 18:30–19:4 advises control of the passions, in the tradition of Hebrew and Egyptian wisdom literature. Those who follow their appetites will end up as the laughing stock of their enemies (Prov 21:17). Gluttonous winebibbers spend money they do not have on eating and drinking (Deut 21:20; Prov 23:20-21). Proper stewardship of one's resources will prevent poverty and its associated shame (40:28-30). Wine and loose women can make a person reckless (Prov 23:31-33; 31:3-5). An admonition against mixing with prostitutes is common in the wisdom literature of Israel (Prov 5:1-6; 23:26-28), as well as in Egypt.

In 19:5-12 the sage urges discipline in speech (5:14–6:1; 22:27–23:3). A person can escape reproach by refusing to repeat an evil report (Prov 25:9-10) and keeping a discreet silence instead. In contrast to the misuse of the tongue to reveal the faults of others inappropriately, Ben Sira advocates a proper use of speech to admonish friends and neighbors (19:13-17). The biblical command to point out the faults of others (Lev 19:17) was taken seriously by many Jewish groups around the first century. Both Jesus and the Qumran community laid down procedures for reproving community members (Matt 18:15-17; 1QS 5.24–6.1). Warning a friend or neighbor may stop the person reoffending (19:13-14). Yet a report of wrongdoing may be false: the wise person will not believe everything said (Prov 14:15; Eccl 7:21). Further caution is needed because an offense may be un-

intentional, and no one is sinless (Eccl 7:20; Ps 143:2). Instead of allowing an unchecked hurt to cause the end of a friendship, a gentle reproof is advisable (Prov 27:5-6), in accordance with the stipulation of Leviticus 19:17. Some later manuscripts have a scribal addition about fearing God and keeping the law (19:18-19).

19:20–20:31 Wisdom and folly in word and deed

Mention of the Torah in 19:17 leads the sage to point out the necessity for the wise person to follow God's law (19:20). True wisdom needs to be directed to a good purpose, because knowing how to be wicked is not wisdom at all. It is better to be considered a fool for keeping free from sin than to cleverly misuse knowledge (19:23). Vigilance is also required, because the wicked person can stealthily gain an advantage (12:10-18). However, aspects of a person's appearance will often indicate whether someone is wise or foolish (13:25-26).

Sirach 20:1-3 discusses the benefits and limits of correcting others. Whereas 19:13-17 encourages prompt reproof of an erring friend, 20:1 notes that some circumstances call for silence rather than a rebuke. Sirach 20:5-8 deals with silence and speech, a favorite theme of ancient wisdom teachers (Eccl 3:7). Silence is appropriate if one has nothing to say (Prov 17:28), or if an answer would be inappropriate at that time (5:12).

In 20:9-12 Ben Sira contrasts appearance and reality, since things are not always what they seem. An experience of failure can lead a person to greater success in the future, while a person's life may be ruined by an apparent success (such as winning the lottery today). Whereas in the ancient orient bribes were intended to benefit the giver (Prov 17:8), some gifts produce no advantage. Because God can raise people up or cast them down (7:11; 11:5), someone may rise "from rags to riches" or from humiliation to honor; see the story of the patriarch Joseph in Genesis 37–50, or Mary's song in Luke 1:47-53.

According to 20:13, wise speech makes one accepted, as Abigail found in 1 Samuel 25:23-34, whereas a fool's words are useless. By expecting too quickly an equivalent reward for kind deeds, fools will be disappointed in friendship. Sirach 20:18 resembles a saying attributed to the Stoic philosopher Zeno of Citium (d. 263 B.C.): "Better to slip with the foot than with the tongue" (Diogenes Laertius 7.26). A fool's proverb is unacceptable because it is uttered on the wrong occasion (Prov 26:9). According to 20:21-23, a false sense of shame can cause harm (4:21), while lying deservedly causes disgrace (Prov 12:22; 13:5).

Sirach 20:27-31 returns to the theme of wisdom that opened this section (19:20-24). Wise speech will lead to advancement (Prov 22:29), as in the biblical stories of Joseph and Daniel (Gen 41:25-36; Dan 2:27-45). Just as a farmer's cultivation of land yields a harvest, so wise people's "cultivation" of their master will lead to atonement for any offenses against him (Prov 14:35). Ben Sira opposes the custom of bribery (Exod 23:8; Prov 18:16) that was widespread in the ancient orient (2 Macc 4:7-8). Concealed wisdom is as unhelpful as buried treasure (Matt 5:15-16; 25:24-30). Whereas folly is best hidden by silence (20:6), wisdom is to be revealed in speech (39:6).

21:1-10 Avoiding sin

Sirach 21:1-2 makes an appeal to flee from sin (17:25-26), so as not to be poisoned by its venomous bite. The mention of the serpent echoes Genesis 3:1-7, where the serpent tempts Adam and Eve. Sin has teeth as sharp as a lion's teeth; note that 1 Peter 5:8 compares the devil to a roaring lion. In another graphic image, sin is like a double-edged sword (Prov 5:4), but its antidote is God's word (Heb 4:12). In 21:4-5 Ben Sira warns against arrogant mistreatment of the poor. The proud use of terror tactics will rebound on the household of the arrogant (10:7-8), whereas God will quickly hear the prayer of the impoverished victim (35:21-25). The God-fearing person heeds warnings to repent (Prov 12:1), but boastful speakers do not recognize their faults.

Sirach 21:8-10 warns of the terrible consequences of sin. One who misappropriates funds to build his own house is constructing his own funerary monument (Jer 22:13-19). A criminal band is as unstable as flammable material, ready to ignite (16:6). The sinner's easy road leads to the nether world (Prov 5:5; 9:18); Ben Sira is referring to an early death rather than to eternal punishment.

21:11–22:18 Wisdom and folly

The section begins by equating observance of the Torah, fearing the Lord, and being wise. The

additional element here is self-control, an important virtue in Ben Sira (22:27–23:6) as well as in St. Paul (Gal 5:23) and in Greek ethics. While one kind of cleverness helps a student to learn, another kind has only bitter fruits (19:23-25). A sage's wise teaching wells up as abundantly as a spring of fresh water (24:25-31), whereas the fool's mind is like a broken vessel (Jer 22:28), unable to contain any useful knowledge. While the intelligent person will learn from a wise saying (Prov 9:9), the pleasure-seeking fool simply discards it unexamined (21:15). Whereas the craftsperson attends to skillful manual work (38:31-34), the sage pays attention to wise public speech (39:6-8). The educational discipline that feels like a fetter to the fool (6:29-30) is like a gold bracelet for the sensible person (21:19-21).

Sirach 21:22-24 considers how to approach someone's home (Prov 25:17). The wise have a proper sense of reserve about entering, whereas fools brazenly enter uninvited. According to 21:26, fools speak before they think, but wise people think before speaking (Prov 14:33). Sirach 21:27-28 indicates that foul speech recoils onto the speaker. When the pagans curse the Jews (regarded as their enemies), their curse comes back on themselves (Gen 12:3; Esth 7:9-10). In attempting to besmirch the reputation of others, slanderers lose their own good name.

According to 22:1, laziness also leads to shame (Prov 24:30-34). In a vivid but disgusting image, Ben Sira then compares the sluggard to a lump of excrement that soils the hand of anyone who comes into contact with it (13:1). Sirach 22:3-6 issues warnings about unruly children. A father's natural pride in begetting a son turns to shame (16:1-2) if the son is undisciplined (Prov 17:21). Whereas Ben Sira chauvinistically considers a daughter's birth to be a loss for her parents, other biblical authors recognize that great blessings come when a woman responds to God's call (Jdt 15:9-10; Luke 1:48-49). While a sensible daughter achieves the blessing of being united with a husband (7:25), a shameless woman causes her parents grief by becoming unmarriageable (42:9-10), according to a patriarchal view of family relationships.

Sirach 22:9-18 employs various comparisons to describe the fool. Teaching someone unwilling to learn is no more successful than gluing together pieces of broken pottery (21:14) or trying to talk to someone who is asleep (Prov 24:33-34). As we weep for someone deceased who has gone from the sun's light (38:16), so we should mourn for the stupid person who has abandoned the light of understanding. Indeed, Ben Sira considers a fool's life to be worse than death. Whereas the customary period of mourning for the dead was traditionally a week in ancient Israel (Gen 50:10; Jdt 16:24), fools deserved to be mourned throughout their lifetime, which was a living death.

Sirach 22:13 advises against becoming the companion of someone unintelligent (the Syriac text says "pig"), so as to avoid being spattered when he shakes himself. Second Peter 2:22 also makes a comparison with a pig, which the Torah regards as an unclean animal (Lev 11:7). Sirach 22:16-18 uses building imagery to describe the solid resolve of the wise, whose firm decision will withstand an earthquake of difficulties (Ps 112:7; Matt 7:24-27), whereas the fool's timid resolve is blown away by fear of trouble.

22:19-26 Preserving friendship

Sirach 22:19-20 warns how easily insensitive behavior can destroy a friendship. In 27:9 birds serve as an image for friends gathering together, but in 22:20 and 27:19 they illustrate how quickly friends can be scared away. Uttering a harsh word or even drawing a sword can be forgiven, if one seeks reconciliation by apologizing, but a complete betrayal of friendship cannot be mended.

In 22:23 the sage urges support of a friend who is currently poor, for the utilitarian benefit of sharing his future prosperity. Though this advice may appear self-serving, it reflects the belief that God rewards good actions (17:22-23). Ben Sira's insistence on fidelity contrasts with the attitude of the fair-weather friend (6:10-11). Despite the widespread shunning of the poor (Prov 19:4, 7), the sage insists that it is no shame to help a friend who needs support (Lev 25:35-36).

22:27–23:27 Control of the tongue and the passions

This poem comprises a double prayer for discipline of the tongue and of the passions (22:27–23:6), plus instruction on controlling the tongue (23:7-15) and the passions (23:16-27). The need for divine help to guard one's mouth echoes Psalm 141:3. In 23:1 (as in 23:4) the sage addresses God as Father (51:10), a rare divine title in the Hebrew

Bible (Isa 63:16; Mal 2:10). Calling God Father is more common in Hellenistic Judaism (Wis 2:16; 14:3) and is Jesus' standard address to God (Luke 11:2; Mark 14:36). In 23:2 the sage recognizes that he needs the "rod of discipline" (Prov 22:15; Ps 141:5) to save him from uncontrolled thoughts and desires, which if unchecked would lead him into sinful shame.

After his prayer, the sage offers teaching on control of the tongue (23:7-15). He urges avoidance of uttering God's holy name in oaths (Exod 20:7; Deut 5:11), which are often an occasion of sin. According to 23:11, there is a danger of a double sin: initially making a rash oath, and then failing to fulfill it (Lev 5:4; Num 30:2). According to some biblical law codes (Lev 24:15-16; John 10:33), blasphemy merits death. Students who forget to discipline their tongue while sitting among the mighty will end up saying something offensive from habit, and will then wish they had never been born (Job 3:3; Jer 20:14) because of the resulting shame to themselves and their family.

In 23:16-27 the sage warns against lack of control of physical passion on the part of a man (23:16-21) or a woman (23:22-26). Ben Sira seems to distinguish between three kinds of male sin (23:16-17). The first is fornication with an unmarried woman, a passion whose fire can be destructive (1 Cor 7:9). The second kind of sin is a sexual relationship with a close relative, as forbidden in the law of Moses (Lev 18:6), a sin that can bring the fire of the divine displeasure (Num 11:1). The third kind of sin, adultery with a married woman (9:9), is like pleasant bread eaten in secret (Prov 9:17; 30:20), but ends in death (Prov 7:22-27).

Sirach 23:18-21 develops the scenario of the third case. Like the sinner in 16:20-21, the adulterer thinks that God will take no notice of him (Job 24:15; Isa 29:15). Yet in fact God is aware of all human activity (17:19-20), even when it is hidden from others (Prov 5:21). Like 42:18, 23:20 asserts that God has advance knowledge of what will happen (Ps 139:1-6). According to 23:21, the unsuspecting adulterer will not escape public punishment (Prov 6:32-35). Indeed, the Torah commanded death by stoning (Lev 20:10; Deut 22:21), although later Jewish law practically eliminated this punishment.

Ben Sira then warns of the evils of a woman's adultery (23:22-27). Her offense is threefold: first, breaking the divine law (Deut 5:18; Exod 20:14);

second, acting unjustly against her husband; and third, bearing children fathered by another man. The adulterous woman will suffer the public punishment of stoning to death (Deut 22:22; Dan 13:36-41), while her hope of numerous successful children and grandchildren will be brought to nothing (Wis 3:16-19; 4:3-6). Instead of leaving a good name behind her, her memory will be a disgrace (41:5-9). Meditating on the fate of the virtuous and sinners will convince the student that there is nothing better in life than fearing God (25:10-11; 40:26-27) and keeping God's commands (Eccl 12:13; Deut 10:12-13).

WISDOM IN DOMESTIC LIFE

Sirach 24:1–32:13

24:1-33 The praise of wisdom

Like Proverbs 8:22-36, this poem is an important witness to Israel's developing theology of wisdom. According to Proverbs 8:22, wisdom came into being as the first of God's works and was present at the creation. Like Baruch 3:37–4:1, Ben Sira specifies that wisdom is found in the law of Moses (24:23). Christian theology has equated wisdom with Christ (1 Cor 1:30). In Catholic piety, the female figure of wisdom in Sirach 24 has also been applied to Mary, seen as "Seat of Wisdom."

Sirach 24:1-2 sets the scene for wisdom's speech to God's people on earth and the heavenly hosts. Although wisdom's first-person declaration (24:3-22) draws on Proverbs 8:12-36, there are also parallels in Greek poems praising the goddess Isis. The first part of wisdom's speech (24:3-12) retells Israel's religious history, starting from creation and moving by way of the exodus to the choice of Jerusalem for the temple.

Sirach 24:3 equates wisdom with God's utterance; similarly, John's prologue describes Jesus as the Word (John 1:1). Whereas other biblical texts speak of creation occurring through God's word (Gen 1:3; Ps 33:6) or God's wisdom (Prov 3:19-20; Wis 9:1-2), here the focus is on divine revelation (Prov 2:6). According to 24:3, this wisdom is spread like a mist over the earth (Gen 1:2; 2:6), though her dwelling is in the height of heaven (Bar 3:29). The pillar of cloud was the means of God's saving presence for the Israelites at the time of the exodus (Exod 13:21-22; 14:19-20). Wisdom has a full experience of the height of heaven and

the depths of the abyss (Prov 8:24-29; Wis 9:16), as well as control of every nation (Prov 8:15-16).

Despite wisdom's cosmic scope (24:7), she is presented as looking for a home on earth (Bar 3:38). This idea is treated differently in 1 Enoch 42:1-2 (perhaps written during the first century A.D.): "Wisdom went out to dwell with humanity, but she found no dwelling place. Wisdom returned to her place and settled permanently among the angels." In contrast, Ben Sira asserts that the Creator finds her an earthly home, since she is told to pitch her tent among the people of Israel (24:8). Similar imagery occurs in John 1:14. Sirach 24:9 states that wisdom was formed from the beginning (Prov 8:22-23) and exists forever (Wis 8:13). She ministered before God like a priest in the "holy tent" or tabernacle in the wilderness after the exodus (Exod 25:8-9), and later came to be established in the temple on Mount Zion. God's love for Jerusalem matches his love for wisdom (Ps 50:2; Prov 8:35), and wisdom holds special authority in the city, because the Torah is its guide (Bar 3:37–4:1). Israel is called the Lord's portion (Deut 32:9), as in 17:17.

Sirach 24:13-14 likens wisdom to six kinds of trees: the majestic Lebanon cedar (1 Kgs 6:9-10), the cypress (2 Kgs 19:23), the palm tree (2 Chr 28:15), the rosebush (Wis 2:8), the olive tree (Judg 9:8), and the plane tree (Ezek 31:8). By comparing wisdom to perfumes and spices, used to make the holy anointing oil and the temple incense (Exod 30:23-38), 24:15 hints at wisdom's priestly attributes. Sirach 24:16-17 then compares wisdom with the terebinth and the vine (Judg 6:11; 9:13). Some later manuscripts include a scribal addition as 24:18.

In 24:19 (as in 6:19 and 51:23) wisdom makes an appeal to her disciples to approach her and receive her fruits (Prov 9:4-6). We may compare Jesus' invitation to come to him for rest (Matt 11:28). Hunger and thirst for divine wisdom will increase the appetite, which will be satisfied only with a further consumption of this food (compare John 6:35). Sirach 24:23 makes a significant theological statement, by connecting wisdom with the covenantal law of Moses (Exod 24:7; Deut 33:4). This linkage occurs elsewhere in Ben Sira (1:26; 19:20) and in other biblical books (Deut 4:5-6; Bar 4:1).

Ben Sira then compares wisdom's abundant life-giving power to six famed rivers, four of which are mentioned in the Genesis creation story (Gen 2:10-14). Though the location of the Pishon is uncertain, the Tigris and Euphrates are great Mesopotamian rivers (Gen 15:8; Dan 10:4). The Gihon is either another name for the Nile (Gen 2:13), or a spring in Jerusalem (1 Kgs 1:38). In 24:28, the first human being who failed to grasp God's wisdom was Adam (Gen 3:17-19). The latest human being (perhaps the author) still has not fathomed the divine wisdom, which is deeper than the abyss (1:3; 43:28).

Sirach 24:30-31 continues the water imagery (Deut 32:2), as the sage seeks to be a channel for the divine wisdom that offers abundant life (Isa 58:11; Ezek 47:1-12). The sage likens his teaching to light that will shine out to a great distance from his base in Jerusalem (Isa 2:3-5; Prov 6:23). At the end of the poem, the Greek adds an extra verse (24:34), almost identical to 33:18, but the New American Bible follows the Syriac by omitting it.

25:1-11 Gifts that bring happiness

More delightful than fraternal harmony and neighborly friendship (Ps 133:1) is a peaceful bond between husband and wife (40:23). More notorious than a proud pauper and a fraudulent magnate is an adulterous old man, since elders were meant to set an example of wisdom for the young (Prov 20:29; Dan 13:5-27). In contrast, Sirach 25:3 advises seeking wisdom in one's youth, while there is still time. The gray hairs of old age are meant to signify the wisdom of experience (Job 12:12), and the greatest glory of the elderly is their God-fearing lifestyle (Prov 16:31; Wis 4:9).

Sirach 25:7-11 describes ten kinds of fortunate people. First comes a parent rejoicing in the gift of children (Ps 127:3-5), then one who sees the downfall of enemies (Ps 112:8). Next the sage notes the happiness of a man dwelling with a sensible wife (Prov 19:14). The yoking together of ox and donkey (Deut 22:10) probably refers to the situation of a man married to two wives (Gen 30:1; 1 Sam 1:6). Sirach 25:8 mentions a person who needs not be ashamed of having spoken unwisely (14:1), nor of having to serve someone considered socially inferior (Eccl 10:5-7; Prov 19:10). The sage also regards as happy someone who has found real friendship (6:14-17), as well as one whose words are listened to (3:29). In conclusion, happy is one who finds wisdom (Prov 4:5-7), but the

greatest happiness lies in showing reverence toward God (40:26-27).

25:13–26:18 Good and bad wives

To the modern Western reader, Ben Sira's view of women appears misogynistic. Despite the praise of the good wife (26:1-4 and 26:13-18), the main emphasis is on the evil wife (25:12-26; 26:5-12). By advising caution in relation to women (9:1-9), Ben Sira follows ancient admonitions to young men. Like Egyptian wisdom literature, the book of Proverbs warns against foreign women, regarded as a source of temptation for men (Prov 5:1-23; 7:1-27).

Biblical tradition also distinguishes between good and bad wives, as seen from the male viewpoint. Besides maxims praising a good wife (Prov 12:4; 18:22) and the acrostic poem celebrating the capable woman (Prov 31:10-31), there are also warnings against the quarrelsome wife (Prov 21:9, 19). More than the book of Proverbs, however, Ben Sira focuses on female faults, perhaps echoing the misogynistic element in eighth- or seventh-century B.C. Greek writers such as Hesiod and Semonides of Amorgos.

Sirach 25:13 links a wound to the heart with the evil done by a woman, to express the emotional pain that men can suffer from women, though the sage ignores the hurt that husbands can cause to their wives. The animal comparisons of 25:15-17 have a generic resemblance to the way Semonides likens women to various kinds of animals (*On Women* 1–82). Sirach 25:19 suggests that the sinful man deserves the evil of an unpleasant wife (Eccl 7:26).

In 25:21 Ben Sira warns his young male students not to be led astray by a woman's beauty or wealth (9:8; 31:6). The inner disposition is important, whereas looks can be deceptive (Prov 11:22; 31:30). According to the patriarchal system of honor, it is shameful when a woman provides her husband's economic support (Tob 2:11-12). In 25:24 the sage asserts that sin's beginning came through a woman (Eve), whose error brought death into the world (Gen 3:1-19; 1 Tim 2:14). Elsewhere, the Bible regards Adam's sin as having introduced death into the world (Rom 5:12-21; 1 Cor 15:22). Ben Sira's portrayal of Eve as the source of the world's troubles may be a distant echo of the Greek legend of Pandora (Hesiod, *Works and Days* 57-104). In 25:25-26 the sage advises his students to divorce an errant wife. The law of Moses allowed divorce if a certificate was given (Deut 24:1-4), though Malachi and Jesus opposed the practice (Mal 2:14-16; Mark 10:2-12).

Ben Sira's discussion of the good wife (26:1-4) praises her for the good she does to her husband. By bringing him long life and joy (Prov 12:4; 18:22), she conveys the blessings promised to the God-fearing person (1:12).

According to 26:5-6, a worse affliction than the slanderous plots of the wicked (51:2-6) is the scourging tongue of a jealous wife in a polygamous marriage. Sirach 26:9 refers to the feminine use of eye make-up as a means of seduction (2 Kgs 9:30; Jer 4:30). For a male in Ben Sira's society, shame was avoided by vigilant control over the female members of the household, whether one's wife or one's daughter (26:10; 42:11). For the modern reader, such an attitude appears an affront to the dignity and freedom of women. According to ancient patriarchal ideology a woman was not unlikely to betray her husband. While the sage speaks obscenely of female lust in 26:12, he does not condemn the male here, although other parts of the book discuss the faults of men (23:16-21; 25:2).

Sirach 26:13-18 again praises the good wife for her grace, thoughtfulness, and modesty. Indeed, a good wife is more valuable to her husband than all other wealth (36:29). Sirach 26:17-18 uses imagery connected with the temple in Jerusalem (24:10-12; 50:5-11). The beauty of a woman's face is like the light on the *menorah* or lampstand (Exod 25:31-40; 1 Macc 4:49-50), while her legs are as fine as the golden columns of the temple (Exod 26:32; 1 Macc 1:21-23). Some later Greek manuscripts add a further nine verses here, contrasting the devout and the impious wife.

26:28–27:15 Warning about sinful persons

The opening numerical saying outlines affronts to the proper order of things, such as the scandal of a righteous person turning to sin (Ezek 18:24). The sage then speaks of the sinfulness that can accompany business ventures (26:29–27:3). A merchant cannot easily remain faultless because of the temptation to dishonesty and the desire to increase profits (Amos 8:4-6; Lev 19:35-36). Love of money can cause many to sin (Prov 28:20; 1 Tim 6:10). A house is built up by God-fearing behavior but destroyed by ungodliness (Prov 12:7; 14:11). Speech tests a person's character (27:4-7), like a sieve that winnows corn or a kiln that fires a potter's jar. Indeed, like the fruit produced by a tree (Luke 6:43-45), speech discloses one's level of self-discipline.

Sirach 27:8-15 contrasts the wise and the foolish. The sage exhorts his students to pursue righteousness (Deut 16:20) so that it becomes their glorious clothing (Isa 61:10; Job 29:14). However, the quest for an upright life cannot be undertaken in isolation (27:9), and indeed "birds of a feather flock together." Whereas the bird is an image for fidelity, the lion symbolizes predatory behavior (21:2), namely, the attack of sin on evildoers (Gen 4:7). Sirach 27:11 praises the consistent wisdom of the devout (5:10-11). Understanding is learned through spending time with wise persons (9:14-16), whereas time spent with a fool brings no insights (22:12). The wicked are known for their offensive talk, callous laughter, wrangling, and cursing (Gal 5:19-21).

27:16–28:7 Avoiding anger

According to 27:16-21, breaking confidences will destroy a friendship (Prov 11:13; 25:9), whereas fidelity will build up a friendly relationship (6:14-17). A friend whose secrets have been disclosed will disappear, just as a bird flies away (22:20) or a gazelle runs from a trap (Prov 6:5). Whereas a friend's hurtful action or abusive talk can be forgiven, revealing secrets will cause the irretrievable breakdown of the friendship (22:22).

Next (27:22-27), the sage advises against associating with evil people (Prov 6:12-15; 1 Cor 15:33). As in 12:16, he warns of the hidden malice of flatterers (Prov 26:24-26). In 27:24 he reveals his own feeling of hatred of such deceitful people, perhaps because they nearly caused his death by denouncing him (51:2-6). As in 12:6, Ben Sira asserts God's hatred of sinners (Prov 6:16-19). Then 27:25-27 provides a reminder of the belief that God will punish evildoers in this life (Prov 6:15). Since those who dig a hole to trap others will fall in it themselves (Prov 26:27), the way to escape receiving evil is to refrain from doing evil (7:1-3).

Sirach 27:28–28:1 consists of warnings against vengefulness. Those who delight in setting traps will be ensnared in them, thereby suffering pain (Ps 7:15-17). The retribution mentioned in 27:29 finds an illustration in the punishment of Haman

(Esth 7:10). Those who take vengeance into their own hands will become victims of divine vengeance (Deut 32:35; Rom 12:19).

Sirach 28:2-7 approaches the tone of Jesus' teaching on forgiveness. Pardoning others is a condition for receiving divine forgiveness (Mark 11:25), whereas refusing mercy to someone else makes it unreasonable to expect mercy from the Lord (Matt 18:23-35). If God forgives offenses (17:29), human beings would do well to act similarly (Luke 6:36-37). The thought of death should turn people away from enmity, since in Ben Sira's view sins are punished before death (7:36; 11:26-28). By remembering the commandment to love one's neighbor as oneself (Lev 19:18), a person will be led to overlook the failings of others.

28:8-26 Quarrelsomeness and evils of the tongue

One way to avoid sinning is to keep away from disputes, since the quarrelsome person will disrupt friendships (Prov 15:18; 16:28). Quarrelers add fuel to the fire (Prov 26:20-21; Jas 3:5-6), particularly if they are rich and powerful (8:1-3; 13:2), and the resulting arguments can even lead to bloodshed (22:24; 27:15). According to 28:12, the same mouth has power either to kindle argument (11:32) or to extinguish it (Prov 15:1; 18:21). A false accusation might even cause an innocent wife to be divorced by her husband.

Sirach 28:17 notes that the tongue can be very hurtful (Prov 25:15; Jas 3:5-8). The burden imposed by slander is as heavy as the iron yoke of Nebuchadnezzar's conquest of Judah (Jer 28:13-14). Slander can make life not worth living (26:5). Because of divine deliverance (51:3-4), the fire kindled by slanderers will ultimately harm the godless but not the just (Isa 43:2; 66:24). According to 28:24, just as a farmer protects his property with a hedge (Isa 5:2), so the wise need to guard their mouths from slander. As a banker weighs and seals moneybags (Job 14:16-17), so sensible students weigh their words and seal their lips (21:25; 22:27). Careless persons, tripped up by their tongues, will fall victim to the onlookers (Prov 13:3; 21:23).

29:1-20 Loans, donations, and guarantees

According to 29:1, it is a kindness to lend to a needy neighbor without demanding interest (Exod 22:24; Lev 25:35-37). Unlike the scoundrel (Ps 37:21), the honest borrower keeps faith with the promise made, by repaying a loan at the required time. Sirach 29:4-6 outlines the common troubles of lenders; far from receiving gratitude, they often suffer grief from the borrowers. Before receiving a loan, the applicant is full of flattery, but when the money is due, the only repayment will be excuses. Even if the debtor can afford to repay, the creditor will be pleased to recover half the loan (8:12), whereas if the debtor cannot afford repayment, the creditor has lost the money and also gained an enemy for no extra cost! If the debtor does repay, it will be with curses rather than with gratitude. Often prudence rather than meanness leads people to refuse to lend.

In case the observations of 29:4-7 seem harsh, 29:8-13 encourages charitable donations. As in 4:1-4, the sage urges helping the poor without delay (Prov 3:28), because the Torah commands offering generous assistance (Deut 15:7-8; Ps 112:5). Instead of leaving money to rot (Matt 6:19; Jas 5:2-3), it is better to use it for the benefit of relatives and friends (14:13). According to 29:11-13 and 40:24, charitable giving will provide deliverance from evil (Prov 19:17; Tob 12:9).

Sirach 29:14-20 speaks of the dangers and benefits of providing collateral guarantees for a neighbor (8:13). A good person will provide the necessary collateral, fully aware of the biblical warnings (Prov 6:1-5; 11:15). The beneficiary of such a guarantee needs to appreciate that the backer has risked his life (Prov 22:26-27), yet the ungrateful person will not acknowledge the help received. Hence, Ben Sira spells out the dangers of providing collateral: financial ruin, and even exile to escape debts. Sirach 29:19 seems to refer to the ambitious guarantor who seeks gain by keeping pledged items such as garments; that person will suffer lawsuits for breaking the rules of the Torah (Exod 22:25; Deut 24:10-13). Hence Ben Sira concludes: be as generous as you can, but also have a prudent regard for your own welfare (Tob 4:8).

29:21–30:13 Household management

Sirach 29:21-28 concerns self-sufficiency. Whereas 39:26 lists ten necessities for life, 29:21 picks out three of them (water, bread, and clothing), and adds housing. While the Stoic philosophers praised self-sufficiency, the aphorism of 29:22 also has biblical parallels (Prov 12:9; 17:1). Sirach 29:23-24 calls on the wise person to be content with a few basic needs (Prov 30:8; 1 Tim 6:8), since it is miserable to always be the guest of other people (Prov 27:8; 2 Kgs 8:1). The visitor is treated like a slave, being told to serve food (Luke 17:8), and moved to an inferior place to accommodate visiting relatives (29:25-27). For the self-respecting student of wisdom, it is painful to be dependent on others for hospitality.

Sirach 30:1-13 deals with the disciplining of sons. The hoped-for benefit of discipline is subsequent good behavior (Prov 10:1; 22:6) that will bring joy to the child's parents (25:7). Indeed, the disciplined son is a worthy replacement for his father (Tob 9:6), in a society esteeming conformity to patriarchal models. Lacking a clear idea of an afterlife (14:16; 17:27-28), Ben Sira considered it important for a male to perpetuate his name by fathering a dutiful son (40:19), as well as by leaving behind a good reputation (41:13; 44:8). Sirach 30:6 sees the son's role as avenging insults offered to his father (Ps 127:5), as well as rewarding kindnesses (1 Kgs 2:7). Ben Sira then warns against pampering a son. The spoiled child foolishly incurs wounds (or inflicts them on others), leaving the father to bandage them. A child needs discipline (Prov 29:15), just as a horse has to be broken in (Prov 26:3). According to 30:9, overindulging a child is a disservice that will eventually bring grief. Hence Ben Sira recommends physical punishment (Prov 13:24; 22:15), though his advice seems harsh for modern readers.

30:14–31:11 Physical and material happiness

Sirach 30:14-25 considers the physical happiness produced by good health and an optimistic outlook. Ben Sira sees health as very important (38:1-15). In regarding death as preferable to a bitter life, he echoes feelings voiced by Moses (Num 11:15), Elijah (1 Kgs 19:4), and Job (Job 3:11-13). A meal presented to someone too sick to eat is as useless as the food that pagans offered to the dead (Deut 26:14; Bar 6:26) or to idols (Ps 115:5-6). A hopeful outlook contributes to good health, just as brooding can lead to depression (Prov 15:13; 17:22). Sirach 30:22-25 advocates enjoying the good things in life (Eccl 9:7-9) but leaving aside resentment, envy, and anger, which cause needless distress (28:6-7).

Sirach 31:1 notes that the worry of the rich about their money often prevents them from sleeping soundly (Eccl 5:11). Whereas the wealthy can enjoy luxury as a result of their work, the poor labor to survive and cannot afford any rest (40:1-2). The sage points out the moral dangers of wealth (31:5-7) and praises the rich person who has maintained virtue (31:8-11). The corrupting power of unfettered wealth is well known to ethical teachers (Prov 28:20; 1 Tim 6:9-10). Because riches can be a temptation (27:1), anyone who is not led astray by wealth deserves praise (Mark 10:23-25).

31:12–32:13 Good manners in eating and drinking

While banquets had long been a feature of the life of the oriental ruling classes (Amos 6:4-6; Esth 1:5-9), Greek tradition placed great importance on the banquet and the ensuing drinking party or symposium. Hence Sirach 31:12-21 advocates moderation in eating. Like 14:9-10 and 37:29, Sirach 31:12-13 advises the avoidance of gluttony (Prov 23:1-3), because danger lurks in the greedy eye (Gen 3:6; 1 John 2:16). Ben Sira urges self-restraint in deference to the feelings of others (Lev 19:18; Rom 15:1-2). Dignified behavior entails being the last to reach out for food and the first to stop eating. For disciplined guests, a moderate amount is enough, so that one will avoid the discomfort resulting from excessive consumption. Sirach 31:21 refers to induced vomiting, commonly practiced by wealthy Romans after overeating.

When advocating self-control in drinking (31:22-31), Ben Sira echoes earlier admonitions about the proper consumption of wine, not only from the Bible (Prov 23:29-35; 31:4-7), but also from the writings of the Greek poet Theognis (497–510). Sirach 31:25 warns against competitive drinking (Isa 5:22; Prov 20:1), since intoxication can lead to many evils (Gen 19:31-36; 1 Macc 16:16). For humanity, a moderate consumption of wine enhances life, by contributing to health and joy (Ps 104:15; 1 Tim 5:23), whereas overindulgence is harmful (31:29-30).

Ben Sira then outlines good table manners for the banquet presider (32:1-2), the elders (32:3-6), the younger guests (32:7-10), and all those invited (32:11-13). The person chosen to preside at dinner is to behave humbly as one of the company (3:17-18), concerned that the guests be satisfied (2 Macc 2:27). The older guests are entitled to share their wisdom (8:8-9; 25:4-6), if they are careful not to interrupt the musical entertainment. The younger guests are to wait until the elders invite them to talk (Job 32:6-7), and then speak briefly. The wise guest also leaves promptly at the proper time for departing. Above all, the virtuous give thanks to God for the gift of food and drink (Deut 8:10; John 6:11).

USING WISDOM TO
MAKE GOOD DECISIONS
Sirach 32:14–38:23

32:14–33:18 Divine providence

Whereas the honest seeker for God is enlightened through study of the law of Moses (32:14-16), sinners reject correction. Sirach 32:18 declares that the sensible person heeds the advice rejected by the arrogant (Prov 12:15; Tob 4:18). According to 32:24, observance of the Torah leads to self-preservation (Prov 19:16). Sirach 33:1-3 contrasts the consistent God-fearing person with unstable apostates, who are tossed about like a ship in a tempest (Jonah 1:5; Eph 4:14). For the wise, God's word is as reliable as the priestly oracle given through the sacred lots of Urim and Thummim (Exod 28:30; Num 27:21).

Having contrasted wise and foolish persons, Ben Sira investigates why the world contains both good and evil people (33:7-15). The sage first considers God's allocation of times (Eccl 3:1-8; Dan 2:21), as seen in the Jewish religious calendar. While in principle every day is of equal value, God has selected some to be special. Days such as sabbaths and festivals are holy (Gen 2:3; Lev 23:2), but other days are ordinary (Rom 14:5; 2 Tim 2:20). So, too, people differ because God has decreed their differing paths (33:10-11). God is like a potter, shaping human beings according to the divine will (Isa 29:16; Rom 9:21). In 33:12 Ben Sira implies that the Israelites are the chosen people whom God has blessed and made holy (Gen 12:2; Exod 19:6). By contrast (according to 16:9), those cursed and dispossessed include the Canaanites (Deut 7:1-2), but the idea of a divine curse on people raises many questions for modern readers of the Bible.

In Ben Sira's scheme here (33:13), God's decree assigns good and evil in a rather deterministic way, as in the Qumran Community Rule (1QS 3:15-4:1). Ben Sira's theodicy is based on a system of paired opposites (42:24-25), such as good and evil (Job 2:10; Eccl 7:13-14; Isa 45:7). Sirach 33:14-15 may be echoing the Stoic philosopher Chrysippus (d. ca. 206 B.C.): "Since goods are opposite to evils, the two must necessarily exist in opposition to each other" (*On Providence*, fragment 1169).

In 33:16-18, Ben Sira concludes this poem on a personal note (24:30-33; 34:12-13), comparing himself to a gleaner following the grape pickers (Lev 19:10; Deut 24:21). His toil has not been simply for his own benefit, but to help everyone seeking wisdom (51:23-28).

33:19–33 Property and servants

Ben Sira's cautious advice is to retain patriarchal control of household power as long as possible (33:20-23), so as to avoid the shame of depending on others for one's livelihood (29:24-28; 40:28-30). Sirach 33:24 even suggests waiting until one's deathbed before distributing property to the heirs (Tob 4:1-2).

Sirach 33:25-33 discusses treatment of slaves, regarded in the ancient world as their masters' property (Deut 5:21). The first part (33:25-30) enjoins harsh treatment, whereas the second part (33:31-33) urges kindness. The saying of 33:25, based on Proverbs 26:3, makes the demeaning comparison of a slave to a beast of burden. Slaves who are forced to work will only look for their rest, but those left idle will seek freedom (Exod 5:4, 17). Sirach 33:27 advocates physical punishment for recalcitrant slaves (Prov 29:19), even confining them in the stocks (Jer 20:2). By contrast, the New Testament letters teach that slaves be treated humanely (Eph 6:9; Col 4:1). Sirach 33:28 warns against leaving slaves unoccupied (Prov 21:25), while 33:30 advises loading the unruly slave with heavy metal fetters (Lam 3:7). Nevertheless, the sage urges the student not to impose his superiority over others, and to do nothing unjust against the law of Moses. In fact, the Torah protected what limited rights slaves had (Exod 21:1-11; Deut 15:12-18).

Ben Sira now echoes the Torah in urging kind treatment for a reliable household slave (33:31-33), who is to be treated like oneself (Exod 21:5-6; Lev 19:18) and regarded as one of the family (7:21). Indeed, treating such a slave like a brother fulfils the Torah (Lev 25:39-40), which urges generous treatment of an impoverished compatriot. Apart from prisoners of war (1 Macc 8:10-11), many slaves were fellow Israelites who had fallen into debt (Prov 11:29). Ben Sira concludes that if such a slave runs away, he is lost forever, since the Torah forbids returning a runaway slave to his master (Deut 23:16-17).

34:1-20 Devout wisdom more reliable than dreams

This poem has three sections: the futility of dreams (34:1-8); the value of wisdom amid life's experiences (34:9-13); and the benefit of fear of the Lord (34:14-20). The ancient Greeks often thought dreams carried messages from the gods (Plato, *Crito* 44a), while Jewish apocalyptic texts told of Enoch's dream visions (1 Enoch 13:10; 83:3). By contrast, Ben Sira adopts the Deuteronomic suspicion of dreams as leading people away from the one true God (Deut 13:2-5; Jer 23:25-32). Trusting in dreams is like chasing the wind (Eccl 5:2). Ben Sira generally links dreams with divinations and omens, which the Torah forbids (Lev 19:26; Deut 18:10-14). However, dreams can be sent by God, as happened to Joseph, Solomon, and Eliphaz (Gen 37:5-10; 1 Kgs 3:5-15; Job 4:12-21). Whereas false dreams have led many astray (Jer 29:8-9), perfect wisdom can be reliably found in the law of Moses.

Sirach 34:9-13 speaks of the wisdom gained through travel (39:4). The understanding that Ben Sira gained on his journeys (possibly to Alexandria) may have included some acquaintance with Greek or Egyptian literature. Another source of wisdom is the testing experience of travel hazards (2 Cor 11:25-26).

In 34:14-20, the sage speaks of the benefits of reverencing the Lord, who supports his followers wherever they are. Indeed, trustful hope in God casts out fear (Ps 23:1-4; 1 John 4:18). The devout are fortunate, because God's eyes are on them to save them (Ps 33:18-19; 128:1). Even for the traveler, God is a shelter and a guard (Ps 121:5-6; Isa 25:4-5).

34:21–35:26 True worship of God

This long section on piety and social responsibility leads into a prayer for divine deliverance of the oppressed Israelites (36:1-22). Sirach 34:21-23 asserts that sacrifice is useless without a concern for justice (Isa 1:14-17; Amos 5:21-24). An offering from ill-gotten goods is unacceptable to God (Prov 21:27; Mal 1:6-8), and a multitude of sin-offerings does not bring forgiveness without repentance (Lev 4:13-21; Hos 8:13).

With prophetic vigor the sage condemns those who offer sacrifices from goods taken from the poor (34:24-27). Seizing a person's livelihood is as bad as slaying a son in his father's presence, the cruel punishment inflicted on Jerusalem's last king Zedekiah (2 Kgs 25:6-7). The God who is father of the poor (Ps 68:6; 103:13) cannot be pleased with sacrifices of goods stolen from the needy. Similarly, depriving laborers of their wages is equivalent to murder (Deut 24:14-15; Jas 5:4-6). In 1514, these verses helped Bartolomé de Las Casas to grasp the harmful effects of the Spanish conquest on the indigenous population of the Americas (*History of the Indies*, bk. 3, ch. 79).

Sirach 34:28-31 condemns insincerity in worship. A builder's labor is wasted if someone else destroys the building (Jer 45:4; Eccl 1:3). Likewise, if the oppressor offers prayers while his poor victims call out to God against him (Exod 22:22), God will hear the cry of the needy, rather than the oppressor's prayers (4:5-6). The law of Moses stipulated a ritual for being cleansed from the impurity contracted by touching a corpse (Num 19:11-12), but the purification rite is wasted if a person touches a dead body afterward (2 Pet 2:22). Likewise, those who fast for the forgiveness of their faults and then return to their sins obtain no benefit from their self-denial (Lev 16:29-30; Isa 58:3-7).

According to 35:1-5, true worship involves upright deeds as well as religious devotion (Jas 1:27). The sage equates keeping the Torah with offering communion sacrifices (Lev 7:29-30; 1 Sam 15:22), while performing kindness is equivalent to presenting a grain offering to God (Lev 2:1-3; Mark 12:32-33). The sacrifice pleasing God is to turn away from evil and injustice (Job 1:1; 28:28).

Sirach 35:6-13 outlines the right attitude for worship. Rather than coming empty-handed (Exod 23:15; Deut 16:16), the person attending the temple liturgy should bring the prescribed offerings (7:29-31). The worship offered by the righteous is acceptable to God, because the sacrifice of their just deeds matches the offerings they make at the temple (Prov 21:3). In 35:10-11, freewill gifts were the priests' portion, while tithes were for the Levites' upkeep (Num 18:8-24; Tob 1:6-8). According to 35:12-13, worshipers can give joyfully because they trust that God will provide for them (Deut 14:22-29; 2 Cor 9:7-8). In response to God's abundant blessings, the sage urges generosity "according to your means" (Lev 5:11; Tob 4:8). As Exodus 20:6 affirms, God rewards people for their good actions (12:2).

Sirach 35:14-22a asserts that the prayers of the needy will not go unheard. God cannot be bribed with sacrifices (Deut 10:17; Gal 6:7), especially offerings derived from inequitable dealings (Prov 15:8). Instead, God upholds justice (Gen 18:25; Deut 10:18) and shows no favoritism (2 Chr 19:7; Acts 10:34-35). Though not unduly partial toward the poor (Lev 19:15), God will certainly hear the cries of the victims of injustice (Prov 22:22-23), especially oppressed widows and orphans (Exod 22:21-22; Luke 18:1-8). Indeed, the pauper's cry pierces the clouds to reach God (Exod 3:9).

Using the image of the divine warrior (Exod 15:3; Isa 42:13), Sirach 35:22b-24 warns that oppressing the weak leads to judgment from the Almighty. Vengeance will come upon the "proud," presumably including the foreign rulers of Palestine in Ben Sira's lifetime (10:8), because God is able to repay people for their wicked deeds (Prov 24:12; Jer 25:14). In 35:25, Ben Sira is confident that God will plead Israel's cause (Isa 51:22) so that they can rejoice in his saving help (Isa 25:9). The Israelites yearn for God's merciful answer to their prayers, just as people long for rain clouds in a time of drought (Zech 10:1).

36:1-22 Prayer for divine deliverance

Although the strong nationalistic tone of this prayer has led some scholars to doubt that Ben Sira wrote it, various factors suggest that he is indeed its author. As in 24:10-11 and 50:1-21, Jerusalem is central in 36:18-19, and the sage's nationalistic feeling is also evident in 50:25-26. The plea for vengeance on the nations arises naturally out of his concern for the oppressed who call on the divine warrior for help (35:21-26). This prayer is in line with pleas for vengeance in the Hebrew Bible (Ps 94:1-7; Jer 10:25), though it differs from Jesus' call to forgive enemies (Matt 5:44). The absence of 36:14-15 does not reflect any missing text but is due to a dislocation in the Greek manuscripts.

The first stanza (36:1-5) prays for divine punishment of the pagan nations, presumably Israel's Hellenistic overlords—either the Ptolemies before 200 B.C. or the Seleucids thereafter. Pleading that the Gentiles be made to dread God, Ben Sira implicitly recalls the exodus and David's victories

(Exod 15:16; 1 Chr 14:17). Whereas God has previously demonstrated justice by punishing the Israelites for their sins, now the prayer asks that God may show them mercy and thereby display holiness (Ezek 36:23). Thus the pagan nations will recognize that there is one true God (Ps 83:19; 1 Chr 17:20).

The second stanza (36:6-12) continues the appeal for divine punishment on Israel's foes. Ben Sira prays for God to renew his wonders, such as those performed through Moses at the time of the exodus (Exod 15:6; Ps 135:9). In 36:8, Ben Sira echoes earlier biblical prayers for God to pour out wrath on pagan nations (Jer 10:25; Ps 79:6). The sage asks God to humble the enemy and defeat the foe, as David had done previously (47:5-7). Mention of the appointed time (36:10) recalls Habakkuk's promise of an occasion when foreign powers would no longer oppress Israel (Hab 2:3).

The third stanza (36:13-19) prays for the regathering of the scattered Israelites, in accordance with the hopes of the prophets (Jer 31:8; Ezek 39:27). Ben Sira begs that the dispersed Jews may inherit the promised land as the early Israelites did under Moses and Joshua (Deut 31:7; Josh 1:6), thereby restoring the situation as in days of old (Isa 51:9; Ps 44:2-4). Israel is called the Lord's people (Deut 28:10; Jer 14:9) and God's firstborn (Exod 4:22; Jer 31:9). Since Jerusalem is the holy city (Isa 52:1; Matt 27:53) and God's dwelling place (Exod 15:17), Ben Sira prays that the temple may be filled with divine glory (1 Kgs 8:11; Hag 2:7).

The final stanza (36:20-22) begs for the fulfillment of the biblical prophecies, so that the nations may recognize the true God (Ezek 36:36). Unlike earlier wisdom books of the Bible, Sirach has an interest in prophecy (48:1–49:10). The "deeds of old" (36:20) cover the divine election of Israel and the exodus (Isa 63:11-12; Ps 74:2). The hope offered by the prophets includes visions of God's rescue of the people from foreign nations (Ezek 34:13; Hab 2:3). As a result of the divine deliverance granted in answer to this prayer, Ben Sira asks that knowledge of the one true God will reach the ends of the earth (Isa 37:20; 45:22).

36:23–37:15 Discernment in relationships

This poem concerns discernment in making important relationships: with a wife (36:26-31), friends (37:1-6), and advisors (37:7-11). To illustrate the need for discernment, Ben Sira begins the poem by referring to the palate's selection of food (Job 12:11; 34:3).

Ben Sira then discusses the choice of wife from a male perspective. Sirach 36:26 indicates the low status of women, who were under the control of male authority figures. In second-century B.C. Jewish culture, men but not women were free to choose their spouse (Tob 7:10-13) because the marriage agreement was usually between the bridegroom and the bride's father. In 36:27 the sage acknowledges the effect that a woman's beauty has on her husband (26:16-18). If in addition she has kindly speech (Prov 15:4), her husband is very fortunate. Sirach 36:29 echoes Proverbs 18:22. As his helpmate and support (Gen 2:20; Tob 8:6), the wife also has a protective role toward her husband, like a vineyard fence defending it from wild beasts. Without a wife, a man can become a homeless wanderer (Gen 4:12). Sirach 36:31 recalls Proverbs 27:8.

In 37:1-6 the sage discusses the need to select friends carefully. Whereas anyone will claim to be loyal (Prov 20:6), some persons are not true friends. Betrayal by a supposed friend can produce a deathly sorrow, as Jesus found in Gethsemane (Matt 26:38). Despite sharing the same table (37:4), the fair-weather friend will be absent in one's time of need (6:10). By contrast, a good friend will come to one's defense against enemies, as David defended his fellow Israelites from the Philistine Goliath (1 Sam 17:32).

Sirach 37:7-11 advocates caution in choosing advisors, since some will offer advice simply out of self-interest. In line with his extreme wariness (6:13; 8:18-19), the sage urges being on guard toward potential advisors until their motives become evident. Despite predicting a happy future, they may easily stand by and watch one's misfortune. Sirach 37:10-11 lists persons from whom it is unwise to seek advice. In 37:11, jealousy caused by polygamy is presupposed in the sage's advice not to consult with a woman about a rival wife (26:6). Wariness is needed with a buyer who is seeking to make a profit (Prov 20:14).

By contrast (37:12), it is wise to consult with a religious person who keeps the commandments (9:15), shares the same outlook, and is sympathetic. It is also important to listen to one's inner instincts, as a late Egyptian wisdom text declares: "One who listens to the judgment of his heart

sleeps untroubled" (*Papyrus Insinger* 21.13). Indeed, a person's conscience is a more useful guide than seven astrologers observing the night sky from an observatory tower (Isa 47:13). Finally, the sage suggests seeking guidance from God, who can lead a person on the right path (Prov 3:6; Tob 4:19).

37:16-26 Wise speech

Sirach 37:16-18 emphasizes the primary role of language in human thought. As Genesis 1 describes God creating by means of the word, so for human beings every action begins with a thought expressed in language. Springing from the mind are four branches (or perhaps measuring sticks): good and evil, and death and life. The wording recalls the choice facing Israel in Deuteronomy 30:15: either life with prosperity (= good) if the people obeyed God, or else death together with doom (= evil) if they were disobedient. In this choice between life and death (Prov 18:21), the tongue has a crucial role (5:13).

Sirach 37:19-26 goes on to explore different kinds of wisdom (19:20-24). Despite seeming wise enough to teach others, individuals may fail to apply wisdom to their own lives, but those who apply good sense to themselves will benefit from it personally. Moreover, if someone deploys wisdom for the benefit of the whole people, the fruits of this knowledge will be enduring (24:33; 33:18). Israelites should use their understanding to help their people, because a person's lifespan is limited, whereas Israel's existence is everlasting (Jer 31:36). According to 37:24, the first to benefit from wisdom will be oneself, through receiving praise from everybody, while those who use wisdom to help the nation will inherit an eternal reputation (Prov 3:35).

37:27–38:23 Health, medicine, sickness, and death

This section comprises four poems: on health (37:27-31), medicine (38:1-8), sickness (38:9-15), and death (38:16-23). Ben Sira begins with personal responsibility for one's health (preventive medicine), before speaking of the benefit of a physician. Sirach 37:27 encourages self-restraint in eating (31:19-20), because not every food benefits everyone (1 Cor 6:12; 10:23). Ben Sira specially addresses his young students, who would be invited to Greek-style banquets where food and drink were plentiful, and so he urges moderate enjoyment of the delicacies offered (Prov 25:16). His warning against overeating (37:30) may be illustrated by the unhappy experience of the grumbling Israelites, who became nauseous from excessive consumption of quail-meat (Num 11:18-20).

Sirach 38:1-8 contains a rare positive portrayal of medical doctors in the Bible (see also the description of Luke in Col 4:14). Because much ancient medicine was connected with pagan belief, King Asa's recourse to physicians (or healers) is viewed as indicating a lack of faith (2 Chr 16:12). However, Ben Sira sees no contradiction between utilizing God-given medicines (38:4) and praying for recovery (38:9). Perhaps the sage has in mind King Hezekiah, who in his sickness used a fig poultice (Isa 38:21) and also prayed earnestly to God (Isa 38:2-3).

Ben Sira regards the medical profession as divinely approved, since a physician's skill derives from God (38:1). Because medicinal herbs come from the Creator (Gen 1:12), they are not to be despised. Sirach 38:5 recalls Moses' action of purifying a foul-tasting water source at Marah by throwing a branch into it (Exod 15:23-25). Ben Sira sees this biblical incident as divine authorization for using medicinal plants. The gift of knowledge enables humanity to benefit from God's great works (42:21-23).

Having praised the physician in 38:1-8, Ben Sira now urges his students to seek healing when required, through prayer (Jas 5:14-16) and through medical assistance (38:9-15). The first step to health is purifying one's heart by turning away from evil and by offering sacrifice for sin (Lev 5:11-13)—though other biblical texts indicate that by no means all sickness is due to sin (Job 2:7-10; John 9:2). After praying, the sick person is advised to seek help from the physician (38:12). Trusting in God and seeking medical help are not incompatible, since God's healing frequently comes through medical means. Indeed, the devout physician also prays to God for success in diagnosing and treating the patient.

After recommending his students to make use of medical help in times of sickness (38:9-15), Ben Sira discusses how to behave when death has occurred (38:16-23). He advises moderation in mourning rather than hoping in a future life (17:27-28; 41:3-4), because no clear doctrine of the

afterlife had developed before his lifetime (Job 14:7-12; Ps 115:17). For Christians, Ben Sira's teaching is completed with the later doctrine of the resurrection (1 Cor 15).

Sirach 38:16 recognizes the rightness of weeping for the dead (22:11) and carrying out a proper funeral (Tob 4:3-4; 14:12-13). It is a mistake to be absent from the burial rites, whether from disregard of the deceased or an unwillingness to make any contribution. The sage advises a couple of days of mourning, presumably for a deceased friend. For family members and important persons (Gen 50:10; Jdt 16:24), the Bible mentions a seven-day period of mourning (22:12). Aware that excessive mourning can bring on depression (Prov 15:13; 2 Cor 7:10), the sage advises a limit to grieving (30:21).

Sirach 38:20-23 cautions against brooding after a bereavement. The deceased person has no hope of returning to earthly life, and the sage offers no expectation of an afterlife (contrast Dan 12:2-3; 1 Thess 4:13-14). Hence, constant thought of the departed person will only cause depression (Gen 44:27-29; 2 Sam 12:23). Ben Sira instead counsels a firm awareness of one's own mortality (7:36; 8:7). Once the deceased has been laid to rest, his or her memory should also be allowed to rest.

DEMONSTRATING THE RESULTS OF WISDOM
Sirach 38:24–42:14

38:24–39:11 Vocations of manual workers and scribes

In order to encourage his students to acquire wisdom through study, Ben Sira praises the scribal profession in comparison with various skilled manual trades (farmer, seal engraver, smith, potter). The incentive for the student is the scribe's honorable status (39:4) and reputation (39:9-11), in contrast with the artisan's hard work (38:25-30) and less honorable position in society (38:32-33).

Ben Sira draws on an ancient Egyptian writing known as the *Satire of the Trades*, which promises wealth for the successful student. Whereas the Egyptian text compares manual laborers unfavorably to the scribe, Ben Sira recognizes the need for such workers in any community (38:31-32), because physical labor was divinely decreed

(7:15). Despite the value and necessity of manual work, Ben Sira begins by asserting the scribe's need for leisure to acquire wisdom (38:24).

In 38:25-30 Ben Sira shows the hardships of four of the eighteen trades listed in the Egyptian text: farmer (1 Kgs 19:19), seal maker (Exod 28:11), smith (Neh 3:32), and potter (Jer 18:2-6). After sampling the work of artisans involved in these four trades, Ben Sira acknowledges that these workers have their own valuable skills (38:31-33). He admits that all these occupations are necessary for the wellbeing of society, much as St. Paul speaks of a variety of roles being needed within the church community (1 Cor 12:27-30). However, 38:33 notes that artisans rarely become prominent in government.

After considering various trades, Ben Sira speaks favorably of the scribal profession (39:1-11). This description is often taken as a self-portrait. The scribe is depicted as giving his whole attention to the revealed word of God (Ps 1:2). In 39:1-2 Ben Sira mentions the "law of the Most High," the "prophecies," and the "discourses of the famous." These categories largely reflect the contents of the Hebrew Scriptures, later divided into three sections (law, prophets, and writings). As noted in 8:8, the learned scribe will gain an honored position in the service of princes (39:4), presumably at court (Prov 22:29). While serving on government missions abroad, the scribe's mind will be broadened, just as Ben Sira himself has gained wisdom through his travels (34:9-13).

Whereas other workers give close attention to their tasks, the scribe's first thought is to seek God in prayer (39:5), aware of the daily need for divine forgiveness (8:5; 17:25). Then the Lord will grant a spirit of wisdom (Isa 11:2; Eph 1:17) and stir up the praise of God (39:15). Through the scribe's teaching, others will benefit from his wisdom (33:18; 51:25-28). Sirach 39:9-11 describes the honorable status achieved by the scribe (37:22-26; 44:13-15).

39:12-35 God as source of everything good

A difficult question for religious believers is the problem of God's justice in the face of evil (theodicy). If God is good, how is it that innocent people suffer? If God created a good world (Gen 1:31), why does evil exist? While some biblical passages suggest that God is the source of every-

thing, evil as well as good (Job 2:10; Isa 45:7), other texts attribute the origin of evil to human sin (Gen 3:17; Rom 5:12) or to the activity of Satan (Wis 2:24; Job 2:7). Since Ben Sira has no doubt about God's goodness, he places his treatment of the question of theodicy within a hymn of praise to God the Creator.

Just as the psalms frequently praise the Lord for being good (Pss 118:1; 136:1), so 39:16 praises God for good deeds (Ps 111:7) and for supplying every need in its own time (Eccl 3:1-8). In the Creator's providence (Ps 33:7), water can serve a good or a bad purpose. God used water to deliver the Israelites from slavery at the exodus but to punish their oppressors (Exod 15:8-10; Wis 11:6-14). In asserting that God has made everything suitable for its purpose (39:21), Ben Sira matches the Stoic view that everything in the universe has its own useful function. Thus, the philosopher Chrysippus (d. ca. 206 B.C.) taught that mice served the purpose of encouraging human beings to be tidy (Plutarch, *On Stoic Self-Contradictions*, 1044D).

Sirach 39:22-24 asserts that both blessing and curse from God serve the divine plan (11:14). The expulsion of the nations (39:23) refers to Joshua's conquest of the promised land (Josh 11:16-23), blamed on the sinfulness of the territory's former inhabitants (Gen 15:16; 1 Kgs 21:26). Just as God's blessing causes dry farmland to be irrigated by seasonal flooding, so God's curse turns fertile soil into a salty waste as a punishment for people's disobedience (Ps 107:33-34).

Right from the beginning God has made good things for good people (39:25). By contrast, the wicked receive not just good things, but bad things as well (40:8-10). Sirach 39:26 lists ten essentials for human life (29:21). Besides drinking water, a person needs fire for heating food, iron for pans, and salt for cooking. Mention of milk and honey together recalls God's promise of the holy land to the Israelites (Exod 3:8), while the "blood of the grape" is a poetic phrase meaning wine (Gen 49:11; Deut 32:14). Clothing is mentioned as a necessity in Genesis 28:20, along with bread.

While God has created all things good, they help the virtuous but ultimately harm the wicked (39:27). There is certainly some truth in this view; for instance, money can serve many useful purposes for someone who knows how to benefit from it, but it can ruin a greedy person (31:5-8). Similarly, wine can bring joy to sensible people but may harm the foolish (31:27-30). Nevertheless, this explanation does not solve all the problems of theodicy.

As a divine punishment (39:28), the winds that normally bring fresh air can become hurricanes. Besides storm winds, Ben Sira lists eight things (39:29-30) which God uses to punish evildoers (Lev 26:14-22; Deut 28:20-24). In the form of lightning, fire can destroy the wicked (2 Kgs 1:10; Luke 9:54). Famine and pestilence were regarded as divine punishments on Israel for failing to keep the Torah (1 Kgs 8:37; Jer 21:9), as also were attacks from wild beasts and snakes (Deut 32:24; 2 Kgs 17:25). Ben Sira regards everything as available for God's use in blessing or punishing (Ps 148:8). So in 39:33 the sage restates his original assertion (39:16): God fulfills every need in its proper time (Eccl 3:1). Hence God deserves to be praised for the providential ordering of the universe (Ps 96:2; 103:1).

40:1-17 Life's burdens

The human life that begins in one's mother's womb (Job 1:21; Ps 139:13) ends with a return to the "mother of all the living"—not a reference to Eve (Gen 3:20) but to mother earth (Gen 3:19). Anxieties affect kings on their thrones (Eccl 1:12-14) as much as poor people sitting on the ground (31:1-4). Sirach 40:5 lists seven causes of anxiety that can even disturb a person's sleep (Eccl 2:23; Job 7:3-4).

After listing these psychological woes, Ben Sira describes external troubles that afflict all human beings, but especially the wicked (40:8-10). The sage asserts that calamities such as war and disease affect the wicked seven times as much as they affect the virtuous (39:28-30). Ben Sira echoes the Torah that lists such punishments for disobeying God's covenant (Deut 28:15-68).

Sirach 40:11-17 depicts the bad effects of evildoing. Human physical life, originally created from the earth (Gen 2:7; 3:19), will go back to the earth (Eccl 3:20; Job 34:15), while the spirit will return to God at death (Eccl 12:7). Far from escaping mortality (Pss 49:14-21; 146:3-4), the impious will die like other mortals, but the deeds of the virtuous will be remembered forever (41:10-11). Wealth gained from injustice (40:13-14) is compared to a desert stream in full spate that quickly dries up (Job 6:15-17). The brief prosperity of the godless is as short-lived as the flourishing of reeds at the riverside (Job 8:11-12; Wis 4:3-5), whereas justice lasts forever (Prov 10:25; Wis 1:15).

40:18-27 A decalogue of good things

Here Ben Sira lists ten of life's good things, culminating in the fear of the Lord. Although profit gained from business and the wages gained from one's labor can sweeten life (Eccl 2:10; 3:12-13), it is better to find a treasure, perhaps a symbol of the gift of wisdom (20:30-31) or a good wife (36:29).

According to 40:19, a person's name can be preserved through offspring (Deut 25:5-6) or through establishing a city (Gen 4:17; 2 Sam 5:9), but a better way to preserve one's good name is by living wisely (44:14-15). Whereas a successful farm produces the nourishment for a healthy life, a better contribution to a man's health comes from a devoted wife (26:13). According to 40:20, more delightful than liquor is "love of friends" (Syriac translation), though the Hebrew text refers to conjugal love (Song 1:2).

A true voice is a more pleasant sound than music (40:21). While human beauty delights the eye, more beautiful are the wild flowers (Matt 6:28-30). Whereas friends may offer temporary advice (37:7), better guidance comes from a prudent wife (Prov 19:14; 31:26). According to 40:24, while brothers and sisters help at a time of trouble (Prov 17:17), charitable giving provides a better protection against distress (Prov 11:4; Tob 12:9).

In spite of denials in Psalm 49:17-21 and Luke 12:15, Sirach 40:25 asserts that money makes a person secure. However, more useful than money are sound judgment and good advice, as the story of King Rehoboam shows (1 Kgs 12:13-15). While economic and physical strength are important, greater security is provided by fear of God (1:11-13; 25:10-11), as earlier biblical teaching notes (Prov 14:26-27; 22:4). Indeed, fear of God is like the garden of Eden before Adam's sin (Gen 2:8-17; Isa 51:3).

40:28–41:15 Life and death

This section concerns the opposite of life, as seen from various viewpoints: begging, which is a life not worth living (40:28-30); death, welcome or unwelcome (41:1-4); and the empty life of the godless (41:5-13). Sirach 40:28 asserts that it is better to die than to beg (29:22-23), because of the associated shame (Luke 16:3). Shameless people find sweetness in food given freely, because they do not have to pay for it, but in the end it will be as destructive as fire (Prov 6:27; Job 20:12-15).

Sirach 41:1-2 notes that death may be welcome to a sufferer but unwelcome to a healthy person (Job 3:21; 21:23-26). Paradoxically (Eccl 3:2), the evil of death can appear good to someone with very poor health (30:17). Ben Sira advises acceptance of death in its time, not because of a hope in the resurrection, but rather because it is the divine decree (14:17; 17:1-2), as Genesis shows (Gen 2:17; 3:19). While death is the universal fate of humanity (14:18; 38:22), Sirach 41:4 suggests that the sage has no hope of an afterlife (Eccl 6:3-6; 9:10), unlike some texts written after the Maccabean revolt (Dan 12:1-3; 2 Macc 7:9; 12:44-45).

Ben Sira now reflects on the unhappy earthly fate of the wicked (41:5-10), whose descendants are unsuccessful and whose name is a disgrace (Job 18:17-21; Ps 21:11). According to the sage, sinners' children lose their power and gain dishonor (Wis 3:17-19; 4:19). Against the usual biblical pattern for family life (Deut 27:16; Prov 31:28), these children will curse a father whose wickedness has caused them disgrace (Wis 12:10-11). Sirach 41:8 laments those who forsake the Torah (49:4), a great temptation to Ben Sira's students because of the strong influence of pagan Greek culture around that time (2 Macc 4:12-17). Whereas the human body decays (41:11), a good reputation is permanent, more precious than treasures (Prov 10:7; 22:1).

41:16–42:8 Appropriate and inappropriate shame

In Ben Sira's culture, shame was a strong motivating force to keep social and moral order, but he did not think people were always ashamed of the right things (4:21), so he lists things that deserve shame (moral lapses and breaches of social etiquette), as well as other items that do not require shame.

Sirach 41:17–42:1 provides a list of twenty disgraceful things. The first seven items all involve a breach of trust in word or deed, while the next five things concern thoughtless or unkind behavior. The following four disgraceful items are sexual misdeeds, starting with looks (Matt 5:28) and ending with deeds (9:8-9), and the last four examples concern breaches of friendship (18:15; 22:22).

After listing actions to be ashamed of, Ben Sira catalogs things for which one need not apologize (42:2-8). The first item is the Torah (42:2). Soon after Ben Sira's day, many Jewish males became ashamed of the Mosaic law and tried to disguise their circumcision (1 Macc 1:15). The second example means perhaps: "Do not be so ashamed of passing judgment that you let someone guilty go unpunished" (cf. Prov 24:23-24). The following six items concern proper business practices: fair division of costs and benefits, honest weights and measures (Prov 11:1; 16:11), and robust commercial dealings (37:11).

The next four items that do not warrant shame concern managing a household (42:5-6), as viewed from a patriarchal standpoint (30:1-13; 33:25-33). Modern appreciation of human dignity means that we find it abhorrent that slaves were beaten and wives "sealed" by keeping them indoors. Mention of a "key" where there are many hands may refer to securing household goods against theft, or could refer to keeping an unmarried girl at home, away from the unwanted attentions of young men. The next two items involve the scribal task of keeping records, while the final pair of items concerns use of wisdom to chastise the foolish and undisciplined (Prov 19:25; Dan 13:52-59).

42:9-14 Paternal concern for daughters

The previous poem on shame leads Ben Sira to consider the care of daughters, since female relatives can bring great honor or dishonor to a male within a patriarchal shame culture. By modern standards, Ben Sira's writing is objectionable. In Hellenistic Judaism, as in Greek society of that time, there was a tendency to confine girls and even women to the home (2 Macc 3:19). Thus, Philo in the first century A.D. wrote: "Women are best suited to the indoor life which never strays from the house" (*Special Laws* 3.169).

Like a man who is sleepless when guarding something precious at home (42:9), a Jewish father in Ben Sira's time keeps anxious watch over a daughter (7:24-25). The patriarchal concern is for her to marry, to remain pure, and to be fertile. The father's worry about her when she is unmarried involves three scenarios (42:9-10): that she does not find a husband, or is defiled by rape or seduction (in which case it would be hard to find a bridegroom for her), or becomes pregnant while still under her father's care.

But when she is married, her father is still concerned that his daughter may disgrace him (42:9-10), though he need not worry about her anymore (7:25). Now the concern involves three other scenarios: that she will be hated by her husband (here the New American Bible has "sterile"), or be unfaithful to him, or prove unable to bear him a child (Gen 30:23; Luke 1:25).

The sage urges paternal vigilance over an unmarried daughter, so as to avoid any family shame (42:11). Indeed, Ben Sira even advises forbidding a lattice in her room, in case a man might see her beauty (Prov 7:6; Song 2:9). Similarly, an Alexandrian Jew of the first century B.C. or A.D. taught: "Guard a virgin in firmly locked rooms, and let her not be seen outside the house until her wedding day" (*Pseudo-Phocylides* 215–16).

Sirach 42:12 also prohibits an unmarried daughter from spending time with married women, presumably because they would talk frankly about their experience of marriage. The sage's chauvinistic view in 42:13 seems to be that corruption is hidden in women like a moth lurking in a garment (Job 13:28; Isa 50:9). While the Masada Hebrew text of 42:14b appears to say: "Better a reverent [or: fearful] daughter than any disgrace," another reading of the manuscript is: "Better a reverent daughter than a shameless son."

WISDOM IN CREATION AND HISTORY

Sirach 42:15–50:24

42:15–43:33 Praise of God's works in creation

As a preparation for the Praise of the Ancestors (44:1–50:24), Ben Sira celebrates God's marvelous creation. According to 42:15, the purpose of the hymn is to recall God's actions (Ps 77:12) and recount what the sage has seen (Job 15:17). God created the universe through the word (Gen 1:3; John 1:3), and the divine glory shines as clearly as sunlight (Ps 19:2-7; Rom 1:20). Despite being in God's presence, angels ("holy ones") are not fully aware of the marvels of divine power (Job 15:15).

The omniscient God searches inscrutable regions (42:18), not only the depths of the sea (Job 38:16), but also the human heart (Prov 15:11; Jdt 8:14). According to 42:18-22, God's knowledge includes the past and the future (Isa 41:21-23), since God sees all the ages (39:20) while remaining unchanging. Hence there is no addition or subtraction with God (Eccl 3:14), nor is there any need for an advisor (Isa 40:13; Rom 11:34).

Ben Sira next acknowledges the beautiful harmony of creation (42:23-25), in which everything created has a stable form of existence. Ben Sira does not mean that every creature lives forever, since both humans and animals die (14:17-18; 41:3). Rather, each creature exists for a particular purpose. In fact, God has created the world with a balance of opposites (11:14; 33:14-15), such as light and darkness (Gen 1:3-5; Isa 45:7).

Next Ben Sira enumerates God's works, visible in the sky and the weather (43:1-22). Whereas Jewish apocalyptic writers and Greek scientists tried in various ways to explain the phenomena of the skies, Ben Sira contented himself with observing creation and praising God for it.

According to 43:2, the sun is not a god as in pagan religion (Egyptian Ra or Greek Apollo), but is rather the work of the Most High. Like a white-hot furnace, the noonday sun scorches the land (Ps 104:32). Sirach 43:5 recalls the ancient picture of the sun as drawn across the sky by horses (2 Kgs 23:11). According to 43:6-7, the moon marks the changing seasons of the Israelite religious calendar (Exod 12:2; Ps 104:19). The beauty of the rainbow (43:11) is a reason for praising its Maker (Gen 9:13; Ezek 1:28).

Sirach 43:13 regards the storm as manifesting God's power (Pss 18:15-16; 104:7), seen in the lightning flashes of divine judgment. In 43:16 the portrayal of the storm echoes earlier biblical depictions (Pss 18:8; 29:8), while the beautiful description of snow and frost (43:17-20) recalls Psalm 147:16-17. Sirach 43:22 speaks of the rain and dew that make the scorched land fertile (Ps 65:10-12).

In 43:23-26, the sage turns to the sea, which the ancient Israelites regarded as terrifying (Ps 107:23-32; Jonah 1:4-16). God's might is evident in God's victory over the ocean's destructive power (Pss 29:3; 89:10-11), especially in the subsiding of the great flood (Gen 8:1-3). Sea voyagers tell of God's marvels that they have witnessed, such as the marine creatures (Ps 107:23-24). Each created being is like a messenger that obediently does God's will (Ps 104:4).

After these descriptions of God's marvelous creatures, Ben Sira turns to praising the Creator (43:27-33). Like Ecclesiastes 12:13, his summary is simple: God is the "all," in other words, the source of all that exists. One of the Dead Sea Scrolls praises God similarly: "Blessed is he who is everything" (4Q267 18.5.9). Ben Sira is not equating God with the created world, since "greater is he than all his works" (43:28). Human beings can praise God only inadequately for God's unfathomable greatness (Pss 106:2; 145:3). However, God does grant wisdom to the devout, some of whom will be celebrated in Sirach 44–50.

44:1–50:24 Praise of Israel's ancestors

Ben Sira's longest composition is a review of Israel's history, extending from the Genesis patriarchs to the contemporary high priest Simeon the Just. Whereas earlier biblical writers had praised God for acting through figures like Moses, Aaron, and David (Pss 77:21; 144:10), Ben Sira actually praises the illustrious figures themselves. This kind of hero list, paralleled in later biblical books (1 Macc 2:51-60: Heb 11:4-38), is patterned on the Greek encomium that mostly celebrated the deeds of male figures. This fact may explain Ben Sira's exclusion of leading female figures from his composition, a serious omission for modern readers.

The whole poem consists of four sections. The introduction (44:1-15) is followed by a longer section focusing particularly on the leading Pentateuchal figures with whom God made a covenant (44:16–45:26), ending with a doxology (45:25-26). The next major section treats figures from Israel's historical and prophetic books, especially prophets and kings (46:1–49:16). The poem is completed by the praise of the recent high priest Simeon (50:1-24), ending with a second doxology (50:22-24).

44:1-15 Praising unnamed heroes of faith

The Praise of the Ancestors begins with an introduction, sometimes used for services commemorating the deceased. Whereas the following sections name specific biblical characters, 44:1-15 offers a general celebration of the dead. The opening words of 44:1 echo the initial phrase of the poem extolling God's works in creation (42:15). The "Most High's portion" from ancient times denotes the people of Israel (Deut 32:7-9). Among the categories of important figures listed in 44:3-6,

priests seem to be absent, though they play a prominent role later on (45:6-26; 50:1-24).

While all these figures were honored in their generation (44:7), some of them have left a reputation (particularly in the biblical narratives), whereas others have left no memorial (44:9). Since he lacks a clear belief in the afterlife (7:17; 17:27-28), Ben Sira wants Israel's heroes kept alive in the memory of their descendants (44:10-15). Accordingly, his characteristic emphasis is on surviving death through one's "name," either with a lasting "reputation" (39:9-11; 41:11-13), or with offspring carrying on the family "name" (16:4; 40:19).

44:16-23 The patriarchs of Genesis

After the introduction, the first part of the Praise of the Ancestors celebrates the Genesis patriarchs. The reference to Enoch in 44:16 (echoing Gen 5:24) may not be original, since this verse is absent from the Masada Hebrew text, and Enoch is also mentioned in 49:14. The Cairo Genizah Hebrew text depicts Enoch here as a sign of knowledge; in other words, a recipient of heavenly secrets (1 Enoch 92:1), whereas the Greek text portrays Enoch as an example of repentance (Wis 4:10-11). To accommodate both senses, the New American Bible offers a paraphrase in 44:16.

Sirach 44:17-23 deals with Noah, Abraham, Isaac, and Jacob, four patriarchs with whom God made or renewed a covenant (Gen 9:9; 17:9; 26:3-5; 28:13-15). Noah is celebrated for his role in enabling the human race to survive the flood (Gen 6:8–9:19; Heb 11:7). Sirach 44:17-18 links the cessation of the flood and God's covenant with Noah (Gen 9:9-11), while the rainbow is the sign that God will never again send a deluge on the entire earth (Gen 9:12-15).

Sirach 44:19-21 concerns Abraham (Gen 11:26–25:10). The sage alludes to the play on words in Genesis 17:4-5, whereby the patriarch's name was changed from Abram (exalted father) to Abraham (father of a multitude). Abraham is praised because his glory was unblemished, while in Hebrews 11:8-19 he appears as an example of faith. The covenant of Genesis 17:9-10 included the sign of circumcision, which is the "ordinance" in Abraham's flesh. In response to the severely testing command to offer his own son (Gen 22:1-2), Abraham was found faithful (Neh 9:8; 1 Macc 2:52). Accordingly, in Genesis 22:15-18 God made an oath to bless nations in his offspring.

In 44:22 Ben Sira mentions Isaac (Gen 21:1–35:29; Heb 11:20). The divine gift to him of a son was because of the promise of a great progeny made to Abraham (Gen 15:1-6; 17:4-8). Sirach 44:23 refers briefly to Isaac's son Jacob (Gen 25:20–49:33; Heb 11:21). The blessing came to rest on the head of Israel (Jacob), though he was younger than Esau, as a result of the trickery suggested by Rebekah (Gen 27:27-29). God gave Jacob his inheritance in terms of offspring, since his twelve sons became ancestors of tribes.

45:1-5 Moses

Chapter 45 considers three Levitical recipients of God's covenants (Moses, Aaron, Phinehas). According to the Hebrew text of 45:1, Jacob became the ancestor of Moses (*Moshe*), a man finding (*motse*) favor with everyone living. As a baby he found favor with Pharaoh's daughter (Exod 2:1-10). While the Greek version says that Moses resembled the angels in honor (45:2), the Hebrew manuscript asserts that Moses was honored like God, alluding to his God-like position toward Pharaoh, with Aaron as his mouthpiece (Exod 4:16; 7:1). The signs worked by Moses included the ten plagues (Exod 7:8–11:10), the exodus event (Exod 14:10-31), and the miracles in the wilderness (Exod 15:22–17:7). Though God's initial commands to Moses concerned the exodus (Exod 3:16-22), the lasting commandments were enshrined in the law (Exod 20:1–23:33). God's glory was also revealed to Moses, especially on Mount Sinai (Exod 24:16; 33:18).

Moses' trustworthiness toward God (45:4) was evident when most of the Israelites worshiped the golden calf (Exod 32:1-20). Although Moses accomplished great things, he was the meekest person on earth (Num 12:3), the most docile to the divine commands. God led him into the dark cloud of the storm-like theophany on Mount Sinai (Exod 19:16-19; 20:21). There God gave him the law of understanding and life (Deut 4:6; 30:15), so that he could teach it to the Israelites (Deut 4:14; Ps 147:19).

45:6-22 Aaron

Compared with Moses, Aaron receives more coverage here, because he more closely anticipates the high priest Simeon (50:1-21). The poem falls into two halves: Aaron's clothing (45:6-13) and his sacrifices (45:14-22). As the first Israelite priest at the time of the exodus (Exod 28:1), Aaron was just as holy as his brother Moses (Ps 106:16).

Sirach 45:6-13 describes Aaron's glory, which consisted in worshiping God in splendid priestly attire according to the perpetual ordinance (Exod 28:2; 29:9). Sirach 45:8-9 portrays the high priest's robes (Exod 28:31-43), which had woven pomegranate shapes and gold bells attached to the hem. The "breastpiece for decision" (45:10) had a pocket containing the sacred lots of Urim and Thummim that were cast to discover God's will in doubtful matters (Exod 28:30). The ephod was a priestly garment like an apron (Exod 28:6-14), while the cincture or sash kept the tunic in place (Exod 28:39; Lev 8:7). On the breastpiece were twelve precious stones, each inscribed with the name of one of the Israelite tribes (Exod 28:17-21; Wis 18:24), while the miter or turban had a gold diadem (Exod 28:36). These high-priestly garments were meant for Aaron and his descendants only (Exod 29:4-9).

The rest of the passage (45:14-22) focuses on the sacrifices offered by Aaron, starting with the grain offering (Lev 6:13-16) that accompanied the regular Tamid sacrifice each morning and evening (Num 28:3-6). Moses ordained Aaron (Exod 28:41; 29:9) by anointing him with sacred oil (Exod 30:30-33). Aaron's tasks included giving the high-priestly blessing (Lev 9:22), offering sacrifices (Lev 2:2), and atoning for the people's sins (Lev 16:32-34). The priests had the role of judging legal cases (Deut 17:8-11) and of instructing the people (Lev 10:11; Deut 33:10). Sirach 45:18-19 alludes to the rebellion of Korah, Dathan, and Abiram, who challenged the unique holiness of Aaron and Moses (Num 16:3). The "marvel" (45:19) was the sudden sinking of the ground that swallowed up the rebels, along with the sudden fire that came from the sanctuary to destroy their supporters (Num 16:31-35).

According to 45:20, Aaron's glory was increased by the allocation of Levites to assist the priests, and by the grant of the priestly share of the sacrifices (Lev 24:5-9; Num 18:6-19). Yet because God was their inheritance, the priests would not inherit any land (Num 18:20).

45:23-26 Phinehas

The zealous priest Phinehas, Aaron's grandson, receives almost as much coverage as Moses. During a time of apostasy, Phinehas killed an

Israelite who had taken a Midianite wife and was engaged in the worship of Baal (Num 25:6-13; Ps 106:30-31). The risk was that the Israelites would be led into pagan practices. According to 45:23, Phinehas's zealous action atoned for Israelite iniquity (1 Macc 2:26). As a reward, he received an eternal covenant, not only to care for the sanctuary, but also to have the high priesthood forever among his descendants (Num 25:12-13; 1 Macc 2:54).

Sirach 45:25 refers to God's covenant with Aaron, contrasted with the Davidic covenant (Ps 89:29-30; 1 Macc 2:57). David's royal line ceased to provide a king for Israel during the Babylonian exile (2 Chr 36:11-19), whereas the high-priestly line still provided Israel with a religious leader (50:1-24). The concluding doxology (45:25-26) is briefer than the one in 50:22-24. According to Ben Sira, if the new priestly leadership after Simeon's death leads the people wisely, their name will live on for generations (44:10-15). Sadly, Simeon's descendants did not maintain the traditional fidelity he had shown toward Israel's God (2 Macc 4:7).

46:1-12 Joshua, Caleb, and the judges

Sirach 46:1 praises Joshua as a warrior (Josh 10:7–11:23) and as Moses' servant (Num 11:28). Using a Hebrew wordplay, Ben Sira notes that Joshua (*Jehoshua*) brought about great salvation (*teshuah*) for the Israelites (1 Macc 2:55). Joshua's task involved both dealing vengeance to Israel's enemies (Josh 10:13) and giving Israel their inheritance (Deut 1:38; Josh 11:23). For modern readers, shocked by the destruction of indigenous peoples, the Bible's praise of Joshua is problematic. In the ancient world, however, his warfare to provide a homeland for his refugee people would have been regarded as natural. Sirach 46:2-3 praises Joshua for brandishing his sword against the city of Ai (Josh 8:18-26) and for fighting God's battles (Josh 1:9; 1 Sam 18:17). In 46:4-6 Ben Sira celebrates Joshua's victory at Gibeon, when the sun stood still at his command, while the enemy was struck with hailstones (Josh 10:7-14).

Joshua is praised because, like Caleb, he fully followed after God (Josh 14:8-9). Significantly (46:7), both men opposed the other Israelite spies who made the people afraid to enter the promised land (Num 14:6; 1 Macc 2:56). As a reward, only these two (out of six hundred thousand) were allowed to enter the land (Num 14:22-38; Josh 14:6-

13). Caleb's family gained a heritage of high ground at Hebron (Josh 15:13-14).

The brief treatment of the judges (46:11-12) praises only those who did not turn away from God; thus, for instance, Samson is probably excluded. It seems that only the minor judges deserve praise (Judg 10:1-5; 12:8-15), since they had offspring and proper burial. Sirach 46:12 wishes that their bones may sprout afresh from their burial place (49:10). Since the sage has no belief in the afterlife (14:16; 41:4), he is praying that worthy successors may continue the judges' good reputation on earth.

46:13-20 Samuel

Like Moses in 45:1, Samuel was esteemed by God and humanity (1 Sam 2:26). After noting that Samuel was pledged in a vow from his mother's womb (1 Sam 1:27-28), Sirach 46:13 refers to his anointing of Israel's first two kings, Saul and David (1 Sam 10:1; 16:13). Ben Sira then praises Samuel for his reliability as a seer (1 Sam 3:20; 9:9). Sirach 46:16-18 recalls the battle with the Philistines at Mizpah (1 Sam 7:7-13), when Samuel offered sacrifice to God, who responded by granting victory to the Israelites. Ben Sira also refers to the dying Samuel's testimony that he was innocent of any wrongdoing against the Israelites (1 Sam 12:3). The final verse speaks of Saul's consultation of the witch of Endor (1 Sam 28:8-19), against the biblical prohibition (Lev 19:31; Deut 18:10-11). The text depicts the dead Samuel as speaking from the grave, prophesying Saul's death in battle (1 Sam 28:13-19).

47:1-11 David

This poem praises King David for winning battles and providing music for divine worship. Ben Sira first mentions the prophet Nathan, whose oracle promised eternal sovereignty to the Davidic line (2 Sam 7:4-17). Sirach 47:2 then likens the king to choice fat from the temple offerings (Lev 4:8-10). Next Ben Sira celebrates David's courage, which enabled him to play with lions and bears (1 Sam 17:34-36; Isa 11:6-7), as well as to defeat Goliath with a sling stone (1 Sam 17:48-51). According to 47:5, David's victory over the Philistine warrior resulted from God's help (1 Sam 17:45-47). Then the Israelite womenfolk sang songs praising David for achieving far more than Saul (1 Sam 18:7; 21:12). When David began his reign, he subdued the surrounding enemies, such as the Philistines (2 Sam 5:17-25). As a result of David's campaigning, the Philistines never again posed a major threat to Israel (2 Chr 17:11; 26:6-7).

Amid his military successes (47:8), David devoutly gave praise to God Most High (Pss 9:2; 34:2). In fact, the Hebrew Psalter associates seventy-three psalms with David. Sirach 47:8-10 depicts David having musical melodies sung before the altar at the temporary sanctuary, before the building of the temple by his son Solomon (1 Chr 22:6). This echoes the Chronicler's tradition that David provided musicians to praise God at the sanctuary (1 Chr 16:4-42; 25:1-7).

In 47:11 the sage alludes indirectly to David's murder of Uriah and adultery with Bathsheba (2 Sam 11) by mentioning that God removed his transgression (2 Sam 12:13; Ps 51:1-4). Accordingly, he figures among Judah's three righteous kings in 49:4. David's strength was exalted "forever," because of the promise of eternal sovereignty to his offspring (2 Sam 7:16; 1 Macc 2:57). Christians see Jesus as fulfilling that promise (Luke 1:32-33).

47:12-25 Solomon and his successors

Ben Sira notes Solomon's great achievements as temple builder and mouthpiece of wisdom, as well as the harmful effects of his marriages to pagan wives. Sirach 47:12 introduces Solomon as David's wise son (1 Kgs 5:21), who reigned in a time of security (1 Kgs 5:5). God had granted Solomon "rest" (1 Kgs 5:18), as a result of his father David's military campaigns (2 Sam 7:1). Solomon constructed a house (= temple) to God's name (2 Sam 7:13; 1 Kgs 8:15-21), intended to last forever (Ps 78:69).

Sirach 47:14 celebrates Solomon's youthful wisdom, granted in answer to his prayer soon after his accession (1 Kgs 3:7-9). Indeed, his wisdom was famous far and wide (1 Kgs 10:24; Matt 12:42). Sirach 47:17 alludes to the biblical statement that Solomon uttered proverbs and songs (1 Kgs 5:12), while Proverbs 1:6 attributes riddles to him. Solomon's glorious name was "Jedidiah" (2 Sam 12:25), meaning "beloved of the Lord." Ben Sira also notes Solomon's amassing of abundant wealth in precious metals (1 Kgs 10:25-27), contrary to the Torah (Deut 17:17).

Despite his wisdom (47:19), he allowed his love of foreign women to lead him into idolatry

(1 Kgs 11:1-13). As in 9:2, critics have noted a misogynistic tone here, when Ben Sira disparages Solomon for letting "women" rule over his body (Prov 31:3). While the book of Kings blames Solomon's idolatry for the breakup of the kingdom (1 Kgs 11:9-11), Ben Sira focuses more specifically on his liaisons with foreign women.

Sirach 47:21 refers to the end of the united monarchy immediately after Solomon's death (1 Kgs 12:1-24). However, 47:22 asserts that despite Solomon's sin, God did not abandon the covenant loyalty, but fulfilled the promise by providing a descendant for David on the throne (2 Sam 7:15; Ps 89:34-38).

Unlike his father Solomon, Rehoboam lacked sense (47:23). He drove the Israelites into rebellion by imposing heavier taxation on them (1 Kgs 12:1-19), allowing "the sinner" (Jeroboam, son of Nebat) to lead the Israelite tribes astray. Jeroboam's sin was to set up golden calves at Dan and Bethel, so that the people would worship there rather than at Jerusalem (1 Kgs 12:26-30). According to 2 Kings 17:21-23, this sin of idolatry ultimately caused the northern Israelites to be exiled by the Assyrians in 722 B.C.

48:1-16 Elijah and Elisha

Sirach 48:1 aptly compares Elijah to fire, recalling the prophet's zealous temperament (1 Kgs 19:14; 1 Macc 2:58), the way he brought down "fire" (= lightning) from heaven (48:3), and the effect of his words like a burning furnace (Mal 3:19). Then 48:2 refers to his calling of a prolonged drought (1 Kgs 17:1; Jas 5:17), causing famine for Israel (1 Kgs 18:2; Luke 4:25). In 48:3 Ben Sira mentions three bolts of lightning that Elijah brought down from the sky; the first fell on the offerings at Mount Carmel (1 Kgs 18:38), while the second and third killed the messengers sent by King Ahab's son Ahaziah (2 Kgs 1:9-14). One of the prophet's awesome deeds was to restore to life the son of the widow of Zarephath (1 Kgs 17:22).

Sirach 48:6 recalls that Elijah foretold King Ahab's death as a punishment for his judicial murder of Naboth (1 Kgs 21:19; 22:34-38). The prophet also predicted the injured King Ahaziah's death, as the penalty for his worship of Baal (2 Kgs 1:16-17). The avenging judgments heard by the prophet on Mount Horeb were against the apostate Israelites (1 Kgs 19:17). To inflict this vengeance, Elijah selected two kings (1 Kgs 19:15-17),

Jehu to unleash a violent campaign against Ahab's son Joram (2 Kgs 9:14-26), and Hazael to cause the death of the Syrian king Ben-hadad (2 Kgs 8:14-15). The prophetic successor anointed by Elijah was Elisha (1 Kgs 19:16).

Like Enoch (49:14), Elijah was taken up to heaven (48:9). The prophet's assumption took place in a whirlwind (2 Kgs 2:11; 1 Macc 2:58), when Elisha saw the fiery horses and chariot. Elijah's future role, written in Malachi 3:23-24, was to put an end to wrath before the final judgment and reconcile parents and children (Matt 17:10; Luke 1:17). The role of reestablishing Israel's tribes echoes the task of God's servant in Isaiah 49:6. The damaged Hebrew manuscript of 48:11 may allude to Elisha, who saw Elijah ascending to heaven (2 Kgs 2:9-12), or else to those who will be alive at Elijah's return to earth (Mal 3:23). However, the Greek version of 48:11 introduces the idea of the afterlife: "Blessed are those who have seen you, and those who have fallen asleep in love, for we too shall certainly live."

Endowed with a double share of Elijah's spirit (2 Kgs 2:9), his successor Elisha performed twice as many miracles (48:12). Thus, whereas Elijah raised the son of the widow of Zarephath (1 Kgs 17:17-24), Elisha raised two persons, the Shunammite woman's son and the corpse thrown into Elisha's grave (2 Kgs 4:32-37; 13:21). The latter event is the subject of 48:13. Because the Israelites in the northern kingdom did not repent despite Elisha's miracles, they were eventually punished by being removed from their land and scattered throughout the Near East (2 Kgs 17:6-12). By contrast, a remnant was left to Judah (Isa 1:8-9). Whereas some of the Judean kings practiced uprightness (such as Hezekiah and Josiah), others (such as Manasseh) were very wicked.

48:17-25 Hezekiah and Isaiah

In praising the good king Hezekiah, Ben Sira first mentions his building work in Jerusalem (as with Nehemiah in 49:13), because such work foreshadowed the achievements of the high priest Simeon (50:1-4) in the sage's own lifetime. Sirach 48:17 makes a Hebrew wordplay on Hezekiah's name: he "fortified" (*hizzak*) his city and also brought water into its midst (2 Kgs 20:20). Next the sage describes Sennacherib's siege of Jerusalem in 701 B.C., mentioning the taunts of the Assyrian commander, the Jerusalemites' fear, the

prayer of Hezekiah, and Isaiah's promise of deliverance (2 Kgs 18:13–19:34; Isa 36:1–38:22). Whereas 2 Kings 19:35 attributes sudden death in the Assyrian camp to the angel of the Lord, 48:21 ascribes it to a plague or epidemic. Sirach 48:22 recalls Isaiah's role in the cure of Hezekiah, along with the associated sign of the shadow's movement on a royal staircase (2 Kgs 20:1-11). Finally the sage refers to Isaiah's visions of the future and his promise of comfort for the mourners in Zion (2 Kgs 20:17; Isa 61:1-3).

49:1-13 From Josiah to Nehemiah

King Josiah (640–609 B.C.) ruled Jerusalem shortly before the Babylonian exile. He was a great religious reformer, because in his reign the law of Moses was rediscovered (2 Kgs 22:8). Accordingly, Josiah's name is compared to blended incense—an appropriate image because of his restoration of temple worship (Exod 30:7). Josiah's grief over Judah's betrayals of God was clear from his penitent reaction to the reading of the Torah scroll (2 Kgs 22:11) and from his subsequent destruction of idols that had even been placed in the temple (2 Kgs 23:4-14).

Ben Sira's verdict on Judah's monarchy (49:4) echoes the view of the books of Kings (2 Kgs 18:3; 23:25). Only David, Hezekiah, and Josiah are judged to have been God-fearing, since all the others tolerated idolatry in their kingdom (including Solomon, according to 1 Kgs 11:5-6). Indeed, the Bible regards the Babylonian exile as divine punishment of the people for disobeying the commandments (2 Chr 36:15-21). Sirach 49:5-6 refers to the events of 587 B.C., when a "foreign nation" (the Babylonians) burned Jerusalem (2 Kgs 25:9).

Sirach 49:7 notes that Jeremiah had been called as a prophet even in his mother's womb (Jer 1:5). His ministry involved both destruction and construction (Jer 1:10; 18:7-10), since he announced Jerusalem's downfall (Jer 7:14-15; 26:6-9) but also its future rebuilding (Jer 29:10-14; 30:17-18). Ben Sira then mentions Jeremiah's contemporary, Ezekiel, whose prophetic call included a vision of God in a heavenly chariot surrounded by various creatures (Ezek 1:4-21). Ezekiel also referred to Job as an example of a very righteous person (Ezek 14:14), famous for persevering in the right path (Job 2:10; Jas 5:11). Sirach 49:10 alludes to the twelve Minor Prophets (Hosea through Malachi), whose writings were collected into one book in

Jewish tradition. As in 46:12, Ben Sira wishes that their bones may sprout afresh from their resting place (49:10); in other words, that worthy successors may continue their good work.

Passing quickly over the exilic period, Ben Sira mentions Israel's civil leader (Zerubbabel) and chief priest (Jeshua) in the early years after the people returned from Babylonian exile (49:11-12). The preciousness of Zerubbabel is indicated by the image of the signet ring (Hag 2:23). Both Zerubbabel and Jeshua (called Joshua in Hag 1:12 and Zech 3:1) were involved in the rebuilding of the Jerusalem temple, completed in 515 B.C. (Ezra 3:2; 6:15). Sirach 49:13 praises Nehemiah, who came from Persia to Jerusalem around 445 B.C. to rebuild the city walls (Neh 2:1-18). Nehemiah's building activity foreshadows the construction works of the high priest Simeon (50:1-4). Strangely, Ben Sira omits the priestly scribe Ezra (Ezra 7:1-6).

49:14-16 Heroes of ancient time

Although Ben Sira began the Praise of the Ancestors with the early patriarchs in Genesis (44:17-23), he unexpectedly kept the earliest Genesis characters until last. Possibly he wished to close the circle of Israel's history, or else to highlight the comparison with Simeon the high priest in 50:1-24.

If the mention of Enoch in 44:16 is a later addition to the text, Ben Sira has deliberately left Enoch till the end (49:14), to downplay his importance as a recipient of divine revelation (as claimed in the book of Enoch). Instead, the sage merely refers to the tradition of Genesis 5:24 that he was taken by God into heaven (Heb 11:5). In 49:15 Ben Sira refers to Jacob's son Joseph, whose bones were carefully brought by the Israelites from Egypt to the promised land (Gen 50:25; Josh 24:32). Sirach 49:16 draws on Genesis 5:1-32 in its mention of three of Adam's descendants: Shem (Noah's son), Seth (brother of Cain and Abel), and Enosh (Seth's son). The most glorious living person was Adam, who initially shared in God's glory, before his sin and expulsion from the garden of Eden (Wis 10:1-2).

50:1-24 Simeon the high priest

Ben Sira's celebration of Simeon II, who had probably recently died, forms the culmination of the Praise of the Ancestors. Simeon (or Simon) was the high priest in Jerusalem at the end of the third century B.C. (approximately 219–196). Since civil government was under the Greek-speaking rulers of Palestine, Simeon was a national figurehead, embodying aspects of Jewish political as well as religious leadership. Sirach 50:1-4 celebrates the high priest's building activities in Jerusalem. Like Jeshua son of Jozadak, he repaired the temple (49:12). Like Hezekiah and Nehemiah, he fortified the walls in Jerusalem (48:17; 49:13). Like Hezekiah, he had a reservoir for water dug (48:17).

Although many scholars have seen 50:5-21 as a description of the Day of Atonement, the details do not match Leviticus 16 or the Mishnaic tractate *Yoma*, and the portrayal is too florid for such a penitential day. Instead, the events generally correspond to the daily whole burnt offering or *Tamid* (Num 28–29; Mishnaic tractate *Tamid* 6.3–7.3). Even the high priest's exit from within the veil (50:5) need not refer to the Day of Atonement (the only day of the year when the high priest went inside the veil to the holy of holies, according to Lev 16:2), since another veil or curtain separated the court of the priests from the outer court.

Sirach 50:5-10 employs poetic imagery to depict the splendor of Simeon appearing for a public sacrifice. Comparison of the high priest with the stars, moon, sun, and rainbow recalls the sage's earlier hymn to the Creator (43:1-12). The likening of the high priest to trees and flowers parallels the portrayal of wisdom in an earlier poem (24:13-15). Fittingly, Ben Sira also compares Simeon to the incense fire (50:9), since the high priest would have burned incense over the grain offering (Lev 2:1-2). The comparison of Simeon II to the luxuriant olive tree echoes Zechariah 4:11-14.

Sirach 50:11-21 describes the high priest's sacrificial service when (like Aaron in 45:8-12) he was dressed in magnificent robes (Exod 28:2-43) for officiating at the bronze altar in the court facing the sanctuary (Exod 27:1-2; 2 Chr 4:1). Sirach 50:14-15 reports the libation of wine, poured out at the foot of the altar (Num 15:5; 28:7), while 50:16 recounts the blast sounded on silver trumpets (Num 10:1-10). According to 50:17, the people fell prostrate in adoration (2 Chr 29:28-29). While the smoke of the sacrifice ascended, the temple singers offered hymns of praise (2 Chr 29:27), as decreed by King David (47:9-10). In an echo of Exodus 34:6, God was invoked as the "Merciful

One." According to 50:20-21, the ceremony concluded with the high priest's blessing of the assembled crowd (Lev 9:22-23; Num 6:23-27), using the sacred name YAHWEH (here translated as LORD). In later tradition the high priest only pronounced the sacred name once a year on the Day of Atonement (*Mishnah Sanhedrin* 10.1), but this was not so in earliest times (2 Sam 6:18).

The poem on Simeon ends with a doxology (50:22-24), resembling the one in 45:25-26. On the basis of 50:22-24 Martin Rinkart (d. 1649) composed the hymn "Now Thank We All Our God." The sage's prayer in 50:23 is for wisdom for the sons of the high priest Simeon (Onias III and Jeshua). In the Hebrew text of 50:24 Ben Sira prays for Simeon's heirs, that God may permanently maintain for them the "covenant with Phinehas." According to this covenant of peace (Num 25:12-13), the divine promise was that the high priesthood would remain in the line of Phinehas forever (45:24). But with the murder of Onias III and the overthrow of his brother Jeshua, now called Jason (2 Macc 4:26, 34), Simeon II's priestly line came to an ignominious end. Hence, the grandson's Greek translation eliminated the covenant with Phinehas and updated 50:24 to match the situation of the late second century B.C.: "May his mercy remain faithful with us, and in our days may he redeem us."

POSTSCRIPTS AND APPENDICES

Sirach 50:25–51:30

50:25-29 Two postscripts

The book's first postscript (50:25-26) records the sage's bitter attack on three neighboring nations: the Idumeans (formerly Edomites) to the south and east of Judea (2 Macc 10:14-17); the Hellenized inhabitants of the western coastal region inhabited formerly by the Philistines (1 Macc 5:68); and the Samaritans centered on Shechem (Nablus) to the north (1 Macc 3:10). Sirach 50:26 calls the Samaritans the "foolish people," echoing Deuteronomy 32:21. Viewing the Samaritans as mixed-race pagans (2 Kgs 17:24-41), the returning Jewish exiles refused to let them assist in rebuilding the Jerusalem temple (Ezra 4:1-3; Neh 3:33-35).

The second postscript (50:27-29) is the author's signature, with an encouragement for readers to practice his teachings.

51:1-12 Hymn of thanksgiving for deliverance

At the opening of the hymn, the sage acclaims the Deity as both savior and king (Pss 18:47; 145:1). The threat to Ben Sira's life came from a slanderous tongue, stirring up a whispering campaign against him (Jer 20:10). The danger became a raging fire (Isa 43:2), like the testing spoken of in 2:5. Mention of the "deep belly of Sheol" (51:5) is reminiscent of the prayer of Jonah, who regarded his stay inside the great fish as time spent in the belly of the nether world (Jonah 2:3).

According to 51:6, Ben Sira felt close to death (Ps 88:4), as did St. Paul in Ephesus, before God rescued him (2 Cor 1:8-10). In his trouble the sage had the terrible experience of feeling alone, without any human helper (Pss 69:21; 142:5). But then he remembered God's past mercies (Ps 25:6; Lam 3:21-23). Hence, from his humble position he raised his voice to God, just as the ailing Hezekiah also prayed from the "gates of Sheol" (Isa 38:10). In 51:10 Ben Sira's prayer is direct: "You are my Father" (Isa 63:16; Ps 89:27). Similarly, an apocryphal Qumran prayer of Joseph for deliverance addresses God as "my Father" (4Q372 1.16), while Jesus' prayer in Gethsemane begins: "*Abba*, Father" (Mark 14:36). Sirach 51:11-12 recounts the sage's deliverance in answer to his prayer (Pss 6:9-10; 18:7) and his fulfillment of his earlier pledge by giving thanks to God (Pss 22:23; 69:31). Perhaps in response to this promise of praise, the Cairo Hebrew manuscript here includes a sixteen-line litany of thanksgiving, omitted from all the Greek and Syriac translations.

51:13-30 An alphabetic wisdom poem

Ben Sira ends his book with a twenty-three-line Hebrew alphabetic poem describing his successful quest for wisdom, personified as a woman (14:20–15:10). The Psalter makes frequent use of such alphabetic poems (acrostics) where each line starts successively with one of the twenty-two letters of the Hebrew alphabet (e.g., Psalms 111, 112, 145). Here (as in Psalm 25) an extra line is added beginning with the letter *pe*.

Though some scholars have questioned the authorship of this poem, indications that the poem is indeed the work of Ben Sira include his characteristic themes of courting Lady Wisdom (51:13-21; 14:20–15:2) and submitting to her yoke (51:26; 6:24, 30). In fact, 51:13-30 also seems to echo the alphabetic poem concluding the book of Proverbs (Prov 31:10-31). Whereas the poem at the end of Proverbs concerns the valiant woman who embodies the fear of the Lord, Ben Sira's composition is about wisdom, personified as a desirable woman.

Sirach 51:13 describes the sage's youthful search for wisdom (6:18), reminiscent of Solomon's early quest for understanding (1 Kgs 3:7-9; Wis 8:2). According to 51:15, already as a young man Ben Sira knew wisdom (Ps 71:17; Mark 10:20), as did Solomon (47:14). Sirach 51:16 notes that a great advance in understanding came from a small amount of attention (6:19). Whereas 1:6 asks who knows wisdom's subtleties, the sage here declares that he came to know her secrets (51:19). Anyone seeking divine understanding needs clean hands and a pure heart (Ps 24:4). Wisdom became Ben Sira's prize possession (Prov 4:7). Like God's servant in the Third Servant Song (Isa 50:4), the sage has been given a tongue to proclaim the divine wisdom and to praise God (39:6).

Then Ben Sira appeals to the uneducated (51:23), echoing the invitation of Lady Wisdom (Prov 1:22-23; 9:4-6). His appeal is that the untutored should lodge in the "house of instruction," a phrase suggesting some kind of educational establishment. In 51:24 Ben Sira asks "how long" his students will lack wisdom's nourishment and drink (Prov 9:5; Isa 55:1).

The image of wisdom's yoke (51:26) develops the thought of an earlier poem (6:24, 30). Sirach 51:26b plays on the Hebrew word *massa*, which means both "burden" (6:21) and "teaching" (Jer 23:33). Wisdom is accessible to those who seek her (Wis 6:12), because God's word is near (Deut 30:14). In practical terms, wisdom will offer material rewards (Prov 8:18), as a result of divine mercy and human diligence (11:1). If the student focuses on the task of acquiring wisdom, God will grant a reward in good time.

THE BOOK OF
ISAIAH

Leslie J. Hoppe, O.F.M.

INTRODUCTION

By any measure the book of Isaiah is among the world's greatest works of religious literature. It probes the mystery of a people's life with God. It is unrelenting in its insistence that the foundation of that life is God's commitment to Jerusalem—God's unwillingness to make judgment on the city's infidelity the last word that its people would hear. The book makes use of a variety of literary techniques—both prose and poetry—to move people to see that Jerusalem did have a future with God. The book's principal characters—the Holy One of Israel, the virgin daughter Zion, and the Servant of the Lord—engage the reader in a drama of great emotion and intensity. Other personalities appear as the book's reflection on Israel's life with God oscillates between judgment and salvation. These include the prophet Isaiah and his two strangely named sons; King Ahaz and his son Hezekiah; Cyrus the Persian; the owner of an unproductive vineyard; the Assyrian army; the nations; the poor; and Immanuel. Justice for the poor is a motif that continually surfaces throughout the book, leading the reader to conclude that Israel's relationship with its God is indirect—that it is a by-product of the creation and maintenance of a just society.

Those who read this book from beginning to end will experience a range of emotions that testify to the book's complexity. They will sympathize with the prophet's friend who expected to find a good harvest of grapes in his vineyard (Isa 5). They will be in awe with the prophet as he experiences the majesty of God (Isa 6). They will puzzle at the obtuseness of Ahaz (Isa 7). They will reel at the intense hatred of the oracles against the nations (Isa 13–27). They will be relieved as they hear of Jerusalem's liberation (Isa 40). They will be shocked at the suffering of the Servant of the Lord (52:13–53:12). They will be happy for mother Zion embraced by her husband and surrounded by her children again (Isa 62, 66). And they will be disappointed by the book's ending (66:24). The last verse is so depressing that when the final verses of Isaiah are read in the synagogue, by custom the reader repeats verse 23, with its more upbeat tone after reading verse 24 so that the book does not end on a negative note.

The book of Isaiah continues to have a profound influence on its readers—especially those who belong to two of the religious traditions that developed from the religion of ancient Israel: Judaism and Christianity. The book of Isaiah is often read in the synagogue as the *Haftarah*, the reading that is meant to parallel and illuminate the reading from the torah. Also, the significance of Jerusalem in the book of Isaiah has helped shaped Judaism's attitude toward this city. Especially significant is the vision of justice and peace with which the city will be blessed (see 2:2-4; 11:6-9).

The Christian confession of Jesus as the Messiah has been shaped significantly by the book of Isaiah. Among the more significant references to

Isaiah in the New Testament is Matthew's citation of the Immanuel prophecy (Isa 7:14; Matt 2:23), Luke's use of elements from the fourth Servant Song to explain the necessity of Jesus' suffering and death (e.g., Isa 53:7-9; Luke 33:27; Acts 8:32-33), and the idea of the New Jerusalem in the book of Revelation (Isa 65:18; Rev 21:2). The church's early theologians referred to the book of Isaiah as "the fifth gospel," because they discerned the significance of this book for the New Testament, which cites Isaiah more often than any book of the Hebrew Bible except the book of Psalms. Isaiah continues to exercise its influence in the church. Passages from Isaiah are read frequently in both the Sunday and weekday lectionaries. The Second Vatican Council cited Isaiah 2:4 and 32:17 in its Constitution on the Church in the Modern World when speaking on social justice and peace (*Gaudium et spes*, 70). Finally, the book's vision for the future has provided liberation theologians with a biblical foundation for their advocacy on behalf of the poor and oppressed.

Modern scholarly interpretation of Isaiah has been shaped by the recognition that the book is a composite work that reflects three different periods of Jerusalem's history. Chapters 1–23 and 28–39 contain material relating to the ministry of the eighth-century prophet, Isaiah, son of Amoz (1:1-2). He condemned the social, political, and economic system of the kingdom of Judah because it created a two-tiered society made up of the very rich and very poor. The rich acquired and maintained their position in Judahite society by taking advantage of the poor. What was even worse was that the temple and its liturgy were used to assure the oppressors that God would continue to protect Judah despite its manifest failure to maintain a community of justice. The prophet believed that the aggressively militaristic Assyrian Empire was God's instrument of judgment on the kingdom of Judah. Chapters 36–39 are taken for the most part from 2 Kings 18:13–20:19, which describes the Assyrian siege of Jerusalem.

Isaiah 40–55 are the product of an anonymous prophet whose ministry took place about 125 years after that of Isaiah, son of Amoz. The message of these chapters is that there is a future for Jerusalem beyond the disaster that occurred when Nabuchadnezzar, king of Babylon, captured Jerusalem, destroyed the temple, ended the Judahite

monarchy and national state, and led off many leading citizens into exile. The rise of Cyrus, the Persian, convinced the anonymous prophet of the exile that Judah's time of judgment was over and that Cyrus was God's chosen instrument to rebuild Jerusalem and its temple (Isa 45). The prophet's exquisite poems helped the people of Judah to make sense of the disaster they experienced and to see that there was a future beyond judgment.

Isaiah 56–66 are a collection of poems that reflected the disillusionment of some when the hopes engendered by Isaiah 40–55 did not materialize. While the temple had been rebuilt, the national state was not restored, the economy was in shambles, and the conflict between the wealthy and the poor resurfaced. Despite the disappointment, the poems of chapters 56–66 expect a full and glorious restoration for Judah (Isa 60).

The final component of Isaiah is found in chapters 24–27. These chapters look forward to a day of judgment when God will finally defeat the powers of evil, vindicate the just, and punish evildoers. The day of judgment will end with all God's people, scattered about the world, returning to worship God in Jerusalem (Isa 27:13).

The circumstances under which the book of Isaiah took the form it now has are not entirely clear. Three fairly complete copies of the book of Isaiah were found among the Dead Sea Scrolls so the book in its present form existed prior to the second century B.C. when the community that produced the scrolls settled near the Dead Sea. The latest components of the book (chs. 24–27) probably date from no later than the fourth century. More precision than this is not possible at present. The book of Isaiah, then, took the form it how has sometime between the fourth and the second centuries B.C., though the earliest components of the book come from the eighth century B.C. What is clear is the book's purpose: to give the people of Judah and Jerusalem hope for the future and the will to re-embrace their ancestral religious traditions. Of course, there were other similar attempts. For example, the Deuteronomic tradition tries to persuade Judah that its future is tied up with careful observance of the norms of traditional Israelite morality as articulated in the book of Deuteronomy. The Chronicler asserts that Judah's future depends upon the legitimacy of its temple rituals as marked by their continuity with preexilic liturgical traditions. The book of Isaiah sees Jerusalem's future as God's "creative redemption." Jerusalem's response to this new act of God is to create and maintain a society based on justice and equity.

While this commentary assumes the composite character of the book, it will approach the work as a whole with a literary and theological integrity of its own. The divisions of the book adopted here are not those reflecting the history of its composition but its literary shape. The book falls into five parts of approximately the same length, which usually begin with an oracle of judgment on pride and arrogance and end with a word of salvation. Also, each of these sections is addressed to Jerusalem. These five sections are chapters 1–12: Jerusalem's Future; chapters 13–27: Jerusalem and the Nations; chapters 28–39: Judgment and Salvation for Jerusalem; chapters 40–55: Jerusalem's Liberation; and chapters 56–66: The New Jerusalem.

There are two principal motifs that are the literary and theological linchpins of the book of Isaiah. The first flows from the distinctive title the book of Isaiah gives for God: "the Holy One of Israel." This unique Isaianic way of speaking about Jerusalem's God was formulated to expand the people's notion of deity. The Lord was unlike any other god and did not act as Jerusalem expected God to act. The holiness of God, then, was not a "moral" quality. It was God's otherness and singularity. It was manifest in the way God acted toward Jerusalem and the nations. In the first three sections of the book (1–12; 13–27; 28–39), God demands that Jerusalem create and maintain a society based on justice. The consequence for failing to do this will be severe judgment including the loss of the state, dynasty, temple, and land. In the fourth section of the book (40–55), there are several instances when "Holy One" is followed by the term "redeemer" (41:14; 43:14; 47:4; 48:17). In the last section, the nations will recognize the holiness of Israel's God because of Jerusalem's commitment to justice (57:15; 60:9, 14).

The second principal motif of the book is Jerusalem/Zion. The portrait that the prophet paints of the city contrasts sharply with that of the "Holy One of Israel." While the Lord demands justice for the poor, Jerusalem and its leaders crush them. While God's holiness has been made known to Israel throughout its history, Jerusalem seeks its security in alliances with other nations and through the worship of other gods. When God declares that Jerusalem has paid for its sins, the people are hesitant to believe. Despite this, God never stops loving Jerusalem and its people. God is determined to provide Jerusalem with a glorious future. The interaction between the Holy One of Israel and Jerusalem is the engine that drives Isaiah.

To appreciate the book's achievement, it is best to read the text straight through first without the commentary. This will allow the reader to get a sense of the book as a whole. Such a sustained reading will evoke from the reader a variety of responses. Reading the commentary then will help the reader probe more deeply into parts of the text that are particularly intriguing, inspiring, or puzzling. The most creative interaction with the text will result from the reader's recognition that the book is an expression of faith—faith in the Holy One of Israel and in the future of Jerusalem. The book is confident that judgment, though deserved by the city, is never God's last word to Jerusalem. The Jewish reader still looks to the final redemption of Jerusalem, while the book's Christian reader looks for the coming of the new and heavenly Jerusalem. The faith of both has been shaped decisively by the book of Isaiah.

COMMENTARY

JERUSALEM'S FUTURE

Isaiah 1:1–12:6

The first section of the book of Isaiah begins with an indictment of Jerusalem's infidelity (1:2-9) and ends with a prayer of thanksgiving for its restoration in the future (12:1-6). Between these two poles, Isaiah alternates between harsh and explicit descriptions of the judgment that awaits Jerusalem for its role in creating an unjust society, and lyrical and touching images of the future beyond judgment that God has for the city and its people. The genius of the prophet was not only his ability to appreciate the realities of the political and military crises in Jerusalem's immediate future but especially his ability to see beyond these to a glorious future for Zion. Still, Isaiah was no Pollyanna as his words make clear. He was certain that Jerusalem was to undergo a severe crisis that included political impotence and military defeat. Even more devastating would be the loss of and exile from the land that God promised to ancient Israel's ancestors. But beyond this judgment on Jerusalem was the promise of a new city ruled by a good king who led a people committed to justice.

1:1 The prophet's name

The book identifies itself as the "vision of Isaiah." It is a vision—the prophet's dream—of what he imagined Jerusalem's future to be. The prophet's name clarifies that vision. The name "Isaiah" means "the Lord saves." The naming of four Judahite kings asserts that what follows was first proclaimed in the eighth century B.C. when Jerusalem faced severe political, economic, and military crises.

1:2-9 God's judgment

The prophet's words begin with a poignant cry of betrayal. That the prophet identifies God as the parent betrayed and Israel as God's guilty children implies that judgment will not be God's last word to Israel. Like the love of parents for their children, God's love for Israel does not fail because of Israel's failures. The second comparison, likening Israel with beasts of burden, suggests that Israel acted out of ignorance, not appreciating the nature of its relationship with God. This also suggests some mitigation of Israel's guilt. Still, this will not prevent Israel from experiencing God's judgment for its infidelity. What the prophet cannot understand is the reason Israel has not learned from experience. Its infidelity continued until its cities were destroyed, its land desolate, and Jerusalem abandoned. Still, God did not allow Israel to destroy itself, but kept a few survivors alive. These survivors have accepted their situation as the Lord's doing, and they recognize the miracle that God worked in keeping them alive.

In verse 9, the prophet introduces what will be a significant theme in the book: the remnant. The survival of the "small remnant" prevented Jerusalem and the other cities of Judah from sharing the fate of Sodom and Gomorrah (see Gen 19:24-25). Paul quotes verse 9 in the course of his impassioned discourse on God's continuing love for the Jewish people (Rom 9:27-29).

1:10-20 Israel's worship

Taking on the persona of God, the prophet picks up on the reference to Sodom and Gomorrah in verse 9 to introduce a critique of Israel's liturgy that has few parallels in comprehensiveness and intensity. God rejects Israel's religious festivals, sacrifices, and acts of personal piety because Israel has not maintained a just society. Without justice, Israel's worship of the Lord is an empty shell. The book of Isaiah ends with another stinging critique of ritual activity (66:1-4). The book, then, is framed by bitter and comprehensive criticisms of ritual because the prophet believed Israel's communal worship facilitated its selective obedience. Israel believed that God must be pleased with it because of its liturgy even though its social, political, and economic life was a mockery of justice. Still, God's judgment is not final because God asks Israel to consider what it has done. Israel has to choose between life and death. Obedience is not a matter of knowledge. It is a matter of will. If Israel chooses to live in obedience, then red can become white. Sin can be countered by repentance.

To put the apocalyptic vision recorded in the book of Revelation into words, John studied the book of Isaiah. In describing the devastation of

Jerusalem at the end of the age, John alludes to verse 10 and the application of the name Sodom to Jerusalem (Rev 11:8). As a book of prophecy, Isaiah assumes that the people of Judah are in control of their future: the choices *they* make will create their future. The prophet's task is to help the people appreciate the consequences of their choices. Because they have created a society based on injustice and oppression, that society will collapse. The book also affirms that judgment will not be the last word that God will address to Judah. God will restore Jerusalem, giving the people another opportunity to create a just society in which all will enjoy God's peace.

The book of Revelation is an example of an apocalyptic worldview that does not envision the triumph of divine justice in *this* world. Apocalyptic looks forward to a new world to be created by the power of God. The climax of the book of Revelation occurs in chapter 21 with its vision of a "*new* heaven and a *new* earth" (Rev 21:1; emphasis added). But like the book of Isaiah, Revelation identifies Jerusalem as the focal point of the new earth (Rev 21:9-27).

1:21-26 Jerusalem's future

At one time, Jerusalem's social and economic system was just. What once was, however, is no more, and the city faces divine judgment. Its political leadership is venal (1:26). The city's leaders should have been protecting the economically vulnerable, but they have used their position to exploit the poor to enrich themselves and thereby have become God's enemies. However, the goal of God's judgment against Jerusalem's elite is not mere vengeance, but the elimination of the city's corrupt political system. With new leadership, Jerusalem can once again be a just and faithful city. Still, the prophet is clear that Zion's current leadership provoked the divine judgment that was coming on Jerusalem. But one day God will provide the city with leaders who have a measure of integrity. The prophet insists that Jerusalem's standing before God is not a consequence of its unique status as the dwelling place of God on earth. Jerusalem's salvation lies in the doing of justice. The city's fate then will be a consequence of its people's commitment to maintaining a just and equitable economic system that protects the most vulnerable people. The future of Jerusalem is in the hands of its people and leaders.

1:29-31 False worship

These verses are likely veiled references to the worship of the goddess Asherah, whose rituals may have involved trees in some way (see Jer 17:2). Asherah was the wife of El, the supreme deity of the Ugaritic pantheon. An inscription found on the Sinai Peninsula suggests that some worshipers of the Lord honored Asherah as the Lord's consort. The prophet objects to worship related to Asherah explicitly in 17:8 and 27:9, and the third part of the book (40–55) is filled with parodies of idol worship. Such worship provided ideological support for an unjust social system based on an elite who controlled the economic lives of the poor. The Lord, however, is a God who takes the side of the poor against those who exploit them.

2:1-4 Jerusalem of the future

The prophet speaks not of the Jerusalem of his day but of Jerusalem in the distant future—a time after the city is purged by the coming judgment. Isaiah is convinced that the city's status will change in the future. However, that status will not be the consequence of God's presence in the temple, but of the city's role as the place to which all peoples will come to learn the torah. The prophet does not speak of the nations as enemies to be defeated but as peoples with whom Judah is to live in peace. The enemy that will be defeated is war. The universal observance of the torah will bring an era of peace. The fourth and fifth sections of the book (40–55; 56–66) develop the themes of the future of Jerusalem and Israel's relations with other peoples.

A variation of this oracle occurs in Micah 4:1-4, while Joel 4:10 turns the oracle's imagery inside out. The book of Isaiah returns to the imagery and thought of 2:1-4 several times, e.g., 5:25; 9:6; 11:6-9; 30:27-28; 51:4; 56:6-8; 60:11-14. These passages underscore the book's purpose of helping its readers appreciate what God has in store for Jerusalem.

2:5-22 The day of judgment

The refrain "the LORD alone will be exalted on that day" (2:11 and 17) sets the tone of this poem on the subject of what lies ahead for Jerusalem. Judgment is coming because of divination, Judah's "prosperity," and idolatry (2:5-11). The Bible is clear about divination: it is forbidden to

Israel (Exod 22:17; Lev 20:27; Deut 18:10-11). The reason for this prohibition is that an unfavorable prediction was followed by the use of prayers and rituals to induce the gods to change the fate of those who have received an unfavorable omen. Judah cannot evade the judgment that is coming on it no matter what rituals may be used to deflect God's will for Israel's immediate future. The country's prosperity benefited the few people at the top of the social and economic hierarchy. The prophet condemned this "prosperity" because it was achieved at the expense of the poor. The worship of gods other than the Lord provided religious support for an unjust social and economic system.

The motif of "the day of the Lord" (2:12) appears frequently in the prophetic tradition (Isa 13:6; Amos 5:18-20; Jer 17:16-18; Ezek 30:3; Joel 1:15). That day was to witness God's final victory over every enemy. What the prophet asserts here is that Israel is among those who will experience God's judgment because of the injustice that the poor must endure. God's ultimate triumph will lead people to cease serving other deities as they finally recognize that Yahweh alone deserves their exclusive service. In describing the terrors of "the day of the Lord," the prophet asserts three times that people will hide themselves among caves and rocks in the attempt to escape judgment (2:10, 19, 21). The book of Revelation uses that same imagery in speaking of the terrors that it sees as coming at the end of the age (Rev 6:15).

3:1-12 The collapse of the political order

The exaltation of the Lord means the collapse of Jerusalem's political order. The country's leaders will be unable to insure that people have the basic necessities for life: bread and water. One consequence will be the breakdown of society's basic structure. Judah will be without competent leaders. This will result in serious and destructive social conflict. The ensuing situation will be so bad that no one will want to accept a position of leadership.

The prophet makes it clear that the cause of this anarchy was the failure of Judah's leaders to maintain a just society. While there were individuals who conducted their affairs with justice, the society as a whole was a distortion of what God wanted Judah to become. While the just can expect to survive the coming judgment, God means

to remake Judahite society by eliminating those responsible for its corruption. In particular, Jerusalem's leaders bear the primary responsibility for the chaos that gripped Judah.

3:13–4:1 Judgment upon the wealthy

The prophet was convinced that the fall of Judah and Jerusalem was the inevitable consequence of decisions made by the people of means. To demonstrate their responsibility, the prophet pictures them on trial before God, who accuses them of oppressing the poor. The prophet singles out rich women flaunting their wealth for all to see. When judgment comes, God will destroy every single bit of finery with which these women flaunt the prosperity gained at the expense of the poor. The rich have stolen from the poor to give themselves the best of everything. Judgment is coming and they will lose everything. The rich will then learn what it means to be poor. War will rob Judah of its young people and plunge it into mourning. Judah's losses in war will turn its women into widows who will contend with one another for the chance to marry the few remaining men.

4:2-6 Jerusalem's restoration

Though the prophet warns Jerusalem of the judgment that is coming upon it, he never claims that judgment is God's last word to the city. On the contrary, Isaiah was able to see beyond the immediate crisis. Of course, the corruption of the city's leadership and the idleness of its wealthy class evoke a purifying visitation from God. Still, the prophet envisions a new city, one that God will create following the terrible judgment that is coming on an economy founded on injustice toward the poor. What the immediate future holds for Jerusalem is the purging that will come with "searing judgment," leaving only a remnant in the city. God will protect those who survive this judgment and then refound Zion.

The temple does not appear to have a significant place in the prophet's vision of a new Jerusalem. Isaiah envisions the Zion of the future with God present not in some grandiose structure but in the humble shelter of the peasant farmer. The judgment that is coming on Jerusalem is not vindictiveness but has as its purpose the preparation of the purified remnant. This remnant will witness God's reestablishment of the city on the basis of justice and equity. While Isaiah condemns the Jerusalem of his day because of its exploitive social and economic system, he sees a new Jerusalem cleansed of the sins of its past.

5:1-7 The song of the vineyard

The prophet returns to words of judgment against Jerusalem and Judah, but this judgment is veiled in an allegory about his "friend's" vineyard (see also Hos 10:1; Jer 2:21; Ezek 19:10-14; Matt 21:33; Mark 12:1; Luke 20:10). The prophet's friend invested time and energy into his vineyard with the expectation of a return on this investment. For crops like grapes, full production did not begin for several years after the vines were planted. The owner of the vineyard had to have confidence and patience that a harvest would come one day. But the song is about disappointment. The anticipated results of the efforts do not materialize: the vineyard produces only bitter grapes. The owner of the vineyard speaks directly to the reader, asking advice because he will have to make a decision about the future of the vineyard soon. The questioning reflects a degree of pathos, since the unspoken answer to the owner's questions is "nothing."

The owner will not tear up the vines and destroy them as one would expect but will rather remove his care and protection from the vineyard. The owner will stop the cultivation of the vineyard and will allow the natural course of events to take place. By tearing down the wall, the owner will open the vineyard to animals that will eat the grapes. Their grazing will put the plants at risk. The owner will not have the vines pruned. They will then grow too long to support the fruit. By failing to hoe, the owner makes it possible for weeds to grow and compete for nutrients and moisture. Eventually, the weeds will dominate the vineyard and the grapevines will become weak and stunted. The prophet implies that divine judgment on Jerusalem is the absence of God's sustaining presence, leaving the city prey to those who will take advantage of its weakness.

The people of Judah have not met God's expectations. They were to be a blessing to the world, i.e., they were to produce fruit. They were to fulfill their calling in the world as the people of God by maintaining a society whose values were shaped by righteousness and justice. The vineyard will be abandoned and without care or cultivation. It will be overrun and eventually destroyed. God will abandon Judah to those who would conquer it.

5:8-23 Judah's crimes

After the allegorical indictment found in the song of the vineyard, the prophet becomes specific. He begins by condemning the large estates of the wealthy (5:8-11). The people of means were able to acquire their large estates by taking advantage of the economic reverses of the poor and confiscating their land for the nonpayment of debts. The wealthy cultivated grapes and olives on their land to increase production of wine and olive oil. The export and sale of these commodities were highly profitable. Because more land was given to the cultivation of crops for export, less land was available for growing grains to feed Judah's people. With less grain available for sale, the price of this staple rose, putting more economic pressure on the poor. This helped create a permanent underclass in Judah. This breach of traditional Israelite morality would bring terrible consequences. The prophet promises that the land will not yield the increase the wealthy were expecting. They will have to face the kind of economic pressures that were part of the daily experience of the poor.

The prophet condemns the extravagant lifestyle of the wealthy (5:11-17). Most Judahite farmers were able to raise enough crops to feed their families and animals, to set aside seed for the next planting, and to have something to offer at the shrines to thank God for the land's fertility. The wealthy lived in excess, but the prophet assures them that they will learn what it means to live on the subsistence level. The people of means were able to acquire their wealth by ignoring God's will, by perverting the values of traditional Israelite morality, by their conceit, and by bribery (5:18-22). Because they have ignored the torah, which makes God's will for Israel clear, they can expect only the worst. Unable to cope, they will die in record numbers and the poor will be able to reclaim their heritage. God will insure that justice triumphs.

5:24-30 The means of judgment

The divine judgment that Judah will experience is coming. The result will be the destruction of the nation that has injustice as its foundation.

The prophet is aware of the expansionist policies of Judah's more powerful neighbors. He sees Judah falling to their military might. What the rich were doing to the poor, Judah's neighbors would shortly do to the nation as a whole. They will destroy a society whose social and economic values are so out of touch with traditional Israelite morality that they deserve the condemnation that the prophet pronounces on them in the name of God.

6:1-13 The call of the prophet

Judgment upon Judah was necessary and inevitable. The prophet was to have a critical role in making the people of Judah aware of that judgment so that when it did come they would recognize it for what it was: judgment on a society whose values were a perversion of God's will for Israel. There was to be no mistaking what was to befall Judah as the result of the military strength of imperialistic neighbors or any inability of Israel's patron deity to protect it against this imperialism. On the contrary, what was to befall Judah was God's own doing, announced by prophets whom God commissioned to bring Judah God's message of judgment. To dramatize Isaiah's role in this terrible encounter between God and Judah, the tradition describes the "call of Isaiah."

The book supplies a date for this call to remind its readers that Isaiah's ministry took place at a turning point in Judah's history (6:1). The forty-year reign of Uzziah (783–742 B.C.) was over. It had been a time of economic expansion and prosperity, though only a few Judahites enjoyed any economic benefits from the boom times of Uzziah's reign. The peasants were left behind. But Judah's economy would never again be as strong as it was under Uzziah, and the specter of the powerful Assyrian army was on the horizon. Judgment was coming.

The setting for the story of Isaiah's call is in the temple. There the prophet sees God accompanied by seraphim. The name "seraphim" recalls the fiery serpents of the wilderness tradition (Num 21:6-9; Deut 8:15). The Hebrew word "seraphim" means "the burning ones" and was used as the name of snakes whose venom caused a burning sensation in a person bitten by them. According to the story in Numbers and Deuteronomy, God used these serpents to punish the Israelites for their murmuring. The seraphim that the prophet sees are harbingers of what is in store for Judah. Their song underscores the basic affirmation that the book makes: God is holy. This holiness requires the purging of all immorality from those who stand in God's presence. Isaiah recognizes this and believes that he will not survive his encounter with God. It is important to note that the prophet stands in solidarity with his people. He does not see himself as a morally upright person who has a right to stand in judgment over others, but the seraphs purge the prophet with a burning coal so that he can begin his mission of announcing God's intention to purge Judah.

In postbiblical Jewish tradition and in medieval Christian tradition, the seraphim form a class of angels. While Isaiah 6 presents the seraphim as winged creatures of the heavenly king, it envisions the seraphim as serpents—not angels. During the time of Isaiah, a bronze serpent was still part of the temple's liturgical accouterments. It was destroyed by King Hezekiah (see 2 Kgs 18:4). The loss of that image and the development of angelology led to the inclusion of seraphim among the "nine choirs of angels" in a noncanonical Jewish book known as *The Testament of Adam* (ch. 4). This latter work rather than the biblical text has shaped the image of the seraphim in Christian art.

What is the prophet's mission? The tradition is aware that Isaiah's ministry did not prevent the destruction of the temple, the scattering of its priesthood, the end of the dynasty nor the end of the national state. Experience has shown that the prophet was not called to keep Israel from its destiny but to make Israel aware of that destiny. The prophet's mission was to delay Israel's comprehension of the divine plan until generations later, after Israel's endurance of not one but two devastations of its land and two exiles. These bitter events whose significance is illuminated by the message of the prophet made it impossible for Israel to evade responsibility for its fate.

John, the visionary in the book of Revelation, sees the glory of God and the Lamb just as the prophet Isaiah did (6:2-3; Rev 4:6-8). Matthew cites verses 9-10 to explain the apparent failure of the crowds to respond to Jesus' mission (Matt 13:13-15), while the prophet's words are implicit in both Mark (4:12) and Luke (8:10). Luke has Paul recite this text at the climax of Acts. Rejected by the Jews of Rome, Paul turns to the Gentiles, convinced that they will listen (Acts 28:23-29). At the end of his narrative of Jesus' public ministry, the author of the Fourth Gospel (not to be confused with the author of Revelation) paraphrases verses 9-10 to explain the failure of Jesus to attract a wide following (John 12:39-41). God tells the prophet Isaiah that his message will fall on deaf ears. People will refuse to see the scenario of their future that the prophet describes. The New Testament sees this as true not only for Isaiah but also for Jesus and Paul.

7:1–8:10 Immanuel—God with us

Again after speaking in generalities, the prophet becomes specific. He just spoke about the purpose of his mission as delaying Judah's comprehension of the divine will until there could be no mistaking the divine intention. Now the prophet describes in detail one instance of that lack of comprehension. The prophet details his encounter with Ahaz, the embattled king of Judah, who was under intense pressure to join a coalition of small national states aligned against the imperial power of Assyria.

The king did not want to be dragged into any military action against Assyria, so he sought Assyria's help in maintaining Judah's independence of action. The prophet recognized that while Ahaz's overtures to Assyria would solve the immediate crisis, their long-term effects would be the opposite of the king's goal of keeping Judah independent. Isaiah advised Ahaz to ignore the threats made against him by the coalition aligned against Assyria since that coalition was certain to fail. The prophet's analysis of the political situation was more astute than that of Ahaz. But the king could not see it nor could he accept the prophet's advice. This he was fated to do (see 6:9-10) since God's goal was the destruction of the Judahite state because of its injustice toward its own citizens. The irony in this passage is the threefold repetition of the Hebrew phrase *immanu el*, which means "God is with us." God is with Judah, but before Judah can experience the saving power of God, it must experience God's judgment on its unjust social and economic system.

This passage is built around several word plays. The first involves the names of Isaiah's sons. God instructed the prophet to take his son and confront Ahaz (7:3). This son's name was *Shear-jashub*, which means "a remnant shall re-

turn." The boy's name implies both judgment and salvation for Judah. Only a few of its people will survive the judgment that will involve the end of Judah's political and religious institutions, but God will insure that there will be survivors who will return and begin again. The passage ends with the naming of another of the prophet's sons, *Maher-shalal-hash-baz*, which means "The spoil speeds, the prey hastens." The son who bears this unwieldy name is a living assurance to Ahaz that his fear of the coalition threatening him is baseless. That coalition will collapse before the child learns to say his first words (8:3-4).

Another wordplay occurs as the prophet concludes his words of assurance to Ahaz in verses 7b-9. One way to preserve that wordplay in English translation is to render verse 9b: "If you do not make yourself *firm* (in the Lord), you will not be *affirmed* (by the Lord)." Note the words for firm/affirmed are forms of the Hebrew root *'mn*, which we know from the word "Amen." The prophet asserts that Ahaz need do nothing to save Judah but have confidence in God's words of assurance. With this confidence, Ahaz's own attempts to find security will come to nothing. But Ahaz felt that he had to do something. He was unwilling to accept the prophet's assurances that the Lord was going to protect Judah. A literal translation of Isaiah 65:16 identifies the Lord as "the God of Amen," i.e., the God of assurance, and Revelation 3:14 identifies Jesus as "The Amen."

The most important of the wordplays in this passage are those involving the Hebrew phrase *immanu el*, which occurs three times: 7:14; 8:8, 10. The prophet attempts to support his words of assurance (7:7-9) that those plotting against Judah are just human beings who will not succeed. Because Ahaz is not content with this assurance, the prophet supports them with a "sign." The prophet calls the king's attention to a pregnant woman that both apparently knew. Isaiah asserts that the crisis will pass before the child, who has yet to be born, is weaned. While the identity of the child is not clear, the significance of the sign is. The prophet advises the king to bide his time and the crisis will pass. He urges Ahaz to regard the birth of the child as a sign of God's presence that will protect Judah from external threats. Matthew (1:22-23) cites this text to underscore the significance of Jesus, whom the evangelist believes to be the very presence of God who has come to save Israel.

The second occurrence of *immanu el* in 8:8 is not as reassuring. The presence it signifies is not a saving presence but one that brings judgment. The prophet affirms that the real danger that Judah faces comes not from the nations allied against it but from an unexpected source. Because the prophet's message has been discounted by king and people, Judah will have to face threats from both Assyria and Egypt (7:18-25; 8:5-8). Still, the prophet is convinced that God's last word to Judah will not be judgment but salvation. While Judah will experience God's judgment through the nations, God will not allow that judgment to consume Judah. The Lord will ever be *immanu el* for Judah (8:9-10).

8:11-15 The futility of intrigue

To recapitulate the message of 7:1–8:10, the prophet speaks about the folly of the political intrigue that Ahaz used to secure his country's future. Isaiah has clearly and forcefully conveyed God's assurances that Judah has nothing to fear from any perceived military or political threats to its existence. Rather than fearing political powers, Judah ought to fear God. It is God who is the enemy of Judah as long as its social and economic practices exploit and oppress its own citizens. Indeed, Judah will have to face an enemy but it will not be a human one. God has always been present to Israel as a rock of salvation. But because of its moral failures, the Lord will now become a "rock for stumbling" (8:14). Both Romans 9:33 and 1 Peter 2:8 quote this text to describe the failure of some people to accept Jesus as God's final word to Israel.

8:16-20 The book of the prophet

This passage gives us a glimpse into the beginnings of the book of Isaiah. The prophet asks that his supporters keep a record of what he said so that people will come to see the significance of his words. The many people who discounted the prophet's message turned to divination for insights into Judah's future. Isaiah wants his words to be preserved so that when his message is confirmed by events of Judah's future, people will know that prophets rather than diviners convey God's word to God's people. Hebrews 2:13 quotes

verses 17-18 in speaking about how Jesus was made perfect through his suffering.

8:23–9:6 From darkness to light

When the prophet envisions the future, he sees beyond the possibilities of the present to an ideal future. Here the prophet looks forward to the day when the two Israelite kingdoms will be united under the rule of a single, glorious ruler from the Davidic dynasty. The prophet begins his ode to Israel's future by mentioning territories in the far north which were among the first threatened by the Assyrians. He describes the rejoicing of the people saved from Assyrian power. The prophet uses several metaphors to describe God's new act of grace for Israel. It will be like the move from light to darkness and like the harvest that brings an end to the threat of hunger and starvation. The joy it brings will be like that of soldiers over the fruits of their victory. It will remind people of the victory of Gideon over the Midianites (Judg 7:15-25)—a victory that came without the need for striking even a single blow. Israel's future will be the result of a similar victory—so complete as to make the donning of warriors' armor no longer necessary.

The prophet's ode to Israel's future continues as he describes the enthronement of the king who will rule over the Israel created by God's new act of grace. This future king will do what Ahaz could not: he will trust in the fidelity and power of the Lord. This king will not need advisors because his faith will guide him wondrously. He will be an authentic representative of God on earth and will bring an all-embracing and a never-ending peace to God's people. His kingdom will be sustained by justice.

Luke 1:78-79 alludes to this text when he has Zechariah speak about what God will do for Israel. Matthew 4:15-16 cites 9:1-2 as he describes the beginning of Jesus' ministry in Galilee—the region where the territories of Zebulon and Naphtali were located.

9:7–10:4 Judgment on Israel

Again the prophet moves back from his vision of the future to his indictment of the present. Though he sees the two Israelite kingdoms united under the rule of the Davidic dynasty some day, for the present the kingdom of Israel has to face judgment. The indictment has four particulars each concluding with the same refrain: "For all this [God's] wrath is not turned back, / his hand is still outstretched!" (9:11, 16, 20; 10:4).

The first particular (9:7-11) denounces Israel for its arrogance. While the houses of the poor built with mud bricks and sycamore timber are collapsing, villas for the wealthy built from cedar and dressed stones are going up. This must end so God is stirring up Israel's neighbors whose military forays will destroy Israel and its corrupt economic and social system. The second particular (9:12-16) singles out Israel's elders and prophets who should have led the people with integrity. Their failure to meet their responsibilities will lead to devastation that will spare no one. Without competent leadership, society as a whole has become corrupt and will suffer under divine judgment.

The third particular (9:17-20) describes a society that is destroying itself through civil strife. Israel's social and economic system has degenerated to the extent that people see each other as enemies. They ought to have considered each other brothers and sisters with whom they are to share the bounty that God has granted the land. Instead of this, they compete with each other for control of the nation's economic resources—a competition that has brought Israel to disaster. The final particular (10:1-4) indicts Israel for creating an economic system that steals from the defenseless. People of means are feeding themselves on the misery of the poor. They are guilty of economic cannibalism. Such a society dooms itself and that doom is what the prophet announced to Israel.

In Romans 9:27-28, Paul cites 10:22 to help explain the failure of the early Christian mission to the Jews. The apostle implies that God's promises never included all the people of Israel.

10:5-34 Assyria—God's instrument of judgment

The great achievement of the prophetic movement was to show the people of Israel that what happened to their two kingdoms fulfilled the purposes of their God. An alternative explanation of events held that the military defeat and political subjection of the Israelite kingdoms were due to the weakness of the Lord compared to the patron deities of the nations. Here the prophet explicitly identifies Assyria as God's instrument

of judgment. The fall of the Israelite kingdoms, then, is not due to any failure on the Lord's part but is the result of Israel's failings.

The militarist and expansionist Assyrian Empire will be the means by which Israel and Judah will experience God's judgment on their social and economic systems. While the Assyrians have their own purposes for their conquest of the two Israelite kingdoms, Isaiah believes that these really serve God's purposes. The Assyrians wanted to take Egypt to secure its resources and to control the trade routes that connected Egypt to Mesopotamia. Between Assyria and Egypt lay the two Israelite kingdoms. These had to be taken in order for the Assyrian army to protect its lines of communication. The overwhelming power of Assyria's military and the confidence of its leaders sealed the fate of the two Israelite kingdoms.

The prophet saw the hand of God in the expansionist policies of the Assyrian Empire (10:5-11). The aberrant religious practices of the Israelite kingdoms served to provide religious support for their unjust social systems. The Israelite people came into existence by rejecting the religious systems of the nations in order to serve a God who took the side of slaves over their masters. The prophet decries the current religious practices of the Israelites who have subjected themselves to gods who support the greed of the people of means as they enrich themselves at the expense of the peasants. At God's direction, Assyria will bring an end to the religious folly of both Israel and Judah.

The Assyrians wished to establish a world empire, but the prophet insists that Israel's God has already done that. Though Assyria's expansionism is the means God has chosen to bring judgment on the Israelite kings, God will deal with Assyria for its arrogance. Assyria will face its own day of judgment (10:12). Before that happens, the Assyrian army will devastate the Israelite kingdoms. God's judgment will be like a forest fire that consumes almost everything in its path. There will be a few trees left, but these will serve simply to mark the movement of the divine judge through the land.

While the devastation of Israel's resources will be horrific, it will not be total. These few trees that survive the fire of God's judgment stand for "the remnant of Israel" that will survive (10:20). Judgment is never God's last word to Israel, and the remnant will be the means of Israel's survival. The importance of this motif for Isaiah is clear from the name he gave to his eldest son: "A remnant shall return" (7:3). Nonetheless, for the prophet the remnant motif involves a proclamation of judgment on unfaithful Judah: 10:19; 17:5-6; 30:17. Faith and conversion are necessary before the remnant can experience God's salvation. This will lead God to restore the remnant to the land from the nations where they have been exiled (11:11). Most of the occurrences of remnant language in Isaiah reflect political usage in which remnant describes what remained of a people who managed to survive a military campaign that aimed at their total destruction.

There are several texts from the book of Isaiah in which the remnant idea is defined as a miraculously preserved minority (4:3; 10:20; and 38:5). This idea meshes with a principal Isaianic theme: Jerusalem is threatened but ultimately delivered. In Isaiah the remnant motif is part of the prophet's call for repentance and faith. Still, Isaiah says practically nothing about the identity of this remnant. Zephaniah, a Judahite prophet who lived about two hundred years after Isaiah, is not so reticent and identifies the remnant with the poor (Zeph 2:3; 3:12-13). They will survive the judgment and be the nucleus of a new people of God.

The poem in verses 28-34 describes with geographical detail the Assyrian advance on Jerusalem from the north. It appears that nothing can stand in the way of the Assyrian invader. Still, God, who is called here "the Lord of hosts" ("host" being a traditional term for "army") prevents the Assyrians from taking Zion. Instead, the Assyrians themselves suffer a great defeat.

11:1-9 The shoot from Jesse

The prophet shifts away from political and military realities back into an idealistic vision of the future. As in 9:2-7, Isaiah gives a central place in that future to an ideal king who will be everything that Judah's actual kings were not.

God's promise regarding Judah's future will find its fulfillment through a descendant of Jesse, the father of David. "The shoot from the stump of Jesse" is an engaging poetic metaphor for an ideal king who will be equipped for his rule by God's spirit. This will insure his success. This savior-king will be known for his judicial wisdom, his ability to translate his decisions into action,

his attitude toward the poor, his readiness to deal harshly with evildoers, his devotion to God, and his righteousness (11:25). The rule of this coming king will please both God and God's people.

The coming of this ideal king will be marked by the taming of wild animals (11:6-8). At present people have to fear for the safety of their domestic animals and their children. The prophet envisions a future when this danger will be removed; however, he is clear that this change will take place only when all people act righteously in accord with the guidance provided by the savior-king (11:9b). The absence of this "knowledge of the LORD" is the reason for alienation from God and the consequent divine judgment (1:3; 5:13; 6:10). The knowledge the prophet speaks of is not information about God but a commitment to God and traditional Israelite moral values.

At the end of his infancy narrative, Matthew states that Joseph settled his family in Nazareth to fulfill the prophetic word that "He shall be called a Nazorean" (Matt 2:23). There is no such text in the Hebrew Bible, though there is a similarity in sound between the Aramaic word for Nazareth and the Hebrew word that the NAB translates as "shoot" in verse 1. Of course, Christian believers have claimed that this prophetic vision of a second David has been fulfilled in Jesus. The expectations of the prophet, however, were not fulfilled in a literal sense but were reinterpreted by people of faith. Religious Jews continue to look for the coming of the king that the prophet describes. Both Jews and Christians together wait for the final revelation of God's power and glory in a completely definitive way.

The redemption that the prophet describes is not directed at the salvation of individual people. The coming of this ideal king will involve the renewal of all creation. Because the world is God's creation, it will not devolve into nothingness, but will be transformed and renewed in the final consummation which both Jew and Christian still await.

11:10-16 Israel and Judah united

Speaking of the rule of the ideal king leads the prophet to speak of the kingdom over which that king will rule. For most of their history, the two Israelite kingdoms were antagonistic to one another with Israel, the more powerful of the two usually taking the upper hand. What the prophet envisions are the two kingdoms united under the rule of a single sovereign from "the root of Jesse," i.e., the Davidic dynasty. Before that vision can find fulfillment, God will first have to gather the remnant of the two kingdoms that have been dispersed through exile. Once this remnant has been assembled, there will be no evidence of the rivalry that had marked the relations between Israel (Ephraim) and Judah. The new united people will enjoy sovereignty over neighboring national states. The prophet compares this future act of deliverance to the exodus from Egypt that transformed the Hebrew slaves into the people of God.

In Romans 15:8-12, Paul cites several texts including verse 10 to emphasize that, while Jesus' being a Jew proves God's fidelity to the promises made to the patriarchs, the salvation promised was for the Gentiles as well.

12:1-6 A hymn of salvation

This is a short hymn of thanksgiving for Jerusalem's deliverance. While Isaiah was certain that Jerusalem was going to experience divine judgment for the failure of its leaders to maintain a just society, he was equally convinced that judgment on Jerusalem was not final. One call to praise and thanksgiving follows another as the prophet exclaims his confidence in Zion's future. One can look beyond judgment to a glorious future for Zion because the Holy One of Israel remains in the midst of the city. While the mission of the prophet was to confront Judah with the consequences of its failure to maintain a just society, there was another aspect to that mission that cannot be ignored. The prophet's mission makes sense only if there is to be a future for Judah. This hymn of salvation expresses the prophet's assurance that divine judgment will not be the end of Judah but the beginning of a new act of salvation.

JERUSALEM AND THE NATIONS

Isaiah 13:1–27:13

The prophets addressed their words to a real people, who lived at a real time and in a real place, and who had to deal with real problems. Among the most serious of these problems were the political and military pressures brought to bear upon the Israelite kingdoms by neighboring national states and imperial powers. Economic and po-

litical realities usually meant that ancient Israel regarded its neighbors as potential threats to its existence. In speaking about Jerusalem's future, Isaiah could not avoid speaking about the nations. In this second section of the book, the dominant attitude toward the nations is negative since these oracles reflect the experience of Israel and Judah with the nations. For most of their history, the two Israelite kingdoms had to contend with the other national states in the eastern Mediterranean region for control of the region's commercial and agricultural resources. The kingdom of Israel's principal rivals were Aram and Moab, while Judah's were the Philistine city-states and Edom. The two Israelite kingdoms contended with each other as well, with Israel having the most success. But it was the rise of the neo-Assyrian and neo-Babylonian empires with their aggressive and expansionist policies that led to the end of first Israel and then Judah as national states.

Oracles against the nations are a prominent feature in several prophetic books, e.g., Amos 1:2–2:3; Jeremiah 46:1–51:64; and Ezekiel 25–32. Indeed, an oracle against Assyria comprises the whole of the book of Nahum. Since the people of the two Israelite kingdoms experienced other nations as threats to their existence, it is not surprising that they called upon their God to defend them from such threats. The oracles against the nations are an expression of ancient Israel's belief that God would never permit these nations to destroy Israel completely. While God has chosen to use these nations to bring judgment upon the Israelite kingdoms for their failure to maintain a just society, God will move against these nations for their failures as well. God's judgment of the nations will mean salvation for Israel.

Some modern readers find these oracles difficult to read. First, the nations against whom the prophet announces God's judgment are simply geographical names devoid of any emotional content. But the prophet's first audience reacted to names like Assyria, Edom, Philistia, and Babylon the same way that the Irish react to England, the Tibetans to China, the Bosnians to Serbia, and the Koreans to Japan. Second, some of the prophet's modern readers are shocked by the harshness of the prophet's words. While the severity of the judgments pronounced by the prophet reflects rhetorical patterns of his culture, also displays an anger that is genuine. There may be a holdover of this attitude toward the nations when Jesus refers to the Syrophoenician woman and her daughter as "dogs" (Mark 7:27-28). Certainly, the book of Revelation is as harsh toward Rome as any of the Old Testament's oracles against the nations.

Like the first section of the book, this one also begins with an oracle of judgment against arrogance and injustice, though here the oracle is addressed to Babylon rather than Judah. Again, as was the case with the previous section, this second section of the book ends on a positive note. The prophet announces salvation for Judah.

13:1–14:23 Against Babylon

First place among the nations under divine judgment is given to Babylon. The events that led to the production of Isaiah as we have it and, indeed, a good part of the Old Testament in its present form were those surrounding the Babylonian conquest of Jerusalem in 587 B.C. and the fall of Babylon less than fifty years later. The fall of this mighty empire and the subsequent restoration of Jerusalem and its temple gave Judah hope for the future. It is fitting, then, that the first of the oracles against the nations has Babylon as its subject. The ascription of this oracle to the eighth-century prophet is appropriate because of his insistence that divine judgment upon Judah, though well deserved, was not God's final word to Jerusalem. While the nations are God's instruments of judgment, they will have to answer for their own excesses, arrogance, and folly.

This poem opens with Babylon's sentinels sounding the alarm as an army of conquest is approaching the city. The marching feet of its immense horde moving toward the city make sounds like the rumble of thunder on a distant mountain as the storm gathers strength and begins its approach. Of course, it is Judah's God who has gathered this mighty force against Babylon, whose military forces desert as the army assembled by God approaches. The portents in the heavens make it obvious that this is no ordinary military adventure, but one directed by God. The devastation will be complete and Babylon will experience the horrors of war. The Medes, who are God's chosen instruments of judgment, will turn Babylon into a wasteland.

The prophet uses a type of hyperbole that often appears in biblical texts with a high emotional content. The poem is trying to revive the spirit of the Judahite community that was devastated by the fall of Jerusalem, the destruction of its temple, and the exile of a sizeable portion of its population. Many of the exiles accommodated themselves to the new realities. The prophet insists that Babylon has no future and implies that its fall is a harbinger of a new future for Judah. The fall of Babylon makes Judah's restoration possible. The prophet elaborates on this reversal of fortunes as he taunts Babylon. He asserts that the exile will be reversed: instead of the people of Israel being led off to Babylon as slaves, the Babylonians will be led to the land of Israel to serve the community restored to its native land. Of course, here the prophet is becoming carried away by his own rhetoric.

The oracle in 14:4b-21 begins by proclaiming the fall of the tyrant responsible for the oppression of many nations, all of whom delight in the tyrant's fall. Peace has come again to the world. The trees of Lebanon's lush forests are personified to represent the nations who are relieved to know there will be no one to cut them down again.

Tyrants of the distant past welcome the king of Babylon to their realm in the nether world. He is now one of them, exchanging the accouterments of a regal life style for the worms that devour the corpses of the dead. Babylon's king did not even have the benefit of a decent burial. His corpse is simply trampled underfoot. This terrible fate is due him because of his failures as a king. His sons will also be killed to insure that his name will be forgotten. The oracle against Babylon concludes with a prose statement (14:22-23) in which God affirms the decision to destroy Babylon totally. The book of Revelation adopts Babylon as its code name for Rome, which it perceived as a threat to the existence of the early Christian community.

The New Testament uses the imagery of 13:10 in speaking about the end of the age (Matt 24:29; Mark 13:24-25; Luke 21:25; Rev 6:12-13; 8:12). In 14:12 the prophet calls the king of Babylon the "Morning Star," which Jerome rendered into Latin as "Lucifer." Patristic and medieval interpreters, influenced by Jerome and connecting Isaiah 14:12 with Luke 10:18, read this passage as a description of the fall of rebellious angels. Of course, this interpretation is an example of creative imagination. Still, Lucifer has passed into popular language as a name for the leader of the fallen angels.

14:24-27 Against Assyria

The aggressively expansionist neo-Assyrian empire made a series of incursions into the territory of the two Israelite kingdoms during the last third of the eighth century B.C. This oracle implies that God would destroy the Assyrian Empire during one of those incursions. While the Assyrian army was besieging Jerusalem in 701 B.C., civil unrest back in Assyria required the return of the army. Perhaps the oracle refers to the lifting of that siege (Isa 37:36-37; 2 Kgs 19:35-37). In any case, the Assyrian Empire fell in 612 B.C. to the Babylonians. Certainly the prophet wanted to insure that the people of Judah would see the working out of a divine purpose in the collapse of that empire. Again, the fall of a great empire was a sign of God's power and determination to rehabilitate Judah and Jerusalem.

14:28-32 Against Philistia

The prophet had already asserted that God used the Philistines to punish Israel for its infidelity (9:11). Now he warns the Philistines that they, in turn, will face their day of judgment. Like all the peoples who lived along the eastern Mediterranean coast, the Philistines were subjugated by Assyria. Though Assyria has fallen, the Philistines should not be too quick to celebrate. Another serpent whose venom is even stronger than that of the Assyrians will strike them. Of course, Babylon, whom the prophet characterizes as a "flying seraph," is that foe from the north who will bring an end to the Philistine cities that harassed Judah in its weakness. Philistia's trouble is Jerusalem's salvation.

15:1–16:14 Against Moab

Moab too had to deal with the Assyrian incursions into its territory. Unlike the two Israelite kingdoms, Moab was much more compliant. It even assisted the Assyrians in dealing with Arab tribes who resisted Assyrian domination. This collaboration with Assyria may have led the prophet to include Moab among the nations that were to experience divine judgment. The oracle likely reflects the result of a later Babylonian campaign in the region that ended the existence of Moab as a political entity. It describes the total devastation that affected every major Moabite city as well as the surrounding countryside. The humiliations that come with occupation led the people to ritual mourning whose purpose was to induce the gods to have pity on them, but it had no effect. Moab's ruination continued and its people fled before the invader, but many did not escape.

Some of Moab's refugees will make their way to Zion, where they will seek to escape the Babylonian forces invading their homeland. Though these refugees will find protection, nothing can be done to stop the total devastation of their homeland. What was once a formidable power in the region will barely survive the Babylonian invasion. The Moabites will lament and pray but without effect. Nothing can stop what will happen to their country. The prophet assures his readers that Moab will indeed experience God's judgment. There will only be a small and weak remnant left of what was once a significant regional power. Of course, the remnant of Judah will be the instrument that God will use to restore Jerusalem.

17:1-6 Against Damascus

Damascus was the capital of Aram (Syria), a one-time rival of the kingdom of Israel and then its ally against the encroachments of the Assyrians. When Ahaz, the king of Judah, refused to join their anti-Assyrian coalition, Aram and Israel were preparing to invade Judah to depose Ahaz and replace him with a more cooperative monarch. Isaiah was certain that these plans would fail (7:1–8:4). The prophet knew the ferocity of the Assyrian military machine. He was sure that the Assyrians would give those arrayed against them no quarter. Hardly anything will be left of Aram and Israel once the Assyrians move against them. The inevitable Assyrian response will cause terrible devastation to cities and villages throughout both Aram and Israel. The destructive forces of the Assyrian army would leave as little behind as do harvesters in a wheat field or on an olive tree.

17:7-11 Against the worship of other gods

The metaphor comparing the Assyrian army to harvesters led the prophet to inveigh against the worship of other gods, which was so offensive to someone who believed in the holiness of Judah's God and in the exclusive claims that God had on Judah. What the people of Judah expected from their God was fertility for the land and protection from enemies. They sought these not only from the Lord, their patron deity, but from other gods as well. Here the prophet mentions the trappings of non-Yahwistic worship as a cause of shame for the people of Judah. The "alien god" of verse 10 is likely Tammuz, a god connected with grain production. The prophet asserts that those who sought to secure a good harvest through rituals associated with Tammuz (see also Ezek 8:14-15) will find that all their activity was in vain and they will enjoy no harvest at all.

The judgment against Israel and Aram will lead Judah to recognize the claims that its national God makes upon it. Judah will see the folly of serving other gods. They will reject all forms of non-Yahwistic religion. Those people who do not will lose their claim to the land just as their ancestors dispossessed earlier inhabitants of the land.

17:12-14 Against the nations

To summarize the oracles against the two great Mesopotamian empires and three local powers, the prophet composed a short poem on the power of God. He used an old metaphor from the ancient Near Eastern religious tradition: the power of God as manifested in the control of the unruly and potentially chaotic sea. The peoples of the ancient Near East believed the greatest manifestation of divine power was keeping the power of the sea in check. The story of creation begins with the "spirit of God" moving over the sea and bringing order and life to what was void and without form (Gen 1:2).

The prophet asserts that God can bring order out of the chaos unleashed by the greed and ferocity of the nations. Though these nations look strong and appear ready to overwhelm Judah, they will not succeed. Their threats will disappear as quickly and suddenly as they appeared. The prophet believes that God will protect Jerusalem (see also Pss 46, 48)—a belief that gave shape to his ministry.

The gospels use this same metaphor centuries later when they testify to Christian belief in the divinity of Jesus. Jesus calms the Sea of Galilee and his disciples marvel at his power asking, "What sort of man is this, whom even the winds and the sea obey?" (Matt 8:27).

18:1–19:25 Against Egypt

The two Israelite kingdoms were sandwiched between Egypt and the Mesopotamian Empires. The goal of the latter was the conquest of Egypt, command of its resources, and control over the trade routes between Egypt and Mesopotamia. Egypt, of course, resisted, and the Israelite kingdoms were caught in the crossfire. There was a particularly destructive escalation of this crossfire in 714 B.C. The Assyrians were poised on the border of Egypt, ready to invade. Egypt wanted a buffer between it and the Assyrian army so it encouraged several Assyrian vassal states in the eastern Mediterranean region to revolt and reassert their independence. What the prophet suggests is that Judah keep away from any such activity.

The prophet was certain that Judah could maintain its political independence if it learned to trust God rather than to engage in futile political and military machinations. It was an open secret that Egypt and Ethiopia were conspiring against the aggression of Assyria. The prophet believed that God determines the course of events—the plans that people make are worthless. God will bring about an end to the Assyrian Empire, but it will come when God chooses. What Judah must do is wait for a sign that God will begin to move against the Assyrians. The victory that God will effect will lead the conspirators to Jerusalem to bring tribute to Judah's God. What Judah must do is wait.

The prophet then becomes specific as he describes some of the signs of God's dominion over Egypt. The first of these are the internal divisions in Egypt that make possible the rise of a new pharaoh (the "cruel master" and "harsh king" of 19:4). The new king that the prophet speaks of is likely Piankhi, the founder of the twenty-fifth dynasty. This Nubian monarch took the throne of Egypt around 714 B.C. and united Egypt, Nubia, and Ethiopia under his rule. An even more serious manifestation of divine power will come when the Nile dries up. The Egyptian economy will collapse because of this disaster. Of course, Egypt's political and economic problems make it an unreliable ally.

Despite these internal difficulties, the pharaoh's advisors urged him to become involved in international politics. Isaiah had little use for the counselors who advised the king of Judah (5:18-25), and he had no respect for the sages of Egypt, even though these sages had a reputation for wisdom. Their advice is necessarily flawed because they do not take into account the judgment of Judah's God on their country. Egypt's political and military leaders will be making decisions based on flawed advice, and these decisions will have disastrous consequences for Egypt and for its allies.

One goal of the Assyrian Empire was to bring Egypt and its wealth under Assyrian control. The two Israelite kingdoms were merely stepping-stones on the way to the real prize. Here the prophet transforms that grand strategy by making Israel the linchpin that will join Egypt and Assyria. These two bitter rivals will find themselves allied in the worship of Israel's God. Again, the prophet is carried away by his own rhetoric and describes a vision that has never been realized.

20:1-6 A dramatic gesture

The prophets tried to persuade people not only with their eloquence but also with their actions. The dramatic gesture became an important part of the prophetic repertoire. Hosea married a prostitute (Hos 1–3). Jeremiah purchased land during the Babylonian siege of Jerusalem (32:1-44). Ezekiel kept silence for seven and one-half years (Ezek 3:26; 24:26-27; 33:21-22). Eclipsing them all was Isaiah's three-year period of nudity. The purpose of this gesture was to dramatize the futility of the anti-Assyrian machinations encouraged by Egypt. The prophet wanted everyone to see what would happen to the Egyptians when Assyria moved against them: they will be carried off into slavery without any clothes to cover their shame.

The Egyptians encouraged the Philistine city-state of Ashdod, which was located on the Mediterranean coast twenty-nine miles south of Jaffa, to rebel against the Assyrians. The territory of Ashdod became incorporated into the Assyrian provincial system in 734 B.C. When Sargon II came to put down the rebellion with overwhelming force, the Egyptians thought the better of challenging him and simply abandoned Ashdod to its fate. The city fell to the Assyrian army in 713 B.C. While Isaiah's advice to Judah was sound, Assyria never conquered Egypt.

21:1-10 Against Babylon

This second oracle against Babylon repeats the message of 13:1–14:22. The title of this oracle is enigmatic. The Greek suggests that the title should read: "An oracle roaring like whirlwinds in the Negev. . . ." The prophet describes the fall

of Babylon. Elam and Media to the east of Babylon are preparing to engulf the ancient Near East in a new wave on conquest. The conqueror will itself be conquered. Everything is in place. The great battle is about to begin. In verses 6-10, the scene shifts. The prophet, like a sentry, is scanning the horizon for a messenger bringing news of Babylon's defeat. Finally the messenger comes: "Fallen, fallen is Babylon." The prophet's words are confirmed by events. The implication is that the reader can have confidence in Judah's prophets.

John of Revelation cites the cry to the messenger who proclaims the fall of Babylon to the prophet (21:9; Rev 14:8; 18:2) to assert his faith in the triumph of Christ and the church over Rome and its emperor.

21:11-12 Against Edom

The prophet returns to the anti-Assyrian revolt encouraged by Egypt and led by Ashdod. Edom was an active participant in that revolt. "Dumah" may be a poetic name for Edom, which came to be known as Idumea in the Greek and Roman periods. This short oracle implies that there will be some respite from Assyrian pressure ("morning comes"), but that it will be followed by a new round of oppression ("also the night").

21:13-17 Against Arabia

After speaking about Edom's future, the prophet turns his attention to Kedar, an association of Arabian tribes living to the east of Edom. That the prophet singles Kedar out for words of judgment shows they were a significant military force, as is confirmed by Assyrian and Babylonian sources. Isaiah announces an end of Kedar's "glory." The prophet wants to impress the people of Judah with the futility of military adventures. This was an important message for the first readers of the book of Isaiah, since Judah had no military power at all. From the prophet's perspective, this did not matter. It was Judah's commitment to justice that was decisive. It was not the Judahite state that would secure Jerusalem's future but a community founded on a just social and economic order.

22:1-14 Against Jerusalem

The prophet was not finished with his comments on the fallout from the failed revolt against

Assyria led by Ashdod. Judah did not join the conspirators, so when Sargon II led his army from Assyria to Ashdod, he bypassed Jerusalem. The city's people celebrated. Isaiah regarded their response to be inappropriate since God's "beloved people" still faced divine judgment. Indeed, judgment was coming because the people of means were guilty of conspicuous consumption—seemingly unmoved by the prophet's warnings. Mercenaries from Elam and Kir will turn the city's "choicest valleys" into highways for an invasion. Though the city will prepare itself for this invasion, these efforts will provide no real security because God is the one planning the city's judgment while its foolish citizens are celebrating their apparent deliverance. Jerusalem, however, will not escape judgment because it has not responded to the prophet's call for justice.

Paul quotes the words of the people of Jerusalem in verse 13 when writing about the significance of the resurrection from the dead. The apostle asserts that without belief in the resurrection, people would think only of their pleasure (1 Cor 15:32).

22:15-25 Against Shebna and Eliakim

The prophet lays the blame for Jerusalem's folly on its leaders for the most part. Here he singles out two royal counselors for particular criticism. Shebna was King Hezekiah's chief of staff. Isaiah saw the impressive tomb that Shebna was preparing for himself. This prompted the prophet to speak about Shebna's certain fall from power. He likely advised Hezekiah to become involved in the anti-Assyrian revolt led by Ashdod. Fortunately for Judah, Hezekiah did not take Shebna's advice and demoted him (36:3). His place as chief of staff was taken by Eliakim. Isaiah expected great things from Eliakim though he too proved to be a disappointment (22:25). Those in a position to bring significant change to Judahite society did nothing to disrupt the economic status quo. They believed that their political and military maneuvering would provide Judah with security. One goal of the prophet's mission was to convince Judah of just the opposite. Only a society based on justice—one that seeks the welfare of the poor—would survive.

The book of Revelation uses the imagery of verse 22 in speaking about Christ to the church of Philadelphia (Rev 3:7).

23:1-18 Against Tyre and Sidon

Tyre and Sidon were commercial centers located on the seacoast north of ancient Israel. Their merchant ships plied the Mediterranean Sea, going as far as Tarshish, located in what is now Spain. By being efficient conduits for international trade, these cities enriched themselves. Their economic resources made them attractive prey for the aggressive Assyrian Empire. The oracles against these cities are intertwined, as was their ultimate fate. The oracle against Sidon (23:1-4, 12-14) asserts that this city would no longer profit from the grain it transported from Egypt to the rest of the ancient Near East. The prophet also proclaims that Tyre will experience divine judgment but for a limited period. Tyre will rise again, but its wealth will be dedicated to the Lord, so that it might support "those who dwell before the Lord." This flight of prophetic fancy is consistent with Isaiah's view of wealth: it is to be shared with those in need rather than being hoarded by the wealthy.

When Jesus condemns the cities of Capernaum, Bethsaida, and Chorazin for their failure to respond to his preaching, he says that the judgment on Tyre and Sidon will be easier than the judgment on them. It is likely that the evangelists were thinking of this oracle against the two Phoenician cities (Matt 11:21-22; Luke 10:13-14).

24:1-23 Judgment upon the whole earth

The oracles of judgment that the prophet utters against the nations of the ancient Near East—including Judah—provide the setting for more general prophecies of a universal judgment that follow in chapters 24–27. In these chapters, the prophet is far less specific and far more pessimistic than in chapters 13–23. Still, the prophet's pessimism is not total. While he speaks about the desolation that comes with divine judgment upon a world without justice, he does hope for a decisive manifestation of divine power that will remake the world into a place where justice triumphs. Readers will be tempted to find precise referents for the nonspecific images that these chapters contain. For example, is the city that the prophet mentions Babylon, Nineveh, Jerusalem, or Samaria? The most plausible answer is that the city is any city and every city founded on injustice and oppression. The nonspecific character of the prophet's words disengages them from a particular time and place and makes their appropriation by readers today easier. On the other hand, the vague generalities of these chapters challenge the reader's attention as the prophet tries to draw a picture of what lies ahead not simply for Babylon, Jerusalem, and Egypt but for the whole world.

Chapters 24–27 have been sometimes called the "Isaiah Apocalypse." They do contain images and motifs that later apocalyptic texts develop. While chapters 24–27 are not full-blown apocalypses, they do share with later apocalyptic texts such as Daniel 7–12 and Revelation the absolute conviction of God's sovereign rule over all creation. They look forward to its coming and await God's final triumph over the power of evil.

The first oracle (24:1-6) envisions the devastation of the earth. All people will be caught up in the destruction that will take place. Those of high social and economic status will find that their wealth will not save them, and those of a lower class will not be exempt from the evil that will come upon all. The prophet gives no specific reason for this universal judgment except for universal disobedience. Only a few people will survive.

This universal judgment will make it impossible for wine to gladden people's hearts—so terrible will be the earth's fate. Carefree hilarity will be replaced by cries of desperation. Still, when judgment comes people will be moved to praise God's righteousness (24:14-16). The theme of universal judgment is picked up again in verses 16b-23. Isaiah sees earthquakes, storms, and astronomical events as the means of divine judgment. Some early Jewish interpreters understood "the host of heaven" to refer to rebellious angels, though this is not explicit here. Most people in the ancient world thought that heavenly bodies were manifestations of deities (see Zeph 1:5; Jer 19:13), so personifying them as "the host of the heavens" (24:21) is something to be expected. The judgment, when it comes, will reveal the power of Judah's God, who will reign in Jerusalem. Human beings are responsible for the coming judgment, but the ultimate purpose of that judgment is not vindictiveness. Its ultimate purpose is to reveal to all the world the justice of God. The prophet envisions the end of the age with God reigning in Jerusalem "in the sight of the elders" (24:23). The book of Revelation sees God's throne sounded by those "twenty-four elders" (Rev 4:4).

25:1-5 A prayer of thanksgiving

This hymn thanks God for a victory over a powerful but unnamed enemy. This victory is another instance of God's marvelous acts on Israel's behalf—acts that stretch back to the distant past. The enemy's capital has been destroyed, leading that "strong people" to recognize the power of Israel's God—a power that was unleashed to protect a helpless Israel. The enemy came upon Israel as an east wind off the desert whose withering heat brings crop failure, famine, and starvation in its wake. God's presence was like a cloud that protected people from the terrible heat of the terrible east wind.

Those protected by God are the "poor" and the "needy." Apocalyptic texts usually address people who consider themselves to be victims of political, social, or economic oppression. It gives their struggles meaning by assuring them that God will take their side against their oppressors. This prayer thanks God for doing just that.

25:6-10a The Lord's feast

Eating sparingly with little variation in diet was the rule for most people in the ancient world. Little wonder then that a lavish banquet became a potent symbol of the restoration of God's rule on the earth (see also Joel 2:24-26; 4:18; Ezra 3:13; Matt 22:1-10; Luke 14:15-24). What is significant about this passage is its assertion that "all nations" will share in that banquet since God will lift the veil that obscures the vision of the nations, bringing an end to that which keeps Israel and the nations apart. They will recognize Israel as God's people. It will be as if death itself were overcome. Here the prophet's words have a double meaning that escapes most readers today. The Canaanite god of the underworld was Mot, whose name is the Hebrew word for "death." Mot was locked in a continuous battle with Baal, the god of fertility. When the prophet asserts that the Lord will destroy death forever, he implies that in the new age there will be no lack of fertility. Hunger will no longer be a threat. People will not have to eat sparingly. This text does not imply that the dead will rise. What it does suggest is that God will make life worth living. Israel will be able to acclaim its God as savior since it is only by the power of God that all this has happened. It is God's doing.

When Paul proclaims God's victory over the power of death (1 Cor 15:54-55), he sees this victory as the fulfillment of Scripture. Though his citations are free and not ascribed to a specific book, it is likely that Paul had verse 8 in mind. The book of Revelation also finds inspiration in the prophet's assertion that God "will wipe away the tears from all faces" (25:8; Rev 7:17).

25:10b-12 Against Moab

The reader's attention is drawn back to the motif of verses 1-5: God's victory over the powerful. Here Moab is the symbol of Israel's powerful enemies. God will frustrate its designs on Israel and it will experience a devastating defeat. This short oracle clashes with what just preceded. In 25:6-8, God will invite all nations to the feast. Once again Israel's attitude toward other people is shaped less by its vision of the future and more by its experience.

26:1-6 The song of the redeemed

When the prophet dreams about the future, his dreams are cast in patterns that try to reestablish Israel in the service of the God who takes the side of the poor against the powerful. This is precisely the imagery behind the prophet's "song of the redeemed." The vision celebrated in this song foresees a future in which the fortunes of the present will be reversed: the mighty will be brought low. The prophet looks toward a time when all Judah will sing a song of victory to God. That song will celebrate Jerusalem—its walls and gates that have withstood the enemy but which welcome and enclose the faithful. The key to the victory was the people's trust in God on whom Judah must always depend. It will be those least able who will seal Judah's victories. Victory will come to the lowly, who will enter the city as victors who have been made such by the power of God alone. The poor and the lowly have no power in the present age, but the future will bring these people total victory over their oppressors.

26:7-19 A psalm celebrating victory

For the prophet, the key to Judah's future was its confidence in its God. The prophet keeps returning to that theme. Military and political realities, of course, made any other source of hope a delusion. The prayer begins by lifting up God's justice and affirms that the righteous may have confidence in it. The wicked, however, never grasp the significance of God's action in the world. The prophet prays that one day they might recognize the meaning of what God will accomplish for Judah. God will bring peace and security for Judah, but its enemies will face destruction. The letter to the Hebrews quotes verse 11 to assure its readers that judgment is coming on those who do not persevere in the faith (Heb 10:27).

Because the promised peace has not come, the just turn to God in their distress. God's people face a very difficult time. It is like the agony of a woman in labor, but at the end of that agony, there is life. The prophet prays that there will be life for Judah. His vision of the future and the ultimate redemption of Judah shapes his attitude toward the present difficulties that the just face. That vision helps the just make sense out of the apparent contradictions of their lives. In his confidence, the prophet prays that Judah's dead also share in God's victory. Is the prophet getting carried away with his rhetoric again, or is verse 19 an expression of faith in the resurrection of the dead? It is difficult to say, but, at the very least, this text provided support for those who held that belief in years to come.

26:20–27:1 The coming judgment

Though the prophet is confident about Judah's future, his attention is drawn to the dire military and political circumstances that it faced. There is death all around, but soon God will reverse Judah's fortunes by destroying those nations allied against it. Giving advice reminiscent of the story of the first Passover (Exod 12), the prophet warns his readers to shut their door until death passes them by.

To express his confidence in God's victory over every evil power, the prophet uses imagery that was ancient but never loses its power to move people. The Canaanites envisioned the creation of the world as following the defeat of a great sea monster that the prophet calls Leviathan. While the Canaanites believed that the decisive defeat of Leviathan took place in the past, leading to the creation of this world, the prophet asserts that this battle has yet to take place. However, he is certain that God will be victorious. Hundreds of years later, the book of Revelation uses similar imagery of a monster from the sea to speak of God's final victory over the power of evil (Rev 13:1).

27:2-6 The Lord's vineyard

The vision of God's final victory over the power of evil leads to another prayer of confidence. The prophet takes up the imagery of 5:1-7 to speak not about God's judgment on the unproductive vineyard that is Israel but about the productivity of that vineyard that is under God's protection. The fruit from the Lord's vineyard will fill "the whole world." Thus the prophet again sounds a note of universalism that will be an important dimension in section four of the book.

27:7-11 The end of idolatry

Israel's salvation will take place because Israel will finally leave the worship of other gods behind. It will recognize that it is the Lord who gives the land its fertility and that it makes no sense to worship other deities. Finally, Israel is faithful to its God alone because God has removed every trace of false worship just as the withering east wind dries up every blade of grass that it touches. Once God delivers Israel, now freed from serving other gods, its enemies will face defeat and destruction.

27:12-13 Israel's restoration

God will pass in judgment one final time over the land of Israel promised to Abraham (see Gen 15:18). The Lord will traverse the full extent of that land from north to south, separating the wicked from the faithful as threshers separate grain from chaff. When that has taken place, the restoration will begin. A trumpet will sound to gather Israel, as happens for every solemn assembly (see Num 10:2-10). This time Israel in exile will assemble to worship God in Jerusalem. Thus the second section of the book of Isaiah ends like the first—with the people of Israel worshiping the Lord, their ancestral God, in Jerusalem.

JERUSALEM'S JUDGMENT AND SALVATION

Isaiah 28:1–39:8

The third section of the book of Isaiah is a series of literary diptychs, one side of which describes divine judgment on the two Israelite kingdoms in general and the city of Jerusalem in particular. The second side of the diptych assures the people of Jerusalem that there is a future beyond judgment. Sometimes this assurance takes the form of an oracle against one of Judah's enemies; other times the prophet proclaims an oracle of salvation for Jerusalem. The final four chapters of this section (Isa 36–39) are narratives taken almost verbatim from 2 Kings 18:13–20:19. But even they replicate this alternation between judgment and salvation. Jerusalem is threatened by the Assyrians and then miraculously saved from their power. Similarly, Hezekiah faces imminent death, but at the last moment his life is spared. But this section ends with the ominous words of the prophet Isaiah, who tells Hezekiah that Babylon will bring an end to Judah's dynasty and state.

28:1-4 The proud crown

As was the case with the two previous sections of the book, this third section begins with an oracle of judgment. This time it is directed at the arrogance of the northern kingdom of Israel. The prophet uses several metaphors in announcing divine judgment on the northern kingdom—here called Ephraim after one of its principal regions. The northern kingdom was blessed with natural beauty and agriculturally valuable land. Isaiah proclaims that its excesses have finally caught up with Ephraim. Its capital, Samaria, was a beautiful city perched on the top of a mountain. The prophet is certain that it is going to fall to its enemies. The prophet compares the city to the wilting blossoms on the crown of a merrymaker after a night of drinking. Like that garland, the city has outlived its usefulness. A storm is coming that will overwhelm it. Assyrian kings on military expeditions often compared themselves to the fury of a storm that would destroy all that stood in its path. Finally, the prophet speaks of Samaria as an early ripening fig, especially attractive to passersby since late summer is the usual time for figs. The reason for Ephraim's predicament is the extravagance of the wealthy. They enjoy lavish meals while those who actually produced the food were living on the subsistence level with barely enough to eat. Isaiah believes that Assyria, God's chosen instrument of judgment, will make short work of Samaria and its proud crown.

28:5-6 A glorious crown

The word of judgment is followed by a word of hope that takes up the image of the crown from the previous unit. The proud crown that is

Samaria is contrasted with the "glorious crown" that is the Lord. The former is facing judgment; the latter brings salvation for the remnant that will survive God's judgment on Israel. The remnant is composed of those who believe that there is a future in Zion despite the disasters that threaten.

28:7-13 Against priest and prophet

The prophet indicts the priests and prophets of his day. They fail in their appointed tasks because they are usually drunk. Here the prophet links his specific criticism with the more general indictment in 28:1. Leviticus 10:8-11 forbids priests on duty to drink. In their drunken state, Israel's religious leaders babble like infants. The quotation of the advice given by Israel's inebriated priests (28:10b) is a succession of nonsense syllables in Hebrew, though the NABRE obscures this. Similarly for those who have rejected Isaiah's indictment of their infidelity, the word of God has become a succession of nonsense syllables. What awaits them is a tragic end. Paul certainly thought of this passage when he was speaking about "the gift of tongues." He freely cites verses 11-12 in 1 Corinthians 14:21-22, although he incorrectly states that the text is from the torah.

28:14-22 Against Jerusalem's political leaders

The actions of Jerusalem's leaders to forestall the inevitable are nothing but a pact with death. Again, the prophet is playing on the name of a Canaanite deity, Mot, the god of the netherworld, whose name means death and whose activity endangers the fertility of the land (see 25:8). Jerusalem's political leaders believe that their leadership will safeguard their city's future, but actually they are only hastening its fall—its death.

The only way that Jerusalem can have any future is if it establishes a just economic system. Trying to protect the city through alliances amounts to little more than suicide. A violent rainstorm that undermined hastily built fortifications around the city gave the prophet the occasion to speak about the solid foundation that God was preparing for the city's future. This foundation is justice. While it is true that Jerusalem was dependent on God's presence in the city, God's presence was, in turn, dependent on the behavior of the city's people—in particular Jerusalem's political leaders. They, however, have not fostered justice—

quite the opposite. This has left God no choice but to begin an "urban renewal project" in the city. The project had to begin with demolition so that the city could be built on the solid foundation of a just economic system.

Jerusalem's leaders believed that strong fortifications would provide all the security the city needed. Isaiah sees devastation ahead since the city will be without the effective protection that justice provides. The prophet stipulates that in the past God fought for Israel against its enemies, the Canaanites (see Josh 10:7-14) and the Philistines (see 2 Sam 5:17-25). But in the coming conflict with Assyria, God will fight against Judah and Jerusalem, something Isaiah characterizes as a "strange deed." There is time to forestall this disaster if the city changes its attitude toward the prophet's message.

At the conclusion of the parable of the Vineyard (Matt 21:33-46), Jesus makes a statement made up of several Old Testament verses strung together to explain the negative reaction to his ministry as a divine necessity. Among those verses is 28:16.

28:23-29 A parable on judgment

Here the prophet uses a succession of rhetorical questions to underscore his message. The judgment that Jerusalem is facing will happen because God acts at the right time for the right purpose. Plowing and planting take place during specific and limited periods according to a plan. Similarly, activities connected with the harvest follow a pattern. The message is clear: all that will happen to Jerusalem will happen at God's discretion for a good reason. Another implication of the parable is that the farmer's various activities, while necessary, have a limited duration so Jerusalem's judgment will be of limited duration as well. While divine judgment is coming, it is not God's final word to Jerusalem.

29:1-8 Jerusalem's judgment and salvation

Isaiah addresses Jerusalem as "Ariel," a name whose significance is unclear. This Hebrew word simply does not occur often enough in the Bible to be sure about its meaning. Ezekiel uses this word to speak of the place of sacrifice, the "altar hearth" where offerings are burnt (Ezek 43:15). If Isaiah understands Ariel in the same way, the prophet may intend this word to imply that Jerusalem will be the setting for the forthcoming sacrifice of Judah's leaders and people. The literal meaning of Ariel is "the lion of God," but the significance of that meaning in this context is also not obvious.

The opening verse of the oracle suggests that the New Year's celebration provided the prophet with an opportunity to speak about what lay ahead for the city. Isaiah declares that a hostile army will surround the city. This siege will lead the people to raise a great lamentation, which will fail to move God since God is intent on making a sacrifice of the city. But the nations chosen to place Jerusalem on the altar of sacrifice will not escape divine judgment. This will not save Jerusalem, but the nations arrayed against it will be judged for their failures as well. Still, the judgment of these nations is a sign of Jerusalem's restoration. Jesus' lament over Jerusalem uses the language and imagery of the prophet's oracle against Ariel (29:3; Luke 19:43).

29:9-16 Against the sages

The prophet, who has already criticized some of Israel's leadership (28:7-22), turns his attention to Jerusalem's sages. He probably has in mind the royal counselors rather than the wise and prudent elders that people sought out for their advice. Like the rest of Jerusalem's leadership, the sages are not fulfilling their responsibilities. The contribution to Judah is as effective as that of a drunk, but they were not drunk with wine like the priests and prophet. They are unable to provide sound advice because God has made it impossible for them to see Jerusalem's true status before God. It is as if all their skill has left them. The prophet blames this on the people of Jerusalem who are content with merely going through the motions during worship. Worst of all, the sages approach the crisis Jerusalem was facing as if it should be handled by diplomatic maneuvering. They do not recognize that the city's future is in God's hands—not theirs. Jesus quotes verse 13 when he criticizes the religious observance of some of his contemporaries (Matt 15:8; Mark 7:6-7). Paul cites verse 16 to affirm the justice of God (Rom 9:21).

29:17-24 A reversal of fortunes

The prophet looks forward to a time when Israel will have the kind of spiritual sensitivity that should mark the people of God. Unfortunately, this is still lacking. There are the devout who tried to live in accord with the Divine Will (the "lowly" and "poorest" of 29:19). Then there are those who led a life that was best described as godless (the "arrogant" of 29:20). Finally, there is a large percentage of "Jacob's children" who are simply ignorant of God's will and promises for Israel (the "blind" and the "deaf" of 29:18). The prophet envisions a time when the latter will be healed, but he appears to intimate that the arrogant are beyond hope. For the prophet a sure sign of God's final act in favor of Israel will be the conversion and incorporation of those who are spiritually insensitive within the community of those already committed to justice.

The social and economic disparity between the poor and the arrogant was serious and it could not go on for much longer. The prophet believed that a reversal of fortunes was coming. God was about to act on behalf of those who were being oppressed. The lowly and poor will find joy, while the arrogant will have gone. When the devout see God's actions on their behalf, their faith will be confirmed and they will be led to an ever greater fidelity to God, for they will stand in awe of God's holiness. The most significant outcome of God's action on behalf of the poor will be the effect it will have on those who "err in spirit" and "find fault." Those people who drag down the spirit of Israel will be transformed and will be firmly convinced that the future belongs to the God of Israel.

30:1-17 Against a compact with Egypt

Conventional wisdom for a small state like Judah caught between two superpowers like Egypt and Assyria was to play off the superpowers against each other. Judah does just that by considering an alliance with Egypt to insure that the Assyrian threat would be neutralized. The prophet consistently advises against this conventional wisdom. Isaiah characterizes Egypt as "Rahab quelled." Rahab is another name for the sea monster that represents the forces of chaos, which God has already defeated (see Job 26:12). The prophet believed that by aligning itself with Egypt, Judah was setting itself up for more severe treatment from Assyria than if it simply submitted. The prophet's strategy in dealing with the Assyrian threat was for Judah to remain passive, making no overt attempts at opposing the unstoppable Assyrian army. He is convinced that the people of Judah will not escape foreign domination because God has chosen Assyria as the instrument of judgment upon Jerusalem.

Isaiah's words reflect his frustration with Judah's political leaders. They look for prophets whose words support their fatally flawed foreign policy. But Isaiah believes that God did not speak through those prophets. Judah has rejected Isaiah's message, which counseled trust in God alone—without relying on alliances, national pride, or armed resistance. The prophet, of course, has made it clear that Judah will not evade divine judgment because of the injustice in Judahite society. But he asserts that submission to Assyria will prevent the total destruction of Judah. The country's leaders, however, labored under the illusion that they could escape judgment. This was their great mistake.

30:18-26 Jerusalem's future

The prophet can envision a glorious future for Jerusalem because he believes that the city's future is not determined by its infidelity but by God's fidelity. After the city experiences God's judgment, there will come deliverance. This oracle begins by identifying the Lord as a "God of justice." The key then to the glorious future that awaits Jerusalem is a just social and economic order—not the city's supposed status as God's dwelling place on earth.

The intensity of Jerusalem's distress at the prospect of Assyrian domination should not lead it to despair but to confident assurance in the coming redemption. God will give to the people all that they need for their life and will insure that the people of Jerusalem have the kind of instruction which, when heard and applied, will keep them from deviating in any way from a life that is in accord with God's will, thus insuring the permanence of the city's deliverance.

The consequence of this new obedience will go beyond the moral order and affect nature; the land will enjoy unparalleled fertility. The contemporary concern for the wise use of natural resources can easily resonate with the prophet's vision which posits a connection between human righteousness and the fruitfulness of the land.

The prophet concludes by using apocalyptic imagery in speaking of Jerusalem's restoration.

The light of the sun and the moon will be so increased that night will be indistinguishable from day and the daylight will be seven times more intense than in the present. When will this happen? The answer is on the day of the "great slaughter" when God will rise up against the enemies of the just and bring down the towers of their strength. In order that the faithful be not afraid of that day, the prophet concludes by describing it as a time when God will heal the wounds of the past that were endured by the just.

30:27-33 Against Assyria

For Jerusalem to live in peace, Assyria will have to fall. Here the prophet asserts that one day this mighty empire will be no more. While Isaiah teaches that God is using the militaristic and expansionist Assyrian Empire as a means to bring down Judah and its unjust social and economic system, the prophet does not endorse the policies of Assyria. Again he makes it clear that Assyria will have to answer for its own crimes. God will descend upon Assyria like a violent winter storm. Assyria will not be able to resist this divine judgment. Of course, Judah will rejoice at Assyria's fall, which is certain to come since God's judgment comes upon injustice and oppression wherever it is found.

31:1-3 Against Egypt

The prophet returns to his attempts to discourage Judah from making an alliance with Egypt against Assyria. An alliance with Egypt appeared to be the right move since Egypt could supply a formidable chariot force which could aid Judah in resisting the Assyrian invaders. Actually, Egypt's chariots would have been of limited use since most of Judah's important cities were in the central highlands where chariots were not maneuverable.

The prophet reasserts the advice he consistently gives to Judah under threat from Assyria: trust in God. God's purposes will be achieved no matter what alliances Judah may make. After all, the Egyptians are human beings and their horses are mere flesh. They could not possibly thwart the plan of God, who has determined to bring an end of Judah's political, religious, and economic institutions because of the injustice that they foster. No chariot army will be able to stop this plan.

31:4-7 God protects Jerusalem

The prophet uses two metaphors to speak of Jerusalem's deliverance. The first is clear enough. God is like a lion which will not surrender its prey though shepherds will try to frighten it off (31:4). The second is more obscure (31:5). The phrasing in the NABRE suggests that God is like birds circling overhead, protecting the city. The Hebrew is not as clear though the parallel with verse 4 suggests that the goal of this imagery is to suggest that God will not abandon Jerusalem. Still, the image of birds circling overhead suggests desolation rather than protection. Of course, this must be seen against the wider backdrop of the Isaianic tradition that affirms that Jerusalem must expect divine judgment because of its oppressive and unjust economic system. Still, the city has a future beyond judgment. What this passage affirms is that God's protection will not allow Jerusalem's total destruction at the hands of its enemies. God's deliverance of the city will finally persuade its people to recognize the claims that God has on their exclusive loyalty. The people will finally stop looking for security by serving gods other than the Lord.

31:8-9 Against Assyria

God's deliverance of Jerusalem can come only at the expense of the Assyrians. Again, the prophet affirms that the time of Assyrian power is limited. When the Assyrian Empire falls, it will be God's doing. The prophet is trying to persuade his readers that their future and the future of their city are in God's hands so they can look toward that future with confidence and assurance. Those who read these words, after the book of Isaiah achieved the shape it now has, lived many years after the Assyrian Empire had fallen to the Babylonian Empire, which, in turn, fell to the Persian Empire. The prophet's audience, however, was still looking for the complete restoration of Jerusalem. Certainly these words were meant to keep their hopes from flagging. After all, Assyria did fall as the prophet said it would. One could have confidence in the prophetic word.

32:1-8 New leadership for Jerusalem

To put a positive spin on his vision of Jerusalem's future, the prophet speaks about leadership. He assures his readers that there will come a time when the current perverse social and economic order will be set aright. Those who have the responsibility for maintaining a just social order will fulfill their responsibilities. In the prophet's day, justice was perverted. People called evil good and fools wise. The poor deserve to have justice done when they are in the right, and apparently there is no one to take their side. But it is not only the poor that suffer. Society itself is transformed into something it should not be. The prophet looks for the day when competent and just political leadership will guide the community. Note there is no hint that this political leadership will come from the Davidic dynasty.

32:9-14 Judgment on Jerusalem

The prophet again shifts his mood abruptly. After describing his vision of a just city led by competent rulers, he moves back to the harsh reality that he has experienced. He speaks to a city under judgment. He turns his attention to the women of the upper classes as he did in 3:16–4:1, because these women were good symbols of the excesses of the wealthy. The prophet warns them that their lives of ease will come to an unexpected end very soon. They ought to be worried. A most appropriate response would be for them to adopt the attitude of mourners with the hope of engaging God's sympathy for their plight. Soon the wealthy will be mourning because their lives of extravagance will end. The soil will lose its fecundity and the cities of Judah will be deserted. The land will revert to the state before human habitation transformed it.

32:15-20 An idyllic future

As quickly as the prophet moved from vision to reality, he shifts back to a vision of an idyllic future. He is convinced that the oracle of judgment he conveyed to the women of the upper classes is not God's final word to Judah. God will send the spirit to make the earth fruitful once again. Human society will be marked by justice. Justice will make it possible for all people to have what they need to lead happy lives. The imagery that the prophet uses here appears to suggest he believes that in the future the people of Judah would be living in small villages. Again, the prophet allows his rhetoric to get the best of him. He expects Jerusalem to be restored. It will be purged of the injustices that have made it the object of divine judgment. The prophet, then, was not one who rejected city life as somehow incompatible to the ideals of traditional Israelite morality. What is essential to the prophet's vision of Judah's future is that justice will lead to peace.

33:1-16 God's justice

This chapter begins with a woe oracle against an unnamed enemy who has threatened Jerusalem—a conventional way of speaking about the city's importance for the future of God's people. The unnamed enemy is the Assyrian Empire, whose demise the prophet announces yet again. The destruction of its enemy means the glorification of Jerusalem, which occupies the prophet's attention in this oracle. That glorification comes because God will rule Jerusalem. God's rule will insure that Zion will be filled with justice and righteousness. These, of course, are prophetic code words for a just social order in which the poor find protection against the greed and arrogance of the rich. Verses 14-16 show how the prophet adapted the question-and-answer pattern of entrance liturgies (e.g., Pss 15, 24) to underscore the importance of justice in the lives of those who would be part of a restored Jerusalem.

33:17-24 A new Jerusalem

The prophet describes Jerusalem after God has removed the Assyrian threat to the city and established justice for the city's poor and oppressed. The prophet uses conventional imagery to speak about God's rule from Zion. The worship of Judah's God will take place without interruption. God's law will guide the city's government, but the prophet allows himself a little poetic license as he speaks of God's dwelling in Zion protected by "broad rivers and streams." There are no rivers or streams in the vicinity of Jerusalem. Finally, sickness and sin will be only a memory. The prophet uses this imagery to move the people to see their future as the work of God rather than the result of political maneuvering.

34:1-17 Against Edom

The prophet turns his attention to the nations again. He does not specify the crimes that the nations have committed, but he promises that God's judgment will be severe and complete. Edom is singled out for harsh judgment because of its proximity to Judah and its behavior when Jerusalem was militarily and politically impotent.

The prophet promises the territory of Edom will become a region without human habitation. Its land will be a haunt for wild creatures once again. Edom will sink into chaos and will be little more than a bad memory for Judah. Its destruction will be as complete as that of Sodom and Gomorrah (Gen 19:24). Nothing can save Edom from its judgment.

Modern readers find the language of this oracle particularly repellant. The prophet's harshness reflects his conviction that the conflict he was describing was not simply between Judah and the nations but a conflict between God and the powers of evil that attempt to frustrate God's rule. It is not just that Assyria or Edom suffers military defeat. The heavens and their host are the opponents that God defeats. In a battle with the powers of evil, God can give no quarter. What happens to the nations is simply the terrible consequence of the conflict that went on in the heavens. The focus on Edom, of course, reflects the pressure that Edom was exerting on Judah. The exaggeration so clearly evident in the oracle is a matter of rhetorical convention and also a genuine ill will that gripped the people of Judah toward Edom.

35:1-10 Zion's joy

The contrast between this passage and the preceding oracle against Edom could not be any stronger. In the previous oracle, nature serves as the means of divine judgment with Edom's territory reverting to a wild state. Here nature is transformed to make the restoration of Jerusalem possible. In both instances, God's power accomplishes the deed. Both the judgment of Edom and the salvation of Jerusalem bring glory to God.

This imagery and the thrust of this oracle are similar to that found in the fourth section of the book, chapters 40–55. The motif of the desert's transformation in verses 1-2 recurs in 40:3; that of God's coming to save in verse 4 in 40:9-10; the healing of the blind in verse 5 and of lame in verse 6 in 40:5 and 42:7; the miraculous highway of verse 8 in 40:3; and the disappearance of sorrow in verse 10 in 51:11. Clearly, this chapter was meant to serve as a bridge to the next section of the book. But why is this chapter placed here, before the chapters (36–39) that end the third section of the book with a historical review of the Assyrian and Babylonian crises? One possibility is that the prophet wished to emphasize that God's plans for Zion transcend history. They are not dependent upon what people do but on the sovereign act of a God who is determined to restore Jerusalem.

The transformation of the desert from an arid, life-threatening place to a fertile, life-supporting place is a common biblical image of salvation. Israel is not blessed with a river system like those in Egypt and Mesopotamia. The threat of drought followed by crop failure, famine, and starvation was always a serious threat. Speaking of God's movement in Israel's life as eliminating that threat was natural for ancient Israel's poets and theologians. The text affirms that the desert and parched lands will become like Lebanon where rains are plentiful, the Carmel range that guards the fertile Jezreel Valley, and Sharon that was a well-watered plain along the coast.

These new circumstances ought to encourage those people who were unable to see any future for themselves as God's people. Similarly, God's movement in their lives will be as miraculous as the opening of blind eyes and the loosing of a mute's tongue. Returning to the metaphor of the transformed desert in verse 7, the prophet asserts that the wilderness will no longer be a dangerous place, the haunt of lions and jackals. There will be a highway there, allowing the people of Judah to return to Jerusalem with joy. The death of Judah's political and religious institutions and the exile of its leading citizens threatened the people's very existence, but God will come with vindication and salvation.

There are at least six allusions to this text in the New Testament: 35:3 (Heb 12:12); verses 5-6 (Matt 11:5; Mark 7:37; Luke 7:22; Acts 26:18); and verse 10 (Rev 21:4). The most striking is the citing of this text by the people who witnessed Jesus' healing of a man with impaired hearing and speaking (Mark 7:37). Though the prophet composed this text to encourage Jews to hold on to their ancestral faith, the New Testament reinterprets this text to proclaim its faith in Jesus.

36:1–37:9a Jerusalem threatened

The third section of the book of Isaiah closes with a prose account of the Assyrian siege of Jerusalem that took place during the reign of Hezekiah (715–698 B.C.). The account is taken from 2 Kings 18:13–20:19 with some notable differences.

The Assyrians, led by their king Sennacherib, began their campaign in Judah by taking forty-six fortified cities. From Lachish, the last of these, Sennacherib sends his Rabshakeh (chief of staff) to Jerusalem, demanding surrender. Meeting with his Judahite counterparts, the Rabshakeh underscores the futility of resistance to the Assyrian forces arrayed against Jerusalem. He asserts that Egypt is an unreliable ally, that Hezekiah's centralization of worship in Jerusalem undermined any religious support he may have enjoyed, and that Jerusalem's fighting forces have been seriously depleted. Finally, the Assyrian asserts that he is following the command of Jerusalem's own God by attacking the city.

The Judahite negotiators are afraid that the Rabshakeh's confident assertions will undermine the morale of Jerusalem's defenders so they ask the Assyrian to speak Aramaic rather than Hebrew, in order to keep the negotiations secret from the people of Jerusalem. This, of course, the Assyrian negotiator refused to do. In fact, he spoke directly to the city's defenders, who had to face the shortages that are inevitable in any siege. The Assyrian demanded the surrender of the city, but he promised to provide an ample supply of food if the people gave up their resistance. He reminded the people of Jerusalem that the gods of many nations proved unable to save their peoples from the Assyrian onslaught, so the likelihood of the Lord saving Judah is remote. The Judahite negotiators were clearly shaken as they made their report to Hezekiah.

When the Judahite negotiators consult Isaiah, he says that Sennacherib will break off the siege, return to Assyria, and be killed there. The prophet asserts that Hezekiah has nothing to fear from the Assyrian threat. When the Rabshakeh returned to Lachish, he found out that Sennacherib had left that city because he heard of Egyptian plans to move against Assyria.

One detail that this account omits from that of 2 Kings 18 is Hezekiah's submission to Sennacherib and the subsequent payment of a heavy indemnity to the Assyrian king (see 2 Kgs 18:14-16). Such action clashes with the advice the prophet gives in verses 6-7. What the Isaianic account underscores is the hopelessness of Jerusalem's situation and Isaiah's confidence in the city's eventual deliverance.

37:9b-36 Jerusalem saved

In what appears to be a parallel account of the Assyrian siege of Jerusalem, Isaiah's role is much more prominent. After receiving a letter from Sennacherib calling for the surrender of Jerusalem, Hezekiah prays that the Lord will do what the gods of the nations could not: halt the Assyrian juggernaut. The prophet responds in poetic form that Sennacherib's plans will fail because the Assyrian king has insulted the Lord. God promises that, despite Sennacherib's earlier conquests, his attempt to take Jerusalem will fail. The prophet also asserts that before Jerusalem's deliverance, it will have to suffer because the normal cultivation of crops will not take place, inducing a famine that will be relieved only after two years. Also, only a remnant of Jerusalem's population will survive this disaster.

The prose accounts end with the prophet's prediction that Sennacherib would never even invade Jerusalem because God will protect it for the sake of David. But the Assyrians did besiege the city, though they did end it and return to Assyria. The narrative underscores the miraculous nature of Jerusalem's deliverance by asserting that an "angel of the Lord" annihilated the Assyrian army in its camp. What actually led to the end of the siege is not known for certain. Most likely Hezekiah paid a heavy price for protection (2 Kgs 18:15-16) and agreed to vassal status. This allowed Sennacherib to break off the siege and return to Assyria so that he could deal with internal unrest, which eventually ended with his assassination.

Over time, the precise circumstances of Jerusalem's deliverance were forgotten. Of course, the city's narrow escape came to support a belief that Jerusalem would never fall because of divine protection. One of Isaiah's contemporaries, Micah, however, announced the city's eventual fall (Mic 3:9-12). Still, most people began to consider it a matter of divine honor for the Lord to keep Jerusalem from all harm. About one hundred years later, Jeremiah was nearly executed for daring to suggest that God would allow Jerusalem to fall (see Jer 26:1-19).

38:1-8 Hezekiah's illness

The experience of Judah is duplicated in the experience of its king. Hezekiah faces certain death but then is spared to live for fifteen more years. The imagery of verse 38 that recounts the reversal of the sun's movement suggests that deliverance will follow upon the crisis facing both Hezekiah and Jerusalem. Of course, this deliverance is only temporary. Hezekiah will die and Jerusalem will fall.

38:9-20 Hezekiah's prayer of thanksgiving

Hezekiah offers a prayer that follows the pattern of other biblical prayers that thank God for deliverance in time of personal peril, e.g., Psalms 6, 13, 22. The prayer begins with words expressing resignation. Death is coming. Though Hezekiah cries for help, he expects his end to be imminent. Still, he cries for help. He wants to live. The king realizes that his illness was a message from God that was not designed to punish but to save him. He thanks God for being rescued from sin and death. The king dedicates his life to the praise of God who saved him from death. If only Jerusalem would have responded to its deliverance in a similar fashion.

39:1-4 The embassy from Babylon

The Babylonians wanted to topple the Assyrians from the position of dominance, so they sent an ambassador to enlist Hezekiah's cooperation in an anti-Assyrian coalition. But Judah had few resources to offer to the enterprise. Hezekiah shows his treasury to the Babylonian ambassador to make it clear how much the Assyrians required in tribute. Isaiah comes to the king to make certain he did not join the coalition, but Hezekiah assured him that all he did was show the Babylonians how little he had to offer.

39:5-8 The exile to Babylon

Of course, the prophet wants to make it clear that Judah's future does not lie with Babylon—no matter how attractive an alliance with it may appear to be. He warns the king that the Babylonians were going to strip the royal family of the little wealth it has remaining and, after doing so, lead the royals into exile where they would be servants of Babylon's kings. The king agrees with the prophet's assessment of the future but is confident that his reign will end before disaster comes upon Judah.

The book of Isaiah does not describe Jerusalem's fall to the Babylonians, though the next section (chapters 40–55) envisions Judah's restoration following the Babylonian conquest of Jerusalem, the destruction of its temple, and the exile of its leading citizens. The prophet's words to Hezekiah about the eventual fall of the city are needed to effect the transition to the next section of the book.

JERUSALEM'S LIBERATION
Isaiah 40:1–55:13

Here begins a thoroughly new message for Jerusalem. Unlike earlier prophets, the author of these words did not ask the people to recognize their failure and confess their infidelity. Before the exile, the prophets had to overcome the people's self-delusion fueled by the existence of the national state, the economic prosperity enjoyed by the powerful, and the active national cult in Jerusalem. The fall of that city made continued denials impossible. Judah's religious, political, and social institutions were no more. The Davidic dynasty was no more, the temple was in ruins and its priesthood scattered, the national state ceased to exist, and Judah's powerful and influential citizens were in exile. Cheap promises and vain expectations were no longer persuasive.

Chapter 40 begins a unique response to the disasters that came upon Jerusalem and its people. Unlike the book of Lamentations, the book of Isaiah does not give voice to the grief of the exiles. Unlike the Deuteronomistic History, this book is explicit about its hope for a new and glorious future for Jerusalem. Of course, the prophet believed that the fall of Jerusalem was an act of divine judgment on the unfaithful city, but he also was certain that the city's glorious and miraculous restoration was imminent. The prophet saw a dramatic upheaval stirring on the political horizon. A new vigorous and powerful ruler was about to bring an end to the vaunted Babylonian Empire. He believed that this was happening for one purpose: God was about to restore Jerusalem.

The prophet uses two metaphors to speak about his beliefs concerning Jerusalem's future: one masculine and the other feminine. The masculine servant metaphor (42:1-4; 49:1-6; 50:4-11; and 52:13–53:12) is the more familiar because of the use the New Testament makes of these passages to express faith in Jesus Christ. Like a king, the servant establishes justice (42:4). He is a

"sharp-edged sword" and a "sharpened arrow" (49:2) whose suffering will benefit many (53:4-5) and who will be vindicated and then will divide out the spoils of war (53:12). The female figure of Jerusalem/Zion is the second linchpin of the prophet's hopes for the future. Beginning in chapter 49 and extending to chapter 66, the reader hears the story of a woman's life from her abandonment by her husband and consequent childlessness to their reconciliation and the birth of many children. The two images parallel one another. For example, in chapter 49 both express doubts about God's presence and power in their lives: the servant in verse 4 and Zion in verse 14. Both the servant and Zion are humiliated and afflicted. Eventually both will experience vindication through their children: the servant in 53:10 and Zion in 66:7-9. The prophet does not tell the story of the servant or of Zion as a continuous narrative but will keep returning to these metaphors in the course of his prophecy.

40:1-11 Jerusalem the herald
The prophet stands as a mute witness as the members of the Divine Council are about to implement God's decision to begin the process of Jerusalem's rehabilitation. The prophet hears a series of commands in the second person plural: "comfort . . . Speak to the heart of . . . proclaim. . . ." He wishes his readers to envision one member of the Divine Council ordering others to take the actions that will mean a new day for Jerusalem. This new day will begin with the news that the city's suffering is about to end. In fact, the order implies that Jerusalem's punishment has been more than its infidelity deserved. Next, the prophet hears one member of the council commanding that another begin preparing the way for God's grand triumphal procession that will bring about the exiles' return and Jerusalem's restoration. The death-dealing nature of the desert must teem with life. The high mountains and deep valleys that would hinder the return of the exiles to Jerusalem must become a level highway.

Jerusalem was not to remain a passive recipient of the good news. The city itself was to become a prophet announcing liberation to the other cities of Judah, which shared its fate during the Babylonian crisis. They too lost many people to exile. Zion is to proclaim the great reversal that God is about to accomplish. God is returning to

Judah at the head of a great throng of exiles, who were coming home where they could live in freedom as God promised their ancestors. In fulfilling its prophetic mission, Jerusalem uses two metaphors to remove the doubts of those who believed that God had no concern for Judah. In verse 10, the city-turned-prophet presents God as a victorious general who is returning home with the exiles—the prize won by defeating the Babylonians. The image in verse 11 is the perfect counterpoint, for it depicts God as a gentle shepherd who takes care of newborn lambs, leading them back to their mothers. Just so God will lead back the exiles of Judah to their mothers—the cities of their homeland. The juxtaposition of these two metaphors affirms that God has the power to change the course of history but is still concerned about the exiles as individuals. The exiles needed to hear what both metaphors implied, since their primary experience of God had been the experience of God's absence. This led them to draw all the wrong conclusions about their future. Jerusalem proclaims that God has the power to end the exile and the love to begin the restoration.

Chapter 40:1-11 sums up the prophet's message in just eleven verses. This text makes the astonishing announcement that God has forgiven Jerusalem and its people. It is Jerusalem's task to proclaim this message to all the cities of Judah. The remainder of chapters 40–55 is simply an elaboration of that message.

Each of the evangelists cites 40:3, applying it to John the Baptist (Matt 3:3; Mark 1:2; Luke 3:4; John 1:23). Of course, this involves a reinterpretation of the prophet's words. No longer do they refer simply to the restoration of Jerusalem but to the redemption of all Israel and all nations. The evangelists wish to portray the Baptist as the herald of this new and universal act of salvation. James alludes to verses 6-7 to speak of the transitory nature of wealth (Jas 1:10) and Peter quotes these verses to underscore the eternal character of God's word (1 Pet 1:24-25).

40:12-31 The Lord, the Creator

To arouse the exiles to believe in a future for Jerusalem, the prophet begins with correcting and expanding their notion of deity. The Lord was not simply a God from the desert who chose to make a nation out of the Hebrew slaves. The Lord is not simply the patron of the two former Israelite kingdoms. By asking a series of rhetorical questions in verses 12-14, the prophet leads the exiles to the conclusion that the Lord is the Creator of the universe. As such, Jerusalem's God controls the destinies of all nations. Of course, the Lord has the power to end the exile and return the people of Jerusalem to their home.

By way of contrast, the gods of the nations are nothing. A second series of rhetorical questions in verses 18-20 parodies the religious beliefs of the nations. The prophet compares the God of Israel, the Creator of the universe, with the gods of the nations who were manufactured by wood and metal workers. Of course, the people of the ancient Near East had a more nuanced view of the relationship between a god and its image than the prophet implies. Still, the prophet's purpose is not to discuss the merits of religions that use images. His purpose is to stimulate his people to believe in their future, a future made possible by the Creator of the universe, who controls the fate of all nations.

The prophet undercuts belief in astral deities by having Israel's God claim credit for the creation of the stars. It is the Lord who maintains the order of the heavens, and every heavenly body is subject to the God who is about to redeem Jerusalem. The profound and distressing experience of God's absence that led the exiles to question the power of the Lord and the relevance of their faith will dissipate in the face of the stirring events that will shortly and dramatically demonstrate the presence and power of the Lord: the fall of Babylon and the restoration of Jerusalem. These events will quicken the spirits of the exiles and prevent Judah from disappearing into the pages of history. The people of God will find new strength as they await their return to the land that God promised to their ancestors.

Paul quotes verse 13 in his hymn to God's mercy and wisdom in Romans 11:34-35. He also cites this text again in 1 Corinthians 2:16 to celebrate the revelation of God's will through Jesus Christ.

41:1–42:9 The nations on trial

A typical prophetic strategy to underscore the sovereignty of God is to describe a trial in which God serves as prosecutor and judge. Here the prophet describes two such scenes in which the nations are on trial. The prophet wants to present the restoration of Judah to its land against a wider backdrop. He calls the nations to hear his message for they too will feel the effects of God's new movement, whose ultimate goal is the redemption of God's people.

The evidence of God's control of events that will lead to Jerusalem's liberation is the rise of the person whom the prophet characterizes as "the champion of justice." He comes not from Judah but from the East (41:2). Cyrus the Persian was on the march, winning victories over the Medes and the Greeks. The prophet was certain that Babylon was about to fall to him as well. This string of victories must mean something. The prophet sees them as a sign of God's movement to save Judah and restore it to its land. It is Judah's God who is transforming the political map of the ancient Near East—all for the sake of Jerusalem. This is certainly evidence of the power of the Lord.

The imminent fall of Babylon is not the end of the first trial scene. The scene ends with a dramatic reassurance for the exiles. The prophet speaks to the exiles in God's name. They have nothing to fear from the military and political upheavals that they are witnessing. On the contrary, all is happening for their sake. God has chosen Israel and has not revoked that choice. The prophet calls the exiles the "offspring of Abraham" because he wishes to underscore the continuing significance of Israel's ancestral religious traditions (41:8). With God's help, Judah will be victorious over all those forces that threaten its existence.

Judah's political impotence will have no bearing on its future. God will be with Judah to insure that it will emerge victorious. It is important to note that the book's favorite term for God, "the Holy One of Israel," is used here with the word "redeemer" (41:14). This will happen several other times in this fourth section of Isaiah (see also 43:14; 47:3-4; 48:17). The book of Isaiah refers to God as "redeemer" more than any other book of the Old Testament. Israel's redeemer will transform it into a power that will overcome those that will try to prevent its restoration. It will emerge with unprecedented power over its enemies. Judah will be able to crush them like a new threshing sledge cuts through the newly harvested shafts of wheat.

God's movement on behalf of the oppressed of Judah will be a miraculous manifestation of God's power. It will be akin to the transformation of the desert into a well-watered garden graced with every beautiful tree and shrub. No one who will witness Judah's restoration will fail to understand who accomplished this miracle—the Holy One of Israel. The results of the trial of the nations will be the restoration of Jerusalem and the universal recognition of its God.

There is a summons to a second trial in 41:21. The prophet begins offering evidence in the next verse. That evidence consists of the rise of Cyrus, the fall of Babylon, and the restoration of Jerusalem. People had recourse to their gods to divine the future. The prophet ridicules the supposed ability of the gods to inform their worshipers about the future. Who would have predicted that Judah would be restored to its land? But that is precisely what is about to take place. The events that are to occur in a short time will shame the so-called gods of the nations. None of their diviners could have foreseen what God has in store for Jerusalem. Events are unfolding. Cyrus is coming to bring an end to Judah's exile. Jerusalem will no longer be a forlorn, abandoned city. It is to be the herald announcing freedom to the exiles. Clearly, the gods of the nations are nothing.

The trial ends with a reaffirmation of the election of Israel as God's people. God's choice of Israel is a fundamental datum of its faith. But this belief was called into question by the fall of the two Israelite kingdoms. The prophet's message implies that Israel's election is not tied to the political status of the two former kingdoms. Judah in exile is still God's servant. It has a destiny to fulfill that cannot be frustrated by political turmoil and military defeat. God will restore Judah to its land so that it can become a model of justice for the nations. The Israelite kingdoms fell precisely because of the failure of the monarchy to maintain a just social and economic system. Judah's mission to establish justice is repeated three times (42:1, 4, 6).

Note that the prophet does not imply that the monarchy will be restored. The establishment and maintenance of a just society were the principal responsibilities of Israel's kings. The book of Isaiah very clearly notes the failure of the monarchy to do this. In fact, Israel's political leadership actually facilitated the oppression of the poor (e.g., 1:21-23; 3:1-12; 28:14-22; 29:14-15). Here the responsibilities of the monarchy fall upon the people as a whole. It will be the responsibility of all the people of Judah to insure "the victory of justice." The trial of the nations ends with an affirmation of God's uniqueness. Only the Lord has announced the liberation of Jerusalem's exiles—something everyone, including those exiles, thought impossible. This shows that the Lord alone is God.

Chapter 42:1-4 is the first of four passages from the book of Isaiah that have become known as the "Servant Songs" (see also 49:1-6; 50:4-11; and 52:13–53:12). While there is some value in isolating these passages, here they will be treated simply as elements in the broader and unified message about Jerusalem's liberation that comprises the fourth section of the book of Isaiah. There has been some controversy about the propriety of isolating these texts from their literary and theological context, and there are several possibilities about the identity of the "servant." Understood in the light of the total argument made in this fourth section, it is most likely that the servant is Judah fulfilling its destiny to be the light to the nations, bringing about the victory of justice. Of course, this is an idealized picture of the potential of the restored community, but the whole of this fourth section of Isaiah is a powerfully constructed and expressed argument by the prophet, who is trying to persuade a thoroughly demoralized people that their God is about to do something wondrous for them and that they have a decisive role in their own restoration.

Matthew has John the Baptist allude to 41:16 to persuade people that God is about to do something decisive through Jesus (Matt 3:12). The evangelist also cites 42:1-4 to show that Jesus' healing ministry fulfilled the words of the prophet and, therefore, show Jesus to be the "servant" about whom the prophet was speaking (Matt 12:15-21). Simeon's canticle in Luke 2:29-32 is a combination of texts taken from the fourth section of the book of Isaiah: 42:6; 46:13; 49:6; 52:10.

42:10-17 The Lord, the Victor

The prophet sings a hymn of praise to the Lord who is about to liberate the exiles of Jerusalem. This, in turn, will lead all nations to acclaim the Lord as God. The hymn is reminiscent of several similar compositions found in the Psalter (Pss 93, 96, 149). The hymn begins with a call to praise that includes all regions of earth and sea—even remote and isolated places like Kedar and Sela.

The call goes out to join in praising the Lord because Israel's God has finally chosen to emerge from self-imposed inactivity. God will now deal with God's enemies. Those who serve other gods will recognize their folly.

Two features of this hymn call for comment because both cause problems for some modern readers of Isaiah. The first is the hymn's military imagery. The people who first heard or read this book felt much more at ease with this imagery than do people today. After all, the origins of Israel were associated with battles that God fought and won: the victory over the Egyptian army at the Red Sea, the victories over the Canaanites during the time of Joshua and the judges, and the victories over the Philistines during the time of David. Judah was in exile because apparently God stopped taking its side against its enemies. This metaphor affirms that God's purposes are fulfilled—even in the wars that people fight over land and resources. It is important to remember that the Lord, the warrior, was not the only way that ancient Israel spoke of its God. The Lord was also the shepherd, who gathers the lambs, carries them gently, and feeds them abundantly (see Isa 40:11). While the New Testament speaks about Jesus as the "good shepherd" (John 10), it also remembers that Jesus said that he came to bring fire on the earth and could not wait until the blaze begins (see Luke 12:49).

A second metaphor in this passage compares the Lord to "a woman in labor" (42:14). Though most of the images that the Bible uses for God are masculine, the book of Isaiah does make use of feminine imagery to speak of the God of Israel (see also 49:15). The prophet did not hesitate to use feminine metaphors to speak of the God of Israel despite the patriarchal bent of his culture.

42:18–43:8 Judah's disabilities

The prophet recognizes to whom he is speaking. His audience is made up of people in shock, people still coping with the loss of the political, social, economic, and religious institutions that gave them identity and purpose. What is worse is that these people fail to recognize that they are responsible for this loss. The prophet calls the people of Judah blind and deaf. These handicaps prevent them from recognizing their true standing before God. They are unable to recognize God's hand in their plight. They fail to see that the loss of their state, national dynasty, temple, and land was due to their refusal to "walk in God's ways," i.e., maintain a society built on justice. They fail to hear the message of the prophets who announced God's judgment on their society and its values.

Still, the prophet believes that Judah's future is not dependent upon its ability to overcome its blindness and deafness. God will save Judah from its own sin. The prophet affirms that God will allow Cyrus to take Egypt and Ethiopia as the price for Judah's freedom. Here the prophet's word reflects the scandal of election: God favors one people over all others. The only explanation that the prophet gives is that God loves the people of Israel and will do anything to save Israel from itself. God assures Judah that the exiles will gather from wherever they have been scattered, even though they still suffer from handicaps.The prophet affirms that God is willing to allow the conquest of nations like Egypt and Ethiopia in exchange for Jerusalem's liberation. How does this relate to the prophet's contention that God's chosen servant is to be a "light to the nations"? The significance of the prophet's concept of Israel's election is one of the principal problems in interpreting this book. Even the New Testament's more consistent inclusiveness does not solve the problem. There God does not give up Egypt, Ethiopia, or any nation for Israel's salvation. But God does not spare Jesus so that all people might be saved. Why was it necessary for Jesus to die in order for the New Israel to be saved from the power of sin? Here we see this important issue in Christian theology presaged in the book of Isaiah.

43:9-15 Judah—God's witness

The prophet returns to the metaphor of a trial. The issue at hand is the Lord's claim to be God. How could people take this claim seriously when Judah was in exile? Of what value is a God who cannot protect or save? The liberation of Jerusalem will change people's views, so it is important that the exiles enthusiastically respond to the prophet's message of their imminent redemption. Of course, no one could have foreseen the circumstances that led to Judah's freedom. The prophet has consistently asserted that judgment was not God's last word to Jerusalem. He described a restored Zion and now his words are about to be fulfilled. The exiles are to put flesh and bone on those words and thereby become God's witnesses.

Judah's witnessing does not consist of providing rational proofs for God's existence. What Judah will show is God's power to save. When Judah had a king, the king's successes manifested God's power. But now the miraculous return of the exiles to Jerusalem will show the nations that Israel's God is God alone. The restoration of Jerusalem will be an irrefutable proof of the Lord's power to save. The fact of the exile appears to have undercut the credibility of Israel's witness. How could Israel's God claim any status given the fall of Jerusalem and the exile of its people? But the exile itself is a testament to God's sovereignty, since it was God who sent Israel to Babylon, but now that tragic episode in Israel's life is about to end. The Babylonians, on the other hand, will lament the fall of their city.

43:16–44:5 Something new

God's victory over the powers of nature during the exodus from Egypt has already shown God's might (Exod 7:8–11:10; 14:21), but these wondrous deeds are not simply memories. God will again act for Israel's sake. For the prophet, the exodus became a prototype of the restoration. Though the two events were separated from each other by hundreds of years, he was certain that the former illuminated the latter. God will free the exiles, lead them through the wilderness again, and bring them back to Jerusalem, where their praise of God's glory will be an effective witness to the one God. This new act of deliverance will be so spectacular that people will no longer remember the exodus but will recall with wonder and praise this new act of God's saving power. Just as the prophet reinterpreted the exodus story in terms of the exiles' experience, so did the New Testament reinterpret that same story as a way to speak of the significance of Jesus. The hymns of the African-American Christian community followed the same pattern, as does the liberation theology of the Americas. The prophet has shown many generations of believers how the exodus can always be something new.

Unfortunately, God's liberation of the Hebrew slaves from Egypt did not produce a grateful people. They constantly murmured in the wilderness on the way to the promised land, and they rebelled against Moses. This pattern continued once Israel arrived in Canaan. Instead of gratitude, Israel burdened God with its sins. At first,

God chose to ignore Israel's sins, but its constant rebellion led God to remember the sins of all Israel—from those of Jacob to those of the present generation. God had no other choice but to abandon Israel. Still, the prophet suggests that Judah not focus on the past but on what God will do in the future. God has taken the initiative in empowering Israel as a witness. God will transform Israel and make it an effective witness though the outpouring of God's spirit into the dispirited exilic community. This community is God's *Jeshurun* (44:2; a Hebrew term translated as "darling" in the earlier NAB). The verbs of verses 4-5 point to some sort of an outward witness, not an inward transformation alone but something that people can see.

44:6-23 A parody on idol worship

The claims of the Lord's sovereignty seemed inflated to many people. After all, the Lord appeared unable to protect Judah from Babylon. At the very least, this must have led most of the prophet's contemporaries to view Israel's God as a second-rate deity. Certainly Marduk, Babylon's god, proved to be more powerful. Flying in the face of these attitudes, the prophet compares the Lord with other gods. The prophet begins by reminding people that the word of the Lord was spoken through the prophets who predicted the restoration of Jerusalem. That restoration is about to happen. This miracle will make the exiles God's witnesses before all peoples.

The prophet's comparison of Israel's God with the nations' gods continues with a parody on idol worship. The religion of ancient Israel was unique among the religions of the ancient Near East because it did not depict its patron deity in plastic form. Archaeologists have uncovered virtually no representations of male gods from the ancient Israelite period, though figurines depicting female deities have been found in surprising numbers. The torah prohibits the use of images of God several times: Exodus 20:4-5, 23; 34:17; Deuteronomy 4:15-18; 5:8; 27:15. The prophet plays on this special feature of Israelite religion to underscore the uniqueness of the Lord.

The prophet's basic point is that the gods of the nations are obviously unable to save because they are merely wooden or metal objects made by human beings. To make his point the prophet misrepresents ancient Near Eastern religious beliefs regarding images of the gods. The ancient peoples were not as naive as the prophet suggests. They believed that after an image was consecrated, the spirit of the god represented by the statue inhabited it. The purpose of the image was to help the god and its worshipers to focus their attention on each other. Some statues even had moving parts, allowing priests to give responses to inquiries made by worshipers. The veneration of icons and statues by Christians shows that images of the sacred have power, though people are aware they are human constructions.

The prophet insists that the reality of the Lord is not manifested through a fabricated image but through real people, who are going to make their way from the land of their exile back to their ancestral homeland. Forgiveness of sins and healing of memories equip Judah to be God's witness. Judah serves a God who forgives sins so that it can look to its past without despair and its future with hope. Judah is to regard its past infidelity like the dew that forms in the mornings of the dry season. It dissipates as soon as the sun rises above the horizon. So God's forgiveness makes Judah's sins just as insubstantial. It is not a statue that is the image of the divine but a living people whom God has redeemed. The calling of Judah is to be the living representation of the Lord. Its singing and rejoicing at the prospect of its impending return ought to stimulate nature to join in the praise of God.

The book of Revelation quotes verse 6, putting the words that the prophet attributes to God on the lips of the risen Jesus (Rev 1:8, 17).

44:24–45:13 God's anointed king

Though the prophet has been speaking about the liberation of Jerusalem as a sovereign act of the Lord, he knows that the actual working out of the divine plan will happen through a human instrument. Abraham, Moses, Joshua, David, and the prophets have all served as the divinely chosen means by which God's will for Israel achieved its ends. Now the prophet is ready to identify the person whom he knows to be the one to effect the newest act of liberation: the redemption of Jerusalem's exiles. The prophet makes a surprising and unexpected identification to say the least.

The prophet begins by repeating the unprecedented nature of what God is about to do. Babylon's diviners did not foresee it. The king's advisors did not even consider the possibility. But it is true that Judah is going to be restored. Its cities—Jerusalem in particular—are going to be rebuilt and repopulated. But who is going to accomplish all this? The surprising answer is Cyrus, the king of Persia. Though the prophet hinted at this earlier (41:2, 25), here he does not use veiled references but makes an explicit identification. In this passage, the prophet mentions Cyrus by name twice (44:28; 45:1) and refers to him with a personal pronoun one more time (45:13).

What is even more surprising, the prophet calls Cyrus the Lord's "messiah" (anointed)—a title that was given to Israel's kings (1 Sam 2:10; 12:3; 2 Sam 23:1; Ps 2:2; 20:7; 132:17). In the book of Isaiah, the term does not have the eschatological connotations that it acquired later. Still, using it to speak of a non-Israelite king is unprecedented. Apparently, the prophet's notion of Jerusalem's liberation did not include the restoration of Judah's native dynasty. God will use Cyrus to free the exiles and enthrone him as king to free the exiles.

Not all the prophet's contemporaries welcomed this message, but he insists that the choice of Cyrus is God's. The only woe oracle that appears in the fourth section of the book (45:8-13) is directed at those who cannot accept the prophet's word about Cyrus. Without the restoration of Judah's native dynasty, there will be no restored Judahite state. By naming Cyrus as God's messiah, the prophet appears to accept a continuing subordinate role for Judah in the political sphere. Though the exiles will be free to return to their land, Judah will remain subject to the Persian king. Apparently, some of the exiles expected that any restoration of Judah would involve the restoration of the Davidic dynasty and Judahite national state.

Another institution of preexilic Israel that apparently does not have a significant place in the prophet's vision of Jerusalem's restoration is the temple. This is the only time the fourth section of the book of Isaiah mentions the temple (44:28). It follows the description of God's victory over chaotic forces represented by the waters of the seas and rivers (44:27). But victory over chaos and temple building are related activities. A temple makes the heavenly victory manifest to people on earth. Also, temple building was an expression of the king's claims to be divinely chosen. In fact,

the decree of Cyrus that allows the exiles to return to Jerusalem states that God chose Cyrus to rebuild the temple of Jerusalem (2 Chr 36:22-23; Ezra 1:2-4).

God's choice of Cyrus as messiah makes it clear that the liberation of Jerusalem does not mean a return to the status quo of Judah's monarchic period. The prophet proclaims that God is about to do something entirely new. The miraculous liberation of Jerusalem will serve to broaden the horizons of Judah's concept of God.

45:14-25 God and the nations

Another important element of the prophet's vision of Jerusalem's future involves the nations. Here too the prophet proclaims something new. The previous sections of the book of Isaiah presented the nations as enemies of Judah bent on its destruction. Though they were instruments of divine judgment, the nations often went beyond their mandate and would themselves experience severe judgment for their excesses. Here the prophet has the nations recognize the Lord's role in the fall of Babylon, the rise of Persia, and the liberation of Jerusalem. By defeating Judah, the nations served God's purposes without knowing it, but this new act of God would make it possible for them to recognize Israel's God as the only God.

The nations confess that it is clear that the Lord alone is God and God's intentions for Judah are clear, whereas once they were hidden. God is "hidden" since God has been with Judah in exile, but now that exile is about to end in a glorious and miraculous way. The peoples of exotic lands will leave their countries in order to come to Jerusalem so that they might see the great victory that God has given to Judah, a victory which has meant defeat for those nations that were threats to Judah's existence.

God asserts that God's intentions have always been clear in the creation of the world and through the demand for justice. God's word was not uttered in some secret place but openly. A similar point is made in the book of Acts. During the controversy regarding the obligation of Gentile converts to Christianity to observe the torah, James notes that the Mosaic law had been proclaimed in every city since Moses "has been read in the synagogues every sabbath" (Acts 15:21). Paul too asserts that what the law requires is written on the hearts of the Gentiles (Rom 2:15). Still, the notion that Israel's God is a "hidden God" does help people to recognize the tentativeness of their insights into God's presence and action in the world. While believers look forward to the day of God's final victory over the powers of evil, they recognize that in the meantime it is not always easy to see God's purposes being fulfilled.

The prophet's vision has the nations joining Judah in acknowledging the Lord as the only God. Jerusalem's liberation, when it did come, did not have the effect on the nations that the prophet anticipated. But 45:23b-24a is cited in both Romans 14:11 and Philippians 2:10-11 for Paul believed that the prophet's vision would find its fulfillment in Jesus and the church.

46:1-13 Salvation in Zion

This passage contrasts Babylon and its gods, Bel and Nebo, with Zion and its God. It opens with Bel and Nebo being led away from Babylon in captivity and ends with the affirmation that God "will put salvation within Zion" (46:13).

Bel was a title given to Marduk, Babylon's patron deity. Nebo was the son of Marduk, whose temple was across the Euphrates from Babylon. These gods had to be carried by their worshipers while the Lord "carries" the people of Judah. In drawing this contrast, the prophet expected that the Persians would follow usual practice by carrying off the images of the gods of the conquered cities, but Cyrus had a different policy. He was as tolerant toward the Babylonians and their religion as he was toward the people of Judah. He tried to show himself to the Babylonians as Marduk's chosen instrument to insure the proper service of that god.

The prophet asserts that the Lord's dominion is not like that of the other gods who cannot save because they are manufactured images and nothing more. This passage again ridicules the worship of other gods in order to eliminate rival claimants for Judah's loyalty. The prophet calls skeptics from both Judah and the nations to remember what God has done. Cyrus is the destroyer of Babylon's military power. The destruction of Babylon and the flight of its helpless gods send a clear message to Israel: do not keep yourselves distant from the shrine of the Lord in Zion. The doubters need to be told that the conquest of Babylon by Cyrus, though apparently unrelated to Judah's destiny, was actually an act of God to restore the people of Judah to Jerusalem. The people then are to attend to the fulfillment of prophecy and the exclusive claims of the Lord as manifest through the rise of Cyrus.

47:1-15 Against Babylon

The only way for the liberation of Jerusalem to proceed is for Babylon to fall. The prophet taunts Babylon by asserting that God will strip it of all prerogatives as a royal city. He declares that this pampered daughter of the Chaldeans, who provided the neo-Babylonian empire with its leadership, will do the work of slaves such as grinding grain into meal. Once an untouchable queen, she will be devastated and subject to sexual harassment like any commoner (compare Hos 2:9-12; Jer 13:20-27). The Lord empowered Babylon to conquer Judah because of the latter's infidelity—not because of Babylon's virtue or because of its military power. Babylon mistook this temporary mission as conferring permanent, privileged status. It thought itself exempt from military defeat and political impotence. It will experience both.

The skills of Babylon's priests and diviners cannot save its empire. Babylon had an international reputation for the skills of its sages and diviners. In the face of the Lord's judgment they are impotent. There are no rituals or charms that can forestall the judgment that awaits Babylon. It is inevitable. Babylon's fall will be quick and spectacular, like fire that consumes dry stubble (47:14). Allies and vassals will leave Babylon to face its fate alone. The book of Revelation imitates the prophet when it taunts Rome, whose fall its author considered inevitable (Rev 17–18). Like Babylon, Rome was the capital of a great empire. Still, both Babylon and Rome were transformed by the power of God. Neither was destroyed, but Babylon became a great center of Jewish learning and Rome became the capital of the Christian world. The visions of both prophets Isaiah and John were fulfilled beyond their expectations.

48:1-22 The power of God's word

The prophet's task is to persuade the exiles that his view of Jerusalem's liberation is not just a flight of fancy but the word of God that is going to be fulfilled and soon. What kept people from accepting the prophet's message was their experience—the harsh realities of their lives in exile. To believe that the Lord, the patron deity of a nation and dynasty that no longer existed, was controlling world events strained the people's credulity. Judah was no longer even a minor player on the stage in the ancient Near East. Babylon, whose material culture, military might, and political power far outstripped that of Judah's best days, could not possibly be threatened by any message from the Lord, no matter how convinced the prophet may be.

In this chapter the prophet is venting his frustration at the exiles' unenthusiastic response to his message. He tries to persuade people that the message he is delivering is the word of God, a word that will find fulfillment. There are two parts in this unit: verses 1-11 and verses 12-21. The first embodies a theory of the connection between God's word and God's deeds, and the second applies this theory to the exilic situation and the rise of Cyrus.

The prophet begins by showing that there is a connection between God's word and Israel's experience, as is clear from Israel's past. The prophet also criticizes a shallow religion that saw Israel's security in its cult and believed that Israel's God had no moral will. He asserts that the word must precede God's actions in Judah's life because of its stubbornness in the past. Judah will know that the Lord is responsible once the word is fulfilled. Unfortunately, the people have shown a tendency to attribute the course of events to some agent other than the Lord. The preexilic prophets contain ample number of threats of judgment on moral grounds, and it was in these that the revealing word of the Lord was contained. The exiles preferred to explain their misfortunes by something other than the moral and religious breakdown of which the prophets spoke.

There is no great act of God without a predictive word to clarify its significance. Judah thinks that it knows who God is and how God acts. It will deny the divine origin of anything that is contrary to its concept of God and the biases connected with it. Of course, this is to be expected since Israel was rebellious from its very beginning. But the Lord is not governed by the conduct of Israel. Whether God judges or saves, the motivation is within God's inner being, i.e., God's name. God does not respond to emotional impulse like human beings. The Lord's work will proceed no matter what the popular reaction is.

In the second part of this passage (48:11-22), the prophet applies what he just said about the power of God's word to the situation that Judah faces. The prophet is providing the word and Cyrus is doing the deed. God chose Cyrus to act against Babylon and has guaranteed his success. The fall of Babylon has no significance apart from its manifestation of God's power.

The speaker of verse 16 is Cyrus, who acknowledges that he will conquer Babylon by the power of God's spirit. The messenger formula in the following verse introduces a statement that offers a perspective similar to that undergirding the book of Deuteronomy: if Israel will learn and observe God's teaching, this will guarantee Israel's prosperity, but the "commandments" in verse 18 probably refer to the prophet's words rather than stipulations of the torah. Israel's future is linked to obedience to the authoritative words of the prophet. Using a series of imperatives in verses 20-21, the prophet calls for a new exodus and a new passage through the desert. The prophet summons Israel to action. Verse 22 appears almost verbatim in 57:21. It is not related to the context here and seems to be a discordant note at the end of a text that shows progressive emotional intensity.

John of Patmos gives advice that is the same as that of the prophet. The book of Revelation calls Christians to "come out" of Rome (Rev 18:4), just as the prophet charges the exiles to leave Babylon (48:20). Believers are called to respond to God's word. They are not to remain passive recipients but active agents of that word. They are to leave behind all that has left them insensitive to the message of God's prophets. John also uses the prophet's epithets "first and last" to speak about Christ (48:12; Rev 1:17; 2:8; see also Isa 44:6).

49:1-6 Israel's mission

The prophet wishes to present his message of Jerusalem's liberation against the widest possible backdrop. It is essential that the exiles do not conceive of their release from captivity as making possible a return to the political, economic, social, and religious conditions of Judah before the fall of Jerusalem. Judah will have a future, but that future consists in bringing the word of God "to the ends of the earth" (49:6). It is for this reason that Israel was chosen as God's people (see Gen 12:3). Jerusalem's restoration will make it possible for the people to present a dramatic and authentic witness of God's power. Luke quotes verse 6 to show that God was controlling the events that led to the decision by Paul and Barnabas to preach to the Gentiles (Acts 13:47) and he sees the church fulfilling Israel's mission to proclaim the word of God "to the ends of the earth" (Acts 1:8).

49:7 The reaction of the nations

There will be a dramatic reversal of fortunes following Jerusalem's liberation. The miracle that God will work in and through Judah will be such that the only possible response will be for kings and princes to acknowledge the sovereignty of Israel's God. While this verse is a testament to the prophet's faith, it was not fulfilled in the way he expected. The restoration never achieved the goals that the prophet had for it. This led to further reflection on and a reinterpretation of the prophet's message. One outcome of this reinterpretation was the appropriation of the book of Isaiah by the writers of the New Testament. They believed that the prophet's words finally found their fulfillment in Jesus and the Gospel.

49:8-26 The reaction of the exiles

While the prophet foresees that princes and kings will prostrate themselves before Judah's God when they witness the fulfillment of God's word, the reaction of God's people to that word is lamentation. The prophet characterizes the days during which he spoke in the name of God as "a time of favor" (49:8). This was the time that the people of Judah were praying for. God was answering their prayers and would lead them back to Zion. The word that God has for the exiles is "Come out!" (49:9). The return to Jerusalem will be less like a wearisome trek and more like a procession led by God, who will guide the people as a shepherd. Judahite exiles from all over the world, not just Babylon, will stream toward their ancient homeland (49:12: Syene is the modern Aswan in Upper Egypt where there was a Jewish colony).

Inanimate nature recognizes Judah's restoration for what it is: a miraculous demonstration of God's power. It responds with uninhibited joy. The liberation of Jerusalem is no mere political event. The cosmos is caught up in this redemptive

act of God that restores the people of Judah not only to their homeland but especially to their unique relationship with God. The people have suffered because of their infidelity, but God's compassion will not allow God's justice to have its full effect on Israel. Judgment was not to be God's last word. The prophet sees the people's redemption on the horizon. Nature too sees this and rejoices.

How do the exiles react to the momentous events in which they are caught up? How do they respond to the prophet's words of hope? Unlike the heavens and the earth, which recognize the significance of God's action, the people of Judah utter words of disbelief. The exiles consider the prophet's message unrealistic—too good to be true. Perhaps they considered them the product of an overwrought religious personality.

To counter the exiles' disbelief, the prophet uses a very poignant metaphor. He asserts that God's love for the people of Judah exceeds that of a nursing mother for her child. While some biblical metaphors can be difficult to understand, the image in verse 15 is impossible to misinterpret. It is difficult to find a more touching image of God's love anywhere else in the Bible. This image underscores the unbreakable bond between God and Israel. While this bond did not exempt Israel from experiencing divine judgment for its infidelity, God's commitment to Israel remains secure. The phrase in verse 16a ("See, upon the palms of my hands I have engraved you . . .") may refer to tattooing, another image of the permanency of God's commitment to Israel. The prophet promises that Jerusalem will be rebuilt and repopulated. He then returns to a familiar motif: the reversal of the fortunes of Judah and Babylon leading all peoples to recognize that the Lord's power saved Judah.

Paul cited 49:8 to urge the people of Corinth to respond to God's grace at work in them (see 2 Cor 6:2). Like the prophet, Paul believed that apart from the believers' response the transforming power of God's word would not have concrete effect.

50:1-3 The purpose of the exiles

To counter the exiles' lack of hope regarding their future, the prophet assures them that the purpose of the exile was not to end Jerusalem's relationship with God but to discipline its people.

Both Hosea and Jeremiah use the metaphor of divorce (Hos 2:4; Jer 3:1, 8) to speak about the consequences that Israel will have to pay for its infidelity, but the prophet rejects this comparison. He maintains that there was no divorce between Jerusalem ("your mother") and God since no bill of divorce was given (see Deut 24:1-4). He also asserts that, despite appearances, the people were not sold into slavery, since that would imply that God needed to sell Israel to settle debts. God has no creditors. What happened to the people of Judah happened because they did not recognize the power of their God, who alone overcame the mighty waters to bring order out of chaos. God's power will now liberate Jerusalem from its exile.

50:4-11 Light and darkness

The prophet identifies himself with all those whom God sent to bring light to those who preferred to live in darkness. This passage is reminiscent of a thanksgiving psalm (e.g., Ps 34) with its description of distress and the affirmation that God saved the prophet. In the midst of humiliating treatment, the prophet asserts that God was with him, so that in the end he will be vindicated. The prophet then turns to his audience and tells them that they may enjoy the same divine protection. The prophet agrees that he walks in the darkness of the exile, but he urges his audience to trust in God so that they might join him in the light. This passage has been listed among the "Servant Songs," though the word "servant" does not appear here.

51:1-8 Salvation is coming

Here the prophet takes a more positive tack as he exhorts his fellow exiles to believe in the future of Jerusalem. He addresses his audience as "you who pursue justice," i.e., those actively committed to the establishment of a just society. He goes on to show that their dreams are realistic despite what appear to be great obstacles to their fulfillment.

Those who believe only a miracle could restore Judah ought to remember the story of Abraham and Sarah, their ancestors. God's promises to them were fulfilled although it appeared impossible for them ever to have children. God will effect another miracle to save the people of Jerusalem in exile. God will transform the city and its people in a way that is similar to the transformation of the desert into a beautiful garden.

Though the prophet uses the mythical image of Eden as a metaphor for the liberated Jerusalem, it is clear that he expects the transformation to take place through justice and the torah. Again recalling the words of 2:2-4, the prophet assures the exiles that all nations will recognize this triumph of justice. Though the heavens suggest permanency, they will be swept away before God's salvation and deliverance for Zion will fail. The people need to live by the torah and be unafraid of those who do not. The latter will be gone soon, but God's deliverance will be lasting. God's victory over the powers of chaos is another reason for the people's confidence. What God did once God can do again.

51:9–52:12 Awake!

The prophet's language is becoming more intense as he urges his fellow exiles to action. Three times in this passage he tells them to awake (51:9, 17; 52:1). The prophet again reminds the exiles of the power of God in creation. First, by using mythological imagery similar to that in 27:1, the prophet wants the exiles to see God as victorious in a primeval combat with the chaos monster Rahab (51:9-16). Confidence in God's power to liberate Jerusalem then is well founded. The exiles will return to Jerusalem. They should not fear what human beings can do to them because of what God promised to do for them. Their oppressors' power will end, and they will be released from captivity very soon. Using the same imagery as in 40:8, the prophet declares that God has assured Zion of its deliverance and the word of the Creator can be depended on.

Second, Jerusalem, which has experienced divine judgment, should realize that judgment was not God's last word to it (51:17-23). Though Jerusalem experienced the loss of its children and military and natural disasters, there is a new day that is about to dawn. Zion will no longer have to drink the cup of judgment. That cup will pass to those nations that have been Zion's tormentors.

Finally, Zion has to rouse itself after the stupor caused by having to drink the cup of judgment (52:1-12). As it rises from the humiliation of captivity, the city will no longer be vulnerable to attack from outsiders. It will no longer be occupied by aliens nor tainted by the ritually impure. The bonds that have kept Zion captive are now falling away. The people whom God abandoned to slavery and captivity will experience the power of God's presence. The deliverance that Zion will experience will testify to the power and presence of God. Those returning from exile will bring good news to Jerusalem. From a distance, those who protect the city from surprise attack will see the procession of Jerusalem's exiles. They will be the first to hear the good news of the city's deliverance, so they will announce that deliverance by singing of God's great victory over the powers that kept Zion in subjection. The people who return must make themselves ritually clean, because they will be entering the city made holy by God's presence.

The book of Revelation assumes that the prophet's vision of a new Jerusalem will be fulfilled only at the end of this age with the descent of the heavenly Jerusalem to earth (52:7; Rev 21:27). In Romans 10:15 Paul applies 52:7 to Christian preachers who bring the good news of Jesus to the Jews.

52:13–53:12 The Suffering Servant

After using feminine metaphors to describe the plight of Zion in some detail in chapters 51 and 52, the prophet returns to the masculine image of the Servant. Taking on the persona of God, the prophet proclaims the exaltation of the servant after his total humiliation. This will happen before the eyes of the kings responsible for the servant's suffering. Again the prophet announces the end of Judah's degradation.

In 53:1, the prophet speaks in the person of the kings who are witnessing the servant's exaltation. They cannot believe what they are seeing since they considered the servant of no account, someone who could be looked upon only with contempt. The kings then make an astonishing statement in verses 4-5. These verses appear to speak of vicarious atonement, i.e., that one person can bear the sin of another so as to remove the guilt of the second person. Such an idea is found nowhere else in the Old Testament. While this does not eliminate the possibility that the prophet was speaking about vicarious suffering, it should lead one to consider other possibilities. Perhaps what the prophet's rhetoric is expressing is an idea similar to that in Lamentations 5:7, i.e., that the preexilic generation actually committed the sin, but the exiles are the ones who have to bear the consequences.

Another way to understand 53:4-5 is to see these verses as the prophet's attempt to broaden his contemporaries' understanding of their suffering beyond punishment for sin. While the prophet did affirm more than once that Jerusalem's suffering was God's judgment on its infidelity (42:18-22, 24-25; 43:24; 47:6), he also maintained that the city's punishment was out of proportion to its guilt (40:2). What then was the point of the exile? Jerusalem's suffering was part of God's work in the world. The nations will see what God has done and will do for Zion and be led to join Judah in the worship of its God. The people's suffering and exaltation then enable them to be God's witnesses (43:9-10) as they fulfill their mission to be "a light to the nations" (42:6; 49:6).

The poem concludes with God speaking in the first person just as the poem began (52:13-14; 53:11-13). God describes the vindication of the servant. In fact, the poem as a whole is a dramatization of the servant's final triumph. This is reminiscent of a thanksgiving psalm, but with certain modifications. In thanksgiving psalms, the person who has been rescued speaks. Here the servant is silent. God describes the servant's vindication. Second, people listen to the testimony of the one rescued in a thanksgiving psalm, but here the people themselves testify to the marvels that they have witnessed.

Of all Isaianic texts, this one has resonated most with the Christian belief in Jesus and in the significance of his suffering and death. There are about forty citations or allusions to this text in the New Testament. This testifies to the power of the prophetic word. Matthew also cites this text in commenting on Jesus' healing of Peter's mother-in-law (Matt 8:17).

The problem of suffering is one of those issues that confronts believers in every religious tradition. It was a special problem for the first Christians, who had to make sense of the tragic death of Jesus. They found this passage especially meaningful. The prophet was able to help the exiles see that their suffering was more than a judgment upon the sins of their elders. It was the means by which Judah could fulfill its mission as a light to the nations. The prophet has articulated one of the great paradoxes of the biblical tradition: victory comes through defeat, exaltation through humiliation, life from death. This is how the first Christians came to understand the cross.

54:1-17 Zion is reconciled with God

The focus of this passage is on reconciliation and its effects. A husband promises never again to lose his temper, never again to walk out on his wife, never again to leave her childless and humiliated. Though the cause of the rift was partly the woman's fault, the husband takes primary responsibility for the tragedy and swears that he will never again be angry with her. The reconciliation makes possible "enduring love" and a "covenant of peace" that is more lasting than the hills (54:8, 10). The woman is physically weaker and is socially and economically dependent on her husband. He has the power to punish, humiliate, and abuse her; he also has the power to make her happy and to give her dignity and freedom. He has to convince her that he really loves her and that she can trust him. The image of God painted by the prophet here is that of a husband who gives in to a temporary fit of anger but whose love of his wife is forever. Of course, Zion represents the exiles as verse 17 makes clear. Also, the verb in verse 7, translated as "I will take you back," is a technical term for the ingathering of the exiles and points to a collective interpretation of the woman.

Following the lead of the Septuagint, Paul applies verse 1 to Sarah (see Gen 15), who becomes the mother of Isaac and ultimately to all the children of the promise as he applies this text to the church, the new Jerusalem (Gal 4:27-28).

55:1-13 The return to Zion

The prophet urges the exiles to return to Jerusalem. His appeal begins with an offer of food and drink to the hungry and thirsty. This food and drink bring life, the source of which is the covenant made between God and those invited to the feast. While the prophet speaks of the "everlasting covenant" made with David, he does not envision the restoration of the Davidic dynasty. He transforms the Davidic covenant by asserting that the role once played by Judah's kings in the past will be fulfilled by a much wider circle in the future. The second person plural "you" in verse 3 makes it clear that the exiles, who are returning to Jerusalem, will be the witnesses to God's power. Those who accept God's invitation to the banquet (the experience of God's presence in Jerusalem) have life through the covenant, which makes God's glory shine through them.

Through the prophet, God summons the exiles to God's sanctuary in Jerusalem. But to enter the sanctuary is to enter into God's presence. Those who come into God's presence must reject patterns of inappropriate behavior (see Pss 15; 25; Isa 33:14-16). While Jerusalem is not mentioned specifically, the clear implication of this text is that an authentic encounter with God can take place only in Zion (see Jer 29:10-14). The time of exile was a special circumstance, but once Babylon has fallen, Jerusalem can be restored to its unique status in Israel. Just as all physical life on earth is dependent upon the moisture that comes from the sky, so Jerusalem's restoration is dependent upon God. But God has spoken. Zion's future is assured.

The prophet calls the exiles to take the first steps back to Jerusalem where the Lord can be found. The desert that stands between Babylon and Judah has been stripped of its power to interfere with the glorious procession that will bring the exiles back to Zion. This is a reprise of the opening vision of the prophecy (40:3-5). The image that the prophet is creating is one which sees God at the head of a great throng of Israelites who are making their way back to their homeland after years of exile. Nature is transformed miraculously to ease their journey. They are returning to Zion where they can seek and find God (see Isa 33:20-22).

Paul quotes verse 10 as he tries to motivate the Corinthians to contribute to the collection that he is making for the poor of Jerusalem (2 Cor 9:10-11).

THE NEW JERUSALEM

Isaiah 56:1–66:24

The image of the Creator who subdued the powers of chaos, leading the exiles back to Jerusalem and initiating a glorious restoration that will amaze the nations, gives way to a more realistic picture in the final section of the book of Isaiah. Some exiles have returned to Jerusalem, but the restoration is sputtering. The prophet observes that the old social trappings are reemerging, that the people are not committed to their identity as Jews, and that their religious observance is inauthentic because it is not founded on a commitment to justice. Despite this, the prophet is still able to speak about the future of Jerusalem in a lyrical and expansive mode. He envisions a new Jerusalem repopulated with those who pursue righteousness and joined in the worship of Yahweh by all nations.

56:1-8 The sabbath

The prophet uses a strategy that presents sabbath observance as an element of Jewish identity and then goes on to expand the parameters of that identity. The observance of the sabbath came to have great significance in the Jewish community as an identity-marker. The preexilic markers of Judahite identity such as the national state and native dynasty were gone. Traditional practices such as sabbath observance, circumcision, and the dietary laws began to take on new significance. This passage mentions the need to keep the sabbath three times (56:2, 4, 6). It also broadens the scope of the people of God. The community, of course, includes the descendants of Abraham (see 48:1; 51:2; 63:16), but also those people who can claim no such descent but who, nonetheless, observe the sabbath and keep the covenant. God will bring these people to Jerusalem and to the temple, which is here called a "house of prayer for all peoples" (56:7; see 1 Kgs 8:41-43). God will not only bring the exiles back to Jerusalem but will call the nations to become part of God's people. What is important for inclusion among this people, then, is not physical descent from a common ancestor but careful observance of God's will.

Verses 3b-5 mention eunuchs, i.e., castrated males. In the monarchic period, eunuchs were members of the royal court (see 1 Sam 8:15; 1 Kgs 22:9; 2 Kgs 8:6). This passage focuses not on their social position but on their physical condition. Deuteronomic law excluded eunuchs from Judah's religious assemblies (Deut 23:1). The prophet did not. Also, eunuchs, who were afraid that they would be forgotten without descendants to remember them, are promised "a monument and a name" in the new Jerusalem. The Hebrew phrase *yad vashem* ("a monument and a name") is the title given to Jerusalem's memorial to the Holocaust. The title is inspired by verse 5 and the memorial is so named because entire families were exterminated in the Holocaust, leaving no one to remember them.

In the story of Jesus' cleansing of the temple, the Synoptic Gospels have Jesus cite verse 7 as a justification for his action, though only Mark cites that part of the prophet's words which call the temple a place of prayer "for all peoples" (Matt 21:13; Mark 11:17; Luke 19:46). But the allusion to the Isaianic text sees the universalism of the messianic age fulfilled through the proclamation of the gospel.

56:9-12 Corrupt leaders

The restored Jerusalem community was not blessed with good leadership. Too often its "watchmen" used their position to enrich themselves at the expense of those over whom they were to watch. What was worse was that their appetite had no limits. The prophet refers to them as "dogs" (56:11). This was a particularly insulting affront. Dogs were not kept as pets but were scavengers living on the outskirts of cities and towns, living off refuse and carrion. The prophet also accuses the community's leaders for toasting to their good fortune and their plans for more profits at the expense of the poor.

57:1-13 Against idolatry

The prophet associates an unjust social system with the worship of other gods. He continues his criticism of a corrupt leadership class by noting that these leaders do not pay any attention to the death of just people. Their passing goes unnoticed by those whose attention is centered on their own aggrandizement. The prophet has no use for Jerusalem's religious leadership and accuses them of idolatry and associated practices including child sacrifice. The intensity of the language here makes it clear that there was a serious division in the Jewish community. Clearly the prophet aligns himself not with the leaders but with those who are oppressed by an incompetent and unjust upper class. The prophet concludes his diatribe by ridiculing idolatry. He claims that gods other than the Lord are powerless to help their worshipers. Only those who remain faithful to Israel's ancestral deity will be secure. Serving other gods is a prelude to destruction.

The prophet's words likely reflect a genuine social and religious conflict between those elements of early Jewish society who wished to remain true to their ancestral religious traditions and those who were ready to accommodate themselves to the political, social, and economic realities of the day. Their accommodation expresses itself in their willingness to abandon their own religious traditions in favor of those of their occupiers.

57:14-21 The two ways

Although the corrupt leadership of Judah had control of the religious symbols of Judaism (e.g., the temple of Jerusalem), the prophet assures people that God dwells with the humble and contrite. The prophet, speaking in the name of God, asserts that the road of repentance is always open to those who have abandoned their religious traditions. Still, the wicked who refuse to repent cannot expect peace from God. The contrast between the "dejected" and the wicked is reminiscent of other descriptions of the "two ways," such as Psalm 1 and Jeremiah 17:5-8. The community in Jerusalem was experiencing a recurrence of the divisions that the prophet believes led to the fall of the city and the end of its political and religious institutions. He reaffirms his belief that God is with the poor and will judge their oppressors.

58:1-12 Fasting

Jerusalem's restoration was not proceeding according to expectations. The people had been fasting to elicit God's mercy, but to no avail. In early Judaism, fasting was not an ascetical practice. It was associated with mourning. The purpose of the fasts that came into vogue during the restoration (see Zech 8:18) was to move God to pity Jerusalem and hasten the day of its complete renewal. What the prophet decries here is not the practice of fasting but the ignorance of those who engaged in this practice. After all that the people of Judah have been through, they still have not learned that God expects them to create and maintain a society of justice and equity for all. The performance of ritual actions, no matter how well intentioned, is not a substitute for such a society. As long as injustice, oppression, and internal conflicts plague Judah, the restoration will be stalled. God wants Judah to "fast" from injustice. God wants the people of means to share their food, clothing, and shelter with their brothers and sisters who lack them. When Judah becomes a society based on compassion rather than oppression, justice rather than injustice, the restoration will go forward. Until then, Judah can expect nothing but divine judgment on an unjust and uncaring society. God will honor a just society with the divine presence.

58:13-14 The sabbath

The observance of the sabbath became a significant form of Jewish self-identity following the return from Babylon. The national state and dynasty were not going to be restored. Despite encouragement and support from the Persians, more than twenty years elapsed before the temple was rebuilt. The sabbath then came to have new meaning. It was not simply a day of rest; it became a symbol of commitment to Judah's ancestral religion. The prophet suggests that if the people of Judah neglect the sabbath, they are rejecting their identity as the people of God. Observance of the sabbath, then, is an essential component of Jerusalem's restoration.

59:1-21 God will establish justice

Though God has ended the power of Judah's enemies and brought back its people from exile, the restoration was a profound disappointment. What was disappointing was not the lack of God's action but the people's response to it. Instead of creating a new society, the people were at war with each other. The old social and economic divisions that tore apart Israelite society in the monarchic period were beginning to reassert themselves. This social conflict had the power to destroy Judah again as it had before.

The first step in reversing this process is the community's confession of sin. People have to take responsibility for creating a society that is self-destructive. The sad state of Judahite society is testimony to the failure of its people to incarnate the prophet's vision, a vision of a society of justice and truth. The people's failures cause God to act since God cannot ignore what the people are doing to themselves. God's judgment will come again on Jerusalem since God always acts for the sake of the oppressed. The prophet affirms that God's intention to restore Judah will not be frustrated by the people's actions. Since God has chosen Zion, God will restore Zion in spite of the failures of some of the people.

In speaking about the universal dominion of sin, Paul strings together several citations from the Old Testament, among them are verses 7-8 (Rom 3:15-17). He also uses the images of "righteousness as a breastplate" and "the helmet of salvation" (59:17) in Ephesians 6:14-17 and 1 Thessalonians 5:8.

60:1-22 The glory of the new Jerusalem

The prophet shifts abruptly from a description of Jerusalem's halting restoration to a utopian picture of the new Jerusalem. Zion here is personified as a woman basking in the glow of God's light. The city, which has been a vassal of more powerful states for more than three hundred years, will be the place from which Yahweh rules the world. In fact, the rulers of those states that held Jerusalem in subjection will serve as workmen in rebuilding the city's walls. The nations will contribute to the outfitting of the new temple. Prosperity and security will be the marks of "the city of Yahweh" and "Zion of the Holy One of Israel." As is clear from chapters 58–59, the prophet's vision has yet to be transformed into reality. Still, he is certain that God will bring all this about "swiftly" (60:22).

Two aspects of the prophet's vision call for comment. First is what has been described as "universalism." The nations are welcomed in Jerusalem. In fact, those nations that do not see the hand of the Lord in Zion's restoration will be no more. The surviving nations, however, are clearly subordinate to Judah. They bring their wealth to Jerusalem and serve its people. What this text reflects is not universalism but religious nationalism.

Second, a critical element in the prophet's vision is his expectation that the people of Jerusalem will be just. This is the foundation of the new Jerusalem. Gone will be the social distinctions of the past, the economic oppression, and the political domination of the poor by the people of means. This new society will be God's doing. Of course, the prophet recognizes that this new society is a long way from being realized. It is not surprising that the book of Revelation uses this text to speak about the heavenly Jerusalem (60:3, 11, 19; Rev 21:23, 25-26).

61:1-3 The prophet's mission

Isaiah describes his mission in terms of justice for the oppressed in language similar to 42:1-4, 49:1-6, and 50:4-11. While the "captives" are the people of Judah still in exile in Babylon, the prophet certainly sees his mission in broader terms. The "afflicted" and the "brokenhearted"

in verse 1 are the victims of the corrupt and incompetent leadership that the prophet condemned in 56:9-12 and 58:1-9. Here he comes back to a significant Isaianic motif: justice for the poor. Judah is condemned to exile because of the injustice of its economic and social system. God will recreate Judahite society according to justice, and the prophet has a central role in the working out of God's plan.

"The Spirit of the LORD" is a characteristic Isaianic expression used to describe the presence and power of God in the world. The prophet uses this phrase to underscore his belief that Jerusalem's liberation and restoration are the work of God, not a human achievement. Jerusalem's future will not be determined by any king, Judahite or Persian. It will be the result of miraculous transformation of society. Though the prophet has a role in that transformation, he exercises that role only because of the anointing of God's Spirit on his life.

Luke has Jesus read this text during synagogue worship and then assert that it had been fulfilled in him (Luke 4:17-19). The evangelist reflects the early Christian belief that God's Spirit has been poured out upon Jesus in a unique way to accomplish the divine plan that will effect the salvation of Israel and the nations. Luke believes that the prophet's vision was fulfilled in Jesus—but fulfilled in a way that far exceeded the prophet's profoundest hopes and wildest expectations.

61:4-11 The priesthood of the poor

The prophet does not describe the political and religious institutions of the new Jerusalem in any detail as Ezekiel does. He prefers language that is more evocative than descriptive. For example, the prophet implies that in the new Jerusalem the role of the king will be taken by the people as a whole (55:3-5). Did this mean that the prophet did not envision the restoration of Judah's native dynasty? Here the prophet speaks to the people of the new Jerusalem and asserts that they "shall be named priests of the Lord" (61:6). Does this mean that he did not envision the restoration of the Zadokite priesthood, the descendants of Aaron and keepers of the temple, to its unique position in the new Jerusalem? What the prophet describes is the priestly role that the people of the new Jerusalem will play in regard to the nations. These "priests" will lead the nations to serve

Judah's God. The rebuilding of the temple and the renewal of priestly service do not appear to be priorities for the prophet. What is more significant for him is the renewal of Judahite society on the basis of justice. A just society brings with it God's blessing and is the embodiment of the covenant between God and Jerusalem.

The prophet understands his mission to Israel to be the creation of a just society, one that will be the envy of the whole world. God has anointed him, i.e., designated him solemnly to overcome the social problems that are keeping Judah from becoming the type of community that can enjoy all God's benefits. Once that new society is created, the people can proceed with the restoration of their villages and cities that were devastated by Judah's political, military, and economic collapse.

Judah can free itself from foreign domination by creating a new society without religious hierarchy and social status. All the people will be priests and all the people will have access to the wealth with which God has blessed Judah. This new society will turn Judah's oppressors into its servants. This new society will bring wealth to its entire people. This new society is precisely what God wants Judah to establish. God will make an everlasting covenant with that new, just community, not with people who are devouring themselves through internal societal conflicts.

The book of Revelation asserts that the members of the Christian community are priests serving their God, thus fulfilling the prophet's vision (61:6; Rev 1:6; 5:10). The Magnificat, Mary's song in Luke, is a collage of Old Testament text that begins with a paraphrase of verse 10 (Luke 1:46).

62:1-5 The new Jerusalem: The Lord's Bride

The prophet recognizes that his vision of a new Jerusalem has not been realized. Instead of retracting or modifying his argument, he restates his points in a more forceful fashion. There will be a new Jerusalem for all peoples to see. Then using feminine grammatical forms for Jerusalem, the prophet addresses the city and asserts that it will be Yahweh's queen. The city's reversal of fortunes will be marked by its new names: "My Delight" and "Espoused" (62:4). The prophet exploits the image of Jerusalem as a woman to speak about the city's coming restoration and glorification. God is being reconciled with Jerusalem as a hus-

band is reconciled with his estranged wife. This union will bring fertility to the land and the rebuilding of the city.

62:6-12 Daughter Zion

The prophet calls upon the people of Jerusalem to remind the Lord of the promises made to Jerusalem. They are to be so intemperate in their pleading that God will have no rest from their petitions. He concludes this chapter by assuring "daughter Zion" that her salvation is coming. The prophet addressed these words to people who considered themselves heirs to the promises made about the restoration of Judah, the liberation of Jerusalem, and the reversal of the fortunes of the poor. Though the prophet's visions have not come to fulfillment, he refuses to abandon them. While Jerusalem and Judah were economically depressed and politically impotent, the prophet speaks of the city's splendor. While that splendor is yet to be revealed, it is coming. The prophet can see God coming; he can see the new Jerusalem.

63:1-6 The Lord, the warrior

It is hard to imagine a more stunning shift in mood than the one that occurs here. The prophet leaves behind the poignant image of a husband reconciling with his wife. In this passage, God is a warrior returning from the battlefield with his clothes soaked with the blood of the enemy. Edom and its capital Bozrah symbolize the forces pressuring Judah and preventing the restoration from proceeding as the prophet envisioned it. But God is determined to restore Judah so that a new, just society can emerge there. God will not allow any interference. Any nation that stands in the way of Judah's restoration will be subject to God's judgment and swept aside. God will accomplish this without the help of anyone—least of all Judah itself which has yet to create the kind of society that God is making possible.

In speaking of the final battle with the powers of evil, the book of Revelation describes the coat of the rider on the white horse as "dipped in blood," implying that the prophet's words will find their fulfillment at the end of this age (63:1; Rev 19:13).

63:7–64:11 A lament

The prophet shifts moods again as he prays for the restoration of Jerusalem. The prophet adopts the lament form which tries to move God to act by reminding God of acts on Israel's behalf in the past and then by describing the difficulties experienced by Zion.

The prophet begins by singing of God's actions for Judah. God has been faithful, loving, and good to Israel. The people of Israel are God's people, so God suffered when they suffered and God saved them when they were about to be extinguished. Despite this, Judah has still continued its path of self-destruction. God did not abandon Judah to its fate but acted toward it as God did toward the exodus generation. That generation too failed to respond faithfully toward the marvelous deeds that God worked for them in freeing them from slavery in Egypt. They murmured in the wilderness. Still, God saved them through Moses. God saved them from themselves.

Just as Moses interceded for the freed but rebellious Hebrew slaves, so the prophet intercedes for the freed but rebellious exiles and their descendants. The prophet calls God the "Father" of the Judahites because their ancient ancestors Abraham and Jacob will not acknowledge them. The prophet is mystified by his people's pattern of rebellion and asks God to be Judah's king by rebuilding the temple so that Judah can once again call on God's name in God's sanctuary. The prophet's cry that God "rend the heavens and come down" (63:19) asks God to take immediate and decisive action to establish the new Jerusalem.

In chapter 64, the prophet continues his prayer on Judah's behalf, pleading that the people experience God's presence and power as their ancestors did long before. The prophet is confident because God saves those who are righteous. Still, the prophet's overwhelming fear is that Israel's infidelity and sin have the power to keep God from restoring Judah. Zion now experiences God's absence because of its infidelity.

The prophet uses all his skill to move God to compassion and forgiveness. The people are God's creation. Can God continue to ignore the fate of the chosen people? Jerusalem and its temple have been devastated. Can God continue to allow these to remain in ruins? God should not allow this terrible situation to continue. Forgiveness and restoration are what the prophet asks of God. In assessing the reasons for the failure of the restoration, the prophet does not find fault with

God but with Judah (64:5), and so has the people confess their sins. Similar confessions became common in early Jewish prayer (e.g., Neh 9:1-37). Also, the prophet does not approach God as a righteous judge who must deal with Judah's sins, but as a father whose love for his erring children remains constant (63:16).

Jesus used this image of God frequently and the prayer that he taught his disciples addresses God as "our father" just as Isaiah's prayer does (see Matt 5:9). In speaking about the spiritual wisdom of the believer, Paul imitates the language of 64:3 (see 1 Cor 2:9).

65:1-16 God's response

The preceding prayer tried to move God to action, but, speaking in the name of God, the prophet affirms that God has always been ready to act. The Judahites themselves ignored their God. But they have done more than this. They have provoked God through aberrant religious practices including the violation of dietary laws that, along with sabbath observance and circumcision, became the marks of Jewish self-identity. By ignoring the dietary laws, some Judahites effectively placed themselves outside the Jewish community. There is only one possible response: divine judgment. Judah experienced it in the past; it will experience it anew. But there are those in the community whom the prophet calls God's "servants." These will not experience judgment but the blessings of the land that will provide what is necessary for their survival, food, and drink.

The Judahites then will not have a single destiny. There are those who "walk in evil paths," and there are God's "servants." Each group will have its own destiny in accordance with its response to the God who freed the exiles of Zion. There are two ways: one leads to life and the other to death. The prophet reminds the wicked what they have to look forward to.

In verses 1-2, the prophet is speaking about God's intention to seek out those Jews who have given up their ancestral religion; Paul applies these verses to the Gentiles whom God has "sought out" through Paul's mission (Rom 10:20).

65:17-25 The new world

The Jerusalem that the prophet envisions is clearly not the city he lives in. It will be part of the new world that God is about to bring into existence. The prophet concluded that this world would not be the place of the ultimate triumph of God's justice. God will create a new world and, of course, a new Jerusalem. This is the first step in the direction of Revelation's "new Jerusalem, coming down out of heaven" (Rev 21:1-3). The new Jerusalem that the prophet expects will be a joy and a delight, not the feeble and forlorn city of this world.

For the prophet, Jerusalem has become a symbol of the new world that God will bring into existence. It is a world in which there will be no infant mortality. People will live into old age. They will enjoy their homes and vineyards and their children will grow into honorable adulthood. God will answer their prayers before they finish making them. In short, this passage describes a perfect world where "the wolf and the lamb pasture together" (65:25), the kind of world the lyrical text of Isaiah 11:6-9 imagines. The utopian visions of chapters 11 and 65 were born of the disappointments experienced by the people of Jerusalem at very difficult periods of their lives. The disappointment of the Jerusalem community made it possible for texts such as 2 Peter 3:13 to reinterpret the prophet's vision of the "new heavens and a new earth" (65:17, see also Isa 66:22) as coming when Jesus returns.

66:1-6 Worship and justice

This text severs the fate of Jerusalem from that of the temple. Verses 1-6 are as negative a statement on temple worship as is found in the Bible. Together with 1:10-20 they frame the book of Isaiah and suggest that one goal of the final form of the book as a whole reflected a conflict within the early Jewish community. On one side were the priests who believed that the rituals of the temple were the guarantees of Israel's future. On the other side were those who believed that a just social and moral order was more significant than any ritual. Verse 5 is a clear reference to that conflict, and the following verse asserts that those for whom the temple is so important will hear the voice of the Lord who comes to redress the injustices done to the poor.

The imagery of verse 1 must have passed into Jewish religious speech since Jesus calls heaven God's "throne" and the earth God's "footstool" (Matt 5:35; 23:22). Stephen cites verses 1-2 to argue that the building of the temple by Solomon was a mistake (Acts 7:49-50).

66:7-17 Jerusalem, our mother

Once Jerusalem is free from those who look to ritual as support for their injustice, Jerusalem will be able to fulfill its destiny as a mother to all believers. After God's judgment has purged the guilty, Jerusalem will give birth miraculously to many children "in a single moment" (66:8). The picture of "mother Zion" surrounded by her children is followed by another announcement of judgment on those who have perverted temple worship. Here the prophet concludes the transformation of Jerusalem from the woman who "was dismissed" (50:1) by her husband to the woman reunited with him and becoming a mother to his children.

66:18-24 The pilgrimage of the nations

The book of Isaiah ends with a familiar Isaianic theme: the pilgrimage of the nations to Jerusalem. They will join Israel in worship at "Yahweh's house," where new priests and Levites will replace those who have been purged because of their venality. This is a part of the new world that God is creating to effect the restoration of Israel— a restoration that will include all humanity except those who have rebelled. Jesus uses the imagery of verse 24 to speak about the punishment of those who lead others into sin (Mark 9:48).

The book ends on a negative note as it speaks about the fate of those who rebel against God. In rabbinic tradition, the public reading of the book of Isaiah concludes with the repetition of verse 23 to leave the hearers on a note of promise, not judgment.

THE BOOK OF

JEREMIAH

Pauline A. Viviano

INTRODUCTION

The historical context

The Assyrian Empire, which dominated the Syro-Palestinian region in the eighth to seventh centuries B.C., gave way to the Babylonian Empire in the late seventh century B.C. shortly after the reign of Josiah, king of Judah (640–609 B.C.). The prophetic call of Jeremiah is dated to the thirteenth year of Josiah's reign, that is, 626 B.C. There are few oracles in the book of Jeremiah that can be dated to Josiah's reign with certainty, but it is possible that the oracles of chapters 2–6 belong to the period when Josiah was king of Judah.

According to 2 Kings 22:3–23:3 a law code was discovered in the temple in 621 B.C.; this law code was authenticated as the word of the Lord by Hulda the prophetess, and King Josiah aligned the reform he had begun with the terms of this law. It is not certain whether the story of the discovery of the law code reflects an actual event or was a story created to support Josiah's reform, but whichever is the case, Deuteronomic law and the theology expressed in that law came to the fore in the late seventh century B.C. and played a major role in the shaping of Israel and its Scriptures in the exilic and postexilic periods. It is thought that the Deuteronomic law code of Deuteronomy 12–26, though in an earlier form, was the law code discovered at the time of King Josiah. The Deuteronomic law code has similarities to Josiah's reform, especially with respect to the centralization of worship. Jeremiah may have supported Josiah's reform, but his prophetic message suggests that the reform of Josiah did not significantly impact the behavior of the people, for they continued to worship other gods at various shrines. The book of Jeremiah shows the influence of Deuteronomic theology and it is generally agreed that the book reached its final form through the hands of Deuteronomic editors.

Most of the book of Jeremiah reflects the period of Babylonian dominance over Judah, especially during the reigns of Jehoiakim and Zedekiah. This was a period of turmoil that resulted from conflicting political policies in the royal court of Judah. Jehoiakim had been placed on the throne by the Egyptian pharaoh Necho II who deposed Jehoahaz. Jehoahaz assumed the throne of Judah upon the death of Josiah in 609 B.C. Josiah had attempted to prevent the Egyptians from assisting the Assyrians against the Babylonians, but he was slain in battle at Megiddo (2 Kgs 23:29). Jehoiakim began his reign as a vassal to Egypt, but when Nebuchadnezzar of Babylon defeated the Egyptians at the Battle of Carchemish (605 B.C.), he became a vassal of Babylon. Jehoiakim was caught between two factions: those who sought to throw off Babylonian rule and those who sought to remain loyal vassals of Babylon. Jeremiah's position is consistent with this latter group. Jehoiakim's policy of vacillation between these factions brought the Babylonian army to Jerusalem in 597 B.C. Jehoiakim died before feeling the full wrath of the Babylonians. Though the Babylonians did not destroy the city at this time, they did take the new king, Jehoiachin, into exile with several thousand leading citizens and they put Zedekiah on the throne of Judah. Zedekiah's reign was marked by the same divided policies of Jehoiakim and, as a result, the Babylonians laid siege against Jerusalem in 588 B.C.; the city and its temple were destroyed in August of 587 B.C. Zedekiah attempted to escape but was captured by the Babylonians. They killed his family in his presence; then he was blinded and taken to Babylon. Jeremiah was most active as prophet during the reigns of Jehoiakim and Zedekiah.

The book of Jeremiah

The book of Jeremiah contains poetic oracles, prose biographical stories about the prophet, and additions from the Deuteronomic compilers of the book. The poetic oracles, particularly those found in chapters 1–25, are thought to contain the heart of Jeremiah's message. The oracles against the nations (chs. 46–51) are also in poetic form, but it is doubtful that Jeremiah authored these oracles. The biographical stories about Jeremiah have been traditionally attributed to Baruch, but they may have developed as the traditions about the prophet grew over time. They are located primarily in chapters 26–45. Most of these stories show the prophet coming into conflict with various groups, performing symbolic acts, or presenting a prophetic message at a particular time and place or addressed to a specific person. The additions attributed to the Deuteronomic compilers appear throughout the book.

That the book of Jeremiah grew over time is clearly evidenced in the differences between the Greek (Septuagint, or LXX) and the Hebrew (Masoretic text) versions of the book. The Greek version is one-eighth shorter than the Hebrew version and the oracles against the nations are found in chapters 26–32 of the LXX, but these oracles are the end of the Masoretic text (chs. 46–51).

As with other prophetic books, the words of the prophet Jeremiah were collected and passed on from one generation to the next. Though the prophet spoke at a particular time and to a particular audience, it was thought that the prophetic word continued to have meaning for subsequent generations. Indeed the book of Jeremiah seemed to have been shaped primarily to address the concerns of the exiles, even though Jeremiah's primary audience lived in the preexilic period. The book of Jeremiah explains the cause of the exile, but at the same time it gives the exiles hope for the future.

The prophet Jeremiah and his poetry

Nowhere in the book of Jeremiah is the prophet described, but we come away from the book with an image of a person who is strong and passionate. This image of Jeremiah is conveyed in his commitment to his message in spite of the suffering that he endured as a result. It is conveyed in his reaction to the painful message he was called upon to proclaim and his complaints to the Lord. It is even conveyed in the style of his poetry, with its often harsh and vehement language. Though poetic devices that play on the repetition of sound are lost in translation, we can still appreciate the vividness of Jeremiah's imagery and become engaged by Jeremiah's frequent use of rhetorical questions. We can be stunned and even outraged by his hyperbole and crude language, but we are drawn to the figure of Jeremiah who came to embody the sorrow and pain of the community that cherished his memory.

COMMENTARY

ORACLES IN THE DAYS OF JOSIAH

Jeremiah 1:1–6:30

The first chapter grounds the entire book of Jeremiah. The central theme of the book is set forth: the Lord will punish the people of Judah for their stubborn persistence in the worship of other gods. Jeremiah is commissioned as the Lord's prophet and, as such, he will come into conflict, especially with the leaders of the community. He will be treated brutally and imprisoned for proclaiming the unwelcome message that the end of the nation is inevitable, but the Lord will stand by the word of Jeremiah and will deliver the prophet from the hands of his enemies.

1:1-3 Introductory verses

The opening verses of the book of Jeremiah situate the activity of the prophet during the reigns of three of the last five kings of Judah: Josiah, Jehoiakim, and Zedekiah. Jehoahaz II (2 Kgs 25:31), who reigned after Josiah, and Jehoiachin (2 Kgs 24:8), who reigned after Jehoiakim, are passed over, probably because both of these kings reigned for only three months. Jeremiah prophesies from 626 B.C. to the fifth month of exile of 587 B.C., roughly the last forty years of the southern kingdom, Judah. These verses identify Jeremiah as a priest, but he functions only as prophet in the book itself. He is from Anathoth, a small village not too far from Jerusalem. It was the village to which Solomon had banished the priest Abiathar. Presumably the descendants of Abiathar's branch of the priestly family continued to live in Anathoth.

1:4-19 Call of Jeremiah

The prophetic call form is an ancient form whose purpose was to underscore that the commissioning of the prophet was done by God and therefore the words of the prophet are to be understood as the words of God. This form consists of several elements, each of which can be found in these opening verses: divine confrontation (1:4), preparatory word (1:5ab), commission (1:5c, 7, 10), objection from the prophet (1:6), divine assurance (1:8), and sign (1:9 or 1:11-14). The divine confrontation in the book of Jeremiah is

very brief. There are no elaborate visions as in the call of Isaiah (Isa 6) or Ezekiel (Ezek 1–3). Visions will play only a minor role in the book of Jeremiah (1:11-12; 13–14; 24:1-10). There is no description of the circumstances surrounding Jeremiah's call as we find with Moses (Exod 3:1-3) and Gideon (Judg 6:1-10). Verse 4 simply announces that the word of the Lord came to Jeremiah.

The preparatory word (1:5ab) is considerably expanded. A call from the womb is unprecedented in the Old Testament, but the birth accounts of Moses, Samuel, and Samson imply a destiny from birth. It is notable that verse 5ab bears a similarity to statements found in ancient Near Eastern texts regarding their rulers. Of Shulgi of Ur (2050 B.C.) it is said, "I, the king, a warrior from the (mother's) womb am I" ("Hymn of Shulgi," in *History Begins at Sumer*, 3rd rev. ed., Samuel Noah Kramer, 285 [Philadelphia: University of Pennsylvania, 1981]); and of Ashurbanipal of Assyria (668–627 B.C.), "Assurbanipal whom . . . the great gods, truly desired (while still) in the womb of his mother, and decreed his rule" (Shalom M. Paul, "Deutero-Isaiah and Cuneiform Royal Inscriptions," *JAOS* 88 [1968]: 184). A close parallel from Egypt regarding Pharaoh Pianchi (751–730 B.C.) reads, "It was in the belly of your mother that I said concerning you that you were to be ruler of Egypt; it was as seed and while you were in the egg that I knew you were to be Lord" (M. Gilula, "An Egyptian Parallel to Jeremiah I 4-5," *VT* 17 [1967]: 114). The "borrowing" of these kinds of statements underscores the importance of Jeremiah and suggests that the prophet has been destined from birth and, in speaking on behalf of the Lord, carries the authority of a king. The use of "know" and "dedicate" in this preparatory word is significant. "Know" in the Old Testament is a relational term that indicates an intimacy between the knower and the known; it is used in covenants and thus carries the notion of a bond between the parties of the covenant. To be "dedicated" is to be consecrated for the Lord's service; the one dedicated belongs to the Lord in a special way.

Jeremiah is "appointed," that is, he is assigned a particular task. Jeremiah is commissioned as "a prophet to the nations" (1:5c), but in the book itself Jeremiah functions as prophet only to Judah. His appointment as prophet "to the nations" may indicate his sphere of activity. As the Lord is active in the affairs of the nations, so Jeremiah as the Lord's prophet will likewise have an impact on the affairs of the nations. Though Jeremian authorship of the "oracles against the nations" (chs. 46–51) is doubtful, these oracles give substance to Jeremiah's role as a "prophet to the nations."

Jeremiah's objection to his commissioning (1:6) echoes statements predicated of Moses, who claims that he has difficulty speaking (Exod 4:10; 6:12, 30), and of Samuel, who is described as a "youth" (1 Sam 3:1, 8) when he received his prophetic call. It may be that Jeremiah was called as a young man, but it may be that the terms of this objection are meant to put Jeremiah in the tradition of Moses and Samuel. It is noteworthy that these two prophets are mentioned by name in the book of Jeremiah (15:1).

The Lord counters Jeremiah's objection using the technical vocabulary found in prophetic call forms for a commissioning: "send"/"go," "command"/"speak" (1:7). The use of this vocabulary underscores that the prophet acts and speaks under divine compulsion. As in verse 6 we find echoes from the traditions surrounding the figure of Moses (cf. Exod 7:2; Deut 18:18). Using a formula drawn from oracles of salvation, "Do not be afraid" (1:8), the Lord assures Jeremiah that God will be with him and will "deliver" him. A similar assurance, "I will be with you," was given to Moses (Exod 3:12) and Gideon (Judg 6:16). The sign, which is a characteristic element of the prophetic call form, may be seen in verse 9, with the transference of the Lord's word to Jeremiah's mouth, or in the two visions that follow (1:11-12 and 1:13-14). Prophecy as the mediation of the divine word represents the Deuteronomic view of prophecy. Indeed the term "to place," found in 1:9 and 5:14, is also found in Deuteronomy 18:18, which speaks of a future prophet who will be like Moses.

In a restatement of the commissioning, the Lord reiterates the appointment of Jeremiah, but now specifies that his task will be "[t]o uproot and to tear down, to destroy and to demolish, to build and to plant" (1:10). Throughout the book of Jeremiah these six verbs will be repeated (12:14-17; 18:7-9; 24:6; 31:4-5, 28, 38, 40; 42:10; 45:4), but it is the Lord who is their subject, not Jeremiah. This underscores the identification of the prophet's words/actions with the Lord's words/actions.

The final verse in this call of Jeremiah anticipates the message of the book of Jeremiah. It is a message announcing a harsh judgment of destruction and exile, but that judgment contains seeds of hope for the future.

The two visions (1:11-12 and 1:13-14) attached to Jeremiah's call address aspects of Jeremiah's prophetic message. In a play on words in the first vision, the "almond tree" (*šāqēd*) becomes a "watching-tree" (*šōqēd*) as the Lord "watches" over the fulfillment of the Lord's word. In the book of Jeremiah this "watching" is to secure destruction, but beyond the time of destruction, Israel "watches" for the fulfillment of the hope announced by Jeremiah. The vision of the boiling pot introduces a concept that will recur in the book of Jeremiah, that is, there is a foe coming from the north against the people of Judah (4:6; 6:1, 22; 10:22; 13:20).

The chapter ends with an oracle that summarizes the contents of the book of Jeremiah: Judah will face destruction (1:15-16a) because the people of Judah are worshiping other gods (1:16). As the book of Jeremiah unfolds, it is clear his message was not well received by leaders and the people; Jeremiah suffered greatly as a result. Verses 17-19 encourage the prophet to stand firm in the face of rejection, for the Lord promises to deliver the prophet. Jeremiah will come into conflict with "kings and princes . . . priests and the people of the land" (1:18); he will also come into conflict with prophets and even the Lord. Nevertheless, he is assured that the Lord is with him to deliver him (1:19).

2:1–3:5 Infidelity of Israel

The opening oracles of Jeremiah read as a divine lament. Reflections on the past are interwoven with complaints about the present; there is an interplay of rhetorical questions and accusations. Relational imagery abounds, but especially that of a marriage that has moved from fidelity to eventual breakdown because of persistent infidelity. The overtly sexual language of Jeremiah is often crude and offensive, but it is used to shock the people into repentance. *Šûb*, the Hebrew word meaning "turn"/"return," is often found in these oracles and throughout the book of Jeremiah. The people "turn" away from the Lord in apostasy (a "turning away"); the prophet calls the people to "return" to the Lord in faithful obedience and exclusive worship of the Lord.

The special relationship between the Lord and Israel is set forth using first a marital image (2:1-2) and then an agricultural image (2:3). As in the book of Hosea (Hos 2:15), the time of wilderness is seen as a time when Israel was the faithful "bride" of the Lord. "Devotion" (*hesed*) refers to a love that is characterized by steadfastness or loyalty. It is the love the Lord has for Israel as its covenant lord and it is the faithful love the Lord expects from Israel in return. Israel is said to be the "first fruits" that are dedicated to the Lord. The guilt of those who "ate of it" is probably in reference to the guilt incurred by those who attacked Israel in the wilderness (e.g., the Amalekites).

In contrast to the memory of Israel's initial fidelity, the oracle shifts to the present broken relationship between the Lord and Israel. Israel's unfaithfulness has a long history; it goes back to Israel's ancestors who rather quickly turned away from the Lord to pursue idols. Idols are here spoken of as "emptiness" and the pursuit of idols makes the pursuers themselves "empty." The exodus, the trek through the wilderness, coming into the Promised Land—all reveal that the Lord has acted on behalf of the people, and so the infidelity of the people is all the more inexplicable. The betrayal of their relationship to the Lord stems from their neglect of the Lord and their enthusiasm for false gods. Israel's turning away from the Lord may have resulted from political alliances with other nations, which are represented by reference to Egypt and Assyria (2:16-18), but it is not just the leaders who stand guilty; the people as well as their leaders are complicit.

As the passage develops, there is an interplay between the Lord's complaint against the people and quotes from the people representing their refusal to serve the Lord, their persistence in the worship of other gods, and their insistence that they are guiltless. The repeated reference to the sinful actions of the people and the vivid use of sexual imagery comparing the people to camels in heat or lustful wild donkeys are certainly meant to shock the people into recognizing the depth of their sin and bringing them to repentance. Sexual imagery dominates much of this section, but the passage draws on other imagery as well to speak of the unfaithfulness of the people: they broke the

yoke of the law; they have become a wild vine; they are permanently stained; they are thieves.

Chapter 3:1 raises the possibility of the Lord's forgiveness, but it is ruled out based on the divorce laws of Deuteronomy 24:1-4: a man was forbidden to remarry a wife whom he had previously divorced. However, as the passage continues in 3:12–4:18, the Lord extends forgiveness to the people, if only they would repent. The accusations against the people draw again on sexual imagery to indict the people: they act as shameless prostitutes. Though they may pray that the Lord's wrath will pass, their persistence in their evil actions shows the hollowness of their prayer.

3:6-10 Judah and Israel

Israel, the northern kingdom, had been destroyed by the Assyrians and its leading citizens were taken into exile in 721 B.C. Thus the northern kingdom was punished for its idolatrous practices. This should have been a warning to Judah, but Judah did not learn. Inexplicably Judah followed Israel in its infidelity to its God and made only a halfhearted move toward repentance. Surprisingly the Lord announces that of the two nations, Israel was more just and the next words are addressed to the northern kingdom.

3:11-18 Restoration of Israel

The harsh tone of the previous passages gives way to the Lord's plaintive longing that Israel return and confess its sin of idolatry so that the Lord can heal them. The language of promise regarding Israel's return and restoration (3:14-18) is grounded in the mercy of the Lord and the Lord's anger will pass (3:12). The ark of the covenant was thought to be the throne of the Lord and, as such, it symbolized the Lord's presence in the midst of the people. The fate of the ark of the covenant is unknown; it was probably taken away or destroyed by the Babylonians. The loss of the ark is assumed in this passage with its assurance that the ark is no longer needed; Jerusalem itself will be the Lord's throne. Even though the northern kingdom had been destroyed about one hundred years earlier, the hope for the reunification of the north and south finds expression here. That all nations will come to honor the Lord in Jerusalem is a theme that recurs throughout the book of Jeremiah.

3:19–4:4 Conditions for forgiveness

The disappointment of the Lord's expectations in making Israel the Lord's people draws on the language of lament and gives a poignant tone to this call for repentance. The pathos of the Lord is revealed as the Lord speaks of inner hopes. Perhaps this will lead the people away from the worship of other gods. It is not clear whether the response of the people indicates a genuine or superficial repentance, but in their confession, the people acknowledge that the Lord alone is their God and that the Lord alone brings salvation. They admit that they have sinned and are deserving of punishment. Their failure to "listen" to the Lord is a frequent complaint that the Lord raises against the people throughout the book of Jeremiah. The final call to repentance in this passage (4:1a) includes what that repentance entails (4:1b-4a), the positive consequence of repentance on the other nations (4:2b), and the negative consequence for the Lord's people if they do not repent (4:4b).

4:5-31 The invasion from the North

A dramatic call to war dominates the opening verses of this passage. War is used here as a means of punishment against the people of Judah and Jerusalem. The people are to prepare for war, but at the same time, the horror of the coming destruction should lead them to acts of penance and mourning. It is the anger of the Lord that has been unleashed and before that anger the leaders of the people will lose courage. It is difficult to determine whether the speaker in several of Jeremiah's oracles is the Lord, Jeremiah, or the people. Jeremiah is probably the speaker in verse 10, but he is giving voice to the people's response to the Lord's announcement of war. The people feel deceived by the Lord because they listened to prophets who proclaimed "peace." The issue of true and false prophecy comes to the fore in the book of Jeremiah, for Jeremiah sees himself as the true prophet announcing that judgment is at hand; he stands against those prophets who speak in the Lord's name a prophecy of peace. It is difficult to know how the people of the day would have viewed this disagreement between prophets, but the test of time supports Jeremiah's claim to be a true prophet.

Though war as punishment dominates this passage, there is a shift in verses 11-12 to the hot desert wind known as sirocco as the means of the punishment to come. Whether through an army or a desert wind, God's judgment against the people is coming. The wickedness of the people arises from the core, their heart (4:14), and is reflected in their rebellion (4:17). Nevertheless, the people are still addressed in a personal way: *my daughter* (4:11). In the midst of this announcement of judgment there is a call to repent and the suggestion that salvation is still possible (4:14). It is characteristic of the book of Jeremiah that in the midst of the announcement of overwhelming and unavoidable devastation, hope is still to be found.

It seems that there is a shift from the Lord's judgment against the people to Jeremiah's response to the coming devastation (4:23-26) and then a return to the Lord's voice in verses 27-31. The ambiguity with reference to speaker may result from the close identity of the prophet with God. The anguish of God over the judgment decreed because of the wickedness of the people is experienced by the prophet himself and finds expression in the prophetic word. The sheer physicality of the prophet's response suggests not only the passionate nature of Jeremiah but also his extreme sensitivity to the suffering that is to come. Using the language of the wisdom tradition, Jeremiah speaks of the foolishness of a people who are wise with respect to evil but without sense when it comes to knowing how to do good.

In terms reminiscent of the creation accounts of Genesis 1 and 2, Jeremiah presents a vision of the uncreation of the world (4:23-26). The word of God resulted in the creation of the world in Genesis 1, but now that world is undone as God's anger is unleashed in judgment. Gone are the light, the mountains, humanity; even the birds have disappeared. The world has returned to the chaos (*tōhû wābōhû*, "waste and void," 4:23) that preceded creation (*tōhû wābōhû*, "without form or shape," Gen 1:2); the garden of Genesis 2:8 returns to its wilderness state as at the beginning of creation. This is a powerful and rhetorically sophisticated passage that confronts the people with the horror of their actions; what they are doing will lead to the undoing of the world.

The Lord's voice reemerges with another announcement of judgment. It is a judgment that is said to be a total destruction (4:27b, 28cd), but the totality of that destruction is offset by a mitigation of that judgment (4:27c). This "total yet not total announcement of destruction" occurs elsewhere in Jeremiah (e.g., 5:18) and may reflect a tendency to hyperbole on Jeremiah's part, but it may also reflect a qualification upon Jeremiah's original statement inserted by later editors who are writing on the other side of survival. The passage returns to the imagery of war, but now focuses on the people's response to the invasion: they take flight, shrink, dress up, and moan in anguish. Yet in the midst of it all Zion is still referred to in personal terms: *daughter* Zion.

5:1-31 Universal corruption

The voices of the Lord, Jeremiah, and the people are found in this passage, but it is not always possible to identify each voice with certainty. The entire chapter is a series of indictments (5:1-5, 10-13, 20-28) that justify the Lord's judgment (5:6-9, 14-17, 29-31) against the people. As is characteristic of Jeremiah's prophetic message, these indictments are in general and specific terms: unjust (5:1), dishonest (5:1), "swear falsely" (5:2) or by other gods (5:7), refuse to repent (5:3), act "foolishly" (5:4), "have broken the yoke" (5:5), commit many crimes (5:6, 25-26), have "rebelled" (5:7, 11, 23), have forsaken the Lord (5:7, 19), "commit adultery" (5:7), are dismissive of the Lord and the prophets (5:12-13), serve other gods (5:19), stubborn (5:23), refuse to fear the Lord (5:24), and neither prophets nor priests do as they should (5:31). Judgment takes the form of attacks by wild animals (5:6), the destruction of the produce of the land (5:10), fire as a metaphor for the Lord's word and for the devastation wrought by war (5:14), war (5:15-17), and exile (5:19). Throughout these indictments and announcements of judgment the passage speaks of a God who tried to discipline the people (5:3), to find anyone among the people and its leaders who was just (5:1, 4-5), and who provided for them in creation (5:22) and harvest (5:24), but nothing has worked. The people continue to deny the Lord (5:12) and ignore the prophets (5:13). The prose of verses 18-19 interrupts the poetic oracles that make up this chapter. These verses serve two functions: to indicate that the destruction of the people is not total and to reiterate a justification for the exile. The Lord's punishment is justified, for the people refuse to worship the Lord and the Lord alone.

6:1-30 The enemy at the gates

The theme of judgment continues in this chapter by focusing on the imminence of an invasion from the north, an invasion that can no longer be held off. An ominous tone pervades this passage as the people prepare for war. From the blowing of the trumpet that announces the coming of war to the siege and destruction of Jerusalem and its people, the passage is dominated by the horror that is to come. The Lord warns the people time and again, but they refuse to pay attention to the prophets or to be obedient to the law. There is no call for the people to mend their ways; indeed their continued refusal to do good seals their fate. The passage ends with the Lord's word directed specifically to Jeremiah. Jeremiah is said to be a "tester" for my people. This is a role that is given to the Lord elsewhere (9:6; 17:10) in the book of Jeremiah. As a refiner tests metal, so Jeremiah is appointed to search and test the way of the people, but here the Lord indicates that the refining process has failed. The people persist in turning away from the Lord; their destruction is inevitable.

ORACLES PRIMARILY FROM THE DAYS OF JEHOIAKIM
Jeremiah 7:1–20:18

This section is a rather eclectic collection of oracles of indictment and judgment against Judah and Jerusalem. The language of lament is drawn into these often harsh oracles, but now and then a brief reference to hope finds expression. Many of the themes of the first six chapters continue to dominate Jeremiah's message in these chapters, but Jeremiah's response to his own suffering receives greater focus as well.

7:1-15 The temple sermon

The temple sermon, which runs from 7:1 to 8:3, is clearly set off from its context as a prose insert into a series of poetic oracles. The entire sermon is most probably a composite work, but taken as a whole the sermon is a series of indictments against the people and the announcement of judgment against them. The sermon betrays the thought and language of the Deuteronomic school, but the core of the chapter reflects a prophetic message similar to that of Jeremiah. All the people of Judah coming to the temple are addressed in verses 1-15. They are coming to worship the Lord of Hosts, but by the end of the sermon it is made clear that in actuality they are worshiping the "host of heaven" (8:2). There are a series of demands made upon the people: "reform your ways," "do not put your trust in . . . deceptive words," "[deal] justly with your neighbor," don't "oppress the alien, the orphan, and the widow," don't "shed innocent blood" (7:3-6). Only by obedience to these demands will the people remain secure in the land given to their ancestors. Attention is drawn to the shocking behavior of the people: "But look at you!" (7:8). By means of rhetorical questions Jeremiah exposes the absurdity of their behavior; they do the opposite of what the Lord has commanded. They "trust in deceptive words," "steal and murder, commit adultery and perjury, sacrifice to Baal," and "follow other gods" (7:8-9). The perverse nature of their actions is seen, not simply in their disobedience, but also by their coming into the temple to worship after sinning, as if temple services alone can make them safe. This section concludes with the announcement of judgment: the fate of Shiloh bears witness that the Lord will destroy the city of Jerusalem and its temple.

7:16–8:3 Abuses in worship

The word of the Lord up to this point in the temple sermon had been directed to the people of Judah, but now the addressee is the prophet himself. Jeremiah is commanded not to intercede on behalf of the people. It is too late. They failed to listen (7:13); now the Lord will not listen. The Lord points to their behavior and speaks of all family members, fathers, mothers, and children, engaged in the worship of the Queen of Heaven and other gods. The description of the worship of this goddess is drawn out at length in contrast to the Decalogue-like listing of 7:8. The focus shifts from a violation of many commandments to the violation of the first commandment: do not worship other gods; for this they stand under judgment. Though verses 21-22 are sometimes taken as a repudiation of the whole sacrificial system, it seems that only certain sacrifices are dismissed. What the Lord requires is obedience, but the history of Israel has been one of a stubborn refusal to faithfully worship the Lord and walk in the ways commanded. Rather than worship the Lord,

the people prefer the high places of Topheth, where they sacrifice their own children by fire in the Valley of Ben-hinnom. The horror of their actions is matched by the horror of what will happen to them on the Day of Judgment. They will be slaughtered, become food for birds of prey, and there will be no burial of their bones. The note of finality in this passage will be countered by hope found in chapters 30–33, but the harsh vehemence of this sermon is meant to awaken the people to repent. Unfortunately it does not do so.

8:4-9 Israel's conduct incomprehensible

There is a pervasive tone of pathos in this indictment of the people. God's anguish over the inexplicable behavior of the people (8:5) is underscored by the use of rhetorical questions (8:4, 5, 8, 9): How is it possible that the people will not repent? The repetition of the term *šûb* ("to turn/return/repent") dominates the opening verses of chapter 8 (six times in vv. 4-6). "To return" gives expression to the hope that the people will repent, but more often it is used as it is here, to speak of the refusal of the people "to turn back" toward the Lord. Chapter 7 brought to the fore the failure of the people in relation to worship, but other areas of Israel's life, specifically law and instruction (8:7-9), have been distorted as well by falsehood and lies. With the refusal of the people to worship properly, to be obedient to the law, and to be truthful in instruction, it is inevitable that they will not know the Lord (8:7) and what the Lord requires of them.

8:10-12 Shameless in their crimes

A severe sentence follows upon the indictment of 8:4-9. Women will be raped, as often happens in war, land will be confiscated (8:10), and all will be lost because everyone, "small and great," has pursued greed. Priest and prophet are singled out for their failure to treat the sins of the people with seriousness and for speaking falsely that peace was at hand (8:11). They have acted shamefully and yet are impervious to feeling shame. Their actions will result in their inevitable punishment.

8:13-17 Threats of punishment

Judgment is announced in verse 13 in agricultural imagery, but this quickly gives way to war imagery (8:15-16). Instead of an abundant harvest in the land, there will be no crops. This passage begins and ends as an "oracle of the Lord," but it is the voice of the people that is heard in verses 14-17. They realize the inevitability of their punishment as they await the arrival of the armies from the north that will devour everything in their path. These armies are moving across the land with war horses eager for battle. Words such as "doomed," "poisoned," no "peace," no "healing," "terror," "shakes," "devour," "no charm will work" suggest the relentless and all-consuming nature of this judgment (8:14-17).

8:18-23 The prophet's grief over the people's suffering

There is an interweaving of the voices of the Lord, Jeremiah, and the people in this passage. Moving away from the images of war, this lament responds to the sense of abandonment expressed by the people (8:19b, 20) and the grief of God or Jeremiah over the refusal of the people to repent and over the suffering the people endure on account of their sinfulness. It is not clear whether Jeremiah is speaking on behalf of God or in his own voice, but the prophet embodies the pathos of God in a way that God's grief becomes his own. The deep pain that finds expression in this passage reveals a God/prophet who suffers with the people.

9:1-8 The corruption of the people

Lament, indictment, and judgment are intertwined, picking up earlier themes but reiterated in different terms. Though the voice of the Lord dominates in this passage, Jeremiah's voice may be evident in the opening verses. The Lord (and/or Jeremiah) longs to put some distance between them and their sinful people (9:1). The opening lament shifts into an indictment that centers on the people's lack of fidelity, expressed primarily as deception and lying and summed up by the phrases "me they do not know" (9:2) and "they refuse to know me" (9:5). The sinfulness of the people is unrelenting as they "go from evil to evil" (9:2) and thus judgment against them is unavoidable (9:6, 8).

9:9-21 Dirge over the ravaged land

The language of lament, picked up from 9:1, pervades these verses that include both indictment and judgment. The horror of the devastation of the land is reiterated over and over again: the land has been "scorched" (2x), is "a waste," and is "ravaged." From the land even the animals "have fled" and in the future Jerusalem will be "a heap of ruins, / a haunt of jackals" (9:9-11). The response to this overwhelming destruction is a call to professional mourners to sing a funeral song (dirge) to give full expression to the depth of the people's grief (9:16-21). Between the poetic oracles that make up this section, a prose explanation draws attention to the cause of this judgment: the people have abandoned the law, did not listen, were stubborn, and followed the Baals. The judgment itself is a reversal of the gifts of manna and water that the Lord bestowed upon the people in the wilderness (Exod 15:22-25; 16:1-35). Now they will eat "wormwood" and drink "poisoned water." The people will be "scatter[ed] among the nations" and killed, in stark contrast to the exodus where the Lord brought the people out of slavery into the Promised Land (9:14-15). The harshness of the punishment is set over against the persistence in sin by the people. Though the Lord is behind their destruction, it is a destruction that causes the Lord grief (9:16-17) and would never have been sent, but for their sins.

9:22-23 True glory

In what may be a response to people who boast in their riches, strength, or wealth, these verses direct the reader to the proper basis for boasting: knowing that the Lord acts with fidelity, justice, and integrity. The locus of the Lord's action is "on earth" (9:23), thus underscoring that the judgment that has come or is coming upon the people is grounded in the actions of a just and faithful deity. Indeed acting with "fidelity, / justice, and integrity" is a "delight" to the Lord (9:23).

9:24-25 False circumcision

The theme of judgment continues in this passage, but judgment comes against even those who are circumcised. Circumcision of the flesh provides no exemption from divine judgment; all stand judged.

10:1-16 The folly of idolatry

With satiric tones the idols of the nations are mocked (10:2-5, 8-9, 11, 14-15) and set in sharp contrast to the incomparable God of Israel (10:6-7, 10, 12-13, 16). The denigration of idols is found in Psalms 115:4-8; 135:15-18; Isaiah 40:18-20; 41:6-7;

46:5-7, but the outright mocking of these idols is mainly represented in Isaiah 44:9-20 and this passage of Jeremiah. Israel is admonished not to fear omens, for the idols of the nations are the work of artisans; they are lifeless and inert, like scarecrows in a field, and they will perish. They cannot do harm or good; they are "nonentities." By way of contrast, the God of Israel is a living God, great and mighty, incomparable, eternal. The Lord is truly God, for God is the creator and the heavens and earth are under God's dominion and judgment. Israel's status as the Lord's elect is brought into the conclusion of this passage: Israel is the Lord's "very own tribe" (10:16).

10:17-22 Abandonment of Judah

It is probably best to assume that Jeremiah is the speaker of this passage, but he brings to the fore the voices of God (10:18) and the people (10:19-20) by quoting them. With the city under siege Jeremiah commands the people to prepare for exile. The response of the prophet to the unleashing of the Lord's judgment against the people mirrors the reaction of the people to the unfolding of their judgment. They are in distress and pain for the loss of their children and thus the loss of their future. For Jeremiah the blame falls upon the behavior of the leaders of the land. They failed to lead the flock and thus the flock has gone astray and will be sent into exile. The advancing armies from the north leave destruction in their path.

10:23-25 Prayer of Jeremiah

This prayer of Jeremiah does not seem to be related directly to the previous passage, but it may represent Jeremiah's response to the coming of the armies from the north. Jeremiah begins with an observation, drawn perhaps from the wisdom traditions of Israel, suggesting that humans are not able to shape their own destiny. Jeremiah petitions the Lord to correct him, that is, to guide his destiny, and to do so with justice, not anger. Then his petition shifts its focus to the nations who have destroyed Israel. Jeremiah wants the Lord's anger not to be set against him but against Israel's enemies.

11:1-14 Plea for fidelity to the covenant

The indictments, announcements of judgment, and laments that have been intermixed in the pre-

vious ten chapters continue in the next ten chapters, but overtones of lament, particularly the laments of the prophet himself, are more evident in this section. A frequent shift from poetry to prose characterizes these chapters. Symbolic actions of Jeremiah (13:1-11, 12-14; 16:1-9; 18:1-12; 19:1-15) receive attention in prose narratives that punctuate this section. Oracles of salvation (13:15-27; 14:10-16; 15:1-4; 16:10-13; 17:1-4; 18:13-17), wisdom sayings (17:5-13), and exhortation (17:19-27) are all represented in these ten chapters.

This first section of chapter 11 has often been identified as a Deuteronomic composition because the language of the passage echoes the language found in writings attributed to Deuteronomic authors, such as, "commanded your ancestors," "brought them up out of the land of Egypt," "you shall be my people," "followed and served other gods" (11:4, 10). This passage is often associated with Josiah's reform, but no explicit connection is drawn between Jeremiah's message and the reform of Josiah in the passage itself. The themes that have dominated Jeremiah's message thus far are brought together in these verses and serve as an introduction to what will follow in subsequent chapters. The certainty of punishment grounds the laments from God, Jeremiah, and the people that are interspersed in the following chapters.

Israel's life as a nation is grounded in the covenant (11:3, 6, 8, 10). In formulaic language the relationship between deity and people is defined: "you shall be my people, and I will be your God" (11:4). It is a relationship that is lived by Israel's listening to and obeying the commands of the Lord. The Lord has shown graciousness to this people by redeeming them from a harsh slavery (Egypt as an "iron furnace," 11:4) and bringing them into a "land flowing with milk and honey" (11:5), but it is reiterated in this passage that the people of Israel have failed to listen and obey. The people, like their ancestors, stubbornly persist in following and serving other gods and therefore the covenant curses are in effect. The threatened disaster will come upon them because of their infidelity; no intercession is now possible (11:14). The command to Jeremiah not to intercede on behalf of the people is a recurring theme in Jeremiah (7:16; 11:14; 14:11; 15:1) and it indicates that it is too late to turn back the punishment.

11:15-17 Sacrifices of no avail

Directly addressing the people, the Lord raises questions about the right of the people to worship in the temple when their actions do not align with their covenant relationship. Though Israel was to be full of life and a source of joy for the Lord ("a spreading olive tree, a pleasure to behold," 11:16), the nation has worshiped other gods, specifically Baal. There is no undoing of the disaster that has been decreed. Yet, in the opening verse of this section, the Lord addresses the people as "my beloved." That punishment is the only recourse left does not mean that the Lord ceases to love the people.

11:18–12:6 The plot against Jeremiah

Six passages (11:18–12:6; 15:10-21; 17:14-18; 18:18-23; 20:7-13; 20:14-18) in the book of Jeremiah have been labeled the "Confessions of Jeremiah." These are called "confessions," not in the sense that Jeremiah is confessing sins or even confessing his faith; they are "confessions" in the sense that Jeremiah is giving expression to his innermost feelings. These passages resemble "laments" and draw heavily from the language of the psalms of lament. There are laments of both God (12:7-13; 14:2-6, 17-18; 15:5-9; 18:13-17) and the people (14:7-9, 19-22) worked into chapters 11–20, but these laments of Jeremiah are unique in prophetic literature. There are no introductions to these six passages; they are set apart because in them we have the voice of the prophet raised in complaint against God and in two of the confessions we have God's response.

Interpretation of these "confessions" have ranged from seeing them as the prophet's personal prayer in response to the difficulties Jeremiah faced in carrying out his prophetic role to formulaic communal laments drawn from worship giving voice to the complaint of the people through the prophet's voice. While we cannot ignore the formulaic language drawn from the laments, there is a personal element in these "confessions" that must be taken into account. These prayers are situated in the life of a person who suffered persecution and rejection delivering God's message and so they are particularly suited to the circumstances of Jeremiah's life. There is no reason to assume that Jeremiah himself could not have voiced his complaint in the formal language of lament.

In the first confession Jeremiah responds to information given to him by the Lord. He had been unaware that some from his hometown of Anathoth were plotting against him (11:18, 21) and indeed that members of his own family were against him (12:6). He calls for vengeance against those who plot against his life. In Jeremiah's call to be prophet in chapter 1, the Lord had assured Jeremiah that the Lord would be with him to defend him and Jeremiah calls upon the Lord to take vengeance upon those who persecute him. Two things are to be noted here: vengeance is the Lord's vengeance and the integrity of the Lord's word is at stake here. Jeremiah does not himself exact vengeance against his enemies; it is up to the Lord to do so. For the integrity of the Lord's word to stand, Jeremiah's enemies must not be allowed to triumph. The Lord responds to Jeremiah, assuring him that those who plot to take his life will be punished, but Jeremiah continues his complaint, raising the issue of why the wicked prosper. In a reversal of Psalm 1, Jeremiah maintains that it is the wicked who are like trees that are planted and flourish, and, even more stridently, Jeremiah says that it is the Lord who plants and nurtures them. Jeremiah is seemingly impatient for justice because the land suffers. The Lord's response is surprising both in form and content. The Lord confronts Jeremiah with rhetorical questions that imply Jeremiah's situation will get worse. If he complains at minor difficulties, how will he manage when the situation gets worse? It is at this point that the Lord reveals to Jeremiah that not only is the town against him but his own family is not to be trusted.

12:7-13 The Lord's complaint

After responding to Jeremiah's lament, the Lord gives expression to sorrow at the condition of the people and their land. The frequent use of "my" (12:7 [3x], 8, 9, 10 [3x]), and terms like "house," "beloved" (12:7), "heritage" (12:7, 8, 9, 10), "vineyard," and "delightful portion" (12:10) lend a certain poignancy to the passage. The Lord's own people, God's own possession, have turned against the Lord who grieves for them and yet must punish them. Throughout much of the book of Jeremiah there is an unrelenting doom that awaits the people, but it is a doom that is brought about by their own actions. The land has been and will be "ravaged," "trampled," "turned into a desert" (12:10) and "a mournful waste" (12:11); there is "no peace" (12:12) or fruitful harvest (12:13). This damage has been caused as punishment for people turning against the Lord, but the Lord is not a cold executioner; rather, the Lord mourns for the land and its people.

12:14-17 Judah's neighbors

The element of hope in these verses contrasts sharply with the harsh judgment that characterizes much of Jeremiah's prophecy. The Lord's people have been uprooted by invading armies as punishment, but those armies will not have the last word. The Lord's judgment will give way to compassion and an uprooted people will be returned to their land and their enemies will be uprooted in turn, but even that uprooting will not be forever, for Israel's enemies will be given the opportunity to learn the ways of the Lord and be restored to their lands.

13:1-11 Judah's corruption

This chapter opens with the first of several symbolic acts of Jeremiah. These symbolic acts add a dramatic element to the proclamation of the prophetic word. The details of what Jeremiah actually does are debated, for he is commanded to go to Babylon twice and it is difficult to see how that could have been accomplished in a three-to-four-month period, given the distance and slow means of travel available at the time. What is clear, however, is the meaning of the symbolic act: the loincloth is a metaphor for the people. The closeness of the loincloth to the body suggests an intimacy between the Lord and the people (13:11), but the rotting of the loincloth represents the judgment that will come upon the people (13:9) because of their refusal to obey the Lord, especially in their persistent worship of other gods (13:10).

13:12-14 The broken wineflask

The proverb regarding a wineflask (13:12) becomes the basis for an announcement of judgment. Wine is often seen as a blessing from the Lord, thus the proverb suggests that Israel should be "filled with" the Lord's blessings, but their actions lead, rather, to their destruction. It is the ill effects of wine (drunkenness) that they experience, rather than its blessing. The harshness of the judgment is characteristic of Jeremiah's prophecy, but it is mitigated to some extent by announce-ments of hope found later in the book (chaps. 30–33).

13:15-17 The last warning

The message of these verses is clear: return to the Lord before it is too late. The complete destruction announced in 13:14 and picked up again in verses 20-27 stands in tension with this call for repentance, but hope may emerge even as darkness begins to descend. It may well be that some of the people will respond and repent, thus sowing the seeds upon which a better future can be built. Jeremiah's own grief is given expression in verse 17.

13:18-19 Exile

The king and queen mother of verse 18 are most likely Jehoiachin and Nehushta (22:24-27; see also 2 Kgs 24:8). Their descent from the throne and the removal of their crowns signifies the end of the king's reign and the end of his mother's position as queen mother. The besieging of the cities of the Negeb suggests that the demise of Jerusalem is close at hand. Judah's rulers will be dethroned and its people forced into exile.

13:20-27 Jerusalem's disgrace

Jerusalem is addressed (13:27b) in this announcement of judgment, but it is a judgment that is intermixed with indictment and lament. The indictment draws upon graphic and offensive sexual imagery to speak of Jerusalem's infidelity to the Lord, and the announcement of judgment borrows the language of sexual violence. This intense rhetoric is presumably aimed at shocking the people into recognizing their sinfulness and repenting, but the passage suggests, rather, that the people of Jerusalem won't change and so there is no other option than a punishment that "fits the crime."

14:1–15:4 The great drought

This section is characterized by a dialogic interplay of the voices of the Lord, Jeremiah, and the people in both poetry and prose. Set against the background of a drought, this prophetic word is dominated by laments from the people (14:7-9, 19-22), the prophet (14:13), and God (14:1-6, 17-18). These laments sometimes merge as in 14:1-6, where the lament of the people is the lament of the Lord. Jeremiah's voice recedes into the background, allowing the voices of God and people to come to the fore. At issue is the anguish of the people who turn to the Lord as their salvation in times of need, but the Lord insists that it is too late. Nothing can turn aside the destruction that will overtake them; it is the inevitable result of their apostasy. The intercession, even of Moses and Samuel, notable prophets of the past, will not work. Offering sacrifice and confessing sin will not be effective. Jeremiah's attempt to excuse the people and blame false prophets is dismissed by the Lord, even though the Lord acknowledges that these false prophets were not personally sent by God; nevertheless the people are accountable. There is no turning the heart of the Lord away from punishment (15:1-4). The vehemence in the description of the devastation to come upon the people is offset by the recognition that the suffering of the people, however much deserved, is a personal source of grief to God (14:17).

15:5-9 Scene of tragedy

The themes of the previous passage continue: the punishment of the people has come about because the people refused to turn from their evil ways. The metaphors of destruction are drawn from farming with its winnowing of the wheat to remove the chaff, and from family life with its cycle of life and death where the death of the young is the source of great grief. There is a sense of finality that pervades this oracle.

15:10-21 Jeremiah's complaint

This is the second of Jeremiah's confessions and, as with the first confession, the Lord responds. It is unusual that Jeremiah addresses his opening words to his mother, but he quickly shifts address to the Lord. Jeremiah's complaint is related to his call to be a prophet, a prophet who has to proclaim the unleashing of the Lord's wrath against the people. It is not Jeremiah who has willed the destruction of his people; indeed he has interceded on their behalf, yet conflict follows him wherever he goes. The Lord responds to Jeremiah's outburst, but the translation of verses 12-13 is not certain. The gist seems to be that the Lord will be with Jeremiah to deliver him. The first "iron" (v. 12) may refer to the "stiff-necked" people of Judah who will not break the "iron from the north," that is, Babylon, and the "bronze" may refer to Jeremiah who will stand firm in the face

of opposition from the people (cf. 1:18; 15:20). If the "you" of verses 13-14 refers to Jeremiah, then the Lord informs Jeremiah that he too will suffer loss in the future, but these verses are often taken as directed to the people as an announcement of judgment against them.

Jeremiah's lament continues by drawing the Lord's attention to the suffering he endures in carrying out his prophetic commission. He embraced his role as messenger of God, but because of his vocation, he has borne insult and was set apart from his people and their celebrations, holding within himself the Lord's rage. From his anguish Jeremiah raises the question, why does he know constant pain? In a stinging reproach Jeremiah even accuses the Lord of failing him as water that cannot be found when needed. The Lord again responds to Jeremiah, but the first part of the response ignores Jeremiah's pain. Rather, the Lord focuses Jeremiah on his task as prophet. He is to come back to the Lord and once again to be the Lord's mouth. Only then does the Lord assure Jeremiah that he will be delivered, reaffirming the promise made at the time of his call (1:18-19).

16:1-13 Jeremiah's life a warning

Jeremiah not only speaks the word of the Lord but he is also called upon by the Lord to embody that word in his life. He is given three commands: do not marry and have children, do not join in mourning, and do not join in celebrations. Each of these commands relates to Jeremiah's message. The command not to marry and have children will protect Jeremiah from grief at the death of his children when children will die of disease, famine, and the violence of war at the time of punishment. Jeremiah is not to express grief, for the Lord has withdrawn peace from the people and Jeremiah is to do likewise. He is not to participate in joyful celebrations, for there will be no cause for joy in the future. The devastation that is coming is so overwhelming that the normal routines of life will be disrupted. Once again when it is asked why this punishment has come upon the people, the answer is the same: the people have abandoned the Lord and turned to other gods in service and worship.

16:14-15 Return from exile

Interrupting the indictments and punishments of the previous and following passages, this passage resounds with hope and counters the un-relenting sense of doom that permeates these chapters. The exodus has been the paradigm for the Lord's gracious act of deliverance, but this passage elevates the rescue and return of the exiles to the Promised Land as the act of the Lord's salvific power that future generations will confess. These verses may represent a later addition drawn from a nearly identical passage in 23:7-8.

16:16-18 Double punishment

Following upon the hopeful statement in verses 14-15, this announcement of punishment may be tempered by the suggestion that the Lord is aware of the people wherever they may be and so will be able to find them and return them to their land, but verse 18 indicates that first they must be held accountable for their sins.

16:19-21 Conversion of the nations

Jeremiah's response opens this section and the Lord's word closes it. After addressing the Lord in conventional language that we find in the psalms (Ps 46:1; see also Pss 27:1; 37:39-40), Jeremiah introduces the notion that the nations will come to the Lord, a notion not foreign to the prophets (Isa 2:3/Mic 4:2; Zech 8:20-23; 14:16-19). Even the nations will see in what has happened to Judah, both in its punishment and its deliverance, the hand of the Lord. They will recognize that their gods are nothing and will come to know the Lord. A characteristic tenet of Old Testament theology is that Israel comes to know the Lord in what the Lord does. This is now extended to the other nations; they too will come to know the Lord in what is done.

17:1-4 The sin of Judah and its punishment

Judah is indicted for the worship of other gods (17:1-3a) and its punishment is the loss of its wealth and land, enslavement, and exile (17:3b-4). That sin is written with an "iron stylus"/"diamond point" suggests the permanence of the people's sin; it is carved into their being and passed on to the next generation ("when their children remember"). The reference to the "horns of their altars" is not clear. The horns of an altar are the projections on the four corners of an altar, but their significance is unknown. A person could claim sanctuary by holding onto the horns of an altar and the passage may suggest that the people will find no sanctuary because of the depth of their sin.

17:5-11 True wisdom

Moving away from indictment and sentence, this passage consists of a collection of wisdom sayings that contrast the fate of those who trust in the Lord with those who trust in human beings or wealth (17:5-8, 10-11). The wisdom tradition is characterized by setting out a choice between two ways: the way of wisdom or the way of folly, but this can also be expressed as a choice between obedience or disobedience, righteousness or wickedness, and, as here, trust in the Lord or trust in humans. Consequences inevitably flow from one's choice and that is the focus of these wisdom sayings. In images drawn from nature those who do not trust in the Lord are like withered shrubs in a barren land, but those who trust in the Lord flourish like well-watered trees. Verse 9 presents a negative reflection upon the nature of the human heart, but it is consistent with Jeremiah's emphasis on the stubborn refusal of the people to return to the Lord. The human heart is open before the Lord and every person is requited in accordance with his or her deeds.

17:12-13 The source of life

In a hymnic interlude these verses reiterate the consequences of forsaking the Lord, the hope of Israel. As in 2:13 the Lord is identified as the source of living waters.

17:14-18 Prayer of vengeance

This third confession of Jeremiah is a prayer for healing and a call for vengeance against those who persecute him. The Lord has promised Jeremiah salvation (15:20) and in confidence Jeremiah petitions the Lord for that salvation. He declares his own innocence, for he has not been the one who has desired the destruction of his people. Indeed, he has interceded on their behalf. The depth of Jeremiah's anguish breaks forth when he cries out that the Lord should not be a terror to him, but his refuge. Jeremiah's call for vengeance may be disconcerting, but what is at stake is Jeremiah's role as prophet. If the word that Jeremiah proclaims is the Lord's word, then those who mock and persecute him are obstructing the Lord's word. For the Lord's word to go forth, Jeremiah's enemies must be stopped.

17:19-27 Observance of the sabbath

It is not clear how this prose sermon fits in its present context. Previous indictments have been focused on the people's turning to other gods, but here the issue is the proper observance of the sabbath. Also, there has been a ring of finality in previous announcements of punishment, but here punishment is not inevitable; the people still have the opportunity to live in accordance with the laws against working on the sabbath. The future is open-ended and will be shaped by what the people do.

18:1-12 The potter's vessel

Jeremiah is commanded to observe a potter at work. The way a potter shapes a pot and reshapes the clay when the pot turns out badly symbolizes the Lord's treatment of Israel. In drawing out the meaning of what Jeremiah observes, the Lord states that all nations are as clay in the hands of the Lord. As bad pots are destroyed and remade, so the nations are destroyed and remade by the Lord when they pursue evil. Jeremiah is commanded to bring this message to Judah and Jerusalem with a call to repentance, but any hope that the people will change is overridden by Jeremiah's insistence that the people will stubbornly refuse.

18:13-17 Unnatural apostasy

A tone of divine lament permeates this announcement of judgment. Through a series of rhetorical questions addressed to the nations, the impossibility of nature to act "unnaturally" is underscored; and yet, Israel has acted "unnaturally" in forgetting the Lord (18:15). The "horrible things" that Israel has inexplicably done will result in the ruin of the land and the exile of the people. Passersby will recognize what has happened and be horrified at the destruction. The severity of the Lord's judgment is suggested by the image of turning the Lord's back to the people.

18:18-23 Another prayer for vengeance

Verse 18 sets the context for the fourth confession of Jeremiah. Three groups are singled out as plotting against Jeremiah: priests, sages, and prophets. They are attentive to Jeremiah's words in order to use his words against him. In response Jeremiah turns to the Lord with another call for vengeance against his adversaries. Jeremiah calls upon the Lord to remember that he has interceded on their behalf, but they repay him with evil. Then Jeremiah unleashes his wrath in a relentless list of horrors that God should bring upon the prophet's enemies. Though Jeremiah's words are particularly harsh, they match the language of judgment found throughout the book of Jeremiah and are similar to the curses upon one's enemies found in laments psalms (Pss 35:4-6, 8; 58:7-11; 109:6-13).

19:1–20:6 Symbol of the potter's flask

The themes of chapter 18 are continued in this prose narrative, which presents another symbolic act that the Lord commanded Jeremiah to perform. After buying an earthenware flask from a potter, Jeremiah is to deliver three announcements of judgment; two are to be given in the presence of some elders and priests (19:3-9, 10-13) and one to the people in the temple courtyard (19:14-15). The first announcement of judgment is delivered near the Valley of Ben-hinnom or Topheth. This valley was the scene of the sacrifice or ritualized initiation of children to the god Molech (2 Kgs 23:10). Jeremiah speaks of it as the valley in which the people burned incense to other gods; the kings of Judah filled the valley with the innocent blood of children sacrificed to Baal. The horror of these actions is matched by the harshness of the judgment. The second announcement of judgment accompanies the breaking of the flask. As the flask has been shattered, so shall the people and their city be shattered. The third announcement of judgment is directed more generally against the people for their stubbornness and disobedience.

The persecution of Jeremiah, which has been a recurring theme in these chapters, is concretized in the actions of Pashhur, the chief officer in the temple. He strikes Jeremiah and puts him in stocks overnight. Jeremiah does not rescind the judgment that he declared the previous day. Rather, he reiterates it, adding that Pashhur himself will bear the name "Terror on every side" because of the "terror" he will experience and witness. "Terror on every side" was a phrase that summarized Jeremiah's word of judgment and it is the phrase with which Jeremiah himself is mocked (20:10). Babylon is identified as the nation through whom the Lord's judgment will be carried out (20:4). On the basis of this verse it is likely that Babylon is to be identified as the unnamed foe "from the north" (1:14; 4:6; 6:1, 22; 10:22; 13:20).

20:7-18 Jeremiah's interior crisis

The fifth and sixth confessions of Jeremiah draw this section of the book of Jeremiah to a close. The intensity of the language with which Jeremiah addresses the Lord in the fifth confession (20:7-13) is striking. He accuses the Lord of seducing or deceiving him (the Hebrew root *pth* carries both meanings) and overpowering him. This strong language suggests that Jeremiah did not realize what he was getting into when he accepted his prophetic role. His life is now defined by mockery and violence precisely because of the message he must proclaim. Jeremiah is caught between the people who persecute him for that message and the Lord who will not allow him to withhold that message. In spite of Jeremiah's bitter outcry against the Lord, he trusts that the Lord will champion his cause against those who persecute him. The abrupt shift from complaint to trust and praise is typical of the form of a lament and so it is not surprising to find a hymn of praise at the end of this confession.

Though the sixth confession (20:14-18) is included among the confessions of Jeremiah, it stands apart from them. There is no address to the Lord or petition here; it echoes the anguish characteristic of laments, but it opens with the curse of the day of his birth. Jeremiah has not only proclaimed the word of the Lord but he has also embodied that word in his life and suffered because of it. It is because of the sorrow and pain he has endured that he cries out against the day of his birth.

ORACLES IN THE LAST YEARS OF JERUSALEM

Jeremiah 21:1–25:38

Prose narratives and prophetic statements are intermixed with poetic oracles in this section, which is thought to be an appendix to the previous chapters. The collection of oracles in chapters 21–23 focus mainly on the kings of Judah, Jerusalem, and the false prophets, and chapters 24–25 look to the future of Judah and the nations.

21:1-10 Fate of Zedekiah and Jerusalem

King Zedekiah consults Jeremiah four times in the book of Jeremiah (21:1-10; 37:3-10, 17-21; 38:14-28), but each time the prophet speaks a message

that is unfavorable. The historical context of this first consultation is the siege of Nebuchadnezzar, king of Babylon, against Jerusalem in 588–587 B.C. King Zedekiah asks Jeremiah to intercede in the hopes that the Lord will cause Nebuchadnezzar to end the siege, but Jeremiah's response is particularly harsh: the Lord will fight against Jerusalem and King Zedekiah will be handed over to the Babylonian king. The only choice that the Lord gives to the people is to remain in the city and die, or leave the city, surrender to the Babylonians, and live. The fall of Jerusalem is certain, for the Lord is firmly against the city.

21:11–22:9 Oracles regarding the kings

Without referring to any specific king, this section is addressed to the royal line of David commanding the king to dispense justice daily. It is implied that the kings did not secure justice for the oppressed (21:12) and they arrogantly dismiss the possibility that this city can be defeated (21:13). However, the Lord's fury will be unleashed against them; the city will fall. A second word (22:1-9) is mediated by Jeremiah to the king and his officials, but this word is conditional. It reiterates the demand for justice, especially for the resident alien, the orphan, and the widow, but the future is open-ended. If they pursue justice, they will continue to rule in Jerusalem; but if they fail in justice, then the city will be destroyed. A short oracle describes this destruction (22:6-7). Consistent with previous passages, the cause of the destruction of Jerusalem is that the people worship other gods, but here this is said to be a desertion of their covenant with the Lord.

22:10-12 Jehoahaz

The command is given not to mourn one who is dead but to mourn one who is going into exile (22:10), but it is not clear who these individuals are until verses 11-12. The one who is dead is presumably King Josiah, and the one who will be exiled is King Jehoahaz (Shallum). It may be that the time for mourning King Josiah is past and whatever hopes were associated with his reign are gone.

22:13-19 Jehoiakim

The oracle concerning Jehoiakim, king of Judah, is an indictment against him for injustice. The specific instance of injustice is that he had built for himself a lavish palace but did not pay the laborers for their work. The indictment is drawn out at length, highlighting the opulence of Jehoiakim's palace built to reflect his exalted status as king. This attention to his palace is set over against his lack of concern for justice, especially to the weak and poor. It is also set over against the justice and righteousness of his father, King Josiah. The prosperity that Josiah enjoyed was the result of his concern for the weak and poor, but Jehoiakim's arrogant disregard for the poor earns him a severe punishment: no one will mourn his death and his corpse will be treated as that of a donkey, that is, it will be discarded and left as food for scavengers.

22:20-30 Jeconiah

The judgment against King Jehoiachin (Jeconiah/Coniah) is preceded by an indictment and judgment against Jerusalem. The oracle against Jerusalem is to be announced upon a mountain for all to hear. It reiterates themes that pervade the book of Jeremiah. Jerusalem is unfaithful and has always been so. The "wind" is used as an agent of judgment against the leaders of the people. They lived in comfort in a palace and temple built with the cedars of Lebanon, but now they will cry out in pain when judgment comes upon them.

There are two oracles that announce judgment against King Jehoiachin, one in prose (22:24-27) and the other in poetry (22:28-30). That the judgment against Jehoiachin is unalterable is underscored by presenting the first oracle as an oath taken by the Lord: Jehoiachin will go into exile and there he will die. No reason is given for this judgment and the severity of this judgment is puzzling in light of the fact that Jehoiachin reigned only three months. The second judgment reinforces the judgment of the prose oracle. Not only has Jehoiachin been cast out and exiled but there will also be no future kings from his line. The question as to why this is so is raised in the opening lines, but it remains unanswered.

23:1-8 A just shepherd

This section consists of brief oracles. The first oracle (23:1-4) is an indictment and judgment that is followed by an announcement of salvation. The indictment is against the leaders of the nation for misleading the people. The failure of the leader

results in the destruction of Judah and the exile of the people. The metaphors of kings as shepherds and Israel as the Lord's flock are found frequently in the Old Testament. The metaphor continues in the announcement of the return and restoration of the people. The Lord will be shepherd to the people, gathering and leading them back to the land where they will be fruitful and multiply. This announcement of salvation borrows from the language of the creation story and the patriarchal promises (Gen 1:28; 17:1-8, 20; 28:3-4; 48:4). Additionally, the Lord will raise up shepherds who will care for the flock.

Another oracle of salvation is introduced in verses 5-6, but here the focus is on one ruler from the line of David. This future king is referred to as a "righteous branch" (23:5; see also 33:15; Zech 3:8; 6:12). The term "branch" will take on messianic overtones in the postexilic period, but here it indicates that the future king will be a legitimate heir to the throne of David. This king will rule with justice and righteousness, that is, he will rule as the Lord rules. The result of his rule will be salvation for Israel and peace in their land. The name of the future king, "The LORD our justice" (23:6), may play off the name Zedekiah, which means "The Lord is my justice." The rule of this future king will be the just rule of the Lord.

A final oracle of salvation (23:7-8) concludes this section. It is an oracle that is nearly identical to 16:14-15, but here it seems to reinforce the hopeful elements of verses 1-6. The return of the people of Israel from exile and their restoration on the land becomes a new salvific action of the Lord to be proclaimed by future generations.

23:9-40 The false prophets

The various poetic and prose oracles in this section are united by a common interest in the topic of false prophets. How does one determine who truly speaks the Lord's word when prophets issue conflicting statements? The book of Deuteronomy attempts to resolve the conflict (Deut 13:1-6; 18:9-22), but looking to the future fulfillment of the prophetic word does not help at the time the word is announced. Jeremiah insists that he is speaking a message on behalf of the Lord, a message that is primarily one of future disaster unless the people repent and surrender to Babylon, but he is countered by prophets who preach "peace." The issue of false prophecy is critical for Jeremiah because false prophets give the people a false hope that will ultimately lead to their destruction.

It seems likely that Jeremiah is the speaker of the opening verse (23:9), but very quickly it becomes difficult to separate the divine voice from the voice of the prophet. As in the confessions, we see into Jeremiah's inner struggle because of the word he must proclaim, a struggle that impacts him both emotionally and physically. Because of infidelity to the Lord and an evil way of life, seen even among the prophets and priests (23:11, 14), disaster will come upon all the people. Verses 13-14 focus on the infidelity of both the prophets of Israel and the prophets of Judah, with the prophets of Judah receiving the harshest judgment; it is judgment as bitter food and poisoned water. The people are likened to the inhabitants of Sodom and Gomorrah who merited only punishment. The failure of the prophets impacts the whole land because the prophets have led the people into ungodliness.

The next oracle (23:16-22) warns the people against false prophets. The people should recognize as false the word of prophets who proclaim a word of peace to those who persist in evil. It was thought that the prophet had access to the council of the Lord. This council was composed of divine beings over whom the Lord presided. The function of the council was to advise the high God (23:18, 22). It was thought that prophets had access to the divine council and thus their words were true. Jeremiah contends that the false prophets have not stood in the Lord's council (23:22) and consequently their words are false. The announcement of judgment (23:19) draws upon imagery of a storm to indicate that the Lord is coming as a warrior against the people. The three rhetorical questions of verses 23-24 make the claim that God is in touch with every sphere of creation.

The final section of this chapter (23:25-40) continues the focus on false prophecy. Jeremiah insists that the way one receives a prophetic word is not as important as the content of that word. Claims to visionary experiences and dreams carry no weight if the Lord did not send the prophet. The words of the false prophets are like straw to wheat; the Lord's word is as a fire. The key to understanding the question of verse 33 is in the word *maśśā'*, which means both "burden" and "oracle." Verses 34-40 attempt to say who is authorized to speak the word of the Lord, but they do not actually give one a way to distinguish true from false prophecy. It simply says that one is not to use "burden/oracle" for any claimed revelation.

24:1-10 The two baskets of figs

Two baskets of figs, one containing good figs and the other bad, provide the controlling metaphor to prophesy concerning the future of two groups: those who had been exiled to Babylon in 597 B.C. and those who remained in the land or escaped to Egypt. The former are the good figs and the Lord will look with favor upon them, return them to the land, and they will flourish. The bad figs represent those who remained in the land, including King Zedekiah and his princes, and those who settled in Egypt. A particularly harsh punishment awaits them in the future. The future of Israel rests with the exiles according to Jeremiah and, indeed, it is the exiles who will lay the foundation for the future of the people.

25:1-14 Seventy years of exile

A summary of twenty-three years of Jeremiah's prophetic message is inserted at this point in the book. It reiterates the main message contained in the oracles of Jeremiah: the people are remiss in worshiping the Lord and the Lord alone, they refuse to change their ways, and thus they stand under judgment. There is surprisingly no reference to the Lord's saving actions of the past; there is only a focus on sin and its inevitable punishment. The only additional element is that seventy years after punishment the Babylonian Empire itself will be the focus of the Lord's judgment. In 29:10 it is the exile itself that is set at seventy years. It is simply not possible, despite some creative attempts, to get seventy years as the period of time that the Babylonian Empire was dominant in the region or that the exile lasted seventy years. It is most likely that the number is simply a round number suggesting a normal life span (cf. Ps 90:10).

25:15-38 The cup of judgment on the nations

It is not clear whether this section is intended as a report of a symbolic act, the expansion of a vivid metaphor, or the explanation of a vision, but the prophetic message itself is clear. The drinking of the cup of wine of wrath sets the context for a severe judgment against the nations. There is no indictment in this section, only an announcement of punishment. The nations will experience the devastation brought by Babylon's armies; they have no choice but to drink the wine of wrath. The Babylonian Empire is bent on conquest and every nation will be defeated by the Babylonian armies, but in the end Babylon itself will fall to the sword. The cryptic reference to Babylon as Sheshach (25:26) is an example of an *atbash* cipher in which the Hebrew letters are substituted in reverse alphabetical order, that is, the first letter of the alphabet is replaced by the last letter, the second letter is replaced by the second last letter, and so forth. Thus Babel (*bbl*) becomes Sheshach (*ššk*). The list of nations is similar to that found in the oracles against the nations (chs. 46–51). Jeremiah had been commissioned as "prophet to the nations" (1:5, 10) and in this passage Jeremiah receives a message from the Lord that is directed to the other nations. It is more likely that Jeremiah carried out the command he is given in a symbolic way than that he traveled from nation to nation carrying a cup of wine for each nation to drink.

Of the two poetic oracles that conclude the chapter, the first (25:30-32) continues the announcement of judgment against the nations. The Lord is imaged as a roaring lion that ravages his flock in stark contrast to the Lord as a protective shepherd. The Lord is also spoken of as a vintager treading grapes and a judge rendering a verdict. The judgment is likened to a storm that has been unleashed against the whole earth. After a prose interlude that speaks of the vast number of the slain who will not be mourned and buried, the second poetic oracle (25:34-38) calls for a lament over the slaughter from which there is no escape. The final verse leads us back to the image of the Lord as a lion on the prowl wreaking devastation across the land.

THE TEMPLE SERMON

Jeremiah 26:1-24; cf. 7:1-15

26:1-19 Jeremiah threatened with death

The negative response to Jeremiah's preaching is no more dramatically presented than in chapter 26 when Jeremiah is put on trial for speaking of the destruction of the temple. A fuller version of the temple sermon is given in chapter 7; the focus of this chapter is the reaction of the religious leaders, specifically the priests and prophets, and the people who hear Jeremiah's announcement of the judgment against the temple.

The substance of the temple sermon is summarized in verses 2-6: if the people turn away from evil, their punishment will be averted; but if they continue to disobey the Lord and not listen to the prophets, then the temple and city will be destroyed. Jeremiah is seized and an impromptu trial begins. The priests, prophets, and people demand a death sentence, which was the punishment for a false prophet (Deut 18:20); the princes of Judah convene to hear the evidence and render a verdict. Jeremiah's defense is to affirm that he was sent by the Lord; the message he speaks is the Lord's message and thus he does not deserve death. The princes of Judah and the people, who seem to have shifted sides, agree that Jeremiah should not be put to death. Some of the elders support this verdict by citing precedent. Micah had prophesied the destruction of Jerusalem and the temple (Mic 3:12), but the king and the people responded to Micah's prophecy by repenting and so the Lord relented.

26:20-24 The fate of Uriah

The trial of Jeremiah continues with a counterprecedent. Another prophet, Uriah, announced the destruction of Jerusalem and the temple, but he was executed by King Jehoiakim. No further report of the proceedings of the trial is given. The passage ends rather abruptly with the notice that Jeremiah was protected by Ahikam, son of Shaphan who had been an official in King Josiah's court. Though Ahikam's office is never given in the Old Testament, it is possible that he was a high-ranking official of the court.

CONTROVERSIES WITH THE FALSE PROPHETS

Jeremiah 27:1–29:32

These three chapters continue to develop the theme of conflict between true and false prophets (14:13-16; 23:9-40). Prophets speak a message regarding the present behavior of the people and the future consequences of such behavior. As prophets claim to be speaking a message from God, a problem arises when prophets make conflicting claims regarding that message. Jeremiah's message was not simply unpopular, but there were prophets who called its validity into question. In the previous chapter Jeremiah was put on trial for the message he proclaimed. In these three chapters Jeremiah insists that his message is authentic and that the prophets who oppose him are lying.

27:1-22 Serve Babylon or perish

The oracles that comprise this chapter are set in the reign of Zedekiah (597–587 B.C.) and are addressed to the kings of the nations surrounding Israel, to King Zedekiah of Judah, and to the priests and all the people. The point of contention is whether or not the nations, including Judah, should rebel against or submit to Babylon. Jeremiah is insistent in calling for submission to Babylon and thus he comes into conflict with those who foment rebellion, especially other prophets. The yoke that Jeremiah is commanded to wear and then to send to the nations is accompanied by the exhortation to serve Babylon, for this is what the Lord wills. The prophets, diviners, dreamers, soothsayers, and sorcerers of these nations are singled out by Jeremiah as prophesying lies, for they encourage the people not to submit to Babylon. The same message is delivered to King Zedekiah, the priests, and all the people. Only in submission to Babylon will they be spared; rebellion will result in further pilfering of the vessels of the temple and the destruction of the city.

28:1-17 The two yokes

Chapter 28 is linked to chapter 27 by being set in the same year. It also echoes the previous chapter in its reference to yokes, temple vessels, and conflicting prophetic messages regarding submission to Babylon. The dramatic character of the confrontation between prophets is heightened by means of symbolic actions done by both prophets in the presence of an audience. Hananiah announces the return of the temple vessels and of the exiles of 597 B.C. Jeremiah responds with the hope that Hananiah's word will come to pass, but he notes that prophets of the past prophesied war and disaster. According to Jeremiah an announcement of peace is to be trusted only if that word is

fulfilled. Hananiah then takes the wooden yoke from around Jeremiah's neck and breaks it, reiterating his prophecy of liberation from Babylon. In a kind of prophetic one-upmanship, Jeremiah returns the next day with an iron yoke to confirm his message that the Lord wills that Judah and the surrounding nations serve Babylon. Jeremiah follows up his encounter with Hananiah with an oracle specifically directed against Hananiah. It is rare to find an announcement of judgment against an individual in the prophetic books and this announcement is particularly harsh: Hananiah will be dead before the year is up. There is a succinct and sober announcement of the fulfillment of this prophecy that concludes the chapter.

29:1-23 Letter to the exiles in Babylon

Those exiled to Babylon in 597 B.C. were not completely cut off from those who remained in Jerusalem. In spite of the distance between the two groups, letters passed between them, as exemplified by the letters sent by Jeremiah to the leaders of the exiles found in this chapter. The occasion for these letters continues the theme of the preceding chapters: conflicting prophetic messages. Jeremiah opposes those prophets who maintain that the period of exile will be short. In a series of oracles relayed by Jeremiah, the Lord commands the people to settle down in the land of exile since they will be there a long time. After seventy years, Babylon will be dealt with, the Lord will favor the people and will return them to their land. (See comments above on 25:14 regarding seventy years.) Jeremiah's letter includes a harsh judgment against King Zedekiah and those remaining in Jerusalem for their failure to listen to the true prophets. A death sentence is given for two false prophets, Ahab, son of Kolaiah, and Zedekiah, son of Maaseiah, who are accused of adultery as well as prophesying falsely.

29:24-32 The false prophet Shemaiah

Jeremiah responds to a letter Shemaiah sent to the priest Zephaniah demanding that Jeremiah be rebuked and confined in stocks for the letter he sent to the exiles. At contention is the length of the exile, which Jeremiah insists will be long (seventy years). Jeremiah denounces Shemaiah as a false prophet and prophesies that he and his descendants will not see the positive future for the people that the Lord has planned.

ORACLES OF THE RESTORATION OF ISRAEL AND JUDAH

Jeremiah 30:1–35:19

Oracles of salvation have been gathered together in chapters 30–33 of the book of Jeremiah. These chapters are often referred to as "the book of consolation" because of the pervasive note of hope that is present. They give evidence of later additions, but the core of these chapters may have originated with Jeremiah. Some of the oracles are addressed to the exiles of the northern kingdom, but in 30:3 the audience is both Israel and Judah. Thus far the book of Jeremiah has been dominated by severe indictments against the people, followed by announcements of a harsh and relentless judgment. It is not clear why the oracles and narratives of hope have been gathered together and inserted at this point in the book of Jeremiah, but it is a welcome respite in the midst of an overwhelmingly negative message. In chapters 34–35 we return to the more negative side of Jeremiah's message.

30:1-24 The restoration

Jeremiah is commanded by the Lord to write down all his past words, for now the fortunes of the people will change. The judgment of the past will give way to the return from exile and restoration on the land that was given to their ancestors. This action is based entirely on the Lord's initiative. The words of hope for the future are in response to the experience of fear and terror of the people. The day of distress is so great that no other day compares with it, but salvation is coming. As the chapter unfolds, the future promise is set against the necessity of the judgment the people have endured. They have sinned grievously; they deserved their punishment, but the God who judges is also the God who saves. The announcement of hope for the future is the undoing of the judgment of the past. Homes and cities will be rebuilt, fortunes will be restored, the population will increase, the people will be ruled by one of their own, and they will rejoice. Once again they will be known as the Lord's people and the Lord will be their God (30:22). The time of their punishment is at an end, but those who have oppressed them will now experience the Lord's wrath. The final two verses (30:23-24) duplicate 23:19-20, but in the context of chapter 23

the object of the Lord's wrath is Judah. In chapter 30 the wrath of the Lord has already been experienced by Judah, so the object of the Lord's wrath must be the enemies of Judah.

31:1-6 Good news of the return

All the families of Israel are addressed in this oracle of salvation. It draws connections between Israel's past and its future. The wilderness period following upon the time of the exodus becomes a metaphor for the exile, but now the Lord's favor will come upon them. Based on the Lord's love, which is characterized as enduring ("age-old") and constant ("mercy" translates *hesed*, which is a love that is characterized by constancy and fidelity), the promises of the past will be realized in the future. Echoing the terminology associated with Jeremiah's call (31:4-5), the time has come for a reversal of judgment. The Lord will "build" up the people and "plant" the land so that it will produce in abundance. The call to go up to Zion indicates that Jerusalem will be rebuilt and it will become the center of worship for Israel.

31:7-14 The road of return

The hymnic language of this oracle suits its message of hope. It calls for a celebration of the deliverance of those who have been exiled. It is to be proclaimed that the Lord has saved the people by bringing them back, not simply from Babylon, "the land of the north" (31:8), but also from all nations. The gathering of those exiled is inclusive: the blind and lame, pregnant women and those about to give birth (31:8), young and old, men and women (31:13). Though this remnant of the people may weep over what has been lost (31:9), that mourning will be turned into joy (31:13). Israel's return to the land will be a time to rejoice because the Lord will guide them and do so with compassion (31:9, 13). Images of the Lord as father (31:9) and shepherd (31:10) replace the image of the Lord as a wrathful judge. The ransoming of Israel will include the fertility of the land and a return to worship (31:12, 14); it will be a time filled with blessings.

31:15-20 End of Rachel's mourning

The mourning of both Rachel (31:15) and Ephraim (31:18-19) at the devastating effects of the judgment against Israel receives a response from the Lord (31:16-17, 20-22). Rachel personifies all the mothers of Israel who grieve over the loss of their children and the loss of the future represented by those children (31:17). Ephraim personifies Rachel's children through Joseph, but probably represents Israel as a whole. Ephraim was one of the major tribes of Israel and it is used often as a synonym for Israel itself (e.g., Hos 5:3, 9). Ephraim's grief is caused by the destruction of Israel, but he acknowledges that the punishment was deserved. He confesses his guilt and repents. To both Rachel and Ephraim the Lord announces a word of hope. Rachel should be comforted, for her children are not wholly lost; they will return from exile. Ephraim/Israel is still the Lord's favored son in whom the Lord delights. The Lord's love remains constant even when forced to punish a disobedient child. The Lord's remembrance of this child is assured and leads to compassion.

31:21-30 Summons to return home

Israel is called upon to begin the journey home (31:21-22). The time for hesitation and rebellion is past, for the Lord is creating a new thing. Only God is the subject of the verb "create" (*bārā'*) in the Old Testament; it is the same term that is used in the opening chapters of Genesis (Gen 1:1). The "new" thing that the Lord is about to do is thus placed on a par with the very act of creation at the beginning of time. It is difficult, however, to determine exactly what that "new" thing is, as the translation of the last phrase in verse 22 is uncertain. It may refer to a new kind of relationship between Israel (the woman) and the Lord (the man), but it may also simply be a reference to the embrace between a man and a woman that results in the conception of a child. The citing of this proverbial statement may then point to the repopulation of Israel in the future.

The next three oracles (31:23-26, 27-28, 29-30) refer to aspects of the restoration to the land. When the fortunes of the people are restored, the people will again refer to the Lord's blessing as a greeting; city folk, farmers, and shepherds, groups often in conflict will dwell in peace; and the Lord will renew the faint and weary (31:23-25). Verse 26 suggests that the content of this oracle was received in a pleasant dream presumably by Jeremiah. The next oracle announces the restoration of both people and animals to the land in language drawn from the call of Jeremiah (1:10). As the Lord "watched" over the word (1:12) to bring

about judgment, so now God is "watching" over the word to bring salvation. The final oracle of this section includes a proverb that Jeremiah says will no longer apply. The proverb, "The parents ate unripe grapes, / and the children's teeth are set on edge" (31:29), has a fatalistic overtone, for it maintains every generation will suffer for the actions of the previous generation. That this proverb will no longer apply in the days to come is often interpreted as an introduction of individualistic judgment into Israel, but it is more likely that it simply means each generation will bear the consequences of its own actions.

31:31-34 The new covenant

The short oracle concerning the new covenant has had a considerable impact on the Dead Sea community, the New Testament (Luke 22:20; 1 Cor 11:25; 2 Cor 3:5-14; Heb 8:8-12; 10:16-17), and later Christian theology. It is tempting to read later theological development back into this passage, but here the focus will be on its meaning in its historical and literary context. Its immediate context is the announcement of the Lord's new salvific action on behalf of the people: God will bring them home from exile. This act of salvation is seen as a major event in Israel's history, an event as fundamental as the exodus, and it will issue in a new covenant. The repopulation of the land (31:27-28) and the rebuilding of Jerusalem (31:38-40) are part and parcel of the return from exile. Thus this new covenant is not spiritualized or universalized but is grounded in the Lord's actions on behalf of the people at this time in their history and these actions will define their future. In spite of their unfaithfulness in the past, Israel's relationship to the Lord has never ceased. They are still "my people" and the Lord is "their God," but now they will be the Lord's people in a new way. The law remains, even in this new covenant, as an identifying characteristic of this people, but that law will no longer exist as an external reality; it will be "in the heart." The people will no longer need to be taught the law, as it will be a part of their being. Because the law is within, all will know the Lord. That "all know the Lord" renders obsolete distinctions between people: "Everyone, from least to greatest," will know the Lord (31:34). Furthermore, integral to this new covenant is that the Lord will forgive the iniquity of the people. Israel's history of sinfulness will be forgotten; it will be left in the past and play no role in the new covenant relationship between the Lord and the people. Knowledge of the Lord and forgiveness are constituent parts of the new covenant.

31:35-37 Certainty of God's promise

The focus of much of the book of Jeremiah is the Lord's actions in Israel's life as a nation, but now the prophet turns to nature to underscore the enduring character of the Lord's relationship to Israel. The Lord is identified as the creator and then, in two "if-then" sentences, impossible situations are imagined: the collapse of the fixed order of the world and measurability of the universe. Even if these impossibilities come to pass, never will Israel and its offspring cease to be the Lord's people. The faithfulness of the Lord and commitment to the people in spite of their sin provide a counterbalance to the many oracles of judgment throughout the book of Jeremiah.

31:38-40 Jerusalem rebuilt

The focus of the last verses of this chapter is the city of Jerusalem. It will be rebuilt and enlarged as the Lord's city, but no temple is mentioned. Valleys and slopes previously contaminated by corpses and ashes will be rendered holy. Remarkably, an unconditional assurance is given that the city will never again be uprooted or demolished.

32:1-44 Pledge of restoration

Hope for the future continues to be the dominant theme as we move from poetic oracles of chapters 30–31 to prose narratives in chapters 32–33. The siege of Jerusalem has begun and Jeremiah has been confined in the "court of the guard," possibly as a result of his arrest for desertion when he attempted to leave Jerusalem to take care of family property in Benjamin (37:11-21). This confinement did allow for some freedom. The message of hope is concretized in a symbolic act that Jeremiah has been commanded by the Lord to perform: he is to purchase a field belonging to a relative. King Zedekiah raised the question of why Jeremiah prophesies as he does against the king and the city. Rather than answer the question directly, Jeremiah is commanded by the Lord to purchase the field in Anathoth, his hometown, and the response to Zedekiah's question comes later in the Lord's response to

Jeremiah's prayer (32:26-44): Jeremiah's message of judgment is the Lord's response to the sinfulness of the people. The significance of Jeremiah's purchase is stipulated in verse 15. What Jeremiah has done testifies to a future beyond the time of destruction when life will return to normal and Israel will once again possess the land.

Jeremiah lifts his voice in prayer recalling the Lord's wondrous deeds in creation and exodus, and God's enduring love. Jeremiah acknowledges that now the Lord has brought judgment against the people. He wonders if the hope for the future symbolized by the purchase of the field has any meaning when the city has already been handed over to the Babylonians (32:16-25). The Lord's answer balances the actions as judge against the people for their infidelity with the refusal to completely abandon the people. The Lord's relationship with Israel will continue, but now that relationship is defined as an everlasting covenant realized in the return of Israel from exile and their restoration in the land (32:26-44). The message of hope symbolized by the purchase of a field is given vivid expression by a God who envisions a future in which God delights in the people and never ceases doing good for them.

33:1-26 Restoration of Jerusalem

These oracles from Jeremiah are linked to the previous chapter, not only by being set in the same historical context, but they also carry forward the same themes of restoration and renewal while presenting them in greater detail. Verses 1-13 are filled with words of promise for the city and its people. The future will reverse the punishment that has decimated the land. There is a piling up of verbs referring to the Lord's actions: "heal," "reveal . . . lasting peace," "restore," "rebuild," "purify," "forgive" (33:6-8)—all images pointing to a glorious restoration. As before, notions of the Lord both as creator (33:2) and savior (33:6ff.) are brought together: the one who creates is the one who saves. This restoration, teeming with abundance, is a source of joy to the Lord and it is an expression of enduring love for the people. The exuberant rejoicing upon restoration is conveyed again by the piling up of songs: "of joy," "of gladness," "of the bridegroom," "of the bride," and "of those bringing thank offerings" (33:11). The second half of the chapter (33:14-26) shifts the focus of promise to the royal and priestly leaders of the land and its people. This section is missing from the LXX and so may represent a later addition to the book of Jeremiah. It begins with the promise of a just and righteous king from the line of David, a passage (33:15-16) that is virtually identical to 23:5-6, but this restatement includes the promise that the Davidic dynasty will never end and the Levitical priests will always stand before the Lord, offering sacrifices. The enduring nature of dynasty and priesthood is grounded in the Lord's enduring covenant with day and night. This may be a reference to the covenant with Noah wherein the Lord guaranteed the order of the universe (Gen 8:21-22; 9:8-17). The passage draws to a close, connecting the permanence of the order of creation with the permanence of the relationship between the Lord and the people. In seeing these promises become reality, the nations who held Israel in contempt will now witness to the Lord's enduring love and mercy.

34:1-7 Fate of Zedekiah

In the midst of oracles of salvation there is a reiteration of the judgment against King Zedekiah similar to that found in 32:1-5. It is, however, difficult to reconcile verses 2-3, a prophecy of the capture and exile of Zedekiah, with the more positive note regarding his death and burial in verses 4-5. Zedekiah was captured, blinded, exiled, and died in prison (52:9-11; 2 Kgs 25:1-7). The details of the prophecy should not be pressed too far, for in general it came to pass.

34:8-22 The pact broken

This story of the unfaithfulness of the citizens of Jerusalem followed by an indictment and judgment stands in contrast to the story in chapter 35 concerning the faithfulness of the Rechabites who receive a promise that their line will never end. In the oracles of Jeremiah the people have been frequently condemned for their unfaithfulness and this story functions as a concrete example of their fickle nature. The people bind themselves in a covenant with King Zedekiah to release their slaves, only to take them back into slavery later. Breaking this covenant is symptomatic of breaking the Lord's covenant. It may be that "freeing the slaves" was a belated attempt by the people to obey the laws of the Lord in the hopes that by their action they could stave off the destruction of the city. However, when the Babylonians

seemed to have abandoned their siege of Jerusalem, the people were no longer motivated to keep the law and took back their slaves. There is no exact parallel to the freeing of all slaves in the law as requested by the king, but Deuteronomy 15:1-11 speaks of the release of slaves who have been in bondage for six years. It may be that this law had not been kept and King Zedekiah endorses freeing all slaves as a way to "catch up" on the law. The Lord affirms that the people did what was right in freeing their slaves (34:15), but their short-lived obedience betrays the lack of fidelity that has been characteristic of Israel throughout its history. The oracle brings in a reference to exodus and covenant (34:13-14). In the exodus the Lord brings freedom to those who were enslaved; in the covenant the Lord is bound in faithful love (*hesed*) to Israel and Israel binds itself to the Lord in love and obedience. Against this history the true horror of the people's actions stands out: they enslave others and in doing so profane the name of the Lord (34:16), a God who is known for the liberation of slaves. The judgment against them fits their crime. They will not "release" their slaves, so they will be "released" to the "sword, starvation, and disease" (34:17); they "passed over" the covenant, so they will be cut apart as the animal they "passed through" was cut apart. The reference here is to part of the ritual that ratified the covenant (Gen 15:7-21). The judgment against the people is that the Babylonian army will return and lay siege again to the city, but this time the army will not leave until the city is destroyed.

35:1-19 The faithful Rechabites

The previous chapters were set in the time of King Zedekiah, but this chapter brings us back ten years earlier to the reign of King Jehoiakim. Though out of chronological sequence, Jeremiah's interaction with the Rechabites is probably placed here to draw a contrast between the unfaithfulness of the citizens of Jerusalem to the Lord's laws and the faithfulness of the Rechabites to the customs established by their founder, Jehonadab. Our knowledge of the Rechabites rests upon only a few passages of the Old Testament: 2 Kings 10:15-17; Jeremiah 35; 1 Chronicles 2:55; and possibly 1 Chronicles 4:11-12 if one accepts the LXX reading of Rechab for Recah of the Hebrew version. A son of Rechab, Jehonadab, called Jonadab in the book of Jeremiah, is presented as a supporter of the rebellion of Jehu, commander of the Israelite army (2 Kgs 10:15-17). Jehu is characterized as a religious zealot; Jehonadab rides in Jehu's chariot in support of Jehu who in a gruesome display of his "zeal for the Lord" has Baal worshipers burned to death in the course of ridding Israel of Baal worship (2 Kgs 10:15-28). Most of our information regarding the Rechabites comes from chapter 35 of the book of Jeremiah. Jonadab prohibited his community from drinking wine, building homes to live in, and owning vineyards or fields or crops. It has been suggested that this lifestyle represents a nomadic ideal whose adherents refused to adopt customs associated with settling in the land, but there is no evidence that such an ideal ever existed. The refusal of the Rechabites to drink wine, live in houses, and engage in agricultural pursuits fits with the lifestyle of ancient metallurgists. Their association with the Kenites (1 Chr 2:55), a tribe whose eponymous ancestor was Cain and whose descendants are noted for working with metal (Gen 4:22), suggests that their lifestyle grew out of the demands of their profession and not out of a nomadic ideal.

Jeremiah is commanded by the Lord to test the resolve of the Rechabites by inviting them to the temple and offering them wine. Their refusal to violate the commands given by their founder becomes an example of fidelity over against the infidelity of Israel. The Rechabites listen/obey (35:8, 10, 14), but Jeremiah's audience does not listen/obey (35:13, 14, 15, 16, 17) in spite of the many warnings they had received through the prophets. A final contrast between the citizens of Judah and Jerusalem and the Rechabites is drawn at the end of the chapter. Judah and Jerusalem stand under judgment, but the Rechabites will survive the destruction of the country. In language reminiscent of the promise given to David and the priestly families, the Rechabites will not "fail [to have] a descendant" (35:19); for all time they will stand in the presence of the Lord.

JEREMIAH AND THE FALL OF JERUSALEM
Jeremiah 36:1–45:5

These chapters continue with narratives reflecting upon the life of Jeremiah, but they focus on the suffering that Jeremiah endured as a prophet. Elements of hope come to the fore (39:15-18; 40:7-12; 42:9-12; 45:5), but they are overshadowed by the imprisonment of Jeremiah and an attempt on his life. Traditionally, Baruch has been identified as the author of these chapters, but there is no evidence to support or refute this claim.

36:1-32 Baruch, the scribe of Jeremiah
The dictation of Jeremiah's oracles to Baruch is set in 605 B.C., when Nebuchadnezzar defeated Egypt at Carchemish. The threat that the Babylonian army posed to Judah may be behind the proclamation of a fast in verse 9, but the focus of the chapter is on the response of King Jehoiakim to the reading of the scroll that Jeremiah had dictated to Baruch and commanded him to read to the people in the temple. Upon hearing the words of the scroll, court officials insist that the scroll be brought before the king, but they also advise Baruch and Jeremiah to go into hiding. King Jehoiakim destroyed the scroll by burning pieces of it as it was read to him. His rejection of Jeremiah's message is given dramatic representation and there is a note of finality in his burning of the scroll. The hope that the people would repent (36:3, 7) is closed off by the actions of the king. Jeremiah is commanded to dictate another scroll, perhaps signifying that the king's actions cannot silence the word of the Lord.

Of particular interest in this chapter are the insights it gives us into the role of scribes, the production of scrolls, and the development of prophetic books. There is considerable debate regarding the relationship of the second scroll that Jeremiah dictated and the book of Jeremiah itself. Many scholars hold that chapters 1–25 contain the contents of the second scroll in some form.

37:1-21 Jeremiah in the dungeon
This episode is the first of three encounters between Jeremiah and King Zedekiah after the Babylonian siege of Jerusalem had begun in 587 B.C. When the Egyptian army set out, possibly to come to the aid of Jerusalem, the Babylonian army withdrew from its assault on Jerusalem to engage the Egyptian army. It is not clear why King Zedekiah appeals to Jeremiah for prayers, for the king does not listen to Jeremiah, nor indeed does anyone else in Jerusalem (37:2). Jeremiah's response to the king underscores that the lull in the

siege is not a sign of hope. The Babylonian army will return and destroy the city, even if only wounded soldiers are all that remain of their army. During the lull in fighting Jeremiah leaves the city to deal with family property in Benjamin and is arrested for treason, beaten, and imprisoned. King Zedekiah secretly sent for Jeremiah, requesting a word from the Lord. The king may have been hoping for a positive message, but Jeremiah reiterates the Lord's earlier judgment against the city. Jeremiah asks the king not to be sent back to where he was held in custody and the king grants his request. Jeremiah will remain in the court of the guard until the Babylonians take the city.

38:1-28 Jeremiah in the muddy cistern

Even though confined, Jeremiah finds an audience for his announcement of judgment against the city of Jerusalem. He insists that only those who leave the city and surrender to the Babylonians will be spared; those who remain in the city will die. Because Jeremiah's message of doom is undermining the resolve of Judah's army, the princes of Judah demand Jeremiah's execution. King Zedekiah hands Jeremiah over to them and they throw Jeremiah into an empty cistern, presumably to starve him to death. The indecisiveness of King Zedekiah is underscored by his capitulation to their demand only to be persuaded by Ebed-melech, an Ethiopian who was a royal official or servant to the king, to have Jeremiah rescued and returned to the court of the guard. King Zedekiah again meets Jeremiah secretly, and again Jeremiah reiterates his message that the only way the city and its people will be spared is if they surrender to the Babylonians. This message applies to the king and his family as well. The weakness of King Zedekiah is apparent in his fear of what will happen to him if he surrenders and in his fear of what the princes of Judah will do if they find out about his meeting with Jeremiah. The princes do find out, but Jeremiah lies to them as he had been advised by the king. It cannot be denied that Jeremiah lies, but given the situation in which he found himself, it is understandable. He opted to protect both the king and himself.

39:1-10 The capture of Jerusalem

The harsh judgment repeatedly announced by Jeremiah comes to pass with the capture and de-struction of the city of Jerusalem, the arrest of King Zedekiah, the execution of his sons and other Judean nobles, and the blinding and exile of King Zedekiah. That verses 4-13 of this chapter are not found in the LXX suggests that this brief history of the last days of Jerusalem was incorporated into the book of Jeremiah. It has been drawn from 52:4-16 and its purpose seems to be not only to confirm the validity of Jeremiah's prophetic word but also to provide the context for the stories that follow.

39:11-14 Jeremiah released to Gedaliah's custody

Jeremiah is released from prison by the captain of the bodyguard at the orders of Nebuchadnezzar, king of Babylon, and entrusted into the hands of Gedaliah. A different version of the release of Jeremiah is found in 40:1-6, but that is probably a variant of this tradition rather than a reference to a later imprisonment and release. There is no explicit reason given for the kindness shown to Jeremiah, but it is likely that Babylonian officials were aware of Jeremiah's pro-Babylonian stance.

39:15-18 A word of comfort for Ebed-melech

Jeremiah announces a word of salvation to Ebed-melech. Though he will see the destruction of Jerusalem, his life will be spared because he trusted in the Lord. No mention is made of Ebed-melech's rescue of Jeremiah (38:7-13). It is not clear why this word of comfort is not attached to the story of chapter 38; it may be here because its fulfillment is at hand.

40:1-12 Jeremiah still in Judah

In this alternate version (cf. 38:11-14) of the fate of Jeremiah after Jerusalem was destroyed, he was taken in chains to Ramah with other exiles, but then was given the choice to go to Babylon, to go wherever he wanted, or to go to Gedaliah, son of Ahikam, who had been appointed governor by the Babylonian king. That Jeremiah chooses to go to Gedaliah in Mizpah, and so remain in Judah, is surprising, for he had prophesied that the future of Israel rests with the remnant that has gone into exile (24:4-7; 29:5-7).

The early days of Gedaliah's governorship appear to go well. When he is met by the military leaders of Judah and their troops, he advises them to return to their lands and harvest their crops, which they do. In the days that follow, peace and abundance seem to have returned to the land of Judah.

40:13–41:10 Assassination of Gedaliah

The rival pro- and anti-Babylonian factions that dominated Judean politics before the fall of Jerusalem did not disappear after the Babylonians destroyed the city. Many accepted Gedaliah's policy of accommodation to Babylonian rule, but others refused to submit. Johanan made Gedaliah aware of a plot against his life that was instigated by the Ammonite king, Baalis, but was to be carried out by Ishmael, a member of the royal line of David (41:1). Gedaliah refuses to take action against Ishmael, and when Ishmael and ten of his men come to him, Gedaliah takes no precautions to protect his life. Ishmael and his forces assassinate Gedaliah, but they also kill Judahites of military age and the Babylonian soldiers at the outpost. The killing spree continues the next day as Ishmael and his men slaughter men from the north who were coming to Mizpah to offer grain offerings and incense. Only men who have hidden provisions to offer as barter for their lives are spared. Ishmael then captures the rest of the people at Mizpah and brings them to Ammon, whose king had supported his rebellion.

41:11–43:7 Flight to Egypt

When Johanan, who had warned Gedaliah of the assassination plot, hears of Ishmael's insurrection, he and those with him confront Ishmael. The captives that had been taken by Ishmael welcome Johanan and join with him. Ishmael and eight of his men escape, never to be heard from again. Johanan and the people with him are afraid of Babylonian reprisals, so they do not return to Mizpah but head for Egypt. Only at this time does Jeremiah return to center stage. The people seek a word of the Lord from Jeremiah regarding the direction the community should take and they vow to follow that word. The first part of the word from the Lord (42:9-12) is consistent with the message that Jeremiah has repeatedly given: if they settle down and submit to Babylon, all will go well for them in the land. The second part of the Lord's word (42:13-17) is an emphatic warning not to go to Egypt, for "sword, famine, and disease" will follow them and they shall die in a

foreign land. The Lord's word is reiterated by Jeremiah in 42:19-22. Underlying the harsh punishment upon those who would go to Egypt is a theological perspective that sees their journey to Egypt as a reversal of the exodus and thus a rejection of the Lord's greatest salvific act on their behalf. Their rejection of Jeremiah's word is surprising in light of their vow to obey whether they agree with the word or not (43:5-6), but it is not surprising in light of the many affirmations throughout the book of Jeremiah that the people time and again refuse to listen to and obey the Lord. It is not clear why Baruch is blamed for inciting Jeremiah against the people, for Jeremiah's position is consistent with his prophetic message. Jeremiah and Baruch will go to Egypt, but it is assumed that they were taken against their will, even though this is not explicitly stated.

43:8–44:30 Jeremiah in Egypt

Even in Egypt Jeremiah continues to function as prophet. He is commanded to perform a final symbolic act; he is to place stones in mortar at the entrance of Pharaoh's house in Tahpanhes. This action is done to affirm the dominance of Babylon, for upon the stones Nebuchadnezzar will place his throne, symbolizing that the Babylonian Empire will rule over Egypt. The last public words of Jeremiah delivered to the Judeans in Egypt are consistent with the prophetic message that he has proclaimed throughout his life. After rehearsing the history of Israel's persistence in the worship of other gods and the judgment visited upon them on that account, Jeremiah raises a series of questions that underscore that even now as refugees in a foreign land the people provoke the Lord's anger by continuing to worship other gods. They have learned nothing from the destruction of Jerusalem and their temple. As before, their sin calls forth punishment, but there will be no remnant left and thus no future for this community of Judeans in Egypt. The Judeans reject Jeremiah's word and insist that they will return to the worship of the Queen of Heaven. They believe their present suffering is the result of abandoning the worship of this goddess, but Jeremiah disagrees. Jeremiah's response is to reiterate the Lord's judgment against them. That all the Judahites in Egypt will be destroyed (44:27) may be hyperbole, for it is countered in the very next verse by a reference to a few who will escape (44:28).

45:1-5 A message to Baruch

The delivery of a message of hope to Baruch is set in the fourth year of the reign of Jehoiakim (605 B.C.), but the basis for Baruch's grief at that time is not clear. Baruch will see the destruction of Jerusalem in 587 B.C. and a few months later he was uprooted from his homeland (43:6); both experiences may provide the basis for his cry of lament in verses 3-4. It is not clear what "great things" Baruch was seeking (45:5). It is unlikely that the Lord is referring to self-serving ambition on Baruch's part; it is more likely that Baruch harbored the hope that through Jeremiah's prophecy and his service to Jeremiah Jerusalem will not be destroyed. The Lord affirms in language drawn from the call of Jeremiah (1:10) that the time of "tearing down" and "uprooting" has come (45:4), but guarantees that Baruch's life will be spared. A similar promise was made to Ebed-melech in 39:18.

ORACLES AGAINST THE NATIONS

Jeremiah 46:1–51:64

The oracles in this section are traditionally called "oracles against the nations" and we find similar oracles in other prophetic books, for example, Isaiah 13–23; Ezekiel 25–32; Amos 1:1–2:3; Nahum; and Obadiah. The origin of oracles against the nations is unknown, but they are linked to the holy war tradition by language and themes. It is doubtful that Jeremiah is the author of these oracles against the nations. The heading (45:1) sets them apart as a separate collection, as does the fact that they have a different placement in the Hebrew text of Jeremiah (chs. 46–51) than in the LXX (after 25:13a). Also it is difficult to reconcile the harsh tone of the oracles against Babylon (chs. 50–51) with Jeremiah's pro-Babylonian stance. These oracles link Jeremiah, who is not presented in the book as prophesying to the nations, to his call to be a "prophet to the nations" (1:5, 10).

The oracles against the nations of chapters 46–49 are distinct from those of chapters 50–51. In the first set of oracles divine judgment is mediated through Babylon against various nations, but in chapters 50–51 Babylon is judged by the other nations. The oracles against Babylon are considerably longer than the oracles of chapters 46–49. The

dating of the oracles from the fourth year of Jehoiakim (605 B.C.; 46:2) to the fourth year of Zedekiah (593 B.C.) provides a suitable context for these oracles, but a preexilic date for the oracles against Babylon (chs. 50–51) is unlikely in view of the pro-Babylonian stance taken by Jeremiah. The judgment against the nations is not because of idolatry; rather it is because of their crimes against other nations and their arrogance. These oracles against the nations do not just announce judgment against the nations but also allow for the restoration of fortunes of these nations after the time of judgment.

46:2-28 Against Egypt

Two oracles against Egypt dominate this section, verses 2-12 and 13-26, though verses 24-26 may constitute a separate oracle. A short final oracle, directly addressed to Israel (46:27-28), concludes the chapter. The first oracle against Egypt is put in the context of the defeat of Egyptian forces at Carchemish in 605 B.C.; the second envisions a later invasion of Egypt that is about to begin or has already begun. In both oracles vivid metaphors concretize the preparation for war and the horror of the experience of war. The war itself is seen as the Lord's judgment upon Egypt, which stands as helpless as Judah in the face of the Lord's vengeance. The final oracle (46:27-28) is virtually identical to 30:10-11 and intrudes into the oracles against the nations with a message of hope for Israel. Israel itself has been judged and exiled, but the judgment against Egypt will open the way for the future restoration of Israel. Israel should not fear, for the Lord is at work in the affairs of the nations to effect what is desired for the people. It was never the Lord's purpose to bring the people to an end but only to punish them for a time, as justice demanded.

47:1-7 Against the Philistines

The opening statement sets this oracle against the Philistines before an attack upon Gaza by a pharaoh, but this verse is missing from the LXX. Pharaoh Neco II led a series of campaigns into the region in 609 B.C., but references to waters "rising from the north" (47:2) and the destruction of Ashkelon (47:5, 7) suggest Babylonian rather than Egyptian involvement. The Babylonian army under Nebuchadnezzar destroyed Ashkelon in 604 B.C. There is no indictment against Philistia in this oracle; there is only a description of the people's reaction to the horrors wrought by an invading army. The Lord is behind this invasion (47:4, 7). There is a certain poignancy that finds expression in questions such as, "[H]ow long?" and "When will you [the sword] find rest?" (47:5, 6). It may be the prophet's voice that comes to the fore asking the sword of the Lord to cease (47:6), even while recognizing that it cannot rest until the Lord commands it (47:7).

48:1-47 Against Moab

There is no superscription that sets these oracles against Moab within a historical context, but the advance of the Babylonian army into the region in the late seventh and early sixth centuries B.C. may be in the background. Moab shared kinship with Israel (Gen 19:37-38), but little is made of that relationship. The focus of these oracles is on the suffering experienced by the Moabites because armies have ravaged its land. The chapter is remarkable in its length and in the language of mourning that is interspersed throughout the oracles. Moab's failings, especially its pride and arrogance (48:7, 14, 26, 29-30, 42), receive some attention, but it is the vivid portrayal of devastation and desolation accompanied by weeping and wailing that pervades the chapter. It is not only Moab that mourns but also its neighbors and even the Lord (48:31-32, 36). The description of Moab's suffering and the mournful tone of the chapter evoke sympathy for its people rather than a vindictive satisfaction in the judgment meted out to them. The oracle ends with the announcement of the restoration of Moab's fortunes.

49:1-6 Against the Ammonites

The Ammonites also shared kinship with the Israelites (Gen 19:38), but there was an ongoing antagonism between these two groups that is evidenced frequently in the Old Testament (e.g., Judg 10–11; 2 Sam 10). The opening verses of this passage allude to a territorial dispute between Israel's tribe of Gad and Ammon as the basis for judgment against Ammon. The Ammonites' reliance on their strength and wealth (49:4) will not prevent their destruction when the Lord's judgment comes upon them (49:5). The destruction of Ammon will be followed by exile; even Ammon's god, Milcom, will go into exile, taking Ammon's leaders with him. This oracle also ends on a posi-

tive note with the restoration of the fortunes of Ammon (49:6).

49:7-22 Against Edom

The absence of a tone of lament from this oracle against Edom may be explained as the result of the frequent and often bitter antagonism between Israel and Edom. Edom is often the object of prophetic denunciations (Isa 34:1-17; 63:1-6; Lam 4:21-22; Ezek 25:12-14; 35:1-15; Amos 1:11-12; Obad; Mal 1:2-5). There are similarities between this oracle and the book of Obadiah (49:9-10a with Obad 5-6; and 49:14-16 with Obad 1-4), but this may be due to the reliance upon a common source rather than direct borrowing of one upon the other. Verses 18-21 are virtually identical to 50:40, 44-46 of the oracle against Babylon and there are marked similarities between what is said of Moab in 48:41-44 and of Edom in 49:22. These parallels suggest that there were stock phrases used in oracles against the nations. There are no historical references in the oracle; rather there is a collage of images assembled to vividly display the destruction of Edom without this destruction being anchored in time. Edom was noted for its wisdom (49:7), but that is now gone as it is judged for its pride. A reference to the incomparability of the Lord stands out in the midst of this judgment against Edom, but it is typical of Israel's prophets to present the Lord as in control of history.

49:23-27 Against Damascus

Damascus, as the capital of Syria, stands in for the nation itself. Syria and Israel were often at war prior to 721 B.C., but their enmity receded into the background after the northern kingdom was destroyed. The inclusion of Syria among these oracles may be due to the help given to Nebuchadnezzar by the Syrian armies when he invaded Jerusalem and Judah in 597 B.C. (35:11), but there is no information in the oracle to locate it as a response to a particular historical situation. The oracle focuses on Syria's fear and distress at the abandonment of its once glorious city and the destruction of its warriors, but no reason is given for the judgment against Syria.

49:28-33 Against Arabia

Little is known of the Arabian tribes located south and east of Canaan. Kedar was noted for its commerce and its people were desert-dwellers, but Hazor, not to be confused with the city in Palestine, is unknown. There is no antipathy against these people expressed here or in the rest of the Old Testament. The reason for judgment against them is perhaps alluded to in verse 31, but it is not clear that there is anything wrong with being a "tranquil nation, living in security," being "[w]ithout gates or bars" and "dwelling alone." It may be that such a description suggests complacency and arrogance. Nebuchadnezzar is explicitly mentioned and it is known that he subjugated the Arabian tribes. The Lord addresses both the Babylonian armies and the people whom they will attack. The Babylonians are commanded to attack and plunder Kedar and Hazor; the people of these tribes are warned to flee. The severity of this judgment is indicated by Hazor becoming "a haunt for jackals" and "a wasteland forever" (49:33).

49:34-39 Against Elam

Unlike the other oracles against the nations, the oracle against Elam is dated; it is set at the beginning of the reign of Zedekiah (49:34). It differs from the other oracles against the nations in other ways as well. There are no direct addresses either to enemies or to the Elamites. Other than Elam there are no place names and there are no references to life in Elam. No one laments; indeed, nothing is said of the actions of anyone other than the Lord. There is no reason given for the announcement of judgment against Elam; the judgment alone dominates the oracle. The subject of each verb is the Lord, as a series of calamities against Elam is announced in terms that echo similar judgments in the book of Jeremiah. The conclusion rather surprisingly makes a brief announcement that the fortunes of Elam will be restored at the end of time.

50:1-46 The first oracle against Babylon

Oracles against Babylon bring the section on the oracles against the nations to a close. These oracles are considerably longer than the others, suggesting the dominance of Babylon in Judah's last days and the importance of the defeat of Babylon for the restoration of the exiles to their land. This first oracle gives a vivid description of the destruction of Babylon, drawing much of its language and imagery from other oracles against the nations. The overriding reason given for Baby-

lon's demise is its arrogance in challenging the Lord (50:24, 31-32). Babylon was the mediator of the Lord's judgment, but it went beyond what the Lord required of it by its brutality against the land of Judah and its people. The destruction of Babylon is linked to a proclamation of hope for the exiles. With the land of their oppressor in ruins the exiles are free to return home.

51:1-58 The second oracle against Babylon

The forcefulness of this second oracle is found in its lengthy description of the total devastation that will be visited upon Babylon. Images of destruction wrought by war dominate, but the unrelenting announcement of judgment is punctuated by a concern for the exiles. Assurance is given that the Lord's people will be vindicated (51:5-6, 10, 11b, 24, 36) because Israel is the Lord's own "portion"/"tribe" (51:18-19). The power of the Lord to carry out the punishment of Babylon is affirmed, for it is God who rules over all of creation (51:14-16, 19).

51:59-64 The prophecy sent to Babylon

Jeremiah's commission to Seraiah is set in the fourth year of King Zedekiah's reign and brings the oracles against Babylon to conclusion. Seraiah is to read a scroll written by Jeremiah announcing judgment against Babylon and then he is to throw the scroll into the Euphrates, symbolizing that Babylon will never rise again.

HISTORICAL APPENDIX
Jeremiah 52:1-34

A shorter version of the destruction of Jerusalem and the capture of King Zedekiah is found in 39:1-10. This longer version is taken from 2 Kings 24:18–25:30 with minor changes. The chapter brings to a close the book of Jeremiah showing the fulfillment of the words of judgment from Jeremiah; Jeremiah's message of hope awaits fulfillment in the future.

52:1-11 Capture of Jerusalem

The punishment of the city of Jerusalem and its kings is the main focus of chapter 52. Typical of the theological perspective of the books of Kings and also of the book of Jeremiah, the disaster is blamed on the evil actions of both king and people. The siege of the city by the Babylonians lasted eighteen months (January 588 B.C.–August 587 B.C.) and resulted in widespread starvation. King Zedekiah and his army escaped but were caught near Jericho by the Babylonian army. The army fled, but the king was forced to see his sons and officers executed. He was blinded, brought to Babylon, and imprisoned for life.

52:12-30 Destruction of Jerusalem

It is not clear why a month passed before the Babylonian army burned down Jerusalem's houses and large buildings, including the temple and palace, and tore down the city walls. Among those exiled were deserters and artisans, but some of the poor were left behind to tend the land. Temple furnishings were broken into pieces and its vessels were carried into exile. References to additional executions and the numbers of those deported bring to a close the Babylonian destruction and decimation of the kingdom of Judah.

52:31-34 Favor shown to Jehoiachin

The final verses, drawn from 2 Kings 25:27-30, take place in the year 561/560 B.C. King Jehoiachin, Zedekiah's predecessor, had been exiled and imprisoned in 597 B.C. (2 Kgs 24:15), but he is now released from prison. He is not allowed to return to Jerusalem, but he enjoys a position of privilege in relation to other exiled kings. He is given new clothes and provisions at the king's table, presumably as signs of his elevated status. Though King Jehoiachin will never return from exile and rule over his people, this final notice is often seen as a sign of hope for the future.

THE BOOK OF

LAMENTATIONS

Irene Nowell, O.S.B.

INTRODUCTION

See "The Festival Scrolls" on page 254.

Name and authorship

In the Hebrew Bible this book is called *Eykah* from the first word of chapters 1, 2, and 4. *Eykah*, an exclamation of astonishment ("how!"), captures the tone. In the Talmud and other early Jewish works it is called *Qinot*, "Lamentations." This title is reflected also in the Greek and Latin translations. Greek and Latin manuscripts also identify Jeremiah as the author, although this late attribution is more symbolic than factual. Jeremiah, who weeps over the impending destruction and exile (Jer 8:23; 9:9, 16, 19), is the "patron saint" of lamenters.

Date and historical background

Both the content and the traditional identification with Jeremiah have associated this book with the destruction of Jerusalem by the Babylonians in 587 B.C. The Septuagint introduces the book thus: "After Israel was taken captive and Jerusalem made desolate, Jeremiah sat weeping and lamenting this lamentation over Jerusalem." Following this tradition, the writing would have been sometime in the sixth century. The style of language is similar to other writers of this period, such as Jeremiah and Ezekiel. There are no specific indications in the content, however, that suggest which tragedy is being lamented. Thus these poems have been applied to many disasters throughout the millennia.

Liturgical use

In the Jewish tradition the book of Lamentations is read on the ninth of Ab to commemorate several tragedies (see introduction to the Festival Scrolls on pages 425–26). Solomon's temple fell to the Babylonians sometime between the seventh and tenth of Ab (see 2 Kgs 25:8-9; Jer 52:12), and the second temple fell to the Romans on the ninth of Ab in A.D. 70. In Christian tradition Lamentations is often used during the Triduum (Holy Thursday to Holy Saturday).

Literary artistry

The five poems in this collection represent both the dirge (chs. 1, 2, 4) and the lament (chs. 3, 5). The dirge, a funeral song, often reports the cry of the mourners, the proclamation of death, and the reaction of the bystanders. The individual lament (ch. 3) usually begins with a cry to God, continues with some of these elements—a description of distress, a plea for help, a demand for vengeance, an attempt to persuade God—and ends with a turn to hope (see, for example, Pss 3; 5; 6). The communal lament contains some of the same elements but is the community's response to a national disaster (see, for example, Pss 74; 79).

Each of these poems is based on the alphabet. The first four are true acrostics. In chapters 1, 2, and 4 the first letter of each three-line verse spells out the Hebrew alphabet in order. The sixty-six verses of chapter 3 represent a more developed acrostic, with three verses for the first letter, three for the second, etc. Chapter 5 has twenty-two verses, suggesting the twenty-two letters of the alphabet, but the first letters of the verses are random. The first three chapters are longer, sixty-six lines each. Chapter 4 has forty-four lines (two lines per verse) and chapter 5 only twenty-two. The predominant rhythm of accents in each two-line unit is 3 accents + 2 accents. This "limping" rhythm is called *qinah* ("lament") because of its association with mourning, although it is found in other contexts also. It is suggested that the three

long chapters of the book followed by the two short chapters is also in imitation of the *qinah* rhythm.

The city is personified as "Daughter," the woman violated, the mother weeping for her children. Two names are used for the city, Zion (see 1:6) and Jerusalem (see 2:13); sometimes the name of the region, Judah, appears (see 1:15). The identification of a city as female is common in the ancient Near East. Four voices are heard in the poems: a narrator, Daughter Zion, a heroic man, and the community. Three of the voices interweave throughout the poems. The heroic man appears only in chapter 3. The voice that is never heard is that of God.

COMMENTARY

THE DESOLATION OF JERUSALEM

Lamentations 1:1-22

In this twenty-two verse acrostic (see Introduction), each verse (except 1:7) consists of three two-line units (called a, b, and c throughout the commentary). The chapter falls into two equal sections: the narrator in verses 1-11 describes the desolation of Jerusalem; Jerusalem herself cries out in lament in verses 12-22.

1:1-11 Jerusalem's desolation

The chapter begins with the cry, *'eykah*, "How"! The cry echoes Isaiah's lament over once-faithful Jerusalem (Isa 1:21). The former glory of Jerusalem, described as a woman, is contrasted with her present desperate state. Those she trusted have abandoned her. "Lovers" and "friends" are covenant terms for political allies. The refrain heard throughout this chapter begins here: "She has no one to comfort her" (1:2; see 1:9, 16, 17, 21).

After suffering the economic devastation of Babylonian rule and the anguish of the siege, Judah has gone into exile. The "rest" promised in the exodus and fulfilled in the land has now been lost (see Deut 12:9; Ps 95:11). The description of her defeat is enclosed by the word "pursuers" (1:3, 6). Her pursuers overtake her in the "narrow straits" (1:3; *metsarim*); the word echoes the

Hebrew term for Egypt (*mitsrayim*), the place where the exodus began. Zion is empty; even the roads and gates grieve (1:4). The people—priests and princes, women and children—are driven into exile (1:6). The enemy has won. But who is the enemy? This affliction comes from God because Jerusalem has rebelled (1:5). This is the first of several admissions of guilt (see 1:8-9, 14, 18). Her glory is lost, and it is her own fault.

Verse 7 is too long for the three-line pattern. Various solutions have been proposed. Some translations omit either the b or c line; others move the b line to verse 6. Perhaps the chapter circulated in two forms, one with the second line, another with the third. The NABRE has chosen to keep all the lines in the order we now have in the Hebrew text. The verse moves to a different perspective. Verses 1-6 described defeat and departure as immediate experiences; in verse 7 Jerusalem remembers what she has lost and what she has suffered. A variation on the refrain bemoaning the absence of a comforter appears: here she has no helper (see Pss 22:12; 72:12; 107:12; Isa 63:5).

The image of Jerusalem in verses 8-9 is that of a demeaned woman. She is shamed by nakedness; her uncleanness (menstrual blood?) is visible on her skirt. She is utterly disgraced. (Compare the prophetic description of the fall of Babylon, Isa 47:1-6.)

The next few verses are set off by an inclusion (the repetition of a word or phrase): Jerusalem herself interrupts the narration of her disaster, crying out to the Lord to look at her misery (see 9c and 11c). The inclusion surrounds further description of the siege and defeat of the city. The enemy has taken her treasures and dared to enter the temple; famine has gripped the people (1:10-11). Her "precious things" are lost: the sacred vessels of the temple taken by the enemy, the children bartered for food.

1:12-22 Jerusalem's cry

Now Daughter Zion begins her lament. The call to witness her pain leads into an accusation of the Lord for inflicting this misery on her. It happened "on the day of his blazing wrath," a day described by the prophets (see Isa 13:9-13; Zeph 2:2-3). She is attacked from within (fire in her bones) and without (a net to trip her up) (1:13). This has happened, however, because of her own sins. God has bound them up into a yoke that presses down on her neck and forces her to the ground (1:14). The judgment against her is described as harvest, a common prophetic image (see Joel 4:13; Hos 6:11). She has been trodden like grapes in the wine press; her young men have been crushed like grain at the feast. God has tossed away her best warriors like chaff and given her into the power of her enemies (1:15).

Jerusalem cries out in agony—no comforter, no children—only tears (1:16). The narrator interrupts to describe Jerusalem's situation and the Lord's decree, summoning her enemies (1:17). Jerusalem ends this accusation against God, not with the turn to hope that is commonly found in the psalms of communal lament but with testimony that God is just in inflicting this suffering on her because of her sins (1:18a).

A new summons to "listen" begins and ends the next section (1:18b and 21a). All those who might have helped, who might have comforted, are listed: the young, political allies, religious leaders. But they are all focused on saving themselves (1:19). So Jerusalem calls again on the Lord to see how she suffers. Again the suffering is described as both within and without (compare 1:13), but now she is like a house with killing outside in the street and death inside (1:20).

The chapter concludes with a prayer for vengeance: may my enemies suffer for their guilt at your hands as I have. Bring on the day the prophets describe (1:21-22). In the final line Jerusalem collapses from her pain.

THE LORD'S WRATH AND ZION'S RUIN
Lamentations 2:1-22

Chapter 2 also has twenty-two verses of three lines each. The beginning letter of each verse spells the alphabet. In this chapter, in contrast to chapter 1, the narrator/poet speaks for the first nineteen verses; in the last three verses Zion cries out in lament. As in chapter 1, Zion is portrayed as a woman. The theme of chapter 2 is clear: The Lord has caused Zion's misery (2:1-9, 17, 20-22). Yet the Lord is Zion's only recourse; only the Lord can help her (2:18-20).

In verses 1-9 the Lord is the subject of almost every sentence; only in verse 7c do the enemies find a voice. The Lord's blazing wrath burns through the section; words for "wrath" or "fury" appear in every one of the first four verses. In verse 4 the Lord, described as a murderous warrior, acts "like an enemy." In verse 5 the poet acknowledges the truth: "The Lord has become the enemy." The Lord has rejected his chosen city and the temple, his footstool (2:1). He has "devoured" (literally, "swallowed up") all Judah's buildings and defenses (2:2, 5). He has crushed the kingdom (2:2), cutting off its strength (the Hebrew idiom is "horn," 2:3). He has "multiplied moaning and groaning"; the Hebrew phrase has the same rhyming effect, *ta'aniyyah wa'aniyyah* (2:5).

Verse 6 returns to the painful truth (see 2:1) that the Lord has destroyed even the sacred places dedicated to his worship; "booth" and "shrine," "altar" and "sanctuary," all suggest the temple. All the liturgical worship—feast day and Sabbath—and the leadership are wiped out. The sacred space is desecrated by the riotous presence of the enemy (2:6-7). The Lord measures Zion like a builder but instead is bent on destroying walls and gates (2:8-9a).

The subject changes in verse 9b; the people respond to the disaster. What was said earlier (1:1, 7) is true: They have no help, no comforter. The leaders are "among the nations," that is, in exile. There is no instruction (Hebrew, *torah*) and the prophets receive no vision. All the people, from old men to young women, respond with traditional mourning rites: silence, sitting on the ground, wearing sackcloth, putting dust or ashes on their heads (see Gen 37:34; Jer 6:26; Job 2:11-13; Esth 4:1-3). But the sight of the starving children brings the poet to bitter grief (2:11). They faint like wounded warriors and die in their mother's arms (2:12).

The poet can find no metaphor to give meaning to Zion's suffering. "Vast as the sea" is another way to say "farther than anyone can imagine" (see Ps 139:9). In chapter 1, Zion acknowledged that the disaster came upon her because of her guilt (1:18). In chapter 2 a reason is given for her guilt: the prophets have prophesied false peace, so Zion did not repent (2:14; see Jer 6:13-15; 14:11-16). Now Zion has become a mockery; passersby taunt her with phrases from the psalms: "perfect in beauty, and joy of all the earth" (2:15; see Pss 48:3; 50:2). The enemies think that they have destroyed Zion by their own power: *They* have devoured; this is *their* day (2:16). But it is really the day of the *Lord's* wrath (see v. 22); it is the *Lord* who has done this (2:17). This restatement of the theme binds verses 1-17 into a unit. It also suggests the reason for Zion's hope: the Lord has struck; only the Lord can heal.

The poet exhorts Zion to cry out to the Lord (2:18-19). Throughout the Old Testament, when Israel cries out in distress, the Lord answers. When they are enslaved in Egypt and cry out, God calls Moses and begins the exodus (Exod 2:23-25). Whenever they are oppressed during the settlement period they cry out and God sends a judge to deliver them (see Judg 3:9, 15; 4:3). The encouragement of the poet is based on precedent. He encourages Zion to pray with tears night and day. It was believed in the ancient world that the heart liquefied with sorrow and that tears were the outpouring of the melted heart (see Ps 22:15; Isa 13:7). Zion is to pray, not for herself but for her children. The fourth line of verse 19 breaks the pattern of three-line verses, but Zion's agony also breaks every pattern.

2:20-22 Zion's lament

The last three verses are Zion's lament. She cries out to the Lord, but her only request is that God take note of the extent of her suffering. The rest of her lament is a description of the disaster. Everything that can be counted on has been lost. Religious leaders are killed even inside the sanctuary and mothers eat their own children. Cannibalism is known to be a horrible result of desperate famine. Young and old lie in the streets. Have they collapsed from hunger? Do they lie there dead and unburied?

Zion concludes her lament with an accusation against God: "You killed them"; "You summoned . . . terrors." The day of the Lord's wrath is mentioned twice (2:21, 22). God has held a terrible festival; Zion's children have been slaughtered as the sacrifice (see Isa 34:1-8; Zeph 1:7-9). The "terrors on every side," announced by Jeremiah, have arrived (see Jer 6:25; 20:3-5). Zion mourns the children destroyed by her enemy; the enemy is God.

THE VOICE OF A SUFFERING INDIVIDUAL
Lamentations 3:1-66

Chapter 3 differs from the previous two chapters in three ways: First, the acrostic is more defined. In contrast to chapters 1–2, where only the first line of each three-line unit formed the acrostic, in chapter 3 *each* line of each three-*verse* unit begins with the appropriate letter of the alphabet. In several instances two or three lines of the three-verse unit even begin with the same word or root. Secondly, the speaker in verses 1-39 is not Zion portrayed as a woman but is an individual man. There is a transition in verse 40 to a lament of the community. In verse 48 the individual voice returns, although the speaker in verses 52-66 sounds more like the speaker in chapters 1–2, an individual as representative of the whole people. Thirdly, only verses 42-51 seem to have a direct connection to the siege and destruction of Jerusalem in 587 B.C.

Verses 1-25 resemble an individual lament with its accusation of God (3:1-16), description of misery (3:17-20), and turn to hope (3:21-25). Verse 1 presents the topic for the first sixteen verses: "I am one [literally, "a man"; Hebrew *geber*] who has known affliction / under the rod of God's anger." In the next fifteen verses only verse 14 does not have God for the subject. But God does not do what he is expected to do. God leads not to security by springs of water (see Isa 49:10) but into darkness (3:2, 6; see Ps 88:7). God has imprisoned the speaker and blocked off his access even to God (3:5, 7-9). God is a wild animal (3:10-11;

see Hos 13:7-8) or a warrior attacking him (3:12-13; see 2:4). God has fed him, not with honey and wheat (see Ps 81:17) nor with blessings (see Jer 31:14) but with bitterness and has broken his teeth with gravel (3:15-16). Oil of wormwood, *Artemesia absinthium*, is bitter. Licking the dust is a common biblical metaphor for humiliation (see Ps 72:9), but here the metaphor is intensified, eating gravel (see Prov 20:17). The description of misery, which was introduced in verse 14, continues in verses 17-20. The speaker is close to despair; his soul is downcast (compare Pss 42:6-7, 12; 43:5).

Like the psalms of lament, this cry to God ends with a turn to hope (3:21-25). These are perhaps the most beautiful verses in this book. Even though God is the one who afflicts, the speaker's hope is grounded in this confession of faith: God's loving compassion does not come to an end (3:22-23). Where else can he go? God is his portion, his lot (3:24). When the land was divided among the tribes, the Levites did not get a share. They were told that the Lord was their portion (Num 18:20; see Josh 18:7). In the psalms the rest of the community claims the Lord as their inherited share (Pss 16:5; 73:26; 119:57; 142:6). Verses 20-22 are striking in their similarity to Psalms 42–43.

3:26-39 A wisdom teaching

The turn to hope leads to a wisdom teaching on perseverance in hope. This instruction is linked to the lament by the catchword, "good." (Throughout this chapter the ideas are not limited to the three-verse alphabetic units.) One can learn to endure suffering (3:26-30) because one hopes in God's enduring love and compassion (3:31-33). God sees the oppression one suffers (3:34-36). There is an echo of Genesis 1 in the recognition that God creates by word (3:37). The ancient idea of causality also appears: if it happened, God did it—whether good or bad (3:38). The implication in these verses is that God has the will and power to save. Therefore it is wise to acknowledge one's own sins, which are the cause of much of one's suffering (3:39). Verse 39 links this section to the beginning with the repetition of *geber*: "What should the living complain about?"

3:40-47 A community lament

The advice to acknowledge and "complain about" one's sins leads to the community's decision to lament (3:40-41). The communal lament, like the individual lament in verses 1-25, begins with an accusation against God (3:42-45). There is a brief confession of sin, but then the complaint begins: "you have not forgiven us." God pursues and kills without pity (3:43; see 2:2, 17, 21). God is wrapped in anger, wrapped in a cloud. The cloud is often a sign of God's presence (see Exod 13:21-22; 24:16-18; 33:9-10; 1 Kgs 8:10-11) but is linked with wrath in the descriptions of the day of the Lord (see Joel 2:2; Zeph 1:15). This time the cloud obscures; God has again blocked himself off from the prayer of the people (see 3:8). Without God they are worthless, as good as trash (3:45). Their description of misery (3:46-47) ends with a statement whose alliteration makes it sound like a proverb (*pahad wapahat, hashshe't wehashshaber*, "Panic and pit," "desolation and destruction").

3:48-51 An individual cry

The catchword, "destruction," links the communal lament to the description of agony that follows. In this section the individual voice is again heard. (Note again that this section begins in the middle of a three-verse unit.) The key image in these verses is that of eyes and sight. The word "eyes" appears in three of the four verses; verse 51 begins literally, "my eyes grieve my soul." My eyes are the source of unceasing tears (3:48-49; see Jer 14:17). I plead with God to look at what I cannot bear to see (3:50-51), the suffering in Jerusalem and its surrounding villages. The villages that depend on a city are often called its daughters (see, for example, Judg 11:26).

3:52-66 A partial psalm of thanksgiving

These verses resemble a psalm of thanksgiving with two missing elements: the opening announcement, "I will give thanks," and the concluding promise of a thanksgiving sacrifice. The central part of a thanksgiving psalm is here: description of recent distress (3:52-53), the quotation of the lament (3:54-55), and the announcement that God has heard and acted (3:56-58). Images of distress echo the psalms—snared by the enemy (3:52; Ps 124:7); in the pit (3:53, 55; Pss 28:1); submerged (3:54; see Ps 69:2). The plea to God and the report of God's action are also reminiscent of psalms: call on the Lord's name (3:55; Ps 116:4); do not be deaf (3:56; see Ps 39:13); you pleaded my case (3:58; Ps 43:1); redeemed my life (3:58; Ps 119:154). God's words in verse 57, "Do not fear," are repeated over and over in prophetic oracles of salvation (for example, Isa 41:13-14).

As the psalms of thanksgiving often do, chapter 3 returns to the lament (3:59-66; see Ps 40). The interpretation of these verses depends on the identification of the speaker. If the speaker is really an individual (perhaps the speaker of vv. 1-25), the enemies seem to be his own people. If the speaker represents the collective voice of Judah (as in chs. 1–2), then the enemies are foreign nations. The accusation against the enemy does not have to do with attack and siege but with plotting, mockery, and injustice (3:59-63). The speaker pleads for retributive justice: do to them what they have done to me (3:64). What the speaker wants done to their hearts in verse 65 is unclear; the Hebrew word occurs only here. It means either "anguish" or "insolence." In any case he wants God to curse them, to pursue them in anger as God has done to him (see 3:43), and to wipe out the sight of them from under the Lord's heaven (see 3:50).

MISERIES OF THE BESIEGED CITY

Lamentations 4:1-22

The pattern of spelling out the alphabet only in the first line of each stanza returns in chapter 4 (see chs. 1–2). The stanzas in this chapter are only two lines each, in contrast to the three-line units in chapters 1–3. Personified Zion does not speak in chapter 4; the only voice is that of the poet who has experienced the siege. Most of the chapter consists of a description of misery; there is no cry to the Lord or petition for help. There is a brief accusation against God and religious leaders (4:11-13), a report of the final days of the siege (4:17-20), and a concluding curse and blessing (4:21-22).

The description of misery (4:1-10, 14-16) lists, group by group, the effects of the siege. Their stories are interwoven. The poet mourns, first of all, that the children of Zion are regarded as worthless (4:1-2). Are the "children" all the people or the young men? The latter is more likely since the women and young children are treated later. The two verses are linked, not only by three different words for "gold" but also by a striking wordplay. "Jewels" are literally "sacred stones"; the Hebrew word for stones (*'abney*) suggests the

word for "children" in the next verse (*beney*). The children of Zion are holy and precious as jewels, but they lie starving or dead at the corner of every street (see 2:19).

The little children and their mothers suffer desperately from the famine resulting from the siege (4:3-4). The starving mothers cannot nurse and so the children starve. The mothers are scorned as cruel by contrast to the most despised animals. The ostrich was widely believed to lay her eggs in the desert sand and then abandon them. Jackals and ostriches live in ruins and deserted places (Isa 34:13), a foreshadowing of what Jerusalem will become, and are associated with lamentation (Mic 1:8).

Verse 5 moves from the image of starving children to a description of the starving rich. Those who not only had enough to eat but who ate delicacies now starve with everyone else; those who were comfortable on fine furniture now pick through the trash. Crimson (or purple) is a sign of wealth because the dye was difficult to obtain; only the wealthy could afford it. This image of the pampered rich leads to a reflection on Daughter Zion (4:6). This is the only suggestion of guilt in this chapter. The contrast drawn is stunning: Zion must be *more* guilty than Sodom because her suffering is long and drawn out. Sodom and Gomorrah (see Gen 19) are metaphors for great guilt and destruction. The prophets accuse the people of being *as* guilty as Sodom (see Jer 23:14) but not *more* guilty. They warn of total destruction like Sodom's (see Isa 1:9; Jer 49:18; 50:40); is there a threat to Jerusalem here?

The poet begins again with the same groups—men, women, and children, those whose suffering is long—but the description is intensified. The starving men are princes (4:7). (Or, since the Hebrew word is *nazir*, they may be Nazirites who have made special promises to God; see Num 6.) The praise of their beauty recalls descriptions of David and the lover in the Song of Songs (see 1 Sam 16:12; Song 5:10-16). But now they are disfigured by starvation (4:8). A proverbial sentence recalls the comparison of Sodom and Zion: It is better to die quickly than to suffer long (4:9). As for the starving women and children, the ravages of famine lead mothers to cannibalism (4:10). Cannibalism is reported as a result of siege in 2 Kings (6:28-29); the prophets threaten that it will come even to Jerusalem (Jer 19:8-9; Ezek 5:10).

The Lord, who has not yet been mentioned in chapter 4, is now accused of bringing this disaster on Zion (4:11). The disaster is so great that not even foreign nations can believe it (4:12). There is an implied contrast with Psalm 48: "See! The kings assembled, / together they advanced. / When they looked they were astounded; / terrified, they were put to flight!" (Ps 48:5-6). A tradition had grown up around Zion that it could not be defeated. The Assyrian king, Sennacherib, could not conquer it at the end of the eighth century (2 Kgs 19:32-36); the psalms declare the invulnerability of the city (Ps 46:5-8). Jeremiah warned, however, that what protected Zion was not the presence of the temple but the presence of God, and God would remain with the people only if they were faithful to the covenant (Jer 7). Ezekiel reports the departure of God from the temple (Ezek 10:18-23).

Verse 13 is incomplete. What happens because of the sins of the religious leaders? Genuine prophets describe the sins of false prophets and priests and their consequences: Priests have rejected knowledge and ignored God's law (Hos 4:4-9). Prophets speak peace to those who feed them and war to those who do not (Mic 3:5). Priests did not seek God; prophets prophesied by idols (Jer 2:8). Therefore the people come to ruin and Jerusalem will be destroyed (Mic 3:12).

Verses 14-16 complete the description of misery by portraying the agony of priests and elders. They, who guarded the sanctuary, now cannot enter it because they are defiled by blood (4:14). Are they simply bloody from the surrounding warfare? This ordinarily would not render them unclean. Or are they guilty of bloodshed because they did not care for the vulnerable in their midst (see Isa 1:15-17)? In Isaiah God says to such people: "Trample my courts no more!" (Isa 1:13-14). They cry out like a leper (Lev 13:45-46) and are shunned even among the nations (4:15). The presence of God was their portion (4:16; see 3:24). Now, since God's face (i.e., presence) is not with them, their faces are not lifted up (i.e., they are not honored).

4:17-20 Jerusalem's fall

The tone changes in the next section. It seems to be a detailed report of the final days of Jerusalem. Similar reports from Jeremiah and 2 Kings help explain these verses. Jerusalem had trusted in Egypt to defend it against the Babylonians (see Jer 37:1-10), but Egypt did not come (4:17). The city walls were breached on the ninth day of the fourth month and the people could no longer walk in the streets (4:18; see 2 Kgs 25:3-4). King Zedekiah and his soldiers left the city by night, "But the Chaldean [Babylonian] army pursued the king and overtook him in the desert near Jericho" (2 Kgs 25:5; see 4:19-20). Like every king of Judah, Zedekiah was anointed, and thus "messiah"; the Hebrew word for "anointed" is *mashiach*. The hopes for every "messiah" are reflected in the way he is named: "lifebreath" and protecting "shade" (see Ps 72). Now that hope is shattered also.

4:21-22 A curse

The last two verses of the chapter are a curse on Edom and a statement of renewed hope for Zion. Edom (another name for Esau), Judah's neighbor to the south, was considered a brother to Israel/Jacob (see Gen 25:30; 32:29). When the Babylonians conquered and destroyed Jerusalem in 587 B.C., the Edomites joined in the pillage. For this they were bitterly hated (Obad 10–14). The poet taunts Edom, in effect saying: "Rejoice now, but your day is coming." The cup of God's wrath is a common prophetic image (see Isa 51:17; Jer 25:15-17). Drunken Edom will be stripped bare—the fate they called down on Jerusalem (Ps 137:7)—and its sins revealed (4:22). For Zion, however, there is hope. From the vantage point of the future, the poet proclaims that her punishment is complete, a promise announced by Isaiah of the exile: "Speak to the heart of Jerusalem, and proclaim to her / that her service has ended, / that her guilt is expiated, / That she has received from the hand of the LORD / double for all her sins" (Isa 40:2).

THE COMMUNITY'S LAMENT TO THE LORD

Lamentations 5:1-22

Lamentations 5 differs from the other chapters in several ways: First, there is no acrostic; the first letters of each line do not spell the alphabet. There are, however, twenty-two lines, recalling the twenty-two letters of the alphabet. Second, each verse has only one line instead of three (chs. 1–2) or two (ch. 3). Third, the meter of the lines is not predominantly 3 + 2 (the *qinah* rhythm; see Introduction) but primarily 3 + 3. Fourth, this chapter fits most closely the pattern and style of the communal lament in the psalms. There is a cry to God, a description of distress, a complaint, and an appeal for help. The turn to hope, however, is very slight if it is there at all. This similarity to the psalms may be the reason chapter 5 has the heading in some Greek and Latin manuscripts: "A Prayer (or Lament) of Jeremiah."

The chapter is framed by two cries to God (5:1, 21). The cry to God in verse 1 is similar to the cry in other chapters (see 1:9, 11; 2:20). But here the people plead with God not only to look but also to remember. Remembering in Hebrew has the connotation of actively making something present. God is asked to take their misery to heart. A major part of their distress in this shame-honor culture is the disgrace they have suffered.

Several elements in this chapter, including the cry to God to remember, suggest Psalm 74, a communal lament over an enemy invasion of the temple (Ps 74:2, 18, 22). Other similarities are: the questions "why" and "how long" (5:20; Ps 74:1, 10-11); the description of the desolation of Mount Zion (5:18; Ps 74:3-7); the plea for restoration (5:21; Ps 74:21); the absence of praise or thanksgiving at the end (5:22; Ps 74:22-23).

5:2-18 A description of distress

Strangers have taken over the land. "Heritage" may mean the whole land (see Num 26:52-56) or it may connote one's individual piece of land (see Judg 2:6). A share in the land is part of the covenant promise (see Gen 12:7; Deut 11:8-9). For this reason Naboth refuses to give his vineyard to King Ahab in the ninth century (1 Kgs 21:1-3). Loss of the land is seen as loss of the covenant. Therefore, the people regard themselves as fatherless (5:3).

Foreign domination also has practical consequences. What once belonged to them they must now buy (5:4). They suffer forced labor without profit (5:5). They are reduced to begging relief from other nations (5:6). "Wood" and "water" (5:4) signify all material needs. "Rest" (5:5) suggests again the loss of the covenant promise, "rest" in the land (see Deut 12:10).

An acknowledgment of guilt interrupts the description of distress (5:7). It is the familiar re-

frain of suffering for the guilt of ancestors (see Ezek 18); later the people will also bemoan their own sins (5:16). The "sins" may be the foreign alliances with Egypt and Assyria (see Isa 8:11-15; 30:1-5; Jer 2:18-19).

The description of distress resumes with a repetition of previous complaints (4:8-9). "Servants," the administrators of the Babylonians, rule them. They not only have to work and to buy what was their own, but they still suffer from famine (5:10). The suffering of various groups of people mentioned in chapter 4 is again described (5:11-13). Even the young men, the people's hope, are forced to do "women's work," grinding grain (v. 13). Joy has departed (5:14-17).

5:18-22 A turn to hope?

The last five verses swing between misery and hope. The sanctuary has been desecrated; Mount Zion has become the haunt of wild animals as the prophets warned (see Jer 9:10; 10:22). But the Lord, not dependent on any place, is enthroned forever (5:19; see Pss 55:20; 102:13). This tiny hymn fragment is as close as this chapter comes to a turn to hope. But immediately the lament returns with its age-old questions: Why? How long? (see Pss 42:10; 79:10; 80:5; 94:3). A second plea to God rings out (v. 21; see 5:1). There are two requests: bring us back, renew us. (The first half of the verse is an almost direct quotation of Jer 31:18.) In chapter 3 the people had resolved to return to the Lord (3:40); here they recognize that they cannot return under their own power. Only God can bring them back (see Jer 31:18; Ps 51:12). Zion and its people have been looking for renewal and revival throughout the book. In chapter 1 the people tried to revive their own lives and Zion tried to find renewal through others (1:11, 16), but neither was successful. In chapter 3 the speaker declared his hope in God's loving mercy, renewed each morning (3:22-23). Now the people beg God to renew them.

This lament does not end with thanksgiving or praise of God for rescue. Instead, like Psalm 88, Lamentations 5 says to God, "Now it's your turn to act." Verse 22 is, in effect, an accusation against God: "We are still suffering and it's your fault." The accusation itself is an expression of faith, recognition that no one but God can relieve this misery. So ends the book of Lamentations.

THE BOOK OF
BARUCH

Pauline A. Viviano

INTRODUCTION

The book of Baruch is found in the Catholic canon of Scripture, but it has not been accepted into either the Jewish or Protestant canons. It is sometimes called 1 Baruch to distinguish it from other works attributed to Baruch. These are 2 Baruch, a Syriac Apocalypse, and 3 Baruch, a Greek Apocalypse. "The *Paraleipomena* of Jeremiah" ("things omitted from the prophet Jeremiah") is sometimes designated 4 Baruch. These works are attributed to Baruch, but it is unlikely that he authored any of them. The Letter of Jeremiah is a separate book in the Septuagint (LXX), where it comes after the book of Lamentations, but the Catholic canon follows the order of St. Jerome's Vulgate and places the Letter of Jeremiah at the end of the book of Baruch.

We know of Baruch from the book of Jeremiah, where he is presented as a scribe and secretary to Jeremiah (Jer 32:10-16; 36:1-31). After the assassination of Gedaliah, Baruch is accused of inciting Jeremiah against military leaders from Judah, who had asked Jeremiah for a word from the Lord (Jer 43:1-3). Both Jeremiah and Baruch are taken to Egypt by these military leaders (Jer 43:5-7), presumably against their will. Baruch is a recipient of an oracle of hope from Jeremiah, assuring Baruch that he would survive the exile (Jer 45:1-5). We have no certain knowledge of what became of Baruch after he was taken to Egypt, but the book of Baruch situates him among the exiles in Babylon. It may be that Baruch played an important role in the postexilic community either among the exiles in Babylon, among the refugees in Egypt, or with those who remained in Jerusalem. He became a significant figure over the next several hundred years. Not only were several books attributed to him but he is also assigned roles beyond that of scribe: biographer, sage, prophet, and apocalyptist.

The author, date, and language

The book of Baruch is composed of four independent sections: 1:1–3:8; 3:9–4:4; 4:5–5:9; 6:1-72. Though traditionally the first three sections have been attributed to Baruch, he is explicitly mentioned only in the introduction (1:1-9) to the first section. The opening verses situate the delivery of Baruch's message in the exilic period, specifically 582 B.C.; the Letter of Jeremiah is said to have been sent by Jeremiah to the Babylonian exiles, though it does not specify whether these are the exiles of 597 B.C. or 587 B.C. These chronological indications cannot be reconciled with the content of the book; for example, the temple cannot be in ruins (presumed in 2:26) and still intact and fully operational (1:10, 14). The identification of Belshazzar as the son of Nebuchadnezzar (1:11) is an error best explained by attributing a late date to the book of Baruch (cf. Dan 5:1-2, where the same mistake is made). The issues and themes taken up in the various sections of the book of Baruch, including the Letter of Jeremiah, reflect the concerns of the late postexilic period and even later. The content of the book betrays a heavy reliance on the Old Testament, especially Second Isaiah (Isa 40–55) and the book of Daniel, which also suggests a late date. It is unlikely that the book was composed prior to 300 B.C., but dates as late as 70 A.D. have been proposed. Our earliest copies of the book of Baruch are in Greek, but it is possible that one or more sections were originally in Hebrew.

Historical situation of the book

The last years of Judah were characterized by political turmoil. It was a vassal of the Babylonian Empire, but after repeated attempts to secure help from Egypt, presumably in a bid for independence, Judah was destroyed by Babylon. The first concerted Babylonian effort against this small kingdom was in 597 B.C. and resulted in the exile of King Jehoiachin and many of Judah's leading citizens, but it was the Babylonian attack of 587 B.C. that resulted in the destruction of the city of Jerusalem and its temple, and another exile. The exile of 587 B.C. was a turning point in the history of Israel. The nation that for centuries had struggled to survive was destroyed. Many were forced into exile to Babylon; others escaped the path of de-

struction and became refugees in foreign lands. The people scattered among the nations became known as the Jews of the Diaspora. Identity and faith became critically important for those separated from their homeland. Without a nation, who were they? Without a temple, where would they worship? How would they worship? Who would lead them? And, perhaps most important, where was God? Had God abandoned them or was God still with them? The book of Baruch addresses some concerns of the Jews of the Diaspora.

The book of Baruch

The first section of the book of Baruch begins with an introduction that sets the historical context (1:1-9) for the confession of guilt (1:10–2:10) and prayer for deliverance (2:11–3:8). The second section is a praise of wisdom that addresses the importance of wisdom (3:9-23), its inaccessibility (3:24-36), and the relation of wisdom and law (3:37–4:4). The third section is a poem of consolation that consists of a series of addresses: Baruch to the Diaspora (4:5-9a), Jerusalem to its neighbors (4:9b-16), Jerusalem to the Diaspora (4:17-29), and Baruch to Jerusalem (4:30–5:9). Finally, chapter 6 purports to be a letter from Jeremiah warning the exiles against idols and idolatry.

COMMENTARY

LETTER TO JERUSALEM

Baruch 1:1–3:8

1:1-9 Historical setting

Baruch reads a scroll to the exiles in Babylon in 582 B.C., five years after the destruction of Jerusalem. The exiles respond with acts of contrition and they take up a collection to send to Jerusalem in support of the temple. The return of the temple vessels may be seen as a fulfillment of the prophecy in Jeremiah 28:1-6, even though that prophecy was uttered by a false prophet.

1:10–2:10 Confession of guilt

The exiles send to the "people back home" the collection with a request for sacrifices to be offered and prayers to be said on their behalf. They also ask that the scroll they are sending be read

aloud. There is no clear beginning of the reading of the scroll itself, but as verse 14 mentions the scroll, presumably it begins in verse 15.

The confession of guilt draws a sharp contrast between God who acts justly (1:15; 2:6, 9) and the people and their leaders who are characterized as "shamefaced" (1:15; 2:6). As the passage develops the people acknowledge their sin and recognize that the punishment they have endured was justified. They recount their sinful actions in general terms: they "sinned" (1:17; 2:5), "disobeyed" (1:18, 19), "have not listened" to the Lord's voice (1:18, 19, 21; 2:5, 10), did not follow the Lord's precepts (1:18; 2:10), "followed the inclinations of [their] wicked hearts" (1:22; 2:7), have "done evil" (1:22), and did not turn "from the designs of [their] evil hearts" (2:8). The only specific sin mentioned is that they "served other gods" (1:22).

The people acknowledge that their sinfulness continued in spite of the warnings they had received from the prophets (1:21). That the Lord carried through with the threats contained in these warnings (1:20; 2:1, 7) is justified, because the people refused to heed these warnings. They knew the precepts of the Lord (1:18; 2:10) but chose to disobey them, as had their ancestors (1:15, 19). Their obstinacy is set against the Lord's actions on their behalf: the exodus (1:19, 20) and the gift of the land (1:20), as well as the repeated warnings that they would be punished if they did not repent.

The horror of the catastrophe is not passed over. It is given expression in a variety of ways: "evils cling to us" (1:20); "curse" (1:20); nowhere has anything like what the Lord did to Jerusalem been done (2:2); we ate the flesh of our sons and daughters (2:3); we are "subject to all the kingdoms around us" (2:4); we are the "object of reproach and horror" (2:4); we have been "brought low" (2:5); "[a]ll the evils . . . have come upon us" (2:7). In spite of the extent of their destruction, it is asserted repeatedly that the Lord is just and the people received the punishment that they deserved. This recounting of sin with references to the warnings of the prophet and to the Lord's past actions on Israel's behalf echoes the language and theology of the Deuteronomic school. It is thought that the prayer of Daniel (Dan 9:4-19) provided a model for this confessional prayer.

2:11–3:8 Prayer for deliverance

The confession of guilt is followed by a prayer for deliverance, which both repeats the confession of guilt and moves beyond it. Once again there are general statements acknowledging the failure of the people: "we have sinned" (2:12; 3:2, 4); "we did not listen" (2:24; cf. 3:4). But additional ways of speaking of the people's sin are now included: "we have committed sacrilege, we have violated all your statutes" (2:12); we did not "serve the king of Babylon" (2:24) as commanded (2:21). It is Jeremiah who insisted that it was the Lord's will that Judah submit to Babylon (Jer 27:1-22).

Also in this section there is another reference to the Lord's actions on Israel's behalf in the exodus (2:11) and against Israel in punishment for the sin of the people (2:20, 23-26). Most dominant in this section, however, is the prayer to the Lord in which the people ask the Lord to pay attention to them and reverse their present situation of exile: "Withdraw your anger" (2:13), hear our prayer (2:14, 16; 3:2), "hear the prayer of the dead" (3:4), "deliver us" (2:14), "look . . . take thought of us" (2:16), "incline your ear" (2:16), "[o]pen your eyes" (2:17), remember not "the wicked deeds of our ancestors" but rather "your power and your name" (3:5). The people plead for mercy (2:19; 3:2) and cry out to the Lord (3:1).

Throughout the prayer the people's requests are expanded by motivation clauses in an attempt to move the Lord to respond to their prayer. A variety of motivations are drawn upon to persuade the Lord to a change of heart: "for we are left few in number" (2:13), "for your own sake" (2:14), so "that the whole earth may know" that the Lord is our God and that Israel "bear[s] your name" (2:15), "for you are . . . merciful" (3:2), "for you are enthroned forever" (3:3), for "we are perishing" (3:3), for our God is the Lord and we will praise the Lord (3:6).

As the prayer draws to a conclusion there is a shift from the people's confession of their sin to blaming their suffering in exile on the sins of their ancestors (3:8). This shift may represent the position of subsequent generations that remained in exile even though they were not responsible for the exile itself.

PRAISE OF WISDOM

Baruch 3:9–4:4

The "Praise of Wisdom" is a poem that speaks of wisdom but also encourages the pursuit of wisdom. The poem begins and ends with exhortations. The first half of the poem is dominated by questions that are answered in the second half of the poem. This intermixing of exhortations with questions and answers prevents the poem from being merely a set of commands. Through the rhetorical device of "question and answer," readers engage dialogically with the poem and become more receptive to its exhortations. The poem draws on themes found elsewhere in the Bible, but it develops these themes with great eloquence.

3:9-23 Importance of wisdom

After exhorting Israel to be attentive to the "commandments of life," the poem turns to the question of the cause of the exile (3:9-11). The prophets attributed the exile to the sinfulness of the people in worshiping other gods and/or in Israel's failure to live in justice, but the author of this poem blames the exile on Israel's abandonment of the fountain of wisdom (3:12). The theory of retribution is underscored in the assertion that if Israel had "walked in the way of God" (3:12) and learned wisdom (3:13), it would have found peace and long life (3:13, 14), but its failure in obedience resulted in its destruction and exile. In a series of rhetorical questions the author implies that rulers and the wealthy have not found wisdom (3:16-19), nor has wisdom been passed onto later generations, even among those whose nations were renowned for their wisdom (3:20-23). Both this section and the next draw upon Job 28 and Isaiah 40:12-31 in speaking of the inaccessibility of wisdom and the incomparability of Israel's God.

3:24-36 Inaccessibility of wisdom

God's dwelling place is not identified as the temple but as the "vast" and "immeasurable" universe (3:24-25). This notion betrays the influence of Greek thought and that of Philo of Alexandria. The poem continues to stress that wisdom has not been found, even by the heroes, the "giants," of the past (3:26-28). Again in a series of rhetorical questions the author highlights the inability of anyone to find wisdom (3:29-31). Only the incomparable, all-knowing creator God knows wisdom (3:32-36).

3:37–4:4 Wisdom contained in the law

The final section of the poem resolves the dilemma raised by exhorting Israel to pursue wisdom and at the same time insisting that wisdom cannot be found: wisdom has appeared on earth in Israel as the torah (3:37–4:1). In the Old Testament the identification of wisdom with the torah is found only here and in Sirach 24:23-29. Wisdom, embodied in the torah, is God's gift to Israel. The final exhortation to Israel is to recognize that it is privileged and blessed, because it knows the will of God (4:3-4).

BARUCH'S POEM OF CONSOLATION

Baruch 4:5–5:9

Often drawing upon the language and imagery of Second Isaiah, this poignant dialogue gives expression to the people's sorrow at the destruc-

tion of Jerusalem and their longing for restoration and salvation.

4:5-9a Baruch addresses Diaspora

The speaker is assumed to be Baruch, even though that is never made explicit in this poem. An opening exhortation to "[t]ake courage" is followed by yet another statement that punishment has come upon the people because they angered God by their actions (4:5-6). It is unusual that the people are accused of sacrificing to demons (4:7), but this probably represents an intensification of the polemic against other gods by equating them with demons. The personification of Jerusalem as a woman begins here and is continued throughout this poem.

4:9b-16 Jerusalem addresses neighbors

Jerusalem expresses her grief over the exile of her citizens. It is the grief of a widow who has lost her children (4:4b-12a, 16). The people have refused to acknowledge and obey the law of God (4:12b-13) and therefore God has made them captives of another nation. Jerusalem calls upon the neighboring countries to remember the destruction and desolation that Israel's God brought upon her (4:14-16).

4:17-29 Jerusalem addresses Diaspora

Jerusalem raises the question as to what she can do, for it is God who must deliver the people and she mourns for her loss by putting on sackcloth and making supplication (4:17-20). With confidence in the mercy of God, Jerusalem encourages the people to call upon God to deliver them (4:21-22). When God's salvation comes, there will be reversals: Jerusalem's mourning will be turned to joy; those who saw the people led away as captives will now see them return (4:23-24). Jerusalem seeks to motivate the people to be patient in their suffering by continuing the contrast between the present and the future: their persecutors will be destroyed; though they were carried off, God will remember them; those who strayed away will turn back to God; the God who brought disaster will bring deliverance (4:25-29).

4:30-5:9 Baruch addresses Jerusalem

Jerusalem is addressed in this final section with a series of exhortations: "Take courage" (4:30); "[l]ook to the east" (4:36); "take off your

robe of mourning and misery" (5:1); "[r]ise up
. . . stand upon the heights; / look . . . and see"
(5:4). All these actions are in response to the salvation that is at hand. As before, a contrast is drawn
between the time of mourning and the triumph
of Jerusalem's enemies, and the time of rejoicing
and the defeat of those who led the Jerusalem's
citizens into exile (4:31-34). The splendor of the
time of salvation is highlighted by terms such as
joy, rejoice, glory, peace, mercy, and justice, which
dominate the last verses of this passage.

THE LETTER OF JEREMIAH

Baruch 6:1-72

This final chapter is said to be a letter from
Jeremiah sent, at God's command, to the people
who had been carried into exile, either the exile
of 597 B.C. or 587 B.C. The letter begins by stating
the reason for the exile (sinfulness, 6:1) and the
duration of the exile (up to seven generations,
6:2), but the rest of the poem is a warning against
idolatry. The pomp and circumstance associated
with the worship of idols made the worship of
other gods attractive to those exiled to Babylon
(6:3), especially if the exiles felt abandoned by
God or thought that their God was powerless
before the gods of their conquerors. Jeremiah's
letter is a sustained warning against the worship
of idols, but it reads more like a caustic sermon
than a letter. It is similar in tone to the mockery
of idols, such as we find in Second Isaiah (40:18-
20; 41:6-7; 44:9-20; 46:5-7), but its mockery is carried to a greater extreme.

There is a great deal of repetition that serves
to underscore the futility of worshiping idols:
"they are not gods" (6:14, 22, 28, 49, 50, 51, 64, 71);
they cannot be "thought," "called," or "claimed"
as gods (6:29, 39, 44, 47, 56, 63, 68); they are "false
gods" (vv. 58 [3x], 62); because idols are not gods,
they are not to be feared (6:14, 22, 28, 64, 68). Interspersed between these assertions are descriptions
of the idols that show why it is ridiculous to worship these false gods. As with the mockery of the
idols in Second Isaiah, the author points out that

the idols are made by artisans (6:7, 45, 50); they
cannot speak (6:7), cannot see (6:18), and cannot
move on their own (6:25, 26). Those who worship
idols do not have sense (6:35-37).

To this modest list from Second Isaiah the
author expands considerably. To the inactivity of
idols the author adds that they cannot dress (6:8-
10) or clean themselves (6:12, 23). Idols are totally
passive; they are subject to rust, corrosion, and
fire (6:11, 23, 56-57); even their clothes rot (6:12,
23, 71). They are consumed by insects (6:19), their
faces get sooty (6:20), and they become a perch
for birds and bats and even for cats (6:21). They
are imprisoned like criminals (6:17), bought (6:24),
handled by the unclean (6:28), stolen (6:56),
stripped (6:57), and thrown away like a corpse
(6:70-71). They cannot feel (6:23) and they have
"no spirit" (6:24). Indeed they are "no better than
stones" (6:38) or scarecrows in a field (6:69). Idols
cannot take action; they cannot do justice (6:13,
33, 63), protect (6:69), heal (6:36, 41), vindicate or
rescue (6:36-37, 53), save or deliver (6:35) even
themselves (6:14, 33), bless with wealth (6:34),
bring rain (6:52), and bestow kingship (6:52). They
are powerless (6:53) and useless (6:6); they are
frauds (6:7, 47, 50). Beasts are better, for they can
help themselves (6:67). Idols do not equal the
forces of nature (the sun, moon, wind, lightning),
which are commanded by God (6:59-62); they cannot even shine like the sun and moon (6:66).

The priests who serve these idols are not left
unscathed by the author of this letter. He accuses
them of stealing gold and silver offered to the
idols and giving it to harlots (6:9-10). They even
steal the clothing of the idols and give it to their
wives (6:32). They sell sacrifices for their own
gain; their wives do not share cured meat with
the poor and weak (6:27). The devotion of the
priests is called into question, for they abandon
their idols when war or fire threatens (6:49, 54).

This rather scathing treatment of idols is meant
to deter the exiles from the worship of other gods;
the Lord alone is to be worshiped (6:5). Only the
God who commands the forces of nature and
brings justice and salvation is worthy of worship.

THE BOOK OF

EZEKIEL

Corrine L. Carvalho

INTRODUCTION

The book of Ezekiel contains the oracles of the prophet Ezekiel, a priest of Jerusalem, who was deported to Babylon in 597 B.C. The date of his deportation implies that he was part of the elite priests who, along with other ruling members of Judean society, posed a threat to Babylon. The book provides dates for many of the oracles, all during his own exile (593–571). The oracles utilize many prophetic forms: a call narrative, vision reports, symbolic acts, lamentations, riddles, etc. Until recently many scholars thought that the book of Ezekiel was a haphazard collection of oracles from a wide variety of time periods; recent studies, however, suggest that the book is a carefully crafted literary whole. Hints to the literary origin of the book include the length of the oracles, the use of dates to guide the reader, and the presence of overarching patterns within the book.

The book has a clear structure: oracles of destruction before the fall of the city (chs. 1–24), oracles against foreign nations (chs. 25–32), the report to the prophet of the fall of Jerusalem (ch. 33), and then oracles of restoration (chs. 34–48). A recurring vision of God's chariot-throne, which represents God's presence, ties these sections together.

Date, Provenance, and Author

Dates for the writing of the book have been as wide ranging as the Babylonian exile until the Maccabean period. However, since the book reflects no hint of the issues facing Judah in the Persian or Hellenistic periods, it probably stems from the period of the exile, with scattered later additions. Some scholars have suggested that the focus of the book on activities in and around Jerusalem demand an author in Judah. Yet, the author of the book nowhere identifies with those left in Judah after either the first deportation or the fall of the city. Instead, the book focuses on those people with access to power: royalty, scribes and sages, priests, and national prophets, the very people exiled to Babylon.

The author of the book is clearly a learned person. He demonstrates knowledge of both Babylonian and Egyptian theology, culture, and history. He is well versed in a variety of Israelite literary traditions, often deliberately playing on earlier themes and motifs. These elements are fully in line with the book's report that Ezekiel was exiled in the first deportation, i.e., that he was a member of the elite who would have had access to a cosmopolitan education.

Although there are undeniable signs of a later revision, the book is presented as if the author is Ezekiel himself. Is the author of Ezekiel the prophet himself, or is the book the product of an anonymous author, who uses the persona of Ezekiel as a focal point of the book (like the author of Daniel)? While the answer is debated, the figure of Ezekiel serves a literary purpose: he both represents the ideal prophet and serves as the eyes through which the viewer sees God.

Historical Background

The use of explicit dates assumes that they mean something to the book's audience. Unfortunately, even with the dates, the exact event that triggered each oracle often remains a mystery. Only a general picture of major events can be reconstructed from various ancient sources.

The book of Ezekiel is set during the height of Babylonian power. Having recently wrestled control over Mesopotamia from the Assyrians, the Babylonian kings sought to expand their power into the Levant, which is the area bordering the Mediterranean Sea on the East from Turkey to Egypt and includes the kingdoms of Judah and Israel. This expansion led to many conflicts with both Egypt and Phoenicia. The fate of Judah was determined by this conflict. After the death of Josiah in 609, Judah had four kings in twenty-two years, each supported by either Egypt or Babylon. The first siege and deportation in 597 came as the result of a rebellion against Babylon. This deportation consisted of only royalty, the army, skilled workers, and "the chiefs of the land" (2 Kgs 24:15-16); Ezekiel was part of this deportation. He dates his oracles with reference to the accession of the exiled king, Jehoiachin, showing that he considered him the only true king of Judah at the time.

Ezekiel's prophetic activity begins four years after this deportation (593). This was around the time when Egypt made a push to gain allies in the Levant. As a result, Zedekiah, the king installed by the Babylonians after the first siege, eventually rebelled against Babylonian control. Babylon retaliated, besieging the city a second time. Although Egypt came to Judah's aid during the eighteen-month siege, they failed, and the city fell to the Babylonians in July 587 (2 Kgs 25:1-4). Although the oracles in Ezekiel 1–32 purport to be from the period before the fall of the city, the book as a whole was written after this second exile and reflects the theological challenges this event posed for Israel.

Major Themes

The literary integrity of the book is demonstrated by its consistent and integrated theology. The main themes of the book are the defiling effect of sin, God's abandonment of the city, and issues about divine power.

The basic outline of the book centers on God's presence and absence. At the beginning of the book, God still resides in the temple in Jerusalem, seated on a cherubim throne fitted with wheels, poised to leave. In Israelite temple theology, the Lord could only be approached by those in a state of ritual purity. Ritual purity stems from the attempt to keep the world as closely aligned with its pristine created state as possible. The impure results of sin can build up, defiling whole clans, lands, and cities. The city of Jerusalem is in such a state at the beginning of the book: the sins of the people are increasing, and the impurity of the city is building up.

Ezekiel denotes this impurity with the word "abomination." Outside of Ezekiel, the word denotes violations of ritual purity in Leviticus, especially of the Holiness Code (Lev 17–26). It is also found in the books of Kings to refer to worship of foreign gods, specifically the Transjordanian gods Chemosh and Molech/Milcom, who were gods associated with child sacrifice (1 Kgs 11:5; 11:7; 2 Kgs 23:13). The use of the term in Ezekiel most closely resembles both uses: abominations are sins against God through violations of purity regulations and worship of other gods.

In the vision of chapters 8–11, Ezekiel sees that this ritual impurity has reached the temple, rendering it unfit to house God's presence. As a result, God puts the chariot-throne in gear and flies out of the city. With God gone, the city has been abandoned. In the ancient Near East, when a god leaves a temple, the city is no longer protected by his or her beneficial powers and so is vulnerable to attack, plagues, pestilence, and defeat. When the Lord leaves the city, its eventual fall is unavoidable. Chapters 11–24 recount the disintegration of the city, the result of the increasing degradation of the people. God's abandonment leaves them in their natural state, a state of utter defilement and debasement.

This view of Israel's "natural" state pervades the book of Ezekiel. Chapters 16 and 23, which personify the city as a female, portray Israel as essentially defiled, a people who have never done anything to deserve God's regard. Israel is depicted as a baby wallowing in its own birth-blood, a defiled creature, unable to purify itself, and even unaware of the need to be cleansed. God sees the baby and purifies it, an act of pure divine initiative. This pattern of divine initiative occurs throughout the book. Israel never purifies itself; even in the oracles of restoration, Israel does nothing to deserve the restoration, nor anything to achieve it. The image of the dry bones illustrates this theme: Israel is as dead as dry bones. God alone acts.

Israel can only respond by acknowledging its own depravity and God's power. A phrase repeated seventy-two times in the book ("that you may know that I am the Lord") conveys this theme. It is clear that this knowledge of God is not an objective recording of facts but a full recognition of the significance of the Lord's character, a transformative awareness of the utterly unbalanced relationship between God and humanity. This "knowledge" of God's greatness will "shame" Israel into righteous behavior.

This theology makes sense when read in light of the historical backdrop of the book. This was a community for whom the very concept of the Lord's power was in question. They had been deported to Babylon, seen their city destroyed, its temple burnt down, their fellow citizens killed, maimed, assaulted, enslaved. The burning question in their minds was where was the Lord when this was happening? Why couldn't God save them? Ezekiel's book addresses this theological crisis by highlighting those elements of Yahwism that allowed the religion to survive. The author's stress on traditions from the past shows that he wants to maintain continuity with Israel's past, even as he plays with those traditions in an attempt to reconceive the implications of God's power.

The Lasting Influence of the Book of Ezekiel

The book of Ezekiel was enormously influential almost from the beginning. Elements of the prophet's visions are echoed in Zechariah in the Old Testament and the Songs of the Sabbath Sacrifice found among the Dead Sea Scrolls. Influence on the New Testament is best seen in the depiction of the holy city in Revelation. Jewish mystical thought found the image of the chariot throne, the *merkabah*, fertile ground for reflection on the experience of the Divine. Christian tradition sees the vision of chapter 1 as a symbol of the Bible itself, the four beings representing the four parts of both the Old and the New Testament, and their four faces allegories for the four gospel writers (Matthew is the angel/human, Mark the lion, Luke the ox, and John the eagle).

COMMENTARY

PART I: CALL OF THE PROPHET

Ezekiel 1:1–3:15

The book begins with an elaborate call narrative, which includes a narrative prologue (1:1-3a), a description of the vision (1:3b-28), an account of God's speech from the apex of the vision (2:1–3:11), and a narrative epilogue that describes the prophet's reaction (3:12-15). This passage contains echoes of the call in Isaiah 6. In both calls the prophets have a vision of God enthroned above angelic beings. In both, the prophets are given judgment oracles to deliver to the nation, and in both the prophets address a community that experiences a siege of Jerusalem. Ezekiel's call narrative, however, expands the description of the vision of God's presence.

The call narrative introduces the reader to the main characters of the book. First, it introduces us to Ezekiel, a priest living in exile. His epithet, a derogatory "Son of man" (2:1, 3, 6, etc.), which can also be translated as "mere mortal," shows that the text does not intend to glorify him. The book consistently keeps its focus on the second character introduced, the Lord God, in Hebrew ʿadonai *Yhwh*, literally translated "my master, YHWH," or in the NABRE, "the Lord GOD" (2:4). Because of the convention of translating "Yahweh" as "LORD," the translation can be misleading. The first word, "Lord," is a title, not the divine name, stressing the higher status of the one addressed. The second word is the divine name "YHWH," translated as "GOD" in the NABRE. The juxtaposition with the derogatory "Son of man" constantly emphasizes the unequal status of God and Ezekiel.

Before "the Lord GOD" speaks, the text's opening vision conveys much about God's character: majestic, loud, bright, enthroned, movable, and ultimately indescribable. This is a god who must be obeyed, whose will cannot be opposed. The interaction between god and human occurs through the "spirit," a divine element that can control human action: setting Ezekiel on his feet (2:2), lifting him up (3:12), and seizing him (3:14). It is paralleled in 3:14 with the "hand of the LORD," an image used to connote divine power.

The last character introduced is "Israel." Its meaning in the book is ambiguous, however. Sometimes the word means the original twelve tribes of Israel. This is especially true in the restoration chapters (34-48) that imagine the reassembly of the whole nation. Most often, especially true in the oracles of condemnation, the prophet speaks only to the citizens of Jerusalem. In this oracle both groups are the subject of God's message of "Lamentation, wailing, woe" (2:10).

1:1-28 God above the cherubim

The vision of God's presence above the cherubim unifies the book. In chapters 8–11, Ezekiel sees the vision abandon the city before its fall, and in chapters 40–48, he witnesses its return to the new temple. The book explores the effect of God's presence and absence on Jerusalem and the nation.

The chapter begins with a typical superscription, telling the reader who Ezekiel was and when he lived. Here we discover that Ezekiel was exiled to Babylon in the first deportation under Nebuchadnezzar in 597 B.C., which suggests he was among the elite of the city. The reader is also told that he is a priest, presumably from among the priestly family in control of the Jerusalem temple. Although this fact is never explicitly confirmed, three factors support this conclusion. First, unlike Jeremiah who was from an outlying priestly family, Ezekiel is identified with those leaders who would be a threat to Nebuchadnezzar. Second, the end of the book glorifies the Zadokite priests, the priestly family most often associated with control of the temple. Third, the book shares the theology and ideology of other texts that arise within the Jerusalem priesthood, such as the Priestly source of the Pentateuch, the Holiness Code (Lev 17–26), and the books of Chronicles.

The meaning of the reference to the "thirtieth year" in Ezekiel 1:1 is debated. While this may be a date displaced from the end of the book, or a reference to the age of Jehoiachin, interpreters as early as Origen favor the view that this refers to the age of the prophet. According to Numbers 4, men from priestly families were ordained into official service at the age of thirty. If this reading is correct, this marks the first of many instances of irony in the book: just when Ezekiel should have been ordained into service at the temple, he finds himself sitting next to a canal in Babylon. Nevertheless, he has an unmediated experience of God's real presence, an experience thought to be limited to the high priest serving at the Jerusalem temple.

The vision itself begins with a "stormwind," a visible manifestation of God also evident in the stories of Elijah (2 Kgs 2:11), Job (38:1), and Jonah (1:4). The creatures described at the beginning of Ezekiel's vision, although not named here, are identified as cherubim in Ezekiel 10:4. These heavenly figures were common in ancient Near Eastern art: winged guardians of entrances and thrones who were part human and part animal. In ancient Israel, they guarded the entrance to Eden (Gen 3:24) and the ark of the covenant. Each of Ezekiel's cherubim has one head with four faces and three pairs of wings.

As the prophet's vision travels up this figure, it becomes clear that the cherubim are not the focal point of the vision. Instead, it is God's presence above them. This follows a west Semitic tradition of representing a deity's presence in a temple with an empty throne. God hovers or sits above that throne, as is clear in Exodus 25:22 and 40:34–38; 1 Samuel 4:4; and Isaiah 6:1. The throne in Ezekiel is portable, as it is in 2 Kings 2.

As Ezekiel's gaze travels up to God, the prophet's speech becomes increasingly inadequate. The Hebrew text reflects the confusion. Ezekiel is unable to give an exact description of what he sees, and instead uses qualifiers to give the reader a general notion of this vision. What is clear is that God's presence is associated with light and splendor. This divine light, called God's *kabod* or "glory" in Ezekiel 1:28, is evident in such diverse places as Exodus 16:9-10, 1 Kings 8:10-11, Isaiah 6:3, and Psalm 29.

2:1-8 God's initial speech

This section begins with Ezekiel's first reaction to the vision: he bows down to the ground in an act of respect. A "spirit" then enters into him and lifts him up on his feet. The spirit reflects Israelite traditions about prophecy: just as prophets are described as prophesying through a "spirit," this spirit has taken hold of Ezekiel. He is a prophet, not by choice but by divine command.

The speech begins with God, not identified until verse 4, calling Ezekiel "Son of man." Within Israelite tradition, prophets such as Elijah were referred to as "son/man of God," but this book will never refer to Ezekiel as a "man of God." The consistent use of the phrase "son of man" drives

home the point that the prophet's authority always derives from God. Verse 5 states that whether or not Israel heeds his message, "they shall know that a prophet has been among them." This is the first of several hints in the book that Ezekiel's prophetic status was in doubt.

In the same verse, Israel is introduced as a "rebellious" nation, a word used four times in this chapter alone. It is a prominent word in the Pentateuch, where it means that they were obstinate, stubborn, and openly hostile to God and God's chosen leaders. The opposition to Ezekiel that permeates the book is therefore tantamount to opposition to God. The text likens the pain of this rebellion to sitting on scorpions (2:6). The initial speech ends with God commanding the prophet not to be rebellious and to eat the scroll that God subsequently presents to him.

2:9–3:4 Ezekiel eats the scroll

Ezekiel sees a hand holding an inscribed scroll. The words translated as "Lamentation, wailing, woe," in 2:10 are three synonyms for mourning. They can also refer to specific types of Israelite lament poetry utilized in other parts of the book (e.g., chs. 19 and 32). Whether these are the exact words he read on the scroll or whether the text is saying these are the types of writing contained on the scroll is unclear. What is clear is that the ingestion of the scroll refers to an internalization of God's message by Ezekiel: the words become part of him. The scroll is said to taste like honey (Ezek 3:3), a parallel to the manna in the wilderness narratives (Exod 16:31). The focus in Ezekiel 2–3 is on the prophet's obedience even in light of both the popular opposition to his ministry and the severity of God's message.

3:5-16 God's speech continues

After Ezekiel eats the scroll, God continues speaking. Ezekiel is warned that Israel will listen to him no more than they listen to God. Yahweh tells the prophet to be as stubborn as they are, "whether they hear or refuse to hear" (3:11). At the end of God's speech, the spirit lifts up Ezekiel, who witnesses God's loud retreat (3:12 and 13). He is then "seized" by this spirit and left "angry and bitter" with the "hand of the LORD" pressing hard upon him (3:14). The prophet is "distraught" for seven days because of the gravity of his mission (3:15).

PART II: ORACLES OF DESTRUCTION
Ezekiel 3:16–24:27

The later editor of Ezekiel places all of the oracles prophesied before the fall of Jerusalem in the first part of the book. This section is bracketed on one side by the narrative of Ezekiel's initial call to be a prophet (1:1–3:15) and on the other side by the oracles prophesying doom on foreign nations (25:1–32:32). While there are a few oracles of hope interspersed among the oracles of destruction, the clear message of this section is unrelenting damnation. The oracles of doom highlight Ezekiel's main themes. Israel is essentially a defiled, sinful nation, from its leaders on down. God alone has been responsible for any good that the nation has experienced, but God abandons the city because Israel's defilement has reached the temple. The city, now without divine protection, is slated for destruction.

Oracles Before God Leaves (3:16–7:27)

3:16-21 The prophet as a watchman
The oracles of destruction begin with a short divine discourse on the nature of the prophetic office. Drawing on a previous prophetic metaphor (see Hos 9:8; Hab 2:1; and Jer 6:17), the text likens the prophet to a sentry or watchman, i.e., a person who sits on the city walls in order to warn the inhabitants of any approaching enemy. If the sentry were to fall asleep on the job, or, worse, see an enemy approach but fail to sound the alarm, then that city's demise would be his fault. So too, a prophet whom God tells of an impending disaster would be responsible for that city's fall if he or she would fail or refuse to warn the city.

The text emphasizes that the sole responsibility of a prophet was to deliver God's message. His efficacy does not depend on the people's response. The metaphor of the prophet as sentry frames the oracles of destruction. It implies that Ezekiel's inability to change his audience does not mean he failed as a prophet. This passage is replicated in Ezekiel 33:1-9, just before the report of the fall of the city.

3:22-27 Ezekiel becomes mute
It is bitterly ironic that in the very next section God commands Ezekiel to stay at home and renders him mute. The exact nature of these re-straints, especially the prophet's dumbness, has been debated. The book does depict Ezekiel's audiences coming to him, suggesting that he did not leave his house. As for Ezekiel's inability to speak, the word translated as "rebuke" in verse 26 can mean that he was unable to intercede on behalf of Israel. This would explain why Ezekiel never argues with God on behalf of the people. In verse 27, God states that Ezekiel can speak only when God gives him a message to deliver. This highlights the trustworthiness of the oracles Ezekiel proclaims. He is no false prophet, pretending to declare messages from God that were, in fact, only his own views, nor does he embellish God's messages with his own words. Every word Ezekiel spoke was from God.

4:1-17 First sign-act: Ezekiel besieges the city
Many scholars have wondered about Ezekiel's sanity. Already by chapter 4 he has eaten a scroll (3:2), laid helpless for seven days (3:15), and been struck with periodic muteness (3:26-27). Now we see him inscribing a clay brick with a representation of the city of Jerusalem and besieging it by lying on his left side for 390 days (probably for the years of sin from Solomon until the fall of the city), and then on his right for 40 days (signifying that the punishment will last one generation). He must also eat only bread cooked on dung. Did Ezekiel really do these actions, and, if so, what are we to think of the state of his mental health?

Whether or not some prophet named Ezekiel performed these actions is less important than the cultural context within which this passage functioned. For the ancient audience, this text reports a sign-act: a public performance of a prophetic message. The performative setting required that the act be shocking, or at least remarkable, in order to incite a viewing audience to understand the divine message. Hyperbole, such as the length of this sign-act, can be a part of the "shock" or effectiveness of a prophetic oracle. Within the literary context of the book, the length of the action conveys what kind of a prophet Ezekiel is: even if God told him to lie on his sides 430 days, he would do this without question.

The one note of protest in the text reinforces this message. Ezekiel requests that his food not be cooked on dung (4:14). It shows that the prophet could, in fact, protest what God commands him to do. God does not rebuke Ezekiel for requesting this revision. Ezekiel, presumably, could have asked for a modification of the action of besieging; his submission is thus reinforced by the one protest he mounts. Yet, the Lord does not give Ezekiel everything that he wants: he only makes the food a bit less impure by having it cooked on animal dung, rather than human feces (4:15).

Prophetic sign-acts are meant to convey a message better than words alone could do. This image of a ritually pure priest lying on his side with ramparts built against a city inscribed on a brick, eating grain cooked on dung, vividly communicates the fate that God predicts for the city: a siege that will leave them eating impure food, a punishment that fits their sins of impurity.

5:1-15 Second sign-act: Ezekiel's shavings

God commands Ezekiel to perform a second symbolic act with the model city. This time he is to shave his beard and divide the hair into three parts: one-third to be burned within the city, one-third to be struck by the sword outside the city, and one-third to be scattered into the wind (5:2). The meaning is transparent and seems to need no further elaboration: Ezekiel describes the fate of those within Jerusalem, some of whom will die fighting outside of the city, some of whom will die when the city walls are breeched, the rest of whom will be exiled. The brief mention of a small bit of hair sewn into the prophet's hem (5:3) refers to the small number of exiles who will survive these disasters.

God elaborates on the meaning of the sign-act (5:5-15). Jerusalem is sinful because, surrounded by foreign nations and utterly reliant on the LORD, she rebels against God's "statutes." God calls this rebellion "abominations" that have defiled the temple (5:9 and 11). The speech further describes the impending punishments. Verse 10 predicts cannibalism, a traditional element in ancient literature describing siege warfare. Verse 12 speaks of disease, famine, and bloodshed, images expanded in verses 16-17. Verses 8 and 14-15, which frame the punishment, show that the aim is not just to destroy the city but to shame it. They become an object lesson for those foreign nations that surround it. The passage ends with the statement, "I, the LORD, have spoken," highlighting the unavoidability of this oracle. God's word stands in judgment (5:15 and 17).

6:1-14 Prophecy against the mountains

The cursing of the mountaintops refers to a condemnation of worship at high places. Some of these high places were associated with groves of sacred trees, as reflected in verse 13. Although some of these cultic areas were used for the worship of the Lord, this oracle is directed against those dedicated to other gods.

Verses 1-7 begin with a condemnation of the mountains of all of Israel. Just as improper worship defiled the land, so God will defile the high places by scattering human bones around their altars. The "lusting hearts" in verse 9, which come to prominence as the book progresses, is an image for the worship of other gods. As the description of the punishment in verse 12 progresses, the prophetic gaze travels through Israel from outside Jerusalem to inside. Those "far off" will die by disease. Those just outside the city walls, or "nearby," will die by the sword (12). Those dwelling within the besieged city will die by famine. The punishment will affect the whole land, from the "wilderness" in the south to Riblah in the north (14).

God states four times that the purpose of this punishment is knowledge of God (6:7, 10, 13, and 14). In verses 8-10, God asserts that those who survive will "know" that their acts were "abominations" and they deserve punishment. In verse 13 this knowledge will come when they see the slain scattered on the old sacred precincts.

7:1-27 Poem on the end

Although not all ancient versions preserve the poetic form of this chapter, the Hebrew text is clearly poetic. The oracle is characterized by the use of short phrases, a high degree of parallelism, and a beautiful play on images that weave the themes into the long passage. This beautiful structure stands in contrast to the horrible message it contains: the end of all they know is close at hand.

Verses 2b-4 start the spiral of images: the end is coming, and God will have no mercy. This oracle is addressed to the very dirt of the nation. The word translated "land" in verse 2 is the same word for the soil out of which Adam was created in Genesis 2:7, not the word used to designate national entities. Here, then, God curses the land of Israel down to its very soil.

Verses 5-27 expand the opening oracle, highlighting the book's concern that the punishment matches the sins. The poem relates this in both its structure and content. The poet states that the end is imminent: their actions demand a requisite response from God. Again the poet plays on a common prophetic image, the "day" of the LORD (7:10). From as early as Amos, the day of the LORD referred to the day when the Lord would appear to carry out a judgment against the wicked.

The people are condemned for three things in this poem: violence or neglect of the law (7:10-11), improper use of wealth (7:12-13 and 19-20), and illicit worship (7:20). These sins are intertwined; for example, one of the improper uses of wealth is to decorate idols. All of these violations are called "abominations" (7:8, 9). The poem repeatedly states that the severity of the punishment will be measured by their sins (7:8, 9, 16, and 27). In addition, the forms of the punishments will match the violations. The people will experience shame for their actions (7:18). Israel will suffer as victims of violence (7:23), their sanctuaries will be destroyed (7:22), and their wealth will fail to save them (7:19). These three punishments are summarized again in verse 24.

The poet connects the poem in chapter 7 to the ones in chapters 5 and 6. In both 5:11 and 7:4 and 9, the Lord will have no mercy. Ezekiel 7:15 reiterates the three punishments mentioned in chapter 6 (sword, disease, and famine). Like Ezekiel 5:13 and 6:7, 13, and 14, the purpose of the punishment is knowledge of the LORD (7:4, 9, and 27).

The poem ends with a description of the ineffectiveness of Judah's leaders in dealing with the impending disaster. Religious leaders, such as prophets and priests, will not be able to help the people avoid the end through visions and "instruction" or torah (7:26). In other words, the people cannot avoid this either by obeying what a prophet may tell them to do or by observing ritual forms of repentance or purification. The same terror awaits all of Israel from its leaders down to the soil.

God Leaves the City (8:1–11:25)

These four chapters return to the opening vision of God on the chariot throne. The material in these chapters forms a unit. This is most evident in the parallels between its beginning (8:1-3) and ending (11:22-25), the progressive movement of the chariot throne (inner gate [8:3], threshold [9:3], and out of the city [11:23]), and the concentric structure of the material.

Once again these chapters describe the prophet's visions, but in these visions he is transported back to the city of Jerusalem. While some scholars have taken this as an indication that someone living in Jerusalem wrote the book of Ezekiel, most recent scholarship concludes that these are not eyewitness accounts, although they were probably based on what the community in exile knew about the events leading to the fall of the city after the second-wave of exiles had joined them in Babylon.

Even so, it would be a mistake to read these visions as literal descriptions of historical events. Rather, the text may conflate events, describe events in hyperbolic language, even envision fictional events that convey more clearly the sins that the prophet wishes to describe. Certainly no historical witness saw a prophet digging through the wall or the cherubim flying out of the temple precinct. In fact, the vision tells the audience something that the people involved did not know: that God had in fact abandoned the city long before the city fell.

Why was it so important to affirm that God had left the city long before its fall? The author wishes to avoid the conclusion that the Lord had failed to defend the city against the Babylonian army. On the contrary, his graphic depiction of the offenses against the LORD serves to highlight God's restraint. The language of these chapters is replete with the terminology of impurity. Judah's sins led to the ultimate defilement of the temple, which forced the LORD to abandon the city. Divine abandonment, therefore, precipitated the final descent towards Jerusalem's ultimate punishment. As the chariot throne flies away, the reader knows that the city is doomed.

8:1-18 Visions of abominations in the temple

The vision is dated to September 592, approximately six years before the fall of the city. The opening verses set the following descriptions within a visionary context. Using descriptive terms parallel to those in 1:26-28, the prophet sees a bright, human-like figure. From the center of the vision, a hand emerges. Although the phrase "hand of the LORD" is usually a metaphor for divine power, here the prophet means a literal hand, which grasps the prophet by the hair and transports him back to Jerusalem.

Once "in" Jerusalem the prophet comes to rest within the temple precincts. Ezekiel's vision suggests that the temple of Jerusalem at this time had at least two courts, an outer one probably accessible to a wide variety of people, and an inner one with access limited in some way. It is unclear from the report of what he sees, however, whether the sins simply entail the activities he describes, or also include the presence of people in parts of the temple where they should not be.

The references to the activities that the book describes are cryptic. Clearly the original audience would have recognized the rituals to which he alludes, but contemporary scholars can only guess at their object and import. First, the text states that he is brought to the seat of "the statue of jealousy that provokes jealousy" (8:3). The god whose jealousy is provoked by the image is the Lord, but it is unclear which god is depicted in the "statue of jealousy." Next, the prophet sees "loathsome beasts" and "idols" carved on the courtyard wall (8:10). The Babylonians carved chaos monsters on the walls of some of their temples, but the text fails to identify either the beasts or the idols. Next the prophet describes ritual activities: incense offerings by the elders (8:11), women weeping for Tammuz (8:14), twenty-five people prostrating to the sun (8:16), and an action involving a branch (8:17). Of these, the only one that can be identified with anything approaching clarity is Tammuz, a Mesopotamian figure whose dying and rising represented cycles of fertility and sterility.

The meaning of the passage luckily does not depend on identifying the deities or rituals involved. The vision clearly communicates that these actions have defiled the temple. The sins are repeatedly referred to as abominations (8:6, 9, 13, 15, and 17). The closing two verses show that the description of the sins serves to justify God's violent anger against Judah.

9:1-11 God sends out the executioners

Chapter 9 gives us a rare glimpse into the Israelite understanding of the mechanics of God's wrath. God, who first removes himself to the outer edge of the temple (9:3a), does not slay evil persons but sends executioners to carry out the punishment. These executioners are called "men"

(9:2), although they are not corporeal beings. Their actions reflect those of minor deities in the religions that surrounded Israel. Here, the "men" have specific functions: the ones who wield the sword are not the same as those marking the foreheads of the righteous. The criterion for righteousness depends on the previous chapter: those who oppose or mourn over the actions described in chapter 8 will receive the "mark" (9:4). The Hebrew in Ezekiel 9:8 is ambiguous; the NABRE translates it as "I was left alone." However, it can also mean, "I alone was left," meaning no one except Ezekiel was deemed righteous enough to receive the mark. Otherwise the text does not state how many were slain, although the text does stress that God will have no mercy (8:18; 9:5 and 10).

The passage seems to depict an immediate slaughter of the wicked. Bodies pile up in the temple precinct, leading to its ultimate defilement. However, this vision probably depicts the fall of the city six years later. The visionary slaughter has a rhetorical function within the book. From this point on, Ezekiel, and thus the reader, knows that the inhabitants of Jerusalem are the walking dead.

10:1-22 The chariot throne departs

The second part of the vision commences with Ezekiel seeing the same chariot throne as he had seen in chapter one. Here for the first time the creatures supporting the throne are specifically called "cherubim" (10:1). God commands the scribe to take burning coals from beneath the chariot wheels and scatter them over the city in an act of destruction (10:2). The description of the chariot throne in verses 9-17 and 20-22 should be read in connection with chapter 1; both utilize the same images and wording. The text stresses God's mobility, especially in verses 18 and 19: the throne lifts up out of the "house" or sanctuary building, flies to the eastern gate of the temple courtyards, and stops momentarily to address the prophet again.

11:1-25 God's last words before departing the city

This chapter does not read as smoothly as the previous three and almost seems to contradict the abiding note of doom in the previous material. Whether this is evidence of secondary additions to the text or the political hand of the author whose agenda includes the elevation of the righteous exiles over the wicked inhabitants of the city is debatable. Verses 14-20, which use language similar to the oracles of restoration in the last third of the book, seem particularly out of place. However, this may be a rhetorical hook or anticipatory device designed to foreshadow later sections of the book.

The description of Judah's sins employs images of violence and bloodshed rather than ritual abomination. The passage plays on two metaphors of destruction: boiling meat (11:3) and bloody death (11:10). The mention of specific people in this chapter suggests that the description of their slaughter in chapters 9 and 10 is wholly visionary, not historical. The real death of Pelatiah in verse 13 causes Ezekiel great grief, representing to him the reality of the utter destruction predicted in previous chapters. His exclamation ("Alas, Lord God! will you utterly wipe out what remains of Israel? You are finishing off what remains of Israel!" [11:13]) shows that he realizes that Pelatiah's death marks the beginning of the fulfillment of the visions.

Those remaining in the city had interpreted the deportation of the elite (king, priests, and bureaucrats) in 597 as evidence of their wickedness (11:15), but verse 16 specifically refutes this. Ezekiel, who knows that God has abandoned the inhabitants of the city, states that the Lord is a "sanctuary" for the exiles instead, meaning God's presence, with its protection and blessings, is with the exiles, not with the remaining city-dwellers.

Once exiled, the entire remnant of Israel is promised restoration. The land will be purged of any residue of abomination (11:18), and the people will be changed in some way so that they will not be able to violate God's laws again. The image used is that of a "new heart" and a "new spirit" (11:19), explained further as a heart of "flesh" that replaces a heart of "stone." While it is tempting to read this passage in light of Jeremiah 31:31-34 that speaks of God's covenant written on the heart, the heart here represents life and death. In Ezekiel, the righteous will "live" (heart of flesh), although they seem to have been "dead" (heart of stone). This new heart will enable them to follow God's commands (11:20).

This large, four-chapter section of the book of Ezekiel ends with the vision of God's departure

(11:22-25). The enthroned God, who has stopped at the eastern gate of the temple court to deliver a final message, lifts up and flies to a mountain east of the city (11:23). Where it goes from there is unclear. The vision ends with the prophet transported back to the river Chebar. God's statement that he would be a sanctuary for the exiles might suggest that the author envisions that the throne proceeds to Babylon. However, the fact that Ezekiel's visions begin with the chariot throne flying to him from the "North" (1:4), and then subsequently departing, suggest that the fullness of God's presence remained elusive for the exiles as well.

Oracles in a Godless Land (12:1–24:27)

The variety of the oracles following God's departure from the city resembles the variety in other prophetic collections; however, Ezekiel's oracles tend to be longer than those from preexilic prophets. Within these chapters, Ezekiel paints vivid metaphors for the rise and fall of Judah's political leaders (chs. 17 and 19), reviews Judah's history of sin (chs.16, 20, and 23), and argues for the culpability of his own generation (ch. 18). The delay between God's abandonment of the city in chapter 11 and its fall in chapter 33 has a twofold rhetorical effect. First, it provides Judah ample opportunity to repent and avoid destruction. Second, the delay makes God look patient and merciful, even in light of the destruction that the Lord ultimately orchestrates.

12:1-20 Another sign-act: Ezekiel flees like a refugee

The audience of this oracle appears to be the inhabitants of Jerusalem. In the sign-act of verses 3-7, the prophet re-enacts the refugee's journey: digging through the wall at night with face covered, presumably to avoid capture by the army surrounding the city (12:12-14). This sign-act describes the attempt of the "prince," Zedekiah, to flee the city (see 2 Kgs 25:4-7). Ezekiel 12:6 and 11 state that Ezekiel is a "sign" to the Israelites, i.e., a concrete symbol of Judah's fate. The book will elaborate on this in Ezekiel 24:15-27.

12:21–13:23 True and false prophecy

The next section deals with the apparent ineffectiveness of Ezekiel's oracles in contrast to the words and actions of the prophets that the people of Judah did heed. The taunt or "proverb" of the people, that "The days drag on, and every vision fails" (12:22), refers primarily to Ezekiel's visions of destruction. Above we noted the discrepancy between the date of the vision of chapters 8–11 and its fulfillment in chapter 33. Assuming that 12:21–13:23 also corresponds to the date in chapters 8–11, Ezekiel's prediction of Jerusalem's fall was still six years in the future. To the people of Judah, Ezekiel is a false prophet: if the destruction has not yet come to pass, it never will.

In answer to this accusation, the passage first notes that the prophecy is not "false" but delayed. It does this by placing the responsibility for the delay squarely in God's hands (12:25 and 28). God's anger, however, had reached the breaking point; there would be no more delay. He has spoken what he has spoken and will do as he speaks. This rhetoric serves three purposes. First, it confirms Ezekiel's prophetic claims. He is not a false prophet but speaks only what God says. Second, it serves a major theme of the book: the preservation of God's power. The delay has been God's choice. Third, it advances the theme that God's ultimate punishment of Israel was not only deserved but, in fact, long overdue.

Chapter 13 takes up the indictment of the false prophets, presumably those whom the Israelites had been following. Verses 1-16 utilize the image of city walls. It is an appropriate metaphor, since Judah falls after its walls have failed to protect the inhabitants (13:14-15). God reminds the prophets that they had not built the walls, meaning that they were not responsible for the city's protection. This message reminds the reader that God's power alone has established and maintained the city of Jerusalem. The prophets will meet their doom because they have led the people astray with untrue oracles. The chapter repeats that these prophets preach "Peace," or a message of assurance that Judah will not be conquered (13:10), even though it is doomed.

Verses 17-23 indict female prophets. We know little about female prophets as a distinct class in ancient Israel, although they were an accepted institution. However, no biblical texts about prophetesses mention distinct dress, unique visions, or special practices of divination. Here Ezekiel does not attack the institution of female prophets per se nor the efficacy of "amulets" and

"veils" (13:17-21). Rather, he condemns their false message (13:19 and 22-23), just as he had condemned the prophets in verse 8; both groups prophesy from "their own thought(s)" (13:2 and 17). While the word "ensnare" in verses 18 and 20 can refer to sexual seduction, it is also a hunting term. The prophecies from these women are a deadly trap for the righteous, because, by prophesying falsely, they have led "the wicked" into the trap of complacency and self-righteousness (13:22).

14:1-11 Moral state of the inquirer

Ezekiel then turns to the question of the moral rectitude of the one seeking a prophetic word. First, God states that if people are unrepentant idolaters then seeking the help of a prophet of the Lord only increases their state of sinfulness. In Ezekiel 14:1-8 the addressees are the exiled elders, not the inhabitants of Jerusalem. The implication is that they have been exiled because of past idolatry, which they had not yet put out of "their hearts" (14:3-4, 7).

Verses 9-11 recognize that other prophets may address these people. Verse 9 states that God is behind the message that these prophets deliver. This suggests that, just like in 1 Kings 22:19-23, the Lord has put a "lying spirit" into the prophets in order to deceive idolaters. In Ezekiel 14:10-11, God removes both idolaters and their prophets from the land, since they defile the nation by their actions.

14:12-23 Will God spare the city for the sake of the righteous?

Verses 12-23 address the problem of the righteous who suffer in the destruction of the city. The passage illustrates the point by referring to three legendary figures: Noah, Daniel, and Job (14:14 and 20). Contemporary readers know all three figures from the Bible, but the traditions to which Ezekiel refers cannot be identical to the biblical texts we now have. Noah certainly refers to the righteous man whom God saved from the flood, but most scholars believe that the whole book of Genesis did not exist when the book of Ezekiel was written. The book of Daniel was not written at the time of the writing of the book of Ezekiel since the Babylonian kings with whom Daniel interacts were alive after the death of Ezekiel. The date of the book of Job is uncertain, but most scholars date it to a time after the exile, again post-dating Ezekiel. These references are either later additions to the book or reflect earlier written or oral traditions of these legendary figures.

The oracle concludes that these men, and thus those who are equally righteous, may be individually saved. However, their presence alone cannot save the city (14:14, 16, 18, and 20) since Jerusalem's fate is unavoidable. There may be a few survivors (14:21-22), but the references to their "ways" and "deeds" are ambiguous (14:22-23). If these are righteous actions, then the survival of the righteous, which contrasts with the wickedness of the punished, proves that God's destruction of Jerusalem was justified (14:23).

15:1-8 Parable of the vine

In Israelite poetic texts, Israel is often called a vine, which God planted in the land. The vine represented the fruitfulness of the country since grape production was an important crop. Ezekiel's oracle inverts this image so that the vine describes the nation's worthlessness. Ezekiel concentrates on the wood of the vine rather than its fruit. This wood is worthless for building (15:3), meaning the country is not strong enough to withstand attack. It burns quickly (15:4-5), meaning Judah will fall to its enemy without much resistance. Jerusalem, the vine that God has planted, will be easily destroyed (15:6-8).

16:1-63 Idolatry as adultery

The longest chapter in Ezekiel focuses on the image of Jerusalem as an adulterous wife, first introduced in Ezekiel 6:9. Ezekiel's particular construal of this metaphor is very difficult for modern readers to appreciate. The passage reveals the accepted misogyny of Israelite culture, as well as its exaltation of physical punishment for sexual offenses. The attribution of sexually explicit, violent, and patriarchal images to God makes it difficult to read this chapter as sacred Scripture. It is particularly imperative, then, that the cultural background of this image is more fully explained.

The depiction of divine sexuality in grandiose and explicit terms was common throughout the ancient Near East, while the practice of referring to the city as the Lord's wife was well known in Israel. The image endured because it was centered on a common social institution (marriage) and its use was adaptable to a number of different situations. It became a root metaphor for the covenant between God and Jerusalem. To fully understand this, it is important to understand ancient Israel's ideology of marriage. In Israel, spouses were not equal partners; women were legally and socially subservient to their husbands. Betrothal and marriage were contractual arrangements by which a woman became the exclusive "property" of her husband, even before the actual marriage. In practical terms, this meant that her husband was her sole sexual partner from the moment of betrothal. Since men could have more than one wife, adultery only occurred when it involved a married woman; it was a crime, punishable by death, against the sole property rights of a wronged husband (Lev 18:20; 20:10; Deut 22:22).

Ezekiel 16 plays on these elements of marriage. God is the one who owns Jerusalem, and Jerusalem owes him her exclusive allegiance and fidelity. Anything less gives him the legal right to punish her. Ezekiel 16 uses hyperbole and inflammatory rhetoric to achieve a shocking literary effect. Here, the author utilizes a common metaphor, the city as God's wife, in ways that border on pornography. (Modern translations tone down the sexually explicit language of the Hebrew texts.) It is an image sure to provoke a response.

The language of adultery within a covenant metaphor does not describe sexual sins but rather idolatry. If a city is the "wife" of a god, then that city should worship that god exclusively. Worshipping other gods is tantamount to adultery, the violation of the strict allegiance to the one god. This passage condemns Jerusalem for violating its exclusive relationship with the Lord by worshipping other gods.

The chapter, although long, forms a coherent unit, examining in detail all the various stages of birth, betrothal, marriage, adultery, punishment, and reconciliation in turn. The passage begins in verses 3-6 with a description of the girl's birth to foreign parents (Amorite or Babylonian; Hittite or Canaanite). The abandonment of the child reflects the accepted practice of exposing unwanted babies. In this case, the Lord, who just happens to be passing by, commands the child, wallowing in its own birth-blood, to live (16:6). This section of the metaphor defines Jerusalem's essential nature: defiled and in need of purification.

In verses 7-14 the girl reaches adolescence: her breasts have grown, and she has body hair. At this point God formally betroths her, spreading his cloak over her as a symbol of sexual intimacy and protection. He makes a formal declaration that may also be translated as "You are mine" (16:8; NABRE has "you became mine"), and he prepares her for marriage by purifying her himself (16:9). The Lord next dresses and adorns the bride and she becomes famous (16:10-14). The covenant with God is an act of pure divine initiative.

The marriage quickly falls apart (16:15-21) as the wife becomes promiscuous (both adulterer and whore). Using hyperbolic language, she not only has intercourse with men other than her husband but she also sets up a public spot to which men can come for her sexual favors, subsidizing this venture with the goods God has given her. The chapter refers explicitly to idolatry in verse 17 ("(you) made for yourself male images"), and verses 20-22 connect these sins with the practice of child sacrifice, an accepted ritual practice among some of Israel's neighbors. While Ezekiel 20:25-26 hints that child sacrifice may have been directed to Yahweh, here the author connects it with the worship of foreign gods.

In addition to the condemnation of idolatry, Ezekiel 16 contains a metaphorical review of Jerusalem's history, one that focuses on her alliances with other nations. Israel's infancy connotes the time before the rise of the monarchy (16:3-7). The betrothal, marriage, and adornment (16:7-14) reflect the reigns of David and Solomon. Subsequent verses, such as 23-35, symbolize Judah's later monarchy, especially its dealings with her "lovers," Assyria, Egypt, and Babylon. These were three great powers to which the city had paid tribute. Assyria was a major threat in the eighth century. From the time of the Assyrian invasion until the fall of Jerusalem to the Babylonians, the city often looked to Egypt for alliances. Lastly, Babylon supported Josiah and Zedekiah, the latter rendering the city a puppet in the Babylonian Empire. Alliances with these nations are "idolatry" because they imply that the Lord alone was not capable of defending the city. God notes that Jerusalem's payment of tribute to these foreign powers, and thus to their foreign gods, makes the city worse than a prostitute. At least prostitutes are paid for their services; Jerusalem instead pays her lovers to come to her.

The next section (16:35-43) provides an explicit description of the wife's punishment. It is not clear whether the description here matches the process of punishment of adulterous women or whether it again uses hyperbole. First the wife is totally stripped, perhaps an expansion of a more limited unveiling of the adulterous wife attested to elsewhere (see Dan 13:31-32). A crowd that includes her lovers then stones her to death, and her place of prostitution is burned to the ground. The gaze of the former lovers who witness her fate serves the purpose of the punishment, that she may become an object lesson. The blame of her fate rests completely on her and not on the Lord. Only after her death is God's anger quieted. The stripping of the wife represents the stripping of the city by the invading army. All those nations in whom she had once trusted for aid now aid Babylon in her destruction. The city is a place of reproach, its destruction so legendarily brutal that people shudder as they think of it.

Verses 44-52 compare Jerusalem to cities that Jerusalemites considered wicked. First, Jerusalem is likened to foreign nations when the passage states, "Like mother, like daughter" (16:44). Next the author compares her to Samaria, the former capital of the northern kingdom, whose destruction was interpreted by some Jerusalemites as God's punishment for the north's breach with Jerusalem. The city is also compared to Sodom, the paradigmatic evil city. Ezekiel states that Jerusalem sinned more than either Samaria or Sodom and their "daughters." Jerusalem's sinfulness makes Samaria and even Sodom appear to be just (16:52).

The last section, verses 53-63, shifts to Ezekiel's view of restoration, a view which includes Sodom and Samaria. The description is typical for Ezekiel, entailing the people's acknowledgement of their sins. Although they had held Sodom "in bad repute" (16:56), Jerusalem's wickedness is now exposed as far worse. Verses 60-63 return to the language that began the oracle. The Lord, as husband, states that he will remember both her youth and his covenant marriage with her. At the same time, Jerusalem will remember her sins and disgrace. She is promised a preeminent status above the other restored cities (16:61), but along with this preeminence comes humility, since she remembers that this is a fate she does not deserve. God states that then she will "know that I am the

Lᴏʀᴅ" (16:62), a statement quite fitting here since "know" is a euphemism for sexual intimacy. The last verse sums up the passage's final point: Jerusalem will be restored but will not forget her transgressions.

17:1-24 Allegory of the eagles and vines

Ezekiel 17:3-10 contains an allegorical riddle, followed by God's explanation of the riddle in verses 11-21. The chapter ends with a shorter allegory, using the same images as the opening riddle, but this time promising restoration instead of destruction (17:22-24).

The riddle describes the captivity of Jehoiachin and his house (17:3-4, 12), the establishment of Zedekiah as his replacement (17:5-6, 13-14), Zedekiah's rebellion against Babylon (17:7-8, 15), and God's prediction of his downfall (17:9-10 and 16-21). The sheer length of this last section shows that this is the focal point of the chapter. Many of the images in this allegory are opaque:

Image	Referent
Great eagle (v. 3)	Nebuchadnezzar
Lebanon (v. 3)	Jerusalem
Topmost branch (v. 4)	Jehoiachin
Land of merchants (v. 4)	Babylon
Native seed (v. 5)	Zedekiah
Another great eagle (v. 7)	Pharaoh Psammetichus II
Vine (vv. 7-8)	Restored Davidic monarchy

The allegory follows the historical record of the period as far as we know it. The Babylonians placed Zedekiah, originally a pro-Babylonian member of the royal family, on the throne after the deportation of Jehoiachin in 597. However, as Egyptian power in west Asia grew, Zedekiah turned to Egypt for support sometime between 593 and 588. Although the details of his contact with Egypt are unknown, it resulted in provoking Nebuchadnezzar's anger, ultimately leading to the fall of the city.

In verses 16-21 the author indicts Zedekiah for breaking his "covenant" or treaty with Nebuchadnezzar. The rupture of this agreement is so heinous that it is equated with breaking an oath sworn to God (17:19). Why does the text state that breaking a treaty with a foreign king is the same as despising an oath sworn to God? First, political

treaties in the ancient world were witnessed by the divine assembly. Presumably any treaty between Zedekiah and Nebuchadnezzar included an invocation for the Lord to witness such an oath.

Second, the book of Ezekiel presumes that Nebuchadnezzar's power derived from the Lord. Although the book of Ezekiel is not explicit about this, the book never clearly condemns either Nebuchadnezzar or Babylon. The claim here is that Babylon's control of Judah and the conditions of Nebuchadnezzar's reign are part of God's plan; Zedekiah's rebellion opposes this plan.

This last idea becomes the basis for the expansion in verses 22-24. Probably a secondary expansion to the text, it does not reflect the actual restoration of the nation during the Persian period. The oracle paints an ideal, ultimate, and lasting restoration of the nation. The Lord transplants a branch of the cedar (nation), which becomes a home for all flying creatures. The final lines of the poem (17:24b and c) focus on the irony of the proposed restoration. This once humble tree triumphs as the high or powerful nations are brought low. Such irony reveals God's power.

18:1-32 Moral responsibility

In one of the most explicit treatises on moral responsibility in the Old Testament, chapter 18 focuses on the extent of personal responsibility and the effectiveness of repentance. To modern ears, the argument that each generation is responsible for its own sins sounds trite, but within the moral tradition of the ancient near east, such conclusions were hardly ordinary. While individuals were certainly held accountable by the gods for their own transgressions, they were also part of a corporate reality, such as the nation or the family, with whom the divine realm more often interacted. For instance, when Achan keeps the banned goods from the city of Jericho, his whole family is stoned to death with him (Josh 7:24-26). Ezekiel does not often challenge this assumption; Zedekiah's sin in chapter 17 is punished by his exile and death, a fate affecting the nation as a whole. (Note, however, that the vision of the angels who mark and spare the innocent in 9:3-7 reveals a concern to protect innocent individuals.)

The passage here focuses on intergenerational punishment, an issue that arose with particular acuteness in response to the fall of Jerusalem.

When Jerusalem fell, it was natural for the community to wonder whose sins were being punished. The same proverb that begins the chapter (18:2) is also debated in Jeremiah 31:29. Several biblical texts accept God's right to inflict punishment onto future generations (see, e.g., Exod 20:5; parallels in Deut 5:9; Num 14:18). Second Kings 24:3-4 holds Manasseh, who was three generations prior to Zedekiah, accountable for the exile. Both Jeremiah and Ezekiel reject this explanation, instead asserting that the exiles themselves deserved this punishment. Ezekiel reinforces this theme by stressing that each person or generation has the opportunity to repent and be freed from the impending punishment. The logical conclusion: the Judahites were sinful both in what they did and in their failure to repent.

The chapter is structured like the disputation of a legal case. First it sets out the principle that each person is morally responsible (18:1-4). From there it describes both the righteous and the evil person (18:5-9 and 18:10-13 respectively), utilizing paradigmatic sins: sexual impurity, idolatry, and economic selfishness. Verses 14-20 deny intergenerational responsibility before discussing what in Hebrew is called "turning" (18:21-28). This has a dual meaning: a sinful person "turns" by repenting, but a righteous person "turns" by acting sinfully. While true repentance redeems one from punishment (18:21-23), past righteous deeds will not save the current sinner (18:24-26). Verses 27-29 reflect the audience's reaction to this new ethic.

The chapter culminates in a call for repentance (18:30-32). The statement is quite powerful not just in what it says but in its placement. God calls on Israel to "make for yourselves a new heart and a new spirit" (31), that is, a complete conversion to a righteous life. On the one hand, the statement is one of profound hope: even with disaster immanent, and sin so pervasive, all that is necessary for God to forgive is conversion, repentance, atonement. In addition, Ezekiel 18:23 and 32 state that God does not take pleasure in the death of the wicked, a merciful portrayal of God. God is not a sadist, even if other parts of the book suggest otherwise.

Ultimately, however, the hope in the passage highlights the tragic nature of Jerusalem's fall. Reading this chapter in light of the book as a whole, the offer of repentance highlights the pointlessness of Jerusalem's fall. The audience knows that, as merciful as God is, Jerusalem will not repent; the disaster was a senseless waste, easily avoided. Like a hero with a fatal flaw that cannot be avoided, Jerusalem marches straight on to its fate.

19:1-14 A lamentation for the leaders of Judah

Chapter 19 contains a single poem, identified at the beginning and end of the chapter as a "lamentation." This Hebrew word sometimes refers to a funeral dirge, other times to the lamentation sung in response to the destruction of a city. Ezekiel plays with this form, ostensibly lamenting the deaths of Judah's princes but implying the eventual fall of the city of Jerusalem.

The poem itself is comprised of two extended metaphors. The first utilizes the imagery of lions, which symbolizes the tribe of Judah in Genesis 49:9. The second image uses the metaphor of the vine, an image usually applied to the nation as a whole (see Ezek 17). While some scholars see the second half of the poem as a secondary addition to the chapter, the whole poem utilizes "macro-parallelism," in which the two halves together play out the meaning of the text.

Both halves are unified by the figure of the "mother." Her identity is ambiguous. Some people believe it refers to a single queen mother, Hamutal, others that it refers to the nation of Judah or Israel, and still others that it is a composite for any queen mother. Similarly, the identity of the lion cubs (19:3 and 5b) and the shoot (19:11) is debated. Most people agree that there is some reference to King Jehoahaz in verse 4 since he was, in fact, taken away to Egypt. Those who hold that the mother lion is Jehoahaz's mother, Hamutal, identify the second cub as her other son, Jehoiakim. Others, especially those who maintain that the mother stands for the nation or city, say the description of the lion's fate in verses 8-9 fits better the fate of Jehoiachin, while the shoot of the vine in verse 11 has been most often identified as Jehoiachin, Zedekiah, or a composite for the fate of the Davidic monarchy. Whatever the specific referent, the meaning of the text is clear: Judah's monarchy will be destroyed.

The poem itself is ironic. The repetition in the material framing the poem that this is and will be a lamentation (19:1 and 14) brings the reader's attention back to the form of the poem itself. The poet laments for people still alive. Rhetorically it is as if Ezekiel has printed the obituary of a living president. The notice also links the poem to the beginning of the book, where God had commanded Ezekiel to eat a scroll filled with "Lamentation, wailing, woe" (2:10).

20:1-44 A history of sin

Chapter 20 contains a lengthy recapitulation of Israel's history from the period of the exodus until their entry into the land. Elders living in Babylon have come to Ezekiel to "consult" the Lord, who refuses to hear their request (20:1-3). Instead, he has Ezekiel pronounce an oracle of destruction based on their history of sinful behavior.

This long oracle opens with a date formula, the first in the book since 8:1. Within the overall structure of the book, the date may signal the beginning of a new section; if so, it marks a final group of oracles of destruction before the announcement of Jerusalem's imminent fall. The date itself places the oracle a little less than a year after the departure of God's presence from the temple in Jerusalem. It may correspond to a visit to Israel by the pharaoh, Psammetichus II, although there is nothing in the oracle itself to suggest this.

What follows is a rewritten history, extending back into the sojourn in Egypt, one unparalleled within the Old Testament. Nowhere else in the Hebrew Bible are the Israelites accused of worshipping Egyptian gods while they were enslaved in Egypt, yet this view of the inherent sinfulness of the people accords with their depiction in the allegorical retelling of Israel's history in chapter 16.

Chapter 20 follows the main outlines of the Pentateuch: sojourn in Egypt (20:5-9), two generations in the wilderness (20:10-17 and 18-26), the revelation of the law in two stages in the wilderness (20:11-12 and 25-26), and then entry into the land (20:28). What is striking, however, is that there is no mention of Moses, Sinai, or the Decalogue. Ezekiel once again takes known traditions and twists them to suit his purposes. By freeing the giving of the law from Sinai and Moses, the reader is prepared for the revelation of new laws at the end of the book.

The retelling of the history presents a troubling view of God. First, the chapter emphasizes that God acts in order to preserve his own reputation ("for the sake of my name"; 20:9, 14, 22, and 44).

What is at stake is God's power. God chooses such a lowly people in order to demonstrate divine power to the world. This refutes the conclusion that Israel's continued existence even after sinning suggests that the Lord was powerless to stop them.

Second, the chapter also stresses God's adherence to judicial procedure. God cannot destroy them until their sins have become great enough to justify their annihilation. In order to speed this process along, God gives them "statutes that were not good" (20:25-26) so that, when they obey them, they will further defile themselves, justifying God's punishment. This shocking statement suggests that God is unfair and manipulative. The irony is that this people, who have never kept the good laws, are now observant of the laws that are not good.

The middle part of the oracle (20:27-31) relates this history to the present generation, who are challenged to break the cycle of sin. In light of chapter 18, which states that each generation is punished for its own sins, the recitation of Israel's history serves two purposes. First, it offers Judah an object lesson that they should not follow. Further, in light of the fact that the city falls, this history implies that the sins of the inhabitants of Jerusalem during the siege were even worse than those that Israel had committed in the past.

The oracle's final section (20:32-44) gives a rare glimmer of restoration. Here God promises a new wilderness-conquest period for the righteous few who will be saved. These verses provide a hook to the rest of the book. Both here and in the oracles of restoration in chapters 34–48, God promises renewal on "my holy mountain" (20:40), not Sinai, but Zion. In both, the restored people are marked by proper worship at this mountain and their avoidance of defilement. In both, Israel must remember the history of sin and defilement in order to avoid it. Yet it is the final verse in the chapter that brings the focus back to God: all of this will be done, not out of love, mercy, or justice, but only because God chooses to act "for the sake of my name" (20:44).

21:1-37 Oracles of the sword

This chapter connects several oracles that use the image of God's sword. In the first poem (21:1-12), the sword is ready to strike against Jerusalem. The second section (21:13-22) celebrates God's sword. The third poem focuses on Nebuchadnezzar's sword (21:23-32), while the chapter draws to a close with a vision of God's sword aimed at Ammon (21:33-37). Each passage repeats images and language found in other parts of the chapter.

The first poem (21:1-12) prophesies a fire throughout the whole land (21:3-4), followed by a short notice that God will bring a sword against Jerusalem (21:6-10). The defeat will be felt most by the temples and the "land," or more literally the "soil" (21:8). The prophet's reaction foreshadows the people's experience (21:11-12). In the middle of this poem (21:5), Ezekiel complains that he is not being taken seriously: "Ah! Lord GOD, they are saying about me, 'Is not this the one who is forever spinning parables?' " (5). The placement of the complaint at this point in the book is important since it addresses the threat to Ezekiel's status posed by the people's failure to repent. This passage asserts that their failure was not the prophet's fault but rather the fault of the audience, who thought he was merely an entertainer. This theme is reiterated in 33:30-33.

The second poem of the chapter, 21:13-22, contains an extended song celebrating God's sword. It is a bitter victory song since it celebrates God's destruction of Judah. Throughout the poem, the poet uses picturesque language to create an image of a battle sword: polished, sharpened, and drawn for battle. Implied is the reality that this sword will return to its sheath bloody, dulled, and sated. Although the Hebrew in this section is often obscure, the image of God could not be clearer: he is a warrior anxious for "slaughter" (21:15). This song heightens the audience's expectation of a violent end.

The third poem (21:23-32) focuses on the human agent of God's destruction: the king of Babylon. The oracle pictures Nebuchadnezzar at a fork in the road: should he go east and attack Ammon or travel west toward Jerusalem? The poet draws the audience into the scene with references to Babylonian instruments of divination, such as divinatory arrows, household gods (teraphim), and liver omens (21:26). The lot falls to Jerusalem not by coincidence but because of the evil of Zedekiah, whom Ezekiel describes as "depraved and wicked" (21:30). As a result, God hands the city over to Nebuchadnezzar (21:32).

The fourth poem (21:33-37) is directed against Ammon, although the references are ambiguous.

On the one hand, it may mean that the Ammonites also wanted to attack Jerusalem but God stayed their hand (21:33-35); instead, God destroys Ammon in their own home (35-37). On the other hand, the poet may only be referring to Ammon as a witness to Nebuchadnezzar's destruction of Jerusalem. If this is the case, then it is Babylon that will be destroyed in verses 35-37. In either case, this is another example of a rhetorical hook, this one foreshadowing the oracles against the nations in chapters 25–32.

22:1-16 The bloody city

Chapter 22 begins with multiple images of the bloody city. On the one hand, the city is "bloody" because of the acts of violence that its inhabitants have committed; on the other hand, the "bloody city" connotes the defiled state that results from its sins (22:3-4). Just as the baby wallowing in its own blood in chapter 16 is defiled, so too the city which is "bloody" is a city that is ritually polluted.

It is this second meaning that is most prominent in this section. When a reader pays close attention to the sins that the prophet lists, violence is not the most prominent one. Instead, the prophet describes acts of idolatry (22:3-4), economic injustice (22:7 and 12), cultic neglect (22:8), and sexual defilement (22:10-11). The image of the blood is a visual symbol of the city's defiled state. The punishment for these crimes is exile, in order to "purge your uncleanness" (22:15).

22:17-31 Two oracles against Israel

The first oracle, 22:17-22, uses the language of a metal refinery to condemn Israel. While fire purifies metal in other biblical texts, here Ezekiel focuses on the "dross" or leftover scrap metal that remains in a smelter at the end of the refining process. This section depicts Jerusalem as the dross, an impurity that must be removed.

The second oracle, 22:23-31, condemns various elite groups: princes (22:25), priests (22:26), officials (22:27), prophets (22:28), and people of the land (22:29). All of them lack integrity. Prophets claim to deliver oracles from God, although they have received no messages. Priests fail to distinguish between the sacred and profane. Princes exploit the very people they should protect, and both the nobles and the "people of the land" oppress the poor. None of them "build a wall" that would avert the Lord's punishment.

23:1-49 A tale of two cities

Chapter 23 reuses the image of Jerusalem as God's unfaithful wife from chapter 16. It also reflects the same view of marriage present there, as well as the same acceptance of corporal punishment for an adulterous wife. Rather than repeat all of that here, I will simply highlight what is unique to this chapter's use of the metaphor.

Ezekiel 23 applies the metaphor to two cities: Samaria and Jerusalem. While chapter 16 shames Jerusalem by stating that she is worse than Samaria, chapter 23 starts with God's "marriage" to Samaria in order to establish a parallel between the histories of the two cities. While chapter 16 focused on Judah's sin of idolatry, the metaphor here is more political, condemning Judah's alliances with foreign nations. This theme is introduced in the depiction of Samaria's payment of tribute to Assyria (23:5-10). The oracle utilizes Ezekiel's trademark irony: Samaria was destroyed by the very "lovers . . . for whom she had lusted" (23:9). Jerusalem not only repeats Samaria's mistakes but she goes further, making alliances with Babylon and yearning for help from Egypt (23:11-21). The hyperbolic sexual language paints a vivid picture of an utterly depraved city.

Like Samaria, Jerusalem is destroyed by both her lovers and those "whom you hate" (23:28), although the poem explicitly states that God is the agent of this violence. This dual agency projects a view of God that is problematic, to say the least. The lovers, acting under God's impetus, physically mutilate the "wife" by cutting off her nose and ears, take away her children (23:25), and publicly strip her (23:26-29). The chapter deliberately blames the victim ("Your depravity and prostitution brought these things upon you" [23:29b-30a]). Once again, it is important to remember that this is metaphorical language. Ezekiel 23 is not about adulterous women (although the literary device is effective because of cultural assumptions about women); it is about the fall of the city. For those in the audience who viewed themselves as innocent victims of Babylonian aggression, this chapter lays the blame squarely on their political decisions (23:31-35).

Verses 36-49 recapitulate the metaphor, this time connecting adultery with religious violations. Here the cities are punished for their idolatry (23:37) and religious irregularities (23:38-39). These religious acts are "adulteries" (23:37, 43, and 45) or covenant violations, for which the women/cities will be punished. At first glance, verse 48 seems to break the frame of the metaphor by addressing real women, but the reference to "all the women" may, just as easily, refer to other cities for which Samaria and Jerusalem have become an object lesson. This interpretation is reinforced in the final phrase of the chapter, "Then you [masculine plural] shall know that I am the Lord God" (23:49).

24:1-14 Allegory of the pot

Chapter 24 is dated to January 588, the beginning of the siege of Jerusalem (see Jer 52:4). The book asserts Ezekiel's knowledge of this event, even while in exile (24:2). The chapter begins with a "parable" depicting Jerusalem as a filthy pot that cannot be properly cleansed. The image of the pot had been introduced in Ezekiel 11:3-12, where the image communicated the people's belief that the city could not be breached. Here, the pot is an image of the city's "uncleanness": bloody and rusty (24:6-8). Furthermore, the chapter combines images seen previously in Ezekiel 21:1-12 and 22:1-16: the bloody and defiled city (24:6), a purifying fire that destroys what cannot be purified (24:11), and a buildup of defilement that can only be destroyed (24:12-13).

24:15-27 A tale of two wives

The book takes up the image of the city as God's wife one last time by imposing on Ezekiel a horrible sign-act. Ezekiel's own wife will die, and he will be prohibited from mourning her. This will be a symbolic act for the death of God's wife, Jerusalem, which should not be mourned. This final chapter in the oracles against Jerusalem places the prophetic narrator right back in the center of the book. The passage states two times that Ezekiel is to be a "sign" to the people (24:24 and 27). A prophetic sign serves two purposes. First, it assures that what the prophet is predicting will come true; for example, when Samuel predicts that Saul will become king, he gives Saul a sign to watch for so that Saul will know that this oracle will come true (1 Sam 10:1-7). The death of Ezekiel's wife should assure the audience that God will destroy Jerusalem. Second, a sign, like a symbolic act, can also symbolize an oracle. Read in this light, Ezekiel's life symbolizes both what will happen to the people and models how they should react. When the book is read in light of this centerpiece, the symbolic acts that the prophet performs in the beginning of the book make more sense. Just as he eats impure food, so too they will eat impure food. Just as he silently accepts God's manipulation of his own life, so too should they be mute in the face of God's punishment. Here, the prophet's silent acceptance of his wife's death serves to highlight God's right to wield life and death.

The editor has placed this chapter here quite deliberately. First, chapters 21–24 pile up images repeated from earlier parts of the book as it approaches the announcement of the fall of the city. This final oracle in the complex is the culmination of the first part of the book, climaxing in the emotional impact of the fall of the city, communicated through the reader's identification with the loss of Ezekiel's wife. Note that it does not build to a final graphic portrayal of violence and bloodshed but to the psychological devastation of loss, the grief of defeat, the unbearable pain of the death of a loved one.

Second, chapters 21–24 contain sections that foreshadow the second half of the book, and the end of the oracle points forward to chapter 33 when the events it predicts come to pass (vv. 21-22 and 25-27). The fulfillment of the oracle is artfully delayed by the insertion of the oracles against foreign nations that intervene. The placement of these oracles just before the report of the fall of the city delays the fall of God's sword, as if the Lord waits one final moment to see if the people will see Ezekiel's sign and repent. The book rhetorically holds its breath. Israel has one last chance . . . and they fail.

PART III:
ORACLES AGAINST FOREIGN NATIONS
Ezekiel 25:1–32:32

Imbedded within several prophetic books is a section of material that modern scholars call "oracles against the nations"—or OAN for short. This material contains a collection of oracles against nations other than Israel and/or Judah. The oracles use the same prophetic forms and style as other oracles, and they are not set off from the material that surrounds them. What makes this material distinctive is its subject matter.

The ancient compilers of prophetic books, who collected this material together, have placed it within the books to serve the needs of the collection as a whole. For instance, the OAN are placed at the beginning of the book of Amos because their primary function is to depict Israel as worse than any of her neighbors. A more common placement between oracles of condemnation and oracles of salvation is seen in Isaiah, Zephaniah, the Greek Bible's version of Jeremiah, and here in Ezekiel. This implies that Israel's restoration depends on the subjugation of its enemies.

While many OAN in Ezekiel are dated, those dates show that the material is not arranged in chronological order. Nevertheless, the collection as a whole shows signs of conscious editing. The section is tied to both the oracles of condemnation and the oracles of restoration through rhetorical hooks; an oracle against Ammon occurs in Ezekiel 21:33-37, while an oracle against Edom can be found in Ezekiel 35:1-14. Similarly, an oracle of restoration is inserted in the OAN (Ezek 28:25-26), while an oracle of condemnation appears on the other side of the OAN (ch. 33).

The material within the OAN is well organized. For instance, there are oracles against seven foreign states (Ammon, Moab, Edom, Philistia, Tyre, Sidon, and Egypt), and the condemnation of the final nation is comprised of seven oracles. There are also seven date formulae. The first six nations are condemned in geographical order, starting with Ammon, and then moving in a counterclockwise direction around Judah, ending in Sidon.

In addition, the compiler of Ezekiel has placed a clue as to the purpose of these oracles in the exact center of the oracles. Ezekiel 28:25-26 contains an oracle of restoration for Israel. It is exactly ninety-seven verses from the beginning of this section, and ninety-seven verses from its end. The editor has used this arrangement to highlight the fact that Israel's restoration depends, in part, on the status of its enemies and God's control of universal history.

Ezekiel's oracles are marked by the use of mythic motifs derived from the cultures he condemns. The oracles drip with sarcasm, irony, and mockery. Images are picked up and reused to form connecting webs which unite each grouping of oracles. Although many people skip over this material, it is some of the best poetry of the book.

It may be surprising that Babylon is not among the condemned nations since it would seem that Israel's restoration would depend first and foremost on the fate of Babylon. Was it not safe for an exiled Ezekiel to utter oracles against Babylon? Did Ezekiel support the Babylonian government? Or did the redactors who gathered the material have a purpose that precluded the inclusion of oracles against Babylon? The answer is not clear. However, the nations that are condemned are all condemned for their opposition to the Babylonians. This is especially true of Tyre and Egypt, objects of lengthy condemnations. At first glance, then, it appears that Ezekiel and/or his followers supported Babylonian aggression.

The key may turn on the theological purpose of the book. For Ezekiel, Babylon is God's sword. The kings of Tyre and Egypt in particular are condemned for elevating themselves to the status of a god. The contrast between the Lord and these false gods keeps the focus on God's divine right and power. Not only does God's will alone determine world history but God has the right to condemn Judah's allies, such as Egypt, and preserve Judah's enemy, i.e., Babylon.

The redactor punctuates these oracles with variations on the recognition formula ("So that X may know that I am the LORD"). For instance, a version of this formula appears in every one of the seven short oracles in the first part of this section and another eight times in the oracles against Egypt. This repetition drives home the point that the purpose of God's violent destruction of Babylon's enemies is to demonstrate divine control of the fate of all nations.

25:1-17 Oracles against Judah's nearest neighbors

This short collection opens Ezekiel's OAN. Before turning to the superpowers that dominated Israel's history, Ezekiel addresses the fate of the nations that shared its borders. This chapter contains four oracles, one each against Ammon (25:1-7), Moab (25:8-11), Edom (25:12-14), and Philistia (25:15-17). A quick glance at the map on p. 1530 shows that the first three lay east and south of Judah, while the last nation was located to the west. These nations were similar in size and strength to Judah. While they had independent political power, the oracles presume that they allied themselves with Babylon, perhaps in order to preserve

themselves. All are depicted as either aiding in or rejoicing over the fall of Jerusalem. The punishment for each of them will come in the form of a military defeat and the possession of their land by a foreign power.

26:1–28:24 Oracles against Phoenicia

The next section includes oracles against both Tyre and Sidon, the two main cities of Phoenicia. Tyre was located on a rocky island in the Mediterranean, just off the coast. Its harbors were the center of Phoenicia's trade. Because the rest of the Levant had few natural harbors in ancient times, Tyre had a monopoly on trade with the islands and coastlands of the Mediterranean. Because of its location as well as its alliance with Egypt, Tyre survived a thirteen-year siege by the Babylonians (586–573). The oracles against Tyre in Ezekiel 26:1–28:19 reflect this history and geography.

Ezekiel 26:1-21 contains four shorter oracles in verses 2-6, 7-14, 15-18, and 19-21. All of them use Tyre's economic prowess as the basis for their condemnations. The first oracle mocks Tyre's location in the middle of the sea. While the Tyrians saw this as a great asset, Ezekiel uses it as an image of destruction. Those cliffs on which the city was built will become bare gleaming rocks where lonely sailors can spread out their nets for drying. The second oracle erroneously predicts Tyre's fall to the Babylonians, while the third and fourth oracles focus on Tyre's demise, first by describing the reaction of the princes of other Phoenician cities (26:16), and then by describing the city's descent into the "netherworld" (26:20).

Next Ezekiel attacks Tyre's trade economy (27:1-36). Chapter 27 begins with praise of the city's splendor, likening it to a finely made ship (27:3-9a), laden with merchandise from around the world (27:19b-25). But just when he has the audience marveling at Tyre's beauty, the poet predicts its demise, like a shipwreck in "the heart of the sea" (27:26-28). The audience experiences the horror of its downfall through the eyes of the onlookers described in verses 29-36.

Ezekiel 28:1-19 seethes with sarcasm. This chapter contains two oracles, both of which focus on the hubris of the Phoenicians. The first oracle (28:2-10) depicts the king exalting himself to the status of a god (28:2 and 6). In verse 3, Ezekiel seems to agree with the king: "Oh yes, you are wiser than Daniel, nothing secret is too obscure for you." But his "wisdom" was spent on making himself rich (28:4-5). He will realize his hubris when he finds himself suffering the same death as his enemies (28:7-10).

In the next oracle (28:11-19), the king of Tyre is likened to the first human, who was surrounded with all good things in the garden of Eden but then cast out because of his own sin. While this story sounds a lot like Genesis 2–3, there are some notable differences. For instance, here Eden is clearly not on earth since the sinful king is cast down onto earth. Eden is characterized not by its abundance of trees as it is in Genesis but by its precious gems. It is likely that Genesis and Ezekiel reflect two different but similar versions of the Israelite traditions about the creation of humanity. The king's violence defiles him, and he must be cast off of God's mountain (28:16). The defilement continues on earth (28:17-18a), leading to his ultimate destruction (28:18b-19).

The final, brief oracle (28:20-24) focuses on Sidon's oppression of Israel. "No longer will there be a thorn that tears or a brier that scratches for the house of Israel" (28:24). This demonstrates that the OAN are really concerned with Israel's security. In pursuit of this, Ezekiel prophesies Sidon's total destruction.

28:25-26 Brief oracle of salvation

The oracles against Phoenicia conclude with a brief note promising a restoration of Israel. The restoration of all twelve tribes in verse 25 is typical of preexilic salvation oracles. The oracle promises a restoration to "the land I gave my servant Jacob" (28:25). The repetition of the recognition formula ("they shall know that I, the LORD, am their God") at the end of this material reminds the reader that both the condemnation of foreign nations, as well as the restoration of Israel, suit God's purposes, not humanity's.

29:1–32:32 Oracles against Egypt

These oracles form the climax of the OAN. Although the individual oracles are dated, the arrangement of the material is not chronological. Instead, the images build in intensity as the collection progresses. The seventh oracle is the turning point, not just of the oracles against Egypt but of the whole section. This section is rich in mythic imagery, most of which have parallels in Egyptian iconography. The condemnation of Egypt reflects the prophet's critique of Judah's bid for Egyptian aid. Each oracle, which characterizes Egypt as overly confident in its power, revels in its ironic demise. The condemnation of their hubris implicitly criticizes Judah's reliance on them.

The oracle in Ezekiel 29:1-16 dates to January 587, one year into the siege of Jerusalem. It predates Pharaoh Hophra's failed attack on the Babylonian forces that were besieging Jerusalem. Here the Pharaoh boasts that he has created the Nile, a boast tantamount to claiming that he created the world. He is pictured as a mythic creature residing in the river's waters. The Hebrew word in verse 3, which the NABRE translates as "dragon," can mean either "crocodile" or "serpent," either of which was associated with the creator god. In the poem, the creature is fished out of the river with nets and flung out into the wilderness with fish, presumably those who rely on Hophra clinging to its scales. The symbolic picture is followed by a political indictment against those who rely on Egypt (29:6b-7), promising the destruction and exile of Egypt (29:8-12). The oracle ends with a small ray of hope for Egypt: a prophecy of restoration after "forty years," or one generation (29:13-16). This restoration, however, is not because of any righteousness on the part of Egypt but simply so that this once great nation can serve as an object lesson within the realm of international politics. This oracle was never fulfilled; Babylon never subdued Egypt.

Dated to April 571, the oracle in 29:17-21 postdates all other oracles in this section by fifteen years. In fact, it is the last oracle ever preached by Ezekiel. In it the prophet revises his erroneous prediction of Babylon's destruction of Tyre (Ezek 26:7-14). The poem describes the weariness of the Babylonian soldiers, with heads gone bald and shoulders injured from the long siege. Instead, God decides to give them Egypt as their consolation prize. This defeat did not take place either, but the fact that the oracle here was not also revised tells us that the text was collected soon after this oracle was composed. The poem ends with a brief prediction of Israel's restoration and the return of speech to the prophet (29:21).

The next undated oracle (30:1-19) uses a classic image seen already in Ezekiel 7:10, the Day of the Lord. The language pictures the Lord as the Divine Warrior leading an attack against Egypt and Ethiopia (30:4-9). Verses 13-18 catalogue the important cities in Egypt that will be destroyed. Again, Egypt is criticized for its pride (30:18), and its destruction will lead to knowledge of the Lord (30:19).

The date of the oracle in Ezekiel 30:20-26 corresponds to Hophra's attack on the Babylonian forces, April 587. The brief oracle uses the image of the "arm" of Pharaoh. In Israelite texts, the "arm" of the Lord is a metaphor for strength and power. In addition, Late Period pharaohs, and Hophra in particular, used the image of the arm in their own titles and iconography. This oracle predicts that God will break the Pharaoh's arm and exile the Egyptians.

The long and complex passage in Ezekiel 31:1-18 likens Egypt to its boastful predecessor, Assyria. Dated two months later, June 587, when Hophra's attack was finally thwarted, the poem makes the fate of the mighty Assyrian empire an object lesson for Egypt. This section slips in and out of poetry, making the oracle difficult to follow. By the end of the section it becomes clear that the tree image, first used to depict Assyria, is now being applied to Egypt, but where the exact shift occurs is open for interpretation. The image of the mythic tree was utilized in both Mesopotamia and Egypt; its height, association with subterranean waters, and fruitfulness all indicate its mythic nature. In both Assyria and Egypt the tree was associated with goddesses: in Asia the tree harbors the wild animals, as reflected in verses 6a and 13, while in Egypt the goddess-tree feeds kings who are protected beneath its boughs. This political significance is prominent in verse 6b as well as 11, 12, 14, 16b, and 18b. But unlike these myths, the Lord does not take on the form of a tree. Rather, the trees are political entities that can be cut down at the Lord's discretion. This manipulation of the image suits the purpose of this passage quite well. The nations of Assyria and Egypt are condemned for their belief that they are invincible and godlike. Through the use of the metaphor, Egypt's Pharaoh, who would have deemed himself a god, is treated like a creature (31:14-15) whom the Lord can destroy.

Dated to March 585, after the fall of Jerusalem to the Babylonians, the oracle in Ezekiel 32:1-16 once again takes up the image of the serpent/monster. This is the second part of a framing device that began with the first oracle against Egypt. Again, the serpent resides in the river, muddying

the waters, and again, God fishes him out of the river, hurling him into the wilderness to be food for wild animals (32:2-6). Verses 9-10 focus on the international reaction to its death, which demonstrates that Egypt's supposed power was a sham. The poem is titled a lament and ends with a reference to female mourners, identified as "the women of all nations" (32:16), meaning that Egypt's demise will be mourned by all of the surrounding nations.

The final poem (Ezek 32:17-32) is a funeral song. Dated to 586, perhaps April of that year (the Hebrew lacks a month), the poem predates the previous one and is closer to the date of the fall of Jerusalem. This lack of chronology again alerts the reader to the fact that the arrangement of these oracles is thematic. This oracle should be read, then, not just as a culmination of the oracles against Egypt but as the climax of the OAN. And what a fitting end! This is a masterfully crafted work, which follows the Egyptians down to Sheol, the underworld. What the poet describes is not the blessed life that Egyptians expected to enjoy after mummification. Rather this is "the pit" (24), peopled by all the wicked nations of the earth. Several of these were in fact "dead" at the time of this prophecy: Assyria had fallen to Babylon in 612; Elam, a country east of Babylon, was defeated by the Assyrians in 650. Others, like Edom, Meshech and Tubal (Asia Minor), and Sidon, still existed. The poem presents an ironic picture of the dead: Egypt holds a premier place, but here it is preeminent among the ineffective dead. The refrain ("slain by the sword") resounds like a death knell. The height of the irony comes in verses 31-32, when Egypt realizes it shares its fate with those Egypt itself has slain by the sword. The nation of Egypt, referred to three times more often than any other nation in Ezekiel, is never again mentioned in the book. Ezekiel has laid this foolish ally to rest.

PART IV: ORACLES OF RESTORATION
Ezekiel 33:1–48:35

The majority of Ezekiel's oracles of restoration are located in the final section of the book. Even though these are oracles of "hope," they lack the uplifting poetry of a Second Isaiah or the pathos of a Jeremiah. Instead, they continue the distinctive rhetoric and accusatory ideology of the first thirty-two chapters.

The editor has integrated these oracles into the book in several ways. First, Ezekiel's oracles of condemnation lurk just below the surface. Yes, God will gather them from exile and return them to the Promised Land, but only so that they can never forget how depraved they are. The oracles of restoration require that the people live in a state of perpetual shame.

Second, God's acts of restoration do not spring from heartfelt love, tearful pain, or kindly mercy. Except for a single mention of divine "pity" (39:25), the Lord acts out of self-interest. God does not weep over the dead bones of chapter 37; God brings them back to life so that "You shall know that I am the LORD" (37:13). This "knowledge" continues to be the universal recognition of God's power.

Third, this final section is integrated into the book through the use of rhetorical devices. Specific images and themes from key points in the book are repeated here. The most obvious of these are the prophet's role as watchman (ch. 33), the need for a new heart (ch. 36), the return of the chariot throne (ch. 43), and the centrality of a purified temple ritual (chs. 43–46). In addition, the redactor continues the use of rhetorical hooks: chapter 33 begins with an oracle of condemnation and chapter 35 contains an oracle against a foreign nation.

While the restoration oracles in Ezekiel may not offer comfort, the intricate way that the author has tied this section to the book as a whole shows a mind of superb literary genius. He does not betray his original message by overturning them with a Pollyanna vision of the future. These oracles continue his main theological point that God's grace alone brings Israel anything that is good. This theology attests to God's right to manipulate history for divine purposes.

33:1-33 The end

It may seem foolish to discuss this chapter as a whole, since it is comprised of five separate parts. However, the whole chapter has a single purpose: to sound the final death knell on Jerusalem. The compiler has tied this death notice to the first thirty-two chapters by echoing earlier portions of the book in each of its five sections:

Passage	Theme	Parallel
33:1-9	The prophet is a watchman.	3:16-21
33:10-20	Individuals are responsible.	18:1-32
33:21-22	The city falls; the prophet can speak.	3:22-27 and 24:15-27
33:23-29	The survivors claim the land.	11:14-21
33:30-33	People misunderstand Ezekiel.	21:5

The repetition of themes in this chapter summarizes the book's main ethical argument. The passage on the watchman repeats that, if a prophet has done his job, then the demise of the people is their own fault. The final section tells us that the people had come in droves to hear Ezekiel, so they had heard his warnings. In addition, the middle section reminds the reader that Ezekiel had been made dumb so that he could only speak what God commanded him. This means that all those songs Ezekiel had been singing were not entertainment but divine oracles. Ezekiel had been effectively delivering God's message to a listening audience; therefore, the guilt is completely on them.

The second section reminds the people that they themselves are responsible for the city's fall. Ezekiel repeats God's message that they suffer for their own sins and for their own unwillingness to repent. This is mirrored by the fourth section, which enumerates their sins, taking up many of the specific accusations found earlier in the book. The fourth section also expresses the claim of those left after the city has fallen that God has given the land to them. The same claim had been made after the first deportation (11:14-21). God's rebuke of this conclusion reinforces the fact that the audience for the subsequent restoration oracles will be the Israelites in exile.

The final section of the chapter, which parallels the first section, asserts that Ezekiel was popular: people were talking about him and lining up to hear his performances. However, while they were titillated by his love songs, they were not chastised. The passage suggests that Ezekiel's rhetoric was so "over-the-top" that people hesitated to view Ezekiel as the watchman warning them of impending disaster. As the final verse spells out, this closing section effectively reinforces Ezekiel's status as a true prophet of God. The audience understood the images; they are consequently indicted for not also perceiving the message.

The third section, sandwiched in the middle of the chapter, is its most important element: the notice that the city has fallen. Ezekiel 33:21 marks this chapter as the end of the oracles against Judah. Just as David stopped repenting when his child died because he knew all further acts of repentance were pointless (2 Sam 12:16-23), the fall of the city means that oracles warning the people will no longer serve any purpose. After this chapter the oracles in the book switch to oracles describing God's vision for Israel's future.

34:1-31 Oracles about the shepherds

This oracle falls into four parallel parts. Verses 1-10 describe Israel's evil human shepherds, while verses 11-16 describe the nation's restoration with God as the true shepherd; verses 17-22 describe the evil shepherds again, while verses 23-31 predict restoration under a new Davidic shepherd. By placing parts two and four in parallel positions, the editor portrays the Davidic shepherd as a king who rules for God. The thrust of this chapter is to affirm that God's covenant with the Davidic monarchy has not been revoked.

The "shepherd" is a royal image used throughout the ancient Near East. The king is like a shepherd who protects his people, the sheep. Shepherds do this in two ways: first by protecting them against natural predators, and second, by keeping them gathered in one place. The evil shepherds in verses 1-10 are condemned for failing on both counts, by living off the fat of the sheep, leaving them vulnerable to enemy attack, and allowing them to roam in the wild. In other words, Israel's kings appropriated the wealth of the nation, failed to protect the people from enemy attacks, and allowed them to be exiled.

The second part of the oracle (34:11-16) reverses this picture. God will gather the sheep together, guard them in a fertile pasture, and heal their wounds. This is perhaps one of the most tender portraits of God in the book of Ezekiel, including, as it does, a condemnation of the "sleek and the strong" (34:16). Yet, again, a careful reading notes that God does not say that he does this out of love for the sheep but simply because that is his duty as shepherd.

The third part of the oracle (34:17-22) contrasts sheep with goats or rams. It is a peculiar contrast since both animals were domesticated. The key lies in the transition at verse 16, which contrasts the weak sheep that God will protect with the "strong," i.e., the elite of society, who had oppressed the weak during the period of the monarchy.

The solution for this imbalance is a classic one in the ancient Near East: the establishment of a just king. In the final part of the oracle (34:23-31), the LORD promises the restoration of a Davidic king who is given the title "prince" (34:24), reinforcing the idea that the true king will be God. This royal restoration is called a "covenant of peace" (34:25-29). In the Near Eastern creation myths that describe the gods' attempts to destroy humanity because of their rebellion, the covenant of peace is the divine promise to end their active hostility toward humans. Therefore, the Lord's covenant of peace promises an end to violent punishment.

35:1–36:15 Condemnation of Edom and restoration of Israel

It may seem odd to find an oracle against a foreign nation so late in the book. While the oracle against Mount Seir in Edom in 35:1-15 shares many of the features of the OAN in chapters 25–32, its placement at this point in the book serves two purposes. First, throughout the Hebrew Bible, Israelite authors seem particularly vexed by Edom's involvement in and/or glee at the fall of Jerusalem. In the final edited form of the book, the OAN are placed before the news of the city's fall. Edom must be condemned again after the notice of the fall. Here, it is because they had assumed that they would take over the land once occupied by Israel. Secondly, the oracle's placement is another example of a rhetorical hook used throughout the book. Just as an oracle against Ammon is found in the first part of the book, so a brief OAN appears in the midst of oracles of restoration.

This particular hook highlights the connection between the OAN and the restoration oracles. Chapter 36:1-15, which reuses the image of the mountain found in chapter 35, depicts Israel's restoration as the answer to the sins of the Edomites (35:2-8). The transition from the condemnation of Israel (ch. 34) to its restoration (ch. 36) passes through the condemnation of an enemy who had hoped to benefit from its demise (ch. 35).

Although God does not act out of mercy or love, the Lord does act out of a sense of justice: Israel will be restored to all that was taken from it (35:8-12). The next chapter, however, cautions the reader against thinking that this is a restoration "owed" to Israel.

36:16-37 Restoration as purification

In the very next section, the book asserts that the restoration is not done because Israel deserves it. "Not for your sake do I act, house of Israel, but for the sake of my holy name which you desecrated among the nations to which you came" (36:22). The language of impurity reminds the nation of the sins for which they were exiled. Yet, even in exile, they continued to "descecrate" God's name, not through their defilement but because their tragedy seemed to negate God's power. Ezekiel 36:20 states that profanation results from attacks on the Lord's reputation: "But when they came to the nations, where they went, they desecrated my holy name, for people said of them: 'These are the people of the Lord, yet they had to leave their land.'" Foreign nations did not see Israel's exile as an example of God's ability to punish them but rather as evidence that the Lord is a weak god. If Jerusalem's destruction called God's power into question and the exile still left the Lord's reputation damaged, the only thing that could recover that reputation was their restoration even when they did not deserve it.

The images of restoration that follow reinforce this message. In verses 24-30 Israel is the passive recipient of God's actions. God gathers them, brings them back to their own land, purifies them, literally recreates them, and then rewards them with fertility. Israel, which initiates none of this, can only react with self-loathing (36:31). Even the notice about the new heart and animating spirit in verses 26-27 connotes God's ultimate removal of human free will, resulting in their inability to disobey God's statutes.

The chapter hammers home the purpose for such a restoration. It is not a blessing for Israel; in fact, it has nothing to do with Israel. The purpose of the restoration is to change public opinion about the Lord. God's name, or reputation, is made holy, or respected, only when the whole world recognizes the Lord as the supreme god. The message is clear: when the Lord can restore a dead and worthless nation like Israel to the status of a world power, then God will be revered in proper measure (36:23).

37:1-14 The valley of dry bones

This oracle, perhaps the most famous in the book, utilizes images of life and death to visualize Israel's restoration. The book of Ezekiel often associates sin and impurity with death, holiness and purity with life. The image of the new heart in the previous chapter, for instance, moves from death (a heart of stone) to life (a heart of flesh). In this chapter Ezekiel is given a vision of dead bodies, which represent the nation. All that is left are dead, dry bones, bleached white by the desert sun. God "re-creates" them, first bringing together the skeletal structure and then clothing the bones with sinews, flesh, and skin. Following the pattern of creation common in the ancient Near East, these bodies are not "alive" until they receive an animating spirit. Just as God has created life, so too can the Lord revivify Israel.

Unlike creation texts, however, the prophet plays a significant role. The actions are precipitated by the prophetic announcement. The prominence of Ezekiel in this chapter means that the audience sees this vision through the character of Ezekiel. His reaction serves as a paradigm for the audience's reactions. God asks Ezekiel, "can these bones come back to life?" Ezekiel provides the audience with the correct answer: "Lord God, . . . you alone know that" (37:3). The final verse attributes this "miracle" to God's power, showing how divine power can be a source of comfort and hope for the enslaved and powerless.

37:15-28 One stick, one nation, one king

The vision of the dry bones is followed by a sign-act. Here the action of the prophet is not miraculous: he holds two inscribed sticks together. This symbolizes the oracle's political message. Each stick is inscribed with one of the names of the two kingdoms: Judah and Joseph/Ephraim. (Joseph and Ephraim are used here for the northern kingdom since Ezekiel uses the term "Israel" to stand for all twelve tribes of a united monarchy.) This sign-act defines the true Israel as a nation of all twelve tribes united under a single king (37:22).

Verses 23-28 connect the sign-act to various parts of the restoration oracles. Verse 23, recapitulating 36:16-32, notes that this will include the cessation of defilement. Verses 24-25 state that the prince will be from the Davidic line, as was noted in 34:23-24. Verse 25 echoes the reference to the eternal promise of land given to Jacob found in 28:25. Verse 26a recalls the covenant of peace of 34:25-29, while verses 26b-27 foreshadow the vision of the temple in chapters 40–48. All of these verses together make clear that the restoration of a united monarchy is not an end in itself but is a necessary step for the restoration of a pure and peaceful land united in the worship of the Lord.

38:1–39:29 God's role in Israel's future

Chapters 38 and 39 appear to address the fate of another of Israel's enemies. However, several things set these chapters apart from the OAN. First, if Magog is a real place, it is not a neighbor of Israel, nor a nation that posed an immediate threat to the nation. Second, the actions for which Magog will be punished will occur in the distant future. The predictive force of these oracles is reinforced in 38:17 when God speaks about the fulfillment of older prophecies. Third, Israel's depiction as an unfortified, unarmed, peaceful people does not match the situation of Judah during the lifetime of Ezekiel. Instead, this oracle drives home the point that the restoration of the nation is not done to benefit the people but rather to make the Lord known.

The oracle begins with a command from God for Ezekiel to prophesy against Gog, a prince of the land of Magog (38:2). Scholars are divided on the identification of Magog. Some believe that it is a mythic enemy. There is some evidence, including Genesis 10:2, that there was a kingdom by this name vaguely known in the ancient Near East, situated "north" in Greece, Anatolia, or modern day Turkey. If this is the nation referred to here, it is still a mythic, far-off country; this mythic quality allows it to function as an empty shell for the prophet's description of a post-restoration attack.

Ezekiel 38:3-9 depicts Gog's attack on a restored Israel in the distant future. This addresses the question, how will a restored nation fare if enemies attack? By picking a far-off, almost mythic enemy, the author has marked Gog as a universal hypothetical enemy. Verses 10-13 portray Gog as not just strong but also wicked: he devises a plan to attack unarmed people solely to make himself rich. The human slaughter serves no noble cause.

In some ways, then, Gog is a mythic Nebuchadnezzar: attacking cities that are clearly weaker only for personal glory.

The oracle begins to turn in the next section (38:14-16). In these verses, God makes clear that even future enemies are brought by the Lord to suit God's purposes, that is, in order to display God's holiness through victory. Verses 18-23 describe the Lord's use of earthquake, pestilence, and bloodshed as the divine arsenal.

Ezekiel 39:1-20 lingers over its depiction of Magog's dead. They too become bones scattered across an empty field, but these bones have no hope of resurrection. Instead, Israelite morticians and gravediggers will spend seven months cleaning up the battlefield and repurifying the land (39:14-16). Even so, there are so many corpses that God issues a lavish invitation to carrion birds and wild beasts to feed on them (39:17-20). The Hebrew word translated as "slaughter" is also the basis for the common word for animal sacrifice. Using dark irony, God is depicted as inviting the animals to the human sacrifice that the Lord offers them.

Ezekiel 39:21-24 is the punch line of this dark joke. "The nations shall know that the house of Israel went into exile because of its sins" (39:23). This statement assumes that the restoration of the nation from its exile alone will not be enough to convince the nations, or Israel perhaps, that the Lord has been in control of Israel's history all along. More proof is needed. When Israel is restored, but weaker than ever (unarmed and unprotected), and a great enemy, stronger, meaner, and more numerous than Babylon, attacks it, God will utterly defeat this great enemy. This will prove that the Lord could have saved Judah from the Babylonians. Judah fell, then, not because God could not stop it but because God allowed it as punishment for Israel's sins.

The whole point of the restoration is to carry through to completion God's plan to be known throughout the world as a strong, powerful god in control of human history. Restoration can only begin once that lesson has been demonstrated. The final speech in these two chapters (39:25-29) begins with the word, "Now." Only now can restoration proceed and God act with pity. God extends this restoration to every single person (39:28). Just as the dry bones come to new life through an animating spirit, Israel's return from exile comes through God's infusion of a divine spirit (39:29). Both Israel and the nations will know God's power when Israel is secure again in their own land (39:28-29).

Vision of the Temple (40:1–48:35)

The final nine chapters of the book describe a vision of a temple. Although Jerusalem is never specifically mentioned in these chapters, the vision locates the temple near the royal palace and the capital city. The length and detail of this material suggest that this vision was not delivered orally. Although there has been a tendency to see these chapters as a secondary addition to the book, recent studies recognize the integral nature of this material to the final form of the book. These chapters finally address the problem of Israel's polluting nature in light of God's promise of a permanent restoration.

The purpose of the vision is less clear, however. Is it a romantic recollection of the first temple, a utopian vision of a heavenly temple, or a program for rebuilding the temple? The text offers conflicting evidence. In Ezekiel 43:10-11 the prophet is instructed to write down the plan of the temple that he sees so that Israelites can "observe" it and be ashamed of their sins. These verses imply that the vision differs from the temple in Jerusalem at the end of the monarchy. In ancient Near Eastern literature, temple visions often provided a glimpse of the heavenly temple, of which the earthly temple was a mere reflection. This might imply that the material has no practical purpose. However, as Ezekiel's vision progresses, the plan addresses very practical concerns, such as where the priests should hang their clothes. Therefore, while this may describe a heavenly or eschatological vision, it may also present a divinely revealed program for the restoration of the national temple. Whether the plan was utopian or practical, however, it has a primarily theological function. It expresses in concrete, spatial terms, God's sovereignty over the nation.

40:1–42:20 The temple buildings

This final vision begins with a date formula, April 573, thirteen years after the destruction of the first temple, yet some forty years before the exiles had any hope of returning to the land. The plan is revealed by a bronze "man" (40:3), who leads the prophet through the temple as it is being finished. This divine messenger, who holds two measuring devices, provides the exact dimensions of the temple plan as they progress. Ezekiel's path starts at the outer east gate, the same gate through which God will soon return. From there, he travels through the outer court (40:17-27), into the inner court (40:28-47), then into the sanctuary building (40:48–41:26). In chapter 42, the prophet returns to the outer court.

The temple plan described in this material reflects Israelite traditions for the layout of the temple of Jerusalem: a sanctuary building divided into three parts (vestibule, nave, and holy of holies), surrounded by one or more courts. Ezekiel's temple has two courts. The nave held tables for offerings, lamps, and incense altars, while the "holy of holies," a cube-shaped room, housed the symbol of God's presence. While other Israelite texts describe a similar sanctuary, Ezekiel's plan spends more time explaining the layout and function of outer elements, such as the gates and side rooms. While each courtyard is a perfect square, its alignment is linear, not concentric. In addition, the stairs at each level assured that a priest would progress into and up toward the divine presence. Ezekiel's vision is especially concerned with a design that will permit the complete separation of sacred from profane (42:20), exemplified by the separation of priests from non-priests (42:1-14).

43:1-12 The return of the Lord

The completion of the sanctuary allows for the return of God's presence. This passage ties the vision most closely to the book as a whole, since the LORD reappears on the same chariot throne as in chapters 1 and 8–11. God's entrance into and enthronement within the temple resembles the Babylonian New Year's rituals that celebrated the enthronement of their chief deity, Marduk. After entering the holy of holies, God states that the divine presence will be enthroned in this temple "forever" (43:7) because Israel will never again defile the temple.

While verses 10-12 suggest that Israel's shame at previous sins will be enough to keep the people in line, God's statement must also be read through the lens of earlier restoration oracles, especially 36:26-27, that describe the people's inability to disobey God's statutes. In 43:10-12 the text states that the revelation of the temple and its ritual laws are the "laws and statutes" that Israel must observe. Ezekiel, functioning like a new Moses, has ascended a high mountain in order to receive the laws, write them down, and deliver them to the people.

43:13-27 The law of the altar

The vision then turns to the laws governing ritual activity. These begin with laws governing the altar used for animal sacrifices. Ezekiel's version of this altar is a large construction, resembling the stair-step pattern of Babylonian ziggurats. Its height would require the priests to ascend to its top in order to offer the slaughtered animals. The placement and detail of this vision denote animal sacrifice as the primary ritual action that would take place at the temple.

44:1–45:8 Human access to the Lord's presence

Throughout the book of Ezekiel the principle problem that led to the fall of the city was the defilement of the first temple through the sins of the people. One of the ways that defilement occurred was through the incursion of the profane into sacred areas. Ezekiel 43:7-9 mentions various actions that had defiled the temple, while Ezekiel 44:7-9 states that defilement arose from the failure to restrict access to the holiest areas of the temple. This material starts with the permanent closing of the eastern gate of the outer court (44:1-3), which signifies God's promise to dwell there forever.

The laws make clear that only priests can enter the inner courtyard of the temple (44:15-19). It distinguishes between Levites—i.e., priests whose lineage derives from the tribe of Levi (44:10-14)—and Zadokite priests—i.e., Levitical priests who can trace their lineage back to the priesthood of the temple during the monarchy (44:15-31). The Levites would serve as assistants to the sacrificial priests, while the Zadokites could perform animal sacrifices and enter the sanctuary itself. The law of the Zadokites describes both their special duties (44:15-19, 23-24), as well as the restrictions necessary to maintain their particular state of purity (44:20-22, 25-31). Ezekiel's distinction between priestly groups represents a change from the monarchic temple, a change that stems from the sins of the Levites before the fall of the city. This material may come from a later hand, however, since nowhere else in the book is there a distinction made among priestly groups.

The final section (45:1-8) provides an overview of the sacred center of the nation: the temple is located in the center (45:1-2), surrounded by a strip of land for the Zakokites (3-4), a strip for the Levites (5), another for the "City" (6), and, finally, two strips for the prince (7-8).

45:9–46:24 Ritual laws

The text next describes the ritual activities that will take place in and around the temple. The section begins by assuring that reliable instruments will be used to measure all offerings (45:9-12). After an overview of who provides the sacrifices (45:13-17), the text describes offerings for various feast days: a day of atonement for the temple (45:18-20), the Passover (45:21-24), the feast of Booths (45:25), the weekly sabbaths (46:1-5), the new moons (46:6-7), and the daily offerings, peace offerings, and freewill offerings of the prince (46:12). On the holy days, the eastern gate of the inner court is opened so that the prince can approach God as far as the doorpost of that gate (46:1-3, 8, and 12). The passage also describes the movement of the people (46:9-10), and laws concerning royal land (46:16-18). The passage ends by describing the kitchens where the priests could prepare the sacrifices without allowing sacred and profane to come into contact (46:19-24).

47:1-12 The river of life

After these very practical ritual laws, the visionary quality of this passage is reinforced in chapter 47 with the description of a river that rises up from beneath the temple. This river flows directly out from the sanctuary, becoming wider and deeper, until it finally empties into the Dead Sea (47:1-8). The vision is a visual expression of the life-giving qualities that God's presence brings to the nation. The riverbanks abound with fruit trees and medicinal plants (47:12). The water is so life-giving that even the Dead Sea becomes fresh water (8), teeming with fish (9-10). Only a section of that sea remains salty, presumably so that salty minerals can still be harvested by the Israelites (11).

47:13–48:35 Political reorganization

The final effects of God's presence will be felt throughout the whole nation. The vision ends with a description of the political reorganization of Israel. Each tribe would have an equal strip of land, which could not be bought or sold. Although the hierarchy of the tribes is represented by their proximity to the sacred area, the vision tries to be as equitable as possible. The city's equitable relationship to the tribes is represented by the equal placement of gates on each side of the city and the attempt to give each tribe an equal amount of land.

The tribal strips, all of which are located west of the Jordan River (47:18), extend out from a central strip, at whose center is the sanctuary (48:8-9). This arrangement of the lands depicts in a concrete way the centrality of God's presence for Ezekiel's vision of a perfect Israel. Reiterating Ezekiel 45:1-8, the central strip also contains the rest of the sacred areas, royal property and the city itself (48:8-22). The capital belongs to no tribe, and even the city workers come from every tribe in the nation (48:19).

This final vision represents the book's understanding of the unique status of Jerusalem within the divine economy. The capital city is not just an urban organization, like other urban locales. Its location in the central strip expresses the fact that it has a special relationship to both the nation and to God. The book as a whole should be read in light of the final verse, where the city is renamed: "The Lord is there" (48:35). This verse explains the book's special focus on the sins taking place within the city of Jerusalem. Since the city should have had a special relationship with God (as God's wife, an intimate partner to God's presence), then sins taking place there are far worse, far more devastating than sins taking place elsewhere.

This urban focus reflects Ezekiel's characterization. As a priest of the temple of Jerusalem, both his oracles of doom and his visions of restoration are concerned with the actions taking place within the city itself in and around the temple. This final section pulls together the book's concern for ritual purity, urban status, and divine presence in a vision that provides a new view of God, city, and nation.

THE BOOK OF
DANIEL

Paul V. Niskanen

INTRODUCTION

Set in Babylon during the time of the exile (ca. 598–538 B.C.), and spanning the reigns of foreign kings from Nebuchadnezzar to Cyrus the Persian, the book of Daniel speaks God's word to a people who have been dispossessed. As the prayer in chapter 3 spells out, the people have "no prince, prophet, or leader, / no burnt offering, sacrifice, oblation, or incense, / no place to offer first fruits, to find favor with [God]" (3:38). Such was the new reality for the Jewish people throughout much of the exilic and postexilic periods. The book of Daniel, which was probably written during the darkest hour of this difficult time (the persecution of the Jews under Antiochus IV from 167–164 B.C.), reaffirms God's constant care for his people and ultimate lordship over history. It is a rousing call to remain faithful to the living God who does not forsake those who hope in him.

The book of Daniel is unique among the books of the Old Testament in that it is often designated as an apocalypse and set apart from historical, prophetic, and wisdom literature. Because of its distinctiveness, its classification within the traditional divisions of the Scriptures is problematic. In the Jewish Bible it is placed not with the prophets but in the collection of writings. Christian Bibles place Daniel after Ezekiel as the fourth major prophet. Ultimately, Daniel is a complex book that defies some of the distinctions we would make between the interwoven strands of biblical thought. When we look at the content of the book

of Daniel, we find narratives reminiscent of biblical histories and folk tales (especially the stories of Joseph in Gen 41–44, Ruth, Tob, Jdt, and Esth). We also find mysterious accounts of symbolic visions similar to parts of Ezekiel and Zechariah. So in spite of its distinctiveness, Daniel shares many common elements with several Old Testament books that precede it.

Daniel also heavily influenced the language and thought of the New Testament that follows it. Jesus' self-designation as "the Son of Man" is based upon the mysterious figure who appears coming on the clouds in Daniel 7:13. Mark's Gospel has Jesus refer to this verse from Daniel twice (Mark 13:26; 14:62) with regard to his coming glory. Jesus' very proclamation of "the kingdom of God" is closely connected to the visions of the coming of God's kingdom in Daniel 2 and 7. In addition to these strong ties to the person and preaching of Jesus, the book of Daniel also profoundly inspired the book of Revelation. The prophetic visions and fantastic imagery in the latter are unmistakably based on those of the former.

Daniel is a strange and puzzling book on many counts. First of all, the book in its present form shows evidence of a complex history of composition. It was written in three languages (Aramaic, Hebrew, and Greek). It is set in Babylon during the time of the exile (sixth century B.C.), but it addresses historical events at the time of the Maccabean revolt (second century B.C.). It can be divided into two roughly equal sections according to genre: chapters 1–6, along with the Greek chapters 13–14, are folk tales told about Daniel in the third person, while chapters 7–12 are symbolic visions recounted by Daniel in the first person. Yet this neat division does not correspond to the break in language used. Daniel 1:1–2:4a is in Hebrew, although it is intimately connected to the Aramaic tales that follow in 2:4b–6:29. Daniel 7 is in Aramaic, although it is a first-person account of Daniel's visions like the Hebrew chapters 8–12.

In spite of these peculiarities, the book of Daniel is a unified composition with a central message that permeates the whole. This message relates to the challenge of living in fidelity to the LORD and to his covenant in a world where Israel is no longer an autonomous nation but is subject to foreign kings and kingdoms. This new situation

begins at the time of the Babylonian exile in which the book of Daniel is set, but for Daniel it does not end with the return from Babylon. Rather, he sees the position of the postexilic Jews who are pawns in the power politics of the world's great empires as equally unacceptable. The book of Daniel addresses difficult questions about the nature of God and God's justice, attempting to discern God's presence and action in this unjust world order. Daniel communicates a vision of world history that unfolds according to the design of God. The present hardships under foreign rule are only temporary and will soon give way to the definitive kingdom of God. This theology, which sees God as supreme ruler and judge, is a continuation of Israelite thought. Daniel builds upon and interprets these earlier biblical traditions for the new world in which the Jews find themselves.

COMMENTARY

THE EXILES OF JUDAH AND THE FOREIGN KING

Daniel 1:1–6:29

1:1-21 Jews in the exile

The opening verses of the book of Daniel set the stage for much of what follows throughout the entire book. The historical background that provides the context for both folktales (chs. 1–6; 13–14) and visions (chs. 7–12) is the period of the exile. Daniel opens with a brief description of the beginning of the exile when Nebuchadnezzar of Babylon captures Jerusalem and deports its leading citizens along with some of the vessels of the temple (1:1-2). Although the historical details are somewhat muddled, the event alluded to is Nebuchadnezzar's first capture of Jerusalem in 598, not the later campaign in 587, when the temple was destroyed and a second wave of exiles deported. The seemingly minor detail of removing some of the vessels of the temple is significant for understanding what the exile means throughout the book of Daniel. We might assume it is merely the period from 598–538, at which time Cyrus of Persia permitted the Jews to return from Babylon

to Judea. However, in Daniel, exile refers not so much to location as to situation. Particularly in regard to the temple, the exile is seen as continuing as long as the temple is defiled and the Jews subjugated by a foreign power.

Chapter 1 introduces the protagonists of the chapters to come: Daniel, Hananiah, Mishael, and Azariah. Their respective Hebrew names mean: "God is my judge," "Yahweh has shown favor," "Who is comparable to God?" and "Yahweh has helped." The names are significant and allude to the challenges to the God of Israel throughout the book: Do kingship and power still belong to Yahweh or to the great kings of the earth? Is God able to favor and help his people in the face of persecution and trial? Who is the true God, and where do power and judgment lie?

The young Jewish exiles are each given a Babylonian name: Belteshazzar, Shadrach, Meshach, and Abednego. This reflects the common usage of two names by Jews in the bilingual environment of the exilic and postexilic periods. They often retained a Hebrew name while also using a name of the dominant language and culture. Well-known New Testament examples of Jews bearing both

Hebrew and Greek names are John Mark (Acts 12:25) and Saul also known as Paul (Acts 13:9).

The first challenge presented to the exiles is that of observing their dietary laws in the foreign court (1:3-16). The issue is not simply that of eating clean or unclean foods as prescribed by Mosaic law (Lev 11:1-47) but that of eating food that has been offered to idols. The same issue is addressed by James (Acts 15:29) and Paul (Rom 14:21; 1 Cor 8:10; 10:28) in the New Testament. Meat in general was not prohibited to Jews, only that of certain animals, and there are no laws against drinking wine. In the ancient world, however, these were the food items that were typically offered in sacrifice to gods. To partake of these items was to acknowledge in some way the god to whom they were offered. Rather than partake of this implicit idolatry, Daniel asks that he and his companions be fed only vegetables and water (1:12). While modern nutritionists might tell us that this is in fact the healthier diet, such was not the ancient view. Thus it may be regarded as somewhat miraculous that after a period on this diet the Jews are healthier in appearance (literally "fatter") than their counterparts (1:15).

2:1-49 Nebuchadnezzar's dream

There are several clues that suggest the story in chapter 2 concerning the dream of Nebuchadnezzar was originally an independent composition. The opening verse situates the events of this chapter in the second year of Nebu-chadnezzar (2:1). This conflicts with the preceding chapter in which Daniel and his companions underwent a training period of three years (1:5). Also, Daniel is introduced to the king by Arioch in verse 25, although a previous introduction is mentioned in Daniel 1:18. Source critics have proposed that the story of the king's dream at the heart of chapter 2 may have its origins in an actual Babylonian prophecy concerning the kings of Babylon. This may indeed be the case, and the use of various source materials appears to offer the best explanation for the discrepancies between different parts of Daniel. Nevertheless, there is a continuity in structure and theme throughout Daniel; whatever sources the author used, he has woven them together into a unified whole with a consistent theological message.

In chapter 2, we can see carried over from the first chapter the element of comparison or competition between Daniel and the various categories of foreign wise men (2:2, 10, 27). Just as Daniel and his companions surpassed the other young men selected for royal service through their fidelity to their God and their laws in chapter 1, here too Daniel's wisdom surpasses that of the Chaldean sages. As Daniel himself asserts, it is not any innate wisdom that he possesses (2:30) but the wisdom that comes from God in heaven (2:28) who has revealed the meaning of the dream. Thus the point is driven home once again: even though the Jews be conquered and exiled, the LORD their God is still God. To God alone belong wisdom and power (2:20), and these gifts he bestows on those who are faithful to him (2:23).

The dream itself presents a vision of a large statue composed of four metals (2:31-33). The head is gold, the arms and chest are silver, the belly and thighs bronze, and the legs iron, while the feet are a mixture of iron and clay. The imagery of four metals corresponds to a well-known motif in antiquity of the declining ages of human beings. Our earliest record of this pattern is found in Hesiod, the Greek poet, who describes successive human races of gold, silver, bronze, and iron, each inferior to the one that preceded it. While this imagery may have been central to an original Babylonian prophecy that saw the reign of Nebuchadnezzar as a golden age, it is obviously incidental to Daniel's purposes. For Daniel, the head of gold no less than the feet of iron and clay represent the foreign powers that have subjugated the Jewish people. They are all only temporary, however, and will be destroyed by another greater power represented by the stone being hewn from a mountain (2:34). The emphasis that this rock is cut not by any hand points to the divine power that will overcome these human kingdoms. The vision thus bears witness to what has been illustrated by the scenes in the royal court. Human power may appear to triumph and hold sway for a time, but the wisdom and power of God ultimately prove superior. Those who remain faithful to God and his laws, though threatened and brought low for a time, are vindicated in the end.

3:1-97 The fiery furnace

Chapter 3 of the book of Daniel is the only one in which Daniel is not mentioned. Rather, we have a short story that focuses exclusively on his three companions: Shadrach, Meshach, and Abednego.

This may be yet another indication of an originally independent account that has been blended into the composition of Daniel. Also telling is the fact that this marks the last mention of these three companions within Daniel. The third chapter presents us with the most direct threat to the Jewish exiles thus far. In the previous chapter we saw Daniel and his friends threatened with death, but this was in their capacity as wise men in Babylon (2:12-13). Now the threat is directly related to the pious Jews' refusal to bow down before an idol (3:10-12). The punishment of death faces the three young men if they persist in worshipping only their God and obeying his commandments (3:15). The counterpart to this scene for Daniel himself will appear in chapter 6, where he too faces death for his refusal to compromise his religion to accommodate the king's law.

While Babylon was famous for its many idols or statues of gods (consider the parody of Babylonian idols in Isaiah 46), it was not Babylonian policy to force its religion on a conquered people. The situation of enforced worship described in Daniel seems rather to fit the time of Antiochus IV (175–164 B.C.), who was the first to place prohibitions on Jewish religious practices, and who established a foreign cult in the Jerusalem temple. The Greek (rather than Babylonian) context can also be noted in the names of the musical instruments mentioned in verse 4. Three of these—the zither, dulcimer, and harp—have distinctively Greek names (the Hebrew text transliterates the Greek *kitharis*, *sambuke*, and *psalterion*) and are in fact Greek instruments known from classical sources.

The story of the fiery furnace emphasizes the importance of worshipping the true God alone (3:95) in keeping with the First Commandment (Exod 20:2-3). In the new world order of the exilic and postexilic periods, when the Jews no longer have political autonomy, new pressures arise that threaten the observance of this commandment. Not only is there the cultural pressure to be like the other nations among whom the Jews now live but there also arises the new specter of religious persecution. Faced with penalties—including death—for the faithful observance of their religion, will the Jewish people still hold fast to their God and law? The reply of the three young men to the king shows the proper attitude to maintain in such circumstances (3:16-18). They will remain

faithful to their God regardless of the circumstances. They see death as a very possible consequence of their stance, and at the same time they affirm the power of their God who can save them if he so wills.

As the story turns out, God does rescue his faithful servants from the fiery furnace by sending them an angel (3:49). This messenger is described as looking "like a son of God" (3:92), that is to say a heavenly being or one belonging to the divine realm. The result is that Nebuchadnezzar reverses his position after witnessing this miraculous deliverance (3:93). Instead of threatening with death those who will not bow before his idol, he threatens with destruction any who would dare to blaspheme the God of Shadrach, Meshach, and Abednego (3:96).

The Prayer of Azariah and the Song of the Three Young Men found in verses 24-90 are additions found in the ancient Greek translation of Daniel. The former contains an acknowledgment of God's justice (3:27-28) and a communal confession of sin (3:29-30) as the rationale for the dire situation not of the three young men in the furnace but of the nation as a whole (3:31-33). It likewise contains a plea for God's mercy and deliverance from oppression (3:34-45). The latter is a hymn of praise to the Lord, the God of Israel, who is "exalted above all forever" (3:52ff). This anticipates Nebuchadnezzar's own confession at the end of the chapter that "there is no other God" comparable to the Lord (3:96).

3:98–4:34 Nebuchadnezzar's second dream

Chapter 4 presents us once again with a tale that is in continuity with, yet quite distinct from, the episodes that precede it. It involves another dream of Nebuchadnezzar (like chapter 2), but this time it is the Babylonian king himself who narrates the events in the form of a letter (3:98). As in chapter 2, the Babylonian wise men come first before the king, but they are unable to provide the dream's interpretation (4:3-4). Daniel, who is more frequently referred to as Belteshazzar in this chapter (4:5), hesitates at first to reveal the dream's meaning because of its indictment of the king (4:16-17). Reassured by the king, he reveals its meaning as a divine judgment on Nebuchadnezzar for his arrogance and presumption in attributing his greatness to his own means rather than giving glory to God (4:17-23). The "holy watcher" (literally "a watcher and a holy one") who appears in the dream (4:10) is one of several angelic agents who figure prominently in the visions of the book of Daniel. This particular designation for an angelic being is also attested in the first book of Enoch, probably written about the same time as Daniel.

The vision of a great tree (4:7) that is in turn cut down is a motif that has parallels both in earlier biblical texts (e.g., Ezek 31:18) and throughout the ancient Near East and Mediterranean world. It is a symbol of strength and stability as well as protection and domination. Its exceeding height, reaching to the heavens, also symbolizes an arrogance that is an affront to God (similar to the tower of Babel in Gen 11:1-9).

The punishment that Nebuchadnezzar receives is the loss of his human reason and a type of banishment in which he lives like a wild animal in the fields (4:30). It has long been recognized that this account bears a striking resemblance to the career not of Nebuchadnezzar but of the last king of Babylon, Nabonidus. Nabonidus removed himself from Babylon for several years and lived in a desert town. Rumor had it that the king was mad. There was an awareness of this tradition among the Jews, as the discovery of the so-called "Prayer of Nabonidus" among the Dead Sea Scrolls confirmed. It may be the case that chapter 4 of Daniel preserves something of this historical account of Nabonidus but has replaced his name with that of the better-known Nebuchadnezzar.

The conversion that takes place at the end of chapter 4 is more personal than the one in chapter 3. There we saw how Nebuchadnezzar pronounced a decree for his kingdom that none should blaspheme the God of the Jewish exiles. Here he goes a step further in blessing and praising the Most High, the King of heaven (4:34). There is no historical evidence to corroborate this account of the conversion of a Babylonian king (whether Nebuchadnezzar or Nabonidus) to confess the God of Israel. Such accounts of conversion on the lips of the Jews' greatest enemy reinforce the theological point being made throughout the book. Their God still reigns supreme in spite of all external indications to the contrary, and ultimately all people—including the greatest kings of this world—must acknowledge the supremacy of God.

5:1-30 The writing on the wall

The positive example of Nebuchadnezzar's repentance is immediately contrasted with the negative example of Belshazzar, who fails to learn from the example of his predecessor. Identified as king (5:1) and Nebuchadnezzar's son (5:2), Belshazzar was actually neither. Rather he was the son of Nabonidus and perhaps reigned as crowned prince or regent in Babylon during his father's prolonged absence. Chapter 5 opens with the scene of a great banquet given by Belshazzar for his nobles (5:1). Immediately we are told that he ordered some of the vessels of the temple that his father had taken to be brought in so that those present might drink from them (5:2). The temple vessels, mentioned in the opening verses of the book of Daniel (1:2), reappear as an important element in the present chapter. The author probably does not have his eye on any actual desecration of these vessels by the Babylonians in the sixth century B.C. Rather, this story can be seen as a parable reflecting on the desecration of the temple by Antiochus IV in 167.

There are a number of parallels between the stories in chapters 4 and 5 of Daniel. As in chapter 4, a judgment is again pronounced against the arrogant and impious king. Once again it is presented in a cryptic manner requiring interpretation. This time it is not an angel but a disembodied hand that writes the message on the wall of the palace (5:5). The king is once more terrified by the revelation—now so much so that he even becomes incontinent (5:6). The Babylonian wise men again fail to interpret the message (5:7-8), and finally Daniel is summoned—here at the queen's advice (5:10-12)—to interpret the writing.

Daniel begins not by interpreting the writing but by scolding Belshazzar for failing to learn from his father's example (5:17-24). Belshazzar is held especially guilty because he knew from the start what his father had to learn the hard way: "that the Most High God is sovereign over human kingship" (5:21). The words that are written—*mene, tekel, peres*—refer to different units of weight (5:25). As interpreted by Daniel, these weight measurements refer to the weighing of Belshazzar's kingdom in the balance and the numbering of its days. It has been given a definite limit by God and will soon come to an end. The final measurement—*peres*—also provides a pun on the word for Persia, as we are told that God has divided Belshazzar's kingdom among the Medes and Persians (5:28). This concern for judging and numbering the days of the sacrilegious king is a foretaste of the visions of Daniel in chapters 7–12. In this the book of Daniel once again affirms that God is the Lord of history, ruling not only over Israel, but over all the kingdoms of the earth.

6:1-29 The lions' den

Perhaps no episode in Daniel is more familiar than that of the lions' den. Even from antiquity it appears that this tale was well known and circulated in various forms, as the parallel account in chapter 14 suggests. The version as found in chapter 6 begins with the mention that Darius the Mede succeeded Belshazzar as ruler of Babylon at the age of sixty-two (6:1). Much ink has been spilled over the problem posed by this reference to Darius the Mede. We know that it was Cyrus the Persian who conquered Babylon and took over its rule from the last Babylonian king. Furthermore, there are no records of any Darius the Mede having ever existed (although three Persian kings after Cyrus did bear this name). Either the author of Daniel was somewhat confused in the details of history, or he was concerned to preserve a schematic picture of history as a succession of world empires that included Media before Persia. This historical scheme is in fact a prominent feature in many Greek historians who speak of the successive empires of Assyria (in which they included Babylon), Media, Persia, and Greece. This is a pattern that Daniel appears to follow both in the visions of chapters 2 and 7 and in the overall structure of the book, dated to the reigns of Babylonian, Median, and Persian kings.

Like the three youths in chapter 3, Daniel, who is one of the king's three highest officials (6:3), is accused by his peers for his refusal to obey a royal ordinance that violated his religious laws (6:5-14). The curious note (6:9) that Mede and Persian law was irrevocable is also witnessed to in the book of Esther (1:19 and 8:8) and indicated by the Greek historian Diodorus Siculus. The decree that no one is to address any petition to god or man for thirty days except to the king (6:8) opposes the First Commandment's obligation to worship the LORD alone. Specifically, we see here the exilic and postexilic emphasis on personal daily prayer as essential to worship. While the ritual sacrifices of the temple figure prominently in Daniel, they do not exhaust the meaning of divine worship. The individual and the communal aspects—the prayer of the heart as well as the public celebrations—are equally important. The connection between these two aspects of worship can be seen in Daniel's praying with his windows open toward Jerusalem (6:11). There does not appear to be a particular Mosaic law prescribing prayer three times a day (6:11), but at some point it became customary to pray in the morning, at midday, and in the evening as attested by later rabbinical literature.

The concerned King Darius (6:15) contrasts sharply with the enraged King Nebuchadnezzar in chapter 3. Darius is not angry that Daniel violated his decree; rather, he regrets having issued it. We get a picture of a different kind of threat to Jewish religious observance here. It is not an intentional or hostile persecution by the king but the jealous maneuvering and scheming of lesser bureaucrats. The king himself is portrayed as being sympathetic, although something of an unwitting bungler. This is similar to the stories we find in Daniel 14 and in the book of Esther.

At the story's conclusion, Daniel is preserved from harm in the lions' den and released (6:20-24). Those who had contrived the trap and accused Daniel then suffer the fate to which they would have condemned him (6:25). Once again, as in chapters 2, 3, and 4, this episode concludes with an account of the king's "conversion." Darius, like Nebuchadnezzar, confesses the God of Daniel as the living God whose kingdom is everlasting and who delivers and saves through marvelous acts of power (6:27-28). What began as a challenge to the God of Israel and a threat to those who serve him ends with the confession and praise of the LORD by his would-be rivals and the deliverance of his faithful servants. The stories of Daniel 1–6 have hammered home their point—the LORD is king. His are dominion and power and wisdom. Even though the Jews have lost their land and king and temple, they may still hold fast to their God—and that is more than enough.

VISIONS OF HISTORY

Daniel 7:1–12:13

Chapter 7 does not pick up the pseudo-chronological sequence from the first six chapters that ends with Cyrus the Persian succeeding Darius the Mede (6:29). Instead, as we begin the accounts of Daniel's visions, we return to the time of King Belshazzar of Babylon (7:1) and repeat the series of Babylon (7:1; 8:1), Media (9:1), and Persia (10:1). The narrative continues in Aramaic as it has since Daniel 2:4b, but now for the first time it is Daniel himself who narrates events in the first person (similar to Nebuchadnezzar's narration of chapter 4). Furthermore, it is no longer the dreams of foreign kings that are interpreted (as in chapters 2 and 4), but the dream of Daniel himself.

7:1-28 Four beasts

The content of Daniel's dream sounds very familiar to those who have read chapter 2. The connection between the two dreams is unmistakable. Both are interpreted to refer to four kingdoms followed by a fifth kingdom established by God. Some have questioned whether these four kingdoms are the same ones referred to by the vision in chapter 2 or even whether the beasts are meant to expressly signify successive kingdoms. We must recognize, however, that there is a certain ambiguity inherent in the use of symbolic imagery. The four kingdoms, which are explicitly successive in chapter 2 (2:39-40), are nonetheless destroyed all at once (2:44). Likewise, the four kingdoms appear to follow one another in chapter 7 (7:4-7), although only the last is definitively destroyed, while the first three are allowed to remain for a while (7:11-12). Perhaps the best solution is to see once again a reference to the four kingdoms running throughout the book of Daniel—Babylon, Media, Persia, and Greece—without overlooking the symbolic value of these kingdoms. They represent the sum of world powers that since the time of the exile has held sway over the Jews. These powers, which reach their climax in Daniel with the fourth beast and its arrogant little horn (7:8), will all ultimately yield to the power and plan of God. Thus, while the historical context of Daniel is fairly transparent as the time of Antiochus IV (the little horn), its message and significance is not limited to that historical moment. The symbolic representations lend themselves to constant reappropriation to our own times and circumstances. Thus early interpreters of Daniel (such as Josephus, *Antiquities*, 10.11.7) saw his visions as relating to their own time of conflict with the Roman Empire. The message of God's sovereignty over the course of human history is universally valid.

If the story of Daniel in the lions' den in chapter 6 is perhaps the most familiar episode from this book, the vision in chapter 7, which culminates with the coming of "One like a son of man" (7:13), is certainly the most significant with regard to the New Testament. This is due not simply to the fact that Jesus referred to himself as the Son of Man. The phrase in and of itself merely refers to one belonging to the human family. Thus, for example, we find in the book of Ezekiel that the prophet is repeatedly called "son of man" by God (e.g. Ezek 2:1). But when during his trial before the Sanhedrin, Jesus tells the high priest that he "will see the Son of Man / seated at the right hand of the Power / and coming with the clouds of heaven" (Mark 14:62), the unmistakable reference to Daniel 7:13 implies much more. The Son of Man in this context is both the representative of God's people and the one who inaugurates God's kingdom.

It is important to recognize that we are dealing with a symbolic vision in Daniel 7. Thus, just as the first three kingdoms are represented as being *like* various beasts (7:4-6)—while the fourth is apparently *unlike* anything (7:7)—the fifth definitive kingdom of God is symbolized by one *like* a human being. There is in Daniel a certain fluidity between these images and the realities they represent. The symbolic world becomes a way of speaking about the unseen spiritual realities that permeate the physical world. (We will see, for example, in chapter 11, how the historical conflict among the nations is expressed in terms of combat between their angelic patrons.) Thus history is shot through with divine purpose and activity, but the divine forces work in and through their earthly counterparts, not over or above them. In other words, the struggle of the Jewish people to remain faithful to their God and their law *is* God's own work represented by the activity of such heavenly beings as "One like a son of man."

Although the kingdom of God in Daniel is viewed as a reality that is yet to come, it would be a mistake to view it as an entirely supernatural kingdom at the end of human history. It is more probable that Daniel means to describe an actual human kingdom within the course of human history to replace the four that preceded it. The "people of the holy ones of the Most High" (7:27) who receive this kingdom are Daniel's own people—the Jews who until now have suffered under foreign rule. The coming kingdom of

God—the particular or terrestrial manifestation of God's reign—will mirror God's universal sovereignty, which has already been acknowledged (3:10; 4:31; 6:27) by likewise being everlasting. It is likely that the Jewish restoration under the Hasmonean Dynasty (142–63 B.C.) was viewed by many as the realization of this vision. The abrupt end to this interlude of Jewish autonomy, brought about by the indomitable might of Rome, probably contributed to the eschatological interpretation of Daniel's visions.

8:1-27 The ram and the he-goat

Although chapter 8 is written in Hebrew, it clearly follows and is dependent upon the Aramaic chapter 7. We have here a second vision of Daniel dated two years later in the third year of Belshazzar (8:1). Once again, kingdoms are represented by animals. This time there are only two mentioned: a ram with two horns (8:3) and a he-goat with one great horn (8:5). The goat overpowers the ram (8:7), but at the height of its power its great horn is shattered and replaced by four others (8:8). Out of one of these four sprouts a little horn as in chapter 7 (8:9; 7:8), and this horn is successful in evildoing for a time (8:9-12; 7:21, 25).

While seeking to understand the vision, Daniel sees Gabriel standing before him (8:15-16). Gabriel, who is described as appearing like a man, explains the vision. The meaning is once again fairly transparent given the context of the book of Daniel. Unlike the interpretation in chapter 7, however, we are explicitly told now that the ram represents the kings of the Medes and Persians (8:20). The familiar combination of these two kingdoms had already been expressed in 5:28 and 6:13. The he-goat represents the king of the Greeks and the great horn on its forehead is the first king, Alexander the Great (8:21). After his death his empire was divided among his generals into four kingdoms, symbolized by the four horns (8:22). Of these four, two proved important for Jewish history. Ptolemy and his successors ruled in Egypt; Seleucus in Syria and Mesopotamia. Palestine was a disputed territory between these two powers. It fell under Ptolemaic rule for most of the third century B.C., but at the turn of the second century it passed to the Seleucids after the successful campaigns of Antiochus III. His son, Antiochus IV, is described as impudent and skilled in intrigue (8:23). The description in verses 23-25 expands upon that of the arrogant little horn in 7:25.

The calculation of 2,300 evenings and mornings as the time in which the temple will be defiled (8:14, 26) equals 1,150 days. This roughly corresponds to the three-year period during which the temple was desecrated. In this it is similar to the year, two years, and a half-year of 7:25. The statement that the vision refers to "the end time" (8:17) is a cause of frequent misunderstanding in Daniel. A more literal translation would be "the vision refers to an end of a time." It is not so much the end of the world or the end of history that is envisioned (although this has become a common perception of what apocalyptic texts are about). Rather, it is the end of a particular period or time of history that is anticipated. Specifically, it is the end of the period of foreign domination and oppression—a period that for Daniel is understood as the exile. This point is made more explicit in chapter 9.

9:1-27 Redefining the exile

Chapter 9 provides a break between the three visions of Daniel in chapters 7–12. Here we have a bit of Scripture study (9:2) and prayer (9:3-20) on the part of Daniel and an interesting biblical interpretation by the angel Gabriel (9:21-27). Following the book of Daniel's chronology from the previous chapter, the vision takes place in the first year of Darius the Mede (9:1). The reference to Jeremiah's prophecy of a seventy-year exile (Jer 25:11; 29:1) as Scripture (9:2) indicates that by the time Daniel was written (ca. 165) the prophetic books had taken their place alongside the Torah as Israel's Scriptures. We have in Daniel 9, then, an early example of biblical interpretation.

The interpretation given by Gabriel is that the seventy years spoken of by Jeremiah signify seventy weeks (9:24)—that is to say seventy weeks of years. We see that in Daniel's perspective the exile did not end with the edict of Cyrus allowing the Jews to return to their land in 538. Rather, the exile is enduring even to the time during which the book of Daniel is written—the persecution of Antiochus IV and the desecration of the temple from 167–164. The defiled state of the temple and the oppression of foreign domination constitute the exile for Daniel, even though the Jews inhabit their own land. This particular type of interpretation, whereby one element (a year) symbolically stands for another (a week) in order to apply an ancient prophecy to a contemporary situation is widely attested among the Dead Sea Scrolls (ca. 150 B.C. to A.D. 50). This type of allegorical interpretation is closely related to patterns we also find in the New Testament and the Fathers of the Church.

The prayer of Daniel in 9:3-19 is interesting for the fact that it doesn't directly request understanding of the Scripture in question and appears somewhat out of context with what precedes and follows it. Nonetheless, it is highly significant not only to this chapter but to the book of Daniel as a whole. Daniel confesses that the disgrace and suffering of the extended period of exile are squarely the result of the people's sins (9:5-7). The seemingly mysterious unfoldings of history are no more than the stipulated penalty for transgressing the covenant (9:12-13). The key, then, for a full return from this state of exile is a full return by the people to their God and his laws. This call for a renewed fidelity rings throughout Daniel. In the face of new historical circumstances that encourage the Jews in ever-greater ways to abandon their God and their religious customs, renewed trust in the mercy and solicitous care of God is needed (9:18-19).

The timeline presented in the interpretation of the seventy weeks is approximate and symbolic since we are in fact dealing with a period of less than 490 years. The first seven weeks correspond to the actual period of exile in Babylon (9:25). The anointed leader who is referred to may be Cyrus (Isa 45:1) or Zerubbabel (Hag 2:21-23) or the high priest Joshua (Zech 3:1-10). The sixty-two weeks (9:26) refer to the postexilic period up to the time of Antiochus IV. The anointed who is cut down is probably the High Priest Onias III who was murdered in 171. The final week (9:27) would roughly encompass the years 170–164. The half week in which the sacrifice is abolished is then the period from 167 when the temple was desecrated to 164 when it was rededicated. Although the numbers do approximate the chronology of events, they are primarily symbolic. Thus, the half-week (or three and a half years) is a period of great evil and distress, being half of seven, the number symbolic of perfection.

10:1–12:13 A theology of history

Chapters 10–12 recount the final vision of Daniel and its interpretation. Dated to "the third

year of Cyrus" (10:1), this vision comes last in chronological sequence. Unlike the previous visions, no details of what Daniel sees are given at all. We are only told that he understands this certainty from his vision: a great war. It is apparently three weeks later (10:3) that Daniel has another vision in which an angelic interpreter once more comes to enlighten Daniel (10:5). The description of the angelic being who speaks to Daniel (10:5-6) is highly reminiscent of passages in Ezekiel, especially its opening vision of God's throne (Ezek 1), where we also find chrysolite, lightning, fiery torches, burnished bronze, and a roaring voice or sound. The awesome nature of the vision causes Daniel's strength to fail and he faints forward to the ground. The human reaction to a divine manifestation is similar to earlier passages in Daniel when it was the foreign kings who were frightened and left weak by various dreams and apparitions (10:8-9; 4:2; 5:5-6).

The angelic figure immediately raises Daniel up and, despite his terrifying appearance, addresses him tenderly and reassuringly (10:10-12). Although the messenger is not named, he is probably to be identified with Gabriel, considering the similarities between this episode and that in chapter 9. The angel is sent by God in response to Daniel's prayer in order to explain to him what will happen to his people (10:14). The references to the princes of Persia and Greece, alongside that of Michael as the prince of Daniel's people, suggest that these "princes" are the heavenly representatives or guardian angels of these respective nations (10:13, 20). The earthly conflict between these states is mirrored in the heavenly realm by angelic combat. It is interesting to note that Persia as well as Greece is portrayed as an adversary. Whereas Isaiah could portray King Cyrus of Persia as the anointed of the LORD for his role in liberating the Jews from their exile in Babylon (Isa 45:1), Daniel is less enthusiastic about any foreign power. The two centuries of Persian rule over the Jews is for him just a part of his expanded understanding of exile. Trading one foreign overlord for another, however benign or benevolent, does not ensure the freedom to serve the LORD that Daniel seeks. This was the lesson in chapter 6, where even the favorably disposed Darius proved to be ultimately inept and inadequate.

After the lengthy prologue of chapter 10, we finally hear in chapter 11 the content of the revelatory vision as described by the divine messenger. This chapter is remarkable in a couple of respects. First of all, it contains one of the most accurate descriptions of secular history found in the Bible. Although this history is recounted in symbolic language and would be incomprehensible to us without external corroboration, such corroboration does exist in several Greek historians, most notably Polybius. Secondly, the scope of this history is a departure from established patterns of biblical writing. Instead of focusing squarely on Israel itself, the orbit has expanded to include universal history. It is then within this wider world history that the place and destiny of the Jewish people is situated.

Recalling that the vision takes place in the third year of the Persian King Cyrus (10:1), the three kings of Persia (11:2) that are yet to come are his successors. The fourth, who grows strong in his riches and provokes Greece, is clearly Xerxes I, who was noted both for his great wealth and his enormous campaign against Greece. Thus the first four Persian kings are indicated—Cyrus, Cambyses, Darius, and Xerxes. Daniel skips over the final seven Persian rulers to then speak of Greece. There are two likely reasons for this omission. First, Xerxes represents the high point of the Persian Empire, and Daniel frequently shifts from speaking about kingdoms to kings, identifying a kingdom with its most representative king (e.g., Babylon = Nebuchadnezzar; see 2:38). Second, the passing of power from Persia to Greece can be seen to have begun with the disastrous defeat of Xerxes' forces to the Greeks at Salamis and Plataea. In the Hellenistic environment in which Daniel was written, these events would be readily known.

As in the vision in chapter 8, the one in chapter 11 begins to speak about Greece with reference to Alexander, the "powerful king" (11:3). Although Alexander is often portrayed quite positively in Jewish literature (see Josephus, *Antiquities*, 11.8.3-5), Daniel sees him as the beginning of the terrible and destructive fourth kingdom. He initiates the wanton violence that will reach its culmination against the Jews in the person of Antiochus IV. His sudden demise may also be read as a judgment and a reminder that power belongs to God alone and that he bestows it on whom he will.

The remainder of the chapter details the careers of the king of the north and the king of the south. These titles refer to the series of rulers of the Seleucid kingdom to the north of Palestine and those of the Ptolemaic kingdom to the south. Beginning in verse 21, Daniel refers to the final king of the north of whom he knows—Antiochus IV. He is described as usurping the kingdom (11:21), which he in fact did. It has been suggested that he was the instigator behind the murder of his brother and predecessor as king, Seleucus IV. He may have also had a hand in the death of Seleucus's son and heir to the throne. He was also behind the murder of the high priest, Onias III, who may be referred to as the "prince of the covenant" (11:22). His rise to power was made possible by the backing of an allied mercenary force from Pergamon (11:23). His robbing of temples and lavish distribution of gifts among his allies and friends (11:24) are also well documented by Greek historians.

After describing Antiochus IV's two campaigns against Egypt and his forced retreat from the second campaign due to Roman intervention (the "ships of the Kittim" in 11:30), Daniel records the actions of the king against the Jerusalem temple and his persecution of the Jewish religion (11:30-35). Daniel 11:36-39 relates some of the idiosyncratic behavior that led some to question the sanity of Antiochus IV. It was not merely Jewish religion and customs that Antiochus flouted; he broke from the traditions of his Seleucid predecessors as well. He disregarded the gods of his ancestors (Apollo was the patron of the Seleucids) and styled himself as *theos epiphanes*—the God manifest. The Greek historian Polybius reports that his detractors deridingly called him *epimanes*—meaning "madman"—a pun on his epithet *epiphanes*.

With verse 40 the historical summary of chapter 11 comes to an end and a nonhistorical account of the king's death is recounted. This break from the historical record has led many (beginning with the neo-Platonist philosopher Porphyry in the third century) to date the book of Daniel to some time between the persecution of the Jews (begun in 167) and the death of Antiochus IV (164), since the author was apparently ignorant of the latter event. We know from both Greek and Jewish sources that Antiochus died while on a campaign in the east and not during a retreat from yet another campaign in Egypt (11:42-44). Daniel's "fictional" account of the king's death between the sea and the glorious holy mountain (11:45) is meant to make a connection between the king's death and his crimes against religion. He dies in the shadow of the temple mount, and thus his death is seen as divine punishment for desecrating that very temple.

Continuing the narrative of the vision from chapter 11, Daniel 12 begins with a reference to the appearance of Michael, who was also mentioned at the beginning of this extended vision in Daniel 10:13. He is described as "the great prince" (12:1), similar to his designation as "one of the chief princes" in Daniel 10:13. Once again he appears in the role of Israel's defender. The time of distress referred to in verse 1 should be understood as corresponding to the appointed time of 11:40 when the impious king of the north comes to his end, but not without first wreaking much destruction. In spite of the great calamity, the angel who has been speaking throughout the vision (presumably Gabriel) assures Daniel that his people will escape, since this has already been written in God's book. Daniel's people should probably be understood as the people of Israel and not a subgroup thereof. This is in keeping with the entirety of the vision, which speaks of whole nations and their patron spirits. Attempts to read these verses in a more sectarian or elitist fashion fail to keep the broader focus of Daniel in mind. There is, to be sure, an individual judgment envisioned in verses 2-3. Those Jews who have forsaken the covenant and collaborated with their persecutors will be punished, while the wise and those who lead many to justice will be rewarded. This is wholly in line with traditional biblical thought, however, and does not warrant a more exclusivist notion of who is among the elect.

The concept of resurrection from the dead (described as awakening from "sleep in the dust of the earth" in 12:2) is explicitly mentioned here for the first time in Scripture. There is likewise the first mention of an eternal reward and punishment. Ezekiel had a vision of a valley of dry bones that come back to life (Ezek 37:1-14), but this was an image for the restoration of Israel. Daniel may be alluding to such a national restoration as well (the "fifth kingdom" in the visions of chapters 2 and 7), but given the time and circumstances in which many Jews died for their fidelity to their beliefs (see 2 Macc 6:18–7:42), it is fair to say he is also envisioning an actual restoration to life for them.

The angelic admonition to keep secret the message and to seal the book until the end time (12:4) is based upon the time lapse between the putative setting of the book during the Babylonian exile and the actual setting and context to which it is addressed. The words of Daniel are addressed in a first moment to those Jews suffering persecution under Antiochus IV, and by extension to the faithful followers of God who suffer persecution or adversity in any age. Daniel would have us situate such adversity within the larger perspective of God's sovereignty over all of history. God's foreknowledge of such events indicates a divine plan for all of history and for each individual that gives us cause for profound hope in spite of difficult circumstances. From God's perspective, the final chapter has already been written, and it entails everlasting life and glory for those who remain faithful. The visions of Daniel encourage us to keep this perspective of eternity, to keep the end in sight and so draw courage and strength to persevere in faithfulness to our God.

The chronological calculations of the last half of Daniel 12 have elicited a variety of interpretations. It may be that we have an initial estimate of the period of persecution as three and a half years (12:7). This is then recalculated as 1,290 days (12:11) and finally as 1,335 days (12:12) as the author (or a later editor) attempts to arrive at a more precise timeline for the actual persecution. More likely is the proposal that we are dealing with symbolic numbers rather than attempts to discern a real chronology. Again, various proposals have been put forward as to the possible symbolic meaning behind these numbers. Unfortunately there is no consensus as to what methods were used to calculate these numbers and what they might mean. They roughly correspond to the three and a half years which, as we have seen, is the "half week" period of great tribulation.

STORIES IN GREEK

Daniel 13:1–14:42

13:1-63 Susanna

The story of Susanna in chapter 13 is preserved only in the Greek translations of Daniel. That it was originally written in Greek and not translated from Hebrew or Aramaic is suggested from the

Greek wordplay in verses 55 and 59, where the sentences Daniel pronounces on the two elders play on the names of the trees under which they claim to have seen Susanna.

In the Greek translation of Theodotion (ca. A.D. 180), the story of Susanna appears before Daniel 1 as a kind of introduction to the whole book. Although set in Babylon (13:1) like the rest of Daniel, this chapter is unique among the individual stories in Daniel in that it takes place within an entirely Jewish context with no mention of the exile or any foreign kings. It introduces Daniel as a young boy (13:45) and establishes his reputation for wisdom among the people (13:64) by his astute handling of Susanna's case.

Susanna is introduced as "a very beautiful and God-fearing woman" (13:2) who had been trained by her parents "according to the law of Moses" (13:3). Her piety is put to the test in this story, as is the law of Moses itself, for the two men who seek to seduce her and then unjustly condemn her are elders and judges of the people (13:5). It is they who are responsible for interpreting and enforcing the law of Moses by judging cases that are brought to them (13:6). They will also seek to manipulate that law by conspiring to condemn the innocent Susanna to death.

Their threat to testify against Susanna if she does not give in to them (13:21) is a threat that is given teeth by the law of Moses. Deuteronomy 19:15 states that, while one witness is not sufficient to bring charges against an individual, the testimony of two or three witnesses does establish a judicial fact (see also Num 35:30 and Deut 17:6 where the death penalty may be applied on the word of two witnesses). Under Mosaic law, the testimony of one woman was no match for that of two elders (and judges as well!). There is a tragic irony that the law to which Susanna is so faithful now menaces her with the prospect of death. Nevertheless, she chooses to adhere to God and his law, whatever the consequences may be. Verse 23 repeats a central theme to the book of Daniel—it is better to remain faithful to God and God's law, even when this means persecution and possibly death at human hands.

After the men proceed with their false testimony against her and succeed in getting the assembly to sentence her to death (13:34-41), Susanna prays aloud to God who responds by "[stirring] up the holy spirit of a young boy named Daniel"

(13:42-45). Nowhere in the book of Daniel is the name of its hero more appropriate. Daniel ("God is my judge") succeeds in revealing God's justice and judgment in Susanna's case. Through Daniel's cross-examination of the elders, he unmasks their perjury and vindicates Susanna. The law of Moses is also vindicated in its proper application by a righteous judge. Daniel fulfills the role of the judge in verifying testimony (13:52-59) and punishing (13:61-62) those who bear false witness as described in Deuteronomy 19:18-19. As in the tale of the three young men in chapter 3 or the lions' den in chapter 6, we once again see that God "saves those that hope in him" (13:60). The story of Susanna is yet another reminder to persevere and remain faithful to God even in the most difficult and dangerous of circumstances.

14:1-42 Bel and the dragon

The final chapter of Daniel contains two short stories with a satirical polemic against idolatry. Verse 1 situates the stories once more within the chronology of Daniel's scheme of four world empires. It appears to pick up where Daniel 6 had left off, with the passing of rule from Media to Persia. Here the last Median king is correctly identified as Astyages, whereas in chapter 6 he was referred to as Darius. Another connection with the tale in chapter 6 is the detail of the lions' den from which God delivers Daniel (14:31-42).

The first story, in which Daniel exposes the deceit of the priests of Bel (14:2-22), is similar to the tale of Susanna in that Daniel uses cunning to expose the duplicity of his opponents. By scattering ashes on the floor of the temple of Bel (14:14), he is able to reveal by their footprints the true consumers of the sacrifices to the idol (14:19-20). Daniel succeeds in exposing Bel as a lifeless idol, and King Cyrus allows Daniel to destroy Bel and its temple (14:22). The superiority of the God of Daniel, "the living God who made heaven and earth and has dominion over all flesh" (14:5) is reaffirmed as in the court tales of Daniel 1–6.

The second panel of this diptych intensifies the message of the first. Now we are confronted with an apparently living god—"a great dragon which the Babylonians revered" (14:23). That the creature is alive is beyond dispute, so Daniel offers to kill the beast, proving it to be mortal (14:24-26). There is no explanation as to why Daniel's strange confection of "pitch, fat, and hair" should cause the dragon to explode (14:27). That Daniel is able to destroy the dragon with neither sword nor club (14:26) but by this absurd recipe heightens the ridiculousness of worshipping anything but the one true God.

The ensuing fear and impotence of the king when confronted by his own subjects (14:28-29) is once again reminiscent of Daniel 6. He is forced to hand Daniel over to his enemies who then throw him into the lions' den (14:30-31). Daniel 14 includes several elements regarding the episode of the lions' den that were not found in chapter 6. These include a stay of six days rather than one night, the enumeration of seven lions, and their usual daily diet of two carcasses and two sheep (14:31-32). Finally, we also have the miracu-

lous transportation of the prophet Habakkuk to Babylon in order to bring Daniel some lunch (14:33-39).

The outcome is by now familiar. Daniel is preserved from harm, thereby proving the power and supremacy of his God (14:40). The king acknowledges the God of Daniel (14:41) and punishes those who would have him killed with the same fate they had planned for him (14:42). The words of the king and the prayer of Daniel drive home once more the message of the book of Daniel: "The king cried aloud, 'You are great, O Lord, the God of Daniel, and there is no other besides you!'" (14:41). "'You have remembered me, O God,' said Daniel; 'you have not forsaken those who love you.'" (14:38).

THE BOOK OF
HOSEA

Carol J. Dempsey, O.P.

INTRODUCTION

The book of Hosea is a complex and highly stylized text. Its backdrop is the rise of the Assyrian Empire in the mid-eighth century B.C. During this time period, Assyria became Israel's greatest threat. Little is known about Hosea, the book's prophet, who exposes Israel's apostasy, idolatry, and transgressions in vivid, metaphorical language that ranges from inferring that Israel is a prostitute (3:1-15) to calling Ephraim a trained heifer (10:11). Hosea's judgment on Israel is relentless (13:1-15), and Israel's transgressions are many (4:1-3). With great poignancy, Hosea captures the vacillation of God's heart as it struggles between bewilderment, remembrance, and sheer frustration only to let go to incredible compassion and understanding (11:1-9). True to his prophetic vocation, Hosea calls the people to repent (6:1-3; 14:1-3) and makes known to them that, indeed, God will heal their brokenness through transformative love (14:5-8). Like many of the other books of the prophets, Hosea closes on a note of hope. A people once forsaken will now become God's own again, living in God's shade and "blossom[ing] like the vine" (14:8).

The historical and social world of Hosea

Interestingly, the book of Hosea does not portray the actual Assyrian invasions of Israel. The text was written, for the most part, in the period following the death of Jeroboam II and just prior to the Assyrian assault in 735–732 B.C. The purpose of this setting was to convince Israel to aban-

don its alliance with Assyria. Furthermore, Hosea seemed to have been in debate over Israel's future from the end of the Jehu dynasty to the emergence of Pekah, who was eventually assassinated by Hoshea during the Assyrians' invasion of Israel.

Like the world of Amos, a contemporary of Hosea, Hosea's world was fraught with idolatry, apostasy, and transgressions. Hosea's primary focus was on the religious state of affairs of Israel and Judah. He condemned Baal worship (2:10, 15, 18, 19; 9:10; 13:1), which also included cultic rites on the high places (4:13; 10:8), pillars (3:4; 10:1-2), divining rods (4:12), images (4:17; 8:4; 14:9), and calf figurines (8:5-6; 10:5; 13:2). All of these elements had, at one time, been part of early Israelite religion and the worship of God. Hosea seems to have been condemning early Yahwism. Like Amos, Hosea dealt with the poverty and injustice of his day, both of which flowed from a time of prosperity and grandeur. Finally, although the text may have been written after the death of Jeroboam II, the text itself seems to reflect the last years of Jeroboam II's reign. Pinpointing actual historical referents within the book, however, is difficult because many of the proclamations are obscure and allusive.

The literary dimensions of the book of Hosea

Perhaps the most striking literary aspect of the book of Hosea is its metaphorical language, with many of the images coming from the natural world and reflective of agriculture and husbandry. God is described as a physician (7:1; 14:5), a shepherd (13:5), and a fowler (7:12). God is also said to be like the dawn (6:3a), spring rains (6:3b), a lion (13:7a), a leopard (13:7b), a bear (13:8), dew (14:6), and an evergreen cypress (14:9). Israel is like a dove (7:11; cf. 9:11), a luxurious vine (10:1), morning cloud (13:3a), dew (13:3b), and chaff (13:3). Hosea 1–3 features an extended metaphor: the infidelity of Gomer mirrors the infidelity of Israel. Hosea 10:1 is another extended metaphor. The book also features warfare imagery that foreshadows impending disaster for Judah (5:8-14; 8:1). Contrasting the warfare imagery is the tender maternal/paternal imagery of a God who remembers caring for Israel as a child (11:1-4) with a heart that now vacillates between anger and compassion (11:9). In the midst of the book's many judgment proclamations are heartfelt pleas for repentance (14:2-3) and promises of healing and renewal (14:5-9). Thus, the style and tone of the book of Hosea shift back and forth from threat to consolation, from frustration to compassion, from impatience to understanding on God's part.

With respect to structure, the book is comprised of two main parts: Hosea's marriage (1–3) and Hosea's prophecies (4–14). The text can be further divided into the following units:

I. Superscription (1:1)

II. Marriage metaphor; Gomer, Hosea, God, and Israel (1:2–3:5)

First judgment speech against Israel (1:2-9)

Word of promise and hope (2:1-3)

Second judgment speech against Israel (2:4-25)

Symbolic action and word of hope (3:1-5)

III. Proclamation against Israel and its leadership (4:1–5:7)

Address to the people of Israel (4:1-3)

Address to Israel's priests (4:4-19)

Address to Israel's priests, kings, and people (5:1-7)

IV. Judgment speech against Israel and Judah (5:8-14)

V. Expression of divine frustration and judgment upon Israel and Judah (5:15–7:2)

VI. Description of failed leadership (7:3-7)

VII. Description of Israel's folly and fate (7:8-12)

VIII. Woe speech against Israel (7:13-16)

IX. Declaration of warfare (8:1-14)

X. Judgment speech against Israel (9:1-6)

XI. Statement of impending divine chastisement (9:7-9)

XII. Description of Israel's crimes (9:10-17)

Crimes at Baal-peor (9:10-14)

Crimes at Gilgal (9:15-17)

XIII. Three metaphors concerning Israel (10:1–11:11)

Israel as a luxuriant vine (10:1-10)

Israel as a trained heifer (10:11-15)

Israel as a child (11:1-11)

XIV. Description of Israel's infidelity (12:1–13:1)

XV. Judgment speech against Israel (13:2–14:1)

XVI. Divine plea and promise of healing, restoration, and new life (14:2-9)

XVII. Epilogue: a word of exhortation (14:10)

Even though the metaphorical language and imagery add color to the text of Hosea, this language and imagery do raise points for further hermeneutical consideration. For example, some of the gender-specific metaphors can be deemed offensive to women. A clear example is the extended marriage metaphor in Hosea 1–3, where the relationship between Hosea and Gomer is supposed to represent the relationship between God and Israel. Hosea and God, the male figures in the text, are the faithful ones; Gomer and Israel, the female figures, are the unfaithful ones. The imagery is difficult because the culture of the day privileged males. Additionally, Gomer remains voiceless in the text. Her experience in the marriage remains unheard. Often in the ancient world, particularly during monarchal times, women were looked upon as subordinate to men.

Furthermore, those metaphors that compare people to animals and plant life deserve further thought and comment. Unless people understand life on the planet as a non-hierarchical relationship among all life forms—truly the interdependence of all life in the web of life—then those metaphors that compare people to animals and plant life can be looked upon as diminution. Finally, the war imagery in the text also reflects the culture of the day and continues to influence readers' political and theological imagination at a time when new paradigms of justice are sorely needed in the search for peace.

The theological dimensions of the book of Hosea

Like his eighth-century-B.C. contemporaries, specifically First Isaiah, Amos, and Micah, the prophet Hosea paints a larger-than-life portrait of God to assert divine authority and sovereignty over all peoples and all gods throughout the entire region. The primary focus of the prophet's message is, however, that God is God of Israel, and Israel is God's people. Covenant love is central to the book. This covenant love entails a bond in love and a strong trustworthiness. The book of Hosea is the first prophetic text to envision covenant love as a marriage, and while the metaphor is effective and lends a personal and intimate dimension to the legal framework of the Mosaic covenant, the metaphor also has its limitations, as noted earlier.

In addition to the focus on divine sovereignty and covenant relationship, the book of Hosea has as its theological fabric a series of blessings and curses reflective of the Mosaic law. Thus, the relationship between covenant and law is paramount in the text and central to the prophet's proclamations. Perhaps the most important theological point that can be gleaned from the book as a whole is Hosea 11:9:

> For I am God and not a man,
>   the Holy One present among you;
>   I will not come in wrath.

Israel's God, though depicted in anthropomorphic, anthropocentric, and androcentric ways, truly is not a human being and does not resolve issues as human beings would and did in the eighth century B.C. Thus, the image of Israel's God as warrior and a fire-and-brimstone God is the product of religious imagination used by the biblical poets to make a specific point in each of the Bible's Prophetic Books. Perhaps the greatest and most accurate quality humans can ascribe to God who is Sacred Mystery is compassion (14:3), which, for believers then and now, is a metaphor that flows from lived experience instead of metaphors that come from having read God and God's ways into life's inevitable events.

Finally, the book of Hosea holds out hope not only for those who are victims of injustice but also for those who cause the injustice. Perpetrators of wickedness and transgressors of covenant and torah are beckoned to return to God (14:2) to meet the face of compassion (14:4) and to experience the profound touch of healing (14:5-8). Thus, the theological message of the book of Hosea is timeless and remains inviting.

COMMENTARY

SUPERSCRIPTION

Hosea 1:1

The book of Hosea opens with a superscription typical of other prophetic books (see, e.g., Isa 1:1; Jer 1:1-3; Amos 1:1; Mic 1:1; Zeph 1:1). This superscription names Hosea's father and situates Hosea's ministry in the mid-eighth century B.C., which was marked by the rise of the Assyrian Empire and the threat it posed to the northern kingdom Israel. According to the list of kings presented in the superscription, Hosea is said to have preached during the reigns of four Judean kings—Uzziah, 783–742 B.C.; Jotham, 742–735 B.C.; Ahaz, 735–715 B.C.; and Hezekiah, 715–687 B.C.—and one Israelite king, Jeroboam II (786–746 B.C.). Supposedly, Hosea's ministry began toward the end of the reign of Jeroboam II. Oddly, only one Israelite king is mentioned, which may, in part, be due to the chaos occurring in the northern kingdom after his reign or, since all the Prophetic Books were edited and passed on in Judah, the listing may reflect a Judean bias in the text. The Israelite northern kingdom was destroyed in 721/722 B.C. Hosea repeatedly warns the inhabitants of Israel about the terror that is about to befall them and pleads with them to restore their covenant relationship with God. Kings not mentioned included Zechariah, Shallum, Menahem, Pekahiah, Pekah, and Hoshea. Only two of them—Menahem and Hoshea—were not assassinated by their successors.

MARRIAGE METAPHOR; GOMER, HOSEA, GOD, AND ISRAEL

Hosea 1:2–3:5

This first major unit of the book of Hosea is couched in metaphorical language and images that describe God's fidelity to the Israelite people despite their infidelities to God, to covenant, and to torah. The poet reminds Hosea's listeners then and now that judgment is never the final word. Hope remains central to the fabric of life and to the prophetic tradition as a whole.

1:2-9 First judgment speech against Israel

Hosea 1:2-9 is the first judgment speech against Israel. In verse 2 the marriage metaphor used to express the relationship between Hosea and Gomer is first introduced, and it represents the marriage between God and Israel. Just as Hosea is to take a wife of prostitution, so God will take back idolatrous, apostate, unfaithful Israel, who has "played the whore" by turning to other gods and trusting in alliances instead of relying on God and focusing on God's ways, covenant, and law.

With respect to the issue of prostitution, within the ancient world this form of conduct was not altogether a lack of moral character but rather a matter of economic necessity if women lacked financial support in the patriarchal social structure in which they found themselves. This structure made women dependent upon male relatives—a father, a husband, a brother, a son, or a next of kin male—for property rights and the produce of the land. If no support was given, then she had to find a way to support herself outside of the normal structure. Quite possibly Gomer may not have been a woman of poor character but rather a woman who had to turn to harlotry in order to support herself. Furthermore, the reference to "children of prostitution" (1:2) does not imply that the children were not Hosea's offspring after he married Gomer. The phrase is merely one that signifies the status of their mother.

In verse 3 the biblical writer features Hosea carrying out God's command without any dialogue or second thought. This verse bolsters the intent of the book as a whole, which is meant to persuade its audience to change its ways so as to avert the disaster and so-called "divine punishment" announced throughout the book. Hosea takes Gomer as his wife; they have relations; she bears him a son, whom he is to name "Jezreel" (1:4), a symbolic appellation of past and future events. "Jezreel" means "God plants" or "God sows." The history behind Jezreel, a place, is rich. Jezreel was a beautiful valley located strategically between the mountains of Galilee and Samaria. There the Jehu dynasty began with the bloody overthrow of the house of Omri. Second Kings 9–10 records the past events that resulted in the assassination of King Joram of Israel, Joram's cousin King Ahaziah ben Jehoshaphat of Judah, and also Jezebel, Joram's mother. After these events, seventy sons of Ahab were killed in Jezreel by the supporters of Jehu, the ancestor of Jeroboam ben Joash (1:1). Jehu is presented in 2 Kings 10:28-31 as someone who did not observe God's commandments. He did, however, destroy the supporters of Baal and consequently eliminated the Omride dynasty and all its supporters. Omri, Ahab, and Jezebel were considered to be evil leaders because they led the people away from God and God's ways. Thus, verses 3-5 foreshadow two points: Jezreel will be avenged and the northern kingdom Israel will be destroyed. The name Jezreel appears later in Hosea where the defeated Jezreel turns into a word of restoration and a new beginning.

Verse 6 describes the daughter born to Gomer and Hosea. Like her brother Jezreel, she too has a symbolic name and function. Gomer and Hosea's daughter is to be named *lo-ruhamah*, "Not-Pitied." God is no longer going to show mercy on the house of Israel, which is a clear reversal of the relationship between God and Israel as laid out in the Mosaic law and tradition. God's love and mercy were foundational to Israel's self-understanding and self-identity.

God, however, has not turned away from the people completely. Judah will experience God's compassion and will be saved by God (1:7). This statement is curious, though, because Judah is eventually destroyed by the Babylonians. The reference could be to the Assyrian invasion led by Sennacherib in 701 B.C. (see 2 Kgs 19:32-37), a time when Jerusalem somehow escaped destruction. The phrase could also have been added into the book before the fall of the southern kingdom of Judah in 587 B.C.

Verses 8-9 describe a third child born to Gomer and Hosea. This child, a son, is to be named *lo-ammi*, "Not-My-People." This name signifies the end of God's covenantal relationship with the people. The phrase "my people" was often used to describe God's covenant with Israel (see, e.g., Exod 6:7; Lev 26:12; Deut 26:17-19; 2 Sam 7:24; Jer 11:4). Thus, the biblical writer portrays God as being thoroughly disgusted with the Israelites.

2:1-3 Word of promise and hope

Hosea 2:1-3 shifts from judgment to promise and hope. Israel's time of chastisement and lamentation will not last forever. Israel's God, although enraged by the people's idolatry, apostasy, and waywardness, will not break covenant. The metaphorical language that describes the number of Israelites in relation to the sand of the sea that can neither be measured nor counted recalls the ancient promises spoken to Abraham and Jacob (see, e.g., Gen 13:16; 22:17; 26:24; 28:13-14).

Finally, Israel and God's estrangement from each other will be reversed. Eventually a new kingdom will emerge, one that combines both the northern kingdom of Israel and the southern kingdom of Judah. Covenant renewal will take place, signified by the reversal of the children's names.

2:4-25 Second judgment speech against Israel

Hosea 2:4-25 is part of a larger unit, chapters 1–3, that focuses on the husband-wife metaphor. The setting for this passage is Hosea's bitter marital experience with Gomer, his promiscuous wife. Like Gomer, Israel has been unfaithful to God, going after and worshiping Canaanite deities and thus breaking covenant.

In verses 4-5 Hosea makes a passionate plea to his children to have them confront their mother about her adulterous ways. Hosea wants Gomer to end her harlotry. The punch line, however, comes in verse 5, where Hosea issues a threat. Either she stops her whoring or he will strip her naked, expose her, make her a wilderness, turn her into a parched land, and kill her with thirst. On one level, these two verses apply to Gomer; on another level, these verses symbolically speak about God's relationship with Israel—Israel's infidelity and what God plans to do to Israel if she does not refrain from her whoring, her idolatrous ways.

Verse 6 continues the series of threats begun in verses 4-5. Hosea/God states that no pity will be given to Gomer's/Israel's children because they are children of prostitution (2:6). Verse 7 expands on verse 4. Hosea/God describes in detail Gomer's/Israel's infidelities.

Verses 8-15 state a series of punishments that husband Hosea/God will inflict on wife Gomer/Israel. Gomer/Israel stands accused of fickleness in infidelity, and ignorance, for she did not know that it was her husband who had given her all sorts of gifts that were later used for Baal (2:10). Perhaps the most graphic and most brutal expression of punishment appears in verses 11-15, where Hosea/God declares that he will (1) take back his grain, wine, and oil, along with his wool and flax that were used to cover her nakedness; (2) uncover her shame in the sight of all her lovers; (3) allow no one to rescue her from his hand; (4) put an end to all her festivals; (5) "lay waste her vines and fig trees"; and (6) punish her for her apostate ways and forgetfulness of Hosea/God.

Following a lengthy judgment speech (2:4-15), Hosea 2:16-17 initiates a shift in tone and images. Having been presented with a picture of an angry God enraged with Israel, expressed through the metaphorical language and imagery of a husband-wife relationship, the section portrays a God who woos Israel with tender words and the promise of a renewed relationship with the land and with God (2:16). After all of the harsh punishments that Gomer/Israel will have to endure, Hosea/God then promises to allure Gomer/Israel into the wilderness so that he can speak tenderly to her, give her vineyards, and thus win her back to himself, with her responding to him as she did in the days of her youth (2:16-17). Thus, in verses 16-17 the poet envisions Israel's turn from apostasy to faithfulness, a turn that God initiates.

Looking at verses 4-17 as a whole, we see that the poet has depicted Hosea/God as an enraged husband whose anger leads to several threats that are punitive and violent emotionally, physically, and psychologically for wife Gomer/Israel, who is to be mercilessly exposed to all "her" lovers. She will then be made to suffer serious consequences for "her" infidelity, only to be wooed again by her husband, whose anger has been expressed abusively. Contemporary believers and readers are faced with a series of ethical and theological considerations, generated first by the initial understanding of covenant as a marital relationship, and second by the gender-specific metaphorical language that brings the marital notion of covenant to life. The question becomes, then, "How humanly and divinely ethical is Hosea's message, which bespeaks of violence being used as a corrective for violence, and how appropriate is this metaphor for today when speaking about covenant and relationships?"

One can conclude that the metaphorical language in Hosea 2:4-17 calls for a reappropriation of the prophet's message in light of contemporary life experiences that reflect situations of violence and abuse, inclusive of marital infidelities and discords that have ended violently. Even though the language of the passage may reflect the social setting and cultural perspectives of its day, such language has the potential to negatively affect one's theological imagination as well as one's understanding of and relationship with God and with other human beings. Thus, Hosea 2:4-17 inspires further ethical and hermeneutical reflection and invites the creation of new metaphors that call people to an abiding sense of respect and integrity in all relationships, even in the face of human frailty and infidelity.

One of the central themes of the Old Testament is covenant. God enters into a covenant with Noah, Abraham, Moses and the Israelites at Sinai, and David, and promises a new covenant to Jeremiah and Hosea. Like the Noahic covenant, the covenant promised in Hosea involves God, people, and the natural world. With this covenant the poet envisions a time when God will restore the land to Israel. God promises to make for the Israelites a covenant "with the wild animals, / With the birds of the air, / and with the things that crawl on the ground" (2:20). This covenant is similar to the covenant that God made with Noah, Noah's descendants, and with every living creature that was with Noah (Gen 9:10). Although the Hosea covenant uses espousal imagery that can be disconcerting for reasons mentioned earlier (see 2:4-17), this new covenant envisions harmonious relationships that flow from the relationship with God. For the people of Hosea's time, this covenant offered tremendous hope.

Verse 20, which is, perhaps, the heart of the pericope, depicts a renewed relationship between human beings and the natural world and an end to violence. Peace and security for all creation (2:20) are intricately linked to the renewal of relationship between God and human beings (2:21-22). Through the redemption and restoration of the Israelite people to their God, the natural world is also redeemed and restored.

Verses 23-25 open with a stock phrase, "On that day" (2:23). The future holds a day of divine blessing and a time of cosmic salvation: heaven and earth will now answer each other, and the earth shall respond to its productivity, which, in turn, will respond to human beings as symbolized by the name of Hosea's child Jezreel, which means "God plants." Finally, God will respond to Hosea's children, that is, the covenant people, in the land. Furthermore, in these verses the poet allows us to see that God will reestablish the divine activities that unite both the natural world and humankind.

Thus, in Hosea 2:20-25, the poet presents a visionary picture that speaks of a new covenant that will affect all creation. The passage depicts a new understanding of the relationship between human beings and the natural world, one that is mutual and interdependent, affirming that the redemption of humanity is connected with the restoration of creation. This divinely promised redemption and restoration leads to a vision of creation that embodies justice, righteousness, peace, and harmonious relationships. Finally, from a hermeneutical perspective, Hosea 2:20-25 challenges contemporary readers to a new ethic, a justice that is not anthropocentric in nature and construct but, rather, one that speaks of justice for all creation. The biblical vision of covenant in Hosea is cosmic and carries with it the potential for a new global ethic.

3:1-5 Symbolic action and word of hope

Hosea 3:1-5 returns to the story of Hosea, and God's desire that Hosea love a woman. In verse 1 the poet depicts God issuing a command to Hosea, telling him a second time to go and love a woman guilty of adultery. The woman is unnamed. She may or may not be Gomer. Most likely, the woman is not Gomer, contrary to popular scholarly thought. The text makes no mention of Gomer being unfaithful to Hosea in 1:1–2:25. There Gomer is described as a woman of prostitution or harlotry. Here this woman is described as an adulterous woman. Thus, this woman mentioned in verse 1 seems to be a different one from Gomer.

In verses 2-5 Hosea complies with God's request and then issues a command to the woman. She is not to practice harlotry nor is she to be with Hosea either. Again, Hosea's actions become an analogy for God's relationship with Israel. A period of separation is to occur that will spark a contrite state on the part of the people. This separation from God will have profound ramifications for Israel. The people will have no king or prince, hence, no government of their own and no public manifestation of worship. This time of separation will be an experience of purification for Israel and, eventually, it will lead to restoration and renewal with a new king—one like David—promised to the people.

Thus, Hosea 1:2–3:5 is highly metaphorical and describes God's agony, disappointment, and rage over Israel's sordid state. Israel's God, however, never abandons covenant. Despite all of the people's failings, God remains faithful to them, even though the relationship may be strained for a while.

PROCLAMATION AGAINST ISRAEL AND ITS LEADERSHIP
Hosea 4:1–5:7

4:1-3 Address to the people of Israel

The prophet Hosea speaks of the suffering of the land in relation to human sinfulness. The most striking passage is Hosea 4:1-3, a judgment speech (a *rib*) against Israel. In verses 1-2 Hosea outlines the grievances that Yahweh has against Israel: lack of fidelity and loyalty, no knowledge of God in the land, swearing, lying, murder, stealing, adultery, and continuous bloodshed. The conjunction "Therefore" in verse 3 begins the description of the land's suffering. Implied is that the suffering will be the result of divine judgment that will take the form of a drought. Hosea draws a connection between the suffering of the land and human sinfulness. Not only is the land affected but also the animals and fish, which, like the land, have done nothing to deserve such painful chastisement. By causing the land to experience a drought, God causes the people to suffer: the land will not be able to produce food or sustain any wildlife, and hence the people will have no food and eventually die. In the ancient world, the people believed that droughts and the like were caused by God and were the effects of divine chastisement for sin.

4:4-19 Address to Israel's priests

Hosea also exposes the complacency of Israel's religious leaders. Following his enumeration of Israel's transgressions (4:1-3), he indicts those priests of his day (4:4-13), while mentioning the prophets (4:5), who have neglected their responsibilities to the detriment of the Israelite community. Part of a longer accusation (4:1-13), verses 4-13 describe God's contention with the priests: they have rejected knowledge and forgotten the law of their God. Consequently, the people are "ruined for lack of knowledge" (4:6). Furthermore, the priests are profiting personally from the people's transgressions since they receive a certain portion of the atonement offerings that the guilty ones would bring to the sanctuaries (4:8).

God's response to the priests' infidelities and deplorable deeds is candid and without compassion. Hosea declares that God will destroy their mothers (4:5), reject them as priests (4:6), forget their children (4:6), "punish them for their ways" (4:9), "repay them for their deeds" (4:9), and allow them to experience no personal satisfaction from their gain or deeds (4:10). Without a doubt, certain religious leaders—here, the priest—have corrupted their office and neglected their responsibilities. For Hosea, the behavior of the priest(s) becomes an ethical issue. Corruption within the priesthood does not go unnoticed by Hosea and, according to the prophet, will not go unchecked by God.

Hosea 4:12-14 describes the actions of the people. They are guilty of consulting pieces of wood and having their wands "make pronouncements for them" (4:12a). The pieces of wood could be a reference to the Canaanite fertility goddess Asherah, but more probably the reference is to the Levitical rod or staff that the Levites and priests carried to symbolize their status. Through the use of such imagery, the poet makes the point that the priesthood is ineffective. Furthermore, the people sacrifice and burn incense on the mountaintops and hills. Thus, the people are guilty of apostasy and probably even pagan worship outside of God's temple (see, e.g., Deut 12:2; 1 Kgs 14:23; Isa 65:7; Jer 2:20; Ezek 18:6, 11, 15 for similar imagery), and because of such a sordid religious state, the people fall into a sordid social state (4:13). All of their actions reap divine judgment (4:14). In sum, the priests were responsible for educating the people in the torah but their failure to do so has led the people into apostasy (here, expressed as prostitution and adultery) and caused them God's wrath.

Words of reproach directed toward the Israelites continue in Hosea 4:15-19. These verses continue themes heard earlier in verses 11-14: whoredom (4:11, 15), drunkenness (4:11, 18), and idolatry (4:13, 17). The mention of Judah in verse 15 is curious. Even though Hosea was a prophet who spoke to the northern kingdom, the book itself is addressed to the southern kingdom Judah in the aftermath of the destruction of the northern kingdom Israel. Finally, Hosea sees Israel as being stubborn (4:16); the kingdom of Israel is joined to idols (4:17); worship has become a mockery (4:18); the people have been caught up by a strange wind, otherwise known as idolatry, and they will suffer consequences (4:19). Thus, the people's lack of knowledge and understanding (4:6, 14) and the corruption of their religious leaders, whose responsibility is to instruct the Israelites in torah, will have severe implications.

To contemporary readers Hosea 4:4-19 suggests that in ancient Israel problems existed within the cult that demanded an ethical response from those prophets who, like Hosea, speak out because of their fidelity to God and the ensuing responsibilities that such a commitment brings. Hosea's ethical response, however, invites continued ethical and theological reflection, particularly with respect to the comment that the priest's mother would be destroyed and the children forgotten (see 4:5, 6). While such metaphorical language intensifies the prophet's message and might even strike the heart of the accused, such language raises a problem: Should others be made to suffer as a chastisement for another's transgression, as the text suggests? Even if the language is metaphorical, it communicates an attitude that sanctions justice at the expense of the society's least powerful and the most vulnerable—women and children.

5:1-7 Address to Israel's priests, kings, and people

Hosea 5:1-7, an address to Israel's religious and political leaders, develops the imagery of Hosea's marriage to Gomer heard earlier in Hosea 1–2. Once again, Israel stands condemned (5:1-2). Israel's deeds (5:3), duplicitous heart and spirit (5:4), and unbridled arrogance (5:5) condemned here are the alliances Israel made with Assyria and Egypt (see 5:13-14; 7:11-12). Israel's inability to see the relationship that needs to exist between worship and how the people live their lives on a daily basis becomes evident in verses 6-7. In these verses the poet portrays the people coming with their flocks and cattle to seek God. Israel's God, however, withdraws from them on account of their betrayal. Significant here is the fact that God does not abandon the people; God "withdraws" from them. To abandon them would be to break covenant, which would go against the promises made to Abraham and Israel's ancestors down through the ages. As the poet reiterates again and again throughout the book of Hosea, God remains faithful to covenant despite the people's infidelity.

JUDGMENT SPEECH AGAINST ISRAEL AND JUDAH

Hosea 5:8-14

In this next unit, Hosea 5:8-14, the focus shifts from idolatry to war (5:8). Israel and Judah must now prepare to do battle with God, who will be "like a lion to Ephraim" and "a young lion to the house of Judah" (5:14). These verses foreshadow the demise of the northern kingdom Israel and the southern kingdom Judah by the Assyrians and the Babylonians, respectively. Israel's lack of trust in God, signified by the alliances made with Assyria (5:13), is a sharp bone of contention with God, who points out the folly of such a choice (5:13-14) that will have consequences (5:9, 11, 13).

EXPRESSION OF DIVINE FRUSTRATION AND JUDGMENT UPON ISRAEL AND JUDAH

Hosea 5:15–7:2

In this next section, the poet portrays Israel's God as being not only disgruntled (5:15) but also frustrated (6:4–7:2) by an untrusting, unfaithful people despite Hosea's words of encouragement (6:1-3).

Hosea 5:15–7:2 opens with God distancing God's self from the people until they decide to make reparation (5:15). This strategy is different from the previous one that promises divine wrath (5:8-14).

Speakers shift from God to Hosea in 6:1-3, a song of penitence, where Hosea exhorts the people to return to God, who will act with compassion to restore and renew them (6:1-2). Hosea also encourages the Israelites to renew their relationship with their God (6:3).

Speakers shift again in Hosea 6:4–7:2. In 6:4-6, the poet features God addressing both Israel and Judah. God directs two rhetorical questions to the two kingdoms to express divine frustration and bewilderment (6:4a). Then, with metaphorical language taken from the natural world, God declares to them the instability and unreliability of their love (6:4b), which, according to covenant, should be loyal and steadfast. Seeing their condition, God next recounts what has been done in the past on their behalf, namely, the exercise of punitive divine justice. The people's disloyalty (6:4) is what has provoked divine wrath (6:5). The passage reaches its climax in verse 6, a verse that makes a sharp theological statement: Israel's God wants loyalty and knowledge of God instead of sacrifices and burnt offerings. Ethical living is more important than religious rituals. True worship is not defined solely by ritual practice; rather, it consists of an attitude and way of life characterized by justice, righteousness, and steadfast love—the hallmarks of covenant and the necessary ingredients for right relationships with all creation (cf. Jer 9:24).

In Hosea 6:7-11, God exposes Israel's crimes, which include violating covenant, betrayal (6:7), murder (6:8-9), and idolatry (6:10). The high point of this unit occurs in verse 11, where God also puts Judah on notice. What Judah has sown, that is, evil, Judah will now reap, that is, evil in return that will take the form of divine judgment (cf. Mic 2:1-5). In Hosea 7:1-2 God continues to upbraid Israel, making known to the people that all their wickedness has not gone unseen by God. The healing reference in verse 1 contrasts with Hosea 5:13, where Israel sought healing from Assyria but to no avail. Thus, none of Israel's or Judah's wrongdoings go unseen by their God, and Israel seems to have lost its conscience: "Yet they do not call to mind / that I remember all their wickedness" (7:2a).

DESCRIPTION OF FAILED LEADERSHIP

Hosea 7:3-7

The central simile in Hosea 7:3-7 is a blazing oven that the poet uses to depict the heated rage of those who not only betray their rulers (7:3-5) but also eventually destroy them (7:6-7). The oven to which the prophet refers was round with a stone or earthen floor. Its dome was made of hardened clay. To whom the king (7:5) and kings (7:7) refer is unclear. Possibilities among those assassinated in Hosea's day include Zechariah (746 B.C.), Shallum (746 B.C.), Pekahiah (737 B.C.), and Pekah (732 B.C.). The oven simile comes into full view in verse 7. Just like one who eats bread from a heated oven, so the conspirators "consume their rulers" (7:7a), which causes the kings to fall (7:7b). The most crucial statement of the passage occurs at the end of verse 7, where God states, "none of them calls upon me." In the midst of Israel's political, social, and religious chaos, the people fail to call upon their God and to rely on God, who is Lord of creation and Lord of history. This God would have come to their aid. Instead, they turn to others. Even the kings themselves believed in their own power as the ultimate source of power and wisdom and failed to recognize God's sovereignty. In sum, Israel has serious internal problems.

DESCRIPTION OF ISRAEL'S FOLLY AND FATE
Hosea 7:8-12

The focus now shifts from Israel's domestic problems that involve conspiracy and assassination (7:3-7) to Israel's alliances with foreign power and politics. Comparing Israel to an "unturned cake," to a "silly and senseless" dove, and to "birds in the air" in general captures the kingdom's sordid state (7:8, 11, 12). Pride and arrogance blind Israel (7:10). Because of these two vices, the people refuse to return to God (7:10), who is their true strength, power, and freedom. As a result of its alliances with foreign powers, and with Egypt and Assyria in particular (7:11), Israel loses both strength and independence. The people's folly will reap them an unfortunate fate (7:12).

WOE SPEECH AGAINST ISRAEL
Hosea 7:13-16

This woe speech develops the earlier picture of Israel's fickleness. Instead of trusting in God, Israel trusts in foreign alliances that, in the end, cannot help Israel in its time of dire need. Israel, because of its poor choices, now stands condemned by God, who is angered by the people's disloyalty, rebellion, betrayal, and evil deeds (7:13-15). The anger of God is both personal and poignant: "they have strayed from me"; "they have rebelled against me"; "they spoke lies against me" (7:13); "They have not cried to me from their hearts"; they rebelled against me" (7:14); "they devised evil against me" (7:15). A people full of potential have now become "useless" and like a "treacherous bow" (7:16a). Israel's rulers are destined for destruction and mockery (7:16b) by the very nation in whom they had trusted.

DECLARATION OF WARFARE
Hosea 8:1-14

Hosea 8:1-14 continues the theme of Israel's idolatry. Comprised of three units—verses 1-3, a cry of warning; verses 4-13, a description of Israel's political and cultic transgressions; and verse 14, a statement of divine judgment—this passage is a vivid example of Israel's breach of covenant relationship and blatant disregard for torah. Similar to Isaiah 1:2-9, Jeremiah 4:1-17, and Ezekiel 6:1-7, it elicits further ethical and theological reflection with respect to the statement of divine judgment in verse 14.

Verses 1-3, the first unit, set the stage for the sequence of events that follow, all of which lead up to the statement of divine judgment in verse 14. Verse 1a opens with a strong imperative spoken by God through the prophet and addressed to an individual: "Put the trumpet to your lips!" The remainder of the verse states the reason for the alarm, "One like an eagle is over the house of the LORD" (8:1ab), and why the people are in danger: "Because they have violated my covenant, / and rebelled against my law" (8:1b). Here, "law" refers to torah as "instruction," as will be seen in verses 4-13. Members of the Israelite community have not followed the teachings and ways of God. In verse 2, God quotes the community. The statement is ironic since in verse 3 God accuses Israel of spurning the good and because of this, the enemy—the "eagle" (8:1)—will pursue Israel and ironically, this enemy—this vulture—is already over the house of Israel.

Verses 4-13 outline the issues and transgressions that violate covenant and law that lead the Israelites away from torah and away from God. First, Israel set up kings independent of God, and princes without God's knowledge. The community had been instructed by God through Moses that the people could indeed set up a king but the person had to be one chosen by God (Deut 17:14-15; see also 1 Sam 16:1-13; 2 Sam 5:3; 1 Kgs 1:11, 18; 19:15-16). Furthermore, the community not only chose a king by themselves but also set up princes without God's knowledge. Hence, political leadership was established without divine initiation, consultation, or approval. Such acts violate covenant.

The indictment against Israel for its idolatry comes in verse 4b: "With their silver and gold /

they made idols for themselves." Idolatry violates the law (see Exod 20:3-4; 34:17; Lev 19:4) and goes against the sense of covenant of which the law is a part. Both covenant and law forbade the construction and worship of idols (see Deut 4:23 and Hos 8:1b).

Verses 5-6 with their reference to the calf of Samaria recall Exodus 32:1-35, when the Israelites made a golden calf from their jewelry while Moses was on Mount Sinai. The verses are addressed to the people of Samaria, the capital city of the northern kingdom, Israel. The "calf of Samaria" (8:6) is to be understood as the bull that Jeroboam I had erected in Bethel (1 Kgs 12:29). The bull is the symbol for the Canaanite god Baal. Just as the people have spurned the good, namely, God and God's ways, so God will reject the people's calf and break it to pieces. Thus, the Israelites live under the shadow of God's judgment, a theme that continues in the next three verses of the passage.

Verses 7-10 describe Israel's political situation. The country is powerless (8:8). Israel has offered tribute to Assyria before the Assyrian invasion, and conquest made it obligatory (8:8-9). Furthermore, Ephraim—the northern kingdom Israel—has "bargained for lovers" (8:9). Despite Israel's negotiations with other countries, it will have to endure God's judgment: God will gather the people up, and they will suffer under the burden of corrupt kings and princes not of their own country (8:10). The verses foreshadow Israel's deportation to Assyria, which, for the Israelite people, could be interpreted as God's curse and judgment for the breach of covenant and the violation of torah (see Deut 28:36-37).

Verses 11-13 shed light on Israel's religious practices and cultic sins. Verse 12, a pivotal verse, features the unit's main point: Israel has disregarded torah—God's instructions are looked upon as a strange thing. Thus, the multiple altars for the expiation of sins become altars of sinning (8:11), and the sacrifices offered to God are consequently rejected by God (8:13a). In verse 13b, divine judgment is cast upon Israel: God will remember the people's iniquity, punish their sins, and they will return to Egypt, to the place where they had once experienced bondage.

The passage closes on a somber note (8:14). Amnesia is the root of all Israel's problems. Israel has forgotten its God and has taken refuge in political and military strength by means of building palaces and multiplying fortified cities. The false security will, however, end in folly at the moment of divine judgment when fire will consume the strongholds.

In summary, Hosea 8:1-14 provides a vivid picture of Israel and its struggles. The nation is (1) guilty of idolatry, (2) considered useless by other nations, (3) disloyal, (4) hypocritical, (5) forgetful, and (6) living under divine judgment. Israel has broken covenant and transgressed the law. For readers then and now, the prophet delivers a powerful message, and yet, one is given to question the ethical aspect of the prophet's word that promises destruction in the face of infidelity.

JUDGMENT SPEECH AGAINST ISRAEL

Hosea 9:1-6

The poet opens this next passage on a somber note. God, the speaker, tells the people not to rejoice or exult like the nations (9:1). Because Israel has abandoned God, Israel will be made to suffer in a myriad of ways: there will be a lack of nourishment (9:2); they will be deported to Egypt and Assyria, where life will be difficult (9:3); celebration will come to an end; ritual sacrifices will be without merit (9:4), which would render food unclean (cf. Num 19:15; Deut 26:14), like bread eaten by mourners (9:4b; cf. Ezek 4:9-17; 24:17, 22) that is not suitable to enter the house of God (9:4c). The question raised in verse 5 is rhetorical. The festival day could refer to one of three pilgrimage festivals: Passover, Shavuot, or Sukkoth. Sukkoth is the most likely reference (see 1 Kgs 8:2, 65; 12:32-33; Ezra 3:4; 6:22). Finally, when Israel flees to a foreign land for protection, Israel will meet its fate (9:6).

STATEMENT OF IMPENDING DIVINE CHASTISEMENT

Hosea 9:7-9

Having exposed Israel's transgressions, and having passed judgment on the guilty parties, God now announces imminent chastisement upon Israel (9:7a, 9b) because of Israel's great iniquity and hostility (9:7c). The "days of punishment," the "days of recompense," have come (9:7). Furthermore, Israel's prophets are unable to deal with the disaster that the people are about to experience (9:7). The comment in verse 7 is also a word of mockery: Israel's prophets are mocked for their attacks on Hosea. In verse 8 the watchman of Ephraim is Hosea himself, the true prophet, against whom a fowler's snare has been set. The image of the "watchman" in verse 8 is a common one applied to other prophets (cf. Jer 6:17; Ezek 3:17; Isa 56:10). God makes clear that Israel has sunk into "the depths of corruption / as in the days of Gibeah" (9:9). The simile probably refers to the violent and shameful deeds that are recounted in Judges 19–21, where the tribe of Benjamin violated a Levite and his concubine at Gibeah. Because of this crime, Benjamin was almost exterminated.

DESCRIPTION OF ISRAEL'S CRIMES

Hosea 9:10-17

The next unit features a series of contrasts that highlight God's graciousness to Israel's wayward response, which results in stirring up God's frustration and anger that causes painful chastisement. In verses 10-13, 15-16 God is the speaker; in verses 14, 17 Hosea speaks.

9:10-14 Crimes at Baal-peor

The opening similes in verse 10 are common ways of correlating nature with Israel to expose God's care for the Israelites just as farmers care for the first harvest of fruit (cf. Exod 23:19; 34:26; Deut 26:2, 10). The similes communicate a sense of divine nostalgia. Israel was God's "first fruits," and now, just like their ancestors, the Israelites of Hosea's day have turned away from God and are guilty of idolatry just like their ancestors (9:10c). The story associated with Baal-peor can be found in Numbers 25:1-9. At Baal-peor, Israel became involved with the worship of a Moabite fertility god known as Baal of peor. Verse 11 describes Israel's fickleness and points out that their idolatry will not bear fruit (9:12). In verse 13 the poet presents an image of promise and pleasure but immediately a contrast is set up to reiterate the passage's basic themes. Speakers shift in verse 14 from God to Hosea. Hosea's appeal to God in verse 14 exposes the prophet's frustration with the people and reverses the expectations of the fertility feast of Sukkoth and the so-called marital relationship between God and Israel. For Hosea, a miscarrying womb and dry breasts are better than having to watch one's children perish.

9:15-17 Crimes at Gilgal

God once again condemns Israel in verses 15-16. For a rich history associated with Gilgal, see 1 Samuel 11; 13:7-15; Joshua 4:19–5:15; 9–10. At Gigal, a shrine had been erected where Israel practiced idolatrous worship (Hos 4:15; 12:11). The unit closes with Hosea announcing God's utter disgust with Israel (9:17). The announcement foreshadows both deportation and later exile.

THREE METAPHORS CONCERNING ISRAEL

Hosea 10:1–11:11

Hosea 10:1–11:11 is composed of three units resplendent in metaphorical language that continues earlier themes heard in the book of Hosea, specifically, God's care for Israel and Israel's idolatrous, apostate, and rebellious nature. The most poignant of all three units (10:1-10; 10:11-15; 11:1-11) is Hosea 11:1-11, a window into the divine heart.

10:1-10 Israel as a luxuriant vine

In Hosea 10:1-10 the poet features God as the speaker, who once again uses natural world imagery to describe Israel's beauty and depravity (cf. Hos 9:10; Isa 5:1-7). The opening verse (10:1) recalls Israel's past when Israel lived in the midst of economic prosperity. The fruit-yielding vine may be a reference to the days of Jeroboam II (786–746 B.C.). The main point in the passage is that Israel's "heart is false" (10:2), and because of Israel's duplicitous heart, the altars and the pillars (10:2), the king (10:3), and even the calf will perish (10:5). Here the calf refers to the calf at Bethel that is mockingly called the "calf of Beth-aven" (10:5), which will be carried to Assyria as tribute to the Assyrian king (10:6a). As a whole, the unit foreshadows the Assyrian invasion and consequential deportation of many of the Israelites to Assyria (10:6-7). The kingdom of Israel will soon stand exposed before God and the nations, and especially before Assyria, without any security or cover available to them (10:8).

10:11-15 Israel as a trained heifer

In these verses the poet uses agricultural life to beckon Israel to return to God, but God's plea goes unheard and unheeded. In verse 12 the poet characterizes God as one calling out to the people of Israel, imploring them to seek the Lord, but nothing moves these wayward ones among the Israelites to change their ways. Thus, the consequences of war will befall them; the Assyrians will invade the land. Here, the Assyrian invasion foreshadowed in verses 14-15 is historically and politically inevitable but portrayed in the text as a form of divine punishment. The poet shows us that even the threat of war does not provoke Israel to change its course of life.

11:1-11 Israel as a child

Hosea 11:1-11 is a poem that might be described as the window to God's heart. Here the poet discloses what could be termed the vacillation of God's heart. In verses 1-4 God remembers how, when Israel was a child, God loved Israel, but how Israel moved farther and farther away, choosing to sacrifice to the Baals and offer incense to idols (11:1-2). The poet uses the metaphor of a parent and child to compare God's relationship with Israel. The allusion to being called out of Egypt (11:1) harks back to the exodus story, where the intimate relationship between God and the Israelites first began. In verses 3-4 the poet next describes God's nurturing and parental love for Israel and provides a contrast to Israel's rejection of God's tender love (11:2). Thus, verses 1-4 provide a glimpse into the heartwarming, heartrending relationship that God has with Israel. God is the one who is "long-suffering" in the relationship, the one who faithfully cares for Israel despite Israel's lack of appreciation of the gift.

In verses 5-7 the poem's focus and tone shift. With love unreturned, God now vows to send Israel back to its days of oppression, which, paradoxically, may already have been occurring (11:6). Verse 7 describes God's frustration with Israel. Verse 8 expresses the folly associated with calling on false gods. Thus far, the poet has portrayed God in a very personable and human way, as one who loves Israel deeply but who gets aggravated with the people's lack of responsiveness and apostasy.

In verses 8-9 the tone shifts again. God uses a series of rhetorical questions to engage in self-reflection. God wonders how Israel could ever be given up, how Israel could ever be handed over, how God could ever make or treat Israel like others. Verse 8c provides a glimpse of God's deepest feelings: God's heart recoils; God's compassion grows tender and warm. Because of God's recoiling heart and warm and tender compassion, God will not execute fierce anger or take any other measures of chastisement (11:9a). The verse ends with a divine self-confession: Israel's God is no mortal; Israel's God is the Holy One in the midst of the Israelites; Israel's God "will not come in wrath" (11:9b).

The poem presents a very human portrait of a loving God with intense feelings for Israel. Throughout many of the passages studied thus far, God has been depicted as possessing many human and culturally conditioned qualities. Sometimes these have prompted the question, "To what extent is God accurately portrayed in and by the biblical text, or to what extent is the texts' depiction merely a projected, historically and culturally limited, image of God?" Verse 9 presents God not coming in wrath or violence but rather, in spite of Israel's unfaithfulness (11:7), God will come with love and compassion. God will refrain from violence. A challenge to traditional Deuteronomistic theology of retribution, verse 9 makes clear that the unfaithful will not receive the punishment their unfaithfulness has warranted; rather, God, despite their offense, will not execute power against them. Is this not an attractive portrait of God, one that, while depicting God's love in human terms, depicts God as not human in refraining from anger and destruction? Thus, in this text the poet provides a vision to which humans, then and now, might well aspire.

In the conclusion of the poem, the poet depicts God metaphorically. God is a lion who roars, whose "children" come frightened from the west like birds from Egypt and like doves from Assyria (11:10-11). God will resettle the Israelites in their homes (11:11). With Israel's return from Egypt and Assyria, the exile (11:5) is reversed. Although verses 10-11 convey hope, they depict God as a ferocious father and the Israelites as children who shake at their father's beckoning. This father-child imagery recalls similar imagery that appeared earlier in the poem, but for modern readers, it suggests a patriarchal and paternalistic relationship, one that betrays religious and cultural attitudes present in Israelite society during the eighth century B.C. and later.

In summary, in Hosea 11:1-11 the poet conveys a very human and divine image of God, but one that is not without its flaws. Central to the passage is the language of relationship—the language of a vacillating heart that moves back and forth from care to frustration to care and compassion with the promise of future restoration. The passage depicts a loving God whose love transcends human love and who will not harm the beloved.

DESCRIPTION OF ISRAEL'S INFIDELITY

Hosea 12:1–13:1

This unit captures many of the themes expressed thus far in the book of Hosea. In the face of God's faithful, gracious love, some among the people of both Israel and Judah have forsaken God and have acted foolishly (12:1-2). Hosea 12:3-7 takes the form of a lawsuit whereby God lays out the case against the two kingdoms (12:3-6) and ends with a strong word of divine exhortation (12:7). Embedded in the lawsuit is a recitation of the Jacob tradition with specific allusions to Genesis 25:19-26; 27:36; 32:27-29. Hosea 12:8-11 continues to describe the foolhardiness of Israel despite God's intervention with prophets (12:11, 14), whom God used to assist, instruct, and woo back the people. God's anger now seems justified but how that anger will be expressed reflects both an underlying theological agenda that reflects the Deuteronomic theology of retribution (see Deut 28) and, perhaps, the poet's desire to pose an incredible divine threat in order to scare the guilty parties into change and reform (12:15). Either way, the historical outcome of the times shows us that such tactics are ineffectual in dealing with a people whose hearts have been hardened and who are caught up in ways that do not lead to and foster right relationship. The passage concludes with a turn of events for Israel that foreshadows the collapse and destruction of the northern kingdom (13:1).

JUDGMENT SPEECH AGAINST ISRAEL

Hosea 13:2–14:1

The poet has announced God's judgment upon Israel, who now lives under divine threat (13:1), and yet, those guilty of transgression continue on in their wayward deeds of idolatry (13:2). Once again, the poet features God threatening to deliver punitive chastisement, a message cast in four descriptive similes (13:3). The voice of Israel's God as the sovereign one, scorned by the people despite the many acts of divine graciousness and tender care (13:4-6), bellows loudly. The one who shepherded Israel will now become a lion, a leopard, poised to attack the people with the ferociousness of a mother bear who has been robbed of her cubs (13:6-8a). The attack will be ruthless and lethal (13:8). The poet's images are horrific, and although they are used to stage divine rage, we need to remember that such texts are imaginatively poetic with a message and purpose directed toward the original audience of the proclamations, living in extremely violent times. The images are images of conquest that reflect the reality of the brutal Assyrian invasion into the northern kingdom Israel in 722 B.C. These images commonly appear in descriptions of brutal oppressors (cf. 2 Kgs 8:12; Isa 13:16, 18; Nah 3:10).

DIVINE PLEA AND PROMISE OF HEALING, RESTORATION, AND NEW LIFE

Hosea 14:2-9

The divine compassion expressed in Hosea 11:1-9 continues in 14:5-9, a divine promise. In verse 5, God promises to heal the Israelites' infidelity and to "love them freely." In verses 6-8, God promises to be "like the dew for Israel"; Israel in turn will "blossom like the lily," "strike root like the Lebanon cedar" (14:6), become beautiful "like the olive tree," smell "like Lebanon cedar" (14:7), "live in [God's] shade," "raise grain," "blossom like the vine," and smell "like the wine of Lebanon" (14:8). Here God resembles Baal, the rain god of fertility. God is about to water Israel to make the land flourish. Verse 9 describes God as an evergreen cypress, from which Israel's faithfulness originates. God, not Baal, is responsible for Israel's future life.

The verses depict God as the sustainer, nurturer, and transformer of life who offers hope to all. Israel is portrayed by means of flourishing natural world imagery. There is a relationship between the restoration of human life and the restoration of the natural world. The text portrays a sense of beauty and peace and speaks to the relationship that God and the Israelite people have with creation. For contemporary readers, the text offers a refreshing message that God desires reconciliation and the well-being and fruitfulness of all creation.

EPILOGUE: A WORD OF EXHORTATION

Hosea 14:10

The poet draws the book of Hosea to a close with a simple exhortation to readers. Those who are wise and perceptive will come to understand the ways of God as laid out in the Hosean text, and they will walk in those ways. Those who are transgressors, who continue in the transgression despite the instruction that has been given through the book of Hosea, will stumble in their own paths. The verse reflects the vocabulary of the wisdom tradition and is most likely the hand of a later editor. In sum, the book of Hosea beckons its readers to remain faithful to covenant, faithful to torah, and faithful to God, who, in the end, waits to forgive, to heal, to renew, and to restore (14:2-9).

THE BOOK OF
JOEL

John J. Collins

INTRODUCTION

The book of Joel appears second in the book of the Twelve Minor Prophets in the Hebrew Bible, between Hosea and Amos. In the Greek translation of the Bible, called the Septuagint, it is placed fourth. In general, the arrangement of the book of the Twelve follows a rough chronological order. The eighth-century prophets Hosea and Amos are placed at or near the beginning, while the postexilic prophets Haggai, Zechariah, and Malachi are at the end. Joel seems to be an exception to this rule, however. While the book provides little specific evidence of its date, it is generally agreed that it is postexilic. Two considerations favor a late date. First, according to Joel 4:6, some Judeans were sold as slaves to Greeks. This reference suggests a date after the Babylonian exile, when Judah was weak and contacts with Greece were increasing. (It does not necessarily require a date after the conquests of Alexander the Great in approximately 330 B.C.) Second, the portrayal of the day of the Lord and the judgment of the nations resembles the kind of eschatological expectation found in other postexilic texts (e.g., Isa 24–27; Ezek 38–39; Zech 14). There are also several echoes of earlier prophetic books, which suggest that Joel was a latecomer in the prophetic tradition. A date about 400 B.C. is a reasonable guess. If this is correct, Joel may be the latest of the prophets, except for the book of Daniel. In any case, it is likely to be one of the latest books in the prophetic corpus. The reason for its place in the Hebrew Bible is that it has the-

matic links with the book of Amos. Joel 4:16, "The LORD roars from Zion, / and from Jerusalem raises his voice," corresponds to Amos 1:2, and the two books also share the theme of the day of the Lord.

Structure and composition

The book falls into two quite distinct parts. 1:1–2:17 contains a description of a plague of locusts and calls on the priests to perform penitential rituals. This is followed by a reply and reassurance from God in 2:18-27. The remainder of the book is concerned with a future time when God will pour out his spirit, save a remnant of the people, and judge the nations. The NABRE follows the Hebrew in distinguishing two more chapters, 3 and 4. Other translations, such as the NRSV, absorb the short chapter 3 into chapter 2 (as 2:28-33). The two parts of the book are linked by the motif of the day of the Lord, but it carries different implications in each section. In the first part of the book, it refers to the plague of locusts. In the second, it is the day of judgment and salvation. There is a clear analogy between the two parts of the book, and it may all be the work of a single prophet. Many scholars, however, think that chapters 3 and 4 are later additions.

The plague of locusts

Locusts have been an affliction in the Near East down to modern times. They are found in North Africa and the Near East, especially in desert regions such as the Sahara and the Arabian peninsula, and also in the Sinai peninsula and the Judean desert. In certain circumstances that are still not fully understood, they swarm and migrate in search of food. The effect of a swarm of locusts is catastrophic. They figure in a vision of Amos (7:1-3), where they eat up all the grass of the land and move the prophet to intercede for the helpless people. Joel gives a particularly vivid account of the plague, comparing the locusts to an invincible army invading the land. We do not know when this particular plague occurred. The account in Joel is remarkable in two respects. First, since the people have no human means of dealing with the locusts, they resort to ritual. The prophet calls on the priests to perform rituals of mourning and cry to the Lord. It is unusual in the Old Testament to find a prophet exhorting priests to perform rituals. More often the prophets were critical of ritual, on the grounds that the true measure of religion was the practice of justice in the marketplace and in social relations. In the postexilic period, the temple cult was of central importance, and we shall see that Haggai and Zechariah were also active in their support of the temple. In face of the plague of locusts, in any case, there was little either priest or prophet could do but cry to the Lord.

It is noteworthy, however, that the ritual does not include any confession of sin. The prophets often view catastrophes, such as the destruction of Jerusalem, as punishment for the sin of the people. In this case, the affliction is certainly viewed as an act of God, but there is little suggestion that it is a punishment for sinful behavior. The only passage that might ground such an interpretation is found in Joel 2:12-13, where the prophet, speaking in the name of God, calls on the people to "return to me with your whole heart." The exhortation to "[r]end your hearts, not your garments" recalls the distrust of ritual that is typical of the preexilic prophets. It is not a repudiation of all ritual, however. The people are urged to "return" "with fasting, weeping, and mourning" (2:12). Moreover, there is no indictment of the people and no indication of why a "return" is necessary. Presumably, there has been a lack of devotion, and the affliction is an occasion to get the people's attention and turn them back to the Lord.

Joel characterizes the invasion of the locusts as "the day of the LORD." This expression occurs five times in Joel (1:15; 2:1, 11; 3:4; 4:14) and some four-

teen times in the other prophets. It always refers to an impending event. The oldest reference is in Amos 5:18. There it is apparent that people were looking forward to the day of the Lord, most probably because it was the designation of a festival. Amos, however, said that the day of the Lord would be darkness and not light, gloom with no brightness. From Amos forward, the day of the Lord became a technical term for a day of divine judgment, on Israel or on the nations. Accordingly, some scholars understand Joel to mean that the locusts are a sign, or forewarning, of a divine intervention that is to come, and that is described in the second part of the book. In chapters 1 and 2, however, the day of the Lord seems to correspond to the invasion of the locusts in itself. So, for example, in 2:2, it is a day of darkness because the locusts spread over the land and block out the light. The day of the Lord was not necessarily the end of the world but simply a day of great catastrophe. It was not necessarily a unique event. There could, in principle, be more than one day of the Lord, although it usually seems to have a definitive character. Joel is the only prophet who applies this language to a natural event. The eschatological associations of the day of the Lord convey vividly the sense of utter catastrophe brought about by the locusts.

The invasion of the locusts, by its nature, was short-lived. According to Joel 2:18, the Lord was stirred by the cries of the people and took pity on them. There follows a prophecy of reassurance, promising a time when the people would eat and be filled and never more be put to shame (2:19b-27).

The day of judgment

The prophet then proceeds to talk about the day of the Lord in its more usual sense in chapters 3 and 4 as the day of divine judgment. The demonstration of the destructive power of the Lord in the locust invasion brings the theme of judgment naturally to mind. Even here, however, Joel differs from earlier prophets such as Amos. For Amos, the day of the Lord was primarily a day of judgment on Israel. For Joel, it is a day of judgment on the nations. For Israel, or at least for the righteous remnant, it is a day of salvation. All who call upon the name of the Lord will be saved. (The idea that only a remnant of Israel would be saved is typical of postexilic prophecy.)

The judgment on the nations is in part related to crimes against Judah. In 4:4-8, Tyre, Sidon, and all the region of Philistia are accused of pillaging Judah and of selling boys and girls as slaves to the Greeks in exchange for wine and prostitutes. The judgment on the nations, however, is not only a matter of revenge on neighboring peoples. It is a universal judgment on "all the neighboring nations" (4:12). This kind of vision of vengeance on all the Gentiles reappears repeatedly in the later prophetic books. Examples can be found in Ezekiel 38–39 and Zechariah 14. It reflects the resentment of a people that was constantly at the mercy of its neighbors. The desire for vengeance is not the most noble of human sentiments, but it is very understandable. It finds a place in the New Testament in the book of Revelation. The sentiment is shared by many people in the developing world in modern times as they look with resentment towards the prosperous and dominant West.

Joel's vision of the future is not only a matter of vengeance, however. After the locust plague, he consoles the people with promises of peace and plenty. In 4:18 he dreams of a day when "the mountains will drip new wine / and the hills flow with milk." In the context of Joel, the remnants of Israel are the primary beneficiaries of these blessings. The hope they express, however, is a universal human yearning that speaks readily to oppressed people of any time or place. A more specifically Jewish hope is expressed in 4:17: "Jerusalem will be holy, / and strangers will never again travel through her." If this hope seems isolationist or xenophobic, we should remember that Gentiles had too often defiled and pillaged Jerusalem in the past and would do so again in the future.

Joel and apocalypticism

The book of Joel and other postexilic prophetic writings, such as Isaiah 24–27 and Zechariah 9–14, are sometimes referred to as "apocalyptic." The reason for this designation is that they bring to mind the book of Revelation in the New Testament by their vision of universal judgment. The earlier prophets were primarily concerned with specific historical crises, such as the invasions of the Assyrians or Babylonians. In the postexilic period, however, the concerns have a less specific, more universal quality. The enemy is not just a specific people but Gentiles at large. Conversely, the hope for the future is not just a restoration to a former state but a radical change in the conditions of life. To be sure, the idea of mountains dripping wine is hyperbolic and not to be taken literally, but the hopes expressed in postexilic prophecy have a more utopian character than those of the earlier prophets.

There remain, however, profound differences between the book of Joel and later apocalyptic texts such as the books of Daniel and Revelation. On the one hand, there is a difference in form. Joel's pronouncements take the form of prophetic oracles. They represent "the word of the LORD" that came to Joel (1:1) just as it had come to Amos or Jeremiah. Daniel and Revelation are primarily visions and, moreover, have a mysterious character that requires interpretation by an angel. On the other hand, there is also a crucial difference in the future hope. The trademark of apocalyptic hope is the resurrection and judgment of the individual dead. (See, for example, Dan 12:1-3; Rev 20:11-15.) There is no hint of such a hope in Joel. The future expectations still concern the people as a group, even if they only apply to a remnant.

Perhaps the most distinctive aspect of Joel's vision of the future is also the most famous. Joel 3:1-5a ("I will pour out my spirit upon all flesh") is quoted in the New Testament, in Acts 2:17-21, in the context of the first Pentecost. The gift of tongues at Pentecost is taken as fulfillment of the prophecy of Joel and as proof that the great and terrible day of the Lord is at hand.

COMMENTARY

1:1 Superscription

The formulaic statement that the word of the Lord came to Joel is a standard opening of a prophetic book. Unlike other such books, however, this one gives no information about the prophet, except the name of his father. Many prophets are dated to the reigns of specific kings, even of foreign kings in the cases of Haggai and Zechariah. In most cases, these prophets are addressing political issues that were specific to their time (the Assyrian or Babylonian invasions, or the Judean restoration under the Persians). The natural disaster which is the point of departure for Joel's prophecy was a recurring phenomenon.

The name Joel means "Yhwh is God." It has the same elements as the name Elijah but in reverse order. The name appears in several genealogies in Chronicles, Ezra, and Nehemiah. The only occurrence in a preexilic context is in 1 Samuel 8:2, where it is the name of the firstborn son of Samuel.

PART I:
THE PLAGUE OF LOCUSTS
Joel 1:2–2:27

The discussion of the plague of locusts falls into two parts, corresponding to the first two chapters of the book.

The first cycle of lamentation (1:2-20)

1:2-14 Call to lament

The prophecy begins with a call to the elders to listen. Such calls are common in both prophetic and wisdom speeches. The elders were the leaders of the community in the postexilic period (cf. Ezra 10:8). It may be, however, that the reference here is simply to "old men," as they are asked whether they remember anything like this in their own days or the days of their fathers. The appeal to the memory of two generations is balanced by a command to pass on the story to the next two generations.

Verse 4 uses four different words for locust. Some scholars have argued that these represent four different species of locust, or four stages of its development. It is characteristic of Hebrew

poetry, however, to say the same thing in different ways. Most probably the variation here is for rhetorical effect: every imaginable kind of locust descended on the land. In verse 6 they are further described as a people who have invaded the land. Traditional interpreters inferred that the locusts provided an allegory for the invasion of human armies. It was not unusual in the ancient Near East to compare invading armies to locusts. In Joel, however, the primary reference is to the locusts, and the armies provide the analogy. The destruction wrought by the locusts is described in verse 7: stripping the bark off trees and destroying vines. The destruction of the vines gives wine drinkers a specific reason to lament.

The call to lament proper begins in verse 5, with the call to the drinkers. There are five imperatives in all, in verses 5, 8, 11, 13, 14. Calls to communal lamentation are found repeatedly in the Hebrew Bible: 1 Kings 21:9, 12; Amos 5:16; Isaiah 22:12; Jeremiah 36:9; Ezra 8:21; 2 Chronicles 20:3.

Verse 8 calls on the people to lament as a virgin might lament for a betrothed spouse who died before the marriage was consummated. The priests mourn because the offerings and libations are not available, due to the destruction of the land. Not only were the priests responsible for making these offerings, but they also received their food from them. These offerings are prescribed in the priestly strand of the Pentateuch (Exod 29:38-42; Lev 23:13, 18; Num 6:15; 15:24; 28:3-9; 29:11, 16-39), which most probably derives from the postexilic period.

Most striking is the statement that "the farmland mourns" (1:10). The earth is often personified in the biblical writings. Compare Isaiah 24:4-5, where the earth mourns and fades and is polluted by the sin of its inhabitants. In Joel, the mourning of the earth is not due to human sin but simply to the natural disaster of the plague of locusts.

Husbandmen and vinedressers (1:11) also have specific reason to mourn because their livelihood is destroyed. Verse 12 ends with a summary statement: "Joy itself has dried up."

Up to this point, the lamentation is simply an acknowledgment of the situation. There is no discussion of cause or responsibility. Lamentation is the only appropriate response to the destruction.

The call to the priests in verse 13 asks them to perform a ritual of mourning by putting on sackcloth and even wearing it during the night. Sackcloth, coarse clothing woven from camel or goat hair, was traditionally worn during mourning for the dead. (Compare the mourning for Abner in 2 Sam 3:31.) The imperative in verse 14 to proclaim a solemn fast also pertains to the priests. Fasting and assembly often went hand in hand in ancient Israel. Compare the story of Naboth's vineyard in 1 Kings 21, where Jezebel gives orders to proclaim a fast and then accuses Naboth before the assembled people. Fasting and sackcloth could be signs of repentance. After the murder of Naboth, Ahab fasts and puts on sackcloth and is granted a reprieve by the Lord because "he humbled himself before me." Such rituals could also be a way of intensifying a petition by demonstrating the seriousness of the petitioner. Ezra proclaimed a fast before setting out on his journey to Jerusalem, "that we might humble ourselves before our God to seek from him a safe journey" (Ezra 8:21). In the context of Joel, the sackcloth and fasting are primarily gestures of mourning, but they also add force to the petition for mercy by demonstrating the abject condition of the people.

Preexilic prophets often looked askance at solemn assemblies and related rituals (see Isa 1:13; Amos 5:21), regarding them as superficial, external gestures that did not necessarily reflect true conversion to justice. Joel, in contrast, has no misgivings about rituals. Some scholars have suggested that he may have been a cult prophet, a person employed by the temple, perhaps even charged with calling solemn assemblies. This is not necessarily the case. He may have been called to prophesy, as Amos had been, by the gravity of the situation. It is remarkable, however, that he does not attribute the catastrophe to some sin of the people or call for repentance as a precondition of deliverance. It is enough that the people demonstrate their distress and call on the Lord. In some part, the difference between Joel's attitude to the cult and that of the earlier prophets can be explained by the changed circumstances of the postexilic period. It is probable, however, that Joel's assumption that prayers and rituals would be effective and that they did not presuppose repentance on every occasion was typical of the cult in all periods. We should also say that Joel was right in not attributing natural disaster to human

sin. This is the lesson of the book of Job, where the friends are rebuked for assuming that suffering is always a punishment for human actions.

1:15-18 Lament for the day of the Lord

Verses 15-18 give the words of the lamentation that priest and people have been exhorted to make. Accordingly, they speak in the first-person plural. After the initial cry of "O! The day!" most of the passage consists of a recitation of the distress that affects the whole land, from the temple cult to the animals. The most striking feature of this passage is the designation of the affliction as "the day of the LORD" that "like destruction from the Almighty is coming!" (1:15).

As we have seen in the Introduction, the "day of the Lord" originally referred to a festival day that was awaited with anticipation (Amos 5:18), but after Amos the expression was taken to refer to a day of judgment, usually a judgment on Israel (Amos 5:18, 20; Ezek 13:5; Zeph 1:7, 14; Mal 3:23) but sometimes on other nations (Isa 13:6; Obad 15). Some scholars understand the reference in Joel 1:15 to mean that the locust plague was a sign that the day of the Lord was at hand. In support of this interpretation, one could argue that the locusts had already arrived, whereas the day of the Lord is near. Nonetheless, it seems more likely that the invasion of locusts is the "destruction from the Almighty" that constitutes the day of the Lord, which has begun but not yet reached its climax. The reasons for seeing the locusts as the actualization of the day of the Lord will become clearer in chapter 2, where the Lord is pictured "at the head of his army" (2:11).

There can be no doubt, however, that the destruction wrought by the locusts is regarded as "destruction from the Almighty." Throughout the Hebrew Bible, bad things as well as good come from the Lord. Compare Amos 3:6: "Does disaster befall a city / unless the LORD has caused it?" Likewise, Job asks his wife: "We accept good things from God; should we not accept evil?" (Job 2:10). As the book of Job makes clear, this does not necessarily mean that every affliction is a punishment. The Lord's ways are mysterious, and Joel makes no attempt to explain them.

1:19-20 A cry for mercy

The first chapter concludes with a plea for mercy. This plea follows on the lament in verses

15-18. If it is spoken by the prophet, it is spoken in the context of the communal lament. Here again there is no confession of sin or expression of repentance. The suffering caused by the locusts is adequate grounds for the plea, and it is expressed even by the animals.

The second cycle of lamentation (2:1-27)

2:1-11 The locust invasion as day of the Lord

Chapter 2 begins by redescribing the invasion of the locusts. The main question about this passage is how it relates to the first chapter. Some scholars have been reluctant to accept that the two descriptions can relate to the same event. Repetition, however, is one of the standard devices of Hebrew poetry, to intensify its impression on the reader. The second account uses verbs in the imperfect tense, whereas the first chapter used the perfect. Again, the variation is rhetorical in effect, and conveys the sense that the invasion is in process. There can be little doubt that this passage refers to actual locusts. While the description prepares us for the prophecy of divine judgment in chapter 4, the concern in this chapter is with the natural catastrophe.

The blowing of the trumpet here is the action of the watchman sounding the alarm at the sight of an approaching army. Compare Jeremiah 4:5 in the context of the Babylonian invasion. For the prophet as watchman, see also Ezekiel 3:17-21; 33:1-9.

The reference to "my holy mountain" shows that the prophet is speaking in the name of the Lord. The idea of a holy mountain, the abode of a deity or deities, is common in the ancient world. Mount Zaphon, in Lebanon, was the holy mountain of Baal. For Mount Zion as the holy mountain of Yhwh, see Psalm 48 and Isaiah 11:9.

Verse 1d could be translated either as "the day of the Lord is coming" (reading a participle), or as "the day of the Lord has come" (reading a finite verb). In either case, the prophet is describing its coming. The day of the Lord is a day of darkness also in Amos 5:18 and Zephaniah 1:15. The imagery is appropriate in this case because the swarm of locusts blocks out the light. This description of the day of the Lord finds a close parallel in Zephaniah 1:14-16, which also refers to trumpet alarms and battle. Joel may have used Zephaniah as a source.

Verse 2:2 emphasizes the unprecedented character of the plague even more strongly than did 1:2. Again, the repetition intensifies the impression. Verse 2:3 refers to fire going before the locusts and also following them. This was suggested already in 1:19. Presumably, the fire is metaphorical. While fire might well follow the locusts, because of the dryness of a land stripped of vegetation, it is difficult to see why fire should precede them. The point seems to be that the destruction wrought by the locusts is like that of fire. The statement that the land before them was like the garden of Eden is not so much a claim of exceptional fertility as a way to maximize the contrast between the land before the locusts and the same land afterwards.

The comparison of the locusts to horses is also found in Revelation 9:7: "The appearance of the locusts was like that of horses ready for battle." In the context of Joel, the point of the comparison lies in the analogy with a military invasion. For a vivid description of horses in a real military invasion see Nahum 3:1-3. The locusts even come in "[t]hrough the windows" (2:9), like Death in Jeremiah 9:20.

The cosmic convulsions in verse 10 have a close parallel in Isaiah 13:10, where the "day of the Lord" refers to the destruction of Babylon. Neither passage implies the end of this world. In Isaiah, the imagery is clearly metaphorical. In Joel, there may be a reference to the actual blotting out of the sky by the swarm of locusts.

Verse 11 makes clear that the invasion of the locusts and the coming of the Lord are the same event: the locusts are the army of the Lord, and he is at their head. No explanation is given as to why the Lord attacks his land in this violent way.

2:12-17 Call to lament

Verses 12-13 are the only verses in Joel that could be construed as a call to repentance. The word "return" (Hebrew *shûbh*) is used repeatedly in the prophets. Amos 4:6-11 cites a list of natural disasters comparable to the one in Joel, after which the people failed to return to Yhwh. Amos, however, is very explicit as to what the people should turn *from*. In contrast, there is no indication of wrongdoing in Joel. In Deuteronomy, the verb sometimes means simply to attend to the Lord and hear his voice (e.g., Deut 30:2, 10). The sense, then, would seem to be to turn to the Lord, rather than to repent of specific conduct. The natural disaster serves to instill the fear of the Lord into the people and heighten their awareness and devotion.

The exhortation to "[r]end your hearts, not your garments" (2:13) is often used in Christian liturgies at the beginning of Lent. It should be noted that it does not imply a rejection of ritual action. People are still supposed to turn to the Lord with fasting, weeping, and mourning. Internal sincerity is not incompatible with external action. Compare the balance of ritual action and purity of heart in Psalm 51.

The purpose of turning to the Lord is to appeal to his mercy. Joel does not regard the plague of locusts as an irrevocable sentence. Joel 2:13 echoes the classic characterization of God in Exodus 34:6: "The LORD, the LORD, a God gracious and merciful, slow to anger and abounding in love and fidelity." The prophet expresses tentative confidence that "[p]erhaps he will again relent"(2:14). Nothing is guaranteed, and the effect of rituals is not automatic, but they express legitimate hope in the mercy of God. The same hope, in language that is almost identical, is placed on the lips of the king of Nineveh in Jonah 3:9.

The call to proclaim a fast and gather an assembly repeats the appeal already expressed in chapter 1. One novel aspect of this section is the grounds that the people give for their appeal. Again, there is no mention of repentance. Instead, the priests are to ask God not to make his heritage a reproach, lest the nations say, "Where is their God?" The same plea is made in Psalm 79:10, with reference to the destruction of the Jerusalem temple. (Compare also Psalm 44:9-16.) This argument does not imply that the people are without sin. It does, however, imply that they are not appealing on their own merits but on the grounds that their misfortune may lead to the mockery of their God.

2:18-27 The Lord's response

The final section of this chapter describes the Lord's response to the prayer. There are several cases in the Psalms where laments or pleas are followed by oracles declaring that the Lord has heard the prayer. (See, for example, Pss 6:9-10; 22:24-25.) Joel presumably delivered this oracle either when the people had performed their liturgy or when the plague of locusts passed.

The oracle of reassurance has several aspects. First, the Lord promises relief from want. Grain, wine, and oil are recognized as the blessings of God already in Hosea 2:10. Future prosperity will compensate the people for all that has been lost to the locusts. Second, there is freedom from fear. The expression "fear not" is typical of Assyrian prophecy and is reflected in the prophecy of Isaiah to Ahaz (Isa 7:4). Here, the freedom from fear is lasting, and it extends to the beasts of the field and to the land itself. Finally, there is freedom from shame, which is closely related to freedom from fear of invasion. The reference to the "northerner" in 2:20 has puzzled commentators. It recalls the prophecy of Jeremiah about evil from the north (Jer 1:11-14). The Assyrian and Babylonian armies that had invaded Judah had traditionally approached from the north. Some scholars infer that the north was the symbolic source of evil and argue that the northerner might even be the swarm of locusts. It seems more likely, however, that a reference to human invaders is intended.

The Hebrew word *moreh* can mean teacher, and the Dead Sea Scrolls use the expression "teacher of righteousness" to refer to a sectarian leader. In this case, however, the reference is to "the early rain," which brought a renewal of fertility after the locusts had passed.

The blessings of the Lord in Joel 2:18-27 are intended for the people of Judah after their time of affliction. They correspond, however, to the aspirations of people in any time and place, and are one of many passages in the Bible that provide a vision of a utopian future and serve as a goal for human hope. Compare Isaiah 11:1-9; 65:17-25.

PART II:
THE DAY OF JUDGMENT
Joel 3:1–4:21

The second section of the book also falls into two parts. The first, in 3:1-5, is preparatory for the day of the Lord. The second, in chapter 4, describes the judgment of the nations and the salvation of Judah and Jerusalem. These oracles are linked to chapters 1 and 2 by the theme of the day of the Lord, but they do not associate that day with a particular disaster, as was the case in chapters 1 and 2. Rather, they project it into the indefinite future.

3:1-5 Signs and upheavals

The expression "After all this," translated as "It shall come to pass" in the NABRE, is one of several expressions used in the Hebrew Bible to introduce oracles about the indefinite future. Other such expressions are "On that day" (Isa 3:18; 4:2; Amos 9:11, and many other passages) and "At the end of days" (or "In days to come": Isa 2:2; Mic 4:1).

The idea that the end time will be marked by an outpouring of the spirit is also found in Ezekiel 36:26-27. The passage from Joel is cited in Acts 2:16-21 in the context of the first Pentecost. It is of interest that the prophetic spirit is said to express itself in dreams as well as in visions. While dreams are a respected means of revelation in Genesis, they are dismissed with contempt in Jeremiah 23:25-32.

The upheavals described in verses 3 and 4 are typical of the "signs of the end" in later apocalyptic literature. A famous example is found in the Gospels, in Mark 13:24-25 and parallels.

According to verse 5, everyone who calls on the name of the Lord will be saved, and these people will constitute a remnant on Mount Zion. This is the first hint in the book of Joel that distinctions are to be made among the people of Judah. The idea of a remnant has its origins in the book of Isaiah. (One of Isaiah's children was named Shear Yashub, a remnant shall return, Isa 7:3.) When Israel and Judah were invaded by the Assyrians, only a remnant survived. Again, only a remnant survived the destruction of Jerusalem by the Babylonians. In the postexilic literature, however, the remnant is not just those who survive physically but the righteous elect. According to Joel, this remnant survives the tribulation on earth. Later apocalyptic texts would locate the survival of the righteous in heaven after death. (See Dan 12:1-3; Rev 14:1-5.)

The idea that those are saved who call upon the name of the Lord is important for the adaptation of this text in Acts. For Joel, the name of the Lord was YHWH. For the early Christians, Jesus was the Lord.

4:1-16 The judgment of the nations

The last section of the book emphatically refers to the eschatological future: "in those days and at that time." Compare Jeremiah 34:15, where this phrase introduces a prophecy reaffirming the restoration of the Davidic line, a prophecy that had been made earlier in Jeremiah 23:5 but that had not been fulfilled.

The most remarkable aspect of this prophecy in Joel is that God will assemble *all* the nations (4:2). The judgment is to take place in the valley of Jehoshaphat, a name that means "The Lord has judged." Some of the nations are indicted for specific offences against Judah. The people of Philistia are accused of selling young Judeans as slaves to the Greeks. The oracle responds by declaring that the Lord will sell their children to the people of Judah, who in turn will sell them to people far away. It is apparent, however, that the judgment is not restricted to nations that have committed wrongs against Judah. All the Gentiles are subject to the judgment of the Lord. The opposition between Jerusalem/Zion on the one hand and the nations on the other is old, and is found already in Psalm 2, where the nations rage against the Lord and his anointed. It becomes more prominent in the postexilic period, as can be seen in passages such as Ezekiel 38–39 (Gog from the land of Magog) and Zechariah 14. The underlying assumption is that Judah will only be safe when all the nations are destroyed. While this assumption may seem paranoid or xenophobic, it was born out of the experience of invasion and conquest at the hands of a series of foreign powers.

Joel 4:10, "Beat your plowshares into swords," reverses a famous prophecy found in Isaiah 2:4 and Micah 4:3, that in a future time people will beat their swords into plowshares. Both prophecies are future projections. The form found in Isaiah reflects the human yearning for peace. The form found in Joel recognizes that conflict is often necessary to bring about the conditions where peace is possible. Joel 4:16, "The Lord roars from Zion," is quoted from Amos 1:2.

The final scenario in the book of Joel is one of security and prosperity in Jerusalem, the holy city. The vision is utopian: the mountains drip wine. We may compare the prophecy in Isaiah 11 of a time when the wolf will lie down with the lamb. More distinctive in this passage is the prediction that "Jerusalem will be holy, / and strangers will never again travel through her" (4:17). The idea of Jerusalem as the perfectly holy city has old roots. It derives from the belief that the Lord made his dwelling in the temple. After the Babylonian

Exile, we find a vision of the ideal restoration of Jerusalem in Ezekiel 40–48. Later in the Second Temple period there was a whole genre of texts describing an ideal Jerusalem. These include the Temple Scroll from Qumran and an Aramaic vision of the New Jerusalem. Finally, in Revelation 21:2, John of Patmos sees "the holy city, a new Jerusalem" coming down from heaven. Where the apocalyptic texts wanted a new, heavenly Jerusalem, however, Joel wanted to see the old Jerusalem transformed. It is in the nature of holy things that they are marked off as different, with limited access. The price of the holiness of Jerusalem is the exclusion of the Gentiles.

There is also a dark side to this final vision. Those who did violence to Judah, such as Egypt and Edom, must be laid waste. (Postexilic Jewish texts often complain about Edom, Judah's neighbor to the south. It is not clear what grounds there are for the indictment of Egypt, unless one thinks back to the time of the Exodus.) Here, as in most of the Old Testament, justice is thought to require vengeance. This idea is rejected in the teaching of Jesus in the New Testament, but it still finds a place in the book of Revelation, a book whose vision of the future has much in common with Joel, although salvation is expected, not in this world or in the old Jerusalem, but in a new creation.

THE BOOK OF
AMOS

Carol J. Dempsey, O.P.

INTRODUCTION

The book of Amos, resplendent with a variety of rhetorical forms expressive of a polished, impassioned, dynamic, and didactic style, captures the imaginations of readers with its straightforward, "in-your-face" message. The prophet wastes no time in drawing attention to the horrific injustices of his day (1:2–5:3; 5:7, 10-13; 5:16–9:10). Such a vision, however, is not without words of encouragement (5:4-9, 14-15) and a vision of future restoration (9:11-15), one that speaks of hope and not despair, life and not death. Amos, the book's prophet, addresses his message to a host of mighty nations guilty of horrendous deeds and horrific injustices (1:3–2:16); to Judah (2:4-5) and Israel (2:6–3:15) for their transgressions; to those living in Samaria who are guilty of oppression and abuse (4:1-3); and to all other Israelites who have failed to keep covenant and live according to God's ways (5:7–6:14). The lot of wayward Israel will be pain, suffering, and devastation at the hand of Israel's God, all of which they will be warned about by the prophet Amos, who will be shown a series of divine visions that outline the impending disasters (7:1–9:10). Despite all of the foreboding news for Israel, the people will not be left without a glimmer of hope. The book of Amos closes on a positive note: in days to come, God will restore the people of Israel (7:11-15). Like so many of the prophets of biblical times, Amos heralds a God who metes out punitive justice for the sake of reestablishing right relationship and re-

storing the people to their land and to covenant fidelity.

The historical and social world of Amos

Whether or not Amos is an actual historical person has been debated among some scholars, but some evidence does exist that suggests he was someone who came from Judah and traveled to Israel, where he conducted his prophetic activity during the first half of the eighth century B.C. Israel's king at the time was Jeroboam II (786–746 B.C.). Judah's king was Uzziah (783–742 B.C.). Jeroboam II was the last king in the northern kingdom's longest dynasty known as the Jehu dynasty. During Jeroboam II's reign, Egypt, Assyria, and Babylon were not yet formidable nations or threats to Israel. The king had successfully subdued the Arameans, who were Israel's most powerful enemy (2 Kgs 14:25-28). Furthermore, no strife between Israel and Judah existed at this time. For Israel, the early part of the eighth century B.C. was a time of prosperity that brought with it, unfortunately, the exploitation of the poor and defenseless by the wealthy and the powerful. With a new economic order came excessive wealth for some Israelites, which, in turn, led to a leisured upper class, many of whom became involved in decadent lifestyles (2:8; 4:1; 6:1-6). Judicial corruption also took root (5:7-12) along with religious hypocrisy. Into this world of affluence, exploitation, and profit stepped Amos, who has long been called God's prophet of social justice.

The literary dimensions of the book of Amos

The book of Amos is a rich literary text that contains a wide variety of forms, such as admonitions (e.g., 5:6, 14-15), laments (e.g., 5:1-17), and narratives (e.g., 7:10-17). The text also features a variety of literary techniques that include the repetition of stock phrases, such as graded numerical sayings (e.g., 1:3, 6, 9, 11, 13; 2:1, 4, 6), rhetorical questions (e.g., 2:11; 3:3-6, 8; 5:18, 25; 6:2; 8:8; 9:7), similes (e.g., 2:13; 5:24; 6:5; 8:8; 9:5, 7), metaphors (e.g., 4:1; 5:2), antitheses (e.g., 5:4-5), and quotations (e.g., 7:1-17). These forms and devices attest to the literary artistry of the text and support its appeal to the ethical consciousness and theological imagination of its readers.

As a literary work, the text can be subdivided into six main literary units and their respective subdivisions:

I. Superscription and introduction (1:1-2)
II. Proclamations concerning the nations (1:3–2:16)
   Concerning Aram/Damascus (1:3-5)
   Concerning Philistia (1:6-8)
   Concerning Tyre (1:9-10)
   Concerning Edom (1:11-12)
   Concerning Ammon (1:13-15)
   Concerning Moab (2:1-3)
   Concerning Judah (2:4-5)
   Concerning Israel (2:6-16)
III. Three words to Israel (3:1–5:6, 8-9)
   First word (3:1-15)
   Second word (4:1-13)
   Third word (5:1-6, 8-9)
IV. Three woes (5:7, 10-17; 5:18-27; 6:1-14)
   First woe (5:7, 10-17)
   Second woe (5:18-27)
   Third woe (6:1-14)
V. Five visions; two judgment speeches (7:1–9:10)
   First vision: locust (7:1-3)
   Second vision: fire (7:4-6)
   Third vision: the plummet (7:7-9)
   First judgment speech concerning Amaziah, his family, and Israel (7:10-17)
   Fourth vision: summer fruit (8:1-3)
   Second judgment speech concerning Israel's unjust inhabitants (8:4-14)
   Fifth vision: God (9:1-10)
VI. Epilogue (9:11-15)

Finally, in order to lend authority and credence to the prophet's words, the poet routinely uses the phrase "Thus says the LORD," which is a traditional prophetic messenger formula added secondarily to the poems themselves. Thus, the poetry of the book of Amos with its defined climactic patterns (for three transgressions . . . and for four) complemented by the text's rich metaphorical language and use of literary devices, is a literary tapestry whose ethical message is both disturbing and hopeful.

The theological dimensions of the book of Amos

Without a doubt, the book of Amos is primarily concerned with social justice. For Amos, this was the God of the poor, the needy, and the oppressed. This God was also "the God of hosts" (3:13)—the commander-in-chief of all that exists in the heavenly court and on earth. This God is sovereign over all territories and peoples (1:3–2:16), over individuals such as Amaziah and his family (7:10-17), and even over Amos himself, insofar as he was called to be a prophet by God quite unexpectedly (7:14-15). This God has the power to depose kings (7:9) and even the people whom this God loves so dearly (8:1-3). This emphasis on sovereignty reflects the poet's agenda to push monotheism in a culture and world where polytheism prevailed even in Judah and in Israel.

From a hermeneutical perspective, the portrait of God as presented in the book of Amos reflects the culture of the day, and, like the other biblical Prophetic Books, the poet's description is anthropomorphic, anthropocentric, and androcentric. Amos's portrayal of God is disturbing, but from a metaphorical perspective, the description is effective in a time when political, social, and religious leaders were amassing more and more power and wealth at the expense of the poor. Israel's larger-than-life God who minces no words and holds back no punitive justice is far more powerful than the greatest of all leaders on earth. Eventually the inevitable will strike Israel, Judah, and the nations—they will suffer defeat at the hands of enemy forces, which the prophet attributes to God. The people of Amos's day live under divine threat, and history bears out that they do not change their ways even when they are being threatened. Israel also lives under promise (9:11-15). Permanent destruction and devastation is not to be Israel and the nations' everlasting lot. Re-creation and restoration is the final word, the final deed, and ultimately the final divine intention of a God whose transformative power continues to bring beauty and life out of ash heaps and ruins.

COMMENTARY

SUPERSCRIPTION AND INTRODUCTION

Amos 1:1-2

The book of Amos opens with a superscription that identifies Amos and his historical times. Both Uzziah and Jeroboam ruled during the eighth century B.C. Both Amos (1:1) and Zechariah (14:5) refer to a literal earthquake during the reign of Uzziah, king of Judah. Neither Amos nor Zechariah gives any further identification of detail about the earthquake except to say that it had happened. This occurrence must have been destructive and familiar to Amos's and Zechariah's readers. The anthropomorphic description of God raising the divine voice from Jerusalem and nature's response sets the tone for what is to follow in the proclamations concerning the nations (1:3–2:16).

PROCLAMATIONS CONCERNING THE NATIONS

Amos 1:3–2:16

This first block of material is a collection of proclamations concerning eight centers of Syria Palestine: Damascus (1:3-5), Gaza (1:6-8), Tyre (1:9-10), Edom (1:11-12), Ammon (1:13-15), Moab (2:1-3), Judah (2:4-5), and Israel (2:6-16). Each proclamation presents heinous examples of violent deeds, done, in particular, against human beings.

1:3-5 Concerning Aram/Damascus

The first proclamation concerns Aram/Damascus, the capital of Syria. The passage describes a violent military campaign launched against Gilead, one of Israel's richest territories, near

Damascus. The brutality of the campaign is described with metaphorical language: "they [the people of Damascus] threshed [the people of] Gilead with sledges of iron" (1:3).

Amos makes known that such brutality will not go unchecked; God promises a fourfold chastisement: (1) to torch the house of Hazael and the strongholds of Ben-hadad; (2) to break Damascus's gate bars; (3) to cut off the inhabitants from the Valley of Aven, along with the one who holds the scepter from Beth-eden; and (4) to exile Aram's people to Kir. Hazael was the name of an Aramean ruler but here the reference is to the kingdom of Aram and not to a specific ruler. Ben-hadad is also the name of an Aramean ruler. Here the reference can be to either a ruler or a dynasty. The exact location of the Valley of Aven is unknown, but Biqaa Valley in present-day Lebanon is a suggested locale. Beth-eden literally means "house of pleasure" and seems to be Bit-Adini, an Aramean state situated between two rivers: the upper Euphrates and the Balih. The exact location of Kir is also unknown, but Mesopotamia is the common consensus among scholars.

The text reveals that Israel's God does not tolerate injustice. The text portrays an extraordinary power play. Because Damascus oppressed Gilead violently, Damascus is to reap what it has sown—violence. The poet describes God as one who will inflict terrible, violent, lethal punishments on Damascus because of the terrible and violent deed it has done to Gilead. Damascus had *power over* Gilead, so God threatens to have *power over* Damascus. God will win for three reasons: (1) God is the all-powerful, sovereign one who acts on behalf of those who have been oppressed; (2) the injustice is done to Gilead, one of Israel's richest territories, and therefore God most certainly will act on behalf of what belongs to God's chosen people, especially since God is Israel's God and this is Israel's story, told from Israel's perspective; and (3) a group of people, expressed collectively through the use of "Damascus," had power over another group of people, so God will indeed have the last word.

In verses 3-5 the poet metaphorically portrays God as "warrior God" who has power over injustice and power over other peoples. As warrior God, God promises to deal with injustice by conquering the enemy, the perpetrator of injustice. In the ancient world, God was imagined as a male deity who was Lord of creation and Lord of history. Furthermore, the historical and cultural times of the prophets were marked by nations in conflict with each other, with Israel being no exception. Consequently, experiences and ideologies of war shaped and informed Israel's self-understanding and poetic expression.

1:6-8 Concerning Philistia

The second proclamation of judgment concerns Gaza, also known as the Philistines. Here the poet uses metonymy: Gaza represents the entire Philistine empire, just as Damascus in verses 3-5 represented all of the Aramean empire. In verse 6, the poet depicts God speaking through the prophet Amos. God accuses Gaza of a crime that it committed against defenseless people: Gaza is guilty of slave trade. Entire communities were carried into exile and handed over to Edom (1:6) so that they could serve the interests of the powerful. Verses 7-8 describe the divine chastisement that will befall Gaza because of its crime. The text depicts the commodification of human beings: people using other people for their own gain, an injustice that existed in the ancient world but also continues today. God is again portrayed as warrior God who will mete out violent punishment to avenge the victims and to strike at the oppressors. As in the oracle against Damascus (1:3-5), the central image of chastisement is fire (1:7). Like verses 3-5, the text makes clear that injustice is not divinely sanctioned; the powerful will be brought low; however, the means will be violent just like it will be for Damascus/Aram.

1:9-10 Concerning Tyre

The third proclamation concerns Tyre, the main city of the Phoenicians during the mid-eighth century. This text is similar to the proclamation concerning Gaza insofar as Tyre stands divinely accused for the same crime as Gaza. Added to the issue of human commodification, however, is the fact that Tyre "did not remember their covenant of brotherhood [kinship]" (1:9b). This reference is a poetic way of saying that Tyre disregarded and violated treaties, with the covenant of kinship being the paradigm of all treaties. Such deeds reap divine anger and the promise of divine chastisement. Justice will be done, but how? The motifs, metaphors, and issues of this passage echo those of verses 3-5 and 6-8.

1:11-12 Concerning Edom

In the fourth proclamation Amos declares Edom guilty of piteously pursuing his brother with the sword. Edom is also guilty of harboring anger and wrath relentlessly. Edom has violated the customary ethos of kinship obligations. The divine chastisement is, once again, fire. For the fourth time, the poet emphasizes the fact that injustice will not be tolerated and that God will deal with the issue albeit with violence. Edom included the region beginning in the north at the River Zered and extended southward to the Gulf of Aqabah. Both Bozrah and Teman were important Edomite cities.

1:13-15 Concerning Ammon

Perhaps one of the most gruesome and violent images in the collection of proclamations concerning the nations is directed against the Ammonites. These people are descendants of Ben-Ammi, Lot's son. Their land was located in the area north and east of Moab. The Ammonites are guilty of ripping open pregnant women in Gilead for selfish reasons: to enlarge their own territory. This atrocity represents the abuse of power and war at its worst. Additionally, women, children, and the poor were considered to be among the most vulnerable members of the society of their day. Amos makes clear to the Ammonites that the punishment threatened will be as violent as the crime itself. Unbridled, selfish human power is checked by divine power but, according to the text, the power exercised is violent and destructive. Lastly, in verses 13-15 power is portrayed as a violent and oppressive force, whether it is exercised unjustly or justly.

2:1-3 Concerning Moab

The repetitious recital of the nations' injustices continues in Amos 2:1-3, the sixth proclamation that is addressed to Moab. The region itself is primarily a high plateau with mountainous areas and deep gorges. Once controlled by Israel before the Moabites gained their independence, the land and its people were later conquered by the Assyrians in 735 B.C. and by invading Arabs in 650 B.C. Moab is guilty of burning to lime the royal bones of the king of Edom. Burning the bones of a human being was considered a severe desecration, especially since within the culture at this time such an act was reserved for the most despicable of criminals (see, e.g., Gen 38:24; Lev 20:14;

21:9). As in the other proclamations, Amos makes clear that such a deed is unacceptable, especially to God, who promises to send fire upon Moab, to cut off the ruler from its midst, and to kill all its officials with him.

Amos's proclamation presents a devastating picture indeed. First, it shows the lack of reverence on the part of some people for the remains of another. Second, the punishment that God promises is similar to that of the other texts—fire—and yet, the chastisement is even more lethal. God promises to cut off Moab's ruler from its midst and to kill all Moab's officials with him. Again, God's promised response to violence is violence, and, once more, we see how the prophet's message reflects the violent culture of the day, whereby God has to be depicted as one stronger than all the enemy nations and their gods if Israel's God is to be understood as "sovereign" and reigning over all gods, all leaders, and all forces.

2:4-5 Concerning Judah

This proclamation concerning Judah is different from the other proclamations concerning the nations. Judah's crime involves no explicit use of power or use of any violence. Rather, Judah has rejected God's law and has gone astray, which is a most egregious offense because torah is connected to the nation's ethical conduct. Forgetfulness of God leads to forgetfulness of God's ways, which, in turn, leads to political, social, economic, and religious disorder and dysfunction. Judah is in complete disarray prior to the nation's complete collapse in 587 B.C. when it was invaded by the Babylonians.

The imagery of fire used in verse 5 reflects the violence of warfare common to Judah, particularly during the eighth to sixth centuries B.C. When used in association with God, fire contributes to the image of a God of wrath who desires to use power to demolish a nation even when that nation has not been indicted for any explicit violent crime. Amos's depiction of God makes clear that God makes no distinctions between the expressions of indictment and their respective punishments. All receive the same threat—fire (1:4, 7, 10, 12, 14; 2:2, 5).

2:6-16 Concerning Israel

In the proclamation concerning Israel, one sees God, through Amos, enumerating the many transgressions of the nation. Each transgression, in some way, is a violation against other people. First, some Israelites are guilty of the economic exploitation of the righteous and needy (2:6). Second, the poor suffer abuse (2:7). Third, the lowly are pushed "out of the way"; in other words, they are denied access to and deprived of fair treatment by the court systems (2:7; see also Isa 3:15 and Prov 22:22 for the abuse of the poor and deprivation of their rights). Fourth, two men—a son and a father—sexually exploited a maiden (2:7). Fifth, debtors are exploited, perhaps poor men and widows specifically (2:8). Law codes restricted the taking of certain items for collateral and also set limits on how long something could be kept. For example, a widow's garment could not be taken from her (Deut 24:17) nor could a poor person's cloak be kept overnight (Exod 22:25-27; Deut 24:12-13). Sixth, others are drinking in holy places the wine that was obtained from fines they imposed, perhaps on the poor (2:8b). Some Israelites are also guilty of making the Nazirites drink wine, thus forcing them to break one of their vows of consecration (see Judg 13:14-15; Num 6:3-4); others silence the prophets (2:12).

Amos exposes an abuse of power on the part of some of the Israelite people. The victims of such abuse, for the most part, are the righteous, the poor, women, and people following a holy way of life. Within Israelite society, these people would be the most vulnerable in terms of political, social, economic, and religious status, and therefore the people most easily abused. The idea of making the Nazirites drink wine and commanding the prophets not to prophesy admits of a certain overt disregard for the explicit honoring of God. Through this proclamation Amos makes clear that the threads of power, domination, and control were part of the fabric of Israelite society.

In verses 13-16 the poet describes God's response. God will come as a foe among those who stepped all over the vulnerable, and God will push them down.

THREE WORDS TO ISRAEL

Amos 3:1–5:6, 8-9

This second block of material consists of "three words" to Israel. Each one of the three units begins with "Hear this word" (3:1; 4:1; 5:1), followed

by a series of proclamations that reveal Israel's waywardness, how God plans on chastising Israel for its transgressions, and how God has already chastised Israel to no avail since Israel has not returned to God. The passages also shed light on Creator God's power (5:8-9). This God remains faithfully committed to Israel despite Israel's shortcomings (5:5, 14).

3:1-15 First word

God's first word to Israel begins on a poignant yet stern note. In verses 1-2 the poet depicts God as being completely frustrated with Israel. Israel shares a special relationship with God, having been rescued from Egyptian slavery by God and having been "known" intimately by God better than all the other families of the earth, and yet, Israel does not turn back to God and does not turn from iniquity.

Verses 3-6 feature a series of rhetorical questions to support the point being made by God in verse 7, namely, that God does, in fact, make known divine plans and intentions before events happen. Through the prophet Amos, and other prophets as well, Israel has been informed of its wrongdoings and has been forewarned about the consequences that will follow. Verses 8-10 bear these points out. Verse 8 features two more rhetorical questions with an implied metaphor that compares God to a lion who has indeed roared/spoken. The word to be proclaimed is revealed in verses 9-10. The prophet is to make known to Assyria and Egypt—Israel's enemies—Israel's wickedness and oppression. Thus, both Assyria and Egypt will be made aware of Israel's discord and lack of unity, which leaves the kingdom ripe for invasion. Following the detailing of transgression is an announcement of judgment in verse 11. The foreshadowed destructive enemy will be Assyria, though Amos never mentions Assyria in his speeches. Isaiah, Amos's contemporary, does mention Assyria as the rod of God's anger that God sends forth (see Isa 10:5). Israel has now been forewarned (cf. 3:7). Israel, and specifically those who dwell in the capital city of Samaria, will not be completely destroyed. A small group—a remnant—will survive the invasion. Here the poet uses a shepherd-lion metaphor. God, as shepherd, will rescue some of the Israelite people from the clutches of the Assyrians, the lion. Lion God in verse 8 will now act as a shepherd, but lion God will also act as a lion in the guise of the Assyrians. Thus, the imagery and metaphorical language in verses 8-12 are rich and multilayered.

Verses 13-15 begin a new proclamation of judgment. To whom the proclamation is addressed is unknown. The anonymous addressee is given a double imperative: to hear (cf. 3:1, 9; 4:1; 5:1) and to witness. The one speaking is the Lord God, the God of hosts, hence, the commander-in-chief of all earthly and heavenly forces. The Israelites are now forewarned again about the divine consequences that they will have to endure because of their transgressions. Their sacred precincts will be destroyed, symbolized by the reference to the altars of Bethel (3:14), and the magnificent residences of the upper wealthy class living in Samaria (cf. 3:9, 12) will be destroyed. Thus, the people will no longer enjoy a life of feasting and prosperity. Israel no longer lives under promise; Israel lives under threat.

4:1-13 Second word

In Amos 4:1-5 the prophet addresses a group of women of Samaria, the pampered darlings of society in Israel's royalist culture. Amos scorns these women because they appear to be guilty of ruthless exploitation of the poor. Perhaps they were not the direct perpetrators of oppression, but as Amos's proclamation shows, they enjoyed a certain type of lifestyle that was due to economic gain received through their husbands (4:1).

As a response to such a situation, Amos announces that God will deal with the situation. These cows of Bashan will be lifted up with hooks and then roasted! Then they will be carried off without any difficulty to Harmon; they will be deported (4:2-3). Amos continues his biting invective in verses 4-5, one of the strongest condemnations of the official cult as sinful, but this time the address is to all the Israelites who practice rites at Bethal and Gilgal, the two major cult sights in Northern Israel. Amos encourages them to sin there so as to exaggerate their corruption. With tongue in cheek, God, speaking through Amos, challenges the Israelites to transgress and even to multiply transgressions while they simultaneously engage in ritual activities (4:4-5a). Verse 5b closes the unit and captures the entire sentiment of divine condemnation. Thus, Amos exposes the disparity between the people's worship and their way of living.

In ancient Israel metaphors provided a foundation for thought and practice in its daily experience and in its religion. The use of metaphors that came from the agricultural world was not uncommon. The Israelites were a people of the land, and many were engaged in animal husbandry. Herds and flocks became the dominant source of metaphors and, thus, their metaphors came from and are reflective of their lived experience. Bovine metaphors were used to express Israel's relationship with God: Israel as a faithful servant is a heifer (Hos 10:11), and a stubborn one at that sometimes (Hos 4:16).

Bashan in Amos 4:1 refers to that plain in Transjordan. It was a famous, lush pasture country (Mic 7:14; Jer 50:19; and Deut 32:14), and its cattle were called "fatlings" (Ezek 39:18). Bashan connoted quality of lifestyle and quality of life. When Amos compares the pampered women of Samaria to the well-fed and pleasantly plump bovines, he introduces the element of imagination and surprise into his oracle. With this metaphor, he makes the point that these women tend to their own self-indulgence, irrespective of the cost to others. Thus, Amos uncovers the role of Samaria's women in the social dynamics of the state's economic aristocracy. They had grown fat on the plunder of the poor and, always wanting more, they hassle their husbands, whom Amos ironically calls "lords," for fresh "drinks"—new acts of injustice. Here, the men appear to be as servants of the women. Thus, with metaphorical language drawn from the culture of his day that appeals to the readers of his day, Amos launches his attack. For his listeners and readers then and now, his point is clear.

The poetic story told in verses 6-13 presents a startling picture. God reiterates all the divinely initiated negative actions that were done against Israel in the hope that Israel would return to God (4:6-13). God withheld rain, struck the people with blight and mildew, laid waste their gardens, had the caterpillar devour fig and olive trees, sent out pestilence, killed the young men with the sword, carried away the people's horses, made a stench go up the people's noses, and overthrew some of them.

In the ancient Israelite world, God's blessing meant fertility, longevity, and prosperity, and God's curse meant famines, plagues, and pestilences. If the people had a lush harvest and plenty of good rain, then they had done something right. If they experienced famine and drought, then they had done something wrong. It was also thought that God would strike the land and other elements in the natural world in order to punish the people for their transgressions. If the grapevines withered by the power of God, then the people had no wine. If pestilence struck a crop of corn, then people had no food. Supposedly, then, they would, in their need, return to God and reform their ways. The text of Amos 4:6-13 reflects these attitudes and beliefs.

In verses 6-10 the poet portrays God as intentionally manipulating various elements in the natural world in a destructive way so as to coax the Israelite people to return to God. The God who once saw the natural world as "good" now turns it into a pawn in an effort to turn human beings from their wretched ways. Of importance here is the fact that nature is affected by Yahweh's punitive deeds because Israel is stubborn. And the question arises, should the land and the gifts of nature be used to incur chastisement?

Even human beings are sacrificed in the course of God's action (4:10-11). Such punitive actions, however, do not succeed in having the people turn back to God. In this regard, the text becomes prophetic on another level: neither punitive measures nor violence succeeds in changing hearts needed for the reform and transformation of attitudes and life.

5:1-6, 8-9 Third word

This third word concerning Israel is as ominous as the other two words. The first unit (5:1-2) takes the form of a dirge that describes the house of Israel as if it had already fallen with no hope of being restored. What follows are two more proclamations, verse 3 and verses 4-9, both of which begin with the traditional prophetic messenger formula "thus says the LORD" (5:3, 4) that lends credence and authority to what the prophet is about to proclaim. In verse 3 the prophet foreshadows the losses that Israel is about to experience during the Assyrian invasion. In the midst of such impending devastation, hope abounds: not all of the people will perish (cf. 3:12).

In verses 4-6 the poet features God speaking through the prophet. The Israelite people are being exhorted to seek God so that they may live (5:4; cf. 5:6). They are encouraged not to seek

Bethel, not to come to Gilgal, and not to cross over to Beer-sheba. Bethel is about nineteen kilometers (twelve miles) north of Jerusalem. After the death of Solomon and during the time of Jeroboam, Bethel became a leading center of idolatry (1 Kgs 13:1-32; 2 Kgs 10:29) and the main sanctuary of Israel (see Amos 7:13). As a religious center, Bethel rivaled the temple in Jerusalem. Like Bethel, Gilgal became a center of idolatry and was condemned not only by Amos but also by his contemporary, Hosea (see Hos 4:15). Gilgal is about one mile northeast of Jericho. The reference to "house of Joseph" is synonymous with "house of Israel" (5:6).

Verses 8-9 establish the credibility and power of Israel's God, who is not only Lord of creation but also Lord of history. This God, who made the stars and galaxies, who summoned sea waters and poured them out over the earth, who brought destruction and ruin, is named LORD.

THREE WOES

Amos 5:7, 10-17; 5:18-27; 6:1-14

Three woe proclamations comprised the third block of material in this next section of the book of Amos. Israel stands condemned for its duplicitous religious rituals. The people worship God in solemn assemblies, offer choice offerings, and yet they neglect the weightier matters of the law, namely, justice and righteousness. Israel's elite also stand condemned for their self-centered, self-indulgent luxurious lifestyle.

5:7, 10-17 First woe

In Amos 5:7, 10-17 the poet casts the first woe proclamation. The central issue is Israel's neglect of justice, righteousness, and truth. In verses 10-13 the prophet condemns the Israelites for those practices that break covenant and exploit neighbors. Earlier, the people were called to seek God; now, they are being called to "[s]eek good and not evil" (5:14). Some among the Israelites are guilty of the inordinate assertion of power. Once again, the poor (5:11), the righteous (5:12), and the needy (5:12) are overpowered and become victims of a whole array of injustices. Yet, God will deliver justice.

5:18-27 Second woe

One of the most gut-wrenching proclamations in the book of Amos is, perhaps, 5:18-27. In verses 18-20, the poet depicts God questioning the Israelites about why they are anticipating the Day of the Lord. This day was, at one point, a positive and liberating time as in the day when Israel was freed from Egyptian bondage. Now, however, the Day of the Lord will be the complete opposite of what the Israelites expect.

In Amos 5:21-24 divine dissatisfaction with the Israelites' rituals is expressed again. Here, God states boldly, "I hate, I despise your feasts, / I take no pleasure in your solemnities" (5:21). Moreover, God rejects the people's burnt offerings, grain offerings, and well-being offerings (5:22). After requesting that all song and music be silenced (5:23), God then calls for justice to "surge like waters, / and righteousness like an unfailing stream" (5:24). Without a doubt, Amos makes the point that God could not care less about the people's offerings and sacrifices, especially when they are being made by a people sunk in the mire of transgression. What God desires is justice and righteousness, hence, right relationships that embrace the spirit of torah with its vision for love and its call to an ethical way of life.

6:1-14 Third woe

In Amos 6:1-14 the prophet rails against those who are complacent in Zion and secure in Samaria (6:1-7). Although the text gives no mention of the economic status of these people, one can presume that the prophet is delivering a woe proclamation to the wealthy upper class of Israelite society (cf. 4:1, 4-7) that, by its complacent and self-indulgent attitude, allows violence to go unchecked (6:3). Would that they had used their power on behalf of justice, but this seems not to have been their choice (6:4-7).

In verses 8-10, the prophet upbraids the Israelites for their pride, a theme that continues in verses 11-14, where they stand condemned for turning justice into poison and righteousness into wormwood, and for taking pride in their own strength without due recognition of God's role in their recent successful military campaign (6:12b-13). The Israelite people are, therefore, guilty of proud self-assertion and a perversion of justice. However, are all of them guilty, as the text would have the reader believe? Underlying their pride

and perversion is the use of power to obstruct and to oppress. To suppress such attitudes, God promises to raise up a nation that will oppress the house of Israel itself. Similar to other texts from Amos, this passage portrays a hierarchical power play that begins and ends with oppression. Additionally, God's power and control comes to the fore: God will use one nation to oppress another. This text reflects attitudes endemic to both patriarchy and hierarchy, characteristic of the culture of the day and attitudes that were likely shared by both the prophet's own theological consciousness and message as well as those of the texts' later editors.

FIVE VISIONS; TWO JUDGMENT SPEECHES
Amos 7:1–9:10

In addition to a series of "three words" and "three woes," the book of Amos also contains five visions (7:1-3, 4-6, 7-9; 8:1-3; 9:1-10), whereby the prophet warns the Israelites of what is about to befall them. Each vision opens with the words "This is what the Lord GOD showed me" (7:1, 4, 7; 8:1), with the exception of the fifth one, which is a vision of God and the destruction of the sanctuary.

7:1-3 First vision: locust

The first vision announces the coming of a swarm of locusts. Locusts are grasshoppers. Their eggs hatch in the springtime, and their shells turn brown from larval friction when they swarm together. In this passage, they represent an uncontrollable agricultural disaster that was due to occur at the second grain and hay growth in the month of April after the times of the "latter rains." The fruit of this second planting was reserved for the farmers themselves who depended on it for themselves, their families, and their livestock. Amos foresees a land soon to be devoid of vegetation (cf. Deut 28:42). Such a vision causes the prophet to make intercession to God on behalf of the sinful people, and God responds favorably.

7:4-6 Second vision: fire

The description of the second vision is similar in pattern to the first vision. This vision of fire recalls Deuteronomy 32:22. The people and their livestock will be left starving. Again Amos makes intercession and God relents.

7:7-9 Third vision: the plummet

In this vision the prophet sees a plummet that God will lay in the midst of the people. A plummet is a small heavy weight at the end of a long cord. Israel's destruction is imminent, particularly for the sanctuaries.

7:10-17 First judgment speech concerning Amaziah, his family, and Israel

Nestled in between the vision reports is a biographical interlude that outlines a dispute between Amos and Amaziah, the priest of Bethel. Amaziah sets up Amos in an attempt to silence him because Amos's word is challenging and uncomfortable. Amaziah, however, is unsuccessful, and Amos's prophecy is later directed against the priest!

8:1-3 Fourth vision: summer fruit

This fourth vision of end-of-the-summer fruit symbolizes that Israel's end is near, and this time God will no longer forgive the people.

8:4-14 Second judgment speech concerning Israel's unjust inhabitants

One of the more vivid passages that describe social injustice within the Israelite community is Amos 8:4-8. In this passage, Amos—direct and unrestrained—addresses a group of Israelites who have acted unethically on several counts. First, they have exploited the poor economically (8:5; cf. 2:6ff.; 4:1; 5:10-13). Torah insists that the Israelites care for the poor and the most vulnerable ones in the society. Second, those doing the exploiting also are selling the sweepings of wheat from their harvests (8:5). This injustice done to the poor is a violation of torah, which insists that the gleanings of the harvest were to be left for the poor (Lev 19:9-10; 23:22). Third, the poor are made into bartered goods in human trade traffic (8:6). Such reprehensible behavior on the part of those possessing greater economic and social advantage and know-how does not go unnoticed. In verses 7-14, God plans to take action against the culprits of injustice whose ruthlessness stems from apostasy and greed (8:5, 13-14).

In verses 7-14, and specifically in verses 9-14, the poet next depicts God's wrath as an earthquake. Retributive measures include the sun going down, feasts turning into mourning and songs into lamentations (8:9-10), sackcloth covering the loins and shaved heads (8:10bc), people deprived of hearing God's words with a resultant aimlessness in their lives (8:11-12), and famine adversely affecting the people (8:13). Injustice will not go without reprimand; unethical behavior is unacceptable.

Similar to Amos 4:6-13, social injustice affected not only human life but also nonhuman life, and, by extension, all creation. For Israel, sin and suffering were linked. According to their worldview, understood and interpreted by their religious imagination that interacted with their life experience, infidelity to God, the breaking of the covenant, and the forgetfulness and transgression of torah led to punitive divine chastisement in the name of justice. Thus, in various prophetic texts, readers hear and see references to the suffering of the natural world, and, specifically, the suffering of the land, as a direct result of God's action. In essence, it was thought that God would or did strike the land in order to punish the people, in an effort to reestablish justice and to woo them back to God through their repentance. Hence, if the land experienced a drought or flood, crops would be destroyed and the people would suffer. Furthermore, when Israel did lose its land to foreign countries, this was also understood as either sanctioned or ordained by God because of the people's transgressions.

In Amos 8:4-14 the poet reveals to people then and now that in a hierarchical society, power is, in fact, connected to one's social and economic status. This power can be used—and many times is—abusively for self-serving purposes that deny others their legal rights and/or human dignity. Yet, this sort of domination will not have the last word; justice will be done. God's power will affect the lives of the offenders in ways that are most uncomfortable. The text suggests that justice will be a corporate experience and not directed solely at the troublemakers. While God's actions here are depicted as less violent and destructive than they are elsewhere, God's wrath is not. The divine wrath and earthquake portrayed here may in fact, however, be symbolic.

Finally, the poet indicates that justice on behalf of the poor will eventually be served. Verses 7-8 feature God taking an oath, swearing never to forget any of the unethical deeds (8:7) and promising to chastise the mercenaries and barterers (8:8; see also 8:9-14).

9:1-10 Fifth vision: God

The theme of divine wrath continues in 9:1-10, the fifth of a series of vision reports in the book of Amos. In this passage Amos tells about a vision he had that concerns God's judgment upon the kingdom of Jeroboam. In this vision, the poet depicts God as one who authorizes power to be used destructively and promises to use it personally in the same way (9:1).

In verses 2-4 Amos describes God's inescapable wrath; the people will be made to suffer. God vows to snatch them from whatever hiding place they choose as an escape. If they dig into Sheol, God's hand will take them; if they climb up to heaven, God's hand will "bring them down" (9:2); if they hide on top of Carmel, God will search them out and take them; if they hide at the "bottom of the sea," God will "command the serpent to bite them" (9:3); if they "go into captivity before their enemies," God will "command the sword"

and it shall kill them (9:4a). God's intentions are stated clearly in verse 4b.

Hence, God's sovereignty becomes an ominous and terrible reality, and God's punishment becomes an absolute finality. God has passed a legal verdict upon Israel for its transgressions, and judgment will be both punitive and intentional.

EPILOGUE

Amos 9:11-15

In Amos 9:11-15, the book's epilogue, a shift in tone occurs. In verses 11-12 Amos speaks of restoration and hope; in verses 13-15 he describes the coming of a new age. In metaphorical language, he announces the restoration of the kingdom of David and Jerusalem, the place of David's reign (9:11). Verse 12 suggests that the restored kingdom's borders will extend to its fullest borders at the time of David. The nations that were part of the Davidic kingdom at its height were all promised to David and his descendants in God's name (2 Sam 7). Lastly, verses 13-15 promise a renewed covenant between God and the land, God and the people, and the people and the land.

THE BOOK OF

OBADIAH

John J. Collins

INTRODUCTION

At twenty-one verses, Obadiah is the shortest book in the Bible. It follows the book of Amos in the arrangement of the twelve prophets in the Hebrew Bible. This placement is due to thematic considerations: Obadiah is largely concerned with Edom, which is mentioned in Amos 9:12. It has been suggested then that Obadiah could be regarded as a virtual commentary on that verse in Amos, although it was not necessarily composed for that purpose. The order in the Greek translation of the Bible (Septuagint) is Hosea, Amos, Micah, Joel, Obadiah. Obadiah is linked to Joel by the motif of the day of the Lord.

Structure and unity

The short book falls into two parts. Verses 1-14 consist of oracles of vengeance against Edom for wrongs done to Judah. Verses 15-21 contain a more general prediction of judgment on all the nations, followed by the restoration of Judah. This structure is quite similar to what we found in the book of Joel: oracles that have a specific historical reference are followed by others that look for a day of the Lord in the indefinite future. Again, it is possible that all of this short book was composed by a single author, but many scholars see the eschatological oracles in verses 15-21 as additions. In the latter view, there was a tendency to add such oracles throughout the prophetic corpus in the course of the editing of the collection. In any case, there is an analogy between the judg-

ment on Edom and the more general judgment on the nations, and this gives coherence to the book.

Historical context

The historical context of the first part of the book can be inferred with some confidence from the accusations against Edom in verse 11: "On the day you stood by, / the day strangers carried off his possessions, / And foreigners entered his gates / and cast lots for Jerusalem, / you too were like one of them." The occasion is one when Jerusalem was destroyed by a third party. By far the most likely occasion is the destruction of Jerusalem by the Babylonians in 586 B.C. Some scholars object that there is no mention of an Edomite invasion in the historical books of the Hebrew Bible, and neither is there any archeological evidence for it. Edom figures prominently, and negatively, however, in the prophetic books of the postexilic period. Jewish resentment against Edom in this period must have had some foundation. Later, in the rabbinic period, Edom is often used as the archetypal enemy of Judaism and becomes a code name for Rome. Some scholars suggest that it was a symbolic enemy already in Obadiah. The charges in verse 11 are quite specific, however, and they probably reflect historical experience. If this is correct, the oracles of Obadiah, or at least those in the first part of the book, were probably composed in Judah after the fall of

901

Jerusalem. They are then contemporary with the Lamentations of Jeremiah and count among the very few witnesses to life in Judah during the Babylonian Exile.

Relation to other prophecy

Obadiah resembles Joel insofar as the book contains no criticism directed against Israel or Judah. Some scholars infer that both were cultic prophets, who saw it as their task to prophesy the well-being of their people and the destruction of their enemies. Obadiah's prophecy stands in the tradition of oracles against foreign nations, which are treated ironically in Amos 1–2 but are amply attested elsewhere in the prophetic corpus (e.g., Jeremiah 46–51). The lack of any criticism of Judah, however, must be seen in light of the situation after the fall of Jerusalem. The people left in the land were already ground down. They needed support and encouragement, not criticism.

Obadiah also shares with Joel a tendency to cite older prophecy. The closest parallels are found in Jeremiah 49:7-22. Compare Obadiah 1-4 with Jeremiah 49:14-16, or Obadiah 5-7 with Jeremiah 49:7-11. We need not necessarily conclude that one of these books borrowed from the other. It may be that both drew on anonymous traditional material. The tendency to quote from older tradition is typical of the later prophetic books.

The theology of Obadiah

Obadiah is in large part a call for vengeance on Judah's enemy Edom. The book has often been criticized for vindictiveness, but the association of justice with vengeance is found throughout the Old Testament and especially in the prophetic corpus. If Obadiah seems especially vindictive, this is due to the brevity of the book, which allows this theme to dominate to an unusual degree. The desire for vengeance was not unprovoked. The underlying assumption is that one people should not exploit the misfortune of another and that such exploitation is especially heinous in the case of neighbors and relatives. By Christian standards, vengeance is never good. The Old Testament also contains a strand that reserves vengeance to God (see Deut 32:35: "Vengeance is mine and recompense"). But vengeance remains a very human emotion, and it is better to acknowledge it and address it than to pretend it does not exist.

Obadiah ends with a prophecy of the restoration of Judah and Jerusalem. As in Joel, the appeal is to the old Zion theology found, for example, in Psalms 46 and 48, that view Zion as the holy mountain of the Lord. In accordance with the usual expectation of postexilic prophecy, only a remnant will be saved, but none at all shall be saved from Edom, the house of Esau (v. 18).

COMMENTARY

PART I: ORACLES AGAINST EDOM

Obadiah 1:1-14

1:1a Title

We are given even less information about Obadiah than we were about Joel. Even his father's name is not given. This is in fact the shortest superscription of any prophetic book. The name, as pointed in the Hebrew text, means "worshiper of YHWH." The consonants could also be read as "servant of YHWH." The name occurs as the servant of Ahab in 1 Kings 18 (the Elijah story). Essentially the same name, with minor variations, is found in 1 Chronicles 9:16 and Nehemiah 11:17.

The prophecy is described as a vision, although no vision is actually described. The word does not necessarily indicate the manner in which Obadiah received his revelation. The prophecy of Isaiah is variously described as a vision (Isa 1:1) and as a word (2:1), and in the latter case Isaiah was said to "see" the word. It would appear that various words for revelation were interchangeable.

1:1b-9 The coming destruction of Edom

In the first oracle, the Lord declares war on Edom. Commentators agree that the phrase "We have heard a message from the LORD" refers to an earlier oracle that Obadiah is citing. There is a close parallel in Jeremiah 49:14-16, but Jeremiah uses the first-person singular: "I have heard." The herald sent among the nations is most probably an angelic figure. Compare the voice crying out in Isaiah 40:3. It is possible that the prophet is referring to an actual campaign against Edom. We do no know much about the history of Edom in this period. It was not destroyed by the Babylonians when they captured Jerusalem. The capital, Bozrah, was destroyed some years later, however, and the kingdom of Edom was brought to an end, possibly by the Babylonian king Nabonidus, who campaigned in northern Arabia about 550 B.C. It is uncertain whether Obadiah actually knew of the destruction of Edom, or whether he is predicting and hoping for it.

This first indictment of Edom conforms to a pattern that occurs frequently in the prophetic books: those who rise too high in their pride will be cast down to the depths. Compare the oracle about Lucifer, son of Dawn, in Isaiah 14:12-20, or

Ezekiel's oracles against Tyre in Ezekiel 27–28. Again in Daniel 8 the "little horn," Antiochus Epiphanes, rises above the host of heaven, only to be cast down. The allusion to the stars in Obadiah 4 recalls Isaiah 14:13, where Lucifer sets his throne above the stars of God. The reverse of this pattern is found in the New Testament in Philippians 2:5-11, which says that Christ abased himself, and was therefore exalted and given a name above every name. The reference here to "mountain crevices" and the comparison with an eagle refers to the rocky terrain of Edom. The arrogance of Edom is reflected in its sense of superiority to Judah after the latter had been destroyed by the Babylonians.

The verbs in verses 5-7 are in perfect tense. Most likely they are prophetic perfects that announce something that has not yet happened as if it had already occurred. These verses suggest that the destruction is exceptionally thorough. It is possible, however, that the prophet is referring to the eventual destruction of Edom by the Babylonians, most probably in the time of Nabonidus (556-539 B.C.).

In verse 6, Edom is identified with Esau, brother of Jacob, and the identification is repeated in verses 18-19. The story of Esau is told in Genesis 27 and 32–33. There he seems more sinned against than sinning. Although Jacob robs him of his birthright, Esau later reconciles with him. Edom is also called Esau in Jeremiah 49:8 and Malachi 1:2-5, which declares that the Lord loved Jacob and hated Esau.

The reference to allies in verse 7 is sometimes interpreted in light of events leading up to the fall of Jerusalem. Edom had been a member of the anti-Babylonian coalition for a time but withdrew from it before the Babylonians invaded. Presumably the other allies resented Edom just as the Judeans did.

Mount Esau is mentioned only here in the Old Testament. Teman is often mentioned as a major city or region in Edom. It was often associated with wisdom. One of the friends of Job, Eliphaz, was a Temanite. Jeremiah 49:7 asks, "Is there no more wisdom in Teman"? The book of Baruch, 3:23, mentions Teman as a place where one might look in vain for wisdom. The "wise men" in verse 8 were probably political counselors, a class that was often at odds with prophets in the Hebrew Bible.

1:10-14 The reason for Edom's destruction

Obadiah's critique of Edom plays on the supposed brotherhood of Esau and Jacob. In this respect, Obadiah follows the lead of Amos 1:11, which indicts Edom "[b]ecause he pursued his brother with the sword, suppressing all pity." Obadiah clearly implies that Edom had collaborated with Babylon in sacking Jerusalem. This does not require that Edom was formally allied with Babylon. Verse 11 rather implies that it stood by and did nothing to help defend Jerusalem. Afterwards, it assumed a more actively hostile role in joining with strangers who entered Jerusalem to pillage. These actions need not have been officially sponsored by the rulers of Edom. Rather, we might suppose that marauding bands from Edom took advantage of the collapse of Judah's defences to take booty from the hapless Judeans. Verse 14 implies that the Edomites killed and despoiled Judean refugees. Although we have no independent evidence for this conduct by the Edomites, we have no reason to doubt its basic reliability. Relations between Judah and Edom were very bad from this time forward, and Obadiah's account offers a plausible explanation of the hostility.

Obadiah clearly implies that it is wrong to rejoice in the misfortune of one's neighbor. Yet he himself seems gleeful at the expected destruction of Edom. His attitude is all the more ironic if the oracle on the destruction of Edom was delivered after Edom had actually been destroyed by the Babylonians.

PART II: THE JUDGMENT OF THE NATIONS
Obadiah 1:15-21

Verses 15-16 announce the coming of the day of the Lord for all nations. Verses 17-21 place the emphasis on the restoration of Jerusalem but also anticipate the destruction of Edom.

1:15-16 The judgment of the nations

Like Joel 3:14, Obadiah sees the day of the Lord as a day of judgment on all the nations and a day of salvation for Israel. This is the reverse of the

way the motif was used by Amos, who insisted that Israel would be the primary subject of the Lord's judgment.

The judgment on the nations is strictly tit for tat. As they have done to Jerusalem, so it will be done to them. Like other prophetic texts of the postexilic period, Obadiah views all the nations as hostile and subject to punishment. This view was hyperbolic, no doubt, but the prophet might have found it difficult to think of any foreign nations that Judah could trust at that time.

The motif of drinking alludes to the cup of the Lord's wrath, a motif that occurs frequently in the prophets, e.g., Isaiah 51:17-23; Jeremiah 25:15-29. The motif also occurs in the oracle against Edom in Jeremiah 49:12-13. There are two possible interpretations of verse 16. The "you" who have drunk on the holy mountain could be Edom if this passage is read in continuity with the preceding oracle. In that case the point would be that as Edom has been punished, so will the other nations be. But it is not clear why Edom should be said to drink the cup on the Lord's holy mountain. More likely, the "you" are the people of Jerusalem, who drank the cup of the Lord's wrath on Mount Zion when the Babylonians conquered it. The point of the oracle, then, is that what the people of Jerusalem suffered once, other peoples will suffer continually.

1:17-21 The salvation of Zion

The reference to a remnant that will be saved on Mount Zion is paralleled directly in Joel 3:5, and the reference to the holiness of Mount Zion is also found in Joel 4:17. Joel 3:5 adds "as the LORD has said," and this may indicate that Joel knew and borrowed from Obadiah. It is possible that the relationship between the two books is more complex. Some scholars have suggested that the reference to holiness was introduced into the text of Obadiah to harmonize it with Joel.

Verse 18 returns to the destruction of Edom. Usually it is the Lord who is like a fire (e.g., Mal 3:2). Here Israel is the devouring flame. In Obadiah's vision of the future, Judah will not only reduce Edom to stubble but will also occupy the territory of Edom. The prophecy that Judah would destroy Edom does not necessarily prove that Obadiah did not know of its destruction by the Babylonians. He may have meant that Judah would join in to pillage Edom as the Edomites had pillaged Judah. But this part of the prophecy is clearly a real prediction that was never fulfilled, not a prophecy after the fact. The Judeans will further spread out into Philistia and the land of the Canaanites and also reclaim the land of northern Israel. The references to the "captives" of Israel and of Jerusalem indicate that Obadiah hoped for a return of the exiles. While we do not know the actual population of Judah during the Exile, it is usually estimated at a few thousand, and it was scarcely sufficient for the land of Judah itself.

While a remnant is left to Jerusalem, Obadiah allows no survivors for the house of Esau (v. 18).

In verse 21, the NABRE follows the Hebrew in reading "deliverers will ascend Mount Zion." Some critics defend this reading, but most emend the Hebrew to a passive form to read "those who have been delivered." The latter reading makes better sense in the context.

The book ends with the affirmation of the kingdom of God on Mount Zion. In this it returns to the old ideology of preexilic Judah. Compare, for example, Psalm 2. This vision of the future glory of Judah and Jerusalem, however, is somewhat spoiled by the resentment against the nations, and especially against Edom. That resentment is entirely understandable in the context of the sixth century B.C., but nonetheless it is not good.

The value of the book of Obadiah is primarily historical as a witness to the distress of the Judean remnant after the fall of Jerusalem. It sheds some light on the feelings of resentment and the desire for vengeance that often animate the wretched of the earth, especially people who have been defeated and humiliated. The prophecy is expressive, a cry from the heart. It is not, however, a text that can provide much moral guidance for later generations.

THE BOOK OF

JONAH

Irene Nowell, O.S.B.

INTRODUCTION

Who is Jonah?

Jonah, son of Amittai, is introduced in the first verse of this book. His identity is mysterious. He is never named as a prophet, but his mission is clearly to deliver God's message to Nineveh (1:1-2). He has a much shorter historical introduction than many other prophets (see, e.g., Isa 1:1; Jer 1:1-3; Ezek 1:1-3; Amos 1:1; Mic 1:1). He is identified only as "son of Amittai," and there is no indication of the period in which he lives.

So who is Jonah, son of Amittai? A prophet by that name appears in the time of Jeroboam II, king of Israel, who ruled for forty-one years (786–746 B.C.; 2 Kgs 14:23-29). His reign was the last period of stability and prosperity for the northern kingdom, although the narrator of 2 Kings condemns him for continuing the worship at Bethel and Dan. The prophet Jonah, named here, is credited with foretelling Jeroboam's acquisition of territory and restoring the earlier boundaries. Is the book of Jonah the story of this eighth-century prophet? The answer is not so simple. There is no historical record of Nineveh turning to worship of YHWH, and the style of the book is not like any other prophetic book. The solution must be sought elsewhere.

Genre and date

The book of Jonah is not the report of the preaching of a prophet at a specific time. Rather it is a fictional tale. It has been called a parable or

a satire or a parody, depending on how one reads it. It has qualities of each of those genres, but none seems to fit the whole work comfortably. Possibly it is woven together from previous pieces and original material. This construction also makes it virtually impossible to date. It must have been written after the period of Jeroboam II, the eighth century, and before the early second century, the time of Sirach, who mentions the Book of the Twelve of which Jonah is a part (Sir 49:10). The portrayal of YHWH as the sole God, sovereign over all nations, supports a postexilic date, possibly around the fifth century B.C.

How does Jonah fit in the Book of the Twelve?

Recent interest in the Book of the Twelve, the collection of shorter Prophetic Books, has highlighted the position of Jonah in this collection. In the Hebrew version, the Masoretic Text, Jonah is the fourth prophet. In the Septuagint, the Greek translation, Jonah is fifth. In both arrangements Jonah is close to Nahum and precedes that prophet. Nahum is seventh in the Masoretic Text and sixth in the Septuagint. The primary message of Nahum is Judah's rejoicing over God's destruction of Nineveh. If the Book of the Twelve is considered as a whole, the message is that God had mercy on Nineveh when it repented (Jonah) but when Nineveh again turned to violence and decimated the northern kingdom of Israel in 722 B.C.,

God destroyed it (Nahum). The message for Judah seems to be that only through repentance will they be saved. The reader knows, however, that the warning will not be heeded. Judah will be attacked by Babylon and most of its people exiled in 587 B.C.

Who is God in this book?

The identity of God in the book of Jonah is complex. God is clearly in charge of creation, bringing a great storm on the sea, commanding a fish to swallow the reluctant prophet and then vomit him up on the shore, bringing up a plant to shade Jonah and then killing it with a worm and strong east wind. God also cares for people other than Abraham's descendants. The Ninevites are worth God's mercy, shown by the warning of a prophet and the lifting of their punishment. God also seems to overreact in threatening disaster for innocent sailors in order to corral one recalcitrant prophet.

The strongest statement about God, however, is found in chapter 4: "gracious and merciful . . . , slow to anger, abounding in kindness, repenting of punishment" (Jonah 4:2; see Joel 2:13). This version of the Old Testament creedal statement is the crux of the book: Jonah is angry because God is forgiving the Ninevites. He declares, "I knew this would happen!" What this book omits from other versions of this description of God is the added phrase, "not declaring the guilty guiltless, but bringing punishment for their parents' wickedness on children and children's children to the third and fourth generation" (Exod 34:7). The Ninevites are forgiven immediately simply because they repented. The message of this book is not punishment and retribution but rather mercy.

COMMENTARY

JONAH'S DISOBEDIENCE AND FLIGHT

Jonah I

The book begins with what seems to be a typical call narrative. "The word of the LORD" comes to Jonah and God gives him a commission to preach. But this is no ordinary call narrative. Ordinarily the person called objects. Moses objects five times when God calls him (Exod 3:11, 13; 4:1, 10, 13). But Jonah outdoes even Moses. He says nothing, but he attempts to flee as far as he can, "away from the LORD" (1:3). He even tells the sailors that this is his intention (1:10). He must know that this flight is futile, since he declares that the God he fears made both "the sea and the dry land" (1:9). His situation is both ludicrous and tragic.

Further exaggeration is found in the vocabulary of this chapter. Everything is oversized. God commissions Jonah to "[s]et out for the *great* city" (1:2, Hebrew *gadol*). When Jonah attempts to flee, God sends a "*great* wind" that stirs up a "*great* storm" (1:4). After Jonah explains his motive, the sailors are "seized with *great* fear" (1:10). Jonah knows that this "*great* storm" is his fault (1:12), so he urges the sailors to hurl him into the sea. Finally, after every other attempt to save themselves, the sailors follow his instructions and the sea grows calm. Then they are "[s]eized with great fear of the LORD" (1:16). The Hebrew word *gadol*, "great," appears fourteen times in this book of forty-eight verses (see also 2:1; 3:2, 3, 5; 4:1, 6, 11). Everything is supersized!

Another literary device in this chapter helps the reader understand what Jonah is doing. In order to get away from God he goes *down* to Joppa and goes *down* into the ship (1:3). Where is he when the storm comes up? He has "gone *down* into the hold of the ship" (1:5, Hebrew *yrd*). Later, in his prayer, he will tell God he "went *down* to the roots of the mountains" (2:7). Meanwhile God is trying to encourage Jonah to get up. God tells him to *get up* and go to Nineveh (1:2, *qwm*), but instead he *gets up* to flee to Tarshish (1:3). During the storm the captain scolds him for sleeping and says, "*Get up*, call on your god!" (1:6). Later God will again tell Jonah to *get up* and go to Nineveh and this second time he does *get up* and go (3:2-3).

The contrast between Jonah and the sailors is also revealing. Jonah is fleeing from God, whereas the sailors turn immediately to their gods during the storm. The sailors cast lots, a typical Jewish action, to discover the reason for the storm. Jonah knows the reason, but hasn't bothered to tell them. When Jonah tells them to fling him into the sea (another flight from God?), they make every effort to avoid harming him, although he has brought great harm upon them. When the sea stops raging, these pagan sailors sacrifice to YHWH. Although Jonah has protested that he fears YHWH (1:9), in the end it is the sailors who are "[s]eized with great fear of the Lord" (1:16).

JONAH'S PRAYER

Jonah 2

Jonah seems to have hoped to die when the sailors tossed him into the sea. That would be the final escape from this commission of God that he fervently desires to avoid. But God does not give up so easily. God sends "a great fish to swallow" the reluctant prophet (2:1). In popular imagination this great fish is thought to be a whale. In the Hebrew text of Jonah, however, this amazing animal is designated only as a fish (Hebrew *dag*). The Septuagint describes it as a sea monster, *ketos*, a word that then appears in the Gospel of Matthew (12:40). In later Greek this word connotes a whale. Jonah is "in the belly of the fish three days and three nights." "Three days" is a common phrase for a long time and sometimes indicates the time span before God will take action (see Gen 40:13; Hos 6:2; Jdt 12:7; Esth 4:16).

Finally, in the belly of the fish, Jonah decides to pray. It would be appropriate for Jonah in this situation to pray a lament. Instead, as if anticipating God, he prays a psalm of thanksgiving. In the Psalter the psalm of thanksgiving usually follows a specific pattern (see, e.g., Pss 116; 118): The person who had been rescued from trouble turns to God and sometimes describes both the distress and the agonized lament. Then the grateful person gathers a crowd in order to tell the story of how terrible the situation was. Finally, the whole crowd goes to offer thanks to God and to celebrate the deliverance.

Jonah begins in typical fashion. He remembers his lament and the relief that God answered him

(2:3). Then he describes his frightening situation and his fear that he will never again be able to praise God (2:4-7). He has not forgotten, however, that God was the cause of this distress (compare Ps 88). But the description of all his suffering is a way to praise God for having heard him and brought him up from the pit (2:3, 7). He intends to go to God's temple (presumably in Jerusalem) and offer the sacrifice he promised when he was in distress (2:8-10).

The fish, which was masculine in 2:1 (*dag*), becomes feminine in 2:2 (*dagah*), so Jonah seems to be carried in her womb (2:1). Is his rescue a new birth? Jonah doesn't see it that way. He finds himself in the "womb of Sheol" (2:3). Sheol was understood as the place to which everyone goes at death. It is described as a place of darkness and stillness, not a place of suffering (see Job 3:17-19). Whether God is there or not is debated (compare Ps 88:10-13 with Ps 139:8). Jonah at least believes that God heard him from there and delivered him. This prophet who was always going down is now brought "up from the pit" (2:7).

The chapter ends with the announcement that God commanded the fish (again masculine) to vomit Jonah up on dry land. The next chapter will indicate that Jonah has been returned to his starting point.

JONAH'S OBEDIENCE AND THE NINEVITES' REPENTANCE

Jonah 3

Once again God summons Jonah. The similarity in wording lulls the reader into thinking that this is a simple repetition of chapter 1. But there are a few differences between this call and the first. God does not tell Jonah to preach against the wickedness of Nineveh, but rather to "announce to it the message that I will tell you" (3:2). Is this a new message? Perhaps not, but it is certainly immediate. The other contrast to chapter 1 is that now Jonah gets up, not to flee, but to go to Nineveh as God commands.

Jonah's message is short and simple, consisting of only five Hebrew words. The prophet does not identify himself or name God. He does not suggest a way to avert the tragedy. The only possible course of action for the Ninevites, it seems, is to be prepared. But these foreign people understand prophetic words better than God's chosen ones. Nineveh is described as "a city great to/for God." Not only does this indicate that it is "an awesomely great city" (3:3), but also suggests that the city is important to God and perhaps ready to turn to God. This is precisely what happens. Even before the news of approaching disaster has reached the king, the common people proclaim a fast and put on sackcloth, the garment of mourning. The king himself is extraordinarily perceptive. Not only does he affirm the action of the people and even extend it to the animals, he also declares the theology underlying this action. He understands the mercy of God.

First, the people must turn away from their evil. This turning, *shub* in Hebrew, was a primary message of Jeremiah (occurring 115 times out of the 314 instances in the Prophetic Books). Second, the people must cry out to God. The wisdom of this action is demonstrated already in the exodus event. As soon as the people cry out to God (Exod 2:23-25), God hears and calls Moses to lead them out of Egypt. Later, in the pioneer period, a pattern emerges: the people sin; God sends an oppressor; they cry out; God raises up a judge to deliver them (see Judg 3:7-9, 12-30, etc.). The king's final statement shows a deep understanding of God: "Who knows? God may again repent" (3:9). This insight also appears often in the prophets. Joel exhorts the people: "Perhaps [God] will again relent / and leave behind a blessing" (Joel 2:14). Two characteristics of God appear in the king's statement. God is not compelled to act if the people mend their ways. "Who knows?" God is still free. But God is very likely to relent or repent (Hebrew *niham*; see Jer 18:18; 26:3, 13, 19; 42:10; Joel 2:13-14; Amos 7:3, 6).

JONAH'S ANGER AND GOD'S REPROOF

Jonah 4

Jonah is defeated by his own success. He is also a failure: he predicted that Nineveh would be destroyed, but because of their repentance God has spared the Ninevites. The Hebrew text of 4:1 reveals a stronger emotion than the NABRE translation: this was exceedingly evil to Jonah and he was on fire with anger. Jonah again prays to the Lord (see 2:2), but this prayer is a challenge to God. He accuses God of setting him up and wants

to die. This wish may have been his desire when he asked the sailors to throw him into the sea (1:12), but now it is more intense: "it is better for me to die than to live" (4:3). God echoes Jonah's words, but goes directly to the root of Jonah's desire: Is it good/better for you to be angry?

The reason for Jonah's anger is God's very nature. Jonah's faith is strong. He firmly believes the teaching of who God is: "gracious and merciful, slow to anger, abounding in kindness, repenting of punishment" (4:2). This description of God occurs in various forms throughout the Old Testament and is found in the Pentateuch, Historical Books, Prophets, Psalms, and Wisdom (Exod 34:6-7; Num 14:18; Neh 9:31; Joel 2:13; Pss 86:5; 103:8; 145:8; Wis 11:23; 15:1; Sir 2:11, 18). The foundational statement in Exodus declares both God's great love and mercy and also God's just punishment for sin (see also Num 14:18; Neh 9:30-31). Jonah, like Joel, emphasizes only God's merciful love (Joel 2:13; see also Pss 86:5; 103:8; 145:8; Wis 11:23; 15:1; Sir 2:11, 18).

Three of the terms used to describe God are "merciful," "kindness," and "repenting." The Hebrew word translated "mercy" (*rahum*) is derived from the word meaning "womb" (*raham*). This word connotes a mother's compassionate care for her child. The Hebrew word translated "kindness" is *hesed*, the deep, faithful, loyal love that is strong as death. The Hebrew word for "repent" or "relent," *niham*, is predicated of God much more often as it is of people. God changes the divine mind far more often than sinners do. Jonah's reason for fleeing to Tarshish showed his great awareness of God's nature. God is indeed far more likely to forgive than to punish.

Now God sets out to be merciful to Jonah and to give Jonah a God's-eye view of the situation with Nineveh (4:5-8). Jonah leaves the "city," a word repeated in 4:5 to remind the reader that the focus of this story is the wicked, repenting city. He builds a hut (Hebrew *sukkah*) and waits to see if God really is going to forgive the city. But God cares as much about Jonah as about Nineveh, so God provides (literally "appoints") a *qiqayon* plant to shade Jonah from the hot sun. (God has already appointed the great fish in ch. 2.) For the first time we hear that Jonah is delighted, rejoicing with a great joy. God is not finished with the lesson, however. God then appoints a worm to destroy the plant. Finally God also appoints a hot east wind.

Jonah is furious. Again he declares that it is better to die than live.

Several terms in this paragraph are significant. Two echo the exodus event. God appoints the *qiqayon* to "deliver" Jonah just as God delivered the people from Egypt (Exod 3:8; 6:6; 12:27; Judg 6:9; 8:34). God also appointed the east wind in Exodus to make a path through the sea (Exod 14:21). God is now attempting to rescue Jonah from his own bad temper. The word *qiqayon* occurs only here in the Hebrew Bible. It is translated variously as "gourd plant," "cucumber," "bush," "ivy." Ironically it sounds in Hebrew like "vomit Jonah." The Hebrew word for "vomit" is *qiq* and *yon* suggests Jonah (Hebrew *yonah*).

Jonah is burning with anger again and God asks the same question: Is it better for you to burn? Jonah replies that it is better, enough to die. Now comes God's lesson for Jonah. Jonah pities the *qiqayon*, for which he expended no effort or care. Should God not pity Nineveh, even the animals who repented along with the people? In the same passage in which he proclaimed God gracious and merciful, the prophet Joel exhorted the people to cry out to God, "Spare your people, LORD!" (Joel 2:17). Here God pities the Ninevites. The implication is that Jonah should not only pity the *qiqayon*, but also Nineveh. The question remains unanswered and so is still addressed to the reader. Who is it that we are now called to pity and forgive?

THE BOOK OF
MICAH

Carol J. Dempsey, O.P.

INTRODUCTION

Railing against the people of Israel and Judah, Micah of Moresheth, the prophet in the book of Micah, is without guile or fear. He does not cower from addressing the power brokers of his day, and he goes to great lengths to make his message heard, even to the point of being willing to run barefoot and naked through the streets. Singing songs of lamentation and proclaiming words of woe, the prophet foreshadows what is about to befall the Israelite community if people do not change their sordid ways. His message, however, is not all doom and gloom. His vision of the mountain of the Lord's house (4:1-4) where all peoples, all nations, will gather and live in abiding peace with mutual respect is a vision that brings hope not only to the people of Micah's day but also to all who continue to listen and ponder his word today. Micah redefines right relationship and makes clear that offering eternal sacrifices to atone for transgression is not what God desires. Instead, God desires ethical praxis and a change of heart and attitude best expressed through acting justly and loving tenderly, the foundation of which is a humble walk with God, which, transformative in itself, will provide the strength and direction needed for right relationship (6:6-8). Perhaps the greatest of all Micah's proclamations comes at the end of the book, where the prophet proclaims who Israel's God truly is—a God of compassion who casts all sins into the depths of the sea and remains faithful and loving toward all people, all creation, for all times (7:18-20).

The world of Micah

The book of Micah presents itself as a word addressed to the people of Israel and Judah in the latter half of the eighth century B.C. during the reigns of Jotham (742–735 B.C.), Ahaz (735–715 B.C.), and Hezekiah (715–686 B.C.). According to the text of Micah, the prophet's career appears expansive but most likely the prophetic activity was confined to the last quarter of the century during the reign of Hezekiah. Together with Amos, Isaiah, and Hosea, Micah was one of the four great prophets of the eighth century B.C. His name means "who is like the Lord." Micah's name was a common one during his time but the phrase "of Moresheth" distinguished him from others who bore the same name.

The book itself reflects a period in Israel and Judah's history that was plagued by Assyrian military invasions. These invasions began with the Syro-Ephraimite War (734–732 B.C.) and continued down through Sennacherib's invasion of Judah in 701 B.C. In the midst of such unrest, Judah did experience religious reforms and an economic revolution. These changes allowed the wealthy landowners to grow in prosperity at the expense of small peasant farmers. Soon religious and political leaders began to view their vocations

911

and positions as business careers. Instead of focusing on serving the people in the communities, they began to assert their power for self-serving purposes and had little regard for the common good. With the abuse of power and idolatry on the rise, right relationship with God and with one another was compromised and gave way to injustice, oppression, and corruption. Assyria was at its zenith of power and influence as Babylon increased in strength. The northern kingdom Israel and the southern kingdom Judah were ripe for invasion. The prophet Micah read the signs of the times, only to have the inevitable eventually occur—the collapse and destruction of the two kingdoms. This catastrophe resulted in Israel's inhabi-tants being deported to Assyria and, later, Judah's inhabitants being exiled to Babylon and Egypt. Into this climate of unrest stepped the prophet Micah, one "filled with power, / with the spirit of the Lord, / with justice and with might; / To declare to Jacob his crimes / and to Israel his sins" (3:8). Ultimately, Micah held out hope to a people loved dearly by their God.

The literary dimensions of the book of Micah

The literary composition of the book of Micah has intrigued scholars for years. In general, scholars have used either a diachronic or synchronic approach to the study of the text, along with other methods of criticism, all of which have yielded many fruitful insights and readings of the text. Much of the contemporary research has focused on the literary and rhetorical coherence and unity of the book as a whole.

With respect to the structure of the book, several proposals have been offered. Based on the literary content and its theological message, the book can be divided as follows:

I. Superscription (1:1)

II. Proclamation of judgment; word of hope (1:2–3:12)

Judgment speech (1:2-7)

Dirge-lament (1:8-16)

Woe proclamation (2:1-5)

Disputation prophecy (2:6-11)

Salvation proclamation (2:12-13)

Address to Israel's political leadership (3:1-4)

Proclamation concerning the prophets (3:5-7)

Interlude: statement of confidence (3:8)

Address to Israel's leadership (3:9-12)

III. Proclamation of future restoration (4:1–5:14)

Prophetic vision (4:1-5)

Divine promise (4:6–5:14)

IV. Words of judgment, lament, trust (6:1–7:20)

Covenant lawsuit (6:1-5)

Torah liturgy (6:6-8)

Judgment speech (6:9-16)

Lament (7:1-6)

Statement of trust (7:7-10)

Divine promise (7:11-13)

Petition (7:14-17)

Statement of divine love (7:18-20)

As a work of literature, Micah 1–3 is generally accepted as authentic Micah material, though Micah 2:12-13 could be received as a later addition, but evidence remains inconclusive. Micah 6:1–7:6 may also be authentic Micah material, with the remainder of the book consisting of an assortment of later additions. Although some of the contents in the book of Micah have been considered authentic Micah material, the larger question remains: Is the prophet Micah truly a historical person or a literary persona representative of a school of prophets that lived and were active during the mid-eighth century B.C.? Scholars continue to debate the question. The fabric of the book as a whole features a wide array of literary forms and techniques such as judgment speeches (1:2-7; 3:1-2), laments (1:8-16; 7:1-7), a lawsuit (6:1-5), prayers (7:14-17, 18-20), reflections (6:6-8), and metaphors (e.g., 1:2-4; 2:12-13; 3:1-3; 4:1-5, 8-13; 7:1), all of which serve to accent and clarify the prophet's message. Finally, the book of Micah sets out to address Jerusalem and Israel's future in the aftermath of the Babylonian exile.

The theological dimensions of the book of Micah

With creativity and boldness, the prophet Micah addressed not only the social and political issues of his day but also the religious issues, all of which portrayed a picture of gross corruption and injustice. Micah rails against the perpetrators of graft (see, e.g., 1–3) while offering not only a vision of a new world order (see 4:1-5) but also a message of hope (e.g., 2:12-13; 4:6-8). Thus, the book of Micah makes clear that Israel's God will not tolerate injustice and oppression rooted in and flowing from apostasy, idolatry, hypocrisy, the disregard for torah, and the break in covenant relationship. Divine justice will be meted out, and yet, the final word of the book as a whole offers a word of universal compassion (7:18-20), but not before the prophet makes intercession on behalf of the people (6:6-8), which yields one of the most often quoted passages of the entire Bible (6:8).

In addition to a focus on justice, salvation, redemption, and compassion, the book of Micah also presents a multifaceted picture of God. This God can be overpowering (1:2-4), retributive (2:1-3, 4-5), enraged (6:9-16), gracious (2:12-13), instructive (6:8), forgiving, and compassionate (7:18-20), much like human beings. This anthropomorphic and anthropocentric portrayal of God reflects the hand of the human biblical poet and, in many ways, this portrait also reflects the human condition. Israel's God has to be stronger and more powerful than all the people, leaders, and forces of the day. Israel's God has to be sovereign over all other gods as well. Divine sovereignty is a core theological theme in the book of Micah, in the other books of the prophets, and in the Bible as a whole. Perhaps the most prophetic statement that can be made of God is stated in Micah 7:18-20, where the prophet acknowledges the compassion, forgiveness, and fidelity of Israel's God, whose love remains ever constant not just for the people of Micah's day but for all people, all creation, down through the ages, to which life itself bears witness.

COMMENTARY

SUPERSCRIPTION

Micah 1:1

The book of Micah opens with a superscription (1:1), typical of many prophetic books (see, e.g., Isa 1:1; Jer 1:1-3; Hos 1:1; Amos 1:1; Zeph 1:1), that situates both prophet and proclamation in a particular time period, and here, specifically in the latter part of the eighth century B.C. All three kings mentioned ruled over Judah. The prophet's proclamation is the result of something that "came" to him, which he "saw" concerning Samaria and Jerusalem, the capital cities of the northern and southern kingdoms, respectfully.

PROCLAMATION OF JUDGMENT; WORD OF HOPE

Micah 1:2–3:12

This first major section of the book includes a proclamation of judgment (1:2–2:11; 3:1-12), and a word of hope (2:12-13).

1:2-7 Judgment speech

In these verses the poet calls his listeners and the whole earth to attention and also calls upon God to be a witness among the inhabitants of the land (1:2). In the Old Testament, God is often called upon to act as a witness (Gen 31:50; 1 Sam 12:5; Jer 42:5). The phrase "from his holy temple" could refer to the temple in Jerusalem/Zion, but here it seems to have in view God's heavenly dwelling place (Ps 11:4) from where God descends.

In metaphorical language, Micah next describes an impending theophany (1:3-4). A theophany is a manifestation of God. The term is derived from two Greek words, "God" and "to show." This theophany highlights the transcendent nature of God. In verse 3 the phrase "the LORD goes out from his place" resumes and advances the thought of verse 2. God who is in the holy temple (1:2) is now going out of that place (1:3). This action on God's part finds an echo in Isaiah 26:21, where God comes out of his place to punish the inhabitants of the earth for their iniquity.

Not only will God go out of the sacred dwelling place but this God will also come down and tread upon the places of the earth. The heights of the earth are sometimes used in connection with God's wrath and sovereignty (Amos 4:1-13). The heights of the earth, literally, "the high places of the earth," is rich in meaning. The Akkadian cognate word for high places means "back, center of the body" (of an animal) but also "ridge" and "high place" as in territory. The high places or "heights of the earth" denoted a certain kind of cultic institution in ancient Israel. These "high places" were homemade constructions most often built on elevated places (Jer 48:35; Isa 15:2) as well as valleys. The houses and shrines of the "high places" were found particularly in the cities of Samaria (1 Kgs 13:32; 2 Kgs 23:19) and in Samaria itself (2 Kgs 17:5-12). The "high places" are associated with apostasy (2 Kgs 23:5-8) and as such are the object of God's wrath (Lev 26:30; 2 Kgs 17:5-23; Ps 78:58).

In Micah 1:3, the meaning of the "heights of the earth" is obscure. The natural assumption would be that they denote the mountains, the "ridges," which are topographically the highest places of the earth. This understanding appears appropriate in light of verse 4. These "high places," however, have a double meaning that becomes clear in verse 5: they will symbolize the capital cities of the northern and southern kingdoms, Samaria and Jerusalem, respectfully. Thus, the coming of God is imminent and will have devastating effects, which the poet captures with vivid natural world imagery and a series of similes. These natural world images are metaphors for both kingdoms, which will eventually be destroyed through military invasions. Together, verses 3-4 disclose the power of God and the powerlessness of creation before God.

In verse 4 the focus is on the mountains and the valleys. The "mountains" symbolize permanence, height, and power from primeval times (Ps 90:2; 95:4; Zech 4:7). The "valleys" or "lowlands" are the fruitful, inhabitable areas preferred by people (Judg 1:19, 34; Hos 2:17; Ps 65:14). God's coming, though described in typical theophanic language (see Ps 18:1-19; 97:1-5), will not bring the people what they experienced in the past as God's chosen people (see Judg 5). This time God's coming will bring the unexpected upon them (Mic 1:6-7, 10-16) because of their attitude (Mic 1:5) and deeds (Mic 2:1-11; 3:1-12) and because God is faithful to the divine word.

With two rhetorical questions (1:5), the poet indicts Israel and Judah, and specifically their capital cities, Samaria and Jerusalem. Both cities were associated with idolatry in the latter part of the eighth century B.C. With regard to Samaria, this point becomes clear in Micah 1:6-7. In the capital cities resided the kingdoms' political leadership charged with the responsibility of upholding torah for the sake of the common good. The poet's inference here is that the community is laden with transgressions due to poor leadership (see Mic 3).

In verses 6-7 God, speaking through the prophet, announces a plan to destroy Samaria because of its transgressions, apostasy, and idolatry. By citing Samaria, the poet uses metonymy. Samaria represents Jacob/Israel, the northern kingdom. Samaria's fate symbolizes the fate of the entire kingdom.

Theologically verses 2-7 present a hierarchical and patriarchal picture of an anthropomorphic, anthropocentric God and God's power. This God who dwells in "his holy temple" (1:2) enthroned in the heavenly court will descend and tread "upon the heights of the earth" (1:3), which is quite a different picture from the God who walked in the garden in the cool of the evening (Gen 3:8) and who spoke with Moses as a friend (Exod 33:11). This God is transcendent and not within reach of the natural world. Such imagery reflects Israel's royal leadership during the monarchical period.

1:8-16 Dirge-lament

Verses 8-16 are a dirge-lament. Verse 8 is a pivotal verse that looks backward to verses 5-7 and forward to verse 9. God "will lament and wail, / go barefoot and naked / . . . utter lamentation like the jackals, / mourning like the ostriches" (1:8) because of the people's transgressions, the impending loss of land and kingdoms, and the sorry state of Jerusalem. "Barefoot and naked" signify mourning (cf. Ezek 24:17-23; Isa 20:2). Nakedness is also associated with sin (see Gen 3:10; 9:20-23). Jackals are smaller than wolves and often prowled among places of ruin and deserted areas. Their food included mammals, poultry,

fish, vegetables, carrion, and refuse. They were sensitive to drought and heat and had a distinctive wailing and howl. Ostriches are two-toed, swift, wingless birds that reside in deserted, uninhabited areas (Job 30:29; Isa 13:21; 43:20; Jer 50:39). Both creatures are associated with desolation and, although they can be signs of joy, here they are signs of barrenness. God will perform all of these actions through the prophet Micah, who is and will be the embodiment of the sinful community. Micah becomes a divine sign for the community and, as prophet, becomes the embodiment of God's presence and God's righteous anger and steadfast love. The incurable wound in verse 9 refers to the blow that Judah and Jerusalem will soon endure, specifically, devastation at the hands of the Babylonians. This incurable wound will be dealt with by God (see Jer 1:14; 15:18; 30:12-15).

Verses 10-15 are the words of the prophet's dirge-lament. They are cast into a funeral song for someone who has already died. All of the cities mentioned are situated in the Shephelah, the lowlands of the region. When God comes down and "treads upon the [high places] of the earth" (1:3), not only will the mountains and hilltops of Samaria and Jerusalem be destroyed but also the lowlands—the Shephelah and all its cities. The historical setting of this dirge-lament is most likely the Assyrian invasion by Sennacherib in 701 B.C. (1:15).

Verse 16 closes the dirge-lament. The verse foreshadows the exile after the fall of Jerusalem in 587 B.C. The use of the perfect tense, otherwise known as the prophetic perfect or tense of vision, for an event that has not yet happened signifies that what has been predicted will, in fact, happen.

2:1-5 Woe proclamation

Chapter 2 opens with a woe proclamation (2:1-5) that conveys a stinging message of judgment. In verse 1 the poet proclaims a warning to those guilty of premeditated injustices, which he enumerates in verse 2.

Verses 3-5 are an announcement of judgment composed of a proclamation of intended chastisement (2:3), a prediction of disaster (2:4), and a threat (2:5). Here the poet depicts God as a schemer of actions that are going to take place to "get even" with those who have transgressed others. Those who have used power oppressively will experience the chastising of God. Those who have taken land will lose their fields (2:4) and will be banned from any further acquisition of property.

Thus Micah 2:1-5 makes clear that God asserts divine power on behalf of those victimized by the abuse of power by others. Verses 1 and 3 exemplify the principle of *lex talionis* (see Lev 24:18-21), which was part of the Israelites' social and legal culture and which became part of its religious culture.

2:6-11 Disputation prophecy

Verses 6-11 are a disputation prophecy. God speaks through the prophet and quotes the prophet's adversaries. The verses describe the strained relationship that exists between God and some of the Israelites because of their smug attitude (2:6) and their deeds of injustice (2:8-9). The rhetorical question in verse 7 highlights how distant the people have become from their God. Verses 8-9 add new transgressions to the list already begun in 2:1-2. The punishment for treachery is expulsion from the land (2:10). Hence, the people's ill-gotten land will provide no place for the guilty to rest. The land has become "unclean," defiled by the people's wickedness (see Lev 18:24-25). The prophecy closes on a note of sarcasm, which is God's final response to the objection raised by the opponents in verse 6 who do not want to hear an honest prophetic word proclaimed.

2:12-13 Salvation proclamation

The tone of the poet's message changes in verses 12-13, a salvation proclamation that promises divine care to the exiled ones of the remnant of "Jacob." Here "Jacob" does not refer to the northern kingdom; instead, "Jacob" refers to Judah as the remnant of Israel, which in turn sets the stage for restoration promised in Micah 4–5. The verses will serve as a consolation for when the people are exiled, if only they will remember.

As a whole, Micah 2:1-13 makes several statements. First, the community addressed is struggling and living under divine threat (2:2-11) and divine promise (2:12-13). Second, even those people closest to God are liable to sin and must accept the consequences of their actions. Third, since land is a divine gift, others' property rights and boundaries must be respected (see Exod 20:15, 17 and Deut 15:4-5). Fourth, power, wealth, and status are not to be used to exploit others.

Lastly, Israel's God is the sovereign one who will not tolerate apostasy or idolatry; Israel's God is a God of justice who will not tolerate injustice.

3:1-4 Address to Israel's political leadership

Having offered a word of hope, the poet now returns to his proclamation of judgment (3:1-12). This new unit consists of an address to Israel's political leaders (3:1-4). Verses 1-4 can be further subdivided into an accusation (3:1-3) and an announcement of judgment (3:4). In these verses, Micah confronts and condemns Israel's political leaders for their brutal treatment of the kingdom's people. The rhetorical question in verses 1-2 articulates plainly the sin of Israel's leadership: they do not act justly (3:1); they are haters of good and lovers of evil (3:2). An extended metaphor follows in verses 2b-3, which vivifies the prophet's message and accentuates the leaders' illicit deeds. Here Micah compares Israel's leaders to savage butchers and voracious cannibals who treat people like animals ready to be consumed. The metaphor crystallizes the extent of injustices within Micah's community, its leadership in particular, and opens eyes wide to the horrendous wickedness of which the political and community leaders are responsible.

Verse 4 presents God's response. Micah declares to the corrupted leaders that God will be unresponsive and somewhat distant from them. The notion of crying out to the Lord is a formulaic expression that occurs often in Deuteronomistic history (see, e.g., Judg 3:9, 15; 10:10). Mention of God's face being hidden from the Israelites also occurs in Ezekiel 39:23-24.

3:5-7 Proclamation concerning the prophets

Following his attack on Israel's political leadership, Micah verbally assaults Israel's prophets (3:5-7). They are guilty of leading the people astray by their false prophecies. They have corrupted their prophetic office for personal satisfaction and gain. Additionally, they respond negatively to their own Israelite audience, who fail to provide them with the expected recompense (3:5). God's response is not to punish others with physical harm but to take away the gifts that are part of their prophetic office. Divine power is used to suppress rather than oppress.

Verses 5-7 have often been treated in terms of an opposition between "true" and "false" prophets. Given the context of the indictment, these prophets are not "false" prophets because they do have, according to the text, prophetic powers that God will take away from them. These prophets being addressed are true prophets who have betrayed their prophetic office and vocation.

3:8 Interlude: statement of confidence

In verse 8 the poet gives a clear picture of power as it related to the prophetic office. After two verbal attacks, Micah takes a reprieve and makes a proclamation about himself. Using the phrase "But as for me," Micah sets himself apart from those he has been attacking, namely, the political and religious leaders of Israel. He boldly states his gifts. To be "filled with power" is to be filled with God's Spirit. This first charismatic gift associates Micah with earlier figures like Saul (1 Sam 10:10; 19:23) and David, who also possessed this gift. To be filled with God's Spirit is also to be filled with justice and might. Justice is what should have been exercised by the political leaders (3:1). "Might," a term associated with military prowess (Judg 8:21), strengthens Micah so he can fearlessly hurl accusations and judgments against Israel's leaders. These gifts are divinely given, and they move the prophet to expose others' injustices to the unjust ones themselves and to those who are victims of injustice. Unlike the political and military leaders of his day whose power and might rest with the sword, Micah's power is his God-given word.

3:9-12 Address to Israel's leadership

In the last segment of Micah 1:2–3:12, Micah again attacks the political and religious leaders of his day. In verses 9-11 he launches his attack and then issues a judgment in verse 12. "Justice" (3:9) recalls 3:1 and 8. The statement that the leaders "abhor justice" reinforces the contrast between the prophet and them. To his list of people, Micah adds the priest (3:11). Spiritual depravity is extensive. Finally, neither the leaders nor the holy city will escape divine retribution: justice will be served. Jerusalem and the temple will be destroyed because leadership has failed to govern with justice and integrity. Despite these harsh words, an element of hope exists. The "plowing" about to take place will be to remove the obstacles

so that new seeds can be planted and can take root (cf. Jer 1:10).

PROCLAMATION OF FUTURE RESTORATION
Micah 4:1–5:14

Words of judgment now turn to words of hope and promise. Devastation will not be the final word for Israel and Judah. All that will transpire will be so that a new order, a new way of life, can be ushered in with the reign of God in the midst of all. This next section consists of a prophetic vision (4:1-5) and a divine promise (4:6–5:14).

4:1-5 Prophetic vision

The next section of the book of Micah opens with a vision of unity and peace. The poem is a prophetic vision that promises peace for the future. The vision closely parallels Isaiah 2:2-4 but stands in contrast to Micah 3:12, where both Jerusalem and the mountain of the house will be leveled. Both Micah 4:1-5 and Isaiah 2:2-4 enjoy lively conversation among scholars, and no conclusive decision has been reached about either text with regard to which one might have been more original, if borrowing has occurred, or if they are from two distinct, independent sources. Most likely the vision was a common one and perhaps part of the tradition to which both Micah and Isaiah appealed.

Although Micah addresses no particular audience here, in the context of the book of Micah as a whole the listeners would seem to be all of Israel, both the northern and southern kingdoms, and especially what would later be the faithful remnant, those once exiled, who would return to the land and through whom God's ongoing vision of world peace will evolve.

The poet begins his vision on a futuristic note, "In days to come" (4:1), and continues with a description of the mountain of the Lord's house that will be the highest of all mountains and hills. Here the poet hints at God's sovereignty, further eclipsed by the picture of all nations streaming to this mountain. Next, the poet envisions what the people who stream to the mountain will say (4:2). Israel's God will be the God of the nations. Thus, there will be one God and one people, and the house of Jacob—the "temple"—will be a house for all nations (cf. Isa 56:7; Mark 11:17). Zion, a city corrupted, will once again be God's dwelling place from where instruction goes forth (4:2c).

In verse 4 the poet offers a stunning portrait of God, who, as judge, does not condemn the nations but sets terms for them. Furthermore, this vision of peace would fulfill one of the Sovereign's main responsibilities, namely, to bring peace and tranquility to all nations (1 Kgs 5:5; Isa 9:7; 11:1-9; Jer 23:5-6; 33:15-16). When arbitration has taken place, when terms have been set, *then* the people will beat their swords into plowshares and their spears into pruning hooks, never again to take up the weapons of war against each other or to learn war. Micah makes clear that the way to peace is not through violence and bloodshed. In a world of peace all peoples, all nations, will enjoy world peace, and all nations, all peoples, will enjoy "the good life." Peace among nations leads to individual peace, symbolized by an agrarian image of security and stability. "Vines" and "fig trees" represent long-term stability, peace, and prosperity (4:4-5).

4:6–5:14 Divine promise

Micah 4:6-8, the opening verses of a divine promise, offers another word of hope that will occur when God draws all nations together, signaled by the phrase "On that day." This promise contrasts with Micah's present wicked days heard in Micah 1–3, with the exception of 2:12-13. These words are ironic. Those who were once the weakest among the Israelites, who endured the perversion of justice, and who are no longer under the oppression of the wicked political, social, and religious leaders of their day because these leaders will be "dethroned," will become the remnant through whom God will gather and establish a new people, a new nation, with God's reign in their midst. Whether or not the lame, scattered, and afflicted refer to the survivors of Judah during Sennacherib's invasion of Judah in 701 B.C. (cf. Isa 11:5-8) or to the Babylonian captivity is unclear and no consensus exists among scholars, though in the context of Leviticus 21:16-23, the mention of these people represents a paradigm shift and a change in Israel's thinking. These people, once prohibited from serving as priests, are now the recipients of God's blessing. Finally, the "tower of the flock" refers to the upper sector of the

capital cities where the palace and other royal buildings stood.

In Micah 4:9-10, God, speaking through the prophet, offers a promise of deliverance. In these verses both present and future time come together. Here daughter Zion refers to Jerusalem and also personifies Jerusalem's inhabitants. The use of a rhetorical question and a simile captures the people's pain and terror, most likely from the invasion of the Babylonians into Jerusalem. The people will writhe and groan like a woman in labor because they will go into exile in Babylon. Yet, this experience will not be permanent; they will be rescued by God from the hands of their enemies (4:10). Hence, embedded in the image of a wailing woman in labor is a word of hope. Although the experience will be painful, the pain will turn to joy. Thus, at this juncture, the people are in a state of transition as they move from devastation to reprieve to restoration.

Just as Micah 4:9-10 begins with the people's present reality of calamity with the hope looming on the horizon, so too Micah 4:11-13 begins with present time, signaled by the time marker "now" (4:11; cf. 4:9). Here the poet describes an imminent attack on Jerusalem and its people (4:11). The irony is that they—the nations—are carrying out a plan designed by Israel's God against God's only people (4:12). The twist of events comes in verse 13. Even though nations are coming to wage war against Zion, Zion will eventually prevail against them, which is also in accord with God's plan. Hence, the nations are being "set up" for defeat by Israel's God, but in the end, they will all be restored to God, together with Israel (4:1-5). Having delivered a futuristic painful yet hopeful word to Zion, the poet returns to present time, "Now" (4:14), wherein the invasion is imminent, at which time Zion will lament, "They have laid siege against us" (4:14a) as the enemies insult and slap on the face of Isaiah's ruler (4:14b). The striking of the cheek was an act of humiliation expressing contempt for a king. Thus, Israel's powerful king will be brought low.

The Israelite people, however, will not be left without a leader. The demise of a corrupt king will give way to a new leader who will come forth from Bethlehem-Ephrathah (5:1). Bethlehem was a small town five miles south of Jerusalem. David, a native of Bethlehem, was anointed there by Samuel (1 Sam 16:1-13). Ephrathah is often identified with Bethlehem (cf. Ps 136:2; Gen 35:16, 19; 48:7; 1 Sam 16:1, 18; 17:12; Ruth 4:11). The relationship between Ephrathah and Bethlehem is unclear. Ephrathah may have been the ancient name for Bethlehem, or it may have been absorbed into Bethlehem. Either way, the town was paradoxically to be the source of salvation. This new leader of Israel will be like a shepherd (Mic 5:3) and not like Israel's former kings, who used their position of authority and power to oppress the people. With this new type of governance will come security, for this new leader will be "peace" (5:4; see also Mic 5:3b; Isa 9:6-7). Hence, the poet sees a new beginning for God's people that would extend throughout the whole earth.

The remainder of verses 4-5 features Israel as the speaker; the subject is the conquest of Assyria. The reference to seven shepherds and eight leaders is a literary device used to indicate that an indefinite yet adequate number of leaders will be roused to defeat the Assyrians on Israel's behalf. The reference to "Nimrod" could refer to Babylon (Gen 10:8-9) but the parallel construction of the verse seems to indicate that the reference is to Assyria. Israel will not be defeated by either the Assyrians or the Babylonians, and the people will one day be blessed with a new just and righteous leader after all their enemies have been defeated and they—the Israelites—have returned from exile.

In Micah 5:5-8, the poet describes the faithful remnant Israel—those people who will survive the invasions and exile. The remnant itself, "[l]ike a lion among beasts of the forest" (5:7), will be victorious over its adversaries. The theme of victory introduced earlier in verse 5 is strengthened in verses 6-8.

The foreshadowed chaos that will come upon both God's people and the enemy nations that the poet proclaimed earlier now comes into full view again in Micah 5:9-14. The poet begins his proclamation with the phrase "On that day," which will not be a time of renewal and restoration (cf. 4:1). Rather, the time will be one of internal purification for Israel and the outpouring of divine wrath for the nations. As part of the messianic restoration, Israel will be stripped of everything that has caused alienation from God, including military ornament, sorcery, and idolatrous worship. The "images" were usually carved or sculptured from stone, metal, or wood. Such representations were forbidden to the Israelites (Exod 20:4; Deut 5:8). "Carved figures" refer to stone monuments with a variety of functions; they may have been symbols of the male deity (Deut 16:22; 1 Kgs 14:23). The "works of your hands" signifies idols sardonically. The "sacred stones" designate wooden cult symbols of the Canaanite mother goddess Asherah. Additionally, those nations who did not obey Israel's God would receive chastisement as well.

WORDS OF JUDGMENT, LAMENT, TRUST
Micah 6:1–7:20

The vision of all nations coming to God followed by a series of divine promises (4:1–5:14) are futuristic proclamations meant to encourage God's people as they go through the painful process of inward and outward purification before restoration can take place. Having given listeners a glimpse of what lies ahead, the poet now returns to Israel's present reality of waywardness while living under the threat of enemy invasion. Despite times of impending disaster about to befall Israel, the people remain favored by God. The poet once again reiterates God's promise of restoration to be accomplished because Israel's God is a God of compassion who remains faithful to Israel as from the days of old.

6:1-5 Covenant lawsuit

Having described the promise of Israel's glorious restoration (4:1-4, 6-8; 5:1-15), Micah once again returns to the problems plaguing Israel in present time. Verses 1-5 are cast into a *rib*, a covenant lawsuit. Micah, acting as an attorney, represents God's case against an ungrateful people. The natural elements are invoked as witnesses (6:1-2; cf. 1:2). In verses 3-5, God states the case against Israel. Instead of presenting the case in juridical language, the poet depicts God using a sorrowful and bewildered tone to confront Israel. The double use of "My people" (6:3, 5) conveys allusions to the exodus, and the plea to remember is the starting point back to right relationship. "King Balak" tried unsuccessfully to persuade the prophet Balaam to curse the Israelite armies (Num 22–24). "[F]rom Shittim to Gilgal" is from the east to the west side of the Jordan. Shittim was the site of Israel's camp under Joshua east of the Jordan River. Gilgal was the site of the Israelite camp after crossing the Jordan (Josh 3–5). The poet makes clear that God does not deserve the Israelites' lack of love, stated so movingly through the double rhetorical question that opens the passage (6:3).

6:6-8 Torah liturgy

Verses 6-8 are a response to God's questions, plea, and demand for an answer. Here Micah appears in a humbled, self-reflective, penitential state, representing his people who have yet to come before God. Micah raises four soul-searching questions aimed at atonement. Each question reflects a willingness to offer some sort of sacrifice, culminating in the offer to sacrifice one's firstborn for the sake of one's sin.

The list of sacrifices reflects Israel's ancient theological tradition. Whole burnt offerings were the typical daily offering at the temple. These offerings maintained the relationship between the Israelites and God. The suggestion of sacrificing one's own firstborn, though, raises two theological questions: (1) Was child sacrifice part of Israel's religious tradition, and (2) did Israel's God want child sacrifice as a sign of oblation?

Human sacrifice was forbidden in ancient Israel and Judah (see, e.g., Lev 18:21; 20:2-5; Deut 12:31; 18:10). In times of crisis, however, this type of sacrifice seems, on occasion, to have occurred, especially prior to the seventeenth century B.C. Human sacrifice did take place in the Canaanite religion, stemming from the god Molech and a human king who had a particular interest in this sort of sacrifice. Elsewhere in the Old Testament God expresses divine outrage at the practice of sacrificing the firstborn because they were "God's" children (Deut 32:16-19; Ezek 16:21). Hence, the reference to the sacrifice of the firstborn is more hyperbolic and metaphorical than actual. Whether or not such a sacrifice would be pleasing to God and suffice for atonement comes clear in verse 8. What God requires is for one to do justice, love kindness, and walk humbly with God. The last is the most important one. Only when one takes a humble walk with God will one come to learn and understand how to do justice and love kindness.

Theologically, justice is identified with the nature of God (Isa 30:18) and is an activity of God

(Gen 18:25; Ps 9:5). Justice is a transformative virtue that seeks to establish or restore community while aiming to balance personal good with the common good. Three types of justice include (1) commutative justice that focuses on relationships between members of the community; (2) distributive justice that functions to ensure the equitable distribution of goods, benefits, and burdens of a community; and (3) social justice that affects the social order necessary for distributive justice. To love kindness involves both affection and ethical love of neighbor and fidelity to covenant and law. To walk humbly with God implies an attitude of reverence and openness coupled with a sense of personal integrity, candidness, and honesty. God's people are called to godliness and to live out the fullness of justice and love.

Finally, the early church fathers have interpreted Micah 6:1-8 in a variety of ways. Cyril emphasizes God's compassion. Tertullian states that God expects people to act with the same divine mercy and compassion that have been bestowed upon them. Both Theodore of Mopsuestia and Augustine note that the love of God, the love of neighbor, and the offering of self in loving service to one another is far superior to any other sacrifice or burnt offering.

6:9-16 Judgment speech

God's tone changes in verses 9-16. No longer sad and bewildered, Israel's God now indicts the wicked ones among the Israelites in Jerusalem because of their social sins (6:9-12) and then casts judgment upon this wayward people (6:13-16). In verses 1-2, the mountains and hills were called to listen to God's case against the people; now Jerusalem and its inhabitants are called to listen to what God has to say (6:9). The divine indictment against the people begins in verses 10-11 with a double rhetorical question that highlights God's intolerance for injustice. The charge is for cheating done with fraudulent weights and measures (Lev 19:35-36; Deut 25:13-16). God will deliver the people from their external enemies, but God will not deliver the people from themselves and their own crimes (6:13).

In verses 14-15 the poet uses a series of five statements to outline the hardships that many of the people will have to endure because of their own wickedness. All of their efforts at trying to feed and sustain themselves will be futile. These curses invoked on the people as a response to their unjust ways are based on the old covenant curses. The first statement reflects Leviticus 26:26b; the second contains overtones of Deuteronomy 28:47-57; the third recalls Leviticus 26:16 and Deuteronomy 28:38; and the fourth corresponds to Deuteronomy 28:40. All of these curses reflect the typical forms of cursing statements found in ancient Near Eastern treaty texts.

Verse 16 is a further indictment against the inhabitants of Jerusalem. Here the poet alludes to two of Israel's wicked kings whose ways the people of Jerusalem have followed. Omri and Ahab were two infamous kings of Samaria who ruled from around 885–850 B.C. Omri was the sixth king of the northern kingdom Israel. He had once commanded Israel's army under King Elah. After a series of events, Omri became king and ruled wickedly. Ahab was Omri's son and successor. The seventh king of Israel (1 Kgs 16:30), he was influenced by his wife Jezebel, who worshiped Baal (1 Kgs 16:31-34; 18). Thus, Ahab gave Baal equal place with God. Ahab also built a temple to Baal in which he erected a wooden image of the Canaanite goddess Asherah (1 Kgs 16:33). Urged by Jezebel, Ahab opposed the worship of God, and killed all God's prophets. He ruled over Israel in Samaria for twenty-two years, from 873–852 B.C. (1 Kgs 16:29). Ahab's loss of right relationship with God led to immoral civil acts, the most famous of which is the takeover of Naboth's vineyard. The heinous deed was done through conspiracy and murder. Ahab murdered Naboth in order to claim his land in the Jezreel Valley (1 Kgs 21). The prophet Elijah opposed Ahab, and through Elijah the wrath of God came down upon Ahab (1 Kgs 21–22). Both Omri and Ahab were guilty of syncretism and apostasy (1 Kgs 16:25-26, 30-33).

In verse 16 the people of Jerusalem stand indicted by their God because they have followed the wicked ways of wicked kings instead of following God and God's ways. Such wickedness led to the demise of the northern kingdom Israel, and these same transgressions of syncretism and idolatry will lead to the demise of the southern kingdom Judah. The inhabitants of Jerusalem and all of Judah will be delivered up to ruin and will become objects of scorn and mockery among the nations (6:16b). Thus, God's people will have to bear the consequences of their own sinfulness.

7:1-6 Lament

Micah 7:1-6 is a poignant lament spoken by the prophet Micah, who feels alone and abandoned as he undertakes the futile task of trying to find one upright person in the land. Abraham before him tried to do the same task (Gen 18:23-33), and Jeremiah and Ezekiel after him also tried to do the same thing (Jer 5:1-5; Ezek 22:30, respectively). In the midst of his dreadful situation, however, the prophet never loses faith and hope in God (7:7). A series of vivid images captures Micah's desperation. His lament begins with a wail—"Woe is me!"—for he sees no one righteous in the land and he finds himself among the violently wicked, the only ones remaining in the land. The summer fruit and the vintage are some of the last crops to be gathered at the end of the harvest season during the late summer and early fall, just before the festival Sukkoth (Tabernacles) takes place, which marks the conclusion of the fruit harvest and the start of the rainy season. Taking the persona of one who goes out into the orchard after the summer fruit has been picked or into the vineyard after the grapes have been gathered, hoping to find some good fruit, Micah complains that just as no clusters or early figs remain, so the "faithful have vanished from the earth" (7:1-2). The only ones remaining in the land are murderers, predators, and thieves who act like animals hunting for their prey (7:2).

Verse 3 recalls Micah 3:11, which speaks of Israel's leaders taking bribes. Corruption runs rampant, beginning with the hierarchy. Those in power assert their power for their own selfish and self-serving interests. No justice exists for those who have little or no money since judges are bought for a price and render judgments for a bribe. These offenses are similar to those heard in Micah 2:2, 8-9; 3:9-11. No honesty and integrity exists in the land. To those who have corrupted their office and have caused pain to others, punishment will be meted out (7:4).

Political and social depravity has led to the breakdown of community and family (7:5-6). Here Micah issues a warning not to trust in friends, companions, or family members because in the depraved state of the land, people turn on one another. In ancient times, betrayal of family members by other family members is a serious situation because the family was a stabilizing and integrating structure within the Israelite society.

The cohesiveness of the family structure and hence the society depended on the absolute authority of paterfamilias and the respect of his children for him and his spouse. Included in the family circle are daughters-in-law because they leave their own families, become attached to their husbands, and remain subject to their husbands' fathers. Thus, human relationship has become sick at the core and no longer functions properly, particularly because of the lack of trust.

7:7-10 Statement of trust

Having expressed the lack of trust that exists among the family and community members (7:6), Micah now utters a word of hope. The phrase "But as for me" (7:7) is a *casus pendens*. It functions to separate Micah from the rest of his dishonorable community members. Having been disappointed by the human condition, Micah places his hope in God. With confidence he will wait for his God who is his salvation. This God will hear him and respond to him just as God has done in the past for Micah's ancestors (Exod 2:24-25; 3:7-10). The triple reference to God attests to Micah's faith. The prophet's statement of trust and confidence in God becomes a lesson and a word of hope for the faithful remnant of the Israelite community, who, for a time, will have to suffer pain and exile.

In verses 8-10 Micah speaks on behalf of his community, who, confident of its deliverance, confesses its transgressions. Assurance in God heard in verse 7 continues in verse 8. The one who will become the taunt of nations (2:4) will be the one to rise in future days, but for now both the prophet and the people will have to bear God's indignation for having sinned. God's indignation refers to all the horror, trauma, calamity, and destruction that will befall the northern kingdom Israel and the southern kingdom Judah. The invasion and collapse of these two kingdoms was inevitable historically, but the prophet sees the demise of the two kingdoms as divinely imposed consequences for sin. The text reflects the community's belief in the Deuteronomistic theory of retribution (see Deut 28). This suffering, however, will have to be endured only for a time because God will vindicate the one being chastised, and those enemies who stand in judgment with mockery and scorn will be put to shame (7:9-10). Finally, verses 8-10 provide a window into the office and vocation of the prophet who is called to make intercession for transgressors, which sometimes entails bearing the pain of not only a community's sin but also the anger and sadness of God at a people who have forsaken God and God's ways.

7:11-13 Divine promise

Words of lament with glimmers of hope interspersed (7:8-10) turn to words of excitement in a vision that describes future restoration and repopulation. Addressed to Jerusalem, the city has endured divine judgment and, as a result of this judgment, has suffered greatly. Now Jerusalem is promised restoration. Here the poet speaks as if the time of restoration is imminent: "It is the day for building your walls" (7:11). When this day dawns, Jerusalem's boundaries will also be enlarged, allowing for two superpower nations, Assyria and Egypt, as well as others, to come to it from near and far. With expanded boundaries, Jerusalem will be the gathering place of the nations, a theme echoed in Micah 4:1-4. This restoration and repopulation will be gradual. The earth itself will be a waste because of the peoples' deeds. Restoration and renewal is a gradual process.

The reference to "the River" (7:12) pertains to the Euphrates River of Mesopotamia (cf. Gen 15:18; Deut 1:7; Josh 1:4; 2 Sam 8:3; 1 Chr 18:3). This reference plays upon Israel's traditional boundaries, which would have extended from the Euphrates to Egypt (Gen 15:18; Num 34; 2 Sam 8; Ezek 47:13-20).

7:14-17 Petition

Words of promise shift to words of petition. Here the poet portrays Micah petitioning God to shepherd the people of Israel and to let them graze in the finest of pastures. The plea to have God act as a shepherd recalls an earlier shepherd metaphor in Micah 2:12-13. There Micah assures the people that God will gather the remnant and lead them out of exile (cf. 4:6-10). Now Micah wants God to lead the people into restoration (cf. 5:4). "Bashan" refers to the plains southwest of Syria that overlook the Sea of Galilee; "Gilead" is the Israelite region of the Transjordan south of the Sea of Galilee and north of the Dead Sea. Both areas are excellent for grazing (cf. Num 32:1; Ps 22:12; Amos 4:1; Ezek 27:6; Song 6:5). Jerusalem and Judah's restoration will astound the nations, and they will stand in humiliation and awe at the power of Israel's God.

7:18-20 Statement of divine love

The poet closes the book of Micah with a word of praise. On behalf of the community, Micah makes a heartfelt confession of faith that acknowledges the true essence of who God is. Israel's God is, ultimately, a God of forgiveness and compassion whose anger is only a passing emotion. This God remains faithful to covenant (Gen 12; 15; 17; 28; 35) and faithful to the people. Here the poet's words echo Exodus 34:6-7. Judgment, destruction, and annihilation are never the final words of God. The final word and work is always forgiveness, always compassion, as Israel's God works continually to restore and transform both the human condition and all of creation.

THE BOOK OF
NAHUM

Carol J. Dempsey, O.P.

INTRODUCTION

With frightful and gruesome images, the prophet Nahum delivers a stinging message to the Assyrian leaders and people and, in particular, to Nineveh, Assyria's capital city. Israel's warrior God is about to destroy Nineveh, the "bloody city" full of lies and plunder "whose looting never stops!" (3:1). A "multitude of slain, / a mass of corpses, / Endless bodies / to stumble upon" will be all that remains (3:3). This message is a harrowing one for Nineveh and Assyria but good news for Judah. Judah's enemy will be squelched, never to rise again. Indeed, for Judah, this impending catastrophic event will be a time of celebration, a time for renewing covenant bonds with God, and a time for long-awaited peace (2:1). The warfare imagery used throughout the book foreshadows the invasion of the Babylonians and Persians who eventually sacked Nineveh. According to the text, this combined assault on Nineveh was in keeping with God's divine intention and orchestrated by God as well. The Assyrians, a people greatly feared in the region, are about to encounter one greater and more powerful than themselves. They are about to experience Israel's God, who will work through the Babylonians and the Medes to accomplish justice for Judah.

The world of Nahum

The book of Nahum offers a word of peril to Assyria and particularly to Nineveh and its in-

habitants, and a word of hope and consolation to Judah, who has long endured the injustices and oppression of Assyria, Judah's enemy nation. Historically, Assyria ruled by brute force and gained power in the region by exacting heavy tributes, deporting entire populations of people, and permitting no compromise or repudiation of treaties. Assyria became known as the lion of the ancient Near East. Assyria's leaders were fearless. Tiglath-pileser III (745–727 B.C.) conquered Israel; Sargon II (721–705 B.C.) and Sennacherib (705–681 B.C.) made Judah a vassal state; and Ashurbanipal (668–627 B.C.) devastated Thebes in Egypt and burned Babylon. When Ashurbanipal died in 627 B.C., coalitions of Medes and Babylonians sought revenge against Assyria. In 612 B.C. the armies of these countries took Nineveh by force and destroyed it. With the destruction of Nineveh came the eventual collapse of the Assyrian Empire, and, remarkably, its rise and fall happened in less than a century and a half. The general consensus among scholars is that Nahum was active as a prophet while Ashurbanipal was reigning, since Nahum 1:12 describes the Assyrians and Nineveh "fully intact and so numerous." During this time, Judah was quite possibly experiencing a period of reform, since Nahum's words allude to Judah having been humbled by God who is now going to liberate the people from their oppressive bonds (1:13). Finally, little is known about Nahum himself, and, like the other prophets mentioned in the Bible's collection of Prophetic Books, whether or not Nahum was an actual historical person continues to be a topic of debate among biblical scholars.

The literary dimensions of the book of Nahum

Perhaps no other book among the prophets has such graphic imagery as the text of Nahum. These images have one single focus and reflect one single purpose: a war about to be waged against Judah's ferocious enemy. Most of these images reflect the culture of the day and life on the battlefield. Some images are drawn from the natual world and used metaphorically to emphasize the force and strength of Israel's God over the Assyrians and, specifically, the inhabitants of Nineveh. Israel's God will be like a lion (2:12), and all of the enemy's fortresses, like fig trees with first-ripe figs, will "fall / into the devourer's mouth" when these fig-tree-like fortresses are shaken (3:12). One of the other striking elements in the book of Nahum is the use of foreshadowing. Through Nahum's prophetic vision, the poet vividly portrays what is about to befall Assyria and Nineveh. Although the book's imagery is effective in establishing its central message, one cannot overlook the inherent violence in the text's images and metaphors. Those images and metaphors are gender specific, as in the case of Nahum 3:5-7, where female imagery is used to describe Nineveh's forthcoming humiliation. Indeed, the prophet is the bearer of good news for Judah, but the poetry, in general, is difficult to hear because its celebratory tone comes at the expense of the complete devastation of another, a scenario that continues to plague contemporary times in search for peace and the transformation of religious imagination.

The book of Nahum can be divided into the following divisions and subdivisions:

I. Superscription (1:1)

II. A hymn to God (1:2-11)

III. A word of good news to Judah (1:12–2:1)

IV. A prophetic vision concerning Nineveh (2:2–3:19)

Proclamation of an impending divine attack against Nineveh (2:2-14)

Proclamation against Nineveh (3:1-17)

Proclamation against the king of Assyria (3:18-19)

Each division and subdivision features an array of literary techniques, in addition to imagery, metaphors, similes, and foreshadowing. The poet is adept at using personification (1:5) and rhetorical questions (1:6; 3:8, 19), and, like many of the other poets of the Prophetic Books, the poet Nahum presents God anthropomorphically and anthropocentrically. Israel's God is like the warriors of old, but warrior God is more powerful than all the human and nonhuman powers on earth. The poet also depicts God as a storm God and a king. All of these techniques contribute to the overall theological message of the book of Nahum, which is that Israel's God does not and will not tolerate injustice.

The theological dimensions of the book of Nahum

For years, Assyria has oppressed kingdoms and countries, Israel and Judah included. Nahum's audience now learns, in gritty detail, that just as Assyria made others suffer, so now Assyria will be made to suffer: Nineveh will be destroyed. In some respects, the portrait of justice depicted in the book of Nahum reflects the old adage "What goes around, comes around." The tone is somber for the Assyrians and Ninevites but jubilant for the Judahites. The "holy war" about to take place will be liberating for those who have long suffered oppression, but this liberation will come at the cost of human life. History has borne out that liberation through violence does not bring lasting peace. Thus, the book of Nahum is about justice, but the way that such justice is achieved invites further critical theological reflection and comment.

COMMENTARY

SUPERSCRIPTION

Nahum 1:1

Verse 1 sets the stage for Nahum's proclamations: they are addressed to Nineveh, the capital of Assyria. The prophet's message is the result of a divine vision, one that was undoubtedly an intuitive experience. The location of Elkosh is unknown. Nahum's name means "the one consoled."

A HYMN TO GOD

Nahum 1:2-11

One of the most vivid and horrifying pictures of the God of justice appears in Nahum 1:2-11. Without reservation, Nahum proclaims that God is about to act on Judah's behalf but to the demise of the Assyrians. This God is a "jealous and avenging God," one who is "full of wrath," who "takes vengeance on his adversaries" (1:2), and who does not clear the guilty (1:3). This God is the storm God who rebukes the sea, dries up all the rivers, and makes the flowers die, the mountains quake, the hills melt, and the earth heave (1:3-5). Bashan (1:4), the district east of Jordan and north of Gilead, was rich in grain and known for its breed of cattle. Carmel (1:4) was a 1,742-feet-high hill associated with the history of Elijah and Elisha (1 Kgs 18; 2 Kgs 2:25; 4:25). Lebanon (1:4) was a long range of hills that rose to about eight or nine thousand feet in the extreme north of Palestine and was known as the land of forests with groves of cedars. Nahum makes clear that divine protection is extended to those who take refuge in God, but God will make a full end of the adversaries and will pursue the enemies (1:8). With this proclamation, Nahum warns the Assyrians and those in Nineveh about Israel's God, who is stronger and more ferocious than the best of the military and political leaders. Those who have plotted and done evil against Israel's God and Israel are about to receive the same treatment (1:11). Nahum's rhetorical question in verse 9 and similes in verse 10 seal Nineveh's fate.

A WORD OF GOOD NEWS TO JUDAH

Nahum 1:12–2:1

With gusto, Nahum proclaims a word of hope to the inhabitants of Judah, announcing the end of their affliction by the Assyrians. The yoke bonds that have bound the country for years are about to be broken. Historically, these verses refer to the conflict between Assyria and Judah (see 1:1). For more than three hundred years, Assyria had controlled the Near Eastern world, including Judah. The Judahites had thought that God had sent the Assyrians against them as a way to chastise them for their apostasy and wickedness. Here the poet depicts God promising to end such affliction. God will now assert divine power for the sake of liberation (1:12-13). The God who once caused Judah to be overpowered now promises to end its distress.

Verse 14 addresses the king of Assyria. To liberate the Judahites, God now promises to destroy the Assyrian ruler, Ashurbanipal, his lineage, and his gods. The Assyrians and their king will be humiliated; their trusted gods will come to naught.

In Nahum 2:1 the prophet exhorts Judah to rejoice. Written in present tense, the poem anticipates the end of Assyrian captivity. The festivals to be celebrated probably are the Passover meal, Pentecost, and Booths that commemorate salvation, liberation, redemption, and a plentiful harvest, respectively. Judah will then be able to celebrate its festivals and fulfill the pledges it has made to God. This, Nahum 1:12–2:1, celebrates the end of Assyrian oppression, an event that Nahum 2 and 3 describe in detail.

A PROPHETIC VISION CONCERNING NINEVEH

Nahum 2:2–3:19

This next section describes the attack on and downfall of Nineveh (2:2–3:17). It also features a proclamation against Assyria's king (3:18-19). With graphic detail, the prophet gives an account of what the battle against Nineveh will entail. The proclamation is futuristic; yet the poet's use of present tense verbs throughout it functions as an assurance to the people of Judah that, indeed, what has been foreseen by Nahum will come to pass.

2:2-14 Proclamation of an impending divine attack against Nineveh

In verse 2 the prophet issues a warning to the Ninevites: they are to prepare for battle. Four rapid-fire imperatives, "guard," "watch," "brace," and "marshal," alert them to be on the defensive. In verse 3 Nahum reveals to this enemy nation who their opponent will be and why they are about to be challenged. Israel's God is about to stop the oppression being done to Judah by the Assyrians, who are indirectly referred to as "ravagers."

Verses 4-14 describe God's warriors and the imminent attack on Nineveh. The warriors will be the Babylonians and the Medes, who, according to the text, will be the warriors God will use to defeat the Ninevites and, essentially, the Assyrian Empire. The crimson shields represent the battle stains from past victories. The soldiers' scarlet uniforms symbolize the brilliance and boldness of the army ready for war. Verse 5 commences the battle: the chariots—the vehicles of devastation—race full force into Nineveh.

Verses 6-11 describe the siege and destruction of Nineveh. A variety of similes and metaphors create a graphic picture of a once fearsome people now taken captive, moaning like doves, and beating their breasts. In verse 8 the "mistress" refers to Nineveh itself, and the "maidservants" is a reference to Nineveh's inhabitants. This invasion of Nineveh will be relentless (2:9), leaving the city devastated and its peoples completely plundered and trembling (2:10-11). A city and a people once so feared have received from another the same kind of treatment that they have done to others for years. Using metaphorical language from the natural world, the poet next features Nahum mocking the false strength of Nineveh (2:12-14), symbolized by the reference to lions. In the Old Testament, the lion evokes ferocity, destructive power, and irresistible strength. It is sometimes described as a bold and valiant warrior (Prov 28:1; 30:30). Lions also symbolize the power of royalty.

In verses 12-14 the den of lions pertains to the royalty of Nineveh—its kings, queens, and princes who exert brute force.

Verse 14 shifts to actual present time. Having proclaimed the vision of the destruction of Nineveh, Nahum now delivers another word from God: "I now come against you" (2:14a). The invasion is imminent. Nineveh will soon meet the "lion" of Judah (cf. Jer 49:19; Hos 11:10; 13:7-8), and what has been foreshadowed in verses 6-11 will surely happen. Nineveh's royalty and all its inhabitants, symbolized by the reference to "young lions," will meet their demise (2:14bc). Israel's God takes full responsibility for the plans, and, by accepting full responsibility, Israel's God asserts divine sovereignty over the strongest of nations. Justice will be meted out punitively, an action that reflects the culture and people's belief in *lex talionis*.

3:1-17 Proclamation against Nineveh

This next section describes further what is about to befall Nineveh. The material is similar to Nahum 2:2, 4-11, but now the images are much more gruesome and include blood, lies, plunder, harlotries, corpses, filth, and sorceries. With respect to imagery, verse 5 presents the most repulsive image not only because of its description but also because it is gender-specific and thus troublesome because of its female reference. The same is true for verse 13 that compares Nineveh's troops to women. The metaphor succeeds in its intent to mock Nineveh, but it remains offensive to women, who are being imaged as weaker than men. Verse 5 echoes 2:14; the destruction of Nineveh draws even closer.

Verses 8-13 begin with an interrogation and contain a variety of metaphors. The prophet reminds Nineveh that No-amon (Thebes), the capital of Egypt and Nineveh's major rival, was devastated despite the city's many natural advantages. Nineveh is no better than Thebes and will suffer the same consequence—destruction, most explicitly captured by the phrase "Even her little ones were dashed to pieces / at the corner of every street" (3:10b). Just as Nineveh's figs are ready to be picked, so the city's fortifications are ripe for the taking (3:12). Just as a swarm of locusts vanish when the sun rises, so the multitudes of Assyrian officials will soon disappear under the heat of invasion (3:17).

3:18-19 Proclamation against the king of Assyria

The focus shifts from Nineveh and the Assyrian officials to the Assyrian king. The imagery denotes not only the ineffectiveness of the king's leaders but also the king himself, which has led to the dissolution of his people. Ultimately, the king has failed at governing well, which leaves open the door for the impending siege. The poem closes on a note of jubilation for Judah: Judah's oppressor will now be oppressed.

THE BOOK OF

HABAKKUK

Carol J. Dempsey, O.P.

INTRODUCTION

Written with brevity and candor, the book of Habakkuk delivers chilling words of judgment upon the people of Judah prior to the destruction and collapse of the holy city Jerusalem, the temple, and the southern kingdom Judah. One of the striking features of the book of Habakkuk is its dialogical style. God and the prophet Habakkuk have an honest, oftentimes heartrending, conversation about life and events in the seventh century B.C. On more than one occasion, Habakkuk complains to God, challenging God about a lack of divine responsiveness to the destruction and violence that surrounds the prophet upon which he must look day after day (1:1-4). Habakkuk's complaints do not go unanswered; God does respond and assures the prophet that, indeed, justice will be served. The book closes on a poignant note: the prophet prays to his God and in his prayer, he acknowledges God's wondrous power. Habakkuk places all his trust in this God who is the prophet's strength and who makes his feet like the feet of deer, swift and agile to "tread upon the heights" (3:19).

The world of Habakkuk

The book of Habakkuk reflects the times of the seventh century B.C. The southern kingdom Judah and its inhabitants stand on the brink of ruin and exile; the fall of Jerusalem and the destruction of the temple are imminently on the horizon. At this time, Babylon is Judah's greatest threat, and ironically, God is said to be rousing up the Babylonians against the Judahites (1:6). Through the brute force of the Babylonians, Israel's God will chastise the inhabitants of Judah because of their injustices, which include greed, theft, embezzlement, extortion, debauchery, and idolatry. Important to note is that the biblical text makes reference to the "Chaldeans," a name used interchangeably and synonymously with the name "Babylonians" (see, e.g., Isa 47:1; Jer 25:12).

During the seventh century B.C. and after the Babylonians' victory over the Egyptians at Carchemish in 605 B.C., the Judahites began paying tribute to the Babylonians. The tide began to turn, however, when Judah's king Jehoiakim rebelled against Babylonian control. As a result of such rebellion, the Babylonians attacked Jerusalem in 597 B.C. and deported both the royal family as well as prominent citizens living in Judah. Succeeding Jehoiakim was Zedekiah, who supported Babylonian control at the beginning of his reign but who later revolted against such control. The revolt triggered the return of the Babylonian armies, who marched into Jerusalem and destroyed it in 587 B.C. This action marked the end of the southern kingdom Judah. The message of Habakkuk is directed to Judah during the time of crisis that led up to Judah's demise by the Babylonians. The actual dating of the book, however, remains a topic of debate.

With respect to the prophet Habakkuk, very little is known about his background, and, like the other prophets of ancient biblical times, whether or not he was an actual historical person is a topic of lively debate. Another topic of discussion is the question of Habakkuk's vocation. Habakkuk may have been a cultic prophet stationed in the temple, or a visionary, or even just an ordinary individual concerned about the events and issues of his day. The general consensus is that Habakkuk was a cultic prophet. Whether or not Habakkuk was an actual person, a cultic prophet, a visionary, or an ordinary human being is second to his profound and prophetic message. Habakkuk is deeply concerned about the injustices he sees within his community, and he is unhappy with the various prophetic theologies of history that resolve the injustices through the use of foreign powers as God's way of chastising Judah.

The literary dimensions of the book of Habakkuk

The text of Habakkuk moves at a lively pace primarily because of the dynamic dialogue that occurs between God and Habakkuk. The addresses and exchanges that take place come to life through the repetitive use of literary techniques such as direct address (1:2; 3:2), which is also achieved by the use of the pronoun "you" (see, e.g., 1:12, 14; 2:10, 16; 3:9, 13), rhetorical questions (see, e.g., 1:3, 12, 17; 2:13, 18, 19; 3:8), the use of imperative verb forms (see, e.g., 1:5; 2:2b, 4), and the cataloging of a series of woe prophecies (2:6b-8, 9-11, 12-14, 15-17, 18-19). Metaphorical language depicts a multifaceted picture of God as "holy God" (1:12), "Rock" (1:12), one who not only listens but also responds (1:2–2:1; 2:2-20), radiant (3:3-4), powerful (3:5-7), and an enraged warrior who will act on behalf of justice (3:2-15). According to the prophet Habakkuk, however, divine justice may not be done in the same direct way as may have been perceived at other junctures of Israel and Judah's history. In the book of Habakkuk, God is seen not so much as a warrior but more like a "commander-in-chief" who will send the Chaldeans (1:6) to deal with the inhabitants and the land of Judah.

With respect to the text's structure, the book of Habakkuk can be divided into the following units and subunits:

  I. Superscription (1:1)

  II. The prophet's first complaint (1:2-4)

  III. A divine response (1:5-11)

  IV. The prophet's second complaint (1:12–2:1)

  V. A divine response: a vision statement with five woes (2:2-20)

  VI. A prophet's prayer (3:1-19)

The theological dimensions of the book of Habakkuk

From the text of Habakkuk, four theological themes emerge: (1) a concern for rampant injustice, (2) an effort at presenting God as powerful and just in the face of injustice, (3) an assertion that righteousness and faith are inseparable, and (4) God as one's hope and salvation in times of trouble. The text's portrayal of God is in need of ongoing critical theological reflection and discussion. For example, the text depicts God in 1:5-11 as one who raises up the Chaldeans, "that bitter and impulsive people," for the purpose of meting out divine punitive justice to Judah because of the land's apostate and lawless ways (see, e.g., 1:2-17). This God has the potential of reducing people to fish and "creeping things" (1:14), as the "wicked devour those more just than themselves" (1:13). Yet this is the same God who empowers the prophet Habakkuk by giving him a vision. This vision is dreadful for the Judahites who oppress others but hopeful for the victims of injustice (see, e.g., 2:2-19). The text also offers a mixed view of divine power. In Habakkuk 3:2-15, the prophet's prayer provides a clear yet metaphorical portrait of God's power in relation to the whole of creation, for instance, how God "shook the earth" and "made the nations tremble" (3:6), how God "came forth" with power to "save [the] anointed one" (3:13), and so forth. According to Habakkuk 3, God has power over heaven, earth, kingdoms, the natural world, and people. All of these elements pale before or on account of such power, with the exception of the prophet, for whom God is his salvation and strength (3:18-19). Thus, the book of Habakkuk presents divine power as a force that has devastating effects. Finally, the book of Habakkuk is a glorious portrait of one person's faith in his God. This faith dares to question and challenge God's actions and motives, and this faith is bold enough and brave enough to let go to God in trust, who will, in the end, save the needy from the hands of evildoers (3:13, 18-19).

COMMENTARY

SUPERSCRIPTION

Habakkuk 1:1

The opening words of the book of Habakkuk introduce and define Habakkuk as a prophet and make clear that what is about to be proclaimed is the contents of a vision (cf. Isa 1:1; Obad 1:1; Nah 1:1). The message is a divine gift.

THE PROPHET'S FIRST COMPLAINT

Habakkuk 1:2-4

With a series of heartrending questions, Habakkuk begins the dialogue with God. In the first two rhetorical questions, Habakkuk asks God why he, the prophet, is not being answered when he cries out for help (cf. Exod 3:7), and why God is not saving him when he shouts out, "Violence!" (cf. Jer 20:7). One can appreciate the prophet's perplexity, especially since he knows from his religious tradition that God has rescued the innocent from the hands of the wicked in the past. Habakkuk poses two more rhetorical questions in verse 3 and asks why he must see iniquity. He also indirectly challenges God by asking why the Holy One of Israel just gazes on evil. Implied is that God sees all the wrongdoing and trouble but does nothing to change the situation of destruction, violence, strife, and discord. In verse 4, he contends that the law is basically useless because it is either misapplied and distorted or not enforced at all. Furthermore, God's failure to act against the wicked renders the Deuteronomic law ineffective with respect to enforcing justice. The identity of the wicked seems to be oppressors within the Judahite community itself. Thus, verses 2-4 are an individual lament that takes the form of a complaint. The phrase "how long" is typical of complaints (cf. Exod 16:28; Num 14:11; Ps 13:1; 62:3; Job 18:2; 19:2).

A DIVINE RESPONSE

Habakkuk 1:5-11

Habakkuk's complaint does not go unheard. Verses 5-11 are God's response to the prophet's lament. Habakkuk learns that God will act on behalf of the suffering righteous by raising up a "bitter and impulsive people"—the Chaldeans—to defeat Judah's wicked (1:5-6). Chaldeans is another term for Babylonians. Verses 6-11 describe the Chaldeans/Babylonians vividly. They are fierce, impetuous, and without a sense of justice. They use their power to oppress others (1:6) and they make up their own rules (1:7). The annual images associated with them denote both speed and ferociousness: they all "come for violence" (1:8-9). No one and nothing will render them powerless (1:10). Their own might is their god (1:11). In response to his complaint, Habakkuk has received a word of judgment that he must now deliver to his people. The passage begs the question: What kind of a God would use an empire, especially a violent and unjust one, to deal with another kingdom's injustices? Historically, Habakkuk's prophecy foreshadows the Babylonian invasion of Judah and its demise, an inevitable event and one that the poet attributes to God in hopes that the wicked in Judah will change their ways. They do not, and the Babylonians do invade Judah in 598 B.C.

THE PROPHET'S SECOND COMPLAINT

Habakkuk 1:12–2:1

Habakkuk is shocked by God's response and in verses 12-14 he once again uses rhetorical questions to reprove God for God's silence and inaction. While God has designated the Babylonians to act against Judah's wicked ones, Habakkuk's question suggests his discomfort with God's plan (1:13). Are not the people of Judah more righteous than their Babylonian enemies? Yet God is silent, allowing the Babylonians to overtake the people of Judah. Habakkuk suggests that they are like fish and crawling things that have no ruler to deliver them (1:14). God's "silence" seems to give more power to the wicked ones. The reference to God as "immortal" in verse 12 may be an allusion to the dying god of the Mot-Baal myth. Israel's God is not supposed to be like Mot-Baal. Israel's God is to be a God of decisive action. The term "Rock," also in verse 12, is a common reference for God (Gen 49:24; Deut 32:4, 15, 18, 30, 31; 2 Sam 22:2; 23:3; Ps 89:26; Isa 30:29, etc.). Clearly, the prophet is disgusted with God's noninvolvement and challenges God's aloofness.

In verses 15-17, Habakkuk metaphorically describes how the king of Babylon treats people—he is like a fisherman who keeps dragging his net again and again to catch more and more fish so that he can increase his own lot. The "net" is an ancient Mesopotamian symbol associated with military power. In the cosmogonic myth, Marduk uses a net to conquer Tiamet. The fisherman attending his net and seine in verse 16 symbolizes the Babylonians' trust in their military power that brought them great wealth at others' expense. Habakkuk persists in questioning God (1:17) to address the fact that God is allowing the Babylonians to kill nation after nation, ruthlessly. How can God allow such things to happen, and are these slaughters truly the way to establishing justice? Habakkuk 2:1 closes the prophet's complaint; Habakkuk remains vigilant.

A DIVINE RESPONSE: A VISION STATEMENT WITH FIVE WOES

Habakkuk 2:2-20

In verses 2-4, God commands Habakkuk to write down the vision, which will consist of five woes (2:5-20). God assures the prophet that indeed the vision is a witness for the appointed time that will surely arrive even if at first it is delayed.

Verses 6-20 are a series of woe sayings. To whom they are addressed is not clear. Possibilities include the Babylonians, Judahites, other foreign countries, or the wicked in general. The first four woes present a picture of how some people have used their power to benefit themselves at the expense of others (2:6-17). The first woe is a word of doom for robbers, thieves, embezzlers, and deceitful ones (2:6-8). The second woe is doom for exploiters and extortionists (2:9-11). The third woe condemns evil and violence (2:12-14). The fourth woe casts judgment on debauchery (2:15-17). The fifth woe condemns idolatry and is different from all the others (2:18-20). In verse 16 the cup is a powerful metaphor. No doubt it is the cup of God's wrath (see Obadiah). Iniquity will not be the final word; justice will prevail. The fifth woe is different. People are upbraided for their trust in idols. Undergirding the expression of justice is the law of retaliation, *lex talionis*. Guilty parties will suffer the same harm they have incurred.

A PROPHET'S PRAYER

Habakkuk 3:1-19

Habakkuk's prayer opens with a simple superscription (3:1). This prayer, on behalf of the king and his people, is an intercessory one meant to be sung by the congregation or one representing the congregation. The superscription is followed by a series of statements that acknowledge God's great deeds and a request that God perform these deeds again but with a spirit of compassion and not wrath (3:2). Verses 3-15 portray God as a warrior and celebrate God's power over creation and nations. Embedded in the warrior God image is the storm god, who often is pictured in Syria-Palestine, standing with a lightning bolt in hand, ready to blaze forth. Waiting for the day of calamity, the prophet becomes queasy and physically uneasy (3:16). The prayer closes on a note of hope (3:17-19). Awaiting justice for those who oppress, the prophet expresses his hope in God, who is the one who saves and the one who strengthens. These verses reflect the richness of Israel's hymnic tradition.

THE BOOK OF

ZEPHANIAH

Carol J. Dempsey, O.P.

INTRODUCTION

Zephaniah was a contemporary of Nahum and Habakkuk, and, like his contemporaries, Zephaniah preached during the Babylonian crisis prior to the fall of Jerusalem in 587 B.C. Like many prophets of his time, very little is known about his background and if, in fact, he was an actual historical figure. The message that Zephaniah delivers is a harrowing one that forewarns about the coming judgment upon Judah (1:1-13), the great Day of the Lord (1:14-18), and judgment on Israel's enemies (2:1-15). Zephaniah also describes the wickedness of Jerusalem (3:1-7) and God's intentions to chastise and transform the nations (3:1-13). He concludes his proclamation with a song of joy (3:14-20) to be sung with gusto because Jerusalem will be restored (3:20). The tone of this prophetic book is foreboding yet hopeful, and, like so many of the other prophetic texts, Zephaniah has its share of violent images that reflect the times and culture of the day. The book is fast-paced and celebrates a God who will not tolerate injustice and transgression, namely, Judah's worship of other gods (1:4-9) and its unjust and abusive leadership (3:1-4).

The world of Zephaniah

The book of Zephaniah opens with a superscription (1:1) that links the prophet Zephaniah to the period when King Josiah reigned (640–609 B.C.). Interestingly, a period of silence existed in the Old Testament prophets, specifically during the first three quarters of the seventh century B.C.

(698–626 B.C.). One possibility for the silence was because of Judah's kings—Manasseh (686–642 B.C.) and Amon (642–640 B.C.)—who were being controlled by the Assyrians and supposedly by the Assyrians' gods. Manasseh's reign was during the zenith of Assyria's power. On the home front, Judah was guilty of ever-increasing persecution, idolatry, and child-sacrifice (2 Kgs 21:1-9, 16).

With respect to Assyria, Sennacherib (705–681 B.C.), one of Assyria's greatest kings, was murdered in 681 B.C. His successor was his son, Esarhaddon (680–669 B.C.), a strong king who extended Assyria's empire as far west as Egypt, which occurred when he captured Memphis in 671 B.C. Esarhaddon's successor was Ashurbanipal (668–627 B.C.). He strengthened Assyria's stronghold on Egypt by conquering Thebes in 663 B.C. After the death of Ashurbanipal around 627 B.C., Assyria's power weakened considerably, which opened the door for Josiah's reforms in Judah, beginning in 621 B.C. Assyria's decline in power also paved the way for the Babylonians to rise to world power under the leadership of Nabopolassar (625–605 B.C.) and Nebuchadnezzar (605–562 B.C.). The text of Zephaniah reflects the Assyrian period and the life of Judah at that time.

The literary dimensions of the book of Zephaniah

The book of Zephaniah moves at a rapid pace. A variety of images, descriptions, and metaphors keep readers enwrapped in God's fury. The repetitious use of the phrase "on that day" and its related references (see 1:9, 10, 14-16, 18; 2:1; 3:11) add cohesion to the series of prophecies of destruction while providing an element of surprise: the Day of the Lord is a time of destruction (1:9-10) that will give way to a time of cleansing and restoration (3:11-13). Throughout the book, the poet also uses the technique of cataloguing— "I will . . ." (1:2-4, 8-9, 12, 17; 3:9-12, 18-20)—to emphasize the power and deeds of Israel's God. The use of quoted speech (1:12; 2:15; 3:7) adds to the drama of the prophet's message as well as the repeated use of vocatives: "O inhabitants" (1:11), "O nation" (2:1), "O Canaan" (2:5), and "O Cushites" (2:12). The poet's metaphors and similes help to create vivid impressions in the imaginations of the hearers and readers of Zephaniah (see, e.g., 1:17; 2:9, 13; 3:14).

With respect to the book's structure, the poetry of Zephaniah can be divided into the following units:

I. Superscription (1:1)
II. Proclamations of judgment and imminent disasters (1:2–3:8)

Against Jerusalem and Judah (1:2–2:3)

Against Philistia (2:4-7)

Against Moab and Ammon (2:8-11)

Against Ethiopia (2:12)

Against Assyria (2:13-15)

III. Statement of reproach against Jerusalem (3:1-7)
IV. Statement of future purification (3:8-13)
V. Proclamation of hope, salvation, and restoration (3:14-20)

Unlike many other prophetic books, Zephaniah features only one main speaker—God, whose speeches reveal a deity full of wrath and hostility toward not only the world's people but also other nonhuman creatures of the earth (1:2-3). This God is completely disgusted with Judah and Jerusalem because of their false and sensual worship (1:4-6; 3:1-5) and is enraged with the nations because of their unjust treatment of Judah (2:8) and their corrupt deeds (3:7). Without a doubt, the book of Zephaniah is a book sure to set one's teeth on edge but, like so many of the Bible's other prophetic books, Zephaniah is not without a word of hope (3:11-20). All of the rage and fury eventually dissipate as daughter Zion looks forward to salvation and restoration in the sight of all peoples.

The theological dimensions of the book of Zephaniah

The most significant theological aspect of the book of Zephaniah is how the prophet portrays Israel's God. Throughout the text, the prophet heralds a fire-and-brimstone God whose quest is for sovereignty over peoples and other gods and whose sense of ethics will not allow for injustice and the inordinate assertion of power of one people over another. In a fit of rage, this God makes no discrimination between the guilty human beings and the nonhumans: all creation will experience the devastating effects of the divine wrath. This divine wrath and anger is understandable, given the state of affairs of Judah, Jerusalem, and the nations in general. What becomes difficult from a hermeneutical viewpoint, however, is the form that the wrath and anger takes: God's actions are destructive and not constructive, punitive and not life-sustaining. These images of an anthropomorphic, androcentric God reflect both the culture of the day and the biblical writer's theological agenda, which is to establish Israel's God not only as sovereign over all nations, peoples, and gods but also as one who is more powerful than the most powerful of nations and peoples on the face of the earth. Israel's God is Lord of creation and Lord of history. Finally, the text makes clear that the divine intent is not for complete annihilation. A remnant will be spared, the nations will be brought into line, and Zion will be restored, but only after all has been divinely chastened and purified, and love is renewed.

COMMENTARY

SUPERSCRIPTION

Zephaniah 1:1

The book of Zephaniah opens with a simple introductory statement that designates the contents of the book as a word from God, identifies who the prophet Zephaniah is by way of his ancestors, and provides a historical framework for Zephaniah's preaching. The fact that the word of the Lord "came" to Zephaniah makes clear that the prophetic word is a gift, usually flowing from an intuitive kind of religious experience, and not something that can be learned or sought after. Zephaniah's name could mean "YHWH hides" or "YHWH treasures." Zephaniah is the name of a Canaanite god, and thus the name could also mean "Zaphon is YHWH." Zephaniah's father is Cushi, his grandfather is Gedaliah, his great-grandfather is Amariah, and his great-great-grandfather is Hezekiah. Very little is known about any of these men except for Hezekiah, whose name means "the Lord is my strength." Hezekiah was the thirteenth king of Judah and was the son of Ahaz and Abi (2 Kgs 18:2). He conducted a reformation that reached beyond Jerusalem to include the cleansing of the land and the tribes of Benjamin, Ephraim, and Manasseh. Hezekiah had a fairly good relationship with the prophet Isaiah. The king had to deal with the aggressive Assyrians and their king, Sennacherib, who was eventually defeated by an angel of the Lord (2 Kgs 19:35). Hezekiah's achievements are recorded in 2 Chronicles 32:27-30. Thus, four generations are represented in the superscription. Zephaniah's roots, then, are in Judah. The prophet is said to have begun his ministry during the reign of Josiah, the sixteenth king of Judah who was the son of Amon and the grandson of Manasseh (2 Kgs 21:23–23:30). Josiah's thirty-one-year reign was characterized by peace, prosperity, and reform. A godly man, he was seriously injured in a battle with the Egyptian pharaoh Necho II and died shortly thereafter. Finally, this superscription is similar to that of Hosea, Joel, Micah, Haggai, and Zechariah, all of which identify the prophetic proclamations as "the word of the LORD."

PROCLAMATIONS OF JUDGMENT AND IMMINENT DISASTERS

Zephaniah 1:2–3:8

The Day of the Lord that Habakkuk was quietly awaiting was drawing near. This day was to be most fierce and terrible, a day of total destruction for Judah, inclusive of human and nonhuman life. Similarly Zephaniah describes a God who is coming with power to deal with the country and Jerusalem's idolatrous and unjust people. In particular, Zephaniah takes issue with Judah's leadership. Some of Judah's officials as well as the king's sons had adopted foreign customs and attire, others engaged in foreign religious practices, and still others were perpetrators of violence and deceit. The historical backdrop to Zephaniah's preaching is the invasion of the Babylonians, whom God is raising up as Judah's enemy to chastise Judah for its transgressions. This section consists of five judgment proclamations that outline imminent disasters for not only Jerusalem and Judah but also for other nations. In these texts one sees an ethnocentric view of God who comes with power to defend Judah by overpowering those countries that have taunted and conquered God's "people." Power is used to overpower, and violence gives birth to more violence.

1:2–2:3 Against Jerusalem and Judah

This first judgment proclamation directed toward Jerusalem and Judah is grand in scope. In verses 2-6 Zephaniah describes the extensive destruction of life that will befall Judah, especially those who have disregarded God and God's ways (1:6). The use of power will be indiscriminate on God's part, and the judgment will be more inclusive than the primeval flood. The reason for such divine wrath is clear from verses 4-6: idolatry, a transgression against the first commandment (Exod 20:2-6). Breach of covenant relationship on the part of human beings reaps repercussions that devastate not only humanity but also the natural world. The reference to Baal in verse 4 is the storm god, the son of El, who is the chief Canaanite god. Baal was the god of rain and the giver of fertility.

He was sometimes referred to as the husband of the land. Originally the word meant "lord" or "owner" (e.g., Exod 21:28-29) or "husband" (e.g., Exod 21:3). By the time of the Late Bronze Age, Baal then became a title for various gods and also the name of El's son. Worship of Baal took place on hills or mountaintops (1 Kgs 12:31; 2 Kgs 17:9-10; 23:8, 13, 15).

Verse 7 contains an admonition to be silent before God, who is close at hand, and is followed by a description of the transgressions of which some members of Judah are guilty. In this verse the prophet also announces what God intends to do to those guilty of transgression. The officials and the king's sons who wear foreign attire are most likely guilty of Baal worship (2 Kgs 10:22) and therefore apostasy. Those who leap over the threshold (1:9) are guilty of a superstition that holds that evil spirits lurk at a doorway, waiting to enter if one steps on the threshold, an act that would let the spirits in. Because these two acts are associated with apostasy, those who engage in them will experience divine punishment. The wealthy who smugly believe that God is indifferent (1:12) will also experience God's punishment: their wealth will be plundered, and their houses and vineyards will come to naught (1:13). The Day of the Lord (1:7, 14) will be a day of divine wrath, sadness, wailing, and economic distress (1:2-13).

In 1:14-16 the description of the Day of the Lord continues. Hastening ever closer, this day will be full of wrath, distress, anguish, ruin, devastation, darkness, gloom, and clouds, with the sound of battle directed against Judah.

The description begun in 1:8-9 of what God plans to do to some people continues in 1:17-18: the inhabitants of the land will lose a sense of direction for their lives and will be slaughtered (1:17). Money will not buy them any security because the whole earth will be consumed (1:18).

This Day of the Lord is hyperbolic and symbolizes God's extraordinary rage over the central sin of some of the people: apostasy. God will not tolerate Judah worshiping other gods. The warfare language emerges from the social location of the Judahites. Finally, the text as a whole portrays God as a violent and somewhat unjust God who threatens to sweep away everything because some people have sinned.

The last section of the poem is an exhortation. The prophet calls Judah to make restitution and to turn back to God before the Day of the Lord and the threatened divine wrath become a reality (2:1-3ab). If the people turn aside from their ways and seek right relationship once more, then perhaps they "will be sheltered on the day of the LORD's anger" (2:3c). The mission of the prophet, then, is not only to expose transgression but also to hold out hope to a struggling people.

2:4-7 Against Philistia

The Day of the Lord will affect not only Jerusalem and Judah but many other nations as well. The first nation to be affected is Philistia (cf. Ezek 25:15-17). Gaza, Ashkelon, Ashdod, and Ekron (2:4) are all cities of the Philistine confederation. The Cherethites (2:5) are a synonym for, or a subdivision of, the Philistines. The Cherethites may be associated with Crete, which is part of the larger Aegean region from where the Philistines came. The Philistine coastal plain will be void of human inhabitants and, thus, the area will become a pastureland where shepherds can pasture their flocks (2:6). The shepherds are Judeans. Interestingly, even though the image in 2:4-5 is one of devastation, the land itself will continue on as a sign of life with life-sustaining possibilities. In 2:7 the plot thickens: the Judeans will not only pasture their flocks on land that once belonged to the Philistines but they will also pasture them by the seacoast, which will become the lot of the Judahites as well (2:7). Thus, embedded in this judgment proclamation against Philistia is a word of hope for Judah (2:6-7).

2:8-11 Against Moab and Ammon

In this third judgment speech the target of God's wrath is Moab and Ammon (cf. Gen 19:30-38; Isa 15; Jer 48–49:6; Ezek 25:1-11). These two nations were Judah's neighbors to the east across the Jordan River. Both the Moabites and the Ammonites have poked fun at the Judahites—God's "people"—and have gloated over their territory (2:8). Therefore Israel's God will deal terribly with these two groups; and ironically, the plunderers will be the ones despoiled by those whom they have attacked (2:9-10). For reference to Sodom and Gomorrah, see Genesis 19:1-29. Israel's God as the sovereign one over all other gods and the conversion of the nations to worshiping God is the focus of 2:11.

2:12 Against Ethiopia

The fourth judgment speech is directed toward Ethiopia (cf. Isa 18:1-6), also known as Cush, whose inhabitants are Cushites who will be slain by the Lord's sword, a dreadful weapon, sharpened, polished, flashing, and always ready for slaughter (cf. Ezek 21:1-17).

2:13-15 Against Assyria

What Nahum foresaw, Zephaniah sees as well—the destruction of Nineveh and the Assyrians. This fifth judgment speech is addressed to Assyria and its capital city Nineveh. Animal imagery reinforces the city's total destruction. Once a secure and exultant city, Nineveh will become a wilderness for animals.

STATEMENT OF REPROACH
AGAINST JERUSALEM

Zephaniah 3:1-7

In Zephaniah 3:1-7, focus shifts from judgment speeches against foreign countries to a statement of reproach against Jerusalem. Verses 1-5 portray God taking Jerusalem to task for a variety of reasons: it is obdurate, belligerent, and distant from God (3:2). Animal imagery metaphorically describes the city's political leadership: officials and judges are ferocious and fierce; they prey on those under their authority (3:3). Its religious leaders are just as bad: the prophets are reckless, treacherous persons; its priests have profaned the sacred and have done violence to the law (3:4). The one who stands in sharp contrast to all of those persons is God, who acts justly every day (3:5). Verse 5 contrasts the unjust with God, imaged metaphorically as a judge.

Verse 6 recalls the types of judgments God has meted out in the past. God has cut off countries, turned battlements into ruins, laid waste streets, and made cities desolate. Historically all of these events reflect the Assyrian devastation of Judah during Hezekiah's reign. The invasion was attributed to God on account of the people's wickedness.

God now hopes that in its present state, Jerusalem will recall this past experience, take note of what happens when one acts wickedly, accept correction, and not lose sight of all that God has brought upon it (3:6-7). God hopes Jerusalem will

learn from the past and fall in line with God's authority and leadership, lest it too will have to suffer more punitive consequences. God, however, observes that Jerusalem's inhabitants have done their corrupt deeds more eagerly (3:7).

STATEMENT OF FUTURE PURIFICATION

Zephaniah 3:8-13

Following the five judgment speeches and a reproach against Jerusalem, Jerusalem is now called upon to wait for the Lord, who will surely pour out divine wrath upon the nations (3:8). The reference to God arising as an accuser hints at a lawsuit that God has against his people. Verse 9 indicates the type of purification that is to occur: the foreign countries will be given pure lips so that they can all worship Israel's God and bring gifts to this God as well (3:10). In verse 11 God, speaking through the prophet, directs attention to Judah. Prior to judgment, the wicked political and religious leaders in Jerusalem were too bold to feel any shame for their behavior even though such behavior turned Jerusalem into a rebellious, polluted, and oppressive city (3:1-5). After God's purifying judgment, the city and its inhabitants will no longer have to feel shame on account of their behavior because their perpetrators will be gone (3:11). The population that will remain in Jerusalem—the remnant—will be a "humble and lowly" people (3:12), a people of integrity who have obeyed God and have sought righteousness (2:3). Their security will be in their God, and they will enjoy abiding peace (3:13).

PROCLAMATION OF HOPE,
SALVATION, AND RESTORATION

Zephaniah 3:14-20

Words of judgment, reproach, and purification lead to words of hope, salvation, and restoration. Addressed to daughter Zion—daughter Jerusalem—now chastened and purified, Zephaniah calls upon the city to shout with joy and sing joyfully (3:14). Why? Because God had removed the judgment against the city, has turned away all the enemies (cf. 1:2–3:8, 15), and now dwells in their midst (3:15). The phrase "On that day" (3:16) is eschatological and points to a future new day for

Jerusalem. No longer will Jerusalem and its inhabitants experience the "Day of the Lord," a day of wrath (1:2–2:3). The phrase "Do not fear, Zion" (3:16) is a typical reassurance formula (cf. Gen 15:1; 21:17; 35:17; Exod 20:20; Isa 7:4; 35:4; 40:9; 41:10; Jer 30:10; Joel 2:21; Hag 2:5; Ruth 3:11). These verses foreshadow the end of the Babylonian exile and the return of the Judahites to their land. Because God dwells in Jerusalem and in its inhabitants' midst (3:17), there is a reason to celebrate. Jerusalem's disgrace will no longer be remembered by others because God is about to remove disaster from the city's midst (3:17d). A city and a people now purified will soon be made glorious through God's transformative love (3:18). Jerusalem is reassured that God will deal with the city's oppressors (3:19a). Verses 19b-20 present a joyous picture. With right relationship renewed, God will gather the peoples together, bring them home, restore them, and make them glorious throughout the earth (3:20). Finally, like all of the prophets in this commentary, Zephaniah's final proclamation is a word of hope, which is at the heart of the prophetic vocation and mission.

THE BOOK OF

HAGGAI

John J. Collins

INTRODUCTION

Unlike Joel and Obadiah, the book of Haggai opens with a very specific indication of the time of the prophet's activity: "On the first day of the sixth month in the second year of Darius the king," or 520 B.C. Moreover, Haggai and Zechariah are among the very few prophets who both have books attached to their names and are mentioned in historical books. (Isaiah is mentioned in 2 Kings 19, in a passage also found in Isaiah 37.) Haggai is mentioned in Ezra 5:1-2: "Then the prophets Haggai and Zechariah, son of Iddo, began to prophesy to the Jews in Judah and Jerusalem in the name of the God of Israel. Thereupon Zerubbabel, son of Shealtiel, and Jeshua, son of Jozadak, began again to build the house of God in Jerusalem, with the prophets of God giving them support." In the following chapter we are told that "[t]he elders of the Jews continued to make progress in the building, supported by the message of the prophets, Haggai and Zechariah, son of Iddo. They finished the building according to the command of the God of Israel and the decrees of Cyrus and Darius" (Ezra 6:14-15). According to this account, Haggai and Zechariah were instrumental in having the temple in Jerusalem rebuilt, some twenty years after the first return of Judeans from the Babylonian Exile. The temple was not finished until the sixth year of Darius, or 516 B.C.

Structure

The book of Haggai contains four oracles, each of which is introduced by a date formula.

The first oracle (1:1-11) is dated to the first day of the sixth month of the second year of Darius (August–September, 520 B.C.). This oracle upbraids the people for their failure to rebuild the temple and claims that the misfortunes they are experiencing are due to this failure. This is followed by a brief narrative (1:12-14) that describes the response of the people under the leadership of the governor Zerubbabel and the high priest Joshua, who proceeded to begin work on the rebuilding.

The second oracle (2:1-9), on the twenty-first day of the seventh month, confronts the disappointment of the people at the scale of the new temple. According to Ezra 3:12-13, many old people who remembered the old temple wept when they saw the foundations of the new one, so that one could not distinguish between the joyful shout of the younger people and the weeping of the elders. Haggai, however, is undismayed. He encourages the governor, high priest, and people to persevere, and promises that the glory of the new temple will yet be greater than that of the old.

The third oracle (2:10-19), dated to the twenty-fourth day of the ninth month in the same year, argues that the offerings of the people are unclean. This might explain why their fortunes were not significantly altered when work on the temple began. Haggai insists, however, that God would bless the people "from this day forward" (2:15).

The final oracle is dated to the same day as the third and is addressed only to the governor

Zerubbabel. The Lord promises to overthrow kingdoms and make Zerubbabel his signet ring. The signet ring gave the official who bore it power to act in the name of the king. Zerubbabel, then, was the instrument through which the authority of God would be exercised. While Haggai is not fully explicit, he strongly suggests that Zerubbabel will be restored to the kingship and be, in effect, the messiah who would restore the kingdom of David.

The entire career of Haggai seems to have lasted less than three months. Some other prophets, such as Amos, may also have had very brief careers, while others, such as Isaiah, were active for decades. Haggai seems to have been called for a very specific purpose to help bring about the rebuilding of the temple. His oracles, however, promise a transformation of life in Judah that never came about. The non-fulfillment of his oracles may have been a factor in the brevity of his career.

The book of Haggai is unified by a clearer historical narrative than that of any other prophet. The oracles are presented in a coherent sequence and held together by prose introductions and the brief narrative in 1:12-15. Such chronological order and logical coherence are without parallel in the other prophetic books. We should infer that the oracles have been carefully edited by someone other than the prophet. The book was most probaby put together very shortly after the oracles were delivered, before it became obvious that its predictions about the transformation of life in Judah would not be fulfilled.

The historical context

The year to which Haggai's oracles are dated, the second year of Darius, or 520 B.C., was a time of upheaval in the Persian empire. Darius did not come to the the throne by peaceful succession. In 522 the throne had been usurped by a man named Gaumata. Darius, who was a member of the ruling Achaemenid family, led a conspiracy to overthrow the usurper. As has often happened throughout history, several subject peoples in the empire seized the opportunity to revolt. Darius had to put down rebellions in Media and Babylon and also, in 519, in Egypt. Many scholars have suspected that these rebellions stirred hopes of independence also in Judah. These hopes were quite unrealistic. It is doubtful whether Zerub-

babel and the high priest Joshua, who derived their authority from the Persians, would have been swept away by revolutionary enthusiasm. But the prophets Haggai and Zechariah could well have entertained such hopes, based not on a realistic assessment of political and military considerations but on their belief in the power of their God. It seems very likely that both prophets hoped for a restoration of the monarchy. We have no record of what the governor and the high priest thought.

It is also possible that the prophets thought that the monarchy could be restored without rebellion against Persia. The Persians had been benefactors of the Jews. They had allowed them to return to Jerusalem and rebuild their temple. They allowed Zerubbabel, who was a descendant of David, to function as governor. It may be that the prophets hoped that they would also allow the restoration of native kingship. Subject peoples often retained their own kings as vassals of the imperial overlord. But the Persians had no intention of letting Judah become independent and were not about to indulge the desire for a restored kingship. We shall reflect on this issue more extensively in connection with the prophecy of Zechariah.

The theology of Haggai

Like Joel and Obadiah, and unlike most pre-exilic prophets, Haggai is very favorably disposed toward the temple cult. He shows an interest in issues of ritual purity that is typical of the Priestly tradition. Such concern is also found in Ezekiel (see especially Ezek 44) but scarcely in any other prophetic book. The most controversial aspect of Haggai's preaching, however, is his assumption that the welfare of the people depends on the temple and its cult. No doubt, this assumption would have been widely shared by the priests who presided over the cult, and by the people who supported it, in any period. Prophets such as Amos and Isaiah, however, were bitterly critical of this belief. (See Amos 5:18-25; Isa 1:12-16.) Jeremiah had derided those who set their trust on "The temple of the LORD! The temple of the LORD!" (Jer 7:4). Even in Haggai's own time this critical tradition was continued by the anonymous prophet of Isaiah 66:1, who has the Lord ask derisively: "The heavens are my throne, / the earth, my footstool. / What house can you build for me?

/ Where is the place of my rest?" It is evident too that most of the people of Judah did not give the rebuilding of the temple the highest priority when they returned from Babylon.

Haggai upbraids the people for putting their own interests first, for building "paneled houses" for themselves while the house of the Lord lay in ruins (1:4). His reasoning was based on ancient mythological ideas that linked the fertility of the land to the cultic worship of the gods. But his argument focuses attention on an interesting problem in the sociology of religion. In a community where resources are scarce, should people attend first to basic human needs, such as housing, or should they give priority to providing for worship and a temple (or church)? The importance of a temple, even from a purely sociological point of view, should not be underestimated. By rebuilding the temple, the people put the community as a whole ahead of their individual needs and create an important symbol for their communal identity. The importance of such symbols can be illustrated vividly from the history of American Catholicism. Immigrant communities made up of very poor people built monumental churches all over the Northeast and Midwest of the United States. These churches proclaimed not only the glory of God but also the cohesiveness and ambition of the immigrant communities themselves. Haggai was no sociologist, but the temple that he helped build would stand as a major symbol of Jewish identity and pride down to the time of King Herod, who would replace it with a grander structure. The contribution of the temple to the cohesion and solidarity of the Jewish people in this period can scarcely be overestimated.

The rhetorical strategy used by Haggai to persuade the people to rebuild the temple was to promise that the Lord would reward them with fertility "from this day" (2:19). This proved to be a risky strategy. The building of the temple did not bring about any obvious change in fertility and prosperity. Haggai was neither the first nor the last prophet to make predictions that were not fulfilled. Later Jewish and Christian history provides abundant examples of people who predicted the end of the world, or the end of history as we know it. The Millerite movement in the 1840s in North America is a famous case in point. Sociologists who study such movements have

pointed out that believers in such predictions often persist in believing that they will yet be fulfilled, even in the face of evidence to the contrary. So it is with Haggai. To those who were discouraged by the small scale of the new temple, or at the fact that the seed did not sprout when the foundations were laid, his response is to tell them to wait and see.

Unfortunately, the book of Haggai only records his preaching over a three-month period. We should like to know how long he persisted in his hope that God would fill the new temple with glory. Jews of later generations might claim that the prophecy was eventually fulfilled, when the temple was enriched by contributions of Jews who lived in other lands but came to Jerusalem on pilgrimage. The original prophecy of Haggai, however, envisioned not only the wealth of the temple but also the subordination of the Gentiles. It is specifically the wealth of the nations that he hoped would be brought to Jerusalem, not just the wealth of Jewish exiles.

A final issue raised by the prophecy of Haggai concerns messianic expectation. The word "messiah" is derived from the Hebrew *mashiach*, which means anointed one. The word Christ is an anglicized form of *christos*, the Greek equivalent. High priests, and possibly some prophets, were anointed, but the anointed of the Lord *par excellence* was the Davidic king. See, for example, Psalm 2, which refers to the king as the Lord's anointed. According to 2 Samuel 7, the Lord had promised to David that one of his descendants would always reign as king in Jerusalem. After the destruction of Jerusalem by the Babylonians in 586, however, there was no longer a Davidic king of Judah. Accordingly, the word messiah came to indicate the hope for a future figure who would restore the kingdom of David.

Christianity claims that this expectation is fulfilled in Jesus, whose kingdom is not of this world. For Jews, however, it can only be fulfilled in this world by a king who would actually restore the kingdom of Israel. Such a king would not necessarily be a supernatural or heavenly figure, and he would not be expected to live and reign forever. He would simply be a king who restored the Davidic line. It should be noted that the word *mashiach* is not used in the Hebrew Bible with reference to a future figure. That usage first appears in the Dead Sea Scrolls and in the Psalms of Solomon, which date from the first century B.C. But the hope for a king who would restore the line of David is well attested in the Hebrew Bible in passages that probably date from the postexilic period (Isa 11; Jer 23:5-6; 33:15-18, etc.). If we say that the fourth oracle of Haggai, in which the Lord says that he will make Zerubbabel his signet ring,

is or may be messianic, all this means is that Haggai expected that Zerubbabel would restore the Davidic line and that his descendants would rule after him as kings in Jerusalem. We do not imply that Haggai thought of Zerubbabel as a supernatural, divine figure in the manner in which Christ is conceived in Christian theology.

COMMENTARY

THE FIRST ORACLE

Haggai 1:1-14

1:1 Introductory statement

Haggai 1:1 identifies the main actors in the drama of which these oracles are part.

Darius is Darius I of Persia (522–486). He was the Persian king whose army was defeated at the battle of Marathon in Greece in 490. He was also famous for organizing the Persian empire in satrapies, or governorships. The second year of his reign was 520, and the sixth month was the month of Elul, in late summer or early fall (August–September).

The name Haggai is derived from the Hebrew word for festival, *hag* (the Muslim festival, the hajj, is derived from the same root). He is the only person with this name in the Hebrew Bible, although some closely related names occur (Haggi, in Gen 46:16; Haggith, wife of David, in 2 Sam 3:4).

Zerubbabel is a fairly common Babylonian name, meaning "seed of Babylon." Zerubbabel is the grandson of King Jehoiachin of Judah, who was taken into exile by the Babylonians. In 1 Chronicles 3:18, he is said to be son of Pedaiah. According to Haggai, he was son of Pedaiah's elder brother Shealtiel. There is no satisfactory solution to this contradiction. Some scholars have supposed that there were two Zerubbabels who were first cousins, but this is not very convincing. Others have suggested that Pedaiah fathered a son by the widow of Shealtiel, in accordance with the marriage laws of Deuteronomy 25 that require

a brother to raise up offspring for a deceased man. More likely, there was some confusion in the sources as to just whose son he was. His father, in either case, was not active in Judah. It is likely that his uncle, who is called Shenazzar in 1 Chronicles 3:18, was identical with Sheshbazzar, the prince of Judah, who led the first group of returning exiles in 538 (Ezra 1:8).

The high priest Joshua also figures prominently in the books of Zechariah and Ezra. The high priest enjoyed much more authority in Judah after the Exile than had been the case before. Since Haggai lists Zerubbabel first, the governor most probably took precedence at this time. We shall see in Zechariah, however, that the governor eventually disappears, and the high priest becomes the primary leader of the Jewish community in the Second Temple period.

Haggai 1:1 mentions only Zerubbabel and Joshua as addressees of the first oracle, but it is clear that it is addressed to the whole people.

1:2-3 The people's objection

The most obvious reason why people would say that the time had not yet come to rebuild the temple is that they did not yet have adequate housing for themselves or did not yet have the necessary resources. There is another possible explanation, however. Jeremiah had prophesied that Jerusalem would be desolate for seventy years (Jer 29:10: "Only after seventy years have elapsed for Babylon will I deal with you and fulfill for you my promise to bring you back to this place." Cf. Jer 25:11-12.) 1 Chronicles 36:22 (= Ezra

1:1) declares that this prophecy was fulfilled when Cyrus of Persia authorized the return to Judah in 538. Strictly speaking, the seventy years did not expire until 516. It is doubtful whether anyone was calculating the years so exactly, but it may be that some people used the prophecy of seventy years as an excuse for inaction. Haggai identifies the real reason for the delay in verse 2. The people think that their own houses should have priority over the house of the Lord. Haggai vehemently disagrees.

1:5-11 The key to prosperity

Haggai develops his argument with a pair of utterances, each of which begins, "Reflect on your experience!" It is noteworthy here that the prophet attempts to reason with the people. Ancient wisdom was based on the assumption that there is a logical connection between act and consequence. The people have been acting in a certain way, attending to their own needs and ignoring the temple. Presumably, they do this because they are concerned about their welfare and they think they can achieve results in this way. Haggai asks them to consider what they have achieved. The picture he sketches is one of people who are hard pressed to eke out a living in difficult circumstances. They do not have quite enough to eat or drink, and their wages are not sufficient to meet their needs. In verses 10-11, we find that the situation is made worse by drought, which affects livestock and crops. The problem is not just that the resources of the people are inadequate or that they are incompetent. The deck is stacked against them by the displeasure of their God. It is he who blows away the fruits of their toil and frustrates their expectations.

Haggai's diagnosis of the cause of this situation is alarmingly simple: it is because the temple has not been rebuilt. The idea that the fertility of the earth depends on the proper observance of the cult is an old one, with roots in the mythological traditions of the ancient Near East. Most of the preexilic prophets are critical of the cult and argue that the prosperity of the people depends on the practice of justice rather than on rituals. Yet we should note that a very similar view of the effects of cultic behavior is found in the eighth-century prophet Hosea and in the stories about the prophet Elijah in 2 Kings. According to Elijah and Hosea, drought and failure of crops came

about when people worshipped Baal rather than the Lord as the source of these things. In Haggai, the problem is not idolatry but neglect, but the logic is the same. The Lord is the source of the grain, wine, and oil. When people fail to acknowledge him, he withholds his blessings. This view of the effects of ritual, or the omission thereof, strikes most modern readers as far too simple, and many of the Hebrew prophets would have agreed. We see the forces of nature as morally neutral. In the words of Jesus in the New Testament, the heavenly father makes his sun rise on the bad and the good and causes his rain to fall on the just and the unjust (Matt 5:45). Haggai, however, insists that the drought and adverse conditions are divine punishment for the failure to build the temple. The implication is obvious; they should go cut timber and build the house so that the Lord would receive his glory.

1:12-15 The response to Haggai's preaching

While Haggai's attempt to give a theological explanation of natural conditions must be considered dubious, it had its desired effect in the short term. The people, led by Zerubbabel and Joshua, took his words to heart and began work on the temple within a month of Haggai's initial preaching. The very appearance of a prophet seems to have put the fear of God into people. Having scolded them into action, Haggai now reassures them that God is with them. The expression "I am with you" in verse 13 recalls the name of the child in Isaiah 7: Immanuel. The belief in the presence and assistance of God was a core element in the ideology of the Davidic line and the Jerusalem temple. (See, for example, Psalm 46).

Nonetheless, the work on the temple evidently went slowly and was not completed until the sixth year of Darius, four years after it was begun (Ezra 6:15). The book of Ezra attributes the delay to the opposition of suspicious Persian officials, but the account is confused. It should also be noted that according to Ezra 5:16, Sheshbazzar had laid the foundations of the temple when he first came from Babylon, although Ezra 3:10 says that this was done under the supervision of Zerubbabel and Joshua. It is likely, of course, that any foundations laid by Sheshbazzar would have fallen into disrepair and would have needed to be relaid by Zerubbabel almost twenty years later.

THE SECOND ORACLE

Haggai 2:1-9

The second oracle is dated approximately one month after the work on the temple had begun. In this case "the remnant of the people" is explicitly mentioned among the addressees (2:2). The remnant presumably consists of those who had returned from the Babylonian Exile.

2:3 Comparison with the former temple

The account of the disappointment of those who remembered the former temple is paralleled in Ezra 3:12-14. It may well be that the account of this incident in Ezra was based on this passage in Haggai.

2:4-5 An oracle of encouragement

Haggai tells the leaders and the people to take courage and not fear. While the Hebrew prophets threaten and scold more often than they reassure, this is a traditional kind of oracle. The words "do not fear" were a trademark of Assyrian prophecy. Isaiah is instructed to deliver such an oracle to Ahaz in Isaiah 7:4. Compare Joel 2:21-22. As we noted above, with reference to Haggai 1:13, the belief that "God is with us" was part of the traditional theology associated with the Jerusalem temple. (See, for example, Ps 46:7.) In light of the strong associations of this phrase with the theology associated with Jerusalem and Mount Zion, it is somewhat surprising that Haggai associates it with the Exodus in 2:5.

There are two possible reasons for invoking the Exodus here. One is that this oracle is dated to the seventh month, and the feast of Tabernacles, or Sukkoth, was celebrated in that month. In Nehemiah 8:14, the celebration begins on the second day of the month. According to Leviticus 23:39, the festival began on the fifteenth day of the seventh month. Leviticus says that the reason for the tabernacles or booths was that the Lord made Israel live in booths when he brought them out of the land of Egypt. The second reason for invoking the Exodus at this point is the analogy between the return from Babylon and the Exodus from Egypt. This analogy is developed especially in Isaiah 40–55.

The pact that God made with the Israelites at the time of the Exodus is usually identified as the Sinai covenant. That covenant, however, was a conditional one and spelled out the commandments that Israel was supposed to keep. In Haggai, however, there is no mention of commandments. The "pact" is simply the assurance that God would be with them. This view of the covenant is closer to the unconditional covenants with Abraham or with David than to the covenant with Moses that is described in Exodus and Deuteronomy. The theology of Haggai remains essentially the Jerusalem theology that centered on the kingship and the promise to David and the temple. This theology emphasized trust in the presence of the Lord rather than the requirements of the commandments.

2:6-9 The coming glory

The promise that the Lord will shake the nations is the subject of a famous solo in Handel's *Messiah*. The opening phrase, "In just a little while," acknowledges that the transformation did not come about immediately when the work on the temple was begun. The prophet reassures the people in face of the delay and calls for patience. His vision of the future is one where the wealth of all nations will be brought to Jerusalem. This is very similar to what we find in the prophets we call Second and Third Isaiah (Isa 40–55, 56–66). Compare especially the rapturous oracle to Zion in Isaiah 60, also made famous by Handel ("Arise, shine, for thy light is come"), and that may be roughly contemporary with Haggai. There we are told that the wealth of the nations will be brought as tribute, including gold and frankincense from Sheba, whose queen had visited Solomon. In this vision of the future, Jerusalem is the center of the earth, like the capital of a great imperial power. Such splendor was a far cry from the depressed state described in Haggai 1:5-11 and was quite unrealistic. Later in the Second Temple period, considerable wealth would flow into Jerusalem from Jews scattered in other lands who came to Jerusalem on pilgrimage. Haggai's prophecy, however, entails not only wealth in Jerusalem but also the submission and subordination of the other nations. This prediction was not a sober assessment of the political prospects. It was something that would require a miracle. But, Haggai insisted, if the gold and silver belong to God, why should that be a problem?

The purpose of the wealth flowing into Jerusalem is not to enrich the residents of the city but to fill the temple with glory. Haggai predicts that the glory of the second temple would surpass that of the first. Whether it ever did so is doubtful. The glory of Solomon's temple is legendary, and we have little reliable information about it. But the second temple would have a glorious history of its own, whether it fulfilled Haggai's expectations or not.

THE THIRD ORACLE

Haggai 2:10-19

2:10-14 Unclean offerings

The discussion of purity and defilement in 2:10-14 is exceptional in Haggai and indeed in the prophetic corpus as a whole. In this case Haggai does not simply deliver a straightforward oracle to other people. Rather, he is himself instructed to enter into a dialogue with the priests, and the dialogue becomes a source of further illumination. The dialogue with the priests begins with a request for a ruling about a question of purity. The priests were the people who had authority to give such rulings. There are two questions here. One concerns the distinction between sacred and profane, while the other deals with the distinction between clean and unclean. These two distinctions overlap, but they are not quite the same. Haggai's point seems to be that holiness does not rub off onto profane things, but uncleanness can be transmitted by contact from one object to another. This point is never made explicitly in Leviticus, where the main biblical discussion of such issues can be found. (Ezek 44:19 implies that priests can transmit holiness to people by contact.) The conclusion in verse 14, however, does not follow logically. We are not told precisely what the people are doing that makes them unclean. Perhaps the point is that they do not purify themselves adequately when they bring offerings to the temple. Consequently their offerings are unclean and unacceptable.

This passage is difficult to understand because of the lack of specificity. In the general context, Haggai is most probably trying to explain why his prophecy remains unfulfilled, by suggesting that the offerings of the people are defiled, but he does not tell us exactly why they are defiled.

2:15-19 Promise of immediate blessings

Haggai's main response to the nonfulfillment of his predictions is not to blame the people, but to reaffirm the prediction. The fulfillment has not come yet, but it will come "from this day forward" (2:15). He does not say "on that day and at that time" in the manner of Jeremiah 33:15, which assigns the restoration of the Davidic line to the indefinite future. Haggai's audience needs more immediate hope. He promises that even though the seed has not sprouted yet, it will do so forthwith. Such specific, verifiable prophecy seems ill-advised in retrospect. We do not know how it fared in this particular case, but there evidently was no reversal of fortunes on the scale that Haggai predicted.

THE PROPHECY TO ZERUBBABEL

Haggai 2:20-23

The final oracle of the book is dated to the same day as the previous one. As in 2:6, Haggai promises that God will shake the heavens and the earth. In this case, however, the concern is with political structures. In 520, the Persian empire was in turmoil, and the overthrow of kingdoms, or would-be kingdoms, was topical news. The reference to the overthrow of chariots and their riders brings to mind the Exodus, when the Lord threw horse and chariot into the sea (Exod 15:1). It also brings to mind the release of the Judeans from Babylon, which was a reenactment of the Exodus according to Second Isaiah (Isa 43:16-19). The idea that the Lord could shake up the political world order did not seem so unreasonable in light of the unexpected fall of Babylon and the struggles for the Persian throne.

Zerubbabel is designated as the servant of the Lord. This phrase could have many different connotations in different contexts. It is often used with reference to a king who is chosen by God. Jeremiah 27:6 declares that Nebuchadnezzar, king of Babylon, is the servant of Yhwh, chosen to exercise dominion over the whole earth. In Haggai 2:23, the motif of servant is complemented by that of "signet ring." The person who wore the signet ring was empowered to use the king's seal. Zerubbabel, however, is not the servant who uses the seal, but the seal itself. The image of signet ring is used in Jeremiah 22:24 with reference to the ill-fated king Jehoiakin: "As I live—oracle of the LORD—even if you, Coniah, son of Jehoiakim, king of Judah, were a signet ring on my right hand, I would snatch you off." The significance of this passage for understanding Haggai is that it shows that the image of the signet ring was applied to the kings of Judah. When Haggai says that God will make Zerubbabel his signet ring, he is prophesying the restoration of the kingship. Zerubbabel is the chosen of the Lord, language that would be used in later times with reference to the messiah. This prophecy was not fulfilled, and Zerubbabel never became king of Judah. Whether he himself had any such aspirations, we do not know. The hope that he might be the one to restore the line of David undoubtedly garnered him support and helped mobilize the people of Judah to rebuild the Jerusalem temple.

The effect of Haggai's prophecy

While his predictions were not fulfilled in any literal way, Haggai's prophecy was effective. He achieved what he set out to do, to have the temple rebuilt. The rebuilding of the temple was beneficial to the Jewish community, even if the conditions of life were not radically transformed. Whether the end justified the means might be debated. Of course, there is no reason to doubt that Haggai was sincere in his predictions and that he expected that a glorious future was at hand. Utopian dreams, however, have proven fickle for many prophets and visionaries besides Haggai. The strength of such visions is that they inspire hope and empower people to act in difficult situations. The danger, however, is that disillusionment may set in when the glorious promises are not fulfilled. Whether this happened in the case of Haggai, we do not know. All his prophecies are dated to the second year of Darius. The rebuilding was not even finished until four years later. On the one hand, the brevity of his career might be taken to indicate that he lost credibility. On the other hand, his prophecies were evidently treasured by the Judean community that preserved them and deemed them worthy to be included with the writings of the great prophets of old.

THE BOOK OF
ZECHARIAH

John J. Collins

INTRODUCTION

The book of Zechariah is one of the longest books in the collection of the Twelve Prophets, being approximately the same length as the book of Hosea. It is also arguably the most complex. Zechariah is mentioned together with Haggai in Ezra 5:1and 6:14, in connection with the rebuilding of the temple. Less than half the material in the book of Zechariah, however, can be attributed to this prophet. It is conventional to distinguish between First or Proto-Zechariah (chapters 1–8) and Second or Deutero-Zechariah (chapters 9–14). Some scholars further distinguish chapters 12–14 as Trito-Zechariah. Even within chapters 1–8, there is editorial material in 1:1-6 and chapters 7–8 that is not the work of the prophet himself. The origin of the oracles in Zechariah 9–14 is quite obscure. These chapters are among the most difficult passages to understand in the entire Hebrew Bible.

FIRST ZECHARIAH

Structure

The prophecies that may be attributed to Zechariah are found in chapters 1–6 of the book, more precisely in 1:7–6:15. Within these chapters there are eight visions and three oracles. The visions are 1:7-17; 2:1-4; 2:5-9; 3:1-5; 4:1-6a, 10b-14; 5:1-4; 5:5-11; and 6:1-8. The first oracle comes between the third and fourth visions (2:10-17). The second is inserted in the middle of the fifth vision,

in 4:6b-10a. The third oracle is found in 6:12-14. It should be noted that the division between chapters 1 and 2 is made differently in some Bibles. Zechariah 2:1-4 in the Hebrew, and also in the NABRE, appears as 1:18-21 in the NRSV and other translations, and the numbering of chapter 2 is different accordingly.

The visions of Zechariah are distinguished by the role of an interpreting angel. In the earliest prophetic visions, in the book of Amos, the prophet speaks directly with God (see Amos 7–8). In Ezekiel 40–48, the prophet has an elaborate vision of the new Jerusalem, in which an angel serves as guide. The interpreting angel is much more prominent in Zechariah than in any earlier prophecy. Later, the interpreting angel becomes a standard feature in apocalyptic visions, such as those we find in Daniel 7–8.

The visions of Zechariah are framed by sermonic material in 1:1-6 and chapters 7–8. This material resembles the Deuteronomistic writings in language and theme. While this material does not come from the prophet himself, it constitutes First Zechariah as a coherent book, with the visions of Zechariah as its core.

The historical context

The historical context of First Zechariah is essentially the same as that of Haggai. Zechariah 1:1 dates the beginning of his prophecy to the eighth month of the second year of Darius, after the second oracle of Haggai but before his third and fourth oracles. Date formulae are found again in Zechariah 1:7 (second year of Darius, twenty-fourth day of the eleventh month) and 7:1 (fourth year of Darius, fourth day of the ninth month). The other visions of Zechariah are not dated, but they are presumably concentrated in a short period, between the second and the fourth years of Darius (520–516).

Although the book of Ezra associates Zechariah with Haggai in rousing the people to rebuild the temple, the rebuilding does not figure so prominently in the book of Zechariah. The fifth vision, in 4:7, says that Zerubbabel will bring out the capstone for the temple. The oracle inserted into this vision is more specific: "The hands of Zerubbabel have laid the foundations of this house, and his hands will finish it" (4:9). Zechariah, however, seems to be concerned more with the status of Joshua and Zerubbabel than with the temple building.

The fourth vision, in chapter 3, presents a defense of the high priest when he is accused by Satan in the heavenly court. Joshua is acquitted, and his guilt is removed. Whatever his shortcomings may have been, Zechariah insists that he should be given unqualified support since he is "a brand plucked from the fire" (3:2). The condition of the small community returned from the Exile is too precarious to allow for criticism of its leaders.

The speech of the angel of the Lord to Joshua in Zechariah 3:6-8 concludes with a promise that "I will surely bring my servant the Branch." The word "Branch" or "Shoot" (Hebrew *tsemach*) is a messianic title. Compare Jeremiah 23:5: "See, days are coming—oracle of the LORD— / when I will raise up a righteous branch for David." Isaiah 11:1 uses different Hebrew words (*choter* and *netzer*) to express the same idea: "a shoot shall sprout from the stump of Jesse, and from his roots a bud shall blossom." In all these cases the imagery is of new growth. The passage in Isaiah envisions a tree that has been cut down, but a new sapling grows up out of it. Later, in the Dead Sea Scrolls, the expression "Branch of David" (*tsemach Dawid*) would become a standard way of referring to the messiah. The promise to "bring my servant the Branch," then, means that God is about to restore the Davidic line. The man who would restore it would be a messiah, in the sense that he would

be an anointed king who would revive the Davidic dynasty.

In the context of Zechariah, there seems little doubt that the figure in question should be identified as Zerubbabel. We have seen that Haggai declared Zerubbabel to be the Lord's signet ring. In Zechariah 4, Zerubbabel is the ceremonial builder of the temple. Temple building was the work of kings in the ancient Near East. While it might seem humanly impossible for Zerubbabel to assume the kingship, this does not bother Zechariah. The kingship will be restored not by an army, nor by might, but by the spirit of the Lord (4:6). Even if the obstacles in the path seemed like mountains, they would become a plain. (Compare the portrayal of the restoration from Babylon in Isaiah 40:3-5: "Every valley shall be lifted up, / every mountain and hill made low.")

The hopes of the Judean community were not entirely focused on Zerubbabel, however. In the restored Judah, the high priest would rival the king in importance. In the the fifth vision, Zechariah 4:3, the prophet sees two olive trees, flanking a lampstand with seven lamps. The two olive trees are identified in Hebrew as "two sons of oil" who stand before the Lord. The expression "sons of oil" is often translated "the anointed" (so both NABRE and NRSV). That translation can be questioned. The Hebrew word for oil in this passage (*yitshar*) is not the word usually used for the oil of anointing (*shemen*). Nonetheless, it seems clear that the two sons of oil here are Joshua and Zerubbabel. Joshua would be anointed as high priest, and Zerubbabel would be anointed if he were to become king. Later, in the Dead Sea Scrolls, we find reference to two messiahs, of Aaron and Israel. Zechariah provides the model for that later expectation. In postexilic Judah, the office of high priest was much more prominent than it had been before the Exile. Henceforth, the ideal Judean community should have two leaders, the high priest as well as the king.

The leadership of a high priest was not especially controversial in the context of the Persian empire. The restoration of the kingship was another matter. In 6:9-15 the prophet is told to collect silver and gold and make crowns. The Hebrew reads the plural, crowns, but it is emended to the singular in the NRSV because the prophet is told to "place (it) on the head of Joshua," the high priest. Presumably, Joshua would only wear one crown. The oracle that follows, however, seems inappropriate for the high priest: "There is a man whose name is Branch—and from his place he will branch out and he will build the temple of the LORD. He will build the temple of the LORD, and taking up the royal insignia, he will sit as ruler upon his throne. The priest will be at his right hand, and between the two of them there will be peaceful understanding." In this passage, the Branch is clearly a royal figure, and he is clearly distinguished from the priest. The reference, then, cannot be to Joshua. Neither is it likely that the prophet would place the crown on the head of the priest in order to signify that a king was about to come. It seems much more likely that this oracle was originally addressed to Zerubbabel. As we have seen, he was credited with building the temple in chapter 4. He was a descendant of David. He is by far the most plausible candidate for identification as the messianic "Branch."

It seems, then, the text of Zechariah 6 has been altered. Originally, the prophet was told to make crowns, presumably one each for Zerubbabel and Joshua. The reference to the crowning of Zerubbabel, however, may have been too much for the Persian authorities, or it may have seemed too risky to the editors of the book of Zechariah. Zerubbabel disappears from the historical record about this time. We do not know whether he was removed by the Persians, died of natural causes, or continued an uneventful life as governor. Neither do we know whether he at all condoned Zechariah's messianic fervor. But he was never crowned king, and the reference to his crowning was edited out of the text of Zechariah. The editing was not very thorough by modern standards. The plural word for crown was allowed to remain, and the oracle now addressed to Joshua seems glaringly incongruous. Ancient editing was seldom thorough. The Bible is full of loose ends that provide grist for the mills of literary critics. In this case, the loose ends give us a fascinating glimpse of a stirring episode in the history of Judah. Some five hundred years would pass before another live human being would be greeted with messianic language in Jerusalem.

The theology of Zechariah

The theme of messianic expectation looms large in the visions of the prophet Zechariah. It is by no means the only theme, however. Perhaps the most striking thing about these visions is their priestly overtones. Zechariah is concerned with the removal of guilt. This is apparent in the trial of the high priest in chapter 3. When Joshua is acquitted, he is clothed with clean, festal garments. The episode is part of a vision, but the symbolism of clothing was very important for the priesthood. (See, for example, Ezek 44:17-19.) Again, the seventh vision, in 5:5-11, imagines the removal of Wickedness, in the form of a woman, from Judah to Babylon. The symbolism of the vision recalls the removal of sin by the ritual of the scapegoat in Leviticus 16. The restoration for which Zechariah hoped was not just political independence, but also the removal of guilt from the land (cf. 3:9). Such priestly concerns were atypical of the earlier prophets, with the notable exception of Ezekiel, who is the prophet most closely related to Zechariah, apart from Haggai.

The sermonic passages that frame the visions in 1:1-6 and chapters 7–8 have a strongly Deuteronomic theology. The introductory passage in Zechariah 1:1-6 strikes a typically Deuteronomic theme by asserting that "the LORD was very angry with your ancestors" and that he would return to Judah if the people returned to him. The Lord had given warning through "my servants the prophets," but the people had failed to heed it. This introduction justifies God's punishment of Judah on the one hand, and on the other hand it warns the reader to pay serious attention to the words of the prophet that follow in this book.

Chapter 7 reports how people came from Bethel to Jerusalem to inquire about mourning and fasting. The response attributed to Zechariah recalls both Deuteronomy and older prophets, from Amos to Jeremiah: the Lord is not concerned with fasting but with kindness and compassion and the protection of the widow, the orphan, and the alien. The woes that have befallen the people are due to the fact that they have not obeyed the Law and the words of the prophets. The tone of this chapter is quite different from the visions of Zechariah and is similar to the sermonic prose sections of Jeremiah.

Zechariah 8 also brings to mind the prose sections of Jeremiah, especially the oracles of hope and consolation in Jeremiah 33. Jeremiah says that the voice of bridegroom and bride will again be heard in the now desolate streets of Jerusalem.

Zechariah looks forward to a time when the city will be filled with boys and girls playing in her streets. These hopeful predictions probably concluded the original book of Zechariah, as it was edited not long after the time of the prophet at the end of the sixth century B.C.

DEUTERO-ZECHARIAH

The last six chapters of the book of Zechariah are among the most obscure and difficult passages in the Hebrew Bible. Although they have been classified as part of the book of Zechariah since the Middle Ages, there is no mention of Zechariah in these chapters. They were simply copied after the oracles of Zechariah on the ancient manuscripts. The material in Zechariah 9–14, and also the book of Malachi, may be regarded as a collection of anonymous oracles that was appended to the collection of Minor Prophets.

Structure

These chapters are punctuated by markers at 9:1 and 12:1. In each case, the heading is "An oracle." The same heading is found in Malachi 1:1. These headings suggest a division of the text, but they do not guarantee that everything between them is coherent. Most of the oracles seem to have been composed with very specific situations in mind, but it is no longer possible to reconstruct these situations with any confidence. Zechariah 9–14 contains numerous echoes of, and allusions to, earlier biblical books, and some scholars have tried to view them as a kind of early biblical interpretation. But they do not present a clear or coherent interpretation of any older texts. These oracles were not composed as works of interpretation. They used allusions to older literature to address problems of their own time and place, just as we have seen in the books of Joel and Obadiah. In some cases, they may have been composed as purely eschatological scenarios that had no reference to any historical events, like Joel chapters 3 and 4.

Themes in Zechariah 9–14

Perhaps the most obvious theme in these chapters is that of kingship. Zechariah 9 begins by predicting that the Lord will destroy many of Israel's neighbors. Then in 9:9 the oracle calls on Zion to rejoice because "your king is coming to you, / a just savior is he, / Humble, and riding on a donkey, / on a colt, the foal of a donkey." The donkey was the vehicle of choice for the judges before the rise of the monarchy in Israel. The passage suggests a throwback to a style of rulership that was more modest than what prevailed under the kings of Israel and Judah. The chapter goes on to describe how God will liberate Jerusalem and manifest himself as the divine warrior.

The theme of rulership appears several other times in these chapters. Zechariah 10 complains that the people "wandered like sheep, / wretched, for they have no shepherd" (10:2). The oracle proceeds to express the anger of the Lord against "the shepherds." The identification of these shepherds is open to question. They are presumably the leaders of Judah in the postexilic period. The theme of the shepherd is taken up again in chapter 11. This passage seems to report a symbolic action by the prophet, in which he enacts the attempt of the Lord to be a shepherd to Israel, ending in the payment of thirty shekels of silver, the price of a slave. The prophet is then told to resume the role of the shepherd because a worthless shepherd will be raised up in the land. All too many rulers of Judah would fit this description. There is another enigmatic oracle against a shepherd in 13:7-9. The passage about the thirty pieces of silver is cited loosely in Matthew 27:9 (the story of Judas), where it is attributed to Jeremiah.

In Zechariah 12, the focus shifts to the house of David. This passage evokes the traditional theme of the assault of the nations against Jerusalem or Mount Zion (e.g., Psalm 2). In 12:3–13:6 we have a series of oracles introduced by the phrase "On that day." This formula is often used to introduce oracles that were added by editors to the prophetic corpus. Several items in these oracles are striking but obscure. The Lord will give victory to Judah first, so that the glory of the house of David and Jerusalem should not be exalted. This passage reflects an awareness of tension between city and countryside that is completely lacking in Zechariah 1–8. Nonetheless, it affirms that the house of David will be "like the angel of the LORD" (12:8). Another striking passage, in 12:10-14, speaks of a spirit of compassion on the house of David and the inhabitants of Jerusalem: "when they look on him whom they have thrust through, they will mourn for him as one mourns for an only child, and they will grieve for him as one grieves over a firstborn." The Hebrew text actually says, "on me, the one whom they have thrust through." Nonetheless, commentators have repeatedly tried to identify a reference to a human figure here. "[H]im whom they have thrust through" is identified with the crucified Jesus in John 19:37. All we can say with confidence is that the oracle looks forward to general reconciliation at some future time. It is uncertain whether the house of David was still an active force in Jerusalem when this oracle was composed. It may be that the whole passage should be read as a hypothetical, eschatological scenario.

One of the most intriguing passages in Zechariah 9–14 is found in 13:2-6. It envisions a time when prophets will be ashamed of their calling and refuse to acknowledge it. The shame surrounding the profession of prophecy probably arose from the conflicts between the prophets in the time of Jeremiah and again in the postexilic period, and also from the discrediting of prophecy because of failed predictions. Too many prophets had spoken lies in the name of the Lord. Prophecy lost its authority in the Persian period. We do not know the names of any Hebrew prophets after Haggai and Zechariah. In the Hellenistic period (after 330 B.C.) revelations were attributed to famous ancient people, such as Enoch or Daniel, rather than to their real authors. Increasingly, in the Second Temple period, religious authority was vested in the scribes, who were the interpreters of the sacred writings, rather than in prophets who claimed new revelation from the Lord.

The book of Zechariah ends in chapter 14 on a note that resembles such passages as Ezekiel's oracle against Gog of the land of Magog (Ezekiel 38–39). This is a purely eschatological fantasy. It has no reference to any historical event. Again, the myth of the assault of the Gentiles on Mount Zion provides the framework. In this case, the city will be taken, as it was by the Babylonians, but then the Lord will arouse himself. His appearance will be followed by earthquake and cosmic convulsions. The Lord will strike all the peoples who fight against Jerusalem, so that their flesh and even their eyes will rot. This violent image of revenge on the nations is followed by a more peaceful conclusion. All who survive of the nations will go up year after year to celebrate the kingship of the Lord at the festival of Tabernacles (Sukkoth) and Jerusalem will be a holy city.

Zechariah 14 is typical of the anonymous oracles that were added to the prophetic books in the Second Temple period. These oracles were not concerned with the events of the time in which they were composed but with the final resolution of history, the end of days. They reflect the gap between the glorious promises of the Scriptures and the paltry existence of Judah under the Persians and later under the Greeks. They express a longing for a time when the kingship of the Lord, God of Israel, would be revealed in all its splendor.

These oracles are sometimes called proto-apocalyptic. They resemble the apocalyptic visions that we find in Daniel or in the book of Revelation, insofar as they envision a definitive end of history. The commonality lies in the tendency to look beyond the particular circumstances of the present and to imagine the end of history as a whole. The apocalyptic literature, however, differs from these late prophetic texts in one crucial respect. In Daniel and Revelation, and in the writings attributed to Enoch, the climax of history is the resurrection and judgment of the dead. There is no hint of such expectation in any part of Zechariah. These oracles, then, are not appropriately described as apocalyptic. Rather they represent the latest phase of biblical prophecy.

COMMENTARY

PROTO-ZECHARIAH

Zechariah 1–8

1:1-6 Introductory oracle

The first six verses of chapter 1 are part of the editorial frame of the book. We are told that the word of the Lord came to Zechariah in the eighth month of the second year of Darius, some two months after Haggai began to prophesy. The actual visions of Zechariah, beginning in 1:7, are dated slightly later than the career of Haggai.

Zechariah is identified here as "son of Berachiah, son of Iddo." In Ezra 5:1 and 6:14, he is identified simply as "son of Iddo." A Zechariah son of Jeberechiah is mentioned in Isaiah 8:2. It may be that a scribe remembered "Zechariah son of Jeberechiah" and "corrected" the text of Zechariah 1:1. It is also possible that Iddo was an ancestor of Zechariah but not his immediate father. According to a priestly genealogy in Nehemiah 12:1-21, Iddo was a priest who "came up" with Zerubbabel and Joshua. In the next generation, Zechariah was the head of the house of Iddo. While there may have been more than one Zechariah son of Iddo in Jerusalem at this time, it seems quite likely that the priest of Nehemiah 12 is the same person as the prophet, especially in view of the latter's priestly theology. The designation of Zechariah as son of Iddo establishes both his priestly connections and his pedigree as being from the stock of the returned exiles. The name Zechariah means "the Lord has remembered" and seems highly appropriate for a prophet of the restoration after the Exile.

The initial oracle of the book has a Deuteronomic ring: return to me and I will return to you. The Deuteronomistic historians who edited the books of Kings had argued that the destruction of Jerusalem was punishment for the sins of previous generations. (See 2 Kgs 24:3-4, where the blame is laid specifically on the sins of the seventh-century king, Manasseh.) A close parallel to this passage in Zechariah is provided by Jeremiah 7:25-26: "From the day that your ancestors left the land of Egypt even to this day, I kept on sending all my servants the prophets to you. Yet they have not listened to me nor have they paid attention; they have stiffened their necks and done worse than their ancestors." The editor of Zechariah, then, subscribes to a theology that laid the blame for the disaster squarely on the people of Judah themselves, and that held that the prophets had given due warning. This theology is expressed many times in the postexilic period in communal prayers of confession: Ezra 9:6-15; Nehemiah 9:6-37; Daniel 9:4-19. The advantage of such a theology was that it instilled in the people a sense of responsibility. They were encouraged to see themselves as responsible for their fate, not victims of blind forces beyond their control. Nonetheless, the assumption that suffering is a punishment for sin is very problematic, as we can see in the book of Job. Whatever their sins, the people of Jerusalem had hardly deserved the destruction visited on them by the Babylonians. A major concern of this passage is to insist on the justice of God, appearances to the contrary notwithstanding. (For the call to "return" compare Jeremiah 18:11; 25:5; 35:15.)

The contrast between ephemeral human beings (the ancestors and the prophets) and the abiding word of the Lord is reminiscent of Isaiah 40:6b and 8b: "All flesh is grass . . . / The grass withers, the flower wilts, / but the word of our God stands forever."

1:7-17 The first vision

The series of visions that begins in 1:7 is also given a date. Hereafter no dates are given until the concluding editorial frame in 7:1. The name for the month is taken from the Babylonian calendar, which marked the new year in the spring.

In this case, the word of the Lord comes in a vision during the night. Night visions can hardly be distinguished from dreams, but they are not called dreams here. Dreams were an old and respected means of revelation in Genesis. Most famously, Joseph prospered in Egypt because of his ability to interpret dreams (Gen 40–41). Dreams were disparaged, however, by Jeremiah, who associated dreams with false prophets (Jer 23:25-28). It may be for this reason that Zechariah refers to his revelations as visions rather than dreams. Dreams are rehabilitated in the book of Daniel, where dreams and visions appear to be interchangeable (Dan 7:1-2).

What Zechariah sees in this vision is a group of four colored horses and their riders. These, he is told, are those whom the Lord sends to patrol the earth. The colors are normal horse colors and do not seem to have any symbolic significance. The number four represents the cardinal points of the compass, north, south, east, and west, with the implication that the Lord has the whole earth patrolled. The use of horsemen to patrol the earth is clearly based on the analogy of the Persian empire. The Greek historian Herodotus reports that people were amazed at the speed of Persian messengers. Fresh horses and riders were stationed at strategic points along their routes. (See Herodotus, *History*, VII, 98.) The horsemen go to and fro on the earth, as Satan is said to do in Job 1:7.

The report of the horsemen is that the whole earth is tranquil and at rest. At the time of Zechariah's vision, some of the rebellions that had greeted the accession of Darius had been put down, but the world was scarcely tranquil or at rest. There was peace in Judah, but this was not entirely a good thing since the restoration was not complete. Hence the question of the prophet: how long will you be without mercy to Jerusalem? The phrase "how long" is a typical element in psalms of lament (e.g., Pss 79:5; 80:5; 90:13). The prophet, like the editor in Zechariah 1:1-6, assumes that the desolation of Jerusalem is due to the anger of the Lord.

In 1:12, the prophet notes that the Lord has been angry with Jerusalem "these seventy years." According to Jeremiah 25:11-12, Judah and other nations would be subject to the king of Babylon for seventy years. Jeremiah 29:10 says that only after seventy years had elapsed for Babylon would the people be brought back to Jerusalem. Less than seventy years elapsed between the destruction of Jerusalem in 586 B.C. and the fall of Babylon in 539. At the time of Zechariah's vision, the seventy years were nearing completion. Zechariah evidently did not consider the initial return of the exiles to be a sufficient fulfillment of Jeremiah's prophecy, and he expected some greater fulfillment at the appropriate time. In 2 Chronicles 36:22 (= Ezra 1:1), the return under Cyrus of Persia in 538 is regarded as the fulfillment of Jeremiah's prophecy. Later, we find that Daniel regards the prophecy as still unfulfilled (Dan 9:2), and so the prophecy is reinterpreted as meaning seventy weeks of years, or four hundred ninety years (Dan 9:24).

Seventy years was a standard period of time in such oracles, perhaps because it roughly represented a lifetime. There is a Babylonian text that says that Marduk decreed seventy years of desolation for Babylon but later relented and shortened the time. Isaiah 23:15 says that Tyre would be forgotten for seventy years.

The force of the reference to the seventy years in Zechariah 1:12 is to suggest that the time should now be up. (Compare Isa 40:2, where Jerusalem is told that her service is at an end.) The calculation is approximate. (586 B.C. was not the only possible starting point. The Babylonians had already captured Jerusalem in 597 and taken some people into exile.) The Lord replies with comforting words (compare Isa 40:1).

The Lord informs Zechariah that whereas he was originally angry with Judah, he is now angry with the nations because the punishment they inflicted was heavier than what had been decreed. Here again Zechariah parallels Second Isaiah, who declared that Jerusalem had received double punishment for all her sins (Isa 40:1). The idea that the nations might incur guilt even when they were inflicting punishment that had been decreed by the Lord receives its classic expression in Isaiah 10:5-19, with reference to Assyria.

The key element in the restoration that was yet to come was the rebuilding of the temple. Without the temple, one could not claim that the Lord had again chosen Jerusalem and made it his dwelling place. The measuring line is stretched over the city for the purpose of rebuilding it. Compare the measuring rod in Ezekiel's vision of the new Jerusalem (Ezek 40:5). The motif of measuring will be taken up in Zechariah 2:5.

2:1-4 The second vision

Zechariah's second vision is much shorter than the first. The prophet sees four horns. It has been suggested that the object in his vision was an altar, with a horn at each corner. Such horned altars were very common in the ancient Near East. The horns are not interpreted with reference to an altar, however. In biblical imagery, horns symbolize might, especially military might, on the analogy of the horns of a bull or an ox. In Psalm 132:17, the Lord promises to make a horn sprout up for David. Deuteronomy 33:17 says of Joseph that his horns are those of a wild ox. Here we are told that the horns represent the power of the nations that scattered Judah. The number four does not refer to specific nations but rather suggests that the enemies of Judah came from the four corners of the earth.

The vision of four horns is followed by a vision of four workmen (some translations read "blacksmiths") who come to cast down the nations. The image of blacksmiths implies that the horns are made of iron or some metal. They will express the anger of the Lord against the nations for their excessive punishment of Judah. This is the shortest and most concise of the visions of Zechariah. In a sense, it complements the first vision that had said nothing about the punishment of the nations, even though the Lord was angry with them.

2:5-19 The third vision

The third vision is also brief, but it is complemented by oracular pronouncements. The vision proper is of a man with a measuring line who says that he is going to measure the length and breadth of Jerusalem. The vision picks up the allusion to a measuring line in 2:16.

Mention of a measuring line inevitably brings to mind the great vision of Ezekiel 40–48, where the visionary is accompanied by an angelic "man" who carries a measuring rod and who measures various structures in the vision. Ezekiel's vision is a utopian proposal for how an ideal Jerusalem should be built. It is a walled city, and access to various areas is carefully controlled to protect holiness and purity. This was one vision of how Jerusalem should be reconstituted after the Exile. It was not the only proposal on offer at the end of the sixth century B.C. The prophet of Isaiah 60–62 (who is variously identified as Second or Third Isaiah) also envisioned walls that would be built by foreigners. But unlike Ezekiel he tells Jerusalem: "Your gates shall stand open constantly; day and night they shall not be closed" (Isa 60:11). The purpose of the open gates is not to restrict access but to ensure that the wealth of the nations could flow into Jerusalem. The Isaianic prophet seems to be much less concerned with purity than was Ezekiel.

Because of their common priestly tradition, we might have expected Zechariah to share Ezekiel's vision of the new Jerusalem, but this is not so. Instead, an angel is sent to tell the "man" with the measuring cord that Jerusalem will be like the open country because of the multitude of its people and livestock. How then will it be protected? The Lord will be for it "an encircling wall

of fire" (2:9). This idea seems to be inspired by a Persian model. The royal city of the Persian kings, Pasargadae, had no walls. In and around it were several fire-altars, which were sacred to the high god of the Persians, Ahura Mazda. The city, then, was thought to be under divine protection. This is also how Zechariah conceives of Jerusalem. The Lord would also be "the glory in its midst" (2:9). The glory of the Lord normally resided in the temple. Here Zechariah imagines the whole city as a virtual temple. This idea is picked up and developed in a radical way in the book of Revelation in the New Testament. There an angel takes a measuring rod to measure the New Jerusalem (Rev 21:15). But there is no temple in that city for it enjoys the immediate presence of the Lord. It will not need the sun or moon, for the Lord will give it light (Rev 21:22). During the day its gates will never be shut, and there will be no night. (Cf. Zech 14:7.)

The brief description of the new Jerusalem is followed by an oracle calling on people to flee from "the land of the north" (2:10). The land of the north is Babylon. Babylon actually lay to the east of Jerusalem, but travelers from Mesopotamia to the Mediterranean seaboard, including invading armies, took a northern route to avoid the desert. Babylon is also "the foe from the north" in Jeremiah 6:22; 10:22. Here, the exiles who remain in Babylon are warned that Babylon is doomed to destruction and that they should flee from it and escape to Jerusalem. The Lord's special concern for Jerusalem is expressed in a striking phrase that has become a modern idiom: whoever touches you touches "the apple of my eye" (Zech 2:12, NAB).

Chapter 2 concludes with a prediction: "Many nations will bind themselves to the LORD" (2:15). Here again Zechariah was staking out a position in a lively debate as to how Judah should be reconstituted after the Exile. According to Ezekiel 44, the admission of foreigners to the temple was a violation of the covenant and a major cause of the disaster that had befallen Jerusalem. The remedy was straightforward: "No foreigners, uncircumcised in heart and flesh, shall ever enter my sanctuary: not even any of the foreigners who live among the Israelites" (Ezek 44:9). A diametrically opposite view is expressed in Isaiah 56: "The foreigner joined to the LORD should not say, 'The Lord will surely exclude me from his people'"

(Isa 56:3). On the contrary, according to this prophet (who is usually designated as Third Isaiah) the Lord will welcome foreigners who want to minister to him and serve him. He will accept their sacrifices and make them joyful in his house of prayer. Again, we might expect that Zechariah would agree with Ezekiel on this issue, in light of his priestly pedigree, but in fact his position seems to be closer to that of Isaiah 56. To be sure, we do not know precisely what it means to "join themselves to the Lord," but the tone of the passage is inclusive rather than exclusive. Like Third Isaiah, Zechariah entertains a vision of the future where foreigners will flock to Jerusalem to worship the Lord. Their presence in Judah will in no way detract from the holiness of the land, which derives not from human regulations but from the presence of the Lord, who will again choose Jerusalem as his dwelling place. The language of "choosing" is part of the traditional theology of the Jerusalem temple. Compare Psalm 132:13: "Yes, the LORD has chosen Zion, / desired it for a dwelling." This language also echoes Deuteronomy, where Jerusalem is "the place which the LORD, your God, chooses as the dwelling place for his name" (Deut 12:11).

This oracle ends with a call to silence before the Lord "who stirs forth from his holy dwelling" (2:17). We might compare Habakkuk 2:20: "But the LORD is in his holy temple; / silence before him, all the earth." In the context in Zechariah, however, the Lord is not in his holy temple because it has not yet been rebuilt. The location of the Lord's current dwelling is uncertain. In several old poetic passages, he is said to come from the mountains of the south. In Deuteronomy 33:1, he comes from Sinai and Seir, in Judges 5:4 from Seir and the mountains of Edom. In other passages, his holy abode is heaven (Deut 26:15; 2 Chron 30:27). It may also be that Zechariah envisions Jerusalem or Zion as the dwelling place of the Lord even before the temple is rebuilt—compare Zechariah 2:9, "I will be the glory in its midst."

3:1-10 The fourth vision

The fourth vision occupies all of the brief chapter 3 and is concerned with Joshua the high priest.

The scene resembles a courtroom: Joshua stands before the angel of the Lord, and his adversary stands at his right hand to accuse him. As

the NABRE translation makes clear, the Hebrew term for "adversary" (*satan*) is not strictly a proper name. The word is used with the definite article: "the satan." It is important to recognize that he is not yet the Devil of later mythology. The word "satan" is used a number of times in the Hebrew Bible for a human adversary. So in 1 Samuel 29:4 the Philistines refer to David as a potential satan. The angel of the Lord acts as a satan to Balaam in Numbers 22:22. In the postexilic period, however, the word comes to be associated with a special supernatural figure who acts as an adversary or troublemaker. The most famous example of Satan's activity is in the prologue of Job, where Satan attends a gathering of "the sons of God" and says that he has been "roaming the earth and patrolling it" (Job 1:6-7). When the Lord boasts of the righteousness of Job, Satan incites him to put him to the test. It is clear, however, that Satan is in the service of the Lord. He is not yet the Prince of Darkness, consigned to the nether regions, as he is in the New Testament. Another example of Satan's activity is found in 1 Chronicles 21:1. The parallel text in 2 Samuel 24:1 says that the Lord incited David to number Israel and Judah. According to Chonicles, it was Satan who incited him.

The judicial role of a satan can be illustrated from Psalm 109:6, where the psalmist complains that his enemies say, "Appoint an evil one over him / an accuser [satan] to stand at his right hand." In the Psalm, the accuser is presumably human. In Zechariah, he is one of the sons of God, as in Job, but he fills the same role of accuser or prosecuting attorney.

"The angel of the Lord" often appears in Genesis, where he is difficult to distinguish from the deity. In the postexilic period, however, angels become increasingly important. In the book of Daniel, they will be given names (Michael, Gabriel) for the first and only time in the Hebrew Bible. The increased importance of angels is evident already in the first two chapters of Zechariah, where they serve as interpreters and dialogue partners for the prophet. The angel of the Lord in chapter 3 is an authoritative figure who acts in the place of the Lord.

This whole scene is a heavenly projection, which dramatizes something that was going on in Jerusalem. Evidently, some people were critical of the high priest Joshua. We are not told what the criticisms were, but it is said that he was standing in filthy clothes, and this may be taken to mean that he was not without fault. In Zechariah 3, Satan becomes the mouthpiece of Joshua's human critics. He and they get short shrift, however. The response of the angel of the Lord is not based on a review of Joshua's conduct to establish guilt or innocence. Rather, any complaint against him is ruled out of order on the grounds that he is "a brand plucked from the fire" (3:2). The point is that the Jewish community had been on the verge of destruction. So little remained that the community could not indulge in the luxury of criticizing its leaders. We can certainly appreciate the logic of this position, but we must also note that Zechariah, like Joshua, belonged to the priestly class and that it was in the interest of that class, as of any people in positions of authority, to preempt criticism whenever possible. The high priest, however, occupied a very sensitive position in the Judean community, especially at this time when the temple cult was being revived. If he should be deemed impure or unclean, the entire cult might be rendered invalid.

The preemptive action of the angel of the Lord is symbolized here by a change of clothing given to Joshua. Clothing is often used to symbolize a change of status. Newly baptized Christians put on white robes. Newly ordained priests put on new vestments. In the case of Joshua, the significance of the new clothes is made explicit by the angel: "Look, I have taken your guilt from you" (3:5). Joshua was not necessarily without fault, but whatever his shortcomings, they would not be held against him. It is sometimes argued that Joshua's filthy clothes represent the sins of the people, which he bears in his capacity as high priest. There is no suggestion in Zechariah, however, that Joshua is bearing the sins of anyone other than himself. The point is that even though some of the accusations against him might be justified in other circumstances, they are disallowed in the present situation. The reclothing of Joshua does not correspond to any known ritual for the removal of guilt in ancient Judaism. The entire episode is a vision, not an historical incident.

The vision is followed by two oracular pronouncements from the angel of the Lord (3:7; 3:8-9). The first of these is an assurance to Joshua that if he walks in the ways of the Lord and performs his duties properly in administering the temple,

which is soon to be rebuilt, "I will give you access to those standing here." Those standing here are the members of the heavenly council or what we would call the angelic host. Prophets in ancient Israel claimed to have access to this heavenly gathering. Prophets are said to be present in the heavenly council in 1 Kings 22 (Micaiah ben Imlah) and Isaiah 6 (Isaiah). Jeremiah dismisses the "false" prophets who opposed him by saying that if they had stood in the Lord's "council" and heard his word, they would have brought the people back to the Lord (Jer 23:22).

The Hebrew Bible does not speak of priests in the heavenly council. In the Second Temple period, however, the heavenly council was itself conceived as a cultic assembly, a heavenly counterpart to what went on in the temple. The sectarian community known from the Dead Sea Scrolls, which had a strong priestly character, claimed to enjoy fellowship with the angels and to participate in the heavenly liturgy. The assurance given to Joshua here is that he will have the highest form of authority available to a human being and that he will have access to the presence of God in ways that are beyond the reach of most human beings.

The second oracular response to Joshua introduces a new subject. God is about to bring his servant, the Branch. As we have seen in the Introduction to Zechariah, the word Branch (Hebrew *tsemach*) has messianic associations: compare Jeremiah 23:5: "See, days are coming—oracle of the LORD— / when I will raise up a righteous branch for David." The promise to Joshua in this context is that the Lord is about to restore the kingship of the Davidic line. The imagery of the branch (shoot) suggests a sapling that sprouts from a tree that has been cut down. (Compare the reference to the stump of Jesse in Isa 11:1.) The language is somewhat veiled and allusive, but it would be clear enough to anyone familiar with the prophecies about the line of David in Jeremiah 23 or Isaiah 11.

We are not given much information about the Branch in Zechariah 3. Here the focus is still on the role of Joshua. The high priest and his associates are told that they are "signs of things to come" (3:8). The implication is that the restoration of the priesthood to Jerusalem is a sign of greater things to come. It will be followed by the rebuilding of the temple and the restoration of the kingship. Joshua and his associates have an important role to play in this development since they perform the rituals that take away the guilt of the land.

The stone placed before Joshua in Zechariah 3:9 has puzzled commentators. There are two possible interpretations. Some scholars identify the stone as part of the high priest's headdress, as described in Exodus 28:36-38: "You shall also make a plate of pure gold and engrave on it, as on a seal engraving, 'Sacred to the LORD.' This plate is to be tied over the turban with a violet ribbon in such a way that it rests on the front of the turban, over Aaron's forehead." Whether this gold plate can be called a stone may be debated. The main point of correspondence with the stone in Zechariah 3:9 is that it is inscribed. Other scholars relate this stone to the "select stone" or "capstone" that is in the hands of Zerubbabel in 4:10 in a passage that also speaks of seven "eyes of the LORD." While the precise significance of this stone is unclear, it evidently has symbolic significance in the construction of the temple. It may be a foundation stone, or it may be a capstone, to be put in place at a later stage of the building. If the latter interpretation is correct, and it seems to be the more plausible of the two, then the symbolic stone is initially placed before Joshua but will eventually be put in place by Zerubbabel. It signifies that the guilt of the land will be taken away when the temple building is completed and the proper rituals are again performed.

The vision of contentment in 3:10, of people sitting under their own vines and fig trees, echoes Micah 4:4 and 1 Kings 5:5. Similar words are attributed to the Assyrian envoy who tries to persuade the defenders of Jerusalem to desert in 2 Kings 18:31.

4:1-6a, 10b-14 The fifth vision

The fifth vision concerns a lampstand and two olive trees. The vision follows the format of the first three visions rather than the fourth: the prophet sees objects and asks the angel who is with him what they mean. Then the angel provides an explanation. In this case, the interpretation is delayed because of an oracle in 4:6b-10a. Commentators agree that this oracle is inserted here secondarily, as it disrupts the connection between the prophet's question and the angel's answer.

The angel awakens Zechariah "like one awakened from sleep" (4:1). Throughout these visions,

it is unclear whether the prophet is awake or asleep, and presumably this would also have been unclear to him. The angel rouses him, but not to his normal daily state of waking. He is awoken to another level of reality. What the angel does is transfer the visionary from one level of reality to another. The visionary state is neither sleeping nor waking in the normal sense of these terms but a third state, where the prophet encounters and talks with an angel.

The golden lampstand with seven lamps is called a *menorah* in Hebrew. In Jewish synagogues, down to the present day, a menorah is a candelabrum with seven lights. The name is normally reserved for a cultic object. (The only exception in the Hebrew Bible is in 2 Kgs 4:10, where it is used for an ordinary lamp.) The first occurrence of a menorah in the Hebrew Bible is in the account of the Tabernacle in Exodus 25:31-40; 37:17-24. There it is specified that it should be made of pure gold and have seven lamps. According to 1 Kings 7:49, Solomon had ten lampstands of pure gold made for the temple (compare 2 Chron 4:7). These lampstands were part of the plunder carried off by the Babylonians in 586 (Jer 52:19). The single menorah of Zechariah's vision recalls the account of the Tabernacle rather than Solomon's temple. The Tabernacle account, although it is found in Exodus, comes from the Priestly writers and is usually dated to the postexilic period. Of course, what Zechariah sees is in a vision, and it is not located either in the Tabernacle or in the temple. It does, however, suggest a cultic context and relates, perhaps, to what the prophet expected the temple to contain when it was rebuilt.

We are given some further details about the structure of the menorah. It has a bowl at the top, which would contain the oil for the lamps. The word translated "spouts" in the NABRE probably refers to the pinched lips (so NRSV) on the rim of the lamps in which the wick might be placed so that it would hang down into the oil. If this is correct, then each lamp could have seven lights. Several examples of such lamps have been found in archeological excavations. Some date as early as the second millennium B.C. The description of the menorah in Zechariah 4 is not nearly as elaborate as the one in the account of the Tabernacle, and it is not clear how far the two descriptions correspond. The menorah in Exodus clearly has seven branches, in the manner that is familiar from later menorahs. The branches are not mentioned explicitly in Zechariah, but they may be implied in the mention of seven lamps.

The seven lamps are explained in 4:10b as "the eyes of the LORD that range over the whole earth." There are many references to "the eyes of the LORD" in the Old Testament. According to Proverbs 15:3, "The eyes of the LORD are in every place, / keeping watch on the evil and the good." No one can hide from the Lord, "[f]or his eyes are upon our ways, / and all our steps he sees" (Job 34:21). According to Jeremiah 32:19, the eyes of the Lord are open to all the ways of men, and so he gives to each according to his ways. A close parallel to Zechariah is found in 2 Chronicles 16:9: "The eyes of the LORD roam over the whole earth, to encourage those who are devoted to him wholeheartedly." In the context of Zechariah, the expression may also be colored by the notion of "the eyes of the king," an expression used to refer to spies and informers in the ancient Near East, and especially in the Persian empire. Moreover, when Darius came to the throne, he was aided by a group of six conspirators, and the Greek historian Herodotus often refers to "the Seven" as an inner circle in the Persian administration. It is possible that the eyes of the Lord bear some analogy to this Persian inner circle, but the number seven often has symbolic significance in the Old Testament, which derives most obviously from the days of the week, or the days of creation in Genesis 1.

The menorah, however, is a cultic object, and its most basic significance is that it represents the presence of God. It has even been suggested that since the lamps are the eyes of the Lord, the candelabrum itself should represent the Lord. Zechariah does not make so direct an association, but the menorah certainly suggests the context of worship in anticipation of the rebuilt temple.

The menorah is flanked by two olive trees. The angel interprets the trees as "two sons of oil." This expression is frequently translated as "two anointed" (so both NABRE and NRSV) and taken to refer to Zerubbabel and Joshua. This interpretation may well be correct, but the matter is more complicated than it may seem at first. The word used for oil is not the usual oil of anointing (*shemen*) but *yitzhar*, a word that is used stereotypically in the context of bountiful harvest: the grain, the wine and the oil (Hos 2:10; Joel 2:19).

When people are symbolized by olive trees in the Hebrew Bible, the symbolism means that they are beautiful, productive, and important. In Jotham's fable in Judges 9:9 the olive tree refuses to leave its fatness, by which gods and men are honored, to rule over the trees. Psalm 128:3 speaks of "children like young olive plants around your table."

The most obvious point of connection between the two trees and the menorah is that the olive trees provide the oil for the lamps. This connection is underlined in verse 12, which speaks of the trees pouring out oil through the channels. We may infer that the two olive trees symbolize people who will provide for the cult. The high priest is a natural candidate, but the vision emphasizes that there are two such trees. In chapter 3 we saw that Joshua was not to be the primary leader of the Judean community. The Lord was about to bring "the Branch," or messianic king. We shall see that dual leadership is also implied in Zechariah 6. If the king is one of the sons of oil, however, the implication is that one of his major responsibilities is to provide for the cult. In fact, this is precisely the role of the prince in another text from the early postexilic period, Ezekiel 40–48. According to Ezekiel 45:17: "It shall be the duty of the prince to provide burnt offerings, grain offerings, and libations on feast days, new moons, and sabbaths, on all the festivals of the house of Israel." So, even if the expression "two sons of oil" does not mean "two anointed ones," the reference here is still to Joshua as high priest and Zerubbabel as governor or as king. Both high priest and king would be anointed, so the usual translation is not so misleading after all. The idea that there should be two anointed ones or messiahs appears again in the Dead Sea Scrolls, where it should be read as a protest against the attempt of the Hasmoneans, the successors of the Maccabees, to combine the offices of king and high priest and exercise both simultaneously.

4:6b–10a The inserted oracle

Into the middle of this vision there has been inserted an oracle addressed to Zerubbabel. It is not at all clear why this oracle should be inserted in this particular place. It may simply have been copied there by mistake in the course of the transmission of the text.

Zerubbabel is told that he is not to rely on human might or power but on the spirit of the

Lord. Scholars often object that no one could have expected Zerubbabel to restore the kingship because of the overwhelming power of the Persian empire. Zechariah, however, was not counting on military power but on the spirit of the Lord. In this respect, Zechariah resembles the earlier Jerusalem prophet, Isaiah, who warned Hezekiah not to rely on Egyptian aid because "the Egyptians are human beings, not God, / their horses flesh, not spirit" (Isa 31:3). Spirit represents the power of God that hovered over the waters at creation, in contrast to the merely human and natural resources of kings and armies. The promise that even mountains would become plains before Zerubbabel recalls the prophecy of Second Isaiah at the time of the restoration from Babylon: "Every valley shall be lifted up, / every mountain and hill made low" (Isa 40:4).

The prophet predicts that Zerubbabel will bring out a special stone for the building of the temple. The Hebrew can be taken to mean the first stone or the head stone (or capstone). This is presumably the same stone that was set before the high priest in Zechariah 3:9. It evidently had some symbolic significance for the temple building. Either it was the foundation stone, or it was a capstone for some part of the building. His action will be met with applause. There is further reference to a special stone in verse 10a. The latter reference is sometimes interpreted as a building deposit. It was traditional in the ancient Near East to deposit metallic tablets with writing on them in the foundations of temples. In the Persian period, the deposits often did not carry inscriptions. The context of 4:10a suggests that this stone or deposit is put in place when the building project is completed, not at its beginning.

However the stone is interpreted, the pronouncement in 4:9-10 is quite clear: "The hands of Zerubbabel have laid the foundations of this house, and his hands will finish it." Temple building was the prerogative of kings in the ancient Near East. It was probably inevitable that Zerubbabel's role in rebuilding the Jerusalem temple raised hopes for the restoration of the kingship. Zechariah is expressing his confidence that Zerubbabel would see the project through. The reference to "such a day of small things" (4:10) recalls the notice in Ezra 3:12-13 that the old people who remembered Solomon's temple wept when they saw the foundations of the new one (compare Hag 2:3). Zechariah expresses his confidence that even such people will rejoice when the project is completed.

5:1-4 The ~~sixth~~ *5th* vision

Zechariah 5 contains two visions that are closely related to each other. In the first he sees a flying scroll. This is a peculiar object for which there is no close parallel in the ancient Near East. It is twenty cubits long (about ten metres) and ten cubits wide. The length is not impossible, but it represents the upper limit of the length of a scroll. The great Isaiah Scroll from Qumran is 7.34 metres long. The main oddity of this scroll, apart from the fact that it is flying, is the ratio of length to width. The Isaiah Scroll from Qumran has a ratio of about 30:1. Zechariah's scroll is 2:1. Since he can see the whole scroll, it is presumably unrolled. This flying scroll, then, is more like a giant billboard than a normal scroll. It has been noted that the dimensions of the scroll are the same as those of the vestibule or porch (*ulam*) of Solomon's temple (1 Kgs 6:3), but it is difficult to see what the significance of this correspondence might be.

The angel interprets the scroll as a curse that is going out over the whole land, which will apply to thieves and other wrongdoers. There is some evidence in the Hebrew Bible for the use of a curse when the person guilty of a crime is unknown. In Judges 17:2 a woman from Ephraim is said to pronounce a public curse on the thief who stole her money. One purpose of the public cursing was to publicize the crime and ask for witnesses to come forward. (Lev 5:1 states that witnesses who have knowledge and fail to come forward are subject to punishment. Compare Prov 29:24.) A written curse was thought to have efficacy of its own. Numbers 5 describes a ritual for testing a woman suspected of adultery. As part of the ritual, the priest puts curses in writing and then washes them off into water that is made bitter with dust (Num 5:23-24). The woman must then drink the water. The curses which have thus gone into her are only supposed to take effect if she is guilty. Again, covenants and treaties were ratified with curses that were written down. Deuteronomy 29:19 says of Israelites who turn aside to serve other gods that "every curse written in this book will pounce on them." The writing down of a curse had a ritualistic effect. It gave the curse a kind of objectivity. The same was true of prophecy.

Compare the futile attempt of King Jehoiakim to destroy the prophecy of Jeremiah by burning it in the fire (Jer 36:23).

The curse written on Zechariah's scroll is said to go forth either over the whole land or over the whole earth. The Hebrew word *eretz* can have either meaning. Zechariah's concern was with the Judean community. He addresses Judeans in Babylon to tell them to go forth in 2:10, but there is nothing to indicate that he was preaching to all the earth. The curse most probably applies to people in the land of Judah. It does not require any human agents to implement it. It enters into the houses of criminals and consumes them. Destruction of a person's house as a punishment is widely attested in the ancient world and is still used by Israeli forces in the Palestinian conflict in the present. A notable parallel to Zechariah is found in the decree of Darius in Ezra 6 authorizing the rebuilding of the Jerusalem temple: "if any man alters this edict, a beam is to be taken from his house, and he is to be lifted up and impaled on it; and his house is to be reduced to rubble for this offense" (Ezra 6:11).

The curse in Zechariah 5 is not related to the temple building, however. It is invoked against ordinary criminals and sinners. We do not know how effectively law was enforced in Judah at this time. Zechariah's vision is an attempt to invoke supernatural deterrence. If people really believed that a curse could follow them into their houses, they would be less likely to engage in wrongdoing.

5:5-11 The seventh vision

The second vision in chapter 5 also has ritualistic overtones. In this case the prophet sees a flying container. It is called an *ephah*, which was a unit of measure, about two-thirds of a bushel. In this case the reference is evidently to a container in which grain might be stored. The angel informs Zechariah that this object contains "their guilt in all the land" (5:6). When the lid is lifted, Zechariah sees a woman sitting inside. She is identified as Wickedness, and she is transported to the land of Shinar. Shinar was the name used for Babylon in the story of the tower of Babel in Genesis 11.

Two aspects of this vision require comment: first the idea that Wickedness can be shipped off in a container, and second the idea that Evil can be symbolized as a woman.

The idea that Wickedness can be shipped away in a container brings to mind the ritual for the Day of Atonement in Leviticus 16. Part of that ritual concerns the scapegoat. The high priest, Aaron, is supposed to lay both hands on the head of a live goat and "confess over it all the iniquities of the Israelites and their trespasses, including all their sins, and so put them on the goat's head. He shall then have it led into the wilderness by an attendant. The goat will carry off all their iniquities to an isolated region" (Lev 16:21-22). The efficacy of such a ritual depends on the participation of the people and their desire to be rid of their sins.

The episode of the woman in the container in Zechariah 5 is not a ritual, but it resembles the ritual of the scapegoat in some respects. It shares with it the idea that wickedness can be treated like an object and physically removed. The Judeans who returned to the land of Judah after the Exile were burdened with a great sense of guilt. We have already seen a reflection of this in chapter 3, where the high priest Joshua was said to be dressed in filthy clothes. Joshua's sins were removed by divine decree. He was not required to repent. It seems as if Zechariah wanted similar absolution for all of Judah.

The Day of Atonement seems to have been a late addition to the cultic calendar of Judaism. It is conspicuously missing from the list of festivals that were observed in the seventh month in Nehemiah 8. In any case, no such rituals could be performed before the temple was rebuilt. Consequently, Zechariah's vision serves as a kind of substitute ritual. If one cannot perform a ritual that enacts physically the removal of evil, one can at least imagine such a removal with the aid of the prophet.

The goat in Leviticus is taken into the wilderness. In Zechariah's vision, wickedness is taken to Babylon and worshipped in a temple. For the survivors of the Exile, Babylon was the antithesis of Judah. If Judah stood for what was right, Babylon could be supposed to worship wickedness. Babylon here is construed as the Other, the dark shadow that is whatever Judah is not. Most peoples in all times and places have developed such negative views of the Other in order to safeguard their own sense of identity. Needless to say, this practice does not contribute much to understanding the Other and doesn't really tell us anything about the Other at all.

The second aspect of the seventh vision that requires comment is the fact that Wickedness is symbolized as a woman. The fact that she is given a temple in Babylon suggests that she is a goddess. The most likely candidates then would be the Babylonian goddess Ishtar or Asherah, who was worshipped widely in Canaan and Israel. The Hebrew word for wickedness, *rish'ah*, could be taken as a wordplay on Asherah. The female figure of Wickedness in a container also brings to mind the Greek story of Pandora's box. Pandora was the first human female, fashioned in the likeness of the goddesses and created to punish Prometheus and mankind. She received gifts from all the gods and was herself sent as a gift to Epimetheus, brother of Prometheus. Then she opened a large jar and released all manner of evils into the world (see Hesiod, *Works and Days*, 55–105). It is unlikely that Zechariah knew the story of Pandora. The fact that both he and Hesiod associate a woman with evil is probably due to the fact that both were men living in patriarchal societies, where men tended to conceive women as Other.

It is sometimes suggested that Zechariah's symbolism implies an interpretation of the story of Adam and Eve. It is true that in later tradition Eve is often blamed for the introduction of evil into the world. Ben Sira, writing in the early second century B.C., says, "With a woman sin had a beginning, / and because of her we all die" (Sir 25:24; compare 1 Tim 2:13-14). But Ben Sira was the first author in Jewish tradition to express such sentiments, and the statement is exceptional even in his book. There is no evidence that anyone associated the beginning of sin with Eve in the time of Zechariah.

Most probably, the symbolism of Zechariah merely reflects the tendency of males in a patriarchal society to project evil onto the other sex, just as Zechariah projects wickedness onto Babylon. Another example of this procedure, from the early postexilic period, is found in Proverbs 7, where temptation is symbolized as an adulterous woman. The fact that women are used to symbolize evil in the biblical writings is very unfortunate and has contributed to prejudice against women down through the centuries. In fairness, however, it should be noted that neither Zechariah nor Proverbs says that women are evil. In Proverbs 8, Wisdom is also personified as a woman. In Zechariah 5, the container with the woman/wickedness is carried away by two women who have wings like storks. These women are not necessarily evil, although not much is said about them at all. The unfortunate tendency to depict wickedness in female form is also found in the New Testament in the image of the whore of Babylon in Revelation 17.

6:1-8 The eighth vision

The final vision of Zechariah rounds out the cycle by using imagery that is closely related to the first vision. Again the prophet sees horses of four different colors. This time they are yoked to chariots. In the ancient world, chariots were the mode of transportation of kings and nobles. They are also the vehicles of gods. Chariots often figure in theophanies of the Lord. So in Isaiah 66:15 we are told that "the Lord will come in fire, / his chariots like the stormwind," and in Jeremiah 4:13, "See! like storm clouds he advances, / like a whirlwind, his chariots." In Psalm 68:18 "God's chariots were myriad, thousands upon thousands" as he advances from Mount Sinai.

In Zechariah's vision, the chariots are sent out by the Lord to patrol the earth, like the horsemen in chapter 1. They are identified with the four winds of heaven. (Compare the association of chariots with stormwinds in Isa 66:15 and Jer 4:13.) The place from which they emerge, between two mountains, is the place of the sunrise in Babylonian mythology. The implication of the vision is that the four winds of heaven are the Lord's patrol, and they signify his complete control over the earth.

The most puzzling statement in this vision is in verse 8: "See, those who go forth to the land of the north provide rest for my spirit in the land of the north." In biblical prophecy, the land of the north is Babylon, its actual location notwithstanding. Compare Zechariah 2:10, where the exiles are told to flee from the land of the north, and the motif of the foe from the north in Jeremiah 6:22; 10:22. This vision, then, continues the concern with Babylon that we saw in chapter 5. There we were told that Wickedness would be made to rest in Babylon. In this vision, the Lord's spirit rests there too. At the end of Zechariah's visions, even Babylon is subject to the Lord's control.

The precise relation between this vision and the prophet's first vision in 1:7-11 is not easy to discern. The two visions are obviously bookends.

The cycle of visions begins and ends with an assertion of divine control. In chapter 1, the state of universal peace provides the occasion for a plea to the Lord to remember Jerusalem and restore it. It may be that a similar plea is implied in chapter 6. If the spirit of the Lord comes to rest in the land of the north, perhaps it will impel the remaining Judean exiles to return home. The implications for the restoration of Judah are then spelled out in Zechariah 6:9-15. This passage complements the final vision in the same way that 1:12-17 complemented the first one.

6:9-15 A final oracle

The word of the Lord that comes to Zechariah in 6:9 is different from the words in 1:14 or 4:8. In this case, the prophet is instructed not only to deliver the oracle but to do something. He is told to take silver and gold from a group of returned exiles and have crowns made. This passage highlights the continued importance of the Babylonian Diaspora for the people who had returned to Judah. The people in Babylon were better off and had more resources. Their reward for their contribution would be that the crowns would be a memorial offering in the temple, honoring the donors. We see here a pattern that would be typical of Judaism in the Second Temple period and that persists in Israel at the present time. Ever after the Babylonian Exile, Jews have been scattered in foreign lands, and those in the Diaspora have often had more resources at their disposal than those who returned to the land of Israel. Throughout the Second Temple period, the prosperity of Jerusalem was enhanced by pilgrims who returned to build the temple. When Zechariah says that "they who are from afar will come and build the temple of the LORD" (6:15), he is recognizing the need of the Jerusalem community for help from their brethren in Babylon. The returnees had struggled for twenty years and had not succeeded in rebuilding the temple. It may be that Zechariah hoped that one of the effects of the spirit of the Lord in the land of the north would be a spirit of generosity on the part of the exiles toward the homeland.

As we have noted in the Introduction to Zechariah above, the Hebrew text says that the prophet was to make crowns, in the plural. We should expect that he would make two crowns, one for Zerubbabel and one for Joshua. As the text stands,

only one figure is crowned, Joshua, but the oracle that is addressed to him seems to have been designed for Zerubbabel.

It should be noted that crowning, in itself, did not have the significance of making someone king in ancient Israel. Not only was a crown as appropriate for a high priest as for a king, but the act of inauguration for either office was anointing rather than crowning. (Crowns did come to signify kingship in the Hellenistic period and were worn by the Hasmoneans, the descendants of the Maccabees, when they restored kingship in Jerusalem around 100 B.C.) Nonetheless, crowns were symbols of great honor, and to place a crown on the head of a governor would indicate that he was being elevated in status.

The oracle addressed to Joshua when the crown is placed on his head was clearly composed with reference to Zerubbabel. The statement "There is a man whose name is Branch" (6:12) can only refer to the person on whose head the crown is being placed. We have seen already that this was a messianic title, as in Jeremiah 23:5, that was used for a king, not a priest. It is clear from 4:6-10a that Zerubbabel was the person credited with rebuilding the temple of the Lord, the task assigned to the Branch here. Moreover, the oracle makes a clear distinction between the Branch, who will sit as ruler on his throne, and the priest, with whom he will have a friendly understanding. The picture here is consistent with what we have found throughout the visions of Zechariah. There were to be two "sons of oil," two leaders in the community, a king and a priest. The king's authority would be somewhat restricted relative to what kings had enjoyed before the Exile, but it would only be qualified by the friendly cooperation of the priest and the heightened responsibility for the temple cult. Presumably, Zechariah had another oracle for the high priest, but this one can only have been intended to encourage Zerubbabel to assume the kingship.

But Zerubbabel never became king. Whether he himself had any aspirations to kingship we do not know. Quite possibly, the Persian authorities got wind of Zechariah's preaching and removed Zerubbabel from the scene. In any case, he disappears from the historical record. The editor of the book of Zechariah discreetly eliminated all explicit reference to Zerubbabel from this passage. Fortunately, he left enough loose ends in the text to make it possible for later generations to reconstruct at least a little of an exciting period in the history of Judah.

7:1-14 A question about fasting

The transition to the prose editorial material in chapter 7 is marked by the first date formula since the introduction of the first vision in 1:7: "In the fourth year of Darius . . . on the fourth day of the ninth month, Kislev." This episode, then, is dated approximately two years after the visions, in December, 418. According to Ezra 6:15, the rebuilding of the temple was not completed until the sixth year of Darius. It may be significant that Darius is here called "the king," as also in Haggai 1:1. In light of the expectation of the Shoot in the actual prophecies of Haggai and Zechariah, it is noteworthy that the editors of these books recognize that, at least for the present, the Persian monarch was *the* king.

This chapter also reports an oracle, but here the oracle is given as a response to an inquiry. The NABRE treats Bethelsarezer as the name of one person who sent another, Regem-melech, to make the inquiry. The Hebrew can be more plausibly translated as "Bethel sent Sar-ezer and Regem-melech," or, in the slightly paraphrasing translation of the NRSV, "the people of Bethel sent . . ." Bethel was about twelve miles from Jerusalem. It was an old cultic site, associated with Jacob (Gen 28). It was the location of one of the state temples of the northern kingdom of Israel (1 Kgs 12:29). Evidently it was still the scene of some kind of worship during the Babylonian Exile.

The two envoys are sent "to implore favor of the Lord." This expression is used to describe seeking divine assistance in face of extreme difficulty, e.g., when Moses seeks the favor of the Lord after the incident of the golden calf in Exodus 32:11. The request is directed to the priests and the prophets, who could act as spokespersons for God. The question is whether the people at Bethel should continue to fast in the fifth month as they had been doing for many years. It was in the fifth month that the Babylonians had burned the temple (2 Kgs 25:8-9), so the fasting was evidently a rite of mourning for the temple. The people wanted to know whether they should continue this ritual now that the rebuilding of the temple was underway. The reference to "seventy years" in the prophet's reply shows that the pe-

riod of mourning corresponded to the time that the temple was in ruins. (On the motif of seventy years, see the note on Zech 1:12 above.) Zechariah's reply also refers to a fast in the seventh month, presumably to commemorate the murder of Gedaliah, the governor appointed by the Babylonians (2 Kgs 25:25).

The prophet's reply seems harsh, questioning the motives of the mourners. Fasting was not what the Lord required. It was a human practice that, somewhat paradoxically, made the mourners feel better about their situation. In the eyes of the Lord, it was no different from eating or drinking. Instead, Zechariah hearkens back to the typical message of the preexilic prophets: what the Lord requires is justice and compassion.

There were certainly honorable precedents for fasting. Joel urges the Judean community to seek relief from the plague of locusts by turning to the Lord "with fasting, weeping, and mourning" (Joel 2:12-13). But Zechariah was not the first prophet to question the practice. Jeremiah 14:2 says that the Lord will not be moved by fasting on the part of the people of Jerusalem. Isaiah 58:4-5, a text that may be roughly contemporary with Zechariah, insists that fasting will not make the voice of the suppliants heard on high. Numerous examples can be cited from the earlier prophets to support Zechariah's view of what the Lord requires. See, for example, Jeremiah 7:5-7: "Only if you thoroughly reform your ways and your deeds; if each of you deals justly with your neighbor; if you no longer oppress the alien, the orphan, and the widow . . . will I let you continue to dwell in this place," or Micah 6:8: "You have been told, O mortal, what is good, / and what the LORD requires of you: / Only to do justice and to love goodness, / and to walk humbly with your God."

The preexilic prophets were very often critical of ritual, on the grounds that it distracted people from the true demands of religion. Such criticism, however, is not typical of Haggai or Zechariah, who were mainly concerned with the restoration of the temple cult. It is very unlikely that the response to the people of Bethel was actually uttered by Zechariah. Rather, what we have here is sermonic prose, colored by Deuteronomic theology, such as we often find in the book of Jeremiah. From the perspective of the Deuteronomistic editors, disaster had befallen Judah because the people would not listen to the words of the prophets, who called them away from ritual to a life of justice. Zechariah 7 thus picks up the message already expressed in 1:1-6. This editorial perspective is rather different from what we have found in the visions and oracles of Zechariah himself. The editors, then, had little patience with the people of Bethel and their worries about fasting. The abrupt response may reflect some tension between the returned exiles and the people who had stayed in the land. The returned exiles typically regarded themselves as the true people of the Lord and looked on the practices of the people who had remained in the land with great suspicion.

8:1-23 The ideal future

Chapter 8 probably concluded the original book of Zechariah. It is appropriate then that it should look to the future, in a spirit of hope. Here again there are close analogies with the sermonic prose in the book of Jeremiah, especially the oracles of hope and consolation in Jeremiah 33. The chapter is made up of a series of short oracles.

The statement that the Lord is jealous for Zion (8:2) echoes a sentiment already expressed in 1:14. Jealousy here is not sexual jealousy. The idea is rather that the Lord cares passionately for Jerusalem. The Lord was famously a jealous God (Exod 20:5) whose "jealousy" was often expressed as anger.

8:3 echoes 1:16 ("I turn to Jerusalem in mercy"). Both verses allude to the dwelling of the Lord on Zion. The "faithful city" recalls Isaiah 1:26: "After that you shall be called / city of justice, faithful city." For Zion as the mountain of the Lord, cf. Isaiah 2:2-4; Micah 4:1-3; Psalm 48:2.

8:4-5 pictures Jerusalem as again inhabited by old and young alike. Compare Jeremiah 33:11, which prophesies that the voices of groom and bride would again be heard in Jerusalem.

The question whether anything is too difficult for the Lord (8:6) is asked in similar terms in Genesis 18:14; Jeremiah 32:17, 27. Compare also the oracle to Zerubbabel in 4:6. The hope for the future of Jerusalem is not based on an assessment of human resources or political probability.

That the Lord should rescue his people from the east is to be expected, but the reference to the west is surprising in this context (8:7). In later times there was a huge Jewish Diaspora in the west. In the late sixth century b.c., the only Judean

exiles who could be said to be in the west were those in Egypt. It may be that the directions are just meant to be inclusive. Compare Isaiah 43:5-6, which also mentions south and north. The statement "I will be their God" implies a renewal of the covenant. Compare Hosea 1:8 (where the covenant is broken off), 2:25.

8:9-13 is an oracle of encouragement, which is also a virtual paraphrase of the oracles of Haggai. Compare especially the encouragement of leaders and people in Haggai 2:4. The implication is that the initial lack of prosperity after the Exile was due to the fact that the temple had not been built. Henceforth, fertility would be restored. 8:14-17, in contrast, links the well-being of Judah to the performance of justice, in the spirit of Jeremiah, and of the response to the people of Bethel in chapter 7. The two oracles are not necessarily incompatible, but they reflect very different emphases. The oracle in 8:9-13 is in line with traditional temple theology, not only in Jerusalem but throughout the ancient Near East. It is certainly the theology of Haggai and probably the theology of the prophet Zechariah. 8:14-17 draws its inspiration rather from Deuteronomy or from the preaching of earlier prophets such as Jeremiah.

The final series of oracles in 8:18-23 picks up the discussion with the men of Bethel in the previous chapter. Verse 19 refers to fasts not only in the fifth and seventh months but also in the fourth and tenth. According to Jeremiah 39:1-2, the wall of Jerusalem was breached by the Babylonians in the fourth month, while the siege had begun in the tenth month (cf. 2 Kgs 25:1-2). In this case, however, the prophet does not disparage the fasting or question its efficacy. Rather, he provides a positive prediction that these days of mourning will yet be turned into joy. Verses 21 and 22 are linked to the mission of the people of Bethel by the phrase "to implore the favor of the LORD." The prophet predicts that at a future time people will come to implore the Lord's favor even when there is no pressing crisis. Moreover, the suppliants will not be confined to the remnants of Israel but will include many peoples and strong nations. This vision of the future is closer to the inclusive vision of Isaiah 60–62 than to the restrictive, exclusive vision of Ezekiel 44.

The conversion of the Gentiles is also suggested in 8:23, the final verse of the chapter. The expression "in those days," like "on that day," often indicates an editorial addition and typically refers to an indefinite future time. Gentiles will be so eager to join themselves to the Judeans that ten will be grabbing at every individual. The term "Yehudi" properly means a person of the province of Judah. It is not quite correct to translate this term as "Jew" in the context of the late sixth century B.C. Even though many people of Judean descent lived outside of Judah at this time and were distinguished by their religious observances, the concept of Judaism as a religion independent of territorial borders did not develop until the time of the Maccabees, in the second century B.C. Zechariah, or rather the editor of the book, evidently shares the view of Isaiah 56 that Gentiles could join themselves to the Lord. This did not mean that they became Jews or Judeans. We do not know just what joining themselves to the Lord would have entailed. The point stressed in this oracle is that Gentiles, no less than Judeans, could seek the Lord and that they should do so by associating themselves with Judeans.

The motif of "people from nations, of every language" is picked up in the New Testament in the story of the first Pentecost in Acts 2.

DEUTERO-ZECHARIAH

Zechariah 9–14

Zechariah is not mentioned in chapters 9–14. The oracles in this section of the book are anonymous, and their place and time of origin is uncertain. The heading "An oracle" that is found in 9:1 is repeated in Zechariah 12:1 and Malachi 1:1.

9:1-8 An oracle against neighbors of Judah

The oracle begins with an assertion of the Lord's sovereignty over Syria (Aram) as well as Israel. In fact, Israelite prophets had always delivered oracles against foreign nations. See Amos 1:1–2:8; Jeremiah 46–51. In the case of Syria, it should be noted that the prophet Elisha exercised the power of his God to heal a Syrian commander, Naaman (2 Kgs 5). It should be noted that while the oracle asserts the sovereignty of the Lord over Syria, it does not predict its destruction.

The name Hadrach does not occur elsewhere in the Hebrew Bible, but it is attested in Assyrian texts from the eighth century as Hatarikka and in an Aramaic inscription as *hzrk*. The reference is apparently to a city in northern Syria. The latest attestation is from the early seventh century B.C. Because of the mention of Hadrach, it has been suggested that this oracle dates from the Assyrian period, but we do not know how long the name remained in use. Damascus was a prominent city throughout the first millennium B.C. It is difficult to imagine why this oracle would have been attached to the book of Zechariah if it dated from the Assyrian period. It is more likely that the prophet knew these places as part of a Persian province in the postexilic period.

The oracle proceeds to list places, moving southward. Hamath was another Syrian city. Solomon's kingdom allegedly extended from the entrance to Hamath to the river of Egypt (1 Kgs 8:65). Tyre and Sidon were the coastal cities of Phoenicia, in modern Lebanon. The wisdom of Tyre is the subject of a taunt song in Ezekiel 28:3: "Oh yes, you are wiser than Daniel, / nothing secret is too obscure for you." Ezekiel held that Tyre should be punished for its arrogance and pride. Here the emphasis is on her wealth, which the Lord would destroy. The Phoenicians were sailors and traders. There was a Tyrian colony in Jerusalem for the purpose of trade in the Persian period (Neh 13:16). Tyre withstood a siege by the Babylonians and was allowed to keep its king. It was besieged and destroyed by Alexander the Great.

The oracle proceeds down the coast to the Philistine cities: Gaza, Ashkelon, Ashdod and Ekron. Philistia is also associated with Phoenicia in Joel 4:4. There is some evidence that the Phoenicians controlled at least some of the Philistine cities. The Philistine cities were conquered by the Babylonians. There was a deportation from Ashkelon to Babylon as there was from Judah. But these cities prospered again under the Persians because of their strategic importance near the border of Egypt. Gaza was the only city in Palestine that opposed Alexander the Great. When it fell, its population was sold into slavery, and Gaza was reconstituted as a Greek city. It prospered again in the Hellenistic period. One could suppose that the prophecy that "[t]he king will disappear from Gaza" (9:5) is related to the Greek conquest, but it does not appear that any of these prophecies of destruction are after the fact or that they were ever fulfilled. Ashkelon did not become uninhabited.

They reflect what a Judean prophet wished would happen to the neighboring cities, not what actually happened.

9:6-7 are the only verses in this passage that give any reason for the destruction of Philistia. They refer to its pride, its bloody meat, and abominations between its teeth. The Philistines did not eat *kosher*; their customs were different from those of the Judeans, and as a result the latter regarded them as impure. The prophet invokes destruction on these cities just because they are different.

This oracle is not entirely destructive, however. It envisions the incorporation of the remnant of Philistia into Judah, as the Jebusites (the Canaanite people of Jerusalem before the time of David) had once been absorbed. The Philistines were not so impure as to be beyond redemption.

The final verse of this oracle, 9:8, says that the Lord will stand guard by his temple in Jerusalem to make sure that it will not again be overrun by foreigners. The sentiment is entirely understandable after the horrors of the Assyrian and Babylonian periods. The immediate context here suggests that the Philistines were perceived as a threat. We do not, however, know of any plausible context when this would have been the case in the period after the Exile. The oracle does not seem to be inspired by any historical grievance as far as we can tell. It seems rather to express resentment toward neighbors who were more wealthy and prosperous than Judah in the postexilic period.

9:9-17 The messianic king

Some scholars see all of chapter 9 as a unified oracle. On this reading, the destruction of Philistia paves the way for the exaltation of Judah. Most scholars, however, see the imperative "Exult" in 9:9 as the beginning of a new oracle. Zion is told to rejoice because the kingship is about to be restored. This theme links this oracle with the original visions of Zechariah. The king who is to come, however, is described as "[h]umble, and riding on a donkey, on a colt, the foal of a donkey." Hebrew poetry often repeats the same thing in slightly different ways. The donkey and the colt are one and the same (although they are interpreted as two animals in Matt 21:1-5). The donkey is a throwback to the period of the Judges, when leaders of the people rode on donkeys. Compare Judges 5:9-10: "My heart is with the leaders of Israel, / with the dedicated ones of the people—

bless the LORD; / Those who ride on white donkeys, / seated on saddle rugs . . . those who travel the road." In the second millennium, even kings rode donkeys. Under the monarchy, however, the preference was for the more powerful horse. Horses were especially desirable for the military.

Even during the period of the kingdoms of Israel and Judah, some prophetic voices were critical of the militarism of the kings. So Isaiah 31:1 cries: "Ah! Those who go down to Egypt for help, / who rely on horses; / Who put their trust in chariots because of their number, / and in horsemen because of their combined power, / But look not to the Holy One of Israel nor seek the LORD!"

The law of the king in Deuteronomy 17:14-20 specifies that the king must not have a great number of horses and must not make people go down to Egypt to acquire them. The choice of the donkey as a mount, then, indicates that this is a chastened kingship. We find the hope for a similarly modest kingship in Micah 5:1-2, which says that the messianic ruler will come from Bethlehem, the traditional home of David's family, rather than from Jerusalem, the traditional home of the kings.

The king envisioned in this oracle is "a just savior" (9:9). The Judges were also saviors of Israel, people who delivered the people from their enemies. The king does not, however, aspire to be a warrior. Rather, he will banish the instruments of war: horse, chariot, and bow. Compare Isaiah 2:4 (Mic 4:3), where swords are beaten into plowshares. The fact that he is said to banish weaponry from Ephraim (the area in the central highlands of Israel that often stands for Israel as a whole), as well as from Jerusalem, probably implies that he will reunite the two kingdoms of Israel. In fact he is promised universal rule, "from the River to the ends of the earth" (9:10). The River is probably the Euphrates, possibly the Nile. This promise corresponds closely to the prayer for the Davidic king in Psalm 72:8: "May he rule from sea to sea, / from the river to the ends of the earth."

In verse 11 the prophet again addresses Zion, in the second-person singular. The "blood of your covenant" is an allusion to Exodus 24:8. The Sinai covenant is the basis of the Lord's obligation to Judah. The second half of the verse should be translated: "I have set free your prisoners from the pit in which there is no water." The release of prisoners recalls the mission of the servant in

Isaiah 42:7. The pit with no water recalls the incarceration of Jeremiah in Jeremiah 38:6.

Verse 12 should be translated: "Return to the stronghold, O prisoners of hope." The NABRE translation of the second part of verse 12, "I am restoring double to you," brings to mind another passage from Second Isaiah, Isaiah 40:2, which says that the Lord has returned to Zion "double for all her sins." The Hebrew words are different, however, and the translation of the verse in Zechariah 9 is uncertain.

Beginning in verse 13, the Lord himself takes on the role of warrior, using Judah and Ephraim as his weapons. The Hebrew text says that he will "rouse your sons, O Zion, against your sons, O Yavan." Yavan is Greece. Many scholars have concluded from this verse that the oracle was composed around the time of the conquests of Alexander the Great. The humble messiah, riding on a donkey, would present a very different view of kingship from that of Alexander. The reference to Greece is uncertain, however. The other verses in the oracle all have two lines (bi-cola). This one has three (a tri-colon). Moreover, the word Yavan, in Hebrew letters, is similar enough to Zion that it could be explained as a scribal error. If the reference to Greece is not original, then we have no idea of the setting of this oracle.

Verse 14 continues the portrayal of the divine warrior in traditional language. The Lord is said to come from the south (Sinai, Edom) in old poetic texts such as Deuteronomy 33:2 and Judges 5:4-5. Lightning is his arrows. Compare the poetic description of the Exodus in Psalm 77:18-19: "your arrows flashed back and forth. / The thunder of your chariot wheels resounded; / your lightning lit up the world."

9:15 describes the battle in which the Lord's people will prevail by his power. The second part of the verse is surprisingly gory, especially in light of the non-violent character of the messiah. They will drink blood like wine and be filled as the receptacles on the altar are filled with the blood of the victims. (The image of drinking blood is also somewhat shocking in a Jewish context.) This verse dispels any illusion that this oracle is pacifistic. The messiah preaches peace to the nations but only after they have been pacified.

The oracle concludes on a more pleasant note by invoking images of youths, new wine, and maidens in a time of peace.

There is very little evidence of messianic hope in Judah between the time of Zerubbabel and the first century B.C. For this reason, it would be very interesting to know the date of Zechariah 9. When messianic hope emerges in the Dead Sea Scrolls, we find a more militant picture of the messiah, and Zechariah 9 is not among the biblical texts cited. It is cited, however, in the New Testament in Matthew 21:5 and John 12:14-15 in the context of Jesus' entry into Jerusalem.

10:1-12 Against the shepherds

The oracle in chapter 10 lacks all historical specificity. It begins by denouncing a pattern of popular religion. People ask the Lord for rain and have recourse to diviners. Teraphim were household cult objects of some sort (see Gen 31:19, 30-35; Judg 17:5). They may have been representations of family ancestors. Divination refers to attempts to discover the future or the will of the gods by ritual means. Most forms of divination are condemned in Deuteronomy 18:9-14. Dreams are regarded with suspicion in Deuteronomy 13:6 and Jeremiah 23:25-32. This oracle, however, says that these people are like sheep who have no shepherd. (Compare 1 Kgs 22:17, where the image is used of an army whose king is killed in battle.) The blame for their conduct, then, falls largely on their leaders.

The shepherd is a popular metaphor for leadership in the ancient Near East. It is used primarily as a royal image, with reference to God (Ps 23:1), or to human kings (Mic 5:3, the messiah; Isa 44:28, Cyrus), but it can also refer to other leaders, such as priests. Jeremiah 3:15 refers to shepherds who will feed you with knowledge and understanding. Both Jeremiah (23:1-4; 25:34-38) and Ezekiel (ch. 34) engage in lengthy diatribes against the shepherds of Israel. In each case the reference is to the rulers, but more than the kings may be included. Since there was no king in Judah in the postexilic period, the reference in Zechariah 10 must be to the ruling class, which would include the chief priests.

The oracle goes on to prophesy that the Lord will assume the role of the shepherd. Then Judah, instead of being sheep, will become a warhorse, and will prevail in battle by the aid of the Lord. (We are not told whom they will fight.) The second half of the chapter is a prophecy of the reunification of Israel (the northern tribes are represented as Joseph and Ephraim) and the ingathering of the exiles. No mention is made of Babylon, but the exiles will come from Assyria and Egypt. Egypt was always a popular destination for Judean exiles. There was a major Jewish community there in the Hellenistic period. The exiles in Assyria would be the lost ten tribes of northern Israel. These returnees would be so numerous that they would spill over into Lebanon. Verse 11 envisions a kind of reverse Exodus, in which the Lord will again smite the sea, but this time it is in order to cross over into Egypt and subdue it. The restored Israel, then, will extend far beyond the bounds of Judah, strong in the Lord and walking in his ways.

11:1-3 An oracle of destruction

This brief oracle is a call to lamentation, addressed to Lebanon and Bashan (northern Transjordan, east of the Sea of Galilee). The central image is the destruction of forests by fire. We do not know whether the reference is to an actual fire or whether the language is metaphorical. The oracle is placed here because it mentions shepherds (who again may be actual shepherds or may refer metaphorically to rulers). Mention of the shepherds links this little oracle both to the preceding oracle in chapter 10 and to the following one in chapter 11.

11:4-17 An allegory of shepherds

The remainder of chapter 11 is taken up with a highly complex oracle. The prophet is told to perform a symbolic action, of the kind that is familiar from the earlier prophets, especially Ezekiel. In this case, he is to take the job of a herdsman taking a flock to market. Sheep were raised for slaughter. It is not remarkable that the shepherds could sell them for that purpose without regret. The incident only becomes remarkable when it is viewed as an allegory for the way rulers treat their people.

The prophet takes two staffs, thereby hinting at the symbolic nature of his action. Normally, a shepherd would only need one staff. The reference to the dismissal of three other shepherds in verse 8 is obscure. At least it shows the Lord's impatience with these shepherds and a rather chilling willingness to let the flock suffer as a result. Each of the staffs symbolizes a covenant. The first, "Delight," represents the covenant with

all the peoples, presumably the covenant with Noah. The second one represents the brotherhood between Judah and Israel. Both staffs are broken, indicating that neither covenant is any longer in effect.

Verses 12-13 provide some reason for the prophet's rather cynical attitude. When he asks for his wages, he is given thirty pieces of silver, the amount of compensation paid when a slave is killed, according to Exodus 21:32. The prophet's reaction makes clear that the amount is trivial. Moreover, the Lord takes this amount as symbolic of the value the people attach to him.

The final action of the prophet is to take the appearance of a foolish shepherd. This indicates that the Lord is going to raise up a ruler who has no regard for the sheep, but this ruler too will be subject to judgment.

Some light may be shed on this oracle by comparing it with Ezekiel 37:15-28. There Ezekiel is told to take two sticks, symbolizing Judah and Israel, and to join them. This action indicates that Judah and Israel would be joined again, under the rule of a messianic king: "David my servant shall be king over them" (Ezek 37:24). The mood in Ezekiel's prophecy is upbeat and positive. Better times are ahead. In contrast, in Zechariah 11 the two sticks are broken, and the shepherd who is to come will be worthless. Zechariah 11, then, seems to be an exceptionally pessimistic, even cynical prophecy. It seems as if the Lord has grown tired of the ways in which human rulers neglect and abuse their flock. Instead of intervening, as in chapter 10, or sending a messianic king, in this case the Lord seems to give up and let human beings wreak destruction as they are inclined to do. This oracle probably reflects the demoralized condition of the Judean community at some point during the Persian period. Fortunately, it is not the last word of the book of Zechariah.

Zechariah 11:12-13, the passage dealing with the thirty pieces of silver, is cited in the New Testament, in Matthew 26:15, with reference to the reward paid to Judas for betraying Jesus.

12:1–13:1 The destiny of Judah and Jerusalem

The last cluster of oracles in the book of Zechariah (chapters 12–14) is framed by two oracles (12:1–13:1 and 14:1-21) that develop the motif of the attack of the nations on Mount Zion or Jerusalem. That motif can be seen in Psalm 2, where the nations are said to rage against the Lord and his anointed, and in Psalm 48, that tells of the panic of the hostile kings when they behold Jerusalem. According to this motif, all the nations would assemble to attack Jerusalem, but they would suffer defeat and consternation. Opinion is divided as to the origin of this motif. Some scholars think that it was inspired by the fact that Jerusalem was not captured when it was besieged by the Assyrian Sennacherib (2 Kgs 18–19; Isa 36–37). Others believe that it was a mythic motif, intrinsically related to the idea of a holy mountain, and that it was propagated as part of the mythology of Jerusalem from the time of David. The idea that Jerusalem could not be conquered because it was the city of the Lord had been shaken by the Babylonian conquest. Nonetheless, the motif survived and provided a storyline for imagining the end of history.

One telling of this story is found in Zechariah 12. The oracle begins by emphasizing the Lord's role as creator and his consequent omnipotence. Then Jerusalem is compared to "a cup of reeling for all peoples," that is to say, a bowl or goblet that will make the nations drunk so that they will stagger. This image is found in Isaiah 51:17, 22, where it refers to the cup of the Lord's wrath. (A different word for cup is used in the Hebrew.) The word translated as "cup" in 12:2 can also mean "threshold," and some scholars have thought that the allusion here is to Amos 9:1, where the Lord strikes the temple at Bethel and makes its threshold shake. A shaking threshold, however, means that the building is about to collapse. In Zechariah 12, the buildings of Jerusalem and its temple are secure. The point is rather that the nations that come against it will stagger like drunken men. A complementary image is found in 12:3: Jerusalem is like a heavy stone. Those who try to lift or move it only hurt themselves. The terror of horse and rider described in verse 4 is typical of the consternation that the nations are supposed to feel when they attack Jerusalem. According to this oracle, all the nations that come against Jerusalem will be destroyed (12:9).

One of the peculiar features of this oracle is the sensitivity to relations between the city of Jerusalem and the countryside of Judah. First, we are told that the siege of Jerusalem will also involve Judah, as it inevitably must (12:2). Then we are told that the leaders of Judah will recognize that the people of Jerusalem draw their strength from the presence of their God (cf. Ps 46). This is a reason for Judah to identify closely with Jerusalem. According to 12:6, the people of Judah will do most of the fighting in the final battle, so that the battle will not affect Jerusalem. But one should not conclude that Judah is subordinate to Jerusalem; the Lord will save Judah first to correct any mistaken impression. There is a hint here of rivalry or tension between Judah and Jerusalem or perhaps of traditional resentment of the pretensions of the monarchy on the part of the rural population. There may have been tensions between Jerusalem and the other towns of Judah in the Persian period. Unfortunately, we do not know the immediate context of this particular oracle.

Verse 8 looks for a transformation of the people of Jerusalem at the time of the final battle. The weakling will become a mighty warrior like David. The house of David will be godlike. In fact, the house of David had always claimed to be godlike. In Psalm 2:7, the Lord addresses the king as "my son"; in Psalm 45:7, the king is addressed as a "god" (Hebrew *elohim*); in Psalm 110:1, the king is enthroned at the right hand of God. In 2 Samuel 14:7, the wise woman of Tekoa says that the king is like the angel of the Lord, knowing good and evil. Such comparisons may be hyperbolic for rhetorical effect. This would at least seem to be the case with the woman of Tekoa. But kings in the ancient world were often thought to be of a higher order of being than mere humanity. This exalted view of the kingship is important background for the Christian belief that the Christ, or Messiah, is divine.

Zechariah 12:1–13:1 refers to the house of David five times. Such mention is rare in postexilic literature. The phrase does not occur at all in Ezra-Nehemiah, Isaiah 56–66, Joel, or Malachi. It is noteworthy that Zechariah 12 does not speak of an individual Davidic king but only of the Davidic house. We do not know how long the Davidic line survived or was traced in Jerusalem after the Babylonian Exile. Zerubbabel, in the late sixth century, is the last representative of the line in a position of authority, but 1 Chronicles 3 presents a genealogy that continues for six generations after Zerubbabel. We do not know, however, that the house of David exercised any leadership in

Jerusalem after Zerubbabel. The author of this prophecy assumes that Jerusalem would not be complete in the end-time without the house of David, however it was restored. Some Jewish writings of the New Testament period suppose that the "son of David" would come from heaven. (See 2 Esdras 12–13.)

The main emphasis in this oracle, however, is not on the future glory of the house of David but on the spirit of reconciliation that will prevail in the last days. The focus of the reconciliation will be a ritual of mourning for "him whom they have thrust through" (12:10). This passage is one of the most puzzling in the whole Old Testament. It has attracted a lot of attention, partly because it is cited in John 19:37, in the context of the crucifixion of Jesus, but also partly because it seems to be a highly specific reference. The Hebrew reads, "they shall look on me, the one whom they pierced, and they shall mourn for him . . ." Some scholars have defended this reading and argued that it is the Lord who has been pierced metaphorically. Most agree, however, that the text should be emended to read, "they shall look on him." In the context, it seems that the people who did the piercing were "the house of David and the inhabitants of Jerusalem" (13:1). Their grief, then, would indicate a great change of heart. No loss would be greater than that of a firstborn or an only son. (This is why the sacrifice of Isaac is so valuable, in Gen 22.)

The grief is compared to "the mourning for Hadadrimmon in the plain of Megiddo" (12:11). Megiddo was a major city in northern Israel. Because of its strategic location it was the scene of many battles and gave its name to Armageddon, the scene of the final apocalyptic battle (Rev 16:16). Haddadrimmon is most easily interpreted as a name for the Canaanite god Baal. Some scholars have attempted to interpret it as a place name, but no such place in the vicinity of Megiddo is known. The myth of Baal, which is now known from the Ugaritic texts, tells how Baal was swallowed up by Death (Mot). While he was dead, there was no rain and the earth shrivelled up, and so there was widespread mourning. Even the Canaanite high god El is said to join in the mourning. Eventually, Baal was rescued from Death by his sister Anath, and nature came back to life. It is quite plausible, then, that there would have been a Canaanite ritual of mourning for Baal, but

we do not have any other evidence that such a ritual was performed in the plain of Megiddo.

Many scholars think that the mourning in question was related to one of the most traumatic events in the history of Judah. In 609 B.C., King Josiah of Judah, the king who had instituted the Deuteronomic Reform, was killed at Megiddo by the Egyptian Pharaoh (2 Kgs 23:29-30). The account in 2 Chronicles 35:22-25 locates his death in "the plain of Megiddo." It also says that "all Judah and Jerusalem mourned him" and "all the male and female singers" recite their laments for Josiah "to this day." Chronicles may have been written about the same time as Deutero-Zechariah. It is difficult, however, to see why mourning for Josiah should be called "the mourning for Hadadrimmon."

Josiah is also sometimes identified as the one "whom they have thrust through," but as we have seen, the context suggests that the figure in question was pierced by members of the house of David, or inhabitants of Jerusalem, presumably close to the time when this oracle was composed. If the reference is to the piercing of a specific individual, then we have no way to make an identification. Some scholars prefer to understand the reference in a collective sense, like the servant of the Lord in Isaiah 53. In this case, the reference would be to dissension within the Judean community during the Second Temple period, and the one who was pierced would symbolize the people who lost out to those in power. There is plenty of evidence of dissension in the Judean community in this period, especially in Isaiah 56–66, and in the books of Ezra, Nehemiah, and Malachi. The house of David, however, is not mentioned in any of these books, and so none of them provide a plausible context for interpreting this passage. Most probably, the reference here is to an incident of which we have no further information, in which members of the house of David, or their supporters, killed or wounded an opponent. The oracle looks to a time when the victors will regret this violence and mourn for the one whom they killed.

The last verses of Zechariah 12 picture a scene of mourning in Jerusalem that will even involve the land itself (12:12). Women played a prominent role in mourning in the ancient world. Therefore the wives of each family are singled out for mention. The families listed are those of David,

Nathan (David's prophet), Levi (the priesthood), and Shimei. The name Shimei is borne by sixteen men or clans in the Old Testament. These include the second son of Gershon, son of Levi (1 Chron 6:2), and a cult musician under David (1 Chron 25:17). The most likely referent here is the Benjaminite kinsman of Saul, who held David responsible for the deaths of Saul's family (2 Sam 16). He cursed David but was spared. He was later killed by Solomon. In the context of Zechariah 12, Shimei symbolizes the kind of ancient feud that would be laid to rest by the eschatological mourning. The references here to houses of Nathan and Shimei suggest that the prophet is using the time of David as a paradigm and that he is not referring to actual families in Jerusalem in his time. Whether "the house of David" refers to the actual descendants of David, or is merely a code name for the people in power, is difficult to decide. In any case, "the house of David" is to be purified from sin in the last days.

13:2-6 The end of prophecy

The following oracle in 13:2-6 is part of the series of oracles introduced by the phrase "On that day" beginning in chapter 12. It may be related to the same eschatological transformation that is described in the previous chapter. This oracle is remarkable in the context of a prophetic book, as the Lord promises to take away not only idols from the land but also prophets. Criticism of prophets is not unusual in the Hebrew Bible, and much of it comes from prophets. Amos denied that he was a prophet, in the sense of membership of a prophetic guild (Amos 7:14). The most famous critique of prophets is found in Jeremiah 23:9-40. Jeremiah was often involved in disputes with other prophets, and it is apparent that such disputes continued in the postexilic period. (Contrast the attitude to the temple in Isaiah 66:1 with that of Haggai and Zechariah.) These disputes eventually undermined confidence in prophecy and led to its decline. The declaration in 13:5, "I am not a prophet. I am a tiller of the soil," closely parallels the disclaimer of Amos 7:14.

This passage is also of interest for the description of prophecy that it gives. Prophets were people who wore hairy mantles, in the tradition of Elijah and Elisha. They were also likely to have wounds on their chests. The origin of such wounds can be seen in the story of Elijah in 1 Kings 18:28, where we are told that the prophets of Baal slashed themselves with swords and spears as was their custom, to work themselves into an ecstatic frenzy. Evidently, prophets of the Lord could engage in such practices too, although they are not documented outside of this passage. This description emphasizes the wilder side of prophecy, which was an ecstatic phenomenon, not an exercise in enlightened rationalism.

13:7-9 Oracle to the sword

This brief oracle seems to have been placed in this context because of the motif of the shepherd, which we have already seen in chapters 10 and 11. Some scholars think that these verses should be connected to 11:4-17, but this is not necessary. The oracle invokes the sword against a shepherd, who is the Lord's associate. As we have seen, the shepherd is a ruler or leader. In the postexilic period, a shepherd who is the Lord's associate might well be a high priest, but we have no way of knowing which individual is in question.

The sword is not only invoked against the leader, however. The thrust of the oracle is that the people are to be winnowed and refined. There is an echo here of Ezekiel's use of the sword as a razor (Ezek 5:1-12) that also divides the people in thirds. In Ezekiel, the survivors are scattered to the winds. In Zechariah, the third category is to be refined and tested. With these people the covenant will be renewed: "They are my people" (13:9). The theme of refining is also found in Daniel 11:35 in connection with the martyrs in the time of persecution.

Zechariah 13:7b ("Strike the shepherd") is cited in Matthew 26:31, in Gethsemane before the crucifixion.

14:1-21 The final battle

The last chapter of Zechariah returns to the theme of the final battle for Jerusalem. In this case, the battle is identified as a day of the Lord, a motif that we have examined in connection with the book of Joel (see Joel 1:15; 2:1). In this case, unlike Zechariah 12, the city is taken and ravaged. This was not part of the old myth of the holy city, but it reflects the historical memory of the fall of Jerusalem, although the oracle may have been composed one or two hundred years after that event. The prophet knew that Jerusalem was not immune to capture, but he still expects the intervention of the Lord to defend it.

14:3-5 presents a strikingly vivid picture of the Lord as divine warrior, with his feet planted on the Mount of Olives, which splits under him. The appearance of the Lord is usually accompanied by convulsions of nature. (See for example the account of the revelation on Mount Sinai in Exodus 19.) The splitting of the mountain is not otherwise attested, but the same verb is used in Micah 1:4 to mean that valleys will burst open. The splitting of the Mount of Olives allows people trapped in the other valleys around Jerusalem (the Hinnom and Kedron valleys) to flee. The actual topography envisioned here is not clear, and it is interpreted in different ways. The Hebrew reads "the valley of my mountains" where the NABRE translates "the valley between the mountains" (14:5). "The valley of my mountains" may itself be scribal error for "the valley of the mountains," the phrase that is then repeated in verse 5. The reference is probably to the valley created by the splitting of the Mount of Olives. The flight from Jerusalem in the midst of this upheaval is compared to the flight from the earthquake in the days of King Uzziah in the eighth century B.C. The earthquake is mentioned in Amos 1:1. It had evidently made a lasting impression on popular memory. It is possible that the valley through the Mount of Olives is meant to serve not only as an escape route but also as the route for the triumphal arrival of the Lord. (Compare the construction of the processional way in Isaiah 40, where every valley is lifted up and every hill brought low.)

The Lord is accompanied by his holy ones. These are not human saints but the heavenly host. A classic description of a theophany, or manifestation of God, is found in Deuteronomy 33:2-3: "The LORD came from Sinai . . . With him were myriads of holy ones." The holy ones often appear in the apocalyptic literature from the second century B.C. onward. A notable occurrence is in Daniel 7:22, 13, where "the holy ones of the Most High" receive the kingdom that is given to the "One like a son of man."

The apparition of the Lord is followed by several major changes. The most fundamental is that the Lord becomes king over the whole earth and henceforward is the only god (14:9). The kingship of the Lord over the whole earth is asserted

repeatedly in the Psalms (see Pss 93, 97, 99) and was evidently celebrated in the temple cult in the preexilic period. This celebration, however, was anticipatory. The Lord was king by right, but his kingship was not yet actualized. Zechariah 14 looks forward to the day when it will no longer be contested.

14:6-7 affirms that there will no longer be inclement weather. Equally there will be no night or darkness. The latter motif is repeated in Revelation 21:25 that explains that the Lord will give light to the new Jerusalem.

The motif of fresh water flowing from Jerusalem is found at length in Ezekiel's vision of the new Jerusalem in Ezekiel 47:1-20. The eastern sea is the Dead Sea. The source of the water is presumably the Gihon spring, which is described in Psalm 46:5: "Streams of the river gladden the city of God." It is water that gives life. There may also be an echo here of the river that flows out of Eden in Genesis 2:10-14.

A final modification of the landscape is described in 14:10-11. The surrounding countryside will be made into a plain so that Jerusalem can be seen to be exalted. Henceforward, it will be secure.

The remainder of the chapter deals with the fate of the nations. All those who fought against Jerusalem will be afflicted with a plague that will cause their flesh to rot. This plague will afflict even the animals. This is the most explicit expression in Zechariah of the motif of vengeance, which we have seen consistently in the postexilic prophetic books.

14:13-14 describes how panic will seize the nations and cause them to fight against each other. This kind of universal conflict is typical of the upheavals of the end time in apocalyptic texts. See, for example, Mark 13:7-8.

It is most surprising in this context, however, to read that Judah will fight against Jerusalem (so NABRE, 14:14). Many scholars regard this statement as a later gloss. Other scholars hold that the verse should be translated "Judah will fight in Jerusalem." The Hebrew preposition b^e that is used in the phrase "fight against," commonly means "in." But it is difficult to see why Judah should be fighting at all in a situation where the nations are turned against each other. The sentence may have been added by a scribe to make the point that everyone will fight with their neighbors without exception. The last part of verse 14 speaks of the riches of the nations without reference to Judah or Jerusalem.

The book ends on a happier note. Not all the nations will be destroyed or afflicted by the curse. Some will be left, and these will come up to Jerusalem to worship the Lord as King and celebrate the feast of Tabernacles. Their attendance will be coerced. If they do not come they will get no rain (14:18). This threat is applied specifically to Egypt. There are several interesting aspects of this scenario. One is the connection between cultic observance and rain and fertility, which was very prominent in the book of Haggai. A second concerns the attitude to the Gentiles. They are cast in a subordinate role, to be sure, but they have a place in the cult of the Lord. This position is affirmed consistently throughout the book of Zechariah. Compare 2:7-9, 15; 8:20-23. It is in accordance with the position of Third Isaiah (Isa 56–66), which also affirms that Gentiles may join themselves to the Lord (Isa 56:1-8), and stands in contrast to the position of Ezekiel 44, where the holiness of Jerusalem has to be preserved by keeping the Gentiles out.

The contrast between Zechariah and Ezekiel in this regard is all the more remarkable in light of the many points of similarity between the two books, not least in their common interest in holiness. The holiness of Jerusalem is vividly expressed in Zechariah 14:20-21. Jerusalem will be so holy that there will be no distinction between ordinary cooking vessels and the temple vessels. Consequently, there will be no need for traders around the temple to provide pilgrims with wares that are appropriate to the temple. The word for "merchant" here originally means Canaanite, but it acquired the meaning "trader" because of the commercial reputation of the Phoenicians, the latter-day Canaanites. In Zechariah 14, the reference is clearly to merchants. This verse is important background to the action of Jesus in the Gospels in driving the merchants out of the temple (Mark 11:15-16 and parallels).

THE BOOK OF
MALACHI

John J. Collins

INTRODUCTION

The oracles that make up the book of Malachi were transmitted anonymously, like those of Deutero-Zechariah. The book is introduced as "An oracle" in Malachi 1:1. Compare Zechariah 9:1; 12:1. The name Malachi is taken from Malachi 3:1, where it means simply "my messenger." Unlike Deutero-Zechariah, however, Malachi is a coherent, well-structured book, which clearly bears the imprint of a distinct prophet. We shall follow the traditional convention and refer to this prophet as Malachi.

Structure

The book consists of six speeches or disputations, with two brief appendices at the end. The units are 1:2-5; 1:6–2:9; 2:10-16; 2:17–3:5; 3:6-12; and 3:13-21. (Some English translations, such as NRSV, divide the book into four chapters. Chapter 4 = 3:19-24 in the Hebrew and NABRE.)

The disputation is often regarded as an adaptation of a legal form, but it can also be modeled on informal disputes between people. There is some precedent for this literary form in earlier prophecy. Micah 6 is a good example. A characteristic feature of the disputation is the citation of the opponents' views. We also find this literary form in wisdom literature. It is especially prominent in the book of Ben Sira (e.g., Sir 15:11-20; 16:17-23).

Historical context

Unlike Haggai or Zechariah, the book of Malachi does not provide explicit dates and has few references to known historical events. The opening oracle (1:2-5) clearly presupposes the destruction of Edom by the Babylonians in the middle of the sixth century B.C. Reference to a governor (1:8) points to the context of the Persian period, after the end of the monarchy. The critique of the priesthood in 1:6–2:9 presupposes the restoration of the temple cult. There is little doubt, then, that the book is postexilic and later than Haggai and Zechariah.

A more controversial indication of date may be found in the discussion of divorce in 2:10-16. This passage also refers to the problem of intermarriage with people of other religions (2:11, according to the most plausible interpretation). We know that intermarriage was an acute problem in the time of Ezra (458) and that Ezra dealt with the problem by requiring the men of Judah to divorce their foreign wives (see Ezra 10). We cannot be sure that Malachi's discussion of divorce was a response to the actions of Ezra, but it would have made excellent sense in that setting. If this is indeed the setting of the oracles, then Malachi was active around the middle of the fifth century B.C., and the book would have been edited not long afterwards.

The fact that the book is placed at the end of the prophetic corpus invites the assumption that it is the latest book in the collection. This is not necessarily so. The book of Joel may well be later, and we have no way of establishing whether the oracles of Deutero-Zechariah are later or earlier.

The book of Daniel is certainly later (second century B.C.). Malachi is, however, one of the latest of the Hebrew prophets. The epilogues that were added to the book by an editor were intended not only as epilogues to the oracles of Malachi but to the entire collection of the twelve minor prophets.

Major themes in Malachi

The first oracle, in 1:2-5, focuses on a popular theme in postexilic prophecy: the punishment of Edom. Compare the discussion of this theme in the book of Obadiah. What we find in Malachi, however, is not an oracle predicting the destruction of Edom but rather a reflection on it after the fact. (Edom was destroyed by the Babylonians about 550.) The reflection is triggered by the question of the Judeans, "How do you love us?" The prophet responds by contrasting the fate of Judah with that of Edom. Judah was destroyed, but it was also restored. Edom, according to Malachi, would remain in ruins. Little is known of the history of Edom in the Persian period. This oracle is concerned less with vengeance against Edom than with reassurance for Judah.

The longest disputation in the book (1:6–2:9) is a critique of the priesthood. Unlike preexilic prophets such as Amos or Micah, or even postexilic oracles such as Isaiah 66, Malachi does not question the value or validity of sacrifice. His critique is that the sacrifices are being carried out improperly and that it would be better to close the temple than to make unworthy offerings. It is noteworthy that he traces the origin of the priesthood to Levi rather than to Aaron: He does not distinguish between Levites and priests who are descendants of Aaron (as in Num 8) or Zadok (as in Ezek 44).

In 1:11, Malachi makes a remarkable claim: "From the rising of the sun, to its setting, / my name is great among the nations; / Incense offerings are made to my name everywhere, / and a pure offering." This is not a claim about the eschatological future but about the prophet's own time. There were some Jewish temples outside the land of Israel in the second temple period. One was at Elephantine, in the south of Egypt, where there was a colony of Jewish mercenaries. Another, later, was at Leontopolis in Egypt, where the high priest Onias IV went into exile at the time of the Maccabean revolt (168–164 B.C.). The Tobiad family may also have had a temple across the

Jordan. These temples were in violation of Deuteronomic law, and it is unlikely that Malachi would have approved of them. It may be that the prophet regarded the worship of the highest God in any religion as worship of the Lord. King Cyrus of Persia is said to refer to the Lord as "the God of heaven" (Ezra 1:2). In Persian religion, the God of heaven was Ahura Mazda, the wise lord. It should be noted that this claim is made as part of a larger argument. The prophet is holding up the example of the nations in order to shame Judah for its shortcomings. Nonetheless, the passage implies a very positive view of the possibility of Gentile worship of the God of Israel.

The third disputation (2:10-16) deals with the problems of intermarriage and divorce. This is a very difficult passage, and the text is partially corrupt. We shall discuss it in some detail in the commentary. The interpretation proposed here is that Malachi disapproved both of intermarriage and of divorce. Intermarriage was a problem because it led people away from the worship of the Lord. (Remember the famous example of Solomon in 1 Kgs 11:1-8.) Divorce, however, was not the solution, as it violated the order of creation established in Genesis. Rather, the solution was to raise godly children and to make sure that the children were not lost to the Judean community because of the foreign wives. This interpretation is admittedly controversial, as any interpretation of this passage must be. It should be noted that Malachi is the only prophet who explicitly disapproves of divorce. The right of a man to divorce his wife in certain circumstances was assumed throughout the ancient Near East, including Israel and Judah. Only rarely was a woman allowed to initiate divorce. (Egypt was an exception in this regard, as was the Jewish community at Elephantine.)

The fifth oracle of Malachi predicts the coming of the Lord to his temple in response to the complaining question, "Where is the just God?" (2:17). The messenger, or angel, sent to prepare the way recalls the angel sent before Israel in the Exodus, and more directly Isaiah 40, where a figure in the divine council is told to prepare a way in the wilderness. The main issue in dispute in this passage is the identity of "the messenger of the covenant" (3:1). In this context, it is difficult to distinguish the messenger from the Lord himself. The "angel of the Lord" is similarly difficult to distinguish from the Lord in Genesis. The main focus of this passage is on the terror associated with the coming of the Lord, which recalls the motif of "the day of the Lord" in the earlier prophets (e.g., Amos 5:18; Isa 2:12-17; see the discussion of the day of the Lord in the commentary on Joel). Malachi's use of the "day of the Lord" resembles that of Amos, insofar as the coming of the Lord is to punish and purify his own people and their cult rather than to judge the other nations.

The fifth disputation (3:6-12) repeats some of the earlier critique of the cult and promises prosperity if the cult is reformed. The final disputation (3:13-21) returns to the question of theodicy and recompense. Noteworthy here is the distinction of a special group within Judah, "those who fear the LORD" (3:16). This group seems to be exempt from the prophet's critique, and was probably the circle to which he belonged. There are signs here of emerging sectarianism: not all Israel or Judah will be saved but only the righteous. This development can also be seen in Isaiah 56–66. The tendency to sectarianism becomes stronger later in the Second Temple period and becomes fully explicit in the Dead Sea Scrolls.

The epilogues

The book of Malachi ends with two short epilogues. The first (3:22) is a reminder to heed "the law of Moses my servant." The oracles of Malachi are not especially Torah-centered, although he was surely aware of the Torah and used it on occasion. The epilogue was added by an editor who wanted to affirm the primacy of the Torah. This epilogue was probably intended to apply to the entire book of the Twelve Minor Prophets.

The second epilogue is more closely related to the oracles of Malachi. In effect, it identifies the messenger who would prepare the way of the Lord with Elijah. Elijah had not died but had been taken up alive to heaven. He was therefore available to return and play a part in the last days. The passage in Malachi is the earliest evidence for the expectation of the return of Elijah. By New Testament times, this expectation was well established. (See Matt 11:14; 17:10-13, where John the Baptist is identified as Elijah.) In Jewish tradition, a place is set for Elijah at the celebration of the Passover.

COMMENTARY

1:1 Superscription

The heading "An oracle" is also found in Zechariah 9:1; 12:1, and suggests that this material circulated anonymously. Zechariah 12:1 similarly says that the oracle is "concerning Israel." In the postexilic period, the people of Judah considered themselves to be the heirs of Israel, even though the name was primarily associated with the northern kingdom.

Malachi is usually treated as a proper name in modern translations, although it is universally recognized that the word just means "my messenger." The Hebrew word *malʾak* is often used to refer to a heavenly messenger, or angel. In this case, it presumably refers to the prophet, who is not otherwise identified.

THE FIRST DISPUTATION

Malachi 1:2-5

1:2-5 Israel and Edom, or Jacob and Esau

The love of the Lord for Israel is asserted in Deuteronomy 7:8; Hosea 11:1. For the people of Judah, in the wake of the destruction of Jerusalem and the Babylonian Exile, the reality of divine love may not have been obvious, and indeed it is often questioned by people who have to deal with adversity. Malachi attempts to deal with this question by comparing Israel and Edom.

Jacob and Esau were regarded as the ancestors of Israel and Edom. Their story is told in Genesis 25–33. (See especially Gen 25:23: "Two nations are in your womb, / two peoples are separating while still within you.") They were twin children of Isaac and Rebekah, but Esau was the firstborn. Yet, with the assistance of his mother who preferred him, Jacob cheated Esau out of his birthright. Not only is Jacob not condemned for his trickery, but through it he obtains a blessing. Malachi goes further than Genesis in declaring, in the name of the Lord: "I loved Jacob, but rejected Esau" (1:3). The story of Jacob is perhaps the clearest illustration in the Bible of the idea of divine election. It is not suggested that Jacob was especially meritorious or that Esau deserved to be hated. (Many translations read "hate" here, but this term in the Hebrew Bible does not always have the same emotional force as its English counterpart and should sometimes be translated as "repudiate" or "reject.") Jewish identity through the centuries has relied heavily on the belief in divine election, and this belief has often been shared and accepted by Christians.

Malachi 1:3b changes the focus from Genesis to contemporary history. Edom has been laid waste, apparently by the Babylonians, about 550 B.C. Naturally, the survivors hoped to rebuild. The Lord declares that he will frustrate that hope. Unlike other prophetic passages that deal with Edom (such as Obadiah), Malachi does not accuse it of crimes that might serve as a justification for its desolation. The Lord is angry with it forever, but this seems to be a way of making the point that he gives Israel preferential treatment. The phrase "territory of wickedness" (1:4) may imply that the Edomites have acted wickedly, but it may just mean that the land is under a curse and suffers an evil fate.

This oracle concludes by declaring that the fate of Edom shows that the Lord is great beyond the boundaries of Israel. We shall find the concern for the Lord's universal rule again in chapter 2. The fate of Edom only proves the point if one assumes, as the prophet does, that the Babylonians were executing the will of the God of Israel when they ravaged Edom. This explanation would hardly have seemed plausible to the Edomites or the Babylonians.

THE SECOND DISPUTATION: THE CRITIQUE OF THE PRIESTHOOD

Malachi 1:6–2:9

The long disputation in 1:6–2:9 is a critique of the priesthood in Jerusalem in the Persian period.

It is not a critique of the cult as such. Malachi's complaint is that the cult is not being performed properly. To make his case, he begins with two analogies. The worshippers should honor the Lord as a son honors his father or a servant honors his master. Compare the argument in Isaiah 1:3 ("An ox knows its owner, and an ass, its master's manger"). This establishes the basic relationship and the honor due to the Lord.

1:7-14 Unworthy offerings

The prophet then accuses the priests of despising his name. The emphasis on the "name" recalls Deuteronomy 12:5 or 1 Kings 8:29. The Lord is present in the temple by making his name dwell there. The priests evidently did not intend to be disrespectful. Malachi makes his point by another analogy. The governor would be offended if someone offered him an animal that was blind or otherwise defective. Yet the priests offer such animals to the Lord. The reasons for such offerings are obvious enough. Animals were expensive, so people tried to economize by offering beasts that were sick and would be lost anyway. Regardless of intentions, such conduct showed that the cult was not being taken seriously. Sacrifices were supposed to cost the person making the offering, and the cost was indicative of the person's respect. The prophet's quarrel is not with people of limited means, who give what they can afford, but with those who do not give the best of their flock to the Lord (1:14).

Malachi declares that it would be better that the temple be closed than that unworthy offerings should be made (1:10). Like Haggai and Zechariah, Malachi took the cult and its rituals very seriously. The problem here is quite different from the one confronted by prophets like Amos in more prosperous times. Amos accused the Israelites of attaching too much importance to sacrifice. Malachi accuses the priests of his day of not treating sacrifice with enough respect.

Malachi 1:11 contains the statement noted in the introduction above, claiming that the Lord's name is great among the nations and that they bring him worthy offerings. As noted in the introduction, the passage is part of a larger argument. The virtues of the Gentiles are exaggerated to shame the Judeans. It is difficult to be sure just what offerings the prophet had in mind. It is unlikely that he was referring to Jewish temples outside of Jerusalem, such as the Jewish temple at Elephantine in southern Egypt. Any Jewish temple outside of Jerusalem was in violation of the law of Deuteronomy 12. The Persian rulers gave some support to the Jerusalem temple, and Isaiah 56:7 says that "my house shall be called / a house of prayer for all peoples," but Malachi states rather emphatically that the Gentiles brought their offerings "everywhere." Moreover, the Hebrew does not say that they offered sacrifices but that "incense offerings are made to my name." The argument requires that the prophet is referring to present practice, not to some future eschatological development. (For the idea that nations will fear the name of the Lord in the future, see Ps 102:15.) The most plausible explanation is that he considers worship of the Most High God in any religion to be, in effect, worship of YHWH. The Persian rulers referred to YHWH as "the God of heaven" (Ezra 1:2), and it may be that the prophet took their professions of respect at face value. We know of some Jewish writers in the Hellenistic period who held this view (a philosopher named Aristobulus and the author of the Letter of Aristeas in the second century B.C.). We find a similar idea in St. Paul's comments on "an Unknown God" in the Areopagus of Athens in Acts 17:23.

Even if the statement is hyperbolic, for polemical purposes, it nonetheless expresses a remarkable openness to the idea of Gentile participation in the cult of the God of Israel. In this respect, Malachi stands in the same tradition as Isaiah 56 and as the book of Zechariah, even though these other prophets only speak of this as a future development.

The entire theology of this section of Malachi is summed up in 1:14: "For a great king am I, says the LORD of hosts." The universal kingship of the Lord was a basic element of the traditional cult in the Jerusalem temple. See, for example, Psalms 47, 48, 93, 96–99. From this it follows that all peoples can and should participate in his worship. But it also follows that he should be shown the highest respect. "The Great King" was the standard way of referring to the Persian king, who was ruler of most of the civilized world at that time. Malachi's point is that the Lord too is a great king, an even greater one. It is unacceptable then to give him offerings that would not be fit even for a provincial governor.

2:1-9 The covenant with Levi

Chapter 2 begins with a threat to the priests. If they do not render sufficient honor they will incur a curse. The nature of the curse is a matter of some dispute. The Greek reads, "I will deprive you of the shoulder" (2:3). The Hebrew reads, "I will rebuke your offspring, or seed." The word for seed (*zera^c*) could be pointed differently (that is, the same consonants could be read with different vowels) as "arm" (*zeroa^c*), and this is probably the way the Greek translator read the text. Also the Hebrew verb can be plausibly emended to mean "cut off." If the reference is to an arm or shoulder, then the point is presumably that the priests will be deprived of the choice portions. The priests got their food, or some portion of it, from the sacrificial animals. According to Numbers 18:8, the offerings of the Israelites were given to the sons of Aaron as a priestly portion in perpetuity. (Compare the story of the sons of Eli in 1 Sam 2:12-17.) If the reference is to seed, then the implication is that the priestly line would be cut off. This is what happened to the family of Eli in 1 Samuel. The Aaronic line was promised a perpetual priesthood (Num 25:13), so any threat to the progeny would put that promise in jeopardy.

Moreover, the Lord threatens to "spread dung" in the faces of the priests (2:3). The Hebrew word translated "dung" is *peres*. It is not the normal word for dung but is used in ritual contexts (Exod 29:14; Lev 4:11; 8:17; 16:27; Num 19:5) to denote the undigested contents of the stomach. "Offal" rather than "dung" would be an appropriate translation. The offal was not burned on the altar but was burned outside the camp along with the animal's head, legs, and entrails (Lev 4:11-12). The offal of your feasts refers to the waste derived from animals sacrificed at festivals. To smear this offal on the faces of the priests would obviously pollute them and make them unfit for service on the altar.

The curses invoked against the priests are grounded in a covenant with Levi (2:4). There is no account of any such covenant in the Hebrew Bible, but its existence may have been inferred from the blessing Levi in Deuteronomy 33:9-11, which says, "they kept your words, / and your covenant they upheld." The passage goes on to speak of the teaching role of the Levites: "They teach your ordinances to Jacob, / and your law to Israel." Malachi 2:6-7 also speaks of a teaching role. There is a perpetual covenant with Phinehas, grandson of Aaron, in Numbers 25:12-13. Jeremiah 33:21 speaks of "my covenant with the priests of Levi," which cannot be broken any more than the covenant with David can be broken. Nehemiah 13:29 refers to "the covenant of the priesthood and the Levites." It seems then that by the Persian period there was believed to be a covenant with Levi, or the Levites, even if it was not explicitly narrated in the Bible. The covenant with Levi is described as one of "life and peace" (Mal 2:5). The covenant with Phinehas was also called a covenant of peace.

At least the covenant with Phinehas is presented in the Bible as an unconditional covenant, or a grant, like the covenants with Abraham and David. Such a covenant could be construed as a blessing. Compare also the priestly portion given to the sons of Aaron as a gift in Numbers 18:8. Malachi, however, views the covenant with Levi as conditional, like the covenant with Moses. The Mosaic covenant entailed curses if it were violated, and blessings if it were observed (see Lev 26; Deut 27–28). Malachi insists that the priests are subject to a curse for failing to observe the covenant with Levi. Moreover, their blessing, the gifts with which they were endowed, would be turned into a curse.

Malachi 2:5-6 offers a sketch of Levi as the ideal priest. He is characterized by fear of the Lord, true doctrine, and integrity. Malachi 2:7, then, extrapolates some characteristics of the true priest. The main emphasis is placed on his teaching role. In preexilic Israel, priests were expected to provide *torah*, but this was primarily a matter of instructing people on matters of ritual and purity. Haggai 2:10-13, where the priests are consulted on an issue of purity, provides a good example of traditional priestly instruction. In the postexilic period, however, the scope of priestly instruction broadened considerably and came to include the Torah in the sense of the full law of Moses.

Most remarkable is the statement at the end of Malachi 2:7: "because he is the messenger of the LORD of hosts." The word "messenger" is *mal²ak*, the word that is used for "angel" and the word from which Malachi takes his name. In Genesis, the messenger of the Lord is difficult to distinguish from the Lord himself. We have seen in Zechariah 12:8 that the house of David would be likened to a messenger or angel of the Lord in the

end time. It is difficult to imagine a more exalted ideal for the priesthood. The use of the term *mal²ak* is especially striking in Malachi since it is used in 3:1 with reference to the angel of the Lord and is used in the superscription of the book with reference to the prophet.

The glowing portrait of Levi only serves as a foil for the condemnation of his descendants. Their instruction leads people astray, and they show partiality in their decisions. Therefore they are held in contempt.

Throughout this discussion of the priesthood, there is no mention of Aaron. This is remarkable since the priesthood in the Second Temple period claimed descent from Aaron and the Levites were relegated to a supporting role (see Num 8:19; 18:1-2; compare Ezek 44:10-27). Malachi does not appear to recognize any distinction between Aaronic priests and Levites. In this respect, Malachi stands in the tradition of Deuteronomy 18, which regards the whole tribe of Levi as priests. We cannot safely conclude that Malachi's criticisms are meant only for the Aaronic priests and not for the Levites. He gives no hint of approval of any of the descendants of Levi. So while he does not appear to recognize the special status of the sons of Aaron, his criticism extends to the entire priestly class, Levites as well as sons of Aaron or sons of Zadok.

THE THIRD THROUGH SIXTH DISPUTATIONS

Malachi 2:10–3:21

2:10-16 Intermarriage and divorce

The third disputation, in 2:10-16, is the most difficult passage in Malachi and one of the most difficult in all the Hebrew Bible. The opening verse hints at division in the community that results from "profaning the covenant of our ancestors" (2:10). Judah has profaned the temple of the Lord and married the daughter of a foreign god. Some scholars take "a daughter of a foreign god" to be a goddess. The mention of a foreign god implies some involvement in pagan worship. The usual view of commentators is that the passage refers to marriage with foreign women, a problem that figures prominently in the book of Ezra. Those who married foreign women were likely to give some recognition to the religious practices of their wives. (Compare the story of Solomon in 1 Kings 11.) It is clear from the passage that the offenders had not abandoned the worship of the Lord but were engaging in mixed worship. It is clear that Malachi completely disapproves of this. He calls on the Lord to cut off anyone who might even befriend anyone who does this.

In 2:13 the prophet moves on to a second problem. The people complain that the Lord no longer accepts their sacrifices or hears their prayers. The reason? "Because the LORD is witness / between you and the wife of your youth / With whom you have broken faith, / though she is your companion, your covenanted wife" (2:14). In view of the reference to the daughter of a foreign god in the previous passage, it is often suggested that Jewish men were divorcing their Jewish wives to marry foreign women, but there is no actual evidence that this was the case. If it were, we should expect that the divorce would be mentioned first, before "a daughter of a foreign god," as the divorce would have cleared the way for the idolatrous marriage. The prophet does not call for the divorce of foreign women or give approval to divorce in any context.

There is explicit mention of divorce in 2:16, but it is obscured by textual difficulties. The usual translation, "I hate divorce," attempts to make sense of a difficult phrase, but there is no first-person pronoun in the Hebrew sentence. The word "hate" is commonly used in marriage contracts in connection with divorce. It means to repudiate one's spouse. Accordingly, the phrase should be translated, "for he has repudiated, sent away . . . and covered his garment with violence." The subject is indefinite. The force of the statement is that to repudiate and divorce (send away) is to commit flagrant injustice. The Lord, according to Malachi, disapproves. So even if the ringing phrase "I hate divorce" is a mistranslation, the passage is nonetheless a remarkable condemnation of divorce.

Divorce was perfectly acceptable in traditional Israelite religion. There is actually no law in the Old Testament regulating it. The passage that serves as a point of reference is Deuteronomy 24, which begins: "When a man, after marrying a woman, is later displeased with her because he finds in her something indecent, and he writes out a bill of divorce . . ." It is assumed that a man has the right to do this. The debate in Jewish tradition has been over the meaning of the phrase "something indecent," which has been inter-

preted in various ways, ranging from adultery to spoiling a meal. Prior to Malachi, no one in the Bible had challenged the right to divorce in principle.

Despite a common assumption, there is no indication that Malachi was only condemning the divorce of Jewish wives. The basis for the condemnation is given in 2:15, but the verse is unfortunately corrupt. Literally it reads, "And not one did, and had a remnant of spirit. And what does the one seek? Godly offspring. Guard your spirit, and let no one be faithless to the wife of your youth." The interpretation of the NABRE, "Did he not make them one, with flesh and spirit?" is probably correct. (This requires a slight emendation from *she'ar*, remnant, to *she'er*, flesh.) This would be a reference to Genesis 2:24, which says that man and wife became "one flesh." The remainder of the verse, "And what does the One require? Godly offspring!" can also be read against the background of Genesis. In Genesis 1:28, the only command given to the first couple is to "be fertile and multiply." On this reading, Malachi sees marriage as a covenant to which God is the witness and which has as its goal the procreation of godly children. One should safeguard that which is one's own—that is, one's wife and children. There is no place for divorce. The opening statement in 2:10 can now be read in a new light: "Have we not all one father?" The appeal is to creation, and it is meant to unify the community, not tear it apart.

The discussion of divorce in Malachi inevitably brings to mind the incident in Ezra 10 that is most probably dated to 458. On his return to Jerusalem, Ezra was horrified to find that Jewish men had married foreign women, and he compelled them to divorce the women and send them away with their children. We do not know the exact date of Malachi, but it clearly dates from the Persian period. If the reading of Malachi proposed here is correct, the prophet would have agreed with Ezra in condemning marriage with foreign women because of the danger of idolatry. But he would have disagreed emphatically with Ezra's solution because he saw divorce as contrary to the order of creation in Genesis. Marriage to foreign women was undesirable, but the real offence lay in turning to the worship of other gods. The solution to intermarriage was to raise godly children, imbued with the fear of the Lord.

Malachi's pronouncements on divorce mark a change in traditional attitudes to marriage. Divorce would still be accepted by mainstream Judaism, but Malachi points to the emergence of a stricter view of marriage as indissoluble. The basis for that view was found in the statement in Genesis that man and wife were one flesh. This stricter view was later developed in the Dead Sea Scrolls and receives a famous endorsement in the New Testament in the saying of Jesus: "what God has joined together, no human being must separate" (Matt 19:6).

2:17–3:5 The coming of the Lord

The fourth disputation is initiated by the people asking: "Where is the just God?" (2:17). There is no reason to regard this question as cynical. It is one that arises often in the Bible. The prophet Habakkuk complained that "the wicked surround the just" and that "justice comes forth perverted" (Hab 1:4). The psalmist of Psalm 73 admits that "I was envious of the arrogant / when I saw the prosperity of the wicked" (v. 3). Job complains bitterly that "the earth is given into the hands of the wicked" (Job 9:24) and that God is responsible. The people of Malachi's time probably had specific grievances, but the prosperity of evildoers is always a challenge for anyone who believes that the world is ruled by a just and omnipotent God.

Psalm 73 takes comfort in the belief that God has set the wicked on a slippery path and that their final destiny is ruin. Unless one believes in judgment after death, however, as the psalmist did not, this belief is difficult to maintain. Malachi takes a different tack. Justice is not a matter of the destiny of individuals but of the society as a whole, and the justice of the society is bound up with its practice of worship. Like many of the prophets before him, Malachi looks for the Lord to manifest himself and come in judgment.

Malachi 3:1 declares that "the lord whom you seek will come suddenly to his temple." "The lord" here does not translate the divine name, as is often the case in the Old Testament, but the Hebrew word *adon*. Nonetheless, there is little doubt that the reference is to YHWH, the God of the temple in Jerusalem. The account of the manifestation of God in 3:1-3 is complicated by the references to a messenger, who goes before the Lord to prepare the way and who is also described

as "the messenger of the covenant." The Hebrew word is *malʾak*, the word from which Malachi takes his name. It can refer either to an angel or to a human messenger. In Exodus 23:20, the Lord promises to send an angel before Israel, to guard it on the way. In that case the *malʾak* has a military function of wiping out the peoples of the land. (Compare the captain of the host of the Lord, who appears to Joshua before the attack on Jericho in Josh 5:13-15.) In Isaiah 40:3, a voice in the Divine Council calls out to prepare the way of the Lord in the desert for the return from Babylon. Again, the reference is most probably to an angel. We should expect, then, that the messenger in Malachi 3:1 is an angel too, despite the fact that the same word is used in the superscription of the book to refer to the prophet.

Scholars are divided as to whether "the messenger of the covenant," mentioned after the coming of the Lord, is the same as "my messenger" in verse 1. It is probably more economical to suppose that the two messengers are one and the same. The phrase "messenger of the covenant" can be taken to mean that this angel enforces the covenant or punishes those who break it. Again, the covenant in question is ambiguous. One thinks first of the Sinai covenant, but Malachi has already spoken of a covenant with Levi and even of a covenant of marriage (2:14). The point may be that this angel is concerned with fidelity to all covenants. The references to the "messenger" are enigmatic, however, and perhaps deliberately so. There would be much speculation on the identity of this figure in later tradition, beginning with the epilogue in Malachi 3:23-24, where he is identified as Elijah.

The main focus of this passage, however, is not on the messenger but on the coming of the Lord, who is compared to a refiner's fire. The whole passage is reminiscent of Amos's oracle on the day of the Lord in Amos 5:18-20. The people long for the day of the Lord's coming, but it will be an overpowering experience. Like Amos, Malachi sees the purpose of the Lord's coming as mainly concerning his own people. In Amos, he comes in judgment, especially on the cult, for which Amos has little use. In Malachi, the Lord also comes in judgment against sorcerers and other wrongdoers. His main purpose, however, is to purify the cult and the temple. This may be a harsh experience, but it is nonetheless redemptive. It will enable the people to offer worthy sacrifices again to the Lord. On the idea of purifying fire, compare Isaiah 6:7, where a seraph touches the prophet's lips with a burning coal. The motif of refining is also used in Daniel 11:35, with reference to the martyrs in a time of persecution.

3:6-12 The conditions of return

The fifth disputation has a strongly Deuteronomistic tone: return to me and I shall return to you. Compare also Zechariah 1:3. The prophet reiterates the charge that people are shortchanging God and repeats the Lord's demand for full measure in tithes and sacrifices. In the spirit of Haggai, Malachi promises that if the offerings are made properly, the floodgates of heaven will open in blessing. The danger of locusts (3:11) is vividly illustrated in the book of Joel. If the people fulfill their obligations they will not only prosper themselves but will also be a light to the nations.

3:13-21 Why serve the Lord?

The last disputation in the book picks up the complaint that was aired briefly in 2:17 about the apparent success of the evildoers and the lack of recompense for those who serve the Lord.

The solution of Malachi is to look for divine intervention and judgment in the future. This in itself was hardly novel. What is distinctive here is that the prophet singles out a group of those who fear the Lord. These people appear to be a minority in the Judah of their day. Compare the servants of the Lord in Isaiah 65:13-16. Here we read for the first time that the Lord keeps a record book recording the deeds of human beings. Later, such books play an important role in the final judgment in apocalyptic literature. (Compare Dan 7:10.) In the apocalyptic literature, the books determine the fate of people after death. Malachi does not envision judgment after death. For him, the purpose of the books is to ensure that justice is ultimately done on earth in a public way so that everyone can see the distinction between the just and the wicked.

The day of judgment is described in terms that are very similar to the day of the Lord's coming in 3:1-3. The Lord comes like fire, and the wrongdoers are burnt to ashes. Those who fear the Lord, however, will experience the fire as a healing sun. There may be some influence here from Persian eschatology. The Persians imagined a fiery judg-ment in which the wicked would be destroyed, while the righteous would experience the fire as if it were warm milk.

THE EPILOGUES

Malachi 3:22-24

3:22 Remember the law of Moses

As noted in the introduction, Malachi concludes with two editorial epilogues. The first calls on the reader to remember the law of Moses. The concerns of Malachi certainly had some basis in the Torah, but they were not simply a blanket appeal to the law, and they were guided by its spirit rather than by the letter. Epilogues such as this one were sometimes added by scribes to bring books into conformity with accepted norms. Another example can be found in Ecclesiastes 12:13: "Fear God and keep his commandments, for this concerns all humankind." While such advice is unexceptional, it tends to distract the reader from the specificity of the particular book and to impose a standardized view of religious observance.

3:23-24 The return of Elijah

The second epilogue is more creative. Here we are told that God will bring Elijah the prophet before the day of the Lord. In effect, the messenger of the covenant in Malachi 3:1 is identified with the returning Elijah. Elijah had been taken up alive to heaven (2 Kgs 2:11) and so had not finished his earthly life. Hence the expectation that he would come back. His assumption to heaven also gave him quasi-angelic status. This is the first time that the legend of Elijah's return appears in the biblical tradition. It would become well established by the turn of the era. According to Mark 9:11 and Matthew 17:10, the scribes taught that Elijah must come first. Presumably this means before the day of the Lord, as in Malachi, although the disciples seem to take it to mean before the coming of the messiah.

The mission of Elijah in Malachi is a remarkably gentle one, to reconcile fathers and children, lest the Lord come and strike the land with doom (3:24). In 1 Kings, Elijah is the model of zeal, and he acts violently in the name of the Lord. (See 1 Kgs 18:40, where he slits the throats of the prophets of Baal.) It is somewhat comforting to find that he is supposed to mellow before he returns for his second tour of duty.

THE
NEW TESTAMENT

THE GOSPEL ACCORDING TO
MATTHEW

Barbara E. Reid, O.P.

INTRODUCTION

In many ways the Gospel of Matthew holds primacy of place for Christians. It is the first book in the New Testament, and in patristic times it was thought to have been the first Gospel written. It was the Gospel most used in worship in the early church. And it has been the one most commented upon and preached, beginning with the first known commentary on the Gospel of Matthew by Origen (ca. A.D. 185–254).

Some of the best-loved passages in Scripture, as well as some of the most difficult sayings and teachings of Jesus, are found in this Gospel. This Gospel is distinctive for its emphasis on the Jewishness of Jesus, as authoritative teacher, whose life and ministry fulfill the Scriptures. Wisdom motifs also mark Matthew's presentation of Jesus. The assurance that Jesus is Emmanuel, "God-with-us," frames the whole Gospel (1:23; 28:20).

Author

Traditionally, the author of the First Gospel has been identified as Matthew, the tax collector who was called by Jesus (Matt 9:9) and sent out as an apostle (10:3). But, like many ancient authors, the evangelist nowhere identifies himself. The apostle Matthew may have been responsible for an earlier stage of the Gospel tradition, or he may have been a missionary to the area where this Gospel was composed. But most scholars agree that he was not the author of the Gospel. The composer copied extensively from the Gospel of Mark; an eye-witness would have told the story in his own words. It is also doubtful that a tax collector would have the kind of religious and literary education needed to produce this Gospel. Finally, the theological concerns in this Gospel are those of second-generation Christians. For the sake of brevity, however, we continue to refer to the author as "Matthew."

The evangelist was likely a Jewish Christian, writing for a community that was predominantly Jewish Christian. The author had extensive knowledge of the Hebrew Scriptures and a keen concern for Jewish observance and the role of the Law. A few scholars hold that Matthew was a Gentile because of his fierce anti-Jewish polemic, especially in chapter 23. In addition, he seems to have been unfamiliar with distinctions between Pharisees and Sadducees (e.g., 16:5-12; 22:23). He also appears to have misunderstood the Hebrew parallelism in Zechariah 9:9, thinking that the prophet is speaking of two beasts (21:1-9).

These, however, are not sure indicators that the evangelist was a Gentile. The anti-Jewish polemic can be explained as part of a Jewish Christian's attempt to define his community in relation to other Jews who have not followed Jesus. Matthew's juxtaposition of "Pharisees and Sadducees" is simply a generic phrase for the religious leaders at a time when Sadducees were no longer functioning. And the apparent misinterpretation of Zechariah 9:9 does not negate the evidence that the evangelist had a thorough knowledge of the Hebrew Scriptures, seen in his frequent biblical citations and allusions.

Date

Allusions to the destruction of the temple in Jerusalem (21:41-42; 22:7; 24:1-2) indicate that Matthew wrote after A.D. 70. A date of approximately A.D. 85 would allow time for circulation of the Gospel of Mark, one of Matthew's sources, which was composed close to A.D. 70.

Setting

We do not know the precise locale of the Matthean community, but a prosperous urban setting is likely from the twenty-six times that Matthew uses the word *polis*, "city" (cf. Mark, four times; Luke, sixteen times) and the twenty-eight times he mentions gold and silver (cf. Mark, one time; Luke, four times). Matthean Christians, like those of other locales, were women and men of diverse social and civic status, ethnic identities, and levels of wealth. They comprised only a small percentage of the total population. It was a mixed community of Jews and Gentiles, striving to work out their identity as the New Israel.

The oldest tradition, and still the most frequently suggested locale for the Matthean community, is Antioch of Syria. As the third largest city of the empire, it had a sizable Jewish population. It was an important center of emerging Christianity (Acts 11:19-26; 13:1-3), where Jewish and Gentile Christians struggled to work out their new relationship in Christ (Gal 2:11-13). Other possible settings include Caesarea Maritima, Sepphoris, Alexandria, Edessa, Tyre, and Sidon.

Jews and Christians

The relationship of the Matthean community to their Jewish counterparts is not entirely clear. Pointing to a rupture between the two groups are references to "their synagogues" (4:23; 9:35; 10:17; 12:9; 13:54), "your synagogues" (23:34), "their scribes" (7:29), "the Jews to the present [day]" (28:15), Jewish persecution of Jesus' followers (10:17; 23:34), and bitter denunciation of the scribes and Pharisees (ch. 23). There are stories of exemplary faith of those who are not Jews: the magi (2:1-12); a Roman centurion (8:5-13); a Canaanite woman (15:21-28); a Roman soldier (27:54). That Jesus' message is for Gentiles is seen

clearly in the final commission (28:19) and more subtly in the inclusion of Ruth and Rahab in Jesus' genealogy (1:5); the coming of the magi to worship Jesus (2:11); the saying "in his name the Gentiles will hope" (12:21); the faith of a Canaanite woman (15:21-28); and in the parables of the tenants (21:33-43) and the marriage feast (22:1-10).

Yet, at the same time Matthew stresses a specific outreach to Israel. Only in Matthew does Jesus tell his disciples to confine their mission to the towns of Israel (10:5-6, 23; 15:24). And Matthew's Gospel, overall, is strongly Jewish in tone, emphasizing the abiding validity of the Law and fulfillment of the Scriptures.

This Gospel is designed to offer Matthew's Jewish Christians an account of Jesus' life and mission that enables them to relate to the two loyalties that pull them. On the one hand, they are Jews who are trying to define themselves in relation to other Jews who have not accepted Jesus. The latter see them as disloyal to the Mosaic covenant, engaged in dangerous partnership with pagans. On the other hand, they are Christians trying to relate to a community in which the majority is now Gentile, for whom the continued adherence of Jewish Christians to Jewish Law and customs would prove problematic. Matthew's Gospel tries to defend and define Jewish Christianity, on the one hand, and unity with Gentile Christians, on the other. It validates the community's continuity with the past promises to Israel, while at the same time justifies their new allegiance to the person of Christ and his mission.

A prime pastoral concern is the impact that Christian use of the Gospel of Matthew has had on Jewish-Christian relations. Statements in the Gospel that reflect the historical tensions of an emerging Jewish Christian community struggling to define itself in relation to other Jews need to be clearly explained as such so that they are not used to fuel anti-Judaism in contemporary contexts.

Composition

Eusebius, our earliest source of information on Matthew, quotes Papias of Hierapolis (ca. A.D. 125) as saying, "Matthew compiled the Sayings *(logia)* in the Hebrew language, and everyone translated them as well as they could" (*H.E.* 3.39.16). Irenaeus and Origen understood Eusebius's statement to mean that Matthew composed the Gospel in Hebrew or Aramaic. There is no firm evidence, however, that Papias was in a position to know the facts of the evangelist's method of composition. Moreover, his statement is full of ambiguities, and there is no indisputable evidence from the Greek text of the Gospel that it was translated from a Hebrew or Aramaic original.

Most modern scholars think that Matthew relied on the Marcan tradition as one of his prime sources. Matthew has retained some 600 of Mark's 660 verses, often streamlining the story and converting narration into dialogue. He follows Mark more closely from chapter 13 onward than in the first twelve chapters. Matthew adds infancy narratives and resurrection appearance stories, and recasts Jesus' teaching into five large blocks of discourse. He adapts the story to his predominantly Jewish Christian community by omitting explanations of Jewish customs (e.g., Matt 15:2; cf. Mark 7:3-4). Matthew also emphasizes more explicitly Jesus' fulfillment of the Scriptures, often citing specific texts from the Old Testament, particularly from the prophet Isaiah (e.g., 3:3; 4:14; 8:17). He gives more attention to the question of the Law and its observance (5:17-48).

Matthew, as well as Luke, also used a source called "Q" (for *Quelle*, German for "source") for some two hundred sayings of Jesus. Although no copy of this collection of sayings has yet been found, its existence can be supposed, due to the similarity in the wording and order of these sayings in the two Gospels. Finally, Matthew also relied on oral and written traditions, designated "M," that are unique to his Gospel.

The evangelist's own words capture well his method of composition: "every scribe who has been instructed in the kingdom of heaven is like the head of a household who brings from his storeroom both the new and the old" (13:52). Matthew both faithfully transmits and creatively shapes the tradition.

Structure

There are various ways to delineate the structure of Matthew's Gospel. Many think that Matthew's organizing principle was to present Jesus as the New Moses, giving five blocks of teaching, corresponding to the five books of the Pentateuch. A concluding formula, "When Jesus finished these words" (7:28; 19:1; cf. 11:1; 13:53; 26:1), marks off each section of narrative and discourse. Framing

the whole are the infancy narratives and the passion-resurrection account. Benjamin W. Bacon was the first to propose this structure (*Studies in Matthew* [London: Constable, 1930]):

I. Infancy Narratives: 1:1–2:23

II. Five Books of Narratives and Discourses

1. The Son Begins to Proclaim the Kingdom
   A. Narrative: Beginnings of the Ministry: 3:1–4:25
   B. Discourse: The Sermon on the Mount: 5:1–7:29

2. The Mission of Jesus and His Disciples in Galilee
   A. Narrative: The Cycle of Nine Miracle Stories: 8:1–9:38
   B. Discourse: The Mission, Past and Future: 10:1–11:1

3. Jesus Meets Opposition from Israel
   A. Narrative: Jesus Disputes with Israel: 11:2–12:50
   B. Discourse: Parables: 13:1-53

4. The Messiah Forms the Church and Prophesies His Passion
   A. Narrative: The Itinerant Jesus Prepares for the Church by His Deeds: 13:54–17:27
   B. Discourse: Church Life and Order: 18:1-35

5. The Messiah and the Church on the Way to the Passion
   A. Narrative: Jesus Leads His Disciples to the Cross as He Confounds His Enemies: 19:1–23:29
   B. Discourse: The Last Judgment: 24:1–25:46

III. Climax: Passion, Death, and Resurrection: 26:1–28:20

One problem with this structure is that it relegates the infancy and passion narratives to a marginal position, when, in fact, they are central to Matthew's story. Not all scholars agree that the motif of Jesus as the New Moses is the central organizing theme.

Some scholars see a chiastic pattern, with chapter 13 as the hinge (e.g., Peter Ellis, *Matthew: His Mind and His Message* [Collegeville: Liturgical Press, 1974]):

a	Narratives	chs. 1–4
b	Sermons	chs. 5–7
c	Narratives	chs. 8–9
d	Sermons	ch. 10
e	Narratives	chs. 11–12
f	Sermon	ch. 13
e'	Narratives	chs. 14–17
d'	Sermons	ch. 18
c'	Narratives	chs. 19–22
b'	Sermons	chs. 23–25
a'	Narratives	chs. 26–28

In this configuration, Matthew 13:35 is the turning point: before it Jesus addresses all Jews; after it he devotes his attention solely to those who have already become his disciples.

Not all scholars see Matthew's structure in such neat patterns. Another approach is to regard Matthew more as a storyteller whose structure has more seams and turns and is determined by his retelling of Mark's story (e.g., Donald Senior, *What Are They Saying About Matthew?* [rev. ed.; New York/Mahwah: Paulist Press, 1996] 34–37):

I. 1:1–4:11 Origin of Jesus

II. 4:12–10:42 Galilean ministry of teaching (chs. 5–7) and healing (chs. 8–9) as a model for disciples' ministry (ch. 10)

III. 11:1–16:12 Varying responses to Jesus (rejection by Jewish opponents, faith of disciples)

IV. 16:13–20:34 Jesus and his disciples on the way to Jerusalem

V. 21:1–28:15 Jerusalem; Jesus' final days of teaching in the temple

VI. 28:16-20 Finale: Back to Galilee; disciples sent to the whole world; Jesus' abiding presence

This outline delineates the major movements and theological motifs of the Gospel, taking into account the fluid nature of narrative, and is the outline adopted in this commentary.

Purpose

This Gospel, with its emphasis on Jesus as authoritative Teacher and its stress on the ethical implications of discipleship, is a powerful catechetical tool. The evangelist may have composed it with the idea of providing a handbook for church leaders to assist them in preaching, teaching, and leading worship. This text is a particularly useful guide for helping believers discern what to keep from tradition and what to let go in changing circumstances. Its strategies for peacemaking, reconciliation, and formation of community make this Gospel a potent pastoral aid. In every age it continues to bring new vision and hope to Christians in mission, inviting them into ever deeper relationship with Jesus, who remains always with them (1:23; 28:20).

The commentaries in this booklet are all primarily based on the Greek text rather than the New American Bible translation. Accordingly, the translation of words or phrases in the commentaries sometimes differs from the translation provided at the top of the page. It is hoped that these complementary translations will enhance understanding of the Gospel.

COMMENTARY

THE ORIGINS OF JESUS

Matt 1:1–4:11

The opening chapters set the stage for the whole Gospel. Matthew, like Luke, begins with two introductory chapters of infancy narratives. The differences between the two accounts indicate that they did not share the same sources for this portion of the story. Matthew tells the story of Jesus' origins, the unusual circumstances surrounding his birth, and the threat to Jesus' life by Herod from the perspective of Joseph. Luke, in contrast, makes Mary central. Beginning with the infancy narratives, Matthew calls attention to the fulfillment of Scripture through Jesus' life and ministry. In the opening two chapters he highlights Jesus' Davidic descent and presents Jesus as recapitulating in his own life important events in the history of Israel. Matthew then situates Jesus in relation to John the Baptist, followed by his account of Jesus' testing in the desert in preparation for his public ministry.

1:1 Book of origins

The title verse introduces motifs that run throughout the whole of the Gospel. The opening phrase, "book of the genealogy *(biblos geneseōs),*" can also be translated "account of the birth" or "book of origin." This same phrase begins the account of creation in Genesis 2:4 (LXX) and the list of descendants of Adam in Genesis 5:1. Matthew narrates a new creative act of God. Three important titles follow. Jesus is *christos,* "messiah," the "anointed" of God. This term designates one who is set apart by God for particular service, such as kings (Pss 2:2; 89:20); priests (Lev 4:3, 5); prophets (1 Kgs 19:16). Some Jewish writings spoke of a coming messiah who would carry out God's purposes in a new way. Expectations surrounding this figure were by no means uniform. "Son of David," one of Matthew's favorite designations of Jesus (1:1, 20; 9:27; 12:23; 15:22; 20:30, 31; 21:9, 15; 22:42-45), underscores Jesus' royal status and also recalls God's choice of unlikely persons for important roles in salvation history. "Son of Abraham" relates Jesus to the prime figure in Israel's history, the one whose struggle to be obedient to God brought blessing for all the peoples on earth.

1:2-17 The genealogy of Jesus (cf. Luke 3:23-38)

The genealogy functions not as a historical record but as a way to situate Jesus in relation to the memorable characters in Israel's history. It tells who he is by recounting who his people are. Drawing on 1 Chronicles 1:28-42; 3:5-24; Ruth 4:12-22, Matthew outlines Jesus' ancestors in three schematized sections of fourteen generations each (v. 17). The progression is from Israel's origin in Abraham to its glorious days under David (vv. 2-6a), then to the disastrous time of the Babylonian exile (vv. 6b-11), and finally to the hope-filled future with the birth of the Messiah (vv. 12-16). The number fourteen is symbolic. Some think that it represents the numerical value of the name David (d + v + d = 4 + 6 + 4 = 14), but more likely it signifies fullness or completion, being double the number seven, which symbolizes perfection in the Bible. A problem is that the last section has only thirteen generations. Matthew simply may have miscounted, or a name may have dropped out in the transmission.

The linear progression of thirty-nine male ancestors is broken at four points by the names of women. They are not the ones who would immediately come to mind as great figures from Israel's past. Each has an unusual twist to her story. Tamar (v. 3), after being widowed, took decisive action to coerce her father-in-law, Judah, to provide an heir for her (Gen 38). She conceived Perez and Zerah, who continued the Davidic line. Tamar is the only woman in the Hebrew Scriptures who is called righteous (Gen 38:26), a term that is of central importance to Matthew. Rahab (v. 5), a prostitute in Jericho (Josh 2), risked disobeying the orders of the king of Jericho and sheltered spies sent from Joshua to reconnoiter the land. She subsequently gave birth to Boaz, the great-grandfather of David. Ruth (v. 5), a Moabite woman, returned with her mother-in-law, Naomi, to Bethlehem, rather than stay with her own people after her husband Mahlon died. In Bethlehem, Ruth presented herself to Boaz at the threshing floor and conceived Obed, who carried forth the Davidic line. Finally, the wife of Uriah (v. 6) is the one who bore David's son Solomon after David arranged to have Uriah killed in battle (2 Sam 11).

Each story speaks of how women took bold actions outside the bounds of regular patriarchal marriage to enable God's purposes to be brought to fruition in unexpected ways. Not only were the circumstances unusual, but some of these women were also outsiders to Israel. Remembering their stories prepares for the extraordinary circumstances of Jesus' birth and the salvation he will ultimately extend to those outside Israel (28:19). The women's presence in the midst of the male ancestors of Jesus also signals the integral role that women disciples play in the community of Jesus' followers. They remind the reader that women are not marginal to the history of Israel or of Christianity.

1:18-25 The birth of Jesus

Both the genealogy and the account of the birth of Jesus stress the theme of continuity and discontinuity. The same faithful God of Israel continues to act with saving grace toward the New People of God in surprising ways. Verses 18-25 explain how Jesus is son of God through the holy Spirit and "son of David" through legal adoption by Joseph.

Marriage in first-century Palestine, usually arranged by the elders of the two families, took place in two steps. There was a formal betrothal before witnesses that was legally binding. The bride remained in her father's home for another year or so until the ceremony of her transfer to the home of her husband. Jesus' conception occurs between these two stages. The agency of the holy Spirit (v. 18) is not sexual; rather, the Spirit is God's life-giving power evident in creation (Gen 1:2; Ps 104:30) and in prophetic speech (22:43). It is the divine power at work in Jesus (3:16; 12:18, 28) and his disciples (10:20).

Joseph is faced with an impossible dilemma (v. 19). He is a righteous (*dikaios*) man, that is, one who is faithful to the demands of the Law. The Law prescribed death for adulterers (Deut 22:23-27). But Joseph is unwilling to publicly denounce his betrothed. A secret divorce is not possible; two witnesses are needed, and Mary's pregnancy would be known by all her relatives and townspeople. Joseph decides on a middle course: he will divorce her quietly (Deut 24:1), without stating the reasons. He will not initiate a public trial (Num 5:11-31). This solution, however, does not prevent Mary from being exposed to public shame. The only way to prevent this would be for Joseph to complete his marriage to her and adopt the child as his own. This is what the angel instructs him to do in a dream (v. 20).

This is the first of four instances in the infancy narratives in which an angel communicates with Joseph through a dream (see also 2:13, 19, 22). This is a common means of divine revelation in biblical tradition (see Gen 16:7-14; 37:5-11), especially to announce the birth of important figures in Israel's salvation (Ishmael, Gen 16:7-12; Isaac, Gen 17:1-19; Samson, Judg 13:3-22). There are usually five elements in annunciations: (1) the angel appears; (2) the person is afraid; (3) the angel gives reassurance, announces the birth, tells the child's name and its meaning, and foretells his great deeds; (4) the person objects; (5) the angel gives a sign. The angel assures Joseph (v. 20) that this child is of God, and not from any act of unfaithfulness. God asks Joseph and Mary to complete their commitment to each other in difficult circumstances. But they also have the promise that God will be with them throughout (v. 23). The angel pronounces and interprets the name of the child, Jesus (v. 21). This derivative of the name Joshua (in Hebrew, *Yeshua* or *Yeshu*) was common in the first century. It means "God helps" but came to be associated with the verb *yšʿ*, which means "God saves." Jesus' saving mission of forgiveness is enacted in healing stories (9:2-8) and is confirmed in his words to his disciples at his final supper with them (26:28).

The first of Matthew's quotations of the Hebrew Scriptures (vv. 22-23) is from Isaiah 7:14. As in 2:15, 17, 23; 4:14; 8:17; 13:35; 21:4; 26:56; 27:9, the citation begins with the formula "this took place to fulfill what the Lord had said through the prophet" (see also the Old Testament citations without this exact formula in 2:5; 3:3; 12:17; 13:14). In Isaiah 7:14 the oracle to King Ahaz refers to the birth of a royal son in the near future who will be a sign of hope to Judah. The Hebrew word *ʿalmâ*, "young woman," refers to the mother's age, not her sexual status (*betulah* is the Hebrew word for "virgin"). The Septuagint, the Greek translation, however, renders this *parthenos*, "virgin." Isaiah is predicting a birth that will come about in a normal way, but Matthew applies it to the virginal conception of Jesus. The promise of Emmanuel, "God is with us" frames the whole Gospel (1:23; cf. 28:20).

Joseph follows the angel's commands and completes the marriage ceremony with Mary (v. 24) and names her son Jesus (v. 25). Again Matthew underscores Mary's virginity at the time of Jesus' conception and birth. Verse 25 is ambiguous; it neither affirms nor denies Mary's perpetual virginity.

In this opening chapter Jesus' identity is established in relation to God, to the royal line of David, and to notable figures of Israel's past. He embodies the faithfulness and startling creativity of God, the kingliness of David, and the bold and socially questionable righteousness of the women in his ancestry and of his legal father, Joseph. In the next chapter the focus is on positive and negative responses to Jesus. Place names figure prominently, linking Jesus with significant events of Israel's history.

2:1-12 Herod and the magi

Matthew does not relate details about Jesus' birth (cf. Luke 2:1-7). What is of interest is the place and the initial reactions to him. Jesus' birth in Bethlehem, the place where David was anointed king (1 Sam 16:1-13), highlights his royal Davidic identity. The reigning king is Herod the Great, who was appointed by the Roman senate to rule Judea in 40 B.C. A power struggle will ensue between Jesus and the Herodian kings over who bears the title "king of the Jews" (v. 2; see 27:11, 29, 37, 42).

The first visitors to the newborn Jesus are exotic characters from the East. The term "magi" originally referred to a caste of Persian priests, who served their king. They were not kings or wise men, but were adept at interpreting dreams. Here they appear to be astrologers who can interpret the movement of the stars. Magi were often associated with sorcery and magic, and were not always held in high regard (e.g., the magicians of Pharaoh, Exod 7–8). Matthew, however, portrays them very favorably. These Gentiles who respond positively to Jesus stand in stark contrast to Herod, the chief priests, and scribes (v. 4), foreshadowing the inclusion of non-Jews in the Jesus movement and the rejection of Jesus by many Jews.

There is much speculation whether the episodes in Matthew 2 have a historical basis or whether they are creations of Matthew to serve his theological purposes. With regard to the star, some think it was Halley's comet, which appeared in 12–11 B.C., others the convergence of Jupiter and Saturn in 7–6 B.C. Alternatively, Matthew may

have created it in conformity with the belief in antiquity that royal births are marked by astrological phenomena. Or Matthew may have intended an allusion to the story of Balaam, a sorcerer from the East, who predicted that a star would come out of Jacob (Num 24:17).

The Scripture quotation in verse 6 is a conflation of Micah 5:1 and 2 Samuel 5:2. Matthew customarily adapts the biblical citations to fit his context and purposes. As Jesus' birthplace, Bethlehem is no longer "too small to be among the clans of Judah" (Mic 5:1), but now is "by no means least among the rulers of Judah" (Matt 2:6). And just as God called David from Bethlehem to shepherd Israel (2 Sam 5:2), so Jesus is shepherd to God's people (9:36; 26:31).

The response of the magi to Jesus matches that of disciples. The magi are overjoyed at the sign of Jesus' birth (2:10), just as disciples' initial acceptance of Jesus is marked by joy (13:20, 44) and is promised as an end-time reward (25:21, 23). The magi bow down in homage to Jesus (v. 11; cf. Herod's insincere desire to do so in v. 8), as do the disciples after the storm (14:33), the Canaanite woman pleading for her daughter (15:25), and the women disciples (28:9) and the Eleven (28:17) when they meet the risen Christ. The magi give to Jesus the most precious gifts they have (v. 11), just as disciples offer him their very selves (4:22; 8:15; 10:37-39). Finally, the magi, like Joseph, are obedient to divine commands conveyed in dreams (v. 12), just as disciples are to obey the covenant and Jesus' word (5:19).

The text does not say how many magi there were or exactly from where they came. The traditional number of three magi is derived from the three gifts that they bear (2:11). It is possible that Matthew has in mind Psalm 72:10, which speaks of the kings of Arabia and Sheba bringing gifts to the newly anointed king. Or he may have intended an allusion to Isaiah 60:6: "All from Sheba shall come / bearing gold and frankincense, / and proclaiming the praises of the LORD." In any case, Matthew sets the stage for all who will come from east and west to dine in the realm of God (8:11; 22:1-14).

2:13-15 The flight into Egypt

Each of the Gospels tells of those who not only reject Jesus but who actively seek to destroy him from the beginning of his ministry. Matthew begins this theme even earlier. From Jesus' very infancy Herod tries to kill him. As an intended victim of violence, the Matthean Jesus teaches his disciples how not to respond in kind to violence, to love their enemies, and to pray for their persecutors (5:38-48). There are circumstances, however, when flight is the necessary course of action (2:13-15).

Joseph takes center stage once again as he obediently fulfills the divine command conveyed in a dream (as also in 1:20-24; 2:19-20, 22). He takes Jesus and his mother to Egypt, a traditional place of refuge for Israelites (Gen 42–48; 1 Kgs 11:40; 2 Kgs 25:26; Jer 26:21; 41:16-18; 43:1-7).

The quotation from Hosea 11:1, "Out of Egypt I called my son" (2:15), seems odd, for the holy family is just going into Egypt. What Matthew presumes is that they will, indeed, leave Egypt, and by doing so Scripture is fulfilled in one more way. The text alludes to the Exodus and identifies Jesus with the paradigmatic saving event for Israel. Here begins Matthew's portrait of Jesus as a Moses-like figure, the authoritative Teacher of the Law.

2:16-18 The slaughter of the children

There is no verification of this event in historical records, but sources do attest to the cruelty of Herod. Josephus (*Ant.* 15; see also *T. Moses* 6:2-7) tells of how Herod, in his paranoia about his power, killed members of his own family. He also ordered the murder of one son from each of the leading families of Judea to ensure that there would be mourning at his funeral. The episode of the slaughter provides another parallel between Jesus and Moses, recalling Pharaoh's murder of the male Hebrew children (Exod 1:15-22). Just as God protected Moses through the actions of Moses' mother and sister and Pharaoh's daughter (Exod 2:1-10), so divine protection surrounds Jesus through the obedient actions of Joseph.

Once again, a citation from the Old Testament underscores the fulfillment of Scripture (2:17-18). Matthew adapts the quotation from Jeremiah 31:15 to fit his context and purpose. Rachel, who died en route from Bethel to Ephrath (which is identified with Bethlehem, Gen 35:16-21), is weeping for all the descendants of Israel who were marched off into exile. Ramah, about five miles north of Jerusalem, was on the route of the exile. Whereas Matthew uses this text to express the bitter lamentation of Israel over its slaughtered children, in Jeremiah it is part of an oracle that promises an end to the suffering and the return of the exiled Israelites (Jer 31:16).

2:19-23 A home in Nazareth

Just as Moses received a divine command to return home after the rulers who sought his life had died (Exod 4:19), so Joseph follows the angel's directive to go home to Israel with his family. Although Herod the Great is dead, his son Archelaus still poses a menace. Archelaus was the eldest of Herod's three sons among whom the kingdom was divided. He ruled Judea, Samaria, and Idumea for ten years (4 B.C.–A.D. 6), while Philip governed the area north and east of the Sea of Galilee, and Herod Antipas (14:1-12) controlled Galilee and Perea. Archelaus followed in his father's footsteps when it came to cruelty, but he did not have his father's administrative ability.

Joseph, once again directed by a dream, takes his family to Galilee (2:22), which enjoyed greater peace than Judea. They settle in Nazareth, some four miles from the city of Sepphoris, which Herod Antipas was building as his capital. It is possible that the availability of work for Joseph, an artisan (13:55), was also a motivating factor for their choice of Nazareth as their new home. Matthew, however, sees this as one more way in which Scripture is fulfilled. There is actually no text in the Scriptures that says "He shall be called a Nazorean" (v. 23). Most likely Matthew sees a wordplay with *nēṣer*, "shoot" or "branch," and intends an allusion to Isaiah 11:1, "A shoot shall sprout from the stump of Jesse." This reference to a Davidic royal heir once again highlights Jesus' identity as king in the line of David (see Rom 15:12; 1 Pet 4:14; Rev 5:5, which also interpret Isaiah 11:1 in relation to Jesus as Messiah). Another possibility is that the wordplay is with *nāzîr*, meaning "one dedicated to God." Nazirites, like Samson (Judg 13:5-7), took a vow, did not cut their hair, and did not drink wine (Num 6:1-21) as a sign that they were set apart for God. Matthew may have in mind an allusion to Isaiah 4:3, "he . . . will be called holy." In any event, this final verse of the infancy narratives rounds out the portrait of Jesus as the fulfillment of all God's promises to Israel.

3:1-12 The proclamation of John the Baptist

The scene switches now to a desert area of Judea, east of Jerusalem, where John is baptizing and preaching repentance. The precise locale of John's ministry is not known. The arid region in the vicinity of the Dead Sea, along the Jordan River (3:6), is likely. John prepares the way, proclaiming the identical message as Jesus, "Repent, for the kingdom of heaven is at hand!" (3:2; 4:17).

The phrase "kingdom of heaven," unique to this Gospel, occurs thirty-two times. While Mark and Luke speak of the "kingdom of God," Matthew avoids using the divine name, much as Jews reading the Torah substitute "Adonai" ("Lord") for "YHWH." The expression "kingdom of heaven" does not connote a geographic area, nor does it refer to something that will be manifest only at a later time in the transcendent realm. The term *basileia*, "kingdom," means "kingly rule" or "reign," not a territory. God's reign is already present and visible here and now with the coming of Jesus (3:2; 4:17; 12:28), though it awaits completion (6:10, 33; 16:27-28).

In the context of first-century Palestine, this proclamation of God's reign was a direct challenge to Roman imperial authority. Jesus and John offer an alternate vision of power—not one based on domination and exploitation, but one in which forgiveness, healing, and well-being are offered to all. "God-with-us" means divine authoritative power over all and empowerment of all who become disciples. It is difficult to find an adequate way to express this in English. The metaphor "kingdom" falls short, evoking an image of male monarchical rule. Other ways to translate *basileia* include "rule," "reign," "realm," or "kin-dom," expressing this powerful and empowering relatedness of God's people in terms that are more inclusive.

John prepares people to recognize this embodiment of God's saving power in Jesus by adapting the words of the prophet Isaiah (40:3). In its original context the prophecy referred to the return of Israel from exile in Babylon, through the desert, to their homeland. Matthew also wants to portray John in the likeness of Elijah, with his ascetic clothing and diet (3:4; 2 Kgs 1:8). Many expected that Elijah would return as precursor and messenger before the end time (Mal 3:1; 4:5-6; Sir 48:10-11). Matthew makes this identification of John with Elijah even more explicit at 11:10, 14; 17:11-13.

With hyperbole, Matthew depicts the response to John as overwhelmingly positive (v. 5). The

baptism John offers differs in several ways from Jewish ritual washing: it is a one-time ritual, not repeated; it is not self-administered, but performed by God's prophet; and it is not for the removal of ritual impurity, but signifies repentance from sin (vv. 2, 6).

Unique to Matthew is the naming of Pharisees and Sadducees among those who come to John to be baptized (v. 7). The Pharisees were lay religious leaders active in Palestine from the second century B.C. until the first century A.D. Their name probably derives from the Hebrew word *perushîm*, "separated ones." They differed from the Sadducees in their oral interpretation of the Law, their more progressive theology, such as belief in resurrection (Matt 22:23; Acts 23:8), and in their accommodation to Hellenism. Sadducees were priests, from a more elite class, based in Jerusalem, whose role disappeared after the fall of the temple in A.D. 70. Their name may have come from the high priestly family of Zadok (1 Kgs 1:26) or from the word *ṣaddîqîm*, "just ones." The Sadducees had influence over the temple personnel and the political elite, whereas the Pharisees appealed to ordinary laypeople, advising them how to live everyday life in faithfulness to the Torah.

Matthew's introduction of these two groups of religious leaders brings onto the stage the prime opponents of Jesus. The Sadducees have a limited role in the Gospel, mentioned again only at 16:1, 6-12, while the Pharisees appear at every turn, challenging Jesus on his table practices (9:11; 15:1), fasting (9:14), the source of his power (9:34; 12:24), sabbath observance (12:2), and his interpretation of the Law (19:3). The Pharisees are the prime movers in the conspiracy to destroy Jesus (12:14; 21:46; 22:15). John's fierce accusation here reveals their insincerity in coming to be baptized and prepares for Jesus' denunciation of their hypocrisy in chapter 23. John insists that anyone who is serious about repentance must demonstrate this visibly in his or her deeds (v. 8), a theme in Jesus' teaching as well (7:21-23). Birth into the people of God is not sufficient for salvation (v. 9). A note of urgency is struck in verse 10. The time for producing "good fruit" (one of Matthew's favorite expressions; see 7:15-20; 12:33-37; 13:8, 22-26; 21:19, 43; 26:29) is now.

After painting numerous parallels between John and Jesus, Matthew now clearly distinguishes the two (vv. 11-12). Jesus is more powerful than John; the baptizer is not even worthy to perform the task of a slave, to carry Jesus' sandals (v. 11). The reference to Jesus baptizing is best understood as a metaphor for his whole ministry of forgiveness, healing, and reconciliation. Only the Fourth Gospel mentions Jesus baptizing (John 3:22; 4:1-2).

Jesus' mission is one that refines with fire (see Zech 13:9; 1 Cor 3:13-15) and empowers people with the holy Spirit. And as a farmer separates wheat from chaff by tossing the harvested grain into the air with a winnowing fork, so Jesus will separate the righteous from the unrepentant at the end time (v. 12; see Jer 15:7). Unquenchable fire metaphorically expresses the unending pain of those whose choices separate them eternally from the love of God (similarly 13:30, 40-43, 49-50).

3:13-17 The baptism of Jesus

This episode further elaborates the relationship between Jesus and John and builds on the identification of Jesus as Son of God that was set forth in the infancy narratives. Only in Matthew's Gospel is there a dialogue between John and Jesus (vv. 14-15). It reflects the difficulties that the early Christians had with Jesus' undergoing John's baptism of repentance. First, if Jesus is greater than John (as John asserted in verse 11), then why does he appear subordinate here? A second problem is that as Christians came to believe in Jesus' sinlessness from birth, they struggled to explain why he would have sought John's baptism of repentance.

In Jesus' reply (v. 15) we find two key Matthean terms: "fulfill" and "righteousness." The theme of fulfillment of God's promises to Israel in the person of Jesus has been stressed from the outset with citations of Scripture (1:22-23; 2:5-6, 15, 17-18, 23) and in the way Jesus' life has replicated the history of his people. Matthew introduced his theme of righteousness when he applied the term to Joseph (1:19); now he affirms Jesus' righteousness. This is also a quality expected of disciples of Jesus (5:6, 10, 20; 6:33). The term *dikaiosynē*, "righteousness," denotes right relationship with God, self, others, and all creation. From a Jewish perspective, righteousness is accomplished through faithfulness to the demands of the covenant, which the Matthean Jesus affirms (5:17-20).

A divine revelation further interprets the happening (vv. 16-17). "Rend[ing] the heavens" is a familiar expression from prophetic literature (Isa 63:19; cf. Ezek 1:1). People in Jesus' day imagined that the world is divided into three tiers: the heavens, the earth, and the underworld. An opening of the heavens signals a moment when human beings are in direct communication with the divine. The descent of the Spirit recalls the messianic prophecies of Isaiah: "the Spirit of the Lord shall rest upon him" (11:2; cf. 61:1) and "the spirit of God" that swept over the waters at creation (Gen 1:2; the Hebrew *rûaḥ ʾelohîm* can also be translated "a mighty wind," as in the NAB).

A heavenly voice (v. 17) is the counterpoint to the voice of John in the desert (v. 3). While in the Gospels of Mark (1:11) and Luke (3:22) the voice is directed only to Jesus: "*You* are my beloved Son," in Matthew the revelation is to all: "*This* is my beloved Son" (v. 17; emphasis added). This declaration carries multiple meanings. In the Hebrew Scriptures "son of God" occurs with three different nuances: (1) a chosen servant of God (the Hebrew *ʿebed*, "servant," is rendered *pais* in the LXX, which can also be translated "child") who will play a saving role for Israel and who will suffer for it (Isa 42:1; see 12:18-21, where Matthew explicitly presents Jesus as fulfilling this text); (2) a royal Davidic son (see Psalm 2:7, a coronation psalm, in which God assures the Davidic king, "You are my son"); (3) Israel is God's first-born son (Exod 4:22-23). The filial relationship between God and Israel is now personified in Jesus. There is also an echo of Genesis 22:2, where God instructs Abraham, "Take your son Isaac, your only one, whom you love" to the land of Moriah to offer him up. There is a foreshadowing that the sacrificial act that God interrupted with Isaac will be fulfilled with Jesus.

Vivid metaphors of the heavens opening, the Spirit descending, and the voice of God speaking (see also 17:5) bring to a dramatic climax a scene that further establishes Jesus' identity as Son of God and Son of David. The baptism scene also points ahead to Jesus' death, where the centurion and his companions affirm, "Truly, this was the Son of God!" (Matt 27:54).

4:1-11 Testing in the wilderness

This is the final episode of the first section of the Gospel, which tells of Jesus' origins, establishes his identity, and sets the stage for the beginning of his public ministry. Matthew, like Luke

(4:1-13), draws both from Mark's brief notice of Jesus' testing in the desert (Mark 1:12-13) and Q (see p. 8), which supplies a dialogue between Jesus and the devil. There is a mythical quality to the scene, as the evangelist has telescoped into one episode temptations that Jesus likely faced repeatedly throughout his life (Heb 4:15). There are also echoes of Israel's sojourn in the desert. But unlike Israel, who proved unfaithful during that time by grumbling against Moses, and testing God, Jesus stays steadfastly faithful to God's word. The fast for forty days and nights (v. 2) echoes that of Moses (Deut 9:18; so also Elijah, 1 Kgs 19:8). The motif of the mountain (v. 8) calls to mind Moses' encounter with God on Mount Sinai. Matthew uses this motif frequently (5:1–8:1; 15:29-31; 17:1-8; 28:16-20) to present Jesus as the authoritative interpreter of the Law.

While the first three chapters clearly establish Jesus' identity as "Son of God" for the reader, the tester (4:3) articulates three fundamental doubts. "*If* you are the Son of God . . ." (vv. 3, 6; emphasis added) functions both to confront the readers about any lingering doubts about what it means for Jesus to be beloved child of God and also demands that they examine their own answers to these tests as followers of God's own beloved. Each cuts to the core of what it means to be faithfully centered on God.

The first temptation is to be intent on gratifying one's own hungers (v. 3). Jesus counters with a quotation from Deuteronomy 8:3. In subsequent episodes Jesus enacts God's care for hungry people by feeding them with both physical and spiritual food (5:1–7:29; 14:31-21; 15:32-39; 26:26-30).

The second test concerns the desire for a showy display of power to prove God's might (v. 5). The devil takes Jesus to the parapet (literally, the "wing") of the temple and urges him to jump off to prove God's ability to rescue. He quotes Psalm 91, which assures that God's angels will let no evil befall the beloved. Jesus counters with another text from Deuteronomy (6:16). As the Gospel continues, Jesus remains true to his mission as "God-with-us," meeting people in their human needs and bringing them healing and empowerment. He does not compel people to believe through flashy displays of power, but in the paradoxical manner of God in human flesh.

The third test concerns idolatrous misuse of power (vv. 8-9). A human face is put on this temp-

tation when Jesus makes the same reply, "Get away, Satan!" (v. 10), to Peter when he rejects Jesus' prediction of his passion (16:21-23). Here Jesus invokes Deuteronomy 6:13, bringing the focus again to true power and worship, which centers on God alone. The same verb, *proskyneō*, "prostrate," (v. 9) is used of the magi's adoration of the infant Jesus (2:2, 8), and of the women disciples' worship at the feet of the risen Christ (28:9).

Although the devil departs at the conclusion of this episode (v. 11), Matthew indicates that these tests haunted Jesus to the end. Even as he was dying a variation on these temptations surfaces: "He trusted in God; let him deliver him now if he wants him. For he said, 'I am the Son of God'" (27:43). The ministrations of angels (4:11) signal that divine protection and power always surround God's beloved ones, no matter how intense the trial.

THE BEGINNINGS OF THE GALILEAN MINISTRY

Matt 4:12–10:42

In the second main section of the Gospel, Matthew narrates the beginnings of Jesus' ministry in Galilee. After his opening proclamation of his mission (4:12-17), Jesus calls the first of his disciples (4:18-22) and begins to preach and heal multitudes of people (4:23-25). Then follows his magisterial teaching in the Sermon on the Mount (5:1–7:28), a series of healing stories (8:1–9:37), and the sending of the disciples in mission (10:1-42).

4:12-17 The announcement of the nearness of God's reign

Matthew, following Mark (1:14), links the beginning of Jesus' public ministry with John's arrest (4:12). He gives a fuller account of John's death at the hands of Herod Antipas at 14:3-12. It seems odd that Jesus would go to Galilee upon news of John's arrest; it may be that Jesus intended to take up the mission where John left off (see John 3:22-23; 4:1-3). The expression "withdrew to Galilee" (v. 12) clashes with Jesus' preaching in public (v. 17), and hints at the danger Jesus faces by ministering there.

Jesus resettles in Capernaum (see also 8:5; 9:1), a fishing village at the northwest corner of the Sea of Galilee. It lay along an important trade route, the *Via Maris*, "the Way of the Sea." This would have ensured a greater audience for his ministry than the tiny village of Nazareth (see 13:53-58, where Jesus is rejected in his hometown). For Matthew, the reason for Jesus' relocation is to fulfill Scripture (vv. 14-16). He adapts an oracle from the prophet Isaiah (9:1-2) to announce the hope that lies beyond death with the coming of Jesus. The oracle was originally addressed to Galilee after the Assyrian invasion in 732 B.C. To make the link, Matthew reminds the reader that Capernaum was in the general region of the territory allotted to the tribes of Zebulun and Naphtali (Josh 19:10-16; 19:32-39). The Matthean Jesus stresses at the outset that his mission is only to Israel (10:5; 15:24). But here again, as in the story of the magi (2:1-12), with the expression "Galilee of the Gentiles" (v. 15) there is a foreshadowing of the expansion of Jesus' mission to the Gentiles (28:16-20).

Jesus' opening proclamation of his mission (v. 17) matches that of John the Baptist (3:2). (See above, at 3:2, for comments on the meaning of "the kingdom of heaven.") The phrase "at hand" translates a word (*engiken*) that is ambiguous in Greek. It can mean "has arrived" or "has drawn near." Matthew (as also Mark 1:15) expresses that there is a new inbreaking of God's reign with the arrival of Jesus, but it is not yet fully accomplished. The expression "from that time on" (v. 17) marks an important transition in the story, as also at 16:21, where the phrase signals a new focus on Jesus' coming passion in Jerusalem.

4:18-22 The call of the first disciples

In this stylized account of the call of Jesus' first followers, Matthew introduces key characteristics of discipleship, which help readers reflect on their own response to Jesus. First, the invitation is initiated by Jesus. Unlike disciples of rabbis, who would seek out the one with whom they wanted to study, these disciples of Jesus are invited by him. They are going about their everyday work, casting their nets into the sea and making repairs to them when Jesus encounters them at the seaside. Far from being "uneducated, ordinary men," as the polemical reference to Peter and John in Acts 4:13 states, these fishermen were savvy businessmen who managed employees (Mark 1:20) and located their industry in an advantageous tax district. Philip and Andrew were originally from Bethsaida (John 1:44), in the territory ruled by

Philip. It is likely that they relocated to Capernaum for a tax break.

Jesus' invitation is to an active mission. Discipleship does not entail merely intellectual assent, but following Jesus in every respect, becoming "fishers" of other persons (see Jer 16:16). There is a stress on the totality and immediacy of the response of these first disciples. The radical changes that the life of discipleship demands are symbolized in the leaving of their nets, their boat, and their father. In the story there is no preparation for this encounter with Jesus. There is something so compelling about his person and message that Peter, Andrew, James, and John immediately follow him.

The communal dimension of discipleship is emphasized by the coming of the call to two sets of brothers. That the call can be rejected is shown in the story of the rich young man (19:16-22). The inclusion of marginalized people in Jesus' entourage is exemplified in the call of the toll collector Matthew (9:9-13). Others for whom there is no call story but who are clearly disciples of Jesus include the women "who had followed Jesus from Galilee, ministering to him" (27:55), among whom were "Mary Magdalene and Mary the mother of James and Joseph, and the mother of the sons of Zebedee" (27:56). Another latecomer in the Gospel is Joseph of Arimathea, whom Matthew also identifies as "a disciple of Jesus" (27:57).

4:23-25 The spreading of Jesus' fame

A summary statement of Jesus' successful ministry of teaching, preaching, and healing makes a bridge between the opening proclamation and initial formation of disciples to the advanced teaching (chs. 5–7) and further healing (chs. 8–9) that precede the sending out of the disciples on mission (ch. 10). Unlike the Gospel of John, which shows Jesus moving between Galilee and Jerusalem, in the Synoptic Gospels Jesus' ministry first centers only on Galilee (v. 23). He makes only one fateful trip to Jerusalem, which begins at Matthew 19:1. Characteristic of Matthew's emphasis on the primacy of Jesus' mission to Israel (10:5; 15:24) is that Jesus teaches in synagogues (v. 23). The expression "their synagogues" reflects the tension in Matthew's day between his predominantly Jewish Christian community and Jews who have not chosen to follow Jesus (see above, "Jews and Christians," in the introductory comments, p. 7).

The geographical sweep indicates those places from which Matthean Christians hailed or places in which the Gospel first circulated. Syria (v. 24) most likely refers to the Roman province by that name, which included Palestine and the other places listed in verse 25. "Decapolis, Ten Cities," most of which were on the east side of the Jordan River, were cities in which Hellenistic culture flourished and which were thought of as Gentile regions. The names thus hint at a mixture of Jews and Gentiles. This great multitude becomes the audience for Jesus' Sermon on the Mount.

THE SERMON ON THE MOUNT

Matt 5:1–7:28

This is probably the best known and most quoted part of the Gospel. Luke has a comparable sermon, but sets it on a plain (6:17-49). Matthew's setting on a mountain (5:1; also at 4:8; 15:29-31; 17:1-8; 28:16-20) makes Jesus a Moses-like figure, but one who exceeds Moses as authoritative Teacher of the Law. This is the first of five major discourses in the Gospel (followed by 10:1–11:1 on mission; 13:1-53 on parables; 18:1-35 on church life and order; 24:1–25:46 on the last judgment). It may have originated as a collection of the core teachings of Jesus, specifically aimed at Jewish Christians, helping them relate their new faith to their Jewish heritage. The emphasis on fulfillment of the Law and the prophets (5:17; 7:12) encircles the whole.

Several ways of outlining the structure of the sermon are possible. The Beatitudes (5:1-12) and parabolic sayings about publicly living and proclaiming them (5:13-16) lead off. Then follow six antithetical statements about the rigorous demands of discipleship (5:17-48). Jesus' interpretation of the Law is more stringent than that of the scribes and Pharisees (5:20). Next are teachings about various attitudes and actions incumbent on disciples (6:1–7:12). A highlight in this section is the Our Father (6:9-15). Rounding out the sermon are concluding exhortations and warnings (7:13-28).

5:1-12 The Beatitudes

The summary statement in 4:23-25 has brought on stage a great multitude who have been healed by Jesus and have heard his teaching. This crowd, along with Jesus' disciples, are now the recipients of detailed instruction. Throughout the Gospel the crowds are generally favorable to Jesus, but at the passion narrative they become adversarial (27:20-26). Jesus assumes a sitting position, typical of teachers (5:1; Ezek 8:1) and of rulers (Matt 27:19).

The Beatitudes have echoes in Wisdom literature and the prophets (e.g., Prov 3:13; 28:14; Sir 25:7-9; 48:1-11; Isa 30:18; 32:20). Matthew casts them in eight parallel statements of blessing and promise in the third person plural (vv. 3-10) and concludes with a ninth beatitude in the second person plural (v. 11). Luke structures them into four blessings followed by four "woes" (6:20-26). Matthew relegates the woes to an extended denunciation of the scribes and Pharisees in 23:13-23. The rewards assured to disciples are already experienced to a degree in the present time ("Blessed *are* . . ."; emphasis added) but await fulfillment at the end time.

In the first blessing (v. 3), *ptōchos* denotes "beggar," that is, one who is destitute. The theme of God's care for the poor is found abundantly in the Old Testament (e.g., Exod 22:25-27; Deut 15:7-11; Isa 61:1). That wealth is an obstacle to discipleship surfaces again in Jesus' teaching at 19:16-30. Matthew's addition of "in spirit" (cf. Luke 6:20) likely reflects the struggle of those in the community with greater material wealth to live as disciples. The assurance of the "kingdom of heaven" frames the Beatitudes (vv. 3, 10).

The second beatitude (v. 4) speaks of comfort to those who mourn. This recalls the comfort Isaiah gives to Zion when mourning the destruction of the temple (Isa 61:1-3). It also points forward to the women who perform the rites of mourning for Jesus surrounding his death (26:6-13; 27:55-56, 61; 28:1-10) and the joy they experience in encountering him once again alive (28:8).

The third beatitude, "Blessed are the meek" (v. 5), does not teach disciples to be shrinking violets; rather, the word *praeis* connotes those who are not overly impressed by their own self-importance—in other words, those who are appropriately humble and considerate. This beatitude echoes Psalm 37:11, where the Hebrew word for meek, *ʿanāwîm*, is essentially equivalent to "poor in spirit." The promise of land has an echo in 1 Enoch 5:7, where the eschatological promise refers not only to Israel but to the whole earth.

In the fourth beatitude there is an allusion to Psalm 107:5, 8-9, in which God satisfies those who hunger and thirst. Matthew adds one of his key terms, "righteousness" (see also 1:19; 3:15; 6:33), that is, right relation with God, self, others, and all creation. Disciples are to seek it actively, "hunger and thirst" for it (v. 6), through faithfulness to the demands of the covenant (5:17-20). However, there is a sober warning in the eighth beatitude that they will be persecuted for the sake of righteousness (v. 10).

The fifth beatitude assures those who exercise mercy that the same will be shown to them (v. 7). A similar assertion is made about forgiveness in the prayer Jesus teaches his disciples (6:12; see also 18:23-35). Twice in conflictual situations Jesus admonishes his opponents to learn the meaning of mercy (9:13; 12:7). At 23:23 Jesus lists mercy, along with judgment and fidelity, as the weightier matters of the Law.

In Psalm 24:4, a hymn for processing into the temple, the "clean of hand and pure of heart" are those who are not idolaters and who have not sworn falsely. They are the ones who are able to stand in the holy place and receive blessings and justice from God. In the sixth beatitude (v. 8) the promise of "seeing God" refers not to encountering God in the temple in Jerusalem (as in Pss 11:7; 17:15; 27:4; 42:3), but is an eschatological promise to be in God's presence face to face (cf. Exod 3:6; 19:21; 33:20, 23, reflecting the belief that human beings could not see God and live).

The seventh beatitude (v. 9) assures those who devote themselves to peacemaking that they will be sons and daughters of God. As Jesus has been shown to be Son of God (1:1; 2:15; 3:17), so too disciples who learn his ways of forgiveness and reconciliation share in the same intimate relationship with God. Jesus gives concrete strategies for peacemaking in 5:38-48 and 18:1-35. In the ears of Jewish Christians, this beatitude would also be evocative of God's gift of *shālôm*, not just the absence of strife, but a pervasive well-being in every arena of life.

The eighth beatitude (v. 10) circles back to the fourth one, regarding righteousness (v. 6), and promises attainment of the reign of God, as does the first (v. 3). The kinds of persecution that Matthean Christians likely faced were economic harassment, conflicts with Jews who did not join them, struggles over the degree of accommodation to Hellenistic culture, and the like. Jesus speaks to his disciples more concretely about the kinds of persecution they may face when he first sends them out on mission (10:16-42).

The ninth beatitude (v. 11) speaks of verbal abuse that disciples suffer because of Jesus. They are to find joy in the midst of such trials through hope in a heavenly reward and from the assurance that they are being prophetic—a ministry that always entails rejection by some (v. 12; 23:29-34).

5:13-16 Salt and light

With two metaphors Jesus speaks to his followers about how they already are salt of the earth (v. 13) and light of the world (v. 14). The first word, *you*, is emphatic in both verses, contrasting Matthean Christians with their counterparts in the synagogue. Salt was a critical necessity in the ancient world (Sir 39:26). It was used for seasoning, preservation, and purifying (2 Kgs 2:19-22). It was used to ratify covenants (Num 18:29; 2 Chr 13:5) and in liturgical functions (Exod 30:35; Lev 2:13; Ezek 43:24; Ezra 6:9). To eat salt with someone signifies a bond of friendship and loyalty (Ezra 4:14; Acts 1:4). Salts in the soil are needed for its fecundity, but soil that is "nothing but sulphur and salt" is a desert wasteland (Deut 29:22; similarly Ps 107:34; Job 39:6; Jer 17:6; Zeph 2:9). Salt scattered on a conquered city symbolically reinforced its devastation (Judg 9:45).

In telling his disciples "You are the salt of the earth," Jesus can draw on any of these symbols. Disciples preserve, purify, and judge, drawing out the savor of God's love in the world. The puzzle about how salt may lose its taste is probably best answered by salt being diluted or dissolved. Coming on the heels of Jesus' exhortation to rejoice when persecuted (vv. 11-12), it is likely a warning to disciples not to let their ardor dissipate under the rigors of persecution.

Disciples are also "the light of the world," like a city set on a mountain that cannot be hidden (v. 14). The metaphor has a political twist, since Cicero (*Cataline* 4.6) described Rome as a "light to the whole world." It is Jesus' beatitudinal way of life that is light to the world, not the imperial domination system. Just as the city on a mountain cannot be hidden, a lamp is not lit and then immediately extinguished (v. 15). One does not waste precious fuel oil this way. Using a vessel (*modios*, literally, a "bushel basket") to put out the light would prevent dangerous sparks from spreading.

These two images speak of the all-encompassing nature of the witness of disciples: as salt and light they influence the whole world. These metaphors also show that the disciples do not draw attention to themselves. Just as salt is most effective when it is not noticed in well-seasoned food and a lamp serves to illumine the other objects in the room, so the effect of disciples' good works is to point to God, who is glorified. In verse 16 Matthew gives the first of many references to God as "Father." See remarks at 6:9-16.

5:17-20 The Law and righteousness

These verses clearly set forth Jesus' relationship to the Law. He is a thoroughly observant Jew who is devoted to keeping the Law. He does not replace the Law, nor does he break it; rather, he fulfills it, bringing it to its intended purpose. He is authentic interpreter of the Law for a changed situation.

5:21-26 On anger

This is the first of six antithetical statements (5:21-48), each of which begins with "You have heard that it was said . . . ," followed by a command introduced with the formula "But I say to you . . ." In each instance Jesus declares a former understanding of the Law inadequate as he places more stringent demands on his disciples. Each of the six examples addresses an aspect of right relation among people in a covenantal faith community. The word *adelphos* in verse 22 refers not only to blood relations but to a Christian "brother or sister."

Killing another person is the epitome of broken relationships. The Law given to Moses forbids killing (Exod 20:13; Deut 5:18). Jesus' command is to defuse anger and work toward reconciliation before the rupture in the relationship reaches a murderous stage. He gives three concrete examples. The first is to avoid insulting one another. *Rēqāʾ* is an Aramaic word meaning approximately the same thing as *morē* in Greek, which is "you fool" (v. 22). Second, liturgical sacrifices do not cover over broken relationships. One must attempt face-to-face reconciliation before making ritual offerings (vv. 23-24; see similar injunctions in Isa 1; Prov 15:8; 21:3, 27; Sir 34:21-27; 35:1-4). The third example warns against letting conflicts escalate to the point of litigation in court (vv. 25-26). For disciples, it is imperative to defuse anger and attempt reconciliation, so that no conflict becomes murderous. One who lets anger simmer and grow will face judgment (v. 22) before God.

The Sanhedrin, Gehenna, and prison are all ways of speaking about judgment. The Sanhedrin was the highest Jewish judicial council (see 26:57-68). Gehenna comes from the Hebrew *gê hinnōm*, "Hinnom valley," which runs south-southwest of Jerusalem. It came to represent the place of fiery judgment, because there the fires of the Molech cult burned, and later, smoldering refuse. Prison was not used to hold debtors or other offenders long term, as verse 26 implies. Once guilt was determined, one would be executed, deported, or sold into slavery. The point is that the consequences for not working at reconciliation are dire. It is not enough for Jesus' disciples to avoid killing; they must actively seek to defuse anger and pursue right relation with all. Here Jesus is not addressing righteous anger, that is, outrage at injustice that gives energy to work toward change.

5:27-30 On adultery

Just as anger is prohibited (vv. 21-26) as the first step toward murder, so the lustful look is condemned as the prelude to adultery. The Law forbids not only adultery (Exod 20:14; Deut 5:18) but also covetousness (Exod 20:17) of another person's spouse and of their possessions. Vivid metaphors of tearing out one's eye and cutting off a hand convey the seriousness of the sin of lust. On Gehenna, see verse 22.

5:31-32 On divorce

The third example builds on the previous one, adding that divorce is also a form of adultery. It is addressed to males and reflects the Jewish custom that only they could initiate divorce. The process for doing so is found in Deuteronomy 24:1. A fuller elaboration of Jesus' teaching on divorce is found in Matthew 19:1-12. Here the reasoning is not given, simply the prohibition, along with the exception for *porneia* (v. 32). Scholars are divided over whether this word connotes sexual misconduct, that is, adultery, or whether it refers to marriage to close kin, which was forbidden in Jewish law (Lev 18:6-18; see also Acts 15:20, 29).

5:33-37 On taking oaths

Now the focus shifts to address honesty in relationships. Whereas Leviticus 19:12 admonished, "You shall not swear falsely by my name, thus profaning the name of your God," Jesus insists that relations among Christians be so transparent as to end the need for taking oaths at all. Just as Matthew uses *the reign of heaven*, avoiding the use of "God" (see comments at 3:2), so here he employs "heaven" (v. 34), "earth" (see Ps 24:1), and "Jerusalem" (v. 35) as euphemisms for God. Verse 36 makes an ironic reference to coloring one's hair, a practice already used in antiquity. Christian integrity must be such that there is need to swear in order to make another believe the veracity of their word.

5:38-42 On nonretaliation

The fifth unit concerns the *ius talionis* (Lev 24:20), which was based on the principle of equal reciprocity. The Law placed limits on retribution, so as to curtail escalating cycles of vengeance. As in the previous four examples, Jesus demands more, thus going to the core of the attitudes and actions necessary to adequately fulfill what the Law intends. The principle is articulated in verse 39a, and four concrete examples follow in verses 39b-42. Verse 39a is best translated "do not retaliate against the evildoer." The verb *antistēnai* most often carries the connotation "resist violently" or "armed resistance in military encounters" (e.g., Eph 6:13).

A command not to resist evil makes little sense on the lips of Jesus, when the whole Gospel shows him doing just the opposite. The issue here is *how* the disciple is to confront evil. The examples that follow show how nonretaliation is a strategy that breaks cycles of violence in confrontations between persons of unequal power and status. In the first three the person addressed is a victim of an injustice inflicted by a more powerful person. Retaliation by the injured party is not a realistic option. The expected response is submission. There is an alternate way to respond by actively confronting the injustice with a positive and provocative act that can break the cycle of violence and begin a different one in which gestures of reconciliation can be reciprocated.

The first example (v. 39b) involves a backhanded slap (only the right hand would be used for striking another), meant to insult and humiliate. Turning the other cheek is a creative response that robs the aggressor of the power to humiliate and shames the one who intended to inflict shame. It interrupts the cycle of violence, which is the first step toward restoration of right relation. It could begin to move the aggressor toward repentance, leading to reconciliation.

In a similar way, a debtor who stands naked in court, after handing over both under and outer garments to a creditor (v. 40), performs a shocking act that places shame on the creditor. See Genesis 9:20-27, which asserts that it is the one who views another's nakedness who is shamed. Isaiah (20:1-6) made use of this strategy. This tactic exposes the injustice of the economic system to which the creditor subscribes and opens the possibility that he may repent, perceiving the common humanity that unites him with those he had exploited.

The third illustration (v. 41) envisions a situation in which a Roman soldier compels one of the subject people to carry his pack. Seizing the initiative, the subjugated person can destabilize the situation, creating a dilemma for the soldier, who worries that he would face punishment for exacting service for excessive distances.

The last example (v. 42) is addressed to the person in a superior economic position. In context it implies a situation in which there is indebtedness due to some injustice. Nonretaliation on the part of the lender would be foregoing the demand that the money or goods be returned.

Each of these illustrations gives an example of how to restore justice by interrupting cycles of violence and enmity and initiating new cycles of generosity that invite reciprocity. In this way the intent of the Law is fulfilled.

5:43-48 Love your enemy

The sixth and last in the series of antitheses deals with the command to love the neighbor (Lev 19:18). Love, as a commandment, concerns not feelings but deeds that reflect faithfulness to the covenant. Nowhere in the Scriptures is there a command to hate the enemy. It was generally understood, however, that Israelites were obliged to practice deeds of covenant fidelity toward one another, but such was not required toward those outside the covenant community. "Hate," *miseō*, not only denotes active hostility but also connotes "love less" (as Matt 6:24). For Jesus this is an inadequate interpretation of the Law. He requires the same treatment for both those inside and outside the covenant community. Concrete ways to love enemies include praying for persecutors (v. 44) and welcoming outsiders (v. 47). "Persecut[ors]" likely refers to fellow Jews who opposed Christian missionaries, as in 10:23; 23:34. The verb *aspazomai*, "greet," in verse 47 connotes welcome and a wish for well-being, not simply a salutation.

While in previous examples the motive was to avoid punishment (vv. 21-26, 29, 30), the reason given for loving enemies (vv. 45-48) is that God acts this way, treating both the just and the unjust with the same gratuitous bounty (v. 45). Giving loving treatment only to one's own people does not adequately fulfill the Law. Verse 48 sums up: "There must be no limits to your goodness, as your heavenly Father's goodness knows no bounds" (cf. NAB: "So be perfect, just as your heavenly Father is perfect"). The word *teleios*, usually translated "perfect," connotes not so much moral perfection as completeness, full maturity, as the Hebrew *tāmîm* does (Deut 18:13).

6:1-18 Almsgiving, prayer, and fasting

There is a shift now away from the antithetical structure of 5:21-48 as this next section addresses three practices that are pillars of Jewish spirituality: almsgiving (vv. 2-4), prayer (vv. 5-15), and fasting (vv. 16-18). All the material, except the Lord's Prayer (vv. 9-13), which stands at the center, is unique to Matthew. Verse 1 sounds the theme and ties this section to the previous one. As recipients of God's limitless graciousness and mercy (5:43-48), disciples are to respond in kind, with generous deeds of righteousness (see 3:15; 5:6, 10, 20) that express and establish right relation. The emphasis in each instance is on the interior disposition. The thread of "who sees" (vv. 1, 4, 5, 6, 16, 18) and the theme of reward (vv. 1, 2, 4, 5, 6, 16, 18) run throughout the section.

6:2-4 On almsgiving

Care for the poor is frequently enjoined in the Scriptures (e.g., Deut 24:19-22; Isa 58:6-8; Prov 25:21; Sir 3:30). In performing deeds of mercy, disciples are not to call attention to themselves. The exaggerated metaphors "blow a trumpet before you" (v. 2) and "do not let your left hand know what your right is doing" (v. 3) underscore the point that almsgiving should be done in an unobtrusive manner. Ostentatious givers already receive the reward of praise from others (v. 2). But such displays further shame the recipient, thus preventing right relation from becoming a present reality. Jesus contrasts the desired behavior of his disciples with that of hypocrites. *Hypocritēs* is the term for an actor who dons a mask (see Jesus'

accusation of the Pharisees as hypocrites in 23:13, 15, 23, 25, 27, 29). It is aptly used here for those who pose as something they are not. The polemic between Matthew's community and the synagogue surfaces again at verses 2 and 5. Hypocrites are found in every religious group, and Christians are no exception. Staying centered on God is the key, as the next section on prayer elaborates.

6:5-15 On prayer

Jesus continues his denunciation of ostentatious shows of pious practices. It is not a critique of praying in a standing position, which was the normal prayer stance both for Jews and early Christians. Nor is Jesus advocating private prayer over communal. In fact, he teaches his disciples a communal prayer to *our* Father (v. 9). As in verse 2, the problematic aspect is the showiness of prayers done to attract the attention of others. Such behavior makes prayer impossible. The purpose of prayer is communication with God, for which one needs to shut out other concerns ("close the door," v. 6) and reach into the depths of spirit ("go to your inner room," v. 6). The reward is deeper communion with God (v. 6) rather than empty praise of human admirers (v. 5).

Furthermore, prayer is not a one-way street, nor does it require multiple words. Matthew stereotypes the prayer of pagans as babbling and criticizes them for thinking that they can manipulate God by deluging God with voluminous words. Jesus emphasizes that God already knows the needs of those who pray and implies that God stands ready to meet those needs (v. 8). Moreover, prayer of petition is only one kind of prayer. Jesus exemplifies prayer that flows from God's gracious initiative and responds in deeds of right relation (14:23; 19:13; 26:36-46). Jesus then teaches his disciples how to pray (vv. 9-13; see also 18:19; 24:20).

As in the rest of this section, the emphasis is on the interior disposition, "how" to pray (v. 9), not the words that are to be used. Luke 11:2-4 has a shorter version. Each evangelist tailors the prayer to his community's needs. The address "Our Father in heaven" is common in Jewish prayers. The pronoun "our" stresses the communal dimension of faith and the oneness of all children of God across all boundaries of difference. Calling God "Father" was not unique to Jesus; there are texts from the Hebrew Scriptures, Qumran, Philo, Josephus, and rabbinic literature in which this metaphor is used of God. Although it is the most frequently used metaphor (fifty-three times) by the Matthean Jesus, it is not the only one. See, for example, 13:33, where Matthew speaks of God as a bakerwoman, or 23:37, where Jesus applies to himself the metaphor used of God in Psalm 91, namely, that of a bird that gathers her fledglings under her wings. For the early Christians, "Father" expressed not so much intimacy as God's power and providence. By addressing God as "Father," they challenged the emperor's claim to be "father of the nation," asserting that only God is the supreme power.

The first three petitions (vv. 9-10) focus on God and are essentially reiterations of one desire, expressed in three ways. "Hallowed be your name" echoes Leviticus 22:32; Deuteronomy 32:51; Isaiah 8:13; 29:23; and is similar to a line from the Jewish *Kaddish* prayer: "May thy great name be magnified and hallowed." God's name is hallowed when people recognize and give praise for divine saving deeds (Isa 29:23) and when they keep God's commands (Lev 22:32). The reign of God is already inaugurated (3:2; 4:17); disciples pray for God to bring it to eschatological fulfillment, according to God's will for salvation and well-being for all realms of creation, "on earth as in heaven" (see 7:21 on God's will).

The remaining petitions (vv. 11-13) ask for divine assistance in satisfying human needs for sustenance, forgiveness, strength in the final testing, and deliverance from evil. "Bread" refers to both spiritual nourishment (e.g., Wisdom's banquet, Prov 9:1-6) and physical nourishment. The meaning of *epiousios*, "daily" or "for the coming day," is ambiguous. It may refer to the food one needs to survive each day, or it may allude to the eschatological Day of the Lord. The prayer recalls God's providing of manna to the Israelites (Exod 16:12-35) and cultivates in disciples this same kind of trust. There are also eucharistic overtones for Christians.

Matthew's keen interest in forgiveness and reconciliation (5:38-48; 18:1-35) is reflected in his expansion of the petition for forgiveness (vv. 12, 14-15). He draws a clear link between one's ability to forgive others and one's ability to be forgiven by God. The two flow from and into each other. Divine forgiveness comes first (18:23-35). After receiving unearned forgiveness from God, disciples are obliged to offer forgiveness to others.

And when disciples forgive others, they are forgiven by God (6:14-15; 18:35). Matthew uses the term *opheilēmata*, "debts," (cf. *hamartias*, "sins," in Luke 11:4), a term that reminds disciples that offenses against others include monetary inequities from systemic injustices. See Deuteronomy 15 for prescriptions for relaxation of debts in the sabbatical year.

The final petition (v. 13) is for God's protection and deliverance both now and at the end time. Until God's purposes are completely accomplished, evil will still exist, ever testing the disciple to be faithful. The language of testing *(peirasmos)* is used not in the sense of God sadistically toying with people, looking for ways to determine their fidelity, but rather it acknowledges the struggle against evil in which disciples engage (as did Jesus, 4:1-11) throughout their earthly sojourn. Jesus teaches his disciples to rely on God's power and faithfulness to bring them through every trial and emerge victorious over evil *(ponēros* can be understood as "evil" or "the evil one," that is, Satan). In Matthew's apocalyptic outlook, there will be a final end-time crisis that will bring this testing to conclusion (chs. 24–25). The whole prayer has an eschatological dimension as well as a present one. Disciples rely on God's power and protection to provide for and save them for all eternity, a reality already tasted in the present.

6:16-18 On fasting

As with almsgiving and prayer (vv. 1-6), Christians who fast are not to call attention to their pious practice. The verb *aphanizō*, "neglect their appearance," literally means "disfigure" or "render unrecognizable." It may refer to covering one's head with a cloth (Jer 14:4) or with ashes (1 Macc 3:47), or neglecting to wash (v. 17). The point is that adulation is its own reward, and no further benefit will accrue to one who is ostentatious in fasting.

6:19–7:12 Ethical sayings

The next sayings are loosely connected by catchwords. Almost all of them have parallels in Luke. They make dualistic contrasts between earth and heaven, light and darkness, love and hate. Such clean separation does not exist in real life. What these pairs underscore is the choice disciples must make to be wholly centered on God while moving toward light, love, and heaven. The prevailing motif is trust in God's providence. The first saying (vv. 19-21) contrasts the corrosive nature of material things with the security of devotedness to God. Treasure on earth, such as clothing and linens, can be consumed by moths or insects or stolen by thieves. They also consume one's attention and one's heart. The lasting treasure is the heart centered on God, which cannot be dislodged.

In this context the saying about the eye being the lamp of the body (vv. 22-23) points out the dangers of eyeing the possessions of others, which incites covetous desire. Evil-eyed envy is one of the attitudes that is most destructive of community. Not only the individual but the whole body of believers is affected by such "darkness." The next saying (v. 24) reprises verses 19-21 with a different image. A word play makes the point all the more sharply. "Mammon," "wealth," is derived from the root *ʾmn,* "trust," the same root from which "amen" comes. God is the only one to whom disciples say "amen."

The last section (vv. 25-34) builds on these sayings, illustrating God's care for birds, wild flowers, and grass of the field, and assures disciples that God knows their needs and provides for them. This passage does not advocate passivity, that is, doing nothing and expecting that God will provide. Nor does it make a judgment on the faith of those whose daily reality is a desperate struggle to survive. The point is that when disciples' whole attention is centered on seeking God's reign and right relation with all creation (5:6, 10, 20; 6:1), then those who have enough of life's necessities do not become obsessed with the quest for material possessions. Rather, they cooperate with God in providing for others (6:1-4), in supplying their daily bread (6:11). Likewise, those who are in desperate straits can let go of their worry. Neither obsessive anxiety about subsistence nor fixated desires on excessive accumulation have a place in the realm of God. Both are reflective of little faith (see also 8:26; 14:31; 16:8).

The present imperative "Stop judging" (7:1) not only warns about avoiding judging others but commands the listeners to desist from what they are in fact doing. As with forgiveness (6:14-15), peoples' actions redound to them in kind. It is not the case that disciples should overlook wrongdoing by another member of the community (*adelphos,* "brother," vv. 3-5). What is forbidden is hypocritical fault-finding. A wooden beam in the

eye (v. 3) is a hyperbolic way of depicting an evil eye (6:23).

The saying in 7:6 is unique to Matthew and somewhat enigmatic. What is holy ("hallowed") in 6:9 is God's name. A pearl can signify the realm of God (see 13:45-46). "Dogs" is likely a reference to outsiders (see also 15:26), since Jews did not keep dogs indoors as house pets. Swine were unclean animals for Jews. So the saying is best understood as an admonition not to preach about the reign of God to Gentiles or pagans, but to concentrate the mission within Israel (similarly 10:5-6). If persecution can be expected in the mission to Israel (5:10; 10:16-36), all the more would such be anticipated with outsiders.

Verses 7-11 circle back to the theme of petitionary prayer. There is a reprise of the image of God as Father (6:9), as the sayings assure that just as human fathers provide good things to their children, so does God. The emphasis (as in 6:25-34) is on God's loving providence. Humans do not manipulate God into giving them what they want, nor does God need reminding of their needs. God does not give stones for bread (Matt 4:3; 6:11; 14:13-21; 26:26-30). When disciples seek foremost God's reign and right relation (6:33), this is readily granted. Askers receive, seekers find, and the door is opened to those who knock, even if the specific things disciples ask for are not always granted.

This loosely connected group of ethical sayings reaches its climax with the "golden rule" (v. 12). There are numerous parallels to this saying in both Jewish and Greco-Roman literature. In the Old Testament there are variations such as "love your neighbor as yourself" (Lev 19:18; see Matt 5:43) and "do to no one what you yourself dislike" (Tob 4:15). Admonitions about forgiveness (6:14-15) and judging (7:1-3) have already been framed in terms of getting back in kind what you do. Now this is offered as the guiding principle that sums up the whole of how disciples are to live according to the Scriptures. It closes the section that began with 5:17-20, on Jesus' fulfillment of the Law and the prophets.

7:13-29 Exhortations and warnings

The final group of sayings and parables are mostly from Q. Using dualistic contrasts, they warn about end-time consequences for doing or not doing what Jesus teaches. The notion of two ways was a common one in Judaism and early Christianity (e.g., Deut 30:15-20; Ps 1:6; Sir 15:14-17). The "narrow gate" (v. 13) and the "constricted road" (v. 14) express the difficulties involved in choosing the way of Jesus. Moreover, there are teachers or pastors ("false prophets" and "ravenous wolves," v. 15) who would lead believers astray. But it is not difficult to determine the right leaders to follow. The effects ("fruits") of their teaching and preaching easily reveal the correctness of their words (vv. 16-18, 20). The theme of bearing good fruit is a favorite of Matthew (see references at 3:10), as is fiery destruction for one who fails to do so (vv. 19; 3:10, 12; 13:40; 18:8; 25:41).

Every major discourse in Matthew's Gospel ends with a warning to put Jesus' teaching into practice (5:2-27; 13:36-43, 47-50; 18:23-35; 24:37–25:46). This is the focus of the sayings in verses 21-23 and the parable of the two builders (vv. 24-27). Saying "Lord, Lord" (vv. 21, 22), either as a cry for help (8:2, 6, 8, 25; 9:28; 14:28, 30; 15:22, 25, 27; 17:15; 20:30, 31, 33) or as a liturgical acclamation (Rom 10:9; 1 Cor 12:3; Phil 2:11) is not sufficient; one must not only acknowledge Jesus' power but also engage it in doing deeds like his own (i.e., doing "the will of my Father in heaven" v. 21; on God's will see also 6:9-10; 12:50; 18:14; 26:39, 42, 44). The opposite is also true. Those who do mighty deeds like those of Jesus must be in intimate relationship with him, or else they risk him declaring at the end time, "I never knew you" (v. 23).

In the parable of the two builders (vv. 24-27) the point is similar. One who hears and puts Jesus' words into practice is like one who builds on a rock foundation (v. 24). This image is often used of God (e.g., Deut 32:4, 18, 31; Pss 18:2; 28:1; Isa 17:10). Now it is applied to Jesus and at 16:18 to Peter. The emphasis on hearing and doing echoes Israel's response at the giving of the Law, "All that the LORD has said, we will heed and do" (Exod 24:7; see also Deut 31:11-12). The emphasis in the parable is on Jesus as authoritative interpreter of the Law—"these words of *mine*" (vv. 24, 26; emphasis added). The conflicts with other religious leaders, both in Jesus' day and in Matthew's, lurk beneath the surface of this parable.

The Sermon on the Mount concludes with the same formula as each of Matthew's major discourses does, "When Jesus finished these words" (7:28; cf. 11:1; 13:53; 19:1; 26:1). The next major section focuses on Jesus' healing ministry.

8:1–9:38 Compassionate healing

Matthew returns to the Markan source, gathering in this section stories of Jesus healing every kind of illness. Two segments dealing with discipleship punctuate these (8:18-27; 9:9-17) and prepare for the commissioning in chapter 10. The healing stories generally have the same form with the following elements: (1) the setting is described; (2) the sick person approaches Jesus and requests healing; (3) the gravity of the illness is depicted, highlighting the healing power of Jesus; (4) Jesus pronounces a word of healing and often touches the person; (5) there is a demonstration of the cure; (6) onlookers react with amazement. The healing stories focus on Jesus' power, but they do not compel people to believe. Some persons are tentative in their requests (8:2), some have great faith before Jesus heals (8:10; 9:22, 29), and others have little faith (8:26). Some reject him (8:34), and others glorify God (9:8) and preach throughout the land about him (9:31).

8:1-4 A person with leprosy

There are three healings in the initial cycle. First is a person with leprosy (vv. 1-4), who prostrates himself before Jesus (see also 2:2, 8, 11; 14:3; 15:25; 28:9). Having just instructed his disciples about doing the will of God (7:21), Jesus now enacts God's will to heal and shows that his own will is one with God's. In Leviticus 13–14 there are detailed prescriptions for dealing with leprosy (a term applied to various kinds of skin ailments, not only what is known today as Hansen's disease). Once again Jesus is intent on fulfilling the Law and sends the healed man to complete the rituals for reincorporation into the community of believers. The detail about telling no one (v. 4) is one that Matthew has preserved from Mark, but the theme of secrecy does not function in Matthew as it does in Mark. In Matthew the crowds are still with Jesus (v. 1), and Jesus' identity has been made public from the start.

8:5-13 A centurion's servant

In the second healing story, set in Capernaum (4:13; 9:1), an officer of the Roman army in charge of one hundred soldiers approaches Jesus, appealing on behalf of his servant (*pais* could also mean "child"). Unlike the episode with the Canaanite woman (15:21-28), Jesus does not rebuff this Gentile. As with her (15:28), Jesus praises the faith of this non-Jew and even contrasts his great faith with that of Israel (v. 10). It is a foreshadowing of the inclusion of Gentiles from all corners of the earth (see Isa 2:2-4; Mic 4:1-4; Zech 8:20-23). Reclining with Israel's ancestors at the eschatological banquet (v. 11) is a frequently used image for the joys of the life that lies beyond (22:1-14; Isa 25:6). Matthew uses his favorite image of "outer darkness, where there will be wailing and grinding of teeth" (vv. 12, cf. 13:42, 50; 22:13; 24:51; 25:30) to contrast the fate of those for whom the eschatological banquet has been prepared but who do not accept Jesus. One unique element in this story is that Jesus heals at a distance and does not personally encounter the sick person. It highlights Jesus' authority (*exousia*, v. 9) but also may reflect a concern for ritual purity by not having Jesus enter a Gentile house.

8:14-15 Peter's mother-in-law

Third in the series of healing stories is the cure of Peter's mother-in-law. There are also elements of a call story. Unlike other healing stories, in which the sick person approaches Jesus, here Jesus takes the initiative. He sees her (*eiden*, v. 14), just as he sees Matthew when he calls him to be a disciple (9:9). Her response, "she rose and waited on (*diakonein*) him" (v. 15), also characterizes discipleship. The verb *diakonein* is used throughout the New Testament for a variety of ministries: table service (Acts 6:2), ministry of the word (Acts 6:4), financial ministry (Luke 8:3; Acts 11:29; 12:25), apostolic ministry (Acts 1:25). Also, in Matthew's version her service is to Jesus alone (cf. Mark 1:31, where she waits on "them"). See 27:55, where the many Galilean women who followed and ministered to Jesus keep vigil at the crucifixion. It is possible that Matthew has blended the story of this woman's healing with that of her call as a disciple. That Simon's mother-in-law may have played a significant role in the early community of disciples is likely from the fact that she is identified (though not by name), whereas other persons who are healed remain completely anonymous.

8:16-17 Summary

Matthew, like Mark, sets this first cycle of healings in one powerful day, rounding it off with a summary statement of all the other cures Jesus did. Typically, he cites Isaiah, drawing attention to how Jesus' healing ministry fulfills the Scriptures. This text (Isa 53:4) is from the Suffering Servant songs and points ahead to the Passion.

8:18-22 The rigors of discipleship

The link between healing and ministry is hinted at in the healing of Simon's mother-in-law (vv. 14-15; see also 9:31). But discipleship demands far more than an attraction to Jesus because of his mighty deeds of healing. To a scribe who wants to follow him, Jesus speaks soberly about the itinerant nature of discipleship (vv. 19-20). For other favorable references to scribes, see 13:52; 23:34. Jesus reminds those who have already become disciples that commitment to following him takes precedence over all other obligations and ties, even to family members. (See Tob 1:16-20 on the obligation to bury the dead; cf. 1 Kgs 19:20.) Jesus' homelessness recalls that of Woman Wisdom (Prov 1:20; Sir 24:7; see other parallels with Wisdom at Matt 11:16, 25-30; 23:34-39).

This is the first instance of the title "Son of Man" in the Gospel. This enigmatic expression is found only on the lips of Jesus. It occurs in contexts where Jesus speaks of his earthly ministry (9:6; 11:19; 12:8, 32; 13:37; 16:13), his passion (12:40; 17:9, 12, 22; 20:18, 28; 26:2, 24, 45), and his future coming and role as judge at the end time (10:23; 13:41; 16:27, 28; 19:28; 24:27, 30, 37, 39, 44; 25:31; 26:64). The phrase *ho huios tou anthrōpou* ("son of man") is found in Daniel 7:14 and in 1 Enoch 37–71 for an end-time agent of salvation and judgment. It may reflect a Semitic expression, *ben ʾādām* in Hebrew, or *bar ʾĕneāsh* in Aramaic, "son of humanity," designating a single member of the human species. Jesus may have used this phrase as a way of speaking of himself simply as a human being. It could be translated as "a certain person" or "someone" or, when used as a self-designation, simply "I." Whatever the provenance and original meaning of the expression, it is clearly used as a christological title in the Gospels.

8:23-27 Stormy fears

Having given orders at verse 18 to cross to the other side of the lake, Jesus now does so with his disciples in tow. These are ones who are willing to give up ties to home and family. But further difficulties lie ahead, symbolized by the "violent storm," literally, *seismos megas*, "a great earthquake" (see 24:7; 27:51; 28:2). The "earthquake" points ahead to the difficulties for disciples surrounding Jesus' passion. Initial enthusiasm for following Jesus can quickly give way to paralyzing fear for one's own life. But Jesus' power to preserve life, already demonstrated in his authority over disease, illness, and demons, now extends even to natural forces (see Pss 65:8; 89:10; 93:3-4; 107:29 for God's power over the threatening waters). The "little faith" of fearful disciples (see also 6:30; 14:31; 16:8; 17:20) gives way to amazement as they focus, not on the seemingly overwhelming obstacles, but on the person of Jesus.

8:28-34 Ministry at the margins

In the next healing story Jesus ventures out on the other side of the lake, which Matthew regards as Gentile territory. Demons and death ("tombs," v. 28) epitomize the forces of evil. Matthew has made the locale Gadara (cf. Gerasa in Mark 5:1), which is some five miles away from the sea. Despite the logistical difficulties, the image of swine (unclean animals) rushing down the steep bank to their watery demise vividly conveys the point. Jesus' power extends over all forces of evil, especially to those on the margins. The deeds expected at the end time (v. 29) are already begun in his earthly ministry. Unlike the story of the Samaritan woman who brings her whole town to believe in Jesus (John 4:39), the swineherds' report to their townspeople causes the opposite reaction (vv. 33-34). Jesus then returns to his home territory (9:1), where he receives a favorable reception (9:8).

9:1-8 Forgiveness with healing

Matthew preserves a tradition from Mark (2:1-12) that reflects the ancient belief that sickness and sin are related. In other New Testament texts (e.g., John 9:3) Jesus clearly asserts that sickness or disability is not due to any one individual person's sin. In a broader sense, sin can be thought of as the mortal condition that holds all people bound, from which only God can liberate. Thus when Jesus forgives the sin of the paralyzed man, some scribes accuse him of blasphemy. A scribe is portrayed favorably in 8:19, but for the remainder of the Gospel scribes are mainly adversaries of Jesus (7:29; 9:3; 12:38; 15:1; 16:21; 20:18; 21:15; 23:13-29; 26:57; 27:41). Blasphemy ordinarily refers to misusing the divine name (Lev 24:15-16; Num 15:30),

but here it refers to Jesus arrogating to himself a power that belongs only to God. This is a charge that resurfaces when Jesus is interrogated by the high priest (26:65).

Not only does Jesus pronounce divine forgiveness, but he also reads others' thoughts (v. 4), another power that belongs only to God (Jer 11:20; Ps 7:9). This episode affirms another dimension of Jesus' power, while also heightening the conflict with Jesus' opponents. In addition, it portrays the important role of the faith community in bringing a person to wellness. It is the faith of the man's friends which Jesus sees (v. 2) and which causes him to act. Finally, it reflects a holistic approach to the person. Jesus heals both body and spirit, allowing the person to arise to a new life (*egeirein*, "rose," v. 7, the same verb used of Jesus' resurrection at 28:6). The crowd reacts (v. 8) in a manner similar to that of 7:28-29.

9:9-13 The call of Matthew

Interjected in a cycle of healing stories that began with Jesus ministering to outsiders (8:28-34) is the call of a tax collector, a marginalized Jew. Matthew has taken the story from Mark (2:13-17), where the tax collector's name is Levi. The change to the name Matthew brings forward the authoritative figure behind this Gospel, one of the Twelve (10:3). As in the call of the first disciples (4:18-22), the response is immediate and total. The remaining verses center on Jesus' close association with many marginalized people (v. 10).

Tax collectors were ostracized by observant Jews for a number of reasons. They were looked upon as collaborators with the Romans, and their work brought them into continuous contact with Gentiles. Moreover, they had a reputation for dishonesty, as they would try to charge more than the amount prescribed (Luke 3:13). "Sinners" (v. 10) refers to Gentiles, who do not know the Law, as well as Jews who miss the mark in keeping the Law, either by immoral acts or because of their profession (tax collectors, shepherds, wool dyers, etc.). Eating with such people was particularly offensive (v. 11), since a shared meal signified intimate relationship. In addition, meals with Jesus foreshadow inclusion in the eschatological banquet (14:32-39; 22:1-14; 26:26-30). Dining with Jesus is not only a social event but also a means of healing (v. 12) and forgiveness (v. 13). Matthew adds a quotation from Hosea 6:6 (v. 13; see also 12:7), which reflects conflict between his community and other Jews about ritual purity. With this story the evangelist legitimates the presence and participation of all kinds of marginalized people in the community of Jesus' followers. Discipleship is offered to all who hunger and thirst for righteousness (5:6); those who think of themselves as already righteous find it difficult to be open to the call (v. 13).

9:14-17 Old and new

Inclusive sharing at table was not the only practice of early Christians that proved problematic. The question of why Jesus did not fast (see also 11:18-19) needed to be explained, as well as why Christians resumed the practice. Jews were obliged to fast only on the Day of Atonement (Lev 16:29; 23:27), but they also fasted in tandem with prayer (Ps 35:13), penance (2 Sam 12:13-25; 1 Kgs 21:27), mourning (2 Sam 1:12; 3:36), and divine revelation (Dan 10:3). The *Didache* (8:1; from the first half of the second century) notes that Pharisees fasted on Mondays and Thursdays (see Luke 18:12), so Christians took up the practice on Wednesdays and Fridays. While the bridegroom (a metaphor used of God, e.g., Hos 2:19; Isa 54:3-6; Jer 2:2, and used again of Jesus in Matt 25:1-13) is still present with the guests, it is not the time for fasting. "The days will come" (v. 15b) is a phrase often used to introduce an oracle of woe (Amos 7:2; Jer 38:31) and hints at the death of Jesus. It echoes Isaiah 53:8, where the Suffering Servant "was taken away." After the death of Jesus it is appropriate for his disciples to fast (see 6:16-18). Metaphors of new cloth and new wine symbolize the new way of Jesus. Yet there is no abandoning what went before. Matthew preserves from the Markan tradition the theme of the incompatibility of the old and the new but adds "and both are preserved" (v. 17).

9:18-26 Tenacious faith

A third cycle of healing stories begins with an account that weaves together the cure of a woman who had suffered from a hemorrhage for twelve years and that of a twelve-year-old girl who has died. Matthew trims away many of Mark's descriptive details (cf. Mark 5:21-43) and adds some that heighten the Jewish ambiance: flute players at the deathbed of the young girl (v. 23), as prescribed for funerals for even the poorest of Jews (*m. Ketub* 4:4); and "tassels" (v. 20) on Jesus' cloak,

worn by Jews to help them remember to keep all God's commandments (Num 15:38-41).

In both stories the healing power of Jesus and the faith of the petitioners is central. The official, despite the fact that his daughter is already dead, prostrates himself before Jesus (as do other characters in 2:2-11; 8:2; 14:3; 15:25; 28:9). And even after twelve years of suffering, the woman with the hemorrhages still musters courageous faith. Jesus, like Elijah (1 Kgs 17:17-24) and Elisha (2 Kgs 4:32-37), has the power to resuscitate those who have died, an act that prefigures his own resurrection.

There are a number of similarities between Jesus and these two women that point ahead to his passion. Like the woman with the hemorrhage, he too suffers, bleeds, does not cry out, stays steadfast in faith, and attains salvation (the Greek word *sōzein*, v. 22, means both "healed" and "saved") by his courageous act. As the child of the ruler, at the time of her death, is surrounded by an unruly crowd, who ridicule Jesus for saying she is not dead, so Jesus, the child of God, is taunted by crowds of passersby, religious officials, and those crucified with him, for his trust in God to bring life from death (27:39-44). And as news spread throughout the land that Jesus had raised up the girl (v. 26), so the Galilean women will spread the news that Jesus has been raised (28:6-8).

9:27-31 Efficacious faith

Matthew brings the cycle of powerful healing stories to a climax as he doubles the number of men (also at 8:28; cf. Mark 5:2) who are blind (cf. Mark 10:46-52; see also Matt 20:29-34) and turns Jesus' question not only toward the ones seeking healing in the narrative but to the reader as well: "Do you believe that I can do this?" (v. 28). A disciple will need to answer this question with a strong affirmative before being able to call on that same power in mission (ch. 10). The men address Jesus with Matthew's favorite messianic title, "Son of David" (v. 27; 1:1; 12:23; 15:22; 20:30, 31; 21:9, 15). The warning not to tell anyone (v. 30) is a holdover from Mark's version; the theme of secrecy does not function in Matthew as it does in Mark (see also 8:4).

9:32-34 Healing and conflict

The final brief healing story reflects ancient belief that disability and illness were caused by demon possession (see also 8:28-34). Matthew keeps the focus on Jesus' mission to Israel (v. 33, as also 10:6; 15: 24). The divided response to Jesus (as in 9:1-8) is a theme that keeps building. The crowds continue to react favorably to him until his passion (27:20-26), while the Pharisees take the role of prime opponents (see 3:7; 5:20; 9:11, 14).

9:35-38 Compassionate shepherd

Concluding this section is a summary statement (as 8:16-17) of Jesus' successful ministry of preaching, teaching, and healing. His focus remains on ministry to his own people (v. 35). This is one of the few times that Matthew does not make the reference to synagogues polemical. The stress is on Jesus' heartfelt compassion for his people. The image of shepherd as religious leader is a familiar one for God (Pss 23; 100; Isa 40:11) and for religious leaders (Ezek 34:8-12) and occurs twice more in the Gospel (10:6; 18:14-16). The metaphor shifts abruptly into agricultural imagery (vv. 37-38), as the image of laborers for the harvest leads into the mission discourse.

10:1-4 Called for mission

The mission discourse is the second of the five major blocks of teaching. It begins with the call and sending of the twelve disciples (vv. 1-15), followed by sober warnings about coming persecutions (vv. 16-25), reassurances about God's protection (vv. 26-33), and further sayings about repercussions, conditions, and rewards of discipleship (vv. 34-42). The central place of this discourse conveys to the reader that all discipleship has a missionary dimension to it. The number twelve is symbolic for the whole of the new Israel, recalling the twelve tribes that constituted the people of the covenant. "Disciples" (*mathētai*, v. 1) designates a wide group of followers (73 times in Matthew). The term "apostle" (*apostolos*, v. 2) means "one sent" and is used only here in the Gospel of Matthew. Jesus' bestowing his authority on his disciples to heal recalls Moses' imparting his spirit to the elders of Israel (Num 11:24-25). The commission to teach comes to disciples only at 28:20.

Matthew relies on Mark (3:13-19) for the list of the Twelve. There are slight variations in the names in Luke 6:12-16 and Acts 1:13. Matthew orders the names in six pairs and adds the designation "the tax collector" to Matthew (v. 3). About many of these figures little is known. Simon Peter always stands at the head and Judas Iscariot at the end. The Twelve (who appear again in 11:1; 19:28; 20:17; 26:14, 20, 47) do not play a major role in this Gospel.

10:5-15 Commissioning

The instructions given to the Twelve speak to all itinerant Christian missionaries as well as to those who receive and support them. They tell Jesus' envoys where and how to travel, how to approach people in new places, what to say and do, and how to handle rejection. For the community that offers hospitality to missionaries, they also provide a way to identify false prophets (7:15-23). Matthew is unique in stressing the mission to Israel (also 15:24). While a few episodes foreshadow a Gentile mission (2:1-12; 8:5-13, 28-33; 15:21-28), this does not become explicit until 28:16-20. Jesus himself likely understood his mission to be only for the renewal of his own people, while his followers subsequently understood it as intended for Gentiles as well.

Christian missionaries make the same proclamation as Jesus (4:17) and John the Baptist (3:2), and they perform the same healing deeds as Jesus (chs. 8–9). By so doing, Christians are the human face of Christ still at work in the world, bringing hope and healing wherever there are illness, death, and manifestations of evil. Missionaries are to present themselves as completely vulnerable—without money, luggage, extra clothing, footwear, or weapons (a walking stick was often used to fend off beasts). They are not self-sufficient; rather, they are totally reliant on God's providence, demonstrated in their dependence on the hospitality of others. While missionaries deserve to be paid (v. 10; similarly 1 Cor 9:14), Jesus instructs them to minister without charge so that the poor are not excluded and so that they are able to proclaim the Gospel with integrity (v. 8b; similarly 2 Cor 11:7). The message cannot be tailored to what those who will give money want to hear. Missionaries are not to move around seeking better accommodations. They are to remain in one house, a visible sign of "God-with-us" (1:23; 28:20), offering peace (see above on 5:9) to all within. Like Jesus, missionaries face acceptance by some and rejection by others. When rejected, they are not to respond violently, but rather they symbolically shake off the vestiges of their encounter. Not to accept the bearers of the Gospel has dire consequences. For the story of Sodom and Gomorrah (v. 15), see Genesis 19.

10:16-42 The cost of missionary life

In addition to the self-imposed rigors outlined in 10:5-15, missionaries also face dangers from without (vv. 16-25). They may be "handed over" (v. 17; as is Jesus in 27:2, 18) to local councils of Jewish leaders, the Roman prefect, or the Herodian king. They may be flogged (v. 17; see 20:19; 23:34; Acts 22:19; 2 Cor 11:24-25) and hated by all (v. 22). Worst of all, members of one's own family or apostates from the Christian community ("brothers" and "sisters"; see v. 21) may denounce them to the authorities.

In response to such perils, missionaries must first remember that they are heralds of the messianic reign of peace, when sheep and wolves can dwell together (Isa 11:6). Even so, they are not naïve about their opponents. When possible, they are to flee persecution (v. 23). When brought before the authorities, they can rely on the Spirit for the words by which they will bear witness. They are to endure "to the end" (v. 22), probably a reference to the eschatological coming of the Son of Humanity rather than to martyrdom. Regarding persecution, see above on 5:10-11. All these tribulations should come as no surprise to Christian missionaries, since they are following in the footsteps of their teacher (vv. 24-25). On Beelzebul (v. 25), see 12:22-37.

Three times Jesus reassures those he sends out not to be afraid (vv. 26, 28, 31). They are to proclaim boldly and openly, since the Gospel is meant for all; it is not esoteric teaching (vv. 26-27). Further, even if their life is taken, it is only their body (*sōma*) that is destroyed, not their soul (*psychē*). Moreover, they are so highly prized in God's sight that God's providential care will never falter (vv. 29-31). One who publicly professes commitment to Jesus can depend on the same unwavering commitment from God through Jesus (v. 32). The only cautions are that there is one who can destroy the whole person in Gehenna (v. 28; see 5:22), and there are eschatological consequences for apostasy (v. 33).

A disparate collection of sayings (vv. 34-42) rounds out the mission discourse. These apply more widely to all disciples. In verses 34-37 Jesus returns to the topic of family divisions that result from allegiance to Jesus. Previously Jesus pronounced peacemakers blessed (5:9) and outlined concrete strategies of nonretaliation of violence (5:38-48). At his arrest he prohibits the use of a sword in his defense (26:52). Verse 34 does not contradict these but rather speaks about the effect of his mission. Jesus' purpose is not to create division, but his coming has provoked opposing responses (see also 4:22; 8:21-22). The "sword" may be an allusion to Ezekiel 14:17, where the prophet speaks of a sword of discrimination that goes through the midst of the people, separating out those destined for destruction from those who will have mercy.

The sayings in verses 37-39 underscore the utter attachment to Jesus that is demanded of a disciple. A disciple who does not love his or her own family members and who does not recognize God's love revealed in those closest at hand will not be able to share that divine love with outsiders. But disciples, especially those called to go away from home on mission, must be willing to subordinate their attachment to what they love best—family and even their own life—for the sake of Jesus and his mission. Taking up one's cross (v. 38) does not refer to accepting suffering in general but refers specifically to the persecutions and sacrifices one endures for the sake of the mission. The paradoxical reward for such self-renunciation is finding life (v. 39).

The last sayings in the discourse shift focus to the receiving communities. Those who accept prophets, righteous ones, and "little ones" (see vv. 40-42; see also 18:6, 10, 14) among the disciples can expect to share in the grace of the one offering such gifts. On reward or punishment for offering a drink, see 25:35, 42.

VARYING RESPONSES TO JESUS

Matt 11:1–16:12

11:1-19 Jesus and John the Baptist

Matthew concludes the second block of teaching (10:1-42) with a transitional sentence, "When Jesus finished . . ." (as in 7:28; 13:53; 19:1; 26:1). Unlike Mark (6:30), Matthew does not recount the return of the Twelve and the success of their first missionary excursion; rather, he focuses on the divided responses to Jesus' mission, which his disciples also experience. The disciples do not always understand, but they, along with the crowds, continue to follow him, while opposition from the religious leaders increases.

This section begins with John's query about Jesus' identity (vv. 2-6), followed by Jesus' testimony about John (vv. 7-11), and concludes with a parable about the rejection both experience (vv. 12-19). The sayings are mostly from Q (parallel in Luke 7:18-35). Matthew noted at 4:12 that John had been arrested, and he will recount the story of John's death at 14:1-12. John's uncertainty about whether Jesus is the "one who is to come" (v. 3) seems to be at odds with the baptismal scene (3:13-17), where John appeared to know that Jesus is the "one coming after" him and is mightier than he is (3:11). The scene in 11:2-6 functions to clarify for the reader that the healings and teaching of Jesus in the previous chapters confirm his messianic identity. The kinds of deeds listed in verse 5 echo Isaiah 35:5-6. Although there is no explicit mention of the Messiah in Isaiah 35, these promises in a postexilic context are heralds of the dawning messianic era. An alternative interpretation is that Jesus is redefining what is to be expected of the Messiah. If some are looking for a military and political leader of the Davidic line such as the *Psalms of Solomon* 17-18 describe, then Jesus corrects their mistaken expectation. It is important to remember, however, that there was a variety of messianic expectations in Jesus' day. The beatitude in verse 6 underlines the paradoxical nature of Jesus' messiahship, at which many will take offense (*skandalizomai*, literally, "be scandalized"; see also 13:21, 57; 15:12; 26:31, 33).

Verses 7-15 shift the focus to Jesus' estimation of John. John is no flighty figure who runs after every would-be messiah who blows into town; rather, he is the one who has correctly identified God's anointed. He is the expected Elijah-like prophet (v. 14; see 17:10-12), the forerunner of the messianic reign. In verse 10 Matthew combines Malachi 3:1 and Exodus 23:30 to show the fulfillment of God's promise to send a messenger (John) to prepare the way for the one who heralds God's reign (Jesus). There may be an implied contrast in verses 7-8 between John and Herod Antipas, as the latter had coins minted with the symbol of a reed at the founding of Tiberias (A.D. 19). John's Elijah-like clothing (3:4) was nothing like Herod's luxurious dress.

John is a hinge figure who both prepares the way for the new era of God's reign (v. 11) and is also part of the reign, as both he and Jesus proclaim its arrival (3:2; 4:17) and suffer violence for its sake (11:12). John's imprisonment is an example of how the reign of God suffers violence at the hands of the violent who attempt to overpower it (v. 12). "The violent" who attempt to lay waste God's rule include not only human opponents, like Herod and those of his ilk, but also the demonic forces with which Jesus contends in his exorcisms and healings. The theme of having "ears . . . to hear" (v. 15) points ahead to the parables discourse (13:9, 13-17, 43).

The parable in verses 11-16 likens "this generation" (a pejorative phrase, as also at 12:39-42; 16:4; 17:17; 23:36) to a group of children who stubbornly refuse to play with another group, whether it is a comic game or a tragic one. Not responding to John's "dirge" nor Jesus' "flute," they instead sit (v. 16) in judgment (see 27:19). Such was also the reception accorded to Woman Wisdom, who called out her invitation to eat and drink (Prov 1:20-21; 9:3-5). But just as Wisdom is rejected by the foolish (Prov 1:23-25; Sir 15:7-8; Wis 10:3; Bar 3:12), so too John and Jesus are rejected. The accusation "glutton and drunkard" (v. 19) alludes to Deuteronomy 21:20, where it connotes a rebellious son. Verse 19b refutes this charge: Jesus is Wisdom incarnate who is vindicated (Prov 8:8, 20) by her works. For other parallels between Jesus and Wisdom, see 8:18-22; 11:25-30; 23:34-36, 37-39.

11:20-24 Consequences of rejection

To reject Jesus' invitation carries weighty consequences. The "mighty deeds" he has done (esp. chs. 8–9) should lead to repentance with understanding that he is the "one who is to come" (11:3) and Wisdom incarnate (11:19b). Capernaum, where Jesus makes his home (4:13; 8:5; 9:1; 17:24), Chorazin, and Bethsaida are villages near the Sea of Galilee. Previously Capernaum had given Jesus a favorable reception (9:8), although after his first powerful deed done there, he already spoke of his rejection by Israel (8:10-12). It is here that Jesus first clashes with the religious leaders (9:3, 11). A taunt to the king of Babylon (Isa 14:12-20) is redirected to Capernaum (v. 23). The coastal cities Tyre and Sidon were frequently denounced by the prophets for their corruption (Isa 23:1-12; Jer 25:22; Ezek 28:11-23). For the story of Sodom (vv. 23-24), see Genesis 19.

11:25-30 The revealer's yoke

This prayer is akin to the *Thanksgiving Hymns* from Qumran and uses language like that of the Fourth Gospel. It stresses the intimate relationship between Jesus and the Creator and Jesus' unique role as revealer. These verses are not to be taken as speaking of predestination or as anti-intellectualism; rather, they speak of how those who are vulnerable and marginalized are the most receptive to the revelation Jesus offers. The word *hēpioi*, "infants," (v. 25) connotes both the dependence of one who is needy as well as the inexperience of the fledgling disciples who have welcomed Jesus' teaching and his saving deeds.

In verses 28-30 Jesus, like Woman Wisdom (Sir 51:23-30), invites those who are oppressed by the yoke of sin, suffering, economic distress, and hard physical labor to take upon themselves his yoke. Rather than taking up the yoke of oppressive rulers such as Egypt (Lev 26:13) or Babylon (Isa 47:6), Israel is to take upon itself that of Yahweh (Jer 2:20). God's "yoke" is study of and obedience to Torah (Jer 5:5). To take up Jesus' yoke is not to reject Torah; rather, it is to live by his interpretation of it (5:17-20). The lightness of Jesus' yoke is not a lax interpretation of the Torah—quite the contrary (5:21-48; 10:16-23)! Accepting its more stringent demands paradoxically leads to liberation from all that oppresses. This is the opposite of what the Pharisaic interpreters do (23:4). "Rest[ing]" connotes that all the created order is in right relationship, and the believing community together delights in its goodness (as God does in Genesis 2:1-3).

12:1-14 Sabbath controversies

Two conflicts between Jesus and the Pharisees advance the theme of rejection and culminate with a death threat (v. 14). In the first conflict Jesus defends his hungry disciples for plucking heads of grain on the sabbath. Deuteronomy 23:25 allows hungry persons to take grain from a neighbor's field, but they may not use a sickle. This saves poor persons from having to beg, while at the same time guaranteeing that they will not take undo advantage of the owner of the field.

The issue in Matthew 12:1-8, however, is that the disciples are breaking the sabbath. Jesus defends his disciples' action by citing two texts of the Torah. In verses 3-4 Jesus interprets 1 Samuel 21:1-6 as an illustration of how an act of compas-

sion to respond to a human need must take precedence over cultic observance. This is reiterated in verse 7 with a quotation from Hosea 6:6. In verse 5 Matthew makes reference to the instructions on the duties of priests described in Leviticus 24:8 and Numbers 28:9-10. Jesus does not dismiss the Law (see also 5:17), but when there are differing interpretations of the Law, it is he who is the authoritative interpreter of the Law.

The second controversy (vv. 9-14), involving a cure on the sabbath, takes place in a synagogue. The question put to Jesus in verse 10 is a trap. Jesus cleverly replies, arguing from the lesser to the greater (as also 6:25, 26, 30; 10:31). His accusers readily recognize that they would rescue a sheep in danger on the sabbath. How much more valuable is a person in need, Jesus advances. The point of debate is whether or not the need is life-threatening, thus warranting saving action on the sabbath, which is allowed. Again, this episode highlights Jesus' authority to interpret the Law and the deadly hostility which that claim provokes.

12:15-21 Approved by God

At the center of the controversy stories in chapter 12 is Matthew's longest fulfillment quotation, that is, the use of citations from the Old Testament to interpret what he is saying about Jesus. The main point of the citation from Isaiah 42:1-4 is to underscore Jesus' identity as the one approved of and chosen by God, even as human authorities reject him and seek to do away with him. There are echoes of God's affirmation of the beloved Son at his baptism (3:17) and transfiguration (17:5). The emphasis is not on the suffering of the servant, but on his meekness and gentleness (11:29; 21:4-5). That Jesus has the spirit of God (v. 18) prepares for the ensuing controversy in 12:22-32.

12:22-37 Power from the Spirit of God

This episode begins with a healing very similar to that in 9:32-34. This time the controversy centers on the source of Jesus' power. The crowd continues to react favorably, though they are uncertain about Jesus' identity (v. 23). The religious leaders, however, continue their offensive, this time accusing Jesus of exorcising by the power of Beelzebul. The etymology of this disdainful name for Satan is uncertain. Most likely it derived from "Baalzebub," "Lord of the Flies," a Philistine deity

(2 Kgs 1:2). The impact of Jesus' reply is that since his deeds of power are destroying Satan's realm, he cannot be using Satan's power. He then turns the tables and suggests that it is his opponents who are in the grip of Satan's power (v. 27). Returning to his own defense, Jesus spells out that it is by the spirit of God that he performs exorcisms (v. 28)—clear signs of the inbreaking of God's realm. Jesus, the stronger one (see 3:11), binds up Satan (v. 29) by his deeds of power.

A series of loosely connected sayings follows. First there is a warning that one cannot stay neutral in this power struggle (v. 30). Then follow ominous sayings about blasphemy against the Spirit (vv. 31-32). This unforgivable sin is attributing to Satan what is truly of God. This is a warning to the religious leaders. They knowingly pit themselves against God by opposing Jesus. By so doing, they close themselves off from God's boundless offer of forgiveness. It is not that God refuses to forgive, but that they have consciously refused to accept forgiveness (see 5:43-48; 18:23-35). Then Matthew uses a favorite metaphor, bearing fruit (vv. 33-37; see also 3:8, 10; 7:16-20; 13:23; 21:19), to unmask further the wickedness of the religious leaders. Their deeds, and especially their spoken opposition to Jesus, reveal their true nature.

12:38-47 An evil generation

A shift of scene brings scribes and Pharisees asking for a sign from Jesus. The many signs Jesus has already performed have not led them to faith; more of the same will likewise have no effect on those who have already chosen evil (v. 39). One final sign remains: that of Jesus' death and resurrection. But even this mighty deed will not convince everyone (27:62-63; 28:17). The theme of outsiders who respond more favorably than Israel, particularly its leaders, surfaces once again (similarly 2:1-11; 8:10-12; 11:20-24), as even Ninevites and the Queen of the South (1 Kgs 10:1-13) will participate in judging the unrepentant.

The saying about the roaming unclean spirit (vv. 43-45) warns that in addition to initial repentance ("swept clean," v. 44), one must become filled with Jesus, allowing him to take possession and dwell within. The religious leaders appear to have everything in order (v. 44), when in fact, they are empty within (similarly 23:27-28). In addition to renouncing evil Jesus' disciples must have a full heart (12:34) that actively seeks the realm of God and a life that produces good fruit.

12:46-50 True family

The final vignette in this section brings Jesus' mother and siblings onto the scene. Matthew does not give a motive for their wanting to speak with him. Are they for him or against him? At 10:34-39 Jesus has spoken about the family divisions that disciples face. Is that the case with his own family? This is the last mention of Jesus' family members. Those bound to Jesus in discipleship are as family to him and to one another.

13:1-53 The parables discourse

The third major block of teaching comprises seven parables, two allegorical explanations (vv. 18-23, 36-43), and a theory on Jesus' use of parables (vv. 10-17, 34-35, 51-52). These puzzling stories use figurative language to speak in everyday terms about the realm of God. Yet there is usually a twist, so that they do not simply tell how life is but challenge the hearer to convert to how life can be in God's realm. They are usually open-ended, allowing for a variety of interpretations.

13:1-9 Parable of the sower, seed, soil, harvest

The scene shifts from the controversies with religious leaders to a large crowd eager for Jesus' teaching (vv. 1-2). Matthew's rendition closely follows that of Mark (4:1-9). A different message comes forth, depending on which "character" is the focus: the sower, the seed, the soil, or the harvest. The sower is usually thought to represent God or Jesus, while the seed is the word of God (vv. 18-23). When focusing on the sower, the central point concerns how the farmer acts: he indiscriminately sows seed on every type of ground, offering the word to everyone, regardless of their potential for accepting it (similarly 5:45). The exhortation in verse 9 recalls the *Shema*, ("Hear O Israel," Deut 6:4-5), prayed each day by observant Jews. This prayer underscores Israel's unique relationship with God, while Jesus' parable widens the invitation to all.

When the seed is the focus, the point shifts to the reliability of the seed to bring forth a yield, even though it first seems that there will be no harvest. The parable echoes Isaiah 55:10-11, assuring that God's word does accomplish its purpose, even though much of it falls on deaf ears.

Shifting attention to the harvest, the point is the assurance not only that the work will eventually bear fruit but that the harvest will explode in staggering proportions. The huge amounts in verse 8 are hyperbolic and propel the hearer into an eschatological scenario. The image of harvest is often used to speak of the end time (see also 13:30, 39; 21:34, 41). A good harvest yields up to tenfold. One that produces one hundred or sixty or thirtyfold is unimaginable. Fulfillment at the end time will far exceed all that we know here and now. Finally, if one focuses on the soil, the message concerns the quality and conditions needed for the word to be nurtured and come to fruition in the lives of disciples. The explanation in verses 18-23 elaborates this interpretation.

13:10-17 The reason for speaking in parables

Matthew, in contrast to Mark (4:1-12), draws a clear division between Jesus' disciples and the crowd. Rather than ask Jesus to explain the parable to them, the disciples ask why Jesus speaks to the crowd in parables (v. 10). Jesus explains that disciples have been given a gift from God to understand the "mysteries of the kingdom of heaven" (v. 11), that is, the presence of God's realm in Jesus and his ministry. Verses 13-17 emphasize human responsibility to respond to God's gift. The effect of the quotation from Isaiah 6:9-10 is to place the blame for not understanding on those who deliberately block their ears to God's word, in contrast to the blessedness of those who do respond to God's grace (vv. 16-17).

13:18-23 Explanation of the parable of the soil

Rarely in the Gospels are parables explained. This and the explanation of the weeds and wheat (13:36-43) are exceptions. Ordinarily parables are open-ended, requiring the hearer to wrestle with their enigmatic challenges. Most likely 13:18-23 represents an interpretation by the early church rather than words from Jesus' lips. The allegorical explanation focuses on the varying levels of receptivity of the four different types of soil, that is, the four types of hearers of the word. The emphasis is on the hearer; each is exhorted to cull out all impediments to becoming "rich soil." The parable also helps explain why some hearers of the word "bear fruit" and others don't.

13:24-30 Weeds among the wheat

This parable, unique to Matthew, wrestles with the questions of who is responsible for evil (vv. 27-28a) and what is to be done about it (vv. 28b-30). The first question is easily answered: an enemy is responsible (v. 28). The more difficult question is what is the best course of action to take with regard to the weeds. The householder's reply is startling, since the best method is to eradicate the weeds as early as possible. To try to separate the two at harvest is difficult and not totally effective. Moreover, to let the two grow together poses danger to the wheat seedlings as they compete for water and nutrients.

The parable does not tell whether the householder's plan succeeded. If one presumes that it did, then the parable assures that the forces of good can withstand the forces of evil, and it advocates patient trust in the One whose job it is to do the separating at the end time. Alternatively, if the householder is seen as a foolish absentee landlord who greedily thinks that even the weeds can bring him benefit as fuel, then the parable speaks of good news to peasants who watch exploitive landowners brought down by one of their own. One other twist may be that the parable invites nonretaliation against an enemy (as 5:43-48), an action that is vindicated in the end time.

13:31-32 Mischievous mustard

The most common interpretation of this parable is that just as a tiny mustard seed grows into a large tree, so the realm of God grows enormously from its small beginnings. But this explanation misses the possible twist and the call for conversion that may lie beneath the surface. That the mustard becomes a large tree *(dendron),* a botanical impossibility, may point to a burlesque of the image in Ezekiel 17, 31, and Daniel 4. Rather than think of the coming reign of God as a majestic cedar tree imported from Lebanon, Jesus uses the image of a lowly garden herb that grows right in one's own backyard. God's realm is not like a dominating empire, but its power erupts out of weakness. Its transformative power comes from unpretentious ventures of faith by Jesus' disciples. Moreover, the uncontrollable growth of mustard, crossing over boundaries to mix with other crops, offers an image for the manner in which Gentile Christians were growing exponentially and intermingling with Jewish believers in the Matthean community.

13:33-35 Hiding leaven

Important to the meaning of this parable is that in every other instance in Scripture in which leaven occurs, it represents evil or corruption (Exod 12:15-20, 34; Mark 8:15; Luke 12:1; 1 Cor 5:6-7; Gal 5:9). The startling message is that the reign of God is like a batch of dough that has been permeated by "corruptive" agents. It offers both hope to those who have been on the margins or excluded and a challenge to those who are in a privileged position. An odd detail is that the woman hides *(kryptō)* the leaven in the dough, which brings out again the paradox of hiddenness and revelation with regard to Jesus and his message (10:26; 11:25; 13:35, 44). It is also important to note that it is the work of a woman that is the vehicle for God's revelation. The amount of flour also indicates a revelation of God is in the offing. Every time a character in the Scriptures bakes with three measures of flour (approximately fifty pounds!), it is in preparation for heavenly visitors (Gen 18:6; Judg 6:19; 1 Sam 1:24). In verses 34-35 Matthew quotes Psalm 78:2 to explain again (as in 13:10-17) that Jesus' disciples have a privileged place of understanding, while the message remains hidden to the crowds.

13:36-43 The weeds and wheat explained

The allegorical explanation of the parable in 13:24-30 is likely not from the lips of Jesus but represents how the early Christians made sense of it (as with 13:18-23). The audience shifts from the crowds to Jesus' disciples (v. 36), as they become privy once again to special understanding. Each detail is given a symbolic meaning. The tone is apocalyptic as evildoers are separated once and for all from the righteous and their opposite fates are sealed. A warning is sounded to anyone who will listen that they be found among the "children of the kingdom" and not among the "children of the evil one." There is a shift from 13:16, where the disciples were blessed *because* they see and hear; now the possibility lies open that a disciple may not hear (v. 43).

13:44-53 Treasure found, stored, and shared

The parables of the buried treasure (v. 44) and the pearl of great price (vv. 45-46) offer two different ways of coming upon the reign of God: finding it unexpectedly or after a diligent search. Both speak of the total response required (as also

4:18-22; 9:9). The emphasis, however, is not on how much one has to give up, but on the immense joy that comes from the complete investment of self and resources in God's realm. The parable of the net (vv. 47-48) and its explanation (vv. 49-50) mirrors that of the weeds and the wheat and its interpretation (13:24-30, 36-43), both in wording and message.

The final verses (51-52) tie together the whole parable discourse in chapter 13. The disciples have a certain privileged level of understanding (13:11-12, 16-17), but their comprehension is by no means complete. The saying about scribes who have been instructed is often thought to be a self-portrait of the evangelist, but it actually characterizes the educated disciple, schooled in Jesus' interpretation of the Law, thus knowing how to preserve what is essential from the old for a new reality.

13:54-58 Rejected prophet

The divided responses to Jesus' teaching play out not only with disciples and crowds, as in the previous discourse on the parables, but also with his own family and neighbors. In a close-knit village, everyone presumes to know everything about Jesus, yet he startles them with his wisdom and mighty deeds. As they puzzle over the source of Jesus' power, the reader is led to supply the answer with a response of faith. The reference to Jesus' siblings has been understood in various ways: as other children of Mary and Joseph, cousins of Jesus, or Joseph's children from an earlier marriage. It is not clear whether Matthew knew the tradition about Mary's perpetual virginity (see 1:25).

14:1-12 Death of John the Baptist

The theme of the rejection of Jesus by his own is heightened as Jesus' likeness to John is voiced by Herod (see also 16:14). John's arrest was the catalyst for Jesus to begin his ministry in Galilee (4:12) and to reveal himself as the coming One and Wisdom incarnate (11:2-19). Like John, Jesus too will be executed and buried by his disciples. Matthew follows Mark 6:14-29 in retelling John's death. He shortens and simplifies the account, shifting the spotlight more toward Herod, not his wife, as the responsible one.

14:13-21 Feeding of the five thousand

In contrast to Herod's deadly banquet, where the king seeks to satisfy his own desires, Jesus hosts a vast multitude, healing and feeding them until they are all satisfied (v. 20). From the midst of his own grief at the death of his mentor (v. 13), his wounded heart fills with compassion for others who are suffering (v. 14). The same faithful God who provided manna and quail for Israel in the wilderness wandering (Exod 16; Num 11:31-35) and who worked through Elisha to feed a hungry crowd (2 Kgs 4:42-44) acts now through Jesus to bring well-being to the people. Jesus' saying that many would come from east and west to eat with Israel's ancestors in the realm of God (8:11) is enacted here. The parable of the great banquet (22:1-10) will also return to this theme. The parallels with the Last Supper (26:26) are unmistakable as Jesus takes, blesses, breaks, and gives the bread. There are also overtones of the eschatological banquet envisioned by Isaiah (25:6-10). In contrast to the disciples' solution to have all in the crowd take care of themselves, Jesus points them toward the abundance—even surfeit—of resources that are already in their midst to be shared (see also 15:32-39). Matthew makes it explicit that the participants in this feast are women and children as well as men (v. 21).

14:22-36 Walking on water

This is the second time that Jesus demonstrates his mastery over the water. In 8:23-27 Jesus calmed the sea and the disciples' dread in the midst of a storm. In this episode Jesus shows himself to be like God, both in his ability to tread on the water (e.g., Ps 77:19; Job 9:8; 38:16) and in his self-identification as *egō eimi*, literally "I am" (v. 27), the self-designation of God to Moses (Exod 3:14). While in the Markan episode the disciples remain uncomprehending and resistant to this epiphany (6:45-52), Matthew adds a poignant vignette that captures the faltering attempts of the disciples, represented by Peter (see also 16:18-19), to overcome their fears and to step out with Jesus in faith. His power to save (1:21; 8:25) takes them beyond their little faith (also 6:30; 8:26; 16:8; 17:20) to the ability to proclaim him "Son of God" (see 3:17; 16:16; 17:5; 27:54).

Jesus continues his saving ministry to all those who are sick. As a pious Jew, he is wearing tassels as a reminder to keep God's commandments (Num 15:38-40; Deut 22:12). Those who want to touch these are expressing their desire to live in the way that is faithful to God, through Jesus (as

also the woman with a hemorrhage, 9:20-22). All who do so are saved (the verb *diesōthēsan*, v. 36, means both "saved" and "healed").

15:1-20 Blind guides

This section begins with a confrontation between Jesus and the religious leaders (vv. 1-9), followed by a declaration of Jesus to the crowd (vv. 10-11), then a discussion between Jesus and his disciples (vv. 12-20). Matthew follows Mark (7:1-23) but makes substantial changes. He tones down Mark's sweeping critique of Jewish practices (7:13), although he does heighten the censure of the Pharisees with his addition of verses 13-14. In contrast to Mark's mostly Gentile community, Matthew's community probably still observed many of the Jewish practices and did not find these incompatible with Jesus' teaching.

The "tradition of the elders" (v. 2) refers to customs and regulations passed down orally, interpreting how to live the Law in everyday life. These began to be codified in written collections around A.D. 200. The debate over the level of authority such traditions carried was a lively one both in Jesus' day and in Matthew's. Jesus denounces those whose interpretation is not in accord with God's intent (vv. 3, 6). As examples, he cites the imposition of purity practices (v. 2), meant only for priests (Exod 30:19; 40:12); distorted use of *korban*, the custom of declaring something dedicated to God (vv. 3-9); and giving cultic purity (regarding unclean foods) priority over moral purity (v. 11). Purity of the heart is fundamental (vv. 17-20); from this all authentic ritual practice flows.

The quotation from Isaiah 29:13 (vv. 8-9) is an invitation to the hearers to open their hearts to Jesus (similarly 13:15, 19). In contrast to Jesus, who leads the blind to sight and faith (9:27-31; 20:30-34), his opponents are blind guides (see also 23:16, 17, 19, 24, 26), taking themselves and others toward disaster and judgment.

15:21-28 Tenacious faith

This is one of the most disturbing episodes in the Gospel. In no other story does Jesus ignore and then insult a person who comes to him in need. Matthew does not say why Jesus is headed toward the pagan coastal region; it is not to extend his mission beyond his own people (v. 24; see also 9:36; 10:6; 18:12). There are two tensions in this story:

they involve crossing both ethnic and gender boundaries. The cry of the Canaanite woman, *eleēson me*, "Have pity on me," recalls Psalm 109:26 and the pleas of the blind men (9:27; 20:30, 31) and the father of the boy with epilepsy (17:15). This is also a liturgical formula, which may reveal tensions in Matthew's community not only over Gentile inclusion but also over the role of women in the liturgical and theological life of the community.

Jesus' retort (v. 26) may allude to Isaiah 56:10, where those who are blind and without knowledge are like "dumb dogs." Or it may allude to the tension between Galileans and coastal peoples, as the Galileans often saw their grain exported to Tyre and Sidon, leaving themselves without enough (see Acts 12:20). The woman's clever response displays her great and tenacious faith (v. 28), which contrasts with that of the disciples, whose fearfulness so often displays their "little faith" (6:30; 8:26; 14:31; 16:8; 17:20). Perhaps Jesus' confrontation with this woman was a turning point in his understanding of his mission to all peoples (28:19).

15:29-39 Healing and feeding more multitudes

This episode replays 14:15-21 with slight differences. Unlike the Markan feeding stories (6:34-44; 8:1-10), where the first takes place in Jewish territory and the second on the Gentile side of the lake, Matthew makes no such distinction. For him, Jesus' mission is still restricted to Israel (10:5; 15:24). As in 14:15-21, the feeding is linked with healing. This time there is also a didactic element. Jesus sits on a mountaintop (v. 29), a teacher akin to Moses (see also 5:1; 17:1; 28:16). The disciples seem to have progressed in their understanding. This time they do not propose to Jesus that the crowd be sent away to find food for themselves. They are ready with seven loaves, and, as before, they help Jesus distribute them. While the same theological motifs are in play as in 14:15-21, there is slightly more emphasis on messianic fulfillment, as the kind of healings Jesus does echo those of the messianic age described in Isaiah 35:5-6. Also, the messianic banquet is to be set on a mountaintop (Isa 25:6-10).

16:1-12 The leaven of the Pharisees and Sadducees

That the feedings of the multitudes were meant to be teaching moments for Jesus' disciples

is clear from the dialogue in verses 5-12. This conversation is preceded by a confrontation between Jesus and the religious leaders. By the time Matthew is writing, the Sadducees are no longer an entity. After the destruction of the temple in A.D. 70, their priestly ministry and power base disappeared. Matthew's linking of Pharisees and Sadducees (as at 3:7-10) is a sweeping expression to include all rival religious leaders. Jesus' denunciation of them reflects the conflicts in Matthew's day between the followers of Jesus and those still adhering to synagogue affiliation. The rival religious leaders question Jesus not with sincerity but with the intent to test *(peirazō)* him, as the devil did (4:1, 3). Even though they have signs, they are predisposed not to respond with faith. See 12:38-47 on the sign of Jonah as a reference to Jesus' death and resurrection.

The disciples, in contrast, struggle to move from "little faith" (v. 8; similarly 6:30; 8:26; 14:31) to understanding and belief. Jesus' query about their not remembering (vv. 5, 9) is not so much pointing out a lapse in memory as it is an accusation of disobedience. Unfaithfulness to the covenant is repeatedly spoken of in the Old Testament as forgetfulness of God or of the commandments (e.g., Deut 4:9; 8:11; 9:7; Isa 17:10; Jer 18:15). The symbol of leaven for corruption occurs often in the Scriptures (see 13:33). In contrast to Mark's version of this episode (8:1-10), Matthew's disciples do finally grasp what it is that Jesus, the authoritative teacher, is telling them (v. 12).

JESUS AND HIS DISCIPLES ON THE WAY TO JERUSALEM
Matt 16:13–20:34

16:13-28 Following the Messiah to the cross

This episode constitutes a major turning point in the Gospel. It begins in the northernmost region of Israel, Caesarea Philippi, a city given to Herod the Great by Augustus and rebuilt by Herod's son Philip, who renamed the city after himself and the emperor. The scene moves from the question of Jesus to his disciples about his identity (vv. 13-20), to the first prediction of the passion (vv. 21-23; reiterated at 17:22-23; 20:17-19), to Jesus' instructions to his disciples about taking up the cross (vv. 24-28). The expression "From that time on" (v. 21) signals a major shift in the story. This same phrase, which introduces Jesus' public ministry in Galilee (4:17), now points attention to Jesus' ministry and death in Jerusalem.

On Jesus' identity as "Son of Man" (v. 13) see the comments on 8:20; for his relationship with John the Baptist and Elijah, see 3:1-17; 4:1-11; 9:18-26; 11:1-19; 14:1-12; 17:9-13. Matthew is unique in drawing parallels between Jesus and Jeremiah through his explicit quotations of the prophet (2:17; 27:9) and his allusions to him (7:15-23; 11:28-30; 23:37-39). The declaration of Jesus' messiahship (v. 16) is not a new revelation in Matthew (see 1:1, 17, 18; 11:2). But the nature of Jesus' messiahship as entailing his suffering and death (v. 21) is articulated here for the first time.

As frequently in Matthew, Peter takes a prominent role as spokesperson for the disciples (see also 14:28; 15:15; 17:4, 24-27; 18:21; 19:27; 26:33). The blessing of Peter in verses 17-19 is unique to Matthew. It plays on the meaning of his name, *Petros* ("rock") in Greek, *Cephas* in Aramaic (1 Cor 15:5), and counters the worship for which Caesarea Philippi was known. It had a sanctuary for the god Pan, with a large rock-faced cliff with carved niches that held statues. Jesus' blessing of Peter exalts the emerging rock-like faith, not only of Peter but of the whole community of disciples. This is the unshakable foundation (see 7:24-27) for those who cling to the "stone that the builders rejected" (21:42; Ps 118:22). Jesus assures the community that God will stand behind their decisions about membership, regulations, and forgiveness (see 18:18, where all the members are given the power to "bind" and to "loose").

Peter's reaction to Jesus' prediction of the passion highlights the fact that the formation of the disciples is not yet complete. The "rock" falters when confronted with the stumbling block (*skandalon*, 18:6, 7) of the passion. Jesus then builds on the instructions begun at 10:38-39 in the mission discourse. To be his disciple entails willingness to lose even life itself. To take up one's cross does not refer to enduring whatever suffering comes in life; rather, it refers specifically to the willingness to suffer the consequences for proclaiming and living the Gospel. So it is not a saying that encourages persons who are victimized or suffering to simply bear it as their way of identifying with Jesus. As we have seen in the Gospel, Jesus always healed and alleviated the suffering of all such persons. Likewise the saying about denial of self

is not simply self-denial in the sense of choosing to giving up certain pleasures; rather, it concerns the disciples' choice to lose themselves entirely in Christ—to take on his way of life and mission and his very identity as one's own. Paradoxically, this is the way that truly leads to life. A reminder about judgment and the imminent coming of the Son of Humanity (vv. 27-28) underscores that the choice to follow Jesus or not carries eternal consequences.

17:1-13 The transfiguration of Jesus and the coming of Elijah

The question of Jesus' identity and what that means continues to loom large in this episode. On the heels of Jesus' teaching that he must suffer and die and then be raised up (16:21), the reader is given utter assurance that Jesus' execution does not mean that he is accursed (Deut 21:23) or in any way rejected by God. The brilliance of his face and clothing (v. 2) indicates his righteousness (see 13:43). The voice from heaven (v. 5) reaffirms the message heard at Jesus' baptism (3:17): he is God's beloved one. The instruction "listen to him" (v. 5) echoes Deuteronomy 18:15 and insists that Jesus is the correct interpreter of the Law and the Prophets, signified by the figures of Moses and Elijah (v. 3).

Matthew further highlights the portrait of Jesus as the new Moses with the details of the high mountain (v. 1; see also 5:1; 15:29; 28:16), Jesus' shining face (v. 2, like that of Moses after his encounter with God on Mount Sinai, Exod 34:29), and the overshadowing cloud (v. 5, like that which signaled God's presence with Israel in their sojourn to freedom, Exod 16:10; 19:9, etc.). Matthew specifically labels this experience a vision (v. 9), and the disciples react in much the same way as Daniel did to his apocalyptic visions (Dan 8:17-18; 10:7-9).

The discussion about Elijah (vv. 9-13) reflects a debate about the correct interpretation of Malachi 4:5 (3:23 Hebrew), which speaks about the coming of Elijah before the Day of the Lord. For Christians this has taken place in the person of John the Baptist (see also 3:1-17; 9:18-26; 11:1-19; 14:1-12).

17:14-20 The power of little faith

The tragic situation of a child who suffers from what is probably epilepsy (the Greek word *selēniazomai* literally means "moonstruck") becomes an occasion for further training for the disciples. The father's plaintive "Lord, have pity" echoes the pleas of other sufferers in the Gospel (8:2, 5-6, 25; 14:30; 15:22, 25; 20:30-31). While the disciples have been given the authority to cure every disease and illness (10:1), Matthew has not yet reported that they were ever able to do so (cf. Mark 6:13, 30). Jesus' harsh words for the disciples echo those of Moses as he voiced his exasperation with Israel (Deut 32:5). Jesus redirects the disciples away from focusing on what they lack, toward claiming and exercising the power they do have with their little faith (see also 6:30; 8:26; 14:31; 16:8; 21:21-22). See 13:31-32 for the parable of the mustard seed.

17:22-23 Second prediction of the Passion

The reaction of the disciples to this second prediction of Jesus' death and resurrection is not denial, as in 16:21-23, but overwhelming grief. Their progress in comprehension and acceptance advances as they move with Jesus toward Jerusalem (contrast Mark 9:2).

17:24-27 The temple tax

This story is peculiar to Matthew's Gospel. The issue is the payment of a yearly tax of a half shekel that was obligatory for all Jewish males over twenty years old (Exod 30:11-16). This served for the upkeep of the temple, as well as a sign of solidarity among Jews both within Israel and in the Diaspora. Controversy over this payment may have stemmed from disapproval over the manner in which the money was used by the Sadducees or the shaming of those who were too poor to contribute. Jesus' exchange with Peter makes it clear that as children of God, whose house the temple is, they are exempt from taxes for the temple. Nonetheless, for the sake of not causing scandal, Jesus pays the money. The fantastic detail of finding a coin in the mouth of a fish gives the story the air of a folktale.

18:1-14 Greatness in God's realm

The fourth great block of teaching concerns life in community. The first section (18:1-14) focuses on the need for humility and for the care of the most vulnerable. The second (18:15-20) outlines a procedure for reconciling aggrieved members

of the community, followed by a parable (18:21-35) about unlimited forgiveness. While these teachings are addressed to "the disciples" (v. 1), the nature of the instruction is to those with leadership responsibility, not to the "little ones."

In the first part (vv. 1-5) Jesus teaches leaders to cultivate humility by consciously identifying themselves with the concerns of the least important in the community. Children are certainly valued in families, but they are the most vulnerable and the least able to contribute to the sustenance of the group, at least until they are older. A second way to exercise humility is by showing hospitality toward those who are "nobodies" (v. 5). Lavishing care on them with the same attentiveness and openness that one would show to an important guest is the way of true leadership. Finally, leaders must be wary of putting any stumbling block (*skandalon*, vv. 6-9) in the way of a "little one." The consequences for doing so are dire. Matthew does not spell out precisely who the "little ones" are. They may be new converts or those whose faith is not yet strong. At 10:42 they are Christian missionaries. One's treatment of "the least" is the basis for reward or punishment at the last judgment (25:40, 45).

A further lesson in prizing each of the "little ones" is presented in the parable of the shepherd who goes to extraordinary lengths to recover a lost sheep (vv. 10-14). Christian leaders are to emulate God's care for Israel (Ps 23; Isa 40:11) and Jesus' compassion for people who are "like sheep without a shepherd" (9:36). They are not to be like the shepherds that Ezekiel (34:12) denounces for placing their own welfare above that of the "flock." They are to seek out the "lost sheep of the house of Israel" (10:6). The emphasis in Matthew's version of the parable is not on the repentance of the sheep (cf. Luke 15:7), but rather on the urgent task of the shepherd who follows God's will and experiences great joy in finding the lost (vv. 13-14).

18:15-20 A process for reconciliation

This section presents steps to be taken in the community when one member sins against another. The first step is direct confrontation, begun by the one who is offended (v. 15) and approaches the other with a willingness to forgive. The best case scenario is that this first confrontation brings about the needed repentance, and then reconciliation results. If it fails, however, the next step is to involve one or two others from the community (v. 16). The aim is to establish the truth, relying on impartial witnesses or facilitators. If this does not work, then the matter is brought before the whole community (*ekklēsia*, "church," used only here and in 16:18 in the Gospels). If that fails, then the person is to be treated like "a Gentile or a tax collector" (v. 17). It is not clear whether this means to exclude the person or to emulate Jesus' practice of befriending such people (see 8:5-13; 9:9-13; 11:19; 15:21-28).

Here Jesus may be advocating that Christians be willing to sit and break bread together, even while they are working toward resolving their differences. Note that Matthew does not indicate the nature of the offense. Such a strategy would not work for every kind of sin. Note that the whole community has a role in binding and loosing offenses (18:18), and the whole body is involved in praying for reconciliation.

18:21-35 Forgiveness aborted

The process sketched above is lengthy and arduous. Peter asks Jesus how often you have to do all this—as many as seven times? In biblical terms, seven is a perfect number, signifying here an endless number of times. Jesus' exhortation to forgive seventy-seven times (v. 22) contrasts with the threat of Lamech, who vowed vengeance "seventy-sevenfold" (Gen 4:24).

The parable plays out in three acts. In the first (vv. 23-27) a king decides to call in his "loan" (*daneion*), that is, the money due him from a slave who is a high-level bureaucrat (indicated by the amounts of money with which he deals, v. 24). This slave is evidently responsible for exacting tribute from other subjects. He builds networks and works the system to his and the king's advantage. The king, in a pure display of power, wants to collect ten thousand talents, approximately six to ten thousand days' wages. His purpose is to remind the servant of his subservience. The slave's response is exactly what the king wanted (v. 26). He does homage to the king and acknowledges his dependence and loyalty. The king is satisfied and returns him to his position. Word will spread both of the king's power and his generosity.

In the second act (vv. 28-30) the forgiven bureaucrat replicates the king's actions with his subordinates. This one owes him one hundred times less than the amount he owed the king. The point is not the difference in amount but that both

are unable to pay. Although the second underling responds in exactly the same way his master did to the king, the latter carries through his threats with a vengeance instead of forgiving the debt.

In the final part (vv. 31-34) the fellow servants report everything to the king, who becomes enraged. If his servant has understood the meaning of his previous actions, then he should have replicated them. If the slave wants loyalty, adulation, and recognition of his power, the king has shown him how to exact it. Instead, he has shamed the king by not imitating him. He has said by his actions that the king's method of exerting power is not effective. If the slave thinks that physical abuse, debasing another, and brutal imprisonment are the ways to gain power, then the king will show him just that. The conclusion (v. 35) was likely added by the evangelist.

As with all metaphors, the king is both like and unlike God. Unlike the monarch in the parable, God does not work for his own self-aggrandizement, but for the well-being of all creation. But like the king, God, through Jesus, has graciously forgiven all debt of sin (for which Jesus teaches the disciples to pray in 6:12). The only response to such mercy is to let it transform one's heart so as to be able to act with the same kind of graciousness toward others. This kind of power is through vulnerability and a willingness to forgo vengeance to work toward reconciliation. Those who do not learn to imitate godly ways in their dealings with one another will be treated by God in the way they have treated others.

19:1-15 Teaching on divorce and blessing of children

In his journey toward Jerusalem, Jesus takes the route along the eastern side of the Jordan River, as did most Jews, to avoid going through Samaria (v. 1). As at 16:1, rival religious leaders put a question to Jesus to test him (*peirazō*, as also 4:1, 3). Jesus' teaching on not divorcing was already introduced in the Sermon on the Mount (5:31-32). Now the question centers on whether there are any exceptions (v. 3). The exchange is cast as a rabbinical debate, such as the one between the first-century rabbis Shammai and Hillel. The latter held that a man could divorce his wife even for spoiling a dish for him, whereas the former argued that only sexual misconduct was grounds for divorce.

In his reply Jesus first cites Genesis 1:27 and then Genesis 2:24, arguing that God's intention from creation is for man and woman to remain united. Jesus' opponents, also citing Scripture, come back with a text from Deuteronomy 24:1-4, where Moses permits a man to divorce his wife by handing her a written bill of divorce. Jesus distinguishes between God's positive command in Genesis, which reveals God's intent, and Moses' concession to Israel because of their inability to achieve the ideal. As at 5:32, Jesus characterizes divorce as adultery, unless the basis for separating is *porneia* (v. 9). The meaning of this word is not certain. It may refer to sexual misconduct, such as adultery or marriage to close kin, which was forbidden in Jewish law (Lev 18:6-18; see also Acts 15:20, 29). If it is the latter, then the question concerns some Gentile converts who wished to become Christian but who were in such forbidden marriages. Would they first have to divorce to enter the community?

The reaction of Jesus' disciples reveals the radical nature of his teaching. "It is better not to marry" (v. 10) is akin to the hyperbole in 18:8-9, which states that it is better to cut off a hand or foot or eye rather than cause a little one to sin. Jesus acknowledges that not all can accept this teaching. It has long been debated whether the saying in verse 12 refers to those who choose to remain celibate or to those who do not remarry after the death or divorce of a spouse. In Jewish tradition marriage was the norm, although some groups, such as the Therapeutae and the Qumranites, evidently practiced celibacy.

The reason why a Christian might make such a choice is for the sake of the mission. Many widows in the early church chose to live together and to devote themselves to ministry rather than remarry (see Acts 9:39, which may refer to such a situation, and 1 Timothy 5:3-16 for regulations regarding them). For women in Jesus' day, his stricter teaching on divorce may often have served a compassionate end, safeguarding women from being cast aside for no good reason and from being placed in a vulnerable position socially and economically. By the same token, painful decisions about divorce in a contemporary context must take into consideration Jesus' prime concern for the well-being of each person as a valued son or daughter of God in the community of believers.

In verses 13-15 the lens widens to the most vulnerable members in the family unit. When linked to the previous scene, Jesus' blessing and prayer for the little ones recognize that they may be the ones who suffer most when the parents are contemplating divorce. A reason why the disciples wanted to prevent the children from coming to Jesus is not given. In a pronouncement reminiscent of 18:3, Jesus speaks about their importance in God's realm.

19:16-30 Discipleship and possessions

The exchange between Jesus and the rich young man and the ensuing discussion with the disciples speak soberly about the obstacle that possessions can pose for discipleship. In Matthew's account (cf. Mark 10:17-31; Luke 18:18-30), the rich man asks Jesus about doing good, one of the evangelist's favorite themes (5:16; 7:17-19; 12:12, 33-35; 13:23, 24; 26:10). Keeping the commandments is a first step in doing good. The young man's question, "Which ones?" rings false, since all the commandments must be kept equally. Jesus' invitation to him to go beyond simply keeping the commandments and to "be perfect" (*teleios*, as also at 5:48) concerns becoming "whole" or "complete." As at 5:48, this is not an invitation for a select few, nor is it presenting a contrast between Judaism and Christianity. In the Old Testament, although riches are regarded as a sign of God's blessing (Deut 28:1-14), there are also the same dire warnings about the corrosiveness of riches (Ezek 7:19; Amos 6:4-8; Prov 15:16).

In Matthew's perspective, being a disciple of Jesus entails faithfulness to the Jewish Law as interpreted by Jesus, which demands radical attachment to him. It is as difficult for a rich person to do this as it is for a camel to squeeze through the eye of a needle (v. 24). The popular interpretation that there was a gate so named in Jerusalem has no basis. Jesus' response to the disciples' astonishment (similarly, 19:10) is to refocus their attention on God's initiative and power with them, enabling them to do what is good—the question with which the rich man began (v. 16). See also the beatitude of the poor in 6:3 and the admonitions that the heart lies where the treasure is (6:21) and that one cannot serve both God and mammon (6:24). The treasure to seek above all is the realm of God (13:44). The theme of reward for disciples runs throughout the Gospel (5:12, 46-47;

6:1-6, 16, 18; 10:39-42; 25:21, 23, 34). Here the focus is eschatological. Disciples share in the glory and the final judgment by the Human One, as their self-emptying for God's realm has prepared them to receive the eternal inheritance God wills for all.

20:1-16 Justice in the vineyard

This parable and the previous episode conclude with the same saying about reversal (19:30; 20:16). This is a floating proverb that is tagged on to various New Testament passages in diverse contexts (see also Mark 10:31; Luke 13:30). It does not supply the meaning for the parable. In the story the first hired are paid last because the point of the story depends on their seeing what the last hired receive. The complaint of the workers in verse 12 voices what is so puzzling about this parable. Does not justice demand that those who worked more earn more? The vineyard owner has promised that he will pay what is just (*dikaios*, v. 4) and insists that he is doing no injustice (*ouk adikō se*, v. 13). He then asks, "Am I not free to do as I wish with my own money? Are you envious because I am generous?" (v. 15).

Two important points are made in the landowner's reply. If he is a figure for God, his actions show that God's generosity, which is not merited, is freely lavished on those most in need. God's generosity does no injustice, but neither can it be calculated or earned. The story *is* about people getting what they deserve: all have the right to eat for the day. From the position of the day laborers, who are on the lowest economic rung and who stand waiting all day (v. 6), wanting to work but not hired, the wage given them enables them to feed their family for one more day. Less than a denarius would be useless. From their perspective, those who were hired at the beginning of the day, though they have worked longer and harder, at least had the satisfaction of knowing all day that come sundown they would be able to feed their families. In God's realm, justice means that all are fed as a sign of God's equal and inclusive love; it does not mean getting what we deserve, either in terms of retribution for wrongdoing or recompense for good deeds.

The second point is that "evil-eye" envy is the most destructive force in a community. The question in verse 15 is, literally, "Or is your eye evil that I am good?" In a first-century worldview of limited good, anyone's gain means another one's

loss. While the grumblers focus on their perceived loss, they miss the limitless goodness and generosity of the landowner. Linked with the previous discussion about the danger of riches, this parable challenges those disciples who have enough to meet their daily needs to reject acquisitiveness and attend to the needs of those who are in desperate straits.

20:17-28 To drink the cup

The third prediction of Jesus' passion is more detailed than the others and occurs as Jesus and his disciples near Jerusalem. In the first prediction (16:21-23) Jesus told his disciples that he would be killed at the hands of the elders, chief priests, and scribes. In fact, the Jewish leaders did not have the authority to carry out capital punishment (see John 18:31). Jesus will actually be handed over to the Gentiles (v. 19), who will put him to death (cf. the second prediction, where Jesus spoke in general terms of being betrayed into human hands, 17:22-23).

It is jarring to have the disciples bickering over the places of honor in the kingdom after this sober prediction. Matthew redacts the story (cf. Mark 10:35-45), so that the mother of James and John makes the request, thus softening the critique of the disciples and making their mother the ambitious one. It is ambiguous whether the other ten are indignant at the audacity of the request or whether they are upset that these two beat them to it (v. 24).

The metaphor "cup" is used often in the Scriptures to speak of the suffering of Israel (Isa 51:17; Jer 25:15; 49:12; 51:7; Lam 4:21; *Mart. Isa.* 5:13). In 26:39 Jesus implores God to let "this cup" pass him by. Jesus then instructs the disciples on the manner of leadership they are to exercise. They are not to "lord it over" any others; rather, like Jesus himself, they are to serve the rest of the community. Jesus' service is service to the death, a giving of his life as ransom for all. The word *polys*, "many," does not exclude anyone. It reflects a Semitic expression where "many" is the opposite of "one," thus the equivalent of "all." The notion of Jesus giving his life as ransom draws on the image of a slave who buys back his freedom for a price. These last verses of the Gospel are aimed at leaders who have some degree of power, privilege, status, and choice. Their choice to take the lowly position of service is liberating when accompanied by empowerment of those who are otherwise powerless. These sayings must not be used to reinforce the servitude of those who are enslaved in whatever way.

20:29-34 A final healing

This is the last healing story in the Gospel. It mirrors the one in 9:27-31, where two blind men also cried out to Jesus, "Son of David, have pity on us!" (see also 12:23; 15:22). After having instructed his disciples on servant leadership (20:25-28), Jesus demonstrates for them the kind of descendant of King David he is. As in 9:27-31, Jesus engages the two men in conversation; he does not merely touch them and keep going. Jesus treats them not simply as objects of compassion but with dignity, as people who are able to articulate their need (v. 32). These two who see and follow (v. 34) model the response needed of disciples as Jesus now prepares to enter Jerusalem as Son of David (21:9, 15) to begin the ordeal that will culminate in his reign with God.

JERUSALEM; JESUS' FINAL DAYS OF TEACHING IN THE TEMPLE
Matt 21:1–28:15

21:1-11 Entry into Jerusalem

Jesus' journey to Jerusalem, begun at 16:21, climaxes with his enthusiastic reception by a very large crowd (vv. 1-11), and his action in the temple (vv. 12-17). Both scenes are eschatological in tone and are heavily interlaced with quotations from the prophets, so that the significance in terms of fulfillment of Scriptures is most evident. Jesus enters the city from the east. The Mount of Olives, according to Zechariah 14:4 is the place where the final eschatological struggle will take place. Matthew seems to speak of two animals (v. 2), but he is preserving the parallelism of Zechariah 9:9 (quoted in v. 5), which actually describes only one beast. The prophet tells of the Messiah entering the city "riding on an ass, / on a colt, the foal of an ass." Jesus' action is a parody of that of a conqueror over a vanquished city. The Hebrew word *hôšiʾânāʾ* means "save, please!" Here it is not so much a plea for help as an acclamation of praise. The shouts of adulation of the crowd (echoing Ps 118:26 in v. 9) contrast with the mounting antagonism of the Jewish leaders. The reaction described in verse 10, "the whole city was shaken (*eseisthē*),"

points ahead to the aftermath of the death of Jesus, when "the earth quaked (*eseisthē*," 27:51).

21:12-17 Confrontation in the temple

In Matthew's account, Jesus' entry into Jerusalem culminates with his action in the temple (cf. Mark 11:15-19, where Jesus waits until the next day). Scholars still speculate on the nature of the abuse that Jesus was protesting. The interpretation of each evangelist differs slightly. In Matthew's account, Jesus interrupts the commercial activity in the temple area (v. 12). Buying and selling of animals was necessary for temple sacrifice. Doves were the poor woman's offering after childbirth (Lev 12:6-8; Luke 2:24). Greek and Roman coins had to be changed into Tyrian shekels, not because they lacked an offensive image, but because they had the highest silver content.

Matthew interprets Jesus' action (v. 13) by combining quotations from Isaiah 56:7and Jeremiah 7:11. The first speaks of the messianic ideal of the temple being a perfect place of prayer for all peoples (though Matthew omits that last phrase; cf. Mark 11:16). The second was a warning to the people of Judah, who continued trusting in the efficacy of temple worship while their deeds toward one another were rampantly unjust. Jeremiah warned that their corruption was defiling their "hideout," the temple, and predicted its destruction. In verses 12-13 Matthew's Jesus is a fiery prophet bent on rectifying abuse. In verses 14-17, unique to Matthew, Jesus is the compassionate healer of those who are least welcome in the temple (see Lev 21:18, where the blind and the lame are forbidden to offer sacrifices).

Jesus fulfills the messianic promise of Isaiah 35:5-6, where all, including those who are blind and lame, are healed and march exultantly into Jerusalem. Typically, the response to Jesus is divided. The leaders become indignant, while the children (see also 18:1-4; 19:13-15) sing "Hosanna to the Son of David" (see the use of this title in healing stories at 9:27; 12:23; 15:22; 20:30, 31). Jesus responds by quoting from Psalm 8:3.

21:18-22 The withered fig tree

This strange story may have evolved from the parable of the fig tree in Luke 13:6-9. Fruitful figs and vines are a symbol of peace and prosperity (1 Kgs 4:25), and Matthew frequently uses the metaphor "bear fruit" to speak of doing righteous deeds (cf. 3:8; 7:15-20; 12:33-37; 13:23; 21:19, 33-43). In the Matthean setting, there are strong eschatological overtones from chapter 21 forward. The time has arrived when there must be evidence of "good fruit," or else there will be destruction of the temple and condemnation of those who lead people astray (see also Jer 8:13; Hos 9:10, 16). The last two verses shift emphasis, so that the story becomes one about the power of faith (see also 7:7-11; cf. 6:30; 8:25, 26; 14:30, 31; 16:8; 17:20, where Jesus chides the disciples for their lack of faith). Jesus does not promise that the object of every prayerful request will be granted; rather, he assures believers that when they pray with faith in God's gracious goodness, God will always be with them (1:23; 28:20). God's power is at work in believers, even when they confront the most insurmountable obstacles.

21:23-27 The authority of Jesus

Throughout Matthew's Gospel, Jesus is portrayed as the authoritative teacher whom many people follow but whom the leaders reject. Now there are open confrontations between Jesus and the religious authorities. The chief priests and elders (v. 23) are the leading opponents in the passion narrative (the Pharisees drop out of view after chapter 23). Their trap backfires, and they themselves are trapped by Jesus' question. Three parables follow, the first two of which indirectly answer the question about the source of Jesus' authority.

21:28-32 Saying and doing

The technique Jesus uses is like that of Nathan (2 Sam 12:1-12), whereby the hearers are asked for their opinion and end by pronouncing judgment on themselves. The parable seems a simple one at first. Both children (the word in verse 28 is *teknon*, "child," not *huios*, "son") fall short of the ideal. But the one who appeared to *do* the father's will was the first.

However, in a culture that highly prizes honor, the answer is not so clear. In some manuscript variants of this parable, the one who gives the correct answer is the second child. The first child shamed the father publicly, a worse fault than failing to carry through on one's word. At 7:21-27 Jesus insisted to his disciples that saying *and* doing are necessary; now he directs this message to religious authorities who do not practice what they preach (23:3). Verses 31-32 contrast the leaders, who should most exemplify righteousness,

with those who are thought least able to do so. But there is still time for the leaders to repent. Those who initially refuse to say yes to Jesus and do the will of God can still change their minds.

21:33-43 Treacherous tenants

Matthew reworks Mark's version (12:1-12), making the parable more allegorical and more pointedly christological. It is a familiar story, echoing Isaiah 5, but with a new ending. In Isaiah 5 Yahweh decides to destroy the vineyard after disappointment over the yield of sour grapes from Israel, the carefully cultivated vine. In Jesus' parable the tenants are destroyed; the vineyard remains and is entrusted to others. The eschatological time (*kairos*, v. 34) demands that fruit be evident now (see 21:18-22). The repeated sending of the servants (vv. 34-39) is like God's repeated sending of the prophets to Israel. Prophets were called "servants" of God (Jer 7:25; 25:4; Amos 3:7; Zech 1:6), and their fates match those in the parable (see Jer 20:2; 26:20-23; 2 Chr 24:21).

The sequence of actions in verse 39 corresponds to the details of Jesus' passion. He is seized (26:50), taken outside the city limits (27:31-32), and then killed (27:35). The murderous plans of the tenants in the vineyard match the intent of the chief priests and Pharisees (21:46; 22:15) toward Jesus. The chief priests and elders pronounce their own self-condemnation (v. 41), but the future tense verbs show that the possibility is yet open so the Jewish leaders can still change their minds (as also 21:29, 32). They could still be among those "other tenants" to whom the vineyard will be entrusted.

Jesus' question in verse 42 (see also 12:3, 5; 19:4; 21:16) underscores the conflict between Jesus' interpretation of Scripture and that of the opposing religious leaders. The quotation from Psalm 118 in verse 42 recalls God's unlikely choice of David as king, the prototype for the Messiah, and points toward the leadership of the new Israel as coming from those rejected as unimportant. At the conclusion (vv. 45-46) the chief priests and Pharisees clearly understand the parable (cf. 13:51), but instead of heeding Jesus' invitation, they plot his arrest.

22:1-14 Dressed for the feast

This is the third of three parables that Jesus addresses to the religious leaders in Jerusalem after they challenged his authority (21:23-27). The parable is highly allegorized and has a number of unrealistic details. The image of a wedding banquet recalls Matthew 9:15, where Jesus was likened to a groom, whose presence demands feasting, not fasting. This metaphor is frequently used in the Scriptures to signify God's abundant care, both now and at the end time (e.g., Isa 25:6-10; 55:1-3). The repeated invitation is reminiscent of the multiple envoys in 21:33-46 and has an echo of Lady Wisdom inviting all to her banquet (Prov 9:5). The custom of a double invitation (see Esth 5:8; 6:14) allowed the potential guest to find out who the other guests were and whether all was being arranged appropriately. It also gave them time to decide if they would be able to reciprocate. The time lapse also allowed the host to determine the amount of food needed.

Unlike Luke 14:15-24, there are no detailed excuses offered by the invitees. Their mistreatment and killing of the king's servants (vv. 5-6) and the king's enraged response (v. 7), are allegorical allusions to the killing of John the Baptist and the prophets and the destruction of Jerusalem in A.D. 70. The king's retaliation can be expected in an honor-and-shame system, in which one responds in kind to an affront. But his second response (vv. 8-10) is shocking. In a first-century Mediterranean world likes eat with likes, since eating together signifies sharing of values and of social position. The king sends his servants out to the places where the main road cuts through the city boundary, going out to the countryside (v. 10). This is where the poorer people lived, while the elite (5 to 10 percent of the population) lived in the center of the city. Like the parables in 13:24-30, 47-50, both "good" and "bad" are gathered in, and then there is sorting out.

The last scene (vv. 11-14) is entirely unrealistic but highlights Matthew's ethical concern: one must be ready at all times for the end-time banquet, clothed with good deeds (similarly Rom 13:14; Gal 3:27; Col 3:12). More is required of a disciple than initial acceptance of the invitation to be a "friend of God and prophets" (Wis 7:27). See also 20:13, where the grumbler is called "friend," as is Judas at the moment of betrayal (26:50). In the Matthean narrative context, the parable is a warning to the religious leaders who are offered repeated invitations to accept Jesus. The seriousness of their refusal is painted with vivid metaphors: they will be cast into the outer darkness (see also 8:12; 25:30), where there is weeping and gnashing of teeth (8:12,

13:42, 50; 24:51; 25:30). The proverbial saying in verse 14 does not entirely capture the meaning of the parable. The focus is on how those who are expected to respond to the invitation (the religious leaders) refuse, while the unexpected invitees (the socially marginal) have accepted.

22:15-22 Taxes to Caesar

This is the first of four more controversies between Jesus and the religious leaders. Their flattering words (v. 16) are true but insincere, as they proceed to lay a deliberate trap (v. 15). The question is a sticky one. Since the Roman occupation of Palestine in 63 B.C., Jews were obliged to pay tribute, or a head tax, in Roman coinage, on each man, woman, and slave. If Jesus opposes this payment, he would be advocating revolt against Rome. If he advocates payment, then he would be seen as a collaborator with the enemy. Jesus sees the malice and hypocrisy of his questioners, who have set this trap (v. 18). His clever response can be understood in one of three ways: (1) one should pay nothing to Caesar because everything belongs to God (Lev 25:23); (2) one should pay the emperor because he is God's representative (as Rom 13:1-7; 1 Pet 2:13-17); (3) one can pay Caesar but recognize that his authority is relative and that loyalty to God takes precedence. The last is the most likely meaning. As in 17:24-27, Jesus advises paying the tax, but this is not a vote of support for the occupying power. The amazed response (v. 22) of the Pharisees' disciples (see also 8:27; 9:33; 15:31; 21:20) underscores Jesus' skill in outwitting his opponents.

22:23-33 The question of resurrection

In this second controversy the Sadducees pose a question that derides belief in the resurrection. Ideas about the afterlife were diverse in Jesus' day. The notion of resurrection of the dead first appears in the book of Daniel (12:2), written in the second century B.C., and was accepted by the Pharisees but not the Sadducees (see Acts 23:6). The situation posed by the Sadducees, citing Deuteronomy 25:5-10, is absurd (although see Tobit 3:8; 6:14, where Sarah, the daughter of Raguel, outlives seven husbands). Like the previous question, it is set up to try to make Jesus contradict his own teaching or the Scriptures. It is a Bible battle in which Jesus emerges as authoritative teacher.

Jesus responds by accusing his opponents of not knowing the Scriptures or the power of God.

He cites Exodus 3:6, 15-16 to argue that Israel's ancestors, who were physically dead at the time that God spoke to Moses, continued to be in relationship with God, and so they were in some sense among the living. Jesus also asserts that the Sadducees do not understand the nature of resurrection. By God's power new life will be created that is continuous in some way with the life we have known, yet it will be brought to fullness in ways we do not yet know.

22:34-40 The greatest commandment

In Mark's account (12:28-34; cf. Luke 10:25), the scribe's question is sincere, but in Matthew it leads to another controversy. The Pharisees gather together (v. 34), signaling a plot against Jesus (see 2:4; 22:41; 26:3; 27:17, 27; 28:12; possibly this also alludes to Ps 2:2). The question they pose is meant to test him (see also 22:15). All commandments are important; all must be kept. The query is not whether some laws can be disregarded, but whether Jesus, like some teachers, would sum up the Torah in a simple statement, as did Rabbi Hillel: "What is hateful to you do not do to your neighbor" (*b. Šabb.* 31a).

Jesus summarizes the whole of the Law in two commandments (see also 7:12). The first, the *Shemaᶜ* (Deut 6:4-9), was recited twice a day by Jews. It enjoins love of God with one's whole heart, soul, and strength. The heart (*kardia*), was considered the seat of all emotions, the soul (*psychē*), the center of vitality and consciousness, and strength (*ischys*) denotes power or might. The second command, love of neighbor, is from the Holiness Code (Lev 19:18), which asserts that love of God is manifest in love toward the neighbor. The modern Western notion of the necessity of self-love would have been a foreign concept to people of the biblical world. They did not understand themselves in individualistic terms, but rather as enmeshed in a particular family, clan, and religious group. Dependent on others for their sense of self-identity, love of self and love of others are inseparable.

22:41-46 David's son

In the fourth and final controversy, Jesus is the one who initiates the questioning. Again, the debate centers on the correct interpretation of Scripture. The text in question is Psalm 110:1, a coronation psalm, in which God assures the new king of special honor (sitting at the right hand) and a vanquishing of his enemies (making them subservient, "under your feet"). The speaker in the psalm is David, who says that the "Lord" (*kyrios*), meaning Yahweh, is speaking to "my lord" (*kyrios*), meaning the new king.

Jesus stumps his opponents by asking that if David, inspired by the Spirit, calls the new king (here equated with the messiah) "lord," then he must be more than simply his son. The notion that the messiah would be a "son of David" is found in Isaiah 11:1, 10; Jeremiah 23:5. Although this is a favorite Matthean title for Jesus (1:1; 9:27; 12:23; 15:22; 20:30, 31; 21:9, 15), "Son of David" is not adequate to express all that Jesus is. This text brings together several important christological titles intimating that Jesus is also Messiah, Son of God, and Lord. The silence of Jesus' opponents indicates a victory for him. There will be no further exchanges with the leaders until the passion narrative, as he speaks now only with the crowds and his disciples.

23:1-12 Warning against hypocrisy

The whole of this chapter is a stinging denunciation by Jesus of the scribes and Pharisees, who have been cast as his opponents throughout the Gospel. Matthew expands a brief critique of scribes from Mark 12:38-40, weaving in material from Q and Luke 11:37-52. In the New Testament, scribes are religious leaders who are learned in Torah. Pharisees, lay religious leaders, differed from Sadducees in their belief in resurrection (see 22:23-33) and in oral interpretation of the Law. The excoriating tone of Jesus' rebuke reflects the vehemence of the conflict between the Christians of Matthew's community, who were predominantly Jewish, and the Jews of emerging rabbinic Judaism.

Jesus takes on the role of a prophet, much like Amos (5:18-20; 6:1-7) or Isaiah (5:8-10, 11-14), who uses the classic "woe" form to denounce the wrongdoing of a group of his own people, with the intent to turn them from evil and toward right relation with God. Jesus' words are a warning to the crowds and his disciples (v. 1) not to follow the hypocritical practices of these leaders, who do not practice what they teach (v. 3). In contrast to Jesus, whose burden is light (11:30), they lay heavy loads on people's shoulders (v. 4). They make their phylacteries and fringes noticeable to all (v. 5). (Phylacteries are leather boxes containing the parchment texts such as Exodus 13:1-16;

Deuteronomy 6:4-9; 11:13-22, which are strapped to the forehead and arm during morning prayer.) Wearing "tassels" or "fringes" at the corners of the outer garments reminds a Jew to observe all God's commands (Num 15:38-39; Deut 22:12; Matt 9:20; 14:36). Jesus also criticizes the leaders' love of places of honor and deferential titles (vv. 6-10)—only he and God are to bear these titles. Like many other reform movements, there was an impulse in early Christianity toward egalitarianism and status reversal (vv. 11-12; see also 18:1-4; 19:13-15; 20:20-28).

23:13-36 Seven woes

In the seven woes that ensue, the religious leaders are repeatedly called "hypocrites"—a term that originally referred to an actor, one who put on a mask to assume another personage. In the first woe (vv. 13-14), Jesus denounces the scribes and Pharisees not only because they fail to enter into God's realm themselves but, worse yet, they block the way for others. The image of unlocking and locking the way to heaven recalls Matthew 16:19, where Peter is given the keys to God's realm. For Matthew's community, Peter and the leaders of the emergent Christian community are the authorities to be heeded rather than those of the synagogue.

The second woe (v. 15) is an accusation that the Gentile converts to Pharisaism are twice as zealous and twice as misguided as their teachers. Jesus warns that in the end they will be "child[ren] of Gehenna" rather than "children of God" (e.g., Matt 5:9, cf. 45). The name "Gehenna" derives from "The Valley (gē) of Hinnom," which runs south-southwest of Jerusalem. It represented the place of fiery judgment, because it was there that fires of the cult of Molech and later, smoldering refuse, were located.

In the third woe (vv. 16-22), Jesus critiques the meaningless distinctions the Pharisees invented in their oath-taking. In Jesus' world, binding obligations were set not by contracts but with one's word, by public swearing. For the most serious agreements, God's name would be invoked. But devout Jews objected to speaking God's name aloud. Just as Matthew substituted "the reign of heaven" for "the reign of God" (see 3:2), so Pharisees would swear on the gold or the gifts of the temple, objects associated with God, as a way to avoid saying the divine name. Jesus says that these fine distinctions are useless; the effect is the same. See Matthew 5:33-37 on not taking oaths at all.

In the fourth woe (vv. 23-24), Jesus accuses the leaders of not being able to distinguish between what is important and what is not. The texts on tithing (see Lev 27:30-33; Num 18:21-32; Deut 14:22-29) prescribe giving one-tenth of one's produce, flocks, wine, grain, and oil to support the temple, the Levites, and the poor. They do not mention herbs, such as mint, dill, and cumin. Jesus teaches his disciples that their observance of the Law must go beyond what is written (Matt 5:21-48), but the point is to arrive at more complete harmony with God and all that God has created (5:20, 48). The Pharisees, by contrast, engage in intensified practices of keeping the Law that lead them away from deeds of justice, mercy, and faith. Thus they become "blind guides," not seeing the way clearly themselves and leading others onto a destructive path. The outrageousness of their practice is captured in the hyperbole "swallow the camel."

The fifth woe (vv. 25-26) contrasts outer practices with inner dispositions. Jesus uses a strong term, harpagēs, "pillage, plunder," to speak of the corrupt inner state of the scribes and Pharisees, who misuse their power to exploit others. He also accuses them of akrasia, "lack of self-control" and "want of power" (see v. 25). The reference is to sexual activity or intemperance in general. By contrast, the interior disposition Jesus has taught his disciples is purity of heart (5:8), the ability to forgive from the heart (18:35), and love of God with all one's heart (22:37).

The sixth woe (vv. 27-28) continues in the same vein as the fifth. The Pharisees and scribes present a lovely exterior, seeming to be in right relation with God and others, while their interior disposition is rotten with hypocrisy and evildoing. Like whitewashed sepulchers, they hide putrid decay within. White-washing sepulchers made them easily visible, so that Jews could avoid contact with them and thus maintain ritual purity (see Lev 21:1, 11).

In the seventh and last woe (vv. 29-36), the Pharisees and scribes pretend to honor the prophets and righteous ancestors with decorated monuments and protest that had they been alive earlier, they would never have done what their ancestors did to the prophets. In truth, Jesus says, they are no different from their forebears. They will kill the prophet Jesus just as their ancestors rid themselves of the pesky prophets who denounced their unrighteousness. They show themselves to be not children of God but children of Gehenna (v. 15) and children of murderers (v. 31), linked to all the innocent blood shed from Abel to Zechariah, the first victim of murder in the Bible (Gen 4:8) to the last. There is some confusion about the identity of Zechariah. The Old Testament prophet Zechariah was the son of Barachiah (Zech 1:1), but as far as we know, he was not murdered "between the sanctuary and the altar" (v. 35), as was Zechariah, son of Jehoiada (2 Chr 24:20-22).

The theme of responsibility for innocent blood is an important one in the passion narrative as Judas tries to return the blood money (27:4), Pilate tries to wash himself of guilt for Jesus' blood (27:24), and the people say to Pilate, "His blood be on us and on our children" (27:25). At the Last Supper Jesus offers to his disciples his "blood of the covenant" (26:28) for the forgiveness of sins.

23:37-39 Lament over Jerusalem

The tone shifts from vehement denunciation of the leaders to profound sadness for the city which destroys God's messengers and which, by Matthew's day, lies in ruins. The poignant image of a mother bird yearning to gather her rebellious young under her wings is a common metaphor in the Scriptures for God's loving care (Deut 32:11; Ruth 2:12; Pss 17:8; 36:7; 57:1; 61:4; Luke 13:34-35). But like a mother who never abandons even the most wayward child, Jesus, quoting Psalm 118:26, holds out the promise that they will see him again when they can receive him as did the disciples when he first entered Jerusalem (21:9).

The denunciations and woes in this chapter must always be read in the context of a bitter internal family dispute between the Jewish Christians and Jews who did not join them in Matthew's day. Jesus is a prophet admonishing his own leaders and inviting them to a change of heart. His words still sound a warning against hypocrisy to any religious leaders.

24:1–25:46 The apocalyptic discourse

Jesus has been teaching his disciples and warning and disputing with other religious leaders since 21:23. He now leaves the temple area and directs his instruction only to his disciples (24:1, 3). He speaks of the calamities that presage the coming of the Human One (24:1-33) and tells three parables (24:45–25:30) that emphasize the need for watchful-

ness. The parable of the final judgment (25:31-46) brings this last block of teaching to a climax.

24:1-14 The beginning of the end

The tension between Jesus and the temple leadership has been mounting. He has performed a prophetic action of purification in the temple (21:12-17), he has engaged in debates with the temple leadership (21:23–22:46), and he has warned his disciples about their hypocrisy (23:1-36). This comes to a head as Jesus now predicts the very destruction of the temple (24:1-2), an occurrence that Jeremiah (7:1-15) associated with the messianic age. In Matthew's day this has already occurred. At his interrogation before the Jewish leaders, false witnesses accuse Jesus of making threats against the temple (26:61) and passers-by deride him about this in the crucifixion scene (27:40).

Jesus then speaks about the signs of the end times. He is seated, as authoritative teacher (see also 5:10; 15:29), on the Mount of Olives, the place associated with the final judgment (Zech 14:4). As in the parable discourse (13:10-17), Jesus' disciples receive private instruction. He paints a picture of massive chaos and destruction, with a proliferation of false messiahs, wars, famines, earthquakes, persecution, hatred because of Jesus' name, sin, betrayal, deception, lawlessness, and loss of fervor. Strife comes both from within and from without.

In almost every age people see these signs and wonder if they herald the end. A similar theme is found in the mission discourse (10:16-25, 34-39), where Jesus also assured his disciples not to fear anything because of God's constant care for them (10:26-33). Here as well, Jesus tells them that if they persevere to the end, they will be saved (v. 13). These birthpangs (v. 8) are the prelude to new life. For Matthew, this end is not imminent—the Gospel must first be preached throughout the whole world (see also 28:16-20).

24:15-31 Signs of the coming of the Human One

There will be unmistakable signs when the end actually does come. It will be as evident as lightning across the sky (v. 27) or vultures circling over a corpse (v. 28). One sign will be like the one spoken of by Daniel, the "desolating abomination" (v. 15; Dan 9:27; 11:31; 12:11). In Daniel this referred to the statue that Antiochus IV Epiphanes placed in the temple in 167 B.C., which sparked the Maccabean revolt. Still fresh in the memories of Matthew's community is that the emperor Caligula threatened a similar action in A.D. 40.

A future event of this caliber will signal the end. This is a time when immediate flight is the response to the danger (as in 2:12-13, 10:23). As is so often the case, it is mothers and children who are the most adversely affected. The disciples are to pray that it not happen at a time when the hardship would be intensified, such as winter or the sabbath. Fleeing on the sabbath (v. 20) may have drawn attention to the community and put them at risk. Or it could be a cause of division if some thought flight would break sabbath observance.

Cosmic signs (as in Isa 13:10; 34:4; Ezek 32:7; Joel 2:10, 31; 3:4; 4:15; Amos 8:9; Hag 2:6, 21) preface the final sign before the coming of the Human One (see comments at 8:20). Why mourning (v. 30) will accompany this sign is not clear—is it because of the tribulations or because people are repenting? The motif of God gathering in the elect at the end time is a common one (Deut 30:3-4; Isa 11:11-12; Ezek 37:21; 39:27-29; Zech 2:6-12).

24:32-51 Parables of watchfulness

A series of parables and figurative sayings exhorts disciples to watchfulness. The fig tree (vv. 32-35), which is different from other trees in Palestine (most are evergreens), sheds all its leaves in winter. Just as its budding is a sign of the arrival of summer, the signs in the previous verses alert disciples to the coming of the Human One. There is a tension between verse 34, which assures that the end is imminent, and verse 14, which asserts that the Gospel first has to be preached to the whole world. Disciples need to be both ready and steadfast, trusting in Jesus' words, which will never pass away (similarly the Torah, 5:18). The timing of the end is unpredictable, so disciples need to stay awake (see also 26:38, 40, 41).

While the previous verses emphasize watchfulness for the coming of the master, the parable of the faithful servant (vv. 45-51) exhorts disciples to vigilance in day-to-day tasks that must be fulfilled in the in-between time. One of these is the daily distribution of food (v. 45). This detail may be an allusion to the difficulties in the early church over food and eating, such as conflicts over Gentile and Jewish Christians eating together (Gal 2:11-14) or having people of differing social status at the same table (22:1-14). Alternatively, giving food may be

understood as a metaphor for teaching (so 1 Cor 3:2; John 6:25-33), and the parable as an exhortation to leaders to exercise their teaching ministry well. The warning to those who gorge themselves on the resources meant for the community is dire; such a one will be dismembered (*dichotomēsei*, literally, "cut in two," v. 51) as a condemned person.

25:1-13 Ready maidens

A second parable advising preparedness for the coming of the Human One casts Jesus in the role of a bridegroom (as 9:15; see Isa 54:5; Jer 31:32; Hos 2:16, where Yahweh is the bridegroom of Israel). In Jesus' day, weddings took place in two stages. First was the betrothal ceremony at the home of the father of the bride, at which the groom presented the marriage contract and the bride price to his future father-in-law. The bride continued to live in her father's house until the second step, when she would move to the home of her husband, about a year later. This is the stage depicted in the parable. The maidens are waiting while the groom and the bride's father hammer out the final negotiations. Upon reaching a final agreement, the wedding party would go in procession to the house of the groom, where the feasting would commence.

The waiting women are friends of the groom; the bride is never mentioned in the story. The word *parthenos* refers to a virgin, a young woman of marriageable age (twelve or in her early teens). The contrast between wise and foolish recalls the builders in 7:24-27. It is not clear whether the women are carrying torches (the usual connotation of *lampades*) wrapped with oil-soaked rags or hand-held oil lamps with lighted wicks. Matthew 5:14-16 provides a clue to interpreting why the women cannot share their oil. There light is equated with good deeds that are visible to others and lead to praise of God. Similarly, at Matthew 7:24-27 the wise are those who hear and act on Jesus' words. Just so, the wise maidens in this parable are those who have faithfully prepared for the end time. No one can supply this preparation for another. One is either ready or not at the eschatological moment.

25:14-30 Investing talents

This parable is often interpreted as an exhortation to use all one's God-given gifts to the full. However, the Greek word *talanton* has no other connotation than a monetary unit or weight measurement. In the parable it denotes a very large sum of money. What the parable depicts are two servants who invest and double the money with which they are entrusted, which wins them their master's approval, a share in his joy, and further responsibility. The third servant, by contrast, buries the money, which was considered the best way of safeguarding valuables in antiquity. Yet he earns harsh punishment from the master.

Key to understanding the parable is that Jesus did not live in a capitalist system, where it was thought that wealth can be increased by investment. Rather, people had a notion of limited good: there is only so much wealth, and any increase to one person takes away from another. The aim in life for a peasant was to have enough to take care of his family. Anyone amassing large amounts for himself would be seen as greedy and wicked. In the parable, then, if the master is not a figure for God, it is the third servant who is the honorable one—only he has refused to collaborate with his master in his unfettered greed. The parable warns rich people to stop exploiting those who are poor, and it encourages poor people to take courageous measures to expose greed for the sin that it is. The last verse is sobering, depicting what can happen to those who oppose the rich and powerful. It can encourage disciples to find ways to stand together as they confront unjust systems. There is still opportunity, since the end time has not yet arrived.

25:31-46 Final judgment

This is the last of Matthew's parables and is unique to this Gospel. The time of judgment has arrived as the Human One comes in his glory (v. 31). This scene is intimately linked with 28:16-20, where Jesus instructs his followers to make disciples of all nations (*panta ta ethnē*, 28:19), a command that this parable presumes has been fulfilled. All the nations (v. 32) are now assembled to render account. The reason why the sheep are separated from the goats is not clear. Both were very valuable. Nor is there any evidence that after pasturing them together during the daytime, a shepherd would separate the two at night. (See 3:12; 13:24-30, 47-50; 24:40-41; 25:1-13 for other images of end-time separation.) Since most people were right-handed and developed greater strength and skill with this hand, the right side came to symbolize favor, blessing, and honor.

The image of Jesus shifts from shepherd to king (v. 34; see 2:2; 21:5). And, like Moses, who

laid out before the Israelites the choice of blessing or curse (Deut 11:26), Jesus separates those "blessed by my Father" (v. 34) from those "accursed" (v. 41). This is not predestined; rather, God's invitation goes out to all (5:45; 13:3-9), and the choice to accept or reject it rests with each. For those who accept the invitation, which is visible in their deeds, blessing and inheritance in God's realm await.

In light of the saying at 24:14, it is likely that Matthew envisions the completion of the great commission (28:16-20); all people, including Israel, Gentiles, and Christians, have heard the Gospel and are now judged according to their deeds. The "least brothers" (v. 40) and "least ones" (v. 45) most likely refer to other Christians rather than to just any person in need. See 11:11; 18:6, 14, where "little ones" and "least" refer to vulnerable members of the Christian community, and 10:41-42, where Jesus promises the reward of a righteous person for those who receive the needy ones sent out on mission. The basis of judgment, then, is how one receives Jesus through his followers who proclaim the Gospel (see 10:40).

26:1–27:66 The passion and resurrection

Matthew's usual formula at the end of a block of teaching, "When Jesus finished . . ." (26:1, as also 7:28; 11:1; 13:53; 19:1), marks the transition to the passion narrative. There is also an echo of Deuteronomy 32:45, where Moses finished his instruction to Israel and then prepared for his death. In these final scenes Matthew follows Mark closely, while adding his own unique touches. Jesus is portrayed as knowing what will happen and as being in control of the events. As Matthew is wont to do, he interprets each action as fulfilling the Scriptures.

26:1-16 Preparation for death: Treacherous plotting and prophetic anointing

For the fourth and last time (16:21; 17:22-23; 20:18-19), Jesus predicts his death. The prime movers are the chief priests and elders (v. 3), along with the high priest, Caiaphas (v. 3), who held office from A.D. 18 to 36. The Pharisees and scribes, who have been Jesus' opponents up to this point in the narrative, drop out of view until 27:62. The people are still basically favorable toward Jesus (v. 5).

In strong contrast to the leaders' treachery is the action of an anonymous woman who anoints

Jesus in the home of Simon the leper. This takes place in Bethany, a village just east of Jerusalem, over the Mount of Olives. In the Gospel of John this is identified as the home of Martha, Mary, and Lazarus (John 11:1–12:12). By anointing Jesus' head, the woman takes on the role of priest and prophet. She both prepares Jesus for burial (v. 12) and commissions him as messianic king (see Sam 16:12-13; 1 Kgs 1:39). Jesus affirms her action, over the objection of the disciples. There is no question of a lack of concern for the poor by Jesus (see 5:3, 42; 6:2-4, 24; 19:21; 25:31-46); rather, the issue is the timing and the woman's recognition of Jesus' fate. She embodies the understanding and loyalty of the women disciples who, in contrast to the others (26:56), remain to see the crucifixion (27:55-56), keep vigil at the tomb (27:61), and are the first to encounter the risen Christ (28:1-10). Her pouring of oil on Jesus' head (v. 6) prefigures Jesus' pouring out of his blood for all (v. 28). While her action is remembered (v. 13), her identity is not.

In strong contrast is the act of Judas (vv. 14-16), who negotiates with the chief priests to hand Jesus over to them. No motive is given (cf. John 12:6). Once again Matthew interprets this deed through Scripture. Thirty pieces of silver is the worth of a slave (Exod 21:32). But probably the allusion is to Zechariah 11:12-13, where this is the amount of a shepherd's wage, which Judas casts back into the treasury (see 27:3-10).

26:17-35 The Last Supper

As the woman prepared Jesus for his passion, so now Jesus prepares his disciples. In the first scene (vv. 17-19), the disciples approach (*prosēlthon*, the reverential stance also of the woman in v. 7; also 4:3, 11; 5:1; 8:2) Jesus and ask about Passover preparations. Jesus' reply has an apocalyptic nuance, as Matthew uses both *kairos*, "appointed time" (8:29; cf. 13:30; 16:3; 21:34), and *engiken*, "draws near" (cf. 3:2; 4:17; 10:7; 21:34; 24:32-33) in reference to the end time.

The meal begins with a notation that Jesus is with his disciples (v. 20). His words and actions interpret for his intimate followers ("Twelve" is symbolic for all, as also 10:1-4) how he is still present with them ("Emmanuel," 1:23; cf. 28:20), even when his earthly life ends. Tragic predictions of betrayal (vv. 20-25) and denial (vv. 31-35) by his closest disciples frame Jesus' eucharistic words and actions (vv. 26-30). In verses 20-25

there is a contrast between the obedience of Jesus (v. 24) and the disobedience of Judas, who calls Jesus "Rabbi" (vv. 25 and 49), after Jesus has instructed his disciples not to use that address (23:8). The allusion to Psalm 41:10 in verse 23 captures the anguish of betrayal by an intimate friend. Typically, Matthew signals the dire consequences of not acting justly with a pronunciation of woe (as 11:21; 18:7; 23:13, 15, 16, 23, 25, 27, 29; 24:19). Unique to Matthew is the personal exchange between Judas and Jesus (v. 25; also 26:49-50). Jesus' enigmatic "you have said so" is the same response he gives to the high priest (26:64) and to Pilate (27:11).

The institution of the Eucharist (vv. 26-29) is the core and climax of this section. Jesus' gift of self in the form of bread is reminiscent of the feedings of the multitudes (14:13-21; 15:32-39) and of the similar actions by Elijah and Elisha (1 Kgs 17:8-16; 2 Kgs 4:42-44), as well as of God's provision of manna in the desert for Israel (Exod 16). The cup in which all participate symbolizes both his death (see 20:22; 26:39, 42) and a ratification of a renewed life in covenantal fidelity. Blood, as the symbol of life (Deut 12:23), was sprinkled by Moses on the altar and on the people (Exod 24:8) to seal the covenant.

A unique element in Matthew's account is the interpretation that this action is "on behalf of many, for the forgiveness of sins" (v. 28). This is an allusion to the servant in Isaiah 53:4-12 (see also 12:17-21; 20:28). The "many" (*pollōn*) is a Semitic expression meaning "all"; no one is excluded from the saving effects of Jesus' death (see 1:21). Forgiveness is possible even for those who hand Jesus over to death. The gift of bread and wine also sounds an eschatological note, as the messianic banquet of Isaiah 25:6-9 is in view. Jesus assures his disciples that while the intimacy of eating and drinking together, which they shared during his earthly life, is ending, they will yet experience this with him in the realm of God (v. 29).

The scene shifts to the Mount of Olives (v. 31; see 24:3), where jubilant singing (Psalms 114–118 are sung at the conclusion of the Passover meal) gives way to a sober prediction by Jesus that all the disciples will have their faith shaken (*skandal-izesthai*, literally, to find Jesus a "stumbling block" or "obstacle." See also 11:6; 13:57; 15:12). A quotation from Zechariah 13:7 that speaks of the disintegration of the community is accompanied by a promise of its renewal. Galilee is the place where Jesus first gathered disciples (4:18-22) and commissioned them (10:1-42) and where he appears to them for the last time, sending them to the whole world (28:16-20). Peter, representative of the whole (see 16:16-23), boasts that this will never happen (vv. 33-35). The irony is strong, as in the next scene the disciples sleep instead of keeping watch (vv. 36-46) and flee (v. 56), while the women disciples stay the course (27:55-56, 61; 28:1-10).

26:36-46 Prayer at Gethsemane

Arriving at Gethsemane (meaning "olive press") with his disciples (v. 36; see 26:20), Jesus separates himself from them to pray, taking along Peter and the sons of Zebedee, namely, James and John. These three were among the first called and sent (4:18-22; 10:2) and were privileged witnesses at the Transfiguration (17:1-8). They are also singled out as the ones who struggled most to understand Jesus' passion (16:22; 20:20-23). The separation of Jesus from the rest of the disciples may be an allusion to Genesis 22:5, where Abraham tells his servants to stay back while he and Isaac pray. While Abraham is exemplary in his faithfulness, he misinterprets what action God desires. Jesus is both faithful to God and understands what action will bring liberation for his people. For him there will be no rescuing angel (26:53).

Three times Jesus implores God (on the metaphor of "Father" for God, see the comments on 6:5-15) to let the cup (a metaphor for death; see 20:22; 26:27) pass from him without drinking it. His grief is extreme (quoting lament psalms 42:4-5; 43:5 at v. 38), and his struggle is real. Jesus is not a puppet in the hand of God. His death is not inevitable. He wrestles with the final choice to proceed with handing over his life.

Jesus' faithfulness in seeking and following God's direction stands in contrast with the frailty of his disciples. They fail to keep watch (see chs. 24–25) and do not pray, as Jesus had instructed (v. 41 and 6:13), to be delivered from the test (*peirasmos*)—both the present crisis and the eschatological trial. Yet they will be restored and empowered by the risen Christ (28:7, 16-20). The final scenes of intimacy between Jesus and his followers began with Jesus noting at the supper that his appointed hour was at hand (26:18). They now close with his declaration that both the hour and the one handing him over are at hand (vv. 45-46).

26:47-56 Jesus' arrest

Jesus' words are immediately fulfilled with the arrival of Judas and a large, armed crowd, who come on the authority of the chief priests and elders. With so many people in the city for the feast, Judas has prearranged a signal so that there will be no confusion. A kiss, normally given by a disciple to a teacher as a sign of respect, turns treacherous. And as at the Last Supper (26:25), Judas addresses Jesus as Rabbi (v. 49), against Jesus' instructions (23:8). The tone of Jesus' response (v. 50) is not clear. It can be understood as an ironic question, "Friend, why are you here?" (KJV) or an instruction that emphasizes Jesus' control of the scene: "Friend, do what you have come for" (NAB). Or, by addressing Judas as "friend," he reminds him of their intimate relationship and holds out to him the possibility of forgiveness, recalling that Judas has partaken in the cup of his blood that is shed for forgiveness of sins (26:28).

A desperate attempt on the part of a disciple to halt the arrest (v. 51) serves to underscore once again a lack of understanding. Jesus has taught his followers not to counter violence with violence (5:38-48), which he reinforces here with a pronouncement unique to Matthew: "all who take the sword will perish by the sword" (v. 52; similarly Rev 13:10). Moreover, Jesus withstands the temptation to call upon angelic rescuers (v. 53, as at 4:6). As always, Matthew explains that all these seemingly incomprehensible events happen to fulfill the Scriptures (v. 54, 56). The fallibility of the disciples culminates with their desertion and fleeing (v. 56; but see 27:55-56, 61; 28:1-10, where the Galilean women continue to follow and serve).

26:57-68 Interrogation before the Sanhedrin

The arresting party brings Jesus to the high priest, scribes, and elders (the Pharisees have dropped from view in the passion narrative and only reappear at 27:62). The mention of Peter (v. 58) prepares for the next scene, in which he denies Jesus (vv. 69-75). The Jewish leaders do not have authority to put a person to death (John 18:31). While Matthew gives the scene the aura of a trial, it is more a strategy session to prepare the case they will present to Pilate. In Christian tradition, the blame for Jesus' death increasingly has been taken off the Romans and put on the Jewish leaders. Matthew paints the Jewish leaders as vile, seeking *false* testimony (v. 59; cf. Mark 14:55) against Jesus.

Two witnesses are necessary for a death sentence (Deut 17:6). The accusation that Jesus said he can destroy the temple and rebuild it (v. 61) is both false and ironically correct. Although he performed a prophetic act in judgment on the temple (21:1-17) and remarked about its coming destruction (24:2), he did not say that he himself would destroy it. But since destruction and restoration of the temple were thought to be a sign of the messianic age, the accusation is actually true. Jesus' initial silence toward the high priest (v. 63) recalls that of the servant in Isaiah 53:7. At 27:40 the charge will be made again by passers-by reviling the crucified Jesus.

The high priest shifts the focus, demanding that Jesus respond under oath to the charge that he is Messiah, Son of God (v. 64). That Jesus is Messiah has been affirmed from the opening line of the Gospel (1:1, 17, 18; 2:4; 11:2; 16:16; 22:42; 23:10). "Son of God" underscores his unique relationship with God (2:15; 3:17; 11:25-27; 17:5), his healing power (8:29), and his authority (see 14:33; 16:20, where the two titles occur in tandem). Jesus had taught his disciples not to take oaths (7:33-37). He replies to the high priest with the same enigmatic phrase, "You have said so" (v. 64), that he had said to Judas (26:25) and to Pilate (27:11). His further response underscores his identity as the coming Human One. Blending Psalm 110:1 and Daniel 7:13, he moves the discussion to an eschatological plane. At this the high priest accuses Jesus of blasphemy, that is, abusing the divine name or insulting God (v. 65), an offense the leaders deem worthy of death (v. 66). They themselves begin to abuse Jesus (cf. Mark 14:65, where it is an anonymous "some") and mock his identity as prophet and Messiah (vv. 67-68), an element unique to Matthew.

26:69-75 Peter denies Jesus

The utter failure of Peter is not unexpected; Jesus has warned that this will happen (26:31-35). Peter has been in the lead as one of the first disciples called (4:18-22) and was a privileged witness at the Transfiguration (17:1-8). He was the spokesperson for the disciples in declaring Jesus "messiah" (16:16), and the one to whom Jesus entrusted the "keys to the kingdom of heaven" (16:19). But he has also been the prime example of a disciple who struggles to understand and fails

miserably (16:22-23; 26:33-35). Not once but three times he denies being with Jesus, and he does so with an oath (see 5:33-37, where Jesus forbids oath-taking). Matthew adds that Peter makes the denial "in front of everyone" (v. 70; cf. 5:16; 10:32-33). This is the last mention of Peter in Matthew's Gospel. Presumably his bitter tears (v. 75) are tears of repentance, and he is among the disciples to whom the women announce the good news (28:7-10) and among those who are commissioned to preach to all the nations (28:16).

27:1-2 The council hands Jesus over

After a night of interrogation and abuse, the chief priests and elders fulfill what Jesus had predicted at 20:18-19. They hand Jesus over (*paradidōmi*, 10:4; 26:15, 25; 27:3, 18, 26) to the Roman governor, Pontius Pilate, who ruled from A.D. 26 to 36.

27:3-10 The death of Judas

Seeing Jesus condemned prompts a change of heart in Judas. Ordinarily the verb *metanoein* is used for repentance, whereas here it is *metamelētheis*, "deeply regretted" (v. 3). But it is likely that Judas' words in verse 4 indicate true repentance and not simply regret. Judas, like the leaders Jesus warned in 23:35-36, is responsible for shedding innocent blood. (See 27:24, where Pilate will try to make himself innocent of Jesus' blood.) The leaders dissociate themselves from Judas' attempt to return the money (see 27:24 for Pilate's use of the same phrase, "Look to it yourselves"). In desperation, Judas flings the money into the temple and tragically ends his life. A rather different version is found in Acts 1:15-20. The quotation in verses 9-10 interpreting the purchase of the "Field of Blood" is actually an adaptation of Zechariah 11:12-13, although Matthew attributes it to Jeremiah. Perhaps Matthew makes the association because of a similarity with the slaughter of the innocents (2:17-18), interpreted with Jeremiah 31:15. Or Matthew may mean to recall Jesus' critique of the temple and its leadership (21:13, quoting Jer 7:11). Alternatively, he may be alluding to the story of the potter's field in Jeremiah 18–19.

27:11-14 Trial before Pilate

Resuming the action begun at verse 2, Matthew now tells of the interrogation by the Roman governor. His question is different from that of the

Jewish authorities and concerns Jesus' kingship. Once again Jesus answers enigmatically, "You say so" (v. 11; see 26:64), and then remains silent when the chief priests and elders testify against him (as also 26:63). Jesus' silence is evocative again of the servant of Isaiah 53:7, whose appearance caused amazement (Isa 52:14-15; v. 14).

27:15-26 Choice of Barabbas

Beyond the Gospel references, there is no other evidence of a custom of releasing a prisoner at Passover. The choice, according to Matthew, is between Jesus Barabbas and "Jesus called Messiah" (v. 17). Matthew heightens the notoriety of the former (v. 16) and names envy as the motive for handing Jesus over (v. 18). Three other unique elements in Matthew serve to shift the blame away from Pilate and onto the Jewish leaders. The first is the dream of Pilate's wife, who urges her husband to "have nothing to do with that righteous man" (v. 19). In the opening chapters, dreams are the means by which Joseph, a "righteous man" (1:19), learns God's desire and by what actions he is to preserve the life of Jesus and his mother (1:20; 2:13, 19, 22). A second element found only in Matthew is Pilate's handwashing (v. 24), a futile attempt to declare his own innocence and to dissociate himself from Jesus' death (similarly the chief priests with Judas, 27:4). A third unique feature of the Matthean account is the climactic cry of the whole people, "His blood be upon us and upon our children" (v. 25).

Until this point the crowds have been basically favorable toward Jesus. Now they demand his crucifixion (vv. 22, 23), and the people as a whole (*laos*, as at 1:21) take upon themselves the responsibility for his blood (v. 25; see Lev 20:9-16; Josh 2:19-20; 2 Sam 1:16; 14:9; Jer 51:35). This verse has been interpreted as a curse upon all Jewish people for all time. This is a grave misinterpretation that Christians have a serious obligation to counter (see the Vatican II document *Nostra Aetate* 4). In the context of Matthew's Gospel, "the whole people" refers to those who opposed Jesus during his lifetime as well as Jewish opponents of the early Christian community. Verse 25 reflects the inner family conflict and the struggle of Jesus' disciples to understand why all Jews did not follow Jesus (similarly Matthew 13; Romans 9–11). Matthew sees a connection between the rejection of Jesus and the events that unfold in the decades following Jesus' death ("upon our children"), particularly the destruction of the temple. The scene concludes with Pilate releasing Barabbas, having Jesus scourged to weaken him, and handing him over (*paradidōmi*, 10:4; 20:18; 26:15, 25; 27:2, 3, 18, 26) for the last time to the soldiers to crucify him.

27:27-31 Mockery by the soldiers

Just as the interrogation before the chief priests and elders ended with them abusing Jesus (26:67-68), so the Roman trial concludes with abuse by the soldiers of the governor inside the praetorium, the governor's official residence. A cohort consisted of six hundred men; in verse 27 it likely refers to simply a large group of soldiers. These would have been local men employed by the Romans. They mock Jesus' kingship, arraying him in scarlet, with a pseudo-crown and scepter. In Mark 15:17 the robe is purple, a color worn by royalty and the rich (see, e.g., Luke 16:19), but Matthew's detail is more realistic. Roman soldiers wore red cloaks; they simply adorn Jesus in one of their own. The crown of thorns was not so much to inflict pain as to imitate that of an emperor with its rays. The acclamation (v. 29) simulates the greeting toward the emperor, "Ave, Caesar!" The derisive mockery turns to physical abuse (v. 30) and ends with Jesus being led to crucifixion.

27:32 Simon of Cyrene

On the way to the site of crucifixion, Simon of Cyrene (a North African city in present-day Libya) is pressed into service to help Jesus carry the cross. Likely he was visiting Jerusalem for the Passover feast. While Jesus has said that those who wish to be his follower must take up their cross (16:24), discipleship motifs are not entirely clear in this scene, especially since Simon is forced into carrying the crossbeam. At the same time, the presence of this Simon is a poignant reminder of the absence of Simon Peter, who has struggled to accept the fact that Jesus would die (16:21-23), then declared he would follow Jesus to the death (26:33-35), but has fled (26:56) and denied that he was ever with Jesus (26:69-75).

27:33-44 Crucifixion and mockery

The place of crucifixion, Golgotha, "Place of the Skull," gets its name either because the hill is skull-shaped or because of the executions that took place there. It was customary to give the condemned person a drink mixed with a narcotic to ease the pain. Matthew makes it wine mixed with gall, so that the action corresponds to what is said in Psalm 69:21.

No details are narrated about the crucifixion itself (v. 35). Matthew's readers are well familiar with what other contemporary writers describe as the most cruel and painful of all punishments. It was used on slaves, violent criminals, and political rebels. Carried out in a public place, it was meant to be a deterrent. Matthew focuses on how to make meaning of this horrible death. He uses the Scriptures, primarily the lament psalms, to interpret each action. In verse 35 the division of Jesus' clothing alludes to Psalm 22:18. The wagging heads of the mockers (v. 39) recalls Psalm 22:7.

For the third time (26:67-68; 27:27-31) Jesus endures mockery. First the passers-by (vv. 39-40) resurrect the charge made before the Sanhedrin (26:61) about the destruction of the temple, an event that Matthew connects with the death of Jesus (21:41, 43). Their taunt, "If you are the Son of God," recalls the same tempting words of Satan (4:3, 6), who urges Jesus to throw himself from the pinnacle of the temple and let God's angels rescue him to prove he is truly God's Son. Both scenes reflect the struggle of believers to explain how Jesus can be the beloved Son of God (2:15; 3:17; 17:5) and yet die such a horrendous death. The taunt of the chief priests, scribes, and elders is a variation of the same (vv. 41-42). The paradox of saving life by losing life (16:25) is visibly played out. It is through losing his life that Jesus "saves his people from their sins" (1:21). While the placard over the cross (v. 37) carries the title "King of the Jews" (the charge made by Pilate, 27:11, and his soldiers, 27:29), the religious leaders use the more messianically charged phrase "King of Israel" (v. 42). Verse 43, unique to Matthew, employs Psalm 22:8 and Wisdom 2:18 to align Jesus with the righteous sufferer whom God will vindicate. Finally, even the bandits crucified with Jesus join in the abuse (v. 44; cf. Luke 23:40-43).

27:45-56 Death of Jesus

An apocalyptic tone is set as darkness spreads over the land for three hours (see Amos 8:9). Jesus cries out in a loud voice (v. 46), once again using the words of Psalm 22. He has been deserted and opposed by Judas (26:14-16, 48-49), the disciples

(26:56), Peter (26:69-75), the religious leaders (26:57-68), the crowds (27:21-22), the Roman authorities (27:1-31), and now even God seems to have abandoned him. His anguished prayer is that of a righteous sufferer. While the end of the psalm, which moves to a note of confident hope in God's power to save, is not spoken, the Gospel will indeed end with Jesus' vindication.

The bystanders either misinterpret or deliberately mock Jesus (v. 47) and think he is calling on Elijah. There was an expectation that Elijah would return before the final judgment (Mal 4:5; Sir 48:10). But John the Baptist has already played this role (Matt 11:14; 17:10-13). It is not entirely clear what prompts the offer of *oxos*, a cheap, sour wine used by the lower classes (v. 48), or whether this is a compassionate or mocking gesture. Most likely Matthew includes it as one more way in which Scriptures (Ps 69:21) are fulfilled. As terse as the notice of Jesus' crucifixion (v. 35) is the statement he "gave up his spirit" (v. 50). This is not a reference to the Holy Spirit but to the life-breath (*pneuma* means both "spirit" and "breath") that Jesus hands back to God. Matthew portrays Jesus not as an unwilling victim but as faithful Son of God who consciously returns to God.

Four apocalyptic signs follow immediately, powerful demonstrations that God did not abandon Jesus:

1) The curtain of the temple, probably the inner veil in front of the holy of holies (Exod 26:31-35), is torn (the passive voice designates this as God's doing) from top to bottom. This can be understood as a portent of the destruction of the temple or as opening access to the God of Israel to all the Gentiles.

2) The earth quakes, a portent of the end of the present age and the beginning of the new (4 Ezra 6:13-16; 2 Apoc. Bar. 27:7; 70:8; Zech 14:4-5; Matt 24:7). Cosmic signs accompany the momentous events of Jesus' birth (2:2), his death, his resurrection (28:2), and his return in glory (24:27-31).

3) Many of the holy dead emerge from their tombs and appear to people in Jerusalem (vv. 52-53). In verse 52, Matthew, in language akin to that of Ezekiel 37, asserts that it is Jesus' death that makes possible the resurrection of the holy ones. The sequence of events becomes confused in verse 53 because Matthew makes a correction: the resurrection of others cannot happen until the resurrection of Jesus, which Matthew has not yet narrated.

4) The centurion and those with him, who had participated in crucifying Jesus, come to believe in Jesus and declare, "Truly this was the Son of God!" (v. 54; cf. vv. 40, 43). This is all the more significant when their employer, the emperor, allocated this title to himself, seeing himself as agent of the gods.

Not only has God not abandoned Jesus but the many Galilean women disciples have also remained faithful to him (vv. 55-56). They are steadfastly keeping watch (as Jesus exhorts disciples to do in chapters 24–25), after having followed Jesus from Galilee and having ministered (*diakonousai*) to him (see 8:15 for various meanings of this verb). Mary Magdalene heads the list (v. 56; as in Matt 27:61; 28:1; Mark 15:40, 47; 16:1, 9; Luke 8:2; 24:10; cf. John 19:25; 20:1-2, 11-18). No information is given about her before this point in the narrative. Only Luke 8:2-3 introduces her before the passion account. The common confusion of her with a prostitute or a sinner has no basis in the Scriptures. The other Mary accompanying her is the mother of James and Joseph (cf. Mark 15:40). At Matthew 13:55 there is the mention of Jesus having siblings named James and Joseph. Possibly Matthew is alluding to the mother of Jesus (cf. John 19:25), but if so, he does not develop the significance. The third figure is the mother of the sons of Zebedee, who at 20:20-21 had wanted places of honor for her sons in Jesus' realm. She drops out of the list in 27:61 and 28:1.

27:57-66 Witnesses at the tomb

Another disciple emerges, a rich man (see 19:16-26, where Jesus elaborates on how difficult it is for a rich person to be a disciple) who offers his tomb for Jesus' burial. There is no mention of Joseph having been part of the Sanhedrin that condemned Jesus (cf. Mark 14:53). There are many limestone quarries in Jerusalem, some of which were used secondarily as cemeteries. A body would be laid in a niche carved in the rock until the flesh decomposed. Then the bones would be gathered into an ossuary ("bone box"), and the niche could be reused for another family member. A tomb complex would have a number of niches. The stone is rolled across the entrance to prevent grave robbers or animals from entering. No anointing of Jesus' body is narrated, since he has already been anointed for burial by an unnamed woman (26:6-13).

Keeping vigil at the tomb (v. 61) are Mary Magdalene and the "other Mary," presumably the mother of James and Joseph named in verse 56. They come again in 28:1 to see the tomb. These witnesses serve to verify that Jesus is truly dead and that there is no mistaking the place of his burial.

Unique to Matthew is the request of the chief priests and the Pharisees (who have been absent since 23:39) to Pilate to set a guard at the tomb (vv. 62-66). Their recollection of Jesus' prediction that after three days he would rise (16:21; 17:23; 20:19) sets the stage for the empty tomb and the resurrection appearances. Their fear of the impact of the disciples' proclamation that Jesus was raised from the dead (v. 64) is ironic, since this is exactly what occurs. The charge that Jesus was an "imposter" (v. 63) and that his disciples stole the body (v. 64) likely reflects the kinds of arguments Matthew's community encountered from their opponents.

28:1-15 The empty tomb

The same two women who witnessed Jesus' crucifixion (27:55-56) and who kept vigil at his burial (27:61) return once again to the tomb. As at the death of Jesus, an earthquake (27:51, 54; see also 24:7), an apocalyptic sign, occurs, accompanied by the descent of an angel from heaven. In the opening chapters an angel conveyed to Joseph the divine interpretation of the puzzling events surrounding Jesus' birth. Similarly, an angel communicates the meaning of the extraordinary aftermath of Jesus' death. In an ironic play on words and images, the guards who were supposed to secure the dead body, themselves become like dead men (v. 4).

The angel assures the women not to fear and announces that Jesus has been raised as he said (16:21; 17:22-23; 20:18-19). The passive voice "he has been raised" (v. 6) connotes that God performs the action. The angel then commissions the women to go quickly to give the message to the disciples and to instruct them to go to Galilee, where they will see him (fulfilling Jesus' words in 26:32). Matthew does not explicitly mention Peter (cf. Mark 16:7; Luke 24:12, 34), though he is presumably among the disciples (v. 7) and the Eleven (v. 16). The women do exactly as instructed; with fear and great joy, they run to announce the message to the disciples (v. 8; cf. Mark 16:8, where they say nothing because of their fear).

Unique to Matthew are verses 9-10, where Jesus meets the women on the way. That they seize his feet is a detail that attests to the reality of his person and his tangibility. He is not a ghost or a spirit; nor is it simply the memory of Jesus that lives on with them. The women worship *(proskynein)* Jesus (see also 2:8, 11; 14:33; 15:25; 28:17). Jesus' repetition in verse 10 of the message they have already received from the angel (v. 7) is significant in that the women are commissioned directly by Jesus, giving them credentials as prime witnesses and apostles. Matthew's account represents a strand of Christian tradition in the same line as that of John 20:1-2, 11-18, where Mary Magdalene goes to the tomb alone and there encounters the risen Christ and is commissioned to announce the good news to the community of brothers and sisters (20:17). By contrast, in Mark 16:1-8 and Luke 24:1-12 the women do not encounter Jesus but only the angel. Peter is given primacy of place by Luke (24:12, 34) and Paul, who does not list the women among those to whom the risen Christ appeared (1 Cor 15:3-8).

Rounding out the story of the guard at the tomb (27:62-66) is their report to the chief priests of all that had happened (28:11-15). Along with the elders, they gather and take counsel (as 27:1). Just as money figured in the plan to hand Jesus over to death (26:14-16; 27:3-10), so did money figure in the false interpretation of his resurrection (v. 12; see 6:19-34; 10:8-9; 13:22; 19:16-30 for warnings about the dangers of money). The ongoing polemics into Matthew's day between followers of Jesus and their opponents are reflected in the remark in verse 15.

FINALE: BACK TO GALILEE; COMMISSION TO THE WHOLE WORLD; JESUS' ABIDING PRESENCE

Matt 28:16-20

28:16-20 The Great Commission

In a scene unique to Matthew, the thread of the story of the women's witness, which left off at verse 10, is resumed. It presumes that they have fulfilled their commission to tell the news of the resurrection to the other disciples and that these have believed them. The juxtaposition of "eleven" with "disciples" creates a tension in the narrative. "Eleven" is a reminder that one of "the Twelve" (see 10:1-4) is no more. Yet "the disciples" (referred to seventy-three times in Matthew) comprised a group larger than the Twelve, among whom were most notably the Galilean women who followed and ministered (27:55). While Matthew has depicted the women as apostles who are commissioned in 28:7-10, he excludes them from the commission to preach to all the nations.

The mountaintop setting (as at 4:8; 5:1; 15:29; 17:1) evokes the image of Jesus as the new Moses. Like the women (28:9), the Eleven worship Jesus, though unlike them, they (it is not clear in the Greek whether it is all or some of them) doubt or hesitate before the challenge *(distazō*, v. 17; also 14:31). Until this point in the Gospel, Jesus had insisted that the mission was restricted to the "lost sheep of the house of Israel" (10:6; 15:24); now the disciples are to go to "all nations" *(panta ta ethnē*, v. 19; see 25:32). Some understand Matthew to be saying that the mission is to be directed from now on to the Gentiles exclusively (i.e., that the mission to Israel has ended). But more likely Matthew's heavily Jewish Christian community sees that Israel is still included among "all [the] nations" to whom they reach out. The mission is to make disciples, to baptize, and to teach.

A liturgical formula from early Christian tradition has been placed on Jesus' lips (v. 19). As Jesus has been depicted as Teacher par excellence, so are his disciples to follow in his footsteps with his authority (v. 18; see 10:1).

The final verse of the Gospel reiterates the assurance given at 1:23 and 18:20: despite the "little faith" and the failures of his followers, Jesus remains always with the community that gathers and ministers in his name. Not even death can break that bond—ever.

THE GOSPEL ACCORDING TO

MARK

Marie Noonan Sabin

INTRODUCTION

Author

The actual author of the Gospel of Mark, like those of all the Gospels, is unknown to us. The manuscripts that survived date from the fourth century; the names of the evangelists were added sometime in the second century. There is reason to believe that the early church was less interested in knowing the actual authorship than in connecting the Gospel narratives with apostolic witnesses. They found the names "Matthew" and "John" within their respective Gospels, and the name "Luke" as one mentioned by Paul as his traveling companion. For Mark they relied on a fragment written by a second-century bishop named Papias, who spoke of Mark as the "interpreter" of Peter. This suggestion dovetailed with the observation in Acts that Peter had visited the home of someone in Jerusalem named "John who is called Mark" (Acts 12:12). Some also found support in the reference in the first letter of Peter to "Mark, my son" (1 Pet 5:13). Not all scholars accept these inferences, yet the link with Peter is supported by internal evidence.

Audience

Since we do not know for certain who wrote the Gospel of Mark, we also cannot be certain of its intended audience. The link with Peter has led some scholars to speculate that it was addressed, like Peter's first letter, to the church in Rome. But there are many other bases for speculating both about Mark's Gospel and Peter's letter. Among them is the fact that Peter is known in Acts as the head of the Jerusalem church; an argument could be made that Mark was a member of that early Jewish-Christian community.

Language

Language offers some internal clues as to both the author and his intended audience. Mark's manuscript, like the other Gospels, has come down to us as a Greek text. Why, one might wonder, would the evangelists have written in Greek instead of in Hebrew or Aramaic, the Semitic idiom common in Galilee? The most probable reason is that from the time that Alexander of Greece conquered the Mesopotamian world, three centuries before the time of Jesus, Greek was the language of educated people. In fact, in the time of Alexander, the Jews translated their Bible into Greek. They called it the "Septuagint" (meaning "seventy"), because they developed a legend that seventy scribes had been asked to do the translation in isolated cells and all came up with identical words, thus proving the inspiration of God. Educated Jews knew the Bible in Greek as well as in Hebrew and Aramaic. There is good evidence that when the evangelists quote or refer to the Jewish Bible, they are following the Septuagint.

Mark's Gospel is not written in fluent Greek, however. Indeed, it contains numerous "semitisms," that is, phrases that are awkward in Greek but would read well if translated into Hebrew or Aramaic. The overall impression it leaves, therefore, is that of an author who thought in one language and was trying to write in another. In addition, Mark's Gospel is the only one that uses Aramaic phrases at key moments of the narrative: *Talitha koum,* meaning "Little girl, rise up!*" (Mark 5:41); *Ephphatha,* meaning "Be released"* or "Be opened" (Mark 7:34); *Abba,* meaning "Father" (Mark 14:36); and *Eloi, Eloi,* meaning "My God, my God" (Mark 15:34).

Date and historical setting

The date of Mark's Gospel is also a matter of speculation. Most, although not all, scholars believe that Mark's was the earliest of the Gospels, written around 70 C.E. and followed in the eighties by Matthew and Luke, and in the nineties by John.

The year 70 was significant for all Jews, including the Jewish followers of Jesus, because it was the year that the Romans destroyed the Temple in Jerusalem. The destruction was the traumatic end to the four-year revolt of the Jews against Rome. The Temple had been destroyed once before by Babylon, six centuries earlier, and the effect had been devastating. The Roman destruction was also a watershed in Jewish history.

This time the Temple was never rebuilt. The leaders of the revolt (the Zealots), along with the temple leaders (priests and Sadducees), disappeared or scattered. Judaism itself might have disappeared had it not been for the Pharisees. The Pharisees' reputation in the New Testament as rigid legalists is ill-deserved. They were, in fact, a devout lay group who had developed a flexible and creative approach to the interpretation of Scripture and had also fostered ways of bringing the prayers of the Temple into Jewish homes. When the Temple was lost, they provided the foundations for a continuing and vital Judaism. As the ancestors of modern rabbinic Judaism, they deserve the respect of modern Christians.

Why, then, are the Pharisees vilified in the New Testament? The answer does not lie in the time of Jesus. Indeed, many of the teachings of Jesus are so close to those of the Pharisees that some scholars have proposed that he is shown arguing with them because he was a member of their school. Judaism before the fall of the Temple was tolerant of many different forms of expression,

and historical studies suggest that Christianity did not begin as a consciously separate religion, but as a new formulation of the ancient Jewish faith. After the Temple fell, however, Judaism regrouped, and the Pharisaic leaders became less tolerant of diversity within their ranks. In that new atmosphere, Jewish followers of Jesus were regarded with suspicion and put out of the synagogues. The Christian-Jewish community responded with anger. In the context of the post-seventies, the Pharisees appeared hostile to Jesus, and it is that hostility (and their own anger) that the evangelists retroactively projected into their accounts of Jesus' time.

Modern Judaism and modern Christianity may have developed along clearly different paths, but readers of the Gospels need to understand that Jesus and his disciples, as well as the evangelists Mark, Matthew, and John (Luke was Gentile), saw themselves as faithful Jews. Matthew's diatribes against "the scribes and the Pharisees" and John's scornful use of "the Jews" must be understood in the context of their own times, not that of Jesus.

The way each Gospel expresses its attitude toward Jews and Judaism is one criterion for dating it. John's denunciation of "the Jews" is one reason for placing his Gospel at the end of the century. Luke's way of distancing Christianity from Judaism (especially in Acts) suggests that he is not writing in its earliest moments. The Gospels of Mark and Matthew, on the other hand, are clearly composed in the context of a deep regard for Judaism itself. So, while all the Gospels are steeped in the Jewish Scriptures, Mark and Matthew especially present Jesus in the light of them.

The relevance of the "Old Testament" to the New Testament

It is helpful to know that in the first century all Jewish thought about God was centered in Scripture. Jews believed that the Bible contained all of God's revelation but that no one person or one faith community could grasp all of that revelation at any single time. It was a pious habit of mind to seek to understand every new and significant person, teaching, and event in Judaism through the lens of Scripture. At the same time, it was a religious task to consider how these new persons, teachings, and events brought to the surface new depths in Scripture hitherto unseen.

It was, in fact, considered important for each new generation to reopen the Scriptures and search for new meanings in the light of its own time. The new meanings that surfaced were not considered replacements of older interpretations but enrichments of them.

Christians reading the New Testament today will miss much of its meaning and most of its richness if they are unfamiliar with the references to the "Old" or First Testament that form its framework and substructure. This commentary, therefore, tries to present the reader with all the scriptural quotes, allusions, and echoes that provide the basis of Mark's theological thought. Some explanation of the full context of these biblical references is always given. For readers who desire more complete understanding, the biblical citations are offered as well.

Readers of Mark's Gospel need to be aware that Genesis is always in the background. Mark is always thinking of God as the Creator, whose primary concern is to create, sustain, and restore life. His Gospel is filled with reminders of "the beginning." It is structured around the idea that God desires to lead us back to the original Garden. Particularly important to Mark is God's creation of human beings in God's image (Gen 1:27). He presents Jesus as a new Adam ("son of man") and as image of the divinity ("son of God").

Mark also connects Jesus to the central prophets of Jewish tradition—Moses and Elijah. In terms of narrative structure, Jesus' relationship to John the Baptist is patterned after the Elijah-Elisha cycle in the two books of Kings, a cycle which, in its own way, echoes biblical narrative from Genesis to Kings. The miracles that Mark shows Jesus performing have their connections to Elijah's raising up a young man from death (1 Kgs 17:17-24), to Elisha's multiplication of loaves (2 Kgs 4:42-44), and to his cleansing of a leper (2 Kgs 5:1-14). When Mark shows Jesus in his state of transfigured glory, he shows him in conversation with Moses, the giver of God's word, and with Elijah, the prophet who, according to biblical legend, never died but was taken up to heaven.

Mark also places Jesus in the tradition of the prophets seeking the reform of the Temple. By means of interweaving quotations from Scripture, Mark links Jesus to the warnings of Jeremiah and the vision of Isaiah. He shows Jesus warning that the Temple would be destroyed unless the Temple authorities gave up their idolatrous connections with foreign power and wealth. At the same time, he shows Jesus sharing Isaiah's vision of a sacred space where all peoples will join together in worshiping the one God.

When Mark composes the narrative of Jesus' death, he makes use of a range of Scriptures that depict God's righteous servant put to death by evil forces. First and foremost, he interprets Jesus' death through the lens of Isaiah's "Suffering Servant." In certain passages known as "The Songs of the Suffering Servant" (Isa 42:1-4; 49:1-7; 50:4-11; 52:13–53:12), Isaiah draws a portrait of God's faithful servant who is tortured, mocked, and killed by the obtuse kings of the world, who do not understand the identity of the one whom they are killing. They also are slow to understand that his death atones for their sins and that after death he will be raised up and exalted by God.

Mark also draws on similar patterns in the Psalms. And he surely had in mind the opening of the Wisdom of Solomon, where "godless men" put "the righteous one" to death because his goodness makes their lives uncomfortable and because "he styles himself a child of the LORD" (Wis 2:13) and "boasts that God is his Father" (Wis 2:16). In this work, the righteous one is not only exalted by God but given immortality as well (Wis 2:23).

In general, the most significant background comes from the Wisdom writings. In Catholic tradition, there are seven Jewish Wisdom writings: Proverbs, Psalms, Job, Ecclesiastes, the Song of Songs, Sirach, and the Wisdom of Solomon. Each of these works is distinct, yet they share certain significant things in common. They are all set in domestic situations and everyday life. Many of them use a pithy, aphoristic style of speech. They are all focused on how to live a wise and holy life. They all agree that "fear of the LORD [in the sense of holy awe] is the beginning of wisdom." Most important, three of them (Proverbs, Sirach, and the Wisdom of Solomon) imagine God's Wisdom as a personified attribute that walks on earth and dwells among human beings. God's Wisdom was there from the beginning and created the world and all that is in it. God's Wisdom is imagined as a maternal figure—life-giving, nurturing and healing, restorative and transfiguring. When Mark wanted to communicate the significance of Jesus, it was quite natural for him to present him as God's Wisdom made flesh.

Genre

A grasp of Mark's overriding reference to Scripture should keep the reader from regarding his Gospel as an eyewitness account or as any conventional form of biography or history. What Mark gives us is far richer. In keeping with the Jewish practices of his time, Mark interprets Jesus in the light of the Hebrew Bible. He uses Scripture as an interpretive framework. At the same time, he shows Jesus reinterpreting Scripture. Out of this two-way exchange, Mark offers us a Wisdom book.

Like other Wisdom books, Mark's Gospel derives its meaning from the Hebrew Bible. It takes place, for the most part, in the everyday settings of sea and synagogue, home and table. Its central figure, Jesus, offers wisdom in parables, riddles, and short pithy sayings called aphorisms. At the same time, Mark shows Jesus to be not only a teacher of Wisdom but Wisdom itself. Jesus calls his followers to an unconventional wisdom, a way of living (and a way of dying) that he himself exemplifies.

In modern terms, Mark's work is theological. As such, it is purposefully put together. An attentive reader cannot fail to notice Mark's craft: the repetition of certain significant words and the shaping of the narrative into symbolic events and meaningful patterns. There is a theological focus to his overall design.

Key words

Mark is given to the repetition of certain key words or phrases. For example, he uses some form of the verb "release" to indicate both the forgiveness of sin and the healing of a disease. In chapter 1 he says that John the Baptist was "proclaiming a baptism of repentance for the *release** of sins" (1:4). Later in the same chapter, when Jesus cures Simon's mother-in-law, Mark says, "the fever *released** her" (1:31). In chapter 2, when Mark describes Jesus' healing of the paralytic, he notes that Jesus said, "Child, your sins are *released*" (2:5). The word is not translated this way because it is not idiomatic English, but the literal meaning conveys two aspects of Mark's interpretation of Jesus. First, it suggests an equation between healing and forgiveness. Second, it indicates Mark's view that

Jesus continually sets people free. At the end of chapter 7, when Mark shows Jesus engaged in a healing action that summarizes much of what has gone before, he calls attention to the importance of the episode by quoting Jesus in Aramaic: *Ephphatha!*—that is, "Be opened" or, literally, "Be *released*"* (7:34).

In chapter 15, Mark returns to the theme, using it in an ironic way as part of the speech of Pilate. As Pilate strives to please the crowd, he keeps asking them which prisoner he should "release" to them (15:9, 11) until he finally "releases" Barabbas (15:15). When Jesus dies, however, Mark says he "released" his last breath (15:37), thus implying that in dying, Jesus himself is set free.

The various forms of "rise up" or "be raised" are significant because together they form a running refrain that points to Jesus' resurrection. Mark uses the phrase "raised up" repeatedly. In chapter 6, for example, when Herod is speculating on the identity of Jesus, he says, "It is John whom I beheaded. He has been raised up" (6:16). By using the word here, Mark hints at the future "raising up" of Jesus. In chapter 14, Mark notes that Jesus says to his disciples, "After I have been raised up, I shall go before you to Galilee" (14:28). At the end of his Gospel, Mark indicates that an angel repeats these words to the women who came to the tomb: "He has been raised; he is not here" (16:6). In other places, Mark consistently uses some form of the same verb to denote the effect of Jesus' healing miracles. Unfortunately, English translations often blur this meaningful refrain by using synonyms. As a consequence, this commentary will go out of its way to call the reader's attention to its presence.

When Jesus heals Simon's mother-in-law, for example, Mark says he "raised her up"* (1:31). When Jesus cures the paralytic, Mark notes that Jesus said, "Rise up"* (2:11). Jesus uses the exact same words to the man with the withered hand (3:3) and to Jairus's daughter, the little girl whom everyone had given up for dead (5:41). By using this word again and again, Mark suggests that Jesus' healing miracles are related to the great miracle of his resurrection.

Another word that is important to Mark is "straightway." The word sounds odd to modern ears, and most English translations, including the New American Bible, either translate it as "immediately" or "at once" or omit it entirely. But it echoes the message of the prophetic voice in chapter 1 that cries out in the desert, telling the people to prepare for God's coming by making "straight" his "ways" (1:3). Mark was so intrigued by this pun (which works in both Greek and English) that he uses it forty-three times in his Gospel.

In the first part of his Gospel (chs. 1–8), Mark uses the word to signal an act of moral urgency. In the first chapter alone, Mark uses this word eleven times. Mark says that Jesus ascended from the baptismal waters "straightway"* (1:10). The Spirit drives Jesus into the desert "straightway" (1:12). When Jesus calls Andrew and Simon, they leave their nets "straightway" (1:18), and Jesus calls to James and John "straightway" (1:20). He goes into the synagogue "straightway" (1:21), where "straightway" he is approached by a man with an unclean spirit (1:23). Jesus' reputation spreads everywhere "straightway" (1:28). When he leaves the synagogue, Jesus proceeds "straightway" to the house of Simon's mother-in-law (1:29), where "straightway" Simon and Andrew tell Jesus about her sickness (1:30). When Jesus touches the leper, "the leprosy left him *straightway*" (1:42), and "being deeply moved," Jesus "*straightway* sent him forth" (1:43). In the first chapter everything happens as it should, and God's ways are made straight.

In the passion narrative of the Gospel, Mark uses the word sparsely and ironically. Judas arrives to betray Jesus "straightway"* (14:43) and approaches him with a kiss "straightway" (14:43). After he has denied Jesus three times, Peter hears the second cockcrow "straightway" (14:72). The high priest calls the council to condemn Jesus "straightway" (15:1). If one recalls Mark's earlier use of the word, the irony here seems heavy. At the same time, by using it Mark is signaling a larger irony by which, in spite of all appearances, God's plan is going straight.

Another key word translated literally in this commentary is *ecstasy*. If one analyzes the elements of this word, one sees that it is made up of two parts—*ek*, which means "out" in Greek, and *stasis*, which is related to the Greek word for "stand." Thus to experience ecstasy means to "stand outside" oneself, to be outside one's normal state of being. Mark uses one form of this word when he wants to indicate that someone is "out of his mind." When Jesus cures the paralytic, for example, Mark first describes his cure as a

kind of resurrection, saying that the man "*rose up*,*" picked up his mat *straightway*, and went away in the sight of everyone" (2:12a). He then says, "They were all *out of their minds** and glorified God, saying, 'We have never seen anything like this' " (2:12b). A similar use occurs in chapter 3 when Mark says that those close to Jesus thought that Jesus was "*out of his mind*" (3:21).

Mark uses a different form of the same word to indicate moments when something Jesus does or says causes people to experience an abnormal state of awareness and joy. He uses both forms of the word to describe the scene in which Jesus raises up the daughter of Jairus. When Jesus arrives, people are already lamenting her death. Then, Mark tells us, "[He] said to her, '*Talitha koum*,' which means 'Little girl, *rise up*!'" Then Mark describes the reaction of those witnessing this event: "The girl, a child of twelve, *rose up straightway** and walked around. At that, they were *out of their minds with ecstasy**" (5:41-42).

At the end of the Gospel, when three women come to Jesus' tomb to anoint him, they discover that his body is not there, and a young man in white tells them, "He has been raised" (16:6). Mark then describes their response as one of "trembling and *ecstasy*" (16:8). Mark has prepared his readers for this response by the earlier episodes. Like the crowd that witnessed the paralytic rise up from his mat and the crowd that saw the dead child come back to life, the women are overwhelmed by joy.

By means of these episodes, linked by the word "ecstasy," Mark indicates the way in which realization of God's power to restore life transforms the human consciousness.

Patterns and design

Mark shapes his narrative in patterns of twos and threes. The reader will be first aware of doublets. Sometimes this is a matter of repeating episodes; sometimes it is a matter of echoing words. There are, for example, two instances in Mark when Jesus calms the sea (chs. 4 and 6). Twice he multiplies bread for a hungry crowd (chs. 6 and 8). There are two occasions when people discuss who Jesus is (chs. 6 and 8). There are two instances in which Jesus gives specific instructions to his disciples (chs. 6 and 8). And there are numerous other examples, which this commentary will point out along the way.

At the end of chapter 8, Mark seems to give a reason for his method when he describes Jesus' healing of a blind man in two stages. Here he dramatizes the idea that the blind man cannot shift from darkness to vision all at once; he needs to go through a process of coming to sight. In the same way, careful readers will find that each repetition enlarges their understanding. At the conclusion of the commentary, we will talk about how Mark's whole Gospel is divided into two parts and how Mark has worked out this structure to shift the reader's perceptions from a conventional to an unconventional way of seeing.

Mark also likes to pattern things in threes. There are three healing miracles, for example, in chapter 1, three questions asked of Jesus in chapter 2, three seed parables in chapter 4. Jesus makes three predictions of his death (in chs. 8, 9, and 10). Three times Mark shows Jesus being called "the beloved son" (in chs. 1, 9, and 12). Jesus has three chief disciples (Peter, James, and John), whom he takes with him on three key occasions (the raising of Jairus's daughter in chapter 5, his transfiguration in chapter 9, and his agony in the garden in chapter 14). There are also three key anonymous women who are healed in the first part of the Gospel (in chs. 1 and 5). In the second part, three women (two Marys and Salome) follow Jesus to Jerusalem, watch where he is laid in the tomb, and then come to anoint him (chs. 15 and 16).

As with the doublets, there are numerous other examples, which we will note as we go along. If readers become alert to this pattern, they will see that Mark always uses the middle of these triads to shed light on the other two. Again at the conclusion of the commentary, we will suggest how Mark's whole Gospel might also be viewed as having three parts. The middle of this large triad, shedding light on both sides, is the scene of Jesus' transfiguration.

Transfiguration at the center

Given Mark's careful choice of words and patterns, it is surely no accident that he places the scene of Jesus' transfiguration exactly in the middle of his Gospel (9:2). The transfiguration of Jesus is Mark's way of imaging his resurrection. On one side of this scene, Mark shows the ecstatic response of those who see the paralytic rise up from his mat and those who witness a little girl rise up from her deathbed. On the other side, he shows the ecstatic response of the women who have come to realize that Jesus himself has been "raised up." The scene of Jesus' transfiguration overshadows both parts of the Gospel, emphasizing God's creative, transforming, transfiguring power to restore life.

Mark's Gospel is sometimes called "the Gospel of the Cross," so it is worth noting that the Transfiguration overshadows the cross. Mark arranges events so that the scene of transfiguration follows right after Jesus speaks to his disciples about taking up the cross, and it completes his meaning. Jesus says: "Whoever wishes to come after me must deny himself, take up his cross, and follow me. For whoever wishes to save his life will lose it, but whoever loses his life for my sake and that of the gospel will save it" (8:34-35). Mark does not explain this saying but dramatizes the paradox it contains by following this call to "lose" one's life with this scene of transfigured life. Mark does not show Jesus elevating the cross for its own sake, but rather embracing it as a means to Transfiguration. In Mark, the whole teaching of Jesus is death-*and-resurrection*, cross-*and-Transfiguration*.

Conclusion

Rich in Scripture, theological in purpose, and brilliant in design, Mark's Gospel invites its readers to become followers of Jesus' transfiguring wisdom.

NOTES ON THE TRANSLATION

Literal or root meanings

The Church encourages translators to return to "the original texts of the sacred books" (*Dei verbum, The Dogmatic Constitution on Sacred Revelation*, #22). That recommendation has been followed scrupulously in this commentary, to the point where the commentator often renders the meaning of the biblical words in a more literal way than the New American Bible translation printed above it. In each instance, the reader should be aware that the commentator has looked at the root meaning of the original word and consciously chosen a more literal translation over one that is more conventional or even more idiomatic. This kind of conscious choice is particularly evident in the four key words listed in the Introduction: "release," "rise up" or "raised up," "straightway," and "ecstasy" or "ecstatic." Liturgical Press believes that its readers will be enriched by being offered these alternative translations.

Capitalization

In some instances, the difference between the commentator's translation and that of the NAB involves capitalization. The reader should know that we have no original manuscripts of the Gospels, and that of those we do possess, the best were written entirely in capital letters called "uncials." Thus all modern capitals are the choice of a later editor. Such editorial emendations are, like translations, forms of interpretation. This commentator has chosen not to capitalize certain words in order to highlight what she believes to be Mark's theological view.

For example, she does not capitalize "son of man" because she believes that it is not used by Mark as a special title, but rather in its usual Hebrew sense of *ben ʿadam,* which literally means "son of Adam" or "human being." (She also sees it as sometimes following the Aramaic custom of using it as an alternative to "I.") She believes that Mark's habit of constantly associating the term with Jesus expresses his theological perception of Jesus as a second Adam. She does not capitalize "messiah" because she wants to emphasize that Mark redefined that term in the process of using it, and she would like to encourage the reader to reflect on that redefinition. She does not capitalize "holy spirit" because she wants to remind the reader of its use throughout the Hebrew Bible. While the modern Christian of course sees this phrase in relation to the Trinitarian understanding of the fourth-century creed, Mark's first-century audience would have heard it in terms of the biblical tradition they knew. Again Liturgical Press hopes that the reader's grasp of the depth of Mark's text will be enhanced by these alternative understandings.

COMMENTARY

BEGINNING

Mark 1:1-45

1:1 Beginning

In the Greek text of Mark, the word "beginning" has nothing in front of it, neither "the" nor "a"; the Gospel starts abruptly with the simple word "Beginning." By this device Mark calls attention to this word and emphasizes it. In this way he recalls the opening of the Hebrew Bible—"In the beginning"—the moment of Creation. In Jewish tradition the word "beginning" was equated with Wisdom, because in the book of Proverbs personified Wisdom says, "The Lord made me *the beginning* of his way" (Prov 8:22). So some Jewish teachers paraphrased Genesis 1:1 to read, "In *Wisdom* God created the heavens and the earth." Mark's opening is thus rich in meaning, identifying the gospel (or "good news") of Jesus with Wisdom, and that Wisdom with a new Creation.

1:2-3 As it is written

Mark brings together here three voices from the Hebrew Scripture. The messenger who "goes ahead" suggests the angel God sent to lead his people to freedom in the story of the Exodus (23:20). The messenger sent to "prepare the way" suggests the figure whom God promises through the prophet Malachi and who will purge the people of their sins (Mal 3:1). The "voice of one crying out in the desert" is the herald described by Isaiah who is to give "comfort" to God's people (Isa 40:1). In just two verses Mark sums up a biblical tradition whereby angelic or human figures are sent to draw the people to God through preparation, through purgation, and through comfort. The messenger here is John the Baptist, who appears, in the next verse, as Isaiah's "voice . . . crying out in the desert."

1:4-8 John the Baptist

The description of John in 1:6 makes him resemble Elijah, who is similarly dressed in the Second Book of Kings (1:8). It was said that Elijah never died but ascended to heaven in a fiery chariot (2 Kgs 2:11). By interpreting John as another Elijah, Mark indicates John's greatness as a prophet. Elijah passed on his gift as a prophet to a successor, Elisha; so here, Mark introduces Elijah as a prophet who will be succeeded by another—Jesus. In the Elijah-Elisha stories, however, Elijah is pictured as the greater prophet; here, John's proclamation about Jesus reverses that order. The Elijah-Elisha context places Jesus in the tradition of the prophets, with their long habit of pressing for religious reform.

1:9-11 The baptism of Jesus

The scene that Mark portrays reinforces the idea that Creation is happening again: as in Genesis 1, God's spirit hovers over the waters. In describing the opening of the heavens, Mark uses an unusual word for that opening that means "rend"* or "split apart"*; he uses the word again near the end of his Gospel when he describes the splitting open of the sanctuary veil after Jesus' death (15:38). The echoing word links the two scenes, suggesting that Jesus is opening up God's dwelling place.

In a Jewish writing of the time (*The Testament of Judah*) the heavens are opened "to pour out the spirit as a blessing of the holy Father." Here God's spirit descends "like a dove," a term used for the beloved in the Song of Songs. The idea of God's beloved becomes explicit here in the "voice from the heavens" saying, "You are my beloved Son; with you I am well pleased."

The phrase "beloved Son" also brings to mind the story of Isaac, where God asks Abraham to "take your son, your only son, your beloved son" and offer him up as a sacrifice (Gen 22:2). In ancient Passover liturgy, Isaac's sacrifice is referred to as a voluntary act on Isaac's part; Isaac merges with the Passover lamb as it is said that Isaac's blood was placed on the doorposts so that the angel of death would spare the Israelites. So the echo here points to Jesus' sacrificial death and its saving consequences.

1:12-13 Temptation in the desert

As the baptism scene recapitulates the opening of Genesis, so the reference to temptation for "forty days in the desert" encapsulates the key experience of Israel in the book of Exodus. There is no suggestion here, however, that Jesus' encounter with Satan involves a struggle. Rather, Mark gives us a static picture, the human figure of Jesus steadfast between "wild beasts" and ministering angels. It is an icon of original humanity, only this time not sinning.

1:14-15 "The gospel of God"

Jesus' ministry picks up where John's leaves off; "the gospel of God" suggests their continuity. While we tend to restrict the term "gospel" to the story of Jesus, Mark uses the term to refer to the broader narrative of all God's deeds among his people; it is the gospel or "good news" of God that both John and Jesus proclaim. Jesus, like John, calls the people to repentance. In both Greek and Hebrew the word translated here as "repent" carries the sense of "turning" or change of heart. Jesus calls people to this change not as a warning but as a promise: it is the "time of fulfillment," the time of God's "kingdom." In biblical thought, God's kingdom is not a particular place but a condition of living according to God's will. While it tends to be projected into the future, it can also denote a timeless state of being. Similarly, the "time of fulfillment" is not restricted to a particular moment but designates a realization of God's presence. Both these ideas are further unfolded in Mark's story.

1:16-20 The call of the first disciples

In the ancient world, it was not customary for teachers to seek their disciples; on the contrary, teachers attracted disciples. Jesus' action here is therefore striking, for it suggests the action of personified Wisdom, who, in the book of Proverbs, does go about calling her followers. Wisdom calls those who are in need of her—"the simple ones" (Prov 1:22). So Jesus here calls simple fishermen. As Wisdom promises her followers a higher life, so Jesus promises his disciples that they will do a more advanced kind of "fishing."

The response of those called is equally striking. Without inquiry or hesitation, they leave both livelihood and family. Their quickness to respond is enhanced by a word omitted in most translations: Mark says that "*Straightway** they left their nets and followed him" (1:18). As we noted in the Introduction (pp. 11–12), the word "straightway" echoes the message of the voice crying in the desert, telling the people to prepare for God's coming by making "straight" his "ways" (1:3). The ready commitment of Simon and Andrew, James and John is thus shown to be the ideal response of anyone called by God. It is worth noting that we never see any of these disciples make this ideal response again. Throughout most of Mark's Gospel they are singularly slow to understand or to follow Jesus. But Mark sets up this opening scene to suggest their ideal capabilities.

1:21-45 Three miracles of healing

Studies of the structure of Mark's Gospel have shown that he likes to link events, teachings, and sometimes words together in a pattern of three. When he does so, the middle event, teaching, or word always functions as the key one, shedding light on the other two. So here, at the conclusion of Mark's opening chapter, when we find three miracles of healing, it is important to notice how and for what purpose they are linked together.

1) The casting out of "an unclean spirit" (1:21-28). Although the NAB caption speaks of the "cure of a demoniac," Mark's text does not use the word "demon" here but "unclean spirit." The use of this term indicates the perception that possession by evil is an unnatural or pathological state, a perception that predominates in Mark's Gospel. In chapter 3, as we will see, Jesus implicitly contrasts possession by an unclean spirit with possession by God's holy spirit (3:29-30). Here in the synagogue, it is because he sees the man's natural state to be a holy one that Jesus heals the man by simply commanding the unclean spirit to leave him.

The unclean spirit, for its part, knows itself to be destroyed by the simple confrontation of "the Holy One of God" (1:24). It is significant that Jesus commands the unclean spirit to depart with the same word that he later uses to command the storm to "be still" (4:39).

The incident is enclosed in descriptions of the people's reaction to Jesus' power. They speak of his act of exorcism as "a new teaching" (1:27). Mark seems to imply that there is something new in Jesus' perception that possession by evil is reversible.

The word that Mark then chooses to describe the crowd's state at seeing the cure (here in verse 27 translated simply as "amazed") is also part of a pattern of three. Mark uses it again to describe the feelings of the crowd that sees Jesus immediately after his transfiguration (9:15) and again to describe Jesus' own disturbed emotions in Gethsemane (14:33). It might best be translated as a state of "shock" or enhanced consciousness.

2) The raising up of Simon's mother-in-law (1:29-31). Short as this incident is, it is the middle and therefore key event of these three healings. Unfortunately, its full drama is obscured by the

translation. The Greek word used to describe the woman's condition (1:30) is frequently used to describe someone already dead, and the Greek word used to describe her cure (1:31) is best translated "raised up."* (It is the same word used to describe Jesus' own resurrection in 16:6.) Finally, the phrase translated as "waited on them" would more accurately be rendered "served"* or "ministered to"* them (the Greek verb used is related to the word for "deacon"). So translated, the incident distills the essence of what Jesus is about: he takes a dead woman by the hand and raises her up, not only to new physical health but to a new spiritual status. Throughout the Gospel of Mark, Jesus says repeatedly that he has come "not to be served but to serve." This woman is the first person in the Gospel to act as Jesus does.

3) The healing of the leper (1:40-45). In his first miracle Jesus heals a man within the synagogue; here he heals a man who has been ostracized from the synagogue because of his illness. Jesus' relation to the synagogue here is complicated. On the one hand, by touching the leper he violates a religious prohibition against touching the "unclean"; on the other hand, Jesus sends the man back to the priests and the prescribed rituals for lepers. To complicate matters further, Jesus tells the healed man to "tell no one anything" (1:44) and yet suggests that the man's healed body will serve as a "proof" or "witness." And in fact the man does become a witness, spreading the word of Jesus' action. Jesus thus heals more than the man's body—he restores him to his community and changes him from someone who was alone and alienated to one who, it seems, cannot help bearing witness to God's healing power.

Summary of the healing miracles (1:21-45)

In the first instance, the unclean spirit within the man cries out upon being confronted by Jesus' holiness; in the second instance, friends bring Jesus to the woman who is sick; in this third incident, the sick man himself approaches Jesus and asks for help. Both the first and last healings involve bringing someone back to acceptance within the synagogue. In the first, Jesus touches uncleanness within; in the last, he touches uncleanness without.

The first and last healings involve people who, because they are considered "unclean," are forced to live on the fringe of Jewish religious society. What point, then, is Mark trying to make by placing the miracle of Simon's mother-in-law in between them? Is he not suggesting that the place of women in this society is on a par with them? The woman, it may be noted, does not even have a name; she is only known by her relationship to a man—in this case, not even her son but her son-in-law. Situated between a demoniac and a leper, the caricature of "the mother-in-law," we might guess, was an ancient joke. But Jesus, we have noted, not only cures her but changes her: he "raises her up."* By his use of this language, Mark signals to us that all of these miracles of healing are forerunners of Jesus' resurrection. Or to put it another way, Jesus' resurrection comprehends the raising up of all humanity.

1:32-39, 45b A rhythm of healing, preaching, and prayer

In between the healing of the mother-in-law and the leper, Mark tells us that Jesus continually healed the sick and drove out demons, and, when he could, withdrew to "a deserted place" to pray. Yet he also tells us that when Simon and others came to tell him that everyone was looking for him, he returned to the villages to preach, noting that this was his purpose. In this way, Mark indicates a tension in Jesus' life between outreach and withdrawal, or a rhythm of action and prayer. In the last part of the final verse, Mark suggests that this division collapses and that even in the desert Jesus is not away from the crowds that need healing.

Summary of chapter 1

In chapter 1, Mark sets out the framework for his whole Gospel: the traditions of Creation and Wisdom. He indicates that in Jesus, God is initiating a new beginning, a new creation. Through Jesus' connection with John and John's resemblance to Elijah, Mark suggests that Jesus is not, however, breaking off from Jewish tradition or the Jewish Bible but is acting in continuity with the prophets. Indeed, Mark suggests in many ways that Jesus is reenacting the history of Israel. In the scene of Jesus' baptism, Mark shows Jesus to be God's "beloved son," as Israel always named itself, and like Isaac, who also represents Israel in Jewish legend, to be a son destined for a sacrificial death that will be saving for many. Through the

brief scene of Jesus' being tempted in the desert, Mark recalls the Israelites' experience of the Exodus.

Mark also shows that Jesus embodies the Wisdom traditions. Through his dramatization of Jesus' calling of his disciples, he suggests the figure of God's Wisdom calling the simple to be her followers. Through his presentation of Jesus as a healer, Mark expands upon the idea of Wisdom as one who seeks to restore God's creation. Although Mark describes Jesus as teaching and preaching, what he actually shows us is Jesus totally given over to making people whole. Through the language of "raising up"* in a key miracle, Mark indicates that he sees resurrection as the ultimate act of Wisdom's way of restoration or re-creation.

JESUS' ACTS OF RESTORATION AND RE-CREATION

Mark 2:1-28

2:1-4 Breaking through the roof

As chapter 1 concludes with the description of a crowd coming to Jesus even in "deserted places," so chapter 2 opens with so many people gathered in Jesus' home that "there was no longer room for them, not even around the door" (2:2). As a consequence, Mark tells us, the four friends bringing a paralytic to Jesus resort to opening up the roof above him (2:2-4). Although the vocabulary is not identical, there is an interesting parallel here to the heavens opening up at Jesus' baptism; it is typical of Mark's theological slant to suggest that Jesus continually opens things up. In the rest of this chapter, Mark shows Jesus opening up new meanings in sinfulness and forgiveness.

2:5-7 "Your sins are released"

It is in keeping with this view that Mark shows Jesus telling the paralytic that his sins are "released"* or "let go."* The word is not translated that way because it is not idiomatic English, but it is literally correct and more accurately reflects Mark's view that evil binds but God sets free. The same verb is used by Mark to describe John's baptism "for the *release** of sins" (1:4), the action of Simon and Andrew in *letting go** of their nets (1:18), and the fever *letting go* of Simon's mother-in-law when Jesus raises her up (1:31).

2:6-7 "Who but God alone can forgive sins?"

This reflection of the scribes is sometimes taken as Markan irony—that is, it is suggested that by phrasing it the way he does, Mark makes the challenge of the scribes unwittingly point to Jesus' special and divine powers. But another possible interpretation is that Mark is making the scribes raise an old theological question so that he can then show Jesus answering it in an unconventional way. When we read the Gospels as eyewitness accounts, we often miss the carefully constructed rhetorical patterns common in the ancient world. It is worth reflecting that from Plato on, it was a common teaching technique to construct a dialogue between a master teacher and an obtuse listener; the questions of the obtuse listener serve to draw out the thought of the master teacher. So here, the question of the scribes serves as a catalyst for Jesus' teaching on forgiveness. And Jesus teaches more than once in Mark's Gospel that human beings are called to forgive one another in imitation of God's forgiveness of them. If one argues to the contrary that only God can forgive, one could use this idea to dodge the obligation to forgive others.

2:9 "Which is easier to say . . . ?"

In typical Jewish fashion, Jesus often answers a question with a question. The question he raises here is something of a riddle, for while forgiving sins is clearly the harder thing to do, it is by far the easier thing to say because it requires no visible proof. (No one can check on whether or not sins have been forgiven, but the cure of paralyzed limbs is either seen or not seen.)

By means of quoting this riddle, Mark also suggests that Jesus equates the act of forgiveness with the act of healing—that is, he shows that Jesus taught that to forgive someone is to heal them. Mark thus implies that all of Jesus' acts of healing are theological symbols of God's desire to forgive us and make us whole. The miracles of healing have a theological dimension.

In the ancient world, moreover, people often believed (as indeed, some people still do) that illness or injury was a punishment inflicted by God for some sin. By coupling forgiveness with healing, Mark shows how Jesus taught that it is God's will to forgive rather than to punish, to heal rather than to hurt.

2:10 "The son of man"

What does Jesus mean by saying that "the son of man has authority to forgive sins on earth"? Many scholars have noted that in Mark, "the son of man" is the way Jesus most often refers to himself; they have then interpreted this phrase as a special title. But recent scholarship has pointed out that in Hebrew and Aramaic the phrase simply means "human being," as in Psalm 8:5:

> What is man that you should be mindful of him,
>   or *the son of man* that you should care for him?

It has also been noted that in Aramaic the phrase was often used as a form of self-reference. Still others note that in Hebrew the phrase literally equals "son of Adam." All these facts suggest that in using it, Mark was not giving Jesus a special title but rather emphasizing his common humanity. If he attaches any special role to it, it is not that of apocalyptic agent but rather that of second Adam, a representative of humanity giving us all a fresh start.

When Mark quotes Jesus saying that "the son of man has authority to forgive sins on earth," he seems to be suggesting that all human beings have the power to forgive and that Jesus as the second Adam is modeling this role for all of us. This function of the phrase "son of man" needs to be kept in mind when we see it again at the end of this chapter (2:27).

2:11-12a "Rise, pick up your mat, and go home"

Once again Mark chooses the same verb for "rise up"* in a healing miracle that he will use to describe the raising up of Jesus. The immediate response of the paralytic is intensified in Mark's text by the additional word "straightway"*; the straightening of the man's limbs is presented as one more instance of "making straight the way of the LORD."

2:12b "They were all astounded . . ."

The word translated here as "astounded" is literally "out of their minds"* or ecstatic. This response of the crowd is echoed in the later response of those who witness the raising up of a little girl (5:42) and, at the very end of the Gospel, in the response of the three women who come to realize the implications of the empty tomb (16:8). The experience of being ecstatic thus forms a pattern in Mark. Its implications need further exploring.

2:13-17 The calling of tax collectors and sinners

This is the second time in Mark's Gospel that Jesus calls disciples to himself; there will be a third calling in chapter 3. The calling of disciples is thus a Markan triad, and knowing the pattern, we can anticipate that the middle incident—which is this one—will be key, shedding light on the meaning of the other two. We have seen that in the first, the disciples respond in ideal fashion ("straightway"). In the third calling (3:13-19), Jesus not only calls disciples to himself but sends them out "to preach and to drive out demons" (3:14-15). We are also given the names of the twelve apostles, including that of Jesus' betrayer. In this middle incident, Mark dramatizes the fact that Jesus calls not saints but sinners.

2:13-14 Levi

The first to be called is Levi, "sitting at the customs post." To understand the implications of this call and why Levi would have been regarded as a public sinner, it is necessary to know something of the history of the Jerusalem Temple and the Jewish priesthood in the time of Jesus and of Mark.

From the eighth century before the time of Jesus until the time of the Gospels, every major power in the Mediterranean world conquered the Jews and occupied Jerusalem: Assyria, Babylon, Persia, Greece, and Rome. Babylon destroyed Solomon's Temple in the sixth century. Under the Persian king Cyrus, the Jews were allowed to rebuild it. In the first century, Herod expanded it, but the Romans destroyed it again in the year 70. Both the Greeks and the Romans were especially hostile to the Jewish faith because they felt that it detracted from their secular power. The Greeks under Alexander III began to undermine the power of the Temple by appointing the high priests. No longer was the priesthood the sacred legacy of Aaron, no longer was it handed down to the special tribe of Levi. It became a political appointment, a job up for sale like any other appointment in the world of power and money.

The most anti-Jewish of the Greek rulers was a man named Antiochus IV. His attempt to wipe out Judaism through the banning of circumcision together with acts of sacrilege in the Temple oc-casioned the revolt of the Maccabees (whose victory and purifying of the Temple is still celebrated each year at Hanukkah). At the time of Jesus and of Mark, the Romans had taken up where the Greeks left off. They continued the practice of appointing the high priests, and they also attempted to desecrate the Temple in other ways.

In this context, tax collectors were hated, not just because they took money but because they took it from the Jewish people for the benefit of Rome. Levi, "sitting at his customs post," is an apt symbol of the Roman corruption of the Jewish priesthood. Instead of being a religious leader as Levites had originally been destined, this Levi has sold out to the enemy and collects taxes for them.

2:15-28 Three questions of Wisdom

1) "Why does he eat with tax collectors and sinners?" (2:15-17). Modern readers sometimes regard this question as one that reveals the Pharisees' legalism and rigidity, but we should recognize it instead as one that is not unnatural for any pious member of a religious community. We might ask ourselves: How readily would today's churchgoers welcome an enemy collaborator into their midst? It also helps our understanding to realize that because the dietary laws were well defined in Judaism, eating with non-Jews was complicated and potentially an occasion for religious backsliding. The question, then, does not reflect so badly on the Pharisees; yet Jesus' response does emphasize his radical inclusiveness.

Jesus' response ("Those who are well do not need a physician, but the sick do," 2:17) is designed by Mark to reveal more of his identity. His reply here is the kind of pithy aphorism that one finds in the book of Proverbs and other Wisdom writings. By showing Jesus speaking in this style, Mark is dramatizing Jesus as a teacher of Wisdom. Even more, when he quotes Jesus as saying, "I did not come to call the righteous but sinners," he is placing Jesus in the role of Wisdom herself, who seeks out all those who have need of her, especially the unwise or the sinner.

Modern readers sometimes interpret Jesus' statement by saying that he really meant the "*self-righteous*." How, they think, could he possibly exclude the righteous? But their thinking betrays a certain literalism. If we realize that Mark is intent upon presenting Jesus to us as God's Wisdom incarnate, then we can hear these words, not as those of an ordinary religious leader, but as the speech of Wisdom herself—Wisdom seeking out the foolish sinner.

2) Feasting or fasting? (2:18-22). The second question asked of Jesus here comes not from the Pharisees but from the people. The question is typical of all people who have made a religious commitment, because it is natural for pious folk to assume that there is a right way and a wrong way of doing things. If they see two religious leaders whom they respect doing things differently, they naturally want to know which one is right. Jesus' indirect reply (again a question answered by a question) suggests that there are no absolutes here but simply seasons of appropriateness. His response is again reminiscent of the Wisdom writings—this time, of Ecclesiastes:

> There is an appointed time for everything . . . .
> A time to weep, and a time to laugh;
> A time to mourn, and a time to dance (Eccl 3:1, 4).

The point is bolstered by two more Wisdom sayings: "No one sews a piece of unshrunken cloth on an old cloak" (2:21) and "No one pours new wine into old wineskins" (2:22).

Like so many of the concise truths of Proverbs, these sayings are homey, seeming to arise from close observation in a domestic setting. They are not in themselves profound, but they support the perspective implicit in the reply about fasting or feasting that there are seasons in the spiritual life. This pair of sayings also suggests that there can be a tension if we try to force a new style upon an old one.

Many Christians have been tempted to read in here a contrast between the "Old Testament" and the New Testament or between Judaism and Christianity, but such contrasts would have made no sense to Mark. At the time Mark was composing, there was no division between testaments; what we now call the "Old" or First Testament constituted all the Scripture there was. There was, moreover, not yet an established Christian church that sharply distinguished itself from Judaism. So the tension between "old" and "new" here cannot be taken as a Jewish-Christian conflict; it is simply a wise observation about the unsettling effects of new patterns upon old ones. It is worth noting, moreover, that Jesus suggests here that his disciples will eventually and appropriately return to

fasting (2:30). The time of the bridegroom is not here permanently—at least, not yet.

The image of the bridegroom suggests the Song of Songs as well as the marriage feast between God and humanity described in Isaiah, some of the other prophets, and some of the psalms. The new clothing and the new wine go along with the image of this feasting. Through this series of aphorisms Mark seems to be suggesting two different time frames—one present and one future. Jesus as "bridegroom" anticipates humanity's future with God, and to the extent that his followers perceive him as such, they feast in the light of this future promise. But that future has not yet arrived, and the dissonance between that future promise and the present reality is experienced as the tension of new cloth pulling at old or new wine causing familiar containers to burst open.

3) "Why are they doing what is unlawful on the Sabbath?" (2:23-28). The third question comes like the first from the Pharisees, and also like the first, it expresses moral outrage. This time the outrage comes from Jesus' direct violation of the Sabbath laws, which forbade all work of any kind, from picking grain to cooking it. Modern Christian readers tend to dismiss these laws as superficial and again condemn the Pharisees as legalists. But the Sabbath laws were designed to foreshadow the end time, when, according to God's promise, there would be no work, no war, no illness, and no distinctions in authority and power, but all—male and female, slave and free—would sit down together as equals at God's banquet and share in God's rest. This "rest" was not conceived of as the mere absence of work but as a joyous sharing in God's timeless presence. One did not heal on the Sabbath because symbolically the Sabbath was a time without illness.

Once again Mark uses a question that gives him the opportunity to set forth Jesus' teaching on the Sabbath. Jesus' teaching indirectly reminds the Pharisees that the essential purpose of the Sabbath is to anticipate and celebrate the wholeness for which God originally created human beings. Thus, he implies, satisfying human hunger is more in keeping with the purpose of the Sabbath than all the rules and rituals, even the sacred bread.

Jesus' final saying, "The Sabbath was made for man, not man for the Sabbath," sums up this idea of original humanity as the apex of God's creation. The final saying, "The son of man is lord even of the Sabbath," should thus not be taken to mean that only Jesus is lord of the Sabbath; rather, it summarizes Jesus' role throughout the Gospel of Mark as the second Adam, the representative of humanity restored to its original wholeness. It is saying that God made the Sabbath for human beings as a symbol of their final destiny—a love feast with him and with one another.

Summary of chapter 2

In chapter 2, Mark dramatizes the way that Jesus, like Wisdom, restores human beings to wholeness, both physical and spiritual. In the opening incident, he shows Jesus equating forgiveness with healing. He next shows Jesus, again like Wisdom, seeking out sinners to be his followers. In particular, he shows Jesus singling out Levi, who stands for all the Jewish religious leaders who were selling out to Rome and thus weakening Jewish faith. By calling him to be his follower, Jesus/Wisdom is implicitly calling him, and Israel in general, to turn away from worldly power and back to the wisdom of their fathers.

Mark then sets up three questions asked of Jesus by perplexed people around him. These questions give Mark the opportunity to set forth Jesus' teaching on sin and forgiveness, religious behavior, and the purpose of the Sabbath. Mark shows Jesus responding in the style of Wisdom, both in terms of his aphoristic speech and in terms of his active seeking out of those who need him. The middle question about fasting or feasting gives Mark the opportunity to indicate the tension Jesus causes by his unconventional ways and how that unconventionality is the result of Jesus' anticipation of the future of humanity, when humankind, restored to original wholeness, will be gathered at the marriage feast of God. By means of the final question, Mark sets forth Jesus' teaching on the Sabbath. In his response Jesus teaches that the Sabbath was created for the benefit of humanity and as a sign and foretaste of its eternal banquet with the divine.

By these means, Mark develops the themes of Wisdom and Creation he introduced in the first chapter. In the second chapter he shows Jesus acting and speaking like God's Wisdom, God's co-creator in Proverbs (Prov 8:30), restoring people to wholeness, unsettling people from their familiar ways, and teaching that human wholeness is central to God's purpose.

JESUS' CHALLENGE OF CONVENTIONAL WISDOM

Mark 3:1-35

3:1-3 Healing the man with a withered hand

The image of something "withered" is a repeated one in Mark; it is part of his Creation theme, contrasting the withering of created things with their intended fruitfulness. In chapter 4, for example, the seed sown in shallow soil withers up (4:6); in chapter 9, "withering away" is one of the effects of an unclean spirit (9:18); in chapter 11, it becomes one of the seasons of the cursed fig tree (11:20-21).

In curing this man's withered arm, Jesus is acting out the restorative role of God the Creator, a role usually assigned to God's Wisdom. Jesus' first act here is to ask the man to "rise up"* (a resurrection word again) and to come forward "into the midst"* of the community. The implication is that the withered arm of the man had alienated him (like the leper) from the religious community, or at least put him on the fringes of it. Jesus' action here thus defies the conventional shunning of the physically disabled; it is doubly restorative.

3:4-5 The purpose of the Sabbath

This scene of healing is also used by Mark as an extension of Jesus' teaching on the sabbath. Mark implies that many who witnessed this healing in the synagogue were once again more concerned about the Sabbath rules than about the purpose of the Sabbath. He shows Jesus challenging them explicitly: "Is it lawful to do good on the Sabbath rather than to do evil, to save life rather than to destroy it?" (3:4) The large and absolute terms Jesus uses here seem to echo the moment in Deuteronomy when God sets before his people the large issues of life and death: "I have set before you life and death. . . . Choose life, then, that you and your descendants may live" (Deut 30:19). Jesus' question here, in other words, is framed so as to echo this proclamation of God. His argument is clearly not a small one over specific rules but a large one over the purpose of human worship.

Mark goes on to describe Jesus as "looking around them with anger and grieved at their hardness of heart" (3:5a). This particular mixture of anger and grief is also reminiscent of God's feelings as they are frequently portrayed in the

Hebrew Bible. God is not portrayed there as un-moved and immovable, but as loving, jealous, angry, grieving, and forgiving. "Hardness of heart," on the other hand—the unmoved and im-movable heart—is a common phrase the Hebrew Bible uses to express the human condition of sin-fulness.

Further, when Mark shows Jesus in the actual act of curing the man, he quotes him as saying, "Stretch out your hand" (3:5b), a phrase that echoes the moment in Exodus when God tells Moses to stretch forth his hand over the sea to prepare a path for the Israelites' escape (Exod 14:16). The echo here is evocative, suggesting that Jesus not only cures the arm but gives the man new freedom. In all these different ways, Mark describes Jesus as a reflection of God.

3:6 The Pharisees and the Herodians

Mark sets up these two groups as particularly in opposition to Jesus. It is a surprising combina-tion. The Pharisees were laypeople and scholars of the Bible. In spite of their later Christian repu-tation, they were in fact flexible interpreters of Scripture, believers in resurrection, and devoted to the cause of bringing Temple holiness into the home. The Herodians, on the other hand, were nominally Jews, but, in practice, collaborators with Rome; they were successively appointed by Rome to be tetrarchs of Palestine. The Romans called each tetrarch "the king of the Jews." The Herodians were obvious opponents of Jesus, but the Pharisees were not. Some scholars have even wondered if Jesus is shown arguing so much with the Pharisees because he belonged generally to their school of thought.

It is worth noting that the Pharisees do not show up again in Mark's description of Jesus' ar-rest and death. Judas makes his deal with "the chief priests" (14:10), with whom the Pharisees were not connected. It is true that the Pharisees do reappear with the Herodians here, trying to entrap Jesus by their question about paying taxes to Caesar (12:13). Yet Mark, more than any other evangelist, seems to implicate Rome in Jesus' death. We know that Matthew's anger against the Pharisees is directed not to those of Jesus' time but to those of Matthew's day who were putting the Jewish followers of Jesus out of the syna-gogues. It is possible that the same phenomenon accounts for their characterization here. Themat-

ically, of course, the plotting of Jesus' death sig-nals their negative response to the choice set before them between death and life.

3:7-10 The crowds that follow Jesus

In between key episodes and teachings, Mark interweaves passages about the crowds that fol-low Jesus. These passages serve to balance the picture of a few Jewish leaders plotting against Jesus with the picture of the large Jewish crowds who push to be close to him.

3:11 The unclean spirits that proclaim Jesus "Son of God"

Throughout the Gospel of Mark, the unclean spirits recognize Jesus' holiness, and even before he commands them to leave, they feel instantly displaced by his presence. We have already heard one such spirit cry out, "What have you to do with us, Jesus of Nazareth? Have you come to destroy us?" (1:24). It is part of Mark's irony that he shows the unclean spirits to have such clarity about Jesus' identity, while he shows the human follow-ers of Jesus to be confused and uncertain. The fact that Mark shows them calling Jesus "Son of God" should not be taken as a proclamation of Jesus' role in the Trinity, because that doctrinal formula-tion was not arrived at until the fourth century. Rather, Mark is indicating that the spirit world saw Jesus clearly as God's image. (There is an early Jewish tradition that when God showed the angels the first human being, they saw God's re-flection so clearly that they knelt in worship.)

3:12 "He warned them sternly not to make him known"

Much has been made by some readers of Mark over the repeated way he shows Jesus trying to silence those who recognize his holiness. This has been interpreted by some to mean that Jesus wanted to keep his identity hidden, and this theory is referred to in some books as "the mes-sianic secret." But such an interpretation assumes that Mark is simply recording what Jesus said and did; it gives no credit to Mark as a shaping author and theologian. If, on the contrary, we assume that Mark has a theological purpose in mind, then we will hear these admonitions to silence differently. They serve two theological functions. First, by showing Jesus repeatedly asking others not to talk about his holiness or his ability to heal, Mark sets

Jesus off from the typical hero who demands recognition of his powers. Second, Mark makes the spread of Jesus' reputation even more significant because it grows in spite of him.

3:13-19 The third calling of disciples

As the last of a triad, this calling should be read in connection with the other two (1:16-20; 2:13-17). As we noted before, in the first calling episode, the disciples appear to be saints responding in an ideal way, but in the second calling scene, it is clear that Jesus is seeking out sinners. This time Mark expands upon the scene by suggesting the purpose of Jesus' calling and by giving us the names of those called. Mark tells us that Jesus "appointed twelve" in order that "he might send them forth to preach and to have authority [or power] to drive out demons." When Mark describes Jesus ascending a mountain to do this, he evokes the memory of Moses; when he emphasizes the number twelve, he evokes the twelve tribes of Israel. He thus implies that Jesus' gathering and sending forth of twelve followers is an act in continuity with Jewish tradition. The actions of preaching and casting out of demons are in continuity with the prophets.

Some of the names of the twelve are also significant. Peter, James, and John are the three whom Jesus will take to see the raising up of a child (5:37), his transfiguration (9:2), and his distress in Gethsemane (14:23). They also are given different names, always a signal in the Hebrew Bible of an inner transformation. Yet at the end we are also given the name of his betrayer. So Mark, in giving us a list of names, is giving us more than practical information. He is confirming what he suggested in the first two calling episodes, namely, that Jesus' disciples are a mixed lot, with one who would ultimately betray him and others who would ultimately be transformed by him. The reappearance of these four in other episodes of Mark's Gospel is worth tracking.

3:20-21 "He is out of his mind"

Once again Mark links episodes with a comment about the crowds pressing in on Jesus, this time to the point where no one could eat. Mark then comments that Jesus' relatives (literally, "those who were close to him," so perhaps his disciples) "set out to seize him, for they said, 'He is out of his mind.'" The Greek word that is trans-

lated "out of his mind" literally means "out of himself"; it is related to the Greek word for "ecstasy," on which we have commented before (see 2:12b). By using it, Mark suggests that Jesus has a more heightened consciousness than those around him.

3:22-30 Satan, forgiveness, and the holy spirit

By quoting the protests of the scribes to Jesus' exorcisms, Mark presents more of Jesus' teaching on forgiveness. The scribes say that Jesus himself must be possessed by Satan in order to drive out demons. Implicit in their statement is the idea that good and evil are so distinct and opposite that the "good" person should not go anywhere near "evil" persons. This thought is a logical extension of the idea that if Jesus were truly a person of God, he would not eat with sinners.

Jesus refutes this point of view in several ways. First he asks the commonsense question, "How can Satan drive out Satan?" He goes on to make the observation that "A kingdom divided against itself cannot stand" (3:23-24). Next he uses the analogy of "the strong man": "But no one can enter a strong man's house to plunder his property unless he first ties up the strong man. Then he can plunder his house" (3:27). Some interpretations of this analogy assert that "the strong man" is Satan, and Jesus is the one who ties him up. But this would turn Jesus into a plunderer as well as a violent enforcer of his will—roles that violate everything we know of Jesus' teachings. Rather, it makes more sense to see that the violent intruder is Satan, and "the strong man" is the normally good person who is bound and robbed by him.

This view is borne out by Jesus' final words here about forgiveness—that "all sins and all blasphemies" will be forgiven except the blasphemy "against the holy spirit" (3:29). What Jesus means by "the sin against the holy spirit" has been puzzled over for centuries. The problem probably arose from capitalizing "holy spirit" and then assuming that "the sin against the Holy Spirit" was a special offense. But Mark would not have been thinking in terms of a Trinitarian formula. He would have been using "holy spirit" to mean simply God's spirit, as it appears in Psalm 51:11:

> Cast me not out from your presence,
> and your holy spirit take not from me.

The clue to Jesus' meaning here lies in the final explanation Mark gives: "For they had said, 'He has an unclean spirit'" (3:30). By means of this explanation, Mark stresses the opposition between an "unclean spirit" and God's "holy spirit." As Psalm 51 attests, it was common Jewish belief that every human being naturally possesses God's holy spirit. Jesus is teaching that the opposite of this state, that is, possession by an "unclean spirit," is thus unnatural or pathological. The "blasphemy against the holy spirit" is the denial of the fact that possession of God's holy spirit is every person's natural state. There is therefore no clearcut division, such as the scribes have implied, between good and evil persons; there are only people in varying states of pathology or wellness.

So Jesus, by driving out the unclean spirits, can restore people to their original wholeness. Sinners are invaded and bound by Satan; Jesus sets them free.

3:31-35 Jesus' "brother and sister and mother"

In the final section of chapter 3, Mark shows Jesus redefining the meaning of family. Mark first shows the crowd around Jesus using the conventional meaning of "family" as those who are related in blood. Mark sets up this usual understanding so that he can present Jesus' unconventional teaching that "whoever does the will of God" is his "brother and sister and mother." This statement does not, of course, denigrate his blood relatives but simply elevates the essential quality of their kinship with him.

Mark initiates here what will become a growing theme in his Gospel, namely, that people cannot be labeled according to prefixed assumptions; they can only be defined by what they do. So no one can presume who constitutes a member of Jesus' family according to some external criterion. Jesus' brothers and sisters are simply those who act like him in relation to God and others. Later in his Gospel, Mark will show that this existential relationship with Jesus also applies to discipleship.

Summary of chapter 3

In chapter 3, Mark shows how Jesus challenges conventional ways of wisdom. Instead of shunning the man who is alienated from the religious community by his physical disability, Jesus summons him to the midst of the synagogue. In curing the man, he not only restores him but restores the Sabbath to its original purpose of celebrating God's creation of human life. Instead of fighting with unclean spirits and demanding their subservience to his powers, Jesus treats them as a human pathology, and once having cast them out of a person, he asks for their silence. For his disciples, he calls together a mixed lot of people, including his future betrayer. He seeks out closeness with people to the point where his family or his disciples consider him "out of his mind." He asserts that all sins will be forgiven except the sin of thinking that the holy spirit is not the natural possession of every human being. He finds his family not in blood bonds but in spiritual kinship. In all these ways, Mark shows Jesus to be at once the restorer of human wholeness and the challenger of conventional wisdom.

JESUS AS WISDOM TEACHER

Mark 4:1-41

4:1-34 The three seed parables

Parables are common to the style of the Wisdom writings, so it is in keeping with Mark's presentation of Jesus that he shows him teaching by means of them. It helps to know that in Jewish tradition a "parable" was a set form with a set purpose, not just an illustrative story. Most often it was a succinct way of suggesting what God, or God's kingdom, is like. And very often it formed this comparison by weaving together small pieces or echoes of Scripture. The suggestive analogy that emerged was one that interpreted the Bible passages at the same time that it used them to point to God's kingdom. The rabbis described parables as "making handles for the Torah," meaning that parables were intended to open up the meaning of the Bible—to help people "get a handle" on it.

Because parables were generally considered interpretations of the Bible, it was common practice for Jewish teachers to place several parables on the same theme next to each other so that the student could reflect on different possibilities of meaning. It was said that they placed them together "like pearls on a string." So when we see three parables on seeds placed together, we should assume that they are intended to be read in relationship to one another. This interrelated reading becomes even more urgent in view of Mark's habit of expressing himself in triads.

4:3-9 The parable of the sower

This parable is based on the common biblical image of God as a farmer sowing his seed. For example, in Isaiah 55:10-11, God says:

> For just as from the heavens
> the rain and snow come down
> And do not return there
> till they have watered the earth,
> making it fertile and fruitful,
> Giving seed to him who sows
> and bread to him who eats,
> So shall my word be
> that goes forth from my mouth;
> It shall not return to me void,
> but shall do my will,
> achieving the end for which I sent it.

And underlying the poetic description of Genesis 1 is a similar image of God creating the whole universe by his word alone. God has only to say "Let there be light" and "there was light" (Gen 1:3). In these passages, God is a sower and his word is the fertile seed that creates the world.

In the parable that Mark shows Jesus telling first, the sower's seed is only partially successful. Unlike God's word in either Genesis or Isaiah, the seed does not entirely "achieve the end" for which God sends it. It is thwarted by birds (4:4), by "rocky ground" (4:5), and by "thorns" (4:7). Only when it falls on "rich soil" does it produce fruit (4:8). This divided result is at odds with the purpose of the Creator in Isaiah and in Genesis.

The vocabulary used to describe these results, moreover, intensifies the division. The birds "consume" the seed (4:4); the sun "scorches" it, so that it "withers" (4:6); the thorns "choke" it (4:7). On the other hand, the seed that falls on good soil yields a superabundant harvest—"thirty, sixty, and a hundredfold" (4:8). The clearcut and exaggerated difference in results suggests an apocalyptic scenario—that is, a frightening view of the end time in which all people are revealed to have been predetermined to either eternal damnation or eternal bliss. Is that the teaching of Jesus here? We need to suspend our judgment until we have read the other two seed parables.

4:26-29 The parable of the seed that grows by itself

This parable is unique to Mark's Gospel. If we read it in connection with the first seed parable,

we find that it offers a picture so opposite that it is comic. In this scenario, the seed is so fertile it sprouts no matter what. Even while the farmer sleeps, the seed goes on growing, "he knows not how" (4:27). The words suggest something that has its own rhythm—"night and day" (4:27)—and cannot be stopped. Indeed, the phrase rendered here as "of its own accord" is literally in Greek "automatically"* (4:28). On automatic, the seed grows larger and larger until "the harvest has come" (4:29).

The first parable would make us wary and worried about our final destiny. This second parable reassures us that all shall be well. This kind of uncalculating trust in God suggests the wisdom that "the Preacher" arrives at in Ecclesiastes, when he says:

> One who pays heed to the wind will not sow,
> and one who watches the clouds will never
> reap.
> Just as you know not how the breath of life
> fashions the human frame in the mother's
> womb,
> So you know not the work of God
> which he is accomplishing in the universe.
> In the morning sow your seed,
> and at evening let not your hands be idle:
> For you know not which of the two will be
> successful,
> or whether both alike will turn out well
> (Eccl 11:4-6).

The first parable presents the scary, apocalyptic view of an end time in which souls are predetermined to eternal bliss or damnation. The second presents the reassuring perspective of Wisdom that in spite of our limited ways, God is making all things work together for good.

This perspective is further emphasized by the fact that the line about wielding the sickle to cut the ripe harvest (4:29) actually echoes a passage in the prophet Joel where the harvest is sin and the sickle represents God's vengeance (4:13). Joel is giving the harvest imagery an abnormal, almost perverse meaning. Mark is reversing this reversal and turning the harvest imagery back into something positive and good.

As the middle parable, this second one is the key to the meaning of the triad. To understand the fullness of what Mark is presenting here as the teaching of Jesus, we need to look at the last one.

4:30-32 The parable of the mustard seed

The mustard seed as "the smallest of all the seeds" was proverbial in Palestine. What grows from it, however, while large for a plant (about eight feet), is not very tall in comparison with a tree. So the oft-repeated interpretation of this parable, that it is about a tiny seed growing into a huge tree, is misleadingly simplistic. Jews in Mark's audience would have been struck by several other aspects of this parable. First, they would have been surprised that anyone would have bothered to plant the mustard seed at all because it was so common. Mustard seed bushes grow all around the Lake of Galilee. Second, in the description of branches large enough to give shade to "the birds of the sky," they would have heard a direct echo of passages in Ezekiel and Daniel.

This echo, in fact, would have given them the real clue to the parable's meaning. In Ezekiel, God plants "a noble cedar" so grand that "beasts and birds dwell in its shade" (Ezek 17:22-23). In context, this grand tree is clearly a symbol of the Davidic kingdom. In the Book of Daniel, King Nebuchadnezzar asks Daniel to interpret a dream that includes this description of a tree:

> I saw a tree of great height at the center of the world. It was large and strong, with its top touching the heavens, and it could be seen to the ends of the earth. Its leaves were beautiful and its fruit abundant, providing food for all. Under it the wild beasts found shade, in its branches the birds of the air nested; all men ate of it (Dan 4:7b-9).

The tree echoes the forbidden tree of Genesis 2, while its heaven-reaching top and nourishing of all flesh suggest "the tree of life" sealed off in the Garden.

By means of these echoes of Ezekiel and Daniel, the parable connects the common mustard seed plant with David's kingdom and with the tree of life in the first Garden. The real surprise in the parable is not the shift from small to large, but the paradoxical joining of the common and the ordinary with the divinely appointed grandeur of David and the divinely created nourishment of the original Garden. Through this imagery from the Bible, the parable suggests that the kingdom of God is analogous to something very common transformed into something grand and divinely life-giving.

Summary of the three parables

If we now read the three parables as a connected unit, we can see how they form a conversation about God's kingdom. The first parable presents a view of God's kingdom that was typical of apocalyptic writing of the time—that is, it suggests that God has created many people in this world but not all of them will be saved or arrive at God's kingdom. Some are destined to be lost. The labored allegorical explanation that is given in 4:14-20 may or may not be Mark's; many scholars think that it was added later. But whether it was or not, the parable itself invites that kind of exposition; it makes salvation the responsibility of the individual soul (or soil). The soil (or soul), moreover, appears predestined. There is no suggestion that the soil could change or that God's grace might intervene.

The second and third parables, however, present an entirely different point of view. The second parable, in fact, as we have seen, functions as a direct, almost comic refutation of the first, suggesting that no matter what, God's seed will grow and God's harvest will come. Its insistence on the unstoppable dynamism of God's seed prepares the way for the third parable, in which God's kingdom grows surprisingly out of common and ordinary seed.

It is worth noting that only the second and third parables are compared to God's kingdom (4:26, 30). As Mark presents Jesus' teaching, he does not introduce the first parable the same way. If we assume that all three parables must be read as a connected whole, then it appears that Jesus is not affirming the apocalyptic view here, but is going to some lengths to refute it. He is doing this in a way that is not familiar to us but would have been to a Jewish audience. He strings together three parables about seeds so his listeners will know they are interconnected. In the first, he gives the view that many of his day believed; in the next two, however, he undermines that view and offers some refuting wisdom. Through the second parable, he reminds his listeners of the wisdom of not trying to control everything, but to let go and trust in God's providence. Through the third parable, he reminds them that God created every human being (not just a few special ones) for the fullness of life.

4:10-13, 21-25 The purpose of the parables

In two different places in the chapter, Mark shows Jesus talking about his reason for teaching in parables. His first response seems almost perverse. He seems to be saying that he teaches in parables because he does not want everyone to understand him. But what he is actually doing is quoting Isaiah, and to understand his meaning, we have to know the context there.

The quotation comes from what is called Isaiah's "call story"—that is, it comes from the place in Isaiah where he recalls how he was first called by God to be a prophet. Every prophet has a similar story, and the stories follow a similar pattern. The prophet is always taken by surprise or put off balance by God's call. He accordingly always resists. Then God acts in some powerful way that makes the prophet realize that he has no choice. In Isaiah's case, he is first given a vision of God seated on a throne, worshiped by seraphim, who cry out, "Holy, holy, holy" while "the frame of the door shook and the house was filled with smoke" (Isa 6:3-4). Isaiah's first response is fear: "Then I said, 'Woe is me, I am doomed! For I am a man of unclean lips, living among a people of unclean lips; yet my eyes have seen the King, the LORD of hosts!' " (Isa 6:5). God then sends one of the seraphim to him with an ember to purge his unclean lips. After that, God asks, "Whom shall I send?" and Isaiah answers, "Here I am . . . . send me" (Isa 6:6-8). At that point, God tells him to "Go and say to this people":

> Listen carefully, but you shall not understand!
>   Look intently, but you shall know nothing!
> You are to make the heart of this people sluggish,
>   to dull their eyes and close their ears;
> Else their eyes will see, their ears hear,
>   their heart understand,
>   and they will turn and be healed (Isa 6:9-10).

In context, God's words are clearly ironic. He is sending the prophet to the people because he wants them to "turn and be healed"; his saying the opposite only underscores how much he wants it. So when Mark shows Jesus quoting that passage here, we should also understand it as irony. Jesus' quotation of Isaiah links him to the prophet's mission and indicates that he, like Isaiah, is speaking so as to touch and heal hearts. He teaches in parables for that purpose.

Mark makes Jesus' intentions clearer a bit later when he has him compare his teaching to a lamp (4:22-25). In the Bible, a "lamp" is frequently used as a metaphor for God's word. The psalmist sings, "Your word is a lamp for my feet" (Ps 119:105), and the author of Proverbs says about one of the commandments, "The bidding is a lamp, and the teaching a light" (Prov 6:23). So here, when Jesus asks if anyone would put a lamp under a bushel basket or a bed, he is suggesting that no one would try to hide God's word. Further, he is indicating that he certainly is not doing so. By implication, he is suggesting that the parable is a "lampstand" that will show off the light of God's word. The rabbis also speak of the parable form as a kind of lamp by which one can read the Bible more clearly.

When Jesus then goes on to say that "there is nothing hidden except to be made visible" and "nothing is secret except to come to light" (4:22), he appears to be expressing the Jewish view that the Bible contains God's revelation and nothing is hidden in the Bible except to be made clear.

The two proverbial sayings that follow—"The measure with which you measure will be measured out to you" (4:24) and "To the one who has, more will be given; from the one who has not, even what he has will be taken away" (4:25)—have a parallel in the Talmud, the most significant collection of the Jewish oral tradition. In the Talmud, it is clear that what is being talked about is the measure of one's understanding of God's word.

4:34-41 Jesus himself as parable

The parable section of the chapter appears to close with Mark telling us that "Without parables he [Jesus] did not speak to them [the crowd], but to his own disciples he explained everything in private" (4:34). The implication of this seems to be that Jesus did not use parables in teaching his disciples. It appears to confirm the earlier statement that Mark quotes Jesus as saying to his disciples: "The mystery of the kingdom of God has been granted to you. But to those outside everything comes in parables" (4:11). Yet the assertion is puzzling, because so far in his Gospel, Mark has not shown us Jesus teaching any other way.

What kind of distinction is Mark trying to make between Jesus' teaching of the crowd and his teaching of his disciples? In what special way has "the mystery of the kingdom of God" been granted to Jesus' disciples? In the closing verses of chapter 4, Mark seems to provide an answer. He shows Jesus himself to be a living parable. That is to say, in the final episode of Jesus' stilling the sea, Mark reveals that the person of Jesus provides an analogy to what God is like.

As in the parables that Jesus tells, this parable that he enacts is composed of echoes of Scripture. In this case, the direct echo is of some of the psalms that reflect on God's power over creation:

> LORD, God of hosts, who is like you? . . .
> You rule the raging sea;
>   you still its swelling waves (Ps 89:9a, 10).
>
> You still the roaring of the seas,
>   the roaring of their waves (Ps 65:8).
>
> [The LORD] hushed the storm to a murmur;
>   the waves of the sea were stilled (Ps 107:29).

Mark, steeped in the Hebrew Bible himself, surely assumed that when he quotes the disciples saying, "Who then is this whom even wind and sea obey?" (4:41), his audience would have heard the answer in their memory of these psalms.

In the first part of chapter 4, Mark shows Jesus teaching in the style of a teacher of Wisdom, teaching in parables. At the end, however, he shows Jesus teaching by his actions. He shows Jesus stilling the sea as God stills the sea in the psalms. He shows Jesus to be "like God." He shows Jesus to be in himself a Wisdom parable. Those who are his disciples have been granted a direct encounter with "the mystery of the kingdom of God."

Summary of chapter 4

In chapter 4, Mark focuses on Jesus' teaching about the kingdom of God. He shows him teaching in the style of a Wisdom teacher, using parables to shed light on God's revelation in Scripture. He does so by following a method common to other Jewish teachers. He strings together three parables linked by the image of seeds. They are all based on the biblical image that expresses God the Creator as God the sower. Yet each one imagines God's sowing and the results differently. The first parable imagines God sowing some seeds that will bear fruit and some that will not. The second parable imagines God's word as a seed that will come to fruition no matter what. The third parable imagines God's word as a seed that is common and

accessible, yet grows to be shade and shelter for all creatures.

In between the parables, Mark shows Jesus commenting on the purpose of parables. He first quotes the passage in Isaiah where God (by ironically saying the opposite of what he means) indicates how much he wants his word to touch and heal the human heart. He next suggests that the parable form is like a lampstand that shows off the light of God's word. He indicates that he speaks in parables in order to bring to light what is hidden in God's revelation.

Mark shows Jesus asking the question of how to find an analogy for God's kingdom. The second and third parables form one kind of answer. But in the final episode of the chapter, when Mark shows Jesus stilling the sea, he provides a different kind of answer. He shows Jesus himself acting the way God does in the psalms. He suggests that Jesus himself is a kind of parable, a living likeness of God. As a parable, he is like a lampstand that makes more visible the light of God's word. He is a living metaphor that serves to bring to light what is hidden in God's revelation.

THE TRANSFORMING EFFECT OF JESUS/WISDOM

Mark 5:1-43

5:1-20 The transformation of the Gerasene demoniac

No one knows exactly what Mark had in mind by "the territory of the Gerasenes," but it was clearly pagan territory, being on "the other side of the sea" from Galilee and inhabited by people who tended pigs (an unclean and forbidden animal to Jews). There are fascinating echoes of Isaiah's description of a pagan people who, he says, were "living among the graves," "eating swine's flesh," and "crying out, 'Hold back, do not touch me!'" (Isa 65:4-5a). So we find here in Mark's narrative a man "dwelling among the tombs" whom "no one could restrain" (5:3), and who was "always crying out" (5:5). He is not said to be "eating swine's flesh," but swine do figure prominently in the story. In Isaiah, these pagan practices enkindle God's wrath (Isa 65:5b). Here, however, Mark shows Jesus treating them as evidence of unclean spirits, a pathological state that can be cured.

The narrative is also suggestive of Jesus' metaphor of "the strong man" in chapter 3. You may remember that there, Jesus observes, "No one can enter a strong man's house to plunder his property unless he first ties up the strong man" (3:27). Here in fact is a strong man, powerful enough to have pulled apart his physical chains (5:4), but nonetheless invaded and plundered by unclean spirits. Jesus' response is not to bind but to free him.

The exchange between Jesus and the unclean spirits reveals something about Mark's view of the nature of evil. First of all, like the unclean spirit in 1:24, the unclean spirits here cry out in protest at Jesus' appearance (5:7). Once again Mark indicates that they feel diminished by Jesus' very presence. Second, it should not be passed over that the name of these unclean spirits, "Legion," is the name of a unit in the Roman army. Surely a Jewish audience would have been amused by this piece of wit at their enemy's expense. Even more, they would have found it a joke that these Roman demons ask to be placed inside a herd of pigs. The final act in this rhetorical comedy is the scene of the pigs rushing headlong into the sea.

The serious side of this story is the pointed suggestion that those who were currently occupying Palestine and meddling with the Temple belong to the devil. At the time that Mark's Gospel was written down (probably the year 70), it would not have been safe or prudent for anyone to have said such a thing directly. But here and elsewhere, as we shall see, Mark insinuates his view of Rome.

After the unclean spirits leave him, the man who had been possessed reappears "clothed and in his right mind" (5:15). The details suggest that before, he had been naked and crazy; in ridding him of his demons, Jesus has restored him to himself. This restoration is such a profound change that it seems like a transformation. The ultimate sign of his transformation appears in the man's going off "to proclaim in Decapolis what Jesus had done for him" (5:20). Like the cured leper in 1:45, this man is transformed from an alienated human being into one who spreads the word of God's goodness.

5:25-34 The transformation of the menstruating woman

The narrative of the woman who was suffering for twelve years from a menstrual disorder is interjected into the story of the twelve-year-old girl who appears to be dead. This structure of interlocking stories is a device Mark uses for a purpose. We will consider later what that purpose is.

The narrative of this woman is striking because in it Mark shows Jesus dealing openly and compassionately with a female condition that was taboo. Menstruating women were considered ritually unclean and excluded from Temple gatherings. Menstruating women were considered sexually unclean, so husbands were forbidden to have intercourse with them. In biblical writings, a menstruating woman is used as a symbol of idolatry. Thus, to describe a woman who had suffered from a flow of menstrual blood over a period of twelve years is to hold up for consideration a woman who in every way sums ups "the unclean" within Judaism—ritually, sexually, and religiously. Her healing contact with Jesus thus has significance far beyond the immediate miracle. Mark suggests that she was changed in two different ways: first, "she felt in her body that she was healed of her affliction" (5:29), and second, she receives an affirmation of her faith (5:34).

There are details in the scene worth noting. First, Mark underlines the spiritual significance of the story by his repeated use of "straightway." He tells us that "*Straightway** her flow of blood dried up" (5:29) and "*Straightway* Jesus was aware that power had gone out from him" (5:30).

Second, Mark says that the woman approached Jesus "in fear and trembling" (5:33). The phrase anticipates the description of the three women before the empty tomb and should be kept in mind as a clue to its meaning. Clearly, the woman here is trembling because she has sensed the power that has healed her body; she is not frightened but in awe of it. When we read later that the women at the tomb were also "trembling" (16:8), we should remember that Mark has used the word here to signify the holy state of being overwhelmed by God's power. Mark confirms this meaning when he quotes Jesus as saying, "Daughter, your faith has saved you" (5:34a). Mark confirms this further by showing Jesus bestowing on her a traditional Jewish blessing: "Go [or walk] in peace . . . ." (5:34a). The woman has been transformed by Jesus from someone who was ostracized as "unclean" into a model of faith.

5:21-24, 35-43 The transformation of the synagogue leader's daughter

After the story of Jesus' transformation of the possessed man in the pagan, Gentile world of the

Gerasenes, Mark says that Jesus crossed the Sea of Galilee again, back to the Jewish side (5:21). Here Mark begins the story of Jairus, the synagogue official who begs for help for his dying daughter (5:22-24). Mark interrupts that narrative to tell the one of the menstruating woman, then returns to it after she has been healed and sent off in peace. The interruption serves two purposes: first, it provides a narrative reason for Jesus' delay in going to see the little girl, an interval that appears to be fatal (5:35), so that, dramatically, Jesus' miracle here has greater dimensions than a simple healing. Second, it makes the story of the older woman shed light on the meaning of the little girl's, and vice versa. Intertwined as narratives, they are also intertwined in meaning. In both cases, a female person is brought back from the brink of death.

Mark shapes the narrative of the little girl so as to show that this is a story of resurrection—one that anticipates Jesus' own. He quotes Jesus as saying three things in the course of the story, each of them pointing to the story's ultimate significance. Jesus says to the synagogue official, "Do not be afraid; just have faith" (5:36). He says to the weeping crowd, "The child is not dead but asleep" (5:39). And he says to the child herself, "Rise up!"* (5:41).

Each one of these comments is geared toward transforming common attitudes toward death. To the synagogue official, death was not only an occasion of sadness but of fear, because it was believed at the time that death rendered the human body "unclean" and so made anyone who touched it ritually unclean. To the crowd "weeping and wailing loudly" (5:38), death was final, and to the child herself, life seemed over. Against these views, Jesus' comments exchange fear for faith, suggest that death is but a temporary and reversible phase, and call the child back to life.

Once again, as in the healing of Simon's mother-in-law (1:31) and the healing of the paralytic (2:11), Mark uses the same word here for "rise" that he uses for Jesus' resurrection. Mark also uses key words to describe the reaction of the witnesses. What is translated here as "They were utterly astounded" (5:42b) is literally "They were out of their minds [or "beside themselves"] with ecstasy."* The phrase "out of their minds" echoes Mark's earlier description of those who witnessed the paralytic rise up (2:12b) and the place where those close to Jesus think he is "out of his mind"

(3:21). Mark will use the word "ecstasy" again at the end of his Gospel to describe the experience of the women overwhelmed by God's power to overcome death.

Summary of chapter 5

In this chapter, Mark shows Jesus having a transforming effect on different states considered "unclean" within Judaism: demon possession, menstruation, and death. Considering these three episodes as another Markan triad, we need to explore how the middle episode is key. The first transforming miracle takes place in the Gentile world; the last is set in the home of a synagogue leader. The first frees a man from his demons and restores him to himself; the last raises up a child thought dead and restores her to her parents. In the middle is the transformation of a Jewish woman whose physical condition has alienated her as completely from Temple and synagogue as demons or death. In curing her, Jesus restores her both to herself and to her religious community. In effect, he brings her back to life.

THE RECOGNITION OF JESUS/WISDOM
Mark 6:1-56

6:1-6 Jesus as too familiar

In the preceding chapters, Mark has repeatedly dramatized how people around Jesus are challenged by his unconventional ways. They are challenged by his "new teaching" (1:27) that possession by demons is a pathological state that can be cured (1:21-28; 3:22-30); by his transforming outreach to "the unclean" (1:40-45; 5:1-43); by his "raising up"* of women (1:29-31; 5:21-43); by his calling of sinners (2:13-17) and his views on sin and forgiveness (3:22-30); by his seeming indifference to religious rules (2:18-28); by his priorities—by the way he continually places human need first (3:1-5); by his redefining the meaning of "family" (3:31-35); by his teaching in parables (4:1-34); by his easy command of demons and storms (1:25; 4:39; 5:8).

At the beginning of chapter 6, Mark dramatizes the opposite: he constructs a scene in which the people in Jesus' hometown find him too familiar to teach them anything. The questions that Mark quotes them as asking are typical of all people who expect (or want) their encounter with the divine to be unusual and spectacular.

Since Mark has been presenting Jesus to his readers as Wisdom herself, there is particular irony in their question "What kind of wisdom has been given him?" (6:2). With further irony, Mark uses their questions to set up Jesus' Wisdom-saying, "A prophet is not without honor except in his native place and among his own kin and in his own house" (6:4). In this pithy observation, Mark shows Jesus also hinting at the destiny of his disciples.

6:7-13, 30-31 The commissioning of the disciples of Jesus/Wisdom

Mark shows that the disciples are instructed to imitate Jesus in preaching repentance, driving out demons, and curing the sick (6:12-13). By implication, the instruction to be detached from their possessions (6:8-9) also reflects the simple lifestyle of Jesus/Wisdom, a point Mark will develop in chapter 10. Mark links this narrative to the scene in Nazareth by showing that Jesus tells them to expect rejection (6:11). Later in the chapter, Mark shows how the disciples return to report and how Jesus invites them to follow him further by withdrawing for prayer (6:30-31).

6:14-29 The death of John the Baptist

As in chapter 5, Mark interweaves different narratives, so that each one comments on the other. As we have seen, one narrative strand is concerned with the disciples—how they are sent forth to be like Jesus and how they return to report. In between we hear the story of John the Baptist. Although at first hearing the transition may seem abrupt and the stories unconnected, with hindsight we can see that Mark has set up the narrative about John and his followers to foreshadow the narrative of Jesus and his disciples. Mark builds upon the original connections he has made between John and Jesus (1:14; 2:18) to achieve this effect.

Mark uses the device of a conversation about Jesus and John to set up the connections. First we hear people in general comparing Jesus with John (6:14), and then we hear Herod making the same comparison (6:16). In both instances, these voices speak of John as "raised from the dead." It is only then, and in retrospect, that we hear how and why John was murdered by Herod.

The story is complex, dramatizing the convergence of many causes. The root cause is classic: a prophet (John) "speaks truth to power." Nonetheless, we are told, Herod himself would not have injured John on that account, because he "feared John" and "liked to listen to him" (6:20). His wife, Herodias, however, angered at being denounced as unlawful, "harbored a grudge" and looked for the chance to avenge herself (6:19). The opportunity presents itself in the form of Herod's birthday party, a seemingly innocuous celebration (6:21). There the dance of a young girl (the daughter of Herodias) leads to Herod's extravagant and thoughtless vow: "I will grant you whatever you ask of me, even to half of my kingdom" (6:23). The plot concludes in a dizzying series of ironies: the young girl acts like a dutiful and docile daughter in repeating to Herod her mother's murderous request for "the head of John the Baptist" (6:24). The king, although "deeply distressed," accedes to the request out of a sense of fidelity to his word (6:26). The girl, dutiful to the end, took the prophet's head and "gave it to her mother" (6:28).

Mark has told the story of John's death in a way that illuminates how it results from a tragic and ironic mixture of vengeful hatred, chance opportunity, filial devotion, and vacillating weakness. As Mark tells the story, it is clear that while there is certainly some real evil at work (the unlawful marriage to begin with, and then the desire for revenge on the part of Herodias), the murder would never have been accomplished without Herod's weak ambivalence. Even though he knew John "to be a righteous and holy man," he had him imprisoned (6:17, 20), and even though he was "deeply distressed" (6:26) by the girl's savage request, he gave the order for John's beheading (6:27).

Mark's narrative and theological purpose in telling this story is revealed in the conclusion: "When his disciples heard about it, they came and took his body and laid it in a tomb" (6:29). Mark has put the story of John's death here as a foreshadowing of Jesus' death. The two stories are not, of course, exactly the same, but there are parallels. In the second part of his Gospel, Mark will show Jesus speaking some unwelcome truths to those in power, and he will suggest how some leaders (both Roman and Jewish) were resentful of this criticism, and so looked for a way to get rid of him. He will show the collaboration between these vengeful people and the opportunist Judas (14:10-11). But above all, he will show how it is Pilate's weakness, especially his desire "to satisfy the crowd," that results in his condemnation of Jesus (15:15).

Mark also uses this story to illuminate the difference between John's disciples and those of Jesus. Unlike John's disciples, Jesus' disciples do not come as a group to ask for his body and bury it. One person, Joseph of Arimathea, does come, but he is a member of the council that condemned Jesus and so a new and unexpected disciple. All the others have fled. It is with pointed irony that Mark makes this story of John and his faithful disciples part of the narrative in which Jesus' disciples receive their instructions.

Finally, Mark uses this story to foreshadow Jesus' resurrection. He does this through the opening speculation by the people and by Herod that Jesus may in fact be John "raised up." Before this, Mark has introduced the motif of resurrection through the vocabulary of "rising up" and "raised up" that he uses for so many of Jesus' miracles. Here Mark makes the resurrection theme explicit.

It is also worth noting that Mark sets up a structure here that he will repeat in connection with Jesus. He gives a hint of John's resurrection before he tells us about his death, just as he will tell of Jesus' transfiguration before he gives an account of his passion. In this way, too, Mark uses John's story to foreshadow that of Jesus.

6:31-44 The feeding of the five thousand

The motif of food and of eating is a recurring one in Mark's Gospel. It causes criticism when Jesus is seen eating with sinners and tax collectors (2:16). It raises questions when Jesus and his disciples feast rather than fast (2:18-19). It occasions moral outrage when Jesus allows his disciples to pick grain on the Sabbath, and the outrage in turn provides the opportunity for Jesus to teach that God's intent for the Sabbath is human wholeness (2:23-28).

All this concern with nurture is part of Mark's portrayal of Jesus as Wisdom—a womanly figure in Proverbs (and elsewhere), who ceaselessly invites guests to the divine banquet. In keeping with these motherly characteristics, Mark shows Jesus' first concern for Jairus's daughter, once he has brought her back to life, is that "she should be given something to eat" (5:43). That verse, which is the conclusion of chapter 5, prepares for Jesus'

concern here for feeding the five thousand who have followed him.

Mark constructs a transition from the narrative of Jesus and the disciples to this narrative by noting that they were surrounded by so many people that "they had no opportunity even to eat" (6:31). There is an echo here of the earlier scene where "the crowds gathered, making it impossible for them even to eat" (3:20). In the earlier instance, Mark tells us that those close to Jesus said, "He is out of his mind" (3:21). In this instance, Mark says that Jesus and his disciples set off "to a deserted place" (6:32) but could not keep the crowds away. Mark then describes a repetition of what happened at the end of chapter 1 when Jesus "remained in deserted places," and yet "people kept coming to him from everywhere" (1:45b). Here again Mark dramatizes that Jesus cannot escape the crowds. They arrive at his destination on foot before he arrives at it by boat (6:32-33).

In the scenes that follow, Mark suggests in several different ways that Jesus is acting the way God acts in the Hebrew Bible. When Mark tells us that Jesus' heart was "moved with pity for them, for they were like sheep without a shepherd" (6:34), he is echoing the place in Ezekiel where God pities the hungry sheep and promises to shepherd them himself (Ezek 34:11-15).

When Mark tells us that Jesus ordered the people to "sit down in groups," the words literally are "meal-sharing groups"* (6:39). This phrasing is suggestive of God's instructions for sharing the Passover meal: "If a family is too small for a whole lamb, it shall join the nearest household in procuring one and shall share in the lamb" (Exod 12:4).

Through the threefold repetition of "deserted place" (6:31a, 32, 35), Mark emphasizes that the setting is similar to the wilderness setting of the Exodus journey.

Mark thus tells the story of Jesus' miraculous feeding of the five thousand in the desert in such a way that it would remind his audience of God's miraculous way of providing his people with manna in the desert. In this context, Jesus' invitation to come to the desert ("Come away . . . and rest a while," 6:31a) is suggestive of God's command not even to gather manna on the seventh day but to share his Sabbath rest (Exod 16:23).

The overall thrust of the book of Exodus is God's providential care for his people, not only in leading them out of slavery but in leading them into a space and time apart from ordinary concerns—into a desert place and Sabbath time where they could learn to become dependent on God for food and life itself. By echoing this crucial time in the history of God's people, Mark suggests how Jesus reflects this nurturing aspect of God.

6:45-52 Walking on water

In describing Jesus' "walking on the sea" (6:48b), Mark shows Jesus acting like God in Job (9:8 and 38:16) and Sirach (24:5-6). Other miraculous actions of Jesus have some precedent in one of the prophets: Elisha multiplies bread (2 Kgs 4:42-44) and cures the leper Naaman (2 Kgs 5:1-14); Elijah raises a young man from the dead (1 Kgs 17:17-24). But no prophet walks on water. In describing this scene, Mark is dramatizing his perception that Jesus resembles God himself. Mark intensifies this perception by showing Jesus still the waters once again as he did at the end of chapter 4. There we noted that Mark, through echoes of Psalm 84, suggests that Jesus is a living parable of what God is like. When Mark repeats the scene here, he makes that likeness clear.

The reaction of the disciples, however, to this second incident of Jesus' stilling the sea is markedly less perceptive than the first time around. This time, when they see Jesus walking to them on the water, they are not awed but terrified. (Here Mark uses a verb that means "fright," not "holy fear.") When the wind dies down, they do not ask, as they did before, "Who then is this, whom even wind and sea obey?" (4:41). In the earlier incident, Mark suggests that they might be coming to a deeper understanding of Jesus' identity. In this scene, however, he says that "they had not understood the incident of the loaves. On the contrary, their hearts were hardened" (6:52).

"Hardness of heart," as we have noted before, is a typical way for the Hebrew Bible to express the obstinate resistance of the sinner to God's outreach. Mark has used it before in his Gospel to describe the Pharisees' cold reaction to Jesus' healing of the man with a withered hand (3:5). It is striking that he uses the same phrase here to describe the obtuse response of Jesus' own disciples.

6:53-56 Recognition of Jesus at Gennesaret

Mark concludes the chapter with a sharply contrasting description of the ordinary crowds.

Most telling is the phrase "people straightway* recognized him" (6:54). It is striking because the chapter opens with Mark dramatizing a scene in Jesus' hometown in which people who "know" him cannot recognize him as anything more than "the carpenter, the son of Mary" (6:3).

The importance of the recognition here is underlined by Mark's use of the word "straightway." While Jesus' own disciples fail to understand anything significant in Jesus' feeding of the five thousand, the crowds scurry to bring their sick, and like the woman with the disordered flow of blood (5:28), they "begged him that they might touch only the tassel on his cloak" (6:56).

Summary of chapter 6

In this chapter, Mark dwells on the theme of people recognizing or not recognizing Jesus as God's Wisdom. In the opening scene, he shows people in Jesus' hometown not recognizing him as anyone special because he is so familiar. In the last scene of the chapter, Mark shows ordinary crowds elsewhere recognizing him "straightway." These two extremes frame the chapter.

In between, Mark dwells on the role of the disciples and their variable responses to Jesus and to his actions. Again there is a framework of two extremes: early in the chapter we see the disciples sent forth to imitate Jesus in his preaching, healing, and exorcising of demons, yet at the end of the chapter we find that "their hearts were hardened," so that they remember neither Jesus' miracle of the loaves nor his earlier command of the sea.

The complicated, uncertain nature of the disciples is further dramatized through Mark's device of interweaving the story of John the Baptist into their story. The narrative of John's death and the possibility of his being "raised up" function as a foreshadowing of the death and resurrection of Jesus. At the same time, Mark sets up the courageous, faithful disciples of John as a contrast to the disciples of Jesus, who, in the end, will become frightened (as they are here) and run away.

And even while he is showing the disciples as repeatedly unable to grasp who Jesus is, Mark is dramatizing more and more clearly that Jesus is the image of God. Jesus feeds the crowds with bread in the desert as God fed the Israelites with manna in the wilderness; he walks on water as God does in Job and Sirach.

JESUS' REDEFINING OF THE "UNCLEAN"

Mark 7:1-37

7:1-13 Discussion of the sacred and the profane

In Jewish tradition, there are clear boundaries between the sacred and the profane, between what is to be consecrated to God and what is to be regarded as secular or "common." The Jewish people see themselves as consecrated to God in accordance with God's blessing of them in Exodus 19:6: "You shall be to me a kingdom of priests, a holy nation." The Ten Commandments of the covenant, as well as the subsidiary laws designed to support and protect them, are considered a gift to be cherished.

The laws concerning food are part of this larger context. Eating kosher food and using kosher dishes are an acknowledgment that all life, as well as the nourishing of it, is sacred to the Lord. The whole discussion in this chapter should be regarded in that context and not as an argument over trivial rules. The Jewish custom of washing their hands before eating, and the vessels before using them, was originally more than good hygiene. They were also acts of ritual purification, signaling Jewish desire to consecrate this most basic of human activities.

Unfortunately, verses 3 and 4, which try to give an explanation for these washing rituals, are flawed in the original manuscript. Verse 3 literally reads, "For the Pharisees and all the Jews do not eat unless they have washed themselves *with the fist** . . . ." Verse 4 literally reads, "And they do not eat from the marketplace unless they immerse themselves, and there are many other traditions they carry out, the immersing of cups and pots and bronze vessels *and beds.**" No translator knows what to do with "the fist" in verse 3 or the "beds" of verse 4. No commentator notes that the word "immerse" here is *baptizo* in Greek. It's a word that Mark uses for baptism but is ill-suited to this context. Many scholars think that this curious explanation of Jewish customs was probably added to Mark's manuscript after the first century. Vincent Taylor, one of the best of these scholars, recommends skipping verses 2-4 entirely.

In any case, Mark uses a favorite device here: he cites a question by the Pharisees in order to set up Jesus' teaching on what is and is not sacred. The Pharisees challenge the eating customs of Jesus' disciples, just as earlier they had challenged their picking grain on the Sabbath (2:24). The language of this challenge highlights what is at stake: "Why do your disciples . . . eat the bread with unclean hands?" (7:5). The word translated "unclean" here could also be translated "common." What is "common" is profane and ordinary, not consecrated and sacred. It is a consistent theme of Mark's that Jesus is like Wisdom, who, in Proverbs, goes into the marketplace to find her followers. Like Wisdom, Jesus does not shun the common and ordinary but seeks to transform it.

In 7:6-7, Jesus critiques his challengers in the language of Isaiah 29:13. In context, Isaiah is expressing God's frustration that the people of Jerusalem do not trust that God will save them from besieging enemies. God finds the root cause in the fact that the people honor him with their lips, not their hearts. Their worship has become merely "routine observance of human precepts."

In 7:8, Jesus carries this accusation even further, saying, "You disregard God's commandment but cling to human tradition." In 7:10-12, Jesus gives a concrete example of this practice. He notes how some fail to honor their parents by withholding support for them on the grounds that the money is "*qorban*," or dedicated to God. How much this was actually done is difficult to determine. But the point of Jesus' criticism is clearly part of the larger theme of the chapter. Jesus is pointing out that human relationships are what is truly sacred, and no religious formula can rationalize that sacredness away.

7:14-23 What defiles a person

Just as Mark uses a question by the Pharisees to set the stage for Jesus' teaching on what is sacred, so here he uses a question by the disciples to open up Jesus' teaching on what is defiling. Jesus says to the crowd that "Nothing that enters one from outside can defile that person" (7:15). Mark calls this a "parable" or "riddle" (7:17), indicating that it is a saying whose full meaning needs to be unpacked.

At first glance, Jesus' saying appears to challenge the Jewish dietary laws. After all, if nothing that one takes in is defiling, then why refuse to eat certain foods? The parenthetical comment "Thus he declared all foods clean" was probably added later and was intended as just such an explanation. We know, however, from Acts 10:1-11 that the question of which foods were unclean went on being debated in the early church. And as Jesus goes on teaching here, we see that he is presenting something more morally complex. The complexity is contained in what comes "from within people, from their hearts" (7:21). If we grasp the saying as a whole, we realize that the emphasis is not on dismissing what enters a person but on demonstrating the greater evil of "what comes out" (7:20). As in much of Jesus' teaching, his intent appears not so much to disregard external rules as to focus on internal realities.

7:24-30 Jesus and the Syrophoenician woman; the healing of the daughter with an unclean spirit

Mark dramatizes Jesus' point here by showing him in pagan or "unclean" territory. Here Jesus converses with a pagan woman and exorcises the unclean spirit that has possessed her daughter. In so doing, Mark is showing Jesus engaged in activities that other pious Jews of his time would have found unconventional, even shocking. Mark softens the shock value of Jesus' outreach to the Gentiles by indicating his reluctance to become involved.

First, Mark tells his audience that Jesus "wanted no one to know about" his journey to Tyre. Second, when the woman asks Jesus to cure her daughter, Mark says that Jesus first put her off by saying, "Let the children be fed first. For it is not right to take the food of the children and throw it to the dogs" (7:27). Jesus' language here indicates that he saw Israel as his priority over the Gentiles. The "children" are the children of Israel. The term "dogs" was a common and insulting way for Jews of the time to refer to Gentiles.

The woman responds in a bold and witty way by accepting these terms and turning them back to Jesus through a play on words and ideas. She says: "Lord, even the dogs under the table eat the children's scraps" (7:28). This kind of playfulness with words is typically Jewish. Mark perhaps wanted to dramatize that even someone as "unclean" as a Gentile woman with a possessed daughter was capable of parrying on equal terms with a Jew. The healing of her daughter (7:30) is linked to Mark's way of showing her, not as unclean Gentile, but as a partner in wit.

There is precedent in Hebrew Scripture for Jewish outreach to the Gentiles. In the Second Book of Kings we hear how Elisha the prophet cured the Syrian king of leprosy (2 Kgs 5:1-19). But Mark uses language that indicates that Jesus' exchange with this woman has more meaning than a simple cure. When the woman first comes to Jesus, Mark says she heard of him "straightway"* (7:25). The word is translated above as "soon," but as we have suggested before, "straightway" is Mark's particular way of indicating moral urgency.

The words of the exchange between Jesus and the woman may also be weighted with special meaning. It was a common Jewish idiom to speak of God's word as "bread." And the word translated here as "food" is literally "bread"* (7:27), so we might understand Jesus to be saying, "It is not right to take God's word [the "bread"] and throw it to the dogs" [that is, to those who do not know how to understand it]. When Mark shows Jesus conceding to the woman's wish, he may be indicating Jesus' willingness to extend God's word to the Gentiles.

7:31-37 Jesus' healing of the deaf-mute

Mark shows that Jesus continued his ministry in Gentile territory, this time on the other side of the Sea of Galilee, in Decapolis. In language that echoes the healing of the paralytic (2:3), Mark tells us that "They brought to him a man that was deaf and mute and begged him that he might lay a hand on him." Mark then describes Jesus' curing the man through a series of ritual actions known to have been used by both Greek and Jewish healers. The Aramaic phrase *ephphatha* literally means "be released,"* which links it to Jesus' saying to the paralytic that his sins are "released" (2:5).

Mark indicates that this healing has moral significance through his use of the word "straightway"* (translated above as "immediately"): "And straightway his ears were opened and his tongue was loosed from chains and he began to speak straight" (7:35).

By the use of the word "straightway," together with the repetition of "straight,"* Mark indicates that more is happening here than a simple cure. The whole event echoes ideas and language in Isaiah, some of which Mark showed Jesus alluding to in 4:10-13. We have noted before that when Jesus is speaking about the purpose of parables, he quotes the place in Isaiah where God says ironically:

You are to make the heart of this people sluggish,
   to dull their eyes and close their ears;
Else their eyes will see, their ears hear,
   their heart understand,
   and they will turn and be healed (Isa 6:9-10).

And as we said earlier, of course God actually hopes the people will see and hear, understand and be healed. In a later book in Isaiah, when God is promising to save his people, God says:

Then will the eyes of the blind be opened,
   the ears of the deaf be cleared;
Then will the lame leap like a stag,
   then the tongue of the mute will sing
      (Isa 35:5-6).

In this concluding episode of chapter 7, Mark shows Jesus doing what God has promised. By showing Jesus healing the deaf-mute, Mark is suggesting that Jesus is opening up people to God's word.

Summary of chapter 7

In this chapter, Mark develops the theme of Jesus' relationship to the "unclean. " It is a theme that Mark touched on in Jesus' first healing of the man with the unclean spirit (1:21-27); in his cure of the leper (1:40-45); in his eating with sinners (2:13-17); in the accusation that Jesus himself has an unclean spirit (3:30); in Jesus' exorcism of the Gerasene demoniac (5:2); and in the power Jesus gives his disciples to drive out unclean spirits (6:7).

This chapter has a triad structure. A homily by Jesus that redefines what makes a person "unclean" (7:14-23) is framed by two conversations on the subject. Before the homily, Jesus has a conversation with men of traditional piety about what is sacred and what is "unclean" or profane (7:1-14). After the homily, he has an unconventional dialogue with a pagan woman and drives out an unclean spirit from her daughter (7:24-30). Mark shows Jesus responding to the challenge of those who think in conventional terms by redefining what is "unclean." Mark dramatizes this redefinition by showing Jesus' outreach to the Gentile woman and her daughter.

In the concluding episode Mark indicates the significance of Jesus' redefinition by showing him engaged in healing a deaf-mute, an action that symbolizes the opening of people's ears to the meaning of God's word.

SECOND SIGHT—A SHARPER FOCUS

Mark 8:1-38

8:1-10 The second feeding of a crowd

Mark designs his Gospel so that themes, images, and even events are repeated more than once. With hindsight the reader becomes aware of a pattern of doublets. There is a theological purpose to this design that chapter 8 points to, which we will discuss later. The doublet at the beginning of chapter 8 is striking: once again a large and hungry crowd is gathered around Jesus, and once again he feeds them with scant supplies. Once again there are baskets left over. (Compare 6:34-44.)

There are also some interesting details of difference. In the first scenario, Jesus is "moved with pity" for the crowd because they "were like sheep without a shepherd" (6:34); his initial compassion is for their spiritual hunger. Here Jesus is concerned about the crowd because they have been with him "for three days and have nothing to eat" (8:2). In the first scene, the disciples approach Jesus about the situation (6:35); here Jesus approaches them (8:1-3). In the first scene, they distribute "five loaves and two fish" (6:38); here they distribute seven loaves and "a few fish" (8:6-7). In both instances, Jesus orders the crowd to sit down to be fed, but in the first one he suggests that they form "meal-sharing groups" (6:39), a detail that is omitted here. In both instances Jesus prays over the bread and then breaks it, but in the first scene Mark specifically says that he "said the blessing" over it (6:41), while in the second, Mark says he "gave thanks" (8:6). In both cases, Mark tells us that the people ate "and were satisfied" (6:42; 8:8). In both scenes, the disciples gather up baskets of leftovers, but in the first instance it is twelve (6:43), while in the second there are seven (8:8).

Is there any significance to these small differences? Many scholars have suggested that the first feeding is suggestive of God feeding his people with manna, while the second is suggestive of the Eucharist. To arrive at this conclusion, they note that the "three days" of chapter 8 suggests Jesus' three days in the tomb; that saying a blessing over the bread is the conventional description of the Jewish grace before meals, while the giving of thanks over it suggests the Eucharist (which literally means "thanksgiving"); that the number twelve in the first episode suggests the twelve tribes of Israel, while the number seven suggests the sacraments of the church. Yet there are many flaws in these arguments: "three days" was a conventional biblical way of indicating a long period of time; the Jewish blessing over food is in fact a prayer of thanksgiving; and the sacraments of the church were not numbered for many centuries. So it would seem that to call the first miracle Jewish and the second one Christian is strained. What is clear is that Mark wanted his audience to be aware of a miraculous event that repeated itself.

8:11-21 Double failures to understand

What follows are two episodes in which first the Pharisees and then Jesus' disciples fail to get the point of the miracle he has just performed. Although they are usually treated separately, it is important to see that they are designed to be parallel. They are also equal in irony.

If one is reading the Gospel as a literal account, one could, of course, shrug off the Pharisees' request for "a sign from heaven" (8:11) by saying that there is no reason to think that the Pharisees were present at the miraculous feeding. But if one agrees that Mark has a theological design, then one perceives the juxtaposition of the feeding miracle and the Pharisees' request for "a sign from heaven" as Mark's way of indicating the Pharisees' obtuseness. When Mark goes on to say that Jesus' response was to sigh "from the depth of his spirit" (8:12), the reader shares that sense of exasperation.

The episode that follows (8:14-23) shows that the disciples have a parallel obtuseness. Mark dramatizes this in several ways. First, he quotes Jesus warning them against "the leaven of the Pharisees and the leaven of Herod" (8:15). Conventionally, "leaven" was considered to be a symbol of puffery or pride, so Jesus is apparently cautioning them against being too self-sufficient to trust in God. The disciples' response misses the point completely. Taking his words literally, "They concluded among themselves that it was because they had no bread" (8:16).

In describing how Jesus reproached them, Mark uses words that repeat earlier moments in the Gospel. At the end of chapter 6, when the disciples are frightened by seeing Jesus walk on the water and still the storm (6:49-51), Mark tells us, "They had not understood the incident of the loaves. On the contrary, their hearts were hardened" (6:52). So here, when Mark shows Jesus saying, "Why do you conclude you have no bread? Do you not yet understand or comprehend? Are your hearts hardened? . . . And do you not remember when I broke the five loaves for the five thousand . . . ?" (8:17-19), we hear a repetition of that earlier moment when the disciples missed the point. The repetition serves to underline the disciples' obtuseness.

8:22-26 The two-stage healing of the blind man

Like the healing of the deaf-mute at the end of chapter 7, the healing of the blind man here has symbolic significance. Particular elements of that earlier healing are repeated here. In both instances, Mark tells us that Jesus took the person aside (7:33; 8:23); in both, Mark indicates a laying on of hands (7:32; 8:25); in both, Mark says that Jesus used spittle as a means of healing (7:33; 8:23). The repeating details are enough to alert the reader to the fact that one healing is linked to the other. On a deeper level, they are linked in terms of the context of Isaiah:

> Then will the eyes of the blind be opened,
> the ears of the deaf be cleared;
> Then will the lame leap like a stag,
> then the tongue of the mute will sing (Isa 35:5-6).

In the earlier healing, Mark shows Jesus clearing the ears of the deaf and opening his mouth; here he shows Jesus opening the eyes of the blind.

The episode here also sheds light on Mark's structural habit of repeating incidents. The blind man does not see clearly right away; it takes a second laying on of hands before he "could see everything distinctly" (8:25). In the same way, Mark repeats incidents so that the reader can see more readily what he is about. So he describes two episodes that show Jesus is in command of the sea (4:35-41; 6:45-51); he twice describes Jesus miraculously feeding the people in the desert; he offers two healing incidents that dramatize how Jesus enacts the words of Isaiah.

This kind of structure may be related to the structure of Hebrew verse, which often repeats an initial thought in varied words. In Psalm 19, for example, we read:

> The law of the LORD is perfect,
> refreshing the soul.
> The decree of the LORD is trustworthy,
> giving wisdom to the simple (Ps 19:8).

The second verse repeats but varies the idea of the first, thereby enriching it. One commentator has described this structure as giving us "A, and what's more, B." In the same way, Mark's second, repeating episodes vary and enrich the significance of the first, making us grasp their meaning more clearly. We will discuss later the way in which the whole second half of Mark's Gospel (chs. 9–16) functions as a second verse, clarifying and enriching the teachings and actions of Jesus in the first half (chs. 1–8).

8:27-33 A second discussion of the identity of Jesus

The question that Mark shows Jesus raising here, "Who do people say that I am?" (8:27), is also a repetition. We have heard it before, although indirectly. In chapter 6, Mark tells us that people are talking about who Jesus is and offering various opinions: "John the Baptist has been raised from the dead . . . . He is Elijah . . . . He is a prophet like any of the prophets" (6:14-15). When Mark gives the disciples' response to Jesus' question here, he shows them repeating these opinions verbatim: "They said in reply, 'John the Baptist, others Elijah, still others, one of the prophets'" (8:28). Mark then shows Jesus asking the question directly of his disciples (8:29).

The response that Mark shows Peter making— "You are the Messiah" (8:29)—is strikingly different from the other speculations. Most Christians accept that response in the light of their own faith today. They also tend to perceive it through the lens of Matthew, who first adds to Peter's confession, "the Son of the living God" (Matt 16:16), and who then shows Jesus responding, "Blessed are you, Simon son of Jonah. For flesh and blood has not revealed this to you, but my heavenly Father. And so I say to you, you are Peter, and upon this rock I will build my church" (Matt 16:17-18). But readers who see the four evangelists as four different theologians will be sensitive to the different nuances in Mark's dramatization of what happens next.

In Mark's version, Jesus does not commend Peter for his reply. Instead, he charges the disciples not to speak about him (8:30) and goes on to tell them, for the first time, how he will suffer, die, and be raised up again (8:31). Mark then describes Peter as so unable to accept this prediction that he "rebuke[s]" Jesus (8:32). Although Mark

does not spell it out, the implication seems to be that Peter cannot accept the idea of Jesus' suffering and death; it does not fit his idea of a "messiah." Mark indicates that Jesus, in turn, cannot accept Peter's interpretation of who he is and that he rebukes him in radically strong language: "Get behind me, Satan. You are thinking not as God does, but as human beings do" (8:33).

Matthew also describes this second exchange between Jesus and Peter, but only after Jesus has commended Peter and told him that he will found his church upon him. What are we to make of this radical difference? If one is reading the Gospels as literal eyewitness accounts, one must resort to examining sources and speculating on how one evangelist took from one source and the other from another. But if one is reading the Gospels as theology (which the church now encourages us to do), one concludes that Mark had a different theological interpretation of this event than Matthew. Since Mark's is the earliest Gospel, one might then conclude that Mark and Matthew were each responding to the theological needs of their own time and respective faith-communities. In Matthew's time (probably a decade later than Mark's), the Christian community was beginning to emerge as a church. (Indeed, the word is used for the first time here in Matthew 16.) Moreover, it was undergoing persecution and needed to be affirmed as a community under God's care. In Mark's time, the Jesus-community saw itself as part of Judaism. The pressing issue was not, therefore, God's providence (which would have been taken for granted), but why Jesus was so important to them and what they meant in calling him "Messiah."

Contrary to popular belief, recent scholarship has shown that there was no single, fixed concept of "the Messiah" within Judaism of the first century. The term, which in Hebrew simply means "the anointed one," was used variably, both in the Hebrew Bible and in other Jewish writings that were contemporaneous with Jesus and Mark. Within the Hebrew Bible, it is most often applied to a king, but also to a high priest or a patriarch. Isaiah applied it to the Persian king Cyrus, who allowed the Jews to go home to Jerusalem from captivity in Babylon (Isa 45:1). In the Jewish writings outside the Bible, the term is variously applied to a teacher, a warrior, and a judge. The Dead Sea Scrolls anticipated the coming of two messiahs, a king and a high priest. In short, one cannot pin the term down to a particular definition but must acknowledge that it was generally used to indicate any figure whom the faith-community saw as God's representative, someone who was doing God's work on its behalf.

The one constant in all these variations was that a "messiah," as God's agent, was always imagined as victorious in his work. When Mark shows Peter rebuking Jesus for telling them he would die, he is showing Peter reacting on the basis of this assumption of victory and triumph. By the same token, when Mark shows Jesus rebuking Peter, he is indicating that Jesus was rebuking him for this assumption. Nowhere in Judaism before Jesus is there evidence of a suffering messiah. (Isaiah's "Suffering Servant" [Isa 52:13–53:12] was not considered messianic.) Only after Christianity was established did the idea begin to develop within Judaism. Here it is Peter's rejection of a suffering messiah that Jesus labels human-minded and not God-minded (8:33).

8:34-38 The second commissioning of Jesus' disciples

Mark shows that in the first commissioning of his disciples, Jesus sends them out to imitate him in preaching repentance, driving out demons, and curing the sick (6:7-13). We noted earlier that when Mark interleaves the story of John the Baptist between this commissioning and the disciples' return from their first efforts (6:14-29), he subtly suggests the destiny of both Jesus and Jesus' disciples. The death of John the Baptist is a foreshadowing of Jesus' death. Since Jesus has just instructed his disciples to imitate him, the placement of John's narrative at this point suggests that they will also be called to imitate him in the yielding of their lives. Here in chapter 8 this indirect suggestion is made clear. Mark shows us Jesus speaking plainly about what is involved in being his disciple: "Whoever wishes to come after me must deny self, take up the cross, and follow me" (8:34).

The chapter concludes with Mark indicating that death, however, is not the end of the story. He has just shown Jesus asserting the paradox that "Whoever wishes to save his life will lose it, but whoever loses his life for my sake and the sake of the gospel will save it" (8:35). Mark develops the implications of this paradox by indicating that at the end of time, Jesus will determine his followers accordingly: "Whoever is ashamed of

me . . . the son of man will be ashamed of when he comes in his Father's glory with the holy angels" (8:38). Some would like to read "son of man" here as the title of triumphant, apocalyptic figure, but as in 2:10, it makes sense to read it instead as the Aramaic form of self-reference. The use of the word "ashamed" emphasizes the fact that the cross is not only a painful death but a shameful one, and the followers of Jesus need to be prepared for worldly shame as well as physical suffering. Yet Mark also shows how Jesus implied that the shame of the cross would one day be replaced by the glory of the Father's presence. Mark thus prepares the reader for the transfiguration of Jesus, which follows in chapter 9.

Summary of chapter 8

In this chapter, Mark repeats some earlier events, images, and ideas. In doing so, he does not present exact repetitions but offers variations on the theme. It is a chapter of doublets. The chapter opens with a second episode in which Jesus feeds a great crowd in a deserted place. It is followed by the double misunderstanding of the miracle both by the Pharisees and by the disciples. It concludes with a second discussion of Jesus' identity and with a second commissioning of his disciples. In describing the disciples' failure to understand, Mark shows Jesus asking, "Are your hearts hardened?" (8:17) thus echoing the language of Jesus' dismay in chapter 6.

In presenting a second discussion of Jesus' identity and a second commissioning of the disciples, Mark sharpens the readers' focus. In the earlier discussions of chapter 6, Mark only hints that suffering and death will be significant parts of their destiny. Mark's main focus is on Jesus' power to heal and restore and on his passing on this power to his disciples. The emphasis is on Jesus as a miracle-worker and his disciples as potentially like him.

In chapter 8, however, Mark reverses the emphasis and begins to show that Jesus sees himself and his disciples as destined for a shameful death. Mark has shown Jesus speaking in parables and riddling sayings before. Here he shows him offering the ultimate paradox of losing one's life in order to save it.

This shift and sharpening of focus is symbolized in the two-stage healing of the blind man, itself a variation on the symbolic healing of the deaf-mute in chapter 7. Both healings take their meaning from the passage in Isaiah where God promises the ultimate healing and restoration of his people. Beyond that, the healing of the blind man has special significance because of the way Mark tells the story. By dramatizing the cure of the blind man in two stages, Mark indicates the theological purpose of his structure of doublets. The second time around, Mark strives to make the meaning of Jesus clearer. In the same way, the whole second half of Mark's Gospel (chs. 9–16) serves to clarify the first. The hinge between the two lies here at the end of chapter 8. When Mark shows Jesus speaking of a time of future glory, he prepares the reader for the scene of Jesus' transfiguration.

TRANSFIGURATION—
NEW PERCEPTIONS

Mark 9:1-50

9:1-7 The Transfiguration

Mark opens this chapter by quoting Jesus' promise that some of those around him will see the kingdom of God before they die (9:1). This assertion is often interpreted to mean that Jesus promised that the end of the world would come soon, or at least that the first followers of Jesus believed that was to happen. But such an interpretation comes from reading the text as a literal account. If instead one sees Mark's shaping hand here, one sees that he was preparing his readers for the transfiguration scene that comes immediately afterward. The Transfiguration does in fact present an imaginative rendering of what God's final kingdom will be like.

The word that is conventionally translated "transfigured" is actually "metamorphosed,"* which indicates not just a change in appearance but a changed state of being. There is a sense of new beginnings. The time frame of "six days" (9:2) is suggestive of the six days of Creation before God's Sabbath rest. Mark intensifies the sense of a new creation when he describes God's voice saying to Jesus the very same words he spoke at the moment of his baptism (compare 9:7 with 1:11).

The reference to "six days" also recalls the period Moses waited before the divine voice called to him on the mountain of Sinai (Exod 24:12-18). Mark further links Jesus to Moses by describing Jesus talking with him. It is significant that Jesus

is pictured conversing with the two greatest figures of Jewish tradition, Moses and Elijah (9:4), representatives of the Law and the Prophets. Jesus, whom Mark has shown to be God's Wisdom, is in conversation with the traditional figures of Jewish wisdom. It is a timeless moment. Mark emphasizes that he sees Jesus as one of them. He perceives Jesus to be a continuation of the wisdom of Israel.

This trio of great figures is matched by a trio of disciples. They are the same three disciples Mark shows Jesus taking with him to witness the raising up of the little girl (5:37); they will be the same three that Mark will show Jesus taking with him into the garden of Gethsemane (14:33). In terms of Markan structure, these episodes form a triad, and the middle or key incident is here in chapter 9. By noting that Jesus took them "up a high mountain" and "apart" (9:2), Mark indicates that Jesus is trying to lead them into his transfigured state. And as Mark describes the scene, they, too, for a brief moment, are changed.

Peter's desire to build three tents (or "booths"*) may seem puzzling unless one is aware of the Jewish feast of Booths (or "Tabernacles"). It is a feast that follows the Jewish New Year and is intended to celebrate the natural harvest as a sign of God's final harvest. It is a feast of the end time. It takes its name from the fact that it is observed by the construction of temporary outdoor huts or "booths," which are decorated with the fruits of the harvest. When Mark shows Peter wanting to build three booths here, he is indicating Peter's perception that he has entered the end time of God's final kingdom.

Unfortunately, this meaning of Peter's question is obscured by the translation "tents." It is also canceled out by the conventional translation, "He hardly knew what to say, they were so terrified" (9:6). The word translated as "terrified" here would be better translated "filled with awe."* If it were, one would hear the echo of the end of chapter 4, where the disciples ask each other, "Who then is this whom even wind and sea obey?" (4:41). That Mark intends to signal awe rather than fright is indicated by the first statement he shows Peter saying: "Rabbi, it is good that we are here!" (9:5). A feeling of goodness is compatible with awe but not with terror. Mark's suggestion that Peter was overwhelmed by the goodness of God's presence is also his way of indicating that Peter, too, has been transfigured, however briefly. As Jesus' transfiguration looks forward to his resurrection, so Peter's state here gives promise of his future glory.

The words Mark uses to describe Jesus' clothing are suggestive of the prophet Malachi's description of God's messenger when he comes at the end of time to judge, purify, and gather God's people (Mal 3:1-3). In that passage God says:

> Lo, I am sending my messenger
>   to prepare the way before me;
> And suddenly there will come to the Temple
>   the LORD whom you seek,
> And the messenger of the covenant whom you
>   desire.
>   Yes, he is coming, says the LORD of hosts.
> But who will endure the day of his coming?
>   And who can stand when he appears?
> For he is like the refiner's fire
>   or like the fuller's lye.
> He will sit refining and purifying,
>   and he will purify the sons of Levi,
> Refining them like gold or silver
>   that they may offer due sacrifice to the LORD.

As we noted at the time, Mark alludes briefly to this passage in the very opening of his Gospel (1:2). Here he comes back to it by describing Jesus' garments as "dazzling white, such as no fuller on earth could bleach them" (9:3). By emphasizing that Jesus' clothing is whiter than "the fuller's lye," Mark links him to Malachi's prophet of the end time.

9:8-10 The descent from the mountain

The vision of future glory fades abruptly: "Suddenly, looking around, they no longer saw anyone but Jesus alone with them" (9:8). Jesus charges them not to tell what they have seen until after he has risen from the dead (9:9). And these disciples, who were the very ones to witness Jesus' raising up of the little girl (5:37), question one another about the meaning of the term "rising from the dead" (9:10). Their descent from the mountain is not only physical but spiritual. They have returned from a brief moment of insight to their usual state of dulled understanding.

9:11-13 Elijah

Elijah is a recurring figure in Mark's Gospel. As we noted earlier, Mark describes John the Bap-

tist in a way that makes him resemble Elijah (1:6). Biblical legend had it that Elijah never died but was taken up to heaven in a fiery chariot (2 Kgs 2:11) and would return some day to prepare God's people for the end time (Mal 3:23). In chapter 6, Mark tells us that people speculated that Jesus might be Elijah come back (6:15). In chapter 8, he indicates that some of the disciples thought the same (8:28). But in the transfiguration scene, Mark shows Jesus talking with Elijah, thus suggesting that Jesus is compatible with Elijah and yet distinct from him.

As further clarification, Mark shows an exchange about Elijah between Jesus and his disciples. The disciples ask why Elijah had to come first (that is, before the end time). Jesus' response falls into three parts. First he echoes the prophecy of Malachi that Elijah has to come "and restore all things" (9:12). Then he turns the question about and asks why he himself ("the son of man") has to suffer. Finally he declares that "Elijah has come and they did to him whatever they pleased" (9:13).

There are gaps in this reply. Nonetheless, Mark seems to be using it to clarify both the similarities and dissimilarities between Jesus and Elijah. First he shows Jesus acknowledging Elijah as a forerunner. At the same time, he shows Jesus comparing his own sufferings to come with those of Elijah.

The reference to Elijah's suffering makes no sense in terms of the narratives concerning Elijah in the Second Book of Kings. The reference only makes sense as an identification of Elijah with John the Baptist. So the exchange serves to confirm what Mark has been doing throughout his Gospel: he has identified John the Baptist with Elijah and shown him to be the forerunner of Jesus, not only in his drawing people to God but also in his unjust suffering and death.

We suggested earlier that in chapter 6 Mark inserts the story of John the Baptist's death into the narrative of the disciples' mission as a subtle forewarning of what they themselves should expect (6:19-29). Here Mark makes the connection clear.

9:14-29 The healing of the boy with a mute and deaf spirit

This healing recapitulates and incorporates a number of healings that Mark has shown Jesus performing in the first half of the Gospel. The exorcism of a "mute and deaf spirit" (9:25) recalls the healing of the deaf-mute in 7:33-37. The violently destructive effects of the unclean spirit (9:18-26) are reminiscent of the demonic possession of the man among the tombs in 5:1-20. Jesus' "rebuke" of the spirit (9:25) echoes his first exorcism of the man in the synagogue (1:25). The corpse-like appearance of the boy and the bystanders' insistence that "He is dead" (9:26) recall the apparent death of Jairus's daughter (5:38-43). And Jesus' gesture of taking the boy by the hand and raising him up (9:27) repeats Jesus' way of raising that little girl and bringing her back to life (5:41). The attentive reader has a sense of déjà vu.

Mark does not simply provide a repetitive incident, however. He adds to it a whole discussion of how unclean spirits can be driven out. Mark tells us first that the crowd, some scribes, and the disciples were all arguing about it (9:14). He notes that the disciples, although commissioned by Jesus to drive out demons (6:7), have failed in this instance. He shows the disciples asking Jesus why they have failed (9:28), and he provides Jesus' answer as the climax to the episode: "This kind can only come out through prayer" (9:29).

Accordingly, Mark places great emphasis here on the importance of faith as part of the healing process. He shows Jesus sighing over the disciples' lack of faith (9:19). He gives Jesus' reply to the boy's father: "Everything is possible to one who has faith" (9:23). He dramatizes the father praying, "I do believe; help my unbelief!" (9:24).

In the first part of his Gospel, Mark shows Jesus performing one miracle after another easily and, as it were, automatically. But here he indicates that miracles are not automatic events; rather, he indicates that healings are a process that involves faith and prayer.

9:30-32 Jesus' second prediction of his death and resurrection

This prediction is the middle of a triad of predictions. The first occurs in 8:31; the third will occur in 10:33-34. The language is almost identical in each case, but not quite. In the first prediction, Mark shows Jesus speaking of being rejected "by the elders, the chief priests, and the scribes" and then being killed. The passive voice used here does not indicate the agent of the killing. In the third prediction, Mark shows Jesus telling his disciples that he will be "handed over to the chief

priests and the scribes" who will, in turn, "hand him over to the Gentiles" who will put him to death. In this middle and key version, Mark quotes Jesus as saying that he will be "handed over to human beings and they will kill him." In this key version, Mark suggests that all humanity rather than a particular agent is responsible for Jesus' death. Mark makes a point of saying that the disciples do not understand (9:32).

9:33-37 "Who is the greatest?"

Mark underlines the disciples' lack of understanding in the next episode. We have seen how twice before, Mark has shown Jesus telling these disciples that he must be rejected, suffer, and die (8:31; 9:31). He has shown Jesus making an explicit connection between his cross and their discipleship (8:34-35). And yet here they are, "discussing among themselves . . . who was the greatest" (9:34).

Mark indicates that they had some sense of the inappropriateness of their discussion by noting that they did not answer Jesus' question but "remained silent" (9:34). Mark then uses their question to set up further teaching by Jesus: "If anyone wishes to be first, he shall be the last of all and the servant of all" (9:35).

It is worth noting that Jesus "called the Twelve" before giving this teaching. This is the third time that Jesus summons and instructs the Twelve; in effect, it is another Markan triad. The first time, Jesus sends them out as apostles "to preach and to have authority to drive out demons" (3:14-15); the second time, he instructs them "to take nothing for the journey but a walking stick" (6:8); here he instructs them to be servants. Mark shows Jesus progressively teaching his disciples how to give up the pursuit of worldly power. He dramatizes Jesus' point by showing him elevate the child (9:36-37).

9:38-40 "Whoever is not against us is for us"

Mark continues in the next episode to stress Jesus' instruction on the yielding of power. He uses the reactions of the disciples as a foil for this teaching. In this scene, the disciples ironically exhibit a worldly sense of competition about the spiritual ministry of exorcism: "Teacher, we saw someone driving out demons in your name, and we tried to prevent him because he does not follow us" (9:38). Mark gives Jesus' response (9:39-40) as further instruction in being one who serves others, not one who seeks to be superior.

9:41-42 The reward of a cup of water

At this point, the text indicates that Jesus said, "Anyone who gives you a cup of water to drink because you belong to Christ . . . will surely not lose his reward." This saying does not seem to fit in here. Instead, it would seem to fit logically after Jesus' statement "Whoever receives one child such as this in my name, receives me" (9:37). This placement is supported by the fact that the phrase that is translated here as "you belong to Christ" literally reads "because in name you are Christ's."

Mark has been showing how Jesus tried to teach his disciples that being like him means being like a child in powerlessness. And so it follows that whoever receives a child in his name—that is, welcomes the powerless in his name—welcomes him. It would make sense for Jesus to then turn it about and speak of his disciples as the "children" being welcomed by others. Assuming that his disciples will become the powerless he has asked them to be, Jesus goes on to say that anyone who welcomes them in his name (even with as little as a cup of water) will be rewarded.

This rearrangement of verses would also make more sense out of Jesus saying, "Whoever causes one of these little ones who believe [in me] to sin, it would be better for him if a great millstone were put around his neck and he were thrown into the sea" (9:42).

The disciples' complaint about someone outside their group driving out demons in Jesus' name (9:38) would then take on even greater irony. Mark would be showing that instead of getting Jesus' point about powerlessness, the disciples (one more time!) had missed the point and latched on to the phrase "in my name" as the key one. Thus the protest against someone driving out demons in Jesus' name who isn't one of "them."

9:43-48 Being ready to give up everything

The list that follows then makes sense as a continuing part of Jesus' instruction to give up things that most people cling to—even, if necessary, one's very limbs. The terse style in which these teachings are phrased is typical of the Wisdom writings, as is the rhythmical pairings of contrasts: "It is better [to do such and such] than to [do this or that]."

9:49-50 Being salted

Being salted "with" fire is a bit puzzling, but there is precedent in the Hebrew Bible for linking both elements with purification. We have already noted the passage in Malachi where he speaks of the final messenger of the covenant being like "the refiner's fire" (Mal 3:2). In both Leviticus and Ezekiel, salt is connected with sacrificial offerings that are burned on the altar. Leviticus speaks of the "salt of the covenant": "Every offering of grain that you present to the Lord shall be seasoned with salt. Do not let the salt of the covenant of your God be lacking from your grain offering" (Lev 2:13). Similarly in Ezekiel, God asks for purifying sacrifices that involve both salt and fire: "When you have finished the purification, bring an unblemished young bull and an unblemished ram from the flock. And present them before the Lord. The priests shall strew salt on them and offer them to the Lord as holocausts" (Ezek 43:23-24).

Mark has just shown Jesus teaching his disciples to be ready to sacrifice their own bodies, if necessary, in order to be his disciples. It would seem to be in keeping with those demands that he speaks of their purifying themselves with salt and fire. When Mark shows Jesus saying in conclusion, "Keep salt in yourselves" (9:50), he would seem to be referring to both "the salt of the covenant" and the fire of self-sacrifice that he himself will model.

Summary of chapter 9

The chapter shifts the readers' focus and makes plain things hidden before. The scene of Jesus' transfiguration begins this shift by revealing the inner and future glory of both Jesus and his disciples. Mark designs this revelation to come before the narrative of Jesus' shameful death so that it will overshadow it. It points to Jesus' resurrection.

At the same time, the chapter is unified by a new perspective on power. The Transfiguration reveals a splendor that will transform the ignominy of rejection and death. The casting out of demons is revealed to be not a matter of super power but of simple faith and prayer. The servant and the child are held up as the greatest. God's power is declared to be inclusive and not restricted to an inner circle. Jesus teaches that it is better to be crippled for God than to remain strong and not be for him. In conclusion, Jesus teaches that the "fire" of sacrificing oneself may be the "salt" needed to season the kingdom.

RETURN TO THE BEGINNING
Mark 10:1-52

10:1-12 "From the beginning of creation"

This discussion of divorce is usually treated apart from Mark's whole Gospel. Abstracted in that way from its context, Jesus' words on marriage appear to be stricter and less flexible than the present teachings of the church. But if the passage is read in its whole setting, a different sense emerges. In the preceding chapter, Mark has shown Jesus elevating a child (9:36-37), and in the passage that immediately follows this one, Mark shows Jesus saying, "Whoever does not accept the kingdom of God like a child will not enter it" (10:15). In fact, the whole of chapter 10 (as we are about to show) is focused on how to live with childlike simplicity. In this passage on marriage, Mark sets up this focus by giving Jesus' reference to "the beginning of creation" (10:6). "The beginning of creation" is the frame for the whole chapter.

In Jewish thought about the end time (that is, the projected moment when, it was believed, the will of God would entirely prevail), there were two distinct strains of thought. One view held that God would prevail as judge, destroying the wicked and preserving the good. The other view held that God would act as a healer and redeemer, restoring his people and leading them back, as it were, to their original state in the Garden of Eden. In the Prophets, one hears a lot about God's judgment on Israel; it is associated with the destruction of Jerusalem and especially the Temple, as well as the defeat and captivity of Israel. In the prophetic imagination, however, God's final judgments are rendered only on the nations that besiege and corrupt Israel. God's judgments on Israel itself are temporary. The prophet always envisions that in the end time God will restore his people to virtue, his Temple to its original state as a house of prayer, and the land to its original condition of abundance and fertility.

In the Wisdom writings, the prevailing imagery is of the Garden. The Psalms sing of how God created human beings for glory ("You have made him a little less than the angels," Ps 8:6); how God preserves his people from destruction (They shall be "like a tree / planted by running water, / That brings forth its fruit in due season," Ps 1:3); how God restores them after a time of wandering or distress ("Beside restful waters he leads me; he refreshes my soul," Ps 23:2-3). The Song of Songs imagines the Garden as the setting for the love affair between God and humanity. The book of Sirach associates the Garden imagery of the Song with the feminine figure of God's Wisdom. The book of Job, for all its tragic disaster, concludes with a reminder of the majesty of creation, the restoration of Job, and a new beginning. The cynical preacher in Ecclesiastes changes from finding that "all is vanity" to a new trust in God's power to create. The author of the Wisdom of Solomon takes the idea of restoration a step further by perceiving that Wisdom in the human soul is a reflection of God's immortality. In all of these writings, while God's judgment on evil is certainly assumed and articulated, there is also a sense that the true human destiny is to return to the original Garden. To say that Mark shows "the beginning of creation" to be the framework for Jesus' teachings is to imply his reference to this whole tradition.

It is this tradition that Mark shows at work here when he tells us that Jesus quoted Genesis 2:24 (10:7-8) and contrasted its ideal of married oneness with the bill of divorce that Moses allowed as a concession to the "hardness of your hearts" (10:5).

Mark has used the phrase "hardness of heart" twice before—once to describe the Pharisees when they begrudge Jesus' healing on the Sabbath (3:5) and again to describe the disciples when they fail to understand the miracle of the loaves (6:52). In all three instances, the phrase does not indicate the commitment of a sin but the failure to measure up to an ideal standard. So here, we may infer, Mark shows Jesus using this phrase to indicate a falling away from the ideal human state.

10:13-16 Children as the ideal members of God's kingdom

In describing Jesus' blessing of the children here, Mark echoes and develops the scene in the previous chapter (9:36-37) where Jesus embraces a child and says, "Whoever receives one child such as this in my name, receives me." As we noted before, in that context Jesus seems to be teaching his disciples the value of powerlessness. This idea seems to be confirmed and clarified by what Mark shows Jesus saying here: "Whoever does not accept the kingdom of God like a child will not enter it" (10:15).

10:17-31 The poor as ideal members of the kingdom

The story of the rich man who cannot follow Jesus is of a piece with this emphasis. The man affirms that he has kept the Ten Commandments from his youth (10:20), a declaration that indicates his essential goodness. And Mark goes on to say that Jesus "loved him" (10:21). Nonetheless, Mark shows Jesus asking more of him: "You are lacking in one thing. Go, sell what you have, and give to the poor, and you will have treasure in heaven; then come, follow me" (10:21).

Just as in the teachings about being faithful in marriage and about becoming childlike, Mark shows Jesus holding up an ideal. It is an ideal that is in keeping with Jesus' other teachings on detachment. Just as Mark shows Jesus teaching his disciples to detach themselves from power by becoming like children, so here he shows Jesus teaching them to detach themselves from possessions. By showing that despite his goodness, this rich man cannot follow Jesus' instruction (10:22), Mark indicates that Jesus is setting up a norm for holiness that demands far more than the conventional one. In the discussion with the disciples that follows (10:23-33), Mark further dramatizes the unconventionality of Jesus' request.

Mark does this by setting up a dialogue between Jesus and his disciples, in which Jesus repeatedly stresses "how hard" it is for the wealthy to enter God's kingdom, while the disciples repeatedly express their astonishment at what he is saying (10:23-26). (Jesus' statement that "It is easier for a camel . . . " has a rabbinic parallel— "It is easier for an elephant . . ."—and so should not be seen as a special riddle of Jesus, but simply as an exaggeration typical of first-century Jewish teachers.)

The climax of this dialogue occurs when the disciples ask, "Then who can be saved?" and Jesus responds, "For human beings it is impossible, but

not for God. All things are possible for God" (10:26-27). In this pithy exchange, Mark shows that Jesus was asking his followers to commit themselves to a way of living that could not be accomplished without God's grace. He was shifting the burden from their need for self-sufficiency to their need for total dependence on God. This acknowledgment of total dependence is, of course, the ultimate poverty, the ultimate detachment.

10:28-31, 35-45 The disciples' failure to understand

In the exchange that follows between Peter and Jesus (10:28-31), Mark shows how little Peter has understood. Peter's response to Jesus' request for this total detachment is to protest that he has already accomplished it: "We have given up everything and followed you" (10:28). Jesus' reply is indirect, not directly disagreeing, and indeed promising rewards in this life and "eternal life in the age to come" (10:30). Yet among his promises, Mark shows Jesus slipping in "persecutions," a reminder that following Jesus will involve following him in the way of suffering. Jesus' final assertion, "Many that are first will be last and [the] last will be first" (10:31), is also a reminder of the paradox of the cross.

Mark particularly dramatizes the disciples' failure to grasp that final lesson when he shows James and John asking to be first in glory (10:37). Mark introduces this ironic question by showing James and John talking to Jesus as if he were their servant: "We want you to do for us whatever we ask of you" (10:35). And he shows Jesus accepting this role: "What do you wish [me] to do for you?" (10:36). In the exchange that follows between Jesus and his disciples, Mark shows the extent of the gap in the disciples' understanding.

The reply that Mark shows Jesus giving here is central to Mark's interpretation of Jesus' theology. First, he shows Jesus speaking cryptically of his "cup" and his "baptism" (10:38-39). In the Psalms, "cup" is figuratively linked to one's inheritance or destiny ("LORD, my allotted portion and my cup," Ps 16:5) and to salvation ("I will raise the cup of salvation and call on the name of the LORD," Ps 116:13). "Baptism" is not a word used in the Hebrew Bible, although the ritual immersion that it connotes was part of Judaism and signified (as it does in Mark) a change of heart. These words take on additional meaning here.

Jesus' use of the word "cup" suggests the cup of wine that he will later designate as the cup of his blood (14:24), and his use of the word "baptism" also suggests a link with his death.

Paul emphasizes this link when he asks, "Are you unaware that we who were baptized into Christ Jesus were baptized into his death?" (Rom 6:3). When Mark shows James and John being quick to accept this "cup" and "baptism" (10:39), he indicates that they are not making these same connections with death. Mark confirms this lack of awareness when he shows Jesus saying, "You do not know what you are asking" (10:38).

By giving the ironic request of James and John, Mark sets the stage for a fuller illumination of Jesus' teaching on worldly power (10:42-45). He shows Jesus here giving his disciples the plainest explanation of what he is about. Mark first shows Jesus distancing himself from the worldly, Gentile conventions of power, in which "those who are recognized as rulers . . . lord it over" others and "make their authority . . . felt" (10:42). Then Mark shows Jesus directly rejecting this approach: "It shall not be so among you" (10:43). Next, he shows Jesus telling them how they should act: "Whoever wishes to be first among you will be the slave of all" (10:43-44). Last, and most important, Mark shows Jesus explaining that by so doing, they will truly be his disciples, because he came expressly "not to be served but to serve" (10:45). Beyond that, Mark suggests by his final phrase that Jesus has come to offer the ultimate service of giving up his life for the sake of others.

The phrase "to give his life as a ransom for many" is a quote from Isaiah 53:11, where God is speaking about his chosen servant, who will offer his life as an atoning sacrifice for the sins of others. This is the last of those passages in Isaiah known as the "Songs of the Suffering Servant." In Isaiah, the Servant is identified as Israel—God's righteous servant among the nations, who is put to death by the kings of the world because they do not understand Israel's God-blessed nature or mission. By quoting this phrase as part of Jesus' self-understanding, Mark suggests that Jesus can be understood through the same lens: he is God's righteous servant; he will be put to death by Gentile powers that fail to understand him; he will offer his life as an atonement for the sins of others; he will ultimately be exalted by God.

10:32-34 Jesus' third prediction of his death

Mark interweaves Jesus' third prediction of his own suffering in between the episodes that show the failure of Peter, James, and John to understand that as Jesus' disciples they have been called to dispossession, service, and death. It is a structure we have seen Mark use before. Just as he placed the story of John the Baptist's death in the middle of the first sending forth of the disciples (6:14-29), so here he places the prediction of Jesus' death between the episode showing Peter's confidence that he has already given up everything and the episode of the request of James and John for glory.

Mark, moreover, shows Jesus being explicit here in a way that he never has been before. In the first prediction, Mark quotes Jesus speaking vaguely about how he must "suffer greatly . . . be rejected . . . be killed . . . and rise after three days" (8:31). In the second prediction, Mark shows Jesus adding the element of betrayal, but generalizing everything else: "The son of man is to be handed over to human beings and they will kill him, and three days after his death he will rise" (9:31). Here Mark shows Jesus speaking specifically about "going up to Jerusalem" and about how he will be handed over "to the chief priests and the scribes," who will, in turn, "hand him over to the Gentiles, who will mock him, spit upon him, scourge him, and put him to death" (10:33-34). If we look at these three predictions as one of Mark's triads, the middle prediction is key, indicating that "human beings" in general are responsible for Jesus' death. But within Mark's narrative, the concreteness of the third prediction is Mark's way of sharpening the irony of the disciples' lack of understanding.

10:46-52 The symbolic cure of the blind man

This is another miracle of healing that has a symbolic and summarizing function. In 8:22-26, Mark shows Jesus healing a blind man in two stages. We noted that the miracle echoes the earlier healing of the deaf-mute (7:33) and completes Jesus' relationship to the passage in Isaiah where "the ears of the deaf" are "cleared" and "the eyes of the blind" are "opened" (Isa 35:5-6). At the same time, the two-stage process alerts the reader to the meaning behind Mark's doublet structure. In the next miraculous healing (9:14-29), a deaf-mute is cured again. In describing this cure, Mark incorporates a number of elements that have been part of several earlier miracles, so that this miracle incorporates what has gone before. In the same way, this cure of the blind man Bartimaeus appears to be a doublet, and more than a doublet, of the cure of the blind man in chapter 8.

Within the immediate narrative, the story of the blind beggar reverses that of the rich man. The rich man could not become a disciple of Jesus because of his many possessions. The beggar has no possessions except his cloak, and he immediately casts that away to come to Jesus (10:50). In the end, the blind man not only receives his sight from Jesus but "followed him on the way" (10:52).

Beyond that, the name Bartimaeus literally means "son of the unclean" in Hebrew, so the name alone has a summarizing function. In the first part of his Gospel, Mark has shown Jesus to be in constant association with "the unclean" of his society—demoniacs, lepers, tax collectors, sinners, a woman with a flow of blood, and a dead body. When Mark shows Jesus healing someone who is named "son of the unclean," he is reminding his readers of them all.

Mark also shows this blind man to have other distinctive characteristics. Unlike the first blind man, who was brought to Jesus by others, this one calls out to him (10:47). Mark shows him addressing Jesus, moreover, as "son of David," a title that indicates he recognizes Jesus as God's chosen agent. There is a certain irony, therefore, in his request to see (10:51), because he seems to already be seeing more than many sighted folk around him. Mark shows Jesus confirming this when he says, "Go your way; your faith has saved you" (10:52). In showing Jesus' cure of Bartimaeus, Mark sums up how Jesus can heal and restore all "the unclean" who have faith in God's outreach to them.

In this summarizing incident, Mark echoes certain words from the first part of his Gospel. When he says that the blind man "began to cry out" (10:47), we hear an echo of the unclean spirit in chapter 5, who also cried out to Jesus (5:5). The intent, however, is the reverse: the unclean spirit wanted Jesus to go away; the blind man wants him to come near. When Mark describes the disciples' telling the blind man to "take courage" (10:49), he uses the same word that he shows Jesus saying to his frightened disciples in chapter 6

(6:50). But again there is a difference: the disciples remain fearful; the blind man seems to need no encouragement, for he springs up and goes to Jesus (10:50). The phrase that is translated here as "get up" (10:49) is in fact "*rise* up"* and thus an echo of Jesus' words to the dead child in chapter 5 (5:41). Jesus' final words to the blind man, "Your faith has saved you" (10:52), repeats his final words to the woman healed of her flow of blood (5:34). In ending this narrative, Mark says that "*Straightway** [translated here as 'immediately'] he received his sight" (10:52). In short, there are enough key words in this short episode to suggest that Mark is loading it with particular significance. It is as though Mark wanted to suggest the possibility of all people—whether blinded by demons or by fear or by "uncleanness" or even by death—to be restored, to have their lives "made straight" again.

Summary of chapter 10

In this chapter, Mark shows Jesus pointing to "the beginning of creation" as revealing God's intended destiny for human beings, and trying to teach his disciples how to return to that state of original simplicity. Mark shows Jesus doing this in several ways. First, he shows Jesus referring to the beginning unity between man and woman as the norm for human relationships. Then he shows him holding up children as models of the detachment from power necessary to enter the kingdom. Next, through setting up a dialogue between Jesus and a rich man, he shows Jesus teaching his disciples that they need to divest themselves of all possessions and learn to depend totally upon God's providence. Mark then indicates the disciples' failure to understand these teachings by showing parallel episodes that involve the three key disciples—Peter first, then James and John. Mark sharpens the irony of the disciples' obtuseness by placing in between these episodes Jesus' third and most explicit prediction of his own suffering and death.

In conclusion, Mark shows the healing of a blind beggar who, out of his powerlessness and poverty, is ready to become a disciple of Jesus. He is a beggar whose name means "son of the unclean" and whose cure, as Mark constructs the story, echoes and summarizes many of Jesus' earlier miracles. When Mark ends this narrative by saying, "Straightway* he received his sight and followed him on the way" (10:52), he affirms the potential for every human being to follow Jesus' way of return to the beginning.

JESUS AND THE TEMPLE AUTHORITIES— NEW UNDERSTANDINGS OF POWER

Mark 11:1-37

11:1-11 Jesus' entry into Jerusalem

In this opening scene, Mark picks up on the cure of the blind beggar by showing the people spreading their cloaks on the ground (11:8) and crying out, "Blessed is the kingdom of our father David that is to come!" (11:10). Their cry also echoes the first proclamation of John the Baptist, "One mightier than I is coming after me" (1:7). Yet Mark modifies the impression of triumphant entry by describing Jesus riding on a colt.

In the whole next section of his Gospel, Mark shows Jesus acting out the new understandings of power he has been trying to teach his disciples. Mark also shifts his style, showing Jesus, like many of the prophets, engaged in symbolic or parabolic action. To begin with, by showing the lengths to which Jesus goes to ride into Jerusalem on a colt (11:1-7), Mark calls attention to the relationship between Jesus and the words of Zechariah:

> See, your king shall come to you;
> a just savior is he,
> Meek, and riding on an ass,
> on a colt, the foal of an ass (9:9).

In Zechariah, the predicted king is unknown and mysterious. One of the most striking details in Zechariah's description is this picture of him entering Jerusalem on "the foal of an ass." The choice of the donkey not only suggests humility but peacemaking; in ancient times war was associated with the horse. Zechariah goes on to say that this king will "banish the horse from Jerusalem" along with "the warrior's bow," and "he shall proclaim peace to the nations" (9:10). The passages that follow in Zechariah are complex, but essentially the coming of this peace-loving king begins the restoration of Jerusalem.

At the same time, Mark echoes, through the images of the people spreading "leafy branches" and crying out "Hosanna" (11:8), the description in the first book of Maccabees of Simon Maccabeus entering Jerusalem "with praise and palm branches" to take back the Temple from the Greek tyrant Antiochus IV (1 Macc 13:47-52).

We have spoken before about how different foreign conquerors of Jerusalem tried to take over the Temple and weaken Jewish religion. One of the most despised was Antiochus IV, a Greek ruler of Palestine two centuries before the time of Jesus. He tried to virtually eradicate Jewish faith in a number of ways. He ordered the substitution of the Greek constitution for the Hebrew Bible. He forbade circumcision, and if mothers violated his edict, he killed their babies and hung the dead infants around their necks. He erected a statue of himself in the Temple. This statue of Antiochus is referred to in Daniel 12:11 as "the abomination of desolation" or "the desolating sacrilege" (a phrase that is used by Mark, as we will see, in chapter 13).

It was the last straw for the Jewish people. They rose up in revolt, led by the seven Maccabee brothers. Their success in restoring the Temple is still celebrated in the annual feast of Hanukkah. The first book of Maccabees records that Simon Maccabeus "cleansed the Temple" of Antiochus's statue and all his other profanities (1 Macc 13:50b).

By using language that would remind his readers of both Zechariah's peace-loving king and of Simon Maccabeus, Mark offers a complex picture of Jesus. Both scriptural passages converge in showing someone who took action to restore the Temple to its original state as a place of worship. Yet there is a tension between the two. As Mark develops his portrait of Jesus' relationship to the Temple, he also continues to show this tension.

11:15-19 Jesus' "cleansing of the Temple"

It is interesting to note that the phrase "cleansing of the Temple" is not used by Mark. The caption is an editor's choice; one can only speculate that the editor was thinking of the book of Maccabees. In any event, the episode that follows, like the opening one of the chapter, is constructed out of interweaving echoes of the Hebrew Scripture. The key echoes occur in what Mark shows Jesus teaching:

> My house shall be called a house of prayer for all peoples.
> But you have made it a den of thieves (11:17).

The first line here is a direct quote from Isaiah 56:7, while the second comes from Jeremiah 7:11. The passage in Isaiah is expressing his vision of a time when God will welcome foreigners to the Temple:

> All who keep the Sabbath free from profanation
> and hold to my covenant,
> Them I will bring to my holy mountain
> and make joyful in my house of prayer (56:6-7).

The passage from Jeremiah comes from what is known as his "Temple sermon." It is a long passage in which the prophet expresses God's anger at the people's breaking of the covenant and his demand for their moral reform:

> Put not your trust in the deceitful words: "This is the Temple of the LORD! The Temple of the LORD! The Temple of the LORD!" Only if you thoroughly reform your ways and your deeds; if each of you deals justly with his neighbor; if you no longer oppress the resident alien, the orphan, and the widow; if you no longer shed innocent blood in this place, or follow strange gods to your own harm, will I remain with you in this place . . . . Are you to steal and murder, commit adultery and perjury, burn incense to Baal, go after strange gods that you know not, and yet come to stand before me in this house which bears my name, and say, "We are safe; we can commit all these abominations again"? Has this house which bears my name become in your eyes a den of thieves? (Jer 7:4-7, 9-11).

In interweaving these two passages, Mark is juxtaposing two very different strands in biblical tradition. The passage from Jeremiah expresses a warning about being corrupted by foreigners who will not only encourage burning incense to a foreign god but will also foster the weakening of covenant commitments. The passage from Isaiah expresses the vision of a time when foreigners will want to join Israel in worshiping the one God, and all people will be joyfully one in prayer. By showing Jesus quoting both these passages at once— indeed, even making one sentence out of them—Mark again suggests a tension and a complexity in Jesus' attitude toward the Temple. On the one hand, the quotation from Jeremiah places him in the tradition of the reforming prophets seeking to purify Temple worship of foreign influences. On the other hand, the quotation from Isaiah places him in the tradition of the visionary prophets seeking to bring all people together by welcoming foreigners into God's house.

When Mark shows Jesus driving out "those selling and buying" and overturning "the tables of the money changers" and not permitting "anyone to carry anything through the Temple area" (11:15-16), these actions must be understood in the context of these prophetic traditions. In the light of these traditions, it does not make sense to assume (as many have) that Mark was indicating that Jesus' actions were hostile to the Temple per se. Nor does it make sense to assume that Jesus was expressing anger at a Temple system that allowed money on the premises.

Some historical background sheds light on the latter. It was customary for Jews to purchase an animal to sacrifice in the Temple, and while they ordinarily used Roman coins in their business transactions, they did not think that appropriate for sacred matters. The Temple authorities accordingly allowed them to exchange their Roman coin for a special Temple coin, which could then be used for their sacrifice. Such a system was no more scandalous than the money collections taken up today in Christian churches.

The prophetic tradition, exemplified in Jeremiah, of criticizing the gap between Temple worship and moral behavior, explains Mark's intent in showing Jesus' anger at the "buyers and sellers" in the Temple. Mark is not suggesting that Jesus was reacting to the custom of money exchange or that he wanted to overturn the whole Temple. Rather, Mark is suggesting that, like reforming prophets before him, Jesus wanted to purify the Temple of the foreign influences that had commercialized it. Under Rome, this commercialization had taken the specific form of turning the priesthood into a political job. The high priests were appointed by Rome and collaborated with the Romans. Some who might have been committed to the Temple became committed instead to collecting taxes for the empire. It is this overall picture of Jewish faith corrupted by venal interests that Mark conveys here. It is opposition to this corruption of faith that Mark shows Jesus symbolizing by overturning the tables of the money changers.

Mark's perspective is signaled by the scriptural contexts he provides for Jesus' action: Maccabees, Jeremiah, Isaiah. By alluding to Maccabees, Mark indicates that Jesus is "cleansing the Temple," as Simon Maccabeus did, from the idolatrous perversion of Jewish worship caused by foreign occupiers. By quoting Jeremiah, Mark indicates that Jesus is angry, as Jeremiah was, at the weakening of the covenant. But by also quoting Isaiah, Mark indicates that Jesus has a countering prophetic vision of a time when foreigners would be included in the covenant.

11:12-14, 20-28 The fig tree

Two episodes involving the fig tree enclose the symbolic action in the Temple. It is a typical Markan structure and indicates a relationship between the scenes. To understand them, it helps to know the symbolism of the fig tree in first-century Jewish thought. First of all, the fig tree was considered to be the tree that was forbidden in the Garden of Eden. (It is an interpretation that makes sense when you consider that fig trees are indigenous to that part of the world, and that Genesis 3:7 says that Adam and Eve sewed together fig leaves for their first form of clothing.) Second, a fig tree in bloom was considered to be a sign of the end time, of God's final kingdom.

It is also important to consider that Jesus' curse of the fig tree is related to God's curse of the ground when Adam and Eve leave the Garden (Gen 3:17). In Genesis, God tells Adam and Eve that the ground will only bring forth "thorns and thistles" for them (Gen 3:18). In Isaiah, however, this curse is explicitly reversed, and God says he will make the cypress grow instead of the thornbush, and the myrtle instead of nettles (Isa 55:13). Jesus' curse is often translated (as it is here) in such a way that it seems irreversible. But some scholars have suggested that the phrasing is more accurately rendered, "May no one ever eat fruit from you *to the end of this age.**" Such a translation leaves open the possibility of a future reversal, and Mark, in a later chapter, refers to the fig tree in bloom (13:28). The possibility of such a reversal also fits better with one of the first things Mark says about the tree: "It was not the season for figs" (11:13). As we have noted before, the Wisdom writings are especially attuned to the idea that human matters are not permanent but seasonable.

The conversation that Mark gives between Jesus and Peter regarding the tree (11:20-25) gives hope for a different season. Peter says, "The fig tree that you cursed has withered" (11:21). Jesus' response, "Have faith in God" (11:22), is usually taken to mean that Jesus is telling Peter he could have the same power as Jesus. If one has been following Mark's view of Jesus, one sees that he

always shows Jesus' power directed toward healing. So here it seems right to understand Jesus' reply as encouragement to have faith in the fig tree's restoration.

Such an understanding is bolstered by two things. First, the term "withered" should remind Mark's readers of the episode where Jesus healed the man with a withered arm (3:1-5). Second, Mark shows Jesus going on here to recommend not only prayer but forgiveness (11:24-25). By providing the context of forgiveness, Mark suggests the possibility of a renewed tree. And as we have just noted above, Mark shows us a renewed fig tree later on.

11:27-32 "By what power . . . ?" (11:28)

The chapter concludes with Mark giving a direct question from the Temple authorities about the source of Jesus' power. Mark then shows Jesus replying with a question that is also something of a riddle: "Was John's baptism of heavenly or of human origin?" (11:30). By showing the authorities' confusion in trying to answer it, Mark indicates their mistake in trying to divide the "human" from the "heavenly." Implied is Mark's view that the figure and actions of Jesus show that they belong together.

Summary of chapter 11

In chapter 10, Mark has shown Jesus teaching his disciples that they should not seek worldly power but rather should follow him in seeking "not be served but to serve." In this chapter, Mark shows the kind of power Jesus does possess. He shows him to be at once forceful and humble.

In the opening verses, Mark shows Jesus entering Jerusalem to the acclaim of crowds, yet riding on a donkey. Through the language he uses to describe Jesus, Mark relates him both to Zechariah's peacemaking king and to Simon Maccabeus in his act of taking back the Temple. Through his description of Jesus' actions in the Temple, Mark further indicates Jesus' relationship to Simon's "cleansing" of the Temple. Through his quotations from Jesus' teaching, Mark places Jesus simultaneously in the tradition of prophetic reform of the Temple (like Jeremiah) and in the tradition of the prophetic vision of restoration of the Temple and universal prayer (like Isaiah).

By enclosing the symbolic action in the Temple with two episodes involving the fig tree, Mark further symbolizes the relationship between Jesus and power. In the first episode, Mark shows Jesus cursing the tree in much the same way that God cursed the ground in Genesis. It is another episode in which Mark shows Jesus reflecting God's action in the Hebrew Bible. Yet in the second episode, Mark shows Jesus encouraging Peter to "have faith" in its restoration. Mark's view is parallel to Isaiah's view of God reversing the original curse and restoring the earth.

Through this conversation with Peter, Mark indicates that Jesus is pointing to the power to move or transform things through faith and prayer and, above all, forgiveness. Through the further exchange between Jesus and the Temple authorities, Mark suggests how it is God's power, especially the power to forgive, that unites the human and the heavenly.

JESUS AS WISDOM IN THE TEMPLE

Mark 12:1-44

12:1-13 Parable of the vineyard

It is striking that Mark shows Jesus once again speaking in parables, a style he has not shown him using since chapter 4. This parable is clearly an allegory, but it is also shaped by pieces of interweaving Scripture. The vineyard as a metaphor for Israel occurs in Isaiah, Jeremiah, Ezekiel, Hosea, and the Song of Songs. In this long tradition, God creates a vineyard that he loves. He is sometimes angry at it, but in the end God always restores it. The opening verses here echo, in a condensed way, the "Vineyard Song" in Isaiah:

> My friend had a vineyard
> on a fertile hillside;
> He spaded it, cleared it of stones,
> and planted the choicest vines;
> Within it he built a watchtower,
> and hewed out a wine press.
> Then he looked for the crop of grapes,
> but what it yielded was wild grapes (Isa 5:1-2).

In Isaiah's song, the "friend" is God, and "the vineyard of the LORD of hosts is the house of Israel" (Isa 5:7). God is angry at his vineyard for only yielding "wild grapes," and he threatens to destroy it (Isa 5:5-6). Much later in Isaiah, when God proclaims a "new heavens and a new earth," he also promises a new vineyard (Isa 65:17-21).

It is important to realize that although Mark is clearly alluding to the first passage in Isaiah,

he is not repeating it. There are key differences: the vineyard here is not yielding "wild grapes" but a good harvest. The anger of the vineyard owner is therefore not directed at the vineyard, but at the tenants who are keeping him from gathering it (12:8b). What we have in Mark is thus not the same plot line as in Isaiah but a rather different story. We cannot hastily conclude (as many have) that it is about God's anger at Israel, because if we are reading carefully, we see that the vineyard (Israel) is not the cause of God's distress.

At the conclusion of the parable, Mark tells us that Jesus said that the owner of the vineyard would "put the tenants to death and give the vineyard to others" (12:9). Mark then shows Jesus quoting Psalm 118:22:

> The stone that the builders rejected
> has become the cornerstone.

Christians of a later time came to identify "the cornerstone" with Christ, and so they interpreted this parable to mean that God would take his vineyard from Jews and give it to Christians. But in the tradition flourishing in Mark's time, the psalm was sung at Passover as a way of rejoicing that Israel, the enslaved people, had become the cornerstone of a nation covenanted to God. Knowing this fact, we need to carefully reexamine all the terms of the parable.

First of all, who are the tenants? The word "tenants" suggests those who have a commercial interest in the property, not a personal one. They are distinguished in the story from the landlord's "servants," whom they beat up and send away, and from his "beloved son," whom they kill. In biblical tradition, a prophet is usually described as God's servant. Israel itself is known as God's servant and also as God's beloved son. The "tenants" are hostile to the servants and the son, and obstructionist in regard to the vineyard. In short, they are hostile to Israel.

The parable, then, is not directed against Israel but against those who would destroy it. Israel, as God's vineyard, is fruitful, but hostile hirelings are preventing God's harvest. God promises to take back the vineyard from them and give it to others who will allow it to come to harvest.

Mark then says, "They were seeking to arrest him, but they feared the crowd, for they realized that he had addressed the parable to them" (12:12). Mark does not explicitly identify whom he means by "them," and there is no direct antecedent. In the following verse, Mark says that "They sent some Pharisees and Herodians to him . . . ." (12:13), so we know that he could not mean either of those two groups. The only plausible group left are the Temple authorities who were questioning Jesus in chapter 11—"the chief priests, the scribes, and the elders" (11:27). In terms of what we know of the historical situation of the Temple in the time of Jesus, the parable is a transparent allegory of the corruption of the Temple by Rome and its Jewish collaborators— that is, the chief priests and some of their associates who had sold out to Rome.

In addition, the reference to the landowner's "beloved son," of course, also suggests Jesus himself, who has been referred to by this phrase twice before at key moments in Mark's Gospel—at his baptism and his transfiguration (1:11; 9:7). In the baptism scene, we have suggested, Jesus is God's "beloved son" in the sense of being a "second Adam," giving hope for a renewed humanity. In the transfiguration scene, Mark shows Jesus addressed by God as "my beloved son" in terms of his inner radiance, which images God's own. At the same time, it is a scene in which Mark shows Jesus in conversation with Elijah and Moses, that is, he shows him in conversation with the greatest prophets of Jewish tradition.

We have noted before that in a Markan triad, the middle episode is the most illuminating one. The transfiguration scene seems to imply that Jesus represents the teachings of Israel in the same way as Moses and Elijah did. So here in this vineyard parable, Jesus stands allied with religious Israel. In predicting the death of "the beloved son" at the hands of outsiders hostile to Israel, the parable is predicting simultaneously the death of Jesus and the destruction of the Temple. By means of this parable, Mark shows how both were destroyed by perverted power. The parable is a fitting conclusion to the discussion of power that runs through both chapters 10 and 11.

12:13-37 The four questions

In this section, Mark shows Jesus answering four questions about the Torah, the first five books of the Bible, or the teachings of Moses. In biblical thought, the Torah was equated with Wisdom. We

have spoken earlier about how, in many different ways, Mark presents Jesus as God's Wisdom. So here, as he shows Jesus in the Temple answering questions about the Torah, Mark suggests that he is responding as Wisdom itself.

It is worth noting, moreover, that the questions involve different schools of thought within Early Judaism—Pharisees, Sadducees, and scribes. David Daube, a Jewish scholar, has suggested that they also represent the four questions asked by four sons in an ancient family liturgy for Passover. The first question is asked by a righteous son on a point of law. The second question is a mocking one, asked by a wicked son. The third question comes from a pious son. Finally, the father of the family gives instruction to a fourth son, who does not know how to ask.

12:13-17 The first response: "Whose image?"

Jesus' response to the Pharisees' question about the lawfulness of the Temple tax is often treated as a statement on the separation of church and state. One of the main causes of Jewish anger at the Caesars was their attempt (like Antiochus IV before them) to put their own image in the Temple. Jesus' response implies that Caesar's image has no place there.

More important, however, is how Mark uses this question (as he has earlier in his Gospel) to illumine Jesus' teaching on some key passage in the Bible. In this case, when Jesus responds to the Pharisees' question with his own question, "Whose image and inscription is this?" (12:16), there is more at stake than money. Mark shows Jesus using language that would have reminded his audience of the most important verse in Genesis: "God created human beings in God's image" (1:27).

What the response implies is this: Caesar's image may be on the coin, but God's image is inscribed on every human being. Jesus' response is first of all a theological one. The theological answer, moreover, touches the core of Mark's Gospel, because Mark has shown Jesus himself to be the image of God.

12:18-27 The second response: "He is not God of the dead but of the living"

The Sadducees were a group particularly in league with the Temple priests. Unlike the

Pharisees, they questioned belief in immortality, and their narrative here is designed to make that belief seem ridiculous. Mark shows Jesus responding in a way that emphasizes God as the Creator. First, he shows Jesus pointing to "the scriptures" and "the power of God" (12:24). Then he shows Jesus spelling out what he has in mind by quoting God's words to Moses at the burning bush: "I am the God of Abraham, [the] God of Isaac, and [the] God of Jacob" (12:26). The meaning of the reply is not obvious, and one has to read between the lines. But Jesus' response implies that by speaking of the patriarchs in the present tense, God indicates that they are still alive, because "He is not God of the dead but of the living" (12:27). Mark shows Jesus suggesting that belief in the Scriptures would lead one to belief in resurrection. Mark also quotes Jesus as saying twice to the Sadducees, "You are misled" (12:24, 27). He implies that not to believe in resurrection is to limit God's power.

To further unpack this passage, Jesus' response seems to be saying that if one believes that God had the power to create life, one should believe that God has the power to re-create it. This point of view is in keeping with the way Mark has depicted Jesus, throughout his Gospel, as healing and restoring life. It is in keeping with the transfiguration scene, in which Mark shows Elijah and Moses fully alive. It is in keeping with the way Mark continually points to Jesus' own resurrection.

12:28-34 The third response: "You shall love the Lord your God . . . ."

The third question is asked by "one of the scribes" (12:28), a group particularly versed in Scripture. The scribe asks the most basic question: "Which is the first of all the commandments?" (12:28).

In his reply, Mark shows Jesus weaving together three essential parts of Judaism. The first part, "Hear, O Israel! The Lord our God is LORD alone" (12:29), is the central "creed" of Judaism, that is, it is an assertion of Jews' central belief in one God. It has always been at the heart of Jewish worship. The second part, "You shall love the Lord your God with all your heart, with all your soul, with all your mind, and with all your strength" (12:30), is a direct quotation from Deuteronomy (6:4). The third part, "You shall love your neighbor as yourself" (12:31), is a direct quotation from Leviticus (19:2).

By interweaving these three parts, Mark shows Jesus speaking as a scribe himself, that is, as a teacher of Scripture. Mark shows Jesus using a method typical of Jewish Scripture scholars and Wisdom teachers of the first century. The effect of this interweaving is to suggest that love of God implies love of neighbor and that both together are what constitute true worship.

It is striking that Mark shows Jesus and the scribe to be in perfect agreement. He shows the scribe repeating what Jesus has said, only adding another quotation from Scripture to further support it: " 'To love your neighbor as yourself' is worth more than all burnt offerings and sacrifices" (12:33).

The last part of the scribe's comment is an allusion to Psalm 40:7-9:

> Sacrifice and offering you do not want . . . .
> Holocausts and sin-offerings you do not require;
> So I said, "Here I am . . .
> To do your will is my delight."

Mark shows that the scribe uses the same method as Jesus, bringing together different parts of the Hebrew Bible to illuminate their meaning.

Mark further indicates the harmony between Jesus and the scribe when he quotes Jesus saying to him approvingly, "You are not far from the kingdom of God" (12:34). The incident stands out because through it Mark shows that Jesus was not at odds with *all* the scribes and Temple authorities. On the contrary, Mark shows Jesus to be in perfect agreement with one who taught the central tenets of Judaism.

12:35-37 The fourth response: "How is he [the messiah] his [David's] son?"

In this passage, Mark shows Jesus posing a riddle about the meaning of "the messiah." He does so by continuing to juxtapose one Scripture passage with another. In this instance, he juxtaposes the tradition based on God's promise to David in the second book of Samuel with a popular interpretation of Psalm 110. In the passage from 2 Samuel, God says to David:

> I will raise up your heir after you, sprung from your loins, and I will make his kingdom firm. It is he who shall build a house for my name. And I will make his royal throne firm forever. I will be a father to him, and he shall be a son to

me. . . . Your house and your kingdom shall endure forever before me; your throne shall stand firm forever (2 Sam 7:12b-14, 16).

In the first century, all the psalms were popularly attributed to David, so he was considered the speaker in Psalm 110. In its opening verse, the words "my lord" were interpreted as a reference to a coming messiah who would be victorious for Israel. Mark shows Jesus putting these two things together and suggesting that they don't add up—that is, he is asking: If the coming messiah is a son of David, how come David calls him "my lord"?

There is no answer to this riddle. By having Jesus pose this riddle, Mark is not intent on giving answers but on raising questions. The riddle raises a question about popular understandings of "the messiah." Earlier in his Gospel, Mark shows that Peter has an understanding that Jesus does not share. Peter thinks that if Jesus is "the messiah," he cannot suffer and die. And as we have seen, Jesus reproaches him (8:29-33). Here Mark shows Jesus using Scripture to reveal the fault line in the tradition. By this means, Mark shows how Jesus raised questions in the minds of his audience. Mark shakes up the popular definition of "the messiah" so that he can dramatize that Jesus is a "messiah" in an unconventional sense.

12:38-44 The rich and the poor in the Temple

Mark concludes the chapter with a contrast between those who use the Temple for their own profit and those who give to it their last coin. The episode sums up and illumines the theme of wealth versus poverty that has run throughout the last three chapters.

We have just noted that Mark shows Jesus in perfect agreement with one of the scribes. But here he shows Jesus denouncing those scribes who use their religion for self-aggrandizement. It is important to see that the scribes who seek "seats of honor" are not unlike James and John, who asked to sit at Jesus' right and left in his glory (10:37). By means of the echo, Mark reminds us of Jesus' teaching that "whoever wishes to be first among you will be the slave of all" (10:44). In addition to seeking glory, we learn, these Temple authorities make venal profit off the needs of poor widows (12:40). The language that Mark shows Jesus using to describe their action—"they *devour* the

house of widows" (emphasis added)—suggests that their greed is the reverse of the nurturing habits of Jesus himself.

The episode of the poor widow has several functions. First of all, it clarifies Jesus' anger at the money changers (11:15-17). By showing Jesus' approval of the widow's contribution to the Temple treasury, Mark indicates that it was not money in the Temple per se that caused Jesus' anger. Rather, as the condemnation of the greedy scribes shows, Jesus was angered by those who used the Temple money for themselves.

At the same time, when Mark shows Jesus praising the poor widow because "she, from her poverty, has contributed all she had" (12:44), he also shows him echoing his instruction to the rich man to sell all he has (10:21). The widow's total self-giving embodies the commandment to "love the Lord your God with all your heart, with all your soul, with all your mind, and with all your strength" (12:30).

Summary of chapter 12

The chapter is unified around the theme of wholehearted love of God versus religion perverted by greed and hypocrisy. The parable of the vineyard contrasts the venal tenants of the vineyard with the vineyard owner's servants and "beloved son." It is a transparent allegory, contrasting the present authorities in the Temple—the Romans and their hirelings—with the prophets and with Jesus.

The parable makes use of the vineyard tradition in the Hebrew Bible, especially Isaiah, to indicate the similarities and differences between Israel's situation now and in the past. As in the past, God is not able to reap from his vineyard (Israel) the harvest he wants from it. Unlike the past, the cause of this is not the vineyard itself but the obstructions placed in the way by the greedy and hostile occupier of the vineyard (Rome).

These "tenants" want whatever "inheritance" there is for themselves. The narrative of the killing of the beloved son, together with the image of the ungathered harvest, suggests that those who now occupy the vineyard are responsible both for the killing of Jesus and for the destruction of the Temple. The quotation from Psalm 110 in the conclusion of the parable suggests that God will vindicate his people (Israel) as he has before.

When Jesus tells this parable, Mark depicts him again as a Wisdom teacher. In the rest of the chapter,

Mark shows Jesus engaged in interpreting the meaning of Scripture to various groups of Jewish scholars in the Temple. By doing this, Mark suggests (as he has earlier) that Jesus is Wisdom itself.

As Wisdom in the Temple, Jesus responds to four types of questions about Jewish teaching. The first question puts forward the relationship between the Temple and worldly power. Jesus' response suggests that worldly power does not belong in the Temple. It also suggests that human beings, as bearers of God's image, belong wholly to God. The second question puts forward the relationship between God and death. Jesus' response indicates that God is concerned with life, not death. God the Creator has the power to go on creating. The third question puts forward the relationship between love of God and love of neighbor. Jesus and the scribe agree that they are inextricably woven together. Love of neighbor (as the Psalms and Prophets have said) is the truest way of loving God. The last question takes the form of a riddle that Jesus himself asks about the meaning of God's "messiah." The riddle raises questions about the conventional understandings of the term and so prepares for an unconventional one.

All of Jesus' responses bear on his identity in Mark's Gospel. Mark presents Jesus as image of God, as one who lives beyond death, as one who has come "not to be served but to serve" (10:45), and as unconventional messiah.

These responses also indicate the kind of Temple reform Jesus stands for. In conclusion, Mark sums up that reform by the contrast Jesus makes between the venal and hypocritical Temple authorities, who use the Temple for their own purposes, and the poor widow, who gives all that she has to sustain it.

JESUS AS PROPHET IN THE TEMPLE

Mark 13:1-37

13:1-2 The prophecy of the destruction of the Temple

In chapters 11 and 12, Mark has shown Jesus pointing to the spiritual devastation of the Temple. Here he speaks of its coming physical destruction. Both kinds of speech belong to the role of the prophet. We have a tendency today to restrict the word "prophet" to one who makes predictions about the future. But the biblical prophets were not soothsayers. They were mes-

sengers of God, reminding the people of God's past word in Scripture and, in the light of it, conveying God's present word on human behavior. They were, in fact, preachers.

The prevailing theme of the prophets is the need for Temple reform. By this they did not so much mean reform of liturgical practices but of people's way of living. They were constantly calling the people back to their commitment to the covenant. They identified the breaking of any of the commandments with idolatry. For example, Jeremiah's "Temple sermon" (see p. 162) equates adultery and perjury with the worship of Baal. They always preached, moreover, in times when Israel was in crisis—either under attack by foreign powers or actually occupied by them. Every foreign power that conquered Jerusalem also took over the Temple. So in such times (which constituted most of Israel's biblical history), the danger of idolatry from within was compounded by foreign influences from without. As a consequence, the prophets warned the people again and again about succumbing to false gods as well as about neglecting their obligations to love their neighbors as themselves.

The Temple building functioned as a key image in these warnings. The prophets expressed God's displeasure with the people by saying either that God would destroy the Temple or that God would leave the Temple. Many scholars think that these imaginative warnings were not so much predicting disaster to the Temple as reflecting on it after the fact. Take Jeremiah, for example. The Temple was destroyed by Babylon in 586 B.C.E., the time of Jeremiah, and the people lived in exile from Jerusalem until 539. When Jeremiah, therefore, tells the people that it is God's will for them to submit to Babylon, is he looking ahead, or is he trying to reassure the exiles that God had a plan in allowing their disaster? Many scholars think it was the latter.

All this background is relevant to the prophecy that Mark shows Jesus making here. For the second time in Jewish history, the Temple was destroyed—this time by the Romans in the year 70 C.E., forty years after the death of Jesus but in the lifetime of Mark. It had a traumatic effect on everyone associated with the Jewish community, including those Jews who were followers of Jesus. Most scholars date the Gospel of Mark around that time, either just before or just after. Mark portrays Jesus, as we have seen, in the role of a prophet, preaching about the corruption of Temple worship. The prophetic tradition raises this question: When Mark shows Jesus saying that the Temple would be destroyed, is he suggesting that Jesus in fact predicted its destruction, or is he imaginatively projecting how Jesus as prophet reflected on its meaning?

In any case, the chapter is carefully designed. Mark opens the chapter by citing the disciples' admiration for the Temple. Their wonder at the great buildings expresses a long tradition of reverence for the Temple as the dwelling place of God. Mark cites Jesus' reply without indicating his tone of voice. Many have assumed that Mark shows Jesus to be angry at the Temple, but we have seen that his anger is tempered by the prophetic vision of reform.

13:4 and 13:32 "When will this happen?"

At the time that Mark was composing, there was a large body of Jewish writings known as "apocalyptic." They were characterized by a number of things. They warned of a final disaster that in some way took the form of a battle between good and evil, that is, directly between God and Satan, or between good and evil nations, or between good and evil forces. (For example, the Dead Sea Scrolls speak of a final clash between "the sons of darkness" and the "sons of light.") They made precise predictions about the time that the world would end. They also projected that there would be particular signs that the end was about to happen. The question raised by the disciples here—"Tell us, when will this happen, and what sign will there be when all these things are about to come to an end?" (13:4)—is typical of these writings. Mark does not give Jesus' reply for many verses, and when he does, he shows him giving an answer that does not fit the apocalyptic perspective: "But of that day or hour no one knows, neither the angels in heaven, nor the Son, but only the Father" (13:32). This exchange functions as the frame for the chapter.

13:5-13 Instructions to the disciples

Mark shows that instead of replying right away to the disciples' question, Jesus instructs them on how to behave in the face of coming disaster. These instructions are a mixture of many things, and they need to be looked at carefully.

Some of what Mark shows Jesus saying are generalized clichés taken from contemporary writing about the end of time. These include the warnings about "wars and reports of wars" (13:7), about nation rising against nation (13:8a), about "earthquakes" (13:8b), about how "brother will hand over brother to death" (13:12).

But most of the warnings Mark places in Jesus' mouth are ones that would only have had meaning for Mark's own community in the year 70 or later. For example, Jesus' warning that "Many will come in my name saying, I am he" (13:5) makes most sense after Jesus' death. Indeed, earlier Mark has shown Jesus refusing to stop someone healing in his name, saying, "Whoever is not against us is for us" (9:40). Similarly, Jesus' warning that "They will hand you over to courts. You will be beaten in synagogues. You will be arraigned before governors and kings because of me" (13:9) does not apply to the disciples of Jesus' time but to his later followers.

It becomes clear that Mark is speaking to his own time when he shows Jesus saying, "But the gospel must first be preached to all the nations" (13:10). So, too, the advice that immediately follows this statement makes sense if it is seen as directed to Mark's community: "When they lead you away and hand you over, do not worry beforehand about what you are to say. But say whatever will be given to you at that hour. For it will not be you who are speaking but the holy spirit" (13:11). Finally, the warning "You will be hated by all because of my name" (13:13a) suggests what was happening in Mark's time, not in that of Jesus.

It is important to realize that Mark is addressing two different periods of time. Otherwise, we might think that the hatred and persecution of Jesus' followers happened while Jesus was still alive. But we know historically that this was not the case. And in other parts of his Gospel, Mark has shown that while some of those in power were hostile to Jesus, the crowds followed him. It is Mark's community, living after the double trauma of the death of Jesus and the destruction of the Temple, that needs encouragement to "persevere to the end" (13:13b).

13:14-27 An apocalyptic end?

This description of the end again makes use of phrases used in apocalyptic writings of the time. These include the warning to flee to the mountains

(13:14), and not to go back to one's house (13:16), the lament for those who are pregnant "in those days" (13:17), and the admonition to "Pray that this does not happen in winter" (13:18).

The reference to "tribulation such as has not been" (13:19) is taken verbatim from Daniel 12:1, where it is indeed predicting a final disaster that will bring about an eternal separation of the good from the wicked:

> Some shall live forever,
>> others shall be in everlasting horror and
>>> disgrace (Dan 12:2).

As in other apocalyptic literature, this moment of doom is precisely timed. In this case, the doom is related to "the abomination of desolation": "From the time that the daily sacrifice is abolished and the abomination of desolation is set up, there shall be one thousand two hundred and ninety days" (Dan 12:11).

The "abomination of desolation" is Daniel's veiled way of speaking about Antiochus's sacrilegious act of placing an image of himself in the Temple. Mark clearly shows Jesus referring to the same act when he uses the very same phrase (13:14a) and then emphasizes that the reference is to a written work ("let the reader understand," 13:14b). By showing that Jesus quotes the book of Daniel, Mark suggests that Jesus, too, perceives sacrilege in the Temple as the cause of the tribulations to come. Only in Mark's time, the veiled reference to sacrilege would have been to that of the Romans.

But Mark also shows that Jesus' perspective is different from that of Daniel and the other apocalyptic writings. He does this in many different ways. First, while Jesus warns, in typical apocalyptic language, of "wars" and "earthquakes" and "famines" (13:7-8), he also comments, "These are the beginnings of the labor pains" (13:8b). The image of "labor pains" or "birth pangs" was often associated with a time when God's kingdom would prevail.

Second, Mark shows Jesus reassuring his followers that God will shorten the days of tribulation (13:20). The description that follows of a darkened sun and stars "falling from the sky" (13:25) also has apocalyptic parallels, but the edge is softened here by the suggestion that this shaking of the heavens is part of God's act of mercy.

Third, Mark shows Jesus telling his disciples that he, the second Adam ("son of Adam" or "son of man"), will return in glory to gather his elect "from the end of the earth to the end of the sky" (13:26-27). Mark has shown Jesus speaking before about his own rising from the dead, but it is the first time that he has shown him promising his disciples some future glory.

In all these ways, Mark shows that while Jesus uses some apocalyptic terms, he does not share that perspective. In chapter 4, we looked at the way Mark shows Jesus telling an apocalyptic parable (the sower), and then two more parables that reverse its meaning (the seed growing secretly and the mustard seed). In the same way here, Mark shows Jesus using the apocalyptic language of some contemporary writers in order to show how he differs from their point of view.

In Mark's Gospel, Jesus does not predict a final battle between good and evil, and he does not believe that anyone can calculate when the end will come. Instead, he says that the suffering to come should be understood as "labor pains" (13:8). He says that God will shorten the suffering (13:20). He says that beyond the suffering there will be glory (13:26). And he says that no one but God the Father can know the time of the end (13:32). Jesus also expresses a non-apocalyptic point of view in his reference to the fig tree and in his parable of the returning lord of the house.

13:28-31 The fig tree blooms again

In chapter 11, Mark shows Jesus first cursing a fig tree that was not in season (11:12-14), and later exhorting Peter to "have faith" in God's power to restore it (11:20-23). These episodes, we suggested, are best understood in terms of God's actions in the Hebrew Bible. In Genesis 3, God curses the ground, but in Isaiah, God reverses that curse (Isa 55:12-13; 65:17-25). Following a similar pattern, Mark shows Jesus speaking here of the fig tree once more in bloom. This image is particularly significant in the light of contemporary Jewish thought, where the fig tree coming back into bloom was considered a sign of God's kingdom.

13:32-37 The lord of the house returns

Mark shows Jesus telling a parable that has significance both for the time of Jesus and for the end time. It has immediate significance for Jesus' disciples because it warns of the lord of the house returning to his servants at "cockcrow" (13:35), a clear foreshadowing of the cockcrow that wakens Peter to remorse for having denied any knowledge of Jesus (14:30, 72).

This parable also bears a significant relationship to the parable of the vineyard (12:1-9). In that parable, the owner of the vineyard goes away and allows hired hands to tend his vineyard. In this parable, the owner also goes off, but he leaves his house in the charge of trusted servants. In both parables, the owner stands for God, and the vineyard or house represents the sacred space where God dwells. In the first parable, the sacred space is violated by hirelings; in the second parable, "the lord of the house" is on his way back home. The parable ends, as it were, with a question: What will the lord of the house find when he returns? And it explicitly ends with the advice to "watch" (13:33, 35, 37), an exhortation that belongs to the Wisdom traditions.

The exhortation to watchfulness appears three times in this chapter. It appears first when Jesus tells the disciples to "Watch out for yourselves" in regard to those who might deceive them (13:9). It occurs a second time in the context of Jesus' warning about "false messiahs and false prophets" (13:22-23). And it is repeated three times in connection with this parable—once at the beginning and twice at the end (13:33, 35, 37).

The word "watch" is the key word of the chapter. It belongs to the Wisdom traditions, because it is in those traditions that the acknowledgment of uncertainty is prized. It is wise to know what one does not know. So here Mark shows Jesus acknowledging that only God the Father can know when the end will come. Not knowing, one must be always on the watch.

Summary of chapter 13

The chapter is unified by the question about "signs." It is framed by the disciples' question that seeks definite signs as to when the end will come and by Jesus' reply that "No one knows," so they must always "watch." An apocalyptic question receives a non-apocalyptic reply.

In between, Mark shows Jesus countering what were conventionally considered the signs of God's coming judgment (war, earthquake, famine, family betrayal, death, and cosmic turmoil) with images that bring hope: giving birth, a merciful shortening of suffering, a glorious ingathering of the elect, a new season in which the fig tree blooms again. In this way, Mark shows Jesus countering the conventional fears of a coming apocalypse with suggestions of a new beginning.

The specific reference to "the beginning of God's creation" (13:19), even though it is made in the context of predicted suffering, is a reminder of God's purpose in creation to "look at everything [that God] had made" and find it "very good" (Gen 1:31). The very word "beginning" reminds Mark's readers of his persistent images of a new creation. The parable of the fig tree in bloom is one more of these images. It is a sign of return to the original Garden.

The glorious ingathering of Jesus as the "son of man" reinforces this sign. We have suggested before that the phrase "son of man" is best understood as "son of Adam." Jesus as "son of Adam" is also a second Adam. Mark presents him as a representative of humanity who has not fallen. As such, he is a representative who perfectly reflects human beings as God intended them to be at the beginning—as image of God.

The central "sign" of the chapter, of course, is the Temple itself. In chapters 11 and 12, Mark has shown Jesus using the language of the prophets to point to its corruption and to hope for its restoration. In this chapter, he shows Jesus borrowing the veiled words of the book of Daniel ("the abomination of desolation") to point to the sacrilegious use of the Temple by the Romans. In the parable of "the lord of the house" returning home, he gives hope that God will come back to his dwelling place.

That hope, without certainty, brings the chapter to its concluding key word, the key word of Wisdom—"Watch!"

THE PASSION NARRATIVE, PART I: PREPARATIONS FOR DEATH AND LIFE

Mark 14:1-52

14:1-2 Preparation for betrayal

In these opening verses, Mark introduces the theme of betrayal that he interweaves throughout the chapter. The Feast of Passover, designed to celebrate the freedom of the people of God, is the setting for the plot to kill Jesus. By means of the plotters' remark that they had better not kill Jesus at the feast (14:2), Mark suggests the tension both between the feast and the plot and between the Temple authorities and the people.

14:3-9 Anointing: preparation for death and life

The next few verses present a counter theme. The setting is "the house of Simon the leper" (14:3). Mark introduces this figure without explanation. The reader only knows the name "Simon" in association with Peter (1:16, 29-30; 3:16). The only leper to appear before is the one cured in 1:40-45. Does Mark intend the reader to make some connection between this Simon and Simon Peter or between this leper and the one who was healed?

The mystery of the scene is compounded by the entry of an anonymous woman carrying an alabaster jar (14:3). Again, Mark makes no attempt to identify this woman. The reader, however, may have a subliminal memory of having encountered before this particular pairing of anonymous woman and leper. In Mark's account of Jesus' first miracles, he tells of Jesus healing "Simon's mother-in-law" (1:29-31), and then a leper (1:40-45). The name "Simon," transposed here to the leper, adds to the impression of déjà vu.

We noted earlier that Mark's language suggests that Jesus did not merely heal the woman physically but "raised her up"* (1:31) to a new status of ministry. It is one in which she "served"* others (1:31). And serving others is how Jesus describes his own way of life (10:45). The leper, too, receives more than a physical cure. Mark tells us that Jesus sent him back to the priest and so to his community. Once there, Mark says, he spread the word of Jesus to such an extent that Jesus could not "enter a town openly" (1:45).

Could it be, then, that Mark intends his readers to regard the woman and leper here as these two persons in their changed state? That supposition is supported by the fact that they act here in unconventional and extraordinary ways. Unlike most lepers, "Simon the leper" is able to open his home to a social gathering. Even more remarkable, Mark shows Jesus saying that what the anonymous woman has done will always be part of the gospel proclamation (14:9).

The leper disappears from the narrative while the woman preoccupies it. It is important to look carefully at how Mark describes her actions. A jar made of "alabaster" suggests something rare and valuable. The perfumed oil that it contains is described by two words, one of which is hard to translate. The first word means "pure"* (trans-

lated above as "genuine"). The other word does not appear in any other piece of writing; it is closest to the Greek word for "faith."* Mark is presenting his readers with a highly symbolic narrative in which the woman is bearing the costly oil of faith.

The woman proceeds to break the jar and pour out the oil (14:3b). The word Mark chooses for "break" here is no ordinary word, but one that means to "shatter" or "to destroy completely." By using it, Mark calls attention to the action. He suggests that this is not a casual or conventional sort of breaking. The word for "poured" has the sense of "poured out." In its root form, it is related to the word associated with a cultic pouring out of blood. Mark uses a variant of it later in the chapter when he describes Jesus saying, "This is my blood of the covenant, which is poured out for many" (14:24). In fact, with hindsight one can see that the woman's gestures here of "breaking" and "pouring out" anticipate the gestures Mark shows Jesus making at the Last Supper. Mark makes the woman's extravagant gestures of breaking and pouring a symbolic foreshadowing of Jesus' extravagant gestures of giving his body to be broken and his blood to be poured out.

By showing the narrow-minded response of some present who view this extravagance as a "waste" (14:4-5), Mark sets the stage for Jesus' praise of this woman's act (14:8-9). Given the symbolic nature of the narrative, every word here is important. When Mark shows Jesus rebuking the protestors by saying, "Let her alone" (14:6), we hear an echo of the scene where Jesus rebukes those who were keeping back the children (10:13-14). When Mark shows Jesus saying, "She has done what she could" (14:8a), we hear an echo of Jesus' praise of the poor widow: "[She] contributed all she had" (12:44).

When Mark shows Jesus saying, "She has anticipated anointing my body for burial" (14:8b), we are forced to consider the different meanings of "anointing." Jesus speaks of anointing here in the context of consecrating the body for death. At the same time, Mark's readers would have been aware that Jesus was referred to as "messiah," a Hebrew word that means "the anointed one." In the Bible and other writings of the time, that term generally referred to someone who was sent to do God's work, and so it was a title associated with glory. But we have already seen that Mark shows

Jesus rebuking Peter for making that association (8:29-33). Mark shows Jesus consistently teaching that God's anointed one should be associated instead with suffering and even death. In this episode in chapter 14, Mark dramatizes that meaning. Jesus becomes "the anointed one" in the context of death.

When Mark shows Jesus saying, "Wherever the gospel is proclaimed to the whole world, what she has done will be told in remembrance* of her" (14:9), what does Mark have in mind? We have suggested that Mark intends a connection between the woman's extravagant gestures of breaking and pouring and Jesus' gestures (later in this chapter) that symbolize his death. In other words, Mark makes her gestures anticipate the eucharistic gestures of Jesus. And those gestures of breaking and pouring are the very ones that, according to Paul, Jesus asked his followers to do *"in remembrance"* of him (1 Cor 11:24-25, emphasis added).

The phrase expresses a concept important to Passover celebrations and also to celebrations of the Eucharist. In both instances, it conveys the sense of doing more than recalling a past event. Rather, it suggests a reliving of a past event in such a way that God's grace is not just recalled but made present. At the end of every Passover meal, the leader prays that God may grant the grace of freedom to every Jew here and now. In the same way, the presider at the Eucharist prays that the freeing grace of Jesus may be made present here and now. The eucharistic act of "remembrance" is not an act of recalling what Jesus did but of making it present once again.

When Mark gives his own account of the first Eucharist (14:22-26), his wording is close to that of Paul's account in First Corinthians. It is therefore striking that Mark does not put the phrase "in remembrance" there. The fact that it is here confirms Mark's intention to link this woman's gestures to the Eucharist. In preparing Jesus' body for burial, she has prepared his body for a death that will be life-giving. It is for her eucharistic gestures that she will be kept *"in remembrance."*

14:10-11 Preparation for betrayal continued

These two verses connect Judas with the plot to kill Jesus. They reintroduce the theme of betrayal. Mark consistently uses the phrase "hand over" to express betrayal. That use carries ironic overtones, because "hand over" can also mean *hand on,* as of a tradition. By his persistent repetition of the phrase, Mark suggests that Jesus is *handing on* the tradition of being *handed over.* It is the same word that Paul uses with the same double meaning when he says that he is *"handing on"* to the Christian community at Corinth what he knows about Jesus' institution of the Eucharist "on the night that he was *handed over"* (1 Cor 11:23).

14:12-16 Preparations for the Passover Supper

The details of this episode again seem both mysterious and symbolic, like the details of the anointing scene. Mark does not identify which disciples were sent or the man "carrying a jar of water" (14:13). Nor does he tell us how the man knows to lead the disciples to the right place. Mark also doesn't identify "the master of the house" nor tell us why he has already prepared a room for Jesus' Passover (14:14-15). The narrative's lack of realistic concreteness suggests that it is also intended to be symbolic.

In fact, many details suggest that Mark intends this narrative to symbolize the Eucharist. By referring to the Passover supper as "the Feast of Unleavened Bread" (v. 12), Mark stresses a detail that would be significant to a eucharistic community. When Mark notes that the disciples set off to prepare the supper on the day "when they sacrificed the Passover lamb" (14:12), he is calling attention to the sacrificial implications of the meal to come.

When Mark speaks of an anonymous man carrying a pottery water jar, the image seems to echo and complement the anonymous woman carrying an alabaster jar of costly ointment. We have noted that the alabaster jar indicates that it contains something precious and that the pouring out of its ointment anticipates Jesus' pouring out of the wine that he calls his blood. The pottery (or earthenware) jar is humble in comparison, and the water is ordinary compared with the precious ointment. One may think of Paul saying, "We hold this treasure in earthen vessels, that the surpassing power may be of God and not from us" (2 Cor 4:7). In any case, by presenting his readers with these different but echoing images, Mark suggests the pairing of water and wine that is part of the eucharistic celebration and proclaims, for the believer, the meeting of humanity with divinity.

In that context, the "large upper room furnished and ready" (14:15) is perhaps suggestive of the house churches that were developing in Mark's time to accommodate the eucharistic gatherings of the early Christian communities. Once again, Mark seems to be projecting his own time frame into the narrative. He is trying to give the reader his own awareness that this last Passover meal of Jesus was also the first Eucharist.

14:22-26 The Passover/Eucharist

In between predictions of betrayal, Mark places his account of the meal that he describes as both Passover and Eucharist. The blessing and breaking of bread, together with the blessing and giving of the cup (14:22-23), suggest the opening prayers of every Passover meal. (These read: "Blessed are you, O God, king of the universe, creator of the fruit of the vine.") It is also usual to conclude the Passover Seder, as they do here, with the singing of a hymn (14:26). What is strikingly different is Jesus' identification of the bread as his body and the wine as his blood (14:22-24). Mark also shows Jesus speaking of his blood as that "of the covenant" (14:24a). That reference suggests both the blood of the Passover lamb that saved the Israelites from destruction (Exod 12:13) and the sacrificial blood that ratified the covenant (Exod 24:8).

In addition, Mark shows Jesus quoting from Isaiah when he speaks of his blood being "shed for many" (14:24b). That phrase is also an echo of what Mark has shown Jesus saying earlier to his disciples about the purpose of his life: "The son of man did not come to be served but to serve and to give his life as a ransom for many" (10:45). In both instances, the phrase is an echo of Isaiah's description of God's justification of his "Suffering Servant":

> Through his suffering, my servant shall justify
> many,
> and their guilt he shall bear (Isa 53:11).

By showing Jesus repeating this phrase, Mark interprets Jesus' death in that tradition of atoning sacrifice. It is also a tradition in which God raises up his servant and exalts him. Like the episode of Jesus' anointing, it is a suggestion of hope in this chapter so seemingly concentrated on betrayal and death.

Another suggestion of hope is given in Jesus' further words that he will not drink "the fruit of the vine" again until the day when he drinks it new "in the kingdom of God" (14:25). Although in one sense it suggests that he is moving toward death, in another sense it offers hope that there will be another time, a new time, in which God's kingdom will at last prevail. And by showing that Jesus speaks of this time as one in which there will be "fruit of the vine" to drink, Mark also suggests that there will be a time when the fruit of God's vineyard will be accessible again to God.

14:17-21, 27-31 Predictions of betrayal

Mark frames the narrative of this Passover/Eucharist with predictions of Jesus' betrayal. The scene he describes before the supper (14:18) echoes a verse in Psalm 41 where the speaker recalls a time when friends as well as foes turned against him:

> Even the friend who had my trust,
> who shared my table, has scorned me (v. 10).

When Mark then shows Jesus saying that his betrayer will be "the one who dips with me into the dish" (14:20), he brings to mind both the dipping gesture characteristic of the Passover Seder and the dipping posture of baptism. By suggesting both simultaneously, Mark suggests that the experience of being betrayed is the tradition of God's servants. (Being *handed over* is being *handed on*).

When Mark shows Jesus saying, "For the son of man indeed goes, as it is written of him" (14:21), he indicates how much his narrative uses Scripture to shape and interpret the story of Jesus' passion. The foretelling of the disciples' betrayal (14:27) is preceded by a passage from Zechariah:

> [I will] strike the shepherd
> that the sheep may be dispersed (Zech 13:7).

In the context of Zechariah, God is saying that he will strike the shepherd *so that* the sheep may be dispersed. God says that he will purge Israel of false prophets and false shepherds so that he can preserve the remnant and make Jerusalem holy again. In Mark, the prophecy is used to indicate how all the Twelve, including Peter, will scatter and leave Jesus without their support.

When Mark shows Jesus making this prediction to Peter, it is even more precise: "Amen, I say to you, this very night before the cock crows twice you will deny me three times" (14:30). Mark thus links Jesus' warning to Peter to his general admonition to "watchfulness" in chapter 13: "You do not know when the lord of the house is coming, whether in the evening, or at midnight, or at cockcrow . . . " (13:35). The vehemence of Peter's refusal to accept himself as a possible betrayer (14:29, 31) intensifies the enormity of his eventual act of betrayal (14:66-72).

Yet even in this context of betrayal, Mark shows Jesus predicting once again that he will be raised from the dead (14:28). In this instance, Mark shows him speaking not only about his being raised but about his life beyond death: "I shall go before you to Galilee." It is striking because his words do not suggest ascension to heaven (like Elijah), but a return to ongoing ministry. And this phrase is the one the women at the tomb are sent to repeat to the disciples after Jesus' death (16:7).

14:32-52 Betrayal in the garden

This betrayal has two parts: (1) betrayal by the three key disciples (14:32-42), and (2) betrayal by Judas (14:43-52).

14:32-42 Betrayal by the disciples. The first part is conventionally labeled "Agony in the Garden," although in fact there is no explicit mention of a garden; the garden setting is inferred from knowledge of Gethsemane. The image of betrayal in a garden fits in with the fact that Creation provides Mark's overall frame of reference. In that context, there is particular irony in Mark showing Jesus, second Adam, betrayed in a garden.

There is also irony within the scene itself. We have noted before that Mark shows Jesus taking these same three disciples with him at three key moments in the Gospel: at the raising up of Jairus's daughter (5:37); at the transfiguration of Jesus (9:2); and here. The first two episodes point toward Jesus' resurrection. In fact, in terms of the overall structure of Mark's narrative, the transfiguration scene takes the place of a resurrection scene. In this scene in the garden, all the elements of the transfiguration scene are reversed. Mark tells us that instead of being radiant and dazzling (9:3), Jesus is "troubled and distressed" (14:33). Instead of ascending up a mountain (9:2), Jesus

falls to the ground (14:35). Instead of being blessed by the Father (9:9), Jesus cries out to the Father to take away his coming suffering and death (14:36). Peter, who is so roused by the moment of transfiguration that he wants to celebrate it (9:5), falls asleep (14:37). It is also significant that Mark shows Jesus not addressing him here as "Peter" but reverting to "Simon," the name he had before he became a disciple.

Mark connects this scene to others in his Gospel as well. By showing that Jesus refers to his suffering as "this cup," Mark links this scene to Jesus' question to James and John: "Can you drink the cup that I drink . . . ?" (10:38). The word is, of course, also linked to the Passover/Eucharist Mark has just described and to the cup of Jesus' blood (14:23-24).

By showing that Jesus cries out "Abba," the Aramaic word for "father" (14:36), Mark indicates the importance of this moment. He shows Jesus using Aramaic only in three other key places: when Jesus raises up the little girl from death (5:41); when Jesus symbolically heals the deafmute (7:34); and when Jesus cries out to God from the cross (15:34).

Most important, Mark shows Jesus using the word "watch" three times in this brief episode (14:34, 37, 38). Like the "cockcrow" (14:30), this refrain links this moment to the warnings at the end of chapter 13 (13:33, 35, 37). There, at the conclusion of the parable of the returning lord of the house, Jesus says to his disciples, "May he not come suddenly and find you sleeping. What I say to you, I say to all: 'Watch!'" (13:36-37). Here Jesus comes back to his disciples three times and finds them asleep.

Jesus' announcement that "the son of man is to be handed over to sinners" (14:41b) picks up the theme of being "handed over." It is full of irony in view of the fact that throughout the Gospel Mark has shown Jesus reaching out to sinners.

The phrase translated above as "Get up!" (14:42) is literally "You are raised up!"* It is again ironic. By means of it, Mark indicates the distance between what the disciples ought to be and what in fact they are.

14:43-52 Betrayal by Judas. The betrayal by Judas follows upon the more subtle betrayals by the three key disciples. It is signaled by Mark's word for moral urgency, "straightway"* (omitted in the translation given here for 14:43). Judas comes as the agent of the Temple authorities—"the chief priests, the scribes, and the elders" (14:43). The crowd that accompanies him is the reverse of "the crowd" we have seen earlier that follows after Jesus. The "sign" that Judas has arranged with them (14:44) is doubly ironic. It is ironic because of the earlier episode where the Pharisees sought "a sign from heaven" (8:11). It is ironic because the sign of betrayal is a kiss (14:44).

Mark's irony continues as he says that Judas approached Jesus "straightway" (again translated as "immediately" above) and addressed him by the honorific "Rabbi" before he kissed him (14:45).

When Mark goes on to say, "they laid hands on him and arrested him" (14:46), the reader hears an ironic echo of Jesus' "laying his hands" on the sick to cure them (6:5).

When Mark shows Jesus asking, "Have you come out as against a robber?" (14:48), the reader hears an ironic echo of Jeremiah's sermon that reproaches the Temple authorities for turning the Temple into "a den of thieves" (11:17).

The reference to the fulfillment of the Scriptures (14:49) should be understood in terms of the passage from Zechariah quoted earlier in this chapter (14:27):

> [I will] strike the shepherd,
> that the sheep may be dispersed.

Mark shows its fulfillment here by the terse statement "And they all left him and fled" (14:50).

The episode concludes with Mark's description of a young man who started to follow Jesus until the crowd seized hold of him; then he left behind the linen cloth on his body "and ran off naked" (14:51-52). The incident dramatizes the kind of situation warned about earlier in 13:14-16: "When you see the desolating abomination . . . a person in a field must not return to get his cloak." By this dramatic image, Mark suggests that the "tribulation" warned about in chapter 13 has begun.

Summary of the passion narrative, Part I (14:1-52)

Part I of the passion narrative interweaves two contrasting themes, one of which leads to death and the other to life. The episodes of the chapter show preparations being made for both.

The negative theme, that of betrayal, appears to dominate. The chapter opens with chief priests and scribes plotting to kill Jesus, and it concludes with his arrest in the garden. In the middle verses, Mark shows Judas joining the conspiracy to kill Jesus. Mark's account of the Last Supper is framed by Jesus' predictions of the betrayals by Judas and Peter. The scene in the garden reverses all the elements of the Transfiguration: Jesus "falls to the ground," while the three key disciples—Peter, James, and John—fail to "watch" with him. After Jesus' arrest, all his disciples desert him. From the point of view of plot, the preparation for Jesus' death appears to be advancing inevitably.

Yet, interwoven into this death-leading plot are events that suggest Jesus' continued life in the Eucharist. First, Mark tells us of an anonymous woman who anoints Jesus for his death. Mark describes her gestures in such a way that they anticipate the Eucharist. The Eucharist is further symbolized by the pairing of this anonymous woman with her alabaster vase of ointment and the anonymous man with his earthenware jar of water. The woman "shatters" the vase and "pours out" the precious ointment. Her extravagant gestures prepare for Jesus' extravagant gestures of breaking and pouring out. The anonymous man with his earthen vessel leads Jesus' disciples to a large room already prepared to receive them. Together, they suggest the early eucharistic communities meeting in house churches and reliving Jesus' gestures "in remembrance" of him.

These episodes introduce the description of the Passover meal in which Jesus speaks of the bread as his body and the wine as his blood. In its introductory blessings and its final hymn, it is a traditional Passover meal, celebrating God's act of freeing his people from slavery. In the midst of this traditional framework, Jesus speaks of his body as the bread to be broken and of the wine as his blood to be "shed for many." In this way he links his blood to the saving blood of the covenant and to the atoning blood of Isaiah's Suffering Servant. He reverses the effect of the vineyard parable by predicting a future day when the vineyard's fruit will again be accessible and God's kingdom will prevail. His words imply the paradox of a death that will be life-giving. After the supper, even while he is predicting the scattering of his disciples, he speaks of his life beyond death.

In Mark's telling of it, Part I of the passion narrative presents episodes and scriptural echoes that prepare simultaneously for Jesus' death and for his new life. The plot seems to be moving inevitably toward his death, but the framework of Passover freedom, together with hints of the kingdom to come, life beyond death in Galilee, and a eucharistic community holding him "in remembrance," points to a dramatic irony in which what looks like the end may in fact be a new beginning.

THE PASSION NARRATIVE, PART II: THE IDENTITY OF JESUS ON TRIAL

Mark 14:53–15:15

14:53-65 Jesus before the high priest

As we read this account, it is important to remember the place of the high priest in Judaism at the time of Jesus. As we explained earlier, the high priest at this time was appointed by the Romans and did not represent the religious leadership of the Jews. The "chief priests and the elders and the scribes" who accompany the high priest here (14:53) should also be understood as part of a group that were collaborating with Rome. Their plot to kill Jesus, therefore, together with their questions and their response to him, must be seen in this context. (Mark has earlier shown Jesus' total agreement with a different sort of scribe in 12:28-34.)

Mark establishes the injustice of the trial by noting that from the outset "the chief priests and the entire Sanhedrin kept trying to obtain testimony against Jesus in order to put him to death, but they found none" (14:55). Mark notes that not having found any valid evidence against Jesus, they offered "false witness" (14:56a). This testimony is further invalidated by the fact that the witnesses did not agree (14:56b, 59). (Having at least two witnesses who agree is a requirement of Deuteronomy 19:15.) The false witness that they offer has to do with the Temple: "We heard him say, 'I will destroy this Temple made with hands and within three days I will build another not made with hands'" (14:58). Mark has earlier given the reader an account of what Jesus said about the Temple (ch. 13), so the reader can judge how false this statement is.

Of course, the reader familiar with the interpretation given in John—"But he was speaking about the Temple of his body" (John 2:21)—may

read this false accusation as containing an ironic truth, but within the framework of Mark's Gospel, Jesus has spoken only of the Temple being destroyed (13:2). Yet the reader who knows the end of the story may be haunted anyway by the ironic mixture here of uncanny truth with deliberate falsehood.

The questions of the high priest also have ironic elements. When the high priest asks, "Are you the Anointed One [the Messiah], the son of the Blessed One?" (14:61), he is asking the key questions of Mark's narrative about Jesus' identity. Mark has earlier shown Jesus reproving Peter for identifying him as a triumphant, non-suffering messiah (8:32). Mark has just shown Jesus becoming "the Anointed One" in the context of death (14:8). He has also just shown that for Jesus, the implication of being "the son of the Blessed One" is acceptance of the Father's will, even to the point of death (14:36).

Jesus' response here, however, does not stress his death but his glory. Mark shows him quoting Daniel 7:13 when he describes himself as "son of man . . . coming with the clouds of heaven." In Daniel's context, the phrase describes an angelic figure who comes in human form ("One *like* a son of man") and who represents the people of God in contrast to worldly kingdoms, described as beasts. We have noted before that Mark shows Jesus applying this phrase to himself as a way of indicating that he represents all humanity. Mark uses the phrase to suggest that Jesus is a second Adam, giving all of us a second chance.

Mark shows Jesus adding to that reference the image of himself "seated at the right hand of the Power" (14:62). The image of someone seated "at the right hand" of God comes from the first verse of Psalm 110, where God is reassuring his anointed king that he will protect him from his enemies:

> The LORD says to my lord:
> "Take your throne at my right hand,
> while I make your enemies your footstool."

In chapter 12, Mark has shown Jesus quoting this psalm in order to raise questions about the nature of the Messiah or Anointed One (12:35-39). Here Mark shows Jesus implicitly identifying himself with this figure. Yet Mark has also shown, through Jesus' rebuke of Peter (8:33), that Jesus defines "messiah" differently from those who associate the term with triumphant power in this world.

Mark shows the high priest responding in a way that reveals he does not share Jesus' understanding of the terms "messiah" or "son of the Blessed One." The high priest responds by tearing his garments and calling Jesus' reply a "blasphemy" (14:64). The high priest implies that it is blasphemous to refer to oneself by either of these terms. But in Jewish law, that was not the case. "Blasphemy" is defined in Leviticus as "cursing" God (Lev 24:15-16), not anything else. Being called "messiah" means being called the one anointed to do God's work; it is hardly a term hostile to God. And being "son of God" was a claim that any pious Jew might make. By this reply, Mark shows the high priest to be either ignorant of Jewish law and custom or indifferent to it. Mark is thus dramatizing the fact that the high priest of that time was not a religious leader but a worldly one. In league with Rome, he did not know or care about Jewish piety.

In addition, Mark constructs the scene of Jesus' trial by interweaving echoes of Scripture that reveal how much it is the pattern for God's just one to be misunderstood and condemned by the powers of the world. First of all, Mark seems to be reenacting the scene in the Wisdom of Solomon where "the wicked" set out to "beset the just one" (Wis 2:12) because "he professes to have knowledge of God and styles himself a child of the LORD" (Wis 2:13) and "boasts that God is his Father" (Wis 2:16b). The "wicked" in the Wisdom of Solomon also go on to condemn the just man "to a shameful death" (Wis 2:20).

Second, by saying that "Some began to spit on him" and "struck him" (14:65), Mark seems also to be summoning up the third song of Isaiah's "Suffering Servant" figure:

> I gave my back to those who beat me,
>   my cheeks to those who plucked my beard;
> My face I did not shield
>   from buffets and spitting (Isa 50:6).

Like "the just one" of the Wisdom of Solomon, the Suffering Servant is mocked and condemned by the obtuse powers of the world, who do not understand his identity as God's servant. By echoing both those works, Mark is providing an interpretive framework for understanding the condemnation and death of Jesus.

14:66-72 Peter denies knowing Jesus

Mark shows the two trials to be about Jesus' identity. He bridges these two trials with the episode in which Jesus' key disciple denies knowing who Jesus is. Peter's presence "in the courtyard" (14:66) picks up an earlier point in Mark's narrative (14:54). The structure is the typical Markan "sandwich" we have noted before, for example in Mark's placement of the story of John the Baptist's death (6:17-29) and in his narrative of the healing of the woman with a menstrual disorder (5:25-34). In each instance, the middle section sheds light on the parts it separates. So here the episode of Peter's denial of Jesus illuminates the trials that center on Jesus' identity.

Both the high priest and Pilate condemn Jesus by misrepresenting his identity as one that claims power. They both function as false witnesses to Jesus. At the other extreme, Mark shows Peter refusing to witness at all.

Ironically, one of the high priest's maids bears witness to Peter's identity ("You too were with the Nazarene, Jesus," 14:67b). This identification of Peter is repeated two more times (14:69-70). Mark creates a triad of true identifications of Peter that balance the triad, under Pilate, of false identifications of Jesus. Peter's denials are incrementally more vehement. The narrative reaches its climax when the cock crows a second time (14:72) and Peter remembers the prediction of Jesus, "Amen, I say to you, this very night before the cock crows twice, you will deny me three times" (14:30). The second cockcrow is prefaced by the key word "straightway"* (translated above as "immediately"). Mark notes that upon hearing it, Peter "broke down and wept" (14:72b). Mark is dramatizing the fact that in denying Jesus, Peter has been denying himself. In Mark's account, Peter's identity is bound to the identity of Jesus. Ironically, too, Peter's denial of himself is not the kind of self-denial that Jesus asked of his followers (8:34). Rather, Mark shows it is the opposite: Peter denies knowing Jesus because he is trying to save himself from a similar fate. Mark's narrative dramatizes the truth of Jesus' wisdom: "Whoever wishes to save his life will lose it" (8:35). The other side of that truth remains for now only in the reader's mind.

15:1-15 Jesus before Pilate

As we have seen, Mark shows the high priest falsely accusing Jesus of blasphemy. His accusation serves to reveal both his ignorance of Jewish religious law and his underlying fear of Jesus' power. Mark shows that he does not understand the terms "messiah" and "son of the Blessed" in a spiritual sense but sees them as a threat to his worldly power. Mark emphasizes the concern of the high priest for worldly power by structuring Jesus' trial before Pilate as a parallel to it. In both instances, Mark shows that the one interrogating Jesus is not interested in what Jesus has done but in who he is and how his identity may threaten their own.

Mark shows Pilate's main concern to be whether Jesus considers himself "the king of the Jews." In Mark's account, Pilate repeats this phrase three times, like a refrain. The first time, Pilate asks the question directly of Jesus (15:2). The second time, he uses the term in a question to the crowd: "Do you want me to release to you the king of the Jews?" (15:9). The third time, Pilate uses it to address the crowd about Jesus' fate: "Then what [do you want] me to do with [the man you call] the king of the Jews?" (15:12).

To grasp the full effect of this refrain, it is helpful for the modern reader to know that the term was in fact a title that the Romans applied to their designated tetrarchs. At the time of Jesus, Herod Antipas was tetrarch of Galilee, while Judea was directly under the administration of Roman procurators like Pilate. Needless to say, ordinary Jews of the time did not like the idea of a Roman appointee being called their "king." Pilate's reference to Jesus by this term was therefore politically charged. By showing Pilate's repeated use of it, Mark indicates that Pilate fired up the crowd to think that Jesus either was a tool of Rome or had claimed such an alliance for himself. While on the surface Mark's narrative seems to suggest that Pilate turned over Jesus' fate to the Jewish crowd, at a more subtle level Mark is showing how Pilate incited the crowd to anger.

Just as Mark shows the high priest trying to turn the religious community against Jesus on the false claim that he had committed some kind of blasphemy, so he shows Pilate trying to turn the crowds against Jesus on the false claim that he had taken to himself a title of Roman power.

The scene has other ironic details worth noting. In the opening verse, Mark says that "the chief priests with the elders and the scribes" held a council about Jesus *"straightway"** (a word omit-

ted in the translation above). Mark repeats the key word of the theme of betrayal by saying they *"handed him over* to Pilate" (15:1b, emphasis added). The word for "release," which Mark has associated before with Jesus' acts of freeing people from physical ailments or from sin, appears here in the question of Pilate: ""Do you want me to release to you the king of the Jews?" (15:9). This question is the middle one of the triad of references to Jesus as "the king of the Jews," thus stressing its irony.

Summary of the passion narrative, Part II (14:53–15:15)

Part II of Mark's passion narrative focuses on the identity of Jesus. There are two balancing scenes in which the identity of Jesus is put on trial. Each trial is characterized by a falsification of who Jesus is; in each case, Jesus is condemned on false grounds. In the trial before the high priest, Jesus is condemned as a blasphemer, although he has said nothing that would constitute blasphemy according to Jewish law. In the trial before Pilate, Jesus is condemned as a would-be "king of the Jews," although he had never claimed that Roman title or sought that Roman power.

In between these matching trials and false witnesses, Mark gives an account of Peter's refusal to witness to Jesus at all. As Mark tells the story, Peter's denial of Jesus is also a denial of himself.

In Mark's narrative, the high priest, Pilate, and Peter are alike in trying to save themselves. As a consequence, each one betrays himself: the high priest betrays that he is not truly a religious leader of the Jews; Pilate betrays that he is not truly an administrator of justice; Peter betrays that he is not truly a disciple of Jesus. Their false witness to Jesus is pivotal to their own identities.

THE PASSION NARRATIVE, PART III: THE DEATH OF JESUS

Mark 15:6-47

15:6 The death sentence

We have already suggested that Mark shows Pilate inciting the crowd by referring to Jesus repeatedly as "the king of the Jews" (15:2, 9, 12). But in fact, Mark is more precise than that. He indicates that Pilate used that title to arouse the chief priests, because "he knew that it was out of envy that the chief priests had handed him over"

(15:10). After that, Mark says, "the chief priests stirred up the crowd to have him release Barabbas for them instead" (15:11).

The release of Barabbas is further Markan irony. It is ironic from the point of view of the Roman trial because Barabbas, Mark tells us, is a known insurgent against Rome and a murderer as well (15:7). And it is ironic from the point of view of the Jewish trial because the name Barabbas means in Hebrew "son of the Father." Jesus, who has no plans to strike against Rome, is put to death, while a convicted rebel against Rome is released. Jesus is condemned for calling himself "son of the Blessed," while one whose very name means the same thing is released.

The word "released" is also used by Mark as an ironic refrain, being repeated three times in this short episode (15:9, 11, 15). The theme that Mark has repeatedly associated with Jesus' acts of forgiveness and healing is repeatedly used here in connection with Jesus' sentence of death.

Mark tells the story of the death sentence in such a way that everyone is implicated: the crowd that shouts "Crucify him" (15:13-14); the chief priests, who have stirred them up to this (15:11); and Pilate, who, "wishing to satisfy the crowd" (15:15), handed Jesus over to be crucified. Although Mark reports the involvement of the crowd, he shapes the narrative to place the greatest blame on the chief priests and Pilate—that is, the agents of Rome. In particular, he indicates the moral weakness of Pilate by showing that he knows Jesus is innocent (15:14) and nonetheless condemns him, just "to satisfy the crowd" (15:15).

15:16-20 The mockery of Jesus

In this description of the Roman soldiers' mockery of Jesus, Mark dramatizes the irony of calling Jesus "king of the Jews" (15:18). He expands upon the image of Isaiah's "Suffering Servant," to which he had alluded earlier (14:64):

> I gave my back to those who beat me,
> my cheeks to those who plucked my beard;
> My face I did not shield
> from buffets and spitting (Isa 50:6).

Here the "buffets and spitting" accompany the elaborate mockery of the purple cloak and crown of thorns (15:17), the mocking salutation (15:18), and posture of kneeling (15:19).

The whole scene also expands upon the brief suggestion in the Wisdom of Solomon of "the wicked" torturing "the just one":

> With revilement and torture let us put him to the
>   test
>   that we may have proof of his gentleness
>   and try his patience.
> Let us condemn him to a shameful death;
>   for according to his own words, God will
>   take care of him (Wis 2:19-20).

The mock homage also ironically recalls three earlier instances in Mark's Gospel where some knelt in all seriousness before Jesus: the leper seeking to be healed (1:40); the demons who recognized him as "son of God" (3:11); and the woman who touched him and was overwhelmed by her cure (5:33).

15:21 Simon forced to take up the cross

The reappearance of the name "Simon" here has symbolic significance. Mark has just shown us Simon Peter denying Jesus while refusing to "deny himself and take up his cross." (The language of denial here explicitly repeats the language of 8:34.) Like Simon the leper, this Simon also functions as his alter ego, forced into doing what Simon Peter the disciple has not been able to do.

The other names in this brief incident are significant as well. "Simon" was a Jewish name, and Cyrene was apparently a Greek colony where many Jews had settled. The names "Alexander" and "Rufus" are, respectively, Greek and Roman. Through these names, Mark suggests how Jesus' followers were eventually to include the Greek and the Roman world.

15:22-32 Crucifixion

Mark translates the name "Golgotha" as "Place of the Skull." His Jewish audience would have known the legend that it was the burial place of Adam's skull. Thus even as he shows Jesus being led to his death, Mark calls attention to the fact that Jesus is a second Adam. Mark thus suggests the cosmic irony of his death.

The "wine drugged with myrrh" (15:23) echoes the distress expressed by the psalmist, who says "I have become an outcast to my kin" because "zeal for your house consumes me" (Ps 69:9-10). In his anguish, he cries out:

Insult has broken my heart, and I am weak.
    I looked for compassion, but there was none,
    for comforters, but found none.
Instead, they put gall in my food;
    for my thirst they gave me vinegar (Ps 69:21-22).

Similarly, the detail about the soldiers' dividing Jesus' clothes (15:24) recalls the agony of the innocent one in Psalm 22:

They stare at me and gloat;
    they divide my garments among them;
    for my clothing they cast lots (Ps 22:18b-19).

The passers-by who shake their heads at Jesus (15:29), along with their mocking taunts to "save yourself" (15:30), also recall Psalm 22:

All who see me mock me;
    they curl their lips and jeer;
    they shake their heads at me (Ps 22:8).

The gesture of head-wagging also echoes the mockery of Jerusalem in the Book of Lamentations:

All who pass by
    clap their hands at you;
They hiss and wag their heads (Lam 2:15).

Mark is clearly summoning up a long biblical tradition in which the servants of God are mocked. He interweaves scriptural references into his narrative as a way of communicating the meaning of Jesus' death.

In this context, it is significant that Mark speaks of the title "the king of the Jews" as an "inscription" on Jesus' cross (15:26). It was common Jewish idiom to speak of Scripture as "what is written" or "what is inscribed." Mark thus suggests that the mockery of Jesus is, in its own right, a "Scripture." He sees Jesus' way of the cross as part of the long tradition of righteous prophets and psalmists who suffered for their zeal for God.

When Mark notes that "With him they crucified two revolutionaries, one on his right and one on his left" (15:27), his phrasing reminds the reader that James and John had once asked to be in those positions (10:37). They thought that being on Jesus' right and left would be places of glory. Mark uses the same phrasing here to reveal to his audience the irony of their request. He shows that

unwittingly they had asked to be placed in the tradition of suffering servants.

Mark shows Jesus being taunted by everyone present: the passers-by (15:30), the chief priests (15:31), and even those crucified with him (15:32). Mark shapes their taunts to underscore the irony of Jesus' plight. The passers-by repeat the earlier false testimony (14:57-58) that Jesus said he "would destroy the Temple and rebuild it in three days" (15:29). Both they and the chief priests ironically suggest that he should "save" himself by "coming down from the cross" (15:30, 32). Mark chooses language that reminds his audience that Jesus has said the opposite: "Whoever wishes to come after me must deny himself, take up his cross, and follow me. For whoever wishes to save his life will lose it, but whoever loses his life for my sake and that of the gospel will save it" (8:34-35). The ultimate irony of Mark's narrative lies in the way he shows that in spite of the appearances of death and defeat, Jesus is accomplishing what he set out to do.

15:33-40 Death

Mark's account of Jesus' death gives details that suggest Creation in the process of being reversed. Light is created at the beginning of Genesis 1; Jesus' death brings darkness (15:33). The loss of light also echoes Jesus' description of the great tribulation, when "the sun will be darkened" (13:24).

Mark next says that Jesus cried out to God (15:34). Significantly, Mark uses Aramaic for the fourth time in the Gospel. The other three times are the raising up of the little girl from death (5:41), the healing of the deaf-mute (7:34), and Jesus' anguished cry to his Father in Gethsemane (14:36)—all key turning points in Mark's Gospel. The words here constitute the opening of Psalm 22, and their significance increases if one knows the whole psalm. It is a psalm in which the speaker begins in despair and moves to an encounter with death, but then is rescued by God, and concludes with thanksgiving and praise. If one knows the whole structure, then the opening verse recalls not only the speaker's initial agony but also his eventual rescue and restoration.

Mark goes on to say that the bystanders are confused by the Aramaic word for "my God" *(Eloi)* and think that Jesus is calling Elijah (15:35). It is worth noting that this is the third time the bystanders have had a place in Mark's account. Each reference indicates a different attitude toward Jesus. The first reference is to Simon of Cyrene, who is forced to help carry the cross (15:21). The second is to the bystanders who revile and taunt Jesus (15:29). In this third reference, the bystanders are simply confused. Their confusion of the word for God with that for Elijah recalls earlier places in Mark's narrative where people confused Jesus' identity with that of Elijah (6:15; 8:28). By repeating the confusion here, Mark suggests that confusion about Jesus' identity remained right up to the end. The episode also serves to clarify the kinship and distinction between Jesus and Elijah. Mark stresses that while Jesus may be like Elijah in many ways, they are not the same.

The next verse repeats the detail, already given in verse 23, of the sour wine offered to Jesus to drink. It is a detail that echoes, as we have noted before, the plight of God's servant in Psalm 69:22. Here this detail is combined with a taunt: "Wait, let us see if Elijah comes to take him down" (15:36). Again the mockery echoes that of the just one in the Wisdom of Solomon:

> Let us see whether his words be true;
> let us find out what will happen to him.
> For if the just one be the son of God, he will
> defend him
> and deliver him from the hand of his foes (Wis 2:17-18).

The precise words that Mark uses to describe the moment of Jesus' death are significant: "Then Jesus, releasing a loud voice, breathed out"* (15:37). This literal translation is not as idiomatic as the conventional one, but it serves to highlight Mark's ultimate use of the theme of *release*. When Jesus cures Simon's mother-in-law, Mark says that "the fever *released** her" (1:31b). When Jesus forgives the paralytic, he says, "Your sins are *released*" (2:5). When Jesus heals the deaf-mute, he says in Aramaic, "Be *released*!" (7:34). And we have just seen how Mark shows Pilate ironically releasing a murderous rebel, but not Jesus, from death (15:6, 9, 15). So it is dramatically effective that Mark uses the verb again here, suggesting that Jesus' final breath is freeing.

The splitting of the sanctuary veil (15:38) must be seen in this context. (The translation "torn" is

misleading.) The word that Mark uses for "split"* here is an unusual one. He has used it once before in his Gospel, when he described the heavens opening up at the moment of Jesus' baptism (1:10). By repeating it here, Mark suggests that a similar event is taking place. In his death, Jesus is opening up the heavens.

This interpretation is strengthened by two details. First, the phrase idiomatically translated here as "top to bottom" is literally "from above to below"*—a wording suggestive of God's creation of the dome of the sky to separate the waters "above" and "below" in Genesis 1:6-8. Second, the unusual word for "split"* is also used in a significant place in the Septuagint (the Greek translation of the Hebrew Bible that the evangelists followed). It appears in a prayer of Isaiah that asks God to split the heavens and come down and take back his sanctuary from Israel's enemies who have trampled it (Isa 63:18–64:1). If we put these details together, we see that Mark's choice of wording suggests that through his death, Jesus is opening up the sacred place of God's dwelling. He is making it accessible.

By immediately following the split veil with the centurion's proclamation of faith in Jesus as "the son of God" (15:39), Mark confirms this understanding. He is suggesting that even the Roman soldier—someone disposed to pollute the Temple with false gods—has come to see the divine image in Jesus' humanity. In his death, Jesus has opened up the heavens even to the Romans.

15:40-41 The watchful women

Before he presents the passion narrative, Mark gives the last word of Jesus to his disciples as "Watch!" (13:37). Mark then shows how Jesus' disciples, particularly his three key disciples, fail to do this (14:32-42). Here Mark introduces a balancing trio of women who do what Jesus has asked. At the same time that Mark shows that all the men have fled (14:50), he also shows that there were women who did not flee but were "seeing* from a distance" (15:40). The verb that Mark uses for "seeing" here is one that implies spiritual insight. The watchful "seeing" of these women stands in contrast to the betrayal by Judas, the denial of Jesus by Peter, and the flight of the other disciples. The women are not labeled "disciples," but Mark describes them acting in the way Jesus has asked his disciples to do. Mark also tells us that they had "followed" Jesus in Galilee and "ministered to him" (15:41a). Mark names three but says there were also many others (15:41b).

The three names that Mark gives are vaguely identified. The first is Mary Magdalene, known in all the Gospels as the first witness to Jesus' resurrection, but not yet called that here. (The idea that she was a "sinful woman" is not in Mark.) The last is Salome, about whom we know nothing. We do know that "Salome" was the name of the daughter of Herodias, who danced for the head of John the Baptist, but in Mark's account of that event, her name is not given (6:17-29). Did Mark assume that his audience knew her name and intended them to infer that she reappears here transformed? The middle woman, described only as "the mother of the younger James and of Joses," is presumably (on the basis of 6:3) the mother of Jesus. It is striking that Mark does not single her out; he treats these women as a generic group. Yet Mark suggests that this generic group of women, in their "following" and "ministering" and, above all, in their watchful "seeing," act in the ways to which Jesus has called all his disciples.

15:42-47 Burial

Mark loads every detail of the burial scene with significance. First, he tells us that "it was the day of preparation, the day before the Sabbath" (15:42). This is usually understood as just a simple reporting of fact. But given Mark's tendency to emphasize symbolic detail, one might surmise that he wants his readers to consider that the burial of Jesus was "a day of preparation" for his resurrection. The "preparation" theme of chapter 14 is being brought to a climax.

Joseph of Arimathea (15:43) is another disciple hitherto unknown in the Gospel, like the anonymous woman and man at the beginning of chapter 14 (14:3-16). He, like they, appears in the narrative suddenly, just as he is needed. Strikingly, he is described as a member of the council that has just condemned Jesus. His action in asking for the body of Jesus (15:43) suggests a transformation in his understanding of Jesus, just as much as the centurion's proclamation (15:39). Together, the Roman centurion and the Jewish member of the Sanhedrin reverse the judgments of the trials against Jesus.

Mark also characterizes Joseph by saying that he was "awaiting the kingdom of God" (15:43). It

is the seventh time that the phrase "kingdom of God" has appeared in Mark's Gospel. The first time is in the preaching of Jesus (1:15). The second, third, and fourth times occur in the chapter containing the seed parables (4:11, 26, 30). The fifth time is when Jesus says approvingly to the scribe, "You are not far from the kingdom of God" (12:34). The sixth time is at the Last Supper, when Jesus says he will "not drink again the fruit of the vine until the day when I drink it new in the kingdom of God" (14:25). "The kingdom of God," in other words, is an important theme throughout the Gospel. When Mark says that Joseph was "awaiting" it, he also picks up on the themes of "watching" and "preparation." Through showing his action of seeking to honor Jesus in death, Mark implies that Joseph now links Jesus with the kingdom.

Pilate's response—wanting to make sure that Jesus was really dead (15:44-45)—confirms the characterization of Pilate that Mark has already given. By means of this detail, Mark again suggests the non-spiritual level on which Pilate exists. In view of Mark's hints of resurrection to come, it is also ironic.

The linen cloth in which Joseph buries Jesus (15:46) is significant because of the way it recalls the young disciple who left his linen cloth behind when he fled the scene of Jesus' arrest (14:51). The reappearance of a "linen cloth" is suggestive of a restoration. The wrapping of Jesus here in a linen cloth reverses that moment of fear and flight. There is also an echo here of the transformed demoniac, who, after his cure by Jesus, is seen "sitting there clothed and in his right mind" (5:15). That man had "lived among the tombs" (5:5) until his encounter with Jesus changed him. The echo of his story, just as Jesus is being laid in a tomb (15:46), is thus something that gives hope.

Further hope appears in the final detail of the two Marys "watching" where Jesus was laid (15:47). Just as Mark speaks of women "watching" or "seeing"* Jesus' crucifixion, so here he describes women again "watching" where Jesus was buried. Watchful women enclose Mark's narrative of Jesus' burial. Mark says that Joseph "rolled a stone" against the "entrance" or "gate"* to the tomb (15:47). The details together recall Jesus' parable of the man who leaves home and "orders the gatekeeper to be on the watch" (13:34). The two Marys here function as gatekeepers, keeping watch for the lord's return.

Summary of the passion narrative, Part III (15:6-47)

Mark's narrative of Jesus' death is carefully crafted. First of all, Mark weaves his narrative out of echoes and patterns of the Hebrew Bible, telling Jesus' story in the light of them. Second, he picks up earlier themes within his own Gospel, repeating them and making their significance more clear. Third and most important, he constructs a structure of dramatic irony, so that what seems to be leading to Jesus' total doom is in fact moving toward his resurrection.

Mark's use of the Hebrew Bible. The details of Mark's narrative are woven out of numerous images in the Hebrew Bible of "the just one" who is persecuted by powerful and obtuse figures of the world because they do not grasp his identity as God's servant. The primary sources here are Isaiah's "Suffering Servant," sent "like a lamb to the slaughter" by the obtuse kings of the world; the "just one "in the Wisdom of Solomon put to death by "the wicked" because he "boasts that God is his Father"; and the persecuted just one in Psalm 22 who is brought to the point of death and despair before he cries out to God and is rescued. The first two sources provide some of the details for Mark's account of the trial by Pilate and the mockery of the Roman soldiers. Along with Psalm 22, they also provide background for the taunts of Jesus on the cross. Psalm 69 adds the detail of the sour wine given to Jesus in his thirst. All of them offer a pattern or structure that Mark wants his readers to find relevant and illuminating. It is the pattern of God's servant, who appears by the world to be doomed but who in the end is exalted by God. It is this structure of dramatic irony that Mark adopts for his narrative.

Mark's repeating themes. Again and again Mark repeats words or images that recall an earlier place in his Gospel. In each case he uses the echo to give an extra dimension to the present scene, sometimes making it fuller and sometimes pointing up its irony.

When he describes Jesus being mocked by the Roman soldiers, for example, he shows them kneeling before Jesus (15:19). It is a detail that ironically summons up earlier moments in the Gospel when people knelt before Jesus in awe (1:40; 3:11; 5:33).

When Mark tells of someone who is forced to carry Jesus' cross, he notes that he was called "Simon," thus reminding his readers of Simon the leper, who welcomed Jesus into his home (14:3), and Simon Peter, who has just denied him (14:66-72). The echoes intensify the irony of Simon Peter's betrayal.

When Mark describes the crucifixion of Jesus, he notes that the Romans crucified two revolutionaries with him, "one on his right hand and one on his left" (15:27). By his phrasing he ironically recalls the request of James and John for just those positions (10:37).

When Mark quotes Jesus' final death cry, he notes that some thought he was calling Elijah (15:34-35), thus repeating earlier stories of how people were confused about Jesus' identity (6:15; 8:28). The repetition underscores Mark's theme of Jesus' mistaken identity.

When Mark describes Joseph of Arimathea "awaiting the kingdom of God" (15:43), he recalls six other mentions of the kingdom (1:15; 4:11, 26, 30; 12:34; 14:25). He thus hints that the kingdom may now be imminent.

When Mark speaks of Joseph wrapping Jesus in a "linen cloth" (15:46), he summons up the stories of the young man who fled (14:51) and the man who had lived "among the tombs" (5:5), whom Jesus transformed (5:15). The echoes provide hope for Jesus' own restoration and transformation.

When Mark uses the verb "release"* to describe Jesus' death (15:37), he chooses a word that he has associated again and again with Jesus' acts of freeing people from sin and from disease (1:31; 2:5; 7:34). He has also placed it as an ironic refrain in Pilate's mouth, in the context of whether or not he should set Jesus free (15:6, 9, 15). By using it as a description of Jesus' last breath, Mark signals that Jesus' death is a freeing act.

Similarly, by using the same words for "splitting open"* the sanctuary veil (15:38) that he has used to describe the "splitting open" of the heavens at Jesus' baptism (1:10), Mark suggests that Jesus' death is not an end but a beginning.

Mark's dramatic irony. Mark tells the story of Jesus' death and burial in such a way that he alerts the reader to the fact that the plot is really moving in the opposite direction than it appears. He does this both by his echoes of the patterns in the Hebrew Bible and by his use of repeating themes.

Mark also hints at a new beginning by the way he frames the narrative of Jesus' burial with descriptions of women who follow Jesus' instruction to "watch." They remind his readers of Jesus' story of the lord who returns to his house.

Summary of the passion narrative, Parts I, II, and III (14:1–15:47)

Part I of Mark's passion narrative focuses on preparations of various kinds. They are ambiguously for both death and life. Part II focuses on Jesus' identity and how he is sentenced because he is mistakenly identified in both his trials. Part III focuses on the dramatic irony of a plot that may seem to be leading to death but is in fact leading to new life.

A NEW BEGINNING: THE RESURRECTION OF JESUS AND THE REVELATION OF WISDOM

Mark 16:1-8

16:1 The women

The same three women who watched Jesus' death (15:40) reappear. Like the anonymous woman at the beginning of chapter 14, they come to anoint the body of Jesus. Mark has shaped his narrative to show that at either end of the passion narrative, there are women coming to anoint Jesus. In Mark's account, their actions claim Jesus as "messiah"—that is, as God's anointed.

16:1-2 The time

Mark says the women came "when the Sabbath was over." In Jewish liturgy, a distinction is made between Sabbath time and "ordinary time." The Sabbath is a time set aside to celebrate God and to reflect his kingdom. The other days are time to journey towards this perfect state of being. The Sabbath liturgy concludes with spices to "hallow" and "sweeten" the ordinary days of the week. Mark may have had this concluding prayer in mind when he describes the women bringing spices at the end of the Sabbath. On the literal level, the spices are for burial; on the symbolic level, they may also signify the transition to "ordinary time."

Mark also says they came "very early, when the sun had risen, on the first day of the week." Each phrase emphasizes, in a different way, a new beginning.

16:3-4 The stone

The "stone" at "the entrance to the tomb" suggests the sealing off of death from life. When the

women say to one another, "Who will roll back the stone for us?" Mark shows their willingness to accept their vulnerability along with their trust that God will provide.

16:5 The young man

The young man "clothed in a white robe" is an angelic figure. The whiteness of his clothing summons to mind the transfiguration of Jesus (9:3), an event that Mark clearly constructed as a foreshadowing of Jesus' resurrection. He also resembles the young man who fled the garden when Jesus was arrested, leaving his linen cloth behind him. The fact that this young man is seen "sitting" also recalls the transformed demoniac, whom the townsfolk found "sitting there clothed and in his right mind" (5:35). Mark's detail about his being "on the right side" further recalls Jesus' proclamation to the high priest that he would "see the son of man seated at the right hand of the Power" (14:62). By means of all these echoes, Mark suggests that this young man represents a transformed life.

16:6 The young man's news

The words that Mark quotes the young man as saying form the heart of his Gospel: "You seek Jesus of Nazareth, the crucified. He has been raised; he is not here." The key words are "crucified" and "raised." Throughout his Gospel, Mark has stressed the necessary connection between Jesus and the cross, and between Jesus and resurrection. In Mark's narrative, it is the paradoxical union of those two seemingly contradictory elements that form his identity. Mark shows that both the high priest and Pilate mistake his being called "messiah" as a sign that he sought power. Mark also shows that both mistook his death as the ending of his power. The phrasing here suggests a paradoxical balance: Jesus is both the suffering, crucified one and the one whom God's power has raised up.

16:7a The commissioning of the women

Mark says that the young man told the women to "go forth."* (The verb is stronger than merely "go.") Mark has shown the women acting all along as disciples. By this act of commissioning, Mark suggests that the women are also sent forth as apostles. They are, moreover, sent forth to the male disciples, even to the head disciple, Peter. The women are sent forth to witness to the men.

What are the implications of the role of men and women in Mark's Gospel? Many readers have observed that Mark shows Jesus' male disciples to be obtuse and foolish. Few seem to have noticed that Mark simultaneously shows that Jesus has female disciples who are insightful and wise. If the Gospel is read on a literal, historical level, it is difficult to know what to make of this. But if the Gospel is read on a symbolic level and in the light of the Wisdom traditions, Mark's purpose becomes clear. We have suggested before the extent to which Mark presents Jesus as God's Wisdom made flesh. In the light of the Wisdom writings, Mark characterizes Jesus as a nurturing, healing, compassionate, and maternal figure, always intent on giving and restoring life. Following the same traditions, Mark sets up a typical contrast in his Gospel between the wise and the foolish. There is a creative logic in his choosing women to be like Woman Wisdom, while their male counterparts act out the part of the foolish. Mark also makes the women's raised status and new ministry a symbol of the new creation that Jesus brings into being.

16:7b The message

Mark indicates that the message the women are sent forth to repeat is not about Jesus' glory but about his ministry. It repeats exactly what Mark has shown Jesus saying on the eve of his crucifixion: "But after I have been raised up, I shall go before you to Galilee" (14:28). It confirms his ongoing life: "there you will see him, as he told you." It sends the disciples back to where the Gospel first began. It suggests a new beginning.

16:8 The revelation to the women

The translation given above is conventional, but unfortunately it is badly misleading. The word translated "bewilderment" is *ekstasis* in Greek. Even someone who has never read Greek can see that its English counterpart is "ecstasy."*

The word "ecstasy" literally means "out of [a normal] state [of being]." In the Septuagint (the Greek translation of the Hebrew Bible that the evangelists followed), the word appears at two key moments in the book of Genesis. When God casts Adam into a "deep sleep" or "trance" while he is creating both man and woman (2:21), the word for "trance" is *ekstasis*. Similarly, when God casts Abraham into a "deep sleep" or "trance"

while he is making the covenant with him (Gen 15:12), the word for "trance" is *ekstasis*. In both instances, the word conveys the action of God creating something new. It also implies a human being undergoing some shock of transition, a human being experiencing a transformation of consciousness.

Mark uses the word "ecstasy" more than once in his Gospel. When he wants to describe the state of the crowd that witnessed the rising up of the paralytic, he says, "They were all ecstatic and glorified God, saying, 'We have never seen anything like this'" (2:12b). When he wants to describe the changed condition of those who have witnessed Jesus' raising up of Jairus's daughter, he says that "They were out of their minds with ecstasy*" (5:42).

Mark also uses a related word to describe Jesus himself. When he wants to describe how "those close to" Jesus thought he was crazy for mingling so closely with the crowds, he says that they thought he was "out of [his] mind" (3:21).

All these earlier uses of the word support its meaning here. The women are, like Jesus, out of their minds at what they have learned from the angel. And like those who witnessed a paralytic rise up from his mat and a child brought back to life, they are in a state of ecstasy at the realization of Jesus' resurrection. The word conveys that they are undergoing some shock of transition. They are experiencing a transformation of consciousness.

It is a sign of this transformed consciousness that "they went out and fled from the tomb." The foolish (male) disciples fled from Jesus. The wise women follow the example of Jesus and flee from the tomb.

"They said nothing to anyone" because they were in a "trance"—like Adam, like Abraham. By his choice of words, Mark suggests that they were in a state of shock, undergoing a transforming experience. Their silence is more, not less, than words.

They are not silent because "they were afraid." This translation is again conventional but unfortunate. Again, Mark has used the word given here twice before in his Gospel—first, to describe the disciples' reaction to Jesus' stilling the storm (4:41), and second, to describe their response to the transfiguration of Jesus (9:6). The New American Bible (which is the translation given above) translates the first instance as "filled with great awe" and the second as "terrified." There is no justification for "terrified" because the context is Peter's exclamation that "It is good that we are here!" (9:5). Both contexts suggest the meaning of awe. The context here of "ecstasy" also supports a translation of "awe."

If we put all these pieces together, we would translate Mark's ending as follows:

> And going out, they fled the tomb, for trembling and ecstasy* possessed them, and they said nothing to anyone because they were filled with awe.*

Such a translation would be a fitting conclusion to a Gospel that presents Jesus as Wisdom and the women as faithful disciples of Wisdom/ Jesus. Throughout his Gospel, Mark has shown that the women disciples of Jesus not only follow after him but follow his example in serving others. Mark has also shown them to be "watchful," which is the way of Wisdom. He thus prepares his readers for an ending in which they begin to comprehend the revelation that Jesus/Wisdom cannot die but is still alive and in their midst. By showing them overcome by awe, Mark is dramatizing the theme of all the Wisdom writings that "Fear of the LORD is the beginning of Wisdom" (Prov 1:7; 9:10; Sir 1:12, 16; Ps 111:10). That fear is not fright but overwhelmed reverence before the divine mystery.

SUMMARY OF THE DESIGN OF MARK'S GOSPEL

Doublets

We suggested earlier that the two-stage healing of the blind man in 8:22-26 is a key to the theological design of Mark's Gospel. That is to say, Mark seems to have designed his Gospel in two parts, with the Transfiguration in the middle. In the first part (chs. 1–8), the reader is like the blind man who at first only sees "people looking like trees" (8:24). In the second part (chs. 9–16), Mark repeats many of the same images, events, and themes, and the reader now sees them more plainly.

The Transfiguration is pivotal because it reveals Jesus' inner glory. We have noted before that Peter's desire to "make three tents" or "booths"* (9:5) suggests the feast of Booths or Succoth, a

harvest feast celebrating the end time of God's kingdom. The Markan text says that Jesus "metamorphosed"* before his disciples (9:2), that is, he changed form entirely. Jesus' "dazzling white" garments (9:3) suggest his relationship to other significant figures (for example, Moses and Elijah) who, in popular nonbiblical writing of the time, are imagined ascending to the heavens clothed like angels. In this literary imagination, resurrection and ascension are similar and intertwined events. Thus to a Jewish audience of the time, this scene of Jesus' total transformation and gleaming garments in an end-time setting would have signified his ascension or resurrection from death to a heavenly state. Mark has not placed the scene of Jesus' resurrection at the end of his Gospel but here in the middle, where it illuminates both halves of his Gospel.

The most crucial difference between the two halves lies in Mark's presentation of the identity of Jesus. In the first part, Jesus reflects God's power in miracles of exorcism and healing, stilling the sea and walking on water, and the multiplication of bread. In the second part, Jesus appears vulnerable to the various plottings against him, and he speaks of dispossession, poverty, and death. In the first part, Jesus calls his disciples to be "fishers" on a grand scale (1:17), to preach and cast out demons (3:14-15; 6:12-13a), and to cure the sick (6:13b). But his instructions to them begin to shift radically at the end of chapter 8 when he says, "Whoever wishes to come after me must deny himself, take up his cross, and follow me" (8:34).

The second part of Mark's Gospel leads inexorably to Jesus' taking up his own cross. And Mark's Gospel is often referred to as the one in which "the cross" is key. But by placing the Transfiguration at the very center of his narrative, Mark signals that the cross is only one part of the story. The whole story involves *cross plus Transfiguration*. In fact, Mark shows that Jesus, in his key statements about the cross, indicates that the cross is *the way* to Transfiguration: "For whoever wishes to save his life will lose it, but whoever loses his life for my sake and that of the gospel will save it" (8:35). The cross is not about suffering in itself or suffering for its own sake. The cross symbolizes how God will transform our suffering. God's creative power to transform or transfigure us from suffering humanity into persons of radiant joy is the key to Mark's theology.

In the first part of his Gospel, Mark shows Jesus reaching out to the most alienated and suffering members of his community—those known to be sinners; those possessed by unclean spirits that deprive them of God's holy spirit; those alienated by leprosy or withered limbs; those who are paralyzed; and women of all kinds and ages who, for various reasons, are kept on the fringes of worship. He reaches out in order to "raise them up," to transform their lives. In the second part of his Gospel, Mark shows Jesus himself to be the one who is alienated and suffering, and then Mark tells us Jesus is also "raised up," transfigured (as he has already shown us) by the will of God.

In the first part of his Gospel, Mark shows Jesus as a teacher of Wisdom, speaking in aphorisms and parables or riddles. Yet at the end of chapter 4, as we have seen, Mark indicates that Jesus himself is a living parable or riddle, pointing to what God is like. In the second part of his Gospel, Mark develops this idea, showing that Jesus in suffering, even more than in power, reveals what God is like. Mark indicates this through the image of the split veil of the sanctuary (15:38), suggesting that Jesus, in his dying, has opened up access to God's dwelling. He confirms it in the cry of the centurion, "Truly this was the son of God" (15:39). In that cry Mark suggests how, in the dying Jesus, even a Roman soldier came to perceive God's image. Through that perception, Mark challenges his readers to understand how God is reflected even in suffering and dying humanity. Jesus as "son of man" represents us all; Jesus as "son of God" represents us all as made in God's image.

There is a mystery here not easily articulated. The first part of Mark's Gospel is filled with the miraculous; the second part is filled with mystery. Having miraculous powers is what we more readily associate with being God's image. It is difficult to see God's image in suffering and death. But throughout the second part of his Gospel, Mark indicates how Jesus shows and teaches that God reverses our natural expectations and gives us a "second sight," as it were, by which conventional human wisdom is turned upside down.

For example, Jesus surprises those who think that entering God's kingdom requires sophisticated learning, by saying that "whoever does not accept the kingdom of God like a child will not enter it" (10:15). He confounds the normal prizing of wealth by instructing the good, rich man to "Go sell what you have" (10:21). He overturns the normal ambitions for power by instructing his disciples clearly that they are not to "lord it over" others (10:42), but rather, "whoever wishes to be great among you will be your servant; whoever wishes to be first among you will be the slave of all" (10:43-44).

Above all, Jesus rebukes those who think that God's anointed ("messiah") should be immune from suffering and death. In chapter 8, he tells Peter explicitly that this way of thinking is "human-minded" and not "God-minded" (8:33). Then in chapters 14–15, Mark shows Jesus undergoing human suffering and death and somehow revealing God in that very process.

Mark shows that Jesus reveals God even in the process of dying because, at the same time that he shows Jesus being betrayed to his death, he indicates how God will transform that death. In chapter 14, Mark hints at this transformation by the way he describes the anointing of Jesus and by the way he links it to Jesus' last meal, which in turn foreshadows the meal of the Eucharist, itself a meal of transformation.

In chapter 16, Mark indicates the transformation of death through the whole episode of the women coming to the tomb. Through the repeated images of a new day (16:2), he projects a new beginning. Through the images of the stone rolled away (16:4) and the women fleeing from the tomb (16:8), he suggests an escape from death. Through the message of the young man in white (16:6-7), he confirms Jesus' own prediction (14:28) that he would be raised up and return to Galilee. Through his description of the women's silent, awed, ecstatic trance (16:8), he indicates their confrontation with the unexpected, overwhelming power of God to transform death itself into ongoing life.

Triad

Another way of seeing Mark's design is to see the whole Gospel arranged as a triad. First of all, the reader should take note that there are three beginnings. The first is the "beginning" of verse 1, suggesting the very opening of Genesis and the idea of God creating "in Wisdom." The second is the return to "the beginning of Creation" in Mark 10:6, which follows upon the transfiguration and introduces Jesus' radical teachings on poverty, powerlessness, and childlikeness. The third is in chapter 16 with its images of a new day and its message of Jesus' return, at what looks like the end, to the beginning of his ministry in Galilee.

From another perspective, there are three sections that each end in a scene of resurrection. The first section, chapters 1–5, concludes with the raising up of the daughter of the synagogue leader Jairus and the image of the witnesses "beside themselves with ecstasy" (5:42). The second section, chapters 6–9:8, concludes with the scene in which Jesus appears before his disciples transfigured in glory. Here Jesus is pictured in conversation with the great prophets Moses and Elijah, who are also portrayed in a transfigured state. In this scene, the three chief disciples are briefly transfigured too, as Peter seeks to build three harvest "tents" or booths to celebrate the end time, and all three are overcome with awe (9:6). The final section runs from 9:9, when Jesus and his disciples descend the mountain, to 16:8. In 16:6 the three women who have been watching learn that Jesus "has been raised," and transfigured by their new understanding, they are overcome with ecstasy and awe.

In all of these configurations, doublet and triad, the re-creative, transfiguring power of God's Wisdom is at the center.

OTHER ENDINGS BY OTHER AUTHORS

Some time after Mark completed his Gospel, three anonymous authors offered other endings to it. The modern reader may well wonder how anyone had capacity, the desire, or the audacity to do such a thing. They had the capacity because texts were not guarded by copyright laws until fairly recent times. They had the desire because the conventional translation of the last verse of Mark's Gospel made it appear to end in failure. They had the audacity because they regarded themselves as guardians of God's word.

Over the centuries, most commentaries have accepted the idea that the women disobeyed the angel's message because they were shaking with fright. Such a conclusion ignores, of course, the linguistic evidence that Mark uses some form of the word *ekstasis* three times in his Gospel, each time to convey the elevated feelings of those who have witnessed a miracle. It ignores as well the significant use of the word *ekstasis* in the Septuagint to indicate a trance or shift in consciousness induced by God.

It also ignores the linguistic evidence of Mark's use of "awe" to indicate key moments of change in Jesus' disciples—first, to describe their response to Jesus' power to still a violent sea (4:41) and then to describe their response to his transfigured glory (9:6). Its use here forms a typical Markan triad, and its meaning here is illumined by its function in the Transfiguration.

Such a conclusion also ignores the role of women throughout the Gospel of Mark: how they are repeatedly "raised up" by Jesus in the first part of the Gospel and how, in the second part, they fulfill the role of true disciples by following, ministering, and "watching," as Jesus has asked. It ignores Mark's use of the Wisdom traditions, where wise people are always contrasted with foolish ones and where Wisdom is portrayed as a woman. Above all, such a conclusion ignores the overall structure of the Gospel, in which God reverses the expected and re-creates all things. If one grasps such a structure, one is open to an ending in which those thought least likely are the ones transformed into witnesses.

It is possible (although not provable) that over the centuries, male leaders in the church have been alarmed at the idea of how a translation using the language of "ecstasy" and "awe" might elevate the role of women. It is possible that male commentators have had a mental block against seeing that while the male disciples in Mark's Gospel are made to look foolish, the female disciples are shown to be wise and faithful witnesses to Jesus' resurrection.

Whatever the cause, the three alternative endings to Mark's Gospel appear in manuscripts known to be faulty. Their dates suggest a limited use by the church. The "Shorter Ending" is dated somewhere between the seventh and ninth centuries. The third ending (called "The Freer Ending" because it is preserved in the Freer Gallery in Washington, D.C.) is not mentioned before Jerome in the fourth century.

The "Longer Ending" is dated from the second century because it was incorporated into a work of the time (Tatian's *Diatessaron)*, but it is not mentioned by either Clement or Origen, significant church fathers of the third and fourth centuries. Tatian's *Diatessaron* was deemed heretical because of its attempt to harmonize all four Gospels. The "Longer Ending" was not made part of the official biblical canon until the Council of Trent in the sixteenth century. It is strange that it was canonized, even though it once formed part of a heretical work, particularly since the ending itself is guilty of trying to blend together different Gospel passages. Even stranger is the fact that although modern scholarship agrees it was not authored by Mark, it is still being printed in most Christian Bibles and used by the Catholic Church as the gospel on the Feast of Saint Mark!

Again the question arises as to why the Council made its decision and why the church has continued to honor it. Again the answer seems to lie in the way Mark's original ending has been translated and understood as signifying the women's failure to witness. Were the ending grasped as a description of the women's stunned awe at the realization of Jesus' resurrection, another ending would not be sought.

The Council perhaps justified its choice of this "Longer Ending" because it makes use of passages from Luke and Matthew. It does not seem to have considered, however, whether these borrowings do justice to the Gospels they are taken from or to the rest of the Gospel of Mark. It is important to look at the "Longer Ending" in detail.

THE LONGER ENDING

16:9-11 The appearance to Mary Magdalene

Some commentators have suggested that this verse rehabilitates Mary Magdalene as a witness because she is described here as giving the angel's message to Jesus' "companions." But the description of her as one who had been possessed by "seven demons" (a reference to Luke 8:2) is denigrating. Her speech here, moreover, is ineffective because "they did not believe" her. In the original Markan ending, as we have read it, Mary Magdalene is a witness to the resurrection and an apostle to the apostles. Here she is a former sinner whose words are not given credibility.

16:12-13 The appearance to two disciples

This is a vague reference to Luke's narrative of two disciples encountering the risen Jesus on the road to Emmaus (Luke 24:13-35). Omitted is Luke's development of this narrative into a eucharistic story in which the disciples recognize Jesus "in the breaking of the bread" (Luke 24:35). As it stands, the narrative here goes nowhere.

16:14-16 The commissioning of the Eleven

Jesus' injunction to "Go into the whole world and proclaim the gospel to every creature" comes from the ending of Matthew's Gospel (28:19). The insistence on baptism as the guarantee of salvation, however, is not in Matthew. And such a rigid distinction between the "saved" and the "condemned" is nowhere to be found in Mark.

16:17-18 "Signs will accompany those who believe"

The only two "signs" in the list that appear in the Gospels are the driving out of demons and the laying of hands on the sick. These are mentioned, however, not as "signs" but as ministries. The speaking "in new languages" is not in any of the Gospels, but in Acts and First Corinthians. The power to "tread on serpents" is mentioned in Luke (10:19), but not the power to pick them up. The power to "drink any deadly thing" without harm is nowhere in the New Testament. (And when these words have been taken literally, they have caused death.) In no Gospel does Jesus advocate the seeking of "signs." In fact, there are several places where Jesus rebukes the Pharisees for "seeking a sign" (Mark 8:11-12; Matt 12:38-39; Matt 16:1-4; Luke 11:16).

16:19-20 The ascension of Jesus

The description of Jesus "taken up into heaven" echoes the ending of Luke (24:51). In Luke, it is part of his way of ending the Gospel on a note of expectation. In the same passage, Luke shows Jesus telling his disciples to go to Jerusalem to await "power from on high" (24:49). In the "Longer Ending" there is no such waiting or expectation of the Spirit.

Instead, the author tidies things up by saying that the disciples "went forth and preached everywhere while the Lord worked with them."

Summary of the "Longer Ending"

The "Longer Ending" pieces together phrases from other Gospels without doing justice to the way they function in their original contexts. In respect to Mark, if one perceives Mark's Gospel in the terms of this commentary, then the "Longer Ending" appears not only unnecessary but offensive because it clashes with the rest of Mark's Gospel.

As a final reflection, you might want to consider all the ways in which this "Longer Ending" undermines Mark's theological point of view:

—How does it undermine the role of women in Mark's Gospel?

—How does the insistence that "whoever does not believe will be condemned" undermine Mark's focus on Jesus' outreach to sinners, his emphasis on forgiveness, his saying that "Whoever is not against us is for us" (9:40), and his emphasis on God's will and power to transform rather than to condemn?

—How does the emphasis here on "signs" undermine Mark's repeated suggestion that God's kingdom is accessible in ordinary ways?

—How does ending with Jesus' ascension into heaven conflict with Mark's emphasis on Jesus' return to Galilee?

—This ending seems to close off discipleship as a thing of the past instead of opening it up to the future. What effect does that have on you as a reader and potential disciple?

THE GOSPEL ACCORDING TO

LUKE

Michael F. Patella, O.S.B.

INTRODUCTION

The Gospel of Luke, the third Gospel in the New Testament canon, has a remarkable place in the study of Sacred Scripture, and this unique position does not stem solely from the fact that it is the only Gospel to have a second volume associated with it, namely, the Acts of the Apostles. Luke engenders a great deal of discussion on the level of New Testament formation, sensitivity to historical data, literary technique, and theological development. This commentary deals with these areas to a greater or lesser degree.

The Gospel message

Each Gospel relates a particular evangelist's theological interpretation of the kerygma, that is, the passion, death, and resurrection of Jesus. To do this, the Gospel writer takes events from Jesus' life as passed down from traditions and sources and composes a Gospel account. Under the inspiration of the Holy Spirit, an evangelist uses his composition to present his particular theology of redemption mediated through Christ's life. Details may or may not be accurate, but the truth of the Gospel goes beyond details. The central focus of this study, therefore, is the theological picture that Luke's Gospel paints of Jesus, his earthly ministry, and the early church.

Matthew, Mark, Luke, and John

Anyone reading the Gospels notices that there are stories within them that overlap, parallel, and seemingly copy each other. The reason for, and explanation of, this problem have been part of the church since the beginning. Scholars such as Origen and Augustine were among the first to develop theories on the formation of the Gospels. In the modern era, new theories have arisen that have continued the dialogue and discussion on the development of the New Testament.

The brevity of this commentary prevents any lengthy discussion of the sources Luke used in writing his Gospel; this question has an involved and complicated history. For simplicity's sake, our commentary notes the names of commonly held sources as well as the familiar vocabulary of biblical scholarship. Knowing the following terms will be most helpful:

- *Canon:* the official collection of books comprising the Bible.

- *Codex Sinaiticus* and *Codex Vaticanus:* two of the most dependable, extant New Testament manuscripts.

- Eschaton: the final times bringing God's eternal plan to fulfillment. The study and interpretation of the eschaton is called eschatology.

- *Evangelist:* the name given to the four Gospel writers: Matthew, Mark, Luke, and John.

- *Kerygma:* the proclamation of the passion, death, and resurrection of Christ that also describes how salvation comes through participation in the same passion, death, and resurrection.

- *Parallel:* a term used to describe a passage in one Gospel that has a like passage in another Gospel.

- *Q:* a hypothetical, oral source that contains material common to Matthew and Luke but not Mark.

- *Synoptics:* the Gospels of Matthew, Mark, and Luke, so named because they share so much of the same narrative line as well as the same material.

- *Textual witness:* early written documents containing all or part of the biblical canon.

Luke the evangelist

Not much is known about the evangelist Luke. The tradition says that he was both a physician and an artist from Syria who completed his Gospel between A.D. 80 and 90. Using Acts 20–28 as a guide, along with Colossians 4:14 and Philemon 1:24, many feel that he may have known Paul. Although it is impossible to prove these claims, the texts that Luke wrote indicate that he was a highly educated person, influential in the early church, aware of geography (outside Palestine anyway) and history, and very much attuned to the dynamic, direction, and development of Christianity.

Sensitivity to historical data

In addition to being considered a doctor and an artist, many have thought of Luke as a historian, because he gives greater attention to historical details than any other evangelist. For example, passages describing the birth of Jesus and the ministry of John the Baptist contain information on emperors, governors, and kings, and a good deal of it is close to accurate. Much of our information about Pontius Pilate comes from Luke. In large part, his information about the Herodian dynasty matches well with the writings of the ancient Jewish historian Flavius Josephus.

Literary technique

Luke is an economical writer. This evangelist avoids repetitions and superfluous information. He tells a story well, with attention given to rising action, climax, and denouement. His use of Greek is among the finest in the New Testament, and he is well-versed in Greco-Roman literary style. His prose has a nobility that has made this Gospel a favorite of many.

Theological development

Luke views the passion, death, and resurrection of Christ as the great salvific act that has affected the whole cosmos. The evangelist expresses this theology by presenting Jesus' earthly ministry as a battle between Christ and Satan. Christ's victory over evil comes with his death and resurrection. In Lukan theology, the death on the cross is actually a transfiguration into glory. Furthermore, by virtue of that death, the same transformative glory is promised to humanity, a concept that came to be known as *theosis*.

In this presentation, Luke relies on literary motifs to relay these key concepts. First, there is the motif of the diabolical force. Every good story needs an antagonist, and Luke elevates Satan to this position. Consequently, Christ's miracles and cures are more than kind deeds; they are attacks against the Evil One and his diabolical force. In other words, Christ is in a relentless pursuit of redeeming the world from Satan's clutches.

Second is the idea of the great reversal, a term used to describe the turn in fortune that will befall all between now and the *eschaton*, that is, the end times: the hungry now will have a banquet, while the rich go hungry; the humble will be exalted, and the exalted will be humbled.

Next, there is the schism motif. Christ will come to all, but some will heed his call to discipleship while others will not.

Finally, there is joy. The word appears more times in the Third Gospel than in any other New Testament work. In Lukan theology, for a world redeemed and transfigured by the blood of Christ, there can be no other Christian response than joy.

COMMENTARY

THE PROLOGUE

Luke 1:1-4

1:1-4 Address to Theophilus

The Gospel opens with a short prologue of a single periodic sentence, a style typical of ancient literature that often sets the tone and purpose of biographies and histories. Josephus and Polybius, for example, show similar introductions. Luke's use of this style often raises the question of whether he sees himself as writing a biography or a history. Opinions favoring one or the other abound. Perhaps the most we can say is that Luke is simply following the literary convention of the day as he writes his two-volume work. The Gospel, neither a biography nor a history, is an evangelical proclamation. A Gentile audience would expect such a prologue, and Luke is simply supplying it.

The identity of Theophilus is unknown. Possibilities range from his being a benefactor of the community, a church leader, or even a civil authority. Perhaps Theophilus is all three. On the other hand, using the name Theophilus (literally, "Beloved of God") universalizes the identity and allows every reader to be the addressee.

The prologue provides hints at the formation of the New Testament as well as the development of the early Christian community. What are the "events that have been fulfilled"? Who are the "eyewitnesses" and "ministers of the word"? Luke describes some of these events and personages within his two-volume work, particularly in the Acts of the Apostles, but how much of it is recoverable is difficult to answer. Of fascinating interest for source critics is Luke's explanation that he has investigated "everything accurately anew, to write it down in an orderly sequence." How many and varied were the initial documents before they saw their final editing at Luke's hand? Extant papyri, lectionaries, and targums certainly bespeak a Christian movement very much in ferment and development. Luke's project replaced the diverse gospel fragments floating around the Greco-Roman world. That this Gospel eventually became part of the New Testament canon attests to its nearly universal use over the course of the first two centuries.

THE INFANCY NARRATIVE

Luke 1:5–2:52

Only Matthew and Luke feature stories of the birth of Christ, although from two different perspectives. Luke centers his account on Mary, while Matthew focuses on Joseph. It is obvious that Matthew and Luke were not copying each other in forming their respective infancy narratives. Nonetheless, they do share some details. Both have an angel relaying the divine plan to the human participants—Joseph in Matthew, Mary in Luke. Both state that this child will be born of the house of David in Bethlehem, that his name will be Jesus, and that these events will occur while Herod the Great is king of Judea (37 B.C.–4 B.C.). Most importantly, despite the many variations in the two different accounts, the two agree on the essential point that Mary is pregnant, and there is no human father.

Luke's purpose for including the infancy narratives is to situate the whole Gospel within the story of God's divine plan. Luke also uses references and allusions to the Old Testament, especially prophetic figures. Furthermore, he has passages dealing with John the Baptist precede those of Jesus. This structure prepares the reader for an account that aims to show Jesus as the one long-promised to deliver humankind from sin and death. Luke's infancy narratives grab the attention of his Gentile audience, catechize them, and graft them to the community of Israel by setting the many references to political events and leaders of the day within the context of the Old Testament. As Simeon proclaims in his canticle (2:29-32), Jesus is "a light for revelation to the Gentiles, / and glory for [the] people Israel" (2:32). Furthermore, this glory will not come easily, for even Jesus' mother, Mary, will be pierced by a sword. Thus, the infancy narratives serve as an abbreviated version of the Gospel and Acts. In the Acts of the Apostles, Luke recounts how Peter, Paul, and the Gentiles receive the light of revelation, but only after hardship and pain. On the final page of Acts, Paul is living, preaching, and teaching in that most Gentile of cities, Rome.

1:5-25 Announcement of the birth of John the Baptist

Luke provides a broad context for Jesus' birth, employing both Old Testament prophecies and typologies. Zechariah and Elizabeth are described as being "advanced in years," and thus past the age of childbearing. The announcement of the Baptist's birth, therefore, is similar to the miraculous birth genre found with Abraham and Sarah (Gen 18:1-15), Manoah and his wife (Judg 13:2-25), and Elkanah and Hannah (1 Sam 1:1-23). In addition, both Zechariah and Elizabeth are of priestly stock, which means that their son John would one day be serving in the temple at Jerusalem. None of the evangelists, however, imply that John the Baptist ever took on this role.

As a priest, Zechariah would take his turn serving in the temple twice a year for a week at a time. This detail no doubt led to the tradition, dating from at least the sixth century, that Ein Karem, with its close proximity to Jerusalem, is the village of John's birth.

Angels are God's messengers and agents, and Luke mentions them twenty-five times in the Gospel. More than half of these occurrences fall within the first two chapters. The presence of an angel at the altar of incense (v. 11) underscores God's role in the events to follow. While in Matthew's Gospel the angel who appears to Joseph (1:20) remains unnamed, Luke specifies the identity of the heavenly messenger who comes to both Zechariah and Mary. The name Gabriel itself is a combination of two Hebrew terms, *Gabur* ("strong man," "warrior"), and *El* ("God"), therefore "Warrior of God." Gabriel has a role in the Old Testament. In the book of Daniel, this angel explains a vision to Daniel (8:17-26) while simultaneously giving Daniel understanding (9:22).

1:26-45 Announcement of the birth of Jesus and Mary's pregnancy

In Luke's chronology, Gabriel's announcement to Zechariah (1:8-20) precedes the one to Mary (1:26-38). Luke is setting the proper sequence of salvation history. If John is the precursor of Jesus in the ministry, he must also come first in the order of birth. In the sixth month of Elizabeth's pregnancy, Gabriel comes to Nazareth to deliver the news to Mary. Of course, Mary is extremely puzzled by this information, and when she expresses her doubt (v. 29), Gabriel encourages her.

When Zechariah doubts, however, he is made mute (vv. 18, 20).

Whatever point Luke is trying to make by this comparison of the two personages, it is not too clear. Perhaps it is another way to indicate the Baptist's subservience to Christ, a point reiterated by the baby's leaping in Elizabeth's womb upon hearing Mary's greeting. Or since the recovery of Zechariah's voice excites wonder in the people (vv. 60-64), Zechariah's muteness reflects Luke's attention to the details of storytelling; it advances the theme and the plot.

1:46-55 The Canticle of Mary

Traditionally called the *Magnificat* in the Western church where it is sung at Evening Prayer, the canticle has all the markings of an early hymn. There are four hymns in these opening narratives, of which this is the first. Grounded in a reference to Abraham and referencing other forebears, this song has a decidedly Jewish-Christian cast. The piece contains the reversal theme found in 1 Samuel 2:1-10, but it is modified. Those who oppress now will be overthrown, and the lowly will be exalted; those who are hungry now will have their fill, but those who are satiated now will be sent away.

1:57-80 The birth of John and the Canticle of Zechariah

Zechariah regains his speech upon acknowledging the divinely given name of his son. The hymn Zechariah sings, also known by its Latin name, the *Benedictus*, the Morning Prayer canticle in the Roman Office, clarifies John the Baptist's role in the sweep of salvation history. He is to "go before the Lord to prepare his ways" (v. 76). The beautiful, poetic images "daybreak from on high will visit us" (v. 78) and "to shine on those who sit in darkness and death's shadow" (v. 79) have their foundation in Isaiah 8:23–9:2. Luke concludes this section on John the Baptist with a brief note placing John in the desert, where the reader will encounter him again at the beginning of chapter 3. The evangelist now moves on to the birth of Christ.

2:1-7 The birth of Jesus

Scholars have often considered Luke's attention to historical detail as one indication of the evangelist's high level of education—not only for the fact that he includes such information but more for the way in which he uses it. Greco-Roman historians wrote their accounts to favor their patrons or the party in power, much the same way as a local chamber of commerce writes about its particular locale today. Thucydides, Tacitus, and Josephus all had a certain editorial slant to their works that supported those who supported them. Luke stands within this tradition, but with an important difference: his bias is toward showing the hand of the holy Spirit at work in both Jewish and Gentile events of the day. Jesus Christ is to be considered the fulfillment of both cultural worlds. We have observed an example of Jewish fulfillment in the stories of Zechariah, Elizabeth, and Mary. In these opening verses of chapter 2, we see the events in the pagan world also cooperating and foretelling the birth of the Messiah in Jesus Christ.

A difficulty enters into this section with the names and dates of the people mentioned. Although the Roman historian Suetonius states that there were registrations of Roman citizens in 28 B.C., 8 B.C., and A.D. 14 (*Divus Augustus* 27.5), there is no record, outside the New Testament, which states that Caesar Augustus (27 B.C.–A.D. 14) decreed the enrollment of the whole empire, that is, non-citizens, for taxation or any other purposes. There were local registrations within various provinces from time to time, and once such census occurred under the Roman legate Quirinius, but he was not made governor of Syria until A.D. 6, when he also took control of Judea at the banishment of Herod's son Archelaus. Since Luke attests that both John the Baptist and Jesus were born under Herod the Great (37 B.C.– 4 B.C.), most scholars concur that it would be impossible for these events to have occurred at a time when Caesar Augustus, Herod the Great, and Quirinius were all simultaneously in power.

For Luke's theological intention, however, the important point is that during the *Pax Romana*, when the Gentile world looked to Augustus Caesar as the prince of peace, Jesus comes into the world as the true Prince of Peace. In fulfillment of the Old Testament prophecies, which establish the messianic line through the house of David, Jesus, a descendant of David, is born in Bethlehem, the city of David. In order to make this point, Luke takes historical facts, such as the census, and reworks them to fit his theological purpose, just

as ancient historians altered details to suit the purposes of their patrons. For contemporary readers, such remolding of details may seem spurious or dishonest, but in the religious tradition, the truth that Jesus is the Savior of the world lies beyond the accuracy of some facts dealing with the reigns of various rulers.

The Greek term *phatnē* is translated as "manger" (v. 7) but can also mean "stable." The Greek *kataluma*, represented here as "inn," specifically means "lodging" or "guestroom," with space for a dining area (*kataluma* is the word employed in Luke 22:11). Reading together both *phatnē* and *kataluma*, we can see that Luke is probably describing the typical house of the day. These homes, built for extended families, had a living space on the upper floors with a stable at ground level. Both Matthew and Luke emphasize Jesus' Davidic lineage through his foster father, Joseph, as well as the fact that Jesus is born in Bethlehem, the city of David. It is reasonable to conclude that Joseph had family in Bethlehem and that he and Mary stayed with them. With all the relatives of the extended family eating and sleeping in the upper *kataluma*, the one private place for Mary to give birth would be in the *phatnē* or stable.

According to Roman, Greek, Coptic, Armenian, and other ancient traditions, the phrase "firstborn son" (v. 7) represents a title of honor. It does not imply that Mary had other children after Jesus.

2:8-20 Angels and shepherds

Once again Luke uses an angel to announce a birth, this time to the shepherds. Shepherds, although not social outcasts, were among the poorest people in the society. A group composed mostly of women and young children, they did not own land or sheep, and they worked for hire. Luke underscores Jesus' salvific role especially for the poor with this annunciation story; the shepherds are the first to hear the good news. With the angelic choir (v. 14) we have the third song in the infancy narratives, the *Gloria*. In Western liturgies this text serves as the foundation for the "Glory to God."

2:21-38 Circumcision, naming, and presentation in the temple

The parallel between John the Baptist and Jesus continues in verse 21. John is circumcised and named eight days after his birth (1:59-60), and now so too with Jesus.

In portraying this section, Luke relies on some elements of the Mosaic Law as well as stories about the prophet Samuel (1 Sam 1:24-28). God commands Abraham to circumcise male descendants and slaves as a sign of the covenant (Gen 17:12), a point the book of Leviticus stipulates (12:3). Although Luke states that both parents must undergo the rites of purification (v. 22), the Levitical prescriptions apply only to the mother (Lev 12:2-5). A Gentile Christian himself, Luke is not always accurate in his explanation of Jewish cultic and legal codes. Luke rightly notes that the firstborn must be consecrated to the Lord (Exod 13:2), but this redemption is accomplished by paying five shekels to a priest (Num 3:47-48). The sacrifice of turtledoves Luke describes is part of a woman's purification rite. These verses serve to emphasize Mary and Joseph as faithful, law-abiding Jews, and with them, Luke underscores the Jewish context of Jesus' birth and mission.

Nothing else is known about the identities of Simeon and Anna other than what this section tells us. Both represent the faithful Israelite who waits and does not lose hope in the coming redemption. Simeon's canticle, or *Nunc dimitiis* (2:29-32), is the fourth and final hymn from the Lukan infancy narratives and has traditionally been part of Compline or night office in the Liturgy of the Hours.

Simeon's words to Mary, ominous though they are, are also highly theological. With verse 34 we see the first instance of the schism motif, which runs throughout Luke's Gospel. Often in Luke's portrayal of Jesus' mission, one party or person will follow him, while another will turn away. One group will be saved, another will fall into perdition. In each case individuals choose their own fate by deciding for or against following Jesus. Simeon states that a sword will pierce Mary's heart as well. The discipleship that Jesus demands extends even to his mother. Not only does Luke indicate through Simeon that discipleship will not be easy, but he also elevates Mary to the role of the model disciple. To love Jesus is to suffer with him.

The widowed state of the prophetess Anna, daughter of Phanuel (vv. 36-38), has made her utterly dependent on God's goodness. Luke tells us that she "spoke about the child to all who were awaiting the redemption of Jerusalem" (v. 38), and thus she is the first evangelist. By starting out with the "redemption of Jerusalem," Luke sets his literary project in order. After the resurrection, the message goes from "Jerusalem, throughout Judea and Samaria, and to the ends of the earth" (Acts 1:8).

2:39-40 Nazareth and Bethlehem

According to the accounts of both Luke and Matthew, Jesus is born in Bethlehem but spends his youth and young adulthood in Nazareth. Mention of these two locales in this manner forms an enigmatic knot that is difficult to unravel. If there are serious questions surrounding the census (see 2:1-7 above), why do Mary and Joseph go to Bethlehem, when we know that Mary is from Nazareth (1:26)? The four Gospels and the Acts of the Apostles refer to "Jesus of Nazareth" but never "Jesus of Bethlehem." Is the whole narrative of the birth at Bethlehem a literary construction serving to demonstrate that Jesus, through his foster father Joseph, is the Son of David who is born in the city of David?

Scripture, history, and archaeology all show that there was a strong Jewish presence in various parts of Galilee, so it would not be a strange place for Jesus to have his upbringing. The most we can say about this puzzlement is that the two sources that mention Jesus' birth, Luke and Matthew, both specifically state that it occurs in Bethlehem. There are no texts that cite Nazareth as Jesus' birthplace. Basing their respective accounts on the oral tradition, the evangelists composed stories that get Mary and Joseph to Bethlehem and then back up to Nazareth. The importance of this Lukan narrative is that Jesus stands in line of the Davidic Messiah, and about that, Luke wants the reader to know, there can be no doubt.

2:41-52 The boy Jesus in the temple

Only Luke contains this story of how Jesus is lost while on the return trip from Jerusalem. Passover was one of the pilgrimage feasts, when devout Jews would go to Jerusalem to celebrate the occasion.

The story itself reflects a theological point that Luke makes explicit in recounting Jesus' earthly ministry: true discipleship goes beyond familial relationships (8:19-21 and 11:27-29). In addition, that this conversation takes place in the temple reflects Luke's ambivalent attitude toward the temple's existence, if not his positive disposition toward it. Luke frequently shows Jesus teaching in the temple up to the final days before his crucifixion. In the Acts of the Apostles, Peter and Paul also preach and teach in the temple.

Jesus returns with his parents to Nazareth, and nothing more is heard about him until he is an adult and begins his ministry. The next time we read of Jesus in Jerusalem will be at his triumphal entry (19:28-39), which leads to his death.

THE PREPARATION FOR THE PUBLIC MINISTRY
Luke 3:1–4:13

John the Baptist is the precursor of Jesus, and Luke shifts the focus from one ministry to the other. This transition entails Jesus' baptism and desert temptation.

3:1-20 The ministry of John the Baptist

Chapter 3, like chapter 1, opens with a periodic sentence, a strong indication that this section is a major literary unit.

As with the birth of Jesus (Luke 2:1-3), Luke situates John the Baptist within a geopolitical framework involving the Roman emperor and his Palestinian-Jewish client states. Tiberius Caesar succeeds Augustus. According to Luke's dating, the word of God comes to the desert-dwelling John the Baptist in A.D. 29.

The nominally Jewish king, Herod the Great, died in 4 B.C. and divided his kingdom among his three sons: Herod Antipas, the tetrarch, or ruler, of Galilee and Perea; Herod Archelaus, ethnarch over Judea, Idumea, and Samaria; and Herod Philip, the tetrarch in charge of Gaulanitis, Trachonitis, and Batanaea. Archelaus's misrule led the emperor Augustus to banish him in A.D. 6, at which time a Roman procurator was appointed to govern his territory. One such procurator was Pontius Pilate, who ruled the area from A.D. 26 to 36, the period Luke is writing about here.

Lysanias is difficult to identify. There is scant information about a person of that name ruling the area of Abilene at this time. Many have speculated on the reason why Luke includes this information. Was he addressing a Christian community based in Abilene (northwest of Damascus), or was he from Abilene himself? We may

never know, but we have here a typical example of the manner in which Luke uses historical data—truth is more important than mere fact.

With the mention of high priests, Annas and Caiaphas, Luke grounds the Baptist's ministry within the history of Jewish Palestine. From John's Gospel (11:49; 18:13), we read that Caiaphas is the priest at the time of Jesus' death. Although only one high priest ruled at a time, Luke may include the reference to Annas simply because Annas was still alive while his son Caiaphas was in charge.

John the Baptist begins the public ministry in the parallel accounts of the other three Gospels as well, but just where John preaches is a question. Mark simply says "in the desert" (1:4). Matthew states "in the desert of Judea" (3:1), which would place him under the jurisdiction of Pontius Pilate. Further on, both Matthew and Mark add that crowds come from Judea and Jerusalem, a region accessible to Perea and Herod Antipas's territory. Luke writes "in the desert . . . [the] whole region of the Jordan" (vv. 2-3), a reading that suggests along the Jordan River, including the Judean side of the river (Roman territory), but in any case, in that area east of Jerusalem as far as the mountains on the east bank. Since Galilee is also under Herod Antipas, Luke seems to introduce the idea that both Jesus and John, each in his proper time, face the same political ruler (see 3:19ff. and 23:6-12).

Luke firmly establishes John as the precursor. Not only does John preach a baptism of repentance for the forgiveness of sins, but the evangelist (vv. 4-6) also interprets the Baptist's role as the fulfillment of Isaiah's prophecy (40:3-5).

Judaism, with its whole tradition of the *mikvah*, or ritual bath, was well acquainted with the water ablutions that John mentions (v. 16). The reference to a baptism "with the holy Spirit and fire" further on in the verse emphasizes that Jesus' action goes beyond religious ritual; it will have an efficacy that will transform the whole created order, just as fire alters the material state of matter. Early Christian mosaics depict this point by presenting Jesus standing in the Jordan River with smiling fish surrounding his feet as the Baptist pours water over Jesus' head.

3:21-22 The baptism of Jesus

John clarifies his subservient role to Christ with his preaching in 3:15-18. From the beginning of

Luke's Gospel, information about John the Baptist has come before the accounts dealing with Jesus. In keeping with this thematic development of the Baptist as precursor, Luke skillfully provides the account of John's arrest (3:19-20) before the narrative surrounding Jesus' baptism (3:21-22).

Luke shows Jesus praying at critical points in his life. To underscore the point that John is lesser than Jesus, Luke recounts the baptism itself in the passive voice. There is no conversation between the two individuals. Jesus is baptized as one among the crowd, the voice from heaven is directed only to him, and it is understood that the others do not hear it. Later, when the Baptist sends messengers to Jesus (7:18-23), there is no indication of his being aware of having baptized Jesus.

To interpret the baptism, Luke relies on a conflation of two Old Testament passages. The first half of the voice from heaven (v. 22) is a paraphrase of Psalm 2:7, while the second half is part of Isaiah 42:1. It should be noted, however, that the textual witnesses for this section display a wide variety of readings. One manuscript, for example, quotes Psalm 2:7 in its entirety: "You are my Son, this day I have begotten you." The version that we have here reflects the evidence from Codices Vaticanus and Sinaiticus, two of the most dependable of the extant Gospel manuscripts. A similar, although not an exact, quotation is found at the transfiguration of Jesus (9:35).

According to the science of the ancients, doves were considered not to have any bile and thus were symbolic of virtue. Not only were they worthy for sacrifice to God, but, as seen here, they also symbolized the divine presence.

3:23-38 The genealogy of Jesus

By setting Jesus' genealogy after the baptism, Luke fashions a twofold theological statement. First, after having seen Jesus' divine sonship pronounced in the voice from heaven (3:22), he now reiterates that point by stating it in verse 38. Second, Luke writes Jesus' ancestral line going all the way back to Adam, and by so doing connects Jesus to all humanity, unlike Matthew, who shows Jesus as descended from Abraham to stress his Jewish background and role (Matt 1:1-17). Luke also underscores Jesus' virginal conception by the use of the parenthetical expression "as was thought" (v. 23).

One theory of the formation of Luke's Gospel holds that the infancy narratives (Luke 1–2) were later additions to a primitive version of the current text (see above). If so, an earlier stage of the Third Gospel began with Jesus' baptism and genealogy. Supporting this possibility is a lack of similar introductory material in the other Gospels (Matthew notwithstanding), as well as use of Luke's Gospel by early Christians and heretics, particularly Marcion, who denied Christ's relationship with anyone in the Old Testament. In any case, in this final redaction Luke does a fine job linking the first two chapters to the third both literarily and theologically.

4:1-13 The temptation in the desert

The Spirit who descended upon Jesus at his baptism now leads him into the desert for forty days.

The desert brings life right to the edge. In the Jewish tradition, it can be a place of divine encounter, such as with Moses and the burning bush (Exod 3:1-14), or it can be the place of death (see Gen 21:14-16). Of course, the forty-year wandering of the Israelites, a communal experience that formed them into the people of God, takes place in the desert. Just so, Jesus' sojourn in the wilderness brings into clearer focus for him what his mission on earth will be.

The Synoptic Gospels all include the desert temptation, but there are differences among them in the telling. Mark's account is the shortest (1:12-13), and Luke's is most similar to Matthew's (4:1-11), but the similarities break down in the respective nuances of each account. In Matthew, the setting of the three temptations goes from the desert, to Jerusalem, to the kingdoms of the world, while in Luke we read desert, kingdoms of the world, Jerusalem. Luke's account has greater internal consistency, for Jesus' ministry will culminate in Jerusalem, and it will be in that city that he meets his greatest temptation as well as his greatest triumph (see below, Luke 22:39-46; 23:44-49; 24). As it stands in this passage, the three temptations are to riches, glory, and power, represented by bread, rule, and defiance of nature respectively. Jesus' reply to each of the temptations, all from the book of Deuteronomy (8:3; 6:13, 16), connects his experience in the desert with that of the wandering Israelites.

For Luke, the devil is a force in the yet unredeemed world of Jesus' ministry. In the Lukan narrative, this encounter in the desert is Jesus' first meeting with the devil, but certainly not the last (v. 13). Jesus will be in hard combat with the devil or Satan from here until his death.

THE MINISTRY IN GALILEE

Luke 4:14–9:50

The Spirit now leads Jesus to Galilee, the area north of Jerusalem and Samaria. This was the district of his upbringing, and he begins his earthly ministry there.

4:14-30 Jesus arrives in Nazareth

From the preceding section we know that Jesus was away from the region and his hometown. What is unclear, however, is how long he was away and why he departed. That he was baptized with all the people somewhere along the Jordan (3:3, 21) has led many to conclude that Jesus was associated with John the Baptist for some time before setting out on his own way.

Jesus reads from Isaiah 61:1-2, a messianic text. Although by the fourth century A.D. the rabbis had adopted a particular order of scriptural pericopes to be read throughout the year, it is uncertain whether such a system was in place in first-century Judaism. If it was, then Jesus demonstrates his authority in bypassing the accepted practice and choosing a passage of his own. His concluding comment (v. 21) allows the listeners to draw their own conclusions.

The reaction of the people in Nazareth reflects the schism motif, which Luke develops from the beginning (see 2:34). Some speak highly of Jesus, while others are filled with resentment at having one of their own preach to them, and Jesus calls them on this point by providing examples from their history when the people acted in like manner. The references to Elijah and Elisha serve to describe the kind of prophet people see in Jesus and, indeed, how he perhaps sees himself. Unlike the prophets of the south, such as Isaiah and Jeremiah, Elijah and Elisha lived in the north, and they, too, made the rounds raising the dead, feeding the poor, and healing the sick (1 Kgs 17:1–2 Kgs 13). Since Galilee is in the north, where much of Jesus' ministry is situated, both the actions and words of Jesus would have special resonance with the people. Jesus' comments draw the obvious conclusion. By their resistance to him, the townspeople are no better than their forebears who did not heed earlier prophets; therefore, they come under the same judgment. Jesus' insinuation enrages the people to the point where they try to kill him.

Nazareth is located on a hill overlooking the Esdraelon Plain. A rocky precipice encircles the southeast section of the town.

4:31-44 Exorcisms, cures, and healings at Capernaum

The central focus of Jesus' ministry is the reclamation of this world for the reign of God, and now the battle begins.

Capernaum lies along the northern shore of the Sea of Galilee, where archaeological evidence points to its being a busy fishing village. Much of Jesus' ministry takes place in this locale.

Unlike the temptation scene in Luke 4:1-13, here Jesus encounters not the devil but an unclean demon. For Luke, both the demon and the devil may represent the same evil force, but they are not one and the same entities. The devil, Satan, and Beelzebul (see 10:18; 11:14-23) are synonymous terms for the Evil One holding creation captive. Demons, on the other hand, play a lesser role and are subject to the devil. That this exorcism as well as the following cure takes place on the sabbath is significant: the reign of God is made manifest on the literal day of the Lord, which, metaphorically speaking, is the *Day of the Lord,* the moment when the end times arrive culminating in the Lord's decisive battle with evil. When the Gospels were written, apocalyptic thought filled the thoughts of Jew and Gentile alike, and this Lukan scene reflects such a mindset. The Gospels are in a large way responsible for the fact that judgment of good and evil is an important part of the Christian theological tradition.

The cure of Simon's mother-in-law follows. The world between sickness, disease, and demonic possession was not so well defined in ancient times. None of it was good, and all of it was evil. Curing a person, therefore, would evoke the same reaction as an exorcism, a point made by the fact that Jesus "rebukes" the fever. Again, the event takes place on the sabbath, leading to the same conclusions as above. From earliest Christianity, a house located in the center of Capernaum has been held as the place of veneration commemorating this miracle, and churches have stood on the spot ever since to accommodate the thousands of pilgrims who continue to visit it.

The sabbath ends at sunset, yet people still come to Jesus for cures and exorcisms. The day of the Lord cannot be confined to the temporal cycle. The passage shows the melding of time with the *eschaton*. The demons always know Jesus' identity, even though the people do not, and these unclean spirits nearly always declare him the Messiah or state his divinity. Jesus prohibits them from speaking in order to demonstrate his power over them and their ruler, the devil.

Jesus leaves Capernaum at daybreak and goes to a deserted place. Tradition has often located this spot along the northeast shore of the Sea of Galilee, a place of volcanic rock and little vegetation. Luke, not known for his accuracy in Palestinian geography, ends the section by saying that Jesus goes to preach in the synagogues of Judea. This point of information is problematic. Judea is in the south. Luke's whole schema has Jesus making only one trip there, and it ends with his passion, death, and resurrection. The earliest manuscripts, Codices Sinaiticus and Vaticanus read "Judea," but another important codex has "Galilee," the district in the north, probably written thus to resolve the narrative contradiction. Most likely Jesus made more than one journey to Judea in his lifetime. Indeed, John's Gospel indicates that Jesus went to Jerusalem at least seven times. This verse (v. 44) reflects such a tradition.

5:1-11 The miraculous draft of fish and the call of Peter

Luke is the only Synoptic writer to include the story of the miraculous catch of fish within the call of Simon, although John's Gospel shows a similar miracle in a resurrection narrative (John 21:1-11).

Lake of Gennesaret is another name for Sea of Galilee (v. 1). Fishing in the Sea of Galilee is done only at night. If the men caught nothing at that time, there was nothing to be had. That they listened to Jesus at all is indicative that they respected Jesus' opinion even when it came to their own profession. There is a tinge of doubt in Simon's reply (v. 5), and his reaction only confirms his initial skepticism (v. 8).

Jesus speaks only to Simon, and Simon is the only one to reply. Luke is preparing the reader for the leadership role that Simon (Peter) will play

throughout the Lukan corpus. We get the impression that the crowd must have been so large that the only way Jesus could be seen and heard without being overwhelmed by the throng was to sit in Simon's boat just off the beach, the same boat that sails out for the catch at the Lord's command. The emphasis on Simon's boat is Luke's way of underscoring the disciple's importance on the symbolic level. Early Christian iconography often used a boat filled with people to depict the church, just as the church has long been called the "bark of Peter."

The miracle excites awe and wonder. Moreover, it represents the multitudinous followers this disciple will "catch" once he becomes a fisher of people in Christ's name. In verse 8 Luke uses the name "Simon Peter" for the only time and shows the disciple moved to repentance. Jesus then speaks directly to Simon in listening distance of the others. Jesus' call results in these fishermen responding immediately. They leave everything and follow, thereby becoming models of the perfect disciples.

5:12-16 The cleansing of a leper

In the Old and New Testaments, the term "leprosy" is used to describe a variety of skin diseases, including leprosy itself. Any skin abnormalities, particularly those ulcerating or scabbing, made ritual purity impossible. Whether or not the disease was contagious, the affliction was considered a sign of sinfulness, and so people so afflicted were separated from the community to prevent physical as well as cultic contamination. After viewing the symptoms of the disease, the priests made the determination on purity or impurity (see Lev 13–14).

The man prostrates himself and acknowledges Jesus' authority both by the title "Lord" and by the supplication "if you wish" (v. 12). His action shows his faith, which Jesus recognizes. Jesus' commanding the cleansing is an affirmation of his lordship. The injunction not to tell anyone echoes the messianic secret found in much of the Gospel of Mark. Of course, it would be impossible to keep. It shows, however, that Jesus prefers that his actions rather than his words speak of his reign. Indeed, Jesus relies on such actions as proof of his being the Messiah (Luke 7:22). As a means of evangelization, the cure has the desired affect of bringing others to Jesus. Rather than portraying

Jesus as being another miracle worker among many, Luke notes that the crowds assembled first "to listen to him." Only then were they "cured of their ailments" (v. 15).

Luke, more than any other evangelist, frequently shows Jesus alone at prayer, an activity hinted at in Luke 4:42. Often Jesus retreats to a deserted place or wilderness after an intense period of preaching, healing, and exorcising, as he does here.

5:17-26 The healing of a paralytic

Although all three Synoptic Gospels have the healing of a paralytic, only Mark and Luke feature the bearers of the stretcher letting the person down through the roof. This story provides a number of details that describe the effect Jesus was having in his ministry.

The crowds he was able to draw must have been exceedingly large. The fact that Jesus teaches from a boat in Luke 5:3 gives us a hint of their size. In this passage the stretcher-bearers cannot possibly make their way through the people gathered in front of the door and must resort to unconventional methods.

Luke shows his Syrian origins here. The Markan parallel to this story says, "After they had broken through" (Mark 2:4), a statement describing better the roofs of Jewish homes in Palestine, which were flat and made of a mud-and-sod mixture resting on wooden beams or stone arches. These roofs often served as terraces on warm summer evenings. To maintain their impermeability during the rainy season, they would be rolled with a large rounded stone to compact the grasses. Burrowing a hole to let down a pallet would have been relatively easy. On the other hand, Luke states "through the tiles" (v. 19), a detail reflecting the domestic architecture stretching from the Golan Heights up into most of Syria, where a series of stone arches commonly support a roof made of shingles.

Although many see this passage as the first of several "conflict stories," there is no reason to conclude that the Pharisees and teachers of the Law are present with bad intentions, for there are no harsh words between them and Jesus until he forgives the paralytic's sins. The Pharisees are correct in their criticism—only God can forgive sins—but they do not know the full meaning of what they say. Jesus, referring to himself as the "Son of Man" for the first time in Luke (v. 24), proves his divinity with the cure, and everyone, including the Pharisees and teachers, is awestruck. Their attitude may change as Jesus progresses in his ministry, but at this point the tension is not evident. In line with the schism motif that Luke has developed (see Luke 2:34), this scene gives reason to believe that this group of Pharisees and scribes are convinced that Jesus does have such authority.

As an Aramaic phrase, the title "Son of Man" can be loosely translated by the pronoun "someone." It is used frequently in the Old Testament, especially in Ezekiel and Daniel. It gains specific import, however, in the latter book, which reads, "As the visions during the night continued, I saw One like a son of man coming, on the clouds of heaven; When he reached the Ancient One and was presented before him, He received dominion, glory, and kinship; nations and peoples of every language serve him. His dominion is an everlasting dominion that shall not be taken away, his kingship shall not be destroyed" (7:13-14). This quotation from Daniel is seminal for formation of the Christian understanding of Jesus' identity, and it is this reference, combined with the cure, which causes the crowd and the Pharisees to be awestruck. They are able to make the connection between the miracle and the person performing it.

The event itself is a good example of the incarnational character of Jesus' mission. Forgiveness of sins and spiritual well-being are not separated from physical wholeness and restoration. The Son of Man does not ignore the material world or the suffering of those living in it. By the double action of forgiving sins and curing the paralysis, Jesus shows that God's beloved creatures are redeemed in this life as well as the next.

5:27-32 The call of Levi, the tax collector

The Jewish people detested tax collectors for good reason. On the religious level, tax collectors made themselves idolaters by cooperating with the Romans; thus they at least tacitly acclaimed Caesar's lordship. Dealing with Roman coinage, which featured an engraving of the emperor, would support such an accusation. On the nationalistic plane, by working for the Romans, Jewish tax collectors betrayed their people. They received their positions by bidding themselves out as agents to the Roman State. The Romans assessed the sum a district should provide to the emperor; the Roman officials demanded a surcharge for themselves, and the collectors were bound to bring in both while taking any extra as their remuneration. They could and would sell whole families into slavery in order to meet their demands. This position made them extortionists, both symbolically and literally.

All three Synoptic Gospels contain this story. Levi sits at the "customs post" (*telōnion* in Greek). This detail tells us that Levi taxed goods going from one political jurisdiction to another. Since nearly eighty percent of Jesus' ministry occurs along the northern shore of the Sea of Galilee, this customs post was most likely located at the mouth of the Jordan River, which formed the border between Galilee, under Herod Antipas, and Gaulanitis, under his brother Philip. The alacrity with which Levi leaves his post at the customs house indicates that his heart was predisposed to conversion before his encounter with Christ; Jesus' call is the catalyst causing the move toward repentance.

Levi's great banquet (*dochē* in Greek) with a large number of invitees underscores his wealth (v. 29). Luke's version differs from the Matthean (9:9-13) and Markan (2:13-17) accounts in several ways. Whereas the other two Synoptics specify that the Pharisees and scribes see Jesus in attendance and then speak to his disciples, Luke simply states that the Pharisees "complained" to his disciples, which leads one to believe that they were at the celebration. Were the Pharisees invited and only saw the rest of the company when they arrived? Would they have gone to a tax collector's banquet in the first place? Whatever the answer, Luke wants the reader to know that the Pharisees were in close proximity to Jesus. Unlike the preceding passage of the paralytic, where friction is not necessarily evident between Jesus and the Pharisees, here Luke describes the encounter between the two with the use of the Greek verb *gongyzō*, "to grumble against someone" or "complain," indicating that some visible tension has arisen between them (v. 30).

The parallel accounts in the other two Synoptics show "Matthew" and "Levi, son of Alphaeus" as the names of the tax collector, but Luke reads "Levi," a name suggesting that he comes from a Levitical family and therefore would have some kind of priestly function (see Deut 31:9; Josh

13:14). Certainly Luke could have shortened Mark's reading by dropping the identifier "son of Alphaeus." The name "Levi" itself, however, contains overtones of the impending messianic age.

In Malachi 3:3 we read, "and he will purify the sons of Levi, / Refining them like gold or like silver / that they may offer due sacrifice to the Lord." This prophet emphasizes the impending Day of the Lord as well as the point that a messenger will come to prepare the way (Mal 3:1). Luke gives attention to John the Baptist as well as to the Day of the Lord. That Levi leaves his functions at the customs post is a sign that this remarkable day has arrived. Hence the feast, which the now repentant Levi holds, prefigures the heavenly banquet. By calling this former tax collector to a new life, the Lord Jesus has purified the sons of Levi. Note as well that with this passage Luke has blended the ministries of the Baptist and Jesus.

5:33-39 Feasting and fasting, new and old

Comparing the three Synoptic versions of this story, we see that Matthew has the disciples of John the Baptist asking Jesus why his disciples do not fast (Matt 9:14). Mark has "people" inquiring, but with a reference to both John's disciples and the Pharisees (Mark 2:18). Luke is obviously editing material that has come through Mark. The antecedent of the pronoun "they" (Luke 5:33) is difficult to identify. Since further on in the verse there is mention of the Pharisees in the third person, "the disciples of the Pharisees do the same," it would seem that the scribes are asking the question. As a professional class of writers who knew the written law, they would not necessarily be as prone to follow the oral traditions promulgated by the Pharisees, even though they may have very well been aware of them.

In addition, the thematic content supports the scribes as the ones interrogating Jesus. This question about eating habits follows within the context of Levi's great banquet (Luke 5:27-32). A similar controversy over feasting and fasting arises further on in Jesus' ministry (Luke 7:31-35). It seems obvious that Jesus has developed a reputation for being one who enjoys good food and wine, and according to the Gospel account, this accusation is not without basis. Not only does he use banquet imagery in much of his preaching, but he is frequently seen at dinner feasts with Pharisees, tax collectors, and sinners. Indeed, Jesus refers to himself as a bridegroom in this passage, thus making his ministry on earth a wedding banquet filled with the joy and the promise of new life. It is the Day of the Lord.

This passage reflects the tensions existing between the Christian movement and Pharisaic Judaism. Although Luke goes to great lengths to demonstrate Christianity's roots in Jewish tradition, particularly in the prophets (see Luke 1–2), the religious practices of the early Pharisees and Christians were incompatible. This irreconcilability stands as the background to the passage.

The parable about new and old patches, cloaks, and wineskins has a twist. The lesson about cloth and wineskins is easy to follow, and the conclusions are based on common sense. One uses old cloth to patch new, not vice versa; the fermentation of new wine needs the elasticity of new skins, not the brittleness of old ones. The summarizing statement, a verse that only Luke shows, however, is ironic: "[And] no one who has been drinking old wine desires new, for he says, 'The old is good'" (v. 39). After a discourse on the desirability of leaving the old for the new, Jesus concludes by admitting that we often prefer the comfort of the old to the challenges of the new, particularly when we see nothing wrong or bad with the old. On the other hand, the examination of the metaphor shows that, in this case, there is something wrong and bad about the old. Threadbare clothing is of little use to anyone, and wineskins can be used only once. We must not let comfort and security blind us to the blessings of the kingdom.

Jesus' point is that the life of a disciple is not a dour regimen of religious protocol, but a life of joy. We should not let self-complacency blind us to the banquet the Bridegroom has ushered in, a banquet that begins now even as we wait to see its fullness in the yet-to-come.

6:1-11 Debates about the sabbath

The Mosaic prohibition against work on the sabbath recurs in many places throughout the Pentateuch. The legislation first surfaces in Exodus 16:23-29, where Moses directs the Israelites on how to collect the manna the Lord has given them. They are to gather enough for the day at hand and leave none for the next day. This instruction is in force until the sixth day, when they are to gather twice as much for the following sab-

bath. Interestingly, when some disobey Moses by keeping some manna longer than they are supposed to, the cache becomes rotten and wormy. When the leftovers are saved for the sabbath, however, the manna remains edible. This Exodus account gives rise to further legislation and consequent debates on what constitutes work on the sabbath.

The controversy revolves around sabbath regulation. If the disciples performed a similar action on any other day of the week, they would have been within their rights (Deut 23:25). Here, however, not only are the disciples in Luke 6:1-5 violating prohibitions against harvesting fields and threshing grain, but by carrying goods, they are also guilty of breaking a sabbath law (see Num 15:32). Jesus' reply to the Pharisees is nearly the same in the other two Synoptic parallels (see Matt 12:1-8; Mark 2:23-28).

The incident to which Luke refers is found in 1 Samuel 21:1-7. Jesus' point is that Pharisees overlook David's infractions, who, with his men, is guilty of breaking more laws than the disciples are. Yet the Pharisees become indignant at Jesus for a less serious offense, and he is the Lord of the sabbath. This moment is one of messianic revelation, but the Pharisees' legalism blinds them to it. The passage ends with "The Son of Man is lord of the sabbath" (v. 5), a verse that introduces another story on violating the sabbath.

The issue at hand is not that Jesus cures but that he cures on the sabbath, something that is considered work. As with the exorcism of the demoniac (Luke 4:31-37), the sabbath or Lord's Day here is also considered the eschatological Day of the Lord, when suffering will cease and wholeness will be restored. Jesus tries to make that point when he addresses the assembly (v. 9), and he proves his lordship in restoring the man's withered hand (v. 10). Seeing that Jesus' argument and actions are unassailable, the scribes and Pharisees become incensed.

It is important to note that Jesus' conflicts with the Pharisees reflect more the tension within the early Christian community concerning Jews and Jewish practice than they do between Jesus and the Jews. Both Jews and Gentiles saw themselves as followers of Christ, and passages such as these show the points of contention both inside and outside the Christian community. Thus, when Jesus castigates the Pharisees in this passage, we see and hear the early debates within the Jewish-Christian community.

6:12-16 The mission of the Twelve

There is a noticeable shift of direction in this scene. Away from the synagogues, towns, and people, Jesus goes "to the mountain to pray" (v. 12) in an all-night vigil. The exact mountain is unknown, though the use of the definite article indicates that Lukan tradition must have had some specific mountain in mind. Galilee has many high places that could qualify as quiet retreats for prayer, but two are the most likely promontories: Mount Hermon, rising from the northeast corner of the Sea of Galilee, and Mount Tabor, south of the sea, visible from Nazareth and on the Jezreel Plain. They both have been traditional places of prayer from earliest antiquity (see Ps 89:13), although Tabor is the more accessible of the two.

Jesus selects from all his disciples twelve men who will have a share in his ministry. The names of the Twelve do not match the lists of the other Gospels, nor do they correspond with what Luke writes in his second volume (see Acts 1:13). In fact, none of the lists in the Synoptics are in exact agreement with each other. How do we account for the fact that the apostles (and only Luke and Matthew call these men apostles) differ, especially when the early church placed so much emphasis on apostolic foundation in determining whether a community was orthodox or that its writings should be included in the canon? One suggestion for the variety of names is that each Gospel writer is recalling the representative figures peculiar to the community for which he is writing. These figures may have known or worked with one or more of what came to be called "the Twelve." All four Gospels agree that Judas Iscariot betrays Jesus, however.

After the night in prayer, Jesus returns to his ministry, except now the people come to him.

6:17-19 Ministering to a great multitude

The crowd's various lands of origin give the reader insight into Luke's geographical understanding as well as his theological agenda. The commission described in Acts 1:8 reads: "you will be my witnesses in Jerusalem, throughout Judea and Samaria, and to the ends of the earth." In the Acts of the Apostles, the apostolic mission follows that trajectory. Here in this passage, however, "Sa-maria" and the "ends of the earth" are not included. The explanation can be found in Luke 9:52-53, where Jesus and his disciples are not welcomed in the Samaritan village. Samaria's time will come, and so will the proclamation to the ends of the earth. For now, Tyre and Sidon, as seaports and in pagan territory, represent for Luke the future direction of the Christian movement. In this passage Luke paints a picture of a mission at the threshold.

6:20-49 Sermon on the Plain

The Sermon on the Plain evidences four sections: the Beatitudes, the exhortations, the analogy of trees and fruit, and the parable of the two houses.

Beatitudes. Jesus descends the mountain before preaching. The Moses typology, so much a part of Matthew's Gospel, does not exist in Luke. He raises his eyes towards his disciples, and addresses the people (v. 20), a simple gesture that calls forth discipleship on the part of the crowd. Because Luke has his Gentile audience in mind, he does not include the *lex talionis* found in Matthew 5:38. Certainly not as quoted or well known as Matthew's Beatitudes, the Lukan redaction is also shorter. Most critics believe that both Matthew and Luke use Q as the source material for their respective versions.

The great reversal theme, first outlined in the *Magnificat* (Luke 1:46-55), recurs here: the poor will inherit the kingdom, the hungry will be satisfied, those weeping will laugh. Luke addresses the people in the second person, whereas Matthew uses the third person. For this reason, some maintain that Luke foresees an immediate resolution to the suffering of the outcast while holding that Matthew pushes justice into the *eschaton*. The interpretation of the Lukan Beatitudes is not that simple, however. Because the Lukan eschatological vision surfaces through the juxtaposition of the Woes in verses 24-26, there is no reason to assume that Luke sees the resolution of the tension between the blessed and the woebegone occurring only within this lifetime. Likewise, Matthew's Beatitudes challenge people to address social injustices in this world.

Luke, like Matthew, places suffering and reward within the context of the Old Testament, in which true prophets faced torture and death, while the false ones found worldly grace and favor. As the Gospel narrative continues, the reader sees Jesus encountering a similar fate. The heart of the message is that we do God's will on earth to relieve suffering and oppression, realizing all along that ultimate mercy and justice will come only with the *eschaton*.

Exhortations. Luke goes to great lengths in explaining love of enemies (vv. 27-38). Human love should match divine love, a love that is "kind to the ungrateful and the wicked" (v. 35). This call to be "merciful, just as [also] your Father is merciful" (v. 36) is a particular Lukan characteristic. Because Luke defines so well the boundless quality of divine mercy, Dante refers to the evangelist as the *Scritsa mansuetudinis Christi*, the "narrator of the sweet gentleness of Christ."

The lesson on judging others is connected to love of enemies. The context surrounding the admonition not to judge others does not refer to assessing the rightness or wrongness of an action or of its moral content; obviously, the whole of the Beatitudes contains elements of judgment. Rather, Luke is addressing those who would play the part of God by judging the salvation or damnation of others, something only God can do. For those who would assume to take on that role, Luke offers a stern warning: they may end up condemning themselves. Similarly, those who extend the benefit of the doubt will have manifold blessings extended to them (v. 38).

Analogy. This comparison of a tree and its fruit is Q material. Matthew contains a nearly identical passage (Matt 7:16-20), but it is not as concise as the one we read here. The image of good and bad fruit and its association with prophecy echo several Old Testament prophetic utterances. Jeremiah performs an action of the good and bad figs (Jer 24:1-10), and a central metaphor for Isaiah (5:1-7) is the vine and grapes. Ezekiel has something similar (Ezek 19:10-14). Thus this short section functions as a reprise for Luke's reference to true and false prophets (vv. 23 and 26).

Parable. The comparison of the two houses (vv. 46-49; Matt 7:21-27) yields readings that reflect the geography of the two different communities. In Syria one would have to dig to reach the bedrock upon which to build; in Palestine and Israel, the bedrock is exposed. Syria has permanent rivers and streams running through it. Indeed, Antioch is situated on the Orontes, just one of several rivers in Syria. On the other hand, the country

about which Matthew writes has only the Jordan, and no real city stands on its banks. The house for Matthew, therefore, is destroyed by wind and rain. The point in both readings, however, is the same: for one to follow Jesus, there must be care, determination, and full intention. The halfhearted who would try to be a disciple will simply wash away.

7:1-10 Healing the centurion's slave at Capernaum

Although Luke shares this story with Matthew, Luke's difference is most notable in that the evangelist includes the Jewish emissaries who are very supportive of the centurion. Several features draw our attention.

The centurion, as the name implies, was in charge of one hundred men. At this time in history, Romans ruled the country through their clients, with Galilee and Perea under the jurisdiction of Herod Antipas. Hence the centurion need not have been a Roman, even though he was a Gentile. That he was a Gentile, however, would have entailed difficulties enough, for a Jew could not enter a Gentile home without becoming ritually impure.

There are two words in Greek used for the term "slave." One is *doulos,* and the other is *pais.* In verses 2, 3, 8, and 10, Luke uses *doulos,* and in verse 7 we read *pais.* Of the two words, the latter, which literally means, "boy" or "youth," describes a more personal, endearing relationship. On the other hand, *doulos* expresses the servility associated with such a state. The translation here, with its use of "slave" and "servant" in the respective verses, shows the nuance between the two words. Luke contrasts the two terms in the narrative. When using indirect address, as in verses 2, 3, and 10, or when the centurion speaks in the abstract, as in verse 8, the text shows *doulos.* When Luke quotes the centurion, however, he employs the term *pais.* From this juxtaposition we can see that Luke is emphasizing the kinship the centurion feels for his servant.

The interplay between the Jewish elders and the centurion is notable. Although the centurion is in service to the nominally Jewish tetrarch, Herod Antipas, he is still a Gentile. Herod Antipas, as a Roman client, has to pay tribute to the Romans, and he passes on this expense by levying heavy taxes upon the population. Nonetheless, the picture we have here shows some semblance of mutual respect between the two parties. The Jewish elders say that the centurion "loves our nation and he built the synagogue for us" (v. 5). Furthermore, the centurion exhibits all the signs of faith in the Lord God that the religious Jew shows. It seems that Luke has described a "God-fearer," a Gentile who found the monotheistic God of the Jews and their moral code appealing, but who was unable or unwilling to separate himself from his own family and ethnic group by dietary laws or circumcision (see Acts 10:22). Thus the Jewish elders in verse 4 can speak highly of the centurion. In addition, knowing that a religious Jew could not enter a Gentile house, the centurion obviates a potentially embarrassing situation by sending a second band of emissaries, this time "friends," with the advice that Jesus perform his deed from afar. Luke probably included this passage to support the place of Gentiles within the Jewish-Christian movement. As Jesus comes to the Gentile centurion, so, too, does he come to Gentiles in the Mediterranean world.

Finally, we see a positive exchange between the Jewish elders and Jesus. Although Luke often describes a great deal of tension between Pharisaical parties and Jesus, the relationship between Jesus and the Jews is not always hostile, as we see here. The elders may not be Pharisees specifically but may have some position of authority in the community, indicating some degree of formal adherence to the Mosaic Law.

The ruins of the second-century synagogue in Capernaum rest on a foundation of an earlier one, which according to one tradition is the synagogue in question here.

7:11-17 The son of the widow of Nain

This story is found only in Luke, and it is the first occurrence of restoring the dead to life found in this Gospel.

Tradition locates Nain on the southwest side of the Carmel mountain range in Galilee. That the prophet Elisha performed a similar miracle in Shunem, on the northeast side of the same mountain range, no doubt influences the response of the crowd here (see 2 Kgs 4:8-37); they exclaim, "A great prophet has arisen in our midst" (v. 16). Some commentators also see an allusion to Elijah's raising the son of the widow of Zarephath, near Sidon in present-day Lebanon (1 Kgs 17:8-24).

In both these accounts the respective prophet resuscitates the dead by lying on top of them several times, and this point highlights the difference they have with the story involving Jesus at Nain. Here Jesus simply commands the young man to rise. The action reflects Jesus' authority, and the crowd recognizes this fact.

7:18-23 The messengers from John the Baptist

This passage is the first formal encounter between John the Baptist and Jesus. Though John baptizes Jesus in 3:21-22, he does so unknowingly. The infancy narratives show the accounts dealing with the Baptist preceding those of Jesus; for example, the annunciation to Zechariah and John's birth come before the annunciation to Mary and Jesus' birth in Bethlehem. This pattern emphasizes that John the Baptist is not the Messiah, but the precursor to the Messiah. Such an understanding is underscored at the baptism and is further clarified here. John the Baptist has seen himself as the forerunner (see 3:16-17). In sending disciples to ask such a question of Jesus now, he seeks confirmation that Jesus is the Messiah for whom he has prepared the way.

The Baptist's disciples in this narrative also play a role for the early church. At this time (A.D. 80–90) and even later, there was tension between the followers of John and those of Jesus. Luke's construction of having John's disciples asking Jesus if they "should . . . look for another" (vv. 19-20) serves as the Christian community's invitation to the Baptist's disciples to join the ranks of Jesus' followers.

Jesus' answer to the Baptist's messengers is based on his ministry thus far, including the raising of the dead, as seen at Nain, which Luke places immediately before this passage. Jesus' response draws on Old Testament prophecy, especially the sayings of the prophet Isaiah (29:18-19; 35:5-6; 61:1), whose preaching is echoed in the synagogue at Nazareth (see Luke 4:18-21). In framing his words by citations from Isaiah, we see how Judaism forms the crucial context for understanding the Gospels and the New Testament.

7:24-35 Jesus and John

Jesus' testimony about John lessens the tensions between their respective disciples as it extends a welcoming embrace to the Baptist's followers. Jesus, the true Messiah, has tremendous regard and respect for John the Baptist: "A prophet? Yes, I tell you, and more than a prophet" (7:26).

The schism motif resurfaces at verses 29-30. Some who had chosen John's baptism see the plan of God fulfilled in Jesus, and others who had rejected John's baptism also reject Jesus and his message. In this latter group, Jesus mentions specifically Pharisees and scholars of the Law. The analogy of the children in the marketplace (vv. 31-32) is apt for them. No matter what the message or the deed, many people will find fault with God's design, because accepting the will of God necessitates a change in one's behavior. It would be wrong to assume that no Pharisees or scribes were disciples either of John or of Jesus; the reign of God split that group as well (see 7:1-10, 36-50; 13:31-33; 14:1-6). The hardness of heart they exhibit here crosses all class divisions.

Lest we tend to overlook the joy Jesus had in his earthly life, it would be good to note that he seems to have had the reputation of relishing good food and drink, as verses 33-34 suggest (see also 5:30; 7:36-50; 10:38-42). In addition, many of his parables and allusions are based on feasting metaphors (see 14:7-14, 15-24). As seen throughout Luke's Gospel, attention to conversion, concern for the poor, and enjoyment of all God's gifts go hand in hand. A dour disciple does not further the reign of God.

7:36-50 The woman of loving gratitude

It is often assumed that the woman is guilty of some kind of sexual sin, yet there is nothing in the text to suggest such a conclusion. The material concerning John the Baptist ("the poor have the good news proclaimed to them"—7:22) forms a good context for this passage. In the tradition this story becomes entangled with Matthew 26:6-13; Mark 14:3-9; John 12:1-8, all recording the anointing at Bethany on the journey to Jerusalem. In Luke, Jesus does not turn toward Jerusalem until 9:51, so this occasion, in the Lukan literary outline at least, is set in Galilee.

Simon the Pharisee's lack of attention to the details of hospitality notwithstanding, such an incident would be shocking in any case. Guests would have been reclining around the outside rim of a *triclinium*, a horseshoe-shaped table. While the left side of their torsos rested on elevated cushions to allow them to take food and drink with their right hand, their feet would be exposed to the wall's perimeter. Before the second century, the Roman custom was to have the *triclinium* open or near the *atrium*. Such an arrangement would explain how the woman gained access to the house. Nonetheless, she would have had to crawl around the outside rim of the table until she found the right set of feet before she could start the anointing. Even with the broadest, most accepting, and opened mind and heart, and even within the public culture of the Mideast, her actions would have been seen as suspicious or at least bizarre. Simon's consternation is understandable, if not permissible.

The text does not mention what kind of ointment the woman uses, but if it is contained in an alabaster jar, it would have been very expensive. The juxtaposition of using this ointment on the feet when the guest should have been anointed on the head accentuates the great release of guilt and shame this woman feels from having encountered Jesus somewhere along the way.

Jesus does not defend the woman by saying that she is sinless; rather, he acknowledges her sins and forgives them. The parable forms the interpretation of the event. Everyone is a sinner and everyone needs forgiveness. Only when we realize that we need the grace of Christ, do we see what a great gift the forgiveness is. This woman becomes the model of the proper response of limitless gratitude all people should show in light of the salvation Christ offers.

Simon's inner thoughts (v. 39) have an ironic twist. Jesus *is* a prophet, and he *does* know what kind of woman this is. That is why he responds in such a manner.

8:1-3 Women disciples from Galilee

Jesus' ministry is sustained and supported by the resources of several wealthy women disciples; three are named here: Mary Magdalene, Joanna, and Susanna. Joanna's marriage to Herod's steward, Chuza, certainly raises speculation on how much Herod and his court would have known about Jesus.

Luke refers to Mary Magdalene as one "from whom seven demons had gone out" (v. 2). The longer ending of Mark is the only other place in the Gospel tradition that describes her similarly (Mark 16:9). Exactly what is meant by the "seven demons" is unclear. If Jesus performed an exorcism over Mary Magdalene, there is no record of it, save for these verses from Luke and Mark; "seven demons" heightens the severity of her earlier possession.

The other evangelists do not name the women disciples until the death account (see Matt 27:56; Mark 15:40; John 19:25). Because he names the women here, Luke, who avoids repetitions, does not identify them at the crucifixion scene. He does name Mary Magdalene and Joanna as witnesses to the resurrection, however (24:10).

This group of men and women will follow Jesus to Jerusalem and remain there through the resurrection, but only the women and some of the men will stand at the cross (23:49).

8:4-18 Parables and response

The parable of the sower and its explanation appear in all three Synoptics. Luke's rendition, as usual, is a more compact version of this familiar story, leaving out the detail about the scorching sun, the shallow depth of rocky soil, and the trampled path. While Matthew 13:2 and Mark 4:1 state that the large crowd forces Jesus to preach from a boat, Luke has Jesus standing in the boat earlier in the Gospel narrative (see 5:1-11). Luke also underscores that the people come to him "from one town after another" (v. 4); Jesus' reputation has spread.

In verses 9-10 Jesus offers an explanation for parables. The "mysteries of the kingdom" (v. 10) are most probably the intuitive knowledge that comes with the intimacy the disciples have with Jesus. Paradoxically, Jesus must still explain the parable to them. This explanation can also be a reference to Isaiah 6:9-10: "Listen carefully, but you shall not understand! / Look intently, but you shall know nothing!"

That this parable is one of the clearest makes Jesus' commenting on it a puzzlement. Surely there are more difficult parables than this one that demand explanations. This dialogue, however, is the logical follow-up to the preceding one concerning the purpose of parables and an example of that intimacy the disciples have with the Lord. Its presence in the text most probably reflects the redaction of the early church in trying to underline the qualities of good disciples.

The term "seed" occurs six times in Matthew and Mark and four times in Luke. Most of the instances are in this parable and its explanation in all three Synoptics. Its use here and elsewhere shows that the word "seed" represents either the word of God or faith.

Naturally, among farmers the image is apt, and particularly so for Luke, who is writing for a community that tradition locates in Syria, one of the ancient world's breadbaskets. The farmers at this time would not plant the seed in rows as is done today; rather, they would walk along broadcasting the seed in front of them.

Any interpretation of this parable should allow for the fact that there is no limit given to the number of times the sower casts the seed. Just as a sower will go out at least once a year to plant, so will the word continue to fall on the soil. The emphasis in the parable is on the soil and the soil's response, not on the seed or the sower.

The connection that the parable of the lamp has with the explanation of the sower and the seed flows smoothly from Luke's hand. In a mixing of metaphors, the seed that has taken root in good soil now becomes a lamp. The knowledge of the mysteries of the kingdom, which we meet in verse 10, is catalyzed by the interpretation in verse 18: "To anyone who has, more will be given, and from the one who has not, even what he seems to have will be taken away." This verse is not describing the moral order; rather, it expresses growth in the word of God. Love and devotion to God build upon themselves and increase within a person to the point that others are drawn to God and the kingdom by the life of those who have let their seed flourish and their light shine. Jesus reiterates this theme when talking about the mustard seed (see Luke 13:19; 17:6).

8:19-21 Jesus and his family

Luke is less harsh in recording this event than either of the other two synoptic writers. Jesus' mother and brothers are unable to reach him "because of the crowd." In the parallel accounts in Matthew and Mark, his mother and brothers come calling for him as if he were a family embarrassment.

The question of Jesus' brothers often arises, especially in the Catholic tradition, which holds that Jesus was the only child of Mary. Explanations that the Greek word for "brother," *adelphos,* can also mean "cousin" are not at all convincing. A better basis for the claim is also founded on tradition, which sees Joseph as a man older than the young woman Mary. This tradition holds that Joseph lost his first wife to childbirth, a death common for women throughout history. Jesus' brothers, then, are really Jesus' half-brothers from Joseph's first marriage. It is impossible to prove or disprove the details of Mary's perpetual virginity. Of course, the virginal conception of Jesus is not the issue under discussion here. Luke is explicit, as is Matthew, that when Mary was pregnant with Jesus, no human father was involved (see above, Luke 1:26-38).

This short passage redefines human relationships under Christ. At this time and place, the extended family was one's first and only locus of identification. To lose or be ostracized from the family was equivalent to losing all personhood. Jesus redefines the lines of association and kinship by broadening the family boundary. Now, the evangelist seems to say, disciples form a new family, which is all-inclusive of those who hear and do the word of God. These new bonds of relationship are developed in Luke's second volume, the Acts of the Apostles.

8:22-25 The calming of the storm

With the phrase "One day" Luke shifts from Jesus' preaching to his performing miracles. The Lake of Galilee, below sea level and surrounded by hills and mountains, is well situated for sudden summer storms to arise without warning. As the hot, humid air rises, the colder air comes rushing in, causing large swells in a very small lake. Recent archaeological finds suggest that the boat would most likely have been between eight to nine meters in length (twenty-six to thirty feet), two to three meters wide (seven to nine feet), and about one to two meters high (four to six feet), certainly enough space for Jesus and a large group of disciples.

Although natural phenomena could explain the miracle—these storms subside almost as quickly as they arise—the miraculous lies at the juncture of human experience and divine intervention. People today still speak of a sudden prayer as saving them from a nearly fatal collision. There is no way to prove whether this event of calming the storm occurred or not. The believer would not be wrong to follow the tradition, which says that it did.

The importance of this story, however, is theological. Up until this point, Jesus has been ministering in the Jewish areas on the western and northern shores of the Sea of Galilee. When he says to his disciples, "Let us cross to the other side of the lake" (8:22), he means the eastern shore, which at that time was in the pagan district of the Decapolis, meaning "Ten Cities." Encountering a storm on the lake while heading toward pagan territory shows Jesus in a battle. He is taking on the cosmic forces arrayed against his ministry, and he will not be cowed by them. Here a storm, which in the pagan culture of the surrounding region would have been associated with the god Baal (see 1 Kgs 18), obeys Jesus' command and everyone is saved. He is the Lord of the cosmos.

The story ends with a question, "Who then is this . . ." (v. 25). Luke has been prompting us all along throughout this narrative with questions or statements concerning Jesus' identity (see 4:22, 34, 41; 5:21; 7:16, 49), and the evangelist will continue to do so (see 9:9) before Peter finally declares him to be the Messiah (9:20).

8:26-39 Exorcising the Gerasene demoniac

Having safely crossed the lake, Jesus and the disciples land on the eastern shore, in pagan territory. Immediately demonic forces again challenge Jesus' lordship, but this time from outside the Jewish districts.

All three Synoptics include this account of the Gerasene demoniac. The name of the locale has its textual problems. In the manuscript tradition, an alternate name for "Gerasene" is "Gadarene," a confusion stemming from the attempts of various scribes to harmonize all three accounts. This attempt at harmonization was further complicated by the fact that Matthew 8:28 reads "Gadarene." The names "Gerasene" and "Gadarene" are based on two separate cities in the Decapolis, Gerasa (or Jerash) and Gadara, respectively. Neither is located on the Sea of Galilee, although Gadara is closer to the lake than Gerasa. Most likely each city's name was used interchangeably as the generic term for the area on the eastern shore, and exacting scribes, trying to address the discrepancies in the text, actually caused more confusion. The tradition locates the site at Kursi, in the northeast quadrant of the Sea of Galilee, which sits on a steep hill above the shoreline.

Not only is the man a demoniac but also, since he lives in tombs, he would be ritually impure to the religious Jews. He calls out to Jesus in a "loud voice" (v. 28), a signal of impending judgment.

Unlike Matthew or Mark, Luke notes that Jesus had commanded the spirit to depart from the man even before the demoniac speaks.

Jesus demands the demons' name in order to show his authority over them, although he uses the singular of the noun. To know a name is to exercise control, and the demons freely give it, recognizing that they must be obedient to him. Luke alone states that the demons beg not to be sent to the abyss (v. 31). The swine, impure animals to the Jews, represent the demons' own uncleanness. In biblical Jewish thought, large bodies of water symbolized the entrance to the abyss, or Sheol. In his exorcism, Jesus sends the demons back to where they come from, the dwelling of the dead. On the one hand, he countermands their wish, and on the other, he proves to all that the demons had actually left the individual.

The pagan man, now free of demons, but bereft of friends and family due to his former state, wants to follow Jesus (v. 38). Jesus turns him into a Gentile missionary going through the city (Gadara? Gerasa?). Thus Luke prepares the reader for the mission to the Gentiles, a major theme in the Acts of the Apostles.

In Luke's narrative of Jesus' earthly ministry, Jesus has been battling the diabolical forces in the world ever since his temptation in the desert. The victory he has with this demoniac functions simultaneously as a realization and as an anticipation of the *eschaton*. In the former, all witness the flight of a legion of evil spirits. Yet the decisive showdown with Satan has yet to occur, and it will not come until Jesus dies and rises in Jerusalem.

8:40-56 Jairus's daughter and the woman with a hemorrhage

Luke follows Mark's order of having one miracle, the hemorrhaging woman, surrounded by another, the raising of Jairus's daughter.

Verse 40 informs us that Jesus has returned to the Jewish districts on the western shore of the Sea of Galilee. Luke, always the evangelist to find joy in the Gospel, specifies that the crowd "welcomed" Jesus. At this point the story of Jairus's daughter is introduced. Verse 42 prepares us for the resolution of the story, when the hemorrhaging woman enters the picture in the next verse and turns our attention.

The woman touches the tassel on Jesus' cloak (v. 44). The term "tassel" most likely refers to the fringes religious Jewish men were commanded to wear on the corners of their outer garment in Numbers 15:38. The Greek Old Testament, or Septuagint, calls these tassels *kraspedon,* the same word Luke employs here. The woman is not merely grabbing at Jesus; she wants to clutch the holiest part of his clothing, a sign of her faith. Fearing rebuke, she falls at Jesus' feet. She bears witness to Jesus' miraculous act in front of all (v. 47), while Jesus commends and blesses her. Her faith opened her to Jesus' cure (v. 48).

Luke keeps the narrative flowing by having a messenger arrive from Jairus's house with the news that the young girl is dead (v. 49) even as Jesus is still speaking. When Jesus states that Jairus' daughter is only sleeping, this crowd, different from the one that initially welcomed Jesus, ridicules him. The comparison between the people in the two groups is noteworthy. The first, not enveloped by the fear and dread of losing a child, are in better straits to receive Jesus and his message with happiness and joy. The second, however, watching the passing of the girl and seeing the suffering of the parents, are too preoccupied to concern themselves with Jesus' visit. The Lord's visitation, however, comes to them, too, with the resuscitation of the daughter. Once again, faith is the operative condition for this miracle (v. 50).

Jesus allows only Peter, John, and James to enter the house with him. These three are selected out from the other members of the Twelve at the transfiguration as well (9:28). Peter occupies a central role in the Acts of the Apostles and the early church. John and James are the sons of Zebedee (5:10); the latter was martyred by Herod Agrippa (Acts 12:2), but what of John? There is a tradition that he is the beloved disciple, the author of the Fourth Gospel (John 13:23; 19:26; 20:2; 21:7, 20-24), but this conclusion cannot be substantiated with absolute certainty. Nonetheless, Paul refers to James, John, and Peter (Kephas) as "pillars" of the church in Jerusalem (Gal 2:9).

9:1-6 The mission of the Twelve

The ninth chapter of Luke introduces a shift in focus. Whereas Luke treats the Galilean ministry in chapters 4 through 8, chapter 9 turns the narrative's attention to the disciples and the beginning of the journey to Jerusalem.

By giving the Twelve authority over the demons, and linking that with the kingdom of God and curing, Luke heightens the eschatological tone of Jesus' ministry. Jesus empowers his followers to join the cosmic battle with Satan. This warfare begins in the temptation scene (Luke 4:1-13) and surfaces throughout the Gospel, coming to a head at the crucifixion.

The injunction to take nothing for the journey ensures complete trust in God. That the Twelve are successful in their curing demonstrates that the kingdom of God has arrived. While this passage is most likely describing the missionary activity of the early church, it does not discount the probability that Jesus had at least the Twelve performing similar deeds in his life on earth. The parallels in the other Synoptics support such an assertion.

The Twelve are commissioned and sent (*apostellō*, 6:2), from which we get the word "apostle." On their names, see Luke 6:12-16.

9:7-9 Herod's thoughts

Herod Antipas was tetrarch of Galilee and Perea. His query in verse 9 echoes that of the disciples in the storm-tossed boat in Luke 8:25 and gives the reader an idea of the questions circulating during Christianity's infancy: Who is Jesus, and, in this case, what is his relationship to John the Baptist? In the Jewish tradition, Elijah is supposed to return to usher in the messianic age. See also 23:6-12.

Herod's wily and suspicious nature comes through in this passage. Unlike Matthew and Mark, Luke does not report Herod's infamous birthday celebration, which leads to the beheading of the Baptist, although earlier in his Gospel the third evangelist notifies the reader that Herod has had John imprisoned (3:19-20). From the Jewish historian Josephus, (*Ant.* 18.5.2) we obtain the information that Herod put John to death at his fortress-palace of Machaerus in the Transjordan.

In this description, Josephus also mentions the important detail that Herod feared John because the Baptist drew large crowds. Crowds could always fall into rioting and insurrection. Eventually both Roman and Jewish authorities will have similar fear of Jesus and will form an alliance to execute him as well.

9:10-17 Return of the Twelve and the feeding of the five thousand

Luke, as well as Mark, juxtaposes the return of the apostles with Herod's questioning about Jesus' identity. Herod tries to suppress the movement even as the movement continues to grow despite his efforts. Bethsaida, a town east of the Jordan River but on the northern shore of the Sea of Galilee, is part of the "Gospel Triangle," that segment of the land about which nearly eighty percent of Jesus' ministry takes place. Just south of the town lies a volcanic deposit of basalt rock and rubble making farming or habitation impossible. Most likely this locale is the "private" area mentioned in verse 10.

The account of the feeding of the five thousand occurs in all four Gospels, though Matthew 15:32-39 and Mark 8:1-10 also feature a feeding of four thousand. The action of first blessing and then breaking the bread has strong eucharistic overtones, and as such, provides eschatological imagery.

Other details play into this imagery as well. Fish, because of their abundance, often symbolize the eschatological banquet. They can also refer to *garum*, a relish made of putrefying fish that was in heavy demand throughout the ancient Mediterranean world. The Greek verb *kataklinō* in verse 14 means to sit or recline at dinner, another reference to the eschatological banquet.

Luke has the crowd gather specifically in groups of fifty, which divides into five thousand evenly. Such a refinement allows Pentecost to function as an interpretive backdrop. In the Jewish tradition at this time, Pentecost was a celebration of the grain harvest and took place fifty days or seven weeks after Passover. In time the feast came to celebrate the giving of the Law to Moses, but whether it commemorated the Sinai covenant at this period is difficult to determine. In any case, the abundance of grain at harvest time symbolizes the abundant blessing of the end times. That five loaves of bread plus two fish equal the number seven underscores the emphasis on Pentecost. Of course, Luke writes about Pentecost in Acts 2, and that feast has prime importance in his work. The feeding of the five thousand, therefore, is one of Luke's ways to foreshadow the *eschaton*.

9:18-27 Peter's confession and the cost of discipleship

Luke is the only evangelist to open Peter's confession scene with Jesus at prayer. Although Matthew has the most elaborate version of Peter's confession, the other synoptic writers recount it. In all three Gospels, Jesus poses the question to the disciples, but Peter is the only one who answers. Their comments about John the Baptist and Elijah recapitulate Herod's thoughts in trying to identify Jesus. Elijah was the prophet whose return would usher in the coming of the Messiah. John the Baptist, as precursor, fits into this category as well, and mention of his name here reflects the early Christian community's appeal to the Baptist's disciples, who still feel that the Baptist is the Messiah.

All Synoptics display a set of three passion predictions. This one is Luke's first (see 9:44; 18:31-33). The context colors the moment. The eschatological overtones in both the feeding of the five thousand and Peter's confession take on a stark reality in the passion prediction. Yes, Jesus is the Messiah ushering in a new age in which all can participate, but that new age comes with a price.

An aphorism encapsulates one of the great paradoxes of Christian life: gain is really loss and loss is really gain (v. 24). In the Lukan narrative, these words prepare the disciples for what lies ahead as it encourages the Lukan community. The eschatological term "Son of Man," along with one of Luke's favorite phrases, "kingdom of God," reaffirms the eschatological dimension that must be a part of any disciple of Christ.

9:28-36 The transfiguration of Jesus

Chapter 9 continues to focus on the small group of disciples, and once again we see Jesus at prayer. The interplay between the mission, eschatological feeding, confession, passion prediction, conditions of discipleship, and now transfiguration form a synthesis of Christian life.

What is the purpose of following Jesus, and where will it all lead? Luke as well as Matthew and Mark answers the question with the transfiguration. Many consider this event to be an account of a post-resurrection appearance. That all three Synoptics situate it within the ministry, however, militates against such an interpretation. It is better to view it as a foreshadowing of the glorification of the resurrection. Placed within this context of passion predictions and discipleship, the transfigured Christ shows the disciples, through Peter, James, and John, the promise that discipleship can bring both to this life and the life to come.

Moses and Elijah, representing the Law and the Prophets, respectively, give their approbation to what the disciples are seeing. Elijah's presence

also has an element of foreshadowing; according to Jewish tradition, he is to usher in the messianic age. Both these worthies speak to Jesus of the "exodus" he is about to accomplish in Jerusalem (v. 31). "Exodus" has a double meaning. Naturally, the reader draws on the account of the Israelites' deliverance from death and slavery in Egypt to freedom and new life in the Promised Land. "Exodus," however, can also refer to death. On this basis, Jesus' death is a deliverance from slavery to new life, and his exodus is completed at the resurrection and ascension. Because so much of the material in this chapter deals with discipleship, the meaning death has for Jesus is the same for those who follow him.

The voice from the cloud resonates with the voice at the baptism (3:21-22), but with two differences. At the baptism, Luke writes, the voice comes from heaven and says, "You are my beloved Son; with you I am well pleased"; but here at the transfiguration, the voice comes from the cloud and says, "This is my chosen Son, listen to him" (v. 35). Because the voice from heaven at the baptism is in the second person, only Jesus hears it. At the transfiguration, the voice is in the third person, allowing the three disciples to hear it as well. The reference to the cloud is an echo from Exodus, where the glory of God's presence (Shekinah) is depicted as a cloud (Exod 13:21). God is present at the transfiguration too.

In Matthew's and Mark's version of the transfiguration, Jesus commands the three disciples not to say anything about what they had seen. Luke simply writes, however, that the three kept silent about the whole event "at that time" (v. 36). Although noting that the place of the transfiguration was of no importance to Luke, the tradition, based on Matthew 17:1 and Mark 9:2, locates it on Mount Tabor.

Placed in the context of the mission, eschatology, passion, and discipleship, the transfiguration becomes part of the promise to those who follow Jesus. As he is transfigured into glory by following the Father's will, so too will each Christian disciple be transfigured.

9:37-50 Exorcism and lessons on the kingdom

This case of demonic possession balances the eschatological tone of transfigured glorification by interjecting an attack from the realm of evil. Though the boy's symptoms seem like a case of epilepsy, and may very well have been, sickness was often attributed to the machinations of the devil. In the sense that goodness is from God and illness is not a good, the ancient interpretation hits the mark. Jesus, the one whom Peter confesses as the Messiah and the one whose glory is seen in the transfiguration, reclaims creation for God in the cure of the possessed boy. Only Luke concludes this story by saying that all were "astonished by the majesty of God" (v. 43). Not only does this bit of editing direct attention to the true source and goal of the exorcism, but it also enables the evangelist to omit verses that underscore the disciples' poor performance (see Matt 17:19-20; Mark 9:28-29). In his harsh words, Jesus shows his frustration in getting the message across to those closest to him (v. 41).

While all are marveling at God's greatness, Jesus predicts his passion for the second time (vv. 45-46). The redemption of creation will not be easy and will not be without suffering and death, a sober reminder after the transfiguration and the exorcism. The Lukan Jesus is emphatic about the suffering he must undergo (v. 44). Matthew and Mark do not include this heightened urgency in their parallel accounts. All three Synoptics, however, show the disciples afraid to ask for clarification about the upcoming passion. Luke states that the meaning was "hidden" from them (v. 45), a comment that ties into Jesus' frustration at verse 41 and leads into the instruction on greatness.

The disciples have difficulty comprehending the meaning behind the life and work of Jesus, as the argument about greatness demonstrates (vv. 46-48). With all they have seen in the ministry, all they have experienced by way of miracles, healings, and for at least three of them, the transfiguration, they still measure success according to the world's standards. The child whom Jesus placed at his side was most probably part of a group of children who would beg, pester, and tag along with these strangers for part of the distance through a town. Receiving a child like this is not always easy to do, yet that is the point of Jesus' action. Furthermore, in the society of that time, children were obligated to show respect to adults, not vice versa. The placement of this pericope after the second passion prediction for a lesson on greatness is particularly apropos.

The account about another exorcist (vv. 49-50) highlights the dispute about prestige and the ri-

valry the disciples have among themselves. The jealousies of the petty despots who ruled all of Palestine often prevented them from working toward mutual self-interest. For the Christian, the horizon line must be higher.

THE JOURNEY TO JERUSALEM
Luke 9:51–19:27

In all three Synoptic accounts, Jesus makes only one trip to Jerusalem, and that journey ends in his passion, death, and resurrection. Luke is the only evangelist, however, to magnify Jerusalem's theological purpose; it is the crucible into which Jesus' whole earthly ministry is funneled. Jerusalem becomes the city of destiny.

This point also marks the beginning of what some scholars call the "Big Interpolation," a large section of material that cannot be linked to Mark and, with few exceptions, has no parallel in Q. The interpolation extends to 18:14.

9:51-56 Departure for Jerusalem and Samaritan inhospitality

Luke describes the shift toward the holy city most dramatically (v. 51). The phrase "When the days for being taken up were fulfilled" signals the end of his Galilean ministry according to a divine plan. "He resolutely determined to journey to Jerusalem" shows an intensity of purpose in completing that divine plan. Luke's vocabulary in verse 51 breathes with metaphor. The Greek for "being taken up, received up" is the word *analēmpsis,* which means both "ascension" and "death." When combined with the "exodus" referred to in the transfiguration (v. 31), there develops the composite picture of death and glorification.

Jesus is going up, both literally and figuratively. Jerusalem is over 900 meters (2700 feet) above sea level, while the Sea of Galilee is nearly 100 meters (300 feet) below; he and his disciples must climb the Judean mountains to reach the city. Metaphorically, after the passion, death, and resurrection, Jesus will ascend to the Father, an ascension that also is his glorification. These events begin and, in a large way, take place within the time frame of Passover, the Jewish commemoration of the Exodus.

Luke's detail about passing through the Samaritan villages raises some questions. Jews in Galilee would avoid passing through Samaria as they made their way south to Jerusalem. The usual route was to walk along the Jordan Valley and begin the ascent at Jericho. It appears that Luke might be relying on some ancient tradition that Jesus passed through, if not ministered in, Samaria. John's story of the Samaritan woman at the well (4:4-41) corroborates Jesus' presence in that territory. Moreover, according to Acts, Samaria was the first non-Jewish region to be converted to Christianity. This short foray into Samaria functions as a foreshadowing of the missionary activity that the Acts of the Apostles will detail. Jesus' rebuke constitutes his stand against vengeance and violence, as well as reflecting his attitude toward missionary activity (see 9:5).

9:57-62 Would-be followers of Jesus

Whereas the disciples have already heard the discourse on the cost of discipleship (see 9:23-27), others joining Jesus have not. Jesus relates the proper comportment in three situations: one to a person who is ready to give all for the kingdom, another to a person who is asked to give all for the kingdom, and still another to one who wants to hold back from giving all to the kingdom. Jesus challenges them by using imagery and hyperbole. The curt answers he gives show the rhythm of someone hurrying with a direct purpose in mind, and the vacillation Jesus encounters with these three would deflect from that purpose.

To the first individual, Jesus underscores that personal comfort will often have to give way to the demands of discipleship. His response to the second may seem harsh, but in no way is it to be understood as negating one's obligations to one's parents or family. Rather, Jesus is seeing through what constitutes a lame excuse while speaking on a symbolic level. To follow Jesus is to enter into a life-giving relationship. There are plenty of people who refuse this relationship, and in this sense they are dead; they can bury the physically dead. The reply to the third individual likewise shows the immediacy of the call. In the Jewish and Hellenistic societies, family bonds were very tight and could hold one back from being a disciple. Jesus first addresses this situation in 8:19-21, and his answer here is similar.

10:1-16 The mission of the seventy-two

The ancient manuscripts are evenly divided over whether the mission involves seventy or seventy-two disciples. Both numbers have a basis in the Old Testament. Seventy-two is a multiple of twelve, the number of the tribes of Israel; thus, by their going forth, a like number of disciples could represent the universalism of Jesus' mission. Alternatively, the narrative in Exodus 24 includes seventy elders who ascend the mountain with Moses, thereby making the disciples representatives of the Mosaic tradition.

Luke is the only evangelist to have a commissioning of a second group. In comparing the directives to the seventy-two disciples with the commissioning of the Twelve (9:1-6), we can see some differences as well as some points of contact. The Twelve are given authority over demons and the ability to cure diseases. Furthermore, they are charged with proclaiming the good news. The seventy-two disciples, on the other hand, travel in pairs as they bring the good news to households and towns. They are told to cure the sick, but Jesus says nothing about exorcizing demons; yet, they also do so (see v. 17).

Both the Twelve and the seventy-two are to travel light and perform with a singularity of purpose. In this section Jesus calls attention to attributes of Middle Eastern hospitality: there will always be someone to invite them into his or her home. The seventy-two are also told not to abuse the hospitality shown them (v. 8). Both groups are to shake the dust from the street of those towns that do not accept them (v. 11). An important difference, however, is that the seventy-two are to go ahead of Jesus and prepare towns for Jesus' eventual visit.

There is much debate on who constitutes the seventy-two. Were the Twelve selected from the seventy-two, or did they stand independent of them? Were there only seventy-two disciples, or were these seventy-two chosen from a much larger group? Were women in the line of Deborah, Hulda, Esther, Miriam, and Ruth involved, or was the mission restricted to men? These questions are difficult to answer. The important point is that Jesus commissions others to do his work on earth, and as such, the church does that work in him and in his name. Indeed, like the seventy-two, the church prepares the world for Jesus' visitation.

Jesus' comment about Sodom places the Christian message in context. To refuse the redemption he offers is a more heinous sin than any transgressions of sexual morality or proper hospitality.

Even the Gentile cities of Tyre and Sidon will fare better, since they can read the signs of the times (v. 13).

10:17-20 Return of the seventy-two

The joy of the seventy-two disciples arises from the power they have over demons, a power given them by Jesus and only in his name. Jesus' response in verse 18 seems awkward to many. Some scholars have suggested that the proper translation should be "They have observed Satan fall like lightning from the sky," with the subject of the imperfect verb, *theōreō* ("observe"), being "demons" in verse 17. Greek grammar can support such a construction. A conclusion can be that since the demons see Satan fall from the sky, they easily submit to the disciples. The disciples, empowered by Jesus, become agents with him in furthering the realm of God.

The section closes with Jesus reaffirming the purpose and direction of the disciples' new power. They are not self-serving magicians or sorcerers; they are participants in Jesus' ministry. The disciples, like Jesus and those whom they help, find their reward in God, a point that gains in importance as they follow him to the cross in Jerusalem.

10:21-24 The prayer of Jesus and blessing of the disciples

Luke frequently shows Jesus at prayer. Reflecting the joy the disciples display in their return, Jesus offers praise and thanksgiving to the Father. Luke connects this joy to the Spirit, who, in the Acts of the Apostles, takes on a greater role of consoling and fructifying (see Acts 2:1-36). Luke's reversal theme is evident in verse 21, with revelation coming to the childlike but not to the wise and learned. The whole monologue appears to come from Q (see Matt 11:25-27; 13:16-17) and is one of the few places in the synoptic tradition that shows Jesus explaining his relationship to the Father in a pattern that seems very Johannine.

The disciples, who went out on the mission without money bag, sack, or sandals, receive a great reward in their experience of life in the Lord. The prophets and kings did not see or hear the Messiah of God (Luke 9:20), but the disciples have seen and heard not only the Messiah but also the works done in his name. These works consist in redeeming the world from Satan's clutches.

10:25-29 The greatest commandment

Jesus answers the "scholar of the law" or lawyer with a question. This tack precludes any trap or misunderstanding by unveiling the true motivation on the lawyer's part. The verb "test" in verse 25 is also applied to the devil in the temptation scene (Luke 4:12), thereby emphasizing the sinister quality of the lawyer's question.

Jesus turns the encounter to his advantage. The law that the lawyer quotes is the Jewish Shema, the prayer a devout Jew would recite everyday (Deut 6:4-5). The second half is found in Leviticus 19:18. By endorsing the lawyer's reply, Jesus proves to him and to all listeners that he and his message are not contrary to the Jewish tradition; rather, Jesus forces the audience to see his teaching as an elaboration or refinement of that tradition.

The scholar of the law, however, presses the point with his next question: "And who is my neighbor?" (v. 29). In this verse Luke states that the lawyer wishes to "justify himself," that is, to prove to Jesus in front of the people that he, the legal scholar, is in good stead in the eyes of God. Jesus challenges the lawyer further by responding with the parable of the Good Samaritan.

10:30-37 The parable of the Good Samaritan

Upon the death of King Solomon, Samaria, the region north of Judea, became the center of the northern kingdom at the division of the united monarchy. The Assyrians conquered it in 722 B.C., carted away most of the Israelite inhabitants, and replaced them with conquered peoples from other parts of their empire. These newcomers married into those Israelites left behind, resulting in a population too mixed for the religious Jews in the south to consider part of the covenant. In addition, these northerners, holding only to the books of Genesis through Deuteronomy, maintained their religious cult on Mount Gerizim in Shechem, whereas the Jews in the south saw true worship as taking place only in Jerusalem. The animosity was mutual, as we see in Luke 9:52-54. Samaritans still live and worship on Mount Gerizim today.

This parable exists only in Luke and reflects the theological direction set out in the Gospel and the Acts of the Apostles. The shock value of using a Samaritan as the protagonist in this parable is twofold. The road from Jerusalem to Jericho is solidly in Judea; thus the Samaritan is an unwelcome foreigner in an unfriendly country. The mention of this road also forces the audience to consider the possibility that he has worshiped in Jerusalem. Secondly, for any Samaritans who might hear this parable, this protagonist, by virtue of his journey to Jerusalem, would be a national traitor. On all fronts, then, he can claim no ethnic allegiance, and no people will claim him.

First the priest and then the Levite happen upon the half-dead victim. As officials in the Jerusalem temple, from which they are most probably returning, their prime concern is maintaining ritual purity. There has been shedding of blood, and if the man is dead, they would disqualify themselves from any temple service until undergoing the proper ritual purification, a time-consuming practice. They both avoid the problem by crossing to the other side of the road. The only one to respond mercifully is the outsider of two closed societies.

The searing lesson of this parable comes in verses 36-37. The lawyer would know from Leviticus 19:18 that a neighbor is defined as one's countryman and is limited by ethnic background. The parable, however, breaks through such an interpretation. The neighbor is the one who acts compassionately toward another, ethnic divisions notwithstanding.

Although the parable is prompted by an antagonistic question from a Jewish scholar, it would be wrong to think that this parable is addressed only to the ancient Jewish audience. In the Acts of the Apostles, Luke has an evangelizing mission to Samaria. This parable would have been as difficult for Samaritans to listen to as it would have been for the Jews. After all, the Samaritan is in Jewish territory returning from a Jewish holy city, and, depending on how one would want to view the tale, he aids a Jewish unfortunate.

The lesson for the Lukan community is the same for today's reader. To be a neighbor forces a Christian to go beyond friend and family and extend welcome and mercy to the outcast and even to one's enemy.

10:38-42 The discipleship of Martha and Mary

Traditionally, many have seen this story, which appears only in Luke, as a comparison between the Christian active life, symbolized by Martha, and the contemplative life, represented by Mary. Some exegetes interpret it as Luke's subtle way of silencing and sidelining women in the Christian ministry. The Lukan context, as others have pointed out, challenges both these assumptions.

Mary and Martha share a common ministry in the church. They are models for both men and women of a partnership in service to the reign of God. In this service the love of God is the source and end of all human endeavor, which Mary remembers but Martha seems to have forgotten. The gentle correction that Jesus offers Martha is a reminder to her that work is nothing without its connection to God. For this reason Martha needs Mary as much as Mary needs Martha.

11:1-13 Teachings on prayer

The Our Father or Lord's Prayer (11:1-4) has a revered place within the Christian tradition. With its references to the "name" (v. 2), "bread" (v. 3), and "sins" (v. 4), this prayer underscores a Jewish background. The differences between the Matthean and the Lukan accounts reflect a different theological nuance. While Luke, for example, does not highlight the separation between heaven and earth, Matthew does so by use of such phrases as "Our Father in heaven" (6:9) and "your will be done, / on earth as in heaven" (6:10). This discrepancy led many ancient scribes to try to harmonize Luke's address with Matthew's by adding the phrase "Our . . . in heaven" to "Father" in their versions of Luke's text. Luke's address here, however, matches all the other instances where the Lukan Jesus prays: "I give you praise, Father, Lord of heaven and earth" (10:21); "Father, if you are willing, take this cup away from me" (22:42); "Father, forgive them, they know not what they do" (23:34); and "Father, into your hands I commend my spirit" (23:46).

The structure is the same in the Lukan and Matthean accounts, subtle differences between the two notwithstanding. They both open by hallowing God's name, thereby affirming the divine majesty. They then move to Christ's intermediary role and conclude with a human petition.

Many see Luke's use of "sins" as his way of demonstrating Christ's efficacy. With his merciful forgiveness manifested in his passion, death, and resurrection, Jesus defeats Satan by breaking the vicious circle of suffering, fear, hate, and revenge the devil uses to hold humankind in thrall. The person at prayer asks Christ to forgive, and Christ has done so; therefore the person must also forgive.

Matthew's version of the Our Father (see Matt 6:9-13) is better known; indeed, this title for the prayer comes from the Matthew's account and not from Luke's. It is Matthew's rendition that also appears to be the basis for the Our Father found in the early Christian work called the *Didache* (8:2). The *Didache*'s version of the prayer became the form used throughout the centuries and includes the doxology that many Christian churches use in their worship. With the Lord's Prayer as a background, Luke continues the teaching on prayer with the parable of the importunate friend, a reading found only in Luke. Luke's wry comparison between divine response and human reaction—"if he does not get up to give him the loaves because of their friendship, he will get up to give him whatever he needs because of his persistence"—is echoed in the Lukan parable of the persistent widow (18:1-8). The point is that if humans will act on behalf of the petitioner solely from self-serving interest, how much more will God act from love. According to the Palestinian-Jewish custom of the day, the whole family slept on floor bedding in a single room, above the animals. To open the door would not only rouse the family but would also cause a fuss with the livestock, and all in the dark.

Luke tells us how prayers are answered (11:9-13). In his schema they have a natural, thematic, and visual flow from the parable. Someone coming at night would have to *seek* the house and door of a friend. Once found, he or she would have to *knock* at the door persistently to rouse the inhabitant to *open* it. The references to a snake and a scorpion provide insight into human response to an answered prayer. The listener or hearer would answer the rhetorical questions in verses 11-12 with a firm "None!" Such imagery, however, calls a person to faith. What might appear to be a snake or a scorpion at first glance might actually be the granted request. Again, the reader encounters Luke's analogical style based on divine response and human reaction (11:13).

11:14-23 The Beelzebul controversy

Each Gospel shows some version of the Beelzebul controversy. Although much of this section is from Q, there is evidence of what is called a "Marcan-Q Overlap"; that is, Q material is intri-

cately tied up with Marcan narrative. A comparison between Matthew 12:29, Luke 11:20-21, and Mark 3:27 is such an example. To be sure, there are no Johannine parallels to the synoptic readings here, but there are certainly traces of such accusations against Jesus at several points in the Fourth Gospel: John 7:20; 8:48-52; 10:20-21. This multiple attestation makes certain the conclusion that Jesus was accused of being in league with the devil during his ministry.

Luke uses this pericope as one of the defining moments in his two-volume narrative. Whereas Matthew and Mark both state that someone must first tie up the strong man, Luke states that someone must overcome or be victorious over the strong man (11:22). There has been evidence of victory all along in the Lukan text.

11:24-26 The return of the evil spirit

Luke sees the contest with Satan as a real battle, and the enemy does not relinquish control easily. The house to which the seven other evil spirits return is the same good one from which the unclean spirit had previously departed. Their roaming through "arid regions searching for rest" stands as a metaphor for those people who do not fill their lives with the goodness of God. Nature abhors a vacuum, and thus seven other wicked spirits find a home within the now empty individual (v. 26). This understanding can be applied to Judas, about whom Luke states that Satan "enter[s]" (22:3). Judas never allowed into his heart the grace that Jesus brings, and thus the wicked spirits take up residence there.

In Luke's Gospel, the battle between Christ and Satan, announced at the birth (1:78-79), begins at the temptation (4:1-13). Jesus has been waging and winning battles against the devil demons all along, but Christ's ultimate victory over Satan, a victory of light over darkness, will come at the cross. This theme continues in the Acts of the Apostles.

11:27-28 True blessedness

The narrative flow forms a juxtaposition of seeming opposites. After the long deliberation about Beelzebul, the strong man, and unclean spirits, a woman in the crowd turns the subject to blessedness, and does so by making a reference to Jesus' mother. Jesus' response, however, demonstrates that his call goes beyond natural kinship;

indeed, natural kinship might even be an impediment (see 8:19-21).

11:29-32 The demand for a sign

Luke avoids redundancy. The narrative sequence has already informed the reader that people are testing and arguing with Jesus (see Luke 11:15), so, unlike Matthew and Mark (12:38; 8:11-12), Luke does not mention Pharisees or scribes badgering Jesus. Jesus simply continues with his teaching.

The book of Jonah forms the necessary background for any interpretation of this passage. The Lukan text in verse 30 is helpful in this regard by supplying the central element of that particular Old Testament work. That Nineveh was the ancient capital of the Assyrians, the people who ravaged the Israelite kingdom under Shalmaneser V in 722 B.C., sharpens the drama of the Jonah story. Jonah is the son of Amittai. Amittai is also the name of one of the prophets from the time of King Jeroboam II (786–746 B.C.). If the name Amittai refers to one and the same person, then it would have been understood that Jonah came from the Israelite kingdom just as the Assyrian Empire was menacing it.

Jonah is sent on a mission, therefore, into absolutely alien and hostile territory, to a land feared and despised by all his compatriots. After fits and starts, including a sojourn in the belly of a great fish (Jonah 2:1), Jonah reaches his destination and preaches judgment, with the result that the whole city of Nineveh, from the king to the lowliest beast, repents. This repentance is the sign of Jonah to which Luke refers in verses 29-30. The explanation continues.

In verse 31 Luke also has a reference to "the queen of the south," or the Queen of Sheba (see 1 Kgs 10:1ff.; 2 Chr 9:1ff.; Matt 12:42). With this allusion the lesson works in reverse: the pagan makes the journey to the land of the true God. In both cases nonbelievers make acts of repentance or faith. Jesus draws a comparison and contrast between those within and those outside the pale of revelation, and in so doing, proclaims the wide invitation of God's love and salvation as well as the breadth of human response to it. In the end Jonah, with his example of the Ninevites, and the queen of the south, with her pilgrimage to Solomon, will stand in judgment of those who reject Jesus.

11:33-36 The visibility of light

These verses are a reprise of the lamp motif seen in 8:16ff. Luke elaborates the analogy here. The discourses about Jonah and the queen of the south in verses 30-31 above provide the example of how "lights" and "lamps" can further evangelization. Matthew uses this Q material as well but places it at two different locations within the Sermon on the Mount (5:13-16 and 6:22-23). Luke, on the other hand, finishes this section with a wonderful simile for a true disciple. The Christian life involves the whole body and all human action. The way people conduct themselves determines the persons they will become. Filled with faith, these people, by their brightness will lead others from darkness into the light of faith. The light and darkness dichotomy in this Q material is reminiscent of John's Gospel.

11:37-54 Denunciation of the legal experts

This section, called the "Woes," has a parallel in Matthew 23:1-38. Differences between the two can be seen in Matthew's concern for and knowledge of the Law, something that Luke, in writing for a Gentile audience, has no need to address.

The Pharisee literally invites Jesus to breakfast, indicated by the Greek verb *aristáō*. If Palestinian social customs of ancient times are in any way similar to those today, the breakfast would be quite substantial and would be taken around ten o'clock in the morning, but it would not be the main meal of the day, which is taken in the evening. The fact that Pharisees and scholars take issue with Jesus in the manner that they do exposes an ulterior motive: they wish to observe his behavior with hopes of gaining evidence against him. If they had really wished to honor him, they would have invited him for the evening repast. Jesus recognizes this plot and responds by revealing their true motives in front of all. He also exhibits the shallowness and hypocrisy of their deeds. Jesus' denunciation at verses 47-51 foreshadows his own death. The system that killed the prophets will also, by implication, kill him, as verses 53-54 substantiate.

It is difficult to identify which Zechariah (v. 51) Luke is referring to. Many see him as Zechariah the priest, son of Jehoiadah (see 2 Chr 24:20-22). Others have seen him as Zechariah the priest, the father of John the Baptist.

12:1-12 In face of persecution

We last read of the crowds in 11:29. Mention of them here returns our focus to Jesus' preaching. The reference to the "leaven . . . of the Pharisees" (v. 1) thematically connects this scene with the meal at the Pharisee's house (11:27-54).

In verse 4 Jesus calls his disciples, and possibly by extension the rest of the people, "friends." This is the only occurrence in all three Synoptic Gospels in which we see this form of address applied to Jesus' followers, and it is another example of a tradition Luke seems to share with John (see John 15:14-15).

In a time of persecution, people generally go into hiding and maintain a secret existence. Jesus' admonition describes a situation in which no hiding will be possible, even if it were desirable. True fear should be reserved for the One who can cast a believer into Gehenna after the body is dead (v. 5). This phrase serves as a circumlocution emphasizing that we need fear only God.

"Gehenna" is a Greek transliteration of the Hebrew *Hinnom,* the name of the valley on the western side of Jerusalem. Often cursed by the Jewish prophets for the child sacrifice that the Jerusalemites practiced there, it is also called Topheth (see 2 Kgs 23:10; Jer 7:31-32; 19:6, 11-14). In time, the Valley of Hinnom functioned as the city garbage dump, thereby making it ritually unclean. In both Jewish and Christian canonical and deuterocanonical texts, Gehenna is the metaphor for hell. As Jesus makes plain in other parts of his ministry, we have a hand in determining our salvation by opting to participate in God's grace. He emphasizes that our salvation lies beyond the reach of any persecutor.

Not even denying Christ in the face of danger and threat will bring eternal condemnation; only a sin against the holy Spirit has that power. The sin against the holy Spirit is the refusal of God's mercy and forgiveness when it is offered. Here, too, by having the choice to accept or reject the love of Christ, we have a role in determining our salvation.

God will not abandon those facing the sword. The holy Spirit will not only be present in fortifying the witnesses to Jesus but will also direct them in their actions and speak on their behalf, as Luke demonstrates in the Acts of the Apostles.

12:13-21 Greed and riches

This section consists of a dialogue followed by a parable. The first half, prompted by someone in the crowd calling out to Jesus, succinctly presents Jesus' true role and ministry while offering an ethical and eschatological lesson.

The person who calls out from the crowd misunderstands Jesus' mission. The person errs by viewing Jesus as an arbiter whose judgment rests on interpreting the intricacies of a legal code. Jesus refuses to be cast in such a position, and he turns the table on the questioner as well as the brother. The issue, Jesus implies, is not who is right or wrong about the inheritance; it is about greed and avarice. If both exhibited less covetousness, one would be inclined to share with the other, and the other would not suspect that he was being cheated. Jesus' ministry is to the lost, and both brothers are sinners. His action allows the two to receive his message. No one loses, and both have the opportunity to enter the kingdom. The parable of the rich fool, which follows (vv. 16-21), illustrates the lesson.

At no point in his discourse does the rich fool credit God for the harvest. Furthermore, he never acknowledges that the bounty should have some purpose other than satisfying his own desires. Because he is so selfish and self-centered, he dies without benefit of both his wealth and God's love. With this parable, Jesus warns the two brothers to guard against ending up like the rich fool—a total loser. An example of how bad it will be for someone like this individual is found in the parable of the rich man and Lazarus (16:19-31).

12:22-34 Trust and faith in God

Matthew places this discourse within the Sermon on the Mount (see Matt 6:25-34), while Luke situates it on the journey to Jerusalem. Nonetheless, the lesson is the same: God's love is so abundant that he looks after every human need. In Luke, this passage provides the proper frame of mind and heart that stands in contrast to the focus of the rich fool seen above (vv. 16-21).

The Greek *korax,* translated here as "ravens" (v. 24), can also mean "crow"; in any case, it refers to a scavenger. Not only was such a creature forbidden as food to Jews, but it was considered a disgusting bird also among Gentile Greeks. Its repulsive character, therefore, makes the comparison all the more striking. Using the rhetorical form of the comparison of the greater, the listener or reader understands that if God tends to the needs of a repugnant carrion-eater, how much more will he care for his beloved people (see also Ps 147:9 and Job 38:41).

This same type of comparison is employed further on in the passage with the flowers, called *krinon* in Greek. Most probably it is the crocus, referred to in other parts of the Bible as the "rose of Sharon" (Song 2:1). Against the green Galilean hillsides in rainy times of the year, these blossoms give a dazzling appearance. Yet the spectacular color of the grass and flowers is short-lived. As soon as the weather turns warm, both the herbage and the blooms shrivel up. In a land with little wood, dried grass is often used for fuel. Once again we hear the comparison of the greater. If God shows so much attention to what ends up in the fire, how much more does he care for his people.

Luke introduces a social justice theme not paralleled in Matthew's version. The "inexhaustible treasure in heaven" (v. 33) comes from almsgiving. Luke underscores the lesson of the discourse with verse 34. If we make ourselves rich in the eyes of God, our hearts and motivation will lead to union with God both in this life and the life to come. Furthermore, by becoming rich in heaven, we relieve ourselves of earthly anxiety.

12:35-48 The need for vigilance

The metaphors for vigilance all make the same point: the Lord's coming, or parousia, will happen when we least expect it. Each of the examples, however, gives a variety of views of what one can expect.

A master returning from a wedding would come with his bride (vv. 35-38). There would be feasting and celebration associated with the homecoming, which the servants should be ready to facilitate. In a role reversal, this master serves the servants. So too will it be at the eschatological banquet, when Jesus will be the host. The Lord's coming will arrive with the shock and surprise of a nighttime thief breaking into a house.

The notion of preparation introduces a paradox: this passage seems to contradict the parable of the rich fool (12:16-21). There readers are told not to worry about the morrow, food, or clothing, but here they are admonished not to take anything for granted, but to be ready for the unexpected. The paradox lies in the fact that adequate preparation is the result of letting go of worldly concerns and values. The prepared person will

not be attached to the concerns of this life, even though she may be immersed in the midst of them.

The parable of the wise and just servant likewise has a strain of irony running through it (vv. 42-48). A good foreman will not take advantage of those under him, and if he does, the master will depose him upon his return. Such a punishment, however, is reserved only for the servant who knew his master's will and acted shamefully. The servant who does not know the master's will and commits the same actions will get off with a lighter punishment. The parable is a lesson in discipleship that parallels Luke 19:11-27. Followers of Christ will be held to a higher standard than nonbelievers.

12:49-59 Division, signs, conduct

Although this section appears to come from Q, verses 49-50 are found only in Luke's Gospel. The evangelist wishes to underscore that discipleship is not without its price, and the world will not gladly welcome the kingdom of God. Fire and water are both elements of destruction and cleansing, and as harsh as the imagery may seem, Luke uses them here to show the immediacy and totality of the impending *eschaton*. The more specific examples of how Christ's message will be received (vv. 51-53) depict a situation in the early church, most probably within the Jewish-Christian synagogues from which the Christians were eventually expelled.

In Israel and Palestine, rain can only come from the Mediterranean and only in the winter, hence the reference to the west wind (v. 54). Similarly, the Sahara, Sinai, and Arabian deserts lie in the south and are the source of the hot, desiccating breeze (v. 55). The signs of the times should be just as obvious.

This discourse works on several levels. The historical signs are the political precariousness of the Jewish state during the intertestamental epoch: Roman occupation, political dissension, and corrupt administration threatened the society to the point of anarchy. On the religious front, the signs of the times were Jesus' ministry (see Luke 4:16-21). These signs are the same no matter what the period in history. Issues of social justice coupled with the religious and spiritual emptiness are signs pointing to the eschatological reign. The Christian is called to respond to them.

The section ends with instruction to the early Christian community itself (vv. 57-59). As a people baptized in Christ's name, they should settle differences within the community and not resort to the pagan law courts. Christians have a new standard of behavior that encompasses personal behavior as well as ways of resolving injustices. These standards extend beyond restitution and include mercy, redemption, and forgiveness. Such an interpretation does not mean covering up shameful or wrongful behavior behind a cloak of secrecy; rather, it means making the community a living symbol of justice and reconciliation (see Matt 5:25-26).

13:1-9 Sin and repentance

The incident involving Pilate referred to here is one of the few places where he is mentioned outside the passion narratives, and it is very telling.

Many see Pontius Pilate as a weak, vacillating governor who feels overwhelmed by the vagaries of the mob, and, against his better judgment, he hands Jesus over to be crucified (see Matt 27:26; Mark 15:15; Luke 23:25; John 19:16). Luke's narrative counters such an assessment by relating this slaughter, for which there is no other record in the Bible or any other extant work. Josephus refers to an uprising of Jews when Pilate uses temple money to build a Jerusalem aqueduct (*Ant.* 18.3.2 and *J.W.* 2.9.4). Pilate ruthlessly suppresses the tumult by having disguised, weapon-bearing Roman soldiers mixed among the Jews. At a given signal, they begin to hack away at the civilian population.

It is quite plausible that both Josephus and Jesus are referring to the same calamity. Likewise, along the southeastern wall of ancient Jerusalem are visible ruins from a collapsed tower (v. 4) dating to the intertestamental period, that is, the two centuries between the composition of the last book of the Old Testament and the first book of the New Testament.

The lesson that Jesus draws from these events releases human suffering from the capricious judgment of wrathful gods, where many of then contemporary pagan cults had placed it, or even from known or unknown sinful behavior, as many in the Jewish religious establishment then taught. Instead, Jesus is saying that suffering comes to good and bad alike, and that all humankind stands in need of repentance and redemption.

Someone's misfortune is not an indicator of moral culpability. John's Gospel (9:2) features a similar lesson in the healing of the person born blind (see also Ps 7:12-13).

With the parable of the fig tree (vv. 6-9), Luke employs a graceful thematic continuity from the stress on repentance to the value of the sinner. The fig tree is highly prized for the luscious texture and sweetness of its fruit (see Judg 9:10-11; 1 Kgs 5:5; 2 Kgs 18:31). Furthermore, the fruit can be dried and preserved for years on end.

The inedible variety of figs looks exactly like the edible kind. Moreover, edible figs can only be pollinated by the female fig wasp (*Blastophaga psenes*), which carries the pollen from the inedible fig and burrows into the buds of the edible one. Hence, for proper cultivation both types of fig trees are necessary. This delicate operation can confuse even the best gardeners, and patience is necessary to ensure a good harvest of the precious fruit. The lesson is that God will not give up on those who struggle with turning toward him. In addition, the great value placed on the fig tree characterizes the value of the sinner in God's eyes—not a reprobate or an outcast, but a prized possession, despite the possibility that the sinner may never "bear fruit."

13:10-17 The cure of the crippled woman on the sabbath

If Jesus was teaching in the synagogue, he must have originally met with respect from the synagogue leader. In fact, the leader reprimands not Jesus but the crowd of people who seemingly have come on the sabbath to be cured. The cause of the leader's discomfort, therefore, is not that Jesus cured but that this curing occurred on the Lord's Day. Healing was seen as work and therefore prohibited. Jesus uses this opportunity to make several points about his identity, his reign, and the world.

The Jewish sabbath, since it commemorates the seventh day on which God rested from all his labors, is literally the Lord's Day. Because of the holy character of the sabbath, the regulations against work were intended to give everyone access to this life in the Lord. Judging from Jesus' response, it appears that in this situation, the sabbath regulations had ceased to provide the spiritual renewal that originally had been associated with them. Jesus' challenge to the custom is successful only because of his authority. He thus gives the sabbath an eschatological dimension. Access to life in the Lord now becomes a foretaste of the heavenly realm, where sin and suffering are put to rout. This interpretation is evident in Jesus' reply (v. 16).

The reference to Satan in verse 16, combined with the setting of the cure on the sabbath, characterizes a central aspect of Lukan eschatology. Sickness and malady are viewed as a part of Satan's malevolent realm, which has made inroads into God's creation. Jesus' role is to redeem creation, to win it back for God. Jesus overpowers the evil forces and ushers in the eschatological reign. No longer dominated by Satan, the crippled woman now has her sabbath rest.

13:18-19 The parable of the mustard seed

All three Synoptics show this parable. The mustard seed was considered the smallest of all possible seeds. The tree itself, the *brassica nigra*, grows wild throughout Palestine and Israel, but farmers also cultivate it. With small, bright yellow flowers and slender, dark green leaves, it can grow to a large, many-branched shrub or tree. As such, it is a metaphor for the small early Christian community, which has an influence on the world going far beyond its size and number to the point that others (symbolized by birds) make their home in it.

13:20-21 The measure of yeast

This parable appears only in Matthew and Luke. The bread of the time would have been sourdough, as most bread was until the development of dry yeast. Once the dough was kneaded, pieces were pulled away, flattened, and laid over a hot metal dome called a *tamboun*. The result was a large, circular crêpe or pita.

Not much yeast was needed to cause a batch of dough to rise, so, like the parable of the mustard seed, the leaven stands as a measure for the Christian community. In this parable the woman who adds the yeast to the flour is the Christ figure.

13:22-30 The narrow door, salvation, and rejection

With this parable Jesus indirectly answers the question put to him. Restrictions to entering the kingdom do not lie with God but with the human response to the divine invitation. Because Luke

recapitulates the point that Jesus is on his way to Jerusalem (v. 22), many consider this section as the beginning of the second half of the journey narrative leading to the city of his death and resurrection.

The conventional city gate during this period had one wide, high central arch flanked by two lower, narrower portals. The main arch permitted camels, carts, and goods to pass. Those who wished to enter and who had no baggage trains could avoid the traffic by walking through either one of the narrow gates.

Applying this daily occurrence to the parable, the lesson seems to be directed to those who drag along their religious or social status, their material possessions, or their own ambitions in seeking easy access to salvation. Jesus counters this attitude by extracting a lesson from a familiar scene. Just as today those who travel light reach their destination more easily than those with much luggage, so too will those who keep their eyes and actions on salvation find the swifter path through the smaller doors. Any attempt to interpret these verses as showing that Gentiles are saved at the expense of the Jews is based on a faulty reading. The setting of the story is Jesus' trip to Jerusalem accompanied by his Jewish disciples, but the Lukan community to whom this story is told is composed mostly of Gentiles. All are instructed, therefore, to enter by the narrow gate, a passage that is difficult but not impossible.

The introduction of mixed metaphors in verses 25-30 is a result of various strands of tradition redacted into one parable. The second lesson is similar to the first: one should not rely on status to enter the kingdom. To use a modern parallel, ticket holders who arrive for a concert at the last minute may still not get in if there is a long line at the gate; their reliance on their ticket stubs proves to be no guarantee of entry. If they had been earnest in their desire, they would have arrived early and waited in line to be sure of getting a seat.

13:31-33 The Pharisees warn about Herod

Do the Pharisees come to Jesus as friends and allies, or are they simply trying to frighten Jesus into submission? In either case, Jesus does not alter his intention to head to Jerusalem. Indeed, he uses the occasion to affirm it—he must go to Jerusalem (v. 33).

Lukan eschatology once again surfaces with the blending of three statements in verse 32. As in the parable of the crippled woman (13:10-17), curing the sick is seen as a successful assault on demonic forces. Furthermore, contained in this statement is a reference to Jesus' passion, death, and resurrection: "On the third day I accomplish my purpose" (v. 32). Jesus predicts his own death with his emphatic resolution to continue to Jerusalem, though, ironically, by traveling to Jerusalem he leaves Herod's jurisdiction.

13:34-35 The lament over Jerusalem

This passage, a rhetorical apostrophe, flows from the scene with the Pharisees immediately above and is a fine example of Luke's narrative finesse. Matthew's Gospel contains a parallel account, but in that Gospel Jesus utters these words after the triumphant entry into Jerusalem (see Matt 23:37-39).

In 13:33 Jesus says that a prophet should not die outside Jerusalem. His words over the city have him identifying with that destiny, and he does so by using a lament, a prophetic genre seen most clearly in Jeremiah and Lamentations. To be sure, prophets were also slain outside Jerusalem, but given the presence of the temple within the city and the city's history with the prophets, Jeremiah and Isaiah make Jerusalem the major symbol of a prophet's destiny (see 1 Kgs 9:7-8; 2 Kgs 21:16; Ps 118:2; Jer 22:5).

In verse 34 the reader should note the feminine imagery inherent in Jesus' self-referential term "hen" (see also Deut 32:11). Contained also is the allusion to his entering the city in 19:28-40.

14:1-6 Healing a man with dropsy on the sabbath

Dropsy, or edema, is characterized by a buildup of fluids, often in the extremities. It is usually symptomatic of a variety of diseases.

There are several similarities between this story and the account of the crippled woman (13:10-17). They are solely Lukan material, and in both cases the miracle occurs on the sabbath. The woman is cured in front of the synagogue leaders, and the man here is restored to health in the presence of leading Pharisees. Furthermore, neither the woman nor the man asks Jesus to be healed; rather, in both instances Jesus, moved by pity, takes the initiative to cure the individual. He ex-

plains his action using the rhetorical device of the comparison of the greater: if the Law makes allowances for saving livestock on the sabbath, how much more should one help a fellow human being on the holy day.

Unlike the passage about the woman, however, there is nothing in this story to indicate that the leaders were angry or that they had duplicitous intentions in "observing him carefully" (v. 1). It seems that the Pharisees here are indeed curious about how Jesus would handle such a case, and, he engages them with his question (v. 3). Because they, too, know the Law and its provisions, they remain silent. Once again, the sabbath setting connects physical well-being with eternal salvation, thereby giving the Lord's Day an eschatological dimension (see also Luke 6:1-11; 11:37-54).

14:7-14 Proper comportment of guests and hosts

With the man now cured of his dropsy, Luke continues to describe the action surrounding the dinner. Jesus observes the customs of courtesy and etiquette and ties these issues of daily protocol to a lesson about the kingdom. Luke calls this lesson a "parable" (v. 7), but its genre is closer to a wisdom saying. Only Luke contains this passage, although a parallel to verse 11 appears in Matthew 23:12, making this aphorism most probably a Q saying. It is also found in Luke 18:14.

The dining room would have been a *triclinium* (see 7:36-50). The host would recline on his left side at the top of the right extension of the table; the opening to the horseshoe-shaped construction would have been to his back. The place of honor would have been at the crossbar, making the position of the honored guest directly perpendicular to the host so that they could talk directly to each other. Succeeding places of honor continued along the crossbar and down the left side, with the lowest place situated at the end of the left extension; the guest would have to constantly readjust his position in order to converse with those in the lowest places. What Jesus notices, therefore, is a stream of guests jockeying for the spot perpendicular to the host while avoiding anything along the left extension, especially the last place.

In the Mediterranean world, an honor-shame based culture, the social gaffe of overstepping one's station, such as Jesus describes, would have been a mortifying experience. On the other hand, being asked to come higher would have been particularly enviable. The lesson goes beyond calculating a social standing among one's peers, however, and points to the proper disposition toward God and how we define our need for God's salvation in our lives. Social self-inflation is equated with spiritual self-righteousness. Those who assume that they are righteous enough to let themselves into the kingdom without any regard for the divine initiative will have to give way to those who know their unworthiness and depend on God's love and grace for everything.

Jesus then turns the lesson to the host. The Roman world ran on the patronage system, in which the rich and influential would curry favor among their constituencies in return for support, respect, and fulfilled obligations. In such a society, a family holding a lavish banquet for notable dignitaries and lesser functionaries would be renowned for their generosity and would thereby garner a great deal of influence in their local area. Such would be their payback.

The true act of generosity in the eyes of God, however, lies in bestowing respect and dignity on those who would not only be unable to repay in kind but whose very social standing carries no prestige whatsoever. The reward one gains in the resurrection of the righteous (Greek: *dikaios*) ties this lesson to the one Jesus teaches to the guests (v. 14). In both instances, then, humility before God becomes the proper comportment for entering the kingdom.

14:15-24 The parable of the great banquet

This parable originates in Q and has a parallel in Matthew (22:1-14).

Banquets in the Gospel tradition always contain a strong eschatological element. Luke's creativity shines in this passage as he situates the banquet parable within the setting of a large dinner and gracefully folds the parable into the scene with the guest's remark in verse 15. The excuses that the original invitees give for not going to the dinner are legitimate. A wedding feast would last for several days, and one who has purchased land or cattle would have a strong desire to examine the sources of his livelihood. But these mitigating circumstances arise after they have presumably already accepted the invitation; it is the summons to enter the feast that they refuse. In a society in

which a patronage system governs many areas of life, their refusals are a disrespectful insult to the host's generosity.

Moreover, the last excuses introduce an eschatological dimension. According to Deuteronomic law, those who have built a house, planted a vineyard, or married a woman did not have to go on a military expedition or engage in any public duty for a period of one year (Deut 20:5-6; 24:5). By using these exemptions to explain why they cannot attend, they call attention to the dinner. The *eschaton* will not arrive without struggle. In order to sit at the banquet table in the kingdom of heaven, one must value it above any other facet of life, and acting on this value will be a struggle of warlike proportions. The banquet therefore becomes a metaphor for victory in the battle on behalf of the kingdom of God. Those refusing to come to the dinner demonstrate that they recognize this point. They simply do not hold the kingdom in as high regard as their daily affairs, as noble as those affairs may be.

The metaphor continues. The rich and wealthy have no need to participate in a banquet. The poor in the nearby city and district, who need the protection and favor of a rich lord, jump at the chance to go. There is still room at the table, so the invitation goes out to those who have no relationship to the host, and thus neither the host nor these guests have anything to gain from each other. The invitation is a purely gracious act.

The lesson of the parable places Jesus' mission in a microcosm. The self-satisfied, self-sufficient, and self-righteous are welcomed into the kingdom, but their self-inflated importance will block their will to enter. Those knowing their spiritual destitution will enter the kingdom willingly, and the Gentiles, who have no legal claim or right to come and dine, will also be invited to fill the dining hall.

14:25-35 The cost of discipleship

The Gospel of Matthew (10:37-38) shows a shortened parallel of verses 25-27. At the core of both accounts is Q source material, which Luke expands. The expansion continues into verses 28-33, a section that has no parallels. Luke concludes with a form of the saying about salt (vv. 34-35), which appears in all three Synoptics.

The language in verse 26 is harsh. In a reflection of the Semitic convention to employ hyperbole in order to make a point, Luke uses the Greek verb *miseō*, a term meaning "detest" or "abhor." The lesson teaches that no earthly attachment to a person, place, or thing should keep us from following God. Discipleship requires singleness of purpose, and this purpose is to go beyond natural ties and allegiances for the sake of the kingdom. Doing so will not be easy (v. 27).

The image seems to switch in verses 28-33, but the purpose of this scene is closely aligned to the preceding material and, in fact, explains it. Constructing a major building or preparing for a military expedition requires a great deal of planning. An architect or a general must calculate losses and the gains and make a decision accordingly. Being a disciple demands at least as much time and consideration. Disciples must acknowledge what they must sacrifice in order to take up the cross (v. 33).

References to building a tower and marching into battle may have been drawn from the life experience of the day. Herod the Great launched major construction in Caesarea Maritima, Jericho, Jerusalem, and even in the desert. Each of these projects involved a tremendous amount of planning to organize both human and material resources. Likewise, there was a major dispute between Herod Antipas and King Aretas of Nabatea, based on the former's divorce of his first wife, who was a Nabatean princess, in order to marry Herod Philip's wife, Herodias. Ultimately, this dispute turned into a war, which ended when Rome intervened and forced King Aretas to give up his plans.

The whole lesson ends with the salt metaphor (vv. 34-35). In order for salt to lose its taste, it would have to cease being sodium chloride. Analogously, disciples who shrug off the cross cease being disciples of Christ.

15:1-32 Parables of the lost

At this point in the journey to Jerusalem, Luke has constructed a series of parables and lessons dealing with sinners and their chance for salvation.

Luke groups together three parables dealing with valuables lost and found. These parables form a unit in which the central personage in each story line is the Christ figure, and the person or object lost is then seen as the sinner. Two of the parables, those of the lost coin and the prodigal son, are found only in Luke's Gospel.

15:1-7 The parable of the lost sheep

Although this parable is Q material, Luke's introduction to it is different from Matthew 18:12-14. In Luke, Pharisees and scribes are grumbling about the tax collectors and sinners who gravitate toward Jesus. Their complaining leads into the parable of the lost sheep. The rhetorical question "What man among you . . . ?" (v. 4) relies on the common sense of the listener to conclude that no one would leave a whole flock to go after one lost sheep. The ridiculousness of leaving ninety-nine sheep in the desert to find a stray defies the imagination, but such ridiculousness is the point of the parable. Nearly equally ridiculous is inviting neighbors and friends to celebrate the return of the stray.

God's love for his creatures is so strong that it includes even the sinners, something that self-righteous individuals have a hard time appreciating. The joy that spreads through heaven also strikes our human ears as overmuch, but it emphasizes the divine welcome given to the repentant sinner.

The Greek uses *anthrōpos* for "man" (v. 4) and thus is a gender-inclusive term. Often in the Holy Land, both in antiquity and now, shepherds are boys, girls, and women, an interesting perspective for the story considering that the shepherd is the Christ figure.

15:8-10 The parable of the lost coin

The Greek for "coin," *drachma*, was of the approximate value of a *denarius* and was worth about one day's wage for a laborer; the woman's diligent search, therefore, is certainly justified. When the object of the search, in this case a coin, is compared to the lost sheep in the previous parable, we can see an increase in the stakes. No matter how valuable one sheep is in earthly terms, it is not worth risking ninety-nine other sheep to find it. In this parable, however, the other nine coins are not placed in jeopardy as the woman seeks out the lost coin.

As with the parable of the yeast (13:20-21), the woman is the Christ figure, and her intense desire to find the lost coin is analogous to God's desire to find the lost sinner. Moreover, the parable says something about the value of the lost sinner in God's eyes. Here the mention of the rejoicing among the angels (v. 10) echoes the heavenly rejoicing found in the parable of the lost sheep

(15:7). In both cases, such a conclusion keeps the eschatological focus of the message.

We read that a woman lights a lamp to sweep the house, a detail that gives evidence of the Syrian origins of Luke's Gospel. Unlike houses in the Judean Hills or even the semi-arid desert fringes of the south, which were constructed of comparatively lightweight limestone or sandstone, allowing for use of windows and other openings, houses on the Syrian plains and heights had a different building material and style altogether. In these areas the common building block was the very heavy, volcanic, black basalt stone. To support upper stories, the walls of these buildings had to be of solid construction and could not contain many, if any, windows. Consequently, interior living spaces were dark, and lighting a lamp would have been necessary, even in broad daylight.

15:11-32 The parable of the prodigal son

This parable has had a great influence on Western art, being depicted in drama, music, ballet, and painting.

The story opens with the younger son asking his father for his share of the inheritance. Of course, it is for the father to decide whether his son deserves it, not the son himself. By his action the younger son communicates that he does not view the inheritance as a gift bequeathed to him because of his father's good graces; rather, he sees it as his due.

According to ancient Jewish custom (Num 27:8-11; 36:7-9), an inheritance is the father's property, which, according to the custom of the day, the father gave to his sons, although he was not bound by any means to do so. When the younger son demands his share of the inheritance, therefore, he is asking the father for a part of the father's life. It is as if the son is requesting the father's very soul, an understanding emphasized by the Greek term for "property," *bios*, the same word used for "life" or "living" (v. 12). By his request, the son is indirectly demanding the father's own death. The father, however, instead of taking insult with his son's effrontery, gives him the inheritance.

The young son squanders the inheritance on "a life of dissipation" (v. 13). The idea is that the son's living is so extravagant, profligate, wasteful, and glitzy, that there is nothing of merit in any of

it. Not only is the son jeopardizing his physical life by dangerous living, but the return of enjoyment on his investment is so meager that it makes the whole venture worthless.

To feed a pig, which represents everything reprehensible to every Jewish sensibility, would be a curse indeed. God-fearing Gentiles in the Lukan community would have been familiar enough with Jewish customs to know how low the young son descended. The son is absolutely alienated from the community. The pods (Greek: *kerátion*) were probably from the carob tree and would be fit for human consumption (v. 16).

With verse 17 the audience is prepared for the next part, where the son acknowledges his sinfulness: "Father, I have sinned against heaven and against you; I no longer deserve to be called your son" (vv. 18b-19). Despite his egregiously bad behavior, he plans to ask for the status of a hired hand, which actually is how his father should have and could have treated him when he asked for the inheritance in the first place.

Father and son meet in verse 20, and the son begins his rehearsed speech, but he does not get to finish it. The father, so moved and filled with emotion at his son's return, does not hear a word he says. He cuts the son off in mid-sentence and tells the servants to prepare for a party, and he explains, "because this son of mine was dead, and has come to life again; he was lost and has been found" (v. 24). Because the son never has the opportunity to call himself a "hired hand," one cannot say that the father is refuting his son's assessment. Rather, we the audience can see that the father has always held this son in high regard and has never stopped loving him. The father's love and generosity toward his lost, now found son so border on the ridiculous that his actions preclude his wayward son's expression of shame and guilt. We have here a loving father whose love exceeds all bounds.

This parable then switches focus to the elder brother (v. 25). By external measure, the elder brother has been obedient and respectful of the father, whom his younger brother has both insulted and grieved. The dialogue between the son and the father, however, challenges such an assumption of his filial relationship.

The elder brother, after citing off his own virtues, explodes in front of his father (vv. 29-30). The father, defending his own act of forgiveness, corrects the elder brother (v. 32). The father insists that the prodigal son is both a son to him and a brother to his other son. The one who has been alienated is now restored to the family.

The elder son is blind to his father's magnanimity. As an elder son, he has a duty to support the father in his decisions, a duty that he obviously shirks. The positions are reversed. Now it is the elder brother who insults and acts disrespectfully, while the younger son, by humbling himself, shows respect. In spite of this, the father still goes on loving, this time toward the elder son (v. 31). The father's forgiveness and charity maintain the ties of a loving relationship toward both his sons. As with all parables, this one turns to the listener, asking us to identify with either the younger son, the elder brother, or the father.

In each of the successive parables of the lost, that which is lost increases in value, from stray lamb, to a drachma, to a son. With such a progression, the worth of the sinner also increases in God's eyes, and the listener is left with the conclusion that God loves all as parents love their children. Furthermore, in the first two parables the shepherd and the woman are the Christ figure, respectively. In the parable of the prodigal son, however, it is not absolutely clear whether the father is Christ or God the Father, and this ambiguity, no doubt, is intentional.

16:1-13 The parable of the dishonest steward

This parable appears only in Luke's Gospel. That the steward is clever to the point of being crafty makes the fact that Jesus commends him difficult for us to appreciate.

Stewards made a living by collecting rents and debts for their masters and charging the debtors interest on the amount owed, which would then go to the stewards' coffers. Here the steward is shameless in the lengths he will go to maintain his position. He is not trying to hide anything from the rich man; indeed, he may even want his employer to find out about his altering the books. His hope is that his cleverness may win back the rich man's favor, and barring that outcome, he will at least have made some grateful constituents to take him in. The steward's audaciousness in achieving his ends calls attention to Jesus' lesson. Anyone of us would go to the greatest lengths, no matter how unsavory, to ensure a secure place in

this world; how much more should we devote our attention to the world to come (v. 8).

Jesus names the problem in verse 9. The term "dishonest wealth" reflects the danger that inheres in worldly goods. Jesus warns the listener to use the wealth, but not to place any trust in it. Only trusting in God will lead to an eternal dwelling; everything else is counterfeit.

The narrative then discusses the conclusions one can draw from the parable by indirectly referring to the description of the steward (vv. 10-13). In verse 1 the steward is accused of "squandering" the master's property. The steward has mismanaged, perhaps through incompetence, the "very small matters" of this world, so there is no reason to trust him in the larger matters of the next one (v. 10). That lesson is turned toward the audience in verse 12. Trust is earned, it is not assumed. Those who deal loosely and unethically with others should not expect others to honor and trust them.

Verse 13 is a Q saying that also appears in Matthew 6:24. "Mammon" (v. 13), a Greek transliteration of the Aramaic word, means more than wealth and riches; it can signify anything of this world that one relies on: titles, positions, privileges, and honors. To be sure, wealth is tied up with many of these perquisites, but mammon is anything which takes our attention away from God, the true source of life.

16:14-15 Encounter with the Pharisees

Luke alone features this reproof, which, with the notice that this particular group of Pharisees "loved money" (v. 14), is tied to the warning about wealth above. Jesus directs the criticism at the human desire for self-justification and public praise. The performance of good deeds, then, goes only as far as human acclaim. In such a case, people will never do an act that may be good but unpopular.

16:16-18 Sayings on the Law and divorce

The "law" in this passage refers to the Mosaic Law, the Jewish religious and cultic legislation, and reflects the context from which the Christian movement emerged. The evangelists and other New Testament writers interpreted the Old Testament, comprised of books both in Hebrew and Greek, as the precursor to the revelation of Christ. Now the "kingdom of God is proclaimed," but the ability to move into a new way of viewing one's relationship with God is not easy; hence "everyone who enters does so with violence" (v. 16). Jewish Christians found that the change from the Mosaic Law to Christ required a major shift in focus, and Gentile Christians, at first not welcome unless they had undergone conversion to Judaism (see Acts 10; 15), put themselves at risk with their pagan neighbors. Luke's Gospel stresses Christ as the ultimate arbiter of any interpretation of the Law (v. 17); in that sense, the law will not pass away, as the next saying demonstrates (v. 18).

Luke and Mark agree against Matthew in their readings on the prohibition of divorce. While Matthew sees unchastity as a mitigating circumstance for dissolving the marriage (see Matt 19:9; Mark 10:11-12), Luke's version of divorce legislation (v. 18) serves as an example of how the Law has lost its validity. According to the Mosaic teaching, a man could divorce his wife by simply signing a statement of dismissal; the woman had no similar option (Deut 24:1-4). Consequently, the woman and her children would be left to fend for themselves by begging and prostitution. Jesus nullifies this legislation by declaring that no one can divorce, and thereby demonstrates that the law and the prophets ended with John (v. 16).

16:19-31 The rich man and Lazarus

This parable appears only in Luke and reflects the evangelist's overriding concern for the poor and for social justice. In the tradition this is also known as the story of Dives and Lazarus, the former name stemming from the Latin *dives*, meaning "rich person." It is one of the best known of all Gospel stories, even prompting Ralph Vaughan Williams to compose a musical score based on this story. The name "Lazarus" itself is the Greek transliteration of the Hebrew abbreviation "Eleazar," a name that means "God has helped." Thematically, it is tied to the saying about God and mammon in 16:13.

The information concerning the rich man's clothing (v. 19) indicates that he is not simply well off—he is excessively wealthy. Purple dye was a costly commodity that very few people even among the rich could afford. These details heighten the contrast between the rich man and Lazarus, who not only has sores that dogs would lick but who even lacks the simplest garment to cover those sores. That Lazarus keeps company with dogs accentuates his dismal state, since dogs were considered filthy, undesirable animals.

Luke illustrates the theme of the great reversal in this parable, first outlined in the *Magnificat* (see Luke 1:46-55). In the parable the hungry are literally "filled with good things," while the rich are "sent away empty" (1:53). The dialogue between Abraham and the rich man amply describes the new state of things. We know that the rich man cannot claim ignorance of the fact that someone hungry is outside his door, for he refers to Lazarus by name (v. 24). There is even an arrogant tone in his request: he does not ask Abraham for the favor but requests that Abraham command Lazarus to come down and refresh him. Most likely he treated Lazarus in a similar fashion when they both were alive.

Abraham, in his reply, ensures that the rich man knows exactly why he is where he is so that neither the rich man, now suffering the flames of the netherworld, nor the audience can conclude that he is a victim of a great misfortune. No, the rich man's lack of charity and responsibility put him there; indeed, the rich man's great sin of omission fashioned the chasm between the two. We are forced to wonder why the chasm cannot be crossed. The answer says a great deal about salvation and damnation.

The lesson is not that God is a God of damnation and punishment, inasmuch as it gives us an example of how much of a role we play in our salvation. The rich man was oblivious to the needs of those around him while he was alive, and now that he is dead, he is still oblivious, as his call for Lazarus's services suggests. Herein lies the danger of wealth that Jesus always preaches: power and wealth blind us to the kingdom of God in this life and in the next. If we are not wide-eyed to the kingdom and its demands now, as Moses and the prophets tell us to be (v. 31), we will not be sensitive to seeing the kingdom after we die. The great irony in the story is that the rich man needs Lazarus in order to be saved. Had he paid attention to Lazarus begging for table scraps at the door of his house, the rich man would not be in the predicament he is in now.

The last verse of the parable, of course, is a reference to Jesus' own resurrection.

17:1-4 Temptations to sin

The journey to Jerusalem continues with further instruction along the way.

Each Synoptic Gospel has a variation of the warning against giving offense. Verses 3-4 parallel

Matthew 18:15, thereby making them Q material. Luke injects a note of reality in verse 1b: as long as there is a believing community, there will be scandals. As great a sin as it is to lead one into temptation, it is far greater to do so to a "little one" (v. 2). Millstones, even one for household use, were heavy and expensive. The punishment suggested is severe indeed.

Where there is sin, there must be forgiveness, and Luke gracefully connects the two. We have another example of the mercy and tenderness that are so much a part of the Third Gospel. This mercy and tenderness, however, are not to be regarded as permission for further injury. Those who sin are to be rebuked, and if sinners repent, they are to be forgiven. The Gospel sees rebuke and forgiveness as a means of achieving both personal salvation and social justice. On the other hand, lest repentance and forgiveness be exercised on a quid pro quo basis, the saying continues with the proviso that because sins or even the same sin will occur numerous times, it must be forgiven each time the sinner repents. We are to imitate divine forgiveness in its limitlessness.

This passage addresses only how to deal with sinful behavior within the church community, but for Luke, mercy extends to those outside the community as well (see Luke 6:27-36).

17:5-6 Saying on faith

Once again, faith is compared to a mustard seed (see Luke 13:19), but the example switches to a sycamine tree (*morus nigra;* read "mulberry" in the text), a large tree with clustered berries. Both Matthew and Luke use the hyperbole from Q to make their point that nothing is impossible to the person who has faith. Matthew's phrase, however, refers to moving a mountain, which most scholars believe to be the original version.

17:7-10 The attitude of a servant

This piece on servants occurs only in Luke.

The social world of the Gospel is particularly evident in this passage dealing with masters and slaves. The lesson is that Christians should not expect praise and honor for performing those duties that they are obligated to perform. Moreover, the saying counters the thought that salvation can be gained on human merit alone and without God's grace. If our own deeds render us unprofitable servants, we have no other recourse for salvation than to depend on the divine initiative.

17:11-19 The cleansing of ten lepers

The prescription to the lepers to show themselves to the priests is found in Leviticus 14:2-9.

The most common route for Jews in Galilee to go to Jerusalem was through the Jordan Valley. Although cutting down through Samaria was not impossible, most Jews preferred to avoid Samaritan territory (see Luke 9:52). Did Jesus ever set foot in Samaria? Verse 11 can be translated "through the region between Samaria and Galilee." This passage is solely Lukan material and shows Luke's proclivity to highlight the faith of the social outcast over that of the established insider. Both Jews (Galileans) and Samaritans compose this group of lepers; both are society's outcasts, and therefore they associate with each other.

Luke's eschatological vision comes into focus with the emphasis on faith in verse 19. Jesus instructs the Samaritan leper, not that his faith has cured him, but that his faith has "saved" him. The leper is not only saved from his leprosy but gains eternal salvation—all from faith. The connection of faith with salvation occurs throughout Luke's Gospel, as we have seen with the woman in the house of Simon the Pharisee (7:50), the cure of the hemorrhaging woman (8:48), and even at the cross (23:43).

17:20-37 The coming of the kingdom and the Son of Man

In verses 20-21 Luke expresses a realized eschatology that supports the vision displayed in the dialogue with the Samaritan leper above. Indeed, the last phrase in verse 21 seems Johannine in its language as it underscores an *eschaton* already present.

The tone and theme switch suddenly to a future-oriented eschatology in verse 22. The opening words of this verse in Greek, which the English translation expresses, indicate a reversal of thought. In this first encounter with Lukan apocalyptic writing, the reading draws a parallel between sudden acts of destruction in the Old Testament and the Son of Man's impending arrival on the earth. Although found far more often in Ezekiel than in Daniel, the latter's use of "Son of Man" has greater bearing on the synoptic understanding of this term, an understanding that Luke shares. The heavily apocalyptic material in Daniel (see Dan 7:13; 8:15-17) is reflected in verse

22 and also figures prominently in the book of Revelation.

Luke includes a warning about following false prophets (as do the parallels in Mark and Matthew), but he also connects the coming of the *eschaton* with the fate awaiting Jesus in Jerusalem (v. 25). Furthermore, Luke builds a sense of urgency by relating Lot's escape from the explosive conflagration that destroyed Sodom; people should be vigilant and anxious. This sense of urgency also has a social justice theme, for injustice and oppression were the reasons for Sodom's obliteration (see Isa 1:9-16; Ezek 16:49-52). Any desire to hold on to the present is discouraged, and Lot's wife stands as an example of what might happen to the one who tarries. Those who make no permanent claims to this life will always be ready for the *eschaton* (v. 31).

To separate Jesus' words from the Gospel writer's is always extremely difficult. In this passage it is impossible. Verse 31 appears to be a prediction after the fact. Josephus describes the sudden arrival of the Romans at the gates of Jerusalem during the First Jewish Revolt (A.D. 66–70; *J.W.* 5.2.3]. Few if any were able to escape the destruction and massacre. The early Christians most likely interpreted the Jewish rebellion and the destruction of Jerusalem with its splendid temple as the fulfillment of Jesus' words, even as those words were mixed into their experiences of the catastrophe. What we have here is an amalgam of Q material, oral tradition, memory, and Lukan editing. (See Luke 21:20-24.)

One cannot take every passage of Scripture literally and apart from a larger theological context. Nowhere is this truer than in apocalyptic literature. Readers should be on guard against determining the saved, the damned, and the rapture by reading this material. Verse 37, in encouraging us to read the signs of the times, advises us to keep the whole Christian tradition in focus as we interpret those signs. And what are the signs? Jesus does not say, and this point is the essential part of the apocalyptic message.

Christians are to concern themselves with doing the will of God, for which Jesus has given his disciples abundant examples: taking care of the poor, trusting in God alone, and forgiving enemies. We are not to waste time trying to predict the future. The paradoxical presentation of the kingdom as already present (v. 21) and not yet

here (v. 30) expresses its true reality. The kingdom will be manifested in living the life of Christ.

18:1-8 The parable of the persistent widow

Situating this pericope after the apocalyptic passage regarding the Son of Man offers the believer the proper way to maintain vigilance for the parousia, or second coming. With prayer and praying mentioned over thirty times in Luke's Gospel and the Acts of the Apostles, the parable of the persistent widow highlights this central feature of Luke's Gospel by emphasizing the necessity and efficacy of constant prayer. Moreover, because widows and orphans were to be special recipients of charity according to Jewish law (Deut 24:17-22), the early Christians would have been particularly attentive to the teaching.

The story appears only in Luke, and there are at least two ways to read it. The first is to see the unjust judge as the protagonist bearing the lesson for the reader. Similar to the literary style found in the parable of the dishonest steward (16:1-8), the intent of the teaching comes through the comparison of the greater: As an unjust judge grants a petition solely for self-serving purposes, how much more will a loving God grant the desires of his beloved petitioner.

A second, feminist interpretation, on the other hand, sees the widow as the protagonist and thus the vehicle for the lesson. In this case, she, in her weakness, becomes the Christ figure who combats evil and injustice on behalf of the poor and neglected. She is unstinting in her efforts, and the unjust judge, the symbol of oppression, is clearly afraid of her, as seen from the Greek verb *hypōpiazō* for "strike" (v. 5), which means to "treat roughly, maltreat, strike under the eye." Here, too, the intent of the teaching surfaces through analogy: As persistent as a widow is to secure her rights, so is God in securing the rights of those petitioning him.

The reference to the Son of Man (v. 8) brings the parable in line with the teaching on the last days (17:22-37): Pray constantly while living and working for the kingdom of God.

18:9-14 The parable of the Pharisee and the tax collector

This parable, also found only in Luke, continues the theme on prayer. Whereas the parable of the persistent widow (18:1-8) shows the necessity of constant prayer, the parable of the Pharisee and the tax collector displays the proper comportment for prayer.

No doubt the Pharisee does everything he says he does. Fasting and tithing are not only good things to do, but the former is also proclaimed by the prophets while the latter is required by the Law (see Deut 14:22-29). The purpose of the parable is not to discourage religious and pious practice; rather, its function is to call into question the reasons why people take on devotional works. The Pharisee gives the reasons for deeds: they are to justify himself in the world's eyes as well as in the eyes of God. Luke underscores this point in verse 9.

In contrast, the tax collector does nothing pious that we know of. In fact, as a tax collector, it would be most surprising if he ever did anything good for anyone. During the Roman occupation, tax collectors were not only traitors to their own people but also extortionists feeding off their compatriots. Furthermore, their dealing with the pagan Romans made them ritually impure, thereby excommunicating themselves from their fellow Jews. Compared with the dedicated, devoted Pharisee, a tax collector would never be considered honest, pious, or holy. Unlike the Pharisee, however, the tax collector knows his sinfulness. He pleads for mercy and demonstrates his need for God. The Pharisee, on the other hand, in singing his own praises, makes God his beneficiary. That the tax collector leaves justified was as shocking to the first-century audience as it is to us. So important is this parable that it sets the tone for those participating in the passion and crucifixion (see 23:48).

18:15-17 Access to the kingdom

This passage stresses that the people brought infants to Jesus, whereas the parallels in Mark and Matthew read only that children came. The mention of infants gives a glimpse of the sociological structure in the ancient world. Conversions were never individualistic or isolated events. If the master or mistress of the household became a follower of Christ, everyone in the extended family and even the slaves did as well. In the Acts of the Apostles we read similar accounts regarding baptism (Acts 16:15, 33; 18:8). Luke's reading could very well reflect and suggest the practice of infant baptism in the early church.

Society today often presents Christianity as a childish, trivial, or trite matter and will use passages like this one to justify doing so. To "accept the kingdom of God like a child," however, means to receive the kingdom of God with an open guilelessness to the gift that God offers, something that requires a healthy maturity. In this case, the tax collector in the preceding passage (18:9-14) is the perfect example of open guilelessness.

18:18-23 The rich official

Although in their respective versions of the story, both Matthew and Mark simply state that a man comes up to Jesus, Luke specifies that the one asking the question is a ruler. Thus Luke informs the reader that the individual is not only rich but also powerful, an important point for the story.

The ruler's fault is one of complacency, and in this regard he is similar to the Pharisee in 18:9-14. When he calls Jesus "Good teacher" (v. 18), Jesus responds in a sharp tone, because he can see through the unctuous language. The ruler hopes that by flattery he can increase in stature to gain eternal life. Jesus continues with listing the prescriptions of the Decalogue. These statutes should recall the whole Exodus experience, in which the people struggle between their ever present faithlessness and their eventual trust in God. The ruler's answer that he has observed all the commandments from his youth demonstrates that he has completely forgotten that covenantal relationship expressed by trust in God.

Jesus concludes by entering the ruler's mindset. The first half of the answer would catch the man's attention, "There is still one thing left for you . . ." (v. 22a). The ruler can handle the challenge; by his wits he has already accumulated wealth and power. Then comes the surprise: "sell all that you have and distribute it to the poor . . . come follow me" (v. 22b). The man's sadness results from a double realization. The first is that he must surrender everything of worth in his life, and the second follows, namely, that everything he thought was of great value both in this life and the next is actually worthless. His life from his youth has been an act of faithlessness. To inherit eternal life, he must stop trusting in what he has trusted and place his trust in God.

18:24-30 On entering the kingdom of God

The dialogue with the rich official prompts Jesus' comment on the ease of a camel going through the eye of a needle, one of the most challenging verses in the Gospel (v. 25). The response from the crowd is certainly understandable: "Then who can be saved?" (v. 26).

A long-standing interpretation of this passage is that there was in Jerusalem a gate called the "Eye of the Needle," which required a cargo-laden camel to rest on all four legs and crawl through the door in order to enter the city. There is no evidence anywhere in the Mideast, however, of any gate called the "Eye of the Needle." In addition, camels are unable to crawl. Jesus is using a form of hyperbole that is a natural part of Semitic speech.

The lesson that arises from this encounter with the ruler is similar to the one taught in the parable of the dishonest steward (16:1-13), where trusting in one's own wealth and accomplishments instead of in God makes salvation difficult if not impossible. In both cases the responsibility for accepting salvation falls on us. Those who place all hope in their own accomplishments will never be open to God's mercy, simply because they have let worldly values blind themselves to it. Since power and wealth are idols, and seductive ones at that, the ruler in the story and others like him cannot even see the way into the kingdom, let alone enter it. In this sense, it is easier for a camel to pass through a needle's eye.

Peter, sensing the meaning of Jesus' hyperbolic example, responds in verse 28. His statement implies that he is looking for an answer as to whether he and the other disciples are saved or not. Jesus does not answer directly; rather, his reply is addressed in the third person (vv. 29-30). Jesus' statement reflects a realized eschatology as well as a future one. Forsaking worldly comfort has a present reward, yet the reward is not fully realized until one reaches eternal life. Unlike the Markan parallel, which speaks of persecutions along with the rewards (Mark 10:30), Luke does not mention such hardships. Because the next passage contains the third prediction of the passion, Luke avoids the redundancy by not including the sobering fact here.

This passage has been used over the centuries as a rationale for religious life.

18:31-34 The third prediction of the passion

Being a disciple has its rewards, but it also has difficulties, as Jesus reminds his band of followers with this third, final, and most vivid prediction of his passion (see 9:22, 44-45; but also 17:25).

Although both Matthew and Mark feature parallels to this passage, only Luke contains information about the prophets (v. 31) and the Twelve's inability to understand what Jesus is saying (v. 34).

18:35-43 The blind beggar of Jericho

Jesus is relentlessly pursuing his intent as described in 9:51. In going from Galilee to Jerusalem through the Jordan Valley, one would turn west at Jericho in order to take the Wadi Qelt road up into the Judean mountains. Jericho, an oasis and a prosperous city in Judea, was also the locale of Herod the Great's winter palace. These facts serve to accentuate the beggar's lowly social position.

All three synoptic accounts contain this story, but only Mark gives the blind man a name (Bartimaeus; see Mark 10:46). Comparisons are very important here. This blind man can "see" Jesus is the Messiah, whereas the Twelve cannot understand what he is saying (v. 34). This paradox fits well within the Gospel tradition, where the blind usually "see," while those who "see" are actually blind.

The beggar uses one of the earliest Christian titles applied to Christ, "Son of David" (v. 38), a title that rarely appears in Luke (see 3:31; 20:41). Jesus hears the distressful cry despite the commotion of the crowd and their efforts to silence the man. Jesus could have walked to the man, but he commands that the beggar be brought to him (v. 40). Among religious people of the time, physical disability was linked to sinfulness. By having the crowd lead the blind man to him, Jesus induces them to take responsibility for healing him, thereby redefining both suffering and sin. Jesus does not assume that the beggar wants to see; rather, he asks him to explicitly state his need (v. 41). Of course, the beggar requests sight, because he knows that Jesus can grant it, and by this action he demonstrates his faith. Hence Jesus can say, "Your faith has saved you" (v. 42). In true Lukan fashion, in the end everyone—beggar and crowd—glorifies God.

19:1-10 Zacchaeus the tax collector

This passage appears only in Luke and concludes what many scholars have called the "Lukan Gospel of the Outcast" (15:1–19:10). Its singular character lies in the fact that Luke, who devotes the whole tone of his Gospel toward embracing the poor and lowly, includes this passage, which focuses on the salvation of the rich and powerful. Unlike the rich official in 18:18-23, Zacchaeus does not depend on his wealth and status but on God's loving mercy to gain entry into the kingdom.

Tax collecting was a lucrative business. Romans used to sell the office to the highest bidder. For his part, the tax collector would then have to pay his contracted amount to the Romans as well as collect the fiscal revenues for them. Anything over and beyond those sums was his to keep. Failing to meet his payments would mean the Romans could confiscate his property and sell him and his family into slavery. Zacchaeus's position as the chief tax collector meant that lesser officials would have bidden for their offices from him, and if they did not produce the payment, Zacchaeus would have applied the appropriate penalties. In a word, Zacchaeus was very wealthy, and the resentment against him would have been very strong.

Despite his occupation, Zacchaeus is determined to see Jesus, even if it means looking foolish in doing so. Scholars are divided on whether to read the verbs "give" and "repay," which grammatically are in the present tense in Greek (v. 8), as present or future. In other words, is Zacchaeus boasting of present practices or making a statement of repentance to guide his future action? His hasty explanation to Jesus is heartfelt, for it would be of no advantage to him, an extortionist, to heed a wandering prophet or wonder-worker. Furthermore, the fact that he does show knowledge of wrongdoing manifests the salvation that is visiting him. If Jesus comes "to seek and to save what was lost" (v. 10), Zacchaeus must be a sinner. Zacchaeus the sinner can make a claim of being a descendant of Abraham, and his earnest desire to get a glimpse of Jesus is proof enough that that is what he desires.

19:11-27 The parable of the ten gold coins

Matthew and Luke differ in the telling of this parable, which, in large part, comes from Q overlapping slightly with Mark 13:34. A major difference between the two is that Luke also has a subtext discussing servants who do not want this particular nobleman to rule over them. This subtext may have as its origin Rome's choice of placing Archelaus, son of Herod the Great, on the throne at the death of his father. Because of his tyrannical and nearly sadistic behavior, the Jews petitioned Rome to have him removed. Rome responded by giving him only one-third of Herod's kingdom and eventually banishing him completely because of his excessive cruelty and incompetence.

Of lesser importance is Matthew's use of *talaton* (25:15) and Luke's *mna* as the denomination of the currency involved, which is translated here as "gold coins" (v. 13). A *mna* ("mina") would be worth about one hundred days' wages, and a *talanton* ("talent") sixty times as much.

Luke introduces the passage by noting that the traveling party was near Jerusalem and that some were supposing that the kingdom of God was about to appear. The parable addresses some of these points. The absentee nobleman returns without notice and thus surprises his servants. The first two servants are prepared for his sudden reappearance and are able to produce interest on the money given them; the third is not so concerned and has only a handkerchief with the original amount. It should be emphasized that the servants are commanded to use the money in such a manner as to earn more; thus the third servant was not only foolish but also disobedient.

As a story that follows the passage about the rich Zacchaeus, this parable gives an example on the proper way to use riches. The metaphor demonstrates that goods are to be employed for the upbuilding of the kingdom, and goods that are not used for this purpose will be taken away, as we see done with the third servant's *mna*.

The Lukan subtext plays a role in this passage by representing absolute refusal on the part of some to acknowledge the kingdom of God at all, whether in Jesus' first coming or in his second. Luke concludes this subtext within the same passage by having the nobleman slay the opposition. Many often cite this passage as an example of Lukan anti-Semitism. There is nothing in it, however, to suggest that those who receive the nobleman/Christ are Gentiles or that those who do not are Jews.

With this parable Jesus' journey to Jerusalem, which begins at 9:51, has reached its destination.

THE TEACHING MINISTRY IN JERUSALEM

Luke 19:28–21:38

Jesus has taught in Galilee, along the road to Judea, and now he will teach in the holy city. He arrives in Jerusalem, the city where he will meet his passion, death, and resurrection. With this background, his teaching takes on urgency.

19:28-40 The entry into Jerusalem

All four Gospels contain the account of Jesus' triumphal entry into Jerusalem. The respective narratives share a great deal of information, and any differences among them are seen in some minor details.

For all three Synoptic writers, this triumphal entry is Jesus' first and only trip to Jerusalem, but John's Gospel, along with some details among the Synoptics, shows evidence that he may have gone to Jerusalem several times during his earthly ministry. The possibility of other sojourns to Jerusalem notwithstanding, what distinguishes this visit from all the others is the reception Jesus receives.

Bethphage and Bethany are both on the Roman road from Jericho to Jerusalem. We know from John 11:17-18 that Jesus has friends at the latter. This detail would explain how he could have made arrangements for the colt beforehand (Luke 19:29-31). All four Gospels show a heavy reliance on the prophecy in Zechariah 9:9 in their depictions of the scene.

In his descent from the Mount of Olives, Jesus encounters a rejoicing crowd. Matthew and Mark mention that the crowd also set garments and branches on the way; John specifies "palm branches" (12:13) but says nothing of garments, while Luke reads "cloaks" but does not include branches (v. 36). That three of the evangelists specify branches is used as evidence by some that the scene of the entry into Jerusalem described here actually refers to an earlier one at the time of the feast of Booths, or Sukkoth, a pilgrimage celebration falling in mid-September. Either Luke's source did not include branches, or Luke saw the reference as a superfluous detail. Whether or not the entry arises from the community's memory of a fall celebration at Sukkoth or a spring feast at Passover, the pertinent detail is that Jesus arrives in Jerusalem with throngs welcoming him.

The other evangelists have the crowd shouting "Hosanna," an Aramaic expression meaning "Save! I pray," a phrase unfamiliar to Luke's Gentile audience. Whereas the other Gospels have *"Blessed is he* who comes in the name of the Lord," Luke reads *"Blessed is the king"* (19:38, emphasis added). Luke's phrasing links Jesus' arrival in Jerusalem to the instruction on the imminent manifestation of the kingdom of God (see 13:35; 16:16; 18:15-17).

As an echo of the angels' hymn at the birth of Jesus (Luke 2:14), the crowd shouts out, "Peace in heaven and glory in the highest" (v. 38). What angels sang at Jesus' birth people now acclaim at his arrival.

Luke's depiction of the Pharisees in the crowd is less harsh than that of Matthew, who locates them in the temple after Jesus has cleansed it (Matt 21:16). Luke situates the Pharisees along the road leading into Jerusalem, and they seem more alarmed than hostile (19:39). Jesus' answer, a hyperbolic statement of fact, also serves as a challenge (19:40).

19:41-44 The lament over Jerusalem

The first lament over the city occurs in Luke 13:34-35 and is a Q saying (see Matt 23:37-39). Here, however, the reading appears only in Luke; both in theme and in imagery it is connected to the third and final reference to Jerusalem's destruction in Luke 21:21-24. Moreover, references to the siege (v. 43) are found in Jeremiah 6:6 and Ezekiel 4:2.

From the slopes of the Mount of Olives, Jesus would have seen the whole city spread out before him on the next hill. The temple with the doors to the holy of holies would have faced him. Tradition commemorates this scene at the Church of Dominus Flevit on the Mount of Olives. Archaeological evidence indicates that the most probable gate of Jesus' entry into the city rests underneath today's Golden Gate, which has been blocked since the eighth century. Today the Palm Sunday procession enters through St. Stephen's Gate, to the north of the Golden Gate along the eastern wall of the city.

19:45-48 The cleansing of the temple

Unlike Matthew or Mark, Luke concludes the entry into Jerusalem with the cleansing of the temple. Luke offers the most economic description of the event by not specifying the money changers, the animals, or even the "whip out of cords" (John 2:15). The phrase "My house shall be a house of prayer, but you have made it a den of thieves" is a blending of Isaiah 56:7 and Jeremiah 7:11.

The business transactions would have taken place in the Court of the Gentiles, surrounded by the Royal Portico, which was constructed for this very purpose. The merchants are not out of place in conducting their affairs in this area. In fact, the temple court served as the ground where worshipers proceeded from secular to sacred space by changing their pagan money to Jewish coins and purchasing ritually pure sacrificial victims. Jesus' anger, therefore, is not so much directed at those who have profaned a sacred zone with their mercantile greed; rather, he seems to be upset that any business should be associated with the temple at all. With incense, animals, oil, grain, and everything else needed for the sacrifices, the temple was a source of great income to the priests who had shares in most of the shops.

The glorious entry into Jerusalem ends on an ominous tone as the "chief priests, the scribes, and the leaders of the people" (v. 47), but not the Pharisees (19:39), plot to put Jesus to death.

20:1-8 Questioning Jesus' authority

It is natural that after such a dramatic action as cleansing the temple, the priests, scribes, and elders would question Jesus' authority. All three Synoptic Gospels feature this account within the same narrative sequence. The authority of Jesus' teaching was a major question throughout his ministry, as the earlier Beelzebul controversy substantiates (Luke 11:14-23).

The temple leaders named here comprise the Sanhedrin, the highest Jewish council. It was composed of three groups: the priests (the high priest as well as the former high priests and family representatives); the scribes (legal scholars); and the elders (the chief members of the leading families and clans). Totaling seventy-one members, this group was the official Jewish court. In Jesus' time it had jurisdiction in religious and secular affairs only in Judea, but capital cases had to be recommended to the Roman governor for approval. It met in Jerusalem within the temple complex.

Jesus' reply is structured to avoid falling into the trap the officials have fashioned. If he were to say that his authority comes from the Lord God, as indeed it does, they could accuse him of blas-

phemy. As it is, Jesus' response insinuates such a conclusion without providing any incriminating evidence. By referring to John the Baptist, Jesus also draws from the prophetic tradition to make his defense. The comments of the temple leaders indicate the great regard for the Baptist that many of the people held. This devotion to John has implications for the development of Christianity.

20:9-19 The wicked tenant farmers

This parable strikes a note of recognition with both the people (v. 16) and the scribes and chief priests (v. 19). The whole piece is an analogy of the prophetic tradition. The one who plants the vineyard represents God; the tenant farmers, the people; the series of servants, the various prophets; the son, Jesus. The vineyard, as a fundamental symbol of Israel, and indeed the parable itself echo Isaiah (5:1-7), but it also surfaces as such in Psalm 80. Matthew (21:39) and Luke (20:15) reflect a literal understanding of the analogy by having the tenants cast the son from the vineyard before killing him (see Mark 12:8). Many think that a redactor tried to align the story with Jesus' crucifixion outside the walls of Jerusalem.

The context of this passage is, of course, the altercation Jesus has with the Sanhedrin in Luke 20:1-8. They refuse to recognize the hand of God in John the Baptist, whom Herod had put to death, and they continue in their refusal to see the hand of God in Jesus. Jesus ties his claim to divine authority by quoting from Psalm 118:22-23 (Luke 20:17), a verse that also resonates with Isaiah 8:14-15.

The schism motif enters here once again (see Luke 2:34). The leaders reject Jesus, but the people do not. God's promise takes root in the vineyard Israel, represented by the people's response, but this vineyard will also be shared with the Gentiles (v. 16).

Luke uses the parable's imagery and interpretation in Acts (18:6; 28:28). It also resurfaces in other New Testament writings, such as Romans 11:17-18 and 1 Peter 2:6-7.

20:20-26 Paying taxes to Caesar

The scribes and the chief priests are relentless in their attempts to trap Jesus by catching him off guard. After being shamed by the parable of the tenant farmers (20:9-19), they now send spies or agents to Jesus with hopes that he might incriminate himself by speaking against the empire. Jesus, however, sees through the ruse (20:23).

Roman coinage was highly symbolic for Jews concerned about paying taxes to the emperor. Engraved on the face of the denarius was the image of Tiberius Caesar—at the very least an offense against Jewish sensibilities, since it would go against the prohibition of graven idols. As a subject people, the Jews were required to use this currency for paying taxes and tribute to their occupiers. The question about the legality of paying taxes, therefore, involves the legality of handling idols to do so; the religious Jew should not be in contact with such pagan objects. Combined with these religious principles was the humiliation of paying the conqueror in the coin that transgressed their law code, thus forcing the Jews to participate in Roman paganism. Jesus' response not only avoids the trap the leaders set for him but also calls into question the meaning of true, righteous behavior.

Jesus gains the upper hand against his adversaries by not pitting allegiance to Rome against fidelity to the Torah (the holy writings of the Jewish religion, especially the first five books of the Old Testament). The lesson is that one is not defiled by paying taxes to Rome. Being righteous before God is an issue deeper than paying taxes to a pagan power.

The idea of rendering to Caesar the things that are Caesar's and to God the things that are God's has often been mistakenly used as an injunction for keeping religious and ethical questions separate from political or secular policies. Correctly read through an eschatological lens, Jesus' aphorism states that the things of this world have an impact on the next, while standards of the age to come should have an influence on this present life.

20:27-40 Sadducees and the resurrection

The Sadducees, opponents of the Pharisees, particularly over the teachings on the resurrection, are the next group to question Jesus with an eye toward tripping him up. Not much is known about them except that they were aristocratic conservatives tied to the temple cult (unlike the Pharisees, who promoted the synagogue movement). The circumstance they describe is based on levirate marriage (Deut 25:5-6), whereby a widow's brother-in-law marries her to ensure that the lands stay in the first husband's family and that his name is carried on. Jesus responds by discussing first the nature of a resurrected life and then the basis of the resurrection in the Jewish tradition.

The resurrected life goes beyond the dimensions of earthly existence. Thus expectations and practices in this world do not hold in the next. Moreover, the resurrected life transcends this one (vv. 35, 36, 38). By citing Moses, Jesus taps the source of Jewish faith as well as the sole component of the Sadducees' teaching, for their belief extended no further than the first five books of Moses, often called the Torah or the Pentateuch.

Jesus' argument is impeccable. The scribes, who along with the Pharisees believe in the resurrection, affirm Jesus' answer; the Sadducees who brought up the matter, on the other hand, are silent (vv. 39-40).

Unlike the parallel accounts in Matthew 22:23-33 or Mark 12:18-27, Luke's version contains a teaching that supports celibate life (v. 35; see also Matt 19:12).

20:41-44 David's Son

Jesus' opponents would want to make sure that there is nothing about him which would suggest that he is the Messiah. At the same time, they have to acknowledge that the people see him as a great man, and therefore he could quite possibly be the one long promised by the prophets. At that time the tradition existed of a Messiah arising from David's line, a belief to which the infancy narratives attest. The narrative here draws on this tradition.

In verse 42 Jesus cites Psalm 110:1, a coronation psalm, which in the Greek Septuagint is reflected in this translation. In Psalm 110 the psalmist is speaking, and "Lord" (uppercase here) refers to Yahweh. The "lord" (lowercase here) is the king whom Yahweh is placing on the throne. In its New Testament interpretation, "Lord" still refers to Yahweh, but David the king is speaking. Consequently, "lord" represents a messianic figure who is greater than David. In these verses Jesus states that the term "lord" refers to himself.

The early church drew on this tradition of a Davidic Messiah both here and elsewhere, and this psalm was used as one of the Old Testament writings prefiguring Christ. The other Synoptics contain passages parallel to this one.

20:45-47 Denunciation of the scribes

Jesus, after defending himself before both the Pharisees and Sadducees, takes the offensive. Scribes, as ones who could read, write, and interpret texts, are synonymous with the Pharisees. As a scholarly religious class who knew the Torah and the oral tradition with all the astuteness of master lawyers, they expected honor and deference as their due. As with all professions, there were good and bad members among them. Even Jesus was considered by his disciples to be a teacher.

The condemnation Jesus levels here (vv. 46-47) is directed toward those who are a part of the temple power structure and use their status and expertise for personal advantage at the expense of the poor and unprivileged. This short passage also reflects the debates between church and synagogue in the early days of the Christian movement. It sets the context for what follows in Luke 21:1-4.

21:1-4 The poor widow's contribution

Luke shares this story with Mark (see Mark 12:41-44). Each coin is a *lepton,* which is worth slightly more than one-hundredth of a denarius. Since a denarius is a day's wage, the widow places about one-fiftieth of a day's living into the treasury, and, as Jesus remarks, this is her whole livelihood.

Many hold that this story shows the widow's pious devotion, and she has become a model of religious dedication in that all should give from their sustenance and not their superfluity. The context, however, suggests another interpretation.

Jesus' first order of business upon entering Jerusalem is to go to the temple and drive out those "selling things" (19:45). His violent response to revenues generated by temple worship in that section of the Lukan narrative would be indicative of anger here. In addition, in the preceding passage Jesus has denounced the scribes for "devour[ing] the houses of widows" (Luke 20:47). Jesus is upset at seeing a poor woman think that God's will demanded making herself destitute so that others could become rich.

21:5-6 The destruction of the temple foretold

All three Synoptics contain the prediction of the temple's destruction. The building of Herod's temple, the edifice under discussion in this passage, began in 19 B.C. and was still under construction during Jesus' lifetime (see John 2:20). The whole complex was completed in A.D. 64, only to be totally razed six years later during the First Jewish Revolt. When it was completed, it was considered one of the most beautiful buildings in the whole Roman Empire. The people's awe and wonder at the stones were totally justified. As the house of God, its destruction would seem like the end of the world in the minds of the people (see Josephus, *Ant.* 15.11.1-7 and *J.W.* 4-5).

Is the prediction of the destruction a *vaticinium ex eventu,* that is, a foretelling after the event? If so, then the writer, Luke, is theologizing about the temple's destruction by placing a prediction of it on the lips of Jesus. On the other hand, anyone sensitive to the political climate of the day would know that the tensions would someday explode, resulting in catastrophic disaster for the nation.

This account forms a bridge between the story of the poor widow (21:1-4) and Luke's apocalyptic section (21:7-36).

21:7-11 The signs of the end

Luke 21:7-36 forms the Lukan apocalypse, but it is not the only place in the Third Gospel where apocalyptic imagery occurs (see Luke 17:22-37). Matthew 24 and Mark 13 have parallel passages.

The great part of the language and metaphor used here is characteristic of apocalyptic writing: signs, natural upheavals, disasters, wars, persecution, and a call to vigilance. Apocalyptic language is often, but not exclusively, associated with eschatological teaching, and in this sense this section is more rightly called the Lukan eschatological discourse. By definition, *eschatology* deals with the interpretation of the end times, the fulfillment of history, and culmination of human destiny. In general, we can say that this section shows eschatological concerns in apocalyptic language.

Rarely has anyone been able to identify conclusively the particular historical references to the events mentioned in verses 7-11. There has never been a time in human history when wars, earthquakes, famines, and plagues have not been a part of the picture. Since any one of these events and phenomena can occur without warning or notice, it is better to be prepared, and preparation consists in always looking for Christ in every person and circumstance.

21:12-19 The coming persecution

The early Christian community faced persecution from the home as well as from rulers of both synagogue and state. These Gospel verses, in non-apocalyptic vocabulary, are meant to console and strengthen the believers facing their tribulation.

Verses 14-15 form a doublet with Luke 12:11-12.

21:20-24 The great tribulation

The words that Jesus speaks in this passage ring true to the history of the destruction of Jerusalem.

The Roman general Titus arrived at Jerusalem and set up his main camp about one mile north of the Mount of Olives at Mount Scopus in the spring of A.D. 70. By July his men set to constructing a siege wall around the city to prevent the people of Jerusalem from escaping while protecting the Roman soldiers from Jewish raiding parties. Since such procedures were standard Roman military operations, the description in these verses need not be considered peculiar to the Roman siege in A.D. 70. Nonetheless, the arrival of the Romans came with unexpected suddenness, and internecine fighting among various Jewish sects had reduced the food stores, so that starvation became a major problem within the city (see Josephus, *J.W.* 5.2-3i). On August 28 (Ninth of Ab, by coincidence the same day the Babylonians breached the city some six hundred years earlier), Jerusalem fell to the Romans. Any Jewish survivors were taken captive, and the city, including the temple, was razed to the ground.

Old Testament prophecies are employed in the description: Hosea 9:7 in Luke 21:22; Sirach 28:18; Deuteronomy 28:64; and Zechariah 12:3 in Luke 21:24. Tradition has it that the Christians in the city fled to the city of Pella in present-day Jordan at the outbreak of hostilities. The "time of the Gentiles" (v. 24) foreshadows the great missionary ventures outlined in the Acts of the Apostles.

21:25-28 The coming of the Son of Man

The scene shifts from Jerusalem to the whole world. The language returns to apocalyptic terminology, drawing on Isaiah, Joel, Zephaniah, and Daniel. What has happened to Jerusalem may be a harbinger of the Son of Man's visitation upon the earth, but it is not an immediate warning signal. The scene is not bleak, however. The astral signs and natural calamities serve to notify that redemption is at hand. Just as the people of Jerusalem were mixed in their reception of Jesus, so too will the world be at his second coming.

21:29-33 The lesson of the fig tree

If people can read the signs in nature, they should be willing and able to read the signs of their deliverance.

The reference to "this generation" (v. 32) is ambiguous. In one sense, there is every reason to believe that many in the then contemporary generation would not pass away until after the First Jewish Revolt. On the other hand, if "all these things" refers to upheavals in nature ushering in the Son of Man, "this generation" is a timeless reference to the world; the *eschaton*, or end time, is always imminent.

21:34-36 Exhortation to be vigilant

One must stand with apocalyptic vigilance. The note of surprise resurfaces here (v. 34). Under an imminent understanding of the *eschaton*, the coming of the Son of Man will always be sudden. The directive to pray (v. 36) is a particularly Lukan concern. Jesus prays in the Garden of Gethsemane (22:39-46), and his note of "tribulations" (v. 36) looks toward his own passion.

21:37-38 Conclusion to the ministry in Jerusalem

During the pilgrimage feasts most people, particularly those without relatives in Jerusalem proper, camped on the fields and hills surrounding the city. The Mount of Olives appears to have been one such place.

Despite the discourse on the temple and Jerusalem, Luke is ambiguous toward both. Jesus teaches in the temple even as he speaks against it. Furthermore, in the Acts of the Apostles the temple becomes the site of many events in the ministry of Peter, Paul, and the other disciples. Jesus' public ministry ends with these verses.

THE PASSION

Luke 22:1–23:56

The passion narrative, the nucleus of the kerygma, forms the oldest part of the Gospel tradition. The accounts of the four evangelists show the greatest similarity with each other in this section.

Nonetheless, each evangelist shapes the information to fit the theological architecture of his respective Gospel. In Luke, the themes found all along reach their climax. The schism motif, the great reversal, and the victory over evil all manifest Jesus' reclamation of the cosmos from Satan's clutches as Christ brings the promise of future glory to all.

22:1-6 The conspiracy against Jesus

The diabolical force that has been mounting challenge against Jesus from the very beginning (Luke 4:1-13) increases in intensity here when Satan "enter[s] into Judas" (v. 3). In Luke's narrative, now is the "time" (4:13) for which the devil has been waiting.

Both priests and scribes are at the center of the conspiracy, but by making Judas his agent, Satan fashions a more serious inroad against Jesus. Hence the passion is not merely a human drama; rather, it is an event that involves the whole cosmos. Luke's account of Jesus' passion, with its collusion between Satan and Judas, departs from the synoptic presentation and aligns itself more closely with the Johannine text, and in so doing respects the cosmological nature of the drama.

One of the major pilgrimage feasts that brought thousands to Jerusalem, the feast of Unleavened Bread was originally an agrarian festival celebrated in the spring during the grain harvest. Passover began as a nomadic feast, also held in the spring, when people took their flocks of sheep and goats from the winter to summer feeding grounds. The Jewish practice at the time of Jesus had joined these two feasts into one commemorating the Exodus from Egypt.

For the Romans, this annual spring holiday posed a major security risk. The throngs of people, coupled with the nationalistic overtones inherent in the Exodus event, set the stage for riots and insurrection. The temple leaders, functioning as colonial lackeys of Rome, were well aware that Jesus was a popular figure who fulfilled the messianic expectations of a great many. A conspiracy between Judas, the chief priests, and the guards that tries to find an opportunity to arrest Jesus away from the crowd is indicative of the volatility of the situation (v. 6).

22:7-38 The Passover meal

According to the synoptic dating, the meal takes place on Passover (v. 7); in John's Gospel (13:1) it is on the day before. Jesus must have had disciples and acquaintances in Jerusalem for him to give such specific instructions to Peter and John (vv. 10-12). For this reason, many scholars believe that Jesus went to Jerusalem on several occasions and not just this once, as Luke and the other Synoptics portray. Since women alone generally carried water jars, a man walking with one would attract attention. Jesus leaves the exact location for the meal unspecified to maintain secrecy in the face of impending danger. The Greek for "guest room" (v. 11) is *kataluma* (see 2:7).

It is nearly impossible to determine with absolute accuracy the Jewish Seder, that is, the Passover meal, at this period of history. Nonetheless, all indications are that it involved a total of three blessings of the cup. Luke mentions two of them—one at the beginning of the meal and one at the end (vv. 17, 20). Paul's version of what has come to be called the "institution narrative" is remarkably similar to that of Luke here (see 1 Cor 11:23-26). The elements of the Exodus sacrifice, such as blood, are reinterpreted in the light of Christ's life. He sheds his blood to ensure the life of God's people (see Exod 12:12-16; 24:5-8).

The mention of the betrayer's hand (v. 21), whom the reader knows to be Judas Iscariot (22:3), sparks an argument at the table. Jesus intervenes with a lesson that continues the reversal theme introduced in the *Magnificat* (Luke 1:46-55). Here at the Last Supper, Jesus gives a more positive rendition of the theme: disciples should reverse the roles themselves in order to further the kingdom. Doing so leads to true greatness (22:24-30).

Just as Jesus predicts the role of Judas, though unnamed (vv. 21-23), so too does he predict Peter's denial (vv. 31-34). The devil has already claimed Judas, and now he is attempting to take the rest of the Twelve, Peter included, as Jesus is well aware. Jesus needs Peter to support the others (v. 32), but Peter will falter, as Jesus predicts. Luke alone acknowledges in this manner the cosmic battle Jesus' life and death entail.

In a crisis one should be sure to prepare for the worst, a worry not present in easier times (vv. 35-37). The Twelve still have difficulty understanding Jesus' teaching and mission. They take his metaphors literally, and he loses patience (v. 38).

22:39-53 The agony and arrest

Jesus goes to the Mount of Olives, as is his custom (21:37-38). Prayer is a key element in the makeup of Luke's Gospel, and at this moment Jesus prays. The disciples, however, oblivious to the seriousness of events, fall asleep.

Many reliable ancient manuscripts do not include verses 43-44, but many other ones, just as reliable, do. Whether these verses belong in the Lukan text is a debated issue, but the balance tips for their inclusion. In Luke's temptation scene (4:1-13), the devil "depart[s] for a time," and because he does, Luke has no need of including the ministering angels found in Matthew 4:11 and Mark 1:13. In Luke's narrative, Satan's time comes at the passion (22:3, 31). With Luke, therefore, the angel comes to minister to Jesus during his agony, the time and place where Satan exhibits his fury; it is Satan's "hour, the time for the power of darkness" (v. 53), an "hour" that will last through the crucifixion (see 23:44).

Jesus' emotional state is fragile, and he prays. The road from Jerusalem to the Judean desert passes up and over the Mount of Olives. He agonizes over a decision on whether to stay or to flee, and the tension brings him to the verge of a nervous breakdown (v. 44). A rare medical condition called "hematidrosis," a bloody sweat, sometimes occurs in people under extreme duress. For this reason some speculate that Jesus actually sweat blood. The text reads, however, that his "sweat became like drops of blood," that is, heavy and thick.

Judas finds his opportunity to hand Jesus over as he had planned with the temple authorities. It is unclear from Luke whether he actually kisses Jesus, although Matthew and Mark say so. Luke, the evangelist of "sweet mercy," is the only Synoptic to have Jesus heal the ear of the high priest's slave, while John's is the only Gospel to state the slave's name (John 18:10). Jesus' followers are ready to fight, but Jesus forbids them (v. 51).

22:54-65 Peter's denial

Peter's denial is recounted in all four Gospels.

Peter, always impetuous, follows as Jesus is led to the house of the high priest. Presumably the other disciples are hiding or at least keeping their distance from Jerusalemites. Fear overpowers Peter's usually forward manner, and he denies any contact or involvement with Jesus. Luke mentions that Jesus looks at Peter once the crowing has stopped. The glance acts as an acknowledgement of the action; Peter cannot hide from Jesus

or himself, so he goes off weeping bitterly. His denial, followed by his remorse, displays Satan's near capture of him as well as the power of Jesus' prayer, for Peter, unlike Judas, will return (22:32).

Jesus spends the night in the house of the high priest, located, according to tradition and some scholars, on the southwestern slope of the city at a site currently called St. Peter in Gallicantu. Other archaeologists place the high priest's house on top of the western hill. Luke mentions only the priests and temple guards as ridiculing and demeaning Jesus here (vv. 64-65); the Romans will have their turn (23:36-37).

22:66-71 Jesus before the Sanhedrin

The Sanhedrin heard all cases dealing with Jewish law but could not inflict capital punishment, the penalty for blasphemy. Thus Jesus also has to undergo proceedings in a Roman court. The Sanhedrin uses this opportunity, therefore, to build their case before presenting him to Pilate, where they supplement the charge against Jesus with treasonable offenses (23:2).

The interrogation scene echoes details from the annunciation of Jesus' birth (1:32, 35). Jesus responds to the questions by quoting from Daniel 7:13, a text that asserts the divinity of the Messiah and thereby places the Sanhedrin under Jesus' judgment. They recognize his ploy immediately and hasten him to Pontius Pilate.

23:1-5 Jesus before Pilate

Like every colonial power in history, the Romans made friends with a certain class of the native population. This enabled them to impose foreign rule by wearing a domestic mask. In Palestine the temple priests were the class whom the Romans supported and who supported the Romans. They received revenues from performing the sacrifices of the people. In addition, they had shares in many of the shops and food providers of Jerusalem, and during the great pilgrimage feasts like Passover, this provided them with a healthy income. Roman stability secured the priests' status.

The Romans, on the other hand, needed the priests to guarantee their legitimacy. The priests enabled the Romans to appear as supporters of the Jewish faith. They acted as mediators between the emperor and the Jewish people, and as such they made Roman tax collection easier.

In sum, there was an elite ruling class composed of Romans and Jews, both of whom had a vested interest in keeping the peace and suppressing any insurrection. Jesus, whose very presence garners crowds and who often questions the abuse by the authorities, presents a major threat to both parties.

Pontius Pilate's official residence was in the cosmopolitan seaport of Caesarea Maritima, Herod the Great's magnificent construction project. Within the amphitheater at the northern end was found a stone tablet incised with Pilate's name. From the Gospel accounts and Josephus, we know that Pilate went to Jerusalem only to strengthen the Roman presence among the crowds of pilgrims visiting the city during the Passover feast.

Pontius Pilate was not the weak, misinformed, and vacillating leader many think he was, and Luke notes his barbarity (13:1). The emphasis in this passage on Jesus' innocence is Luke's way of stressing that Jesus was not crucified for being a common insurrectionist (although that is the accusation), as many early Christian detractors at that time were saying.

In all of ancient literature, the only extant record of a Roman criminal court proceeding is the New Testament account of Jesus' trial before Pilate. Despite the variations of the trial among the four evangelists, their narrative lines are all quite similar: questioning by Pilate along with hesitancy on his part over Jesus' guilt; release of a criminal named Barabbas in Jesus' place; and a handing over of Jesus for crucifixion.

23:6-12 Jesus before Herod

Luke alone features this account. Herod Antipas, the son of Herod the Great, is the Jewish client-king of Galilee and Perea, and he is probably in Jerusalem for the Passover feast. Because Jesus is originally from Galilee, Pilate sends him to Herod as a diplomatic courtesy. The two leaders had been at enmity with each other, probably because of Pilate's slaughter of Galileans (13:1), but Pilate's action here reconciles the two.

Herod has an interest in Jesus (9:9), and it appears that he wishes to see some spectacle (23:8). Jesus never indulges in such displays. Consequently, Herod and his soldiers mock Jesus, as the Roman soldiers will do in 23:36. Jesus is returned to Pilate, where he is condemned. The Christian tradition sees this episode as a prophetic fulfillment of Psalm 2:1-2. See Acts 4:25-28.

23:13-25 The sentence of death

The Gospel presentation of a vacillating Pilate is most apparent in this scene. Any information about releasing a prisoner in honor of the holiday we have from Matthew, Mark, and John, but not Luke (ancient and dependable manuscripts omit v. 17, which appears to have been an added gloss prompted by the readings in Matthew 27:15 and Mark 15:6). Luke simply mentions that Pilate releases Barabbas (v. 25). The Gospels are the only source we have that mentions this custom; ancient Roman historians never refer to such a policy. Is Luke, or the other evangelists for that matter, relating a historical fact? Scholars are divided on the issue. In any case, the guilty Barabbas serves as a point of comparison with the innocent Jesus.

23:26-32 The way of the cross

Crucifixion was a feared form of execution that the Romans reserved for slaves, subject populations, and the lowest criminals. The vertical shaft of the cross usually remained standing at the place of execution for successive use and to serve as a grim warning to the resident population. To add to their shame, the condemned were stripped naked and made to carry their own crossbeam amidst the jeers, taunts, and jabs of the crowd.

The Romans press Simon the Cyrenian into service, not because they pitied Jesus, but because they wanted to ensure that he lived long enough to undergo the ignominious death. By following behind Jesus, Simon becomes a model disciple, a point that would be important for the Cyrenians who formed part of the early Christian community (Acts 11:20; 13:1). The Gnostics, who denied the humanity of Jesus, will claim that Jesus was swept into heaven at the crucifixion and that Simon was mistakenly nailed to the cross, an interpretation that early Christian writers effectively counter.

People are following Jesus on the way (v. 27), and Luke's schism motif again surfaces; some are disciples, others are not. Luke often shows people divided along lines of discipleship, and this episode provides an example of that theme. The words to the "daughters of Jerusalem" (vv. 28-30), who bear a strong resemblance to a Greek chorus, reflect the scene described in the Lukan apocalyptic material (21:6-28). Here the context is one of forgiveness.

23:33-43 The crucifixion

Luke does not use the term "Golgatha"; he simply calls the area of crucifixion the "place called the Skull" (v. 33), which at the time of Christ was located outside the walls of Jerusalem. The spot of both the crucifixion and burial have been venerated as such since the second century, and the Basilica of the Holy Sepulchre has covered the place since the time of Empress Helena. The biblical, historical, and archaeological records confirm the area marked by the basilica as the true spot of Jesus' death, burial, and resurrection.

In this section there is another bracketed verse: "Father, forgive them, they know not what they do" (23:34), probably one of the most gentle verses in the whole Bible. Nearly the same manuscripts that do not include 22:43-44 are the ones that also exclude this one. Although scholars are also divided on whether this verse should be part of the original text, a strong case can be made for its inclusion. In addition to its presence in dependable manuscripts, the verse certainly fits with the theme of forgiveness that runs through Luke's whole Gospel, including the passion (22:49-51).

While Luke has Herod's men alone ridiculing Jesus in 23:11, the evangelist situates the mocking by the Roman soldiers here at verses 36-37. Matthew and Mark mention that the two criminals revile Jesus, but only Luke provides a dialogue in which one criminal reprimands the other. At this point Jesus again utters words of mercy, and again we see the schism motif, with one criminal acknowledging Jesus and the other cursing him.

Throughout the crucifixion and death, there are intentional echoes from Psalm 22, Isaiah 53, Wisdom 2–3. These Old Testament works become the lens through which the kerygma is interpreted.

23:44-49 The death of Jesus

Luke's portrayal of the death of Jesus has important differences from the other two Synoptics. As the scene opens, we read of the description of the three hours of darkness. Luke adds the detail about the eclipse of the sun (v. 45). An eclipse is impossible during a full moon, which would have been the case during Passover. This verse should be read, therefore, as a circumstantial phrase well

translated as "while the sun's light failed." If there is any historical background to three hours of darkness, it is most likely attributable to a dust storm coming from the desert, which is a common occurrence in this area during the spring of the year. The important point, however, is to see this passage as an echo of the many apocalyptic prophecies and writings that describe the Day of the Lord as one in which the sun will not shine (see Isa 13:10; Amos 8:9).

The tearing of the temple veil in Luke comes before the death of Jesus and not after it, as it does in Matthew and Mark. Luke is a fine literary artist, and by such a placement of the verse, he constructs the ripping of the curtain as a part of the buildup to the death of Jesus, the climax of the passage. The tearing of the veil itself is laden with a great deal of Old Testament symbolism. We really have no way of knowing to which of the several veils in the temple Luke (or the other evangelists) is referring. The bigger question is whether Luke sees the tearing as a means to let the divine presence out or the means to allow humans in. Since this Lukan version occurs before the death of Jesus, letting the divine presence out is the better conclusion. This is the day of the Lord, and God's presence, his judgment, now centers on the cross.

Among the four Gospels, there are three versions of Jesus' last words from the cross. In each case Christ's final utterance is an expression of each evangelist's theology, which for Luke is trust in God. Jesus shows absolute confidence in the Father during this last moment, a mood quite different from his prayer on the Mount of Olives (22:39-46). With the word "Father," Luke connects this last prayer with the two other prayers Jesus has spoken throughout his passion: the agony (22:42) and the prayer for forgiveness (23:34). See also the prayer for the disciples (10:21) and the Lord's Prayer (11:2).

The centurion offers the first reaction and therefore the first interpretation of Jesus' death in verse 47. The statement that Jesus is innocent (or righteous, just) recalls the deliberations of the Sanhedrin, Pilate, and Herod. On another level, the use of "innocent/righteous/just" harks back to the passage from Wisdom 3:1-3: "But the souls of the just are in the hand of God, / and no torment shall touch them. / They seemed, in the view of the foolish, to be dead; / and their passing away was thought an affliction / and their going forth from us, utter destruction. / But they are in peace." Luke sees the centurion's statement as an act of glorification of God. Jesus has accomplished his "exodus," which he set out to do in 9:31. The "hour . . . of darkness" (22:53) has passed; it is now the hour of the Lord's glorification, ushered in by Jesus' loud cry from the cross (v. 46), a paraphrase of Psalm 31:6.

In the last two verses of the death scene, Luke portrays another dichotomy among several people; he separates the disciples and acquaintances from onlookers and mockers. The emphasis on the eyewitnesses will become an important point for the early church and will be used against those Gnostic detractors who would deny Jesus' actual death by crucifixion.

The Lukan proclivity to emphasize God's mercy becomes evident with the breast-beating onlookers as they return to their homes. The only other occurrence in Luke of breast-beating is in the parable of the Pharisee and the tax collector (18:9-14). In that parable the tax collector knows his sinfulness and asks for forgiveness. The onlookers, like the tax collector, know their sinfulness and depart asking for forgiveness. From Jesus' prayer from the cross, "Father, forgive them, they know not what they do" (23:34), we know that forgiveness is already there.

In Christian piety, verses 34, 43, and 46 are counted among the seven last words of Christ (see also Matt 27:46/Mark 15:34; John 19:26, 28, 30).

23:50-56 The burial of Jesus

The inclusion of the detail "a rock-hewn tomb in which no one had yet been buried," mentioned in some fashion in all four Gospels, underscores that Jesus' body is not laid in a tomb as part of a multiple burial. The evangelists stress that the tomb is new and unused. This detail later becomes important for the early church in countering Gnostic and Jewish charges that Jesus' body was confused among the corpses. All the activity has to be completed before the sabbath begins at sundown.

Joseph of Arimathea, like Simeon and Anna in the infancy narrative (2:25-38), awaits the "kingdom of God" (v. 51). With him, Jesus' universal message penetrates the Sanhedrin and, ironically, has a positive effect there. Joseph's concern for extending the legal prescriptions regarding burial

of the dead ensures that Jesus is not totally excommunicated from his own nation. The women disciples from Galilee (8:1-3) are faithful throughout Jesus' ministry, are present at the crucifixion, and for the burial (v. 56).

THE RESURRECTION

Luke 24:1-53

Discrepancies among the four Gospel accounts reflect the oral transmission of the stories. Each Gospel account relates the respective evangelist's theological interpretation of the fact that Jesus bodily rose on the first day of the week.

Resurrection accounts among the four Gospels can be arranged in several categories. First, there are those dealing with the empty tomb on the first day of the week. Second, there are Jesus' appearances in Jerusalem and environs. And third, there are his appearances in Galilee. All four Gospels feature accounts of the empty tomb, and, to a greater or lesser extent, they all recount appearances in Jerusalem. Luke's is the only one, however, that does not contain any narratives of the Galilean appearances. On the other hand, the most protracted Jerusalem story (24:13-35) is found only in the Third Gospel. Because the second volume to the Lukan corpus, the Acts of the Apostles, relates the whole missionary venture of the church as starting in Jerusalem and from there "throughout Judea and Samaria, to the ends of the earth" (Acts 1:8), Christ's presence in Galilee is simply folded into the broader picture with references to the spice-bearing women (23:55-56) and the "men of Galilee" (Acts 1:11).

24:1-12 The resurrection of Jesus

Tombs were often sealed with a large, wheel-like stone that was rolled in a carved trench in front of a rectangular doorway. Several strong men were needed to move it. The lowly status of women in ancient society not only kept them from politics, but it also meant that they were not to be taken seriously. Paradoxically, this condition gave them some power, since they could come and go in the most volatile areas without raising suspicion, as their standing at the crucifixion and their visit to the tomb attest. Mary Magdalene is the only woman witness common to all four Gospels. For this reason, she has been called *apostola apostolorum*, the "apostle of the apostles."

That the stone has been rolled away when the women arrive is the first sign of something out of the ordinary. Luke has men, described in angel-like terms, stilling the women's fear and placing the resurrection in the context of Jesus' teaching and ministry. The men do not command the women to tell the others, but the women do so out of their own joy and enthusiasm, a truly Lukan ideal of the faithful disciple, and these women have not yet seen the risen Lord. Unfortunately, the men remain incredulous of the women's story, although Peter finds it sufficiently convincing to see for himself.

24:13-35 The road to Emmaus

The spice-bearing women have spread the word concerning the empty tomb, so the disciples in town know about it (24:9). One of the disciples along the road is called Cleopas (v. 18), a name similar to Klopas, the husband of one of the women at the cross, according to John's Gospel (19:25). Many have speculated with good reason that the two mentioned here are married to each other.

Luke is the only Gospel to present this passage, and there may be historical accuracy associated with it. At least three towns lay claim to being the Emmaus of this pericope. The text says that it is situated sixty stadia from Jerusalem, which is the distance for the round trip between the city and Emmaus, a walk one could make at that hour of the day, especially if as excited and enthusiastic as these two disciples. The Emmaus matching most of the criteria lies opposite present-day Moza, whose ruins from the 1948 war are still visible.

The reply to Jesus' questions summarizes the ministry as disciples would have seen and understood it (vv. 17-24). Jesus' explanation places all the events within the context of Old Testament prophecies and Jewish experience (vv. 25-27). They recognize him in the breaking of the bread, a detail reiterated when they relate the story to the Eleven and the others. They can fully *see* who Jesus is, however, and therefore *believe* in him only once the "traveling companion" explains the Law and the prophets. None of this information is new to these disciples; they are merely hearing it again as though for the first time, and the little hope they may have had has blossomed into faith: "Were not our hearts burning [within us] while

he spoke to us on the way and opened the scriptures to us?" (v. 32). This passage presents a balance between the word (vv. 25-27) and sacrament (vv. 30-32), and as such, it is highly eucharistic and liturgical. See also Mark 16:12-13.

By specifically using "eleven" (v. 33) instead of "apostles," Luke highlights Judas's betrayal and prepares the narrative for the election of his replacement in Acts 1:15-26.

24:36-49 The appearance in Jerusalem

Maintaining that the resurrected Jesus is a ghost is more comprehensible to the disciples than believing that he is risen. With this Jerusalem appearance, paralleled in John 19:19-29, Luke presents an apology for those who deny the reality of the resurrection. He does so by having Jesus call the question on the nature of his current existence (v. 39a). Jesus then allows the disciples to feel his flesh and bone while he presents the marks of the crucifixion (vv. 39b-40). Finally, he expresses hunger, and they give him fish to eat. Because it symbolizes overabundance, fish is a sign of the eschatological age, which Jesus' resurrection has indeed ushered in.

As he does with the disciples on the road to Emmaus, Jesus here explains his life, ministry, and resurrection in light of the Old Testament prophecies and experience. The role of the disciples as witnesses to these events is emphasized. They are to start in Jerusalem before heading to the nations. This geographical plan is restated in Acts 1:8. The "power from on high" (v. 49) is the Holy Spirit, who descends upon them in Jerusalem (Acts 2:1-13).

This passage introduces the nature of the glorified body, a reality that goes to the heart of Christian belief. The resurrected life that Christ initiates goes beyond spiritual existence in eternity. It is a new life involving the glorified body that is not immediately recognizable to friends and loved ones, and therefore different from the mortal body, yet this glorified body has continuity with the mortal one. The glorified body transcends the limits of time and space, and yet it is physical. Wounds and blemishes are apparent, yet they do not scar or cause pain. Not much more can be said on the nature of the resurrected body than what Luke describes here. Luke wants faithful believers to know that the same destiny awaits them (see Acts 2:14-41).

24:50-53 The ascension

Luke recapitulates the ascension in the Acts of the Apostles (1:6-12), with some additions. The two ascension stories serve as a bridge connecting the two-volume work. Here it occurs on the same day as the resurrection; in Acts, it begins the apostolic ministry. This ascension account completes the journey to Jerusalem (9:51), while it also ends the Gospel. Jesus' exodus, first voiced in 9:31, is completed with the glorious ascension.

The road to Bethany passes over the Mount of Olives. Jesus was last on the mount during his agony and arrest, when the hour of the "power of darkness" held sway (22:53). His presence on the Mount of Olives now is the triumph over the dark power of Satan.

In Scripture, the Mount of Olives is considered the hill of God's judgment and glorification, and it takes on that role here. Jesus raises his hands in the Old Testament priestly blessing, he ascends gloriously into heaven, and the disciples are filled with joy. Although the Spirit does not come until they are gathered together at Pentecost (Acts 2:1-4), they participate even now in Christ's glorification by praising God in the temple (v. 53). They are the models for all Christians who await the fullness of Christ's reign.

THE GOSPEL ACCORDING TO
JOHN

Scott M. Lewis, S.J.

INTRODUCTION

At first glance the Gospel of John seems deceptively simple and straightforward. As we read and study the text carefully, however, it becomes obvious that there is more to the text than we thought. John is a master of irony, and as the privileged readers we are in a position to appreciate the irony-laden words and actions of the Gospel's characters. John's Jesus uses ordinary words in a manner charged with different layers of meaning, which his listeners usually misunderstand. Water is not just water, nor is bread only bread. Finally, many concepts with which we are familiar are used in a unique way. The word "truth" in verse 14 of the prologue will be unfolded along with the narrative of the Gospel. We are familiar with the word "life," which is used fifty times in the Gospel of John. Its Johannine meaning, however, dances tantalizingly beyond our immediate comprehension. It is wise not to approach the text with preconceived ideas, but as if we are reading it for the first time. Let the text provoke, challenge, and enlighten you. Don't be afraid to question the text or argue with it.

One of the most striking features of the Gospel of John is its different portrayal of Jesus. In the Synoptic Gospels (Matthew, Mark, and Luke), we see much more of the humanity of Jesus. In John, Jesus is a majestic, serene figure, omniscient and totally in control of his destiny at all times. One scholar described John's Jesus as "God striding across the face of the earth." There are no exorcisms in John, and only seven miracles are described. Important miracles such as the raising of Lazarus in John 11 are absent in the other Gospels.

It is likely that John represents a parallel but independent tradition and is not dependent on the Gospel of Mark, as in the Synoptic tradition. Although the name "John" is ascribed to the Gospel, the actual author is unknown, the text referring to him merely as the "disciple whom Jesus loved" (see 13:23; 19:26; 21:7, 20). The text as we have it went through at least three stages of development and represented the tradition and teaching of the Johannine community rather than just one individual.

The Gospel of John reflects the tensions, pressures, and influences of the time and place in which it was written. John has a very black-and-white view of the world: good and evil, light and darkness, spirit and flesh. His narrative is not given to the sort of nuance that we would normally expect and can seem unduly harsh and abrasive at times. Scholars tell us that the Gospel was written around A.D. 90, while the community was involved in acrimonious polemics with fellow Jews. The term "the Jews" (hoi ioudaioi) is often used in a very pejorative way, usually to describe the enemies of Jesus. It is important to remember that the author and his community were also Jews. We should not assume that the historical Jesus vilified or rejected his people.

Likewise, John reserves his strongest vitriol for fellow Christians who differ with him in matters of theology, especially those that relate to Jesus (christology). This is especially evident in the First Letter of John. Reading the text in a superficial and unquestioning manner often leads to sectarian or anti-Judaic misuses of the Gospel. Tragically, this has occurred often in our history. As we study the text, it is helpful to put ourselves in the shoes of the "enemies" of Jesus. What does the world look like through their eyes? Why did they respond as they did? Would we respond differently if we were in their place?

The famous prologue (1:1-18) is often described in terms of the overture to an opera, giving the reader a foretaste of the themes that will be developed at length through the rest of the Gospel. It contains John's theology in a compact form and introduces us to the plot of the Gospel

narrative. Matthew and Luke narrate the earthly birth of Jesus, but John develops the theme of preexistence and takes us back to the very beginning, before the world was ever created. We as readers know where Jesus is really from, while most of the characters of the Gospel of John do not. John's Jesus is not the product of human societies; he is a stranger and alien in the world, even though it was created at his hands. The prologue introduces the theme of the descent and ascent of the emissary of God, as well as the opposition arrayed to thwart the mission of the Word made flesh, an opposition that is represented by the "world" and the "Jews." Finally, it contains the promise that the revelation and perfection of God's gifts brought by the eternal Word will make it possible to become children of God.

COMMENTARY

PROLOGUE

John 1:1-18

1:1-3 In the beginning

The phrase "In the beginning" in verse 1 echoes Genesis 1:1 and alerts the reader to the new creation motif present in the Gospel. The "Word" (*Logos*) is present in the Old Testament as the creative energy of God, as in Genesis 1 and Isaiah 55. The Greek term *logos,* a widely used philosophical term meaning "order," "reason," or "harmony," was chosen to express this aspect of God. The role of the *Logos* is parallel to that of divine Wisdom in the late Old Testament, as in Psalm 33:6; Wisdom 7:25; 8:5; 9:1; 9:9-11; and Proverbs 8:22-31. These passages describe a feminine Wisdom figure who is the divine artisan and co-creator and who was with God before creation. The *Logos* in John is the one through whom all things were created and who was with God and turned toward God even before creation. This is not a simple identification of God and the *Logos,* but a statement that what God was, the *Logos* also was.

1:4-5, 9 Life, light, and darkness

In verse 4 the theme of "life" (*zōē*) is introduced. Jesus has the power of life in him and is

able to impart it to whomever he chooses (5:24; 11:25; 14:6). John sees the world in a stark contrast of light and darkness (vv. 4 and 9). The light comes from above, while darkness is from below (3:19; 8:12; 9:5; 12:46). The contrasting themes of light and darkness would have been readily understood by people in a variety of religious and philosophical traditions.

1:6-8, 15 John the Baptist

Verses 1:6-8 and 15 represent an "intrusion," meaning that they break the flow of the poem and possibly represent a later insertion. They emphasize the subordinate status and supporting role of John the Baptist. There was some rivalry between the disciples of Jesus and John the Baptist (see 3:22-36 and 4:1-2). His role was not completely clear in the first century, and many continued to follow him (Acts 19:1-7).

1:10-11 Opposition to the light

Rejection by both the world and "his own"—presumably the "Jews"—is introduced in verses 10 and 11. Opposition will intensify as Jesus approaches the climax of his mission. This resistance will be present in almost every encounter that

Jesus has with people and represents John's stark contrast between the world above and the world below.

1:12-13 Divine empowerment

Believing in the one from above is the key to empowerment, the power to become children *(tekna)* of God (vv. 12-13). This will be expressed in extended form in chapters 14–17. People are not children of God by nature; it is what they become when they are born from above (3:3), and it is by divine initiative, not human. For John, this is a status to be experienced in this life. It is not necessary to wait until the end times or death, as in traditional eschatology. This is similar to the principle of adoption and empowerment by the Spirit found in Romans 7–8.

1:14 The incarnation

This verse contains the most theologically provocative statement in the Gospel. The one who is the object of faith is described: the Word became flesh and dwelt among us. The Greek word that describes the dwelling of the Word literally means "to pitch one's tent" and possibly alludes to the instances in the Old Testament where Yahweh is said to dwell in the tent or tabernacle (Exod 25:8; 29:46; Zech 2:14; Sir 24:8).

The notion of the divine becoming flesh was a scandal to Greeks, who devalued the flesh and exalted the spirit or the mind, as well as to Jews, who safeguarded the oneness and transcendence of God. It is the concept of the incarnation that separates Christianity from both Judaism and Islam. Its vigorous assertion by John's community resulted in its marginalization from other groups of followers of Jesus. In addition to the notion of a physical body, flesh also means the limits of time and space, as well as mortality. With the incarnation, Jesus becomes the point of unity between the world above and the world below.

In the Old Testament, God's glory *(kabod)* is divine power perceptible on a human level (Exod 33:22; 40:34-35), and is all that human beings can bear. Verse 14 insists that they have seen his glory *(doxa)*, signifying that God's power has become visible in and through a human being. "Grace and truth" is an attribute of God found in Exodus 34:6 *(hesed w-emet)*. Grace is both a sign of God's favor and a description of God's goodness and kindness. John's definition of truth will unfold, as in

4:24; 8:32; 18:37-38. Truth is part of John's high christology, which unmasks the world and its pretensions.

1:16-17 God's gifts

This fullness of grace and truth has bestowed grace (or gift) in place of (or upon) grace (v. 16). This does not imply an inferior status of the previous gift, but its perfection or completion in the new. In verse 17 law is juxtaposed with grace and truth in a way that suggests the theme of fulfillment and perfection of Judaism in Jesus present in nearly every scene of the Gospel.

1:18 The unknown God

No one has ever seen God, who cannot be known through normal human means. All human claims about God are erroneous or incomplete. Human limitations are such that God is unknowable unless the doors of perception are cleansed, which can only be accomplished by the Spirit given through Jesus. In every scene Jesus reveals a God whom we have never known, and this will be reflected in the use of language that emphasizes the sharp dichotomy between above and below, spirit and flesh, light and darkness. There are similar ideas present in Gnostic literature and the Odes of Solomon (late first or early second century A.D.). They share the notion of a redeemer/revealer who reveals the unknown God and awakens humanity to its true origin and destiny. Gnostic groups who shared these ideas made liberal use of the Gospel of John, and it is for this reason that this Gospel was viewed with suspicion by many communities in the early church.

THE BOOK OF SIGNS

John 1:19–12:50

Many scholars believe that this section of the Gospel draws on a preexistent collection of miracles or signs. The evangelist selected and refined only seven of the miracles of Jesus. In the Synoptic Gospels, they are deeds of power *(dynamis)* and reveal the arrival of the reign of God. In John, however, they are called signs *(semeia)* and are a revelation of the identity of Jesus as the one sent from the Father above. Verses 1:29, 35, and 43 begin with "the next day," which is clearly an artificial literary device. Some are able to discern a pattern of seven days, which, coupled with 1:1, seem to signify the seven days of creation. This pattern is rather strained in some places, and there are other possibilities. Others see a three-day preparation patterned after Exodus 19, with God's glory being revealed on the fourth day (2:1-12). We will assume this pattern.

1:19-28 Day One

This interrogation of John at the hands of the Jerusalem delegation is unique to John. In verse 20 the Baptist himself denies a messianic status and admits a secondary status with regard to Jesus (cf. vv. 6-8, 15). He denies that he is Elijah (v. 21), but it is interesting to note that in Mark 9:11-12, Jesus reveals that John the Baptist was indeed Elijah. Elijah was the prophet who was expected to reappear in the last days to prepare the way for the Messiah (Mal 4:5-6; Sir 48:9). His replies "I am not" *(ouk eimi)* parallel the many "I AM" *(ego eimi)* statements of Jesus throughout the Gospel. The "prophet" referred to in verse 25 is one promised in Deuteronomy 18:15, 18 and amplified in the Dead Sea Scrolls from Qumran (1QS 9:11; 4Q Flor). The self-declaration from Isaiah 40:3 (vv. 23-27) and John's assertion of his baptism of water are paralleled in the Synoptic Gospels (Mark, Matthew, and Luke).

1:29-34 Day Two

John the Baptist witnesses to Jesus, beginning with a proclamation that he is the Lamb of God (v. 29) who takes away the sin of the world. John portrays Jesus as the paschal lamb (19:36) described in Exodus 12, although the paschal lamb of Exodus did not take away sin but was a sign of reconciliation. The paschal lamb imagery is also used in Revelation 5 and 1 Corinthians 5:7. Jesus came after John but ranks ahead of him because he existed before him (v. 30). This refers to the preexistence of the *Logos* in 1:1-3 and alludes to his divine status. The Spirit descending on Jesus is witnessed by John the Baptist rather than Jesus or the crowds, as in the Synoptic accounts (Mark 1:10; Matt 3:16; Luke 3:22). In verse 34 the Baptist acclaims Jesus the Son of God, the second in what will become a string of titles.

1:35-42 Day Three

Again John the Baptist recognizes the role of Jesus as the Lamb of God. Two of his disciples follow Jesus. In the Synoptic Gospels it is Jesus who seeks out and calls his disciples, while in John it is the disciples who search for Jesus. When Jesus asks them what they want, they ask, "Where are you staying *(menein)*?" The word is identical to that used in chapter 15 with the parable of the vine, when Jesus promises that the believer who remains or abides in him *(menein)* will enjoy the indwelling of Jesus and the Father.

The question has levels of meaning, and that is confirmed when Jesus invites the disciples to "come and . . . see." Verbs of perception in John have a deeper meaning than the mere physical. Here they are an invitation to the two disciples as well as John's readers to experience and comprehend where Jesus truly abides—with God. Andrew, one of the two disciples, proclaims to his brother Simon that they have found the Messiah. When he brings his brother Simon to Jesus, he immediately receives the nickname Cephas (Peter, meaning "rock"). In Mark 8:27-30, this occurs after Peter's confession that Jesus is the Messiah and occurs halfway through his ministry.

1:43-51 Day Four

In verse 43 Philip is the only disciple directly called by Jesus, and the command "Follow me" is the formulaic call to discipleship present in all four Gospels. Philip proclaims to Nathanael that they have found the one prophesied by Moses and the prophets and that he is the son of Joseph from Nazareth (v. 45). His insistence is met with a contemptuous retort, "Can anything good come from Nazareth?" (v. 46), reflecting the unimportance of Nazareth in the first century. In the ancient Mediterranean world, it was sufficient to know one's village of origin and the name of one's father to place one in society. The irony is that Jesus as the Word made flesh is not from Nazareth, and his Father is God, which we already know as privileged readers.

Jesus addresses Nathanael as a true Israelite, with no duplicity or guile in him (v. 47). This is unlike Jacob (Gen 27:35) and is in line with a similar description in Psalm 32:2: "in whose spirit is no deceit." When Nathanael asks Jesus how he knows him, Jesus replies that he saw him under the fig tree even before Phillip called him, clearly an instance of supernatural sight (vv. 48-49). In amazement, Nathanael proclaims him Son of God and King of Israel (v. 50). All these titles—Lamb of God, Son of God, King of Israel—are true only to a certain point, but they are human categories and therefore inadequate. Jesus will transcend even these, and in a solemn pronouncement Jesus declares that they will see even greater things— the sky opened and the angels of God ascending and descending on the Son of Man (v. 51). This is a variation on Jacob's dream in Genesis 28:12-13, an important theme in rabbinic literature. Rents in the veil separating the physical and spiritual worlds are a favored aspect of apocalyptic theology, as in the baptism of Jesus in Mark 1:10, where the "heavens [were] torn open." Jesus is the bridge between heaven and earth, as well as the gateway.

2:1-3 A wedding banquet

It is the third day after the four-day preparation. This is the first of seven signs that the evangelist presents to disclose the divine identity of Jesus and is present only in John's Gospel. The wedding celebration would have lasted for several days, and the family honor would have depended on providing an adequate feast for the guests. The mother of Jesus is never referred to by name in the Fourth Gospel, nor is the Beloved Disciple, for it is discipleship rather than individual personalities that is important.

2:4-5 A request and a strange answer

When Jesus' mother brings to his attention the fact that the hosts have no more wine, he replies in what seems to us a very brusque manner. The address "Woman" in verse 4 sounds rude to modern ears, but it is actually an Aramaic form that is not disrespectful, although rather formal. "How does your concern affect me?" (*Ti emoi kai soi:* literally, "What do you have to do with me?") is an idiom found in both Aramaic and Greek and expresses defensiveness in the face of attack, as with the demons in Mark 1:24; 5:7, or a concern that someone is forcing an issue or intruding into one's private business.

There is a bit of tension in the story, for Jesus remains slightly aloof from the situation. It is clear that he is defined by his relationship with God the Father and not earthly family ties. His insistence that his hour has not yet come is an indication that he must adhere to the divine timetable. His hour is defined throughout the Gospel as the glorification or crucifixion (12:23), although in this context it probably also alludes to the first public

manifestation of his power—he does not feel that the time is right to manifest himself. His mother does not doubt at all that Jesus will respond, and her order to the waiters to do whatever he says displays the absolute trust that is taken as an exemplar of discipleship.

2:6-12 The stone jars

Verse 6 describes six stone jars, each holding approximately twenty-four gallons. Stone jars were often used because, unlike pottery, they did not transmit impurity or defilement. The water that is drawn out of the jars has become wine (vv. 8-9). The steward's statement about the good wine being saved until now (v. 10) suggests John's theme of fulfillment and perfection (1:17), bolstered by the fact that six jars were used in Jewish rituals, one short of the number of perfection and fulfillment. The miracle seems unimportant and even trivial in itself, but it is symbolic of a change of the eon, a new world, and the advent of the Messiah. In Amos 9:11, 13; Joel 3:18; Isaiah 25:6, the advent of the messianic age is signified by an abundance of rich and sweet wine. Through this sign Jesus reveals his glory (v. 11) or divine power (*doxa;* 1:14; 5:41-44; 7:18; 11:4, 40; 12:43; 17:5, 22-24), and his disciples begin to believe in him.

2:13-17 The cleansing of the temple

In the Synoptic Gospels the cleansing of the temple is almost the last public act of Jesus and occurs after his triumphal entrance into Jerusalem, preceding his arrest (Mark 11:15-17; Matt 21:12-13; Luke 19:45-46). In John's Gospel it is one of the first public acts and takes place at the beginning of Jesus' ministry, during one of his three trips to Jerusalem. There is no way to reconcile this discrepancy other than to acknowledge that John's Gospel is an independent witness to the life of Jesus and orders the events in accordance with its own theological concerns and literary structure.

This is the first instance of opposition on the part of the "Jews." Jesus drives out the sellers of oxen, sheep, and doves, along with the money-changers. In a rather violent Johannine twist, he uses a whip of cords and overturns tables and coins in the process. The quotations in verses 16-17 are from Zechariah 14:21 and Psalm 69:9 instead of Jeremiah, as in Mark 11:17 and contain no references to thieves. The offense is turning his Father's house into a marketplace.

2:18-22 A new temple

Jesus is asked for some sort of sign to authenticate his prophetic behavior (v. 18), which is consistent with an Old Testament prophet such as Jeremiah. His reply (v. 19) is "Destroy this temple and in three days I will raise it up." Thinking that he is referring to the Jerusalem temple (v. 20), they object that the temple has been under construction for forty-six years, and his claim must have seemed ludicrous. The rebuilding of the temple began in 20–19 B.C. and was completed and finished in the sixties of the first century. Forty-six years would have placed this event in A.D. 28.

This is one of many instances in which Jesus speaks on a symbolic higher plane but is misunderstood by people who interpret his words in literal and mundane ways. He is speaking of the temple of his body (v. 21), and of course the three days becomes a prediction of his resurrection. Two words for "temple" are used. The first, *hieros*, possibly refers to the entire temple precincts. The temple of Jesus' body is described with the Greek word *naos*, usually referring to the inner sanctuary, where the image of the god is to be found. This is written after the destruction of the temple, and Jesus is seen by John's community as the new temple *(naos)* or place of encounter with God. The final verse (v. 22) is a perfect illustration of how the Gospels were written. The words and deeds of Jesus are remembered after the resurrection and interpreted in light of that experience.

2:23-25 Imperfect faith

Although it appears that many begin to believe in Jesus because of the signs, Jesus is not convinced, as he is all too cognizant of the vagaries of human nature. The dangers of superficial or incomplete belief will be a recurrent theme in the rest of the Gospel.

3:1-2 Nicodemus by night

The introduction of Nicodemus in verses 1-2 is linked with the description of people with imperfect faith in 2:23-25. Nicodemus, a Pharisee and leader of the Jews, plays a symbolic role. He represents those who possess a natural human understanding of reality, as well as those who are sympathetic to Jesus but lack the conviction to make a full and unequivocal stand in faith. He appears again in 7:50 and 19:39 as a well-intentioned but rather timid figure.

In John's uncompromising polemic, Nicodemus is used to challenge followers to make a public commitment and face the cost; he cannot straddle two different worlds. Nicodemus comes by night (v. 2), which here accentuates his limited human understanding and his attraction to the light represented by Jesus. He acknowledges that Jesus is a teacher come from God, for the common expectation is that the ability to perform signs is proof of the presence and approval of God.

3:3-6 Second birth

The reply of Jesus is almost a non-sequitur (v. 3). He makes a solemn pronouncement that no one can "see" the kingdom of God (cf. 1:12-13) without being born from above *(anothēn)*. To "see" means to experience and understand, and the "kingdom of God" is not a place but a state of being. The word *anothēn* has two meanings—"again" and "from above." The theme of spiritual rebirth is widespread in ancient mystery religions and esoteric philosophies. Nicodemus takes it in the first sense (v. 4), which leads him to an absurdity, for Jesus is speaking on a spiritual plane but is understood in the physical or natural sense, a consequence of the natural barrier to knowing God described in 1:18.

Jesus rephrases the need for rebirth (v. 5) and insists that one enters rather than sees the kingdom of God, but only after being born both of water and Spirit. Does water mean normal human birth or baptism? Although the latter is likely, the first meaning is not thereby excluded. Additionally, the kingdom of God is also represented by the community of believers, and one receives the new life promised by Jesus by entrance into the group by means of baptism. The chasm between the earthly and human and the heavenly and divine is stated emphatically (v. 6). Those who are of the flesh judge according to the senses (7:24; 8:25). The Spirit, however, provides believers with a new mode of perception and understanding.

3:7-8 Wind and Spirit

Jesus explains this necessity in terms of wind and Spirit—the Greek word for both is *pneuma*. The Spirit, like the wind, is mysterious and cannot be controlled by human beings (Eccl 11:5; Sir 16:21), since it does not originate from them. Nicodemus's puzzled question is met with a rebuke from Jesus (vv. 9-12). Nicodemus represents the best of a religious tradition, but he does not have a deep understanding of the "earthly things," which were part of his own tradition, so Jesus questions whether he can comprehend the "heavenly things" that he will reveal. The status of Jesus is unique, for as the divine emissary (v. 13), he is the only one to have been in God's presence (see 1:18). Even the great spiritual figures who had ecstatic or revelatory experiences (Moses, Abraham, Enoch, etc.) are unqualified to reveal what Jesus can, because he has descended from above.

3:14-15 Lifted up

In his portrayal of the salvific nature of Jesus' death, John uses the story of Moses and the fiery serpents from Numbers 21:8-9. The Greek word *(hypsōsen)* means both "lifted up" and "exalted," representing a Johannine double meaning. The crucifixion is referred to in this Gospel as the exaltation or glorification of Jesus. The serpent's venom is human death, and Jesus follows with a discussion of the cure, which is eternal life through belief in the one sent from above.

3:16-17 God's love

Verse 16 is one of the most famous passages in the New Testament. Despite the many negative references to the "world" *(kosmos)*, here it is an object of God's love. It is unclear whether "perish" means through death or apocalyptic judgment, as in 5:28-29; both eschatologies are present in John. The incarnation is for salvation rather than condemnation (v. 17).

3:18-21 The mystery of belief and unbelief

One's salvation or condemnation depends on belief in the name of the Son of God. Belief is not intellectual assent to doctrine, but total surrender and openness to the object of belief. Verses 19-21 reflect the prologue, especially verses 10-11. Rejection of Jesus and a refusal to believe reflect the inner state of the individual. Those who are evil in orientation will not come to the light, while those who live the truth welcome it. Our modern awareness of human psychology and the dynamics of faith and doubt are more subtle and sophisticated, but John has a dualistic, either-or worldview.

3:22-36 Rivalry

Clumsiness in wording and transition indicates that verses 22-36 probably comprise several traditions. Verse 22 is evidence that Jesus is as-

sociated with John the Baptist, possibly as a disciple, and that they have gone their separate but harmonious ways. Both Jesus and John work in concert and appear to make a deep impression on many people. It is clear that Jesus is baptizing, but contrast this statement with 4:2. The locations of Aenon and Salim (v. 23) are unknown, although several sites have been proposed.

The dispute that arises between the disciples of John and a Jew is over ceremonial washings (v. 25). In the Synoptic Gospels, the disciples of Jesus are criticized for not washing their hands. A similar criticism is perhaps at the core of the disagreement, because in verse 26 the disciples of John complain to him that Jesus is baptizing independently and is gathering a following of his own. John replies that any power or influence can only be that which is granted by God (v. 27), similar to Jesus' reply to Pilate in 19:11. This reflects a strong current of divine predetermination throughout the Gospel of John, one also present in the sectarian writings of Qumran. John reconfirms his testimony from 1:19-34 (v. 28); his only role is to witness to Jesus (1:6-8, 15).

Verse 29 is similar in nature to an incident from Mark 2:18-20, which was also in the context of a controversy between disciples, although over the issue of fasting. Here the parable is interpreted in a manner that stresses the secondary and supportive role of John the Baptist. Recognizing the power granted to Jesus from above, John begins his fading exit from the scene (v. 30). He clearly is totally open to the Word of God, and he proves this by insisting to his own disciples that both he and Jesus are part of the same mission, which should eliminate any reason for resentment or competition.

3:31-36 The one from above

Verses 31 and 32 place Jesus in a completely different category. He has come from above and is above all, and he reveals what is from above and out of the reach of ordinary earthly people and will be rejected by many for precisely that reason (cf. 1:11). Jesus speaks for God (vv. 33-36), who has given over everything to him, and to accept the words of Jesus is to accept the God who sent him (cf. Luke 10:22). The promise of eternal life is again given for those who believe in the one who has been sent (v. 36). There is an ominous note: those who reject Jesus will not receive eternal life, and the wrath of God remains on them (cf. Rom 2:5), which presumably includes judgment and punishment.

4:1-6 The new spiritual order

The story of the encounter of Jesus with the Samaritan woman expands on the dawn of the messianic age revealed in 2:1-12. Verses 1-3 explain why Jesus leaves Judea and heads to Galilee. The Pharisees have heard that Jesus appears to be outstripping John the Baptist in baptisms, although the evangelist (or someone much later) adds that Jesus himself did not do any baptizing, leaving that to his disciples. The number of disciples who are baptizing indicates the birth and spread of a new movement, and this is disquieting to the Pharisees. Jesus must pass through Samaria (v. 4), the region in central Israel and the habitation of the Samaritans. They enter Sychar (v. 5), near the ancient city of Shechem and site of Jacob's well (Gen 33:19 and 48:22). At noon Jesus sits down to rest by the well.

4:7-9 The woman at the well

When the Samaritan woman comes to draw water, Jesus asks her to give him a drink (v. 7). By entering a Samaritan village and speaking with this woman, Jesus has crossed ethnic, religious, and gender boundaries. The Samaritans were seen as ethnically impure, having intermarried with colonizers after the Assyrian invasion in 722 B.C. They were religiously suspect, worshiping in a different manner and having their own version of the Torah. And it would have been considered scandalous for him to speak directly to a woman, especially alone. Verse 8 underscores the fact that his disciples are not present, and he is alone with the woman. Her response is rather surly and aggressive (v. 9), emphasizing that Jesus is a Jew and she is a woman and a Samaritan. "Jews use nothing in common with Samaritans" is an understatement, for there was strong animosity between the two groups. The Greek wording is stronger: "Jews do not associate with Samaritans."

4:10-15 Living water

The preliminaries over, Jesus begins probing by stating that if she recognized who he is and understood the transcendental nature of the water he is offering, she would be asking *him* for a drink (v. 10). He promises "living water," which in a technical sense is any water that is flowing and not stored in cisterns or stagnant. As in other scenes, Jesus is using an ordinary word in a spiritual and transcendental sense, and at first the woman understands only on a mundane and human level (v. 11). She assumes that Jesus means some sort of water from the well in front of them. Her question in verse 12 is ironic: "Are you greater than our father Jacob?" John would answer in the affirmative, consonant with 1:17.

The symbolic use of the well becomes apparent in verse 13, as Jesus states that the water from the well will leave one thirsty again, representing the received religious tradition. The water that Jesus will give, on the other hand, will satisfy fully and abolish thirst forever. It will be a spring of water welling up to eternal life (cf. 1:4). In the Jewish tradition, the Torah was likened to living water. "The words of Torah are received into the heart till the Torah becomes a flowing spring" (*Yalkut Shimoni* 2, 480).

Water is used as the symbol of life in countless instances in the Old Testament, but it is used in an eschatological sense in the prophets (Zech 14:8; Ezek 47:1-12; Isa 44:3-4; Jer 2:13; 17:13f.) to symbolize the outpouring of the Spirit of God. That this is the meaning intended is clarified in 7:37-39, where Jesus makes an identical proclamation in the temple, with a parenthetical comment from the narrator that he was speaking of the Spirit. It is clear that although she is intrigued, the woman has still not caught the deeper meaning of the words, thinking only of an inexhaustible supply of water (v. 15). She addresses him as "Sir," which is a progression from her rather rude initial response.

4:16-19 A prophet

When Jesus tells the Samaritan woman to call her husband and come back (v. 16), she replies that she does not have a husband (v. 17). Jesus affirms the truth of her words in an ironical sense (v. 18), for she has had five husbands and is living with a man to whom she is not married. His words are not condemning, but merely a statement of fact. Stunned, the woman replies that he is a prophet (v. 19), and she moves closer to her recognition of his identity. This provides a transition from the dialogue about the living water to the verses that follow, which discuss proper worship in the new age.

4:20-24 Burning religious questions

The woman seeks a definitive answer about the correct place of worship: the center of Jewish worship is in the temple of Jerusalem, while Samaritans worshiped on Mount Gerizim (v. 20). In reply, Jesus informs her that the hour is very close when both forms and places of worship will be transcended by a new and universal spiritual order (v. 21).

Verses 23-24 are the essence of this scene's revelation. "The hour is coming" represents the traditional eschatology: the final days and the new age are in the future on the horizon, but Jesus adds, "and is now here," meaning that in his person the new order is present. A true worshiper is one who worships the Father in Spirit and truth, and they are the particular focus of God's attention. "Truth" refers to Jesus himself, who is filled with truth, as in 1:14, 17. Jesus promises to impart the Spirit—the Living Water—4:13-14 and 7:37-39, as well as the Paraclete in 14:15-17, 25-26; 15:26-27; 16:7-11, 12-15. The locus of the encounter of God is being shifted from particular places such as the temple or Mount Gerizim to Jesus himself, who provides access to the Father. Since God is Spirit, God must be worshiped in Spirit (v. 24), which Jesus alone imparts to believers.

4:25-30 Messianic expectations

The woman voices a messianic expectation, possibly a Samaritan variation referred to as the *taheb*, or restorer, of the prophetic figure foretold by Moses in Deuteronomy 18:15-18 (v. 25). This messianic figure is to have a teaching function, as in 14:25; 16:13-15; and Qumran 1QS 9:1. Jesus affirms that he is in fact this messianic figure.

The disciples return from town and are not a little shocked and scandalized that Jesus is conversing with a woman, but no one has the courage to challenge him (v. 27). The woman leaves everything and relates the event to those in the town, and the foreknowledge of Jesus seems to have been the crucial element in her hesitant question about the possibility of his being the Messiah (vv. 28-29).

4:31-34 Divine sustenance

When the disciples urge Jesus to eat something in verse 31, he replies cryptically that he has food from another source unknown to them (v. 32). The disciples, of course, interpret this in a literal and physical way, assuming that someone has been providing him with food on the side (v. 33). Jesus has to be very explicit as he insists that doing the will of the One who sent him is in itself sustaining, for the mission on which he has been sent is the work of God and is all-consuming (v. 34).

4:35-43 The harvest

This rendition of the proverb found in Matthew 9:37-38 is meant to heighten the sense of urgency concerning the mission. The eschatological harvest is ready now, not in the future, as the openness of the Samaritans to the Word of God proves. In verse 38, Jesus says that the way has already been prepared by others, probably alluding to John the Baptist and Jesus himself. Non-Jews—Samaritans—have responded to the words of Jesus in faith and are being welcomed, and the followers of Jesus are invited to take part in the harvest. The new universal order described in verses 21-24 is making its appearance.

It is possible that these verses are addressing a situation in John's community around A.D. 90, namely, a number of Samaritan converts who might not have been welcomed enthusiastically by everyone. The message is clear: the Samaritans are the first to receive the words of Jesus and believe. The woman's testimony about Jesus' knowledge of the details of her life is convincing for her and apparently for many others (v. 39). Jesus accepts an offer of hospitality from the Samaritans and stays with them for two days (v. 40). Many come to faith independent of the testimony of the woman, believing that Jesus is "the savior of the world" (v. 42). The coupling of "world" with "savior" is found only here and in 1 John 4:14. After two days Jesus departs for Galilee (v. 43).

4:44-45 Uncertain welcome

The proverb in verse 44 is present in the Synoptic tradition (Matt 13:57; Mark 6:4; Luke 4:24) but seems strangely out of place here, since Jesus has been welcomed in Samaria and the next few verses relate his welcome in Galilee. The people of Galilee welcome him (v. 45); many of them saw what he had done in Jerusalem (see 2:13-25). But Jesus did not trust the people in Jerusalem who were dazzled by his signs (2:23-25). He saw them as fickle and imperfect in faith, and this rather ominous note could refer to future trouble.

4:46-54 Healing of the royal official's son

Jesus returns to Cana for his second sign, completing a cycle that began in 2:1-12. This is a different rendition of the healing of the centurion's son reported in Matthew 8:5-13 and Luke 7:1-10. When a royal official asks Jesus to come and heal his son, Jesus responds with a rebuke of people requiring signs and wonders in order to believe (v. 48). The man persists; Jesus tells him to go and his son will live (v. 49). When the official returns home and discovers that his son has been healed, he and his entire household believe. He is most likely a Gentile, and he comes to an authentic faith when faced with the sign that Jesus has performed, unlike many others in a similar situation.

In the context of four Jewish feasts (5:1–10:42), opposition to Jesus increases in tempo and vehemence. Jesus will be portrayed as the perfection and fulfillment of four feasts: Sabbath (5:1-47); Passover (6:1-72); Tabernacles (7:1–10:21); and Dedication (10:22-42).

5:1-9 The healing

The feast is not specified; the sabbath is most likely (v. 1). There are three variations to the name—Beth Zatha, Bethesda, and Bethsaida, but most commentators accept Beth Zatha (v. 2). The pools were thought to have curative powers, even in Canaanite times. The remains of the pool and its structures have been excavated near St. Anne's Church in Jerusalem. Some later manuscripts, none dating before the fifth century, describe an angel who stirs up the water periodically, providing healing for the first person to enter the agitated waters (v. 4). It was most likely a later explanation of the rather cryptic response in verse 7, and the verse is omitted in modern translations. Jesus seeks out the man who has been ill for thirty-eight years rather than the usual supplication from the sufferer (v. 6). Asking if he wants to be well is likely an attempt to evoke some sort of response on the man's part. The man seems to dodge Jesus' question and does not respond with any sort of faith or even a request (v. 7). His reply is more of a complaint. Jesus orders the man to rise, take up his mat, and walk in a manner reminiscent of Mark 2:9-12 (v. 8), and the man complies. The statement that it was a sabbath is the transition to the next part of the narrative, the controversy and the descriptions by Jesus of his relationship to God the Father (v. 9).

5:9-18 Controversy over the sabbath

The focus shifts to the "Jews," who object because the healing took place on the sabbath. Work is forbidden on the sabbath, which is to be kept holy. This is one of the Ten Commandments and is central to Israel's religion (Exod 20:8-11 and Deut 5:12-15). Israelites have even died rather than violate the sabbath, as when they refused to fight on a sabbath during the Maccabean Revolt (1 Macc 2:29-41).

The man immediately shifts the responsibility to Jesus (v. 11). The Jews begin interrogating him to determine the identity of his benefactor (v. 12). The man does not know who it was, both in the ordinary and the deeper sense (v. 13); in fact, he does not seem to be affected at all by the physical healing. Unlike the Samaritan woman in chapter 4, his encounter with Jesus has not resulted in faith or even curiosity. Jesus warns him not to sin anymore, implying that there is a link between sin and illness, as in Mark 2:5-7 (v. 14). This link is denied in the case of the man born blind in chapter 9, suggesting that Jesus' warning is meant for this man in particular and is not to be taken as a universal statement.

In a striking instance of ingratitude, the man informs the authorities that it was Jesus who healed him and commanded him to walk (v. 15). The authorities then begin to harass Jesus for his sabbath activities (v. 16). This represents the core of the passage and is the key for its interpretation. Since his Father continues to work, so must he; as the Son, Jesus can only do what his Father does (v. 17). Jesus does not deny or denigrate the sabbath, but because of his status transcends it. Birth and death occur even on the sabbath; therefore a long Jewish tradition insists that God continues to sustain and give life and to judge. This incites the authorities to a murderous rage, for in addition to breaking the sabbath, Jesus appears to have uttered blasphemy by making himself equal to God (v. 18).

5:19-24 Jesus answers the charges

In this verse and those that follow, Jesus does not deny the charge but enhances and clarifies his relationship with God, which empowers him to give life and to judge (v. 19). It was widely believed that a true son behaves in a manner that mirrors his father. This issue of paternity is also at the center of the debate in 8:31-59. The relationship between the Father and the Son is described in terms of love, which is at the core of the new divine-human relationship described in 14:10-14 and 15:9-11 (v. 20). The powers and prerogatives of the Father are shared with the Son, which in turn are shared with believers who abide in the Son. Jesus also shares in the divine power of giving life, continuing the theme of 1:4 and culminating in 11:25-44 (v. 21). God the Father is the sole judge of humanity, but being the emissary of God, Jesus shares the divine prerogatives, standing in the place of the one who sent him. Rejection or acceptance of Jesus is at the same time rejection or acceptance of God (vv. 22-23).

The exalted rhetoric associated with the identity of Jesus is not meant for christological speculation or doctrinal definition but describes the mission of Jesus and his role as revealer and giver of eternal life. Those who hear the word and believe in Jesus thereby believe God and already have eternal life. By belief in Jesus, one passes into a new order or relationship with God even before death (v. 24). The reference to condemnation anticipates the verses that follow.

5:25-30 The eschaton

Coupled with verses 28-29, this formal pronouncement (v. 25) is a reinterpretation of the traditional eschatology. It combines the coming eschatological judgment with what is called a "realized eschatology" ("the hour is coming, and is now here"—see 4:23). The *eschaton* and judgment have arrived with Jesus. Those who hear his voice and believe will live, while those who reject it continue in the realm of death. Only God the Father has life within himself (v. 23), but this is shared with the Son (see 1:4; 5:21; 11:25-44). The power of judgment has been given to the Son of Man, but this should be compared with the description of judgment in 3:17-21 (v. 27). Verses 28-29 represent a traditional eschatology with its roots in Daniel 12:1-3. The resurrection is for both the good and the wicked—the first for reward, the second for punishment. The power of Jesus lies in his complete openness and transparency to God, as well as his total harmony with the divine will (v. 30).

5:31-47 Witnesses

Jesus continues his defense against the charge of blasphemy and violation of the sabbath. Ac-

cording to both the Old Testament (Num 35:30; Deut 17:6) and the later rabbinic tradition, at least two witnesses are required for testimony in capital cases. John the Baptist was a witness (vv. 33-35), but they were content to rejoice in his light, not realizing that Jesus bears the greater light. Jesus has performed works (v. 36) that testify that the Father has sent him. His primary witness is God the Father (vv. 37-38), but they have never heard his voice or seen his form (cf. 1:18), and they do not recognize that Jesus himself is the voice and word of God. Even though the Scriptures witness to Jesus, they fail in their studies to recognize him (v. 39).

Finally, their unbelief is the result of not having the love of God within them, and the reason is that they have opted for human glory *(doxa)*, which is only esteem and praise, rather than the divine glory revealed in Jesus (vv. 41-44). Moses will be their accuser, for if they had really believed and interiorized the law of Moses, they would recognize who Jesus really is. This alludes to 1:17: the gift of Moses and the gift of Jesus are not in conflict with each other, for belief in the former prepares one to receive the latter.

The miraculous feeding is followed by an interlude with Jesus walking on the sea (vv. 16-21) and concluded with the "bread of life" discourse (vv. 25-59) and a conversation between Jesus and his disciples, with a confession of faith by Peter (vv. 60-71). John does not have an institution narrative of the Eucharist at the Last Supper, so many see this chapter as eucharistic in intent. Although it was certainly fruitful in later reflections on the meaning of the Eucharist, its *primary* meaning concerns the identity and mission of Jesus.

6:1-15 The miraculous feeding (cf. Mark 6)

Jesus has just been in Jerusalem and now suddenly turns up in Galilee (vv. 1-3). In chapter 7 he will be back in Jerusalem, leading some scholars to speculate that chapters 5 and 6 may have been transposed at some stage. Tiberias is mentioned only here in the New Testament and was a city founded by Herod Antipas in A.D. 20 in honor of Tiberius Caesar. The crowds follow Jesus because of the many signs he has been performing with the sick, evidence that his work extended far beyond the seven miracles presented in the Gospel.

The feeding of the multitude will evoke memories of God's providing manna for the Israelites during their desert journey, as well as the imagery in Psalm 23. In the Synoptic accounts, there is no mention of Passover, and the concern for food occurs at the end of a long day of teaching, the issue being raised by the disciples rather than Jesus (vv. 4-5). Jesus is testing the disciples, for he is always in complete control of the situation and omniscient (v. 6). Philip responds with the enormity and seeming hopelessness of the situation (v. 7).

After the boy produces the five barley loaves and two fish, Jesus takes the loaves and gives thanks *(eucharistein),* suggesting a connection with the Eucharist (v. 11). There is a striking parallel with the account of the prophet Elisha in 2 Kings 4:42-44:

> A man came from Baal-shalishah bringing the man of God twenty barley loaves made from the first-fruits, and fresh grain in the ear. "Give it to the people to eat," Elisha said. But his servant objected, "How can I set this before a hundred men?" "Give it to the people to eat," Elisha insisted. "For thus says the LORD, 'They shall eat and there shall be some left over.'" And when they had eaten, there was some left over, as the LORD had said.

The Elijah/Elisha cycle forms a thematic backdrop for the New Testament portrayal of Jesus. Gathering up the fragments so that nothing may be lost is subject to several interpretations (v. 12). "Gathering" and "fragments" are eucharistic terms found in early patristic literature. In the *Didache* 9:4, the Eucharistic Prayer echoes similar concerns: "As this broken bread was scattered upon the mountains, but was brought together and became one, so let thy Church be gathered together from the ends of the earth into thy kingdom." It can therefore also refer to believers, as Jesus is concerned that he might lose nothing of what has been given to him (see 6:39 and 18:9) "Twelve" usually symbolizes the twelve tribes of Israel, but the emphasis is on the abundance of the food provided by Jesus.

As a result of this sign, the people acclaim Jesus as the prophet like Moses foretold in Deuteronomy 18:15 (vv. 13-14). He is the fulfillment of prophetic expectation; there is no mention of a Messiah. The sign has dazzled the crowds, and their faith and understanding are defective and incomplete, as is often the case in John. This de-

ficient understanding is borne out by their desire to make him a king (v. 15). Since Jesus is aware of their intentions, he withdraws to the mountain to be alone and to escape them.

6:16-21 Interlude: Encounter on the sea

Verses 16-21 represent an interlude and a transition to the discourse back in Capernaum. They parallel the encounter on the sea after the feeding of the multitude in Mark 6:45-52 and Matthew 14:22-23. The disciples leave by boat without Jesus and soon find themselves in the midst of a storm (vv. 17-18). The appearance of Jesus walking toward them on the sea arouses fear (v. 19). His reply of "It is I" *(ego eimi)* can be construed as a simple identification of self or as a divine predicate, as in 6:35; 8:12, 58; 11:25; Exod 3:14; Isa 41:10 and 43:10 (v. 20). In Isaiah 41:10, *ego eimi* is even coupled with the injunction "Fear not." Given the importance of "I AM" statements in John, it is more likely a divine predicate, indicating that the presence of Jesus is also the presence of God. The crowd notices that Jesus did not leave with his disciples in the boat, and when they can't find him, they converge on Capernaum looking for him (vv. 22-25).

6:25-29 The bread from heaven

Jesus accuses the crowd of lacking comprehension of the signs and pursuing him only because of their satisfaction with the miraculous food (v. 26). He exhorts them to raise their sights higher and to seek lasting spiritual sustenance that only he can give (v. 27). God has set his seal on the Son of Man, signifying his authentic and unique status as an emissary from God. The crowd's question is a perennial one: what must we do to please God? Here it is phrased rather strangely as the "works of God" (v. 28). The "work of God" is singular in nature, namely, to believe in the one sent by God. Belief in the one sent by God is not mere intellectual assent but a complete reorientation of one's life and a personal relationship with him (v. 29).

6:30-33 Request for a sign

Since Jesus has challenged the Mosaic tradition, the crowd asks for an authenticating sign (v. 30) to justify his actions. Signs were supposed to lead one to faith (Gen 9:12-17; Exod 4:8-9; Isa 7:11-14). The crowd refers to the archetypal feeding miracle, the gift of manna in the desert (v. 31). The phrase "He gave them bread from heaven to eat" is not found in the Old Testament but probably echoes Exodus 16:4, 15; Nehemiah 9:15; and Psalm 78:24. The rest of the chapter is an exegesis (what the Jews would call a "midrash") of that passage. The true bread is that which only God can give, giving life to the entire world, not just Israel. The manna in the desert cannot even approach this (vv. 32-33), as it is temporary and perishable.

6:34-40 The bread from heaven

The crowd understands in a literal and physical way, as did the Samaritan woman in the case of the living water (4:15), so they ask that Jesus give them this bread always (v. 34). In a solemn pronouncement, Jesus declares that *he* is the bread of life (v. 35), providing food and drink that will never leave one hungry or thirsty (4:14; 7:37). In the Old Testament tradition, Wisdom is depicted as providing nourishment (Sir 24:21; Isa 49:10), but as sustainer and life-giver, Jesus perfects and surpasses both Wisdom and the Torah. He is aware that some do not believe or have incomplete faith (v. 36). The universal nature of God's gift of life is emphasized by words such as "anyone," "everyone," and all (vv. 37, 40). God's will is that all people who believe in Jesus receive eternal life and be raised up on the last day (vv. 36-40).

6:41-51 Murmuring and rebellion

The bystanders begin "murmur[ing]," which calls to mind the rebellious behavior of the Israelites in the desert (Exod 16:2-12; Num 14:2-29). Interpreting Jesus' words literally as Nicodemus did, they marvel at the impossibility of his coming down from heaven. Their familiarity with the family of Jesus and his earthly origins becomes an issue as in Mark 6:3; Matthew 13:53-57; and Luke 4:16-30 (vv. 41-42), although the privileged reader knows that his descent is from the Father. The universal thread is taken up again from Isaiah 54:13. "They shall all be taught by God" (v. 45) signifies that anyone who has really understood or listened to God will believe in Jesus. As the living bread that came down from heaven, Jesus grants eternal life to those who eat this bread. This bread given for the life of the world is his flesh (v. 51), which alludes to his impending death.

6:52-59 Eat my flesh and drink my blood

Drinking blood would have been unthinkable for a Jew, especially in view of the strong prohibition in Leviticus 17:10-14. Likewise with eating flesh; the image is made even more graphic by the use of a different verb for eating that describes munching or chewing. This invitation to ingest eternal life through the flesh and blood of Jesus is explained further in verse 57: Jesus has life in him from the Father; the one consuming his flesh and blood will therefore have that same life.

The primary focus is on the broken body and spilled blood of Jesus that is given over in order to give life to and nourish the world. But the language is also eucharistic in nature, evoking Mark 14:22-25 and 1 Corinthians 11:23-28. The discourses in chapters 13–17 suggest that being nourished and sustained by Jesus, while including the Eucharist, does not exclude many other aspects of the Christian life (vv. 53-57). One must assimilate Jesus as one would food, allowing his life-giving presence to become the very fiber of one's being. In the context of the Passover, in which Jews celebrate God's gift of the manna in the desert, Jesus claims to transcend and perfect even this gift.

6:60-71 The first defections

In verses 60-66, many of the disciples take offense at the words of Jesus and his claim to be the source of life. The insistence that the spirit gives life but the flesh is of no avail signifies the limitations of human understanding. The words of Jesus are of a different order and represent both spirit and life, but many of his disciples leave because they cannot go beyond human categories and receive his words. Jesus asks the Twelve, the inner circle, whether they also want to leave, but Peter affirms their faith (v. 67). His confession of faith in verses 68-69 makes it very clear that there are no other possibilities; Jesus alone has the words of eternal life. It is not that they completely understand his teachings, but they trust him enough to know that their understanding will grow during their journey with him. The Twelve not only have come to believe, but they now know that Jesus is the Holy One of God—the One from above. Even this is open to question, for Jesus knows that Judas is going to betray him (vv. 70-71).

7:1-9 Jesus and his brothers

In chapters 7 and 8, Jesus goes to Jerusalem during the feast of Tabernacles, and his visit to the temple provokes threats, accusations, and attempted arrests. In several places Jesus states that the "Jews" were trying to kill him (5:18; 7:19). This prevents him from moving freely about, and Judea appears to be a place of danger (see 11:7-8). This is the feast of Tabernacles or Booths (Sukkoth), a popular annual harvest festival that celebrated God's care and guidance while the Israelites were in the wilderness (v. 2). The feast takes place on the fifteenth day of the seventh month, Tishri (September–October), and is described in Exodus 23:16; 34:22; Deut 16:13-15; Lev 23:39-43. The feast became increasingly eschatological in orientation, pointing toward God's redemptive action at the end time.

Jesus' brothers advise him to go to Judea to show his works to his disciples. But this would be garnering human rather than divine glory. This attempt on their part to goad Jesus into making a public splash by performing miracles is evidence of their lack of understanding and true faith, and the narrator states tersely that they did not believe in him (vv. 3-5). That there may have been tensions and misunderstandings among Jesus' family members is probably more accurate than later piety would admit, for this is corroborated by Mark 3:21, 31-35, and 6:1-6, where his family is depicted in rather negative terms.

Jesus refuses, stating that his hour has not yet come, as in 2:4 (v. 6). The time is always right for his brothers; the world does not hate them because they have given it no reason to do so. Jesus, however, is hated because he is from above, and his presence shows the works of the world for what they are. Refusing to go, Jesus insists that they go on their own, stating that his time has not yet been fulfilled (v. 8). This initial reluctance to accede to the requests of others is also found in 2:4-7 and 4:48-50, which is indicative of the fact that his mission is totally defined by his relationship with the Father and obedience to the divine will.

7:10-36 Jesus goes to the feast

Jesus asserts his complete autonomy in verse 10 by his decision to go to Jerusalem alone. There is an air of expectancy surrounding his arrival, and a division has already occurred among the people. Some are open to his message, while others think that he is a deceiver (vv. 11-13). As Jesus begins to teach in the temple, his knowledge of the Scriptures evokes amazement from the crowd (vv. 14-15), questioning the origin and legitimacy of his teaching. Although the literacy and education of Jesus are debated by scholars, he is presented in John and in Luke (4:16-30) as being literate and conversant with the written tradition. Jesus insists that his teaching is not his own or a matter of learning but is of God, and this is obvious to anyone who seeks to do God's will (vv. 16-18).

The controversy in verses 19-36 centers on the origins of the Messiah. The argument Jesus has with the crowd concerns his healing in 5:9-10, which he defends on the basis of law and practice with respect to circumcision. Just as the sabbath is technically violated in order to do the will of God, Jesus does so in order to give life. He challenges the crowd to judge justly rather than by appearances; that is, sense data and rationality (vv. 19-24). They engage in speculation about the identity and possible messianic status of Jesus, but militating against this is their assertion that they know his origins, whereas the origins of the Messiah will be unknown. This is Johannine irony, for they don't really know where he is from; his origins and identity are not defined by earthly categories (1:1-3) but by God. There is also an extrabiblical tradition of the Messiah's hidden nature in *1 Enoch* 48:6 and *4 Ezra* 13:51-52.

Their failure to discover and accept his origins prevents them from believing in him. Again they try to arrest him, but his fate is determined by a divine timetable rather than a human one (vv. 25-31). Some of the crowd appears to be swayed by his signs, causing the chief priests and the Pharisees to send guards to arrest him. Jesus' enigmatic words about his departure and the inability of others to come will be repeated in 13:33. They of course misunderstand, believing that he is going to the Greeks (Gentiles) in the Diaspora, when in fact he is returning to the Father (vv. 32-36).

7:37-39 Last day of the feast

Jesus' solemn revelatory statement in verses 37-39 is an amplification of 4:13-14 and occurs in the context of the celebration of the feast of Sukkoth in the temple. Twigs of myrtle, palm, willow, and a citron are bound up in what is called a *lulab,* which is waved during processions around the altar while Psalms 113–118 are sung. A ceremonial water libation for abundant rain is celebrated on the eighth day. A procession to the Pool of Siloam brings back water in a golden vessel through the Water Gate to the temple for pouring onto the altar (*m. Sukkah* 4:9; Josephus, *Ant.* 3:245, 247). This was a ritualization of the prophecies in Zechariah 14:6 and Ezekiel 47:1-11, which spoke of water pouring out from the temple, the center of the world, and giving life wherever it flowed.

By naming himself as the source of living water, Jesus claims to be the fulfillment and embodiment of what is symbolized in the Sukkoth ritual, and the origin of the life-giving water is shifted from the temple to him. There is an ambiguity in the Greek in verse 38 that allows for a translation that describes the rivers of living water flowing from either Jesus or the believer. In either case, Jesus is the ultimate source, and he shares this with those who believe. A parenthetical comment explains that the living water is the spirit and that it was only given after the glorification (crucifixion) of Jesus (cf. 19:34).

7:40-52 A division in the crowd

Some in the crowd respond to Jesus' words with a proclamation of him as "the Prophet" (see 1:21; Deut 18:15), while others proclaim him Messiah. But many reject Jesus because he is from Galilee, and the Messiah is supposed to come from Bethlehem. John does not tie Jesus in any way to Bethlehem, but the tradition in Matthew and Luke must have been widely known. Either way the statement is ironical: in one tradition Jesus was born in Bethlehem, while in John he is from above (vv. 40-43).

The guards sent to arrest Jesus are impressed by his words, earning the contempt of the Pharisees and an accusation that they, too, have been deceived by him. They also show a common contempt for the people of the land as being ignorant and accursed. Nicodemus reappears and seeks a fair hearing for Jesus in accordance with the law. The authorities chide him for being sympathetic to what is perceived as a Galilean movement, and they again assert that no prophet arises from Galilee (vv. 44-52).

7:53–8:11 The story of the woman taken in adultery

This incident is not included in the earliest handwritten manuscripts of John's Gospel, and in some later manuscripts it is placed either in other locations within John's Gospel or in the Gospel of Luke. It is probably an independent, free-floating tradition about Jesus.

The story focuses on the murderous impulses of the crowd and their projection of their own darkness on a helpless victim or scapegoat. A woman has been taken in adultery and is liable to stoning according to Leviticus 24:1-16; Deuteronomy 13:10; 17:2-7. She is being used by the Pharisees as a means of trapping Jesus into denying the law of Moses. He has been aware of their murderous impulses for some time, and hatred is equated with murder itself.

Jesus refuses to take the bait and merely writes in the sand and invites those who are sinless to cast the first stone. We cannot know what he wrote, and it does not matter, for it was sufficient to trigger a remembrance of sin on the part of the bystanders. Those present have been brought to an awareness of their own inner darkness. This story is more about non-condemnation than forgiveness, for Jesus only admonishes her not to sin again.

8:12-30 The light of the world

Verses 12-59 relate a long polemical encounter between Jesus and "the Jews," some of whom are initially open to his words. In the course of the encounter, Jesus echoes the "I AM" epiphany in Exodus 3:14 four times. The first three instances provoke controversy, the last an attempted stoning for blasphemy.

In verse 12, Jesus proclaims that he is "the light of the world," an image usually ascribed to God, as in Psalm 27:1. The light of life that his followers will have resonates with a passage in one of the Dead Sea Scrolls from Qumran (1QS 3:7) concerning God, as well as their self-description as "the sons of light." This proclamation is in the context of the Sukkoth ceremony of light (*m. Sukkah* 5:1-4). Four huge menorah or candlesticks were placed in the Court of the Women, and it was said that the light was sufficient to illuminate all Jerusalem, calling to mind Zechariah 14:6. The Torah was described in terms of light for the world in Wisdom 18:4; Proverbs 6:23; Psalm 119:105; and Baruch 4:2, as well as in the rabbinic tradition.

John is portraying Jesus as the embodiment and fulfillment of these passages and as an expression of the light coming into the world in 1:4-5.

People bring judgment on themselves by their acceptance or rejection of this light (3:19-21). The Pharisees question the validity of his testimony, to which Jesus claims the Father as a corroborating witness (vv. 13-18), necessary under a tradition in which two or more witnesses are required (Num 35:30; Deut 17:6; 19:15) and no one can testify on his or her own behalf (*m. Ketub* 2:9). Jesus insists that the root problem is that the crowd does not know him or the Father (cf. 1:18; 14:7); indeed, they do not do so because they are from "below," with all the accompanying ignorance and limitation, while Jesus is from "above" (vv. 19-24). Verses 24 and 28 link the "I AM" assertion with life-giving power to overcome sin and Jesus' revelation of the Father. The final instance (v. 58) refers to the preexistence of Jesus, as revealed in 1:1-3.

8:31-59 Son of Abraham, Son of God

The sharp exchange between Jesus and a group of halfway believers has for centuries provided fuel for anti-Semitic theological attitudes. It is important to place it in the context of the struggle of John's community with Jewish authorities toward the end of the first century. The negative images and statements should be understood as the rhetorical devices of the author and not a condemnation of the Jewish people by Jesus.

Addressing those who had begun to believe in him (v. 30), Jesus exhorts them to remain or stand fast (Greek: *menein;* cf. 15:10) in his word in order to be truly liberated, for their incipient faith still has a long way to go. The truth that they will then know will make them free (v. 32). This truth consists in knowing God through Jesus (1:14; 4:23-24; 14:6) and has nothing to do with human or conceptual knowledge. Taking his statement literally, they retort that they have never been enslaved, conveniently forgetting the sojourn in Egypt and their current occupation by the Romans.

But sin itself is slavery (Rom 6), and in order to be truly free, they need to be liberated by a son who abides or remains in God's household (Rom 7). The crowd first claims to be offspring of Abraham, then of God. By denying that they are illegitimate in verse 41, they are possibly impugning the parentage of Jesus. Jesus rejects both of their paternal claims, for parentage is revealed in the behavior and attitudes of offspring. Abraham was noted for his faith and openness to God; if they

were his offspring, they would believe in Jesus, since he was sent from God. If God were their Father, they would love Jesus as the one sent from God. Since they reject Jesus and want to kill him, they are displaying deceitful and murderous behavior, proving that the devil rather than God or Abraham is their father (vv. 41-44). Those who reject Jesus do not belong to God (v. 47).

Amid accusations of being a Samaritan or possessed (v. 48), Jesus insists that he honors his Father and is in turn glorified by him. When Jesus proclaims that whoever keeps his word will never die (v. 51), derision and an accusation that he is trying to make himself greater than Abraham (vv. 49-55) are the response (cf. the ironical question concerning Jacob in 4:12). His statement that Abraham rejoiced to see his day and that he existed even before Abraham (1:1) results in an attempt on his life, leading Jesus to flee (vv. 56-59).

9:1-7 The healing of the man born blind

The healing is the mere prelude to the extended controversy between the blind man and the Pharisees in verses 8-34. The blind man and the Pharisees move in opposite directions—the man toward the sight of faith, and the latter deeper into the sightless darkness of willful ignorance. The disciples ask the perennial question concerning the blind man: Whose fault is it? "Who sinned, this man or his parents?" (v. 2). It was traditionally held that physical infirmity was the result of sin on the part of the individual or his parents (Exod 20:5; Luke 13:1-5). Jesus rejects this explanation (vv. 3-4); the man was born blind in order to play a role in revelation of the works of God.

With a reference to 8:12 and an allusion to his approaching death, Jesus declares that he is the light of the world as long as he is in the world and so must act accordingly (vv. 3-4). After anointing the man's eyes with a paste of saliva and mud, he tells him to wash in the Pool of Siloam (vv. 6-7), which, according to a loose etymology, means "sent." Jesus, of course, is the one who is "sent," indicating that it is by means of an encounter of faith with him that human eyes are opened to the truth.

9:8-23 Controversy

People first question whether the man who now has his sight is in fact the same one who used to sit and beg, then whether he was actually blind or not (vv. 8-13). The healing, performed on a sabbath, sparks a tremendous controversy with the Pharisees. They question the man's parents concerning his blindness, but they refuse to answer (vv. 18-23). Their fear that they will be expelled from the synagogue reflects the situation in the eighties and nineties rather than during the lifetime of Jesus. The main objection on the part of the Pharisees is that Jesus sinned by healing on the sabbath, so God cannot be with him (vv. 16, 24).

9:24-34 Second interrogation

The Pharisees' insistence that they do not know where Jesus is from (v. 29) is ironic, for that is the crux of the problem. Had they recognized his divine origin, they would have been open to his message. The man grows bolder as the interrogation continues: in verse 17 he proclaims that Jesus is a prophet, while in verses 30-32 he insists that God must be with Jesus for him to be able to restore his sight. He has read the meaning of the sign correctly and his conclusion is self-evident. But he is ridiculed, called one born in sin, and expelled from their presence.

9:35-38 Coming to faith

Jesus finds the man and asks him if he believes in the Son of Man. Strangely, there is no mention of the Messiah. "Son of Man" refers to Jesus and describes his human revelatory role (1:51; 3:13-14; 5:27; 6:27, 53, 62). When the man asks who the Son of Man is so that he might worship him, Jesus reveals himself, and the man does reverence. His journey has been from blindness to sight in many respects, and from unbelief to faith. Throughout the controversy the man repeatedly admitted his ignorance on many matters, but he was spiritually open and astute enough to read the meaning of the sign that Jesus performed, while the others plunged deeper into darkness and ignorance.

9:39-41 Blindness

The proclamation in verse 39 is the core of the story: Jesus came for judgment, in the sense that those who are blind but open to God's word might see, while those who claim to have sight will be shown to be completely blind. When some of the Pharisees take umbrage at the suggestion that they are blind, Jesus responds that blindness is not a sin; the greatest sin is to claim to see (and under-

stand) when one does not. The presence of Jesus as the light provokes judgment in the acceptance or rejection of others (1:9-11; 5:27; 8:12; 12:46-48). The story is the antidote for dogmatism of any sort and can be understood on one level as a metaphor for humanity, for only by admitting "blind[ness]" can humanity receive the sight that Jesus offers.

10:1-16 Good and bad shepherds

The extended metaphor in verses 1-16 is opaque and puzzling, even for the immediate audience (v. 6). Who are the ones referred to in the metaphor? Are the thieves, robbers, and hirelings messianic prophets and pretenders, the current Jewish leadership, or members of other Christian communities? The images from the Old Testament are clear enough: bad shepherds, representing the compromised leadership of Israel, are portrayed in Jeremiah 23:1-8; Ezekiel 22:27; Zephaniah 3:3; Zechariah 10:2-3, 11:4-17. Numbers 27:16-17 speaks of the need for a leader to lead the people in and out, ensuring that they are not like sheep without a shepherd. There is an extended tirade against bad shepherds in Ezekiel 34:1-11, but God promises to seek out his sheep and place a Davidic shepherd over them (Ezek 34:23-24).

In the New Testament the followers of Jesus are sheep (John 21:16-17). In the Synoptic tradition a number of instances refer to the lost sheep of the house of Israel or sheep without a shepherd (Mark 14:27; Matt 9:36/ Mark 6:34; and Mark 15:24). Although the metaphor could be directed at other Christian groups, the most likely targets are the Pharisees and Jewish leaders, especially since chapter 9 ended with their condemnation by Jesus. They have already been shown to be blind; now John will portray them as deaf to the word of God. Using the "I AM" proclamation (vv. 7, 11), Jesus establishes that he is both the shepherd and the gate for the sheep. Those sheep that truly belong to God and to Jesus will hear his voice and follow, and will not listen to those who are not from God and do not have the well-being of the people in mind. This is understood more clearly in the context of the intracommunal struggle depicted in 1 John. Jesus provides access to God by being the gate (Ps 118:20), the mediator between God and humanity. Those who enter through the gate will have life in abundance (1:4; 3:16; 5:21; 11:25-44). The other sheep that do not belong to the fold (v. 16) possibly represent the

Gentiles (17:20-23) but can also refer to other Christian groups. The motif of one shepherd drawing others into the fold of the one God is found in Micah 5:3-5; Jeremiah 3:15; 23:4-6; Ezekiel 34:23-24.

10:17-21 Laying down one's life

Jesus is loved by the Father because he willingly lays down his life and takes it up again in fulfillment of the Father's command. He is not a victim; his death is a deliberate act of self-giving love. The claims of Jesus provoke another controversy (vv. 19-21).

10:22-42 A Hanukkah encounter

The feast of Hanukkah (vv. 22-23) probably occurred in December, and the encounter takes place in the Portico of Solomon (Acts 3:11). Hanukkah celebrates the rededication of the Temple in 164 B.C., as recounted in 1 Maccabees 4:52-59. A long argument erupts over whether Jesus is truly the Messiah, to which he offers as evidence the works he has performed. The sheep that hear his voice follow, and he will give them eternal life, so that they will never perish. No one can take them away, because they have been given to Jesus by the Father, who is greater than all (vv. 24-29). He follows that with an assertion that he is one with the Father (v. 30), but in 14:28 he states that the Father is greater than he. The assertion of unity refers to the mutual indwelling and relationship of the Father and the Son and should not be seen as a metaphysical statement concerning the divine nature.

The bystanders attempt to stone Jesus for blasphemy (vv. 31-33), because as a man he has tried to make himself God. In reply, Jesus quotes Psalm 82:6, in which heavenly beings *(elohim)* are addressed as gods. If those to whom the word of God came could be addressed as gods, he reasons, then it is not outrageous to do so for one consecrated and sent into the world as the Son of God. The crowd is not impressed with his exegesis and tries to arrest Jesus, but he escapes across the Jordan. Many begin to believe in him, noticing that John the Baptist performed no signs, but that what he said about Jesus is true.

11:1-16 A delayed mission of mercy

The raising of Lazarus is found only in John's Gospel, although Jesus restores life to the son of the widow of Nain in Luke 7:11-17. In the Synoptic tradition it is the incident in the temple that pushes the authorities to move against Jesus, whereas John represents this as the last sign and defining act of the public ministry of Jesus. This is the first mention of Mary and Martha in John (cf. Luke 10:38-42), and the anointing of Jesus by Mary is mentioned, although it will not appear until chapter 12.

When Jesus receives word from the sisters that his friend Lazarus is ill, he echoes the reason for the illness given in the case of the blind man in 9:3: the glory of God and his Son. Jesus loved Lazarus and his sisters, so his intentional two-day delay upon hearing of Lazarus's illness is shocking and baffling from the human point of view. His disciples are appalled at his intention to return to Judea (v. 8), for his life has been in danger there.

Jesus continues with the symbolism of light as in 8:12 and implies urgency in his intention. The disciples still do not understand, and when Jesus states that Lazarus is asleep, they take his words literally. Jesus has to tell them bluntly that Lazarus is dead (vv. 11-15). Thomas expresses a resigned willingness to return with Jesus and die with him, ironical in light of later events (v. 16). The prelude in verses 1-16 makes it clear that the situation that greets them on their arrival in Bethany is the result of a deliberate decision by Jesus.

11:17-33 Jesus encounters Martha and Mary

Jesus will encounter Martha in verses 17-27 and Mary in verses 28-37. Upon arrival, they are greeted with the news that Lazarus is dead and has been in the tomb for four days (v. 17). This underscores the fact that he is definitively dead, for according to rabbinic tradition the spirit of the departed hovered around the body for three days. The "Jews" who have come to mourn with the sisters are here portrayed in a positive manner. Martha's pointed greeting in verse 21 expresses disappointment and perhaps even a bit of reproach, but she is still hopeful in verse 22. In reply to Jesus' reassurance that her brother will rise, Martha acknowledges the conventional Jewish (Dan 12:2) and early Christian (Mark 12:18-27; 1 Thess 4:13-18; John 5:28-29) view of the resurrection as occurring in the future on the last day (vv. 23-24).

Jesus' "I AM" statement in verse 25 is unequivocal: as the one who is the resurrection and the life, he has the power of life within him (1:4; 5:24-26). Life *(zōē)* is used thirty-six times in John, seventeen of these with the modifying word "eternal." This is the life not of the world to come but of the world above and does not apply only to the afterlife. The promise of life to the believer in verses 25-26 seems nonsensical if it is taken to refer to biological life and death. But spiritual and biological life and death are contrasted in a manner to convey the promise to the believer that he or she will never be separated from God, even by death. Eternal life, which is direct knowledge of God, begins in the present rather than in some distant future.

Martha responds in faith to Jesus by acknowledging him as the Messiah, Son of God, and the "one . . . coming into the world," which is probably a prophetic figure as in Deuteronomy 18. Mary confronts Jesus with the same words as Martha did in verses 21-22, but she kneels at his feet in reverence.

11:33-37 A puzzling grief

Jesus is moved and upset by the weeping of Mary and the Jewish mourners with her, and he begins to weep (v. 35), which is puzzling considering the deliberate nature of his delay, his intention to restore the life of Lazarus, and his complete foreknowledge. Although some remark at how much Jesus loved Lazarus, others comment that given what he had done for the blind man, he should have been able to help his friend.

11:38-44 Roll away the stone

Jesus orders the stone to be removed from the tomb despite Martha's protestations that there will be a stench after four days in the tomb (vv. 38-39). The prayer of Jesus in verses 41-42 is for the benefit of the crowd so that they might believe. After his command to Lazarus to come out, the man appears still bound hand and foot with his face wrapped in a cloth. This is not a resurrection but the resuscitation or reanimation of a corpse. Lazarus will have to die a second time. The resurrection involves a qualitative change in the nature of the body. When Jesus rises from death, the face-covering is rolled up and placed to one side in a definitive gesture (20:7), while Lazarus is still bound.

11:45-54 Panic in high places

The raising of Lazarus brings many to faith (v. 45). When the news is related to the Pharisees, the lights burn late in the Sanhedrin as the Pharisees and chief priests meet to decide what to do about Jesus. Verses 47-48 are both poignant and ironic: the chief priests and Pharisees are afraid that Jesus, left unchecked, would attract many followers, causing the Romans to deprive them of their land and nation. This, of course, is written after that had become a fact.

Caiaphas, high priest from A.D. 18–36, makes his first appearance in verses 49-50. His comment is meant as a solution for ridding themselves of a meddlesome prophet. With Johannine irony, he unwittingly prophesies in his office as high priest that Jesus would die on behalf of the people and the whole nation. John adds that his death is also to gather into one the dispersed children of God, possibly referring to the Jews in the Diaspora, although Gentiles may also be included (v. 52).

From that day on, there is a plot to kill Jesus (vv. 53-54), causing Jesus to hide in a town called Ephraim. He in effect becomes a hunted man. The crowd heading for Jerusalem for Passover asks aloud whether he will make an appearance or not, and the chief priests seek to arrest him. The tension builds for the transition to entrance into Jerusalem and the passion in chapter 12.

12:1-9 The anointing at Bethany

There are parallels to this anointing (vv. 1-8) in Mark 14:3-9; Matthew 26:6-13; and Luke 7:36-50, although they vary in form. John's version is unique in many respects: the one raising objections is named as Judas, the woman performing the anointing as Mary, and the location of the dinner as the home of Lazarus and his sisters rather than Simon the Leper or Simon the Pharisee.

Anticipating the impending death of Jesus, Mary anoints him as an act of love and devotion, as well as a proleptic preparation for burial. Judas cannot comprehend this act of love and objects to the expense and the possibility of giving the money to the poor. But the poor are not at the heart of his concern, only his own lack of love and the gathering momentum of evil in his life (v. 6).

12:12-16 The entrance into Jerusalem

Jesus' messianic entrance is essentially identical in all four Gospels, but in John it represents his third trip to Jerusalem (2:13; 7:10), and there is no cleansing of the temple. The crowd cries "Hosanna," meaning "Save," which is taken from Psalm 118:25-26. A royal messianic acclamation is indicated, but Zechariah 9:9 is the prophetic passage used to modify the description of the entrance, depicting Jesus seated upon an ass's colt rather than mounted or riding a chariot. This can signify the distinctively nonpolitical nature of his messianic status or emphasize the universal elements found in Zechariah. This reinterpretation is a post-resurrection theological insight by the disciples (cf. 2:22).

12:9-11, 17-19 The whole world goes after Jesus

The presence of Lazarus causes a sensation and attracts many to faith in Jesus (vv. 9-11; 17-19). The fear of the Pharisees in verse 19 that the "whole world" is going after Jesus is well-founded and fulfills the fears voiced in 11:50-52. If this is accurate, it is hard to understand why there is no mention of Lazarus in the other Gospels.

12:20-33 The hour of the Son of Man

The "whole world" is indeed going after Jesus, which is indicative of his universal mission and the ingathering of the scattered children of God (11:52). This is confirmed by a request via Philip and Andrew (vv. 20-22) from a group of visiting Greeks (Hellenes) to "see" Jesus. The Greeks were likely "God-fearers"—Gentiles attracted to Judaism and its practices but not full members. This is the trip wire that signals that the hour for the Son of Man to be glorified has arrived (v. 23). His hour was always associated with his future glorification (2:4; 4:23; 7:30; 8:20).

The image of the grain of wheat (vv. 24-25) dying and bearing fruit is also found in some Greek mystery religions but is also similar to the seed analogy used by Paul in 1 Corinthians 15:36. This grain of wheat expresses the principle of death and life and the necessity of the earthly to give way to the heavenly. It is coupled with the pronouncement about loving one's life and losing it, hating it and preserving it for eternal life (v. 25), which counsels a "letting go" of one's life rather than a fearful grasping. This principle is a fundamental and well-attested element in early Christian tradition: Mark 8:35; Matthew 16:25; Luke 9:24, as well as a parallel tradition in Matthew 10:39 and Luke 17:33.

Likewise, verse 26 is similar in some ways to the command to take up one's cross found in Mark 8:34; Matthew 16:24; and Luke 9:23. John does not portray Jesus as the Man of Sorrows but the Lord of Glory. Jesus admits to being troubled in verse 27, but his request for the cup to pass from him in Mark 14:36 is here only a brief rhetorical question, followed by an assertion that this hour is his sole reason for being there.

Jesus' request to the Father to glorify him (v. 28) is answered by an affirmative voice from heaven. Some of the crowd hear thunder, others an angel; not all are attuned to heavenly realities. There is some similarity to a *bat qol* ("daughter of a voice"), which Jewish tradition believed to be a heavenly voice that declares God's will, teachings, or commandments to individuals or groups. Jesus' death is a judgment on the world (v. 31), which will be one of the dimensions of his trial. Being "lifted up" (3:14; 8:28) from the earth is clearly his impending crucifixion. As a result, he will draw all people to himself, which, coupled with 3:16, implies a more universal mission than Israel alone.

12:34-36 The light will soon depart

Puzzlement is the reaction of the crowd in verses 34-36. Tradition depicts the Davidic Messiah as remaining forever, but Jesus insists that the Son of Man will be lifted up, which contrasts popular expectations with the early Christian reinterpretation of the messianic tradition. There is a warning: the light (Jesus) will not be around much longer, so his listeners are encouraged to believe while they can, lest they walk in darkness. Believing in the light will enable them to become children of the light, which is echoed in Luke 16:8; 1 Thess 5:5; and especially in the literature of the Qumran community (1QS 1:10; 1QM 1:1).

12:37-50 Human praise and the glory of God

In spite of Jesus' signs, most have not believed, and Isaiah 53:1 (v. 38) and 6:1-10 (v. 40) are invoked to explain their unbelief. This is repeated elsewhere in the New Testament: Rom 10:16; Mark 4:11-12; Acts 28:26-27. The revelation of God's glory is a thread running throughout Isaiah (6:1-10; 40:5; 42:8; 48:11; 60:1), so John is able to assert that Isaiah saw the preexistent glory of Jesus (v. 41). Among those who have come to believe in Jesus are many authorities, but with a fear reminiscent of 9:22, they refuse to do so openly for fear of expulsion from the synagogue, as in the case of Nicodemus and Joseph of Arimathea (3:2; 19:38).

John's accusation that they preferred human praise to the glory of God depicts a conflict in the Gospel between the transcendent and earthly, the human and the divine, and those who are open to God's revelation and those who cling to human traditions and perceptions. Such examples can be found in every age and in every religion. The gauntlet is thrown down in verses 44-50: since Jesus represents the Father who sent him, rejection of him is rejection of the Father. Those who refuse to believe are not condemned by Jesus, who did not come for that purpose (3:18-21), but will be judged by the word revealed by him on the last day. Today we would have a much more nuanced explanation of conversion and the dynamics of faith and doubt, and it is hoped that we do not condemn those who do not share our views. These words conclude the section of the Gospel designated by scholars as "The Book of Signs."

THE BOOK OF GLORY

John 13:1–20:31

Scholars designate chapters 13:1–20:31 as "The Book of Glory" because they describe the glorification of Jesus and his return to the Father. The farewell discourse that follows the meal is in the ancient tradition of testaments of famous men (see Gen 49; Josh 22–24; Deut; Socrates in Plato's *Phaedo*; *Testaments of the Twelve Patriarchs*). These testaments usually consisted of exhortations, prayers, consolation of followers, predictions of the course of future events, and the appointment of a successor. Chapters 13–17 are a composite work, woven together artistically from collections of teachings. This is reflected in their repetitious quality and by "seams" in the discourse. For instance, at the end of 14:31, Jesus says, "Get up, let us go!" but the discourse continues for three more chapters. The discourses describe the impending departure of Jesus and the change of mind, heart, and behavior necessary to overcome the world as he has. The union of Jesus with the Father is dying to the world; the union of the believer with Jesus is the same, and these teachings provide the means. Love is the path to God, but John's depic-

tion of love is very specific: laying down one's life for others.

John's version of the Last Supper is comparable to those of the Synoptic tradition (Matt 27:17-29; Mark 14:19-25; Luke 22:7-38), but with some significant variations. John does not describe the preparations for the meal, and it is not a Passover meal, for Jesus dies on the day of preparation for Passover (19:31, 42). Jesus himself is the Paschal Lamb (1:29; 19:36), although the paschal lamb for Passover does not have an expiatory function. The account of the foot-washing takes the place of the Synoptic institution of the Eucharist. The practice of the Eucharist by the Johannine community is assumed (6:55-58), so the foot-washing becomes an interpretation of the Eucharist's significance.

13:1-5 Fully aware and deliberate

In keeping with the theme of the omniscience and foreknowledge of Jesus (6:6; 12:30), he is fully conscious of his heavenly origin and destiny. Throughout the Gospel Jesus moved about with an awareness that his hour had not yet come (2:4; 7:30; 8:20), but now he fully realizes that it has arrived. His love for his own in the world has been to the end or utmost *(telos)*, and the end is his self-giving death (v. 1), which Jesus demonstrates with the foot-washing. Judas, as the tool of Satan and the forces opposed to God, has already decided on his treacherous mission (v. 2). Speculation concerning the motives of Judas is futile, for the four Gospels give different reasons. For Matthew, money is the reason, while John ascribes the instigation to Satan.

13:5-11 The foot-washing

Foot-washing was a job considered too menial for a Jewish slave to perform, and it was usually reserved for the lowliest slaves of the household. It is similar to the pattern of the descent and humiliation of the Son as he assumes the condition of a slave that is described in Philippians 2:1-11. For John, however, it is a pattern of self-giving love. Peter objects to being washed (vv. 6-8) because he does not understand the meaning of Jesus' death. One of the things that he does not understand is that Jesus' action bears witness to a rejection of worldly honor and shame values of domination and subservience. He replaces it with a new model for human relationships: loving and humble service and laying down one's life for others (15:13; 16:2; 21:19; 1 John 3:16). The egalitarian nature of the early Johannine community reflects this model. It is later that he and the others will understand, as is often the case (2:17, 22; 7:39; 12:16; 14:29).

The foot-washing symbolizes the salvific death of Jesus, so when Jesus tells Peter that unless he is washed he will have no part in him, the laying down of one's life for others comes to mind (15:13), as well as the kind of death Peter himself will later experience (21:19). The insistence on being washed (vv. 8, 10) likely evokes the baptism that is the rite of passage into the community and a sharing in Jesus' death.

13:12-17 A model of discipleship

As teacher and lord, Jesus was willing to wash their feet; how much more they should be willing to do the same for one another. The foot-washing is given as a model or paradigm not only of humble and loving service, but of self-sacrificing love. He is not proposing an anemic Holy Thursday ritual, but a pattern or model to be imitated in every aspect of life, from small acts of kindness to sacrificial death. It only has the power to bless when it is understood and put into practice (v. 17).

13:18-30 A traitor in their midst

Jesus is again troubled, as in 12:27, but this time it is because of his knowledge that there is a traitor in their midst (cf. Matt 16:21; Mark 14:18). When the disciples want the identity of the traitor, they must go through an intermediary—the Beloved Disciple (vv. 23-25). This disciple reclines with his head on Jesus' chest, but the word used is *kolpos*, which means "bosom." The same word describes the close relationship that exists between Jesus and the Father (1:18), suggesting that the Beloved Disciple was believed by his community to enjoy an analogous relationship with the Lord, endowing him with more authority and respect.

Jesus reveals the identity of the traitor by giving him a morsel to eat (v. 26). The significance of the morsel is open to interpretation: some see it as a sign of the unfailing love of Jesus even to the one who betrays him (see Ps 41:9-10), while others detect hints of early eucharistic practices. After Judas accepts the morsel, Satan enters him (v. 27). Jesus orders him to do quickly what he has

planned to do, making Jesus fully in control of his fate. Even at this stage, none of the disciples have any understanding of these words or actions (v. 28); awareness will come after the fact. After Judas leaves, the narrative states tersely that it was night, for on a deeper level the darkness has the upper hand (v. 30).

13:31-35 Something new, something old

In verses 31-33 Jesus enigmatically refers to his departure and the inability of others to find him or follow him (7:33-36; 8:21-22), underscoring his divine and otherworldly origin. He gives his "new" commandment (vv. 34-35) as a parting legacy that is in effect a summation of the foot-washing and his impending death. The love commandment is not new, for Jesus quotes Deuteronomy 6:5 and Leviticus 19:18 in Mark 12:28-34. The author of the Johannine letters admits as much (1 John 2:7; 3:11); it has been told from the beginning. Its newness here is its eschatological nature and its radical definition: laying down one's life for others. This is the guiding principle for the dawning messianic age.

Love in John is not emotion, sentiment, or personal attraction, but very practical, dynamic, and demanding. Jesus himself is the revelation of God's love (3:16; 1 John 3:16) in his ministry and in his death (15:12-13). Love will now be the distinguishing mark of disciples of Jesus (v. 35) rather than dress, diet, rituals, or observance of the law, as Christians are always in need of calling to mind.

13:36-38 Peter's boast

Simon Peter wants to follow Jesus and can't understand why he cannot. The cross is where Jesus is going, and Peter will follow later (21:19). Peter's brash promise that he will lay down his life for Jesus reveals just how little he understands the meaning of the foot-washing and the new commandment, and it is met with the prediction of his threefold denial before the cock crows (vv. 37-38).

14:1-4 The departure of Jesus

Jesus gives words of consolation and encouragement to his disciples, who are still captives of their ignorance and lack of comprehension. They continually ask where he is going and why they are unable to go. At this stage it is a solitary journey; Jesus has descended from the Father and is now returning to him. Jesus reassures them that there are many dwelling places in his Father's house and that after preparing a place for them, he will return and take his followers with him (vv. 2-4).

14:5-7 The way

Jesus' assertion that the disciples know the way is met with puzzlement by Thomas, which provides Jesus with the opportunity to declare, "I am the way and the truth and the life" (v. 6). The "Way" is the self-designation of the early Christian movement in Acts 9:2; 19:9, 23; 22:4; and 24:14, 22. Additionally, the term was used in the Qumran community (1QS 9:16-21) and in a stream of Jewish writings known as "two-way" spirituality, for example, the *Didache* (chs. 1 and 5). Jesus is a manifestation of the truth (1:14, 17), and knowing him sets one free (8:32), but not all are able to accept it (18:38). "Life" has been a constant thread throughout the Gospel, and the granting of eternal life is the root mission of Jesus (1:4; 3:16; 5:24-26; 11:25-26).

The association of all three terms—"the way and the truth and the life"—with the person of Jesus is a christological proclamation that asserts the utter uniqueness of Jesus and the inability of anyone to come to the Father except through him. This exclusive and sectarian statement was probably generated in the Johannine community's struggle with the synagogue and with other Christian groups. From our own historical vantage point, it is possible to broaden our understanding. Jesus can also be defined as "the way and the truth and the life" with respect to his example of complete self-giving, love, and service to humanity. Although Jesus is the gate to the Father, it is in the living out of this spiritual path or pattern that one has access to God, regardless of who one is.

14:8-14 The indwelling and empowerment

Knowing Jesus is the same as knowing the Father, since Jesus manifests him perfectly in his own person (v. 8). This is not understood by Philip, whom Jesus chides for his inability to get it despite his long association with him. In verses 10-12 Jesus elaborates on his words, insisting that he dwells in the Father and the Father dwells in him, the evidence being the works that the Father performs in him. But this divine empowerment is also available for those who believe in him (v. 12); in fact, believers will be able to do even greater things.

This stunning promise is given scant attention in modern church settings, much to our spiritual detriment. Even though Jesus is returning to the Father, his disciples are expected to continue his work. This will be developed in chapters 15–17. Jesus will also do anything that is asked in his name (vv. 13-14). To pray in the name of Jesus has nothing to do with a quasi-magical power in pronouncing a name; it means to ask for something with the same mind and heart as Jesus and presupposes abiding in him through the Spirit, as commanded in chapter 15.

14:15-24 The love commandment revisited

Loving Jesus is only accomplished by keeping his commandments (vv. 15, 21, 23, 24). Although Jesus gave his disciples only one commandment—to love one another—it is clear from other passages and the letters of John that the other commandment is to believe that Jesus is the one sent from God. Love is a mode of knowing God as well as an empowering principle, for both Jesus and the Father will love and reveal themselves to those who love Jesus. All these things are possible through the sending of the "Advocate" (Paraclete), which is a fulfillment of the requirement for rebirth in the Spirit in 3:1-8 (cf. 20:22). It will be the alter ego of Jesus and his continuing and permanent presence in the community (14:15-17, 25-26; 15:26-27; 16:7-11, 12-15).

"Paraclete" was originally a legal term meaning advocate, counselor, or stand-in. It fulfills a variety of functions: teaching, 14:17 and 15:4; prophecy, 14:2-3 and 16:13-15; witness, 8:17-18 and 15:26. Its origin is God (15:26 and 16:28), and the world cannot receive it (14:17). It is clear that John's community is a Spirit-filled community in which teaching and revelation are continuous.

14:25-30 Jesus' gift of peace

Jesus bestows his peace on the disciples, signaling his departure. He makes it clear that it is not an earthly peace, which is merely the temporary absence of violence. This is God's peace—wholeness or *shalom*—given through the Spirit to abolish fear and the sense of distance or separation from God. Because of this gift of peace, Jesus is able to repeat the opening line of the chapter: "Do not let your hearts be troubled or afraid" (v. 27). All other forms of peace depend on this transcendent peace. He assures them that he will come back (v. 28) and observes that they should rejoice that he is going to the Father, "for the Father is greater than I," which contradicts 10:30. The ruler of this world—Satan—is now coming in the context of the impending passion, but he has no power whatsoever over Jesus, who goes to the cross to prove to the world that he loves the Father and is totally obedient to his will (v. 30).

15:1-11 Abiding in Jesus, the true vine

Jesus promised that he would always be present in the community. Now he relates how the members of this community will continue to be sustained and nourished with life and power. In describing the nature of the union of the disciples with Jesus and the Father (vv. 1-11), Jesus utilizes the metaphor of the vine, which was a well-known Old Testament symbol for Israel (Ps 80:8-19; Isa 5:1-7; Jer 2:21; Ezek 17:6-8; 19:10-14; Hos 10:1; Eccl 24:27). Since Jesus declares in an "I AM" statement that he is the true vine (v. 1), it is probable that the followers of Jesus are being depicted as the true Israel. The image of vine is similar to that of Body of Christ used in 1 Corinthians 12:12-27; Col 1:18; Eph 1:22-23, although these instances stress the element of interdependence and equality more than the image of the vine does.

In verses 1-11 the word "remain," or as it is often translated, "abide" *(menein)* appears ten times, illustrating the mutual indwelling and continuous union with Jesus, not just at key moments in one's life. Those who remain connected to the vine are sustained and nourished, while those who do not remain on the vine wither and die and are useless (vv. 4-6). In the metaphor of the vine, branches, and vine grower, it is clear that they refer to Jesus, his believers, and the Father, but the meaning of the pruning and burning is unclear. Jesus' disciples have already been cleansed by his words (13:10), but the pruning can also refer to those with imperfect faith, such as those the author of the epistles rails against.

The branches are judged according to the fruit produced, which is similar to the means of discerning false prophets in Matthew 7:15-20; Luke 6:17-44; and 1 John. The fruit would be the good works done in obedience to the commandments of Jesus. By remaining in Jesus, his words remain in believers, and anything they ask will be done for them (v. 7). It is in this indwelling and the bearing of its fruit that God the Father is glorified (v. 8). To "remain" assumes fulfilling the love commandment of Jesus (vv. 12-14). Love is the golden thread that binds Jesus, his followers, and the Father (vv. 9-10), who is love itself (1 John 4:8, 16).

15:12-17 Love and the new relationship

All this changes radically the relationship between believers and Jesus. No longer are they servants or slaves but friends (vv. 13-15). This friendship is epitomized by the personal experiential knowledge of the activity and purpose of Jesus, as well as cognizance of everything that Jesus has heard from the Father (vv. 14-15). Nothing is to be hidden; nor is there any sense of the vertical or hierarchical, which is also the model of John's community. This is dependent on obedience to the commandments of Jesus (v. 14). It was Jesus who chose his followers, although chapter 1 depicts them as seeking him out. But now they are appointed to go and bear lasting fruit (20:21), receiving from the Father whatever they ask in Jesus' name (v. 16). Repeating verse 12, they are commanded to love one another, for this is what makes the indwelling possible (v. 17).

15:17-27 The world's hatred

Since the disciples and Jesus abide in one another, the world will hate the disciples just as it hated Jesus (v. 18). Recalling 13:16, Jesus reminds the disciples that they are not greater than the master, so they can expect the same treatment (v. 20). Those who reject Jesus have no excuse, for he has spoken his words to them and performed signs in their midst (vv. 21-24). Hatred of Jesus is equal to hatred of the Father (v. 23) and is the fulfillment of Psalms 35:19 and 69:4 (v. 25). These verses reflect the alienation and sense of being under siege that was felt by John's community. The Advocate (Spirit) that Jesus will send will continue his work and will give testimony through his followers, presumably in the form of good works and signs (v. 26).

16:1-3 Dubious favors for God

Jesus continues in this vein by giving his disciples ample warning of the world's hostility (v. 1).

Expulsion from the synagogue (cf. 9:22; 12:42) reflects the experience of the Johannine community after the Jewish self-definition at Jamnia following the destruction of the temple in A.D. 70. Although the *birkath ha-minim* recited in synagogues toward the end of the first century contains a prayer for the destruction of the *minim* (heretics) and the Nazarenes (Christians), there is little documented evidence outside the New Testament of actual killing. The stoning of Stephen in Acts 7:58–8:1 is immediately linked with the zealous persecution of Paul (9:1-9), who admits to having been a violent persecutor of the church of God (Gal 1:13; 1 Cor 15:9). He warns that there will be a time when those who kill them will think that they are offering worship to God (v. 2).

Killing out of a warped sense of devotion or piety has been an unhappy reality in all ages and in all religions, and our own age is certainly no different. The reason, according to Jesus, is that the perpetrators have never known him or the Father (15:21; v. 3). Their murderous hatred is proof of their unbelief, for those who truly know and love God are not captive to murderous impulses. Throughout the controversies Jesus has repeatedly accused his tormentors of plotting to kill him, and it is clear that his disciples can expect the same treatment.

16:4-20 The departure of Jesus

The departure of Jesus has been mentioned in 13:36; 14:5; and 16:5, always accompanied by incomprehension on the part of the disciples. Jesus assures them that it is advantageous for them that he go away (vv. 5-7), for this is necessary for the Advocate to come (cf. 7:39). The Advocate or Spirit of truth (vv. 12-15) will act as an intermediary between Jesus and John's community, declaring all that Jesus has received from the Father. It will remind them of the words that Jesus spoke during his ministry, and it is implied that in leading them to all truth, it will also declare things that have not yet been spoken.

But most of all, the Spirit of truth (cf. Qumran texts 1QS 3:19) will prove the world wrong about sin, righteousness, and judgment, all three of which are aspects of the world's rejection of Jesus. For John, unbelief is synonymous with sin, while righteousness is the vindication of Jesus by his being raised from the dead and returning to the Father. The world judges incorrectly by refusing

to recognize Jesus as being sent from the Father and by its inability to penetrate beyond external appearances.

Jesus toys with the phrase "a little while" (vv. 16-19) to refer to his impending death and the time before his reappearance after the resurrection, which causes puzzlement and consternation among the disciples. By way of explanation, the grief that they will feel upon his death is contrasted with the joy (15:11; 16:20, 22; 17:13) they will experience "on that day" (14:20; 16:23, 26) when they will see him again. Although most scholars take "on that day" to refer to the resurrection, a reference to a second coming is not excluded, for the traditional eschatology (cf. 21:22-23) and John's realized eschatology coexist in the same Gospel.

The alternating joy and sorrow on the part of the world and the disciples over the death of Jesus is a perfect example of the vast chasm that separates worldly and divine perceptions (v. 20). At that time they will have no more questions, for all will be clear, and whatever they ask the Father in Jesus' name will be given to them (vv. 23-26). The "complete . . . joy" signals the access to God that they will enjoy and the mutual indwelling that they will experience.

16:21-24 Messianic birth pangs

The image of the woman giving birth in verses 20-22 has a long biblical tradition and is used to denote the travail of messianic struggle (Isa 26:16-19; 66:7-11; Mark 13:19, 24; Matt 24:9, 21, 29; Acts 14:22; 1 Cor 7:26; 10:11; 2 Cor 4:17; Rom 8:22; Rev 12; Mic 4:10). John uses the image of new birth twice (1:13 and 3:38) to signify the new stage in the soul's journey. Here it refers to the birth of the new age, which is accomplished in Jesus and the accompanying suffering and tribulation.

The disciples think that they now understand (vv. 29-30); they see that Jesus knows everything, so they now believe that he came from God. Jesus is not impressed, and in a parallel to his response at Peter's confident boast in 13:38, he informs them that they will desert him and leave him alone. Verse 33 acts as an *inclusio* with verse 1, that is, creating a frame or bracket by placing similar material in both verses. Jesus has informed them beforehand of all the troubles they will have, but they should have courage because he has conquered the world, which is an anticipatory reference to his approaching death. As followers of Jesus encounter struggles, this should be kept in mind so that they do not lose heart.

Chapter 17, sometimes called a "prayer of ascent" or the "priestly prayer of Jesus," brings together the elements introduced in the prologue and unfolded during the account of the ministry of Jesus. The scope of Jesus' prayer encompasses the time before the foundation of the world, when he was in God's presence, and the accomplishment of his earthly ministry. His prayer also stretches toward the future and those who will come to faith.

Compared with the Gospel of Luke, Jesus does not appear to pray as often, for John only depicts Jesus doing so here and at the tomb of Lazarus. But John's Jesus enjoys an intimacy with God that is so close and immediate that prayer, which supposes a distance or absence, becomes secondary. Verses 1-26 are more in the form of a blessing than a personal prayer, for Jesus is mostly concerned with the disciples he is leaving behind, who have reached a stage of reception of his words and belief that he came from God. It is the prayer of one who is supremely confident, in complete control of his destiny, and aware that he has completed his mission satisfactorily.

17:1-8 Glorification

The mutual glorification of the Father and the Son is the focus of verses 1-5. Aware that the hour has come, Jesus lifts his eyes heavenward, as in 11:41, and asks for God's glory so that he may in turn glorify the Father. Although Jesus has been given authority over all people, he gives eternal life to those whom the Father has given him—in other words, those who believe that he has come from God (1:4, 9-13; 3:14-21, 31-36; 4:13-14; 5:24-25; 6:35; 7:37-38; 8:12; 10:27-29; 11:25-26; 12:47; 14:6-7). He is crystal clear in defining eternal life: to know the Father, who is the only true God, and the one sent by God, Jesus the Christ. A core element of John's Gospel is the insistence that Jesus Christ is the only means of access to God (see 10:25-29; 14:6) and to eternal life. He asks again (v. 5) for the glory he had before the world began (1:1-3), thereby returning to his divine origins after the completion of his mission. The disciples have received and accepted all God's words that Jesus passed on to them, as well as his divine origin (vv. 7-8).

17:9-19 Prayer for his disciples

Jesus' concern for his disciples is the central focus of verses 9-19. He prays for their protection (vv. 9-10) rather than for the world. Since he is returning to the Father and in one sense already has departed this world, they will be his presence and instruments in the world (v. 11). He prays that they continue to be protected in the name of God which Jesus has received (vv. 11-12) and which he revealed (v. 26). Revealing God's name is better understood as disclosing the essence, nature, and quality of God rather than repetition of a proper name. The complete joy (v. 13) that the disciples share is the result of knowing God directly and continually (15:11; 1 John 1:4; 2 John 12) through the Spirit. The presence of unaffected joy authenticates spiritual and religious claims, which should cause all Christian communities to pause and reflect.

Jesus addresses the Father as "holy" (v. 11), which is the characteristic of God in the Old Testament and sets him apart (Isa 5:16; 6:3). Those who worship God are commanded to be holy as God is (Lev 11:44; 19:2; 20:7; 1 Pet 1:15-16). He therefore prays that since they are in the world, they be kept one as Jesus and the Father are (v. 11) in a unity of holiness. To this end, he prays that they be "consecrate[d]" (which can also be translated as "sanctified") in the truth, which is God's word (v. 17) embodied in Jesus (1:9, 17; 8:31-32). They must be protected in the divine name (v. 12) and from the Evil One (v. 15), who is the negative ruler of this world (12:31; 14:30; 16:11).

The disciples do not belong to the world; in fact, the world hates them because of the presence of the light within their community (v. 14) and because they have received God's words from Jesus (vv. 14-17). He therefore prays that they be consecrated or set apart in the truth that is God's word, for they are being sent into the world with the same message as Jesus (v. 18; 20:21). The glorification of Jesus is his death and resurrection, for it is in this that he reveals God and fulfills God's will. The disciples glorify Jesus when they continue his mission of divine revelation, and that indeed is their mission (v. 18; 20:21).

17:20-26 That they may be one

The prayer in verses 20-26 is directed toward those who will be brought to faith by the witness of the disciples. Jesus' prayer for unity signifies far more than institutional solidarity; he prays that they may all be one, but it is a special sort of unity, a mysticism of love. Jesus shares the glory given to him by the Father with the disciples and invites them to experience God's love in the same way that he does (vv. 22-24). This perfection of unity and love is the palpable presence of God that reveals God to the world and continues the mission of Jesus. It is this visible manifestation of God's love in the community and its members that both reveals God and draws others to faith. Jesus closes his prayer (vv. 25-26) by again insisting that the world does not know God, but he does. He has revealed the name of God, and the same love with which the Father loved the Son will be present among his followers.

THE PASSION NARRATIVE

John 18:1–19:42

The long-predicted hour of Jesus has arrived (3:14; 8:28; 12:32-33) when he will be "lifted up" for the sake of all humanity. While the other Gospels portray the crucifixion as terrible and tragic, for John it is the glorification of Jesus. Jesus scarcely seems to suffer—he is not a helpless victim (10:18), for this is not Mark's man of sorrows. Although John's account of the passion of Jesus parallels the Synoptic accounts in many respects, there are some important variations. Comparing John's account with the others is interesting and enlightening, and a "Parallel Gospel" book is very useful for this purpose.

For instance, the trial before Pilate is structured and long, with Jesus interacting with Pilate in a manner very different from his laconic responses in Mark. Objections have been raised by some that the passion narratives, especially John's, have little basis in fact and are nothing more than an attempt to give historical expression to prophetic texts from the Old Testament. That represents an extreme position, for mainstream scholarship recognizes that while the passion narrative should not be considered a court record or a narration of brute facts, it does rest on a solid framework of tradition. It is a theological interpretation of the death of Jesus; the passion is therefore refracted through the prism of John's theological concerns.

This is a very important issue, as the Johannine passion narrative plays a prominent part in the spiritual and liturgical life of the Church. John uses strident language and negative imagery in his depiction of "the Jews," and this has helped fuel hateful and sometimes violent behavior and attitudes toward Jewish people and their faith. We must remember that in John's narrative, the term "the Jews" denotes those who were actively opposed to Jesus. The narrative cannot be taken at face value: Pilate was not a benign, well-intentioned man led astray by a violent crowd, and any Jewish complicity is limited to a particular handful of individuals who desired Jesus' death.

18:1-12 The arrest

Crossing the Kidron valley is associated with death (cf. 1 Kgs 2:37), made more so by the darkness and the presence of tombs. Gethsemane means "oil press"; John is alone in referring to it as a garden. The prayer for the cup passing from Jesus (but cf. 12:27) and its associated anguish over his impending death are lacking. Soon Judas arrives with a cohort of troops, along with the temple guards and the Pharisees. Since a cohort consisted of six hundred men, it is likely that it was a small detachment of soldiers. Interestingly, John alone reports that the Pharisees took an active role in the arrest. No kiss from Judas betrays Jesus in John's story, for Jesus is majestic and in total control of the situation and has complete knowledge of the events that are going to unfold (v. 4).

When Jesus asks the arresting party whom they are seeking, they reply, "Jesus the Nazorean." To this he replies, "I AM" (Exod 3:14), and the force of the divine name knocks them to the ground. This should be understood as a theological rather than a historical statement. Clearly Jesus is in full possession of his divine status even at the point of his arrest. In the scuffle with the sword, John identifies the attacker as Simon Peter and the victim as Malchus, slave of the high priest. In Matthew, Jesus rebukes them with the admonition that those who take up the sword will die by it (Matt 26:52), while in Luke he simply heals the slave's severed ear. For John, Peter's action interferes with the divine plan, and Jesus has to insist that he is to drink of the cup the Father has given him. Jesus tells his arresters to let the others go, fulfilling his own words (6:39; 10:28; 17:12) about not losing any of those given to him by the Father.

18:13-27 Interrogation before the high priest

Jesus is taken to Annas, the high priest from A.D. 6 to 15 and father-in-law of Caiaphas, the current high priest. Reference is made to Caiaphas's unwitting prophecy in 11:49-50. Mark depicts Jesus as being dragged before a nocturnal plenary session of the Sanhedrin, but the summary session before a handful of officials described in John is probably closer to the truth.

During the drama of Peter's threefold denial, the scene shifts from the courtyard to the interrogation room, then back to the courtyard for the remainder of his denials. The identity of the "other disciple" in verses 15-16 who gains access to the proceedings because of his acquaintance with the high priest is unclear, but in all probability it is the Beloved Disciple, also not named in the Gospel. While Jesus is being interrogated, Peter undergoes one of his own interrogations (vv. 17-18). His reply to the maid's question about whether he is a disciple of Jesus is "I am not," sharply contrasting with the "I AM" of Jesus in the garden.

Jesus was questioned about his disciples and his teaching, but not about any messianic claims or alleged threats against the temple. His reply is sharp and rather combative: he has taught openly, saying nothing in secret. Since he has openly proclaimed God's word to the world, they have no excuse. He also invites the high priest to ask those who heard him, meaning his followers and disciples, who are now bearers of his words (vv. 20-21). His boldness earns him a blow and a rebuke from one of the temple guards (v. 22) for showing disrespect (Exod 22:7; Lev 19:14; 20:9; Isa 8:21).

Jesus is then transferred to Pilate for further questioning (v. 24), but no formal charges have been brought, nor is there any condemnation for blasphemy or any other charge, although he has been accused of this throughout the Gospel, beginning in 5:18. The scene shifts again to the courtyard, where Peter is asked twice about being a disciple of Jesus and being seen with him in the garden (vv. 25-27). Again he mirrors the "I AM" of Jesus with "I am not." The last question was from a relative of Malchus, making Peter's denial even more ridiculous and mendacious. As the cock crows, Jesus' predictions of denial and flight in 13:38 and 16:32 come to mind.

18:28–19:15 The trial before Pilate

In the dramatic trial before Pilate, two trials are taking place. The first is the apparent trial of Jesus, while on another level, "the Jews," Pilate, and all humanity are on trial, being given the op-

portunity to choose either God's kingdom as revealed in Jesus or the world, which is opposed to God. The structure of the trial is carefully crafted and highly symbolic. In seven brief scenes (18:29-32, 33-38a, 38b-40; 19:1-3, 4-7, 8-11), Pilate shuttles back and forth between the inside of the praetorium, where Jesus is being held, and the crowd in the outer courtyard. These symbolize respectively the spiritual realm that Jesus represents and the world that rejects his revelation. Pilate is caught between these two worlds, feeling the pull of both, but in the end he opts for the world of Caesar rather than that of God.

18:28-32 Before Pilate

As they arrive at the praetorium, it is morning (v. 28), the beginning of the new day of redemption, and in sharp contrast to the "night" that fell when Judas departed the upper room to betray Jesus. With a touch of Johannine irony, the Jewish authorities refuse to enter the praetorium, for Passover is approaching and they do not want to defile themselves. They are worried about committing sacrilege but are ignorantly preparing to perform the greatest sacrilege of all, the killing of the Lamb of God. Pilate asks them what the charges are (v. 29), but they answer evasively (v. 30), insisting that the fact that he is here is proof enough that he is a criminal.

Pilate is massively uninterested in judging the case and demands that they judge him themselves (v. 31), but they correctly point out that under Roman occupation they do not have the right to judge capital crimes. The stoning of Stephen in Acts 7:54–8:1 can be seen as an extra-judicial murder or mob violence rather than an execution. The Romans were indifferent to the variety of religious beliefs in their empire, and subject people were permitted to continue their worship unhindered. In Acts 18:12-17 the Roman proconsul Gallio deems religious questions outside his jurisdiction and tosses Paul's case out of court. To the question "Why was Jesus put to death?" we might look to 11:47-53, where the Jewish authorities are fearful that Jesus and his movement will disrupt the delicate balance with the Roman authorities and invite harsh reprisals.

18:33-38a The kingdom of Jesus

Entering the praetorium, Pilate begins a private interrogation of Jesus (vv. 33-38). He asks Jesus whether he is King of the Jews. This is the first mention of this charge, although there is a basis for it (1:49; 12:13), and it hints at the religious and political nature of the accusations against Jesus. His reply is a question (v. 34): Did you figure this out on your own, or did others tell you this? The contemptuous retort of Pilate places the onus for the charges back on the Jewish authorities, and he asks Jesus what he has done (v. 35).

By explaining that his rule or kingdom is not of this world, Jesus means that its origin, values, and methods are from God rather than the world (v. 36), evidenced by the refusal of the use of force and violence to defend himself. He is not referring to a place or calling for a turning away from the concerns of life in this world. Pilate's uncomprehending conclusion that Jesus is indeed a king is met by refusal on the part of Jesus, and an insistence that his sole reason for coming into the world was to testify to the truth (v. 37), and anyone belonging to the truth listens to him—even Pilate himself if he so chooses. Pilate shows himself to be far from the truth with his famous query in verse 38: "What is truth?" The irony is that "truth" is literally staring him in the face!

18:38b-40 Barabbas or Jesus

Pilate declares Jesus innocent (cf. Luke 23:4, 14, 22) and offers to release a prisoner in honor of the Passover (cf. Mark 15:6-14; Matt 27:15-23), asking the crowd if they want him to release the King of the Jews. There is no historical record of any such Passover custom. The crowd makes its choice: Barabbas (v. 40), who is a revolutionary, a man of violence representing the kingdom of the world. The crowd has made its first choice.

19:1-7 The scourging

Pilate has Jesus scourged (v. 1), as in Matthew 27:26-31 and Mark 15:15-20, while Barabbas disappears from the scene. As the soldiers parody royal trappings and hail Jesus as King of the Jews, they are unwittingly doing obeisance to a real king (v. 3). In Luke's Gospel it is not until Jesus is before Herod Antipas (23:6-12) that he is dressed in royal garb. The Son of God is contrasted with the humanity of Jesus as Pilate proclaims, "Behold, the man!" Judging by external appearances, Pilate and the others do not see anything divine, but the Johannine claim of the incarnation is clear (v. 5).

Three times Pilate declares that he finds no evidence of wrongdoing in Jesus (18:38; 19:4, 6),

as in Luke 23:4, 14, 22. This heightens the sense of guilt on the part of the "Jews," as John takes great pains to shift the bulk of the responsibility onto them. Pilate is portrayed as a tragic and vacillating figure who is the victim of circumstance. He was even venerated as a saint in the early Coptic church. We know from Philo and Josephus that Pilate was in fact a venal and ruthless individual, who ruled with an iron fist and was not reluctant to spill blood. The "Jews" declare that Jesus has to die for violating the law by making himself the Son of God (v. 7). This alludes to the punishment for blasphemy set forth in Leviticus 24:16 and repeated in the rabbinical tradition. Jesus' claim to a filial relationship with God represents the core of John's Gospel and almost resulted in stoning on numerous occasions.

19:8-12 Where are you from?

But when Pilate hears the statement that Jesus ought to die (v. 8), it strikes fear into him, for "Son of God" could mean many things in the Greco-Roman world, including a divine or semi-divine being. Pilate does not want to run afoul of the gods and their many powers. Hastening back into the praetorium, he asks Jesus where he is from, probably indicating a desire to know if he is of human or divine origins (vv. 8-9). The readers of the Gospel, of course, are fully aware of Jesus' origins, for this has been a point of contention throughout the Gospel.

Jesus refuses to answer, for Pilate has already had his chance to receive the revelation of God through Jesus and showed himself to be closed to that reality (18:37-38). Pilate impatiently reminds Jesus that he has absolute power of life and death over him (v. 10), and so Jesus would do well to answer his questions. But his earthly power is illusory, Jesus claims, for he can only do what is permitted by God (vv. 11-12). Similar views were expressed by John the Baptist in 3:27, reflecting the current of predetermination that runs throughout this Gospel. Jesus makes an ambiguous comment about the one who handed him over being guilty of the greater sin. This has traditionally been thought to refer to Judas, but Caiaphas and the Jewish authorities are also strong candidates.

19:13-16 Whose friend?

Pilate tries all the harder to release Jesus, and the crowd resorts to a form of blackmail, claiming that if he does, then he is no friend of Caesar. Anyone making himself king opposes Caesar (v. 12). They are speaking the language of power, which the Romans understand and respect well. "Friend of Caesar" is an honorific title given by the emperor as a sign of special favor, and to lose that status can only mean that one is an enemy of Caesar, not a healthy thing to be. Jesus calls his followers friends, too, but Pilate chooses to be the friend of an earthly king, preferring human power and glory. The fear factor is decisive, and the possibility of lost prestige and security pushes him over the edge. He seats himself on the judge's bench and in a mocking (but ironically true) fashion presents Jesus to the crowd as a king (vv. 13-14). They make their choice of kingdoms by calling for the crucifixion of Jesus, at the time of the preparation day for the Passover, clearly underscoring the role Jesus plays as the Lamb of God.

When an incredulous Pilate asks if he should crucify their king, the chief priests (not the crowd) answer, "We have no king but Caesar!" These are shocking words, implying a preference for an earthly and pagan king to the king sent by God and can be interpreted as a definitive rejection of the kingdom of God. Although it calls to mind 1 Samuel 8:7, where the Israelites are said to have rejected God by demanding a king like the pagan nations, it is hard to envision the chief priests publicly repudiating their God and traditions in such a manner.

19:17-30 The crucifixion of Jesus

John's theological hand is evident in his version of the crucifixion account. Pilate hands Jesus over to be crucified (v. 16), but in Johannine fashion, Jesus carries his own cross—he is in command of his destiny—and Simon of Cyrene (Mark 15:21) does not make an appearance. As in the Synoptics, the two others are crucified on either side of him, but they do not revile him (v. 18), and they are not called bandits or thieves. The inscription placed on the cross in three languages—Hebrew, Latin, and Greek—is most likely intended to convey a universal sense of God's revelation to the world through the crucified Jesus (vv. 19-22), for he has been "lifted up" and is drawing all people to himself (12:32). But the chief priests are outraged and protest vehemently to Pilate that it should not state that Jesus was the King of the Jews but merely a claimant to the title. Pilate

stands his ground, and his adamant "What I have written, I have written" gives a definitive and unalterable sense to the crucifixion. Again Pilate is portrayed as at least ambiguous about his condemnation of Jesus, and here he appears to have the final word in the matter.

The soldiers cast lots for the garments of Jesus (vv. 23-25) in fulfillment of Psalm 22:19. John informs us that the garment was seamless, perhaps suggesting the garment of the high priest, which, according to Josephus, is seamless (*Ant.* 3:161). Jesus would then be a priestly mediatory figure between God and humanity, fitting well with John's theology. Jesus' relationship with the Father was expressed in terms of oneness, and Jesus prayed for the oneness and unity of his disciples (17:11, 22-24). This suggests that the seamless robe can also symbolize the community of disciples, an interpretation favored by the church fathers.

The Synoptic accounts merely relate that a group of women looked on from a distance, but here the mother of Jesus and the Beloved Disciple stand at the foot of the cross, along with several women. The mother of Jesus, unnamed in the Gospel, appears at the beginning (2:1-11) and the end of the mission of Jesus. The Beloved Disciple plays a prominent role in the passion narratives (13:23; 21:24-25) and is claimed to be the source of the Gospel witness. His appearance at the foot of the cross underscores his special relationship to Jesus and his uncommon loyalty in the hour of his death; in fact, he is portrayed as the model disciple. His identity is illusive, and it is not even certain that he was one of the Twelve. The dying Jesus commends his mother to the care of the Beloved Disciple, asking that their relationship be that of mother and son (vv. 26-27). The community of disciples, the mother of Jesus, the Beloved Disciple, and all who come to faith are joined together in the new family of believers whom Jesus leaves behind.

Fully aware and in command to the very end (v. 28), Jesus exclaims, "I thirst," in order to fulfill Psalm 69:22. Common wine is given to him on a sprig of hyssop (v. 29), which is used to smear the blood over the lintels before Passover (Exod 12:21-23). After receiving the wine, he declares, "It is finished," denoting that he has accomplished everything that the Father has sent him to do (17:4), and his mission is complete (v. 30). He has truly "loved them to the end" (13:1). After bowing his head, he hands over the spirit, signifying both his death and the release of the Spirit promised in 7:39 and 14:16-17. The absence of a cry of divine abandonment, darkness at noon, the rending of the temple veil, earthquakes, a loud cry at the moment of death, or a declaration by a centurion (Mark 15:33, 34, 37, 38, 39) is striking.

19:31-37 The piercing of the side of Jesus

In John's idiosyncratic chronology of the events of the passion, the death of Jesus occurs on the day of preparation. This is before the start of the sabbath and Passover, which in that year coincided, making it a particularly solemn occasion. An exposed corpse would be particularly defiling (Deut 21:23), so the "Jews" ask Pilate to authorize the coup de grâce in the form of the breaking of the legs, which causes suffocation, and the taking down of the bodies. This is done to the other two who were crucified with Jesus, but it was unnecessary in the case of Jesus, since he is already dead (vv. 32-33). A soldier pierces the side of Jesus and blood and water flow out (v. 34). It is seen as the fulfillment of Scripture (Exod 12:10, 46; Num 9:12; Ps 34:20-21), which prohibits broken bones in the lamb sacrificed for Passover, which is an amplification of John's portrayal of Jesus as the Paschal Lamb. The piercing of the side is an expression of the messianic text Zechariah 12:9-13.

This incident, unique to John, is layered with meaning. In Christian tradition this has been seen as the release of the Spirit and divine life for the church. The blood and water have been associated with the Eucharist (cf. Mark 14:24) and baptism. The solemn witness offering testimony in verse 35 is probably none other than the Beloved Disciple himself. He is testifying to three things: it was Jesus on the cross; he was human; he really died. These things may seem self-evident to us, but all three have been denied then as well as today, as a visit to the religion section of any modern bookstore will show. Some groups denied that Jesus was really a human being; he just appeared to have a body. Others denied that Jesus died on the cross, claiming that someone died in his place. John insists on the incarnation (1:14; 1 John 4:2-3) as well as the witness of blood and water (1 John 5:6-7).

19:38-42 The burial of Jesus

Joseph of Arimathea is mentioned in all four Gospels, but John adds that he was a secret fol-

lower for fear of the Jews (v. 38). In John's eyes, this is a particularly egregious failing, and to drive the point home, Nicodemus is the next person to appear in the narrative. He came to Jesus by night in 3:2 and did not fare well in his encounter with him; in 7:50-52 he offers hesitant support of Jesus before his fellow Pharisees. John insists that public and unequivocal profession of belief in Jesus is necessary, ruling out any sort of fence-sitting. By their bold and public actions, both men seem to be moving toward full and explicit faith. Joseph has obtained the body of Jesus from Pilate, and Nicodemus brings one hundred pounds of myrrh and aloes. They bind the body of Jesus along with the spices according to custom. It is an unhurried and well-prepared burial. The other Gospels have Jesus placed hastily in a tomb, so that the women head for the tomb on Sunday morning to anoint the body with the spices. A new tomb in which no one has ever been buried is in a garden very close to the place of crucifixion, and that is where Jesus is laid.

20:1-10 The empty tomb

Mary Magdalene is present in all four Gospels, but here she is alone, before sunrise. In Mark 16:1 and Luke 24:1 the women are heading for the tomb to anoint the body of Jesus with spices; in John, it has already been done (19:40). When Mary Magdalene saw that the stone has been removed, she runs to tell Simon Peter and the Beloved Disciple, assuming that someone has taken the body from the tomb, as was the case in Matthew 27:64; 28:13-15. Both disciples run to the tomb (vv. 3-5). The Beloved Disciple arrives first but, possibly out of deference, does not enter, although he looks in and sees the burial cloths. There is a bit of tension between the two disciples, and it is clear that in this Gospel the Beloved Disciple is the star and is highly esteemed and beloved by Jesus. But in this chapter and in chapter 21, Peter's leadership is recognized.

As Simon Peter enters the tomb (vv. 6-7), he sees the burial cloths, and the cloth covering the face of Jesus is carefully rolled up and placed to one side in a separate place. Such a detail likely illustrates that the resurrection is a very deliberate and definitive conquest of death, for we remember that in 11:44 Lazarus exited the tomb still bound in the burial cloths. Additionally, the Greek grammatical construction points to God as the source of the action. When the Beloved Disciple enters the tomb, he sees and believes, implying that Peter has somehow failed to comprehend the significance of the burial cloths.

There is a strange statement (v. 9) that they did not yet understand the Scripture that Jesus had to rise from the dead. The early Christian tradition claims that the resurrection was foretold in the Scriptures (Acts 2:24-27; 1 Cor 15:4), but it is not clear to which passages they refer. In John's Gospel many things in the life of Jesus and in Scripture are clarified only after the sending of the Spirit (2:27; 12:16). Obviously, the Beloved Disciple believes in Jesus and that he is somehow alive. But there were many theological currents in the first century concerning the afterlife, which is illustrated in Mark 9:10, as the disciples discuss what rising from the dead might mean.

20:11-18 Jesus and Mary Magdalene

This resurrection encounter (vv. 11-18) between Jesus and Mary Magdalene is unique to John. Mary Magdalene remains alone outside the tomb weeping (v. 11). She looks into the tomb and sees two angels in white on either end of where the body had been (v. 12). They were not present when the two disciples were there; it is possible that the Mary story was a separate account joined to the race to the tomb by the evangelist. All the Gospels report figures in the tomb, but with variation in details.

The angels ask Mary a pointed question (v. 13): "Woman, why are you weeping?" Implied in the question is the assumption that if she really believed and understood the significance of what had transpired, she would not weep (16:20-22). She merely repeats her fears that the body has been stolen.

Jesus appears and asks her exactly the same question but adds, "Whom are you looking for?" recalling 1:38; 6:24, 26; 7:34, 36; 12:21; and 18:4. Still uncomprehending and unable to recognize Jesus, thinking him to be the gardener, she asks about the location of the body (v. 15). It is only when Jesus speaks her name (v. 16), recalling the Good Shepherd in 10:3-5, that she recognizes him with the exclamation "Rabbouni!" Jesus' admonition not to hold on to him has puzzled people for centuries (other translations say "Don't touch me," implying that she has not yet done so). After all, he invites Thomas to touch his wounds in

20:27. But it is clear that at this point the mission lacks one final step: ascension to the Father, and it is for this reason that he asks her to let go of him (v. 17). This is not like the raising of Lazarus, for Jesus does not just resume his life as it was three days ago. After his return to the Father, he will appear to his disciples (vv. 19-31; 1 Cor 15:3-8; Acts 9:3-6). It is not a rebuke, and she is granted the singular honor, earning her recognition as the apostle to the apostles, of carrying an electrifying message to the others.

Through the Gospel the relationship of Jesus to God the Father has been exclusive (see 1:18). Those from below are incapable of knowing or comprehending God. But now, with the impending completion of the mission, that relationship has been radically altered, for he refers to "my Father and your Father, my God and your God," implying that they are now his brothers and sisters. Those who believe in Jesus (and potentially all humanity) can experience the same relationship with God as Jesus does (14:18-24; 16:16-24; 17:6-19). Seeing Jesus is of supreme importance in post-resurrection faith, and it means far more than mere sense perception. It implies understanding and believing. Mary's proclamation in verse 18, "I have seen the Lord," speaks of a life-transforming experience.

20:19-23 The upper room

The disciples have not been transformed, for they have not seen Jesus. They are behind locked doors for fear of the Jews (7:13; 9:22; 19:38) when Jesus stands in their midst, presumably without the use of the door (v. 19). He greets them with a traditional greeting of "Peace" *(Shalom),* but in view of the peace promised in 14:27 and 16:33, it is God's peace that he brings. Showing them his hands and feet (v. 26) parallels Luke 24:36-43 and serves to confirm his humanity and identity, as in 19:34 and 1 John 4. Uttering the peace blessing again, he gives them the same mission that the Father gave him for the sake of the world (3:16; 17:18). They will be the instruments by which others come to saving faith, for as bearers of the Spirit, they will make God present to the world for generations to come.

The opening words of both the book of Genesis and John's Gospel speak of a beginning, and as Jesus breathes the holy Spirit into the community of believers, it is clear that God is creating them anew. The Hebrew word *ruah* means "breath," "wind," or "spirit." The Spirit was promised in 14:16-17, 26; 15:26; 16:7-15, and it will provide the powers needed to continue Jesus' ministry, as well as interpreting the meaning of his ministry to his followers. Matthew's Jesus gives the power of the binding and loosing of sins to Peter (16:19) and the community (18:18). John confers this authority on the entire community of disciples, for it is the consequence of the divine Spirit dwelling within the community.

20:24-29 Doubting Thomas

Thomas was not present when Jesus came, and when the transformed community exclaims, "We have seen the Lord!" he refuses to believe unless he can actually see and touch the nail marks and the wound in the side of Jesus (vv. 25-26). A week later, when Thomas was present, Jesus repeats his appearance and greeting of peace, then invites Thomas to place his finger within his wounds and to cease his lack of faith and believe. It is not clear whether Thomas actually does so, but he eloquently confesses faith in Jesus as Lord and God—a more exalted profession than anyone else in the Gospel made.

Thomas is known to history as "doubting Thomas," but this obscures the fact that alone in the Gospel of John he is given a significant role (11:16; 14:5; 21:2), and in early Christian tradition he carried the gospel to India. He was of sufficient stature that some Christians even attached his name to a collection of sayings known to us as the Gospel of Thomas. In verse 29 Jesus seems to chide Thomas a bit for believing on the basis of proofs and declares blessed those who have not seen but believe, a statement clearly aimed at the second- or third-generation Christians in the time of the Gospel's composition. Temporal proximity to Jesus is of no particular advantage; in fact, our own faith is in many ways a greater witness, since we have not been given the visual proofs available to the original disciples.

20:30-31 First ending

The primitive form of the Gospel likely ended with verses 30-31, in which John declares that there were many other signs that Jesus performed that are not written in this book. The few presented in the book serve but one purpose: to bring others to faith (or to help those already believing

to continue) that Jesus is the Messiah and Son of God, and through this belief receive life in his name.

We have seen how the original Gospel seems to end with 20:30-31, complete with the purpose of its composition. Chapter 21 is likely an epilogue, although some scholars maintain its unity with the entire Gospel. Several independent elements have been woven together to form the chapter. Unresolved issues are dealt with, most notably Peter's estrangement from Jesus following his threefold denial as well as some tension between Peter and the Beloved Disciple and their respective supporters. Readers will of course recognize the story of the miraculous catch from the story of Jesus' calling of the disciples in Luke 5:1-11, but this is probably a parallel tradition rather than a direct literary dependence.

EPILOGUE: THE RESURRECTION APPEARANCE IN GALILEE
John 21:1-25

21:1-14 Appearance at the Sea of Tiberias

The story opens on the Sea of Galilee (here called Tiberias, after the city). In Mark 14:28 and 16:7, Jesus has promised that they will see him in Galilee, so from the standpoint of coherence, this story fits better with Mark. All the appearances of the risen Christ have been in Jerusalem. Simon Peter and six other disciples have fished all night, catching nothing. At dawn Jesus stands on the shore, but the disciples fail to recognize him, in a manner similar to the appearance to the disciples on the road to Emmaus (Luke 24:13-35) and the appearance to Mary Magdalene (20:15). Addressing them as "Children," Jesus quizzes them and then directs them where to put down their nets, resulting in a huge haul of fish.

It is no surprise that the Beloved Disciple is the first to recognize Jesus and exclaims, "It is the Lord!" Peter impetuously jumps into the water and arrives at the shore before the heavily laden boat. They discover that Jesus has prepared a fire, along with fish and bread. At the direction of Jesus, Peter drags the net to shore, and the narrator reports that it held 153 fish. This obsessive attention to detail has excited the curiosity of exegetes for two thousand years. Many have searched for symbolic or esoteric meaning.

Augustine points out that the sum of the numbers from 1 to 17 equals 153, while for Jerome 153 equals the number of types of fish known to ancient natural science. The Hebrew numerological system for finding hidden meanings and truths within words *(gematria)* has yielded inconclusive results. Those wishing to follow the arguments can consult a detailed commentary.

The full meaning is perhaps inaccessible in our age. For us, the most likely and useful answer is that it is a symbol of universality and completeness and involves the quest to bring souls to God. In Mark 1:17 and Luke 5:10, Jesus promises to make the disciples "fishers of men," and the metaphor was widely used in an eschatological sense to mean the ingathering at the end of time. In fact, verse 11 states that although there were so many fish, the net was not torn, implying a seamlessness and limitless capacity.

Jesus invites the disciples to have breakfast (vv. 12-13) and distributes bread and fish, suggesting both 6:1-15 and the eucharistic practices of the early community. It is supposedly the third postresurrection appearance to the disciples (v. 14) but should be the fourth if Mary Magdalene is counted as a disciple. We wonder why they returned to their former occupations after the appearance in the upper room and the gift of the Spirit, and indeed they act as if the risen Jesus is unfamiliar to them. This would seem to indicate an independent tradition that has been incorporated into the Gospel.

21:15-19 The rehabilitation of Peter

Peter denied Jesus three times, as foretold in 13:38 (18:17, 25-27). After the breakfast Jesus puts Peter on the spot with a rigorous and uncomfortable examination. He addresses him formally as "Simon, son of John" rather than "Cephas," for his fidelity and performance have not lived up to his appellation of Peter (meaning "rock"). Jesus asks him if he loves him "more than these." This last phrase is ambiguous; it can mean "more than you love these other disciples" or "more than these others love me." Most exegetes favor the latter meaning, for it would be more in keeping with the context of the story.

Peter's painful grilling continues; three times he must respond affirmatively to the poignant question Jesus addresses to him, matching his threefold denial. His affirmations are met only

with the command "Feed my lambs" and "tend my sheep." It is clear that humble service is the leadership model in the Johannine community. The third time that Jesus fires the question at him, Peter is hurt and responds that Jesus knows everything, including the fact that he loves him, for Jesus is omniscient throughout the Gospel. Jesus then uses the occasion to tell Peter that his life will no longer be his own and that he will be led where he does not want to go, referring to Peter's eventual martyrdom in Rome, the way in which he will glorify God, as did Jesus.

This didactic story draws on the Good Shepherd (10:1-6, 11-18) and the love commandments (13:14-15, 34; 14:15, 21, 23-24; 15:12-14), all of which portray the full expression of love as laying down one's life for others. Peter is now rehabilitated, and the story ends with Jesus uttering the invitation and command of discipleship found in Mark 1:17 and 2:17: "Come, follow me!"

21:20-23 Rivalry and misunderstanding

Packed into verses 20-23 are two problems facing the community. The first is the rivalry between Peter and the Beloved Disciple. Peter turns and sees the Beloved Disciple following them, and the narrator refers back to the Last Supper to remind the reader of who he is. Peter's plaintive, very human question is "What about him?" Peter wants to know if the Beloved Disciple is going to suffer martyrdom too!

Jesus is rather brusque in his response, basically telling Peter that it's none of his business, and that if Jesus wants the Beloved Disciple to remain until his return, it is no concern of Peter's. He should worry about his own discipleship, and Jesus repeats the command (v. 22): "*You* follow me!" (emphasis added). But this gives rise to a misunderstanding that is soon widespread, namely, that the Beloved Disciple would not die. It is obvious that the recent death of the Beloved Disciple, whoever he might have been, has caused consternation within Johannine communities. The author of this story takes pains to set the record straight: Jesus did not say that the disciple would not die, only "What if I want him to remain until I come?"

Both Paul and Mark expected the imminent return of Jesus, the parousia, and their eschatology and ethics reflected that expectation (1 Thess 4:13-18; 1 Cor 15; Mark 13). The passage of time and the delay of the return of Jesus generated theological tensions and difficulties of faith within early Christian communities (1 Thess 4:13-18; 2 Pet 3:3-10). In the Gospel of John two eschatologies are allowed to coexist—the traditional one oriented toward the future and the "realized eschatology" of John, depicting the presence of the end-time realities in the person of Jesus (5:24-27; 11:23-25; 14:22-24). This passage may reflect a Johannine eschatological reinterpretation more in harmony with the rest of the New Testament, necessitated by the delay of the parousia.

21:24-25 Second and final ending

The final ending refers to the many other things that Jesus did and, in a possible allusion to the other Gospels, speculates that the whole world would not be sufficient to contain the books that would be required. But we wish that the author had not been so reticent.

THE ACTS OF
THE APOSTLES

Dennis Hamm, S.J.

INTRODUCTION

Welcome to a sequel. If the Acts of the Apostles were a contemporary film rather than an ancient document, they might call it "The Gospel of Luke: Part Two," for this book of the New Testament is clearly a sequel to the Third Gospel. The easiest way to recognize that fact is to read the first four verses of Luke's Gospel, where the author addresses one Theophilus (likely a new convert and possibly the sponsor of the publication—the one who paid the copyists) and then to flip forward to the opening phrase of Acts: "In the first book, Theophilus . . ." That should be enough to indicate that we are dealing with a two-volume work. Those who study and write about Luke's work are so conscious that his contribution to the New Testament canon—that is, the collection of books accepted by the church as inspired by God—is a two-volume project, deserving to be treated as a single masterpiece, that they commonly refer to it simply as Luke-Acts, as we shall do in this commentary.

This obvious fact of the unity of Luke-Acts has long escaped most readers because the conventional ordering of printed editions of the New Testament separates Luke's Gospel from its sequel by placing the Gospel of John between them. Those who chose that sequence had a perfectly good reason: the arrangement keeps the four canonical stories of Jesus together as a bundle. That way, Acts makes an appropriate bridge from the stories about Jesus to the letters of Paul. But this arrangement also has a downside: it has accidentally distracted readers from recognizing the continuity between the two parts of Luke's work.

During the last third of the twentieth century, biblical scholars have focused less on the study of discrete segments of texts and more on the form and meaning of entire documents. That focus has produced a fresh appreciation of the integrity and artistry of the work now commonly called Luke-Acts.

How does Luke himself understand his project? Luke expresses his intentions regarding the whole of Luke-Acts in the four-verse introduction at the head of his Gospel.

> [1]Since many have undertaken to compile a narrative of the events that have been fulfilled among us, [2]just as those who were eyewitnesses from the beginning and ministers of the word have handed them down to us, [3]I too have decided, after investigating everything accurately anew, to write it down in an orderly sequence for you, most excellent Theophilus, [4]so that you may realize the certainty of the teachings you have received.

Notice that the subject of his work is "the events that have been fulfilled among us." The phrase "events fulfilled" suggests that those events were not simply happenings but truly fulfillments of the Scriptures of Israel. The "us" in question is the Christian community of Luke's own time, a group far enough removed in time (at least by forty or fifty years) from the life, death, and resurrection of Jesus that they needed the testimony of eyewitnesses and preachers of the word to learn about those events. And yet the "us" was in such continuity with that first generation of Christians (the eyewitnesses) that those events could be understood as fulfilled among *us*. In other words, Luke's audience could still think of the past events as having been fulfilled among *them*. This also applies to subsequent readers, including us.

Did Luke think that such "fulfillment" events were still occurring in his own time? Yes. Other parts of Luke-Acts indicate this awareness quite clearly. Consider Jesus' final words at the close of Luke's Gospel: "Thus it is written that the Messiah would suffer and rise from the dead on the third day, *and that repentance, for the forgiveness of sins, would be preached in his name to all the nations, beginning from Jerusalem*" (Luke 24:46-47, emphasis added). Notice that what is said to fulfill the Scriptures here is not only the death and resurrection of the Messiah but also the preaching of repentance in the name of Jesus to all the nations, which is precisely what Acts is all about. So "the events that have been fulfilled among us" include not only the story of Jesus (told in the Third Gospel) but also the story of the church (the subject of Acts) as it continues to unfold in Luke's own generation. By the extension implied in his vision, our generation is included as well. This awareness of the end-time fulfillment occurring in the time of the church comes through strongly in an assertion in Peter's speech in Acts 3:24: "Moreover, all the prophets who spoke, from Samuel and those afterwards, also announced these days."

Are there other clues to the unity of Luke-Acts? There are many. Take, for example, the words that Gabriel speaks to Mary at the annunciation.

> "He will be great and will be called Son of the Most High, and the Lord God will give him the throne of David his father, and he will rule over the house of Jacob forever . . ." (Luke 1:32-33).

It is instructive to see what happens to those predictions throughout the remainder of Luke-Acts. In the world of first-century Judaism, the word about Jesus' inheriting David's throne meant becoming the Messiah, the end-time political and religious leader of a restored people of Israel.

When does Luke show Jesus taking up that role? Certainly not in the Gospel. Nowhere in Luke's narrative of Jesus's life, death, and resurrection does Jesus become king in that conventional sense. Indeed, talk of kingship occurs only ironically—in the accusations of the Sanhedrin, in the mockery of the leaders and soldiers under the cross, and in the inscription on the cross: "This is the king of the Jews." But the implication of these ironic references is that Jesus has failed to inherit the throne of David in the conventional sense. His kingship turns out to be far grander than that.

The reader has to begin reading the second volume, the Acts of the Apostles, to learn Luke's understanding of how Jesus inherits David's throne. In Peter's speech at Pentecost, we hear Peter recite a psalm of David, Psalm 16, in which the speaker of the prayer expresses the hope that his flesh will not "see corruption." Peter then asserts that these words of David were not spoken about himself but about the Messiah. Psalm 16, Peter says, must be interpreted in the light of 2 Samuel 7:12 and Psalm 132:11 in a way that points only to Jesus. Jesus now reigns over end-time Israel, not from an earthly throne in Jerusalem but as risen Lord of the Christian community. That is just one example of the careful continuity between the Gospel of Luke and the Acts of the Apostles. This commentary will highlight many more such links between the first and second parts of Luke's two-volume work.

Why did Luke's readers need a sequel? These preliminary observations may begin to suggest some of the reasons why Luke added a sequel to his new edition of the story of Jesus.

A church increasingly composed of non-Jews (Gentiles) needed help in understanding how Gentiles could claim the heritage of Israel. Luke tells the story of the church to demonstrate that their experience is the fruition of "the light to the nations" (Isa 49:6) that the People of God was always meant to be.

People living after the generation of the original eyewitnesses needed a way of understanding how the life of Jesus still had relevance in their own lives. Luke shows how the life of Christians, individually and communally, is always some kind of replay of the life of Jesus. Thus Stephen's death parallels Jesus' death, and the travels and trials of Paul mirror the travels and trials of Jesus.

As a community spreading throughout the Roman Empire, the church needed an account of itself that demonstrated honorable roots (origins in the ancient people of Israel) and posed no political threat to Roman law and order. And so Luke stresses biblical fulfillment and underscores the innocence of Jesus and his followers in the courts of Roman officials.

A growing church needed models for interacting with the worlds it was encountering. And so Luke told its early history not simply as reminiscences of "the way we were" but in the form of episodes that could model "the way we *are.*" Indeed, that is why the Acts of the Apostles has been of permanent value to the church. While we can never succeed in simply replicating the early days of the church, we can always find reminders of what has been permanently important to the life of the church in Luke's portrayal of those early days.

What are we to make of all those short speeches? A good third of the content of the Acts of the Apostles consists of brief speeches. Often readers have taken these to be something like "tapes" of the apostolic preaching. Intense study of the Greek-writing historians of the first century has, however, led scholars to another conclusion. One of the tools of history writing in the Mediterranean world of those days was the composition of speeches put on the lips of key figures to interpret the meaning of the events narrated. In other words, even when Hellenistic (Greek) historians had verbatim records of what an important person said on a particular occasion, they would consider it part of good history writing to use the benefit of hindsight, along with the sources at their disposal, and compose a speech that captured the essential truth of what was happening. Most Lukan scholars judge that the speeches in Acts represent that kind of history writing, that is, Luke, drawing upon the tradition handed down from the apostles, composes speeches and puts them on the lips of Peter, Paul, and Stephen to explain to his readers the meaning of the history he is telling.

To those of us who thought we were hearing in those speeches the very words of Peter and Paul, this way of understanding the speeches was, at first, disappointing. But in the end, taking Luke to be writing speeches in the manner of his peer historians makes better sense of the material. For each of those speeches makes more sense as addressed to Luke's readers rather than as addressed to the audience within the plot line of the narrative. Indeed, the speeches build on one another and presume an audience that has read the Third Gospel and the rest of the Acts of the Apostles.

What we have in those cameo speeches, then, is not a set of tapes that we have to sort out for ourselves (like editors working with Richard Nixon's White House tapes); rather, what we have are Luke's authoritative interpretations of the early history of the church. Because of their content, they also give us examples of the early church's use of Scripture in proclaiming the good news. At the end of the day, this is a more satisfying and instructive way of reading those speeches. This commentary aims to make that apparent.

Outline. Many commentators have observed that Jesus' words to the disciples before his ascension contain a kind of outline of Acts: "You will be my witnesses in Jerusalem, throughout Judea and Samaria, and to the ends of the earth" (Acts 1:8). That observation is illustrated in the following outline:

I. The Risen Christ and the Restoration of Israel in Jerusalem (1:1–8:3).

II. The Mission in Judea and Samaria (8:4–9:43).

III. The Inauguration of the Gentile Mission (10:1–15:35).

IV. The Mission of Paul to the Ends of the Earth (15:36–28:31).

This way of outlining the major movements of Luke's history also reflects one of the main texts from the Scriptures that he uses to interpret what is going on in the early history of the church:

> For now the LORD has spoken
> who formed me as his servant from the womb,
> That Jacob may be brought back to him
> and Israel gathered to him;
> And I am made glorious in the sight of the LORD,
> and my God is now my strength!
> It is too little, he says, for you to be my servant,
> to raise up the tribes of Jacob,
> and restore the survivors of Israel;
> I will make you a light to the nations,
> that my salvation may reach to the ends of the earth. (Isa 49:5-6)

Notice that this prophecy about Servant/Israel entails two stages: first, the restoration of Israel (the twelve tribes of Jacob); second, becoming a "light to the nations." In the Acts of the Apostles, Luke shows how this prophecy is fulfilled.

Isaiah's first stage, the end-time restoration of Israel, unfolds in the first two movements in Acts—first in the formation of the Jerusalem community out of Jews from all nations (1:1–8:3), then in their outreach to Jews in the surrounding area and to Samaritans (8:4–9:43).

Isaiah's second stage, becoming a "light to the nations," unfolds in two further movements— first in the inauguration of the mission to the Gentiles (10:1–15:35), then in Paul's mission to "the ends of the earth" (15:36–28:31).

This commentary will highlight the two continuities sketched in this introduction: (1) the continuity between the story of Jesus and the story of the church, and (2) the continuity between the Christian story as a whole and the longer story of Israel's life with God, as told in the Greek version of the Hebrew Scriptures. The importance of this approach was underscored by the recent document of the Pontifical Biblical Commission, "The Jewish People and Their Sacred Scriptures in the Christian Bible" (Vatican City: Libreria Editrice Vaticana, 2002; available at http://www.libreriaeditricevaticana.com).

Although the format of this commentary does not allow for footnotes, the author's dependence on prior commentators will be obvious to those familiar with Lukan scholarship. Readers who wish to pursue their study of Luke-Acts more deeply should consult the following: Luke Timothy Johnson, *The Acts of the Apostles* (Collegeville, Minn.: Liturgical Press, 1992); James D. G. Dunn, *The Acts of the Apostles* (Valley Forge, Pa.: Trinity Press, 1996); Joseph A. Fitzmyer, S.J., *The Acts of the Apostles,* Anchor Bible 31 (New York: Doubleday, 1998); and Ben Witherington, III, *The Acts of the Apostles* (Grand Rapids, Mich.: William B. Eerdmans, 1998).

Now let us begin to read Luke's sequel.

COMMENTARY

THE RISEN CHRIST AND THE RESTORATION OF ISRAEL IN JERUSALEM

Acts 1:1–8:3

Luke shows how Jesus' mission to initiate the end-time restoration of Israel finds expression in the emergent, Spirit-filled Christian community in Jerusalem.

1:1-5 Introduction: "As I was saying, Theophilus . . ."

Luke introduces this sequel to his Gospel by addressing Theophilus, as he did in the prologue to his Gospel (Luke 1:1-4), indicating that this is a continuation of the same project described there. Literally, the Greek of verse 1 says, "I dealt with all that Jesus *began* to do and teach," implying that Acts will treat what Jesus *continues* to do and teach through the apostolic church. And the phrase "through the holy Spirit" more naturally modifies "chosen"—that is, "after giving instruc-

tions to the apostles whom he had chosen through the holy Spirit." For Luke, alone among the Synoptic writers, notes that Jesus chose the Twelve after spending the night in prayer (Luke 6:12-13), which for Luke often precedes a special empowerment by the Spirit (see Luke 3:21, leading to 4:18; Acts 1:14, leading to 2:1-4; and Acts 4:23-31).

As in the Gospel, the centerpiece of Jesus' teaching remains the kingdom of God. Jesus' reference to "the promise of the Father" alludes to at least three passages in the Third Gospel: (1) Luke 11:13: "If you then, who are wicked, know how to give good gifts to your children, how much more will the Father in heaven give the holy Spirit to those who ask him?"; (2) Luke 12:32: "Do not be afraid any longer, little flock, for your Father is pleased to give you the kingdom"; (3) Luke 24:49: "And [behold] I am sending the promise of my Father upon you; but stay in the city until you are clothed with power from on high." The gift of the Spirit at Pentecost will also signal a further manifestation of the kingdom of God already inaugurated in the ministry of Jesus (see Luke 11:20 and 17:21).

Linking this blessing with John the Baptist's prophecy about being "baptiz[ed in] the holy Spirit" (Luke 3:16) also ties this promise to Ezekiel's promise of a cleansing restoration of the people of Israel that will accompany the gift of the divine Spirit (Ezek 36:24-27).

1:6-12 The ascension of Jesus

Since the disciples are Jews who have identified Jesus as their long-awaited Messiah, it is reasonable for them to ask if Jesus will now restore the kingdom to Israel (v. 6). After all, he has been speaking to them for forty days about the kingdom of God, which, in the common expectation of the day, is supposed to be a restoration of the nation to what it was when David reigned a millennium before. Jesus does not deny the appropriateness of the question; he simply refuses to reveal to them the divinely decreed schedule (v. 7). Jesus also reinterprets their implied notion of the kingdom; it is not going to be a matter of nationalism but a new kind of unity empowered by the holy Spirit, as foreshadowed by the new "family" portrayed in Luke 8:1-21.

In this, Jesus echoes what he had said to them on Easter Sunday (Luke 24:49). When he tells them that the Spirit's power will enable them to be his witnesses from Jerusalem "to the ends of the earth" (v. 8), he alludes to Isaiah 49:6, where the Lord tells his Servant that he will not only restore the tribes of Jacob but will also be a light to the nations, "that my salvation will reach to the ends of the earth."

Although the traditional word for the withdrawal of Jesus' physical presence from the apostles is "the ascension," it might be more accurate to describe Luke's description of this event as an "assumption," since the author portrays it as an act of the Father. To describe this departure, Luke draws upon the biblical traditions about the assumptions of Enoch (Gen 5:23-24; Sir 49:14b) and Elijah (2 Kgs 2:9-11; Sir 48:9). To interpret the event, he adds what have been called "apocalyptic stage props"—the movement upward into the heavens, a cloud as vehicle, and the interpreting angels.

This is Luke's second account of the ascension. The first account, given at the end of Luke's Gospel (24:50-51), sets the event on Easter Sunday and describes Jesus in details that recall the description of the high priest Simon II in Sirach 50:1-24. Like Simon, Jesus' presence occasions worship (Sir 50:17, 22); he raises his hands and pronounces a blessing (Sir 50:20), and this is followed by references to the community's blessing God and rejoicing in the temple (Sir 50:22-23). In so doing, Jesus is acting like the temple priest at the end of the daily Whole-Offering (also called the Tamid, or "regular," service; Exod 29:38-42; Num 2:1-10). And within the Gospel narrative, Jesus is doing what the priest Zechariah was unable to do at the end of the Tamid service, whose incense ritual is the scenario briefly portrayed at the beginning of Luke's Gospel. By alluding in this manner to Sirach 50, Luke was celebrating Jesus the way Ben Sira celebrated Simon II as the climax of his Praise of the Ancestors (Sirach 44–50). For Luke, it is Jesus, not Simon II, who is the climax of Israel's history; and so Luke chooses to end his first volume by portraying Jesus' departure on Easter Sunday with those overtones.

Why, then, does Luke take the liberty to narrate this event so differently as he begins his second volume? Some scholars suggest that in Acts Luke has expanded the time frame of Luke 24 to the round (and biblically symbolic) number forty, in order to associate the ascension closely with the outpouring of the Spirit on the fiftieth day, Pentecost (the Jewish feast of the giving of the Law on Mount Sinai). The apocalyptic stage props serve four purposes: (1) to recall the transfiguration (Luke 9:18-36, another mountain episode, when the disciples could not pray, as now they can); (2) to look forward to the outpouring of the Spirit and the mission that follows; (3) to recount the departure of Jesus in a way that recalls 2 Kings 2:9-12 (another narrative about the transmission of spirit for prophetic succession); and (4) to point toward the final coming (described already in Luke 21:27 as coming "in a cloud," alluding to the cloud imagery of Daniel 7:13, but in the singular, to prepare for Acts 1:9). Thus Luke is able to speak of one reality, the final departure of Jesus from his assembled followers, from two interpretive points of view. Luke 24 alludes to the ascension as a fitting ending of the story of Jesus; Acts 1 narrates the same event as the beginning of the story of the mission of the Church, initiated by the risen Lord and empowered by the gift of the Spirit.

1:13-26 The community gathers to restore "the Twelve" by electing Matthias

The apostles (minus Judas Iscariot) whom Luke had carefully called "the eleven" at Luke 24:33 gather with the "women, and Mary the mother of Jesus, and his brothers" (v. 14). This group, numbered at 120 in verse 15 (notice the multiple of 12), comprises the nucleus of the church that will become the heart of restored Israel in chapter 2.

"The women" no doubt included Mary Magdalene, Joanna, Susanna, and Mary the mother of James, and the many other women who had accompanied Jesus and the Twelve and had "provided for them out of their resources" (Luke 8:3). They are the ones "who had come from Galilee with him" (Luke 23:55) and, coming to anoint the body of Jesus in the tomb, discovered it empty and became the first witnesses to the resurrection (Luke 24:10, 22-23).

His "brothers" are the very ones who, together with Jesus' mother, were last seen in Luke 8:19-21, standing at the edge of a crowd around Jesus when he said, "My mother and my brothers are those who hear the word of God and act on it" (v. 21). Whatever the ambiguity of their status then, now they are at the center of the believing community. Like Jesus after the water immersion by John and before his special anointing by the Spirit (Luke 3:21), the community is immersed in prayer.

Jesus' prayer that Simon Peter, even after denying Jesus, will turn back and strengthen his brothers (Luke 22:32) begins to be fulfilled, as Peter now asserts his leadership (Acts 1:15).

The first agenda item to be addressed by the community is the replacement of Judas Iscariot, who had been "numbered" among the core group (v. 17). Because of the symbolic meaning of Jesus' choice of twelve, indicating the restoration of the twelve tribes of the people of God, "the eleven" (Luke 24:33) must again become the Twelve.

The importance of the number twelve becomes clear when one recalls the words of Jesus at the Last Supper: "And I confer a kingdom on you, just as my Father has conferred one on me, that you may eat and drink at my table in my kingdom; and you will sit on thrones judging the twelve tribes of Israel" (Luke 22:29-30). Whatever Matthew's parallel saying may mean in the context of his Gospel (Matt 19:28), for Luke this is a reference to the leadership of the Twelve in the Jerusalem church after Pentecost. "Judging" here has the sense it has in the book of Judges, which features twelve charismatic leaders who led the tribes of Israel before the time of the monarchy. The reconstituted Twelve will similarly "judge" (that is, exert Spirit-filled leadership among) the reconstituted people of Israel after Pentecost.

The way the words of Peter (1:16-20) and the prayer of the community (1:24-25) speak of Judas's death is full of irony. Abandoning a community that will soon express its unity and detachment from material possessions by selling fields, with no one calling anything his own, Judas invested his blood money in a field ("turned away . . . to his own place," v. 25) and died there in a horrible, isolated death. Whereas Matthew's account of Judas's death (Matt 27:5) parallels the suicide-by-hanging of David's betrayer Ahithophel (2 Sam 17:23), Luke's version reflects the punitive death-by-falling that was Antiochus IV's end (2 Macc 9:12-14).

The community makes sure that Judas's replacement will be a qualified witness to the resurrection by choosing two candidates who were present with Jesus from the baptism of John through the ascension. Then, having done their human best, they put the final choice out of their hands, leaving it up to God through the device of casting lots. Thus Matthias is chosen to restore the Twelve.

2:1-13 The coming of the Spirit

Pentēcostēs (literally "fiftieth") is the Greek name for the Israelite feast of Weeks (*Shavuʿot* in Hebrew). The second of the three classical pilgrim feasts of Israel—Unleavened Bread/Passover, Weeks, and Booths (see Exod 23:14-17; 34:22; Deut 16:16)—the feast of Weeks was called "Fiftieth" in Greek because it occurred seven weeks, or fifty days, after the feast of Unleavened Bread/Passover. Originally an agricultural feast celebrating the end of the grain harvest, Pentecost eventually came to be associated with the giving of the Law at Sinai.

Luke narrates the Pentecost events in words and images that evoke the revelation at Mount Sinai. The reconstituted Twelve (among the 120) are gathered like the twelve tribes at Sinai. The sounds from heaven, the filling of the *whole* house (like the shaking of the *whole* mountain in Exodus 19:18), and the fire recall the theophany (appearance of God) at

Sinai. The tongues of fire symbolize the reality that the powerful presence of God (like fire) will find expression in human words, the prophetic ministry of the disciples. The appearance of fire also corresponds to John the Baptist's prediction that Jesus would baptize "with the holy Spirit and fire" (Luke 3:16). In the fuller sweep of the narrative, the parallel between Jesus and Moses is evident in that Jesus ascends with a cloud (1:9) and then mediates the gift of the prophetic word of God to the people (2:4, 11, 18, 33). Thus Luke underscores the fact that on the feast of the giving of the Law (the privileged communication of God's word) comes the end-time gift of the holy Spirit to empower a fresh expression of the divine word in the ministry of the apostles.

The list of nations from which the Jewish pilgrims and converts come symbolizes the future implications of what is happening here. By highlighting this inclusive gathering, Luke proclaims that this is in fact the fulfillment of the expected end-time ingathering of Israel. The Pentecostal gift is destined for Jews first, but then also for the "ends of the earth" (Acts 1:8), "those far off" (2:39; see Isa 57:19).

When Luke says that they "were *confused* because each one heard them speaking in his own language" (v. 6, emphasis added), he appears to be alluding to the story of the tower of Babel (in its Septuagint version, that is, the Greek translation of the Hebrew Old Testament). Whereas Genesis 11 tells of a sinful people who wish to make a name for themselves and are scattered in confusion and lose their ability to communicate (literally "to *hear* one another"), Acts 2 tells of a people of many languages who gather, are "confused" by a new ability to "hear," and are empowered to become a new community as they repent of their sins and call upon the name of the Lord. The likelihood of the allusion becomes even stronger when one notes that the name Babel is rendered *Sygchysis* ("Confusion") in the Septuagint.

2:14-36 Peter explains: the Spirit of God is restoring end-time Israel, and the crucified Jesus is its risen Messiah and Lord!

In this speech of Peter to the festival crowd, Luke employs a kind of biblical interpretation that the Dead Sea Scrolls have taught us to call a *pesher*. The word *pesher* is simply Aramaic for "interpre-

tation." But in the hands of the Essenes, an ascetical community that lived at Qumran, a *pesher* meant understanding a biblical passage as fulfilled in the present or recent history of their own community. Luke now has Peter explain the significance of the Pentecost events in a series of such *peshers*.

After a deft and humorous remark about the enthusiastic behavior of the community (they are not drunk; it's only nine in the morning, v. 15), Peter quotes Joel 3:1-5, joining it with a crucial phrase from the Greek version of Isaiah 2:2 ("in the last days"). He says, in effect, that what has been happening in Jerusalem is the fulfillment of these end-time prophecies. Whereas Israel had experienced a special infusion of God's spirit on an occasional king or prophet, now "in the last days" the gift of the prophetic spirit has been made available in a surprisingly inclusive way, transcending gender ("your sons and daughters," "my servants and my handmaids") and age ("young," "old," v. 17).

In true *pesher* fashion, Peter proceeds to apply specific phrases to recent and current events. He interprets the phrase "wonders . . . and signs" of verse 19 as the wondrous deeds God had done through Jesus. As his story continues to unfold, it will become clear that Joel's reference to those "who calls on the name of the Lord" will be applied to those who call upon the name of the Lord *Jesus* in Christian faith (see 9:14, 21; 22:16). And so the quotation from Joel 3, fortified by Isaiah 2:2, interprets *what time it is:* it is the inauguration of the long-awaited end-time, begun by God in Jesus and continued by God through the church.

But this outpouring of the Spirit on the community of believers is more than a sign of the end times; it is also a sign of the resurrection and enthronement of Jesus. To make this point, Luke (through Peter) enlists the last third of Psalm 16, which contains the clause " . . . you will not abandon my soul to the nether world, / nor will you suffer your holy one to undergo corruption" (1970 version). With the traditional understanding that all the psalms come from David, Peter argues that since David himself died and therefore *his* flesh obviously "saw corruption," the words must apply to someone else. Add to this the prophecy of Psalm 132:11 that God would set one of David's descendants on his throne, and these texts turn out to apply to the Messiah *in his resurrection*. It is in this sense, as risen king of restored Israel, that Jesus can be called "the Anointed One" ("Messiah" in Hebrew, "Christ" in Greek).

Then, to show how the risen Jesus is entitled also to the name "Lord" (used in the quotation from Joel 3 in Acts 2:21), Peter enlists the first verse of Psalm 110: "The LORD said to my Lord, 'Sit at my right hand / till I make your enemies your footstool'" (1970 version). The final verse of the speech (2:36) summarizes the whole speech succinctly.

2:37-41 The response to the proclamation

When the people ask Peter what they should do, he invites them to repent and be baptized in the name of the Lord Jesus (which, in the light of the preceding speech, means belief in the resurrection of Jesus). And when Peter promises that they will receive the "gift of the holy Spirit," we now understand that the events of Acts 2 are the fulfillment of John the Baptist's promise that one mightier than he would baptize "in the holy Spirit and fire" (Luke 3:16; see also Acts 1:5). Mission to the Gentiles is already glimpsed when Peter joins "you and . . . your children" with "and to all *those far off*" (Isaiah's phrase for Gentiles in Isaiah 57:19, emphasis added). Jewish and Gentile Christians alike will qualify as those ". . . whom the LORD shall call" (Joel 3:5).

2:42-47 The first Christian community

Although the portrait of the *koinōnia*, or communal life, of the Jerusalem Christian community (vv. 42-47) has often been used to illustrate the ideals of vowed religious life, Luke clearly means it to portray the Christian community of Jerusalem as restored Israel. Each of the details is powerfully suggestive, describing who they are and what they are about.

The "teaching of the apostles" to which they devote themselves no doubt refers to the teaching of Jesus and the kind of biblical interpretation regarding Jesus just displayed in Peter's Pentecost speech. Since "the breaking of the bread" (v. 42) refers to the practice of the Lord's Supper, "the prayers" are likely the traditional prayers of Jewish life, such as the *Shema* (Deut 6:4-9; note the reference to the Christians regularly gathering in the temple area in verse 46, presumably for prayer, as in 3:1). That the apostles are said to

perform "wonders and signs" (v. 43) reinforces the continuity between their ministry and that of Jesus, just described as commended by God with "wonders and signs" in verse 22. Their sense of mutual service (see Luke 22:25-27) leads them spontaneously to share their possessions, even to sell property to meet one another's needs (v. 45). That they continue to meet in the temple area is consistent with the description, at the end of Luke's Gospel, that "they were continually [or regularly] in the temple praising God" (Luke 24:53). The Jewish Christians' allegiance to Jesus as Lord and Messiah has not meant severance from the life of the temple.

Finally, notice that verse 47b describes this Christian communal life as "being saved"—an explication of a phrase from Joel quoted in verse 21 ("everyone *shall be saved* who calls on the name of the Lord"; emphasis added). The awe (*phobos*, literally "fear") that comes upon everyone is reminiscent of the fear that God sent upon the nations as they witnessed the progress of the Exodus and Conquest (Exod 15:16; 23:27; Deut 2:25; 11:25; 32:25; Josh 2:9). This awe is a continuation of the people's response to the new Exodus already begun in the story of Jesus (see Luke 1:12, 65; 2:9; 5:26; 7:16; 8:37; 21:26).

This cameo picture of the life of the Jerusalem Christian community reflects the fulfillment of the jubilee theme struck in the quotation of Isaiah 61:2 at Luke 4:19.

3:1-26 The healing of the man born lame and Peter's explanation

Having referred to "many wonders and signs worked through the apostles" (2:43), Luke now describes in detail one such sign—the healing of the lame man at the temple gate. As in the case of the Pentecost events, he also provides a speech that interprets the significance of that sign.

Consistent with the statements that the disciples, after the resurrection, were regularly in the temple (Luke 24:53) and that they continued to meet in the temple precincts (Acts 2:46), Luke shows Peter and John going up to the temple "at the ninth hour, the hour of prayer," that is, at the time of the regular afternoon Tamid service (see Luke 1:10 and Acts 10:30), what we call 3 P.M.

Why Luke foregrounds this particular healing becomes evident when we attend to the details. What unfolds here interrupts routine. The friends of the beggar carry the immobile man and prop him up at the gate, a daily drill for them. And Peter and John are entering the temple precincts for their customary participation in the mid-afternoon liturgy (see Luke 24:53). When the beggar, apparently without looking, begs for alms (*eleēmosynē*), Peter commands him to look at them. Gaining his attention, he commands him to walk, using language that contrasts the power of silver and gold with the power of the name of Jesus. Something astoundingly new breaks the routine of daily begging.

In the Greek Bible (the Septuagint, whose conventional sign is LXX), *eleēmosynē* sometimes means "alms," but more often it means "the mercy of God" (as in LXX Isa 1:27 and LXX Ps 23:5). The original readers of Luke's Greek would have been aware of a kind of pun here: the beggar was expecting *eleēmosynē* in the sense of mere alms; what he receives is a surprising *eleēmosynē*, the mercy of God in the form of liberation from lameness.

Luke emphasizes the fact that the man not only stands and walks—he *leaps*, a detail mentioned *twice* in verse 8. This stress on leaping recalls the only other place where the Bible mentions the lame leaping, Isaiah 35:6: "Then will the lame leap like a stag." Now it becomes clear why Luke chooses precisely this healing as the one to highlight in the context of his description of the birth of the church. Isaiah 35:5-6 is a prophetic description of the restoration of Israel, now understood as fulfilled in the Jerusalem messianic community.

Just as the Fourth Gospel, where faith in Jesus is the deepest kind of seeing and thus we are *all* born blind in that sense, highlights the healing of a man born *blind*, so Luke highlights this healing of a man born *lame*.

What the healing account itself began, with its allusion to Isaiah 35 in the language of leaping, the speech continues in its further interpretation of the healing, using still more references to the Scriptures.

First, who did it? When the crowds attribute the healing to the apostles, Peter announces that this was the work of "the God of Abraham, of Isaac, and of Jacob," who has "glorified his servant Jesus." Since this way of referring to God echoes the call of Moses in Exodus 3:6, Peter may be implying that this healing is a sign that God is working a new Exodus through the long-awaited

prophet-like-Moses, who is Jesus (recall the "wonders and signs" language of 2:19, 22).

This identification of Jesus is further underscored by the *pesher* citation of Deuteronomy 18:15, 18-19 at verses 22-23. Regarding the person who fails to respond to ("hear") God's words spoken by that prophet, Luke replaces Deuteronomy's vague warning ("I myself will make him answer for it") by substituting Leviticus's stiffer sanction for failing to participate in the liturgy of the Day of Atonement (Lev 23:29): "[that person] shall be cut off from his people." Notice that, as Luke understands it, Jews who accept Jesus as the Messiah do not divorce themselves from the people of Israel; rather, they constitute the true Israel, and those who fail to accept Jesus are, in effect, excommunicated.

This healing is also a sign of the end times: "*All* the prophets who spoke, from Samuel and those afterwards, also announced *these days*" (v. 24, emphasis added). Further, this healing is a sign that what is unfolding here in Jerusalem is a fulfillment of God's ancient promise to Abraham: "In your offspring all the families of the earth shall be blessed" (v. 25, alluding to Gen 22:18; and see 12:3; 26:4). In the final verse of the speech, Luke makes a clever play on the words "raise up" that were just heard in the quotation from Deuteronomy 18:15: God has indeed "raised up" his servant Jesus, not simply in the sense of commissioning him but also in the new sense of resurrection from the dead. Now the risen Lord is working through the likes of Peter and John, offering new opportunities for conversion to the life of the Spirit.

4:1-22 The temple authorities confront the apostles on the question of authority

The spectacle of Jesus' followers teaching crowds in the temple precincts ("Solomon's Portico," 3:11) alarms the temple authorities. Not only are these Galileans usurping their teaching authority with the people, they are proclaiming in Jesus "the resurrection of the dead," which, for the Sadducees, was one of the false doctrines of the Pharisees. The Sadducees held as true only what could be found in a strict reading of the Pentateuch (the first five books of the Old Testament), and they found no teaching about immortality or resurrection in those five scrolls (see Luke 20:27-40).

When the rulers and elders gather to meet as the Sanhedrin, they raise the same question they had earlier raised with Jesus after he had driven out the sellers and continued teaching daily in the temple area (Luke 20:1-8), namely, the question of authority. This time their question is about the power that healed the lame man: "By what power or by what name have you done this?" (v. 7). It is the same issue raised by the healing and addressed by Peter in the previous speech (3:12-13). And the answer is the same here. The healing was an act of God done in the name of Jesus; the healing showed that the Sanhedrin's judgment (Jesus was an offender deserving death) has been overruled by the "higher court" of God, as confirmed by the resurrection of Jesus.

Peter's empowerment by the holy Spirit fulfills Jesus' promise to his disciples in Luke 12:11-12. To drive home that this victory of God's power and authority is greater than any earthly authority, Peter cites a favorite psalm used by the church to celebrate God's action in the death and resurrection of Jesus (see Luke 20:17 and 1 Pet 2:7). Paraphrasing Psalm 118:22, Peter says to the assembly, "He is 'the stone rejected by you, the builders, which has become the cornerstone.'" In the context of Psalm 118, the rejected stone refers to Israel, cast aside by imperial power yet rescued by God, who will use it as a cornerstone. This verse serves wonderfully as a Christian *pesher* because it is not only an apt celebration of the death and resurrection of Jesus, but it also evokes the image of the end-time temple interpreted as the Christian community.

What is more, the theme of the psalm—that God's power to *save* is greater than imperial power—provides the background for Peter's wordplay on the theme of healing/saving. The Greek word for "heal" and "save" in verses 9 and 12 is *sōzō*, which can mean any aspect of the whole range of rescuing, from physical healing to eschatological salvation. In verse 9 it denotes the physical healing of the paralytic, whereas in verse 12 it apparently refers to ultimate salvation. Thus the physical cure of the man born lame becomes not only a sign of the restoration of Israel but also of the full salvation of all who believe: "There is no *salvation* through anyone else, nor is there any other name under heaven given to the human race by which we are to be *saved*" (v. 12, emphasis added).

Although that verse is sometimes applied to the uniqueness of Jesus within the context of religious pluralism, a different context may be operating here. For an audience familiar with the claim of Roman emperors to the title of *sōtēr* ("Savior"), the mention of *sōtēria* ("salvation") suggests a contrast between the imperial power that controls the temple officials and the divine power working through Jesus. As in Psalm 118, true power and authority come not from worldly empire but from God's power, here exercised in the name of the risen Lord Jesus.

When the Sanhedrin orders the apostles "never again to speak to anyone in this name" (v. 17), Peter and John say, "Whether it is right in the sight of God for us to obey you rather than God, you be the judges." It is a clear assertion that these religious officials have lost whatever religious authority they had. The behavior of the Sanhedrin has shown that these men are more interested in preserving their own control than in serving the authority of God. That the healing of the beggar at the temple gate is "a remarkable sign" they readily admit, but they choose to ignore its significance. Luke underscores the public nature of this event in the closing statement in the episode: "For the man on whom this sign of healing had been done was over forty years old" (and therefore well known to frequenters of the Temple Mount).

4:23-31 The prayer of the community and God's response

Luke portrays Peter and John returning and reporting to "their own" (Luke could mean anything from the Twelve, to the 120 of Acts 1:15, to the 5000 "men" [*andres*] mentioned at 4:4) what the chief priests and elders had told them. What follows is either (a) a miracle of choral speaking, in which this large group improvises a *pesher* interpretation in unison or (b) a prayer-speech that historian Luke composes (in *pesher* style) to convey how the early community understood persecution and responded to it in their prayer and action. The latter seems more likely.

This episode presents us with one of the most striking examples of *pesher* interpretation in the entire New Testament. Luke introduces it by having the group invoke God as creator (v. 24b: "Sovereign Lord, maker of heaven and earth and the sea and all that is in them"). Then they quote the first two verses of Psalm 2. The community then proceeds to apply the references to persons and actions of the initial verses in Psalm 2 to the actors and happenings of their recent experience in Jerusalem. "The Gentiles" are of course the Romans. "The peoples"—in the context of the psalm, a parallel expression for the Gentiles—now becomes "the peoples of Israel" (note that Luke retains the plural, "people*s*," to echo the wording of the psalm). As for "the kings of the earth," Herod Antipas was the king before whom Jesus was arraigned (see Luke 23:6-12), and Pilate was the representative of the "king" of the Roman Empire. The "rulers" are the Sanhedrin leaders (see vv. 5 and 8) who had also just forbidden them to speak any more about Jesus. And they had indeed "gathered in this city against your holy servant Jesus whom God had *anointed*" ("christed" catches the overtones of the Greek).

When we hear "And now, Lord, take note of their threats" (v. 29), knowing the thrust of the rest of Psalm 2, we might expect something like "shatter them like an earthen dish" (Ps 2:9b). Instead, we hear quite the opposite: "Enable your servants to speak your word with all boldness, as you stretch forth [your] hand to heal, and signs and wonders are done through the name of your holy servant Jesus" (vv. 29-30). In response to the official crucifixion of Jesus and the present resistance of the rulers, they pray for empowerment to continue the mission of Jesus in word and work, especially preaching and healing. The divine response to their prayer (v. 31) is the "mini-Pentecost" that follows.

4:32–5:11 Life in the Christian community

Acts 4:32-35 provides another cameo picture of the Jerusalem Christian community. With Acts 2:42-47, it makes a frame around the intervening episodes, which exemplify how God has worked through the leadership of the apostles (Peter and John) to continue Jesus' preaching and healing ministry. The description of the community as being "of one heart and mind" and holding everything in common embodies the Greek ideal of friendship. And the statement that "there was no needy person among them" alludes to the Hebrew ideal of covenant justice expressed in Deuteronomy 15:4. The jubilee note struck here echoes the jubilee theme of the passage from Isaiah 61 that Jesus read at his debut in the Nazareth syna-

gogue (Luke 4:18-19). This spontaneous "faith sharing" of material goods to meet the needs of all is mediated through the leadership, a fact that is signified by their laying the proceeds of real estate sales "at the feet of the apostles" (v. 37).

To show that even from the beginning it was a struggle to live out the ideals of Christian community life, Luke now presents examples. First he offers a good example in Joseph Barnabas, who did it right (4:36-37). Then comes a dramatic account of a bad example, the deceptive behavior of Ananias and Sapphira (5:1-11).

The reference to Barnabas introduces one who will emerge as a key player in the Jerusalem Christian community and its mission. (So important does this coworker of Paul become that the second-century *Epistle of Barnabas* was attributed to him.)

The sin of Ananias and Sapphira lies not so much in possessiveness as in their deception. As Peter himself grants, the property was theirs to keep or sell as they wished. But pretending that they were donating the whole proceeds, when in fact they were holding back part—this was nothing less than lying to the holy Spirit! Ironically, Luke notes that Sapphira falls dead "at the feet" of Peter as punishment for deceptively laying "at the feet of the apostles" only part of the property proceeds from the sale of their property. What is done to the community is done to the Spirit of God. The whole episode echoes another famous holding back, that of Achan, who, after the battle of Jericho, kept for himself some of the banned goods (Josh 7).

5:12-16 Another summary

The Jesus group continues to assemble in the temple precincts (see 3:11). And the "signs and wonders" that God had done through Jesus (2:22), for the continuation of which they had prayed (4:30), continue to happen through the apostles. As contact with the mere tassel of Jesus' garment was enough to occasion healing in his ministry (Luke 8:43-44), now people seek even Peter's passing shadow as a medium of healing and deliverance from evil spirits.

5:17-42 Testing the mission: the work of God or human beings?

With divine help, the apostles move from prison to preaching. Strikingly, when the angel of the Lord opens the prison gates for them, he instructs them to go and take their stand in the temple and tell the people all about "this life." Like their Master, who entered the temple not simply to expel the vendors but also to take his stand there and teach the people daily (Luke 19:45–21:38; and see Luke 2:46, where the twelve-year-old Jesus teaches in the temple), the apostles, too, continue the mission in what remains for them their sacred center, the temple area. Like Jesus, they *occupy* the temple precincts as the right place to do God's will by teaching the people (5:21, 42; see Luke 20:1).

This miraculous "jail break" strikes the theme of the unhindered word that will be reprised in the great escape of Acts 12. Indeed, the final word of the book is *akōlytōs* ("without hindrance"), describing Paul's preaching the kingdom of God and the Lord Jesus Christ even while under house arrest (28:31).

When they are accused of disobeying orders, Peter and the apostles repeat what Peter and John had said once before to the Sanhedrin, namely, that when divine and human orders collide, they must obey God rather than human beings (v. 29; see 4:19-20). To justify this response, they cite the ruling of a "higher court." Drawing upon what will become a traditional Christian application of Scripture, they announce that in the resurrection God has over-ruled the curse of crucifixion (death by "hanging . . . on a tree"; see Deut 21:23 and Gal 3:13) by exalting Jesus to his "right hand" (Ps 110:1). And the purpose of this is to renew the people of God, Israel.

Then comes the famous intervention of Rabbi Gamaliel, whom Paul will name as his mentor in Acts 22:3. Citing the short-lived movements of other would-be messiahs—Theudas and Judas the Galilean—Gamaliel argues that obedience to false prophets comes to nothing; so let (divinely guided) history show whether this Jesus movement is of God or not. The implication is that Jesus will be shown to be another false prophet. The Sanhedrin chooses to listen to a man, Gamaliel, rather than to the evidence of God demonstrated in the signs and wonders done through the apostles. At the same time, Gamaliel's wait-and-see approach exemplifies the kind of openness that led to others of the house of Israel eventually accepting Jesus as their Messiah.

Acts 6:1-7 Crisis and solution: choosing the Seven
No sooner had the Jerusalem church dealt with challenges from the outside than it had to deal with an internal conflict—a quarrel between "Helle-nists" and "Hebrews" regarding an alleged neglect of the widows among the Hellenists. The "Helle-nists" are best understood as Greek-speaking Jews, probably people who grew up in the Diaspora (Jewish communities scattered outside Palestine beginning after the Babylonian Exile) and later im-migrated to Judea. "Hebrews," then, would be indigenous, Aramaic-speaking Jews. We have evi-dence, even as far back as the Maccabees (ca. 170 B.C.), that there had long been tension between the Jews who had taken on the language and even some of the customs of the Hellenistic world, on the one hand, and the more traditional Jews who preferred to speak Aramaic and avoid Hellenistic ways, on the other. This passage lets us know that the infant Christian community of Jerusalem in-cluded Jews from both subgroups and that becom-ing Christian did not automatically remove the "liberal" or "conservative" baggage that they brought with them.

Luke informs us that the community had set up a daily dole (of food, presumably) to take care of the needy among them, especially widows. But the widows of the Greek-speaking group were somehow being neglected. Luke does not mention the cause of the neglect. (Was it a combination of scarcity and prejudice—the ["Hebrew"] Twelve favoring their own kind? Or were they too busy to oversee the distribution properly?) Whatever the source of the problem, the Twelve apply a fa-miliar practical solution: they increase the staff. Too busy with the service (*diakonia*) of the word to tie up their time with serving at table, they call the entire community together (here called "dis-ciples" for the first time in Acts) and charge them to select seven good men to carry out this other *diakonia*. That the seven chosen all have Greek names suggests a kind of affirmative action on the part of the community: they choose members of the Greek-speaking group, thereby assuring that the neglect of the Hellenists' widows would be remedied.

Although the word for the service (of both word and table) is *diakonia*, the Seven are not called *diakonoi* (from which comes the English word "deacons"). Moreover, the service per-formed by Martha (Luke 10:40), the Twelve (Acts 1:12, 25), and Peter and Silas (12:25) is also termed *diakonia*, indicating that the term has not yet ac-quired its technical sense. Still, although Luke is probably not describing the creation of the office of deacon here, this episode points toward the later three-tier structure of bishop-priests-deacons reflected in the writing of Ignatius of Antioch. For that reason, this passage has traditionally been associated with the church office of deacon.

This freeing up of the Twelve leads to a continuing rapid growth of the church, even attracting some of the temple priests to the fold.

6:8-15 Stephen accused

Curiously, after Stephen has been commissioned as one of the Seven to "serve at table," thereby freeing the apostles for the service of the word, Luke proceeds to show Stephen engaged in precisely that apostolic work. Like the Twelve (2:43; 4:30; 5:12) and like Jesus before them (2:22), he is filled with power to do "wonders and signs" (6:8). What Luke describes is more a matter of prophetic succession than delegation: Jesus to the Twelve, then the Twelve to the Seven, exemplified by Stephen. Luke will indicate in Stephen's speech that the line of succession reaches back to Moses and the patriarchs, even as it reaches forward to the church of Luke's day (and ours). The same Spirit that empowered Jesus and the Twelve to preach and heal empowers Stephen to do the same.

As in the case of Jesus and the Twelve, the exercise of that prophetic ministry meets opposition, arrest, and a hasty "trial." Whereas Luke had omitted any mention of false witnesses in his very brief account of the Sanhedrin's investigation of Jesus (Luke 22:66-71), as he also omits in his presentation of the crucifixion Mark's taunt of the head-wagging passers-by about destroying and building the temple, he does introduce here some false witness against Stephen. Like the witnesses at the trial of Jesus in Mark and Matthew, they accuse their adversary of threatening the holy place (the temple). They also make him out to be an enemy of the Law of Moses. The discourse that follows in the next chapter will do much more than simply rebut those charges. It will show how the Law and the temple reach fulfillment in Christian life and worship.

7:1-53 Stephen addresses the Sanhedrin

In Luke's Gospel the risen Jesus spoke to his disciples about the fulfillment of things written about him in the Law of Moses, the prophets, and the psalms (Luke 24:27, 44). Our author has already shown us how the events of Jesus' life, especially his death and resurrection (Luke 24:46), fulfill the Law of Moses (the Torah, or first five books of the Bible). Peter's speech in Acts 3:22 gave one example: Jesus is the prophet-like-Moses whom God would "raise up," alluding to Deuteronomy 18:15.

Now, in the first half of Stephen's speech, the longest speech in Acts (more than twice as long as Peter's Pentecost speech), we hear Torah narrative applied to Jesus at length. Without explicitly mentioning the name of Jesus Messiah—"the righteous one" at verse 52 being as close as he comes—Stephen retells the stories of Abraham, Joseph, and Moses in ways that point to Jesus' death and resurrection and to the post-Easter church.

Just as the canticles of Mary and Zechariah celebrated the conception of Jesus and the birth of John the Baptist as leading to the fulfillment of God's promises to Abraham (Luke 2:55 and 73), Stephen tells of God's promise to Abraham that he would give the land to his descendents through a process that would entail rescue from slavery "in a land not their own" (v. 6) to freedom to "worship me in this place" (v. 7). In that last phrase Luke alludes to God's promise to *Moses* regarding worship at *Sinai* (Exod 3:12) and makes *this place* refer to *Jerusalem*. The remainder of Acts will portray true worship centered on the risen Jesus (recall that the disciples had worshiped the risen Lord on Easter Sunday near Bethany, Luke 24:52).

The brief account of the Joseph story then serves to illustrate how God begins to fulfill the promises to Abraham by rescuing his descendants from famine by means of a person who was first rejected and later emerges as their savior. The brother they had sold to slave traders eventually rose to become a prime minister whose grain reserve program saved their lives.

This pattern of God working through a rejected-one-become-savior is elaborated more fully in the rendition of the story of Moses that follows. And here Luke chooses words even more carefully to highlight the parallels between Moses and Jesus. The young Moses was "powerful in his words and deeds" (v. 22; see Luke 24:19 regarding Jesus). Like Jesus, Moses was misunderstood by his kin (v. 25). As Moses was asked, "Who appointed you ruler and judge over us?" (v. 27), so too was Jesus (Luke 12:14). Luke then becomes more richly specific in verses 35-36: "This Moses whom they had rejected . . . God sent as [both] ruler and deliverer. . . . This man led them out, performing *wonders and signs* in the land of Egypt, at the Red Sea, and in the desert for forty years" (emphasis added). Note how Acts uses the phrase "wonders and signs," first found in the quotation of Joel in Acts 2:19, both for what God did through Jesus (Acts 2:22) and for what God now does through the apostles (2:43; 4:30).

If readers have not grasped the connection with Jesus by this time, our author makes it crystal-clear with the reference to Deuteronomy 18:15 at verse 37: "God will raise up for you, from among your own kinsfolk, a prophet like me." That this applies to Jesus was already established in Peter's speech (Acts 3:22).

Thus far Stephen has dealt with the charge that he speaks against the Law; indeed, he has shown how the message about Jesus fulfills the thrust of the narratives about the ancestors and Moses. Now the speech takes up the matter of the temple, which this discourse takes to be really a question of what makes for true worship. If God promised Abraham that Israel would come to "worship . . . in this place" (v. 7), how has that promise been fulfilled? Stephen says that the people have been disobedient in the matter of worship from the beginning. First there was the idolatry of the golden calf (vv. 39-41). Then God gave them over to worship of the gods of the nations, as exemplified in the Greek version of Amos 5:25, which Luke applies to the whole period before their exile in Babylon by changing Amos's reference to exile beyond Damascus to exile beyond Babylon. The speech makes the case that the move beyond the divinely mandated portable tent of testimony (the desert tabernacle, the place of the divine presence) to the fixed and solid temple built by Solomon was misunderstood by some in Israel as a way of magically confining God to that space. That misunderstanding was a step in the direction of idolatry and an attempt to box God, who "does not *dwell* in houses made by human hands," as illustrated by the quotation from Isaiah 66:1-2 (emphasis added).

By this time in the speech, Stephen has moved from a story about "*our* ancestors" (v. 39) to one about "*your* ancestors" (v. 52, emphasis added).

His climactic word to those who have accused him of speaking against the Law is to accuse them of not observing it themselves.

7:54-60 The martyrdom of Stephen

If the charges brought against Stephen had suggested a parallel with the synoptic tradition of the trial of Jesus, the death of Stephen clearly and powerfully mirrors the death of Jesus—and also responds to the question of true worship. When Stephen announces a vision of the heavens opening and the Son of Man standing at the right hand of God (v. 56), his adversaries take him outside of the city to kill him, just as they did to his Master. And just as Jesus commended his spirit to the Father, Stephen can pray, "Lord Jesus, receive my spirit" (v. 59; see Luke 23:46). As Jesus prayed to God to forgive his crucifiers, so Stephen prays to *Jesus*, "Lord, do not hold this sin against them" (v. 60).

Two themes shine through this narrative: (1) the follower of Jesus relives the story of Jesus, sometimes quite literally; (2) Stephen answers the question about true worship with his prayer to Jesus as Lord and with the giving up of his life.

8:1-3 Saul (Paul) spearheads the persecution of the church

Saul, first mentioned as minding the cloaks of Stephen's stoners at 7:58, is said to approve this extra-judicial execution (8:1), which triggers a persecution of the church in Jerusalem. Thus begins a scattering of "Jews for Jesus" throughout Judea and Samaria. The note that the apostles were exempt from the persecution suggests that it was the Hellenists who are scattered.

THE MISSION IN JUDEA AND SAMARIA

Acts 8:4–9:43

In the remainder of chapter 8 and all of chapter 9, Luke presents Philip evangelizing the margins of Israel among the Samaritans and with the Ethiopian eunuch. Then comes the conversion/ call of Saul on the road to Damascus and, finally, Peter's work among his fellow Jews, just before his dramatic experience with Cornelius's household draws him into mission to the Gentiles. In germ, these two chapters describe the major transitions announced in Acts 1:8: "You will be my witnesses in Jerusalem, throughout Judea and

Samaria, and to the ends of the earth." Philip, Saul (Paul), and Peter take the last three steps.

8:4-25 Philip the evangelist versus Simon the magician

We saw that Stephen was a mouthpiece for Lukan Christology (the doctrines of the person and works of Christ) and also an example of the imitation of Christ. Now another member of the Seven, Philip, enters the scene as another kind of example. The first episode featuring Philip demonstrates how the Christian mission extends beyond Judea into the realm of the "heretical" (from the Jewish point of view) Samaritans and how that mission trumps the pagan magic typified by Simon Magus.

To describe the outreach of the mission beyond Jerusalem to the margins of the people of Israel, Luke five times uses his favorite word for that—*euangelizomai*, from which we get our word "evangelize." Luke found it in his Greek Bible, especially in Isaiah (40:9; 52:7; 60:6; 61:1), where the prophet speaks of announcing the coming saving power of God. Luke employs the word to describe the preaching of angels (Luke 1:19; 2:10), of John the Baptist (3:18), of Jesus (4:18 [Isa 61:1]; 4:43; 7:22; 8:1; 9:6; 16:16; 20:1), of the apostles (Acts 5:42); and in the present episode, the word describes the mission of the whole dispersed church (8:4), of Philip (vv. 12, 35, 40), and of Peter and John (v. 25). It is all a matter of telling what God is doing.

After describing the preaching and healing of Philip in words that recall the work of Jesus and the apostles (8:7), Luke speaks of the conversion of one Simon. Though he had gained an enthusiastic following as a magician before Philip's arrival, even he is converted by Philip's evangelizing (vv. 9-13). (Our word "simony," denoting the purchase or sale of spiritual things, derives from Simon Magus, alluding to his misguided attempt to buy the power to mediate the holy Spirit [vv. 18-19].)

Curiously, only when the apostles Peter and John come down from Jerusalem to pray for and lay hands on the Samaritan converts do they receive the holy Spirit (vv. 14-17). Luke here distinguishes between baptism "in the name of the Lord Jesus" and this infusion of the Spirit. A similar distinction will be made later—but in reversed order (Spirit baptism, then baptism in the name of Jesus)—in the conversion of Cornelius and his household (10:44-49).

Though some Christian groups have turned this narrative distinction into a doctrine of two baptisms (water baptism and Spirit baptism), Luke, followed by the Catholic tradition, presents as normative Peter's description of baptism and reception of the holy Spirit as one unified event (2:38). Where Luke narratively separates Spirit and baptism, he seems to be making a special point in each case. Here the point is to underscore the privileged role the apostles have in affirming the mission to the Samaritans through their mediation of the Spirit.

8:26-40 Philip and the Ethiopian eunuch

In this episode Philip is drawn, by both an angel of the Lord and the Spirit of the Lord, even further toward the margins of the house of Israel. The fact that the next candidate for conversion and baptism is a eunuch has important prophetic resonances. For example, Isaiah 56:3-5, part of a vision of the restoration of Israel that Jesus quoted in his takeover of the temple (Luke 19:46), speaks of eunuchs finding a home and an imperishable name in the coming restoration. Since Luke will treat the later conversion of the centurion and his family as the breakthrough to the Gentiles, our author would have us understand the eunuch as a convert to Judaism. Yet his ethnicity as an Ethiopian is important to Luke's theme of the universality of the church's mission.

The text that the eunuch is reading aloud (v. 28) is Isaiah 53:7-8, from the famous fourth Servant Song, which Luke quotes only here in his two volumes. It is important to note that this is the Septuagint version, whose wording here differs significantly from the Hebrew. The wording of the Old Greek is peculiarly open to being understood as applicable to the death and resurrection of Jesus. The rendering of Luke Timothy Johnson, in his *Acts of the Apostles* (Collegeville, Minn.: Liturgical Press, 1992), illustrates this well: "As a sheep led to the slaughter, and as silent as a lamb before its shearer, so he does not open his mouth. In his lowliness his judgment was taken away. Who will recite his generation? For his life is taken away from the earth." The application of this text to the childless Jesus would have a special appeal for the eunuch. Jesus' "generation" after he was "taken away" in resurrection is his growing band of post-Easter disciples, now including this eunuch.

Though he went to Jerusalem "to worship" (v. 27), as a eunuch he was explicitly prevented from entering beyond the Court of the Gentiles (see Deuteronomy 23:2, where eunuchs are banned from "the community of the Lord"). How different here, where his reception of the gospel of Jesus leads him to ask, "What is to prevent my being baptized?" Thus the one banned will indeed become a member of the community of the Lord.

Along with illustrating the spread of the word (1:8), this episode demonstrates the process of interpreting the Scriptures that Luke surely had in mind when he spoke of Jesus explaining to the disciples at Emmaus what referred to him in all the Scriptures "beginning with Moses and all the prophets" (Luke 24:27).

9:1-19 The conversion and commissioning of Saul

Although this key episode in the history of the church is traditionally called the "conversion" of Paul, it is not a conversion in the sense of changing from one religion to another, for Saul/Paul does not cease to be a Jew; he moves from being a Jew who persecutes the growing "Jews for Jesus" group to being a Jew for Jesus himself.

Is this a conversion in another sense, namely, turning from an immoral life to a moral one? Even in his persecution of the church, Paul is zealously pursuing what he understands to be the will of God. Yet Luke describes Saul as "breathing murderous threats," which is at odds with the commandment against murder. And Luke's description of the martyrdom of Stephen (7:54–8:1) showed Saul minding the cloaks of those performing the "extralegal" stoning and "consenting to this execution."

Further, the change from persecutor to promoter is surely some kind of transformation and reorientation. This has led some to call what happens to Paul a prophetic commissioning, for he is stopped in his tracks to be sent on a mission. Maybe it is best to say that this is both a conversion and a commissioning.

Luke describes the event as a theophany. It parallels the encounter of Moses with the divine Presence in Exodus 3. Like Moses, Saul is startled with a manifestation of brightness, hears his name called twice, hears the voice identify itself, and receives a commission.

The revelation that he receives, "I am Jesus, whom you are persecuting," is a striking summation of a major theme of Paul's letters: the identification of the risen Lord with his church, which Paul elaborates in his treatment of the Christian community as the body of Christ, especially in Romans and 1 Corinthians.

When Paul addresses the voice in the vision as *Kyrie*, it most likely means "Lord" in the full sense of the appellation. The identification of that Lord as Jesus, then, parallels Stephen's calling Jesus "Lord" (7:59). That this title recurs twelve more times in this chapter suggests that Luke would have us understand this beginning of the mission to the Gentiles as a special manifestation of the lordship of the risen Jesus. For references to this experience in Paul's own words, see 1 Corinthians 9:1 ("Have I not seen Jesus our Lord?"); 2 Cor 4:4:6; Gal 1:12.

To this paradox of the enemy of the Christian movement becoming its greatest promoter, Luke adds another: when his eyes were opened, he could see nothing (v. 8). Though he became temporarily blind, he really did have, in a deeper sense, an "eye-opening" experience. The cure from that physical blindness that accompanies his baptism underscores his spiritual enlightenment. Luke will elaborate on this imagery in the later retellings of this episode in chapters 22 and 26.

Notice that our author has four different and suggestive ways of naming the growing church in this passage: "the disciples of the Lord" (v. 1); "the Way" (v. 2); "all who call upon your name" (v. 14, echoing Joel 2:32 quoted in Acts 2:21; and see Romans 10:13); and "the holy ones" (v. 13, a Jewish term for Israel set apart for the Lord's service, here appropriated by Christian Jews, as Paul will do in his letters).

9:19b-31 Saul preaches in Damascus and visits Jerusalem

The adversary turned promoter begins his apostolic life right there in Damascus by preaching in the local synagogues that Jesus is the long-awaited Christ (Greek for the Hebrew term *Messiah*, or "Anointed One"). When Luke says that Saul proclaimed Jesus as the Son of God, he probably means this title in the same sense, that is, as Messiah (see Psalm 2:7). Later theology will apply it in the full sense of divinity, as in John 1:1, 18.

How Saul "will have to suffer" for the name of Jesus (v. 16) is soon demonstrated in the plot by the Jews of Damascus against his life (v. 23) and then in the similar efforts of the Jerusalemite Hellenists (v. 29). In Jerusalem, it takes Barnabas's testimony to render him credible and acceptable to the local disciples. As in the case of Philip (8:14-17), the mission of the one whom later tradition will call "the Apostle" needs the seal of approval from the Jerusalem leadership. This Jerusalem sojourn is possibly the visit to which Paul refers, with a different emphasis, in Galatians 1:18-20.

In contrast to the cloak-and-dagger escapades that characterized Paul's debut as an apostle, the one-line summary at verse 31 describes the growth of the church throughout the entire area as peaceful and abundant.

9:32-43 Peter heals at Lydda and Joppa

Just how that growth mentioned in the summary of verse 31 occurred is illustrated by two episodes from Peter's healing ministry. Visiting a Christian community ("the holy ones") in the plains town of Lydda, he heals a long-term paralytic named Aeneas. The sight of old Aeneas healed moves "all the inhabitants" to "turn to the Lord" (now shorthand for coming to Christian faith). Another exemplary disciple, Tabitha, falls sick and dies, apparently prematurely. Her resuscitation at Peter's command occasions the conversion of many in Joppa.

Commentators have noticed that the language Luke uses to describe these healings is reminiscent of the Deuteronomic historian's description of the wonder-working of Elijah and Elisha (1 Kgs 17:17-24; 2 Kgs 4:31-37). This further underscores Luke's presentation of the disciples as prophetic successors of Jesus, just as he is the prophet-like-Moses. They are not, however, successors in the sense of replacing Jesus; their ministry is an expression of the risen Lord Jesus working through them.

THE INAUGURATION OF THE GENTILE MISSION
Acts 10:1–15:35

Although Luke knows of others who brought the gospel to Gentiles (see the reference to Cypriot and Cyrenean Christians who evangelized Greeks in Antioch at 11:20), he chooses to focus on the experience of Peter, who was divinely led in this direction in dramatic ways. The accounts of Herod Agrippa's persecution of Christians, followed by his own punitive death, then the first

mission of Paul (Acts 13–14), all lead naturally to the Council of Jerusalem (Acts 15), which resolves an important policy question raised by this unexpected success among the nations.

10:1-33 Visions and revisions: the mission of Peter to Cornelius

To describe the change that Peter undergoes in chapter 10 as a "conversion" might seem strange to our way of thinking, but Luke clearly sees this transformation of Peter as parallel to Paul's "conversion" in importance. Paul changed from seeing the Jesus movement as a threat to the will of God to seeing it as the very fulfillment of God's plan. Similarly, Peter is moved from perceiving the messianic movement as a Jews-only affair to understanding it as God's blessing for Gentiles as well. Although this vision is implied in Peter's second speech (see 3:25), it takes the divine interventions portrayed in the present chapter to enable Peter to see the practical consequences of the promise to Abraham that his descendants would be a blessing for "all the nations of the earth" (Gen 18:18; 22:18). Thus, as in the case of Paul's transformation, Luke will tell the story of Peter's change three times. In both transformations, the initiative is not human but divine.

Cornelius is a "God fear[er]." This is not a formal social classification but a description of a Gentile who, without formally joining the people of Israel (entailing circumcision for males), has taken on Jewish beliefs and pious practices such as almsgiving and prayer at the hour of temple worship.

Luke underscores the fact that the actions of both Cornelius and Peter are divinely prompted by linking their actions to interlocking visions. The angel of God makes it clear to Cornelius that the intervention is a response to his prayer and tells him to send for Peter at Simon the tanner's place. Peter's vision confronts him (three times!) with a powerful puzzlement: shown a sheet full of clean and unclean animals, he is instructed to kill and eat. In effect, this is a command to ignore a primary Jewish identity marker. (It also evokes the cosmic covenant God made with Noah in Genesis 9, where Noah and family, representing all humanity, were given "every creature that is alive" to eat, Gen 9:3.)

When the messengers from Cornelius, presumably Gentiles, arrive at Simon's place with the account of their master's visions, Peter's readiness to offer them hospitality indicates that he has begun to learn the lesson of the animal vision: if all animals are clean, the major social barrier between Gentile and Jew has been eliminated. Peter himself states at verse 28 that he has learned this lesson.

Several elements suggest that, though he is only a "God-fear[er]" (a Gentile worshiper of YHWH, but not a full-fledged convert), Cornelius's piety has achieved a kind of temple intimacy with God. The angelic vision happens "about three o'clock" (vv. 3 and 30; literally "the ninth hour," the time of the afternoon sacrifice, in the spirit of Psalm 141:2, Judith 9:1, and Daniel 9:21). His prayers and almsgiving have reached God "as a memorial offering before God" (v. 4; and see v. 31), and he can refer to his own "non-kosher" home as "here in the presence of God" (v. 33, a phrase whose Old Testament connotation is the temple presence of God, as in Leviticus 4:4, 18, 24). Sacred space now extends to wherever people respond to the will of God.

10:34-48 Peter evangelizes Cornelius and his household

Peter's speech to the household of Cornelius is a rich résumé of Lukan theology. God shows no partiality, but whoever fears him and acts uprightly is acceptable to God (*dektos*, "acceptable," or "accepted," like a valid temple sacrifice). This principle does not address the contemporary question of religious pluralism but rather the first-century question of who is a candidate for God's messianic blessing. The reference is to persons like Cornelius and company: no matter what their ethnic identity, as long as they are receptive to God's revelation through the people Israel and do what is right, they are acceptable to God.

Peter can speak of the whole life of Jesus as God proclaiming "peace through Jesus Christ" (v. 36, alluding to Isa 52:7). When he refers to "how God *anointed* Jesus of Nazareth with . . . Spirit and power" (v. 38, emphasis added), he is rooting Jesus' title of "Christ" in the prophetic anointing for mission interpreted by Isaiah 61:1 at Luke 4:18. Fittingly for this context, he calls Jesus "Lord of *all*" and "the one appointed by God as judge of the living and the dead" (emphasis added).

The action of the Spirit is said to interrupt Peter's speech, but in fact Luke has communicated fully to his readers. The *shalom* ("peace") that God

has proclaimed to Israel through Jesus is meant for all. And God presently demonstrates that thesis by way of the endowment of the Holy Spirit upon Cornelius's receptive household. Pointedly, Luke notes that "the circumcised believers who had accompanied Peter were astounded that the *gift of the holy Spirit* should have been *poured out* on the Gentiles also, for they could hear them *speaking in tongues* and glorifying God" (v. 45, emphasis added). The language is carefully chosen to recall the Pentecostal outpouring of the holy Spirit in chapter 2 (see 2:17, 18, 33, 38). That the gift of the Spirit should precede baptism in the name of Jesus demonstrates, again, that the mission to the Gentiles is God's will. It also shows that circumcision is not required for entry into the messianic people of God.

Christian tradition will honor another person, Paul, as the Apostle to the Gentiles par excellence (indeed, Paul identifies himself that way in Galatians 2:7), but Luke has made it clear that that mission was authenticated by no less a person than the chief of the apostles, Peter. And Peter was simply responding to the initiative of God.

In the broader framework of the narrative in Acts, Peter's journey from Jewish Joppa to Roman Caesarea (10:23-24) is a miniature of the word journey from Jerusalem to Rome.

11:1-18 Peter explains God's actions to the Jerusalem authorities

As Simon Peter needed three similar visions to begin to fathom God's intentions regarding Jewish-Christian relations to the Gentiles, so Luke himself deems it necessary that this turn to the Gentiles be told three times. As in the case of Saul's conversion/call, our author first narrates the events directly (Acts 10) and then provides two interpretations of those events in subsequent speeches (chs. 11 and 15).

Since Peter's acceptance of Gentile hospitality is a violation of Jewish law, and his extension of the messianic renewal to the Gentiles was done without authorization from the Jerusalem church authorities, the apostles rightly demand an explanation. The recital of Peter's rooftop visions of the menagerie in the linen sheet, the embassy from Cornelius's house, the visit, the account of Cornelius's vision—all this is familiar enough to us who have read chapter 11. But what follows presents five fresh elements of interpretation.

First, the experience of Cornelius's household in their response in faith to the preaching of Peter is described as being "saved" (v. 14; compare with Acts 2:47). Second, Peter equates their experience of the holy Spirit with the apostles' own experience on Pentecost, pointedly referred to as "the beginning" (v. 15). Third, these endowments of the Spirit are, for the first time, described as what John the Baptist and Jesus meant by being "baptized with the holy Spirit" (v. 16; see Luke 3:16 for John's word and Acts 1:5 for Jesus'). Fourth, Peter refers to the Pentecost experience as the moment when he and the rest of the Twelve "came to believe in the Lord Jesus Christ" (v. 17); this implies that their initial discipleship during Jesus' earthly ministry had not yet constituted full Christian faith. Full Christian faith requires acceptance of Jesus as risen Lord and the gift of the holy Spirit. Finally, the Jerusalem leaders view the Cornelius episode not simply as a singular episode but as a paradigm of what God wills: "God has then granted life-giving repentance to the Gentiles too" (v. 18).

11:19-30 The Antioch mission

Although Luke has highlighted Peter's encounter with Cornelius as the paradigmatic and authoritative breakthrough, this passage makes it clear that the word has been reaching the Gentiles through other agents as well. In the wake of the persecution that followed the martyrdom of Stephen, Jerusalem messianists (Christians) brought the word to Greek-speaking Jews from Cyprus and Cyrene, and these in turn evangelized Greeks (Gentiles) up in Antioch of Syria.

As in the case of Peter and Cornelius, this outreach to Gentiles in Antioch is ratified by Jerusalem authorization: the elders send Barnabas, who in turn enlists the help of Saul of Tarsus. When Luke says Barnabas "encouraged" the people to remain faithful (v. 23), he may be hinting at the meaning of his nickname (Barnabas = "son of consolation"), which he said the apostles applied to this Levite from Cyprus (see 4:36).

In Paul's letter to the Galatians, he refers to himself as "entrusted with the gospel to the uncircumcised, just as Peter to the circumcised" (Gal 2:7). If this seems to be at odds with Luke's portrayal of Peter's evangelization of the household of Cornelius, it should be noted that Paul nowhere claims to be the *first* missioner to the Gentiles. And Luke does give us significant episodes about

Peter's evangelizing the circumcised (Acts 2–5; 9:32-43). Nor do we hear of Peter spending much more time among the uncircumcised.

Having described the developments of a mixed (Jewish-Gentile) church in Antioch, which is emerging as an entity distinct enough to warrant a special name, *hoi Christianoi* ("Christians," the first use of the name), Luke illustrates their solidarity with the Jewish-Christian brothers and sisters in Judea. Responding to Agabus's prophecy about imminent widespread famine, the Antiochenes send relief to the Jerusalem elders.

12:1-25 Great reversals: Peter's escape and Herod's death

This book called the Acts of the Apostles turns out to be mainly about the acts of *two* apostles, Peter and Paul. Up to this point, Peter has dominated the stage. In the present chapter, Luke rounds off the story of Peter before taking up in earnest the missions of Paul.

Using as his centerpiece a favorite genre of Hellenistic entertainment, the "great escape" story, Luke vividly illustrates divine power at work through accounts of vivid reversals and transitions.

First there is the transition from James to James. The third of four Herods mentioned in Luke-Acts, Herod Agrippa I, the grandson of Herod the Great, has James of Zebedee, one of the Twelve, killed by the sword. No motive is given. Before the chapter closes (v. 17), it is clear that the key Jerusalem leader is not one of the Twelve but another James, the brother of the Lord. To underscore the fact that the followers of Jesus relive his story (recall especially the martyrdom of Stephen in chapters 6 and 7), Luke notes that this persecution by Herod occurs during Passover time.

Divine power and justice are displayed in the dramatic reversal experienced by Herod. The chapter begins with the king's arrogant and violent exercise of power in arbitrary persecution, execution, and arrest; it ends with Herod's being hailed as a god, only to suffer an ignominious death. Notice that this idolatry occurs in the secular capital, Caesarea (Maritima), and the idolaters are a pagan embassy from Tyre and Sidon. This is one of a series of examples in Acts showing how Gentiles can be idolatrous in their theism. And Tyre was famous for its propensity to treat a man as a god (see Ezek 28).

Another subtle transition that Luke signals here is the growing division between the minority group called "the church" (vv. 1 and 5) and the Jewish majority. At the end of his Gospel and the beginning of Acts, Luke was careful to stress that the first Christians were, and remained, practicing Jews. Then, describing the plot of the Jewish community in Damascus against Paul, Luke could state simply, "the Jews conspired to kill him" (9:23). Now here in chapter 12 Luke can refer to Agrippa's persecution of the church as "pleasing to the Jews" (v. 3), and Peter can speak of his rescue "from the hand of Herod and from all that the Jewish people had been expecting" (v. 11). While Jews will continue to join the growing church, the hostility between this minority and the majority begins to deepen.

These transitions and reversals frame the marvelous escape of Peter. Luke's interest in paralleling God's work in the mission of Jesus and the church with the divine liberating action of the Exodus continues here. As in Exodus (3:2; 4:24 LXX; 14:19; 23:20, 23; 32:34), an angel of the Lord is instrumental in leading the action (vv. 7-11, 15, 23). The biblical word for smiting (*patassō*) is used playfully here to point up the contrast between the gentle smiting that the angel uses to awaken Peter (v. 7) and the fatal smiting of Herod at the end (v. 23), reminiscent of the smiting of Sennacherib's troops by the angel of the Lord in 2 Kings 19. As in the story of God's dealings with Israel in the Hebrew Bible (Old Testament), the same divine power continues to bring both liberation and reprisal. Luke's dwelling with such zest on these events fits well the spirit of a book whose final word, describing Paul's unstoppable preaching while under house arrest, is *akōlytōs* ("unhindered").

The return of Barnabas and Saul to Antioch after completing their "relief mission" (*diakonia*) to the poor of Jerusalem (v. 25) completes the excursion begun at 11:30. This is likely the visit to which Paul refers in Galatians 2:1-10, when "the pillars" (James, Cephas, and John) urged Paul to continue being "mindful of the poor."

Acts 13:1-3 From five leaders, two missioners: the sending of Barnabas and Saul

Having rounded off the story of Peter's leadership of the early church, Luke now picks up the story of Paul, which will dominate the remainder of the book. Indeed, this second half of the history

could well be called "The Acts of Paul." An illustrious quintet of church prophets and teachers—including one Simeon called *the black* (Niger), an African (Lucius from Cyrene), and a childhood companion of Herod Antipas—are pictured here fasting and praying. Barnabas and Saul are chosen by the holy Spirit (in prophecy, presumably) and sent off to do what the Spirit calls "the work." The work, of course, is what the quotation from Habakkuk at verse 41 calls what God is doing and something that the scoffers will never believe.

13:4-13 Barnabas, Saul, and John Mark evangelize Cyprus

This first outreach of the person that Christian tradition will call "the Apostle to the Gentiles" is a reprise of elements that characterized the first outreach of Philip to the Samaritans and then that of Peter to the Gentile household of Cornelius. As Philip met, in the person of Simon Magus, the power of evil present in the pagan world of magic and overcame that power with the Spirit of God, here the three Antiochene missioners encounter that same dark power in the person of a magician who happens to be an apostate Jew, Elymas bar-Jesus. Note that the Apostle, first introduced with his Jewish name, Saul, at the stoning of Stephen (Acts 7:58), is now called by his Latin name, Paul (v. 9; possibly a nickname, since *paulus* means "little"), probably because his mission will mainly address Gentiles from now on.

Paul taunts the magician, accusing him of reversing the plan of God, "twisting the straight paths of [the] Lord" (compare Luke 3:5, quoting Isaiah 40:3-5, "winding roads shall be made straight"). And Elymas's punishment of blindness parallels Paul's temporary fate when he was stopped in his tracks bent on resisting the plan of God in the community of the Way in Damascus (see Acts 9:6-11, where Paul, temporarily blinded, is sent to Straight Street!). Luke says that they evangelize the island from stem to stern (from Salamis in the east to Paphos in the west), but he details only the conversion of the island's governor, Sergius Paulus, Paul's first Gentile disciple. Sergius is for Paul what Cornelius was for Peter.

13:14-52 Paul preaches in a synagogue in Pisidian Antioch

Although the name Galatia does not appear during this first missionary journey, Paul and

Barnabas's ministry in Antioch of Pisidia (to be distinguished from Antioch of Syria, some three hundred miles to the east), and then in Iconium, Lystra, and Derbe, takes them into the southern part of that Roman province. Since we have no evidence that Paul evangelized farther north in Galatia, these are likely the "churches of Galatia" that Paul addressed in his famous letter by that name (Gal 1:2 and see 1 Cor 16:1).

As Peter began his post-Easter apostolic career with a speech proclaiming the life, death, and resurrection of Jesus in the light of the Hebrew Scriptures (Acts 2), Paul now does the same. Like Peter, Paul first addresses his message to his fellow Jews and to Gentile "God fear[ers]." As in the case of Peter's Pentecost speech, we can detect the hand of historian Luke employing the *pesher* technique, that is, using ancient texts to interpret recent events in the life of the community in the light of Easter faith.

The scene is reminiscent of Jesus' speech in the synagogue at Nazareth (Luke 4:14-30). The local Jewish community is gathered for readings from Scripture followed by interpretive preaching. In broad strokes Paul rehearses the familiar highlights of God's special relationship with Israel: the exodus from Egypt, the desert period, the conquest, and the kingship (Saul and David). Then he "fast forwards" to the coming of Jesus as savior of Israel, heralded by John. The phrase "according to his promise" (v. 23), in this context referring to Jesus as descendant of David, seems to have Nathan's prophecy to David especially in view (2 Sam 7:12-14).

The second half of the speech, concerning the death and resurrection of Jesus and the mission of the church, draws even more heavily on biblical references to interpret the Christian experience.

As we have come to expect from Luke, blame for the death of Jesus is assigned to both Jewish and Roman leaders. Yet the death is interpreted as the fulfillment of "the oracles of the prophets" and "all that was written about him" (vv. 27, 29). Earlier parts of Luke-Acts have taught us some of the Scripture passages to which such statements refer—for example, Isaiah 53:7-8 (Acts 8:32-33); Psalm 31:6 (Luke 23:46); and the stories of Joseph and Moses in the Torah exemplifying the pattern of the rejected leader who becomes a savior (Acts 7:9-38).

When it comes to the resurrection, the Old Testament references become more abundant and explicit. Reference to "raising up" the son of David (v. 33), also to be known as Son of God, gives new meaning to 2 Samuel 7:12-14 ("I will raise up your heir after you. . . . I will be a father to him, and he shall be a son to me"). The quotation of Psalm 2:7 in verse 33 ("You are my son; this day I have begotten you") interprets the resurrection as a moment of accession to the throne as king of Israel. Thus the same verse that we first heard at the scene by the Jordan ("You are my beloved Son," Luke 3:22), referring there to divine sonship and introducing a genealogy extending back to "Adam, son of God," here takes on a further dimension—the messianic one.

The quotation of Isaiah 55:3 ("I shall give you the benefits assured to David") becomes even more meaningful when we discover that the immediate context of that verse in Isaiah includes reference to an everlasting covenant (v. 2) and a mission to the Gentiles (v. 4). As in Luke 24:46-47, all three realities—the death and resurrection of the Messiah and the mission of the church—are grounded in Scripture. The use of Psalm 16:7 ("You will not suffer your holy one to see corruption"), fulfilled not in David but in the resurrection of Jesus, echoes the interpretation that Peter made at the heart of his Pentecost speech (Acts 2:25-31).

The language about justification through faith in verses 38-39 shows Paul using language that is characteristic of his letters, especially Romans and Galatians.

Although this speech gets a positive response and "many" in that synagogue congregation follow Paul and Barnabas, when "almost the whole city" (v. 44) turns out, no doubt including a majority of Gentiles, the (unpersuaded) Jews begin to contradict Paul. This prompts a final invocation of Scripture, announcing both continuity and novelty. The passage from Isaiah that Simeon alluded to in his canticle at the presentation of Jesus in the temple (Luke 2:29-32) Paul quotes in full (v. 47): "I have made you a light to the Gentiles, that you may be an instrument of salvation to the ends of the earth" (Isa 49:6b). What Simeon applied to Jesus, Paul now applies to himself and Barnabas as exponents of the Christian mission. Indeed, Paul had just declared, ". . . through him [Jesus] forgiveness of sins is being proclaimed to you"

(v. 38). That is, the risen Lord Jesus is now working through the likes of Paul and Barnabas. The novelty is that Jewish rejection of the good news triggers a turn to the Gentiles (v. 46).

With painful irony Luke shows that what was originally understood as the Jewish mission to be a "light to the Gentiles" now leaves many Jews behind. That Paul and Barnabas can later return to Pisidian Antioch to strengthen the disciples there and appoint elders (14:21-23) indicates that they left behind a community of believers (presumably composed of the Jews and converted Gentiles mentioned in 13:43) when they first left this town.

Does the strong language of Paul in verses 46-47 mean that God has abandoned the chosen people because of their unbelief? That interpretation has been the first step of Christian anti-Semitism. Luke's point is rather that which is reflected in Paul's own letters: the gospel is meant for Jews first, then Gentiles (see Rom 1:16; 9:24; 10:12). Another purpose is to present a paradigm of early Christian mission experience: the message will be accepted by some Jews and Gentiles and rejected by others, but God will use this rejection as an occasion for the advance of the mission (which is also Paul's interpretation in Romans 11). Paul will continue to address Jews first as his mode of operating, for example, in Iconium (14:1), Thessalonica (17:1), Beroea (17:10), Athens (17:17), Corinth (18:4), and Ephesus (18:19).

In shaking the dust off their feet (v. 51), Paul and Barnabas act on the advice Jesus gave to the Twelve (Luke 9:5) and the Seventy-two (Luke 10:10-11). And the rejoicing of the disciples in the midst of rejection and persecution acts out the fourth Beatitude of the Sermon on the Plain (Luke 6:23).

14:1-28 Paul and Barnabas, from Antioch to Antioch

Before zooming in on the marvelous details of the healing of the lame man at Lystra, Luke sketches the experiences of Paul and Barnabas in Iconium to highlight what is characteristic of their mission. (Uniquely in Acts, they are called "apostles," at verse 4 and again at verse 14, probably more to acknowledge their being on a mission [13:2] than to indicate special status.) Here they draw a positive response from "a great number of Jews and Greeks [Gentiles]." As in the work

of the Twelve in Jerusalem, the Lord confirms the word through signs and wonders. As in Pisidian Antioch, the response of the larger population is divided and evokes persecution from Gentiles and Jews alike.

When we come to the dramatic events at Lystra, there can be no doubt that Luke has chosen to foreground this healing by highlighting parallels with the healing done through Peter and John in Acts 3. As in the case of that first major healing in the life of the Jerusalem church, here we have a healing of a man born lame sitting outside a temple, done with a verbal command, and resulting not only in standing and walking but even in leaping. Both healings are interpreted as a sign of the salvation that comes through faith (3:16; 14:9). Thus the first Gentile healing matches the first Jewish healing. The work of the second great leader (Paul) is inaugurated by a healing that parallels the dramatic healing of the first great leader of the Church (Peter). And the responses are similar. As Peter and John had to deflect the adulation of the crowd in the Jerusalem Temple, so Paul and Barnabas, taken by the pagans for Zeus and Hermes, are compelled to dodge the blasphemy of having sacrifice offered to them!

The brief speech attributed to both Barnabas and Paul invokes a strategy of evangelization that has typified missionary work at its best. Instead of moving directly to the fulfillment of messianic expectations (nonexistent for the pagans of Lystra), the apostles proclaim the "living God," the creator revealed in the good gifts of nature that they celebrate in their own sacrifices—the rains and the fruitful seasons. This acknowledgment of God as creator and sustainer of all life is, of course, at the heart of Jewish monotheism; now Christianity makes it a necessary foundation of its proclamation of the gospel. Appreciation of Jesus requires knowledge and acceptance of God the creator.

The would-be stoners from Iconium, joined by adversaries from Pisidian Antioch, finally catch up with the apostles in Lystra (v. 19) and manage to carry out their intentions on Paul, leaving him for dead. Supported by the disciples, he is able to return to town and to continue his mission the next day. It is a sign of their courage that they are able to act in the spirit of the motto expressed in verse 22 and circle back through the very towns from which their persecutors came. In Lystra,

Iconium, and Antioch they find Christian communities large and stable enough to require the appointment of elders (presbyters) for their governance. Luke has no trouble portraying a church that is at once charismatic and prophetic, and, at the same time, requiring the structure of appointed officers (recall the conjunction of teachers and prophets among the five named at 13:1 and the appointment of *diakonoi* in chapter 6; and see the discussion of 20:17 and 28 regarding *episcopoi, presbyteroi,* and *diakonoi*).

We sense a kind of symmetry in the narrative as the apostles return to the community that commissioned them in Syrian Antioch. This first mission commenced at the beginning of chapter 13 with mention of offices (prophets and teachers), prayer and fasting, and designation of chosen persons for "the work" with a laying on of hands and a send-off. Now that mission comes to a close with mention of officers (elders) appointed and commissioned with prayer and fasting and a reference to "the work" Paul and Barnabas have now accomplished (14:22-26). Luke has been careful to show that this first mission was not so much what Paul and Barnabas had done but "what God had done with them and how he had opened the door of faith to the Gentiles" (v. 27).

15:1-35 The "Council" of Jerusalem. The early church resolves its first big crisis: must Gentile converts become Jews?

This account of the early church responding to and resolving its first major crisis displays at its best Luke's genius as a historian. If you have ever been a part of a leadership committee, recall a time when that group met to resolve a major policy issue. No doubt that process entailed more than one meeting, and those meetings took hours before all sides of the issue were voiced. Full resolution and implementation likely required more hours of meeting, debate, and work.

By analogy with that contemporary experience, consider what the fledgling church was facing at this point and how Luke describes its response. Becoming disciples of Jesus as the Christ had been largely a Jewish matter. It was natural, then, for the Jewish Christians to expect Gentile converts to do what Gentile converts had always done, namely, undergo circumcision (for males) and keep the full 613 laws of Moses. Obvi-

ously, those who had specialized in teaching and living the Torah, like the converts who belonged to the party of the Pharisees, would be inclined to see it this way. Others, however, such as Paul and Barnabas, who were more broadly experienced in what God had been doing among the Gentiles, were convinced that a Gentile should not have to become a Jew to become a Christian.

Remarkably, Luke manages to present the resolution of this crisis in a passage that takes only five minutes to read! In thirty-five verses, our author cuts to the essence of the matter and, in the telling of it, provides a paradigm of ecclesial decision-making that has subsequently characterized the church at its best.

Verses 1-2 present the "state of the question": visitors from the Jerusalem headquarters challenge the lenient practice of the Antioch community (not requiring circumcision of male Gentile converts), and Paul and Barnabas promptly oppose the Jerusalem people. (Although Luke does not mention Peter at this point, this confrontation could well be the altercation that Paul himself describes, for another purpose than Luke's, in Galatians 2:11-14. This is one way of reconciling the accounts of Acts 15 and Galatians 2.)

Recognizing that this is an issue that needs to be resolved at a higher level, the local church sends Paul, Barnabas, and some other representatives to Jerusalem. Their trip up to Jerusalem ("up" because topographically one always goes *up* to Jerusalem even when the trip is a north-south journey) is punctuated by their regaling the disciples with stories of the conversion of the Gentiles. Though the Antiochene party is graciously received, the Pharisee Christians firmly restate their position: Gentile converts must get circumcised and observe the Mosaic Law.

Since the Antioch delegation is meeting with "the apostles and presbyters [elders]," this is not a plenary session of the whole church but a leadership meeting. As any recorder of minutes will recognize, the phrase "after much debate had taken place" saves Luke an enormous amount of ink and parchment. Then Luke has Peter get up and retell what we who have read Acts 10 and 11 recognize as the story of Cornelius and his household. This time the words of Peter highlight new dimensions of that experience. He says that God purified their hearts by faith, alluding to Ezekiel 36:25-26. He argues that God's endowment of the holy Spirit upon those Gentiles shows that salvation comes by "the grace of the Lord Jesus" (v. 11). The argument against the Jerusalem policy is clinched with Paul and Barnabas describing the "signs and wonders God had worked among the Gentiles through them," which we readers recognize as a reference to the events narrated in Acts 13–14.

The clincher comes, surprisingly, from the mouth of James, the leader of the Jerusalem church, that is, the one we would most expect to support the "conservative" policy of circumcising Gentile converts. His argument turns out to be a *pesher*, that is, an application of Scripture to current events, such as we have met in the speeches of Peter and the one of Paul in Pisidian Antioch. James finds confirmation of the position represented by Paul and Barnabas in the Greek version of Amos 9:11-12.

As in the case of the other *peshers*, the interpretation here requires the Greek version (Septuagint) of the prophet. This part of Amos 9 is about the restoration of Israel. But where the Hebrew text has *edom* (Edom), the Septuagint translator has read *'adam* (humanity), so that a statement about the conquest of a remnant of Edom becomes one about "the rest of humanity" seeking the Lord. How does James (or Luke) find in this passage from the Greek Bible an affirmation of an unhindered mission to the Gentiles? It reflects the same two-stage mission that the early community found in Isaiah 49:5-6, namely, (1) restoration of the tribes of Israel ("the fallen hut of David") and (2) the reception of the Gentiles ("the rest of humanity").

James's solution is to acknowledge that the mission to the Gentiles is God's will but also to maintain some continuity with the past by insisting that they should require from Gentile converts what Israel had always required of resident aliens, as spelled out in Leviticus 17–18. As a sign that they are joining a community with Israelite roots, Gentile converts should follow the usual rules for resident aliens and "abstain from meat sacrificed to idols, from blood, from meats of strangled animals, and from unlawful marriage" (v. 29). (Alternatively, a convincing case can also be made that the issue here was not so much menu as venue, that the four items of the apostolic decree referred simply to the behavior involved in participating in pagan temple feasts, and that Gentile believers were hereby warned to make a clean break from such places.)

Notice that Luke's crisp account of what must have been a more extended process provides a paradigm for problem solving and decision-making in the church. It comes down to three movements:

1. Conduct a full hearing of the community's experience of what they understand God to be doing among them (here, the accounts of Peter, Paul, and Barnabas).

2. Try to understand that experience against the faith-community's tradition as currently understood (here, James's citation of Greek Amos 9).

3. Make a practical policy decision that affirms the values evoked in steps 1 and 2 (here, the decision to free Gentile converts from unnecessary obligations, but requiring them at least to keep the Levitical rules for resident aliens—or, on the alternative interpretation, to cease frequenting pagan temple feasts).

This very human problem-solving process is something that the community can boldly describe with the words "It is the decision of the holy Spirit and of us . . ." (v. 28).

THE MISSION OF PAUL TO THE ENDS OF THE EARTH
Acts 15:36–28:31

The travels described in Acts 16–20 cover two more distinct journeys, the second and third missionary journeys of Paul (and companions). And each journey has a distinct geographical center of gravity: as the first addressed communities in southern Galatia, the second concentrates on major cities in Macedonia and Achaia, and the third centers in, and radiates from, the great Ephesus.

Like the first journey described in chapters 13–14, the second and third also begin and return to Syrian Antioch and include one major speech by Paul—the only address to a Gentile audience (in Athens, 17:22-31) and the farewell address at Miletus to the Ephesian elders (20:18-35). Yet because these two journeys are separated by what is only a brief return to Syrian Antioch (18:22), it may be helpful (and even more faithful to Luke's narrative) to think of the activities recounted in these five chapters as the Aegean mission. Together, these travels form a whole, moving from what Paul himself refers to as "the beginning of the gospel" at Philippi (Phil 4:15) to Paul's "last will and testament" addressed to the Ephesian elders at Miletus (Act 20:17-38). The remainder of the book (Acts 21–28) is a distinct segment devoted to journeys related to Paul's Jewish and Roman imprisonment and "trials" (really hearings) in Jerusalem and Caesarea Maritima, and finally house arrest in Rome.

15:36-41 Paul and Barnabas separate

Luke's delicate treatment of the interplay between the human intentions and divine will continues to unfold dramatically. What will eventually become Paul's greatest missionary expansion begins simply with the intention of revisiting and strengthening the churches he had founded in the first mission (Acts 13–14). That God can work with the results of human frailty is implied in Luke's notice that Paul and Barnabas had a "disagreement" (whose depth is suggested by the Greek word here, *paroxysmos*, v. 38, from which the English "paroxysm" derives) about whether Mark, who had deserted the previous mission at Pamphylia, should be allowed to accompany them. Thus the breakup of the first team leads to the formation of a powerful new team—Paul and Silas. First introduced in verses 22-32 as a leader in the Jerusalem community and a prophet, Silas is usually taken to be the same person as the Silvanus mentioned in the New Testament epistles.

16:1-5 Timothy joins Paul and Silas

This brief passage shows Paul's nuanced approach to Jewish/Gentile relations in the Christian mission. Even as he continues to promulgate the apostolic decree of the Council of Jerusalem (15:23-29), which frees Gentile converts from having to become Jews, he can still insist that Timothy undergo adult circumcision. Apparently Timothy was raised Jewish by his mother (named Eunice, we learn in 2 Timothy 1:5) but had never been circumcised (prevented by his Greek father?). That Paul convinced him to get circumcised, even though he was now a Christian, suggests that Paul still considered mission to Jews important enough to take this surprising step to make Timothy more acceptable to his fellow Jews.

16:6-10 The call to Macedonia

The movement of this team of three into fresh mission territory presents again the delicate interface of the divine and human in their decision-

making. As they move westward, they are prevented from moving south by the holy Spirit and from moving north by "the Spirit of Jesus." When Paul receives a dream vision of a Macedonian calling for help, that call still requires ratification by human decision (v. 10).

A note on the "we" passages

The introduction of the first person plural ("we") in verse 10 signals the first of the famous four "we" sections in Acts (16:10-17; 20:5-15; 21:1-18; 27:1–28:16). To account for this phenomenon, commentators have noted that the first person plural was sometimes used in ancient travel narratives as a literary device to evoke immediacy. However, this does not appear to be the case with Acts, a work of history. The abruptness of the shifts from third-person narrative to first-person (and back again) is more easily accounted for as deriving from the actual involvement of the author (or his sources). Moreover, ancient historians were eager to indicate their presence at the events they described when they had grounds to make such a claim. We have no evidence of their making such claims groundlessly.

16:11-15 The conversion of Lydia and her household

Seeking a Jewish house of prayer, Paul, Silas, Timothy (and Luke, if we understand "we" historically) encounter a group of women gathered by the riverside. With marvelous economy of words, Luke describes one Lydia. She is a businesswoman, a dealer in the luxury item of purple cloth, a God fearer, and wealthy enough to be mistress of a household. Such is her openness and response to Paul's sharing of the word that Luke describes it in language reminiscent of the conversion of the Emmaus pair in Luke 24:31-32: "The Lord opened her heart." Conversion and baptism lead immediately to generous hospitality. Since the missioners later return to "Lydia's house" (v. 40) after their release from prison, she may well have emerged as the leader of the first house church of Philippi (and thus the first in what will later be known as Europe).

16:16-40 Further adventures in Philippi: deliverance, imprisonment, and further deliverance

On his way to the house of prayer, Paul encounters some unsolicited and annoying advertising. A slave girl with a mantic spirit goes around shouting what is in fact the truth: "These people are slaves of the Most High God, who proclaim to you a way of salvation" (v. 17). Though true enough in a Christian context, the ambiguous language would have been heard by pagans as announcing Paul and Silas as promoting a new cure in the name of the god that they promote as the top god of the pagan pantheon. When Paul puts a stop to this with a command in the name of Jesus and the woman is delivered of the oracular spirit, her exploiters, distressed by the loss of business, bring the missioners before the Roman magistrates. The charge: illegal (anti-imperial) proselytizing.

The twosome are stripped, beaten, and imprisoned. During the night an earthquake opens the jail doors and unchains the prisoners. When the jailer finds the missioners freed but still present, he responds to these portents by falling on his knees and asking, "What must I do to be saved?" And they say, "Believe in the Lord Jesus and you and your household will be saved." As in the case of Lydia, openness leads to conversion of a household, hospitality, and baptism.

When the Roman authorities realize their mistake and try to dismiss Paul and friends discreetly, Paul confronts the police. He and his men are Roman citizens, and he insists that their beating and imprisonment without trial are a miscarriage of justice that ought to be reversed, not secretly but officially. This elicits a sheepish apology from the magistrates, who come to apologize and to ask them to leave town. This they do, but not without stopping at Lydia's place to encourage the budding Philippian community.

17:1-15 From Thessalonica to Beroea, with mixed reviews

Although Luke treats Paul's mission in Thessalonica (some hundred miles west of Philippi) as a brief, three-week encounter, the community he founded there was significant enough to receive the earliest letter we have from the Apostle's hand, 1 Thessalonians.

The events here are described in language that resonates with the Third Gospel. When Luke notes that Paul joined the local synagogue community according to "his usual custom," he could be referring to Paul's usual missionary strategy. He could as well mean that Paul attended syna-

gogue as his Jewish practice, much as Jesus attended the Nazareth synagogue "according to his custom" (Luke 4:16). His teaching in that house of prayer and study is summarized in words that reflect the message of Jesus to the disciples on Easter Sunday ("The Messiah had to suffer and rise from the dead," v. 3; see Luke 24:26, 46-47). And when those in the Jewish community who find Paul's message a threat drag to the magistrates some of the small Christian community growing in Jason's place, their accusations echo those leveled against Jesus: "They all act in opposition to the decrees of Caesar and claim instead that there is another king, Jesus" (v. 7; see Luke 23:2).

Some sixty miles to the southwest, Paul and Silas find a much more receptive synagogue in Beroea, where people engage the missioners in biblical study, not just on the Sabbath but "daily" (v. 11). But the zealous Thessalonian adversaries soon arrive to stir up the crowds against them, much as the pre-Christian Paul (Saul) traveled distances to block the spread of what he had determined was a dangerous Jewish heresy, "the Way" (Acts 9:2).

17:16-34 Paul in Athens

In this episode Luke presents Paul giving the only fully developed speech to a Gentile audience. He describes that audience with care when he highlights the Stoics and Epicureans in verse 18 (both named only here in the New Testament). The mere mention of the names evokes stereotyped philosophical positions regarding humanity, nature, and the gods. Stoics perceived reality as a unified, organic cosmos in which the divinity inhered pantheistically as a kind of "law." Humanity was part of that cosmos and found happiness by harmonizing with that essentially benevolent law of the cosmos.

Epicureans, on the other hand, had a more mechanistic notion of the world, in which the divine was conceived in a "deistic" way at best (the divinity causing the cosmos but remaining uninvolved with it). Epicureans expected mere dissolution after death and, meanwhile, sought happiness by prudently doing what was most sensibly pleasant. It makes sense, then, for Luke to describe the crowd reactions as divided. On the one hand, there were those who heckled Paul, dismissing him as a "seed-pecker," a reaction that fits the Epicureans, who would have found Paul's teaching radically incompatible with their own. On the other hand, there were those who were initially confused (thinking Paul to be speaking of new gods, *Iēsous* and *Anastasis* ["Resurrection," mis-heard as the name of the divine consort of *Iēsous*?]) yet remained open to the preacher and wanted to hear more. And this reaction fits the Stoics, who would have found some tantalizing convergences with their worldview and lifestyle and would have been drawn to further inquiry.

The notion that the deity is not captured in sanctuaries and does not need human worship (see 7:48) would have been congenial to Stoics and Epicureans alike. But against Stoic pantheism, Paul asserts the biblical notion of a transcendent creator who *made* everything and, moreover, sustains everything. Paul reminds them of the common origin of the human family ("made from one"—compatible with the biblical account of origin from Adam and also the fresh beginning with Noah). Echoing his brief proclamation to the Lycaonians at Lystra, Paul remodels LXX Isaiah 42:5 and calls them to contemplate the earth with its seasons as a habitat for humanity and a revelation of the Creator's care.

Where he might have cited Scripture for a synagogue audience, here Paul enlists instead an ancient Stoic poet from his region, Aratus ("for we too are his offspring"), and he also quotes a sixth-century B.C. author, Epimenides of Knossos: "In him we live and move and have our being." Thus Luke appropriates Hellenistic language to assert against Stoic pantheism what we might call a biblical pan*en*theism. Against the Stoic notion of endless cycles of cosmic rebirth and death, he announces the biblical doomsday. Against the coldness of Epicurean "deism," he asserts the biblical notion of God's intimate involvement with creatures. If Luke has said in verse 24 that human handicraft cannot *house* God, in verse 29 he argues that human skill and wit cannot *image* the divinity. The unexpressed element of the argument is the biblical idea that the only adequate image of the living God is living human beings, who are images of the King of the universe insofar as they are stewards of the earth.

If Jesus is going to be the ultimate judge of the human family, it would follow that the criteria are what we have heard him teach in the Third Gospel, especially in the Sermon on the Plain (Luke 6:20-49).

Commentators have noted that Paul is portrayed using this philosophical "natural theology" approach just this once in Acts. And in his first letter to the Corinthians, he makes a point of not coming to them with the wisdom of philosophers but simply with the "foolishness" of a crucified Messiah. Was the approach of Paul in Athens simply a failed strategy, never to be repeated? It would seem, rather, that the church has seen in this episode a model of how Jerusalem can speak to Athens. Thomas Aquinas, for example, used the philosophical categories of a rediscovered Aristotle to speak to his European culture. And theology has always been an effort to recast the givens of revelation in the language of one's own time and place. One can even see in this brief masterpiece hints of the basis for the interreligious dialogue that challenges us today.

18:1-17 Paul in Corinth

Because the New Testament contains two of the letters that Paul later wrote to the Christian community in Corinth, we know more about this community than any of the other churches that Paul founded. The correspondence that we call 1 and 2 Corinthians gives us a privileged window on the texture and tensions of this vibrant community in the middle fifties of the first century. In the first half of Acts 18, Luke, apparently working from sources other than Paul's letters, sketches the beginnings of that fascinating church. Some of the strokes of that sketch provide precious contact with historical data; other strokes limn Luke's inspired interpretation of those events, showing what God is doing through human failures and successes in that busy crossroads of the ancient world.

Acts 18 offers two important links with secular history. The Roman historian Suetonius tells us that the emperor Claudius expelled members of the Jewish community of Rome because of an "uproar" caused by one "Chrestus" in A.D. 49. Scholars have taken that to be a garbled reference to *Christos*. It would seem to refer to a stir caused by Jewish Christians from Jerusalem preaching Jesus as the Messiah. Priscilla and Aquila, then, seem to be part of that group expelled from Rome. They are "Jews for Jesus" who host Christian meetings at their house (1 Cor 16:19), as they will later do in Rome, when Nero allows Jews to return five years later (see Rom 16:5). This enterprising couple takes in as houseguest Paul, their fellow tentmaker and messianic missioner. An inscription found at Delphi dates the proconsul of Achaia, Gallio, to A.D. 51–52, thus providing another link to secular history.

But it is sacred history that most interests Luke. He shows that the whim of an emperor and the adjudication of a proconsul can play into the divine project. Aquila and Prisca (Priscilla) become two of Paul's principal coworkers, and their hospitality enables the Apostle to settle into what was (next to his twenty-seven-month stay in Ephesus; see 19:10) his second most extended sojourn in a single town, lasting some eighteen months.

Paul's extended sessions at the local Jewish house of study, with Gentile God-fearers as well as Jews in attendance, issue in the usual mixed results. Most Jews reject the novelty of a crucified craftsman proclaimed as the Messiah and "the Lord." But there are notable exceptions: Crispus, the synagogue leader, and one Titus Justus, the God-fearer who owned the house next door to the synagogue. Paul's work is affirmed by a night vision of Jesus assuring him in language that recalls the divine promise of support to the prophets Isaiah and Jeremiah ("I am with you").

Tellingly, the mixed Christian community is called the Lord's "people" (*laos*, the biblical word for the people of the covenant; source of our word "laity"). When Paul's Jewish adversaries bring him before the bench of the proconsul Gallio, he unwittingly affirms that "covenantal peoplehood" of the Christians by dismissing their charges against Paul as a matter of Jewish doctrine, titles, and law (v. 15).

18:18-28 Further mission notes and the integration of Apollos

Luke's intent in the remainder of chapter 18 seems mainly to give a summary of activity occurring between Paul's work in Corinth and his work in another major urban center, Ephesus (to be treated in Acts 19). The résumé highlights features that are key to Luke's interpretation. (1) Paul continues to operate as a Jew (see the reference to the Nazirite haircut, v. 18; for background, see Num 6:1-21). (2) He continues his mission to fellow Jews (he dialogues with the Ephesian synagogue congregation). (3) He stays in touch with church officials at the Jerusalem headquarters (v. 22). (4) The Christian mission continues in an

orderly way. For example, Paul revisits and affirms communities established in Phrygia and Galatia. And when Apollos, a skilled rhetorician from the Hellenistic Christian/Jewish community of Alexandria, arrives in Ephesus and begins to preach the "Way of the Lord" with enthusiasm, but incompletely, Paul's co-workers, Priscilla and Aquila, explain the Way to him more fully. Apollos's move from Ephesus to Achaia is done with the recommendation of the Ephesian Christians.

(The power of Apollos's ministry was such that some of those he trains will form a kind of "I had the great Apollos as my personal trainer" faction, and Paul will have to address this issue in 1 Corinthians 1–3. See especially 1 Corinthians 3:6: "I planted, Apollos watered, but *God* caused the growth," emphasis added).

19:1-40 Paul in Ephesus: the Way of the Lord Jesus versus magic and idolatry; evangelizing from the Asian capital (19:1-12)

Paul's encounter with twelve Ephesian "disciples" who had not received the holy Spirit provides an instructive parallel with the previous episode—Priscilla and Aquila's instruction of Apollos. Both involve the instruction of disciples who are somehow incomplete. Apollos's incompleteness was subtle: although he had been instructed in the Way of the Lord (vv. 25-26; see 9:2; 14:16; 16:17) and taught accurately about Jesus and was ardent in spirit, he knew only the baptism of John, was not described as filled with the Spirit, and needed to be taught *more* accurately about the Way. Similarly, these twelve Ephesians, who seem to have missed the training of Aquila, Priscilla, and the reformed Apollos, also knew only John's baptism and had not even heard that there was a holy Spirit.

As in the case of the conversion of Cornelius's household (10:44-46), a "mini-Pentecost" follows. These two descriptions of "regularizing" disciples tell us two interesting things about the emergent church: (a) that the influence of John the Baptist was more powerful than we usually give him credit for, and (b) unity of belief and practice within the church had been a struggle from the beginning.

The summary description in verses 8-12 portrays the shape of the next twenty-seven months of Paul's evangelization. Despite past rejections, his serious effort to bring the Good News to his fellow Jews first continues with a three-month colloquium in the Ephesian synagogue. That this effort was not entirely without success is hinted at in the reference to the *disciples* whom Paul took with him after a nasty confrontation compelled him to change his venue to the hall of Tyrannus.

During the next two years Ephesus becomes a mission center from which the whole province of Asia is evangelized, "Jews and Greeks alike." The description of healings occasioned even by cloth or aprons touched to Paul's skin demonstrates that the healing ministry begun in Jesus (Luke 8:44-47, the woman with the flow of blood) and continued through Peter (Acts 5:15-16) persists in the Apostle to the Gentiles. See Paul's own reference to his work as "what Christ has accomplished through me to lead the Gentiles to obedience by word and deed, by the power of signs and wonders . . ." (Rom 15:18-19; see also 2 Cor 12:12).

19:13-20 The power of Jesus' name versus demons and magic

The power of the risen Lord Jesus over the competing powers of this world is now illustrated by two vivid and entertaining anecdotes regarding demons, magic, and idolatry.

When the seven sons of the high priest Sceva attempt to deliver a man from demonic oppression by using Jesus' name in a magical way, they themselves are rebuked, overpowered, and sent packing, naked and wounded. The spiritual power of the name of the Lord Jesus, properly used, is dramatized by the immense commercial value of books burned by those converted from their magical practices (v. 19).

19:21-40 A confused assembly confronted

The Way of the Lord Jesus continues to have practical consequences. The silversmiths of Ephesus riot when their livelihood (selling silver models of the world-famous temple of the goddess Artemis) appears to be threatened by the Christian preaching against idolatry. (Archaeology helps us to picture the structures involved here. One of the "seven wonders of the ancient world," the temple of Artemis, the Artemision, was four times the size of the Parthenon, with 127 sixty-foot pillars. The dimensions alone help us understand why silver models of the place were

such hot items in the religious tourism trade. And the "theater" was not like your local movie house but a magnificent amphitheater carved into a mountainside, 495 feet in diameter.) Two important points emerge from Luke's account of this disruption. First, the intervention of the town clerk models the way for Roman officials to work out tensions with Christians: ("let the matter be settled in the lawful assembly," v. 39).

Second, some of Luke's word choices hint that he is making a subtle contrast between pagan chaos and Christian order. Describing the riot, Luke says that the city was filled with *synchysis* ("confusion"—v. 29). Used only once in the New Testament, this is a deftly chosen word, for it is the word used in the Septuagint at Genesis 11:9 (the sole occurrence in the Greek version of the Torah) to translate the name "Babel." And Luke has already used the verbal form of the word to describe the Pentecost experience as a reversal of Babel's confusion (Acts 2:6), Pentecost being the occasion when people are confused by their ability to understand!

The contrast is further enhanced by Luke's using *ekklēsia* to describe the confused assembly in verses 32, 39, and 41. Apart from Acts 7:38, where the word refers to the assembly of the Hebrews at Sinai, *ekklēsia* elsewhere in Acts always means the community of the church. Only in this passage is the word used for a non-ecclesial assembly. For the original readers of Acts, this word choice could only have pointed up the contrast between the two kinds of "assembly"—the confused riot of the silversmiths versus the orderly growth of the church (vv. 10-17, 20). The final two occurrences of *ekklēsia* in Acts turn up in the very next chapter, in verses 17 and 28, where they describe the Ephesian church as an assembly driven by motives quite other than idolatry, greed, and anxiety.

20:1-16 Journeying toward Jerusalem (and the resuscitation of "Lucky")

In a note between the episodes of the triumph over the exorcists and the riot of the silversmiths (19:21), Luke had already referred to Paul's decision to travel to Jerusalem (and then move on to Rome). Although Paul later (24:17) refers to the purpose of this journey as the bringing of alms to Jerusalem (the collection referred to in his letters to Corinth and Rome—for instance, Romans 15:25-28), there is no mention of the collection here in chapter 20. Perhaps the delivery of the

Jerusalem relief fund was not the public-relations success Paul had hoped for.

After a farewell tour of churches in Macedonia and three months in "Greece" (Achaia, centering, no doubt, around unnamed Corinth), Paul, intending to join what was apparently a pilgrim group of Jews sailing for Syria, learns of a plot against him and decides to take a more indirect route, looping back around the Aegean basin. The seven names listed (plus the author or his source, since the second "we" section begins in verse 5) comprise a delegation representing most of the sectors of Paul's mission. This delegation fits the notion that this is indeed the "Jerusalem relief fund" trip (see Rom 15:25-27).

The colorful anecdote about the resuscitation of Eutychus (aptly named "Lucky," the meaning of his name in Greek) may well be included here simply for its entertainment value and its parallel with the account of Peter's raising of Tabitha (9:36-43). But given Luke's careful choice of words and phrases—"on the first day of the week" (v. 1; see Luke 24:1); "upstairs room" (v. 8; see 1:13; 9:37, 39); "break[ing] bread" (vv. 7, 11; see Luke 22:19; 24:30; Acts 2:46); a fallen youth taken up "dead" (v. 9) and revived by Paul imitating the gestures of Elijah and Elisha and taken away as a *pais zōnta* ("living lad"), it is hard to dismiss the possibility that the author intends the reader to reflect on the story's symbolic resonances, especially when one notices that the event sits between references to Passover ("the feast of Unleavened Bread," v. 6) and Pentecost (v. 16). For the Christian practice of the breaking of the bread on the first day of the week (Sunday) is always a celebration of death and restoration to new life, precisely as these things are interpreted in the light of the Jewish feasts of Passover and Pentecost.

As for the detailed itinerary surrounding this anecdote, the listing of places could simply be explained as evidence of an eyewitness's passion for detail. It could also reflect Luke's intention to show how Jesus' heroic follower Paul imitates his master even in his making an extended final journey to Jerusalem, where he too will be interrogated by Jewish and Gentile officials.

20:17-38 Paul's testament to the Ephesian elders

Paul makes a point of bypassing Ephesus (to avoid those plotting against him?), but he is eager to summon the elders of that community to Miletus, some forty miles to the south, so that he can bid them farewell. What follows is the only speech in Acts that Paul addresses to a Christian audience.

The speech follows the conventions of other biblical testaments, touching on the topics of a review of the speaker's life, commissioning of successors, encouragement and warnings regarding the future, farewell and blessing. Like other classic farewell addresses, it serves both to present the speaker as a model for the readers/auditors and also to address the historical aftermath of the speaker and interpret what is going forward historically.

In the context of Luke-Acts, the speech is a privileged moment in Paul's own imitation of Christ. Like Jesus, he makes his own "passion prediction" on the way to Jerusalem. And his farewell address to the Ephesian elders has much in common with Jesus' own farewell address to the apostles at the Last Supper (Luke 22:25-38). Like Jesus at the supper, Paul characterizes authority in the messianic community as one of humble service, focuses on the kingdom, encourages his listeners to care for those left in their charge (Jesus: "Strengthen your brothers"; Paul: "Help the weak"), and warns of future challenges. That Paul can serve as model to the extent that he himself has imitated Jesus is suggested by explicit reference to Jesus in the beatitude that climaxes the speech: "It is more blessed to give than to receive" (v. 35).

Several things about the language of this speech are worth noting. Along with Luke's calling the group "presbyters" (*presbyteroi*, or "elders," v. 17), the usual term in Acts for leaders other than the apostles in the churches, Paul calls them "overseers" (v. 28, translating *episkopoi*, the word rendered "bishops" in later Christian writings). This reflects the apparent equivalence of those terms as found, for example, in Titus 1:5-7. In the ordinary Greek of the day, *episkopos* meant "superintendent" or "guardian" in any of a variety of social settings. In first-century Christian writings it serves as a Hellenistic equivalent of the more Judean term "elder," which Luke uses for both Jewish and Christian leaders throughout Luke-Acts. In the second century these terms will be used to designate distinct roles in the evolving three-tier hierarchical structure of a single local bishop (*episkopos*), directing a number of elders (*presbyteroi*, from which the English words "priest" and "presbyterate" derive), supported by a further group of *diakonoi*, or deacons.

One remarkable verse (v. 28) deserves special attention: "Keep watch over yourselves and over the whole flock of which the holy Spirit has appointed you overseers, in which you tend the church of God that he acquired with his own blood." This translation, which renders straightforwardly what scholars generally agree is the best reading of the Greek text, raises the question of what it can mean to speak of God's blood. An early response to this problem was the introduction of the variant reading "church of the Lord" for "church of God," which was open to the understanding that "his blood" referred to the blood of the Lord Jesus. But the more difficult reading, "church of God," does appear to be the more authentic one. A possible solution of this crux is to translate the final phrase, "the blood of his Own" (referring to the Son, Jesus). In any case, with the references to "holy Spirit," "God," and "blood," we have in this verse a rare New Testament adumbration of the later, more developed doctrine of the Trinity. Using phrases that catch important aspects of Paul's theology as it is expressed in the Pauline letters (conversion to God, faith in the Lord Jesus, the power of the Spirit to form community, the gospel of God's grace, the plan of God, the importance of perseverance), this speech is a fitting conclusion to Luke's narrative of Paul's intra-Christian ministry.

21:1-14 Paul and the delegation continue the journey to Jerusalem

After departing from Ephesus, Paul and companions continue the journey to Jerusalem. This stage of the journey comprises the third "we" section in Acts (vv. 1-18), implying the author's presence during this part of the journey. The summary gives us a glimpse of how people got about the Mediterranean in those days: they hung around a port until they found a cargo ship going in the general direction of their intended destination.

The fact that Paul and his entourage find communities of Christians in Tyre and Ptolemais indicates that the evangelization of Phoenicia, to which Luke referred in 11:19, took root and flourished. Indeed, the intensity of communion with the disciples at Ptolemais is enough to warrant

the same kind of prayerful seaside send-off they received at Ephesus (20:36-38).

These episodes illustrate that hearing and following the Spirit are not a simple matter. Although the Tyrian Christians keep telling Paul "through the Spirit" not to embark for Jerusalem, he continues. Obviously, he feels they have misinterpreted the Spirit in this case. And when Agabus, who prophesied accurately the famine during the reign of Claudius (Acts 11:28), acts out symbolically what he perceives to be the Spirit's message regarding Paul's fate in Jerusalem, he gets it only partly right: Paul will indeed be bound in Jerusalem, but by Romans, not by Jews. Faced with Paul's determination to go to Jerusalem even if it means death, it is the companions, not Paul, who imitate Jesus' struggle in facing the prospect of death (Luke 22:39-42), first with resistance, then acceptance.

21:15-26 Paul has his Jewish fidelity challenged

When Paul and company arrive in Jerusalem, James and a plenary session of the Jerusalem elders hear Paul's report about what God has been doing through his ministry among the Gentiles. The Jerusalem Christian authorities are happy enough with that good news, but they inform Paul that the success among the Gentiles has raised concerns among the "many thousands" (v. 20) of Jewish Christians in the area who have gotten the idea that he is urging all the Jews in the Diaspora to abandon the Mosaic practices. Although nothing we have read in Acts supports this charge, Paul's own letter to the Romans shows that the notion that he was denigrating the Mosaic Law was prevalent enough to warrant the full-scale defense that he makes in that major letter.

James's strategy for damage control in this regard—having Paul accompany four men to the temple and sponsor the ceremonies fulfilling their nazirite vows (see Num 6:3-20 for the nazirite ritual)—seems promising. Twentieth-century digs to the south of the Temple Mount have revealed the *mikvaot* (immersion baths), where pilgrims ritually purified themselves before climbing the stairs leading up into the temple precincts. The public nature of this purification, along with Paul's sponsoring of the sacrifices (twelve animals, three apiece for four men) would offer a clear rebuttal to the accusations that Paul was discouraging observance of the Torah.

The reference in verse 25 to the policy regarding Gentile converts expressed in the apostolic decree of the Jerusalem Council (Acts 15:23-29) strikes an odd note here. Paul, after all, played a major part in that meeting and, indeed, helped promulgate its policy regarding Gentile converts (16:4). But the notice serves to remind the reader that the present issue, Paul's attitude toward Jewish observance of the Torah, is something other than what is expected of Gentile Christians.

Given Paul's own language about "[dying] to the law" (Gal 2:19), some commentators find Luke's portrayal here of Paul's "compromise" implausible. Yet it can be argued that Paul is acting in a way wholly consistent with the policy he articulates in 1 Corinthians 9:19-21: "Although I am free in regard to all, I have made myself a slave to all so as to win over as many as possible. To the Jews I became like a Jew to win over Jews; to those under the law I became like one under the law—though I myself am not under the law—to win over those under the law. To those outside the law I became like one outside the law—though I am not outside God's law but within the law of Christ—to win over those outside the law."

Sadly, in the end the strategy fails, for in the events that follow, nothing indicates that Paul's Jerusalem relief fund was accepted, and no one in the Jerusalem Christian community comes to his rescue in the confrontation that continues to unfold. The Jerusalem church, so robustly present in the early chapters of Acts and now grown to "many thousands," disappears from view during the final seven chapters.

21:27-36 Romans rescue Paul from an attempted lynching

In addition to the local members of the sect of the Nazarene, other Jews, pilgrims from the province of Asia, mount an attack against Paul. Having recognized their fellow provincial, the Gentile Trophimus, some had jumped to the conclusion that Paul had taken this man into the court of Israel on the Temple Mount, thereby breaching the barrier separating Gentiles from the space reserved for Israelites. Signs posted on the balustrade forbade Gentiles to pass this point on pain of death. The rioting crowd falls upon Paul, haul him out of the sacred space, and try to kill him on the spot.

At this point the cohort commander intervenes with centurions and soldiers, who bring him to "the compound," a reference to the Antonia fortress, the military headquarters and barracks contiguous with the northwest corner of the temple platform. The shout of the crowd—"Away with him!"—echoes the cry at the trial of Jesus before Pilate (Luke 23:18).

21:37-40 Paul identifies himself

When Paul identifies himself as a Jew and a Roman citizen to the cohort commander, the latter is relieved that he is not "the Egyptian"—the last rabble-rouser the Romans had to deal with. The reference fits Josephus's account of an "Egyptian false prophet" who, a few years earlier, had led thirty thousand (Josephus's number) to the Mount of Olives to wait for Jerusalem to fall like Jericho in the days of Joshua. Paul and his purpose are something else entirely, as his ensuing speech will reveal. Having spoken to the commander in Greek, the *lingua franca* of that part of the empire, he now proceeds to address the crowd in what Luke calls "Hebrew"—almost certainly a reference to Aramaic, the mother tongue of Jesus and the common language of Judea.

22:1-21 Paul's first defense speech

Paul's exchange with the cohort commander had raised questions of ethnicity and status. Paul is a Jew, not "the Egyptian." He speaks Greek as well as Aramaic. And he is a Roman citizen. Now as he begins his speech, he makes it clear that he speaks as a Jew to Jews ("My brothers and fathers"). The clause "what I am about to say in my defense" renders the word *apologia*, the classical term for a legal defense, thereby setting the agenda for the final seven chapters of Acts. Facing a crowd driven by the zeal for the Mosaic Law—who are attacking Paul because they think he has violated that Law—he makes the perfect move to win their good will. He displays his Jewish pedigree, citing his Jewish upbringing, his training in the Law, even describing his own past persecution of "this Way" as stemming from precisely the "zeal . . . for God" that they are presently demonstrating in their persecution of him.

Just as Luke repeated twice the story of Peter's first mission to Gentiles in his encounter with Cornelius's household (in Acts 10, 11, and 15), so he retells the story of Paul's conversion/commission here, for the second in what will be another series of three accounts. No clumsy redundancy, these repetitions are the author's way of underscoring the importance of these pivotal events. As in the case of Peter's encounter with Cornelius, each retelling comes with variations and developments that fit the immediate context and help the reader fathom the significance more deeply.

In this version of Paul's encounter with the risen Jesus, the brightness is enhanced: at the most brilliant time of day, *noon*, Paul experiences a brightness that outshines the noontime sunlight! His visual impairment is not called blindness here but is simply ascribed to the brightness of the light. Whereas in the account of Acts 9 the companions heard the voice but see no one, here they see the light but hear no voice.

These are not the discrepancies of a negligent author but variations of an artist in full control of his material. Saying that "the Lord" answered Paul enhances the nature of the vision as a theophany, that is, a manifestation of God. (It is not impossible that Luke's emphasis on blindness in the midst of brightness is prompted by his perception that Paul here experiences the noontime blindness that Deuteronomy 28:28 promises Israel if it does not hearken to the voice of the Lord.)

The Jewishness of Ananias is enhanced. He is a "devout observer of the law" (v. 12). And he announces that their ancestral God has designated Paul to witness (what he had seen and heard) "before *all*" (emphasis added) about "the Righteous One," an eminently Jewish title for Jesus, denoting fidelity to the covenant and echoing Luke's unique version of the confession of the centurion under the cross (Luke 23:47: "This man was *dikaios*" ["innocent," "righteous"]). Here there is less emphasis on the physical cure from blindness; restored vision simply follows upon Ananias's word.

If Paul's adversaries are challenging his mission to Gentiles, the final part of the speech claims that the outreach to the nations was far from the action of an apostate. Like the great prophet Isaiah, Paul "saw the Lord" in the temple, protested his unworthiness, and received his mandate there, at the liturgical heart of Israel (v. 18; see Isa 6:1). In response, the crowd repeats the rejection of 21:36.

22:22-29 Paul imprisoned

Just as the tribune was caught in a false assumption about Paul earlier (that he was "the

Egyptian," 21:38), now he is caught in another mistake about the Apostle's identity—assuming that this Jew is not a Roman citizen. Wrong again. This vivid drama, with Paul stretched out for interrogation under the lash and then rescued at the last minute, is more than good storytelling. It also demonstrates for Luke's readership that Paul, as a Roman citizen, is eminently qualified to mediate the gospel to the Roman world as well as to the Diaspora.

22:30–23:11 The investigation continues: Paul before the Sanhedrin

Having learned of Paul's Roman citizenship, the commander (Claudius Lysias, we learn in verse 26) tries a gentler mode of getting to the facts of the charges against Paul. He orders the chief priests and the full Sanhedrin to convene for a hearing. Notice that these people are not necessarily gathered as adversaries of Paul; they comprise the official Jewish body that the commander now looks to in order to discover whether Paul is a danger to Roman law and order. Thus we are not yet dealing with a trial; Lysias is still conducting a Roman investigation to see if Paul has done something that warrants a Roman trial.

Paul's declaration that he has always conducted himself with a clear conscience before God surely applies to his whole life and supports the notion that his experience on the road to Damascus is better understood as a prophetic call rather than a conversion, at least in the moral or religious sense.

The exchange between Paul and the high priest Ananias is loaded with irony. Paul comes across as a better exponent of the Law than does its official guardian. His assertion that he did not realize Ananias was the high priest implies that the latter's behavior, punishing an unconvicted person, was hardly the deportment expected of a person in that office.

Before any formal inquest begins, Paul asserts that he is a Pharisee (v. 6) and makes a simple proclamation of the gospel: "I am on trial for the hope in the resurrection of the dead." Commentators note Paul's shrewdness in playing the afterlife card, a key point of division between the two parties. As Jesus' controversy with the Sadducees in Luke 20:27-40 demonstrated, Sadducees denied the resurrection. And as Luke notes here in a rare aside, neither did they believe in postmortem survival as "angel" or "spirit." For the Sadducees, if you could not find it in the Torah, it didn't count. This, of course, splits the Sanhedrin, with the Pharisees refusing to condemn Brother Paul.

But more is going on here than clever forensic strategy. By the time of Luke's writing of Acts, the high priest Ananias has indeed been "struck," assassinated in A.D. 66, according to Josephus. The Sadducees have ceased to exist as authorities, having lost their power base with the destruction of the temple by the Romans in A.D. 70. This leaves the Pharisees, the current leaders of formative Judaism, as the most important figures for Luke's readers. They emerge in this episode not so much as defenders of Paul but rather as men acting in bad will. Though they accept "the resurrection of the dead" as a hope, they resist Paul's testimony that the hoped-for resurrection has already begun concretely in Jesus of Nazareth.

It is this, rather than Paul's legal guilt or innocence, that will remain the issue for the remainder of the book. It is really the gospel that is on trial. In the context of the narrative, Paul's focus on the resurrection makes it clear to the Roman tribune (the most important auditor of this hearing) that the charges against Paul are Jewish matters, nothing of concern to imperial governance.

23:12-35 A plot to assassinate Paul and a Roman rescue

A group of more than forty of Paul's co-religionists make a pact not to eat or drink until they have killed him. Luke offers no motive for such fanaticism. One can only surmise that these men exhibit the kind of rebellious zealotry that will come to expression some ten years later in the Zealot revolt against Rome in A.D. 67–70. They may have perceived in Paul's messianic mission to the Gentiles (and his rumored "watering down" of Jewish practices) a vitiation of Judean nationalism.

Tipped off by Paul's nephew regarding the plot to ambush his prisoner (v. 16), Lysias moves to place him in the protective custody of an armed cavalry, who are to escort him safely to the governor Felix (in office A.D. 52–59, the sixth prefect after Pontius Pilate).

Luke gives us the gist of the report Lysias sends to Felix. Given that our author has already provided his version of the events reported in the message, Luke no doubt expects the reader to smile at the way this Roman official tweaks the truth to put the best possible face on his conduct. We know from 21:27-40 that Lysias first quelled the riot, arrested Paul, and eventually ordered him interrogated under the lash. Only *then*, when Paul announced his citizenship, did the tribune first learn of it. As Lysias tells it in his report, his action with Paul was from the beginning a bold rescue of a known Roman citizen. In his favor, his present "protective custody" action has in fact become such a rescue.

We may wonder why Felix, when he learns that Paul is from Cilicia, does not send him there for trial. In fact, Syria-Cilicia is a double province at this time (Vespasian will split it later), and Felix governs the area in which the charges have been brought against the accused. So he is responsible for the trial.

24:1-27 Paul is heard before Felix, in public and privately

Finally, with the arrival from Jerusalem of Ananias and some elders with their attorney, Paul faces a formal trial before the procurator Felix. After paying unctuous compliments to the governor, Tertullus, the prosecuting attorney, levels a set of broad and, as we readers know, unfounded charges against Paul: (a) he sows dissension among Jews all over the world [empire] (*oikoumenē*) and (b) he tried to profane the temple. Tertullus even tries to dignify with the term "arrest" (v. 6) what we know to have been an attempt at mob lynching.

As in his speech on the Antonia barracks steps to the crowd of would-be lynchers (Acts 22), Paul answers these false charges by rehearsing the facts that establish his exemplary and eminently traditional Jewish behavior. Far from desecrating the temple, he went there to worship their ancestral God. He is still a Torah-keeping Jew who worships the God he has always served in good conscience, except that now it is according to "the Way" that his adversaries dismiss as a "sect." Their charges are hearsay and therefore without merit. The original plaintiffs were the "Jews from . . . Asia" (21:27), but they are not present to testify. And the only thing that the present plaintiffs have witnessed was his proclamation that he is on trial "for the resurrection of the dead" (v. 21; see 23:6).

Paul's claim to have come "to bring alms for my nation and offerings" (v. 17) is the sole reference in Acts to his transmission of the Jerusalem relief fund (see Rom 15:25-26) as the main motive for his presence in Jerusalem. By calling the collection "alms for my nation" and linking it with his sponsoring of sacrifices for the nazirites fulfilling their vows, he casts those actions in language that associates them with the essence of Jewish piety. Felix's knowledge that Paul, as bearer of these funds, controls a substantial amount of money may well be what generated the governor's hope for a bribe (v. 26).

Since Felix is informed about "the Way" (through his Jewish wife Drusilla?), and since he has perhaps decided that the Way is no threat to Roman social order, he postpones judgment, pending further (unnecessary) consultation with Lysias. Felix allows two years to elapse without coming to judgment. Like most of the leaders in Luke-Acts, Jewish or Roman, Felix wants chiefly to look after his own interests. (Regarding Felix's administration, the Roman historian Tacitus observes, "He exercised the power of a king with the spirit of the slave.")

25:1-12 Paul appeals to Caesar and comes before Agrippa

This chapter of Acts functions mainly as a transition. Luke is setting the scene for Paul's climactic speech before Agrippa in chapter 26. As he does so, he strengthens two themes important to his history: (a) the controversy regarding Paul and the Christian Way is a thoroughly Jewish matter, and (b) the legal structure and personnel of the Roman Empire are functioning at this time as instruments of divine Providence.

When Jewish leaders present their (now two-year-old) case against Paul and request that he be sent to them in Jerusalem (to be ambushed and killed along the way), Festus asserts his imperial authority. If they have charges to bring against a man in Roman custody, let them do it on the procurator's turf, before his tribunal in Caesarea (v. 5). Luke reflects Paul's adversaries' charges in Paul's response: he has done nothing against the Torah or against the temple *or against Caesar*. "Against Caesar" is a new note, paralleling the charges of the Sanhedrin against Jesus before Pilate (Luke 23:2). When Festus offers Paul the option of facing a formal trial before the Sanhedrin in Jerusalem, he appeals to Caesar. This allows Festus to unburden himself of this case, and he decides to send Paul to Rome.

25:13-27 Paul before Agrippa

Enter King Agrippa and his twice-widowed sister Bernice. Agrippa—Herod Agrippa II—is the fourth Herod to appear in Luke's work. Herod the Great, the famous builder of Caesarea and Masada and spectacular renovator of the second temple, reigned at the time of the infancies of John the Baptist and Jesus (Luke 1:5). Herod the Tetrarch (Antipas), son of Herod the Great, ruled Galilee and Perea during the rest of Jesus' life. Herod Agrippa I (ruled A.D. 41–44), grandson of Herod the Great, appeared (and died) in Acts 12. Now we meet the great-grandson, Herod Agrippa II (who ruled after A.D. 50). We learn nothing new in Festus's report to Agrippa, but the way the report is expressed is telling. Festus characterizes the elders' charges as entirely a Jewish affair— "some issues . . . about their own religion"— much as Gallio spoke when he dismissed the Corinthian Jews' quarrel with Paul in Acts 18:15 and as Lysias wrote in his report to Felix (23:29). There is a nice irony in the title used for the emperor in v. 26. The Greek word that our New American Bible version translates (accurately, in this context) as "our sovereign" is *ho kyrios* (literally, "the lord"). Given that the last instance of that word was a title for the risen Jesus (23:11) and the next instance, a few verses later, again refers to Jesus (26:15), the use of the title here (for Nero!) highlights the irony that the true lord of this history is not the emperor but Jesus—an irony that the book of Revelation will exploit richly.

When Festus invites Agrippa to interrogate Paul, it is not as a formal trial but rather as a hearing in the service of the Roman process; Festus hopes the Jewish king will come up with something substantive to report to Rome. This move also gives Luke the opportunity to underscore another parallel between the experience of the Apostle and his Master: as Procurator Pilate sent Jesus to the then current Jewish king (Herod Antipas) for a kind of hearing, so Procurator Festus presents Paul to another Jewish king. In Jesus' case, of course, Pilate was attempting to shunt the accused off to another jurisdiction. Festus, however, does not intend to let his charge slip out of Roman custody.

Verses 23-27 set the stage for Paul's final extended apologia in chapter 26. Luke packs the audience hall with an entourage that includes "cohort commanders and the prominent men of the city" (v. 23). Thus Paul will be addressing, along with Festus, Agrippa, and Bernice, powerful members of Caesarea's Gentile community.

26:1-23 The inquest before Governor Festus and King Agrippa

The speech that Paul gives to these powerful representatives of the Jewish and Gentile communities is, like the speeches in Acts 2, 3, 13, and 17, one of Luke's theological masterpieces. Much of what we denote by the post-biblical terms "ecclesiology" (theology of church), "Christology" (how Jesus is the Messiah), and "soteriology" (theory of salvation) Luke communicates through this speech.

First, Luke highlights Paul speaking as an expert Jew (a Pharisee, and therefore one highly trained in Israelite tradition) to a well-informed Jewish leader (Agrippa was completing the project of his great-grandfather, the renovation of the Second Temple). Moreover, Paul had demonstrated his zeal for his people's tradition in his efforts against what he had at first perceived as a threat to those traditions, the Way of the Jesus people. To top it off, the centerpiece of his teaching and preaching is the essence of Jewish hope—resurrection from the dead. The unmentioned novelty, of course, is that Paul and the rest of the people of the Way have been announcing that the expected end-time general resurrection has been stunningly anticipated by the resurrection of a single person, Jesus of Nazareth (see the reference to "the first to rise from the dead" at verse 23).

Paul then recounts for the second time the experience on the road to Damascus, making it the third time for us readers (who first heard of it in the original narrative of Acts 9 and then in the speech of Acts 22). The variations in the details and language in this third telling are far more than an effort at literary variety. The language about light, darkness, and seeing participates in a consistent symbolic theme carrying powerful implications.

This time the light from the sky *is brighter than the noonday sun*, flattening *everyone* to the ground. And the language about blindness—which was quite literally physical in the Acts 9 account, then muted in the Acts 22 version—is not even applied to Paul here. That imagery now describes the experience of Gentile converts. Here the emphasis is on the fact that Paul will witness to what he *has seen* and that he is being missioned to *open the eyes*

of the Gentiles so that *they* may *turn from darkness to light*. Thus what Paul first experienced literally in his physical blindness in the first account becomes a metaphor for the Christian mission to the nations in this third account. This metaphor is developed further at the climax of the speech: Paul is saying "nothing different from what the prophets and Moses foretold, that the Messiah must suffer and that, as the first to rise from the dead, he would *proclaim light both to our people and to the Gentiles*" (vv. 22-23, emphasis added).

And how, precisely, does Luke understand that the risen Messiah "proclaims light" after the resurrection? The whole of Luke-Acts answers that question, especially in its use of quotations of Isaiah. At Luke 2:30-32, during the presentation in the temple, when Simeon takes the child Jesus into his arms and sings his famous *Nunc Dimittis*, he draws upon Isaiah's imagery of vision and light: "for my eyes have seen your salvation [LXX Isa 40:5] / which you prepared in sight of all the peoples, / a light for revelation to the Gentiles [Isa 42:6; 49:6], / and glory for your people Israel."

At his debut in Nazareth, Jesus employs LXX Isaiah 61:1-2 to characterize his mission, and the center of that quotation is "He has sent me to proclaim . . . recovery of sight to the blind" (Luke 4:18). Jesus does indeed give sight to the blind in the physical cure of the blind in his pre-Easter activity (Luke 7:21; 18:35-43), but it takes the post-Easter activity of the church in Acts to fulfill the promise of the Servant functioning as a light to the Gentiles. Luke makes that quite explicit when, at the synagogue in Pisidian Antioch, he has Paul and Barnabas (both!) say, "We now turn to the Gentiles. For so the Lord has commanded us, 'I have made you a light to the Gentiles, that you may be an instrument of salvation to the ends of the earth'" (Acts 13:46-47; see Isa 49:6). Strikingly, language describing the Servant of Yahweh in Isaiah, earlier applied to Jesus by Simeon, is now applied to the post-Easter continuation of Jesus' mission by his followers. Thus when we hear the reference to the risen Christ proclaiming "light to the Gentiles" at the climax of Paul's speech in Acts 26, we know that what Paul and the rest of the church are doing is not only in continuity with Jesus' mission but their work is somehow the work of the risen Lord himself.

This was the import of Paul's vision on the road to Damascus ("Saul, Saul, why are you persecuting me?"—v. 14b). The risen Lord is identified with the believing community, and through them he opens the eyes of the nations and brings them from darkness to light. At the end of the book, Luke will have Paul use Isaiah 6:9-10 ("They have closed their eyes, / so that they may not see with their eyes") to characterize those of Israel who, like Saul before his conversion, fail to respond to the mission.

Whereas Festus responds to the defense simply with amazement ("You are mad, Paul") and Agrippa with cynicism, Festus, Bernice, and the rest comment that Paul is doing nothing that deserves death or imprisonment (v. 31). Thus, like Jesus (see Luke 23:4, 14, and 22), Paul is declared innocent three times by Roman officials and a Jewish king (Lysias, 23:29; Festus, 25:25; and Agrippa, 26:31-32). And also like (and with) Jesus, he is fulfilling Servant Israel's vocation to be a light to the nations.

27:1-44 To Rome: storm, shipwreck, and survival

As he nears the end of his history, Luke gives us a whopping good sea adventure. Some recent commentators have wondered why Luke, who can be so sparse in his treatment of such momentous events as, for example, the early spread of the Christian mission into the Hellenistic world (11:20-21), decides at this point to spend so much parchment on the details of Paul's voyage to Rome. Some scholars, subscribing to the theory that the "we" sections are a literary convention and noting resonances with other ancient accounts of shipwreck, have suggested that Luke has imaginatively embellished some minimal facts available to him regarding Paul's voyage. Others, noting the abundance of nautical technical terms, posit that Luke took over an available voyage account and applied it to Paul.

It is, however, simpler and more reasonable to presume that Luke is sparse when his sources are sparse and that he willingly shares details when he has access to them, especially when he was an eyewitness to the events he describes. The first-person plural of this final "we" section (27:1–28:16) supports such an interpretation. Moreover, we have no evidence of the "we" form used as a literary convention in ancient history writing by authors who are not describing their own experience.

That Paul himself was richly experienced in sea travel and its dangers is clear from his remark in 2 Corinthians 11:25: "Three times I was shipwrecked, I passed a night and a day on the deep . . . ." And the tradition that Luke was a close companion of Paul is firm (Phlm 24; Col 4:14; and 2 Tim 4:11). There is no reason to presume that he was inexperienced in sea travel or lacked the vocabulary to describe it. Of course, master storyteller that he is, he knows he has a "good yarn" here. He tells it with relish and in a way that serves his history of what God has accomplished in and through these events, which could be called the passion and vindication of the Apostle Paul.

As a Roman citizen, Paul, accompanied by his faithful companion Aristarchus (see 19:29; 20:4; Col 4:10; and Phlm 24) and the narrator (presumably Luke), is placed under the protective custody of a centurion, one Julius. There being no commercial passenger ships in antiquity, Julius books passage on a ship returning to the Aegean area. The "philanthropic" (*philanthropos*) Julius allows Paul to visit friends, probably Christians, during a stop at Sidon. Because of the late fall weather, the ship hugs the coast, passing behind the shelter of Cyprus. At Myra they transfer to an Alexandrian grain ship headed for Italy. When they put in at Fair Havens, in the mid-south side of the island of Crete, Paul advises wintering there, since continuing now would entail loss of cargo and lives—reasonable advice that will turn out, in the end, to be only partly accurate.

When the voyage continues and a hurricane wind (a "northeaster") forces them dangerously off course, Paul provides quite a different sort of message. A dream vision enables him to urge courage and to predict (more accurately than his earlier commonsense prediction) safety to all aboard. The God he belongs to and serves would save them. It is significant that he says "God" rather than "the Lord Jesus" here; it is language that a pagan audience would more easily understand, and Luke is emphasizing that it is the maker of heaven and earth who is managing what is going forward in the midst of this chaos of nature.

Speaking of Luke's use of language, one cannot help noting that the description of Paul, acting in the manner of the host presiding at a Jewish meal (taking bread, thanking God, breaking the bread), evokes the language of the Last Supper and Christian Eucharist. Most commentators rightly insist that Luke surely does *not* mean to say that Paul, attended by his two Christian companions, is presiding at a Christian celebration of the Lord's Supper before a "congregation" of 273 pagans! At the same time, Luke the savvy wordsmith surely knows that his Christian readers (or hearers) would catch the resonance with the Christian liturgy (and with Luke 5:16 and 22:19).

Indeed, once that resonance is heard in verse 35, further resonances abound. For example:

1) Immediately before this mealtime blessing, Paul had said, "Not a hair of the head of anyone of you will be lost." This, of course, repeats what Jesus had said in his end-time discourse (Luke 21:18), which also speaks of "signs in the *sun*, the moon, *and the stars*," and asserts that "on earth nations will be in dismay, *perplexed by the roaring of the sea and the waves*" (Luke 21:25, emphasis added). In this literal experience of such a sea, Luke has made a point of noting that "neither the sun nor the stars were visible for many days" (Acts 27:20).

2) In a way that is more obvious in Greek than in English translation, Luke uses "salvation" language suggestively. The words used to describe physical survival of storm and shipwreck in this account (*sōzō* in vv. 20, 31; *sōtēria* in v. 34) are, to be sure, the usual words for describing rescue and survival; but in Luke's work, they are also used for salvation in the ultimate (eschatological) sense (e.g., *sōtēria*, "salvation," at Luke 1:77 [forgiveness of sins]; at 19:9 [Zacchaeus's conversion]; and at Acts 4:12; 13:26, 47; *sōtērion*, "salvation," at Luke 2:20 and 3:6 [Isa 40:5]; *sōzō*, the verbal form of "save," at Luke 7:50; 8:12; 13:23; 17:19; 18:26; 19:10; Acts 2:21 [Joel 3:5]; 2:47; 4:12; and 15:1, 11). That diction makes it easy, even inevitable, that readers will hear salvation overtones in the storm and shipwreck account of Acts 27.

3) Finally, in an extended work that has thematized the importance of detachment from material goods on the Christian journey of following Jesus, all the literally realistic details of dumping cargo, jettisoning gear, cutting off the dinghy, and abandoning anchors point to the need for traveling light to achieve salvation. (See Luke 10:4; 14:33; 18:25-27: "'For it is easier for a camel to pass through the eye of a needle than for a rich person to enter the kingdom of God.' Those who heard this said, 'Then who can be saved?' And he said, 'What is impossible for human beings is possible for God.'")

This is not to say that Luke has composed an allegory of Christian life in Acts 27. Rather, he has reported this tale of God's care of Paul and his mission in such a way that the historical account of nautical disaster and survival resonates with and alludes to the end-time situation of the church and the world. (We are "all in the same boat," and God is our only hope.) A further clue that Luke has this resonance in mind may be the fact that only his version of the synoptic tradition of the stilling of the storm pictures Jesus and the disciples as *sailing* (*pleontōn*, Luke 8:23).

28:1-10 Malta: hospitality, vindication, and healing

The story of the sea travel, including the "we" section that tells it, continues through the arrival in Rome (in verse 16, where the New American Bible translates "he entered," the Greek has "*we* entered"). The safe arrival of all 276 on the shore of Malta leads to a supreme irony. Everything has been building, we readers have been led to believe, to a trial and judgment by the highest authority of the secular world, Caesar. But Luke will end his second volume without any mention of that Roman trial (which, tradition tells us, resulted in Paul's death). Instead, we are told of judgment by a lower, more spontaneous "court," reflecting the higher, divine judgment.

In Mediterranean antiquity, survival of disaster demonstrated divine favor. Luke calls the hospitable Maltese natives *barbaroi* (that is, non-Greek-speakers), but he speaks of their uncommon *philanthropia*. When they see Paul attacked by a snake, they interpret that as a sign of divine disfavor—indeed, proof that Paul is a murderer (v. 5). However, when he fails to swell up and drop dead, they call him a god! An overreaction, to be sure, but a powerful point has been made. As God had vindicated Jesus through resurrection, so he vindicates Paul through rescue from storm and snakebite. Further affirmation comes by way of Paul's ability to extend Jesus' healing ministry to the father of Governor Publius and other sick of the island who come to him.

28:11-31 Arrival in Rome and testimony to Jews

How a work ends is a matter of great importance to any careful author, especially in antiquity (recall Aristotle's stress on the importance of a beginning, middle, and end of a work). Luke chooses to end his two-volume work, not, as we already observed, with the expected Roman trial, but with several encounters between Paul and local Jewish leaders. Because these dialogues issue in "mixed reviews" at best and end with Paul quoting Isaiah 6:9-10 and turning once again to Gentiles, some commentators have read this as a declaration that God has, at this point, severed his covenant relationship with the Jews. Since this kind of interpretation has supported Christian anti-Judaism, it is important to read Luke's narrative ending carefully, on its own terms.

The first contact that Paul and his two companions make on Italian soil is with people in Puteoli, whom Luke calls "brothers." Since it is the Gentile Luke who refers to them as brothers, the presumption is that they are fellow Christians. After a week of enjoying their hospitality (the Roman guard himself apparently glad for the break), they move on to the Forum of Appius and then to the rest stop called Three Taverns. At both places brothers come down from Rome to meet them. Paul's response to the brothers ("Paul gave thanks to God and took courage," v. 15) confirms the likelihood that these are also Christians. (The Christian community in Rome had been founded by others than Paul or Peter, possibly by the "travelers from Rome" [2:10] who had witnessed the birth of the church at Pentecost.)

The author James D. G. Dunn makes a charming interpretive conjecture regarding Luke's inclusion of the name of the Alexandrian ship that takes Paul's party to Rome, the *Dioscuri* ("Zeus's Boys," that is, Castor and Pollux, twin sons of the god Zeus). Noting that Luke uses "brothers" four times in the next few verses, first of Christians then of Jews, this author suggests that Luke calls attention to the name of the ship because for him the Christian and Jewish "brothers" that Paul is about to encounter are "indeed twin children of the one God, brothers of Paul, and so of one another."

Once established in Rome, apparently under house arrest in his own rented lodgings (v. 28), Paul calls together (non-Christian) Jewish leaders, who are also called "brothers" (vv. 17 and 21). His purpose is a kind of preemptive defense. Since the plaintiffs in his case are the Jerusalem Jews, he presents his apologia to their Roman counterparts. For us readers, the defense is familiar: the

Roman authorities in Caesarea have not found him guilty of anything warranting the death penalty, and his behavior is perfectly Jewish: he preaches "the hope of Israel." What is new is his hinting at the possibility (not pursued) of a countersuit (v. 19). They reply that they have heard nothing bad about him, by letter or hearsay. But they have heard about this controversial "sect" that he promotes, and they do want to learn more about that.

To this end, Paul holds an all-day conference with an even greater number of Jewish leaders, focusing on the heart of the matter: the kingdom of God and Jesus as fulfillment of the Scriptures. Some are convinced, others are not, and they leave without agreeing among themselves. As commentary on this divided response, Paul invokes Isaiah 6:9-10, implying that those who have failed to accept Jesus as the hope of Israel have fulfilled that prophecy. He adds, alluding to LXX Isa 40:5 (quoted earlier at Luke 3:6), that "this salvation of God has been sent to the Gentiles; they will listen."

Does this final word of Paul mean that the door is closed to further mission to Israel? No more than the presence of Isaiah 6:9-10 in the original commission of Isaiah of Jerusalem indicated that he had no mission to his people (belied by the sixty chapters that follow in the scroll of Isaiah). The rejection of the gospel by the majority of historical Israel is, for Luke, a fact to be faced. But this fact, and the turn to the Gentiles, is no more a definitive dismissal of the Jews than are the parallel moments in the synagogues of Pisidian Antioch (13:46-47) or Corinth (18:6). In ending with this episode, Luke has helped his (largely Gentile) readers understand (a) their relationship to historical Israel, (b) the majority of Israel's rejection of its Messiah, and (c) how the Gentiles have become beneficiaries of Israel's vocation to be a "light to the nations" (Isa 49:6).

Meanwhile, in the spirit of the parables of the barren fig tree (Luke 13:6-9) and two lost sons (Luke 15:11-32), the door remains open. In Paul's continued ministry during his house arrest, he receives "*all* who came to him" (emphasis added). He models the community's ongoing mission as "he proclaimed the kingdom of God and taught about the Lord Jesus Christ with boldness of speech [*meta parrēsias*], without hindrance [*akōlytōs*]" (v. 31, my translation). Note that the last

two words powerfully affirm the theme of freedom running through the whole of Acts; *parrēsia*
is that same freedom and boldness of speech for
which the community prayed in Acts 4:29 and
which the leaders exhibit throughout Acts (2:29;
4:13, 31; 9:27-28; 13:46; 14:3; 18:26; 19:8; and 26:25).
And the final word, *akōlytōs* ("without hindrance") reminds us that neither the one who was
sent to proclaim release to prisoners (Luke 4:18)
nor his Spirit-led followers were hindered by imprisonment or even death.

Luke's two-volume work, which began in the
Jerusalem temple, ends with the mission continuing unabated in a rented Roman apartment. In the
end, Luke's history is not so much about Peter or
Paul as about the fidelity of God and the continuing prophetic mission of the followers of Jesus. If
the ending of Acts surprises us by failing to include the martyrdom of Paul (which was surely
known to Luke), that very inconclusiveness serves
to remind us that we are invited to continue the
story with our lives.

THE PAULINE LETTERS

Vincent M. Smiles

INTRODUCTION

On his own admission, Paul once tried to destroy the church, but because of "a revelation of Jesus Christ" (Gal 1:11-16) he became in many respects the greatest of the apostles (1 Cor 15:8-10) and the most important witness of early Christianity. His conversion to become "an apostle of Christ Jesus" (1 Cor 1:1) happened about three years after Jesus' death (c. A.D. 33); he then worked as an apostle for about thirty years, until his own death in Rome during the persecutions of Nero (c. A.D. 64).

By far the most important source for knowledge of Paul is his own letters. The Acts of the Apostles, written by the same author as the Gospel of Luke, also provides an important history, but "history" in the modern sense of the term, that is, having a strong focus on factual information, was not Luke's primary purpose. As in the Gospel, Luke's *primary* concerns were theological, to provide "assurance" about Jesus' life, death, and resurrection (Luke 1:4; Acts 2:36).

Neither Luke nor Paul knew Jesus personally. It is *possible* that Luke knew Paul personally, as the famous "we" passages in Acts suggest (Acts 16:10-17; 20:5-8, 13-15; 21:1-18; 27:1–28:16). However, those passages may be stylistic devices rather than proof of eyewitness participation in Paul's ministry, and in various ways Luke seems *not* to have known Paul well: his letters are never mentioned or quoted, his attitude to the law and his Pharisaic past (Gal 3:1-29; Phil 3:2-6) are not

understood (e.g., Acts 23:6; 26:5), and Luke has Paul in Jerusalem more frequently than Paul's own report allows (Acts 9:23-26; 11:27-30; 12:25; 15:1; cf. Gal 1–2). Therefore, though Acts is valuable, Paul's own letters remain the decisive source for knowledge of his ministry.

There are thirteen letters that bear Paul's name, and the letter to the Hebrews has also been attributed to Paul, but that was doubted as early as Origen (about A.D. 200), and today there is virtual consensus that Paul had no role in its composition. Of the thirteen, there is general agreement that Paul wrote Romans, 1 and 2 Corinthians, Galatians, Philippians, 1 Thessalonians, and Philemon. The other six letters divide into two groups: Ephesians, Colossians, and 2 Thessalonians, which in the view of *most* scholars Paul probably did not write, and 1 and 2 Timothy and Titus (the Pastoral Letters), which *nearly all* scholars believe Paul did not write. Reasons for doubting Paul's authorship of Ephesians, Colossians, and 2 Thessalonians will be given in the introductions to those letters. Authorship, however, is a complex matter. Paul wrote in the name of his coworkers (e.g., Timothy and Silvanus), indicating their support for the letter. When others wrote in his name, they did so because of some connection, however remote, with his authority and tradition.

Paul's original seven letters (epistles) were written between the late forties and early sixties

A.D., *before* any of the four Gospels (A.D. 65 to 90). The letters are very *circumstantial,* meaning that Paul composed them to respond to particular situations that he and his churches faced. That is why his letters are such valuable witnesses of early Christianity. Interpretation of the letters must always take these circumstances into account. This is also true, for the most part, of the letters that Paul probably did not write. Ephesians is the exception in that it appears to be a general treatise on the church, written with a broad audience in mind rather than a particular community. Colossians and 2 Thessalonians, however, were composed in light of real problems facing churches that looked to Paul as *"the* apostle," as he was known to later generations. The authors wrote in Paul's name because it evoked great authority and trust.

The most important circumstance of Paul's time that we must bear in mind was his presumption that the end of human history (the *eschaton*) was at hand (see 1 Cor 7:29-31). Although later he was not so sure (Phil 1:20-24), early in his ministry Paul was convinced that he would be alive at "the coming of the Lord" (1 Thess 4:15). When "with the voice of an archangel and with the trumpet of God" the Lord Jesus himself would "descend from heaven," Paul expected that he would be among those "still alive," who would be "caught up together" with the dead "to meet the Lord in the air" (1 Thess 4:15-17). From such texts (e.g., also Mark 13:26-27; Matt 24:40-41), some modern Christians have developed the notion of "the rapture," and have combined it with the presumption that Paul and the evangelists were not talking about expectations of the first century but about the end of the world in the twentieth, and now twenty-first, century.

This is naïve, not to say shallow and self-serving, interpretation. How can we presume that Paul wrote primarily for us today? What about the people to whom he actually wrote, not to mention all the centuries in between? A full reading of the letters shows that Paul and his later disciples wrote entirely for the people and circumstances of their own time. The Scriptures are relevant today because the theologies, principles, and values they enunciate are foundational for the church in every age. Taking texts out of context and isolating chosen ideas for literal fulfillment today (what about the dragon of Revelation 12:3-4?) does no justice to the intentions of the biblical authors. That Paul and others were wrong about the near end of the world is only another indication that the Scriptures, like Jesus, have to do with "the weak flesh of humanity" as well as with the divine Spirit of inspiration (see Vatican II, Dogmatic Constitution on Divine Revelation, art. 13).

The value of Paul's letters for the church today is as great as the challenges the church faces. For questions of doctrine and morality, in debates about the nature of the church and of ministry, and facing questions about evangelization and mission, the church now, as always, has to turn to Jesus and to the church's original foundation and inspiration. Paul is particularly important as the witness of how the earliest churches first enfleshed the gospel of Jesus. His descriptions of the church, particularly as "the body of Christ" (1 Cor 12:27); his instructions about the Eucharist (1 Cor 10–11) and inclusion of women among church leaders (e.g., Rom 16:1-7); his recounting of major incidents (Gal 1:13–2:14); and his christological understanding (e.g., Phil 2:6-11)—these and many other aspects of his letters, and of the letters written in his name, are primary texts for the church today. The best approach to the letters requires prayer, an open mind, and careful study both of their individuality and of the conversation, and sometimes vigorous debate, that together they represent.

THE LETTER TO THE

ROMANS

Robert J. Karris, O.F.M.

INTRODUCTION

Dr. Karris recommends a pronoun-rich reading of Romans

How should you approach Romans? Nibble on it piecemeal as the Lectionary does? Or meet it head on? I recommend the courageous second approach. Begin reading chapter 1 and go straight through to chapter 16. Along the way make a detailed list of the personal pronouns Paul uses. How often does he use "I" or "we" or "you" or the third person? Why, for example, does the personal pronoun "we" dominate Romans 5:1-11 and 8:31-39? Who is the "I" of Romans 7:7-25? Why does "I" occur so poignantly and so frequently in Romans 9–11? Who is the "you" of Romans 6:12-23? Why are there so many imperatives in Romans 12:1–15:13?

Further, as you mosey through the text, take a close look at the way Paul begins (1:1-16) and ends (15:14-33) his letter proper and how he insists on his role as the apostle to the Gentiles (1:5, 13; 15:16, 18, 27). In your reading you can't but notice how often Paul buttresses his presentation with quotations from the Greek or Septuagint translation of Scripture, for example, Romans 3:11-17, and you may be envious of the scriptural literacy of the first hearers of his letter.

Be sure not to miss the numerous questions with which Paul energizes his text. For example, Romans 4:1: "What then can we say that Abraham found, our ancestor according to the flesh?" and Romans 11:1: "I ask, then, has God rejected his people? Of course not!" Do you have the feeling that Romans 8:31-39 or Romans 11:33-36 forms a grand conclusion or peroration and are puzzled why Paul soldiers on after these two magnificent confessions of faith?

Although you're tired, struggle through the Roman directory of Romans 16. From a careful reading of 16:1-16, scholars have discerned that there were some five house churches in Rome and that women played a major role in earliest Christianity. If you're not too weary, you may ask why Paul ends his letter with a doxology (16:25-27) rather than a simple wish, as in 1 Corinthians 16:24: "My love to all of you in Christ Jesus." From this courageous and careful hands-on approach you will be in a very good position to ask and test the answers to such questions as the literary form, addressees, purpose, and messages of Romans.

Check the background you bring to your reading of Romans

Against what background should I read Romans? Various church traditions have provided us with backgrounds. For example, there is the Lutheran background of underscoring human dependence upon God's grace and faith over against legalism in all its forms. Unfortunately, most Roman Catholics bring little informed background to Romans, for Paul's letters, especially Romans, are rarely preached upon during Sunday Mass. Contemporary scholars successfully interpret Romans as a story of God's dealings with humankind going back to Adam, Abraham, the giving of the law, the death and resurrection of the Lord Jesus Christ, and final glory. Others make some good sense of Romans as the gospel of God's love and peace over against the Roman imperial gospel of peace and prosperity.

In this commentary I follow Stanley K. Stowers in reading Romans against the background of the Jewish view of Gentiles. Paul states this Jewish viewpoint very clearly in Galatians 2:15: "We, who are Jews by nature and not sinners from among the Gentiles." This Jewish view of Gentiles is manifest in a passage from the religious romance *Joseph and Aseneth*, which dramatically portrays Joseph's abhorrence of kissing the pagan Aseneth: "It is not fitting for a man who worships God, who will bless with his mouth the living God and eat blessed bread of life . . . to kiss a strange woman who will bless with her mouth dead and dumb idols and eat from their table bread of strangulation and drink from their libation a cup of insidiousness" (8.5-7 in C. Burchard's translation).

The Jewish philosopher Philo of Alexandria champions the view that the law of Moses frees Gentiles from their desires, so that they can achieve their goal of self-mastery over their passions. In Book IV.55 of his *Special Laws*, Philo comments: "The law thinks that all those who adhere to the sacred constitution, established by Moses, ought to be free from all unreasonable passions, and from all wickedness" (C. D. Yonge translation). 4 Maccabees 1:16-19 maintains that wisdom derived from the law is the master of human passions:

> Reason, I suggest, is the mind making a deliberate choice of the life of wisdom. Wisdom, I submit, is knowledge of things divine and human, and of their causes. And this wisdom, I assume, is the culture we acquire from the law, through which we learn the things of God reverently and the things of men to our worldly advantage. The forms of wisdom consist of prudence, justice, courage, and temperance. Of all these prudence is the most authoritative, for it is through it that reason controls the passions (NRSV).

With the above background in mind, we will be able to glimpse how Paul maintains that the Gentile believers' new life in Christ, not works of the law, has given them control over their passions (see 6:12-23). We will better appreciate Paul's indictment of the Gentiles in Romans 1:18-32, his dramatization of the Gentile "I" in 7:7-25, and his exhortations in 12:1–15:13, for example, 12:2: "Do not conform yourself to this age but be transformed by the renewal of your mind, that you may discern what is the will of God, what is good and pleasing and perfect." In brief, we will be better able to understand all of Romans, which reveals the gospel of the Apostle to the Gentiles.

The literary form and purposes of Romans

Scholars have called Romans a letter essay or an ambassadorial letter. I treat Romans as a letter of persuasion, technically a protreptic letter. Its main purpose is to persuade the Gentile Christians in Rome about the truth of Paul's gospel for/to the Gentiles. If they accept Paul's gospel to the Gentiles, they may also be willing to help support Paul's mission to the Gentiles in Spain (15:22-24) with personnel and money.

In writing an account of his gospel to the Gentiles, Paul has one eye on Jerusalem. He is anxious that the saints in Jerusalem accept the money that he has collected from Gentile converts and its symbolism of the unity of his law-free gospel with the gospel preached by Jerusalem. Perhaps this aspect of Paul's purposes accounts for the many quotations from Scripture in Romans, for the Judean Christians could be persuaded by arguments from Sacred Scripture. While it seems clear to me that Paul knew something about the situation in Rome, I am not fully persuaded that a purpose of Romans was to settle the so-called controversy between "the weak" and "the strong" in Romans 14:1–15:13. Why would Paul write the weighty first thirteen chapters of Romans to handle such a relatively small problem? We usually don't eliminate a mosquito with a blunderbuss.

What makes Romans tick?

Those who have taken my earlier recommendation and persevered through a pronoun-rich reading of Romans have gone beyond the spoon-fed selections of Romans from the Sunday Lectionary and are ready for the strong food of rhetorical criticism. The cement that holds the various sections of Romans together is formed from the three ingredients of Paul's rhetoric. Although it is clear that the Roman Christians know who Paul is and that he knows something about them and their circumstances, Paul has to establish his position as a person of integrity, trust, authority, and goodwill, especially in the light of possible slurs about the truth of the gospel he preaches (see Rom 3:7-8). This ingredient of Paul's rhetoric is called *ethos* and is especially prominent in his use of "I" in his introduction to and conclusion of Romans, and I would venture to suggest that Romans 9–11, which uses "I" twenty-seven times, contains much *ethos* (besides considerable *pathos*).

As a superb letter writer, Paul makes his points according to *the logic* of his time. Our preliminary reading has repeatedly discovered one component of Paul's logic, namely, his reliance of the authority of Sacred Scripture. As a matter of fact, it has been calculated that fifty-one of the eighty-nine quotations of Scripture found in Paul's letters occur in Romans, and thirty-nine percent of Romans 9–11 consists of citations from Sacred Writ. Paul normally uses the third person for these quotations.

Sometimes the reason for Paul's use of Scripture is relatively clear to us moderns. For example, the chain of quotations in Romans 3:10-18 refers to the entirety of the thinking, willing, articulate, and acting human being: throats, tongues, lips, mouths, feet, eyes. In Romans 15:9-12 Paul makes his case about the Gentiles by quoting the entirety of Scripture, that is, its three major portions: Law, Prophets, Writings. It goes without saying that Paul expects his hearers to know their Bible.

In our preliminary reading of Romans, we have frequently stumbled across another major component of Paul's logic when we encountered questions such as "What are we to say?" (Rom 4:1; 6:1; 7:7; 8:31; 9:14, 30), or exclamations such as "Of course not" (Rom 3:4, 6, 31; 6:1, 15; 7:7, 13; 9:14; 11:1, 11), or second-person addresses to an imaginary conversation partner, such as Romans 9:19-21:

> You will say to me then: "Why does he still find fault? For who can oppose his will?" But who indeed are you, a human being, to talk back to God? Will what is made say to its maker: "Why have you created me so?" Or does not the potter have a right over the clay, to make out of the same lump one vessel for a noble purpose and another for an ignoble one? (trans. H. Anderson, p. 545; other examples in Rom 2:1-5, 17-29; 8:2; 11:17-24; 14:4, 10).

Technically speaking, this component of Paul's logic bears the name of diatribe, which unfortunately for our understanding has the meaning in contemporary English of "a bitter verbal or written criticism." Stanley Stowers defines ancient diatribe in this way: "A term for teaching activity in the schools, literary imitations of that activity, or for writings which employ the rhetorical and pedagogical style typical of diatribes in the schools." Typical of the diatribe in the schools were intense dialogues, questions, and answers.

Those familiar with teaching in the Middle Ages recognize a cousin of the diatribe in the "sic et non" and "quaestiones" traditions of the scholastics, as they raised questions and provided answers for and against an interpretation. Contemporary classrooms provide a distant cousin of the diatribe when they feature questions and answers. Finally, it should be noted that the goal of the diatribe modality is pedagogical and hortatory, not polemical, that is, it is motivated by a concern that students learn; it does not arise from Romans' contempt of false opinions. Finally, as Stowers maintains: "It is also a misunderstanding to read dialogical features (e.g., objections) as references to actual groups in the Roman church." I invite advanced students to explore the diatribe style manifested in Epictetus's "Concerning Anxiety" in Book II.13 of his *Discourses*.

Surely the vast majority of us readers are not trained in reading a text that contains a heavy component of the teaching style called diatribe. So we will have to take our time and exercise great patience. To me, this component of Paul's logic shows how carefully he constructed Romans and how he endeavored to engage his hearers and to win them over to full acceptance of his gospel to the Gentiles. Further, just think of how skilled a reader Phoebe was to proclaim Paul's complex letter intelligently and persuasively (Rom 16:1-2).

Lastly, Paul uses *pathos* to influence the minds of his hearers through engaging their hearts and emotions. Who can miss the *pathos* that floods through Romans 9:1-5; 10:1; 11:1-2; for example, Romans 9:3: "For I could wish that I myself were accursed and separated from Christ for the sake of my brothers, my kin according to the flesh"?

Further, Leander E. Keck has pointed to another dimension of *pathos:* The speaker or author should experience in himself the same emotions he wants to inspire in his hearers. In Book II.47.195

of his *Concerning the Orator,* Cicero writes of how he defended Manius Aquilius in court:

> For here was a man whom I remembered as having been consul, commander-in-chief, honored by the Senate, and mounting in procession to the Capitol. On seeing him cast down, crippled, sorrowing and brought to the risk of all he held dear, *I was myself overcome by compassion before I tried to excite it in others* (Loeb translation modified).

It seems that this characteristic of *pathos* may stand behind Paul's frequent use of "we," for example, in Romans 5:1-11; 7:5-6; 8:31-39, and the exhortatory materials in 12:4; 13:11-12; 14:7-8, 10, 12, 13, 19; 15:1-2, as Paul demonstrates that he shares the same emotions that he wants to evoke in his hearers.

Finally, I invite my readers to take another glance at Romans 15:30-33. Paul is not looking forward to his confrontation with the Judean believers and wants the Romans to join him in the struggle by their prayers on his behalf. In this passage Paul's *ethos* and *pathos* embrace and invite the hearers to storm heaven for his deliverance.

The messages of Romans

In the exposition of individual passages, I will have an opportunity to describe the various messages of Romans. According to my count, there are 146 references to "God" in the sixteen chapters of Romans. This overwhelming number tells me that Romans is about God. In particular, it explains God's actions in the face of apparent injustice. Or as Luke Timothy Johnson says so well: "The argument of Romans is, at root, simple. God is one and God is fair."

A simple outline of Romans

I wholeheartedly encourage my readers to engage in a serious, continuous, and pronoun-rich reading of Romans, and I have composed my commentary to aid such a reading. The following outline presents a basic road map through this long, intricate, and richly rewarding letter that Paul wrote from Corinth about A.D. 57.

Romans 1:1-15 Beginning

Romans 1:16-17 Theme

Romans 1:18–11:36 Body

Romans 12:1–15:13 Exhortations

Romans 15:14-33 Conclusion

Romans 16:1-27 Greetings, a warning, final doxology

COMMENTARY

ADDRESS

Romans 1:1-15

1:1-7 The apostle to the Gentiles introduces himself and his gospel

In these compact verses Paul introduces himself, his gospel, and the gist of his message. He did not take it upon himself to speak for God and God's Son as their apostle. God called him, a zealous persecutor of the church, to be an apostle to the Gentiles (see Gal 1:11-24). I pause here and urge my readers to go back to my Introduction (p. 439) to see what I have to say about the Jewish view of Gentiles: They are sinners. Yet God has called the Jew Paul to preach the gospel to these sinners.

The good news or gospel that Paul preaches is not totally new but has antecedents in the Scriptures (1:2). We will be frustrated if we look exclusively for individual verses in the Old Testament. Paul is looking more to the broad sweep of God's purpose of giving life to women and men. Paul will refer again to God's salvific purpose when he considers Abraham (Rom 4), Adam (Rom 5:12-21), the gift of the law (Rom 7:1–8:30), those powers that try to separate us from God (Rom 8:31-39), and God's election of Israel (Rom 9–11).

The gospel is about God's Son, born a Jew from a royal house, and "established as Son of God in power according to the spirit of holiness through resurrection from the dead, Jesus Christ our Lord"

(1:4). Paul makes no mention here that this royal figure was crucified by Roman power. Instead, he uses the eschatological category of resurrection from the dead to indicate that God has done something new and final in Jesus. Death has not conquered Jesus. God has exalted him to be Lord.

Richard A. Horsley has been reminding us that Paul's gospel stands in radical contrast to the imperial gospel, inaugurated by Caesar Augustus, whose victories and rule were considered good news. Augustus was hailed by an inscription at Priene as "[a Savior] who has made war to cease and who shall put everything [in peaceful] order" (F. W. Danker). It is not happenstance that Paul will follow his introduction with an indictment of Gentile idolatry and vices (1:18-32). Jesus, Son of David, Son of God, is Savior and Lord, not Caesar.

It is also significant that Paul exhorts his hearers in Romans 5:1: "Let us have peace with God through our Lord Jesus Christ" (author's translation). Americans who think that emperor worship, bread, and circuses are beyond their ken should take a closer look at American Civil Religion and the United States' multiple shrines dedicated to pleasure, consumerism, and the fountain of youth.

God has called Paul "to bring about the obedience of faith" (1:5). Paul announces here a major theme of Romans, which he will develop at great length with the example of Abraham, who was a Gentile, an ungodly person, but who believed (4:5). Already we hear the briefest of hints about theodicy: Should we Gentiles believe in a God who seems not to have been faithful to the people God first called? If God were not faithful to them, how can we Gentiles have confidence that God will be faithful to us? See Romans 9–11.

1:8-15 Paul gives thanks and states that he worships God through preaching

My sole comment here is on Romans 1:9: "God is my witness, whom I worship with my spirit in proclaiming the gospel of his Son" (author's translation). Paul uses the Greek verb *latreuein*, "to worship." His worship of God is through his missionary activity of proclaiming the gospel of the Lord Jesus, not through emperor worship. In Romans 12:1 Paul tells the Romans how to worship: "I urge you therefore, brothers, by the mercies of God, to offer your bodies as a living

sacrifice, holy and pleasing to God, your spiritual worship."

In Romans 15:16 Paul again uses worship terminology to describe his preaching of the gospel: "to be a minister of Christ Jesus to the Gentiles in performing the priestly service of the gospel of God, so that the offering up of the Gentiles may be acceptable, sanctified by the holy Spirit." It does not seem to me that Paul is merely using worship language in a figurative way.

HUMANITY LOST WITHOUT THE GOSPEL
Romans 1:16–3:20

1:16-17 Paul states the theme of his letter

My readers can peruse all thirteen of Paul's letters and not find another instance where Paul announces the theme of his letter as he does here, for Romans alone is modeled after a scholastic diatribe or instruction (see Introduction, pp. 442–43). Paul will explicate this theme in the rest of Romans, often by using the questions of scholastic diatribe. While the gospel is God's power for the salvation of all people, it is meant first for God's elect people.

I borrow from two renowned commentators to define "God's righteousness." Joseph A. Fitzmyer accentuates it as an attribute of God who is judge for God's people: "It is a quality whereby God actively acquits his sinful people, manifesting towards them his power and gracious activity in a just judgment. . . ." Ernst Käsemann underscores God's dominion over the world: "God's sovereignty over the world revealing itself eschatologically in Jesus . . . the rightful power with which God makes his cause to triumph in the world which has fallen away from him and which yet, as creation, is his inviolable possession."

I believe that we can capture some of the nuances of "from faith to faith" if we look at Paul's quotation from Habakkuk. I translate the Septuagint of Habakkuk 2:4: "The righteous person will live because of my faithfulness." The reference behind "my" is God, who is faithful to the person who has kept right relationship with God. Although Paul has dropped "my," it seems that the background of Habbakuk is still in his mind. The Greek word *pistis*, which is regularly translated by "faith," also means "faithfulness" and "trust."

God's righteousness reveals God's faithfulness to God's chosen people and to creation and leads to a faithful response. Would that sermons were preached on the gospel of God's righteous fidelity to God's elect and God's creation!

1:18-32 The plight of the Gentiles

I ask you to skip ahead to Romans 3:21-24. Read that passage carefully: "But now the righteousness of God has been manifested . . . the righteousness of God through faith in Jesus Christ for all who believe. For there is no distinction; all have sinned. . . . They are justified freely by his grace through the redemption in Christ Jesus." It would seem that Romans 3:21-24 is the "logical" next paragraph after Paul's theme sentence in Romans 1:16-17. But before Paul could arrive at this "solution," he had to state the "problem": All have sinned. Put another way, in the style of a scholastic diatribe Paul develops his theme of "God's righteousness unto salvation" by contrasting it with its antithesis: sin's domination over humans (see 3:9) and the law's inability to cope with sin (3:20).

The dominant Jewish view of Gentiles pulses through this passage. Later on, in Romans 6:17, Paul will remind his Gentile hearers that they were formerly in the same boat of lacking mastery over self, because they "were once slaves of sin." From the key sin of idolatry all other sins cascade forth. As Wisdom 14:12 states:

> For the source of wantonness is the devising of
>   idols;
>   and their invention was a corruption of life.

And Wisdom 14:25-27 continues:

> And all is confusion—blood and murder, theft and
>   guile,
>   corruption, faithlessness, turmoil, perjury,
> Disturbance of good men, neglect of gratitude,
>   besmirching of souls, unnatural lust,
>   disorder in marriage, adultery and
>   shamelessness.
> For the worship of infamous idols
>   is the reason and source and extremity of all
>   evil.

There is no excuse for such behavior: "For although they knew God they did not accord him glory as God or give him thanks" (1:21; see 1:32).

Contemporary society almost forces us to bypass the capital sins and even murder in Romans 1:29-31 and to focus on what Paul says about same-sex love in 1:24-28. As Richard B. Hays and others have shown, there is no doubt that Paul condemns these actions that are willingly chosen. Luke Timothy Johnson formulates the question for contemporary application: "Or is it [same-sex love], as some studies and many people claim, the 'natural' mode of sexual expression for a small portion of the world's population?"

2:1-5 The Gentile who boasts

In the very beginning of my Introduction (p. 439), I asked my readers to make their way through all of Romans by asking questions such as: What personal pronouns does Paul use? Romans 2:1-5 is a very important case in point, for Paul changes from the third person pronouns of 1:18-32 to "you" singular. The NAB's translation of Romans 2:1 and 3 masks Paul's use of the Greek *ō anthrōpe*, which is used in scholastic diatribe and means "fellow" or, in our parlance, "guy." I render Romans 2:1, which continues Paul's discussion of how passions rule Gentiles: "Therefore, you are without an excuse, guy, like anyone who judges." Paul's diatribal address picks up "the insolent, haughty, and boastful" Gentiles of Romans 1:30 and skewers them. For they, too, are sinners. Romans 2:4 finds a parallel in Wisdom 11:23:

> But you [God] have mercy on all, because you can
>   do all things;
>   and you overlook the sins of men that they
>   may repent.

2:6-16 Three key teachings

Gentiles are still very much in Paul's eyes as he refers to two fundamental beliefs about God that are based in the Scriptures. God "will repay everyone according to his works" (2:6). Proverbs 24:12 states: God "will repay each one according to his deeds." Romans 2:11 confesses: "There is no partiality with God." Sirach 35:12 professes: "For he is a God of justice, / who knows no favorites." The Gentile is judged by deeds, but so too is the member of God's chosen people, for God is impartial.

A further fundamental belief is imbedded in Romans 2:16: "according to my gospel, God will judge people's hidden works through Christ

Jesus." The gospel, for which Paul fought so un-compromisingly in Galatians, is that Gentiles do not have to become Jews and observe the law in order to be justified in God's sight. In turn, Christ Jesus will not judge them on the basis of their observance of Jewish covenantal law but on the observance of the law in their hearts. As Charles H. Talbert comments, "A pervasive belief existed among ancient Jews as well as pagans that all people had some elemental knowledge of moral-ity for which they were responsible."

2:17-29 A pretentious teacher, who is a Jew and would teach Gentiles

Again, note the change of personal pronoun, as third person gives way to "you" singular. Stanley Stowers has helped me to see this passage as a diatribal attack on the pretentious teacher, who happens to be a Jew and is not the "typical Jew." I recall many of J. F. Powers's short stories that featured Roman Catholic clergy. Clergy who read these stories were up in arms, for they mistakenly thought that Powers was attacking them, whereas he was pointing his literary finger at people, lay or clergy, who were greedy, self-centered, and lazy.

A compelling parallel to what Paul is doing in this passage occurs in what Epictetus writes in his discourse: "To those who take up the teachings of the philosophers only to talk about them." Epicte-tus addresses the would-be teacher, whose deeds are evil: "For your own evils are enough for you: your baseness, your cowardice, the bragging that you indulged in when you were sitting in the lec-ture room. Why did you pride yourself on things that were not your own?" (*Discourses* 2.19.19, in Loeb translation). Instead of teaching Gentiles the true way to God, this vain teacher leads them away from God. Indeed, Isaiah 52:5 is verified here, for the Gentiles revile God's name because of what the Jewish teacher has done or failed to do.

3:1-9 God's chosen people, although sinners, are still advantaged

Paul continues his scholastic diatribe with a series of five objections or questions. Each objec-tion is twofold. See 3:1, 3, 5, 7-8a, 9a for these questions and 3:2, 4, 6, 8b, and 9b for Paul's re-sponses. Although this series of questions and answers functions very well here, it is a foretaste of Paul's extensive discussion in Romans 9–11 about God's fidelity in the face of the nonbelief in

Jesus the Christ on the part of most of the chosen people.

I focus on Paul's responses in 3:4 and 3:6 and then on both question and answer in 3:9. Romans 3:4 reads: "God must be true." God's truthfulness refers to God's covenant fidelity to the chosen people. See Psalm 89:2: "The promises of the LORD I will sing forever, / proclaim your loyalty [truth-fulness] through all ages." Romans 3:6 proclaims that God is judge of the world. Psalm 94:2 pleads with God: "Rise up, judge of the earth; / give the proud what they deserve." Romans 3:9a is surely a difficult sentence, especially since the anteced-ent "we" of 3:8 is ambiguous. If the "we" includes both Paul and his imaginary Jewish interlocutor, then the translation is: "What then? Are we [Jews] disadvantaged? Not at all." If the "we" refers solely to Paul, then F. W. Danker's translation makes sense: "What then? Am I protecting my-self? Am I making excuses? Not at all."

Readers should not miss the occurrence of the noun "sin" for the first time in Romans 3:9b. Through the use of personification, Paul paints sin as a master who dominates Jew and Gentile. What irony for those who believed they had achieved self-mastery.

3:10-20 Observance of the law does not lead to justification

If my readers have an image of Paul rapidly dictating this letter to his scribe Tertius (see 16:22), this passage should cause a drastic revision of that image. For nowhere in Scripture are these ten quotations found together in the same book. They seem to have been composed beforehand. Take 3:13, for example. "Their throats are open graves; / they deceive with their tongues" (author's translation) is found in the Septuagint of Psalm 5:10. The next line of 3:13, however, comes from the Septuagint of Psalm 139:4: "The venom of asps is on their lips." The motif of "no one, not one" surges through 3:10-12, and the full involvement of the human person (from head to toe) seems to be the ordering principle for 3:13-18.

Paul's long chain of Scripture quotations should not distract us from the conclusion he draws in 3:20: "No human being will be justified in his [God's] sight by observing the law." That is, neither the chosen people nor the Gentiles find justification in the law. Romans 3:21-26 will state where justification may now be found.

JUSTIFICATION THROUGH FAITH IN CHRIST

Romans 3:21–5:21

3:21-26 The soteriological heart of Romans

Having argued his thesis by means of its antithesis in 1:18–3:20, Paul now formulates it positively in a section that is soteriologically and christologically significant but dense. I highlight five key points and leave to advanced students an investigation of the likelihood that Paul adapted earlier tradition in 3:24-26. First, the law does not bring about justification, although it testifies to it (3:21). Paul will address the role of the law in Romans 4 and 7–11, for "the law is holy, and the commandment is holy and righteous and good" (7:12).

Second, "[all sinners] are justified freely" (3:24), that is, God has declared them to be acquitted of their sin.

Third, Christ's death on the cross is front and center stage in the words "by his blood" (3:25). Christ's shedding of his blood has brought about redemption, an image that denotes being ransomed from the slavery and domination of sin (see 3:9).

Fourth, 3:25 employs another image—that of expiation. God has set forth Jesus Christ on the cross as the new expiatory sacrifice that takes away sin through the shedding of his blood. The Old Testament background seems to be Exodus 25:17 ("You shall then make an expiating cover") and Leviticus 16:15-16: "Then he (Aaron) shall slaughter the people's sin-offering goat, and bringing its blood inside the veil, he shall do with it as he did with the bullock's blood, sprinkling it on the expiatory and before it. Thus he shall make atonement for the sanctuary because of all the sinful defilements and faults of the Israelites" (author's translations).

Fifth, four times in this passage "faith" or "to believe" occurs (3:22). Justification, redemption, expiation are not forced upon men and women. They have to respond in faith to God who has done these things for them through Jesus Christ.

3:27–4:2a A person is justified by faith

This section is yet another dialogue in diatribe modality. In it Paul leads his readers to appreciate the centrality of faith for both Jew and Gentile.

God who is one does not require two ways but only one—that of faith. The section begins with "boasting," ends with "boasting," and leads to the example of Abraham (4:2b-25), whose faith was credited to him as righteousness (4:9).

I lay out this dialogue, modifying the NAB translation above and indicating the interlocutor by "I" and Paul by "P." Paul formulates the interlocutor's questions in such a way as to lead to his key theological teachings.

I: Is there reason to boast?

P: It is ruled out.

I: By what principle? That of the law?

P: No, rather by the principle of faith. For we consider that a person is justified by faith apart from works of the law. Does God belong only to Jews? Does he not belong also to Gentiles?

I: Yes, also to Gentiles.

P: For God is one and will justify the circumcised on the basis of faith and the uncircumcised through faith.

I: Are we then annulling the law by faith?

P: Of course not. On the contrary, we are supporting the law.

I: What then are we to say? Have we found Abraham, to be our forebear by his own efforts? For if Abraham was justified on the basis of his works, he has reason to boast.

All of Romans 4:2b-25 will give Paul's response: Faithful Abraham has no reason to boast.

4:2b-25 Abraham's faith and the God who justifies the ungodly

Romans 4:2b-25 provides Paul's reasons why Abraham has no reason to boast: he did nothing to earn justification. Put positively and compactly, Abraham, a Gentile, believed God despite all evidence to the contrary. In fashioning his final answer to the diatribal dialogue that commenced in 3:27, Paul utilizes another feature of the scholastic diatribe: teaching by means of examples. For instance, Epictetus draws upon luminaries of the philosophical tradition such as Plato, Diogenes, and Epicurus to paint positive and negative examples. Paul reaches back into the Jewish tradition to forebear Abraham. It is very important to note what characteristics of Abraham are of theological interest to Paul and what Abraham's example says about God.

Recall what Paul says about the sins of the Gentiles in 1:18-32. Abraham was a Gentile, an idolater, an ungodly person when God called him out of Ur of Chaldea. Drawing upon Genesis 15:16, Paul notes: "Abraham believed God, and it was credited to him as righteousness" (Rom 4:3). Abraham hadn't undergone the rite of circumcision when he believed (Gen 17). Nor was he being rewarded for having offered gracious and generous hospitality to strangers (Gen 18). He had not yet been obedient to God in his willingness to sacrifice his only son, Isaac, the carrier of God's praises (Gen 22). Abraham was the recipient of a gift (Rom 4:4). Why did God do this? The reason is found in God's nature: God justifies the ungodly (4:5). Earlier, in 3:10-18, Paul displayed one of his ways of interpreting Scripture as he strung together quotations from various parts of Scripture in a chain. In 4:7-8 Paul follows another method, namely, citing a Scripture passage that contains the same key word. Both of these passages, then, interpret each other. In this instance Paul quotes Psalm 31:1-2 in the Septuagint because it contains the same key verb "to credit." The NAB's "does not record" (4:8) masks this point. Through God's act of justification, God forgives iniquities. In 4:9-12 Paul draws yet another point from Abraham's faith: Through his faith Abraham is the father of both the uncircumcised and the circumcised.

In Romans 7–8 Paul will pay close attention to, and argue extensively about, the role of the law. In 4:13-16 Paul whets his hearers' appetites with apodictic statements, the key of which is: "If those who adhere to the law are the heirs, faith is null and the promise is void" (4:14).

In 4:17-22 Paul moves away from his earlier, more abstract consideration of Abraham as a model of faith and gets specific. Again Paul confesses a cardinal point of his and our faith: God "who gives life to the dead and calls into being what does not exist" (4:17). Through this faith Abraham was empowered to trust God's word and promise. Abraham's God has given life to his almost dead body and to the dead womb of his wife, Sarah. In 4:23-25 Paul moves from Abraham's faith in the God who justifies the ungodly and gives life to the dead and draws himself and his hearers into the story. Notice the change of

personal pronouns in 4:24-25: "It was also for *us* . . . *our* Lord . . . for *our* transgressions . . . for *our* justification" (emphasis added).

Scholars who interpret Romans from a story perspective have hit pay dirt in Romans 4. The story of Abraham and Sarah captivates believers, who are led to see in these forebears their stories of hoping against hope (4:18), believing that God draws life out of death and trusting that God justifies ungodly people such as us who may have been overcome by sin.

5:1-11 God's many gifts through Jesus Christ our Lord

This is an exceedingly rich passage. I offer six considerations. First, I urge my readers to note Paul's use of "we." I count seventeen uses of "we/ our." I would venture to say that Paul is including himself with his Gentile hearers, and his main purpose is *pathos*. In my Introduction (p. 443) I stated that the author experiences the emotion that he wants his listeners to experience. In this passage the "emotions" are the entire gambit of God's gifts: peace, love, boasting, hope, reconciliation, the Holy Spirit.

Second, in this passage Paul often makes reference to teachings he presented earlier. Boasting (5:2, 3, 11), which Paul and his society considered good as long as it was done decently, stands in stark contrast with the illegitimate boasting of 3:17 and 4:2 and ties this passage to what preceded it. Because of God's many gifts, the Gentiles can toot their own horn, and do so to God's honor. The peace (5:1) that the Gentiles are experiencing is not that created by Caesar Augustus but by Jesus Christ our Lord (see 1:7). In 1:16 Paul proudly proclaimed that he was not ashamed of the gospel of Jesus Christ, crucified as a criminal but raised by God from the dead. Romans 5:5 contains the same verb "to shame": Hope does not shame because of the reality of God's gift of absolutely gratuitous love (see 5:5).

Third, in 5:3-5, Paul displays his literary prowess as he fashions a *sorites* (literally: "a heap"), as he moves from affliction to endurance to proven character to hope.

Four, notice how many times Paul refers to Jesus Christ (5:1, 2, 6, 8, 9, 10, 11). Jesus Christ is God's Son (5:10). Through the shedding of his blood we have reconciliation with God, that is, enemies have turned their tanks into plows. In

Jewish tradition there is the story of a mother and seven sons who resisted the tyrant Antiochus and preserved their faith and ancestral customs, even though they were mercilessly tortured and killed for their fidelity. Their deaths were of great benefit to the entire nation. 4 Maccabees 17:22 reads: "Through the blood of these devout ones and their death as an atoning sacrifice, divine Providence preserved Israel which had previously been mistreated" (NRSV modified). Jesus' death is of even greater benefit to humanity.

Fifth, the multiple gifts that Gentile believers experience do not come from their own inner strength but through God's Spirit, who is other and holy (5:5).

Finally, Paul's "how much more" argument in 5:10 prepares his hearers for his argument in 5:12-21. See, for example, 5:15. God's gifts through Jesus Christ enable people to attain the self-mastery that they and their culture have been longing for.

5:12-21 The wondrous consequences of the obedience of Jesus Christ

In Romans 5:12 the "we" style vanishes (except for the use of "our" in the formulaic ending of 5:21: "through Jesus Christ *our* Lord"; emphasis added), and Paul adopts the discursive third person style. If you ask how 5:12-21 connects with what has preceded, I give two answers. It gives an analysis of sin that is more profound than that given in 1:18–3:20. Further, it praises the wondrous gifts that have come about through the faithful obedience of Jesus Christ and thus continues the general thematic of 5:1-11. Paul may have composed this passage on another occasion and saw how fitting it was for this letter.

It is important to quote two Scripture passages as background to Romans 5:12-14. Genesis 2:16-17 states: "The LORD God gave man this order: 'You are free to eat from any of the trees of the garden except the tree of knowledge of good and bad. From that tree you shall not eat; the moment you eat from it you are surely doomed to die'" (NAB). Adam's sin of disobedience brings about death. Wisdom 2:23-24 speaks of the reign of death: "For God formed man to be imperishable; / the image of his own nature he made him. / But by the envy of the devil, death entered the world, / and they who are in his possession experience it" (NAB). As Luke Timothy Johnson writes: "Everyone has

sinned the way Adam did, so that the effect of Adam's sin continues, and continues to be symbolized by the death experienced by all humans."

But as Paul teaches through the extensive comparisons of 5:15-21, Adam's disobedience is not the end of the story. Paul makes his point much more succinctly in 1 Corinthians 15:45: "So, too, it is written, 'The first man, Adam, became a living being,' the last Adam a life-giving spirit." The risen Lord Jesus stands at the beginning of the new creation. While on the side of Adam are disobedience, transgression, and death, on the side of the New Adam there are obedience, acquittal, life, and grace. "In conclusion, just as through one transgression condemnation came upon all, so through one righteous act acquittal and life came to all" (5:18). In Romans 6–8 Paul will spell out the meaning of incorporation into the life of the New Adam through baptism (Rom 6), the role of the law (Rom 7), and the driving force of God's Spirit (Rom 8).

Advocates of the story approach to Romans are happy that Paul has finally shown the narrative that lies below the surface of his discursive soteriology and christology. Jesus, God's Son, has redeemed believers not from one single sin but from the power of sin and death. Those who experienced the power of Osama bin Ladin on 9/11/01 have no doubt that the transgression of one single individual has a negative effect on millions. Even the musical *Beauty and the Beast* teaches us that the selfish, heartless action of one individual has consequences for an entire household. On the positive side, the narrative of the life of Francis of Assisi (d. 1226) continues to breathe fresh life into countless people of all faiths.

JUSTIFICATION AND THE CHRISTIAN LIFE

Romans 6:1–8:39

6:1-14 Baptism and the newness of life

Paul develops the points he has been making in Romans 5:12-21 by means of an objection by an imaginary interlocutor in 6:1-2. Throughout 6:2-14, Paul will be answering the absurd question of 6:1: "Shall we persist in sin that grace may abound?" The attentive reader will note Paul's use of "we" in 6:1-9 and his use of "you" plural in 6:11-14. What the Gentile believers in Romans experienced in baptism Paul also experienced.

Thus Paul engages in *pathos* or exhorting his hearers on the basis of common experience. Finally, from his description of baptism (6:2-5), Paul will draw upon some common principles (6:6-10) and then apply them (6:11-14).

The ritual of infant baptism and especially the baptism of adults at the Easter Vigil give us some inkling of Paul's view of baptism. The immersion of the baptizand is likened to Christ's death and burial; the lifting up out of the water is likened to Christ's resurrection. The change of clothing points to the newly baptized's change of status.

Although I have been trying to interpret Romans without explicit reference to Galatians, I believe that some verses from this earlier letter help us to appreciate what Paul means here by baptism. Galatians 3:1-5 very clearly points to the explosive nature of the Christian experience of baptism. See especially Galatians 3:5: "Does, then, the one who supplies the Spirit to you and works mighty deeds among you do so from works of the law or from faith in what you heard?" Baptism may very well have been the occasion for the display of the multiple gifts of the Spirit (see 1 Cor 12–14), the time when the love of God was manifestly "poured out into our hearts through the holy Spirit" (Rom 5:5) and the time when the newly baptized cried out "Abba, Father!" (Gal 4:6; Rom 8:15) as a profession of their new status as children of God.

Romans 6:6-10 largely consists of "principles." Paul's use of "for" in 6:5, 7 announces principles. For example, 6:7 states that the person who has died has lost the very means of sinning, namely, "our sinful body" (6:6). The "if" sentences of 6:5, 8 formulate principles. The "we know" sentences of 6:6, 9 remind listeners of principles.

Romans 6:11-14 applies these principles to Paul's Gentile listeners, who were quite aware of the vices that dominated their society (see Rom 1:18-32). "Therefore, sin must not reign over your mortal bodies so that you obey their desires" (6:12). In Romans 8 Paul will spend considerable time on the role of the Holy Spirit in believers' everyday lives of living out the newness of baptismal life.

6:15-23 Be addicted to the Lord Jesus Christ

Paul develops his teaching some more by means of another rhetorical question in the first person: "What then? Shall we sin because we are not under the law but under grace? Of course not!" (6:15). With the exception of 6:19, where Paul uses "I," this entire section is in the second person and is addressed to Gentile believers who once engaged in sins of which they are now ashamed (6:21; see 1:24-28).

To me, the best contemporary analogy to the master-slave relationship that Paul utilizes in this section is addiction. We all know of individuals who are addicted to gambling or alcohol or drugs and will do just about anything to get their daily "fix." These individuals are in thralldom, in slavery to their addiction. Even though they realize in their sober moments that they are destroying their lives and those of the people they love, they cannot help themselves. They are very clever at hiding their addiction and at making excuses for their conduct.

If we apply this analogy to 6:16-23, we realize that because of all that God has done for us in Jesus Christ—justification, redemption, gift of the Holy Spirit, baptism—we are now to be addicted to righteousness, sanctification, and life. We are to be "obedient from the heart to the pattern of teaching to which [we] were entrusted" (6:17). The reference here is most likely to the core of teaching given at the time of baptism in the midst of one's brothers and sisters. In 6:19, 22 Paul introduces a new term, "sanctification." Just as their God is holy or "other," the lives of believers are to be "other." How "other"? Paul's reference back to the sins of Romans 1:18-32 gives a glimpse of what has to be left behind in believers' new addiction to Jesus Christ.

This section ends with a rousing summary: "The wages of sin is death, but the gift of God is eternal life in Christ Jesus our Lord" (6:23). I conclude by accentuating the plural number of the "you" that Paul employs in this section. Individuals do not come out of addiction by themselves. They need outside help, community, loved ones. In this instance, they need the Christian community or local house church.

7:1-6 The role of the law: Part I

As Paul has been making his case that new life in Christ has freed believers from the power of sin and death, he has often dropped hints about the role of the Mosaic law. I mention some of Paul's earlier pronouncements about the law. See 3:20:

"no human being will be justified in his sight by observing the law; for through the law comes consciousness of sin." In Romans 4:14-15 Paul states: "For if those who adhere to the law are the heirs, faith is null and the promise is void. For the law produces wrath; but where there is no law, neither is there violation." After mentioning the law in 5:13, Paul says in 5:20: "The law entered in so that transgression might increase but, where sin increased, grace overflowed all the more." Finally, Romans 6:14-15 reads: "For sin is not to have any power over you, since you are not under the law but under grace. What then? Shall we sin because we are not under the law but under grace?" These hints have whetted our appetites. Now Paul sets the table for a full course on the law.

Again, I invite my readers to check Paul's personal pronouns. Romans 7:2-3 is an illustration in the third person. Romans 7:1 and 4 have "you" plural and the fictive kinship term "brothers [and sisters]." Romans 7:4c-6 employs "we" pronouns as Paul identifies himself with his Gentile hearers.

The illustration is pretty straightforward, as it talks about the binding force of law for a married couple while both partners are alive. It presupposes that this married union will result in the bearing of fruit (children; see 7:4-5). Once the husband has died, the law of marriage for the wife ceases. She is free to marry another.

Paul introduces the application of this illustration by the words "in the same way" in 7:4, but note the ways in which he transfers the terms of the illustration. See, for example, 7:4: "You also were put to death to the law through the [crucified] body of Christ, so that you might belong to another, to the one who was raised from the dead in order that we might bear fruit for God." It is clear that believers now belong to another, namely, Jesus Christ. It is also clear that the death of Jesus Christ has destroyed the power of law over believers. When we were without the Spirit, that is, in the flesh (see Romans 8 for more detail), the law awakened sinful passions by forbidding certain actions. Like people caught in a bad marriage, we were held captive to destructive forces. But now that the law is dead, we may serve "in the newness of the spirit" (7:6).

7:7–8:2 The role of the law: Part II

Paul develops his thought here about the relationship between law and sin by means of two diatribal objections and answers in 7:7a and 7:13a. Each answer is developed further in what follows. I am indebted to Stanley Stowers for the interpretation that the "I" that occurs in virtually every verse of 7:7-25 is an instance of what the Greeks called *prosopopoiia*, or "speech in character." Finally, 7:25a and 8:1-2 are Paul's remarks to the "I."

Speech in character "is a rhetorical and literary technique in which the speaker or writer produces speech that represents not himself or herself but another person or type of character." Thus the "I" is not Paul nor a Jew nor a Christian; rather the "I" is the Gentile striving to attain self-mastery by means of observance of the Mosaic law. In his own way, Joseph A. Fitzmyer is on the same wavelength as Stowers when he comments that the "I" is: "unregenerate humanity faced with the Mosaic law—but as seen by a Christian."

Key verses in this interpretation are 7:15 and 7:19, which are paralleled in Greek literature and philosophy. Romans 7:15 reads: "What I do, I do not understand. For I do not do what I want, but I do what I hate." Romans 7:19 states: "For I do not do the good I want, but I do the evil I do not want." Such was the situation of Medea in Greek tragedy, who, overcome by anger and the desire for revenge, killed her own children. In Euripides' *Medea* the main character wails: "I am overcome by evil. Now, now, I learn what horrors I intend, but passion overpowers sober thought, and this is the cause of the direst evils for men and women" (1077–1080; Loeb modified). Medea, a pagan, is the model for lack of self-mastery.

There is a heart-rending version of Medea in Samuel Barber's "Medea's Dance of Vengeance." See also the Roman poet Ovid, who in his *Metamorphoses* comments: "I see the better and approve it, but I follow the worse" (7.20-21; Loeb). In his *Discourses* the Stoic philosopher Epictetus writes: "What he wants to do he doesn't do, and what he doesn't want he does" (2, 26.4; Loeb modified).

Into this pagan situation of being mastered by the passions, Jewish apologists such as Philo of Alexandria proclaimed that the Jewish Mosaic law made Jews more self-controlled, better able to control their passions. In Book IV.55 of his *Special Laws*, Philo praises the Mosaic law: "The law thinks that all those who adhere to the sacred constitution, established by Moses, ought to be free from all unreasonable passions, and from all wickedness" (C. D. Yonge translation).

Paul agrees that "the law is holy, and the commandment is holy and righteous and good" (7:12). But he also realizes that sin has overwhelmed the law: "For sin, seizing an opportunity in the commandment, deceived me and through it put me to death" (7:11). If Gentiles cannot turn to the Mosaic law for liberation from the powers of sin, death, and flesh, they must turn and have turned to Jesus Christ. Before the "I" of the "speech in character" has a chance to complete its tale of woe and misery, Paul, the author of this letter, interrupts and exclaims: "Thanks be to God through Jesus Christ our Lord" (7:25a).

In Romans 8:1-2 the author Paul again returns from using "speech in character" and in 8:2 addresses the "I," now turned to "you" singular: "For the law of the spirit of life in Christ Jesus has freed *you* from the law of sin and death" (emphasis added). That is, Paul does not immediately turn to the hearers of his letter by using "you" plural. He is completing his theological thought and captivating his hearers by using the artistry of "speech in character."

8:3-13 The life of God's Spirit in the believer

All of Romans 8 addresses the question: If the law is unable to give life, then whence comes life? In this section Paul answers this question by pointing to the Gentile believers' experience of the Spirit. I invite my readers to once again look carefully at the pronouns in this section. Although "us" occurs in 8:4, I would suggest that 8:12 contains the key "we" statement: "Consequently, brothers [and sisters], we are not debtors to the flesh, to live according to the flesh." Paul expresses his teaching about the flesh and the Spirit in the third person in 8:5-8. Romans 8:9-11, 13 captures the attention of Paul's Gentile listeners at Rome, as Paul uses "you" plural. Self-mastery does not come from the law but from the Spirit. Romans 8:13b reads: "If by the spirit you put to death the deeds of the body, you will live."

For the rest I focus on two points. Romans 8:3 contains a lapidary statement about Paul's view of God, who has given life to believers by "sending his own Son in the likeness of sinful flesh and for the sake of sin." God's own Son has become human and through his death has taken away humanity's sin. My second point deals with Paul's contrast between flesh and Spirit. For Paul "the

flesh" is not to be confused or equated with sexual sins. "The flesh" is the entire human person, turned away from God and turned toward self. Paul's discussion of the flesh and the Spirit in Galatians 5:19-23 is very illuminating. In Galatians 5:19-21 Paul lists among "the works of the flesh" such human intellectual and willful actions as "idolatry, sorcery, . . . envy, . . . acts of selfishness." For Paul, "the Spirit" comprises God's actions toward the world, God's presence in the world, for God's people, in a creative way. Galatians 5:22-23 is very enlightening, for Paul lists among "the fruit of the Spirit" such creative actions as "love, . . . generosity, . . . self-control."

8:14-30 The future of believers is now

I formulate the theme that courses through this long section in this way: What believers experience now is the foretaste, the firstfruits, the down payment of what is to come. In more technical terminology, Paul is talking about eschatology in the process of realization. Scholars who pursue a story approach to Romans rightly note that Paul seems to momentarily draw the curtain back from the end time to show believers what it will be like. At the same time, Paul stresses that believers are already experiencing in the Spirit, in hope, what God's gracious purpose has in store for them. They have been saved—in hope (8:24). I also invite my readers to see how often Paul joins hands with the experience of the Gentile believers in Romans by frequently using "we." I refer to 8:16, 17, 18, 22, 23, 24, 25, 26, 28.

Here are the believers' present experiences that point to the future. They are "children of God," sons and daughters of God, brothers and sisters of Jesus. Romans 8:15 says pointedly: "*You* received a spirit of adoption, through which *we* cry, *Abba,* 'Father'" (emphasis added to "you" and "we"). The Holy Spirit has brought about this experience of adoption into God's family (see 8:16). Amidst present sufferings, glory awaits believers. That is their hope, for they are not like the pagans, "who have no hope" (1 Thess 4:13). They await what Revelation 21:1 refers to as "a new heaven and a new earth," that is, a time when God's curse upon humanity and the earth is lifted. See Genesis 3:17-19: "Cursed be the ground because of you! / In toil shall you eat its yield / all the days of your life. / Thorns and thistles shall it bring forth to you. . . . / By the sweat of your face / shall you get bread to eat." Believers await in groaning the fulfillment of the firstfruits of the Spirit, namely, the redemption of their entire selves (8:23).

Among the vicissitudes of human life and the life of faith, the Spirit comes to believers' aid and intercedes with God for them. As James D. G. Dunn says so well: "The Spirit is seen here as typically active not so much in the heights of spiritual rapture as in the depths of human inability to cope." In 8:28-30 Paul captures the final experience believers have: It is the confidence born of their faith "that all things work for good for those who love God" (8:28). Glorification is the ultimate destiny of all who have faith in Jesus Christ as their Lord (8:30). Paul speaks of it as already present.

8:31-39 A hymn to the God who is for us

I have counted a dozen occurrences of "we/our/us" in the Greek of this relatively short passage. Paul again engages in *pathos* and identifies himself with his listeners. To what does "this" in 8:31 refer? Is it a reference to the sufferings Paul mentions in 8:18-25? I would suggest that it's a reference to the various battles which believers wage against the powers of sin, death, and the flesh and which Paul has treated in Romans 5:11–8:30.

Paul once again adopts the style of a scholastic diatribe and raises questions in 8:31, 32, 33, 34, 35. The scene is the courtroom of the Last Judgment. Paul's answers seem like an early creed and reveal deep faith in what God has done for believers: God is for us; God lovingly handed his Son over for our salvation; God acquits the ungodly; Christ Jesus died, was raised, is at the right hand of the Father, and intercedes for us; we conquer overwhelmingly through the God who loves us; God loves us in Christ Jesus our Lord. The trials that Paul experienced as a missionary and apostle do not have the power to separate him from the love of Christ (8:35). It is for God's sake that Paul endures all this, as he demonstrates from Psalm 43:23 in the Septuagint. No creature whatsoever, no matter how fearsome, is able to separate believers from God's love, manifested in Christ Jesus our Lord (8:38-39).

This hymn has provided courage to believers after national, community, and personal disasters. People battling cancer have drawn tremendous strength by looking at God through the lens of this hymn. Believers of all stripes rejoice that Paul

shared his experience of God, which forms the basis for our experience of God.

JEWS AND GENTILES IN GOD'S PLAN
Romans 9:1–11:36

9:1-5 Paul's ethos, pathos, and logic on dress parade in the service of theodicy

I make four opening remarks for all of Romans 9–11. The rousing hymn in praise of God that Paul created in Romans 8:31-39 almost seems to defy any new thoughts. Shouldn't Paul conclude his letter, send greetings, and call it quits? If Paul were only dealing with the salvation of humankind, he might very well stop with 8:39. But in Romans Paul is concerned with God and how justification by faith for both Gentiles and Jews accords with God's earlier choice of Israel as God's special people. Remember that the theme sentence of Romans goes: The gospel "is the power of God for the salvation of everyone who believes: for *Jew first*, and then Greek" (1:16; emphasis added).

Second, Paul, a fervent Jew, the apostle to the Gentiles, bares his heart *(pathos* and *ethos)* on the question: Has the word of God failed? (9:6). Twenty-seven times, compared with eight in Romans 1:18–8:39, Paul uses "I." Stanley Stowers captures Paul's *pathos* and *ethos* well: "Even his mission to the Gentiles turns out to be an episode in the self-story of an Israelite acting for the sake of his people."

Third, the *logic* of Paul's argument in these three chapters is thoroughly scriptural—almost 40 percent of these ninety verses. James W. Aageson has well said: "The reliability of *God's word* to Israel was at stake; and it was to *God's word*, the Scriptures, that Paul turned to argue that it had not failed." In my commentary I will be tracking Paul's use of Scripture and implore my readers to be patient as they gradually discern how Paul is joining Scripture texts via themes. At the same time I advise my readers that Paul, even in Romans 9–11, does not neglect scholastic diatribe, for example, Romans 11:17-24.

Finally, although Paul is truly a religious genius, it is difficult to imagine him composing Romans 9–11 off the top of his head. Paul has frequently wrestled with and anguished over the issues of these chapters and may have preached a sermon or two about them.

In 9:1-5 Paul engages in deep and sincere *pathos* ("great sorrow and constant anguish") over his fellow Jews, the majority of whom have not believed in the gospel of Jesus as Messiah and Lord. God has gifted them so generously. While nothing can separate believers from the love of Christ (8:35), Paul, similar to Moses in Exodus 32:32, is willing to be "separated from Christ for the sake of" his brothers and sisters, his kin according to the flesh.

9:6-13 Paul's thesis and scriptural arguments from the patriarchs

In 9:6 Paul states the proposition that he will be defending from God's word throughout Romans 9–11: The word of God has not failed. The word of God's promise (9:9) and God's call (9:7, 12) are determinative of who God's children are. For example, "This means that it is not the children of the flesh who are the children of God, but the children of the promise are counted as descendants" (9:8). Paul's Scripture quotations come from Genesis 21:12; 18:10, 14; 25:23, the earliest narratives of God's people. Even the citation from a prophetic text (Mal 1:2-3 in Rom 9:13) refers back to the very beginnings of Israel. In this first section of Scripture argumentation, Paul has introduced in 9:7b and 12 a theme that he will pick up in Romans 9:24-26, namely, the theme of "call." The citation from Genesis 21:12 in Romans 9:7b should be translated: "In Isaac your offspring will be called."

9:14-18 God is not unjust; God is sovereign

After using elements of scholastic diatribe throughout Romans 1–8, Paul does not think it time to put it to bed. It has been so useful in helping him engage his listeners. Although God has chosen one and not another, God surely is not unjust. In Romans 9:15 Paul proves God's sovereignty by quoting Exodus 33:19 exactly as it is in the Septuagint: "I will show mercy to whom I will. I will take pity on whom I will" (author's translation).

In 9:16 Paul draws his conclusion by picking up the theme of God's mercy: "So it depends not upon a person's will or exertion, but upon God, who shows mercy." Paul's quotation from Exodus 9:16 is almost verbatim as it describes God's power over Pharaoh. Using the same inferential words he did in 9:16 (*ara oun*), Paul draws his conclusion in 9:18, again emphasizing God's

mercy: "Consequently, he has mercy upon whom he wills, and he hardens whom he wills." Having employed the theme of God's call in 9:6-13, Paul now joins it to the theme of God's mercy: God is the one who calls in God's mercy. The astute reader will notice that Paul is joining Scripture quotations together by means of identical words and themes.

9:19-29 God's mercy, call, and ultimate fidelity

The questions/objections of scholastic diatribe hold 9:19-22 together. Paul combines citations from Isaiah 29:16 and Job 9:12 to answer these objections. How dare a human being even raise such objections! In 9:23 Paul resumes his theme of "mercy" and in 9:25-26 his theme of "call" to show that not only Jews but also Gentiles receive mercy and are called. But God has foreseen through Isaiah that not all is lost for Israel, which has not responded positively to the gospel. Quoting Isaiah 10:22, Paul says: "'Although the number of the Israelites were like the sand of the sea, a remnant will be saved'" (author's translation). The theme of "remnant," introduced here, will reappear in Romans 11:5. Key, too, are words from Isaiah 1:9 in Romans 9:29: The Lord has left us descendants (literally: "a seed").

9:30-33 Surprisingly pagans have faith; unfortunately Israel has not

Paul moves his considerations along by two more questions in 9:30 and 32 and by adding in 9:31-32 the way God has chosen both Jews and Gentiles, that is, through faith and not by works. Paul buttresses his considerations with a combined citation from two passages in Isaiah where he finds the same words. The words "whoever *believes* in him shall not be put to shame" come from Isaiah 28:16, which also contains the word "stone" (emphasis added). Isaiah 8:14 in the Septuagint also contains the word "stone" as well as "stumble" and "rock." Paul's interpretation of these two passages is daring and christological, for the stone laid by God in Zion as a sure foundation has become the stumbling stone, Jesus Christ. See 1 Peter 2:6-8 for a similar use of Isaiah 28:16 and 8:14.

10:1-13 Righteousness through faith

Romans 10:1-4 continues Paul's discussion of righteousness, and 10:5-13 provides scriptural support. Paul's concern for his fellow Jews is palpable (10:1). He does not slander them, for they manifest zeal for worshiping God and obeying God's law that is genuine (10:2). See, for example, 1 Maccabees 2:27: "Then Mattathias went through the city shouting, 'Let everyone who is zealous for the law and who stands by the covenant follow after me.'" But they have not submitted to the righteousness of God that has been revealed in Christ Jesus and in the gospel. Through Jesus Christ God has acquitted believers. What the law tried to accomplish, God has accomplished in Jesus Christ. Thus he is the end and goal of the law.

The Scripture citation of Leviticus 18:5 in Romans 10:5 is verbatim and supports the view that righteousness comes from the law. Paul's Scripture citations in Romans 10:6-8 stem from Deuteronomy 9:4; 30:12-14, and Psalm 106:26 in the Septuagint. Although the passages from Deuteronomy talk about God's gift of the law, Paul has interpreted them christologically via his "that is" clauses in 10:6-8.

Paul's main point about the righteousness that comes from faith is evidenced in his explicit quotation of Deuteronomy 30:14 in Romans 10:8: "'The word is near you, / in your mouth and in your heart' / (that is, the word of faith that we preach)." In Romans 10:9 Paul interprets "mouth" from Deuteronomy 30:14, and in 10:10 he explains "heart" from Deuteronomy 30:14 and does so by relying upon early confessions of faith: Jesus is Lord; God raised Jesus from the dead. In 10:11 Paul recycles and universalizes the quotation from Isaiah 28:16 he quoted earlier in 9:33. Paul's final citation in this section is verbatim from Joel 3:5. It is God who is described as calling in Romans 9:7, 12, 24, 25, 26. Now Gentile and Jewish believers do the calling.

10:14-21 God's chosen people have been disobedient while the senseless Gentiles have believed

This section shows that God's chosen people have no excuse for not believing the gospel. As is his custom, Paul makes his case by means of the questions of scholastic diatribe and his responses, which are largely taken from Scripture, especially Isaiah. One theme that joins this passage to the previous section is that of *word*. See 10:8: "'The word is near you, / in your mouth and in your

heart' / (that is, the word of faith that we preach)." See also 10:17: "and what is heard comes through the word of Christ," and 10:18: "and their words to the end of the world." While Paul underscores the belief of the foolish Gentiles (10:19-20) and chastises Israel's disobedience (10:21), he announces in advance his "solution" to the nonbelief of God's chosen people. Quoting Deuteronomy 32:21, Paul says: "I will make you jealous of those who are not a nation" (Rom 10:19). See Romans 11:11-15 for Paul's treatment of this theme of jealousy.

11:1-10 Israel's rejection is partial

By means of diatribal questions and quotations from Scripture, Paul continues to present his resolution of the place in God's plan of Israel's failure to believe in Jesus Christ. Paul's own experience as a Jew who is a Christian (11:2) answers the first question (11:1). Paul cites the example of the seven thousand who remained faithful during Elijah's time as further proof. Just above the verbs "I alone *am left*" (11:3) and "I *have left* for myself" (11:4) hovers the theme that Paul introduced earlier in Romans 9:27—the remnant (emphasis added). In 11:5 Paul makes the connection explicit: "So also at the present time there is a remnant, chosen by grace."

Paul concludes this section by referring to the Law (Deut 29:3), the Prophets (Isa 29:10), and the Writings (Ps 68:24 in the Septuagint) and links all three by the catchword "eyes." James D. G. Dunn helpfully maintains that the adverbial phrase *dia pantos,* with which Paul concludes this section, "is better translated 'continually' than 'for ever.'" The very existence of a remnant indicates that the rejection is only partial.

11:11-24 Paul censures Gentile Christian arrogance

Paul's main point about the destiny of God's chosen people comes across loud and clear: God has not abandoned them. See, for example, 11:24: "how much more will they who belong to it by nature be grafted back into their own olive tree." In making this point, Paul addresses his Gentile listeners and censures them for possible arrogance against unbelieving Israel.

Readers who have been diligently tracking Paul's use of Scripture quotations in Romans 9–11 may have had the same experience I did, that is, the realization that Paul does not cite a single word of Scripture in this section. Rather, elements from scholastic diatribe dominate this passage, for example, 11:11 and 11:17-24. In 11:13-16 Paul addressed the Gentile Christians in the second person plural. In 11:17 he begins to use the second person singular in his personification of the wild olive shoot and in doing so hones in on possible boasting and arrogant taunting on the part of Gentile Christians. Note how Paul singles out the imaginary person in 11:17 by using "you." Romans 11:18 continues to address the imaginary person with imperatives. Verses 19-24 formulate a dialogue between Paul and his imaginary person. Of course, Paul's responses and imperatives carry the day.

11:25-32 God has mercy on all

Paul's Scripture citation in Romans 11:26-27 is a combination of Isaiah 59:20-21 and Isaiah 27:9. Most important is Paul's modification of Isaiah 59:20, where the Greek of the Septuagint reads *heneken* ("for the sake of"), that is, "The deliverer will come for the sake of Zion" (author's translation). By exchanging *ek* ("out of") for *heneken*, Paul makes a potent christological statement: Christ is the deliverer and has come from Zion (and indeed for Zion's sake).

Throughout this section, which has Gentile believers in mind, there is an ebb and flow between universality and particularity. Three statements point to universality: "the full number of the Gentiles" (11:25), "thus all Israel will be saved" (11:26), and "that he might have mercy upon all" (11:32). Romans 11:29 breathes particularity: "For the gifts and the call of God are irrevocable." How God holds together universality and particularity is being revealed now as God lets men and women in on his mystery, and we frail human beings struggle mightily and sometimes sin grievously in our attempts to fathom and live by this mystery.

11:33-36 Praise to God

Paul's Scripture citation in Romans 11:34 is verbatim from Isaiah 40:13. Scholars are unsure to what extent Paul cites Scripture and what Scripture he cites in Romans 11:35. Job 41:3 has been proposed. These verses are justifiably called hymnic. In Greek the rhyme of 11:33 sounds forth: *ploutou, theou, autou, autou, anex-, anex-*. The rhyth-

mic driving force of 11:36 even roars through the English: "From him and through him and for him are all things." Paul's use of quotations from Scripture and rhyme and rhythm serve one purpose: the praise of God, whose ways he has been describing since Romans 1:16. Human beings stand in awe and in worship of this gracious and merciful God.

THE DUTIES OF CHRISTIANS
Romans 12:1–15:13

12:1-3 The overture to Paul's exhortations

I offer three preliminary considerations for all of Romans 12:1–15:13. First, those of us who have been paying close attention to Paul's use of pronouns will notice how frequently he employs imperatives in Romans 12:1–15:13. For example, 12:2: "Do not conform yourself to this age," and 15:2: "Let each of us please our neighbor for the good, for building up."

Second, I supply some background material so that we may be better able to recognize the similarities and differences between the block of exhortations in 12:1–15:13 and those in other writings. The exhortations that Paul artistically presents in 12:9-21 have some parallels in Jesus' Sermon on the Mount. Compare Matthew 5:44: "Love your enemies, and pray for those who persecute you," and Romans 12:14: "Bless those who persecute [you], bless and do not curse them."

An example of a very common "two ways teaching" is found in a section of the *Didache*, which dates to the same time as Romans. The *Didache* reads:

> There are two ways, one of life and one of death, and the difference between the two ways is great. This then is the way of life. First, love the God who made you, and second, your neighbor as yourself. And whatever you do not want to happen to you, do not do to another. . . . And now the second commandment of the teaching. Do not murder, do not commit adultery, do not engage in pederasty, do not engage in sexual immorality. Do not steal, do not practice magic, do not use enchanted potions, do not abort a fetus or kill a child that is born (1:1-2 and 2:1-2; Loeb translation modified).

The *Didache* continues:

And the way of death is this. First of all it is evil and filled with a curse: murders, adulteries, passions, sexual immoralities, robberies . . . deceit, arrogance, malice, insolence. . . . It is filled with persecutors of the good, haters of the truth. . . . Murderers of children and corruptors of what God has fashioned, who turn their backs on the needy, oppress the afflicted, and support the wealthy (5:1-2; Loeb modified).

Although Paul has some items in common with the "two ways teaching," he did not see fit to adopt this very popular "ethical" schema.

Third, one of the reasons Paul does not adopt such traditional materials as the "two ways teaching" is that he is spelling out the practical implications of his theology of love (12:9-21; 13:8-10; 14:1–15:13) and the Spirit (12:4-8) and of faith (12:3, 6; 14:1, 22-23). In brief, he is telling the Romans in 12:1–15:13 what Romans 5:5 means: "the love of God has been poured out into our hearts through the holy Spirit that has been given to us."

I make three points about Romans 12:1-3. First, 12:1-3 and what follows are not independent of what has gone before in the previous eleven chapters. Paul uses his authority (his *ethos*) and draws inferences ("therefore") from what he has previously stated and now summarizes in the phrase "by the mercies of God."

Second, there is a very close connection between what Paul says in 12:1 ("offer your bodies as a living sacrifice") and what he had said earlier, for instance, in 1:24: "Therefore, God handed them over to impurity through the lusts of their hearts for the mutual degradation of their bodies." Paul's Gentile listeners are now worshiping God (12:1) rather than creatures (1:25).

Third, behind the command "Do not conform yourself to this age" (12:2) stands the eschatological perspective that has dominated Romans 1–11; for example, 3:21: "But *now* the righteousness of God has been manifested" (emphasis added). The eschatological dimension of 12:2 also points ahead to 13:11-14, which deals with the perspective of the end time and rounds off this section of exhortations. Technically, 12:2 and 13:11-14 form a thematic *inclusio,* that is, the placement of similar material at the beginning and end of a section.

12:4-8 One body with many gifts

In 1 Corinthians 12–14 Paul wrote a far more extensive treatment of the one body with many

parts and of the gifts *(charismata)* of the Holy Spirit. Although here in Romans 12:4-8 Paul does not say that the "gifts" (12:6) come from the Holy Spirit, expressions such as "according to the grace given us" seem to presuppose the Holy Spirit (12:6). "Prophecy in proportion to the faith" (12:6) invites special comment. Prophecy is not so much foretelling the future but forthtelling, and could very well blend with the gift of exhortation (12:8).

"In proportion to the faith" is a phrase that resonates in Christian communities across the ages. One believer looking at a text of Scripture may see a valid but surface meaning, whereas the prophet may see far deeper and speak more challengingly about the same Scripture text. The development of Paul's thought in 1 Corinthians 12–14 may also give us a clue as to why Paul in Romans 12:9-21 gives exhortations about love. Paul's hymn to love in 1 Corinthians 13 occurs after a detailed discussion of the body of Christ and the gifts of the Spirit. The Corinthians are to pursue love in exercising their gifts (1 Cor 14:1).

12:9-21 The path of love

It is certainly easier to delve into the literary structure and theology of this passage than to abide by its thirty injunctions. Yes, thirty. That's what Philip F. Esler maintains. I just counted them, and he's right. For example, 12:11 has three: "Do not grow slack in zeal, be fervent in spirit, serve the Lord"; 12:16 has four: "Have the same regard for one another; do not be haughty but associate with the lowly; do not be wise in your own estimation."

With its flowing translation, the NAB translation of 12:16 hides some of its artistry. Here Paul uses the same Greek verb *(phronein)* three times ("have the same regard; do not be haughty; do not be wise"). Paul's artistry also shines forth in the connection between 12:13-14, where the same Greek verb *(diokein)* occurs and stands behind "*exercise* hospitality" and "bless those who *persecute*" (emphasis added). Paul's sprinkling of similar mnemonic devices throughout 12:9-16 has led Esler to suggest that we have here "a precious fragment of Paul's oral proclamation on the subject of the love that must characterize the life and identity of Christ-followers."

The injunctions of Romans 12:17-21 deal with peace, forgiveness, and non-retaliation. They are different, too, in that they contain the only explicit citations of Scripture in this section: Deuteronomy 32:35 in Romans 12:19 and Proverbs 25:21-22 in Romans 12:20. Giving food and drink to an enemy (12:19) has the result of heaping "burning coals upon his head" (12:20). Obviously, we are not to take "heaping burning coals upon" someone's head literally. I rely on Frederick W. Danker's interpretation of this obscure action: to "cause a person to blush with shame and remorse." In our language, especially in certain regions, there are expressions that are opaque to outsiders. For example, the first time I heard "The pastor threw a ram," I had little idea what it meant and tried to visualize an elderly pastor throwing cattle around. I was told that the pastor was very angry. I had to convert "ram" into an expression for "anger." Similarly, we have to convert "heaping burning coals upon" into an expression for "shaming a person."

Some years ago my work took me to a diocese where the Scripture adopted for reflection and implementation for the entire year was Romans 12:9-21. What a whale of an agenda for any church, local or diocesan!

13:1-7 Civil authority and the believer

Why does Paul say what he does in this passage and why now? The answer to "why now" is easier to provide. In this section Paul is tidying up some loose ends from what he has just said in 12:17-21. If Christians are not to exact revenge for evil done them (12:19), who is? They are to leave "room for the wrath" (12:19), which God will exercise through legitimate civil authority. See how "wrath" recurs in 13:4-5, for example, 13:4: "It is the servant of God to inflict wrath on the evildoer." Paul is also providing some extra specificity to what he said in 12:9: "Hold on to what is good." Notice that the word "good" occurs three times in 13:3-4 in verses couched in the diatribal "you" singular style. For instance, 13:3: "Then do what is good and you will receive approval from it."

Paul was raised in a hierarchical and patriarchal society and was heir to views of the role of government in God's created order. In its address to kings and magistrates, Wisdom 6:3 expresses something very similar to what Paul says in Romans 13:1: "Because authority was given you by the LORD and sovereignty by the Most High." But Wisdom 6:3 immediately characterizes God as the

One "who shall probe your works and scrutinize your counsels!"

Paul does not give absolute authority to the Roman emperors who ruled the roost in his day. Such rulers are "servant[s] of God" (13:4), not gods to be worshiped. Luke Timothy Johnson has expressed well the hermeneutical implications of 13:1-7: "If all civil authority is from God and ordered under God, then it equally follows that a civil authority that does not respond to God's will can be considered disqualified as a true authority, and so could be resisted 'for conscience's sake.'"

13:8-10 Love your neighbor as yourself

Paul continues what has been called his "general exhortations" by double linking Romans 13:8-10 to what has gone before. The immediate connection is between 13:7 and 13:8, where the same Greek root *(opheil)* appears. In 13:7 the NAB translates it by "due[s]"; in 13:8 by "owe." Variations of "love one another" (13:8) occur in 12:5: "So we, though many, are one body in Christ and individually parts of one another"; 12:10: "Love one another with mutual affection; anticipate one another in showing honor"; and 12:16: "Have the same regard for one another." Further, Paul introduced the thirty injunctions of Romans 12:9-21 with "Let love be sincere."

In listing specific commandments of the Decalogue in Romans 13:9, Paul follows the order of Deuteronomy 5:17-21. Leviticus 19:18 supplies Paul with the commandment of love of neighbor. After much discussion of the role of the law earlier in Romans 1–11, Paul sums it up. What people tried to accomplish by living the Mosaic law Christian believers now accomplish by their faith-filled lives of loving their neighbors as themselves.

13:11-14 A passage that led to St. Augustine's conversion

This passage connects with the earlier eschatological passage of Romans 12:2: "Do not conform yourself to this age but be transformed by the renewal of your mind." Thus 13:11-14 forms an *inclusio* (see p. 469) with the opening gambits of Paul's general exhortations. Romans 13:13-14 echoes with earlier passages in Romans. Romans 6:13 reads: "And do not present the parts of your bodies to sin as weapons for wickedness, but present yourselves to God as raised from the dead to life and the parts of your bodies to God as weapons for righteousness." See also Romans 8:12-13. In an earlier letter Paul also used the contrast between night/darkness/evil deeds and day/light/good deeds (1 Thess 5:4-11). Believers are to put on the Kevlar body armor of light (13:12) and the attitude of the Lord Jesus (13:14; see Phil 2:5-11).

In Book 8.12 of his *Confessions,* St. Augustine tells the story of hearing a young child's sing-song of "Take and read, take and read." He went back to the place where he had put Paul's text. He writes: "I snatched it up, opened it and in silence read the passage upon which my eyes first fell." The passage was Romans 13:13-14. St. Augustine continues: "I had no wish to read further, and no need. For in that instant, with the very ending of the sentence, it was as though a light of utter confidence shone in all my heart, and all the darkness of uncertainty vanished away" (F. J. Sheed translation). Augustine was on the threshold of casting off the desires of the flesh and giving himself over to the fruit of the Spirit.

14:1–15:13 Principles that govern conduct with regard to indifferent matters

Scholars are divided on the question of whether in Romans 14:1–15:13 Paul is addressing a concrete situation in the Roman house churches. I, for one, do not think so. Nor do I think that Paul is specifically addressing a situation where "the weak" are Jewish Christians and "the strong" are Gentile Christians. After making two methodological points, I treat the principles that Paul enunciates in this section.

A number of my readers may have already perused my commentary on Galatians in this booklet. In that letter it was fairly clear that Paul was engaged with teachers/influencers who were championing circumcision and observance of the Mosaic law. See, for example, Galatians 6:15: "For neither does circumcision mean anything, nor does uncircumcision, but only a new creation." In 1 Corinthians 8:7 the situation is clear and deals with meat sacrificed to idols: "But not all have this knowledge. There are some who have been so used to idolatry up until now that, when they eat meat sacrificed to idols, their conscience, which is *weak,* is defiled" (emphasis added).

However, when we take a close look at Romans 14:1–15:13, it is very difficult to ascertain what was going on. Eating and drinking (14:2, 21),

special days (14:5-6), and clean and unclean food (14:14) are vague and insufficient evidence on which to depict a battle over indifferent matters that was actually raging in or among the Roman house churches.

Moreover, I challenge my readers to find multiple references to "the weak" and "the strong" and to their positions in this passage. Romans 14:1 and 15:1 are the only two verses that refer to "the weak," while Romans 15:1 is the only verse that addresses "the strong." In our quest for finding or making order out of what Paul says, we are the ones who create the camp of "the weak" and the camp of "the strong."

As J. Paul Sampley has shown, this is indeed Paul's goal in writing so obliquely rather than directly, as he did in Galatians and 1 Corinthians. Sampley writes: "Direct speech is argumentative and confrontational while figured speech is allusive and evocative; direct speech needs proofs, while figured speech invites the hearer to establish its veracity by self-application." I might add that Paul's two diatribal questions in 14:4, 10 help him get his listeners to apply his teaching to themselves.

If this lengthy passage doesn't deal with specific questions in the Roman house churches, then what's it all about? It's about the principles to be applied in those multiple situations that involve indifferent matters, that is, not questions of faith and morals, but which nonetheless can create ugly stains on the fabric of community life. Paul has arrived at these principles from previous experiences with communities, especially in Corinth. N. T. Wright's comment about 14:1–15:13 is helpful: "This is what justification by faith looks like when it sits down at table in Christian fellowship."

I give a few of the principles that course through this section and invite my readers to discover others as they explore Paul's interchange of the personal pronouns "you" and "we" and engage in their own self-application of Paul's teaching. "We shall all stand before the judgment seat of God" (14:10). "Nothing is unclean in itself" (14:14). "The kingdom of God is not a matter of food and drink, but of righteousness, peace, and joy in the holy Spirit" (14:17). Paul appeals not only to principles but also to the example of Jesus Christ: "For Christ did not please himself" (15:3); "Welcome one another, then, as Christ welcomed you" (15:7). Finally, in 15:9-12 he appeals to all of

Sacred Writ—the Law, the Prophets, and the Writings—to show the universality of God's welcome.

During the course of my work, I have traveled to different cultures and experienced firsthand the struggle involved in realizing that what I thought was "universal law" was an indifferent matter. St. Peter's in Rome doesn't have kneelers, yet I thought that such a practice was de rigueur. I was pleasantly surprised when I was served pea soup with ham in a German friary on a day of abstinence: "Ach, what is pea soup without ham?"

CONCLUSION
Romans 15:14–16:27

15:14-24 Paul needs the assistance of the Roman believers in spreading his gospel to Spain

I make three observations. As Paul concludes his rich letter to the Romans, he repeats three times that his gospel is for the Gentiles (15:16, 18). It is the gospel he has been preaching throughout this very letter.

Second, Paul's description of having preached the gospel of Christ "from Jerusalem all the way around to Illyricum" (15:19) should be taken in a global sense, for Paul has not preached to every individual or in every town.

Finally, 15:24 should not be read as if Paul were alerting the Roman house churches that he planned to visit them during a whistle stop. The Greek behind "to be sent on my way" really means to supply food, money, companions, means of travel, and such. The Roman believers could not make all these arrangements overnight. Also, according to Joseph A. Fitzmyer, "there is thus far no evidence of Jewish habitation in Spain prior to the third century A.D." So Paul could not follow a procedure of preaching first in a Jewish synagogue. Moreover, as Robert Jewett surmises, Paul had to have the Scriptures translated "into the Celt-Iberian dialects still employed by most of the population in Spain." The nice things that Paul says about the Roman believers in 15:14, 22-24 (technically: *captatio benevolentiae*) are in service of winning them over to the task of preaching his gospel.

15:25-33 Paul's anxiety about his reception in Jerusalem

In Romans 12:8 Paul mentions the gift of generosity: "if one contributes, in generosity." Romans 12:13 exhorts: "Contribute to the needs of the holy ones." Paul is taking the collection he gathered from Gentile Christians to fulfill the pledge he made in Galatians 2:10 to help the poor among the Jerusalem Christians. This money, however, is not just alms. It is a symbol of the unity of the churches: The Gentile Christians "decided to do it, and in fact they are indebted to them, for if the Gentiles have come to share in their spiritual blessings, they ought also to serve them in material blessings" (15:27).

Paul's words in 15:30-31 reveal the apprehension he has about his upcoming journey to and meeting in Jerusalem: "Join me in the struggle by your prayers to God on my behalf, that I may be delivered from the disobedient in Judea." Jews may well consider Paul, a former zealot, to be a turncoat. Jewish Christians, who are zealous for the Mosaic law, may view Paul's law-free gospel for the Gentiles as repugnant. Would the Jerusalem Christians actually reject the collection and its symbolism?

16:1-16 Five house churches and leadership roles for women

To some, Romans 16:1-16 may appear to be as inspiring as reading a church directory. To others it has become a window into Romans and the early church. Behind 16:5, 10, 11, 14, 15 there is evidence of at least five house churches in Rome, or more probably tenement house churches. See, for example, 16:5: "Greet also the church at their house," that is, the house of Prisca and Aquila.

There are eight women mentioned as active in promoting the gospel: Phoebe, Prisca, Mary, Junia, Tryphaena, Tryphosa, Persis, and Rufus's mother. I single out Phoebe and Junia for further comment. Phoebe is a wealthy woman who is a *diakonos* and *prostatis* (16:1-2). The first term may be translated as "minister" and indicates a position of responsibility in the church. Archbishop Rabanus Maurus (d. 856) commented: "This passage teaches by apostolic authority that women are also constituted in the ministry of the church" (PL 111:1605D). The second term may be translated as "benefactor," if one understands that this term indicates a person of enormous prestige and influence.

It is highly likely that Phoebe not only carried Paul's letter to the Romans to the house churches but also read it to them. You see, Phoebe was likely among the five percent of the population who could read. Further, in reading Romans, she surely had to know what it was about. Ancient letters (and manuscripts) did not have spacing, chapters and verses, and subheadings. I give a simple example. Suppose I put a recent headline in capital letters without spacing: FLORIDAKEY-DEERREBOUNDS. Without too much effort you read: Florida key deer rebounds. But is "key" an adjective meaning "principal"? Does "key" refer to the Florida Keys? Is "key deer" a technical name for a special species of deer? The reader would have to know answers to these questions in order to read this simple sentence out loud meaningfully. Just think of the skill Phoebe must have if she is to navigate successfully through all the elements of scholastic diatribe that Paul used in composing his letter!

I make three points about Junia (16:7). First, she is a woman. St. John Chrysostom (d. 407), who was proficient in Greek and was a misogynist, commented: "To be an apostle is something great. But to be outstanding among the apostles, just think of what a wondrous song of praise that is. . . . Truly, how great the wisdom of this woman must have been that she was even deemed worthy of the title of apostle." Second, the fathers of the church and Greek grammar indicate that Junia is an apostle and outstanding among the apostles and not merely held in high regard by male apostles.

Third, Junia was not an apostle of a church, for nowhere in 16:7 does Paul refer to her as such. Contrast 2 Corinthians 8:23 and Philippians 2:25. I am of the opinion that Junia is an apostle in the same sense as Paul, who had seen the risen Lord (1 Cor 9:1) but was not one of the Twelve. She may have been among the five hundred who saw the risen Lord (1 Cor 15:6).

16:17-27 Final goodbye with warning and doxology

There are three strange elements in Romans 16. In the previous passage we encountered the first one. Nowhere else in his letters does Paul extend greetings to twenty-four people. He des-perately wants to establish a home base among the Roman Christians for his evangelical mission to Spain.

In 16:17-20 we run into the second extraordinary element in the farewell section of a Pauline letter. Paul now warns the Romans of people who "do not serve our Lord Christ but their own appetites" (16:18). One is reminded of Philippians 3:19, where Paul warns of false teachers, whose "God is their stomach."

Words we hear or speak during a farewell provide a contemporary analogy to Paul's seemingly unmotivated warning in these verses. Sometimes farewell words do not seem motivated by the event. After the magnificently glorious celebrations that surrounded my First Mass in my parish church, I was leaving home. My father kissed me and said, "Don't forget where you've come from." To this day I remember and abide by this unmotivated farewell reminder not to overly honor myself and thereby dishonor my parents. In this warning Paul is indeed speaking "rather boldly" (15:15).

Paul ends Galatians with: "The grace of our Lord Jesus Christ be with your spirit, brothers. Amen" (6:18). He concludes his other letters in a similar fashion. But once again, Romans is strange. Paul finishes with a doxology. It is fitting that Paul concludes by praising and honoring God, for God has been the theme of this very long letter. It is fitting that at the conclusion of a letter whose main purpose is to reveal God's plan for the Gentiles Paul praises God for revealing this very plan. I. Howard Marshall rightly contends that doxologies also have a hortatory purpose. Romans 16:25 asks for strengthening and perseverance and repeats some of the themes of Romans 8:25-27.

In my final comment I persevere to the end with my reading program for Romans and invite my readers to check the pronouns of this doxology: "you" and "I." Paul has the Romans ("you") at heart. At the same time, this is his doxology. He is the one who is praising and honoring God, revealing his *ethos,* showing his true colors.

BIBLIOGRAPHY

James W. Aageson, "Scripture and Structure in the Development of the Argument in Romans 9–11," *Catholic Biblical Quarterly* 48 (1986) 265–289.

Frederick W. Danker, *Benefactor: An Epigraphic Study of a Graeco-Roman and New Testament Semantic Field*. St. Louis: Clayton Publishing Co., 1982.

James D. G. Dunn, *Romans 1–8, 9–16*. Word Biblical Commentary 38AB. Dallas: Word Books, 1988.

Philip F. Esler, *Conflict and Identity in Romans: The Social Setting of Paul's Letter*. Minneapolis: Fortress, 2003.

Joseph A. Fitzmyer, *Romans*. Anchor Bible 33. New York: Doubleday, 1993.

A Greek-English Lexicon of the New Testament and other Early Christian Literature. Third edition (BDAG). Revised and edited by Frederick W. Danker. Chicago: University of Chicago Press, 2000.

Robert Jewett, "Romans," in *The Cambridge Companion to St. Paul*. Edited by James D. G. Dunn. Cambridge: Cambridge University Press, 2003, pp. 91–104.

Luke Timothy Johnson, *Reading Romans: A Literary and Theological Commentary*. Macon, GA: Smyth & Helwys, 2001.

"Joseph and Aseneth," A new translation and introduction by C. Burchard in *The Old Testament Pseudepigrapha II*. Edited by James H. Charlesworth. Garden City, NY: Doubleday, 1985, pp. 177–247.

Ernst Käsemann, " 'The Righteousness of God' in Paul," in *New Testament Questions of Today*. Philadelphia: Fortress, 1969, pp. 168–182.

Leander E. Keck, "*Pathos* in Romans? Mostly Preliminary Remarks," in *Paul and Pathos*. Edited by Thomas H. Olbricht and Jerry L. Sumney. Atlanta: Society of Biblical Literature, 2001, pp. 71–96.

I. Howard Marshall, "Romans 16:25-27—An Apt Conclusion," in *Romans and the People of God: Essays in Honor of Gordon D. Fee on the Occasion of His 65th Birthday*. Edited by Sven K. Soderlund and N. T. Wright. Grand Rapids: Eerdmans, 1999, pp. 170–184.

Paul and Empire: Religion and Power in Roman Imperial Society. Edited by Richard A. Horsley. Harrisburg: Trinity Press International, 1997, pp. 1–8.

J. Paul Sampley, "The Weak and the Strong: Paul's Careful and Crafty Rhetorical Strategy in Romans 14:1–15:13," in *The Social World of the First Christians: Essays in Honor of Wayne A. Meeks*. Edited by L. Michael White and O. Larry Yarbrough. Minneapolis: Fortress, 1995, pp. 40–52.

Stanley K. Stowers, "The Diatribe," in *Greco-Roman Literature and the New Testament: Selected Forms and Genres*. Edited by David E. Aune. Atlanta: Scholars Press, 1988, pp. 71–83.

———. *A Rereading of Romans: Justice, Jews, and Gentiles*. New Haven: Yale University Press, 1994.

Charles H. Talbert, *Romans*. Smyth & Helwys Bible Commentary. Macon, GA: Smyth & Helwys, 2002.

N. T. Wright, "The Letter to the Romans," in *The New Interpreter's Bible*. Volume X. Nashville: Abingdon Press, 2002, pp. 393–770.

THE LETTERS TO THE
CORINTHIANS

Maria A. Pascuzzi, C.S.J.

INTRODUCTION

First and Second Corinthians are literary windows affording readers a "Paul's-eye" view into the life and development of one very dynamic Christian community. As we peer through them, what we see can quickly challenge idealized notions about the cohesiveness and harmony of the earliest communities of believers (cf. Acts 4:32). The way Paul tells it, the community at Corinth was characterized by rivalry (1 Cor 1:12); obsession with status and superior wisdom leading to arrogance (1 Cor 1–4); disregard for the less spiritually enlightened and gifted (1 Cor 8:1-13; 12–14) as well as for the economic have-nots (1 Cor 11:17-22); sexual immorality (1 Cor 5:1-13; 6:12-20); assertiveness with regard to individual rights (1 Cor 6:12-13); and, as time went on, a suspicious and disdainful attitude toward Paul himself (2 Cor 1:12–2:12; 10–12).

Such behavior serves to remind the reader that conversion did not produce an immediate social and moral transformation to a new way of life rooted in gospel values. Paul had to deal with this reality, and in his correspondence he commands, exhorts, persuades, threatens, does everything possible to refocus the community on the gospel and bring about transformed gospel living.

While these letters serve as windows on the past, they also reflect back to us much that still characterizes Christian living today. As we attempt now to understand the conflicting impulses, values, and behavior that gave rise to what

Paul perceived as inauthentic Christian living at Corinth, perhaps we can better understand what contributes to inauthentic Christian living in our own day. We may also find in Paul's exigent call to the Corinthians to transform their lives the impetus for our own continued transformation in light of the gospel. Before examining each letter, some preliminary information about Corinth, Paul's work there, and the nature and purpose of the letters is needed to establish a context in which these letters can be more adequately understood.

The city of Corinth and its citizens

Corinth was strategically located on a narrow isthmus that linked mainland Greece to its north with the Peloponnesus to its south. The city was also an important east-west axis, located within a few miles of two great harbors: Cenchreae, which handled commerce to and from points east, and Lechaeum, which handled commerce to and from points west. This Greek city flourished from the fifth century B.C. until it was left in near ruin by the Romans in 146 B.C. A century passed before Corinth was refounded as a Roman colony in 44 B.C. The city was rebuilt according to Roman architectural patterns, reorganized politically in line with Roman government structures, and repopulated with Rome's urban poor, freedmen (former slaves), and slaves from among its conquered populations, as well as immigrants from the east, including Jews. Greek descendants of those who had survived Corinth's assault continued to live amidst its ruins. However, in this new Roman Corinth, they were regarded as resident aliens.

Within a few decades of its refounding, Corinth became the capital of the new Roman province Achaia. By the time Paul arrived, about A.D. 50/51, Corinth was emerging as Greece's premier city and the commercial, manufacturing, and cultural megacenter of the entire eastern Mediterranean. The stamp of Imperial Rome, as well as the influx of tradespersons, merchants, and tourists who came to visit Corinth's numerous shrines or to attend the Isthmian games, philosophers, and orators were all factors that contributed to the variety of ideas, mores, and perspectives that gave Corinth its vitality and appeal.

Paul's move to Corinth was probably calculated. The city's pluralistic and cosmopolitan character was clearly advantageous to him. He would no doubt get a hearing, and even a modestly successful mission among such sophisticated city-dwellers could lend credibility to his gospel of a crucified Messiah and validate his Gentile mission.

However, pluralism and sophistication were only two aspects of the social and the cultural ethos that dominated Corinth. The Corinthians were known to be fiercely competitive, driven by the desire for status, wealth, honor, and power. The route to these involved navigating the Roman patronage system, a network of hierarchically ordered patron-client relations. In return for the benefactions and enhanced social status gained through access to a rich patron's circle of influence, clients supported and promoted the patron, bolstering his status and ultimately widening his sphere of power.

Judging from Paul's description of the situation in the community, as noted above, it appears that these ingrained primary social and cultural values were carried over into the Christian community by the newly converted, with negative consequences. Their behavior, still conditioned by Corinth's secular values and aspirations, was destroying God's *ekklēsia*, a microsociety whose unity and holiness were to distinguish it from the macrosociety from which the converts came.

In these letters Paul negotiates the problems arising from this clash of values and deals with their negative impact on the life of the community.

However, his greater concern is to further the process of resocialization by inculcating a perspective rooted in the gospel and the values and behavior consonant with that. This was no easy task, since Paul needed to remove Corinth's ethos from the Corinthians without removing the Corinthians from pagan Corinth (see 1 Cor 5:9-10)!

Paul's mission in Corinth and the Corinthian church

The Acts of the Apostles, a key secondary source for Paul's life and work after his own letters, provides scant information about Paul's founding mission in Corinth. He came to Corinth after a short and largely unsuccessful stay in Athens (Acts 17:15-34). He found lodging and work as a tentmaker with Priscilla and Aquila, a Jewish-Christian couple, and was soon joined by his coworkers Silas and Timothy (Acts 18:1-5). According to Luke, Paul began evangelizing in the synagogue, but as Jewish opposition increased, he refocused his efforts on the Gentiles and moved his ministry base to the home of a Gentile believer, Titus Justus (Acts 18:5-8). Luke reports that Paul ministered at Corinth for a year and a half (Acts 18:11), but without specifying dates for this sojourn. The mention of Paul's arraignment before Gallio (Acts 18:12-17), proconsul of Achaia from either A.D. 50 to 51 or 51 to 52, has figured significantly in attempts to date Paul's ministry in Corinth, which many scholars place sometime between A.D. 50 and 52.

More insight about Paul's life and ministry at Corinth and the composition of the community is gained from the Corinthian correspondence itself. Paul declares that he had come to preach, not baptize, though he admits baptizing a few, perhaps in the earliest days of his ministry (1 Cor 1:14-17). By deliberate choice, he preached his gospel without eloquence (1 Cor 1:17; 2:1-5). Just how rhetorically unimpressive Paul was is hard to say. However, he may have been outclassed in the eyes of the community by a certain Apollos, famed for eloquence, who preached at Corinth after Paul's departure (Acts 18:24; 19:1; 1 Cor 3:6). Paul testifies that he worked to support himself so that he could preach his gospel to all free of charge (1 Corinthians 9). This may reflect his deliberate choice to avoid entanglement in the patronage system with its obligation. Both Paul's choice to forego financial support as well as his alleged lack of rhetorical prowess are issues that will surface again in 2 Corinthians 10–12.

With regard to the community, composed of Jews and Gentiles, the latter apparently predominated, judging by the decidedly pagan aspect of the issues Paul treated, for example, food sacrificed to idols and attendance at pagan temple feasts (1 Cor 8–10), as well as references to their former idolatrous way of life (1 Cor 6:10; 8:7; 12:2). Past assumptions that community members were drawn from Corinth's lower classes, largely based on remarks about their insignificant origins and status (1 Cor 1:26-31), have been modified in view of recent research into the social composition of urban Christian communities. It is now acknowledged that along with the economically poor, the Corinthian community included others disadvantaged because of ethnicity, class, or gender biases, and still others considered to be persons of some means and social stature who are mentioned in the text (e.g., 1 Cor 1:14; 16:17, 19; see further Rom 16:1, 21-23).

Given the diversity of this community, estimated to number anywhere from fifty to two hundred persons, scholars prefer to speak of it as "socially stratified." This socioeconomic diversity probably accounts for community tensions at the Lord's Supper, where the poor were disregarded (1 Cor 11:17-22), and other situations where some members may have used their means or status to the detriment of others (e.g., 1 Cor 6:1-11) or to exempt themselves from certain moral dictates (e.g., 1 Cor 5:1-13).

The nature and purpose of Paul's Letters to the Corinthians

Paul wrote 1 Corinthians from Ephesus about A.D. 55/56. Second Corinthians was written a year or so later from Macedonia after Paul received Titus's update on the situation at Corinth. Evidence in these letters indicates that Paul had actually written more than two letters to this community. In 1 Corinthians 5:9, Paul states that he had written a previous letter, no longer extant, containing information relevant to an issue he was now writing about in 1 Corinthians 5. Then, in 2 Corinthians 2:1-4, he speaks of a "tearful letter," obviously predating 2 Corinthians. Attempts have been made to identify this "tearful letter" with 1 Corinthians or with 2 Corinthians 10–13. However, both identifications have been seriously questioned, and the

possibility that the "tearful letter" is also lost cannot be excluded.

Many scholars have argued that 2 Corinthians is a combination of at least two letters: 2 Corinthians 1–9 plus 2 Corinthians 10–13. Others have suggested five or six. What is important to recognize here is that 1 and 2 Corinthians are only part of a continuous dialogue between Paul and this community. Fortunately, they are preserved in the canon of the New Testament, where they are designated "first" and "second" in view of their respective lengths. However, they were not necessarily letters one and two in Paul's ongoing correspondence with the community, which included at least four letters.

First and Second Corinthians are true letters reflecting contemporary Greco-Roman conventions of letter writing. Each letter has an opening section with its requisite features, a body, the main part of the letter, where key matters are taken up, and a conclusion. These and other formal and stylistic features will be noted in the course of the commentary. Here it is important to underscore that in Paul's day the letter functioned as a substitute for personal presence when this was not possible (1 Cor 5:3) or, in some cases, not desirable (2 Cor 2:1-2). In 1 and 2 Corinthians, we read what Paul wanted to say about issues and developments in the community articulated from his point of view. In other words, we read only one-half of a dialogue between partners involved in an ongoing relationship. Many details and facts already known to Paul and the Corinthians are omitted. At times Paul quotes the Corinthians (e.g., 1 Cor 6:12; 7:1) and offers clues about the evolving situation there (e.g., 2 Cor 11:4-15). These do illumine some Corinthian views and some of the content and contours of Paul's own remarks. However, a fuller picture of the situation depends, to a large extent, on the piecing together of textual and extratextual clues.

It is a commonplace in Pauline studies to refer to Paul's writings as "occasional letters." What is recognized in the use of this term is that his letters were prompted, or occasioned, by particular circumstances, questions, or behavior arising in the daily life of the communities Paul had founded that necessitated a response from him. They are not sustained and systematic expositions of Paul's accumulated theological insights. Even Romans, the one letter written by Paul to a community he had not founded, is now considered to have more of an occasional character than previously assumed.

Thus, what we find in 1 and 2 Corinthians are *ad hoc* responses intended primarily for a particular community and its peculiar needs. This is not to suggest that Paul lacked any theological framework within which he formulated his responses. Rather, it is to caution against assuming that what we read is Paul's coherently articulated and exhaustive last word on all issues. It is more likely we are reading Paul's first word on a variety of issues, most of which arose only after he had moved on to evangelize elsewhere.

Though a letter and a speech were not identical, the letter substituted for speech, as noted above. In Paul's day, speech was of utmost importance. Political leaders, as well as those who claimed to teach religious and philosophical truths, were expected to speak eloquently and persuasively. Rhetoric, the study of how to argue persuasively in a given situation, was a main component of Greco-Roman education. Though it was primarily concerned with techniques for researching, constructing, and ultimately delivering a winning speech, its aims and conventions also affected how people wrote. Given this overlap between speech and letter and the fact that Paul designed his letters to be read aloud (Phlm 2; 1 Thess 5:27), it is reasonable to expect that Paul employed contemporary techniques of argumentation to make as persuasive a case as possible for his own points.

Speeches, or arguments, were classified according to three types, each ordered to a distinct purpose and appropriate to a different setting. The forensic or judicial speech, proper to the courtroom, was used to defend or accuse someone in view of a past action. The deliberative speech, for use in the assembly, sought to persuade or dissuade about future courses of action. Finally, epideictic speech, appropriate for a variety of public occasions, employed praise or blame to affirm important values and reinforce the audience's current adherence to them. Speeches nor-

mally began with an introduction and concluded with a recapitulation of key points. In between, other standardized components were incorporated depending on the type of argument. However, every argument had two indispensable parts: a statement of the thesis/point to be proved, followed by the proofs. Persuasion, regardless of the speech type, ultimately depended on three factors: the moral character of the speaker, or proof based on *ethos;* the ability to evoke the proper emotional response from the audience, or proof based on *pathos;* and finally logical arguments, or proof based on *logos.*

With regard to the Corinthian correspondence, the deliberative type of argument is dominant in 1 Corinthians, where Paul frequently attempts to persuade or dissuade the community about possible courses of action in view of what is advantageous to the community (e.g., 1 Cor 7; 8–10; 12–14). At certain points, he also introduces forensic and epideictic rhetoric as the situation demands (e.g., 1 Cor 5; 9; 13).

In 2 Corinthians we come across a changed situation. A wedge has been driven between Paul and the community by outsiders. Speaking in his own defense, Paul employs forensic rhetoric at 2 Corinthians 1:1–7:6 and again at 2 Corinthians 10–13. In 2 Corinthians 8–9, Paul deliberates with the community, urging it to go forward with a planned collection that will benefit both the impoverished community at Jerusalem and the Corinthians themselves, who will be distinguished for their generosity.

Throughout these two letters Paul's appeals to his own character and to the emotions of the community are deftly interwoven with logical arguments, evidencing both Paul's rhetorical sophistication and his intention to persuade rather than simply impose his will. Recognition of the rhetorical nature of 1 and 2 Corinthians contributes to a more informed and profitable reading of these letters, which are composed of discreet argumentative units where Paul is engaged in persuasion.

THE FIRST LETTER TO THE

CORINTHIANS

Maria A. Pascuzzi, C.S.J.

INTRODUCTION

The occasion and structure of
1 Corinthians

Sometime after Paul had left Corinth and was settled into his ministry at Ephesus, oral and written reports about a number of developments in the community at Corinth reached him. Through "Chloe's people," that is, members of her household, Paul was orally apprised of rivalries within the community (1 Cor 1:11). He says that he had also heard about a case of sexual immorality (1 Cor 5:2) and divisions at the Eucharist (1 Cor 11:18). Chloe's people or others could have been the source of this information. Other information, whose source is unspecified, concerning lawsuits (6:1-11), fornication (6:12-20), inappropriate attire at the liturgy (11:2-16), and disagreement over the resurrection (1 Cor 15) may have also been referred to Paul orally.

Paul's second source of information was a letter written by the Corinthians asking his advice on various issues (1 Cor 7:1). Their questions related to matters ranging from sex within marriage, which, apparently, some wanted to renounce (1 Cor 7:2-6), to the advisability of marriage (7:7-40), to whether one could eat food offered to idols (1 Cor 8), to the use of spiritual gifts (1 Cor 12–14). This letter was brought to Paul by community delegates, presumably the persons Paul mentions at 1 Corinthians 16:17. In addition to Chloe's people, this delegation may also have supplied some of the oral information. As a response to the information that had reached him, Paul composed 1 Corinthians.

To explain the ideological basis that influenced the thought and motivated the behavior reflected in 1 Corinthians, some scholars have hypothesized that some group (e.g., Gnostics or Judaizers) or person (e.g., Apollos) from outside the community introduced ideas at variance with what Paul had preached. Others explain the problems as deriving from "overrealized eschatology," that is, the Corinthians misinterpreted Paul's message, incorrectly assuming that they were already fully transformed and free of all moral constraints. Another explanation holds that the Corinthians understood Paul, lived according to what he had preached, but that Paul, for political reasons, changed his mind about things and now saw their behavior as a problem.

Each theory has been subjected to scrutiny and found to be inadequate. What seems apparent from 1 Corinthians is that here we encounter real flesh-and-blood people working out the implications of their new faith. In light of more recent investigations into the social and cultural ethos of the Corinthians, it is possible to understand the Corinthian situation as testimony to the difficulties that accompanied the planting of the Christian gospel in a pagan environment such as Corinth, where environmental influences were still strong. The difficulties Paul addresses in this letter are not between the community and himself, but rather within this nascent community struggling with its own identity, ethos, and behavior.

In 1 Corinthians, Paul deals with a larger number of disparate issues than in any other of his letters. The variety of issues, along with what scholars perceived as multiple literary and logical incongruities (e.g., contradictory responses on idol meat at chs. 8 and 10), led to speculation that 1 Corinthians was a compilation of letters. This hypothesis has proved to be unwarranted, especially in view of more recent insights about how Paul unfolds his arguments. Most scholars now affirm the literary unity of first Corinthians.

Nonetheless, it is still not easy to fathom the letter's logic as Paul shifts from topic to topic. A variety of ways of understanding the letter's structural organization have been proposed. Many understand 1 Corinthians to consist of an introduction (1:1-9) and conclusion (16:1-21) enclosing the body of the letter, which is envisioned according to a two-part structure: responses to matters referred orally to Paul (1:10–6:20), followed by responses to the Corinthians' letter (7:1–15:58). The phrase "now in regard . . . " (e.g., 7:1, 25; 12:1) is usually taken to signal the beginning of Paul's response to a question or issue raised in the letter.

Currently, there is a growing tendency to understand the structure of 1 Corinthians along the lines of a deliberative speech. Paul's exhortation "that there be no divisions . . . that you be united in the same mind and in the same purpose" (1:10) is construed as his major thesis. The body of the letter consists of a series of rhetorical proofs or demonstrations in support of the thesis (1:11–15:58). The thesis plus demonstrations are encompassed by the exordium at 1:1-9 (the rhetorical equivalent of the literary introduction) and the recapitulation at 16:13-18 (the argument's conclusion). Understood from the vantage point of rhetoric, 1 Corinthians is a sustained argument on the single theme of unity, cast in the form of a deliberative speech.

The two-part literary schema and the rhetorical schema are both useful for understanding the letter's structure, provided we recognize that neither accounts perfectly for its structure and we do not adhere too rigidly to either one. In the case of the two-part schema, an "oral matter" intrudes on the written responses at 11:18. Additionally, there is no indication that the discussion on hair-

styles at 11:2-16 or on the resurrection at chapter 15 is actually a response to a written inquiry. In the case of the rhetorical schema, while chapters 1–4 clearly relate to the problem of factionalism and support Paul's call for unity, not every piece of advice or resolution of a problem found throughout 1 Corinthians 5–16 is constructed in view of resolving the problem of factionalism (e.g., ch. 7). In fact, in 1 Corinthians 5–16, Paul is not always deliberating (e.g., chs. 5, 9, and 13). Thus, rather than insisting on either structural schema, it may be more useful to focus on the discrete units or blocks of argumentation contained in 1 Corinthians. Careful examination of their content, as well as Paul's persuasive strategy, should allow us to apprehend Paul's major concerns in this letter.

A final point of consideration regarding the structure of 1 Corinthians concerns a compositional pattern Paul uses to arrange his thought, which is especially recurrent in this letter. The pattern is evidenced when Paul introduces a topic, (A), shifts to another topic, (B), then returns to his original topic, (A'); hence the designation ABA', or concentric pattern. 1 Corinthians 8–10 is a good example. Paul discusses idol meat in chapter 8, (A), shifts to discuss his apostolic rights in chapter 9, (B), then returns to idol meat in chapter 10, (A'). As scholars now recognize, the B section, once perceived to rupture the flow of Paul's thought, actually reinforces the point being made in the adjacent A and A' sections. The B section is an example of the rhetorical technique "digression," an insertion into an argument to amplify or support the main point. This way of unfolding an argument clearly contrasts with a linear arrangement of ideas to which modern readers are accustomed. However, it accorded with the accustomed literary and rhetorical methods of Paul's day. Once we understand Paul's method of unfolding an argument, both its coherence and its point become more readily apparent.

Paul's theological perspective in 1 Corinthians

Paul's responses to the Corinthians were shaped by the dialogue between himself and them, but they were rooted in Jewish tradition, enriched by Paul's understanding of what God had done in Christ. Paul shared with other Jews an apocalyptic view centered on the hope that

God would intervene to overthrow the evil order now reigning in the world, after which a new order under God's sovereignty would be ushered in. According to Paul, God had powerfully intervened as hoped, but in an unexpected and paradoxical way through the mystery of Christ crucified (1:18). Christians were therefore living at a crucial juncture point: the world in its present form was passing away (7:31; 10:11), the new order was beginning (2 Cor 5:17b). For Paul, this entire transition hinged on Christ's death and resurrection, the eschatological (end-time) salvation event through which humanity gained the renewed existence that Jewish tradition associated with the end-time. The inauguration of the end-time would be signaled by the outpouring of the Spirit (1:7; 2:12; 3:16). Coincident with this salvation event, God was now calling into Christ's fellowship the new, end-time community (1:9).

Since Paul believed that all this had been accomplished through Christ, to whom the Corinthian community owed its existence, he brings his christological insights to bear on his responses to this community. Their human wisdom is revalued in light of God's wisdom and power shown forth in Christ crucified (1:18). Their boasting is shown to have no foundation, since everything comes from God in Christ (3:21-23; 4:7). Through Christ's death they have been washed, redeemed, sanctified (1:30; 5:7; 6:11) and brought back for God (6:19-20; 7:23). They are now the "church of God" (1:2), "God's temple" (3:17).

As a result, how the Corinthians behave can never be independent of God, under whose sovereignty they stand and by whose will they are called and empowered by the Spirit to live lives of holiness (1:2). In Christ, believers formed one body (12:12), a unity effected through baptism and manifested and reinforced by the Eucharist (10:16-17). Immorality that threatened the community's holiness had to be avoided (5:13; 6:18; 10:14). Likewise, unity-destroying distinctions and behavior, whether based on status (11:17-24), knowledge (ch. 8), or spiritual endowment (chs. 12 and 14), had to be abandoned. The well-being of the whole church would form the context for discernment and behavior (6:12b; 8:3; 10:24, 31-33; 14:12), motivated by love (ch. 13).

Paul stresses throughout 1 Corinthians that this eschatological existence is not yet complete (1:7-8). That would come in the future, when death would be conquered, physical bodies would be transformed into glorious resurrection bodies, and all things would be subjected to God through Christ (ch. 15). In the meantime, the Corinthians were to use the freedom wrought by Christ to preserve their holiness and unity, the twin hallmarks of God's eschatological community (see, e.g., Ezek 37:15-28). The extent to which Paul's commands and exhortations throughout 1 Corinthians are concerned with the true nature of the community underscores the centrality of ecclesiology in this letter. How should this community, poised between the event of Christ's death and resurrection and the promise of future glory, live in the present? Paul's concern in 1 Corinthians is to help the community with this perennially difficult question.

OUTLINE OF FIRST CORINTHIANS

COMMENTARY

INTRODUCTION

1 Corinthians 1:1-9

1:1-3 Greeting

The opening section of an ancient letter consisted of three parts: the name of the sender, the name of the recipients, and a greeting. Paul follows this convention, naming himself and Sosthenes as the letter's co-senders. Co-sender need not imply that Sosthenes was co-author of this letter. Throughout 1 Corinthians, the first person "I" dominates. This suggests that a single author, Paul, was responsible for the composition and content of the letter. Moreover, even when the plural is used, what is usually intended is the whole community of Christians, for example, "are we provoking the Lord?" (10:22).

Paul adds a description of himself that is brief but dense with insight into his self-understanding. He is first of all an "apostle," a term that is both a title and a description of a function. It derives from the Greek verb *apostellō*, which means "to send." Used in conjunction with the phrase "of Jesus Christ," here the term "apostle" denotes Paul's function as one sent out on behalf of, or as an envoy of, Jesus Christ. Paul does not appropriate this function for himself; rather, it is enjoined on him as one "called" to be Christ's envoy "by the will of God" (see further Gal 1:15). By underscoring the divine initiative, Paul reminds the Corinthians that he is an authorized envoy of Christ, in whose name and by whose authority he worked among them and now writes to them. Stated from the perspective of rhetoric, Paul has established his *ethos* here. This will serve as an important argument throughout the letter.

Unless the Sosthenes mentioned in 1:1 is the same Sosthenes named in the Acts of the Apostles, we have no information concerning his identity. In Acts 18:17, Sosthenes, a synagogue official at Corinth, is mentioned in the context of Paul's arraignment before Gallio, the proconsul. After Gallio had refused to hear the case against Paul brought by the Jews and had ejected them from the tribunal (Acts 18:15-16), the Jews seized Sosthenes and beat him. Whether Sosthenes was beaten because he was sympathetic to Paul is not known. Nor is it ever recounted in Acts or elsewhere that this particular Sosthenes converted to

Christianity. Thus there are no compelling reasons to identify the Sosthenes of Acts 18:17 with the person mentioned at 1:1 who is also called by this commonly used name. The most we can deduce from 1:1 is that this Sosthenes was in Ephesus with Paul. Given the fact that Paul adds no other information about him, either here or in the rest of 1 Corinthians, it is also reasonable to deduce that the Corinthian community was familiar with this Sosthenes, called "our brother," a term used for fellow believers and coworkers.

Paul identifies the recipients of this letter as the "church of God that is in Corinth" (1:2). The term *ekklēsia*, which can be translated "church," "assembly," or "congregation," was used in secular Greek to refer to a political assembly. Paul distinguishes his addressees as the *ekklēsia* "of God," which exists not by self-determination or in view of common political concerns, but because God has called it into being.

This theological qualification of the community is augmented by three others. First, the community is sanctified, that is, made holy or set apart for God in Christ Jesus, through whom they have received this new identity. Second, they are called to be holy. This is not a mere rephrasing of the previous qualification; rather, it defines how the community must live in view of the fact that it has been sanctified. Finally, the community at Corinth does not exist independently but is part of a universal fellowship of believers who call upon the name of the Lord and are subject to his authority. These theological, christological, and ecclesiological qualifications ascribed to the community at the outset of the letter influence all that follows.

Paul concludes this opening section with his characteristic grace and peace greeting. Rather than the usual Greek *chair* ("to rejoice"), Paul substitutes *charis* ("grace") and adds the Jewish greeting *shalom* ("peace"). *Charis* expresses Paul's understanding of how God acts toward humanity, in infinite generosity. *Shalom* expresses the result of God's generous activity, humanity's entire well-being that comes from God through Christ.

1:4-9 Thanksgiving

Paul's thanksgiving section adheres to the ancient letter form in which some type of thanksgiving followed the opening formula. Paul's thanks are directed to God, the source and be-stower of the grace the Corinthians have received. This grace has taken the form of enrichment in every spiritual gift, especially in "discourse" (speech) and "knowledge." Paul, who is himself spiritually enriched (14:18), is genuinely grateful to God that the Corinthians enjoy such blessing. Indeed, these gifts confirm Paul's testimony to Christ and verify that the gospel has taken root among the Corinthians (1:6). Yet Paul knows that the full outworking of God's purposes lies beyond the present and the Corinthians' current state of spiritual endowment. The Corinthians must still await the final revelation of Jesus Christ and con-tinually rely on the work of Christ to keep them irreproachable until that day of judgment (1:7-8). Paul's thanksgiving ends on a note of confidence, because "God is faithful" and called the Corin-thians into fellowship *(koinōnia)* with Jesus Christ.

Within this section Paul introduces some key theological points that anticipate issues to be ad-dressed in this letter. His thanksgiving to God for the bestowal of grace contrasts with the Corin-thians' boastful attitude, for which Paul will re-peatedly chide the community, reminding them that everything they have is a gift from God through Christ (4:7). The very gifts for which Paul expresses thanks will unfortunately turn out to be a source of division in the community. Paul will have to address this and remind the Corin-thians that every gift comes from the same Spirit (12:4), is set at the service of the same Lord (12:5), and is ordered to the welfare of the whole body of believers (12:12-26).

Likewise, the eschatological perspective that circumscribes the thanksgiving will be brought forward in Paul's attempts to redress the problems that derive from the Corinthians' over satisfaction with their current spiritual status. Paul will repeat-edly remind the community that the future escha-tological event impinges on how they live and behave in the present (4:5; 6:13-14; 7:29-35). Finally, of overriding importance in the rest of 1 Corinthians is the fact that the Corinthians are divinely created in fellowship with Christ. This fellowship with, or participation in, the life of the risen Jesus is the basis for their hope of future glory (15:20). However, par-ticipation also enjoins upon each believer the on-going task of realizing this fellowship. In some way or another, the reality of this fellowship will per-vade Paul's responses throughout the letter.

ARGUMENT FOR UNITY IN THE COMMUNITY

I Corinthians 1:10–4:21

This first major section of the letter body forms a coherent unit revolving around Paul's call for unity in the face of reported divisions within the community. Apparently, multiple factors are be-hind the divisiveness: attachment to particular teachers, pursuit of wisdom apart from the wis-dom of the crucified Christ that Paul has preached, and boasting in status. In his effort to move the Corinthians to restore unity, Paul will have to clear up two misconceptions—one relating to the nature of the gospel, the other to the role of ministers.

Divisions in the community (1:10-17)

1:10-17 Report of rivalries

Paul begins with an urgent plea in the name of the Lord Jesus, under whose authority the Co-rinthians stand, that they let go of their divisions and be united. "United" translates a Greek verb that literally means "restore." Thus Paul is not urging the Corinthians to do something new but to restore the unity of mind and purpose proper to those called into fellowship with Christ. The source of Paul's information about the community situation is disclosed immediately—"Chloe's people." These associates of Chloe were likely traveling on her behalf from Ephesus to Corinth, where they observed the situation.

Returning to Ephesus, they reported to Paul, informing him of rivalries stemming from alle-giances to particular persons. Some were identify-ing themselves with Paul, others with Apollos, others with Cephas, and some even claimed al-legiance to Christ alone. The phrases "I belong to Paul . . . Cephas," etc., have been taken as the slogans of actual parties at Corinth, and great ef-fort has been exerted to reconstruct the particular ideological bias of each group. However, Paul's use of these phrases may simply be his way of putting into his own words his understanding or interpretation of the situation. In fact, Paul's use of the introductory words "I mean that . . ." (v. 12) just before the mention of the so-called parties seems to indicate that we are hearing Paul's rearticulation of the report about rivalries which he construes in relation to four figures.

Clearly there were divisions in the community that may have revolved around the favoring of some person over another (vv. 11-13), which may have been linked to who baptized whom (vv. 13-16). Additionally, Paul's contrast between the cross of Christ and the wisdom of human eloquence (v. 17) suggests that this, too, was at the root of the divisions. However, that the community was actually divided into four clearly delineated groups does not seem to have been the case. In fact, Paul never refers to them again in the letter. Paul's characterization of the situation in this way allows him to set the stage for his handling of the problem of disunity.

For Paul, it is simply inconceivable that Christians be divided at all, let alone on account of allegiance stemming from baptism, the sacrament that unites all believers to Christ and to one another. The series of rhetorical questions in 1:13 underscores the absurdity of partisanship. Christ is not divided, and neither can those baptized into Christ be divided! In an aside (vv. 14-16), Paul dissociates himself from baptism-based partisanship by disclaiming any extensive personal role in baptizing. This disclaimer introduces an opening for Paul to highlight what he is called and sent to do as an apostle: preach the gospel, and "not with the wisdom of human eloquence" (v. 17). With this negation, Paul rejects persuasive wisdom as antithetical to the wisdom of the cross that he preaches. This opposition seems to be at the root of divisions in the community that Paul deals with in the next step of his argument, where he will set out the essence of his gospel.

The wisdom of the cross (1:18–2:5)

In the foreground of this section of Paul's argument is the paradoxical message of the cross, God's wisdom and power (1:18-25). The Corinthians themselves are testimony to this message (1:26-31); its very essence accounts for Paul's preaching without persuasive words (2:1-5). Divisions, though not directly mentioned in this subsection, are in the background, since vain pursuit of human wisdom and boasting about those who make the best case for it are fundamental to the divisiveness.

1:18-25 The paradox of the cross

The gospel Paul preaches is Christ crucified, God's wisdom and power. God's cross-revealed wisdom defies human wisdom and divides humanity into two groups: the perishing, who reject this message as foolishness, and those being saved,

for whom it is the power of God. The divine overthrow of human wisdom foretold by Isaiah (Isa 29:14) was taking place in the cross. Even the wise man, scholar, and philosopher, representatives of the sharpest thinkers of this age, are incapable of fathoming God's wisdom and power revealed in Christ crucified because theirs is human wisdom, originating in this age, which God has made foolish (1:21). According to human categories, crucifixion, epitomizing weakness and suffering, simply cannot cash out as any kind of wisdom or power, let alone divine wisdom and power!

Humankind's objections to this message are ethnically and historically particularized in the reactions of Jews and Greeks. Jews want signs. Accustomed to a God who had worked wonderfully and powerfully to deliver and save Israel in the past, Jews simply cannot see in a crucified Messiah the power and wisdom of God. For them, the cross is an affront, a stumbling block (see Rom 9:32-33; 11:11). Greeks, on the other hand, want wisdom, that is, the insights and strategies that lead to power, success, and honor. In Greco-Roman society in general, and in Corinth in particular, these were considered the manifestations of the truly wise person. For such as these, the cross signified everything that was counter to wisdom; cross-wisdom was an oxymoron, sheer foolishness. Despite the fact that Jews and Greeks differed with regard to how divine wisdom and power should be authenticated, they were in agreement that it would have to be authenticated by something other than the mind-boggling paradox of the cross.

Yet, it is precisely through what both reject that both Jews and Greeks are saved. Therefore, despite their expectations, Paul insists, "we" preach Christ crucified, a message that disregards humanly established ways of knowing God's power and wisdom, which are known in the cross or not at all. Humans must either give up their categories and accept the crucified Christ as the means of salvation or keep to their own standards, rejecting the message of the cross and perishing. In summarizing his reflections, Paul restates the paradox of the cross. Its very weakness is God's power, more powerful than human strength. Its very absurdity is God's wisdom, wiser than human wisdom. This is the gospel. It runs counter to the world's wisdom. It is fathomed by those willing to see differently and able to live in the tension of this paradox.

1:26-31 The experience of the Corinthians

This paradox is now considered in light of the Corinthians' own experience. Before their call, many were the world's nobodies. So little is there to recommend them that Paul can describe them only by what they were not: not wise, not powerful, not of noble birth. But now they, too, are signs of God's power, with Christ the crucified one as the source of their power. God did not choose them according to the standards of the world. God's wisdom does not correlate, nor has it ever correlated (see Deut 7:7), with the social hierarchy established by humans. It defies human categories, demolishes human standards, and inverts human hierarchies. Now the wise are shamed. The nobodies are chosen by God to undo the somebodies, to reduce to nothing the world's standards, which are incapable of comprehending God's wisdom.

In God's choice of the Corinthians, God reveals an authority to act in a way that is independent of the world and what it thinks or how it judges things ought to be. As a result, no human being has any grounds for boasting. Self-satisfaction and arrogance are eliminated, because everyone obtains grace and salvation in the exact same way. No one has an upper hand, a more superior way or insight into God's wisdom, a higher status meriting a more privileged place within God's plan of salvation. There is only one way to know God and God's salvation: the paradox of the cross, which is God's wisdom and power. Thus competition and boasting and the resultant divisions in the community are excluded.

Paul appropriates words from Jeremiah 9:23 to conclude this subsection. Within the context of this letter, these words constitute a radical challenge to the Corinthians to let go of their boasting in human words of wisdom and human categories and begin to live out their dependence on God's grace, the source of their salvation.

2:1-5 The preaching of Paul

Since the content of the gospel message is Jesus Christ and him crucified, when Paul came to Corinth he deliberately put aside grandiose speech and the use of powerful rhetorical strategies to persuade the Corinthians of this mystery. Considering that the idea of Christ crucified, source of salvation and the very revelation of God's wisdom and power, was (and still is!) such a hard sell, one

would think that Paul would have pulled out all his rhetorical stops to convince the Corinthians of the truth of this message. Instead he comes in "weakness and fear and much trembling" (v. 3) and speaks his message and proclamation without persuasive words of wisdom. Paul's emphatic "my" message and "my" proclamation" (v. 4) is apparently intended to distinguish himself from skilled orators and their message.

Why Paul voluntarily puts himself at such apparent rhetorical disadvantage becomes clear in verses 4-5. True understanding of God's wisdom can never come through human wisdom, which it transcends, nor through mere human articulation, which it eludes. It comes only through the power of the Spirit. Ironically, despite his apparent rhetorical disadvantage, Paul is the most advantaged because his proclamation is powered by the Spirit (v. 4), who brings about faith that rests, appropriately, on God's power.

Paul's lack of rhetorical prowess, like the Corinthians' lack of social status, illustrates again the paradoxical nature of God's wisdom, which defies human reason and subverts human standards of judgment. As God's grace does not take account of social standing, neither does it rely on the persuasive ability of the messenger and words of human wisdom for its actualization in the life of the believer. The implications for the Corinthians are clear: attachment to rhetorically skilled ministers and captivation with their hollow human wisdom leads only to vain boasting and division.

The wisdom of the mature (2:6–3:4)

Paul clears up misconceptions about wisdom, its attainment, and what constitutes true spiritual maturity (2:6-16). Unfortunately, the Corinthians who have received the Spirit persist in their immaturity, running after wisdom that sounds reasonable and is persuasively presented. As long as they persist on this course, they cannot benefit from the spiritual instruction and true wisdom that Paul is capable of imparting (3:1-4).

2:6-16 True wisdom

In an apparent reversal of what he has just stated, Paul announces that he actually does speak a wisdom to the mature. Paul's about-face has so baffled interpreters that some regarded this subunit as originally not part of the letter. Others read it as an indication of Paul's inconsistency and insincerity. Many now read Paul's about-face as intentional irony, to wit: You want wisdom! I have wisdom for the mature. Then, having set up the spiritual snobs in the community for his esoteric message, Paul dismisses them as total infants, too stupid and immature to attain to such wisdom! Whether Paul's intention was to humiliate, as suggested by this view, is not altogether certain.

What we learn from the text is that here Paul deals with wisdom and spiritual maturity. These were of great importance not only to this community but also to Paul. However, Paul meant something radically different by these terms. Here he reconsiders both terms in light of the gospel in order to instruct the community concerning true wisdom and how it is attained, to deal with divisions caused by the spiritually enlightened, and ultimately to advance his argument for unity.

Paul begins by affirming that he does preach a wisdom, something that he has overtly claimed from the outset of this letter (1:17-18). However, this wisdom differs from that to which the Corinthians aspire. A variety of religious and philosophical currents had made their way to Corinth, but Paul does not specify the type or content of the wisdom being pursued by some in the community. He simply associates it with the "wisdom of this age" (2:6), which is opposed to God's secret and hidden wisdom. The rulers of this age, operating with its wisdom, are incapable of penetrating God's wisdom; otherwise they could never have crucified the Lord of glory. The fact that they did simply illustrates that the pursuit of human wisdom leads to utter ignorance, not spiritual insight. Corinthian Christians who pursue the wisdom of this age through human reason are likewise incapable of penetrating God's wisdom, remain unenlightened, and are spiritually immature, despite their claims to the contrary.

The true wisdom to be pursued, which brings knowledge and enlightenment, is beyond what the human mind and heart can conceive and hence unattainable through human reason. It is knowable, as Paul already stated at 2:4, only through the agency of the Spirit. Paul supports his point by a commonsense argument based on human experience. The Corinthians would no doubt agree with him that one's inner workings are really scrutinized and known only by one's self. Arguing by analogy, Paul says, so it is with

God. God's own Spirit scrutinizes the depths of God. Whoever would apprehend God's wisdom must be in touch with the Spirit of God and equipped with the categories and language of spiritual realities, because this is what the Spirit reveals. Paul and the Corinthians have received the Spirit of God. They are spiritual and equipped to speak of and understand God's wisdom in Spirit-taught language. Once this wisdom, summed up in the message of the cross, is understood, the criteria by which humans judge are radically changed.

3:1-4 Continued Corinthian immaturity

Paul now explains that he could not impart to the Corinthians the spiritual knowledge and insight they so desired. This was not due to any inability on his part or to any innate lack on the Corinthians' part. They had received the Spirit. They should have been able to handle Spirit-taught words, understand spiritual realities, and live as mature persons, that is, spiritual persons. But they were acting in a "fleshly" way, that is, contrary to the Spirit who unifies, still judging according to human criteria, as demonstrated by their unity-destroying behavior. While they persisted in jealousy and rivalries, they were showing themselves to be all too human. Viewed from a spiritual angle, they were still spiritual infants, unable to absorb the mysterious wisdom of the cross, the solid food reserved for spiritual adults. They had not been ready for solid food in the past, and their current wrangling over wisdom and wisdom teachers and superior status proves that they are still not ready!

The community and its leaders (3:5-23)

Paul's next step in his argument for unity deals with misunderstandings revolving around the role of community leaders. Their distinctive tasks are complementary (3:5-9); indeed, every member of the community whose foundation is Christ must contribute to its unity and holiness, in view of which one will be judged (3:10-17). Since all belongs to God in Christ, only God's wisdom revealed in Christ counts (3:18-23).

3:5-9 Paul and Apollos: coworkers in God's field

The opening rhetorical question underscores the absurdity of the partisanship that has grown up around certain ministers. Paul and Apollos are mere farm hands, working at different but equal tasks in God's field, the community, whose growth depends on God alone. The insignificance of ministers, implied in the rhetorical question, is reinforced through this metaphor and serves to warn the Corinthians against attaching too much importance to any one minister. Moreover, since, as the metaphor implies, ministers work for the same boss and undertake complementary tasks directed to the same goal, to oppose one minister to the other is to undermine God's own work.

3:10-17 Everyone's work will be fire-tested

At the end of 3:9, Paul changes metaphors, describing the community as God's building, and now advances his argument employing construction imagery (3:10-15). Paul, the wise master builder, laid the foundation for God's building, Jesus Christ. As a foundation determines the contours and shape of the concrete structure arising from it, so must the community of believers, whose oneness is underscored by the term "building," be determined by its foundation, Christ. Each member builds up from this one foundation and must take care that the contribution made is consistent with it and ordered to the building's unity. Paul directs this warning not to Apollos and himself but to the Corinthians. They can build on the foundation with precious stones, or with perishable materials such as wood or hay, by which Paul means the fleeting and fatuous stuff of human wisdom. The latter will not stand the fire test, that is, the day of judgment, when retribution or salvation will be awarded in light of one's work.

Indeed, if anyone destroys this building, now further qualified as God's temple (3:16-17), God will destroy that person. Paul uses the Greek term *naos,* translated "temple," which actually referred to a particular place within the temple—the inner sanctuary where God's holiness dwelt. Thus the Corinthian community, *corporately as a community,* indwelt by God's own Spirit, is now the living locus of God's holiness. As a result, each member's behavior must be oriented from and toward the community's holiness.

3:18-23 All belong to God in Christ

In concluding this subunit of argumentation, Paul once again takes up the themes of wisdom

and folly and very bluntly addresses the Corinthians. The world's wisdom is mere craftiness, a human construct of hollow notions, two facts attested by the Scriptures Paul cites (Job 5:13 and Ps 94:11).

If you think yourself wise in view of that standard, your self-perception is actually self-deception! Give up that standard! Accept and submit to the inverted order that is paradoxically God's wisdom, epitomized in the cross, and then, though the world considers you a fool, paradoxically, you will be truly wise!

Within this paradoxical perspective, the futility of exalting any one minister over another and divisive boasting over human wisdom becomes apparent. Every minister plays an equal and complementary part in unfolding God's plan, and all ministers are at the service of the Corinthians, who together have "everything" (3:21). Here Paul cites a popular maxim of his day summarizing all the privileges believed to accrue to the ideal wise person, a completely self-sufficient person of superior status who was beyond the petty rules and regulations that applied to the less enlightened.

In contradistinction to this privilege and autonomy, Paul reminds the Corinthians that together, as a community, they are co-sharers and co-inheritors of all things in and with Christ. As such, no one can use his or her freedom and privilege for individual self-promotion and boasting, or toward whatever destroys the unity of the community in Christ through which these privileges exist. Moreover, the Corinthian community ultimately stands in and through Christ in direct and subordinate relationship *to God* (3:23). The Corinthians must ultimately live in faithful obedience to God and answer to God, not Paul or Apollos or Cephas, not even Christ, but God who holds all together and judges all according to the wisdom made manifest in the cross.

Cross-wisdom: the ultimate critique (4:1-21)

In this final step of his argument, Paul returns to the role of ministers and appropriates another set of metaphors that stress the subordinate role of ministers and the singular character upon which they are to be judged—trustworthiness (4:1-5). This is followed by a stinging critique of the Corinthian community in light of cross-wisdom. Judged by the criterion of the cross, their lives are shown to be a repudiation of God's counter-order wisdom (4:6-13). Paul's highlighting of their failure to live lives transformed by the gospel of the cross is intended to restore a sense of realism to the situation so that the Corinthians can go forward to restore the unity of the community.

4:1-5 Ministers are required to be trustworthy

Changing metaphors, Paul now describes ministers as "servants" and "stewards," persons who work under the authority of a master and are accountable to the master's standards. The singular requirement to which they are held is trustworthiness, that is, they must be faithful to the proclamation of Christ crucified, God's wisdom. In context, this statement should probably be understood as an implicit critique of the standard of judgment applied to ministers by the Corinthians. They were impressed by parcels of wisdom and grandiose speech, the wrong criteria applied by some Corinthians, who had wrongly arrogated to themselves the right to judge ministers. It was not that ministers were beyond judgment. But they were accountable to God, not the Corinthians.

Even the fact that Paul is the founding apostle of this community in no way invests the Corinthians with any particular right to judge him or any other minister of God. The right to judge and the criterion for judgment are God's alone. So much so is this the exclusive prerogative of God that Paul, who is spiritually mature, does not even bother to judge himself. (How much less should the spiritually immature judge others?) Besides, Paul knew that even were he to find himself beyond reproach by the light of his own conscience, it was not one's conscience but only God who is the ultimate arbiter of truth and under whose eschatological judgment everyone must pass. God's future judgment is the only thing that counts, and God's verdict depends not only on what one does in the present but also on one's hidden motivations!

4:6-13 Cross-wisdom: the ultimate critique

Paul now explains that he has discussed these things by way of reference to Apollos and himself in order to teach the Corinthians a beneficial lesson about how they are to act among themselves. Through the example of Apollos and himself, Paul

was able to underscore the cooperative and complementary character of ministry. Neither he nor Apollos does anything that is self-serving; rather, both work toward the same common purpose. Neither is a Hellenistic wise man to be made a rallying point for partisan allegiance; rather, both are servants and stewards whose allegiance is directed to God.

The Corinthians are to learn from this "not to go beyond what is written" (4:6). The meaning of "what is written" is a matter of speculation. It could refer to the Scriptures in general, to the gospel of the cross, to all Paul has thus far written in this letter, or to the specific sections of Scripture he has so far cited. The whole phrase, "not to go beyond what is written," could also be Paul's adaptation of an adage connoting something like "stick to the guidelines."

Whatever the case, Paul's clear intention is stated in the rest of verse 6, namely, that they desist from the divisive behavior caused by their pitting one leader against another. This is accompanied by prideful boasting ("inflated with pride," literally being "puffed up"). As the image suggests, they are "puffed up" by empty wind, mere pretentiousness but no substance.

Paul's three questions in verse 7 serve as a reality check. There is nothing different or special about the Corinthians. Anything they have is a gift, made possible by the cross of Christ. Yet, rather than living an existence consonant with that reality, characterized by the paradoxical wisdom of the cross, the Corinthians live another triumphant existence guided and evaluated in view of other standards. They claim to have it all, to be rich in spiritual-intellectual assets, and to have been already empowered to reign. In philosophical circles, especially among the Stoics, to be rich and to reign were applied to intellectual-spiritual status and represented the prerogatives of the ideal wise person. Apparently, the Corinthians were still aspiring to the values of their world, mixing up the goals of gospel living with society's goals and using the standard of judgment applied by society to measure their own wisdom and spiritual maturity.

In his critique of the Corinthians, Paul transposes the whole problem to a theological key. In that key the problem is presented as rooted in a premature arrogating of the full privileges of end-time living and the status of the spiritually perfect by the community. Paul goes on to contrast the Corinthians' grandstanding with the lot of apostles with purposeful irony aimed at Corinthian pretentiousness. Apostles are weak and considered fools; their lives are characterized by hardship and deprivation. So low is their social status that Paul likens apostles to "the world's rubbish, the scum of all" (4:13)! All this is in contradistinction to the lot of the Corinthians, who, Paul mockingly observes, are wise, strong, and esteemed. Judged by the world's standards, apostles are nothing and the Corinthians are everything! But when each stands under the critique of the cross, all such judgments are reversed. By their vain boasting and glorying in their own achievements, the Corinthians repudiate God's wisdom and the suffering and crucified Christ in whom this wisdom was revealed. In the starkest possible terms, Paul makes it clear that true ministers, indeed every true follower of Christ, must be co-sharers not only in Christ's glory but in his sufferings and status as one rejected by the world.

4:14-21 Concluding admonition

Having just taken the Corinthians down a few pegs, Paul now explains that his harsh rhetoric was not intended to shame but to admonish and refocus the perspective of the Corinthians, whom he genuinely loves. Whereas in 3:1-5 Paul referred to his relationship with the community using the maternal imagery of nourishing, here he refers to himself metaphorically as their "father" (4:15), giving expression to the intimate relationship between himself and this community engendered through his preaching of the gospel. Paul's paternal intervention and call for the community to be imitators of him (4:16) could be read as the ultimate expression of patriarchal arrogance. However, read in context, Paul's call for imitation is contingent upon his own imitation of Christ and refers to the pattern of renunciation, suffering, and servant-model type of leadership that he undertakes for the sake of the gospel. Here Paul's own *ethos* becomes a powerful appeal to the Corinthians to transform their own lives. In Paul's absence, he sends Timothy as one who will model this life pattern ("my ways in Christ Jesus," 4:17) for the community. This manner of life is not a distinct imposition on the Corinthians, but the pattern of life required of all Christians everywhere. Here again Paul reminds the Corinthians

that they are no maverick community of elite spiritualists, but part of a universal fellowship.

Despite the arguments that Paul has set out in this first major unit of the letter, he is concerned that some will persist in the behavior that has been a source of division in the community. He has already made it eminently clear that God's wisdom and power are not compatible with human words, no matter how elegant and persuasive the articulation. Here he contrasts empty words and true power again, and if need be, Paul will come and reveal the impotence of the empty talkers.

With this final warning, Paul concludes the first major argument of this letter. Throughout this argument for unity, he has applied the scandalous and paradoxical lens of the cross to the situation of this community. Through that lens, it becomes clear that the Corinthians are still dominated by the values and presuppositions of their culture. They are still searching for the human wisdom that will unlock the door to power and status, still judging people by the secular categories of prestige and success. They remain impressed by elegant words and controlled by the desire for enhanced status afforded by attachment to the best purveyor of human wisdom. The Corinthians' culturally conditioned living of the gospel had emptied the cross of Christ of its power and value and resulted in the problems that were threatening to destroy Christianity at Corinth. The restoration of the community's unity, as Paul has demonstrated, would require nothing less than the entire realigning of its values with God's countercultural cross-wisdom.

ARGUMENTS CONCERNING IMMORALITY WITHIN THE COMMUNITY AND RELATIONSHIPS WITH THOSE OUTSIDE THE COMMUNITY

1 Corinthians 5:1–6:20

Paul now takes up three ethical issues, beginning with a case of sexual immorality at 1 Corinthians 5. The logical disjuncture between the previous discussion in chapters 1–4 and its themes and this new one, focused on an individual case of sexual immorality, has contributed to the speculation that 1 Corinthians is not one unified literary composition. However, this is too radical an assessment since there are word links—for example, to boast, to judge—between 1 Corinthians 5 and the chapters that precede it. Nonetheless, it is clear that chapters 5–6 do form a distinct macro-unit, structured according to the ABA' pattern. Sexual immorality is introduced in 5:1-13 (A). Then Paul discusses Christian recourse to pagan courts in 6:1-11 (B), before again dealing with sexual immorality in 6:12-20 (A').

Why Paul introduces these three topics here can perhaps be best explained in view of their rhetorical-pedagogic function in the letter. As 1 Corinthians progresses, Paul takes up a variety of questions for which there are no black-and-white answers. Instead, the community has to consider not only the good but also the better courses of action that they as Christians must adopt in view of the well-being of the whole community. Multiple criteria have to be considered, and keen powers of discernment are needed to weigh the options.

A closer look at 1 Corinthians 5–6 reveals the community's incompetence to handle matters where clear-cut decisions are called for. In the face of this, here in chapters 5–6, Paul first reorders the Corinthians' focus within the fundamental boundaries of absolute good and evil as a prelude to assisting them with decisions on issues that admit of shades of gray. If the community cannot judge black-and-white cases of community-destroying behavior, how can Paul expect them to be able to discern what is best for the community?

Argument against sexual immorality (5:1-13)

In this subunit of argumentation, Paul deals with a blatant case of sexual immorality within the community. It was apparently tolerated rather than dealt with and stopped. Paul's unequivocal judgment is that the offender needs to be expelled from the community to protect its holiness. The decision to excommunicate, however, ultimately remains with the community. In this compact unit, Paul argues to persuade the Corinthians to take the prescribed action.

5:1-5 The community's failed judgment

Whatever the exact contents of the report Paul heard, he states the problem this way: "there is immorality *(porneia)* among you (plural)." This manner of articulating the problem indicates that Paul's overriding concern is with the community, which has allowed the situation to go unchecked.

The Greek term *porneia* is a comprehensive term covering all forms of sexual immorality. By adding the phrase "a man living with his father's wife," Paul qualifies the immorality as incest. "Father's wife" was used to distinguish one's stepmother from one's biological mother (Lev 18:7-8).

What Paul says, literally, is that the man "is having" his stepmother, a verb normally used to indicate a sexual relationship, which, in view of the present tense, should be considered ongoing. Such a relationship, proscribed by both Jewish and Roman law, is simply wrong, even if the offender's father is dead. Thus there is no need to argue for the man's guilt. Yet, the community has failed to judge the situation for what it is—a case of rank evil in its midst—and has allowed the brother to carry on unimpugned. Not only that, they are inflated with pride either because of the relationship or perhaps despite it. Whatever the case, their haughty attitude is the real cause of Paul's consternation and the bigger issue circumscribing the problem addressed in this chapter.

Since the Corinthians have failed to judge correctly and do the obvious, Paul, who has judged correctly, outlines the action that ought to be taken. The exact punishment envisioned by him is unclear. He could be intending physical death, or physical punishment coupled with expulsion, or simply expulsion from the community. When all the data is assessed, it seems more likely that Paul intends the latter. Banished from the community, presumably the offender will come to his senses and repent. Whatever the punishment, one thing is clear: it is ultimately ordered to the benefit of the offender so that "his spirit may be saved on the day of the Lord" (v. 5). Here Paul is not deliberating with the community among possible courses of action. This is the only course possible, and it is imperative that the community carry it out.

Paul obviously realizes that commanding alone will not move the community to take action, and so he couches his call for expulsion in three distinct arguments. The first argument is introduced with his remark that such behavior is not found even among the pagans! This statement is no doubt an exaggeration. However, the exaggerated comparison between the pagans and the Corinthians functions as an appeal to their emotions (argument based on *pathos*). The community should be ashamed of itself for disregarding a common standard of decency that even pagans are capable of observing. Appeals to the emotions, especially shame, were considered among the most powerful arguments to induce a person or group to change judgments, if for no nobler reason than simply to avoid being disgraced. To the Corinthians, who lived in an honor/shame culture, saving face was of utmost importance.

5:6-8 "you are unleavened"

After dismissing the Corinthian boasting as not good, Paul proceeds to appeal to the Corinthians' reason. Using a commonsense maxim, he takes up the metaphoric language of dough and yeast and argues on analogy that the evil one's presence is corrupting and compromising the entire community's true character of sinlessness. Since the community is sinless, it cannot at the same time have sin in its midst. This incompatibility demands that the sinner be expelled, metaphorically expressed in the command to "clear out the old yeast" (v. 7). Paul explains why sinlessness is the character of Christian existence and necessitates this cleansing in one brief phrase: "for our paschal lamb, Christ, has been sacrificed." The mention of the paschal lamb and unleavened bread recalls the rites of the Jewish Passover, which Paul symbolically interprets and transposes to a moral key. Through Christ's blood, Christians are morally cleansed, constituted holy, a condition willed by God (see 1 Thess 4:2). This is the core of Paul's reasoning and the ultimate ground of the specific command to expel the sinner. Paul concludes this section by exhorting the community to live in a manner consistent with its own sinless/holy character.

5:9-13 The community's failed judgment

Paul returns to the community's failed judgment by referring to his previous letter to the Corinthians. They had missed Paul's point. He was not prohibiting social interaction with the immoral of the society at large but, as he now clarifies, with anyone calling himself a brother who perpetrated any of the vices Paul now lists in verse 11. The introduction of the list of vices allows Paul to class the offending brother with egregious sinners. By doing so, he again appeals to the community's emotions, to elicit a sense of abhorrence for and alienation from "such a person," which should move them to judge and expel him. The vice-list makes clear that there is no double-standard. A vice-doer who is a brother is not a brother but a sinner. Here Paul draws the line not between Christians and pagans but between Christians and pseudo-Christians. There can be no social contact with the latter!

In conclusion, Paul disclaims any obligation to judge those outside the community. As outsiders, they cannot corrupt the community's holiness. But those within can, and so he reminds the community of its obligation to judge the sinners within the community and, as this case warrants, "purge the evil person from your midst" (v. 13). This paraphrase of a formula repeated in Deuteronomy (e.g., Deut 17:7; 19:19; 21:21; 22:21, 22, 24) echoes the punishment prescribed in the Torah for egregious sins and evokes Jewish abhorrence for sexual sin, especially incest, considered the characteristic practice of pagans (Lev 18:1-3).

Thus, by Jewish lights and by the standards of common decency of society at large, incest is intolerable. Christians cannot ignore these standards as a baseline for their own behavior. However, what ultimately must guide Christian behavior is the person of Christ and the event of his death, on account of which the community's corporate identity as sanctified is established. This ecclesial identity is linked to ethical behavior, which must be ordered to safeguarding the sanctified life of the community.

Since Paul does not discuss the reasons why the offending brother undertook this relationship or why the community tolerated his presence, speculation abounds concerning their motives. In view of the discussion in 1 Corinthians 1–4, where it appears that some had arrogated to themselves the status and prerogatives of the ideal wise person, perhaps their complacent disregard for this violation of the standards of common decency, or even boasting about it, was intended to demonstrate that they had arrived at a state of perfection that allowed them to transcend all the conventions to which the unenlightened were obligated. If so, then here again some community members confused the standard of human wisdom and the exercise of privileges reserved for the world's wise with the standards that must guide Christians and the privilege of sanctified life in Christ, which enjoins on each member the obligation to live as a sanctified member of a sanctified community.

Argument against recourse to pagan courts (6:1-11)

Having brought up the need for the community to exercise jurisdiction for internal matters, Paul leaves aside the issue of sexual immorality and excoriates the community for abdicating this responsibility and allowing the adjudication of internal community issues to take place before pagan courts. Paul does not say how he learned about this situation. However, he argues against such recourse on two grounds. First, Christians are competent to adjudicate their own disputes (6:1-6), and second, Christians ought not to have such disputes requiring litigation in the first place (6:7-8). In concluding, Paul reminds the community that certain forms of behavior are simply incompatible with its new corporate ecclesial identity (6:9-11).

6:1-6 Competence to judge

Paul first expresses his shock in a rhetorical question, one of the nine such questions that he will use in this subunit to bring his argument forward. Explicit in this first question is the community's failure to carry out its responsibility by going before the "unjust" (v. 1). Although the Roman court system was known for its corruption and favoring of the well-to-do in its exploitation of the poor, in context "unjust" is probably to be taken less as a moral evaluation and more as a term to distinguish those outside from those inside the communion of the holy ones.

In the next two rhetorical questions Paul reminds the community of its judicial prerogatives. The belief that the holy ones would judge the world was rooted in Jewish apocalyptic eschatology, which envisioned the role of judgment as one of the prerogatives of God's elect (Dan 7:21-22). Many later Jewish writings also anticipate the participation of the holy ones in the final judgment (e.g., Wis 3:7-8; Sir 4:11).

Paul goes further in his next question to suggest that they will even judge the angels (v. 3), presumably the fallen ones, who were expected to undergo judgment (2 Pet 2:4). By reminding them of their prerogatives as holy ones, Paul builds an argument from greater to lesser to point up both the absurdity and inappropriateness of recourse to pagan courts. If in their glorious eschatological future they will sit in judgment on the world (including, obviously, the ones to whom they now hand over their judgments) and even angels, how much more so should they be capable of handling minor and ordinary everyday cases in the present! Paul does not specify what type of cases, but his choice of words underscores their inconsequential nature.

Why, then, Paul continues, do you elevate to the role of judges "people of no standing in the church"? (v. 4). It would be bad enough had the community simply failed to perform its duty, but it has actually ceded its privilege to a secular system and its standards of judgment. This act of submission to that system indicates that the community is still tied to the social conventions of the world and has yet to redirect its total allegiance to the community of faith. Paul's explicit intent to shame the community should at least awaken their concern to save face, and indeed they have much to be ashamed about. The need to take inconsequential cases before unbelievers seems to point up the community's deficiency when it comes to judiciousness, despite all the claims to be truly wise!

6:7-8 Renouncing litigation

With two more questions Paul advances his argument in another direction. Community members should renounce their right to litigate to the detriment of other community members and, instead, endure injustice and defrauding. This idea had great currency among philosophers who held that a truly wise person was above injury or insult. Seeking redress would simply negate this claim, and the wise one would show himself or herself to be no better than anyone else! Paul may be playing off Corinthian arrogance at this point.

Beyond that, it is important to recognize that what Paul says here is quite consistent with what he says elsewhere about how Christians must comport themselves (Rom 12:17) and, though unstated, is obviously rooted in the example of Christ, who endured injustice without seeking redress. But not only have the Corinthians paraded their problems before the unjust, but in the very act of doing this they have become perpetrators of injustice and cheating against their own family. The distinction between the world and the family of faith has been blurred.

6:9-11 Final warning

Paul's final rhetorical question insinuates that the glorious eschatological destiny that awaits the

Corinthians will not be had simply by waiting. In fact, if they do wrong they risk sharing the lot of those who will not inherit the kingdom. Paul again cautions them against self-deception (v. 9; cf. 3:18) and lists the vices that characterized some of their former lives as pagans. They have to continuously renounce all such behavior and live as those who are washed, sanctified, and justified. Together these three terms express the fullness of the transformation that has taken place in the lives of believers, who are now in Christ and made one and holy by the indwelling of the Spirit of God. In this one family of believers, brothers cannot go against brothers, nor can the holy ones mix with the unjust.

Argument against sexual immorality (6:12-20)

Paul now returns to the topic of sexual immorality. However, here there is no indication that the type of *porneia* under discussion, that is, extramarital sexual unions, perhaps with prostitutes, represents the actual behavior of some community members or simply behavior that could hypothetically result from the exercise of freedom understood apart from a theological context. In the form of a dialogue between himself and an imaginary dialogue partner, Paul engages and corrects the Corinthians' errant thinking and then, through a series of rhetorical questions, moves his argument against fornication forward. He frames this entire discussion within two important parameters: Christians are free (6:12), but they belong to God (6:19).

6:12-14 Everything is lawful for me

The phrase "Everything is lawful for me," marked off in the biblical text with quotation marks, is a Corinthian principle or slogan cited by Paul. Paul had indeed preached freedom from sin as one of the hallmarks of new Christian existence (1 Cor 6:11; Gal 5:1). However, once again it appears that the Corinthians had interpreted Paul's freedom teaching apart from its theological and ethical significance and in accord with societal ideas and categories. According to the philosophers, freedom was the authority to act on one's own, the quintessential right and privilege of the ideal wise person. Especially among the Stoics, it was believed that this freedom was manifested in one's acting according to nature.

After qualifying the use of freedom in view of what is beneficial, presumably for the whole community, and the need for self-control, Paul moves closer to the heart of the matter in verse 13, where he quotes another Corinthian slogan: "Food for the stomach and the stomach for food." In other words, as the Corinthians saw it, the sating of the stomach was considered a natural biological necessity. Moreover, they obviously held that no moral value could be attached to acts of natural biological necessity, because the body was meant ultimately for destruction, which proved its moral insignificance.

The Corinthians presumably transferred this way of thinking to sex to argue that it was merely another natural biological necessity, no more than the functioning of morally insignificant parts of a morally insignificant body. The blatant disregard for the body manifested in such thinking accorded very well with the view of the body expressed by the philosophers, especially the Stoics, who looked forward to death as the release of the soul from one's paltry body.

Here Paul's concern is that the inferior status accorded to the body could lead to fornication, and so he insists that the body is not meant for immorality but for the Lord! Moreover, against nature which destroys, Paul establishes the power and purpose of God, who raised Jesus and who will raise us. That future glorious eschatological destiny imbues the body with moral value and impinges on what one does in the body in the present. The reality of the resurrection, which grounds Paul's argument here, anticipates his fuller argument for the resurrection in chapter 15.

6:15-20 You are not your own

Through a series of rhetorical questions, Paul now adds to this argument, rooted in the resurrection destiny of the body, an argument rooted in the believers' union with Christ and another rooted in a consideration of the body as the temple of the holy Spirit. Picking up on his statement that the body is for the Lord, Paul now reminds the Corinthians of their union with Christ, a union so intimate that Paul uses the imagery of sexual union to describe it. As unthinkable as it would be for a man or woman to take his or her body, which is one with his or her spouse, and unite it sexually to another, so also is it unthinkable for a Christian who is one with Christ ("one spirit with him," v. 17) to form another union. This union of believers with Christ in one holy body precludes immoral unions between a believer and a prostitute, which constitute a defilement of the whole Christian community. Thus Paul commands believers to flee immorality!

Before discussing the sanctifying role of the Spirit, Paul counters another Corinthian argument to the effect that the physical body has nothing to do with sin. This squares well with the Corinthian argument that bodily actions were deemed to have no moral significance, which Paul has already countered. It may also underscore how much the Corinthians' thinking was influenced by the philosophers of the day, since the argument that the body has nothing to do with sin fits very well with the Stoic idea that sin is not in the performance of any particular external act but is a matter of interior intention. Paul does not recognize this dichotomy between act and intention. His reaction is clear: a fornicator defiles not only the community but himself or herself, who is indwelt by the Spirit.

Here Paul returns to the image of the temple of God. At 3:16-17 Paul spoke of the Spirit who indwells the community as a whole, and now he applies this metaphor to every member individually. As the entire community must safeguard its holiness, so must each individual believer, whose body is no longer his or her own to use at will but is the sacred place of God's dwelling. Thus the Corinthians, corporately and individually, are free, but they are not totally autonomous. God has a claim on them. They have been bought at the price of Christ's death.

For Corinthians, exposed to the buying and selling of slaves in the marketplace, the implications of this metaphoric language would have been clear. They now belong to God and stand under God's authority and will. To accept the offer of freedom that comes through Christ is to stand in a new relationship, to accept a new bondage with ethical implications. Therefore the freedom exercised by those in Christ is never absolute freedom but freedom exercised within the parameters of belonging to God in Christ and ordered to God's glory. It was this relationally circumscribed and theologically inflected understanding of freedom that the wise ones at Corinth apparently failed to perceive.

In both 1 Corinthians 5 and here in 6:12-20, Paul does not treat sexual morality as a purely individual matter of choice, with only individual consequences. Since the community forms one sanctified whole, the immorality of one member can damage the sanctified life of the whole body. The community as a whole must be vigilant about this holiness and take responsibility to cleanse itself from whatever mars that holiness (5:1-13). The individual, too, must be vigilant for the life of the whole and avoid through his or her own exercise of freedom any defilement of the community's sanctified life (6:12-20). By the holiness of its life, manifested at the level of moral existence, the community of believers must glorify God and distinguish itself from the world. To bring community issues before outsiders blurs the distinction between this holy community and the world, dishonors God, and shows the community to be incapable of the reconciling love demanded by the cross-wisdom that must guide this community (6:1-11).

CONCERNING MARRIAGE AND SEXUAL RELATIONS
1 Corinthians 7:1-40

Having just discussed immoral sexual relations outside marriage, Paul now turns to discuss the question of sexual relations within marriage, offering advice to the married as well as to the unmarried and widows (7:1-16). This is followed by an apparent digression relating to social status (7:17-24). Then Paul redirects himself to virgins, widows, and married women.

It is important to remember when reading 1 Corinthians 7 that Paul is not writing a systematic treatise on marriage but is responding to questions posed by the community (see 7:1). His answers are conditioned by his belief that the community is living in the last days of the end-time and that the Lord's second coming is quickly approaching. Unfortunately, Paul's advice here has been mistakenly read as a devaluation of marriage and human sexuality and expressive of an overall contempt of women. Once one recognizes the occasional nature of Paul's responses and the eschatological urgency that conditioned them, it is quite clear that this presentation of Paul and his teaching is a distortion in service of a negative agenda about marriage, sexuality, and women that was not Paul's.

To appreciate Paul's discussion, some information about currents of discussion in Paul's day will be helpful. Among the philosophers, the relative merits of marriage were a regular topic of discussion, and written record reveals their ambivalence about it. While it was conceded that marriage was good for the ordinary citizen and promoted the well-being of society, some argued that marriage, with all its obligations and strains, was ill-suited to the ideal wise one and hindered the pursuit of wisdom. For such a one, it was argued, to remain unmarried, which did not imply sexually chaste, was a better option.

Some of the Corinthians who fancied themselves as spiritually enlightened seem to have taken up the lines of this debate with regard to their own situation. Some may have thought that sexual asceticism would further their pursuit of wisdom and establish their superior status as those dedicated to spiritual matters rather than the mundane preoccupations of the less enlightened. In any event, the community directs the matter to Paul, who does not have black-and-white answers to these issues. Rather, he considers with the community what is preferable, balancing his answers between what is practically doable in the particular situation in which members find themselves and the urgency of the present eschatological situation.

7:1-16 Advice to the married, unmarried, and widows

Paul begins by citing another Corinthian slogan. This one is concerned with "touch[ing] a woman," a euphemism for sexual intercourse. Apparently some proposed the renunciation of sexual relations within marriage in view of their new spiritual status or even the renunciation of marriage and sex altogether in preference for celibacy. While Paul clearly prefers the latter, he clarifies that within the married state, one cannot renounce sexual activity in order to be more spiritual, because this misplaced asceticism could wind up leading to immorality! Far from denouncing erotic pleasure within marriage, Paul urges married people to do what is proper to married people. Marriage enjoins on both man and woman equal obligation and equal rights over their sexual relationship. Neither can unilaterally withdraw from these obligations except for prayer, an option afforded by Jewish law, which Paul seems to have in mind here. But even this must be by mutual agreement. It is possible that

some at Corinth were appealing to Paul's own celibacy to justify sexual asceticism. However, he makes it clear that celibacy is a gift from God. Since celibacy cannot be self-imposed or externally imposed, for Paul it follows that not marrying is possible and preferable only if one is gifted with celibacy by God.

To the unmarried and widows, Paul does cite his own celibacy as a model to be followed, although he is well aware that the sexual drive may prove to be too much for some, in which case he counsels marriage. To the married, Paul specifies that he repeats the Lord's own instruction, that is, the prohibition of divorce. Though Paul cautions both men and women against divorce, his remark, addressed specifically to women (v. 11), seems to take for granted that some women are divorcing or are intending to do so. Whether women are contemplating divorce as a way to free themselves for spiritual pursuits or to free themselves from husbands whose spiritual pursuits preclude sexual relations is not certain. Paul's reminder to women that they should not attempt to remarry (to avoid adultery) seems to support the latter scenario.

Paul's next set of counsels concerns believers who are married to unbelievers. There is no reason for one who has become a believer to divorce an unbelieving spouse unless the unbeliever finds the believing partner's faith to be a problem and chooses to initiate the divorce. Then the believer is not bound. Otherwise, such marriages can be occasions of grace and holiness even for the nonbeliever and the couple's children.

7:17-24 Advice on one's social status

Although Paul may appear to digress in this subsection with the introduction of contrasting religious/ethnic statuses (circumcised-uncircumcised/Jew-Gentile) and social statuses (slave-free), this shift in focus allows Paul to continue to address the Corinthian situation from another angle. Apparently, some at Corinth are operating with the conviction that to really pursue the spiritual concerns proper to one's new Christian identity, one needs to change one's life circumstances or status, as if there were only one right or true life context or status appropriate to an authentic Christian life. By underscoring the insignificance of ritual identity markers/ethnicity and social status as a gauge for one's faithful obedience to God, Paul is able to illustrate the general principle he announces both at the beginning and the end of this subsection. This principle challenges the Corinthian assumption by establishing the fact that one's particular life context or social status in no way jeopardizes one's Christian freedom or ability to lead an authentic Christian existence. Thus there is no need for married people or any others to divest themselves of their particular set of circumstances.

7:25-40 Advice to virgins/engaged couples, married women, and widows

In the remaining verses, Paul's advice is directed alternately to virgins/engaged couples (7:25-28 and 36-38), married women and widows (7:39-40), with a brief interlude (7:29-35) in which he offers an explanation for his consistent counsel to celibacy.

The question concerning virgins probably relates to whether an engaged but not yet married girl should proceed with marriage or remain unmarried. Paul advises celibacy but in the end leaves the decision up to the engaged couple, who do well whether they marry or not. Paul's insertion of the remark that the choice to marry is not a sin may have been necessitated by a contrary claim that marriage was sinful, an idea not unknown among early Christians (see 1 Tim 4:1-5). Paul's second reminder against divorce, now exclusively addressed to married women, may underscore the reality of wife-initiated divorce within the community. It is Paul's opinion that it is better for widowed women to remain unmarried.

Paul explains his preference for celibacy in view of the unfolding eschatological plan, an event of cosmic proportion. The world in its present form is passing away; human existence, with its characteristic forms, institutions, and priorities, is now relativized. Time is growing short, and the pressures will be intense in this brief interval before the unfolding begins. It is in light of this exigent situation that Paul counsels those who are unmarried to remain as they are, contrasting what he envisions as their total devotion to the Lord with the divided attention that characterizes the married. Indeed, Paul prefers that all persons be free from the legitimate distractions of daily life in anticipation of the imminent coming of the Lord. Since Paul was not gifted with the charism of marriage, it is important to keep in

mind that he speaks from the biased vantage point of a celibate. Clearly, stress, strain, and distraction are not the exclusive domain of the married. Thus we have to keep in mind that by Paul's best lights and in view of the eschatological exigency, he counsels celibacy as the better choice.

ARGUMENT CONCERNING FOOD OFFERED TO IDOLS
1 Corinthians 8:1–11:1

In pagan cities such as Corinth, a good part of social life involved participation in cultic banquets at the temple, where meat sacrificed to idols was consumed, or at private dinner parties, where hosts served their guests sacrificed meat that went from the temple to local butcher shops, where it was purchased for consumption in private settings. Did the Corinthians, now converted from their former pagan ways, need to refrain from eating this meat? The community was divided in its response to this question, with its complicated theological and social implications, and apparently referred the issue to Paul, who responds from the angle of Christian knowledge and the exercise of rights and responsibility. In terms of literary composition, this unit is arranged according to the A (ch. 8) B (ch. 9) A' (ch. 10) pattern. In terms of rhetoric, there are four movements plus a summary which need to be considered.

8:1-13 Concern for others trumps knowledge as a criterion for action

Paul begins by citing another Corinthian slogan but notes that knowledge is not an unqualified good. It can puff up with pride, whereas love builds up. Paul even registers doubt that the enlightened ones' knowledge is as complete as they claim. Apparently some Corinthians, presumably those whom Paul had already chastised for their arrogance, argued in view of their superior knowledge that there was no reason to forego eating meat sacrificed to idols. An idol had no existence; therefore, so-called idol meat was just meat.

Judging from Paul's remark at verse 10 about reclining at table in the temple, it appears that the enlightened were arguing in view of their knowledge that they could continue to participate in the cultic banquets at the temple. However, "the weak" (in context, the less intellectually sophisticated) understood such eating to be charged with religious significance. They were apparently shocked that others would continue this practice. Perhaps they were even shocked at the continued social intermingling with pagans that this practice would presumably entail.

In principle, Paul agrees with the intellectuals. They are operating with sound theological principles. Idols do not exist. There is only one God. Objectively speaking, Paul could even agree that a decision to continue eating idol meat followed logically from what they and he knew to be true. Thus Paul is not questioning the legitimacy of their right in regard to idol meat. However, he makes it clear that knowledge, even when rooted in sound theological principle, is not the exclusive criterion for determining praxis. Concern for other members of the community must take precedence over the exercise of a legitimate individual right.

Earlier Paul reminded the enlightened that their exercise of freedom was circumscribed by their belonging to God in Christ (6:19). Here he explicitly adds the other dimension that circumscribes the Christian exercise of freedom—the community. To scandalize any member of the community by the arrogant and complacent exercise of a right, which in the case of eating idol meat brings no benefit to anyone (v. 9) and scandal to some, simply because it can be justified in principle, amounts to a sin against the weaker brother, indeed against Christ. The phrase "against Christ" refers to the whole communion of believers, who together are later identified as the body of Christ (12:12). Thus Paul firmly warns against exercising rights, no matter how legitimate, to the detriment of one member, which is to say, to the detriment of all. He concludes this subunit of argumentation in the first person, injecting the course of action he would follow, which clearly depends on renouncing one's right out of love and concern for the entire community.

9:1-27 Renunciation of rights: an illustration based on Paul's praxis

Chapter 9 appears to be a departure from Paul's discussion of the right to eat idol meat. A closer look at this subunit reveals that it is an integral part of his argument. Here Paul problematizes his apostolic freedom in order to stress his renunciation of this freedom and thus provide a model of Christian praxis for the community. With regard to the right to eat idol meat, Paul has

just argued that Christians must consider not only their freedom to exercise this right but also the possibility of freely renouncing that right when it negatively impacts others in the community. Indeed, this is what Paul said he would do (8:13).

Now, in chapter 9, Paul provides a model of renunciation in view of his own apostolic lifestyle and practice. He begins by building a strong case for his apostolic right to financial support. He is free. He is an apostle, and he has all the rights of every other apostle.

Paul first establishes these rights by reference to apostolic practice in verses 4-6, followed by simple examples based on the soldier, the vine planter, and the shepherd in verse 7. All these are supported by their trade. Paul supplements his argument by reference to a Mosaic law that prescribes recompense in the form of food even for oxen (vv. 8-9)! In verses 10-11, Paul further establishes his rights in view of the extent and the quality of his relationship with the Corinthians. Paul has shared spiritual blessing with them and is entitled to material recompense, even more so than other ministers.

After interjecting that he has renounced all these rights for the sake of the gospel (v. 12), Paul resumes the case for his own rights in view of a tradition associated with both Jewish and pagan practice, namely, the recompense of temple personnel who carried out the sacrifices at the altar. They were entitled to a portion of the sacrifice.

The final argument Paul calls upon to establish his right to support is the command of the Lord (see Luke 10:7) concerning recompense for the preachers of the gospel.

With his rights firmly established, Paul again affirms that he has freely given up the exercise of these rights (v. 15) and makes it clear that his purpose in writing about this is not to oblige the community to recompense him. He then proceeds in a roundabout way to explain his motives for setting aside his rights. In effect, he says that he did not undertake the work of preaching the gospel of his own volition; instead, it was an obligation imposed on him by God. Paul will do this, whether willingly or unwillingly, because he is compelled by God. Thus there is no cause for boasting in this. But he is quite proud of the fact that he has not taken advantage of the right to support that comes with this commission. On the contrary, he says that the only recompense he desires is no recompense at all! In offering the gospel free of charge, Paul renounces his right to support and presents himself as an exemplar of renunciation of rights.

Paul's argument becomes clearer in verses 19-23. In a series of rhetorical statements, he describes his missionary strategy of adaptability in order to accomplish his goal of winning as many as possible to the gospel. He presents himself as willingly living by the cultural, ethnic, and intellectual constraints of others in the service of the gospel; hence his reference to having become a "slave." To the intellectually sophisticated at Corinth, for whom freedom and the exercise of rights go hand in hand, the idea of renouncing one's rights can only appear to be weakness and foolishness. But Paul's slavish freedom is, paradoxically, true freedom manifested in the ability to adapt one's self to the needs of others. While the intellectuals at Corinth exercise their rights to the scandal and destruction of the weak, Paul's renunciation of rights, a true act of freedom, is ordered to the opposite end, namely, to save.

After using his own apostolic lifestyle as a model of freedom for the renunciation of rights, Paul now concludes this subunit of argumentation by exhorting the community to a life of discipline and self-control that supersedes the immediate concern of idol meat and its renunciation (vv. 24-27). The sports imagery employed by Paul makes perfect sense to anyone aware of the rigors of an athlete's life and would not be lost on the competitive Corinthians, whose city was home to the famous Isthmian games. Calling to mind the extent to which athletes train and discipline themselves in order to win a crown woven of perishable leaves, Paul exhorts the Corinthians to exercise and discipline themselves all the more, since they aspire to an imperishable crown. The Corinthians cannot be complacent as if they were running without a purpose or simply punching at air; rather, they must train and drive themselves to win this crown. In context, the self-discipline that Paul exhorts is aimed, above all, at the Corinthian intellectuals. Rather than complacently exercising their rights to the detriment of others, they need to practice restraint for the sake of the whole community.

10:1-13 Complacency and God's wrath: an example based on Israel's past

Paul's account of his own apostolic practice was intended as an exemplary lesson on the exercise of Christian freedom and served to develop and illustrate the point made in 8:13. Now Paul directs his attention to the complacent attitude of the Corinthian intellectuals, whose self-satisfaction with their own knowledge and exercise of rights is bringing them to flirt with idolatry. In addition to the problem of scandal, Paul is concerned that the Corinthian intellectuals are courting disaster by frequenting pagan temples, believing that they are beyond polytheistic superstitions and practices. Paul considers their actions a preamble to their own undoing. To illustrate and warn against such an outcome, he cites the example of Israel, whose complacency incurred the wrath of God.

In 1 Corinthians 10:1-4, Paul showcases the spiritual endowments of Israel. These verses contain allusions to select episodes from Israel's exodus (see Exod 13–14) and wilderness experience (see Exod 16–17; Num 20–21). Paul retells the stories, stressing the fact that all the Israelites enjoyed God's deliverance and protection, and all were sustained on the wilderness journey by God's providence. In his retelling of these episodes, Paul uses language that is clearly anachronistic, referring to Israel's exodus as a "baptism," specifically a baptism into Moses (v. 2), and their nourishment as a type of unifying spiritual communion underscored by the repetition of "all" and "the same" (v. 3). Paul even metaphorically identifies Christ with the water-giving rock which, according to Jewish legend, followed Israel in the desert.

Paul's point here is not to suggest that the Israelites had Christian sacraments; rather, he is attempting to create an analogy between the experience of Israel and that of the Corinthians. Though seemingly complicated in its presentation, the point is simple. As one people, Israel experienced powerful spiritual signs of God's favor and all the spiritual nourishment necessary to sustain them. Yet, despite such spiritual endowments, they still incurred God's wrath and were destroyed (v. 5). Israel took God's gifts for granted as signs of immunity from God's wrath and continued in idolatrous and immoral ways.

In a series of examples underscoring Israel's self-destructive behavior (vv. 6-10), Paul warns the Corinthians to avoid this kind of presumptuous conduct. The reference to Israel's sitting down to eat and drink (v. 7) recalls the erection of an altar of sacrifice to the golden calf (Exod 32) and Israel's subsequent feasting and rising up to revel (i.e., worship) this idol. This is a particularly apt reference for the Corinthians, who think they are secure in their knowledge and immune from idolatry. However, by going off to apparently innocuous feasting with their pagan friends in the venues associated with their former pagan lives, they are not above becoming entangled in idol worship. Moreover, as no amount of spiritual security saved the Israelites, who persisted in sexual immorality (v. 8), so likewise, if the Corinthians persist in sexual immorality, neither will they be saved. In case the self-styled intellectuals at Corinth could possibly miss the point of this storytelling, Paul makes it clear: If you think you stand secure in your knowledge, watch out! Others who believed themselves just as secure fell (v. 12).

Though Paul's concluding words of reassurance appear to, they do not negate the stern warning. On the contrary, the reassurance makes the warning all the more urgent. God is faithful and will assist the Corinthians with the testing and trials that they are bound to encounter. However, when through their arrogant reliance on their own power and knowledge rather than on God's power and wisdom they bring upon themselves testing and trials, then they are certain to fall as Israel did! Hence, rather than boasting in the exercise of this right to eat idol meat, which is intended to showcase their superior knowledge and unconstrained freedom, they ought to shun the practice.

10:14-22 Against communion with idols: judge for yourselves

As chapter 9 looked back to the discussion of chapter 8 and served to illumine and illustrate the need for renunciation of rights, 1 Corinthians 10:1-13, with its warning rooted in the example of Israel, looks forward to 1 Corinthians 10:14-22, where Paul now argues against participation at temple banquets. After the command to flee idolatry, Paul appeals to the Corinthians as "sensible people," a phrase that may be laced with sarcasm. Whatever the case, in view of the analogical argument he is about to set forth, Paul expects them to judge for themselves whether frequenting temple banquets is an innocuous practice.

Paul begins with what he and the Corinthians would agree on: participation in the Lord's Sup-

per is an actual sharing in the blood and body of Christ, which effects a solidarity or bonding among believers and with Christ. The emphasis here is on the "sharing" and the oneness or solidarity effected (v. 18). Thus one cannot participate and intend non-solidarity, since the very act of participation produces it. It is clear that Paul does not recognize any dichotomy between the act of participation and the participant's intention.

As a second example of the bonding and solidarity effected through meal participation, Paul cites the historical example of the Jews ("Israel according to the flesh," v. 18). Their participation in the "altar" is Paul's way of saying they joined themselves to God. Both examples illustrate that eating a meal in the presence of God effects a solidarity between the community and God whom it worships.

Now Paul can go forward to draw a conclusion based on analogy: if eating a meal sacrificed to God effects solidarity with God, then eating a meal sacrificed to idols effects communion with idols. But Paul cannot draw this conclusion without contradicting what he had said previously (8:1-6). Aware of this (v. 19), he restates the conviction that an idol is nothing, and moves the analogy forward by substituting the term "demons" (v. 20). In referring to demons, Paul probably has in mind Deuteronomy 32:16-17. Based on this text, a Jewish tradition evolved which, while discounting the existence and divinity of anyone or thing but God alone, acknowledged the existence of demonic powers, variously referred to as gods or "idols," that actively opposed the purposes of God in the world. Apparently picking up on this tradition, Paul denies the existence of actual pagan idols but acknowledges the existence of supernatural powers. Since the absolute exclusiveness of the solidarity with God in Christ precludes any other union, the enlightened ones have to make a choice: participation at the table of demons or the table of the Lord. The Corinthians cannot have it both ways.

Paul concludes this section with two rhetorical questions. The first reverts back to the example of Israel set out in 10:1-13 and recalls the destruction that accompanied their complacency. Lest any of the enlightened ones doubt a similar outcome if they continue at cultic banquets, Paul leaves them with a final question that puts their presumed knowledge and power in perspective. Perhaps they are intellectually stronger than the weak. But are they stronger than the Lord? The answer is clear.

10:23–11:1 Summary: seek the good of others

In his argument so far, Paul gives a single response, in light of two separate criteria, to the question of participation in temple banquets. First, the practice should be renounced out of love and concern for the other members of the community (8:1-13 argument plus 9:1-27 example). Second, the practice should be renounced because participants in temple banquets implicate themselves in idolatrous worship and risk incurring God's wrath (10:1-13 example plus 10:14-22 argument).

Now, in the final subsection of this extended argument concerning food offered to idols, Paul considers whether meat sacrificed to idols can be consumed in non-cultic, private settings. Paul's discussion is framed by two concerns: that freedom is exercised in view of what is upbuilding for the community (v. 24) and that whatever activity is undertaken should be directed to the glory of God (v. 31). Within this framework, Paul considers the eating of previously sacrificed meat purchased at the market and eaten in a believer's own home or at a dinner party in the home of an unbeliever to be a legitimate practice, which, of itself, does not contravene either of the two concerns. Presumably, the enlightened at Corinth already know this. It is the weak who need to understand that eating sacrificed meat in private venues is a legitimate exercise of freedom. Thus informed, the weak need to overcome their scruples and cease to create problems where they do not exist.

In verses 28-29 Paul adds a proviso enjoining renunciation if "someone" in any private setting calls attention to the meat's origin. Paul does not identify the informer as a believer. Regardless, this proviso is part of the ethic of concern for others that Paul is attempting to instill in the community. Modeled on Christ's example of selfless love, Christian freedom seeks the good of others and the glory of God. It is neither constrained by unwarranted scrupulosity nor simply ordered to self-satisfaction. As one whose praxis is rooted in imitation of Jesus, who sought the salvation of many, Paul's call to the Corinthians to imitate him is ultimately a call to live Christlike lives.

ARGUMENTS CONCERNING ASPECTS OF COMMUNITY WORSHIP
1 Corinthians 11:2–14:40

In this next major section of 1 Corinthians, Paul sets out three separate arguments that are linked by the fact that each concerns problematic behavior affecting the community's worship. Without mentioning the source of his information, he first deals with a problem relating to the hairstyles of some community members praying and prophesying at the liturgical assembly (11:2-16). A more serious problem, which Paul has learned of through oral sources, concerns abuses and divisions at the Eucharist, the very sign and source of the community's unity, which is being negated by their behavior (11:17-34). Finally, in a lengthy argument concerning spiritual gifts (12:1–14:40), a topic presumably raised by the Corinthians in their letter, Paul deals with the problems created by the misguided desire of some to show their superior spiritual status by flaunting certain spiritual gifts and deprecating others.

Argument concerning hairstyles (11:2-16)
11:2-16 Liturgy and hair etiquette

The logical sequel to Paul's remark at 11:2, concerning traditions, seems to be the discussion at 11:17-34. Though the community is faithful to the traditions, which earns Paul's praise (11:2), their behavior at the Eucharist, not their hairdos, is an exception to this fidelity to tradition, which earns Paul's censure (11:17). Thus 11:3-16 appears to be out of place in its current literary context. Not surprisingly, some commentators argue that verses 3-16 were a later insertion into the text. However, this need not be the case. If the Corinthians had raised this issue, Paul may have felt compelled to give a response, which, however awkwardly, he locates here along with other responses about issues affecting community worship. In addition to the awkward fit, the exact nature of the problem is somewhat obscure, as is Paul's argumentation.

What can be inferred from 11:3-16 is that in the context of the liturgical assembly some women *and* men, as is clear from 11:4, were transgressing codes relating to hair etiquette, which apparently upset others in the community. Contrary to custom, some women were praying and prophesying with their hair unbound, while some men, likewise engaged, wore their hair long. The mention of having one's hair cut off (vv. 6-7) and the later references to long hair (vv. 15-17) suggest that hairstyles, not head coverings or veils, are under discussion. Why some in the community felt free to abandon this custom is a matter of speculation. Some hypothesize that the transgressors were attempting to concretely express the extinction of ethnic, status, and gender distinctions presumed to be the intent of Paul's baptism/new creation preaching (see, e.g., Gal 3:27-28; 2 Cor 5:16-17). Regardless of their motivation, Paul rejects the abandonment of the custom relating to hairstyles.

To make his case, Paul begins his argument by establishing a schema of relationships (vv. 3-4). Obviously, Paul does not intend the word "head" in the literal sense. As a metaphor, it is most often understood to stand for "authority over" or "source of," although other renderings are possible. Whatever the case, in Paul's schematic formulation, the point is that one member of the pair is precedent and preeminent with regard to the other. Within this logic Paul insists that how one acts either honors or dishonors one's figurative head/source. Men who transgress the hair etiquette dishonor Christ, while women dishonor the men of the community (vv. 4-6).

Paul does not explain why a particular hairstyle is an occasion of dishonor to one's figurative head/source. However, it requires no stretch of the imagination to get the connection. Even in our own day, clothing, hairstyles, tattoos, body piercing, and the like are often construed as positive or negative reflectors of parents, schools, or other institutions thought to have some investment in the person under scrutiny. In the Mediterranean culture of Paul's day, unbound hair on a woman was associated with sexual permissiveness, and short-cropped hair was associated with lesbianism and prostitution, while men with long hair were thought to be effeminate.

With regard to the presence of a woman with unbound hair at the assembly, Paul would be objecting to her appearance as a sexually loose or available woman. In reference to men praying and prophesying with long hair and women with cropped hair, if the latter was an actual case (which is not clear from the text), Paul would be objecting to the blurring of gender distinctions caused by the adoption of inappropriate hairstyles.

A second argument is unfolded in verses 7-12. The contrast stated in verse 7 is explicated in verses 8-9, where, in reference to the account of creation in Genesis 2, Paul explains his claim that woman is the reflected glory of man in view of her having been made from him. Consequently, a woman is expected to avoid anything that dishonors a man. Thus she must keep her hair bound.

What Paul intends in verse 10 is an enigma. It is not certain whether he is expressing an additional claim that a woman needs her hair bound because of "the angels" or whether verse 10 is an implication deriving from verses 8-9. Paul could be alluding to the belief that angels, considered the protectors of the order of creation, were present as the custodians of the liturgy. The enigmatic expression "have authority over her head" may mean that the woman should take charge of her own head and keep her hair bound in view of the order and decorum of the liturgy, over which the angels stood guard.

Paul's statements stressing the reciprocity between man and woman (vv. 11-12) need not be taken as a contradiction of what he has previously argued; rather, Paul makes two equally valid observations. Men and women are equal and interdependent. As such, they have an equal right to pray and prophesy in the church, and hence to assume roles of liturgical leadership. This equality, however, does not allow for the abandonment of social norms or for the abolition of gender differences, which Paul believes are to be maintained through external markers, namely, long, bound hair for women and short hair for men. Paul's assertion of the equality and interdependence of men and women, notwithstanding gender difference, is usually overlooked by those who view this entire passage as a statement of the absolute subordination of women.

In the concluding verses, Paul adds a third and fourth argument, neither of which is developed. The third argument appeals to what nature teaches, by which Paul must mean that long hair is inappropriate for men and appropriate for women (vv. 14-15). The fourth and final argument appeals to the custom of the churches of God (v. 16). In case the Corinthians are not persuaded by his three preceding arguments, Paul adds this last appeal to remind the Corinthians that, in any case, they ought to conform their practice to that of all believers.

Argument concerning division and abuses at the Lord's Supper (11:17-34)

11:17-22 Your meetings do more harm than good

Paul's commendation of the Corinthians at 11:2 was perhaps part of his rhetorical strategy to prepare the community for the rebuke with which he begins his discussion of their behavior at the Eucharist (v. 17). Paul's next statement, namely, that he has heard about divisions within the community (v. 18)—as if he were unaware of such divisions—has led many to conclude that 1 Corinthians must be a composite of at least two letters. However, the additional remark "and to a degree I believe it" is a bit of mocking sarcasm. Paul knows well the extent of the divisiveness in the community. Since it has invaded even their Eucharist assembly, Paul now observes that more harm than good results from this coming together. Verse 19 should probably be taken as a continuation of Paul's mocking. What else can be expected but divisions when some community members are still concerned only about their own individual status, well-being, and self-satisfaction!

To understand Paul's comments, it is helpful to recall that in earliest Christianity the Lord's Supper was not the highly ritualized, one-hour event in a church to which we are accustomed. Smaller assemblies of believers at Corinth would gather at the home of the head of one such assembly, whose house would have been large enough to accommodate the entire community. There all believers gathered as one to eat an actual meal, during which they shared the bread and cup of the Lord's Supper, the sign and source of their unity. But Paul says even though they are assembled for this purpose, each comes to eat "his own supper," not to eat the "Lord's supper" (v. 20), with the result that some are sated while others go without and are even made to feel ashamed (v. 22).

Sometimes Paul's rhetoric is taken as a description of the economic disparity within the community that is thought to underlie the problem discussed here. However, economic disparity is only one aspect of a much larger picture. Established social convention dictated that rank and status be acknowledged by one's place at table and the amount and quality of food and drink one was apportioned. When this larger picture is considered, it appears that Paul's overriding concern is that societal norms are being used as the standard of comportment at the Eucharist. These norms encourage divisions and self-aggrandizement and promote self-serving behavior, all of which undermine the unity of the community and negate the whole purpose of the Eucharist. If members' only purpose in coming is to serve their own needs and eat to their own satisfaction, then they ought to stay in their own homes (v. 22). Whatever the Corinthians think of themselves, Paul makes it clear that he cannot praise them.

11:23-26 The tradition of the institution

To call the Corinthians back to their senses, Paul reminds them of the tradition concerning the founding of this communal meal (vv. 23-26). Since Paul's letter antedates Mark, the first Gospel, by almost fifteen years, we have here the earliest preserved account of the institution of the Eucharist. Paul employs the technical terms "received" and "handed on" used in Jewish culture for the transmission of important traditions. This tradition is "from the Lord," meaning that the origin of this tradition of sharing the cup and bread is with the Lord himself. The community gathers in the *present* to observe *the Lord's* last supper, to recall the *past* historical event of Jesus' betrayal and self-sacrificing love symbolized in the bread and cup, and to proclaim this death until his *future* coming.

For Paul, the whole point of this coming together is to remember (vv. 25-26) the death of Christ and to allow the reality and meaning of that death to take form in their own lives. What matters to Paul is not the words of the tradition per se, but that the Corinthians live as one saved community rooted in the self-sacrificing love of Christ! Their self-serving behavior betrays Christ's self-sacrificing love and destroys the reality effected through his death. As such, they are not eating the "Lord's supper" (v. 20) but continuing in their own community-destroying ways.

11:27-32 The tradition and the situation in the Corinthian community

Paul now applies the tradition to the specific situation of abuse and division at the Lord's Supper. In context, verses 27-28 refer neither to a person's moral condition nor to the discernment of the Real Presence. Rather, to eat unworthily means to behave in a way that promotes divisions that are antithetical to the whole purpose of the Eucharist. Unworthy participants are responsible for the body and blood of the Lord, in the sense that they are held responsible for offending the community of believers who are the body of Christ. To eat and drink without "discerning the body" refers to the self-serving behavior that disregards the well-being and unity of the whole body of believers. Such blatant disregard is an act of self-incrimination (v. 29) through which those who eat unworthily bring God's judgment on themselves.

Exactly what Paul means in verse 30 remains an enigma. It seems, however, that he takes the illness and death of some members of the community as a sign that God's judgment has already befallen the community. Apparently Paul expects this to be taken as a warning by the Corinthians to discontinue their abusive behavior in order to avoid future condemnation (v. 32).

11:33-34 Practical advice

Paul concludes his discussion with pragmatic instructions in which he prescribes the behavior appropriate to Christians gathered to celebrate the source and sign of their unity. Above all, each one's behavior is to be characterized by consideration for the other. Temporal waiting is obviously a first step in showing consideration. However, beyond mere waiting, Paul probably also has in mind a true openness to and receptivity of the other born of the selfless love and desire for unity that the Eucharist is meant to symbolize and engender. Paul's notice in verse 34 that he defers the treatment of other unspecified matters to a future visit underscores the importance of this discussion about behavior at the Eucharist.

Argument concerning spiritual gifts (12:1–14:40)

The expression "Now in regard to" at 12:1 indicates that Paul is about to begin a new argument, which extends from 12:1 through 14:40. This is Paul's final and lengthiest argument relating to a matter affecting community worship. In this particular argument, concerned with "spiritual gifts" (Greek: *pneumatika*), Paul addresses a problematic situation involving the use and abuse of spiritual gifts (Greek: *charismata*). Though Paul does not say, it is likely that he became aware of this situation from the Corinthians' letter to him.

What can be inferred from the argument is that competitiveness in the community revolving around the possession and manifestation of spiritual gifts deemed to be more superior, especially the much-vaunted gift of tongues, was threatening the unity of the community (ch. 12) and creating disorder and chaos at the community's prayer assembly (ch. 14). In response, Paul unfolds an argument in three segments, forming an ABA' pattern. Section A (= 12:4-31a) contains a general discussion that stresses both the need for unity in diversity and diversity in unity, while the A' section (= 14:1-40) is more specifically focused on the advantage of prophecy over speaking in tongues and the order that must obtain within the prayer assembly. In the middle B section (= 12:31b—13:13), a rhetorical digression, Paul develops and discloses the key motive that must inform the exercise of spiritual gifts, namely, Christian charity.

The whole issue under discussion in chapters 12–14 presumes a situation in the community at Corinth in which extraordinary spiritual gifts and their manifestation were an everyday reality in the life of the community. It is important to remember when reading the argument here that Paul is grateful for and acknowledges the inherent goodness of each spiritual gift with which the community has been endowed, including the gift of speaking in tongues (see 1:5). Unfortunately, some viewed their gifts, especially speaking in tongues, as tokens of superior spiritual status, exercised for self-aggrandizement. It is this skewed view and abusive use of the gifts that Paul rejects and seeks to correct by his discussion of the relative significance of each gift, whose exercise must be ordered to the upbuilding and unity of the whole community.

A variety of gifts from the same Spirit for the common good (12:1-31a)

In this first subunit of argumentation, Paul introduces the new topic (vv. 1-3) and then locates the origin of all spiritual gifts in the same divine source (vv. 4-11). A body analogy, commonly used in Greco-Roman speech to illustrate the relationship of the one and the many, is employed by Paul in verses 12-26 to stress the diversity and interdependence of community members. In conclusion, Paul applies this analogy directly to the situation at Corinth and ranks members in view of gifts and roles (vv. 27-31a).

12:1-3 Introduction

Paul's desire that the Corinthians not "be unaware" implies a certain ignorance about spiritual realities, despite the fact that some in the community are apparently posing as authorities on the subject, believing that the mere manifestation of certain spiritual gifts, especially ecstatic utterances, somehow makes them authentic spiritual persons. Paul corrects this assumption in the next two verses. In their former lives as pagans, the Corinthians may have been caught up in the thrill of ecstasy, but it was all futile, since they were swept off to dumb idols (v. 2). Thus their own experience underscores the fact that ecstatic experience and accompanying utterances, of themselves, cannot be the measure of what it means to be an authentically spiritual person.

The true test of whether one is guided by the Spirit of God is that one is able to confess that "Jesus is Lord" (v. 3). Paul contrasts this confession with the statement "Jesus be accursed." Rather than an actual utterance heard in the Corinthian prayer assembly, the latter statement should probably be taken as a rhetorical counterpoint introduced by Paul to dramatize the antithesis between what is authentically Spirit-empowered and what is not. For Paul, the acknowledgment of the Lordship of Jesus alone is the criterion by which one judges who lives in the realm of the Spirit and is authentically Spirit-inspired.

12:4-11 Manifestations of the Spirit

Up until this point in his argument, Paul has spoken of spiritual realities *(pneumatika)*. Here in verse 4 he introduces the word "gifts" *(charismata)* for the first time. By redefining authentic spiritual realities as "gifts," Paul indirectly undermines Corinthian arrogance. No one has merited such gifts, and since each community member's gift derives from the same source, none is inherently inferior to another. Along with the diversity of gifts inspired by the Spirit, there are also various forms of service and workings that are also divinely ordained. All these gifts in all their diversity ultimately derive from God and are given through the agency of the Spirit. To each member of the community is given some manifestation of the Spirit (v. 7). Since the Spirit is manifest in the manifold gifts, services, and workings, any claim that any one particular gift, service, or working

is a fuller manifestation of the Spirit is simply unwarranted. Moreover, to devalue any gift is to devalue the work of the Spirit. Thus, as arrogance is undermined by virtue of the fact that any manifestation of the Spirit is a gift, so also is the competitiveness that derives from the false assumption that certain manifestations are superior to others.

In the second half of verse 7, Paul now adds a second criterion for determining who is authentically spiritual and what is authentically Spirit-inspired. That which is an authentic manifestation of the Spirit must in some way benefit others. The manifestations are given neither for self-glorification nor for advancing one's own status but for the common good. When the latter is not the end toward which the public manifestation of the Spirit is ordered, it cannot be an authentic Spirit-inspired manifestation, nor can the person be authentically spiritual.

With these two criteria established, Paul proceeds to give a representative listing (compare with the list at 12:28 and Rom 12:6-8) of the manifestations of the Spirit in verses 8-11. In all, Paul mentions nine examples of the Spirit's manifestations in these three verses, portraying them as common occurrences in the community at Corinth. "Faith" (v. 9) is apparently a reference to a particular endowment for a special service (although Paul does not specify), and not the saving faith common to all believers.

Judging by Paul's discussion in chapter 14, it was the gift of tongues that was apparently creating most of the disturbance in the community. Paul's careful listing of these distinct yet all Spirit-inspired gifts at work in the community is probably intended to put this particular gift of tongues in its proper context. It is only one among many. The repetition of "to one/to another" and the "same/one Spirit" underscores both the activity of the Spirit, the source of each gift, and the importance of each individual member of the community whose gift, though different from that of another, contributes to and is necessary for the common good.

In verse 11, Paul concludes this subsection on gifts and succinctly restates the key points he has made so far: every distinct gift is the work of the Spirit. It is a gift freely given to individual believers through God's generous grace, to be exercised in the service of the church for the promotion of the common good.

12:12-26 Diversity in unity, unity in diversity

Paul now carries his points forward by means of an analogy between the church and the body. The body analogy was a common figure of speech in political discourse in antiquity. Human societies were compared to a body, whose well-being depended on each member of society knowing his or her place. Usually the analogy was employed to conserve the status quo, especially as a means to keep the lower classes in their place and dissuade them from dissent or rebellion that could upset the balance of power. Paul uses the analogy not to subordinate but to stress the diversity, interdependence, and importance of all the members of the community, who together form one body.

The analogy is introduced in 12:12, which concludes with the phrase "so also Christ," not with "so also the community/church" as one might expect. For Paul, the body of believers is Christ, or the body of Christ, a metaphoric expression he employs to express what he believes to be the reality of Christian existence. Believers are bound in a living unity with the risen Lord, which is effected through the unifying activity and presence of the Spirit in baptism (v. 13). Hence, though many, they form one body, the body of Christ.

Having established the analogy, Paul now stresses the need for diversity within this unity by means of an absurd staging of talking body parts announcing their liberation from the body (vv. 14-16)! The result of the withdrawal of any part, either in view of its superiority or inferiority to the other parts, would be a distorted entity, but not a body which, of its very nature, requires the diversity of parts (vv. 19-20). Paul's lesson is clear. A human body cannot be a body without the diversity of parts. Likewise, the body of Christ cannot be a body without each distinct believer, whose place and function in the body depend on God (v. 18). Hence the diversity within the community is not a reality to be obliterated, nor even merely tolerated. It is essential.

Whereas in verses 14-20 Paul's stress is on the necessity of diversity in unity, in verses 21-26 the accent falls on the need to maintain unity amidst the diversity. No member of the community can afford to scorn any other member or set up divisive distinctions. The "weaker" and "less honorable" parts probably allude to community members who were looked down on either because of social sta-tus or lack of intellectual and spiritual sophistication or both. Paul reminds the arrogant of the community, who likely associate themselves with the more "presentable" or "honorable" parts, that those they scorn need to be honored and cared for. God has not differentiated among members as a basis for division, for there can be no division in the body, which relies on the interdependence of its parts for its functioning. Moreover, not only are the weakest links indispensable to the life of the community, but it is to these that God has given greater honor (v. 24). Thus if there is division and discord, the whole body suffers, because no member is independent of the other in the body of Christ.

12:27-30a Application to the church

The analogy is now directly applied to the community of believers, who are Christ's body. Within this body, God has gifted members with diverse gifts and functions. As with the preceding list (vv. 8-10), here, too, in verse 28, Paul seems to provide a representative rather than exhaustive list. He numerically ranks the first three. There is no way of knowing if the enumeration is intended to suggest a hierarchy of authority among these three. Minimally speaking, the enumeration suggests that Paul considered these three very important ministries.

The other gifts or functions, introduced by "then," parallel each other's importance, though they are probably of lesser importance than those enumerated. Once again Paul lists varieties of tongues last (see 12:10), apparently to reinforce the fact that tongues are only one among many gifts bestowed for the common good. Each of the concluding rhetorical questions begins with the Greek negative *(mē)*, which always expects the answer no! No, all cannot have the same gift or perform the same function, and no one person can have all the gifts and perform all the functions. Here again Paul emphasizes the necessity for diversity in unity. Against the arrogant in Corinth, who apparently measure a member's spiritual endowment and worth in view of *one* gift, speaking in tongues, Paul asserts that diversity is not only good but necessary! Some of the Corinthians have unfortunately mistaken uniformity for unity. Paul wants the latter, which is only truly achieved when each member's distinct contribution is valued and incorporated with all others to build up the whole body.

Love, the more excellent way (13:1-13)

This poetic encomium (speech) in praise of love is often taken as an abstract meditation on love, with little connection to the discussion of spiritual gifts. However, in context this encomium is actually an integral part of Paul's argument in chapters 12–14, through which he presents love as the quality of Christian life par excellence and the absolute norm that must govern the exercise of the gifts of the Spirit. Verse 31 of chapter 12 introduces this poetic interlude, which begins at 13:1.

13:1-3 Gifts without love are of no account

Using himself as a hypothetical example, Paul asserts that without love the exercise of gifts is futile and empty. The first gift Paul mentions is tongues. Exercised apart from love, the tongues-speaker produces only a strident noise, like brass instruments struck without purpose. Though Paul begins with the Corinthians' prized gift, we must not hastily assume that his sole purpose here is to deflate the arrogant Corinthians by devaluing what is most important to them. This becomes apparent in verses 2-3, where Paul considers other gifts and practices. Even if one should prophesy, a gift Paul considers superior to tongues (see 14:5), or have extraordinary faith, without love this person is nothing. Likewise, should one choose a life of self-abnegation and hardship, as Paul himself did (see ch. 9), without love such practices are of no account. In sum, all gifts and religious practices are equally of no account unless motivated and informed by love.

13:4-7 In praise of love

Paul's praise of love personified begins with two positive statements in the first half of verse 4 and ends with one long verse extolling four of love's positive features (v. 7). From the second half of verse 4 through verse 6, Paul focuses on what love is not or does not do. In all, there are eight negative statements. Most of the negatives correspond directly or indirectly to actual behavior of the Corinthians already criticized by Paul. For example, "jealous" and "inflated" (v. 4b) recall behavior and attitudes that Paul castigated in chapters 1–4 and 5. To "rejoice over wrongdoing" (v. 6) probably alludes to behavior censured in chapters 5 and 6. "Does not seek its own interest" (v. 5) evokes Paul's discussion of meat offered to idols and the renunciation of one's rights in the interest of others (chs. 8–10).

Thus Paul's list of negatives is not merely a poetic extolling of the abstract notion of love but a rather pointed indictment of the Corinthians' behavior. By all counts, Corinthian behavior is devoid of Christian love. In view of the assertions of verses 1-3, the Corinthians should realize that their exercise of gifts and other religious practices is entirely void. They have gained nothing by their displays. They are nothing, despite their own exalted self-perception.

In verse 7, Paul summarizes positively the character of love. Belief and hope are focused on the future. Strengthened by them, Christians are enabled to bear and endure in the present. Especially in view of the repeated "all things," Paul's statement in verse 7 can unfortunately be read as an exhortation to suffer any kind of abuse, believe anything, or maintain hope at all costs, even when unrealistic. Far from promoting abusive, self-destructive, or self-deceptive behavior, here Paul advocates behavior governed by love that transcends the self-interest, jealousy, and competitiveness leading to strife and division and promotes reconciliation and unity.

13:8-13 The abiding nature of love

Paul now advances his argument for the preeminence of love in view of its enduring character in contrast to gifts, all of which are temporal. Paul singles out prophecy, tongues, and knowledge, underscoring their transitory, incomplete, and imperfect nature (vv. 8-9). Given this, these revelatory gifts allow the Corinthians only a partial understanding of the mysteries of God in the present. Unfortunately, the Corinthians pride themselves on their possession of such gifts and assume that they offer complete access to divine mysteries. However, complete access and understanding are a future reality associated with the end-time. When the *eschaton* arrives, these limited gifts will lose whatever partial significance they now have, since the perfect will replace and fulfill the partial (v. 10).

To illustrate his point, Paul uses an analogy (v. 11). As childhood values, behavior, and ways of thinking are abandoned as one matures into adulthood, so are the lesser or partial spiritual gifts abandoned at the *eschaton*. Prizing and boasting in partial spiritual gifts, just like prizing and boasting in certain ministers (see 3:1-4), again shows that the Corinthians are spiritually immature, despite their claims to the contrary.

In verse 12, Paul reinforces his point with one more analogical argument. Like indistinct mirror images, the insights acquired through temporal spiritual gifts are useful now but nothing at all compared with the perfect (face-to-face) vision promised at the *eschaton*. Faith, hope, and love are all hallmarks of Christian life in the present. Love is the greatest both because it is the supreme motive that allows Christians to use all the Spirit's gifts for the end toward which God has ordained them and because it alone endures eternal.

The use of spiritual gifts in the context of worship (14:1-40)

Having discussed the necessity of diverse gifts (ch. 12) and established love as the absolute criterion for evaluating the use of gifts (ch. 13), Paul now focuses specifically on the problems occurring at community worship deriving from the exercise of spiritual gifts. Apparently, those in the community fixated on speaking in tongues as a demonstration of spiritual superiority are causing chaos in the community. In chapter 14, Paul first unfolds a sustained argument for the desirability of prophecy over speaking in tongues (vv. 1-25) and then lays down instructions regulating community worship (vv. 26-40).

14:1-25 Argument in favor of prophecy

Paul's preference for prophecy is predicated on two main arguments enunciated in verses 2-5 and developed in verses 6-25. First, what is articulated through prophecy is directed to human beings and is intelligible to the entire assembly, whereas tongues are directed to God and are not intelligible to all (vv. 2-3). Second, prophecy builds up the community, whereas tongues is an exercise in self-edification (v. 4). In verse 5, Paul restates his points, insisting that prophecy is the greater gift, although he acknowledges that tongues could have edifying value if they are interpreted.

Paul develops his argument that tongues are unintelligible in verses 6-12. With the exception of verse 6, where Paul offers an autobiographical reflection, perhaps hypothetical or perhaps an actual comment on his strategy at Corinth (see 2:1), this subsection is constructed around three analogies

(vv. 7-11). In the first, tongues are likened to isolated notes sounded by a flute or harp. Unless the notes form a coherent pattern, no intelligible melody is produced and listeners are at a loss. Likewise, if a bugle is made to emit a series of random sounds, troops would not know they are being called to assemble for battle. In this second case, the lack of intelligibility is not merely benign. Paul's third analogy turns on the variety of languages. When no common language exists to unite two people, they remain estranged, an unfortunate outcome. For Paul, speaking in tongues amounts to unintelligibility (v. 9), on a par with the three examples cited. Paul concludes by positively acknowledging the zeal of the Corinthians. It is good, but it needs to be directed toward acquiring the gifts that build up the whole community (v. 12).

The lack of intelligibility and its consequences are now considered in view of the community's worship assembly (vv. 13-19). Without the complementary gift of "interpretation," for which speakers in tongues should pray, tongues do not edify. The Corinthians may feel that truly genuine spiritual experience transcends the human mind. However, Paul suggests that in some way their experience in the Spirit must be translated into what is intelligible with the mind, because only in this way is the community built up (vv. 14-15). Additionally, when intelligibility is lacking, community members cannot authentically participate in community prayer. They can say "Amen," but since they have no idea what they affirm, their prayer and praise are rendered inauthentic. In concluding, Paul claims that he could outdo any of the Corinthians when it comes to speaking in tongues (v. 18). However, he again sets an example of renunciation for the benefit of others, consistent with what he had recommended in chapters 8–10.

Paul now turns to his second concern: the effect of tongues and prophecy on outsiders/unbelievers. In verse 21, Paul cites Isaiah 28:11-12. An interpretation of this text then follows in verse 22, which states, in effect, that tongues are for unbelievers, while prophecy is for believers. In all probability, verse 22 represents the view of some Corinthians who claim that their dazzling displays of ecstatic speech would win over unbelievers. Paul challenges and corrects this view in verses 23-25, insisting that tongues negatively impact unbelievers, while prophecy brings them to recognize the presence of God. However we construe these verses, Paul's view is clear in verses 24-25: prophecy is also better for unbelievers.

14:26-40 Regulating community worship

The varieties of gifts spoken of in chapter 12 are evident when the Corinthians congregate for worship, which Paul here describes as a lively, Spirit-filled assembly of believers, each bringing some spiritual gift. To ensure that every gift, including tongues, is directed to its proper end, that is, the upbuilding of the community (v. 26), Paul proposes some rules of order. He first regulates the use of tongues, which some apparently exercised in an uncontrolled manner, monopolizing the community's assembly time and creating disorder. As a gift, tongues cannot be excluded, but Paul sets three controls on their use. He limits the number of contributions from those gifted with tongues, prohibits simultaneous speaking in tongues, and enjoins the speaker of tongues to exercise this gift in silence if there is no interpreter (vv. 27-28).

With regard to prophecy, Paul also limits the number of contributions to two or three. However, Paul allows that as many as have a revelation may speak, as long as no two speak simultaneously, so that each may listen to and learn from the other (vv. 29-31). These controls may sound reasonable to modern readers accustomed to ordered and decorous worship assemblies, in which everyone's place and time to speak are predetermined. However, some of the Corinthians who like to show off their spiritual gifts may perceive these controls as contrary to the free flow and spontaneous activity of the Spirit. Who is Paul to constrain the Spirit? Paul seems to anticipate and eliminate this type of objection by reminding the community that God's Spirit cannot inspire any disorder or chaos, since God is a God of peace (v. 33).

At 1 Corinthians 11:5, Paul indisputably takes for granted that women pray and prophesy in the assembly. Is he now contradicting himself in verses 34-35 by enjoining silence on women, commanding their subordination to their husbands, to whom they are instructed to direct inquiries? Some commentators suggest that verses 34-35 are an interpolation (later insertion) dating from the late first century, more akin to the view expressed by the author of 1 Timothy as found, for example,

at 1 Timothy 2:11-12. Others who take these verses as original offer a variety of suggestions. Some argue that male elitists in the Corinthian community, not Paul, held the view expressed in verses 34-35, which Paul actually challenges here, although no text evidence supports this suggestion. Moreover, it depends on an interpretation of verse 36 as a sarcastic rejoinder by Paul to the elitists. Some claim that Paul addresses only married women, though this distinction is not evident from the text. Still others argue that verses 34-35 contain Paul's real position, while 11:2-6 represent his concession to some women whom he allows to speak, but with restrictions.

Given the limited evidence, it may remain impossible to determine which suggestion accurately accounts for verses 34-35. In the end, the greater problem presented by these verses is not whether Paul did or did not write them, but how they are interpreted and applied. Responsible interpretation requires that these verses be considered in view of Paul's larger vision of church as the union of all men and women using their gifts and talents to advance the gospel of Jesus Christ.

As Paul concludes, he backs the Corinthian spiritualists into a corner (v. 37). Either they recognize what he has written (ch. 14 and maybe chs. 12–13) as a commandment of the Lord, or they are not the genuine prophets and spiritual people they claim to be. Then, without singling anyone out, Paul announces the consequence for noncompliance (v. 38) before succinctly reiterating in verses 39-40 what he has argued in chapter 14.

ARGUMENT FOR THE RESURRECTION
1 Corinthians 15:1-58

Paul's last major argument of 1 Corinthians is a lengthy defense of the resurrection of the dead. As we have seen throughout this letter, exclusive concern for the spiritual and disregard for the physical underlie many of the behavioral problems Paul has addressed. In this particular argument, the focus is on errant thought not problematic behavior as Paul now considers the Corinthians' spirit-body dualism vis à vis the question of the resurrection. In line with their dualistic beliefs, it appears that some Corinthians consider eternal life an entirely spiritual existence, experienced apart from the body left behind at death. The paltry body has no place in this exclusively spiritual dimension of future existence (see above at 6:12-20), hence the denial of the resurrection of the dead (v. 12).

Against this view, Paul develops a three-stage argument. He first rehearses the tradition concerning Christ's resurrection (vv. 1-11). Next he argues for the resurrection in view of three factors (vv. 12-34). In the third subsection, Paul discusses the manner in which the dead are raised (vv. 35-49). He concludes this argument by affirming that the resurrection is a mystery apprehended through faith (vv. 50-58).

15:1-11 The resurrection of Christ: rehearsing the facts

Paul begins by reminding the Corinthians that what he preached to them was nothing other than the central gospel tradition concerning Jesus' death and resurrection, a tradition he himself had "received" and "handed on" (see 11:23). This tradition was articulated in an ancient Christian creed, which Paul now cites in verses 3b-5. The central faith conviction professed in this creed by the earliest Christians was fourfold: Christ died, he was buried, he was raised, he appeared.

Paul's recitation of the tradition serves two purposes here. First, it serves to remind the Corinthians that they cannot simply reject, alter, or hold a belief contrary to any of the foundational elements of the Christian faith. It is on this complete profession of faith, not just one or two elements of it, that they presumably took their stand. Moreover, it is through this faith that they and all believers are saved. If any aspect of this central faith conviction is altered or rejected, their faith would be in vain, a possibility Paul hopes to avert.

Second, the recitation provides Paul with the opportunity to introduce historical testimony to Christ's resurrection (vv. 5-8). This testimony is essential to his argument for the resurrection of the dead. It is important to observe that Paul insists that Jesus "appeared to" the witnesses, not that they saw Jesus. This is intended to underscore the fact that the risen Jesus was not a construct of the witnesses' imagination. Peter is listed as the first to whom Jesus appeared, a privilege that contributed to his status in the early church; then come the "Twelve," Jesus' inner circle of disciples, who exercised an authoritative and foundational role in earliest Christianity. The circle of

witnesses widens as Paul mentions more than five hundred brethren, then Jesus' brother James, a prominent leader in the Jerusalem community (see Acts 15), then "all the apostles"(v. 7), obviously a reference to a group larger than the Twelve. Paul finally lists himself as the last and least of those to whom Jesus appeared (see 1 Cor 9:1; Gal 1:16; Acts 9:3-5). The autobiographical aside "as to one born abnormally" (v. 8; literally "born of an abortion") is a strange expression, probably inserted to emphasize Paul's exceptional route to apostleship.

Notably absent from Paul's list of witnesses are women, who according to all four Gospels (see Mark 16:1-8; Matt 28:1-10; Luke 24:1-9; John 20:1-18) were the first to witness to the resurrection. Whatever the reason for the omission, which is a matter of speculation, Paul has compiled what he considers to be a list of witnesses sufficient to verify that Jesus who died and was buried was indeed raised from the dead!

15:12-34 The reality of the resurrection of the dead

Paul now moves to the specific controversy in the Corinthian community, which becomes explicit in verse 12: some deny the resurrection of the dead. To counter this claim, Paul advances three arguments in verses 12-34. First, he exposes both the logical inconsistency of their claim in view of the testimony to the resurrection and the chain of absurd conclusions one would have to draw if one were to reason based on the Corinthians' premise (vv. 13-19). In verses 13-14, Paul lists each of these conclusions. To reinforce his point, he restates the same chain of conclusions in verses 15-17 but in the reverse order, adding that the Corinthians would still be in their sin (v. 17)! Moreover, the dead in Christ would simply have perished (v. 18). With this first argument Paul sets out the devastating consequences of the Corinthians' claim and, as a final reinforcement, notes how utterly sham is their hope and how pitiable they indeed are if there is no future resurrection (v. 19).

Paul's second argument (vv. 20-28) begins with the attested reality of Christ's resurrection (v. 20), based on which he draws out the key consequence of this central gospel conviction for believers: they, too, will be raised through Christ. Paul illustrates this fact in two ways. First, Christ is the "firstfruits." The ripening of the firstfruits signaled that the rest of the fruit would also ripen and would soon be ready for harvest. Paul metaphorically applies this idea to illustrate that Christ's own resurrection guarantees and heralds the resurrection of all believers (v. 20). Second, Christ is the antitype of Adam. Whereas through Adam death became the destiny of all, through Christ all believers are destined to life (vv. 21-22). Then, in language rooted in Jewish apocalyptic, Paul describes the events that will transpire at the Lord's second coming (vv. 23-28).

The resurrection of believers is a future event coinciding with Christ' s second coming, not before. When the resurrection is completed, then comes the "end," that is, the fulfillment of God's salvific plan in Christ, which entails the subduing and destruction of all powers hostile to God and the establishment of God's reign. This work begun through Christ's death and resurrection will come to completion at his second coming. Every sovereignty, authority, and power (v. 24)—terms referring to hostile cosmic powers and perhaps more pointedly to the political leaders and corrupt structures of Roman Corinth—will be destroyed. Death is personified as the last enemy, the quintessential symbol of all resistance to God, since it is the lot of all those under the reign of sin (v. 26).

Christ must reign until he has subdued all these enemies and they are subjected to him. This idea is expressed in verses 25 and 27, where Paul alludes to and christologically reinterprets Psalm 8:7 and Psalm 110:1 to confirm the necessity of Christ's reign and his ultimate victory over all things, including death. While it is difficult to know whether by "him" in verse 27 Paul means Christ or God, the psalm allusions suggest that Paul intends that all is made subject to Christ through God, who is the One exempt from subjugation. Indeed, in the end Christ himself will be subjected to the One so that God may be all in all (v. 28).

In phases one and two of his argument against the Corinthian denial of the resurrection, Paul first showed the absurdity of their denial and then established the certainty of the future resurrection of all believers, which is guaranteed through Christ's own resurrection. In this third step (vv. 29-34), Paul marshals two *ad hominem* arguments to complete his case against the Corinthian position. Paul first alludes to a practice apparently common among the Corinthians, namely, vicarious baptism on behalf of the dead. Though such a practice is not attested elsewhere in the New Testament, Paul's reference here indicates that it was a practice in Corinth. He does not opine about the value of vicarious baptism or inform us about the extent of this practice at Corinth. In view of his overall argument, he simply insinuates that the practice is useless if there is no future resurrection of the dead. By practicing vicarious baptism while simultaneously denying the resurrection, the Corinthians simply demonstrate their own logical inconsistency.

Paul's second argument concerns suffering. He continuously puts his own life in jeopardy and suffers for the sake of the gospel (see, e.g., 2 Cor 4:8-11; 6:3-10; Acts 18:23-40). Why would he do this if there were no hope of future resurrection? But Paul does suffer hardship, and this attests to the truth of the resurrection. Otherwise, he says, with a dash of sarcasm, the only wisdom to live by is that of self-fulfillment, which characterizes life without hope. This wisdom is encapsulated in the maxim Paul cites in verse 32, which was associated with the Epicurean school of philosophy. For Paul, this is no wisdom, because it fails to reflect the central Christian conviction that believers are destined to life through Christ. Paul concludes with sharp commands to the Corinthians to come to their senses. Citing a popular maxim attributed to the Greek poet Menander (v. 33), Paul warns the whole Corinthian community to stay away from those who deny the resurrection of the body. Since Paul has just cited the useless wisdom of Greek philosophy in verse 32, it may be that he is warning the Corinthians against dangerous dabbling in Greek philosophical ideas that subvert the gospel. If the Corinthians do this, they are not unlike those who are ignorant of God, that is, the pagans. Paul's concluding remark (v. 34c) sets recourse to pagan ideas on a par with recourse to pagan courts (see 6:5). Both are shameful!

15:35-49 The resurrection body

The two questions posed in verse 35 expose the basis of the Corinthians' qualms about the resurrection. They cannot understand how the dead are raised, nor can they imagine what a resurrected body will be like. In verses 35-49, Paul deals with the second question and leaves the other until verses 50-58. In his response to the question about the form the resurrection body will take, he employs a variety of analogies to argue that the resurrected body is a transformed spiritual body. Since a sown seed must die in order to become a full-grown plant, a fact that Paul presents as perfectly obvious to anyone capable of observing nature, the Corinthians are just plain fools to assume, as Paul implies they do, that a resurrected body is just a reanimated dead body (v. 36)!

Paul develops the seed analogy and through it establishes the crucial point that the sowing/fruition process is one that includes both transformation and continuity. The sown seed that must die does not come forth at harvest time as a reanimated seed; rather, it undergoes a radical transformation and continues its existence in a new and distinct body. Yet this body is necessarily organically linked to the seed because each seed transforms into a body peculiar to that seed (vv. 37-38). The mention of different kinds of seeds with different bodies leads to a new analogy in view of distinctions concerning flesh (v. 39), and finally to another analogy based on distinctions between terrestrial and celestial bodies, each with its own peculiar manifestation (vv. 40-41).

The application of the analogies set out in verses 36-41 now begins with Paul's statement, "So also is the resurrection of the dead" (v. 42). The contrast/continuity between sown seed and full-grown plant is still at the basis of the four new sets of contrasting pairs now introduced: corruptible/incorruptible (v. 42), dishonorable/glorious (v. 43), weak/powerful (v. 43b), natural body/spiritual body (v. 44). The human person will continue in embodied existence, but as the contrasts make clear, the new body will be incorruptible, glorious, constituted in power, and above all a spiritual body, which does not imply some vague, ethereal existence but rather a body animated by the Spirit of God.

A new analogy built on an Adam/Christ contrast is introduced in verses 45-49 to further the natural/spiritual body contrast set out in verses 42-44. Paul begins with the observation that the first man was gifted only with physical, natural life (see Gen 2:7), whereas Christ was a life-giving spirit (v. 45). The one kind of body and existence that humans inherit from Adam precedes the other, spiritually animated existence that comes through Christ (v. 46). In and through Christ, the Corinthians will attain and live this completely transformed spiritual existence, but it is a future eschatological reality that must be awaited.

In view of the context, the contrast between "earthly" Adam and "heavenly" Christ (v. 47) should probably be understood as a restatement and reinforcement of the contrast already made between the natural life inherited through Adam versus the spiritual life inherited through Christ. Paul makes it clear in verse 48 that Christians are indebted to both the first and the last Adam. During their earthly existence, their likeness is to the earthly Adam; however, in their future eschatological existence in their resurrected bodies, believers will bear the likeness of Christ, whose resurrection is the guarantee of their own future resurrection. How will this happen? This first of the two questions with which Paul began this subsection at verse 35 is now taken up in the concluding section of chapter 15.

15:50-58 The resurrection event

Paul's last section begins with a bold declaration that, at first, seems to play right into the hands of the Corinthians. Part of their problem with the resurrection is that they cannot fathom how anything corruptible and corporeal squares with future spiritual existence. However, Paul is not sustaining their argument. Rather, by underscoring the incompatibility of future eschatological existence with present existence, Paul actually argues for the absolute necessity of the resurrection. Without it, one cannot participate in future eschatological existence! But how will it take place?

The answer is a mystery, an insight about God's preordained plans hidden from the world (see 2:7) that Paul now unfolds in charged apocalyptic language and imagery. As Paul writes, he considers the second coming of Christ imminent. He and others ("we") who will not have died at the second coming, along with all those who are already dead in Christ, will be changed and resurrected into God-given spiritual bodies. Paul uses typical apocalyptic motifs and images (e.g., suddenness, the sound of the trumpet, awakening of the dead) to describe the end-time resurrection scenario. With the exception of the description of the Lord's arrival, Paul's revelation here is comparable to that found in 1 Thessalonians 4:13-18, the only other place in his writings where a revelation of this kind is unfolded.

In verses 53-54, Paul introduces a new metaphor to ensure that the Corinthians understand that the body will not be discarded or annihilated at death to give way to the eternal existence of the soul alone. He insists that the corruptible/mortal body will clothe itself in incorruptibility/immortality. Hence resurrected life will still be an embodied existence, but our flawed natural bodies will undergo a total transformation. When this occurs, the promise of victory over sin and death will have been fulfilled, not because of any human merit but because of what God has done in Christ (vv. 55-57).

Paul's concluding exhortation sounds rather general and disconnected from the whole preceding argument. However, it actually follows from the argument. The reality of the resurrection, which Paul has just argued in fifty-seven verses, is, in the final analysis, that which sustains Christians in their faith and their work of living and spreading the gospel. With this surety, neither their hope, faith, or labor is in vain!

Paul's argument in chapter 15 is not a self-contained theological treatise on the reality of the resurrection but rather the culmination of all the preceding arguments in 1 Corinthians. Throughout this letter Paul has challenged the community to eschew behavior motivated by the ideas, values, and structures of pagan Corinth. As he now makes eminently clear in chapter 15, it is the reality of Christ's resurrection and the prospect of their own that constitute the moral compass that must guide and shape the Corinthians' lives. Their behavior must be compatible with the new moral order whose inauguration begins in the mystery of Jesus' death and resurrection and culminates in the mystery of their own resurrection, when God's purposes in history will be fully realized. The fact of the resurrection requires a radical reorientation of the lives of all believers, in the body, in the present, in anticipation of the future resurrection.

CONCLUSION

1 Corinthians 16:1-24

With the major problems and issues of the Corinthian community now addressed, culminating in the extended discussion of the resurrection, Paul now brings up three final matters: the collection for the saints, his travel plans, and Apollos. Each is briefly treated in the first half of this chapter (vv. 1-12). In the second half of chapter 16, following the ancient letter form, Paul formally concludes this letter with a few exhortations and greetings typical of his own letter closings (13:23). In both verses 1 and 12, Paul begins with the formula "Now in regard to," first used at 7:1, which may indicate that his comments on the collection (vv. 1-4) and Apollos (v. 12) are responses to questions posed by the Corinthians in their letter to Paul.

16:1-12 The collection, Paul's travel plans, Apollos

Background information about this collection and the reason for it are not provided here. Paul assumes that the Corinthians know about this collection for the saints, meaning the Jerusalem community, as is clear from verse 3. Elsewhere, at Galatians 2:1-10, Paul recounts a visit to Jerusalem and his meeting with the church's leaders. After sanctioning his mission to the Gentiles, the leaders asked Paul to remember the poor, presumably of the Jerusalem community, which he said he was eager to do (v. 10). Thus the contribution for Jerusalem's poor, which Paul urged on all his Gentile communities, was apparently Paul's way of honoring that request. Writing a few years later in his letter to the Romans, he explains why the Gentile Christians ought to make this contribution. It is a debt owed by them to Jewish Christians, through whom they have become beneficiaries of Israel's spiritual blessings. Hence Jewish Christians should share in and benefit from the material blessings of Gentile believers (see Rom 15:27).

In addition to this express purpose, Paul may have viewed the collection as a way to foster unity between Gentile and Jewish Christians and to develop within the communities he founded a sense of benevolent regard for all believers everywhere. Paul's instructions, in line with those given in Galatia and presumably in Macedonia (see 2 Cor 8), underscore the fact that the collection was a part of Paul's missionary practice and not an imposition on this one community. At this time there was obviously no centralized system of collection in Corinth. However, no one was exempt from putting money aside privately and on a regular weekly basis, as clear from verse 2. Paul expects all collecting to be completed before his arrival, at which point the funds would be entrusted to the community's own appointees, whom Paul would provide with letters of recommendation, a common practice at the time to ensure the status of the envoys (see 2 Cor 8:16-24). Paul's final remark reveals his hesitancy to go to Jerusalem, although he apparently did go, bringing funds from

Macedonia and the province of Achaia, of which Corinth was capital (see Rom 15:26).

In verse 5 Paul switches to a discussion of his travel plans. He assures the Corinthians that he will return to them, but not right away. He intends to stay in Ephesus, whence he writes this letter, to capitalize on evangelizing opportunities, notwithstanding opposition (vv. 8-9). The mention of Pentecost, a Jewish feast celebrated in late spring, places Paul's departure from Ephesus for the region of Macedonia in early summer. Only after visiting the communities of Macedonia, presumably at Philippi and Thessalonica, would Paul come down to Corinth to stay with them at some length, perhaps the entire winter (vv. 5-6).

After mentioning his own plans, Paul speaks of Timothy, who is apparently being dispatched by Paul to Corinth (see 4:17). Timothy's youth (see 1 Tim 4:12) and perhaps inexperience probably explain Paul's reminders to the community about how Timothy should be treated.

Paul concludes this first half of chapter 16 with the mention of Apollos, whom the Corinthians hoped would return to Corinth (v. 12). Some claim that verse 12 belies a real rivalry between Apollos and Paul and interpret Paul's comments as an attempt to dispel suspicions that he was obstructing Apollos's return out of jealousy. However, in view of Paul's description of the collaborative character of his relationship with Apollos at 3:5-9, it seems reasonable to take verse 12 at face value as an indication that there was no rivalry between the two co-workers. Whether Apollos ever did return to Corinth is not known.

16:13-23 Concluding exhortations and greetings

With five terse exhortations, Paul begins the formal conclusion to 1 Corinthians. As he does elsewhere (e.g., 1 Thess 5:6; Rom 13:11-14), he exhorts the Corinthians to "be on guard," a phrase freighted with eschatological significance. The day of judgment is imminent, and eschatological urgency is the framework of believers' lives. Therefore, believers must be on guard for the arrival of the day of judgment and vigilant over their conduct as they await the second coming. "Be courageous" and "be strong" are rather general appeals, while the remaining two exhorta-

tions appear to be directed specifically to the Corinthian situation. By denying the resurrection, some were straying from the faith, in which, Paul now exhorts them to stand firm. The final exhortation that every "act should be done with love" recalls not only chapter 13 but the whole ethic of love and concern for others, rooted in the example of Christ, which Paul has sought to inculcate through his responses in 1 Corinthians.

After these brief exhortations, Paul singles out for praise some model members of the community who have used their gifts to serve the other members of the community (v. 15). He then exhorts the community to be "subordinate" to them (v. 16). This deference is not owed in view of any hierarchical office those praised occupy within the community. Rather, it is the witness of their lives spent in service to others that calls forth the community's respect and recognition (v. 18).

The passing on of greetings (vv. 19-20) is part of Paul's strategy to maintain communication between the churches and to reinforce the sense that all believers everywhere are joined in one new family of faith. Prisca and Aquila, who had arrived in Corinth shortly before Paul and offered him work (see Acts 18:1-3), are now living in Ephesus and are apparently leaders within the local church there. The greetings include a kiss, a public sign of the unity and reconciliation that existed among community members. The addition of the word "holy" (v. 20) need not imply that Paul has in mind here some type of greeting reserved for the liturgy.

Paul adds a postscript in his own handwriting, unusual with regard to ancient letter writing conventions and something Paul did only occasionally (see Gal 6:11-18), presumably to ensure his personal concern. Even more unusual in these final verses is the inclusion of a conditional curse (v. 22), which serves to reinforce the series of strict warnings Paul has already enunciated in this letter. The curse is followed by a prayer, *Marana tha*, "Come, our Lord," and then a typical grace benediction. Paul concludes with an assertion of personal love for the community, which is unique to this letter. This expression of love allows Paul to recall one of the letter's major themes and reinforce his own *ethos* as a loving, caring father, a powerful argument indeed for why the community should heed his advice, admonitions, and appeals.

THE SECOND LETTER TO THE

CORINTHIANS

Maria A. Pascuzzi, C.S.J.

INTRODUCTION

Occasion and purpose

When we turn to 2 Corinthians, it is evident that the solid relationship between Paul and the Corinthian community, presupposed in 1 Corinthians, is no longer intact. Rather, the community's trust in Paul has eroded, and their relationship is seriously strained. Paul now finds himself in a defensive position, reflected in the letter's rhetoric, which is largely apologetic, struggling to win back the trust and esteem of the community.

Since there is no independent account of what precipitated this crisis and elicited 2 Corinthians, the situation must be reconstructed. A likely scenario based on the text evidence runs as follows: Paul had promised to return to Corinth for a lengthy visit after concluding his ministry in Ephesus and then visiting Macedonia (1 Cor 16:5-7) but did not do as promised. Rather, sometime after sending 1 Corinthians, he apparently changed his mind, deciding to stop at Corinth once on his way to Macedonia and again on his return from Macedonia, after which he would bring the Corinthians' collection for the poor to Jerusalem (2 Cor 1:15).

Paul did not follow through on these plans either. Evidently, he learned that the troubles in the Corinthian community had escalated, even though he had sent Timothy (1 Cor 4:17) and dispatched 1 Corinthians to deal with key problems. This troublesome situation was further exacerbated when rival missionaries arrived in Corinth.

They discredited Paul and instigated a crisis between the community and him (2 Cor 11:4). To remedy the situation, Paul made an unscheduled, "pain[ful]" visit to Corinth, where he was publicly humiliated (2:5). Once back in Ephesus, he wrote the now lost tearful letter (2:4) and sent it to the community via Titus. Anxious to hear the community's reaction to this severe letter, Paul left Troas and met up with Titus in Macedonia (2:12-13). Titus reported that many in the community had realigned themselves with Paul (7:5-16), although doubts lingered about his trustworthiness, since he had changed plans and failed to make the promised visit (1:12–2:4). Apparently, others remained under the influence of the intruders, allied with them against Paul. In response to this situation, Paul composed 2 Corinthians.

Second Corinthians is our only source of information about the intruders. Paul's counter brag at 11:22, that he is as much a Hebrew and Israelite as the intruders, indicates that he regards them as Jewish Christians. Apart from this, Paul says only that they are "false apostles" (11:13) who preach a gospel different from his (11:4-5). They have "letters of recommendation" (3:1) and are supported by the community (11:7-12). They evidently boast about their rhetorical skills and knowledge (10:10; 11:6), appealing to their supernatural power (12:12) and visions (12:1) as proof of the superiority of their gospel and ministry.

Unfortunately, this information is too general, and probably too biased, to allow for a definite identification of the intruders. Though scholarly speculation abounds, perhaps the most that can be safely stated is that the intruders were Jewish Christians. Paul considers them adversaries and holds them responsible for having driven a wedge between himself and the community. As he tells it, they alleged that he was a frail and gutless preacher, forceful only on paper (10:1-18), deficient in speech (11:6), and without "letters of recommendation" (3:1-3). They apparently cited Paul's refusal of Corinthian financial support as testimony that he was no true apostle (11:7) and raised the suspicion that he was deceitfully intending to profit from the collection he promoted (12:12-16). Paul's failure to demonstrate the power of his message with miracles and signs and his lack of ecstatic visions (12:1-10) were also apparently evinced as confirmation of his inferior status.

The intruders were clearly attempting to dismantle Paul's apostolic authority and invalidate his ministry. They probably found a receptive audience among the spiritual elitists in the community, whose captivation with eloquent speech and boasting in ecstatic gifts and knowledge had already been a source of discord at Corinth (see 1 Cor 8–14). Although Paul reserves his most direct and vehement attack on the intruders until chapters 10–13, they are in the background of his argument throughout the letter.

The unity of 2 Corinthians

Scholars who claim that 2 Corinthians is a composite of letters or letter portions usually cite three blocks of text as evidence to support this claim: (1) 6:14–7:1; (2) chapters 8–9; and (3) chapters 10–13. They argue that these text blocks differ so significantly from their immediate literary context in either content or tone that they must have been once-independent letters or pieces of letters occasioned by separate circumstances. Some would even argue that chapters 8 and 9 were each originally separate letters. Additionally, some maintain that at 2:13 Paul unexpectedly breaks his narrative, resuming it at 7:5. They point to the intervening material, that is, 2:14–7:4, as further evidence that 2 Corinthians is a composite. In view of these arguments, 2 Corinthians could be a combination of anywhere from two (chs. 1–9 and 10–13) to six letters or letter fragments.

However, the case for the composite nature of 2 Corinthians may not be as strong as it seems. First of all, the manuscript evidence supports the letter's compositional integrity. Second, as our study of 1 Corinthians has shown, digressions are not always signs of later insertions, nor does change of tone or topic necessarily signal a new letter or letter fragment. Third, when Paul's rhetorical strategy is considered, 2 Corinthians appears less disjointed and incoherent than is insisted by those who divide it.

Beyond these three observations, the fact that there is no scholarly agreement on the number of separate letters allegedly contained within 2 Corinthians is itself telling. Moreover, those who insist on dividing the letter are obliged to answer two crucial questions: What circumstances occasioned the writing of each presumably independent letter, and why were they stitched together to form canonical 2 Corinthians? So far the answers have not been compelling enough to warrant abandoning attempts to understand this letter as a coherent whole.

In its final canonical form, 2 Corinthians displays the typical features of an ancient letter. It has an opening section complete with name of sender, addressees and a greeting (1:1-2), and a blessing of God in place of the usual thanksgiving (1:3-11). The body of the letter extends from 1:12 through 13:10, after which there is a formal conclusion (13:11-13), with exhortations, greetings, and a benediction typical of Paul's endings of his letters.

From a rhetorical perspective, 2 Corinthians can be considered a defense speech (forensic rhetoric) within which Paul includes one hortatory unit concerning the collection (chs. 8–9). After the opening (1:1-11), Paul attempts to dispel doubts about his sincerity by clarifying the motives behind his change in travel plans and to showcase his good character in order to gain the community's good will (1:12–2:16). Then he goes to the heart of the matter—the defense of his ministry, which has come under attack. After dissociating himself from charlatans who peddle God's word (2:17), Paul follows with a series of arguments that underscore the validity of his ministry and his apostolic authenticity (3:1–7:16). Having worked to win back the community's support and esteem, he feels confident enough to solicit the community with regard to the collection for the saints, a matter of great concern to him (chs. 8–9). Then he directly confronts those whom he holds responsible for exacerbating matters and instigating the crisis at Corinth. In four stinging chapters, Paul attacks the intruders, unfavorably comparing their ministry and motives to his own to show that they, not he, are the real charlatans (2 Cor 10–13:10). After this climactic counterattack, there follows a standard epistolary conclusion (13:11-13).

Key theological ideas

The First Letter to the Corinthians focused on various colorful problems pertaining to life in the community and community life in relation to the world outside. In contrast, 2 Corinthians focuses almost exclusively on the issue of legitimate Christian apostleship and the true character of ministry in the service of the gospel. Paul's understanding of apostleship is rooted in his theology of the gospel, specifically in the dialectic between weakness and power (see 1 Cor 1:18-31), which he applies to his own life and ministry. In his abundant suffering, Paul shares in the sufferings of Christ (2 Cor 1:5), and in his own afflicted body he carries about the dying of Jesus (4:10-11). These sufferings do not undermine his apostolic legitimacy but authenticate it, since it is precisely through weakness and suffering that God's divine power to save is made manifest (4:7). That is why Paul never attempts to overcome his weakness or shrink from suffering; rather, he boasts in it (see 11:30; 12:5), since it indisputably distinguishes him as a true minister of the glorious new covenant in Christ (2:14) through whom God has reconciled the world, inaugurating the new creation (5:11-21). In addition to his suffering, Paul also points to his sincerity (2:17), his willingness to forgive (2:10), his selfless concern for the Corinthians (12:11-18), and his moral integrity (8:20-21). All are a piece of the cruciform existence that characterizes the apostle's life and distinguishes and authenticates Paul as a true minister of the gospel.

This same cruciform existence must be the hallmark of every Christian life. Paul does not recommend weakness, suffering, death, or poverty to the Corinthians as ends in themselves (see 1:3-6; 4:10-12; 8:8-15). Rather, he insists that receptivity to the gospel message, the story of God's power and glory paradoxically manifested in Christ crucified, is demonstrated in one's acceptance of suffering, one's glorying in weakness, and one's selfless service to others for the sake of Christ, whose love constrains us to live no longer for ourselves (2 Cor 5:14-15).

OUTLINE OF SECOND CORINTHIANS

COMMENTARY

INTRODUCTION

2 Corinthians 1:1-11

1:1-2 Greeting

Paul's self-identification as an apostle of Christ Jesus by God's will underscores the authoritative basis of his ministry, which is the result of God's initiative. Timothy, who had evangelized with Paul at Corinth (1:19), is mentioned as co-sender of this letter. Whether this implies coauthor is not certain. The letter is addressed to the "church of God . . . in Corinth." The addition of "with all the holy ones throughout Achaia" allows Paul to accent universality, as he did at 1 Corinthians 1:2. Given the Corinthians' behavior, the designation "holy ones" seems ill-fit. However, this is their vocation (1 Cor 1:2), of which Paul again reminds them. The salutation, where Paul typically combines Greek *charis* (grace) and Hebrew *shalom* (peace), expresses his understanding of God's generous gifting of humanity with and through Christ and the well being or *shalom* that results.

1:3-11 Blessing

Paul begins with a typical Jewish benediction (vv. 3-4), blessing God who graciously comforts him in all his afflictions. Paul turns this experience into an opportunity to comfort others, becoming the conduit of God's comfort for those in need. Though the blessing proper does not extend beyond these two verses, two key terms, "affliction" and "encouragement" (Greek: *paraklēsis*, also rendered "encouragement" or "consolation") are repeated in verses 5-7. Here the focus is on Paul's relationship with the community, and the general notion of affliction is now subsumed under Christ's sufferings. As co-participants in Christ's sufferings, Paul and the community are bound to each other. Although Paul's share of Christ's suffering is "overflowing" (v. 5), he accepts this in view of its positive benefit for other Christians who must also endure suffering.

In verses 8-11, Paul concludes by appealing to the Corinthians for their prayers, reminding them of sufferings he endured in Asia, which left him so despairing that he had resigned himself to death. Beyond speculation that Paul here alludes to some experience in Ephesus (see, e.g., 1 Cor 15:32; Acts 19:23-40), it is impossible to know, based on the scant text information, to what traumatic experience he refers. Nonetheless, Paul makes clear that the experience did not nullify his faith. Rather, it resulted in his complete reliance on God and a more profound faith that, in the future, God would rescue him from death through the resurrection.

Why Paul begins with this blessing of God and emphasis on his suffering needs to be considered within the context of the whole argument he unfolds in this letter. As noted, the rival apostles had apparently cited Paul's suffering and weakness as evidence of his inferiority. Rather than deny his suffering, Paul subverts this criticism by identifying his suffering as a participation in the sufferings of Christ. Paul is not incapacitated by it; on the contrary, his suffering enables him to act as an agent of comfort to community members in their time of affliction. Suffering, the common lot of Paul and the community, cannot be a source of alienation between them, since their co-participation in Christ's suffering bonds them further to each other. Moreover, suffering has brought Paul to a more complete reliance on God and has increased his hope in God. What could be wrong with the apostle's suffering? Clearly, nothing!

It is important to underscore that Paul does not promote suffering as an absolute good but values his suffering insofar as it serves his ministry. Indeed, it is in Paul's "overflowing" suffering, identified with Christ's suffering, that God's saving grace overflows and not, as the rivals would have the Corinthians believe, in demonstrations of power! Thus suffering cannot be discounted as a mere sign of weakness, and the Corinthians, far from taking offense at Paul's suffering, should bless God too! They should see in it the degree to which God is at work in Paul and find in his suffering both a source of comfort and union between themselves and their apostle, whose ministry they are called to share and support through prayer (v. 11).

PAUL'S TRUE MOTIVES AND CHARACTER

2 Corinthians 1:12–2:16

Circumscribed within the accusations brought against Paul by the outsiders and the larger controversy they have instigated is the community's own questioning of Paul's sincerity in view of his apparent failure to keep his word and visit them. If not addressed, this issue risks being magnified by the larger controversy. Therefore, before Paul tackles the major bone of contention raised by the intruders, that is, the legitimacy of his apostleship (v. 17), he first deals with this issue to make sure he has the community on his side. Paul begins by boasting of his sincerity especially toward the community (1:12-14). After showing that he has legitimate motives for foregoing his promised visit (1:15–2:4), Paul returns to the fate of the offender (2:5-11) before giving thanks for the positive outcome to this particular crisis and posing a final question that provides the opening for Paul to defend his ministry before the Corinthian community (2:12-16).

1:12-14 Paul is sincere and reliable

In verses 12-14 Paul transitions from the opening blessing but keeps the focus on the mutually beneficial relationship between himself and the community, boasting of his candid and sincere conduct "especially toward you"(v. 12). Paul is certain of this because what he says and writes he does by the "grace of God," that is, as one divinely commissioned to reveal God's wisdom in a completely intelligible way (v. 13). Not only can the Corinthians put away their doubts, but they can enjoy with Paul a relationship of mutual understanding and pride that will grow until "the day of [our] Lord Jesus" (v. 14). The benefit to the community accruing from Paul's sincere and candid preaching of the gospel justifies Paul's boasting and the community's boasting in him. This clearly distinguishes Paul from the false preachers, whose ministry is a vehicle for self-promotion.

1:15–2:4 The motives for Paul's change in travel plans

At issue here is Paul's failure to go forward with his planned double visit to Corinth (v. 16). He had not followed through on previously announced travel plans (1 Cor 16:5) nor on his new modified plans. The Corinthians are understandably irked and have begun to wonder whether Paul can be trusted.

In response, Paul offers two reasons for his change of plans. The first is unfolded in verses 15-22, where Paul begins with the positive statement that the purpose of the visit was to be of benefit (a double favor) to the community (v. 15), something with which the Corinthians presumably agree. Then in verse 17 Paul poses two questions, to which some Corinthians were likely to respond yes! Yes, you did act lightly! Yes, you are a vacillator, saying yes one day and no the next day! But Paul insists on his trustworthiness, which is guaranteed in view of two certainties: God's faithfulness (v. 18) and the constancy of Jesus (vv. 19-20). If Paul is commissioned by God who is faithful to preach the gospel of the Son of God who is ever constant, then Paul, too, must be trustworthy. Thus, the source of Paul's commission and the very commission with which he is entrusted both demand and attest to his own constancy and not simply with regard to his travel plans. The Corinthians should have no problem agreeing with this, since, as Paul reminds them, when they say "Amen," a reference to a liturgical formula, they put their faith in Christ in whom all the promises of God are fulfilled and thereby ultimately express their faith in the constancy of God.

Paul presents the second motive for his change of travel plans in 1:23–2:4. Not only is Paul constant, he is also pastorally concerned for the community with which he is bound in Christ through his apostolic commissioning (v. 21). Since his work is to advance the community's joy (1:24), and they his, the Corinthians should realize that Paul had their best interests at heart when he decided to forego another potentially painful visit (2:1). Instead, Paul substituted the planned visit with a letter, (the now lost "painful" or "tearful" letter), the purpose of which was to express his "abundant love" for the community (2:4).

2:5-11 The fate of the offender

The disclosure of the second motive brings Paul back to the painful visit and the fate of the one offending him (2:5-11). Most scholars assume that when Paul made his unscheduled visit to Corinth to address the crisis, some community member publicly challenged his authority. The fact that Paul reminds the Corinthians that this act of effrontery was not simply a cause of personal pain but an offense against the whole body of believers at Corinth (v. 5) may indicate that some in the community did not see it this way at all. However, "the majority" apparently did and acted to discipline the offender (v. 6).

Although no details about the disciplinary action are disclosed, Paul interprets the action as a demonstration that the community is "obedient in everything" (v. 9) and now asks that they forgive the offender (vv. 7-8). Neither the offender's identity nor the exact nature of the offense is mentioned. Attempts to identify the offender here with the community member censured for immorality (see 1 Cor 5:1-13) have failed to convince for a number of reasons. For example, Paul's approach to the offender here is quite lenient in comparison with his severe posture toward the offender of 1 Corinthians 5. Moreover, the roles attributed to Satan in each situation are substantially different. At 1 Corinthians 5:5, Satan was to destroy the offender's flesh. Here at 2:11, Satan is a potential threat to the community if the offender is not forgiven. Since Paul elsewhere associates the false apostles with Satan (11:13-14), his concern here may be that the intruders/Satan will seize upon this situation to sow further discord within the community and between the community and Paul; hence Paul's recommendation to forgive and restore the offender to fellowship.

2:12-16 A positive outcome

Paul now recalls how he had come to hear that the majority of Corinthians did the right thing and disciplined the offender (vv. 12-13). Having decided to send Titus to Corinth with the tearful letter, Paul went on to Troas to evangelize. While there, he was so distracted by his concern over the unfolding of events in Corinth that he aborted his evangelizing mission and went to Macedonia to catch Titus as he was returning from Corinth. Paul's relief at the positive outcome and his joy that the gospel was being advanced led him to express words of thanks to God (v. 14).

The metaphoric language introduced here touches on Paul's apostolic self-understanding, his role and his adequacy to perform that role, which he will defend at length beginning in 2:17. The first metaphor is drawn from the practice of triumphal processions in which conquering generals paraded their captives (v. 14). Here Paul's apostolic self-understanding emerges as he metaphorically presents himself as a captive paraded about by the victor, God. Paul, the itinerant missionary, is not at liberty to be self-directing (see 1 Cor 9:16-17). Rather, as a captive, dragged about by God, he exudes "the odor of the knowledge"

of God in every place (2:14). The imagery of "odor" may derive from Sirach 24:15, where God's wisdom is referred to as a scent or fragrance. If so, then Paul presents himself as the shamed and afflicted apostle/captive who emanates God's odor/wisdom. Since Christ is the wisdom and, therefore, the true aroma of God, the apostles who proclaim Christ are indeed the "aroma of Christ" (v. 15) exuding the message of Christ crucified, God's wisdom. As one bound to fulfill this role, Paul acknowledges its serious implications. To some, through faith, what the apostle secretes will be the scent of salvation leading to life; to others, it is the odor of death leading to destruction (see 1 Cor 1:18). Paul's concluding question, "Who is qualified for this?" underscores how crucial the ministry of the gospel is. The question remains unanswered here, but the implication is clear. No one is fit for the task, save whomever God captures and equips to execute it.

PAUL DEFENDS HIS MINISTRY
2 Corinthians 2:17–7:16

So far Paul has attempted to allay doubts about his reliability, reestablish his good character, and regain the community's good will. All this paves the way for his engagement with the major point of controversy: the validity and authenticity of his ministry. Though the controversy is ostensibly between Paul and the community, lurking in the background of his comments are the intruders. Their arrival and style of ministry have precipitated the crisis, since Paul is being unfavorably compared with them.

Paul begins by refuting a double charge and launches the first step of his defense, which is built around the contrast between his and Moses' ministry (2:17– 4:6). Having established the superiority of the ministry of glory with which he is entrusted, Paul argues that this ministry is characterized by afflictions that, paradoxically, constitute the credentials of a true apostle (4:7–5:10). He continues the characterization of his ministry as one of reconciliation (5:11–6:10), which climaxes with a personal appeal to the Corinthians (6:11-13). At this point Paul introduces a brief digression (6:14–7:1) before resuming his appeal (7:2-4), after which he expresses his complete confidence in the community (7:5-16).

2:17–4:6 Ministers of a new covenant

Based on his opening statements, it appears that two charges were laid against Paul, both relating to the validity of his ministry: one concerned his refusal of financial support (2:17); the other, letters of recommendation (3:1). As already discussed, the financing of teachers and preachers by well-to-do patrons was customary in Paul's day. Though Paul accepted financial patronage from some congregations (see Phil 4:16; 2 Cor 11:9), his refusal of Corinthian support (1 Cor 9:1-18) galled this community. Besides suspecting Paul of hypocrisy, the Corinthians were evidently not convinced by his argument that the nature of the gospel demanded that it be preached gratis (1 Cor 9:15-18). They operated with the notion that only paid ministers were quality ministers who could be expected to give their all (see 12:13 and 11:7-12). To make matters worse, Paul lacked "letters of recommendation." In antiquity, great value was placed on the testimony of authoritative figures who vouched for others' credentials through letters. Paul knew the importance of this social convention and, when necessary, could invoke his own authority to recommend others (see Rom 16:1 and 1 Cor 16:3).

In response to the first charge, Paul berates financed ministers as hucksters who "trade on the word of God" (2:17). He dissociates from them, contrasting their profit-driven ministry with his own, which is carried on in sincerity, to which God witnesses. For Paul, this is sufficient. As for letters of recommendation, here, too, Paul distinguishes himself from "others." That he would need to provide such credentials "again" is preposterous, as his question underscores (3:1), precisely because his relationship with this community, metaphorically referred to as a letter that Paul carries about in his heart for all to read, testifies to the authenticity of his ministry. This letter/relationship owes its origin to Christ and pertains to the new covenant, powered by the Spirit and written on hearts of flesh (see Jer 31:33; Ezek 11:19; 36:26), of which Paul is a minister. He would not be adequate to the task except that God has qualified him for it; hence he takes no credit—perhaps in contrast to "some others"—for the success of his ministry, which is "not of letter but of spirit" (3:6).

The contrast introduced here is not between a spiritual reading of the Old Testament versus a literal one, as often assumed, but between two possible principles by which the new covenant is to be animated: the Mosaic law, which drove the old covenant but brought death, or the Spirit who gives life (v. 6b). This contrast, in which the law is deprecated and by extension the entire old covenant, raises questions about God's purposes in giving the law, which Paul does not pursue here. Instead, he goes forward with the old/new antithesis by contrasting his ministry with that of Moses. The contrast builds on Paul's interpretation of Exodus 34:1-4, 29-35, the account of Moses' ascent to Sinai to receive the stone tablets on which the law was engraved. A key element in this account, taken up by Paul in verses 7-11, is the glory of the Lord reflected on the face of Moses, which became so resplendent as a result of his encounter with the Lord that the Israelites could not stare at Moses unless his face was veiled. In light of this, Paul reasons that if the Mosaic covenant, pejoratively termed the "ministry of death," was attended by such glory, albeit a glory destined to fade, then the ministry of the Spirit, a ministry of righteousness destined to endure, must be all the more glorious. Paul further insists that the greater glory of the new covenant has nullified whatever glory once attended the old covenant.

Confirmed in this hope, Paul contrasts his ministry, characterized by openness, with that of Moses, characterized by covertness, as symbolized by the veil. Paul claims that Moses donned this veil to keep the Israelites from acknowledging the abrogation of this whole old covenant, whose vanishing glory was visible on his face (vv. 12-13). Paul's aim here is not to charge Moses with deception but, as is clear from verse 14, where the veil becomes a metaphor for Israel's blindness, to impugn the Israelites for their hardened minds. Paul then transfers his remarks about historical Israel to his Jewish contemporaries, hardened still. Though Paul condemns them for failing to acknowledge that the old covenant is abrogated through Christ, he also appeals to them to "turn to" (convert to) the Lord, identified with the eschatological Spirit of freedom, which all believers experience (cf. Rom 8:2). Conversion removes the veil.

In verse 18, Paul reprises the key elements that have been part of his argument so far: veil, face, glory. Implicit in this verse is the contrast between the superior experience of all believers who pass "from glory to glory" and are progressively transformed into the image of God and the vanishing glory of Moses and the Mosaic covenant. In short, Paul has argued that what the Spirit accomplishes in believers through the ministry of the Spirit, of which he is a qualified minister, eclipses the ministry of Moses, a ministry of law carved in stone, which was impotent to save. Though harsh in his denigration of the law and law-based ministry, Paul's views here are consistent with those he expresses elsewhere, especially in Galatians and Romans. It has been suggested that Paul's rivals in Corinth were Jewish Christians who insisted on the continuing validity of the law. Whether they in fact espoused this position is not certain. What is certain is that here Paul seems to refute such a view.

Paul wraps up this first phase of his argument by reaffirming that his ministry has its origin in God's mercy (4:1-6). Though the stakes attached to this ministry of glory are high (see 2:15-16), he is not discouraged. On the contrary, commissioned and qualified by God, he is a confident minister of the gospel. He has no need to resort to deception and cunning, practices he renounces as contrary to the gospel; rather, he ministers in openness and honesty, not compromising the truth of the word of God. This truthful manner of ministry, configured to the truth of the gospel, validates Paul's ministry and justifies his self-commendation.

Paul's admission that his gospel appears veiled to some (4:3) raises the possibility that his detractors accused him of being less transparent and sincere than he claimed. However, Paul denies that his preaching style leads to incomprehension. If some fail to perceive the light of the gospel, it is because the "god of this age" (Satan; 4:4) has blinded them. Paul knows himself to be above reproach in this matter because he preaches only Jesus Christ, in whom the light of the knowledge of the glory of God is revealed.

4:7–5:10 A ministry of affliction

In this second phase of his defense, Paul reflects on the paradoxical nature of authentic Christian ministry. Logically, the treasure, that is, this great ministry of glory, ought to be entrusted to a robust and resilient minister equal to the task. But it has been entrusted to Paul, weak and frag-ile as a common clay jar with a short shelf life. This paradoxical arrangement is not accidental but essential. Paul's weakness attests that apostolic ministry is powered by God and not the apostle, a fact borne out in the four antitheses set out in verses 8-9. In the course of his ministry, Paul survived potentially devastating adversities, not by the dint of his own inner resources but by the power of God. Paul's sufferings and weakness also attest to his union with Christ, whose suffering and death, Paul firmly believes, are being replicated in his own life of suffering and always with the paradoxical result that life triumphs.

This is evidenced among the Corinthians themselves. Life is at work in them, while, and precisely because, death is at work in Paul (vv. 10-12). However much Paul's suffering demonstrates God's power, affirms his union with Christ, and is the source of life for others—all good things—what ultimately makes his suffering bearable is the knowledge that he and all believers will be raised and brought into the presence of God and Christ. This certainty is rooted in the belief Paul shares with the Corinthians that God who raised Jesus will also raise them (vv. 13-14). Verse 15 expands the thought of verse 12. Everything Paul suffers is for the community, so that the life that more and more of them come to experience will occasion praise and thanks to God.

Paul's firm hope in the resurrection and his present lived experience of inner renewal, even while his body is consumed by the rigors of ministry, bring him to affirm again, "we are not discouraged" (4:16; see also 4:1). In verse 17, Paul introduces a present/future contrast as he considers his sufferings in the context of the coming glory. By comparison with that future glory, eternal and weighty, Paul's suffering is light and momentary, further qualified in verse 18, as visible and transitory. Hence his focus must not be on his present suffering but on what is invisible and everlasting.

The mention of eternal glory leads Paul to reflect on his future destiny beginning at 5:1. This destiny concerns all believers, who are included in the "we." Paul's greatest desire is to be with the Lord permanently, which he speaks of as being at "home" (5:8). At present, he says, our "earthly dwelling," that is, the physical body, is a tent, a temporary home. When death destroys it "we have" (v. 1), Paul declares with certainty, a more permanent building, a spiritual or resurrection body awaiting us in heaven.

But how do believers exist between death and resurrection? For Paul, a disembodied existence, here negatively represented in the terms "naked" and "unclothed" (vv. 3, 4) was unthinkable. Though he considers the physical body/tent a weight (v. 4), Paul does not want the disembodied, "unclothed" state that death effects, which can reasonably be taken to mean he does not want to die. Instead, he prefers that his body be "further clothed" (v. 4), in other words, progressively transformed until the mortal is swallowed up by life (see also 1 Cor 15:53-54). The Spirit is already enabling this progressive transformation from death to life (see 3:15; 4:16), guaranteeing (see 1:21-22) God's future and complete transformation of what is mortal. Until then, Paul acknowledges that the body is an obstacle to complete and permanent union with the Lord, who is known now through faith and not by sight in that direct face-to-face way that Paul desires (see 3:18 and 1 Cor 13:13).

This yearning for the Lord apparently outweighs Paul's misgivings about death as he now declares his preference to leave the body to be at home with the Lord. Paul's discussion of the impermanent, burdensome, and limiting character of the physical body could reinforce the view of some Corinthians, earlier refuted by Paul, that the body has no moral value (see 1 Cor 6:12-20). Here Paul concludes by pointedly reminding them that the Lord will judge each of them in view of the good or evil done "in the body," the only place where ethical behavior and moral purpose are manifested.

In this second phase of his defense, Paul has provided the Corinthians with a new framework for evaluating valid ministry and authentic apostleship. Within this framework, weakness and suffering necessarily, even though paradoxically, constitute the hallmarks of a genuine minister because the gospel is paradox. In Christ, God manifests power in weakness, glory through apparent shame, and brings life from death (see 1 Cor 1:18-30). In Paul, an apostle of Jesus Christ, God's glory and power are again made manifest in the apostle's weakness, sufferings, and death. The Corinthians are not only joined to Paul in suffering (1:7), but through his ministry of hardship they are already experiencing life.

5:11–6:10 A ministry of reconciliation

At the end of the previous argument, Paul's focus shifted to the future of all Christians. Now at verse 11 he returns to his self-defense, beginning a third phase in this long argument for the legitimacy and authenticity of his apostolic ministry. He addresses the community from beginning to end ("you," v. 12 and v. 20), though clearly with an eye to his rivals. Paul admits that his task is "to persuade" others (v. 11), yet he implicitly distinguishes himself from his rivals by emphasizing his transparency before God, which he hopes the Corinthians will also recognize. Despite his claim to the contrary, Paul is, in fact, commending himself, but not for selfish reasons. His purpose is to give the Corinthians reason to take pride in him, a man of substance (heart) and to rebut those who are all show, able to boast only in externals, perhaps even in ecstatic experiences (see 12:1) and miracle-working (see 12:12). Besides, as Paul makes clear, ecstatic experiences are private matters between an individual and God (see further 1 Cor 14:2). They are irrelevant to ministry, which is "for you" (v. 13). Paul provides this information to enable the Corinthians to make an informed choice between himself and his opponents.

Paul continues by appealing to the community's identification with the death of Christ and then draws out the implications of this event (5:14-17), whose universal significance is underscored in Paul's statement "one died for all" (v. 14b). How Christ's death benefits all humanity is assumed but not explained here. Rather, Paul is concerned to draw out the implications of Christ's death for all believers, about which the Corinthians obviously need to be reminded. First, all believers owe their new life to Christ and so must pattern their lives after his. Second, as a result of Christ's death, believers no longer belong to the realm of the flesh, that old existence of corruption and death that heretofore characterized human existence. Thus it follows that as those now "in Christ" (v. 17), the Corinthians can no longer know or judge Christ or anyone else "according to the flesh" (v. 16), that is, according to their old criteria.

Paul cites his own example to show how standards and values once considered important are now invalid (v. 16). Christ's self-emptying love is the basis of reconciliation and unity. This love has made possible the existence of this community, and Christ's love must be what compels the community to act and to judge. Since the Corinthians and Paul now know from the same perspective in Christ and are expected to judge based on the same criterion, namely, Christ, it is clear that the community's negative assessment of Paul according to the old standards of power and prestige obviously needs to be reconsidered!

Believers belong to a "new creation" (v. 17), an entirely new order in which cosmic brokenness is now being reversed by the cosmic reconciliation willed and set in motion by God, who has "reconciled us to himself through Christ" (v. 18). Reconciliation is what God alone accomplishes through the agency of Christ. God, through Christ, rights the relationship between all creation and God's-self and all creation with itself, no longer counting believers' trespasses against them (v. 19). Paul is tasked with making known God's reconciling activity in Christ. However, he is no mere bearer of a message about a past event. Through his own ministry it is "as if God were appealing" (v. 20). Paul clearly understands himself as an agent of God's ongoing reconciling work, mediated in the present through his apostolic life and ministry. Thus he appeals to the Corinthians to be reconciled to God, which implies reconciliation among themselves and with Paul, God's minister of reconciliation.

Paul again directs the Corinthians' attention to what God has done in Christ, this time focusing on God's intention that believers "might *become* the righteousness of God" (v. 21, emphasis added). "Becoming" God's righteousness suggests that while God's salvific purposes are made known in Christ, believers are called to respond to God's offer by choosing to live out this righteousness. If so, a certain moral connotation seems to be attached to the notion of righteousness and needs to be manifested in holy living. Knowing well the Corinthians' practical lapses both with regard to unity/reconciliation (see 1 Cor 1–4) and holiness (see 1 Cor 5–6; 8–10), Paul justifiably fears that the community has received the grace of God in vain (6:1). He therefore appeals to them to turn and respond to that grace. Though Isaiah, cited here in support of this appeal (6:2a; see Isa 49:8), envisioned the day of salvation as a future event, Paul believed that with the advent of the Messiah, that day had come. Salvation was a present offer, a grace to which the Corinthians needed to respond.

Paul brings the discussion of his ministry of reconciliation to a close by underscoring his own *ethos.* Neither he nor his co-workers has done anything to impede the Corinthians from responding to God's grace and fully partaking of this reconciliation. To reinforce his point, Paul briefly recaps how he has lived and worked among them. He has demonstrated endurance in the face of numerous difficulties (see also 4:8-10; 11:23-29; 12:10). Some hardships were inflicted by others (e.g., beatings, imprisonments); some were self-imposed (labors, vigils, and fasts). But Paul has not simply endured the hardships. He has acted with "purity," a reference to his selfless motives, and has demonstrated many other virtues (vv. 6-7a) that attest to his authenticity as an apostle.

That Paul is able to withstand whatever befalls him is due to God who equips Paul "with weapons of righteousness at the right and at the left" (v. 7). The mention of the right and left could simply mean that Paul is fully prepared. In the context of the military metaphor, we should probably understand that Paul is prepared for both the offense and the defense, since the right hand wielded the sword and the left held the shield. Responses to Paul's ministry have alternated between extremes from glory to dishonor, from insult to praise (v. 8a). Whatever the response, Paul is prepared to fight whatever battles he must to spread the gospel.

Having once again demonstrated the authenticity of his ministry, Paul now introduces a final set of seven contrasts (vv. 8b-10), through which he deals with the negative assessments that have plagued his ministry. The first statement of each pair contains a negative evaluation of Paul, most likely reflecting the views of some in the Corinthian community. Paul simply counters each one by offering his own positive view of himself without adding any criticism of the Corinthians. The latter is unnecessary. In the end, the Corinthians' negative appraisal of their apostle shows that many are still attached to their former way of knowing and to judging "according to the flesh" (see 5:16). This again confirms their spiritual immaturity (see 1 Cor 3). If they were truly spiritual people, they would understand God's wisdom manifested in Christ crucified (1 Cor 1:18-31). With Christ as their standard of judgment, they would share Paul's positive assessment of his life and ministry, recognizing God's paradoxical wisdom at work in him.

6:11-13 A personal appeal

In a spirit of reconciliation, Paul now makes a personal and emotionally charged appeal to the Corinthians, in which he stresses his openness and affection for them and asks that they reciprocate by making room in their hearts for him. Rather than chastise the community, Paul speaks as a parent and guide to the Corinthians, whom he considers his beloved children in Christ (see 1 Cor 4:15).

6:14–7:1 A call to holiness

Having focused so far on his own ministry and relationship to the community, Paul now turns to the community's relation to the world outside. This shift in focus, coupled with the presence of some ideas and vocabulary not typical of Paul, have led many scholars to conclude that 6:14–7:1 is a non-Pauline fragment inserted by an editor. However, no manuscript evidence indicates an insertion here, and as many scholars now recognize, the passage is sufficiently Pauline in vocabulary and construction to be reasonably considered authentic. In fact, as with other Pauline digressions, closer examination often reveals logical links to the surrounding context. For example, at 6:1 Paul had already expressed concern that the Corinthians had received the grace of God in vain; hence this brief section in which Paul exhorts the community to recall its true identity and reaffirm its exclusive allegiance to God and Christ is entirely consonant with that concern.

Additionally, having just underscored his pedagogical relationship to the community in 6:13, Paul now assumes a teaching role at 6:14. He instructs and warns about alliances still maintained by some in the community that contravene allegiance to Christ and undermine the reconciliation achieved through Christ. This is especially evident in their strained relationship with Paul, God's minister of reconciliation.

Paul begins with a command that echoes the Old Testament prohibition (see Lev 19:19; Deut 22:9-11) against mismatching or, in the case of animals, misyoking pairs that do not naturally go together. The command is followed by six rhetorical questions containing six antithetical pairings: righteousness/lawlessness, light/darkness, Christ/Beliar, (an alternate term for Satan), believer/unbeliever, and the temple of God/idols (6:14b-16a). Through this series of questions, Paul again stresses the exclusive character of Christian existence (see 1 Cor 10:21). Implicitly, he exhorts the Corinthians to dissociate themselves from all that is pagan and to ally themselves exclusively with God, Christ, righteousness, light, etc.

Paul was quite aware that Christians would necessarily maintain contacts with unbelievers (see 1 Cor 5:9-10) and, in some cases, be married to them without necessarily compromising their relationship with Christ (1 Cor 7:12-14). Thus he cannot have intended here an absolute prohibition of all contact with non-believers. The point, rather, is that the believer's exclusive aligning of self to God in Christ necessitates the renunciation of all activity involving alliances which compromise the believer's relationship with God and Christ and which defile the community, now identified as "the temple of the living God" (v. 16b). For Paul, the community constituted the spiritual temple of God in virtue of its being indwelt by the Spirit of God (1 Cor 3:16-17).

In verses 16b-18, Paul links a series of Old Testament references (Lev 26:12; Ezek 37:27; Jer 31:33c; Isa 52:11; Ps 2:7; Jer 31:9c) that underscore the reciprocal and exclusive relationship between God and the community. This radically exclusive relationship with God marks off true believers from unbelievers, whether within or outside the community, whose allegiance is divided. Moreover, it enjoins on each member of the community the obligation to be cleansed of all defilement in order to maintain the holiness of the community (7:1).

The function of this brief digression is to remind those in the community, probably the same spiritual elitists Paul criticizes in 1 Corinthians, that their continued courting of danger in pagan temples and their rabid pursuit of superficial, transient realities are at the heart of the problems in Corinth. They are responsible for compromising their relationship with Christ through the *koinonia* they establish with pagan idols in pagan temples. In their pursuit of external manifestations of wisdom and power, they show themselves attached to the conventions of the world and thus misjudge true ministers and misinterpret true ministry.

7:2-4 Paul resumes his appeal

Having implicitly inculpated the Corinthians for their tenuous relationship with Christ and near-ruptured relationship with himself, Paul resumes the plea begun above at 6:11-13, exhorting the community to make room for him. Once again he underscores his good faith toward them. He has not wronged, ruined, or taken advantage of anyone, in contrast, perhaps, to those who, in Paul's estimate, were taking financial advantage of the community (see 2:17; 11:19-20).

Though the Corinthians misjudge and malign Paul, he assures them that his intention is not to condemn them (v. 3a). On the contrary, as he has "already said" (v. 3b; obviously a reference to 6:11) and now repeats, he holds them in his heart, and his affection for them is so deep that he desires to die and live with them. Here Paul adopts, but inverts, a classic expression, "to live together and die together" (see 2 Sam 15:21) to articulate his own deepest desire to be fully reconciled with the community and share with them full partnership in the gospel. Despite the strained relationship with the community and the affliction Paul experiences, he expresses optimism that the Corinthians will reciprocate and that their relationship with Paul will be fully restored.

7:5-16 Paul's complete confidence in the Corinthians

Since Paul now picks up on points previously narrated at 2:5-13, many scholars assume that 7:5-16 originally followed on 2:13. Grammatically speaking, this position is difficult to sustain. Paul speaks in the first person singular ("I") at 2:13 and the first person plural ("we") at 7:5. If 7:5 had originally followed 2:13, why the switch from "I" to "we"? Additionally, certain vocabulary employed from 6:11 through 7:4 (e.g., affection, boasting, consolation, joy, distress), recurs in 7:5-16, suggesting more continuity between this unit and what immediately precedes it than is usually admitted.

Moreover, the claim that 7:5 is the direct continuation of 2:13 requires assuming either (a) that Paul abruptly broke off the story at 2:13 to focus on his own ministry until 7:5, at which point he just as abruptly returned to the thought of 2:13, or (b) that 2:14–7:4 is another original Pauline letter or letter fragment inserted here by a later, albeit inept, editor unconcerned about coherency!

Assumption (a) implies that Paul was an erratic thinker/writer; assumption (b) implies that the letter lacks literary integrity. Both are drastic and, from the perspective of Paul's rhetorical goals and strategy, unnecessary.

It is important to bear in mind that at 7:5 Paul has reached a new point in his argument. So far he has carefully unfolded a defense of his ministry, which began at 2:14. At 8:1 he will begin his appeal to the Corinthians for money. The success of his collection drive clearly depends on the degree to which the Corinthians are well disposed to him. If they are not, Paul has little reason to hope that they will entrust their money to him, especially given the misgivings they had about his sincerity (see 1:15-24).

To ensure that there were no residual hard feelings over the painful letter that could compromise his collection appeal and the continuation of his defense, Paul again focuses on the painful letter and his anxiety over it, which he only briefly mentioned at 2:1-13. Here, however, he speaks about the letter and its purpose, as well as his encounter with Titus, much more extensively and with new emphases. This elaboration of previously but briefly narrated points in the service of advancing one's argument at a later stage is an example of the rhetorical technique known as *amplificatio* ("amplification"). In its present position in the letter, this amplification functions as a hinge text. Through it, Paul continues and intensifies the optimistic line introduced at 7:4 and paves the way for his collection appeal in chapters 8–9.

Three smaller units comprise 7:5-16. In the first unit, vv. 5-7, Paul describes the terrible state he was in at Macedonia before Titus came. The "fear" Paul experienced (v. 5) was probably due to his uncertainty about how the Corinthians would react to his "tearful letter" sent via Titus. Having written a stinging letter rebuking the community over the offense he suffered during his unexpected visit to Corinth, Paul knew that his letter had as much potential to alienate the community as it had to elicit their support and action on his behalf. Titus's arrival brings Paul a triple dose of encouragement (vv. 6-7). Beyond the joy of Titus's company, Paul is further encouraged to learn that Titus has not been rebuffed but edified by the Corinthians. The source of Titus's edification, the Corinthians' heartfelt concern for their apostle and remorse over the offensive incident, is the good news that relieves Paul of his anxiety and moves him to rejoice. As delighted as Paul is at this outcome, he is not insensitive to the pain he caused the community.

In the next unit (vv. 8-13a), Paul apologizes, but not without first distinguishing between "worldly sorrow" and "godly sorrow" (7:10). Paul truly regrets the former, by which he means whatever momentary indignation the Corinthians experienced. But he does not regret the latter, because "godly sorrow" induces repentance, which is ultimately beneficial to the Corinthians (v. 10). It has awakened their sense of earnestness and an appropriate sense of indignation against the one who offended Paul, as well as their yearning to patch things up with Paul (v. 11). From Paul's perspective, the severe letter accomplished what he had intended, namely, that the Corinthians would show themselves truly Christian in the sight of God by their concern for his minister, Paul (v. 12). Thus Paul has good reason to be encouraged (v. 13a).

In the final subunit, vv. 13b-16, Paul again speaks of Titus. His success among the Corinthians was a source of joy to Paul, who had not lost face! The Corinthians had come through for him, having more than vindicated his boasting about them. All this joy and encouragement move Paul to express his complete confidence in the community (v. 16).

In this unit Paul has amplified the bare facts narrated earlier at 2:5-13, stressing every positive outcome of a situation that could have ended badly but, fortunately, did not. The Corinthians have shown themselves to be spiritually mature and have benefited from their repentance. Titus accomplished his task unscathed, returning to Macedonia impressed by the Corinthians' obedience and concern for Paul. Paul is encouraged and optimistic about his relationship with the Corinthians.

THE COLLECTION FOR JERUSALEM

2 Corinthians 8:1–9:15

Having praised and flattered the Corinthians to the point of declaring his full confidence in them, Paul now banks on the hope, engendered by Titus's report, that mutual trust has been restored to press his case for the collection. The collection, for reasons already discussed (see 1 Cor 16:1-4), was of singular importance to Paul's gos-

pel. If he has overestimated the Corinthians' good will, he could railroad his own cause. If, however, his optimistic assessment is correct, then this is the time to launch his appeal!

8:1-8 The example of the Macedonians

These first six verses constitute an introduction to Paul's argument. He is about to ask the community for money. This is never an easy task, and though Paul is hopeful that his reconciliation with the community is solid, he has to be cautious and avoid awakening any suspicions or hostile feelings. Thus he wisely begins by focusing on God, the Macedonians, and Titus. In this way Paul keeps himself out of the spotlight and lets the story of the Macedonian Christians rouse the Corinthians' emotions.

Despite their utter poverty, the Macedonians did not view the collection as an imposition but as a privilege through which they could express their fellowship with the "holy ones" (v. 4). They not only insisted on participating, but given the opportunity, they contributed "beyond their means" (v. 3) in a spirit of joy and generosity (v. 2). Paul attributes this abundant generosity not merely to the Macedonians' own goodness or sense of justice nor to anything he himself did or said, but to the grace (*charis*) of God (v. 1). In responding to this gift of grace, the Macedonians have shown their devotion to the Lord (v. 5). Their good example prompts Paul to urge Titus to go to Corinth (v. 6).

Whether Titus had been initially responsible for the collection drive among the Corinthians is unclear. There is no mention of him in conjunction with the collection instructions at 1 Corinthians 16:4. What we do know is that Titus had success among the Corinthians over other delicate issues, is purportedly well disposed toward them (see 7:7, 13b, 15), and is obviously equal to the task. By putting Titus in charge of the collection, Paul minimizes his own role and keeps himself in the background.

This story of the Macedonians' heroic generosity is quite moving and should have accomplished the desired effect of rousing the Corinthians' feelings of admiration or even envy, given their proud and competitive spirit. In either case, Paul has captured their attention and takes the occasion to exhort them not merely to participate in the collection but to excel in this gracious act (*charis*) of giving (v. 7). *Charis* can mean both "grace" and "gift" and is Paul's preferred term for the "collection." At verse 1 he used *charis* to refer to God's gift of grace given to the Macedonians, which enabled their own giving. Since, as Paul understands it, giving flows from being gifted, the Corinthians, who have been abundantly gifted by God, as underscored in verse 7, should naturally give freely and abundantly without being prodded. In fact, Paul refuses to mandate giving (v. 8), not because he fears their disobedience but because the gracious act/collection *(charis)* flows from the graces/gifts *(charismata)* received.

8:9-15 Motives for giving

Paul first relies on the example of Christ's own self-emptying gift *(charis)* to support his exhortation. His unique interpretation of Christ's self-emptying in terms of rich/poor is probably influenced by the current discussion and should not be taken as an indication of the historical Jesus' economic situation. At Philippians 2:6-11, we learn that Christ's self-emptying love demonstrated itself not only in the fact of incarnation but in the taking on the form of a "slave" and the subsequent total impoverishment that resulted from death on a cross. As a result of Jesus' self-emptying love, the Corinthians have been rescued from the poverty of alienation from God and restored to God's friendship (see 5:7-19). They are rich now. Paul proposes that they emulate Christ by manifesting their own love in their own self-emptying for the sake of enriching others. On a practical level, Paul would like to see this love be manifest in their participation in the collection. Thus he encourages them to complete what they had already begun, assuring them that whatever they contribute, if properly motivated, will be deemed acceptable (vv. 11-12).

In addition to the example of Christ's love, which should be the Corinthians' primary motivation, Paul invokes the principle of equality as another motive for giving. Relatively speaking, the Corinthians are better off than the members of the Jerusalem community. Paul clarifies that he is not suggesting that the Corinthians disadvantage themselves (v. 13). Rather, by giving of their current surplus, they would be supplying what the poor lack. It is important to note that Paul does not advocate self-impoverishment as an end in itself but in view of fostering an equitable balance of goods necessary for living. He apparently intends that

this principle of equality will be an ever-present motivating factor in all Christian communities, since he assures the Corinthians that if they were to fall on hard times, their needs would likewise be met in view of this same principle (v. 14). The citation from Exodus 16:18 recalls the distribution of manna in the desert according to need and serves to illustrate and support Paul's point (v. 15).

8:16–9:5 Titus, his collaborators, and the collection drive at Corinth

Paul now discloses the practical steps that will be taken to ensure that the Corinthians will heed his exhortation and come through on the collection. Paul renounces a direct role in the collection to avoid eliciting criticism that could undermine the collection (vv. 20-21). Instead, a delegation of three will be sent to Corinth to oversee the project. Paul delegates Titus, who has already had success among the community and is apparently anxious to go back and undertake this task. The identity of the second and third delegates is a matter of speculation. The second is simply referred to as "the brother," someone well known to all the churches and famed for his preaching (v. 18). He has been appointed "by the churches" (v. 19), though Paul does not say which churches. The third delegate, referred to as "our brother," that is, a member of Paul's entourage, is recommended for his earnestness (v. 22).

Paul returns in verse 23 to underscore Titus's status as his coworker and to qualify the other two delegates as representatives of the churches. If the Corinthians respond enthusiastically with regard to the collection, it will stand as a testimony to their love and be known to all the churches. Moreover, their cooperation will further vindicate Paul's boast, which can only serve to advance and strengthen the reconciliation between Paul and them (v. 24).

At 9:1 Paul now protests that it is superfluous to write to the Corinthians about the collection for the saints. It is not necessary to assume that this statement signals the start of a new, once originally independent letter. On further consideration, it becomes apparent that the mention of the collection allows Paul to reintroduce the topic of the Macedonians, but in such a way as to instigate the Corinthians to get onboard with the collection and cooperate with the delegates. Paul says that he has boasted to the Macedonians of the Corinthians' year-old eagerness to participate in the collection. He also reports that the Corinthians' example stirred the Macedonians' zeal for the collection and prompted them to contribute (v. 3). In fact, both Paul and the Corinthians know that they had done next to nothing about the collection since the previous year. Thus Paul gives the Corinthians fair warning that with the arrival of the advance delegation in Corinth, they had better expedite the project and be ready for Paul's arrival in the event that any Macedonians accompany Paul (vv. 3-4). Failure on the Corinthians' part would bring shame not only on themselves for being less generous than the poorer Macedonians, but on Paul too (v. 4). Yet Paul is hopeful that motives other than the desire to avoid shame will induce the proud Corinthians to attend earnestly to the collection. This is why he has sent an advance delegation. Their purpose is to encourage and help the Corinthians arrange for their "promised gift" so that it will be ready as a "bountiful gift" and not a last-minute act of begrudging giving (exaction) in order to save face (9:5).

9:6-15 The rewards of giving

Paul now offers a theological foundation, supported by scriptural citations, for his collection project. Picking up on the term "bountiful," he begins with a commonsense statement about sowing and harvesting (v. 6). Applied metaphorically to the topic of giving, what Paul suggests is that bountiful giving will produce bountiful rewards. But if generosity has its own rewards, the Corinthians need to realize that generous giving is made possible by God, who first provides the abundance, so that with their own needs met, the Corinthians can give from their abundance (v. 8). This statement reinforces the theological idea already present at 8:1-7, namely, that God is the one who graces/gifts and whose grace enables our gracious giving. That God is the source of all good works is reinforced at verse 9 with a citation from Psalm 111:9 and further reinforced in verse 10a, where the influence of Isaiah 55:10-11 is discernible. Here God is described as not only supplying the seed (grace), that is, creating the possibility of giving, but sustaining this good work of giving by continually multiplying the seed and increasing the "harvest of your righteousness" (v. 10; see Hos 12:10).

At verse 11, Paul reminds the Corinthians that they have already been richly endowed precisely for the sake of being generous "through us," that is, Paul and his collection project. Once the collection is distributed and the poor are assisted, they will give thanks to God for the generosity of the Corinthians, which God has enabled (v. 12), and ultimately God will be glorified (v. 13). Thus the Corinthians are again exhorted to contribute to the collection, not only for their own advantage but because in doing so they demonstrate their obedience to the gospel (v. 13). This authentic expression of Christianity, manifested in generous giving, will bring forth thanks to God for "his indescribable gift" (v. 15).

PAUL'S COUNTERATTACK ON THE INTRUDERS
2 Corinthians 10:1–13:10

Apart from some indirect gibes and insinuations apparently aimed at the rival apostles (see, e.g., 2:17; 3:1; 4:2; 7:2), Paul's primary focus up to this point in the letter has been his conflicted relationship with the community. His goal has been to overcome their differences and restore trust; in consequence, Paul was able to renew his appeal to the Corinthians concerning the collection. Now he turns to confront the intruders, who were attempting to upstage him and capitalize on the strained relationship to promote themselves.

This final unit serves as a kind of rhetorical knockout punch, packed with invective and sarcasm. Paul refutes accusations leveled against him (10:1-18) and positively contrasts himself with his rivals, who are exposed as charlatans (11:1–12:10). Paul then recaps his major points and brings up the subject of his imminent third visit to Corinth (12:11-21). With the mention of the visit, Paul transitions to the final chapter, where he issues a series of warnings to the community (13:1-10), which are followed by the epistolary conclusion (13:11-13). Throughout this unit Paul takes on his rivals, but his remarks are addressed to the Corinthians. Ultimately, his concern is to safeguard this community and bring about their obedience to the gospel so that when he returns to Corinth, he and they may again enjoy full partnership.

Paul refutes his opponents' accusations (10:1-18)

Two subunits are distinguishable in this opening segment of Paul's argument. The first, verses

1-11, begins and ends with the intruders' criticism of Paul in regard to rhetorical competence. In the second subunit, verses 12-18, Paul is concerned about territorial jurisdiction, around which he develops the theme of boasting in preparation for chapters 11–12.

10:1-11 Spiritual weapons

Paul begins with an exhortation, pointing to the gentleness and clemency of Christ (v. 1a), but quickly alludes to a criticism brought forth by his opponents (v. 1b). Paul denies that he lacks boldness. If he is meek and humble, it is in imitation of Christ. But he is quite prepared to deal boldly with his opponents, who claim that he walks "according to the flesh" (v. 2). In Paul, this phrase usually means to live a sinful life. However, beginning in verse 3, the context requires that the phrase be taken to mean according to human arguments/persuasive strategies. Paul renounces such cunning (see 4:2) and battles with spiritual weapons (literally "weapons powerful to God"), which will be so effective against the slick but vacuous arguments of his opponents that Paul will take every thought captive in obedience to Christ (vv. 4-5). In this battle Paul expects to overpower his smooth-talking opponents and win back the Corinthians to complete obedience to Christ, which also means full fellowship with Paul. When this occurs, Paul will punish his opponents, who subvert the gospel (v. 6).

As Paul continues, he commands the Corinthians to face the facts (v. 7a). It is doubtful that someone has accused him of not being Christian; rather, Paul's opponents probably alleged that he was not a true apostle and hence without authority. This seems to be supported by verse 8, where Paul boasts of the authority given him by the Lord. If the opponents were connected to the Jerusalem church, they may have claimed that they were possibly commissioned by Jesus himself (see 5:16) during his earthly ministry or by his immediate disciples. Since Paul cannot claim to have received his apostolic commission in this way, his opponents may have used this fact to discredit his apostolic legitimacy. Yet Paul insists that his claim to be "of Christ" is valid, and his exercise of apostolic authority is genuine, since it is ordered to building up the community (v. 8).

In verses 9-11, Paul returns to allegations concerning his weak personal presence and lack of rhetorical competence and assures the Corinthians that when he arrives, the allegations will be shown to be baseless.

10:12-18 Paul boasts in his own labors

After his ironic jab at his self-commending opponents (v. 12a), who use only one another as a basis of comparison and risk deluding themselves (v. 12b), Paul criticizes his opponents for overstepping boundaries by coming to Corinth to minister. This is not just a matter of guarding his own turf for selfish reasons. Corinth, a Gentile city, was part of Paul's ministerial jurisdiction to the Gentiles, apportioned to him and his co-workers by God (v. 13) and confirmed by the apostles at the Jerusalem council (see Gal 2:6-10).

Apparently, in Paul's mind the two broad ministerial jurisdictions established at this council along ethnic lines of demarcation—one for the circumcised/Jews, the other for the Gentiles—also implied geographical lines of demarcation. Unlike his opponents, who did not honor these boundaries, Paul did not overreach his territorial limits (v. 14) or build on anyone else's labors (v. 15). Thus Paul, who is approved by the Lord and whose work has been done within the limits established by God, is the one with the legitimate right to boast in what has been accomplished at Corinth (vv. 17-18).

The "fool's speech" (11:1–12:10)

In view of the recurrence of the words "fool," "foolishness," and "foolish," this segment of Paul's argument is usually referred to as the "fool's speech." Paul first explains why it is necessary that he engage in a little foolishness (11:1-21a) and then indulges in his own foolish boasting (11:16–12:10). Throughout this speech Paul deftly uses the rhetorical skill he was said to lack to deride his opponents and their claims.

11:1-21a A "little foolishness"

Though Paul considers boasting foolishness, he finds it necessary to engage in a "little foolishness" (v. 1) of his own, since the Corinthians not only tolerate the boasting of his opponents but also are swayed by them to accept a different gospel to their own peril (v. 4). Like the father of a bride, responsible for safeguarding the virginity of his daughter until she wed her betrothed, Paul's apostolic task is to preserve the community incorrupt for Christ alone. However, he fears that like Eve, seduced and deceived by Satan disguised as a serpent, the community was allowing itself to be seduced and corrupted by these superapostles. In comparison with these, Paul is in no way inferior (v. 5). Though he concedes that he lacks training in the art of oratory, he denies lacking knowledge, which he has abundantly demonstrated (v. 6).

In bringing up his practice of preaching the gospel free of charge (v. 7), Paul seems to have abruptly changed topics. However, this issue is closely linked to the charge of inferiority, since in Paul's day it was assumed that preachers without financial backing were second-rate. Paul now appears to be second-guessing himself, questioning whether his choice was a mistake, since it could be cited as further proof of his inferiority. If he were a true apostle, he should have taken the support due to him. He had already explained why he renounced his apostolic right to financial support (1 Cor 9) and does not repeat those reasons here. Here he simply asserts that he has not and will not burden the Corinthians (v. 9).

That the Corinthians continue to find grounds in this for despising Paul as inferior is not his problem. He will not allow his preaching of the gospel to be compromised by the patronage system and intends to boast of his independence from such social conventions. And he will continue to operate this way! This is not because he disdains the Corinthians, whom he assures of his love (v. 11). Rather, his goal is to stop the superapostles from using the Corinthians' financial support to feign friendship and manipulate allegiance when their real intention is to supplant Paul and boast of the successful mission at Corinth as if it were the result of their work and not his (v. 12). Paul's verbal assault on these predators is vehement. He rejects them as false apostles and deceivers. Masquerading as apostles of Christ, they are actually ministers of Satan. According to Jewish tradition, Satan disguised himself as an angel of light (see *Apocalypse of Moses* 17:1-2). Thus, like Satan, so his followers. Paul concludes this tirade with a short eschatological statement obviously intended as a threat. In the end, they will be unmasked, and their judgment will correspond to their deeds.

After ten verses of defense and attack, Paul reminds his readers that he is going to begin his "fool's speech," even though it goes against his own better judgment (v. 16). The circumstances require that he take on the role of a boaster. By doing this, he risks being considered foolish, but he fears far greater risks to the community if he does not. The Corinthians should be able to deal with him in this assumed role, since they gladly put up with *real* fools (v. 19)! This stinging sarcasm continues as Paul describes the excessive tolerance of the "wise" Corinthians, who put up with the worst abuses at the hands of their ministers (v. 20)! Paul's mocking depiction of the Corinthians as gullible pawns is intended to force them to realize how foolish is their attachment to his opponents, who actually victimize the community. Paul concludes with an admission of weakness, but this is probably intended ironically, since he is about to boast quite boldly.

11:21b–12:10 Paul's foolish boasting

The fool's speech proper begins here. The agenda for this bragging contest is set by the opponents. Whatever they dare boast of, Paul will too (v. 21b). The contest begins with a focus on titles. On the first point, Paul can equally claim the three titles Hebrew, Israelite, descendant of Abraham, which are claimed with boastful pride by his opponents (v. 22). Ethnically, culturally, and religiously, there is simply no disparity between himself and the rivals.

When it comes to the next title, "ministers of Christ," Paul ironically stakes his claim to this title, not on powerful deeds or notable accomplishments, as his rivals did, but on suffering—and Paul's were unparalleled (v. 23b)! He lists them in spades, bragging about all the dangers, hardships, beatings, deprivation, and humiliation he has endured throughout his ministry (vv. 24-28). All this suffering, which had been cited by his opponents to discredit his apostolic authority and ministry, Paul now shamelessly showcases as that which legitimates his claim to the title "minister of Christ." Paul is clearly the supersufferer! Since suffering and affliction, paradoxically, constitute the credentials of a true apostle and authentic minister (see 4:7– 5:10), the Corinthians should recognize Paul's apostolic legitimacy.

In this clever and ironic twist, Paul has pulled the rug out from under his opponents, who consider demonstrations of power authenticators of apostolic ministry. Paul knows very well that his opponents would never admit of, let alone boast of, weakness, even if they had suffered! Thus the irony of his question, "Who is weak, and I am not weak?" (v. 29)!

Since Paul must boast, he boasts of another episode of weakness and indignity—his escape from Damascus (vv. 30-33; see also Acts 9:23-25). His purpose in adding this particular example to the catalogue of hardships already recited is illumined by the contemporary Roman military practice of awarding the "wall crown" to the first soldier to scale the enemy's wall. By contrast, Paul is but a weakling, an anti-hero being shuttled down the wall in a basket! Paul's intentional spoof on the practice of recognizing and rewarding displays of power is a perfect lead-in to the last item of comparison in the fool's speech (12:1-10).

Apparently the superapostles had impressed the Corinthians with displays of spiritual power and descriptions of ecstatic experiences. Paul knows that comparing such experiences serves no purpose (v. 1), since weakness, rather than displays of power, authenticates ministry. However, having been forced into this boasting contest, Paul has no choice but to recount a revelatory experience of his own. His reluctance is evident in the fact that he speaks in the third person. This is a rhetorical device that allows him to distance himself from this visionary episode, which, though extraordinary, has little to do with the authenticity of his daily ministry. Only God knows how "this person" was transported to Paradise, the highest of heavens, where he was granted special revelations meant to be kept secret (vv. 3-4). About "this person" Paul has reason to boast (v. 5), since he has been granted access to a place few have been permitted to enter and has been privy to ineffable revelations.

But at this point Paul again subverts the boasting contest by introducing his own terms: "about myself I will not boast, except about my weaknesses" (v. 5b). Were he to boast about his experience to impress the Corinthians, he would be telling the truth, since he has had an "abundance of the revelations" (vv. 6-7a). But he will not boast, because he has been given a "thorn in the flesh." Though the exact nature of this affliction is not certain, its purpose is. Paul twice emphasizes that this "thorn" was given to him precisely to prevent his being "too elated" (v. 7). Paul's thrice-repeated plea that he be relieved of this suffering is reminiscent of Jesus' supplication in the garden (see

Matt 26:39-44). The Lord's answer (v. 9), presented as authoritative divine revelation, reminds Paul that the only thing that counts is God's grace—not mystical experiences or human displays of power, but God's grace.

Moreover, God's "power" (v. 9; here a synonym for grace) is brought to perfection in weakness. Thus Paul need not seek to overcome weakness and avoid suffering. When he is weakest, as measured by human standards, he is strongest, not by the dint of his own resources but by the grace/power of God paradoxically manifested in weakness. Rather than despising Paul, the Corinthians ought to recognize that his weakness is powerful testimony that God is at work in their apostle's life and ministry. In light of this revelation, Paul's conclusion makes perfect sense: he will boast of his weakness and be content with his hardships (vv. 10-11).

In the end, even though Paul's revelatory experience ironically turned out to be another affirmation of his weakness, he has won this boasting contest. He has won not on his opponents' terms nor even on his own, but ultimately on God's terms. God manifested his power and wisdom in the weakness and folly of the cross (see 1 Cor 1:18-31), and God continues to do so in the weakness and suffering of his ministers, whose lives are conformed to the life of Jesus (see 4:10-11).

12:11-21 Epilogue and transition

The fool's speech is over, and as if embarrassed by his own peacock performance, Paul reminds the Corinthians that their failure to support him forced him into foolish self-commendation (v. 11). Having excused himself, Paul now recaps major points made in the two preceding sections. He is not inferior. Opponents may call him a "nothing," but no number of insults can change the fact that he is a true apostle (v. 11c). Though Paul refrains from saying that he accomplished signs among the Corinthians, he insists that they "were performed among you" (v. 12). The use of the passive may be intended to underscore the power of God at work through the apostle's weakness. Paul then restates his motive for refusing their support (v. 13). His request that they forgive him for this "wrong" is pure sarcasm.

Paul is ready to go back to the community and announces an imminent visit (v. 14a). His founding visit to Corinth was followed by a second, "painful" visit (chs. 1–2). This will be his third (v. 14). His refusal to accept their financial support remains a delicate issue. Paul tries to dispel the rancor about his praxis by showing that his motives, unlike those of his opponents, who are indirectly impugned here, are selfless. First he stresses that his interest is in them and not their possessions (v. 14b). Then he points to the customary financial setup between children and parents. In view of this, it is clear that Paul alone behaves as a true parent to the Corinthians, while his opponents subvert this natural order of things by taking. While they live off Paul's spiritual children, he is impelled by his profound love for the Corinthians "to spend" himself and be "spent" for them (vv. 14c-15).

The comparison between Paul and his opponents is implicit in his emotionally charged question, "If I love you more, am I to be loved less?" (v. 15c). If the Corinthians are honest, they will have to admit that they have been shortchanging Paul when it comes to love and support. They will also have to grant that Paul has truly never burdened them (v. 16a). However, Paul knows that his opponents have planted the suspicion that he is deceitfully living off the Corinthians by covertly siphoning money from what they had put aside for the collection (v. 16b). Paul denies doing this. In fact, he has opted out of direct involvement in the collection and is sending Titus (see 8:16-24). On a previous mission to Corinth, Titus had been positively impressed by the Corinthians, who apparently felt comfortable and confident enough with him to admit their error (see 7:5-15). If the community has confidence in Titus, who shares with Paul the "same" values and approach to ministry, to suspect Paul of dishonesty is not only unfounded but also illogical.

Paul knows that what he has said sounds like a defense, and in many ways it has been, but he hastens to add that his testimony before God in Christ (see 2:17) is part of his apostolic service to upbuild the community (see 10:8). Paul's apprehension about this trip derives from concerns about what he may discover upon his return to Corinth. His fear is that the unity and holiness of the community are still being compromised by the same litigious and immoral behavior (vv. 21-22) that he had already addressed in 1 Corinthians. If so, Paul also fears that he may be in for

another humiliating experience, comparable to what occurred on his second visit. His announcement of an imminent visit, his expressed fear that the Corinthians had still not conformed their lives to the gospel, and his mention of unrepentant sinners provide the transition to the concluding chapter.

13:1-10 Final warnings

The juridical significance of the qualifier "third" (v. 1a) is made clear in v. 1b, where Paul cites a legal prescription which states that the testimony of at least two or three witnesses is required to convict an alleged wrongdoer (see Deut 19:15). Paul had witnessed wrongdoing and served warning on his second visit, which he now repeats in absentia (v. 2a). Should he again find anyone persisting in wrongdoing on this third visit, Paul's case against the wrongdoers would be conclusively established (v. 2b). Paul will not be lenient in dealing with unrepentant sinners and offers this as proof to the community that Christ is speaking through him (vv. 2c-3a). As Paul's weakness testified to his conformity to Christ, so also does his power. Paul will come in the power of Christ and deal boldly with the Corinthians (v. 4).

In the next series of admonitions (vv. 5-9), Paul, who has been under intense scrutiny with regard to his apostolic authenticity, turns the tables and admonishes the Corinthians to scrutinize themselves about their own authenticity. Examine and test yourselves, Paul cautions. Are you living in the faith, that is, do your lives conform to the gospel? Would your lives show that Christ is in you?

Though Paul expresses himself in a somewhat convoluted way in verses 6-9, the import of these statements is this: what the Corinthians think of Paul is less important than whether they advance in their life in Christ and commitment to the gospel. If this occurs, it does not matter to Paul whether or not he is judged an authentic apostle by their criteria. He has acted according to the truth and rejoices when the Corinthians are strong even if he is weak. Paul can and does pray for the community. However, in the end it is up to the Corinthians to renew their commitment to Christ and to live as true Christians. Paul's hope is that this severe written warning will be effective. Otherwise, despite claims to the contrary (see 10:10), Paul will be severe when he is again present among them and will exercise his apostolic authority to build up this community, which risks destroying itself.

EPISTOLARY CONCLUSION

2 Corinthians 13:11-13

After bidding the Corinthians to rejoice, Paul exhorts them to mend their ways, encourage one another, agree with one another, and live in peace (v. 11). These exhortations recall the situation of 1 Corinthians, where Paul had to deal with immoral lives in need of reform (1 Cor 5–6); disedifying rather than mutually upbuilding behavior (1 Cor 8–10); disagreement (1 Cor 1–4); and discord (1 Cor 12–14). The reader who gets the impression that the situation at Corinth has not significantly improved is probably right. Paul has tirelessly preached the gospel and labored to create a community of believers at Corinth. In the end, though, it is the responsibility of each believer to make Christian community a reality at Corinth. Whether Paul is absent or present, the Corinthians, who are Paul's partners in the work of the gospel, are responsible for the continual renewal of their lives and the work of reconciliation (see 5:17-20). Once they are a community of love and peace, then the God of love and peace will dwell among them.

After hearing this letter read to them, the Corinthians were to exchange a "holy kiss," a symbol of each member's willingness to heed Paul's exhortation and to work toward unity and reconciliation. Paul typically closes his letters with a blessing, but this is the only time he invokes the blessings of the Lord Jesus Christ, God, and the holy Spirit (v. 14). While the prayer is Trinitarian in structure, it does not necessarily express all that is understood about the nature of God as enunciated in the doctrine of the Trinity. In the context of this letter, what the prayer does express is Paul's sincere desire that through the outpouring of Christ's grace, through which the community has come to know the love of God, they may live in the fellowship of the holy Spirit, who indwells each of them and is the source and sustainer of their unity in Christ.

THE LETTER TO THE

GALATIANS

Robert J. Karris, O.F.M.

INTRODUCTION

I write this commentary for beginners and those who want a quick refresher course for preaching. But this is not a "commentary for dummies," for I envision my beginning readers as people who want clear but not simplistic exposition. I stand on the shoulders of other commentators and will acknowledge them, especially the premier commentator of our era, J. Louis Martyn.

To get us thinking about the complex thought world behind the letter to the Galatians, I tell the story of the poor friars who planned to raise money for a new bell tower by selling flowers from the friary garden. Their business became so popular that it adversely affected the trade of the local florist, who tried by various means to get the friars to sell honey or bread instead. Finally, he hired the local thug, Hugh McNails, who beat up the friars and persuaded them to close their flower shop. The moral of the story is: Only Hugh can prevent florist friars.

Readers from the United States might groan over the moral of this story, but they would get the pun. But readers from Europe would have a hard time understanding what was going on. You see, for some sixty years the Ad Council, along with the federal and state governments, has been so successful in promoting a slogan that 95 percent of U.S. adults and 77 percent of children recognize Smokey Bear and his slogan: "Only you can prevent forest fires." So it is understandable that Americans would recognize the pun.

In reading Galatians, we Americans are often like people from Europe who have not been exposed to Smokey Bear's slogan. When Paul talks about "the elemental powers" in Galatians 4:9, people of his time would know what he is referring to, whereas we scratch our heads in wonderment. The Jews of Paul's day would have little difficulty picking up on Paul's references to Abraham in Galatians 3–4, whereas Gentiles at that time and we today might be left in the dark.

Let me take the Smokey Bear slogan a step further. Behind that slogan stand an entire governmental structure and a view of society. Who has the power to influence 280 million people to hold such name recognition if not the federal government, which promotes freedom of speech and which has power across state lines? The appeal to "you," an individual, and not to communities is quintessentially American. In a similar way, behind the phrase "the elemental powers" stands a view of reality in which the four powers of water, air, earth, and fire are the elementary building blocks of the world. Behind the name "Abraham" stands the entire story of God's dealings with the chosen people. In brief, this commentary aims to see what stories are at work in Galatians.

What makes Galatians tick?

Galatians is so short that readers sometimes think that it will be a breeze to read and comprehend. But after Paul's relatively simple narrative account in chapters 1 and 2, readers may stumble through the rest of the letter. Let me isolate the building blocks of Galatians and point to the cement that holds these blocks together.

The master plan of Galatians is that of an R&R letter: rebuke, which commences at 1:6, and request, which begins at 4:12. The most evident building blocks of this master plan are its beginning in 1:1-5 and its conclusion in 6:11-18. As we will see in the commentary proper, astute readers can pretty well discover the main thrust of Galatians from these two blocks of material. Paul tells the Galatians what he wants to say, then says his piece, and summarizes what he has said.

The largest building blocks are twofold: situational and preformed. What I call the preformed materials comprise the vast majority of Galatians: Paul's apologetic autobiography in 1:11–2:21, his argument from Scripture in 3:5–4:7, his scriptural allegory in 4:21-31, and his exhortations in 5:1–6:10. While these materials are not exactly cookie-cutter pieces, they give the impression that Paul has used them before. On the other hand, the situational building blocks are the means by which Paul makes Galatians and its preformed materials distinct, much as exterior and interior designs make "seen-one-seen-them-all" houses distinct in large subdivisions. Also, it is from these situational sections that we glimpse what is going on behind the scenes in Galatians 1:1-5; 1:6-10; 3:1-5; 4:8-11; 4:12-20; 5:2-12; 6:11-18.

The cement that holds these building blocks together consists of the three components of Paul's rhetoric. Like any good speaker or writer, Paul has to establish or reinforce his position as a person of trust, integrity, and goodwill. The Greeks called this *ethos,* from which our word "ethics" derives. Paul consumes almost all of Galatians 1–2 reestablishing his trustworthiness: his gospel is from God, not from human beings.

As a good speaker, Paul argues his case according to the *logic* of the time. He uses the argument of examples. He himself and Abraham are examples in Galatians 1–3. Paul also argues from accepted principles of faith. I give two examples. In 5:1 Paul first states the premise and then draws the conclusion, introducing it with the inferential adverb "so" (*oun* in Greek): "For freedom Christ set us free; *so* stand firm and do not submit again to the yoke of slavery." Sometimes Paul states his conclusion first and then enunciates his premise. A good example occurs in 5:4-6. In 5:4 Paul gives his conclusion from the two principles of faith he first articulates in 5:5-6. I put in italics the inferential particle "for" (*gar* in Greek):

> 5:4. You are separated from Christ, you who are trying to be justified by law; you have fallen from grace. 5. *For* through the Spirit, by faith, we await the hope of righteousness. 6. *For* in Christ Jesus, neither circumcision nor uncircumcision counts for anything, but only faith working through love.

Finally, Paul uses *pathos* to engage the hearts of his listeners. I give two quick examples. Who can read Galatians 4:13-20 and not realize that Paul is smuggling himself into the hearts of his beloved Galatian brothers and sisters: "So now have I become your enemy by telling you the truth?" (4:16). Galatians 1:6 is a wake-up slap in the face: "I am amazed that you are so quickly forsaking the one who called you!!" I recall in this context a cartoon that shows Paul with a startled look on his face as he reads a letter: "You have time to write to the Corinthians, the Thessalonians, the Philippians, but I'm amazed that you're too busy to sit down and write a simple letter to your mother!"

These three ingredients of Paul's rhetoric are operative today. Analyze any president's State of the Union address, and you'll see ethos, logic, and pathos on dress parade. This example also prepares us for reading Galatians, for not everyone on both sides of the aisle will be giving a standing ovation for every argument the president makes. Did all Galatians applaud Paul's letter to them? Were the teachers/influencers won over by Paul's argumentation?

The teachers or influencers from outside

I agree with contemporary scholars who avoid the labels "Judaizers" or "opponents" to talk about the people behind the scenes who occasioned Galatians. I will follow J. Louis Martyn and Mark D. Nanos, who call these outsiders "the teachers" and "the influencers" respectively. The scholarly community mainly uses the method of mirror reading to ascertain what these teachers/influencers were advocating. That is, scholars accentuate the situational building blocks and from them try to discern why Paul is using the preformed materials he selects. Finally, they reconstruct through these mirrors what was happening in the Galatian churches.

For example, in the situational materials on Galatians 1:1-5, Paul underscores his call to be an apostle from Jesus Christ and not from human beings. So the inference is made that the teachers/ influencers were saying that the gospel Paul preaches to the Gentiles is of human origin. The pre-formed materials of Galatians 1–2 seem to corroborate that inference, for Paul argues mightily that his gospel came from divine revelation and not from the earlier apostles, who, indeed, did not force him to alter his gospel.

Another example occurs in Galatians 3:1-5, where Paul argues that the Galatians' faith came from Paul's preaching and the Spirit and not from works of the law (including circumcision). The remainder of chapter 3 will deal with the case of Abraham, to whom the promise was made before the mandate of circumcision. In brief, we infer from these indications that the teachers/influencers asserted that the Galatian Christian males had to be circumcised and that all Galatian Christians had to observe the Jewish law to be true Christians.

Date and destination

I date Galatians between A.D. 50 and 55, and thus before Romans. I tend to agree with J. Louis Martyn that Paul wrote it to his converts in North Galatia, or the territory of Galatia, and not to his converts in South Galatia, or the Roman province of Galatia.

COMMENTARY

ADDRESS

Galatians 1:1-5

1:1-5 Salutation and anticipation of the letter's theme

If you compare this salutation with the salutations of the other genuine Pauline letters, except the letter to the Romans, you will note that Paul has expanded his normal greeting. Take, for example, the salutation in 1 Thessalonians 1:1: "Paul, Silvanus, and Timothy to the church of the Thessalonians in God the Father and the Lord Jesus Christ: grace to you and peace." Galatians 1:1-5 retains the skeleton of the typical Pauline greeting: "Paul to . . ., grace to you and peace," but has much more.

Galatians 1:1 makes two key points. First, Paul underlines the fact that he is the one sent, the apostle of Jesus Christ and God the Father, and not the emissary of some human being, no matter how exalted. Paul will focus on this factor in even greater detail in 1:11–2:21. The second point that Paul makes in Galatians 1:1 is that God the Father raised Jesus from the dead. What had been expected to occur at the end of time in Jewish eschatological expectation, namely, the resurrection of the dead, has broken into time and space now in the resurrection of the Jewish Messiah, Christ Jesus. In the light of this event, can business in the Jewish and Christian communities be conducted as usual?

The second notable expansion of Paul's normal greeting is found in Galatians 1:4, where he probably quotes an early confession that uses sacrificial terminology and then modifies it with one that employs apocalyptic terms. The confession reads: The Lord Jesus has given himself to take away our sins, that is, to eliminate the death-bearing effects of our sins. Implied is the fact that Jesus the Lord did this through the sacrifice of himself on the cross and not through obedience to the law. Using apocalyptic expressions, Paul states that the result and purpose of Jesus' death are our rescue from the present evil age.

Further, Jesus' death has end-of-the-world implications, for it has rescued believers, both Gentiles and Jews, from the present evil age, where sin and death roam about and take captive for their purposes even such a good thing as the law, God's gift to Israel. In brief, Paul anticipates his theme. With the death and resurrection of Jesus, the end of time has come forward and the new creation has begun (see Gal 6:15).

LOYALTY TO THE GOSPEL

Galatians 1:6-10

1:6-10 The beginning of the rebuke part of Galatians

While other letters in antiquity and Paul's letters follow the greeting with a thanksgiving period, Galatians does not. Was Paul so angry with the Galatians that he shot right past the normal courtesy of a thanksgiving? No, he adapted the rebuke statement that was also common in letter writing after the greeting. I paraphrase a pertinent example: "I am amazed that after all my instruction, you have botched the job, etc." The rebuke presupposes some close relationship between the sender and the recipient of the letter. Paul will be spelling out the reasons for his rebuke right up to 4:12, where he makes his request.

In Galatians 1:6 Paul makes it very clear that some of the Galatians are in the process, not of forsaking him and his preaching, but of forsaking God and the new creation they are enjoying. In the situational verse, Galatians 1:7, he also provides another hint of what is happening among the Galatians, for "some . . . are disturbing" them. The "disturbance" in question is not a telemarketer calling at dinnertime or someone playing loud music at two in the morning. Rather the disturbance is moral, on the level of conscience.

I find a wonderful parallel in 1 Thessalonians 1:9-10, where Paul reminds his Gentile converts that they "turned to God from idols to serve the living and true God and to await his Son from heaven, whom he raised from [the] dead, Jesus, who *delivers us from the coming wrath*" (emphasis added). It seems that the teachers/influencers are telling the Galatians that Paul's gospel will not deliver them from God's wrath. In our terms, unless the Galatians supplement Paul's teaching with theirs, they're going to hell.

PAUL'S DEFENSE OF HIS GOSPEL AND HIS AUTHORITY

Galatians 1:11–2:21

1:11-24 Paul, zealot for ancestral traditions, becomes apostle to Gentiles

Among the major points in Galatians 1:11–2:21 is Paul's example. Paul insists: Even though I was a zealot for Judaism and its ancestral traditions, I gave it all up. Thus this section prepares for Paul's plea in 4:12: "Be as I am, because I have also become as you are." Paul is saying: "You Galatians are trying to go back to where I was before Christ's revelation of a new creation to me. Don't do it." Parallels to Paul's call are best found in Philippians 3:4-16, where Paul accentuates his zeal for observance of the law: "In righteousness based on the law I was blameless" (Phil 3:6).

Another major point in this section is Paul's insistence that his gospel for and to the Gentiles did not come to him from human agency or human tradition, even that of Cephas (Peter), but from revelation. It was God who called Paul as God earlier had called prophets such as Jeremiah and revealed his Son to Paul (1:15-16). From Galatians 1:4 we know that the word "Son" is shorthand for the Son's significance in the story of humankind: The Son, who died for our sins and was raised from the dead, rescues Jews and Gentiles from this evil age.

2:1-14 Paul fights for inclusive table fellowship

As Paul continues his apology for his apostolic ministry and gospel to the Gentiles, we should keep in mind the wise counsel of George Lyons: "Ancient autobiographies were more concerned with ethical characterization and edification than with chronology and exactitude" (p. 60). So Luke's account in Acts 15 and Paul's account here of what happened at the Council of Jerusalem may both be true, since they are told from two different perspectives.

Paul's main points are threefold. The first point concerns the rite of circumcision, by which males entered into the chosen people and committed themselves to observe God's gift of the law. The leaders of the Jerusalem church did not compel Paul to circumcise Titus (2:3) or add the ritual of circumcision to his apostolic ministry (2:6).

The second point occurs twice, in 2:5 and 2:14: "the truth of the gospel." While the good news or gospel at Paul's time might refer to a military victory or the birth of an emperor who would change the world and effect lasting peace, for Paul the gospel of Jesus Christ has the power to save through the gift of the Spirit and effects a new creation amidst the old structures of the world. The new creation effected by the gospel has replaced any distinction based on circumcision and uncircumcision: "For neither does circumcision mean anything, nor does uncircumcision, but only a new creation" (Gal 6:15). This is the truth of the gospel; this is "our freedom that we have in Christ Jesus" (2:4). In Paul's view, the teachers/influencers want to liberate the Galatians from this freedom and enslave them by means of circumcision and observance of the law (2:4).

A question introduces the third point: Why the big fuss over who eats what with whom? I answer that food and drink are languages. Do you eat hot dogs on Christmas? Do you toast the bride and groom with water at a wedding? Indeed, not all days are equal; some should be celebrated with better-quality food and drink. Religion also enters into the area of food and drink, as Christians quickly realize when they reflect on the eucharistic bread and wine and Roman Catholics recall their obligation to fast and abstain on Good Friday.

As is the case today, during Paul's time the quality and quantity of food and drink were also social markers. Even at the same symposium, which consisted of eating, a libation to the gods, and drinking with conversation, the patron may have received better food, while his clients were given inferior fare. Jews may have sat in the same room with Gentiles but dined at their own table on specially prepared kosher food and drink. It seems to me that Philip Esler has provided a very helpful way to view what was happening during table fellowship in Antioch. As Jewish and Gentile Christians shared one loaf and one cup, some Jewish Christians were overwhelmed with the fear that a Gentile Christian, not having completely forgotten idolatrous ways, may have secretively offered a drop of eucharistic wine to a god. How could a person put oneself in the position of participating in such idolatry?

2:15-21 Righteousness, the works of the law, and faith

There are three issues in Galatians 2:16. The meaning of righteousness or justification is the first one. The image seems to stem from the criminal law court system, where a person (or a people) is acquitted, vindicated, judged in the right. Helpful background is Psalm 143:1-2:

> LORD, hear my prayer;
> in your faithfulness listen to my pleading;
> answer me in your justice.
> Do not enter into judgment with your servant;
> before you no living being can be just.

When sinful human beings as God's elect appear before God's law court, God in gracious mercy acquits them; they do not justify or acquit themselves. Modern computer technology has come to our interpretive aid in this matter by supplying the example of word-processing programs that justify margins, that is, they make them straight. Without word processing, the words on this page would not have straight left and right margins but would be out of order, in chaos.

The second issue concerns the meaning of "the works of the law." From the immediate context of Galatians 1–2, it seems that the phrase "the works of the law" refers to those things that distinguish Jews from Gentiles, namely, circumcision, dietary laws, and festivals. But from Galatians 3–4 it seems better to take "the works of the law" in a more comprehensive sense to refer to observance of the law.

In the third issue, grammar and christology hold hands: Is the Greek genitive *Iesou Christou* objective, subjective, or authorial? For years scholars have taken it to be objective, that is, "faith in Jesus Christ." A more appealing interpretation is to take this genitive to be subjective, that is, "the faithfulness that Jesus Christ manifested in his death on the cross for us." If the genitive is authorial, then Jesus Christ is the author of both his and the Christians' faith.

From these three considerations I draw some conclusions. Paul is not attacking the Jews as an arrogant people who are trying to earn heaven by their meritorious deeds. Paul gives himself as an example of how a Jewish zealot became the preacher of a law-free gospel to Gentiles. Through Christ's death and resurrection for us, God has shown a new way of being righteous with God's people. Men do not need to be circumcised, people do not need to observe dietary laws and the sabbath to become members of God's people in Christ. As we will soon see in chapter 3, Paul deals with the big picture—the story of how God fashions a community of faith by liberating people from the powers of the old age and inaugurating a new creation.

FAITH AND LIBERTY

Galatians 3:1–4:31

3:1-5 The Spirit's role in Christian life

Galatians 3:1-5 begins another long section of rebuke and personal example. In a culture that cherished wisdom, Paul's rebuke of the foolishness of the Galatians is harsh. The example that follows throughout chapter 3 is that of Abraham, who was justified without circumcision. Galatians 3:1-5, along with 3:6-29, allows us to glimpse the preaching of the teachers/influencers, who are championing "the works of the law," especially circumcision. Paul reminds the Galatians that in a very graphic way he had preached Jesus Christ crucified to them and that they listened to this message, which elicited faith. Their faith did not come from "the works of the law," about which they had not yet heard. The gifts of God's powerful Spirit did not come to them from their performance of "the works of the law," about which they were blissfully ignorant.

Paul draws the logical conclusion from his argument based on the Galatians' actual experience: Are you so stupid that you don't recognize that you have already received God's eschatological gift of the Spirit and don't need to complete your faith or membership in God's people with "the works of the law"? With a telling play on two meanings of the word "flesh," that is, flesh as circumcision of the foreskin and flesh as the realm of human weakness, Paul further castigates the Galatians for their stupidity of beginning in the ways of God's powerful Spirit and ending with the flesh. In 5:13–6:10 Paul will return to this contrast of flesh and Spirit when he gives guidance about Christian conduct.

3:6-29 The story of Abraham, the law, Abraham's seed, and us

There are many starting points for the story of St. Francis of Assisi. Some authors start with Christ's command to Francis: "Repair my house." Others commence with Francis's overcoming of his dread of lepers, pariahs of his society. Still others underscore Francis's profound experience of God, who to Francis was "My God and my All." The stories told from these starting points will have many things in common, for example, the economic situation of the time, the importance of Lateran Council IV, the crusades against another pariah of that society, the Muslim. Each story, however, will end up with its singular view of Francis of Assisi and what his life meant then and might mean now.

In 3:6-29 Paul is telling the story of Abraham, the law, Abraham's Seed, which is Christ Jesus,

and us. His telling of this story seems very different from the way the teachers/influencers were telling it. Yet both they and Paul were using the same common materials, that is, Israel's Scriptures in their Greek version, the Septuagint. Whereas Paul's starting point is Christ Jesus and his faithfulness, the starting point of the teachers/influencers seems to have been God's covenant made with Abraham, which was sealed by circumcision and in which believers remained by faithfully observing the law.

Notice how often Paul refers in this passage to Jesus Christ, who is Paul's real starting point and the goal of the story of Abraham. See, for example, Galatians 3:16, where Paul interprets God's promise to Abraham and his seed to refer to Christ. Galatians 3:23-29 is permeated with references to Christ Jesus. For example, 3:23 reads: "Before faith came, we were held in custody under law, confined for the faith that was to be revealed." As Sam K. Williams says so well, the word "faith" here is best translated as "Jesus-Christ-faith."

From his starting point of Jesus Christ, Paul returns to the story of Abraham. It seems that the teachers/influencers commenced their story with Genesis 17:10-11, where God instructs Abraham: "And this is the covenant that you shall keep between me and you and your seed after you for their generations. Every male among you will be circumcised . . . this circumcision will be a sign of the covenant between me and you" (author's translation). Paul, however, commences his story of Abraham by quoting Genesis 15:6: "Abraham believed God, and it was credited to him as righteousness" (3:6; author's translation). By selecting Genesis 15:6 as his key text, Paul scores the big point that Abraham is the father of faith, not of circumcision, for he believed and was declared righteous before he or his descendant was even circumcised.

Having made his point that God justified Abraham by faith, Paul then turns back to the promise God made to Abraham in Genesis 12:3: "All the nations will be blessed through you" (author's translation). By means of his citations of Genesis 15:6 and 12:3, Paul can conclude against the teachers/influencers: "Consequently, those who have faith [the Gentiles] are blessed along with Abraham who had faith" (Gal 3:9).

In Galatians 3:10-25 Paul uses Scripture and human analogies to deal with the role of God's gift of the law. In 3:10-14 Paul uses four Scripture texts to attack the teachers'/influencers' reading of Deuteronomy that God's blessings descend upon those who obey the law. Against their reading Paul quotes Deuteronomy 27:26: "Cursed be everyone who does not persevere in doing all the things written in the book of the law" (author's translation). Implied is that no one can fully obey the law and therefore falls under the curse. Paul supports his case in 3:11 by quoting Habakkuk 2:4 about the centrality of faith, not the law: "The one who is righteous by faith will live" (author's translation).

Then, in 3:12 Paul summons the Pentateuch to ground his position, as he cites Leviticus 18:5: "The one who does these things [the matters of the law] will live by them" and not find true life. Finally, in a daring soteriological move Paul returns to Deuteronomy 27:26 to pick up the theme of "cursed be everyone" and to integrate it with another passage in Deuteronomy that speaks of "cursed be everyone": "Cursed be everyone who hangs on a tree" (Deut 21:23; author's translation). Paul then professes his faith: "Christ ransomed us from the curse of the law by becoming a curse for us" (3:13).

In Galatians 3:15-18 Paul builds his argument about the deficiency of the law by using an analogy and Scripture. Paul's analogy of a human will and testament employs the same Greek word behind "covenant" (diatheke) and depends upon the legality that no one can annul or amend the will once it has been ratified. Reading the Septuagint of Genesis 13:15, 17:8, 24:7, Paul states that God's promise was to Abraham and to his "descendant" in the singular. Of course, in Paul's eyes that singular descendant is Christ (3:16). Calculating the time between Abraham and the Sinai covenant, Paul makes his case that the law, which came 430 years later (see Exod 12:40), cannot annul God's promises made to Abraham and through him to the Gentiles.

In Galatians 3:19-25 Paul gives two answers to his question: "Why, then, the law?" (3:19). Galatians 3:19-22, especially 3:19, provides the first answer: "It was added for transgressions." The context indicates that the law was added to restrain transgressions. In this sense it was the disciplinarian of which Paul talks in 3:24-25. In 3:19 Paul masks God's action in giving the law: "It was promulgated by angels at the hand of a mediator." As Leviticus 26:46 clearly indicates, the mediator was Moses. The role of the angels in the giving of the law finds a parallel in the Septuagint of Deu-

teronomy 33:2 at the giving of the law: "the angels were with God at God's right hand" (author's translation). See also Acts 7:53.

In a mini-summary of the points he has been making from verse 10 onward, Paul writes: "For if a law had been given that could bring life, then righteousness would in reality come from the law. But scripture confined all things under the power of sin, that through the faithfulness of Jesus Christ the promise might be given to those who believe" (3:21-22; author's translation). Paul will have more to say about the law in Romans 7:12: "So then the law is holy, and the commandment is holy and righteous and good."

In Galatians 3:23-25 Paul gives a second answer to the question "Why the law?" He uses two images: imprisonment (confined in custody) and that of a disciplinarian. Both of these images are severe but point to a temporary reality, until Jesus-Christ-faith has come onto the scene.

Paul concludes his argument with the teachers/influencers by calling the Galatians' attention to baptism, by which they become one in Christ Jesus, who is Abraham's descendant. Galatians 3:28 is most likely a liturgical formula that describes the new eschatological reality of Christian community effected by Christ's death and resurrection and the gift of the promised Spirit. For Paul's purposes, the first line is most important: "There is neither Jew nor Greek"/Gentile. Christian communities are still wrestling with the implementation of the vision of this confessional statement of the new reality in Christ Jesus: "There is neither slave nor free person, there is not male and female; for you are all one in Christ Jesus."

If we go back to my opening example of stories about Francis of Assisi, I would say that one major criterion by which we can judge the truth of each story is this: Does it give life? Using this criterion, I would have to say that Paul's story is true, because it has already given life to the Galatians, who had received the Spirit through Paul's preaching of this story as gospel. The question remains: Will the Galatians reaffirm Paul's story or accept that of the teachers/influencers?

4:1-11 Elemental powers of the world, heirs, and the Spirit's cry of "Abba, Father"

I treat three points. While Galatians 3:23-29 and 4:1-11 repeat certain themes, for example, both refer to baptism (3:27-28; 4:4-8), what is surely different between them is Paul's reference to "the elemental powers of the world" (4:3; see 4:9). In my Introduction (pp. 581–82) I mentioned that when we are faced with this type of jargon, we are like foreigners coming to the United States and trying to figure out the meaning of the pun "Only Hugh can prevent florist friars." I provide the following three parallels. Wisdom 13:1-5 is invective against people who worship the four elements of fire, water, earth, and air and do not infer from these good things the God who made them. Wisdom 13:1 states: "For all people . . . were in ignorance of God, and who from the good things seen did not succeed in coming to the knowledge of the one who is" (author's translation).

In their stories of Abraham, both Philo of Alexandria and Josephus, contemporaries of Paul, depict Abraham as overcoming the pagan worship of the elements as gods and coming to the worship of the true God. In Book I.155–156 of his *Jewish Antiquities*, Josephus writes:

> Abraham determined to renew and to change the opinion all people had then concerning God. For he was the first . . . to publish . . . that there was but one God, the Creator of the universe. . . . This opinion was derived from the irregular phenomena that were visible both at land and sea, as well as those that happen to the sun, and moon, and all the heavenly bodies (modified translation of William Whiston).

With the above background in mind, we begin to glimpse what was going on behind the scenes in Galatia. The teachers/influencers congratulated the Galatians on giving up their worship of the elements and the festivals associated with their worship and invited them to imitate Abraham, who explored the heavenly bodies to ascertain "days, months, seasons, and years" (4:10). What Abraham discovered is contained now in the Jewish sacred times. Paul's attack on the teachers/influencers and the Galatians is radically christocentric. As he says in 4:3: "In the same way we [Paul the Jew included] also, when we were not of age [and before God sent his Son], were enslaved to the elemental powers of the world." If the Galatians return to observing sacred days, after having received Paul's law-free gospel, they are turning back again to "the weak and destitute elemental powers" (4:9).

The figure of Abraham, the first Gentile believer, is one link between Galatians 4:1-11 and 3:6-29. Another is "heir" (Gal 3:29 and 4:1-2). The law's time to be guardian is over, for God has sent God's Son, born as a human being, born as a Jew, to ransom those under the law, so that both Jews and Gentiles might receive full legal rights as heirs (4:5).

Galatians 4:6 is vitally important: "As proof that you are sons, God sent the Spirit of God's Son into our hearts, crying out, 'Abba, Father'" (author's translation). Here Paul is using the same argument he used so powerfully in 3:1-5: the experience of the Galatians. Paul seems to be making another point by his interchange of pronouns "*you* are sons" and "into *our* hearts." Both Gentile Christians and Jewish Christians (Paul included) are heirs together. Both have the same Father, whose name is given in both Aramaic ("Abba") and Greek.

It is fitting that Paul concludes the "rebuke" part of his letter with a sarcastic rebuke: "Do you want to be slaves to them [the elemental powers] all over again?" (4:9). Paul now turns to his "request."

4:12-20 Paul begins his request and appeals to the affections of his friends

G. Walter Hansen and Richard N. Longenecker make a good case that Paul commences the request section of his letter with Galatians 4:12, which contains the first imperative of the entire letter. Hansen notes that a rebuke letter often concluded with a request for renewal of friendship and a change of conduct. These components are obvious in the short papyrus letter contemporaneous with Paul. I adapt Hansen's text:

> I am amazed (rebuke; see Gal 1:6) that you did not see your way to let me have what I asked you to send by Corbolon, esp. when I desired it for a festival. I beg you (request) to buy (imperative) me a silver seal and to send (imperative) it to me posthaste.

In the midst of expending much energy on showing his integrity *(ethos)* and arguing from Scripture and from the Galatians' experience (logic), Paul now wears his emotions on his sleeve *(pathos)*. He is tender as he addresses his converts as "brothers and sisters" (4:12) and "my children" (4:19). Like the good wisdom and evangelical teacher that he is, Paul's first exhortation is: "Be as I am" (4:12). In other words, Paul is not telling the Galatians to do something that he doesn't do himself. In the context of this letter, the focus of this appeal is on Paul's self-sacrificing relinquishment of Jewish conduct that separated Jews from Gentiles (circumcision, dietary laws, sabbath) and his adaptation of Gentile ways.

Paul further appeals to the generous and gracious acceptance he received from the Galatians when he appeared on their doorsteps with a weakness of the flesh. Might this weakness of the flesh be the wounds Paul received for preaching the gospel? See 2 Corinthians 11:24-25: "Five times at the hands of the Jews I received forty lashes minus one. Three times I was beaten with rods, once I was stoned." The Galatians did not spit on Paul and reject him, but would have spent an arm and a leg to assist him.

Galatians 4:17 provides a hazy snapshot of the teachers/influencers: "They show interest in you, but not in a good way; they want to isolate you, so that you may show interest in them." It seems that the teachers/ influencers are courting the Galatians, so that they might separate them from their fellow Gentile Christians and include them in the exclusive club of the Jewish Christians who observe the law. Paul is the champion of inclusivity, not exclusivity. He wants both Jewish and Gentile Christians around the same table.

I recall an experience I had some time ago when I went to a restaurant with an African-American confrere. The owner stopped us near the entrance, looked me in the eye, and addressed me: "This is an exclusive club. You can get a membership card immediately and be seated." I was being courted to leave my confrere behind and enjoy exclusive table fellowship. My confrere and I walked out of the restaurant together and sought an inclusive table. Will the Galatians leave their friend Paul standing at the door as they rush to fill a table in an exclusive club?

4:21-31 You are children of the promise and of the Spirit

There are four keys to unlock the meaning of this troublesome passage. The first key is the supposition that Paul is swept into his interpretation of Sarah, Hagar, and their sons because the teachers/influencers were using these figures to instruct the Galatians to follow the path of Sarah's

son, Isaac, whom Abraham circumcised and who inherited the promise. Paul turns the exegetical tables on these teachers/influencers and uses Sarah's son for his purposes of proclaiming that the Gentiles, like Isaac, are heirs of the promise (4:28).

The second key is the meaning of "allegory" (4:24). The Greek verb Paul uses here has the generic meaning "to use analogy or likeness to express something." Like any good preacher, Paul is finding an analogy between the historical events of Genesis 21 and the historical events of his own time. As R.P.C. Hanson says: "He (Paul) is doing what he is doing in his scriptural expositions of I Cor. 9 and 10 and II Cor. 3. . . . He is envisaging a critical situation which took place under the Old Covenant . . . as forecasting and repeated by a situation under the New Covenant" (p. 82).

The third key is the Greek verb that stands behind Galatians 4:25: "It *corresponds*" (emphasis added). Literally the Greek verb *systoichei* means "stands in line with." The reader is to imagine two lines over against each other: the troops of General X are arrayed against the troops of General Y. Or the lines may be drawn according to radical contrasts: flesh on one side, Spirit/promise on the other side; slavery on one side, freedom on the opposite side; Hagar on one side, and Sarah on the other. So standing in line with "slave" are Hagar, Ishmael (although never named), flesh, Mount Sinai, the present Jerusalem. Standing in line with "free" are Sarah (although never named), Isaac, promise/Spirit, the Jerusalem above.

The fourth key is Paul's quotation of Isaiah 54:1 in 4:27. As Richard B. Hays says: "Paul's major purpose for citing Isa 54:1 is to evoke Deutero-Isaiah's central theme of God's gracious eschatological restoration of Israel and a universal embrace of the nations" (p. 304). Put briefly, the New Jerusalem, which apocalyptic texts such as Revelation 21 expected at the end of time, has appeared because of the boundary-breaking death and resurrection of Christ Jesus. In it are Gentiles who live without the law.

Now that we have used these four keys to gain entrance to Paul's extended analogy, we are somewhat prepared to appreciate the three conclusions he draws for the Galatian Gentiles. The first is that the Galatians are like Isaac and are children of the promise (4:28). The second depends upon acquaintance with a Targumic tradition that Ishmael harassed Isaac because he was circumcised willingly at age thirteen and therefore was more righteous than Isaac, who was circumcised after a mere eight days (see 4:29). The third is found in the one and only quotation from the law in this passage (see 4:21): "'Drive out the slave woman and her son. / For the son of the slave woman shall not share the inheritance with the son' / of the freeborn." Paul uses Scripture to convince his Galatian converts to do something they should have done at the very beginning: Throw the teachers/influencers out of your community!

EXHORTATION TO CHRISTIAN LIVING

Galatians 5:1–6:10

5:1-12 Paul's authoritative appeal that the Galatians stand firm in freedom

Paul's appeals in this section tell us much about Christian freedom, Christian community, and the message of the teachers/influencers. If we go back to my introductory gambit about the slogan "Only you can prevent florist friars (forest fires)," we realize that this makes sense in our American culture of rampant individualism. For the "you" that Smokey Bear is pointing to is an individual, not a community. Paul's view of freedom should be seen from the way Paul uses this term in Galatians. Christians are free to form an inclusive community (3:26-28). They have freedom from the power of sin (3:22), from the power of the law (3:23), from the elemental powers of the world (4:3). As Sam K. Williams says: Christians are free "from the religious and cultural prisons whose darkness breeds prejudice, suspicion, and resentment" (3:26-28).

If the Galatians are circumcised, they will join an exclusive club and be obligated to fulfill all its regulations (5:3). Being circumcised or not being circumcised is no longer a way of joining community, but rather "faith working through love" (5:6). Those who are inspirited by Christ's Spirit through faith manifest Christ's self-sacrificing love for one another in community (see Gal 2:20). If one tries to supplement Christian faith with the ethnic marker of circumcision and tries to be justified by observance of the law, that person has fallen from grace (5:4). "A person is not justified by works of the law but through the faithfulness of Jesus Christ" (2:16; author's translation).

From this passage it is very clear that the teachers/influencers were trying to persuade the Galatians to fully join the Christian community by being circumcised (5:2). They are "a little yeast" that is negatively influencing "the whole batch of dough" (5:9). They are causing headaches and heartaches of faith for the Galatians (5:10).

Paul displays angry humor in 5:12. Deuteronomy 23:2 provides the best interpretive parallel: "No one whose testicles have been crushed or whose penis has been cut off, may be admitted into the community of the Lord." Paul says: Those who are cutting off foreskins so that others may gain definitive entry into the community should have their own penises cut off and thus be banned from belonging to the community. Is there any doubt that community is a dominant theme of this passage?

5:13-26 Part One of Paul's ethical appeal: The apocalyptic battle between Flesh and Spirit

Behind this passage another aspect of Paul's confrontation with the teachers/influencers seems to be raging. These teachers/influencers are saying to the Galatians that once they have been circumcised and become members of the Israel of God, they will have the law to guide them in their moral lives and the community of the law to support them when the evil spirit has led them into sin. To Paul this approach to the ethical life is eschatologically outdated and christologically deficient. I call my readers' attention to Galatians 1:4: The Lord Jesus Christ "gave himself for our sins that he might rescue us from *the present evil age*" (emphasis added). Rescue from the present evil age is not by means of the law but by means of God's Spirit (4:6, 29; 5:16-24). I make three explanatory remarks.

First, J. Louis Martyn is indeed correct to see that Paul is using apocalyptic language here to describe what the results in the moral sphere are of Christ's incursion into "the present evil age." He writes:

> The Spirit's war against the Flesh . . . was declared by God when he sent his Son and the Spirit of this Son into the territory of the Flesh. This war is, then, the new-creational struggle, the apocalyptic war of the end-time, the war in which God's forces are the ones on the march. . . ." (pp. 530–531).

Paul's apocalyptic imagery of warfare is clear in Galatians 5:13, for the Greek word behind "opportunity" literally means "a staging area for an army." Galatians 5:17 describes the warfare between flesh and Spirit, which "are opposed to each other." Just as in a real war one's options are curtailed in this war, so that "you may not do what you want." The stakes in this warfare are very high, for "inherit[ance of] the kingdom of God" is the goal and prize. We do a disservice to Paul's thought when we take flesh in either its capitalized or noncapitalized form to refer to sins of the flesh. Flesh is the entire world turned against God; flesh refers to human beings turned in upon themselves and away from God.

Although Paul does not invoke the entire law for moral guidance, he is not antinomian. Through the eschatological experience hoped for in Jeremiah 31:33-34, the Galatians have knowledge of what God wants written on their hearts. As James D. G. Dunn says, they depend "more on inward apprehension of what is the appropriate conduct than on rule book or tradition" (p. 296). Further, "the whole law is fulfilled in one statement, namely, 'You shall love your neighbor as yourself' " (5:14). The Galatian Christians are to be slaves to "one another through love" (5:13), as Paul turns the slave/free dichotomy on its head and says in effect: Sure, you are free, free to be in bondage by love to one another. The first fruit of the Spirit is "love" (5:22). People do not need the law to discern the works of the flesh, for they are "obvious" (5:19). Against the fruit of the Spirit "there is no law" (5:23), as if a generous grocer who is feeding the poor were responding to her complaining neighbors: "Is there a law against helping the poor?"

Finally, the flesh destroys community. See the "vices" in the middle of the "works of the flesh": "hatreds, rivalry, jealousy, outbursts of fury, acts of selfishness, dissensions, factions, occasions of envy" (5:20-21). See also the anti-community behavior Paul rebukes in Galatians 5:13 and 5:26. But the fruit of the Spirit fosters community: "peace, patience, kindness, generosity, faithfulness, gentleness, self-control" (5:22).

Throughout the centuries Christians have been heirs to the battle Paul is waging in Galatians 5:13-26. One side says: They need detailed laws and regulations to prevent them from sinning. Another side states: They need to be genuinely attentive to the Spirit. For those old enough to remember the immediate post-Vatican II days, I invoke the battles between those who cherished the detailed instructions given in the moral manuals and those who championed works such as Bernard Haring's *The Law of Christ*, which stressed the role of the Spirit in moral life.

6:1-10 Part Two of Paul's ethical appeal: The serious consequences of behavior within the household of faith

I take Galatians 6:10, which Hans Dieter Betz has called the summary and conclusion of Galatians 5:1–6:9, as my starting point. Paul's ethical appeal ends with a universal dimension "do good to all," and with a particular dimension, "especially to those who belong to the family of the faith." This is not a natural family or household, but one formed by faith. In this household there are people who teach and lead their fellow members into a deeper understanding of Christian life (6:6). In it there is fraternal correction, done in a spirit of gentleness and love, as members are socialized into appropriate Spirit-led conduct (6:1). In imitation of Christ's self-sacrificing love manifested in his death on the cross for us (Gal 2:20), members of the faith community bear one another's burdens and thus fulfill the only true law, the law of Christ (6:2).

As a modern example of what Paul is saying, I think of my own religious community of Friars Minor, who are white, African American, Hispanic, and Asian, and who are socialized into what it means to be a community of brothers not so much by rules and regulations, but by the example of fellow friars who have faithfully and creatively followed the guidance of the Spirit.

In Galatians 6:7-9, Paul again reveals the apocalyptic bent of his theology. There are ultimate consequences from deeds sown in the flesh and in the Spirit. But Paul ends his serious reminder with a note of encouragement: "Let us not grow tired of doing good, for in due time we shall reap our harvest, if we do not give up" (6:9).

CONCLUSION

Galatians 6:11-18

6:11-18 Postscript and summary of the letter

As Paul summarizes his message, there are pathos and ethos in his description of himself: I bear in my body the brand marks of Jesus Christ (6:17). Paul's scars are signs of his love for Christ Jesus and the Galatians. Paul continues to attack the teachers/influencers who champion circumcision as the saving supplement to Paul's gospel (6:11-13). In my tradition, it's as if someone were to accost a regular church member and say that he will only be saved if he recites the Novena to St. Anthony of Padua every Tuesday. It is not circumcision that is foundational but the cross. What God has done to Sin and Flesh and Law by the death and resurrection of his Son has changed the world and transformed Paul (6:14).

In Galatians 6:15 Paul introduces the term "new creation." I find a compelling parallel to "new creation" in one of my favorite books from New Testament times. *Joseph and Aseneth* tells the story of the conversion of the Gentile Aseneth so that she could marry Joseph (see Gen 41:45). In Joseph's prayer over Aseneth, I have italicized the "new creation" words: "Lord God of my father Israel, the Most High, the Powerful One of Jacob, who gave life to all things, and called them from darkness to light, and from error to truth, and from death to life, you, Lord, bless this virgin and *renew* her by your spirit, and *form her anew* by your hidden hand, and *make her alive again* by your life" (8.9; modified translation of C. Burchard).

The death and resurrection of the Lord Jesus and the sending of his creative Spirit have brought about the new creation. This new creation, however, is not just revealed in individuals but also and especially in the household of faith, where Jew and Gentile, male and female, slave and freeborn are sitting at the same table, enjoying their freedom in the Spirit, in the midst of the present evil age, and awaiting God's righteousness in hope.

BIBLIOGRAPHY

Hans Dieter Betz, *Galatians*. Hermeneia. Philadelphia: Fortress, 1979.

James D. G. Dunn, *The Epistle to the Galatians*. Black's New Testament Commentary. Peabody, MA: Hendrickson, 1993.

G. Walter Hansen, *Galatians*. The IVP New Testament Commentary Series. Downers Grove, IL: InterVarsity Press, 1994.

R.P.C. Hanson, *Allegory and Event*. Louisville: Westminster John Knox Press, 2002.

Richard N. Longenecker, *Galatians*. Word Bible Commentary 41. Dallas: Word Books, 1990.

George Lyons, *Pauline Autobiography: Toward a New Understanding*. Atlanta: Scholars Press, 1985.

J. Louis Martyn, *Galatians*. Anchor Bible 33A. New York: Doubleday, 1998.

Mark D. Nanos, *The Irony of Galatians: Paul's Letter in First-Century Context*. Minneapolis: Fortress, 2002.

Sam K. Williams, *Galatians*. Abingdon New Testament Commentaries. Nashville: Abingdon, 1997.

THE LETTER TO THE
EPHESIANS

Vincent M. Smiles

INTRODUCTION

Authorship and destination

Ephesus, on the west coast of Asia Minor (Turkey), was in Paul's day a large seaport city. Paul stayed there for about three years (Acts 20:31) and undoubtedly wrote some of his letters from there, but whether he wrote the letter to the Ephesians is a matter of some doubt.

Ever since the sixteenth century, scholars reading Ephesians in Greek have wondered whether Paul could be its author. Even reading the text in English, those familiar with Paul's letters find reasons to wonder: its ornate, elevated style (especially in chapters 1–3), its purely universal view of "the church," the focus on Christ's cosmic victory over "the powers" with little stress on Christ's death, the comparative lack of apocalyptic expectation combined with a view of salvation already accomplished, the absence of "brothers" as a form of address and of any personal expressions of affection, and the obvious dependence on Colossians—all give reason to question whether Paul is the author. The evidence against Paul as the author is so strong that today about 75 percent of scholars regard Ephesians as pseudonymous.

As with Colossians, however, the issue of authorship may be more complicated. Some, who accept that Paul did not write Colossians, think nevertheless that he may have had some input into that letter. Similarly, with respect to Ephesians, it is possible that the author knew Paul personally—he or she certainly knew Paul's letters (not only Colossians)—or may have written Ephesians expanding on a text written by Paul himself. That text might simply have been Colossians, but a further theory is that Ephesians is an enlarged version of the letter to Laodicea (see Col 4:16). On balance, however, the evidence favors more distance between Paul and Ephesians than these latter theories allow, especially given that Colossians also was probably not composed by the apostle himself.

This commentary will presuppose that Ephesians was written by an admirer of Paul, about twenty or thirty years after his death (i.e., A.D. 80– 90). The writer knew Colossians very well, but was also well acquainted with Paul's other letters. Whether Ephesians was originally addressed to Ephesus is doubtful, since first, the words "in Ephesus" (1:1) are missing from the best and earliest manuscripts of the letter, and second, both 1:15 and 3:2 suggest that Paul and the readers had only "heard" of one another, as though Paul had never been there. Whereas Paul's letters always speak to the *particular* circumstances of individual churches, providing specific instructions, Ephesians envisions Paul writing from prison (3:1; 4:1) in *general* terms about challenges for "the church" at large. Ephesians, therefore, is often viewed as a kind of encyclical letter to Paul's churches in general, in Ephesus and elsewhere.

The relationship with Colossians and the purposes of Ephesians

The closeness between Colossians and Ephesians is far more obvious than is the similarity between any other two Pauline letters. This is not to say that they were written by the same author; they probably were not. More probably, the writer of Ephesians composed freely, with major ideas and phrases of Colossians making their presence felt naturally. Some obvious similarities are noted in the commentary on 4:17–5:20. Other passages where similarities are easily detected include:

Ephesians	Colossians	Topic
1:7	1:14	redemption— forgiveness
1:21-23	1:16-19	Christ's victory as head—fullness of God
2:5	2:13	dead made alive
3:2-3	1:25-26	hidden mystery revealed to Paul
5:22–6:9	3:18–4:1	Wives, husbands, children, slaves
4:15-16	2:19	Christ the head—body bound together
6:21-22	4:7-8	Tychicus, the news-bearer

Major themes of Ephesians, most notably the cosmic Christ as head of the universal church, were evidently largely inspired by Colossians; the connection is beyond dispute.

On the other hand, Ephesians is quite different from Colossians in what it says about Judaism. Colossians contests "the philosophy" (Col 2:8), evidently deriving mainly from Judaism, that required obedience to certain laws (2:16-23). Such laws, says Colossians, are mere "human tradition" (2:8, 22), having to do with "the elements of the world" (2:8, 20), which Christ has defeated (2:14-15, 20). Judaism is not specifically mentioned in Colossians, but these warnings portray the Jewish law in a rather negative light; only 3:11 ("no longer Greek and Jew") suggests the possibility of Jewish and Gentile believers living peacefully within the one body.

Ephesians 2:11-18, on the other hand, presumes a very high estimation of Judaism; theirs are "the covenants," to which Gentiles are joined by faith in Christ. The language of "those far off" being brought "near" is Jewish terminology for conversion to Judaism. Most significant is the triple mention of Christ's achieving "peace" (2:14, 15, 17), reconciling Jews and Gentiles "in one body" (2:15-16). It has, therefore, been suggested that Ephesians was written, in part, to reach out to Jewish Christians and present to them a friendly understanding of Paul, softening some of his harshness (e.g., Gal 3:1-21). At the same time, it appeals to Gentile believers to be welcoming of Jewish Christians. In any event, it is clear that Ephesians has a keen concern for the unity of all believers under "one faith" (4:1-6). The primary purpose for its composition, therefore, was to provide a vision of Christ and of "the church" that would make unity among "the churches" and their various believers possible.

The value of Ephesians today

The author of Ephesians lived in a time of transition. The foundational "apostles and prophets" (2:20) had all died. The church, therefore, or better "the churches," had to adjust. Ephesians represents a second/third generation voice that reminds the various churches that they are God's "handiwork, created in Christ Jesus" (2:10) and that they must "live worthily" of their "calling" (4:1). As Paul himself had done, so also the Ephesians writer reminds believers of the fundamentals: they belong together as one body in Christ.

The Catholic Church of the twenty-first century has its own transitions and tensions: What and who is "the church"? How is it to fulfill its mission? Who is to be included in deciding such questions? For all its emphasis on the universal church, Ephesians agrees with the rest of the New Testament that "the church" is the community of the baptized, whether a local congregation (e.g., Col 4:15), "the churches" of a particular region (e.g., Gal 1:2), or the church in general (as in Ephesians). In each manifestation the church is "the body of Christ" (1 Cor 12:27; Eph 1:23), both a physical and a spiritual reality. But in the minds of far too many Catholics, "the church" really only comprises the pope, bishops, and priests; they do not see themselves as truly "the church." Ephesians and the entire New Testament are a corrective to this distortion. Similarly, Ephesians' view of ministry, that it is the task of *all* the baptized (4:11-12), needs to be reaffirmed, as it was by the Second Vatican Council.

Ephesians was written by one of the baptized, a man or woman, perhaps a "teacher," some decades after Paul's death. It represents the voice of the faithful struggling under new and difficult circumstances to recall and remain faithful to the original inspiration of the gospel. The unfathomable "love of Christ" (3:19) is still with the church; Ephesians invites a continuing rediscovery of the ancient tradition so that that love can be more vibrant in the church and so that the church can reach out more effectively to the world.

COMMENTARY

1:1-2 Greeting

The opening is very similar to that of 1 Corinthians and nearly identical with that of Colossians. Except for Galatians, Paul's letters always describe believers as "holy," but Ephesians refers to believers as "holy" nine times (e.g., 1:4, 18; 3:8, cf. 2:21; 4:24), proportionally more frequently than any other letter; this accords with the letter's strong ethical emphasis (4:1–6:9). The greeting (1:2) is identical with the longer greeting of Paul's own letters (e.g., Rom 1:7), "grace" being an especially important theological term (see 2:5-8).

1:3-14 A blessing prayer

After the opening, most of Paul's letters have a "thanksgiving," but Ephesians (also 2 Cor 1:3) first has a traditional opening of Jewish prayer, "Blessed be God . . ." (1:3), and then also, quite uniquely, a "thanksgiving" (1:16). Both give thanks by recalling the actions and gifts of God. This "blessing" uses liturgical language; much of its phrasing is hymn-like. There are lots of repetitions: "in Christ" ("in him") occurs nine times, ten times if we include "in the beloved" (1:6); the phrase "for the praise of his glory" occurs three times (1:6, 12, 14). The section comprises a single sentence in Greek and features the sort of effusive language that is also found in Colossians (e.g., Col 1:9-20) but is even more prominent here. Phrases like "blessed us with every spiritual blessing" (1:3), "favor of his will" (1:5), "intention of his will" (1:11), and synonymous verbs (e.g., "chose," 1:4; "destined" 1:5, 11) combine to emphasize the abundance of God's favors.

The theological perspective, taking off from Colossians, emphasizes the initiative of God (2:5-10) which in Christ and beyond human calculation "chose" believers "before the foundation of the world" for holiness (1:4; 2:21), "adoption" (1:5), and "redemption" (1:7, 14; Col 1:14). God had always planned for "the gospel of salvation" (1:13); "the mystery of God's will" was "made known" to the faithful (cf. 3:5; Col 1:26), and it was "set forth" (accomplished) in Christ (1:9). God's "plan" and "purpose" were "to sum up all things in Christ" (1:10-11), that is, "to bring all things under Christ as head" (cf. 1:20-22; 4:15), a further key theme taken from Colossians (1:20-22; 4:15, cf. Col 1:18; 2:10).

God's purpose that believers be "holy and blameless" (1:4) consumes the entire second half of the letter (4:1–6:17). But, in a sense, God's purpose has *already* been fulfilled; believers "*have* redemption [and] the forgiveness of sins" (1:7; Col 1:14). And yet, for all the emphasis on the *present fulfillment* of blessings, there remains an echo of Paul's point (Rom 8:23; 2 Cor 1:22; 5:5) that the "the holy Spirit" is "the first installment" of coming redemption, not yet its completion (1:14; cf. 4:30).

1:15-23 A thanksgiving prayer

Whereas the "blessing" focuses on what God has accomplished in Christ, this "thanksgiving" is more a prayer that believers will appropriate the gifts they have received. If the letter was addressed to Ephesus, then Paul himself could hardly be the author of the opening sentence ("*hearing* of your faith"; also 3:2), since he spent about three years in the city (Acts 20:31). The prayerful thanks, however, are no less sincere, as also the prayer that God will grant them "a spirit of wisdom and revelation by knowledge" of God

(1:17). As in Colossians 1:9-10, this prayer highlights the importance of sound knowledge, but here also it is not intellectual knowledge that is primary, but rather deep spiritual recognition, with "the eyes of the heart" (1:18, cf. 3:18-19).

Among the prophets, "knowing God" was the key to the covenant (e.g., Hos 6:6; Isa 11:2; Jer 31:31-34). Here "knowledge" of God involves knowing all the blessings which God has granted in Christ and which this writer delights in listing in heaps of words: "hope," "call," "riches of glory," "inheritance," "the surpassing greatness of God's power" (1:19-20). Believers "know" God's "power," which is at work *now* (in every generation), as it also "worked in Christ," not only "raising him from the dead" but also "seating him" above all powers in the universe (1:20-21). This develops the theme taken over from Colossians (Col 2:15), namely, that Christ's victory, which for Paul would be complete only at the second coming (1 Cor 15:24, cf. Rom 8:38), is complete *now*; God "put all things beneath [Christ's] feet." Dramatic though that is, even more so is the statement that "God gave Christ as head over all things to *the church*" (1:22).

This is the first of nine times that "the church" is mentioned (also 3:10, 21; 5:23-32), and in every instance it refers to the *universal* church, as opposed to a local congregation (e.g., Rom 16:1, 5; Col 4:15). As in Colossians (Col 1:18), the church is a cosmic entity, but this writer expands this idea: as Christ is "head" of the church, so he is the head of all creation (1:10). By virtue of Christ, the church has an extraordinary status and role; according to God's eternal purpose, it is the means by which "God's wisdom is made known" to all the powers of the universe (3:10-11). The church also is "seated with [Christ] in the heavens" (2:5-6). To be sure, the writer recognizes that for believers themselves, the victory is not complete (6:10-17). Nevertheless, the vision of a present realization of salvation is extraordinary; Paul's expectation of Christ's imminent return (e.g., 1 Thess 4:13-17) has faded, and suffering is virtually unmentioned (only 3:13; cf. Rom 5:3; Phil 1:29-30). Rather, the church is Christ's (glorified) "body" and his "fullness" within history (1:23; 4:10).

The Greek phrasing of 1:23 is very difficult. The New American Bible translation is possible (see 4:10), but more natural, given the form of the verb, is: "the fullness of the one who *is filled* with respect to all things in every way." As Christ was "raised" and "seated" in heaven (1:20), so also Christ "is filled" with "all the fullness of God" (Col 1:19; 2:9) and will in turn fill believers (3:19; 4:10, 13; Col 2:10). Either way, the vision of the church is breathtaking. Though Christ is head of the universe, only the *church* is Christ's body and fullness. The church, therefore, is the destiny of the universe! Though this is a beautiful spiritual vision, once the church gained power in history, the vision became susceptible to distortion, particularly the notion that all peoples and beliefs must surrender to the church. The church today must be far more humble!

2:1-10 From death to life

The opening phrase (also 2:5) is strongly reminiscent of Colossians 2:13. "The age of this world" and "the ruler of the power of the air" (2:2) presuppose (as does Colossians) that "this world" is dominated by spiritual forces which are beyond human control but which Christ has defeated (Col 2:15). Those evil powers account for the "disobedience" of non-believers (2:2), and "all of *us*"—strongly emphasized in the Greek—were once like them and were destined for "wrath" (2:3, cf. 1 Thess 1:10). But God's "great love" seized the initiative and "brought us to life with Christ" (2:4-5) and "seated us with him in the heavens" (2:6). God's cosmic victory in Christ means that "the coming ages"—perhaps spiritual forces, not just time periods—will see "the richness of [God's] grace" to believers (2:7), who have their home in the heavens (cf. Col 3:3-4).

The writer is at pains to emphasize that God's action was a matter of grace, not of human deserving (cf. Rom 3:27; 4:4-5; Gal 2:16-19). What Paul had said in the context of a debate over Jewish law, this writer applies to "works" in general, so that there will be no "boasting." Paul would agree with the sentiment (e.g., Rom 3:27–4:5); faith itself and the living of it have to do with God's power (Gal 3:23-25; Phil 1:29; 2:13). The point is *not* that humans have no responsibility (Phil 2:12; Gal 5:13–6:10), but simply that neither law nor human action defines the relationship with God (Gal 3:1-14; Eph 2:15; Col 2:14). Believers, as believers, are God's "handiwork." God even "prepared" our "good deeds" in advance! What could emphasize the point more?

2:11-22 The one people of God

As believers had once been "dead in sins," so also they had once been "distant" from the chosen people. There is a switch in this section from God to Christ as the primary actor. The writer displays a high regard for Israel and seems oblivious to any hostility with Jews or the problem of Jews rejecting the gospel. All of this contrasts markedly with Paul's own situation (cf. 1 Thess 2:14-16; 2 Cor 11:24; Rom 9:1-3; 10:1). But this writer says simply that God has "made the two into one new humanity, creating peace" (2:15), as though there was no division between "circumcision" and "uncircumcision" (2:11).

In being "without Christ" Gentiles, as Gentiles, had also been "alienated" from Israel and its "covenants of promise" and therefore were "without hope" (2:12). The writer shares with Paul that, by God's design, Israel, Christ, and the church are intimately connected (cf. Rom 9:1-4; 11:21-31). "But now," "by the blood of Christ" Gentiles have the blessings of Israel. This passage (2:13-16; cf. 1:7) is the closest this letter comes to sustained reflection on the sacrificial death of Jesus; for Paul himself, "Christ crucified" was always the starting-point (e.g., Rom 3:24-26; 1 Cor 1:17–2:2; Gal 3:1-3).

In any event, Christ remains the key. The blessings of Israel are the prize, but the means is Christ, not the law (2:14-15). This is the point of division from Judaism, which believers must recognize while retaining the deepest respect for Judaism and the law, as Paul did (Rom 7:12). Ephesians is implicitly appealing for unity between Jewish and Gentile Christians.

The text again becomes reminiscent of Colossians in seeing Christ's death as destroying "the dividing wall" (2:14), "the law with its . . . legal claims" (2:15; cf. Col 2:14). It is *different*, however, in that here there is no debate with some "philosophy" insisting on laws (cf. Col 2:16-23). This writer sees "the two," Jews and Gentiles, reconciled "to God in one body" (2:16). "In one body" is best understood, in the context, as a reference to the church and perhaps reflects the thought of Colossians, and of Paul himself, that in Christ "there is no longer Greek [Gentile] and Jew" (Col 3:11; Gal 3:28). In other words, the writer is dwelling on the reality of Jews and Gentiles within the church, not on the external relationship of the church with Judaism. Christ "destroyed enmity"

and "preached peace" to both Jews and Gentiles (2:17), and "through Christ" all have "access" to God (2:18).

The conclusion is that enmity has been destroyed, at least within the church. All believers, whether Jews or Gentiles, belong to God's household (2:19); reconciliation with God means reconciliation with one another. The writer images the church as an organic, not a static, building; the whole is "jointed together" and "is growing" into a "holy temple" (2:21). This latter phrase would have a particular poignancy, especially for Jews, in light of the destruction of the Jerusalem temple by the Romans in A.D. 70.

The image of the "apostles and prophets" (2:20) as the church's foundation contrasts with Paul's image of "Jesus Christ" as the church's sole foundation (1 Cor 3:11). Ephesians seems deliberately to recall and to nuance Paul's idea. The church is in a new situation: the foundational generation has died, and the church, no longer expecting Christ's imminent return, must look to how it will endure through history. Christ remains "the capstone" (or "keystone") of the building (2:21). In remaining faithful to the "apostles and prophets," the church remains "apostolic" (and prophetic), as it is also "one, holy, and catholic" (universal). All the baptized together are God's "one building in the Spirit" (2:22).

3:1-13 Remembering Paul's ministry

Though not a member of the Twelve, Paul was by far the most important of the apostles within the New Testament (Acts 13–28), but there were many other "apostles and prophets," men and women alike, who had "labored together in the gospel" (Phil 4:2-3; cf. Rom 16:1-15). But the writer now remembers Paul as the apostle par excellence "for you the Gentiles" (3:1); he had been a prisoner and suffered many times "on your behalf" (also 3:13; 2 Cor 11:21-33). Paul was God's reliable instrument; he had received "God's grace" (3:2, 7; Rom 15:15; Gal 2:9) "for your benefit" (3:2), and "the mystery of Christ" "by revelation" (3:3-4, cf. Gal 1:11-12). The writer knew Paul's letters (not only Colossians), and believers could "read" them (not only Ephesians) "to understand [Paul's] insight" (3:4) for themselves.

This passage (3:2-7) recalls and develops Colossians 1:25-27. It presupposes, in the manner of apocalyptic literature (e.g., Dan 8:17-19), that

God's plan of salvation is ancient, but "in other generations" (3:5) had been kept secret until the appointed time (cf. 3:9). In Colossians the recipients of "the mystery" are all the baptized (Col 1:26), but here, consistent with their founding role, the primary recipients are "the holy apostles and prophets" (3:5), that is, Paul himself and those who worked with him. The content of "the mystery" recalls 2:11-18: "the Gentiles," "through the gospel," share in the fulfilled "promise" to Israel. It was this gospel—the inclusion of the Gentiles—for which Paul was commissioned by God's "power" (3:7; cf. Gal 1:16).

For a third time Paul's apostolate is referred to as "the grace given" by God (3:8; cf. 3:2, 7), and again it is emphasized that Paul received this apostolate "to preach to the Gentiles." Why such emphatic repetition was thought necessary is impossible to know. During his ministry Paul had not been accepted by all as an "apostle" (1 Cor 9:1-2; Gal 1:1–2:9) and had conceded that he was "the last of the apostles" (1 Cor 15:9). Here he is referred to as "the least of all the saints" (3:8), which brings into sharp relief how great was God's grace. Paul had highlighted the same contrast in his autobiographical accounts (1 Cor 15:8-10; Gal 1:13-16). He knew from personal experience that God often chooses the most unlikely instrument to advance the gospel (1 Cor 1:27-29).

It is a unique thought that the purpose of Paul's apostolate was so that "God's manifold wisdom might be made known to the heavenly principalities and authorities," those powers that Christ had defeated (1:20-22). Indeed, this had happened "through the church," which means that now the church participates with Christ in the continuing mop-up campaign against "the devil" (6:11-12). "By God's eternal purpose, made effective in Christ" (3:11), the church can be "bold" in this endeavor (3:12) and should not be discouraged at the thought of Paul's "afflictions" (3:13).

3:14-21 A prayer

The intensity of already intense language is now increased as the writer breaks into prayer that God will enable believers to have greater and greater power in the Spirit "to know" the unknowable "love of Christ" (3:19). The prayer has two parts: a petition (3:16-19) and a doxology (3:20-21).

"For this reason" recalls 3:1 and that this is "Paul" at prayer, on his "knees" before "the Father" of the universe. The heart of Christian spirituality is caught in the petition; the "power" derives purely from "the Spirit," but it is not a power for doing (cf. 2:8-9) so much as for *surrendering* "by faith," so that "Christ may well in your hearts" (2:16-17). This is reminiscent of Paul's great claim, "I no longer live, rather Christ lives within me" (Gal 2:20), which he claimed for believers generally, not just himself (cf. Rom 6:8-11). All believers are to "be rooted and founded in love" (cf. Col 1:23; 2:7). This means primarily "the love" that Christ has shown (2:4; cf. Gal 2:20; 1 John 4:10), as the next part of the petition indicates, but believers' love for others (4:2, 15; 5:2) and for "the Lord" (6:24) is also envisioned. Believers do "know" that love, but the prayer asks for their (ongoing) "strengthening" to plumb the unfathomable "love of Christ" in all its dimensions (3:18-19). The end of the journey is "to be filled" by Christ (1:23) "with all the fullness of God" (cf. 4:10-13; Col 1:19; 2:9-10).

As the petition hints at the cosmic reach of Christ's love, so the doxology praises God, who, as "Father" of the universe (3:15), can (and will) "accomplish far more than all we ask or imagine" and whose "glory" both "in the church" and "in Christ Jesus" exceeds the universe and all the powers within it (3:20-21).

4:1-16 Growing to maturity in Christ

"The church" is not explicitly mentioned in this section, but the focus on "unity" (4:3-6, 13) and "ministry" (4:11-12) as the means for "the whole body" (4:16) to grow to maturity in Christ shows that the church and how it functions are the main concerns. But this is not mere description; rather, the writer proclaims that the church must "live" by these ideals if it is to be true to its "calling" (4:1, 4). Though there is now emphasis on human responsibility, the priority of "grace" (as in 2:8) remains prominent (4:7-11).

The reminder of Paul's being "a prisoner" adds deep feeling to the "appeal" (cf. Rom 12:1) that believers "live in a manner worthy" of their "call" (4:1). The narrative of God's "call" filled the first part of the letter and now leads to the imperative of believers' existence. And the first imperative is to be "humble," "gentle," "patient," and "loving" toward one another; only so will true "unity" be maintained. "Unity" is a gift of "the Spirit," but it can be destroyed; "the bond of peace" is a way of summarizing all the qualities needed to preserve it. Thus "the spirit" in "the unity of the spirit" is both human and divine; even God's gifts sometimes need human cooperation. Unity here and now ("one body") is to mirror "the one hope" (redemption, 1:14) to which believers "were called" (4:4).

The early churches were inevitably quite diverse in many respects. There was, for instance, more than one baptismal formula. Matthew's (Matt 28:19) finally became standard, but it is not the same as Paul's (Gal 3:28; cf. 1 Cor 12:13), which itself was not fixed (cf. Col 3:11). Ephesians (4:4-6) reflects a further formula or, at least, additional liturgical language of baptism. The insistence here that there must be "one faith, one baptism" (4:5) bespeaks attempts of the early churches, no matter how diverse or scattered, to be "one body." The emphasis here on God as the "one God" of the entire universe (4:6) furthered these efforts considerably. For the New Testament (e.g., John 17:20-23), Christians being divided among themselves is unthinkable.

The writer now picks up a theme well known in Paul's own writing, namely, that "to each one" in the church God has given some "measure of Christ's gift" (4:7; cf. Rom 12:3-8; 1 Cor 12:4-11). This is reinforced by reference to Psalm 68:19, which, in the context of recounting God's saving deeds for Israel, actually speaks of God's "receiving gifts" from Israel's, and God's, enemies. Jewish tradition applied the psalm to *Moses* "ascending" Mount Sinai and receiving gifts from God. Ephesians seems to reflect that idea but switches the text to speak of *Christ's* "ascending" and "*giving* gifts" to the church. As the writer sees it, it was Christ who "ascended on high and took captivity captive," the same victory that was earlier described as *God's* action (1:20-22). Having despoiled the powers, Christ distributed the enemy's wealth, so to speak, to the church (cf. Mark 3:27).

The writer pauses to dwell further on the psalm in relation to Christ: he who "ascended" and "filled" the universe with his presence (4:10) first "descended to the lower regions of the earth" (4:9). This is sometimes interpreted to refer to Christ "descending to the dead" (as in the Apostles' Creed; cf. 1 Pet 3:19), but far more likely, it refers to the incarnation (as in John 3:13).

Christ's gift of "apostles" and "prophets" and other primary ministers (4:11) was bestowed so that the church might be the fully functioning "body of Christ" (4:12, 16). It is perhaps important to emphasize that women, as well as men, were such primary ministers (e.g., Rom 16:1-12; Phil 4:2-3; Acts 2:17-18; 21:9). Paul had taught that "God designated some in the church to be, first, apostles; second, prophets; third, teachers" (1 Cor 12:28), but that listing followed on his insistence that *every* member of the church had some "spiritual gift" or "ministry" "for the common good" (12:4-7) and that no one's contribution was to be neglected or despised (12:14-27). Both Paul and Ephesians agree that the primary ministers are not to be the only ministers, but are rather "to equip the *holy ones for the work of ministry*" (4:11-12), an emphasis taken up vigorously by the Second Vatican Council, but sometimes, even today, forgotten. The writer adds "the evangelists [and] the pastors" (4:11) to Paul's list, which reflects the new situation of ministry toward the end of the first century. Later "bishop," "presbyter," and "deacon" became established titles (e.g., 1 Tim 3:1-13; Titus 1:5), and, sadly, women were increasingly excluded from leadership (1 Tim 2:11-15).

All gifts and ministries have the same aims (4:13), which, in various ways, have already been named: "building of the body" (2:21-22), "unity of faith" (4:5), maturity and "the fullness of Christ" (1:23; cf. 3:19). The purpose of leadership is then stated in negative terms so that the church will not be tossed about "by every wind of teaching" arising from "human trickery" (4:14). To the contrary, the church is to be characterized by "speaking the truth in love" so as "to grow into Christ, the head, in every way" (4:15; cf. 1:22).

Paul himself had not extended the image of "the body of Christ" (1 Cor 12:27) to Christ being its "head." Later on this notion, especially in combination with 5:23 ("wives subordinate to their husbands"), contributed to a very patriarchal view of the church. As used here, however, it is a beautiful, dynamic notion of the church organically growing toward Christ and his "fullness." The church not only grows into Christ, it also grows from him, as well as from the functioning of all its members, and so "builds itself up in love" (4:16). The key to the whole is the unity of believers with one another and with Christ (4:3-6, 13, 16).

4:17–5:20 Once darkness, not light

This very long section of ethical exhortation is, in part, dependent on Colossians but also has some unique concerns and images. The dependence on Colossians is apparent in a long list of words, phrases, and concepts that are sometimes almost identical with the earlier letter. Examples include: "old self"—"new self" (4:22-24; Col 3:9-10); "forgive as God forgave you" (4:32; Col 3:13); "greed" as "idolatry" (5:5; Col 3:5); "wrath" for the "disobedient" (5:6; Col 3:6); "psalms, hymns and songs" (5:19; Col 3:16), and so on. Ephesians is unique, however, in its much stronger use of the imagery of "light" versus "darkness" (4:18; 5:8-9, 11-14, cf. Col 1:12-13), its concern for "anger" and proper speech among believers (e.g., 4:31), and a stronger emphasis on separation from outsiders (5:6-7; cf. Col 4:5-6).

The writer solemnly warns believers ("I testify in the Lord") that they must be different from "the Gentiles." Most readers, though not all, were "Gentiles," in the sense that their natural heritage was not in Judaism (3:1; 2:11); but "Gentiles," even in Paul's time (e.g., 1 Cor 5:1), was used to refer to non-believers, who, unlike Jews and Christians, did not acknowledge the one God (1 Thess 4:5). As the imminent expectation of Christ's return receded and the church, though still a small minority, became a *part of* society, as opposed to watching and waiting for its destruction (see 1 Cor 1:18; 7:29-31), it became increasingly necessary for Christians to distinguish themselves from the dominant culture, although living within it. Baptism and other rituals, as well as "the faith," were essential boundary markers, but on a day-to-day basis even more important was (and is) "living" by the highest ethical ideals.

The writer vividly portrays "Gentile" behavior as "futile" ("foolish"), having no understanding of "the life of God" (the life that God enables) because of "the hardness of their hearts" and their consequent surrender of themselves to "every kind of impurity" (4:17-19). Such negative evaluations of "outsiders" by "insiders" inevitably arise among emerging religious groups; they change, however, if a group—as happened with Christianity—itself becomes dominant. Power changes perspectives. Believers today have to be humble in their evaluations of "outsiders" and have to apply to *themselves* Scripture's many warnings about "ignorance" and "excess" (4:18-19).

When believers "learned Christ" (a completely unique expression), the learning had nothing to do with being either "callous" or "impure" (4:19-20), and therefore the transformation from "the old self" to "the new" must mean putting aside "deceitful desires" and turning to "holiness" (4:22-24). The dependence on Colossians 3:8-11 shows that baptism is in mind here. The "new self, created by God's design" (4:24), transforms the relationship with God and with others.

The next paragraph (4:25-32) follows a pattern of mentioning, first, the vice to be avoided and then the good to be espoused. There is clear encouragement for truthful and loving words, as there is also, throughout the letter, a deep concern about "falsehood" (4:14, 22, 25; 5:6) and about the misguided "impulses" (2:3) and "futile thinking" (4:17-18), which impede true knowledge and understanding (e.g., 4:13-14; 5:17-18). The writer quotes Zechariah 8:16 to urge believers to "speak the truth" and adds as motivation, "For we are members of one another" (4:25, cf. Rom 12:5). Psalm 4:5 is quoted to make the point that "anger" (though inevitable) must not become "sin"; "Do not let the sun set on your anger" was proverbial even then. "Anger" here denotes the "fury" that leads to "bitterness" and "shouting" (4:31) and provides "an opportunity for the devil" (4:27; cf. 6:11; 2 Cor 2:11). Far from "stealing," all must "work with their own hands" (cf. 1 Thess 4:11) and be prepared "to share with anyone in need" (4:28).

"Foul speech" ought to have no place among believers (5:3-4), but speech must rather be "good" for "building" the church and "imparting grace" (4:29). The injunction not to "grieve the holy Spirit" reflects Isaiah 63:10, which recalls Israel's "provoking God's holy Spirit" by disobedience. The rest of that verse (4:30) repeats the thought of 1:13-14, namely, that by faith believers were "sealed with the holy Spirit" as a "pledge" of the coming "redemption." Meanwhile, destructive anger and the bitter words that accompany it must be "removed" (4:31); in their place belong kindness, compassion, and "forgiving one another" as God has forgiven us (4:32, cf. Col 3:13; Matt 6:14).

To forgive as God forgives leads naturally to the thought that believers become "imitators of God" (cf. Matt 5:48), living like God's "beloved children" (5:1) and like Christ who "loved us" to the point of "surrendering himself for us" as a "sacrifice to God" (5:2). Paul urged his churches to "imitate" himself (e.g., 1 Cor 11:1; Phil 3:17); the exhortation to imitate God is unique to this letter. The following warnings focus especially on sexual morality (actions and speech) and on "greed," which is equated with "idolatry" (5:5; Col 3:5). The repeated warning against "obscenity . . . or suggestive talk" (5:4; cf. 4:29) perhaps indicates that the writer had witnessed or at least heard of such inappropriate speech among the churches. "Thanksgiving" should better characterize their conversation, as well as the awareness that immorality forfeits salvation (5:5).

Perhaps a particular person or teaching is in mind with the warning against "empty arguments." That warning and the explanation that such things bring "the wrath of God on the disobedient" (5:6) closely imitate Colossians (Col 2:8; 3:6), where a particular problem was in view. In any event, the writer wishes for there to be a clear boundary between the church and, at least, the "immoral" ones in society who were alluded to in the previous warnings—"do not be associated with them" (5:7; cf. 5:11). This compares interestingly with Paul's words to the Corinthians, distinguishing between the "immoral of this world," with whom association was unavoidable, and the "immoral" within the church (1 Cor 5:9-13). For Paul, it was the latter that were the real threat.

The contrast this writer draws between the church and the larger society is abundantly apparent in the following verses (5:8-14) with their imagery of "light" and "darkness." Prior to "learning Christ" (4:20), believers were "darkness," but now "in the Lord" they *are* light" and must "live as children of light," which recalls 5:1: "Be imitators of God." "Light" as a metaphor for God and the realm of God is very common in Scripture (e.g., Ps 27:1; 44:4; Isa 9:2; 60:1, 19-20; Mic 7:8; John 1:4-9; 8:12). The darkness is not beyond God's realm, but it resists God's invitation (cf. John 3:20-21). Light, on the other hand, produces every kind of goodness (5:9), discerns "what is pleasing to the Lord," and "exposes" the "hidden, shameful" deeds of darkness as evil (5:10-12).

The next verses (5:13-14) are difficult, and interpretation has to squeeze out of the text what it does not precisely say. To "be exposed by the light" and thus to "become visible" means to

"come into the light," which presumably has something to do with conversion. Indeed, perhaps the writer is suggesting that believers have an obligation so to "expose" and indict as evil "the fruitless works of darkness" (5:11) that evildoers will come to the light of Christ. It is perhaps in that sense that "what [or whoever] becomes visible *is* [or 'becomes'?] light" (5:14) and is identified with Christ. The quotation supports this interpretation, since it is almost certainly a baptism hymn (cf. Rom 6:3-4) and addresses the newly baptized: "Awake, O sleeper, and arise from the dead, and Christ will shine on you" (cf. Isa 60:1). Ephesians, of course, intends the reminder for more than just the newly baptized. Ultimately, believers, like Jesus (John 8:12), are to be "the light of the world" (Matt 5:16).

The whole congregation is to see that they "walk" as "wise ones" (5:15), "making the best of the opportunity" (Col 4:5) in the midst of the present "evil days" (5:16; cf. 6:13). Neither being "ignorant" ("foolish") nor "getting drunk" will enable the proper "understanding" that is so essential (4:17-18, cf. 3:18-19; 4:13-14). This long section comes to an end by again borrowing from Colossians (Col 3:16), exhorting believers, "filled with the Spirit" (5:18), to share "psalms and hymns" with one another (such as 5:14) and constantly to "give thanks . . . to God the Father" (5:19-20).

5:21–6:9 Household rules

This section obviously corresponds to, and is a development of, Colossians 3:18–4:1. The development is noteworthy. Ephesians dwells at far greater length on men's obligation to love their wives and, in comparing that love to Christ's love for the church, produces an impressive meditation on the relationship between Christ and the church. Nevertheless, the same enormous problems regarding the "subordination" of wives and the "obedience" of slaves exist for Ephesians as for Colossians. Both presuppose the unquestioned patriarchal structure of first-century society.

Whereas, in other respects, Ephesians wants the church to be different from the rest of society (5:7, 11) and probably sees these instructions also as furthering that purpose, society's template with regard to marriage and slavery remains unchanged. For Ephesians, the "difference" is a greater measure of "love" for wives (5:25) and less "bullying" ("threatening") for slaves (6:9). It has taken until modern times for the *structures* of society and for the church itself to change, and the process is not even yet complete. We cannot, therefore, judge them; we have to turn the eye of discernment onto ourselves, and how we interpret and apply these verses is a test for that discernment.

Verse 21, grammatically, could as well be included with the previous section as with this one, but its verb ("be subordinate") is intended to be applied in a special way to "wives" (5:22). The author assumes that wives ought to "subordinate" themselves to their husbands (cf. 1 Pet 3:1-6) and, going beyond Colossians, strengthens this idea by weaving it into the theme of Christ as "the head of the church" (5:23). The *distortion* of this text that sometimes leads women to think they must stay with an abusive husband or men to think they have a right to hit their wives (!) has been criticized strongly by the American Catholic bishops. It intends, in fact, to make Christian marriage into a model of the love Christ has for the church and probably also into a demonstration of the goodness of Christian faith. We can certainly affirm that intention and that spouses should subordinate themselves to *one another* (5:21; 1 Cor 7:4).

The idea that Christ's death was, specifically, "for the sake of" the *church* (5:25) is unique to this letter. Paul's emphasis—the two thoughts are not contradictory—was that Christ died "for the ungodly" (Rom 3:23-26; 5:6-8), outsiders being more clearly included. That sacrifice is to be a model, for wives and husbands alike, of how they are to love one another. Christ "sanctified" the church, "cleansing" it both by his death and by baptism (5:26). The church is imaged here as Christ's bride (cf. Ezek 16:8-9), whom he will espouse to himself at the final judgment "in splendor," "holy and blameless" (5:27).

To love one's spouse is also to "love oneself" (5:28), one's own "body" and "flesh" (5:29). That, says the writer, was how "Christ loved the church, since we are members of his body" (5:29-30; cf. 1 Cor 12:27). Mention of "flesh" prepares for the quotation from Genesis 2:24, which is the climax of the second creation story (the first = Gen 1:1–2:4). That story focuses primarily on humans and the creation of sex and marriage (Gen 2:20-24). Ephesians takes that text—most notably, "the two shall become one flesh"—and applies it, as "a great

mystery . . . to Christ and to the church" (5:31-32) and the "marriage" between them. How ironic and tragic that such a beautiful image has sometimes been a device for violence, including the violence of the subordination of women to men. The writer returns to the theme of marriage in the church and emphasizes that "each man should love his wife as himself" and, as ancient society would expect, that "the wife should respect [literally 'fear'] her husband" (5:33). *Mutual love* and respect would properly be our modern emphasis.

The command that children should "obey" their parents (6:1) is nearly identical with Colossians 3:20 but adds motivation by quoting Deuteronomy 5:16 (cf. Exod 20:12). Different words (from Colossians) are used to instruct "fathers"—we would say "parents"—not to "provoke children to anger" (6:3). The command to "raise children in the instruction of the Lord" (6:4) is unique to Ephesians. The lengthy instructions to "slaves" (6:5-8), as in Colossians 3:22-25, probably indicate both the presence of slaves among the readers and the need to make slavery compatible with faith. "There is no longer slave nor free" (Gal 3:28) is being compromised. As the husband is likened to Christ (5:23), so also is the slave master (6:5), with terrible effects in later history. We can apply to ourselves the exhortations to serve "in sincerity of heart," rather than for "currying favor" (6:5-6), and fruitfully be aware that there is one God "in heaven" over all, no matter status or identity (6:8-9).

6:10-20 Final exhortations

In this final section the writer envisions Christian life as a great battle against "the evil spiritual powers" (6:12) that Christ has defeated (1:20-22). The battle continues because believers *are* "flesh and blood," but the evil they battle is not (6:12). Ultimately, in spite of 2:4-8, even Ephesians knows that the process of salvation is not yet complete. Therefore, especially through prayer (6:18-20), believers need *God's* "strength" and "armor" to withstand "the tactics of the devil" (6:11-13). "The evil day" (6:13) is the time of "temptation" ("testing") and "evil," from which we also pray to be delivered in the Lord's Prayer (Matt 6:13).

Drawing on Old Testament texts listing the weaponry of God (Isa 11:5; 59:16-17; Wis 5:16-23), the writer describes the (primarily defensive) armor that will see believers through the fight:

"the girdle of truth," "the breastplate of righteousness," and so on (6:14-17). "The gospel of peace" (6:15) might better be translated "the *proclamation of peace*," meaning that believers must be "ready" to witness to the "peace" that God gives and thereby to "extinguish the flaming arrows" aimed at them (6:16). This passage, in other words (cf. 5:11-14), might be a hint of some concern for defense of the gospel among non-believers. The only *offensive* weapon in the believer's armor is "the sword of the Spirit, which is the word of God" (6:17); evangelization, that is, sharing the gospel, is part of the believer's task. "The word" is not to be identified with the Bible or any part of it; "the word" is "alive and active" (Heb 4:12) in and among believers. The Bible enables us to recognize "the word," but it does not define it.

It is for continued, vigorous sharing of "the mystery of the gospel" (6:19) that the writer asks the recipients to pray, as they also pray for themselves and "for all the holy ones" (6:18), that is, the church. The final reminder of Paul's "imprisonment" keeps the great apostle's memory present as the letter draws to a close (6:20).

6:21-24 Conclusion

The note about Tychicus's bringing "news" of Paul and "that he may encourage your hearts" (6:21-22) is nearly word-for-word identical with Colossians 4:7-8. The letter concludes, wishing "peace to believers." "Love with faith" (6:23) is unique to Ephesians, as is the final blessing. On the other hand, "grace" was a key term in Paul's theology (e.g., Rom 3:24; 11:6, cf. Eph 2:8) and in all his final blessings. Paul and Ephesians agree: "grace" is the beginning and the end of Christian existence, and our only hope for "immortality" (6:24). Many manuscripts add "Amen."

THE LETTER TO THE

PHILIPPIANS

Vincent M. Smiles

INTRODUCTION

The importance of Philippi

Philippi was located about 110 miles northeast of Thessalonica in Macedonia. It got its name in 360 B.C. from Philip II of Macedon, father of Alexander the Great. In 42 B.C. it was the scene of a great battle to decide the successor of Julius Caesar; Caesar Augustus, the emperor at the time of Jesus' birth, was the victor. In 31 B.C. he made Philippi a Roman colony, permitting army veterans to settle there. Philippi, therefore, enjoyed special status; it came under Italian law and was exempt from various taxes. Paul was aware of its prestige (see 3:20; 4:22).

According to Acts 16:9, a vision summoned Paul to preach the gospel in Macedonia. From the very beginning Paul's relations with Philippi were warm and affectionate; it was the one church that consistently supported him in his apostolic work (4:15-16, cf. 1:5). Its founding members and leaders included a number of women (4:2-3; Acts 16:13-15), but unlike other cities of Paul's mission, Philippi seems not to have included a synagogue or any large Jewish population. The issue of when and where Paul wrote his letter to the Philippians takes us into its particular difficulties.

Challenges for interpretation

Scholars are agreed that Paul wrote Philippians, but most also believe that the letter we have was originally two or three separate letters. The most obvious seam is between 3:1 and 3:2; the switch of mood is so abrupt that even those who defend the unity of the letter struggle to explain the transition. Another difficulty is the delayed thank-you (4:10-20), which interrupts what looks like a standard ending of a letter (4:8-9, 21-23).

These and other observations have given rise to numerous theories about the original *letters* to Philippi and, of course, such theories affect the question of when and where Paul wrote. A common theory of multiple letters regards 4:10-20 as *letter A*, written from prison in Ephesus, about A.D. 55. *Letter B*, from prison a few weeks later, comprises 1:1–3:1a, 4:4-7, 21-23, and *letter C* includes the polemical 3:1b–4:3, 8-9 after Paul's release and was written perhaps from another city (Corinth?). A more simple theory would be: *letter A* = 1:1–3:1; 4:1-7, 10-23 (from Ephesus, about 55), and *letter B* = 3:2-21; 4:8-9 (from Corinth, about 56). All such theories presuppose that an editor, for some reason, conflated the original two or three letters and in doing so chopped off the openings and endings of one or more letters to avoid needless repetition.

Those who reject such theories insist that, in spite of difficulties, the letter is coherent and should be read as a unity, and certainly it *can* be read as a unity. The commentary to follow will do so, without denying that the theories of division are, at least from a historical perspective, very valuable. Assuming its unity, where was Paul when he wrote Philippians? The traditional view is that he wrote from Rome in the early sixties while under house arrest (Acts 28:16-31). Philippians, however (see 1:12-20; 2:17), envisions more than house arrest, and travel between Rome and Philippi was more difficult than the ease of communication that is presumed in the letter (2:19-30). Some scholars think Ephesus was the more likely place of writing, some time in the mid-fifties.

There is no explicit record of Paul being imprisoned in Ephesus, but that is not an insurmountable problem (see 2 Cor 1:8; 11:23; 1 Cor 15:32). The best guess, therefore, is that Philippians comprises one or more letters written from prison in Ephesus in the mid-fifties and perhaps also from Corinth a year or so later.

COMMENTARY

1:1-2 Greeting

The opening is brief and simple but includes interesting details. Timothy is named as co-sender, but he probably had little to do with the actual composition of the letter. From 1:3 Paul speaks in terms of his particular experience (e.g., 1:12-17); this letter, like the others that are original to Paul (Romans, 1 and 2 Corinthians, Galatians, Philippians, 1 Thessalonians, Philemon), bears the imprint of one very strong personality. It is unusual that Paul here does not claim the title "apostle." It was sometimes important for him to do so (e.g., Rom 1:1; Gal 1:1-12), but in the warm relationship he shared with Philippi, there was no such need. "Slaves" recalls Jesus' instruction about leadership (Mark 10:44).

Even more interesting, but also strange, is Paul's special mention of "the overseers and ministers." The Greek terms (*episkopos* and *diakonos*) are sometimes translated "bishop" and "deacon" (e.g., 1 Tim 3:2, 8), but in his list of primary church functions (1 Cor 12:28), these titles have no place, and in fact "overseers" are never mentioned again in the original letters. He uses "minister" (*diakonos*) to describe, among others, himself and other leading "ministers" of the gospel (1 Cor 3:5; 2 Cor 3:6), but only in the case of Phoebe (Rom 16:1) does it have an official ring to it. These titles are so unusual that some scholars think the phrase was inserted by an editor, but this is doubtful. They must have been leaders of various house-churches—people like Euodia, Syntyche, and Clement (4:2-3).

The letter is addressed to "*all* the holy ones" (the baptized); he greets them with the standard but significant formula he employs in all his letters: "Grace to you and peace . . ." Though Paul addresses the community six times as "brothers" (e.g., 1:12), it is important to note that he is addressing women and men alike (note 4:2-3). *Adelphoi* ("brothers") in this context is best translated "believers."

1:3-11 The thanksgiving

The warmth of Paul's relationship with the Philippians is evident here: "I thank my God at *every* remembrance of you, praying *always* with joy at my *every* prayer for *all* of you." In Greek the italicized words all begin with the letter "p," increasing the emotional and rhetorical effect. "My God" (also 4:19; Rom 1:8) denotes a personal relationship and is quite common in the psalms (e.g., Ps 22). "Joy" characterizes this letter throughout (1:18; 2:2, 17; 3:1; 4:1, 4, 10).

As a "thanksgiving," the passage is a standard feature of letter writing (cf. Rom 1:8-15; 1 Cor 1:4-9, etc.), but there is nothing standard or merely formal about Paul's "joyful" remembrance of the Philippians and of their "partnership in the gospel from the first day until now" (1:5). "Partnership" (or "participation"—see 2:1; 3:10; 4:15) refers both to their spiritual and their material sharing in the task of the gospel (see 4:15). They "defend and confirm" (1:7) the gospel by living it and by "struggling together" for its progress (1:27). They have also generously enabled Paul's missionary endeavors by their gifts to him (4:16); the phrase "until now" may refer to Paul's having just received their latest contribution.

The beginning of the "good work" that God "will continue" in them was that "first day," when Paul came to Philippi and was received, according to Acts 16:11-15, by Lydia and the other women at the "place of prayer." Lydia herself is not mentioned in Philippians, but the leadership of women seems to have remained important (4:2-3) in the intervening years. Lydia was from Thyatira (northwest Asia Minor), says Luke (Acts 16:14), so she may no longer have been in Philippi.

The "day of Christ" is the first of several references to the expected return of Jesus (see 1:10; 2:16; 3:20-21). Some years earlier Paul had fully expected to be alive for Jesus' return (1 Thess 4:15-17), but now he realizes that he may die first (1:20-23). Nevertheless, the end will come soon, and Paul's confident prayer (1:9) is that, at the judgment, the believers of Philippi will be "pure and blameless" (1:10). In the meantime, he says, he "longs for them with the affection of Christ Jesus" (1:8); Paul's love for his churches was unmistakable (1 Thess 2:7-8; 2 Cor 11:11). His final prayer is that they "will be filled with the fruit of righteousness" (1:11). Paul will resume this theme of "righteousness through Christ" in the fiery words of 3:2-9.

Although he was in prison (1:7, 13-17), the apostle was joyful and confident. Epaphroditus, who has delivered the Philippians' gift (4:18), remains with Paul, recovering, we will discover later, from a near brush with death (2:25-30). Also with Paul is Timothy, of whom Paul will speak affectionately (2:22).

1:12-26 The irresistible progress of the gospel

The first paragraph here (1:12-18) is remarkable, speaking as it does of the effect of Paul's imprisonment, first among "the praetorium and all the rest" (1:13), probably denoting non-believers, and second, among believers also (1:14-18). "The praetorium" (palace guard) refers not to a place but to the soldiers and others of "Caesar's household" (4:22). Paul wants the Philippians to know that his imprisonment, although on the surface a disadvantage, "served to advance the gospel." This goes along with Paul's optimistic tone, in spite of the most difficult circumstances. Even among non-believers it has become known that Paul's imprisonment is "in Christ," meaning that they see Paul, not as a common criminal, but as a witness of Christ. And "most of the believers," far from being intimidated by his imprisonment, have gained greater confidence "to speak the word fearlessly" (1:14).

It is amazing that Paul has such equanimity in the circumstances he describes next. "Some," he says, "proclaim Christ because of envy and rivalry" (1:15), "thinking to cause me trouble in my imprisonment" (1:17). We know, then, that these opponents were Christians, but it is impossible to know much else about them or what sort of "trouble" (or "affliction") they might cause for Paul. Because he was a champion of the freedom of Gentile believers from the Jewish law, Paul ran into opposition many times, including in Antioch, Jerusalem (Gal 2:1-14; Acts 15:1-5), Galatia (Gal 1:6-9; 6:12-16), and Philippi (Phil 3:2-9; cf. Rom 3:8; 6:1-15).

The "trouble" these people sought to cause was perhaps simply distress in Paul's own mind. Their intention, however, may have been even more sinister, hoping to make his imprisonment worse and more protracted. Whatever the case, Paul refused to see it as a defeat. There was no trouble that could subdue his joy and confidence in Christ! Especially encouraging for him are those believers who preach Christ "for the sake of God's will" (1:15, not merely human "good will") and "out of love," aware that Paul was in prison "in defense of the gospel" (1:16). All that matters for Paul, whether to his advantage or not, is that "Christ is proclaimed; in that," he says, "I rejoice"!

"And I will continue to rejoice," he insists, "because I know that 'this will result in deliverance for me.'" These last words are from the book of Job (13:16). Whether or not the Philippians would recognize the reference—Philippians is almost devoid of Old Testament quotations—it seems clear that Paul sees in Job's words a reason for confidence. In the text in question, Job rebukes his friends because they have presumed to speak for God. Job, however, is convinced that they do not understand God's ways and that God, somehow, will vindicate him and bring him "deliverance" (or "salvation"). In applying this text to himself, Paul appears to be saying that he "knows" what will happen to him. In reality, however, he does not even know whether the outcome will be "life or death" (1:20). Either alternative will be "deliverance"!

"The prayer" of his friends in Philippi and the "support of the Spirit of Jesus Christ" (1:19) are further reasons that Paul is confident. In fact, his confidence extends to "eager expectation and hope" (1:20). "Hope" here denotes the biblical virtue that "waits with eager longing" (Rom 8:19); it is not to be understood, as so often in modern speech, as a vague and anxious desire ("I hope the weather will be nice"). Paul fully "expects" his hope to be fulfilled. "I shall not be put to shame," he says, "in any way," meaning that there is nothing his enemies can do to defeat him. That is true for the simple reason that Paul has let go of any personal gain or advantage; all that matters is that "Christ is glorified," and whether that happens by Paul's "life or death" (1:20), it is all he desires.

Indifference to death is difficult to understand. We associate such indifference with the depths of despair and pain, but here it arises in a letter which, more than any other, exudes hope and joy. This gives a glimpse into Paul's spirit and into what motivated his long and difficult ministry. For Paul, "life" itself is nothing other than "Christ," and therefore "to die is gain" (1:21). To the Galatians he had said, "I have been crucified with Christ. I no longer live, rather, Christ lives within me" (Gal 2:19-20; cf. Rom 8:10-11). His entire life and identity are enfolded in his allegiance to Jesus. He is, therefore, content "to live in the flesh" for the sake of "fruitful labor" (1:22) for the gospel. On the other hand, he has a great desire "to depart this life and be with Christ—which is far better" (1:23). Nevertheless, he knows that it may be "more necessary for [their] benefit" to remain (1:24) and, for some reason, he seems convinced that this is the more likely outcome.

In fact, Paul is sure that he will "remain and abide with" them for their "progress and joy in the faith" (1:25), "so that" the Philippians "may boast in Christ Jesus" when Paul comes to them again. "Boasting" is closely related to the joyful hope that so fills this letter. Paradoxically, there is no such thing for Paul as "boasting" (Rom 3:27; 4:2; 1 Cor 1:29), as though humans could somehow be independent of God. On the other hand, within the relationship of faith, Paul often speaks of the joyful boast that believers can have because of what God enables within them (e.g., Rom 5:2-3; 2 Cor 1:12-14; Phil 2:16; 1 Thess 2:19).

1:27–2:18 Encouragement and instructions

Paul now changes his tone. In a long, complex sentence (vv. 27-30), he turns emphatically to instruction: "Only [one thing]—conduct yourselves worthily . . ." "Conduct yourselves" could be translated "be citizens" (cf. 3:20) and would be relevant in Philippi, which, as a Roman colony, was proud of its full citizenship rights. Believers, however, now are citizens under "Christ's gospel," and Paul's wish is that whether he can "come and see" them or not (2:12), he should "hear about" them that they "stand in one spirit" (1:27). "Spirit" might include reference to the Holy Spirit, but the parallel phrase "one mind" shows that Paul is primarily thinking of the spiritual unity of believers. "The faith of the gospel" (1:27) is a unique phrase; it probably means "the faith that arises from the gospel." Though the Philippians are being persecuted, they are not to "be startled in any way by the opponents" (1:28), the latter referring probably to unbelievers, the probable source of the trouble Paul himself experienced in Philippi (1 Thess 2:2).

The next part of this complex sentence gets even more difficult. "This," he says, "is proof to them of destruction, but of your salvation" (1:28). "This" must refer to the whole situation of belief opposed by unbelief. The next two phrases ("proof to them of destruction, but of your salvation") could mean (1) that unbelievers think that the outcome will be "destruction" for the church, with Paul, however, assuring believers that in reality it will be their "salvation." Alternatively, (2) Paul assures the church that the present situation shows that unbelievers are bound for destruction (cf. 1 Cor 1:18; 2 Cor 4:3), but believers for salvation (1:28; cf. Rom 8:28). "And this," he concludes, "is from God," meaning not only salvation but also the mysterious outworking of things that, on either interpretation, unbelief cannot fathom.

The next two verses (1:29-30) assert that *everything* derives from God, both the capacity "to believe"—faith is a gift (cf. Gal 3:23-25)—and "to suffer" for Christ. The Philippians share "the same struggle" which they saw in Paul when he was persecuted in Philippi (1 Thess 2:2; Acts 16:20-24) and which they now hear about as he languishes in prison. For Paul, to suffer for Christ is a privilege (Rom 5:3) and an opportunity to experience grace (2 Cor 12:8-10).

Paul's rhetoric rises to a higher pitch as he reminds the Philippians of the fundamental qualities of life "in Christ" and appeals to them to live these out in full. "If there is . . ." is purely rhetorical; there is no question of whether these qualities are present (cf. 4:8). The passage is carefully and artistically phrased, so that commentary might obscure rather than clarify. Verses 1-4 prepare for the exhortation of verse 5 and the uniquely beautiful, but also deeply theological hymn of verses 6-11. Because of its unusual wording and rhythm, some scholars believe that Paul *quotes* a hymn that he did not himself compose. In any event, he found it deeply meaningful.

The crucial phrases parallel and reinforce one another, but not merely for rhetorical effect. Paul may have in mind emerging tensions within the Philippian churches (4:2-3), which he wishes to forestall. "Encouragement in Christ" and "comfort of love" (2:1) are synonymous; "love" refers both to the love Christ has for believers and to the love he inspires in them for one another (Gal 2:20; Phil 1:9). "Participation (or 'fellowship') in the spirit" recalls Paul's blessing that has been adopted into the liturgy (2 Cor 13:13) and, more clearly than 1:27 ('in one spirit'), alludes to the Spirit of God that believers share. The words "compassion (or 'affection') and mercy" reflect Paul's insistence elsewhere on the primacy of the love-command (Rom 13:8-10; Gal 5:14).

"Complete my joy" (2:2) finishes the thought begun with all those "ifs" and recalls the great joy Paul felt with regard to the Philippians (1:4; 4:1). Being "in Christ," believers can be of "the same mind" and have "the same love," that is, mutual love for one another. The next phrases—"united in heart (or 'mind'), thinking one thing"—repeat and reinforce the same notion. The words "Do nothing" (2:3) are actually not in the Greek text, though it is reasonable to supply them. Paul simply says, "Nothing out of selfishness nor from vainglory ('conceit'), but with humility regard others as more important . . ." "Others" here refers to believers; elsewhere Paul extends this love to outsiders (4:5; Gal 6:10; 1 Thess 3:12; 5:15). "Humility" and making others' interests more important than one's own (2:4, cf. 1 Cor 10:24, 33; 13:5) are not to be understood as groveling subservience; being humble has nothing to do with being a doormat (John 18:22-23). The humility Paul describes is self-sacrifice for others born out of unity in Christ. The basis for such humility is what Paul turns to in the Christ-hymn that follows.

Paul introduces the hymn with a third use of the verb *phronein* ("think") in this immediate pas-

sage (2:1-5; see 3:15); the related noun is part of the word "humility" ("lowly thinking"—2:3). It denotes an attitude or mindset more than "thought." The New American Bible translation may be correct, but more probably Paul is simply pointing to "the attitude that is also in Christ Jesus" himself (2:5), as the opening lines of the hymn suggest. Paul presents Christ's loving and humble attitude as the model for Christian morality. The hymn itself is almost impossible to interpret in a short space; we will confine ourselves to a few essentials.

Whether the hymn is poetry as such or simply rhythmic, exalted prose, it is constructed around balanced, pregnant phrases that tell and celebrate the stages of Christ's redemptive acts for the world. It can be divided into six stanzas of three lines each, dealing with: beginning—emptying—dying—being exalted—being named—being glorified. The first half comprises Christ's actions, the second half God's. The central point is the little phrase "death on a cross." The hymn evokes and may, in some respects, be modeled on the great Servant Song of the Good Friday liturgy (Isa 52:13–53:12).

The major problem of the first three lines (2:6) is whether they envisage Christ in divine preexistence ("in the form of God"), analogous to John 1:1, or as the antitype to Adam, who also was "in God's image" (Gen 1:26-27), but who, unlike Christ, "grasped at" equality with God and was disobedient (Gen 3:1-19). There are strong arguments on both sides. It is also possible—and an easy way out—that Paul might have entertained aspects of both interpretations. Other texts (notably 2 Cor 8:9; Gal 4:4; Col 1:15-17) show that the preexistence of Christ was not foreign to Paul, but Christ as the antitype of disobedient Adam is even more clearly attested (Rom 5:12-21; 1 Cor 15:22). A great deal depends on how individual phrases are translated and interpreted. "Equality with God" as "something to be *grasped at*" suggests the Adamic interpretation, but the crucial Greek word *(harpagmon)* could also be rendered "something to *be held on to*" or *"be taken advantage of."* Overall, the Adamic interpretation is more likely, but certainty is impossible.

The next stanza ("emptying") has three phrases describing Christ's entrance into the human condition (2:7). The preexistence interpretation sees here the description of the incarnation, as in John 1:14

("the Word became flesh") and can properly say that it was precisely in being a "slave" (not in spite of it) that Jesus revealed who God is. "Emptied himself" evokes 2 Corinthians 8:9 ("though he was rich, Christ became poor for your sake"). The Adamic view focuses on the contrast between human arrogance ("You will be like gods"—Gen 3:5) and Christ's humility.

The final stanza of the hymn's first part describes Christ's self-sacrificial death (2:7-8). All can agree that Christ's "obedience to death" is, for Paul, the heart of the gospel, and, as here, he sometimes focuses on Jesus' death without explicit mention of the resurrection (e.g., 1 Cor 2:2; Gal 2:19-20). In the immediate context, Christ's self-emptying death provides the basis for the self-sacrifice that Paul wants the Philippians to practice toward one another (2:3-4). The nadir of the hymn is the little phrase "death on a cross," which many interpreters understand to be Paul's addition to the hymn he is quoting. That view may be correct; the phrase breaks the rhythm. On the other hand, standing at the center, it may be intended to stand alone as the turning point. Paul was not bound by rules as he either quoted or composed. However understood, it is a stark but powerful image: Christ crucified, the one on whom human redemption turns, seemingly abandoned (Mark 15:34; Gal 3:13).

"Because of this" (2:9) recalls the similar turning point in the hymn of the Suffering Servant (Isa 53:11-12) and does not primarily envisage reward for suffering but points to the *ways* of God, victory *through* suffering. God reveals in Jesus the *reversal* of human expectations by highly exalting the Crucified and bestowing on him "the name above every other name." This may refer to the exalting of the name "Jesus" itself (2:10), but probably it envisages God conferring on Jesus the name "Lord." Throughout the Old Testament, "Lord" *(kyrios)* is the translation for the sacred name YHWH, the sacred name for God (Exod 3:14; 20:7). The preexistence view of the hymn sees Jesus being raised again to his previous exalted status (cf. John 17:5). The Adamic view takes at face value that God "highly exalted" Jesus and "gave him a name" he did not previously have (cf. Acts 2:36; Rom 1:3-4). The latter view is not, of course, a denial of Jesus' divine nature but simply says that it was *not yet so fully* articulated. That Paul saw Jesus as "the Son of God" is quite clear

(e.g., Rom 8:2, 32; Gal 4:4), but in Paul's time the formulations of the Nicene Creed were far in the future.

Be that as it may, the present text provides clear precedent for later formulations. Isaiah 45:23, clearly quoted in 2:10-11 ("every knee shall bend . . . every tongue confess") applies to Jesus words that the text from Isaiah uses of God; all creation and all parts of creation will own and confess that "Jesus is Lord" (Rom 10:9; 1 Cor 12:3) and in glorifying Jesus will glorify "God the Father." So concludes this remarkable hymn. Its second half is not as relevant to Paul's point that believers are to imitate the humility of Jesus. Nevertheless, in depicting also the final stage of Christ's self-sacrifice, it enables believers to have a greater vision of the path of faith.

In the next paragraph (2:12-18) Paul uses the example of Christ to exhort the Philippians to both greater effort and a deeper vision. Of great interest is the command "Work out your own salvation." It arises from mention of Paul's "absence." When present, *he* worked for their salvation; now "all the more" he throws the responsibility on them. It is a remarkable command, however, because usually salvation, for Paul, is exclusively *God's* work (e.g., 1 Thess 5:9) and, in fact, he hastens to correct any misunderstanding by emphasizing that "*God* is the one who . . . works in you both to desire and to work" for salvation (2:13; cf. 1:29). Nevertheless, Paul also knows that humans have a part in the salvation of themselves and of those close to them (Rom 11:14; 1 Cor 7:16; 9:22); believers' conduct does matter.

The difference, therefore, between believers and the world ought to be apparent. Believers "shine like stars in the cosmos" (2:15), but not if "quarrels and disputes" (2:14) mark their behavior. The world, says Paul, is "crooked and perverse"; believers are to be "innocent." This can come across as an idyllic, unrealistic vision, but Paul presupposes a community where *every* member "works for salvation." There is here no handing over of responsibility to a class of "ministers and overseers" (1:1); all together "hold on to the word of life" and will prove the value of Paul's "labor" on "the day of Christ" (2:16). Meanwhile, for all his apparent optimism (1:25; 2:24), Paul acknowledges that he may be "poured out as a libation," almost certainly a reference to martyrdom (2 Tim 4:6). "Sacrifice and service" is the language of temple worship and is used elsewhere both of Paul (Rom 15:16) and of believers generally (Rom 12:1; 15:27; Phil 2:30; 4:18). Paul would find death a reason for "rejoicing" (1:23; cf. 3:10), and if it happens, he asks that the Philippians "rejoice with" him (2:18)!

2:19–3:1 Travel plans

Paul often includes, usually toward the end of his letters (see Rom 15:14-32; 1 Cor 16:5-12), some indication of the travel plans for himself and others. He hopes "to send Timothy soon" (2:19) so that he will be able to bring back good news. Paul takes this occasion to speak very warmly of Timothy (1:1; Acts 16:1), who was like a devoted child to the apostle (1:22). Paul also hopes that he himself will soon be able to come to Philippi (1:24).

He thinks it even more urgent "to send Epaphroditus," who came as "an apostle" of the Philippians (2:25), bearing their gift (4:18). The next verses suggest regular communications between Paul in prison and the Philippians. They have heard that Epaphroditus fell seriously ill ("close to death"—2:27, 30), and word has come back of their concern, so that now Epaphroditus is concerned for *them* (2:26, 28). Though he figures nowhere else in the New Testament, he was a "co-worker" with Paul for a while (2:25). Paul regarded it as a mercy of God that Epaphroditus recovered from his illness (2:27) and is concerned that the Philippians should receive him warmly and "hold such people in high regard" (2:29; cf. 1 Thess 5:13). He "risked his life" both "for the work of Christ" and for the "service" the Philippians wished to render to Paul (2:30).

The word "finally" (3:1) can signal the near conclusion of a letter (2 Cor 13:11; cf. Eph 6:10; 2 Thess 3:1) or the conclusion of one topic and transition to another (1 Cor 7:29; 1 Thess 4:1). Here, following "travel plans," the letter should be drawing to a close, but it does not, and it is unusual that there is a second "finally" (4:8). Further, the natural sequence of "Rejoice in the Lord" (3:1) is either 4:1 or 4:4, certainly not 3:2! These observations have convinced scholars either that Philippians comprises more than one letter (the majority view) or that something has caused Paul to create a very awkward transition after 3:1. In any event, 3:1 or at least the command to "rejoice in the Lord" concludes the first (half of the) letter, recalling one of its major themes. It is "no burden" to him to

repeat himself (about joy), but it is rather a "safeguard" for them (cf. Neh 8:10; Pss 81:1; 21:1).

3:2-11 An urgent warning against false faith

This paragraph shows how Paul's feelings of affection can burst into anger at those who would threaten the direction of believers' faith in Christ. The threat probably comes from conservative Jewish Christians, similar to those he contended with in Galatians. In that case the opponents were already present (Gal 1:6-7; 6:12). In this case Paul seems simply to be afraid of their imminent arrival in Philippi, and he uses harsh invectives to emphasize that such persons are not to be trusted. In calling them "dogs," he turns on them a common Jewish epithet directed at Gentiles (Mark 7:27); "evildoers" may be an ironic twist on their claim to be "law-doers," and "mutilation" *(katatome)* is a sarcastic reference to their insistence on "circumcision" *(peritome*—3:2; cf. Gal 6:12). *They* are not the true "circumcision," says Paul; *"we are,"* we "who worship through the Spirit of God" (3:3).

The opponents claim that with their adherence to the traditions and laws of Israel, *they* represent the true "Israel" ("descendants of Abraham" — Gal 3:6-9, 29). Paul insists that they are nothing of the kind and sees this as an urgent issue, because it has to do with whether believers have "confidence" in Christ—note the repetition of this word (3:3-4)—or implicitly regard Christ's death as worthless (cf. Gal 2:20-21). By his conversion Paul was convinced that the covenant, from Abraham on, was founded simply on grace and faith (Rom 4:1-5; 9:6-16); the law was secondary (Rom 4:13-17; Gal 3:15-17).

Paul's critique of these Jewish-Christian opponents must *not* be taken as a critique of Judaism, as has too often been the case. Paul's love of his heritage (e.g., Rom 9:1-5) and his confidence that God would be faithful to the covenant with them (Rom 11:1-2, 29) are well attested. The enduring value of God's covenant with the Jews was also strongly affirmed at the Second Vatican Council. This polemic has to do with particular circumstances in Philippi, not with Judaism as such.

Paul presents himself as the model to follow. If circumcision or law-obedience were crucial, Paul would have "even more" reason for "confidence" than the opponents (3:4). There follows in verses 5-6 his recounting of the privileges he enjoyed by birth and his chosen way of life as a "Pharisee," all of which attest to his unique pedigree as a devoted member of the chosen people. His "zeal" for the law, in which he had been "blameless" (3:6), had even extended to persecution of the church (cf. 1 Cor 15:9; Gal 1:13-14; Acts 7:58–8:3; 9:1-2). But what he had once thought of as "gains," now "because of Christ" he reckons as "loss" (3:7). No human privilege or achievement "counts" for anything when compared with "the supreme good of knowing Christ Jesus my Lord" (3:8).

The key issue for Paul in all his letters is the nature of the divine-human relationship—specifically, by what is it characterized? As here, he rejects law and tradition as its foundation; elsewhere he rejects human wisdom or any kind of superior status, whether religious or social (Rom 2:17-29; 1 Cor 1:18-31). All such "gains" are simply "so much rubbish"; what matters is to "know Christ" (3:8), which means to have "faith in" him (3:9), in the sense of joyful trust. To "be found in him" looks forward to the judgment, when those who are "in Christ" will have no reason for fear (2:16).

Verses 9-11 describe the purpose of letting go of former privileges and status: it is "to know him and the power of his resurrection" (3:10). "Resurrection," however, is not merely in the future; it is a *present* experience, even in the midst of suffering (2 Cor 4:7-18; 5:17). To be "in Christ" is already to "walk in newness of life" (Rom 6:4; cf. 7:6). None of this, however, is a human accomplishment. The relationship ("righteousness") believers enjoy with God derives from a "righteousness" gained by Christ that is conferred as a gift; it is not essentially dependent on law or tradition (3:9). Even "faith" (3:9) is not the *condition* of "righteousness" but simply the *way it is lived*.

3:12-21 The ongoing journey toward Christ

Having stressed again *God's* initiative (cf. 1:29; 2:13), Paul turns emphatically to the theme of human responsibility, though even here Christ's action is prominent. He uses a series of verbs ("received," "made perfect," "pursue") to describe the *process* of "straining forward" toward "perfection" in Christ. He is at pains to say that, to be sure, he is not totally "perfected," but that, as he wishes them to do, he makes maximum effort to "possess" that for which he is already "possessed by Christ" (3:12). Therefore, he lets go of "the

past" and sets his sights only on "the prize of God's upward calling" (3:13-14). Paul may again have death in mind (cf. 1:23; 2:17), but "calling" is an important word in his letters to denote both the event of conversion and the life of faith to which it leads (e.g., Rom 4:17; 8:30; 1 Cor 1:9, 26; 7:15-24). Paul considers himself and others as, in a sense, "perfect" (3:15, cf. 1 Cor 2:6; Matt 5:48), but this perfection consists in the "attitude," which he wants the Philippians to have, of *striving* for perfection! If some are inclined to disagree (cf. 1 Cor 11:16), Paul is sure that he is right and that "God will reveal this also" to them. Meanwhile they should remain constant in the progress already attained (3:16) and join together in being "imitators" of Paul and of those whose behavior is a true model.

Paul's confidence in himself, that he is a proper guide and "model" for believers, should not be seen as arrogance. The ultimate example he has in mind is Christ in his self-emptying death (2:6-8), to which all believers are to seek to be "conformed" (3:10). Paul's self-assurance derives from long years of having lived in imitation of the self-sacrificial example of Jesus. On the other hand, "there are many" whose behavior makes them "the enemies of the cross" (3:18). Paul had "often" told the Philippians of such people; they, therefore, must have known who they were. We, however, can only plead ignorance. Perhaps they are the opponents Paul inveighs against in 3:2, but that is not clear. The criticisms of them are very vague, but they may indicate moral laxity of some kind. A warning against laxity also appears in Galatians (Gal 5:13-26) following that letter's stern teaching against being overly concerned with law. The pattern here is similar.

By contrast with such people, whose "minds are set on earthly things" (3:19), "*our* citizenship is in heaven, from where we await a *savior*, the *Lord*." "Citizenship" (cf. 1:27) and "savior" are never found again in Paul's own letters; they are suited very specifically for this city with its "Roman" citizenry, which acknowledged the *emperor* (probably Nero) as "Lord" and "Savior." The contrasting of the emperor with Jesus is undoubtedly deliberate, though Paul is not preaching political rebellion (cf. Rom 13:1-7). His point is precisely that believers' hope is *not* in politics. Believers' hope is in Christ, who will, at his coming, "change our lowly body to conform with his glorified body" (3:21), a theme that Paul develops at length elsewhere (1 Cor 15:35-57). The *present* experience of *gradually* "being transformed" into the image of the Lord (2 Cor 3:18) anticipates that future "change" at the resurrection. Gradual transformation is what Paul has largely had in mind since 3:10.

4:1-9 Final appeals and exhortations

The opening demonstrates once again Paul's deep affection for, and joy in, the Philippians. We never hear elsewhere of Euodia and Syntyche. The appeal to them to "have the same mind" is the same plea of 2:2 (Rom 15:5). Paul asks his "true yokemate" (*Syzygos*—perhaps a proper name) to "assist them," probably meaning to act as an arbitrator. They were important leaders of the church in Philippi, having been foundational, along with Lydia (Acts 16:13-15), in establishing the church there. We cannot know what their dispute was, and in any case it was not overly serious; Paul has confidence that they will work it out. We also do not know anything more about "Syzygos." The word (name?) is masculine; this is not a reference, as is sometimes supposed, to Paul's wife.

Paul exhorts them all yet again to "rejoice." In that joy their "kindness" (or "gentleness") can and should "be known to all" (4:5). "The Lord is near" refers to the soon-expected "day of Christ" (2:16; cf. 3:20). In the meantime they must not "worry"; that would be the opposite of joy. They must simply make their prayers and requests known to God (4:6), and "the peace of God" (cf. John 14:27), which has to do with far more than the absence of conflict or suffering (1:29), "will guard their hearts and minds" (4:7). "Peace" is the gift that flows from "grace" (1:2; Rom 5:1-11). "Finally" Paul exhorts them simply to hold fast to all that is good and repeats again the theme of learning from and imitating his manner of following Christ. The "peace" blessing is also found elsewhere (Rom 15:33; 2 Cor 13:11).

4:10-20 Thanks for the Philippians' generosity

Many commentators regard this section as "letter A," sent before the other letter(s) as a thank-you note. That could be correct, but this is not the first time Paul has received a gift from the Philippians (4:16; cf. 2 Cor 11:9); this is the "revival" of their generosity—not that their concern had flagged, but they "lacked the opportunity" to show it (4:10). Now, however, Epaphroditus has delivered their gift (4:18), and Paul rejoices at their concern and, as is typical, not only gives thanks for the material blessing but also reflects on the spiritual riches he has in Christ (4:13). As elsewhere, Paul can appear slightly arrogant as he assures them that he has "learned" to be "self-sufficient" (4:11-12). He just barely says "thanks" (4:14), but his tone is not so much arrogant as embarrassed.

Elsewhere, especially in the Corinthian letters (1 Cor 9:3-18; 2 Cor 12:13-16), Paul refused to exercise his "right" to be paid for his apostolic work, "working night and day" rather than be a burden on anyone (1 Thess 2:9). For some reason, however, he had long ago entered into a financial arrangement with the Philippians (4:15) but was hesitant to accept their money. It might appear that he wanted their *possessions* rather than *themselves* (2 Cor 12:14) and be no better than other "peddlers of the word of God" (2 Cor 2:17). Further, his enemies might say that he appropriated for himself (2 Cor 8:20-21) money he had promised to collect for Jerusalem (Gal 2:10; Rom 15:25-26). So he assures the Philippians that he is "not eager for the gift" but for "the profit that accrues to *their* account" (4:17). The money is fully adequate to his needs, but, more important, it is "an acceptable sacrifice, pleasing to God" (4:18). And God will also fill their every need "according to his wealth in glory" (4:19). Paul concludes his thank-you in the manner of a prayer, giving glory to God (4:20).

4:21-23 Final greetings and blessing

The sending of greetings is common enough (see 1 Cor 16:19-20; 2 Cor 13:12), but particular here is the mention of greetings from some in "Caesar's household" (4:22), which to many suggests that Paul was in Rome. This is possible, but Caesar's officials and servants were in major cities throughout the empire, including Philippi. The mention of Caesar (only here in Paul's letters; cf. Rom 13:1-7) would be meaningful for this Roman colony. Paul ends the letter with his standard blessing (1 Cor 16:23; Gal 6:18); it echoes his opening greeting (1:2). "Grace" is the beginning and end of Christian existence.

THE LETTER TO THE
COLOSSIANS

Vincent M. Smiles

INTRODUCTION

Colossians among Paul's letters

Among the thirteen letters that bear Paul's name, Colossians has a unique place. Seven letters are universally accepted as written by Paul (Romans, 1 and 2 Corinthians, Galatians, Philippians, 1 Thessalonians, Philemon). A large majority think that Paul did not write the Pastoral Letters (1 and 2 Timothy, Titus) or Ephesians, and a growing majority think the same regarding 2 Thessalonians. That leaves Colossians. A small majority favor the conclusion that Paul himself is not the author, but a number of them think that Paul was still alive and may have had some say in the letter's composition. In this case, someone like Timothy was the main author, with Paul providing input. Just about all would agree with one author's description of Colossians as a "bridge" between Paul himself and those who continued his ministry and wrote further letters in his name.

Colossians certainly bears many striking similarities to Paul's letters, but with regard to style and theology and the absence of some key Pauline terms (e.g., "righteousness," "law," addressing the readers as "brothers"), its distinctiveness is very apparent. The image of Christ and the church as cosmic entities is particularly distinctive, as also is the style of lengthy sentences overflowing with synonymous expressions. Whoever wrote Colossians knew Paul's letters, and perhaps Paul himself, quite well but also had developed a unique style and theological view. Paul sometimes wrote in the name of his coworkers; here

one of them or someone associated with them has written in Paul's name.

The close connections between Colossians and Ephesians is discussed in the commentary on Ephesians (see p. 1337).

When and why was Colossians written?

A reasonable hypothesis is that the letter was written from Ephesus, perhaps while Paul was in prison in Rome or shortly after his death (i.e., early to late sixties A.D.). It has two main purposes: first, to respond to the challenge presented by "the philosophy" (2:8), and second, to provide some support for Epaphras (1:7; 4:12-13) and others in their furthering of Paul's ministry. "The philosophy" probably had its home in Judaism (note 2:11, 16, 21) and invoked ideas from popular philosophy, such as "the elements of the world" (2:8), which were identified with spiritual "powers" (2:10, 15, 18). Colossians has none of the polemic of Galatians, but as in that case, the law was being introduced as a necessary factor between believers and God, as though the divine-human relationship required a legal code (see 2:13-15). Like Paul in Galatians, this writer insists that believers live "in Christ" (2:7) and indeed "in God" (3:3) and have no need of any such intervening power (cf. Gal 2:19-21).

The value of Colossians for today is in that teaching. Believers in every generation need to remember that nothing is to displace the primacy of a direct relationship with God "in Christ."

COMMENTARY

1:1-2 Opening greeting

The opening verse is identical to the opening words of 2 Corinthians 1:1. In Corinth (1 Cor 9:1-5; 2 Cor 11:5-33) and in Galatia (Gal 1:1–2:14), Paul had to defend his apostolate. In Colossae his apostolate seems to have been unchallenged, but the words "apostle of Christ Jesus by the will of God" might have been necessary because the Colossian churches did not know him by sight (2:1) and also he wanted to make more effective the commendation of those who would continue his ministry (1:7; 4:7-14). Timothy had long been a major partner in Paul's mission (1 Thess 1:1; 3:2; Acts 16:1-3). Although the addressees are "the believers in Colossae" (1:2), the letter is intended also for other churches (4:13-15). The greeting here is shorter than usual (cf. Rom 1:7; 1 Cor 1:3).

1:3-8 Thanksgiving

In Greek this thanksgiving comprises just one sentence. Generally, it echoes Paul's thought and language well; "giving thanks," "praying," and recalling of the recipients' coming to faith are all characteristic of Paul's thanksgivings (e.g., Phil 1:3-5; 1 Thess 1:2-5). Further, faith, love, and hope are featured here, as in 1 Thessalonians, but whereas, for Paul, hope is a quality that enables "eager expectation" for the coming reward (Rom 8:18-25; Phil 1:20), here it suggests not expectation but the reward itself "reserved for you in heaven" (1:5).

The Colossians "heard" the gospel from Epaphras and recognized in it "the grace of God." Epaphras had established the church in Colossae (1:7-8; 4:12-13) and had been imprisoned with Paul (Phlm 23); he also provided the news of the Colossians' faith (their "love in the Spirit") and (probably) of the competing "philosophy" (2:8). The strong commendation ("our beloved fellow slave . . .") unites Epaphras closely with Paul, confirming his fidelity to Christ *"on your behalf"* (cf. 1:24; 2:1); the latter phrase is otherwise used most often of *Christ's* sacrifice (e.g., Rom 5:8; 8:32; 1 Cor 11:24). The gospel, says the writer, "has come to you" and indeed to "the whole world," something of an exaggeration in the first century (1:23)! In any event, the gospel is "bearing fruit" among the Colossians (1:6); the writer is not fearful for them (2:5), as Paul was for the Galatians (Gal 4:11).

1:9-14 Prayer for the Colossians

This section also comprises one long sentence. It describes an enthusiastic prayer for the Colossians' growth in faith. "From the day" Paul and his companions "heard" about it, they have been praying (the verbs express continuous action) that the Colossians "might be filled" with all necessary spiritual gifts (1:9-11). There is a strong emphasis on gifts of "knowledge" and "wisdom" (1:9-10), which goes along with this letter's contesting of "a philosophy" (2:8) and with the description of Paul and his companions as those who "teach with all wisdom" (1:28). Faith has everything to do with commitment and right action, another strong emphasis of this letter (1:10, 21-22; 3:1–4:6), but faith must also be intelligent both to direct behavior (2:16-23) and for the sake of witness to outsiders (4:5-6). Behavior and knowledge are virtually inseparable (1:10).

The second half of the prayer shows that *what* believers "know" goes far beyond mere intellectual knowledge; it has to do with knowing the dignity that God bestows on believers, already granting them "a share with the saints in light" and transferring them "to the kingdom of his beloved Son" (1:12-13). Such language of future blessings realized *now* contrasts with Paul's own theology (2:12; 3:1, cf. Rom 6:5), but it reminds the Colossians that "the reality" is already theirs (2:17).

The prayer witnesses to the charismatic enthusiasm that also characterized Paul's experience of church prayer (e.g., 1 Cor 14:1-19). It conveys the thankful "joy" (1:11-12) of being in Christ; "in him" they "have redemption, the forgiveness of sins" (1:14). "Forgiveness" is virtually unmentioned in Paul's own letters (only Rom 4:7). Paul's theology deals more with God's *gifts* in Christ (Spirit, freedom, adoption) than with sins removed. Here the prayer, which has become a celebratory recounting of God's action (1:12-14), prepares for a glorious hymn in praise of the cosmic Christ.

1:15-20 The cosmic Christ

These verses encapsulate a hymn or spiritual song (3:16, cf. John 1:1-18; Phil 2:6-11), older than the letter itself, that was incorporated here, with a few editorial touches, by the letter's author. As it stands, it has two main parts: describing Christ's role in creation (1:15-17) and in reconciliation (1:18-20). Its editing is not easily distinguished from the original. Still, scholars have ventured some educated guesses, which can illustrate the kind of development that may account for this difficult but profound text.

1. "Of the church" (1:18a) breaks the established rhythm and restricts "all things" to "the church." Probably "the head of the body" originally envisaged "the body" of *creation*, applying to Christ language that, in the wider Greco-Roman culture, was sometimes used of Zeus. "Of the church" was added to prepare for subsequent teaching (2:19).

2. In 1:16b the "powers" listed correspond precisely to the "powers" which are a part of the competing teaching and which God "stripped away" and defeated (2:8-10, 15). They may have been added to 1:16 to emphasize their subordination to Christ.

3. Probably the hymn originally spoke of God ("the fullness," cf. 2:9), by means of Christ's *resurrection* ("the firstborn from the dead," 1:18), "reconciling all things through him" (1:20; cf. 2 Cor 5:18-19). The reference to Christ's death ("the blood of his cross") *after* the resurrection is awkward and looks like an editorial addition.

It is reasonable to think that the original hymn might have looked something like the following. If the bracketed lines are omitted, we end up with two stanzas of four lines each (italicized text); one theory does just that and *could* be correct.

1:15 *He is the image of the invisible God* (2 Cor 4:4),
firstborn of all creation (Prov 8:22-31; Rev 3:14),
[16] *for in him all things were created* (1 Cor 8:6; John 1:3)
(in the heavens and upon the earth) (Phil 2:10)
all things were created through him and for him (cf. Rom 11:36)
[17] (and he is before all things
and all things hold together in him
[18a] and he is the head of the body). (Eph 4:15)
[18b] *He is the beginning,*
firstborn from the dead (1 Cor 15:20),
(that he might be the first among all)
[19] *for in him all the fullness was pleased to dwell* (2:9-10)
[20] *and through him to reconcile all things* (2 Cor 5:18-19),
(whether things on earth or things in heaven).

As edited by the letter writer, this was a Christian hymn, but several scholars maintain, with good reason, that it was either modeled on an earlier Jewish hymn in praise of Wisdom (cf. Prov 8:22-31) or was inspired by applying Wisdom traditions to Christ (e.g., Wis 7:22-30), as in John 1:1-18.

The hymn was adapted to provide a theological base from which to fight "the philosophy" (2:8). If we could know this (probably Jewish) "philosophy" as the Colossians did, we would, undoubtedly, recognize some measure of sincerity and goodness in its teachers. Paul had described even Peter as "clearly wrong" and a "hypocrite" (Gal 2:12-14); so here, these teachers are described in negative terms (2:8, 18) but were not necessarily evil. Nevertheless, their teaching compromises the gospel. It seems to have involved "the elements of the world" (2:8, 20), "the principalities and powers" (2:10, 15), which humans were to obey by certain ascetic practices (2:21-23). However, the fault was not asceticism (note Matt 6:16-18; 1 Cor 7:29-35), but requiring trust to be placed in "principalities," as though they could produce what Christ had *already* accomplished. The "powers" were, in effect, becoming rivals of Christ.

The hymn, therefore, makes clear that Christ is the ruler of the *cosmos*; all powers, including angels (2:18), are subject to him. He is "the image of the invisible God, the firstborn of all creation" (1:15). The hymn has a very high view of the divinity of Christ, but it is a step in the development of doctrine, not its completion; it has not reached the level of the Nicene Creed. And yet, in both parts of the hymn (1:15, 18), Christ is supreme over creation, both its agent and its goal (1:16), the one in whom "all things hold together" (1:17). What elsewhere is said of God (Rom 11:36) is ascribed here to Christ (1:16d), who is clearly understood as preexistent before the rest of creation (1:17-18).

It is very important in this letter that Christ is "the head" not only of creation but also "of the church" (1:18). "The church" here, like Christ, is a cosmic entity, since it is "his body" (1:24). The major focus, however, remains on Christ; "in him all the fullness was pleased to dwell and, through him [Christ] to reconcile all things to him" (i.e., "to God," 2 Cor 5:19, but see 1:22). "The fullness" evidently refers to God (cf. 2:9), or at least that's the way the writer of the letter sees it. In the original it might simply have referred to "the fullness" of spiritual reality (cf. John 1:14, 16). "Full-ness" is an important concept in both Colossians and Ephesians (Eph 1:23). As Christ bears "the fullness" of God, so believers are to "be filled with all the fullness of God" and "of Christ" (Col 2:9; Eph 3:19; 4:13).

"Reconciliation," though using a slightly different Greek word, was also important in Paul's own letters (Rom 5:10-11; 2 Cor 5:18-20). There, as here, it denotes God's action in and through Christ, but whereas "the world," for Paul (2 Cor 5:19), meant simply human beings, estranged by sin from God (e.g., Rom 5:12; cf. Col 1:22), here "all things" includes the universe itself, which the ancient world sometimes saw as out of balance. They admired its beauty and order, but natural and moral evils suggested that the "body" of the *cosmos* needed the *logos* of God—reconciliation. Once again, this answers "the philosophy"; believers do not need lesser authorities ("the principalities and powers"). In Christ "the head," God has "reconciled all things" (1:20), including by "the blood of his cross" (cf. 2:14-15!).

1:21-23 The meaning of the hymn for Colossae

The amended hymn is immediately applied to the Colossians; they once were "alienated" (from God) and "hostile in mind." "Mind" has more to do with attitude than with intellect; proper "understanding" in that broader and deeper sense is crucial (e.g. 1:9-10). "Evil deeds" (1:21) are both the cause and the demonstration of minds out of tune with God (cf. Rom 1:18-32). "But now" (cf. Rom 3:21; 6:22) Christ has "reconciled" them "in his fleshly body through death" (1:22). "Fleshly body" (cf. 2:11) is a strange phrase; both terms were important for Paul (e.g., Rom 6:6, 12; 7:4; 1 Cor 12:13, 27; Rom 7:5; 8:3), but he never combined them as here. In the present context "body" recalls, and contrasts with, 1:18. The cosmic Christ is "head" of both the universe and the church, but Jesus, in his own *"fleshly* body through death," achieved reconciliation. In baptism believers "strip off" the "fleshly body" (2:11).

Christ's purpose is to "present" the reconciled before God (cf. 1:28) like a "holy, unblemished" sacrifice (cf. Rom 12:1), "irreproachable" at the judgment (1:22) in spite of their sinful past. They, of course, must "persevere in the faith"; all is not yet complete. They must remain

"firmly grounded, not shifting from the hope" that the gospel produced. The gospel of the cosmic Christ has been "proclaimed in all creation under heaven," a considerable exaggeration (as in 1:6), but aiming to demonstrate that the gospel, contrary to "the philosophy," is in accordance with God's plan for the universe "from all eternity" (1:25-26). This exaltation of the gospel, and of Paul as its "minister" (*diakonos*—cf. 1:25), goes beyond anything that Paul himself said (cf. Rom 1:16-17; 15:19), but it furthers the Colossians' idea of Christ and the church as cosmic entities. It also prepares for the next section.

1:24–2:5 Paul, his coworkers, and God's eternal plan

If Colossians was written, in part, to establish the authority of those who continued Paul's ministry, this purpose is largely accomplished here. To "rejoice in sufferings" echoes Paul's tendency to see suffering, and even death, as nothing in comparison with the joy of being in Christ (e.g., Rom 8:18; Phil 1:19-23). The following claim for Paul's sufferings, as "completing what is lacking [!] in the afflictions of Christ" (1:24), is surprising and, on the face of it, shocking. The notion that somehow Christ's death might be inadequate was anathema to Paul (Gal 2:21); it is inconceivable that such a claim is intended here. Rather, dwelling on Paul's thoughts about his sufferings as an apostle (especially 2 Cor 4:7-10), the writer sees them as having a role "for your sake . . . on behalf of [Christ's] body, the church," which, like all creation, continues to "groan" as it awaits "the redemption of our bodies" (Rom 8:18-25). It might be, as one author has suggested, that the crucial phrase should be hyphenated: "I am completing what is lacking in *Christ's-afflictions-in-my-flesh* for the sake of his body." In this case, it is not Christ's own sufferings that might be lacking, but rather the sufferings of Paul for the sake of Christ and the church.

This emotional recalling of Paul's sufferings "for your sake" and the reminder that he was the church's "minister according to God's stewardship" (1:25) shed a favorable light also on Paul's co-workers, "we" who aid him in "proclaiming" and "instructing" (1:28). "We," strongly emphasized in the Greek, includes Timothy, Epaphras, and Tychicus (1:1, 7-8; 4:7-14). Paul had "fulfilled for you the word of God," the word that was an ancient and "hidden mystery, but now is manifested to God's holy ones" (1:26). "Holy ones" (cf. 1:2) denotes *all* the baptized, but here there is some emphasis on the preachers.

"Hidden mystery" is apocalyptic language. "Apocalypse" is the Greek word for "revelation," and in apocalyptic literature (especially Daniel and Revelation; cf. Mark 13; Matt 24), God's ancient plan for the world is "revealed" to a seer (Daniel, Enoch, John, the apostles), who then imparts it to others through speech or writing (e.g., Dan 2:19-28; cf. 7:1-28; Rev 1:1, 9-11). The plan ultimately always has to do with the *eschaton*, the end of the world ("the hope of glory," 1:27). However, here the expectation of the end is not as imminent as for Paul himself (e.g., 1 Cor 7:29-31; 1 Thess 4:13-17), though it has not disappeared, as it mostly has today.

Colossians strikes a wonderful balance: the "mystery" is "Christ in you," an experience here and now that anticipates "the glory" hoped for. The apostles proclaim the gospel "so that," at the judgment, they will be able to "present everyone perfect in Christ" (cf. 1:22; Phil 2:16). That was the reason for Paul's "labor and struggle," and that, indeed, was the purpose of Christ's "power working within me" (1:29).

As there is a strong emphasis on the "power" of Christ at work within Paul (1:29), so there is also emphasis on his "struggle for your sake (cf. 1:24) and for those in Laodicea" (2:1). Epaphras (1:7-8) had acted as Paul's emissary, but Paul remained the key authority. Paul's concern for his churches (see 2 Cor 11:28) was important to emphasize, especially for those who had never known him personally (2:1). His struggle had been for their encouragement, their "unity in love," and, returning to a prominent theme, their "understanding" (cf. 1:9-10). Neither Paul nor his co-workers own and control the gospel; their purpose is that believers attain "all the richness of fully assured understanding and knowledge" (2:2). It is the entire community that is to understand "the mystery of God, Christ."

"Mystery" recalls 1:27 (above). The phrase "God, Christ" is confusing; the ancient manuscript copiers produced fifteen variations on this phrase in their attempts to explain it (e.g., "God the Father," "God, the Father of Christ")! It is not impossible that Christ is called "God" here, but "the God of Christ" (cf. 1:3; 2 Cor 1:3) is also pos-

sible, or perhaps the thought is that "Christ" is the content of "God's mystery." This goes along well with "the mystery, which is Christ in you" (1:27) and is perhaps the best we can do. In any event, it is "in him" that "all the treasures of wisdom and knowledge are hidden" (2:3), and therefore for believers they are not hidden at all (cf. 2 Cor 4:1-6).

The writer hints for the first time at the presence of some threatening ideas. Their "knowledge" of Christ should keep them safe from seemingly persuasive but actually "specious arguments" (2:4). Though Paul cannot be with them "in the flesh," he is with them "in the spirit" (cf. 1 Cor 5:3). If he were with them, he would rejoice at "the strength" of their "faith in Christ" (2:5). The writer's confidence, in spite of the threat, is notable.

2:6–3:4 Hold to "the faith"; no further "philosophy" is needed

The writer now turns to countering the threat of alternative ideas, doing so first by general encouragement that sets the theme for the major sections to come. Just as they "received Christ" and were "rooted and established in him," so they must "walk" (2:6-7). There is first a constant reminder of what believers *already have* in Christ and why no further teachings or dictates (2:14, 20) are required. "The faith" here denotes *what* "you were taught," the message as preached by Epaphras (1:7), but faith as *trust* and *relationship* (2:5) is by no means separate from the message (cf. Rom 10:9), an important point for the church today. Faith in its fullness leads naturally to fullness of "thanksgiving" (*eucharistia*, 2:7).

Whether the writer has a specific "someone" in mind is difficult to say (see 2:16-18). Certainly there is no one in Colossae comparable to the opponents in Galatia (Gal 1:7). Nevertheless, there is the seductive power of some "philosophy," which the writer regards as based in "human tradition," having to do with "the elementary powers of the world" (2:8, 10, 15; cf. 1:21). The "elements" (earth, air, fire, water) were widely thought to be the foundational components of the universe and were sometimes regarded as personal forces (e.g., Wis 13:2; Gal 4:3; 2 Pet 3:10-12); in Judaism they could be associated with angels and the giving of the law (Acts 7:53; Gal 3:19; 4:9-10).

The attraction of such teaching is that it takes seriously the invisible and unpredictable "powers" that affect human existence. Further, it prescribes practices (2:21), in the manner of the sacred laws of Judaism, for dealing with those forces. In this regard there is a link between the problem envisioned here and that in Galatia. And, as in Galatia, the solution is to recall the status already attained in Christ (e.g., Gal 4:1-7). Thus whatever is "not according to Christ" is to be rejected (2:8; cf. Gal 5:2-4).

"In him"—the tenth occurrence of this idea so far—"dwells the whole fullness of the deity bodily" (2:9), a very strong statement of Christ's identity with God (cf. 1:19; John 1:1, 14). The present tense is important; this was not merely something that happened in the past, when Christ was on earth. It is true now, and believers, who are "in Christ," already "share in this fullness" of divinity (2:10; cf. John 17:20-23). There can be no improvement, says Colossians, on Christ as the means of access to God. Christ is "the head of every principality"; the "elements" have nothing to add.

The next paragraph employs a series of metaphors, focused largely around baptism, to bring out the meaning of being "in him." Jewish writers sometimes spoke of "circumcision" as the "stripping away" of vice; circumcision ultimately had to involve the "circumcision of the heart" (Deut 30:6, cf. Rom 2:29). Such circumcision "was not administered by hand." The "stripping off of the fleshly body" (cf. 1:22) could be achieved only "by the circumcision of Christ," that is "by baptism." In baptism believers were "buried with" Christ and even "raised with" him "by faith in the power of God." (2:12). That believers are *already* "raised" goes notably beyond what Paul himself said (cf. Rom 6:5; 8:11; 2 Cor 4:14), but it makes the point about what believers have in Christ.

The baptismal imagery continues, employing perhaps language of the liturgy and highlighting the transformation from a life "dead in transgressions" (Eph 2:1) to one in which God "brought you to life with him" (cf. Rom 6:4), "forgiving us all our transgressions" (2:13; cf. 1:14). These are already vivid metaphors, but now they pile up even further, going beyond the language of baptism. Verses 14-15 contain six verbs ("obliterating," "removed," "nailing," "despoiling," "made a spectacle" and "leading in triumph"). Presum-

ably their subject, following the sequence from 1:13, is God rather than Christ. It is also possible that the writer is content to be ambiguous, permitting the imagery to have its effect regardless. Probably at least 1:14 describes God's action.

God "obliterated the bond" that, with its "legal claims," held sinful humans in debt. "The bond" is the legal document listing human failures. The image is like the slave with the impossible debt in Jesus' parable (Matt 18:21-35). When human behavior is stacked beside the demands of the law, then humans deserve condemnation. In freeing humans, God did not obliterate the law—the law is "holy" (Rom 7:12)—but rather the condemnation that it produces (cf. Rom 8:1-4). God "removed [the bond] from our midst, nailing it to the cross" (2:14), a powerful way to speak of God in Christ making peace with the world (1:20, 22; 2 Cor 5:18). If God is the subject, then "in him" (not "by it") God "despoiled," more literally *stripped away,* the principalities and powers, made a public spectacle of them, and paraded them" in a victorious procession, like a general with prisoners of war (2:15).

It would, therefore, be nonsense for believers to revert to a position from which God has set them free (cf. Gal 4:8-10) and permit anyone to "pass judgment" on them with regard to religious rules and regulations (2:16). Such things are "a shadow" in comparison with "the substance," literally "the *body* of Christ" (2:17; cf. 1:24). The word "disqualify" is related to the word for "prize" in Philippians 3:14, but here the thought is that someone might "deny [believers] the prize" of being "in God" (3:3).

There is further difficult use of multiple images with no agreement on precisely what the writer means. In discussion with the competing philosophy, some advantage seems to have been claimed for ascetic practices (cf. 1:23) that enable "self-abasement" ("humility," cf. 3:12) not only by obeying regulations but also by "the worship of angels," meaning probably by being able to *join in with* "the worship of angels" (cf. Isa 6:2-3; Dan 7:10; Rev 4:9-10; 7:11-12). This is what the "visions" were probably about as the person was "entering into" worship (not "taking his stand"). The claims made were probably impressive and attractive.

The writer, however, is quite scathing in evaluating these claims, whatever they are. Such a person is "inflated [conceited] without reason," not genuinely "humble" at all (cf. Phil 2:1-5). This is not true spiritual understanding but suggests only "a fleshly mind" (2:18). Such a person—a believer is envisaged—ought rather to "hold on to the head" (1:18; 2:10), who alone guarantees the proper "support" and "growth" of the body (2:19). The main point is repeated and emphasized: if believers "died with Christ" (cf. 2:11-12; Rom 6:2, 8), being liberated "from the elements," it is nonsense to return to "regulations." Far from taking believers into heavenly worship, that only projects them back into the insecurities of "living in [this] world" (2:20, cf. 3:1); they are back again to being dictated to, and "the glorious freedom of the children of God" (Rom 8:21) is lost!

The divine-human relationship does not rest on law but on God's love and compassion (Rom 5:6-8; 9:16; Gal 2:11-21). Regulations have a place; this writer will soon provide more than enough (3:18–4:1)! But such rules ("Don't touch, don't eat"), like the things they deal with, "are bound for destruction"; ultimately they are only "human precepts" (2:22; cf. Mark 7:7). They have "a semblance of wisdom," a passing usefulness (2:23), but Jesus did not come with a system of law—"the sabbath is for people, not people for the sabbath" (Mark 2:27). In any context, ancient or modern, this is quite a radical stance and by no means easily maintained. It nevertheless reflects well both Jesus and Paul.

In conclusion, believers "were raised with Christ" (3:1; cf. 2:12), who is "seated at God's right hand" (3:1; cf. Ps 110; Matt 22:44; Acts 2:34; 1 Cor 15:25). Their focus is not to be on "things of earth" (3:2), religion and rules that skew the relationship with God. Having "died" with Christ (cf. Gal 2:19-20), the "life" of the baptized is now "hidden with Christ in God" (3:3). "Hidden" evokes God's ancient "mystery" and "wisdom" (2:3) manifested to believers (1:26-27), but now believers are themselves a *part of the mystery*, so that at the end, "when Christ, your life, appears," they also "will appear with him in glory" (3:4). Why bother with "angels" when you already commune with God?

3:5-17 Reject evil, do good

Having reminded believers that they "died and were raised with Christ" (2:12, 20; 3:1), the author now tells them to "put to death the parts of you that are earthly" (3:5). Now the rubber, so

to speak, hits the road: believers do in fact "live in the world" (2:20) and indeed "in the flesh" (cf. 2:23)! Paul himself had faced the same irony (e.g., Gal 5:1, 13-17). Though believers have "stripped off the old self . . . and put on the new" (3:9-10), they remain "in the flesh" (Gal 2:20), and its temptations are always at hand (see Rom 8:3-8). God's reconciling of humans does not eliminate their freedom or their capacity to reject goodness.

The first list of vices (3:5) centers mostly on sexual sins (cf. 1 Thess 4:3-4) but culminates with "greed," which some ancient writers regarded as among the worst evils (cf. Luke 12:15). Here it is equated with "idolatry." Such things earn "the wrath of God" (cf. Rom 1:18). The Colossians are again reminded (cf. 2:13) that their own lives were once characterized by such vices, but now "they must put them all away"; there follows a further list centering on vices that disrupt friendship and community, culminating with the command to "stop lying."

The language next recalls baptism (cf. 2:11-12) and, as earlier, uses the metaphor of "stripping off." Baptism involved disrobing before entering into the baptismal pool and then "putting on" a new garment to symbolize "putting on Christ" (Gal 3:27; Rom 13:14). The "new self," says the writer, "is *being* renewed [an *ongoing* process!] for knowledge (cf. 2:3), according to the image of its creator" (3:10; cf. 1:15; Gen 1:26-27). It is not just a matter of virtues but of an entirely "new self," "new creation" (2 Cor 5:17). As the perversion of "knowledge" had distorted humanity (Rom 1:18-23), so genuine knowledge will characterize the new humanity.

Baptismal language continues. Apparently, in Paul's churches the baptismal formula included something like "In Christ there is no longer Greek and Jew" (3:11; cf. 1 Cor 12:13; Gal 3:28). This expressed succinctly the new reality created in baptism and experienced within the church, where all races, classes, and genders were able to be together as "one body" (3:15; 1 Cor 12:12-27). The formula predated Paul, but he used it because it suited so well his desire to break down the barrier in the church between the Jews ("circumcision," Gen 17:9-14), the original chosen people, and all the rest (see Eph 2:11-18). That also means that all other barriers of privilege and status are abolished in Christ; *all* who have faith—even the barbarous "Scythians"—"are clothed with Christ," are members of the same body.

But, of course, there is tremendous tension here, both for the ancient churches and today. Slavery, for example, continued to be practiced even within the church (3:22-25; Eph 6:5-9; 1 Tim 6:1-2; Titus 2:9-10; 1 Pet 2:18-20)! It took Christianity many more centuries to recognize fully the social implications of the gospel. And, truth be told—not least in relation to the full equality of women—the church continues to struggle even today. In any age, what ultimately matters is "Christ," who "is all and *is in all*" (3:11).

As "God's chosen ones," believers must "clothe themselves" with virtues (3:12); this list features qualities of compassion and gentleness, stresses the obligation to forgive "as the Lord forgave you" (3:13; cf. Matt 6:12; 18:21-22), and culminates with "love, the bond of perfection" (3:14). "The peace of Christ" (cf. Phil 4:7) is to "reign in your hearts," and indeed it was into peace "in one body" that believers "were called" (3:15). There is emphasis again on "wisdom" (cf. 2:3) and mutual instruction, but not only in an intellectual sense; "psalms, hymns and spiritual songs" are also to flavor their conversation (3:16). They are to do everything "in the name of the Lord Jesus, giving thanks . . . through him" (3:17).

3:18–4:6 Household rules

Having put "human precepts" in their place (2:22), the writer now provides several precepts as a guide for Christian households. The difference is that these are not offered as essential in themselves; they also, as history has shown, are "shadows" rather than "reality" itself (2:17). This is particularly clear with respect to the instructions to slaves and slave owners. All of these commands presuppose a patriarchal society in which "the master" had legal rights of control and possession with respect to his wife, children, and slaves.

Such "household codes" were quite well known in the ancient world generally and had a considerable impact on the later writings of the New Testament (Eph 5:21–6:9; 1 Pet 2:18–3:7). Particular effort was made to enforce the submission of wives to husbands (Titus 2:5; 1 Cor 14:34-35) and to stop women from being leaders of house-churches (1 Tim 2:11-15). That women were such leaders is beyond question (e.g., Rom 16:1-15: note Phoebe, Prisca, and Junia; Phil 4:2-3).

The first command here is specifically to "wives" (3:18), not women in general. Single

women and widows, particularly if they were wealthy (e.g., Lydia, Acts 16:14), could operate reasonably independently and themselves be heads of households (e.g., Nympha, 4:15). Nowadays husbands and wives properly are "subject to one another" (Eph 5:21, cf. 1 Cor 7:2-5), should "love" and "not be bitter" toward one another, and mothers as well as "fathers" should not "provoke" or "embitter" their children. The command to "obey parents" (3:20) derives from Exodus 20:12 (cf. Mark 10:19).

Most problematic is the command to "slaves" to "obey your human masters in everything" (3:22). Slave owners made full use of such texts to insist that slavery was a divinely ordained institution. Needless to say, this is a "human command" that has thankfully been destroyed (cf. 2:22). The instructions for slaves are lengthier, probably because there were slaves among the letter's recipients—Onesimus, one of those who delivered the letter (4:9), was a slave (Phlm 10-16). Further, Christian faith was already beginning to expose slavery as morally questionable (3:11!) and provided some opportunity for slaves to attain freedom (1 Cor 7:21); 1 Timothy 6:1-2 shows that bitterness could arise between slaves and their Christian masters. The church, however, had no power (yet!) to alter the economic structure of the Roman Empire; it had to conform in order to be accepted (4:5; cf. 1 Tim 6:1; Titus 2:5). The command to "masters" to treat their slaves "justly and fairly" (4:1) was intended to eliminate cruelty, at least among Christian "masters" (cf. 1 Pet 2:18-20).

The remaining exhortations turn first to the theme of constant, thank-filled prayer (4:2; cf. 1 Thess 5:17-18) and include the request that the Colossians should "pray also for us." Once again (as in 1:24-29) Paul and his co-workers are closely associated in the task of proclaiming "the mystery of Christ," for which Paul suffered imprisonment (4:3) and for which he had primary responsibility (4:4; cf. Eph 3:1-7). The command "Conduct yourselves wisely toward outsiders" shows that the church was already becoming a sufficiently public entity that its reputation was important. "Making the most of the opportunity" (or "time") has in mind that time is short before the end (1 Cor 7:29-31). The relationship with outsiders is especially in mind in the final words of instruction; "gracious speech, seasoned with salt" means conversation with others that is wise, good-humored, and interesting. Believers are not to be insipid and boring and certainly not closed off from the world. They must be able rather "to respond to each one," particularly with respect to faith (1 Pet 3:15).

4:7-18 Commendation of co-workers and final greetings

This section seems to require accepting the letter to the Colossians as Paul's own composition, since it is so detailed and personal. Most of the names here also appear in Philemon 23-24. But if such details were enough to make a text original to Paul, then 2 Timothy and Titus would also be his compositions, but very few scholars think that they are. These greetings and commendations make sense when we remember that Paul's mission had always been a team effort. The persons named were part of that team, at least for a short time. If the team—what scholars call "the Pauline school"—and individuals within it were to continue Paul's ministry, they had to assume the authority he exercised and continue the mission in his name. This section says what the writer believes Paul would have said if he could personally greet the Colossians and commend his co-workers to them. The more personal notes regarding Mark (4:10) and Archippus (4:17) deal with real people in real circumstances but do not require Paul himself as author.

Tychicus seems to have joined the team late (Acts 20:4; 2 Tim 4:12; Titus 3:12). He not only brought news of Paul but was also "to encourage [the Colossians'] hearts" (4:8), corresponding exactly to a description of Paul's ministry (2:2). Tychicus carried the letter and would also read it to the gathered community. Onesimus (Phlm 10) was to accompany him; he was from Colossae or thereabouts (4:9). If Colossians was written while Paul was alive, as some think, then it was delivered when Onesimus returned to Philemon.

Aristarchus was from Thessalonica, had traveled with Paul, and had been in prison with him (Acts 19:29; 20:4). "Mark, cousin of Barnabas," accompanied Paul and his cousin during early missions (Acts 12:12; 13:5, 13) and was the cause of a disagreement between Paul and Barnabas (Acts 15:37-39). Barnabas (Acts 4:36-37) was the one who brought Paul into the circle of the apostles (Acts 9:26-27) and was Paul's major companion in the early days (11:29-30; 13:1–15:38), but they had a

serious disagreement when Barnabas sided with Peter in Antioch (Gal 2:11-14), and they went their separate ways. This verse (4:10) suggests reconciliation with Mark. "Jesus [a common Jewish name in those days], known as Justus," along with Mark, was "of the circumcision" (i.e., were Jews); they—Mark and Justus—were the "only" Jews who worked with Paul "for the kingdom of God." They were "a comfort" (4:11) in that Paul suffered great distress at the resistance to the gospel among Jews generally (see Rom 9:1-4; 10:1). Other "Jews" had worked with Paul (e.g., Prisca and Aquila, Acts 18:2; Rom 16:3-5); the writer must mean that these were the Jews presently in "the Pauline school." Mention of them supports the letter's point that the Colossians need add no Jewish observances to their life in Christ.

Epaphras was a key figure for the Colossians (1:7). Like Onesimus, he was from Colossae. The description of him as "a slave of Christ" (cf. Rom 1:1; Phil 1:1), "striving for you in his prayers" (4:12) and bearing "much labor" (the word also denotes "distress") amounts to a very strong commendation (4:13). "Luke, the beloved physician" (2 Tim 4:11; Phlm 24) and "Demas" round off the group sending greetings. There is a later tradition that "Demas deserted" Paul (2 Tim 4:10). Finally, greetings are also sent to "the believers in Laodicea" and to "Nympha and the church in her house" (4:15). Later copiers of the letter changed the text to read "Nymphas and the church in *his* house," since they could not accept that a woman was apparently named as the leader of a church. She probably functioned in a manner similar to Phoebe (Rom 16:1), Stephanas, and others (1 Cor 16:15-18; 1 Thess 5:12-13), that is, as leader of a house-church. "Church" here denotes a small congregation (twenty to forty people?), whereas in 1:18 it means "the church universal."

There is a final command that there must be a sharing of letters. The letter to the Colossians is to be read in Laodicea, the Laodicean letter (presumably from Paul) in Colossae (4:16). The letter to the Laodiceans, of course, is unknown, though there is an apocryphal letter of that name (easily found on the Web). Some think that the letter to the Laodiceans is actually Ephesians or the text on which Ephesians is based. Archippus (4:17) was perhaps Philemon's son (Phlm 2) or, at any rate, was a member of that house-church. In Philemon 2 he is described as Paul's "fellow soldier," but he may have shown some unwillingness to "fulfill the ministry which he received" (4:17).

The greeting in "my [Paul's] own hand" (cf. 1 Cor 16:21; Gal 6:11) assures the readers that the letter is genuinely "from Paul," at least in the sense that it represents well what he would say in these circumstances. The reminder of his imprisonment secures an emotional bond with the recipients. The closing blessing is extremely brief; later copiers added "Amen."

THE FIRST LETTER TO THE
THESSALONIANS

Vincent M. Smiles

INTRODUCTION

The importance of I Thessalonians, and its place and date of writing

The First Letter to the Thessalonians is the earliest of all the New Testament writings. It was probably composed in Corinth—perhaps Athens—in A.D. 49 or maybe even earlier (41–44?). Thirteen letters bear Paul's name; of them, scholars agree that Paul wrote at least seven (Romans, 1–2 Corinthians, Galatians, Philippians, 1 Thessalonians, Philemon); the authenticity of each of the others (Ephesians, Colossians, 2 Thessalonians, 1–2 Timothy, Titus) is disputed. Paul was martyred (probably) in Rome in the early sixties; he wrote all his letters, therefore, before any of the Gospels were written (Mark—c. 70—being the first Gospel). This makes Paul the earliest witness of Christianity, and 1 Thessalonians the earliest part of Paul's testimony.

Thessalonica (modern-day Thessaloniki or Salonika) is located at the far northwestern end of the Aegean Sea. In Paul's time it was the principal city of the Roman province of Macedonia. According to the more traditional reconstruction of his apostolic journeys (following the outline of the Acts of the Apostles), Paul ventured into Macedonia and Achaia (Greece) in the late forties, after a long ministry in Syria and Asia Minor that was based in Antioch (c. 34–48). It is possible, however—some think probable—that he began his westward journeys earlier, reaching Greece as early as 41. Whatever the date, he arrived there from Philippi (1 Thess 2:2; Acts 16:11–17:1) and subsequently traveled south to Beroea (Veria), Athens, and Corinth (1 Thess 3:1; Acts 17:10–18:1).

The evidence of Acts

As indicated, Acts also recounts these travels, but there is not always complete consistency between Acts and Paul's own letters. Acts was written about twenty years after Paul's death (about 85) and is primarily a *theological* narrative about the early church. It contains some valuable historical information, but exact history is not its primary purpose. In the case of Paul's mission in Thessalonica, there are some clear contrasts between Acts and 1 Thessalonians: Acts 17 (a) has Paul in Thessalonica only three weeks; (b) envisions mostly Jewish converts; and (c) does not mention Timothy being in Thessalonica. The letter, however, (a) implies a more substantial stay than three sabbath sermons (2:9; see also Phil 4:16); (b) envisions a mostly Gentile community (1:9, "turned from idols"); and (c) makes clear that Timothy was a primary missionary (1:1; 3:2-6). In all cases the letter to the Thessalonians, written by an eyewitness, is to be preferred over Acts, which is an important but secondary source. Acts, therefore, is not a major help either in reconstructing this part of Paul's history or in understanding the letter. While not dismissing Acts, interpreters of Paul must focus *primarily* on the texts of his letters.

The occasion and purpose of 1 Thessalonians

Fortunately, 1 Thessalonians provides valuable clues to its context, and its purpose is substantially clear. Paul, Silvanus, and Timothy had labored long and hard in Thessalonica (2:9) and had successfully established house-churches there (5:27), which yet were sufficiently united that Paul could refer to them as "the church of the Thessalonians" (1:1). The letter does not say why the "apostles" (2:7) left Thessalonica, but given the letter's focus on "affliction" (1:6; 3:3-7), it probably had to do with local opposition (2:14); in this regard Acts 17:5-9 may well be correct. In other words, the missionaries probably left before they wanted to. Paul, then, was anxious about this fledgling church; would they be able to persevere?

In Athens the apostles decided that Timothy must return "to find out about [their] faith" (3:5). The news he brought back elated Paul, and he set about writing this letter of thanksgiving and encouragement. Timothy also seems to have relayed to Paul some questions and concerns, both from the Thessalonians themselves and, perhaps, from his own observations. Most notably, they seem to have asked about whether believers who had died would be included in the resurrection of the dead (4:13-18). There may also have been questions about marriage (sex?—4:3-7), and some members of the community may have been faltering in their commitment to Christ (5:14). It must be said, however, that detecting real problems behind Paul's advice is extremely difficult; not every exhortation from Paul necessarily corresponds to some issue among the readers.

Does 1 Thessalonians comprise one letter or two?

Such reconstructions of what was going on in Thessalonica become all the more tenuous when we take into account the views of some experts that 1 Thessalonians actually comprises more than one letter. The theory goes that 1 Thessalonians 2:13–4:2 was originally a separate (earlier) letter, written shortly after Paul had left Thessalonica, and that when Paul's letters were gathered together, this shorter letter was incorporated into the "second letter," comprising 1:1–2:12 and 4:3–5:28. The strongest argument in favor of this theory is the second "thanksgiving," which begins in 2:13. This is unique among the letters certainly

written by Paul (cf. 2 Thess 2:13). There is also some tension between 2:6-7, which suggests some lapse of time since Paul's founding visit, and 2:17, which speaks of being absent from Thessalonica "for a short time."

These arguments cannot lightly be dismissed, but they have not convinced most scholars who continue to take the letter *mostly* as it is. "Mostly" signals a problem, and the problem is 2:13-16, particularly 2:14-16. The latter three verses, which feature very harsh language against "the Jews who killed the Lord Jesus," have been debated vigorously for many years. As the commentary will show, there are substantial reasons for thinking that they (along with 2:13?) may have been added to the letter in the late first century.

Again, however, most scholars are not convinced of this. The policy adopted here is to acknowledge the weight of these important questions about the letter's integrity, but nevertheless to interpret the text as it has come to us from ancient tradition. The minority view may yet prove to be correct, but for now the weight of the evidence is that 1 Thessalonians has come to us essentially as Paul wrote it.

The importance of 1 Thessalonians for the church today

For the life of the church, this is by far the most important question. The letter's history is essential for a basic understanding of what the letter *meant* to its first audience, but it is because of what the letter *means* today that believers still read it. Historical study is essential to a modern reading, but it is not the whole of it. Present meaning, however, is largely determined by present questions and concerns; every generation will hear somewhat differently based on its circumstances. The following are some obvious themes that are important for the church today.

1. *The church as a local community:* In spite of the Second Vatican Council (e.g., the Dogmatic Constitution on the Church), "the church" today still connotes, for a large number of believers, the institutional church and the hierarchy. For Paul and the New Testament as a whole, there was no such connotation. In those days "the church" meant everything from a house-church (e.g., Rom 16:5; Gal 1:2) to that whole collection of "the

churches" that had been established in various cities of the Roman Empire (see 2 Cor 8:24; Col 1:24). Paul's authentic letters are all addressed to the men and women of the community, whether Thessalonica, Corinth, or elsewhere. This was true whether the community was to be praised for its faith (e.g., 1 Thessalonians, Philippians) or corrected for its abuse of the Eucharist (1 Cor 11:17-34) or some other fault. "The church of the Thessalonians" had its leaders (see 5:12-13), but Paul's primary concern was "the church," from which its leadership and ministry arose.

2. *Leadership in the church:* Male, ordained clergy have dominated leadership in the church for so many centuries that modern readers inevitably read the New Testament as though it presupposed the same structure. This, however, is not the case. We know nothing specific about the leaders whom Paul mentions in 1 Thessalonians 5:12-13, but from Paul's other letters we know that women were included among the primary leaders of the churches (see Rom 16:1-7; Phil 4:2-3; Col 4:15). And though Acts (14:23) says that Paul "appointed presbyters in each church," in the authentic letters "presbyters" are never mentioned. Ministry in Paul's churches did not primarily depend on "appointment" (ordination) but on the charisms of the Spirit (1 Cor 12). This means that structures of ministry, even today, are susceptible to change.

3. *The ongoing power of the gospel:* Finally, it should be noted that Paul was vividly aware of the *presence* of God's action in believers' lives and of the ongoing power of the gospel. After so many centuries of history, believers have a tendency to look to the past as the source of inspiration and revelation. This, of course, is correct as far as it goes, but it misses Paul's emphasis that the word of God *"is now* at work" among believers (1 Thess 2:13), that *"now* is the day of salvation" (2 Cor 6:2). The inspiration of the Bible is to be found not only in its writers but also in its readers.

COMMENTARY

1:1 Greeting

Paul associates Silvanus and Timothy (Acts 16:1-3) with himself in the writing of the letter. Silvanus ("Silas" in Acts) was from Jerusalem; Paul met him there at the conference (about A.D. 48) when the status of Gentiles in the church was discussed (Acts 15:1-27). Subsequently, he replaced Barnabas as Paul's traveling companion after Paul and Barnabas had a disagreement (15:36-40). He then traveled with Paul through Asia Minor and assisted in establishing churches in Galatia (16:6), Philippi (16:11-29), Thessalonica (17:1-4), and Corinth (18:5; 2 Cor 1:19). After Corinth he is no longer mentioned in association with Paul, but 1 Peter 5:12 associates him with Peter and the writing of that letter.

Timothy was extremely important to Paul (see Phil 2:19-23). It was Timothy whom Paul sent back to Thessalonica to find out how the church was doing (1 Thess 3:2, 5); that "sending" confirms that Paul was the leader of the team. Timothy joined Paul's mission shortly after Silas (Acts 16:1-3) and then remained throughout Paul's apostolate (Rom 16:21; Acts 20:4), probably until the imprisonment that ended with Paul's death in Rome. Though the letter speaks throughout in terms of "we" (except 3:5; 5:27), there is no reason to doubt that Paul is the primary and perhaps the sole author of the letter. Nevertheless, the collaborative nature of his leadership is important to note, and it may, in part, help to explain why his companions and successors felt free, after his death, to write letters in his name (e.g., Ephesians, Colossians, 2 Thessalonians).

The addressee is "the church of the Thessalonians." We should envisage a house-church or several of them (5:27), a fairly small community by modern standards. "Church" in the New Testament always designates a community of people, whether a house-church (e.g., Rom 16:3-5; Acts

2:46), the believers of a city (1 Cor 1:2), or the church as a worldwide community (Eph 1:22-23); it never designates an abstract institution, nor is it ever identified simply with its leadership. The church exists *"in* God the Father and the Lord Jesus Christ." The greeting is brief (cf. Rom 1:7; 1 Cor 1:3), with "grace" *(charis)* being an especially important term for Paul—a near one-word summary of his gospel (Rom 5:15-21; 11:6; 1 Cor 15:10; Gal 1:6; 5:4). Paul inserts *charis* ("grace") where standard Greek letters had *chairein* ("greetings"), and he adds "peace" (Hebrew *shalom*), perhaps reflecting a greeting found in Jewish letters.

1:2-10 Thankful remembrance of preaching in Thessalonica

This is similar to the "thanksgiving" sections of Paul's other letters (e.g., Rom 1:8-15; 1 Cor 1:4-9; Phil 1:3-11), but here he is particularly enthusiastic and joyful, because in spite of persecution (1:6; 2:14; 3:6-8), they have persevered in the "work of faith, the labor of love, and the endurance of hope" (1:3). This triad (faith, love, hope) is recalled later (5:8: "the breastplate of faith and love, helmet of hope"). In fact, a major reason for the letter is Paul's desire to encourage them in faith and love, but most especially in hope, in the face of persecution and the death of loved ones (4:13-18). Paul recalls here their positive reception of "the gospel" (1:5) and reminds them of their "election" and that they are "loved by God" (1:4).

Election, more commonly referred to as God's "call," is a key idea in Paul's letters (see Rom 9:7-26; 11:26; 1 Cor 7:18-24), this one in particular (2:12; 4:7; 5:24). It is the starting point for much of Paul's theology, pointing as it does to God's initiative of love and grace. The election takes place apart from human expectation or calculation (see Rom 5:6-8: "while we were sinners"), and indeed, even "apart from the law" (Rom 3:21). The Thessalonians "knew *that*" (rather than *how*) they "were chosen" in "the gospel" that Paul and his companions preached (1:5).

"Gospel" in the New Testament never refers to a book, nor does it refer to any particular doctrines. It refers simply to the *act* of proclamation, which was not "in word alone" but was a matter of "power" and "the holy Spirit" and "conviction" (1:5). For Paul, the gospel always has about it immediacy and living power; it happens "today" (2 Cor 6:2: *"now* is the day of salvation") and has

powerful effects. In other words, *God enables* faith (Phil 1:29) and the "knowing of election" (1:4); behind true preaching there is always the loving action of God.

The effect among the Thessalonians was that they "became imitators of [the apostles] and of the Lord" both in "affliction" and in "joy" (1:6). More than that, they became "a model" for believers throughout the region. Their gracious "reception" of the apostles became legendary, so that others reported how the Thessalonians "turned from idols to serve the living and true God" (1:8-9). The abandonment of traditional religions was one of the most difficult and amazing acts of ancient believers. In the context of modern freedoms, it is difficult to appreciate that such "turning" required great courage, since it inevitably caused social disruptions, even in families (1 Cor 7:12-15; Luke 12:51-53: "father against son, son against father") and was the source of persecution both from locals (2:14; Acts 17:5-9) and, ultimately, from the Romans.

Verse 10 explains their motivation. It is an important verse, since it is the earliest summary of what believers preached and believed. "Awaiting [God's] Son from heaven" points to the very apocalyptic atmosphere of early Christian experience. Paul and others expected to be "alive" at "the coming of the Lord" (4:15), which is also described as "the coming wrath" (1:10). But for believers this will not mean "condemnation" (Rom 8:1), but rather "rescue" at the hands of God's resurrected "Son." How and when Jesus will come again is an important issue in 1 Thessalonians (2:19; 3:13; 4:13–5:11; 5:23), but later it recedes in importance (e.g., in Ephesians).

Such expectation, however—a vibrant awareness of the nearness of God—holds rich vitality for spiritual life and should not simply be dismissed as outdated. Investments in this world (marriage, business) have their own goodness, but their value is better seen in the light of the world to come, "for the framework of this world [and all our investments] is passing away" (1 Cor 7:31).

2:1-12 Paul's defense of the apostles' preaching in Thessalonica

As already in 1:4 Paul addresses the community as "brothers," but this does not mean he intends the letter only for men; the term *adelphoi* is best translated "believers." Paul presupposed the patriarchal culture of his world (e.g., 4:4; 1 Cor 11:2-16: "husband, the head of his wife," 11:3), but he also knew that "in Christ" such patriarchy has no place (Gal 3:26-28: "no longer male and female" in Christ), and, to some extent, working with women in leadership, he did overcome patriarchal biases. It is inaccurate, therefore, to portray Paul as a misogynist; the evidence that women worked with him in his apostolic labors is unmistakable (e.g., Rom 16:1-7, 12-15: Phoebe, Prisca, Junia; Phil 4:2-3: Euodia, Syntyche).

Paul turns to a defense of the apostles' behavior while in Thessalonica. "Defense" suggests there had been accusations, but there is no direct evidence of this. Elsewhere Paul, when attacked, was not shy about directly rebuffing his detractors (2 Cor 10–13; Gal 2:11-14). In Thessalonians, for some reason, Paul fears being thought of as one of those preachers of his time who represented themselves as experts in some religion and traveled around making money from their converts. He acknowledged that apostles had the right to material support (1 Cor 9:3-7), but he also knew of Christian preachers who, in his view, were greedy "peddlers of the word of God" (2 Cor 2:17) and whom he contrasted with himself in his preaching of the gospel "without charge" (2 Cor 11:7; 1 Cor 9:12).

Paul had come to Thessalonica by way of Philippi, where he also had encountered opposition (2:2). In reminding the Thessalonians of his conduct, he says five times what it did *not* involve: deception, people-pleasing, flattery, greed, and being a (financial) burden (2:5-9). It's a veritable catalog of what preachers should avoid. It was rather a matter, "through our God" (2:2), of great "struggle," of "toil and drudgery, working night and day, in order not to burden any of you" (2:9). "As apostles of Christ, we could," he says, "have imposed our weight, but we were gentle [or 'infants'] among you, like a nursing mother cherishing her children" (2:7). It is interesting here to recall Jesus' words: "Among the nations those who are seen as rulers over the Gentiles lord it over them. . . . But it shall not be so among you. Rather, whoever wishes to be great among you will be your servant" (Mark 10:42-43). Paul's actual conduct accords with Jesus' instruction.

In 2:11 Paul changes the image, comparing Silvanus, Timothy, and himself to a "father, ex-

horting and encouraging each one as his own children." Against any possible detractors, Paul insists that their conduct was devout, just, and blameless (2:10) as they taught the community that their conduct also must be "worthy of the God who [even now] calls [them] into his kingdom" (2:12). It is important to note the *present* tense—the gospel is not a thing of the past.

2:13-16 Four problematic verses

This paragraph, especially verses 14-16, is much disputed in modern scholarship, the dispute being whether this generalizing and harsh condemnation of "the Jews" is authentic or was added later in light of persecution by Jews (e.g., John 16:2) and the destruction of Jerusalem by the Romans in A.D. 70. Paul's letters were indeed collected and edited. Second Corinthians, for instance, may be a conflation of at least two letters to Corinth (2 Cor 1–9 and 10–13), and 1 Corinthians 14:33b-36 may be an editorial addition to that letter. However, here, as also in those cases, the ancient manuscripts are as they are, and scholars, no matter what their convictions, cannot cut and paste the Bible as they choose.

The evidence that 2:(13?)14-16 is a later addition has some weight:

1. It does not fit well into the flow of the letter, much less into the sequence of Paul's ministry. "God's wrath has come upon them" (2:16) does not fit well into this early period; it might fit better after Jerusalem was destroyed in A.D. 70.

2. It contains some (for Paul) unusual ideas (e.g., that Jews were responsible for Jesus' death; cf. 1 Cor 2:8, where "rulers of this world" does *not* designate Jews).

3. It seems harshly anti-Jewish, especially in light of Paul's affection for his heritage (e.g., Rom 9:1-5: "I could wish that I myself were accursed for the sake of my people"; 11:1-2).

On the other hand, the arguments in favor of its authenticity are also persuasive:

1. All ancient manuscripts contain the passage.

2. Its unusual features may derive from the use of traditional language by Paul (cf. Luke 11:47-51).

3. The critique is not *anti*-Jewish so much as *intra*-Jewish, not unlike the harsh words of the prophets (e.g., Jer 7:33-34) or Jesus (Matt 23:29-33).

4. Though he loved his heritage, Paul was quite capable of harsh critique of Jews with whom he disagreed (see Rom 2:17-24). In the presence of such uncertainty, it is foolish to be dogmatic one way or the other, though the case for authenticity does seem slightly stronger.

As the letter stands, 2:13 accords well with the theme of 1:5, namely, that the gospel, though proclaimed by human agency, ultimately derives its power from the "word of God, which is now at work in you who believe." "Word of God" here does not mean words *about* God, but rather the word that *God speaks* now, in every generation, the word that "is active and alive" (Heb 4:12). Paul's angry language in 2:14-16 gives no warrant whatsoever to anti-Semitism and, in some respects, is rather questionable. The primary responsibility for the death of Jesus lay with the Roman authorities, crucifixion being a Roman punishment. And the accusations that Jews "do not please God and are opposed to everyone" (2:15) are more reflective of the anti-Jewish propaganda of ancient authors than of the esteem for Jews that Paul elsewhere demonstrates.

The horror of Christians using Scripture to justify unspeakable cruelty toward innocent people must be forever rejected. If Paul did indeed write these words, he intended to assure the Thessalonians that they were suffering just like "the churches of God in Judea" (2:14), and his anger no doubt derived, in part, from the harsh treatment that he received in some synagogues (2 Cor 11:24: "five times I received thirty-nine lashes from the Jews"). But his very accepting of that punishment witnesses that he remained connected to Judaism. He longed for Jews to accept the gospel (Rom 9:1-3; 10:1), and he lived out his belief that "the gifts and call of God" to Israel "are irrevocable" (Rom 11:29).

2:17–3:13 The difficulty and the joy of recent events

Paul now resumes his expressions of affection and longing for the Thessalonians. Such emo-

tional outpouring may seem strange today. His language, in part, is conventional—he also tells believers in Rome that he "long[s] to see" them (Rom 1:11), though he had never even met them; he calls the Philippians also his "joy and crown" (Phil 4:1), and he tells the Corinthians (2 Cor 1:14) and Philippians (Phil 2:16) as well as the Thessalonians that they will be his "boast at the coming of the Lord" (2:19).

But convention alone does not explain his language. The range of strong emotions in Paul's letters is considerable—joy, gratitude (Phil 4:10-14); rage (Gal 3:1; 5:12!); outrage (2 Cor 11:13-15); sorrow (2 Cor 2:1-4); and exhilaration (Phil 4:4-7). The list could go on. But for all his churches, even when he was angry at them (Gal 4:19-20), he clearly held a sincere affection (2 Cor 11:11: ". . . because I do not love you? God knows that I do!").

That affection is nowhere more evident than here. Away from Thessalonica, the apostles felt "orphaned" (2:17). Paul himself had tried twice to return to them, "but Satan prevented us" (2:18). Satan is mentioned again in 3:5 as "the tempter" who might do harm to the community's faith. In both cases Paul may have seen "Satan" in the political opposition which he himself had encountered in Thessalonica (see Acts 17:6-7) and which now harassed the believers and prevented Paul's return. This forced separation, whatever its cause, became completely unbearable for Paul, and while in Athens they determined that Timothy must return to find out whether the Thessalonians' faith was holding up under the pressure (3:1, 5). Why Timothy could make the journey and Paul could not is impossible to answer. Timothy's mission was "to strengthen and encourage" and especially to see to it that "no one was disturbed" by the persecutions and other "afflictions" they were enduring (3:2-3). Paul had warned them that suffering is inevitable in the life of faith, and now they have experienced it for themselves (3:4).

"Just now," however—as though he had just walked through the door!—Timothy has brought "the good news of [their] faith and love," and Paul, suffering some distress of his own (whether in Athens or, more likely, Corinth), is "consoled by [their] faith" (3:6-7). Indeed, for him this good news of their "standing in the Lord" is "life" itself (3:8). It may be significant that though Timothy recounted their "faith and love," he could not speak of their "hope" (1:3; 5:8). It has been suggested that "hope" was the one thing that was "lacking in [their] faith" (3:10), and that may well have been. Harassment from other citizens and the death of loved ones (4:13) must have been a heavy burden. Whatever the circumstances, the Thessalonians were enduring well, and Paul now simply breaks into prayer, wondering what "thanksgiving" he can possibly render for the joy he feels on their account (3:9).

What he comes up with are two petitions. Predictably, he prays first that "God and our Lord Jesus" will make it possible for himself, Silvanus, and Timothy to visit Thessalonica soon (3:10-11). His second prayer is addressed to "the Lord" (Jesus) alone, a telling indication of how closely, even in the earliest theological reflection, Jesus was identified with God. He prays that Jesus will "increase [their] love" and "strengthen [their] hearts" to be "blameless" at his "coming with all his holy ones" (3:12).

What Paul means by "holy ones" is not immediately obvious. We naturally think of angels (Matt 16:27), and that may well be correct, but elsewhere Paul never mentions angels or "holy ones" (saints) at the Lord's coming. For Paul, "holy ones" always refers to *believers* (e.g., Rom 1:7; 12:13; 15:25-26); he regularly addresses his letters (this one being the exception) "to the saints" of Rome, Corinth, and so on. But the language Paul uses here is traditional; he quotes from Zechariah 14:5, which speaks of God's coming "and all his holy ones with him." The tradition Paul employs, therefore, certainly envisions angels, as also most probably Paul himself does. It would be nice to think that Paul has in mind the believers of Thessalonica who have died (4:13; note 4:14b), but 4:16 says "they will rise" when the Lord "will descend from heaven." The whole picture is a further reminder of the deeply apocalyptic character of this letter and of early Christian experience in general.

4:1-12 Exhortation to holiness

Just as the thanksgiving in this letter is inordinately extended, so also are the exhortations to good behavior, this being the first such section, 5:12-22 the second. Extended exhortation, however, is not unusual for Paul (Rom 12:1–13:14; Gal 5:13–6:10) and makes sense, given his aim of "strengthening" in this letter.

There are several difficulties for interpreters, most especially in verses 3-6. The biggest problem

is the interpretation of verse 4, which very literally reads: ". . . that each of you know how to obtain (control?) his vessel in holiness." All agree that this metaphor ("vessel") has to do with proper sexual conduct, but does Paul mean (a) to obtain a *wife* or (b) generally to control *sexual behavior*? The first option (as in the New American Bible) is not popular these days, but that, of course, is not a reason to reject it. It is also *possible* that Paul is referring to, and forbidding, consanguineous marriages (Lev 18:6-18), which Greek society permitted in order to keep the woman's inheritance in the family. If this is the case, then the injunction "not to exploit a brother in this matter" (4:6) refers to the business contract involved in transferring the woman's property to her husband. In any event, 4:3-7 almost certainly intends to warn the Thessalonians against sexual "impurity"; the latter word, in Paul, regularly refers to sexual misconduct (e.g., Rom 1:24; Gal 5:19).

The alternative is that both men and women are being told to "control [their] sexual behavior" and that 4:6 either reinforces this by forbidding any sexual irregularities or, perhaps (but less likely), introduces the different issue of justice in business practices ("do not defraud"). Overall the first option ("obtain a wife"), whether we like it or not, seems more likely. If this is correct, then this is one of those texts where Paul's, and his society's, patriarchal biases show (cf. 1 Cor 11:2-16), and modern believers are not bound to first-century cultural standards. In any event, believers are not called to "uncleanness," a general term for various types of immorality (2:3), but to "holiness" (3:13).

Paul speaks here—and 4:8 strongly confirms this—as one who represents Christ ("in the Lord"), so that to ignore him is tantamount to "ignoring God" (cf. Luke 10:16). Paul was always adamant that his apostolic authority derived from God (Gal 1:6-12); it was not, he acknowledged, from official channels and was not always recognized by others (1 Cor 9:2); it was nevertheless real and effective (1 Cor 15:10). "The will of God" for the Thessalonians is their "holiness" (4:3-4), by which he means that they are to live by "the holy Spirit that God gives [them]" (4:8; again, note the present tense). "Holiness" (4:7) is not primarily something to be attained, as though they did not have it, but is a gift they are to practice. Already, he says, they know his instructions—they are "God-taught"—and he has no need to tell them about love, which they practice "toward all the believers" (4:9-10). He concludes the section by urging them to "live quietly, mind [their] own business, and work with [their] own hands" so as to provide for their needs and be on good terms with outsiders (4:11-12).

4:13-18 The hope of faith in the face of death

This is one of the most fascinating apocalyptic texts in the entire New Testament and, for study purposes, should be compared with similar texts (e.g., Mark 13; Matt 24; Rev 21). We learn here that Paul and his contemporaries expected Jesus' second coming in the very near future, and, indeed, Paul expected to be "alive" for the event (4:15). By the time he wrote Philippians 1:21-24 (six to ten years later), he could anticipate that he might be dead before the end, but a vivid expectation of Jesus' return never left him.

Occasionally, believers are disconcerted at the early church's "mistake" in expecting Jesus to return "soon" (Rev 1:1-3), and critics sometimes make it a basis for discrediting Christian faith. Imminent expectation was not, however, foundational to faith. The delay of the end did, understandably, disturb some early believers (2 Pet 3:3-10), but then as now faith's primary focus was on being "God's children" and on living out that reality in the here and now.

The pressing circumstance in Thessalonica, about which the Thessalonians had probably questioned Timothy, was the death of some of their loved ones; would they also "be with the Lord" at his coming (4:14, 17)? Paul is interestingly inconsistent in his answer: 4:14b ("God *will bring* [them] *with* Jesus") does not quite jibe with 4:16 ("the dead in Christ *will arise*" *at his descent* "from heaven"). This slight confusion reminds us not to be too caught up in the details of what will happen at the end; there are many differing descriptions in the New Testament.

The point Paul makes is that believers' grief should be tempered by the hope of the resurrection and the awareness that God is very near. The basis of this hope is the power of Jesus' death and resurrection (see 1 Cor 15:12-19). That power reaches beyond death, so that those "who are left alive at the Lord's coming" will have no advantage over "the dead in Christ" (4:15). God will "take up" the living and "raise up" the dead, and "thus we shall always be with the Lord" (4:16-17).

Modern readers of 4:17 ("we will be caught up with them in the clouds") need to beware of fundamentalist interpretations which insist that this text foretells a very literal "rapture" (snatching up) of Christians into heaven at the end of the world. Those who interpret the text this way often also insist that "these are the last days," as though they had some knowledge denied to everyone else. Mark 13:32 insists to the contrary that "no one—not the angels, not even the Son—knows that day or hour." Paul, like Jesus (Matt 24:40-41), used the imagery of apocalyptic literature in accordance with the culture of his time; but believers are bound by faith, not by particular cultural ideas, whether of marriage (4:4; Col 3:18, "wives, be subordinate"), slavery (Col 3:22, "slaves, obey your masters"), or apocalypticism. Bumper stickers that claim, "When the Rapture comes, you take the wheel!" are cute at best; at worst, they are a serious misreading of Scripture, not to say arrogant. Paul's major point, speaking to believers grieving at the death of loved ones, is that God is very close to the living and the dead, both now and in eternity.

5:1-11 Further instructions about the coming end

The apocalyptic atmosphere continues unabated in this next section, with Paul suggesting (as in 4:1-2, 9) that the Thessalonians know everything he might tell them about "times and seasons." Evidently this was already discussed at some length when he, Silvanus, and Timothy were with them. The imagery Paul uses ("thief in the night," "birth pangs") is also found in other apocalyptic texts, both Christian (Matt 25:43; Mark 13:8) and Jewish (1 Enoch 62:4), and "the day of the Lord" recalls prophetic texts of God's coming judgment (Joel 2:1; Amos 5:18-20). Paul's point here is that believers have nothing to fear; they are "children of light and the day" and so live by a different code than "the rest" of the world that are "in darkness" (5:4-6).

We encounter here the dualism of apocalyptic thinking, namely, the idea that "we, who are being saved" stand over against "them, who are perishing" (1 Cor 1:18; 2 Thess 2:10). The division of time into "this age" and "the age to come," and of humanity into the "saved" and the "lost," was a regular feature of apocalypticism long before the time of Jesus (e.g., Dan 12:1-3). To this day, such language convinces some Christians that outside of Christian faith there is no salvation, but the question of whether unbelievers can be saved is answered both in Scripture (Matt 25:31-46) and in church teaching (Dogmatic Constitution on the Church, art. 16) with a clear yes. Paul, to be sure, thought that unbelievers were headed for "the coming wrath" (1:10), but in this, as in other things, believers must exercise discernment, relying not only on Scripture but also on God-given intelligence, on the guidance of the Spirit, church tradition, and, as Vatican II reminds us, "the secular sciences" (The Church in the Modern World, art. 62).

The strength of Scripture is in the great principles it enunciates of love and justice and its revelation that all people are created "in God's image" and are God's children. A strict application of the Bible's laws and its pronouncements of judgment has never served the church well. Paul's knowledge of the world and history was far more restricted than ours, as also therefore was his context. It is essential that we keep these things in view as we evaluate Paul's text.

For their part, believers are to avoid idle carousing; they are to be clothed with faith, love, and hope as they await the fullness of salvation (5:8-9). Paul recalls again Jesus' "dying for us," which is the basis of Christian hope (5:10; see 4:14). Paul, in fact, recalls the power of that death over and over in his letters (e.g., Rom 3:25; 4:25; 14:9; 1 Cor 1:18-25; Gal 2:19-21). It binds us to God, so that "whether we live or die," there is no separation (5:10).

5:12-22 Final instructions and exhortations

The exhortations here are universal in scope, applicable to any church in any age. And yet they witness to essential, fundamental truths of faith about both church order and Christian morality. In 5:12-13 we have the earliest text ever on church leadership. Paul addresses the entire community, asking them to "acknowledge those who labor among you." These were the women and men who functioned as primary leaders by virtue of their spiritual gifts and faith-commitment. The presumption of some that women were not church leaders has to do with our patriarchal his-

tory and bias, not with historical accuracy. The Pontifical Biblical Commission acknowledged already in 1976 that "some women collaborated in *the properly apostolic work*" and named Prisca (Rom 16:5), Euodia and Syntyche (Phil 4:2-3), Phoebe and Junia (Rom 16:1-2, 7) as examples. Paul urges the church to hold such people in high esteem and to show them love. And that is all; leaders are essential, but the task of ministry belongs fundamentally to the church as the body of Christ (1 Cor 12:7, "to each is given the manifestation of the Spirit for the common good").

Having described the leaders as "those who admonish (instruct) you," Paul goes on to tell the whole community to "admonish the disorderly" (not "the idle," though note 2 Thess 3:6-12). He may have a specific problem in mind here, but what that was we cannot know. The same is true regarding the commands to "encourage the fainthearted [and] support the weak" (5:14). Perhaps these are believers who are timid in the face of persecution. Whatever the case, it is the task of the church to support them. It is also everyone's responsibility to "ensure that no one repays evil for evil"; they are rather to seek the good of all, including outsiders (5:15; cf. 4:12).

The series of rapid-fire commands that follows in 5:16-22 reads like poetry; only the added sentence in 5:18 ("this is God's will for you in Christ Jesus") disturbs the rhythm and rhyme of the Greek text. Theology and spirituality can be much enriched by meditation on these exhortations. In spite of all the hardships that so preoccupy this letter, Paul insists that believers "rejoice always, pray unceasingly, in every circumstance give thanks." The charismatic character of early Christianity is apparent in the command not to "extinguish the Spirit," the Spirit being envisaged as a flaming fire (cf. Acts 2:3, "tongues as of fire"). A primary gift of the Spirit was prophecy, which, though much valued by Paul (1 Cor 14:1-5, 29-33), was subject to abuse and therefore required discernment (5:21). Paul's concern for the church's public image is again apparent in the final command, "Avoid every appearance of evil" (5:22).

5:23-28 Final greeting and blessing

Finally, Paul once again breaks into prayer (cf. 4:11-13) and, once again, the "holiness" and "blamelessness" of the Thessalonians are what he requests (5:23). Their sanctification to the point of being "perfect" is not something they can accomplish of themselves, and thus Paul asks God to accomplish this in them. "Holiness" is not primarily a human endeavor (cf. 4:3). The prayer looks forward to "the coming of our Lord Jesus Christ," when their divinely gifted integrity of "body, mind and spirit" will be apparent. The "God who calls [them] is faithful and will accomplish this" (5:24).

Paul asks for their prayers and, as elsewhere, he instructs them to greet one another "with a holy kiss" (5:26; Rom 16:16; 1 Cor 16:20; cf. 1 Pet 5:14). He then solemnly puts them on oath to "make sure the letter is read to all the believers" (5:27), meaning probably that there were several house-churches within the church of Thessalonica, as was also true in other places (Gal 1:2; Col 4:15). His final blessing is the same as at the end of all his letters. Its fullest form, which we still use today at the beginning of our liturgies, is found in 2 Corinthians 13:13, and as was the case at the beginning, he wishes them "the grace of our Lord Jesus Christ." So ends the very earliest piece of Christian literature—a powerful witness of what the church was and is always to be, a *community* of "faith, love and hope" (1:3; 5:8).

THE SECOND LETTER TO THE
THESSALONIANS

Vincent M. Smiles

INTRODUCTION

The challenges of 2 Thessalonians

For being such a short letter, 2 Thessalonians presents a surprising number of challenges for modern interpreters. A primary issue is whether or not the letter was written by Paul himself, with most scholars these days believing that it was not. A second major issue is the letter's situation: when was it written, who were its intended recipients, what were their problems, and where were they located? Those problems are difficult enough and also have to be answered for a few other New Testament books, but they pale in comparison with the difficulty of understanding what the author says in the central part of the letter. What is meant by "the restrainer" in 2:6-7? Is this a good or an evil power? In fact, is "restrainer" even the correct translation of the Greek term? And who is "the rebel" (or "the lawless one") in 2:3-9, whose coming "springs from the power of Satan"? These problems of 2:3-9 will be dealt with in the commentary itself; the other problems need to be clarified, as far as possible, immediately.

Who wrote 2 Thessalonians?

There are several New Testament letters which the ancient church accepted as written by Paul but which modern scholarship, for good reasons, believes he did not write. Almost all scholars have long regarded the Pastoral Epistles (1 and 2 Timo-

thy and Titus) as not written by Paul; Ephesians, Colossians, and 2 Thessalonians comprise a middle group, whose authenticity has been doubted. Complete certainty is impossible, but in recent years *most*, though not all, scholars have come to accept that 2 Thessalonians was not written by Paul.

Although, superficially, the letter appears to be authentic, closer examination shows that it uses Paul's style and vocabulary in a strange way. It imitates and even, at points, copies from the earlier letter, using it as a model. For example, 2 Thessalonians 1:1 repeats the opening of 1 Thessalonians almost word for word, a practice otherwise unknown among Paul's letters. Even 2 Corinthians 1:1-2, initially almost identical to 1 Corinthians 1:1-3, ultimately differs substantially. The second letter (2 Thess 2:13) has a second thanksgiving, imitating a unique feature of 1 Thessalonians, and the prayers in 2:16 and 3:16 appear to be modeled on prayers in the earlier letter (1 Thess 3:11; 5:23). Furthermore, 2 Thessalonians 3:8 largely repeats 1 Thessalonians 2:9. Such similarities might ordinarily be expected to indicate the same author, but actually copying and imitating his own writing is not a feature of Paul's certainly authentic letters.

In addition to such unexpected imitation, there are also some unexpected stylistic differences. In 2 Thessalonians there is a strange predominance of long, complex sentences (e.g., 2 Thess 1:3-10—one sentence in Greek!) and of long noun-phrases (e.g., 2:8-10). To be sure, such features also appear in the certainly authentic letters, but not to this extent. In a detailed examination of such stylistic peculiarities, one author has shown that 2 Thessalonians resembles Colossians and Ephesians, whose authenticity is also doubted.

In addition to these stylistic observations, the theology of 2 Thessalonians does not appear authentic; most notably, its central section (2:1-12) clashes strangely with Paul's eschatological teaching in 1 Thessalonians 4–5. The latter presupposes that the end is very close (e.g., 4:15, "we who are *alive,* who *remain* at the coming of the Lord") but envisages no way to calculate the time of the end (5:1-3). This is consistent with Paul's views elsewhere (e.g., Rom 13:11-12; 1 Cor 7:29) and with Mark 13:32 ("About that day or hour no one knows, not the angels in heaven nor even the Son"). However, 2 Thessalonians 2:1-6 presupposes that such calculation is possible and even claims that Paul had instructed the readers about it (2:5).

Furthermore, for being such a short letter, 2 Thessalonians has an unusual number of appeals to the letters and tradition of Paul and his companions (2:2, 15; 3:6, 14, 17) and an unusual number of reminders of when Paul was with them (2:5; 3:10, cf. 2:14). The impression is that the writer of 2 Thessalonians had to go to unusual lengths to "authenticate" this letter as being from "Paul." This is consistent with the situation at the end of the first century, twenty to thirty years after Paul's death, when the apostle had become a revered figure and it was important to appeal to his authority to settle difficult questions.

In this regard, one author has noted that Paul himself, when giving information about "the end," did so not only on his own authority but also by appeal to "a mystery" or "a word of the Lord" (note 1 Cor 15:51; 1 Thess 4:15), which is in line with apocalyptic writing in general (e.g., Dan 7:15-16; Rev 1:2; 22:16). In 2 Thessalonians 2:3-12, however, the only source is "Paul" himself. For this writer, Paul has become the higher authority, and thus a letter in his name will suffice to settle the present crisis about an apocalyptic question.

Further, though pretending to derive from Paul, 2 Thessalonians is unusually lacking in expressions of love. In the authentic letters Paul is effusively affectionate (e.g., Phil 1:8; 2:12; 4:1),

and, in fact, nowhere is this more evident than in 1 Thessalonians (e.g., 1 Thess 2:7-8, 17). Even when angry, Paul expresses affection (1 Cor 4:14-15; 10:14; 2 Cor 11:11; Gal 4:19-20). That Paul would write to the Thessalonians at a time when they were suffering greatly and would not express personal affection is unthinkable.

In modern culture, to write a text and place someone else's name on it comes across as fraudulent, but in the ancient Greco-Roman world it was not so unusual, and, in fact, the character of Paul's ministry makes such letters unsurprising. First, like many others, Paul *dictated* his letters to secretaries, people like Tertius (Rom 16:22, "I, Tertius, who wrote this letter greet you in the Lord"). Such secretaries could sometimes have an influence on the way things were expressed.

Second, and more important, Paul included others, named and unnamed (1 Thess 1:1, "Timothy, Silvanus"; Gal 1:2, "all the believers with me"), among the senders of his letters, though he himself seems to have been the only real author in most cases. This reflects the collaborative nature of Paul's missionary endeavors. Therefore, just as it was natural for Paul to write in their names, so it was natural, when Paul was not around, for them to write in his name, even after his death.

And third, both Jewish and Greco-Roman societies knew of many examples of texts being written in the name of famous dead people (e.g., Psalms of Solomon, Letters of Plato). As in many of those cases, so in the case of Paul's co-workers and successors, the purpose was not fraud for profit, but simply to appeal to the apostle's authority to help those who stood in the tradition of his teaching.

It is, of course, impossible to prove in any definitive way whether or not Paul wrote this letter. People of good faith can reasonably disagree on this matter, as is also the case with other disputed books. Modern believers properly focus, not on such historical questions, but on the theology and spirituality of the texts. However, in our attempts to understand Paul, it is perhaps important to realize that not everything that goes under his name necessarily conveys an accurate portrait of him and his theology.

The situation of the letter

Who, then, did write 2 Thessalonians and, more important, when and under what circumstances?

Evidently the letter intends to guide believers "about the coming of our Lord Jesus" (2:1) in the context of persecution (1:4) and particularly to warn them against those who claim that "the day of the Lord is [already] here" (2:2). After the destruction of Jerusalem by the Romans (A.D. 70), confusion and speculation about the time of the end were rife (e.g., Mark 13:5-7; 2 Pet 3:3-10). The book of Revelation suggests (e.g., 13:7) that in the nineties (under the emperor Domitian) persecution of believers in Asia Minor was a major problem. Many scholars think that this may be the context also of 2 Thessalonians. If so, then the letter was written to a real situation, but not to a specific community. It is meant to remind believers in various churches (see Rev 2–3) of established apostolic tradition (2:15) so that they are not "shaken out of [their] minds" by the claims of more recent teachers (2:2).

This need to appeal to authoritative tradition explains why the author used 1 Thessalonians as a model and insisted that what he wrote truly came from the apostle's hand (2 Thess 3:17). Such appeals to older authority are found elsewhere in Scripture (e.g., Daniel, Pastoral Epistles).

Interpreting 2 Thessalonians in the church today

The debate about authorship and the uncertainties of it remind us to be humble in the face of questions we cannot definitively settle and to maintain a careful balance in interpreting Scripture. Reason, as well as faith, is a gift of God, and reason, along with tradition and doctrine, is to guide interpretation of the Bible. Regardless of authorship, 2 Thessalonians is sacred Scripture that can still speak to the heart of the church.

"Literal" interpretations, which imagine that biblical texts were written with the early twenty-first century in mind, only introduce the sorts of confusions that 2 Thessalonians warns against. A true "literal" interpretation never forgets the letter's first-century context and what the author wanted to accomplish in that time among those believers. It also does not forget the limited perspective and knowledge of the ancient writer, who, like Paul himself, expected the end to come very soon. It is not a disparagement of the ancient texts when we admit that such expectations were mistaken. The texts have remained valuable in every generation for their spiritual wisdom and their witness to the faith-experience of first-century believers; their value does not reside either in exact recall of historical events or in precise delineations of God's future plans. The Scriptures, though inspired, have their limitations, just as we, in the midst of our limitations, are not without divine inspiration.

The church today is not, for the most part, persecuted, as was the church to which this letter was addressed. But the church today has its own sufferings and perplexities and can gain much from contemplating the courage and perseverance of ancient believers. We cannot identify with everything this letter has to say, but if we look carefully beneath the surface, we can discover that the same divine Spirit that urged and consoled believers then is still with us in the modern world.

COMMENTARY

1:1-2 Prescript and greeting

The prescript (1:1), which, in accordance with ancient style, includes the sender's and recipient's names, is an exact copy of 1 Thessalonians 1:1, adding only the word "our." If Paul is not the real author, it is *possible* that either Silvanus or Timothy might be. The greeting (1:2) is identical to the longer greeting of Paul's authentic letters and, in that regard, differs slightly from 1 Thessalonians. This may indicate that the author knew the other letters; the model for this one, however, is certainly 1 Thessalonians. "Grace and peace" (2:16; 3:16) were primary theological terms, being respectively the foundation and the fruit of the gospel (e.g., Rom 5:1-2).

1:3-12 The (first) thanksgiving

Proportional to the length of the letter, this is an amazingly long thanksgiving (cf. Rom 1:8-15), and, even more remarkable, 1:3-10 comprises in Greek one long, very complex sentence. This is one of the reasons for thinking that Paul did not write it. Nevertheless, it contains a number of challenging ideas, which in part reflect 1 Thessalonians and in part are somewhat unique. "We *ought* to give thanks" (also 2:13) is awkward phrasing, never used by Paul himself, but the reasons for thanks are very much in Paul's tradition, in that fidelity to the gospel (Phil 1:5) and the fruitfulness of God's gifts among believers (1 Cor 1:4) were always important for the apostle. In this case the writer especially commends believers for their growth in faith and love, even in the midst of "persecutions and afflictions." The themes of faith and love (1:3), of the Thessalonians as model believers (1:4), and of looking forward to Christ's coming judgment (1:7, 9) are all reminiscent of the initial thanksgiving in 1 Thessalonians and were important ideas for Paul himself.

Not typical of Paul is the lengthy dwelling here on the theme of divine retribution for "those who are afflicting you" (1:6). Presumably the latter are identical with those who "do not acknowledge God and do not obey the gospel" (1:8), though it is possible the writer has different groups in mind. The idea of severe retribution appears again in 2:10-12, making this letter far harsher and more vengeful in its tone than any other letter under Paul's name. Such passages are usually, and un-

derstandably, not popular, and care is indeed needed in their interpretation.

Harsh, condemnatory warnings, however, are found throughout Scripture, including sayings from Jesus (e.g., Luke 13:1-9); they are not confined, as is sometimes imagined, to the Old Testament. They express God's rejection of evil and bias for justice, but also the human authors' anger, especially in the face of persecution. They are, it must be emphasized, more than outweighed by expressions of God's love and mercy (e.g., Exod 34:6-7; Luke 15:11-32) and by the demand that believers must love their enemies (e.g., Lev 19:33-34; Matt 5:31-38). The harshness of this letter undoubtedly reflects the bitter experience of religious persecution.

The consolation for believers is that God's judgment is just (1:5), as is shown in their being "considered worthy of the kingdom of God" for which they suffer (cf. 1:11, praying "that our God make you worthy of the call"). Behind this is the idea, important for Paul himself, that salvation derives "not from human desiring or striving, but from God who has mercy" (Rom 9:16; cf. Eph 2:8-9). "The revelation of the Lord Jesus from heaven with his mighty angels" (1:7) recalls 1 Thessalonians 3:13 and various other apocalyptic texts (e.g., Matt 24:31). Also typical of apocalypticism is the expectation of "blazing fire" at the end (e.g., 1 Cor 3:13-15; Isa 66:15-16), delivering punishment for the "disobedient," who will be "separated from the presence of the Lord." On the other hand, "on that day" of judgment the Lord will "be glorified among his holy ones" and "be marveled at by all who have believed" (1:10).

The writer personalizes this general description by saying that the reason for the "glorifying" and "marveling" was that "our testimony to *you* was believed" (1:10); believers will be a cause for celebration on judgment day. "Holy ones" here, as in 1 Thessalonians 3:13, probably refers to "his mighty angels" who will accompany him (1:7), so that the writer envisages the earthly believers joining the heavenly host in triumphant praise of the Lord (see Phil 2:10-11; Rev 7:9-17).

The thanksgiving concludes with a prayer that is somewhat reminiscent of 1 Thessalonians 1:2-3. The prayer asks that God "might make believers worthy" and "complete" their "every good purpose and work of faith." The latter phrase is also found in 1 Thessalonians 1:3 but otherwise is slightly unusual for Paul (cf. Rom 3:27-28; 9:32).

2:1-12 The central problem: Is this the end of the world?

After that long thanksgiving, finally the heart of the matter: "the coming *(parousia)* of our Lord Jesus Christ and our being gathered to him" (not "with him"). The readers have been radically "shaken out of [their] minds" by the claim that "the day of the Lord is here" (not merely "at hand"). The writer does not know whether it is some spirit-filled utterance that has disturbed them or a "word" of prophecy or even a "letter" claiming to be from Paul. Whatever it is, it is deceitful. This imprecision, with the writer covering all bases, suggests that the letter is not written to a specific, known situation but is intended to respond to some end-of-the-century situation(s) in which persecutions had convinced believers that history was all but over.

Verse 2 provides glimpses into early church worship that enable us to see how ecstatic speech and prophecies, while deeply valued, also had to be regulated and subjected to discernment (cf. 1 Cor 14:29-32). First Thessalonians 5:19-21 also advises, "Do not extinguish the spirit, do not despise prophecies, but *test everything*"! The human condition is such that "spirit" and prophecy are inevitably ambiguous; not everything that claims to be from God necessarily is so. The readers are envisioned as profoundly shaken by some communication, possibly even "a letter pretending to be from Paul," that has them convinced that the end of the world is already here! In 3:11 it appears that some have even ceased working because of this conviction.

The writer urges the Thessalonians not to be deceived "in any way" and then begins an explanation (vv. 3-8) of why they should realize that "the day of the Lord" has not yet come (cf. Mark 13:5-7, "Beware, lest anyone deceive you . . . the end is not yet!"). This explanation is very difficult to interpret. It begins with, "For unless the apostasy comes first, and the rebel (lit. 'the lawless one') is revealed," but then the sentence becomes simply an extended description of "the rebel" and remains unfinished. It should probably be understood as meaning, "For *the end is not here*, unless the apostasy . . ." "Apostasy" refers to the defec-

tion of believers. Since some inevitably faltered in the face of persecution, it was commonly accepted that the great "temptation" (testing) at the end would produce considerable apostasy (1 Tim 4:1, cf. Mark 13:13, 20); thus the prayer "Lead us not into [the] temptation [of the last days]" (Matt 6:13).

The long description of "the rebel, the one doomed to destruction" is reminiscent of various Old Testament texts, most notably Daniel 11:36-37 ("He shall exalt himself, making himself greater than any god"), describing the arrogant King Antiochus, who in 167 B.C. had desecrated the temple sanctuary and viciously persecuted the Jewish people (1 Macc 1:41-63). The whole passage (2 Thess 2:3-9) is full of elements commonly found in apocalyptic texts about the signs of the end of the world: the rebel "seat[ing] himself in the sanctuary" is reminiscent of "the abominating desolation" in Daniel 9:27 (a further reference to King Antiochus) and Mark 13:14, and the theme of deception and apostasy recalls Mark 13:22 (see 1 Tim 4:1 and 2 Tim 4:4). In other words, the writer knows the apocalyptic traditions well and employs them here in full measure to demonstrate, by expert knowledge, that the readers have been deceived. This is not the end of the world! Not yet!

The most difficult problem in this very complex passage is "the restrainer." In verse 6 "what is restraining" *(to katechon)* is an impersonal (neuter) power, but in verse 7 "it" becomes "he" *(ho katechon)* who is active "until he *passes from* the scene" (not "is removed"). The New American Bible, along with the majority of scholars, ancient and modern, takes "the restrainer" to be a benevolent power that holds back "the rebel" until the latter is finally "revealed." What or who "the restrainer" is supposed to be is impossible to know; suggestions include the Roman Empire, angelic powers, or the gospel that must be preached to all nations before the end (Matt 24:14). Until that time "the mystery of rebellion is already at work, but only until the restrainer passes away," and then, simultaneously it would seem, "the rebel will [both] be revealed" and will be killed by "the Lord Jesus, with the breath (or Spirit) of his mouth." This "coming" *(parousia)* of the Lord is the true end for which the readers should wait. This interpretation may be correct, but its major weakness is that "restrainer" may not be the best translation of the Greek term.

An alternative interpretation, found in the notes of the New American Bible, is very different. The Greek word for "the restrainer" *(katechon)* is ambiguous; elsewhere it usually means "possess" or "seize." If that is the meaning here, then "the possessing power" *(katechon)* is probably not benevolent but is some evil force (person) that anticipates the coming of the final, more terrible evil one. In this case verses 5-7 read:

> Do you not recall that while I was still with you, I told you these things; and now you know the "possessing power," so that the rebel might be revealed in his own time, for the mystery of rebellion is already at work, but let the "possessor" be for the moment, until he passes away.

Believers here are told to wait; "the rebel" will soon enough be revealed and destroyed after the "possessing power passes from the scene." Both interpretations agree that believers are told to wait and hold on to the instruction given long ago. Though now is the *beginning* of the end (see 1 Thess 1:10; 4:13-18), the *end* of the end will be the "coming" *(parousia)* of "the Lord Jesus" and not before. It is impossible to know for sure which interpretation is correct, but overall evidence favors the first.

The passage continues, in tones reminiscent of the harsh words of 1:6 and 8-9, to talk not only of "the lawless one," whose "coming" *(parousia)* "springs from the power of Satan," but also of those who "are perishing, because they have not accepted the love of truth." Though they were deceived by Satan's displays of "power and signs and false wonders" (2:9), the writer insists that they themselves bear responsibility for not accepting the truth. In its reasoning the passage is similar to Romans 1:18-32, which condemns human refusal to "glorify or give thanks" to God, even though knowledge of God was easily available, so that God "gave them up to their passions" and permitted their sins to be their punishment. Here God is envisaged as sending "a deceiving power so that unbelievers might believe the falsehood" and be condemned (2:11-12). Such judgmental, apocalyptic language needs careful evaluation and application. Its rather narrow context is not to be forgotten; certainly a fundamentalist interpretation, which would view all "unbelievers" as necessarily "condemned," would be a misuse of this text. "Love of truth" is

a universal value, but complete clarity about "the truth" remains beyond our grasp.

2:13-17 A second thanksgiving and prayer

In contrast to the harsh condemnation of unbelievers in 2:10-12, the writer turns to a prayer of thanksgiving for salvation and does so with precisely the same phrase as in 1:3 ("We ought to give thanks to God"). The "choosing" of believers here is a near synonym of God's making them "worthy of the kingdom" (1:5) and "calling" them (1:11). Once again, fully consistent with Paul's own theology, there is a strong emphasis on God's initiative in preparing believers for salvation. "First fruits" (1:13), for Paul himself (e.g., Rom 8:23; 11:16; 1 Cor 15:23), usually suggests the early harvest of something that promises more to come; the meaning here is less clear. It is possible, however, that instead of "first fruits" *(aparchen)*, the text should actually read "from the beginning" *(ap'arches)*, which would emphasize the foresight of God's plan.

In any event, God prepared believers "through sanctification by the Spirit" (God's work) and "belief in truth" (human response). One of the things that distinguishes this letter from 1 Thessalonians is a strong concern with the acceptance of "the truth" (2:10, 12, 13) and the danger of "deceit" (2:9, 11). Neither word is found in 1 Thessalonians. This writer sees "the truth" as coming "through the gospel" (preaching) of Paul and his companions. It is belief in this truth that will lead to possessing "the glory of our Lord Jesus Christ," and therefore believers must "stand firm and hold fast to the [apostolic] traditions" they have received "whether through oral statement or letter" (2:15; cf. 2:2).

The further prayer in 2:16-17 is curiously similar, in a couple of phrases, to that in 1 Thessalonians 3:11-13. The content, however, is different, with this prayer once again emphasizing God's initiative in "loving us [in Christ] and giving eternal consolation and good hope through grace" (2:16). Paul's idea that God enables "every good deed" in believers (2 Cor 8:9) is one that later writers especially liked to repeat (2:17; cf. Eph 2:10; Col 1:10; 2 Tim 3:17).

3:1-16 Final instructions and prayers

In a letter filled with prayers, the writer now asks believers to "pray for us, that the word of the Lord might speed forward (literally 'run') and be glorified" (3:1). There is no way of knowing who "the perverse and wicked persons" (3:2) might be who are envisioned as harassing Paul and his companions. Paul suffered a great deal in his ministry (2 Cor 11:23-33), including in Thessalonica (1 Thess 1:6; Acts 17:5-10), and this writer effectively reminds readers of that fact. That "not all have faith" helps explain this suffering, but "the Lord is faithful who will strengthen you and guard you from the evil one" (3:3). Similarly the writer expresses confidence that the believers are, and will remain, true to the instructions Paul provided, and once again breaks into prayer that "the Lord may direct their hearts" to the greatness of God's love and Christ's endurance in his suffering (3:5).

There follows a lengthy paragraph of instructions that appear to respond to a real situation of Paul's ministry, and some see this as evidence that Paul did indeed write this letter. However, the writer knew 1 Thessalonians and easily reproduces the situation of Paul's letter in order to invoke Paul's authority for the sake of his troubled readers at the end of the first century. Furthermore, though the letter is only fictively addressed to Thessalonica, it is by no means impossible that the very real situation addressed included the kinds of problems identified here. Expectation of the world's imminent end must indeed be a very disruptive experience.

The writer warns the community to avoid any persons who are disruptive and not obedient to "the tradition they received from us" (3:6), once again a focus on apostolic tradition! Believers are to recall Paul's own behavior; he and his companions were models to be imitated. In pursuit of this portrayal, 3:8 borrows both verbally and conceptually from 1 Thessalonians 2:9, that Paul and his co-workers "labored night and day so as to be a burden to no one," in spite of their considerable "authority" (3:9, cf. 1 Thess 2:7). Paul lived out the servant-leadership of Jesus (Mark 10:42-45; John 13:12-14) and is thus a model to be imitated (3:9).

The injunction that "if anyone is unwilling to work, neither should that one eat," (3:10) is quite believable as a tradition that might have come from Paul, given his own self-reliance. It is probably also an allusion to sharing all things in common (Acts 2:44). What the writer is primarily concerned about is the "disorderly" conduct of those who are not doing productive work (3:11) but are being busy-

bodies, perhaps fomenting speculation about the end of the world. Such people are solemnly warned that they are to "work quietly and eat their own food" (3:12). The community as a whole is to persevere in doing good (3:13).

There follows a solemn instruction to the community that "if anyone does not obey our word through this letter, [they are to] take note of, and not associate with, such a person" (3:14). This harsh treatment, however, does not mean they are to excommunicate the person permanently. The language here recalls Paul's instruction in 1 Corinthians 5:9 regarding believers who were guilty of serious immorality. The instruction "Do not regard the offender as an enemy, but warn as speaking to a brother or sister" (3:15) also recalls Matthew 18:15-18, where a process is established for dealing with offenses and reconciliation within church communities. It is instructive to recall that these are the origins of the sacrament of reconciliation, with private confessionals not originating until many centuries later. The paragraph closes with yet another prayer that "the Lord of peace give you peace always and in every way."

3:17-18 Further "proof" of Paul's authority and final blessing

In conclusion the writer tries very hard—one might say, too hard—to convince the readers that this letter indeed derives from Paul himself (3:17). His purpose, of course, is to appeal to Paul's authority in order to reassure churches that are suffering in very difficult persecutions and need encouragement and instruction. Paul himself did authenticate his letters with his own handwriting (2 Cor 16:21; Gal 6:11; Phlm 19), but never three times over! The text, however, is Sacred Scripture, regardless of its author, as is also true of other biblical texts. The Scriptures arise from the church and from the faith of believers, and the church did not disappear with the deaths of the apostles. This letter arises from a church that is suffering and witnesses that, even in the absence of Paul, believers held onto faith and enabled the church to grow.

The final blessing (3:18, "The grace of our Lord Jesus Christ be with you all") corresponds with Paul's standard final words in his letters (e.g., 1 Thess 5:28; 1 Cor 16:23; Gal 6:18) and is now used in the liturgy.

THE FIRST LETTER TO
TIMOTHY

Terence J. Keegan, O.P.

INTRODUCTION

The First Letter to Timothy is the first of three letters usually referred to as the Pastoral Letters because they deal with matters concerning the leadership and organization of the Christian community. While some think that Paul may have composed 2 Timothy and possibly the others as well, most scholars believe that they come from a period after the death of Paul, probably composed by followers of Paul who were concerned that his legacy be handed on to the next generation of Christians. The practice of ascribing later writings to an earlier major figure was common in the ancient world; it can be found in the writings of the Old Testament and other ancient Jewish writings, as well as in the literature of ancient Greece and Rome.

Regardless of who wrote them, all agree that these letters are presented as having the authority of Paul and that they are generally consistent with themes that appear in other Pauline letters. Ultimately, however, the question of authorship does not affect their authoritative status, for, whoever wrote them, they are part of the inspired scriptural conversation between God and God's people.

Similarities among all three Pastoral Letters have led many scholars to consider them together when dealing with questions of authorship as well as interpretation. While there are striking similarities between 1 Timothy and Titus, there are striking differences between these two and 2 Timothy. 1 Timothy and Titus were written in an ancient letter form known as "commandments of a ruler," a letter from a ruler to a delegate and his community. Both of these letters deal with leadership roles in the community, the responsibilities of various groups within the community, and the threat of some kind of Jewish Christian false teaching. 2 Timothy deals with none of these matters but instead is a personal letter exhorting Timothy, by imitating Paul, to be the person through whom authentic Pauline teaching is to be transmitted to future generations. It makes no mention of offices within the community or the responsibilities of community members. Timothy is charged to combat false teaching, but the false teachings are nowhere described as Jewish.

While 2 Timothy may not have been written by Paul during his life, it was composed in the style of a distinctively Pauline letter and contains passages and biographical material that many feel are authentically Pauline. 1 Timothy and Titus depart in significant ways from the Pauline letter form, and their similarities indicate that they were composed probably subsequent to 2 Timothy and possibly by a different person or persons.

These three letters, like Philemon but unlike the other Pauline letters, are each addressed to a single person. The intended audience, however, is not just Timothy or Titus (the ones to whom these letters are addressed) but the larger

Christian community (the implied reader). Paul had preached in all the communities to which he wrote letters, with the exception of the Roman community, and even there he was known to many members of the community and would shortly be visiting that community. Unlike these letters, the Pastoral Letters are addressed to church leaders and members of a later generation that may not have known Paul personally. Addressing these letters to Timothy and Titus not only suited the content and purpose of these letters (orderly succession of leaders and correctness of teaching) but also extended the authority of Paul, through persons known to him in his lifetime, to communities of a later generation.

Interestingly, Timothy and Titus are both presented as young men and are instructed to serve as models of behavior for young men in their communities (1 Tim 4:12; Titus 2:7). The historical figures were indeed young men when Paul first encountered them early in his ministry. They would have been much older toward the end of Paul's ministry, where some scholars attempt to locate the Pastoral Letters.

Timothy appears in all of Paul's undisputed letters except Galatians and frequently appears in the Acts of the Apostles. He is listed as Paul's coauthor in most of the letters that include a coauthor (2 Cor 1:1; Phil 1:1; Col 1:1; 1 Thess 1:1; 2 Thess 1:1; Phlm 1). Titus appears only in 2 Corinthians and Galatians. They both appear as trusted companions of Paul, true to his teachings. "For this reason I am sending you Timothy, who is my beloved and faithful son in the Lord; he will remind you of my ways in Christ [Jesus], just as I teach them everywhere in every church" (1 Cor 4:17). "As for Titus, he is my partner and co-worker for you . . ." (2 Cor 8:23).

According to the narrative of 1 Timothy, Paul had gone to Macedonia, leaving Timothy temporarily in charge of the community at Ephesus. At some later date, whether in Macedonia or elsewhere, he wrote to Timothy, charging him to fulfill his responsibilities until he, Paul, returned. In detailing Timothy's responsibilities, the letter deals with the organization of the community, the roles of its leaders and all the other members of the community. It also explains how to handle the problem of false teachers, including those who, in their asceticism and renunciation of marriage, claimed Paul as their champion. While both 1 Timothy and Titus deal with false teachings and church order, in 1 Timothy the false teachings are more complex and the church organization further developed.

One of the reasons so many scholars are convinced that 1 Timothy was written long after the death of Paul is that it, like Titus, seems to address a period in the development of the early church when concern is for settled order and correct transmission of doctrine. The great Pauline themes of faith, righteousness, and grace, in dynamic development in Paul's early letters, appear here in fixed formulas. The apostolic and charismatic leadership of the early church is past, and the present need is for order, discipline, and virtue in a stable church structure. These letters shift away from Paul's perspective on believers living in a world that is in tension with the coming age. They appropriate the Pauline tradition for a new situation to refute false teachers and to establish the church as the kind of community that can carry the Pauline tradition forward into future generations. The shift apparent in these letters is somewhat comparable to that called for in the document The Church in the Modern World issued by the Second Vatican Council, calling on the church to become more fully engaged with contemporary secular society.

The emphasis of 1 Timothy on God's universal saving intention (2:4-6; see also Titus 2:11-14), as well as its positive view of creation (4:3-4), served to bring the Pauline gospel into the mainstream of contemporary society. While its moral vision of the compatibility of the ethics of church with that of society is somewhat at odds with the perspective of social alienation found in the book of Revelation, both of these parts of the New Testament, each in its own way, challenge the contemporary reader to find ways in which to engage society without betraying the integrity of the gospel message.

COMMENTARY

1:1-2 The opening

Ancient letters usually began with an identification of the sender and the recipient, followed by a short greeting. This letter begins by identifying its sender, "Paul"; his position, "apostle of Christ Jesus"; and the source of his authority, "God our savior and Christ Jesus our hope." This way of identifying the sender also focuses on an important theme both of this letter and of the letter to Titus—the theme of hope. In this letter and especially in Titus, God is the ground and object of hope, which is fulfilled in the gift of eternal life (1 Tim 4:10). God is the source of hope insofar as he saves us by being faithful to the divine promises, sending Christ Jesus to redeem us and form us into a chosen people (Titus 2:14).

The recipient is identified as "Timothy, my true child in faith." This expression illustrates an understanding of the church as a genuinely new family that needs to be nurtured and protected as it grows and matures, as well as designating Timothy as the legitimate representative authorized to minister in Paul's name. The expression "true child" is also used of Titus in the letter addressed to him (Titus 1:4), but in 2 Timothy, Timothy is addressed as "dear child" (2 Tim 1:2). The language in 1 Timothy and Titus emphasizes the authentication of Timothy and Titus. They are teachers in whom communities can put their trust. The greeting expands the typical Pauline greeting, "grace and peace," by the addition of "mercy," perhaps in anticipation of the stress on mercy in the thanksgiving at 1:13.

SETTING THE CONTEXT

1 Tim 1:3-11

1:3-7 Defend against false teaching

As Paul goes off to Macedonia, Timothy is left behind in Ephesus and given responsibility to exercise leadership in Paul's absence. While in 2 Timothy Paul entrusts his gospel to Timothy (2 Tim 1:14; 2:2), in 1 Timothy it is Paul to whom the gospel has been entrusted (1:11; 2:7). Paul remains in control and continues to exercise his responsibilities (3:14; 4:13). Timothy, as his representative, is charged to counter with correct instruction the false teaching that has arisen at Ephesus. The purpose of the instruction, however, is not simply to negate the false teaching but to "love from a pure heart, a good conscience, and a sincere faith" (1:5). Here, as elsewhere in 1 Timothy and Titus, there is a clear connection made between correct doctrine and a morally and religiously integrated life.

The "myths and endless genealogies" (1:4) that are being taught by these "teachers of the law" (1:7) are probably the same as what the letter to Titus calls "Jewish myths and regulations of people" (Titus 1:14). Some think that "genealogies" (1:4; see Titus 3:9) in the false teachings indicate some kind of gnostic speculation. More likely, however, they concern speculations on the lineage of the patriarchs. Here and in Titus there is lack of specificity on these false teachings, both because there is no need to provide a hearing for dangerous opinions and because the real point of the letters is to promote a well-integrated life for members of well-ordered communities.

1:8-11 The value and function of the law

The law referred to in these verses is the Jewish Law, concerning which Paul had said, "a person is not justified by works of the law but through faith in Jesus Christ" (Gal 2:16). Nevertheless, he also maintained that "the law is holy, and the commandment is holy and righteous and good" (Rom 7:12). The law was able to point out sinfulness, although it lacked the power to save. 1 Timothy 1:8-11 is saying essentially what Paul had said. A concern of this letter is with those who continue to oppose Paul by imposing Jewish legal obligations or who misrepresent Paul by teaching a kind of libertinism that gives free rein to all kinds of behavior.

These verses employ a common feature of popular moral preaching, namely, a listing of typical vices. The list here is based on the core of the Old Testament law, the Ten Commandments. The vices listed are said to be opposed to "sound teaching" (1:10; 4:6), which, like "sound words" (6:3), refers in 1 Timothy and Titus to the kind of teaching that leads to correct moral behavior (see Titus 1:9, 13; 2:1, 2, 8).

OPENING BRACKET

1 Tim 1:12-20

This passage and another similar passage near the end of the letter (6:11-16, 20-21a) bracket the body of the letter (2:1–6:10, 17-19). These bracketing passages focus on the overall purpose of the letter: the entrusting of Paul's gospel to Timothy for the purpose of protecting it from false teachers. In the opening bracket more emphasis is placed on Christ Jesus appointing Paul to his ministry (1:12), while the closing bracket emphasizes Timothy's responsibility to guard what has been entrusted to him (6:20) "until the appearance of our Lord Jesus Christ" (6:14). Both, however, focus on the charge entrusted to Timothy (1:18; 6:20), both times using the Greek vocative case (indicating the person addressed, "Timothy"), a case rarely used in the New Testament and used only these two times in this letter, a clear indication of their parallel and bracketing function.

In both passages Timothy's responsibilities are set in the context of community attestation: "prophetic words" (1:18) and "many witnesses" (6:12). In both Timothy is encouraged with metaphors of competition: to "fight a good fight" (1:18) and to "compete well for the faith" (6:12). In both Timothy is warned about the dangerous opposition that threatens the faith (1:19-20; 6:21). The special bracketing function of these passages is further highlighted by the fact that both include a doxology, an act of praise (1:17; 6:15-16). Both doxologies emphasize the uniqueness of God: "the only God" (1:17) and "the only ruler" (6:15), which provides the basis for the letter's emphasis on universal salvation (2:3-6). God's desire that all be saved is the reason why Paul was appointed an apostle (2:7) and the reason why Timothy is being charged to defend Paul's gospel in the face of opposition.

1:12-17 Prayer of thanksgiving

Pauline letters typically have a passage immediately after the opening in which Paul gives thanks to God for what God has done for the community or person to whom the letter is addressed. While 2 Timothy has the characteristic Pauline thanksgiving (2 Tim 1:3-5), it is lacking in both 1 Timothy and Titus. The belated thanksgiving in the present passage is addressed to Christ rather than to God, and the thanksgiving is for what Christ has done for Paul, not for what God has done for the letter's recipient. The present passage is actually more like the interjected thanksgivings in Paul's letters in which Paul thanks God for favors to himself (Rom 7:25; 1 Cor 15:57).

This thanksgiving, as part of the opening bracket, does serve as a foundation for the main themes of the letter and is appropriately placed after the passages that deal with false teaching and immorality. Paul himself was "once a blasphemer and a persecutor and an arrogant man" (1:13). Subsequently, by grace and faith, he became a Christian leader and "an example for those who would come to believe in [Christ]" (1:16). Paul serves as an example for readers up to the present day of how "the grace of our Lord" (1:14) can transform even the most arrogant person into a servant of Christ. The remainder of the letter will continue these themes, that is, upright living that follows from correct understanding of Christian doctrine as well as the proper exercise of leadership and authority in the Christian community.

The Christian doctrine at the heart of this passage, "Christ Jesus came into the world to save sinners" (1:15), is introduced by "this saying is trustworthy," a phrase regularly used in the Pastoral Letters to identify a basic truth of early Christian faith (1 Tim 3:1; 4:9; 2 Tim 2:11; Titus 3:8). The passage concludes with a doxology which, like the doxology found at the end of the letter (6:15-16), includes all four elements usually found in New Testament doxologies: the object of praise, "the king of ages, incorruptible, invisible, the only God"; an expression of praise, "honor and glory"; an indication of time, "forever and ever"; and a response, "Amen." Interestingly, while the thanksgiving is addressed to Christ Jesus (1:12), the doxology is addressed to God.

1:18-20 Timothy's responsibilities

The mention of Timothy's name in verse 18 is a departure from the style of letter writing in the Hellenistic world. Names of recipients would normally appear only in the opening and closing of the letter. Mention of his name at this point serves the bracketing function of this passage and refocuses the letter on Timothy (the recipient) after the thanksgiving has been focused on Paul, highlighting the seriousness of the challenge Timothy is facing in opposing error in the church. He is to take up this challenge "in accordance with the prophetic words once spoken about you" (1:18). Prophecy—words uttered by God's spokesperson—is the only charism that appears in all of Paul's lists of spiritual gifts (Rom 12:6; 1 Cor 12:10, 28, 29; see 1 Cor 13:2; 14:6, 22). Here and at 4:14

prophecy is associated with the charismatic authorization of Timothy's ministry, a ministry here described as fighting a good fight with the weapons of faith and a good conscience.

While the opponents Timothy is to deal with are never identified and their teaching is only vaguely described, two individuals are cited with whom Paul presumably had to deal. They are cited here as examples of the kinds of persons Timothy is to beware. Both names appear in 2 Timothy. Hymenaeus said that the resurrection has already taken place, (2 Tim 2:17-18), and Alexander the coppersmith did Paul a great deal of harm (2 Tim 4:14). Their use here may be an indication that 2 Timothy preceded and influenced 1 Timothy. Both men have been "handed over to Satan" (1:20), the procedure indicated for the incestuous man in 1 Corinthians 5:1-5. In both places the procedure—what today would be called excommunication—is not punitive but educative and should lead to conversion. A similar procedure appears in Titus 3:10-11. Support for this procedure emphasizes the overall concern of 1 Timothy and Titus with correct teaching and good order in the community.

THE HOUSEHOLD OF GOD

1 Tim 2:1–3:15

2:1-7 Universal salvation and good citizenship

After the opening bracket, the four main sections of the letter deal with good order in the community, true devotion as opposed to false teaching, the responsibilities of Timothy as a community leader, and dealing with false teachers. False teaching threatens the stability of the community both in itself and with respect to the surrounding secular world. Praying for everyone, from kings on down, serves a dual purpose and is rooted in the fundamental doctrinal truth that "there is also one mediator between God and the human race, / Christ Jesus, himself human, / who gave himself as ransom for all" (2:5-6). First, it furthers God's purpose, for which Paul is appointed preacher and apostle, that everyone be saved and come to a knowledge of the truth. Emphasis on God's desire to save all people is as important for the contemporary reader of this letter as it was for the original readers in their

situation. Nowhere in the New Testament is this desire more explicit than in 1 Timothy 2:4.

Second, it furthers the desire of the developing Christian community to have its members accepted as good citizens in civil society. The quiet, tranquil lives desired is described using a technical term, "devotion" (2:2), sometimes translated "religion." It is the word used in the Roman world for reverence for the gods and respect for traditional values and practices, a combination of piety and correct behavior. This much esteemed virtue receives little notice in the rest of the New Testament but is prominent in 1 Timothy and Titus (2:2; 3:16; 4:7, 8; 6:3, 5, 6, 11; Titus 1:1; 2:12). It is a virtue that pertains to the special concern of 1 Timothy and Titus that Christians lead lives worthy of their calling, lives that can be held in high esteem by the surrounding world. This passage illustrates a developing understanding of the church, not as an isolated and dangerous sect but as a community that is open to all, and of Christian life as fully compatible with good citizenship.

2:8-15, 3:1a How men and women are to pray and live

In the introduction to this letter, Paul spoke of Timothy as "my true child in faith" (1:2), indicating an understanding of the church as a genuinely new family. Here and later in the letter (6:1-2, 17-19) there is a list of duties, often called a "household code." Such lists in other writings (Eph 5:22–6:9; Col 3:18–4:1; 1 Pet 2:13–3:8) focused on members of a familial household; here, however, the whole church, the household of God, is addressed.

The concern of these verses is with community worship that is filled with factions and quarreling. Men are addressed in 2:8 and simply told to pray "without anger or argument." The remainder of the chapter concerns women's behavior in the assembled community. Women are not only admonished about appropriate dress and conduct, but they are also forbidden "to teach or to have authority over a man" (2:12). It is not clear why women are singled out for such extensive treatment, but all three Pastoral Letters seem to accept the widespread belief at that time that women were notoriously unable to control their sexual passions (1 Tim 5:11-15; 2 Tim 3:6-7; Titus 2:4-5). The belief that women were weak-willed and easy prey to false teachers probably influenced the prohibition on public teaching and the requirement that they remain completely silent in the Christian assembly (2:11-12; 1 Cor 14:34-35). While some have suggested that the injunction to "be quiet" (2:12) refers not to prayer but to aggressive confrontations, this passage has provoked more discussion than any other in the Pastoral Letters in recent years. It must be acknowledged that great harm has come upon women throughout the history of the church because of understandings of this passage.

While women are in some ways subordinate to men in Paul's letters, one does find there women prophets (1 Cor 11:1-13) and a degree of equality among men and women (Gal 3:28). The unusual interpretation of the Adam and Eve story (Gen 2) used to support the subordination of women is likewise contrary to Paul's teaching, for Paul clearly speaks of Adam's sin, not Eve's (Rom 5:12-19). 1 Timothy's inventive interpretation of Genesis 2 (2:13-14) is, interestingly, a clear example of scriptural warrant for interpretive strategies that go beyond the original meaning of the text. One needs to go beyond the original meaning of 2:11-12 by reading this passage with a hermeneutic of suspicion. Hermeneutics involves the methods used to interpret a text. The apparent meaning of a text is often colored by cultural presuppositions that are now known to have been mistaken. A hermeneutics of suspicion is a method that questions the validity of these cultural presuppositions and seeks a deeper meaning in the text. This method enables contemporary readers to arrive at fresh meanings of the text that are free from the cultural assumptions of the past.

At the same time, one must recognize that just as past assumptions about family structures and power relationships were not absolute but rather culturally conditioned, the same can be said for what contemporary society regards as appropriate about family structures and power relationships. Reading the Pastoral Letters with a hermeneutic of suspicion can help contemporary readers go beyond the culturally conditioned values of both past and present centuries.

The message of this passage for the church of the first century as well as for the church today is that good order based on sound doctrine needs to be maintained in the church. Women throughout history have spoken powerfully for the kind of sound doctrine promoted by 1 Timothy. The church

was blessed because St. Catherine of Sienna did not take the injunction to silence literally when she persuaded Pope Gregory XI to return from Avignon to Rome in 1376. She was clearly more interested in what is a primary concern of 1 Timothy, the preservation of authentic Christian tradition.

The final verse in the passage on women emphasizes the role of motherhood in the salvation of women (2:15). Childbearing, however, fits in with God's plan for salvation only when it is accompanied by faith and love, the hallmarks of Christian existence; by holiness, the condition of belonging to the Lord; and self-control, a quality valued in Hellenistic society and a continuing motif in 1 Timothy and Titus (2:9, 15; 3:2; Titus 1:8; 2:2, 5); qualities equally expected of women as well as of men. "This saying is trustworthy" (3:1a) pertains to what precedes rather than to what follows. This is the second use of this phrase in the Pastoral Letters, a phrase which usually signals a basic truth of early Christian faith (1 Tim 1:15; 4:9; 2 Tim 2:11; Titus 3:8). Like every other use of this phrase in the Pastoral Letters, it is connected with a statement on salvation. In this case it is used to ratify the previously expressed teaching on the salvation of Christian women and more broadly the teaching on salvation which began in 2:3-4 affirming that God "wills everyone to be saved and to come to knowledge of the truth" (2:4).

3:1b-7 Qualifications for bishops

After spelling out the duties of men and women in the community, the letter continues with listings of the qualifications for leadership positions in the community. The purpose of this passage is to provide a stable structure for the community in the face of forces that have the potential to cause its disintegration. The qualifications listed here, like the previous treatment of the role of women, are culturally conditioned and concerned with public respectability in the context of a particular culture. The only uniquely Christian features in these lists are the requirements that the bishop "not be a recent convert" (3:6) and that deacons hold "fast to the mystery of the faith with a clear conscience" (3:9).

The list contains no specification of the actual roles of bishops and deacons in the community, and apart from the two items mentioned above, the qualifications listed are typical of what would be expected of pagan and Jewish officials. All these qualifications, however, are in keeping with two major concerns of 1 Timothy and Titus, namely, that the community be well ordered under reliable leadership and that the Christian community, by reason of its integrity, be respected by the surrounding world (3:7). One qualification that appears in the lists for both bishop and deacon is that they not be lovers of money (3:3) or greedy for sordid gain (3:8). Leaders who are mercenary would clearly detract both from good order within the community as well as from the reputation of the community in the surrounding world. This characteristic is specifically attributed to false teachers who are harming the community (6:5; see Titus 1:11).

It is tempting to see in the offices of bishop and deacon their well-defined positions as they appear in the developed church of the second century. Nevertheless, it is far from clear just how well defined these positions had become in the context of 1 Timothy and Titus. Another group that appears in these letters are the presbyters, who seem to be synonymous with bishops (5:17, 19; Titus 1:5-6). Timothy and Titus have significant administrative and teaching authority, and Titus himself is given the authority to appoint presbyters (Titus 1:5), but nowhere are Timothy and Titus called bishops. Whether bishops have the kind of authority described for Timothy and Titus is not clear.

3:8-13 Qualifications for deacons

How the office of deacon differs from that of bishop/presbyter is similarly unclear. The qualifications are similar, and the functions are not mentioned. The fact that they are listed second might indicate that here, just as in the later church, their role is subordinate to that of bishop. Even more problematic is the reference to women in verse 11. Some hold that this passage refers to deaconesses like Phoebe (Rom 16:1), but what her role was or what the role of these women were is not clear. It is possible that this verse refers not to deaconesses but to the wives of deacons, who, like their husbands, must have qualities that contribute to the good order of the community and its reputation in the surrounding world.

3:14-15 Conclusion on the household of God

These verses bring to conclusion the first main section of the letter on the household of God

(2:1–3:15) and serve as a transition to what follows. "These matters" (3:14) refers to all that has preceded in this section in the same way that "these things" (4:11) refers to all that precedes in each of the next two main sections of the letter. In this first main part of the letter Paul detailed Timothy's responsibilities for the household of God. While Timothy is temporarily in charge, Paul continues to be responsible for the community (1:11; 2:7) and plans to return (3:14). Paul's plans to visit his communities are often noted in his letters (Rom 15:24; 1 Cor 4:19; Phlm 22). Mention of these plans gives added importance to the letter, which is to take the place of Paul's authoritative presence, supporting 1 Timothy's intention of serving as a kind of church constitution for a developing Christian community. The good order that precedes and the opposition to false teaching that will follow are what Paul intends for the Christian community.

The Christian community is then described using two images, "the household of God" and "the church of the living God, the pillar and foundation of truth" (3:15). The first image treats the church as a well-ordered structure exhibiting proper behavior, the main concern of the passages that preceded. The second image focuses on the church as a living faith-community whose organization and moral life are based on the solid foundation of sound doctrine, the concern of the second main section of the letter.

SOUND DOCTRINE OF DEVOTION/RELIGION

1 Tim 3:16–4:11

3:16 Mystery of devotion

The second main section of the letter begins by providing the theological basis for this solid foundation of truth by using what appears to be a passage from a liturgical hymn. The letter speaks of this solid foundation as "the mystery of devotion" (3:16), the second use of this technical term in this letter (see 2:2). The hymn sums up the content of Christian faith on which Christian living is based. The use of passages from hymns or confessions is common in New Testament letters and serves to remind readers of the fundamental truths that they believe and express in their community worship. A similar passage from a hymn is used in 1 Peter 3:18-19, 22.

An indication that the passage in 1 Timothy is taken from a hymn is the fact that it consists of three balanced couplets: flesh-spirit (contrast), seen-proclaimed (complementary), world-glory (contrast). This passage summarizes the church's authentic faith in the paschal mystery: Jesus died on the cross (his manifestation in the flesh) and rose from the dead. He was first seen by angels then proclaimed by apostles to the Gentiles. People all over the world have come to believe in Jesus, who is now enthroned as Lord of the church and will come again to judge the living and the dead.

4:1-5 Problems in later times, apostasy

The letter here turns attention to the fundamental problem mentioned at the start of the letter—people teaching false doctrines (1:3), doctrines opposed to the fundamental truths of Christian faith just summarized in the hymn (3:16). False teachers, upsetting the lives of the faithful and dividing communities, had been a problem from the earliest days of Christianity. Paul dealt with false teachings in his early letters and communities. False teachers became especially troublesome as the church attempted to settle into a structured and sustainable existence.

So important is the matter of correct teaching that the author has raised the stakes from a simple contrast between truth and falsehood to an end-time contrast between the forces of good and the forces of evil (cf. 2 Tim 3:1-9). He appeals to the prophetic Spirit to set the stage for the end-time conflict, clearly the same Spirit who had vindicated the crucified Jesus in the preceding hymn (3:16). References to the Spirit are rare in the Pastoral Letters, with each reference emphasizing a different aspect of the Spirit (see 2 Tim 1:14; Titus 3:5). Here the prophetic Spirit foretells the end-time conflict with "deceitful spirits and demonic instructions" (4:1).

The notion that deceit is characteristic of the end times was common in the New Testament era. It is found in the Marcan apocalypse (Mark 13:5-6, 22) as well as in parallel passages in Matthew and Luke. False teachings are referred to elsewhere in the Pastoral Letters, but only here are specific issues identified, which are then refuted with an explicit argument. These two issues—"they forbid marriage and require abstinence from foods" (4:3)—are similar to problems Paul encountered at Corinth about marriage (1 Cor

7:1-3) and food (1 Cor 8:4-13; 10:23-33). The problem here might also be related to the claim by Hymenaeus (see 1 Tim 1:20) that the "resurrection has already taken place" (2 Tim 2:18). This claim is consistent with the teachings of a later heretical group, the Gnostics, who viewed the material world as evil. If those transformed by the saving grace of Jesus were already "resurrected," already living full spiritual lives, abstinence from physical pursuits such as sex, marriage, and food would be consistent with their denigration of the material world.

These errors are refuted by appealing, as Paul did (1 Cor 8:6; 10:26), to the one God who created all that is. "Everything created by God is good" (4:4) echoes the words of Genesis 1:31: "God looked at everything he had made, and he found it very good." The goodness of God's creation was tainted by sin, but the redemption won by Jesus has overcome all the evil caused by sin. Nevertheless, powerful sects preaching that the material world is evil have arisen throughout the history of the church. These included the Gnostics of the early church; the Manichees, among whom St. Augustine once was numbered; and the thirteenth-century Albigensians, against whom St. Dominic preached, to name but a few. According to 1 Timothy, everything created by God is not only good, but "it is made holy by the invocation of God in prayer" (4:5). This powerful assertion about the goodness of all that God creates is as important today as it has been throughout the history of Christianity. Receiving God's good creation in prayer pertains clearly to the common Christian practice of thanking God in prayer before meals, but it can pertain equally to the use of sex within marriage or to any other good thing.

4:6-10 Training for devotion, false versus true teachers

After reflecting on the conflicts of the end times (4:1-5), Paul addresses a charge to Timothy that involves a contrast between the true teacher exemplified in the person of Timothy and the false teachers discussed in 4:1-3. "These instructions" (4:6) probably refers to the previous instructions on the goodness of creation. False teachers are concerned with "profane and silly myths" (4:7; see 1:4), while true teachers are concerned with "the words of the faith and of the sound teaching" (4:6). False teachers require unwarranted asceticism based on a false understanding of resurrection and the spiritual life (4:3). True teachers train for devotion (4:7), knowing that future life is still a promise (4:8, 10). Christians trained in devotion would lead lives that could be held in high esteem by the surrounding world. Training for devotion is somewhat like, but far more important than, physical training. "Devotion is valuable in every respect, since it holds a promise of life both for the present and for the future" (4:8).

This statement on the importance of devotion is the third of the trustworthy sayings to appear in the letter (see 1:15; 3:1). This saying is unique among the trustworthy sayings in the Pastoral Letters, since only here are specific implications of the saying spelled out. The first implication is "toil and struggle" (4:10). God has promised the life to come, but the path to that life will involve effort. There is, however, no suggestion here or elsewhere in this letter that the author is thinking of the kind of hardship and persecution that is discussed in 2 Timothy (2 Tim 3:10-12; 4:5). The second implication concerns Christian hope, an important theme in both this letter and in Titus (1 Tim 1:1; 4:10; 5:5; Titus 1:2; 2:13; 3:7). God is the ground and object of hope, which is fulfilled in the gift of eternal life. The final implication is God's gift of salvation. Every time a trustworthy saying appears in the Pastoral Letters it refers to some aspect of salvation. God wills that all people be saved, but God also wills that they come to a full knowledge of the truth (2:4). Those who do so are the faithful, whom God particularly wills to be saved. These are the ones who toil and struggle for devotion.

4:11 Conclusion

This second main section of the letter concludes with an instruction to "command and teach these things" (4:11; see 3:14; 6:2), a reference to all that has preceded in this section. Timothy is charged to command and teach about training for devotion and the rejection of teaching that is opposed to the fundamentals of Christian faith.

INSTRUCTIONS ABOUT LEADERSHIP
1 Tim 4:12–6:2

4:12-16 Timothy's duties

After a discussion of true and false teachings, the third main section of the letter focuses on the duties of the leader of the community. In the pre-

vious verses Timothy was encouraged to "give these instructions" (4:6) and to "train yourself for devotion" (4:7). This section further expands on these two fundamental duties of a community leader. He is the church's authorized teacher and guardian of its faith, and he is to witness to that faith in the way he lives and performs his duties.

The overall concern of 1 Timothy and Titus for a stable Christian community with an authorized leadership is here manifest in the solemn description of Timothy's authorization for ministry: "through the prophetic word with the imposition of hands of the presbyterate" (4:14). This is the only passage in 1 Timothy dealing with how leaders assume their positions. It differs significantly from 2 Timothy, where Paul imposes hands on Timothy (2 Tim 1:6), transmitting his own authority. It differs as well from Titus, where Titus appoints presbyters (Titus 1:5). The intent of the present passages is to establish both the charismatic and the transmitted authority of the church leader. The charge "let no one have contempt for your youth" (4:12) is reminiscent of what Paul wrote about Timothy to the Corinthians: "no one should disdain him" (1 Cor 16:11). The narrative of the letter presumes that he is still a young man who has been raised up by the presbyterate to a position of leadership and enabled by the gift of the Spirit to "attend to the reading, exhortation, and teaching" (4:13).

The list of five qualities that Timothy is to model (4:12) are noteworthy, since they significantly differ from the list of six qualities in 2 Timothy that are observed in Paul (2 Tim 3:10-11). Common to both lists are faith and love, the hallmarks of Christian existence (see 1:14; 2:15; 6:11). 2 Timothy also lists patience, endurance, persecutions, and sufferings, qualities important for the character and purpose of that letter. Instead of these, 1 Timothy lists speech, conduct, and purity, qualities more specific to the nature and purpose of 1 Timothy.

The passage concludes with a series of imperatives directed at Timothy: "be diligent . . . be absorbed . . . attend . . . persevere " (4:15-16), which emphasize the importance of his position and the seriousness of his responsibilities. He is to do these things for two reasons: first "so that your progress may be evident to everyone" (4:15). "Progress" is a technical term employed by Stoics and other philosophers, but appearing elsewhere in the New Testament only in Philippians 1:12, 25 (interestingly, the only book in the New Testament besides 1 Timothy that speaks of both bishops and deacons). "Progress" refers to a person's moral and spiritual evolution. For Plutarch, progress comes between natural dispositions and perfection. Virtues important in the surrounding world are important as well for 1 Timothy and Titus. Timothy's moral and religious development should not only inspire the Christian community but also bring credit to the community in the eyes of others. The second reason he is to do these things is to "save both yourself and those who listen to you" (4:16). God is the savior of all, but Timothy has been brought into this plan by reason of his authorization and spiritual gifts.

5:1-2 Respect for men and women, old and young

The instructions to Timothy continue, but the focus shifts from how he is to deal with false teaching to how he is to deal with the members of the household of God. The present section differs from earlier sections dealing with household members (2:8–3:13). There a household code (2:8-15) dealt with the behavior of various members of the community, followed by a section (3:1-13) dealing with qualifications and responsibilities for positions of leadership. The present section deals with how Timothy and others are to treat various members of the community, first considered in terms of age and sex. Greater attention is paid to older men, continuing an Old Testament concern for men in their old age (Sir 3:12-14), but all are to be treated with respect and kindness. Within the household of God, obligations toward one's immediate family are to be extended to all members of the community.

5:3-16 Rules regarding widows

This long section addresses the place of widows in the community, obviously a matter of concern in the church at the time the letter was written. As with all members of the community, widows are to be treated with the respect that is owed them (5:3). There are, however, different categories of widows. First and foremost is "the real widow, who is all alone, has set her hope on God and continues in supplications and prayers night and day" (5:5). Christians have an obligation to provide for family members who become widows (5:4, 8, 16), but those left with no one to

provide for them become the responsibility of the community. These real widows are to be "enrolled," a term which probably indicates not only that they are being provided for but also that they have some official role in the community. The qualifications laid down for being enrolled (5:9-10) are similar to qualifications listed for bishops and deacons (3:2-3, 8-9).

Besides these "real widows," there are the widows who have families that can provide for them, widows of any age who are self-indulgent (5:6), and younger widows, "less than sixty years old" (5:9), who might not be self-indulgent but might become so. The advice given about younger widows manifests concerns raised elsewhere in the Pastoral Letters. Women are especially prey to false teachers disturbing the church (2 Tim 3:6-7). Rather than risk succumbing either to the desire for marriage or to the wiles of false teachings (see Titus 1:11), it would be better for them to marry and manage a home and children (5:14). The recommendation to remarry should also be seen in connection with the false teachers' attack on marriage in 4:3. An additional concern of these letters is the repute of the community in the surrounding world. Young widows should marry lest they fall into kinds of behavior that bring disrepute on the community (5:14).

5:17-22 Rules regarding presbyters

After dealing with those older widows who serve a special function within the community, the letter now deals with older men, presbyters, who have a special function in the community. It is not clear how the presbyters dealt with here are any different from the bishops of chapter 3. Titus 1:5-9 uses "bishop" and "presbyter" almost interchangeably, the term "presbyter" referring to the person's status within the community, a respected member of the community, and the term "bishop" referring to his function, exercising oversight and leadership in the community. Like Timothy, presbyters have a responsibility for teaching and preaching, what the qualifications for bishops state they must be able to do (3:2; Titus 1:9). Like widows, they are to be provided for by the community. In fact, presbyters "deserve double honor" (5:17). The scriptural basis provided in the next verse appears in two parts. The first is clearly from Deuteronomy 25:4 (see 1 Cor 9:9), but the second is a saying of Jesus (Matt 10:10; Luke 10:7). While some believe that only the first is referred to as Scripture, others feel that this passage may be early evidence for the conferral of scriptural status on New Testament literature or sources.

Just as there was a concern with widows who stray and bring disrepute on the community, there is an even greater concern with presbyters who sin. When accusations are brought against presbyters, they are entitled to what today would be called "due process." Those who indeed do sin, however, are to be reprimanded publicly, "so that the rest will also be afraid" (5:20). The need for harsh treatment of errant church leaders is all too evident in the contemporary church.

The admonition that care should be taken not to "lay hands too readily on anyone" (5:22) could refer to the ordination of presbyters (see 4:14), but in the present context it more likely refers to the laying on of hands involved in the reconciliation of sinners. Timothy is exhorted not to play favorites but to reconcile to the community only those who have fully repented of their sins. The bottom line is a word of advice to Timothy, which applies, through him, to all with positions of leadership: "keep yourself pure" (5:22).

5:23-25 Timothy's duties

The final comment in verse 22, "keep yourself pure," connects as well to the verse that follows. Timothy bears a heavy responsibility for the church at Ephesus and must be both spiritually and physically fit for the task at hand. The rejection of a false dietary asceticism (4:3-4) is here reinforced by the recommendation to make proper use of the good things, like wine, created by God for one's physical well being (5:23). This advice to Timothy parallels the advice given earlier to young widows about remarriage (5:14), rejecting false teaching and extolling God's good creation. The emphasis on the public character of both sin and good deeds relates to the overall concern of 1 Timothy and Titus for the public perception of the Christian community. The behavior of Christian leaders, good or bad, will affect the public perception of the community. Whether or not their deeds are public, they will not long remain hidden.

6:1-2 Conclusion on slaves

In chapters 2 and 3 the letter had addressed the responsibilities and qualifications of various members of the community in the "household of God"—husbands and wives, bishops, and dea-

cons. The previous chapter shifted the focus and looked at the way the community and its leaders should deal with certain members—older men, widows, and presbyters. Here the focus seems to shift back to the responsibilities of certain members within the community. Just as bishops and deacons are to conduct themselves in ways that bring honor to the Christian community, slaves are charged with a similar responsibility.

There is no suggestion here, nor generally in the New Testament, that the Christian community was to overthrow the social structures of society. In 1 Timothy and Titus especially, Christians are charged to behave as good citizens in what was considered a well-ordered society. Slaves are encouraged to fulfill their responsibilities to their masters, even to their Christian masters, "so that the name of God and our teaching may not suffer abuse" (6:1). The motive for similar advice to slaves in Titus is expressed positively: "so as to adorn the doctrine of God our savior in every way" (Titus 2:10).

Dealing with slaves at this point in the letter, shifting back to responsibilities of certain members of the community, is not really out of place. This third main section of the letter is concerned with the responsibilities of leaders in the community. Timothy is, as Paul describes himself in Titus 1:1, a slave of God, as are all those who exercise leadership roles. Timothy, above all, as a slave, must fulfill his responsibilities to his master. The final words of verse 2, "teach and urge these things" (cf. 3:14; 4:11), conclude this third main section of the letter. These words, which are unfortunately and inexplicably missing from many editions of the New American Bible, refer not just to the advice to slaves but to all the responsibilities that Timothy and other leaders, slaves of God, have been charged with in this section of the letter.

FALSE TEACHING AND TRUE WEALTH
1 Tim 6:3-10, 17-19

6:3-10 The evils of false teaching exposed

The focus of the letter now shifts from the responsibilities of true teachers to a criticism of false teachers in this fourth and final main section of the letter. As in chapter 4, Timothy is advised to beware of false teachers and to be strong in adhering to correct doctrine, the doctrine that leads to religion/devotion (6:3; see 2:2; 3:16; 4:7, 8; 5:4; 6:5,

6, 11). In this chapter the correct understanding of religion is contrasted with the understanding of those who think that religion can be a source of material gain (6:5; cf. Titus 1:11). These are the people who fall into erroneous beliefs and end up experiencing a host of vices—"envy, rivalry, insults, evil suspicions, and mutual friction" (6:4-5). They are the ones referred to earlier in the letter who have "turned to meaningless talk" (1:6) and are "paying attention to deceitful spirits and demonic instructions through the hypocrisy of liars with branded consciences" (4:1-2). "Religion with contentment" (6:6) expressed the Stoic ideal of being content in any situation, but here it expresses a perspective on life restored by the saving mission of Christ. Religion is indeed a source of great gain if it leads to a Christian appreciation for moderation and sufficiency. Those, however, who use religion to achieve material wealth will stray into error and encounter an array of evils, for "the love of money is the root of all evils" (6:10).

6:17-19 Conclusion on the wealthy

While this passage appears after the first part of the closing bracket (6:11-16), it serves to conclude the fourth and final section of the body of the letter on false teachers. This passage deals with a final group within the household of God not yet treated in the letter—the rich. They are fittingly dealt with here and told not to be proud (6:17), after the emphasis on the overarching power of God in the final doxology (6:15-16). While it is wrong to use religion to pursue wealth, it is admirable to use wealth in the service of religion, recognizing that the ultimate source of security is not transient wealth but the eternal God. As with the earlier section on slaves, this passage dealing with the wealthy is really not out of place, since it concludes the previous section, which dealt with the connection of false teaching and the inappropriate pursuit of wealth (6:5).

In a broader perspective, wealth is viewed in the same light as were marriage and food. "Everything created by God is good, and nothing is to be rejected when received with thanksgiving" (4:4). Just as Timothy and all Christian leaders are slaves of God, they are to rely on God for all the good things they need to fulfill their ministries. The reason for the proper use of riches, like the reason for all the moral exhortations in this letter, is "to win the life that is true life" (6:19).

CLOSING BRACKET

I Tim 6:11-16, 20-21a

6:11-16 Timothy's responsibility and accountability

While the false teacher's misuse of religion leads to ruin, the true teacher's correct pursuit of religion leads to eternal life. This passage, together with 6:20-21a, closely parallels the opening bracket of the letter (1:12-20). That bracket appeared after the formal opening (1:1-2) and an expression of concern for the problem of false teachings (1:3-11). It began with a thanksgiving for the mercy and promise of eternal life extended to Paul, the true teacher (1:12-17).

In this final bracket Timothy is encouraged to follow the example of Paul, to "compete well for the faith" (6:12; see 1:18) and "to keep the commandment without stain or reproach" (6:14). His role of being a faithful witness parallels not only Paul's but also that of Jesus before Pilate (6:13). In the opening of the letter Timothy was addressed by Paul as "my true child in the faith" (1:2); here he is addressed as "man of God" (6:11), an expression used in the Old Testament for a person with a prophetic function (1 Sam 2:27; 1 Kgs 13:1). Its use recalls the prophetic charge to Timothy in the opening bracket (1:18).

Timothy is charged to keep "the commandment" (6:14), a term that appears nowhere else in the Pastoral Letters. In this context, however, it likely refers to the tasks entrusted to Timothy at the laying on of hands (4:14). It would involve both his teaching responsibilities as well as his responsibility to provide moral leadership by his own good example. He is to keep this commandment "until the appearance of our Lord Jesus Christ" (6:14), a reference to the eschatological parousia (second coming) of the risen Lord, similar to 1 Thessalonians 3:13; 5:23, but without suggesting that the appearance will occur during Timothy's lifetime.

This final charge to Timothy concludes with a doxology (6:15-16) that is strikingly similar to the doxology that concludes the thanksgiving in the opening bracket (1:17). Like that earlier doxology, it includes all four elements usually found in New Testament doxologies: the object of praise, "the King of kings and Lord of lords, who alone has immortality, who dwells in unapproachable light, and whom no human being has seen or can see";

an expression of praise, "honor and eternal power"; an indication of time, "eternal"; and a response, "Amen."

Unlike the doxology at 1:16 and unlike all the other New Testament passages that are commonly identified as doxologies, this one in chapter 6 is the only one that does not use the Greek word for "glory," *doxa*. Instead, this final doxology uses the word "power." While 1 Timothy and Titus respect the power of earthly rulers, their power is subject to God's, and only his is an "eternal power" (6:16).

6:20-21a Final recommendation

The final words of Hellenistic letters usually recapitulate and emphasize the main themes of the letter. The final words here complete the closing bracket by summarizing the advice given to Timothy throughout the letter, addressing Timothy directly, as in the opening bracket (1:18). They renew the warning about the dangerous opposition that threatens the faith (6:21; see 1:19-20). Timothy is to "guard what has been entrusted" (cf. 1:18) and "avoid profane babbling" (cf. 4:7).

BLESSING

1 Tim 6:21b

This letter's closing is, curiously, the shortest of all such closings in the New Testament. Both 2 Timothy and Titus, like Paul's authentic letters, include second- and third-person greetings as well as references to travel plans prior to the final blessing. These omissions serve only to reinforce the focus of this letter on the singular responsibility of Timothy, the community leader, to overcome opposition by adhering to sound doctrine in promoting the internal life of the community as well as in securing its good reputation in the surrounding world. The blessing itself, "grace be with all of you," is identical to that found at the end of 2 Timothy. Titus and most of Paul's letters have longer blessings, but all, except Romans, use the identical words found in 1 Timothy. In all these letters, including Philemon, the blessing is addressed to "you" in the plural, an indication that even those letters addressed to individuals were intended to be heard by the larger community.

THE SECOND LETTER TO

TIMOTHY

Terence J. Keegan, O.P.

INTRODUCTION

Of the three Pastoral Letters, 2 Timothy contains by far the greatest amount of biographical material about Paul. Most agree that it contains material dating from Paul, and some feel that it was written by Paul himself. It was probably the first of the Pastoral Letters to be written, possibly by someone other than the author of 1 Timothy and Titus. One of the most noticeable differences between 2 Timothy and the other Pastoral Letters is the large number of references to persons and places, but there are other, more significant differences. Unlike these other letters, 2 Timothy has no codes of behavior for community members, no discussion of qualifications for various ministries, and no element of anti-Jewish polemic.

2 Timothy is essentially a reflection on the ministry of Paul and on how that ministry is to be continued after his death. Timothy is the person closely associated with Paul's ministry and has become his designated successor. The two focuses of this letter, Paul and Timothy, highlight the succession of the latter in the ministry of the former. Though there is mention of Timothy's responsibility to instruct others who will in turn become teachers (2:2), the letter is mainly concerned with Timothy's own vocation and ministry. Fidelity to his vocation demands that he follow the sound teaching he learned from Paul. Timothy is to be loyal to his faith and not ashamed of bearing witness either to the Lord or to Paul. The letter's emphasis on suffering contrasts with the goal in

1 Timothy and Titus of leading quiet and peaceable lives in society.

In 2 Timothy Paul is presented as imprisoned and in chains, deserted by others because of the shame brought on by his chains. Paul is nonetheless confident of the salvific effects of his prolonged imprisonment and proclaims Christ as sovereign judge over all. Paul's fearlessness in the face of evil is the basis of the advice to Timothy to protect his community from the impact of false teaching (2:14–3:9) without fearing the personal attacks that may result (3:10-12). Paul is presented as the model for Timothy in both word (1:13; 2:2; 3:14) and deed (3:10-11). There is no suggestion, however, that Timothy should be a model, as in the other Pastoral Letters, where Timothy and Titus are to serve as models for the communities they lead (see 1 Tim 4:12-15; Titus 2:7-8). The advice in 2 Timothy focuses primarily on Timothy. Not only are there no specific directions concerning the community, but there is no indication of where Timothy is presumably located. While 1:18 might be read as a hint that the community he is leading is Ephesus, 4:12 indicates that although he may once have been there, he no longer is.

While 1 Timothy and Titus are concerned with the organization of the church in the post-Pauline era and were probably written later than 2 Timothy, both presume that Paul is still active and free to travel. Since 2 Timothy is chronologically located near the end of Paul's life, its position after

1 Timothy seems natural. This letter reads like Paul's last will and testament, containing the parting advice of one convinced that his present imprisonment will end with his death. While addressed to Timothy, it speaks powerfully to a modern culture that needs to regain its focus on the value of loyalty, fidelity, and suffering for the sake of the gospel.

COMMENTARY

1:1-2 The opening

The letter opens, as is typical of Hellenistic letters, with the identification of both the sender and the receiver, followed by a greeting. The sender, Paul, is identified as "an apostle of Christ Jesus by the will of God for the promise of life in Christ Jesus." The first part, "an apostle of Christ Jesus by the will of God," is identical to the identification at 2 Corinthians 1:1 (cf. 1 Cor 1:1). This identification echoes Paul's conviction that the will of God determined the shape of his life and his work as an apostle. The identification in this letter, however, continues by focusing on "the promise of life" as the purpose of Paul's apostolate. The phrase "promise of life" is an expression used only in the Pastoral Letters (cf. 1 Tim 4:8). God has promised and guarantees the gift of eternal life. Just as the hope of eternal life motivated the apostolate of Paul, this hope should motivate Timothy and the readers of this letter.

Timothy, the receiver of the letter, is identified as "my dear child." In 1 Timothy he is called "my true child in faith" (1 Tim 1:2), similar to what Titus is called, "my true child in our common faith" (Titus 1:4). "True child" suits the purpose of these letters as mandates to Timothy and Titus to minister in Paul's name. "Dear child" in 2 Timothy uses the language denoting deep friendship that Paul had used of Timothy (1 Cor 4:17). Its use in 2 Timothy suits the purpose of the letter as a reflection on Paul's ministry in the context of a personal farewell and a designation of Timothy as the legitimate and faithful heir who will carry on the Pauline legacy. The opening concludes with the greeting typical of all Paul's letters, but with the addition of "mercy" to the typical Pauline "grace and peace." Both 1 and 2 Timothy add this word to the greeting, but not Titus.

1:3-5 Thanksgiving

Pauline letters typically have a passage immediately after the opening in which Paul gives thanks to God for what God has done for the community or person to whom the letter is addressed. These thanksgivings also serve to summarize the main themes of the letter. 2 Timothy, alone among the Pastoral Letters, has this characteristic Pauline thanksgiving. While 1 Timothy has a kind of belated thanksgiving (1 Tim 1:12-17), it is different in form and function from the typical Pauline thanksgiving. The thanksgiving in 2 Timothy is more typical, although the words used, *echō charin* (cf. 1 Tim 1:12), are different from the Pauline *eucharistō* (Rom 1:8; 1 Cor 1:4; Phil 1:3; 1 Thess 1:2; Phlm 4).

This thanksgiving stresses the double focus of the letter, Paul and Timothy, by thanking God for Timothy's faith (1:5) and expressing Paul's desire to see Timothy once more (1:4). Paul's desire to see Timothy actually frames and colors the entire letter. In the final chapter Timothy is urged to come quickly and to bring Mark (4:9, 11, 21). Timothy, the other focus of the letter, is presented as one in whom the true faith lives on, though the emphasis on faith and the desire for the visit suggests that Timothy's faith may have been a matter of concern.

TIMOTHY'S VOCATION AND PAUL'S SUFFERING

2 Tim 1:6-18

1:6-14 Pauline model of vocation

The dual focus of this letter is evident in the sequencing of four exhortations to Timothy to carry on Paul's ministry (1:6-14; 2:1-7; 2:14-26; 3:10-17). These exhortations are separated by doctrinal material and sections dealing with Paul's life and imminent departure. This first exhortation deals with Timothy's vocation, which flows from and is modeled on Paul's. An interesting feature of this exhortation is the frequent use of the first person plural pronoun. Paul and Timothy are viewed together, especially in the center of this chiastically arranged exhortation (1:9-10) as saved and called to their vocations by the saving grace of Christ's death and resurrection.

The exhortation begins and ends by speaking of their common vocation as based on the gift of the Spirit, a gift that is transmitted from Paul to Timothy (1:6-7, 13-14). Just before the center Paul encourages Timothy to bear the hardships of his ministry, not being ashamed either of his testimony to his crucified Lord or of Paul, now a chained prisoner (1:8). Right after the center Paul notes how he has suffered for his ministry, not being ashamed either of his sufferings or of his Lord (1:11-12). In 2 Timothy and in the undisputed letters, but not in 1 Timothy or Titus, suffering is integral to Paul's self-understanding (Rom 8:35-39; 1 Cor 4:9-13; 2 Cor 4:7-11; Gal 6:14-17; Phil 3:8-11; 1 Thess 2:2).

The exhortation opens with a reference to the transmission of office from Paul to Timothy "through the imposition of my hands" (1:6), a transmission that involved the gift of the Spirit. The term used here, *charisma,* was coined by Paul to distinguish real gifts of the Spirit from ecstatic phenomena, *pneumatika* (see 1 Cor 12:1, 4). It is a term used in the New Testament only in the letters of Paul and in the literature dependent on him, a term that highlights the gratuitous nature of the gifts and points to their ecclesial function. Everywhere in Paul and in the Pastoral Letters the gift of the Spirit is for building up the church as the body of Christ.

A similar passage in 1 Timothy speaks of Timothy's gift being conferred through the imposition of hands of the presbyterate (1 Tim 4:14). In 2 Timothy it is Paul alone who imposes hands. Both passages refer to the practice attested to elsewhere in the New Testament and the early church of using the imposition of hands for the transference of power, the appointment to office, and the conferral of the gift of the Spirit.

The differences between the passages illustrate the differences between these two letters. 1 Timothy is concerned with the community as a whole

and shows Timothy being brought into the ministry by a group of elders to share in their responsibility for leading an orderly Christian community. 2 Timothy is concerned with the specific role of the departing Paul in designating Timothy as his successor, who, like him, will be expected to accept his share of hardship for the gospel. The advice in verse 8 flows from the previous verses. Because of the strength that comes from God's gift of the Spirit transmitted by Paul, Timothy can endure the hardships involved in testifying to the Lord, not being ashamed either of the Lord or of Paul.

The hymn-like central section of this exhortation (1:9-10) attributes three qualities to God's saving purpose. First, it is gratuitous. Like Paul in the letter to the Romans, this letter establishes a clear contrast between human works and divine grace. Second, it is accomplished in Christ Jesus, and third, the initiative derives from all eternity. Even though this salvation was made manifest in the saving work of Jesus Christ, it was willed by God from all eternity. This brief passage is an interesting condensation of the theology, Christology, and eschatology of the Pastoral Letters. The one God establishes his purpose for salvation from all eternity. That salvation is made manifest by Christ's "appearance," which here refers to the past appearance of the Savior Christ Jesus, who destroyed death and brought life and immortality. Later in the letter the eschatological picture will be completed when the same term "appearance" is used to refer to a future appearance of Christ Jesus, who is to judge the living and the dead (4:8; cf. 1 Tim 6:14; Titus 2:13). Christian life, for the Pastoral Letters, lies between these two appearances of Christ Jesus.

This life is now available through the gospel for which Paul "was appointed preacher and apostle and teacher" (1:11). As he hands on his ministry to Timothy, Paul expresses confidence that Christ Jesus is able to guard what has been entrusted to Paul "until that day" (1:12), a clear reference to the final day when Christ will be revealed as God's eschatological agent (cf. 1:18; 4:8). The exhortation concludes with the mandate to Timothy to "guard this rich trust with the help of the holy Spirit" (1:14). The confidence that Christ will guard this trust between his two appearances is based on the belief that Timothy and those who follow him will be aided by the holy Spirit in transmitting the true gospel of Jesus Christ. Here 2 Timothy expresses the distinctively Pauline idea of the indwelling of the holy Spirit (1 Cor 3:16; 6:19) more clearly than do the isolated references to the Spirit in the other Pastoral Letters (1 Tim 4:1; Titus 3:5).

1:15-18 False and faithful friends

This passage is the first of several biographical passages in this letter. Together with the last such passage, 4:16-18, it speaks of Paul's being without human contact, a lonely prisoner about to die. These two passages, just after the beginning and just before the end, share in the framing function of the appeals for Timothy to visit Paul (1:4; 4:9, 11, 21) and help define the letter as a testamentary farewell. The mention of Onesiphorus in both passages contributes to their framing function. Ephesus (1:18) in Asia (1:15) was where Paul exercised much of his apostolate and where he left a thriving Christian community. Ephesus was also where almost everyone abandoned him on his arrest. Now in Rome he draws on this experience to encourage Timothy, who once was in Ephesus but probably no longer is there (see 4:12). Onesiphorus,who alone was not ashamed of Paul's chains, can serve as a model for Timothy not to be ashamed either of Paul or of his "testimony to our Lord" (1:8).

This passage contains two prayers for mercy—one for the family of Onesiphorus (1:16), the other for Onesiphorus himself (1:18). These prayers for mercy recall the note in Philippians that God had shown mercy to Epaphroditus because of his service to Paul (Phil 2:25-27). They also relate to the addition of "mercy" to the greeting at 1:2. The first prayer was for mercy in the present, but the second is for mercy in the eschatological future, "that day," which Paul had spoken about in reference to himself (1:12). The second prayer might imply that Onesiphorus is already dead, in which case it would be one of the earliest examples of Christian prayer for the dead.

EXHORTATION TO BE STRONG AND ENDURE SUFFERING

2 Tim 2:1-13

2:1-7 The hardships of faithful ministry

Like the first exhortation, this second exhortation begins and ends with a reference to what the Lord has given to Timothy (1:6, 14; 2:1, 7). However, while the first exhortation focused on the gift of God through the holy Spirit, this exhortation emphasizes the task that has been entrusted to Timothy. Timothy, with "the grace that is in Christ Jesus" (2:1), is to entrust to others what he has learned from Paul. These others, in turn, will be able to continue the chain of faithful transmission.

Significantly, 2 Timothy uses a technical term for "entrust" that in ancient times was used to refer to some kind of treasure, such as a valuable item or a sacred story, that was entrusted to another. This sacred trust, the gospel of salvation, is referred to three times in this letter as that with which Paul has been entrusted (1:12), that which Timothy is to guard with the help of the holy Spirit (1:14), and finally that which Timothy is to hand on to others who will continue its transmission (2:2). This term is used only once in the other Pastoral Letters, in the conclusion to 1 Timothy, where Timothy is urged to "guard what has been entrusted to you" (1 Tim 6:20).

These other letters use different language to speak of that with which Paul has been entrusted (1 Tim 1:11; Titus 1:3) and what Paul entrusts to Timothy (1 Tim 1:18), but they never speak of Timothy or Titus entrusting it to others. While Titus is to appoint leaders for orderly community life (Titus 1:5), the transmission of Paul's gospel to future evangelists is a concern only of 2 Timothy. Timothy is not alone in passing on Paul's teaching. There were "many witnesses" (2:2), but clearly not all of them remained faithful witnesses. Timothy's task is to establish a chain of transmission involving faithful witnesses, a task that will involve hardships like those Paul is enduring (cf. 1:12).

The hardships to be endured are compared to the hard work associated with soldiers, athletes, and farmers. Athletes compete to achieve "the winner's crown" (2:5). If Timothy bears the hardships of his ministry "like a good soldier of Christ Jesus" (2:3), he is assured that the Lord will give him the understanding needed to fulfill the task of faithful transmission (2:7). While 1 Timothy uses the athletic image in discussing training for devotion (1 Tim 4:7-8) and metaphors of competition (1 Tim 1:18; 6:12), neither 1 Timothy nor Titus suggests that Christian life will involve suffering. In both these letters advice is given to be under the control of authorities (Titus 3:1) and to pray for kings that "we may lead a quiet and tranquil life" (1 Tim 2:2). 2 Timothy alone among the Pastorals links fidelity to the gospel to a life that will involve hardship and suffering. Here Paul's suffering is presented as the model for Timothy (2:3, 8-9; cf. 3:12).

2:8-13 The gospel and its reward

The letter next identifies the message to be transmitted: the gospel for which Paul is suffering, "Jesus Christ, raised from the dead, a descendant of David" (2:8). Being introduced with "remember," these words are clearly an early creedal formulation that uses terminology employed in Paul's letters. "Raised from the dead" is language Paul commonly uses to refer to the resurrection. In Romans 1:3 Paul uses the phrase "descended from David" to identify Jesus as the Messiah, the expected ideal king of Israel. These expressions are not used elsewhere in the Pastoral Letters. They are used here to recall the traditional faith of the church with which Timothy has been entrusted. Paul is suffering in chains for these words, but the words are not chained. Timothy's task is to continue the transmission of these words so that others may "obtain the salvation that is in Christ Jesus."

This passage concludes with another selection of traditional material, probably a section of a hymn, assuring Timothy and the readers of the letter that fidelity with Christ means victory with the Lord (2:11-13). It is introduced by "this saying is trustworthy," a phrase regularly used in the Pastoral Letters to introduce a basic truth of early Christian faith (1 Tim 1:15; 3:1; 4:9; Titus 3:8). The four-line selection opens with the Pauline notion that Christian life can be spoken of as dying with Christ (cf. Rom 6:3; Gal 2:19-20). The four lines from this hymn have a recurring pattern that would lead one to expect the final phrase to be "he will be unfaithful." Surprisingly, it is instead "he remains faithful, / for he cannot deny himself" (2:13).

Paul often affirms the absolute fidelity of God (see 1 Cor 1:9). Here the absolute fidelity of God is attributed to Christ Jesus. This section, whose purpose is to exhort Timothy to be strong and endure hardships for the gospel, concludes with an assurance of the absolute fidelity of Christ. While the immediate concern of this passage is with the responsibilities of a first-century evangelist, its message applies equally well to people living out their Christian vocation in any way in any age. Jesus, the Savior and Judge, remains true to his people regardless of how faithful they may or may not be.

DANGER OF FALSE TEACHING
2 Tim 2:14–3:9

2:14-26 Dealing with false teachers

The first exhortation to Timothy focused on the gift of God through the holy Spirit (1:6-14), and the second on the task entrusted to Timothy (2:1-7). This third exhortation deals with how he is to fulfill the charge to entrust to faithful people what he has heard from Paul in light of the ever-present danger of false teaching. The danger arises because people dispute about words (2:14), quarrel because of foolish and ignorant debates (2:23), and become more and more godless as a result of profane and idle talk (2:16).

Paul's advice to Timothy for dealing with this problem is twofold. First, he must be pure in himself. "Turn from youthful desires and pursue righteousness, faith, love, and peace, along with those who call on the Lord with purity of heart" (2:22). If he can present himself "as acceptable to God, a workman who causes no disgrace" (2:15), he will be able to impart "the word of truth without deviation" (2:15). Second, he must himself "avoid foolish and ignorant debates" (2:23) and then be able to charge others to stop engaging in useless disputes.

The basis for this advice is found in the center of this passage, where Old Testament texts are cited as "God's solid foundation" (2:19). "The Lord knows those who are his" is quoted from Numbers 16:5, where it dealt with a revolt against Moses. God will protect and empower those who are doing his work, not the false teachers. The second quote is even more important. "Let everyone who calls upon the name of the Lord avoid evil" (2:19) is a combination of allusions to Isaiah 26:13 and Sirach 17:21. God calls whom he wills, but humans must accept the call by themselves calling "on the Lord with purity of heart" (2:22) and avoiding the kind of behavior that is harmful to the gospel. The next chapter has the familiar verse on the inspiration and usefulness of Scripture (3:16-17), but the passage in 2:19 is the only Old Testament passage actually cited in this letter. The following two verses (2:20-21) clearly anticipate the passage in

3:16-17. Timothy and others entrusted with Paul's gospel are compared to various kinds of vessels that, when cleansed, become vessels "for lofty use, dedicated, beneficial to the master of the house, ready for every good work" (2:21).

The next verse encapsulates an aspect of this letter that has timeless significance for Christians—the essential link between Christian faith and the life of virtue. Timothy and all Christians can and should lead lives of exemplary virtue precisely because they have called "on the Lord with purity of heart" (2:22). For Christians, their pattern of behavior is an expression of their deepest convictions.

While this exhortation is primarily concerned with Timothy and others entrusted with Paul's gospel, it does shed some light on the false teachers. Just before the center of this passage, two of them, Hymenaeus and Philetus, are identified, as well as their false teaching "that [the] resurrection has already taken place" (2:18). While specific moral issues appear elsewhere (see 1 Tim 4:3), this is the only precise false doctrine identified in any of the Pastoral Letters. Hymenaeus and Alexander (cf. 4:14) were identified as enemies of Paul in 1 Timothy 1:20, although their errors were not mentioned there.

Paul had taught that in baptism we die and rise with Christ (Rom 6:8; cf. 2 Cor 6:14-15). Some in Corinth had distorted Paul's teaching by denying the future resurrection of the dead (1 Cor 15:12), probably maintaining what was being taught by Hymenaeus and Philetus, that is, that Christians already enjoyed the fullness of resurrected life. Paul, as well as the Pastoral Letters, clearly teaches that although we have died with Christ and now live with him, there will be a future resurrection when all will be judged on the life they have led (Rom 14:10, 12; 1 Tim 6:12-16; 2 Tim 4:1, 8).

The exhortation concludes with advice on dealing with false teachers, correcting them with kindness so that "they may return to their senses out of the devil's snare" (2:26), advice that sounds less harsh than what Paul is said to have done in 1 Timothy, handing them "over to Satan to be taught not to blaspheme" (1 Tim 1:20; cf. Titus 3:10-11).

3:1-9 False teaching in the last days

In the previous exhortation Timothy was urged to "pursue righteousness, faith, love, and peace, along with those who call on the Lord with

purity of heart" (2:22), in contrast to false teachers who taught that the resurrection had already occurred. Here the contrast is intensified by advancing the context to the last days (cf. 1 Tim 4:1-5). The last days are distinguished from "that day" (1:18; 4:8), the day when the Lord will appear as just judge. The last days precede "that day." They will be dangerous times; the church will be beset by people who will harm the faithful with cruelty, violence, and aggressiveness. Here, as elsewhere in the Pastoral Letters, false teaching leads to base morality, just as good teaching leads to good morality. False teaching can be easily recognized as such by the results it produces.

The virtue of religion/devotion, prominently treated in 1 Timothy (1 Tim 2:2; 3:16; 4:7, 8; 6:3, 5, 6, 11), is here mentioned in terms of its false understanding: "they make a pretense of religion but deny its power" (3:5). In 1 Timothy it was observed that some think religion can be a source of material gain. These are people who fall into erroneous beliefs and end up experiencing a host of vices: "envy, rivalry, insults, evil suspicions, and mutual friction" (1 Tim 6:4-5). In 2 Timothy the list is longer and the evils more intense (3:2-4).

The danger posed by false teachers is further illustrated by the evil influence they are able to exert on impressionable women. These women, eager to learn but lacking the erudition to distinguish true from false teaching, are led by their passions to accept appealing but perverse teachings (3:6-7). All three Pastoral Letters seem to accept the widespread belief at that time that women were notoriously unable to control their sexual passions (1 Tim 5:11-15; Titus 2:4-5). The false teachers who impress women are compared to the Egyptian magicians who were clever enough to impress Pharaoh but opposed the truth that came from God (3:8-9). They turned their staffs into snakes, as had Aaron, but Aaron's staff swallowed their staffs (Exod 7:11-12).

PAUL'S EXAMPLE AND TIMOTHY'S COMMISSION
2 Tim 3:10–4:8

3:10-17 Imitation of Paul and the role of Scripture

The previous description of intensified evil in the end times sets the stage for this fourth and final exhortation to Timothy. With the approach of the end times, wicked people will become even more so (3:13) and good people will be persecuted (3:12). Interestingly, the term used to describe the good people who will be persecuted is the same term, "religion/devotion," which in 1 Timothy and Titus is that all-important virtue that will secure respect for the Christian community in the surrounding world.

Timothy is reminded about what he knows of Paul and is encouraged to remain faithful in following him (3:14). Timothy is reminded of nine important aspects of Paul's heritage that he is to follow (3:10-11). First among these is his teaching, the subject of much of this letter (1:13-14; 2:2, 8-9). Timothy is also aware of Paul's way of life and purpose. Timothy is aware as well of the six qualities that characterized Paul's life: the Christian virtues of faith, patience, love, and endurance (3:10), which were the basis of his teaching, life, and purpose, and the persecutions and suffering (3:11) that were the inevitable result. Just as Paul had responded to God's call to work as an apostle, so too should Timothy. In the Acts of the Apostles Paul is said to have visited the three cities mentioned here—Antioch, Iconium, and Lystra (Acts 13:1–14:23)—and to have commented, "It is necessary for us to undergo many hardships to enter the kingdom of God" (Acts 14:22). It is interesting to note that Timothy came from one of these cities, Lystra, born of a Jewish mother who became a believer, and a Greek father (Acts 16:1).

Timothy's faith, a faith that he received from his mother and grandmother, was mentioned in the first chapter (1:5). Presumably it was from them that he first learned the Sacred Scriptures, the Scriptures of Judaism. It was clearly from Paul, however, that Timothy learned how the Sacred Scriptures could give "wisdom for salvation through faith in Christ Jesus" (3:15). How Timothy is to use the Sacred Scriptures is spelled out in the final two verses, beginning with the observation that "all scripture is inspired by God" (3:16). The more than one hundred citations of these verses in the writings of the patristic period show that they were generally understood to mean that each and every part of Scripture comes from God. At the same time, however, these writings emphasize the usefulness of Scripture far more than its inspiration and the variety of interpretive techniques used by the Fathers indicates that they had a far broader understanding of inspiration than the narrow literalism of contemporary fundamentalism.

Timothy is instructed to use the Scriptures, as Paul had, creatively guided by the Spirit, to fulfill the ministry with which he has been charged thus far in this letter. He is to use the Scriptures in teaching the sound doctrine he has received from Paul, handing it on to other faithful ministers (2:2). He is to use the Scriptures to refute the false teachers who have already become active (2:14) and whose activity will intensify in the final days (3:5). He is to use the Scriptures to correct his "opponents with kindness" when it is possible to lead them "to knowledge of the truth" (2:25). Finally, he is to use the Scriptures for training in righteousness. In order to accomplish his ministry, Timothy must himself be pure (2:22). He will then belong to God, be able to impart "the word of truth without deviation" (2:15), "be competent, equipped for every good work" (3:16; cf. 2:21).

4:1-8 Timothy's solemn commission

After the preceding sequence of instructions and exhortations, the main body of the letter comes to a close with a solemn commissioning in which Paul hands over his ministry to Timothy. The solemnity of the commissioning is emphasized by the charge being given "in the presence of God and of Christ Jesus" (4:1; cf. 1 Tim 5:21). This commissioning begins and ends with a reference to the final appearance of Christ Jesus as judge (4:1, 8), providing an eschatological context for the seriousness of Timothy's ministry.

Here, as earlier in the letter, the end time, "that day," is distinguished from the "last days," the dangerous times for which Timothy is now being prepared. These are the times, mentioned earlier, when "people will not tolerate sound doctrine . . . will accumulate teachers . . . and will be diverted to myths" (4:3-4; cf. 2:18; 3:6-7). Sound doctrine is a major concern throughout the Pastoral Letters, but its meaning varies. In 2 Timothy it is the words of Paul that serve as the basis for the missionary activity charged to Timothy and others (1:13; 4:3). In 1 Timothy and Titus, sound doctrine has become the moral content of Paul's gospel, involving both accuracy in teaching and the proper morality to which it leads (1 Tim 1:10; 4:6; 6:3; Titus 1:9, 13; 2:1, 2, 8).

The solemn commissioning begins with the charge "proclaim the word" (4:2). The ministry of the word is a ministry without which a Christian community cannot exist. In Acts, Paul's ministry is summarized as "preach[ing] the kingdom" (Acts 20:25; 28:31). Except for Philemon, Paul wrote about his preaching in all his letters, most eloquently in Romans 10:14-15. The charge continues with four more imperatives, all of which entail Timothy's emulating Paul and carrying on his ministry.

After a digression in which Timothy is warned about the threat of people succumbing to false teachers in the times to come (4:3-4), there is another series of four imperatives exhorting Timothy to follow Paul's example. These imperatives are introduced by "but you" (4:5), contrasting what is expected of Timothy with the expected failures of others. Timothy is to be "self-possessed in all circumstances" (4:5), a quality expected of a bishop in 1 Timothy (1 Tim 3:2). He is to "put up with hardship" (4:5), just as he had known Paul to endure persecutions and suffering (3:11). According to 1 Timothy, Christ Jesus had appointed Paul to the ministry (1 Tim 1:12). Now that Paul is about to depart, it is Timothy's turn to "perform the work of an evangelist" (4:5), a dominant theme in 2 Timothy that is all but absent in 1 Timothy and Titus. The final imperative sums up all those that have gone before and sums up the entire message of this letter: "fulfill your ministry" (4:5).

The message of this letter is clearly intended for all Christians of all times. The challenge to Timothy to fulfill his ministry challenges all Christians to consider the demands of their Christian vocations. For him as for all, fulfilling one's ministry involves fidelity much more than success. It involves being willing to suffer for the gospel, recognizing that the reward for fidelity is sharing in the life of the resurrection. Timothy is not urged to settle into a secure and comfortable life; rather, he and all are urged to witness, in word and deed, to the truth that is Christ in the midst of a world that prefers to follow its own desires (4:3).

The final three verses complete this final exhortation by providing the reason for the exhortation and for the letter: Paul is about to die (4:6). Just as Paul used the metaphor of athletic competition (2:5) when he urged Timothy to "bear your share of hardship" (2:3), he here applies the athletic metaphor to himself (4:7). Paul has competed well. He has kept the faith, both in the sense that he has been faithful in his office as preacher and teacher

and also in the sense that he has carefully handed on the gospel and its solid doctrine to his successor. Interestingly, denial of belief in a future resurrection was the only doctrinal matter explicitly attributed to the false teachers (2:18). This autobiographical reflection fittingly ends by affirming Paul's expectation of his vindication in the future resurrection of the dead for himself as well as for all who long for the Lord's appearance (4:8).

PERSONAL POSTSCRIPT
2 Tim 4:9-18

After the conclusion of the main body of the letter, Timothy is urged four times to visit Paul (4:9, 11, 13, 21). The alleged reason is Paul's loneliness in the final days of his imprisonment before his impending death. The appeal in this section of the letter, however, provides additional biographical information about Paul, information that further supports the overall purpose of the present letter. An overarching concern of the letter is that Paul's legacy be continued (1:6; 4:1-2).

The geographical places named in this section provide a summary of the areas evangelized by Paul that now are to be cared for by his successors. Most of the persons named are associates of Paul who will be responsible for carrying on his ministry in these various regions. It is not known where Timothy presently is, but he must be somewhere other than Ephesus, otherwise he would already know that Tychicus (Titus 3:12) had been sent there (4:12).

Two of those named are cast in a negative light in ways that are significant for the letter as a whole. Demas, who was "enamored of the present world" (4:10), deserted Paul. In Acts, Demas was once a companion of Paul (Col 4:14; Phlm 24), but in the apocryphal Acts of Paul he is said to have rejected Paul's teaching on the future resurrection, saying that "it has already taken place in the children whom we have, and that we are risen again in that we have come to know the true God" (Acts of Paul 3:14). This false teaching is what led Demas to be enamored of the present world and to have deserted Paul, who is in prison and about to die. The whole thrust of 2 Timothy is toward the future resurrection which motivates the steadfastness in ministry and endurance of hardships that Paul exemplifies and which he encourages in his successors.

The other person treated negatively is Alexander the coppersmith (4:14). Just as Paul expects the Lord, the just judge, to award the crown of righteousness to himself and to "all who have longed for his appearance" (4:8), others, like Alexander, will be repaid according to their deeds. He is probably the same Alexander mentioned in 1 Timothy as an opponent of Paul (1 Tim 1:20). He is here described as having "resisted our preaching" (4:14). Timothy is warned to be on guard against him as he takes on responsibility for the ministry of preaching.

An interesting feature of this passage is Paul's request that Timothy bring the cloak, papyrus rolls, and parchments from Troas (4:13). The importance of the Scriptures for Timothy's ministry has already been noted (3:14-17). The cloak may be related to Elisha's succession to Elijah, which was symbolized by the assumption of his mantle (2 Kgs 2:11-14). Paul's request for his cloak and Scriptures might indicate his desire to transfer to Timothy the symbols of his ministry.

As this section draws to a close, Paul recalls his earlier trial, when everyone deserted him. He was lonely then as he is now, but then as now his strength was from the Lord. It is in this strength that he is able to say "may it not be held against them" (4:16), recalling the words of Jesus on the cross (Luke 23:34). In that earlier trial the Lord had rescued Paul (4:17), just as the Lord had rescued him in previous difficulties (3:11). This time he expects to die, but he can use the same language to describe what is to come: "the Lord will rescue me from every evil threat and will bring me safe to his heavenly kingdom" (4:18). The doxology concluding this section, like the doxologies in 1 Timothy (1 Tim 1:17; 6:15-16), contains the four elements of the classic New Testament doxology: the object of praise, "to him"; an expression of praise, "be glory"; an indication of time, "forever and ever"; and a confirmatory response, "Amen" (4:18).

THE CLOSING
2 Tim 4:19-22

As is typical in New Testament letters, the conclusion of this letter begins with a series of greetings, naming both those to be greeted, "Prisca and Aquila and the family of Onesiphorus" (4:19), as well as those in Rome sending greetings, "Eubulus, Pudens, Linus, Claudia, and all the brothers" (4:21). The closing greeting is interrupted by additional personal and place names, continuing the thoughts expressed in 4:9-13 and adding a final plea for Timothy to come to Rome (4:20-21). Prisca and Aquila were frequent coworkers with Paul (Acts 18:2; Rom 16:3; 1 Cor 16:19). Onesiphorus had served Paul both in Ephesus and Rome (1:16-18). However, none of the four sending greetings from Rome appear elsewhere in the New Testament, and their mention here is surprising, since, according to 4:11, only Luke was with Paul in his imprisonment, and Paul is pleading for Timothy to join him. Possibly they are Christians in Rome who, while not ministering to Paul in prison, will provide leadership to the Roman community after his death. Linus appears in early church traditions as the successor to Peter as leader of the church in Rome.

The letter ends with a blessing, as do all Paul's letters. Unlike the blessings at the end of 1 Timothy and Titus, this blessing is in two parts. "The Lord be with your spirit" (4:22) is in the singular, addressing Timothy, the recipient of this letter, and emphasizing the intensely personal nature of this letter. "Grace be with you all" (4:22), the blessing found at the end of 1 Timothy, is in the plural. Only these stylized closing words interrupt the letter's consistent focus on Timothy as an individual. Nevertheless, they indicate that this highly personal letter, addressed to Paul's designated successor, is intended to be read by a larger community.

THE LETTER TO
TITUS

Terence J. Keegan, O.P.

INTRODUCTION

The letter to Titus is similar to 1 Timothy in content and purpose. While it is addressed to a different person, Titus, who has responsibility for a different community, Crete, it is concerned, like 1 Timothy, with pastoring the communities in the post-Pauline era. Like 1 Timothy, but unlike 2 Timothy, it provides qualifications for community leaders, codes for members of the community, and directives on ensuring that the community maintain a good reputation in the surrounding secular world. Its similarity to 1 Timothy in both language and content indicates some kind of relationship between these two letters. They may have been written by the same person or, at the very least, one was influenced by the other.

While Titus and 1 Timothy are quite similar in content and purpose, Titus addresses a situation less developed and complex than that addressed in 1 Timothy. Unlike the situation in 1 Timothy, where bishops/ presbyters and deacons were already in place, in this letter Titus is charged to appoint the bishops/presbyters for the communities on Crete, a place, according to Acts, that Paul had stopped at only briefly as a prisoner on his way to Rome (Acts 27:7-15). This letter deals with a newly founded form of Christianity, unlike the situation in 1 Timothy, where it could be said that a bishop should not be a recent convert (1 Tim 3:6).

While the opponents referred to in 1 Timothy included some with Judaizing tendencies, that is,

Jewish Christians who believed that Gentile converts should be made to observe Jewish religious laws and customs, in Titus the treatment of opponents is almost entirely focused on those with Judaizing tendencies (1:10, 14; 3:5, 9). The more clearly delineated threat of opponents is also more decisively dealt with. The letter to Titus links the reason for appointing leaders to the threat of Judaizing false teachers. But because the opponents threaten the good order of the community, greater emphasis is placed on behavior within the community than on the responsibilities of the newly appointed leaders. Church structures in Titus are fewer and simpler than those described in 1 Timothy, but Titus is richer in theological elaboration and the household codes are more fully developed. In this theological elaboration, Titus provides an explanation for the basis of Christian behavior, namely, the gift of God given in Christ through the power of the holy Spirit.

While Titus is the shortest of the Pastoral Letters, its opening is by far the longest. In fact, apart from that found in Romans (Rom 1:1-6), Titus's description of the sender (1:1-3) is the longest of any New Testament letter. Furthermore, this description of Paul, the sender, contains the most comprehensive description of the apostolate in the New Testament. For this reason, some suggest that Titus may have preceded 1 Timothy, introducing Paul and his apostolate and explaining how that apostolate is to be carried on by others in a particular local church setting. The present order of the Pastoral Letters in the New Testament is due to the ordering principle used at the time the scrolls of the various books were gathered together and bound into a single volume. At that time the supposed Pauline corpus was organized with the letters to churches preceding letters to individuals, and letters within these two groups organized according to length. Hence Titus was placed between 2 Timothy and Philemon.

COMMENTARY

1:1-4 The opening

Like most ancient letters, this letter begins with an identification of the sender and the recipient followed by a short greeting. This letter begins by identifying its sender, "Paul"; his position, "a slave of God and apostle of Christ Jesus"; and the purpose of his apostolate (1:1-3). The purpose of Paul's apostolate here, as elsewhere, involves faith in Jesus Christ. This letter and 1 Timothy, however, are concerned not only with faith but with the proper appreciation of that faith, that is, "religious truth" (1:1), which involves both correct belief and appropriate behavior. The term used here for "religious," elsewhere translated as "devoutly" (2:12), is the word used in the Roman world for reverence for the gods and respect for traditional values and practices. This much esteemed virtue receives little notice in the rest of the New Treatment but is important in Titus and especially in 1 Timothy (1 Tim 2:2; 3:16; 4:7, 8; 6:3, 5, 6, 11).

An important element in that correct belief and the motivation for appropriate behavior is the hope for a future resurrection. The letter's restrained eschatology (1:2; 2:13; 3:7) implies that the letter was written for a Christian community that no longer lived in imminent expectation of the parousia. In its more settled state, the community needed proper instruction in the fine points of Christian faith. The "hope of eternal life that God, who does not lie, promised before time began" (1:2) is what is proclaimed in the word with which Paul has been entrusted. God our savior, "who wills everyone to be saved and to come to knowledge of the truth" (1 Tim 2:4), has entrusted this proclamation to Paul. As God's slave (1:1), Paul is bound—to fulfill his appointed task. That task involves the salvation of God's people.

The recipient is identified as "Titus, my true child in our common faith." This expression illustrates an understanding of the church as a genuinely new family that needs to be nurtured and protected as it grows and matures, as well as designating Titus as the legitimate representative authorized to minister in Paul's name. The greeting begins with the typical Pauline greeting, "grace and peace" but continues with "from God the Father and Christ Jesus our savior" (1:4).

THE NEED FOR CAPABLE, AUTHORIZED LEADERSHIP
Titus 1:5-16

1:5-9 Appointment of presbyters/bishops

Omitting the thanksgiving that is common at this point in letters (cf. 2 Tim 1:3-5), the letter identifies its purpose as charging Titus with the good order of the church at Crete. Titus's charge is twofold: to "set right what remains to be done" and to "appoint presbyters in every town" (1:5). This section dealing with "presbyters" (1:5) and a "bishop" (1:7) is the only section in the entire letter dealing with church leaders. Unlike 1 Timothy, this letter says nothing about deacons (cf. 1 Tim 3:8-13) or widows (cf. 1 Tim 5:3-10). In Titus the presbyters and bishops are clearly identical. The presbyter appointed in each town (1:5) is the bishop of that town. The term "presbyter" refers to the person's status within the community, a respected member of the community, while the term "bishop" refers to his function, exercising oversight and leadership in the community.

The list of qualifications for the presbyter/ bishop in 1:6-8 is almost identical to the list of qualifications for the bishop in 1 Timothy 3:2-4. For 1 Timothy and Titus, he must be an effective leader whose personal character is a credit to the community he leads. While the qualifications are similar to what would be expected of any reputable official in the secular world, the duties of such a leader are specific to the needs of the community, "holding fast to the true message as taught so that he will be able both to exhort with sound doctrine and to refute opponents" (1:9). These duties overlap those ascribed to presbyters in 1 Timothy, "preaching and teaching" (1 Tim 5:17), but the specific charges to exhort (1 Tim 4:13; Titus 2:15) and to refute opponents (2 Tim 2:25; Titus 2:15) are elsewhere ascribed only to Timothy and Titus.

Charging newly appointed presbyters with these responsibilities is an indication of the critical threat facing the community addressed by this letter. Throughout 1 Timothy and Titus there is a concern for sound doctrine or teaching (1 Tim 1:10; 4:6; 6:3; Titus 1:9, 13; 2:1, 2, 8), a concern related to the need for stability and order as the church faces an immediate doctrinal and moral threat. This concern should not be read, however, as a prohibition of innovative thinking, but only of erroneous teaching that harms the community. In 1 Timothy and Titus sound doctrine means the kind of well-grounded, correct doctrine that results in correct moral behavior.

1:10-16 Silencing false teachers

The first part of the charge to Titus, to "set right what remains to be done" (1:5), is what is of concern in most of the rest of this letter. Titus is here charged to do what the presbyter/bishops he appoints will be expected to do—"to refute opponents" (1:9). The immediate problem is the false teaching of the Jewish Christians, which is upsetting whole families (1:10-11). The church in Crete, which included a large number of Jewish Christians, likely encountered a problem similar to one Paul had to deal with—Gentile converts being required to observe elements of the Jewish Law like circumcision and dietary restrictions (cf. Gal 5:1-2; Phil 3:1-4). A similar problem is dealt with in 1 Timothy (1 Tim 1:7; 4:3-4). There the concern about dietary restrictions is dealt with by affirming the goodness of all of God's creation, including foods and sex (1 Tim 4:4). The response in Titus, "to the clean all things are clean" (1:15) echoes the response of Paul in his letter to the Romans: "nothing is unclean in itself" (Rom 14:14).

What specifically was being taught in Crete is not clear other than that it involved "Jewish myths and regulations" (1:14) that had to do with some things being declared unclean. The false teachers are characterized as failing in one of the qualities just ascribed to a bishop, "teaching for sordid gain" (1:11; cf. 1:7; 1 Tim 3:8). In this regard they are like the false teachers dealt with in 1 Timothy, "supposing religion to be a means of gain" (1 Tim 6:5). As in 1 Timothy, the false teachers are further described as failing not only in their teaching but also in their lives (1 Tim 6:3-5). False beliefs lead to immoral behavior. "They are vile and disobedient and unqualified for any good deed" (1:16). The rhetorical device of ascribing a list of vices to the false teachers discredits these opponents. Those who had been influential insiders are now treated as outsiders.

An indication of the critical nature of the problem confronted is the harshness with which the false teachers are to be dealt. Titus and the newly appointed presbyters are to "silence them" (1:11) and "admonish them sharply" (1:13). As his mandate for dealing with issues in the community is being summed up, Titus is told to "let no one look down on you" (2:15). A similar authoritarian stance is recommended for Timothy in 1 Timothy, but it is more concerned with dealing with behavior within the community (1 Tim 4:12; 5:20) than with the threat of opponents. The harsh, authoritarian stance in both these letters contrasts with the kind and gentle approach recommended in 2 Timothy (2 Tim 2:24-26).

PROPER BEHAVIOR IN THE CHRISTIAN COMMUNITY
Titus 2:1–3:8

2:1-10 The church and social structures

Setting right what remains to be done (1:5) involves not only correct doctrine but also good order in the community that is "consistent with sound doctrine" (2:1). These verses (2:2-10) are the first part of the "household code" for the church at Crete, a code that continues at 2:15–3:3. The reason given for this code is twofold: "so that the opponent will be put to shame without anything bad to say about us" (2:8) and "so as to adorn the doctrine of God our savior in every way" (2:10). Behavior consistent with sound doctrine will adorn that doctrine, enhancing the reputation of the Christian community in the surrounding world. A radically new religious community might be suspected of being a threat to civil order. Christians behaving in accord with sound teaching will lay to rest any such concerns.

Like the household codes in 1 Timothy (2:8-15; 6:1-2, 17-19), this code pertains to the entire community as the household of God, unlike the codes in other letters that focus on the family group (Eph 5:22–6:9; Col 3:18–4:1; 1 Pet 2:13–3:8). Titus, however, goes beyond 1 Timothy in that all members of the community are not only expected to exhibit certain qualities but are also expected to play important roles in the furtherance of the community. Older men, like the bishop in 1 Timothy (1 Tim 3:2; cf. Titus 1:8), are expected to exhibit social qualities found in leading citizens; they are to be "temperate, dignified, self-controlled" (2:2). They are also to possess specific Christian virtues by being "sound in faith, love, and endurance" (2:2). Paul had identified these three virtues as the qualities in the Thessalonians for which he thanked God: "your work of faith and labor of love and endurance in hope" (1 Thess 1:3). While Paul will later place love in the final, emphatic position (1 Cor 13:13), putting "endurance in hope" last expressed his concern in his letter to the Thessalonians about life beyond the grave and the future coming of Christ. The letter to Titus is also concerned with the future coming of Christ (2:13), but here the quality in the final position is simply "endurance."

A concern for future generations is evident in the rest of this section. The qualities expected of older women are specifically intended to enable them to "train younger women" (2:4) to be good wives and mothers so that Christianity might be perceived as contributing to the stability of society (2:5). Just as Timothy is urged to "set an example for those who believe" (1 Tim 4:12), Titus himself is to serve as a model for younger men, teaching them by word and deed to live in such a way that no one will be able to speak ill of the Christian community (2:6-8). This letter's concern that young people become respectable members of society is not found elsewhere in the New Testament but is consistent with the overall concern of 1 Timothy and Titus for the continuing life of the community.

Slaves deserve special mention (2:9-10; cf. 1 Tim 6:1-2), because in those days the vast majority of the population in urban areas were slaves. While many were well educated and some even held powerful positions, their civil status was that of slaves. Here, as elsewhere, the concern of 1 Timothy and Titus is that Christian faith should enable members of the community to become even better members of society, adhering to accepted norms of behavior, "to adorn the doctrine of God our savior in every way" (2:10).

2:11-14 Salvation

The reason for the previous household code stressing good Christian and civil behavior among all members of the community is that "the grace of God has appeared, saving all" (2:11). The verses that follow summarize Christian belief in the two-fold appearance of Christ. Just as Paul is described in the identification at the start of this letter as being between the past revelation of the word and the future hope of eternal life (1:2-3), so the later Christian community lives between the two appearances of Christ. In his first appearance he saved us by his redemptive death; he "gave himself for us" (2:14). By baptism and the holy Spirit Christians are cleansed and empowered to live lives worthy of their faith as they await the future coming of Christ.

This theologically dense passage on the appearances of Christ Jesus is the most thorough treatment of the basic Christian kerygma in the Pastoral Letters. Unlike 1 Timothy, which speaks only of the end-time appearance of Christ Jesus, Titus stresses both Christ's future appearance (1:13) and the salvific nature of his past appearance (2:11; 3:4). Unlike 1 Timothy, where only God is called "savior" (1 Tim 1:1; 2:3; 4:10), in Titus the term is used both for God (1:3; 2:10; 3:4) and Christ (1:4; 2:13; 3:6), although the two are clearly differentiated in 1:3-4 and 3:4-6. God is the source of hope insofar as he saves us by being faithful to his promises, sending Christ Jesus to redeem us and form us into his chosen people (2:14). We are saved by the past appearance of Christ, but it is the future appearance that is the source of the hope (2:13) that is the basis for the household code. While future hope is more prominent in Titus (1:2; 2:13; 3:7), this same theological foundation is found in 1 Timothy, though it is not as fully expressed in that letter (1 Tim 2:3-6).

2:15–3:3 Exhortation to good citizenship

The household code (2:1-10), interrupted by providing its theological foundation (2:11-14), is here concluded by explicitly charging Titus to exhort the community to good citizenship. "These things" (2:15) that Titus is to say are the things he is told to say in 2:1-10. He is further charged to "exhort and correct" (2:15), doing what the presbyter/bishop he will appoint will be expected to do (1:9). Furthermore, he is told to "let no one look down on you" (2:15), just as Timothy was told to "let no one have contempt for your youth" (1 Tim 4:12). Both Timothy and Titus are presented in these letters as younger companions of Paul who are placed in positions of authority in their respective communities.

After the personal charge to Titus, the preceding household code is then summarized in terms that make explicit that, as a whole, it is to be understood as a charge to good citizenship. The "them" in 3:1 refers to all those whose behavior was commented on in chapter 2. In 1 Timothy, Christians were urged to pray "for kings and for all in authority" (1 Tim 2:2). Here they are to be "under the control of magistrates and authorities" (3:1). The charge to obey civil authority is found elsewhere in the New Testament (Rom 13:1-7; 1 Pet 2:13-17), but in 1 Timothy and Titus it is integral to the moral exhortations throughout the letters. These letters urge Christians to participate fully in civic life through gainful employment, respect for neighbors, and obedience to civil authority.

3:4-8 Baptismal hymn

These verses contain language used nowhere else in the Pastoral Letters, most likely because they are part of a preexisting hymn. The previous passage on salvation (2:11-14) offered a kind of commentary on this hymn and provided the theological basis for the exhortation in the household code. Now the letter presents the hymn itself, labeling it as a trustworthy saying (3:8; cf. 1 Tim 1:15; 3:1; 4:9; 2 Tim 2:11), a phrase regularly used in the Pastoral Letters to identify a basic truth of early Christian faith.

The present passage provides a brief synthesis of Pauline theology. Apart from Romans 6:3-11, it contains the most important statement on baptism in the New Testament. Through baptism Christians are no longer slaves to sin but are reborn by the holy Spirit as heirs in hope of eternal life. This hymn situates its teaching on baptism in the context of the two appearances of Christ, the context for all the exhortations of Titus. It further presents the Pauline teaching on justification as the basis

for the baptismal lives now led in hope. The use of this hymn allows the letter to Titus to connect its treatment of the Jewish Christian problem to that confronted by Paul. In Galatians and again in Romans, Paul confronted those who felt that people could be saved by their own righteous deeds. For Paul as well as for the letter to Titus, people are "justified by his grace" (3:7) and not by "any righteous deeds" (3:5).

The previous passage on salvation (2:11-14) explained what is involved in living lives based on baptismal conversion, denying impiety and worldly passions while living modestly, justly and piously and waiting in hope for the appearance of Christ. This hymn makes explicit the early Christian teaching that baptismal lives are led by the power of the holy Spirit. Only here and in 2 Timothy 1:14 is the role of the holy Spirit in Christian living explicitly mentioned in the Pastoral Letters. While teachings about the holy Spirit are not emphasized in these letters, the theological concerns of these letters are firmly grounded in the early traditions about the holy Spirit.

FINAL DIRECTIVES TO TITUS
Titus 3:8-11

As the letter draws to a close, the main points of the letter are summarized. What Titus was told to say in chapter 2 (2:1, 15) he is here told to insist on, that is, that people do good and avoid evil (3:8-9). Avoiding evil involves specifically the kinds of evil promoted by the Judaizing opponents at Crete (1:10-16), like arguing about genealogies. The tasks assigned to bishops and to Titus as well, to exhort and refute opponents (1:9; 2:15), are here given further specification, consistent with what Paul is said to have done in 1 Timothy (1 Tim 1:20). Excommunication is to be used as a last resort in dealing with one who upsets the community. Calling the person a "heretic" and further pointing out that the person is "perverted and sinful and stands self-condemned" (3:10-11) gives expression to the overall perspective of 1 Timothy and Titus, linking belief, true or false, with behavior, good or bad.

FINAL REMARKS AND FAREWELL
Titus 3:12-15

Mention of travel plans is a common feature at the end of Paul's letters. Here the mention of travel plans, those of Paul and of others, are presented in a way that illustrates authorization for ministry, one of the overarching concerns of 1 Timothy and Titus. Paul is now about to send either Artemis or Tychicus to Crete to replace Titus while Titus visits Paul at Nicopolis (3:12). In 2 Timothy 4:12, Paul had sent Tychicus to Ephesus. Just as Paul has sent Titus, Timothy, and others to administer churches, Titus is now charged to send others, Zenas and Apollos, to exercise their ministries in other places (3:13). They, like Titus and Timothy, are to devote themselves to their ministries (3:14; cf. 1 Tim 4:6, 16; 2 Tim 2:15; 4:2; Titus 1:5). While verse 14 continues the instruction on the two missionaries, the phrase "our people" can be understood as applying to the entire community.

The letter concludes with a greeting and a final blessing, both typical of the way Paul concludes his letters. While the greeting is addressed to Titus ("you" in the singular), who is then to extend Paul's greeting to others, the blessing is addressed to "all of you," an indication that the blessing and indeed the entire letter is intended not for a single person, Titus, but for the whole church.

THE LETTER TO
PHILEMON

Terence J. Keegan, O.P.

INTRODUCTION

The letter to Philemon is the shortest but one of the most intriguing letters in the New Testament. Almost all scholars agree that it was written by Paul himself during one of his imprisonments. It provides one piece of an extended conversation involving Paul, Onesimus, Philemon, and others. The information the other parts of the conversation would provide remain a mystery and have been the subject of much conjecture. Fortunately most of this missing information, while interesting, is not crucial for appreciating the ongoing significance of this short and beautiful letter.

Paul is clearly in prison at the time of the letter, but the where and when of the imprisonment are not known. Discussions on these questions are usually linked to discussion about his imprisonment at the time he wrote his letter to the Philippians, and answers vary widely. Were both letters written from Rome and hence later than the letter to the Romans? Were one or both written from Ephesus or some other location? Was one written from an earlier or later imprisonment than the other? It seems most likely but hardly certain that Philemon was written during an earlier imprisonment, possibly at Ephesus, from which Paul expected to be released, and hence be able to visit Philemon and continue his ministry. Travel for both Onesimus and Paul from Ephesus to Colossae, the usually assumed location of Philemon's home, would be relatively easy, since they are only about a hundred miles apart.

Onesimus is a slave belonging to Philemon and is, at the time of the letter, with Paul. Why he has left his owner and is with Paul is also the subject of much speculation. He has done something to offend his owner, which could have been some inappropriate act while he was in his service or which may simply have been his running away. While he may have been a runaway slave, the prevailing opinion is that he was visiting Paul to appeal to him for advice and assistance in his difficulty with his owner. Some have even suggested that Philemon sent his pagan slave to minister to Paul in prison. It is also not certain what Paul expects Philemon to do. He is clearly asking him to receive Onesimus back as a brother in the Lord and to charge Paul for whatever debt Onesimus owes. Paul, however, also says that he would like Onesimus to be able to serve him and seems to be suggesting that Philemon do even more than he is explicitly asked to do, perhaps even give Onesimus to Paul as his slave.

This letter, like others in the New Testament, simply accepts slavery as an institution without discussing its morality. This letter does, however, recognize the tension that exists between the liberating message of the gospel (cf. Gal 3:26-28; 1 Cor 12:13) and the slavery that society accepted. In its treatment of Christian brotherly love, it provides a basis for later Christian understanding of the slavery issue. It calls for a reordering of relationships on a higher plane than those possible within secular society. While many questions will remain unanswered, the letter to Philemon can be read by Christians of all ages as an exposition on the new relationship that exists among people as a result of their incorporation into Christ. This relationship, which transcends all other relation-ships, including that of master and slave, is based on the new life that all Christians share by reason of the grace that comes from Christ. This new life involves both mutual love and partnership in promoting the gospel.

COMMENTARY

THE OPENING

Phlm 1-3

1-2 Senders and recipients

Like all Paul's letters, the letter to Philemon opens by identifying both the senders and the recipients. The senders are Paul and Timothy. Elsewhere Paul calls himself "an apostle of Christ Jesus" (1 Cor 1:1) or "a slave of Christ Jesus" (Rom 1:1), but here he identifies himself a "a prisoner for Christ Jesus" (1). This identification refers not only to his actual status as a prisoner but even more to the reason for his being a prisoner—his preaching of the gospel of Christ—and most es-pecially, in the context of the purpose of this letter, to Christ's total, authoritative claim on Paul and Paul's dedication to that claim. Timothy's being called a "brother" establishes his close relation-ship with Paul and also prepares for Paul's ad-dressing Philemon as "brother" (7, 20) and his appealing to Philemon to accept Onesimus as a "brother" (16).

The main recipient of the letter is Philemon, but the letter is also addressed to other key in-dividuals in his community, Appia and Archip-pus, and to the whole community. In the early church, communities were usually small enough to gather for worship in a private home, often that of a leading citizen like Philemon. While the immediate purpose of the letter is to persuade Philemon to do a good deed, the argument of the letter involves Philemon's understanding of his and Onesimus's relationship within the whole community. Using the terms "brother" and "sis-ter" as well as "co-worker" sets the stage for the new relationship Paul seeks to bring about be-tween Philemon and Onesimus. Addressing the letter to the whole community provides greater incentive for Philemon to comply with the let-ter's request. It also gives the letter applicability, beyond Philemon himself, to the whole commu-nity as well as to Christian communities of future generations.

3 Greeting

The formal greeting is similar to those used in Paul's other letters and has the same wording as the greeting in Paul's other letter from prison (Phil 1:2). While formal, this greeting, together with the formal blessing at the end (25), frames the body of the letter within the context of God's grace. Paul's theology of grace is nowhere developed in this letter, nor are other aspects of his theology. It is reasonable to assume, however, that Philemon and his community, having been converted by Paul, are familiar with the main aspects of Paul's teaching. God's graciousness toward Philemon and his community should inspire their gracious-ness toward one another.

THANKSGIVING

Phlm 4-7

4-5 Philemon's love and faith

The thanksgiving, which follows the opening greeting in all Paul's letters except Galatians, usu-ally involves thanking God for some quality in the letter's recipient and serves to introduce the main themes of the letter. Here Paul thanks God for Philemon's love and faith, qualities that will be the basis of Paul's appeal in the body of the letter. Paul sees in Philemon's faith not just his assent to the gospel but the way his vital faith has been operative in his life—"faith working through love" (Gal 5:6). Philemon's love "for all the holy ones" (5) includes those in "the church at your house" (2), Paul himself (7), and will shortly be extended to include Onesimus (16).

6-7 Effects of Philemon's love and faith

In the opening of the letter, Paul referred to Philemon as "our co-worker" (1). He now strengthens that designation by referring to him as "brother" (7), associating him more closely with himself and with "Timothy our brother" (1), the co-author of the letter. Paul suggests that he and Philemon together can now do even more good for the holy ones than what Paul has already seen Philemon doing. Thus far, Paul has drawn an extremely positive picture of Philemon. As the letter develops, Philemon will be expected to live up to this positive picture. The themes of prayer (4), love (5, 7), partnership (6), good (6), and refreshing the heart (7) will all be used as Paul develops his argument.

APPEAL ON BEHALF OF ONESIMUS
Phlm 8-21

8-12 Paul appeals out of love

Paul claims the right to order Philemon to do the good he is about to propose, but refrains from exercising this right. This right probably derives from Paul's apostolic authority, although Paul called himself a prisoner rather than an apostle in the introduction to the letter. Because of the encouragement he has felt on the basis of the good that has come from Philemon's love, rather than order him to do what is proper, Paul urges him "out of love" (9). The love here referred to is both Philemon's love for all the holy ones (5) and Paul's and Timothy's love for Philemon (1). Paul refers to himself as an old man and as a prisoner (9) as motivation for Philemon to extend to Paul the love he has for the holy ones.

Having established the basis of his appeal as the love relationship that exists between himself and Philemon and their mutual love for the holy ones, Paul now identifies the object of his appeal. Whatever he may have been, Onesimus has become Paul's child in prison. By bringing him into Christianity, Paul has become his "father." Paul will describe him as "my own heart" (12). Onesimus has become one of the holy ones mutually loved by Paul and Philemon. Significantly, the term "child," which Paul uses to refer to Onesimus and often to Christians in general, is used in

his letters for only one other individual, namely, Timothy (1 Cor 4:17; Phil 2:22), Paul's partner in spreading the gospel and a co-author of this letter.

The extensive use of family language in this letter indicates that a new model of mutual relationships has already been established within the Christian community, a model of relationships that is in tension with the master/slave relationship accepted in Roman society. Paul does not advocate the overthrow of the institution of slavery, but he does advocate overcoming the tension by fully incorporating the Christian slave into the familial relationships within the Christian community. In at least two ways Paul has described a new household in tension with the structured household of Philemon. First, in this new household Paul, not Philemon, is the head; both Philemon and Onesimus are his children. Second, Paul's father/child relationship with Onesimus has priority over Philemon's master/slave relationship with Onesimus.

The name Onesimus, a common name for slaves, means "the useful one," enabling the play on words in verse 11. Away from Philemon, Onesimus was useless to him. Now a Christian devoted to Paul, he has become useful both to Paul and to Philemon. He will become useful to Philemon when Paul sends him back, but his real usefulness to both Philemon and Paul will become clear later in the letter.

13-14 Philemon's voluntary good deed

Paul never explicitly states what it is that he expects Philemon to do. He had said that he had a right "to order you to do what is proper" (8), but here says he wants the good Philemon will do to be voluntary (14), a good deed on the part of Philemon in response to the grace of God. He says he would have liked Onesimus to remain with him, serving him in prison for the gospel, an indication that Onesimus, like many slaves at that time, was well educated and hence equipped to be of service to Paul and the gospel. However, he sends him back to Philemon and apparently expects Onesimus to be with Philemon when he is released from prison and visits Philemon (22).

15-18 Paul's request

Paul appears to be asking Philemon to receive his slave back, charging Paul for anything that Onesimus might owe as a result of previous misdeeds or his temporary absence. Paul, however, is asking for much more. He is asking that Philemon receive Onesimus back not only as a slave but also as a brother in the Lord. He is asking that he receive Onesimus both as a man, that is, as a fellow Christian who is his slave, and in the Lord, that is, as a co-worker in the gospel. Most of all, Paul is asking that Philemon receive Onesimus back just as warmly as he would welcome Paul. Onesimus has become Paul's "own heart" (12). Just as Philemon is Paul's co-worker in the gospel (1), so too Philemon should regard Onesimus as a co-worker, like Paul, in the gospel. Verse 17 implies that Paul's primary concern was to effect a reconciliation between Philemon and Onesimus.

Modern readers are often disappointed that Paul does not ask Philemon to grant freedom to his slave. While some scholars think that there are passages (16, 21) that can be read as hinting that Paul desires Onesimus's freedom, most do not, and all agree that the letter falls far short of reconsidering the practice of slavery. In fact, recent studies in cultural anthropology have shown that Philemon's simply freeing his slave would not have fundamentally altered his relationships within the household. Paul wants to alter these relationships. The letter offers a model for transforming the way Christians view one another, now seeing other human beings with eyes reconditioned by faith in Jesus Christ. The transforming power of God's grace, personally experienced by Paul, led to his conviction about God's ability to make all things new (2 Cor 5:17). Paul was actually asking Philemon for something far more radical than freeing his slave. Paul's declaration that Onesimus is Philemon's brother both "as a man and in the Lord" (16) indicates not merely a spiritual reevaluation in the sight of the Lord but a real change in the social relationship between slave and owner.

As the father of Onesimus (10), Paul now accepts responsibility for the debts of his son. In so accepting this responsibility, however, Paul is emphasizing the intensity of his relationship with Onesimus and setting the stage for the implied request at the end of the letter. Martin Luther saw in Paul's letter to Philemon a parallel to the kenotic hymn Paul quotes in Philippians (Phil 2:6-11), his other letter from prison. Christ emptied himself of his right with the Father and instead died to bring us into favor with God. As Christ pleads our cause and takes our part, so too Paul has emptied himself of his rights and takes the place of Onesimus in order to get Philemon to waive his right to punish Onesimus and instead welcome him as a brother.

19-21 Personal appeal

Paul's letters were dictated by him and written by a scribe, but he would sometimes add a note at the end in his "own hand" (19; cf. 1 Cor 16:21; Gal 6:11). By writing in his own hand he is concluding his appeal by making his request intensely personal. He now not only restates his agreement to pay Onesimus's debt but also reminds Philemon of the debt he owes to Paul. The new life in Christ that Philemon now lives he owes to Paul, that is, he owes Paul his "very self" (19). With this comment Paul draws Philemon into the creditor-debtor relationship as a debtor as well as a creditor. The sphere of mutual relationships is expanded. Philemon, in fact, has the same relationship to Paul as does Onesimus. For both, Paul is their father in faith. For both, Paul is their partner in the gospel (1; 13).

Paul is expecting Philemon to reflect on the significance of these relationships when Paul asks to "profit from you in the Lord" (20), followed by his appeal to Philemon to "refresh my heart in Christ" (20). Paul is expecting Philemon to reflect on his love for Paul and his partnership with him in the gospel and to consider what he can do to further support him in his ministry. Near the beginning of the letter Paul thanked God for Philemon's love, faith, and partnership, noting that "the hearts of the holy ones have been refreshed by you" (7). He identified Onesimus as "my own heart" (12) and now asks Philemon to "refresh my heart" (20). Paul concludes this personal appeal by expressing his confidence that Philemon will not only do what Paul has explicitly asked, that is, receive Onesimus back as a brother in the Lord, but will do even more (21).

Paul is certainly expecting that Philemon will accept Onesimus not only as a returned slave and a brother in the Lord but also as a beloved co-worker in the gospel, a partner with Paul and Philemon. He may also be expecting that Philemon will refresh his heart by granting the wish Paul had earlier expressed: "that he might serve me on your behalf" (13). Philemon indeed may have Onesimus back forever by giving him to Paul as their mutual partner in the gospel.

This letter calls not only Philemon but all Christians to adopt new patterns of mutual respect, mutual responsibility, and mutual concern. This letter can help Christian communities today to reflect on the roles and concerns of minorities and others who might be marginalized. Accepting the transforming power of God's grace will not only alter relationships but can offer new possibilities for living out Christian faith in freedom and joy.

CONCLUSION

Phlm 22-25

22 Travel plans

Travel plans are a common feature of Paul's letters, appearing just before the final greetings and blessing. Here Paul indicates his hope to be able to visit Philemon. There must have been a realistic prospect of his being released from prison, a development for which he asks the prayers of Philemon and his community. His arrival at the home of Philemon would be an appropriate occasion for Philemon to refresh his heart by granting him Onesimus. To this point in the letter, "you" has been in the singular, referring to Philemon alone. The request for prayers, however, uses "your" in the plural, indicating not only that Paul is asking for the prayers of the community but also that this personal letter to Philemon is intended to be read to the entire community.

23-25 Greeting and blessing

Greetings are another common feature of Paul's letters, appearing just before the final blessing. The greetings from Paul's fellow prisoner, Epaphras, and four fellow workers are addressed to "you" in the singular, that is, to Philemon alone, possibly because they were personally known by Philemon. The final blessing, however, is addressed to the entire community, using the blessing formula similar to those found in Paul's other letters and identical to that in Paul's other letter from prison, the letter to the Philippians (Phil 4:23).

THE LETTER TO THE

HEBREWS

Daniel J. Harrington, S.J.

INTRODUCTION

Among the books of the New Testament, the Letter to the Hebrews stands out for its rhetorical and theological brilliance. It is arguably the greatest Christian sermon ever preached or written. Its author deserves to be revered as the patron saint of preachers. He has presented the essential claim of Christian faith that Christ died for our sins in a persuasive argument with a deep emotional appeal. One way to introduce this book is to describe Hebrews as a sermon in written form, of uncertain origin, intended to encourage perseverance in Christian faith.

A sermon in written form

The author describes his work as a "message of encouragement" (13:22), which most interpreters take to mean a speech or sermon in written form. The only literary features that might qualify Hebrews as a letter or epistle are the travel plans and personal greetings that appear in 13:23-24. These features may have been attached to the sermon as it was sent from one community to another. Or perhaps they were interpolated into the text to promote its association with the corpus of Pauline letters.

Hebrews is no ordinary sermon. Indeed, it is a highly literary and rhetorical sermon that is at once simple and subtle. The basic theological point is simple: Christ is both the perfect sacrifice for sins and the priest who offers himself as a sacrifice. The work's sophisticated use of the Greek language indicates a high level of education on the author's part. As a good preacher, the author interweaves expositions of biblical texts and exhortations to faith and good actions. While he sometimes appears to make a formal delineation between exposition and exhortation, he always joins the two. Exposition leads into exhortation, and exhortation leads to further exposition. He announces his main themes beforehand, repeats keywords, begins and ends units in similar ways (a technique called inclusion), and uses various rhetorical devices (alliteration, arguments "from the lesser to the greater," etc.).

The rhetorical handbooks of the Greco-Roman world distinguished three kinds of speeches: forensic or judicial (used in accusing or defending someone in a legal trial), deliberative (used in persuading a public assembly to take action), and epideictic (used at public memorial occasions to confirm a community's values by praise or blame).

Hebrews best fits the conventions of epideictic rhetoric. It celebrates the greatness of Jesus as the Son of God and as the great high priest and promotes the values that he stood for. It offers comparisons with the angels, Moses, the priests of the old covenant, and Melchizedek to extol the greatness of Jesus. It praises and blames those who are being addressed and seeks to confirm their positive beliefs in the hope of rousing them from spiritual sluggishness and of rescuing them from the danger of falling away from the Christian faith.

The basic outline of Hebrews is clear enough. The first main part (1:1–4:13) establishes Jesus' superiority as God's Son to the angels and to Moses and uses various biblical texts to explore Jesus' significance and the need for persevering in Christian life. The second main part (4:14–10:18) concerns the high priesthood of Christ and the perfect sacrifice of Christ. The third main part (10:19–13:25) reflects on the nature of Christian life and the need for perseverance and endurance in the face of suffering. There are many much more elaborate outlines. But even the simple tripartite outline is not entirely adequate, since the author is so skilled in making transitions, in anticipating themes to be developed later, and in integrating biblical expositions and exhortations.

Of uncertain origin

The authorship of Hebrews has always been controversial. The early church writer Origen said: "But who wrote the epistle, in truth God knows" (Eusebius, *Ecclesiastical History* 6.25.14). Although the reference to "our brother Timothy" in 13:23 might suggest Pauline authorship, the language, literary style and form, and theology are very different from those of Paul's genuine letters. The attributions to Barnabas (see Acts 4:36) and Apollos (see Acts 18:24) are at best guesses.

The sermon in written form is anonymous. The author never names himself, nor does he reveal much personal information. But some reliable statements can be made about his identity. The author had sophisticated knowledge of the Old Testament in its Greek translation and displays a good familiarity with the techniques of Jewish biblical interpretation. He must have been Jewish. Nevertheless, he was convinced that God had done something so dramatically new and significant through the life, death, resurrection, and exaltation of Jesus that the institutions of the old covenant with Israel through Moses on Mount Sinai were no longer effective. They were only types or shadows of the realities fulfilled in Christ. As he addresses his audience, the author seeks to serve as their teacher and pastoral guide. To respect the mixed genre of Hebrews as a sermon in written form, I refer in the commentary to the author, the writer, and the preacher alternatively, as well as to the readers, the congregation, the community, and the audience.

Those originally addressed in Hebrews seem to have been Jewish Christians who had em-braced Christianity with enthusiasm but were wavering and in danger of giving into discouragement and falling away, especially in the face of suffering (see 12:3-11). It is very tempting to locate the community in Rome on the basis of 13:24 ("those from Italy send you greetings") and the earliest attestations of Hebrews in Clement of Rome's first letter to the Corinthians (1 Clement). But there is no certainty here. Neither is the date of composition certain, since practically anytime between A.D. 50 and 100 is possible. The absence of any reference to the destruction of the Jerusalem temple in A.D. 70 might suggest an early date (the fifties or sixties), though one must admit that the author is more interested in explaining Scripture than in commenting on contemporary events. With these cautions in mind, the hypothesis that Hebrews was addressed to a Jewish Christian community at Rome in the late fifties or early sixties of the first century A.D. remains nonetheless the most attractive setting.

Uncertainty also surrounds the history-of-religions background of Hebrews, so much so that this issue is often called "the mystery of Hebrews." Although some of the author's biblical expositions sound something like what one finds in the writings of Philo of Alexandria, he seems more interested in typology than in allegory. The portrayal of Melchizedek as a heavenly figure in some Dead Sea Scrolls was initially thought to illumine Hebrews 7. But it now appears that the author simply gives his own christological readings of the pertinent biblical texts. Concepts that developed in Gnosticism are sometimes read back into Hebrews, but again the results only highlight the author's theological originality. The New Testament document that is closest to Hebrews is 1 Peter. It is a sermon addressed to alienated and suffering Christians, who are urged to find encouragement and hope in the example of Christ the Suffering Servant. While those addressed in 1 Peter were mainly Gentile Christians, the main audience for Hebrews appears to have been Jewish Christians.

To encourage perseverance

Hebrews is a sustained theological reflection on the very early Christian confession of faith that Christ died for us and for our sins. This confession appears both in Paul's writings (see Gal 1:4; 3:13; 2 Cor 5:14, 21; Rom 5:6; 14:15) and in the pre-Pauline creedal formulas that Paul quotes (see 1 Cor 11:24; 15:3; Rom 3:25-26).

The author of Hebrews shares and develops the idea of the sacrificial nature of Christ's death and its atoning value. However, his most distinctive theological contribution is the concept of the high priesthood of Christ. According to early Christian tradition (see Mark 10:45; 14:24; and especially 14:36), Jesus willingly offered himself in death. Since the one who offers a sacrifice is a priest, the author endeavors to show that Christ can be called a priest despite the fact that he was not born into the Jewish priestly tribe of Levi. The basic theological claim of Hebrews is that Christ is both the perfect sacrifice for sins and the priest who offered himself as that sacrifice.

In developing this thesis, the author assumes that Christ is the key to the Old Testament Scriptures. Not content to leave behind the Old Testament, he argues that the words of Scripture only make sense when attributed to Christ or applied to him. His favorite texts are the messianic Psalms 2 and 110, and in his exhortations he calls upon Psalms 8 and 95 among others. The description of the Day of Atonement ritual in Leviticus 16 is the basic source for establishing Christ's sacrifice and priesthood.

The author insists on the superiority of Christ as the Son of God over the angels and over Moses. Because Christ is both the high priest and the perfect sacrifice, his saving action—his death, resurrection, and exaltation taken as a single event—has made possible the forgiveness of sins, confident access to God, and hope for eternal life with God.

The people addressed in Hebrews seem to be having a hard time in accepting the absolute sufficiency of Christ's perfect sacrifice on the cross. If they are to persevere in Christian faith, they need a spiritual renewal. At various points the author addresses their situation directly with stern warnings and words of encouragement. Most of all, he hopes that his biblical-theological presentation of Christ's sacrifice and priesthood will give them the appropriate theological framework to put aside their doubts and spiritual sluggishness and to revitalize their Christian faith and practice.

To that end the author portrays Christ as the pioneer (the one who has already gone before us) and the leader for those who follow him on the way to eternal life with God. The risen and ex-alted Christ remains a mediator on our behalf in the present (9:24) and will appear again to bring salvation in the future (9:28). His perfect sacrifice renders unnecessary the sacrifices and priests of the old covenant. In fact, these persons and institutions were at best types or signs that have received their full definition in Christ.

Two hard questions

Does Hebrews illumine the Christian priesthood? The work is mainly concerned with the priesthood of the Old Testament and the priesthood of Christ. It does not speak directly about the communal priesthood of all Christians (see 1 Pet 2:9; Rev 1:6; 5:10; 20:6) or about the Christian ministerial priesthood. However, many Christians have found in Christ's priesthood an apt metaphor for describing Christian life in general. It has also been traditional among Catholics and other Christians to find in Christ's priesthood the model and dynamism for the ministerial priesthood. But some Protestants regard Christ's priesthood to be the end of all claims to priesthood, since his perfect "once for all" sacrifice has rendered unnecessary all other sacrifices and priesthoods. The problem is that Hebrews is silent on this important question and can be (and has been) read as supporting or denying all the various positions about priesthood.

Is Hebrews anti-Jewish? Since both the author and his audience seem to have been Jews, such a charge seems unfair and anachronistic. In fact, Hebrews is an interpretation of Judaism in the light of Christ. Without the authoritative Scriptures of Israel and the great heroes and institutions of the biblical tradition, there would be little substance to Hebrews. And yet perhaps more than any other New Testament writer, the author of Hebrews insists that the old covenant, priesthood, and sacrificial system have been superseded through Christ. Modern Christian readers need to respect the historical (Jewish) setting of Hebrews and to be sensitive to the anti-Jewish potential of the text when it is taken out of its first-century Jewish Christian context.

Reading Hebrews

Hebrews is a sermon in written form. It presents a sustained theological argument, and so it may be helpful to read it straight through at one sitting. Its rhetoric and theology are highly sophisticated and difficult for modern readers, and therefore it deserves careful study, with the commentary that follows as a guide. It may be helpful to look up the Old Testament texts that the author quotes in order to appreciate how he handles these texts from his christological perspective. One must be aware, however, that the author used the ancient Greek version (Septuagint) of the Old Testament, which often differs from the Hebrew text on which

our modern translations are based. A communal reading of this sermon in written form might serve as a final exercise. A well-prepared and reverent group reading of the whole text takes about fifty minutes. The exercise will help those who have worked through this difficult text to appreciate better the truth of the author's own comment: "The word of God is living and effective, sharper than any two-edged sword" (4:12).

COMMENTARY

GOD'S SON AND GOD'S WORD

Heb 1:1–4:13

1:1-4 Prologue: Jesus as the climax of divine revelation

The prologue serves as an introduction or overture to the entire sermon by calling attention to major themes and to the pivotal place of Jesus in the history of salvation. Using the device of alliteration, in which several words begin with the same letter ("past . . . partial . . . prophets"), the author begins in 1:1-2a by showing how Jesus continues the story of God's communication to Israel and brings it to a definitive point or climax. He develops the idea by four contrasts. (1) Whereas God spoke "in times past," now he has spoken "in these last days" (the new era ushered in by Jesus and issuing in the fullness of God's kingdom). (2) Whereas God spoke "to our ancestors" (historic Israel), now he has spoken "to us" (the Christian community). (3) Whereas God spoke "through the prophets" (including Moses, Joshua, and David, as well as those known traditionally as the prophets), now he has spoken through "a son" (Jesus). (4) Whereas God spoke "in partial and various ways," now he has spoken in a full and definitive way (through Jesus).

In describing the person and work of Jesus in 1:2b-3, the author highlights his identity as the Messiah and as Wisdom. Jesus' identity as the Messiah is developed with the help of two psalms (2 and 110) that serve as major texts throughout the sermon. Both psalms originated in the ritual associated with the coronation of kings in ancient

Israel. The king was "anointed" as part of his coronation, and the word "Messiah" means "the anointed one." By declaring Jesus as "heir of all things" (see Ps 2:8) and as taking his seat at God's right hand (Ps 110:1), the author tells us right away that Jesus is the Messiah of Jewish expectations. What historic Israel hoped from its kings, Jesus has provided.

Jesus' identity as the Wisdom of God is established by evoking terms and motifs from various Old Testament passages in which Wisdom is portrayed as the agent of God in creation (see Proverbs 8, Sirach 24, and Wisdom 7). The author affirms that Jesus was God's agent in creating the universe ("through whom he created the universe," see Prov 8:30; Wis 7:22), that he reflects God's glory and represents God's being (see Wis 7:26), and that he carries on God's work of creation ("who sustains all things"). The motif of Jesus as the Wisdom of God is prominent in early Christian hymns preserved in other New Testament books, most notably Colossians 1:15-20 and John 1:1-18.

While identifying Jesus as God's Messiah and Wisdom, the author also introduces his major theme of Jesus' role in the "purification from sins," a work accomplished through his sacrificial death on the cross and his subsequent exaltation to the heavenly throne of God. Likewise, in 1:4 he announces the theme that will be developed in what follows immediately: the superiority of Jesus to the angels. This theme is related to the superior "name" that Jesus bears as the Son of God. The author's task will be to show why the Son should be regarded as superior to the angels.

1:5-14 Jesus as superior to the angels

Why the author felt compelled to take on this task is not certain. There is some evidence in the Dead Sea Scrolls and other early Jewish texts for veneration of angels. And some early Christians may have regarded Jesus as an angel. Or the issue may have been entirely theoretical.

The device that the author uses to establish Jesus' superiority to the angels is a chain (or *catena*) of biblical quotations. While the *catena* genre was used by Jewish writers of the times, the author of Hebrews makes it serve his christological purpose. For him, Christ is the key to the Scriptures, and so all the biblical texts that he quotes are assumed to speak to or about Christ. There are three pairs of quotations (1:5, 6-7, 8-12), along with a single quotation of Psalm 110(109):1 (1:13).

The introduction to the *catena* in 1:5a ("to which of the angels did God ever say") establishes that the purpose is to prove the superiority of the Son. The concluding comment in 1:14 about the angels as servants is a case of "inclusion," in which an argument is begun and ended in similar ways.

In 1:5 the first pair of quotations—Psalm 2:7 and 2 Samuel 7:14—serve to identify Jesus as God's Son and Messiah: "You are my son . . . he shall be a son to me." The assumption is that God is the speaker and addresses Jesus as his Messiah/Son. Part of the ideology of kingship in ancient Israel was that the king became God's "son" at his accession to the throne. And so when applied to Jesus, the terms "Messiah" and "Son" are synonyms.

In 1:6-7 the second pair of quotations—Deuteronomy 32:43/Psalm 97(96):7 and Psalm 104(103):4—establish the inferiority of the angels to the Son of God. The assumption is that God spoke these words when Jesus the Wisdom of God took on human flesh ("when he leads the firstborn into the world") and that these words concern the Son of God. The first text says that the role of the angels is to worship the Son, and the second text presents the angels as instruments of God ("winds . . . a fiery flame").

In 1:8-12 the third pair of quotations—Psalm 45(44):7-8 and Psalm 102(101):26-28—takes texts originally addressed to God and applies them to the Messiah/Son ("your throne, O God . . . O Lord, you established"). The emphasis is on the eternity of Jesus' reign as God's Messiah/Son

("forever and ever . . . God, your God, anointed you . . . your years will have no end"). While such things cannot be said of angels, applying these biblical affirmations about God to Christ suggests his own authority, eternity, and even divinity.

In 1:13 the final (single) quotation—Psalm 110(109):1—applies what was said by God to the king at his coronation ("sit at my right hand / until I make your enemies your footstool") to the resurrected and exalted Messiah/Son. Throughout Hebrews, the center of attention will be Jesus' death, resurrection, and exaltation understood as one great event. The *catena* concludes in 1:14 with a comment about the role of the angels as servants of God ("ministering spirits") on behalf of all those who seek salvation.

2:1-4 A call to commitment and responsibility

At many points in his sermon the author addresses his audience directly and challenges them to apply his message about Christ to their own situation. Even in his exhortations, however, he injects new theological considerations based on the Old Testament and on God's saving activity in Jesus.

As a good preacher, the author moves in 2:1 from the *catena* of biblical quotations to their significance for Christian life and includes himself among those being addressed ("therefore we must attend . . ."). The expression "what we have heard" may refer to the gospel message in general, to the biblical passages applied to Christ in 1:5-14, or to Jesus as the Word of God—or all three at once. The danger that the audience faces is expressed by the phrase "so that we may not be carried away," which evokes the image of a ship failing to reach its harbor safely. The author fears that his people may drift away from the gospel that they had once embraced.

The warning in 2:2-3a builds on the case developed about the Son's superiority to the angels. It employs the rhetorical device of arguing "from the lesser to the greater" and assumes that the law was given to Moses on Sinai through the mediation of angels (see Acts 7:53; Gal 3:19). If the Mosaic Law given through angels punishes each and every transgression, how much more will God punish neglect of the salvation given through Christ. The logic is that the greater revelation (the gospel) given through the greater revealer (Christ) will exact greater punishment from those who fail to attend to it.

Having raised the threat of severe punishment, the author in 2:3b-4 reminds his audience about the nature of the salvation brought by Christ. It was announced by Jesus ("the Lord") and confirmed by the apostolic witnesses and by God through miracles ("signs, wonders, various acts of power") and through the gifts of the holy Spirit (not a major figure in Hebrews). Note the "trinitarian" dimension that serves as the framework for describing the saving work of Christ.

2:5-9 Jesus as the Son of Man

Having reflected on the significance of the salvation brought by Jesus for the community of faith, the author takes up again the theme of Jesus' superiority to the angels. According to a biblical tradition (see Deut 32:8; Dan 10:20-21; 12:1), God placed the world in the present age under the governance of angels. According to early Christian faith, however, the new age or "world to come" (2:5) has already been inaugurated in and through Christ. But the quotation of Psalm 110(109):1 in Hebrews 1:13 ("until I make your enemies your footstool") could give the impression that Christ's reign was still future. And so the author contends that Christ's reign is both present and future and that it began with Jesus' incarnation, death, and exaltation.

The biblical vehicle for the author's argument is Psalm 8:5-7(4-6), which is part of a meditation on the great dignity of human beings. The psalmist ("someone . . . somewhere") praises God ("you") for God's care and love for humankind ("man . . . the son of man") and observes that God has placed human beings a little lower than the angels and given them stewardship over the world (see Gen 1:26, 28).

True to his interpretive principle that Christ is the key to the Scriptures, the author assumes that Psalm 8 speaks about Christ as the "son of man." In his interpretation (2:8b-9), he affirms that God has already placed all creation under the governance of Christ as the Son of Man. The problem is that humans do not yet perceive Christ's sovereignty, though they surely will do so in the fullness of God's kingdom. What is now perceived through faith is the risen and exalted Christ ("crowned . . . with glory and honor"). His glo-

rification followed from his suffering and death, when he was lower than the angels "for a little while" (the adverb is interpreted chronologically rather than qualitatively). The paradox is that Christ's humiliation in his passion became the occasion for the exaltation of us all. The idea that Christ's death was the perfect sacrifice for sins and opened up the possibility for the salvation of all humans is introduced by the concluding clause: "that by the grace of God he might taste death for everyone" (2:9).

2:10-18 Christ in solidarity with humans

The fundamental affirmation of Hebrews is expressed in 2:10: God ("for whom and through whom all things exist") made Jesus the pioneer or champion ("leader") to bring all humans to salvation, and the way by which this goal was achieved was through the cross, in which Christ was made "perfect through suffering." This statement captures the self-sacrifice involved in Jesus' death on the cross as well as the atoning value of his death for others. Thus Jesus can be understood (as we will see) as both the priest (because he offered himself willingly) and the sacrifice (because his death was for us and for our sins).

Jesus' solidarity with humans and his special relationship with God are established in 2:11-13 by a series of Old Testament quotations. Both Christ ("he who consecrates") and humans ("those who are being consecrated") share a common origin in God and in humanity. And so Christ can call other humans "brothers." The first biblical quotation is Psalm 22:22(23)—from the prayer of the righteous sufferer, which is also the source of Jesus' last words on the cross, according to Mark (15:34) and Matthew (27:46). In the author's christological framework, Jesus ("I") confesses and praises God ("you") among his fellow humans ("to my brothers"). In the second biblical quotation (Isa 8:17-18), Christ ("I") professes trust in God ("in him") and identifies himself with other humans ("I and the children God has given me"). Thus Christ is the link or mediator between God and humans.

The classic question, Why did Christ become human? is taken up in 2:14-18. By sharing our humanity, Christ was able to render inoperative the devil as the one who has power over death and to free us from the fear of death that makes us slaves (2:14-15). The object of Christ's saving work was the "descendants of Abraham," which includes not only Israel as the chosen people of God but also the many nations of which Abraham was the father (2:16). Only by being fully human could Christ be both our priest ("a merciful and faithful high priest") and our sacrifice ("to expiate the sins of the people"). Only by being tested through suffering could Christ help us as we are being tested. These ideas about the priesthood of Christ will be developed at great length in chapters 5–10.

3:1-6 Jesus as superior to Moses

The preacher returns in 3:1 to direct address. He reminds his congregation that as "brothers" of Christ and of one another, they share in the holiness that reflects God the holy one par excellence and in the call to eternal life with God. Identifying Jesus as "the apostle" (the one "sent" from God—the only New Testament application of this title to Christ) and "high priest" (a title already introduced in 2:17 and soon to become the center of attention), the author in 3:2 focuses on Jesus' fidelity to God as "the one who appointed him." He also introduces the figure of Moses and the characterization of Moses as "faithful in all his house."

This description of Moses comes from Numbers 12:7(8): "Not so with my servant Moses! / Throughout my house he bears my trust." In the Old Testament context, Moses appears as the instrument of God's revelation who is superior to Aaron, Miriam, and all other recipients of divine revelation. The "house" is Israel as the people of God, where Moses functioned as the "servant" of God.

In comparing Moses and Christ in 3:3-6, the author is more concerned to praise Christ than to denigrate Moses. He proceeds on two fronts: the house (3:3-4) and the servant (3:5-6). Just as the architect-builder of a house deserves more praise than the house itself, so God (and Christ as God's agent) deserves more praise than Moses in founding the people of God. Just as in a large household a son is more important than a servant, so Christ the Son is more important than Moses the servant in the people of God. Whereas Moses was a servant "in" God's house, Christ was a son placed "over" the house. Thus Jesus' faithfulness as God's Son was superior to the faithfulness of God's servant Moses.

The preacher concludes in 3:6b by identifying the Christian community as the "house" or people of God ("we are his house") and by warning the community to retain their confidence and pride in what God has done and continues to do for them through Christ the Son. Otherwise they may cease to be God's house.

3:7-19 The negative example of Israel in the wilderness

A good preacher frequently offers a congregation positive examples to be imitated and negative examples to be avoided. As a way of challenging the congregation to emulate the fidelity displayed by Christ, the author presents the negative example of ancient Israel wandering in the wilderness between the exodus from Egypt to the entrance into the land of Canaan.

The main biblical text is Psalm 95(94):7b-11 (which is read in light of Numbers 14). The text is introduced as having logical significance ("therefore") and as being from God ("as the holy Spirit says"). In Psalm 95 the admonition to be faithful follows an invitation to worship God, most obviously at the Jerusalem temple (Ps 95:1-7a). The admonition itself recalls the episode of Israel's rebellion in the wilderness (see Exod 17:1-17; Num 14:21-23). The place in which the rebellion took place was called in Hebrew "Massah" (meaning "testing") and "Meribah" (meaning "quarreling"). The text begins with a call to hear God's voice "today" (Heb 3:7b = Ps 95:7b). Then there is a warning to avoid the rebelliousness displayed by the Exodus generation in the wilderness for forty years (Heb 3:8-9 = Ps 95:8-9). Finally, God recalls his anger at that generation and his resolve that they would not find "rest" in the land of Canaan (Heb 3:10-11 = Ps 95:10-11).

Having quoted this biblical text at length, the author in 3:12-15 makes an application to the situation of his audience in the first century A.D. First, in 3:12 he warns them against falling away from the living God, as the Exodus generation did, through "an evil and unfaithful heart." Then, in 3:13 he encourages them to regard every day as "today" and not to allow their hearts to be hardened. Finally, in 3:14-15 he warns them again that their partnership with Christ depends on remaining faithful "until the end." The final warning and the application in general are underscored by a repetition of Psalm 95:7b-8 and by bringing back the key words ("today . . . hear his voice . . . harden not your hearts . . . rebellion").

The application is an example of the actualization of Scripture. Just as the psalmist used the negative example of the Exodus generation to motivate people in his own generation, so the author of Hebrews applies both the example and the biblical text to early Christians in his own day. This process of actualization is carried on whenever the letter to the Hebrews is proclaimed today, since "the word of God is living and effective" (4:12).

Still another rhetorical device in the preacher's repertoire is his use of rhetorical questions. From what had been said and from the way in which the questions are asked, it is clear what answers the preacher expects. The first two questions (3:16 and 3:17) are answered by two more questions, while the final question (3:18) receives a response by means of a declarative sentence (3:19).

The first pair of questions (3:16) establish that those who had rebelled were those Israelites who came out of Egypt with Moses. Their disobedience is the main topic in Psalm 95:7b-11. The second pair of questions (3:17) indicate that God was angry with those people because they sinned in putting God to the test and in rebelling against God. The punishment for that generation's rebelliousness was death in the wilderness before any could enter "rest" in the land of Canaan (see Num 14:29-30).

The third question (3:18) affirms that God swore an oath against the disobedient Israelites, so that they could not enter his rest. And the concluding comment (3:19) attributes their failure to "lack of faith." The author has made two important rhetorical moves here. He has linked disobedience to lack of faith as effect and cause (see Num 14:22-23). And he has repeated the word "rest" several times, thus preparing the listener to ask whether it may refer to something beyond life in the land of Canaan.

4:1-13 The abiding promise of sabbath rest

Having explained Psalm 95:7b-11 in terms of the disobedience and lack of faith shown by the Exodus generation, the preacher in 4:1-2 moves to the congregation that he addresses ("Therefore, let us . . .") and tells them that God's promise of entering "rest" remains a possibility in the present.

He warns them to be on guard lest they fail to have that promise brought to fulfillment. Like the Exodus generation, they have received the "good news" (the same word as "gospel"). Like the Exodus generation, they run the risk of failure if they do not respond in faith. What they should learn from the negative example of the Exodus generation is the pivotal importance of faith issuing in obedience. Only then can they hope to enjoy the "rest" that God has promised.

What is this "rest"? It is not simply life in the land of Canaan after the Exodus from Egypt. Indeed, it remains a present possibility for the early Christians as God's people ("we who believed"). To clarify the meaning of "rest," the author in 4:3-5 uses the Jewish interpretive technique of explaining one verse in Scripture by another linked to the first by a common word. Part of the author's main text has been Psalm 95:11: "As I swore in my wrath, / 'They shall not enter into my rest.'" Genesis 2:2 is another text that mentions "rest": "And God rested on the seventh day from all his works." The second text, of course, is from the biblical account of creation and expresses God's plan for creation. The combination of the two texts suggests that "rest" really refers to eternal life with God. The "rest" denied the Exodus generation was but a shadow of the rest that God has enjoyed since the beginning of creation and that God makes available to all who believe.

In 4:6-8 the author makes clear that God's promise of rest remains valid, despite the failure of the Exodus generation to attain to it because of their disobedience. The key word in this section is "today," which suggests that God's promise of rest remains a possibility even after the Exodus generation. Here the author works with the traditional ascription of the psalms to David (see 4:7). Now David lived long after Joshua, the one who finally did lead God's people into the promised land of Canaan. If Joshua had given genuine rest to God's people, David would not have been able to speak about "today" as the time to hear God's voice and so enjoy rest with God. In Greek the names Joshua and Jesus are the same. But the rest that God's people enjoyed under Joshua's leadership was but a shadow or type of the genuine rest that is now available to God's people through Jesus' leadership.

Finally, in 4:9-10 the author brings together what he has been saying about rest: "a sabbath rest still remains for the people of God" (4:9). This sabbath rest is God's own sabbath rest on the seventh day of creation (see Gen 2:2); it is not simply life in the land of Canaan or even observance of the sabbath day. Rather, it is sharing in God's sabbath rest, which began on the seventh day of creation and lasts forever. It is fullness of life with God.

And yet, as 4:11 makes clear, the enjoyment of God's own rest demands a deliberate choice ("let us strive to enter into that rest") to avoid the kind of disobedience displayed by the Exodus generation ("so that no one may fall").

The preacher ends the first main part of his sermon in 4:12-13 with reflections on the word of God and the omniscience of God. The word of God (4:12) is more than the book we call the Bible. Because it comes from the living God, the word of God is living and active. Throughout his sermon thus far, the preacher has been concerned to show that the Scriptures can speak effectively to people in his own time. They are not simply witnesses to the past but rather have significance for "today." So effective are the Scriptures in addressing the concerns of people today that they can be compared to a sharp ("two-edged") sword that can penetrate into a person's inmost self ("between soul and spirit, joints and marrow") and can distinguish among thoughts and intentions.

In 4:13 the subject changes from the word of God to God ("him"), or more precisely, to the omniscience of God. Nothing can remain hidden from God. And to God everyone must be ready to render an accounting as to a judge. Thus the author seeks to motivate his congregation to strive ever more vigorously for eternal life with God ("rest") by reminding them of the possible consequences of not doing so.

THE PRIESTHOOD AND SACRIFICE OF CHRIST

Heb 4:14–10:18

4:14–5:10 Jesus as the compassionate high priest

The author began his sermon by establishing Jesus' identity as the Son of God. In the central section of his sermon, he will show how the Son of God is also the great high priest. The material in 4:14-16 serves as the link between the first two main sections, and enables the preacher to ad-

vance his argument about the saving significance of Jesus' death and resurrection. The reuse of many of the same words and ideas in 10:19-23 will in turn enable him to round off (by the device of "inclusion") the second part and move to the third and final part.

True to his craft as a preacher, the author in 4:14-16 alternates between theological statements about Jesus' high priesthood (4:14a, 15) and exhortations ("let us . . . ," 4:14b, 16). The first theological statement (4:14a) must be understood against the background of the Jewish Day of Atonement ritual described in Leviticus 16. There the Jewish high priest is instructed to pass through the curtain in front of the Holy of Holies and to offer sacrifice on behalf of the sins of the people. But Jesus the Son of God "has passed through the heavens" in his resurrection and exaltation. Whereas the Jewish high priest entered only the earthly symbol of God's presence, Jesus has entered the real abode of God (heaven). More than anyone else, therefore, Jesus deserves the title of "great high priest." The first exhortation (4:14b) concerns perseverance in the confession of faith in the saving significance of Jesus' death "for us" and "for our sins."

The second theological statement (4:15) again takes as its premise an idea in Leviticus 16—that the high priest is a sinner and makes atonement for his own sins. Though Jesus was "without sin," he nonetheless experienced the moral and physical testing (see Mark 1:12-13; Matt 4:1-11; Luke 4:1-13) that is part of the human condition. As fully human, the Son of God can "sympathize with our weaknesses." The second exhortation (4:16) moves beyond "holding on" and urges the readers to approach God's throne with boldness. This confidence is based on the new relationship made possible through Jesus' activity as "our great high priest" in his sacrificial death and in his exaltation. While the motif of God's throne might imply judgment and condemnation, now through Christ it has become a "throne of grace" (a place of divine favor) from which one can expect mercy and grace from God. It is Christ who makes possible this access to God's throne and this confident attitude among those who approach God.

But how can Jesus of Nazareth be called a high priest at all? In ancient Israel only men from the tribe of Levi who could trace their heritage back to Aaron were qualified to serve as high priests. As the author freely admits in 7:14, Jesus was descended from Judah and so had no earthly claim to the Jewish priesthood. The answer to the question resides in the different qualifications for priesthood developed in 5:1-10 and in the different priesthood explained in 7:1-28. (Note the reuse of terms from 5:1-3 in 7:27-28.) The intervening exhortation in 5:11–6:20 spells out the consequences of Jesus' different high priesthood for Christian life.

The high priest is first of all (5:1) a mediator between God and humans. As a human himself, he represents other humans before God, especially in his task of offering sacrifices for sins. Secondly (5:2-3), the high priest stands in solidarity with other humans because he shares their weakness. Thus he can show compassion to "the ignorant and erring." And as he offers the atoning sacrifices, he does so both for his own sins and for the sins of others. Thirdly (5:4), the high priest is called by God as Aaron was (see Exod 28:1) and does not take up the office on his own. More important than Aaronic/levitical descent for establishing Jesus' right to priesthood are the criteria of mediatorship, solidarity with others, and divine appointment. According to these criteria, it is possible to call Jesus "our great high priest."

The author applies these criteria in reverse (or chiastic) order. The divine appointment of Christ as high priest is established in 5:5-6 by means of quotations from the author's favorite biblical passages—Psalms 2 and 110. The author assumes that the speaker is God and the one addressed is Christ. Both psalms were used in coronation rituals for kings in ancient Israel, and so can be called "messianic." Since for the author and other early Christians the key to the Scriptures is Christ, these two oracles are understood to concern Christ. The first oracle (Ps 2:7 = Heb 5:5) establishes that Christ is God's Son (see Heb 1:5), and the second oracle (Ps 110:4 = Heb 5:6) introduces the idea (to be developed at great length in Hebrews 7) of the eternal priesthood of Christ "according to the order of Melchizedek." The two quotations interpreted from a christological perspective are put forward as proof that God has called and appointed Christ to be the great high priest.

Christ's solidarity with other humans is established in 5:7-8 by reference to his suffering—a

universal human experience: "he learned obedience from what he suffered." The description of Christ's suffering most vividly evokes the episode in Gethsemane (see Mark 14:32-42; Matt 26:36-46; Luke 22:39-46) but probably also takes in all of his passion and death and indeed his entire life "in the flesh." The reference to his "prayers and supplications with loud cries and tears" places Jesus in the context of the many Old Testament lament psalms (see Psalms 3, 5, etc., and especially Psalm 22). From the author's christological perspective on biblical interpretation, Christ has become the speaker par excellence of the lament psalms. And in his case "because of his reverence" his prayers were heard, and he was vindicated through his resurrection and exaltation.

Christ's mediatorship, according to 5:9-10, surpasses that of any other priest: "when he was made perfect, he became the source of eternal salvation for all who obey him." The reference to Christ's being made perfect alludes to his having reached his "goal" through his death and resurrection, which in turn has made possible "eternal salvation for all who obey him." No other priest could bring about eternal salvation. The best that the Old Testament priests could do was the annual Day of Atonement ritual with its hope that the people's sins of the past year would be wiped away. The final verse (5:10) anticipates the full treatment of the different priesthood of Christ "according to the order of Melchizedek" in chapter 7.

5:11–6:12 A call to Christian maturity

Hebrews is not simply a theological treatise. It is a sermon that interweaves biblical exposition and theology with reflections on the spiritual condition of the audience. Between his discussions of Christ's high priesthood in 4:14–5:10 and 7:1-28, the author issues a call to spiritual maturity (5:11–6:12) and offers an assurance about God's promises (6:13-20).

The call to Christian maturity in 5:11–6:12 consists of a reprimand (5:11–6:3), a stern warning (6:4-8), and a word of hope and encouragement (6:9-12). In the first part of the reprimand (5:11-14) the author admits that his topic of Christ's priesthood is "difficult to explain." But he locates the difficulty not so much in the material but rather in the audience ("you have become sluggish in hearing"). He goes on in 5:12 to scold them for failing to advance in Christian life. By this time they should have become teachers but in fact they stand in need of learning again the basic elements (the ABCs) of Christian faith. They remain in Christian infancy: "You need milk, [and] not solid food." In 5:13-14 he develops the contrast between the spiritually immature as lacking "experience of the word of righteousness" and the spiritually mature who can "discern good and evil." The Christian ideal is the integration of doctrine and practice.

The second part of the reprimand (6:1-3) challenges the congregation to move forward in their theological education and practice. The author urges them not to remain at the basic level, without of course neglecting the basics entirely—no more than one can neglect one's ABCs in writing or reading. The list of basics in 6:1b-2 is founded on "repentance from dead works and faith in God." Initiation into Christian life is covered by "baptisms and laying on of hands," while life-after-death is treated in "resurrection of the dead and eternal judgment." As they became Christians, the members of the congregation learned the distinctively Christian interpretations of Jewish beliefs and practices. Even though they seemed to be wavering about these matters, the author hopes that by moving them forward to "advanced" teaching about Christ's priesthood and sacrifice all these issues will fall into place again for them. As a good preacher, however, he acknowledges in 6:3 that their progress depends ultimately on God ("if only God permits").

The stern warning in 6:4-8 (see 10:26-31) is intended to shock the community into recognizing the seriousness of turning aside from Christian faith. The author declares that repentance after apostasy is impossible for those who have been "enlightened and tasted the heavenly gift and shared in the holy Spirit"—a general description of Christian initiation (which need not be broken down into the separate sacraments of baptism, Eucharist, and confirmation)—and "tasted the good word of God and the powers of the age to come"—a reference to God's word encountered in the Old Testament and in the preached gospel and to the signs and wonders that were part of early Christian experience. Those who fall away from Christian faith are said to be recrucifying the Son of God and holding him up to contempt. The theology of this stern warning seems to be that

since Christ's death has made possible the forgiveness of sins, those who reject its saving significance have nowhere else to go for repentance and forgiveness. The rhetorical force of the warning seeks to awaken the community to recognize the seriousness of their situation.

The stark choice that is before the community is illustrated in 6:7-8 by the contrast between the good soil and the bad soil (see Mark 4:3-9; Matt 13:3-9; Luke 8:4-8). Whereas the good soil that produces useful crops receives a blessing from God (see Gen 1:11-12), the bad soil that produces only thorns and thistles is cursed (see Gen 3:17-18) and burned off. This dramatic contrast underscores how serious a decision lay before the wavering Christians. Will they produce good fruits and be blessed by God in Christ? Or will they produce thorns and thistles, and so share in the curse imposed upon Adam?

Having gotten the congregation's attention by his stern warning, the preacher in 6:9-12 offers some mitigating words of hope and encouragement. He first expresses in 6:9-10 confidence that his dear friends will enjoy the "better things related to salvation" because God will surely recognize their good works and the love that they have shown in serving their fellow Christians ("the holy ones"). Then in 6:11-12 he expresses his personal solicitude ("we earnestly desire") that they will persevere and so come to the fullness of what they can hope for in Christ. The stern warning of 6:4-8 has been replaced by the soothing talk of 6:9-12. But as the final comments in 6:12 indicate, the problem of spiritual sluggishness remains. If they are to enjoy what God has promised, they need to imitate the faith and patience shown by their spiritual forebears—a theme developed at length in Hebrews 11.

6:13-20 An assurance about God's promises

The reference to "inheriting the promises" in 6:12 provides the occasion for an assurance about God's promises in 6:13-20, which in turn prepares for the reflection in 7:1-28 about God's promise of a priest "according to the order of Melchizedek" in Psalm 110:4.

The key biblical text in the assurance is Genesis 22:16-17 in which God, impressed by Abraham's willingness to sacrifice his son Isaac, promises to Abraham many descendants. The two key points in the text for the author of Hebrews according to 6:13-15 are the content of the promise and the oath formula by which it is introduced ("he swore by himself"). The content of the promise is " 'I will indeed bless you and multiply' you." The oath formula is distinctive precisely because God "swore by himself." And the result is that Abraham obtained the promise "after patient waiting"—mostly likely not through Isaac alone but superabundantly through Christ.

In 6:16-18 the preacher continues his reflection on the oath and the promise of Genesis 22:16-17. In 6:16 he sets forth two basic principles of law: We humans customarily swear an oath by someone greater ("so help me God"), and we use an oath to end an argument ("I swear to God"). Then in 6:17-18 he refers back to Genesis 22:16-17 to make the case that God's promise is based not only on the content of the promise itself but also on the oath that precedes it. We can trust God's promise to Abraham and his descendants (in Christ) because it is based on "two immutable things"—God's word and God's oath. The significance of these reflections will become clearer in the meditation on Psalm 110:4 in chapter 7.

The final two verses (6:19-20) bring the listeners back to the topic of the high priesthood of Christ, which will be treated at length in chapter 7. They also introduce two striking images. God's promise fulfilled in Christ is "an anchor of the soul" (6:19), and Jesus is the "forerunner"— the leader who has gone before us to eternal life with God (6:20). As the high priest of Leviticus 16 entered the Holy of Holies on the Day of Atonement, so Christ has gone before us to enter God's heavenly court.

7:1-28 Jesus as a priest according to the order of Melchizedek

After moving from the first reflection on Christ's priesthood in 4:14–5:10 to exhortation in 5:11–6:20, the author returns to his main theological topic: Jesus' priesthood according to the order of Melchizedek.

In the Old Testament Melchizedek appears only in Genesis 14:17-20 and Psalm 110:4. These two passages will serve as the biblical basis for the author's argument about the superiority and eternal character of the priesthood of Christ. Although there were some speculations about Melchizedek in early Jewish and Christian writings, here the author is concerned only with establishing his points on the basis of these two biblical texts. How he handles them reveals much about Jewish biblical interpretation in the first century A.D. and about the Christian conviction that Christ is the key to the Scriptures.

The reflection on Genesis 14:17-20 in Hebrews 7:1-10 seeks to show the superiority of Christ's priesthood to the Jewish levitical priesthood. In 7:1-2a the author introduces Melchizedek as "king of Salem and priest of God Most High" and focuses on the two matters of greatest importance to his argument: Melchizedek blessed Abraham as he returned from battle, and Abraham gave to Melchizedek a tithe or "tenth of everything."

In 7:2b-3 the author considers the person of Melchizedek. His name can be interpreted in Hebrew to mean "king of righteousness" or "righteous king." Likewise, the name of his city "Salem" (which was most likely Jerusalem) can be associated with the Hebrew word for "peace." As righteous king and king of peace, Melchizedek was a type of Christ. Moreover, in Genesis 14:17-20 Melchizedek comes out of nowhere. He is given no genealogy ("without father, mother, or ancestry"), and nothing is said about his birth or death ("without beginning of days or end of life"). This argument from silence contributes to the author's case that Melchizedek prefigures Jesus the Son of God. But the real focus of attention is the superior priesthood of Melchizedek and Christ.

The rest of the argument on the basis of Genesis 14:17-20 in 7:4-10 focuses on the acts of blessing and tithing. By Jewish custom the superior figure blesses the inferior figure. By Jewish custom all the other tribes pay a tithe or tax to support the priestly tribe of Levi (see Num 18:21-24). But according to Genesis 14:17-20 Abraham gave a tenth of all his spoils (a tithe) to Melchizedek, who had blessed Abraham. Both actions show the superiority of Melchizedek to Abraham. Since the patriarch Levi—from whom the Jewish levitical priests traced their lineage—was a descendant of Abraham, these two actions, according to the reasoning of the author of Hebrews, suggest the anteriority and superiority of Melchizedek's priesthood to that of Levi. It is as if Levi, before he was born, had already acknowledged the superiority of Melchizedek and so of Christ. The next step in the argument is to prove that Christ's priesthood is the priesthood of Melchizedek.

The reflection on Psalm 110:4 in Hebrews 7:11-28 seeks to establish the eternal character of Christ's priesthood. The text is quoted in 7:17: "You are a priest forever / according to the order of Melchizedek." The oracle is introduced by an oath formula, which is quoted in 7:21: "The Lord has sworn, and he will not repent: / 'You are a priest . . .'" The author contends that the promise (ratified by an oath) of an eternal priesthood in Psalm 110:4 has been fulfilled in Christ.

Having established the anteriority and superiority of Melchizedek's priesthood in 7:1-10, the author now argues that the priesthood of Melchizedek has found its fulfillment in Christ, and that Christ's priesthood has superseded that of Levi. Whereas the events described in Gen 14:17-20 preceded chronologically the law of Moses and the levitical priesthood, the oracle in Psalm 110:4 (whose origin in David's time is assumed) came later than the law of Moses and the levitical priesthood.

In 7:11 the author reasons that if the levitical priesthood brought "perfection" (see 7:28), there would have been no need for God to promise another priesthood in Psalm 110:4. He observes in 7:12 that a change of priesthood implies a change of law. This is part of his argument that Christ represents better promises and a better covenant.

There was, however, an obvious obstacle to calling Jesus a priest in a Jewish context. Jesus did not belong to the priestly tribe of Levi. Rather, he belonged to the royal tribe of Judah through King David. The author freely admits this fact in 7:13-14. How then could Jesus be called a priest? This was made possible through Jesus' resurrection from the dead. Jesus became a priest "by the power of a life that cannot be destroyed" (7:16), thus fulfilling the promise of an eternal priesthood ("forever") in Psalm 110:4. His priesthood replaced the weak and imperfect priesthood of Levi. Because Christ's priesthood has provided an access to God that was impossible under the old priesthood, it has introduced "a better hope" (7:18-19), which is eternal life with God.

The eternal priesthood of Christ is based according to 7:20-22 not only on the promise of God ("You are a priest forever") but also on the oath of God ("The Lord has sworn, and he will not repent"). At this point the author builds on his reflections about two immutable things—God's promise and God's oath—in 6:13-20. Just as

Christ's priesthood means "a change of law" (7:12) and "a better hope" (7:19), so it is also "the guarantee of an [even] better covenant" (7:22). The levitical priesthood was not eternal, since the levitical priests died (7:23). But since the risen Christ lives forever, his priesthood is eternal (7:24) and so is "always" able to make intercession with God (which is what priests do) for "those who approach God through him" (7:25).

The concluding reflection in 7:26-28 highlights the heavenly character of Christ's priesthood. He is "holy, innocent, undefiled, separated from sinners, higher than the heavens" (7:26). His death on the cross represents the one, perfect sacrifice. And so he has no need to offer sacrifices every day for his own sins and the sins of others. In describing the perfect sacrifice of Christ in 7:27 the author summarizes the theology of his entire work: "he did that once for all when he offered himself." Christ is both the priest (the one who offers sacrifice) and the victim (what is offered), and his sacrifice has value "once for all." There is no need for other sacrifices or other priests in the light of Jesus' one, perfect sacrifice.

The final verse (7:28) argues for the superiority and eternal character of Christ's priesthood on three counts. Whereas the law merely "appoints" high priests, the oracle about Christ's priesthood in Psalm 110:4 is accompanied by a divine oath. Whereas the levitical high priests were subject to "weakness," the risen Christ is the Son of God "made perfect forever." Whereas the levitical priesthood was part of the law of Moses, Christ's priesthood which came later than the law not only with regard to Christ but also to Psalm 110:4 is the key to the better covenant—the primary topic of chapter 8.

8:1-6 Jesus' heavenly priesthood

Having established the eternal character of Christ's priesthood on the basis of Psalm 110:4, the author argues that the place of Christ's priesthood and sacrifice is heaven. As a good preacher, he offers in 8:1 both a recapitulation ("we have such a [great] high priest") and a transition to the next topic (heaven as the locus of Christ's priestly ministry). Here Psalm 110:1 ("The LORD said to my Lord: 'Sit at my right hand . . .'"), which was already cited in 1:13 (see also 1:3), serves as one starting point. The other starting point is the early Christian belief that Jesus, having really died, was raised from the dead and now lives with God in glory ("at the right hand of the throne of the Majesty in heaven").

The two main topics of 8:2-5 are the sanctuary and the sacrifices associated with Christ's priesthood. The sanctuary where Christ ministers has been established by God, not by human beings. It is therefore the "true tabernacle" in the sense that every earthly sanctuary is a copy and shadow of the heavenly sanctuary. This theme is developed in 8:5.

Before that, however, the author must treat in 8:3-4 the heavenly nature of Christ's sacrifices. If Christ were on earth, he would not be offering sacrifices since by the definition of the law of Moses he would not be a priest (because he was from the tribe of Judah, not of Levi). But of course, the sacrifice of Christ was his own self in his death on the cross. Those priests who function on earth do so at an earthly sanctuary and offer earthly gifts and sacrifices to God. Their sanctuary is only "a copy and shadow of the heavenly sanctuary" (8:5).

Such language is reminiscent of Plato's teaching that the visible world is but a copy and shadow of the ideal world. A more likely source, however, is God's instruction to Moses in Exodus 25:40 when Moses began to construct the tabernacle: "See that you make everything according to the pattern shown you on the mountain." The idea is that God gave Moses a "blueprint" or prototype of the tabernacle on Mount Sinai. The heavenly sanctuary of Christ's priesthood is "the real thing," and other sanctuaries are at best poor imitations. Since the author had already established the "better promises" and the "more excellent" character of Christ's ministry, 8:6 functions as another summary. It also serves as a transition, since it introduces the theme of a "better covenant."

8:7-13 The old and new covenants

This section contains the longest continuous Old Testament quotation in the New Testament. The text is the prophecy of God's new covenant with his people that appears in Jeremiah 31:31-34. The historical background is the prophet's recognition that soon Jerusalem and its temple would be captured and destroyed by the Babylonians in the early sixth century B.C. While often described as a prophet of doom, Jeremiah was also a prophet of hope. His hope was based on God's fidelity to

his people and to his promises, not on the strength of Judah's armies and kings. His prophecy of a new covenant looks forward to a restored and superior relationship between God and Israel, one more perfect than anything that Israel had yet experienced.

The author in 8:7 introduces the quotation by observing that if the first covenant had been perfect and without blemish, there would have been no need for a second or new covenant. At this point and 8:13, his only explicit interest is with the word "new" in the promise of a new covenant. Nevertheless, there are other themes in Jeremiah 31:31-34 that are also important, especially the ideas of God's renewed relationship with Israel, the internal appropriation of the new covenant ("in their minds . . . upon their hearts"), and the forgiveness of sins.

The concluding comment in 8:13 explores the implications of the "new" covenant. Such language, according to the author, makes the first covenant "obsolete." He goes on to qualify that strong term by explaining that "what has become obsolete and has grown old is close to disappearing." That was the perspective of the prophet Jeremiah, for he recognized the catastrophe that would soon fall upon Judah in the early sixth century B.C. Is it also the perspective of the author of Hebrews? If so, to what does he refer? Could it be the Jerusalem temple (which was destroyed in A.D. 70), the institutions of the Old Testament (priesthood, sanctuary, sacrifices, etc.), or Judaism in general? Why are they said to be "close to disappearing," instead of already "disappeared"?

9:1-10 The earthly sanctuary

Having argued that the sanctuary of Christ's priesthood is in heaven, the author explains that the earthly sanctuary described in Exodus 25–26 was a shadow or "parable" of the real thing. He also prepares for the characterization of Christ's perfect sacrifice in 9:11–10:18 in terms of the rituals of the Day of Atonement (Leviticus 16).

The "earthly sanctuary" of the first covenant is described in 9:1-5 in terms of its "regulations" (which in 9:10 are called "regulations concerning the flesh"). Taking his information from Exodus 25–26, the author first in 9:2 mentions the outer tent or tabernacle, with its furnishings consisting of the lamp-stand, the table, and the bread of offering. The name of the outer tent is "the Holy

Place." The inner tent is called "the Holy of Holies," the place where only the high priest could enter once a year on the Day of Atonement (9:3-5). Its furnishings—the gold altar of incense, the gilded ark of the covenant, a gold jar containing manna, Aaron's staff, and the tablets of God's covenant with Moses—are more exotic and elaborate than those of the Holy Place. The list is drawn from the book of Exodus and from popular traditions, not necessarily from the realities of the Second Temple. The most important feature of the inner tent, however, is "the place of expiation" (often translated as "the mercy seat"), the place in the Holy of Holies that was sprinkled with blood by the high priest on the Day of Atonement (see Lev 16:14-15; Rom 3:25). Recognizing that prolonging these descriptions might lead to distraction, the author in 9:5 abruptly breaks off his treatment ("now is not the time . . .").

To highlight further the importance of the rituals of the Day of Atonement, the preacher in 9:6-7 contrasts what happened in the outer tent and what happened in the inner tent. Whereas in the Holy Place many priests repeatedly performed their sacrifices for sins, only the high priest might enter the Holy of Holies once a year for the purpose of sprinkling blood there "for himself and for the sins of the people."

However important the rituals of the Day of Atonement might seem, they were inadequate when compared with the perfect sacrifice of Christ (9:8-10). These institutions of the old covenant were used by the holy Spirit to foreshadow the genuine "way into the sanctuary" that Christ the high priest would reveal (9:8). They belonged to "the present time" and could not perfect persons in the depth of their being ("in conscience"). They were "regulations concerning the flesh" that were in force "until the time of the new order" or "the age to come" that has been inaugurated by Christ's life, death, resurrection, and exaltation. They functioned as symbols or parables, dealt with earthly things (food, drink, ablutions, etc.), were open to only a select few (the priests), and were imperfect by nature. They pointed to the perfect sacrifice of Christ offered in his death on the cross for us and for our sins.

9:11-28 The efficacy of Christ's blood

The essence of the Day of Atonement ritual was the high priest's sprinkling of animal blood inside the Holy of Holies. Based on the idea of blood as a symbol of life and as an agent of purification, this action was believed to take away the past sins of the people (including those of the high priest himself) and to prepare them for renewed life before God in the new year. For the author of Hebrews, Christ is both the perfect high priest and the perfect sacrifice (in his death on the cross). His blood, shed only once, accomplished what the blood of animals shed annually could not achieve.

In 9:11-14 the author affirms that Christ the "high priest of the good things that have come to be" ("the age to come," which is already here) has entered the divinely constructed tent (heaven) with his own blood (not animal blood) as the perfect sacrifice offered once for all, with "eternal redemption" as its result. He celebrates the greater efficacy of Christ's sacrifice by arguing in 9:13-14 "from the lesser to the greater." If the animal blood used in earthly sacrifices had any efficacy with regard to the body, how much more has Christ's perfect sacrifice on the cross ("the blood of Christ") cleansed consciences from sins and made it possible to worship the living God. By entering the heavenly sanctuary with his blood, Christ provided an effective cleansing from sin and made possible right relationship with God (what Paul calls "justification").

In 9:15-22 the author contends that the blood of Christ has inaugurated the new covenant prophesied by Jeremiah. Christ is the mediator of that new covenant through his death on the cross (9:15). To explain this point in 9:16-17, he plays on the double meaning of "testament," which can refer to a "covenant" and to a "last will and testament." Just as a last will is activated only when the person dies, so the promise of the new covenant has been activated through the death of Christ. The result is redemption from sins under the old covenant and participation in the eternal inheritance. Just as the old covenant given to Moses on Sinai was ratified by the sprinkling of blood upon an altar (see Exod 24:3-8), so the new covenant has been ratified by the shedding of Christ's blood on the cross. In 9:22 the author describes blood as a means of purification and of forgiveness, and observes that "without the shedding of blood there is no forgiveness" (see Lev 17:11).

In 9:23-28 the author argues that by approaching God in the heavenly sanctuary with his own blood Christ brought about a complete purification of sins. But Christ's work is not simply a past event ("once for all," see 9:12). Rather, Christ the high priest continues to exercise a priestly ministry in heaven: "that he might now appear before God on our behalf" (9:24). Moreover, Christ the high priest will exercise a priestly ministry at the last judgment when he "will appear a second time" (9:28). Since he has already taken away sins by his death on the cross, then his task will be "to bring salvation to those who eagerly await him." Thus there are three phases in the priestly work of Christ: cleansing from sin (past), ongoing mediation on our behalf (present), and final deliverance (future).

10:1-18 Christ as the effective priest and sacrifice

As he reaches the close of his reflections on the priesthood and sacrifice of Christ, the author in 10:1-4 insists that the repeated sacrifices under the law of Moses were ineffective. At best they were "a shadow of the good things to come" as opposed to the true form or image, and so they were incapable of making perfect those who offered them at the Day of Atonement (10:1). The very fact that these sacrifices were repeated every year shows their inability to bring about real atonement for sins (10:2-3). Finally the author asserts in 10:4 that the blood of bulls and goats cannot take away sins.

Next in 10:5-10 the author contends that the many sacrifices offered according to the law of Moses have been superseded by the one perfect sacrifice of Christ. To make this point he places the words of Psalm 40:5-7 in the mouth of Christ "when he came into the world" (the incarnation) as a statement of Christ's vocation and the superiority of his sacrifice. In 10:8 the author identifies the sacrifices of Psalm 40 with those offered according to the law of Moses. Then in 10:9-10 he goes on to contrast those sacrifices with the one perfect sacrifice of Christ's body offered on the cross. His sacrifice has superseded and even abolished the animal sacrifices. Only the one perfect sacrifice of Jesus Christ was able to make people holy ("consecrated"). That sacrifice was offered in a spirit of faithful obedience to God's will: "Behold I come to do your will."

Just as the many sacrifices under the law have been superseded by the one sacrifice of Christ, so

according to 10:11-14 the many priests have been replaced by the one priest. Under the law of Moses there were many priests who offered the same sacrifices over and over without being able to take away sins (10:11). However, Christ the one great high priest "offered one sacrifice for sins" (in his death on the cross) and has been exalted to God's right hand (Jesus' resurrection and ascension, described in terms of Ps 110:1). The one perfect sacrifice of Christ is summarized as follows: "For by one offering he has made perfect forever those who are being consecrated."

Whereas the repeated sacrifices by the priests of the old covenant were ineffective, the one sacrifice of Christ the priest of the new covenant brings about the forgiveness of sins. The motif of the new covenant is introduced by quotations from Jeremiah 31:31-34 in 10:15-17. The new covenant that is inscribed on hearts and minds matches the total interior obedience of Christ ("I come to do your will"). The new covenant wipes away sins and allows God's people to make a new start. So effective is the one perfect sacrifice of Christ in forgiving sins that there is no need for any more sacrifices: "Where there is forgiveness of these, there is no longer offering for sin" (10:18). Thus the sacrificial system of the old covenant, which was at best a "shadow" of Christ's sacrifice, has been superseded. From now on the forgiveness of sins is necessarily linked to Jesus' sacrificial death for us and for our sins. Other sacrifices have been rendered unnecessary.

PERSEVERANCE IN CHRISTIAN LIFE
Heb 10:19–13:25

10:19-39 A call to persevere in faith

Following a pattern set in 5:11–6:12, this passage consists of an appeal (10:19-25), a stern warning (10:26-31), and a word of encouragement (10:32-39). It ends on a note of faith, which prepares for the catalogue of the heroes of faith in chapter 11.

Using language reminiscent of 4:14-16, the author in 10:19-21 provides a theological foundation for his appeal by affirmations about what has happened through Jesus' death, resurrection, and exaltation. Through the blood of Christ we have access to the heavenly sanctuary and have a great high priest who mediates with God on our behalf. The three appeals in 10:22-25 feature the virtues of faith, hope, and love. The call to approach God in faith ("with a sincere heart and in absolute trust") in 10:22 builds upon the conviction that Christ's perfect sacrifice has brought about the forgiveness of sins—an experience that is symbolized in baptism. The call to persevere in Christian hope in 10:23 builds on the trustworthiness of God and of God's promises. The call to live in love with fellow Christians in 10:24-25 builds upon the need for Christian community to be the place where Christians encourage one another to love and to do good works in preparation for the Day of the Lord (judgment). The passing observation that some were absenting themselves from the Christian assembly (10:25) is another symptom of the ecclesial situation of the community to which the author wrote.

The stern warning in 10:26-31 (see 6:4-8) again concerns a post-baptismal sin of the most serious kind—apostasy (see 10:29). If one rejects Christ after having embraced Christian faith, there is no effective sacrifice for one's sins because the sacrifices of the old covenant have been superseded and the all-sufficient sacrifice of Christ has been rejected. All that remains for such persons is the "fearful prospect" of judgment and punishment. The seriousness of their sin is highlighted by another argument "from the lesser to the greater." If according to Deuteronomy 17:6 a person may be put to death for idolatry or blasphemy on the testimony of two or three human witnesses, how much greater will the punishment be for those who spurn the Son of God, profane the blood of God's covenant, and commit outrages against the holy Spirit. The fearsome character of God's judgment is reinforced by quotations from Deuteronomy 32:35-36: "Vengeance is mine; I will repay . . . The Lord will judge his people." This stern warning concludes with one of the most menacing sentences in Scripture: "It is a fearful thing to fall into the hands of the living God" (10:31).

As in 6:9-12, the stern warning is balanced by a word of hope and encouragement in 10:32-39. The author in 10:32-34 urges the community to recall what they suffered shortly after having become Christians ("after you had been enlightened"). The way in which these sufferings are described—public abuse, imprisonment, and confiscation of property—may reflect conditions that prevailed at Rome for some Christians in the late fifties or early sixties of the first century A.D.

The preacher's point is that the new Christians endured these sufferings joyfully because they were convinced that they had "a better and lasting possession" (10:34). He goes on in 10:35-36 to exhort these people to confidence and endurance in the present situation out of the conviction that they will surely be rewarded by God ("great recompense . . . receive what he has promised"). Then in 10:37-38 he appeals to the second coming of Christ with a christological interpretation of Isaiah 26:20 ("he who is to come shall come") and urges perseverance in faith by quoting Habakkuk 2:4 ("my just one shall live by faith"). He ends in 10:39 by counting himself and his community "among those who have faith and will possess life," thus preparing for the catalogue of biblical exemplars of faith in chapter 11.

11:1-40 Examples of persevering faith

To explain what it means to be "among those who have faith and will possess life" (10:39), the author presents a catalogue of figures from the Old Testament who provide models of persevering faith in God's promises. Similar lists of biblical heroes can be found in Sirach 44–49 and Wisdom 10:1–11:4. What distinguishes the list in Hebrews 11 is the resolute emphasis on "by faith." For the author of Hebrews, faith involves the knowledge of unseen realities, a generous response to God's call, a hopeful trust in God's promises, and faithful endurance in the face of suffering and death.

What may appear to be an abstract definition of faith in 11:1-2 is more a programmatic statement to be illustrated by the examples that follow. That faith involves trust in God's promises ("what is hoped for . . . things not seen") is clear. The problem comes with the Greek words *hypostasis* ("realization") and *elenchos* ("evidence"), and whether they are to be taken as objectively as those translations suggest or in a more subjective way ("assurance . . . conviction"). Of course, faith involves both objective and subjective dimensions, as the following examples will show.

The first examples (11:3-7) correspond to events and figures in Genesis 1–11. The work of creation described in Genesis 1 (11:3) was carried out by the power of God's word, and we understand this to be so "by faith." The reason why God accepted the sacrifice of Abel rather than that of Cain (see Gen 4:1-7) is attributed in 11:4 to Abel's superior faith and righteousness. The reason why Enoch was taken up into heaven (see Gen 5:24) was his great faith, according to 11:5. The case of Enoch leads to a brief reflection in 11:6 on the life of faith as the only life that is pleasing to God and on the necessity for belief in God and in God's desire to reward those who seek him. In the cases of creation, Abel's sacrifice, and Enoch's assumption, the author has provided an interpretation ("by faith") that is not explicit in the biblical texts. In the case of Noah (11:7) he has a strong biblical example of faith. According to Genesis 6:8-22, Noah obeyed God's command to build an ark on the strength of his trust in God's promises "about what was not yet seen" and he was rewarded by "the salvation of his household." Noah's act of faith was both a witness against the corrupt world and a foreshadowing of Abraham's "righteousness that comes through faith."

A second set of biblical examples of faith is provided by Abraham and other patriarchs in 11:8-22. According to 11:8-10, faith is what motivated Abraham to leave his homeland and to enter the promised land of Canaan (see Gen 12:1-4), even though he did not know where he was going. And yet by "dwelling in tents" he acknowledged that the promised land of Canaan was not to be his perfect and final abode. Rather, it was a sign or shadow of the heavenly city of God, "the city with foundations, whose architect and maker is God." Faith, according to 11:11-12, is what enabled Abraham and Sarah to accept the promise (see Gen 17:15-22) that despite their advanced ages and her sterility they would have a son named Isaac, and that their descendants would be as many as "the stars in the sky" and "the sands on the seashore." Abraham's faith rested on the person of God: "for he thought that the one who made the promise was trustworthy" (11:11).

In 11:13-16 the author interrupts his list for a reflection on the as-yet-unfulfilled or eschatological nature of the faith displayed by Abraham and Sarah and indeed by all the great Old Testament exemplars of faith. Since "all these died in faith," they failed to enjoy during their lifetimes on earth the fullness of life with God—something that has been made possible through Jesus' death, resurrection, and exaltation. Rather, they remained "strangers and aliens on earth" (11:14; see Gen 23:4) in search of a homeland. However, they recognized that their true homeland was not the land from which they came (and to which they could return) but rather the city that God had prepared for them in heaven. What these heroes of faith hoped for has become a reality through Christ.

The theme of the as-yet-unfulfilled character of the patriarchs' faith is developed by further examples in 11:17-22. Faith moved Abraham to offer his son Isaac as a sacrifice to God, despite the fact that God's promise of many descendants was to be through Isaac (11:17-19). What made Abraham willing to obey God's command was, according to the author, a belief in God's power to raise the dead back to life, and so Isaac was a symbol foreshadowing the resurrection of Jesus. The blessings bestowed by Isaac and Jacob (11:20-21) were signs of their hopes for future generations. The observation that Jacob gave his blessing while "leaning on the top of his staff" (see Gen 47:31 in the Greek version) adds to the "pilgrim" motif of faith. The fact that Joseph gave instructions about the Exodus from Egypt and about moving his bones out of Egypt (11:22; see Gen 50:24-25) indicates the incomplete nature of what he experienced and his trust that there would be much more to the promises of God.

The faith displayed by the patriarchs was also at work in Moses and the Exodus generation according to 11:23-31. Faith led Moses' parents to conceal him in defiance of Pharaoh's decree to kill the male infants of the Hebrews (11:23; see Exod 2:1-10). Faith led Moses to identify himself not with the royal household of Egypt but rather with Israel as the people of God (11:24-27; see Exod 2:11-15), even though this meant suffering "the reproach of the Anointed" and so prefiguring the sufferings of Christ. Faith led Moses to command the elders of Israel in Egypt to sprinkle blood from the Passover lambs at the doors of the residences of the Hebrews (11:28; see Exod 12:21-23). He had no guarantee beyond his faith in God's promises that this action would protect the Israelites from "the Destroyer of the firstborn." Faith led Moses and others to cross the Red Sea with the conviction that they would emerge safely and that the Egyptians would not do so (11:29; see Exod 14:22-28). Faith led Joshua to trust that the walls of Jericho would fall (11:30; see Josh 6:12-21), and faith led the Gentile prostitute Rahab to ally herself with the people of God by protecting the Israelite spies (11:31; see Josh 2:1-21; 6:22-25).

A good preacher knows when to bring a topic to its conclusion ("What more shall I say?"), and so in 11:32-38 he summarizes the subsequent history of God's people. After a list of heroes (11:32), he gives examples of triumphant faith in 11:33-35a and still more examples of endurance in the face of suffering in 11:35b-38. These heroes bore their sufferings out of faith in the resurrection (see 11:35a), which was appropriate since this world "was not worthy of them" (11:38a).

However great was the faith that these heroes displayed, they nonetheless did not yet receive what had been promised (11:39-40). What God promised was forgiveness of sins and eternal life with God—something made possible through Jesus' death, resurrection, and exaltation. By contrasting the heroes of Old Testament faith and "us" (Christians), the author suggests that "we" have received what God promised and so are in a superior position to them.

12:1-17 A call to persevere in faith

The heroes of faith celebrated in chapter 11 constitute a "cloud of witnesses" for Christians (12:1). Nevertheless, the Christians addressed in this sermon are still engaged in a struggle or race that demands endurance and discipline. In this contest they have the good example of Jesus as "the leader and perfecter of faith" (12:2). What is especially significant for them is Jesus' own willingness to endure the suffering and shame of the cross in full expectation of his exaltation to God's throne (see Ps 110:1) and the perfect joy of life in heavenly glory. For Jesus, the cross was a trial to be endured in the hope of glory.

In 12:3-4 the preacher addresses the community's own situation in the light of Christ's example. His endurance of hostility from sinners should inspire them to "not grow weary and lose heart" (12:3). Moreover, their situation, however serious it may seem, in fact has not yet reached the point of "shedding blood" (12:4), which suggests that they have not yet faced martyrdom.

To help the community to understand its present sufferings and to encourage them to persevere in faith, the author offers a reflection on the theme of suffering as a discipline, with Proverbs 3:11-12 as his main text. His emphasis is on the educative or formative (rather than punitive) value of suffering. In the biblical passage quoted in 12:5-6 the sage directs his student ("my son")

to accept the divine discipline as a sign of God's love and concern for him. In the biblical world a father had the ultimate responsibility for child rearing (especially in the case of sons). In his first application in 12:7-8 the preacher suggests that their present sufferings are proof that God regards the Christians as legitimate "sons" for whom he takes responsibility.

He goes on in 12:9-11 to compare the discipline applied by earthly fathers with the discipline applied by God. If earthly fathers win respect from the sons whom they discipline, how much more should we respect "the Father of spirits" in our sufferings (12:9). Moreover, the benefits from divine discipline—sharing in God's holiness, and "the peaceful fruit of righteousness"—in the present and the future far outweigh the benefits that may come from a human father's application of discipline. Divine discipline is superior to human discipline in forming children of God.

Rather than obsessing over their present sufferings, the addressees need to get back on the "way" of discipleship. Using language from Isaiah 35:3 and Proverbs 4:26, the preacher in 12:12-13 urges them to pull themselves together and walk along the straight path with renewed spiritual energy. They also need to remove whatever hinders their spiritual progress. Therefore, according to 12:14, they need to strive for the peace and holiness that come from God and that bears witness to God in the world. They need to guard against the "bitter root" (see Deut 29:18) of division that can harm the life of the whole community (12:15). And they need to learn from the negative example of Esau who because of his impatience and desire for momentary gratification (see Gen 25:29-34) sold his birthright to Jacob and could not get it back when he sought Isaac's blessing (see Gen 27:30-45). The case of Esau reiterates in a subtle way the author's previous stern warnings about the impossibility of repentance after apostasy (see 6:4-8 and 10:26-31).

12:18-29 A call to heavenly worship

Through Christ's priestly sacrifice on the cross, we have access to God. What the institutions and rituals of the old covenant were powerless to do, Christ has accomplished by making possible right relationship with God (justification) and participation in the heavenly worship of God.

This point is developed in 12:18-24 by contrasting the old worship symbolized by Mount Sinai

(12:18-21) and the new worship symbolized by Mount Zion (12:22-24). The description of Mount Sinai is taken mainly from Exodus 19 (see also Exod 20:18-21 and Deut 4:10), though what appears to be awesome in Exodus 19 is interpreted negatively as terrifying in Hebrews. The Sinai experience was full of violent images of storms, fire, and trumpet blasts. It featured a command (Exod 19:12-13) to stone any animal that touched the sacred mountain. Even Moses the mediator of the Sinai covenant confessed that he was "terrified and trembling" (Deut 9:19). By contrast, the new heavenly worship symbolized by Mount Zion is peaceful and joyful. Here Mount Zion is not the earthly city of Jerusalem but rather the heavenly Jerusalem (see Revelation 21–22), "the city of the living God." It is inhabited by angels, "the firstborn enrolled in heaven" (perhaps the saints of the Old Testament, Christian martyrs, or Christians who had already died), God the judge of all, and Jesus the mediator of a new covenant. Whereas Abel's blood bore witness against Cain's guilt and cried out for vengeance (see Gen 4:10), Jesus' blood spoke more eloquently in that it won forgiveness of sins and brought about perfect reconciliation with God.

The contrast is followed by an admonition not to reject God's warning (12:25-29). In the new covenant of Mount Zion/heavenly Jerusalem it is God who speaks. If the people of the Sinai covenant refused to listen to Moses and were punished for their obduracy, how much more punishment can Christians expect if they fail to heed the heavenly voice of God and his Son (see 6:4-8; 10:26-31; 12:15-17).

While the author of Hebrews is generally concerned with realized eschatology (the present benefits of Christ's saving action) and spatial eschatology (heaven and earth), he does occasionally engage in temporal eschatology (as in 10:27-28). Here in 12:26-28 his biblical text is from Haggai 2:6: "I will once more shake not only earth but heaven." The earth shook at the giving of the old covenant at Mount Sinai (see Exod 19:18). But the sixth-century prophet Haggai spoke of a future shaking that would involve both earth and heaven. At God's future eschatological intervention both earth and heaven will shake. Nevertheless, the final shaking will be good news for those who have persevered in faith and in the worship of God. The result will be the removal of "shaken,

created things" (12:27). Then the kingdom of God will be "the unshakable kingdom" in which the worship of God will be conducted "in reverence and awe." To those consoling and encouraging words, the preacher adds a concluding comment designed to bring his audience back to the serious challenge that faced them in the present: "For our God is a consuming fire" (12:29; see Deut 4:24; Isa 33:14).

13:1-6 General instructions

Under the heading "let mutual love continue" (13:1), the author encourages the cultivation of the human virtues of hospitality, compassion, chastity, and avoidance of greed. In each case he provides a theological motivation.

As Acts and the New Testament epistles show, there was an extensive network of communication among early Christians. The virtue of hospitality toward emissaries (apostles) and other travelers was essential to its smooth functioning. The theological motive about receiving angels attached to the admonition not to neglect hospitality (13:2) alludes to episodes involving Abraham and Lot in Genesis 18 and 19. The directive to be mindful of prisoners and victims of torture (13:3) is accompanied by an appeal to human solidarity. The call to respect marriage and to avoid adultery (13:4) invokes God's judgment against fornicators and adulterers (see 1 Cor 5:13; Eph 5:5). The rejection of greed (13:5) is balanced by contentment with what God gives. The theological motive for such an attitude is trust in God as expressed in God's own promise according to Deuteronomy 31:6, 8. The concluding confession in 13:6 quotes Psalm 118(117):6 to the effect that confidence in God casts out all fear. In this short instruction the motives are quite varied: biblical precedents, human solidarity, divine judgment, and trust in God. The absence of a direct appeal to Christ in these instructions is unusual in a work that is so directly centered on Christ as Hebrews is.

13:7-17 Community life and worship

This section begins and ends with instructions about "leaders" (13:7-9 and 13:17), and contains an intervening reflection on worship (13:10-16). The leaders "who spoke the word of God to you" may include not only those who actually evangelized the group addressed in this work but also the apostles and even the Old Testament heroes of faith celebrated in chapter 11. The statement in 13:8 that "Jesus Christ is the same yesterday, today, and forever" sounds like an early Christian confession of faith, and at the same time fits well with the emphasis in Hebrews on Christ as the eternal leader of God's people. This confession is followed by a warning in 13:9 not to be swayed by "strange teaching." The example of "foods, which do not benefit those who live by them" may refer to the Old Testament sacrifices or to the Jewish food laws. If, however, Hebrews was directed to a Jewish Christian community at Rome (as many scholars think likely), then there may be an allusion to the struggle between the "weak" and the "strong" treated by Paul in Romans 14–15. The author of Hebrews clearly takes the side of the "strong."

The intervening section on worship (13:10-16) begins in 13:10 by making a distinction in the worship of the old covenant and the new covenant. The "altar" refers more likely to the heavenly sanctuary at which Christ the high priest presides than to a church building or even to community celebrations of the Eucharist. Those who continue to "serve the tabernacle" (under the old covenant) have no right to the "altar" of Christ (under the new covenant). If (as seems likely) the original addressees were Jewish Christians, this statement expresses a sharp distinction between "old covenant" Judaism and "new covenant" Jewish Christianity.

In 13:11-12 the author makes a final attempt to explain Jesus' death in terms of sacrifice. According to Leviticus 16:27, the carcasses of the animals whose blood was used in the Day of Atonement ritual were to be taken outside the camp and burned. In Jesus' time it was forbidden to hold an execution within the city walls of the holy city of Jerusalem. Therefore Jesus was crucified at Golgotha, a small hill which was outside the city walls. Thus according to 13:12 Jesus suffered "outside the gate" in accord with the type or pattern laid out in Leviticus 16. His death was the perfect atoning sacrifice. In light of this typology, the author invites the community to "go to him outside the camp" (13:13) and thus share in the shame that Jesus suffered in his crucifixion. Such action will confirm that their true city is the heavenly Jerusalem ("the one that is to come") and that they have "no lasting city" on earth.

What is true worship for these Jewish Christians? It is not to be found in the sacrifices of the

old covenant. Rather, according to 13:15-16, Christian worship is preeminently the praise of God and good deeds. Only here does the author "spiritualize" the concept of sacrifice and relate it to acts of public worship ("a sacrifice of praise") and to good works done by Christians ("God is pleased by sacrifices of that kind," 13:16). Elsewhere, the focus has been on the material sacrifices of the old covenant and the death of Christ interpreted as the perfect sacrifice of the new covenant. The extent to which the "sacrifice of praise" might refer to the Eucharist remains uncertain.

The section ends in 13:17 by returning to the topic of "leaders." Here the leaders are clearly those who presently exercise oversight in the Christian community addressed in this work. The author urges respect for and cooperation with these leaders as being most beneficial for both the leaders and the community.

13:18-25 Final prayers and greetings

The author first in 13:18-19 requests prayers on his own behalf. He attests to the purity of his own intentions ("we have a clear conscience") and hopes to meet soon with the community in person. He clearly knows these people personally, and may well count himself among their leaders (see 13:17).

Then in 13:20-21 the author formulates a prayer on behalf of the community. He prays first (13:20-21a) that God may enable them to do God's will, and then (13:21b) he asks that God may carry out in them what is pleasing to God. God is the beginning and the end of all their good works. The description of Jesus as "the great shepherd of the sheep" is unique in Hebrews (but see John 10:11 and 1 Pet 5:4), whereas the reference to Jesus' resurrection and to "the blood of the eternal covenant" are prominent themes throughout the work.

The request for a favorable reception in 13:22 consists of what is generally regarded as the author's own description of his sermon in written form ("this message of encouragement") and a somewhat disingenuous comment about his having written "rather briefly." The personal information in 13:23 provides a reference to Timothy that is the work's only real link to Paul. Assuming that this is Paul's co-worker, we may suppose that the author knew Timothy. Or perhaps the reference to Timothy was interpolated later to make a connection with Paul and his circle.

The greeting in 13:24a is directed to both the "leaders" (see 13:7, 17) and "all the holy ones" (a common way of referring to Christians). Many scholars find in 13:24b ("those from Italy send you greetings") grounds for supposing that the recipients are in Italy (most likely in Rome), and that the author is conveying greetings from Italians who are living where he is (outside Italy). The text, however, is ambiguous, and it could be read in the opposite way to indicate that the sermon in written form was sent from Italy to another place outside Italy.

The final blessing in 13:25 ("grace be with all of you") is both formulaic (see Titus 3:15) and at the same time expressive of the author's theology of Christ's priestly sacrifice as the ultimate and effective manifestation of God's favor toward humankind.

THE GENERAL LETTERS

Patrick J. Hartin

The term "catholic letters" has traditionally been used to designate a group of seven New Testament writings: James, 1 and 2 Peter, 1, 2, and 3 John, and Jude as distinct from the writings of Paul. In the Eastern church the word "catholic" (used in the sense of "universal") was applied to these seven writings. This was an outgrowth of the theological understanding that they were writings addressed, not to any specific church, but to the church at large. This designation indicated the encyclical nature of the letter in that it was intended to be circulated among many churches. In the Western church the designation for these writings was "canonical epistles" *(epistolae canonicae)* indicating the idea that they were letters approved for reading in the liturgy throughout the Christian world.

When Bishop Athanasius of Alexandria issued his Easter letter containing the list of New Testament books in A.D. 367, the catholic letters were placed immediately after the Acts of the Apostles and before the letters of Paul. This same order can be found in many ancient lists of the New Testament canon. It seems that this was the traditional order. The Codex Sinaiticus and the Latin Vulgate adopted a different order, with Paul's letters following the Acts of the Apostles and the catholic letters placed after Paul's writings. The very influential role that the Latin Vulgate played ultimately established this sequence as the traditional one followed today.

THE LETTER OF
JAMES

Patrick J. Hartin

INTRODUCTION

Author

The author identifies himself as "James" (Greek, *Iakōbos*), recalling the Hebrew name Jacob, father of the "twelve tribes of Israel." This name was very common in the biblical world. Three significant members of the early Christian community bore this name: James, son of Zebedee, apostle and brother of John (Mark 1:19), executed by Herod Agrippa about A.D. 44 (Acts 12:2); James, son of Alphaeus, also an apostle (Mark 3:18); and James, "brother of the Lord" (Gal 1:19).

Some information regarding the author can be deduced from the text: (a) *He is at home within the world of Judaism.* He makes great use of the Wisdom traditions of Israel. His thought betrays the concrete mentality of the Hebrew Scriptures rather than the abstract thinking of the Greek. (b) *He is also at home within the world of nascent Christianity.* He shows numerous relationships with the thought and traditions of the Gospels, particularly the Sermon on the Mount. (c) *He writes with the authority of a teacher* (3:1). (d) *He does not appear to be an apostle.* The letters of Paul and Peter carefully indicate their role as apostles in their opening greetings (1 Cor 1:1; 1 Pet 1:1). Instead, the author refers to himself as "a slave of God and of the Lord Jesus Christ" (1:1).

James, "the brother of the Lord" and head of the Jerusalem church, appears to fit best the picture of the author that emerges from the text. He was equally at home in the world of Judaism and the world of early Christianity. Paul indicates that this James was among those who were privileged to witness the risen Jesus (1 Cor 15:7). He exercised an important position within the early Christian community in Jerusalem (Acts 12:17). He was an influential figure at the Council of Jerusalem (A.D. 49). Paul refers to him as one of "the pillars" of the church (Gal 2:9). He remained leader of the Jerusalem church until his martyrdom in A.D. 62. The Jewish historian Josephus also mentions him.

One major difficulty with this suggestion is *the excellent quality of the Greek*—it is among the best in the entire New Testament. Stylistically, the writer shows great finesse at using literary devices to make his argument succinctly. This demands someone well educated in Greek rhetorical skills.

The best way to harmonize the evidence is to understand the reference to James (1:1) as demonstrating the writer's desire to invoke James as the authority behind this letter. He must be someone who was closely associated with James. The writer sends this letter in James's name ("the brother of the Lord") shortly after James's death to encourage Jewish-Christian communities in the Diaspora (particularly in the area of Syria or northern Palestine) to hold on to his traditions and teachings and to remind them of the importance they have as "the firstfruits of his [God's] creatures" (1:18).

The term "brother of the Lord" has been variously interpreted in the Christian tradition (see discussion in Patrick J. Hartin, *James,* Sacra Pagina Series 14 [Collegeville: The Liturgical Press, 2003] 16–25). However, it is best to see the word "brother" as referring to a broader understanding of kinship (rather than to a physical brother of Jesus). For two reasons: First, degrees of kinship were more loosely defined in the ancient world than they are today. (See, for example, John the Baptist's condemnation of Herod Antipas: "It is not lawful for you to have your *brother's* wife" [Mark 6:16; see also Luke 3:19]. Here, Herod Antipas was only the *step-brother* of Herod Philip.) Second, the above argument supports the Catholic tradition that Mary remained a virgin after giving birth to Jesus.

It is in this sense that this commentary refers to the author as "James, the brother of the Lord."

Hearers/readers

The text identifies the hearers/readers very graphically: "to the twelve tribes in the dispersion" (1:1). The best understanding of this phrase emerges from the hope for the restoration of the twelve-tribe kingdom of Israel. The Exile marked the beginning of the *dispersion* of the people of Israel, and the word "dispersion" (or *Diaspora*) became a technical term for those Israelites living outside Palestine. During the Exile the prophets proclaimed the restoration of this twelve-tribe kingdom. This became a central conviction in late Jewish eschatology and apocalyptic literature. It also lies behind Jesus' call to repentance (Matt 4:17). In Matthew 15:24 Jesus countered the appeal of the Syrophoenician woman with these words: "I was sent only to the lost sheep of the house of Israel." This passage conveys Jesus' mission as gathering in and reconstituting the twelve-tribe kingdom of Israel.

In addressing his hearers/readers in this way, James describes his task as similar to that of Jesus. They constitute the beginning of the restoration of the house of Israel. In line with 1:18, James sees that those who now belong to the new Israel are the "firstfruits" and represent a foretaste of the future, final restoration of God's people.

Genre and purpose

The letter of James belongs to the general class of Wisdom literature that proliferated throughout Israel and the ancient Near East in the first two centuries B.C. While Martin Dibelius classified James as *paraenesis* (a collection of moral exhortations), some modern scholars have proposed that it should be viewed more precisely as *protreptic discourse,* that is, a discourse containing sustained arguments that strive to develop a theme more thoroughly. Since the purpose of protreptic discourse is that of *social formation,* James aims at reminding his hearers/readers of those values that give them their identity as the twelve-tribe kingdom and separate them from the wider society.

Major themes

While the name of Jesus occurs only twice (1:1; 2:1), references to God are far more numerous. The concept of God is at home in the world and belief of Judaism in the first century A.D. In line with the Jewish profession of faith, God is one (2:19). God is merciful and compassionate (5:11); the Father of lights, the creator of the world (1:17); the champion of the poor (5:1-6); and the lawgiver and the judge (4:12; 5:9).

James's message calls believers to harmonize their faith and action. James's ethic was not meant to be read in an individualistic sense, but rather in a communitarian way. James lies squarely in the tradition of the prophets before him in giving expression to the voice of the poor and the marginalized in society. In line with Jesus' teaching, James promises the poor the inheritance of the kingdom (Jas 2:5; Luke 6:20) and challenges the conscience of every hearer/reader to respect the poor.

COMMENTARY

1:1 Greetings

This opening follows the usual structure of a first-century letter by mentioning the author, those to whom it is written, and concluding with greetings. The writer identifies himself simply as James. Since he does not identify himself further, the reader associates him with the most important James in the early church, the leader of the church in Jerusalem, "James, the brother of the Lord" (see Introduction, pp. 768–69). Rather than speak from above, the author chooses the term "slave of God," which recalls the long biblical tradition that identifies leaders of the people in this way, such as Moses (1 Kgs 8:53), David (1 Kgs 8:66), and the prophets (Jer 7:25). It is used in the sense of obedience to God's will and loyalty to God's service (see also Phil 2:7; 1 Pet 2:16).

The community to whom the author writes is identified as "the twelve tribes in the dispersion." By this term the readers are described as the fulfillment of Israel's hopes in the restoration of God's twelve-tribe kingdom in the eschatological age. The long-awaited hopes of the past are now being realized with these Christian communities that are emerging from the people of Israel. The word "dispersion" (literally, Diaspora) means "scattering" and refers to those areas outside Palestine where the people of Israel had been scattered (see Deut 30:4; Neh 1:9; see Introduction, p. 769). Undoubtedly, James is writing to Jewish Christians, who see their community as the beginning of these hopes, for they are the "firstfruits" (1:18). The author intends to outline the type of life this newly constituted Israel is called to embrace. This writing helps readers of every age to see themselves as true heirs of Israel's traditions. He uses the standard form of "greeting" that opens Greco-Roman letters *(chairein)*. He deliberately uses this brief greeting in order to connect with the word for "joy" *(charan)* in the next verse. This is part of James's style of using catchphrases to develop the letter.

1:2-11 Testing, wisdom and the lowly

In place of the traditional thanksgiving section that characterized a Pauline letter, the letter of James introduces two sections expressing joy (1:2-11) and blessing (1:12-27), which present the major themes that will unfold throughout the letter.

The first introductory section (1:2-11) begins with a call to the community to *"consider it all joy"* (1:2; emphasis added) when they experience *the testing of their faith* (1:2-4, *the first theme*). Faith is as important for James as it is for Paul, occurring some sixteen times in this short letter (1:3, 6; 2:1, 5, 14[twice], 17, 18[three times], 20, 22[twice], 24, 26; 5:15). Whenever believers, individually or as a group, are involved in the ordeal of suffering, they should accept it joyfully. As gold is tested and purified by fire, so believers will be purified by trials. Testing produces steadfastness, which in turn leads to wholeness or integrity *(perfection,* 1:3-4). It reminds the reader of Matthew's Jesus in the Sermon on the Mount exhorting his hearers: "So be perfect, just as your heavenly Father is perfect" (Matt 5:48).

A second theme emerges in 1:5-8 with the request for wisdom. In the biblical traditions God is the source of all wisdom: "The beginning of wisdom is the fear of the LORD" (Prov 9:10). The gift of wisdom enables people to act in the midst of trials so that their actions lead to wholeness *(perfection).* "Indeed, though one be perfect among the sons of men, / if Wisdom, who comes from you, be not with him, / he shall be held in no esteem" (Wis 9:6). Wisdom is that one gift needed for perfection understood as wholeness, completion, and integrity. James instructs his hearers/readers that if they lack wisdom, they are to ask God, for God is the only one who can grant it. This is similar to the command of Jesus, "Ask and it will be given to you" (Matt 7:7). The believer must pray to God for wisdom, for the knowledge of how to act correctly. For James the root cause of unanswered prayer is lack of faith in God. One is "of two minds" (1:8), having a divided loyalty, as Jesus indicates in Matthew's Sermon on the Mount: "No one can serve two masters. . . . You cannot serve God and mammon" (Matt 6:24). This is a central theme for James, who calls on his readers to make a choice between friendship with God and friendship with the world (4:4).

James introduces a third theme here that has importance throughout the letter, namely, *the contrast between rich and poor* (1:9-11). Both the poor and rich are called upon to "take pride" or to boast in what God does for them. The background for this concept of boasting lies in the Hebrew Scriptures, where God is the source of all blessings (see Jer 9:22-23). The lowly are to rejoice because God has given them an exalted status within the Christian community, where they experience equality with one another. The rich, on the other hand, are those who have lost their position within the wider community, only to discover a true status within the Christian community. True humility finds favor with God (see Sir 3:18). The rich recognize the fragility of life: those who place confidence in their own "pursuits" will waste away suddenly like a wild flower burnt up by the scorching heat (1:11).

1:12-27 Testing, hearers and doers of the word

A second introductory section, introduced with the word "Blessed," again announces major themes that will be taken up in the body of the letter. The first theme expressed here (*endurance under testing brings with it the crown of life,* 1:12-18) is parallel to the first theme of the previous section. Essentially James is saying: "Blessed is the person who withstands trial; that person is progressing toward salvation" (1:12). This is similar to the Beatitudes described in Matthew 5:3-12. James wishes to emphasize that present trials will effect their reward ("the crown of life," 1:12), because such trials give believers the chance to show their love for God.

The trials that are experienced are not to be regarded as temptations sent by God (1:13). The Gospel tradition holds that temptations do not come from God but from the devil (e.g., Jesus' temptations in the Synoptic Gospels). James continues in the same tradition. The truth is that people are tempted by desires that entice them. The consequence of desiring is described in terms of the image of giving birth (1:14-15): when desire conceives, it gives birth to sin; and when it is fully mature, it gives birth to death in its turn.

James's image of God emerges clearly from this section. God is not the source of evil but the origin of everything that is good (1:16-17). James describes God as the "Father of lights" (1:17). Unlike the heavenly bodies, whose movements result in variations of the light they send out, their creator, God, is unchanging. God's love for humanity is always constant. God's greatest gifts to humanity have been those of creation and rebirth as "the firstfruits of his [God's] creatures" (1:18). This connects back to the opening of the letter to

"the twelve tribes in the dispersion." God's gift of rebirth is meant to encompass all humanity: the first implies that others will follow.

A series of sayings brings this introductory section to a conclusion (1:19-27): be slow to anger (1:20-21); quick to hear (1:22-25); and slow to speak (1:26-27). They contain wisdom advice for the hearer/reader on how to lead life in order to be counted among those who are blessed. The hearers/readers are admonished first of all to be *"slow to wrath"* (1:19; emphasis added), because human anger does not conform to God's righteousness, the moral standards set by God. "The word that has been planted in you" (1:21) refers to the word of the gospel that was implanted in the hearts of the believers when they came to rebirth as God's creatures. They are to welcome this word by putting it into practice in their lives. For James salvation requires a response on the part of the believer that is demonstrated in action led according to the moral standards set by God.

Next, James takes up his call to "be quick to hear" (1:19; emphasis added), which focuses on putting faith into action: *"Be doers of the word and not hearers only"* (1:22; emphasis added). This phrase is a suitable summary of the whole letter, expressing the central call to the believer. The word is God's will expressed also in the biblical law (or Torah). The word of the gospel, the message of Jesus, the biblical law—these are all expressions for God's word, God's moral law for God's people. They are different stages of the same reality. Jesus' message captures the heart of the biblical law in the "royal law . . . 'You shall love your neighbor as yourself'" (2:8). James illustrates his call to put faith into action by means of a brief parable. The point is captured in 1:24: those who do not follow God's word in their lives are like those who glance briefly at themselves in a mirror and immediately forget what they looked like.

Finally, the saying "be slow to speak" (1:19; emphasis added) is taken up in 1:26-27. In effect, James says: "If you think you are religious but you lack control of speech, you deceive yourselves and your religion is worthless." James is concerned with the inconsistency between belief and speech and returns to this theme elsewhere throughout this letter (2:14-17; 3:9-10; 4:3). This leads him to provide a definition of religion in terms of action (1:27). It is expressed first in terms of caring for widows and orphans. Believers are called upon to imitate God in their actions. The community shows its true relationship with God by reaching out to the least members of society. *Orphans and widows* were symbolic for the most unfortunate members and a reminder of God's care for their community in the past: "You shall not violate the rights of the alien or of the orphan, nor take the clothing of a widow as a pledge. For, remember, you were once slaves in Egypt, and the LORD, your God, ransomed you from there; that is why I command you to observe this rule" (Deut 24:17-18; see also Exod 22:20-23; Ps 94:1-23). The affliction of orphans and widows came from their lack of protection and legal status when the head of the family died. James adds a further identifying marker for his community: religious people should also keep themselves from the defilement of the world (1:27). The call is made not to be conformed to the standards of this world but to take one's values from the gospel message, which continues God's will as expressed in the biblical Torah.

Five themes from this introductory section will be explored throughout the letter: endurance through trial (1:2-4; 12-18; 5:7-11); asking for wisdom (1:5-8; 3:13-18; 4:1-10); the contrast of rich and poor (1:9-11; 2:1-13; 5:1-6); being doers of the word (1:22-25; 2:14-26; 4:13-17); and control of the tongue (1:26-27; 3:1-12; 4:11-12).

2:1-13 Do not show favoritism

James begins the body of the letter by taking up the theme of the contrast between rich and poor introduced before (1:9-11). He envisages a context in which the rich exploit their positions to oppress the powerless. Discrimination against people is incompatible with the faith of Jesus Christ. This is the second of only two explicit references to Jesus in the letter (1:1). The phrase "faith in our glorious Lord Jesus Christ" is difficult to translate. Literally it reads: "the faith of our Lord Jesus Christ of the glory." In referring to the "faith of our Lord Jesus Christ," James refers to Jesus' faithfulness to the Father's will through the obedience of his life. Jesus' faithfulness becomes an example for all believers. In the letter of James faith is directed toward the Father rather than toward Jesus (see 2:19, 23).

James goes on to paint a vivid picture of discrimination: favoritism shown to the rich at the expense of the poor (2:2-4). Even worse, this dis-

crimination is within the assembly, where it ought not occur. James calls the gathering place of Christians an "assembly" (literally, "synagogue," 2:2). The choice of the word "synagogue" in preference to the more customary Christian designation of *ekklesia* is interesting. This is the only time in the New Testament where a Christian gathering is identified as a "synagogue," indicating the closeness of James's community to its roots within the world of Israel.

James provides an example of such atrocious behavior that every reader has to concur that this is not the way the community should behave as followers of Jesus (2:2-4). In a sense, James challenges the accepted values of his own world, in which honor is bestowed upon the rich and powerful. This example also challenges every succeeding generation to reevaluate its own treatment of people and to root out every form of discrimination. Indirectly, James reminds them of Jesus' teaching: the poor are promised the inheritance of the kingdom (2:5; see Matt 5:3).

James provides further support for his call not to discriminate in 2:5-13. He begins by providing an argument based upon God's actions: God has chosen "the poor in the world to be rich in faith and heirs of the kingdom" (2:5). Discrimination also transgresses the royal law, namely, "You shall love your neighbor as yourself" (2:8). James insists that those who belong to a community guided by "the royal law" of love cannot discriminate. The law of love is the true law guiding every aspect of life. Just as Jesus presented the law of love as the epitome of the law itself (see Matt 22:36-40), so James sees it fulfilling the same role. To discriminate breaks Jesus' command to love and makes one a transgressor of the law (2:9). One is called on to carry out the whole law (2:10-11).

Jesus' teaching in the Sermon on the Mount upholds the same vision of carrying out the whole law: "Do not think that I have come to abolish the law or the prophets. I have come not to abolish but to fulfill. Amen, I say to you, until heaven and earth pass away, not the smallest letter or the smallest part of a letter will pass from the law, until all things have taken place" (Matt 5:17-18). This is not casuistry, but rather an understanding of what the law (Torah) is all about. The law (Torah) is the expression of God's will for humanity. One's whole life must be orientated toward implementing God's will completely.

James's thought concludes with an expression of general principles of judgment and mercy (2:12-13). Mercy triumphs over judgment: for those who have practiced mercy, there is no need to fear judgment (see Jesus' parable on the judgment of the nations, Matt 25:31-46).

2:14-26 Doers of the word / faith and works

This passage continues the line of thought of the previous passage (2:1-13), in which James had stressed that an imitation of Jesus' faithfulness (2:1) excluded discrimination against others. Now, in 2:14-26, this same faith is examined more fully, especially insofar as it expresses itself in action. He presents the theme of the whole argument in 2:14. Faith that is alive needs to demonstrate itself in action—that is the type of faith that saves. In the style of a Greek diatribe, James uses an imaginary example to illustrate the type of faith that saves (2:15-17). On its own faith without works is dead.

James describes a situation in which a living faith will manifest itself in appropriate deeds. His illustration of a brother or sister lacking clothing or food is reminiscent of the parable of the judgment of the nations in Matthew 25:31-46. James concludes with a brief summary of what he had stated in the opening thesis (2:14): faith without works is dead (2:17). He repeats the same refrain again in 2:26. By way of offering proof for his argument, James invents an imaginary opponent to whom he issues the challenge: "Demonstrate your faith to me without works" (2:18). The implication in this challenge is that of course he cannot. Then James offers to show him his faith from his works (2:18). The very heart of the Jewish profession of faith in God as one (the *Shema Israel* expressed in Deuteronomy 6:4-5) required a response in active love. Jesus stressed the same concept that this profession of faith needed to be demonstrated in love of neighbor (Matt 22:36-40). James continues these traditions by showing that true faith needs a response of love (2:18-19); otherwise it is a dead faith, in the same category as the faith of the demons, who believe that God is one "and tremble" (2:19).

To support his perspective (2:20-25), James turns to the Scriptures. Abraham's exemplary behavior is used to support his thesis that good works are necessary. The choice of the example of Abraham is deliberate. As the forefather of Israel,

he is also the father of James's community as heir of Israel's traditions. Abraham was justified not by faith alone but rather through his works, seen especially in his willingness to offer his beloved son Isaac on the altar. A conclusion is drawn from the scriptural reference. What was true in the case of Abraham is true universally (2:24): faith unaccompanied by works is not genuine. Abraham is characterized here as "the friend of God" (2:23). This is significant because James wishes to draw a sharp distinction between those who seek friendship with God and those who find friendship with the world (see 4:4 and the comment on 1:8).

In addition to the holy patriarch, James gives a further example from the Scriptures of someone whose faith flowed forth into works, namely, the prostitute Rahab (2:25). Matthew's early Christian traditions held her in high regard, as can be seen through her incorporation into the genealogy in Matthew's Gospel as an ancestor of Jesus (Matt 1:5). Her hospitality to the messengers of God's people is held up for imitation. She exemplified what James said earlier about caring for widows and orphans (1:27). Christian congregations ought to receive representatives of the church in the same way. Rahab becomes a type of the Christian congregation. James finally clinches his basic thesis with a statement that harks back to the opening of this passage (2:14, as well as to 2:17): "just as a body without a spirit is dead, so also faith without works is dead" (2:26).

Most attention in the letter of James has been focused on this passage because of its seeming conflict with Paul's thought regarding the relationship between faith and works. However, James and Paul are considering two very different issues. James is speaking about *works of faith*, whereas Paul has in mind *works of the law* (Rom 3:28). James's focus is on living out faith in action: "Be doers of the word and not hearers only" (1:22). Faith needs to demonstrate through works that it is alive. Paul, on the other hand, was concerned with a different issue, namely, the question of how one arrives at faith: not through the Jewish law, but through God's free gift. Paul was contrasting *faith with the law*, while James was contrasting *an active faith with a dead faith*.

3:1-12 The tongue and speech

Chapter 3 turns attention to the teacher and the wise person. Once again James takes up themes mentioned in the introductory sections. In the spirit of the Wisdom literature, James gives advice on how to lead life in harmony with faith. An admonition on not becoming a teacher forms the introduction to the discussion on the tongue (3:1). This consideration is particularly appropriate for the role of a teacher within the community. Teaching was exercised chiefly through the oral word of instruction rather than through the written word. The teacher's role in the early church was vital for the development and growth of the community. It could be either positive (building up the community) or negative (undermining or destroying the community).

The role of teachers is often mentioned in the early church (see Acts 13:1; 1 Cor 12:28; Eph 4:11). Teachers focused attention on guiding the community to remain true to their traditions, while showing how these traditions could be newly interpreted and applied to the new situations of the Christian communities. In speaking of the teacher, James does not have an office in mind, but rather a function that is being exercised. James himself functions as a teacher for his community in that he endeavors to apply the Torah and Jesus' teachings to the situation of his own community. For James, the reason people should not become teachers is that "we all fall short in many respects"—in other words, "all of us make many mistakes" (3:2). This theme is common in Hellenistic writings and is also found in the Scriptures (Sir 19:15; Eccl 7:20; 1 John 1:8 and 10). Only "the perfect [person]" (3:2) is able to control speech.

Once again James introduces the theme of perfection or wholeness (see 1:4; 1:25; 2:22). The believer strives for wholeness or integrity in every dimension of life, including speech. James adds image to image, building up the picture of the evil perpetrated by the unguarded tongue (3:3-5a). Like the charioteer, who controls a horse through a small bit, or the pilot, who guides the ship by means of a tiny rudder, so the small tongue controls and guides the whole body, for good or evil. Using language derived from philosophy that had become part of popular culture, James speaks of the evil influence that the tongue exercises on human life at every stage of its development (3:6). James concludes pessimistically that "no human being can tame the tongue" (3:8).

The letter further develops the dangers of the tongue (3:5b-10) by using two frightening images:

the tongue is a fire, and the tongue is a cosmic force (3:6). The tongue of the natural, unredeemed person cannot be tamed; it is a "restless evil, full of deadly poison" (3:8). James goes on to speak of the contradictory work of the tongue: we bless God and curse one another (3:9-12). To bless God is the greatest function of the human tongue: thrice daily the devout Jew praised God. But at the same time this tongue is used to curse one another. James emphasizes that the person who is the object of the curse "is made in the likeness of God" (3:9). Consequently, the curse is directed at God.

3:13–4:10 Call to friendship with God

A feature of ancient instruction was the use of what is termed a *topos,* that is, the systematic development of a theme or topic in a standard way. Two such *topoi* lie behind James's instruction: the *topos* of speech (in the previous passage, 3:1-12) and the *topos* of envy (in the present passage, 3:13–4:10). For this reason 3:13–4:10 is judged to be a single unit as it deals clearly and systematically with the topic of envy. Attention now shifts from the teacher to the wise person. This section opens with the rhetorical question: "Who among you is wise and understanding?" (3:13) and introduces the argument that a believer's whole life must demonstrate works/deeds that are inspired by wisdom from above (3:13).

True disciples know that it is characteristic of truly righteous persons to be inspired by divine wisdom. In this way they show dependence on God. James illustrates a twofold lifestyle for his readers: the one is led without the wisdom from above and is characterized by a life full of "bitter jealousy and selfish ambition" (3:14), which is "earthly, unspiritual, demonic" (3:15). In contrast to this "non-wisdom," James sketches a lifestyle influenced by true wisdom from above (3:17): it is "pure, peaceable, gentle, compliant, full of mercy and good fruits, without inconstancy or insincerity" (3:17). Jesus taught in Matthew's Sermon on the Mount that "by their fruits you will know them" (Matt 7:16). Genuine believers will always exhibit wisdom by the kind of life they lead, which will bring them righteousness (3:18).

James continues to expand the argument by developing this *topos* of envy (jealousy) in 4:1-10. His reference to conflicts and wars (4:1) is characteristic of this *topos* of envy. James is not saying that wars and conflicts have occurred within his community. Instead, he is using a rhetorical device to draw attention to the consequences of envy. James 4:2 is a difficult verse to translate. The New Revised Standard Version (NRSV) offers a more logical option than the New American Bible (NAB): "You want something and do not have it; so you commit murder. And you covet something and cannot obtain it; so you engage in disputes and conflicts." The reason for preferring this translation to the NAB comes from the reference "You kill (murder)." In the NAB translation (see text above) this phrase stands on its own, whereas in the NRSV translation it is understood as a consequence of the inordinate desire of envy, which is the main theme of this whole section.

The heart of James's letter occurs in 4:4 with the contrast drawn between friendship with the world and friendship with God. A choice is given to the hearer/reader: you have to decide between friendship with God or with the world. This reaches back to the opening of the letter (1:8), where reference was made to the "man of two minds." Jesus offers the same choice in the Sermon on the Mount: "You cannot serve God and mammon" (Matt 6:24). The opening word of 4:4 ("Adulterers") underscores the seriousness of this choice, since it recalls breaking the covenant relationship between God and God's people. Throughout the Hebrew Scriptures the breaking of the covenant relationship is compared to the rupture of the marriage bond through adultery.

As he has done previously, James offers two scriptural quotations to support his argument. The first quotation (4:5) is difficult to identify: "The spirit that he has made to dwell in us tends toward jealousy." Probably James is quoting a text from memory, which makes identification difficult. James adds a second quotation: "God resists the proud, / but gives grace to the humble" (4:6, which comes from Proverbs 3:34).

From discussing the causes of strife, James turns attention to its remedies (4:7-10). One is asked to submit to God and to resist the devil (4:7). The call to "cleanse your hands . . . and purify your hearts" (4:8) symbolizes a call to pay attention to both actions ("hands") and thoughts ("hearts"). See Sirach 38:10: "Let your hands be just, / cleanse your heart of every sin." "You of two minds" (4:8) again refers to 1:8 and 4:4: you cannot vacillate in allegiance to God. James con-

cludes his argument (4:10) with a saying that is reminiscent of the Jesus saying: "Whoever exalts himself will be humbled; but whoever humbles himself will be exalted" (Matt 23:12; see Luke 14:11; 18:14). Humility is not a social condition but a moral and spiritual one.

4:11-12 Speaking evil against another

For the third time James returns to the theme of speech (see 1:26; 3:1-12). Those who set themselves over against their brothers and sisters by criticizing and judging them also speak against the law and pass judgment on the law. Jesus utters similar instructions not to judge another in the Sermon on the Mount (Matt 7:1). Slander is a serious breach of the command to love one's neighbor (2:8; see also Lev 19:16-18). God is the lawgiver, and humanity is called to be a doer of the law. The concept of God as lawgiver and judge is fundamental to the Hebrew Scriptures. Humanity must be careful not to usurp God's role. James sums up the argument with a rhetorical question: "Who then are you to judge your neighbor?" (4:12). Paul asks a similar question in Romans 14:4: "Who are you to pass judgment on someone else's servant?"

4:13–5:6 Judgment on the rich because of friendship with the world

Here James reflects on a major theme in this letter: the choice between friendship with the world and friendship with God. Two examples (4:13-17; 5:1-6) show how a choice for the world leads to certain consequences. James returns to the theme of the rich for the final time (see 1:9-11; 2:1-13). Merchants are viewed as examples of those who seek friendship with the world (4:13-17). James condemns them for their presumption in laying plans without any reference to God or God's will (4:15). James concludes with a statement that implies responsibility for one's actions (4:17).

In 5:1-6 James changes focus from merchants to the rich, landowning class. When James calls upon the rich to "weep and wail over your impending miseries" (5:1), he is not addressing them (the rich) directly, but his own community. As with the prophets before him, this exhortation is intended to encourage the hearers/readers to remain faithful by showing what is about to befall those outside the community (namely the rich).

James's first attack is against the substance of the rich persons' wealth: it is valueless (5:2-3). In mentioning the coming misfortunes, the author presents them as having already occurred: their garments are damaged; their gold and silver have been destroyed. Matthew 6:19-20 (Luke 12:33-34) presents an interesting parallel to this text: "Do not store up for yourselves treasures on earth, where moth and decay destroy, and thieves break in and steal. But store up treasures in heaven, where neither moth nor decay destroys, nor thieves break in and steal. For where your treasure is, there also will your heart be."

James levels three accusations against the rich: they have defrauded the day-laborers out of their just wage (5:4); they have lived their lives in luxury and self-indulgence; and they have brought the innocent or "righteous one" into court for trial, so that he has been condemned (5:6). Once again the rejection of God's power forms the basic indictment James levels against the rich. They have made a choice for friendship with the world and have usurped everything to suit their own prosperity. The rich have yet to discover and experience the reality of God's power acting on behalf of the poor and oppressed (5:4). The oppressed do not resort to violence; instead they place their confidence in God's judgment at the end of time (5:5-6). This passage brings the body of James's letter to an end.

5:7-11 Call to patient endurance

In concluding the letter (5:7-20), James does not use the customary method of ending letters. Instead, he uses other approaches also evident in Hellenistic letters. In this passage the theme of eschatology is taken up. Many New Testament letters contain eschatological references in their conclusions (see 1 Cor 16:22; 2 Pet 3:12-14; and Jude 18-21).

At the same time James connects back to themes that appeared explicitly in the introductory section, namely, steadfastness and endurance during trial (1:2-4 and 1:12-18). He urges the readers to have patient endurance until "the coming of the Lord" (5:7). This reference speaks of an imminent expectation for Jesus' coming at the end of time: "Behold, the Judge is standing before the gates" (5:9). This would indicate an early date for the writing. James helps his readers to see themselves as belonging to that long line of witnesses, the prophets, who remained ever faithful and persevered in their allegiance to the Lord (5:10).

They are a prophetic community with values different from those of the world.

A second example of faithful perseverance is offered, namely, that of Job (5:11). James shows a reliance on the way the traditions about Job had developed in the intertestamental period, that is, the period of two centuries between the composition of the last book of the Old Testament and the first book of the New Testament. In the biblical book bearing his name, Job is hardly a patient person. However, in the intertestamental period (see the *Testament of Job* 1:5; 4:6; 27:6-7) he is presented this way. James uses this popular image of Job to challenge his hearers/readers to a life of patience and perseverance when faced with their own suffering and trials.

5:12 Call to avoid taking oaths

In this single verse James condemns the taking of oaths and appeals once again to his readers to examine their speech (see 1:26; 3:5-12; 4:11-12). In the Christian community one's word should be one's bond. There should be no need for taking oaths, since one should be able to presume truthfulness. The words "either by heaven or by earth" are substitutes for the original form of the oath and are used intentionally to avoid the validity of the oath, and hence its binding force. Jesus in the Sermon on the Mount speaks similarly about avoiding the taking of oaths (Matt 5:33-37).

5:13-18 Prayer

This concentration on the theme of prayer forms a fitting end to the letter, creating an "inclusion" with the opening, that is, the repetition, at the end of a section, of a word or phrase used at its beginning—in this case, prayer. In 1:5 James spoke about asking God for wisdom; now he argues that the way to obtain wisdom is through prayer. Not only is prayer the major theme of this section, but the various words for prayer are the controlling structural elements in its development. In every situation and need the appropriate response is that of prayer. In both suffering and joy people should raise their voices to God in prayer (5:13). The response of the sick is to call in the presbyters (or elders) of the church (5:14-15), who will pray over them and anoint them with oil in the name of the Lord.

James must be reflecting here some ritual in use in his community. Anointing with oil reminds the hearer/reader of the disciples' anointing the sick and casting out demons with the use of oil (Mark 6:13). When ill, one turns to God and asks the support of the community in praying to God for healing. The power of prayer cannot be measured.

Finally, Elijah, the prophet, is portrayed as a man of prayer. The effectiveness of Elijah is not related to any superhuman gifts or qualities he possessed, but to the fact that he prayed with great intensity and sincerity (5:17-18).

5:19-20 The great commission

The letter concludes somewhat abruptly with an admonition to bring back those who err from the error of their ways. 1 John 5:16 and Jude 22-23 also call on the community to pray that those who sin will change their ways. These three writings (James, 1 John, and Jude) bear witness to the existence of other ways of concluding ancient letters. Once again the community dimension of the letter shines through. Every member of the community shares a responsibility for one another. The commission with which James entrusts his hearers/readers is one that is confined to his own community. James wishes to ensure that those who belong to his community continue to remain true to their commitment. The call to conversion brings together everything that has been said throughout the letter. The hearers/readers are to take the author's instructions and put them into practice. The letter ends on a high note of confidence and assurance in the work of God's salvation.

THE FIRST LETTER OF

PETER

Patrick J. Hartin

INTRODUCTION

Author

The writer identifies himself as "Peter, an apostle of Jesus Christ" (1:1). He also says that he was a witness to Christ's sufferings (5:1) and shares "in the glory to be revealed" (5:1). Although he addresses fellow elders (literally "presbyters"; 5:1), he speaks with authority, showing that he holds a position in the early Christian church that makes his voice respected.

At first glance the identification of the author with Peter, leader of the Twelve and witness to Christ's sufferings, seems justified. His position of authority within the early Christian community, his knowledge and use of the Old Testament, his association with both Silvanus and Mark as well as with the city of Rome—all these agree with what is known about Peter.

However, two major difficulties call this identification into question: *(a) the outstanding quality of the Greek* makes it among the best in the New Testament; *(b) the letter's theology bears a resemblance to Paul's theological ideas*, for example, some typical Pauline phrases appear: *in Christ* (3:16; 5:10, 14); *to serve* (1:12; 4:10). Paul's underlying stress on the importance of Jesus' death and resurrection is also well reflected in the thought of First Peter.

The above arguments militate against the writing coming directly from Peter. As with the letter of James, the writer invokes Peter's authority to resolve issues that had arisen after the apostle's death (A.D. 64). The letter probably originated from a circle of Peter's disciples in Rome, using the help of Silvanus and Mark (5:12-13), who account for some themes that were at home in Paul's thought. The letter was probably written in the early seventies, shortly after the destruction of Jerusalem in A.D. 70. The reference to Rome in a symbolic way as "Babylon" (5:13) would be a veiled reference to the Roman destruction of the city of Jerusalem (just as Babylon some five centuries earlier had destroyed Jerusalem). The attitude toward the state that First Peter endorses is very similar to Paul's views as expressed in Romans 13:1-7: they both uphold the state's authority (see 1 Pet 2:13-17).

Hearers/readers

The first letter of Peter identifies the hearers/readers as "the chosen sojourners of the dispersion in Pontus, Galatia, Cappadocia, Asia, and Bithynia" (1:1). The letter uses the reference to the dispersion differently from the way it occurs in the letter of James, where it refers to the scattering of Jewish-Christians outside the land of Palestine. In First Peter the term is used metaphorically, referring to Gentile Christians, who, as God's own people (2:9), are scattered like strangers in this world. Their real homeland is not here but in heaven. The places mentioned (Pontus, Galatia, Cappadocia, Asia, and Bithynia) are names for Roman provinces situated in the northern, central, and western parts of Asia Minor north of the Taurus Mountains. This territory covered an area of some 128,000 square miles. The address (1:1) indicates that this letter was meant to be circulated throughout the provinces of this region. The sequence of names probably indicates the route along which this letter would be circulated.

Major themes

First Peter is a very pastoral letter. The writer aims at strengthening the faith of his hearers/readers. He begins by recalling the Christian hope and inheritance based upon Jesus' resurrection from the dead (1:3-7). Jesus' sufferings are pre-

sented as a model for the hearers/readers, who themselves are enduring hostilities and suffering. They can be certain that just as Jesus' sufferings led to glory, so will theirs (1:11). The letter uses some remarkable imagery to describe the dignity of Christian believers: they are true heirs of the inheritance of God's people, Israel: the community is "a living stone" (2:5); "a chosen race, a royal priesthood, a holy nation, a people of his [God's] own" (2:9). This vision of their identity helps them face the challenges of living in a hostile world. Drawing upon well-known household codes, the writer gives direction on how to lead faithful Christian lives within this context.

COMMENTARY

1:1-2 Greetings

The writer opens the letter using the traditional Greco-Roman formula for a letter that identifies the sender, mentions the recipients, and concludes with a form of greeting. Referring to himself as "Peter, an apostle of Jesus Christ," the writer identifies himself with the leader of the original apostles (Mark 3:16). While the apostle Peter is unlikely to have actually written this letter himself (see Introduction, p. 784), the writer invokes Peter's authority for this letter. It is in this sense that this commentary refers to the author as Peter.

The readers are identified as "the chosen sojourners of the dispersion." The "dispersion," or Diaspora, is a technical term referring to Jews living outside their homeland, Palestine. However, the implied readers are certainly not Jews, nor are they Jewish Christians; rather, they are Christians who have come from the Gentile world. As such, this designation should be understood metaphorically as referring to Gentile Christians, who are "sojourners" here on earth, exiles from their true homeland in heaven. The writer uses the term "dispersion" differently from its usage in James 1:1.

The location of the recipients is more specifically identified as "Pontus, Galatia, Cappadocia, Asia, and Bithynia," names of Roman provinces in Asia Minor. The concept of "sojourners" im-

plies that the way of life of these followers of Jesus is different from that of the world around them. They are also called "chosen sojourners," indicating that their identity comes from God's choice of them to become part of God's people. The writer refers to this same concept later when he identifies them as "a chosen race, a royal priesthood, a holy nation, a people of his own" (2:9), using the words of the Exodus covenant (see Exod 19:6).

Finally, the writer mentions the role of the Father, the Spirit, and Jesus Christ in the work of salvation. In doing so, he shows the basis for their identity as God's chosen ones: their choice is founded upon the Father's "foreknowledge" (1:2), particularly the Father's will and intention, to make them into his new people. God's choice of them also involves their "sanctification by the Spirit" (1:2), whose power enables them to lead their lives according to their new dignity. God's choice also includes their "sprinkling with the blood of Jesus Christ" (1:2). Just as Moses ratified the covenant of Sinai with the blood that he sprinkled on the altar (symbolizing God) and the people (Exod 24:3-8), now the new covenant is ratified with Jesus' blood that is sprinkled upon these hearers/readers. This phrase also prepares the reader for one of the major themes that runs throughout this letter, namely, the redemptive work of Jesus and its significance for believers (see 1:18-21; 2:21, 24; 3:18; 4:1, 11). The writer concludes with a prayer that grace and peace be multiplied among the hearers/readers.

1:3-12 Praise for salvation given by the Father, through the Son, and by the Spirit

In place of the traditional thanksgiving section found in Paul's letters, the writer immediately moves to the body of the letter. In the first part of the body the author reflects on the theme of the believer's identity (1:3–2:10). He begins by praising God the Father for the great gift of salvation. This blessing bears notable similarities to the opening of the letter to the Ephesians: "Blessed be the God and Father of our Lord Jesus Christ, who has blessed us in Christ with every spiritual blessing in the heavens" (Eph 1:3). The hearers/readers are reminded that they have been born to a new life through Jesus' resurrection (1 Pet 1:3).

This metaphor of new birth (1:3) has led some commentators to see this as a reference to baptism and to postulate that this writing was based upon an original baptismal homily. While this reads too much into the metaphor, the theology of baptism certainly influences this writer's thought. This new birth gives rise to the hope in an imperishable inheritance in heaven (1:3-5), and for this God is protecting them (1:5). The future hope is contrasted with their present experiences of suffering (1:6), which reveals the genuineness of their faith (1:7). Like precious gold that is purified by fire, so their new faith experiences testing or purification in order to prepare them for the coming of Jesus Christ (1:7).

The writer reminds the hearers/readers, who have not seen Jesus, how they love him and believe in him (1:8). Long ago the prophets of the Hebrew Scriptures foretold this salvation for which the believers are now hoping (1:10). These prophets were led by the Spirit to announce the message of the sufferings of Christ and his subsequent glory (1:11). The prophets show that the path from suffering to glory is the center of Jesus' saving work and the heart of the Christian way of life. This message clearly speaks to Peter's present readers, who are experiencing sufferings and trials. It reminds them that their rebirth in faith is more precious than gold, that it was foretold in the past and looks forward to a future glory.

1:13–2:3 Call to lead a holy life

The hearers/readers need also to respond to the new life they have received through a life that is worthy of their faith (1:13-14). Holiness should dominate their lives. The imagery of the Passover seems to lie behind this section. At Sinai, the LORD God was identified as the Holy One, who called on the Israelites to be holy: "For I, the LORD, am your God; and you shall make and keep yourselves holy, because I am holy" (Lev 11:44; 19:2). First Peter quotes this text and addresses the same call to holiness to his hearers/readers: they are to imitate God in all their actions (1:16). To be holy means to be different, to be set apart. The Israelites were a nation set apart for the worship of God alone. The same is true of Christians: they are called to be different in that their way of life sets them apart from the nations around them (as the writer indicated in the opening of the letter when he referred to them as "sojourners" [1:1]). Their values do not come from the world, but have God as their source. Their new life of holiness enables them to address God as "Father," which inspires an attitude of "reverence" (1:17) for the mystery of God's love and rule over all.

The author goes on to remind the hearers/readers of certain truths they have accepted. Continuing with the Passover theme, he reminds them that just as the Israelites were ransomed from slavery, so have they been ransomed "with the precious blood of Christ" (1:19), not with precious metals "like silver or gold" (1:18). They have been ransomed from the futile way of life they inherited from their pagan ancestors (1:18). First Peter compares the work of Jesus to that of "a spotless unblemished lamb" (1:19): they have received their redemption through the blood of the spotless lamb (Isa 53:7-10). This is a further reminder of the Passover motif (Exod 12:1-30). Through his death, Jesus has ransomed Christians, enabling them to place their trust, their faith, and their hope in God (1:21).

The author repeats many of the themes introduced at the beginning of the letter (1:22–2:3). They are called to "love one another intensely" (1:22). This love is a response to Christ's work, which planted "the imperishable seed" in them (1:23). In support, the author quotes Isaiah 40:6-8, which contrasts the frailty and transitory nature of human life and its accomplishments with the word of the Lord, which remains forever (1:24-25).

Their faith endures forever because God is trust-worthy. Their growth in new life involves two dimensions: first of all, the stripping away of all vices (2:1) hindering that growth, and the nourishment and enjoyment of the new life they have received (2:2-3). The author concludes with an allusion to Psalm 34:9: "Taste and see how good the LORD is; / happy the man who takes refuge in him."

2:4-10 A holy people

Two metaphors dominate this passage: that of a living stone (2:4-8) and that of a people (2:9-10). The author uses numerous texts from the Hebrew Scriptures to illustrate his vision. The image of a living stone is applied to his hearers/readers. While humanity has rejected them, God has specially chosen them as "living stones" (2:5). They should allow God to build them into a spiritual household to become a holy priesthood able to offer acceptable sacrifices to God through Jesus Christ (2:4-5) who is a "living stone" (2:4).

Three quotations from the Hebrew Scriptures illustrate the meaning. Christ is the "cornerstone" or foundation stone (see Isa 28:16), and whoever places trust in him will be supported (2:6). Further, this living stone (which is Christ) was rejected (2:7) but has become the cornerstone (see Ps 118:22). Finally, he uses Isaiah 8:14 very freely to indicate how Jesus becomes an obstacle and a stumbling block for some (2:8). This metaphor of the living stone and its supportive Hebrew Scripture texts illustrates two things: it shows, first of all, how Jesus Christ is the model for the believing community: just like Jesus, believers are chosen by God but rejected by humanity, especially the world of the pagans. Secondly, since Christ is the cornerstone and foundation for faith, believers are being built in him into a spiritual house as a holy priesthood offering true spiritual worship to God (2:5).

The second metaphor of a holy people (2:9-10) expressing the true identity of Christian believers is revealed in four phrases: a chosen race, a royal priesthood, a holy nation, God's own people. These phrases are all derived from Exodus 19:5-6. Christians as God's possession give worship to God through the power of Jesus' death and resurrection. Their most important characteristic is that they have become "God's people," just as Israel of old was chosen as God's people (2:10). Reflect-

ing on Hosea 1:6-9 and 2:25, the writer proclaims that the readers were originally separated far from God, but now they have been brought into God's household to become God's people (2:10).

2:11-12 Conduct in a pagan environment

The author now begins a second major theme of the letter, namely, the Christian life of witness in the context of a Gentile world (2:11–4:11). The readers are to consider themselves as "aliens and sojourners" in this present world (2:11). Since their true homeland is to be found in heaven (1:1), they are to conduct themselves in this world as though they are just passing through. Their way of life should bear witness to their beliefs among Gentiles (2:12). Even though Gentiles abuse them, Christians are called to respond in a manner worthy of their beliefs. This witness should bring the Gentiles to revise their view of Christians and ultimately to confess and praise their God at the end of time.

2:13-17 Respect for civil authorities

This passage considers the principles outlined above (2:11-12), which called believers to lead lives as "aliens and sojourners" in this world. This is not a call for believers to become a withdrawal sect such as the Qumran community; rather, Christians are called upon to honor civil authorities. Belief in the Lord Jesus should lead Christians to accept the authority of the emperor and governors, acknowledging their right to punish wrongdoers and to reward those who act for good (2:13-14). This witness should silence those who are suspicious of Christians (2:15; see 2:12). The best answer to those hostile to the Christian community is the life-witness of obedient Christians (2:15). Baptism has set believers free from the stipulations of the Jewish Torah (as Paul indicates forcefully in Gal 3:23-27), as well as from slavery to the elemental powers of the world (in the context of a pagan world [Col 2:20-23]). This freedom is not a freedom for license, but a freedom to lead one's life under God's rule (2:16).

The first letter of Peter upholds a positive relationship between Christians and the state; Christians are urged to acknowledge and to give honor to all: the community, God, and the emperor as supreme ruler (2:17). The letter gives expression to a consciousness of the Christian's double obligation of fulfilling God's will as well as the demands of political authority. It is the same issue addressed in the saying of Jesus: "Repay to Caesar what belongs to Caesar and to God what belongs to God" (Mark 12:17). Clearly, First Peter reflects a situation very different from that of the book of Revelation, where Christians are being persecuted by the state for not participating in emperor worship, a context that First Peter does not envisage here. The thoughts of First Peter are very similar to those found in Romans 13:1-7, which may indicate evidence of a common tradition that both First Peter and Paul are using independently.

2:18–3:7 Household instructions

First Peter uses the literary form of "household codes" to express his instructions. A number of such codes or lists appear in the New Testament letters (for example, Col 3:18–4:1; Eph 5:21–6:9; 1 Tim 2:8-15; 5:1-2; 6:1-2; and here 1 Pet 2:18–3:7). These lists describe the ethical obligations members of a household have toward one another. Such lists embrace every possible relationship within society and were very popular among the philosophers of that time.

The developing Christian communities drew up similar ethical lists depicting the way their members should interact with one another as well as with every level of society. The need for such directions was felt most urgently in largely Gentile Christian communities. They wanted to witness to their faith in Jesus Christ in such a way that the wider society would see their faith influencing them to become valuable citizens within society. These lists are an illustration of how the Lordship of Jesus Christ transforms the lives of believers to affect every relationship and to attract others to make a similar confession in the Lord Jesus Christ. In this household list First Peter gives attention to the relationships of slaves, wives, and husbands. When interpreting these household codes, they must be read in the context of their own world and not simply transposed into a twenty-first-century society that would describe these relationships very differently.

2:18-25 Attitude of slaves toward their masters

According to First Peter, belief in God should lead slaves to accept their masters' authority and to endure suffering even when innocent (2:18-19).

First Peter differs from the traditional advice to slaves by focusing on the difficult lot of slaves and by considering situations where they suffer unjustly. They are invited to view their unjust sufferings in the light of the unjust suffering of Christ. In such situations, they are called to unite with the sufferings of Christ by following the example that he set. The description of the suffering and death of Christ on our behalf (2:22-24) is presented in terms of the Suffering Servant of Isaiah 52:13–53:12. Christian slaves are called upon to live out their commitment to Christ in a concrete way by imitating his suffering. Christ obtained salvation through suffering for sinners, so Christian slaves can bring others to salvation through the witness of their sufferings. No mention is made here of the responsibilities of masters toward their slaves!

3:1-7 Attitude of wives and husbands

First Peter continues the household code with reference to wives and husbands. Again its thoughts are rooted in the social structure and attitudes of the first century A.D. Christian wives are instructed on how to relate to their husbands who are not believers (3:1). By the witness of their lives and through their belief in Christ, they hope ultimately to win over their husbands to the Christian faith (3:1-2). The wives' concern should not focus on extravagant externals, such as "braiding the hair, gold jewelry, or dressing in fine clothes" (3:3); instead, they should cultivate a gentle internal disposition at peace with God and one another (3:4). Reaching back into the tradition of the Hebrew Scriptures, First Peter holds up Sarah for imitation because of the way in which she respected Abraham by calling him "lord" or "master" (3:6; see Gen 18:12 LXX), a term that indicates respect and honor for the husband. Likewise the wives of pagan husbands should demonstrate respect and honor for their husbands, showing that they are daughters of Sarah (3:6). Abraham and Sarah were important figures in the world of early Christianity (Rom 4:19-25; 9:9; Gal 4:22-31).

Husbands are also instructed to examine their relationship with their wives (3:7). While the cultural view of women dominates this picture ("showing honor to the weaker female sex"), yet the equality of women with men is acknowledged, since in the life of Christ "we are joint heirs of the gift of life" (3:7; see also Gal 3:28: "There is neither Jew nor Greek, there is neither slave nor free person, there is not male and female; for you are all one in Christ Jesus"). First Peter shows that proper relationships cannot be separated from a relationship with God that is expressed in prayer (3:7).

3:8-12 General advice to the whole community

This section brings the household instructions to an end. Generally, household codes would turn to consider the relationship of parents and children at this point. Instead, First Peter turns attention to relationships within the entire community and urges unity and love for one another so that their way of life will truly reflect a Christian community (3:8). Instead of returning evil for evil, they are called to react with a blessing (3:9). That is the way Jesus acted, and they are called to act in like manner (see 2:21-25). Their unity with Christ gives direction to the way they lead their lives. First Peter quotes Psalm 34:13-17 to remind the community that "whoever would love life . . . must turn from evil and do good" (3:10-11).

3:13-17 Christian attitude toward suffering

The Christian is exhorted to have confidence in the midst of suffering. The sufferings envisaged here do not necessarily point to some state persecution, as was the case with the book of Revelation. It seems that Gentiles living in the same society with Christians cannot understand their lifestyle and values. The Gentiles respond with abuse and ridicule, and ostracize them because of their commitment to the Lord Jesus, but this should not cause them to be afraid (3:14). When challenged, Christians should be ready to witness to their faith (3:15). First Peter calls on Christians to make their defense in gentleness and with respect, while being willing to accept suffering, if that is God's will (3:16-17).

3:18-22 Example of Christ

Jesus suffered as an innocent person for the guilty. His death is the reason the hearers/readers and indeed all Christians are now able to approach God (3:18). His suffering led to the ultimate experience of death. But death was not the end. He "was brought to life in the spirit" (3:18)

and went "to preach to the spirits in prison" (3:19). It is not too clear who these spirits were. Possibly First Peter has in mind an interpretation of Genesis 6:1-4, where evil angels were held responsible for leading humanity astray into an ever greater wickedness that ultimately provoked God's righteous judgment in sending the flood. These evil angels were imprisoned in a pit after their sin with women. Jesus' proclamation to them by his death and resurrection is a way of demonstrating his victory over the forces of evil: these evil spirits no longer have power over humanity.

This example of Christ's suffering and consequent triumph in the resurrection gives hope to Christians who innocently endure suffering and persecution. Because Christ's triumph over evil is complete, Christians have nothing to fear. Christ has redeemed them from the powers of evil and death and has given them future hope through their new birth in Christ. Reference to Noah (3:20) is also significant. First Peter argues that just as God rescued the faithful Noah from the evil world by means of water, so too God liberates faithful Christians from the evils of their world by means of the waters of baptism (3:21). Jesus' resurrection makes the waters of baptism effective and brings salvation to those who accept it (3:21). Through his resurrection, Jesus Christ shares God's power, and all authority in the universe is subjected to him (3:22). Behind this beautiful description of the saving work of Christ lies a creedal formula in use in the early church. Not only does First Peter use the Hebrew Scriptures as a source to support his teaching, he also uses the language of the liturgy that permeates the Christian community:

> Put to death in the flesh, brought to life in the spirit, he went to preach to the spirits in prison, and having gone into heaven, he is at the right hand of God, making angels, authorities and powers subject to him (3:18, 19, 22; see also 1 Tim 3:16).

This passage has enormous importance for Christian believers. Just as Christ's death brings life, so too Christian suffering is considered life-generating. Christians participate in Christ's death and resurrection through baptism. As Christ "was put to death in the flesh" and "was brought to life in the spirit" (3:18), so Christians die to their sins and are made alive in the spirit through baptism. Christian believers are made aware that they share both in Christ's sufferings and in his resurrection.

4:1-6 Christians live according to God's will

First Peter connects back to the previous section by stressing that Christians who lead a life of suffering with Christ are also dedicated to avoiding a life of sin (4:1) and living according to God's will (4:2). Their lifestyle distances them from the way of life of their Gentile neighbors. First Peter presents a list of vices (4:3) similar to the lists that Paul used in his letters (see Rom 1:29-31; 1 Tim 1:9-10; 2 Tim 3:2-5). The vices described here reflect the type of feasts that pagans used to celebrate. Before becoming Christians, First Peter's hearers/readers used to participate in these celebrations, but now, having embraced Christ and become God's people, they distance themselves from such activities (4:4).

Further, First Peter envisages a preaching of the good news to those who have died (4:6). While Peter does not mention who does the preaching, it seems that he has 3:18-20 in mind, where Jesus preaches after his death. This time, however, the preaching is not to the powers of evil but to those who have died. While the exact reference of "the dead" is disputed, the best explanation is that "the dead" are Christians who had heard and accepted the gospel message but subsequently died before Christ's return.

For early Christians this was an enormous problem, since many believed that Christ would return during their own lifetime. Here First Peter assures his hearers/believers that while in the eyes of the world these Christians have ended up in death in the same way as those who have not believed ("condemned in the flesh in human estimation"), they now share in Christ's triumph over death through resurrection ("they might live in the spirit in the estimation of God," 4:6). First Peter assures his hearers/readers that as Christ triumphed over the powers of evil (3:18-22), so those who believed in him and his message would share with him in that triumph in the resurrection.

4:7-11 Living with the expectation of the end time

With this passage the author brings to an end the second major theme of the letter, namely, the Christian life of witness in the context of a Gentile world (2:11–4:11). First Peter reminds the hearers/readers that the eschatological hour is near (4:7). Consequently, the community must lead its life marked by prayer (4:7), love (4:8), hospitality (4:9), and service of one another (4:10). First Peter presents love as the central virtue "because love covers a multitude of sins" (4:8). This maxim appears in the Hebrew Scriptures (Prov 10:12; Ps 32:1), as well as elsewhere in the New Testament (Jas 5:20) and in early Christian literature (*1 Clem* 50:5).

First Peter's quotation of Proverbs 10:12 is closer to the Hebrew text, although he usually quotes from the Greek translation (LXX). This could indicate that he is relying upon the way in which it was being quoted in early Christian tradition. While the exact meaning of this proverb is somewhat vague, the general intent is clear: in loving others one fulfills the essence of the gospel call to love God and neighbor. Consequently, one experiences God's forgiveness for all sins. This passage culminates in a doxology to the praise of God (4:11).

4:12-19 Suffering as a Christian

The writer begins the third and final section of the letter (4:12–5:11) taking up themes that were introduced elsewhere in the letter. All the themes bear a strong eschatological emphasis. First Peter 4:12 returns to the theme of suffering that has dominated the letter. The readers are invited to see their sufferings as a purification (4:12) and as a sharing in Christ's sufferings (4:13). That should be cause for rejoicing, because those who have suffered are promised that they will share in Christ's glory (4:14). The present sufferings initiate the eschatological judgment within God's household (4:17). The prospect of suffering should not cause fear among Christians; rather, it should be seen to be "in accord with God's will" (4:19), and consequently they should place themselves in the care of their ever "faithful creator" (4:19).

5:1-5 Exhortation to the leaders of the community

The author identifies himself as a "fellow presbyter and witness to the sufferings of Christ" (5:1). The term "presbyter" or "elder" reflects the Jewish world, where the leaders of the community were identified by this term. It referred not simply to age but rather to the role exercised by leaders within a community. As such, First Peter exhorts his fellow elders (or leaders) to take care of the community that has been entrusted to them (5:1-2).

In offering advice to the elders, the writer uses traditional imagery. Earlier in the letter First Peter had referred to Christ as the "shepherd and guardian of your souls" (2:25). Now the leaders of the community are called to care for "the flock of God" that has been entrusted to them (5:2). First Peter defines the type of leadership they should exercise through a number of contrasts: they should carry out their leadership role "willingly" (not "by constraint") (5:2). They should not be inspired by greed, but by a desire for service (5:2). Finally, they should "not lord it over" those in their care, but should be examples to the community ("the flock," 5:3). Finally, First Peter uses the image of Christ the shepherd to encourage them to act like shepherds toward those entrusted to their care (4:4). This brings the author to address a universal appeal to the members of the community: "God opposes the proud, but bestows favor on the humble" (4:5; see Prov 3:34).

5:6-11 Final exhortations: trust God

This section draws the body of the letter to a conclusion. The readers are called to humble themselves (5:6); to cast all their anxiety upon God (5:7), to keep alert (5:8). The devil, like a roaring lion (see Ps 22:14), is inciting the Gentiles to persecute the Christians. What First Peter's readers are experiencing is not unique, because Christians throughout the world are enduring similar sufferings and persecutions (5:9). A doxology concludes the body of the letter. The author promises that Christ will support and strengthen them in this struggle (5:10-11).

5:12-14 Final greeting

The letter concludes in the traditional way with personal greetings. Silvanus is identified either as the bearer of the letter or the one who acted as Peter's scribe in writing it (5:12). Greetings are sent from "the chosen one at Babylon" (5:13), referring to the church in Rome (see Introduction, p. 784; the book of Revelation also refers to Rome as Babylon in 14:8; 17:5; 18:2). Greetings also comes from "Mark, my son," referring probably to John Mark from Jerusalem (Acts 12:12-17) and indicating that Peter was responsible for his conversion to the Christian faith ("my son," 5:13). The Christian greeting "Peace to all of you who are in Christ" concludes the letter.

THE SECOND LETTER OF
PETER

Patrick J. Hartin

INTRODUCTION

Relationship between Second Peter and Jude

Virtually the whole of the letter of Jude is incorporated into Second Peter. Of Jude's twenty-five verses, no less than nineteen reappear in some form in Second Peter. A brief overview of this relationship can be seen from the following chart:

- 2 Peter 2:1-18 reproduce Jude 4-16
- 2 Peter 3:2-3 correspond to Jude 17-18
- 2 Peter 3:14 and 18 parallel Jude 24-25
- 2 Peter 1:1-2 echo Jude 1-2

That Second Peter used the letter of Jude appears evident from the above comparison. Second Peter is not an exact reproduction of Jude, but rather an adaptation and expansion. For example, the exclusion of the references to the apocryphal books of the *Assumption of Moses* and *1 Enoch* (Jude 9 and 14-15) is more easily understandable if we imagine the writer of Second Peter deliberately dropping Jude's references because they were not universally accepted as part of Scripture.

Author

This writing states that it is from "Symeon Peter, a slave and apostle of Jesus Christ" (1:1). The author is further acknowledged to be a witness to the transfiguration (1:16-18), implying that the author is Peter. There is also a reference to First Peter (3:1). Despite these indications, it is impossible to identify the author with the apostle Peter for the following reasons: (a) *The relationship between Second Peter and Jude:* Since Jude is a late writing and Second Peter has made use of Jude, Second Peter must be even later. (b) *There are also indications that the first generation of Christians had by now passed away:* "From the time when our ancestors fell asleep" (3:4). The writer belongs either to the second or third generation of Christians. (c) *The writings of the apostle Paul have been made into a collection and are considered as Scripture:* ". . . beloved brother Paul, according to the wisdom given to him, also wrote to you, speaking of these things as he does *in all his letters.* In them there are some things hard to understand that the ignorant and unstable distort to their own destruction, just as they do *the other scriptures*" (2 Pet 3:15-16; emphasis added). (d) *Concern for the time of the second coming:* In the early decades after Jesus' death and resurrection, the first followers expected his imminent return (see 1 Cor 7:29-31). When this did not happen, the question of his return became increasingly important. We seem to be at a late period in the early church when the teaching regarding the Second Coming was under major attack.

This writing breathes an atmosphere that is at home at the end of the first century A.D. Since Peter died around A.D. 64, the apostle Peter could not have written it. As with First Peter, the author of Second Peter was probably one of Peter's disciples. He invoked Peter's authority to stress the traditional belief of the Christian faith and to correct the inroads of false teachers in areas and communities where the apostle Peter had originally taught. By invoking Peter's authority, he reminds his hearers/readers of Peter's teaching and speaks in the way Peter would have spoken in order to solve the problems these new teachers were raising. It is in this sense that this commentary refers to the author as Peter. It is best to see this letter coming from around the close of the first century or the beginning of the second century A.D.

Hearers/readers

The address is very "catholic," that is, universal: "To those who have received a faith of equal value to ours" (1:1). Since 3:1 refers to First Peter, perhaps the author is addressing the same readers in Asia Minor who are referred to in 1 Peter 1:1. It also presumes an audience that is very familiar with the writings of Paul and upholds Paul's authority (3:15-16). This indicates areas of Asia Minor where both Paul and Peter were active. The actual place of origin does not greatly matter, but since the author wrote in the name of Peter, he must have been associated with the same sphere of influence as Peter, probably Rome.

Literary form

The external form appears to be that of a letter (1:1-2). Instead of personal greetings at the end,

the writing concludes with a brief doxology (3:18). Indications of a personal relationship between the sender and the recipients, so characteristic of a letter, are also lacking.

The literary form seems to be better suited to *the form of a testament,* a type of writing very popular in Christian and Jewish circles. The setting for a testament depicts someone who bids farewell to his intimate associates. He speaks about his imminent death and offers admonitions and edifying words, preparing them for calamities that are about to come when he departs. Examples of such testamentary farewell speeches abound throughout the biblical writings. The most characteristic of these are the speeches of Jacob (Gen 47:29–49:33); Moses (Deut 29–31); Joshua (Josh 23–24); and the twelve patriarchs (in the apocryphal writing *Testaments of the Twelve Patriarchs).* In the Christian context there are the final farewell discourses of Jesus (John 13–17); and Paul (Acts 20:18-38). The writing of Second Timothy also falls into this category of a farewell testament. Since the characteristic features of a testament are all evident in this writing, it is justified in designating Second Peter as a "testament" or farewell speech that is sent (hence the letter form at the beginning) to encourage Christians to remain true to the teachings of the apostle Peter (and Paul) and to warn them against accepting the novel heresies that are currently being propagated.

COMMENTARY

1:1-2 Greetings

The writing opens with the usual epistolary features naming the author, the recipients, and extending greetings. However, these are the only specific features of the letter format. The writer identifies himself as "Symeon Peter" (1:1), using the Semitic form of his name Symeon to remind the hearers/readers that he was one of the original followers of Jesus. This form Symeon also occurs in Acts 15:14. He is further identified as "a slave and apostle of Jesus Christ" (1:1). This designation shows his relationship to Jesus as his "slave" (see commentary on Jas 1:1) as well as his

relationship to the spread of Christianity as an apostle.

The readers to whom this writing is addressed are not clearly defined: "to those who have received a faith of equal value to ours" (1:2). However, the writer stresses the essential equality between the faith of the apostles and that of the second- and third-generation Christians.

Finally, greetings are sent, using the phraseology of 1 Peter 1:2 "May grace and peace be yours in abundance." (Note a similar phrase in Jude 2: "May mercy, peace, and love be yours in abundance.") To this Second Peter adds the phrase "through knowledge of God and of Jesus our Lord" (1:2). As this is an important theme that is developed throughout this letter, it is introduced here at the beginning to draw the attention of the hearers/readers to this theme. Paul was also accustomed to use the opening greetings as a way of introducing important themes to his hearers/readers (see Rom 1:1-7).

1:3-4 Main theme announced

In place of the thanksgiving found in Paul's letters as well as Greco-Roman letters, Second Peter introduces the main ideas of this writing. God's power is the source and foundation for the Christian life. This power has communicated to believers everything they need for "life and devotion" (1:3). God has also bestowed great promises on believers (1:4), promises that are challenged by the opponents, especially those relating to the parousia (3:3-4). The whole purpose of God's promises is for believers to come "to share in the divine nature" after escaping the corruption of the world (1:4).

Second Peter is using vocabulary that is at home in the Hellenistic world to give expression to the work of God and of Christ. This shows that the writer seeks to express his thoughts in language that the Greco-Roman world would understand. This concept of sharing in the divine nature would be developed later in the writings of the church fathers to extol the concept of human divinization through the work of God and of Christ. Essentially, Second Peter is stating his theme that one overcomes the corrupting influence of this world through God's gift in Christ to share in God's nature.

1:5-11 Exhortation to remain firm in their call

The way of life of the believers is expressed through a number of virtues that the writer lists: faith, virtue, knowledge, self-control, endurance, devotion, mutual affection, love (1:5-7). The list begins with the virtue of faith and ends with love. The enumeration of virtues (and vices) was a popular way of presenting moral teaching in the Greco-Roman world. Paul reflects this mode of teaching well in his ethical instructions (e.g., Phil 4:8; 1 Tim 3:1-12). The positive exhortation is interrupted with one negative note where the author warns that whoever does not strive to embrace

these virtues is "blind and shortsighted" (1:9). This foreshadows one of the major concerns of this letter, namely, the false teachers who exemplify this spirit of blindness. For the writer, perseverance in remaining true to one's call is essential for the Christian (1:10-11).

1:12-15 Peter's testament

The writer speaks in the manner of the apostle Peter, who sees his death approaching (1:14). He wants to leave behind for his hearers/readers a reminder of what he had taught (1:15). This shows the nature of this present writing as a "testament," a very popular literary genre in the ancient world in which a famous person leaves behind a document that testifies to his enduring teaching (see Introduction, pp. 798–99). Perhaps, it would be best to identify Second Peter as a "testamentary letter." Here Peter, as the implied author, is aware that his death is imminent ("since I know that I will soon have to put it aside," 1:14). He refers to his human life as a "tent" (1:13), in the manner of Isaiah 38:12, which will be discarded in death. This letter, then, becomes a way in which Peter can remain with them after death: "I will always remind you of these things" (1:12); "to stir you up by a reminder" (1:13); "I shall also make every effort to enable you always to remember these things after my departure" (1:15).

1:16-21 Defense of prophecy concerning Jesus' second coming

In traditional testaments, reference to the leader's life would be given as an example for his hearers/readers. This section does exactly this by referring to events in Peter's life, such as being a witness to the transfiguration (1:17). This aspect of a testament will recur again in 3:1-3. This section gives attention to the major reason for this writing: to present Peter's defense against false teachers. The traditional faith of the community is under attack. The essence of the attack relates to belief in Jesus' second coming (*parousia*). Peter defends his (and his fellow apostles') proclamation against two charges by the opponents: the second coming of Christ is a myth (1:16-18), and the prophecy of the second coming is not a true prophecy (1:20-21).

Second Peter denies both charges. In the first instance, the second coming is not based on "cleverly devised myths" (1:16), but on preaching that was based upon eyewitness experiences of God's own revelation when God testified to Jesus as God's own Son at the transfiguration (1:17). The appeal to the authority of the transfiguration serves as a defense for the teaching on the parousia (second coming). The transfiguration foreshadows the second coming of Jesus.

The second defense (1:20-21) concerns the truth of prophecy. The writer presents a memorable definition of biblical prophecy: ". . . *there is no prophecy of scripture that is a matter of personal interpretation, for no prophecy ever came through human will; but rather human beings moved by the holy Spirit spoke under the influence of God*" (1:20-21; emphasis added). For Second Peter, the interpretation of prophecy must rest upon a communal understanding rather than simply an individual feeling. The divine inspiration of the Hebrew Scriptures is clearly attested. The Hebrew prophets were divinely inspired witnesses to the coming of the Lord (1:21).

2:1-10a Defense against the false teachers

A characteristic feature of the genre of a testament is that a leader makes prophecies about the future. Second Peter presents the apostle Peter looking into the future and foreseeing the emergence of false teachers (2:1). While the characteristic of a testament was to present the prophecy (in this instance, the coming of false teachers) as an event to come in the future, it becomes clear from the rest of this chapter that these false teachers are already a problem within the community. The writer compares the false teachers that have appeared in their midst to the false prophets in the Hebrew Scriptures (2:1). The writer offers a long illustration from the Hebrew Scriptures to show how the wicked are punished and the righteous vindicated (2:4-10a).

This lays the groundwork for the argument that the future parousia brings with it reward and punishment (3:3-10). All the illustrations are taken from the letter of Jude. In fact, nineteen of Jude's twenty-five verses are taken over by Second Peter either in their entirety or in part (see Introduction, p. 797). In this section Second Peter makes use of Jude 4-8 and changes it in a number of ways. He puts all the examples from the Hebrew Scriptures in their chronological order as they appear in the Bible: rebellious angels, the flood, and Sodom and

Gomorrah. In addition, Second Peter adds the two positive examples of Noah and Lot (2:5, 7-8) so that the hearer/reader sees clearly that God rewards those who stand up against false teachers. Second Peter argues this quite strongly in 2:9: just as God rescued the two righteous men (Noah and Lot) in the past and punished those who did evil (the rebellious angels, the people of Sodom and Gomorrah), so God will act in a similar way in the future. God will rescue "the devout" and punish "the unrighteous" (2:9), namely, those who do evil, identified later as the false teachers.

2:10b-16 Denunciation of the false teachers

The writer points out how the false teaching gives rise to an evil way of life. Again, most of this material comes from the letter of Jude 8-16 and is adapted to suit Second Peter's context. The first example (2:10b-11) concerns reviling "glorious beings," that is, the angels. The false teachers deny that the angels have any influence on humanity. Second Peter leaves out Jude's example of Michael and Satan because it does not fit his context. According to the understanding of the time, one of the roles of angels was to report to God about the actions of human beings (see Job 1:6-12). The angels should by rights have brought accusations against the false teachers before God's throne, but they did not do so (2:11).

The second example (2:12-14) shows how the immoral lives of the false teachers reflect the lives of animals rather than human beings (2:12). Second Peter seeks to warn his hearers/readers against any association with these false teachers, since they draw others into their evil ways (2:14).

The final example in this section is that of Balaam (2:15-16, taken from Jude 11). For Second Peter, the example of Balaam illustrates a false prophet who strayed from the true message. Even his donkey rebuked him (2:16; see Num 22:23-35). Balaam becomes a further example to the hearers/readers of the punishment of an evildoer.

2:17-22 Further denunciations

Second Peter accuses his opponents of being people who lack direction. They act like "waterless springs and mists driven by a gale" (2:17). In the first instance, Second Peter shows the harmful effects these false teachers have on others (2:17-19). Again the writer is relying upon Jude 12-13, 16.

The effect of their teaching is to seduce Christians, especially those who have recently converted from paganism: "Those who have barely escaped from people who live in error" (2:18). Second Peter shows the consequences of what happens when belief in the second coming of Christ is denied together with belief in reward and punishment at the last day. Since there is no final judgment, they give themselves over to a life that knows no restrictions, as is seen in leading a life devoted to the "licentious desires of the flesh" (2:18).

Second Peter then considers how the teaching of the false teachers harms themselves (2:20-22). When they became Christians, they "escaped the defilements of the world through the knowledge of [our] Lord and savior Jesus Christ" (2:20). Now their teaching has drawn them back, and their situation is worse than it was previously (2:21).

Finally, the author uses two well-known parables to arouse revulsion in the minds of his hearers/readers: he compares these false teachers to a dog that returns to its own vomit and to a sow that returns to wallow in mud (2:22). The first proverb comes from Proverbs 26:11: "As the dog returns to his vomit, / so the fool repeats his folly." In the world of the first century, a dog was not the well-received, domesticated animal of today. A "dog" was generally a word used to insult someone. So the two animals (dog and sow) would evoke the same feelings of revulsion in the hearers/readers. The source of the second proverb is unknown; it was probably a traditional proverb found in their culture.

3:1-10 Defense regarding the delay of the parousia

The writer opens this passage in a formal way (3:1-2), reminding the faithful of Peter's authority. It is also a reminder of the genre of a testament. He deliberately associates this writing with First Peter by identifying it as his "second letter" (3:1). As with a testament, this letter serves to take the place of Peter's physical presence among them. A further dimension of the genre of a testament is found in the rest of this passage, where the writer, using the figure of Peter, looks into the future and speaks about these false teachers who are to come (3:3), a vision that has now been realized within the community.

This section considers the heart of the opponents' teaching. The writer begins with a call to

remember the tradition, particularly the teachings both of the prophets and of Jesus, whose message his apostles handed on (3:2). Previously the false teachers had accused Peter of inventing myths (1:16). Second Peter again reiterates that his teaching is based upon the word of Christ passed on through the apostles (3:2). He spells out clearly the heart of the opponents' rejection: the return of Christ (3:4). The question "Where is the promise of his coming?" (3:4) is a typical biblical question, implying doubt and derision on the part of the one asking the question (see also Judg 6:13; Isa 36:19).

The basis for the opponents' objections rests on the perceived permanence of the world: "From the time when our ancestors fell asleep, everything has remained as it was from the beginning of creation" (3:4). They claim that God has not been actively involved in the world, so why should God begin now? To this Peter gives a number of responses taken from biblical history:

- By God's word, the creation occurred and earth was formed from water (3:5; see Gen 1:9-10). The concept that all things were derived from water as the original element was also a Greek philosophical understanding.
- By God's word, the world was destroyed by water (3:6; see Gen 7:4).
- By God's word, the earth and everything on it will be destroyed by fire (3:7; the biblical roots of this belief in the destruction of the world by fire are found in late Hebrew writings such as Isaiah 66:15-16 and Malachi 3:19. The source for this biblical view is probably to be traced back to the Persians.)
- The delay in the parousia only appears to be a delay from the human perspective. With God time does not matter: "With the Lord one day is like a thousand years and a thousand years like one day" (3:8; this saying finds its origin in Psalm 90:4).
- The delay is actually a sign of God's patience, making it possible for more people to repent (3:9). This statement is a deduction from the very definition of God as a God of mercy and compassion (Exod 34:6).
- Finally, as Jesus predicted in Mark 13:32-37, the day of the Lord will come unexpectedly, like a thief in the night (3:10).

Second Peter rests his argument on the understanding that since the world has already undergone change through the power of God's word (in the creation and in the flood), so too it is to experience change in the future with the return of Jesus and a final judgment. While the end of the world is a certainty, Second Peter (as with the rest of the New Testament) gives no speculation on when this will occur.

3:11-13 Consequences of this teaching

Because the world will end in such a cataclysmic way, the readers should lead lives that strive after "holiness and devotion" (3:11). This call is set within the context of apocalyptic language that sees the destruction of the world (3:12) and the emergence of "new heavens and a new earth" (3:13). This description of the destruction of the world by means of fire is found only here in the New Testament; nevertheless, it was a common cultural view of the first century A.D.

3:14-16 Even Paul agrees with this teaching

Second Peter appeals to Paul's letters for support, since Paul taught the same things that Second Peter is teaching. Paul taught that there would be a judgment of all at the end of time (Rom 14:10-12). Paul also envisaged the delay of judgment as a time for repentance (Rom 2:4-5). In appealing to Paul's support, Second Peter makes three important observations. He understands that Paul was inspired in the writing of his letters ("according to the wisdom given to him," 3:15). Secondly, he shows that there was a tendency within the early church to collect Paul's letters ("in all his letters," 3:16). Thirdly, Paul's letters are considered to have an authority equal to that of the Hebrew Scriptures ("the other scriptures," 3:16). Consequently, the hearers/readers can rely on this teaching concerning the parousia, since it is the traditional teaching of the church, and the two greatest apostles, Paul and Peter, also bear witness to this traditional belief.

3:17-18 Final exhortation and doxology

The writer makes a final appeal to his hearers/readers to be on guard against the deceptions of the false teachers (3:17). He addresses his hearers/readers as "beloved" (3:17), a term that he had used frequently throughout this final chapter (3:1, 8, 14). In a positive way, he returns to his opening statement (1:2), where he encouraged his readers to grow in the "knowledge of God and of Jesus our Lord." This final appeal reminds the reader of the importance of the traditional teaching and knowledge about Jesus and his preaching, especially as it relates to his second coming and the end of the world: You can be sure that Jesus Christ will return. Finally, Second Peter ends with a doxology in praise of the Lord Jesus Christ. This praise is meant to be addressed to Jesus from now until eternity (3:18).

THE LETTERS OF
JOHN

Scott M. Lewis, S.J.

INTRODUCTION

The First, Second, and Third Letters of John were written after the Gospel of John, possibly around A.D. 100–115. They were written by an anonymous Presbyter, or elder (2 John 1; 3 John 1) and intended for the various house churches comprising the Johannine communion. First John is not written in the style of an ancient letter. Its repetitious and circular nature suggest a homily, possibly intended to be read to the assembled community to which it is addressed. Second and Third John, on the other hand, are short and terse and follow the conventions of ancient letter writing.

The letters are examples of parenesis, or moral exhortation. The Presbyter wants not only to encourage and strengthen his fellow believers but also to ensure that they continue to believe and behave in a manner consistent with the faith in which they stand. The three letters were probably written by the same author, although he was not necessarily the author of the Gospel, since the letters differ on some theological points, such as the atoning and expiatory nature of Jesus' death (1 John 1:7; 2:2; 4:10).

Church communities were no different in the first century than they are in the twenty-first; there were problems, disagreements, and divisions. The much idealized view of Christian living presented in chapters 14–17 of the Gospel has given way to human realities, and now the elder who writes these letters must deal with a major crisis. A serious schism has arisen, and the unity of the communities has been broken (1 John 2:18-27; 4:16; 2 John 7-11). Those who deny Jesus the Christ in any way are antichrists, liars, and false prophets (1 John 2:18, 22; 4:1, 3).

Additionally, it is apparent that many of the discourses in the Gospel, especially chapters 14–17, are subject to misinterpretation, especially those dealing with sin, Christian living, and the ongoing role of the Spirit. It appears that some believed that the Spirit was leading them in new directions. The elder seeks to set the record straight. He reiterates forcefully the essential elements of the Gospel revelation, especially the importance of the incarnation, the love commandment, the Spirit, the nature of sin, and eschatological expectations. The stark contrast between light and darkness, truth and falsehood, love and hate characterizes the letters, reflecting the dualism of the Fourth Gospel and its community. One stands with light or darkness—there is no middle ground. Readers wishing to delve into the history of the Johannine community and its struggles will profit from Raymond Brown's *The Community of the Beloved Disciple*.

THE FIRST LETTER OF

JOHN

Scott M. Lewis, S.J.

COMMENTARY

PROLOGUE

1 John 1:1-4

1:1-4 The Word of Life

As in the Gospel (1:1), the opening line speaks of the "beginning," referring here primarily to the revelation of God in Jesus in which the Christian community has placed its faith. The Word of Life—the *Logos* (John 1:1)—is not some abstraction or concept but was made real and concrete for the world. It was seen (John 1:39; 14:9; 19:35; 20:18, 25) and touched (John 20:27), signifying that Christ truly came in the flesh (4:2; 2 John 7). Since the author's community has seen and touched the Word of life, his testimony carries weight, and he gives this testimony so that the readers may have fellowship or sharing *(koinonia)* with his community. Fellowship with his community includes the experience of the mutual indwelling of the Father and the Son (17:11, 21, and 23) and is the source of complete joy that he wishes for his readers (15:11; 17:13). Breaking the unity of the community is tantamount to breaking communion with God.

GOD AS LIGHT

1 John 1:5–3:10

1:5–2:2 Light and darkness

The core of the message is verse 5: God is light, and in him there is no darkness at all. Light must be understood in the ethical sense. Jesus revealed the God whom no one had ever seen (John 1:18). Hatred, violence, greed, selfishness, and so on are alien to God; when they are attributed to God, they are a human projection. This is connected to the statement that God is love (4:8-9), demonstrated by his revelation in Jesus and the expiation of our sins.

This entire section will consist of the logical consequences of that first principle. If God is light, then those who claim fellowship with him must be light; if there is no darkness in God, then those who claim fellowship with him must not have darkness within them. What is demanded is an imitation of God himself, which would be impossible without the transforming power of the Spirit.

Verses 6, 8, and 10 begin with the conditional "If," representing those things for which the author reproaches his opponents. They all involve denying sin in one's life and claiming fellowship with God while walking in darkness. Those who do this lie and do not act in truth (v. 6). Walking (a Jewish term for how one lives one's life) in the light and acting in truth, however, result in fellowship with one another (v. 7), as well as the washing away of all sins with the blood of Jesus. This affirms the importance of the death or exaltation of Jesus, and the blood of Christ is explicitly linked to the forgiveness of sins (1 John 2:2, 12; 3:5, 8; 4:10; 5:6-8).

Walking in the light does not mean that one is perfect, and it is only realistic to admit that even the best people will sin. Claiming to be sinless when one is not is self-deception and lying, which is characteristic of Satan in John 8:34, and in so doing we cut ourselves off from God. Acknowledgment of sins results in forgiveness and cleansing, because Jesus is our Advocate with the Father and expiation for both our sins and those of the whole world (1:8–2:3). The reference to the sins of the whole world is a universalistic element that probably draws on John 1:29 and 20:23 and is a welcome counterbalance to the usual Johannine sectarianism. In the Gospel of John the Advocate (Paraclete) refers to the Spirit, while here it is applied to Jesus.

2:3-11 Walking in the light

The litmus test for knowing Jesus is simple: anyone claiming to do so must keep his commandments (v. 3) and live just as Jesus lived (v. 6). Knowing God has nothing to do with intellectual or factual knowledge but is a deep and personal relationship. If God is love, then those claiming to know God must manifest this love in their lives. With a backward glance at the "new" commandment in John 13:34, the author admits that it is not new, but a very old commandment, whose origins stretch back to the creation and which has been proclaimed anew (v. 7) by Jesus. It is an eschatological commandment; the new age of light is dawning, and the darkness is passing away. The true light (see John 1:9)—Jesus and the community of believers—is already shining (v. 8). Walking in the light is equated with loving one's brother or sister; the one who does that is in the light and will not fall, while the one hating his brother truly walks in darkness (vv. 8-11).

2:12-14 Family of believers

The author addresses his words in a figurative fashion to the broad generational spectrum of the community, stretching back to its foundation: children, fathers, and young men (vv. 12-14). He reminds them of what they have received and encourages them to stand fast: their sins have been forgiven; they know both Jesus and the Father; they are strong and the word of God remains in them; and they have conquered the evil one (John 17:15).

2:15-17 Denunciation of the world

Verse 15 makes the startling statement that if anyone loves the world, "the love of the Father is not in him," which seems strange in view of John 3:16. There is a stern warning not to love the world or the things of the world; they are snares and allurements, ephemeral in nature, and tainted with sin (vv. 16-17). In John 3:16, however, the "world" is the created order and humanity, while here it describes all those things that are opposed to God. God is the only enduring reality; all else is fleeting and can be taken away. Therefore, those who do the will of God remain forever.

2:18-23 The last hour

Eschatology is suddenly center stage: it is "the last hour." This represents a more traditional apocalyptic eschatology, anticipating the return of Jesus. In the Gospel it is alluded to only in 5:26-29 and 14:1-3. Not only is the antichrist coming but now many antichrists have appeared (v. 18). These antichrists are, of course, those who have broken with the author's community, for he states that "they went out from us" (v. 19), but their desertion proves that they never really belonged anyway, for they were on the side of darkness.

The issue appears to be one of christology: the liar is one who denies that Jesus is the Christ (v. 22), and anyone denying the Son is also denying the Father. We have only one side of this controversy, so it is unclear in what sense they are denying the Son. John is not an example of theological moderation; for him, even those who adhered to a more moderate christology are counted among the unbelievers.

2:24-27 Anointed with the Spirit

The members of the community are well armored, being anointed by the holy one and possessing all knowledge (vv. 20, 27). This anointing of the Spirit will teach them to discern true and false and, in fact, will teach them everything. Since through the anointing they already know the truth, there is no danger as long as they stand fast in what they have heard from the beginning (v. 26).

2:28–3:10 Children of God

In John 1:12-13 those who believe in Jesus are promised the opportunity to become children of God. In John 3:3 Jesus insists that only those who have been born "from above" *(anothen)* can see the kingdom of God. The author of 1 John encourages the "children" (v. 28) of the community to stand fast, for those who are righteous are begotten by God. The fact that they are children of God is proof of the Father's great love for them (1 John 3:1).

There is a tradition of adoption by God as sons and daughters (Gal 4:15; Rom 8:15), but the Johannine tradition posits an actual transformation as God's children now, but it will be complete only at the time of Jesus' return. The hope is that when what we are to become is revealed, we shall see God as he is; since he is pure, we must be pure (3:2-3).

The focus changes in verse 4 to the one who sins: he is lawless; he does not know God. The one who acts righteously and loves his brother belongs to God and is begotten by him, and whoever sins belongs to the devil (v. 8), for parentage is determined by one's visible life (cf. John 8:34). Continuing with the language of birth and generation, it is clear that no one begotten by God sins or can sin, because "God's seed remains in him" (v. 9). This is incomprehensible in light of 1 John 1:8-10, and there have been countless attempts to resolve the contradiction. Misunderstandings of verses such as this one can lead to questionable behavior. God's seed can be taken to mean the divine principle implanted in someone by the Spirit; one is in the process of transformation and cannot sin insofar as he or she is in God. One who is truly and completely in God cannot sin.

LOVE FOR ONE ANOTHER

1 John 3:11–5:12

3:11-18 The love commandment revisited

We return to the love commandment in verse 11 (John 13:34; 15:12), the fundamental principle of the community. But here love is contrasted with evil and murder, with Cain as an example (v. 12). The presence of hate within an individual renders him a murderer, and no murderer has eternal life (v. 15), a replay of the argument that Jesus had with some of the "Jews" in John 8:44. Hatred is equated with murder in Matthew 5:21-22; this explains why Jesus often accused his opponents in the Gospel of John of wanting to kill him despite the absence of overt violence. The world is likened to Cain, for its deeds are evil, and hatred is what the followers of Jesus can expect (John 3:19-21; 7:7; 15:18-20; 16:18-25; 17:14). Their belief in Jesus and their living of the love commandment expose the hidden hatred and negativity of the world.

In John 5:24 Jesus promises that those who believe in him have already passed from death to life; in 1 John 3:14, the fact that they love their

brothers is proof that this has occurred. It was through the exemplar of Jesus laying down his life for them that they came to know love. To live one's life as Jesus did means to lay down one's life for one's brothers (v. 16), and this includes tending to the needs of others. In a question similar to that posed in James 2:15-17, the author asks how the love of God can remain in one who passes by someone in need and refuses compassion (v. 17), which is always concrete and practical. This is followed by the exhortation to love in deeds and in truth rather than mere words (v. 18). The poor and the needy are usually the losers when a community becomes elitist and self-absorbed in an overly interiorized and privatized spirituality. Love for the Johannine community is not sentiment or feeling, but practical and demanding living for others.

3:19-24 The heart as judge

How can one be sure of belonging to the truth and being right with God? Verses 19-22 propose the heart as the judge; if one is not condemned by the heart, then confidence in God is the result. This is rather vague, but is developed a bit in 4:18, which states that perfect love casts out fear. If one still fears God's judgment, that is evidence that one must still grow in love. If the heart is not afraid, that is an indication that one's heart is right with God. That God is greater than our hearts and knows everything is not intended to induce fear but a sense of freedom and peace for the believer. God is fully aware of our real intentions and our desire to do his will.

The central theme of the letter is hammered home again in verses 23-24: the commandments of God are to believe in the name of his Son, Jesus Christ (John 1:12; 3:16; 14:1; 20:31), and to love one another (13:34; 15:12). Those who obey these two inextricably linked commandments will continue to experience the mutual indwelling of Jesus, with the presence of the Spirit as confirmation. There is an echo of the great love commandment in Mark 12:18-34, but with the addition of the faith requirement.

4:1-6 Testing the spirits

In a Spirit-filled, charismatic community, the question of the discernment of spirits is extremely important. In our own time the failure to exercise discernment in cases of the claims of charismatic leaders has often resulted in tragedy. All sorts of things can be said under the seeming influence of the Spirit by many different people, a problem faced in 1 Corinthians 12:3, 1 Thessalonians 5:11-22, and Revelation 2:2. In John 14:26 and 16:13, a teaching function is ascribed to the Spirit, and many of the author's opponents appear to have taken that very seriously.

By what standard can their accuracy be measured? The author warns his audience to be wary and to test the spirits, since so many false prophets have gone out into the world, certainly referring to his opponents (v. 1). In Deuteronomy 13:1-5 and 18:20-22, the false prophet is one who speaks the names of unknown gods. In a similar vein, those spirits that acknowledge that Jesus Christ has come in the flesh belong to God, while those not doing so are the spirit of the antichrist (vv. 2-3). Fidelity to the primal revelation is crucial. The emphasis on "come in the flesh" (v. 2) might indicate that some were denying the salvific value of the humanity or "flesh" of Jesus. The full incarnation of the Word *(Logos)* is manifested in the human and social sphere in care for the poor and the weak and the needs of others—in other words, in concrete acts of love.

It is obvious to the author that those who do not acknowledge Jesus belong to the world, for the world eagerly accepts their teachings, while the truth concerning Jesus is a sign of contradiction and an occasion of opposition from the world (vv. 4-5). The writer claims that "we," meaning his community, belong to God, as does anyone who listens to them, while those who do not belong to God refuse to do so. This is a question of the correct interpretation of the Christian revelation and message, and the author takes the correctness of his community's proclamation as his point of departure. The spirit of truth he equates with the stance of his community, while the spirit of deceit describes his opponents. In an intriguing parallel, the Qumran community believed in the opposition of two spirits, truth and injustice (1QS 3:13-20), while deceit or falsehood was the characteristic of those opposed to God.

4:7-18 God is love

"Love" appears twenty-seven times in this short section. Verse 7 exhorts us to love one another because love is of God (v. 8). Everyone who loves is begotten by God and knows God; in fact,

God is love. God took the initiative with love, and this was accomplished through the sending of his only Son into the world (cf. John 3:16) as expiation for our sins and so that we might have life through him (vv. 9-10). This is not a poetic flight of fancy or speculation, for God is known to be love by his actions, as in the faithful covenant loyalty of the Old Testament *(hesed)*. Love is not a noun or adjective but a verb and describes both God and the response of believers in Jesus. Since God has loved us in such a fashion, we must love one another (v. 11) in order to be of God.

The nature of the unseen God dominates the next portion, framed by verses 12 and 20: no one has ever seen God (v. 12), but if we love one another, we will know God, and his love will be brought to perfection in us, with the presence of the Spirit as proof (v. 13). This describes a transformative process, for the source of the love is God, not humans. The presence of this perfected love in us removes whatever fear of the day of judgment we might have had, for we have become the love that is God (v. 17). Perfect love (God) and fear cannot coexist; if we are not afraid of the judgment, it is proof that we are in God, while the presence of fear is evidence that our transformation is incomplete (v. 18). A reflection on this section should encourage Christian preaching and teaching that focus more on actualizing the transformative love of God than on morbid or fearful images of God and punishment and judgment.

4:19-21 The unseen God

We are able to love because God has first loved us—this is not a massive self-help project (v. 19). The unseen God is loved in other people; hating others while claiming to love God is an absurdity and a lie. The quality of the communal relationship with God is reflected in the interpersonal relationships of its members, a constant challenge to all church congregations.

5:1-5 Loving God

Almost like a refrain, the author repeats his belief that all who believe that Jesus is the Christ or who love the Father are begotten by him. Loving God and obeying his commandments empower one to love the children of God, presumably only members of the community. The love of God is synonymous with obeying his commandments, and his commandments are not burdensome, which finds agreement in the entire biblical tradition (Deut 30:11-14; Matt 11:28-30). Those begotten by God conquer the world (John 16:33) by means of faith in Jesus as the Son of God and share in his victory (vv. 4-5).

5:6-12 Testimony and witnesses

Jesus Christ has three impeccable witnesses that are in agreement: water, blood, and the Spirit (vv. 6-7), possibly to satisfy the requirement in Deuteronomy 19:15 for at least two witnesses. Testimony is also crucial throughout the Gospel of John. The witnesses of blood and water resonate with the witness from the foot of the cross (John 19:34-35) and address the objections of those opponents who deny that Jesus has come in the flesh. The blood and water also represent the baptism and death of Jesus, that is, his earthly and incarnate ministry. The Spirit is the third witness, and its presence within the community continues to testify to the blood and water, and it is the Spirit of truth. Older English translations of verse 7 add "in heaven: the Father, the Word, and the Holy Spirit; and these three are one." This phrase was added by copyists during the christological controversies of the fourth and fifth centuries and is not present in the oldest manuscripts that we possess.

EPILOGUE

1 John 5:13-21

5:13-21 Sin, prayer, and final reflections

The author of the Gospel of John writes so that his readers will come to believe in Jesus as the Messiah and Son of God and that through believing they might *have* life in his name (John 20:31). The elder writes this letter so that his readers might *know* that they have eternal life (v. 13), and all the exhortation and testimony are to affirm what they have already received. With this confidence, believers can ask for anything in accordance with the will of God and be assured of being heard (vv. 14-15).

One of the first things one should pray for is any brother or sister who is committing sin, and if this is done, God will grant life to the sinner. The fact that believers can sin has already been acknowledged in 1:5–2:2, although 2:28–3:10 seems to rule it out. In 2:1 Jesus is the one who intercedes on behalf of sinners, but here other

Christians make intercessory prayers, presumably through Jesus. But the proviso is that the prayers should only be for those whose sins are not "deadly," for although all wrongdoing is sin, not all sin is deadly. This echoes the unforgivable blasphemy against the holy Spirit in Mark 3:28-30, as well as the Jewish tradition that placed the worship of other gods or the rejection of God in this category. It is not clear what constitutes a "deadly" sin, but given the repetitious warnings in these letters, the most likely candidate is a denial that Jesus is the Son of God or that he has come in the flesh. There is the rather shocking statement that one should not pray for one whose sin is deadly. It would seem that this is the person most in need of prayers, but the dualistic worldview of the Johannine community will not admit any middle ground or equivocation.

In John 17:9 Jesus states his intention not to pray for the world but only for those given to him by God. It is only in the context of his farewell prayer that his prayers are solely on behalf of his followers, but a literal or superficial understanding of this and similar passages can generate a narrow and overrigorous exclusivism. Fortunately, we also have passages like John 3:16 and 12:47, which assure us that God's action in Jesus is not to condemn the world but to save it. Verse 18 asserts that no one begotten by God sins, being protected by God from the clutches of the evil one (cf. John 17:15). Even though the members of the community belong to God, the whole world is under the power of the evil one, which is a disturbing statement in view of Jesus' claim that the ruler of this world will be driven out (John 12:31) and that believers have conquered the evil one (1 John 2:12-13). This stark dualism seems more in keeping with the Dead Sea community at Qumran or the later Gnostic groups. The action of Jesus Christ has given us the ability to discern the one who is true, and that one is Jesus himself, who is true God and eternal life (v. 20).

The letter ends with the incongruous admonition to be on guard against idols—this has not been mentioned in the Gospel or the other letters. In what sense is it a threat? For John's community, the true God has been revealed to them in Jesus Christ, and the refusal to believe in him is tantamount to idolatry. In both the Old and New Testaments, idolatry is the root human sin and by far the gravest.

THE SECOND LETTER OF
JOHN

Scott M. Lewis, S.J.

COMMENTARY

The Second Letter of John is in the form of a conventional Hellenistic letter. The author—presumably the Presbyter (elder) of 2 and 3 John—is writing to one of the sister communities in order to warn them against his opponents, the "deceivers" and "antichrists," who are spreading what he deems to be false teachings.

1-3 Address and greeting

The Presbyter writes to the "chosen Lady" and "her children," whom he loves in the truth. Some have taken the "chosen Lady" to be an actual person, but most assign metaphorical value to the address. He is referring to one of the communities, which he holds in very high regard. Her "children" are those believers who are walking in truth and love.

4-11 Body of the letter

The Presbyter rejoices to find that "some" of her children are walking in truth, which eases in to the warning that he has for them. Addressing the Lady directly (v. 5), he exhorts her to live the fundamental commandment from the beginning (John 13:34; 1 John 2:7-8, 24), namely, to love one another. Love is walking according to his commandments, and as he made clear in the previous letter, this includes correct belief concerning Jesus Christ. The reason for his concern (v. 7) is that many "deceivers" have gone out into the world

and do not acknowledge Jesus as "com[ing] in the flesh" (1 John 4:2). Some have suggested that this refusal refers to the return of Christ, but it is more likely that it involved a denial of the incarnation or full humanity of Christ (John 1:14), or a separation of the Christ from the human Jesus.

For the Johannine community, knowing and adhering to the truth received in the beginning (v. 5; 1 John 2:24) is synonymous with salvation and eternal life (John 6:27, 29; 20:31; 1 John 2:25). The writer warns them (vv. 8-9) that straying from the truth can cost them eternal life, for those who do not remain in the teaching of the Christ do not have God. The word translated as "progressive" in verse 9 is more correctly understood as "going too far" or "going beyond" what is proper or right. The author is uncompromising and asks the community not to receive or grant hospitality to anyone who arrives bearing these false teachings, in fact not even to greet them. Since those who were missionaries or itinerant teachers relied on hospitality, he hopes that these harsh measures will hinder the growth of his opponents' teachings.

The Johannine community's sectarian nature is quite evident in this form of excommunication or shunning. The false teachers are believed to belong to the realm of the world and darkness, and anyone who even greets them is tainted by their evil works (v. 11). It is distressing that dialogue and mutual respect are so lacking in these letters as well as in the Gospel. It seems that the love commandment in the Johannine tradition applies to fellow Christians, and more precisely, other Johannine Christians (1 John 2:9-11; 3:11, 23). Assigning those outside of our group to a lesser status is a form of tribalism that is the bane of all religious traditions, to which our own history bears painful and tragic witness.

12-13 Closing

Using a conventional ending, the author claims to have much more to tell the community members but will wait for an opportunity to visit in person so that "our joy may be complete," which is a Johannine expression indicating the joy resulting from a communion or fellowship in love and in truth. The "children," or members of his community, also send greetings.

THE THIRD LETTER OF
JOHN

Scott M. Lewis, S.J.

COMMENTARY

The Third Letter of John was also written by the Presbyter, but this time to a named individual. Despite being the shortest letter in the New Testament—and one that fails to mention Jesus directly—it is intriguing in that it gives us a momentary and partial glimpse into the tensions of the Johannine communities. In this letter the author's opponent even has a name—Diotrephes.

More of a private and personal letter, it does not address the theological tensions of 1 and 2 John. Governance and authority in the community are its overriding concerns, and we can even detect elements of a power struggle between the Presbyter and Diotrephes.

1-4 Address and greeting

The Presbyter's addressee is an individual named Gaius, a common Roman name, which prevents an identification with others of the same name in the New Testament (Acts 19:29; 20:4; Rom 16:25; 1 Cor 1:14). That Gaius is esteemed by the Presbyter is clear: he is addressed as "beloved," he is loved "in truth," and his "soul is prospering." These are indications that he walks in the truth and in love, that is, he has remained faithful to the correct christology, and he extends loving hospitality to members of the Johannine communion, who also walk in the truth. Love is the nature of God, and this God has been revealed in Jesus. This is the "truth" in which believers are invited to participate.

5-12 Body of the letter

Hospitality is a privileged expression of love and walking in the truth (vv. 5-8). Gaius has been exemplary in this practice, and glowing reports from traveling brothers have been received by the Presbyter. He hints that these travelers are missionaries or teachers of a sort, for they are completely dependent on community members and receive nothing from outsiders. This is for the sake of the Name, most likely an allusion to Jesus. He urges continuous support of them so that they all may be "co-workers in the truth" (v. 8), which in this context is the work of proclaiming the Johannine Gospel message.

The Presbyter names and describes his adversary, a man named Diotrephes (vv. 9-10), about whom we know nothing other than what is present in this letter. It appears that he exercises some authority or control in the community, although it is unclear whether he actually holds any sort of office. The "church" (ekklesia) to which the Presbyter writes (v. 9) signifies the congregation rather than an extended institution or structured community. Gaius appears to be a loyal member of that community, one whom the Presbyter can trust.

The Presbyter describes Diotrephes: he loves to dominate; he does not acknowledge the Presbyter's authority; he spreads "evil nonsense" about him; and most of all, he refuses to extend hospitality to emissaries from the Presbyter's community. On top of that, he prevents members of his community from doing so and expels those who do. Some scholars see this as reflecting the rise of the early episcopate, but this is unlikely. The early Johannine communities were egalitarian in nature, and house congregations were united in a communion of unity in Jesus Christ and the path of love.

This appears to be more of a personal power struggle. The Presbyter paints a negative portrait of Diotrephes, but we must remember that we are hearing only one side of the story; a letter from Diotrephes would probably present a very different point of view. Although the Presbyter rages at Diotrephes for refusing hospitality to his emissaries, in 2 John 10-11 the Presbyter commanded the "chosen Lady" to treat his theological opponents in exactly the same way! A standard exhortation to do good and avoid evil in order to be of God (v. 11) is followed by praise for Demetrius, although the nature of the good report concerning this person is not clear.

13-14 Closing

The author insists on waiting for a personal visit to relate other matters to Gaius. He closes with a peace salutation and a greeting from the friends of his community to those in Gaius's, each by name. It is interesting that the term "friends" is used rather than "children." "Friends" would be more in keeping with John 15:14, indicating that they are keeping the commandments of Jesus.

THE LETTER OF
JUDE

Patrick J. Hartin

INTRODUCTION

The letter of Jude, one of the shortest New Testament writings, is also one of the most intriguing. It was taken up almost in its entirety into Second Peter. Its place in the canon has often been challenged, not least of all by the early church, which was concerned with its usage of the apocryphal books of *1 Enoch* and the *Assumption of Moses.*

Author

The writer of the letter identifies himself as: "Jude, a slave of Jesus Christ and brother of James" (v. 1). In the New Testament world the name Jude (or more accurately "Judas") was quite common. Matthew 13:55 notes that James, "the brother of the Lord" and leader of the Jerusalem church, had a brother named Judas: "Is not his mother named Mary and his brothers James, Joseph, Simon, and Judas?" The writer, then, identifies himself with this James, the leader of the Jerusalem church and "brother of the Lord."

However, the information we glean about the author from the text presents some difficulties in making this identification: (a) *The writer's vocabulary shows a good knowledge of Greek*—some twenty-two words occur only in this letter in the New Testament (excluding Second Peter's borrowing from Jude). (b) *The opening greetings,* "May mercy, peace, and love be yours in abundance" (v. 2), differ from the common Pauline greetings: "Grace . . . and peace" (e.g., Phil 1:2). However there are similarities with the opening of a number of other New Testament letters. For example, a threefold listing of "grace, mercy, and peace" occurs in 1 Timothy 1:2; 2 Timothy 1:2; and 2 John 3. The letters of Peter have the greetings as "May grace and peace be yours in abundance." The opening of Polycarp's letter to the Philippians (written before A.D. 155) also has a similar form: "Mercy and peace from God Almighty and Jesus Christ our Savior be multiplied to you." All this shows that a variation of the form used by Jude was common in the post-apostolic period. (c) *The writer comes from a period after the apostles:* In verses 17-18 the author does not include himself in the group of apostles but gives the impression that he belongs to a later generation.

All these arguments point to the letter coming from a second-generation Christian at the end of the first century. As with the letters of James and First Peter, the writer invokes the name of Jude because he wishes to endorse his authority in settling problems that have arisen in a certain area of the Christian church.

Hearers/readers

The letter is an immediate response to a sudden danger arising within certain Christian communities. Intruders entering the communities are undermining their traditional faith as well as their morals. It is addressed: "To those who are called, beloved in God the Father and kept safe for Jesus

Christ" (v. 1). The writing does not provide a detailed description of the readers or of their opponents. From the letter some information can be deduced about the first hearers/readers of this letter. From its tone the letter seems to be directed to a definite church or group of churches. The use of the Hebrew Scriptures and apocryphal allusions indicate a Jewish-Christian community. The writer's identification of himself as "brother of James" must indicate a community in which James's authority was recognized. The cultural mixture of Jewish and Greek elements in this letter is similar to that of the letter of James and would perhaps argue for a similar destination. Given this information, the area of Syria or northern Palestine would seem to be the most likely destination.

Genre and main thoughts

While this writing commences with the traditional opening formula of a letter, it lacks final personal greetings and ends with a doxology praising God. A close reading reveals that the literary form of a letter suits it best. In verses 3-4 the writer shows his pastoral intent of writing to a group of Christians for whom he holds responsibility. He aims at helping them meet the new challenges arising from the inroads of intruding teachers within their community. Drawing upon their common heritage, the writer warns his hearers/readers about the dangers they face. It is a wonderful record of an early Christian church struggling to hold firm to the traditional faith, while at the same time opening up to the new culture around it.

COMMENTARY

Verses 1-2 Greetings

Using the customary format of a letter, the writer refers to himself as Jude, "a slave of Jesus Christ" (see Jas 1:1; Titus 1:1). This phrase "slave of Jesus Christ" recalls the biblical tradition that identifies figures like Moses (1 Kgs 8:53) and David (1 Kgs 8:66) as a "slave of God." As with the letters of James and First Peter, the writer invokes the authority of an apostolic figure, Jude, for this letter (see Introduction, pp. 822–23). It is in this sense that this commentary refers to the author as Jude. Since he is less well known, he identifies himself further as the "brother of James" (probably James "the brother of the Lord," Gal 1:19). This would imply that he is writing to Jewish Christians, since James was an important figure in their world. The writer identifies the readers in a general sense as "those who are called." Paul refers to his hearers/readers in Rome in a similar way (Rom 1:6). Finally, he extends greetings: "may mercy, peace, and love be yours in abundance" (v. 2; see 1 Tim 1:2; 2 Tim 1:2).

Verses 3-4 Occasion for the letter

The usual thanksgiving section is missing. The author intended to write to his readers about their common salvation, but a more urgent topic arose. Many false teachers have entered the community of his hearers/readers and are distorting their faith, especially their belief in Jesus Christ. The writer urges the hearers/readers "to contend for the faith" (v. 3). This image is taken from the world of athletic contests. Since only one person can win the prize, Jude exhorts his readers to be the ones who win in this struggle. He says two things about these intruders (v. 4): they "pervert the grace of our God into licentiousness," implying their moral degeneration into sexual immorality; and they "deny our only Master and Lord, Jesus Christ," implying doctrinal teaching that refuses to acknowledge the Lordship of Jesus and his teaching.

Verses 5-7 God punishes those who are unfaithful

The phrase "I wish to remind you" is a marker identifying the beginning of the argument based on past examples. Using three examples, Jude reminds his hearers/readers of figures who fell from positions of favor with God and were punished because of their sins.

His first reference is to God's chosen people, whom God liberated from slavery in Egypt. They complained against God in the desert and were destroyed because of their lack of faith (v. 5; see Num 14).

In the second example, angels of God came down to earth to seek out women (Gen 6:1-4). They were punished by God in chains and darkness until the judgment day (v. 6; see *1 Enoch* 10:4-6, 12-13).

Thirdly, Sodom and Gomorrah were punished in eternal fire because of their "sexual promiscuity" (v. 7).

Verses 8-9 Application

These verses consider the intruding teachers: they "defile the flesh" (like Sodom and Gomorrah, they practice sexual immorality); they "scorn lordship" (like the Israelites at the time of the Exodus, they reject God's covenant and authority); and they "revile glorious beings" (like the angels, they refuse to serve and obey God). The implication is that these false teachers will experience similar judgments and punishments.

In verse 9 Jude cites a story taken from an apocryphal Jewish writing, *The Assumption of Moses* (though many modern scholars prefer to name it more correctly *The Testament of Moses*). This work exists in only one Latin manuscript text, dated from the sixth century A.D. Unfortunately this manuscript ends before the description of the death of Moses. The story that Jude narrates here is presumed to refer to the lost ending of this manuscript.

The book of Deuteronomy says that Moses died and was buried in the land of Moab, "but to this day no one knows the place of his burial" (Deut 34:6). Jude's quotation fills in details surrounding Moses' death and envisages a struggle between Michael and Satan over the body of Moses. Satan argued that Moses did not deserve burial because he had once killed an Egyptian (see Exod 2:12). Michael did not condemn Satan but simply said: "May the Lord rebuke you!" leaving judgment to the Lord. The point of this story is that the archangel Michael did not take on himself the power of passing judgment but left judgment to the Lord. Likewise, Jude says that God is the final judge and God will pass judgment on these intruding teachers.

Verses 10-13 Further examples of God's punishment

Jude turns now to consider the intruding teachers, who act like irrational animals (v. 10).

They despise what they do not understand. Jude sees that their irrational attitudes will eventually lead to their own destruction (v. 10). Three more examples of sinners are taken from the biblical tradition and applied to the intruders (v. 11): Cain, Balaam, and Korah.

These false teachers are walking in *"the way of Cain"* (emphasis added). Cain murdered his brother Abel (Gen 4:8), so these intruding teachers are committing spiritual murder against the community.

The intruders are also practicing *"Balaam's error"* (emphasis added). From references to Balaam in the book of Numbers (22–24; 25:1; 31:16-18), the implication emerges that Balaam led the Israelites into sin. In like manner these intruding teachers are leading the community that Jude addresses into sin.

Finally, *"the rebellion of Korah"* (emphasis added) refers to a revolt that Korah led against the authority of Moses and Aaron (Num 16). In like manner these intruding teachers are fomenting a rejection of Jude's authority and teaching. In the tradition these three examples symbolize those who lead the community into error and reject the duly appointed leaders of the community. These examples are certainly apt for the dangers these intruders pose to the community that Jude addresses.

Even the early Christian meals that remember the Lord's supper (called *agapai,* or "love feasts") have been infiltrated by these intruding teachers (v. 12). In graphic imagery, Jude uses four images drawn from nature (vv. 12-13) to describe these intruding teachers. Common to these images is the concept that they do not act according to their nature. Instead they create chaos: "waterless clouds"; "fruitless trees"; "wild waves of the sea" splashing foam everywhere; and "wandering stars" (vv. 12-13). The implication for Jude's hearers/readers is clear: they are to avoid all contact with the intruding teachers because these teachers do not act according to the ways set by God. Instead they cause chaos by leading people astray.

Verses 14-19 Further warnings of judgment

Jude shows that the rise of these intruding teachers had been foretold in the past by both the prophets and the apostles. Jude refers to the example of Enoch (Gen 5:21-24), who was taken up to be with God without dying. He became an important figure in Jewish tradition between the testaments, as is seen from the influential apocryphal writing *1 Enoch*. Jude quotes from this writing to assure his hearers/readers that God will execute judgment on these intruding teachers: "Behold, the Lord has come with his countless holy ones to execute judgment on all" (vv. 14-15; see *1 Enoch* 1:9). This quotation lies closer to the text of *1 Enoch* discovered in Qumran than to other extant texts. The quotation's purpose is to stress the traditional teaching of divine judgment (Matt 16:27; 25:31-46).

Jude adds further support from Christian tradition by quoting a saying from the apostles: "In [the] last time there will be scoffers who will live according to their own godless desires" (v. 18). Since no such quotation appears in the rest of the New Testament, its origin must belong to the wider world of Christian tradition. The point of these references to *1 Enoch* and the apostles is clear: the presence of these intruding teachers was foretold in the past, and one can be certain that God's punishment and judgment await them.

Verses 20-23 Build up your faith

These verses present the climax of the letter. Jude spells out clearly why he has written them. He wants to build up the community's faith (v. 20). The way to accomplish this is through prayer in the Spirit, remaining in God's love, and relying upon Christ's mercy as they await the coming of the Lord (v. 21). For this reason they are to guard against the evil teachings of the intruders. It is not sufficient for the community and individuals to protect themselves from these false teachers.

While verses 22-23 contain a number of very difficult textual problems, nevertheless the basic meaning is clear: Jude reminds the members of his community of their responsibility to reach out to those who are wavering (v. 22) and "to save others by snatching them out of the fire" (v. 23). This is somewhat similar to the conclusion to the letter of James, where the hearers/readers are instructed that "whoever brings back a sinner from the error of his way will save his soul from death and will cover a multitude of sins" (Jas 5:20).

Verses 24-25 Final doxology

The letter concludes without any personal greetings so characteristic of Paul's letters. Instead, it ends with a hymn of praise (a doxology) in honor of God through Jesus Christ. God keeps the community from harm and brings them morally blameless into God's presence. This community praises this one God, the Savior, for God's glory, majesty, power, and authority that was in the past, is now, and will continue to be "for ages to come."

THE BOOK OF
REVELATION

Catherine A. Cory

INTRODUCTION

More than any other part of the New Testament, the book of Revelation evokes greatly varying reactions among its readers. Some find it surreal and confusing or simply silly and therefore want to ignore it completely. Others find it endlessly fascinating because of its many colorful and sometimes grotesque images. Others, fearful about the future, view the book as an illustrated timeline that will help them better prepare for the events of the end of the world. Still others see it as a kind of "war manual," explaining how they should conduct themselves in the impending battle between the righteous ones and the forces of evil in the world.

But is there more to the book of Revelation? Does Revelation have anything to say to believers who are not fixated on determining the date of the end time and instead want to read the Scriptures to hear God's voice in the present time, to inspire faith, and challenge themselves and their faith communities to right behavior, now, in the midst of the activities of their everyday lives? To some people's surprise, the answer is yes, provided we seek to understand the book of Revelation from within the social and historical context in which it originated and as the type of literature it is—apocalyptic. The Second Vatican Council's *Dei Verbum* and the Roman Catholic Pontifical Biblical Commission's "Interpretation of the Bible in the Church" strongly encourage this approach to the study of Scripture, and nowhere is it more important than in our study of the book of Revelation.

As a first step to reading and interpreting any piece of literature, it is important to learn something about its author and the place and time in which the author wrote. This information helps us determine the author's point of view. We must also take into account any historical circumstances or cultural differences that may have affected his or her approach to the topic. Although Sacred Scripture is different from other literature in the sense that Christians believe it to be inspired of God, its human authors are true authors. Since the word of God is mediated through these human authors' historical and cultural circumstances, we need to ask similar questions about the identity of the biblical author and the place and time in which he lived. Therefore, we will begin this commentary by asking what we know about the author of the book of Revelation and the time and place in which he wrote.

Another thing we need to know when we sit down to read a piece of literature is its genre or literary form. Only then do we know what expectations to have about its meaning. For example, if we know that a particular story is a fable, we can expect to read about talking animals, and we know that we should look for its moral or central teaching. However, we would *not* expect a fable to give us a scientific study or a lesson in history. When we read the Gospels of the New Testament, we can expect to hear the story of Jesus. We know that the narratives will be realistic, having some of the features of a history or biography, but hopefully we also know that they were written for the primary purpose of proclaiming faith in Jesus as the messiah of God. The word "gospel" means "good news." To expect something different—for example, a documentary on the life of Jesus—is to seriously misunderstand the author's intention and, as a consequence, misinterpret the meaning of the biblical text. Therefore, before beginning our reading of the book of Revelation we also need to ask about its genre.

Authorship

The author of the book of Revelation does not tell us much about himself, except that his name was John and that he saw himself as God's servant (1:1). Two early church writers, Justin Martyr (c. A.D. 160) and Irenaeus (c. A.D. 180), associated the author of this book with the apostle John and with the writer of the Fourth Gospel, also known by that name (see *Dial.* 81 and *Adv. haer.* 3.11.1-3; 4.20.11). However, most biblical scholars today think that the author of the book of Revelation was neither an apostle of Jesus nor the author of the Gospel of John. The reasons for this view have to do with differences in the style of writing and the probable date of composition of this book. At most, we can say that the author of the book of Revelation was an early Jewish Christian prophet by the name of John, otherwise unknown in early Christian literature.

Date of composition and location of the work

John tells his readers that he received the visions about which he writes while residing on Patmos, a small island in the Aegean Sea. Further, he tells us that he was there because he "proclaimed God's word and gave testimony to Jesus" (1:9). Thus we can probably assume that his exile on Patmos came as a result of his preaching activity. He also incorporates letters to seven churches of Asia Minor (modern Turkey) into his work. Therefore, we can locate this work in the eastern Mediterranean.

Concerning the date of composition of the book of Revelation, the text itself provides few clues. The most important piece of evidence is the author's use of the term "Babylon" for Rome

(18:2). In other Jewish literature written toward the end of the first century A.D., this term is used to describe Rome, but only after the Roman armies had destroyed Jerusalem and the temple in A.D. 70 (see *2 Esdr.* 3:1-2, 28-31; *2 Apoc. Bar.* 10:1-3; 11:1; 67:7; *Sib. Or.* 5:143, 159). Recall that the Babylonians had destroyed the Jerusalem temple in the sixth century B.C. and deported the people of Judea, throwing them into the darkest period of their history. Because the book of Revelation also makes this connection between Rome and Babylon, scholars generally agree that it had to have been written after A.D. 70. The early church writer Irenaeus (*Adv. haer.* 5.30.3) suggests that Revelation was written toward the end of Domitian's reign (A.D. 81–96), so, without other evidence to the contrary, a date of A.D. 95–96 is reasonable. This means that the book of Revelation is among the last books to be written in the New Testament. This book was commonly accepted as Sacred Scripture by the latter half of the second century.

The genre of the book of Revelation

What can we say about the genre of the book of Revelation? John describes his work as a prophecy, even though he never actually calls himself a prophet (1:3). A careful reader of this book will notice right away that we do not have a continuous story as we find in the Gospels. Instead, John records the visions (images) and auditions (voices) that came to him through a divine being, usually an angel. The subject matter of these visions and auditions are "heavenly things" and future events. This kind of work is generally described as an "apocalypse," from a Greek word that means "revelation." In fact, in some Bible translations the book of Revelation is given the title "Apocalypse."

Typical of this genre, the seer (that is, the recipient of the visions) receives revelations through mediation of some sort and then records them in writing. The revelations involve secrets of the *cosmos* (the workings of the heavenly bodies, the fixing of the calendar, names and activities of angelic beings, places of reward and punishment) and secrets about the future (political and historical events, the destiny of God's people, etc.). Sometimes the seer is allowed to journey to the heavenly locations. In those cases the apocalypse also describes the details of the heavenly journey.

Most apocalypses also include a command to the seer to seal up the written account of the visions for some future time.

If we assume that the book of Revelation belongs to the genre "apocalypse," what then are we to understand about its interpretation? Some people read the book of Revelation to find out what will happen when this physical world is destroyed or to discover when it will come to an end—in other words, as a roadmap of the end time. However, we can be quite certain that the author of the book of Revelation did not write it for that purpose and that the original audience did not understand it in that way. Therefore, we would be seriously misled about its meaning if that is what we seek to learn from it today.

Perhaps the best way to understand apocalypses is to investigate the precursors or forerunners of the genre. In recent decades scholars have been debating whether apocalypses have their roots in the writings of the prophets or in Wisdom literature. This question arose out of the fact that one can see features of both genres in a wide variety of Jewish and Christian apocalypses and, in particular, in the book of Revelation.

As mentioned above, John himself describes his book as a prophecy (1:3; 22:7, 10, 18, 19). Nowhere in Revelation does he distinguish Jewish prophets of old from Christian prophets. Therefore, it is reasonable to assume that he understood his prophecy to function in the same way as the prophets before him. Whereas we tend to think of prophets primarily as predictors of the future, the prophets of the Old Testament were better known as spokespersons of God on behalf of the covenant. In that capacity the prophet brought accusations against Israel and Judah when they failed to keep the covenant and warned of God's punishment against wrongdoers. The prophet also brought a message of consolation when, in the midst of their suffering, they thought God had abandoned them or when they repented of their sin.

Thus the Old Testament prophets' message was principally a call to conversion and a divine consolation in times of trouble. The prophets also complained against the people, saying that God would punish them if they continued in their wicked ways, but the prophets did not engage in fortunetelling or what modern people understand as predicting the future.

Another important aspect of biblical prophecy is its grounding in a particular place and time. In other words, the prophetic author's original, intended meaning is closely connected to the historical circumstances out of which he wrote. For the book of Revelation this means that we ought to read it as a call to conversion and a message of consolation written first for the churches of Asia Minor, in *their* historical and cultural situation, and now reinterpreted for *our* historical and cultural situation. This is a process that requires prayerful reflection, but it is also in keeping with our understanding of the prophets' role as the conscience of the people.

Other scholars argue that the genre "apocalypse" has its roots in Wisdom literature. The Old Testament books included in this category are Proverbs, Job, and Ecclesiastes, along with Sirach (also known as Ecclesiasticus) and Wisdom of Solomon. While Wisdom literature covers a wide variety of topics, it is principally concerned with questions about universal truth, the meaning of life (and death), and what constitutes human good. As one might expect, then, it also addresses issues of theodicy (response to the problem of evil): Why do the righteous suffer without warrant? Why do the wicked appear to go unpunished? What is the meaning of human suffering, and where is God's justice? All of us can relate to these questions, especially when the difficulties of life become too much to bear.

How have these theodicy questions traditionally been addressed within Judaism and Christianity? Needless to say, answers have never come easily. The reason? Jewish and Christian respondents must come to terms with two interrelated and sometimes apparently contradictory assertions: God is sovereign (all-powerful and in control) and God is just. If we acknowledge the existence of evil in the world, we are forced to question whether or to what extent God has power over evil. On the other hand, if we assert the sovereignty of God, then we must wonder about God's justice, since experience shows us that evil does indeed go unpunished at times, and good people do suffer harm.

The sages (wise teachers) of the Old Testament Wisdom literature wrestled with similar questions. The book of Job is an excellent example. If we accept that the genre of the book of Revelation has roots in Wisdom literature, we can see how it treats questions of theodicy by repeatedly asserting that God is sovereign, reigning supreme not only over the heavenly realm but also over the earthly realm and even the underworld. In addition, it repeatedly asserts that God is just, promising reward to God's holy ones and punishment of the wicked. This message of hope and consolation is especially powerful if the audience for which it is intended is experiencing persecution for its faith.

Finally, as mentioned above, the apocalyptic genre does not presuppose a sustained story line that extends from the beginning to the end of the book. Likewise, the reader of the book of Revelation will observe that the book is not organized chronologically. Rather, its author describes a collection of visions, some of which are situated in the heavenly realm and others on earth; some pertaining to the believing community as it anticipates persecution, others relating to those who have endured the suffering and proved themselves faithful. Often the author will introduce a particular idea or image in an early vision and then return to it later in a series of expanded visions or auditions. For these reasons the reader must resist the temptation to impose a chronology on the book. Any attempt to see the book as a linear map of the events of the end time will necessarily lead to misunderstanding of its message.

Biblical scholars have not yet conclusively answered the question about the origins of the apocalyptic genre. However, its parallels with biblical prophecy and Wisdom literature give us a clearer sense of what to expect when we read apocalypses. To sum up, apocalypses do three things: (1) they console people in situations of persecution; (2) they present a particular interpretation of historical events that focuses on the justice and sovereignty of God and the triumph of good over evil; (3) they persuade their hearers to keep covenant with God, that is, to live in a way that assures that they will be among God's elect in the end time.

Outline of the book of Revelation

Anyone who has done any in-depth study of the Bible knows that there are almost as many outlines of a given book as there are scholars studying it. Unfortunately, the authors of these biblical books did not provide us with their outlines, so modern readers use whatever clues they

can find in the text to uncover the author's intent and then construct an outline accordingly. In turn, the outline provides a map for studying the book in an organized way. The outline provided here is designed to highlight the patterns of the symbolic number seven in the book of Revelation.

I. Rev 1:1-8 Introductory materials
II. Rev 1:9–11:19 First cycle of visions
  A. Rev 1:9-20 Initial vision of one like the son of man
  B. Rev 2:1–3:22 The seven letters to the seven churches of Asia Minor
  C. Rev 4:1–5:14 The vision of God's throne and the Lamb
  D. Rev 6:1–7:17 The opening of the seven seals
  E. Rev 8:1–11:19 The seven trumpets
III. Rev 12:1–20:15 Second cycle of visions
  A. Rev 12:1-18 Vision of the woman and the dragon
  B. Rev 13:1-18 Vision of the beasts of the sea and the land
  C. Rev 14:1-20 Vision of the Lamb and imminent judgment
  D. Rev 15:1–16:21 Visions of the seven bowls
  E. Rev 17:1–18:24 Fall of Babylon (interlude)
  F. Rev 19:1–20:15 Seven visions of the last things
IV. Rev 21:1–22:5 Vision of the New Jerusalem
V. Rev 22:6-21 Concluding materials

The commentary that follows is organized according to this outline, with additional subdivisions as needed. However, before beginning our analysis of the book of Revelation, a brief introduction to the symbolism of its colors and numbers is in order.

Symbolic numbers in the book of Revelation

Numbers are used liberally throughout the book of Revelation, and readers sometimes mistakenly take them literally rather than symbolically, as intended by the author. Here are the most commonly cited numbers and their symbolic meanings:

- Three = a number suggesting a few, a limited number, or a limited time.
- Four = fullness, especially as it relates to the breadth of the universe (e.g., four corners of the world); universality.
- Seven = perfection, fullness, perfect orderedness. In the book of Genesis it is the number of the completeness of creation.
- Ten = sometimes denoting a limited number, other times recalling the ten kings of Daniel 7:24, who oppress the holy ones of God in the period before God's reign is finally established.
- Twelve = fullness or completeness, especially bringing diversity into unity. Israel was made up of twelve tribes. The calendar year consists of twelve months, and the day has two sets of twelve hours.
- Thousand = a number signifying myriads, a number too large to count.

These numbers, as well as multiples, combinations, or fractions of these numbers, occur throughout the book of Revelation. In each case the context will help us understand their significance.

Symbolic colors in the book of Revelation

Like numbers, the colors in the book of Revelation are also symbolic. Again, the context will help us understand their significance, but this list of color symbols will help us get started.

- White = victory, triumph
- Red = bloodshed, violence
- Scarlet = royalty, bloodshed
- Purple = royalty
- Black = famine
- Pale green = death

The exalted Christ is frequently represented as wearing white, as are the martyrs who make up his heavenly army. The dragon that wreaks havoc on the earth is red, and the whore Babylon wears scarlet and purple. Thus the first thing the reader will observe is that the colors in the book of Revelation mark out the two sides in a great battle between good and evil.

COMMENTARY

INTRODUCTORY MATERIALS

Rev 1:1-8

The introductory section of this book consists of a prologue (1:1-3), from which the title of the book is derived, followed by what appears to be the "address" portion of a letter (1:4-8).

1:1-3 Prologue

The first word of the document, *apocalypsis*, means "revelation." Thus the book is known as Revelation or the Apocalypse. The author of the book, who is also the recipient of the revelation, identifies himself as John and describes his purpose in writing: to witness to "the word of God and to the testimony of Jesus Christ" (1:2). He also describes his work as prophecy (1:3). Notice the relationship of parties involved in the transmission of this revelation. The revelation belongs or pertains to Jesus Christ (1:1). It is given by God but is mediated through an angel to John, who in turn reported what he saw to others (the community of believers, 1:1-2). The prologue concludes with a beatitude (a saying that begins, "Blessed is the one ... . ") for those who hear the word and act upon what they hear (1:3). This is a prophet at work, acting as spokesperson for God and calling people to conversion.

1:4-8 The "address"

This subunit looks like the "address" portion of a letter, but it is somewhat misleading because the letter form is abandoned almost immediately. The author, again identified as John, says that he is writing to the seven churches of Asia. However, he may not have had exactly seven in mind, since seven is a symbolic number representing fullness or perfection. In fact, he may have been referring to *all* the churches of first-century Asia, now Turkey.

This opening of the letter contains an extended greeting, beginning with the words "grace to you and peace" (1:4). Notice John's use of patterns of three. This grace and peace has a threefold source: God, the seven spirits before God's throne, and Jesus. Further, God is identified with three tenses of the verb "to be"—"who is and who was and who is to come" (1:4)—an expansion of the divine name "I AM," revealed to Moses at the burning bush (Exod 3:14). Finally, Jesus is described in terms of three roles or functions: "faithful witness, the firstborn of the dead and ruler of the kings of the earth" (1:5). His activities on the community's behalf are also enumerated in a pattern of three: he loves us, freed us from sin, and made us a kingdom and priests of God (1:5-6). In these very succinct statements, John is asserting God's sovereignty, Jesus' triumph over evil and death, and the believers' reason for hope and consolation. As we shall see later, these are the primary elements of John's theodicy (response to the problem of evil).

Finally, the opening of the letter contains a prayerlike expression of confidence in Jesus' return (1:7). The text of the prayer is constructed of quotations from the Old Testament books of Daniel and Zechariah. Daniel 7:13 describes a vision of "one like a son of man" (a heavenly being who has the appearance of a human) who comes before God's throne in heaven to receive, from God, an everlasting dominion and kingship over all the earth. In the interpretation of Daniel's vision (Dan 7:15-27), this heavenly being is shown to be a symbol of the holy ones of God (Dan 7:18, 22). However, here, in the book of Revelation, the one who will come on the clouds is Jesus Christ.

In Zechariah 12:10 the prophet speaks on behalf of God, saying that God will pour out a spirit of compassion on Judah and Jerusalem, so that they will mourn over the one whom they have pierced. Here, in the book of Revelation, the message continues to be one of hope and consolation, but with an added emphasis on the revelation of Christ as the "pierced" one.

This section ends with a declaration of the sovereignty of God, who is almighty, the beginning and end of all things (1:8). Alpha is the first letter of the Greek alphabet, and Omega is the last.

FIRST CYCLE OF VISIONS
Rev 1:9–11:19

This first cycle of visions consists of an initial vision (1:9-20) followed by seven letters to the churches of Asia Minor (2:1–3:22), a vision of God's throne and the Lamb (4:1–5:14), the opening of seven seals (6:1–7:17), and the blowing of seven trumpets (8:1–11:19).

INITIAL VISION OF "ONE LIKE A SON OF MAN"
Rev 1:9-20

After the prologue and the opening, John recounts a vision of a heavenly being (1:9-20). He begins by affirming his relationship with his hearers in terms of what they share in Jesus. Again, notice the use of the pattern of three: "I John . . . who share with you the distress, the kingdom, and the endurance we have in Jesus" (1:9). Taken together, these three expressions speak to John's understanding of what it means to participate in the Christian life. The word translated here as "distress" can also mean "persecution" or "tribulation," referring to the end time. The word translated as "kingdom" can also mean "kingly reign" or "sovereignty" and should be taken to refer to the hope the hearers share in the full manifestation of God's power over evil in the end time. Finally, the word "endurance," also translated "patient endurance," is key to understanding John's message. The word appears seven times in Revelation (1:9; 2:2, 3, 19; 3:10; 13:10; 14:12), and in each case it describes how Christians ought to respond to the troubles they face *because* they are Christian. Later, in 3:10, John is quite explicit that he associates these troubles with the end time.

Next, John provides the temporal and spatial setting for the vision (1:10-11). The "Lord's day" or "the day (dedicated) to the Lord" is most likely a reference to Sunday, the first day of the week and the day on which early Christians gathered to celebrate Eucharist (see Acts 20:7; 1 Cor 16:2). On this day he was "caught up in spirit," that is, under the influence of the Spirit, perhaps in a trance of some sort, when he heard a great trumpetlike voice. In the first century A.D., the trumpet was used in cultic (worship) settings to signal different elements of the worship service or to announce the beginning of festivals or other public events.

Some biblical scholars have seen in John's description of the setting of his first vision some parallels with the call narratives of the Old Testament prophets (cf. Isa 6; Jer 1; Ezek 1–3). If Revelation 1:9-10 is the setting for John's call to prophesy, then the command to write down the words of the vision and distribute them to seven churches (1:11) describes his first task as prophet. All these churches were located in what is now Turkey.

The vision that follows consists of three parts: the account of the vision itself (1:12-16); John's response to the vision (1:17-18a); and an interpretation of the vision (1:18b-20). The imagery of the vision is highly symbolic, much of it coming from the writings of Daniel and Ezekiel. The "one like a son of man" (a heavenly being in human form) is an allusion to Daniel 7:13 (see comments on 1:7 above, p. 836). The mention of his snow-white hair parallels that of the Ancient of Days [God] in Daniel 7:9. Other details of John's description of the heavenly being—dressed in a long robe with a golden sash, with feet that gleamed like polished metal and eyes that blazed like fire (1:13-15)—have parallels with Daniel's vision of a heavenly being in human form who comes to deliver a message about the conflict of nations (Dan 10:5-6).

This description of "one like a son of man" is also reminiscent of Ezekiel's visions of God on the throne. In both cases, what would have been God's torso is said to gleam like amber, and what would have been God's feet has the appearance of fire (see Ezek 1:27; 8:2). Ancient peoples believed that one's power to act resided in the hands and feet and that one's will, intellect, and judgment resided in the eyes and heart. Thus John's heavenly being manifests full power, intellect, and judgment through his unusual feet and eyes (1:14-15).

Finally, the long robe and girdle with which the heavenly being is clothed (1:13) are reminiscent of the dress of the priests of the Jerusalem temple (see Exod 28:4; 39:29; Wis 18:24). Perhaps John is suggesting that this heavenly being has been set apart for some special function in the divine liturgy. This would be consistent with his mention of the trumpet in 1:10. In apocalyptic literature the two-edged sword is a symbol of eschatological (end-time) judgment. The fact that it comes from the heavenly being's mouth means that his *words* are judgment (1:16).

John's terrified response (1:17) and the consolation that follows (1:17-18) are typical of visions of this sort. See, for example, Daniel's response to the vision of the "man" dressed in linen (Dan 10:8-9) and the heavenly being's words of comfort given in response to his alarm (Dan 10:10-12). In the interpretation of John's vision (1:18-20), the heavenly being reveals himself as the resurrected Christ, the one who was dead but now lives (1:18). The resurrected Christ explains that the seven stars in his hand are the guardian spirits of the seven churches (ancient peoples believed that cities prospered because their guardian angels protected them), and the seven golden lamps are the seven churches (1:20).

The number seven is especially significant here. In Greco-Roman culture the rainbow was thought to consist of seven colors. In the second century A.D., some of the Roman emperors included seven stars on their minted coins as a symbol of world domination. Thus the message of this vision is ultimately one of hope and confidence in the One who possesses power over anything that might affect the churches. Just as the heavenly being in the vision walks among the lamps, the risen Christ continues to dwell among them, and just as he holds the stars in his hand, the risen Christ continues to be responsible for their guardianship.

LETTERS TO THE SEVEN CHURCHES
Rev 2:1–3:22

John goes on to record seven letters to the churches of Asia Minor (2:1–3:22). The letters follow a very strict literary pattern, with few variations.

Form of the letters to the seven churches:

• To the spirit of the church in _____

• write this: _____ says this:

• I know . . . _____ (message of consolation)

• yet I hold this against you: _____ (accusation)

• To the victor I will give _____

• Whoever has ears ought to hear what the Spirit says to the churches.

In the opening address of each letter, after the church is identified, the writer describes the source of his prophetic message, namely, the exalted Christ. Notice that almost all the descriptions of Christ are taken from the initial vision, suggesting that we ought to see the letters as part of a larger unit that begins with the vision of "one like a son of man" (1:9-20). In the body of each letter, the church is either consoled on account of the sufferings they endure, or scolded for their offenses against God. In most cases they are both consoled and scolded!

From these letters we can discover what the author thinks are the problems of the churches in his day. Pay careful attention to the section of each letter that begins "Yet I hold this against you . . ." As we read these letters, we might also want to think about whether these problems have any counterpart in the lives of today's faith communities.

The command to listen, which is found in the conclusion of each letter, is typical of prophetic literature. The phrase "to the victor," also in the conclusion of each letter, describes the rewards that faithful ones will receive on account of their devotion to Christ who has conquered; those who shed their blood for the ransom of the saints will be exalted by God (5:5, 9-10). At the conclusion of the book of Revelation, in the vision of the New Jerusalem, we learn that those who conquer (i.e., the victors) will inherit the fullness of covenant relationship with God (cf. 21:7).

What, then, is John doing by including these seven letters in the first major unit of the book of Revelation? On one level he is simply playing the part of a scribe, writing down the words dictated by the exalted Christ. However, we cannot neglect the fact that he is also acting as prophet or spokes-person of God, delivering messages of consolation and warning. In fact, this is the perspective from which the whole of the book of Revelation ought to be read. These are communities that were apparently well known to John and for which he felt responsibility, much as the prophets of the Old Testament felt responsible to call the Israelites to conversion.

2:1-7 Message to the church at Ephesus

Because of its location on the western coast of Asia Minor and at the mouth of the river Cayster, Ephesus was an important commercial center for the eastern part of the Roman Empire in the first century A.D. It was also considered to be among the largest cities of the province, with a population estimated at 250,000. The city played an important role in the life of first-century Judaism and Christianity. The Jewish historian Josephus, for example, notes that there was a substantial Jewish population in Ephesus. The Acts of the Apostles suggests that Paul used Ephesus as his base of operations for two years during his missionary activity (Acts 19:1-41). In addition, early traditions associate John, the author of the Fourth Gospel, with Ephesus. It is also said that Mary, the mother of Jesus, lived there for a time and died at Ephesus.

The city contained shrines in honor of a full range of Greek and Roman deities. Its most important religious site was the temple of Artemis, a Greek mother-goddess and goddess of fertility, which was considered to be one of the Seven Wonders of the World. There was also a 25,000-seat theater in Ephesus. The library of Celsus was located there, along with temples for the imperial cult and shrines of the Egyptian deities. The city had also gained a reputation as a place to study magic, so it was not uncommon to find exorcists there.

In this letter John praises the church at Ephesus for their faithful endurance in the face of deception by false apostles and their heresies (2:2-3). However, he warns them that their initial love (zeal?) has waned, and they are now in danger of losing their faith unless they reform their ways (2:4-5). John's choice of description for the exalted Christ—holding the seven stars and walking among the seven lampstands (see the commentary on 2:1)—is especially appropriate for the church at Ephesus because it was a rich and powerful city, and many biblical scholars think that the church at Ephesus was the mother church of the area. However, John may also want to remind the faithful that the exalted Christ continues to be present among them and therefore knows their deeds, both good and bad.

The promise made to those who conquer (2:7) is reminiscent of the second creation story in Genesis, in which Adam and Eve were barred access to the tree of life after their sin (Gen 3:24). In this letter, those who will be allowed to eat of the tree of life are being restored to an intimate relationship with God such as Adam and Eve enjoyed in paradise. The "tree of life" imagery in Genesis may have been introduced here as a counterpoint to the sacred tree of the cult of Artemis.

2:8-11 Message to the church at Smyrna

The city of Smyrna was located on the western coast of Asia Minor, north of Ephesus. It had a good harbor, and its location at the end of a major east-west road made it an important commercial city in the first century A.D., though its origins date back to 1000 B.C. Along with Ephesus, Sardis, and Pergamum, it was one of four centers of the provincial assembly of Asia Minor and the first in the province to build a temple to the goddess Roma (Rome). In A.D. 26 the city built a temple to Tiberius, making it second only to Pergamum as a center for the emperor cult (worship of the emperor as a manifestation of the Roman deities). Although we know relatively little about life in Smyrna in the first century, evidence from the second century indicates that the city was suffering under many conflicts—between Christians and non-Christians, between rich and poor, and between local government authorities and Roman

provincial authorities. Bishop Polycarp was martyred at Smyrna in A.D. 155.

This letter differs from the form outlined above in that there is no accusation of the community, presumably because the author has nothing with which to charge them. He acknowledges their economic poverty, calling them rich, presumably rich in faith (2:9). Further, he encourages them to stand firm in the face of persecution and not to fear the suffering that is about to befall them (2:10). They will be arrested, he says, and some will even be put to death, but those who are faithful to the end will survive the "test[ing]" and will be rewarded with eternal life. Thus the description of the exalted Christ as the one who "once died but came to life" (2:8) is consistent with John's expectations for the future of the community at Smyrna.

The source of the Christian community's persecution appears to have been the Jewish synagogue ("assembly") in Smyrna (2:9), further suggesting an intra-family fight between Jews and Christian Jews, that is, Jews who accepted Jesus as the messiah. The ten days of tribulation (2:10) may be an allusion to the story of Daniel and his friends, who were tested for ten days when they refused to eat the king's food, which had been dedicated to idols (Dan 1:12-15; cf. 5:3-4). The promise that those who conquer will escape the "second death" (2:11) is a reference to final judgment (see 20:11-15).

2:12-17 Message to the church at Pergamum

Like many of the major cities in Asia Minor, Pergamum's history is very long. During the Hellenistic period, in the early third century B.C., it became famous as the capital of an independent kingdom in western Asia Minor. However, on the death of its last king, King Attalus III, in 133 B.C., the kingdom was bequeathed to the Romans, and shortly after that time Pergamum became the capital of the Roman province of Asia Minor. During the reign of the Roman emperor Augustus (31 B.C.–A.D. 14), the province was reconstituted, and perhaps at that time Ephesus became its capital, but Pergamum likely retained some of its special status for imperial authorities, being the first to build a temple to Augustus.

Throughout this period the city of Pergamum was known as an important center of learning, having one of the largest libraries in the world, and a center for the arts, including a famous school of sculpture. Pergamum also possessed a sanctuary of Asclepius, a Greek god of healing, where people could obtain medical care and where they studied rhetoric. The famous medical doctor Galen was from Pergamum. Temples to several other deities were located here, including a temple to Zeus, the highest deity in the Roman pantheon. The city was also known for its silver mines and for the making of textiles and parchment. Agricultural work flourished here as well.

In this letter the exalted Christ is described as having a sharp, two-edged sword, suggesting judgment, either of the Christian community or of the city itself (2:12; cf. Isa 11:4; 49:2). The author of the letter begins by acknowledging the difficult situation of the community: they live in the place where Satan has his throne (2:13). This is likely a reference to the position of esteem that Pergamum held in the emperor cult and in the worship of Roman deities. It is interesting to note that the previous letter calls the synagogue at Smyrna the "assembly of Satan" (2:9), suggesting some kind of collusion between the Roman authorities and the synagogue. Here, too, the Christian community is praised for standing firm in the face of persecution (2:13).

However, all is *not* well. John accuses the Christian community of harboring some who teach that it is permissible to compromise their faith and participate in idol worship (2:14). (For the story of Balak and Balaam, see Num 22:1–25:3.) They also tolerate the teachings of the Nicolaitans, who apparently hold a similar view on participating in pagan cults (2:15; 2:6). In other words, they have accommodated the practice of their faith to the demands of the wider culture to such an extent that they have compromised the integrity of their faith. Needless to say, the author of the letter considers this to be a very serious problem! Hence the description of the exalted Christ as having a sharp, two-edged sword, the symbol of judgment (2:12).

The promise made to the ones who conquer (2:17) has messianic and salvific overtones. Jewish apocalyptic literature describes an expectation that the manna of the Exodus will return in the messianic age. The meaning of the white stone (2:17) likely has something to do with victory, and the new name signals a new destiny or a new way of life.

2:18-29 Message to the church at Thyatira

The city of Thyatira was located in Lydia in the western part of Asia Minor. Although few artifacts remain today, the city is believed to have played an important role in the civic life of the area from the second century B.C. through the third century A.D. Apparently it was also an important center for the making and trading of wool. The Acts of the Apostles tells a story about a woman named Lydia, who was from Thyatira and was baptized by Paul after listening to his preaching (Acts 16:11-15). Lydia was a dealer in expensive purple dyes. Like several of its neighbors, Thyatira had religious sites associated with the emperor cult and shrines to the Greek and Roman deities.

In this letter the exalted Christ is described as the Son of God, with eyes of fire and shining feet (2:18), perhaps in contrast to the sun god Helius, whose devotees had a shrine in Thyatira. The members of the Christian community are praised for their love, above all, and for the fact that they continue to grow in holiness (2:19). However, they are scolded for enduring the influence of a prophetess who deceives people and lures them into idolatry (2:20). It is likely that she is a Nicolaitan (see 2:12-17). The name Jezebel is a reference to a Canaanite queen of King Ahab, who established the cult of Baal (worship of any of various local fertility or nature gods among Semitic peoples) in Israel and doomed Ahab's dynasty (2 Kgs 10:7). Fornication and adultery should be understood metaphorically to describe participation in idol worship.

Finally, a double promise is made to the victors (2:26-28). First, they will be given authority over the nations, an allusion to Psalm 2, which, already by the first century B.C., was thought to refer to the Jewish messiah. Second, they will be given the morning star. The meaning of the latter is uncertain.

3:1-6 Message to the church at Sardis

Sardis was located in Asia Minor, approximately sixty miles inland from Smyrna and Ephesus. Along with Ephesus, Smyrna, and Pergamum, it was one of four centers of the Roman provincial assembly of Asia and the regional capital of Lydia. The Jewish historian Josephus mentions the existence of a large Jewish community there in the first century A.D. However, we know little about the Christian community in Sardis until the second century, and then primarily through the writings of Melito, the bishop of Sardis. Apparently, persecutions of Christians were conducted in Sardis during that period. The city was founded in the third century B.C.

In this letter the description of the exalted Christ appears to build upon the mention of the morning star at the end of the previous letter, but like the other letters, it also includes details from the initial vision of "one like a son of man" (3:1; see 1:16, 20). Again, like the earlier letters, the author begins, "I know your works . . . " (3:1). However, he has nothing positive to say about this community. They may have a reputation of goodness, but they are in fact as good as dead! Thus he tells them that they better wake up and strengthen what still survives of their faith (3:2). If they do not, he will come when they least expect and inflict judgment on them (3:3).

The promise to the victors is a robe of victory (3:4-5; see "colors" in the introduction to this commentary, pp. 834–35) and assurance that their names will always be found in the book of life (3:5), an allusion to the book of names of the holy ones in 20:12.

3:7-13 Message to the church at Philadelphia

Philadelphia was located in western Asia Minor, along a route between Smyrna and Sardis. The city was founded in the second century B.C. by one of the kings of Pergamum, when the area was still an independent kingdom. Because of the fertile farmland around it, Philadelphia became a center of agriculture, as well as leather working and textile making. However, the area was also prone to earthquakes, and Philadelphia was hit especially hard in the early part of the first century, leaving significant damage to city buildings and walls. It suffered another setback when, in A.D. 92, during the reign of Domitian, the provinces were ordered to destroy half of their vineyards and were not allowed to plant new ones. This city's most important deity was Dionysius, the god of wine. Some from among the Christian community at Philadelphia were martyred along with Polycarp at Smyrna in A.D. 155.

Breaking with the pattern of the previous letters, the description of the exalted Christ in the letter to the Philadelphians does not go back to

the initial vision of "one like a son of man," except for the mention of keys (3:7; cf. 1:18). Here the key is the key of David, suggesting authority that is granted them because of their faith in the messiah of the Jews. The open door is a metaphor for opportunity (3:8). The writer acknowledges that the community has little power right now, but he tells them that eventually their opponents—the "assembly (synagogue) of Satan" is a derogatory reference to the Jewish community at Philadelphia—will come to their way of thinking (3:9).

Although hinted at in other letters, here the theme of theodicy is made explicit: God will vindicate the righteous and make the wicked see the error of their ways. The promise given to this community is an anticipation of the final vision of the book of Revelation, the New Jerusalem (3:12). As we shall see later, the New Jerusalem will have no need of a temple because the whole city and its inhabitants will constitute the temple of God and the Lamb (see 21:2, 22-23).

3:14-22 Message to the church at Laodicea

Located southeast of Philadelphia, Laodicea was a major commercial city in the first century A.D. Because it was not far from Hierapolis, the waterfall that emptied out of the hot springs of that city apparently could be seen in Laodicea. It had been founded during the reign of the Greek king Antiochus II (261–246 B.C.) and, under Roman rule, had grown into a manufacturing center for clothing and carpets made from a special type of black wool produced in the area. Laodicea boasted a medical school known for the healing of eye diseases, and it served as a major banking center. The city itself was very wealthy, as evidenced by the fact that it rebuilt quickly and without aid from outside sources after a devastating earthquake in A.D. 60.

In the opening of this letter, the exalted Christ is given three attributions, none of which is connected to the initial vision of the "one like a son of man" (3:14; see 1:9-20). Here we find the only reference in the New Testament to Christ as the "Amen," meaning "So be it." This attribution suggests a position of great authority, much like the third attribution, "source of God's creation" (3:14). The Greek word *archē*, here translated as "source," can also mean "ruler" or "beginning." The second attribution, "faithful and true witness," recalls 1:5 and anticipates 19:11, where Christ is similarly described.

Unlike most of the other letters, the phrase "I know your works" (3:15) is not an introduction to praise or consolation, but rather an indictment. Using the imagery of water, perhaps the now tepid, sulfurous water descending from the hot springs at Hierapolis, the writer says he is about to spit them out of his mouth because, comfortable in their riches, they are disgustingly lukewarm in their faith (3:15-17). Worse yet, they have deluded themselves into thinking that they are among the spiritual elite, people of admirable faith (3:17). This letter, then, is intended as a rude awakening to the church at Laodicea!

With an ironic twist, the message quickly turns to consolation. Their spiritual poverty will be remedied by a gift of fire-refined gold (3:18), an Old Testament image for the purifying effects of suffering (Mal 3:2). They will be relieved of their nakedness with garments of victory, the reward of the martyrs, and they will be given new sight through the saving ointment that Jesus brings (3:18). Recall that these are the things for which this city is renowned: riches, fine clothing, and medicine for eyes. Again the author draws upon the image of an open door—opportunity—and promises that anyone who opens to Jesus will dine with him, a clear allusion to Eucharist (3:20). Finally, the victor is promised a seat on God's throne (3:21). We will return to both of these images—the open door and the throne of God—in the next section of this book.

THE VISION OF GOD'S THRONE AND THE LAMB

Rev 4:1–5:14

There are several types of visions in the book of Revelation. This vision is a theophany, that is, a revelation or manifestation of God. The Greek word *theos* means "God." Typically, theophanies have a mountain setting. The seer (i.e., the recipient of the vision) is taken to, or otherwise allowed to see, where God resides. The vision is accompanied by heavenly voices and cosmic manifestations of the power of God, like lightning, fire, and thunder. The seer usually describes himself as being in a trance, and time appears to stand still, at least momentarily. In this theophany

John sees an open door and is told, "Come up here . . . " (4:1; see 3:20).

The throne that John is allowed to see derives its imagery from the Hellenistic royal court. Hence the description of the immense throne at the end of the throne room and the floor that looked like a sea of glass (4:2, 6). In ancient cultures the throne was the symbol of the king's authority. Therefore, the more intimidating it was, the more it said about the king's authority. Interestingly, in this vision the one seated on the throne (4:3) is described, not in anthropomorphic terms, as one might expect, but by analogy to precious stones, perhaps to suggest that God's kingly splendor surpasses that of any earthly king.

The identity of the twenty-four elders (4:4) is unknown, though scholars have suggested that they represent the sum of the twelve tribes of Israel and the twelve apostles. The same two groups appear together in the final vision of the New Jerusalem in Revelation 21–22. Twenty-four, being a multiple of twelve, represents fullness or perfection. They are dressed in white, symbolizing victory, and they wear crowns of gold, symbolizing their royal authority (4:4). The seven spirits of God are the angels of the presence, who stand before God's throne (4:5).

The "four living creatures" (4:6) are called watchers, or *merkabah* angels, in the Jewish hierarchy of angels. These watchers are sometimes portrayed as angels of fire who support God's throne or as heavenly beings covered with eyes, with which they constantly keep watch over the throne. The notion probably originated with the Jewish idea of the cherubim, who were part of the throne of the ark of the covenant in the holy of holies. In distinguishing these watchers as the four different animal creatures (4:7-8), John most likely was influenced by Ezekiel 1:5-14. In later Christian theology the symbols of the four living creatures become associated with the four Gospels: the lion (Mark), the ox (Luke), the man (Matthew), and the eagle (John).

The watchers' prayer of praise recalls the description of God in the opening of the book of Revelation: "The Lord God almighty, / who was, and who is, and who is to come" (4:8; cf. 1:8). Each time the watchers give glory to God, the twenty-four elders bow down in homage to God (4:10). The casting down of their crowns (4:10) is similar to Hellenistic oriental kingship rituals in which vassal kings cast their crowns at the emperor's feet to declare their allegiance and identify themselves as the emperor's vassals. The proclamation, "Worthy are you" (4:11), was the standard way that the Roman emperor was addressed as he entered the throne room. All this is to say that John's audience would have readily understood the message of this vision: God is, always was, and always will be all-powerful and king over all that exists.

John signals a new scene in his vision of the heavenly throne room when he says, "[Then] I saw . . ."(5:1). The first scene shows that God is sovereign; this second scene will address the question of God's justice. The description of the One on the throne holding a scroll (5:1) resembles depictions of the Roman emperor seated on his throne as judge and holding a *libellus*, a petition or letter in the form of an open scroll. The seer, John, first experiences extreme pain when he fears that no one is able to open the scroll and thereby dispense justice (5:4). However, when one of the elders tells him that the lion of the tribe of Judah and the root (i.e., descendant) of David will open the seals, we also learn about his qualifications to do so—he has triumphed (5:5)! The Greek word is *nikē*, meaning "to win," "to triumph," or "to win the right." But over what did he triumph?

Suddenly John sees a Lamb standing in the midst of (or as part of) the throne (5:6). This is no ordinary lamb! John says that it "seemed to have been slain" (5:6), meaning that it has the marks of having been slaughtered, but it is, in fact, alive! John observes that the Lamb has seven horns and seven eyes. Horns were thought to contain the power of an animal or an object: in this case the Lamb possesses the fullness of power (5:6). It also has seven eyes, symbolizing full knowledge or insight (5:6). Ancient people thought that an individual was able to see, not because of the light that came into the eye, but because of light that was *inside* the person. These eyes, John says, are the seven spirits of God. They are sent out into the world, bringing knowledge of all that is happening on earth (5:6).

When the Lamb steps up to receive the scroll (5:7), the four living creatures and the elders reveal in song how the Lamb won the right to open the scroll (5:8). Three actions are attributed to him: (1) he was slaughtered (i.e., crucified); (2) he ransomed the holy ones (i.e., the Christian believers); (3) he made them a kingdom and priests for God

(5:9-10). Now he stands before God's throne, ready to dispense justice on God's behalf by vindicating the holy ones: they may be oppressed now, but they will reign on earth (5:10). God's holy ones are not present in heaven, but their prayers are represented before God by the four living creatures and the elders (5:8).

The scene concludes with everyone in the heavenly throne room singing in praise of the Lamb and the One seated on the throne (5:11-12). The heavenly choir numbers not in the thousands but *thousands* of thousands, suggesting a number too great to count. Everyone in the heavenly realm participates in this divine liturgy, creating a scene of perfect harmony, with no hint of suffering, pain, injustice, or evil. Finally, as if to crown this glorious moment, John observes that all created beings—those in heaven, on earth, and under the earth—join in the cosmic song of praise to God and the Lamb (5:13). The four living creatures confirm the event by saying, "Amen," meaning "So be it," and the elders worship their king (5:14).

THE SEVEN SEALS

Rev 6:1–7:17

The contents of the scroll, which the Lamb received in the previous vision, cannot be revealed until all of its seals are broken. Thus the cycle of the seven seals is closely connected to the vision of God's throne and the Lamb. Scrolls sent by kings or important dignitaries carried the seal of the sender to verify their authenticity. The seal also ensured that only the intended recipient would have access to the contents of the scroll. The four living creatures are the ones to announce the opening of the first four seals (6:1, 3, 5, 7). As each seal is broken, John receives yet another revelation. Although his vantage point for these visions is in the heavenly realm, all the activity associated with the opening of the seals takes place on earth.

6:2-8 The first four seal visions

The first four visions associated with the opening of the seals come in rapid succession. The first, the rider on the white horse, represents victory in war (6:2). Several scholars of the book of Revelation suggest that John has in mind the Parthians, whose equestrian armies were known for their skill with the bow and who were long-standing enemies of the Romans. John observes that he *was given* a crown (6:2). The passive verb form does not reveal the giver, but John's audience would have understood it to be God. That is, God allowed the war and God handed over the defeat of the Romans to the Parthians. However, we should not understand this to mean that God is responsible for evil. Rather, John is saying that nothing happens that is outside God's control; God is sovereign in all things!

The second horse, bright red, represents bloodshed (6:4). Its rider wields his sword *by permission* (6:4), suggesting again that God is firmly in control of these earthly events. The rider takes peace from the earth, in this case, Rome, and makes people slaughter one another (6:4), a reference to the civil strife that often follows war.

When the third seal is opened and the black horse appears, John observes that its rider carries a scale for buying and selling (6:5), thus revealing another consequence of war, namely, famine. Food shortages that require someone to pay a day's wages for a day's worth of bread are extreme, to be sure. The words that announce this famine come from the midst of the four living creatures (6:6), perhaps from God or the Lamb, suggesting that God is permitting the famine or at least knows of it. The command not to damage the oil and the wine (6:6) may simply mean that God will not allow this famine to end in total annihilation. However, some scholars have suggested that oil and wine were not principally food but objects for religious ritual, and were excluded from the famine for that reason.

The opening of the fourth seal brings another horse, sickly green, the color of death (6:7-8). Its rider and Hades, the place of the dead, are given power by God to unleash all the consequences of war—killing by sword, famine, pestilence, and wild animals—on one-fourth of the earth, suggesting that their effects are comprehensive and yet limited (6:8).

John may have borrowed his imagery of four horses and their horsemen from the book of Zechariah. The prophet describes a vision of four horsemen sent by God to patrol the earth, that is, the nations that were complacent while Jerusalem suffered (Zech 1:8-17). At this point an angel appears and asks God how long Jerusalem must wait for God's mercy (Zech 1:12). The question is one of theodicy. The angel tells Zechariah to prophesy,

declaring to the people that God is moved to compassion for Jerusalem and angry at the nations that did not come to its aid. The point of the prophecy of Zechariah is this: God is sovereign, but also just and merciful. So, too, in the book of Revelation: the horsemen are sent out, under God's authority, to take away the peace of Rome. In the next vision, the opening of the fifth seal, the faithful will ask how long it will be before God avenges their suffering. As he watches these visions unfold, one can imagine John being quietly gleeful, since, as we discover later, he perceives Rome to be the ultimate foe of the believing community.

6:9-11 The fifth seal vision

With the opening of the fifth seal, the scene shifts to the faithful martyrs residing under God's altar in the heavenly realm (6:9). The martyrs praise God's sovereignty and at the same time ask when God's justice will be manifest on their behalf (6:10). In response, they are given white robes, signifying victory, and told to enjoy their rest until the full number of martyrs has been reached (6:11). This is not to say that God is responsible for the martyrs' deaths, but rather that their deaths are somehow part of God's larger plan in the battle of good over evil.

6:12-16 The sixth seal vision

The opening of the sixth seal is accompanied by cosmic signs that are typical of apocalyptic literature: an earthquake, the sun turning black and the moon turning to blood, stars dropping from the heavens, and mountains falling down (6:12-14). Thus the action has shifted again to the earthly realm, though it appears that John is still in the heavens. John tells us that people of *every* social status responded to the cosmic signs with fright, begging for the earth to swallow them to protect them from God's wrath and the wrath of the Lamb (6:15-16). His point, of course, is that no one was unaffected by these phenomena. However, the intense cosmic activity (6:12-14) also suggests that all of creation is working on *God's* behalf, not theirs.

John also observes that these people are trying to avoid the *wrath* of the Lamb (6:16). A wrathful lamb is a strange paradox, because we tend to think of lambs as cute and cuddly, but already we know that it is no ordinary lamb, since earlier it was identified as the lion of the tribe of Judah and the root of David (5:5) and described as having seven horns and seven eyes (5:6). This sixth vision ends with the peoples exclaiming, "Who can withstand it?" (6:17), because it appears that *no one* will escape God's wrath.

7:1-17 Interlude between the sixth and seventh seal visions

The situation seems dire, but there is reason for hope. In a two-part interlude between the sixth and seventh seal visions—7:1-8 and 9-17—John witnesses God's protective action on behalf of the tribes of Israel, which represent the believing community. Like the previous vision, the setting is the earthly realm. First, John sees four angels holding back the forces of destruction, perhaps another reference to the four horsemen, so that they can do no harm to the universe (7:1; see 6:1-8). When the announcing angel orders them to hold back the forces of destruction a little longer, it becomes clear that this process of marking the servants of God with a seal (7:2-3) is for their protection. In the Greco-Roman world, people branded slaves on the forehead to indicate ownership. Likewise, in Ezekiel 9:1-3 the Lord tells Ezekiel to put a mark on the forehead of the people who grieve over the terrible things that were happening in Jerusalem. Thus the sealing of the servants of God sets them apart as belonging to God and, therefore, under God's protection. The number sealed—144,000, or 12,000 from each tribe—should be understood symbolically: perfection or fullness (12) multiplied by fullness (12), multiplied again by a number too great to count (1,000). In other words, John is not witnessing the sealing of a relatively small gathering of the elect, but an unbelievably massive crowd of people, a sea of humanity!

The second part of this interlude (7:9-17) is introduced by John's observation of a great multitude standing before the throne of God and the Lamb (7:9). The crowd that John sees is most likely the 144,000 who were sealed in the preceding scene (see 7:1-8). They are wearing robes of victory and crying out in praise and thanksgiving for the source of their salvation, namely, God and the Lamb (7:9-10). Their palm branches are symbols of victory in war (cf. 1 Macc 13:51; 2 Macc 10:7) but are also reminiscent of the feast of Tabernacles, when Jews gathered in Jerusalem to celebrate the harvest festival and build booths or tents in remembrance of God's loving care during the

Exodus. This feast also anticipates the messianic age, when God's kingdom will be fully manifest and everyone will come to Jerusalem to worship God, and the whole city will be as holy as the temple (see Zech 14:16-21). In the concluding vision of the book of Revelation, the New Jerusalem (21:1–22:5), John will provide us with a fuller version of this Tabernacles motif.

Again John is permitted to witness the heavenly liturgy, with all the angels surrounding the throne, the four living creatures, the elders, and now the crowd too big to count gathering to worship God in song (7:11-12; see 5:9-14). It should be noted that their prayer contains exactly seven words of honor, symbolizing the fullness of praise to God (7:12).

Almost as if interrupting the liturgy, one of the elders asks John the identity of the ones in white robes. John defers to the elder, who then provides interpretation for him: these are the ones who have come through the persecution as martyrs, joining their blood with Christ's (7:13-14). What follows is a prophecy of consolation: they will no longer need to build tabernacles (tents) for themselves because *God* will tabernacle (i.e., shelter) them (7:15). Echoing the prophet Isaiah, the elder further declares that the white-robed crowd will never again suffer hunger, thirst, heat, or grief and, instead, will be led to springs of life-giving water (7:15-17; see Isa 49:10; 25:8).

Imagine how the elder's prophecy must have sounded to John and those soon to be martyrs! It is a profoundly moving message of hope. In fact, this entire interlude (7:1-17) would have been seen as a defiantly faith-filled response to the problem of theodicy: despite appearances to the contrary, God is absolutely sovereign and just! God protects the holy ones and will surely rescue them from their sufferings, so that they can participate in this glorious liturgy of praise. John will return to these images once again in the vision of the New Jerusalem at the end of the book of Revelation (21:2–22:5).

THE SEVEN TRUMPETS

Rev 8:1–11:19

After the intense drama created by the opening of the previous six seals, finally the seventh and last seal is opened (8:1). The scroll could have been unrolled at this point. This is what one might have expected, especially after John's lament in

Revelation 5:1-5 about finding no one worthy to open the scroll. However, surprisingly, there is no reading of its contents. Instead, there is silence in the heavens (8:1), perhaps the silence that one encounters in worship or in the presence of the divine. The rhetorical effect is to create an atmosphere of heightened anticipation. Thus the reader is forewarned that there is even greater drama to come!

Breaking the silence, John is given another vision (8:2-5), in which seven angels, probably the archangels of Jewish tradition, are given seven trumpets, a traditional symbol of the announcement of God's judgment (see Isa 27:13; Joel 2:1; Zeph 1:16). Is this the content of the scroll, revealed not in words but in visions? Perhaps, but the text does not tell us. John's vision continues when another angel is given incense with which to offer up the prayers of the believing community (8:3-4). These prayers, now rising up to God, were first voiced in Revelation 6:10—"How long will it be, holy and true master, before you sit in judgment and avenge our blood on the inhabitants of the earth?"

The angel then fills the censer with fire from the altar—God's holy fire—and throws it down to earth, where it manifests in imagery associated with apocalyptic judgment (8:5). Again the issue is theodicy. The author is asserting that nothing happens without God's permission and that God, who is sovereign, will ultimately vindicate the faithful ones.

8:6-12 The first four trumpet visions

The setting for John's visions has shifted again from the heavenly to the earthly realm (8:6), where, with the blowing of each trumpet, plagues are inflicted upon the earth. Scholars have observed that these plagues are similar in content to the plagues of the Exodus. For example, the first vision, which describes hail and fire mixed with blood being cast upon the earth, recalls the seventh plague of hail and fire in the Exodus story (8:7; see Exod 9:23-26). Likewise, the second vision describes the sea turning to blood, recalling the first plague of the Exodus story, in which the Nile River is turned to blood (8:9; see Exod 7:20). This recollection of the Exodus is interesting, especially in light of the last scene of the previous cycle of visions (7:9-17), in which the believing community and all the heavenly beings celebrate the fullness of the feast of Tabernacles, also recalling the Exodus.

The seven angels who stand closest to God's throne are the ones to announce the plagues (8:2, 7, 8, 10, 12), signaling that the plagues originate with God and descend upon the earth by God's permission. Recall that the plagues of the Exodus story were plagues only for the Egyptians; for the Hebrew peoples they were miracles, a central feature of God's liberating activity on their behalf. Likewise, by comparison, the plagues of the book of Revelation are miracles and part of God's larger plan for the salvation of the community of believers. This understanding of the plagues is confirmed by the scene that precedes the blowing of the trumpets: the offering of the prayers of the saints, who cry, "How long, O Lord?" (see 8:4).

Like the pattern established in the visions of the four horsemen, the first four visions of the trumpets are described very briefly and follow one another in rapid succession (8:6-13; cf. 6:1-8). However, in contrast to the visions of the four horsemen, the Roman Empire is no longer the object of destruction, but the earth itself. The destruction is substantial, and yet limited in scope, since one-third of the created world is affected by each plague (8:7, 8, 10, 11, 12). As yet, there is no mention of harm coming to the believing community or even to humanity in general. Rather, in systematic fashion, first the things of the earth are affected, then the things of the sea, followed by the things of the fresh waters, and finally the things of the heavens.

In the vision of the third trumpet, "Wormwood" is the name of the star that makes the fresh waters bitter. In the book of Jeremiah, wormwood is described as a bitter poison that God uses to punish wrongdoers (Jer 9:15; 23:15).

8:13 Interlude between the fourth and fifth trumpet visions

In a brief interlude between the fourth and fifth trumpets (8:13), John sees and hears a bird of prey flying in the sky. The Greek word *aetos* is sometimes translated as "eagle," but "vulture" is more accurate for its connotations of impending doom. The bird cries out "Woe" three times, anticipating the three trumpets still to come, much like the prophets who cried "Woe" when they announced God's judgment against the wrongdoers. See, for example, Isaiah 3:9, 11; 45:9-10; Jeremiah 13:27; 22:13; 23:1; 48:46; Ezekiel 13:18; 16:23; 24:9.

9:1-12 The fifth trumpet vision

When the fifth trumpet is blown (9:1), we quickly learn that the woes are directed at humanity itself. The fallen star is a traditional symbol for a fallen angel or Satan (9:1; see Isa 14:12-15; Luke 10:18; Jude 13). The abyss generally refers to Sheol, the place of the dead, also called Hades. However, in Revelation it is the place where the fallen angels are imprisoned until the end-time judgment (see 17:8; 20:1-3). The key that was given to the fallen angel (9:1) is a symbol of power over the abyss, and even though God is not named, the passive form of the verb "to give" indicates that God is the giver of the key.

When the fallen angel opens the abyss, smoke pours out (9:2)—later we will see that the source of the smoke is a pool of fire within the abyss (see 20:7-10)—followed by an army of locusts (9:3). These are not ordinary locusts, because they do not eat vegetation; rather, they sting their human prey like scorpions (9:5). No one escapes their sting, except those who had been marked with the seal of God on their foreheads (9:4; see 7:1-8). In the ancient world both insects were considered offensive to humans, much as some people today feel about snakes or rats (see Luke 10:19).

John's description of the locust-scorpions—looking and sounding like horses and chariots, having crowns on their heads, and military armor where their chests should be (9:7, 9)—is reminiscent of the imagery used in the vision of the first horseman, a symbol of the Parthians (cf. 6:1-2). The "hair like women's hair" (9:8) may also refer to the Parthians, whose men were known to wear their hair long. Their reign of terror is limited to five months—half of ten—meaning a short time (9:5, 10). The name of their king, in both Hebrew and Greek, is translated as "Destruction" (9:11).

Indeed, the state of affairs looks desperate for humanity; suffering and destruction are everywhere! And yet, the careful reader will observe that God is still in control of this situation. The angel who unlocked the abyss received the key from God (9:1). The passive verb forms used to describe the activity and limitations of the locust-scorpions—"were given" (9:3), "were told" (9:4), and "were not allowed" (9:5)—all suggest that God is the all-powerful One, permitting the locusts to inflict pain and suffering. However, this is not to say that God is the cause of suffering. Rather, John is saying that evil has a *human* face

(9:7), and in its destructive rampage it inflicts suffering on the whole human race. The book of Joel describes a similar plague of locusts, which God allowed for the purpose of calling people to repent (Joel 1:6-7, 15; 2:1-11; cf. Exod 10:12-15). Remember, too, that God has arranged in advance for the protection of the holy ones; they have the seal of God on their forehead (see 9:4). Thus, even in this terrible scene of destruction, John asserts that God is sovereign and just, calling people to conversion and protecting the chosen ones.

9:13-21 The sixth trumpet vision

Immediately afterward, the sixth angel-trumpeter announces another vision: the release of the destructive forces associated with the four angels located at the four directions of the universe (9:13-21). Although John does not specifically mention it, this may be the vulture's second woe (8:13; see 11:14): The order for their release comes from a voice located among the four horns of God's altar (9:13). In ancient religions the power of the deity was thought to reside in the horns of its altar. Therefore, this order comes directly from God. The fact that the angels are held ready for the exact date and time (9:15) also indicates that what is about to happen is completely under God's control. Again, the object of God's wrath is humanity, and like the previous vision, its scope is limited (one-third means a limited number; see 9:15). However, unlike the earlier vision, the angels are released not simply to harm their victims but to *kill* them (9:15).

Suddenly a cavalry of immense proportions appears on the scene (9:16): as a symbolic number, 200 million is double the product of ten thousand times ten thousand, which signifies fullness on top of fullness, multiplied by numbers too great to count. They come from the Euphrates River (9:14), which, in the late first-century A.D., was the eastern boundary of the Roman Empire. The horses are monstrous, with lionlike heads and serpent tails, complete with stinging mouths (9:17-19). What a nightmare! Their riders wear red, blue, and yellow armor, and the plagues they bring are fire (red), smoke (blue), and sulfur (yellow; 9:17-18). The symbolic meaning of these plagues is unclear, except that they probably represent the abyss and they kill. The purpose of the vision is revealed finally at its end. God allowed the destruction of one-third of wicked humanity in the hope that the rest would repent (9:20-21). However, they do not repent, and so we move to the next vision.

10:1–11:14 Interlude between the sixth and seventh trumpet visions

The next two visions form an interlude between the sixth and seventh trumpets, much like the interlude we saw between the opening of the sixth and seventh seals (7:1-17). The literary effect is to create a "pregnant" pause in the action, heightening the reader's anticipation for what is to come. We also have a change of setting here. In the previous six trumpet visions, John was in the heavenly realm observing what was taking place on earth. Now he is back on earth watching a mighty angel come down from heaven (10:1).

The first of these two visions (10:1-11) is reminiscent of the throne vision in Revelation 4, especially in the mention of the rainbow or halo and thunder (10:1, 3; see 4:3, 5). This angelic being also shares some features with the earlier "one like a son of man," namely, a face like the sun and legs like columns of fire (10:2; cf. 1:14-15). Apart from this angel, only two other angels in the book of Revelation are called "mighty": the angel who issued the challenge for a worthy one to come forward to open the scroll held by the One seated on the throne (5:2) and the angel who will throw a stone into the sea as a prophetic action against "Babylon" (18:21). Who is the mighty angel in 10:1? Most likely it is not "one like a son of man." However, it is reasonable to conclude that it is closely connected with God's glory, and that it comes with divine authority to deliver a message.

Unlike the scroll of the earlier throne vision, we are told that the scroll held by this angel is open, not closed (10:2; cf. 5:1). However, we are not told the content of the scroll. Although all the angels in the book of Revelation speak with a loud voice, this one reveals his high status through his lionlike voice and the response he receives from the seven (symbolizing fullness or perfection) thunders (10:3). When the thunders "speak" John's impulse is to write down what he hears, but he is told by another voice not to write but to "seal up" what was said (10:4). The significance of this command is unclear, except to say that humans will not be allowed access to this part of John's vision.

Then the mighty angel raises his right hand toward heaven—the traditional position of oath-taking—and swears by the eternal One that there will be no more delay (10:5-6). He swears on God who *created heaven, earth, and sea*, thus explaining why the angel stands as he does, with one foot on the sea and the other on the land, while pointing toward the heavens. In other words, the message he delivers pertains to the entire created order! When the seventh angel sounds his trumpet, the mystery of God will come to completion (10:7). The Greek word *mystΣrion* usually means *hidden purposes*, referring to something hidden from view.

Again John hears a heavenly voice; it is the angel who told him not to write what the seven thunders said (10:8). Now he is told to take and eat the scroll that the mighty angel is holding. The scene is reminiscent of Ezekiel, who is handed a scroll and told to eat it (Ezek 2:9–3:15). Ezekiel's scroll contains words of lament, mourning, and woe. When he first eats it, it is sweet in the mouth, but later he learns that it is directed against Israel and he goes off, in bitterness and anger, to do what God commands. For John, too, the prophecy he must deliver will at first taste sweet but in the end will bring him bitterness (10:9-10). Thus the eating of the scroll is accompanied by the command to prophesy (10:11).

Immediately John takes up his mandate, and so begins the second vision of this interlude (11:1-14). His first task is to measure the inner parts of the Jerusalem temple, excluding the outer court of the Gentiles and those who worship there (11:1-2). The prophetic act, also seen in Ezekiel 40–43 and Zechariah 2:1-5, symbolically marks out the space where God's glory resides on earth. It also identifies the boundaries of protection for God's people.

What follows then is a message of consolation for the believers. They are told that the holy city will be overrun, but for a limited time—three and a half years, half of seven, the number representing fullness or completion (11:2). The number *three and a half* is also an allusion to Daniel 7:25 and the cruel reign of King Antiochus IV, who persecuted Jews a little more than two centuries earlier for "a year, two years, and a half-year." In the concluding vision of the book of Revelation, the city will be measured again and established forever as the dwelling place of God and the Lamb (21:15-27).

John is now told about two unnamed witnesses (the Greek word is *martyria*), who will prophesy for forty-two lunar months, or three and a half years—the same amount of time that the city will be overrun—while wearing sackcloth, the coarse dress of prophets and a sign of repentance (11:3). The witnesses, who are further described as two olive trees and two lamps (11:4), recall Zechariah 4–6. The two images are related, of course, because lamps were fueled by the oil from pressed olives. In the book of Zechariah the olive trees represent Zerubbabel, the anointed king of Israel and the one who laid the foundations of the temple, and Joshua, the high priest who was responsible for building the temple. These two were anointed—*messiah* means "anointed"—"who stand by the Lord of all the earth" (Zech 4:14). Similarly, in Revelation the witnesses are said to "stand before the Lord of the earth" (11:4).

Although they are unnamed in the book of Revelation, these two witnesses appear to have connections to Elijah and Moses because of the things they are able to do to those who harm them (11:5-6). In the Old Testament stories Moses is identified with the plagues of the Exodus, especially changing water to blood (Exod 7:14-25). Elijah was said to have words like fire (Sir 48:1) and the ability to close up the heavens so that it would not rain (1 Kgs 17:1). According to the prophet Malachi, Elijah was expected to return to preach repentance before the end-time Day of Judgment (Mal 3:23-24). Deuteronomy 18:15-22 describes God's promise to raise up a prophet like Moses from among the people. Therefore the original readers of the book of Revelation would have readily recognized the connections that John was making between the witnesses in his vision and Moses and Elijah.

Without transition, the voice from heaven tells John that the witnesses, when they complete their testimony, will be attacked by the beast from the bottomless pit (11:7). We will learn more about the beast later in 13:1-8. For now, it is sufficient to say that it is the embodiment of evil. What follows is a story of the trial, unjust punishment, rescue, and vindication of the witnesses. The story follows the pattern of the Wisdom tale, which can be found throughout Jewish Wisdom literature. See, for example, the story of the vindicated righteous one in Wisdom 2:10–3:12 and some of the stories of Daniel in the book of Daniel. The Wisdom tale provides a fitting answer to the problem of the unwarranted suffering of God's holy ones,

because it carries a message of consolation and hope for the persecuted: as God rescued and vindicated the righteous one in the story, so we can trust that God will rescue and vindicate us!

Here is how the Wisdom tale unfolds. As soon as the witnesses have completed their testimony, the beast conquers them and kills them (11:7). Their unburied corpses are left in the street of the "great city," probably Rome, to be viewed by passersby as a mockery and disgrace (11:8-9). The inhabitants of the earth, probably those who are in allegiance with Rome, celebrate and gloat over the destruction of the witnesses because their testimony was torment to them (11:10). Horrors! The witnesses could not have come to a worse end! But three and a half days later (symbolic of a limited time), the voice says, God comes to their rescue (11:11). God's own breath (*pneuma*, also translated "spirit") of life enters into them, and the inhabitants of the earth hear God's voice calling the witnesses, "Come up here." All the while their enemies are watching! (11:11-12). They respond with fear as they see the witnesses' restoration (11:11) because they realize the full extent of their wrongdoing, and they know that they are about to experience the full fury of God's punishment. We can almost hear their lament, "Oh, no! What did we do?" An enormous number of people (seven thousand, or a full number too great to count) fall victim to God's punishing wrath (11:13). But God's rage is also restrained—only a tenth of the population is killed. Those who remain repent and give glory to God. Thus the Wisdom tale teaches that God is sovereign and just; God will rescue the holy ones and punish the wicked. But God is also merciful and will not destroy creation forever.

A brief note on the city's symbolic names: "Sodom" and "Egypt" suggest that the city has a reputation for immorality (see Gen 18:22-32; Exod 1:11-14; and Isa 1:10). Also, the phrase "where . . . their Lord was crucified" does not refer to a place but to the forces that oppose the Christian believers (i.e., Rome; see 1 Cor 2:6-8). Parallels between the story of the two witnesses and the story of the death and resurrection of Jesus are unavoidable and probably intentional. The reader is reminded that Jesus Christ is "*the* faithful witness" (1:5; emphasis added) of whom they are disciples.

At this point the narrator of the book of Revelation announces that the second woe has passed and the third is about to come (11:14). However, we cannot be certain which is the second woe—perhaps the releasing of the four angels at the four corners of the universe (9:13-19) or the story about the vindication of the two witnesses (11:1-13). Likewise, as we shall see, John does not clearly identify the third woe. What follows is a scene of triumph, not woe.

11:15-19 The seventh trumpet vision

When the seventh angel blows his trumpet (11:15), a heavenly voice announces that God's kingdom has replaced the kingdom of the world (i.e., the Roman Empire). The setting has again shifted to the heavenly realm. The twenty-four elders, who were first introduced in the throne vision of Revelation 4, fall down in worship, praising and thanking God for asserting the fullness of power against evil and rescuing the righteous believers (11:16-18). John's mention of the destroyers of the world (11:18) is probably a reference back to the king of the locust-scorpions, identified as Abaddon or Apollyon (see 9:1-12). However, it may also be a reference forward to the dragon and its two beasts that will be revealed in Revelation 12 and 13.

Suddenly the heavenly temple, even the holy of holies, is opened so that all believers can see and enjoy God's unmediated presence (11:19). The ark of the covenant, which once contained the tablets of the Sinai covenant, was lost when Solomon's temple was destroyed in 587 B.C. but is now restored in the heavenly temple (11:19). This detail recalls a legend about Jeremiah hiding the ark of the covenant and other artifacts of the temple for the day when God "gathers his people together again and shows them mercy" (2 Macc 2:7). The thunder, flashes of lightning, and other cosmic happenings (11:19) confirm that John is experiencing a theophany, that is, a manifestation of God. Thus ends the first half of the book of Revelation.

SECOND CYCLE OF VISIONS

Rev 12:1–20:15

The second half of the book of Revelation begins with an intercalation, that is, a vision inserted within another vision. This literary technique suggests that the two visions are to be interpreted together as a single, interrelated unit. The outer vision (12:1-6 and 13-17) begins in the heavens

and eventually shifts to the earthly realm. Likewise, the inner vision (12:7-12) begins in the heavens and ends with a transition to earth. The outer vision (12:1-6, 13-17) describes an immense dragon attacking an unnamed woman enthroned in the heavens. The inner vision describes a war in heaven in which the angel Michael throws the dragon down to earth (12:7-12). The two visions work together to explain, in symbolic imagery, how the forces of evil came down upon God's holy ones. We will examine each vision separately, and in their parts, and then look at them together.

VISION OF THE WOMAN AND THE DRAGON

Rev 12:1-18

12:1-6 Part one of the vision of the woman and the dragon

In the opening scene of this vision, John sees an unnamed woman with the sun as her raiment, the moon as her footstool, and twelve (symbolizing fullness or perfection) stars as her crown (12:1). Without warning, the beauty and serenity of this scene are shattered by the realization that the woman is in the throes of childbirth, a traditional image for the sudden and unexpected arrival of the end time (12:2). Adding to the drama, an enormous red dragon is waiting in earnest for the child to be born so that he can eat it as soon as it is born! (12:3-4). In Revelation, red is the color of violence and bloodshed.

The dragon's ten horns (12:3) recall the book of Daniel, in which a ten-horned, devouring beast symbolizes the kingdom of the Greeks, who persecuted the Israelites because they refused to give up their Jewish cultural and religious practices (see Dan 7:1-28). The seven diadems or crowns (12:3) on the dragon's seven heads also signal kingship. However, the identity of the kingdom that is associated with the dragon will not be revealed until 17:1-6, where she is described as Babylon.

The message of the vision is one of consolation in the face of persecution. The woman is in a truly difficult situation, but the child born to her is male (12:5); in a patriarchal culture a male child was considered to be a sign of God's blessing. We also learn that he is destined to rule with great strength (12:5). The Greek version of Isaiah (LXX Isa 66:7) and Psalm 2:7-9 both express hope in a king who would be God's son and rule with a rod of iron.

As the vision progresses, the message of hope continues to play out in dramatic fashion. The child is rescued from the jaws of the dragon, snatched up to God (12:5), while the woman escapes to the desert, where God had made a place for her (12:6). God harbors her for a period of 1,260 days (i.e., 42 months, or three and a half years), symbolizing a limited time (12:6; see 11:3-14). Thus, although the desert is often a place of danger, here it is a place of protection.

12:7-12 Vision of the war in heaven

John leaves us wondering about the woman in the desert and now turns our attention to the inner vision (12:7-12). Immediately, the reader learns that war is about to break out in heaven (12:7). The war is quick and decisive: the dragon and his angels are soundly defeated by the archangel Michael and his angels (12:7-8) and then tossed out of the heavenly realm (12:9)! The apocalyptic sections of the book of Daniel likewise describe the archangel Michael as a warrior prince who battles against the enemies of God's people and utterly destroys them (Dan 10:10-21; 12:1-4). Almost as a side note, we learn the dragon's names and the activity by which he is known: "the ancient serpent (referring to the snake who seduced Eve in Genesis 3:1-6), . . . the Devil (literally 'slanderer' or 'enemy') and Satan ('accuser' in Hebrew), who deceived the whole world" (12:9).

A heavenly voice confirms what John has just witnessed: the salvation, power, and sovereignty of God are now manifest (12:10a), and the accuser (i.e., prosecutor) of the woman's offspring—the persecuted believers—has been driven out of the heavens, conquered by the blood of the Lamb, Jesus Christ (12:10b-11). But the heavenly voice also warns that the dragon still needs to be driven from the other two cosmic realms, the earth and sea, and his rage will be especially intense because he knows his end is soon! (12:12).

12:13-18 Part two of the vision of the woman and the dragon

But what about the woman, whom John last saw in the desert, and how did she make her way from the heavens to the desert? The second half of the outer vision (12:13-18) provides an explanation. Unable to capture the woman's child, who was immediately taken up into heaven (12:5), the dragon is now in hot pursuit of the woman

(12:13). But God rescues her, giving her two wings of an enormous bird, so that she can fly away to safety (12:14). Suddenly the great dragon becomes a huge water serpent, something like the mythical Leviathan, spewing a flood of water after her (12:15). Now God's creation comes to the woman's rescue: the earth comes alive, opening its mouth to swallow the river (12:16). Good news: the woman has escaped! One can almost imagine the dragon stomping away in fury!

At the conclusion of the vision, John observes that the dragon has turned his rage to the rest of the woman's children, the Christian believers (12:17). The reader is expected to understand, finally, the significance of the three and a half years (12:6, 14). Yes, it is the time that the woman is protected in the desert, but it is also the length of time that her children will suffer persecution. Half of seven, their persecution will be comprehensive but limited. In other words, there is reason for hope even in the midst of suffering.

But why did the author of the book of Revelation link these two visions together in this manner? Jewish tradition and Jewish apocalyptic literature in particular saw a direct connection between what was happening on earth and what was happening in the heavens. In fact, the rabbis had a saying, "As in heaven, so on earth." Thus this inner vision explains the source of the believers' persecution on earth, namely, the dragon and his angels who were thrown out of the heavenly realm, but it also promises that these evil powers will be defeated on earth just as quickly and dramatically as they were defeated in the heavens.

Given the high level of drama contained in these two visions, the reader should not be surprised that they ought to be interpreted symbolically rather than literally. We have already identified the woman's other offspring as the persecuted believers. Who, then, is the woman? John does not tell us her identity, but interpreters of the book of Revelation have advanced at least three possibilities. Some argue that the woman is Eve, because of allusions to Genesis 3:14-16, in which God curses the serpent, promising enmity between it and the woman and her offspring, and then tells the woman that her childbearing pain will intensify because of what she had done (see 12:2, 4, 9, 10).

Others argue that the woman is Mary, because the child that is snatched up to heaven is the messiah and the Lamb, by whose blood the believers are saved, that is, Jesus Christ (see 12:10-11). Still others argue that the woman represents the church, since her offspring are the persecuted believers (12:17).

The problem, of course, is that none of these identifications fit every detail of both visions. Perhaps the reader is expected to recall all three possibilities simultaneously, making these two visions a multilayered story of salvation.

Both of the visions described in Revelation 12 conclude with a reference to the dragon's fury being unleashed on earth and sea, thus anticipating the next two visions: the vision of the beast of the sea (13:1-10) and the vision of the beast of the land (13:11-18).

THE VISION OF THE BEASTS OF THE SEA AND THE LAND

Rev 13:1-18

13:1-10 The beast of the sea

John's next vision is of a beast emerging from the sea. In the ancient world the sea was seen as hostile and chaotic. The four great beasts of the book of Daniel also came from the sea (Dan 7:1-8). In fact, many of the descriptors of Revelation's beast from the sea are similar to those associated with the four beasts in Daniel. For example, Daniel's fourth beast has ten horns, which represent ten kings of the Greek empire (Dan 7:7-8, 23-24). In Revelation the diadems on the ten horns also represent kingship.

Other aspects of Revelation's beast of the sea (13:2) appear to relate to the first three of Daniel's beasts: the body of a leopard (cf. Dan 7:6), the feet of a bear (cf. Dan 7:5), and the head of a lion (cf. Dan 7:4). In the book of Daniel these three beasts represent three of the great empires of history—the Babylonian empire (winged lion), the Median empire (bear), and the Persians (leopard). Thus, given John's apparent familiarity with Daniel, we should conclude that Revelation's beast of the sea also symbolizes a very powerful empire. In John's historical context, this would be the Roman Empire (see also 6:1-8).

John describes the beast of the sea in considerable detail, but the details are to be understood metaphorically. Its seven heads (13:1) describe the fullness of power. The blasphemous name on its heads (13:1) probably refers to titles regularly given to the Roman emperors of John's day—"Lord," "Lord and God," and "Savior of the World"—all of which the Christian believer would have considered to be blasphemies against God. The blasphemies it utters (13:5) refer to its offenses against God and the Christians who worship God.

Regarding the detail about the beast's head seeming to have been "mortally wounded, but this mortal wound was healed" (13:3), some scholars conclude that the beast is the emperor Nero (d. A.D. 68), who committed suicide, leaving the empire in civil war for a year before Vespasian took the throne and restored the empire in A.D. 69. However, it is also likely that John is making a parody on the Lamb "that seemed to have been slain" (5:6). Thus, with much disdain, he writes that the people of the whole earth are completely enamored of the Roman Empire. They worship the Roman Empire, saying that there is no other like it and no one can stand against it, and they worship the dragon (i.e., Satan), from whom the Roman Empire gets its authority (13:3-4). But all this is so much foolishness! *God* is the one they should worship. And the Lamb, who gets its authority from God, is the one against whom no one can stand!

Worship of the dragon and the beast (13:4) is probably a reference to the emperor cult, in which people were obligated to offer sacrifices to the emperor in order to ensure the empire's prosperity. Christians who refused to participate were considered a threat to the empire. However, John reminds his readers that Rome has no power except what was given it by God. For this reason, John uses the passive forms of the verbs "to give" and "to permit." The beast, John says, "*was given* authority to act" (13:5; emphasis added), "*was also allowed* to wage war against the holy ones" (13:7; emphasis added), and "*was granted* authority over every tribe, people, tongue, and nation" (13:7). Thus John is asserting that God is sovereign over everyone and everything, even as the Roman Empire reigns over the whole world and God's holy ones are being killed by its emperor.

The holy ones, however, should be consoled by the fact that the time of their suffering is limited: Rome can act for only three and a half years, half of seven, the number of fullness (13:5). They should also be consoled by the fact that the names of the ones who worship the beast will *not* be found in the Lamb's book of life (13:8), while theirs most surely will be, as long as they remain faithful.

Thus John concludes this vision with a prophetic admonition directed to the Christian community. He begins with a riddle (13:10) that sounds like some kind of teaching on predestination, but most scholars agree that it is not; rather, it is a call for endurance and trust, no matter what the cost. If the Christian community opposes the beast (i.e., the Roman Empire) and refuses to worship it, they should expect suffering and even death, because it is an inevitable outcome of their opposition. However, that is not their concern. Whatever happens, their only response should be faithful perseverance (13:10).

13:11-18 The beast from the earth

Immediately following the vision of the beast from the sea, John receives a vision of a beast rising from the earth (13:11-18). Like the beast from the sea, this beast is related to the dragon. In fact, it *speaks* like the dragon (13:11). Further, it exercises all the authority of the first beast, which received *its* authority from the dragon (13:12). Therefore, if the first beast is the Roman Empire, then the second must be its representative, the emperor.

The narrator of John's vision makes clear that this beast is a deceiver. He has horns that make him look like a lamb, but he has the voice of the dragon, the embodiment of all that is evil (13:11). He works miracles like the prophets of Israel, even like Elijah, the prophet who could call down fire from heaven and who was expected to return in the end time (Rev 13:13-14; see 1 Kgs 18:38; 2 Kgs 1:10; and Rev 11:3-14 on the two witnesses who were prophets). In sum, he is a false prophet whose goal it is to deceive the whole world. Although John does not use the term, some scholars have called this beast the anti-Christ, because it gives the *appearance* of being the Christ ("anointed"), but clearly is not.

Again John uses the passive form of certain verbs to indicate that the beast acts with God's permission. Thus the narrator of this vision says that the beast "was allowed" to perform miracles (13:14) and give life to the image (i.e., statue) of the beast (13:15). In effect, John is saying that the deceptive activity of the beast is somehow part of God's plan. However, we should not interpret this

to mean that God is the source of evil. Rather, John is asserting that God remains sovereign over all things, even over the emperor, despite appearances to the contrary.

John indicates that the stranglehold of the emperor extended beyond religion to politics and economics, since everyone was required to have the mark of the beast on their right hand and on their head (13:16). The mark on the head recalls the first-century A.D. practice of branding slaves on the forehead to show whose property they were. Thus the mark of the beast is most likely a reference to the official seal of the emperor, which was used to authenticate imperial documents and identify the emperor's property. The image of the emperor was also imprinted on all the coins of the empire, so a person could not even buy or sell without indirectly participating in the emperor cult (see 13:17). Again, the reader should not take this talk of branding literally. Rather, John intends that we treat it metaphorically and contrast this mark of the beast with the mark of the Lamb that was placed upon the forehead of God's holy ones (see 7:2-3). Either you belong to the Lamb or you belong to the beast! If you belong to the Lamb, you are protected from the catastrophes of the end time; but if you belong to the beast, you will suffer the same fate that he will suffer.

At the conclusion of this vision, John adds a note to his readers concerning the identity of the beast from the earth (13:18). To appreciate what John is saying here, we must imagine a community that already knows the identity of the beast and, together with John, shares a bit of "naughty" delight in talking about the beast behind his back! The practice in which John is engaged is called *gematria*. Jewish rabbis of the ancient world were skilled at it, but non-Jewish people in the Greco-Roman world enjoyed it too. It was a process of assigning numbers to letters of a word or a name and using the resulting number to designate something about the holder of that name.

Because Latin, Hebrew, and Greek do not have separate sets of symbols for numbers, people used the individual letters and combinations of letters to designate quantities. It became quite natural, then, to refer to a person by their number, particularly among friends who wished to share a "secret" that they wanted to keep from outsiders. People who already knew the name could very quickly discern the number, but those who did not would find it almost impossible to solve the riddle. Sometimes the number also has symbolic meaning, as in the case of 666. Six is one short of perfection or fullness and therefore means imperfection or evil. Thus John is saying to his audience, "Here is this beast who has deceived and enamored the whole world, but *we* know who he really is—he is evil itself!"

What, then, is the name of the beast? Since he appears to be one of the emperors of Rome, and presumably someone known to John, our choices have been narrowed considerably. Most scholars believe him to be Nero, since his Greek name and title, transliterated into Hebrew, adds up to 666: N(50) + r(200) + o(6)+ n(50) + Q(100) + s(60) + r(200), while his Latin name and title, transliterated into Hebrew, adds up to 616: N(50) + r(200) + o(6) + Q(100) + s(60) + r(200), which is a variant reading found in some of the manuscripts (handwritten copies) of the book of Revelation. Nero was already deceased at the time of John's writing, but because of the legend associated with his departure and because he, like Domitian after him, also persecuted Christian believers, some have concluded that Domitian was Nero returned to life.

VISION OF THE LAMB AND IMMINENT JUDGMENT

Rev 14:1-20

14:1-5 Vision of the Lamb on Mount Zion

As a counterpoint to the visions of the dragon and its two beasts, John has another vision—this time of the Lamb standing on Mount Zion, also known as Jerusalem (14:1-5). Instead of the inhabitants of the world who wear the mark of the beast, John sees the 144,000—fullness upon fullness multiplied by a number too great to count—wearing the mark of the Lamb and his Father (14:1; cf. 13:16-17). These are the same 144,000 who were sealed in 7:1-8. In constructing this image, the author may have in mind Psalm 2: "I myself have installed my king / on Zion, my holy mountain" (Ps 2:6). In traditional Judaism this is the place where the remnant of Israel would be gathered together in the messianic age (Joel 3:5; Obad 17; Mic 4:6-8; Zeph 3:12-20).

As the vision proceeds, John hears sounds—something like rushing water, thunder, and harps (14:2)—that are usually associated with theoph-

any (i.e., manifestation of God; cf. 1:15; 5:8; 15:2; 19:6). Further, the mention of the throne, the elders, and four living creatures (14:3) recalls the throne vision of Revelation 4, suggesting some direct connection between Zion (Jerusalem) and the heavenly throne room. Again, in contrast to the multitudes who worship the beast in the preceding vision (13:8), John sees the 144,000 singing a "new hymn" in praise of God and the Lamb (14:3). The "new hymn" is probably the same one sung by the heavenly court in 5:8-10. In it the heavenly host praised the Lamb, who is deemed worthy to break the seals on God's scroll because he redeemed all peoples and nations by his blood.

John observes that not everyone, but only the 144,000 who have been "ransomed from the earth" (14:3), can learn this song. They are the ones who were marked on their foreheads with the seal of God before the destructive forces were unleashed from the four corners of the world (7:3). Here, John adds, they "follow the Lamb wherever he goes" (14:4), most likely a reference to their perseverance, even to the point of suffering and death (14:3-4). Pure in every way, they are God's perfect sacrifice; they are the firstfruits, the first and best of the harvest, offered on behalf of all God's people (14:4-5). For persecuted Christians, this is the motivation for their faithful endurance: the opportunity to participate in the true heavenly liturgy.

The significance of the detail about the 144,000 who had not defiled themselves with sexual activity (14:4) is not altogether clear. Some scholars have suggested that this vision represents the gathering of God's army in anticipation of holy war, since soldiers who engaged in holy war were expected to abstain from sexual activity during military service. Others have argued that sexual abstinence is consistent with their role as priests in this heavenly liturgy. Still others have suggested that the virginal state of the 144,000 should be viewed as a metaphor for their refusal to participate in the emperor cult, since Jewish and early Christian writings often describe idol worship in terms of prostitution and adultery. Whether one or all of these meanings are intended, we can be quite sure that it should not be taken literally, so as to say that only celibate Christians are redeemed.

14:6-20 Visions of imminent judgment

Three more "mini" visions, or perhaps extensions of the previous vision, now follow in rapid succession (14:6-13, 14-16, 17-20). Together they represent the "good news" of God's coming judgment.

The first of these visions is introduced with the phrase "I saw another angel" (14:6), which will be repeated two more times before its end, as a second and third angel appear. The first angel flies into the midheaven announcing (literally, "evangelizing") an eternal gospel (literally, "good news"; the Greek word is *euangelion*) for all people (14:6). It is a call to repentance and an invitation to worship the one true God, who made the heavens, the earth, and the sea—the place from which the dragon was thrown down and the places where the beast of the earth and the beast of the sea currently reside, though not for long! The good news is that the time for God's judgment has come (14:7). The reader will recall that the great-winged vulture, who announced the three woes, also flew in the midheaven (see 8:13). It was understood to be the place that stretched across the entire created world.

A second angel appears with a prophetic message of doom for Babylon: the "great" city that made its peoples drunk on its enticements and practices of idol worship has fallen! (14:8). In 1 Peter 5:12 Rome is referred to as "Babylon," and there is every reason to suppose the same meaning is intended here.

The third angel appears with an admonition: whoever gives in to the enticements of the Roman Empire and participates in its cultic practices will also experience the full force of the wrath of God (14:9-10). Of whom is he speaking? Fellow Christians? This is certainly possible! One can probably imagine a situation in which a person decides to keep quiet and go along with the crowd rather than risk persecution or death. For this reason, John again calls his hearers to faithful endurance (14:12) by warning them what is in store if they fail in their perseverance (14:10-11). A heavenly voice adds authority to John's admonition with a beatitude: "Blessed are the dead who die in the Lord" (14:13). The Spirit confirms it with a second blessing: the dead will be able to rest, knowing that their deeds (i.e., their witness to the faith) will follow them after death (14:13).

In the next vision John sees "one who looked like a son of man" seated on a white cloud (14:14). The crown on his head represents kingship. The sickle, necessary equipment for harvesting grain, is also a traditional symbol of God's judgment

(see Isa 17:5; 27:12; Jer 51:33; Joel 3:13). The color white signals victory (14:14). Although the "one who looked like a son of man" is unnamed, we may safely conclude that he is Jesus Christ, because of the initial vision, in which he is revealed to be the risen Jesus (1:13). The imagery is borrowed from Daniel 7:9-14, a vision in which "one like a son of man" comes on the clouds and is presented before the "Ancient One" and given dominion over all nations and peoples. His will be an everlasting kingdom, in contrast to the kingdom of the fourth beast, who made war on the "holy ones" of God and reigned with terrifying strength, but only until the Ancient One arrived and pronounced judgment in favor of the "holy ones." In Daniel the fourth beast is the Greek empire and its king, Antiochus IV, who was notorious for his persecution of the Jewish people.

One can easily imagine John juxtaposing his own "one like a son of man," a heavenly warrior and deliverer of justice, against Rome and its emperor, represented by the great dragon and its beasts. In John's vision "one like a son of man" waits, poised for the harvest, until he hears the angel's command to begin the reaping (14:14-16). On first view, it might seem strange that Jesus Christ has to wait for the angel's command, but the angel is merely God's messenger (the Greek word *angelos* means "messenger"). It is God who is in charge! This harvest appears to refer to the gathering in of all humanity, because no distinction is made between righteous and wicked.

Another vision, also of judgment, follows immediately (14:17-20). In it John sees another angel wielding a sickle (14:17). The angel's job is to harvest the grapes of the earth, and his orders came from the angel in charge of the fire of the altar (14:18). The angel at the altar is the one who earlier offered up the prayers of the "holy ones" and then filled the censer with fire and threw it on the earth (8:3-5). Recall, also, that the souls of the martyrs have been resting under the altar, waiting for the day when God will vindicate them (6:9-10). Thus this vision is another response to the question raised by the martyred souls: "How long will it be . . . before you sit in judgment and avenge our blood on the inhabitants of the earth?" (6:10). They need not wait any longer because the time of judgment has come!

The angel's activity of harvesting the grapes and throwing them into the "great wine press of

God's fury" (14:19) is a traditional metaphor for judgment. See, for example, Isaiah 63:1-6, Joel 4:13, and Jeremiah 25:30. Although the narrator of the vision does not make it explicit, this judgment imagery is double-edged. For the owners and recipients of the fruits of the vineyard, harvest and winemaking are joyous events. But there can be no wine without first smashing the grapes and extracting their blood (i.e., juice). Therefore this harvest also involves suffering and pain.

John observes that God's wrath is so furious and God's judgment so comprehensive that the "blood" runs like a river, as deep as a horse's bridle and as far as two hundred miles (literally, 1,600 *stadia*; 14:20). Again, for the owner of the vineyard this is an astounding amount of wine, indicative of intensive and long-lasting joy! The Greek *stadion* (sing.) measures about 606 feet, so 1,600 *stadia* total approximately 183 miles. More important, however, are the symbolic meanings of this number. It is 40 multiplied by 40, with 40 symbolizing a period of transition or transformation. It is also 4 multiplied by 4 multiplied by 10 multiplied by 10, with 4 being the universal number and 10 representing fullness or completion. In other words, this judgment is wholly transformative and/or fully comprehensive, and God's power over evil is absolute.

VISIONS OF THE SEVEN BOWLS

Rev 15:1–16:21

John signals a transition to a new and important series of visions with the phrase "Then I saw in heaven another sign, great and awe-inspiring" (15:1). Elsewhere the word "sign" is used only of the woman enthroned in the heavens (12:1) and the great dragon (12:3). This third series of seven visions—the first was the opening of the seals (6:1–7:17), and the second the visions of the trumpets (8:1–9:19)—will be the last because, the reader is told, God's wrath is coming to completion in them (15:1).

15:2-8 Another vision of heavenly liturgy

Before these seven bowls of the seven plagues are unleashed, John is privileged to witness again the heavenly liturgy. The floor that looks like a sea of glass (15:2) is reminiscent of the throne vision in Revelation 4. The fact that it is mingled with fire (15:2) may indicate that God's judgment

is about to be rendered, or it may signal that only those tried by fire—the persecuted—may enter. The latter view is supported by John's observation that the singers who hold God's harps are the ones who endured faithfully against the wicked enticements of the dragon and his two beasts (15:2-3). They were earlier identified as the 144,000 who were sealed with the name of God on their forehead (7:1-8; 14:1-5).

The "song of Moses" (15:3) is an allusion to Exodus 15:1-18, the song that Moses and the Israelites sang in praise of God, who rescued them by unleashing the plagues on the Egyptians. John's version of the song is made up of phrases from throughout the Old Testament (Rev 15:3-4; see Ps 111:2; 139:14; Amos 4:13; Ps 145:17; Deut 32:4; Jer 10:7; Ps 86:9; Mal 1:11; Ps 98:2), making it a song in praise of God's justice and sovereignty. It also proclaims the goal of God's mighty deeds: that all God's peoples come together in worship.

The preparations for the release of the seven plagues are now underway. John sees the opening of the tent of witness, an allusion to the tent of meeting of the Exodus (15:5; see Exod 33:7-11). The seven angels who emerge (15:6) are wearing golden sashes, reminiscent of the priests of the temple, but also like the "one like a son of man" in Revelation's initial vision (see 1:6). Their white linen robes are a symbol of victory (see also 19:8, 14). They come out of the temple with seven plagues and then receive the implements of judgment—the bowls of the wrath of God—from one of the four living creatures who stand before the altar of God. The point of the vision is this: God is the source of these plagues. The smoke in the temple (15:8) suggests that God now inhabits it and will remain there until the seven angels complete their assigned task. This is why no one can enter the temple until the plagues are finished (15:9).

16:1-9 The first four bowl visions

The "loud voice" (16:1) that speaks from the temple, issuing the order to pour out the plagues, presumably is God's (see 15:8). Like the first four visions of the seals series (6:1-8) and the trumpets series (8:6-12), the pouring out of the first four bowls comes in rapid succession. Further, like the trumpets series, these visions recall the plagues of the Exodus. Thus the first bowl is poured out on earth, and people whose allegiance is with the dragon and its beasts develop boils and other skin diseases (16:2; see Exod 9:10-11). The second is poured into the sea, the sea turns to blood, and everything in it dies (16:3). The third is poured into the rivers and fresh water springs, and they, too, turn to blood (16:4-7; Exod 7:17-21).

Suddenly the angel of the waters (ancient peoples believed that there were heavenly beings in charge of the various elements of creation, like guardian angels) breaks out in a prayer in praise of God's justice (15:5). Those who killed the holy ones and prophets have received their just "reward," he says. They now have only blood to drink! (15:6). As this vision closes, the altar itself joins in the angel's prayer of praise. Of course, altars cannot talk, so the author may be using the literary technique of personification to refer to the angel of the altar or the souls of the martyrs who have been waiting *under* the altar for God to avenge their deaths (6:9-11). The altar's words, "Your judgments are true and just" (16:7), would suggest that the martyrs are now satisfied that God has answered their plea.

When the fourth bowl is poured out on the sun, scorching the people of the earth, John observes that its victims cursed the name of God (16:8-9). The language is reminiscent of the beast of the sea that blasphemes against God (13:1, 5-6) and also anticipates the description of the whore Babylon, who rides a beast covered in blasphemies (17:3). By cursing God the people identify themselves with the dragon and the beasts that get their authority from the dragon. However, the mention of repentance also recalls Pharaoh's response to the Exodus plagues: he expresses the desire to repent until the plague is removed and then returns to his obdurate behavior. Whatever the response of the people, the goal of God's wrath is clear: to call people to repentance and to worship of the one true God. These plagues are not simply gratuitous violence on God's part, but rather a tool for conversion. But the people do not repent or give God glory (16:9).

16:10-21 The last three bowl visions

The fifth bowl, which is poured upon the throne of the beast, results in darkness over its entire kingdom (16:10; cf. Exod 10:21). This is not the peaceful darkness of sleep, but a desperate darkness that drives people to great anguish, even to swearing against God, as their suffering from the earlier plagues is intensified. The narrator adds, "But they did not repent of their works" (16:11). As we shall see in Revelation 17–18, these people are the worshipers of Babylon (i.e., Rome), and their works are the activities that support the power of the beast, namely, politics, commerce, and cultic practices of the Roman Empire.

The sixth bowl is poured out in the Euphrates River, then the eastern border of the Roman Empire, and it dried up, so that armies from the East could enter the empire (16:12). John probably has in mind the Parthians, who were longtime enemies of the Romans (see also 6:1-2 and 9:14). Suddenly John sees unclean spirits emerge from the mouths of the dragon, the beast of the sea, and the beast of the land (here called "the false prophet" because of his deception, 16:13; cf. 12:3; 13:1, 11, 14). The narrator adds that they are "demonic" (that is, deceptive) spirits. John compares the demonic spirits to frogs, recalling the locust-scorpions in Revelation 9:1-9, which elicit feelings of disgust or dislike, but also suggesting the Exodus plague of frogs (Exod 7:25–8:15). The "kings of the whole world" (16:14) probably refers to the kings of the *Roman* world, as distinct from the kings of the East. As John describes it, the three unclean spirits are responsible for all the kings of the earth rallying to war; their assembly will mark the great day of God's justice and judgment (16:14).

The next statement is directed toward John's audience, the believing community, and presented as the words of Jesus: You will not know when or how I will come, so be alert and ready! (16:15). John's comment about being caught naked (16:15) should not be taken literally, but rather as a metaphor for the believers making themselves vulnerable to shame if they have not properly prepared for Jesus' return. In honor-shame cultures, one's honor is more valuable than any other possession a person might have.

The narrator concludes this vision by saying that the unclean spirits assembled the armies at Armageddon (16:16). In Hebrew, this is *har Megiddo*, which means "mountain of Megiddo." Strategically located between Mount Carmel and the Jordan River in the northern part of Israel, it was the entryway for invading armies from the north and east, and therefore the location of some especially fierce battles in Israel's history. However, for John, Armageddon is not so much a place but a symbol of the battle to end all battles!

Finally the seventh bowl is poured out into the air (16:17). The voice from the temple, the same voice that gave the command for the bowls to be poured out, shouts, "It is done," that is, the full measure of God's wrath is completed (16:17). Again John sees and hears the signs of theophany—thunder, lightning, earthquake, and the sounds that accompany them (16:18). As a result, the great city Babylon (i.e., Rome) was broken into three parts by the earthquake, people were pelted by enormous hailstones weighing a hundred pounds each, and the features of the land were so changed as not to be recognizable anymore (16:19-21). The storm and earthquake were fearful, that is, awesome and of catastrophic proportions! But the people did not repent. Rather, their hearts were hardened, so that they cursed God (16:21).

THE FALL OF BABYLON
Rev 17:1–18:24

Before the book's final series of visions, which describe the judgment of the world and the establishment of God's kingdom, Revelation provides a long interlude in which the judgment against the whore Babylon, that is, Rome, is described in great detail. This topic is not new to the readers of the book of Revelation. The seven bowl visions (16:1-21) that immediately precede this section are a final call to repentance for all who have fallen under the spell of the dragon, that is, Rome, and those who pay allegiance to her. However, Rome's fate was sealed already when the angel-prophet of Revelation 14:8 proclaimed, "Fallen, fallen is Babylon the great." These next two chapters are an elaboration of that prophecy.

17:1-18 Vision of the whore Babylon

The connection with the previous series of bowl visions is established in John's mind by the reappearance of one of the angels who held the seven bowls (17:1). The angel takes John to the wilderness, a place of safety in Revelation 12, but here it is also a vantage point from which he can see everything that is happening on the earth (17:3). From this place the angel invites John to view the verdict issued against the great harlot seated on many waters (17:1).

Although today's reader might be stymied by the metaphor of harlotry, John's readers likely understood that he was referring to the city of Rome. Prostitution and fornication (17:1-2) are metaphoric terms that were regularly used to describe idol worship and the material excesses associated with the Roman Empire (see 2:19-23). Likewise, the phrases "kings of the earth" and "the inhabitants of the earth" (17:2) are symbolic descriptors of those who have pledged allegiance to Rome.

The whore Babylon wears purple, a symbol of royalty, and scarlet, suggesting violence (17:4). The beast on which she rides is the beast of the sea (17:3; see 13:1), previously identified as the Roman Empire. However, now the beast is scarlet, perhaps recalling its connection to the red dragon of Revelation 12. Instead of blasphemous names on its heads (13:1), it now wears *many* blasphemous names *all over its body* (17:3). John continues to describe the harlot, saying that she has a name of mystery on her forehead—Babylon (17:5). The term *mystērion* usually refers to something that is secret or hidden, but in Revelation it also suggests an allegorical interpretation, making Babylon a metaphor for Rome.

The description of Rome as the one "who lives near the many waters" (17:1), who holds "a gold cup" in her hand (17:4), and whose inhabitants are drunk with the wine of her fornication (Rev 17:2), may be borrowed from Jeremiah's prophecy against Babylon (Jer 51:7, 13). Jeremiah describes Babylon's impending downfall as God's vengeance for the destruction of the temple (Jer 51:11). In the same spirit, the author of the book of Revelation attributes God's vengeance against Rome to its role in the death of the martyrs (17:6).

As John marvels over what he was seeing, one of the angels holding the seven bowls becomes the interpreter of his vision (17:6-7). The angel tells him that the beast is the one "who was and is *not* and is to rise" (17:8; author's translation), an obvious spoof on the name of God in the introduction of the book of Revelation: the one "who is and who was and who is to come" (1:4). If we are correct in assigning Nero's name to the beast in Revelation 13, then the same should apply here. Thus John is saying that Nero was (i.e., he reigned), and is not (i.e., he died), and is to come (i.e., either he or a reign like his will return). See Revelation 13:3 and 13:14. This beast is about to rise from the abyss—the place with which it is regularly associated—and is going to perdition—a fate to which it is regularly assigned (17:8; see 11:7). The angel also tells John that the dwellers of the earth who do not have their names in the book of life will marvel over the beast (17:8), presumably because they pay allegiance to the beast and do not associate themselves with the Lamb.

The angel alerts John to pay careful attention to the next part of his interpretation, saying, "Here is a clue for one who has wisdom" (17:9; see 13:8). The "seven hills" are the seven hills on which Rome is seated (17:9). The reader might be tempted to think of the "seven kings" in historical terms, too, but the angel's riddle is vague, and the list of first-century Roman emperors does not correspond to the riddle. At a minimum, we can say that the five fallen kings describe a series of emperors who preceded the currently reigning emperor, the sixth king (17:10). The seventh king will reign for a limited time, and then an eighth will rise to the throne, who is like one of the seven (17:11). Scholars suggest that Nero (the beast personified) is the sixth king and that Domitian (A.D. 81–96) is the eighth king, whom second-century Roman historians described as a tyrant and a megalomaniac. However, little can be said beyond that. It is possible that the seven kings simply signify the full measure of kingship, since seven is the symbol of fullness.

The angel continues his interpretation, explaining that the "ten horns" are the ten kings still to come, who will have authority and be of one mind with the beast (17:12-13). For a short time they will make war on those who are faithful to the Lamb, but in the end the Lamb will be victorious, because he is sovereign over even the most powerful of kings. The ones who are with him need not fear, because they are called and chosen (17:14).

Finally, the angel explains that the "waters" are the peoples of the Roman Empire (17:15). Eventually, the beast and the ten kings who have authority with the beast will turn their hatred on Rome and shame her, devour her, and utterly destroy her (17:16). This is what evil does; it destroys everything, even its own. But as the beast and the kings allied with him rampage, God remains sovereign, because they are actually fulfilling God's purpose and will continue to do so until God's will is accomplished (17:17).

18:1-8 Babylon's fall

John's next vision is of an angel of great authority (18:1-3). The angel apparently originated from beside the heavenly throne, because his reflected glory lights up the earth (18:1). The angel's speech is a prophecy that is delivered in the form of a dirge (i.e., funeral song). The opening statement, "Fallen, fallen is Babylon" (18:2) recalls another angel's prophecy in Revelation 14:8, also against Rome. Rome's fornication involves both idolatry and material excess. The language and imagery of this dirge are similar to that found in Isaiah and Jeremiah (Isa 21:9; Jer 25:15, 27; 50:39).

In addition to the destruction of Rome, the angel prophesies that Rome's vassal kings (18:3) will suffer punishment because they participated in her fornication and will lament her passing (see 18:9-10). Likewise, the merchants of her empire (18:3) will pay a price; they have grown rich on her excess, so they, too, will grieve for her (see 18:11-17). A second voice urges God's people to leave Rome before they are drawn into her sinful ways (18:4; see Isa 48:20; Jer 50:8). Thus John's vision makes clear that sinful activity *will* result in punishment despite appearances to the contrary. Rome revels in her false glory and thinks herself a queen with no reason to mourn, but God remembers her wicked deeds and *in a single day* she will suffer double for her sins (18:5-7). Further, the intensity of God's vengeance will demonstrate that the One who judges is sovereign (18:8).

Finally, the angel prophesies that Rome's vassal kings, merchants, and seafarers will mourn over her destruction. Echoing the words of the prophet Ezekiel in his dirge over Tyre, the angel announces that Rome's vassal kings will weep and wail over the once powerful city, their terror rooted in the fact that they deserve the same fate, since they were wanton with her (18:9-10; see Ezek 26:16-17). Likewise, the merchants will mourn because no one buys Rome's riches anymore. All of her luxuries, excesses, and splendid dainties are destroyed, never to be restored (18:12-14; see Ezek 27:12-22). They fear her torment because they became wealthy on account of her (18:15; see Ezek 27:31-36). Finally, the captains of ships, sailors, and sea traders mourn and weep over Rome's burning, because they had grown rich from her wealth (18:17-19; see Ezek 27:30-34).

All three groups express terror over Rome's destruction, not in sympathy with Rome but because of their own self-interest. They understand that they will suffer because Rome suffers. Moreover, all three groups marvel over the swiftness of

God's judgment—in a single hour! (18:10, 17, 19). Of course, John's audience would have heard this prophecy of doom as a message of hope, since it asserts unequivocally that God is just, and God's justice, when it comes, will be swift. The message of the prophecy is confirmed, at the conclusion of the lamentations, when John exhorts his hearers— the holy ones, apostles, and prophets—to rejoice because God has given judgment against Rome *on their behalf* (18:20).

Finally, John sees another angel described as "mighty" (18:21). This angel issues a prophecy of doom in both word and action. Taking a stone that resembled a great millstone used for grinding grain into flour, the angel threw it into the sea, where it quickly sank to the bottom. "With such force shall Babylon the great city be thrown down," the angel says, "and will never be found again" (18:21). Thus begins a litany whose antiphon is "No . . . will ever be heard in you again" (18:22-23).

What are these things that will no longer be seen or heard in Rome? They are the instruments of joy and merriment, the craftspeople that sustain the quality of life of the society (18:22), the grinding stones that help put bread on the table (18:22), the lights that brighten people's homes (18:23), and the bride and bridegroom whose marriage provides offspring for the future (18:23). As a literary technique, the litany booms like a solemn drumbeat or death knell: Rome will be no more! Finally, the mighty angel reveals the reason for this massive and pervasive destruction: the merchants deceived people with their sorcery and, more importantly, the blood of the martyrs was found in the great city that was Rome (18:24). In other words, God is about to avenge the death of his holy ones!

SEVEN VISIONS OF THE LAST THINGS

Rev 19:1–20:15

The book of Revelation concludes with a final series of visions that describe the judgment that is about to come upon the wicked and the reward that is promised to the righteous. All of these visions are presented in highly mythical language. Therefore, they should be interpreted as symbolic and not historical descriptions. However, the message is clear: God is just and God is sovereign. God will *indeed* vindicate the righteous and punish the wicked.

19:1-10 The heavenly liturgy

As a prelude to the visions of the last things, once again John is allowed to witness the heavenly liturgy (cf. 7:9-12; 14:1-5). The great multitude (19:1) described here is apparently the same as the great multitude who earlier stood before God's throne, dressed in white robes and with palm branches in their hands (cf. 7:9). They shout, "Alleluia," which translates "Praise Yнwн," and they sing a song of victory on account of God's true and just condemnation of the whore Babylon, i.e., Rome, and God's avenging of the death of the martyrs (19:2-3; cf. 6:10). Again, they shout "Alleluia" and affirm the final end of Rome by saying that the smoke from the city goes up forever and ever (19:3). John's mention of the twenty-four elders and the four living creatures who joined in worship of God, who is seated on the throne, again recalls the throne vision of Revelation 4.

Suddenly a voice from the throne calls everyone in heaven to offer praise to God (19:5), and the multitude responds with a sound so deafening that it resembles rushing water and thunder crashing (19:6). Again, they shout "Alleluia" and assert that God, the Almighty One, reigns as king (19:6), and they announce with great joy that it is time for the marriage of the Lamb. The bride, whose identity has not yet been revealed, has completed her wedding preparations (19:7). Her bridal gown, which is made of fine, costly, bright white linen (a type found only in Egypt), symbolizes her holiness (19:8). The gown *is given* (passive verb form) to her, meaning that it is a gift *from God* and God is the source or cause of her holiness. John adds that the bridal gown is the righteous deeds of the holy ones (19:8; cf. 15:6). Therefore, we can conclude that the bride is a metaphor for the church, and the holy ones are the members of the church. For a long time they waited under God's altar, demanding God's vengeance on those who killed them (6:9-11). Now they rejoice because the time of God's vindication has finally come (19:6-7).

John goes on to say that he heard the voice from the throne tell him to write the very words of God, "Blessed are those who have been called to the wedding feast of the Lamb" (19:9). This beatitude is about the establishment of God's kingdom, and being *the very words of God*, it carries divine authority. Elsewhere in the New Testament, imagery of a marriage feast is likewise associated with the coming of God's kingdom (Matt 7:11; 22:1-14; 25:1-13).

John falls down to worship the angel, but the angel stops him, telling him that he is not a deity. Rather, he is a fellow servant who holds the testimony of (i.e., concerning) Jesus (19:10). The Greek is difficult to translate into English here, but basically the angel is saying that he, like John himself and others like him, is a prophet who witnesses to Jesus by speaking his word (19:10; cf. 1:1-3). But they must worship only God! (19:10).

After this glorious vision of heavenly worship, John witnesses in rapid succession seven visions of vindication and final judgment. These are all cosmic in scope, embracing heaven and earth and even the space under the earth. The imagery is extremely graphic, but it should not be taken literally. Rather, using metaphorical language, John is asserting that God is sovereign and just and that God rewards the righteous and punishes the wicked.

19:11-16 Vision of the white horse and rider

In the first of seven concluding visions, John sees heaven opened, and again a white horse and rider appear. However, this time the rider is not the Parthian army that made war on Rome (6:2); this one is "Faithful and True" (19:11; cf. 3:14). Because he is described as having eyes of fire with a sword coming from his mouth (19:12, 15), the reader should conclude that the rider is the risen Jesus of the initial vision of this book (see 1:14, 16). He rides a beast of war, the horse, but his is a war of righteousness (19:11). The "many diadems" on his head (19:12) signify supreme kingship. Recall that the dragon wore seven diadems (12:3), and the beast wore ten (13:1). The "name . . . that no one knows" (19:12) means that he has absolute authority, and no one has ownership over him (19:12; cf. 14:1; 17:5), though later he is identified as "Word of God" (19:13), which symbolizes divine authority. The blood-washed robe (19:13) is a symbol of victory in battle (Isa 63:1-3; Wis 18:14-16), and "tread[ing] the wine press" (19:15) describes the wrath of . . . God on judgment day—God will crush the wicked so hard that their lifeblood will spurt out and run like a river! (see Isa 63:1-3). The heavenly army of the risen Jesus is also victorious, dressed in white linen robes (19:14), much like those of the bride

in the preceding vision (cf. 7:9). These are the martyrs who had washed their robes in the blood of the Lamb and now no longer hunger or thirst or suffer grief (cf. 7:9-17).

19:17-18 Vision of the great supper of God

The second vision takes place in the midheaven (i.e., the sky). An angel standing in the sun invites all the birds of the sky to enjoy God's banquet (19:17). The banquet imagery is borrowed from Ezekiel's prophecy against Gog of the land of Magog (Ezek 39:17-20) and is typical of apocalyptic literature. However, for the novice reader, the imagery can be appalling! The birds are invited to dine on the flesh of kings, captains, soldiers, horses, and riders (19:18). Imagine the perverse delight of John's audience, thinking about how their persecutors would be eaten alive—banquet food for birds of prey! Thus God punishes the wicked.

19:19-21 Vision of the destruction of the beast and the false prophet

Without transition, suddenly John observes the beast and the kings of the earth gathering for battle against the Word of God and his army (19:19). This is the preparation for Armageddon (see 16:16). But the war is swift. The beast and the false prophet—the beasts of Revelation 13—are captured without incident, suggesting that they have little power when confronted by the risen Christ and the army of God (19:20). The lake of fire into which they are thrown symbolizes their final destruction (19:20). The slaying of the "rest" (19:21) explains how the kings, military officers, warriors, horses, and riders came to be table fare for God's banquet. Later they, too, will be thrown into the lake of fire (see 20:15).

20:1-10 The "thousand-year" visions

The fourth and fifth visions in this series are sandwiched together into an intercalation. The seer John begins by narrating the first part of the outer vision, then breaks away to describe the inner vision, and finally returns to complete the narration of the outer vision. The reader should think of the two visions as taking place at the same time. While the inner vision takes place in heaven, the outer vision spans all three realms of the created world.

In the outer vision (20:1-3, 7-10), the dragon (see Rev 12) is taken captive by the angel who descends from heaven with the key to the bottomless pit (see Rev 9). The angel hurls the dragon into the pit and seals it for a thousand years (20:2-3). Note the three other names by which the dragon is known: the ancient serpent, the devil, and Satan (20:2; cf. 12:9). The dragon's capture marks the end of his "short while" on earth (cf. 12:12). But this is not *the* end, for John is told that the dragon must be released for a little while after the thousand years are finished (20:3). The verb of necessity, *dei* in Greek, suggests that this is part of God's plan. Therefore God's holy ones should not be fearful.

Leaving the reader in suspense about the dragon, John abruptly shifts to the fifth vision (20:4-6), the thousand-year reign of Christ and those who had been martyred in his name. John sees thrones and, seated upon them, the ones who were given authority to judge (20:4). These are the souls of those who were martyred for their testimony to Jesus. God rewards them with resurrection so that they can share in Christ's reign (20:4). This, the reader learns, is the first resurrection (20:5). Those who enjoy the first resurrection are blessed because the second death (i.e., the general judgment, here associated with the lake of fire) will bring them no harm (20:6). Thus John asserts that God is just and God will reward the righteous.

Finally, John returns to the second half of the fourth vision (20:7-10). Satan is now released from his thousand-year bondage to gather his armies from the four corners of the earth (20:7). John's reference to Gog and Magog (20:8) comes from Ezekiel 38, in which the prophet rails against Gog, the king of Magog, who came from the far northern regions to wage war against Israel. The prophet promises that God's wrath will fall on Gog, and he and his armies will be utterly destroyed. Why? It is to show that God is great and holy and to make God known to the whole world! (Ezek 38:23). Here John describes Magog not as Gog's kingdom but as a person who is in alliance with Gog. However, the message is the same as Ezekiel's: God is sovereign, and God will destroy the wicked.

With his vast armies coming from all over the world, Satan is ready to make war against God's people (20:8). John's use of the phrase "camp of the holy ones" (20:9) may be intended to recall the wilderness camp of the Israelites during the Exodus (e.g., Exod 19:16-17). The "beloved city" is Jerusalem (20:9). The holy ones are the members of the church (20:9). This is the battle of Armageddon, which John first mentioned in 16:14-16 and again in 17:14 and 19:11-21. The name is derived from the Hebrew *har Megiddo,* which means "mountain of Megiddo." Historically, it was the location of some of Israel's fiercest battles. Here it takes on cosmic and mythical proportions. The battle is swift and decisive! God intervenes on behalf of the holy ones, sending fire on the earth (20:9; cf. Ezek 38:22). Satan is thrown into the lake of fire, where the beast and the false prophet have already met their end (20:10).

20:11-15 Vision of judgment before God's throne

This throne vision has a link back to the fifth vision of the last things, in which the martyrs are described as seated on thrones in order to share judgment with the risen Christ (20:4), but it also recalls the throne vision of Revelation 4. Thus, as we arrive at the end of the book of Revelation, we have come full circle to a vision of the sovereign God seated on the throne of glory. Given the pervasiveness of the parallel theme of God's justice, the reader should not be surprised that this sixth (and second to the last) vision is one of judgment.

God's throne is white (20:11), signifying victory over the forces of evil. The earth and sky have fled (20:11), presumably because nothing tainted by evil can exist in this holy place, but also in anticipation of the final vision of this book, the New Jerusalem (see 21:1–22:5). Then John sees the dead as they emerge from the sea and the underworld (Hades) to stand before God, who will judge them based upon what is contained in the book of deeds and the book of life (20:12-13). Some, though not all, first-century Jews believed in a general resurrection of the dead at the end time, in which people would be judged on the basis of their deeds (see, for example, Dan 7:10). In this vision those whose names are not in the book of life are sentenced to the second death, the lake of fire (20:15). When the general judgment of human beings is complete, Death (personified; the consequence of evil) and Hades (the place of the dead) are also thrown into the lake of fire (20:14). John does not mention the fate of the holy ones, because they already enjoy resurrection with Christ (see 20:6). Thus John asserts God's power over the forces of evil and his justice in punishing the wicked. In sum, the slate has been wiped clean for the transformed *cosmos* (universe), which is about to appear.

VISION OF THE NEW JERUSALEM
Rev 21:1–22:5

The vision of the New Jerusalem is the seventh in this sequence of visions of the last things and the final vision of the book of Revelation. It can be divided into three parts based upon the three images used to describe this transformed universe: the bride and wife of the Lamb (21:1-8), the new temple (21:9-27), and the new creation (22:1-5).

21:1-8 The bride and wife of the Lamb

In the preceding vision (20:11-15), John narrated a scene in which the palette of God's creation has been wiped clean. Now he sees a *new* heaven and a *new* earth and the holy city, a *new* Jerusalem, coming out of heaven from God (21:1-2). The reader should notice that this vision is not about the coming of an otherworldly reality, but the restoration of a transformed *this*-worldly reality. John compares it to a bride who has prepared herself for her husband (21:2). The imagery is traditional. The prophets of the Old Testament used the bridal image to describe the restoration of the historical Jerusalem, when God's people would return from the Babylonian exile. See, for example, Isaiah 49:18: "Look about and see; / they are all gathering and coming to you. / As I live, says the LORD, / you shall be arrayed with them all as with adornments, / like a bride you shall fasten them on you." See also Isaiah 52:1 and Isaiah 61:10.

The voice that John hears explains the significance of the vision: this is God's dwelling, and the people who reside in this city are God's people (21:3). The relationship, which the voice describes, is *covenant*. The language is almost identical to that of Ezekiel: "I will make with them a covenant of peace . . . . My dwelling shall be with them; I will be their God, and they shall be my people" (Ezek 37:26-27). As narrated in the previous vision (20:11-15), the old order, dominated by the dragon, the beasts of the land and sea, Death and Hades, has passed away. Therefore there is no suffering

or death in this new order (21:4). This, too, is traditional imagery for the restoration of Jerusalem. See, for example, Isaiah 25:7-8: "On this mountain . . . the Lord GOD will wipe away the tears from all faces."

Now God speaks: "They are accomplished," that is, "the transformation is complete" (21:6; see 21:5). God's declaration, "I [am] the Alpha and the Omega" (the first and last letters of the Greek alphabet; 21:6), is an assertion of sovereignty over all things. Thus God promises to the thirsty (i.e., those who have committed themselves in covenant with God) the water of life *as a gift* and reaffirms his covenant with the holy ones (21:6-7). Again, the imagery is traditional. See, for example, Isaiah 55:1, 3: "All you who are thirsty, / come to the water! / You who have no money, / come, receive grain and eat; / . . . / I renew with you the everlasting covenant, / benefits assured to David." Other examples of water associated with life in the messianic age include Isaiah 41:17-18; Isaiah 44:3-4; Ezekiel 47:1-12; Zechariah 13:1; and Zechariah 14:8. The phrase to "the victor" (21:7) recalls the promises at the conclusion of the letters to the seven churches in Revelation 2–3. The reference to those who are doomed for the lake of fire (21:8) is a reminder that nothing evil can reside in this transformed city, the bride of the Lamb.

21:9-27 The new temple

When one of the angels of the seven plagues approaches John and invites him to see the bride of the Lamb (21:9), John is transported to a high mountain—most likely the location of the historical Jerusalem—where he can see the New Jerusalem coming out of heaven from God (21:10). In ancient Judaism the Jerusalem temple was the symbol of God's covenant, its worship center, and the place where God's glory resides on earth. Here John will use the temple as a metaphor for the New Jerusalem.

Again, the imagery is traditional. The new city is radiant with God's glory (21:11; cf. Isa 60:1-2; Ezek 43:2-5; Zech 2:5). Its cubic shape mirrors the holy of holies in Solomon's temple (21:16; cf. 1 Kgs 6:20; 2 Chr 3:8f.), and the plan of the temple, including its three gates on each of four walls, recalls Ezekiel's plan of the temple (21:12-13; cf. Ezek 41:21; 43:16; 45:1; 48:20). The twelve precious stones of the foundation of the walls (21:19) recall the high priest's breastplate, which was to have twelve stones representing the twelve tribes (cf. Exod 28:17-21). They also recall the promise of Jerusalem's restoration contained in both Tobit and Isaiah (Tob 13:15-17; Isa 54:11-12).

Some of the details of John's vision remind the reader that although the New Jerusalem is this-worldly, it also has a cosmic and mythical dimension. Its walls, for example, measure 144 cubits in height and thickness (21:17). A cubit was measured from the elbow to the tip of one's finger, approximately 18 inches, so 144 cubits is approximately 72 yards. More importantly, 144 is the total of 12 multiplied by 12, or perfection squared. Since the city walls were its first line of protection against attackers, this one is perfectly protected! The city itself measures four-square, 12,000 *stadia* on a side and 12,000 *stadia* high (21:16). A *stadion* measured approximately 606 feet, so 12,000 *stadia* is approximately 1,377 miles. A city this size is not feasible, but the symbolism is important. A four-square city, characterized by perfection (12) multiplied by a number too great to count (1,000), suggests one that is perfect in its dimensions, comprehensive, and all-inclusive. Consistent with this view of the city is the description of its walls being made of jasper, its streets paved in gold, and each of its gates crafted of a single pearl! (21:18, 21).

Other details in John's vision of the New Jerusalem are reminiscent of the throne vision of Revelation 4. For example, the city having the radiance of jasper (21:11) recalls the description of the One seated on the throne, who appeared "like jasper and carnelian" (4:3). Likewise, the names of the twelve tribes of Israel inscribed on the gates of the city (21:12) and the names of the twelve apostles inscribed on the foundation stones (21:14) recall the twenty-four elders who were situated on thrones surrounding the throne of God (4:4). Thus the reader should not be surprised when John announces that he saw no temple in the new city. God and the Lamb reside directly—that is, without the mediation of a temple—in the city (21:22). God's glory and the radiance of the Lamb provide the city's light, and because God is forever faithful, there is no need to fear danger because the city will never have darkness in it (21:23, 25). Moreover, God's radiance will attract all nations into the city, and nothing unclean will enter it (21:24, 26-27). In sum, the New Jerusalem is God's dwelling place on earth.

22:1-5 The new creation

In the third segment of this vision, the angel of the seven plagues takes John to see the river of the water of life coming out of the throne of God and the Lamb, which is now inside of the city (22:1). Again, the imagery is traditional. The river recalls the second creation story in Genesis, which provided the setting for God's creation of a human from the dust of the earth (cf. Gen 2:9-10), as well as Ezekiel's vision of a river of water flowing from the temple (Ezek 47:1-12) and Zechariah's vision of water coming from Jerusalem when God's day of judgment comes (Zech 14:8). John's observation that there is a tree of life on each side of the river (22:2) recalls the tree of life that God placed in the garden, also from the second creation story (cf. Gen 2:9). It is the same tree from which Adam and Eve were banished after their sin (Gen 3:22). In other words, John's vision of the New Jerusalem is paradise restored!

John further observes that these trees produce fruit twelve months of the year, and they have leaves that are good for healing of the nations (22:2). The language is closely related to that of the prophet Ezekiel: "Their leaves shall not fade, nor their fruit fail. Every month they shall bear fresh fruit, for they shall be watered by the flow from the sanctuary. Their fruit shall serve for food, and their leaves for medicine" (Ezek 47:12). The point of this part of the vision: God will provide all they need for nourishment and for well-being. John adds "for *the nations*," making the vision all-inclusive (emphasis added). John's observation that there is nothing accursed in the city (22:3) and no darkness (22:5) recalls an end-time prophecy about the lifting of the curse on Jerusalem, so that it can finally live in safety (cf. Zech 14:7-11). In sum, John's vision of the New Jerusalem is the establishment of a new creation, or better, a return to the first creation, before there was sin and evil in the world. It is a return to the Garden of Eden.

CONCLUDING MATERIALS
Rev 22:6-21

Revelation ends with a collection of warnings, beatitudes, and exhortations, some of which recall earlier sections of the book. Several refer to the prophetic character of the book.

The heavenly being who is speaking to John (22:6) appears at first to be one of the seven angels who hold the seven bowls (21:9). However, some of the later sayings in this section are clearly those of the risen Christ (e.g., 22:12-13). Perhaps we have sayings from a variety of sources, without regard to the identity of the speaker, collected together at the end of this document. The description of these words as "trustworthy and true" (22:6) is an assertion of their authenticity, as is the statement that God sent his angel to tell his prophets what must take place soon (22:6). John made a similar statement in the opening of the book (see 1:1).

The declaration "I am coming soon!" (22:7) most likely comes from the risen Christ (cf. 3:11). It will appear two more times in this section, in 22:12 and 22. The beatitude about keeping the message of this book is a short form of the first beatitude of the book of Revelation (1:3).

Now John speaks, identifying himself again as the recipient of the revelation (22:8; cf. 1:1, 9). He also recalls his encounter with the angel messenger in 19:10, with a few variations: "the brothers" of the earlier recollection are now "the prophets," and "the testimony concerning Jesus" is now "the message of this book."

This next saying is directed to John and most likely comes from the angel of verse 6. The command *not* to seal the words of the book (22:10) signals the immediacy of the end (cf. Dan 8:26). The saying about letting the wicked still act wickedly may sound like determinism, but since the book of Revelation allows for the possibility of repentance (see, for example, 14:6), that interpretation is unlikely. Instead, we should understand it as a warning not to be complacent but always to be ready, for the end is near.

The saying that begins "I am coming soon" (22:12) signals that the risen Christ is now speaking and that he brings rewards for believers according to their works. The attribution "Alpha and Omega" (22:13) is used elsewhere in the book of Revelation only for God (1:8; 21:6). The beatitude that follows, "Blessed are they who wash their robes . . . " (22:14), is most likely a recollection of 7:14, in which the angel explains to John the identity of the 144,000. The "tree of life" and the gates of the city are probably allusions to the vision of the New Jerusalem (21:24-27; 22:2). The saying about "dogs, the sorcerers, the unchaste . . . and all who love and practice deceit" (22:15) recalls those who are not allowed into the New Jerusalem, since it is the place where God and the Lamb reside (see 21:8, 27). It also suggests those who have made allegiance with the dragon and its beasts (see 13:6-8).

Jesus continues, providing further authentication for the book of Revelation, here called "testimony for the churches" (22:16). His authority to speak lies in the fact that he is the messiah: thus the reference to the root of David and the bright morning star (see Isa 11:1; Num 24:17).

The statement about the Spirit and the bride (22:17) has all the flavor of a call to worship, and some scholars have suggested that the author's liturgical allusion was intentional. The Spirit is the one who speaks to the churches through the prophets (see 2:7; 19:10). The bride is the New Jerusalem (see 21:2, 9). The one "who hears" is the one who reads and takes to heart the words of the book of Revelation. All say, "Come," addressed to the risen Jesus. He is the coming one. The invitation for the thirsty to come (22:17) is reminiscent of the promise made to the inhabitants of the New Jerusalem that they will have access to "the fountain of the water of life" (cf. 21:6).

The book ends with a warning to would-be editors not to add to, take away from, or otherwise alter the contents of this book (22:18). Certainly such things happened because ancient religious documents were considered to be community expressions of faith and recollections of larger oral or written traditions. Therefore, if a scribe found that something was missing or thought that a clarification of meaning was necessary, he would simply make the change. However, this warning might also serve to assure the reader that the content of the book is reliable, much like the statements of authenticity we have seen throughout this section. See, for example, 22:7, 12, and 20. In sum, whatever the involvement of the human author, the book of Revelation is reliable because God is its source (see 1:1).

Once again Jesus promises, "I am coming soon!" (22:20), to which the author, on behalf of the readers, answers, "Amen," meaning, "So be it." Certainly this is a message of hope for the persecuted! However, the time is *coming;* it is not yet here. Therefore the author adds a prayer of petition, "Come, Lord Jesus" (in Aramaic *marana tha*).

Finally, the book ends as it began—with literary features of a letter. Thus we see a closing greeting, wishing the grace (i.e., gift) of Jesus on all (22:21). Amen. So be it!

Contributors

Dianne Bergant, C.S.A., is professor of Old Testament studies at Catholic Theological Union in Chicago. She is a member and past president of the Catholic Biblical Association of America and is an active member of the Chicago Catholic/Jewish Scholars Dialogue. She has published numerous works, including *Scripture: History and Interpretation*, and *The Song of Songs* in the Berit Olam series, both published by Liturgical Press.

Thomas M. Bolin is associate professor of religious studies at St. Norbert College in De Pere, Wisconsin. His research focuses on ancient Israelite history and religion, wisdom literature, postexilic texts, and theological hermeneutics.

Corrine L. Carvalho received her doctorate from Yale University and is professor of theology at the University of St. Thomas, St. Paul, Minnesota. She is the author of *Encountering Ancient Voices: A Guide to Reading the Old Testament* (St. Mary's Press, 2006).

Richard J. Clifford, S.J., is professor of Old Testament at Boston College School of Theology. He taught biblical studies at Weston Jesuit School of Theology in Cambridge from 1970 to 2008. His doctorate is from Harvard University. He was general editor of the *Catholic Biblical Quarterly* and is a former president of the Catholic Biblical Association. As well as teaching and lecturing in scholarly circles, he is active in adult education in various New England dioceses.

John J. Collins is Holmes Professor of Old Testament at Yale Divinity School. A native of Ireland, he has a doctorate from Harvard University, and earlier taught at the University of Chicago, and the University of Notre Dame. He has published widely on the subjects of apocalypticism, wisdom, Hellenistic Judaism, and the Dead Sea Scrolls and served as president of both the Catholic Biblical Association and the Society of Biblical Literature.

Joan E. Cook, S.C., teaches Scripture at Georgetown University in Washington, DC. She is author of *Hannah's Desire, God's Design* (Sheffield Academic Press, 1999) and *Hear, O Heavens and Listen, O Earth: An Introduction to the Prophets* (Liturgical Press, 2006), which won a first-place Catholic Press Association award in 2007. Cook has also written numerous articles on biblical women and biblical prayer.

Jeremy Corley is a Catholic priest of the Diocese of Portsmouth, UK. Following several years of parish ministry, he completed a doctorate in biblical studies at the Catholic University of America. He has published books and articles on biblical topics, especially the book of Sirach, and now teaches Scripture at St. Patrick's College, Maynooth, Ireland.

Catherine A. Cory is an associate professor in the theology department at the University of St. Thomas, St. Paul, Minnesota. She is the author of two textbooks, *Voyage through the New Testament* (Pearson) and, with David T. Landry, *The Christian Theological Tradition* (Prentice-Hall).

Gregory W. Dawes is senior lecturer in both religious studies and philosophy at the University of Otago (New Zealand). He undertook graduate study at the Pontifical Biblical Institute in Rome, where he completed the Licentiate degree, before receiving a PhD from the University of Otago in 1995. He has written several books, the most recent being *The Historical Jesus Question: The Challenge of History to Religious Authority* (Westminster John Knox, 2001). He is currently researching Christian responses to the work of Charles Darwin.

Carol J. Dempsey, OP, is professor of biblical studies at the University of Portland, Oregon, with special expertise in Old Testament and prophets. She holds a PhD in biblical studies from The Catholic University of America and has authored several books including *Jeremiah: Preacher of Grace, Poet of Truth* (Liturgical Press, 2007), and *Reading the Bible, Transforming Conflict* (Orbis, 2011).

John C. Endres, S.J., has been teaching Old Testament / Hebrew Bible at the Jesuit School of Theology (in Berkeley) of Santa Clara University since 1982. He was chief editor of *Chronicles and Its Synoptic Parallels in the Books of Samuel, Kings, and Related Biblical Texts* (Liturgical Press). He also writes and teaches on the Psalms, the deuterocanonical books, Dead Sea Scrolls, and the Book of Jubilees.

Roland J. Faley, T.O.R., was a Franciscan friar and biblical scholar who taught in seminaries and universities in the United States and abroad. With degrees from Catholic University, St. Thomas University in Rome, and the Biblical Institute in Rome, Fr. Faley was the minister general of his religious order and was the author of *Footprints on the Mountain; Bonding With God;* and *Apocalypse Then and Now* (all Paulist Press).

Dennis Hamm, S.J., since 1975 has taught Scripture at Creighton University and since 2004 has held the Graff Faculty Chair of Catholic Theology. He is author of the various journal articles and reviews, as well as the three-volume *Let the Scriptures Speak*, published by Liturgical Press. He is also a coeditor, along with Leonard Greenspoon and Bryan J. LeBeau, of *The Historical Jesus through Catholic and Jewish Eyes*.

Daniel J. Harrington, S.J., was professor of New Testament at the Boston College School of Theology and Ministry. With a doctorate in biblical languages and literatures from Harvard University, Fr. Harrington served as president of the Catholic Biblical Association and wrote many books on the Old and New Testament, including the New Collegeville Bible Commentary on *The Letter to the Hebrews* (Liturgical Press, 2006).

Patrick J. Hartin is an ordained priest of the Diocese of Spokane, Washington. He presently teaches courses in the New Testament and in Classical Civilizations at Gonzaga University. He is a contributor to *Give Us This Day* and the author of numerous books, published by Liturgical Press, including: *A Spirituality of Perfection: Faith in Action in the Letter of James*, *James* (Sacra Pagina series), *James of Jerusalem: Heir to Jesus of Nazareth* (Interfaces series), *Apollos* (Paul's Social Network series), *Exploring the Spirituality of the Gospels*, and *A Window into the Spirituality of Paul*.

Katherine M. Hayes is professor of sacred Scripture at the Seminary of the Immaculate Conception in Huntington, New York, where she has taught since 1997. She also teaches, since 2012, at St. Joseph Seminary in Yonkers, New York. She is author of *"The Earth Mourns": Prophetic Metaphor and Oral Aesthetic* (Society of Biblical Literature/Brill, 2002) and articles and reviews in a variety of scholarly and pastoral publications, including *Catholic Biblical Quarterly*.

Leslie J. Hoppe, O.F.M., is an adjunct professor at Catholic Theological Union after serving on its faculty for twenty-four years and serves as the provincial minister of the Assumption Province Franciscans. He has written several books on biblical studies and archaeology, including *The Holy City: Jerusalem in the Theology of the Old Testament* (Liturgical Press, 2000). He is a former editor of *The Bible Today* and currently serves on its editorial board.

Robert J. Karris, O.F.M., is professor emeritus and former head of research at The Franciscan Institute of St. Bonaventure University. He is a past president of the Catholic Biblical Association and the author of *Jesus and the Marginalized in John's Gospel* and *Symphony of New Testament Hymns*, both published by Liturgical Press.

Terence J. Keegan, O.P., serves as the executive vice president and treasurer at Providence College, Providence, Rhode Island.

Alice L. Laffey, S.S.D., is associate professor in the Department of Religious Studies at the College of the Holy Cross, Worcester, Massachusetts. Trained in the modern historical-critical study of the Deuteronomistic History, she has expanded her study of the Old Testament to include postmodern feminist and ecological approaches.

Scott M. Lewis, S.J., is vice president and dean at Regis College, Toronto, where he also serves as associate professor of New Testament and is engaged in retreat ministry.

Feidhlimidh Magennis is a priest of the Diocese of Dromore, Ireland. After completing his License in Sacred Scripture at the Pontifical Biblical Institute, Rome, he taught in Ireland and Canada. He is currently a principal lecturer in religious studies at St. Mary's University College, Belfast.

Paul V. Niskanen is associate professor of theology at the University of St. Thomas, St. Paul, Minnesota. He is the author of *The Human and the Divine in History: Herodotus and the Book of Daniel* (T&T Clark, 2004).

Irene Nowell, O.S.B., of the Benedictine community of Mount Saint Scholastica in Atchison, Kansas, is a member of the translation team of the revised Old Testament of the New American Bible. She teaches Scripture courses at Saint John's School of Theology•Seminary, Collegeville, Minnesota. Nowell is a member of the Committee on Illuminations and Texts for The Saint John's Bible and a past president of the Catholic Biblical Association. She is author of *Pleading, Cursing, Praising: Conversations with God through the Psalms; Sing a New Song: The Psalms in the Sunday Lectionary;* and *Women in the Old Testament,* all published by Liturgical Press.

Kathleen M. O'Connor is author of several books including *Jeremiah: Pain and Promise* (Fortress, 2012), *Lamentations and the Tears of the World* (Orbis, 2004), and *The Wisdom Literature* (Liturgical Press, 1990). She is the William Marcellus McPheeters Professor of Old Testament, emerita, at Columbia Theological Seminary, Decatur, Georgia, and also taught at the Maryknoll School of Theology in Ossining, New York. She is active in the Catholic Biblical Association of America and the Society of Biblical Literature.

J. Edward Owens, O.SS.T., is currently Minister Provincial of the US Province of Trinitarians. Previously, he was a professor of biblical studies at St. John's Seminary in California and then Oblate School of Theology in Texas. He has written numerous articles in academic and pastoral publications, including *The Bible Today, Human Development,* and *The Catholic Biblical Quarterly* Monograph Series.

Maria A. Pascuzzi, C.S.J., is associate dean for undergraduate studies at the Immaculate Conception Seminary School of Theology at Seton Hall University, NJ. Previously she was a tenured associate professor of biblical studies at the University of San Diego. During her tenure there, she was also the founding director of the University's Center for Catholic Thought and Culture. She is the author of *Paul: Windows on His Thought and His World* (Anselm Academic, 2014).

Michael F. Patella, O.S.B., is a professor of New Testament at the School of Theology•Seminary of Saint John's University, Collegeville, where he also serves as seminary rector. He is the author of *The Death of Jesus: The Diabolical Force and the Ministering Angel* (Paris: Gabalda, 1999), *The Lord of the Cosmos: Mithras, Paul, and the Gospel of Mark* (T&T Clark, 2006), *Word and Image: The Hermeneutics of the The Saint John's Bible* (Liturgical Press), and *Angels and Demons: A Christian Primer of the Spiritual World* (Liturgical Press). He has been a frequent contributor to *The Bible Today* and also served as chair of the Committee on Illumination and Text for *The Saint John's Bible.* He is a member of the Catholic Biblical Association.

Barbara E. Reid, O.P., professor of New Testament at Catholic Theological Union in Chicago. She is the author of *Parables for Preachers, Choosing the Better Part?,* and co-editor of the *Collegeville Pastoral Dictionary of Biblical Theology,* published by Liturgical Press. She has also published various journal articles on New Testament topics.

Marie Noonan Sabin has taught the Gospel of Mark at Bangor Theological Seminary; an earlier book on Mark, *Reopening the Word*, was published by Oxford University Press in 2002.

Vincent M. Smiles is professor of theology at Saint John's University, Collegeville, Minnesota. He is author of *The Gospel and the Law in Galatia* and *The Bible and Science: Longing for God in a Science-Dominated World*, both published by Liturgical Press.

Mark S. Smith is Skirball Professor of Bible and Ancient Near Eastern Studies at New York University. Previously he taught at Yale University, Saint Joseph's University in Philadelphia, and Saint Paul Seminary in Saint Paul, Minnesota. Author or co-author of eighteen books, he is past president of the Catholic Biblical Association of America.

Pauline A. Viviano is an associate professor of theology at Loyola University Chicago. She received her doctorate in biblical languages and literature from St. Louis University. Besides articles in academic and popular journals, her publications include reading guides for the books of Joshua, Judges, First and Second Samuel, First and Second Kings, and Ruth for the *Catholic Study Bible* published by Oxford University Press, and *Collegeville Bible Commentary Volume 2: Genesis* (Liturgical Press, 1985). In addition to university teaching she often lectures at parishes in and around Chicago.

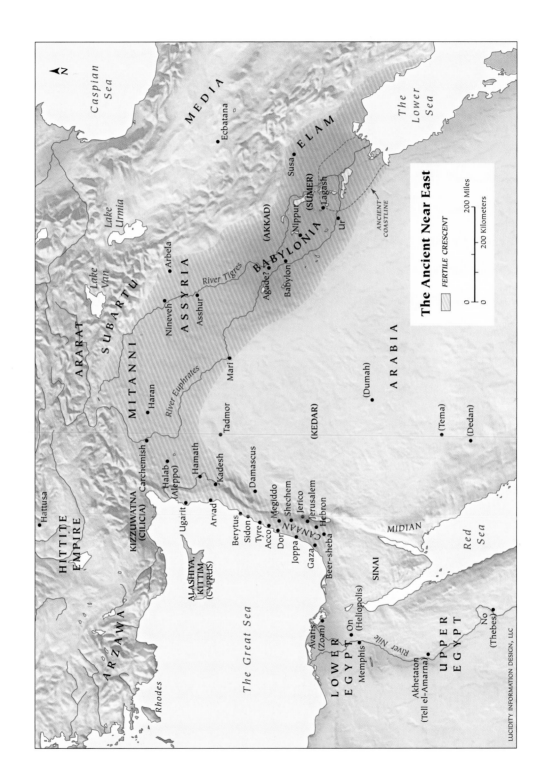

The Ancient Near East

FERTILE CRESCENT

200 Miles
200 Kilometers

N

Caspian Sea

MEDIA

Ecbatana

Lake Urmia

ELAM

Susa

The Lower Sea

Lake Van

SUBARTU

ARARAT

Arbela

ASSYRIA

(SUMER)

Nippur

Lagash

Ur

ANCIENT COASTLINE

River Tigres

(AKKAD)

BABYLONIA

Agade?

Babylon

MITANNI

Nineveh

Asshur

River Euphrates

Haran

Mari

ARABIA

(Dumah)

Tadmor

(KEDAR)

(Tema)

(Dedan)

KIZZUWATNA (CILICIA)

Carchemish

Halab (Aleppo)

Hamath

Kadesh

Damascus

HITTITE EMPIRE

Hattusa

Arvad

Megiddo

Shechem

Jerico

Jerusalem

Hebron

Ugarit

Berytus

Sidon

Tyre

Acco

Dor

Joppa

Gaza

Beer-sheba

CANAAN

MIDIAN

ALASHIYA, KITTIM (CYPRUS)

ARZAWA

Rhodes

The Great Sea

SINAI

Red Sea

LOWER EGYPT

Avaris (Zoan)

On (Heliopolis)

Memphis

River Nile

UPPER EGYPT

Akhetaton (Tell el-Amarna)

No (Thebes)

LUCIDITY INFORMATION DESIGN, LLC

1523

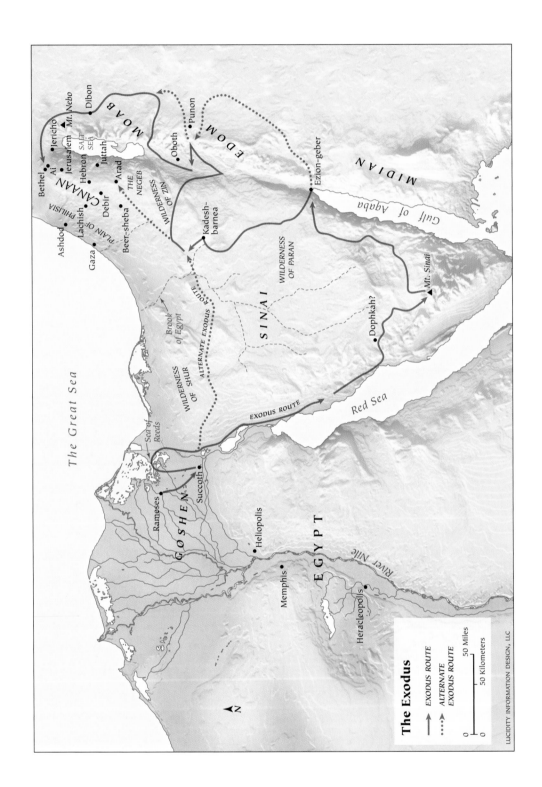

The Exodus

→ EXODUS ROUTE
⋯▸ ALTERNATE EXODUS ROUTE

50 Miles
50 Kilometers

LUCIDITY INFORMATION DESIGN, LLC

1524

Israel Settled in Canaan

········· APPROXIMATE BOUNDARY OF
         ISRAEL'S TRIBES
    ○   CITIES OF REFUGE

0 ————————————————— 30 Miles
0 ————————————————— 30 Kilometers

Sidon

Mt. Lebanon

Mt. Hermon

Damascus

Tyre

Dan
(Laish)

Kedesh

ARAM

ASHER

NAPHTALI

Hazor

Acco

Achshaph

ZEBULUN

Sea of
Chinnereth

Golan

Ashtaroth

Mt.
Carmel

The Great
Sea

Shimron

Mt.
Tabor

ISSACHAR

Edrei

Dor

Megiddo

Shunem

Ramoth-gilead

Wadi Kishon

Taanach

Mt.
Gilboa

Beth-
shean

MANASSEH

MANASSEH

Thebez

Zaphon

Mt. Ebal

Shechem

River Jabbok

Mt. Gerizim

River Jordan

Joppa

Shiloh

GAD

EPHRAIM

Bethel

Rabbah

DAN

BENJAMIN

Jericho

Gezer

Gibeah

Bezer

AMMON

Ashdod

Ekron

Jerusalem

Mt. Pisgah

Mt. Nebo

Ashkelon

Beth-
shemesh

Bethlehem

PHILISTINES

REUBEN

Gath

Gaza

Hebron

The Salt Sea

Debir

JUDAH

Dibon

Ziklag

River
Arnon

Beer-
sheba

MOAB

Brook
Besor

SIMEON

The Negeb

Brook Zered

EDOM

LUCIDITY INFORMATION DESIGN, LLC

1525

United Monarchy of Israel

- – – – MAXIMUM EXTENT OF THE UNITED MONARCHY
- AREAS OF INFLUENCE
- CONQUERED AREAS
- ■ SITES FORTIFIED BY SOLOMON
- ASHER ISRAELITE TRIBES
- MOAB NON-ISRAELITE GROUPS

0   30 Miles
0   30 Kilometers

Sidon

SIDONIANS

Mt. Lebanon

Mt. Hermon

Damascus

Tyre

Abel-beth-maccah

Dan

SYRIA (ARAM)

N

ASHER

NAPHTALI

Hazor

Acco

Cabul

Chinnereth

Sea of Chinnereth

Ashtaroth

Helam

Mt. Carmel

ZEBULUN

Mt. Tabor

Jokneam

ISSACHAR

MANASSEH

Dor

Megiddo

Jezreel

Wadi Kishon

Beth-shean

Rogelim

Ramoth-gilead

Taanach

Mt. Gilboa

The Great Sea

Hepher?

ISRAEL

Abel-menolah

MANASSEH

Samaria

Tirzah

Mt. Ebal

Shechem

Mahanaim

Mt. Gerizim

River Jabbok

Zarethan?

River Jordan

Joppa

Shiloh

GAD

EPHRAIM

Beth-horon

Bethel

Rabbah

Baalath?

Gezer

BENJAMIN

Jericho

AMMON

Ashdod

Ekron

Gibeah

Jerusalem

Mt. Pisgah

Ashkelon

Gath?

Beth-shemesh

Bethlehem

Mt. Nebo

PHILISTINES

Gaza

Hebron

Dibon

Gerar

Carmel

The Salt Sea

JUDAH

Ziklag?

Beer-sheba

Arad

MOAB

River Arnon

SIMEON

Kir-hareseth

Brook Besor

The Negeb

Zoar

Brook Zered

Tamar

EDOM

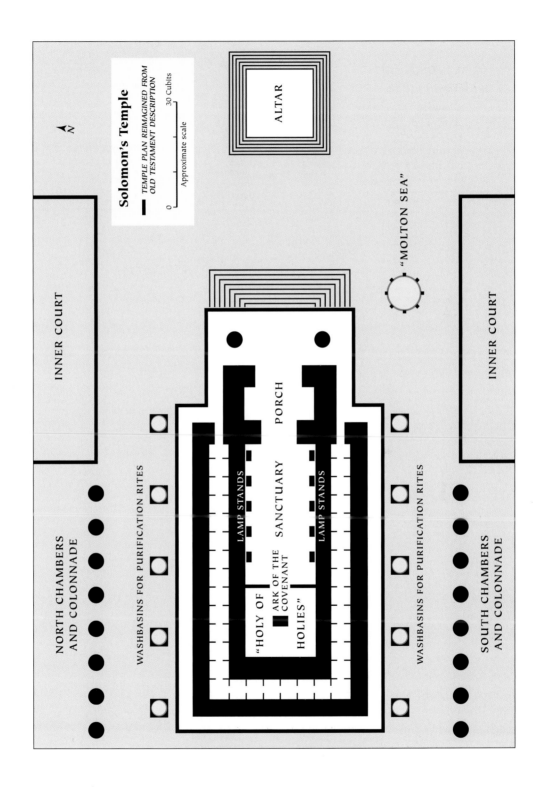

Solomon's Temple

TEMPLE PLAN REIMAGINED FROM OLD TESTAMENT DESCRIPTION

Approximate scale

0   30 Cubits

N

ALTAR

INNER COURT

INNER COURT

"MOLTON SEA"

NORTH CHAMBERS AND COLONNADE

SOUTH CHAMBERS AND COLONNADE

WASHBASINS FOR PURIFICATION RITES

WASHBASINS FOR PURIFICATION RITES

PORCH

SANCTUARY

LAMP STANDS

LAMP STANDS

ARK OF THE COVENANT

"HOLY OF

HOLIES"

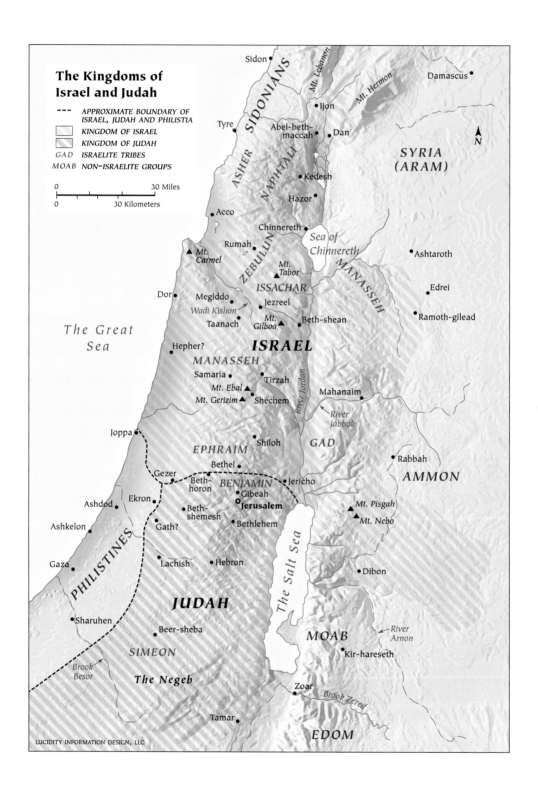

The Kingdoms of Israel and Judah

- - - APPROXIMATE BOUNDARY OF ISRAEL, JUDAH AND PHILISTIA
KINGDOM OF ISRAEL
KINGDOM OF JUDAH
GAD ISRAELITE TRIBES
MOAB NON–ISRAELITE GROUPS

0   30 Miles
0   30 Kilometers

Sidon

SIDONIANS

Mt. Lebanon

Mt. Hermon

Damascus

Ijon

Tyre

ASHER

Abel-beth-maccah

Dan

SYRIA (ARAM)

N

Kedesh

NAPHTALI

Hazor

Acco

Chinnereth

Sea of Chinnereth

Ashtaroth

Rumah

ZEBULUN

Mt. Carmel

Mt. Tabor

MANASSEH

Edrei

Dor

ISSACHAR

Megiddo

Jezreel

Ramoth-gilead

Wadi Kishon

Taanach

Mt. Gilboa

Beth-shean

The Great Sea

Hepher?

ISRAEL

MANASSEH

Samaria

Tirzah

River Jordan

Mahanaim

Mt. Ebal

Mt. Gerizim

Shechem

River Jabbok

Joppa

EPHRAIM

Shiloh

GAD

Bethel

Rabbah

Gezer

Beth-horon

BENJAMIN

Jericho

AMMON

Gibeah

Ashdod

Ekron

Jerusalem

Beth-shemesh

Mt. Pisgah

Mt. Nebo

Ashkelon

Gath?

Bethlehem

PHILISTINES

Gaza

Lachish

Hebron

The Salt Sea

Dibon

JUDAH

Sharuhen

Beer-sheba

MOAB

SIMEON

Kir-hareseth

River Arnon

Brook Besor

The Negeb

Zoar

Brook Zered

Tamar

EDOM

1528

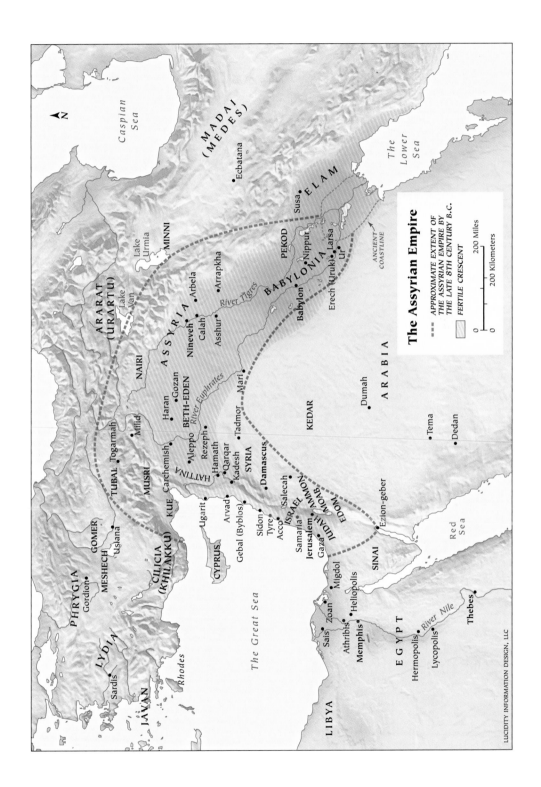

The Assyrian Empire

- - - APPROXIMATE EXTENT OF
THE ASSYRIAN EMPIRE BY
THE LATE 8TH CENTURY B.C.

▨ FERTILE CRESCENT

200 Miles

200 Kilometers

Caspian
Sea

MADAI
(MEDES)

Ecbatana

ELAM

Susa

MINNI

PEKOD

Lake
Urmia

BABYLONIA

Nippur

ARARAT
(URARTU)

Lake
Van

Arbela

Arrapkha

Larsa

Ur

Erech (Uruk)

River Tigris

The
Lower
Sea

ANCIENT
COASTLINE

NAIRI

ASSYRIA

Nineveh

Calah

Asshur

Babylon

Haran

Gozan

BETH-EDEN

River Euphrates

Mari

Tadmor

ARABIA

Dumah

Milid

Togarmah

TUBAL

Aleppo

Rezeph

Hamath

Qarqar

Kadesh

SYRIA

KEDAR

Tema

Dedan

MUSRI

Carchemish

HATTINA

KUE

Ugarit

Arvad

Damascus

Acco

Salecah

ISRAEL

AMMON

MOAB

EDOM

GOMER

MESHECH

Ushana

Gebal (Byblos)

Sidon

Tyre

Samaria

Jerusalem

JUDAH

Gaza

Ezion-geber

PHRYGIA

Gordion

CILICIA
(KHILAKKU)

CYPRUS

SINAI

Red
Sea

LYDIA

Sardis

JAVAN

Rhodes

The Great Sea

Migdol

Heliopolis

Zoan

Sais

Athribis

Memphis

Hermopolis

River Nile

Lycopolis

Thebes

EGYPT

LIBYA

LUCIDITY INFORMATION DESIGN, LLC

1529

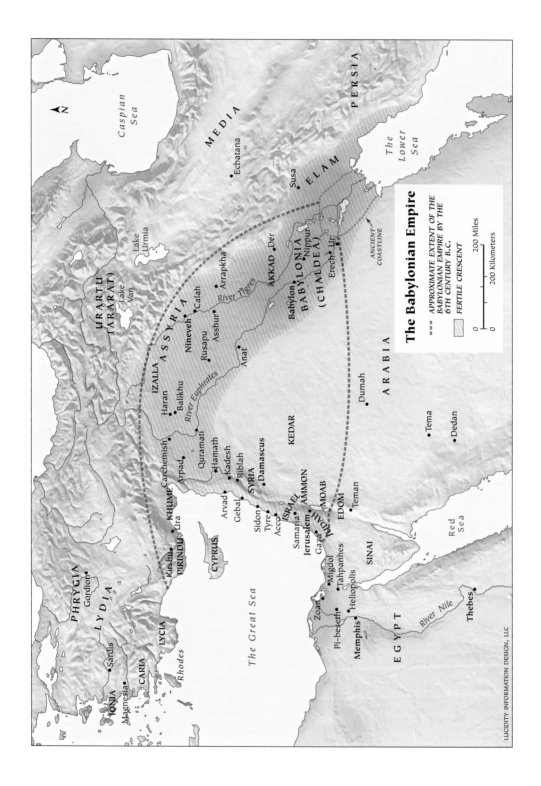

The Babylonian Empire

LUCIDITY INFORMATION DESIGN, LLC

Legend:
- APPROXIMATE EXTENT OF THE BABYLONIAN EMPIRE BY THE 6TH CENTURY B.C.
- FERTILE CRESCENT

0   200 Miles
0   200 Kilometers

N

Caspian Sea

MEDIA

PERSIA

Ecbatana

The Lower Sea

Susa

ELAM

URARTU (ARARAT)

Lake Urmia

Lake Van

ASSYRIA

IZALLA

Der

AKKAD

Nippur

BABYLON

BABYLONIA (CHALDEA)

Erech

Ur

Arrapkha

Calah

River Tigres

Nineveh

Rusapu

Asshur

Anat

Haran

Balikhu

River Euphrates

ANCIENT COASTLINE

ARABIA

Dumah

KEDAR

Carchemish

Quramati

Hamath

Arpad

Kadesh

Riblah

Damascus

SYRIA

KHUME

Ura

Arvad

Gebal

Sidon

Tyre

Acco

Samaria

ISRAEL

Jerusalem

JUDAH

AMMON

MOAB

EDOM

Teman

Gaza

Tema

Dedan

Red Sea

Kirshu

PIRINDU

CYPRUS

Rhodes

PHRYGIA

Gordion

LYDIA

Sardis

LYCIA

CARIA

Magnesia

IONIA

The Great Sea

Migdol

Tahpanhes

SINAI

Zoan

Pi-beseth

Heliopolis

Memphis

EGYPT

River Nile

Thebes

The Persian Empire

APPROXIMATE EXTENT OF
THE PERSIAN EMPIRE BY
THE 5TH CENTURY B.C.

300 Miles

300 Kilometers

LUCIDITY INFORMATION DESIGN, LLC

MASSAGETIA

SOGDIANA

GANDARA

BACTRIA

ARACHOSIA

CHORASMIA

Oxus River

Indus River

ARIA

DRANGIANA

GEDROSIA

SCYTHIA

Aral
Sea

PARTHIA

SAGARTIA

CARMANIA

Erythraean
Sea

HYRCANIA

Pasargarda

Persepolis

PERSIA

Caspian Sea

MEDIA

Ecbatana

Susa

ELAM

The Lower Sea

SAUROMATIA

CAUCASUS MTNS.

ARMENIA

Arbela

BABYLONIA

Ur

River Tigres

Nineveh

ASSYRIA

Babylon

Black Sea

Sinope

Haran

River Euphrates

KEDAR

ARABIA

CAPPADOCIA

Tarsus

SYRIA

Damascus

DASCYLIUM

Byzantium

PHRYGIA

Gordion

CILICIA

PHOENICIA

Thapsacus

THRACE

Cyprus

Sidon

Tyre

Jerusalem

MACEDONIA

LYDIA

Sardis

CARIA

Ephesus

The
Upper Sea

Red Sea

Ister River
(Danube)

GREEK
STATES

Athens

Crete

Naucratis

Memphis

EGYPT

River Nile

Thebes

Syene

ETHIOPIA

LIBYA

1531

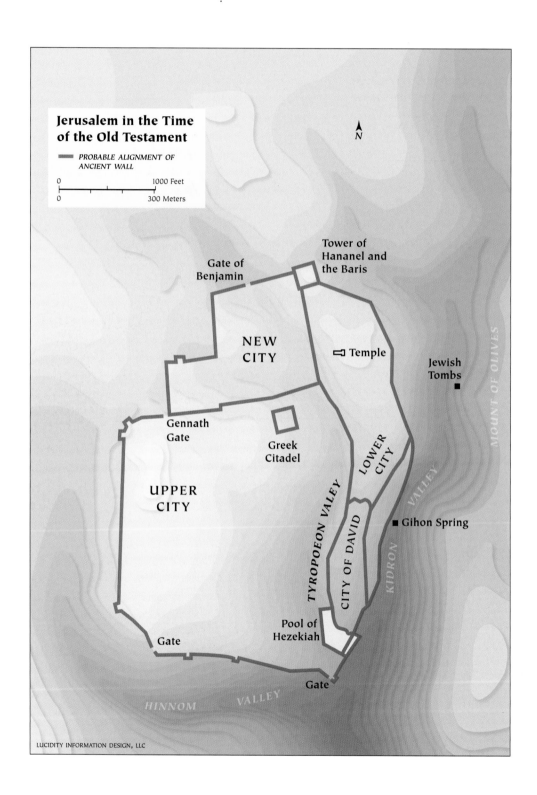

Jerusalem in the Time of the Old Testament

PROBABLE ALIGNMENT OF ANCIENT WALL

0   1000 Feet
0   300 Meters

N

Gate of Benjamin

Tower of Hananel and the Baris

NEW CITY

Temple

Jewish Tombs

MOUNT OF OLIVES

Gennath Gate

Greek Citadel

LOWER CITY

UPPER CITY

TYROPOEON VALEY

CITY OF DAVID

KIDRON VALLEY

Gihon Spring

Pool of Hezekiah

Gate

Gate

HINNOM VALLEY

LUCIDITY INFORMATION DESIGN, LLC

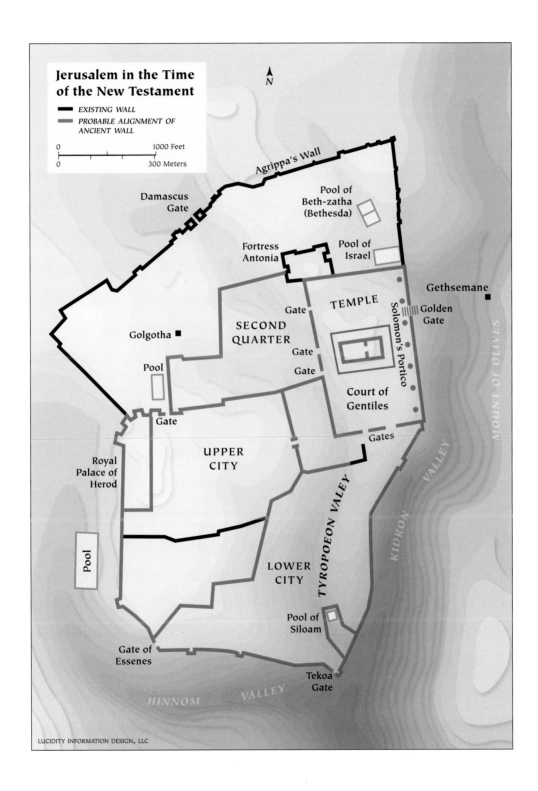

EXISTING WALL

PROBABLE ALIGNMENT OF
ANCIENT WALL

0   1000 Feet

0   300 Meters

N

Agrippa's Wall

Damascus
Gate

Pool of
Beth-zatha
(Bethesda)

Fortress
Antonia

Pool of
Israel

TEMPLE

Gethsemane

Golgotha

SECOND
QUARTER

Gate

Solomon's Portico

Golden
Gate

Pool

Gate

Gate

Court of
Gentiles

MOUNT OF OLIVES

Gate

UPPER
CITY

Gates

Royal
Palace of
Herod

TYROPOEON VALEY

KIDRON VALLEY

Pool

LOWER
CITY

Pool of
Siloam

Gate of
Essenes

Tekoa
Gate

HINNOM   VALLEY

Palestine in the Time of Jesus

- - - BOUNDARY OF HEROD'S KINGDOM
○ CITIES OF THE DECAPOLIS
■ FORTRESS

0   30 Miles
0   30 Kilometers

Sidon

PHONECIA (TYRE)

Mt. Lebanon

Mt. Hermon

Damascus ○

Tyre

PROVINCE OF SYRIA

○ Caesara Philippi

N

GALILEE

TETRARCHY OF PHILIP

Ptolemais •

Chorazin •
Capernaum •
Gennesaret •
Bethsaida-Julias •

○ Raphana

Cana •
Magdala •

Sea of Galilee

Mt. Carmel ▲
Sepphoris •
Tiberias •

Hippos ○

○ Dion

The Great Sea

Nazareth •
▲ Mt. Tabor

Gadara •

Abila ○

Dora •

Nain •

Wadi Kishon

Scythopolis •
▲ Mt. Gilboa
Pella ○

Caesarea Maritima •

DECAPOLIS

SAMARIA

Seabaste •
Neapolis •
▲ Mt. Ebal
▲ Mt. Gerizim

○ Gerasa

Antipatris •

Alexandrium ■

River Jabbok

Joppa •

Arimathea •

Ephraim •

PEREA

Philadelphia ○

Lydda •

Bethel •

JUDEA

Emmaus •

Jericho •
Cyprus ■

Mt. Pisgah ▲

Azotus •
Ekron •

Jerusalem ○
Bethany •
Bethlehem •
Hyrcania ■

Mt. Nebo ▲

Ashkelon •

Herodium ■

Machaerus ■

Gaza •

Hebron •

River Jordan

The Salt Sea

River Arnon

Masada ■

Areopolis •

Beer-sheba •
Malatha •

NABATAEAN KINGDOM

Brook Besor

IDUMEA

Brook Zered

LUCIDITY INFORMATION DESIGN, LLC

The Roman Empire

*APPROXIMATE EXTENT
OF THE ROMAN EMPIRE
AT THE TIME OF THE
NEW TESTAMENT*

400 Miles

400 Kilometers

N

Atlantic
Ocean

Caspian Sea

Black Sea

Mediterranean Sea

Red Sea

PARTHIAN
EMPIRE

ARABIA

MESOPOTAMIA

Babylon

ARMENIA

ASSYRIA

Damascus

SYRIA

Antioch

Jerusalem

JUDEA

Thebes

EGYPT

Memphis

Alexandria

CAPPADOCIA

CILICIA

Tarsus

Cyprus

LYCIA

ASIA

Ephesus

Pergamum

Crete

BITHYNIA and PONTUS

GALATIA

CYRENAICA

Cyrene

Leptis
Magna

SARMATIA

DACIA

Danube River

MOESIA

THRACE

Byzantium

Philippi

MACEDONIA

EPIRUS

ACHAIA

Athens

Brundisium

Syracuse

SICILY

Carthage

NUMIDIA

MAURETANIA

GAETULIA
(AFRICA)

GERMANIA

Vindobona

Aquincum

RAETIA

ILLYRICUM
(DALMATIA)

CISALPINE
GAUL

ITALIA

Rome

Pompeii

CORSICA

SARDINIA

BELGICA

Lutetia

GAUL

LUGDUNENSIS

AQUITANIA

Lugdunum

NARBONENSIS

Tolosa

Tarraco

TARRACONENSIS

Salmantica

HISPANIA

LUSITANIA

Toletum

Corduba

BAETICA

BRITANNIA

LUCIDITY INFORMATION DESIGN, LLC

1535

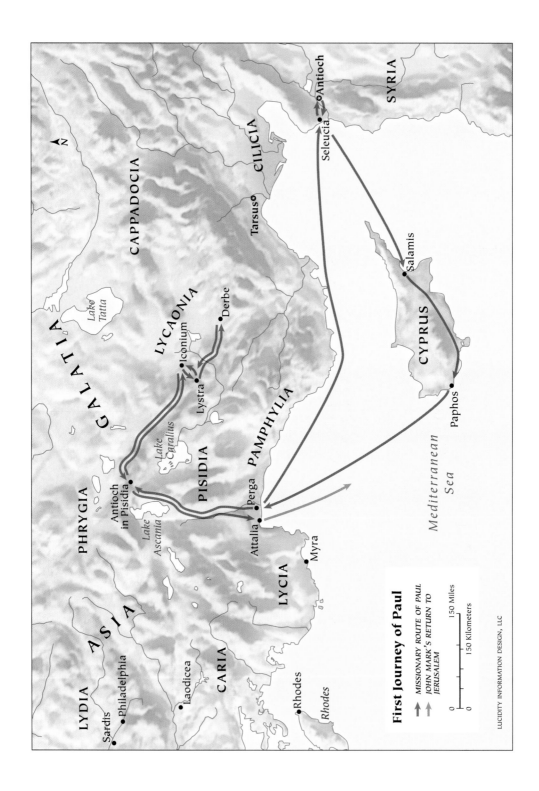

First Journey of Paul

MISSIONARY ROUTE OF PAUL
JOHN MARK'S RETURN TO JERUSALEM

150 Miles

150 Kilometers

LUCIDITY INFORMATION DESIGN, LLC

N

SYRIA
Antioch
Seleucia
CILICIA
Tarsus
Salamis
CYPRUS
Paphos
Mediterranean Sea

CAPPADOCIA

GALATIA
Lake Tatta
LYCAONIA
Derbe
Iconium
Lystra
PHRYGIA
Antioch in Pisidia
Lake Caralitis
Lake Ascania
PISIDIA
Perga
PAMPHYLIA
Attalia
Myra
LYCIA

ASIA
LYDIA
Sardis
Philadelphia
Laodicea
CARIA
Rhodes
Rhodes

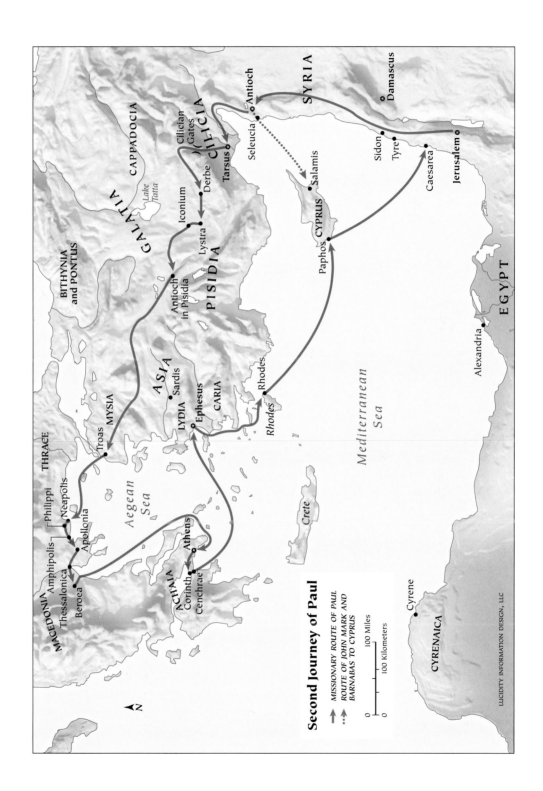

Second Journey of Paul

MISSIONARY ROUTE OF PAUL

ROUTE OF JOHN MARK AND
BARNABAS TO CYPRUS

100 Miles

100 Kilometers

LUCIDITY INFORMATION DESIGN, LLC

SYRIA

Antioch

Damascus

Seleucia

Tarsus

Cilician
Gates

CILICIA

Salamis

Sidon

Tyre

CYPRUS

Paphos

Caesarea

Jerusalem

Derbe

Iconium

Lystra

PISIDIA

Antioch
in Pisidia

CAPPADOCIA

GALATIA

Lake
Tatta

BITHYNIA
and PONTUS

ASIA

Sardis

LYDIA

Ephesus

CARIA

Rhodes

Rhodes

MYSIA

Troas

THRACE

Philippi

Neapolis

Amphipolis

Apollonia

MACEDONIA

Thessalonica

Beroea

Aegean
Sea

ACHAIA

Athens

Corinth

Cenchrae

Mediterranean
Sea

Crete

EGYPT

Alexandria

Cyrene

CYRENAICA

N

Third Journey of Paul and His Voyage to Rome

MISSIONARY ROUTE OF PAUL
PAUL'S VOYAGE TO ROME
ROUTE OF TIMOTHY AND
ERASTUS TO MACEDONIA

0   200 Miles

0   200 Kilometers

N

Euxine Sea

BITHYNIA and PONTUS

GALATIA

Lake Tatta

THRACE

MACEDONIA

Thessalonica

Philippi

Aegean Sea

Troas
Assos
Mitylene

Pergamum

Sardis

ASIA

Ephesus

Miletus

Cos
Cnidus

Rhodes

Iconium

Antioch in Pisidia

Lystra

Derbe

PAMPHYLIA

Cilician Gates

Tarsus

CILICIA

Antioch

SYRIA

Damascus

Tyre

Sidon

Ptolemais

Caesarea

Jerusalem

CYPRUS

Paphos

Myra

Patara

Salmone

Crete

Phoenix

Lasea

Fair Havens

Cauda

Athens

Corinth

ACHAIA

Adriatic Sea

Rhegium

Syracuse

Malta

Puteoli

Three Taverns

Rome

Forum of Appius

Tyrrhenian Sea

Mediterranean Sea

EGYPT

Alexandria

Cyrene

CYRENAICA

(STORM AT SEA)

1538